THE TREASURY
OF
DAVID

CONTAINING

AN ORIGINAL EXPOSITION OF THE BOOK OF PSALMS;

A COLLECTION OF ILLUSTRATIVE EXTRACTS FROM THE
WHOLE RANGE OF LITERATURE;

A SERIES OF HOMILETICAL HINTS UPON ALMOST EVERY
VERSE;

AND LISTS OF WRITERS UPON EACH PSALM

IN THREE VOLUMES

C. H. Spurgeon

VOLUME THREE
PSALM CXI to CL

HENDRICKSON
PUBLISHERS
PEABODY, MASSACHUSETTS 01961-3473

ISBN 0-917006-25-9

PREFACE.

At length I am able to present to the Christian public another part of "The Treasury of David." It has demanded longer labour than its predecessors, but that labour has been freely given to it ; and to the utmost of my ability I have kept the volume up to the level of those which have gone before. In the production of this exposition I had far rather be long than lax ; for I know by experience the disappointment which comes to readers when, after a promising beginning, they see a serious declension towards the end. The general acceptance given to this Commentary has placed me under a heavy obligation to do my best even to the end. Towards that end I am still proceeding with all possible diligence, and it is with great pleasure that I look forward to the speedy issue of the last volume of the work. Many labours distract me from this favourite employment, but I hope to press on with more speed than of late, if my life be spared. It would be imprudent to make too sure of *that ;* for the most fragile Venice glass is not more brittle than human life :

> "The spider's most attenuated thread
> Is cord, is cable, to the tender film
> Which holds our soul in life."

I have been all the longer over this portion of my task because I have been bewildered in the expanse of the One Hundred and Nineteenth Psalm, which makes up the bulk of this volume. Its dimensions and its depth alike overcame me. It spread itself out before me like a vast, rolling prairie, to which I could see no bound, and this alone created a feeling of dismay. Its expanse was unbroken by a bluff or headland, and hence it threatened a mono-tonous task, although the fear has not been realized. This marvellous poem seemed to me a great sea of holy teaching, moving, in its many verses, wave upon wave ; altogether without an island of special and remarkable state-ment to break it up. I confess I hesitated to launch upon it. Other Psalms have been mere lakes, but this is the main ocean. It is a continent of sacred thought, every inch of which is fertile as the garden of the Lord : it is an amazing level of abundance, a mighty stretch of harvest-fields. I have now crossed the great plain for myself, but not without persevering, and, I will add, pleasurable, toil. Several great authors have traversed this region and left their tracks behind them, and so far the journey has been all the easier for me ; but yet to me and to my helpers it has been no mean feat of patient authorship and research. This great Psalm is a book in itself : instead of being one among many Psalms, it is worthy to be set forth by itself as a poem of surpassing excellence Those who have never studied it may pronounce it commonplace, and complain of its repetitions ; but to the thoughtful student it is like the great deep, full, so as never to be measured ; and varied, so as never to weary the eye. Its depth is as great as its length ; it is mystery, not set forth as mystery, but concealed beneath the simplest statements ; may I say that it is experience allowed to prattle, to preach, to praise, and to pray like a child-prophet in his own father's house ?

My venerable friend, Mr. Rogers, has been spared to help me with his admirable suggestions ; but Mr. Gibson, who so industriously translated from the Latin authors, has fallen asleep, leaving behind him copious notes upon the rest of the Psalms. Aid in the homiletical department has been given me by several of the ministers who were educated at the Pastor's College, and their names are duly appended to the hints and skeletons which they have supplied. In this department the present volume is believed to be superior to the former ones. May it prove to be really useful to my brethren, and my desire is fulfilled. I know so well the use of a homiletic hint when the mind is in search for a subject, that I have felt peculiar pleasure in supplying my readers with a full measure of such helps.

In hunting up rare authors, and making extracts from them, Mr. Keys has rendered me great assistance, and I am also a debtor to others who have cheerfully rendered me service when I have sought it. Burdened with the care of many institutions, and the oversight of a singularly large church, I cannot do such justice to my theme as I could wish. Learned leisure would be far more accurate than my busy pen can ever hope to be. If I had nothing else to think of, I would have thought of nothing else, and undivided energies could have accomplished what spare strength can never perform. Hence, I am glad of help ; so glad, that I am happy to acknowledge it. Not in this thing only, but in all other labours, I owe in the first place all to God, and secondarily, very, very much to those generous friends who find a delight in making my efforts successful.

Above all, I trust that the Holy Spirit has been with me in writing and compiling these volumes, and therefore I expect that he will bless them both to the conversion of the unrenewed and to the edification of believers. The writing of this book has been a means of grace to my own heart ; I have enjoyed for myself what I have prepared for my readers. The Book of Psalms has been a royal banquet to me, and in feasting upon its contents I have seemed to eat angels' food. It is no wonder that old writers should call it,— the school of patience, the soul's soliloquies, the little Bible, the anatomy of conscience, the rose garden, the pearl island, and the like. It is the Paradise of devotion, the Holy Land of poesy, the heart of Scripture, the map of experience, and the tongue of saints. It is the spokesman of feelings which else had found no utterance. Does it not say just what we wished to say ? Are not its prayers and praises exactly such as our hearts delight in ? No man needs better company than the Psalms ; therein he may read and commune with friends human and divine ; friends who know the heart of man towards God and the heart of God towards man ; friends who perfectly sympathize with us and our sorrows, friends who never betray or forsake. Oh, to be shut up in a cave with David, with no other occupation but to hear him sing, and to sing with him ! Well might a Christian monarch lay aside his crown for such enjoyment, and a believing pauper find a crown in such felicity.

It is to be feared that the Psalms are by no means so prized as in earlier ages of the Church. Time was when the Psalms were not only rehearsed in all the churches from day to day, but they were so universally sung that the common people knew them, even if they did not know the letters in which they were written. Time was when bishops would ordain no man to the ministry unless he knew "David" from end to end, and could repeat each Psalm correctly ; even Councils of the Church have decreed that none should hold ecclesiastical office unless they knew the whole Psalter by heart. Other practices of those ages had better be forgotten, but to *this* memory accords an honourable record. Then, as Jerome tells us, the labourer, while he held the plough, sang Hallelujah; the tired reaper refreshed himself with the Psalms, and the vinedresser, while trimming the vines with his curved hook, sang something of David. He tells us that in his part of the world, Psalms were the Christian's ballads; could they have had better? They were the love-songs of the people of God; could any others be so pure and heavenly? These sacred hymns express all modes of holy feeling; they are fit both for childhood and old age; they furnish maxims for the entrance of life, and serve as watchwords at the gates of death. The battle of life, the repose of the Sabbath, the ward of the hospital, the guest-chamber of the mansion the church, the oratory, yea, even heaven itself may be entered with Psalms,

Finally, when I reach the last Psalm, it is my firm conviction that I shall find no truer closing words for myself than those of Bishop Horne, which I take liberty here to quote, using them as if they were my own, since they admirably express my present feelings and past experiences :—

" And now, could the author flatter himself that anyone would take half the pleasure in reading the following exposition which he hath taken in writing it, he would not fear the loss of his labour. The employment detached him from the bustle and hurry of life, the din of politics, and the noise of folly. Vanity and vexation flew for a season, care and disquietude came not near his dwelling. He arose fresh as the morning to his task; the silence of the night invited him to pursue it; and he can truly say, that food and rest were not preferred before it. Every Psalm improved infinitely upon his acquaintance with it, and no one gave him uneasiness but the last; for then he grieved that his work was done. Happier hours than those which have been spent on these meditations on the songs of Zion he never expects to see in this world. Very pleasantly did they pass, and they moved smoothly and swiftly along; for when thus engaged, he counted no time. The meditations are gone, but have left a relish and a fragrance upon the mind, and the remembrance of them is sweet."

Reader,

I am,

Thine to serve

For Christ's sake,

PSALM CXI.

There is no title to this Psalm, but it is an alphabetical hymn of praise, having for its subject the works of the Lord in creation, providence, and grace. The sweet singer dwells upon the one idea that God should be known by his people, and that this knowledge when turned into practical piety is man's true wisdom, and the certain cause of lasting adoration. Many are ignorant of what their Creator has done, and hence they are foolish in heart, and silent as to the praises of God : this evil can only be removed by a remembrance of God's works, and a diligent study of them; to this, therefore, the Psalm is meant to arouse us. It may be called THE PSALM OF GOD'S WORKS *intended to excite us to the work of praise.*

DIVISION.—*The Psalmist begins with an invitation to praise, verse 1 ; and then proceeds to furnish us with matter for adoration in God's works and his dealings with his people, 2—9. He closes his song with a commendation of the worship of the Lord and of the men who practise it.*

EXPOSITION.

PRAISE ye the LORD. I will praise the LORD with *my* whole heart, in the assembly of the upright, and *in* the congregation.

1. *"Praise ye the* LORD," or, *Hallelujah!* All ye his saints unite in adoring Jehovah, who worketh so gloriously. Do it now, do it always : do it heartily, do it unanimously, do it eternally. Even if others refuse, take care that ye have always a song for your God. Put away all doubt, question, murmuring, and rebellion, and give yourselves up to the praising of Jehovah, both with your lips and in your lives. *"I will praise the* LORD *with my whole heart."* The sweet singer commences the song, for his heart is all on flame : whether others will follow him or not, he will at once begin and long continue. What we preach we should practise. The best way to enforce an exhortation is to set an example ; but we must let that example be of the best kind, or we may lead others to do the work in a limping manner. David brought nothing less than his whole heart to the duty ; all his love went out towards God, and all his zeal, his skill, and his ardour went with it. Jehovah the one and undivided God cannot be acceptably praised with a divided heart, neither should we attempt so to dishonour him ; for our whole heart is little enough for his glory, and there can be no reason why it should not all be lifted up in his praise. All his works are praiseworthy, and therefore all our nature should adore him. *"In the assembly of the upright, and in the congregation"* ;—whether with few or with many he would pour forth his whole heart and soul in praise, and whether the company was made up of select spirits or of the general mass of the people he would continue in the same exercise. For the choicest society there can be no better engagement than praise, and for the general assembly nothing can be more fitting. For the church and for the congregation, for the family or the community, for the private chamber of pious friendship, or the great hall of popular meeting, the praise of the Lord is suitable ; and at the very least the true heart should sing hallelujah in any and every place. Why should we fear the presence of men ? The best of men will join us in our song, and if the common sort, will not do so, our example will be a needed rebuke to them. In any case let us praise God, whether the hearers be a little band of saints or a mixed multitude. Come, dear reader, he who pens this comment is in his heart magnifying the Lord : will you not pause for a moment and join in the delightful exercise ?

2 The works of the LORD *are* great, sought out of all them that have pleasure therein.

3 His work *is* honourable and glorious : and his righteousness endureth for ever.

4 He hath made his wonderful works to be remembered : the LORD *is* gracious and full of compassion.

5 He hath given meat unto them that fear him : he will ever be mindful of his covenant.

6 He hath shewed his people the power of his works, that he may give them the heritage of the heathen.

7 The works of his hands *are* verity and judgment ; all his commandments *are* sure.

8 They stand fast for ever and ever, *and are* done in truth and uprightness.

9 He sent redemption unto his people : he hath commanded his covenant for ever : holy and reverend *is* his name.

2. *"The works of the* LORD *are great."* In design, in size, in number, in excellence, all the works of the Lord are great. Even the little things of God are great. In some point of view or other each one of the productions of his power, or the deeds of his wisdom, will appear to be great to the wise in heart. *"Sought out of all them that have pleasure therein."* Those who love their Maker delight in his handiworks, they perceive that there is more in them than appears upon the surface, and therefore they bend their minds to study and understand them. The devout naturalist ransacks nature, the earnest student of history pries into hidden facts and dark stories, and the man of God digs into the mines of Scripture, and hoards up each grain of its golden truth. God's works are worthy of our researches, they yield us instruction and pleasure wonderfully blended, and they grow upon, appearing to be far greater, after investigation than before. Men's works are noble from a distance ; God's works are great when sought out. Delitzsch reads the passage, " Worthy of being sought after in all their purposes," and this also is a grand truth, for the end and design which God hath in all that he makes or does is equally admirable with the work itself. The hidden wisdom of God is the most marvellous part of his works, and hence those who do not look below the surface miss the best part of what he would teach us. Because the works are great they cannot be seen all at once, but must be looked into with care, and this seeking out is of essential service to us by educating our faculties, and strengthening our spiritual eye gradually to bear the light of the divine glory. It is well for us that all things cannot be seen at a glance, for the search into their mysteries is as useful to us as the knowledge which we thereby attain. The history of the Lord's dealings with his people is especially a fit subject for the meditation of reverent minds who find therein a sweet solace, and a never failing source of delight.

3. *"His work is honourable and glorious."* His one special work, the salvation of his people, is here mentioned as distinguished from his many other *works*. This reflects honour and glory upon him. It is deservedly the theme of the highest praise, and compels those who understand it and experience it to ascribe all honour and glory unto the Lord. Its conception, its sure foundations, its gracious purpose, its wise arrangements, its gift of Jesus as Redeemer, its application of redemption by the Holy Ghost in regeneration and sanctification, and all else which make up the one glorious whole, all redound to the infinite honour of Him who contrived and carried out so astounding a method of salvation. No other work can be compared with it : it honours both the Saviour and the saved, and while it brings glory to God it also brings us to glory. There is none like the God of Jeshurun, and there is no salvation like that which he has wrought for his people. *"And his righteousness endureth for ever."* In the work of grace righteousness is not forgotten, nor deprived of its glory ; rather, it is honoured in the eyes of the intelligent universe. The bearing of guilt by our great Substitute proved that not even to effect the purposes of his grace would the Lord forget his righteousness ; no future strain upon his justice can ever be equal to that which it has already sustained in the bruising of his dear Son ; it must henceforth assuredly endure for ever. Moreover, the righteousness of God in the whole plan can never now be suspected of failure, for all that it requires is already performed, its demands are satisfied by the double deed of our Lord in enduring the vengeance due, and in rendering perfect obedience to the law. Caprice does not enter into the government of the Lord, the rectitude of it is and must for ever be beyond all question. In no single deed of God can unrighteousness be found, nor shall there ever be : this is the very glory of his work, and even its adversaries cannot gainsay it. Let believers, therefore, praise him

evermore, and never blush to speak of that work which is so honourable and glorious.

4. *"He hath made his wonderful works to be remembered."* He meant them to remain in the recollection of his people, and they do so : partly because they are in themselves memorable, and because also he has taken care to record them by the pen of inspiration, and has written them upon the hearts of his people by his Holy Spirit. By the ordinances of the Mosaic law, the coming out of Egypt, the sojourn in the wilderness, and other memorabilia of Israel's history were constantly brought before the minds of the people, and their children were by such means instructed in the wonders which God had wrought in old time. Deeds such as God has wrought are not to be admired for an hour and then forgotten, they are meant to be perpetual signs and instructive tokens to all coming generations ; and especially are they designed to confirm the faith of his people in the divine love, and to make them know that *"the LORD is gracious and full of compassion."* They need not fear to trust his grace for the future, for they remember it in the past. Grace is as conspicuous as righteousness in the great work of God, yea, a fulness of tender love is seen in all that he has done. He treats his people with great consideration for their weakness and infirmity ; having the same pity for them as a father hath towards his children. Should we not praise him for this ? A silver thread of lovingkindness runs through the entire fabric of God's work of salvation and providence, and never once is it left out in the whole piece. Let the memories of his saints bear witness to this fact with grateful joy.

5. *"He hath given meat unto them that fear him."* Or *spoil*, as some read it, for the Lord's people both in coming out of Egypt and at other times have been enriched from their enemies. Not only in the wilderness with manna, but everywhere else by his providence he has supplied the necessities of his believing people. Somewhere or other they have had food convenient for them, and that in times of great scarcity. As for spiritual meat, that has been plentifully furnished them in Christ Jesus ; they have been fed with the finest of the wheat, and made to feast on royal dainties. His word is as nourishing to the soul as bread to the body, and there is such an abundance of it that no heir of heaven shall ever be famished. Truly the fear of the Lord is wisdom, since it secures to a man the supply of all that he needs for soul and body. *"He will ever be mindful of his covenant."* He could not let his people lack meat, because he was in covenant with them, and they can never want in the future, for he will continue to act upon the terms of that covenant. No promise of the Lord shall fall to the ground, nor will any part of the great compact of eternal love be revoked or allowed to sink into oblivion. The covenant of grace is the plan of the great work which the Lord works out for his people, and it will never be departed from : the Lord has set his hand and seal to it, his glory and honour are involved in it, yea, his very name hangs upon it, and he will not even in the least jot or tittle cease to be mindful of it. Of this the feeding of his people is the pledge : he would not so continually supply their needs if he meant after all to destroy them. Upon this most blessed earnest let us settle our minds ; let us rest in the faithfulness of the Lord, and praise him with all our hearts every time that we eat bread or feed upon his word.

6. *"He hath shewed his people the power of his works."* They have seen what he is able to do and what force he is prepared to put forth on their behalf. This power Israel saw in physical works, and we in spiritual wonders, for we behold the matchless energy of the Holy Ghost and feel it in our own souls. In times of dire distress the Lord has put forth such energy of grace that we have been astonished at his power ; and this was part of his intent in bringing us into such conditions that he might reveal to us the arm of his strength. Could we ever have known it so well if we had not been in pressing need of his help ? We may well turn this verse into a prayer and ask to see more and more the power of the Lord at work among us in these latter days. O Lord, let us now see how mightily thou canst work in the saving of sinners and in preserving and delivering thine own people. *"That he may give them the heritage of the heathen."* He put forth all his power to drive out the Canaanites and bring in his people. Even thus may it please his infinite wisdom to give to his church the heathen for her inheritance in the name of Jesus. Nothing but great power can effect this, but it will surely be accomplished in due season.

7. *"The works of his hands are verity and judgment."* Truth and justice are conspicuous in all that Jehovah does. Nothing like artifice or crooked policy can ever be seen in his proceedings ; he acts faithfully and righteously towards his people,

and with justice and impartiality to all mankind. This also should lead us to praise him, since it is of the utmost advantage to us to live under a sovereign whose laws, decrees, acts, and deeds are the essence of truth and justice. *"All his commandments are sure."* All that he has appointed or decreed shall surely stand, and his precepts which he has proclaimed shall be found worthy of our obedience, for surely they are founded in justice and are meant for our lasting good. He is no fickle despot, commanding one thing one day and another another, but his commands remain absolutely unaltered, their necessity equally unquestionable, their excellence permanently proven, and their reward eternally secure. Take the word *commandments* to relate either to his decrees or his precepts, and we have in each case an important sense; but it seems more in accordance with the connection to take the first sense and consider the words to refer to the ordinances, appointments, or decrees of the great King.

> " Whate'er the mighty Lord decrees,
> Shall stand for ever sure,
> The settled purpose of his heart
> To ages shall endure."

8. *"They stand fast for ever and ever."* That is to say, his purposes, commands, and courses of action. The Lord is not swayed by transient motives, or moved by the circumstances of the hour; immutable principles rule in the courts of Jehovah, and he pursues his eternal purposes without the shadow of a turning. Our works are too often as wood, hay, and stubble, but his doings are as gold, silver, and precious stones. We take up a purpose for a while and then exchange it for another, but he is of one mind, and none can turn him: he acts in eternity and for eternity, and hence what he works abides for ever. Much of this lasting character arises out of the fact which is next mentioned, namely, that they *"are done in truth and uprightness."* Nothing stands but that which is upright. Falsehood soon vanishes, for it is a mere show, but truth has salt in it which preserves it from decay. God always acts according to the glorious principles of truth and integrity, and hence there is no need of alteration or revocation; his works will endure to the end of time.

9. *"He sent redemption unto his people."* When they were in Egypt he sent not only a deliverer, but an actual deliverance; not only a redeemer, but complete redemption. He has done the like spiritually for all his people, having first by blood purchased them out of the hand of the enemy, and then by power rescued them from the bondage of their sins. Redemption we can sing of as an accomplished act: it has been wrought for us, sent to us, and enjoyed by us, and we are in very deed the Lord's redeemed. *"He hath commanded his covenant for ever."* His divine decree has made the covenant of his grace a settled and eternal institution: redemption by blood proves that the covenant cannot be altered, for it ratifies and establishes it beyond all recall. This, too, is reason for the loudest praise. Redemption is a fit theme for the heartiest music, and when it is seen to be connected with gracious engagements from which the Lord's truth cannot swerve, it becomes a subject fitted to arouse the soul to an ecstacy of gratitude. Redemption and the covenant are enough to make the tongue of the dumb sing. *"Holy and reverend is his name."* Well may he say this. The whole name or character of God is worthy of profoundest awe, for it is perfect and complete, whole or holy. It ought not to be spoken without solemn thought, and never heard without profound homage. His name is to be trembled at, it is something terrible; even those who know him best rejoice with trembling before him. How good men can endure to be called " reverend " we know not. Being unable to discover any reason why our fellow-men should reverence *us*, we half suspect that in other men there is not very much which can entitle them to be called reverend, very reverend, right reverend, and so on. It may seem a trifling matter, but for that very reason we would urge that the foolish custom should be allowed to fall into disuse.

10 The fear of the LORD *is* the beginning of wisdom: a good understanding have all they that do *his commandments*: his praise endureth for ever.

10. *"The fear of the LORD is the beginning of wisdom."* It is its first principle, but it is also its head and chief attainment. The word " beginning " in Scripture sometimes means the chief; and true religion is at once the first element of wisdom, and its chief fruit. To know God so as to walk aright before him is the greatest of

all the applied sciences. Holy reverence of God leads us to praise him, and this is the point which the psalm drives at, for it is a wise act on the part of a creature towards his Creator. *"A good understanding have all they that do his commandments."* Obedience to God proves that our judgment is sound. Why should he not be obeyed? Does not reason itself claim obedience for the Lord of all? Only a man void of understanding will ever justify rebellion against the holy God. Practical godliness is the test of wisdom. Men may know and be very orthodox, they may talk and be very eloquent, they may speculate and be very profound; but the best proof of their intelligence must be found in their actually doing the will of the Lord. The former part of the Psalm taught us the doctrine of God's nature and character, by describing his works: the second part supplies the practical lesson by drawing the inference that to worship and obey him is the dictate of true wisdom. We joyfully own that it is so. *"His praise endureth for ever."* The praises of God will never cease, because his works will always excite adoration, and it will always be the wisdom of men to extol their glorious Lord. Some regard this sentence as referring to those who fear the Lord—their praise shall endure for ever: and, indeed, it is true that those who lead obedient lives shall obtain honour of the Lord, and commendations which will abide for ever. A word of approbation from the mouth of God will be a mede of honour which will outshine all the decorations which kings and emperors can bestow.

Lord, help us to study thy works, and henceforth to breathe out hallelujahs as long as we live.

EXPLANATORY NOTES AND QUAINT SAYINGS.

Whole Psalm.—This is the first alphabetical Psalm which is regular throughout. The four former alphabetical Psalms, namely, ix. and x., xxxiv. and xxxvii., are irregular and defective in many particulars, for the rectification of which neither Hebrew MS. editions nor ancient versions afford sanction and authority. It is singular that not only are Psalms cxi. and cxii. perfectly regular, but, furthermore, that not one various reading of note or importance occurs in either of these Psalms.—*John Noble Coleman.*

Whole Psalm.—The following translation is given to enable the reader to realize the alphabetical character of the Psalm. It is taken from " The Psalms Chronologically Arranged. By Four Friends."

All my heart shall praise Jehovah,	1
Before the congregation of the righteous;	
Deeds of goodness are the deeds of Jehovah,	2
Earnestly desired of all them that have pleasure therein;	
For his righteousness endureth for ever,	3
Glorious and honourable is his work;	
He hath made his wonderful works to be remembered,	4
In Jehovah is compassion and goodness;	
Jehovah hath given meat to them that fear him,	5
Keeping his covenant for ever,	
Learning his people the power of his works,	6
Making them to possess the heritage of the heathen;	
Nought save truth and equity are the works of his hands,	7
Ordered and sure are his commands,	
Planted fast for ever and ever,	8
Righteous and true are his testimonies;	
Salvation hath he sent unto his people,	9
Their covenant hath he made fast for ever;	
Upright and holy is his name,	10
Verily, the fear of the Lord is the beginning of wisdom,	
Yea, a good understanding have all they that do thereafter;	
Zealously shall he be praised for ever.	

Whole Psalm.—The general opinion of interpreters is, that this and some of the following Psalms were usually sung at the eating of the Paschal lamb, of which custom mention is also made, Matt. xxvi., tnat Christ and the disciples sang a hymn before they went out into the garden.—*Solomon Gesner*.

Whole Psalm.—The two Psalms, cxi. and cxii., resemble one another in construction, alphabetical arrangement, and general tone and manner. They are connected in this way : Ps. cxi. sets forth the greatness, mercy, and righteousness of God : Ps. cxii. the reflection of these attributes in the greatness, ver. 2, mercy, ver. 5, and righteousness, ver. 4, 9, of his chosen. The correspondence of purpose in the two Psalms is important to the right appreciation of some difficulties connected with the latter Psalm.—*Speaker's Commentary*.

Whole Psalm.—The scope of this Psalm is to stir up all to praise God, and that for so many reasons as there are verses in the Psalm. The exhortation is in the first words, *"Praise ye the Lord."* The reasons follow in order. The Psalm is composed so after the order of the Hebrew alphabet, as every sentence or half verse beginneth with a several letter of the A B C in order, and all the Psalm is of praise only. Whence we learn in general, 1. Sometimes it is expedient to set all other things apart, and employ ourselves expressly to proclaim the praises of the Lord only ; for so is done in this Psalm. 2. The praises of the Lord are able to fill all the letters and words composed of letters, in all their possible junctures of composition ; for so much doth the going through all the letters of the A B C point out unto us, he is Alpha and Omega, and all the middle letters of the A B C of praise. 3. The praises of the Lord are worthy to be kept in memory : for that this Psalm may be the better remembered, it is composed after the manner of the A B C, and so it insinuateth thus much to us.—*David Dickson*.

Verse 1.—*"Praise ye the* LORD*,"* etc. The exhortation is immediately succeeded by the expression of a firm resolve ; the Psalmist having commenced by urging the duty of gratitude upon others—*"Praise ye the Lord,"* forthwith announces his determination to act upon his own advice—*"I will praise the Lord with my whole heart."* Such a conjunction of ideas is fraught with several most important lessons. 1. It teaches us, very emphatically, that our preaching, if it is to carry weight and conviction, must be backed and exemplified by our conduct ; that we need never expect to persuade others by arguments which are too weak to influence ourselves. 2. Another inference is similarly suggested—that our own decision should be given without reference to the result of our appeal. The Psalmist did not wait to ascertain whether those whom he addressed would attend to his exhortation, but, before he could receive a reply, declared unhesitatingly the course he would himself adopt.— *W. T. Maudson, in a Sermon on Thanksgiving*, 1855.

Verse 1.—*"With my whole heart."* That is, earnestly, and with a sincere affection ; meaning also, that he would do it privately, and, as it were, within himself, as by the next words he noteth that he will do it openly.—*Thomas Wilcocks*.

Verse 1.—*"With my whole heart."* We see the stress here laid upon a whole heart, and the want of which is the great canker of all vital godliness. Men are ever attempting to unite what the word of God has declared to be incapable of union—the love of the world and of God—to give half their heart to the world, and the other half to God. Just see the energy, the entireness of every thought and feeling and effort which a man throws into a work in which he is deeply interested ; the very phrase we use to describe such an one is, that " he gives his whole mind to it." Attempt to persuade him to divert his energies and divide his time with some other pursuit, and he would wonder at the folly and the ignorance that could suggest such a method of success. " Just take a hint from Satan," says some one; " see how he plies his powers on the individual, as if there were but that one, and as if he had nothing else to do but to ruin that one soul." It was a holy resolution of the Psalmist that he would praise God ; and a wise one to add, *"with my whole heart."* And we have the result of this determination in the following verses of the Psalm.—*Barton Bouchier*.

Verse 1.—Two words are used, *"assembly"* and *"congregation."* The former implies a more private meeting of worshippers, the latter the more public. The former may apply to the family circle of those who were celebrating the passover, the latter to the public worship connected with the feast.—*W. Wilson*.

Verse 2.—*"The works of the* LORD *are great."* Their greatness is known from comparison with the works and powers of men, which, verily, die and perish quickly. We should, therefore, admire, fear, confide, obey.—*Martin Geier*.

Verse 2.—*"The works of the* LORD *are great,"* etc. Their greatness is equally manifest when we turn from the *immensity* to the *variety* of his works. . . . . How great are the works of him who gives to every plant its leaf and flower and fruit ; to every animal its faculties and functions ; to every man his understanding, affections, and will. What an accumulative idea of the magnitude of his works do we gather from the innumerable multitudes and endless diversities of being called into existence by his powers.—*Samuel Summers,* 1837.

Verse 2.—*"The works of the* LORD *are great."* The workman who never makes a small article, an inferior article, but makes all his articles both great and valuable, deserves much praise ; and any one that will study God's works, which we think so little of by reason of their being so constantly before us, cannot fail to behold God's infinite power and wisdom in every one of them, even though he cannot comprehend them.—*Robert Bellarmine.*

Verse 2.—*"Great."* The word גדול (gadol) *"great,"* has in the Hebrew so extensive a range of meaning, that in the English there is no single substitute expressive enough to take its place. It denotes greatness and augmentation of various kinds. In this passage " the works of Jehovah " are described as greatly *"magnified or augmented "* in their influences and effects on the minds of men who behold them. The *greatness* ascribed to these works, is a greatness in number, in character, in dignity, in beauty, in variety, in riches.—*Benjamin Weiss.*

Verses 2, 4.—*"Great . . . sought out."* *"Remembered."* The works of Jehovah surpass the reach of human discovery, but are yet searched and explored with delight by all the members of his church ; for if they are too great to be understood, they are also too great to be forgotten.—*Edward Garrard Marsh.*

Verse 2.—*"Sought out."* To see God in his creatures, and to love him and converse with him, was the employment of man in his upright state. This is so far from ceasing to be our duty, that it is the work of Christ, by faith, to bring us back to it ; and therefore the most holy men are the most excellent students of God's works ; and none but the holy can rightly study or know them. Your studies of physics and other sciences are not worth a rush, if it be not God by them that you seek after. To see and admire, to reverence and adore, to love and delight in God appearing to us in his works, and purposely to peruse them for the knowledge of God ; this is the true and only philosophy, and the contrary is mere foolery, and so called again and again by God himself.—*Richard Baxter,* 1615—1691.

Verse 2.—It does not follow, that because the study of nature is now of itself an insufficient guide to the knowledge of the Creator and the enjoyment of eternal felicity, such studies are either to be thrown aside, or considered as of no importance in a religious point of view. To overlook the astonishing scene of the universe, or to view it with indifference, is virtually to " disregard the works of Jehovah, and to refuse to consider the operations of his hands." It is a violation of Christian duty, and implies a reflection on the character of the Deity, for any one to imagine that he has nothing to do with God considered as manifested in the immensity of his works ; for his word is pointed and explicit in directing the mind to such contemplations. " Hearken unto this, stand still, and consider the wonderful works of God." " Lift up thine eye on high, and behold who hath created these orbs." " Remember that thou magnify his works which men behold." " Great and marvellous are thy works, Lord God Almighty ! Thy saints shall speak of the glory of thy kingdom and talk of thy power, to make known to the sons of men thy mighty operations and the glorious majesty of thy kingdom."—*Thomas Dick* (1772—) *in* "*The Sidereal Heavens."*

Verse 2.—*"Sought out of all them that have pleasure therein."* This is a true characteristic of the upright and pious. The works of God are said to be *"sought out of them,"* when they regard them, call them to mind, and carefully, taking them one by one, investigate them ; and at the same time explain them to others, and recount them : all which is included in the verb דרש ; for that verb, properly is *"trivit "* [to rub, beat, or bray] hence by thrashing and grinding he has *investigated* perfectly, and has *rubbed* out the *kernel of it* for the use and profit of another : whence it is used for *concionari,* etc.—*Hermann Venema.*

Verse 2.—*"Sought out,"* . . . . *" have pleasure therein."* Philosophy seeks truth, Theology finds it, but Religion possesses it. Human things must be known to be loved, but divine things must be loved to be known.—*Blaise Pascal,* 1623—1662.

Verses 2—4.—*"Sought out."* . . . *"The* LORD *is gracious and full of compassion."* This is the grand discovery of all the searching, and therein lies the glory that is the conclusion of all. As in searching into any experiments in nature, there is an infinite pleasure that accompanies such a study to them that are addicted thereunto ; so to him that hath pleasure in the works of God, and is addicted to spy out his kindness in them, there is nothing so pleasant as the discovery of new circumstances of mercy that render his work *"glorious and honourable."* Get, therefore, skill in his dealings with thee, and study thy friend's carriage to thee. It is the end why he raised thee up, and admitted thee into friendship with him, to show his art of love and friendship to thee ; to show, in a word, how well he could love thee.—*Thomas Goodwin.*

Verse 3.—"His work is honourable and glorious." The first thing that we notice is, that whereas the preceding verse spoke of the Lord's *"works"* in the *plural* number, this speaks of his *"work"* in the singular number ; it would seem as if the Psalmist, from the contemplation of the works of the Lord in general, was, as it were, irresistibly drawn away to the study of one work in particular ; his mind and whole attention, so to speak, absorbed in that one work : a work so pre-eminently glorious and divine, that it eclipses, at least in his eyes, all the other works, although he has just said of them that they are great, and sought out of all them that have pleasure therein. " The works of the Lord are great. His work is honourable and glorious." My next remark is, that the words used in the original are different, and as the former more strictly signifies *makings*, or *things made*, so the word in this verse more properly imports a *doing* or a *thing done*, and this, perhaps, is not without its significance. It leads me to the inference, that from the contemplation of the great works of creation, God's makings, wonderful, and interesting, and useful as they are, the spiritual mind of God's servant rapidly passes to some greater deed which the Lord hath done, some more marvellous act which he has accomplished, and which he designates as an honourable and a glorious deed. Now, since I consider that he spoke before of Christ, as the visible and immediate agent in creation, without whom was not anything made that was made, can we hesitate long as to this greater work, the rather as to it is immediately subjoined the suggestive sentence, " And his righteousness endureth for ever." Is not this doing, the making an end of sin, and the bringing in of an everlasting righteousness ? Is it not the great mystery, in which, as in creation, though the Eternal Father is the Fountain source, the Original Contriver, He, the co-eternal Son, is the Doer the Worker ? Is it not, in short, *salvation*, the all-absorbing subject of God's people's wonder, love, and praise ?—*James H. Vidal, in "Jesus, God and Man,"* 1863.

Verse 4.—"He hath made his wonderful works to be remembered." The *memorials* of the Divine benefits are always valued greatly by a grateful heart, as making present with us the things which transpired ages before : such under the Old Testament was the sacrament of the paschal Lamb ; but now the sacred Supper under the New Testament. Therefore, whatever recalls the Divine works to the *memory*, e.g. the *ministry of the church*, also the *Sacred Scriptures*, are worthy of the highest reverence.—*Martin Geier.*

*Verse 4.—*The sweet spices of divine works must be beaten to powder by meditation, and then laid up in the cabinet of our memories. Therefore, says the Psalmist here, *"God hath made his wonderful works to be remembered"*; he gives us the jewels of deliverance, not (because of the commonness of them) to wear them on our shoes, as the Romans did their pearls ; much less to tread them under our feet ; but rather to tie them as a chain about our necks. The impression of God's marvellous acts upon us must not be like that which the stone makes in the water, raising circles, beating one wave on another, and for a time making a noise, but soon after it sinks down, and the water returneth to its former smoothness ; and so we, while judgment is fresh, are apt to publish it from man to man, but soon after we let it sink into the depth of oblivion, and we return to our old sins.—*Abraham Wright.*

Verse 4.—"Made his wonderful works to be remembered." The most amazing perverseness in man is proven by the fact that he does not remember what God has so arranged that it would seem impossible that it should be forgotten.—*William S. Plumer.*

Verse 4.—

> For wonderful indeed are all his works,
> Pleasant to know and worthiest to be all
> Had in remembrance always with delight.

> —*John Milton.*

Verse 5.—The first hemistich is the consequence of what is stated in the second, *i.e., because* God remembered his covenant, *therefore* he gave food to them who fear him.—*George Phillips.*

Verse 5.—"*He hath given meat,*" etc. The "*meat*" here mentioned is supposed to respect the paschal lamb, when they were to remember the works of God.—*Thomas Manton.*

Verse 5.—"*Meat.*" Literally, *booty* or *spoil*: the *spoil* (Exod. xii. 36) brought by Israel out of Egypt, as God had engaged by "covenant" to Abraham, Gen. xv. 14, "They shall come out with great *substance*" (Kimchi). Rather the *manna* and *quails*, which to the hungry people were like a booty thrown in their way. The word is used for "*meat*" in general, in Prov. xxxi. 15 ; Mal. iii. 10.—*A. R. Fausset.*

Verse 5.—"*He hath given meat.*" I rather choose to render it *portion*, in which sense it is taken in Prov. xxx. 8, and xxxi. 15 ; as if he should say, that God has given his people all that was needful, and that, considered as a portion, it was large and liberal ; for we know that the people of Israel were enriched, not in consequence of their own industry, but by the blessing of God, who, like the father of a family, bestows upon his household everything necessary for their subsistence. In the following clause of the verse, he assigns as the reason for his care and kindness his desire of effectually demonstrating that his covenant was not null and void.—*John Calvin.*

Verse 5.—"*He will ever be mindful of his covenant.*" This clause would seem to be introduced parenthetically—a passing thought, a happy thought, presenting itself spontaneously to the Psalmist's mind, and immediately expressed with his lips. It will be observed it is in the future tense, while all the other clauses are in the past— "He *hath made* his wonderful works to be remembered" ; "He *hath given* meat unto them that fear him" ; "He *will ever be* mindful of his covenant" ; not *he hath ever been*. Dwelling on these past favours of God to Israel, it is his joy to think that they were but partial fulfilments of a covenant promise, which still remained, and in its highest sense should remain for ever ; and that covenant itself the memorial or type of the better, the spiritual covenant, the gospel. So out of the abundance of the heart his mouth speaketh, and he celebrates God's promised truth to Israel as the memorial and pledge of his eternal faithfulness to the New Testament Israel, his blood-ransomed church.—*James H. Vidal.*

Verse 6.—"*He hath shewed his people,*" etc. The Prophet indicates the unbelief of the Jews, who murmured against God in the desert, as if he could not enable them to enter into the promised land, and possess it, because the cities were walled, and the inhabitants strong, and giants dwelt in it. "*He shewed,*" he says, *i.e.*, he placed before their eyes, "*the power of His works,*" when he gave the lands of the heathen to be inhabited by his own people.—*Wolfgang Musculus.*

Verse 6.—"*He hath shewed his people the power of his works.*" So he hath showed his works of power to his people in Gospel times, as the miracles of Christ, his resurrection from the dead, redemption by him, and the work of grace on the hearts of men in all ages.—*John Gill.*

Verse 6.—"*He hath shewed his people,*" etc. To them it is given to see, but not to others who are delivered up to a judicial blindness. "Call unto me, and I will answer thee, and show thee great and mighty things, which thou knowest not." Jer. xxxiii. 3.—*John Trapp.*

Verse 6.—"*To give them the heritage of the heathen.*" The heathen themselves are bequeathed to God's people, and they must take possession of this inheritance to draw them to themselves.—*Richter, in Lange's Commentary.*

Verse 7.—The works of God expound his word, in his works his word is often made visible. That is an excellent expression, "*The works of his hands are verity and judgment.*" *The acts of God are verity*, that is, God acts his own truths. As the works of our hands ought to be the verity and judgments of God, (every action of a Christian ought to be one of Christ's truths), so it is with God himself ; the works of his hands are his own verity and judgments. When we cannot find the meaning of God in his word, we may find it in his works : his works are a comment an infallible comment upon his word.—*Joseph Caryl.*

Verses 7, 8.—God is known to be faithful and just both in his works and in his word, insomuch that the most beautiful harmony is apparent between the things he has spoken and those he has done. This wonderfully confirms the hope and faith of the godly.—*Mollerus.*

Verse 8.—*"They stand fast for ever and ever."* סְמוּכִים, *semuchim,* they are *propped up, buttressed for ever.* They can never fail ; for God's power supports his works, and his providence preserves the record of what he has done.—*Adam Clarke.*

Verse 8.—*"They stand fast,"* are established, *"for ever and ever,"* etc. This verse seems to have reference to the works of God mentioned in the former. His doings were not the demand of an occasion, they were in unison with a great and extensive purpose, with respect to the people of Israel and the Messiah. Not one jot or tittle shall pass from the law of his mouth, till all be fulfilled.—*W. Wilson.*

Verse 8.—*"They are done in truth."* It is impossible that any better way should be directed, than that which the Lord useth in the disposal of all things here below, for all the works of the Lord are done in truth. As the word of God is a word of truth, so all his works are works of truth ; for his works are nothing else but the making good of his word, and they are answerable to a threefold word of his. First, to his word of *prophecy.* Whatsoever changes God makes in the world, they hit some word of prophecy. Secondly, the works of God are answerable to his word for *threatening.* God threatens before he smites, and he never smote any man with a rod or sword, but according to his threatening. Thirdly, the works of God are answerable to his word of *promise.* All mercies are promised, and every work of mercy is the fulfilling of some promise. Now seeing all the works of God are reducible, either to prophecies, threatenings, or promises ; they *"are done in truth"* ; and what can be better done than that which is done in truth ? The Jewish doctors observe, that the word *emeth* here used for truth, consists of *aleph,* the first letter of the alphabet, *mem,* the middle letter thereof, and *tau,* the last ; to shew, that as God is *alpha* and *omega,* so the truth of God is the all in all of our comfort. Grace and truth by Christ is the sum of all the good news in the world.—*Abraham Wright.*

Verse 8.—*"Are done."* Verses 7 and 8 contain a precious meaning for the soul whose rest is the finished work of Christ. Jehovah has commanded, giving it in trust to Jesus to make sure, in perfect obedience, the word of truth and holiness. The commandment therefore has been *"done."* It has been done *"in truth and uprightness"* by him whose meat it was to do it ; who willingly received it with a knowledge of its end, and in whose accomplishment of it the believing sinner finds his assurance and eternal peace. John xii. 50. Jesus held the law within his heart, to keep it there for ever. As the fulfiller in truth of the commandment, he has become its end for righteousness to every believer in his name.—*Arthur Pridham.*

Verse 9.—*"He sent redemption to his people."* Once out of Egypt, ever out of Satan's thraldom.—*John Trapp.*

Verse 9.—*"Sent redemption"* . . . . *"commanded his covenant."* The deliverance was the more thankworthy, as being upon a covenant account ; for thus every mercy is a token of the Lord's favour to his favourite : it is this which makes common mercies to become special mercies. Carnal men, so that they enjoy mercies, they mind not which way they come in, so as they can but have them ; but a child of God knows that everything that comes through the Redeemer's hands and by his covenant is the better for it, and tastes the sweeter by far.—*William Cooper, in the Morning Exercises.*

Verse 9.—*"Redemption."* Praise our Triune Jehovah for his redemption. Write it down where you may read it. Affix it where you may see it. Engrave it on your heart that you may understand it. It is a word big with importance. In it is enfolded *your* destinies and those of the Church, to all future ages. There are heights in it you never can have scaled, and depths you never can have fathomed. You have never taken the wings of the morning, and gained the utmost parts of earth, to measure the length and breadth of it. Wear it as a seal on your arm, as a signet on your right hand, for Jesus is the author of it. O ! prize it as a precious stone, more precious than rubies. . . . Let it express your best hopes while living, and dwell on your trembling lips in the moment of dissolution ; for it shall form the chorus of the song of the redeemed throughout eternity.—*Isaac Saunders,* 1818.

Verse 9.—*"He hath commanded his covenant for ever."* As he covenanted, so he looketh that his covenants should be respected, which are as binding to us, as his covenant is to him ; and, through grace, his covenant is as binding to him, as those are to us.—*John Trapp.*

Verse 9.—*"Holy and reverend, or, terrible, is his name."* " Holy is his name," and therefore *"terrible "* to those who, under all the means of grace, continue unholy. —*George Horne.*

Verse 9.—*"Holy and reverend is his name."* Which therefore we should not presume on a sudden to blurt out. The Jews would not pronounce it. The Grecians (as Suidas observeth), when they would swear by their Jupiter, forbare to mention him. This should act as a check to the profaneness common amongst us. Let those that would have their *name reverend*, labour to be *holy* as God is holy.—*John Trapp.*

Verse 10 (*first clause*).—In this passage *"fear "* is not to be understood as referring to the first or elementary principles of piety, as in 1 John iv. 18, but is comprehensive of all true godliness, or the worship of God.—*John Calvin.*

Verse 10.—*"The fear of the LORD is the beginning of wisdom,"* etc. The text shows us the first step to true wisdom, and the test of common sense. It is so frequently repeated, that it may pass for a Scripture maxim, and we may be sure it is of singular importance. Job starts the question, " Where shall wisdom be found ? and where is the place of understanding ? " He searches nature through in quest of it, but cannot find it : he cannot purchase it with the gold of Ophir, and its price is above rubies. At length he recollects the primitive instruction of God to man, and there he finds it : " To man he said, Behold, the fear of the Lord, that is wisdom ; and to depart from evil is understanding."—Job xxviii. 28. Solomon, the wisest of men, begins his Proverbs with this maxim, " The fear of the LORD is the beginning of knowledge," Prov. i. 7. And he repeats it again : " The fear of the LORD is the beginning of wisdom ; and the knowledge of the holy," (the knowledge of those that may be called *saints* with a sneer), " is understanding," Prov. ix. 10. *"The fear of the LORD "* in Scripture signifies not only that pious passion or filial reverence of our adorable Father who is in heaven, but it is frequently put for the whole of practical religion ; hence it is explained in the last part of the verse by *"doing his commandments."* The fear of the Lord, in this latitude, implies all the graces and all the virtues of Christianity ; in short, all that holiness of heart and life which is necessary to the enjoyment of everlasting happiness. So that the sense of the text is this : To practise religion and virtue, to take that way which leads to everlasting happiness, is *wisdom*, true wisdom, the *beginning* of wisdom, the first step towards it : unless you begin here you can never attain it ; all your wisdom without this does not deserve the name ; it is madness and nonsense. *"To do his commandments "* is the best test of a *"good understanding "* : a *"good "* sound *"understanding "* have *"all they "* that do this, *"all "* of them without exception : however weak some of them may be in other things, they are wise in the most important respect ; but without this, however cunning they are in other things, they have lost their understandings ; they contradict common sense ; they are beside themselves. In short, to pursue everlasting happiness as the end, in the way of holiness as the mean, this is *"wisdom,"* this is common sense, and there can be none without this.—*Samuel Davies, A.M.* (1724—1761) *President of Princeton College, New Jersey.*

Verse 10.—*"The fear of the LORD is the beginning of wisdom."* Now, then, I demand of the worldling what is the most high and deep point of wisdom ? Is it to get an opulent fortune, to be *so wise as fifty thousand pounds ?* Behold, " godliness is great gain," saith Paul, and the Christian only rich, quoth the renowned catechist [Clement] of Alexandria. Is it to live joyfully, (or to use the gallant's phrase) jovially ? Behold, there is joyful gladness for such as are true hearted, Ps. xcvii. 11. A wicked man in his mad-merry humour for a while may be *Pomponius Lætus*, but a good man only is *Hilarius ;* only he which is faithful in heart is joyful in heart. Is it to get honour ? *the praise of God's fear* (saith our text) *endures for ever.* Many worthies of the world are most unhappy, because they be commended where they be not, and tormented where they be ; hell rings of their pains, earth of their praise ; but " blessed is the man that feareth the Lord " (Ps. cxii. 1), for his commendation is both here lasting, and hereafter everlasting ; in this world he is renowned among men, in the next he shall be rewarded amongst saints and angels in the kingdom of glory.—*John Boys.*

Verse 10.—*"The fear of the LORD is the beginning of wisdom."* It is not only the

beginning of wisdom, but the middle and the end.   It is indeed the Alpha and
Omega, the essence, the body and the soul, the sum and substance.   He that hath
the fear of God is truly wise. . . .   It is surely wisdom to love that which is most
lovable, and to occupy our hearts with that which is most worthy of our attachment,
and the most capable of satisfying us.—*From the French of Daniel de Superville,*
1700.

Verse 10 (*first clause*).—Fear is not all then ; no, for it is but the beginning.
God will have us begin, but not end there.   We have begun with *qui timet Eum,*
" who fears him ; " we must end with *et operatur juslitiam,* " and does justice," and
then comes *acceptus est Illi,* and not before.   For neither fear, if it be fear alone ;
nor faith, if it be faith alone, is accepted of Him.   If it be true fear, if such as God
will accept, it is not *timor piger,* " a dull lazy fear " ; his fear that feared his lord and
" went and digged his talent into the ground," and did nothing with it.   Away with
his fear and him " into outer darkness."—*Lancelot Andrewes.*

Verse 10.—Can it then be said that the non-religious world is without wisdom ?
Has it no Aristotle, no Socrates, no Tacitus, no Goethe, no Gibbon ?   Let us understand what wisdom is.   It is not any mere amount of knowledge that constitutes
wisdom.   Appropriate knowledge is essential to wisdom.   A man who has not the
knowledge appropriate to his position, who does not know himself in his relation
to God and to his fellow-men, who is misinformed as to his duties, his dangers, his
necessities, though he may have written innumerable works of a most exalted
character, yet is he to be set down as a man without wisdom.   What is it to you
that your servant is acquainted with mathematics, if he is ignorant of your will,
and of the way to do it ?   The genius of a Voltaire, a Spinoza, a Byron, only makes
their folly the more striking.   As though a man floating rapidly onwards to the
falls of Niagara, should occupy himself in drawing a very admirable picture of the
scenery.   Men who are exceedingly great in the world's estimation have made the
most signal blunders with regard to the most important things ; and it is only
because these things are not considered important by the world, that the reputation
of these men remains.

If you have learned to estimate things in some measure as God estimates them,
to desire what he offers, to relinquish what he forbids, and to recognise the duties
that he has appointed you, you are in the path of wisdom, and the great men we
have been speaking about are far behind you—far from the narrow gate which you
have entered.   He only is wise, who can call Christ the wisdom of God.—*George
Bowen.*

Verse 10.—"*The beginning of wisdom.*"   That is, the principle whence it springs,
and the fountain from which it flows.—*William Walford.*

Verse 10.—As there are degrees of wisdom, so of the fear of the Lord ; but there
is no degree of this fear so inferior or low, but it is a beginning, at least, of wisdom ;
and there is no degree of wisdom so high or perfect, but it hath its root in, or beginning, from this fear.—*Joseph Caryl.*

Verse 10.—"*Beginning of wisdom.*"   The word translated *beginning* is of uncertain
sense.   It may signify the *first* in *time* only, and so the rudiments, first foundation,
or groundwork, and so though the most necessary, yet the most imperfect part of
the work.   And if it should thus be understood here and in other places, the sense
would be no more but this, that there were no true *wisdom,* which had not its foundation in piety and fear of God.   But the word signifies the *first* in *dignity* as well as
in order of time, and is frequently used for the chief or principal of any kind. . . .
And thus it is to be understood here, that "*the fear of the Lord*" (which signifies all
piety) *is the principal or chief of wisdom,* as *sapientia prima* in Horace is the *principal*
or most excellent wisdom ; according to that of Job xxviii. 28 : " Unto man he
said, Behold, the fear of the Lord, that is wisdom ; and to depart from evil is understanding," *that,* by way of eminence, the most excellent *wisdom* and understanding.—
Henry Hammond.

Verse 10.—"*A good understanding have all they that do his commandments.*"   They
which *do* the commandments have a good understanding ; not they which speak
of the commandments, nor they which write of the commandments, nor they which
preach of the commandments, but they which do the commandments, have a good
understanding.   The rest have a false understanding, a vain understanding, an
understanding like that of the scribes and pharisees, which was enough to condemn
them, but not to save them.—*Henry Smith.*

Verse 10.—"*A good understanding have all they that do,*" etc.   So much a man knoweth in true account, as he doth ; hence understanding is here ascribed to the will ; so Job xxviii. 28. Some render it *good success.—John Trapp.*

Verse 10 (last clause).—*"The praise of it endures for ever" ;* or as other translations, *"his praise" ;* referring it either to God, or else to the man who fears God. Some divines ascribe this praise to God alone, because *tehilla* properly signifieth only that kind of praise which is due to God ; and so they make this clause to contain both a precept and a promise. *Precept,* exhorting us to praise God with all our heart, both in the secret assemblies of the faithful and in the public congregation. And lest any man in executing this office should be discouraged, the prophet addeth a promise, " God's praise doth endure for ever " ; as if he should have said, " The Lord is King, be the people never so impatient ; the Lord is God, albeit the Gentiles furiously rage together, and the Jews imagine a vain thing ; the kings of the earth stand up, and the rulers combine themselves against him," Ps. xcix. 1 ; xviii. 31 ; ii. 1. He that dwelleth in heaven hath all his enemies in derision, and makes them all his footstool ; his power is for ever, and so consequently his praise shall endure for ever ; in the militant church, unto the world's end ; in the triumphant, world without end.

Most interpreters have referred this unto the good man who fears the Lord, yet diversely. S. Augustine expoundeth it thus, *"his praise,"* that is, his praising of the Lord, *"shall endure for ever,"* because he shall be one of them of whom it is said (Ps. lxxxiv. 4) " Blessed are they that dwell in thy house : they will be still praising thee." Others understand by *"his praise"* the commendation of the good man, both in the life present and in that which is to come, for his righteousness shall be had in an everlasting remembrance. Ps. cxii. 6.—*John Boys.*

Verse 10 (second clause).—Where the fear of the Lord rules in the heart, there will be a constant conscientious care to keep his commandments : not to talk them, but to do them ; and such *"have a good understanding,"* i.e., First, They are well understood, their obedience is graciously accepted as a plain indication of their mind, that they do indeed fear God. Secondly, They understand well. 1. It is a sign they do understand well : the most obedient are accepted as the most intelligent. They are wise that make God's law their rule, and are in everything ruled by it. 2. It is the way to understand better. " A good understanding are they to all that do them " ; *i.e.,* the fear of the Lord, and the laws of God give men a good understanding, and are able to make them wise unto salvation.—*Condensed from Matthew Henry.*

HINTS TO PREACHERS.

Verse 1.—*"Praise ye the Lord" ;* there is an exhortation. *"I will praise the Lord ; "* there is a vow. It shall be *"with my whole heart" ;* there is experimental godliness. It shall be *"in the assembly of the upright" ;* there is a relative position occupied along with the family of God.—*Joseph Irons.*

Verse 1.—*"With my whole heart."* This includes spirituality, simplicity, and earnestness.—*Joseph Irons.*

Verse 1.—I. Who are the upright ? II. What are they doing ? Praising God. III. What shall I do if I am favoured to stand among them ? " I will praise the Lord."

Verse 1.—Where I love to be, and what I love to do.

Verse 2.—The Christian philosopher. I. His sphere : " The works of the Lord." II. His work : " Sought out." III. His qualification : " Pleasure therein." IV. His conclusion : " Praise," as in verse 1.

Verses 2—9.—The Psalmist furnishes us with matter for praise from the works of God. 1. The greatness of his works and the glory of them. 2. The righteousness of them. 3. The goodness of them. 4. The power of them. 5. The conformity of them to his word of promise. 6. The perpetuity of them.—*Matthew Henry.*

Verse 3 (last clause).—As an essential attribute, as revealed in providence, as vindicated in redemption, as demonstrated in punishment, as appropriated by believers.

Verse 4.—The compassion of the Lord as seen in aiding the memories of his people.

Verses 4, 5.—God's marvels ought not to be nine-day wonders. I. *It is God's design that his wonders should be remembered,* therefore, 1. He made them great. 2. He wrought them for an undeserving people. 3. He wrought them at memorable times. 4. He put them on record. 5. He instituted memorials. 6. He bade them tell their children. 7. He so dealt with them as to refresh their memories. II. *It is our wisdom to remember the Lord's wonders.* 1. To assure us of his compassion : " The Lord is gracious." 2. To make us consider his bounty : " he hath given meat." 3. To certify us of his faithfulness : " he will ever be mindful of his covenant." 4. To arouse our praise : " Praise ye the Lord."

Verse 5.—There is, I. Encouragement from the past : " He hath given meat," etc. II. Confidence for the future : " He will ever be mindful," etc.—*G. R.*

Verse 6.—The power of God an encouragement for the evangelization of the heathen.

Verse 9.—*Redemption.* Conceived, arranged, executed, and applied by God. By price and by power. From sin and death. That we may be free, the Lord's own, the Lord's glory.

Verse 9.—*Redemption.* I. Its author : " He sent." II. Its objects : " Unto his people." III. The pledge it gives us : " He hath commanded his covenant," etc. IV. The praise it creates in us.

Verse 9.—*"Holy and reverend."* I. The holiness of God the object of our reverence. II. Such reverence has much useful influence over us. III. It should always accompany our faith in redemption and covenant. See preceding clauses of verse.

Verse 10.—I. The beginner in Christ's school. II. The man who has taken a degree : " a good understanding," etc. III. The Master who receives the praise.

Verse 10.—I. The beginning of wisdom : " the fear of the Lord "—God is feared. II. Its continuance : " a good understanding have all they that do his commandments "—when the fear of the Lord in the heart is developed in the life. III. Its end, praising God for ever : " his praise," etc.—*G. R.*

PSALM CXII.

TITLE AND SUBJECT.—*There is no title to this Psalm, but it is evidently a companion to the hundred and eleventh, and, like it, it is an alphabetical Psalm. Even in the number of verses, and clauses of each verse, it coincides with its predecessor, as also in many of its words and phrases. The reader should carefully compare the two Psalms line by line. The subject of the poem before us is*—the blessedness of the righteous man, *and so it bears the same relation to the preceding which the moon does to the sun ; for, while the first declares the glory of God, the second speaks of the reflection of the divine brightness in men born from above. God is here praised for the manifestation of his glory which is seen in his people, just as in the preceding Psalm he was magnified for his own personal acts. The hundred and eleventh speaks of the great Father, and this describes his children renewed after his image. The Psalm cannot be viewed as the extolling of man, for it commences with "Praise ye the Lord ; " and it is intended to give to God all the honour of his grace which is manifested in the sons of God.*

DIVISION.—*The subject is stated in the first verse, and enlarged upon under several heads from 2 to 9. The blessedness of the righteous is set forth by contrast with the fate of the ungodly in verse* 10.

EXPOSITION.

PRAISE ye the LORD. Blessed *is* the man *that* feareth the LORD, *that* delighteth greatly in his commandments.

1. "*Praise ye the LORD.*" This exhortation is never given too often ; the Lord always deserves praise, we ought always to render it, we are frequently forgetful of it, and it is always well to be stirred up to it. The exhortation is addressed to all thoughtful persons who observe the way and manner of life of men that fear the Lord. If there be any virtue, if there be any praise, the Lord should have all the glory of it, for we are his workmanship. "*Blessed is the man that feareth the Lord.*" According to the last verse of Psalm cxi., " the fear of the Lord is the beginning of wisdom " ; this man, therefore, has begun to be wise, and wisdom has brought him present happiness, and secured him eternal felicity. Jehovah is so great that he is to be feared and had in reverence of all them that are round about him, and he is at the same time so infinitely good that the fear is sweetened into filial love, and becomes a delightful emotion, by no means engendering bondage. There is a slavish fear which is accursed ; but that godly fear which leads to delight in the service of God is infinitely blessed. Jehovah is to be praised both for inspiring men with godly fear and for the blessedness which they enjoy in consequence thereof. We ought to bless God for blessing any man, and especially for setting the seal of his approbation upon the godly. His favour towards the God-fearing displays his character and encourages gracious feelings in others, therefore let him be praised. "*That delighteth greatly in his commandments.*" The man not only studies the divine precepts and endeavours to observe them, but rejoices to do so : holiness is his happiness, devotion is his delight, truth is his treasure. He rejoices in the precepts of godliness, yea, and delights *greatly* in them. We have known hypocrites rejoice in the doctrines, but never in the commandments. Ungodly men may in some measure obey the commandments out of fear, but only a gracious man will observe them with delight. Cheerful obedience is the only acceptable obedience ; he who obeys reluctantly is disobedient at heart, but he who takes pleasure in the command is truly loyal. If through divine grace we find ourselves described in these two sentences, let us give all the praise to God, for he hath wrought all our works in us, and the dispositions out of which they spring. Let self-righteous men praise themselves, but he who has been made righteous by grace renders all the praise to the Lord.

2 His seed shall be mighty upon earth : the generation of the upright shall be blessed

3 Wealth and riches *shall be* in his house : and his righteousness endureth for ever.

4 Unto the upright there ariseth light in the darkness : *he is* gracious and full of compassion, and righteous.

5 A good man sheweth favour, and lendeth : he will guide his affairs with discretion.

6 Surely he shall not be moved for ever : the righteous shall be in everlasting remembrance.

7 He shall not be afraid of evil tidings : his heart is fixed, trusting in the LORD.

8 His heart *is* established, he shall not be afraid, until he see *his desire* upon his enemies.

9 He hath dispersed, he hath given to the poor ; his righteousness endureth for ever ; his horn shall be exalted with honour.

2. *"His seed shall be mighty upon earth,"* that is to say, successive generations of God-fearing men shall be strong and influential in society, and in the latter days they shall have dominion. The true seed of the righteous are those who follow them in their virtues, even as believers are the seed of Abraham, because they imitate his faith ; and these are the real heroes of their era, the truly great men among the sons of Adam ; their lives are sublime, and their power upon their age is far greater than at first sight appears. If the promise must be regarded as alluding to natural seed, it must be understood as a general statement rather than a promise made to every individual, for the children of the godly are not all prosperous, nor all famous. Nevertheless, he who fears God, and leads a holy life, is, as a rule, doing the best he can for the future advancement of his house ; no inheritance is equal to that of an unblemished name, no legacy can excel the benediction of a saint ; and, taking matters for all in all, the children of the righteous man commence life with greater advantages than others, and are more likely to succeed in it, in the best and highest sense. *"The generation of the upright shall be blessed."* The race of sincere, devout, righteous men, is kept up from age to age, and ever abides under the blessing of God. The godly may be persecuted, but they shall not be forsaken ; the curses of men cannot deprive them of the blessing of God, for the words of Balaam are true, " He hath blessed, and I cannot reverse it." Their children also are under the special care of heaven, and as a rule it shall be found that they inherit the divine blessing. Honesty and integrity are better corner-stones for an honourable house than mere cunning and avarice, or even talent and push. To fear God and to walk uprightly is a higher nobility than blood or birth can bestow.

3. *"Wealth and riches shall be in his house."* Understood literally this is rather a promise of the old covenant than of the new, for many of the best of the people of God are very poor ; yet it has been found true that uprightness is the road to success, and, all other things being equal, the honest man is the rising man. Many are kept poor through knavery and profligacy ; but godliness hath the promise of the life that now is. If we understand the passage spiritually it is abundantly true. What wealth can equal that of the love of God ? What riches can rival a contented heart ? It matters nothing that the roof is thatched, and the floor is of cold stone : the heart which is cheered with the favour of heaven is " rich to all the intents of bliss." *"And his righteousness endureth for ever."* Often when gold comes in the gospel goes out ; but it is not so with the blessed man. Prosperity does not destroy the holiness of his life, or the humility of his heart. His character stands the test of examination, overcomes the temptations of wealth, survives the assaults of slander, outlives the afflictions of time, and endures the trial of the last great day. The righteousness of a true saint endureth for ever, because it springs from the same root as the righteousness of God, and is, indeed, the reflection of it. So long as the Lord abideth righteous he will maintain by his grace the righteousness of his people. They shall hold on their way, and wax stronger and stronger. There is also another righteousness which belongs to the Lord's chosen, which is sure to endure for ever, namely, the imputed righteousness of the Lord Jesus, which is called " everlasting righteousness," belonging as it does to the Son of God himself, who is " the Lord our righteousness."

4. *"Unto the upright there ariseth light in the darkness."* He does not lean to injustice in order to ease himself, but like a pillar stands erect, and he shall be found so standing when the ungodly, who are as a bowing wall and a tottering fence, shall lie in ruins. He will have his days of darkness, he may be sick and sorry, poor and pining, as well as others; his former riches may take to themselves wings and fly away, while even his righteousness may be cruelly suspected; thus the clouds may lower around him, but his gloom shall not last for ever, the Lord will bring him light in due season, for as surely as a good man's sun goes down it shall rise again. If the darkness be caused by depression of spirit, the Holy Ghost will comfort him; if by pecuniary loss or personal bereavement, the presence of Christ shall be his solace; and if by the cruelty and malignity of men, the sympathy of his Lord shall be his support. It is as ordinary for the righteous to be comforted as for the day to dawn. Wait for the light and it will surely come; for even if our heavenly Father should in our last hours put us to bed in the dark, we shall find it morning when we awake. *"He is gracious, and full of compassion, and righteous."* This is spoken of God in the fourth verse of the hundred and eleventh Psalm, and now the same words are used of his servant: thus we are taught that when God makes a man upright, he makes him like himself. We are at best but humble copies of the great original; still we are copies, and because we are so we praise the Lord, who hath created us anew in Christ Jesus. The upright man is " gracious," that is, full of kindness to all around him; he is not sour and churlish, but he is courteous to friends, kind to the needy, forgiving to the erring, and earnest for the good of all. He is also " full of compassion "; that is to say, he tenderly feels for others, pities them, and as far as he can assists them in their time of trouble. He does not need to be driven to benevolence, he is brimful of humanity; it is his joy to sympathize with the sorrowing. He is also said to be " righteous ": in all his transactions with his fellow men he obeys the dictates of right, and none can say that he goes beyond or defrauds his neighbour. His justice is, however, tempered with compassion, and seasoned with graciousness. Such men are to be found in our churches, and they are by no means so rare as the censorious imagine; but at the same time they are far scarcer than the breadth of profession might lead us to hope. Lord, make us all to possess these admirable qualities.

5. *"A good man sheweth favour, and lendeth."* Having passed beyond stern integrity into open-handed benevolence he looks kindly upon all around him, and finding himself in circumstances which enable him to spare a little of his wealth he lends judiciously where a loan will be of permanent service. Providence has made him able to lend, and grace makes him willing to lend. He is not a borrower, for God has lifted him above that necessity; neither is he a hoarder, for his new nature saves him from that temptation; but he wisely uses the talents committed to him. *"He will guide his affairs with discretion."* Those who neglect their worldly business must not plead religion as an excuse, for when a man is truly upright he exercises great care in managing his accounts, in order that he may remain so. It is sometimes hard to distinguish between indiscretion and dishonesty; carelessness in business may become almost as great an evil to others as actual knavery; a good man should not only *be* upright, but he should be so discreet that no one may have the slightest reason to suspect him of being otherwise. When the righteous man lends he exercises prudence, not risking his all, for fear he should not be able to lend again, and not lending so very little that the loan is of no service. He drives his affairs, and does not allow them to drive him; his accounts are straight and clear, his plans are wisely laid, and his modes of operation carefully selected. He is prudent, thrifty, economical, sensible, judicious, discreet. Men call him a fool for his religion, but they do not find him so when they come to deal with him. " The beginning of wisdom " has made him wise, the guidance of heaven has taught him to guide his affairs, and with half an eye one can see that he is a man of sound sense. Such persons greatly commend godliness. Alas, some professedly good men act as if they had taken leave of their senses; this is not religion, but stupidity. True religion is sanctified common sense. Attention to the things of heaven does not necessitate the neglect of the affairs of earth; on the contrary, he who has learned how to transact business with God ought to be best able to do business with men. The children of this world often are in their generation wiser than the children of light, but there is no reason why this proverb should continue to be true.

6. *"Surely he shall not be moved for ever."* God has rooted and established

him so that neither men nor devils shall sweep him from his place. His prosperity shall be permanent, and not like that of the gambler and the cheat, whose gains are evanescent : his reputation shall be bright and lustrous from year to year, for it is not a mere pretence ; his home shall be permanent, and he shall not need to wander from place to place as a bird that wanders from her nest ; and even his memory shall be abiding, for a good man is not soon forgotten, and *"the righteous shall be in everlasting remembrance."* They are of a most ancient family, and not mushrooms of an hour, and their grand old stock shall be found flourishing when all the proud houses of ungodly men shall have faded into nothing. The righteous are worth remembering, their actions are of the kind which record themselves, and God himself takes charge of their memorials. None of us likes the idea of being forgotten, and yet the only way to avoid it is to be righteous before God.

7. *"He shall not be afraid of evil tidings."* He shall have no dread that evil tidings will come, and he shall not be alarmed when they do come. Rumours and reports he despises ; prophecies of evil, vented by fanatical mouths, he ridicules ; actual and verified information of loss and distress he bears with equanimity, resigning everything into the hands of God. *"His heart is fixed, trusting in the Lord."* He is neither fickle nor cowardly ; when he is undecided as to his course he is still fixed in heart : he may change his plan, but not the purpose of his soul. His heart being fixed in solid reliance upon God, a change in his circumstances but slightly affects him ; faith has made him firm and steadfast, and therefore if the worst should come to the worst, he would remain quiet and patient, waiting for the salvation of God.

8. *"His heart is established."* His love to God is deep and true, his confidence in God is firm and unmoved ; his courage has a firm foundation, and is supported by omnipotence. He has become settled by experience, and confirmed by years. He is not a rolling stone, but a pillar in the house of the Lord. *"He shall not be afraid."* He is ready to face any adversary—a holy heart gives a brave face. *"Until he see his desire upon his enemies."* All through the conflict, even till he seizes the victory, he is devoid of fear. When the battle wavers, and the result seems doubtful, he nevertheless believes in God, and is a stranger to dismay. Grace makes him desire his enemies' good : though nature leads him to wish to see justice done to his cause, he does not desire for those who injure him anything by way of private revenge.

9. *"He hath dispersed, he hath given to the poor."* What he received, he distributed ; and distributed to those who most needed it. He was God's reservoir, and forth from his abundance flowed streams of liberality to supply the needy. If this be one of the marks of a man who feareth the Lord, there are some who are strangely destitute of it. They are great at gathering, but very slow at dispersing ; they enjoy the blessedness of receiving, but seldom taste the greater joy of giving. " It is more blessed to give than to receive "—perhaps they think that the blessing of receiving is enough for them. *"His righteousness endureth for ever."* His liberality has salted his righteousness, proved its reality, and secured its perpetuity. This is the second time that we have this remarkable sentence applied to the godly man, and it must be understood as resulting from the enduring mercy of the Lord. The character of a righteous man is not spasmodic, he is not generous by fits and starts, nor upright in a few points only ; his life is the result of principle, his actions flow from settled, sure, and fixed convictions, and therefore his integrity is maintained when others fail. He is not turned about by companions, nor affected by the customs of society ; he is resolute, determined, and immovable. *"His horn shall be exalted with honour."* God shall honour him, the universe of holy beings shall honour him, and even the wicked shall feel an unconscious reverence of him. Let it be observed, in summing up the qualities of the God-fearing man, that he is described not merely as righteous, but as one bearing the character to which Paul refers in the memorable verse, " For scarcely for a righteous man will one die : yet peradventure for *a good man* some would even dare to die." Kindness, benevolence, and generosity, are essential to the perfect character ; to be strictly just is not enough, for God is love, and we must love our neighbour as ourselves : to give every one his due is not sufficient, we must act upon those same principles of grace which reign in the heart of God. The promises of establishment and prosperity are not to churlish Nabals, nor to niggard Labans, but to bountiful souls who have proved their fitness to be stewards of the Lord by the right way in which they use

10 The wicked shall see *it*, and be grieved; he shall gnash with his teeth, and melt away: the desire of the wicked shall perish.

The tenth and last verse sets forth very forcibly the contrast between the righteous and the ungodly, thus making the blessedness of the godly appear all the more remarkable. Usally we see Ebal and Gerizim, the blessing and the curse, set the one over against the other, to invest both with the greater solemnity. " *The wicked shall see it, and be grieved.*" The ungodly shall first see the example of the saints to their own condemnation, and shall at last behold the happiness of the godly and to the increase of their eternal misery. The child of wrath shall be obliged to witness the blessedness of the righteous, though the sight shall make him gnaw his own heart. He shall fret and fume, lament and wax angry, but he shall not be able to prevent it, for God's blessing is sure and effectual. " *He shall gnash with his teeth.*" Being very wrathful, and exceedingly envious, he would fain grind the righteous between his teeth; but as he cannot do that, he grinds his teeth against each other. " *And melt away.*" The heat of his passion shall melt him like wax, and the sun of God's providence shall dissolve him like snow, and at the last the fire of divine vengeance shall consume him as the fat of rams. How horrible must that life be which like the snail melts as it proceeds, leaving a slimy trail behind. Those who are grieved at goodness deserve to be worn away by such an abominable sorrow. " *The desire of the wicked shall perish.*" He shall not achieve his purpose, he shall die a disappointed man. By wickedness he hoped to accomplish his purpose— that very wickedness shall be his defeat. While the righteous shall endure for ever, and their memory shall be always green; the ungodly man and his name shall rot from off the face of the earth. He desired to be the founder of a family, and to be remembered as some great one: he shall pass away and his name shall die with him. How wide is the gulf which separates the righteous from the wicked, and how different are the portions which the Lord deals out to them. O for grace to be blessed of the Lord! This will make us praise him with our whole heart.

EXPLANATORY NOTES AND QUAINT SAYINGS.

Whole Psalm.—The hundred and eleventh and the hundred and twelfth Psalms, two very short poems, dating apparently from the latest age of inspired psalmody, present such features of resemblance as to leave no doubt that they came from the same pen. In structure they are identical; and this superficial resemblance is designed to call attention to something deeper and more important. The subject of the one is the exact counterpart of the subject of the other. The first celebrates the character and works of *God;* the second, the character and felicity of *the godly man.*—*William Binnie.*

Whole Psalm.—Here are rehearsed the blessings which God is wont to bestow on the godly. And as in the previous Psalm the praises of God were directly celebrated, so in this Psalm they are indirectly declared by those gifts which are conspicuous in those who fear him.—*Solomon Gesner.*

Whole Psalm.— This Psalm is a banquet of heavenly wisdom; and as Basil speaketh of another part of Scripture, likening it to an apothecary's shop; so may this book of Psalms fitly be compared; in which are so many sundry sorts of medicines, that every man may have that which is convenient for his disease.— *T. S.,* 1621.

Whole Psalm.—The righteousness of the Mediator, I make no doubt, is celebrated in this Psalm; for surely that alone is worthy to be extolled in songs of praise: especially since we are taught by the Holy Ghost to say, " I will make mention of thy righteousness, even of thine only." I conclude, therefore, that in this alphabetical Psalm, for such is its construction, Christ is " the Alpha and the Omega." —*John Fry.*

Verse 1.—This Psalm is a praising of God for blessing the believer, and the whole Psalm doth prove that the believer is blessed: which proposition is set down in verse 1, and confirmed with as many reasons as there are verses following. Whence learn, 1. Albeit, in singing of certain Psalms, or parts thereof, there be nothing directly spoken of the Lord, or to the Lord, yet he is praised when his truth is our song, or when his works and doctrine are our song ; as here it is said, " *Praise ye the Lord.*" and then in the following verses the blessedness of the believer taketh up all the Psalm. 2. It is the Lord's praise that his servants are the only blessed people in the world. " *Praise ye the Lord.*" Why ? because " *Blessed is the man that feareth the Lord.*" 3. He is not the blessed man who is most observant to catch opportunities to have pleasure, profit, and worldly preferment, and careth not how he cometh by them : but he is the blessed man who is most observant of God's will, and careful to follow it.—*David Dickson.*

Verse 1.—" *Blessed is the man that feareth the Lord.*" It is not said simply, *Blessed is the man who fears :* for there is a fear which of itself produces misery and wretchedness rather than happiness. It has to do, therefore, chiefly with what is feared. To fear when it is not becoming, and not to fear when fear is proper, these are not blessedness for a man, but misery and wretchedness. The prophet, therefore, says rightly, " Blessed is the man that feareth *the Lord* " : and in the 7th and 8th verses he says of this blessed one that he shall not be afraid of evil tidings. Therefore, he who fears God and, according to the exhortation of Christ, does not fear those who can kill the body, he truly may be numbered among the blessed.— *Wolfgang Musculus.*

Verse 1.—" *Feareth the Lord.*" Filial fear is here intended. Whereby we are both restrained from evil, Prov. iii. 7 ; and incited unto well doing, Eccles. xii. 13 ; and whereof God alone is the author, Jer. xxxii. 39, 40 ; A duty required of every one, Ps. xxxiii. 8 ; Early, 1 Kings xviii. 12 ; Only, Luke xii. 5 ; Continually, Prov. xxiii. 17 ; With confidence, Ps. cxv. 11 ; With joyfulness, Ps. cxix. 74 ; With thankfulness, Rev. xix. 5.—*Thomas Wilson, in "A Complete Christian Dictionary,"* 1661.

Verse 1.—" *That delighteth greatly in his commandments.*" The Hebrew word רפֵח, *chaphets*, is rather emphatical, which is, as it were, to *take his pleasure*, and I have rendered it *to delight himself.* For the prophet makes a distinction between a willing and prompt endeavour to keep the law, and that which consists in mere servile and constrained obedience.—*John Calvin.*

Verse 1.—" *That delighteth greatly in his commandments*"—defining what constitutes the true " fear of the Lord," which was termed " the beginning of wisdom," Ps. cxi. 10. He who hath this true " fear " *delights* (Ps. cxi. 2) not merely in the theory, but in the practice of all " the Lord's commandments." Such fear, so far from being a " hard " service, is the only " blessed " one (Jer. xxxii. 39). Compare the Gospel commandments, 1 John iii., 23, 24 : v. 3. True obedience is not task-work, as formalists regard religion, but a " delight " (Ps. i. 2). Worldly delights, which made piety irksome, are supplanted by the new-born delight in and taste for the will and ways of God (Ps. xix. 7—10).—*A. R. Fausset.*

Verse 1.—" *In his commandments.*" When we cheerfully practise all that the Lord requireth of us, love sweeteneth all things, and it becomes our meat and drink to do his will. The thing commanded is excellent, but it is sweeter because commanded *by him*—" *his* commandments." A man is never thoroughly converted till he delighteth in God and his service, and his heart is overpowered by the sweetness of divine love. A slavish kind of religiousness, when we had rather not do than do our work, is no fruit of grace, and cannot evidence a sincere love.—*Thomas Manton.*

Verse 2.—" *His seed.*" If any one should desire to leave behind him a flourishing posterity, let him not think to accomplish it by accumulating heaps of gold and silver, and leaving them behind him ; but by rightly recognising God and serving Him ; and commending his children to the guardianship and protection of God.— *Mollerus.*

Verse 2.—" *The generation of the upright*"—the family ; the children—" *shall be blessed.*" Such promises are expected to be fulfilled *in general ;* it is not required by any proper rules of interpreting language that this should be universally and always true.—*Albert Barnes.*

Verse 2.—" *The generation of the upright shall be blessed.*" Albeit, few do believe it, yet is it true, that upright dealing hath better fruits than witty projecting and cunning catching.—*David Dickson.*

Verses 2, 3.—It is probable that Lot thought of enriching his family when he chose the fertile plains of wicked Sodom, yet the event was very different ; but Abraham " feared the Lord, and delighted greatly in his commandments," and his descendants were " *mighty upon earth.*" And thus it will generally be, in every age, with the posterity of those who imitate the father of the faithful ; and their disinterested and liberal conduct shall prove, in the event, a far preferable inheritance laid up for their children, than gold and silver, houses and lands, would have been.— *Thomas Scott.*

Verse 3.—" *Wealth and riches shall be in his house, and his righteousness endureth for ever.*" He is not the worse for his wealth, nor drawn aside by the deceitfulness of riches, which yet is hard and happy.—*John Trapp.*

Verse 3.—In the lower sense, we may read these words literally of abundant wealth bestowed on the righteous by God, and used, not for pride and luxury, but for continual works of mercy, whence it is said of the person so enriched, that " *his righteousness endureth for ever.*" But the higher meaning bids us see here those true spiritual riches which are stored up for the poor in spirit, often most needy in the prosperity of the world ; and we may come at the truest sense by comparing the words wherein the great apostle describes his own condition, " As poor, yet making many rich ; as having nothing, and yet possessing all things." 2 Cor. vi. 10. For who can be richer than he who is heir of God and joint heir with Jesus Christ ?—*Agellius, Chrysostom, and Didymus, in Neale and Littledale.*

Verse 3.—"*His righteousness endureth for ever.*" It seems a bold thing to say this of anything human, and yet it is true ; for all human righteousness has its root in the righteousness of God. It is not merely man striving to copy God. It is God's gift and God's work. There is a living connexion between the righteousness of God and the righteousness of man, and therefore the imperishableness of the one appertains to the other also. Hence the same thing is affirmed here of the human righteousness which in cxi. 3 is affirmed of the Divine.—*J. J. S. Perowne.*

Verse 3.—"*His righteousness endureth for ever.*" We are justified before God by faith only : Rom. iii. 4 : but they are righteous before men, who live honestly, piously, humbly, as the law of God requires. Concerning this righteousness the Psalmist says that *it endureth for ever*, while the feigned and simulated uprightness of hypocrites is abominable before God, and with men speedily passes away.— *Solomon Gesner.*

Verse 4.—"*Unto the upright there ariseth light in the darkness.*" The arising of light out of darkness, although one of the most common, is one of the most beautiful, as it is one of the most beneficent natural phenomena. The sunrise is a daily victory of light over darkness. Every morning the darkness flees away. Heavy sleepers in the city are not apt to be very well acquainted with the rising sun. They know the tender beauties of the dawning, and the glories of sunrise by poetical description, or by the word of others. The light has fully come, and the day has long begun its work, especially if it be summer time, before ordinary citizens are awake ; and, unless on some rare occasions, the millions of men who, every day, see more or less the fading of the light into the dark, never see the rising of the light out of the dark again ; and, perhaps, seldom or never think with what thankfulness and joy it is hailed by those who need it—by the sailor, tempest-tossed all night, and driven too near the sand-bank or the shore ; by the benighted traveller lost in the wood, or in the wild, who knows not south from north until the sun shall rise ; but the night watcher in the sick room, who hears, and weeps to hear, through the weary night, the moaning of that old refrain of sorrow, " Would God it were morning ! " What intensity of sorrow, fear, hope, there may be in that expression, " more than they that watch for the morning ; I say, more than they that watch for the morning " ! Now I make no doubt that there is at least somewhat of that intenser meaning carried up into the higher region of spiritual experience, and expressed by the text, " Unto the upright there ariseth light in the darkness." . . . Sincerity : an honest desire to know the truth : readiness to make any sacrifice in order to the knowledge : obedience to the truth so far as it is known already— these will bring the light *when nothing else will bring it.*—*Alexander Raleigh, in* "*The Little Sanctuary and other Meditations,*" 1872.

Verse 4.—"*Unto the upright there ariseth light in the darkness.*" The great lesson taught by this simile is the connection which obtains between integrity of purpose and clearness of perception, insomuch that a duteous conformity to what is right, is generally followed up by a ready and luminous discernment of what is true. It tells us that if we have but grace to *do* as we ought, we shall be made to *see* as we ought. It is a lesson repeatedly affirmed in Scripture, and that in various places both of the Old and New Testament : " The path of the just is as the shining light, that shineth more and more unto the perfect day " ; " The righteousness of the upright shall deliver them " ; " Light is sown for the righteous, and gladness for the upright in heart " ; or still more specifically, " To him that ordereth his conversation aright will I shew the salvation of God."—*Thomas Chalmers*, 1780—1847.

Verse 4.—"*Unto the upright there ariseth light in the darkness*" : that is, comfort in affliction. He hath comforted others in affliction, and been light to them in their darkness, as is showed in the latter end of the fourth verse, and in the fifth, and therefore by way of gracious retaliation, the Lord will comfort him in his affliction, and command the light to rise upon him in his darkness.—*Joseph Caryl.*

Verse 4.—"*Light.*" "*Darkness.*" While we are on earth, we are subject to a threefold "*darkness*"; the darkness of error, the darkness of sorrow, and the darkness of death. To dispel these, God visiteth us, by his Word, with a threefold "light"; the light of truth, the light of comfort, and the light of life.—*George Horne.*

Verse 4.—"*Gracious, and full of compassion, and righteous*"—attributes usually applied to *God*, but here said of "*the upright.*" The children of God, knowing in their own experience that God our Father is " gracious, full of compassion, and righteous," seek themselves to be the same towards their fellow men from instinctive imitation of him (Matt. v. 45, 48 ; Eph. v. 8 ; Luke vi. 36).—*A. R. Fausset.*

Verse 5.—"*A good man sheweth favour,*" etc. Consider that power to do good is a dangerous ability, unless we use it. Remember that it is God who giveth wealth, and that he expecteth some answerable return of it. Live not in such an inhuman manner as if Nabal and Judas were come again into the world. Think frequently and warmly of the love of God and Jesus to you. You will not deny your crumbs to the miserable, when you thankfully call to mind that Christ gave for you his very flesh and blood. Consider as one great end of poverty is patience, so one great end of wealth is charity. Think how honourable it is to make a present to the great King of the world ; and what a condescension it is in his all-sufficiency to do that good by us, which he could so abundantly do without us.—*Thomas Tenison*, 1636—1715.

Verse 5.—"*Lendeth.*" The original word here, לוה, *lavah*, means to join oneself to any one ; to cleave to him ; then to form the union which is constituted between debtor and creditor, borrower and lender. Here it is used in the latter sense, and it means that a good man will accommodate another—a neighbour—with money, or with articles to be used temporarily and returned again. A man who always *borrows* is not a desirable neighbour ; but a man who never lends—who never is willing to accommodate—is a neighbour that no one would wish to live near—a crooked, perverse, bad man. True religion will always dispose a man to do acts of kindness in any and every way possible.—*Albert Barnes.*

Verse 5.—Charity though it springs in the heart should be guided by the head, that it may spread itself abroad to the best advantage. "*He will guide his affairs with discretion,*" and no affairs are so properly the good man's own as the dispensation and stewardship of those blessings which God has entrusted him with, for "*it is required in stewards that a man be found faithful.*"—*Michael Cox*, 1748.

Verse 5.—"*He will guide his affairs with discretion.*" Just as a steward, servant, or agent in any secular concern has to feel that his *mind* is his master's, as well as his hands, and that his attention, thought, tact, and talent, should be vigorously and faithfully given to the interests of his employer ; so the Christian stewardship of money, demands on the part of God's servant, in respect to every form of its use and disposal, the exercise of reflexion ; a reference to conscience ; the recollection of responsibility to God ; attention to the appeals of humanity is addressed to the ear of justice and love. Everything is to be weighed as in the balance of the sanctuary ; a decision formed ; and then energy, skill schemes, and plans wisely constructed, prudential limitations or beneficent liberality as may seem best. Spending, saving, giving, or lending, all being done so as best to meet what may be felt to be the Master's will, and what may best evince at once the wisdom and the fidelity of his servant.—*Thomas Binney, in "Money : a Popular Exposition in Rough Notes,"* 1865.

Verse 5.—"Discretion." There is a story, concerning divers ancient Fathers, that they came to St. Anthony, enquiring of him, what virtue did by a direct line lead to perfection, that so a man might shun the snares of Satan. He bade every one of them speak his opinion ; one said, watching and sobriety ; another said, fasting and discipline ; a third said, humble prayer ; a fourth said, poverty and obedience ; and another, piety and works of mercy ; but when every one has spoken his mind, his answer was, That all these were excellent graces indeed, but discretion was the chief of them all. And so beyond doubt it is ; being the very *Auriga virtutum*, the guide of all virtuous and religious actions, the moderator and orderer of all the affections ; for whatsoever is done with it is virtue, and what without it is vice. An ounce of discretion is said to be worth a pound of learning. As zeal without knowledge is blind, so knowledge without discretion is lame, like a sword in a madman's hand, able to do much, apt to do nothing. *Tolle hanc et virtus vitium erit.* He that will fast must fast with discretion, he must so mortify that he does not kill his flesh ; he that gives alms to the poor, must do it with discretion, *Omni petenti non omnia petenti*—to every one that doth ask, but not everything that he doth ask ; so likewise pray with discretion, observing place and time ; place, lest he be reputed a hypocrite ; time, lest he be accounted a heretic. Thus it is that discretion is to be made the guide of all religious performances.—*Quoted by John Spencer, 1658.*

Verse 6.—What doth the text say ? *"The righteous* (that is the bountiful) *shall be in everlasting remembrance."* God remembers our good deeds, when he rewards them (as he does our prayers, when he hears them). If to remember, then, be to reward, an everlasting reward is our everlasting remembrance. . . . Now in those who are to be partakers of mercy, the divine wisdom requires this congruity, that they be such as have been ready to show mercy to others.—*Joseph Mede, 1586—1638.*

Verse 6.—"The righteous shall be in everlasting remembrance." The stately and durable pyramids of Egypt have not transmitted to posterity even the names of those buried in them. And what has even embalming done, but tossed them about, and exposed them to all the world as spectacles to the curious, of meanness, or horror ? But the piety of Abraham, of Jacob, of David and Samuel, of Hezekiah, Josiah and others, is celebrated to this very day. So when pyramids shall sink, and seas cease to roll, when sun and moon and stars shall be no more, *"the righteous shall be in everlasting remembrance."—John Dun, 1790.*

Verse 7.—"He shall not be afraid of evil tidings." How can you affright him ? Bring him word his estate is ruined ; " yet my inheritance is safe," says he. Your wife, or child, or dear friend is dead ; " yet my Father lives." You yourself must die ; " well, then, I go home to my Father, and to my inheritance."

For the public troubles of the Church, doubtless it is both a most pious and generous temper, to be more deeply affected for these than for all our private ones ; and to sympathise in the common calamities of any people, but especially of God's own people, hath been the character of men near unto him. Observe the pathetical strains of the prophet's bewailing, when he foretells the desolation even of foreign kingdoms, much more of the Lord's chosen people, still mindful of Sion, and mournful of her distresses. (Jer. ix. 1, and the whole Book of Lamentations.) Yet even in this, with much compassion, there is a calm in a believer's mind ; he finds amidst all hard news, yet still a fixed heart, trusting, satisfied in this, that deliverance shall come in due time, Ps. cii. 13, and that in those judgments that are inflicted, men shall be humbled and God exalted, Isaiah ii. 11, and v. 15, 16 ; and that in all tumults and changes, and subversion of states, still the throne of God is fixed, and with that the believer's heart likewise, Ps. xciii. 2. So Ps. xxix. 10.—*Robert Leighton.*

Verse 7.—"He shall not be afraid," etc. If a man would lead a happy life, let him but seek a sure object for his trust, and he shall be safe : *"He shall not be afraid of evil tidings : his heart is fixed, trusting in the Lord."* A man that puts his confidence in God, if he hears bad news of mischief coming towards him, as suppose a bad debt, a loss at sea, accidents by fire, tempests, or earthquakes, as Job had his messengers of evil tidings, which came thick and threefold upon him, yet he is not afraid, for his heart is fixed on God : he hath laid up his confidence in God, therefore his heart is kept in an equal poise ; he can say, as Job, " The Lord gave, and the Lord hath taken away ; blessed be the name of the Lord," Job i. 21. His comforts did not ebb and flow with the creature, but his heart was fixed, trusting in the Lord.—*Thomas Manton.*

Verse 7 (first clause).—The good man will not be alarmed by any report of danger, whilst the dishonest man, conscious of his wickedness, is always in a state of fear.—*George Phillips.*

Verse 7.—"*His heart is fixed*," or prepared, ready, and in arms for all services ; resolved not to give back, able to meet all adventures, and stand its ground. God is unchangeable ; and therefore faith is invincible, for it sets the heart on him ; fastens it there on the rock of eternity ; then let winds blow and storms arise, it cares not.—*Robert Leighton.*

Verse 7.—"*His heart is fixed*"—established fearlessly. So Moses, with the Red Sea before and the Egyptian foes behind (Exod. xiv. 13) ; Jehoshaphat before the Ammonite horde of invaders (2 Chron. xx. 12, 15, 17) ; Asa before Zerah, the Ethiopian's " thousand thousand, and three hundred chariots " (2 Chron. xiv. 9—12). Contrast with the persecuted David's fearless trust, Saul's panic-stricken feeling at the Philistine invasion, inasmuch as he repaired for help to a witch. How bold were the three youths in prospect of Nebuchadnezzar's fiery furnace ! How fearless Stephen before the council ! Basilius could say, in answer to the threats of Cæsar Valens, " such bug-bears should be set before children." Athanasius said of Julian, his persecutor, " He is a mist that will soon disappear."—*A. R. Fausset.*

Verse 7.—"*Trusting in the Lord*," I need not prove that a man can have no other sure comfort and support. For what can he confide in ? His *treasure* ? This may soon be exhausted, or it may awaken the avarice or ambition of a powerful enemy, as Hezekiah's did the king of Babylon, and so instead of being a defence, prove the occasion of his ruin. Can he confide in *power* ? Alas, he knows that when this is grown too big to fall by any other hands, it generally falls by its own. Can he finally confide in worldly *wisdom* ? Alas, a thousand unexpected accidents, and unobserved latent circumstances, cross and frustrate this, and render the Ahithophels not only unfortunate, but often contemptible too.—*Richard Lucas,* 1648—1715.

Verse 8.—"*His heart is established.*" Happy, surely, is the man whose heart is thus established. Others may be politic, he only is wise ; others may be fortunate, he only is great ; others may drink deeper draughts of sensual pleasure, he only can eat of the tree of life, which is in the midst of the paradise of God. He is an image of that great Being whom he trusts . . . . and in the midst of storms, and thunders, and earthquakes sits himself serene and undisturbed, bidding the prostrate world adore the Lord of the universe.—*George Gleig,* 1803.

Verse 8.—"*Until he see his desire upon his enemies.*" His faith will not fail, nor shrink, nor change, while one by one his enemies are brought to the knowledge of the truth and the love of Christ, and he shall see his heart's desire fulfilled upon them, even that they may be saved.—*Plain Commentary.*

Verse 8.—"*Until he see his desire upon his enemies.*" Or, according to the original, *Until he looks upon his oppressors ;* that is, till he behold them securely, and, as we say, confidently *looks in their faces ;* as being now no longer under their power, but being freed from their tyranny and oppression.—*Thomas Fenton.*

Verse 9.—When all the flashes of sensual pleasure are quite extinct, when all the flowers of secular glory are withered away ; when all earthly treasures are buried in darkness ; when this world, and all the fashion of it, are utterly vanished and gone, the bountiful man's state will be still firm and flourishing, and "*his righteousness shall endure for ever.*" "*His horn shall be exalted with honour.*" A horn is an emblem of *power ;* for it is the beast's strength, offensive and defensive : and of *plenty,* for it hath within it a capacity apt to contain what is put into it ; and of *sanctity,* for in it was put the holy oil, with which kings were consecrated ; and of *dignity,* both in consequence upon the reasons mentioned (as denoting might, and influence, and sacredness accompanying sovereign dignity) and because also it is an especial beauty and ornament to the creature which hath it ; so that this expression, "*his horn shall be exalted with honour,*" may be supposed to import that an abundance of high, and holy, of firm and solid honour shall attend upon the bountiful person. . . . God will thus exalt the bountiful man's horn even here in this world, and to an infinitely higher pitch he will advance it in a future state.—*Isaac Barrow,* 1630—1677.

Verse 9.—"*For ever.*" The Hebrew phrase in this text is not עוֹלָם, *in seculum,* which is sometimes used of a limited eternity, but עַד, *in eternum*, which seems more expressive of an endless duration, and is the very same phrase whereby the duration of God's righteousness is expressed in the foregoing Psalm at the third verse.— *William Berriman*, 1688—1749.

Verses 9, 10.—These words are an enlargement of the character, begun at the first verse, of the blessed man that feareth the Lord, that delighteth greatly in his commandments. The author closes that character with an amiable description of his charity, and so leaves on our minds a strong impression, that benevolence of heart when displayed in the benefaction of the hand is the surest mark and fairest accomplishment of a moral and religious mind; which, whether it rewards the worthy, or relieves the unworthy object, is the noblest imitation of the dealings of God with mankind. For he rewardeth the good if any can be called so but himself, (though the name *good* is but *God* spread out). He beareth even with the wicked and stretcheth out his hand to save even them.—*Michael Cox*.

Verse 10.—*"The wicked."* The word רָשָׁע, *the wicked*, is used emphatically, by the Jews, to denote him who neither gives to the poor himself, nor can endure to see other people give; while he who deserves but one part of this character is only said to have *an evil eye in regard of other people's substance, or in regard of his own*.—*Mishna*.

Verse 10.—*"The wicked shall see it and be grieved,"* etc.—The sight of Christ in glory with his saints, will, in an inexpressible manner torment the crucifiers of the one, and the persecutors of the other; as it will show them the hopes and wishes of their adversaries all granted to the full, and all their own " desires " and designs for ever at an end; it will excite envy which must prey upon itself, produce a grief which can admit of no comfort, give birth to a worm which can never die, and blow up those fires which nothing can quench.—*George Horne*.

Verse 10.—*"The wicked shall see it, and be grieved,"* etc. It is the property of the Devil, not to mistake the nature of virtue, and esteem it criminal, but to hate it for this reason, because it is good, and therefore most opposite to his designs. The wicked, as his proper emissaries, resemble him in this, and grieve to have the foulness of their vices made conspicuous by being placed near the light of virtuous example. . . . They may, like the giants of ancient fable, attempt a romantic war with heaven; but all their preparations for that purpose must recoil with double force upon themselves, and cover them with shame and confusion. . . . If such be the effect of their malice in the present life, that, instead of injuring those they rage against, it usually turns to their own vexation, how much more, when the scene shall open in the life to come. . . . They shall continue then to gnash their teeth (the wretched amusement of that cursed state) as well in grief and anguish for their own torments, as in rage and envy at the abundant honour which is done the saints.—*William Berriman*.

Verse 10.—*"The wicked shall see it, and be grieved"*; that is, he shall have secret indignation in himself to see matters go so; *"he shall gnash with his teeth, and melt away."* Gnashing of teeth is caused by vexing the heart; and therefore it follows, *" he melts away"*; which notes (melting is from the heart) an extreme heat within. The sense is very suitable to that of Eliphaz (Job v. 2) " wrath slayeth the foolish," or wrath makes him melt away, it melts his grease with chafing, as we say of a man furiously vexed. Hence that deplorable condition of the damned, who are cast out of the presence of God for ever, is described by " weeping, and wailing, and gnashing of teeth "; which imports not only pain, but extreme vexing at, or in themselves. These finally impenitent ones shall be slain for ever with their own wrath, as well as with the wrath of God.—*Joseph Caryl*.

Verse 10.—*"The wicked shall see it."* The Psalm which speaks of the blessedness of the saints also bears solemn testimony to the doom of the wicked. Cowper sings as if this verse was before his eyes.

> . . . The same word, that like the polished share
> Ploughs up the roots of a believer's care,
> Kills, too, the flow'ry weeds where'er they grow,
> That bind the sinner's Bacchanalian brow.
> Oh that unwelcome voice of heavenly love,
> Sad messenger of mercy from above,
> How does it grate upon his thankless ear,
> Crippling his pleasures with the cramp of fear·

His will and judgment at continual strife,
That civil war embitters all his life ;
In vain he points his pow'rs against the skies,
In vain he closes or averts his eyes ;
Truth will intrude.

Verse 10.—"*He shall gnash with his teeth.*" An enraged man snaps his teeth together, as if about to bite the object of his anger. Thus in the book *Rāmyanum*, the giant Rāvanan is described as in his fury gnashing together his " thirty-two teeth ! " Of angry men it is frequently said, " Look at the beast, how he gnashes his teeth ! " " *Go near that fellow !* not I, indeed ! he will only gnash his teeth."— *Joseph Roberts.*

Verse 10.—"*He shall gnash with his teeth, and melt away.*" The effect of envy, which consumes the envious. Thus the poet : " Envy is most hateful, but has some good in it, for it makes the eyes and the heart of the envious to pine away."— *John Le Clerc*, 1657—1736.

HINTS TO PREACHERS.

Verse 1.—"*Praise ye the LORD.*" I. Who should be praised ? Not man, self, wealth, etc., but God only. II. Who should praise him ? All men, but specially his people, the blessed ones described in this Psalm. III. Why should they do it ? For all the reasons mentioned in succeeding verses. IV. How should they do it ? Chiefly by leading such a life as is here described.

Verse 1 (*second clause*).—I. Fear of the Lord ; what it is. II. Its connection with the delight mentioned. III. The qualities in the commandments which excite delight in godfearing minds.

Verse 2.—The real might of the holy seed and their true blessedness.

Verse 3.—The riches of a Christian : content, peace, security, power in prayer, promises, providence, yea, God himself.

Verse 3.—The enduring character of true righteousness. 1. Based on eternal principles. 2. Growing out of an incorruptible seed. 3. Sustained by a faithful God. 4. United to the everliving Christ.

Verse 3.—Connection of the two clauses—How to be wealthy and righteous. Note the following verses, and show how liberality is needful if rich men would be righteous men.

Verse 4 (*whole verse*)—I. The upright have their dark times. II. They shall receive comfort. III. Their own character will secure this.

Verse 4 (*first clause*).—I. The character of the righteous : " upright," " gracious," etc. II. His privilege. 1. Light as well as darkness. 2. More light than darkness. 3. Light in darkness : inward light in the midst of surrounding darkness. Light seen above, when all is dark below. Even darkness itself becomes the harbinger of day.—*G. R.*

Verse 4 (*last clause*).—A Trinity of excellencies found in true Christians, in Christ, and in God : their union forms a perfect character when they are well balanced. Show how they are exemplified in daily life.

Verse 5.—I. A good man is benevolent, but a benevolent man is not always good. II. A good man is prudent, but a prudent man is not always a good man. There must first be goodness and then its fruits. " Make the tree good," etc.— *G. R.*

Verse 5.—"*Lending.*" I. It is to be done. II. It is to be done as a favour ; borrowing is seeking alms. III. It should be done very discreetly. Add to this a homily on borrowing and repaying.

Verse 6.—I. In this life the Christian is, 1, Steadfast ; 2, Calm ; 3, Unconquerable : and II. When this life is over his memory is, 1, Beloved ; 2, Influential ; 3, Perpetual.

Verse 6.—I. The character of the righteous is eternal : " surely," etc. II. His influence upon others is eternal : " shall be had," etc.—*G. R.*

Verse 7.—1. "*He shall not be afraid,*" etc. : peaceful. 2. "*His heart is fixed*" : restful. 3. "*Trusting in the Lord*" : trustful ; the cause of the former.

Verse 7.—I. The waves : " evil tidings." II. The steady ship : " he shall not be afraid." III. The anchor : " his heart is fixed, trusting." IV. The anchorage : " in the Lord."

Verse 8.—Heart establishment, the confidence which flows from it, the sight which shall be seen by him who possesses it.

Verse 8.—I. The security of the righteous : " his heart is established." II. His tranquillity : " he shall not be afraid ; " and, III. His expectancy : " until," etc. —*G. R.*

Verse 9.—Benevolence : its exercise in almsgiving, its preserving influence upon character, and the honour which it wins.

Verse 10.—I. What the wicked must see, and its effect upon them. II. What they shall never see (their desire), and the result of their disappointment.

PSALM CXIII.

TITLE AND SUBJECT.—*This Psalm is one of pure praise, and contains but little which requires exposition ; a warm heart full of admiring adoration of the Most High will best of all comprehend this sacred hymn. Its subject is the greatness and condescending goodness of the God of Israel, as exhibited in lifting up the needy from their low estate. It may fitly be sung by the church during a period of revival after it has long been minished and brought low. With this Psalm begins the Hallel, or Hallelujah of the Jews, which was sung at their solemn feasts : we will therefore call it* THE COMMENCEMENT OF THE HALLEL. *Dr. Edersheim tells us that the Talmud dwells upon the peculiar suitableness of the Hallel to the Passover, "since it not only recorded the goodness of God towards Israel, but especially their deliverance from Egypt, and therefore appropriately opened with 'Praise ye Jehovah, ye servants of Jehovah,'—and no longer servants of Pharaoh." Its allusions to the poor in the dust and the needy upon the dunghill are all in keeping with Israel in Egypt, and so also is the reference to the birth of numerous children where they were least expected.*

DIVISION.—*No division need be made in the exposition of this Psalm, except it be that which is suggested by the always instructive headings supplied by the excellent authors of our common version : an exhortation to praise God, for his excellency, 1—5 ; for his mercy, 6—9.*

EXPOSITION.

PRAISE ye the LORD. Praise, O ye servants of the LORD, praise the name of the LORD.

2 Blessed be the name of the LORD from this time forth and for evermore.

3 From the rising of the sun unto the going down of the same the LORD's name *is* to be praised.

4 The LORD *is* high above all nations, *and* his glory above the heavens.

5 Who *is* like unto the LORD our God, who dwelleth on high,

6 Who humbleth *himself* to behold *the things that are* in heaven, and in the earth !

7 He raiseth up the poor out of the dust, *and* lifteth the needy out of the dunghill ;

8 That he may set *him* with princes, *even* with the princes of his people.

9 He maketh the barren woman to keep house, *and to be* a joyful mother of children. Praise ye the LORD.

1. "*Praise ye the LORD,*" or Hallelujah, praise to JAH Jehovah. Praise is an essential offering at all the solemn feasts of the people of God. Prayer is the myrrh, and praise is the frankincense, and both of these must be presented unto the Lord. How can we pray for mercy for the future if we do not bless God for his love in the past ? The Lord hath wrought all good things for us, let us therefore adore him. All other praise is to be excluded, the entire devotion of the soul must be poured out unto Jehovah only. "*Praise, O ye servants of the LORD.*" Ye above all men, for ye are bound to do so by your calling and profession. If God's own servants do not praise him, who will ? Ye are a people near unto him, and should be heartiest in your loving gratitude. While they were slaves of Pharaoh, the Israelites uttered groans and sighs by reason of their hard bondage ; but now that they had become servants of the Lord, they were to express themselves in songs of joy. His service is perfect freedom, and those who fully enter into it discover in that service a thousand reasons for adoration. They are sure to praise God best who serve him best ; indeed, service is praise. "*Praise the name of the Lord*" : extol his revealed character, magnify every sacred attribute, exult in all his doings, and reverence the very name

by which he is called. The name of Jehovah is thrice used in this verse, and may by us who understand the doctrine of the Trinity in Unity be regarded as a thinly-veiled allusion to that holy mystery. Let Father, Son and Holy Spirit, all be praised as the one, only, living, and true God. The close following of the words, "Hallelu-jah, Hallelu, Hallelu," must have had a fine effect in the public services. Dr. Edersheim describes the temple service as responsive, and says " Every first line of a Psalm was repeated by the people, while to each of the others they responded by a 'Hallelu-Jah' or 'Praise ye the Lord' thus—

The Levites began : *'Hallelujah'* (Praise ye the Lord).
The people repeated : *'Hallelu Jah.'*
The Levites : ' Praise (*Hallelu*), O ye servants of Jehovah.'
The people responded : *'Hallelu Jah.'*
The Levites : ' Praise (*Hallelu*) the name of Jehovah.'
The people responded : *'Hallelu Jah.'* "

These were not vain repetitions, for the theme is one which we ought to dwell upon ; it should be deeply impressed upon the soul, and perseveringly kept prominent in the life.

2. *"Blessed be the name of the LORD."* While praising him aloud, the people were also to *bless* him in the silence of their hearts, wishing glory to his name, success to his cause, and triumph to his truth. By mentioning *the name*, the Psalmist would teach us to bless each of the attributes of the Most High, which are as it were the letters of his name ; not quarrelling with his justice or his severity, nor servilely dreading his power, but accepting him as we find him revealed in the inspired word and by his own acts, and loving him and praising him as such. We must not give the Lord a new name nor invent a new nature, for that would be the setting up of a false god. Every time we think of the God of Scripture we should bless him, and his august name should never be pronounced without joyful reverence. *"From this time forth."* If we have never praised him before, let us begin now. As the Passover stood at the beginning of the year it was well to commence the new year with blessing him who wrought deliverance for his people. Every solemn feast had its own happy associations, and might be regarded as a fresh starting-place for adoration. Are there not reasons why the reader should make the present day the opening of a year of praise ? When the Lord says, " From this time will I bless you," we ought to reply, " Blessed be the name of the Lord from this time forth."

"And for evermore" : eternally. The Psalmist could not have intended that the divine praise should cease at a future date however remote. " For evermore " in reference to the praise of God must signify endless duration : are we wrong in believing that it bears the same meaning when it refers to gloomier themes ? Can our hearts ever cease to praise the name of the Lord ? Can we imagine a period in which the praises of Israel shall no more surround the throne of the Divine Majesty ? Impossible. For ever, and more than " for ever," if more can be, let him be magnified.

3. *"From the rising of the sun unto the going down of the same the LORD's name is to be praised."* From early morn till eve the ceaseless hymn should rise unto Jehovah's throne, and from east to west over the whole round earth pure worship should be rendered unto his glory. So ought it to be ; and blessed be God, we are not without faith that so it shall be. We trust that ere the world's dread evening comes, the glorious name of the Lord will be proclaimed among all nations, and all people shall call him blessed. At the first proclamation of the gospel the name of the Lord was glorious throughout the whole earth ; shall it not be much more so ere the end shall be ? At any rate, this is the desire of our souls. Meanwhile, let us endeavour to sanctify every day with praise to God. At early dawn let us emulate the opening flowers and the singing birds,

" Chanting every day their lauds,
While the grove their song applauds ;
Wake for shame my sluggish heart,
Wake and gladly sing thy part."

It is a marvel of mercy that the sun should rise on the rebellious sons of men, and prepare for the undeserving fruitful seasons and days of pleasantness ; let us for this prodigy of goodness praise the Lord of all. From hour to hour let us renew the strain, for each moment brings its mercy ; and when the sun sinks to his rest, let us not cease our music, but lift up the vesper hymn—

> " Father of heaven and earth !
> I bless thee for the night,
>   The soft still night !
> The holy pause of care and mirth,
>   Of sound and light.
> Now far in glade and dell,
>   Flower-cup, and bud, and bell
> Have shut around the sleeping woodlark's nest,
>   The bee's long-murmuring toils are done,
>   And I, the o'erwearied one,
> Bless thee, O God, O Father of the oppressed !
>   With my last waking thought."

4. *"The* LORD *is high above all nations."* Though the Gentiles knew him not, yet was Jehovah their ruler : their false gods were no gods, and their kings were puppets in his hands. The Lord is high above all the learning, judgment, and imagination of heathen sages, and far beyond the pomp and might of the monarchs of the nations. Like the great arch of the firmament, the presence of the Lord spans all the lands where dwell the varied tribes of men, for his providence is universal : this may well excite our confidence and praise. *"And his glory above the heavens : "* higher than the loftiest part of creation ; the clouds are the dust of his feet, and sun, moon, and stars twinkle far below his throne. Even the heaven of heavens cannot contain him. His glory cannot be set forth by the whole visible universe, nor even by the solemn pomp of angelic armies ; it is above all conception and imagination, for he is God—infinite. Let us above all adore him who is above all.

5. *"Who is like unto the* LORD *our God?"* The challenge will never be answered. None can be compared with him for an instant ; Israel's God is without parallel ; our own God in covenant stands alone, and none can be likened unto him. Even those whom he has made like himself in some respects are not like him in godhead, for his divine attributes are many of them incommunicable and inimitable. None of the metaphors and figures by which the Lord is set forth in the Scriptures can give us a complete idea of him : his full resemblance is borne by nothing in earth or in heaven. Only in Jesus is the Godhead seen, but he unhesitatingly declared " he that hath seen me hath seen the Father." *"Who dwelleth on high."* In the height of his abode none can be like him. His throne, his whole character, his person, his being, everything about him, is lofty, and infinitely majestic, so that none can be likened unto him. His serene mind abides in the most elevated condition, he is never dishonoured, nor does he stoop from the pure holiness and absolute perfection of his character. His saints are said to dwell on high, and in this they are the reflection of his glory ; but as for himself, the height of his dwelling-place surpasses thought, and he rises far above the most exalted of his glorified people.

> " Eternal Power ! whose high abode
> Becomes the grandeur of a God :
> Infinite lengths beyond the bounds
> Where stars revolve their little rounds.

> " The lowest step around thy seat
> Rises too high for Gabriel's feet ;
> In vain the tall archangel tries
> To reach thine height with wond'ring eyes.

> " Lord, what shall earth and ashes do ?
> We would adore our Maker too ;
> From sin and dust to thee we cry,
> The Great, the Holy, and the High ! "

6. *"Who humbleth himself to behold the things that are in heaven, and in the earth ! "* He dwells so far on high that even to observe heavenly things he must humble himself. He must stoop to view the skies, and bow to see what angels do. What, then, must be his condescension, seeing that he observes the humblest of his servants upon earth, and makes them sing for joy like Mary when she said, " Thou hast regarded the low estate of thine handmaiden." How wonderful are those words of Isaiah, " For thus saith the high and lofty One that inhabiteth eternity, whose name is Holy ; I dwell in the high and holy place, with him also that is of a contrite and humble spirit, to revive the spirit of the humble, and to revive the heart of the contrite ones." Heathen philosophers could not believe that the great God was observant of the small events of human history ; they pictured him as abiding in serene indifference to all the wants and woes of his creatures. " Our Rock is not as their rock " ; we have a God who is high above all gods, and yet who is our Father, knowing what we have need of before we ask him ; our Shepherd, who supplies our needs ; our Guardian, who counts the hairs of our heads ; our tender and considerate Friend, who sympathizes in all our griefs. Truly the name of our condescending God should be praised wherever it is known.

7. *"He raiseth up the poor out of the dust."* This is an instance of his gracious stoop of love : he frequently lifts the lowest of mankind out of their poverty and degradation, and places them in positions of power and honour. His good Spirit is continually visiting the down-trodden, giving beauty for ashes to those who are cast down, and elevating the hearts of his mourners till they shout for joy. These upliftings of grace are here ascribed directly to the divine hand, and truly those who have experienced them will not doubt the fact that it is the Lord alone who brings his people up from the dust of sorrow and death. When no hand but his can help he interposes, and the work is done. It is worth while to be cast down to be so divinely raised from the dust. *"And lifteth the needy out of the dunghill,"* whereon they lay like worthless refuse, cast off and cast out, left as they thought to rot into destruction and to be everlastingly forgotten. How great a stoop from the height of his throne to a dunghill ! How wonderful that power which occupies itself in lifting up beggars, all befouled with the filthiness in which they lay ! For he lifts them *out of* the dunghill, not disdaining to search them out from amidst the base things of the earth that he may by their means bring to nought the great ones, and pour contempt upon all human glorying. What a dunghill was that upon which we lay by nature ! What a mass of corruption is our original estate ! What a heap of loathsomeness we have accumulated by our sinful lives ! What reeking abominations surround us in the society of our fellow men ! We could never have risen out of all this by our own efforts, it was a sepulchre in which we saw corruption, and were as dead men. Almighty were the arms which lifted us, which are still lifting us, and will lift us into the perfection of heaven itself. Praise ye the Lord.

8. *"That he may set him with princes."* The Lord does nothing by halves : when he raises men from the dust he is not content till he places them among the peers of his kingdom. We are made kings and priests unto God, and we shall reign for ever and ever. Instead of poverty, he gives us the wealth of princes ; and instead of dishonour, he gives us a more exalted rank than that of the great ones of the earth. *"Even with the princes of his people."* All his people are princes, and so the text teaches us that God places needy souls whom he favours among the princes of princes. He often enables those who have been most despairing to rise to the greatest heights of spirituality and gracious attainment, for those who once were last shall be first. Paul, though less than the least of all saints was, nevertheless, made to be not a whit behind the very chief of the apostles ; and in our own times, Bunyan, the blaspheming tinker, was raised into another John, whose dream almost rivals the visions of the Apocalypse.

> " Wonders of grace to God belong,
> Repeat his mercies in your song."

Such verses as these should give great encouragement to those who are lowest in their own esteem. The Lord poureth contempt upon princes ; but as for those who are in the dust and on the dunghill, he looks upon them with compassion, acts towards them in grace, and in their case displays the riches of his glory by Christ Jesus. Those who have experienced such amazing favour should sing continual hallelujahs to the God of their salvation.

9. *"He maketh the barren woman to keep house, and to be a joyful mother of children."* The strong desire of the easterns to have children caused the birth of offspring to be hailed as the choicest of favours, while barrenness was regarded as a curse ; hence this verse is placed last as if to crown the whole, and to serve as a climax to the story of God's mercy. The glorious Lord displays his condescending grace in regarding those who are despised on account of their barrenness, whether it be of body or of soul. Sarah, Rachel, the wife of Manoah, Hannah, Elizabeth, and others were all instances of the miraculous power of God in literally fulfilling the statement of the Psalmist. Women were not supposed to have a house till they had children ; but in certain cases where childless women pined in secret the Lord visited them in

mercy, and made them not only to have a house, but to keep it. The Gentile church is a spiritual example upon a large scale of the gift of fruitfulness after long years of hopeless barrenness ; and the Jewish church in the latter days will be another amazing display of the same quickening power : long forsaken for her spiritual adultery, Israel shall be forgiven, and restored, and joyously shall she keep that house which now is left unto her desolate. Nor is this all, each believer in the Lord Jesus must at times have mourned his lamentable barrenness ; he has appeared to be a dry tree yielding no fruit to the Lord, and yet when visited by the Holy Ghost, he has found himself suddenly to be like Aaron's rod, which budded, and blossomed, and brought forth almonds. Or ever we have been aware, our barren heart has kept house, and entertained the Saviour, our graces have been multiplied as if many children had come to us at a single birth, and we have exceedingly rejoiced before the Lord. Then have we marvelled greatly at the Lord who dwelleth on high, that he has deigned to visit such poor worthless things. Like Mary, we have lifted up our Magnificat, and like Hannah, we have said "There is none holy as the Lord ; for there is none beside thee : neither is there any rock like our God."

"*Praise ye the* LORD." The music concludes upon its key-note. The Psalm is a circle, ending where it began, praising the Lord from its first syllable to its last. May our life-psalm partake of the same character, and never know a break or a conclusion. In an endless circle let us bless the Lord, whose mercies never cease. Let us praise him in youth, and all along our years of strength ; and when we bow in the ripeness of abundant age, let us still praise the Lord, who doth not cast off his old servants. Let us not only praise God ourselves, but exhort others to do it ; and if we meet with any of the needy who have been enriched, and with the barren who have been made fruitful, let us join with them in extolling the name of him whose mercy endureth for ever. Having been ourselves lifted from spiritual beggary and barrenness, let us never forget our former estate or the grace which has visited us, but world without end let us praise the Lord. Hallelujah.

EXPLANATORY NOTES AND QUAINT SAYINGS.

Whole Psalm.—With this Psalm begins the *Hallel*, which is recited at the three great feasts, at the feast of the Dedication (*Chanucca*) and at the new moons, and not on New Year's day and the day of Atonement, because a cheerful song of praise does not harmonise with the mournful solemnity of these days. And they are recited only in fragments during the last days of the Passover, for " my creatures, saith the Holy One, blessed be He, were drowned in the sea, and ought ye to break out into songs of rejoicing ? " In the family celebration of the Passover night it is divided into two parts, the one half, Ps. cxiii. cxiv., being sung before the repast, before the emptying of the second festal cup, and the other half, Ps. cxv.—cxviii., after the repast, after the filling of the fourth cup, to which the ὑμνήσαντες (Matt. xxvi. 30, Mark xiv. 26), or singing a hymn, after the institution of the Lord's Supper, which was connected with the fourth festal cup, may refer. Paulus Burgensis styles Ps. cxiii.—cxviii. *Alleluja Judæorum magnum.* (The great Alleluiah of the Jews). This designation is also frequently found elsewhere. But according to the prevailing custom, Ps. cxiii.—cxviii., and more particularly Ps. cxv.—cxviii., are called only *Hallel* and Ps. cxxxvi., with its " for his mercy endureth for ever " repeated twenty-six times, bears the name of "*The Great Hallel*" (הַלֵּל הַגָּדוֹל).—*Frank Delitzsch.*

Whole Psalm.—The Jews have handed down the tradition, that this Psalm, and those that follow on to the cxviiith, were all sung at the Passover ; and they are denominated "*The Great Hallel.*" This tradition shows, at all events, that the ancient Jews perceived in these six Psalms some link of close connection. They all sing of God the Redeemer, in some aspect of his redeeming character ; and this being so, while they suited the paschal feast, we can see how appropriate they would be in the lips of the Redeemer, in his Upper Room. Thus—

In Psalm cxiii., he sang praise to him who redeems from the lowest depth.

In Psalm cxiv., he sang praise to him who once redeemed Israel, and shall redeem Israel again.

In Psalm cxv., he uttered a song—over earth's fallen idols—to him who blesses Israel and the world.

In Psalm cxvi., he sang his resurrection-song of thanksgiving by anticipation.

In Psalm cxvii., he led the song of praise for the great congregation.

In Psalm cxviii. (just before leaving the Upper Room to go to Gethsemane), he poured forth the story of his suffering, conflict, triumph and glorification.—A. A. Bonar.

Whole Psalm.—An attentive reader of the Book of Psalms will observe, that almost every one of them has a view to Christianity. Many, if not most of the Psalms, were without doubt occasioned originally by accidents of the life that befell their royal author ; they were therefore at the same time both descriptive of the situation and life, the actions and sufferings, of King David, and predictive also of our Saviour, who was all along represented by King David, from whose loins he was descended according to the flesh. But *this* Psalm appears to be *wholly* written with a view to Christianity. It begins with an exhortation to all true servants and zealous worshippers of God, to *"praise his name,"* at all times, and in all places ; *"from this time forth and for evermore,"* and *"from the rising of the sun unto the going down thereof."* And the ground of this praise and adoration is set forth in the following verses to be,—first, the glorious majesty of his Divine nature ; and next, the singular goodness of it as displayed to us in his works of providence, particularly by exalting those who are abased, and his making the barren to become fruitful. His lifting the poor out of the mire, and making the barren woman to become fruitful, may, at first sight, seem an odd mixture of ideas. But a right notion of the prophetic language will solve the difficulty ; and teach us, that both the expressions are in fact very nearly related, and signify much the same thing. For by the *"poor"* are here meant those who are destitute of all heavenly knowledge (the only true and real riches) and who are sunk in the mire and filth of sin. So, again, his making *"the barren woman to keep house, and to be a joyful mother of children,"* is a prophetic metaphor, or allusion to the fruitfulness of the Church in bringing forth sons or professors of the true religion. My interpretation of both these expressions is warrantable from so many parallel passages of Scripture. I shall only observe that here the profession of the Christian faith throughout the whole earth is foretold ; as also the particular direction or point of the compass, toward which Christianity should by the course of God's providence be steered and directed, *viz.,* from East to West, or *"from the rising of the sun unto the going down of the same."—James Bate,* 1703—1775.

Verse 1.—"Praise ye the LORD." "Praise." The הללו is repeated. This repetition is not without significance. It is for the purpose of waking us up out of our torpor. We are all too dull and slow in considering and praising the blessings of God. There is, therefore, necessity for these stimuli. Then this repetition signifies assiduity and perseverance in sounding forth the praises of God. It is not sufficient once and again to praise God, but his praises ought to be always sung in the Church.—*Mollerus.*

Verse 1.—"Praise ye the LORD." This praising God rests not in the mere speculation or idle contemplation of the Divine excellence, floating only in the brain, or gliding upon the tongue, but in such quick and lively apprehensions of them as to sink down into the heart, and there beget affections suitable to them ; for it will make us love him for his goodness, respect him for his greatness, fear him for his justice, dread him for his power, adore him for his wisdom, and for all his attributes make us live in constant awe and obedience to him. This is to praise God, without which all other courting and complimenting of him is but mere flattery and hypocrisy. . . . God Almighty endowed us with higher and nobler faculties than other creatures, for this end, that we should set forth his praise ; for though other things were made to administer the matter and occasion, yet man alone was designed and qualified to exercise the act of glorifying God. . . . In short, God Almighty hath so closely twisted his own glory and our happiness together, that at the same time we advance the one we promote the other.—*Matthew Hole,* 1730.

Verse 1.—"Praise, O ye servants of the LORD." From the exhortation to praise God, and the declaration of his deserving to be praised ; learn, that as it is all men's duty to praise the Lord, so in special it is the duty of his ministers, and officers of his house. First, because their office doth call for the discharge of it publicly. Next, because as they should be best acquainted with the reasons of his praise, so also should they be the fittest instruments to declare it.   And lastly, because the ungodly are deaf unto the exhortation, and dumb in the obedience of it ; therefore when he hath said, *"Praise ye the Lord,"* he sub-joineth, *"Praise, O ye servants of the Lord."—David Dickson.*

Verse 1.—*" Ye servants of the* Lord.*"*—All men owe this duty to God, as being the workmanship of his hands ; Christians above other men, as being the sheep of his pasture ; preachers of the word above other Christians, as being pastors of his sheep, and so consequently patterns in word, in conversation, in love, in spirit, in faith, in pureness. 1 Tim. iv. 12.—*John Boys.*

Verses 1—3,

> Hallelujah, praise the Lord
> Praise, ye servants, praise his name !
> Be Jehovah's praise ador'd,
> Now and evermore the same !
> Where the orient sun-beams gleam,
> Where they sink in ocean's stream,
> Through the circuit of his rays
> Be your theme Jehovah's praise.

Richard Mant.

Verse 2.—*"Blessed be the name of the* Lord.*"*   Let then, O man, thy labouring soul strive to conceive (for 'tis impossible to express) what an immense debt of gratitude thou owest to him, who, by his creating goodness called thee out of nothing to make thee a partaker of reason, and even a sharer of immortality with himself ; who, by his preserving goodness, designs to conduct thee safe through the various stages of thy eternal existence ; and who, by his redeeming goodness, hath prepared for thee a happiness too big for the comprehension of a human understanding. Canst thou receive such endearments of love to thee and all mankind with insensibility and coldness ? . . .   In the whole compass of language what word is expressive enough to paint the black ingratitude of that man, who is unaffected by, and entirely regardless of, the goodness of God his Creator, and the mercies of Christ ?—*Jeremiah Seed,* 1747.

Verse 2.—*"Blessed be the name of the* Lord,*"* etc.   No doubt the disciples that sat at that paschal table, would repeat with mingled feelings of thanksgiving and sadness that ascription of praise.   *"Blessed be the name of the* Lord *from this time forth and for evermore."*   But what Israelite, in all the paschal chambers at Jerusalem on that night, as he sang the Hallel or hymn, or which of the disciples at the sorrowing board of Jesus, could have understood or entered into the full meaning of the expression, *"from this time forth?"*   From what time?   I think St. John gives us a clue to the very hour and moment of which the Psalmist, perhaps unconsciously, spake. He tells us, that when the traitor Judas had received the sop, he immediately went out ; and that when he was gone out to clench as it were and ratify his treacherous purpose, Jesus said, *"Now* is the Son of man glorified, and God is glorified in Him."   From that time forth, when by the determinate counsel and foreknowledge of God, the Son of man was about to be delivered into the hands of wicked men, and crucified and slain, as Jesus looked at those around him, as sorrow had indeed filled their hearts, and as with all-seeing, prescient eye he looked onwards and beheld all those that should hereafter believe on him through their word, with what significance and emphasis of meaning may we imagine the blessed Jesus on that night of anguish to have uttered these words of the hymn, *"Blessed be the name of the* Lord *from this time forth and for evermore"* !   "A few more hours and the covenant will be sealed in my own blood ; the compact ratified, when I hang upon the cross." And with what calm and confident assurance of triumph does he look upon that cross of shame ; with what overflowing love does he point to it and say, " And I, if I be lifted up, will draw all men unto me " !   It is the very same here in this Paschal Psalm ; and how must the Saviour's heart have rejoiced even in the contemplation of those sufferings that awaited him, as he uttered this prediction, *"From the rising of the sun unto the going down of the same the* Lord's *name is to be praised"* ! " That which thou sewest is not quickened except it die : " and thus from that hour to the present the Lord hath added daily to the church those whom in every age and in every clime he hath chosen unto salvation, till, in his own appointed fulness of time, from the east and from the west, from the north and from the south, all nations shall do him service, and the earth be filled with the knowledge of the Lord as the waters cover the sea."—*Barton Bouchier.*

Verse 2.—"From this time forth and for evermore." The servants of the Lord are to sing his praises in this life to the world's end ; and in the next life, world without end.—*John Boys.*

Verse 3.—"From the rising of the sun unto the going down of the same." That is everywhere, from east to west. These western parts of the world are particularly prophesied of to enjoy the worship of God after the Jews which were in the east ; and these islands of ours that lie in the sea, into which the sun is said to go down, which is an expression of the old Greek poets ; and the prophet here useth such a word in the Hebrew, where the west is called, according to the vulgar conceit, the sunset, or the sun's going down, or going in.—*Samuel Torshell,* 1641.

Verses 4, 5.—"The Lord is high." ... *"The Lord our God dwelleth on high."* But how *high* is he ? *Answer* I. So high, that all creatures bow before him and do homage to him according to their several aptitudes and abilities. John brings them all in, attributing to him the crown of glory, putting it from themselves, but setting it upon his head, as a royalty due only to him. (Rev. v. 13). 1. Some by way of *subjection,* stooping to him : angels and saints worship him, acknowledging his highness, by denying their own, but setting up his will as their supreme law and excellency. 2. Others acknowledge his eminency by their *consternation* upon the least shining forth of his glory ; when he discovers but the emblems of his greatness, devils tremble, men quake, James ii. 19 ; Isai. xxxiii. 14. Thirdly, even inanimate creatures, by *compliance* with, and ready subjection to, the impressions of his power, Hab. iii. 9—11 ; Isai. xlviii. 13 ; Dan. iv. 35. ... II. He is so high that he surmounts all created capacity to comprehend him, Job. xi. 7—9. So that indeed, in David's phrase, his greatness is *"unsearchable,"* Ps. cxlv. 3. In a word, he is so high, 1. That no bodily eye hath ever, or can possibly see him. 2. Neither can the eye of the understanding perfectly reach him. He dwells in inaccessible light that no mortal eye can attain to.—*Condensed from a sermon by Thomas Hodges, entitled,* "A Glimpse of God's Glory," 1642.

Verse 5.—"Who is like unto the Lord our God ?" It is the nature of love, that the one whom we love we prefer to all others, and we ask, *Who is like my beloved ?* The world has not his like. Thus love thinks ever of one, who in many things is inferior to many others ; for in human affairs the judgment of love is blind. But those who love the Lord their God, though they should glow with more ardent love for him, and should ask, Who is as the Lord our God ? in this matter would not be mistaken, but would think altogether most correctly. For there is no being, either in heaven or in earth, who can be in any way likened unto the Lord God. Even love itself cannot conceive, think, speak concerning God whom we love as he really is.—*Wolfgang Musculus.*

Verse 5.—"Who is like unto the Lord our God," etc. Among the gods of the nations as Kimchi ; or among the angels of heaven, or among any of the mighty monarchs on earth ; there is none like him for the perfections of his nature, for his wisdom, power, truth, and faithfulness ; for his holiness, justice, goodness, grace, and mercy. Who is eternal, unchangeable, omnipotent, omniscient, and omnipresent ? Nor for the works of his hands, his works of creation, providence, and grace ; none ever did the like. What makes this reflection the more delightful to truly good men is, that this God is their God ; and all this is true of our Immanuel, God with us, who is God over all, and the only Saviour and Redeemer ; and there is none in heaven and earth like him, or to be desired beside him.—*John Gill.*

Verse 5.—"The Lord our God who dwelleth on high." God is on high in respect of place or dwelling. It is true he is in the aërial and starry heaven by his essence and power ; but the heaven of the blessed is his throne : not as if he were so confined to that place as to be excluded from others, for " the heaven of heavens cannot contain him " ; but in respect of manifestation he is said to be there, because in that place he chiefly manifests his glory and goodness. In respect of his essence he is *high* indeed, inexpressibly high in excellency above all beings, not only in Abraham's phrase, *"The High God,"* but in David's, *"The Lord most High."* Alas ! what are all created beings in respect of him, with all their excellences, but nothing and vanity ? ... For these excellences are divers things in the creatures, but one in God ; they are accidents in the creatures, but essence in God ; they are in the creature with some alloy or other, they are like the moon when they shine brightest, yet are spots of imperfection to be found in them. In respect to measure, he is infinitely above them all. Alas, they possess some small drops in respect to the fountain, some poor glimmering rays in respect to this glorious sun ; in a word, he is an infinite ocean of perfection, without either brink or bottom.—*Thomas Hodges*, in a *Sermon preached before the House of Commons*, 1642.

Verse 5.—God is said not only to be on high, but to "*dwell*" on high ; this intimates *calm and composed operation*, and it is proper for us to take this view of the character of God's administration. You recollect that in all ages unbelief has been in some respect rendered plausible by the delays of God in the accomplishment of his designs. So, in St. Peter's time, it would seem that because the apostles and preachers of Christianity had dwelt much on Christ's coming to judgment, they cried out, " Where is the promise of his coming, for since the fathers fell asleep, all things continue as they were from the beginning of the creation ? " What is the apostle's answer to this ? His first answer, I grant, is, that all things have not continued as they were from the creation, for there was a flood of waters, and those who said, Where is the promise of his coming ? in the days of Noah were at last answered by the bursting earth and the breaking heavens. . . . That was his first answer ; but his second answer contains the principle that, " One day is with the Lord as a thousand years, and a thousand years as one day." The Being who is from everlasting to everlasting is under no necessity to hurry his plans ; therefore he hath fixed the times and the seasons—they are all with him, and *he dwelleth on high.*—*Richard Watson*, 1831.

Verses 5, 6.—The philosophy of the world, even in the present day, has its elevated and magnificent views of the Divine Being ; yet it would seem uniform, whether among the sages of the heathen world or among the philosophers of the present day, that the loftier their views are even of the Divine nature, the more they tend to distrust and unbelief ; and that, just in proportion as they have thought nobly of God, so the impression has deepened—that, with respect to individuals at least, they were not the subjects of his immediate care. The doctrine of a particular providence, and the doctrine of direct divine influence upon the heart of man, have by them always been considered absurd and fanatical. Now, when I turn to the sages of inspiration—to the holy men of old, who thought and spoke as they were moved by the Holy Ghost, I find quite a different result—that in proportion to the views they had of the glory of God, so was their confidence and hope.

That two such opposite results should spring from the same order of thoughts with respect to the Divine Being, is a singular fact, which demands and deserves some enquiry. How is it that, among the men of the world, wise as they are, in proportion as they have had high and exalted views of God, those lofty ideas tend to distrust ; while just in proportion as we are enlightened on the very same subjects by the Scriptures of truth, rightly and spiritually understood, that we as well as the authors of these sacred books, in proportion as we see the glory and the grandeur of God, are excited to a filial and comforting trust ? There are two propositions in the text which human reason could never unite. "*Who dwelleth on high* "—but yet he "*humbleth himself to behold the things that are in heaven, and in the earth.*" And the reason why the mere unassisted human faculties could never unite these two ideas is, that they could not, in the nature of things, be united, but by a third discovery, which must have come from God himself, and show the two in perfect harmony—the discovery that " God so loved the world that he gave his only begotten Son, that whosoever believeth in him should not perish, but have everlasting life."—*Richard Watson*, 1831.

Verses 5, 6.—The structure of this passage in the original is singular, and is thus stated and commented on by Bp. Lowth, in his 19th Prælection :—

Who is like Jehovah our God ?
Who dwelleth on high.
Who looketh below.
In heaven and in earth.

The latter member is to be divided, and assigned in its two divisions to the two former members ; so that the sense may be, " who dwelleth on high in heaven, and looketh below on the things which are in earth."—*Richard Mant.*

Verse 6.—"*Who humbleth himself.*" Whatever may be affirmed of God, may be affirmed of him infinitely, and whatever he is, he is infinitely. So the Psalmist, in this place, does not speak of God as humble, but as infinitely and superlatively so, humble beyond all conception and comparison ; he challenges the whole universe of created nature, from the highest immortal spirit in heaven to the lowest mortal on earth, to show a being endued with so much humility, as the adorable majesty of the great God of Heaven and earth. . . . If some instances of the Divine humility surprise, the following may amaze us :—To see the great King of heaven stooping from his height, and condescending himself to offer terms of reconciliation to his rebellious creatures ! To see offended majesty courting the offenders to accept of pardon ! To see God persuading, entreating and beseeching men to return to him with such earnestness and importunity, as if his very life were bound up in them, and his own happiness depended upon theirs ! To see the adorable Spirit of God, with infinite long-suffering and gentleness, submitting to the contempt and insults of such miserable, despicable wretches as sinful mortals are ! Is not this amazing ?— *Valentine Nalson*, 1641—1724.

Verse 6.—*"Who humbleth himself to behold."*—If it be such condescension for God to behold things in heaven and earth, what an amazing condescension was it for the Son of God to come from heaven to earth and take our nature upon him, that he might seek and save them that were lost ! Here indeed he humbled himself.— *Matthew Henry.*

Verse 7.—*"He raiseth up the poor,"* etc. There is no doubt a reference in this to the respect which God pays even to the lower ranks of the race, seeing that " he raiseth up the poor, and lifteth up the needy." I have no doubt there is reference throughout the whole of this Psalm to evangelical times ; that, in this respect, it is a prophetic psalm, including a reference especially to Christianity, as it may be called by eminence and distinction the religion of the poor—its greatest glory. For when John the Baptist sent two disciples to Jesus, to know whether he was the Messiah or not, the answer of our Lord was, " The blind see, the lepers are cleansed, the dead are raised "—all extraordinary events—miracles, in short, which proved his divine commission. And he summed up the whole by saying, " The poor have the gospel preached unto them ; " as great a miracle as any—as great a distinction as any. There never was a religion but the true religion, in all its various dispensations, that had equal respect to all classes of society. In all others there was a privileged class, but here there is none. Perhaps one of the most interesting views of Christianity we can take is its wonderful adaptation to the character and circumstances of the poor. What an opportunity does it furnish for the manifestation of the bright and mild graces of the Holy Spirit ! What sources of comfort does it open to mollify the troubles of life ! and how often, in choosing the poor, rich in faith, to make them heirs of the kingdom, does God exalt the poor out of the dust, and the needy from the dunghill !—*Richard Watson.*

Verse 7.—*"He raiseth up the poor,"* etc. Gideon is fetched from threshing, Saul from seeking the asses, and David from keeping the sheep ; the apostles from fishing are sent to be " fishers of men." The treasure of the gospel is put into earthen vessels, and the weak and the foolish ones of the world pitched upon to be preachers of it, to confound the " wise and mighty " (1 Cor. i. 27, 28,) that the excellency of the power may be of God, and all may see that promotion comes from him.—*Matthew Henry.*

Verse 7.—*"He raiseth up the poor."* The highest honour, which was ever done to any mere creature, was done out of regard to the lowest humility ; the Son of God had such regard to the lowliness of the blessed virgin, that he did her the honour to choose her for the mother of his holy humanity. It is an observation of S. Chrysostom, that that very hand which the humble John Baptist thought not worthy to unloose the shoe on our blessed Saviour's feet, that hand our Lord thought worthy to baptize his sacred head.—*Valentine Nalson.*

Verse 7.—*"And lifteth the needy out of the dunghill" ;* which denotes a mean condition ; so one born in a mean place, and brought up in a mean manner, is sometimes represented as taken out of a dunghill ; and also it is expressive of a filthy one ; men by sin are not only brought into a low estate, but into a loathsome one, and are justly abominable in the sight of God, and yet he lifts them out of it : the phrases of *raising up* and *lifting out* suppose them to be fallen, as men are in Adam, fallen from a state of honour and glory, in and out of which they cannot deliver themselves ; it is Christ's work, and his only, to raise up the tribes of Jacob, and to help or lift up his servant Israel. Isa. xlix. 6 ; Luke i. 54 ; see 1 Sam. ii. 8.— *John Gill.*

Verse 7.—"The poor . . the needy." Rejoice, then, in the favourable notice God taketh of you. The highest and greatest of beings vouchsafes to regard *you.* Though you are poor and mean, and men overlook you ; though your brethren hate you, and your friends go far from you, yet hear ! God looketh down from his majestic throne upon you. Amidst the infinite variety of his works, you are not overlooked. Amidst the nobler services of ten thousand times ten thousand saints and angels, not *one* of your fervent prayers or humble groans escapes his ear.—*Job Orton*, 1717— 1783.

Verse 7.—Almighty God cannot look above himself, as having no superiors ; nor about himself, as having no equals ; he beholds such as are below him ; and therefore the lower a man is, the nearer unto God ; he resists the proud, and gives grace to the humble, 1 Pet. v. 5. He pulls down the mighty from their seat, and exalteth them of low degree. The Most High hath special eye to such as are most humble ; for, as it followeth in our text, *"he taketh up the simple out of the dust, and lifteth the poor out of the dirt."—John Boys.*

Verse 7.—"Dunghill." An emblem of the deepest poverty and desertion ; for in Syria and Palestine the man who is shut out from society lies upon the *mezbele* (the dunghill or heap of ashes), by day calling upon the passers-by for alms, and by night hiding himself in the ashes that have been warmed by the sun.—*Franz Delitzsch.*

Verse 7.—"Dunghill." The passages of the Bible, in which the word occurs, all seem to refer, as Parkhurst remarks, to the stocks of cow-dung and other offal stuff, which the easterns for want of wood were obliged to lay up for fuel.—*Richard Mant.*

Verses 7, 8.—These verses are taken almost word for word from the prayer of Hannah, 1 Sam. ii. 8. The transition to the *"people"* is all the more natural, as Hannah, considering herself at the conclusion as the type of the church, with which every individual among the Israelites felt himself much more closely entwined than can easily be the case among ourselves, draws out of the salvation imparted to herself joyful prospects for the future.—*E. W. Hengstenberg.*

Verse 8.—"Even with the princes of his people." It is the honour that cometh from God that alone exalts. Whatever account the world may take of a poor man, he may be more precious in the eyes of God than the highest among men. The humble poor are here ranked, not with the princes of the earth, but with *"the princes of his people."* The distinctions in this world, even among those who serve the same God, are as nothing in his sight when contrasted with that honour which is grounded on the free grace of God to his own. But here, also, the fulness of this statement will only be seen in the world to come, when all the faithful will be owned as kings and priests unto God.—*W. Wilson.*

Verse 9.—"He maketh the barren woman to keep house," etc. Should a married woman, who has long been considered sterile, become a mother, her joy, and that of her husband and friends, will be most extravagant. " They called her *Malady,"* that is, " Barren," " but she has given us good fruit." " My neighbours pointed at me, and said, *Malady* : but what will they say now ? " A man who on any occasion manifests great delight, is represented to be like the barren woman who has at length borne a child. Anything which is exceedingly valuable is thus described : " This is as precious as the son of the barren woman " ; that is, of her who had long been reputed barren.—*Joseph Roberts.*

Verse 9.—"He maketh the barren woman to keep house," etc. As baseness in men, so barrenness in women is accounted a great unhappiness. But as God lifteth up the beggar out of the mire, to set him with princes, even so doth he *"make the barren woman a joyful mother of children."* He governs all things in the private family, as well as in the public weal. Children and the fruit of the womb are a gift and heritage that cometh of the Lord, Ps. cxxvii. 3 ; and therefore the Papists in praying to S. Anne for children, and the Gentiles in calling upon Diana, Juno, Latona, are both in error. It is God only who makes the barren women *"a mother,"* and that *"a joyful mother."* Every mother is joyful at the first, according to that of Christ, " a woman when she travaileth hath sorrow, because her hour is come : but as soon as she is delivered of the child, she remembereth no more the anguish, for joy that a man is born into the world."

Divines apply this also mystically to Christ, affirming that he made the church of the Gentiles, heretofore *"barren," "a joyful mother of children,"* according to that of the prophet : " Rejoice, O barren, that didst not bear ; break forth into joy and rejoice, thou that didst not travail with child : for the desolate hath more children than the married wife, saith the Lord," Isai. liv. 1. Or it may be construed of true Christians : all of us are by nature barren of goodness, conceived and born in sin not able to think a good thought (2 Cor. iii. 5) ; but the Father of lights and mercies makes us fruitful and abundant always in the work of the Lord (1 Cor. xv. 58) ; he giveth us grace to be fathers and mothers of many good deeds, which are our children and best heirs, eternizing our name for ever.—*John Boys.*

Verse 9.—*"The barren woman"* is the poor, forsaken, distressed Christian church, whom the false church oppresses, defies, and persecutes, and regards as useless, miserable, barren, because she herself is greater and more populous, the greatest part of the world.—*Joshua Arndt,* 1626—1685.

Verse 9.—*"Praise ye the LORD."* We may look abroad, and see abundant occasion for praising God,—in his condescension to human affairs,—in his lifting up the poor from the humblest condition,—in his exalting those of lowly rank to places of honour, trust, wealth, and power ; but, after all, if we wish to find occasions of praise that will most tenderly affect the heart, and be connected with the warmest affections of the soul, they will be most likely to be found in the domestic circle—in the mutual love—the common joy—the tender feelings—which bind together the members of a family.—*Albert Barnes.*

Verse 9.—*"Praise ye the LORD."* The very hearing of the comfortable changes which the Lord can make and doth make the afflicted to find, is a matter of refreshment to all, and of praise to God from all.—*David Dickson.*

HINTS TO PREACHERS.

Whole Psalm.—The Psalm contains three parts :—I. An exhortation to God's servants to praise him.   II. A form set down how and where to praise him, ver. 2, 3.   III. The reasons to persuade us to it.   1. By his infinite power, ver. 4, 5.   2. His providence, as displayed in heaven and earth, ver. 6.—*Adam Clarke.*

Verse 1.—The repetitions show, 1. The importance of praise.   2. Our many obligations to render it.   3. Our backwardness in the duty.   4. The heartiness and frequency with which it should be rendered.   5. The need of calling upon others to join with us.

Verse 1.—I. To whom praise is due : " the Lord."   II. From whom it is due : " ye servants of the Lord."   III. For what is it due : his " name."   1. For all names descriptive of what he is in himself.   2. For all names descriptive of what he is to his servants.—*G. R.*

Verses 1, 9.—" Praise ye the Lord."   I. Begin and end life with it, and do the same with holy service, patient suffering, and everything else.   II. Fill up the interval with praise.   Run over the intervening verses.

Verse 2.—I. The work of heaven begun on earth : to praise the name of the Lord.   II. The work of earth continued in heaven : " and for evermore."   If the praise begun on earth be continued in heaven, we must be in heaven to continue the praise.—*G. R.*

Verse 2.—1. It is time to begin to praise : " from this time."   Is there not special reason, from long arrears, from present duty, etc. ?   2. There is no time for leaving off praise : " and for evermore."   None supposable or excusable.

Verse 3.—God is to be praised.   1. All the day.   2. All the world over.   3. Publicly in the light.   4. Amidst daily duties.   5. Always—because it is always day somewhere.

Verse 3.—1. Canonical hours abolished.   2. Holy places abolished—since we cannot be always in them.   3. Every time and place consecrated.

Verses 5, 6.—The greatness of God as viewed from below, ver. 5.   II. The condescension of God as viewed from above, ver. 6.   1. In creation.   2. In the Incarnation.   3. In redemption.—*G. R.*

Verses 5, 6.—The unparalleled condescension of God.   1. None are so great, and therefore able to stoop so low.   2. None are so good, and therefore so willing to stoop.   3. None are so wise, and therefore so able to " behold " or know the needs of little things. 4. None are infinite, and therefore able to enter into minutiæ and sympathize with the smallest grief : Infinity is seen in the minute as truly as in the immense.

Verse 6.—I. The same God rules in heaven and earth. II. Both spheres are dependent for happiness upon his beholding them. III. They both enjoy his consideration. IV.—All things done in them are equally under his inspection.

Verse 7.—The gospel and its special eye to the poor.

Verses 7, 8.—I. Where men are ? In the dust of sorrow and on the dunghill of sin. II. Who interferes to help them ? He who dwelleth on high. III. What does he effect for them ? " Raiseth, lifteth, setteth among princes, among princes of his people."

Verse 8.—Elevation to the peerage of heaven ; or, the Royal Family increased.

Verse 9.—For mothers' meetings. " A joyful mother of children." I. It is a joy to be a mother. II. It is specially so to have living, healthy, obedient children. III. But best of all to have Christian children. Praise is due to the Lord who gives such blessings.

Verse 9.—I. A houschold God, or, God in the Household : " He maketh," etc. Have you children ? It is of God. Have you lost children ? It is of God. Have you been without children ? It is of God. II. Houschold worship, or, the God of the Household : " Praise ye the Lord." 1. In the family. 2. For family mercies.— *G. R.*

PSALM CXIV.

SUBJECT AND DIVISION.—*This sublime* SONG OF THE EXODUS *is one and indivisible. True poetry has here reached its climax : no human mind has ever been able to equal, much less to excel, the grandeur of this Psalm. God is spoken of as leading forth his people from Egypt to Canaan, and causing the whole earth to be moved at his coming. Things inanimate are represented as imitating the actions of living creatures when the Lord passes by. They are apostrophised and questioned with marvellous force of language, till one seems to look upon the actual scene. The God of Jacob is exalted as having command over river, sea, and mountain, and causing all nature to pay homage and tribute before his glorious majesty.*

EXPOSITION.

WHEN Israel went out of Egypt, the house of Jacob from a people of strange language ;

2 Judah was his sanctuary, *and* Israel his dominion.

3 The sea saw *it*, and fled : Jordan was driven back.

4 The mountains skipped like rams, *and* the little hills like lambs.

5 What *ailed* thee, O thou sea, that thou fleddest ? thou Jordan, *that* thou wast driven back ?

6 Ye mountains, *that* ye skipped like rams ; *and* ye little hills, like lambs ?

7 Tremble, thou earth, at the presence of the Lord, at the presence of the God of Jacob ;

8 Which turned the rock *into* a standing water, the flint into a fountain of waters.

1. "*When Israel went out of Egypt.*" The song begins with a burst, as if the poetic fury could not be restrained, but overleaped all bounds. The soul elevated and filled with a sense of divine glory cannot wait to fashion a preface, but springs at once into the middle of its theme. Israel emphatically came out of Egypt, out of the population among whom they had been scattered, from under the yoke of bondage, and from under the personal grasp of the king who had made the people into national slaves. Israel came out with a high hand and a stretched-out arm, defying all the power of the empire, and making the whole of Egypt to travail with sore anguish, as the chosen nation was as it were born out of its midst. "*The house of Jacob from a people of strange language.*" They had gone down into Egypt as a single family—" the house of Jacob " ; and, though they had multiplied greatly, they were still so united, and were so fully regarded by God as a single unit, that they are rightly spoken of as the house of Jacob. They were as one man in their willingness to leave Goshen ; numerous as they were, not a single individual stayed behind. Unanimity is a pleasing token of the divine presence, and one of its sweetest fruits. One of their inconveniences in Egypt was the difference of languages, which was very great. The Israelites appear to have regarded the Egyptians as stammerers and babblers, since they could not understand them, and they very naturally considered the Egyptians to be barbarians, as they would no doubt often beat them because they did not comprehend their orders. The language of foreign taskmasters is never musical in an exile's ear. How sweet it is to a Christian who has been compelled to hear the filthy conversation of the wicked, when at last he is brought out from their midst to dwell among his own people !

2. "*Judah was his sanctuary, and Israel his dominion.*" The pronoun " his " comes in where we should have looked for the name of God ; but the poet is so full of thought concerning the Lord that he forgets to mention his name, like the spouse in the Song, who begins, " Let *him* kiss me," or Magdalene when she cried, " Tell me where thou hast laid *him*." From the mention of Judah and Israel certain critics have inferred that this Psalm must have been written after the division

of the two kingdoms ; but this is only another instance of the extremely slender basis upon which an hypothesis is often built up. Before the formation of the two kingdoms David had said, " Go, number Israel and Judah," and this was common parlance, for Uriah the Hittite said, " The ark and Israel, and Judah abide in tents " ; so that nothing can be inferred from the use of the two names. No division into two kingdoms can have been intended here, for the poet is speaking of the coming out of Egypt when the people were so united that he has just before called them " the house of Judah." It would be quite as fair to prove from the first verse that the Psalm was written when the people were in union as to prove from the second that its authorship dates from their separation. Judah was the tribe which led the way in the wilderness march, and it was forseen in prophecy to be the royal tribe, hence its poetical mention in this place. The meaning of the passage is that the whole people at the coming out of Egypt were separated unto the Lord to be a peculiar people, a nation of priests whose motto should be, " Holiness unto the Lord." Judah was the Lord's " holy thing," set apart for his special use. The nation was peculiarly Jehovah's dominion, for it was governed by a theocracy in which God alone was King. It was his domain in a sense in which the rest of the world was outside his kingdom. These were the young days of Israel, the time of her espousals, when she went after the Lord into the wilderness, her God leading the way with signs and miracles. The whole people were the shrine of Deity, and their camp was one great temple. What a change there must have been for the godly amongst them from the idolatries and blasphemies of the Egyptians to the holy worship and righteous rule of the great King in Jeshurun. They lived in a world of wonders, where God was seen in the wondrous bread they ate and in the water they drank, as well as in the solemn worship of his holy place. When the Lord is manifestly present in a church, and his gracious rule obediently owned, what a golden age has come, and what honourable privileges his people enjoy ! May it be so among us.

3. "The sea saw it, and fled" ; or rather, " The sea saw and fled "—it saw God and all his people following his lead, and it was struck with awe and fled away. A bold figure ! The Red Sea mirrored the hosts which had come down to its shore, and reflected the cloud which towered high over all, as the symbol of the presence of the Lord : never had such a scene been imagined upon the surface of the Red Sea, or any other sea, before. It could not endure the unusual and astounding sight, and fleeing to the right and to the left, opened a passage for the elect people. A like miracle happened at the end of the great march of Israel, for "Jordan was driven back." This was a swiftly-flowing river, pouring itself down a steep decline, and it was not merely divided, but its current was driven back so that the rapid torrent, contrary to nature, flowed up-hill. This was God's work : the poet does not sing of the suspension of natural laws, or of a singular phenomenon not readily to be explained ; but to him the presence of God with his people is everything, and in his lofty song he tells how the river was driven back because the Lord was there. In this case poetry is nothing but the literal fact, and the fiction lies on the side of the atheistic critics who will suggest any explanation of the miracle rather than admit that the Lord made bare his holy arm in the eyes of all his people. The division of the sea and the drying up of the river are placed together though forty years intervened, because they were the opening and closing scenes of one great event. We may thus unite by faith our new birth and our departure out of the world into the promised inheritance, for the God who led us out of the Egypt of our bondage under sin will also conduct us through the Jordan of death out of our wilderness wanderings in the desert of this tried and changeful life. It is all one and the same deliverance, and the beginning ensures the end.

4. "The mountains skipped like rams, and the little hills like lambs." At the coming of the Lord to Mount Sinai, the hills moved ; either leaping for joy in the presence of their Creator like young lambs ; or, if you will, springing from their places in affright at the terrible majesty of Jehovah, and flying like a flock of sheep when alarmed. Men fear the mountains, but the mountains tremble before the Lord. Sheep and lambs move lightly in the meadows ; but the hills, which we are wont to call eternal, were as readily made to move as the most active creatures. Rams in their strength, and lambs in their play, are not more stirred than were the solid hills when Jehovah marched by. Nothing is immovable but God himself : the mountains shall depart, and the hills be removed, but the covenant of his grace abideth fast for ever and ever. Even thus do mountains of sin and hills of trouble

move when the Lord comes forth to lead his people to their eternal Canaan. Let us never fear, but rather let our faith say unto this mountain, " Be thou removed hence and cast into the sea," and it shall be done.

5. *"What ailed thee, O thou sea ? "* Wert thou terribly afraid ? Did thy strength fail thee ? Did thy very heart dry up ? " What ailed thee, O thou sea, *that thou fleddest ? "* Thou wert neighbour to the power of Pharaoh, but thou didst never fear his hosts ; stormy wind could never prevail against thee so as to divide thee in twain ; but when the way of the Lord was in thy great waters thou wast seized with affright, and thou becamest a fugitive from before him. *"Thou Jordan, that thou wast driven back ? "* What ailed thee, O quick descending river ? Thy fountains had not dried up, neither had a chasm opened to engulph thee ! The near approach of Israel and her God sufficed to make thee retrace thy steps. What aileth all our enemies that they fly when the Lord is on our side ? What aileth hell itself that it is utterly routed when Jesus lifts up a standard against it ? " Fear took hold upon them there," for fear of HIM the stoutest hearted did quake, and became as dead men.

6. *"Ye mountains, that ye skipped like rams ; and ye little hills, like lambs ? "* What ailed ye that ye were thus moved ? There is but one reply : the majesty of God made you to leap. A gracious mind will chide human nature for its strange insensibility, when the sea and the river, the mountains and the hills, are all sensitive to the presence of God. Man is endowed with reason and intelligence, and yet he sees unmoved that which the material creation beholds with fear. God has come nearer to us than ever he did to Sinai, or to Jordan, for he has assumed our nature, and yet the mass of mankind are neither driven back from their sins, nor moved in the paths of obedience.

7. *"Tremble, thou earth, at the presence of the Lord, at the presence of the God of Jacob."* Or " from before the Lord, the Adonai, the Master and King." Very fitly does the Psalm call upon all nature again to feel a holy awe because its Ruler is still in its midst.

" Quake when Jehovah walks abroad,
Quake, earth, at sight of Israel's God."

Let the believer feel that God is near, and he will serve the Lord with fear and rejoice with trembling. Awe is not cast out by faith, but the rather it becomes deeper and more profound. The Lord is most reverenced where he is most loved.

8. *"Which turned the rock into a standing water,"* causing a mere or lake to stand at its foot, making the wilderness a pool : so abundant was the supply of water from the rock that it remained like water in a reservoir. *"The flint into a fountain of waters,"* which flowed freely in streams, following the tribes in their devious marches. Behold what God can do ! It seemed impossible that the flinty rock should become a fountain ; but he speaks, and it is done. Not only do mountains move, but rocks yield rivers when the God of Israel wills that it should be so.

" From stone and solid rock he brings
The spreading lake, the gushing springs."

" O magnify the Lord with me, and let us exalt his name together," for he it is and he alone who doeth such wonders as these. He supplies our temporal needs from sources of the most unlikely kind, and never suffers the stream of his liberality to fail. As for our spiritual necessities they are all met by the water and the blood which gushed of old from the riven rock, Christ Jesus : therefore let us extol the Lord our God.

Our deliverance from under the yoke of sin is strikingly typified in the going up of Israel from Egypt, and so also was the victory of our Lord over the powers of death and hell. The Exodus should therefore be earnestly remembered by Christian hearts. Did not Moses on the mount of transfiguration speak to our Lord of " the exodus " which he should shortly accomplish at Jerusalem ; and is it not written of the hosts above that they sing the song of Moses the servant of God, and of the Lamb ? Do we not ourselves expect another coming of the Lord, when befor his face heaven and earth shall flee away and there shall be no more sea ? We join hen with the singers around the Passover table and make their Hallel ours, for we too have been led out of bondage and guided like a flock through a desert land, wherein the Lord supplies our wants with heavenly manna and water from the Rock of ages. Praise ye the Lord.

EXPLANATORY NOTES AND QUAINT SAYINGS.

Whole Psalm.—The cxivth Psalm appears to me to be an admirable ode, and I began to turn it into our own language.   As I was describing the journey of Israel from Egypt, and added the Divine Presence amongst them, I perceived a beauty in this Psalm, which was entirely new to me, and which I was going to lose ; and that is, that the poet utterly conceals the presence of God in the beginning of it, and rather lets a possessive pronoun go without a substantive, than he will so much as mention anything of divinity there.   " Judah was his sanctuary, and Israel his dominion " or kingdom.   The reason now seems evident, and this conduct necessary ; for, if God had appeared before, there could be no wonder why the mountains should leap and the sea retire ; therefore, that this convulsion of nature may be brought in with due surprise, his name is not mentioned till afterwards ; and then with a very agreeable turn of thought, God is introduced at once in all his majesty.   This is what I have attempted to imitate in a translation without paraphrase, and to preserve what I could of the spirit of the sacred author.

When Israel, freed from Pharaoh's hand,
Left the proud tyrant and his land,
The tribes with cheerful homage own
Their King, and Judah was his throne.

Across the deep their journey lay,
The deep divides to make them way ;
The streams of Jordan saw, and fled
With backward current to their head.

The mountains shook like frightened sheep,
Like lambs the little hillocks leap ;
Not Sinai on her base could stand,
Conscious of sovereign power at hand.

What power could make the deep divide ?
Make Jordan backward roll his tide ?
Why did ye leap, ye little hills ?
And whence the fright that Sinai feels ?

Let ev'ry mountain, ev'ry flood,
Retire, and know th' approaching God,
The King of Israel ! see him here :
Tremble, thou earth, adore and fear.

He thunders—and all nature mourns ;
The rock to standing pools he turns ;
Flints spring with fountains at his word,
And fires and seas confess their Lord.

Isaac Watts, in "The Spectator," 1712.

Verse 1.—*"When Israel went out of Egypt."*   Out of the midst of that nation, that is, out of the bowels of the Egyptians, who had, as it were, devoured them ; thus the Jew-doctors gloss upon this text.—*John Trapp.*

Verse 1.—*"Israel went out of Egypt."*   This was an emblem of the Lord's people in effectual vocation, coming out of bondage into liberty, out of darkness into light, out of superstition, and idolatry, and profaneness, to the service of the true God in righteousness and true holiness ; and *from a people of strange language* to those that speak the language of Canaan, a pure language, in which they can understand one another when they converse together, either about experience or doctrine ; and the manner of their coming out is much the same, by strength of hand, by the power of divine grace, yet willingly and cheerfully, with great riches, the riches of grace, and a title to the riches of glory, and with much spiritual strength ; for though weak in themselves, yet they are strong in Christ.—*John Gill.*

Verse 1.—*"The house of Jacob."*   The Israelites though they were a great number when they went forth from Egypt, nevertheless formed one house or family ; thus the church at the present time dispersed throughout the whole world is called one house : 1 Tim. iii. 15 ; Heb. iii. 6 ; 1 Pet. ii. 5 : and that because of one faith, **one** God, one Father, one baptism, Ephes. iv. 5.—*Marloratus.*

Verse 1.—*"A people of strange language."* When we find in verse 1, as in Psalm lxxxi. 5, Egypt spoken of as a land where the people were of a *"strange tongue,"* it seems likely that the reference is to their being a people who could not *speak of God,* as Israel could ; even as Zeph. iii. 9 tells of the *"pure lip,"* viz. the lip that calls on the name of the Lord.—*Andrew A. Bonar.*

Verse 1.—*"A people of strange language."* Mant translates this *"tyrant land,"* and has the following note :—" The Hebrew word here rendered " tyrant," has been supposed to signify " barbarous " ; that is, " using a barbarous or foreign language or pronunciation." But, says Parkhurst, the word seems rather to refer to the " violence " of the Egyptians towards the Israelites, or " the barbarity of their behaviour," which was more to the Psalmist's purpose than " the barbarity of their language " ; even supposing the reality of the latter in the time of Moses. The epithet " barbarous " would leave the same ambiguity as Parkhurst supposes to belong to the text. Bishop Horsley renders " a tyrannical people."

Verse 1.—*"A people of strange language."* The strange language is evidently an annoyance. Israel could not feel at home in Egypt.—*Justus Olshausen.*

Verse 2.—*"Judah was his sanctuary, and Israel his dominion."* These people were God's *sanctification and dominion,* that is, witnesses of his holy majesty in adopting them, and of his mighty power in delivering them : or, his *sanctification,* as having his holy priests to govern them in the points of piety ; and *dominion,* as having godly magistrates ordained from above to rule them in matters of policy : or, his *sanctuary,* both actually, because sanctifying him ; and passively, because sanctified of him. . . . This one verse expounds and exemplifies two prime petitions of the Lord's Prayer. " Hallowed be thy name, thy kingdom come " : for *Judah* was God's sanctuary, because *hallowing his name ;* and *Israel* his dominion, as desiring his *kingdom to come.* Let every man examine himself by this pattern, whether he be truly the servant of Jesus his Saviour, or the vassal of Satan the destroyer. If any man submit himself willingly to the domineering of the devil, and suffer sin to reign in his mortal members, obeying the lusts thereof, and working all uncleanness even with greediness ; assuredly that man is yet a chapel of Satan, and a slave to sin. On the contrary, whosoever unfeignedly desires that God's kingdom may come, being ever ready to be ruled according to his holy word, acknowledging it a lantern to his feet, and a guide to his paths ; admitting obediently his laws, and submitting himself alway to the same ; what is he, but a citizen of heaven, a subject of God, a saint, a *sanctuary* ?—*John Boys.*

Verse 2.—*"Judah was his sanctuary,"* etc. Reader, do not fail to remark when Israel was brought out of Egypt the Lord set up his tabernacle among them, and manifested his presence to them. And what is it now, when the Lord Jesus brings out his people from the Egypt of the world ? Doth he not fulfil that sweet promise, " Lo, I am with you alway, even unto the end of the world " ? Is it not the privilege of his people, to live *to* him, to live *with* him, and to live *upon* him ? Doth he not in every act declare, " I will say, it is my people ; and they shall say, the Lord is my God " ? Matt. xxviii. 20 ; Zech. xiii. 9.—*Robert Hawker.*

Verse 2.—*"Judah was his sanctuary."* Meaning not the tribe of Judah only, though they in many things had the pre-eminence ; the kingdom belonged to it, the chief ruler being out of it, especially the Messiah ; its standard was pitched and moved first ; it offered first to the service of the Lord ; and the Jews have a tradition, mentioned by Jarchi and Kimchi, that this tribe with its prince at the head of it, went into the Red Sea first ; the others fearing, but afterwards followed, encouraged by their example. In this place all the tribes are meant, the whole body of the people.—*John Gill.*

Verse 2.—One peculiarity of the second verse requires attention. It twice uses the word *"his,"* without naming any one. There are two theories to account for this circumstance. One is that Psalm cxiv. was always sung in immediate connection with cxiii., in which the name of God occurs no less than six times, so that the continuance of the train of thought made a fresh repetition of it here unnecessary. But this view, to be fully consistent with itself, must assume that the two Psalms are really one, with a merely arbitrary division, which does not, on the face of the matter, seem by any means probable, as the scope of thought in the two is perfectly distinct. The other, which is more satisfactory, regards the omission of the Holy

Name in this part of the Psalm as a practical artifice to heighten the effect of the answer to the sudden apostrophe in verses five and six. There would be nothing marvellous in the agitation of the sea, and river, and mountains in the presence of God, but it may well appear wonderful till that potent cause is revealed, as it is most forcibly in the dignified words of the seventh verse.—*Ewald and Perowne, in Neale and Littledale.*

Verse 3.—*"The sea saw it"* : to wit this glorious work of God in bringing his people out of Egypt.—*Matthew Pool.*

Verse 3.—*"The sea saw it."* Saw there that " Judah " was " God's sanctuary," " and Israel his dominion," and therefore *"fled"* ; for nothing could be more awful. It was this that *drove Jordan back,* and was an invincible dam to his streams ; God was at the head of that people, and therefore they must give way to them, must make room for them, they must retire, contrary to their nature, when God speaks the word.—*Matthew Henry.*

Verse 3.—*"The sea saw it, and fled."*

> The waves on either side
> Unloose their close embraces, and divide,
> And backwards press, as in some solemn show
> The crowding people do,
> (Though just before no space was seen,)
> To let the admirèd triumph pass between.
> The wondering army saw, on either hand,
> The no less wondering waves like rocks of crystal stand.
> They marched betwixt, and boldly trod
> The secret paths of God.
>
> *Abraham Cowley, 1618—1667.*

Verse 3.—*"Jordan was driven back."* And now the glorious day was come when, by a stupendous miracle, Jehovah had determined to show how able he was to remove every obstacle in the way of his people, and to subdue every enemy before their face. By his appointment the host, amounting probably to two millions-and-a-half of persons (about the same number as had crossed the Red Sea on foot), had removed to the banks of the river three days before, and now in marching array awaited the signal to cross the stream. At any time the passage of the river by such a multitude, with their women and children, their flocks and herds, and all their baggage, would have presented formidable difficulties ; but now the channel was filled with a deep and impetuous torrent, which overflowed its banks and spread widely on each side, probably extending nearly a mile in width ; while in the very sight of the scene were the Canaanitish hosts, who might be expected to pour out from their gates, and exterminate the invading multitude before they could reach the shore. Yet these difficulties were nothing to Almighty power, and only served to heighten the effect of the stupendous miracle about to be wrought.

By the command of Jehovah, the priests, bearing the ark of the covenant, the sacred symbol of the Divine presence, marched more than half-a-mile in front of the people, who were forbidden to come any nearer to it. Thus it was manifest that Jehovah needed not protection from Israel, but was their guard and guide, since the unarmed priests feared not to separate themselves from the host, and to venture with the ark into the river in the face of their enemies. And thus the army, standing aloof, had a better opportunity of seeing the wondrous results, and of admiring the mighty power of God exerted on their behalf ; for no sooner had the feet of the priests touched the brim of the overflowing river, than the swelling waters receded from them ; and not only the broad lower valley, but even the deep bed of the stream was presently emptied of water, and its pebbly bottom became dry. The waters which had been in the channel speedily ran off, and were lost in the Dead Sea ; whilst those which would naturally have replaced them from above, were miraculuosly suspended, and accumulated in a glassy heap far above the city Adam, that is beside Zaretan. These places are supposed to have been at least forty miles above the Dead Sea, and may possibly have been much more ; so that nearly the whole channel of the Lower Jordan, from a little below the Lake of Tiberias to the Dead Sea, was dry. . . . . . What a glorious termination of the long pilgrimage of Israel was this ! and how worthy of the power, wisdom, and goodness of their Divine Protector ! " The passage of this deep and rapid river," remarks Dr. Hales, " at the most unfavourable season, was more manifestly miraculous, if possible, than that of the Red Sea ; because here was no natural agency whatever employed ; no mighty wind to sweep a passage, as in the former case ; no reflux of the tide, on which minute philosophers might fasten to depreciate the miracle. It seems, therefore, to have been providentially designed to silence cavils respecting the former ; and it was done at noon-day, in the face of the sun, and in the presence, we may be sure, of the neighbouring inhabitants, and struck terror into the kings of the Canaanites and Amorites westward of the river."—*Philip Henry Gosse, in "Sacred Streams,"* 1877.

Verse 3.—*"Jordan was driven back."* The waters know their Maker : that Jordan which flowed with full streams when Christ went into it to be baptized, now gives way when the same God must pass through it in state : then there was use of his water, now of his sand. I hear no more news of any rod to strike the waters ; the presence of the ark of the Lord God, Lord of all the world, is sign enough to these waves, which now, as if a sinew were broken, run back to their issues, and dare not so much as wet the feet of the priests that bare it. How subservient are all the creatures to the God that made them ! How glorious a God do we serve ; whom all the powers of the heavens and elements are willingly subject unto, and gladly take that nature which he pleaseth to give them.—*Abraham Wright.*

Verse 3.—*"Jordan was driven back."* It was probably at the point near the present southern fords, crossed at the time of the Christian era by a bridge. The river was at its usual state of flood at the spring of the year, so as to fill the whole of the bed, up to the margin of the jungle with which the river banks are lined. On the broken edge of the swollen stream, the band of priests stood with the ark on their shoulders. At the distance of nearly a mile in the rear was the mass of the army. Suddenly the full bed of the Jordan was dried before them. High up the river, " far, far away," " in Adam, the city which is beside Zaretan," " as far as the parts of Kirjath-jearim " (Josh. iii. 16), that is, at a distance of thirty miles from the place of the Israelite encampment, the waters there stood which " descended " " from the heights above,"—stood and rose up, as if gathered into a waterskin ; as if in a barrier or heap, as if congealed ; and those that " descended " towards the sea of " the desert," the salt Sea, " failed and were cut off." Thus the scene presented is of the " descending stream " (the words employed seem to have a special reference to that peculiar and most significant name of the " Jordan "), not parted asunder, as we generally fancy, but, as the Psalm expresses it, " turned backwards " ; the whole bed of the river left dry from north to south, through its long windings ; the huge stones lying bare here and there, imbedded in the soft bottom ; or the shingly pebbles drifted along the course of the channel.—*Arthur Penrhyn Stanley, in "The History of the Jewish Church,"* 1870.

Verse 4.—*"The mountains skipped like rams,"* etc. The figure drawn from the *lambs* and *rams* would appear to be inferior to the magnitude of the subject. But it was the prophet's intention to express in the homeliest way the incredible manner in which God, on these occasions, displayed his power. The stability of the earth being, as it were, founded on the mountains, what connection can they have with rams and lambs, that they should be agitated, skipping hither and thither ? In speaking in this homely style, he does not mean to detract from the greatness of the miracle, but more forcibly to engrave these extraordinary tokens of God's power on the illiterate.—*John Calvin.*

Verse 4.—*"Skipped."* A poetic description of the concussion caused by the thunder and lightning that accompanied the divine presence.—*James G. Murphy.*

Verse 4.—At the giving of the law at Sinai, Horeb and the mountains around, both great and small, shook with a sudden and mighty earthquake, like rams leaping in a grassy plain, with the young sheep frisking round them.—*Plain Commentary.*

Verses 4—6.—When Christ descends upon the soul in the work of conversion, what strength doth he put forth ! The strongholds of sin are battered down, every high thing that exalts itself against the knowledge of Christ is brought into captivity to the obedience of his sceptre, 2 Cor. x. 4, 5. Devils are cast out of the possession which they have kept for many years without the least disturbance. Strong lusts are mortified and the very constitution of the soul is changed. *"What ailed thee, O thou sea, that thou fleddest ? thou Jordan, that thou wast driven back ? ye mountains, that ye skipped like rams ?"* etc. The prophet speaks those words of the powerful entrance of the children of Israel into Canaan. The like is done by Christ in the conversion of a sinner. Jordan is driven back, the whole course of the soul is altered, the mountains skip like rams. There are many mountains in the soul of a sinner, as pride, unbelief, self-conceitedness, atheism, profaneness, etc. These mountains are plucked up by the roots in a moment when Christ begins the work of conversion. —*Ralph Robinson*.

Verse 5.—

> Fly where thou wilt, O sea!
> And Jordan's current cease!
> Jordan, there is no need of thee,
> For at God's word, whene'er he please,
> The rocks shall weep new waters forth instead of these.
>
> *Abraham Cowley*.

Verses 5, 6.—A singular animation and an almost dramatic force are given to the poem by the beautiful apostrophe in verses 5, 6, and the effect of this is heightened in a remarkable degree by the use of the present tenses. The awe and the trembling of nature are a spectacle on which the poet is looking. The parted sea through which Israel walks as on dry land, the rushing Jordan arrested in its course, the granite cliffs of Sinai shaken to their base—he sees it all, and asks in wonder what it means ?—*J. J. Stewart Perowne*.

Verses 5, 6.—This questioning teaches us that we should ourselves consider and inquire concerning the reason of those things, which we see to have been done in a wondrous way, out of the course of nature. There are signs in the sun, moon, stars, heaven, etc., concerning which Christ has spoken. Let us inquire the reason why they are, that we be not stupid and inaccurate spectators. The things which are done miraculously do speak : and they can give answer why they are done. Nay, rather, portents, signs, earthquakes, extraordinary appearances are loud-speaking, and they declare from themselves what they are : namely, that they are prophetic of the anger and future vengeance of God. Such inquiry as this is not prying curiosity, but is pious and useful, working to this end, that we become observant of the judgments of God, with which he visits this world, and yield ourselves to his grace, and so we escape the coming vengeance.—*Wolfgang Musculus*.

Verses 5, 6.—

> What ails thee, sea, to part,
> Thee, Jordan, back to start ?
> Ye mountains, like the rams to leap,
> Ye little hills, like sheep ?
>
> *John Keble*.

Verse 7.—"*Tremble, thou earth.*" Hebrew, *Be in pain*, as a travailing woman ; for if the giving of the law had such dreadful effects, what should the breaking thereof have ?—*John Trapp*.

Verse 7.—

> " At the presence of the Lord be in pangs, O earth.'

"*Lord,*" *Adon*, the Sovereign Ruler. "*Pangs,*" *Chuli* : Mic. iv. 10. The convulsions of nature, which accompanied the Exodus, were as the birth-throes of the Israelite people. "A nation was born in a day." But the deliverance out of Babylon saw the prelude to a far more wondrous truth ;—that of him, in whom nature was to be regenerated.—*William Kay*.

Verses 7, 8.—"*Tremble,*" etc. This is an answer to the preceding question : as if he had said, It is no wonder that Sinai, and Horeb, and a few adjoining hills should tremble at the majestic presence of God ; for the whole earth must do so, whenever he pleases.—*Thomas Fenton*.

Verse 8.—"*Which turned the rock into a standing water.*" *Into a pool.* The divine poet represents the very substance of the rock as being converted into water, not literally, but poetically ; thus ornamenting his sketch of the wondrous power displayed on this occasion.—*William Walford*.

Verse 8.—The remarkable rock in Sinai which tradition regards as the one which Moses smote, is at least well chosen in regard to its situation, whatever opinion we may form of the truth of that tradition, which it seems to be the disposition of late travellers to regard with more respect than was formerly entertained. It is an isolated mass of granite, nearly twenty feet square and high, with its base concealed in the earth—we are left to conjecture to what depth. In the face of the rock are a number of horizontal fissures, at unequal distances from each other ; some near the top, and others at a little distance from the surface of the ground. An American traveller* says : " The colour and whole appearance of the rock are such that, if seen elsewhere, and disconnected from all traditions, no one would hesitate to believe that they had been produced by water flowing from these fissures. I think it would be extremely difficult to form these fissures or produce these appearances by art. It is not less difficult to believe that a natural fountain should flow at the height of a dozen feet out of the face of an isolated rock. Believing, as I do, that the water was brought out of a rock belonging to this mountain, I can see nothing incredible in the opinion that this is the identical rock, and that these fissures, and the other appearances, should be regarded as evidences of the fact."— *John Kitto.*

Verse 8.—Shall *the hard rock be turned into a standing water, and the flint-stone into a springing well ?* and shall not our hard and flinty hearts, in consideration of our own miseries, and God's unspeakable mercies in delivering us from evil, (if not gush forth into fountains of tears) express so much as a little *standing water* in our eyes ? It is our hard heart indeed, *quod nec compunctione scinditur, nec pietate mollitur, nec movetur precibus, minis non cedit, flagellis duratur,†* etc.   O Lord, touch thou the mountains and they shall smoke, touch our lips with a coal from thine altar, and our mouth shall show forth thy praise. Smite, Lord, our flinty hearts as hard as the nether millstone, with the hammer of thy word, and mollify them also with the drops of thy mercies and dew of thy Spirit ; make them humble, fleshy, flexible, circumcised, soft, obedient, new, clean, broken, and then " a broken and a contrite heart, O God, shalt thou not despise." Ps. li. 17. " O Lord my God, give me grace from the very bottom of my heart to desire thee ; in desiring, to seek thee ; in seeking, to find ; in finding, to love thee ; in loving, utterly to loathe my former wickedness ; " that living in thy fear, and dying in thy favour, when I have passed through this Egypt and wilderness of this world, I may possess the heavenly Canaan and happy land of promise, prepared for all such as love thy coming, even for every Christian one, which is thy *"dominion "* and *"sanctuary."*‡—*John Boys.*

Verse 8.—The same almighty power that turned waters into a rock to be a wall to Israel (Exod. xiv. 22), turned the rock into waters to be a well to Israel. As they were protected, so they were provided for, by miracles, standing miracles ; for such was the standing water, that fountain of waters, into which the rock, the flinty rock, was turned " and that rock was Christ," 1 Cor. x. 4. For he is a fountain of living waters to his Israel, from whom they receive grace for grace.—*Matthew Henry.*

Verse 8.—*"The flint into a fountain of waters."* The causing of water to gush forth out of the flinty rock is a practical proof of unlimited omnipotence and of the grace which converts death into life. Let the earth then tremble before the Lord, the God of Jacob. It has always trembled before him, and before him let it tremble. For that which he has been he still ever is ; and as he came once he will come again. —*Franz Delitzsch.*

HINTS TO PREACHERS.

Verses 1, 2.—The time of first delivery from sin a season notable for the peculiar presence of God.

Verses 1, 2.—The Lord was to his people—I. A deliverer. II. A priest—" his sanctuary." III. A king—" his dominion."

Verses 1, 7.—" The house of Jacob " and " the God of Jacob," the relation between the two.

Verse 2.—The church the temple of sanctity and the domain of obedience.

---

* Dr. Olin.　　　　† Bernard　　　　‡ Augustine.

Verse 3.—The impenitence of sinners rebuked by the inanimate creation.

Verse 3.—"Jordan was driven back," or death overcome.

Verse 4.—The movableness of things which appear to be fixed and settled. God's power of creating a stir in lethargic minds, among ancient systems, and prejudiced persons of the highest rank.

Verses 7, 8.—Holy awe. I. Should be caused by the fact of the divine presence. Should be increased by his covenant character—"the God of Jacob." III. Should culminate when we see displays of his grace towards his people—"which turned," etc. IV. Should become universal.

Verse 8.—Wonders akin to the miracle at the rock. I. Christ's death the source of life. II. Adversity a means of prosperity. III. Hard hearts made penitent. IV. Barrenness of soul turned into abundance.

Verse 8.—Divine supplies. 1. Sure—for he will fetch them even from a rock 2. Plentiful—"a mere or standing water." 3. Continual "fountain of waters.". 4. Instructive. Should create in us holy awe at the power, etc., of the Lord.

PSALM CXV.

Subject.—*In the former Psalm the past wonders which God had wrought were recounted to his honour, and in the present Psalm he is entreated to glorify himself again, because the heathen were presuming upon the absence of miracles, were altogether denying the miracles of former ages, and insulting the people of God with the question, "Where is now their God?" It grieved the heart of the godly that Jehovah should be thus dishonoured, and treating their own condition of reproach as unworthy of notice, they beseech the Lord at least to vindicate his own name. The Psalmist is evidently indignant that the worshippers of foolish idols should be able to put such a taunting question to the people who worshipped the only living and true God; and having spent his indignation in sarcasm upon the images and their makers, he proceeds to exhort the house of Israel to trust in God and bless his name. As those who were dead and gone could no longer sing Psalms unto the Lord among the sons of men, he exhorts the faithful who were then living to take care that God is not robbed of his praise, and then he closes with an exulting Hallelujah. Should not living men extol the living God?*

Division.—*For the better expounding of it, the Psalm may be divided into an entreaty of God to vindicate his own honour, verses 1, 2; a contemptuous description of the false gods and their worshippers, 3—8; an exhortation to the faithful to trust in God and to expect great blessings from him, 9—15; an explanation of God's relationship to their present condition of things, verse 16; and a reminder that, not the dead, but the living, must continually praise God here below, 17, 18.*

EXPOSITION.

Not unto us, O Lord, not unto us, but unto thy name give glory, for thy mercy, *and* for thy truth's sake.

2 Wherefore should the heathen say, Where *is* now their God?

1. It will be well to remember that this Psalm was sung at the Passover, and therefore it bears relationship to the deliverance from Egypt. The burden of it seems to be a prayer that the living God, who had been so glorious at the Red Sea and at the Jordan, should again for his name's sake display the wonders of his power. *"Not unto us, O Lord, not unto us, but unto thy name give glory."* The people undoubtedly wished for relief from the contemptuous insults of idolaters, but their main desire was that Jehovah himself should no longer be the object of heathen insults. The saddest part of all their trouble was that their God was no longer feared and dreaded by their adversaries. When Israel marched into Canaan, a terror was upon all the people round about, because of Jehovah, the mighty God; but this dread the nations had shaken off since there had been of late no remarkable display of miraculous power. Therefore Israel cried unto her God that he would again make bare his arm as in the day when he cut Rahab and wounded the dragon. The prayer is evidently tinctured with a consciousness of unworthiness; because of their past unfaithfulness they hardly dared to appeal to the covenant, and to ask blessings for themselves, but they fell back upon the honour of the Lord their God—an old style of argument which their great lawgiver, Moses, had used with such effect when he pleaded, "Wherefore should the Egyptians speak and say, For mischief did he bring them out, to slay them in the mountains, and to consume them from the face of the earth? Turn from thy fierce wrath, and repent of this evil against thy people." Joshua also used the like argument when he said, "What wilt thou do unto thy great name?" In such manner also let us pray when no other plea is available because of our sense of sin; for the Lord is always jealous of his honour, and will work for his name's sake when no other motive will move him.

The repetition of the words, "Not unto us," would seem to indicate a very serious desire to renounce any glory which they might at any time have proudly appropriated to themselves, and it also sets forth the vehemence of their wish that God would at any cost to them magnify his own name. They loathed the idea of seeking their own glory, and rejected the thought with the utmost detestation ; again and again disclaiming any self-glorifying motive in their supplication. *"For thy mercy, and for thy truth's sake."* These attributes seemed most in jeopardy. How could the heathen think Jehovah to be a merciful God if he gave his people over to the hands of their enemies ? How could they believe him to be faithful and true if, after all his solemn covenant engagements, he utterly rejected his chosen nation ? God is very jealous of the two glorious attributes of grace and truth, and the plea that these may not be dishonoured has great weight with him. In these times, when the first victories of the gospel are only remembered as histories of a dim and distant past, sceptics are apt to boast that the gospel has lost its youthful strength and they even presume to cast a slur upon the name of God himself. We may therefore rightly entreat the divine interposition that the apparent blot may be removed from his escutcheon, and that his own word may shine forth gloriously as in the days of old. We may not desire the triumph of our opinions, for our own sakes, or for the honour of a sect, but we may confidently pray for the triumph of truth, that God himself may be honoured.

2. *"Wherefore should the heathen say, Where is now their God ? "* Or, more literally, "Where, pray, is their God ? " Why should the nations be allowed with a sneer of contempt to question the existence, and mercy, and faithfulness of Jehovah ? They are always ready to blaspheme ; we may well pray that they may not derive a reason for so doing from the course of providence, or the decline of the church. When they see the godly down-trodden while they themselves live at ease, and act the part of persecutors, they are very apt to speak as if they had triumphed over God himself, or as if he had altogether left the field of action and deserted his saints. When the prayers and tears of the godly seem to be unregarded, and their miseries are rather increased than assuaged, then do the wicked multiply their taunts and jeers, and even argue that their own wretched irreligion is better than the faith of Christians, because for the present their condition is so much preferable to that of the afflicted saints. And, truly, this is the very sting of the trials of God's chosen when they see the veracity of the Lord questioned, and the name of God profaned because of their sufferings. If they could hope that some good result would come out of all this they would endure it with patience ; but as they are unable to perceive any desirable result consequent thereon, they enquire with holy anxiety, " Wherefore should the heathen be permitted to speak thus ? " It is a question to which it would be hard to reply, and yet no doubt there is an answer. Sometimes the nations are permitted thus to blaspheme, in order that they may fill up the measure of their iniquity, and in order that the subsequent interposition of God may be rendered the more illustrious in contrast with their profane boastings. Do they say, " Where is now their God ? " They shall know by-and-by, for it is written, " Ah, I will ease me of mine adversaries " ; they shall know it also when the righteous shall " shine forth as the sun in the kingdom of their Father." Do they say, " Where is the promise of his coming ? " That coming shall be speedy and terrible to them. In our own case, by our own lukewarmness and the neglect of faithful gospel preaching, we have permitted the uprise and spread of modern doubt, and we are bound to confess it with deep sorrow of soul ; yet we may not therefore lose heart, but may still plead with God to save his own truth and grace from the contempt of men of the world. Our honour and the honour of the church are small matters, but the glory of God is the jewel of the universe, of which all else is but the setting ; and we may come to the Lord and plead his jealousy for his name, being well assured that he will not suffer that name to be dishonoured. Wherefore should the pretended wise men of the period be permitted to say that they doubt the personality of God ? Wherefore should they say that answers to prayer are pious delusions, and that the resurrection and the deity of our Lord Jesus are moot points ? Wherefore should they be permitted to speak disparagingly of atonement by blood and by price, and reject utterly the doctrine of the wrath of God against sin, even that wrath which burneth for ever and ever ? They speak exceeding proudly, and only God can stop their arrogant blusterings : let us by extraordinary intercession prevail upon him to interpose, by giving to his gospel such a triumphant vindication as shall utterly silence the perverse opposition of ungodly men.

3 But our God *is* in the heavens : he hath done whatsoever he hath pleased.

4 Their idols *are* silver and gold, the work of men's hands.

5 They have mouths, but they speak not : eyes have they, but they see not :

6 They have ears, but they hear not : noses have they, but they smell not :

7 They have hands, but they handle not : feet have they, but they walk not : neither speak they through their throat.

8 They that make them are like unto them ; *so is* every one that trusteth in them.

3. *"But our God is in the heavens "*—where he should be ; above the reach of mortal sneers, over-hearing all the vain janglings of men, but looking down with silent scorn upon the makers of the babel. Supreme above all opposing powers, the Lord reigneth upon a throne high and lifted up. Incomprehensible in essence, he rises above the loftiest thought of the wise ; absolute in will and infinite in power, he is superior to the limitations which belong to earth and time. This God is *our* God, and we are not ashamed to own him, albeit he may not work miracles at the beck and call of every vain-glorious boaster who may choose to challenge him. Once they bade his Son come down from the cross and they would believe in him, now they would have God overstep the ordinary bounds of his providence and come down from heaven to convince them : but other matters occupy his august mind besides the convincement of those who wilfully shut their eyes to the super-abundant evidences of his divine power and Godhead, which are all around them. If our God be neither seen nor heard, and is not to be worshipped under any outward symbol, yet is he none the less real and true, for he is where his adversaries can never be—in the heavens, whence he stretches forth his sceptre, and rules with boundless power.

"He hath done whatsoever he hath pleased." Up till this moment his decrees have been fulfilled, and his eternal purposes accomplished ; he has not been asleep, nor oblivious of the affairs of men ; he has worked, and he has worked effectually, none have been able to thwart, nor even so much as to hinder him. " Whatsoever he hath pleased " : however distasteful to his enemies, the Lord has accomplished all his good pleasure without difficulty ; even when his adversaries raved and raged against him they have been compelled to carry out his designs against their will. Even proud Pharoah, when most defiant of the Lord was but as clay upon the potter's wheel, and the Lord's end and design in him were fully answered. We may well endure the jeering question, " Where is now their God ? " while we are perfectly sure that his providence is undisturbed, his throne unshaken, and his purposes unchanged. What he hath done he will yet do, his counsel shall stand, and he will do all his pleasure, and at the end of the great drama of human history, the omnipotence of God and his immutability and faithfulness will be more than vindicated to the eternal confusion of his adversaries.

4. *"Their idols are silver and gold."* mere dead inert matter ; at the best only made of precious metal, but that metal quite as powerless as the commonest wood or clay. The value of the idol shows the folly of the maker in wasting his substance, but certainly does not increase the power of the image, since there is no more life in silver and gold than in brass or iron. *"The work of men's hands.".* Inasmuch as the maker is always greater than the thing that he has made, these idols are less to be honoured than the artificers, who fashioned them. How irrational that men should adore that which is less than themselves ! How strange that a man should think that he can make a god ! Can madness go further ? Our God is a spirit, and his hands made the heavens and the earth : well may we worship him, and we need not be disturbed at the sneering question of those who are so insane as to refuse to adore the living God, and yet bow their knees before images of their own carving. We may make an application of all this to the times in which we are now living. The god of modern thought is the creation of the thinker himself, evolved out of his own consciousness, or fashioned according to his own notion of what a god should be. Now. it is evident that such a being is no God. It is impossible that there should be a God at all except the God of revelation. A god who can be fashioned by our own thoughts is no more a god than the image manufactured or produced by our own hands. The true God must of necessity be his own

revealer. It is clearly impossible that a being who can be excogitated and comprehended by the reason of man should be the infinite and incomprehensible God. Their idols are blinded reason and diseased thought, the product of men's muddled brains, and they will come to nought.

5. *"They have mouths, but they speak not."* The idols cannot utter even the faintest sound, they cannot communicate with their worshippers, they can neither promise nor threaten, command nor console, explain the past nor prophesy the future. If they had no mouths they might not be expected to speak, but having mouths and speaking not, they are mere dumb idols, and not worthy to be compared with the Lord God who thundered at Sinai, who in old time spake by his servants the prophets, and whose voice even now breaketh the cedars of Lebanon. *"Eyes have they, but they see not."* They cannot tell who their worshippers may be or what they offer. Certain idols have had jewels in their eyes more precious than a king's ransom, but they were as blind as the rest of the fraternity. A god who has eyes, and cannot see, is a blind deity ; and blindness is a calamity, and not an attribute of godhead. He must be very blind who worships a blind god : we *pity* a blind man, it is strange to *worship* a blind image.

6. *"They have ears, but they hear not."* The Psalmist might have pointed to the monstrous ears with which some heathen deities are disfigured,—truly they *have* ears ; but no prayer of their votaries, though shouted by a million voices, can ever be heard by them. How can gold and silver hear, and how can a rational being address petitions to one who cannot even hear his words ? *"Noses have they, but they smell not."* The Psalmist seems to heap together these sentences with something of the grim sardonic spirit of Elijah when he said, " Cry aloud : for he is a god ; either he is talking, or he is pursuing, or he is on a journey, or peradventure he sleepeth, and must be awaked." In sacred scorn he mocks at those who burn sweet spices, and fill their temples with clouds of smoke, all offered to an image whose nose cannot perceive the perfume. He seems to point his finger to every part of the countenance of the image, and thus pours contempt upon the noblest part of the idol, if any part of such a thing can be noble even in the least degree.

7. *"They have hands, but they handle not."* Looking lower down upon the images, the Psalmist says, " They have hands, but they handle not," they cannot receive that which is handed to them, they cannot grasp the sceptre of power or the sword of vengeance, they can neither distribute benefits nor dispense judgments, and the most trifling act they are utterly unable to perform. An infant's hand excels them in power. *"Feet have they, but they walk not."* They must be lifted into their places or they would never reach their shrines ; they must be fastened in their shrines or they would fall ; they must be carried or they could never move ; they cannot come to the rescue of their friends, nor escape the iconoclasm of their foes. The meanest insect has more power of locomotion than the greatest heathen god. *"Neither speak they through their throat."* They cannot even reach so far as the guttural noise of the lowest order of beasts ; neither a grunt, nor a growl, nor a groan, nor so much as a mutter, can come from them. Their priests asserted that the images of the gods upon special occasions uttered hollow sounds, but it was a mere pretence, or a crafty artifice: images of gold or silver are incapable of living sounds. Thus has the Psalmist surveyed the idol from head to foot, looked in its face, and sounded its throat, and he writes it down as utterly contemptible.

8. *"They that make them are like unto them."* Those who make such things for worship are as stupid, senseless, and irrational as the figures they construct. So far as any spiritual life, thought, and judgment are concerned, they are rather the images of men than rational beings. The censure is by no means too severe. Who has not found the words leaping to his lips when he has seen the idols of the Romanists ? *"So is every one that trusteth in them."* Those who have sunk so low as to be capable of confiding in idols have reached the extreme of folly, and are worthy of as much contempt as their detestable deities. Luther's hard speeches were well deserved by the Papists ; they must be mere dolts to worship the rotten relics which are the objects of their veneration.

The god of modern thought exceedingly resembles the deities described in this Psalm. Pantheism is wondrously akin to Polytheism, and yet differs very little from Atheism. The god manufactured by our great thinkers is a mere abstraction : he has no eternal purposes, he does not interpose on the behalf of his people, he cares but very little as to how much man sins, for he has given to the initiated " a larger hope " by which the most incorrigible are to be restored. He is what the last set of critics chooses to make him, he has said what they choose to say, and he will do what they please to prescribe. Let this creed and its devotees alone, and they will work out their own refutation, for as now their god is fashioned like themselves, they will by degrees fashion themselves like their god ; and when the principles of justice, law, and order shall have all been effectually sapped we may possibly witness in some form of socialism, similar to that which is so sadly spreading in Germany, a repetition of the evils which have in former ages befallen nations which have refused the living God, and set up gods of their own.

9 O Israel, trust thou in the LORD : he *is* their help and their shield.

10 O house of Aaron, trust in the LORD : he *is* their help and their shield.

11 Ye that fear the LORD, trust in the LORD : he *is* their help and their shield,

12 The LORD hath been mindful of us : he will bless *us ;* he will bless the house of Israel ; he will bless the house of Aaron.

13 He will bless them that fear the LORD, *both* small and great.

14 The LORD shall increase you more and more, you and your children.

15 Ye *are* blessed of the LORD which made heaven and earth.

9. "*O Israel, trust thou in the LORD.*" Whatever others do, let the elect of heaven keep fast to the God who chose them. Jehovah is the God of Jacob, let his children prove their loyalty to their God by their confidence in him. Whatever our trouble may be, and however fierce the blasphemous language of our enemies, let us not fear nor falter, but confidently rest in him who is able to vindicate his own honour, and protect his own servants. "*He is their help and their shield.*" He is the friend of his servants, both actively and passively, giving them both aid in labour and defence in danger. In the use of the pronoun " their," the Psalmist may have spoken to himself, in a sort of soliloquy : he had given the exhortation, " trust in Jehovah," and then he whispers to himself, " They may well do so, for he is at all times the strength and security of his servants."

10. "*O house of Aaron, trust in the LORD.*" You who are nearest to him, trust him most ; your very calling is connected with his truth and is meant to declare his glory, therefore never entertain a doubt concerning him, but lead the way in holy confidence. The priests were the leaders, teachers, and exemplars of the people, and therefore above all others they should place an unreserved reliance upon Israel's God. The Psalmist is glad to add that they did so, for he says, "*He is their help and their shield.*" It is good to exhort those to faith who have faith : " These things have I written unto you that believe on the name of the Son of God ; . . . that ye may believe on the name of the Son of God." We may stir up pure minds by way of remembrance, and exhort men to trust in the Lord because we know that they are trusting already.

11. The next verse is of the same tenor—"*Ye that fear the LORD, trust in the LORD,*" whether belonging to Israel, or to the house of Aaron, or not, all those who reverence Jehovah are permitted and commanded to confide in him. "*He is their help and their shield.*" He does aid and protect all those who worship him in filial fear, to whatever nation they may belong. No doubt these repeated exhortations were rendered necessary by the trying condition in which the children of Israel were found : the sneers of the adversary would assail all the people, they would most bitterly be felt by the priests and ministers, and those who were secret proselytes would groan in secret under the contempt forced upon their religion and their God. All this would be very staggering to faith, and therefore they were bidden again and again and again to trust in Jehovah.

This must have been a very pleasant song to households in Babylon, or far away in Persia, when they met together in the night to eat the Paschal supper in a land which knew them not, where they wept as they remembered Zion. We seem to hear them repeating the three-fold word, " Trust in Jehovah," men and women and little children singing out their scorn of the dominant idolatry, and declaring their adhesion to the one God of Israel. In the same manner in this day of blasphemy and rebuke it becomes us all to abound in testimonies to the truth of God. The sceptic is loud in his unbelief, let us be equally open in the avowal of our faith.

12. *"The Lord hath been mindful of us,"* or *"*Jehovah hath remembered us." His past mercies prove that we are on his heart, and though for the present he may afflict us, yet he does not forget us. We have not to put him in remembrance as though he found it hard to recollect his children, but he hath remembered us and therefore he will in future deal well with us. *"He will bless us."* The word *"us"* is supplied by the translators, and is superfluous, the passage should run, *"He will bless ; he will bless the house of Israel ; he will bless the house of Aaron."* The repetition of the word *"* bless *"* adds great effect to the passage. The Lord has many blessings, each one worthy to be remembered, he blesses and blesses and blesses again. Where he has once bestowed his favour he continues it ; his blessing delights to visit the same house very often and to abide where it has once lodged. Blessing does not impoverish the Lord : he has multiplied his mercies in the past, and he will pour them forth thick and threefold in the future. He will have a general blessing for all who fear him, a peculiar blessing for the whole house of Israel, and a double blessing for the sons of Aaron. It is his nature to bless, it is his prerogative to bless, it is his glory to bless, it is his delight to bless ; he has promised to bless, and therefore be sure of this, that he will bless and bless and bless without ceasing.

13. *"He will bless them that fear the Lord, both small and great."* So long as a man fears the Lord it matters nothing whether he be prince or peasant, patriarch or pauper, God will assuredly bless him. He supplies the want of every living thing, from the leviathan of the sea to the insect upon a leaf, and he will suffer none of the godly to be forgotten, however small their abilities, or mean their position. This is a sweet cordial for those who are little in faith, and own themselves to be mere babes in the family of grace. There is the same blessing for the least saint as for the greatest ; yea, if anything, the " small " shall be first ; for as the necessity is the more pressing, the supply shall be the more speedy.

14. *"The Lord shall increase you more and more, you and your children."* Just as in Egypt he multiplied the people exceedingly, so will he increase the number of his saints upon the earth ; not only shall the faithful be blessed with converts, and so with a spiritual seed ; but those who are their spiritual children shall become fruitful also, and thus the multitude of the elect shall be accomplished ; God shall increase the people, and shall increase the joy. Even to the end of the ages the race of true believers shall be continued, and shall growingly multiply in number and in power. The first blessing upon mankind was, " Be fruitful, and multiply, and replenish the earth " ; and it is this blessing which God now pronounces upon them that fear him. Despite the idols of philosophy and sacramentarianism, the truth shall gather its disciples, and fill the land with its defenders.

15. *"Ye are blessed of the Lord which made heaven and earth."* This is another form of the blessing of Melchizedek : " Blessed be Abram of the Most High God, possessor of heaven and earth " ; and upon us through our great Melchizedek this same benediction rests. It is an omnipotent blessing, conveying to us all that an Almighty God can do, whether in heaven or on earth, This fulness is infinite, and the consolation which it brings is unfailing ; he that made heaven and earth can give us all things while we dwell below, and bring us safely to his palace above. Happy are the people upon whom such a blessing rests ; their portion is infinitely above that of those whose only hope lies in a piece of gilded wood, or an image of sculptured stone.

16 The heaven, *even* the heavens, *are* the Lord's : but the earth hath he given to the children of men.

16. *"The heaven, even the heavens, are the Lord's."* There he specially reigns, and manifests his greatness and his glory : *"but the earth hath he given to the children of men."* He hath left the world during the present dispensation in a great measure under the power and will of men, so that things are not here below in the same perfect order as the things which are above. It is true the Lord rules over all things by his providence, but yet he allows and permits men to break his laws and persecute his people for the time being, and to set up their dumb idols in opposition to him. The free agency which he gave to his creatures necessitated that in some degree he should restrain his power and suffer the children of men to follow their own devices ; yet nevertheless, since he has not vacated heaven, he is still master of earth, and can at any time gather up all the reins into his own hands. Perhaps,

however, the passage is meant to have another meaning, viz., that God will increase his people, because he has given the earth to them, and intends that they shall fill it. Man was constituted originally God's vicegerent over the world, and though so yet we see not all things put under him, we see Jesus exalted on high, and in him the children of men shall receive a loftier dominion even on earth than as yet they have known. " The meek shall inherit the earth ; and shall delight themselves in the abundance of peace " : and our Lord Jesus shall reign amongst his ancients gloriously. All this will reflect the exceeding glory of him who reveals himself personally in heaven, and in the mystical body of Christ below. The earth belongs to the sons of God, and we are bound to subdue it for our Lord Jesus, for he must reign. The Lord hath given him the heathen for his inheritance, and the uttermost parts of the earth for his possession.

17 The dead praise not the LORD, neither any that go down into silence.
18 But we will bless the LORD from this time forth and for evermore. Praise the LORD.

17. *"The dead praise not the LORD "*—so far as this world is concerned. They cannot unite in the Psalms and hymns and spiritual songs with which the church delights to adore her Lord. The preacher cannot magnify the Lord from his coffin, nor the Christian worker further manifest the power of divine grace by daily activity while he lies in the grave. *"Neither any that go down into silence."* The tomb sends forth no voice ; from mouldering bones and flesh-consuming worms there arises no sound of gospel ministry nor of gracious song. One by one the singers in the consecrated choir of saints steal away from us, and we miss their music. Thank God, they have gone above to swell the harmonies of the skies, but as far as we are concerned, we have need to sing all the more earnestly because so many songsters have left our choirs.

18. *"But we will bless the LORD from this time forth and for evermore."* We who are still living will take care that the praises of God shall not fail among the sons of men. Our afflictions and depressions of spirit shall not cause us to suspend our praises ; neither shall old age, and increasing infirmities damp the celestial fires, nay, nor shall even death itself cause us to cease from the delightful occupation. The spiritually dead cannot praise God, but the life within us constrains us to do so. The ungodly may abide in silence, but we will lift up our voices to the praise of Jehovah. Even though for a time he may work no miracle, and we may see no peculiar interposition of his power, yet on the strength of what he has done in ages past we will continue to laud his name " until the day break, and the shadows flee away," when he shall once more shine forth as the sun to gladden the faces of his children. The present time is auspicious for commencing a life of praise, since to-day he bids us hear his voice of mercy. " From this time forth " is the suggestion of wisdom, for this duty ought not to be delayed ; and it is the dictate of gratitude, for there are pressing reasons for prompt thankfulness. Once begin praising God and we have entered upon an endless service. Even eternity cannot exhaust the reasons why God should be glorified. *"Praise the LORD,"* or Hallelujah. Though the dead cannot, and the wicked will not, and the careless do not praise God, yet we will shout " Hallelujah " for ever and ever. Amen.

EXPLANATORY NOTES AND QUAINT SAYINGS.

Whole Psalm.—Several manuscripts and editions, also the Septuagint, the Syriac, and many of the old translators join this Psalm to the preceding, and make one of them. But the argument and the arrangement of the two Psalms do not allow of the least doubt as to their original independence of each other.—*Justus Olshausen.*

Verse 1.—*"Not unto us, O LORD, not unto us, but unto thy name give glory."* The Psalmist, by this repetition, implies our natural tendency to self-idolatry, and to magnifying of ourselves, and the difficulty of cleansing our hearts from these self-reflections. If it be angelical to refuse an undue glory stolen from God's throne,

Rev. xxii. 8, 9 ; it is diabolical to accept and cherish it. "To seek our own glory is not glory," Prov. xxv. 27. It is vile, and the dishonour of a creature, who, by the law of his creation, is referred to another end. So much as we sacrifice to our own credit, to the dexterity of our hands, or the sagacity of our wit, we detract from God.—*Stephen Charnock.*

Verse 1.—*"Not unto us, but unto thy name give glory,"* etc. This is not a doxology, or form of thanksgiving, but a prayer. Not for our safety or welfare, so much as for thy glory, be pleased to deliver us. Not to satisfy our revenge upon our adversaries ; not for the establishment of our own interest ; but for the glory of thy grace and truth do we seek thine aid, that thou mayest be known to be a God keeping covenant ; for mercy and truth are the two pillars of that covenant. It is a great dishonouring of God when anything is sought from him more than himself, or not for himself. Saith Austin, it is but a carnal affection in prayer when men seek self more than God. Self and God are the two things that come in competition. Now there are several sorts of self ; there is carnal self, natural self, and glorified self ; above all these God must have the pre-eminence.—*Thomas Manton.*

Verse 1.—There are many sweet and precious texts of Scripture which are so endeared, and have become so habituated to us, and we to them, that one cannot but think we must carry them with us to heaven, and that they will form not only the theme of our song, but a portion of our blessedness and joy even in that happy home. . . . But if there be one text which more especially belongs to all, and which must, I think, break forth from *every* redeemed one as he enters heaven, and form the unwearying theme of eternity, it is the first verse of this Psalm. I am sure that not one of the Lord's chosen ones on earth, as he reviews the way by which he has been led, as he sees enemy after enemy prostrate before his utter feebleness, and has such thorough evidence and conviction that his weakness is made perfect in the Lord's strength, but must, from the very ground of his heart, say, *"Not unto us, O Lord, not unto us, but unto thy name"* be the praise and the glory ascribed. And could we see heaven opened—could we hear its glad and glorious hallelujahs —could we see its innumerable company of angels, and its band of glorified saints, as they cast their crowns before the throne, we should hear as the universal chorus from every lip, *"Not unto us, O Lord, not unto us, but unto thy name give glory, for thy mercy, and for thy truth's sake."* I know not why this should not be as gladly and as gratefully the angel's song as the song of the redeemed : they stand not in their own might nor power,—they kept not their first estate through any inherent strength of their own, but, like their feebler brethren of the human race, are equally "kept by the power of God " ; and from their ranks, I doubt not, is re-echoed the same glorious strain, *"Not unto us, O Lord, not unto us, but unto thy name give glory."* Even our blessed Lord, as on that night of sorrow he sung this hymn of praise, could truly say, in that nature which had sinned, and which was to suffer, " Not unto us,"—not unto man, be ascribed the glory of this great salvation, which I am now with my own blood to purchase, but unto thy name and thy love be the praise given.—*Barton Bouchier.*

Verse 1.—*"Non nobis, Domine, sed tibi sit gloria."* A part of the Latin version of this Psalm is frequently sung after grace at public dinners, but why we can hardly imagine, except it be for fear that donors should be proud of the guineas they have promised, or gourmands should be vainglorious under the influence of their mighty feeding.—*C. H. S.*

Verses 1, 2.—He, in a very short space, assigns three reasons why God should seek the glory of his name in preserving his people. First, because he is merciful ; secondly, because he is true and faithful in observing his promise ; thirdly, that the Gentiles may not see God's people in a state of destitution, and find cause for blaspheming him or them. He therefore says, *"for thy mercy, and for thy truth's sake,"* show thy glory, or give glory to thy name, for it is then thy glory will be exhibited when thou showest mercy to thy people ; and then thou wilt have carried out the truth of the promise which thou hast made to our fathers. *"Lest the Gentiles should say, Where is their God ? "* lest the incredulous Gentiles should get an occasion of detracting from thy power, and, perhaps, of ignoring thy very existence.—*Robert Bellarmine.*

Verses 2, 3.—If God be everywhere, why doth Christ teach us to pray, " Our Father which art in heaven " ? And when the heathen made that scoffing demand, *"Where is now their God ? "* why did David answer, *"Our God is in the heavens " ?*

To these and all other texts of like import we may answer ; *heaven* is not there spoken of as bounding the presence of God, but as guiding the faith and hope of man. " In the morning " (saith David, Ps. v. 3) " will I direct my prayer unto thee, amd will look up." When the eye hath no sight of any help on earth, then faith may have the clearest vision of it in heaven. And while God appears so little in any gracious dispensation for his people on earth, that the enemy begins to scoff, *"Where is now their God ? "* then his people have recourse by faith to heaven, where the Lord not only is, but is glorious in his appearings. From whence as he the better seeth how it is with us, so he seems to have a position of advantage for relieving us.—*Joseph Caryl.*

Verses 2—8.—Contrast Jehovah with any other God. Why should the heathen say, *"Where, pray, (אֵ) is your God ? "* Take up Moses' brief description in Deut. iv. 28, and expand it as is done here. Idols of gold and silver have a *mouth*, but give no counsel to their worshippers ; *eyes*, but see not the devotions nor the wants of those who serve them ; *ears*, but hear not their cries of distress or songs of praise ; *nostrils*, but smell not the fragrant incense presented to their images ; *hands*, but the thunderbolt which they seem to hold (as Jupiter Tonans in after days), is a *brutum fulmen*, they cannot launch it ; *feet*, but they cannot move to help the fallen. Ah ! they cannot so much as whisper one syllable of response, or even mutter in their throat ! And as man becomes like his God, (witness Hindoo idolaters whose cruelty is just the reflection of the cruelty of their gods,) so these gods of the heathen being " soul-less, the worshippers become soul-less themselves " (Tholuck).—*Andrew A. Bonar.*

Verse 3.—*"And our God (is) in heaven ; all that he pleased he has done."* The word *"and,"* though foreign from our idiom, adds sensibly to the force of the expression. They ask thus, as if our God were absent or had no existence ; and yet all the while our God is in heaven, in his exalted and glorious dwelling-place.—*Joseph Addison Alexander.*

Verse 3 (*first clause*).—It would be folly to assert the like concerning idols ; therefore, if the heathen say, *Where is your God ?* we reply, *He is in heaven*, etc. : but where are your idols ? In the earth, not making the earth, but made from the earth, etc.—*Martin Geier.*

Verse 3.—*"But our God is in the heavens."* When they place God in heaven, they do not confine him to a certain locality, nor set limits to his infinite essence ; but on the contrary they deny the limitation of his power, its being shut up to human instrumentality only, or its being subject to fate or fortune. In short, they put the universe under his control ; and teach us that, being superior to every obstruction, he does freely everything that may seem good to him. This truth is still more plainly asserted in the subsequent clause, *"he hath done whatsoever he hath pleased."* God then may be said to dwell in heaven, as the world is subject to his will, and nothing can prevent his accomplishing his purposes.—*John Calvin.*

Verse 4.—*"Their idols are silver and gold."* Can there be anything more absurd than to expect assistance from them, since neither the materials of which they are formed, nor the forms which are given them by the hand of men possess the smallest porton of divinity so as to command respect for them. At the same time, the prophet tacitly indicates that the value of the material does not invest the idols with more excellence, so that they deserve to be more highly esteemed. Hence the passage may be translated adversatively, thus, Though they are of gold and silver, yet they are not gods, because they are the work of men's hands.—*John Calvin.*

Verse 4.—*"Their idols are silver,"* etc. They are metal, stone, and wood. They are genererally made in the form of man, but can neither see, hear, smell, feel, walk, nor speak. How brutish to trust in such ! and next to them, in stupidity and inanity, must they be who form them, with the expectation of deriving any good from them. So obviously vain was the whole system of idolatry that the more serious heathens ridiculed it, and it was a butt for the jests of their freethinkers and buffoons. How keen are these words of Juvenal !

Audis,
Jupiter, hæc ? nec labra moves, cum mittere vocem
Debueras, vel marmoreus vel aheneus ? aut cur
In carbone tuo charta pia thura soluta
Ponimus, et sectum vituli jecur, albaque porci
Omenta ? ut video, nullum discrimen habendum est
Effigies inter vestras, statuamque Bathylli.   Sat. xiii., ver. 113.

"Dost thou hear, O Jupiter, these things? nor move thy lips when thou oughtest to speak out, whether thou art of marble or of bronze? Or, why do we put the sacred incense on thy altar from the opened paper, and the extracted liver of a calf, and the white caul of a hog? As far as I can discern, there is no difference between thy statue and that of Bathyllus."

This irony will appear the keener, when it is known that Bathyllus was a fiddler and player, whose statue, by the order of Polycrates, was erected in the temple of Juno at Samos.—*Adam Clarke.*

Verse 4.—"*Idols.*" Idolators plead in behalf of their idols, that they are only intended to represent their gods, and to maintain a more abiding sense of their presence. The Spirit, however, does not allow this plea, and treats their images as the very gods they worship. The gods they profess to represent do not really exist, and therefore their worship is altogether vain and foolish. Must not the same be said of the pretended worship of many in the present day, who would encumber their worship with representative rites and ceremonies, or expressive symbols, or frame to themselves in their imaginations a god other than the God of revelation?—*W. Wilson.*

Verse 4.—"*Silver and gold*"—proper things to make money of, but not to make gods of.—*Matthew Henry,*

Verse 4.—"*The work of men's hands.*" The following advertisement is copied from a Chinese newspaper:—" Archen Tea Chinchin, sculptor, respectfully acquaints masters of ships, trading from Canton to India, that they may be furnished with figure-heads of any size, according to order, at one-fourth of the price charged in Europe. He also recommends for private venture, the following idols, brass, gold, and silver: the hawk of Vishnoo, which has reliefs of his incarnation in a fish, boar, lion, and turtle. An Egyptian apis, a golden calf and bull, as worshipped by the pious followers of Zoroaster. Two silver mammosits, with golden ear-rings; an aprimanes, for Persian worship; a ram, an alligator, a crab, a laughing hyena, with a variety of household gods on a small scale, calculated for family worship. Eighteen months' credit will be given, or a discount of fifteen per cent. for prompt payment of the sum affixed to each article. Direct, China-street, Canton, under the marble Rhinoceros and Gilt Hydra."—*Arvine's Anecdotes.*

Verse 4.—"*The work of men's hands.*" Works, and not the makers of works.—*Adam Clarke.*

Verse 4.—"*The work of men's hands.*" And therefore they must needs be goodly gods, when made by bunglers especially, as was the rood of *Cockram*, which if it were not good enough to make a god would make an excellent devil, as the Mayor of Doncaster merrily told the complainants.—*John Trapp.*

Verses 4—7.—A beautiful contrast is formed between the God of Israel and the heathen idols. He made everything, they are themselves made by men; he is in heaven, they are upon earth; he doeth whatsoever he pleaseth, they can do nothing; he seeth the distresses, heareth and answereth the prayers, accepteth the offerings, cometh to the assistance, and effecteth the salvation of his servants; they are blind, deaf, and dumb, senseless, motionless, and impotent. Equally slow to hear, equally impotent to save, in time of greatest need, will every worldly idol prove, on which men have set their affections, and to which they have, in effect, said, "Thou art my God."—*George Horne.*

Verses 4—7.—In Alexandria there was a most famous building called the *Serapion*, a temple of *Serapis*, who presided over the inundations of the Nile, and the fertility of Egypt. It was a vast structure of masonry, crowning a hill in the centre of the city, and was ascended by a hundred steps. It was well fortified and very handsome. The statue of the god was a colossal image, which touched with outstretched hands, both sides of the building, while the head reached the lofty roof. It was adorned with rich metals and jewels.

The Emperor Theodosius, having commanded the demolition of the heathen temple, Theophilus, the bishop, attended by the soldiers, hastened to ascend the steps and enter the fane. The sight of the image, for a moment, made even the Christian destructives pause. The bishop ordered a soldier to strike without delay. With a hatchet he smote the statue on the knee. All waited in some emotion, but there was neither sound nor sign of divine anger. The soldiers next climbed to the head and struck it off. It rolled on the ground. A large family of rats, disturbed in their tranquil abode within the sacred image, poured out from the trembling statue and raced over the temple floor. The people now began to laugh, and to destroy with increased zeal. They dragged the fragments of the statue through the streets. Even the Pagans were disgusted with gods who did not defend themselves. The huge edifice was slowly destroyed, and a Christian church was built in its place. There was still some fear among the people that the Nile would show displeasure by refusing its usual inundation. But as the river rose with more than usual fulness and bounty, every anxiety was dispelled.—*Andrew Reed, in "The Story of Christianity,"* 1877.

Verses 4—8.—Theodoret tells us of S. Publia, the aged abbess of a company of nuns at Antioch, who used to chant, as Julian went by in idolatrous procession, the Psalm, " Their idols are silver and gold, the work of men's hands. . . . They that make them are like unto them ; so is every one that trusteth in them " ; and he narrates how the angry Emperor caused his soldiers to buffet her till she bled, unable as he was to endure the sting of the old Hebrew song.—*Neale and Littledale.*

Verse 5.—*"Mouths, but they speak not."* The noblest function of the mouth is to speak. Eyes, ears, and nose are the organs of certain senses. The mouth contains the organ of taste, and the hands and feet belong to the organ of touch, but speech is the glory of the mouth.—*James G. Murphy.*

Verse 6.—*"They have ears, but they hear not."* But are as deaf as door-nails to the prayers of their suppliants. The Cretians pictured their Jupiter without ears, so little hearing or help they hoped for from him. Socrates, in contempt of heathen gods, swore by an oak, a goat, a dog ; as holding these better gods than those.—*John Trapp.*

Verse 7.—*"They have hands, but they handle not."* Even their artist therefore surpasseth them, since he had the faculty of moulding them by the motion and functions of his limbs ; though thou wouldest be ashamed to worship that artist. Even thou surpassest them, though thou hast not made these things, since thou doest what they cannot do.—*Augustine.*

Verse 7.—*"Neither speak they through their throat."* Yehgu ; not so much as the low faint moaning of a dove. Isaiah xxxviii. 14.—*William Kay.*

Verse 7.—*"Speak,"* or, as the Hebrew word likewise signifies, *breathe.* They are not only irrational, but also inanimate.—*Thomas Fenton.*

Verse 8.—*"They that make them are like unto them."* They that make them *images* show their ingenuity, and doubtless are sensible men ; but they that make them *gods* show their stupidity, and are as senseless, blockish things as the idols themselves.—*Matthew Henry.*

Verse 8.—*"They that make them are like unto them."* They are like idols, because, though they hear and see, it is more in appearance than in reality ; for they neither see nor hear the things that pertain to salvation, the things that only are worth seeing, so that they may be said more to dream than to see or hear ; as St. Mark has it, " Having eyes ye see not, having ears ye hear not."—*Robert Bellarmine.*

Verse 8.—*"Like unto them,"* etc. Every one is just what his God is ; whoever serves the Omnipotent is omnipotent with him : whoever exalts feebleness, in stupid delusion, to be his god, is feeble along with that god. This is an important preservative against fear for those who are sure that they worship the true God. —*E. W. Hengstenberg.*

Verse 8.—*"Like unto them."* Namely, " hollowness," vanity, unprofitableness (*tohu*). Isaiah xliv. 9, 10.—*William Kay.*

Verse 8.—They that serve a base god cannot but be of a base spirit, and so can do nothing worthily and generously. Every man's temper is as his god is.—*Thomas Manton.*

Verse 9.—*"He is their help."* We should rather have expected, " Our help and our shield," etc. But the burden thrice introduced, appears to be a well-known formula of praise. *"Their,"* i.e., " of all who trust in him." The verses contain a climax : (1) Israel in general is addressed ; (2) the priests or ministers of God's service ; (3) the true Israelites ; not only chosen out of all people, or out of the chosen people for outward service ; but serving God in sincerity of heart.—*Speaker's Commentary.*

Verse 10.—*"He is the help"* of his people ; they are helpless in themselves, and vain is the help of man, for there is none in him ; there is no help but in the Lord, and he is a present, seasonable, and sufficient help. Jehovah the Father has promised them help, and he is both able and faithful to make it good ; he has laid help upon his Son for them ; and has set up a throne of grace, where they may come for grace to help them in time of need. Christ has helped them out of the miserable estate they were fallen into by sin ; he helps them on in their way to heaven, by his power and grace, and at last brings them thither. The Spirit of God helps them to the things of Christ ; to many exceeding great and precious promises ; and out of many difficulties, snares and temptations ; and he helps them in prayer under all their infirmities, and makes intercession for them, according to the will of God ; and therefore they should trust in the Lord, Father, Son, and Spirit.—*John Gill.*

Verse 12.—*"The* LORD *hath been mindful of us : he will bless us."* God hath, and therefore God will, is an ordinary Scripture argument.—*John Trapp.*

Verse 13.—*"He will bless . . . . both small and great."* Mercy, according to the covenant of grace, giveth the same grounds of faith and hope to everyone within the church ; so that whatever of favour is shown to one of God's people, it is of a general use and profit to others. This Scripture sheweth that as the duty of trusting in the Lord is common to all sorts of persons, so the blessing of trust is common, and doth belong to all sorts of believers, small and great. God's Israel consists of several degrees of men. There are magistrates who have their peculiar service ; there are ministers who intercede between God and man in things belonging to God, and there are the common sort of them that fear God, and are admitted to the honour of being his people. Now these have all the same privileges. If God be the help and shield of the one, he will be the help and shield of the other ; if he bless the one he will bless the other. Every one that feareth God, and is in the number of the true Israelites, may expect his blessing as well as public persons ; the meanest peasant as well as the greatest prince, as they have leave to trust in God, so they may expect his blessing. The reason is that they have all an equal interest in the same God, who is a God of goodness and power, able and willing to relieve all those that trust in him. He is alike affected to all his children, and beareth them the same love.—*Thomas Manton.*

Verse 13.—He says, *" both small and great,"* by which circumstance he magnifies God's paternal regard the more, showing that he does not overlook even the meanest and the most despised, provided they cordially seek his aid. Now as there is no acceptance of persons before God, our low and abject condition ought to be no obstruction to our drawing near to him, since he so kindly invites to approach him those who appear to be held in no reputation. The repetition of the word *"bless"* is intended to mark the uninterrupted stream of his loving-kindness.—*John Calvin.*

Verse 14.—*"The* LORD *shall increase you,"* etc. This is expressive of the further and increasing blessing of Jehovah on his Israel, upon his ministers, and upon the whole church. They are to be increased in light and knowledge, in gifts and graces, in faith and utterance, in numbers and multitude.—*Samuel Eyles Pierce.*

Verse 14.—

> The Lord will heap his blessings upon you,
> Upon you and your children.

—*William Green, in "A New Translation of the Psalms,"* 1762.

Verse 15.—*"Blessed are ye,"* etc. Ye are the people blessed of old in the person of your father Abraham, by Melchizedek, priest of the Most High God, Creator of heaven and earth," Gen. xiv. 19. *"Of Jehovah,"* literally, *to Jehovah,* as an object of benediction to him. Or the Hebrew preposition, as in many other cases, may be simply equivalent to our *by.* The creative character of God is mentioned, as ensuring his ability, no less than his willingness, to bless his people.—*Joseph Addison Alexander.*

Verse 16.—*"The heaven, even the heavens, are the* LORD'S." He demonstrates, that, as God has his dwelling-place in the heavens, he must be independent of all worldly riches ; for, assuredly, neither wine, nor corn, nor anything requisite for the support of the present life, is produced there. Consequently, God has every resource in himself. To this circumstance the repetition of the term *"heavens"* refers. *The heavens, the heavens are enough for God ;* and as he is superior to all aid, he is to himself instead of a hundred more.—*John Calvin.*

Verse 16.—*"The earth hath he given,"* etc.—This verse is full of beauty, when read in connection with what follows, as a descriptive declaration of the effect of " the regeneration " on this lower scene. For until then, man has rather been given to the earth than the earth to the sons of men. It is but a place of graves, and the day of death seems better than the day of birth, so long as men walk in no brighter light than that of the sun.—*Arthur Pridham.*

Verse 17.—*"The dead praise not the LORD,"* etc. David considers not here what men do, or do not, in the next world ; but he considers only that in this world he was bound to propagate God's truth, and that he could not do so if God took him away by death. Now there is a double reason given of David's and other holy men's deprecation of death in the Old Testament ; one in relation to themselves, *qui promissiones obscuræ*, because Moses had conveyed to those men all God's future blessings, all the joy and glory of heaven, only in the types of earthly things, and said little of the state of the soul after this life. And therefore the promises belonging to the godly after this life, were not so clear that in the contemplation of them they could deliver themselves confidently into the jaws of death : he that is not fully satisfied of the next world, makes shift to be content with this. The other reason was *quia operarii pauci,* because God had a great harvest in hand, and few labourers in it, they were loth to be taken from the work ; and this reason was not in relation to themselves, but to God's church, since they would not be able to do God's cause any more good here. This was the other reason that made those good men so lothe to die. *Quid facies nomini tuo ?* says Joshua in his prayer to God. If the Canaanites come in to destroy us, and blaspheme thee, what wilt thou do unto thy mighty name ? What wilt thou do unto thy glorious church, said the saints of God under the Old Testament, if thou take those men out of the world, whom thou hast chosen, enabled, and qualified, for the edification, sustentation, and propagation of that church ? Upon this account David desired to live, not for his own sake, but for God's glory, and his church's good ; neither of which could be advanced by him when he was dead.—*Abraham Wright.*

Verse 17.—*"The dead praise not the LORD,"* etc. Who are here meant by *"the dead " ?* I cannot rest in the view taken by those who consider this verse simply as a plea by those who use it, that they may be saved from death. They are words provided for the church at large, as the subsequent verse proves. By *"the dead,"* then, I understand those who descend to the silence of eternal death, who have not praised God, and never can. For them the earth might seem never to have been given.—*W. Wilson.*

Verse 17.—*"Into silence."* Into the grave—the land of silence. Ps. xciv. 17. Nothing is more impressive in regard to the grave than its utter *silence.* Not a voice, not a sound, is heard there,—of birds or men—of song or conversation—of the roaring of the sea, the sighing of the breeze, the fury of the storm, the tumult of battle. Perfect stillness reigns there ; and the first sound that shall be heard there will be the archangel's trump.—*Albert Barnes.*

Verses 17, 18.—The *people* of God cannot die, because the *praise* of God would die with them, which would be impossible.—*E. W. Hengstenberg.*

Verses 17, 18.—It is not to be overlooked that there do occur, in certain Psalms, words which have the appearance of excluding the hope of eternal life.* . . . Yet it is a very significant fact, that in all the Psalms in question, there is an earnest solicitude expressed for the glory of God. If death is deprecated, it is in order that the Lord may not lose the glory, nor his church the services which a life prolonged might furnish. This is well exemplified in the hundred and fifteenth, which I the rather cite because, being the sole exception to the rule, that the dark views of death are found in Psalms of contrition and deep sorrow ; it is the only Psalm to which the preceding observations are inapplicable. It is a tranquil hymn of praise.

> 17. It is not the dead who praise Jah :
>   Neither any that go down into silence.
> 18. But WE will bless Jah,
>   From this time forth and for evermore.
>   Hallelujah !

The Psalm thus closed, was one of the Songs of the Second Temple.

---

* Psalm vi. 5, xxx. 9, lxxxviii. 10, 12, lxxxix. 47, cxv. 17.

What we hear in it is the voice of the church, rather than of an individual soul. And this may assist us in perceiving its entire harmony with faith in the heavenly glory. It much concerns the honour of God that there be continued, on the earth, a visible church, in which his name may be recorded from generation to generation. That is a work which cannot be performed by the dead. Since, therefore, the uppermost desire of the church ought ever to be that God's name may be hallowed, his kingdom advanced, and his will done in the earth ; it is her duty to pray for continued subsistence here, on the earth, to witness for God. And it is to be carefully observed, that not only in this passage, but in all the parallel texts in which the Psalmists seem to speak doubtfully or disparagingly of the state of the departed, it is in connection with the interest of God's cause on the earth. The thought that is uppermost in their hearts is, that " in death there is no commemoration " of God—no recording of his name for the salvation of men. This single circumstance might, I think, suffice to put the reader on his guard against a precipitate fastening on them of a meaning which would exclude the hope of eternal life. It goes far to show that what the Psalmist deprecates, is not death simply considered, but premature death. Their prayer is, " O my God, take me not away in the midst of my days." Ps. cii. 24. And I do not hesitate to say that there are men so placed in stations of eminent usefulness, that it is their duty to make the prayer their own.—*William Binnie.*

HINTS TO PREACHERS.

Verse 1.—The passage may be used as, I. A powerful plea in prayer. II. An expression of the true spirit of piety. III. A safe guide in theology. IV. A practical direction in choosing our way of life. V. An acceptable spirit when surveying past or present success.

Verse 1.—I. No praise is due to man. Have we a being ? Not unto us, etc. Have we health ? Not unto us, etc. Have we outward comforts ? Not unto us, etc. Friends ? Not unto us, etc. The means of grace ? Not unto us, etc. Saving faith in Christ ? Not unto us, etc. Gifts and graces ? Not unto us, etc. The hope of glory ? Not unto us, etc. Usefulness to others ? Not unto us, etc. II. All praise is due to God. 1. Because all we have is from mercy. 2. Because all we expect is from faithfulness.—*G. R.*

Verse 2.—A taunting question, to which we can give many satisfactory replies.

Verse 2.—Why do they say so ? Why doth God permit them to say so ?—*Matthew Henry.*

Verses 2, 3.—I. The inquiry of heathens : ver. 2. 1. Of ignorance. They see a temple but no god. 2. Of reproach to the people of God when their God has forsaken them for a time : " While they say daily unto me, where," etc. II. The reply to their inquiry : ver. 3. Do you ask where is our God ? Ask rather where he is not ? Do you ask what he has done ? " He has done whatsoever he hath pleased."—*G. R.*

Verse 3.—I. His position betokens absolute dominion. II. His actions prove it. III. Yet he condescends to be " our God."

Verse 3 (*second clause*).—The sovereignty of God. Establish and improve the great scriptural doctrine, that the glorious God has a right to exercise dominion over all his creatures ; and to do, in all respects, as he pleases. This right naturally results from his being the *Former* and the *Possessor* of heaven and earth. Consider (1) He is infinitely wise ; he perfectly knows all his creatures, all their actions, and all their tendencies. (2) He is infinitely righteous. (3) He is infinitely good.—*George Burder.*

Verses 4—8.—I. The character of idol gods. Whether our gods are natural objects or riches or worldly pleasures, they have no eye to pity, no ear to hear petitions, no tongue to counsel, no hand to help. II. The character of the true God. He is all eye, all ear, all tongue, all hand, all feet, all mind, all heart. III. The character of the idol worshippers. All become naturally assimilated to the objects of their worship.

Verse 8.—The likeness between idolators and their idols. Work it out in the particulars mentioned.

Verse 9.—The living God claims spiritual worship ; the life of such worship is faith ; faith proves God to be a living reality—" He is their help," etc. Only elect Israel will ever render this living worship.

Verses 9—11.—I. The reproof. " O Israel ! " " O house of Aaron ! " " Ye who fear the Lord." Have you been unbelieving towards your God ? II. The correction or admonition. " Trust in the Lord." Have you trusted in the true God as others have in their false gods ? III. The instruction. " He is their help," etc. Let churches, ministers, and all who fear God know that at all times and under all circumstances he is their help and their shield.—*G. R.*

Verse 10.—I. Those who publicly serve should specially trust. " O house of Aaron, trust." II. Those who are specially called shall be specially helped. " He is their help." III. Those who are specially helped in service may be sure of special protection in danger—" and their shield."

Verse 11.—Filial fear the foundation of fuller faith.

Verse 12.—What we have experienced. What we may expect.—*Matthew Henry.*

Verses 12, 13.—I. What God *has done* for his people : " He hath been mindful of us." 1. Our preservation proves this. 2. Our mercies. 3. Our trials. 4. Our guidance. 5. Our consolations. Everything, even the minutest blessing, represents a thought in the mind of God respecting us. " How precious are thy thoughts concerning me, O God, how great," etc., and those thoughts go back to an eternity before we came into being. " The Lord hath been mindful of us " ; then should we not be more mindful of him ? II. What he *will do* for his people—" He will bless us." 1. Greatly. His blessings are like himself, great. They are blessed whom he blesses. 2. Suitably. The house of Israel, the house of Aaron, all who fear him, according to their need, both small and great. 3. Assuredly. " He will," " he will," " he will," " he will." With one " will " he curses, with four " wills " he blesses.—*G. R.*

Verse 13.—I. The general character—" fear the Lord." II. The degrees of development—" small and great." III. The common blessing.

Verse 14.—I. Gracious increase—in knowledge, love, power, holiness, usefulness, etc. II. Growing increase—we grow faster, and advance not only more, but more and more. III. Relative increase—our children grow in grace through our examples, etc.

Verse 14.—The blessings of God are, I. *Ever-flowing*—" more and more." II. *Over-flowing*—" ycu and your children." Let parents seek more grace for themselves for the sake of their children. 1. That they may be more influenced by their example. 2. That their prayers may be more prevalent on their behalf. 3. That their children may be more blessed for their sakes.—*G. R.*

Verse 15.—A blessing. I. Belonging to a peculiar people—" ye." II. Coming from a peculiar quarter—" of the Lord," etc. III. Bearing a peculiar date—" are." IV. Stamped with peculiar certainty—" Ye are blessed." V. Involving a peculiar duty—" Bless the Lord now and evermore."

Verse 15.—The Creator's blessing—its greatness, fulness, variety, etc.

Verse 16.—Man's lordship over the world, its limit, its abuse, its legitimate bound, its grand design.

Verses 17, 18.—I. Missing voices—" The dead praise not." II. Their stimulus upon ourselves—" But we." III. Their cry to others—" Praise ye the Lord." Let us make up for the silent voices.

Verses 17, 18.—I. They who do not praise God here will not praise him hereafter. No reprieve therefore from punishment. II. They who praise God in this life will praise him for evermore. Hallelujah for this. " Praise the Lord."—*G. R.*

Verses 17, 18.—A new year's sermon. I. A mournful memory—" the dead." II. A happy resolve—" but we will bless the Lord." III. An appropriate commencement—" from this time forth." IV. An everlasting continuance—" and for evermore."

PSALM CXVI.

SUBJECT.—*This is a continuation of the Paschal Hallel, and therefore must in some measure be interpreted in connection with the coming out of Egypt. It has all the appearance of being a personal song in which the believing soul, reminded by the Passover of its own bondage and deliverance, speaks thereof with gratitude, and praises the Lord accordingly. We can conceive the Israelite with a staff in his hand singing, "Return unto thy rest, O my soul," as he remembered the going back of the house of Jacob to the land of their fathers; and then drinking the cup at the feast using the words of the thirteenth verse, "I will take the cup of salvation." The pious man evidently remembers both his own deliverance and that of his people as he sings in the language of the sixteenth verse, "Thou hast loosed my bonds"; but he rises into sympathy with his nation as he thinks of the courts of the Lord's house and of the glorious city, and pledges himself to sing "in the midst of thee, O Jerusalem." Personal love fostered by a personal experience of redemption is the theme of this Psalm, and in it we see the redeemed answered when they pray, preserved in time of trouble, resting in their God, walking at large, sensible of their obligations, conscious that they are not their own but bought with a price, and joining with all the ransomed company to sing hallelujahs unto God.*

Since our divine Master sang this hymn, we can hardly err in seeing here words to which he could set his seal,—words in a measure descriptive of his own experience; but upon this we will not enlarge, as in the notes we have indicated how the Psalm has been understood by those who love to find their Lord in every line.

DIVISION.—*David Dickson has a somewhat singular division of this Psalm, which strikes us as being exceedingly suggestive. He says, "This Psalm is a threefold engagement of the Psalmist unto thanksgiving unto God, for his mercy unto him, and in particular for some notable delivery of him from death, both bodily and spiritual. The first engagement is, that he shall out of love have recourse unto God by prayer, verses 1 and 2; the reasons and motives whereof are set down, because of his former deliverances, 3—8; the second engagement is to a holy conversation, verse 9; and the motives and reasons are given in verses 10 to 13; the third engagement is to continual praise and service, and specially to pay those vows before the church, which he had made in days of sorrow, the reasons whereof are given in verses 14—19."*

EXPOSITION.

I LOVE the LORD, because he hath heard my voice *and* my supplications.

2 Because he hath inclined his ear unto me, therefore will I call upon *him* as long as I live.

3 The sorrows of death compassed me, and the pains of hell gat hold upon me : I found trouble and sorrow.

4 Then called I upon the name of the LORD ; O LORD, I beseech thee, deliver my soul.

5 Gracious *is* the LORD, and righteous ; yea, our God *is* merciful.

6 The LORD preserveth the simple : I was brought low, and he helped me.

7 Return unto thy rest, O my soul ; for the LORD hath dealt bountifully with thee.

8 For thou hast delivered my soul from death, mine eyes from tears, *and* my feet from falling.

1. "*I love the* LORD." A blessed declaration : every believer ought to be able to declare without the slightest hesitation, " I love the Lord." It was required under the law, but was never produced in the heart of man except by the grace of God, and upon gospel principles. It is a great thing to say " I love the Lord "; for the sweetest of all graces and the surest of all evidences of salvation is love. It is great goodness on the part of God that he condescends to be loved by such poor

creatures as we are, and it is a sure proof that he has been at work in our heart when we can say, "Thou knowest all things, thou knowest that I love thee." *"Because he hath heard my voice and my supplications."* The Psalmist not only knows that he loves God, but he knows why he does so. When love can justify itself with a reason, it is deep, strong, and abiding. They say that love is blind ; but when we love God our affection has its eyes open and can sustain itself with the most rigid logic. We have reason, superabundant reason, for loving the Lord ; and so because in this case principle and passion, reason and emotion go together, they make up an admirable state of mind. David's reason for his love was the love of God in hearing his prayers. The Psalmist had used his *"voice"* in prayer, and the habit of doing so is exceedingly helpful to devotion. If we can pray aloud without being overheard it is well to do so. Sometimes, however, when the Psalmist had lifted up his voice, his utterance had been so broken and painful that he scarcely dared to call it prayer ; words failed him, he could only produce a groaning sound, but the Lord heard his moaning voice. At other times his prayers were more regular and better formed : these he calls *"supplications."* David had praised as best he could, and when one form of devotion failed him he tried another. He had gone to the Lord again and again, hence he uses the plural and says " my supplications," but as often as he had gone, so often had he been welcome. Jehovah had heard, that is to say, accepted, and answered both his broken cries and his more composed and orderly supplications ; hence he loved God with all his heart. Answered prayers are silken bonds which bind our hearts to God. When a man's prayers are answered, love is the natural result. According to Alexander, both verbs may be translated in the present, and the text may run thus, " I love because Jehovah hears my voice, my supplications." This also is true in the case of every pleading believer. Continual love flows out of daily answers to prayer.

2. *"Because he hath inclined his ear unto me "* :—bowing down from his grandeur to attend to my prayer ; the figure seems to be that of a tender physician or loving friend leaning over a sick man whose voice is faint and scarcely audible, so as to catch every accent and whisper. When our prayer is very feeble, so that we ourselves can scarcely hear it, and question whether we do pray or not, yet God bows a listening ear, and regards our supplications. *"Therefore will I call upon him as long as I live,"* or, " in my days." Throughout all the days of my life I will address my prayer to God alone, and to him I will unceasingly pray. It is always wise to go where we are welcome and are well treated. The word " call " may imply praise as well as prayer : calling upon the name of the Lord is an expressive name for adoration of all kinds. When prayer is heard in our feebleness, and answered in the strength and greatness of God, we are strengthened in the habit of prayer, and confirmed in the resolve to make ceaseless intercession. We should not thank a beggar who informed us that because we had granted his request he would never cease to beg of us, and yet doubtless it is acceptable to God that his petitioners should form the resolution to continue in prayer : this shows the greatness of his goodness, and the abundance of his patience. In all days let us pray and praise the Ancient of days. He promises that as our days our strength shall be ; let us resolve that as our days our devotion shall be.

3. The Psalmist now goes on to describe his condition at the time when he prayed unto God. *"The sorrows of death compassed me."* As hunters surround a stag with dogs and men, so that no way of escape is left, so was David enclosed in a ring of deadly griefs. The bands of sorrow, weakness, and terror with which death is accustomed to bind men ere he drags them away to their long captivity were all around him. Nor were these things around him in a distant circle, they had come close home, for he adds, *"and the pains of hell gat hold upon me."* Horrors such as those which torment the lost seized me, grasped me, found me out, searched me through and through, and held me a prisoner. He means by the pains of hell those pangs which belong to death, those terrors which are connected with the grave ; these were so closely upon him that they fixed their teeth in him as hounds seize their prey. *"I found trouble and sorrow,"* trouble was around me, and sorrow within me. His griefs were double, and as he searched into them they increased. A man rejoices when he finds a hid treasure ; but what must be the anguish of a man who finds, where he least expected it, a vein of trouble and sorrow ? The Psalmist was sought for by trouble and it found him out, and when he himself became a seeker he found no relief, but double distress.

4. *"Then called I upon the name of the LORD."* Prayer is never out of season, he

prayed *then*, when things were at their worst. When the good man could not run to God, he *called* to him. In his extremity his faith came to the front : it was useless to call on man, and it may have seemed almost as useless to appeal to the Lord ; but yet he did with his whole soul invoke all the attributes which make up the sacred name of Jehovah, and thus he proved the truth of his confidence. We can some of us remember certain very special times of trial of which we can now say, "*then* called I upon the name of the Lord." The Psalmist appealed to the Lord's mercy, truth, power, and faithfulness, and this was his prayer,—"*O Lord, I beseech thee, deliver my soul.*" This form of petition is short, comprehensive, to the point, humble, and earnest. It were well if all our prayers were moulded upon this model ; perhaps they would be if we were in similar circumstances to those of the Psalmist, for real trouble produces real prayer. Here we have no multiplicity of words, and no fine arrangement of sentences ; everything is simple and natural ; there is not a redundant syllable, and yet there is not one lacking.

5. "*Gracious is the* LORD, *and righteous.*" In hearing prayer the grace and righteousness of Jehovah are both conspicuous. It is a great favour to hear a sinner's prayer, and yet since the Lord has promised to do so, he is not unrighteous to forget his promise and disregard the cries of his people. The combination of grace and righteousness in the dealings of God with his servants can only be explained by remembering the atoning sacrifice of our Lord Jesus Christ. At the cross we see how gracious is the Lord and righteous. "*Yea, our God is merciful,*" or compassionate, tender, pitiful, full of mercy. We who have accepted him as ours have no doubt as to his mercy, for he would never have been our God if he had not been merciful. See how the attribute of righteousness seems to stand between two guards of love :— gracious, *righteous*, merciful. The sword of justice is scabbarded in a jewelled sheath of grace.

6. "*The* LORD *preserveth the simple.*" Those who have a great deal of wit may take care of themselves. Those who have no worldly craft and subtlety and guile, but simply trust in God, and do the right, may depend upon it that God's care shall be over them. The worldly-wise with all their prudence shall be taken in their own craftiness, but those who walk in their integrity with single-minded truthfulness before God shall be protected against the wiles of their enemies, and enabled to outlive their foes. Though the saints are like sheep in the midst of wolves, and comparatively defenceless, yet there are more sheep in the world than wolves, and it is highly probable that the sheep will feed in safety when not a single wolf is left upon the face of the earth : even so the meek shall inherit the earth, when the wicked shall be no more. "*I was brought low, and he helped me,*"—simple though I was, the Lord did not pass me by. Though reduced in circumstances, slandered in character, depressed in spirit, and sick in body, the Lord helped me. There are many ways in which the child of God may be brought low, but the help of God is as various as the need of his people : he supplies our necessities when impoverished, restores our character when maligned, raises up friends for us when deserted, comforts us when desponding, and heals our diseases when we are sick. There are thousands in the church of God at this time who can each one of them say for himself, "*I* was brought low, and he helped *me.*" Whenever this can be said it should be said to the praise of the glory of his grace, and for the comforting of others who may pass through the like ordeal. Note how David after stating the general doctrine that the Lord preserveth the simple, proves and illustrates it from his own personal experience. The habit of taking home a general truth and testing the power of it in our own case is an exceedingly blessed one ; it is the way in which the testimony of Christ is confirmed in us, and so we become witnesses unto the Lord our God.

7. "*Return unto thy rest, O my soul.*" He calls the rest still his own, and feels full liberty to return to it. What a mercy it is that even if our soul has left its rest for a while we can tell it—" it is thy rest still." The Psalmist had evidently been somewhat disturbed in mind, his troubles had ruffled his spirit ; but now with a sense of answered prayer upon him he quiets his soul. He had rested before, for he knew the blessed repose of faith, and therefore he returns to the God who had been the refuge of his soul in former days. Even as a bird flies to its nest, so does his soul fly to his God. Whenever a child of God even for a moment loses his peace of mind, he should be concerned to find it again, not by seeking it in the world or in his own experience, but in the Lord alone. When the believer prays, and the Lord inclines his ear, the road to the old rest is before him, let him not be slow to follow it. "*For the* LORD *hath dealt bountifully with thee.*" Thou hast served a good

God, and built upon a sure foundation ; go not about to find any other rest, but come back to him who in former days hath condescended to enrich thee by his love. What a text is this ! and what an exposition of it is furnished by the biography of every believing man and woman ! The Lord hath dealt bountifully with us, for he hath given us his Son, and in him he hath given us all things : he hath sent us his Spirit, and by him he conveys to us all spiritual blessings. God dealeth with us like a God ; he lays his fulness open to us, and of that fulness have all we received, and grace for grace. We have sat at no niggard's table, we have been clothed by no penurious hand, we have been equipped by no grudging provider ; let us come back to him who has treated us with such exceeding kindness. More arguments follow.

8. *"For thou hast delivered my soul from death, mine eyes from tears, and my feet from falling."* The triune God has given us a trinity of deliverances : our life has been spared from the grave, our heart has been uplifted from its griefs, and our course in life has been preserved from dishonour. We ought not to be satisfied unless we are conscious of all three of these deliverances. If our soul has been saved from death, why do we weep ? What cause for sorrow remains ? Whence those tears ? And if our tears have been wiped away, can we endure to fall again into sin ? Let us not rest unless with steady feet we pursue the path of the upright, escaping every snare and shunning every stumblingblock. Salvation, joy, and holiness must go together, and they are all provided for us in the covenant of grace. Death is vanquished, tears are dried, and fears are banished when the Lord is near.

Thus has the Psalmist explained the reasons of his resolution to call upon God as long as he lived, and none can question but that he had come to a most justifiable resolve. When from so great a depth he had been uplifted by so special an interposition of God, he was undoubtedly bound to be for ever the hearty worshipper of Jehovah, to whom he owed so much. Do we not all feel the force of the reasoning, and will we not carry out the conclusion ? May God the Holy Spirit help us so to pray without ceasing and in everything to give thanks, for this is the will of God in Christ Jesus concerning us.

9 I will walk before the LORD in the land of the living.
10 I believed, therefore have I spoken : I was greatly afflicted :
11 I said in my haste, All men *are* liars.
12 What shall I render unto the LORD *for* all his benefits toward me ?
13 I will take the cup of salvation, and call upon the name of the LORD.

9. *"I will walk before the LORD in the land of the living."* This is the Psalmist's second resolution, to live as in the sight of God in the midst of the sons of men. By a man's walk is understood his way of life : some men live only as in the sight of their fellow men, having regard to human judgment and opinion ; but the truly gracious man considers the presence of God, and acts under the influence of his all-observing eye. " Thou God seest me " is a far better influence than " My master sees me." The life of faith, hope, holy fear, and true holiness is produced by a sense of living and walking before the Lord, and he who has been favoured with divine deliverances in answer to prayer finds his own experience the best reason for a holy life, and the best assistance to his endeavours. We know that God in a special manner is nigh unto his people : what manner of persons ought we to be in all holy conversation and godliness ?

10. *"I believed, therefore have I spoken."* I could not have spoken thus if it had not been for my faith : I should never have spoken unto God in prayer, nor have been able now to speak to my fellow men in testimony if it had not been that faith kept me alive, and brought me a deliverance, whereof I have good reason to boast. Concerning the things of God no man should speak unless he believes ; the speech of the waverer is mischievous, but the tongue of the believer is profitable ; the most powerful speech which has ever been uttered by the lip of man has emanated from a heart fully persuaded of the truth of God. Not only the Psalmist, but such men as Luther, and Calvin, and other great witnesses for the faith, could each one most heartily say, " I believed, therefore have I spoken." *"I was greatly afflicted."* There was no mistake about that ; the affliction was as bitter and as terrible as it well could be, and since I have been delivered from it, I am sure that the deliverance is no fanatical delusion, but a self-evident fact ; therefore am I the more resolved

to speak to the honour of God. Though greatly afflicted, the Psalmist had not ceased to believe : his faith was tried but not destroyed.

11. *"I said in my haste, All men are liars."* In a modified sense the expression will bear justification, even though hastily uttered, for all men will prove to be liars if we unduly trust in them ; some from want of truthfulness, and others from want of power. But from the expression, " I said in my haste," it is clear that the Psalmist did not justify his own language, but considered it as the ebullition of a hasty temper. In the sense in which he spoke his language was unjustifiable. He had no right to distrust all men, for many of them are honest, truthful, and conscientious ; there are faithful friends and loyal adherents yet alive ; and if sometimes they disappoint us, we ought not to call them liars for failing when the failure arises entirely from want of power, and not from lack of will. Under great affliction our temptation will be to form hasty judgments of our fellow men, and knowing this to be the case we ought carefully to watch our spirit, and to keep the door of our lips. The Psalmist had believed, and therefore he spoke ; he had doubted, and therefore he spoke in haste. He believed, and therefore he rightly prayed to God ; he disbelieved, and therefore he wrongfully accused mankind. Speaking is as ill in some cases as it is good in others. Speaking in haste is generally followed by bitter repentance. It is much better to be quiet when our spirit is disturbed and hasty, for it is so much easier to say than to unsay ; we may repent of our words, but we cannot so recall them as to undo the mischief they have done. If even David had to eat his own words, when he spoke in a hurry, none of us can trust our tongue without a bridle.

12. *"What shall I render unto the LORD for all his benefits toward me ? "* He wisely leaves off fretting about man's falsehood and his own ill humour, and directs himself to his God. It is of little use to be harping on the string of man's imperfection and deceitfulness ; it is infinitely better to praise the perfection and faithfulness of God. The question of the verse is a very proper one : the Lord has rendered so much mercy to us that we ought to look about us, and look within us, and see what can be done by us to manifest our gratitude. We ought not only to do what is plainly before us, but also with holy ingenuity to search out various ways by which we may render fresh praises unto our God. His benefits are so many that we cannot number them, and our ways of acknowledging his bestowments ought to be varied and numerous in proportion. Each person should have his own peculiar mode of expressing gratitude. The Lord sends each one a special benefit, let each one enquire, " What shall *I* render ? What form of service would be most becoming in me ? "

13. *"I will take the cup of salvation."* " I will take " is a strange answer to the question, " What shall I render ? " and yet it is the wisest reply that could possibly be given.

> " The best return for one like me,
> So wretched and so poor,
> Is from his gifts to draw a plea
> And ask him still for more."

To take the cup of salvation was in itself an act of worship, and it was accompanied with other forms of adoration, hence the Psalmist says, *"and call upon the name of the LORD."* He means that he will utter blessings and thanksgivings and prayers, and then drink of the cup which the Lord had filled with his saving grace. What a cup this is ! Upon the table of infinite love stands the cup full of blessing ; it is ours by faith to take it in our hand, make it our own, and partake of it, and then with joyful hearts to laud and magnify the gracious One who has filled it for our sakes that we may drink and be refreshed. We can do this figuratively at the sacramental table, we can do it spiritually every time we grasp the golden chalice of the covenant, realizing the fulness of blessing which it contains, and by faith receiving its divine contents into our inmost soul. Beloved reader, let us pause here and take a long and deep draught from the cup which Jesus filled, and then with devout hearts let us worship God.

14 I will pay my vows unto the LORD now in the presence of all his people.

15 Precious in the sight of the LORD *is* the death of his saints.

16 O LORD, truly I *am* thy servant : I *am* thy servant, *and* the son of thine handmaid : thou hast loosed my bonds.

17 I will offer to thee the sacrifice of thanksgiving, and will call upon the name of the LORD.

18 I will pay my vows unto the LORD now in the presence of all his people,

19 In the courts of the LORD's house, in the midst of thee, O Jerusalem. Praise ye the LORD.

14. *"I will pay my vows unto the LORD now in the presence of all his people."* The Psalmist has already stated his third resolution, to devote himself to the worship of God evermore, and here he commences the performance of that resolve. The vows which he had made in anguish, he now determines to fulfil : " I will pay my vows unto the Lord." He does so at once, *"now,"* and that publicly, " in the presence of all his people." Good resolutions cannot be carried out too speedily ; vows become debts, and debts should be paid. It is well to have witnesses to the payment of just debts, and we need not be ashamed to have witnesses to the fulfilling of holy vows, for this will show that we are not ashamed of our Lord, and it may be a great benefit to those who look on and hear us publicly sounding forth the praises of our prayer-hearing God. How can those do this who have never with their mouth confessed their Saviour ? O secret disciples, what say you to this verse ! Be encouraged to come into the light and own your Redeemer. If, indeed, you have been saved, come forward and declare it in his own appointed way.

15. *"Precious in the sight of the LORD is the death of his saints,"* and therefore he did not suffer the Psalmist to die, but delivered his soul from death. This seems to indicate that the song was meant to remind Jewish families of the mercies received by any one of the household, supposing him to have been sore sick and to have been restored to health, for the Lord values the lives of his saints, and often spares them where others perish. They shall not die prematurely ; they shall be immortal till their work is done ; and when their time shall come to die, then their deaths shall be precious. The Lord watches over their dying beds, smooths their pillows, sustains their hearts, and receives their souls. Those who are redeemed with precious blood are so dear to God that even their deaths are precious to him. The death-beds of saints are very precious to the church, she often learns much from them ; they are very precious to all believers, who delight to treasure up the last words of the departed ; but they are most of all precious to the Lord Jehovah himself, who view the triumphant deaths of his gracious ones with sacred delight. If we have walked before him in the land of the living, we need not fear to die before him when the hour of our departure is at hand.

16. The man of God in paying his vows re-dedicates himself unto God ; the offering which he brings is himself, as he cries, *"O LORD, truly I am thy servant,"* rightfully, really, heartily, constantly, I own that I am thine, for thou hast delivered and redeemed me." *"I am thy servant, and the son of thine handmaid,"* a servant born in thy house, born of a servant and so born a servant, and therefore doubly thine. My mother was thine handmaid, and I, her son, confess that I am altogether thine by claims arising out of my birth. O that children of godly parents would thus judge ; but, alas, there are many who are the sons of the Lord's handmaids, but they are not themselves his servants. They give sad proof that grace does not run in the blood. David's mother was evidently a gracious woman, and he is glad to remember that fact, and to see in it a fresh obligation to devote himself to God. *"Thou hast loosed my bonds,"*—freedom from bondage binds me to thy service. He who is loosed from the bonds of sin, death, and hell should rejoice to wear the easy yoke of the great Deliverer. Note how the sweet singer delights to dwell upon his belonging to the Lord ; it is evidently his glory, a thing of which he is proud, a matter which causes him intense satisfaction. Verily, it ought to create rapture in our souls if we are able to call Jesus Master, and are acknowledged by him as his servants.

17. *"I will offer to thee the sacrifice of thanksgiving."* Being thy servant, I am bound to sacrifice to thee, and having received spiritual blessings at thy hands I will not bring bullock or goat, but I will bring that which is more suitable, namely, the thanksgiving of my heart. My inmost soul shall adore thee in gratitude. *"And will call upon the name of the LORD,"* that is to say, I will bow before thee reverently, lift up my heart in love to thee, think upon thy character, and adore thee as thou dost reveal thyself. He is fond of this occupation, and several times in this Psalm

declares that " he will call upon the name of the Lord," while at the same time he rejoices that he had done so many a time before. Good feelings and actions bear repeating : the more of hearty callings upon God the better.

18. *"I will pay my vows unto the* Lord *now in the presence of all his people."* He repeats the declaration. A good thing is worth saying twice. He thus stirs himself up to greater heartiness, earnestness, and diligence in keeping his vow,—really paying it at the very moment that he is declaring his resolution to do so. The mercy came in secret, but the praise is rendered in public ; the company was, however, select ; he did not cast his pearls before swine, but delivered his testimony before those who could appreciate it.

19. *"In the courts of the* Lord's *house " :* in the proper place, where God had ordained that he should be worshipped. See how he is stirred up at the remembrance of the house of the Lord, and must needs speak of the holy city with a note of joyful exclamation—*"In the midst of thee, O Jerusalem."* The very thought of the beloved Zion touched his heart, and he writes as if he were actually addressing Jerusalem, whose name was dear to him. There would he pay his vows, in the abode of fellowship, in the very heart of Judea, in the place to which the tribes went up, the tribes of the Lord. There is nothing like witnessing for Jesus, where the report thereof will be carried into a thousand homes. God's praise is not to be confined to a closet, nor his name to be whispered in holes and corners, as if we were afraid that men should hear us ; but in the thick of the throng, and in the very centre of assemblies, we should lift up heart and voice unto the Lord, and invite others to join with us in adoring him, saying, *"Praise ye the* Lord," or Hallelujah. This was a very fit conclusion of a song to be sung when all the people were gathered together at Jerusalem to keep the feast. God's Spirit moved the writers of these Psalms to give them a fitness and suitability which was more evident in their own day than now ; but enough is perceptible to convince us that every line and word had a peculiar adaptation to the occasions for which the sacred sonnets were composed. When we worship the Lord we ought with great care to select the words of prayer and praise, and not to trust to the opening of a hymn-book, or to the unconsidered extemporizing of the moment. Let all things be done decently and in order, and let all things begin and end with Hallelujah, Praise ye the Lord.

EXPLANATORY NOTES AND QUAINT SAYINGS.

Whole Psalm.—A Psalm of Thanksgiving in the Person of Christ. He is imagined by the prophet to have passed through the sorrows and afflictions of life. The atonement is passed. He has risen from the dead. He is on the right hand of the Majesty on High ; and he proclaims to the whole world the mercies he experienced from God in the day of his incarnation, and the glories which he has received in the kingdom of his Heavenly Father. Yet, although the Psalm possesses this power, and, by its own internal evidence, proves the soundness of the interpretation, it is yet highly mystic in its mode of disclosure, and requires careful meditation in bringing out its real results. Its language, too, is not so exclusively appropriate to the Messiah, that it shall not be repeated and applied by the believer to his own trials in the world ; so that while there is much that finds a ready parallel in the exaltation of Christ in heaven, there is much that would seem to be restrained to his condition upon earth. It therefore depends much on *the mind* of the individual, whether he will receive it in the higher sense of the Redeemer's glory ; or restrict it *solely* to a thanksgiving for blessings amidst those sufferings in life to which all men have been subject in the same manner, though not to the same extent as Jesus. The most perfect and the most profitable reading would combine the two, taking Christ as *the exemplar* of God's mercies towards ourselves.

1. Enthroned in eternity, and triumphant over sin and death—I—Christ—am well pleased that my Heavenly Father listened to the anxious prayers that I made to him in the day of my sorrows ; when I had neither strength in my own mind, nor assistance from men ; therefore *"through my days "*—through the endless ages

of my eternal existence—will I call upon him in my gratitude, and praise him with my whole heart.

3. In the troublous times of my incarnation I was encircled with snares, and urged onwards towards my death. The priest and ruler ; the Pharisee and the scribe ; the rich and the poor, clamoured fiercely for my destruction. The whole nation conspired against me. *"The bands of the grave"* laid hold of me, and I was hurried to the cross.

4. Then, *truly* did Christ find heaviness and affliction. " His soul was exceeding sorrowful, even unto death." He prayed anxiously to his Heavenly Father, that " the cup might pass from him." The fate of the whole world was in the balance ; and he supplicated with agony, that his *soul* might be delivered.

5. The abrupt breaking off in this verse from the direct narrative of his own sorrows is wonderfully grand and beautiful. Nor less so, is the expression *"our* God " as applied by Christ to his own disciples and believers. *" I called,"* he states, *"on the name of the* LORD." But he does not yet state the answer. He leaves that to be inferred from the assurance that God is *ever* gracious to the faithful ; yea, *"our* God"—the protector of the Christian church, as well as of myself—*"our God is merciful."*

6. Instantly, however, he resumes. Mark the energy of the language, " I was afflicted ; and he delivered me." And how delivered ? The soul of Christ has returned freely to its tranquillity ; for though the body and the frame perished on the tree, yet the soul burst through the bands of death. Again in the full stature of a perfect man Christ rose resplendent in glory to the mansions of eternity. The tears ceased ; the sorrows were hushed ; and henceforward, through the boundless day of immortality, doth he " walk before Jehovah, in the land of *the living."* This last is one of those expressions in the Psalm which might, without reflection, seem adapted to the rescued believer's state on earth, rather than Christ's in heaven. But applying the language of earthly things to heavenly—which is usual, even in the most mystic writings of Scripture—nothing can be finer than the appellation of *"the land of the living,"* when assigned to the future residence of the soul. It is the noblest application of the metaphor, and is singularly appropriate to those eternal mansions where death and sorrow are alike unknown.

10. This stanza will bear an emendation.

> I felt confidence, although I said,—
> " I am sore afflicted."
> I said in my sudden terror,—
> " All mankind are false."—*French.*

It alludes to the eve of his crucifixion, when worn down with long watchfulness and fasting, his spirit almost fainted in the agony of Gethsemane. Still, oppressed and stricken as he was in soul, he yet trusted in Jehovah, for he felt assured that he would not forsake him. But, sustained by God, he was deserted by men, the disciples with whom he had lived ; the multitudes whom he had taught ; the afflicted whom he had healed, *"all* forsook him and fled." Not one—not even the " disciples whom he loved "—remained ; and in the anguish of that desertion he could not refrain from the bitter thought, that all mankind were alike false and treacherous.

12. But that dread hour has passed. He has risen from the dead ; and stands girt with truth and holiness and glory. What then is his earliest thought ? Hear it, O man, and blush for thine oft ingratitude ! I will lift up *"the cup of deliverance"* —the drink-offering made to God with sacrifice after any signal mercies received— and bless the Lord who has been thus gracious to me. In the sight of the whole world will I pay my past vows unto Jehovah, and bring nations from every portion of the earth, reconciled and holy through the blood of my atonement.

The language in these verses, as in the concluding part of the Psalm, is wholly drawn from earthly objects and modes of religious service, well recognized by the Jews. It is in these things that the *spiritual* sense is required to be separated from the external emblem. For instance, the sacramental cup was without a doubt drawn and instituted from the cup used in commemoration of deliverances by the Jews. It is used figuratively by Christ in heaven ; but the reflective mind can scarcely fail to see the beauty of imagining it in his hand in thankfulness for his triumph, *because* " he has burst his bonds in sunder " : the bonds which held him fast in death, and confined him to the tomb : the assertion that " precious in the sight of Jehovah is the death of his saints " *specially includes* the sacrifice of Christ within its more general allusion to the blood shed, in such abundance, by prophets and martyrs to the truth. In the same manner the worship of Jehovah in the courts of his temple at Jerusalem is used in figure for the open promulgation of Christianity to the whole world. The temple services were the most solemn and most public which were offered by the Jews ; and when Christ is said to " offer his sacrifices of thanksgiving " to God *in the sight of all his people*, the figure is easily separated from the grosser element ; and *the conversion* of all people intimated under the form of Christ *seen* by all.—*William Hill Tucker.*

Verse 1.—"*I love.*" The expression of the prophet's affection is in this short abrupt phrase, "*I love*," which is but one word in the original, and expressed as a full and entire sentence in itself, thus—"*I love because the Lord hath heard*," etc. Most translators so turn it, as if, by a trajection, or passing of a word from one sentence to another, this title Lord were to be joined with the first clause, thus— (אֲהַבְתִּי כִּי־יִשְׁמַע יְהֹוָה), "*I love the* LORD, *because he hath heard*," etc. I deny not but that thus the sense is made somewhat the more perspicuous, and the words run the more roundly ; yet are they not altogether so emphatical. For when a man's heart is inflamed, and his soul ravished with a deep apprehension of some great and extroardinary favour, his affection will cause interruption in the expression thereof, and make stops in his speech ; and therefore this concise and abrupt clause, "*I love*," declareth a more entire and ardent affection than a more full and round phrase would do. Great is the force of true love, so that it cannot be sufficiently expressed.—*William Gouge*, 1575—1653.

Verse 1.—"*I love the* LORD." Oh that there were such hearts in us that we could every one say, as David, with David's spirit, upon his evidence, "*I love the* LORD" ; that were more worth than all these, viz. ; First, to know all scerets. Secondly, to prophesy. Thirdly, to move mountains, etc., 1 Cor. xiii. 1, 2, etc. "*I love the* LORD" ; it is more than I know the Lord ; for even castaways are enlightened, (Heb. vi. 4) ; more than I fear the Lord, for devils fear him unto trembling (James ii. 19) ; more than I pray to God (Isai. i. 15). What should I say ? More than all services, than all virtues separate from charity : truly say the schools, charity is the form of all virtues, because it forms them all to acceptability, for nothing is accepted but what issues from charity, or, in other words, from the love of God.—*William Slater*, 1638.

Verse 1.—"*I love the* LORD, *because*," etc. How vain and foolish is the *talk*, " To love God for his benefits towards us is mercenary, and cannot be pure love ! " Whether pure or impure, there is no other love that can flow from the heart of the creature to its Creator. " We love him," said the holiest of Christ's disciples, " because he first loved us ; " and the increase of our love and filial evidence is in proportion to the increased sense we have of our obligation to him. We love him for the benefits bestowed on us.—*Love begets love.*—*Adam Clarke.*

Verse 1.—"*He hath heard my voice.*" But is this such a benefit to us, that God hears us ? Is his hearing our voice such an argument of his love ? Alas ! he may hear us, and we be never the better : he may hear our voice, and yet his love to us may be but little, for he will not give a man the hearing, though he love him not at all ? With men perhaps it may be so, but not with God ; for his hearing is not only voluntary, but reserved ; *non omnibus dormit :* his ears are not open to every one's cry ; indeed, to hear us, is in God so great a favour, that he may well be counted his favourite whom he vouchsafes to hear : and the rather, for that his hearing is always operative, and with a purpose of helping ; so that if he hear my voice, I may be sure he means to grant my supplication ; or rather perhaps in David's manner of expressing, and in God's manner of proceeding, to hear my voice is no less in effect than to grant my supplication.—*Sir Richard Baker.*

Verse 1.—"*Hath heard.*" By hearing prayer God giveth evidence of the notice which he taketh of our estates, of the respect he beareth to our persons, of the pity he hath of our miseries, of his purpose to supply our wants, and of his mind to do us good according to our needs.—*William Gouge.*

Verses 1 and 2.—The first יִשְׁמַע is more of an aorist. The Lord hears always ; and then, making a distinction הֵמָּה אֲוֹנִי. He has done it hitherto ; אֶקְרָא Therefore will I call upon him as long as I live, cleaving to Him in love and faith ! It should be noticed, in addition, that קְרָא here is not simply the prayer for help, but includes also the praising and thanksgiving, according to the twofold signification of קְרָא בְּשֵׁם יְהֹוָה, in verses 4, 13, and 17 : therefore, Jarchi very excellently says : *In the time of my distress I will call upon Him, and in the time of my deliverance I will praise Him.—Rudolph Stier.*

Verses 1, 2.—"I love." "Therefore will I call upon him." It is love that doth open our mouths, that we may praise God with joyful lips ; " I will love the Lord because he hath heard the voice of my supplications " ; and then, ver. 2, " I will call upon him as long as I live." The proper intent of mercies is to draw us to God. When the heart is full of a sense of the goodness of the Lord, the tongue cannot hold its peace. Self-love may lead us to prayers, but love to God excites us to praises : therefore to seek and not to praise, is to be lovers of ourselves rather than of God.—*Thomas Manton.*

Verses 1, 12.—"I love." "What shall I render?" Love and thankfulness are like the symbolical qualities of the elements, easily resolved into each other. David begins with, *"I love the Lord, because he hath heard my voice"* ; and to enkindle this grace into a greater flame, he records the mercies of God in some following verses ; which done, then he is in the right mood for praise ; and cries, *"What shall I render unto the Lord for all his benefits?"* The spouse, when thoroughly awake, pondering with herself what a friend had been at her door, and how his sweet company was lost through her unkindness, shakes off her sloth, riseth, and away she goes after him ; now, when by running after her beloved, she hath put her soul into a heat of love, she breaks out in praising him from top to toe. Cant. v. 10. That is the acceptable praising which comes from a warm heart ; and the saint must use some holy exercise to stir up his habit of love, which like natural heat in the body, is preserved and increased by motion.—*William Gurnall.*

Verse 2.—"He hath inclined his ear unto me." How great a blessing, is the inclining of the Divine ear, may be judged from the conduct of great men, who do not admit a wretched petitioner to audience : but, if they do anything, receive the main part of the complaint through the officer appointed for such matters, or through a servant. But God himself hears immediately, and *inclines his ear*, hearing readily, graciously, constantly, etc. Who would not pray ?—*Wolfgang Musculus.*

*Verse 2.—*And now *because he hath inclined his ear unto me*, I will therefore *call upon him as long as I live :* that if it be expected I should call upon any other, it must be when I am dead ; for as long as I live, I have vowed to call upon God. But will this be well done ? May I not, in so doing, do more than I shall have thanks for ? Is this the requital that God shall have for his kindness in hearing me, that now he shall have a customer of me, and never be quiet because of my continual running to him, and calling upon him ? Doth God get anything by my calling upon him, that I should make it a vow, as though in calling upon him I did him a pleasure ? O my soul, I would that God might indeed have a customer of me in praying : although I confess I should not be so bold to call upon him so continually, if his own commanding me did not make it a duty : for hath not God bid me call upon him when I am in trouble ? and is there any time that I am not in trouble, as long as I live in this vale of misery ? and then can there be any time as long as I live, that I must not call upon him ? For shall God bid me, and shall I not do it ? Shall God incline his ear, and stand listening to hear, and shall I hold my peace that he may have nothing to hear ?—*Sir Richard Baker.*

Verse 2.—"Therefore will I call upon him." If the hypocrite speed in prayer, and get what he asks, then also he throws up prayer, and will ask no more. If from a sick bed he be raised to health, he leaves prayer behind him, as it were, sick-abed ; he grows weak in calling upon God, when at his call God hath given him strength. And thus it is in other instances. When he hath got what he hath a mind to in prayer, he hath no more mind to pray. Whereas a godly man prays after he hath sped, as he did before, and though he fall not into those troubles again, and so is not occasioned to urge those petitions again which he did in trouble, yet he cannot live without prayer, because he cannot live out of communion with God. The creature is as the white of an egg, tasteless to him, unless he enjoy God. David saith, *"I love the Lord, because he hath heard my voice and my supplications,"* that is, because he hath granted me that which I supplicated to him for. But did this grant of what he had asked take him off from asking more ? The next words show us what his resolution was upon that grant. *"Because he hath inclined his ear unto me, therefore will I call upon him as long as I live" :* as if he had said, I will never give over praying, forasmuch as I have been heard in prayer.—*Joseph Caryl.*

Verse 2.—*"As long as I live."* Not on some few days, but every day of my life; for to pray on certain days, and not on all, is the mark of one who loathes and not of one who loves.—*Ambrose.*

Verse 3.—Here beginneth the exemplification of God's kindness to his servant; the first branch whereof is a description of the danger wherein he was and out of which he was delivered. Now, to magnify the kindness of God the more in delivering him out of the same, he setteth it out with much variety of words and phrases.

The first word חֶבְלֵי, *"sorrows,"* is diversely translated. Some expound it snares, some cords, some sorrows. The reason of this difference is because the word itself is metaphorical. It is taken from cruel creditors, who will be sure to tie their debtors fast, as with cords, so that they shall not easily get loose and free again. The pledge which the debtor leaveth with his creditor as a pawn, hath this name in Hebrew; so also a cord wherewith things are tied fast; and the mast of a ship fast fixed, and tied on every side with cords; and bands or troops of men combined together; and the pain of a woman in travail, which is very great; and destruction with pain and anguish. Thus we see that such a word is used here as setteth out a most lamentable and inextricable case.

The next word, *"of death"* מָוֶת, sheweth that his case was deadly; death was before his eyes; death was as it were threatened. He is said to be *"compassed"* herewith in two respects: (1) To show that these sorrows were not far off, but even upon him, as waters that compass a man when he is in the midst of them, or as enemies that begird a place. (2) To show that they were not few, but many sorrows, as bees that swarm together.

The word translated *"pains,"* מְצָרֵי, in the original is put for sacks fast bound together, and flint stones, and fierce enemies, and hard straits; so that this word also aggravateth his misery.

The word translated *"hell,"* שְׁאוֹל, is usually taken in the Old Testament for the grave; it is derived from שָׁאַל, a verb that signifieth to crave, because the grave is ever craving, and never satisfied.

The words translated *"gat hold on me,"* מְצָאוּנִי, and *"I found,"* אֶמְצָא, are both the same verb; they differ only in circumstances of tense, number, and person. The former showeth that these miseries found him, and as a serjeant they seized on him; he did not seek them, he would wittingly and willingly have escaped them, if he could. The latter sheweth that indeed he found them; he felt the tartness and bitterness, the smart and pain of them.

The word translated *trouble*, צָרָה of צַר, hath a near affinity with the former word translated pain, מֵצַר of צוּר, and is used to set out as great misery as that; and yet further to aggravate the same, another word is added thereto, *"sorrow."*

The last word, *"sorrow,"* יָגוֹן of יָגָה, importeth such a kind of calamity as maketh them that lie under it much to grieve, and also moveth others that behold it much to pity them. It is often used in the Lamentations of Jeremiah. Either of these two last words, trouble and sorrow, do declare a very perplexed and distressed estate; what then did both of them joined together? For the Holy Ghost doth not multiply words in vain.—*William Gouge.*

Verse 3.—*"Gat hold upon me."* The original word is, *found me*, as we put in the margin. They found him, as an officer or serjeant finds a person that he is sent to arrest; who no sooner finds him, but he takes hold of him, or takes him into custody. When warrants are sent out to take a man who keeps out of the way, the return is, *Non est inventus*, the man is not found, he cannot be met with, or taken hold of. David's pains quickly found him, and having found him they gat hold of him. Such finding is so certainly and suddenly followed with taking hold, and holding what is taken, that one word in the Hebrew serves to express both acts. When God sends out troubles and afflictions as officers to attack any man, they will find him, and finding him, they will take hold of him. The days of affliction will take hold; there's no striving, no struggling with them, no getting out of their hands. These divine pursuivants will neither be persuaded nor bribed to let you go, till God speak the word, till God say, Deliver him, release him. *"I found trouble and sorrow."* I found trouble which I looked not for. I was not searching after sorrow, but I found it. There's an elegancy in the original. The Hebrew is, *"The pains of hell found me."* They found me, I did not find them;

but no sooner had the pains of hell found me, than I found trouble and sorrow, enough, and soon enough.—*Joseph Caryl.*

Verse 3.—See how the saints instead of lessening the dangers and tribulations, with which they are exercised by God, magnify them in figurative phraseology: neither do they conceal their distress of soul, but clearly and willingly set it forth. Far otherwise are the minds of those who regard their own glory and not the glory of God. The saints, that they may make more illustrious the glory of the help of God, declare things concerning themselves which make but little for their own glory.—*Wolfgang Musculus.*

Verses 3—7.—Those usually have most of heaven upon earth, that formerly have met with most of hell upon earth. *"The sorrows of death compassed me, and the pains of hell gat hold upon me: I found trouble and sorrow:* (as Jonas crying in the belly of hell). But look upon him within two or three verses after, and you may see him in an ecstasy, as if he were in heaven; verse 7: *"Return unto thy rest, O my soul; for the* LORD *hath dealt bountifully with thee."*—*Matthew Lawrence.*

Verse 4.—*"The name of the* LORD." God's name, as it is set out in the word, is both a glorious name, full of majesty; and also a gracious name, full of mercy. His majesty worketh fear and reverence, his mercy faith and confidence. By these graces man's heart is kept within such a compass, that he will neither presume above that which is meet, nor despond more than there is cause. But where God's name is not rightly known, it cannot be avoided but that they who come before him must needs rush upon the rock of presumption, or sink into the gulf of desperation. Necessary, therefore, it is that God be known of them that pray to him, that in truth they may say, *"We have called upon the name of the* LORD." Be persuaded hereby so to offer up your spiritual sacrifice of supplication to God, that he may have respect to your persons and prayers, as he had respect to Abel and his offering. Learn to know the name of God, as in his word it is made known; and then, especially when you draw near to him, meditate on his name. Assuredly God will take good notice of them that take due notice of him, and will open his ears to them by name who rightly call upon his name.—*William Gouge.*

Verse 4.—*"O* LORD, *I beseech thee, deliver my soul."* A short prayer for so great a suit, and yet as short as it was, it prevailed. If we wondered before at the power of God, we may wonder now at the power of prayer, that can prevail with God, for obtaining of that which in nature is impossible, and to reason is incredible.—*Sir Richard Baker.*

Verse 4.—We learn here that there is nothing better and more effectual in distressing agonies than assiduous prayer—*"Then called I upon the name of the* LORD;" but in such prayers the first care ought to be for the salvation of the soul—*"I beseech thee, deliver my soul";* for, this being done, God also either removes or mitigates the bodily disease.—*Solomon Gesner.*

Verse 5.—*"Gracious is the* LORD," etc. He is *gracious* in hearing, he is *"righteous"* in judging, he is *"merciful"* in pardoning, and how, then, can I doubt of his will to help me? He is righteous to reward according to deserts; he is gracious to reward above deserts; yea, he is merciful to reward without deserts; and how, then, can I doubt of his will to help me? He is gracious, and this shews his bounty; he is righteous, and this shews his justice; yea, he is merciful, and this shews his love; and how, then, can I doubt of his will to help me? If he were not gracious I could not hope he would hear me; if he were not righteous, I could not depend upon his promise; if he were not merciful, I could not expect his pardon; but now that he is gracious and righteous and merciful too, how can I doubt of his will to help me?—*Sir Richard Baker.*

Verse 5.—The first attribute, *"gracious,"* (חַנּוּן) hath especial respect to that goodness which is in God himself. The root (חָנַן) whence it cometh signifieth to do a thing gratis, freely, of one's own mind and goodwill. This is that word which is used to set out the free grace and mere goodwill of God, thus (וְחַנֹּתִי אֶת־אֲשֶׁר אָחֹן), " I will be gracious to whom I will be gracious," Exod. xxxiii. 19. There is also an adverb (חִנָּם) derived thence, which signifieth gratis, freely, as where Laban thus speaketh to Jacob, " Shouldst thou serve me for nought?" Thus is the word opposed to merit. And hereby the prophet acknowledged that the deliverance which God gave was for the Lord's own sake, upon no desert of him that was delivered.

The second attribute, *"righteous"* or just, (צַדִּיק), hath particular relation to the promise of God. God's righteousness largely taken is the integrity or equity of all his counsels, words, and actions. . . . Particularly is God's righteousness manifested in giving reward and taking vengeance. Thus it is said to be " a righteous thing with God to recompense tribulation to them that trouble you ; and to you who are troubled rest," 2 Thess. i. 6, 7. . . . But the occasion of mentioning God's righteousness here in this place being to show the ground of his calling on God, and of God's delivering him, it must needs have respect to God's word and promise, and to God's truth in performing what he hath promised.—*William Gouge.*

Verse 5.—"*The Lord* " ; "*our God.*" The first title, "*Lord,*" sets out the excellency of God. Fit mention is here made thereof, to shew the blessed concurrence of greatness and goodness in God. Though he be Jehovah the Lord, yet is he gracious, and righteous, and merciful. The second title, "*our God,*" manifesteth a peculiar relation betwixt him and the faithful that believe in him, and depend on him, as this prophet did. And to them in an especial manner the Lord is gracious, which moved him thus to change the person ; for where he had said in the third person " the Lord is gracious," here, in the first person, he says, "*our God,*" yet so that he appropriateth not this privilege to himself, but acknowledgeth it to be common to all of like character by using the plural number, "*our.*"—*William Gouge.*

Verse 5.—The " Berlenburger Bibelwerk " says, " The righteousness is very significantly placed between the grace and the mercy : for it is still necessary, that the evil should be mortified and driven out. Grace lays, as it were, the foundation for salvation, and mercy perfects the work ; but not till righteousness has finished its intermediary work."—*Rudolph Stier.*

Verse 5.—"*Our God is merciful.*" Mercy is God's darling attribute ; and by his infinite wisdom he has enabled mercy to triumph over justice without in any degree violating his honour or his truth. The character of merciful is that by which our God seems to delight in being known. When he proclaimed himself amid terrific grandeur to the children of Israel, it was as " the Lord, the Lord God merciful and gracious, pardoning iniquity, transgression, and sin." And such was the impression of this his character on the mind of Jonah that he says to him, " I knew that thou wert a merciful God." These, however, are not mere assertions—claims made to the character by God on the one hand, and extorted without evidence from man on the other ; for in whatever way we look upon God, and examine into his conduct towards his creatures, we perceive it to bear the impression of mercy. Nor can we more exalt the Lord our God than by speaking of his mercy and confiding in it ; for our " Lord's delight is in them that fear him, and put their trust in his mercy."—*John Gwyther,* 1833.

Verse 6.—"*The Lord preserveth the simple.*" God taketh most care of them that, being otherwise least cared for, wholly depend on him. These are in a good sense simple ones ; simple in the world's account, and simple in their own eyes. Such as he that said, " I am a worm, and no man ; a reproach of men, and despised of the people." Ps. xxii. 6. And again, " I am poor and needy, yet the Lord thinketh on me." Ps. xl. 17. These are those poor ones of a contrite spirit on whom the Lord looketh. Isai. lxvi. 2. Of such fatherless is God a father ; and of such widows a judge. Read Ps. lxviii. 5, and cxlvi. 7, 8, 9. Yea, read observantly the histories of the Gospel, and well weigh who they were to whom Christ in the days of his flesh afforded succour, and you shall find them to be such simple ones as are here intended.

By such objects the free grace and merciful mind of the Lord is best manifested. Their case being most miserable, in reference to human helps, the greater doth God's mercy appear to be ; and since there is nothing in them to procure favour or succour from God, for in their own and others' eyes they are nothing, what God doth for them evidently appeareth to be freely done.

Behold here how of all others they who seem to have least cause to trust on God have most cause to trust on him. Simple persons, silly wretches, despicable fools in the world's account, who have not subtle brains, or crafty wits to search after indirect means, have, notwithstanding, enough to support them, in the grand fact that they are such as the Lord preserveth. Now, who knoweth not that " It is better to trust in the Lord, than to put confidence in man ; it is better to trust in the Lord, than to put confidence in princes " ? Ps. cxviii. 8, 9.—*William Gouge.*

Verse 6.—"*The Lord preserveth the simple.*" How delightful it is to be able to reflect on the character of God as *preserving* the soul. The word properly signifies to defend us at any season of danger. The Hebrew word which is translated *"simple,"* signifies one who has no control over himself, one that cannot resist the power and influence of those around, and one, therefore, subject to the greatest peril from which he has naturally no deliverance. " The Lord preserveth." : his eye is upon them, his hand is over them, and they cannot fall. The word *"simple"* signifies likewise those that are ignorant of their condition, and not watching over their foes. Delightful thought, that though we may be thus ignorant, yet we are blessed with the means of escape ! We may be simple to the last extent, and our simplicity may be such as to involve our mind in the greatest doubt : the Lord preserveth us, and let us rest in him. It is delightful to reflect, that it is the simple in whom the Lord delights, whom he loves to bless. We are sometimes especially in the condition in which we may be inclined to make the inquiry, how we may be saved. We suppose there are many truths to be apprehended, many principles to be realized before we can be saved. No ; " the Lord preserveth the simple." We may be able to reconcile scarcely any of the doctrines of Christianity with each other ; we may find ourselves in the greatest perplexity when we examine the evidences on which they rest ; we may be exposed to great difficulty when we seek to apply them to practical usefulness ; but still we may adopt the language before us : *"The* LORD *preserveth the simple : I was brought low, and he helped me. Return unto thy rest, O my soul."—R. S. M'All,* 1834.

Verse 6.—*"The* LORD *preserveth the simple."* The term *simple* equals the " simplicity " of the New Testament, namely, that pure mind towards God, which, without looking out for help from any other quarter, and free from all dissimulation, expects salvation from him alone.—*Augustus F. Tholuck.*

Verse 6.—*"The simple."* They are such as honestly keep the plain way of God's commandments, without those slights, or creeks of carnal policy, for which men are in the world esteemed wise ; see Gen. xxv. 27, where Jacob is called a plain man. Simple or foolish he calls them, because they are generally so esteemed amongst the wise of the world ; not that they are so silly as they are esteemed ; for if the Lord can judge of wisdom or folly, the only fool is the Atheist and profane person (Ps. xiv. 1) ; the only wise man in the world is the plain, downright Christian (Deut. iv. 6), who keeps himself precisely in all states to that plain, honest course the Lord hath prescribed him. To such simple ones, God's fools, who in their misery and affliction keep them only to the means of deliverance and comfort which the Lord hath prescribed them, belongs this blessing of preservation from mischief, or destruction : so Solomon (Prov. xvi. 17), " The highway of the upright is to depart from evil." " He that keepeth his way preserveth his soul " ; see also Prov. xix. 16, 23 ; for exemplification see in Asa, 2 Chron. xiv. 9—12, and xvi. 7, 8, 9, read the excellent speech of Hanani the seer.—*William Slater,* 1638.

Verse 6.—*"I was brought low."* By affliction and trial. The Hebrew literally means to hang down, to be pendulous, to swing, to waive—as a bucket in a well, or as the slender branches of the palm, the willow, etc. Then it means to be slack, feeble, weak, as in sickness, etc. It probably refers to the prostration of strength by disease. *"And he helped me."* He gave me strength ; he restored me.—*Albert Barnes.*

Verse 6.—*"I was brought low, and he helped me."* The word translated *"brought low,"* דַּלֹּתִי *à* דָּלָה , properly signifieth to be drawn dry. The metaphor is taken from ponds, or brooks, or rivers that are clean exhausted and dried up, where water utterly faileth. Thus doth Isaiah use this word, " The brooks shall be emptied and dried up," Isai. xix. 6, דָּלְלוּ וְחָרְבוּ יְאֹרֵי . Being applied to man, it setteth out such an one as is spent, utterly wasted, or, as we use to speak, clean gone, who hath no ability to help himself, no means of help, no hope of help from others.

The other word whereby the succour which God afforded is expressed, and translated *"helped"* יְהוֹשִׁיעַ *ab* יָשַׁע, signifieth such help as freeth out of danger. It is usually translated " to save."—*William Gouge.*

Verse 6.—*"I was brought low, and he helped me."* Then is the time of help, when men are brought low : and therefore God who does all things in due time when I was brought low, then helped me. Wherefore, O my soul, let it never trouble thee how low soever thou be brought, for when thy state is at the lowest, then is God's assistance at the nearest. We may truly say, God's ways are not as the ways of the world, for in the world when a man is once brought low, he is commonly trampled upon, and nothing is heard then but, " down with him, down to the ground " : but with God it is otherwise ; for his delight is to raise up them that fall, and when they are brought low, then to help them. Hence it is no such hard case for a man to be brought low, may I not rather say his case is happy? For is it not better to be brought low, and have God to help him, than to be set aloft and left to help himself? At least, O my body, this may be a comfort to thee: for thou art sure to be brought low, as low as the grave, which is low indeed: yet there thou mayest rest in hope; for even there the Lord will not fail to help thee.—*Sir Richard Baker.*

Verse 6.—*"He helped me."* Helped me both to bear the worst and to hope the best; helped me to pray, else desire had failed; helped me to wait, else faith had failed.—*Matthew Henry.*

Verse 7.—*"Return unto thy rest, O my soul."* The Psalmist had been at a great deal of unrest, and much *off the hooks,* as we say; now, having prayed (for prayer hath *vim pacativam,* a pacifying property), he calleth his soul to rest; and rocketh it asleep in a spiritual security. Oh, learn this holy art; acquaint thyself with God, acquiesce in him, and be at peace; so shall good be done unto thee. Job xxii. 21. *Sis Sabbathum Christi.* Luther.—*John Trapp.*

Verse 7.—Gracious souls rest in God; they and none else. Whatever others may speak of a rest in God, only holy souls know what it means. *"Return unto thy rest, O my soul,"* to thy rest in calm and cheerful submission to God's will, delight in his service, satisfaction in his presence, and joy in communion begun with him here below, which is to be perfected above in its full fruition. Holy souls rest in God, and in his will; in his will of precept as their sovereign Lord, whose commands concerning all things are right, and in the keeping of which there is great reward; in his will of providence as their absolute owner, and who does all things well; in himself as their God, their portion, and their chief good, in whom they shall have all that they can need, or are capable of enjoying to complete their blessedness for ever.—*Daniel Wilcox.*

Verse 7.—*"Return unto thy rest."* Return to that rest which Christ gives to the weary and heavy laden, Matt. xi. 28. Return to thy Noah, his name signifies *rest,* as the dove when she found no rest returned to the ark. I know no word more proper to close our eyes when at night when we go to sleep, nor to close them with at death, that long sleep, than this, *"Return unto thy rest, O my soul."*—*Matthew Henry.*

Verse 7.—*"Return unto thy rest."* Consider the variety of aspects of that rest which a good man seeks, and the ground upon which he will endeavour to realize it. It consists in, 1. Rest from the perplexities of ignorance, and the wanderings of error. 2. Rest from the vain efforts of self-righteousness, and the disquietude of a proud and legal spirit. 3. Rest from the alarms of conscience, and the apprehensions of punishment hereafter. 4. Rest from the fruitless struggles of our degenerate nature, and unaided conflicts with indwelling sin. 5. Rest from the fear of temporal suffering and solicitude arising from the prospect of danger and trial. 6. Rest from the distraction of uncertainty and indecision of mind, and from the fluctuations of undetermined choice.—*R. S. M'All.*

Verse 7.—*"Return,"* שׁוּבִי. This is the very word which the angel used to Hagar when she fled from her mistress, " Return," Gen. xvi. 9. As Hagar through her mistress' rough dealing with her fled from her, so the soul of this prophet by reason of affliction fell from its former quiet confidence in God. As the angel therefore biddeth Hagar " return to her mistress," so the understanding of this prophet biddeth his soul return to its rest.—*William Gouge.*

Verse 7.—*"Rest."* The word *"rest"* is put in the plural, as indicating complete and entire rest, at all times, and under all circumstances.—*A. Edersheim.*

Verses 7, 8.—*"For the LORD hath dealt bountifully with thee."* He hath dealt indeed most bountifully with thee, for where thou didst make suit but for one thing, he hath granted thee three. Thou didst ask but to have my soul delivered, and he hath delivered mine eyes and my feet besides; and with a deliverance in each of them the greatest that could be: for what greater deliverance to my soul than to be delivered from death? What greater deliverance to my eyes than to be delivered from tears? What to my feet than to be delivered from falling? That if now, O my soul, thou return not to thy rest, thou wilt show thyself to be most insatiable; seeing thou hast not only more than thou didst ask, but as much indeed as was possible to be asked.

But can my soul die? and if not, what bounty is it to deliver my soul from that to which it is not subject? The soul indeed, though immortal, hath yet her ways of dying. It is one kind of death to the soul to be parted from the body, but the truest kind is to be parted from God ; and from both these kinds of death he hath delivered my soul. From the first, by delivering me from a dangerous sickness that threatened a dissolution of my soul and body ; from the other, by delivering me from the guilt of sin, which threatened a separation from the favour of God ; and are not these bounties so great as to give my soul just cause of returning to her rest ?—*Sir Richard Baker.*

Verses 7, 9.—*"Return unto thy rest, O my soul."* . . . *"I will walk."* How can these two stand together ? *Motus et quies private opponuntur*, saith the philosopher, motion and rest are opposite ; now *walking* is a *motion*, as being an act of the loco-motive faculty. How then could David *return* to his rest and yet *walk ?* You must know that *walking* and *rest* here mentioned, being of a *divine* nature, do not oppose each other ; *spiritual rest* maketh no man *idle*, and therefore it is no enemy to walking ; *spiritual walking* maketh no man *weary*, and therefore it is no enemy to rest. Indeed, they are so far from being opposite that they are subservient to each other, and it is hard to say whether that *rest* be the *cause* of this *walking*, or this *walking* a *cause* of that *rest*. Indeed, both are true, since he that *rests* in God cannot but *walk before him*, and by *walking before*, we come to *rest in God*. *Returning to rest* is an act of *confidence*, since there is no rest to be had but in God, nor in God but by believing affiance in, and reliance on him. *Walking before God* is an act of *obedience* ; when we disobey we wander and go astray, only by obedience we walk. Now these two are so far from being enemies, that they are companions and ever go together ; confidence being a means to quicken obedience, and obedience to strengthen con-fidence.—*Nathanael Hardy.*

Verse 8.—*"Thou hast delivered my soul from death, mine eyes from tears, and my feet from falling."* Lo, here a deliverance, not from one, but many dangers, to wit, *"death," "tears," "falling."* Single deliverances are as threads ; but when multiplied, they become as a cord twisted of many threads, more potent to draw us to God. Any one mercy is as a link, but many favours are as a chain consisting of several links, to bind us the closer to our duty ; *vis unita fortior.* Frequent droppings of the rain cannot but make an impression even on the stone, and renewed mercies may well prevail with the stony heart. Parisiensis relateth a story of a man whom (notwithstanding his notorious and vicious courses) God was pleased to accumulate favours upon, so that at last he cried out, *"Vicisti, benignissime Deus, indefatigabili sua bonitate,* Most gracious God, thy unwearied goodness hath overcome my obstinate wickedness "* ; and from that time devoted himself to God's service. No wonder, then, if David upon deliverance from such numerous and grievous afflictions, maketh this his resolve, to *"walk before the Lord in the land of the living."*—*Nathanael Hardy.*

Verse 8.—As an humble and sensible soul will pack up many troubles in one, so a thankful soul will divide one mercy into sundry particular branches, as here the Psalmist distinguisheth, the delivery of his soul from death, of his eyes from tears, and of his feet from falling.—*David Dickson.*

Verse 8.—Some distinguish the three particulars thus : *"He hath delivered my soul from death,"* by giving me a good conscience ; *"mine eyes from tears,"* by giving a quiet conscience ; *"my feet from falling,"* by giving an enlightened and assured conscience.—*William Gouge.*

Verse 8.—*"My feet from falling."* Whether means he, into penal misery and mischief, or into sin ? There is a *lapsus moralis*, as 1 Cor. x. 12. Err I ? or would David here be understood of sinning ? So Ps. lxxiii. 2 : " My feet were almost gone ; my steps had well nigh slipped." And if I be not deceived, the text leans to that meaning, rising still from the less to the greater. First. It is more bounty to be kept from grief than from death, for there is a greater enlargement from misery. It is not more bounty to be kept from the sense of affliction than to be kept from death, which is the greatest of temporal evils ; but it is more bounty in a gracious eye to be kept from sin than from death. Secondly. How his eyes from tears ? If not kept from sin ? That had surely cost him many a tear, as Peter (Matt. xxvi. 75). But understand it *de lapsu morali*, so the gradation still riseth to enlarge God's bounty ; yea, which I count the greatest blessing, in these afflictions he kept me steady in my course of piety, and suffered not afflictions to sway my heart from him. Still, in a gracious eye, the benefit seems greater to be delivered from sinning than from the greatest outward affliction. That is the reason Paul (Rom. viii. 37) triumphs over all afflictions. 2 Cor. xi. and xii. He counts them his glory, his crown ; but speaking of the prevailing of corruption in particular, he bemoans himself as the miserablest man alive. Rom. vii. 24.—*William Slater.*

Verse 9.—*"I will walk,"* etc. It is a holy resolution which this verse records. The previous verse had mentioned among the mercies vouchsafed, " Thou hast delivered my feet from falling"; and the first use of the restored limb is, "*I will walk before the LORD.*" It reminds one of the crippled beggar at the Beautiful Gate of the temple, to whom Peter had said, " In the name of Jesus Christ rise up and walk "; and "immediately his ancle-bones received strength, and he leaping up stood and walked, and entered with them into the temple, walking, and leaping, and praising God." It is a very sure mark of a grateful heart to employ the gift to the praise of the giver, in such a manner as he would most wish it to be employed.— *Barton Bourchier.*

Verse 9.—When thou, my soul, returnest to this rest, thou shalt walk in order that thou mayest have some exercise in thy rest, that thy resting may not make thee restive. "*I will walk before the LORD in the land of the living.*" For now that my feet are delivered from falling, how can I better employ them than in walking ? Were they delivered from falling that they should stand still and be idle ? No, my soul, but to encourage me to walk : and where is so good walking as in the land of the living ? Alas ! what walking is it in the winter, when all things are dead, when the very grass lies buried under ground, and scarce anything that has life in it is to be seen ? But then is the pleasant walking, when nature spreads her green carpet to walk upon, and then it is the land of the living, when the trees shew they live, by bringing forth, if not fruits, at least leaves ; when the valleys shew they live, by bringing forth sweet flowers to delight the smell, at least fresh grass to please the eyes. But is this the walking in the land of the living that David means ? O my soul, to walk in the land of the living is to walk in the paths of righteousness : for there is no such death to the soul as sin, no such cause of tears to the eyes as guiltiness of conscience, no such falling of the feet as to fall from God : and therefore, to say the truth, the soul can never return to its rest if we walk not withal in the paths of righteousness ; and we cannot well say whether this rest be a cause of the walk, or the walking be a cause of the resting : but this we may say, they are certainly companions the one to the other, which is in effect but this—that justification can never be without sanctification. Peace of conscience, and godliness of life, can never be one without the other. Or is it perhaps that David means that land of the living where Enoch and Elias are living, with the living God ? But if he mean so, how can he speak so confidently, and say, "*I will walk in the land of the living"?* as though he could come to walk there by his own strength, or at his own pleasure ? He therefore gives his reason : "*I believed, and therefore I spake,*" for the voice of faith is strong, and speaks with confidence ; and because in faith he believes that he should come to walk in the land of the living, therefore with confidence he speaks it, "*I will walk in the land of the living."—Sir Richard Baker.*

Verse 9.—"*I will walk before the LORD in the land of the living,*" i.e., I shall pass the whole of my life under his fatherly care and protection. The prophet has regard to the custom of men, and chiefly of parents : for those who ardently love their children have them always in their thoughts and carry them there, never ceasing from care and anxiety about them, but being always attentive to their safety. *Omnis enim in natis chari stat cura parentis.* Children are, therefore, said to walk before and in the sight of their parents, because they have them as constant guardians of their health and safety. Thus also the godly in this life walk before God, that is to say, are defended by his care and protection.—*Mollerus.*

Verse 9.—"*I will walk before the LORD.*" According to a different reading of the first word, "*I shall,*" and, "*I will,*" the clause puts on several senses ; if read "*I shall walk,*" they are words of *confident expectation ;* if "*I will,*" they are words of *obedient resolution.* According to the former, the Psalmist promiseth somewhat to himself from God ; according to the latter, he promiseth somewhat of himself to God. Both these constructions are probable and profitable. "*Before God";* that is, in his service ; or, "*before God,*" that is, under his care. Let us consider both senses. 1. "*I shall walk before the LORD in the land of the living" ;* that is, by continuing in this world, I shall have opportunity of doing God service. It was not because those holy men had less assurance of God's love than we, but because they had greater affections to God's service than we, that this life was so amiable in their eyes. To this purpose the reasonings of David and Hezekiah concerning death and the grave

are very observable. " Shall the dust praise thee ? shall it declare thy truth"?
so David, Ps. xxx. 9. " The grave cannot praise thee, death cannot celebrate thee";
so Hezekiah, Isai. xxxviii. 18. They saw death would render them useless for
God's honour, and therefore they prayed for life.

It lets us see why a religious man may desire life, that he may *"walk before the
Lord,"* and minister to him in the place wherein he hath set him. Indeed, that joy,
hope, and desire of life which is founded upon this consideration is not only lawful,
but commendable : and truly herein is a vast difference between the wicked and
the godly. To walk in the land of the living is the wicked man's desire, yea, were
it possible he would walk here for ever ; but for what end ? only to enjoy his lusts,
have his fill of pleasure, and increase his wealth : whereas the godly man's aim in
desiring to live is that he may *"walk before God,"* advance his glory, and perform
his service. Upon this account it is that one hath fitly taken notice how David
doth not say, I shall now satiate myself with delights in my royal city, but, *"I shall
walk before the Lord in the land of the living."*

2. And most suitably to this interpretation, this *"before the Lord,"* means *under
the Lord's careful eye.* The words according to the Hebrew may be read, *before the
face of the Lord,* by which is meant his presence, and that not general, before which
all men walk, but special, before which only good men walk. Indeed, in this sense
God's face is as much as his favour ; and as to be cast out of his sight is to be under
his anger, so to walk before his face is to be in favour with him : so that the meaning
is, as the Psalmist had said, I shall live securely and safely in this world under the
careful protection of the Almighty ; and this is the confidence which he here seemeth
to utter with so much joy, that God's gracious providence should watch over him
the remainder of his days.—*Nathanael Hardy, in a Sermon entitled "Thankfulness
in Grain,"* 1654.

Verse 9.—*"In the land of the living."* These words admit of a threefold interpretation, being understood by some, especially for *the land of Judea.* By others,
erroneously for *the Jerusalem which is above.* By the most, and most probably, for
this *habitable earth,* the *present world.*

1. That exposition which Cajetan, Lorinus, with others, give of the words, would
not be rejected, who conceive that by *"the land of the living"* David here meaneth
Judea, in which, or rather over which being constituted king, he resolveth to walk
before God, and do him service. This is not improbably that *"land of the living"*
in which the Psalmist when an exile " believed to see the goodness of the Lord";
this is certainly that *"land of the living"* wherein God promiseth to " set his glory";
nor was this title without just reason appropriated to that country. (1.) *Partly,*
because it was a *"land"* which afforded the most plentiful supports and comforts
of natural life, in regard of the wholesomeness of the climate, the goodness of the
soil, the overflowing of milk and honey, with other conveniences both for food and
delight. (2.) *Chiefly,* because it was the *"land"* in which the living God was worshipped, and where he vouchsafed to place his name ; whereas the other parts of
the world worshipped lifeless things, of which the Psalmist saith, " They have mouths,
and speak not ; eyes, and see not ; ears, and hear not."

2. *"The land of the living"* is construed by the ancients to be that *heavenly
country,* the place of the blessed. Indeed, this appellation does most fitly agree
with heaven : this world is *desertum mortuorum,* a desert of dead, at least, dying
men ; that only is *regio vivorum,* a region of living saints. " He who is our life "
is in heaven, yea, " our life is hid with him in God," and therefore we cannot be said
to live till we come thither. . . . In this sense no doubt that devout bishop and martyr,
Babilas, used the words, who being condemned by Numerianus, the emperor, to an
unjust death, a little before his execution repeated this and the two preceding verses,
with a loud voice. Nor is it unfit for any dying saint to comfort himself with the
like application of these words, and say in a confident hope of that blessed sight,
"I shall walk before the Lord in the land of the living."

3. But doubtless the literal and proper meaning of these words is of *David's
abode in the world ;* during which time, wheresoever he should be, he would *"walk
before God" ;* for that seems to be the emphasis of the plural number, *lands,*
according to the original. The world consists of many countries, several lands,
and it is possible for men either by force, or unwillingly, to remove from one country
to another : but a good man when he changeth his country, yet altereth not his
religion, yea, wherever he is he resolveth to serve his God.—*Nathanael Hardy.*

Verse 9.—*"Land of the living."* How unmeet, how shameful, how odious a thing it is that dead men should be here on the face of the earth, which is *"the land of the living."* That there are such is too true. "She that liveth in pleasure is dead while she liveth," 1 Tim. v. 6 ; Sardis had a name that she lived, but was dead, Rev. iii. 1 ; "The dead bury their dead," Matt. viii. 22 ; all natural men are "dead in sins," Eph. ii. 1, 2 Cor. v. 14.—*William Gouge.*

Verses 9, 12, etc.—The Hebrew word that is rendered *walk,* signifies a continued action, or the reiteration of an action. David resolves that he will not only take a turn or two with God, or walk a pretty way with God, as Orpah did with Ruth, and then take his leave of God, as Orpah did of her mother, Ruth i. 10—15 ; but he resolves, whatever comes on it, that he will walk constantly, resolutely, and perpetually before God ; or before the face of the Lord. Now, walking before the face of the Lord doth imply a very exact, circumspect, accurate, and precise walking before God ; and indeed, no other walking is either suitable or pleasing to the eye of God. But is this all that he will do upon the receipt of such signal mercies ? Oh, no ! for he resolves to take the cup of salvation, and to call upon the name of the Lord, and to offer the sacrifice of thanksgiving, vers. 13, 17. But is this all that he will do ? Oh, no ! for he resolves that he will presently pay his vows unto the Lord in the presence of all his people, vers. 14, 18. But is this all that he will do ? Oh, no ! for he resolves that he will love the Lord better than ever and more than ever, vers. 1, 2. He loved God before with a real love, but having now received such rare mercies from God, he is resolved to love God with a more raised love, and with a more inflamed love, and with a more active and stirring love, and with a more growing and increasing love than ever.—*Thomas Brooks.*

Verse 10.—*"I believed, therefore have I spoken."* It is not sufficient to believe, unless thou also openly confessest before unbelievers, tyrants, and all others. Next to believing follows confession ; and therefore, those who do not make a confession ought to fear ; as, on the contrary, those should hope who speak out what they have believed.—*Paulus Palanterius.*

Verse 10.—*"I believed, therefore have I spoken."* That is to say, I firmly believe what I say, therefore I make no scruple of saying it. This should be connected with the preceding **verse**, and the full stop should be placed at "spoken."—*Samuel Horsley.*

Verse 10.—*"I believed,"* etc. Some translate the words thus : *I believed when I said, I am greatly afflicted :* I believed when I said in my haste, *"all men are liars"* ; *q.d.,* Though I have had my *offs* and my *ons,* though I have passed several frames of heart and tempers of soul in my trials, yet I believed still, I never let go my hold, my grip of God, in my perturbation.—*John Trapp.*

Verse 10.—The heart and tongue should go together. The tongue should always be the heart's interpreter, and the heart should always be the tongue's suggester ; what is spoken with the tongue should be first stamped upon the heart and wrought off from it. Thus it should be in all our communications and exhortations, especially when we speak or exhort about the things of God, and dispense the mysteries of heaven. David spake from his heart when he spake from his faith. *"I believed, therefore have I spoken."* Believing is an act of the heart, "with the heart man believeth" ; so that to say, *"I believed, therefore have I spoken,"* is as if he had said, I would never have spoken these things, if my heart had not been clear and upright in them. The apostle takes up that very protestation from David (2 Cor. iv. 13) : "According as it is written, I believed, and therefore have I spoken ; we also believe, and therefore speak" ; that is, we move others to believe nothing but what we believe, and are fully assured of ourselves.—*Joseph Caryl.*

Verse 10.—*"I was greatly afflicted."* After that our minstrel hath made mention of faith and of speaking the word of God, whereby are to be understood all good works that proceed and come forth out of faith, he now singeth of the cross, and sheweth that he was very sore troubled, grievously threatened, uncharitably blasphemed, evil reported, maliciously persecuted, cruelly troubled, and made to suffer all kinds of torments for uttering and declaring the word of God. *"I believed,"* saith he, *"therefore have I spoken ; but I was very sore troubled."* Christ's word and the cross are companions inseparable. As the shadow followeth the body, so doth the cross follow the word of Christ : and as fire and heat cannot be separated, so cannot the gospel of Christ and the cross be plucked asunder.—*Thomas Becon* (1511—1567 or 1570).

Verses 10, 11.—The meaning seems to be this—I spake as I have declared (ver. 4) because I trusted in God.   I was greatly afflicted, I was in extreme distress, I was in great astonishment and trembling (as the word rendered *"haste"* signifies trembling as well as haste, as it is rendered in Deut. xx. 3;) and in these circumstances I did not trust in man ; I said, *"all men are liars"*—*i.e.*, not fit to be trusted in ; those that will fail and deceive the hopes of those who trust in them, agreeable to Psalm lxii. 8, 9.—*Jonathan Edwards.*

Verse 11.—*"I said in my haste, All men are liars,"* Rather, in an ecstacy of despair, I said, the whole race of man is a delusion.—*Samuel Horsley.*

Verse 11.—*"All men are liars."*   That is to say, every man who speaks in the ordinary manner of men concerning happiness, and sets great value on the frail and perishable things of this world, is a liar ; for true and solid happiness is not to be found in the country of the living.   This explanation solves the sophism proposed by St. Basil.   If every man be a liar, then David was a liar ; therefore he lies when he says, every man is a liar—thus contradicting himself, and destroying his own position.   This is answered easily ; for when David spoke he did so not as man, but from an inspiration of the Holy Ghost.—*Robert Bellarmine.*

Verse 11.—*"All men are liars."*   Juvenal said, " Dare to do something worthy of transportation and imprisonment, if you mean to be of consequence.   Honesty is praised, but starves."   A pamphlet was published some time ago with the title, *"Whom shall we hang?"*   A very appropriate one might *now* be written with a slight change in the title—*"Whom shall we trust?"*—*From " A New Dictionary of Quotations,"* 1872.

Verses 11—15.—It seems that to give the lie was not so heinous an offence in David's time as it is in these days ; for else how durst he have spoken such words, *"That all men are liars,"* which is no less than to give the lie to the whole world ? and yet no man, I think, will challenge him for saying so ; no more than challenge St. John for saying that all men are sinners, and indeed how should any man avoid being a liar, seeing the very being of man is itself a lie ? not only is it a vanity, and put in the balance less than vanity ; but a very lie, promising great matters, and able to do just nothing, as Christ saith, " without me ye can do nothing " : and so Christ seems to come in, to be David's second, and to make his word good, that *all men are liars.*   And now let the world do its worst, and take the lie how it will, for David having Christ on his side, will always be able to make his part good against all the world, for Christ hath overcome the world.

But though all men may be said to be liars, yet not all men in all things ; for then David himself should be a liar in this : but all men perhaps in something or other, at sometime or other, in some kind or other.   Absolute truth is not found in any man, but in that man only who was not man only ; for if he had been so, it had not perhaps been found in him neither, seeing absolute truth and deity are as relatives, never found to be asunder.

But in what thing is it that all men should be liars ?   Indeed, in this for one ; to think that God regards not, and loves not them whom he suffers to be afflicted ; for we may rather think he loves them most whom he suffers to be most afflicted ; and we may truly say he would never have suffered his servant Job to be afflicted so exceeding cruelly, if he had not loved him exceeding tenderly ; for there is nothing lost by suffering afflictions.   No, my soul, they do but serve to make up the greater weight of glory, when it shall be revealed.

But let God's afflictions be what they can be, yet I will always acknowledge they can never be in any degree so great as his benefits : and oh, that *I could think of something that I might render to him for all his benefits :* for shall I receive such great, such infinite benefits from him, and shall I render nothing to him by way of gratefulness ?   But, alas, what have I to render ?   All my rendering to him will be but taking more from him : for all I can do is but to *"take the cup of salvation, and call upon his name,"* and what rendering is there in this taking ?   If I could take the cup of tribulation, and drink it off for his sake, this might be a rendering of some value ; but this, God knows, is no work for me to do.   It was his work, who said, " Can ye drink of the cup, of which I shall drink ? "   Indeed, he drank of the cup of tribulation, to the end that we might take the cup of salvation ; but then in taking it we must call upon his name ; upon his name and upon no other ; for else we shall make it a cup of condemnation, seeing there is no name under heaven, in which we may be saved, but only the name of Jesus.

Yet it may be some rendering to the Lord if I pay my vows, and do, as it were, my penance openly ; *"I will therefore pay my vows to the LORD, in the presence of all his people."* But might he not pay his vows as well in his closet, between God and himself, as to do it publicly ? No, my soul, it serves not his turn, but he must pay them in the presence of all his people ; yet not to the end he should be applauded for a just prayer ; for though he pay them, yet he can never pay them to the full ; but to the end, that men seeing his good works, may glorify God by his example. And the rather perhaps, for that David was a king, and the king's example prevails much with the people, to make them pay their vows to God : but most of all, that by this means David's piety may not be barren, but may make a breed of piety in the people also : which may be one mystical reason why it was counted a curse in Israel to be barren ; for he that pays not his vows to God in the presence of his people may well be said to be barren in Israel seeing he begets no children to God by his example. And perhaps, also, the vows which David means here was the doing of some mean things, unfit in show for the dignity of a king ; as when it was thought a base thing in him to dance before the ark ; he then vowed he would be baser yet : and in this case, to pay his vows before the people becomes a matter of necessity : for as there is no honour to a man whilst he is by himself alone, so there is no shame to a man but before the people : and therefore to shew that he is not ashamed to do any thing how mean soever, so it may tend to the glorifying of God ; *"he will pay his vows in the presence of all his people."* And he will do it though it cost him his life, for if he die for it he knows that *"Precious in the sight of the LORD is the death of his saints."* But that which is precious is commonly desired : and doth God then desire the death of his saints ? He desires, no doubt, that death of his saints which is to die to sin : but for any other death of his saints, it is therefore said to be precious in his sight, because he lays it up with the greater carefulness. And for this it is there are such several mansions in God's house, that to them whose death is precious in his sight he may assign the most glorious mansions. This indeed is the reward of martyrdom, and the encouragement of martyrs, though their sufferings be most insufferable, their troubles most intolerable ; yet this makes amends for all ; that *"Precious in the sight of the LORD is the death of his saints."* For if it be so great a happiness to be acceptable in his sight, how great a happiness must it be to be precious in his sight ? When God, at the creation looked upon all his works, it is said he saw them to be all exceeding good : but it is not said that any of them were precious in his sight. How then comes death to be precious in his sight, that was none of his works, but is a destroyer of his works ? Is it possible that a thing which destroys his creatures should have a title of more value in his sight, than his creatures themselves ? O, my soul, this is one of the miracles of his saints, and perhaps one of those which Christ meant, when he said to his apostles, that greater miracles than he did they should do themselves : for what greater miracle than this, that death, which of itself is a thing most vile in the sight of God, yet once embraced by his saints, as it were by their touch only, becomes precious in his sight ? To alter a thing from being vile to be precious, is it not a greater miracle than to turn water into wine ? Indeed so it is ; death doth not damnify his saints, but his saints do dignify death. Death takes nothing away from his saints' happiness, but his saints add lustre to death's vileness. It is happy for death that ever it met with any of God's saints ; for there was no way for it else in the world, to be ever had in any account : but why say I, in the world ? For it is of no account in the world for all this : it is but only in the sight of God ; but indeed this only is all in all ; for to be precious in God's sight is more to be prized than the world itself. For when the world shall pass away, and all the glory of it be laid in the dust ; then shall trophies be erected for the death of his saints : and when all monuments of the world shall be utterly defaced, and all records quite rased out ; yet the death of his saints shall stand registered still, in fair red letters in the calendar of heaven. If there be glory laid up for them that die in the Lord ; much more shall they be glorified that die for the Lord.

I have wondered oftentimes, why God will suffer his saints to die ; I mean not the death natural, for I know *statutum est omnibus semel mori ;* but the death that is by violence, and with torture : for who could endure to see them he loves so cruelly handled ? But now I see the reason of it ; for, *"Precious in the sight of the LORD is the death of his saints."* And what marvel then if he suffer his saints to die ; when by dying they are wrought, and made fit jewels to be set in his cabinet : for as God has a bottle which he fills up with the tears of his saints, so I may say he hath a cabinet which he decks up with the deaths of his saints : and, O my soul, if thou couldst but comprehend what a glory it is to serve for a jewel in the decking up of God's cabinet, thou wouldest never wonder why he suffers his saints to be put to death, though with never so great torments, for it is but the same which Saint Paul saith : " The afflictions of this life are not worthy to be compared with the glory that shall be revealed."—*Sir Richard Baker.*

Verse 12.—*"What shall I render unto the* LORD *?"* Rendering to the true God, in a true and right manner, is the sum of true religion. This notion is consonant to the scriptures : thus : "Render unto God the things that are God's." Matt. xxii. 21. As true loyalty is a giving to Cæsar the things that are Cæsar's, so true piety is the giving to God the things that are God's. And so, in that parable of the vineyard let out to husbandmen, all we owe to God is expressed by the *rendering the fruit of the vineyard ;* Matt. xxi. 41. Particular acts of religion are so expressed in the Scriptures Psalm lvi. 12 ; Hosea xiv. 2 ; 2 Chron. xxxiv. 31. Let this, then, be the import of David's מָֽה־אָשִׁיב לַֽיהֹוָה, *"What shall I render unto the* LORD *?"* " In what things, and by what means, shall I promote religion in the exercise thereof ? How shall I show myself duly religious towards him who hath been constantly and abundantly munificent in his benefits towards me ? "—*Henry Hurst.*

Verse 12.—*"All his benefits toward me."* What reward shall we give unto the Lord, for all the benefits he hath bestowed ? From the cheerless gloom of non-existence he waked us into being ; he ennobled us with understanding ; he taught us arts to promote the means of life ; he commanded the prolific earth to yield its nurture ; he bade the animals to own us as their lords. For us the rains descend ; for us the sun sheddeth abroad its creative beams ; the mountains rise, the valleys bloom, affording us grateful habitation and a sheltering retreat. For us the rivers flow ; for us the fountains murmur ; the sea opens its bosom to admit our commerce ; the earth exhausts its stores ; each new object presents a new enjoyment ; all nature pouring her treasures at our feet, through the bounteous grace of him who wills that all be ours.—*Basil, 326—379.*

Verse 12.—*"All his benefits."* As partial obedience is not good, so partial thanks is worthless : not that any saint is able to keep all the commands, or reckon up all the mercies of God, much less return particular acknowledgment for every single mercy ; but as he " hath respect unto all the commandments " (Ps. cxix. 6), so he desires to value highly every mercy, and to his utmost power give God the praise of all. An honest soul would not conceal any debt he owes to God, but calls upon itself to give an account for all his benefits. The skipping over one note in a lesson may spoil the grace of the music ; unthankfulness for one mercy disparageth our thanks for the rest.—*William Gurnall.*

Verse 13.—*"I will take the cup of salvation."* It may probably allude to the libation offering, Numb. xxviii. 7 ; for the three last verses seem to intimate that the Psalmist was now at the temple, offering the meat-offering, drink-offering, and sacrifices to the Lord. *"Cup"* is often used by the Hebrews to denote plenty or abundance. So, " the cup of trembling," an abundance of *misery ;* " the cup of salvation," an abundance of *happiness.*—*Adam Clarke.*

Verse 13.—*"Cup of salvation."* In holy Scripture there is mention made of drink-offerings, Gen. xxv. 14 ; Levit. xxiii. 13 ; Num. xv. 5 ; which were a certain quantity of wine that used to be poured out before the Lord ; as the very notation of the word importeth, coming from a root נָסַךְ, *effudit,* that signifieth to pour out. As the meat-offerings, so the drink-offerings, were brought to the Lord in way of gratulation and thanksgiving. Some therefore in allusion hereunto so expound the text, as a promise and vow of the Psalmist, to testify his public gratitude by such an external and solemn rite as in the law was prescribed. This he termeth *a cup,* because that drink-offering was contained in a cup and poured out thereof ; and he adds this epithet, " salvation," because that rite was an acknowledgment of salvation, preservation and deliverance from the Lord.

After their solemn gratulatory sacrifices they were wont to have a feast. When David had brought the ark of God into the tabernacle, they offered burnt offerings and peace offerings, which being finished, " he dealt to every one of Israel, both man and woman, to every one a loaf of bread, and a good piece of flesh, and a flagon of wine." 1 Chron. xvi. 3. Hereby is implied that he made so bountiful a feast, as he had to give thereof to all the people there assembled. In this feast the master thereof was wont to take a great cup, and in lifting it up to declare the occasion of that feast, and then in testimony of thankfulness to drink thereof to the guests, that they in order might pledge him. This was called a cup of salvation, or deliverance, because they acknowledged by the use thereof that God had saved and delivered them. Almost in a like sense the apostle styleth the sacramental cup, the cup of blessing. Here the prophet useth the plural number, thus, " cup of *salvations*," whereby, after the Hebrew elegancy, he meaneth many deliverances, one after another ; or some great and extraordinary deliverance which was instead of many, or which comprised many under it. The word translated *take* (אֶשָּׂא *a* אֶשָּׂא) properly signifieth to lift up, and in that respect may the more fitly be applied to the forementioned taking of the festival cup and lifting it up before the guests. Most of our later expositors of this Psalm apply this phrase, " I will take the cup of salvation," to the forenamed gratulatory drink-offering, or to the taking and lifting up of the cup of blessing in the feast, after the solemn sacrifice. Both of these import one and the same thing, which is, that saints of old were wont to testify their gratefulness for great deliverances with some outward solemn rite.—*William Gouge.*

Verse 13.—*"Cup of salvation."* *Yeshuoth :* Ps. xviii. 50, xxviii. 8, liii. 6. The *cup* of salvation, symbolized by the eucharistic cup of the Passover Supper.—Zion that had drunk of the " cup of trembling " (Isai. li. 17, 22) might now rise and drink of the cup of salvation.

To the church these words have had a yet deeper significancy added to them by St. Matt. xxvi. 27. Jesus, on that Passover night, drank of the bitter wine of God's wrath, that he might refill the cup with joy and health for his people.—*William Kay.*

Verses 13, 14, 17—19.—A fit mode of expressing our thanks to God is by solemn acts of worship, secret, social, and public. " The closet will be the first place where the heart will delight in pouring forth its lively joys ; thence the feeling will extend to the family altar ; and thence again it will proceed to the sanctuary of the Most High." (*J. Morison*). To every man God has sent a large supply of benefits, and nothing but perverseness can deny to him the praise of our lips.—*William S. Plumer.*

Verse 14.—A man that would have his credit as to the truth of his word kept up, would choose those to be witnesses of his performing who were witnesses of his promising. I think David took this heed in his rendering and paying his vows : *"I will do it,"* saith he, *"now in the presence of all his people."* The people were witnesses to his straits, prayers, and vows ; and he will honour religion by performing in their sight what he sealed, signed, and delivered as his vow to the Lord. Seek not more witnesses than providence makes conscious of thy vows, lest this be interpreted ostentation and vain self-glorying : take so many, lest the good example be lost, or thou suspected of falsifying thy vow. Brifley and plainly : Didst thou on a sick bed make thy vow before thy family, and before the neighbourhood ? Be careful to perform it before them ; let them see thou art what thou vowedst to be. This care in thy vow will be a means to make it most to the advantage of religion, whilst all that heard or knew thy vow bear thee testimony that thou art thankful, and thus thou givest others occasion to glorify thy Father who is in heaven.—*Henry Hurst* (1690) *in "The Morning Exercises."*

Verse 14.—*"I will pay my vows,"* etc. Foxe, in his Acts and Monuments, relates the following concerning the martyr, John Philpot :—" He went with the sheriffs to the place of execution ; and when he was entering into Smithfield the way was foul, and two officers took him up to bear him to the stake. Then he said merrily, What, will ye make me a pope ? I am content to go to my journey's end on foot. But first coming into Smithfield, he kneeled down there, saying these words, " I will pay my vows in thee, O Smithfield."

Verse 15.—*"Precious in the sight of the LORD is the death of his saints."* It is of value or importance in such respects as the following :—(1) As it is the removal of another of the redeemed to glory—the addition of one more to the happy hosts above ; (2) as it is a new triumph of the work of redemption,— showing the power and the value of that work ; (3) as it often furnishes a more direct proof of the reality of religion than any abstract argument could do. How much has the cause of religion been promoted by the patient deaths of Ignatius, Polycarp, and Latimer, and Ridley, and Huss, and Jerome of Prague, and the hosts of martyrs ! What does not the world owe, and the cause of religion owe, to such scenes as occurred on the death-beds of Baxter, and Thomas Scott, and Halyburton, and Payson ! What an argument for the truth of religion,—what an illustration of its sustaining power,—

what a source of comfort to those who are about to die,—to reflect that religion does not leave the believer when he most needs its support and consolation ; that it can sustain us in the severest trial of our condition here ; that it can illuminate what seems to us of all places *most* dark, cheerless, dismal, repulsive—" the valley of the shadow of death."—*Albert Barnes.*

Verse 15.—*"Precious in the sight of the* LORD *is the death of his saints."* The death of the saints is precious in the Lord's sight. First, because he "seeth not as man seeth." He judgeth not according to the appearance ; he sees all things as they really are, not partially : he traces the duration of his people, not upon the map of time, but upon the infinite scale of eternity ; he weighs their happiness, not in the little balance of earthly enjoyment, but in the even and equipoised balance of the sanctuary. In the next place, I think the death of the saints is precious in the Lord's sight, because *they are taken from the evil to come ;* they are delivered from the burden of the flesh ; ransomed by the blood of the Redeemer, they are his purchased possession, and now he receives them to himself. Sin and sorrow for ever cease; there is no more death, the death of Christ is their redemption; by death he overcame him that had the power of death ; therefore, they in him are enabled to say, " O death, where is thy sting ? O grave, where is thy victory ? " Again, the death of the saints is precious in the Lord's sight, for in it *he often sees the very finest evidences of the work of his own Spirit upon the soul ;* he sees faith in opposition to sense, leaning upon the promises of God. Reposing upon him who is mighty to save, he sees hope even against hope, anchoring the soul secure and steadfast on him who is passed within the veil ; he sees patience acquiescing in a Father's will—humility bending beneath his sovereign hand—love issuing from a grateful heart. Again, the death of the saints is precious in the Lord's sight, *as it draws out the tendernesses of surviving Christian friends*, and is abundant in the thanksgivings of many an anxious heart ; it elicits the sympathies of Christian charity, and realises that communion of saints, of which the Apostle speaks, when he says, " if one member suffer, all the members suffer with it ; if one rejoice they all joy." . . . The death of saints is precious, because the sympathy of prayer is poured forth from many a kindly Christian heart. . . . Nor is this all—the death of saints is precious, for *that is their day of seeing Jesus face to face.*—*Patrick Pounden's Sermon in "The Irish Pulpit,"* 1831.

Verse 15.—*"Precious."* Their death is precious (*jakar*) ; the word of the text is, *in pretio fuit, magni estimatum est.* See how the word is translated in other texts. 1. Honourable, Isai. xliii. 4 (*jakarta*) ; " thou wast precious in my sight, thou hast been honourable." 2. Much set by, 1 Sam. xviii. 30 ; " His name was much set by." 3. Dear, Jer. xxxi. 20. *An filius* (*jakkir*) *pretiosus mihi Ephraim :* " Is Ephraim my dear son ? " 4. Splendid, clear, or glorious, Job xxxi. 16. *Si vidi lunam* (*jaker*) *pretiosam et abeuntem :* " the moon walking in brightness."

Put all these expressions together, and then we have the strength of David's word, *"The death of the saints is precious " ;* that is, 1. honourable ; 2. much set by ; 3. dear ; 4. splendid and glorious in the sight of the Lord.—*Samuel Torshell, in "The House of Mourning,"* 1660.

Verse 15.—*"Precious."* It is proper to advert, in the first place, to the apparent primary import of the phrase, namely, *Almighty God watches over, and sets a high value upon the holy and useful lives of his people*, and will not lightly allow those lives to be abbreviated or destroyed. In the second place, the words lead us to advert to *the control which he exercises over the circumstances of their death.* These are under his special arrangement. They are too important in his estimation to be left to accident. In fact, chance has no existence. In the intervention of second causes, he takes care always to overrule and control them for good. Let the weakest believer among you be quite sure, be " confident of this very thing," that he will never suffer your great enemy to take advantage of anything in the manner of your death, to do you spiritual harm. No, on the contrary, he takes all its circumstances under his immediate and especial disposal. The sentiment will admit, perhaps, of a third illustration ; *when the saints are dying, the Lord looks upon them, and is merciful unto them.* Who can say how often he answers prayer, even in the cases of dying believers ? Never does he fail to support, even where he does not see good to spare. By the whispers of his love, by the witness of his Spirit, by the assurance of his presence, by the preparatory revelation of heavenly glory, he strengthens his afflicted ones, he makes all their bed in their sickness. Ah ! and when, perhaps, they scarcely possess a bed to languish upon, when poverty or other calamitous circumstances leave them, in the sorrow of sickness, no place of repose but the bare ground for their restless bodies, and his bosom for their spirits, do they ever find God fail them ? No ; many a holy man has slept the sleep of death with the missionary Martyn, in a strange and inhospitable land, or with the missionary Smith, upon the floor of a dungeon, and yet

> " Jesus has made their dying bed
> As soft as downy pillows are."

When no other eye saw, when no other heart felt, for these two never-to-be-forgotten martyrs, murdered men of God, and apostles of Jesus, then were they precious in God's sight, and he was present with them.　And so it is with all his saints, who are faithful unto death.　Fourthly, we are warranted by the text and the tenor of Scripture, in affirming that *the Lord attaches great importance to the death-bed itself.* This is in his estimate—whatever it may be in ours—too precious, too important, to be overlooked ; and hence it is often with emphasis, though always with a practical bearing, recorded in Scripture.　It is possible, certainly, to make too much of it, by substituting, as a criterion of character, that which may be professed under the excitement of dying sufferings, for the testimony of a uniform, conspicuous career of holy living.　But it is equally indefensible, and even ungrateful to God, to make too little of it, to make too little account of a good end, when connected with a good beginning and with a patient continuance in well-doing.

> " The chamber where the good man meets his fate
> Is privileged beyond the common walk of virtuous life."

Its transactions are sometimes as fraught with permanent utility as with present good.　The close of a Christian's career on earth, his defiance, in the strength of his Saviour, of his direst enemy, the good confession which he acknowledges when he is enabled to witness before those around his dying bed, all these are precious and important in the sight of the Lord, and ought to be so in our view, and redound, not only to his own advantage, but to the benefit of survivors, " to the praise of the glory of his grace."—*W. M. Bunting, in a Sermon at the City Road Chapel*, 1836.

Verse 15.—Why need they beforehand be afraid of death, who have the Lord to take such care about it as he doth ?　We may safely, without presuming, we ought securely without wavering, to rest upon this, that our blood being precious in God's eyes, either it shall not be split, or it is seasonable, and shall be profitable to us to have it spilt.　On this ground " the righteous are bold as a lion," Prov. xxviii. 1. " Neither do they fear what man can do unto them."　Heb. xiii. 6.　Martyrs were, without question, well instructed herein, and much supported hereby.　When fear of death hindereth from any duty, or draweth to any evil, then call to mind this saying, "*Precious in the sight of the* LORD *is the death of his favourites.*"　For who would not valiantly, without fainting, take such a death as is precious in God's sight.—*William Gouge.*

Verse 15.—"*His saints*" imports *appropriation.*　Elsewhere Jehovah asserts, " All souls are mine."　But he has an especial property in—and therefore claim upon—all saints.　It is he that made them such.　Separate from God there could be no sanctity.　And as his right, his original right, in all men, is connected with the facts of their having been created and endowed by his hand, and thence subjected to his moral government, so, and much more, do all holy beings, all holy men, who owe to his grace their very existence as such, who must cease to be saints, if they could cease to be *his* saints, whom he has created anew in Christ Jesus by the communication of his own love, his own purity, his own nature, whom he continually upholds in this exalted state, so, and much more, do such persons belong to God. They are " *his* saints " through him and in him, saints of his making, and modelling, and establishing, and therefore *his* exclusively.　Let this reference to the mighty working of God by his Spirit in you, your connection, your spiritual connection, with him, and your experience of his saving power,—let this reference convert the *mystery* into the *mercy* of sanctification in your hearts.

"*His* saints " denotes, in the second place, *devotedness.*　They are saints not only *through* him, but *to* him ; holy unto the Lord, sanctified or set apart to his service, self-surrendered to the adorable Redeemer.

"*His* saints " may import *resemblance*—close resemblance.　Such characters are emphatically *God-like*, holy and pure ; children of their Father which is in heaven ;

certifying to all around their filial relationship to him, by their manifest participation of his nature, by their reflection of his image and likeness.

"*His* saints " suggests associations of *endearment*, of complacency. " The Lord taketh pleasure in them that fear him, in all them that hope in his mercy " ; " a people near unto him " ; " the Lord's portion is his people " ; and " Happy is that people that is in such a case, yea, happy is that people whose God is the Lord."—*Condensed from a Sermon by W. M. Bunting*, 1836.

Verse 15.—"*Saints.*" The persons among whom implicitly he reckons himself, styled *saints*, are in the original set out by a word (חֲסִידִים) that importeth an especial respect of God towards them. The root whence that word issueth signifieth *mercy* (חָסַד *consecravit, benefecit*). Whereupon the Hebrews have given such a name to a stork, which kind among fowls is the most merciful ; and that not only the old to their young ones, as most are, but also the young ones to the old, which they use to feed and carry when through age they are not able to help themselves.

This title is attributed to men in a double respect ; 1. Passively, in regard of God's mind and affection to them ; 2. Actively, in regard of their mind and affection to others. God's merciful kindness is great towards them ; and their mercy and kindness are great towards their brethren. They are, therefore, by a kind of excellency and property styled " men of mercy." Isai. lvii. 1. In regard of his double acceptation of the word, some translate it, " merciful, tender, or courteous," Ps. xviii. 25. Others with a paraphrase with many words, because they have not one fit word to express the full sense, thus, " Those whom God followeth with bounty, or to whom God extendeth his bounty." This latter I take to be the most proper to this place ; for the word being passively taken for such as are made partakers of God's kindness, it sheweth the reason of that high account wherein God hath them, even his own grace and favor. We have a word in English that in this passive signification fitly answereth the Hebrew, which is this, *favourite.*—*William Gouge.*

Verse 15.—*Death* now, as he hath done also to mine, has paid full many a visit to your house ; and in very deed, he has made fell havoc among our comforts. We shall yet be avenged on this enemy—this King of Terrors. I cannot help at times clenching my fist in his face, and roaring out in my agony and anguish, " Thou shalt be swallowed up in victory ! " There is even, too, in the meantime, this consolation ; " O Death, where is thy sting ? " " Precious in the sight of the Lord is the death *for* his saints," in the first place ; in the second place, and resting on the propitiatory death, " Precious in the sight of the Lord is the death *of* his saints." The Holy Ghost, Psalm cxvi. 15, states the first ; our translators, honest men, have very fairly and truly inferred the second. We are obliged to them. The death of your lovely child, loveliest in the beauties of holiness, with all that was most afflictive and full of sore trial in it, is nevertheless, among the things in your little family which are right precious in the sight of the Lord ; and this in it, is that which pleases you most ; precious, because of the infinite, the abiding, and the unchanging worth of the death of God's own holy child Jesus. The calm so wonderful, the consolation so felt, yea, the joy in tribulation so great, have set before your eyes a new testimony, heart-touching indeed, that, after eighteen hundred years have passed, *"the death of his saints "* is still precious as ever in the sight of the Lord. Take your book of life, sprinkled with the blood of the covenant, and in your family record, put the death of Rosanna down among the precious things in your sight also—I should rather have said likewise.

Present my kindest regards to Miss S- -. Tell her to wipe that tear away—Rosanna needs it not. I hope they are all well at L—, and that your young men take the way of the Lord in good part. My dear Brother, " Go thy way, thy child liveth," is still as fresh as ever it was, from the lips of Him that liveth for ever and ever, and rings with a loftier and sweeter sound, even than when it was first heard in the ears and heart of the parent who had brought and laid his sick and dying at the feet of Him who hath the keys of hell and of death.—*John Jameson, in "Letters ; True Fame," etc.*, 1838.

Verse 16.—"*O LORD, truly I am thy servant.*" Thou hast made me free, and I am impatient to be bound again. Thou hast broken the bonds of sin ; now, Lord, bind me with the cords of love. Thou hast delivered me from the tyranny of Satan, make me as one of thy hired servants. I owe my liberty, my life, and all that I have, or hope, to thy generous rescue : and now, O my gracious, my Divine Friend and Redeemer, I lay myself and my all at thy feet.—*Samuel Lavington*, 1728—1807.

Verse 16.—"*I am thy servant.*" The saints have ever had a holy pride in being God's servants ; there cannot be a greater honour than to serve such a Master as commands heaven, earth, and hell. Do not think thou dost honour God in serving him ; but this is how God honours thee, in vouchsafing thee to be his servant. David could not study to give himself a greater style than—" O Lord, or, truly I am thy servant, and the son of thy handmaid," and this he spake, not in the phrase of a human compliment, but in the humble confession of a believer. Yea, so doth the apostle commend this excellency, that he sets the title of servant before that of an apostle ; first servant, then apostle. Great was his office in being an apostle, greater his blessing in being a servant of Jesus Christ : the one is an outward calling, the other an inward grace. There was an apostle condemned, never any servant of God.—*Thomas Adams.*

Verse 16.—"*I am thy servant.*" This expression of the king of Israel implies (1). *A humble sense of his distance from God and his dependence upon him.* This is the first view which a penitent hath of himself when he returns to God. It is the first view which a good man hath of himself in his approaches to, or communion with God. And, indeed, it is what ought to be inseparable from the exercise of every other pious affection. To have, as it were, high and honourable thoughts of the majesty and greatness of the living God, and a deep and awful impression of the immediate and continual presence of the heart-searching God, this naturally produces the greatest self-abasement, and the most unfeigned subjection of spirit before our Maker. It leads to a confession of him as Lord over all, and having the most absolute right, not only to the obedience, but to the disposal of all his creatures. I cannot help thinking this is conveyed to us in the language of the Psalmist, when he says, "*O LORD, truly I am thy servant.*" He was a prince among his subjects, and had many other honourable distinctions, both natural and acquired, among men ; but he was sensible of his being a servant and subject of the King of kings ; and the force of his expression, "*Truly, I am thy servant,*" not only signifies the certainty of the thing, but how deeply and strongly he felt a conviction of its truth.

This declaration of the Psalmist implies (2) *a confession of his being bound by particular covenant and consent unto God,* and a repetition of the same by a new adherence. This, as it was certainly true with regard to him, having often dedicated himself to God, so I take it to be confirmed by the reiteration of the expression here, "*O LORD, truly I am thy servant; I am thy servant.*" As if he had said, " O Lord, it is undeniable ; it is impossible to recede from it. I am thine by many ties. I am by nature thy subject and thy creature ; and I have many times confessed thy right and promised my own duty." I need not mention to you, either the example in the Psalmist's writings, or the occasions in his history, on which he solemnly surrendered himself to God. It is sufficient to say, that it was very proper that he should frequently call this to mind, and confess it before God, for though it could not make his Creator's right any stronger, it would certainly make the guilt of his own violation of it so much the greater.

This declaration of the Psalmist is (3) *an expression of his peculiar and special relation to God.* "*I am thy servant, and the son of thine handmaid.*" There is another passage of his writings where the same expression occurs : Ps. lxxxvi. 16. " O turn unto me, and have mercy upon me ; give thy strength unto thy servant, and save the son of thine handmaid." There is some variation among interpreters in the way of illustrating this phrase. Some take it for a figurative way of affirming, that he was bound in the strongest manner to God, as those children who were born of a maid-servant, and born in his own house, were in the most absolute manner their master's property. Others take it to signify his being not only brought up in the visible church of God, but in a pious family, and educated in his fear ; and others would have it to signify still more especially that the Psalmist's mother was an eminently pious woman. And indeed I do not think that was a circumstance, if true, either unworthy of him to remember, or of the Spirit of God to put upon record. —*John Witherspoon, 1722—1797.*

Verse 16.—O Lord, *I am thy servant* by a double right ; (and, oh, that I could do thee double service ;) as thou art the Lord of my life, and I am the son of thy handmaid : not of Hagar, but of Sarah ; not of the bondwoman, but of the free ; and therefore I serve thee not in fear, but in love ; or therefore in fear, because in love : and then is service best done when it is done in love. In love indeed I am bound to serve thee, for, "*Thou hast loosed my bonds*"; the bonds of death which compassed me about, by delivering me from a dangerous sickness, and restoring me to health : or in a higher kind ; thou hast loosed my bonds by freeing me from being a captive to be a servant ; and which is more, from being a servant to be a son : and more than this from being a son of thy handmaid, to be a son of thyself.— *Sir Richard Baker.*

Verse 16.—Bless God for the privilege of being the children of godly parents. Better be the child of a godly than of a wealthy parent. I hope none of you are of so vile a spirit as to contemn your parents because of their piety. Certainly it is a great privilege when you can go to God, and plead your Father's covenant : *"Lord, truly I am thy servant ; I am thy servant, and the son of thy handmaid."* So did Solomon, 1 Kings viii. 25, 26, " Lord, make good thy word to thy servant David, my father." That you are not born of infidels, nor of papists, nor of upholders of superstition and formality, but in a strict, serious, godly family, it is a great advantage that you have. It is better to be the sons of faithful ministers than of nobles.— *Thomas Manton, in a Sermon preached before the Sons of the Clergy.*

Verse 16.—*"Thou hast loosed my bonds."* Mercies are given to encourage us in God's service, and should be remembered to that end. Rain descends upon the earth, not that it might be more barren, but more fertile. We are but stewards ; the mercies we enjoy are not our own, but to be improved for our Master's service. Great mercies should engage to great obedience. God begins the Decalogue with a memorial of his mercy in bringing the Israelites out of Egypt,—" I am the Lord thy God, which brought thee out of the land of Egypt." How affectionately doth the Psalmist own his relation to God as his servant, when he considers how God had loosed his bonds: *"O LORD, truly I am thy servant ; thou hast loosed my bonds !"* the remembrance of thy mercy shall make me know no relation but that of a servant to thee. When we remember what wages we have from God, we must withal remember that we owe more service, and more liveliness in service, to him. Duty is but the ingenuous consequent of mercy. It is irrational to encourage ourselves in our way to hell by a remembrance of heaven, to foster a liberty in sin by a consideration of God's bounty. When we remember that all we have or are is the gift of God's liberality, we should think ourselves obliged to honour him with all that we have, for he is to have honour from all his gifts. It is a sign we aimed at God's glory in begging mercy, when we also aim at God's glory in enjoying it.[1] It is a sign that love breathed the remembrance of mercy into our hearts, when at the same time it breathes a resolution into us to improve it. It is not our tongues, but our lives must praise him. Mercies are not given to one member, but to the whole man.— *Stephen Charnock.*

Verse 17.—*"The sacrifice of thanksgiving."*

" When all the heart is pure, each warm desire
Sublimed by holy love's ethereal fire,
On winged words our breathing thoughts may rise,
And soar to heaven, a grateful sacrifice."

James Scott.

Verse 18.—*"Vows."* Are well-composed vows such promoters of religion ? and are they to be made so warily ? and do they bind so strictly ? Then be sure to wait until God give you just and fit seasons for vowing. Be not over-hasty to vow : it is an inconsiderate and foolish haste of Christians to make more occasions of vowing than God doth make for them. Make your vows, and spare not, so often as God bids you ; but do not do it oftener. You would wonder I should dissuade you from vowing often, when you have such constant mercies ; and wonder well you might, if God did expect your extraordinary bond and security for every ordinary mercy : but he requires it not ; he is content with ordinary security of gratitude for ordinary mercies ; when he calls for extraordinary security and acknowledgment, by giving extraordinary mercies, then give it and do it.—*Henry Hurst.*

Verse 18.—*"Now."*—God gave an order that no part of the thankoffering should be kept till the third day, to teach us to present our praises when benefits are newly received, which else would soon wax stale and putrefy as fish doth. *"I will pay my vows now,"* saith David.—*Samuel Clarke (1599—1682) in "A Mirrour or Looking-glasse, both for Saints and Sinners."*

Verse 18.—*"In the presence of all his people."* For good example's sake. This also was prince-like, Ezek. xlvi. 10. The king's seat in the sanctuary was open, that all might see him there, 2 Kings xi. 14, and xxiii. 3.—*John Trapp.*

Verse 18.—*"In the presence of all his people."* Be bold, be bold, ye servants of the Lord, in sounding forth the praises of your God. Go into presses of people ; and in the midst of them praise the Lord. Wicked men are over-bold in pouring forth their blasphemies to the dishonour of God ; they care not who hear them. They stick not to do it in the midst of cities. Shall they be more audacious to dishonour God, than ye zealous to honour him ? Assuredly Christ will shew himself as forward to confess you, as you are, or can be to confess him. Matt. x. 32. This holy boldness is the ready way to glory.—*William Gouge.*

Verse 19 (*second clause*).—He does not simply say in the midst of Jerusalem : but, *"in the midst of thee, O Jerusalem."* He speaks to the city as one who loved it and delighted in it. We see here, how the saints were affected towards the city in which was the house of God. Thus we should be moved in spirit towards that church in which God dwells, the temple he inhabits, which is built up, not of stones, but of the souls of the faithful.—*Wolfgang Musculus.*

HINTS TO PREACHERS.

Verses 1, 2.—I. Present—" I love." II. Past—" He hath." III. Future—" I will."

Verses 1, 2.—Personal experience in reference to prayer. I. We have prayed, often, constantly, in different ways, etc. II. We have been heard. A grateful retrospect of usual answers and of special answers. III. Love to God has thus been promoted. IV. Our sense of the value of prayer has become so intense that we cannot cease praying.

Verses 1, 2, 9.—If you cast your eyes on the first verse of the Psalm, you find a *profession of love*—*"I love the LORD"* ; if on the second, a *promise of prayer*—*"I will call on the LORD"* ; if on the ninth, a *resolve of walking*—*"I will walk before the LORD."* There are three things should be the object of a saint's care, the devotion of the soul, profession of the mouth, and conversation of the life : that is the sweetest melody in God's ears, when not only the voice sings, but the heartstrings keep tune, and the hand keepeth time.—*Nathanael Hardy.*

Verse 2.—" He hath," and therefore " I will." Grace moving to action.

Verses 2, 4, 13, 17.—Calling upon God mentioned four times very suggestively—I will do it (verse 2), I have tried it (4), I will do it when I take (13), and when I offer (17).

Verses 2, 9, 13, 14, 17.—The " I wills " of the Psalm. I will call (verse 2), I will walk (9), I will take (13), I will pay (14), I will offer (17).

Verses 3, 4, 8.—See Spurgeon's Sermon, " To Souls in Agony," Metropolitan Tabernacle Pulpit, No. 1216.

Verses 3—5.—The story of a tried soul. I. Where I was. Verse 3. II. What I did. Verse 4. III. What I learned. Verse 5.

Verses 3—6.—I. *The occasion.* 1. Bodily affliction. 2. Terrors of conscience. 3. Sorrow of heart. 4. Self-accusation : " I found," etc. II. *The petition.* 1. Direct : " I called," etc. 2. Immediate : " then," when the trouble came ; prayer was the first remedy sought, not the last, as with many. 3. Brief—limited to the one thing needed : " deliver my soul." 4. Importunate : " O Lord, I beseech thee." III. *The restoration.* 1. Implied : " gracious," etc., v. 5. 2. Expressed, v. 6, generally : " The Lord preserveth," etc. ; particularly : " I was brought low," etc. : helped me to pray, helped me out of trouble in answer to prayer, and helped me to praise him for the mercy, the faithfulness, the grace, shown in my deliverance. God is glorified through the afflictions of his people : the submissive are preserved in them, and the lowly are exalted by them.—*G. R.*

Verse 5.—I. Eternal grace, or the purpose of love. II. Infinite justice, or the difficulty of holiness. III. Boundless mercy, or the outcome of atonement.

Verse 6.—I. A singular class—" simple." II. A singular fact—" the Lord preserveth the simple." III. A singular proof of the fact—" I was," etc.

Verse 7.—*"Return unto thy rest, O my soul."* Rest in God may be said to belong to the people of God on a fourfold account. I. By designation. The rest which the people of God have in him is the result of his own purpose, and design, taken up from his mere good pleasure and love. II. By purchase. The rest which they wanted as *creatures* they had forfeited as *sinners*. This, therefore, Christ laid down his life to procure. III. By promise. This is God's kind engagement. He has said, " My presence shall go with thee, and I will give thee rest," Exod. xxxiii. 14. IV. By their own choice gracious souls have a rest in God.—*D. Wilcox.*

Verse 7.—*"Return unto thy rest, O my soul."* When, or upon what occasion a child of God should use the Psalmist's language. I. After converse with the world in the business of his calling every day. II. When going to the sanctuary on the Lord's-day. III. In and under any trouble he may meet with. IV. When departing from this world at death.—*D. Wilcox.*

Verse 7.—I. The rest of the soul : " My rest," this is in God. 1. The soul was created to find its rest in God. 2. On that account it cannot find rest elsewhere. II. Its departure from that rest. This is implied in the word " Return." III. Its return. 1. By repentance. 2. By faith, in the way provided for its return. 3. By prayer. IV. Its encouragement to return. 1. Not in itself, but in God. 2. Not in the justice, but in the goodness of God : " for the Lord," etc. " The goodness of God leadeth thee to repentance."—*G. R.*

Verse 8.—The trinity of experimental godliness. I. It is a unity—" Thou hast delivered " ; all the mercies come from one source. II. It is a trinity of deliverance, *of* soul, eyes, feet ; *from* punishment, sorrow, and sinning ; *to* life, joy, and stability. III. It is a trinity in unity : all this was done for me and in me—" my soul, mine eyes, my feet."

Verse 9.—The effect of deliverance upon ourselves. " I will walk," etc. I. Walk by faith in him. II. Walk in love with him. III. Walk by obedience to him.—*G. R.*

Verses 10, 11.—I. The rule : " I believed," etc. In general the Psalmist spoke what he had well considered and tested by his own experience, as when he said, " I was brought low and he helped me." " The Lord hath dealt bountifully with me." II. The exception : " I was greatly afflicted, I said," etc. 1. He spoke wrongfully : he said " All men are liars," which had some truth in it, but was not the whole truth. 2. Hastily : " I said in my haste," without due reflection. 3. Angrily, under the influence of affliction, probably from the unfaithfulness of others. Nature acts before grace—the one by instinct, the other from consideration. —*G. R.*

Verse 11.—A hasty speech. I. There was much truth in it. II. It erred on the right side, for it showed faith in God rather than in the creature. III. It did err in being too sweeping, too severe, too suspicious. IV. It was soon cured. The remedy for all such hasty speeches is—Get to work in the spirit of verse 12.

Verse 12.—Overwhelming obligations. I. A sum in arithmetic—" all his benefits." II. A calculation of indebtedness—" What shall I render ? " III. A problem for personal solution—" What shall *I* ? " See Spurgeon's Sermon, No. 910.

Verses 12, 14.—Whether well-composed religious vows do not exceedingly promote religion. Sermon by Henry Hurst, A.M., in " The Morning Exercises."

Verse 13.—Sermon on the Lord's supper. We take the cup of the Lord—I. In memory of him who is our salvation. II. In token of our trust in him. III. In evidence of our obedience to him. IV. In type of communion with him. V. In hope of drinking it new with him ere long.

Verse 13.—The various cups mentioned in Scripture would make an interesting subject.

Verse 14.—*"Now."* Or the excellence of time present.

Verse 15.—I. *The declaration.* Not the death of the wicked, nor even the death of the righteous is in itself precious ; but, 1, because their persons are precious to him. 2. Because their experience in death is precious to him. 3. Because of their conformity in death to their Covenant-Head ; and 4. Because it puts an end to their sorrows, and translates them to their rest. II. *Its manifestation.* 1. In preserving them from death. 2. In supporting them in death. 3. In giving them victory over death. 4. In glorifying them after death.

Verse 15.—See Spurgeon's Sermon, " Precious Deaths," No. 1036.

Verse 16.—*Holy Service.* I. Emphatically avowed. II. Honestly rendered— " truly." III. Logically defended—" son of thine handmaid." IV. Consistent with conscious liberty.

Verse 17.—This is due to our God, good for ourselves, and encouraging to others.

Verse 17.—"*The sacrifice of thanksgiving.*" I. How it may be rendered. In secret love, in conversation, in sacred song, in public testimony, in special gifts and works. II. Why we should render it. For answered prayers (verses 1, 2), memorable deliverances (3), choice preservation (6); remarkable restoration (7, 8), and for the fact of our being his servants (16). III. When should we render it. *Now*, while the mercy is on the memory, and as often as fresh mercies come to us.

Verse 18.—I. How vows may be paid in public. By going to public worship as the first thing we do when health is restored. By uniting heartily in the song. By coming to the communion. By special thankoffering. By using fit opportunities for open testimony to the Lord's goodness. II. The special difficulty in the matter. To pay them *to the Lord*, and not in ostentation or as an empty form. III. The peculiar usefulness of the public act. It interests others, touches their hearts, reproves, encourages, etc.

Verse 19.—The Christian at home. I. In God's house. II. Among the saints. III. At his favourite work, " Praise."

PSALM CXVII.

SUBJECT.—*This Psalm, which is very little in its letter, is exceedingly large in its spirit ; for, bursting beyond all bounds of race or nationality, it calls upon all mankind to praise the name of the Lord. In all probability it was frequently used as a brief hymn suitable for almost every occasion, and especially when the time for worship was short. Perhaps it was also sung at the commencement or at the close of other Psalms, just as we now use the doxology. It would have served either to open a service or to conclude it. It is both short and sweet. The same divine Spirit which expatiates in the 119th, here condenses his utterances into two short verses, but yet the same infinite fulness is present and perceptible. It may be worth noting that this is at once the shortest chapter of the Scriptures and the central portion of the whole Bible.*

EXPOSITION.

O PRAISE the LORD, all ye nations : praise him, all ye people.

2 For his merciful kindness is great toward us : and the truth of the LORD endureth for ever. Praise ye the LORD.

1. *"O praise the LORD, all ye nations."* This is an exhortation to the Gentiles to glorify Jehovah, and a clear proof that the Old Testament spirit differed widely from that narrow and contracted national bigotry with which the Jews of our Lord's day became so inveterately diseased. The nations could not be expected to join in the praise of Jehovah unless they were also to be partakers of the benefits which Israel enjoyed ; and hence the Psalm was an intimation to Israel that the grace and mercy of their God were not to be confined to one nation, but would in happier days be extended to all the race of man, even as Moses had prophesied when he said, " Rejoice, O ye nations, his people." (Deut. xxxii. 43), for so the Hebrew has it. The nations were to be his people. He would call them a people that were not a people, and her beloved that was not beloved. We know and believe that no one tribe of men shall be unrepresented in the universal song which shall ascend unto the Lord of all. Individuals have already been gathered out of every kindred and people and tongue by the preaching of the gospel, and these have right heartily joined in magnifying the grace which sought them out, and brought them to know the Saviour. These are but the advance-guard of a number which no man can number who will come ere long to worship the all-glorious One. *"Praise him, all ye people."* Having done it once, do it again, and do it still more fervently, daily increasing in the reverence and zeal with which you extol the Most High. Not only praise him nationally by your rulers, but popularly in your masses. The multitude of the common folk shall bless the Lord. Inasmuch as the matter is spoken of twice, its certainty is confirmed, and the Gentiles must and shall extol Jehovah—all of them, without exception. Under the gospel dispensation we worship no new god, but the God of Abraham is our God for ever and ever ; the God of the whole earth shall he be called.

2. *"For his merciful kindness is great toward us."* By which is meant not only his great love toward the Jewish people, but towards the whole family of man. The Lord is kind to us as his creatures, and merciful to us as sinners, hence his merciful kindness to us as sinful creatures. This mercy has been very great, or powerful. The mighty grace of God has prevailed even as the waters of the flood prevailed over the earth : breaking over all bounds, it has flowed towards all portions of the multiplied race of man. In Christ Jesus, God has shown mercy mixed with kindness, and that to the very highest degree. We can all join in this grateful acknowledgment, and in the praise which is therefore due. *"And the truth of the LORD endureth for ever."* He has kept his covenant promise that in the seed of Abraham should all nations of the earth be blessed, and he will eternally keep every single promise of that covenant to all those who put their trust in him. This should be a cause of constant and grateful praise, wherefore the Psalm concludes as it began, with another Hallelujah, *"Praise ye the LORD."*

EXPLANATORY NOTES AND QUAINT SAYINGS.

Whole Psalm.—A very short Psalm if you regard the words, but of very great compass and most excellent if you thoughtfully consider the meaning. There are here five principal points of doctrine.

First, *the calling of the Gentiles*, the Apostle being the interpreter, Rom. xv. 11 ; but in vain might the Prophet invite the Gentiles to praise Jehovah, unless they were to be gathered into the unity of the faith together with the children of Abraham.

Second, *The summary of the Gospel*, namely, the manifestation of grace and truth, the Holy Spirit being the interpreter, John i. 17.

Third, *The end of so great a blessing*, namely, the worship of God in spirit and in truth, as we know that the kingdom of the Messiah is spiritual.

Fourth, *the employment of the subjects of the great King* is to praise and glorify Jehovah.

Lastly, *the privilege of these servants :* that, as to the Jews, so also to the Gentiles, who know and serve God the Saviour, eternal life and blessedness are brought, assured in this life, and prepared in heaven.—*Mollerus.*

Whole Psalm.—This Psalm, the shortest portion of the Book of God, is quoted, and given much value to, in Rom. xv. And upon this it has been profitably observed, " It is a small portion of Scripture, and as such we might easily overlook it. But not so the Holy Ghost. He gleans up this precious little testimony which speaks of grace to the Gentiles, and presses it on our attention."—*From Bellett's Short Meditations on the Psalms, chiefly in their Prophetic character,* 1871.

Whole Psalm.—The occasion and the author of this Psalm are alike unknown. De Wette regards it as *a Temple-Psalm*, and agrees with Rosenmüller in the supposition that it was sung either at the beginning or the end of the service in the temple. Knapp supposes that it was used as an intermediate service, sung during the progress of the general service to vary the devotion, and to awaken a new interest in the service, either sung by the choir or by the whole people.—*Albert Barnes.*

Whole Psalm.—In God's worship it is not always necessary to be long ; few words sometimes say what is sufficient, as this short Psalm giveth us to understand. —*David Dickson.*

Whole Psalm.—This is the shortest, and the next but one is the longest, of the Psalms. There are times for short hymns and long hymns, for short prayers and long prayers, for short sermons and long sermons, for short speeches and long speeches. It is better to be too short than too long, as it can more easily be mended. Short addresses need no formal divisions : long addresses require them, as in the next Psalm but one.—*G. Rogers.*

Verse 1.—"*O praise the* LORD," etc. The praise of God is here made both the beginning and the end of the Psalm ; to show, that in praising God the saints are never satisfied with their own efforts, and would infinitely magnify him, even as his perfections are infinite. Here they make a circle, the beginning, middle, and end whereof is *hallelujah*. In the last Psalm, when David had said, " Let everything that hath breath praise the Lord," and so in all likelihood had made an end, yet he repeats the *hallelujah* again, and cries, " Praise ye the Lord." The Psalmist had made an end and yet he had not done ; to signify, that when we have said our utmost for God's praise, we must not be content, but begin anew. There is hardly any duty more pressed in the Old Testament upon us, though less practised, than this of praising God. To quicken us therefore to a duty so necessary, but so much neglected, this and many other Psalms were penned by David, purposely to excite us, that are the *nations* here meant, to consecrate our whole lives to the singing and setting forth of God's worthy praises.—*Abraham Wright.*

Verse 1.—"*All ye nations.*" Note : each nation of the world has some special gift bestowed on it by God, which is not given to the others, whether you have regard to nature or grace, for which it ought to praise God.—*Le Blanc.*

Verse 1.—"*Praise him.*" A different word is here used for "*praise*" than in the former clause : a word which is more frequently used in the Chaldee, Syriac, Arabic, and Ethiopic languages ; and signifies the celebration of the praises of God with a high voice.—*John Gill.*

Verse 2.—*"For his merciful kindness is great toward us."* We cannot part from this Psalm without remarking that even in the Old Testament we have more than one instance of a recognition on the part of those that were without the pale of the church that God's favour to Israel was a source of blessing to themselves. Such were probably to some extent the sentiments of Hiram and the Queen of Sheba, the contemporaries of Solomon ; such the experience of Naaman ; such the virtual acknowledgments of Nebuchadnezzar and Darius the Mede. They beheld " his merciful *kindness* " toward his servants of the house of Israel, and they praised him accordingly.—*John Francis Thrupp.*

Verse 2.—*"For his merciful kindness is great toward us."* Albeit there be matter of praise unto God in himself, though we should not be partakers of any benefit from him, yet the Lord doth give his people cause to praise him for favours to them in their own particular cases.—*David Dickson.*

Verse 2.—*"For his merciful kindness is great."* גבר, *gabar,* is *strong :* it is not only *great* in *bulk* or *number ;* but it is *powerful ;* it prevails over sin, Satan, death and hell.—*Adam Clarke.*

Verse 2.—*"Merciful kindness . . . . and the truth of the LORD."* Here, and so in divers other Psalms, God's mercy and truth are joined together ; to show that all passages and proceedings, both in ordinances and in providences, whereby he cometh and communicateth himself to his people are not only mercy, though that is very sweet, but truth also. Their blessings come to them in the way of promise from God, as bound to them by the truth of his covenant. This is soul-satisfying indeed ; this turns all that a man hath to cream, when every mercy is a present sent from heaven by virtue of a promise. Upon this account, God's mercy is ordinarily in the Psalms bounded by his truth ; that none may either presume him more merciful than he hath declared himself in his word ; nor despair of finding mercy *gratis,* according to the truth of his promise. Therefore, though thy sins be great, believe the text, and know that God's mercy is greater than thy sins. The high heaven covereth as well tall mountains as small molehills, and mercy can cover all. The more desperate thy disease, the greater is the glory of thy physician, who hath perfectly cured thee.—*Abraham Wright.*

HINTS TO PREACHERS.

Whole Psalm.—The universal kingdom. I. The same God. II. The same worship. III. The same reason for it.

Verse 2.—*"Merciful kindness."* In God's kindness there is mercy, because, I. Our sin deserves the reverse of kindness. II. Our weakness requires great tenderness. III. Our fears can only be so removed.

Verse 2 (last clause).—I. In his attribute—he is always faithful. II. In his revelation—always infallible. III. In his action—always according to promise.

PSALM CXVIII.

AUTHOR AND SUBJECT.—*In the book of Ezra, iii. 10, 11, we read that "when the builders laid the foundation of the temple of the Lord, they set the priests in their apparel with trumpets, and the Levites the sons of Asaph with cymbals, to praise the Lord, after the ordinance of David king of Israel. And they sang together by course in praising and giving thanks unto the Lord ; because he is good, for his mercy endureth for ever toward Israel. And all the people shouted with a great shout, when they praised the Lord, because the foundation of the house of the Lord was laid." Now the words mentioned in Ezra are the first and last sentences of this Psalm, and we therefore conclude that the people chanted the whole of this sublime song ; and, moreover, that the use of this composition on such occasions was ordained by David, whom we conceive to be its author. The next step leads us to believe that he is its subject, at least in some degree ; for it is clear that the writer is speaking concerning himself in the first place, though he may not have strictly confined himself to all the details of his own personal experience. That the Psalmist had a prophetic view of our Lord Jesus is very manifest ; the frequent quotations from this song in the New Testament prove this beyond all question ; but at the same time it could not have been intended that every particular line and sentence should be read in reference to the Messiah, for this requires very great ingenuity, and ingenious interpretations are seldom true. Certain devout expositors have managed to twist the expression of the seventeenth verse, "I shall not die, but live," so as to make it applicable to our Lord,* who did actually die, and whose glory it is that he died ; but we cannot bring our minds to do such violence to the words of holy writ.*

The Psalm seems to us to describe either David or some other man of God who was appointed by the divine choice to a high and honourable office in Israel. This elect champion found himself rejected by his friends and fellow-countrymen, and at the same time violently opposed by his enemies. In faith in God he battles for his appointed place, and in due time he obtains it in such a way as greatly to display the power and goodness of the Lord. He then goes up to the house of the Lord to offer sacrifice, and to express his gratitude for the divine interposition, all the people blessing him, and wishing him abundant prosperity. This heroic personage, whom we cannot help thinking to be David himself, broadly typified our Lord, but not in such a manner that in all the minutiæ of his struggles and prayers we are to hunt for parallels. The suggestion of Alexander that the speaker is a typical individual representing the nation, is exceedingly well worthy of attention ; but it is not inconsistent with the idea that a personal leader may be intended, since that which describes the leader will be in a great measure true of his followers. The experience of the Head is that of the members, and both may be spoken of in much the same terms. Alexander thinks that the deliverance celebrated cannot be identified with any one so exactly as with that from the Babylonian exile ; but we judge it best to refer it to no one incident in particular, but to regard it as a national song, adapted alike for the rise of a chosen hero, and the building of a temple. Whether a nation is re-founded by a conquering prince, or a temple founded by the laying of its corner-stone in joyful state, the Psalm is equally applicable.

DIVISION.—*We propose to divide the Psalm thus, from verses 1 to 4 the faithful are called upon to magnify the everlasting mercy of the Lord ; from 5 to 18 the Psalmist gives forth a narrative of his experience, and an expression of his faith ; in verses 19 to 21 he asks admittance into the house of the Lord, and begins the acknowledgment of the divine salvation. In verses 22 to 27 the priests and people recognize their ruler, magnify the Lord for him, declare him blessed, and bid him approach the altar with his sacrifice. In the two closing verses the grateful hero himself exalts God the ever-merciful.*

EXPOSITION.

O GIVE thanks unto the LORD ; for *he is* good : because his mercy *endureth* for ever.

2 Let Israel now say, that his mercy *endureth* for ever.

3 Let the house of Aaron now say, that his mercy *endureth* for ever.
4 Let them now that fear the LORD say, that his mercy *endureth* for ever.

1. "*O give thanks unto the LORD.*" The grateful hero feels that he cannot himself alone sufficiently express his thankfulness, and therefore he calls in the aid of others. Grateful hearts are greedy of men's tongues, and would monopolize them all for God's glory. The whole nation was concerned in David's triumphant accession, and therefore it was right that they should unite in his adoring song of praise. The thanks were to be rendered unto Jehovah alone, and not to the patience or valour of the hero himself. It is always well to trace our mercies to him who bestows them, and if we cannot give him anything else, let us at any rate give him our thanks. We must not stop short at the second agent, but rise at once to the first cause, and render all our praises *unto the Lord* himself. Have we been of a forgetful or murmuring spirit? Let us hear the lively language of the text, and allow it to speak to our hearts: "Cease your complainings, cease from all self-glorification, and give thanks unto the Lord." "*For he is good.*" This is reason enough for giving him thanks; goodness is his essence and nature, and therefore he is always to be praised whether we are receiving anything from him or not. Those who only praise God because he *does* them good should rise to a higher note and give thanks to him because he *is* good. In the truest sense he alone is good, "There is none good but one, that is God"; therefore in all gratitude the Lord should have the royal portion. If others seem to be good, he *is* good. If others are good in a measure, he is good beyond measure. When others behave badly to us, it should only stir us up the more heartily to give thanks unto the Lord, because he is good; and when we ourselves are conscious that we are far from being good, we should only the more reverently bless him that "he is good." We must never tolerate an instant's unbelief as to the goodness of the Lord; whatever else may be questionable, this is absolutely certain, that Jehovah is good; his dispensations may vary, but his nature is always the same, and always good. It is not only that he was good, and will be good, but he *is* good, let his providence be what it may. Therefore let us even at this present moment, though the skies be dark with clouds, yet give thanks unto his name.

"*Because his mercy endureth for ever.*" Mercy is a great part of his goodness, and one which more concerns us than any other, for we are sinners and have need of his mercy. Angels may say that he is good, but they need not his mercy and cannot therefore take an equal delight in it; inanimate creation declares that *he is good*, but it cannot feel his *mercy*, for it has never transgressed; but man, deeply guilty and graciously forgiven, beholds mercy as the very focus and centre of the goodness of the Lord. The endurance of the divine mercy is a special subject for song: notwithstanding our sins, our trials, our fears, his mercy *endureth for ever*. The best of earthly joys pass away, and even the world itself grows old and hastens to decay, but there is no change in the mercy of God; he was faithful to our forefathers, he is merciful to us, and will be gracious to our children and our children's children. It is to be hoped that the philosophical interpreters who endeavour to clip the word "for ever" into a mere period of time will have the goodness to let this passage alone. However, whether they do or not, we shall believe in endless mercy—mercy to eternity. The Lord Jesus Christ, who is the grand incarnation of the mercy of God, calls upon us at every remembrance of him to give thanks unto the Lord, for "he is good."

2. "*Let Israel now say, that his mercy endureth for ever.*" God had made a covenant with their forefathers, a covenant of mercy and love, and to that covenant he was faithful evermore. Israel sinned in Egypt, provoked the Lord in the wilderness, went astray again and again under the judges, and transgressed at all times; and yet the Lord continued to regard them as his people, to favour them with his oracles, and to forgive their sins. He speedily ceased from the chastisements which they so richly deserved, because he had a favour towards them. He put his rod away the moment they repented, because his heart was full of compassion. "His mercy endureth for ever" was Israel's national hymn, which, as a people, they had been called upon to sing upon many former occasions; and now their leader, who had at last gained the place for which Jehovah had destined him, calls upon the whole nation to join with him in extolling, in this particular instance of the divine goodness, the eternal mercy of the Lord. David's success was mercy to Israel, as well as mercy to himself. If Israel does not sing, who will? If Israel

does not sing of mercy, who can? If Israel does not sing when the Son of David ascends the throne, the very stones will cry out.

3. *"Let the house of Aaron now say, that his mercy endureth for ever."* The sons of Aaron were specially set apart to come nearest to God, and it was only because of his mercy that they were enabled to live in the presence of the thrice holy Jehovah, who is a consuming fire. Every time the morning and evening lamb was sacrificed, the priests saw the continual mercy of the Lord, and in all the holy vessels of the sanctuary, and all its services from hour to hour, they had renewed witness of the goodness of the Most High. When the high priest went in unto the holy place and came forth accepted, he might, above all men, sing of the eternal mercy. If this Psalm refers to David, the priests had special reason for thankfulness on his coming to the throne, for Saul had made a great slaughter among them, and had at various times interfered with their sacred office. A man had now come to the throne who for their Master's sake would esteem them, give them their dues, and preserve them safe from all harm. Our Lord Jesus, having made all his people priests unto God, may well call upon them in that capacity to magnify the everlasting mercy of the Most High. Can any one of the royal priesthood be silent?

4. *"Let them now that fear the Lord say, that his mercy endureth for ever."* If there were any throughout the world who did not belong to Israel after the flesh, but nevertheless had a holy fear and lowly reverence of God, the Psalmist calls upon them to unite with him in his thanksgiving, and to do it especially on the occasion of his exaltation to the throne; and this is no more than they would cheerfully agree to do, since every good man in the world is benefited when a true servant of God is placed in a position of honour and influence. The prosperity of Israel through the reign of David was a blessing to all who feared Jehovah. A truly God-fearing man will have his eye much upon God's mercy, because he is deeply conscious of his need of it, and because that attribute excites in him a deep feeling of reverential awe. " There is forgiveness with thee that thou mayest be feared."

In the three exhortations, to Israel, to the house of Aaron, and to them that fear the Lord, there is a repetition of the exhortation to *say*, " that his mercy endureth for ever." We are not only to believe, but to declare the goodness of God; truth is not to be hushed up, but proclaimed. God would have his people act as witnesses, and not stand silent in the day when his honour is impugned. Specially is it our joy to speak out to the honour and glory of God when we think upon the exaltation of his dear Son. We should shout " Hosannah," and sing loud " Hallelujahs " when we behold the stone which the builders rejected lifted into its proper place.

In each of the three exhortations notice carefully the word *"now."* There is no time like time present for telling out the praises of God. The present exaltation of the Son of David now demands from all who are the subjects of his kingdom continual songs of thanksgiving to him who hath set him on high in the midst of Zion. *Now* with us should mean always. When would it be right to cease from praising God, whose mercy never ceases?

The fourfold testimonies to the everlasting mercy of God which are now before us speak like four evangelists, each one declaring the very pith and marrow of the gospel; and they stand like four angels at the four corners of the earth holding the winds in their hands, restraining the plagues of the latter days that the mercy and long-suffering of God may endure towards the sons of men. Here are four cords to bind the sacrifice to the four horns of the altar, and four trumpets with which to proclaim the year of jubilee to every quarter of the world. Let not the reader pass on to the consideration of the rest of the Psalm until he has with all his might lifted up both heart and voice to praise the Lord, " for his mercy endureth for ever."

> " Let us with a gladsome mind
> Praise the Lord, for he is kind;
> For his mercies shall endure
> Ever faithful, ever sure."

5 I called upon the Lord in distress: the Lord answered me, *and set me* in a large place.

6 The Lord *is* on my side; I will not fear: what can man do unto me?

7 The Lord taketh my part with them that help me: therefore shall I see *my desire* upon them that hate me.

8 *It is* better to trust in the LORD than to put confidence in man.

9 *It is* better to trust in the LORD than to put confidence in princes.

10 All nations compassed me about : but in the name of the LORD will I destroy them.

11 They compassed me about ; yea, they compassed me about : but in the name of the LORD I will destroy them.

12 They compassed me about like bees ; they are quenched as the fire of thorns : for in the name of the LORD I will destroy them.

13 Thou hast thrust sore at me that I might fall : but the LORD helped me.

14 The LORD *is* my strength and song, and is become my salvation.

15 The voice of rejoicing and salvation *is* in the tabernacles of the righteous : the right hand of the LORD doeth valiantly.

16 The right hand of the LORD is exalted : the right hand of the LORD doeth valiantly.

17 I shall not die, but live, and declare the works of the LORD.

18 The LORD hath chastened me sore : but he hath not given me over unto death.

5. *"I called upon the* LORD *in distress,"* or, *"*out of anguish I invoked Jah." Nothing was left him but prayer, his agony was too great for aught beside ; but having the heart and the privilege to pray he possessed all things. Prayers which come out of distress generally come out of the heart, and therefore they go to the heart of God. It is sweet to recollect our prayers, and often profitable to tell others of them after they are heard. Prayer may be bitter in the offering, but it will be sweet in the answering. The man of God had called upon the Lord when he was not in distress, and therefore he found it natural and easy to call upon him when he was in distress. He worshipped, he praised, he prayed : for all this is included in calling upon God, even when he was in a straitened condition. Some read the original " a narrow gorge"; and therefore it was the more joy to him when he could say " The Lord answered me, and set me in a large place." He passed out of the defile of distress into the well-watered plain of delight. He says, " Jah heard me in a wide place," for God is never shut up, or straitened. In God's case hearing means answering, hence the translators rightly put, " The Lord answered me," though the original word is *"heard."* The answer was appropriate to the prayer, for he brought him out of his narrow and confined condition into a place of liberty where he could walk at large, free from obstruction and oppression. Many of us can join with the Psalmist in the declarations of this verse : deep was our distress on account of sin, and we were shut up as in a prison under the law, but in answer to the prayer of faith we obtained the liberty of full justification wherewith Christ makes men free, and we are free indeed. It was the Lord who did it, and unto his name we ascribe all the glory ; we had no merits, no strength, no wisdom, all we could do was to call upon him, and even that was his gift ; but the mercy which is to eternity came to our rescue. we were brought out of bondage, and we were made to delight ourselves in the length and breadth of a boundless inheritance. What a large place is that in which the great God has placed us ! All things are ours, all times are ours, all places are ours, for God himself is ours ; we have earth to lodge in and heaven to dwell in,—what larger place can be imagined ? We need all Israel, the whole house of Aaron, and all them that fear the Lord, to assist us in the expression of our gratitude ; and when they have aided us to the utmost, and we ourselves have done our best, all will fall short of the praises that are due to our gracious Lord.

6. *"The* LORD *is on my side,"* or, he is " for me." Once his justice was against me, but now he is my reconciled God, and engaged on my behalf. The Psalmist naturally rejoiced in the divine help ; all men turned against him, but God was his defender and advocate, accomplishing the divine purposes of his grace. The expression may also be translated " to me," that is to say, Jehovah belongs to me, and is mine. What infinite wealth is here ! If we do not magnify the Lord we are of all men most brutish. *"I will not fear."* He does not say that he should

not suffer, but that he would not fear : the favour of God infinitely outweighed the hatred of men, therefore setting the one against the other he felt that he had no reason to be afraid. He was calm and confident, though surrounded with enemies, and so let all believers be, for thus they honour God. *"What can man do unto me ? "* He can do nothing more than God permits ; at the very uttermost he can only kill the body, but he hath no more that he can do. God having purposed to set his servant upon the throne, the whole race of mankind could do nothing to thwart the divine decree : the settled purpose of Jehovah's heart could not be turned aside, nor its accomplishment delayed, much less prevented, by the most rancorous hostility of the most powerful of men. Saul sought to slay David, but David outlived Saul, and sat upon his throne. Scribe and Pharisee, priest and Herodian, united in opposing the Christ of God, but he is exalted on high none the less because of their enmity. The mightiest man is a puny thing when he stands in opposition to God, yea, he shrinks into utter nothingness. It were a pity to be afraid of such a pitiful, miserable, despicable object as a man opposed to the almighty God. The Psalmist here speaks like a champion throwing down the gauntlet to all comers, defying the universe in arms ; a true Bayard, without fear and without reproach, he enjoys God's favour, and he defies every foe.

7. *"The LORD taketh my part with them that help me."* Jehovah condescended to be in alliance with the good man and his comrades ; his God was not content to look on, but he took part in the struggle. What a consolatory fact it is that the Lord takes our part, and that when he raises up friends for us he does not leave them to fight for us alone, but he himself as our chief defender deigns to come into the battle and wage war on our behalf. David mentioned those that helped him, he was not unmindful of his followers ; there is a long record of David's mighty men in the book of Chronicles, and this teaches us that we are not to disdain or think little of the generous friends who rally around us ; but still our great dependence and our grand confidence must be fixed upon the Lord alone. Without him the strong helpers fail ; indeed, apart from him in the sons of men there is no help ; but when our gracious Jehovah is pleased to support and strengthen those who aid us, they become substantial helpers to us.

"Therefore shall I see my desire upon them that hate me." The words, "my desire," are added by the translators ; the Psalmist said, " I shall look upon my haters : I shall look them in the face, I shall make them cease from their contempt, I shall myself look down upon them instead of their looking down upon me. I shall see their defeat, I shall see the end of them." Our Lord Jesus does at this moment look down upon his adversaries, his enemies are his footstool ; he shall look upon them at his second coming, and at the glance of his eyes they shall flee before him, not being able to endure that look with which he shall read them through and through.

8. *"It is better to trust in the LORD than to put confidence in man."* It is better in all ways, for first of all it is wiser : God is infinitely more able to help, and more likely to help, than man, and therefore prudence suggests that we put our confidence in him above all others. It is also morally better to do so, for it is the duty of the creature to trust in the Creator. God has a claim upon his creatures' faith, he deserves to be trusted ; and to place our reliance upon another rather than upon himself, is a direct insult to his faithfulness. It is better in the sense of safer, since we can never be sure of our ground if we rely upon mortal man, but we are always secure in the hands of our God. It is better in its effect upon ourselves : to trust in man tends to make us mean, crouching, dependent ; but confidence in God elevates, produces a sacred quiet of spirit, and sanctifies the soul. It is, moreover, much better to trust in God, as far as the result is concerned ; for in many cases the human object of our trust fails from want of ability, from want of generosity, from want of affection, or from want of memory ; but the Lord, so far from failing, does for us exceeding abundantly above all that we ask or even think. This verse is written out of the experience of many who have first of all found the broken reeds of the creature break under them, and have afterwards joyfully found the Lord to be a solid pillar sustaining all their weight.

9. *"It is better to trust in the LORD than to put confidence in princes."* These should be the noblest of men, chivalrous in character, and true to the core. The royal word should be unquestionable. They are noblest in rank and mightiest in power, and yet as a rule princes are not one whit more reliable than the rest of mankind. A gilded vane turns with the wind as readily as a meaner weathercock. Princes are

but men, and the best of men are poor creatures.   In many troubles they cannot help us in the least degree ; for instance, in sickness, bereavement, or death ; neither can they assist us one jot in reference to our eternal state.   In eternity a prince's smile goes for nothing ; heaven and hell pay no homage to royal authority.   The favour of princes is proverbially fickle, the testimonies of worldlings to this effect are abundant.   All of us remember the words put by the world's great poet into the lips of the dying Wolsey ; their power lies in their truth :—

> " O how wretched
> Is that poor man that hangs on princes' favours !
> There is betwixt that smile we would aspire to,
> That sweet aspect of princes, and their ruin,
> More pangs and fears than wars or women have ;
> And when he falls, he falls like Lucifer,
> Never to hope again.'

Yet a prince's smile has a strange witchery to many hearts, few are proof against that tuft-hunting which is the index of a weak mind.   Principle has been forgotten and character has been sacrificed to maintain position at court ; yea, the manliness which the meanest slave retains has been basely bartered for the stars and garters of a profligate monarch.   He who puts his confidence in God, the great King, is thereby made mentally and spiritually stronger, and rises to the highest dignity of manhood ; in fact, the more he trusts the more is he free, but the fawning sycophant of greatness is meaner than the dirt he treads upon.   For this reason and a thousand others it is infinitely better to trust in the Lord than to put confidence in princes.

10. "*All nations compassed me about.*"   The hero of the Psalm, while he had no earthly friend upon whom he could thoroughly rely, was surrounded by innumerable enemies, who heartily hated him.   He was hemmed in by his adversaries, and scarce could find a loophole of escape from the bands v'.ich made a ring around him.   As if by common consent all sorts of people set themselves against him, and yet he was more than a match for them all, because he was trusting in the name of the Lord.   Therefore does he joyfully accept the battle, and grasp the victory, crying, "*but in the name of the LORD will I destroy them*," or " cut them in pieces." They thought to destroy *him*, but he was sure of destroying *them ;* they meant to blot out his name, but he expected to render not only his own name but the name of the Lord his God more illustrious in the hearts of men.   It takes grand faith to be calm in the day of actual battle, and especially when that battle waxes hot ; but our hero was as calm as if no fight was raging.   Napoleon said that God was always on the side of the biggest battalions, but the Psalmist-warrior found that the Lord of hosts was with the solitary champion, and that in his name the battalions were cut to pieces.   There is a grand touch of the *ego* in the last sentence, but it is so evershadowed with the name of the Lord that there is none too much of it.   He recognized his own individuality, and asserted it : he did not sit still supinely and leave the work to be done by God by some mysterious means ; but he resolved with his own trusty sword to set about the enterprise, and so become in God's hand the instrument of his own deliverance.   He did all in the name of the Lord, but he did not ignore his own responsibility, nor screen himself from personal conflict, for he cried, "*I* will destroy them."   Observe that he does not speak of merely escaping from them like a bird out of the snare of the fowler, but he vows that he will carry the war into his enemies' ranks, and overthrow them so thoroughly that there should be no fear of their rising up a second time.

11. "*They compassed me about ; yea, they compassed me about.*"   He had such a vivid recollection of his danger that his enemies seem to live again in his verses. We see their fierce array, and their cruel combination of forces.   They made a double ring, they surrounded him in a circle of many ranks, they not only talked of doing so, but they actually shut him up and enclosed him as within a wall.   His heart had vividly realized his position of peril at the time, and now he delights to call it again to mind in order that he may the more ardently adore the mercy which made him strong in the hour of conflict, so that he broke through a troop, yea, swept a host to destruction.   "*But in the name of the LORD will I destroy them.*"   I will subdue them, get them under my feet, and break their power in pieces.   He is as certain about the destruction of his enemies as he was assured of their having compassed him about.   They made the circle three and four times deep, but for all that he felt confident of victory.   It is grand to hear a man speak in this fashion when it is not boasting, but the calm declaration of his heartfelt trust in God.

12. *"They compassed me about like bees."* They seemed to be everywhere, like a swarm of bees, attacking him at every point ; nimbly flying from place to place, stinging him meanwhile, and inflicting grievous pain. They threatened at first to baffle him : what weapon could he use against them ? They were so numerous, so inveterate ; so contemptible, yet so audacious ; so insignificant and yet so capable of inflicting agony, that to the eye of reason there appeared no possibility of doing anything with them. Like the swarm of flies in Egypt, there was no standing against them ; they threatened to sting a man to death with their incessant malice, their base insinuations, their dastardly falsehoods. He was in an evil case, but even there faith availed. All-powerful faith adapts itself to all circumstances, it can cast out devils, and it can drive out bees. Surely, if it outlives the sting of death, it will not die from the sting of a bee. *"They are quenched as the fire of thorns."* Their fierce attack soon came to an end, the bees lost their stings and the buzz of the swarm subsided : like thorns which blaze with fierce crackling and abundant flame, but die out in a handful of ashes very speedily, so did the nations which surrounded our hero soon cease their clamour and come to an inglorious end. They were soon hot and soon cold, their attack was as short as it was sharp. He had no need to crush the bees, for like crackling thorns they died out of themselves. For a third time he adds, *"for in the name of the LORD will I destroy them,"* or ''cut them down,'' as men cut down thorns with a scythe or reaping-hook.

What wonders have been wrought in the name of the Lord ! It is the battle-cry of faith before which its adversaries fly apace. '' The sword of the Lord and of Gideon '' brings instant terror into the midst of the foe. The name of the Lord is the one weapon which never fails in the day of battle : he who knows how to use it may chase a thousand with his single arm. Alas ! we too often go to work and to conflict in our own name, and the enemy knows it not, but scornfully enquires, '' Who are ye ? '' Let us take care never to venture into the presence of the foe without first of all arming ourselves with this impenetrable mail. If we knew this name better, and trusted it more, our life would be more fruitful and sublime.

> "Jesus, the name high over all,
>   In hell, or earth, or sky,
> Angels and men before it fall ;
>   And devils fear and fly."

13. *"Thou hast thrust sore at me,"* '' Thrusting, thou hast thrust at me.'' It is a vigorous apostrophe, in which the enemy is described as concentrating all his thrusting power into the thrusts which he gave to the man of God. He thrust again and again with the keenest point, even as bees thrust their stings into their victim. The foe had exhibited intense exasperation, and fearful determination, nor had he been without a measure of success ; wounds had been given and received, and these smarted much, and were exceeding sore. Now, this is true of many a tried child of God who has been wounded by Satan, by the world, by temptation, by affliction ; the sword has entered into his bones, and left its mark. *"That I might fall."* This was the object of the thrusting : to throw him down, to wound him in such a way that he would no longer be able to keep his place, to make him depart from his integrity, and lose his confidence in God. If our adversaries can do this they will have succeeded to their heart's content : if we fall into grievous sin they will be better pleased than even if they had sent the bullet of the assassin into our heart, for a moral death is worse than a physical one. If they can dishonour us, and God in us, their victory will be complete. '' Better death than false of faith '' is the motto of one of our noble houses, and it may well be ours. It is to compass our fall that they compass *us ;* they fill us with their venom that they may fill us with their sin. *"But the LORD helped me";* a blessed '' but.'' This is the saving clause. Other helpers were unable to chase away the angry nations, much less to destroy all the noxious swarms ; but when the Lord came to the rescue the hero's single arm was strong enough to vanquish all his adversaries. How sweetly can many of us repeat in the retrospect of our past tribulations this delightful sentence, '' But the Lord helped *me.''* I was assailed by innumerable doubts and fears, but the Lord helped me ; my natural unbelief was terribly inflamed by the insinuations of Satan, but the Lord helped me ; multiplied trials were rendered more intense by the cruel assaults of men, and I knew not what to do, but the Lord helped me. Doubtless, when we land on the hither shore of Jordan, this will be one of our songs, '' Flesh and heart were failing me, and the adversaries of my soul surrounded me in the swellings of Jordan, but the Lord helped me. Glory be unto his name.''

14. *"The Lord is my strength and song,"* my strength while I was in the conflict, my song now that it is ended ; my strength against the strong, and my song over their defeat. He is far from boasting of his own valour ; he ascribes his victory to its real source, he has no song concerning his own exploits, but all his peans are unto *Jehovah Victor*, the Lord whose right hand and holy arm had given him the victory. *"And is become my salvation."* The poet warrior knew that he was saved, and he not only ascribed that salvation unto God, but he declared God himself to be his salvation. It is an all-comprehending expression, signifying that from beginning to end, in the whole and in the details of it, he owed his deliverance entirely to the Lord. Thus can all the Lord's redeemed say, " Salvation is of the Lord." We cannot endure any doctrine which puts the crown upon the wrong head and defrauds the glorious King of his revenue of praise. Jehovah has done it all ; yea, in Christ Jesus he *is* all, and therefore in our praises let him alone be extolled. It is a happy circumstance for us when we can praise God as alike our strength, song, and salvation ; for God sometimes gives a secret strength to his people, and yet they question their own salvation, and cannot, therefore, sing of it. Many are, no doubt, truly saved, but at times they have so little strength, that they are ready to faint, and therefore they cannot sing : when strength is imparted and salvation is realised then the song is clear and full.

15. *"The voice of rejoicing and salvation is in the tabernacles of the righteous."* They sympathised in the delight of their leader and they abode in their tents in peace, rejoicing that one had been raised up who, in the name of the Lord, would protect them from their adversaries. The families of believers are happy, and they should take pains to give their happiness a voice by their family devotion. The dwelling-place of saved men should be the temple of praise ; it is but righteous that the righteous should praise the righteous God, who is their righteousness. The struggling hero knew that the voice of woe and lamentation was heard in the tents of his adversaries, for they had suffered severe defeat at his hands ; but he was delighted by the remembrance that the nation for whom he had struggled would rejoice from one end of the land to the other at the deliverance which God had wrought by his means. That hero of heroes, the conquering Saviour, gives to all the families of his people abundant reasons for incessant song now that he has led captivity captive and ascended up on high. Let none of us be silent in our households : if we have salvation let us have joy, and if we have joy let us give it a tongue wherewith it may magnify the Lord. If we hearken carefully to the music which comes from Israel's tents, we shall catch a stanza to this effect, *"the right hand of the Lord doeth valiantly" :* Jehovah has manifested his strength, given victory to his chosen champion, and overthrown all the armies of the foe. " The Lord is a man of war, the Lord is his name." When he comes to blows, woe to his mightiest opponent.

16. *"The right hand of the Lord is exalted,"* lifted up to smite the foeman, or extolled and magnified in the eyes of his people. It is the Lord's *right* hand, the hand of his skill, the hand of his greatest power, the hand which is accustomed to defend his saints. When that is lifted up, it lifts up all who trust in him, and it casts down all who resist him. *"The right hand of the Lord doeth valiantly."* The Psalmist speaks in triplets, for he is praising the triune God, his heart is warm and he loves to dwell upon the note ; he is not content with the praise he has rendered, he endeavours to utter it each time more fervently and more jubilantly than before. He had dwelt upon the sentence, " they compassed me about," for his peril from encircling armies was fully realised ; and now he dwells upon the valour of Jehovah's right hand, for he has as vivid a sense of the presence and majesty of the Lord. How seldom is this the case ; the Lord's mercy is forgotten and only the trial is remembered.

17. *"I shall not die, but live."* His enemies hoped that he would die, and perhaps he himself feared he should perish at their hand : the news of his death may have been spread among his people, for the tongue of rumour is ever ready with ill news, the false intelligence would naturally cause great sorrow and despondency, but he proclaims himself as yet alive and as confident that he shall not fall by the hand of the destroyer. He is cheerfully assured that no arrow could carry death between the joints of his harness, and no weapon of any sort could end his career. His time had not yet come, he felt immortality beating within his bosom. Perhaps he had been sick, and brought to death's door, but he had a presentiment that the sickness was not unto death, but to the glory of God. At any rate, he knew that he should

not so die as to give victory to the enemies of God ; for the honour of God and the good of his people were both wrapped up in his continued success. Feeling that he would live he devoted himself to the noblest of purposes : he resolved to bear witness to the divine faithfulness, *"and declare the works of the LORD."* He determined to recount the works of Jah ; and he does so in this Psalm, wherein he dwells with love and admiration upon the splendour of Jehovah's prowess in the midst of the fight. While there is a testimony for God to be borne by us to any one, it is certain that we shall not be hurried from the land of the living. The Lord's prophets shall live on in the midst of famine, and war, and plague, and persecution, till they have uttered all the words of their prophecy ; his priests shall stand at the altar unharmed till their last sacrifice has been presented before him. No bullet will find its billet in our hearts till we have finished our allotted period of activity.

> " Plagues and deaths around me fly,
> Till he please I cannot die :
> Not a single shaft can hit,
> Till the God of love sees fit."

18. *"The LORD hath chastened me sore."* This is faith's version of the former passage, " Thou hast thrust sore at me ; " for the attacks of the enemy are chastisements from the hand of God. The devil tormented Job for his own purposes, but in reality the sorrows of the patriarch were chastisements from the Lord. " Chastening, Jah hath chastened me," says our poet : as much as to say that the Lord had smitten him very severely, and made him sorrowfully to know the full weight of his rod. The Lord frequently appears to save his heaviest blows for his best-beloved ones ; if any one affliction be more painful than another it falls to the lot of those whom he most distinguishes in his service. The gardener prunes his best roses with most care. Chastisement is sent to keep successful saints humble, to make them tender towards others, and to enable them to bear the high honours which their heavenly Friend puts upon them. *"But he hath not given me over unto death."* This verse, like the thirteenth, concludes with a blessed " but," which constitutes a saving clause. The Psalmist felt as if he had been beaten within an inch of his life, but yet death did not actually ensue. There is always a merciful limit to the scourging of the sons of God. Forty stripes save one were all that an Israelite might receive, and the Lord will never allow that one, that killing stroke, to fall upon his children. They are " chastened, but not killed " ; their pains are for their instruction, not for their destruction. By these things the ungodly die, but gracious Hezekiah could say, " By these things men live, and in all these things is the life of my spirit." No, blessed be the name of God, he may chastise us, but he will not condemn us ; we must feel the smarting rod, but we shall not feel the killing sword. He does not give us over unto death at any time, and we may be quite sure that he has not done so while he condescends to chasten us, for if he intended our final rejection he would not take the pains to place us under his fatherly discipline. It may seem hard to be under the afflicting rod, but it would be a far more dreadful thing if the Lord were to say, " He is given unto idols, let him alone." Even from our griefs we may distil consolation, and gather sweet flowers from the garden in which the Lord has planted salutary rue and wormwood. It is a cheering fact that if we endure chastening God dealeth with us as with sons, and we may well be satisfied with the common lot of his beloved family.

The hero, restored to health, and rescued from the dangers of battle, now lifts up his own song unto the Lord, and asks all Israel, led on by the goodly fellowship of the priests, to assist him in chanting a joyful Te Deum.

19 Open to me the gates of righteousness : I will go into them, *and* I will praise the LORD :

20 This gate of the LORD, into which the righteous shall enter.

21 I will praise thee : for thou hast heard me, and art become my salvation.

19. *"Open to me the gates of righteousness."* The grateful champion having reached the entrance of the temple, asks for admission in set form, as if he felt that he could only approach the hallowed shrine by divine permission, and wished only to enter in the appointed manner. The temple of God was meant for the righteous to enter and offer the sacrifices of righteousness, hence the gates are called the gates of righteousness. Righteous deeds were done within its walls, and righteous teachings sounded forth from its courts. The phrase " the gate " is sometimes used to signify power or empire ; as, for instance, " the Sublime Porte " signifies the seat of empire of Turkey ; the entrance to the temple was the true Sublime Porte, and what is better, it was the *porta justitiæ*, the gate of righteousness, the palace of the great King, who is in all things just. *"I will go into them, and I will praise the Lord."* Only let the gate be opened, and the willing worshipper will enter ; and he will enter in the right spirit, and for the best of purposes, that he may render homage unto the Most High. Alas, there are multitudes who do not care whether the gates of God's house are opened or not ; and although they know that they are opened wide they never care to enter, neither does the thought of praising God so much as cross their minds. The time will come for them when they shall find the gates of heaven shut against them, for those gates are peculiarly the gates of righteousness through which there shall by no means enter anything that defileth. Our champion might have praised the Lord in secret, and doubtless he did so ; but he was not content without going up to the assembly, there to register his thanksgivings. Those who neglect public worship generally neglect all worship ; those who praise God within their own gates are among the readiest to praise him within his temple gates. Our hero had also in all probability been sore sick, and therefore like Hezekiah he says, " The Lord was ready to save me : therefore we will sing my songs to the stringed instruments all the days of my life in the house of the Lord." Public praise for public mercies is every way most appropriate, most acceptable to God, and most profitable to others.

20. *"This gate of the Lord, into which the righteous shall enter."* The Psalmist loves the house of God so well that he admires the very gate thereof, and pauses beneath its arch to express his affection for it. He loved it because it was the gate of the Lord, he loved it because it was the gate of righteousness, because so many godly people had already entered it, and because in all future ages such persons will continue to pass through its portals. If the gate of the Lord's house on earth is so pleasant to us, how greatly shall we rejoice when we pass that gate of pearl, to which none, but the righteous shall ever approach, but through which all the just shall in due time enter to eternal felicity. The Lord Jesus has passed that way, and not only set the gate wide open, but secured an entrance for all those who are made righteous in his righteousness : all the righteous must and shall enter there, whoever may oppose them. Under another aspect our Lord is himself that gate, and through him, as the new and living Way, all the righteous delight to approach unto the Lord. Whenever we draw near to praise the Lord we must come by this gate ; acceptable praise never climbs over the wall, or enters by any other way, but comes to God in Christ Jesus ; as it is written, " no man cometh unto the Father but by me." Blessed, for ever blessed, be this wondrous gate of the person of our Lord.

21. Having entered, the champion exclaims, *"I will praise thee,"* not " I will praise the Lord," for now he vividly realizes the divine presence, and addresses himself directly to Jehovah, whom his faith sensibly discerns. How well it is in all our songs of praise to let the heart have direct and distinct communion with God himself ! The Psalmist's song was personal praise too :—"*I will* praise thee " ; resolute praise, for he firmly resolved to offer it ; spontaneous praise, for he voluntarily and cheerfully rendered it, and continuous praise, for he did not intend soon to have done with it. It was a life-long vow to which there would never come a close, " I will praise thee." *"For thou hast heard me, and art become my salvation."* He praises God by mentioning his favours, weaving his song out of the divine goodness which he had experienced. In these words he gives the reason for his praise,—his answered prayer, and the deliverance which he had received in consequence. How fondly he dwells upon the personal interposition of God ! *"Thou* hast heard *me."* How heartily he ascribes the whole of his victory over his enemies to God ; nay, he sees God himself to be the whole of it : *"Thou* art become my salvation." It is well to go directly to God himself, and not to stay even in his mercy, or in the acts of his grace. Answered prayers bring God very near to us ; realised salvation enables us to realise the immediate presence of God. Considering the extreme distress through which the worshipper had passed, it is not at all wonderful that he should feel his heart full of gratitude at the great salvation which God had wrought for him, and should at his first entrance into the temple lift up his voice in thankful praise for personal favours so great, so needful, so perfect.

22 The stone *which* the builders refused is become the head *stone* of the corner.

23 This is the LORD's doing ; it *is* marvellous in our eyes.

24 This *is* the day *which* the LORD hath made ; we will rejoice and be glad in it.

25 Save now, I beseech thee, O LORD : O LORD, I beseech thee, send now prosperity.

26 Blessed *be* he that cometh in the name of the LORD : we have blessed you out of the house of the LORD.

27 God *is* the LORD, which hath showed us light : bind the sacrifice with cords, *even* unto the horns of the altar.

This passage will appear to be a mixture of the expressions of the people and of the hero himself.

22. *"The stone which the builders refused is become the head stone of the corner."* Here the people magnify God for bringing his chosen servant into the honourable office, which had been allotted to him by divine decree. A wise king and valiant leader is a stone by which the national fabric is built up. David had been rejected by those in authority, but God had placed him in a position of the highest honour and the greatest usefulness, making him the chief corner-stone of the state. In the case of many others whose early life has been spent in conflict, the Lord has been pleased to accomplish his divine purposes in like manner ; but to none is this text so applicable as to the Lord Jesus himself : he is the living stone, the tried stone, elect, precious, which God himself appointed from of old. The Jewish builders, scribe, priest, Pharisee, and Herodian, rejected him with disdain. They could see no excellence in him that they should build upon him ; he could not be made to fit in with their ideal of a national church, he was a stone of another quarry from themselves, and not after their mind nor according to their taste ; therefore they cast him away and poured contempt upon him, even as Peter said, " This is the stone which was set at nought of you builders " : they reckoned him to be as nothing, though he is Lord of all. In raising him from the dead the Lord God exalted him to be the head of his church, the very pinnacle of her glory and beauty. Since then he has become the confidence of the Gentiles, even of them that are afar off upon the sea, and thus he has joined the two walls of Jew and Gentile into one stately temple, and is seen to be the binding corner-stone, making both one. This is a delightful subject for contemplation.

Jesus in all things hath the pre-eminence, he is the principal stone of the whole house of God. We are accustomed to lay some one stone of a public building with solemn ceremony, and to deposit in it any precious things which may have been selected as a memorial of the occasion : henceforth that corner-stone is looked upon as peculiarly honourable, and joyful memories are associated with it. All this is in a very emphatic sense true of our blessed Lord, " The Shepherd, the Stone of Israel." God himself laid him where he is, and hid within him all the precious things of the eternal covenant; and there he shall for ever remain, the foundation of all our hopes, the glory of all our joys, the uniting bond of all our fellowship. He is " the head over all things to the church," and by him the church is fitly framed together, and groweth unto a holy temple in the Lord. Still do the builders refuse him : even to this day the professional teachers of the gospel are far too apt to fly to any and every new philosophy sooner than maintain the simple gospel, which is the essence of Christ : nevertheless, he holds his true position amongst his people, and the foolish builders shall see to their utter confusion that his truth shall be exalted over all. Those who reject the chosen stone will stumble against him to their own hurt, and ere long will come his second advent, when he will fall upon them from the heights of heaven, and grind them to powder.

23. *"This is the LORD's doing."* The exalted position of Christ in his church is not the work of man, and does not depend for its continuation upon any builders or ministers ; God himself has wrought the exaltation of our Lord Jesus. Considering the opposition which comes from the wisdom, the power, and the authority of this world, it is manifest that if the kingdom of Christ be indeed set up and maintained in the world it must be by supernatural power. Indeed, it is so even in the smallest detail. Every grain of true faith in this world is a divine creation, and every hour

in which the true church subsists is a prolonged miracle. It is not the goodness of human nature, nor the force of reasoning, which exalts Christ, and builds up the church, but a power from above. This staggers the adversary, for he cannot understand what it is which baffles him : of the Holy Ghost he knows nothing. *"It is marvellous in our eyes."* We actually see it ; it is not in our thoughts and hopes and prayers alone, but the astonishing work is actually before our eyes. Jesus reigns, his power is felt, and we perceive that it is so. Faith sees our great Master, far above all principality, and power, and might, and dominion, and every name that is named, not only in this world, but also in that which is to come ; she sees and marvels. It never ceases to astonish us, as we see, even here below, God by means of weakness defeating power, by the simplicity of his word baffling the craft of men, and by the invisible influence of his Spirit exalting his Son in human hearts in the teeth of open and determined opposition. It is indeed " marvellous in our eyes," as all God's works must be if men care to study them. In the Hebrew the passage reads, *"It is wonderfully done "* : not only is the exaltation of Jesus of Nazareth itself wonderful, but the way in which it is brought about is marvellous : it is wonderfully done. The more we study the history of Christ and his church the more fully shall we agree with this declaration.

24. *"This is the day which the* LORD *hath made."* A new era has commenced. The day of David's enthronement was the beginning of better times for Israel ; and in a far higher sense the day of our Lord's resurrection is a new day of God's own making, for it is the dawn of a blessed dispensation. No doubt the Israelitish nation celebrated the victory of its champion with a day of feasting, music and song ; and surely it is but meet that we should reverently keep the feast of the triumph of the Son of David. We observe the Lord's-day as henceforth our true Sabbath, a day made and ordained of God, for the perpetual remembrance of the achievements of our Redeemer. Whenever the soft Sabbath light of the first day of the week breaks upon the earth, let us sing,

> ' This is the day the Lord hath made,
> He calls the hours his own ;
> Let heaven rejoice, let earth be glad,
> And praise surround the throne."

We by no means wish to confine the reference of the passage to the Sabbath, for the whole gospel day is the day of God's making, and its blessings come to us through our Lord's being placed as the head of the corner. *"We will rejoice and be glad in it."* What else can we do ? Having obtained so great a deliverance through our illustrious leader, and having seen the eternal mercy of God so brilliantly displayed, it would ill become us to mourn and murmur. Rather will we exhibit a double joy, rejoice in heart and be glad in face, rejoice in secret and be glad in public, for we have more than a double reason for being glad in the Lord. We ought to be specially joyous on the Sabbath : it is the queen of days, and its hours should be clad in royal apparel of delight. George Herbert says of it :—

> " Thou art a day of mirth,
> And where the week-days trail on ground,
> Thy flight is higher as thy birth."

Entering into the midst of the church of God, and beholding the Lord Jesus as all in all in the assemblies of his people, we are bound to overflow with joy. Is it not written, " then were the disciples glad when they saw the Lord " ? When the King makes the house of prayer to be a banqueting house, and we have grace to enjoy fellowship with him, both in his sufferings and in his triumphs, we feel an intense delight, and we are glad to express it with the rest of his people.

25. *"Save now, I beseech thee, O* LORD." Hosanna ! God save our king ! Let David reign ! Or as we who live in these latter days interpret it,—Let the Son of David live for ever, let his saving help go forth throughout all nations. This was the peculiar shout of the feast of tabernacles ; and so long as we dwell here below in these tabernacles of clay we cannot do better than use the same cry. Perpetually let us pray that our glorious King may work salvation in the midst of the earth. We plead also for ourselves that the Lord would save us, deliver us, and continue to sanctify us. This we ask with great earnestness, beseeching it of Jehovah. Prayer should always be an entreating and beseeching. *"O* LORD, *I beseech thee, send now prosperity."* Let the church be built up : through the salvation of sinners may

the number of the saints be increased ; through the preservation of saints may the church be strengthened, continued, beautified, perfected. Our Lord Jesus himself pleads for the salvation and the prosperity of his chosen ; as our Intercessor before the throne he asks that the heavenly Father would save and keep those who were of old committed to his charge, and cause them to be one through the indwelling Spirit. Salvation had been given, and therefore it is asked for. Strange though it may seem, he who cries for salvation is already in a measure saved. None can so truly cry, " Save, I beseech thee," as those who have already participated in salvation ; and the most prosperous church is that which most imploringly seeks prosperity. It may seem strange that, returning from victory, flushed with triumph, the hero should still ask for salvation ; but so it is, and it could not be otherwise. When all our Saviour's work and warfare were ended, his intercession became even more prominently a feature of his life ; after he had conquered all his foes he made intercession for the transgressors. What is true of him is true of his church also, for whenever she obtains the largest measure of spiritual blessing she is then most inclined to plead for more. She never pants so eagerly for prosperity as when she sees the Lord's doings in her midst, and marvels at them. Then, encouraged by the gracious visitation she sets apart her solemn days of prayer, and cries with passionate desire, " Save now," and " Send now prosperity." She would fain take the tide at the flood, and make the most of the day of which the Lord has already made so much.

26. *"Blessed is he that cometh in the name of the LORD."* The champion had done everything "in the name of the Lord": in that name he had routed all his adversaries, and had risen to the throne, and in that name he had now entered the temple to pay his vows. We know who it is that cometh in the name of the Lord beyond all others. In the Psalmist's days he was The Coming One, and he is still The Coming One, though he hath already come. We are ready with our hosannas both for his first and second advent ; our inmost souls thankfully adore and bless him and invoke upon his head unspeakable joys. " Prayer also shall be made for him continually ; and daily shall he be praised. ' For his sake everybody is blessed to us who comes in the name of the Lord, we welcome all such to our hearts and our homes ; but chiefly, and beyond all others, we welcome *himself* when he deigns to enter in and sup with us and we with him. O sacred bliss, fit antepast of heaven ! Perhaps this sentence is intended to be the benediction of the priests upon the valiant servant of the Lord, and if so, it is appropriately added, *"We have blessed you out of the house of the LORD."* The priests whose business it was to bless the people, in a sevenfold degree blessed the people's deliverer, the one chosen out of the people whom the Lord had exalted. All those whose high privilege it is to dwell in the house of the Lord for ever, because they are made priests unto God in Christ Jesus, can truly say that they bless the Christ who has made them what they are, and placed them where they are. Whenever we feel ourselves at home with God, and feel the spirit of adoption, whereby we cry, " Abba Father," the first thought of our hearts should be to bless the elder Brother, through whom the privilege of sonship has descended to such unworthy ones. In looking back upon our past lives we can remember many delightful occasions in which with joy unutterable we have in the fulness of our heart blessed our Saviour and our King ; and all these memorable seasons are so many foretastes and pledges of the time when in the house of our great Father above we shall for ever sing, " Worthy is the Lamb that was slain," and with rapture bless the Redeemer's name.

27. *"God is the LORD, which hath shewed us light,"* or " God is Jehovah," the only living and true God. There is none other God but he. The words may also be rendered, " Mighty is Jehovah." Only the power of God could have brought us such light and joy as spring from the work of our Champion and King. We have received light, by which we have known the rejected stone to be the head of the corner, and this light has led us to enlist beneath the banner of the once despised Nazarene, who is now the Prince of the kings of the earth. With the light of knowledge has come the light of joy ; for we are delivered from the powers of darkness and translated into the kingdom of God's dear Son. Our knowledge of the glory of God in the face of Jesus Christ came not by the light of nature, nor by reason, nor did it arise from the sparks which we ourselves had kindled, nor did we receive it of men ; but the mighty God alone hath showed it to us. He made a day on purpose that he might shine upon us like the sun, and he made our faces to shine in the light of that day, according to the declaration of the twenty-fourth verse. Therefore,

unto him be all the honour of our enlightenment.   Let us do our best to magnify the great Father of lights from whom our present blessedness has descended.   *"Bind the sacrifice with cords, even unto the horns of the altar."*   Some think that by this we are taught that the king offered so many sacrifices that the whole area of the court was filled, and the sacrifices were bound even up to the altar ; but we are inclined to keep to our own version, and to believe that sometimes restive bullocks were bound to the altar before they were slain, in which case Mant's verse is correct :—

> " He, Jehovah, is our Lord :
> He, our God, on us hath shined :
> Bind the sacrifice with cord,
> To the hornèd altar bind."

The word rendered " cords " carries with it the idea of wreaths and boughs, so that it was not a cord of hard, rough rope, but a decorated band ; even as in our case, though we are bound to the altar of God, it is with the cords of love and the bands of a man, and not by a compulsion which destroys the freedom of the will.   The sacrifice which we would present in honour of the victories of our Lord Jesus Christ is the living sacrifice of our spirit, soul, and body.   We bring ourselves to his altar, and desire to offer him all that we have and are.   There remains a tendency in our nature to start aside from this ; it is not fond of the sacrificial knife.   In the warmth of our love we come willingly to the altar, but we need constraining power to keep us there in the entirety of our being throughout the whole of life.   Happily there is a cord which, twisted around the atonement, or, better still, around the person of our Lord Jesus Christ, who is our only Altar, can hold us, and does hold us : " For the love of Christ constraineth us ; because we thus judge, that if one died for all, then all died ; and that he died for all, that they that live should not henceforth live unto themselves, but unto him which died for them, and rose again."   We are bound to the doctrine of atonement ; we are bound to Christ himself, who is both altar and sacrifice ; we desire to be more bound to him than ever, our soul finds her liberty in being tethered fast to the altar of the Lord.   The American Board of Missions has for its seal an ox, with an altar on one side and a plough on the other, and the motto " Ready for either,"—ready to live and labour, or ready to suffer and die.   We would gladly spend ourselves for the Lord actively, or be spent by him passively, whichever may be his will ; but since we know the rebellion of our corrupt nature we earnestly pray that we may be kept in this consecrated mind, and that we may never, under discouragements, or through the temptations of the world, be permitted to leave the altar, to which it is our intense desire to be for ever fastened.   Such consecration as this, and such desires for its perpetuity, well beseem that day of gladness which the Lord hath made so bright by the glorious triumph of his Son, our covenant head, our well-beloved.

28 Thou *art* my God, and I will praise thee : *thou art* my God, I will exalt thee.

29 O give thanks unto the LORD ; for *he is* good : for his mercy *endureth* for ever.

Now comes the closing song of the champion, and of each one of his admirers. 28. " *Thou art my God, and I will praise thee,*" my mighty God who hath done this mighty and marvellous thing.   Thou shalt be mine, and all the praise my soul is capable of shall be poured forth at thy feet.   " *Thou art my God, I will exalt thee.*"   Thou hast exalted me, and as far as my praises can do it, I will exalt thy name.   Jesus is magnified, and he magnifies the Father according to his prayer, " Father, the hour is come ; glorify thy Son, that thy Son also may glorify thee." God hath given us grace and promised us glory, and we are constrained to ascribe all grace to him, and all the glory of it also.   The repetition indicates a double determination, and sets forth the firmness of the resolution, the heartiness of the affection, the intensity of the gratitude.   Our Lord Jesus himself saith, " I will praise thee " ; and well may each one of us, humbly and with confidence in divine grace add, on his own account, the same declaration, " *I* will praise thee."   However others may blaspheme thee, I will exalt thee : however dull and cold I may sometimes feel myself, yet will I rouse up my nature, and determine that as long as I have any being that being shall be spent to thy praise.   For ever thou art my God, and for ever I will give thee thanks.

29. *" O give thanks unto the* LORD *; for he is good : for his mercy endureth for ever."* The Psalm concludes as it began, making a complete circle of joyful adoration. We can well suppose that the notes at the close of the loud hallelujah were more swift, more sweet, more loud than at the beginning. To the sound of trumpet and harp, Israel, the house of Aaron, and all that feared the Lord, forgetting their distinctions, joined in one common hymn, testifying again to their deep gratitude to the Lord's goodness, and to the mercy which is unto eternity. What better close could there be to this right royal song ? The Psalmist would have risen to something higher, so as to end with the climax, but nothing loftier remained. He had reached the height of his grandest argument, and there he paused. The music ceased, the song was suspended, the great *hallel* was all chanted, and the people went every one to his own home, quietly and happily musing upon the goodness of the Lord, whose mercy fills eternity.

EXPLANATORY NOTES AND QUAINT SAYINGS.

Whole Psalm.—This is the last of those Psalms which form the great *Hallel,* which the Jews sang at the end of the passover.—*Adam Clarke.*

Whole Psalm.—The whole Psalm has a peculiar formation. It resembles the *Maschal* Psalms, for each verse has of itself its completed sense, its own scent and hue ; one thought is joined to another as branch to branch and flower to flower.—*Franz Delitzch.*

Whole Psalm.—Nothing can surpass the force and majesty, as well as the richly varied beauty, of this Psalm. Its general burden is quite manifest. It is the prophetic expression, by the Spirit of Christ, of that exultant strain of anticipative triumph, wherein the virgin daughter of Zion will laugh to scorn, in the immediate prospect of her Deliverer's advent, the congregated armies of the Man of Sin (verses 10—13).—*Arthur Pridham.*

Whole Psalm.—The two Psalms, 117th and 118th, are placed together because, though each is a distinct portion in itself, the 117th is an exordium to that which follows it, an address and an invitation to the Gentile and heathen world to acknowledge and praise Jehovah.

We are now arrived at the concluding portion of the hymn, which Christ and his disciples sung preparatory to their going forth to the Mount of Olives. Nothing could be more appropriate or better fitted to comfort and encourage, at that awful period, than a prophecy which, overleaping the suffering to be endured, showed forth the glory that was afterwards to follow, and a song of triumph, then only recited, but in due time to be literally acted, when the cross was to be succeeded by a crown. This Psalm is not only frequently quoted in the New Testament, but it was also partially applied at one period of our Saviour's sojourn on earth, and thus we are afforded decisive testimony to the purpose for which it is originally and prophetically destined. It was partially used at the time when Messiah, in the days of his humiliation, was received with triumph and acclamation into Jerusalem ; and we may conclude it will be fully enacted, when our glorified and triumphant Lord, coming with ten thousand of his saints, will again stand upon the earth and receive the promised salutation, " Blessed be the King that cometh in the name of Jehovah." This dramatic representation of Messiah coming in glory, to take his great power and reign among us, is apportioned to the chief character, " the King of kings and Lord of lords," to his saints following him in procession, and to priests and Levites, representing the Jewish nation.

The Conqueror and his attendants sing the 117th Psalm, an introductory hymn, inviting all, Jews and Gentiles, to share in the merciful kindness of God, and to sing his praises. It is a gathering together of all the Lord's people, to be witnesses and partakers of his glory. The first, second, and third verses of the 118th Psalm are sung by single voices. As the procession moves along, the theme of rejoicing is announced. The first voice repeats, *" O give thanks unto the* LORD *; for he is good, because his mercy endureth for ever."* Another single voice calls on Israel to acknowledge this great truth ; and a third invites the house of Aaron, the priesthood, to acknowledge their share in Jehovah's love. The fourth verse is a chorus ; the whole procession, the living, and the dead who are raised to meet Christ (1 Thess. iv. 16), shout aloud the burden of the song, verse 1. Arrived at the temple gate, or rather, the gate of Jerusalem, the Conqueror alone sings, verses 5, 6, 7. He begins by recounting the circumstances of his distress. Next, he tells of his refuge : I betook me to God, I told him my sorrows, and he heard me. The procession, in chorus, sings verses 8 and 9, taking up the substance of Messiah's chaunt, and fully echoing the sentiment, *"It is better to trust in the LORD than to put confidence in princes."* The Conqueror alone again sings verses 10, 11, 12, 13, 14. He enlarges on the magnitude of his dangers, and the hopelessness of his situation. It was not a common difficulty, or a single enemy, whole nations compassed him about. The procession in chorus, verses 15, 16, attributes their Lord's great deliverance to his righteous person, and to his righteous cause. Justice and equity and truth, all demanded that Messiah should not be trodden down. " Was it not thine arm, O Jehovah, which has gotten thee the victory ? " Messiah now takes up the language of a conqueror, verses 17, 18, 19. My sufferings were sore, but they were only for a season. I laid down my life, and I now take it up again : and then, with a loud voice, as when he roused Lazarus out of the grave, he cries to those within the walls, " *Open to me the gates of righteousness : I will go into them, and I will praise the LORD."* The priests and Levites within instantly obey his command, and while they throw open the gates, they sing, " *This is the gate of the LORD, into which the righteous shall enter."* As he enters, the Conqueror alone repeats verse 21. His sorrows are ended, his victory is complete. The objects for which he lived and died, and for which his prayers were offered, are now fulfilled, and thus, in a few short words, he expresses his joy and gratitude to God. The priests and Levites sing in chorus verses 22, 23, 24. Depositaries and expounders of the prophecies as they had long been, they now for the first time, quote and apply one, Isai. xxviii. 16, which held a conspicuous place, but never before was intelligible to Jewish ears. " The man of sorrows," the stone which the builders refused, is become the headstone of the corner. The Conqueror is now within the gates, and proceeds to accomplish his good purpose, Luke i. 68. " *Hosannah, save thy people, O LORD, and send them now prosperity,"* verse 25. The priests and Levites are led by the Spirit to use the words foretold by our Lord, Matt. xxiii. 39. Now at length the veil is removed, and his people say, " *Blessed be he that cometh in the name of the LORD,"* verse 26. The Conqueror and his train (verse 27) now praise God, who has given light and deliverance and salvation, and they offer to him the sacrifice of thanksgiving for all that they enjoy. The Conqueror alone (verse 28) next makes a solemn acknowledgment of gratitude and praise to Jehovah, and then, all being within the gates, the united body, triumphant procession, priests and Levites, end, as they commenced, " *O give thanks unto the LORD ; for he is good : for his mercy endureth for ever."—R. H. Ryland, in " The Psalms restored to Messiah,"* 1853.

Whole Psalm.—It was Luther's favourite Psalm, his beauteous *Confitemini,* which " had helped him out of what neither emperor nor king, nor any other man on earth, could have helped him." With the exposition of this his noblest jewel, his defence and his treasure, he occupied himself in the solitude of his Patmos (Coburg).—*Franz Delitzsch.*

Whole Psalm.—This is my Psalm, my chosen Psalm. I love them all ; I love all holy Scripture, which is my consolation and my life. But this Psalm is nearest my heart, and I have a peculiar right to call it mine. It has saved me from many a pressing danger, from which nor emperor, nor kings, nor sages, nor saints, could have saved me. It is my friend ; dearer to me than all the honours and power of the earth. . . . But it may be objected, that this Psalm is common to all ; no one has a right to call it his own. Yes ; but Christ is also common to all, and yet Christ is mine. I am not jealous of my property ; I would divide it with the whole world. . . . And would to God that all men would claim the Psalm as especially theirs ! It would be the most touching quarrel, the most agreeable to God—a quarrel of union and perfect charity.—*Luther. From his Dedication of his Translation of Psalm CXVIII. to the Abbot Frederick of Nuremberg.*

Verse 1.—" *For he is good."* The praise of God could not be expressed in fewer words than these, " *For he is good."* I see not what can be more solemn than this brevity, since goodness is so peculiarly the quality of God, that the Son of God himself when addressed by some one as " Good Master," by one, namely, who beholding his flesh, and comprehending not the fulness of his divine nature, considered him as man only, replied, " Why callest thou me good ? There is none good but one, that is God." And what is this but to say, If thou wishest to call me good, recognize me as God ?—*Augustine.*

Verse 1.—" *His mercy endureth for ever.*" What the close of Ps. cxvii. says of God's truth, viz., that it endureth for ever, the beginning of Ps. cxviii. says of its sister, his mercy or loving-kindness.—*Franz Delitzsch.*

Verses 1—4.—As the salvation of the elect is one, and the love of God to them one, so should their song be one, as here four several times it is said, " *His mercy endureth for ever.*"—*David Dickson.*

Verses 1—4.—Because we hear the sentence so frequently repeated here, that " *the mercy of the* LORD *endureth for ever,*" we are not to think that the Holy Spirit has employed empty tautology, but our great necessity demands it : for in temptations and dangers the flesh begins to doubt of the mercy of God : therefore nothing should be so frequently impressed on the mind as this, that the mercy of God does not fail, that the Eternal Father wearies not in remitting our sins.—*Solomon Gesner.*

Verse 2.—" *Let Israel now say.*" Albeit all the elect have interest in God's praise for mercies purchased by Christ unto them, yet the elect of Israel have the first room in the song ; for Christ is first promised to them, and came of them according to the flesh, and will be most marvellous about them.—*David Dickson.*

Verse 2.—" *Let Israel now say, that his mercy endureth for ever.*" Let such who have had an experience of it, acknowledge and declare it to others ; not only believe it with their hearts, and privately give thanks for it, but with the mouth make confession of it to the glory of divine grace.—*John Gill.*

Verses 2, 3, 4.—" *Now.*" Beware of delaying. Delays be dangerous, our hearts will cool, and our affections will fall down. It is good then to be doing while it is called *to-day,* while it is called *now.* *Now, now, now,* saith David ; there be three nows, and all to teach us that for aught we know, it is *now* or never, to-day or not at all ; we must praise God while the heart is hot, else our iron will cool. Satan hath little hope to prevail unless he can persuade us to omit our duties when the clock strikes, and therefore his skill is to urge us to put it off till another time as fitter or better. Do it anon, next hour, next day, next week (saith he) ; and why not next year ? Hereafter (saith he) it will be as well as now. This he saith indeed, but his meaning (by hereafter) is never : and he that is not fit to-day, hath no promise but he shall be more unapt to-morrow. We have neither God nor our own hearts at command ; and when we have lost the opportunity, God to correct us perhaps will not give us affections. The cock within shall not crow to awaken us, the sun shall not shine, and then we are in danger to give over quite ; and if we come once to a total omission of one duty, why not of another, and of another, and so of all ? and then farewell to us.—*Richard Capel* (1586—1656) *in " Tentations, their Nature, Danger, Cure.*"

Verse 4.—" *Them that fear the* LORD.*" Who were neither of " the house of Aaron," that is, of the priests or Levites ; nor of " the house of Israel," that is, native Jews ; yet might be of the Jewish religion, and " *fear the* LORD.*" These were called *proselytes,* and are here invited to praise the Lord.—*Joseph Caryl.*

Verse 4.—" *God's mercy endureth for ever.*" That is, his covenant mercy, that precious church privilege : this is perpetual to his people, and should perpetually remain as a memorial in our hearts. And therefore it is that this is the foot or burthen of these first four verses. Neither is there any idle repetition, but a notable expression of the saints' insatiableness of praising God for his never failing mercy. These heavenly birds having got a note, sing it over and over. In the last Psalm there are but six verses, yet twelve Hallelujahs.—*Abraham Wright.*

Verse 5.—Perhaps verse 5, which says, " *I called upon the* LORD *in distress* " (literally, out of the narrow gorge), " *and the* LORD *answered me on the open plain* " —which describes the deliverance of Israel from their captivity,—may have been sung as they defiled from a narrow ravine into the plain ; and when they arrived at the gate of the temple, then they broke forth in full chorus into the words, " Open to me the gates of righteousness " (ver. 19).—*Christopher Wordsworth.*

Verse 5.—It is said, " *I called upon the* LORD.*" Thou must learn to call, and not to sit there by thyself, and lie on the bench, hang and shake thy head, and bite and devour thyself with thy thoughts; but come on, thou indolent knave, down upon thy knees, up with thy hands and eyes to heaven, take a Psalm or a prayer, and set forth thy distress with tears before God.—*Martin Luther.*

Verse 5.—*"The LORD answered me, and set me in a large place."* It may be rendered, *The LORD answered me largely;* as he did Solomon, when he gave him more than he asked for; and as he does his people, when he gives then a sufficiency and an abundance of his grace; not only above their deserts, but above their thoughts and expectations. See Eph. iii. 20.—*John Gill.*

Verse 6.—*"The LORD is on my side."* The reason which the Psalmist gives here for his trusting, or for his not fearing, is the great fact, that the Lord is on his side; and the prominent idea which this brings before us is *Alliance; the making common cause,* which the great God undoubtedly does, with imperfect, yet with earnest, trusting man.

We know very well the great anxiety shown by men, in all their worldly conflicts, to secure the aid of a powerful ally; in their lawsuits, to retain the services of a powerful advocate; or, in their attempts at worldly advancement, to win the friendship and interest of those who can further the aims they have in view. When Herod was highly displeased with the armies of Tyre and Sidon, they did not venture to approach him until they had made Blastus, the king's chamberlain, their friend. If such and such a person be on their side, men think that all must go well. Who so well off as he who is able to say, *"The LORD is on my side"?—Philip Bennet Power, in "The I Will's of the Psalms,"* 1861.

Verse 6.—God is with those he calls and employs in public service. Joshua was exhorted to be strong and of good courage, " For the Lord thy God is with thee " (Josh. i. 9). So also was Jeremiah, " Be not afraid of their faces; for I am with thee to deliver thee " (Jer. i. 8). God's presence should put life into us. When inferior natures are backed with a superior, they are full of courage: when the master is by, the dog will venture upon creatures greater than himself and fear not; at another time he will not do it when his master is absent. When God is with us, who is the supreme, it should make us fearless. It did David; *"The LORD is on my side; I will not fear what man can do unto me."* Let him do his worst, frown, threat, plot, arm, strike; the Lord is on my side, he hath a special care for me, he is a shield unto me, I will not fear, but hope; as it is in the next verse, " I shall see my desire on them that hate me," I shall see them changed or ruined. Our help is in the name of the Lord, but our fears are in the name of man.— *William Greenhill.*

Verse 6.—*"I will not fear."* David, (or God's people, if you will,) being taught by experience, exults in great confidence, but does not say, the Lord is my helper, and I shall suffer no more, knowing that while he is a pilgrim here below he will have much to suffer from his daily enemies; but he says, *"The LORD is my helper, I will not fear what man can do unto me."—Robert Bellarmine.*

Verse 6.—*"Man"* does not here mean *a man,* but *mankind,* or man as opposed to God.—*Joseph Addison Alexander.*

Verse 8.—It may perhaps be considered beneath the dignity and solemnity of our subject to remark, that this 8th verse of this Psalm is the middle verse of the Bible. There are, I believe, 31,174 verses in all, and this is the 15,587th. I do not wish, nor would I advise you to occupy your time in counting for yourselves, nor should I indeed have noticed the subject at all, but that I wish to suggest one remark upon it, and that is, that though we may generally look upon such calculations as only laborious idleness,—and they certainly have been carried to the most minute dissection of every part of Scripture, such as to how many times the word " Lord," the word " God," and even the word " and," occurs,—yet I believe that the integrity of the holy volume owes a vast deal to this scruple-weighing of these calculators. I do not say, nor do I think, that they had such motives in their minds; but whatever their reasons were, I cannot but think that there was an overruling Providence in thus converting these trifling and apparently useless investigations into additional guards and fences around the sacred text.—*Barton Bouchier.*

Verse 8.—*"It is better to trust in the LORD,"* etc. Luther on this text calleth it, *artem artium, et mirificam, ac suam artem, non fidere hominibus,* that is, the art of arts, and that which he had well studied, not to put confidence in man : as for trust in God, he calleth it *sacrificium omnium gratissimum et suavissimum, et cultum omnium pulcherrimum*, the most pleasant and sweetest of all sacrifices, the best of all services we perform to God.—*John Trapp.*

Verse 8.—*"It is better to trust in the* LORD.*"* All make this acknowledgment, and yet there is scarcely one among a hundred who is fully persuaded that God alone can afford him sufficient help. That man has attained a high rank among the faithful, who resting satisfied in God, never ceases to entertain a lively hope, even when he finds no help upon earth.—*John Calvin.*

Verse 8.—It is a great cause oftentimes why God blesseth not means, because we are so apt to trust in them, and rob God of his glory, not waiting for a blessing at his hands. This causeth the Lord to cross us, and to curse his own benefits, because we seek not him, but sacrifice to our own nets, putting confidence in outward means. Therefore when we hope for help from them, God bloweth upon them, and turneth them to our hurt and destruction.—*Abraham Wright.*

Verse 8.—When my enemies have been brought to contempt, let not my friend present himself unto me as a good man, and bid me repose my hope in himself ; for still must I trust in the Lord alone.—*Augustine.*

Verses 8, 9.—Nothing is more profitable than dwelling on familiar truths. Was there ever a good man who did not believe that it was better to trust in Jehovah than rely on any created arm ? Yet David here repeats this truth, that if possible it may sink deep into every mind.—*William S. Plumer.*

Verse 9.—*"It is better to trust in the* LORD *than to put confidence in princes."* David knew that by experience, for he confided in Saul his king, at another time in Achish, the Philistine, at another time in Ahithophel his own most prudent minister, besides some others ; and they all failed him ; but he never confided in God without feeling the benefit of it.—*Robert Bellarmine.*

Verse 9.—*"It is better,"* etc. Literally, " Good is it to trust in Jehovah more than to confide in man." This is the Hebrew form of comparison, and is equivalent to what is stated in our version. " It is *better*," etc. It is better, (1) because man is weak,—but God is Almighty ; (2) because man is selfish,—but God is benevolent ; (3) because man is often faithless and deceitful,—God never ; (4) because there are emergencies, as death, in which man cannot aid us, however faithful, kind, and friendly he may be,—but there are no circumstances in this life, and none in death, where God cannot assist us ; and (5) because the ability of man to help us pertains at best only to the present life,—the power of God will be commensurate with eternity.—*Albert Barnes.*

Verse 9.—*"Than to put confidence in princes."* Great men's words, saith one, are like dead men's shoes ; he may go barefoot that waiteth for them.—*John Trapp.*

Verse 9.—They who constantly attend upon God, and depend upon him, have a much sweeter life, than those that wait upon princes with great observance and expectation. A servant of the Lord is better provided for than the greatest favourites and minions of princes.—*Thomas Manton.*

Verse 10.—*"All nations compassed me about."* A multitude of enemies everywhere cannot hinder the presence of God with us. Acts xvii. 28. They are without ; He is within, in our hearts ; They are flesh ; He is Spirit : they are frail ; He is immortal and invincible.—*Martin Geier.*

Verse 11.—Whether Tertullus persecute the church with his tongue, or Elymas with his hand, God hath the command of both. Indeed the wicked are the mediate causes of our troubles : the righteous are as the centre, the other the circumference ; which way soever they turn, they find themselves environed ; yet still the centre is fixed and immovable, being founded upon Christ. It is good for some men to have adversaries ; for often they more fear to sin, lest they should despise them, than dislike it for conscience, lest God should condemn them. They speak evil of us : if true, let us amend it ; if false, contemn it ; whether false or true, observe it. Thus we shall learn good out of their evil ; make them our tutors, and give them our pupilage. In all things let us watch them, in nothing fear them : " which is to them an evident token of perdition, but to us of salvation," Phil. i. 28. The church is that tower of David ; if there be a thousand weapons to wound us, there are a thousand shields to guard us, Cant. iv. 4.—*Thomas Adams.*

Verse 12.—*"They compassed me about like bees."* Christ's enemies are so spiteful, that in fighting against his kingdom, they regard not what become of themselves, so they may hurt his people ; but as the bee undoeth herself in stinging, and loseth her life or her power with her sting, so do they. All that the enemies of Christ's church can do against his people is but to trouble them externally ; their wounds are like the sting of a bee, that is, unto pain and swelling, and a short trouble only, but are not deadly.—*David Dickson.*

Verse 12.—*"They compassed me about like bees."* Now, as the north-east wind of course was adverse to any north-east progress, it was necessary that the boat should be towed by the crew. As the rope was being drawn along through the grass on the banks it happened that it disturbed a swarm of bees. In a moment, like a great cloud, they burst upon the men who were dragging ; everyone of them threw himself headlong into the water and hurried to regain the boat. The swarm followed at their heels, and in a few seconds filled every nook and cranny of the deck. What a scene of confusion ensued may readily be imagined.

Without any foreboding of ill, I was arranging my plants in my cabin, when I heard all around me a scampering which I took at first to be merely the frolics of my people, as that was the order of the day. I called out to enquire the meaning of the noise, but only got excited gestures and reproachful looks in answer. The cry of " Bees ! bees ! " soon broke upon my ear, and I proceeded to light a pipe. My attempt was entirely in vain ; in an instant bees in thousands are about me, and I am mercilessly stung all over my face and hands. To no purpose do I try to protect my face with a handkerchief, and the more violently I fling my hands about, so much the more violent becomes the impetuosity of the irritated insects. The maddening pain is now on my cheek, now in my eye, now in my hair. The dogs from under my bed burst out frantically, overturning everything in their way. Losing well nigh all control over myself, I fling myself into the river ; I dive down, but all in vain, for the stings rain down still upon my head. Not heeding the warnings of my people, I creep through the reedy grass to the swampy bank. The grass lacerates my hands, and I try to gain the mainland, hoping to find shelter in the woods. All at once four powerful arms seize me and drag me back with such force that I think I must be choked in the mud. I am compelled to go back on board, and flight is not to be thought of. . . . I felt ready, in the evening, for an encounter with half a score of buffaloes or a brace of lions rather than have anything more to do with bees ; and this was a sentiment in which all the ship's company heartily concurred.—*George Schweinfurth, in "The Heart of Africa,"* 1873.

Verse 12.—David said of his enemies, that they came about him like *"bees" ;* he doth not say like *wasps.* For though they used their stings, yet he found honey in them too.—*Peter Smith,* 1644.

Verse 12.—*"They compassed me about like bees."*

As wasps, provoked by children in their play,
Pour from their mansions by the broad highway,
In swarms the guiltless traveller engage,
Whet all their stings, and call forth all their rage,
All rise in arms, and with a general cry,
Assert their waxen domes, and buzzing progeny ;
Thus from the tents the fervent legion swarms,
So loud their clamours, and so keen their arms.

—*Homer.*

Verse 12.—*"They are quenched as the fire of thorns."* The illustration from the *"fire of thorns "* is derived from the fact that they quickly kindle into a blaze, and then the flame soon dies away. In Eastern countries it was common to burn over their fields in the dry time of the year, and thus to clear them of thorns and briers and weeds. Of course, at such a time they would kindle quickly, and burn rapidly, and would soon be consumed. So the Psalmist says it was with his enemies. He came upon them, numerous as they were, as the fire runs over a field in a dry time, burning everything before it.—*Albert Barnes.*

Verse 12.—*"In the name of the* LORD.*"* This has been understood as the *tessera,* the sentence of attack, or signal to engage, like those of Cyrus—Jupiter is our leader and ally—Jupiter our captain and preserver. Cyropæd. l. 3 and 7 ; and Gideon, Judges vii. 18. This interpretation being only founded on the repetition, may it not more probably be designed as suited to the musical performance ?—*Samuel Burder.*

Verse 13.—"*Thou hast thrust sore at me that I might fall.*" The apostrophe is strong, and probably directed to some particular person in the battle, who had put David in great danger.—*Samuel Burder.*

Verse 13.—"*Thou hast thrust sore at me that I might fall.*" Thou hast indeed. Thou hast done thy part, O Satan, and it has been well done. Thou hast known all my weakest parts, thou hast seen where my armour was not buckled on tightly, and thou hast attacked me at the right time and in the right way. The great Spanish poet, Calderon, tells of one who wore a heavy suit of armour for a whole year, and laid it by for one hour, and in that hour the enemy came, and the man paid for his negligence with his life. " Blessed is the man that endureth temptation ; for when he is tried he shall receive the crown of life, which the Lord hath promised to them that love him."—*John Mason Neale.*

Verse 14.—"*The* LORD *is my strength and song, and is become my salvation.*" "*My strength,*" that I am able to resist my enemies ; "*my salvation,*" that I am delivered from my enemies ; "*my song,*" that I may joyfully praise him and sing of him after I am delivered.—*William Nicholson, 1662.*

Verse 14.—Good songs, good promises, good proverbs, good doctrines are none the worse for age. What was sung just after the passage of the Red Sea, is here sung by the prophet, and shall be sung to the end of the world by the saints of the Most High.—*William S. Plumer.*

Verse 14.—"*And is become my salvation.*" Not that he hath become anything which he was not before, but because his people, when they believed on him, became what they were not before, and then he began to be salvation unto them when turned towards him, which he was not to them when turned away from himself.—*Augustine.*

Verse 15.—"*The voice of rejoicing and salvation is in the tabernacles of the righteous.*" Every one should be careful that his dwelling is one of the *tabernacles of the righteous,* and that he himself together with his household should walk in righteousness (Luke i. 75). And he should be so diligent in hymns and sacred songs, that his rooms should resound with them.—*Martin Geier.*

Verse 16.—"*The right hand of the* LORD *doeth valiantly.*" Thrice he celebrateth God's right hand, to set forth his earnest desire to say the utmost ; or, in reference to the Sacred Trinity, as some will have it.—*John Trapp.*

Verse 17.—"*I shall not die, but live.*" As Christ is risen, " we shall not die, but live " ; we shall not die eternally, but we shall live in this world, the life of grace, and in the world to come, the life of glory ; that we may in both declare the " works " and chant the praises of God our Saviour. We are " chastened " for our sins, but " not given over to death " and destruction everlasting ; nay, our being " chastened " is now a proof that we are not so given over ; " for what son is he whom the father chasteneth not ? " Heb. xii. 7.—*George Horne.*

Verse 17.—"*I shall not die, but live.*" To live, signifies, not barely to live, but to live comfortably, to have content with our life ; to live is to prosper. Thus the word is often used in Scripture. "*I shall not die, but live.*" David did not look upon himself as immortal, or that he should never die ; he knew he was subject to the statute of death : but the meaning is, I shall not die now, I shall not die by the hands of these men, I shall not die the death which they have designed me to ; or when he saith, "*I shall not die, but live,*" his meaning is, I shall live comfortably and prosperously, I shall live as a king. That which we translate (1 Sam. x. 24) " God save the king," is, " Let the king *live,*" that is, let him prosper, and have good days ; let him have peace with all, or victory over his enemies.—*Joseph Caryl.*

Verse 17.—"*I shall not die,*" etc. The following incident is worth recording : " Wicliffe was now getting old, but the Reformer was worn out rather by the harassing attacks of his foes, and his incessant and ever-growing labours, than with the weight of years, for he was not yet sixty. He fell sick. With unbounded joy the friars heard that their great enemy was dying. Of course he was over-whelmed with horror and remorse for the evil he had done them, and they would hasten to his bedside and receive the expression of his penitence and sorrow. In a trice a little crowd of shaven crowns assembled round the couch of the sick man —delegates from the four orders of friars. ' They began fair,' wishing him ' health and restoration from his distemper"; but speedily changing their tone, they exhorted him, as one on the brink of the grave, to make full confession, and express his unfeigned grief for the injuries he had inflicted on their order. Wicliffe lay silent till they should have made an end, then, making his servant raise him a little on his pillow, and fixing his keen eyes upon them, he said with a loud voice, ' I shall not die, but live, and declare the evil deeds of the friars.' The monks rushed in astonishment and confusion from the chamber.—*J. A. Wylie, in "The History of Protestantism."*

Verse 17.—*"I shall not die,"* not absolutely, for see Psalm lxxxix. 48 ; Heb. ix. 27 ; but not in the midst of my days, Psalm cii. 24 ; nor according to the will of mine enemies, who *"thrust at me that I might fall,"* verse 13. *But,* on the contrary, *I shall live,* not simply as he had hitherto lived, in the greatest distress, which would be a wretched life, a living death : but lively, joyous, happy. Of this, he says he is secure ; this the word asserts. On what foundation does he rest ? Verses 14, 15, *"Because God had become his salvation,"* and *"the right hand of the Lord doeth valiantly."* —*Jacob Alting.*

Verse 17.—*"And declare the works of the Lord."* Matter of praise abounds in all the divine works, both of the general creation and preservation and of the redemption of our souls : chiefly, that God, besides the life of nature, has given to us the life of grace, without which we could not properly praise God and declare his works.—*Rivetus.*

Verse 17.—*"And declare the works of the Lord."* In the second member of the verse, he points out the proper use of life, God does not prolong the lives of his people, that they may pamper themselves with meat and drink, sleep as much as they please, and enjoy every temporal blessing ; but to magnify him for his benefits which he is daily heaping upon them.—*John Calvin.*

Verse 17.—According to Matthesius, Luther had this verse written against his study wall.

Verse 18.—*"The Lord hath chastened me sore."* Strong humours require strong physic to purge them out. Where corruption is deeply rooted in the heart, a light or small matter will not serve the turn to work it out. No ; but a great deal of stir and ado must be made with it.—*Thomas Horton.*

Verse 18.—*"But he hath not given me over unto death."* It might have been worse, may the afflicted saint say, and it will be better ; it is in mercy and in measure that God chastiseth his children. It is his care that " the spirit fail not before him, nor the souls which he hath made," Isai. lvii. 16. If his child swoons in the whipping, God lets fall the rod, and falls a kissing it, to fetch life into it again.—*John Trapp.*

Verse 19.—*"Open to me the gates of righteousness."* The gates won by his righteousness, to whom we daily say, " Thou only art holy"; the gates which needed the " Via Dolorosa " and the cross, before they could roll back on their hinges. On a certain stormy afternoon, after the sun had been for three hours darkened, the world again heard of that Eden from which, four thousand years before, Adam had been banished. " Verily I say unto thee, this day shall thou be with me in paradise." O blessed malefactor, who thus entered into the heavenly gardens ! O happy thief, that thus stole the kingdom of heaven ! And see how valiantly he now enters it. *"Open to me the gates of righteousness."* Not " God be merciful to me a sinner " ; not " Lord, if thou wilt, thou canst make me clean." But this is what is called the suppliant omnipotency of prayer. " Blessed are they that do his commandments, that they may have right to the tree of life, and may enter in through the gates into the city.—*John Mason Neale.*

Verse 21.—*"I will praise thee : for thou hast heard me."* There is a point which we would especially notice, and that is, praise for *hearing* prayer. In this point, almost above all others, God is frequently robbed of his praise. Men pray ; they receive an answer to their prayers ; and then forget to praise. This happens especially in small things ; we should ever remember that whatever is worth praying for, is worth praising for also. The fact is, we do not recognize God in these small things as much as we should ; if we do praise, it is for the receipt of the blessing, with which we are pleased, leaving out of account the One from whom the blessing has come. This is not acceptable to God ; we must see him in the blessing, if we would really praise. The Psalmist says, "*I will praise thee: for thou hast heard me*"; he praised not only because he had *received*, but also because he had *heard*— because the living God, as a hearing God, was manifested in his mercies. And when we know that God has heard us, let us not delay our praise; if we put off our thanksgiving until perhaps only the evening, we may forget to praise at all; and if we do praise, it will in all probability be with only half the warmth which would animate our song at first. God loves a quick return for his blessings; one sentence of heartfelt thanksgiving is worth all the formalism of a more laboured service. There is a freshness about immediate praise which is like the bloom upon the fruit; its being spontaneous adds ineffably to its price.

Trace, then, dear reader, a connection between your God and your blessing. Recognize his hearing ear as well as his bounteous hand, and be yours the Psalmist's words, "*I will praise thee: for thou hast heard me.*"—*Philip Bennet Power.*

Verse 22.—"*The stone.*" "*The head stone of the corner.*" Christ Jesus is a stone: no firmness, but in him. A fundamental stone: no building, but on him. A corner stone: no piecing nor reconciliation, but in him.—*James Ford, 1856.*

Verse 22.—"*The Stone which the builders rejected,*" etc. To apply it to Christ "*The Stone*" is the ground of all. Two things befall it; two things as contrary as may be,—1. *Refused*, cast away; then, called for again, and *made head of the building*. So, two parts there are to the eye. 1. The *refusing*; 2. the *raising*; which are his two estates, his *humiliation*, and his *exaltation*. In either of these you may observe two degrees, *a quibus*, and *quosque*, by whom and how far. *By whom refused?* We weigh the word, *ædificantes:* not by men unskilful, but by workmen, professed *builders;* it is so much the worse. *How far?* We weigh the word,—*reprobaverunt; usque ad reprobari*, even to a reprobation. It is not *improbaverunt, disliked*, as not fit for some eminent place; but *reprobaverunt, utterly reprobate*, for any place at all.

Again, *exalted*, by whom? The next words are *a Domino*, by God, as good a *builder*, nay, better than the best of them; which makes amends for the former. And *How far?* Placed by him, not in any part of the *building;* but in the part most in the eye (*the corner*), and in the highest place of it, *the very head.*

So *rejected*, and that by the *builders*, and to the *lowest estate:* and from the *lowest estate exalted, in caput anguli*, to the chiefest place of all; and that by God himself.—*Lancelot Andrewes.*

Verse 22.—"*The stone which the builders refused,*" etc. We need not wonder, that not only the powers of the world are usually enemies to Christ, and that the contrivers of policies, those builders, leave out Christ in their building, but that the pretended builders of the church of God, though they use the name of Christ, and serve their turn with that, yet reject himself, and oppose the power of his spiritual kingdom. There may be wit and learning, and much knowledge of the Scriptures, amongst those that are haters of the Lord Jesus Christ, and of the power of godliness, and corrupters of the worship of God. It is the spirit of humility and obedience, and saving faith, that teach men to esteem Christ, and build upon him. The vanity and folly of these builders' opinion appears in this, that they are overpowered by the great Architect of the church: his purpose stands. Notwithstanding their rejection of Christ, he is still made the head corner stone. They cast him away by their reproaches, and by giving him up to be crucified and then cast into the grave, causing a stone to be rolled upon this *stone* which they had so rejected, that it might appear no more, and so thought themselves sure. But even from thence did he arise, and "*became the head of the corner.*"—*Robert Leighton.*

Verse 22.—"*The stone which the builders refused,*" etc. That is to say, God sent a living, precious, chosen stone on earth; but the Jews, who then had the building of the church, rejected that stone, and said of it, " This man, who observeth not the Sabbath, is not of God "; and, " We have no king but Cæsar," and, " That seducer said, I will arise after three days "; and many similiar things beside. But this stone, so rejected by the builders as unfit for raising the spiritual edifice, "*is become the head of the corner*"; has been made by God, the principal architect, the bond to connect the two walls and keep them together; that is to say, has been made the head of the whole church, composed of Jews and Gentiles; and such a head, that whoever is not under him cannot be saved; and whoever is built under him, the living stone, will certainly be saved. Now all this "*is the Lord's doing,*" done by his election and design, without any intervention on the part of man, and therefore, *"it is wonderful in our eyes."* For who is there that must not look upon it as a wonderful thing, to find a man crucified, dead and buried, rising, after three days, from the dead, immortal, with unbounded power, and declared Prince of men and angels, and a way opened through him for mortal man, to the kingdom of heaven, to the society of the angels, to a happy immortality ?—*Robert Bellarmine.*

Verse 22.—*"The stone which the builders refused."* Here we behold with how strong and impregnable a shield the Holy Ghost furnishes us against the empty vauntings of the Papal clergy. Be it so, that they possess the name, " chief-builders"; but if they disown Christ, does it necessarily follow that we must disown him also ? Let us rather contemn and trample under our feet all their decrees, and let us reverence this precious stone upon which our salvation rests. By the expression, *"is become the head of the corner,"* we are to understand the real foundation of the church, which sustains the whole weight of the edifice ; it being requisite that the corners should form the main strength of buildings.—*John Calvin.*

Verse 22.—*"The stone,"* etc. That is I, whom the great men and rulers of the people rejected (1 Sam. xxvi. 19), as the builders of a house reject a stone unfit to be employed in it, am now become king over Israel and Judah ; and a type of that glorious King who shall hereafter be in like manner refused (Luke xix. 14, and xx. 17), and then be by God exalted to be Lord of all the world, and the foundation of all men's happiness.—*Thomas Fenton.*

Verse 22.—*"The stone."* The author of *Historia Scholastica* mentions it as a tradition that at the building of the second temple there was a particular *stone* of which that was literally true, which is here parabolically rehearsed, viz., that it had the hap to be often taken up by the builders, and as oft rejected, and at last was found to be perfectly fit for the most honourable place, that of the *chief corner-stone*, which coupled the sides of the walls together, the extraordinariness whereof occasioned the speech here following : *"This is the LORD'S doing ; it is marvellous in our eyes."*—*Henry Hammond.*

Verse 22.—*"The head stone of the corner."* How of the *"corner"* ? The *corner* is the place where two walls meet : and there be many twos in this *building :* the two walls of nations, *Jews* and *Gentiles ;* the two of conditions, *bond* and *free ;* the two of sex, *male* and *female :* the great two (which this [Easter] day we celebrate) of the *quick* and the *dead ;* above all, the greatest two of all, *heaven* and *earth.*—*Lancelot Andrewes.*

Verse 22.—*"Is become the head stone of the corner."*

> Higher yet and ever higher, passeth he those ranks above,
> Where the seraphs are enkindled, with the flame of endless love
> Passeth them, for not e'en seraphs ever loved so well as he
> Who hath borne for his beloved, stripes, and thorns, and shameful tree ;
> Ever further, ever onward, where no angel's foot may tread,
> Where the four-and-twenty elders prostrate fall in mystic dread :
> Where the four strange living creatures sing their hymn before the throne,
> The Despised One and rejected passeth, in his might alone ;
> Passeth through the dazzling rainbow, till upon the Father's right
> He is seated, his Co-equal, God of God, and Light of Light.

R. F. Littledale.

Verse 22.—*"Head stone of the corner."* It is now clear to all by divine grace whom Holy Scripture calls the corner-stone. Him in truth who, taking unto himself from one side the Jewish, and from the other the Gentile people, unites, as it were, two walls in the one fabric of the Church ; them of whom it is written " He hath made both one " ; who exhibited himself as the Corner-stone, not only in things below, but in things above, because he united on earth the nations of the Gentiles to the people of Israel, and both together to angels. For at his birth the angels exclaimed, " On earth peace, good will toward men."—*Gregory, quoted by Henry Newland,* 1860.

Verse 22.—*"The corner."* By Bede it is rendered as a reason why the Jewish builders refused our Saviour Christ for the *head*-place, *Quia in uno pariete, stare amabant.* They could endure no *corner ;* they must stand alone upon their own single wall ; be of themselves, not join with Gentiles or Samaritans. And Christ they endured not, because they thought if he had been *head* he would have inclined that way. *Alias oves oportet me adducere* (John x. 16). *Alias* they could not abide. But sure, a purpose there must be, *alias oves adducendi,* of bringing in others, of joining a *corner*, or else we do not *facere secundum exemplar*, build not according to Christ's pattern ; our fashion of fabric is not like his.—*Lancelot Andrewes*.

Verses 22—27.—By the consent of all expositors, in this Psalm is typed the coming of Christ, and his kingdom of the gospel. This is manifested by an *exaltation*, by an *exultaton*, by a *petition*, by a *benediction*. The *exaltation : ver*. 22, "*The stone which the builders refused is become the head stone of the corner.*" The Jews refused this stone, but God hath built his church upon it.

The *exaltation : ver*. 24, "*This is the day which the* LORD *hath made ; we will rejoice and be glad in it.*" A more blessed day than that was wherein he made man, when he had done making the world ; "*Rejoice we, and be glad in it.*"

The *petition :* ver. 25, "*Save now, I beseech thee, O* LORD *: O* LORD, *I beseech thee, send now prosperity.*" Thy justice would not suffer thee to save without the Messiah ; he is come, "*Save now, O* LORD, *I beseech thee.*" Our Saviour is come, let mercy and salvation come along with him.

The *benediction* makes all clear : ver. 26, "*Blessed be he that cometh in the name of the* LORD." For what David here prophesied, the people after accomplished Matt. xxi. 9, "Blessed is he that cometh in the name of the LORD." The corollary or sum is in my text : ver. 27, "*God is the* LORD, *which hath shewed us light : bind the sacrifice with cords, even unto the horns of the altar.*"—*Thomas Adams*.

Verse 24.—"*This is the day which the* LORD *hath made.*" 1. Here is the doctrine of the Christian sabbath : "*it is the day which the* LORD *hath made,*" has made remarkable, made holy, has distinguished it from other days ; he has made it for man ; it is therefore called the Lord's day, for it bears his image and superscription. 2. The duty of the Sabbath, "*we will rejoice and be glad in it*" ; not only in the institution of the day, that there is such a day appointed, but in the occasion of it, Christ's becoming "*the head of the corner.*" This we ought to rejoice in, both as his honour and our advantage. Sabbath days must be rejoicing days, and then they are to us as the days of heaven. See what a good Master we serve, who having instituted a day for his service, appoints it to be spent in holy joy.—*Matthew Henry*.

Verse 24.—"*This is the day,*" etc. The " queen of days," as the Jews call the Sabbath. Arnobius interpreteth this text of the Christian Sabbath ; others, of the day of salvation by Christ exalted to be the head corner-stone ; in opposition to that dismal day of man's fall.—*John Trapp*.

Verse 24.—Because believers have ever cause for comfort, therefore they are commanded always to rejoice, Phil. iii. Whether their sins or sufferings come into their hearts, they must not sorrow as they that have no hope. In their saddest conditions, they have the Spirit of consolation. There is seed of joy sown within them when it is turned under the clods, and appears not above ground. But there are special times when God calls for this grain to spring up. They have some red letters, some holy days in the calendar of their lives, wherein this joy, as wine at a wedding, is most seasonable ; but among all those days it never relisheth so well, it never tasteth so pleasantly, as on a Lord's-day. Joy suits no person so much as a saint, and it becomes no season so well as a Sabbath.

Joy in God on other days is like the birds chirping in winter, which is pleasing ; but joy on the Lord's-day is like their warbling times and pretty notes in spring, when all other things look with a suitable delightful aspect. "*This is the day which the* LORD *hath made,*" (he that made all days, so especially this day, but what follows ?) "*we will rejoice and be glad in it.*" In which words we have the church's solace, or joy, and the season, or day of it. Her solace was great : "*We will rejoice and be glad.*" Those expressions are not needless repetitions, but shew the exuberancy or high degree of their joy. The season of it : "*This is the day which the* LORD *hath made.*" Compare this place with Matt. xxi. 22, 23, and Acts iv. 11, and you will find that the precedent verses are a prophetical prediction of Christ's resurrection, and so this verse foretells the church's joy upon that memorable and glorious day. And, indeed, if " a feast be made for laughter," Eccles. x. 19, then that day wherein Christ feasteth his saints with the choicest mercies may well command their greatest spiritual mirth. A thanksgiving-day hath a double precedency of a fast-day. On a fast-day we eye God's anger ; on a thanksgiving-day we look to God's favour, In the former we specially mind our corruptions ; in the latter, God's compassions ; —therefore a fast-day calls for sorrow, a thanksgiving-day for joy. But the Lord's-day is the highest thanksgiving-day, and deserveth much more than the Jewish Purim, to be a day of feasting and gladness, and a good day.—*George Swinnock*.

Verse 24.—*"Day which the* LORD *hath made."* As the sun in heaven makes the natural day by his light, so does Christ the Sun of Righteousness make ours a spiritual day.—*Starke.*

Verse 24.—*"Day which the* LORD *hath made."* Adam introduced a day of sadness, but another day is made by Christ : Abraham saw his day from afar, and was glad ; we will walk even now in his light.—*Johann David Friesch*, 1731.

Verse 25.—*"Save."* With the Hebrews *salvation* is a wide word, comprising all the favours of God that may lead to preservation ; and therefore the Psalmist elsewhere extends this act both to man and beast, and, as if he would comment upon himself, expounds σῶσον *save*, by εὐόδωσον *prosper*. It is so dear a title of God, that the prophet cannot have enough of it.—*Joseph Hall.*

Verse 25.—*"Save now, I beseech thee, O* LORD." Let him have the acclamations of the people as is usual at the inauguration of a prince ; let every one of his loyal subjects shout for joy, *"Save now, I beseech thee, O* LORD." This is like *vivat rex*, and speaks both a hearty joy for his accession to the crown, an entire satisfaction in his government, and a zealous affection to the interests and honour of it. Hosanna signifies, *"Save now, I beseech thee."* Lord, save me, I beseech thee ; let this Saviour be my Saviour ; and in order to that my Ruler ; let me be taken under his protection, and owned as one of his willing subjects. His enemies are my enemies ; Lord, I beseech thee, save me from them. Send me an interest in that prosperity which his kingdom brings with it to all those that entertain it. Let my soul prosper and be in health, in that peace and righteousness which his government brings. Ps. lxxii. 3. Let me have victory over those lusts that war against my soul, and let divine grace go on in my heart, conquering and to conquer.—*Matthew Henry.*

Verse 25.—*"Save now,"* or, *hosanna.* Our thanksgivings on earth must always be accompanied with prayers for further mercies, and the continuance of our prosperity ; our hallelujahs with hosannas.—*Ingram Cobbin.*

Verse 25.—*"Save now, I beseech thee, O* LORD," etc. Hosanna. The cry of the multitudes as they thronged in our Lord's triumphal procession into Jerusalem (Matt. xxi. 9, 18 ; Mar. xi. 9, 15, John xii. 13) was taken from this Psalm, from which they were accustomed to recite the 25th and 26th verses at the Feast of Tabernacles. On that occasion the great *Hallel*, consisting of Psalms cxiii.—cxviii. was chanted by one of the priests and at certain intervals the multitudes joined in the responses, waving their branches of willow and palm, and shouting as they waved them, Hallelujah, or *Hosanna*, or "O LORD, *I beseech thee, send now prosperity."* This was done at the recitation of the first and last verses of Ps. cxviii. ; but according to the school of Hillel, at the words *"Save now, we beseech thee."* The school of Shammai, on the contrary, say it was at the words, *"Send now prosperity."* Rabban Gamaliel and R. Joshua were observed by R. Akiba to wave their branches only at the words, *"Save now, we beseech thee "* (Mishna, *Succah*, iii. 9). On each of the seven days during which the feast lasted the people thronged the court of the temple, and went in procession about the altar, setting their boughs bending towards it ; the trumpets sounding as they shouted *Hosanna.* But on the seventh day they marched seven times round the altar, shouting meanwhile the great Hosannah to the sound of the trumpets of the Levites (Lightfoot, *Temple Service*, xvi. 2). The very children who could wave the palm branches were expected to take part in the solemnity (Mishna, *Succah*, iii. 15 ; Matt iii. 15). From the custom of waving the boughs of myrtle and willow during the service the name Hosannah was ultimately transferred to the boughs themselves, so that according to Elias Levita (*Thisbi*. s. v.), "the bundles of the willows of the brook which they carry at the Feast of Tabernacles are called Hosannahs."—*William Aldis Wright, in "Smith's Dictionary of the Bible,"* 1863.

Verse 25.—*" Send now prosperity."* God will send it, but his people must pray for it. " I came for thy prayers," Dan. x. 12.—*John Trapp.*

Verse 26.—*"Blessed is he that cometh in the name of the* LORD." The difference between Christ and Antichrist is to be noticed, because Christ did not come in his own name, but in the name of the Father ; of which he himself testified, John v., *"I am come in my Father's name, and ye receive me not ; if another shall come in his own name, him ye will receive."* Thus all faithful ministers of the Church must not come in their own name, or the name of Baal, or of Mammon and their own belly, but in the name of God, with a lawful call ; concerning which see **Heb. v.**, Rom. x. and xv.—*Solomon Gesner.*

Verse 27.—*"God is the* LORD, *which hath shewed us light."* The Psalmist was clearly possessed of light, for he says, *"God is the* LORD, *which hath shewed us light."* He was evidently, then, possessed of light ; and this light was in him as " the light of life." This light had shone into his heart ; the rays and beams of divine truth had penetrated into his conscience. He carried about with him a light which had come from God ; in this light he saw light, and in this light he discerned everything which the light manifested. Thus by this internal light he knew what was good and what was evil, what was sweet and what was bitter, what was true and what was false, what was spiritual and what was natural. He did not say, This light came from creature exertion, this light was the produce of my own wisdom, this light was nature transmuted by some action of my own will, and thus gradually rose into existence from long and assiduous cultivation. But he ascribes the whole of that light which he possessed unto God the Lord, as the sole author and the only giver of it. Now, if God the Lord has ever showed you and me the same light which he showed his servant of old, we carry about with us more or less of a solemn conviction that we have received this light from him. There will indeed, be many clouds of darkness to cover it ; there will often be doubts and fears, hovering like mists and fogs over our souls, whether the light which we have received be from God or not. But in solemn moments when the Lord is pleased a little to revive his work ; at times and seasons when he condescends to draw forth the affections of our hearts unto himself, to bring us into his presence, to hide us in some measure in the hollow of his hand, and give us access unto himself, at such moments and seasons we carry about with us, in spite of all our unbelief, in spite of all the suggestions of the enemy, in spite of all doubts and fears and suspicions that rise from the depths of the carnal mind, in spite of all these counter-workings and underminings, we carry about with us at these times a solemn conviction that we have light, and that this light we have received from God. And why so ? Because we can look back to a time when we walked in no such light, when we felt no such light, when everything spiritual and heavenly was dark to us, and we were dark to them.

Those things which the Spirit of God enables a man to do, are in Scripture sometimes called *sacrifices.* " That we may offer," we read, " spiritual *sacrifices* acceptable to God by Jesus Christ." The apostle speaks of " receiving of Epaphroditus the things which were sent from the brethen at Philippi ; an odour of a sweet smell ; a *sacrifice* acceptable and well-pleasing to God." Phil. iv. 18. So he says to the Hebrew church : " But to do good and to communicate (that is, to the wants of God's people), forget not ; for with such *sacrifices* God is well pleased." Heb. xiii. 16. Well, then, these spiritual sacrifices which a man offers unto God are bound also *to the horns of the altar.* They are not well-pleasing in the sight of God, except they are bound to the horns of the altar, so as to derive all their acceptance from the altar. Our prayers are only acceptable to God as they are offered through the cross of Jesus. Our praises and thanksgivings are only acceptable to God as they are connected with the cross of Christ, and ascend to the Father through the propitiation of his dear Son. The ordinances of God's house are only acceptable to God as spiritual sacrifices, when they are bound to the horns of the altar. Both the ordinances of the New Testament—baptism and the Lord's supper —have been bound by the hands of God himself to the horns of the altar ; and no one either rightly went through the one, or rightly received the other, who had not been first spiritually bound by the same hand to the horns of the altar. Every act of liberality, every cup of cold water given in the name of a disciple, every feeling of sympathy and affection, every kind word, every compassionate action shown to a brother ; all and each are only acceptable to God as they ascend to him through the mediation of his dear Son. And, therefore, every sacrifice of our own comfort, or of our own advantage, of our own time, or of our own money, for the profit of God's children, is only a spiritual and acceptable sacrifice so far as it is bound to the horns of the altar, linked on to the cross of Jesus, and deriving all its fragrance and odour from its connection with the incense there offered by the Lord of life and glory.—*J. C. Philpot.*

Verse 27.—How comfortable is the light ! 'Tis so comfortable that light and comfort are often put for the same thing : " *God is the* LORD, *which hath shewed us light,"* that is, the light of counsel what to do, and the light of comfort in what we do, or after all our sufferings. Light is not only a candle held to us to do our work by, but it comforts and cheereth us in our work. Eccl. xi. 7.—*Joseph Caryl.*

Verse 27.—" *Shewed us light* : " " *bind the sacrifice.*" Here is somewhat received ; somewhat to be returned. God hath blessed us, and we must bless God. His grace and our gratitude, are the two lines my discourse must run upon. They are met in my text ; let them as happily meet in your hearts, and they shall not leave you till they bring you to heaven.—*Thomas Adams.*

Verse 27.—"*Bind the sacrifice with cords,*" etc. The sacrifice we are to offer to God, in gratitude for redeeming love, is ourselves, not to be slain upon the altar, but " living sacrifices " (Rom. xii. 1) to be bound to the altar ; spiritual sacrifices of prayer and praise, in which our hearts must be fixed and engaged, as the sacrifice was bound " with cords to the horns of the altar."—*Matthew Henry.*

Verse 27.—"*Bind the sacrifice,*" etc. 'Tis a saying among the Hebrews, that the beasts that were offered in sacrifice, they were the most struggling beasts of all the rest ; such is the nature of us unthankful beasts, when we should love God again, we are readier to run away from him ; we must be tied to the altar with cords, to draw from us love or fear.—*Abraham Wright.*

Verse 27.—"*With cords.*" This word is sometimes used for thick *twisted cords*, Judges xv. 13 ; sometimes for *thick branches* of trees, used at some feasts, Ezek. xix. 11, Levit. xxiii. 40. Hereupon this sentence may two ways be read ; *bind the feast with thick branches*, or *bind the sacrifice with cords* ; both mean one thing that men should keep the festivity with joy and thanks to God, as Israel did at their solemnities.—*Henry Ainsworth.*

Verse 27.—"*Even unto the horns of the altar.*" Before these words must be understood, *lead it* : for the victims were bound to rings fixed in the floor. "*The horns* " were architectural ornaments, a kind of capitals, made of iron or of brass, somewhat in the form of the curved horns of an animal, projecting from the four angles of the altar. The officiating priest, when he prayed, placed his hands on them, and sometimes sprinkled them with the blood of the sacrifice : compare Exod. xxx. 3 ; Lev. iv. 7, 18. At the end of this verse the word *saying* must be supplied.—*Daniel Cresswell.*

Verse 27.—"*Unto the horns.*" That is, all the court over, until you come even to the horns of the altar, intending hereby many sacrifices or boughs.—*Henry Ainsworth.*

Verse 28.—"*God.*" The original for "*God* " gives force to this passage : Thou art my "*El* "—the Mighty One ; therefore will I praise thee : my "*Eloah* "—a varied form with substantially the same sense, " and I will extol thee "—lift thee high in glory and honour.—*Henry Cowles.*

Verse 28.—This " extolling the Lord " will accomplish one of the great ends of praise, viz., his exaltation. It is true that God both can and will exalt himself but it is at once the duty and the privilege of his people to exalt him. His name should be upborne and magnified by them ; the glory of that name is now, as it were, committed to them : what use are we making of the opportunity and the privilege ?—*Philip Bennet Power.*

HINTS TO PREACHERS.

Verses 1—4.—I. The subject of song—" O give thanks unto the Lord, for he is good." II. The chorus—" His mercy endureth for ever." III. The choir— " Let Israel now say," etc. ; " Let the house of Aaron," etc. ; " Let them that fear the Lord," etc. IV. The rehearsal—" Let them *now* say," that they may be better prepared for universal praise hereafter.

Verse 5.—I. The season for prayer—" in distress." II. The answer in season —" The Lord answered me." III. The answer beyond the request—" And set me," etc.

Verse 6.—I. When may a man know that God is on his side ? II. What confidence may that man enjoy who is assured of divine aid ?

Verse 7.—I. The value of true friends. II. The greater value of help from above.

Verses 8, 9.—*"Better."* It is wiser, surer, morally more right, more ennobling, more happy in result.

Verse 10.—Take a wide range and consider what has been done, should be done, and may be done " in the name of the Lord."

Verse 12.—I. Faith's innumerable annoyances. II. Their speedy end. III. Faith's complete victory.

Verse 13.—I. Our great antagonist. II. His fierce attacks. III. His evident object: "that I might fall." IV. His failure: "but the Lord helped me."

Verse 14.—I. Strength under affliction. II. Song in hope of deliverance. III. Salvation, or actual escape out of trial.

Verse 15.—The joy of Christian households. It is joy in salvation: it is expressed,—" The voice ": it abides: " the voice *is* " *:* it is joy in the protection and honour given by the Lord's right hand.

Verses 15, 16.—I. True joy is peculiar *to* the righteous. II. *In* their tabernacles: in their pilgrimage state. III. *For* salvation: rejoicing and salvation go together. IV. *From God*: " the right hand," etc.: three right hands; both the salvation and the joy are from the hand of the Father and the Son and the Holy Ghost; the right hand of each doeth valiantly.—*G. R.*

Verse 17.—I. Good men are often in special danger: Joseph in the pit; Moses in the ark of bulrushes; Job on the dunghill; David's narrow escapes from the hand of Saul; Paul let down in a basket; what a fruit basket was that! How much was suspended upon that cord! The salvation of how many! II. Good men have often a presentiment of their recovery from special danger: " I shall not die, but live." III. Good men have a special desire for the preservation of their lives: " live and declare the works of the Lord."—*G. R.*

Verses 17, 19, 22.—The victory of the risen Saviour and its far-reaching consequences: (1) Death is vanquished; (2) the gates of righteousness are opened; (3) the corner-stone of the church is laid.—*Deichert, in Lange's Commentary.*

Verse 18.—I. The afflictions of the people of God are chastisements. " The Lord hath chastened me." II. Those chastisements are often severe: " hath chastened me *sore*." III. The severity is limited: " it is not unto death."—*G. R.*

Verse 19.—I. Access to God desired. II. Humbly requested: " Open to me." III. Boldly accepted: " I will go into them." IV. Gratefully enjoyed: " And praise the Lord."

Verse 22.—In these words we may notice the following particulars. I. The metaphorical view in which the church is here represented, namely, that of a *house* or *building*. II. The character that our Immanuel bears with respect to this building; he is *the stone* in a way of eminence, without whom there can be no building, no house for God to dwell in among the children of men. III. The character of the workmen employed in this spiritual structure; they are called *builders*. IV. A fatal error they are charged with in building the house of God; they *refuse* the stone of God's choosing; they do not allow him a place in his own house. V. Notice the place that Christ should and shall have in this building, let the builders do their worst; he *is made the head stone of the corner*. The words immediately following declare how this effected, and how the saints are affected with the views of his exaltation, notwithstanding the malice of hell and earth: " This is the Lord's doing, and it is wonderful in our eyes."—*Ebenezer Erskine.*

Verses 22, 23.—I. The mystery stated. 1. That which is least esteemed by men as a means of salvation is most esteemed by God. 2. That which is most esteemed by God when made known is least esteemed by man. II. The mystery explained. The way of salvation is the Lord's doing, therefore marvellous in our eyes.—*G. R.*

Verses 22—25.—I. Christ rejected. II. Christ exalted. III. His exaltation is due to God alone. IV. His exaltation commences a new era. V. His exaltation suggests a new prayer. See Spurgeon's Sermon, No. 1,420.

Verse 24.—I. What is spoken of. 1. The gospel day. 2. The sabbath day. II. What is said of it. 1. It is given by God. 2. To be joyfully received by man.—*G. R.*

Verse 25.—What is church prosperity? Whence must it come? How can we obtain it?

Verse 25.—I. The object of the prayer. 1. Salvation from sin. 2. Prosperity in righteousness. II. The earnestness of the prayer : " I beseech thee, I beseech thee." III. The urgency of the prayer, " now—now "—now that the gates of righteousness are open, now that the foundation stone is laid, now that the gospel day has come—now, Lord ! now !—*G. R.*

Verse 27.—"*Bind the sacrifice,*" etc. Devotion is the mother, and she hath four daughters. 1. Constancy : " Bind the sacrifice." 2. Fervency : Bind it " with cords." 3. Wisdom. Bind it " to the altar." 4. Confidence. Even to the " horns " of the altar.—*Thomas Adams.*

Verse 27.—"*Bind the sacrifice with cords,*" etc. I. What is the sacrifice ? Our whole selves, every talent, all our time, property, position, mind, heart, temper, life to the last. II. Why does it need binding ? It is naturally restive. Long delay, temptations, wealth, rank, discouragement, scepticism, all tend to drive it from the altar. III. To what is it bound ? To the doctrine of atonement. To Jesus and his work. To Jesus and our work. IV. What are the cords ? Our own vows. The need of souls. Our joy in the work. The great reward. The love of Christ working upon us by the Holy Spirit.

Verse 28.—I. The gladdest fact in all the world : " Thou art my God." II. The fittest spirit in which to enjoy it : " Praise thee."

Verse 28.—I. The effect of Christ being sacrificed for us : " Thou art my God." II. The effect of our being offered as an acceptable sacrifice to him. " I will praise thee, I will exalt thee." Or, I. The covenant blessing : " Thou art my God." II. The covenant obligation : " I will praise thee."—*G. R.*

Verse 29.—I. The beginning and the end of salvation is mercy. II. The beginning and end of its requirements is thanksgiving.—*G. R.*

PSALM CXIX.

TITLE.—*There is no title to this Psalm, neither is any author's name mentioned. It is* THE LONGEST PSALM, *and this is a sufficiently distinctive name for it. It equals in bulk twenty-two Psalms of the average length of the Songs of Degrees. Nor is it long only ; for it equally excels in breadth of thought, depth of meaning, and height of fervour. It is like the celestial city which lieth four-square, and the height and the breadth of it are equal. Many superficial readers have imagined that it harps upon one string, and abounds in pious repetitions and redundancies ; but this arises from the shallowness of the reader's own mind : those who have studied this divine hymn, and carefully noted each line of it, are amazed at the variety and profundity of the thought. Using only a few words, the writer has produced permutations and combinations of meaning which display his holy familiarity with his subject, and the sanctified ingenuity of his mind. He never repeats himself ; for if the same sentiment recurs it is placed in a fresh connection, and so exhibits another interesting shade of meaning. The more one studies it the fresher it becomes. As those who drink the Nile water like it better every time they take a draught, so does this Psalm become the more full and fascinating the oftener you turn to it. It contains no idle word ; the grapes of this cluster are almost to bursting full with the new wine of the kingdom. The more you look into this mirror of a gracious heart the more you will see in it. Placid on the surface as the sea of glass before the eternal throne, it yet contains within its depths an ocean of fire, and those who devoutly gaze into it shall not only see the brightness, but feel the glow of the sacred flame. It is loaded with holy sense, and is as weighty as it is bulky. Again and again have we cried while studying it, " Oh the depths ! " Yet these depths are hidden beneath an apparent simplicity, as Augustine has well and wisely said, and this makes the exposition all the more difficult. Its obscurity is hidden beneath a veil of light, and hence only those discover it who are in thorough earnest, not only to look on the word, but, like the angels, to look into it.*

The Psalm is alphabetical. Eight stanzas commence with one letter, and then another eight with the next letter, and so the whole Psalm proceeds by octonaries quite through the twenty-two letters of the Hebrew alphabet. Besides which, there are multitudes of appositions of sense, and others of those structural formalities with which the oriental mind is pleased,—formalities very similar to those in which our older poets indulged. The Holy Spirit thus deigned to speak to men in forms which were attractive to the attention and helpful to the memory. He is often plain or elegant in his manner, but he does not disdain to be quaint or formal if thereby his design of instruction can be the more surely reached. He does not despise even contracted and artificial modes of speech, if by their use he can fix his teaching upon the mind. Isaac Taylor has worthily set forth the lesson of this fact :—" In the strictest sense this composition is conditioned ; *nevertheless in the highest sense is it an utterance of spiritual life ; and in thus finding these seemingly opposed elements, intimately commingled as they are throughout this Psalm, a lesson full of meaning is silently conveyed to those who shall receive it—that the conveyance of the things of God to the human spirit is in no way damaged or impeded, much less is it deflected or vitiated by its subjugation to those modes of utterance which most of all bespeak their adaptation to the infancy and the childlike capacity of the recipient."*

AUTHOR.--*The fashion among modern writers is, as far as possible, to take every Psalm from David. As the critics of this school are usually unsound in doctrine and unspiritual in tone, we gravitate in the opposite direction, from a natural suspicion of everything which comes from so unsatisfactory a quarter. We believe that David wrote this Psalm. It is Davidic in tone and expression, and it tallies with David's experience in many interesting points. In our youth our teacher called it " David's pocket book," and we incline to the opinion then expressed that here we have the royal diary written at various times throughout a long life. No, we cannot give up this Psalm to the enemy. " This is David's spoil." After long reading an author one gets to know his style, and a measure of discernment is acquired by which his composition is detected even if his name be concealed ; we feel a kind of critical certainty that the hand of David is in this thing, yea, that it is altogether his own.*

SUBJECT.—*The one theme is the word of the Lord. The Psalmist sets his subject* in many lights, and treats of it in divers ways, but he seldom omits to mention the word of the Lord in each verse under some one or other of the many names by which he knows it ; and even if the name be not there, the subject is still heartily pursued in every stanza. He who wrote this wonderful song was saturated with those books of Scripture which he possessed. Andrew Bonar tells of a simple Christian in a farmhouse who had meditated the Bible through three times. This is precisely what this Psalmist had done,—he had gone past reading into meditation. Like Luther, David had shaken every fruit-tree in God's garden, and gathered golden fruit therefrom. " The most," says Martin Boos, " read their Bibles like cows that stand in the thick grass, and trample under their feet the finest flowers and herbs." It is to be feared that we too often do the like. This is a miserable way of treating the pages of inspiration. May the Lord prevent us from repeating that sin while reading this precious Psalm.

There is an evident growth in the subject matter. The earlier verses are of such a character as to lend themselves to the hypothesis that the author was a young man, while many of the later passages could only have suggested themselves to age and wisdom. In every portion, however, it is the fruit of deep experience, careful observation, and earnest meditation. If David did not write it, there must have lived another believer of exactly the same order of mind as David, and he must have addicted himself to psalmody with equal ardour, and have been an equally hearty lover of Holy Writ.

Our best improvement of this sacred composition will come through getting our minds into intense sympathy with its subject. In order to this, we might do well to commit it to memory. Philip Henry's daughter wrote in her diary, " I have of late taken some pains to learn by heart Psalm CXIX., and have made some progress therein." She was a sensible, godly woman. Having done this, we should consider the fulness, certainty, clearness, and sweetness of the word of God, since by such reflections we are likely to be stirred up to a warm affection for it. What favoured beings are those to whom the Eternal God has written a letter in his own hand and style. What ardour of devotion, what diligence of composition can produce a worthy eulogium for the divine testimonies ! If ever one such has fallen from the pen of man it is this CXIX. Psalm, which might well be called the holy soul's soliloquy before an open Bible.

This sacred ode is a little Bible, the Scriptures condensed, a mass of Bibline, Holy Writ rewritten in holy emotions and actions. Blessed are they who can read and understand these saintly aphorisms ; they shall find golden apples in this true Hesperides, and come to reckon that this Psalm, like the whole Scripture which it praises, is a pearl island, or, better still, a garden of sweet flowers.

NOTES RELATING TO THE PSALM AS A WHOLE.

Eulogium upon the whole Psalm.—This psalm shines and shows itself among the rest.

Velut inter ignes
*Luna minores.**

a star in the firmament of the Psalms, of the first and greatest magnitude. This will readily appear if you consider either the manner it is composed in, or the matter it is composed of. The manner it is composed in is very elegant. The matter it is composed of is very excellent. 1. The manner it is composed in is very elegant; full of art, rule, method; theological matter in a logical manner, a spiritual alphabet framed and formed according to the Hebrew alphabet. 2. The matter it is composed of is very excellent; full of rare sublimities, deep mysteries, gracious activities, yea, glorious ecstacies. The Psalm is made up of three things,—1. prayers, 2. praises, 3. protestations. Payers to God; praises of God; protestations unto God.—*Rev. W. Simmons, in a sermon in the " Morning Exercises,"* 1661.

Eulogium.—This Psalm is called the Alphabet of Divine Love, the Paradise of all the Doctrines, the Storehouse of the Holy Spirit, the School of Truth, also the deep mystery of the Scriptures, where the whole moral discipline of all the virtues shines brightly. And as all moral instruction is delightsome, therefore this Psalm because excelling in this kind of instruction, should be called delightsome, inasmuch as it surpasses the rest. The other Psalms, truly, as lesser stars shine somewhat; but this burns with the meridian heat of its full brightness, and is wholly resplendent with moral loveliness.—*Johannes Paulus Palanterius,* 1600.

Eulogium.—In our German version it has the appropriate inscription, " The Christian's golden A B C of the praise, love, power, and use of the Word of God."—*Franz Delitzsch,* †1871.

Eulogium.—It is recorded of the celebrated St. Augustine, who among his voluminous works left a Comment on the Book of Psalms, that he delayed to comment on this one till he had finished the whole Psalter; and then yielded only to the long and vehement urgency of his friends, " because," he says, " as often as I essayed to think thereon, it always exceeded the powers of my intent thought and the utmost grasp of my faculties." While one ancient father † entitles this Psalm " the perfection of teaching and instruction "; another ‡ says that " it applies an all-containing medicine to the varied spiritual diseases of men—sufficing to perfect those who long for perfect virtue, to rouse the slothful, to refresh the dispirited, and to set in order the relaxed; " to which might be added many like testimonies of ancient and modern commentators on it.—*William De Burgh,* 1860.

Eulogium.—In proportion as this Psalm seemeth more open, so much the more deep doth it appear to me; so that I cannot show how deep it is. For in others, which are understood with difficulty, although the sense lies hid in obscurity, yet the obscurity itself appeareth; but in this, not even this is the case; since it is superficially such, that it seemeth not to need an expositor, but only a reader and listener.—*Augustine,* 354—430.

Eulogium.—In Matthew Henry's " Account of the Life and Death of his father, Philip Henry," he says: " Once, pressing the study of the Scriptures, he advised us to take a verse of this Psalm every morning to meditate upon, and so go over the Psalm twice in the year; and that, saith he, will bring you to be in love with all the rest of the Scriptures. He often said, " All grace grows as love to the word of God grows."

Eulogium.—It is strange that of all the pieces of the Bible which my mother taught me, that which cost me most to learn, and which was to my child's mind most repulsive—the 119th Psalm—has now become of all the most precious to me in its overflowing and glorious passion of love for the law of God.—*John Ruskin, in " Fors Clavigera."*

Eulogium.—This Psalm is a prolonged meditation upon the excellence of the word of God, upon its effects, and the strength and happiness which it gives to a

---

* And like the moon, the feebler fires among,
Conspicuous shines." —*Horace.*

† St. Hilary. ‡ Theodoret.

man in every position. These reflections are interspersed with petitions, in which the Psalmist, deeply feeling his natural infirmity, implores the help of God for assistance to walk in the way mapped out for him in the divine oracles. In order to be able to understand and to enjoy this remarkable Psalm, and that we may not be repelled by its length and by its repetitions, we must have had, in some measure at least, the same experiences as its author, and, like him, have learned to love and practise the sacred word. Moreover, this Psalm is in some sort a touch-stone for the spiritual life of those who read it. The sentiments expressed in it perfectly harmonise with what the historical books and other Psalms teach concerning David's obedience and his zeal for God's glory. There are, however, within it words which breathe so elevated a piety, that they can have their full sense and perfect truthfulness only in the mouth of Him of whom the prophet-king was the type.—*From the French of Armand de Mestral*, 1856.

Eulogium.—The 119th Psalm has been spoken of by a most distinguished living rationalistic critic (Professor Reuss) as "not poetry at all, but simply a litany— a species of chaplet." Such does not seem to be the opinion of the angels of God, and of the redeemed spirits, when that very poem supplies with the language of praise—the pæan of victory, "Just and true are thy ways" (Rev. xv. 3) ; the cry of the angel of the waters, "Thou art righteous, O Lord !" (Rev. xvi. 5) ; the voice of much people in heaven, "True and righteous are his judgments" (Rev. xix. 2) ; what is this but the exclamation of him, whoever he may have been, who wrote the Psalm—"Righteous art thou, O Lord, and upright are thy judgments" (Psalm cxix. 137).—*William Alexander, in "The Quiver,"* 1880.

Incident.—In the midst of a London season ; in the stir and turmoil of a political crisis, 1819 ; William Wilberforce writes in his Diary—"Walked from Hyde Park Corner repeating the 119th Psalm in great comfort."—*William Alexander, in "The Witness of the Psalms."* 1877.

Incident.—George Wishart, the chaplain and biographer of "the great Marquis of Montrose," as he was called, would have shared the fate of his illustrious patron but for the following singular expedient. When upon the scaffold, he availed himself of the custom of the times, which permitted the condemned to choose a Psalm to be sung. He selected the 119th Psalm, and before two-thirds of the Psalm had been sung, a pardon arrived, and his life was preserved. It may not be out of place to add that the George Wishart, Bishop of Edinburgh, above referred to, has been too often confounded with the godly martyr of the same name who lived and died a century previously. We only mention the incident because it has often been quoted as a singular instance of the providential escape of a saintly personage ; whereas it was the very ingenious device of a person who, according to Woodrow, was more renowned for shrewdness than for sanctity. The length of this Psalm was sagaciously employed as the means of gaining time, and, happily, the expedient succeeded.—*C. H. S.*

Alphabetical Arrangement.—It is observed that the 119th Psalm is disposed according to the letters of the Hebrew alphabet, perhaps to intimate that children, when they begin to learn their alphabet, should learn that Psalm.—*Nathanael Hardy,* 1618—1670.

Alphabetical Arrangement.—True it is that the verses indeed begin not either with the English or yet the Latin letters, but with the Hebrew, wherein David made and wrote this Psalm. The will and purpose of the Holy Ghost is to make us to feel and understand that the doctrine herein contained is not only set down for great clerks which have gone to school for ten or twenty years ; but also for the most simple ; to the end none should pretend any excuse of ignorance.—*From Calvin's Two-and-Twenty Sermons upon the cxixth Psalm,* 1580.

Alphabetical Arrangement.—There may be something more than fancy in the remark, that Christ's name, "*the Alpha and Omega*"—equivalent to declaring him all that which every letter of the alphabet could express—may have had a reference to the peculiarity of this Psalm,—a Psalm in which (with the exception of ver. 84 and 122, exceptions that make the rule more marked) every verse speaks of God's revelation of himself to man.—*Andrew A. Bonar,* 1859.

Alphabetical Arrangement.—Origen says it is alphabetical because it contains the elements or principles of all knowledge and wisdom ; and that it repeats each letter eight times, because eight is the number of perfection.

Alphabetical Arrangement.—That the unlearned reader may understand what is meant by the Psalm being alphabetical, we append the following specimen upon the section *Aleph :*—

A blessing is on them that are undefiled in the way
   and walk in the law of Jehovah ;
A blessing is on them that keep his testimonies,
   and seek him with their whole heart ;
Also on them that do no wickedness,
   but walk in his ways.
A law hast thou given unto us,
   that we should diligently keep thy commandments.
Ah ! Lord, that my ways were made so direct
   that I might keep thy statutes !
And then shall I not be confounded,
   while I have respect unto all thy commandments.
As for me, I will thank thee with an unfeigne heart,
   when I shall have learned thy righteous judgments.
An eye will I have unto thy ceremonies,
   O forsake me not utterly.

From " *The Psalms Chronologically Arranged. By Four Friends.*" 1867.

Author and Subject.—This is a Psalm by itself, it excels them all, and shines brightest in this constellation. It is much longer than any of them ; more than twice as long as any of them. It is not making long prayers that Christ censures ; but making them for a pretence ; which intimates that they are in themselves good and commendable. It seems to me to be a collection of David's pious and devout ejaculations, the short and sudden breathings of his soul to God, which he wrote down as they occurred, and towards the latter end of his time gathered them out of his day-book where they lay scattered, added to them many like words, and digested them into this Psalm, in which there is seldom any coherence between the verses ; but, like Solomon's proverbs, it is a chest of gold rings, not a chain of gold links. And we may not only learn by the Psalmist's example to accustom ourselves to such pious ejaculations, which are an excellent means of maintaining constant communion with God, and keeping the heart in frame for the more solemn exercises of religion ; but we must make use of the Psalmist's words, both for the exciting and the expressing of our devout affections. Some have said of this Psalm, He that shall read it considerately, it will either warm him or shame him ; and this is true.—*Matthew Henry,* 1662—1714.

Author and Subject.—This very singular poem has descended to us without name or title ; and with some difficulty in fixing its date. It is by many critics supposed to have been written by King David ; and there is in it so much of the peculiar language and strain of feeling that distinguish his compositions, with so perpetually shifting a complication of every condition of life through the whole scale of adversity and prosperity, that seems to distinguish his own history from that of every other individual, as to afford much reason for adopting this opinion, and for inducing us to regard it as a series of poems composed originally by David, at different times under different circumstances, or collected by him, and arranged in their present form, from floating passages of antecedent bards, that were in danger of being lost or forgotten. If this view of the subject approaches to correctness, it may constitute one of the poems which Josephus tells us David gave to the public on the re-establishment of tranquillity after the discomfiture of the traitor Sheba, and the return of the ten refractory tribes to a state of loyalty.

This poem, or rather collection of poems, is designed for private devotion, alone ; and we have, here, no distinct reference to any historical or national event, to any public festival, or any place, of congregational worship ; though a few general hints are occasionally scattered upon one or two of these points. We have nothing of David or Solomon, of Moses or Aaron, of Egypt or the journey through the wilderness ; nothing of Jerusalem, or Mount Zion, or Ephrata ; of the temple, or the altar, of the priests or the people. It consists of the holy effusions of a devout soul, in a state of closet retirement, unbosoming itself in blessed communion with its God, and descanting on the holy cycle of his attributes, and the consolations of his revealed will under every trial to which man can be exposed.

The form of this Psalm is singular ; and, though alphabetical, it is without an exact parallel in any of the others. It is, in truth, a set or collection of canticles, or smaller poems, each forming a literal octrain or range of eight couplets ; the first octrain taking the first letter of the Hebrew alphabet for the opening letter of every line ; the second, the second letter, and in the same manner proceeding through the whole extent of the twenty-two letters that constitute the alphabet of the Hebrew tongue ; and consequently extending the entire poem to twenty-two octrains or discourses of eight lines each. Poetical collections of this kind are still common in the East, and especially among the Persian poets, who distinguish their separate poems, or canticles, by the name of gazels, and the entire set of fasciculus by that of diwan. By the Arabian poet Temoa they are happily denominated strings of pearls : an idea which the Persian poets have caught hold of, and playfully illustrated in various ways.

From this peculiarity of construction the couplets of Psalm cxix. may, in the Hebrew tongue, be committed to memory with far more ease than in any modern language : for, as each versicle under every octrain commences with the same letter, and the progressive octrains follow up the order of the alphabet, the letter becomes a powerful help to the memory of the learner, and enables him to go through the whole without hesitation.—*John Mason Good*, 1764—1827.

Author and Subject.—It is at least possible that the plaited work of so long a Psalm, which, in connection with all that is artificial about it from beginning to end gives us a glimpse of the subdued, afflicted mien of a confessor, is the work of one in prison, who whiled away his time with this plaiting together of his complaints and his consolatory thoughts.—*Franz Delitzsch*, 1871.

Subject.—The 119th Psalm is the appropriate sermon, after the Hallel, on the text which is its epitome (Ps. i. 1, 2), " Blessed is the man that walketh not in the counsel of the ungodly . . . . . but his delight is in the law of the Lord." Except in two verses (122, 132), the law is expressly extolled in every verse.—*Andrew Robert Fausset, in " Studies in the CL. Psalms,"* 1876.

Subject.—Every verse contains in it either a praise of God's word, from some excellent quality of it ; or a protestation of David his unfeigned affection towards it ; or else a prayer for grace, to conform himself unto it ; for unto one of these three, —*praises*, *prayers*, or *protestations*, may all the verses of this Psalm be reduced.— *William Cowper.*

Subject.—I know of no part of the Holy Scriptures where the nature and evidences of true and sincere godliness are so fully and largely insisted on and delineated as in the 119th Psalm. The Psalmist declares his design in the first verses of the Psalm, keeps his eye on it all along, and pursues it to the end. The excellency of holiness is represented as the immediate object of a spiritual taste and delight. God's law —that grand expression and emanation of the holiness of God's nature, and prescription of holiness to the creature—is all along represented as the great object of the love, the complacence, and the rejoicing of the gracious nature, which prizes God's commandments " above gold, yea, the finest gold ; " and to which they are " sweeter than honey and the honey-comb."—*Jonathan Edwards*, 1703—1758.

Subject and Connection of its parts.—This Psalm, no less excellent in virtue than large in bulk, containeth manifold reflections on the nature, the properties, the adjuncts, and effects of God's law ; many sprightly ejaculations about it, conceived in different forms of speech ; some in way of petition, some of thanksgiving, some of resolution, some of assertion or aphorism ; many useful directions, many zealous exhortations to the observance of it ; the which are not ranged in any strict order, but, like a variety of wholesome herbs in a fair field, do with a grateful confusion lie dispersed, as they freely did spring in the heart, or were suggested by the devout spirit of him who indited this Psalm, where no coherence of sentences being designed, we may consider any one of them absolutely, or by itself.—*Isaac Barrow*, 1630—1677.

Subject and Connection.—Upon considering the matter of this Psalm, it will be found that the stanzas beginning with the same letter have very little, and sometimes not the least connection with each other ; and the praises of Jehovah, the excellencies of his law, and supplications, are mingled together without order or coherence. Hence I have been led to think, that the Psalm was never intended for an ode to be performed at one time, *tout de suite*, but was a collection of stanzas of prayer and praise arranged in alphabetical order, from which the pious worshipper might select such as suited his situation and circumstances, using, as he saw fit, either one line or two lines of each stanza, and uniting them together so as to make a connected and coherent composition proper for the occasion and the circumstances in which he was.—*Stephen Street*, 1790.

Subject and Connection.—In view of the alphabetic or acrostic arrangement of this Psalm, Dr. Adam Clarke ventures the following remark :—" All *connection*, as might naturally be expected, is sacrificed to this artificial and methodical arrangement." This is hardly probable, as Dr. Clarke himself felt when he endeavoured in his Analysis " to show the connection which the eight verses of each part have among themselves." Each group of eight verses seems to have a theme or subject common to itself, and while the peculiar structure of the Psalm has obscured this arrangement, so that it is sometimes difficult to trace, it must not be said that the connection is destroyed.—*F. G. Marchant, of Hitchin*, 1879.

Subject and Connection.—In stanza *Aleph* the blessedness of walking in the way of God's word is declared ; in *Beth*, that word is pronounced to be the only safeguard of the young against sin ; in *Gimel*, is a pious resolve to cleave to the word, in spite of the sneers of the world. *Daleth* expresses a longing for the consolation of God's word to fortify good resolutions ; *He* declares an earnest desire for grace to obey the word ; *Vau* expresses firm trust and intense delight in God's word, and an earnest desire to see its full accomplishment ; *Zain* describes the blessed comfort derived from God's word in evil days ; *Cheth* utters the joy which is inspired by the consciousness that God is his portion, and by communion with those that love his word, and by a persuasion that all things work for good to all who love him ; *Teth* describes the blessed effects of affliction, as described in God's word, in weaning the soul from the world and drawing it nearer to him ; *Jod* represents the example of the resignation and piety of the faithful, especially in affliction, as gently drawing others to God ; *Caph* is an expression of intense desire for the coming of God's kingdom, and the subjection of all things to him, according to the promises of his word. *Lamed* declares that the word of God is everlasting, immutable, and infinite in perfection : and, therefore, in *Mem* it is asserted that God's word is the only treasure-house of true wisdom ; and in *Nun*, that it is the only beacon-light in the darkness and storms of this world ; and in *Samech*, that all sceptical attempts to undermine men's faith in that word are hateful and deadly, and will recoil with confusion on those that make them ; and in *Ain*, is a prayer for steadfastness and soundness of heart and mind, amid all the impiety and unbelief of a godless world ; which is followed by an assurance in *Pe*, that the word of God brings its own light and comfort with it to those who earnestly pray for them, and fills the heart with compassion for those who despise it. In *Tzaddi* is a declaration that even the youthful soul may stand strong and steadfast, if it has faith in the purity, and truth, and righteousness of God's law ; and therefore in *Koph*, is an earnest prayer for the grace of faith, especially, as is expressed in *Resh*, in times of affliction, desolation, and persecution, as *Schin* adds, from the powerful of this world ; but even then there is peace, joy, and exultation for those who love God's word. And therefore the Psalm concludes, in *Tau*, with an earnest prayer for the bestowal of the gifts of understanding, assistance, and grace from God, to the soul which owns its weakness, and rests on him alone for support.—*Christopher Wordsworth*, 1872.

Subject and Connection.—This Psalm has been called *Psalmus literatus*, or *alphabetites ;* and the Masora calls it alpa betha rabba. The name Jehovah occurs twenty-two times in the Psalm. Its theme is the word of God, which it mentions under one of the ten terms, תּוֹרָה, *law ;* דֶּרֶךְ, *way ;* עֵדָה, *testimony ;* פִּקּוּד, *precept ;* חֹק, *statute ;* מִצְוָה, *commandments ;* מִשְׁפָּט, *judgment ;* דָּבָר, *word ;* אִמְרָה, *saying ;* אֱמֶת, *truth ;* in every verse except 122. The last of these terms is scarcely admissible as a term for the *word ;* but it has to suffice only in verse 90. According to this alphabetical series of eight stanzas, the word is the source of happiness to those who walk by it (*aleph*), of holiness to those who give heed to it (*beth*), of truth to those whose eyes the Lord opens by his Spirit (*gimel*), of law to those whose heart he renews (*daleth*), begets perseverance by its promises (*he*), reveals the mercy and salvation of the Lord (*vau*), awakens the comfort of hope in God (*zayin*), presents the Lord as the portion of the trusting soul (*cheth*), makes affliction instructive and chastening (*teth*), begets a fellowship in the fear of God (*jod*), and a longing for the full peace of salvation (*kaph*), is faithful and immutable (*lamed*), commands the approval of the heart (*mem*), is a light to the path (*nun*), from which to swerve is hateful (*samek*), warrants the plea of innocence (*ayin*), is a testimony to God's character and will (*pe*), is a law of rectitude (*tsade*), warrants the cry for salvation (*qoph*), and payer for deliverance from affliction (*resh*), and from persecution without a cause (*shin*), and assures of an answer in due time (*tau*).   There is here as much order as could be expected in a long alphabetical acrostic.—*James G. Murphy, in a " Commentary on the Book of Psalms,"* 1875.

Whole Psalm.—Dr. Luther and Hilary, and other excellent men, think that here a compendium of the whole of theology is briefly set forth : for the things which are said, generally, about the Scripture, and the word of God, and theology, are helpful to the examination of doctrinal questions.   In the first place, it speaks of the author of that doctrine.   Secondly, of its authority and certainty.   Thirdly, it is declared that the doctrine, contained in the Apostolic and Prophetic books, is perfect, and contains all things which are able to give us instruction unto everlasting salvation. Fourthly, it affirms the perspicuity of the Scripture.   Fifthly, its usefulness.   Sixthly, its true and saving knowledge and interpretation.   Lastly, it treats of practice ; how, for instance, the things which we are taught in the word of God are to be manifested and reduced to practice, in piety, moderation, obedience, faith, and hope, in temptations and adversities.—*Solomon Gesner, 1559—1605.*

Names given to the Law of God.—The things contained in Scripture, and drawn from it, are here called, 1. God's *law*, because they are enacted by him as our Sovereign.   2. His *way*, because they are the rule both of his providence and of our obedience.   3. His *testimonies*, because they are solemnly declared to the world, and attested beyond contradiction.   4. His *commandments*, because given with authority, and (as the word signifies) lodged with us as a trust.   5. His *precepts*, because prescribed to us, and not left indifferent.   6. His *word*, or saying, because it is the declaration of his mind, and Christ the essential, eternal Word is all in all in it.   7. His *judgments*, because framed in infinite wisdom, and because by them we must both judge and be judged.   8. His *righteousness*, because it is all holy, just, and good, and the rule and standard of righteousness.   9. His *statutes*, because they are fixed and determined, and of perpetual obligation.   10. His *truth* or *faithfulness*, because the principles upon which divine law is built are eternal truths.—*Matthew Henry.*

Names given to the Law of God.—The next peculiarity to be observed in this Psalm is, the regular recurrence of nine characteristic words, at least one or other of which is found in each distich, with one solitary exception, the second distich of the 12th division.   These words—*law, testimonies, precepts, statutes, commandments, judgments, word, saying,* and a word which only twice occurs as a characteristic— *way.*

These are, doubtless, all designations of the Divine Law ; but it were doing a deep injury to the cause of revealed truth to affirm that they are mere synonyms ; in other words, that the sentiments of this compendium of heavenly wisdom are little better than a string of tautologies.   The fact is, as some critics, both Jewish and Christian, have observed, that each of these terms designates the same law of God, but each under a different aspect, signifying the different modes of its promulgation, and of its reception.

Each of these words will now be examined in order, and an attempt will be made to discriminate them.

1. " *Law.*"   This word is formed from a verb which means to direct, to guide, to aim, to shoot forwards.   Its etymological meaning, then, would be a rule of conduct, a κανών σαφής.   It means God's law in general, whether it be that universal rule called the law of nature, or that which was revealed to his Church by Moses, and perfected by Christ.   In strictness, the law means a plain rule of conduct, rather placed clearly in man's sight, than enforced by any command ; that is to say, this word does not necessarily include its sanctions.

2. " *Testimonies* " are derived from a word which signifies to bear witness, to testify.   The ark of the tabernacle is so called, as are the two tables of stone, and the tabernacle ; the earnests and witnesses of God's inhabitation among his people. Testimonies are more particularly God's revealed law ; the witnesses and confirmation of his promises made to his people, and earnests of his future salvation.

3. " *Precepts*," from a word which means *to place in trust*, mean something entrusted to man, " that is committed to thee " ; appointments of God, which consequently have to do with the conscience, for which man is responsible, as an intelligent being.

4. " *Statutes.*"   The verb from which this word is formed means to engrave or

inscribe. The word means a definite, prescribed, written law. The term is applied to Joseph's law about the portion of the priests in Egypt, to the law about the passover, etc. But in this Psalm it has a more internal meaning ;—that moral law of God which is engraven on the fleshy tables of the heart ; the inmost and spiritual apprehension of his will : not so obvious as the law and testimonies, and a matter of more direct spiritual communication than his precepts ; the latter being more elaborated by the efforts of the mind itself, divinely guided indeed, but perhaps more instrumentally, and less passively employed.

5. " *Commandments*," derived from a verb signifying to command or ordain. Such was God's command to Adam about the tree ; to Noah about constructing the ark.

6. " *Judgments*," derived from a word signifying to govern, to judge or determine, mean judicial ordinances and decisions ; legal sanctions.

7. " *Word*." There are two terms, quite distinct Hebrew, but both rendered " word " in each of our authorised versions. The latter of these is rendered "*saying*" in the former volume of this work. They are closely connected : since out of twenty-two passages in which " word " occurs, in fourteen it is parallel to it, or in connection with, " *saying*." From this very circumstance it is evident they are not synonymous.

The term here rendered " *word* " seems the Λογος, or Word of God, in its most divine sense ; the announcement of God's revealed will ; his command ; his oracle ; at times, the special communication to the prophets. The ten commandments are called by this term in Exodus ; and דְּבִיר is the oracle in the temple. In this Psalm it may be considered as,—(1) God's revealed commandments in general. (2) As a revealed promise of certain blessings to the righteous. (3) As a thing committed to him as the minister of God. (4) As a rule of conduct ; a channel of illumination.

8. As to the remaining word " *way*," that occurs but twice as a characteristic word, and the place in which it occurs must rather be considered as exceptions to the general rule ; so that I am not disposed to consider it as intended to be a cognate expression with the above. At all events, its meaning is so direct and simple as to require no explanation ; a plain rule of conduct ; in its higher sense, the assisting grace of God through Christ our Lord, who is the Way, the Truth, and the Life. *John Jebb*, 1846.

EXPOSITION OF VERSES 1 TO 8.

BLESSED *are* the undefiled in the way, who walk in the law of the LORD.

2 Blessed *are* they that keep his testimonies, *and that* seek him with the whole heart.

3 They also do no iniquity : they walk in his ways.

4 Thou hast commanded *us* to keep thy precepts diligently.

5 O that my ways were directed to keep thy statutes !

6 Then shall I not be ashamed, when I have respect unto all thy commandments.

7 I will praise thee with uprightness of heart, when I shall have learned thy righteous judgments.

8 I will keep thy statutes : O forsake me not utterly.

These first eight verses are taken up with a contemplation of the blessedness which comes through keeping the statutes of the Lord. The subject is treated in a devout manner rather than in a didactic style. Heart-fellowship with God is enjoyed through a love of that word which is God's way of communing with the soul by his Holy Spirit. Prayer and praise and all sorts of devotional acts and feelings gleam through the verses like beams of sunlight through an olive grove. You are not only instructed, but influenced to holy emotion, and helped to express the same.

Lovers of God's holy words are blessed, because they are preserved from defilement (verse 1), because they are made practically holy (verses 2 and 3), and are led to follow after God sincerely and intensely (verse 2). It is seen that this holy walking must be desirable because God commands it (verse 4) ; therefore the pious soul prays for it (verse 5), and feels that its comfort and courage must depend upon obtaining it (verse 6). In the prospect of answered prayer, yea, while the prayer is being answered the heart is full of thankfulness (verse 7), and is fixed in solemn resolve not to miss the blessing if the Lord will give enabling grace (verse 8).

The changes are rung upon the words " *way* "—" undefiled in the way," " walk in his ways," " O that my ways were directed " ; " *keep* "—" keep his testimonies," " keep thy precepts diligently," " directed to keep," " I will keep " ; and " *walk* "— " walk in the law," " walk in his ways." Yet there is no tautology, nor is the same thought repeated, though to the careless reader it may seem so.

The change from statements about others and about the Lord to more personal dealing with God begins in the third verse, and becomes more clear as we advance, till in the later verses the communion becomes most intense and soul moving. O that every reader may feel the glow.

1. " *Blessed.*" The Psalmist is so enraptured with the word of God that he regards it as his highest ideal of blessedness to be conformed to it. He has gazed on the beauties of the perfect law, and, as if this verse were the sum and outcome of all his emotions, he exclaims, " Blessed is the man whose life is the practical transcript of the will of God." True religion is not cold and dry ; it has its exclamations and raptures. We not only judge the keeping of God's law to be a wise and proper thing, but we are warmly enamoured of its holiness, and cry out in adoring wonder, " Blessed are the undefiled ! " meaning thereby, that we eagerly desire to become such ourselves, and wish for no greater happiness than to be perfectly holy. It may be that the writer laboured under a sense of his own faultiness, and therefore envied the blessedness of those whose walk had been more pure and clean ; indeed, the very contemplation of the perfect law of the Lord upon which he now entered was quite enough to make him bemoan his own imperfections, and sigh for the blessedness of an undefiled walk.

True religion is always practical, for it does not permit us to delight ourselves in a perfect rule without exciting in us a longing to be conformed to it in our daily lives. A blessing belongs to those who hear and read and understand the word of the Lord ; yet is it a far greater blessing to be actually obedient to it, and to carry out in our walk and conversation what we learn in our searching of the Scriptures. Purity in our way and walk is the truest blessedness.

This first verse is not only a preface to the whole Psalm, but it may also be regarded as the text upon which the rest is a discourse. It is similar to the benediction of the first Psalm, which is set in the forefront of the entire book : there is a likeness between this 119th Psalm and the Psalter, and this is one point of it, that it begins with a benediction. In this, too, we see some foreshadowing of the Son of David, who began his great sermon as David began his great Psalm. It is well to open our mouth with blessings. When we cannot bestow them, we can show the way of obtaining them, and even if we do not yet possess them ourselves, it may be profitable to contemplate them, that our desires may be excited, and our souls moved to seek after them. Lord, if I am not yet so blessed to be among the undefiled in thy way, yet I will think much of the happiness which these enjoy, and set it before me as my life's ambition.

As David thus begins his Psalm, so should young men begin their lives, so should new converts commence their profession, so should all Christians begin every day. Settle it in your hearts as a first postulate and sure rule of practical science that holiness is happiness, and that it is our wisdom first to seek the Kingdom of God and his righteousness. Well begun is half done. To start with a true idea of blessedness is beyond measure important. Man began with being blessed in his innocence, and if our fallen race is ever to be blessed again, it must find it where it lost it at the beginning, namely, in conformity to the command of the Lord.

" The undefiled in the way." They are in the way, the right way, the way of the Lord, and they keep that way, walking with holy carefulness and washing their feet daily, lest they be found spotted by the flesh. They enjoy great blessedness in their own souls ; indeed, they have a foretaste of heaven where the blessedness lieth much in being absolutely undefiled ; and could they continue utterly and altogether without defilement, doubtless they would have the days of heaven upon the earth. Outward evil would little hurt us if we were entirely rid of the evil of sin, an attainment which with the best of us lies still in the region of desire, and is not yet fully reached, though we have so clear a view of it that we see it to be blessedness itself ; and therefore we eagerly press towards it.

He whose life is in a gospel sense undefiled, is blessed, because he could never have reached this point if a thousand blessings had not already been bestowed on him. By nature we are defiled and out of the way, and we must therefore have been washed in the atoning blood to remove defilement, and we must have been converted by the power of the Holy Ghost, or we should not have been turned into the way of peace, nor be undefiled in it. Nor is this all, for the continual power of grace is needed to keep a believer in the right way, and to preserve him from pollution. All the blessings of the covenant must have been in a measure poured upon those who from day to day have been enabled in perfect holiness in the fear of the Lord. Their way is the evidence of their being the blessed of the Lord.

David speaks of a high degree of blessedness ; for some are in the way, and are true servants of God, but they are as yet faulty in many ways and bring defilement upon themselves. Others who walk in the light more fully, and maintain closer communion with God, are enabled to keep themselves unspotted from the world, and these enjoy far more peace and joy than their less watchful brethren. Doubtless, the more complete our sanctification the more intense our blessedness. Christ is our way, and we are not only alive in Christ, but we are to live in Christ ; the sorrow is that we bespatter his holy way with our selfishness, self-exaltation, wilfulness, and carnality, and so we miss a great measure of the blessedness which is in him as our way. A believer who errs is still saved, but the joy of his salvation is not experienced by him ; he is rescued but not enriched, greatly borne with, but not greatly blessed.

How easily may defilement come upon us even in our holy things, yea, even in the way. We may even come from public or private worship with defilement upon the conscience gathered when we were on our knees. There was no floor to the tabernacle but the desert sand, and hence the priests at the altar were under frequent necessity to wash their feet, and by the kind foresight of their God, the laver stood ready for their cleansing, even as for us our Lord Jesus still stands ready to wash our feet, that we may be clean every whit. Thus our text sets forth the blessedness of the apostles in the upper room when Jesus had said of them, " Ye are clean."

What blessedness awaits those who follow the Lamb whithersoever he goeth, and are preserved from the evil which is in the world through lust. These shall be the envy of all mankind " in that day." Though now they despise them as precise fanatics and Puritans, the most prosperous of sinners shall then wish that they could change places with them. O my soul, seek thou thy blessedness in following hard after thy Lord, who was holy, harmless, undefiled ; for there hast thou found peace hitherto, and there wilt thou find it for ever.

"*Who walk in the law of the Lord.*" In them is found habitual holiness. Their walk, their common everyday life is obedience unto the Lord. They live by rule, that rule the command of the Lord God. Whether they eat or drink, or whatsoever they do, they do all in the name of their great Master and Exemplar. To them religion is nothing out of the way, it is their everyday walk : it moulds their common actions as well as their special devotions. This ensures blessedness. He who walks in God's law walks in God's company, and he must be blessed ; he has God's smile, God's strength, God's secret with him, and how can he be otherwise than blessed ?

The holy life is a walk, a steady progress, a quiet advance, a lasting continuance. Enoch walked with God. Good men always long to be better, and hence they go forward. Good men are never idle, and hence they do not lie down or loiter, but they are still walking onward to their desired end. They are not hurried, and worried, and flurried, and so they keep the even tenor of their way, walking steadily towards heaven ; and they are not in perplexity as to how to conduct themselves, for they have a perfect rule, which they are happy to walk by. The law of the Lord is not irksome to them ; its commandments are not grievous, and its restrictions are not slavish in their esteem. It does not appear to them to be an impossible law, theoretically admirable but practically absurd, but they walk by it and in it. They do not consult it now and then as a sort of rectifier of their wanderings, but they use it as a chart for their daily sailing, a map of the road for their life-journey. Nor do they ever regret that they have entered upon the path of obedience, else they would leave it, and that without difficulty, for a thousand temptations offer them opportunity to return ; their continued walk in the law of the Lord is their best testimony to the blessedness of such a condition of life. Yes, they are blessed even now. The Psalmist himself bore witness to the fact : he had tried and proved it, and wrote it down, as a fact which defied all denial. Here it stands in the forefront of David's *magnum opus*, written on the topmost line of his greatest Psalm—" BLESSED ARE THEY WHO WALK IN THE LAW OF THE LORD." Rough may be the way, stern the rule, hard the discipline,—all these we know and more,—but a thousand heaped-up blessednesses are still found in godly living, for which we bless the Lord.

We have in this verse blessed persons who enjoy five blessed things, A blessed way, blessed purity, a blessed law, given by a blessed Lord, and a blessed walk therein ; to which we may add the blessed testimony of the Holy Ghost given in this very passage that they are in very deed the blessed of the Lord.

The blessedness which is thus set before us we must aim at, but we must not think to obtain it without earnest effort. David has a great deal to say about it ; his discourse in this Psalm is long and solemn, and it is a hint to us that the way of perfect obedience is not learned in a day ; there must be precept upon precept, line upon line, and after efforts long enough to be compared with the 176 verses of this Psalm we may still have to cry, " I have gone astray like a lost sheep ; seek thy servant ; for I do not forget thy commandments."

It must, however, be our plan to keep the word of the Lord much upon our minds ; for this discourse upon blessedness has for its pole-star the testimony of the Lord, and only by daily communion with the Lord by his word can we hope to learn his way, to be purged from defilement, and to be made to walk in his statutes. We set out upon this exposition with blessedness before us ; we see the way to it, and we know where the law of it is to be found : let us pray that as we pursue our meditation we may grow into the habit and walk of obedience, and so feel the blessedness of which we read.

2. "*Blessed are they that keep his testimonies.*" What ! A second blessing ? Yes, they are doubly blessed whose outward life is supported by an inward zeal for God's glory. In the first verse we had an undefiled way, and it was taken for granted that the purity in the way was not mere surface work, but was attended by the inward truth and life which comes of divine grace. Here that which was implied is expressed. Blessedness is ascribed to those who treasure up the testimonies of the Lord : in which is implied that they search the Scriptures, that they come to an understanding of them, that they love them, and then that they continue in the practice of them. We must first get a thing before we can keep it. In order to keep it well we must get a firm grip of it : we cannot keep in the heart that which we have not heartily embraced by the affections. God's word is his witness or testimony to

grand and important truths which concern himself and our relation to him : this we should desire to know ; knowing it, we should believe it ; believing it, we should love it ; and loving it, we should hold it fast against all comers. There is a doctrinal keeping of the word when we are ready to die for its defence, and a practical keeping of it when we actually live under its power. Revealed truth is precious as diamonds, and should be kept or treasured up in the memory and in the heart as jewels in a casket, or as the law was kept in the ark ; this however is not enough, for it is meant for practical use, and therefore it must be kept or followed, as men keep to a path, or to a line of business. If we keep God's testimonies they will keep us ; they will keep us right in opinion, comfortable in spirit, holy in conversation, and hopeful in expectation. If they were ever worth having—and no thoughtful person will question that—then they are worth keeping ; their designed effect does not come through a temporary seizure of them, but by a persevering keeping of them : " in keeping of them there is great reward."

We are bound to keep with all care the word of God, because it is *his* testimonies. He gave them to us, but they are still his own. We are to keep them as a watchman guards his master's house, as a steward husbands his lord's goods, as a shepherd keeps his employer's flock. We shall have to give an account, for we are put in trust with the gospel, and woe to us if we be found unfaithful. We cannot fight a good fight, nor finish our course, unless we keep the faith. To this end the Lord must keep us : only those who are kept by the power of God unto salvation will ever be able to keep his testimonies. What a blessedness is therefore evidenced and testified by a careful belief in God's word, and a continual obedience thereunto. God has blessed them, in blessing them, and will bless them for ever. That blessedness which David saw in others he realized for himself, for in verse 168 he says, " I have kept thy precepts and thy testimonies," and in verses 54 to 56 he traces his joyful songs and happy memories to this same keeping of the law, and he confesses, " This I had because I kept thy precepts." Doctrines which we teach to others we should experience for ourselves.

"And that seek him with the whole heart." Those who keep the Lord's testimonies are sure to seek after himself. If his word is precious we may be sure that he himself is still more so. Personal dealing with a personal God is the longing of all those who have allowed the word of the Lord to have its full effect upon them. If we once really know the power of the gospel we must seek the God of the gospel. " O that I knew where I might find HIM," will be our whole-hearted cry. See the growth which these sentences indicate : first, in the way, then walking in it, then finding and keeping the treasure of truth, and to crown all, seeking after the Lord of the way himself. Note also that the further a soul advances in grace the more spiritual and divine are its longings ; an outward walk does not content the gracious soul, nor even the treasured testimonies ; it reaches out in due time after God himself, and when it in a measure finds him, still yearns for more of him, and seeks him still.

Seeking after God signifies a desire to commune with him more closely, to follow him more fully, to enter into more perfect union with his mind and will, to promote his glory, and to realize completely all that he is to holy hearts. The blessed man has God already, and for this reason he seeks him. This may seem a contradiction : it is only a paradox.

God is not truly sought by the cold researches of the brain : we must seek him with the heart. Love reveals itself to love : God manifests his heart to the heart of his people. It is in vain that we endeavour to comprehend him by reason ; we must apprehend him by affection. But the heart must not be divided with many objects if the Lord is to be sought by us. God is one, and we shall not know him till our heart is one. A broken heart need not be distressed at this, for no heart is so whole in its seekings after God as a heart which is broken, whereof every fragment sighs and cries after the great Father's face. It is the divided heart which the doctrine of the text censures, and strange to say, in scriptural phraseology, a heart may be divided and not broken, and it may be broken but not divided ; and yet again it may be broken and be whole, and it never can be whole until it is broken. When our whole heart seeks the holy God in Christ Jesus it has come to him of whom it is written, " as many as touched him were made perfectly whole."

That which the Psalmist admires in this verse he claims in the tenth, where he says, " With my whole heart have I sought thee." It is well when admiration of a virtue leads to the attainment of it. Those who do not believe in the blessedness of seeking the Lord will not be likely to arouse their hearts to the pursuit, but he who calls another blessed because of the grace which he sees in him is on the way to gaining the same grace for himself.

If those who *seek* the Lord are blessed, what shall be said of those who actually dwell with him and know that he is theirs ?

> " To those who fall, how kind thou art !
> How good to those who seek
> But what to those who find ? Ah ! this
> Nor tongue nor pen can show !
> The love of Jesus—what it is,
> None but his loved ones know."

3. *" They also do no iniquity."* Blessed indeed would those men be of whom this could be asserted without reserve and without explanation : we shall have reached the region of pure blessedness when we altogether cease from sin. Those who follow the word of God do no iniquity, the rule is perfect, and if it be constantly followed no fault will arise. Life, to the outward observer, at any rate, lies much in doing, and he who in his doings never swerves from equity, both towards God and man, has hit upon the way of perfection, and we may be sure that his heart is right. See how a whole heart leads to the avoidance of evil, for the Psalmist says, " That seek him with the whole heart. They also do no iniquity." We fear that no man can claim to be absolutely without sin, and yet we trust there are many who do not designedly, wilfully, knowingly, and continuously do anything that is wicked, ungodly, or unjust. Grace keeps the life righteous as to act even when the Christian has to bemoan the transgressions of the heart. Judged as men should be judged by their fellows, according to such just rules as men make for men, the true people of God do no iniquity : they are honest, upright, and chaste, and touching justice and morality they are blameless. Therefore are they happy.

" They walk in his ways." They attend not only to the great main highway of the law, but to the smaller paths of the particular precepts. As they will perpetrate no sin of commission, so do they labour to be free from every sin of omission. It is not enough to them to be blameless, they wish also to be actively righteous. A hermit may escape into solitude that he may do no iniquity, but a saint lives in society that he may serve his God by walking in his ways. We must be positively as well as negatively right : we shall not long keep the second unless we attend to the first, for men will be walking one way or another, and if they do not follow the path of God's law they will soon do iniquity. The surest way to abstain from evil is to be fully occupied in doing good. This verse describes believers as they exist among us : although they have their faults and infirmities, yet they hate evil, and will not permit themselves to do it ; they love the ways of truth, right and true godliness, and habitually they walk therein. They do not claim to be absolutely perfect except in their desires, and there they are pure indeed, for they pant to be kept from all sin, and to be led into all holiness.

4. *" Thou hast commanded us to keep thy precepts diligently."* So that when we have done all we are unprofitable servants, we have done only that which it was our duty to have done, seeing we have our Lord's command for it. God's precepts require *careful* obedience : there is no keeping them by accident. Some give to God a careless service, a sort of hit or miss obedience, but the Lord has not commanded such service, nor will he accept it. His law demands the love of all our heart, soul, mind, and strength ; and a careless religion has none of these. We are also called to *zealous* obedience. We are to keep the precepts abundantly : the vessels of obedience should be filled to the brim, and the command carried out to the full of its meaning. As a man diligent in business arouses himself to do as much trade as he can, so must we be eager to serve the Lord as much as possible. Nor must we spare pains to do so, for a diligent obedience will also be *laborious and self-denying.* Those who are diligent in business rise up early and sit up late, and deny themselves much of comfort and repose. They are not soon tired, or if they are they persevere even with aching brow and weary eyes. So should we serve the Lord. Such a Master deserves diligent servants ; such service he demands, and will be content with nothing less. How seldom do men render it, and hence many through their negligence miss the double blessing spoken of in this Psalm.

Some are diligent in superstition and will worship ; be it ours to be diligent in keeping God's precepts. It is no use travelling fast if we are not in the right road. Men have been diligent in a losing business, and the more they have traded the more they have lost : this is bad enough in commerce, we cannot afford to have it so in our religion.

God has not commanded us to be diligent in *making* precepts, but in *keeping* them. Some bind yokes upon their own necks, and make bonds and rules for others : but the wise course is to be satisfied with the rules of holy Scripture, and to strive to keep them all, in all places, towards all men, and in all respects. If we do not this, we may become eminent in our own religion, but we shall not have kept the command of God, nor shall we be accepted of him.

The Psalmist began with the third person : he is now coming near home, and has already reached the first person plural, according to our version ; we shall soon hear him crying out personally and for himself. As the heart glows with love to holiness, we long to have a personal interest in it. The word of God is a heart-affecting book, and when we begin to sing its praises it soon comes home to us, and sets us praying to be ourselves conformed to its teachings.

5. " *O that my ways were directed to keep thy statutes !* " Divine commands should direct us in the subject of our prayers. We cannot of ourselves keep God's statutes as he would have them kept, and yet we long to do so : what resort have we but prayer ? We must ask the Lord to work our works in us, or we shall never work out his commandments. This verse is a sigh of regret because the Psalmist feels that he has not kept the precepts diligently, it is a cry of weakness appealing for help to one who can aid, it is a request of bewilderment from one who has lost his way and would fain be directed in it, and it is a petition of faith from one who loves God and trusts in him for grace.

Our ways are by nature opposed to the way of God, and must be turned by the Lord's direction in another direction from that which they originally take or they will lead us down to destruction. God can direct the mind and will without violating our free agency, and he will do so in answer to prayer ; in fact, he has begun the work already in those who are heartily praying after the fashion of this verse. It is for present holiness that the desire arises in the heart. O that it were so now with me : but future persevering holiness is also meant, for he longs for grace to keep henceforth and for ever the statutes of the Lord.

The sigh of the text is really a prayer, though it does not exactly take that form. Desires and longings are of the essence of supplication, and it little matters what shape they take. " O that " is as acceptable a prayer as " Our Father."

One would hardly have expected a prayer for direction ; rather should we have looked for a petition for enabling. Can we not direct ourselves ? What if we cannot row, we can steer. The Psalmist herein confesses that even for the smallest part of his duty he felt unable without grace. He longed for the Lord to influence his will, as well as to strengthen his hands. We want a rod to point out the way as much as a staff to support us in it.

The longing of the text is prompted by admiration of the blessedness of holiness, by a contemplation of the righteous man's beauty of character, and by a reverent awe of the command of God. It is a personal application to the writer's own case of the truths which he had been considering. " O that *my* ways," etc. It were well if all who hear and read the word would copy this example and turn all that they hear into prayer. We should have more keepers of the statutes if we had more who sighed and cried after the grace to do so.

6. " *Then shall I not be ashamed.*" He had known shame, and here he rejoices in the prospect of being freed from it. Sin brings shame, and when sin is gone, the reason for being ashamed is banished. What a deliverance this is, for to some men death is preferable to shame ! " *When I have respect unto all thy command-ments.*" When he respects God he shall respect himself and be respected. Whenever we err we prepare ourselves for confusion of face and sinking of heart : if no one else is ashamed of me I shall be ashamed of myself if I do iniquity. Our first parents never knew shame till they made the acquaintance of the old serpent, and it never left them till their gracious God had covered them with sacrificial skins. Disobedience made them naked and ashamed. We, ourselves, will always have cause for shame till every sin is vanquished, and every duty is observed. When we pay a continual and universal respect to the will of the Lord, then we shall be able to look ourselves in the face in the looking-glass of the law, and we shall not blush at the sight of men or devils, however eager their malice may be to lay somewhat to our charge.

Many suffer from excessive diffidence, and this verse suggests a cure. An abiding sense of duty will make us bold, we shall be afraid to be afraid.   No shame in the presence of man will hinder us when the fear of God has taken full possession of our minds.   When we are on the king's highway by daylight, and are engaged upon royal business, we need ask no man's leave.   It would be a dishonour to a king to be ashamed of his livery and his service ; no such shame should ever crimson the cheek of a Christian, nor will it if he has due reverence for the Lord his God.   There is nothing to be ashamed of in a holy life ; a man may be ashamed of his pride, ashamed of his wealth, ashamed of his own children, but he will never be ashamed of having in all things regarded the will of the Lord his God.

It is worthy of remark that David promises himself no immunity from shame till he has carefully paid homage to all the precepts.   Mind that word " *all*," and leave not one command out of your respect.   Partial obedience still leaves us liable to be called to account for those commands which we have neglected.   A man may have a thousand virtues, and yet a single failing may cover him with shame.

To a poor sinner who is buried in despair, it may seem a very unlikely thing that he should ever be delivered from shame.   He blushes, and is confounded, and feels that he can never lift up his face again.   Let him read these words : " Then shall I not be ashamed."   David is not dreaming, nor picturing an impossible case.   Be assured, dear friend, that the Holy Spirit can renew in you the image of God, so that you shall yet look up without fear.   O for sanctification to direct us in God's way, for then shall we have boldness both towards God and his people, and shall no more crimson with confusion.

7. "*I will praise thee.*"   From prayer to praise is never a long or a difficult journey.   Be sure that he who prays for holiness will one day praise for happiness. Shame having vanished, silence is broken, and the formerly silent man declares, " I will praise thee."   He cannot but promise praise while he seeks sanctification. Mark how well he knows upon what head to set the crown.   " I will praise *thee*." He would himself be praiseworthy, but he counts God alone worthy of praise.   By the sorrow and shame of sin he measures his obligations to the Lord who would teach him the art of living as that he should clean escape from his former misery.

" *With uprightness of heart,*"   His heart would be upright if the Lord would teach him, and then it should praise its teacher.   There is such a thing as false and feigned praise, and this the Lord abhors ; but there is no music like that which comes from a pure soul which standeth in its integrity.   Heart praise is required, upright- ness in that heart, and teaching to make the heart upright.   An upright heart is sure to bless the Lord, for grateful adoration is a part of its uprightness ; no man can be right unless he is upright towards God, and this involves the rendering to him the praise which is his due.

" *When I shall have learned thy righteous judgments.*"   We must learn to praise, learn that we may praise, and praise when we have learned.   If we are ever to learn, the Lord must teach us, and especially upon such a subject as his judgments, for they are a great deep.   While these are passing before our eyes, and we are learning from them, we ought to praise God, for the original is not, " when I have learned," but, " in my learning."   While yet I am a scholar I will be a chorister : my upright heart shall praise thine uprightness, my purified judgment shall admire thy judg- ments.   God's providence is a book full of teaching, and to those whose hearts are right it is a music book, out of which they chant to Jehovah's praise.   God's word is full of the record of his righteous providences, and as we read it we feel compelled to burst forth into expressions of holy delight and ardent praise.   When we both read of God's judgments and become joyful partakers in them, we are doubly moved to song—song in which there is neither formality, nor hypocrisy, nor lukewarmness, for the heart is upright in the presentation of its praise.

8. " *I will keep thy statutes.*"   A calm resolve.   When praise calms down into solid resolution it is well with the soul.   Zeal which spends itself in singing, and leaves no practical residuum of holy living, is little worth : " I will praise " should be coupled with " I will keep."   This firm resolve is by no means boastful, like Peter's " though I should die with thee, yet will I not forsake thee," for it is followed by a humble prayer for divine help, " *O forsake me not utterly.*"   Feeling his own incapacity he trembles lest he should be left to himself, and this fear is increased by the horror which he has of falling into sin.   The " I will keep " sounds rightly enough now that the humble cry is heard with it.   This is a happy amalgam : resolution and depen- dence.   We meet with those who to all appearance humbly pray, but there is no force of character, no decision in them, and consequently the pleading of the closet is not

embodied in the life : on the other hand, we meet with abundance of resolve attended with an entire absence of dependence upon God, and this makes as poor a character as the former. The Lord grant us to have such a blending of excellences that we may be " perfect and entire, wanting nothing."

This prayer is one which is certain to be heard, for assuredly it must be highly pleasing to God to see a man set upon obeying his will, and therefore it must be most agreeable to him to be present with such a person, and to help him in his endeavours. How can he forsake one who does not forsake his law ?

The peculiar dread which tinges this prayer with a sombre hue is the fear of utter forsaking. Well may the soul cry out against such a calamity. To be left, that we may discover our weakness, is a sufficient trial : to be altogether forsaken would be ruin and death. Hiding the face in a little wrath for a moment brings us very low : an absolute desertion would land us ultimately in the lowest hell. But the Lord never has utterly forsaken his servants, and he never will, blessed be his name. If we long to keep his statutes he will keep us ; yea, his grace will keep us keeping his law.

There is rather a descent from the mount of benediction with which the first verse began to the almost wail of this eighth verse, yet this is spiritually a growth, for from admiration of goodness we have come to a burning longing after God and communion with him, and an intense horror lest it should not be enjoyed. The sigh of verse 5 is now supplanted by an actual prayer from the depths of a heart conscious of its undesert, and its entire dependence upon divine love. The two " I wills " needed to be seasoned with some such lowly petition, or it might have been thought that the good man's dependence was in some degree fixed upon his own determination. He presents his resolutions like a sacrifice, but he cries to heaven for the fire.

NOTES ON THE VERSES.

The first eight verses commence with Aleph, and may be alphabetically rendered thus :—

1. All they that are undefiled in the way, walking in the law of the Lord, are blessed.
2. All they that keep his testimonies, and that seek him with the whole heart, are blessed.
3. Also they do no iniquity : they walk in his ways.
4. All thy precepts diligently to keep thou hast commanded us.
5. Ah, Lord ! that my ways were directed to keep thy statutes !
6. Ashamed I shall never be, when I have respect unto all thy commandments.
7. Always will I praise thee, with uprightness of heart, when I shall have learned thy righteous judgments.
8. All thy statutes will I keep : O forsake me not utterly.

Pastor Theodore Kübler, of Islington, 1880.

Whole eight verses, 1—8.—Every line begins with Aleph, to which the Jews ascribe the meaning of *an ox,* that is, the beast of useful service, and thus of many blessings. Key of the section : " O the blessings."—*F. G. Marchant.*

Whole eight verses, 1—8.—These eight verses teach that true piety is sincere, consistent, practical, hearty, intelligent, earnest, active, stirring, diligent, humble, distrustful of itself, systematical, guileless, unspotted from the world, self-renouncing, confident in God, delighting in thankfulness, fully purposed to keep the law, and as ready to confess that without divine grace it can do nothing.

They also teach us how great is the sin of not believing God's word. As it is a law, the faithless refuse to walk by it ; as it is a testimony, they refuse to believe their Maker ; as it demands righteousness, they refuse to seek it ; as it gives precepts, they will not obey them ; as it ordains statutes, they rebel against them ; as it has excellent commandments, they stand out in opposition to them ; as it abounds with righteous judgments, they refuse to stand by them. They will not pray for grace ; they will not praise God for mercies received ; they do not feel their dependence or impotence, and they never look to the Father of lights from whom cometh down every good and perfect gift.—*William S. Plumer,*—1880.

Verse 1.—" *Blessed.*" The Psalmist beginneth with a description of the way to true blessedness, as Christ began his Sermon on the Mount, and as the whole Book of Psalms is elsewhere begun. Blessedness is that which we all aim at, only we are either ignorant or reckless of the way that leadeth to it, therefore the holy Psalmist would first set us right as to the true notion of a blessed man : " *Blessed are the undefiled in the way, who walk in the law of the* LORD."—*Thomas Manton,* 1620—1677.

Verse 1.—" *Blessed.*" Here the Lord, who in the last day will pronounce some to be blessed and some to be cursed, doth now tell us who they are. What can comfort them to whom the Lord shall say, Depart from me, ye cursed ? Where away shall they go when the Lord shall command them to depart from him ? And what greater joy can come to a man, than to hear the Judge of all saying unto him, Come to me, ye blessed ? Oh that we were wise in time, to think of this, that so we might endeavour to become such men as God in his word hath blessed !—*William Cowper,* 1566—1619.

Verse 1.—The Scripture speaketh of blessedness two ways ; *casually,* in reference to that which is the cause whereby we get a right to this blessed estate ; and in this sense it is attributed to faith in Christ, to forgiveness of sin, and to justification of life which we obtain in Christ. Sometimes the Scripture speaketh *formally* of blessedness, in order to the actual execution of it ; and thus it pronounceth them blessed who are perfect in their course ; for this is a blessedness actually executed, and doth fit us to have the full execution and consummation of blessedness begun in us ; thus they are blessed who endure patiently, who are poor in spirit, who are merciful, who are peacemakers, etc. If I speak of a sick man, and say he is happy, for he hath met with a good physician ; here I pronounce him blessed because he hath found one who will restore him to health. If I say of the same man, he is a happy man, he can now digest very well what he eateth, he can sleep, and walk abroad ; I speak of him now as actually blessed with health of body.

The end of everything being the good of that thing, and the prosperity of everything being the end of it,—to attain in some latitude this perfection of action must needs make a man actually blessed. Hence blessedness is ascribed to *walking* in God's way. If we have not the habit of doing anything, we do it with difficulty, we are ready to cease from doing it ; as a horse will continually break out of the pace to which he is not perfectly broken. Thence it is that the saints find their estate miserable till they form the habit which maketh them with facility and constancy *walk* with God ; there being no greater misery than to see themselves doing good duties uncheerfully, no sooner entering them than out again, and desisting from them. On the contrary, they count it of all things most blessed to have attained some degree of permanent habit in godliness. The blessedness which is here spoken of is the actual execution of that blessedness which comes to us by faith in Christ.—*Paul Bayne,* —1617.

Verse 1.—" *The undefiled.*" You ask, Why does God will that we be undefiled ? I reply, because he has chosen us for himself, for servants, for spouses, for temples. These three privileges or names mean that all defilement must be shunned by us.— *Thomas Le Blanc.*

Verse 1.—" *Undefiled in the way.*" In the 1st Psalm it was " Blessed is the man that walketh not in the counsel of the ungodly " ; but who could think to walk in that way, and not have his feet soiled ? " Who could go upon hot coals and his feet be not burned ? " Here, however, the caution is, to take heed not to get any soil or defilement " *in the way,*"—in the Lord's way. Oh ! what an insight does this give us of the pit-falls and snares that beset us in the road, and of the plague and evil of our own hearts, that even in the midst of holy things, somewhat of stain, or spot, or wrinkle will stick to us !—*Barton Bouchier,* 1856.

Verse 1.—" *The undefiled in the way.*" How can our feet be undefiled ? How can our garments be unsoiled ? We cannot guide ourselves. Unaided, we stumble into sloughs of defilement. But all help is near. Jesus is at hand to keep us by his mighty power. Let us lean on his supporting arm at every step, and when we fall let us rise and wash our robes in his all-cleansing blood. So may we ever be among " *the undefiled in the way*" ; and let the law of the Lord, lovely in purity, glorious in holiness, perfect in love, be the path in which our feet advance. Jesus is our model and our all. God's law was in his heart.—*Henry Law, in* " *Family Devotion,*" 1878.

Verse 1.—" *In the way.*" They are blessed who are in *the* way, not *a* way, any chance or uncertain road, but " the King's Highway " ; that path which the Lord himself has declared to us, saying, " I am the way."—*Hilary and Theodoret, quoted by Neale and Littledale.*

Verse 1.—" *The way.*" There is much ado now about the way : many say, " Which is the way ? " Some say, " This " ; some, " That." Would you not mistake, inquire for " the old way, the way of holiness," and follow it, and thou shalt not perish. Some would go a new way ; some a shorter, some an easier way. Do you go the holy way.—*John Sheffield (about* 1660), *in* " *The Morning Exercises.*"

Verse 1.—" *Who walk.*" In this way there must be no standing, sitting, or reclining, but *walking,* so that all our movements may be regular, going on unto perfection : Matt. v. 48 ; 1 Cor. xiv. 20 ; James i. 4 ; Heb. vi. 1.—*Martin Geier,* 1614—1681.

Verse 1.—" *Who walk in the law of the* LORD." To go on with liberty in good duties is a point of blessed perfection. He is not truly able to *walk* who can only go twice or thrice about his chamber, or stir himself on some plain ground for a quarter of an hour ; but he which can go strongly and freely up a hill in ways craggy and uneven : so Christians who can go while God maketh their way inoffensive, putting everything away which might hinder, but presently give over if ought disturbeth, they are not come to this free walking in which standeth a traveller's perfection. Look at those who are fat at heart, pursey (as we say), or have inward lameness, and ache of joints, or have caught a thorn from without, so that they are forced to lie by, and cannot walk ; or those whose limbs are so feeble, that they cannot trip upon anything, but down they come ;—all these lame folk do esteem other travellers to be happy who are able to exercise themselves in walking at will. Thus, when Christians find themselves hindered, and wearied, and stumbling, they deem others blessed who can go on constantly in their holy course, through good report and evil report, in want, in abundance, in every estate and condition. Wherefore, let us strive after this blessed walking.—*Paul Bayne.*

Verse 1.—" *Who walk in the law of the* LORD." Who walk towards heaven in heaven's way, avoiding the corruptions that are in the world through lust.—*John Trapp,* 1611—1662.

Verse 2.—The doubling of the sentence, "*Blessed*," "*Blessed*," in the first verse and second, is to let us see the certainty of the blessing belonging to the godly. The word of God is as true in itself when it is once spoken, as when it is many times repeated : the repetition of it is for confirmation of our weak faith. That which Isaac spake of Jacob,—" I have blessed him, and he shall be blessed," is the most sure decree of God upon all his children. Satan would fain curse Israel, by the mouth of such as Balaam was ; but he shall not be able to curse, because God hath blessed.—*William Cowper.*

Verse 2.—" *Blessed are they that keep his testimonies, and that seek him with the whole heart.*" In the former verse a blessed man is described by the course of his actions, " Blessed are the undefiled in the way : " in this verse he is described by the frame of his heart.—*Thomas Manton.*

Verse 2.—" *Keep his testimonies.*" The careful keeping in mind of God's testimonies is blessedness ; for though there is a keeping of them in conversation mentioned in the former verse, here another thing is intimated diverse from the former ; he that keepeth this plant or holy seed so that the devil cannot take it out of his heart, he is happy. The word here used signifieth such a careful custody as that is wherewith we use to keep tender plants.—*Paul Bayne.*

Verse 2.—" *Testimonies.*" The notion by which the word of God is expressed is " testimonies " ; whereby is intended the whole declaration of God's will, in doctrines, commands, examples, threatenings, promises. The whole word is the testimony which God hath deposed for the satisfaction of the world about the way of their salvation. Now because the word of God brancheth itself into two parts, the law and the gospel, this notion may be applied to both. First, *to the law*, in regard whereof the ark was called " the ark of testimony " (Exod. xxv. 16), because the two tables were laid up in it. *The gospel* is also called the testimony, " the testimony of God concerning his Son." " To the law, and to the testimony " (Isa. viii. 20) ; where testimony seems to be distinguished from the law. The gospel is so called, because therein God hath testified how a man shall be pardoned, reconciled to God, and obtain a right to eternal life. We need a testimony in this case, because it is more unknown to us. The law was written upon the heart, but the gospel is a stranger. Natural light will discern something of the law. and pry into matters which are of a moral strain and concernment ; but evangelical truths are a mystery, and depend upon the mere testimony of God concerning his Son.—*Thomas Manton.*

Verse 2.—" *Testimonies.*" The word of God is called his testimony, not only because it testifies his will concerning his service, but also his favour and goodwill concerning his own in Christ Jesus. If God's word were no more than a law, yet were we bound to obey it, because we are his creatures ; but since it is also a testimony of his love, wherein as a father he witnesseth his favour towards his children, we are doubly inexcusable if we do not most joyfully embrace it.—*William Cowper.*

Verse 2.—" *Blessed are they . . . . that seek him with the whole heart.*" He pronounces " blessed " not such as are wise in their own conceit, or assume a sort of fantastical holiness, but those who dedicate themselves to the covenant of God, and yield obedience to the dictates of his law. Farther, by these words, he tells us that God is by no means satisfied with mere external service, for he demands the sincere and honest affection of the heart. And assuredly, if God be the sole Judge and Disposer of our life, the truth must occupy the principal place in our heart, because it is not sufficient to have our hands and feet only enlisted in his service.—*John Calvin, 1509—1564.*

Verse 2.—" *The whole heart.*" Whosoever would have sound happiness must have a sound heart. So much sincerity as there is, so much blessedness there will be ; and according to the degree of our hypocrisy, will be the measure of our misery.—*Richard Greenham, 1531—1591.*

Verses 2, 3.—Observe the verbs *seek, do, walk*, all making up the subject to whom the blessedness belongs.—*Henry Hammond, 1605—1660.*

Verse 3.—" *They also do no iniquity.*" If it be demanded here, How is it that they who walk in God's ways work no iniquity ? Is there any man who lives, and sins not ? And if they be not without sin, how then are they to be blessed ? The answer is, as the apostle says of our knowledge, " We know but in part : " so is it true of our felicity on earth, we are blessed but in a part. It is the happiness of angels that they never sinned ; it is the happiness of triumphant saints, that albeit they have been sinners, yet now they sin no more ; but the happiness of saints militant is, that our sins are forgiven us ; and that albeit sin remains in us, yet it reigns not over us ; it is done in us, but not by our allowance : " I do the evil which I would not." " Not I, but sin that dwells in me," Rom. vii. 17.

To the *doing of iniquity*, these three things must concur ; first, a purpose to do it ; next, a delight in doing it ; thirdly, a continuance in it ; which three in God's children never concur ; for in sins done in them by the old man, the new man makes his exceptions and protestations against them. It is not I, says he ; and so far as he from delighting in them, that rather his soul is grieved with them ; even as Lot, dwelling among the Sodomites, was vexed by hearing and seeing their unrighteous deeds. In a word, the children of God are rather sufferers of sin against their wills than actors of it with their wills ; like men spiritually oppressed by the power of their enemy ; for which they sigh and cry unto God. " Miserable man that I am ! who shall deliver me from the body of this death ? " And in this sense it is that the apostle saith, " He who is born of God sinneth not " (1 John iii. 9).—*William Cowper.*

Verse 3.—" *They also do no iniquity.*" The blessedness of those who walk in the law : they do—or have done—no wickedness : but walk—or have always walked —in his ways. Throughout the Psalm it may be noticed that sometimes the present tense is employed indicating present action : sometimes the perfect to indicate past and present time verses 10, 11, 13, 14, 21, 51—61, 101, 102, 131, 145, 147.—*The Speaker's Commentary*, 1873.

Verse 3.—" *They also do no iniquity.*" That is, they make not a trade and common practice thereof. Slip they do, through the infirmity of the flesh, and subtlety of Satan, and the allurements of the world : but they do not ordinarily and customably go forward in unlawful and sinful courses. In that the Psalmist setteth down this as a part (and not the least part neither) of blessedness, *that they work none iniquity, which walk in his ways :* the doctrine to be learned here is this, that it is a marvellous great prerogative to be freed from the bondage of sin.—*Richard Greenham.*

Verse 3.—" *They do no iniquity.*" All such as are renewed by grace, and reconciled to God by Christ Jesus ; to these God imputeth no sin to condemnation, and in his account *they do no iniquity.* Notable is that which is said of David. " He kept my commandments, and followed me with all his heart, and did that only which was right in mine eyes " (1 Kings xiv. 8). How can that be ? We may trace David by his failings, they are upon record everywhere in the word ; yet here a veil is drawn upon them ; God laid them not to his charge. There is a double reason why their failings are not laid to their charge. *Partly, because of their general state*, they are in Christ, taken into favour through him, and " there is no condemnation to them that are in Christ " (Rom. viii. 1), therefore particular errors and escapes do not alter their condition ; which is not to be understood as if a man should not be humbled, and ask God pardon for his infirmities ; no, for then they prove iniquities and they will lie upon record against him. It was a gross fancy of the Valentinians, who held that they were not defiled with sin, whatsoever they committed ; though base and obscene persons, yet still they were as gold in the dirt. No, no, we are to recover ourselves by repentance, to sue out the favour of God. When David humbled himself, and had repented, then, saith Nathan, " The Lord hath put away thy sin " (2 Sam. xii. 13). *Partly, too, because their bent and habitual inclination is to do otherwise.* They set themselves to comply with God's will, to seek and serve the Lord, though they are clogged with many infirmities. A wicked man sinneth with deliberation and delight, his bent is to do evil, he makes "provision for lusts " (Rom. xiii. 14), and " serves " them by a voluntary subjection (Titus iii. 3). But those that are renewed by grace are not " debtors " to the flesh, they have taken another debt and obligation, which is to serve the Lord (Rom. viii. 12).

Partly, too, because their general course and way is to do otherwise. Everything works according to its form ; the constant actions of nature are according to the kind. So the new creature, his constant operations are according to grace. A man is known by his custom, and the course of his endeavours shows what is his business. If a man be constantly, easily, frequently carried away to sin, it discovers the habit of his soul, and the temper of his heart. Meadows may be overflowed, but marsh ground is drowned with every return of the tide. A child of God may be occasionally carried away, and act contrary to the inclination of the new nature ; but when men are drowned and overcome by the return of every temptation, it argues a habit of sin. *And partly, because sin never carries sway completely, but it is opposed by dislikes and resistances of the new nature.* The children of God make it their business to avoid all sin, by watching, praying, mortifying : " I said I will take heed to my ways, that I sin not with my tongue " (Ps. xxxix. 1), and thus there is a resistance of the sin.   God hath planted graces in their hearts, the fear of his Majesty, that works a resistance ;   and therefore there is not a full allowance of what they do.   This resistance sometimes is more strong, then the temptation is overcome : " How can I do this wickedness, and sin against God ? " (Gen. xxxix. 9).   Sometimes it is more weak, and then sin carries it, though against the will of the holy man : " The evil which I hate, that do I " (Rom. vii. 15, 18).   It is the evil which they hate; they protest against it ; they are like men which are oppressed by the power of the enemy.   And then there is a remorse after the sin : David's heart smote him.   It grieves and shames them that they do evil.   Tenderness goes with the new nature : Peter sinned foully, but he went out and wept bitterly.—*Thomas Manton.*

Verse 3.—They that have mortified their sins live in the contrary graces.   Hence it is that the Psalmist said, that " *they work no iniquity, but walk in thy paths.*"   First they crucify all their sins, "*they do no iniquity*:"   secondly, as they do no iniquity, so they follow all the ways of God, contrary to that iniquity : as they *give up all* the ways of sin, so they *take up all* the ways of grace.   It is a rule in divinity, that *grace takes not away nature ;* that is, grace comes not to take away a man's affections, but to take them up.—*William Fenner,* 1600—1640.

Verse 3.—" *They walk in his ways.*"   It reproves those that rest in negatives. As it was said of a certain emperor, he was rather *not vicious* than virtuous.   Many men, all their religion runs upon *nots :* " I am *not* as this publican " (Luke xviii. 11). That ground is naught, though it brings not forth briars and thorns, if it yields not good increase.   Not only the unruly servant is cast into hell, that beat his fellow-servant, that ate and drank with the drunken ; but the idle servant that wrapped up his talent in a napkin.   Meroz is cursed, not for opposing and fighting, but for not helping (Judges v. 23).   Dives did not take away food from Lazarus, but he did not give him of his crumbs.   Many will say, I set up no other gods ; ay, but dost thou love, reverence, and obey the true God ?   For if not, thou dost fail in the first commandment.   As to the second, thou sayest, I abhor idols ; but dost thou delight in ordinances ?   I do not swear and rend the name of God by cursed oaths ; ay, but dost thou glorify God, and honour him ?   I do not profane the Sab-'>ath ; but dost thou sanctify it ?   Thou dost not plough and dance ; but thou art idle, and toyest away the Sabbath.   Thou dost not wrong thy parents ; but dost thou reverence them ?   Thou dost not murder ; but dost thou do good to thy neighbour ?   Thou art no adulterer ; but dost thou study temperance and a holy sobriety in all things ?   Thou art no slanderer ; but art thou tender of thy neighbour's honour and credit, as of thy own ?   Usually men cut off half their bill, as the unjust steward bade his lord's debtor set down fifty when he owed a hundred. We do not think of sins of omission.   If we are not drunkards, adulterers, and profane persons, we do not think what it is to omit respect to God, and reverence for his holy Majesty.—*Thomas Manton.*

Verse 3.—" *They walk in his ways.*"   Not in those of his enemies, nor even in their own.—*Joseph Addison Alexander,*—1860.

Verse 3.—" *They walk in his ways.*"   Habitually, constantly, characteristically. They are not *merely* honest, upright, and just in their dealings with men ; but they walk in the ways of God ; they are *religious.*—*Albert Barnes,* 1798—1870.

Verse 4.—" *Thou hast commanded us to keep thy precepts diligently.*"   It is not a matter ἀδιάφορος, and left to the discretion of men, either to hear, or to neglect sacred discourses, theological readings, and expositions of the Sacred Book ; but God has commanded, and not commanded cursorily when speaking of another matter, but צִוִּיתָה, earnestly and greatly he has commanded us to keep his precepts. There should be infixed in our mind the words found in Deut. vi. 6, " *My words shall be in thy heart ;* " in Matt. xvii., " *Hear ye him* : " in John v., " *Search the Scriptures.*"   Above all things, students of theology should remember the Pauline rule in 1 Tim. iii., " *Give attention to reading.*"—*Solomon Gesner.*

Verse 4.—" *Thou hast commanded us,*" etc.   Hath God enjoined us to observe his precepts so exceeding carefully and diligently ?   Then let nothing draw us therefrom, no, not in the least circumstance ; let us esteem nothing needless, frivolous, or superfluous, that we have a warrant for out of his word ; nor count those too wise or precise that will stand resolutely upon the same : if the Lord require anything, though the world should gainsay it, and we be derided and abused for the doing of it, yet let us proceed still in the course of our obedience.—*Richard Greenham.*

Verse 4.—" *Diligently.*" For three causes should we keep the commandments of the Lord with diligence : first, because our adversary that seeks to snare us by the transgression of them is diligent in tempting, for he goes about, night and day, seeking to devour us ; next, because we ourselves are weak and infirm, by the greater diligence have we need to take heed to ourselves ; thirdly, because of the great loss we sustain by every vantage Satan gets over us ; for we find by experience, that as a wound is sooner made than it is healed, so guiltiness of conscience is easily contracted, but not so easily done away.—*William Cowper.*

Verse 4.—" *Diligently.*" In this verse he reminds the reader how well he knew that this study of the divine law must necessarily be severe (earnest), since God has commanded that it should be observed diligently ; that is, with the profoundest study ; as that which alone is good, and as everything is good which it commands.—*Antonio Brucioli,* 1534.

Verse 4.—The word translated " *diligently,*" doth signify in the original tongue *wonderful much,* so that the words go thus : " *Thou hast commanded to keep thy precepts wonderful much.*"—*Richard Greenham.*

Verses 4, 5.—" *Thou hast commanded us to keep thy precepts diligently,*" verse 4 ; this is God's imperative. " *O that my ways were directed to keep thy statutes !* " verse 5 ; this should be our optative.—*Thomas Adams,* 1614.

Verses 4, 5.—It is very observable concerning David, that when he prayeth so earnestly, " *O that my ways were directed to keep thy statutes,*" he premiseth this as the reason, " *Thou hast commanded us to keep thy statutes diligently,*" thereby intimating that the ground of his obedience to God's precepts was the stamp of divine authority enjoining him. To this purpose it is that he saith in this same Psalm, ver. 94, " *I have sought thy precepts,*" thereby implying that what he sought in his obedience was the fulfilling of God's will. Indeed, that only and properly is obedience which is done *intuitu voluntatis divinæ,* with a respect to and eye upon the divine will. As that is only a divine faith which believeth a truth, not because of human reason, but divine revelation, so that only is a true obedience which conformeth to the command, not because it may consist with any selfish ends, but because it carrieth in it an impression of Christ's authority.—*Nathanael Hardy.*

Verse 5.—In tracing the connection of this verse with the preceding, we cannot forbear to remark how accurately the middle path is preserved, as keeping us at an equal distance from the idea of self-sufficiency to " *keep the Lord's statutes,*" and self-justification in neglecting them. The first attempt to render spiritual obedience will quickly convince us of our utter helplessness. We might as soon create a world as create in our hearts one pulse of spiritual life. And yet our inability does not cancel our obligation. It is the weakness of a heart that " cannot be subject to the law of God," for no other reason than because it is " carnal," and therefore " enmity against God." Our inability is our sin, our guilt, our condemnation, and instead of excusing our condition, stops our mouth, and leaves us destitute of any plea of defence before God. Thus our obligation remains in full force. We are bound to obey the commands of God, whether we can or not. What, then, remains for us, but to return the mandate to heaven, accompanied with an earnest prayer, that the Lord would write upon our hearts those statutes to which he requires obedience in his word ? " *Thou hast commanded us to keep thy statutes diligently.*" We acknowledge, Lord, our obligation, but we feel our impotency. Lord, help us ; we look unto thee. " *O that my ways were directed to keep thy statutes.*"—*Charles Bridges,* 1849.

Verse 5.—" *O that,*" etc. In the former verse the prophet David observes the charge which God gives, and that is, that his commandments be diligently kept : here, then, he observes his own weakness and insufficiency to discharge that great duty, and therefore, as one by the spirit desirous to discharge it, and yet by the flesh not able to discharge it, he breaketh out into these words, " *O that my ways were directed,*" etc. Much like unto a child that being commanded to take up some great weight from the ground, is willing to do it, though not able to do it : or a sick patient advised to walk many turns in his chamber, finds a desire in his heart, though inability in his body to do that which he is directed unto.—*Richard Greenham.*

Verse 5.—" *O that my ways,*" etc. It is the use and duty of the people of God to turn precepts into prayers.   That this is the practice of God's children appeareth : " Turn thou me, and I shall be turned ; for thou art the Lord my God " (Jer. xxxi. 18).   God had said, " Turn you, and you shall live," and they ask it of God, " Turn us," as he required it of them.   It was Austin's prayer, *Da quod jubes, et jube quod vis,* " Give what thou requirest, and require what thou wilt."   It is the duty of the saints ; for, 1st, *It suiteth with the Gospel-covenant,* where precepts and promises go hand in hand ; where God giveth what he commandeth, and worketh all our works in us and for us.   They are not conditions of the covenant only, but a part of it. What God hath required at our hands, that we may desire at his hands.   God is no Pharaoh, to require brick where he giveth no straw.   *Lex jubet, gracia juvat.*   The articles of the new covenant are not only put into the form of precepts, but promises. The law giveth no strength to perform anything, but the Gospel offereth grace. 2ndly, Because, *by this means, the ends of God are fulfilled.*   Why doth God require what we cannot perform by our own strength ?   He doth it, (1.) To keep up his right.   (2.) To convince us of our impotency, and that, upon a trial, without his grace we cannot do his work.   (3.) That the creature may express his readiness to obey.   (4.) To bring us to lie at his feet for grace.—*Thomas Manton.*

Verse 5.—" *O that,*" etc.   The whole life of a good Christian is *an holy desire,* saith Augustine ; and this is always seconded with endeavour without the which, affection is like Rachel, beautiful, but barren.—*John Trapp.*

Verse 5.—" *O that my ways were directed,*" etc.   The original word כון, *kun,* is sometimes rendered to *establish,* and, accordingly, it may seem as if the prophet were soliciting for himself the virtue of perseverance.   I am rather inclined to under-stand it as signifying *to direct ;* for, although God is plainly instructing us in his law, the obtuseness of our understanding and the perversity of our hearts constantly need the direction of his Spirit.—*John Calvin.*

Verse 6.—" *Then shall I not be ashamed.*"   No one likes *to be ashamed* or *to blush :* therefore all things which bring shame after them must be avoided : Ezra ix. 6 ; Jer. iii. 25 ; Dan. ix. 7, 9.   As the workman keeps his eye fixed on his pattern, and the scholar on the copy of his writing-master ; so the godly man ever and anon turns his eyes to the word of his God.—*Martin Geier.*

Verse 6.—There is a twofold shame ; the shame of a guilty conscience ; and the shame of a tender conscience.   The one is the merit and fruit of sin ; the other is an act of grace.   This which is here spoken of is to be understood not of a holy self-loathing, but a confounding shame.—*Thomas Manton.*

Verse 6.—" *Then shall I not be ashamed,*" etc.   Then shall I have confidence both towards God and man, and mine own soul, when I can pronounce of myself that my obedience is impartial, and uniform, and universal, no secret sin reserved for my favour, no least commandment knowingly or willingly neglected by me.— *Henry Hammond.*

Verse 6.—" *Then shall I not be ashamed,*" etc.   You ask, Why is he not ashamed who has " *respect unto all the commandments of God ?* "   I answer, the sense is, as if he had said, The commandments of God are so pure and excellent, that though thou shouldest regard the whole and each one of them most attentively, thou wouldest not find anything that would cause thee to blush.   The laws of Lycurgus are praised ; but they permitted theft.   The statutes of Plato are praised ; but they commended the community of wives.   " *The law of the Lord is perfect, converting the soul :* Ps. xix. 7.   It is a mirror, reflecting the beautiful light of the stars on him who looks into it.—*Thomas Le Blanc.*

Verse 6.—The blessing here spoken of is freedom from shame in looking unto *all* the commandments.   If God hear prayer, and establish the soul in this habit of keeping the commandments, there will be yet this further blessing of being able to look unto every precept without shame.   Many men can look at *some* commandments without shame.   Turning to the ten commandments, the honest man feels no shame as he gazes on the eighth, the pure man is free from reproach as he reads the seventh, he who is reverent and hates blasphemy is not rebuked by the thought that he has violated the third, while the filial spirit rather delights in than shuns the fifth.   So on with the remainder.   Most men perhaps can look at some of the precepts with comparative freedom from reproof.   But who can so look unto them all ?   Yet this, also, the godly heart aspires to.   In this verse we find the Psalmist consciously anticipating the truth of a word in the New Testament : " He that offendeth in one point is guilty of all."—*Frederick G. Marchant.*

Verse 6.—" *Ashamed."*

> I can bear scorpion's stings, tread fields of fire,
> In frozen gulfs of cold eternal lie ;
> Be toss'd aloft through tracts of endless void.
> But cannot live in shame.

Joanna Baillie, 1762—1851.

Verse 6.—" *When I have respect unto all thy commandments."* Literally, " In my looking at all thy commandments." That is, in his regarding them ; in his feeling that all were equally binding on him ; and in his having the consciousness that he had not intentionally neglected, violated, or disregarded any of them. There can be no true piety except where a man *intends* to keep ALL the commands of God. If he makes a selection among them, keeping this one or that one, as may be most convenient for him, or as may be most for his interest, or as may be most popular, it is full proof that he knows nothing of the nature of true religion. A child has no proper respect for a parent if he obeys him only as shall suit his whim or his convenience ; and no man *can* be a pious man who does not purpose, in all honesty, to keep ALL the commandments of God ; to submit to his will *in everything.—Albert Barnes.*

Verse 6.—" *All thy commandments."* There is the same reason for obedience to one command as another,—God's authority, who is the Lawgiver (James ii. 11) ; and therefore when men choose one duty and overlook others, they do not so much obey the will of God, as gratify their own humours and fancies, pleasing him only so far as they can please themselves too ; and this is not reasonable ; we never yield him a " reasonable service," but when it is universal.—*Edward Veal (1632— 1708), in " The Morning Exercises."*

Verse 6.—" *All thy commandments."* A partial obedience will never satisfy a child of God. The exclusion of any commandment from its supreme regard in the heart is the brand of hypocrisy. Even Herod could " do many things," and yet one evil way cherished, and therefore unforsaken, was sufficient to show the sovereign power of sin undisturbed within. Saul slew all the Amalekites but one ; and that single exception in the path of universal obedience marked the unsoundness of his profession, cost him the loss of his throne, and brought him under the awful displeasure of his God. And thus the foot, or the hand, or the right eye, the corrupt unmortified members, bring the whole body to hell. Reserves are the canker of Christian sincerity.—*Charles Bridges.*

Verse 6.—" *Unto all thy commandments."* *Allow* that *any* of God's commandments *may* be transgressed, and we shall soon have the whole decalogue set aside.— *Adam Clarke, 1760—1832.*

Verse 6.—Many will do some good, but are defective in other things and usually in those which are most necessary. They cull out the easiest and cheapest parts of religion, such as do not contradict their lusts and interests. We can never have sound peace till we regard all. " *Then shall I not be ashamed when I have respect unto all thy commandments."* Shame is fear of a just reproof. This reproof is either from the supreme or the deputy judge. The supreme judge of all our actions is God. This should be our principal care, that we may not be ashamed before him at his coming, nor disapproved in the judgment. But there is a deputy judge which every man has in his own bosom. Our consciences do acquit or condemn us as we are partial or sincere in our duty to God, and much dependeth on that. 1 John iii. 20, 21, " For if our heart condemn us, God is greater than our heart, and knoweth all things. Beloved, if our heart condemn us not, then have we confidence towards God." Well, then, that our hearts may not reprove or reproach us, we should be complete in all the will of God. Alas, otherwise you will never have evidence of your sincerity.— *Thomas Manton.*

Verse 6.—Such is the mercy of God in Christ to his children, that he accepts their weak endeavours, joined with sincerity and perseverance in his service, as if they were a full obedience. . . . O, who would not serve such a Lord ? You hear servants sometimes complain of their masters as so rigid and strict, that they can never please them ; no, not when they do their utmost ; but this cannot be charged upon God. Be but so faithful as to do thy best, and God is so gracious that he will pardon thy worst. David knew this gospel indulgence when he said, " *Then shall I not be ashamed, when I have respect unto all thy commandments,"* when my eye is to all thy commandments. The traveller hath his eye on or towards the place he is going to, though he be as yet short of it ; there he would be, and he is putting on all he can to reach it ; so stands the saint's heart to all the commands of God ; he presseth on to come nearer and nearer to full obedience ; such a soul shall never be put to shame.—*William Gurnall*, 1617—1679.

Verse 7.—" *I will praise thee . . . . when I shall have learned,*" etc. There is no way to please God entirely and sincerely until we have learned both to know and do his will. Practical praise is the praise God looks after.—*Thomas Manton.*

Verse 7.—" *I will praise thee.*" What is the matter for which he praises God ? It is that he has been taught something of him and by him amongst men. To have learned any tongue, or science, from some school of philosophy, bindeth us to our alma mater. We praise those who can teach a dog, a horse, this or that ; but for us ass-colts to learn the will of God, how to walk pleasing before him, this should be acknowledged of us as a great mercy from God.—*Paul Bayne.*

Verse 7.—" *Praise thee . . . when I shall have learned,*" etc. But when doth David say that he will be thankful ? Even when God shall teach him. Both the matter and the grace of thankfulness are from God. As he did with Abraham, he commanded him to worship by sacrifice, and at the same time gave him the sacrifice : so doth he with all his children ; for he gives not only good things, for which they should thank him, but in like manner grace by which they are able to thank him.—*William Cowper.*

Verse 7.—" *When I shall have learned.*" By learning he means his attaining not only to the knowledge of the word, but the practice of it. It is not a speculative light, or a bare notion of things : " Every man therefore that hath heard, and hath learned of the Father, cometh unto me " (John vi. 45). It is such a learning as the effect will necessarily follow, such a light and illumination as doth convert the soul, and frame our hearts and ways according to the will of God. For otherwise, if we get understanding of the word, nay, if we get it imprinted in our memories, it will do us no good without practice. The best of God's servants are but scholars and students in the knowledge and obedience of his word. For saith David, " *When I shall have learned.*" The professors of the Christian religion were primitively called disciples or learners : Τὸ πλῆθος τῶν μαθητῶν, " the multitude of the disciples " (Acts vi. 2.)—*Thomas Manton.*

Verse 7.—" *Learned thy righteous judgments.*" We see here what David especially desired to learn, namely, the word and will of God : he would ever be a scholar in this school, and sought daily to ascend to the highest form ; that learning to know, he might remember ; remembering, might believe ; believing, might delight ; delighting, might admire ; admiring, might adore ; adoring, might practise ; and practising, might continue in the way of God's statutes. This learning is the old and true learning indeed, and he is best learned in this art, who turneth God's word into good works.—*Richard Greenham.*

Verse 7.—" *Judgments of thy righteousness* " are the decisions concerning right and wrong which give expression to and put in execution the righteousness of God.—*Franz Delitzsch.*

Verse 8.—This verse, being the last of this portion, is the result of his meditation concerning the utility and necessity of the keeping the law of God. Here take notice :—1. Of his resolution, " *I will keep thy statutes.*" II. Of his prayer, " *O forsake me not utterly.*" It is his purpose to keep the law ; yet because he is conscious to himself of many infirmities, he prays against desertion. In the prayer more is intended than is expressed. " *O forsake me not ;* " he means, strengthen me in this work ; and if thou shouldst desert me, yet but for a while, Lord, not for ever ; if in part, not in whole, Four points we may observe hence :—1. That it is a great advantage to come to a resolution as to a course of godliness. 2. Those that resolve upon a course of obedience have need to fly to God's help. 3. Though we fly to God's help, yet sometimes God may withdraw, and seem to forsake us. 4. Though God seem to forsake us, and really doth so in part ; yet we should pray that it may not be a total and utter desertion.—*Thomas Manton.*

Verse 8 with 7.—" *I will keep thy statutes,*" etc. The resolution to " *keep the Lord's statutes* " is the natural result of having " *learned his righteous judgments.*" And on this point David illustrates the inseparable and happy union of " simplicity " of dependence, and " godly sincerity " of obedience. Instantly upon forming his resolution, he recollects that the performance of it is beyond the power of human strength, and therefore the next moment he follows it with prayer : " *I will keep thy statutes ; O forsake me not utterly.*"—*Charles Bridges.*

Verse 8.—"*I will.*" David setteth a personal example of holiness. If the king of Israel keep God's statutes, the people of Israel will be ashamed to neglect them. Cæsar was wont to say, Princes must not say, *Ite*, go ye, without me ; but, *Venite*, come ye, along with me. So said Gideon (Jud. v. 17): " As ye see me do, so do ye."—*R. Greenham.*

Verse 8.—"*Forsake me not utterly.*" There is a total and a partial desertion. Those who are bent to obey God may for a while, and in some degree, be left to themselves. We cannot promise ourselves an utter immunity from desertion ; but it is not total. We shall find for his great name's sake, " The Lord will not forsake his people " (1 Sam. xii. 22), and, " I will never leave thee nor forsake thee " (Heb. xiii. 5). Not utterly, yet in part they may be forsaken. Elijah was forsaken, but not as Ahab : Peter was forsaken in part, but not as Judas, who was utterly forsaken, and made a prey to the Devil. David was forsaken to be humbled and bettered ; but Saul was forsaken utterly to be destroyed. Saith Theophylact, God may forsake his people so as to shut out their prayers (Ps. lxxx. 4), so as to interrupt the peace and joy of their heart, and abate their strength, so that their spiritual life may be much at a stand, and sin may break out, and they may fall foully ; but they are not *utterly* forsaken. One way or other, God is still present ; present in light sometimes when he is not present in strength, when he manifests the evil of their present condition, so as to make them mourn under it ; and present in awakening their desires, though not in giving them enjoyment. As long as there is any esteem of God, he is not yet gone ; there is some light and love yet left, manifested by our desires of communion with him.—*Thomas Manton.*

Verse 8.—"*Forsake me not utterly.*" The desertions of God's elect are first of all *partial*, that is, such as wherein God doth not wholly forsake them, but in some part. Secondly, *temporary*, that is, for some space of time, and never beyond the compass of this present life. " For a moment (saith the Lord in Esay) in mine anger I hid my face from thee for a little season, but with everlasting kindness will I have mercy on thee, saith the Lord thy Redeemer." And to this purpose David, well acquainted with this matter, prayeth, " *Forsake me not overlong.*" This sort of desertions, though it be but for a time, yet no part of a Christian man's life is free from them ; and very often taking deep place in the heart of man, they are of long continuance. David continued in his dangerous fall about the space of a whole year before he was recovered. Luther confesseth of himself, that, after his conversion, he lay three years in desperation. Common observation in such like cases hath made record of even longer times of spiritual forsakings.—*Richard Greenham.*

Verse 8.—"*O forsake me not utterly.*" This prayer reads like the startled cry of one who was half afraid that he had been presumptuous in expressing the foregoing resolve. He desired to keep the divine statutes, and like Peter he vowed that he would do so ; but remembering his own weakness, he recoils from his own venturesomeness, and feels that he must pray. I have made a solemn vow, but what if I have uttered it in my own strength ? What if God should leave me to myself ? He is filled with terror at the thought. He breaks out with an " O." He implores and beseeches the Lord not to test him by leaving him even for an instant entirely to himself. To be forsaken of God is the worst ill that the most melancholy saint ever dreams of. Thank God, it will never fall to our lot ; for no promise can be more express than that which saith, " I will never leave thee, nor forsake thee." This promise does not prevent our praying, but excites us to it. Because God will not forsake his own, therefore do we cry to him in the agony of our feebleness, " O forsake me not utterly."—*C. H. S.*

EXPOSITION OF VERSES 9 TO 16.

WHEREWITHAL shall a young man cleanse his way? by taking heed *thereto* according to thy word.

10 With my whole heart have I sought thee : O let me not wander from thy commandments.

11 Thy word have I hid in mine heart, that I might not sin against thee.

12 Blessed *art* thou, O LORD : teach me thy statutes.

13 With my lips have I declared all the judgments of thy mouth.

14 I have rejoiced in the way of thy testimonies, as *much as* in all riches.

15 I will meditate in thy precepts, and have respect unto thy ways.

16 I will delight myself in thy statutes : I will not forget thy word.

9. " *Wherewithal shall a young man cleanse his way?* " How shall he become and remain practically holy ? He is but a young man, full of hot passions, and poor in knowledge and experience ; how shall he get right, and keep right ? Never was there a more important question for any man ; never was there a fitter time for asking it than at the commencement of life. It is by no means an easy task which the prudent man sets before him. He wishes to choose a clean way, to be himself clean in it, to cleanse it of any foulness which may arise in the future, and to end by showing a clear course from the first step to the last ; but, alas, his way is already unclean by actual sin which he has already committed, and he himself has within his nature a tendency towards that which defileth. Here, then, is the difficulty, first of beginning aright, next of being always able to know and choose the right, and of continuing in the right till perfection is ultimately reached : this is hard for any man, how shall a youth accomplish it ? The way, or life, of the man has to be cleansed from the sins of his youth behind him, and kept clear of the sins which temptation will place before him : this is the work, this is the difficulty.

No nobler ambition can lie before a youth, none to which he is called by so sure a calling ; but none in which greater difficulties can be found. Let him not, however, shrink from the glorious enterprise of living a pure and gracious life ; rather let him enquire the way by which all obstacles may be overcome. Let him not think that he knows the road to easy victory, nor dream that he can keep himself by his own wisdom ; he will do well to follow the Psalmist, and become an earnest enquirer asking how he may cleanse his way. Let him become a practical disciple of the holy God, who alone can teach him how to overcome the world, the flesh, and the devil, that trinity of defilers by whom many a hopeful life has been spoiled. He is young and unaccustomed to the road, let him not be ashamed often to enquire his way of him who is so ready and so able to instruct him in it.

Our " *way* " is a subject which concerns us deeply, and it is far better to enquire about it than to speculate upon mysterious themes which rather puzzle than enlighten the mind. Among all the questions which a young man asks, and they are many, let this be the first and chief : " Wherewithal shall I cleanse my way ? " This is a question suggested by common sense, and pressed home by daily occurrences ; but it is not to be answered by unaided reason, nor, when answered, can the directions be carried out by unsupported human power. It is ours to ask the question, it is God's to give the answer and enable us to carry it out.

" *By taking heed thereto according to thy word.*" Young man, the Bible must be your chart, and you must exercise great watchfulness that your way may be according to its directions. You must take heed to your daily life, as well as study your Bible, and you must study your Bible that you may take heed to your daily life. With the greatest care a man will go astray if his map misleads him ; but with the most accurate map he will still lose his road if he does not take heed to it. The narrow way was never hit upon by chance, neither did any heedless man ever lead a holy life. We can sin without thought, we have only to neglect the great salvation and ruin our souls ; but to obey the Lord and walk uprightly will need all our heart and soul and mind. Let the careless remember this.

Yet the " *word* " is absolutely necessary ; for, otherwise, care will darken into morbid anxiety, and conscientiousness may become superstition. A captain may watch from his deck all night ; but if he knows nothing of the coast, and has no pilot on board, he may be carefully hastening on to shipwreck. It is not enough to desire to be right ; for ignorance may make us think that we are doing God service when we are provoking him, and the fact of our ignorance will not reverse the character of our action, however much it may mitigate its criminality.   Should a man carefully measure out what he believes to be a dose of useful medicine, he will die if it should turn out that he has taken up the wrong vial, and has poured out a deadly poison : the fact that he did it ignorantly will not alter the result.   Even so, a young man may surround himself with ten thousand ills, by carefully using an unenlightened judgment, and refusing to receive instruction from the word of God.   Wilful ignorance is in itself wilful sin, and the evil which comes of it is without excuse.   Let each man, whether young or old, who desires to be holy have a holy watchfulness in his heart, and keep his Holy Bible before his open eye.   There he will find every turn of the road marked down, every slough and miry place pointed out, with the way to go through unsoiled ; and there, too, he will find light for his darkness, comfort for his weariness, and company for his loneliness, so that by its help he shall reach the benediction of the first verse of the Psalm, which suggested the Psalmist's enquiry, and awakened his desires.

Note how the first section of eight verses has for its first verse, " Blessed are the undefiled in the way," and the second section runs parallel to it, with the question " Wherewithal shall a young man cleanse his way ? "   The blessedness which is set before us in a conditional promise should be practically sought for in the way appointed. The Lord saith, " For this will I be enquired of by the house of Israel to do it for them."

10. " *With my whole heart have I sought thee.*"   His heart had gone after God himself : he had not only desired to obey his laws, but to commune with his person. This is a right royal search and pursuit, and well may it be followed with the whole heart.   The surest mode of cleansing the way of our life is to seek after God himself, and to endeavour to abide in fellowship with him.   Up to the good hour in which he was speaking to his Lord, the Psalmist had been an eager seeker after the Lord, and if faint, he was still pursuing.   Had he not sought the Lord he would never have been so anxious to cleanse his way.

It is pleasant to see how the writer's heart turns distinctly and directly to God. He had been considering an important truth in the preceding verse, but here he so powerfully feels the presence of his God that he speaks to him, and prays to him as to one who is near.   A true heart cannot long live without fellowship with God.

His petition is founded on his life's purpose : he is seeking the Lord, and he prays the Lord to prevent his going astray in or from his search.   It is by obedience that we follow after God, hence the prayer, " *O let me not wander from thy commandments ;* " for if we leave the ways of God's appointment we certainly shall not find the God who appointed them.   The more a man's whole heart is set upon holiness the more does he dread falling into sin ; he is not so much fearful of deliberate transgression as of inadvertent wandering : he cannot endure a wandering look, or a rambling thought, which might stray beyond the pale of the precept.   We are to be such whole-hearted seekers that we have neither time nor will to be wanderers, and yet with all our whole-heartedness we are to cultivate a jealous fear lest even then we should wander from the path of holiness.

Two things may be very like and yet altogether different : saints are " strangers " —" I am a stranger in the earth " (verse 19), but they are not wanderers : they are passing through an enemy's country, but their route is direct ; they are seeking their Lord while they traverse this foreign land.   Their way is hidden from men ; but yet they have not lost their way.

The man of God exerts himself, but does not trust himself : his heart is in his walking with God ; but he knows that even his whole strength is not enough to keep him right unless his King shall be his keeper, and he who made the commands shall make him constant in obeying them : hence the prayer, " *O let me not wander.*" Still, this sense of need, was never turned into an argument for idleness ; for while he prayed to be kept in the right road he took care to run in it, with his whole heart seeking the Lord.

It is curious again to note how the second part of the Psalm keeps step with the first ; for where verse 2 pronounces that man to be blessed who seeks the Lord with his whole heart, the present verse claims the blessing by pleading the character : " *With my whole heart have I sought thee.*"

11. When a godly man sues for a favour from God he should carefully use every

means for obtaining it, and accordingly, as the Psalmist had asked to be preserved from wandering, he here shows us the holy precaution which he had taken to prevent his falling into sin. " *Thy word have I hid in mine heart.*" His heart would be kept by the word because he kept the word in his heart. All that he had of the word written, and all that had been revealed to him by the voice of God,—all, without exception, he had stored away in his affections, as a treasure to be preserved in a casket, or as a choice seed to be buried in a fruitful soil : what soil more fruitful than a renewed heart, wholly seeking the Lord ? The word was God's own, and therefore precious to God's servant. He did not wear a text *on* his heart as a charm, but he hid it *in* his heart as a rule. He laid it up in the place of love and life, and it filled the chamber with sweetness and light. We must in this imitate David, copying his heart-work as well as his outward character. First, we must mind that what we believe is truly God's word ; that being done, we must hide or treasure it each man for himself ; and we must see that this is done, not as a mere feat of the memory, but as the joyful act of the affections.

" *That I might not sin against thee.*" Here was the object aimed at. As one has well said,—Here is the best thing,—" thy word ; " hidden in the best place,—" in my heart ; " for the best of purposes,—" that I might not sin against thee." This was done by the Psalmist with personal care, as a man carefully hides away his money when he fears thieves,—in this case the thief dreaded was sin. Sinning " against God " is the believer's view of moral evil; other men care only when they offend against men. God's word is the best preventive against offending God, for it tells us his mind and will, and tends to bring our spirit into conformity with the divine Spirit. No cure for sin in the life is equal to the word in the seat of life, which is the heart. There is no hiding from sin unless we hide the truth in our souls.

A very pleasant variety of meaning is obtained by laying stress upon the words " thy " and " thee." He speaks to *God*, he loves the word because it is *God's* word, and he hates sin because it is sin against *God* himself. If he vexed others, he minded not so long as he did not offend his God. If we would not cause God displeasure we must treasure up his own word.

The personal way in which the man of God did this is also noteworthy : " With my whole heart have *I* sought thee." Whatever others might choose to do he had already made his choice and placed the Word in his innermost soul as his dearest delight, and however others might transgress, his aim was after holiness : " That *I* might not sin against thee." This was not what he purposed to do, but what he had already done ; many are great at promising, but the Psalmist had been true in performing : hence he hoped to see a sure result. When the word is hidden in the heart the life shall be hidden from sin.

The parallelism between the second octave and the first is still continued. Verse 3 speaks of doing no iniquity, while this verse treats of the method of not sinning. When we form an idea of a blessedly holy man (verse 3) it becomes us to make an earnest effort to attain unto the same sacred innocence and divine happiness, and this can only be through heart-piety founded on the Scriptures.

12. " *Blessed art thou, O Lord.*" These are words of adoration arising out of an intense admiration of the divine character, which the writer is humbly aiming to imitate. He blesses God for all that he has revealed to him, and wrought in him ; he praises him with warmth of reverent love, and depth of holy wonder. These are also words of perception uttered from a remembrance of the great Jehovah's infinite happiness within himself. The Lord is and must be blessed, for he is the perfection of holiness ; and this is probably the reason why this is used as a plea in this place. It is as if David had said—I see that in conformity to thyself my way to happiness must lie, for thou art supremely blessed ; and if I am made in my measure like to thee in holiness, I shall also partake in thy blessedness.

No sooner is the word in the heart than a desire arises to mark and learn it. When food is eaten, the next thing is to digest it ; and when the word is received into the soul the first prayer is—Lord, teach me its meaning. "*Teach me thy statutes*" ; for thus only can I learn the way to be blessed. Thou art so blessed that I am sure thou wilt delight in blessing others, and this boon I crave of thee that I may be instructed in thy commands. Happy men usually rejoice to make others happy, and surely the happy God will willingly impart the holiness which is the fountain of happiness. Faith prompted this prayer and based it, not upon anything in the praying man, but solely upon the perfection of the God to whom he made supplication. Lord, thou art blessed, therefore bless me by teaching me.

We need to be disciples or learners—" *teach me ;* " but what an honour to have God himself for a teacher : how bold is David to beg the blessed God to teach him! Yet the Lord put the desire into his heart when the sacred word was hidden there, and so we may be sure that he was not too bold in expressing it.   Who would not wish to enter the school of such a Master to learn of him the art of holy living ?   To this Instructor we must submit ourselves if we would practically keep the statutes of righteousness.   The King who ordained the statutes knows best their meaning, and as they are the outcome of his own nature he can best inspire us with their spirit. The petition commends itself to all who wish to cleanse their way, since it is most practical, and asks for teaching, not upon recondite lore, but upon statute-law.   If we know the Lord's statutes we have the most essential education.

Let us each one say, " *Teach me thy statutes.*"   This is a sweet prayer for everyday use.   It is a step above that of verse 10, " O let me not wander," as that was a rise beyond that of 8, " O forsake me not utterly."   It finds its answer in verses 98— 100 : " Thou through thy commandments hast made me wiser than mine enemies," etc. ; but not till it had been repeated even to the third time in the " Teach me " of verses 33 and 66, all of which I beg my reader to peruse.   Even after this third pleading the prayer occurs again in so many words in verses 124 and 139, and the same longing comes out near the close of the Psalm in verse 171—" My lips shall utter praise when thou hast taught me thy statutes."

13. " *With my lips have I declared all the judgments of thy mouth.*"   The taught one of verse 12 is here a teacher himself.   What we learn in secret we are to proclaim upon the housetops.   So had the Psalmist done.   As much as he had known he had spoken.   God has revealed many of his judgments by his mouth, that is to say, by a plain and open revelation ; these it is our duty to repeat, becoming, as it were, so many exact echoes of his one infallible voice.   There are judgments of God which are a great deep, which he does not reveal, and with these it will be wise for us not to intermeddle.   What the Lord has veiled it would be presumption for us to uncover, but, on the other hand, what the Lord has revealed it would be shameful for us to conceal.   It is a great comfort to a Christian in time of trouble when in looking back upon his past life he can claim to have done his duty by the word of God.   To have been, like Noah, a preacher of righteousness, is a great joy when the floods are rising, and the ungodly world is about to be destroyed.   Lips which have been used in proclaiming God's statutes are sure to be acceptable when pleading God's promises. If we have had such regard to that which cometh out of God's mouth that we have published it far and wide, we may rest quite assured that God will have respect unto the prayers which come out of our mouths.

It will be an effectual method of cleansing a young man's way if he addicts himself continually to preaching the gospel.   He cannot go far wrong in judgment whose whole soul is occupied in setting forth the judgments of the Lord.   By teaching we learn ; by training the tongue to holy speech we master the whole body ; by familiarity with the divine procedure we are made to delight in righteousness ; and thus in a threefold manner our way is cleansed by our proclaiming the way of the Lord.

14. " *I have rejoiced in the way of thy testimonies.*"   Delight in the word of God is a sure proof that it has taken effect upon the heart, and so is cleansing the life. The Psalmist not only says that he does rejoice, but that he has rejoiced.   For years it had been his joy and bliss to give his soul to the teaching of the word.   His rejoicing had not only arisen out of the word of God, but out of the practical character-istics of it.   The Way was as dear to him as the Truth and the Life.   There was no picking and choosing with David, or if indeed he did make a selection, he chose the most practical first.   " *As much as in all riches.*"   He compared his intense satisfaction with God's will with that of a man who possesses large and varied estates, and the heart to enjoy them.   David knew the riches that come of sovereignty, and which grow out of conquest ; he valued the wealth which proceeds from labour, or is gotten by inheritance : he knew " all riches."   The gracious king had been glad to see the gold and silver poured into his treasury that he might devote vast masses of it to the building of the Temple of Jehovah upon Mount Zion.   He rejoiced in all sorts of riches consecrated and laid up for the noblest uses, and yet the way of God's word had given him more pleasure than even these.   Observe that his joy was personal, distinct, remembered, and abundant.   Wonder not that in the previous verse he glories in having spoken much of that which he had so much enjoyed : a man may well talk of that which is his delight.

15. *"I will meditate in thy precepts."*   He who has an inward delight in anything will not long withdraw his mind from it.   As the miser often returns to look upon his treaure, so does the devout believer by frequent meditation turn over the priceless wealth which he has discovered in the book of the Lord.   To some men meditation is a task ; to the man of cleansed way it is a joy.   He who has meditated will meditate ; he who saith, " I have rejoiced," is the same who adds, " I will meditate." No spiritual exercise is more profitable to the soul than that of devout meditation ; why are many of us so exceeding slack in it ?   It is worthy of observation that the preceptory part of God's word was David's special subject of meditation, and this was the more natural because the question was still upon his mind as to how a young man should cleanse his way.   Practical godliness is vital godliness.

" *And have respect unto. thy ways,*" that is to say, I will think much about them so as to know what thy ways are ; and next, I will think much of them so as to have thy ways in great reverence and high esteem.   I will see what thy ways are towards me that I may be filled with reverence, gratitude, and love ; and then, I will observe what are those ways which thou hast prescribed for me, thy ways in which thou wouldest have me follow thee ; these I would watch carefully that I may become obedient, and prove myself to be a true servant of such a Master.

Note how the verses grow more *inward* as they proceed ; from the speech of verse 13 we advanced to the manifested joy of verse 14, and now we come to the secret meditation of the happy spirit.   The richest graces are those which dwell deepest.

16. " *I will delight myself in thy statutes.*"   In this verse delight follows meditation, of which it is the true flower and outgrowth.   When we have no other solace, but are quite alone, it will be a glad thing for the heart to turn upon itself, and sweetly whisper, " I will delight myself.   What if no minstrel sings in the hall, I will delight myself.   If the time of the singing of birds has not yet arrived, and the voice of the turtle is not heard in our land, yet I will delight myself."   This is the choicest and noblest of all rejoicing ; in fact, it is the good part which can never be taken from us; but there is no delighting ourselves with anything below that which God intended to be the soul's eternal satisfaction.   The statute-book is intended to be the joy of every loyal subject.   When the believer once peruses the sacred pages his soul burns within him as he turns first to one and then to another of the royal words of the great King, words full and firm, immutable and divine.

" *I will not forget thy word.*"   Men do not readily forget that which they have treasured up, that which they have meditated on (verse 15), and that which they have often spoken of (verse 13).   Yet since we have treacherous memories it is well to bind them well with the knotted cord of " I will not forget."

Note how two " I wills " follow upon two " I haves." We may not promise for the future if we have altogether failed in the past ; but where grace has enabled us to accomplish something, we may hopefully expect that it will enable us to do more.

It is curious to observe how this verse is moulded upon verse 8 : the changes are rung on the same words, but the meaning is quite different, and there is no suspicion of a vain repetition.   The same thought is never given over again in this Psalm ; they are dullards who think so.   Something in the position of each verse affects its meaning, so that even where its words are almost identical with those of another the sense is delightfully varied.   If we do not see an infinite variety of fine shades of thought in this Psalm we may conclude that we are colour-blind ; if we do not hear many sweet harmonies, we may judge our ears to be dull of hearing, but we may not suspect the Spirit of God of monotony.

NOTES ON VERSES 9 TO 16.

The eight verses alphabetically arranged :—

9. By what means shall a young man cleanse his way ? By taking heed thereto according to thy word.
10. By day and by night have I sought thee with my whole heart : O let me not wander from thy commandments.
11. By thy grace I have hid thy word in my heart, that I might not sin against thee.
12. Blessed art thou, O Lord : teach me thy statutes.
13. By the words of my lips will I declare all the judgments of thy mouth.
14. By far more than in all riches I have rejoiced in the way of thy testimonies.
15. By thy help I will meditate in thy precepts, and have respect unto thy ways.
16. By thy grace I will delight myself in thy statutes : I will not forget thy word.

Theodore Kübler.

Whole eight verses, 9—16. Every verse in the section begins with ב, *a house.* The subject of the section is, The Law of Jehovah purifying the Life. Key-word, זכה (*zacah*), *to be pure*, to make pure, to cleanse.—*F. G. Marchant.*

Verse 9.—Whole verse. In this passage there is, (1) A question. (2) An answer given. In the question, there is the person spoken of, "*a young man*," and his work, "*Wherewithal shall he cleanse his way ?*" In this question there are several things supposed. 1. That we are from the birth, polluted with sin ; for we must be cleansed. It is not *direct* " his way," but " cleanse his way." 2. That we should be very early and betimes sensible of this evil ; for the question is propounded concerning the young man. 3. That we should earnestly seek for a remedy, how to dry up the issue of sin that runneth upon us. All this is to be supposed.

That which is enquired after is, What remedy there is against it ? What course is to be taken ? So that the sum of the question is this : How shall a man that is impure, and naturally defiled with sin, be made able, as soon as he cometh to the use of reason, to purge out that natural corruption, and live a holy and pure life to God ? The answer is given : "*By taking heed thereto according to thy word.*" Where two things are to be observed. 1. The remedy. 2. The manner how it is applied and made use of.

1. The remedy is the word ; by way of address to God, called " *Thy word ;* " because, if God had not given direction about it, we should have been at an utter loss. 2. The manner how it is applied and made use of, " *by taking heed thereto,*" etc. ; by studying and endeavouring a holy conformity to God's will.—*Thomas Manton.*

Verse 9.— ' *Wherewithal shall a young man cleanse his way ?*" etc. Aristotle, that great dictator in philosophy, despaired of achieving so great an enterprise as the rendering a young man capable of his ηθικα ακροαματα, "his grave and severe lectures of morality ; " for that age is light and foolish, yet headstrong and untractable. Now, take a young man all in the heat and boiling of his blood, in the highest fermentation of his youthful lusts ; and, at all these disadvantages, let him enter that great school of the Holy Spirit, the divine Scriptures, and commit himself to the conduct of those blessed oracles ; and he shall effectually be convinced, by his own experience, of the incredible virtue, the vast and mighty power, of God's word, in the success it hath upon him, and in his daily progressions and advances in heavenly wisdom.—*John Gibbon (about 1660) in " The Morning Exercises."*

Verse 9.—" *A young man.*" A prominent place—one of the twenty-two parts—is assigned to young men in the 119th Psalm. It is meet that it should be so. Youth is the season of impression and improvement, young men are the future props of society, and the fear of the Lord, which is the beginning of wisdom, must begin in youth. The strength, the aspirations, the unmarred expectations of youth, are in requisition for the world ; O that they may be consecrated to God.—*John Stephen, in " The Utterances of the cxix. Psalm," 1861.*

*Verse 9.—*For " *young man,*" in the Hebrew the word is נער, *naar, i.e.,* " *shaken off ;* " that is to say, from the milder and more tender care of his parents. Thus Mercerus and Savallerius. Secondly, *naar* may be rendered " *shaking off ;* " that is to say, the yoke, for a young man begins to cast off the material, and frequently the paternal, yoke.—*Thomas Le Blanc.*

Verse 9.—" *Cleanse his way.*" The expression does not absolutely convey the impression that the given young man is in a corrupt and discreditable way which requires cleansing, though this be true of all men originally : Isaiah liii. 6.   That which follows makes known that such could not be the case with this young man. The very inquiry shows that his heart is not in a corrupt state.   Desire is present, direction is required.   The inquiry is—How shall a young man make a clean way—a pure line of conduct—through this defiling world ?   It is a question, I doubt not, of great anxiety to every convert whose mind is awakened to a sense of sin—how he shall keep clear of the sin, avoid the loose company, and rid himself of the wicked pleasures and practices of this enslaving world.   And as he moves on in the line of integrity—many temptations coming in his way, and much inward corruption rising up to control him—how often will the same anxious inquiry arise : Romans vii. 24. It is only in a false estimate of one's own strength that any can think otherwise, and the spirit of such false estimate will be brought low.   How felt you, my young friends, who have been brought to Christ, in the day of your resolving to be his ? But for all such anxiety there seems to be an answer in the text.

" *By taking heed thereto according to thy word.*"   It is not that young men in our day require information : they require the inclination.   In the gracious young man there are both, and the word that began feeds the proper motives.   The awful threatenings and the sweet encouragements both move him in the right direction. The answer furnished to this anxious inquiry is sufficiently plain and practical.   He is directed to the word of God for all direction, and we might say, for all promised assistance.   Still the matter presented in this light does not appear to me to bring out the full import of the passage.   The inquiry to me would seem to extend over the whole verse.*   There is required the cleansing that his way be according to the Divine Word.   The enquiry is of the most enlarged comprehension, and will be made only by one who can say that he has been honestly putting himself in the way, as the young man in the 10th and 11th verses ; and it can be answered only by the heart that takes in all the strength provided by the blessed God, as is expressed here in the 12th verse.   The Psalmist makes the inquiry, he shows how earnestly he had sought to be in the right way, and immediately he finds all his strength in God. Thus he declares how he has been enabled to do rightly, and how he will do rightly in the future.—*John Stephen.*

Verse 9.—Instead of question and answer both in this one verse, the Hebrew demands the construction with question only, leaving the answer to be inferred from the drift of the entire Psalm—thus : " *Wherewithal shall a young man cleanse his way to keep it according to thy word ?* "   This translation gives precisely the force of the last clause.   Hebrew punctuation lacks the interrogation point, so that we have no other clue but the form of the sentence and the sense by which to decide where the question ends.—*Henry Cowles,* 1872.

Verse 9.—" *His way.*"   ארח, *orach,* which we translate *way* here, signifies a *track,* a *rut,* such as is made by the wheel of a cart or chariot.   A *young sinner* has no *broad beaten* path ; he has his *private ways* of offence, his *secret pollutions ;* and how shall he be cleansed from these ?   how can he be saved from what will destroy mind, body, and soul ?   Let him hear what follows ; the description is from God.

1. He is to *consider* that his way is *impure ;* and how abominable this must make him appear in the sight of God.   2. He must examine it *according to God's word,* and carefully hear what God has said concerning *him* and *it.*   3. He must *take heed* to it, לשמר, *lishmor,* to *keep, guard,* and *preserve his way*--his general course of life, from all defilement.—*Adam Clarke.*

Verse 9.—" *By taking heed,*" etc.   I think the words may be better rendered and supplied thus, *by observing* what is *according to thy word ;* which shows how a sinner is to be cleansed from his sins by the blood of Christ, and justified by his righteousness, and be clean through his word ; and also how and by whom the work of sanctification is wrought in the heart, even by the Spirit of God, by means of the word, and what is the rule of a man's walk and conversation : he will find the word of God to be profitable, to inform in the doctrines of justification and pardon, to acquaint him with the nature of regeneration and sanctification ; and for the correction and amendment of his life and manners, and for his instruction in every branch of manners : 2 Tim. iii. 16.—*John Gill,* 1697—1771.

Verse 9.—" *By taking heed.*"   There is an especial necessity for this " *Take heed,*" because of the proneness of a young man to thoughtlessness, carelessness,

---

* This opinion is confirmed by the quotation which follows from Cowles.

presumption, self-confidence. There is an especial necessity for "*taking heed*," because of the difficulty of the way. "Look well to thy goings;" it is a narrow path. "Look well to thy goings," it is a new path. "Look well to thy goings;" it is a slippery path. "Look well to thy goings;" it is an eventful path.—*James Harrington Evans*, 1785—1849.

Verse 9.—"*According to thy word.*" God's word is the glass which discovereth all spiritual deformity, and also the water and soap which washeth and scoureth it away.—*Paul Bayne.*

Verse 9.—"*According to thy word.*" I do not say that there are no other guides, no other fences. I do not say that conscience is worth nothing, and conscience in youth is especially sensitive and tender; I do not say that prayer is not a most valuable fence, but prayer without taking heed is only another name for presumption; prayer and carelessness can never walk hand in hand together; and I therefore say that there is no fence nor guard that can so effectually keep out every enemy as prayerful reading of the word of God, bringing every solicitation from the world or from companions, every suggestion from our own hearts and passions, to the test of God's word :—What says the Bible? The answer of the Bible, with the teaching and enlightenment of the Holy Spirit, will in all the intricacies of our road be a lamp unto our feet and a light unto our path.—*Barton Bouchier.*

Verse 9.—"*Thy word.*" The word is the only weapon (like Goliath's sword, none to equal this), for the hewing down and cutting off of this stubborn enemy, our lusts. The word of God can master our lusts when they are in their greatest pride : if ever lust rageth at one time more than another, it is when youthful blood boils in our veins. Youth is giddy, and his lust is hot and impetuous : his sun is climbing higher still, and he thinks it is a great while to night; so that it must be a strong arm that brings a young man off his lusts, who hath his palate at best advantage to taste sensual pleasure. The vigour of his strength affords him more of the delights of the flesh than crippled age can expect, and he is farther from the fear of death's gun-shot, as he thinks, than old men who are upon the very brink of the grave, and carry the scent of the earth about them, into which they are suddenly to be resolved. Well, let the word of God meet this young gallant in all his bravery, with his feast of sensual delights before him, and but whisper a few syllables in his ear, give his conscience but a prick with the point of its sword, and it shall make him fly in as great haste from them all, as Absalom's brethren did from the feast when they saw Amnon their brother murdered at the table. When David would give the young man a receipt to cure him of his lusts, how he may cleanse his whole course and way, he bids him only wash in the waters of the word of God.—*William Gurnall.*

Verse 9.—The Scriptures teach us the best way of living, the noblest way of suffering, and the most comfortable way of dying.—*John Flavel*, 1627—1691.

Verse 10.—"*With my whole heart have I sought thee.*" There are very few of us that are able to say with the prophet David that we have sought God with our whole heart; to wit, with such integrity and pureness that we have not turned away from that mark as from the most principal thing of our salvation.—*John Calvin.*

Verse 10.—"*With my whole heart have I sought thee.*" Sincerity is in every expression; the heart is open before God. The young man can so speak to the Searcher of hearts. . . . . Let us consider the directness of this kind of converse with God. We use round-about expressions in drawing nigh to God. We say, With my whole heart would I seek thee. We are afraid to be direct. . . . . See how decided in his conscious actings is the young man before you, how open and confiding he is, and such you will find to be the characteristic of his pious mind throughout the varied expressions unfolded in this Psalm. Here he declares to the Omniscient One that he had sought him with all his heart. He desired to realize God in everything.—*John Stephen.*

Verse 10 (first clause).—God alone sees the heart; the heart alone sees God.—*John Donne*, 1573—1631.

Verse 10.—"*O let me not wander from thy commandments.*" David after he had protested that he sought God with his whole heart, besought God that he would not suffer him to decline from his commandments. Hereby let us see what great need we have to call upon God, to the end he may hold us with a mighty strong hand. Yea, and though he hath already mightily put to his helping hand, and we also know that he hath bestowed upon us great and manifest graces; yet this is not all: for there are so many vices and imperfections in our nature, and we are so feeble and weak that we have very great need daily to pray unto him, yea, and that more and more, that he will not suffer us to decline from his commandments.—*John Calvin.*

Verse 10.—The more experience a man hath in the ways of God, the more sensible is he of his own readiness to wander insensibly, by ignorance and inadvertency, from the ways of God ; but the young soldier dares run hazards, ride into his adversary's camp, and talk with temptation, being confident he cannot go wrong ; he is not so much in fear as David who here cries, " *O let me not wander*."—*David Dickson*, 1583—1662.

Verse 11.—" *Thy word have I hid in mine heart, that I might not sin against thee.*" There laid up in the heart the word has effect. When young men only read the letter of the Book, the word of promise and instruction is deprived of much of its power. Neither will the laying of it up in the mere memory avail. The word must be known and prized, and laid up in the heart ; it must occupy the affection as well as the understanding ; the whole mind requires to be impregnated with the word of God. Revealed things require to be seen. Then the word of God in the heart— the threatenings, the promises, the excellencies of God's word—and God himself realized, the young man would be inwardly fortified ; the understanding enlightened, conscience quickened—he would not sin against his God.—*John Stephen.*

Verse 11.—" *Thy word have I hid in mine heart, that I might not sin against thee.*" In proportion as the word of the King is present in the heart, " *there* is power " against sin (Eccles. viii. 4). Let us use this means of absolute power more, and more life and more holiness will be ours.—*Frances Ridley Havergal*, 1836—1879.

Verse 11.—" *Thy word have I hid in mine heart.*" It is fit that the word, being " more precious than gold, yea, than much fine gold," a peerless pearl, should not be laid up in the porter's lodge only—the outward ear ; but even in the cabinet of the mind.—*Dean Boys, quoted by James Ford.*

Verse 11.—" *Thy word have I hid in mine heart.*" There is great difference between Christians and worldlings. The worldling hath his treasure in jewels without him ; the Christian hath them within. Neither indeed is there any receptacle wherein to receive and keep the word of consolation but the heart only. If thou have it in thy mouth only, it shall be taken from thee ; if thou have it in thy book only, thou shalt miss it when thou hast most to do with it ; but if thou lay it up in thy heart, as Mary did the words of the angel, no enemy shall ever be able to take it from thee, and thou shalt find it a comfortable treasure in the time of thy need.— *William Cowper.*

Verse 11.—" *Thy word have I hid in mine heart.*" This saying, *to hide*, importeth that David studied not to be ambitious to set forth himself and to make a glorious show before men ; but that he had God for a witness of that secret desire which was within him. He never looked to worldly creatures ; but being content that he had so great a treasure, he knew full well that God who had given it him would so surely and safely guard it, as that it should not be laid open to Satan to be taken away. Saint Paul also declareth unto us (1 Tim. i. 19) that the chest wherein this treasure must be hid is a good conscience. For it is said, that many being void of this good conscience, have lost also their faith, and have been robbed thereof. As if a man should forsake his goods and put them in hazard, without shutting a door, it were an easy matter for thieves to come in and rob and spoil him of all ; even so, if we leave at random to Satan the treasures which God hath given us in his word, without it be hidden in this good conscience, and in the very bottom of our heart as David here speaketh, we shall be spoiled thereof.—*John Calvin.*

Verse 11.—" *Thy word have I hid in mine heart.*"—Remembered, approved, delighted in it.—*William Nicholson* (—1671), *in " David's Harp Strung and Tuned.*"

Verse 11.—" *Thy word.*" Thy saying, thy oracle ; any communication from God to the soul, whether promise, or command, or answer. It means a direct and distinct message, while " word " is more general, and applies to the whole revelation. This is the ninth of the ten words referring to the revelation of God in this Psalm.— *James G. Murphy*, 1875.

Verse 11.—" *In my heart.*" Bernard observes, bodily bread in the cupboard may be eaten of mice, or moulder and waste : but when it is taken down into the body, it is free from such danger. If God enable thee to take thy soul-food into thine heart, it is free from all hazards.—*George Swinnock*, 1627—1673.

Verse 11.—" *That I might not sin against thee.*" Among many excellent virtues of the word of God, this is one ; that if we keep it in our heart, it keeps us from sin, which is against God and against ourselves. We may mark it by experience, that the word is first stolen either out of the mind of man, and the remembrance of it is away ; or at least out of the affection of man ; so that the reverence of it is gone, before that a man can be drawn to the committing of a sin. So long as Eve kept by faith the word of the Lord, she resisted Satan ; but from the time she doubted of that, which God made most certain by his word, at once she was snared.—*William Cowper.*

Verse 12.—*" Blessed art thou, O Lord : teach me thy statutes."* This verse contains a prayer, with the reason of the prayer. The prayer is. *" Teach me thy statutes ; "* the reason, moving him to seek this, ariseth of a consideration of that infinite good which is in God. He is a blessed God, the fountain of all felicity, without whom no welfare or happiness can be to the creature. And for this cause David earnestly desiring to be in fellowship and communion with God, which he knows none can attain unto unless he be taught of God to know God's way and walk in it ; therefore, I say, he prayeth the more earnestly that the Lord would teach him his statutes. Oh that we also could wisely consider this, that our felicity stands in fellowship with God.—*William Cowper.*

Verse 12.—In this verse we have two things, 1. An acknowledgment of God's blessedness, *" Blessed art thou, O Lord ; "* i.e., being possessed of all fulness, thou hast an infinite complacency in the enjoyment of thyself ; and thou art he alone in the enjoyment of whom I can be blessed and happy ; and thou art willing and ready to give out of thy fulness, so that thou art the fountain of blessedness to thy creatures. 2. A request or petition, *" Teach me thy statutes ; "* q.d., seeing thou hast all fulness in thyself, and art sufficient to thy own blessedness ; surely thou hast enough for me. There is enough to content thyself, therefore enough to satisfy me. This encourages me in my address.

Again,—Teach me that I may know wherein to seek my blessedness and happiness, even in thy blessed self ; and that I may know how to come by the enjoyment of thee, so that I may be blessed in thee. Further,—Thou art blessed originally, the Fountain of all blessing ; thy blessedness is an everlasting fountain, a full fountain ; always pouring out blessedness : O, let me have this blessing from thee, this drop from the fountain.—*William Wisheart, in " Theologia, or, Discourses of God,"* 1716.

Verse 12.—Since God is blessed, we cannot but desire to learn his ways. If we see any earthly being happy, we have a great desire to learn out his course, as thinking by it we might be happy also. Every one would sail with that man's wind who prospereth ; though in earthly things it holdeth not alway : yet a blessed God cannot by any way of his bring to other than blessedness. Thus, he who is blessedness itself, he will be ready to communicate his ways to other : the excellentest things are most communicative.—*Paul Bayne.*

Verse 12.—*" Teach me."* He had Nathan, he had priests to instruct him, himself was a prophet ; but all their teaching was nothing without God's blessing, and therefore he prays, *" Teach me."*—*William Nicholson.*

Verse 12.—*" Teach me."* These words convey more than the simple imparting of knowledge, for he said before he had such, when he said he hid God's words in his heart ; and in verse 7 he said he *" had learned the judgments of his justice : "* it includes grace to observe his law.—*Robert Bellarmine,* 1542—1621.

Verse 12.—*"Teach me."* If this were practised now, to join prayer with hearing, that when we offer ourselves to be taught of men, we would therewith send up prayer to God, before preaching, in time of preaching and after preaching, we would soon prove more learned and religious than we are.—*William Cowper.*

Verse 12.—*" Teach me thy statutes."* Whoever reads the Psalm with attention must observe in it one great characteristic, and that is, how decisive are its statements that in keeping the commandments of God nothing can be done by human strength ; but that it is he who must create the will for the performance of such duty. The Psalmist entreats the Lord to open his eyes that he may behold the wondrous things of the law, to teach him his statutes, to remove from him the way of lying, to incline his heart unto his testimonies, and not to covetousness, to turn away his eyes from beholding vanity, and not to take the word of truth utterly out of his mouth. Each of these petitions shows how deeply impressed he was of his entire helplessness as regarded himself, and how completely dependent upon God he felt himself for any advancement he could hope to make in the knowledge of the truth.   All his studies in the divine law, all his aspirations after holiness of life, he was well assured could never meet with any measure of success, except by the grace of God preventing and co-operating, implanting in him a right desire, and acting as an infallible guide, whereby alone he would be enabled to arrive at the proper sense of Holy Scripture, as well as to correct principles of action in his daily walk before God and man.— *George Phillips,* 1846.

Verse 12.—" *Teach me thy statutes.*"—If it be asked why the Psalmist entreats to be taught, when he has just before been declaring his knowledge, the answer is that he seeks instruction as to the practical working of those principles which he has learnt theoretically.—*Michael Ayguan* (1416), *in Neale and Littledale.*

Verse 13.—" *With my lips have I declared,*" etc.   Above all, be careful to talk of that to others which you do daily learn yourself, and out of the abundance of your heart speak of good things unto men.—*Richard Greenham.*

Verse 13.—Having hid the purifying word in his heart, the Psalmist will *declare it with his lips ;* and as it is so pure throughout, he will declare all in it, without exception.   When the fountain of the heart is purified, the streams from the lips will be pure also.   The declaring lips of the Psalmist are here placed in antithesis to the mouth of Jehovah, by which the judgments were originally pronounced.— *F. G. Marchant.*

Verse 13.—As the consciousness of having communicated our knowledge and our spiritual gifts is a means of encouragement to seek a greater measure, so it is an evidence of the sincerity and fruitfulness of what knowledge we have : " *Teach me thy statutes.   With my lips have I declared all the judgments of thy mouth.*"—*David Dickson.*

Verse 13.—" *With my lips,*" etc.   The tongue is a most excellent member of the body, being well used to the glory of God and the edification of others ; and yet it cannot pronounce without help of the lips.   The Lord hath made the body of man with such marvellous wisdom, that no member of it can say to another, I have no need of thee ; but such is man's dulness, that he observes not how useful unto him is the smallest member in the body, till it be taken from him.   If our lips were clasped for a time, and our tongue thus shut up, we would esteem it a great mercy to have it loosed again ; as that cripple, when he found the use of his feet, leaped for joy and glorified God.—*William Cowper.*

Verse 13.—" *Declared all the judgments.*"   He says in another place (Ps. xxxvi. 6), " *Thy judgments are like a great deep.*"   As the apostle says (Rom. xi. 33, 34), " *O the depth of the wisdom and knowledge of God ! how unsearchable are his judgments, and his ways past finding out.   For who hath known the mind of the Lord ?* " If the judgments are unsearchable, how then says the prophet, " *I have declared all the judgments of thy mouth ?* " We answer, —peradventure there are judgments of God which are not the judgments of his mouth, but of his heart and hand only.

We make a distinction, for we have no fear that the sacred Scripture weakens itself by contradictions.   It has not said, The judgments of his mouth are a great deep ; but " *Thy judgments.*"   Neither has the apostle said, The unsearchable judgments of his mouth ; but " *His unsearchable judgments.*"   We may regard the judgments of God, then, as those hidden ones which he has not revealed to us ; but the judgments of his mouth, those which he has made known, and has spoken by the mouth of the prophets.—*Ambrose,* 340—397.

Verse 14.—" *I have rejoiced in the way of thy testimonies,*" etc.   The Psalmist saith not only, " I have rejoiced in thy testimonies," but, " in the *way* of thy testimonies."   Way is one of the words by which the law is expressed.   God's laws are ways that lead us to God ; and so it may be taken here, " the way which thy testimonies point out, and call me unto ; or else his own practice, as a man's course is called his way ; his delight was not in speculation or talk, but in obedience and practice : " *in the way of thy testimonies.*"   He tells us the degree of his joy, " *as much as in all riches :* " " as much," not to show the equality of these things, as if we should have the same affection for the world as for the word of God ; but " as much," because we have no higher comparison.   This is that which worldlings doat upon, and delight in ; now as much as they rejoice in worldly possessions, so much do I rejoice in the way of thy testimonies.   For I suppose David doth not compare his own delight in wealth ; but his own choice and delight, with the delight and choice of others. If he had spoken of himself both in the one respect and in the other, the expression was very high. David, who was called to a crown, and in a capacity of enjoying much in the world, gold, silver, land, goods, largeness of territory, and a compound of all that which all men jointly, and all men severally do possess ; yet was more pleased in the holiness of God's ways, than in all the world : " For what shall it profit a man, if he shall gain the whole world, and lose his own soul ? " (Mark viii. 36).—*Thomas Manton.*

Verse 14.—" *The way of thy testimonies.*" The testimony of God is his word, for it testifies his will ; the " *way* " of his testimony is the practice of his word, and doing of that which he hath declared to be his will, and wherein he hath promised to show us his love. David found not this sweetness in hearing, reading, and professing the word only ; but in practising of it ; and in very deed, the only cause why we find not the comfort that is in the word of God is that we practise it not by walking in the way thereof. It is true, at the first it is bitter to nature, which loves carnal liberty, to render itself as captive to the word : *laboriosa virtutis via,* and much pains must be taken before the heart be subdued ; but when it is once begun, it renders such joy as abundantly recompenses all the former labour and grief.—*William Cowper.*

Verse 14.—Riches are acquired with difficulty, enjoyed with trembling, and lost with bitterness.—*Bernard,* 1091—1157.

Verse 14.—A poor, good woman said, in time of persecution, when they took away the Christian's Bibles, " I cannot part with my Bible ; I know not how to live without it." When a gracious soul has heard a profitable sermon, he says, " Methinks it does me good at heart ; it is the greatest nourishment I have : " " *I have rejoiced in the way of thy testimonies, as much as in all riches.*"—*Oliver Heywood,* 1629—1702.

Verse 15.—" *I will meditate in thy precepts,*" etc. All along David had shown what he *had* done ; now, what he *will* do. Verse 10, " I have sought ; " verse 11, " I have hid ; " verse 12, " I have declared ; " verse 14, " I have rejoiced." Now in the two following verses he doth engage himself to set his mark towards God for time to come. " *I will meditate in thy precepts,*" etc. We do not rest upon anything already done and past, but continue the same diligence unto the end. Here is David's hearty resolution and purpose, to go on for time to come. Many will say, Thus I have done when I was young, or had more leisure and rest ; in that I have meditated and conferred. You must continue still in a holy course. To begin to build, and leave unfinished, is an argument of folly.—*Thomas Manton.*

Verse 15.—" *I will meditate in thy precepts.*" Not only *of* thy precepts or concerning them, but *in* them, while engaged in doing them.—*Joseph Addison Alexander.*

Verse 15.—" *I will.*" See this " I will " repeated again and again (verses 48, 78). In meditation it is hard (sometimes at least) to take off our thoughts from the pre-engagements of other subjects, and apply them to the duty. But it is harder to become duly serious in acting in it, harder yet to dive and ponder ; and hardest of all to continue in an abode of thoughts, and dwell long enough, and after views to make reviews, to react the same thinkings, to taste things over and over, when the freshness and newness is past, when by long thinking the things before us seem old. We are ready to grow dead and flat in a performance except we stir up ourselves often in it. It is hard to hold on and hold up, unless we hold up a wakeful eye, a warm affection, a strong and quick repeated resolution ; yea, and without often lifting up the soul to Christ for fresh recruits of strength to hold on. David, that so excellent artist in this way, saith he *will meditate,* he often saith *he will.* Doubtless, he not only said " I will " when he was to make his entrance into this hard work ; but likewise for continuance in it, to keep up his heart from flagging, till he well ended his work. It is not the digging into the golden mine, but the digging long, that finds and fetches up the treasure. It is not the diving into the sea, but staying longer, that gets the greater quantity of pearls. To draw out the golden thread of meditation to its due length till the spiritual ends be attained this is a rare and happy attainment.—*Nathanael Ranew,* 1670.

Verse 15.—" *I will meditate.*" How much our " *rejoicing in the testimonies* " of God would be increased by a more habitual meditation upon them ! This is, however, a resolution which the carnal mind can never be brought to make, and to which the renewed mind through remaining depravity is often sadly reluctant. But it is a blessed employment, and will repay a thousandfold the difficulty of engaging the too backward heart in the duty.—*Charles Bridges.*

Verse 15.—Meditation is of that happy influence, it makes the mind wise, the affections warm, the soul fat and flourishing, and the conversation greatly fruitful.—*Nathanael Ranew.*

Verse 15.—" *Meditate in thy precepts.*" Study the Scriptures. If a famous man do but write an excellent book, O how we do long to see it ! Or suppose I could tell you that there is in France or Germany a book that God himself wrote, I am confident men may draw all the money out of your purses to get that book. You have it by you : O that you would study it ! When the eunuch was riding in his chariot, he was studying the prophet Isaiah. He was not angry when Philip came and, as we would have thought, asked him a bold question : " Understandest thou what thou readest ? " (Acts viii. 27—30) ; he was glad of it. One great end of the year of release was, that the law might be read (Deut. xxxi. 9—13). It is the wisdom of God that speaks in the Scripture (Luke xi. 49) ; therefore, whatever else you mind, really and carefully study the Bible.—*Samuel Jacomb* (1629—1659), *in " The Morning Exercises."*

Verse 15.—" *I will have respect.*" The one is the fruit of the other : " *I will meditate ;*" and then, " *I will have respect.*" Meditation is in order to practice ; and if it be right, it will beget a respect to the ways of God. We do not meditate that we may rest in contemplation, but in order to obedience : " Thou shalt meditate in the book of the law day and night, that thou mayest observe to do according to all that is written therein " (Joshua i. 8).—*Thomas Manton.*

Verse 15.—" *And have respect unto thy ways.*"—As an archer hath to his mark.—*John Trapp.*

Verse 15.—" *Respect unto thy ways.*" It is not without a peculiar pleasure, when travelling, that we *contemplate* the splendid buildings, the gardens, the fortifications, or the fine-art galleries. But what are all these sights to the *contemplation of the ways of God*, which he himself has traversed, or has maked out for man ? And what practical need there is that we consider the way, for else we shall be as a sleepy coachman, not carefully observant of the road, who may soon upset himself and his passengers.—*Martin Geier.*

Verse 15.—" *Thy ways.*" David's second internal action concerning the word is consideration ; where mark well, how by a most proper speech he calls the word of God the *ways* of God ; partly, because by it God comes near unto men, revealing himself to them, who otherways could not be known of them ; for he dwells in light inaccessible ; and partly, because the word is the *way* which leads men to God. So then, because by it God cometh down to men, and by it men go up unto God, and know how to get access to him, therefore is his word called his *way.*—*William Cowper.*

Verses 15, 16.—The two last verses of this section present to us a threefold internal action of David's soul toward the word of God ; first, meditation ; secondly, consideration ; thirdly, delectation ; every one of those proceeds from another, and they mutually strengthen one another. Meditation brings the word to the mind ; consideration views it and looks at length into it, whereof is bred delectation. That which comes into the mind, were it never so good, if it be not considered, goes as it came, leaving neither instruction nor joy ; but being once presented by meditation, if it be pondered by consideration, then it breeds delectation, which is the perfection of godliness, in regard of the internal action.—*William Cowper.*

Verse 16.—" *I will delight myself,*" etc. He protested before that he had great delight in the testimonies of God : now he saith he will still delight in them. A man truly godly, the more good he doth, the more he desireth, delighteth and resolveth to do. Temporisers, on the contrary, who have but a show of godliness, and the love of it is not rooted in their heart, how soon are they weary of well-doing ! If they have done any small external duty of religion, they rest as if they were fully satisfied, and there needed no more good to be done by them. True religion is known by hungering and thirsting after righteousness, by perseverance in well-doing and an earnest desire to do more.

But to this he adds that *he will not forget the word*. The graces of the Spirit do every one fortify and strengthen another ; for ye see meditation helps consideration. Who can consider of that whereof he thinks not ? Consideration again breeds delectation ; and as here ye see, delectation strengthens memory : because he delights in the word he will not forget the word ; and memory again renews meditation. Thus every grace of the Spirit helps another ; and by the contrary, one of them neglected, works a wonderful decay of the remnant.—*William Cowper.*

Verse 16.—" *I will delight myself.*" When righteousness, from a matter of constraint, becomes a matter of choice, it instantly changes its whole nature, and rises to a higher moral rank than before. The same God whom it is impossible to move by law's authority, moves of his own proper and original inclination in the very path of the law's righteousness. And so, we, in proportion as we are like unto God, are alive to the virtues of that same law, to the terror of whose severities we are altogether dead. We are no longer under a schoolmaster ; but obedience is changed from a thing of force into a thing of freeness. It is moulded to a higher state and character than before. We are not driven to it by the God of authority. We are drawn to it by the regards of a now willing heart to all moral and all spiritual excellence.—*Thomas Chalmers,* 1780—1847.

Verse 16.—Meditation must not be a dull, sad, and dispirited thing : not a driving like the chariots of the Egyptians when their wheels were taken off, but like the chariots of Amminadib (Cant. vi. 12) that ran swiftly. So let us pray,—Lord, in meditation make me like the chariots of Amminadib, that my swift running may evidence my delight in meditating. Holy David makes delight such an ingredient or assistant here, that sometimes he calls the exercise of meditation by the name of " *delight,*" speaking in the foregoing verse of this meditation, " *I will meditate of thy precepts,*" and in the 16th verse, " *I will delight myself in thy statutes ; *" which is the same with meditation, only with superadding the excellent qualification due meditation should have ; the name of delight is givn to meditation because of its noble concomitant—holy joy and satisfaction.—*Nathanael Ranew.*

Verse 16.—" *Delight myself.*" The word is very emphatical : אשתעשע, *eshtaasha,* *I will skip about and jump for joy.*—*Adam Clarke.*

Verse 16.—" *I will not forget.*" Delight preventeth forgetfulness : the mind will run upon that which the heart delighteth in ; and the heart is where the treasure is (Matt. vi. 21). Worldly men that are intent upon carnal interests, forget the word, because it is not their delight. If anything displeases us, we are glad if we can forget it ; it is some release from an inconvenience, to take off our thoughts from it ; but it doubleth the contentment of a thing that we are delighted in, to remember it, and call it to mind. In the outward school, if a scholar by his own averseness from learning, or by the severity and imprudence of his master, hath no delight in his book, all that he learneth is lost and forgotten, it goeth in at one ear, and out at the other : but this is the true art of memory, to cause them to delight in what they learn. Such instructions as we take in with sweetness, they stick with us, and run in our minds night and day. So saith David here, " *I will delight myself in thy statutes ; I will not forget thy word.*"—*Thomas Manton.*

Verse 16.—" *Forget.*" I never yet heard of a covetous old man, who had forgotten where he had buried his treasure.—*Cicero de Senectute.*

EXPOSITION OF VERSES 17 TO 24.

D EAL bountifully with thy servant, *that* I may live, and keep thy word.

18 Open thou mine eyes, that I may behold wondrous things out of thy law.

19 I *am* a stranger in the earth : hide not thy commandments from me.

20 My soul breaketh for the longing *that it hath* unto thy judgments at all times.

21 Thou hast rebuked the proud *that are* cursed, which do err from thy commandments.

22 Remove from me reproach and contempt ; for I have kept thy testimonies.

23 Princes also did sit *and* speak against me : *but* thy servant did meditate in thy statutes.

24 Thy testimonies also *are* my delight *and* my counsellors.

In this section the trials of the way appear to be manifest to the Psalmist's mind, and he prays accordingly for the help which will meet his case. As in the last eight verses he prayed as a youth newly come into the world, so here he pleads as a servant and a pilgrim, who growingly finds himself to be a stranger in an enemy's country. His appeal is to God alone, and his prayer is specially direct and personal. He speaks with the Lord as a man speaketh with his friend.

17. " *Deal bountifully with thy servant.*" He takes pleasure in owning his duty to God, and counts it the joy of his heart to be in the service of his God. Out of his condition he makes a plea, for a servant has some hold upon a master ; but in this case the wording of the plea shuts out the idea of legal claim, since he seeks bounty rather than reward. Let my wages be according to thy goodness, and not according to my merit. Reward me according to the largeness of thy liberality, and not according to the scantiness of my service. The hired servants of our Father have all of them bread enough and to spare, and he will not leave one of his household to perish with hunger. If the Lord will only treat us as he treats the least of his servants we may be well content, for all his true servants are sons, princes of the blood, heirs of life eternal. David felt that his great needs required a bountiful provision, and that his little desert would never earn such a supply ; hence he must throw himself upon God's grace, and look for the great things he needed from the great goodness of the Lord. He begs for a liberality of grace, after the fashion of one who prayed. " O Lord, thou must give me great mercy or no mercy, for little mercy will not serve my turn."

" *That I may live.*" Without abundant mercy he could not live. It takes great grace to keep a saint alive. Even life is a gift of divine bounty to such undeserving ones as we are. Only the Lord can keep us in being, and it is mighty grace which preserves to us the life which we have forfeited by our sin. It is right to desire to live, it is meet to pray to live, it is just to ascribe prolonged life to the favour of God. Spiritual life, without which this natural life is mere existence, is also to be sought of the Lord's bounty, for it is the noblest work of divine grace, and in it the bounty of God is gloriously displayed. The Lord's servants cannot serve him in their own strength, for they cannot even live unless his grace abounds towards them.

" *And keep thy word.*" This should be the rule, the object, and the joy of our life. We may not wish to live and sin ; but we may pray to live and keep God's word. Being is a poor thing if it be not well-being. Life is only worth keeping while we can keep God's word ; indeed, there is no life in the highest sense apart from holiness : life while we break the law is but a name to live.

The prayer of this verse shows that it is only through divine bounty or grace that we can live as faithful servants of God, and manifest obedience to his commands. If we give God service it must be because he gives us grace. We work *for* him because he works *in* us. Thus we may make a chain out of the opening verses of the three first octaves of this Psalm : verse 1 blesses the holy man, verse 9 asks how we can attain to such holiness, and verse 17 traces such holiness to its secret source, and shows us how to seek the blessing. The more a man prizes holiness and the more earnestly he strives after it, the more will he be driven towards God for help therein, for he will plainly perceive that his own strength is insufficient, and that he cannot even so much as live without the bounteous assistance of the Lord his God.

18. "*Open thou mine eyes.*" This is a part of the bountiful dealing which he has asked for ; no bounty is greater than that which benefits our person, our soul, our mind, and benefits it in so important an organ as the eye. It is far better to have the eyes opened than to be placed in the midst of the noblest prospects and remain blind to their beauty. "*That I may behold wondrous things out of thy law.*" Some men can perceive no wonders in the gospel, but David felt sure that there were glorious things in the law : he had not half the Bible, but he prized it more than some men prize the whole. He felt that God had laid up great bounties in his word, and he begs for power to perceive, appreciate, and enjoy the same. We need not so much that God should give us more benefits, as the ability to see what he has given.

The prayer implies a conscious darkness, a dimness of spiritual vision, a power-lessness to remove that defect, and a full assurance that God can remove it. It shows also that the writer knew that there were vast treasures in the word which he had not yet fully seen, marvels which he had not yet beheld, mysteries which he had scarcely believed. The Scriptures teem with marvels ; the Bible is wonder-land ; it not only relates miracles, but it is itself a world of wonders. Yet what are these to closed eyes ? And what man can open his own eyes, since he is born blind ? God himself must reveal revelation to each heart. Scripture needs opening, but not one half so much as our eyes do : the veil is not on the book, but on our hearts. What perfect precepts, what precious promises, what priceless privileges are neglected by us because we wander among them like blind men amongst the beauties of nature, and they are to us as a landscape shrouded in darkness !

The Psalmist had a measure of spiritual perception, or he would never have known that there were wondrous things to be seen, nor would he have prayed, " open thou mine eyes ; " but what he had seen made him long for a clearer and wider sight. This longing proved the genuineness of what he possessed, for it is a test mark of the true knowledge of God that it causes its possessor to thirst for deeper knowledge.

David's prayer in this verse is a good sequel to verse 10, which corresponds to it in position in its octave : there he said, " O let me not wander," and who so apt to wander as a blind man ? and there, too, he declared, " with my whole heart have I sought thee," and hence the desire to see the object of his search. Very singular are the interlacings of the boughs of the huge tree of this Psalm, which has many wonders even within itself if we have opened eyes to mark them.

19. "*I am a stranger in the earth.*" This is meant for a plea. By divine com-mand men are bound to be kind to strangers, and what God commands in others he will exemplify in himself. The Psalmist was a stranger for God's sake, else had he been as much at home as worldlings are ; he was not a stranger to God, but a stranger to the world, a banished man so long as he was out of heaven. Therefore he pleads, "*Hide not thy commandments from me.*" If these are gone, what have I else ? Since nothing around me is mine, what can I do if I lose thy word ? Since none around me know or care to know the way to thyself, what shall I do if I fail to see thy com-mands, by which alone I can guide my steps to the land where thou dwellest ? David implies that God's commands were his solace in his exile : they reminded him of home, and they showed him the way thither, and therefore he begged that they might never be hidden from him, by his being unable either to understand them or to obey them. If spiritual light be withdrawn the command is hidden, and this a gracious heart greatly deprecates. What would be the use of opened eyes if the best object of sight were hidden from their view ? While we wander here we can endure all the ills of this foreign land with patience if the word of God is applied to our hearts by the Spirit of God ; but if the heavenly things which make for our peace were hid from our eyes we should be in an evil case,—in fact, we should be at sea without a compass, in a desert without a guide, in an enemy's country without a friend.

This prayer is a supplement to " open thou mine eyes," and, as the one prays to see, the other deprecates the negative of seeing, namely, the command being hidden, and so out of sight. We do well to look at both sides of the blessing we are seeking, and plead for it from every point of view. The prayers are appropriate to the characters mentioned : as he is a servant he asks for opened eyes that his eyes may ever be towards his Lord, as the eyes of a servant should be ; as a stranger he begs that he may not be strange to the way in which he is to walk towards his home. In each case his entire dependence is upon God alone.

Note how the third of the second octave (11) has the same keyword as this third of the third octave : " Thy word have I hid," " Hide not thy commandments from me." This invites a meditation upon the different senses of hiding *in* and hiding *from*.

20. " *My soul breaketh for the longing that it hath unto thy judgments at all times.*" True godliness lies very much in desires. As we are not what we shall be, so also we are not what we would be. The desires of gracious men after holiness are intense,— they cause a wear of heart, a straining of the mind, till it feels ready to snap with the heavenly pull. A high value of the Lord's commandment leads to a pressing desire to know and to do it, and this so weighs upon the soul that it is ready to break in pieces under the crush of its own longings. What a blessing it is when all our desires are after the things of God. We may well long for such longings.

God's judgments are his decisions upon points which else had been in dispute. Every precept is a judgment of the highest court upon a point of action, an infallible and immutable decision upon a moral or spiritual question. The word of God is a code of justice from which there is no appeal.

> " This is the Judge which ends the strife
> Where wit and reason fail ;
> Our guide through devious paths of life,
> Our shield when doubts assail."

David had such reverence for the word, and such a desire to know it, and to be conformed to it, that his longings caused him a sort of heart-break, which he here pleads before God. Longing is the soul of praying, and when the soul longs till it breaks, it cannot be long before the blessing will be granted. The most intimate communion between the soul and its God is carried on by the process described in the text. God reveals his will, and our heart longs to be conformed thereto. God judges, and our heart rejoices in the verdict. This is fellowship of heart most real and thorough.

Note well that our desire after the mind of God should be constant ; we should feel holy longings " *at all times.*" Desires which can be put off and on like our garments are at best but mere wishes, and possibly they are hardly true enough to be called by that name,—they are temporary emotions born of excitement, and doomed to die when the heat which created them has cooled down. He who always longs to know and do the right is the truly right man. His judgment is sound, for he loves all God's judgments, and follows them with constancy. His times shall be good, since he longs to be good and to do good at all times.

Remark how this fourth of the third eight chimes with the fourth of the fourth eight. " My soul breaketh ; " " my soul melteth." There is surely some recondite poetic art about all this, and it is well for us to be careful in studying what the Psalmist was so careful in composing.

21. " *Thou hast rebuked the proud that are cursed.*" This is one of God's judgments : he is sure to deal out a terrible portion to men of lofty looks. God rebuked Pharaoh with sore plagues, and at the Red Sea " the foundations of the world were discovered at thy rebuke, O Lord." In the person of the haughty Egyptian he taught all the proud that he will certainly abase them. Proud men are cursed men : nobody blesses them, and they soon become a burden to themselves. In itself, pride is a plague and torment. Even if no curse came from the law of God, there seems to be a law of nature that proud men should be unhappy men. This led David to abhor pride ; he dreaded the rebuke of God and the curse of the law. The proud sinners of his day were his enemies, and he felt happy that God was in the quarrel as well as he.

" *Which do err from thy commandments.*" Only humble hearts are obedient, for they alone will yield to rule and government. Proud men's looks are high, too high to mark their own feet and keep the Lord's way. Pride lies at the root of all sin : if men were not arrogant they would not be disobedient.

God rebukes pride even when the multitudes pay homage to it, for he sees in it rebellion against his own majesty, and the seeds of yet further rebellions. It is the sum of sin. Men talk of an honest pride ; but if they were candid they would see that it is of all sins the least honest, and the least becoming in a creature, and especially in a fallen creature : yet so little do proud men know their own true condition under the curse of God, that they set up to censure the godly, and express contempt for them, as may be seen in the next verse. They are themselves contemptible, and yet they are contemptuous towards their betters. We may well love the judgments of God when we see them so decisively levelled against the haughty upstarts who would fain lord it over righteous men ; and we may well be of good comfort under the rebukes of the ungodly since their power to hurt us is destroyed by the Lord himself. " The Lord rebuke thee " is answer enough for all the accusations of men or devils.

In the fifth of the former octave the Psalmist wrote, " I have declared all the judgments of thy mouth, and here he continues in the same strain, giving a particular instance of the Lord's judgments against haughty rebels. In the next two portions the fifth verses deal with lying and vanity, and pride is one of the most common forms of those evils.

22. " *Remove from me reproach and contempt.*" These are painful things to tender minds. David could bear them for righteousness' sake, but they were a heavy yoke, and he longed to be free from them. To be slandered, and then to be despised in consequence of the vile accusation, is a grievous affliction. No one likes to be traduced, or even to be despised. He who says, " I care nothing for my reputation," is not a wise man, for in Solomon's esteem " a good name is better than precious ointment." The best way to deal with slander is to pray about it : God will either remove it, or remove the sting from it. Our own attempts at clearing ourselves are usually failures ; we are like the boy who wished to remove the blot from his copy, and by his bungling made it ten times worse. When we suffer from a libel it is better to pray about it than go to law over it, or even to demand an apology from the inventor. O ye who are reproached, take your matters before the highest court, and leave them with the Judge of all the earth. God will rebuke your proud accuser ; be ye quiet and let your advocate plead your cause.

" *For I have kept thy testimonies.*" Innocence may justly ask to be cleared from reproach. If there be truth in the charges alleged against us what can we urge with God ? If, however, we are wrongfully accused our appeal has a *locus standi* in the court and cannot be refused. If through fear of reproach we forsake the divine testimony we shall deserve the coward's doom ; our safety lies in sticking close to the true and to the right. God will keep those who keep his testimonies. A good conscience is the best security for a good name ; reproach will not abide with those who abide with Christ, neither will contempt remain upon those who remain faithful to the ways of the Lord.

This verse stands as a parallel both in sense and position to verse 6, and it has the catchword of " testimonies," by which it chimes with 14.

23. " *Princes also did sit and speak against me.*" David was high game, and the great ones of the earth went a hawking after him. Princes saw in him a greatness which they envied, and therefore they abused him. On their thrones they might have found something better to consider and speak about, but they turned the seat of judgment into the seat of the scorner. Most men covet a prince's good word, and to be spoken ill of by a great man is a great discouragement to them, but the Psalmist bore his trial with holy calmness. Many of the lordly ones were his enemies, and made it their business to speak ill of him : they held sittings for scandal, sessions for slander, parliaments of falsehood, and yet he survived all their attempts upon him.

" *But thy servant did meditate in thy statutes.*" This was brave indeed. He was God's servant, and therefore he attended to his Master's business ; he was God's servant, and therefore felt sure that his Lord would defend him. He gave no heed to his princely slanderers, he did not even allow his thoughts to be disturbed by a knowledge of their plotting in conclave. Who were these malignants that they should rob God of his servant's attention, or deprive the Lord's chosen of a moment's devout communion. The rabble of princes were not worth five minutes' thought, if those five minutes had to be taken from holy meditation. It is very beautiful to see the two sittings : the princes sitting to reproach David, and David sitting with his God and his Bible, answering his traducers by never answering them at all. Those who feed upon the word grow strong and peaceful, and are by God's grace hidden from the strife of tongues.

Note that in the close of the former octave he had said, " I will meditate," and here he shows how he had redeemed his promise, even under great provocation to forget it.   It is a praiseworthy thing when the resolve of our happy hours is duly carried out in our seasons of affliction.

Verse 24. " *Thy testimonies also are my delight and my counsellors.*"   They were not only themes for meditation, but " also " sources of delight and means of guidance.   While his enemies took counsel with each other the holy man took counsel with the testimonies of God.   The fowlers could not drive the bird from its nest with all their noise.   It was *their* delight to slander and *his* delight to meditate. The words of the Lord serve us for many purposes ; in our sorrows they are our delight, and in our difficulties they are our guide ; we derive joy from them and discover wisdom in them.   If we desire to find comfort in the Scriptures we must submit ourselves to their counsel, and when we follow their counsel it must not be with reluctance but with delight.   This is the safest way of dealing with those who plot for our ruin ; let us give more heed to the true testimonies of the Lord than to the false witness of our foes.   The best answer to accusing princes is the word of the justifying King.

In verse 16 David said, " I will delight in thy statutes," and here he says " they are my delight : " thus resolutions formed in God's strength come to fruit, and spiritual desires ripen into actual attainments.   O that it might be so with all the readers of these lines.

NOTES ON VERSES 17 TO 24.

Verse 17.—"*Deal bountifully with thy servant,*" etc. These words might be—Render unto thy servant, or upon thy servant. A deep signification seems to be here involved. The holy man will take the responsibility of being dealt with, not certainly as a mere sinful man, but as a man placing himself in the way appointed for reconciliation. Such we find to be the actual case, as you read in the 16th verse, in the Part immediately preceding —" I will delight myself in thy statutes ; I will not forget thy word." Now, the statutes of the Lord referred pre-eminently to the sacrifice for sin, and the cleansings for purifications that were prescribed in the Law. You have to conceive of the man of God as being in the midst of the Levitical ritual, for which you find him making all preparations : 1 Chron. xxii., xxiii., xxiv. Placing himself, therefore, upon these, he woud pray the Lord to deal with him according to them ; or, as we, in New Testament language, would say,—placing himself on the great atonement, the believer would pray the Lord to deal with him according to his standing in Christ, which would be in graciousness or bounty. For if the Lord be just to condemn without the atonement, he is also just to pardon through the atonement ; yea, he is just, and the justifier of him that believeth in Jesus.—*John Stephen.*

Verse 17.—"*Deal bountifully,*" etc. O Lord, ı am constantly resolved to obey and adhere to thy known will all the days of my life : O make me those gracious returns which thou hast promised to all such.—*Henry Hammond.*

Verse 17.—"*Deal bountifully . . . that I may keep thy word,*" etc. A faithful servant should count his by-past service richly rewarded by being employed yet more in further service, as this prayer teacheth ; for David entreats that he may live and keep God's word.—*David Dickson.*

Verse 17.—"*Bountifully.*" And indeed, remembering what a poor, weak, empty, and helpless creature the most experienced believer is in himself, it is not to be conceived that anything short of a *bountiful* supply of grace can answer the emergency.—*Charles Bridges.*

Verse 17.—"*Thy servant.*" That he styles himself so frequently the servant of God notes the reverent estimation he had of his God, in that he accounts it more honourable to be called the servant of God who was above him than the king of a mighty, ancient, and most famous people that were under him. And indeed, since the angels are styled his ministers, shall men think it a shame to serve him ? and especially since he of his goodness hath made them our servants, " ministering spirits " to us ? Should we not joyfully serve him who hath made all his creatures to serve us, and exempted us from the service of all other, and hath only bound us to serve himself ?—*William Cowper.*

Verse 17.—"*That I may live.*" As a man must " live " in order to work, the first petition is, that God would " deal with his servant," according to the measure of grace and mercy, enabling him to " live " the life of faith, and strengthening him by the Spirit of might in the inner man.—*George Horne,* 1730—1792.

Verse 17.—"*That I may live, and keep thy word.*" David joins here two together, which whosoever disjoins cannot be blessed. He desires to live ; but so to live that he may keep God's word. To a reprobate man, who lives a rebel to his Maker, it had been good (as our Saviour said of Judas) that he had never been born. The shorter his life is, the fewer are his sins and the smaller his judgments. But to an elect man, life is a great benefit ; for by it he goes from election to glorification, by the way of sanctification. The longer he lives, the more good he doth, to the glory of God, the edification of others, and confirmation of his own salvation ; making it sure to himself by wrestling and victory in temptations, and perseverance in well doing.—*William Cowper.*

Verse 18.—"*Open thou mine eyes.*" Who is able to know the secret and hidden things of the Scriptures unless Christ opens his eyes ? Certainly, no one ; for " No man knoweth the Son but the Father ; neither knoweth any man the Father save the Son, and he to whom the Son will reveal him." Wherefore, as suppliants, we draw near to him, saying, " *Open thou mine eyes,*" etc. The words of God cannot be kept except they be known; neither can they be known unless the eyes shall be opened,—hence it is written, " *That I may live and keep thy word ;* " and then, " *Open thou mine eyes.*"—*Paulus Palanterius.*

Verse 18.—" *Open thou mine eyes.*"   " What wilt thou that I shall do unto thee ? " was the gracious inquiry of the loving Jesus to a poor longing one on earth.   " Lord ! that I may receive my sight," was the instant answer.   So here, in the same spirit, and to the same compassionate and loving Lord, does the Psalmist pray, " *Open thou mine eyes;* " and both in this and the preceding petition, " Deal bountifully with thy servant, " we see at once who prompted the prayer.—*Barton Bouchier.*

Verse 18.—" *Open thou mine eyes.*"   If it be asked, seeing David was a regenerate man, and so illumined already, how is it that he prays for the opening of his eyes ? The answer is easy : that our regeneration is wrought by degrees.   The beginnings of light in his mind made him long for more ; for no man can account of sense, but he who hath it.   The light which he had caused him to see his own darkness ; and therefore, feeling his wants, he sought to have them supplied by the Lord.—*William Cowper.*

Verse 18.—" *Open thou mine eyes.*"   The saints do not complain of the obscurity of the law, but of their own blindness.   The Psalmist doth not say, Lord make a plainer law, but, Lord, *open mine eyes :* blind men might as well complain of God, that he doth not make a sun whereby they might see.   The word is " a light that shineth in a dark place " (2 Pet. i. 19).   There is no want of light in the Scripture, but there is a veil of darkness upon our hearts ; so that if in this clear light we cannot see, the defect is not in the word, but in ourselves.

The light which they beg is not anything besides the word.   When God is said to enlighten us, it is not that we should expect new revelations, but that we may see the wonders in his word, or get a clear sight of what is already revealed.   Those that vent their own dreams under the name of the Spirit, and divine light, they do not give you *mysteria*, but *monstra*, portentous opinions ; they do not show you the wondrous things of God's law, but the prodigies of their own brain ; unhappy abortives, that die as soon as they come to light.   " To the law and to the testimony : if they speak not according to this word, it is because there is no light in them " (Isaiah viii. 20).   The light which we have is not without the word, but by the word.

The Hebrew phrase signifieth " *unveil mine eyes.*"   There is a double work, negative and positive.   There is a taking away of the veil, and an infusion of light. Paul's cure of his natural blindness is a fit emblem of our cure of spiritual blindness : " Immediately there fell from his eyes as it had been scales : and he received sight forthwith " (Acts ix. 18).   First, the scales fall from our eyes, and then we receive sight.—*Thomas Manton.*

Verse 18.—The Psalmist asks for no new revelation.   It was in God's hand to give this, and he did it in his own time to those ancient believers ; but to all of them at every time there was enough given for the purposes of life.   The request is not for more, but that he may employ well that which he possesses.   Still better does such a form of request suit us, to whom life and immortality have been brought to light in Christ.   If we do not find sufficient to exercise our thoughts with constant freshness, and our soul with the grandest and most attractive subjects, it is because we want the eyesight.   It is of great importance for us to be persuaded of this truth, that there are many things in the Bible still to be found out, and that, if we come in the right spirit, we may be made discoverers of some of them.   These things disclose themselves, not so much to learning, though that is not to be despised, as to spiritual sight, to a humble, loving heart.

And this at least is certain, that we shall always find things that are new to *ourselves.*   However frequently we traverse the field, we shall perceive some fresh golden vein turning up its glance to us, and we shall wonder how our eyes were formerly holden that we did not see it.   It was all there waiting for us, and we feel that more is waiting, if we had the vision.   There is a great Spirit in it that holds deeper and even deeper converse with our souls.

This further may be observed, that the Psalmist asks for no new faculty.   The eyes are there already, and they need only to be opened.   It is not the bestowal of a new and supernatural power which enables a man to read the Bible to profit, but the quickening of a power he already possesses.   In one view it is supernatural, as God is the Author of the illumination by a direct act of his Spirit ; in another it is natural, as it operates through the faculties existing in a man's soul.   God gives " the spirit of wisdom and revelation in the knowledge of Christ, that the eyes of man's understanding may be enlightened." (Eph. i. 17.)   It is important to remember this also, for here lies our responsibility, that we have the faculty, and here also is the point at which we must begin action with the help of God.   A man will never grow into the knowledge of God's word by idly waiting for some new gift of discernment, but by diligently using that which God has already bestowed upon him, and using at the same time all other helps that lie within his reach. There are men and books that seem, beyond others, to have the power of aiding insight. All of us have felt it in the contact of some affinity of nature which makes them our best helpers ; the kindred clay upon the eyes by which the great Enlightener removes our blindness (John ix. 6). Let us seek for such, and if we find them let us employ them without leaning on them. Above all, let us give our whole mind in patient, loving study to the book itself, and where we fail, at any essential part, God will either send his evangelist Philip to our aid (Acts. viii) or instruct us himself. But it is only to patient, loving study that help is given. God could have poured all knowledge into us by easy inspiration, but it is by earnest search alone that it can become the treasure of the soul.

But if so, it may still be asked what is the meaning of this prayer, and why does the Bible itself insist so often on the indispensable need of the Spirit of God to teach ? Now there is a side here as true as the other, and in no way inconsistent with it. If prayer without effort would be presumptuous, effort without prayer would be vain. The great reason why men do not feel the power and beauty of the Bible is a spiritual one. They do not realize the grand evil which the Bible has come to cure, and they have not a heart to the blessings which it offers to bestow. The film of a fallen nature, self-maintained, is upon their eyes while they read : " The eyes of their understanding are darkened, being alienated from the life of God " (Eph. iv. 18). All the natural powers will never find the true key to the Bible, till the thoughts of sin and redemption enter the heart, and are put in the centre of the Book. It is the part of the Father of lights, by the teaching of his Spirit, to give this to the soul, and he will, if it humbly approaches him with this request. Thus we shall study as one might a book with the author at hand, to set forth the height of its argument, or as one might look on a noble composition, when the artist breathes into us a portion of his soul, to let us feel the centre of its harmonies of form and colour. Those who have given to the Bible thought and prayer will own that these are not empty promises.—*John Kerr, in a Sermon entitled, " God's Word Suited to Man's Sense of Wonder,"* 1877.

Verse 18.—O let us never forget, that the wonderful things contained in the divine law can neither be discovered nor relished by the " natural man," whose powers of perception and enjoyment are limited in their range to the objects of time and sense. It is the divine Spirit alone who can lighten the darkness of our sinful state, and who can enable us to perceive the glory, the harmony, and moral loveliness which everywhere shine forth in the pages of revealed truth.—*John Morison,* 1829.

Verse 18.—" *Uncover my eyes and I will look—wonders out of thy law.*" The last clause is a kind of exclamation after his eyes have been uncovered. This figure is often used to denote inspiration or a special divine communication. " *Out of thy law,*" i.e., brought out to view, as if from a place of concealment.—*Joseph Addison Alexander.*

Verse 18.—" *Wondrous things.*" Many were the signs and miracles which God wrought in the midst of the people of Israel, which they did not understand. What was the reason ? Moses tells us expressly what it was : " Yet the Lord hath not given you an heart to perceive, and eyes to see, and ears to hear, unto this day " (Deut. xxix. 4). They had sensitive eyes and ears, yea, they had a rational heart or mind ; but they wanted a spiritual ear to hear, a spiritual heart or mind to apprehend and improve those wonderful works of God ; and these they had not, because God had not given them such eyes, ears, and hearts. Wonders without grace cannot open the eyes fully ; but grace without wonders can. And as man hath not an eye to see the wonderful works of God spiritually, until it is given ; so, much less hath he an eye to see the wonders of the word of God till it be given him from above ; and therefore David prays, " *Open thou mine eyes, that I may behold wondrous things out of thy law.*" And if the wondrous things of the law are not much seen till God give an eye then much less are the wondrous things of the Gospel. The light of nature shows us somewhat of the Law ; but nothing of the Gospel was ever seen by the light of nature. Many who have seen and admired, some excellencies in the Law could never see, and therefore have derided, that which is the excellency of the Gospel, till God had opened their heart to understand.—*Joseph Caryl,* 1602—1673.

Verse 18.—" The word is very nigh " unto us ; and, holding in our hand a document that teems with what is wonderful, the sole question is, " Have we an eye to its marvels, a heart for its mercies ? " Here is the precise use of the Holy Spirit. The Spirit puts nothing new into the Bible ; he only so enlightens and strengthens our faculties, that we can discern and admire what is there already.   It is not the telescope which draws out that rich sparkling of stars on the blue space, which to the naked eye seem points of light, and untenanted : it is not the microscope which condenses the business of a stirring population into the circumference of a drop of water, and clothes with a thousand tints the scarcely discernible wing of the ephemeral insect.   The stars are shining in their glory, whether or no we have the instruments to penetrate the azure ; and the tiny tenantry are carrying on their usual concerns, and a rich garniture still forms the covering of the insect, whether or no the powerful lens has turned for us the atom into a world, and transformed the almost imperceptible down into the sparkling plumage of the bird of paradise.   Thus the wonderful things are already in the Bible.   The Spirit who indited them at first brings them not as new revelations to the individual ; but, by removing the mists of carnal prejudice, by taking away the scales of pride and self-sufficiency, and by rectifying the will, which causes the judgment to look at truth through a distorted medium,—by influencing the heart, so that the affections shall no longer blind the understanding,— by these and other modes, which might be easily enumerated, the Holy Ghost enables men to recognize what is hid, to perceive beauty and to discover splendour where all before had appeared without form and comeliness ; and thus brings round the result of the Bible, in putting on the lip the wonderful prayer which he had himself inspired : " *Open thou mine eyes, that I may behold wondrous things out of thy law*,"—*Henry Melvill*, 1798—1871.

Verse 18.—The " *wondrous things* " seem to be the great things of an eternal world—he had turned his enquiring eyes upon the wonders of nature, sun, moon, and stars, mountains, trees, and rivers.   He had seen many of the wonders of art ; but now, he wanted to see the spiritual wonders contained in the Bible.   He wanted to know about God himself in all his majesty, purity, and grace.   He wanted to learn the way of salvation by a crucified Redeemer, and the glory that is to follow.

" *Open mine eyes*."—David was not blind—his eye was not dim.   He could read the Bible from end to end, and yet he felt that he needed more light.   He felt that he needed to see deeper, to have the eyes of his understanding opened.   He felt that if he had nothing but his own eyes and natural understanding, he would not discover the wonders which he panted to see.   He wanted divine teaching—the eye-salve of the Spirit ; and therefore he would not open the Bible without this prayer, " *Open thou mine eyes*."—*Robert Murray M'Cheyne*, 1813—1843.

Verse 18.—" *Wondrous things*."   Wherefore useth he this word " *wondrous ?* " It is as if he would have said, Although the world taketh the law of God to be but a light thing, and it seemeth to be given but as it were for simple souls and young children ; yet for all that there seemeth such a wisdom to be in it, as that it sur-mounteth all the wisdom of the world, and that therein lie hid wonderful secrets.— *John Calvin*.

Verse 18.—" *Thy law*."   That which is the *object* of the understanding prayed for, that in the knowledge whereof the Psalmist would be illuminated, is תּוֹרָה.   The word signifies instruction ; and being referred unto God, it is his teaching or instruc- tion of us by the revelation of himself, the same which we intend by the Scripture. When the books of the Old Testament were completed they were, for distinction's sake, distributed into תּוֹרָה, כְּתוּבִים and נְבִיאִים, or the " Law," the " Psalms," and the " Prophets," Luke xxiv. 44.   Under that distribution *Torah* signifies the five books of Moses.   But whereas these books of Moses were, as it were, the foundation of all future revelations under the Old Testament, which were given in the explication thereof, all the writings of it were usually called " the Law," Isaiah viii. 20.   By the *law*, therefore, in this place, the Psalmist understands all the books that were then given unto the church by revelation for the rule of its faith and obedience. And that by the *law*, in the Psalms, the written law is intended, is evident from the first of them, wherein he is declared blessed who " meditateth therein day and night," Ps. i. 2 ; which hath respect unto the command of reading and meditating on the *books thereof* in that manner, Josh. i. 8.   That, therefore, which is intended by this word is the entire revelation of the will of God, given unto the church for the rule of its faith and obedience—that is, the holy Scripture.

In this law there are נִפְלָאוֹת " *wonderful things*," פָּלָא signifies to be " wonderful," to be " hidden," to be " great " and " high ; " that which men by the use of reason cannot attain unto or understand (hence נִפְלָאוֹת are things that have such an impression of divine wisdom and power upon them as that they are justly the object of our admiration) ; that which is too hard for us ; as Deut. xvii. 8, כִּי־יִפָּלֵא מִמְּךָ דָבָר—" If a matter be too hard for thee," hid from thee. And it is the name whereby the miraculous works of God are expressed, Ps. lxxvii. 11, lxxviii. 11. Wherefore, these " wonderful things of the law " are those expressions and effects of divine wisdom in the Scripture which are above the natural reason and understanding of men to find out and comprehend. Such are the mysteries of divine truth in the Scripture, especially because Christ is in them, whose name is " Wonderful," Isa. ix. 6 ; for all the great and marvellous effects of infinite wisdom meet in him.—*John Owen*, 1616—1683.

Verse 18.—" *Wondrous things.*" There are promises in God's word that no man has ever tried to find. There are treasures of gold and silver in it that no man has taken the pains to dig for. There are medicines in it for the want of knowledge of which hundreds have died. It seems to me like some old baronial estate that has descended to a man who lives in a modern house, and thinks it scarcely worth while to go and look into the venerable mansion. Year after year passes away and he pays no attention to it, since he has no suspicion of the valuable treasures it contains, till, at last, some man says to him, " Have you been up in the country to look at that estate ? " He makes up his mind that he will take a look at it. As he goes through the porch he is surprised to see the skill that has been displayed in its construction : he is more and more surprised as he goes through the halls. He enters a large room and is astonished as he beholds the wealth of pictures on the walls, among which are portraits of many of his revered ancestors. He stands in amazement before them. There is a Titians, there a Raphael, there is a Correggio, and there is a Giorgione. He says, " I never had any idea of these before." " Ah," says the steward, " there is many another thing that you know nothing about in the castle," and he takes him from room to room and shows carved plate, and wonderful statues, and the man exclaims, " Here I have been for a score of years the owner of this estate, and have never before known what things were in it." But no architect ever conceived of such an estate as God's word, and no artist, or carver, or sculptor, ever conceived of such pictures, and carved dishes, and statues as adorn its apartments. It contains treasures that silver, and gold, and precious stones are not to be mentioned with.— *Henry Ward Beecher*, 1872.

Verse 18.—" *That I may behold wondrous things.*" The great end of the Word of God in the Psalmist's time, as now, was piactical ; but there is a secondary use here referred to, which is worthy of consideration,—its power of meeting man's faculty of wonder. God knows our frame, for he made it, and he must have adapted the Bible to all its parts. If we can show this, it may be another token that the book comes from Him who made man . . . . That God has bestowed upon man the faculty of wonder we all know. It is one of the first and most constant emotions in our nature. We can see this in children, and in all whose feelings are still fresh and natural. It is the parent of the desire to know, and all through life it is urging men to enquire.—*John Ker*.

Verse 18.—" *Wondrous things out of thy law.*" In cxviii. we had the " wondrous " character of redemption ; in cxix. we have the " wonders " (verses 18, 27, 129), of God's revelation.—*William Kay*, 1871.

Verses 18, 19.—When I cannot have Moses to tell me the meaning, saith Saint Augustine, give me that Spirit that thou gavest to Moses. And this is that which every man that will understand must pray for : this David prayed for ;—" *Open thou mine eyes that I may see the wonders of the Law ;* " and (verse 19) " *hide not thy commandments from me.*" And Christ saith, " If you, being evil, can give good gifts to your children ; how much more shall your heavenly Father give his Holy Spirit to them that ask him ? " so that then we shall see the secrets of God.—*Richard Stock* (—1626).

Verse 19.—" *I am a stranger in the earth.*" David had experience of peace and war, of riches and poverty, of pleasure and woe. He had been a private and public person ; a shepherd, a painful calling ; a soldier, a bloody trade ; a courtier, an honourable slavery, which joineth together in one the lord and the parasite, the gentleman and the drudge ; and he was a king,—a glorious name, filled up with fears and cares. All these he had passed through, and found least rest when he was at the highest, less content on the throne than in the sheepfolds. All this he had observed and laid up in his memory, and this his confession is an epitome and brief of all ; and in effect he telleth us, that whatsoever he had seen in this his passage, whatsoever he had enjoyed, yet he found nothing so certain as this,—that he had found nothing certain, nothing that he could abide with or would abide with him, but that he was still as a passenger and " *stranger in the earth.*"—*Anthony Farindon*, 1596—1658.

Verse 19.—" *I am a stranger in the earth,*" etc.   As a sojourner, he hath renounced the world, which is therefore become his enemy ; as " *a stranger* " he is fearful of losing his way ; on these accounts he requesteth that God would compensate the loss of earthly comforts by affording the light of heaven ; that he would not " *hide his commandments,*" but show and teach him those steps, by which he may ascend toward heaven, rejoicing in hope of future glory.—*George Horne*, 1730—1792.

Verse 19.—" *I am a stranger in the earth.*"   This confession from a solitary wanderer would have had little comparative meaning ; but in the mouth of one who was probably surrounded with every source of worldly enjoyment, it shows at once the vanity of " earth's best joys," and the heavenly tendency of the religion of the Bible.—*Charles Bridges.*

Verse 19.—" *I am a stranger in the earth,*" etc.   1. Every man here upon earth (especially a godly man) is but a stranger and a passenger.   2. It concerns him that is a stranger to look after a better and a more durable state.   Every man should do so.   A man's greatest care should be for that place where he lives longest ; therefore eternity should be his scope.   A godly man will do so.   Those whose hearts are not set upon earthly things, they must have heaven.   The more their affections are estranged from the one, the more they are taken up about the other (Col. iii. 2) ; heaven and earth are like two scales in a balance, that which is taken from the one is put into the other.   3. There is no sufficient direction how to obtain this durable estate, but in the word of God.   Without this we are but like poor pilgrims and wayfaring men in a strange country, not able to discern the way home.   A blessed state is only sufficiently revealed in the word : " Life and immortality is brought to light through the gospel " (2 Tim. i. 10).   The heathens did but guess at it, and had some obscure sense of an estate after this life; but as it is brought to light with most clearness in the word, so the way thither is only pointed out by the word.   It is the word of God makes us wise to salvation, and which is our line and rule to heavenly Canaan ; and therefore it concerns those that look after this durable state to consult with the word.   4. There is no understanding God's word but by the light of the Spirit. " There is a spirit in man : and the inspiration of the Almighty giveth them understanding " (Job xxxii. 8).   Though the word have light in it, yet the spirit of man cannot move till God enlightens us with that lively light that makes way for the dominion of the truth in our hearts, and conveyeth influence into our hearts.   This is the light David begs when he says, " *Hide not thy commandments from me.*"   David was not ignorant of the Ten Commandments, of their sound ; but he begs their spiritual sense and use.   5. If we would have the Spirit we must ask it of God in prayer ; for God gives the " Spirit to them that ask him " (Luke xi. 13) ; and therefore we must say, as David, " O send out thy light and thy truth : let them lead me : let them bring me unto thy holy hill, and to thy tabernacles " (Ps. xliii. 33).—*Thomas Manton.*

Verse 19.—" *I am a stranger in the earth,*" etc.   When a child is born, it is spoken of sometimes under the designation of " a little stranger ! "   Friends calling will ask if, as a privilege, they may " see the little stranger."   A stranger, indeed ! come from far.   From the immensities.   From the presence, and touch, and being of God !   And going—into the immensities again—into, and through all the unreckonable ages of duration.

But the little stranger grows, and in a while begins to take vigorous root.   He works, and wins, and builds, and plants, and buys, and holds, and, in his own feeling, becomes so " settled " that he would be almost amused with anyone who should describe him as a stranger now.

And still life goes on, deepening and widening in its flow, and holding in itself manifold and still multiplying elements of interest.   Increasingly the man is caught by these—like a ship, from which many anchors are cast into the sea.   He strives among the struggling, rejoices with the gay, feels the spur of honour, enters the race of acquisition, does some hard and many kindly things by turns ; multiplies his engagements, his relationships, his friends, and then—just when after such preparations, life ought to be fully beginning, and opening itself out into a great, restful, sunny plain—lo ! the shadows begin to fall, which tell, too surely, that it is drawing fast to a close.   The voice, which, soon or late, everyone must hear, is calling for " the little stranger," who was born not long ago, whose first lesson is over, and who is wanted now to enter by the door called death, into another school. And the stranger is not ready. He has thrown out so many anchors, and they have taken such a fast hold of the ground that it will be no slight matter to raise them. He is *settled*. He has no pilgrim's staff at hand ; and his eye, familiar enough with surrouding things, is not accustomed to the onward and ascending way, cannot so well measure the mountain altitude, or reckon the far distance. The progress of time has been much swifter than the progress of his thought. Alas ! he has made one long mistake. He has " looked at the things which are seen," and forgotten the things which are not seen. And " the things which are seen " are temporal, and go with time into extinction ; while " those which are not seen, are eternal." And so there is hurry, and confusion, and distress in the last hours, and in the going away. Now, all this may be obviated and escaped, thoroughly, if a man will but say—" *I am a stranger in the earth : hide not thy commandments from me.*"—*Alexander Raleigh, in " The Little Sanctuary, and other Meditations.*" 1872.

Verse 19.—" *I am a stranger in the earth,*" etc. In the law, God recommends strangers to the care and compassion of his people ; now David returns the arguments to him, to persuade him to deal kindly with him.—*Robert Leighton, 1611—1684.*

Verse 19.—" *In the earth.*" He makes no exception here ; the whole earth he acknowledged a place of his pilgrimage. Not only when he was banished among the Moabites and Philistines was he a stranger; but even when he lived peaceably at home in Canaan, still he thinks himself a stranger. This consideration moved godly Basil to despise the threatening of Modestus, the deputy of Valens the emperor, when he braved him with banishment. *Ab exilii metu liber sum, unam hominum cognoscens esse patriam, paradisum omnem autem terram commune naturæ exilium.* And it shall move us to keep spiritual sobriety in the midst of pleasures, if we remember that in our houses, at our own fireside, and in our own beds, we are but strangers from which we must shortly remove, to give place to others.—*William Cowper.*

Verse 19.—" *Hide not thy commandments from me.*" The manner of David's reasoning is this. I am here a stranger and I know not the way, therefore, Lord, direct me. The similitude is taken from passengers, who coming to an uncouth country where they are ignorant of the way, seek the benefit of a guide. But the dissimilitude is here : in any country people can guide a stranger to the place where he would be ; but the dwellers of the earth cannot show the way to heaven ; and therefore David seeks no guide among them, but prays the Lord to direct him.—*William Cowper.*

Verse 19.—" *Hide not thy commandments from me.*" There is a hiding of the word of God when means to hear it explained by preachers are wanting ; and there is a hiding of the comfortable and lively light of the Spirit, who must quicken the word unto us. From both those evils we may, and we should, pray to be saved.—*David Dickson.*

Verse 20.—" *My soul breaketh,*" etc. Here is a protestation of that earnest desire he had to the obedience of the word of God ; he amplifies it two ways : first, it was no light motion, but such as being deeply rooted made his heart to *break* when he saw that he could not do in the obedience thereof what he would. Next, it was no vanishing motion, like the morning dew ; but it was permanent, *omni tempore*, he had it *at all times.*—*William Cowper.*

Verse 20.—" *My soul breaketh for the longing,*" as one that with straining breaks a vein.—*William Gurnall.*

Verse 20.—" *My soul breaketh,*" etc. This breaking is by rubbing, chafing, or crushing. The spirit was so *fretted* with its yearning desire after the things which Jehovah had spoken, that it was broken as by heavy friction. The " *longing* " to find out and follow the hidden wonders was almost unbearable. This *longing* continued with the Psalmist " *at all times,*" or " in every season." Prosperity could not make him forget it ; adversity could not quench it. In sickness or health, in happiness or sadness, in company or alone, nothing overcame that *longing*. "*The wondrous things*" were so wonderful, and still so hidden. To see a little of " the beauty of the Lord " is to get to know how much there is which we fail to see, and thus to *long* more than ever. He who pursues ardently the wonders of the word of the Lord, will never set that *longing* at rest as long as he remains " in the earth." It is only when we shall " be like him," and " shall see him as he is," that we shall cry " Enough, Lord ! " " I shall be satisfied when I awake in thy likeness."—*F. G. Marchant.*

Verse 20.—"*My soul breaketh for the longing.*" For the earnest desire. "That it hath *unto thy judgments at all times.*" Thy law; thy commands. This was a constant feeling. It was not fitful, or spasmodic. It was the steady, habitual state of the soul on the subject. He had never seen enough of the beauty and glory of the law of God to feel that all the wants of his nature were satisfied, or that he could see and know no more; he had seen and felt enough to excite in him an ardent desire to be made fully acquainted with *all* that there is in the law of God.—*Albert Barnes.*

Verse 20.—"*My soul breaketh for the longing,*" etc. The desire after God's appointments becomes painfully intense. A longing—an intense longing—for the judgments of the Lord at all times. These are the particulars of his breaking soul. His whole mind is toward the things of God. He prays that he may behold the wondrous things of Jehovah's law, and that he may not hide his commandments from him; and here his soul breaks for longing towards his judgments at all times. The state of the Psalmist's mind would not lead us here to suppose that he was awaiting the manifestation of the Lord's judgments in vindicating his cause against ungodly men, or that he was longing for opportunity of fulfilling all the deeds of righteousness towards his fellow-men; for this he was doing to the utmost. Evidently he is intent upon the ordinances of religion, which were called "*judgments*" in reference to the solemn sanctions with which they were enjoined. The man of God so longed to join with the Lord's people in these, that his heart was ready to break with desire, as he was forced from place to place in the wilderness. The renewed heart is here. Another might long to be delivered from persecution, to be at rest, to be restored to home, relations, and comfort. The man of God could not but desire those natural enjoyments; but, over all, his holy mind longed with ardour for the celebration of Jehovah's worship.—*John Stephen.*

Verse 20.—"*Thy judgments.*" God's judgments are of two sorts : first, his commands ; so called because by them right is judged and discerned from wrong. Next, his plagues executed upon transgressors according to his word. David here refers to the first. Let men who have not the like of David's desire, remember, that they whose heart cannot break for transgressing God's word because they love it, shall find the plagues of God to bruise their body and break their heart also. Let us delight in the first sort of these judgments, and the second shall never come upon us.—*William Cowper.*

Verse 20.—Mark that word, "*at all times.*" Bad men have their good moods, as good men have their bad moods. A bad man may, under gripes of conscience, a smarting rod, the approaches of death, or the fears of hell, or when he is sermon sick, cry out to the Lord for grace, for righteousness, for holiness ; but he is the only blessed man that hungers and thirsts after righteousness at all times.—*Thomas Brooks, 1608—1680.*

Verse 20.—"*At all times.*" Some prize the word in adversity, when they have no other comfort to live upon ; then they can be content to study the word to comfort them in their distresses ; but when they are well at ease, they despise it. But David made use of it "*at all times ;*" in prosperity, to humble him ; in adversity, to comfort him; in the one, to keep him from pride; in the other, to keep him from despair in affliction, the word was his cordial; in worldly increase, it was his antidote; and so at all times his heart was carried out to the word either for one necessity or another.—*Thomas Manton.*

Verse 20.—"*At all times.*" How few are there even among the servants of God who know anything of the intense feeling of devotion here expressed ! O that our cold and stubborn hearts were warmed and subdued by divine grace, that we might be ready to faint by reason of the longing which he had "*at all times*" for the judgments of our God. How fitful are our best feelings ! If to-day we ascend the mount of communion with God, to-morrow we are in danger of being again entangled with the things of earth. How happy are they whose hearts are "*at all times*" filled with longings after fellowship with the great and glorious object of their love !—*John Morison, 1829.*

Verse 20.—If you read the lives of good men, who have been, also, intellectually great, you will be struck, I think, even to surprise, a surprise, however, which will not be unpleasant, to find them, at the close of life, in their own estimation so ignorant, so utterly imperfect, so little the better of the long life-lesson. Dr. Chalmers, after kindling churches and arousing nations to their duties, summed up his own attainments in the word "desirousness," and took as the text that best described his inner state, that passionate, almost painful cry of David, " *My soul breaketh for the longing that it hath unto thy judgments.*" But how grand was the attainment ! To be in old age as simple as a little child before God ! To be still learning at threescore years and ten ! How beautiful seem the great men in their simplicity !—*Alexander Raleigh, in " The Little Sanctuary,"* 1872.

Verse 21.—" *Thou hast rebuked the proud that are cursed.*" If the proud escape here, as sometimes they do, hereafter they shall not ; for, " *the proud man is an abomination to the Lord ;* " Prov. xvi. 5. *God cannot endure him ;* Ps. ci. 5. And what of that ? *Tu perdes superbos,* Thou shalt destroy the proud. The very heathens devised the proud giants struck with thunder from heaven. And *if God spared not the angels,* whom he placed in the highest heavens, *but* for their pride *threw them down headlong to the nethermost hell,* how much less shall he spare the proud dust and ashes of the sons of men, but shall cast them from the height of their earthly altitude to the bottom of that infernal dungeon ! " Humility makes men angels ; pride makes angels devils ;" as that father said : I may well add, makes devils of men. Αλαζονείας ούτις εκφευγει δικην, says the heathen poet, Menander ; " Never soul escaped the revenge of pride," never shall escape it. So sure as God is just, pride shall not go unpunished. I know now we are all ready to call for a bason, with Pilate, and to wash our hands from this foul sin. Honourable and beloved, this vice is a close one ; it will cleave fast to you ; yea, so close that ye can hardly discern it from a piece of yourselves : this is it that aggravates the danger of it. For, as Aquinas notes well, some sins are more dangerous, *propter vehementiam impugnationis,* " for the fury of their assault ; " as the sin of anger : others for their correspondence to nature ; as the sins of lust : other, *propter latentiam sui,* " for their close skulking " in our bosom ; as the sin of pride. Oh, let us look seriously into the corners of our false hearts, even with the lanthorn of God's law, and find out this subtle devil ; and never give peace to our souls till we have dispossessed him. Down with your proud plumes, O ye glorious peacocks of the world : look upon your black legs, and your snake-like head : be ashamed of your miserable infirmities : else, God will down with them and yourselves in a fearful vengeance. There is not the holiest of us but is this way faulty : oh, let us be humbled by our repentance, that we may not be brought down to everlasting confusion : let us be cast down upon our knees, that we may not be cast down upon our faces. For God will make good his own word, one way ; " A man's pride shall bring him low."—*Joseph Hall,* 1574—1656.

Verse 21.—" *Thou hast rebuked the proud.*" Let the histories of Cain, Pharaoh, Haman, Nebuchadnezzar, and Herod, exhibit the proud under the rebuke and curse of God. He abhors their persons and their offerings : he "knows them afar off :" he " resisteth them : " he scattereth them in the imaginations of their hearts." Yet more especially hateful are they in his sight, when cloaking themselves under a spiritual garb,—" which say, Stand by thyself, come not near to me : for I am holier than thou. These are a smoke in my nose, a fire that burneth all the day." David and Hezekiah are instructive beacons in the church, that God's people, whenever they give place to the workings of a proud heart, must not hope to escape his rebuke. " Thou wast a God that forgavest them, though thou tookest vengeance on their inventions : " Ps. xcix. 8.—*Charles Bridges.*

Verse 21.—" *Thou hast rebuked the proud.*" David addeth another reason whereby he is more enflamed to pray unto God and to address himself unto him to be taught in his word ; to wit, when he seeth that he hath so " *rebuked the proud.*" For the chastisements and punishments which God layeth upon the faithless and rebellious should be a good instruction for us ; as it is said that God hath executed judgment, and that the inhabitants of the land should learn his righteousness. It is not without cause that the prophet Isaiah also hath so said ; for he signifieth unto us that God hath by divers and sundry means drawn us unto him, and that chiefly when he teacheth us to fear his majesty. For without it, alas, we shall soon become like unto brute beasts : if God lay the bridle on our necks, what license we will give unto ourselves experience very well teacheth us. Now God seeing that we are so easily brought to run at random, sendeth us examples, because he would bring us to walk in fear and carefully.—*John Calvin.*

Verse 21.—" *The proud.*" This is a style commonly given to the wicked ; because as it is our oldest evil, so is it the strongest and first that strives in our corrupt nature to carry men to transgress the bounds appointed by the Lord. From the time that pride entered into Adam's heart, that he would be higher than God had made him,

he spared not to eat of the forbidden tree.   And what else is the cause of all transgression, but that man's ignorant pride will have his will preferred to the will of
God.—*William Cowper.*

Verse 21.—" *The proud.*"   Peter speaks of the proud, as if they did challenge
God like champions, and provoke him like rebels, so that unless he did resist them,
they would go about to deprive him of his rule, as Korah, Dathan, and Abiram under-
mined Moses.   *Num.* xvi.

For so the proud man saith, I will be like the highest, Isa. xiv., and, if he could,
above the highest too.   This is the creature that was taken out of the dust, Gen. ii. 7,
and so soon as he was made, he opposed himself against that majesty which the angels
adore, the thrones worship, the devils fear, and the heavens obey.   How many sins
are in this sinful world ! and yet, as Solomon saith of the good wife, Prov. xxxi. 29,
" Many daughters have done virtuously, but thou surmountest them all ; "   so may
I say of pride, many sins have done wickedly, but thou surmountest them all ;   for
the wrathful man, the prodigal man, the lascivious man, the surfeiting man, the
slothful man, is rather an enemy to himself than to God ;   but the proud man sets
himself against God, because he doth against his laws ;   he maketh himself equal with
God, because he doth all without God, and craves no help of him ;   he exalteth himself
above God, because he will have his own will though it be contrary to God's will.
As the humble man saith, Not unto us, Lord, not unto us, but to thy name give
the glory, Ps. cxv. i. ;   so the proud man saith, Not unto Him, not unto Him, but
unto us give the glory.   Like unto Herod which took the name of God, and was
honoured of all but the worms, and they showed that he was not a god, but a man,
Acts xii. 21.   Therefore proud men may be called God's enemies, because as the
covetous pull riches from men, so the proud pull honour from God.   Beside, the
proud man hath no cause to be proud, as other sinners have ;   the covetous for riches,
the ambitious for honour, the voluptuous for pleasure, the envious for wrong, the
slothful for ease ;   but the proud man hath no cause to be proud, but pride itself,
which saith, like Pharaoh, " I will not obey," Exod. v. 2.—*Henry Smith, 1560—1591.*

Verse 21.—" *Proud that are cursed.*"—Proud men endure the curse of never
having friends ;   not in prosperity, because they know nobody ;   not in adversity,
because then nobody knows them.—*John Whitecross, in " Anecdotes illustrative of the
Old Testament."*

Verse 21.—This use of God's judgments upon others must we make to ourselves ;
first, that we may be brought to acknowledge our deserts, and so may fear ;   and,
next, that we may so behold his justice upon the proud that we may have assurance
of his mercy to the humble.   This is hard to flesh and blood ;   for some can be brought
to rejoice at the destructon of others, and cannot fear ;   and others, when they are
made to fear, cannot receive comfort.   But those which God hath joined together
let us not separate :   therefore let us make these uses of God's judgments.—*Richard
Greenham.*

Verse 22.—" *Remove from me reproach and contempt.*"   Here David prays against
the reproach and contempt of men ;   that they might be *removed,* or, as the word is,
rolled from off him.   This intimates that they lay upon him, and neither his greatness
nor his goodness could secure him from being libelled and lampooned :   son.e despise
him and endeavoured to make him mean, others reproached him and endeavoured
to make him odious.   It has often been the lot of those that do well to be ill spoken
of.   It intimates, that this burden lay heavy upon him.   Hard words indeed and
foul words break no bones, and yet they are very grievous to a tender and ingenuous
spirit :   therefore David prays, Lord, " remove " them from me, that I may not be
thereby either driven from any duty, or discouraged in it.—*Matthew Henry.*

Verse 22.—" *Remove from me reproach and contempt,*" etc.   In the words (as
in most of the other verses) you have,—1. A request :   " *Remove from me reproach
and contempt.*"   2. A reason and argument to enforce the request :   " *For I have
kept thy testimonies.*"

First, for the request, " *Remove from me reproach and contempt ;* "   the word
signifies, Roll from upon me, let it not come at me, or let it not stay with me.   And then
the argument :   " *for I have kept thy testimonies.*"   The reason may be either thus :
(1) He pleads that he was innocent of what was charged upon him, and had not
deserved those aspersions.   (2) He intimates that it was for his obedience, for this
very cause, that he had kept the word, therefore was reproach rolled upon him.   (3)
It may be conceived thus, that his respect to God's word was not abated by this

reproach, he still kept God's testimonies, how wicked soever he did appear in the eyes of the world. It is either an assertion of his innocency, or he shows the ground why this reproach came upon him, or he pleads that his respect to God and his service was not lessened, whatever reproach he met with in the performance of it. The points from hence are many. 1. It is no strange thing that they which keep God's testimonies should be slandered and reproached. 2. As it is the usual lot of God's people to be reproached ; so it is very grievous to them, and heavy to bear. 3. It being grievous, we may lawfully seek the removal of it. So doth David, and so may we, with submission to God's will. 4. In removal of it, it is best to deal with God about it ; for God is the great witness of our sincerity, as knowing all things, and so to be appealed to in the case. Again, God is the most powerful asserter of our innocency ; he hath the hearts and tongues of men in his own hands, and can either prevent the slanderer from uttering reproach, or the hearer from the entertainment of the reproach. He that hath such power over the consciences of men can clear up our innocency ; therefore it is best to deal with God about it ; and prayer many times proves a better vindication than an apology. 5. In seeking relief with God from this evil, it is a great comfort and ground of confidence when we are innocent of what is charged. In some cases we must humble ourselves, and then God will take care for our credit ; we must plead guilty when, by our own fault, we have given occasion to the slanders of the wicked : so, " Turn away my reproach which I fear ; for thy judgments are good " (Ps. cxix. 39). " My reproach," for it was in part deserved by himself, and therefore he feared the sad consequences of it, and humbled himself before God. But at other times we may stand upon our integrity, as David saith here : *" Turn away my reproach which I fear : for thy judgments are good."—Thomas Manton.*

Verse 23.—" *Princes also did sit,*" under the shadow of justice, "*and speak against me.*" Now this was a great temptation to David, that he was not only mocked and scorned at the taverns and inns, being there blazoned by dissolute jesters and scoffers, and talked of in the streets and market-place ; but even in the place of justice (which ought to be holy) ; it could not therefore be chosen but that they also would utterly defame and slander him, and condemn him to be, as it were, a most wicked and cursed man. When David then did see that he was thus unjustly entreated and handled, he maketh his complaint unto God and sayeth, " O Lord, the princes and governors themselves do sit and speak evil against me ; *and yet for all that I have kept thy testimonies.*" Here in sum we are to gather out of this place, that if it so fall out, when we have walked uprightly and in a good conscience, that we are falsely slandered, and accused of this and that whereof we never once thought ; yet ought we to bear all things patiently ; for let us be sure of that, that we are not better than David, whatever great protestation of our integrity and purity we may dare to make. —*John Calvin.*

Verse 23.—" *But thy servant did meditate in thy statutes.*" As husbandmen, when their ground is overflowed by waters, make ditches and water-furrows to carry it away ; so, when our minds and thoughts are overwhelmed with trouble, it is good to divert them to some other matter. But every diversion will not become saints, it must be a holy diversion : " In the multitude of my thoughts within me thy comforts delight my soul " (Psalm xciv. 19). The case was the same with that of the text, when the throne of iniquity frameth mischief by a law ; as you shall see here, when he had many perplexed thoughts about the abuse of power against himself. But now where lay his ease in diversion ? Would every diversion suit his purpose ? No ; " *Thy* comforts,"—comforts of God's allowance, of God's providing, comforts proper to saints. Wicked men in trouble run to their pot and pipe, and games and sports, and merry company, and so defeat the providence rather than improve it : but David, who was God's servant, must have God's comforts. So, elsewhere, when his thoughts were troubled about the power of the wicked : " I went into the sanctuary of God ; then understood I their end " (Psalm lxxiii. 17). He goeth to divert his mind by the use of God's ordinances, and so cometh to be settled against the temptation.—*Thomas Manton.*

Verse 23.—" *But thy servant did meditate in thy statutes.*"—Perceive here the armour by which David fights against his enemy. *Arma justi quibus omnes adversariorum repellit impetus,* his weapons are the word and prayer. He renders not injury for injury, reproach for reproach. It is dangerous to fight against Satan or his instruments with their own weapons ; for so they shall easily overcome us. Let us fight with the armour of God—the exercises of the word and prayer : for a man may peaceably rest in his secret chamber, and in these two see the miserable end of all those who are enemies to God's children for God's sake.—*William Cowper.*

Verse 23.—" *Thy statutes.*"   It is impossible to live either *Christianly* or *comfortable* without the daily use of Scripture.   It is absolutely necessary for our direction in all our ways before we begin them, and when we have ended them, for the warrant of our approbation of them, for resolving of our doubts, and comforting us in our griefs.   Without it our conscience is a blind guide, and leadeth us in a mist of ignorance, error, and confusion.   Therein we hear God speaking to us, declaring his good will to us concerning our salvation, and the way of our obedience to meet him in his good will.   What book can we read with such profit and comfort ?   For matter, it is wisdom : for authority, it is divine and absolute : for majesty, God himself under common words and letters expressing an unspeakable power to stamp our heart. Where shall we find our minds so enlightened, our hearts so deeply affected, our conscience so moved, both for casting us down and raising us up ?   I cannot find in all the books of the world, such an one speak to me, as in Scripture, with so absolute a conquest of all the powers of my soul.

Contemners of Scripture lack food for their souls, light for their life, and weapons for their spiritual warfare ; but the lovers of Scripture have all that furniture.   Therein we hear the voice of our Beloved, we smell the savour of his ointments, and have daily access unto the art of propitiation.   If in our knowledge we desire divinity, excellency, antiquity, and efficiency, we cannot find it, but in God's word alone.   It is the extract of heavenly wisdom, which Christ the eternal Word brought out of the bosom of his Father.—*William Struther,* 1633.

Verses 23, 24.—The two last verses of this section contain two protestations of David's honest affection to the word.   The first is, that albeit he was persecuted and evil spoken of, and that by great and honourable men of the world, such as Saul, and Abner, and Ahithophel ; yet did he still meditate in the statutes of God. It is a hard temptation when the godly are troubled by any wicked men ; but much harder when they are troubled by men of honour and authority.   And that, first, by reason of their *place :* the greater *power* they have, the greater *peril* to encounter with their displeasure ;   therefore said Solomon, " The wrath of a king is as messengers of death."   Next, because authorities and powers are ordained by God, not for the terror of the good, but of the evil : Rom. xiii. 3.   And therefore it is no small grief to the godly, when they find them abused to a contrary end : that where a ruler should be to good men like rain to the fields new mown, he becomes a favourer of evil men and a persecutor of the good.   Then justice is turned into wormwood ; that which should bring comfort to such as fear God, is abused to oppress them. And therefore it should be accounted a great benefit of God, when he gives a people good and religious rulers.—*William Cowper.*

Verses 23, 51.—If the 119th Psalm came from the pen of David, as multitudes believe, then I do not wonder that many have connected its composition with his residence in the school of the prophets of Naioth.   The calm in which he then found himself, and the studies which he then prosecuted, might well have led his musings in the direction of that alphabetic code, while there are in it not a few expressions which, to say the least, may have particular reference to the dangers out of which he had so recently escaped, and by which he was still threatened.   Such, for example, are the following: "*Princes also did sit and speak against me: but thy servant did meditate in thy statutes.*"   " *The proud have had me greatly in derision : yet have I not declined from thy law.*"—*William M. Taylor, in " David King of Israel ; his Life and its Lessons.*"   1880.

Verse 24.—*Thy testimonies also are my delight and my counsellors.*"   His delight and his counsellors, that is, his delight *because* his counsellors ;   his counsellors, and therefore his delight.   We know how delightful it is to any to have the advantage of good counsel, according to the perplexities and distractions in which they may be. " Ointment and perfume rejoice the heart : so doth the sweetness of a man's friend by hearty counsel," says Solomon, Prov. xxvii. 9.   Now this is the sweetness of Divine communion, and of meditation on God and his word ; it employs a man with *seasonable counsel,* which is a very great refreshment to us.—*T. Horton,* 1673.

Verse 24.—" *Thy testimonies also are my delight,*" etc.   Those that would have God's testimonies to be their delight, must take them for their counsellors and be advised by them ; and let those that take them for their counsellors in close walking, take them for their delight in comfortable walking.—*Matthew Henry.*

Verse 24.—" *Thy testimonies also are my delight and my counsellors.*" What could we want more in a time of difficulty than comfort and direction ? David hath both these blessings. As the fruit of his " meditation in the Lord's statutes," in his distress they were his " *delight ;* " in his seasons of perplexity they were his "*counsellors,*" directing his behaviour in the perfect way.—*Charles Bridges.*

Verse 24.—" *My counsellors.*" In the Hebrew it is, " the men of my counsel," which is fitly mentioned, for he had spoken of princes sitting in council against him. Princes do nothing without the advice of their Privy-Council ; a child of God hath also his Privy-Council, God's testimonies. On the one side there was Saul and his nobles and counsellors ; on the other side there was David and God's testimonies. Now who was better furnished, think you, they to persecute and trouble him, or David how to carry himself under this trouble ? Alphonsus, king of Arragon, being asked who were the best counsellors ? answered, " The dead (meaning books), which cannot flatter, but do without partiality declare the truth." How of all such dead counsellors, God's testimonies have the pre-eminence. A poor, godly man, even then when he is deserted of all, and hath nobody to plead for him, he hath his senate and his council of state about him, the prophets and apostles, and " other holy men of God, that spake as they were moved by the Holy Ghost." A man so furnished, is never less alone than when alone ; for he hath counsellors about him that tell him what is to be believd or done ; and they are such counsellors as cannot err, as will not flatter him, nor applaud him in any sin, nor discourage or dissuade him from that which is good, whatever hazard it expose him to. And truly, if we be wise, we should choose such counsellors as these : " *Thy testimonies are the men of my counsel.*"—*Thomas Manton.*

Verse 24.—" *My counsellors.*" See here a sentence worthy to be weighed of us, when David calleth the commandments of God his " *counsellors.*" For, in the first place, he meaneth that he might scorn all the wisdom of the most able and most expert men in the world, since he was conducted by the word of God, and governed thereby. In the second place, he meaneth that when he shall be so governed by the word of God, he would not only be truly wise, but that it would be as if he had all the wisdom of all the men in the world, yea, and a great deal more.—*John Calvin.*

EXPOSITION OF VERSES 25 TO 32.

M Y soul cleaveth unto the dust : quicken thou me according to thy word.
    26 I have declared my ways, and thou heardest me : teach me thy statutes.

27 Make me to understand the way of thy precepts : so shall I talk of thy wondrous works.

28 My soul melteth for heaviness : strengthen thou me according unto thy word.

29 Remove from me the way of lying : and grant me thy law graciously.

30 I have chosen the way of truth : thy judgments have I laid *before me*.

31 I have stuck unto thy testimonies : O Lord, put me not to shame.

32 I will run the way of thy commandments, when thou shalt enlarge my heart.

Here, it seems to me, we have the Psalmist in trouble bewailing the bondage to earthly things in which he finds his mind to be held. His soul cleaves to the dust, melts for heaviness, and cries for enlargement from its spiritual prison. In these verses we shall see the influence of the divine word upon a heart which laments its downward tendencies, and is filled with mourning because of its deadening surroundings. The word of the Lord evidently arouses prayer (25—29), confirms choice (30), and inspires renewed resolve (32) : it is in all tribulation whether of body or mind the surest source of help.

This portion has D for its alphabetical letter : it sings of Depression, in the spirit of Devotion, Determination, and Dependence.

25. " *My soul cleaveth unto the dust.*" He means in part that he was full of sorrow ; for mourners in the east cast dust on their heads, and sat in ashes, and the Psalmist felt as if these ensigns of woe were glued to him, and his very soul was made to cleave to them because of his powerlessness to rise above his grief. Does he not also mean that he felt ready to die ? Did he not feel his life absorbed and fast held by the grave's mould, half choked by the death-dust ? It may not be straining the language if we conceive that he also felt and bemoaned his earthly-mindedness and spiritual deadness. There was a tendency in his soul to cling to earth which he greatly bewailed. Whatever was the cause of his complaint, it was no surface evil, but an affair of his inmost spirit ; his *soul* cleaved to the dust ; and it was not a casual and accidental falling into the dust, but a continuous and powerful tendency, or *cleaving* to the earth. But what a mercy that the good man could feel and deplore whatever there was of evil in the cleaving ! The serpent's seed can find their meat in the dust, but never shall the seed of the woman be thus degraded. Many are of the earth earthy, and never lament it ; only the heaven-born and heaven-soaring spirit pines at the thought of being fastened to this world, and bird-limed by its sorrows or its pleasures.

" *Quicken thou me according to thy word.*" More life is the cure for all our ailments. Only the Lord can give it. He can bestow it, bestow it at once, and do it according to his word, without departing from the usual course of his grace, as we see it mapped out in the Scriptures. It is well to know what to pray for,—David seeks quickening : one would have thought that he would have asked for comfort or upraising, but he knew that these would come out of increased life, and therefore he sought that blessing which is the root of the rest. When a person is depressed in spirit, weak, and bent towards the ground, the main thing is to increase his stamina and put more life into him : then his spirit revives, and his body becomes erect. In reviving the life, the whole man is renewed. Shaking off the dust is a little thing by itself, but when it follows upon quickening, it is a blessing of the greatest value ; just as good spirits which flow from established health are among the choicest of our mercies. The phrase, " according to thy word," means.—according to thy revealed way of quickening thy saints. The word of God shows us that he who first made us must keep us alive, and it tells us of the Spirit of God who through the ordinances pours fresh life into our souls ; we beg the Lord to act towards us in this his own regular method of grace. Perhaps David remembered the word of the Lord in Deut. xxxii. 39, where Jehovah claims both to kill and to make alive, and he beseeches the Lord to exercise that life-giving power upon his almost expiring servant. Certainly, the man of God had not so many rich promises to rest upon as we have, but even a single word was enough for him, and he right earnestly urges " according to thy word." It is a grand thing to see a believer in the dust and yet pleading the promise, a man at the grave's mouth crying, " quicken me," and hoping that it shall be done.

Note how his first verse of the 4th octonary tallies with the first of the third (17). —" That I may live : " . . . " Quicken me." While in a happy state he begs for bountiful dealing, and when in a forlorn condition he prays for quickening. Life is in both cases the object of pursuit : that he may have life, and have it more abundantly.

26. " *I have declared my ways.*" Open confession is good for the soul. Nothing brings more ease and more life to a man than a frank acknowledgment of the evil which has caused the sorrow and the lethargy. Such a declaration proves that the man knows his own condition, and is no longer blinded by pride. Our confessions are not meant to make God know our sins, but to make us know them. " *And thou heardest me.*" His confession had been accepted ; it was not lost labour ; God had drawn near to him in it. We ought never to go from a duty till we have been accepted in it. Pardon follows upon penitent confession, and David felt that he had obtained it. It is God's way to forgive our sinful way when we from our hearts confess the wrong.

" *Teach me thy statutes.*" Being truly sorry for his fault, and having obtained full forgiveness, he is anxious to avoid offending again, and hence he begs to be taught obedience. He was not willing to sin through ignorance, he wished to know all the mind of God by being taught it by the best of teachers. He pined after holiness. Justified men always long to be sanctified. When God forgives our sins we are all the more fearful of sinning again. Mercy, which pardons transgression, sets us longing for grace which prevents transgression. We may boldly ask for more when God has given us much ; he who has washed out the past stain will not refuse that which will preserve us from present and future defilement. This cry for teaching is frequent in the Psalm ; in verse 12 it followed a sight of God, here follows from a sight of self. Every experience should lead us thus to plead it with God.

27. " *Make me to understand the way of thy precepts.*" Give me a deep insight into the practical meaning of thy word ; let me get a clear idea of the tone and tenor of thy law. Blind obedience has but small beauty ; God would have us follow him with our eyes open. To obey the letter of the word is all that the ignorant can hope for ; if we wish to keep God's precepts in their spirit we must come to an understanding of them, and that can be gained nowhere but at the Lord's hands. Our understanding needs enlightenment and direction : he who made our understanding must also make us understand. The last sentence was, " teach me thy statutes," and the words, " make me to understand," are an instructive enlargement and exposition of that sentence : we need to be so taught that we understand what we learn. It is to be noted that the Psalmist is not anxious to understand the prophecies, but the precepts, and he is not concerned about the subtleties of the law, but the commonplaces and everyday rules of it, which are described as " the way of thy precepts."

" *So shall I talk of thy wondrous works.*" It is ill talking of what we do not understand. We must be taught of God till we understand, and then we may hope to communicate our knowledge to others with a hope of profiting them. Talk without intelligence is mere talk, and idle talk ; but the words of the instructed are as pearls which adorn the ears of them that hear. When our heart has been opened to understand, our lips should be opened to impart knowledge ; and we may hope to be taught ourselves when we feel in our hearts a willingness to teach the way of the Lord to those among whom we dwell.

" *Thy wondrous works.*" Remark that the clearest understanding does not cause us to cease from wondering at the ways and works of God. The fact is that the more we know of God's doings the more we admire them, and the more ready we are to speak upon them. Half the wonder in the world is born of ignorance, but holy wonder is the child of understanding. When a man understands the way of the divine precepts he never talks of his own works, and as the tongue must have some theme to speak upon, he begins to extol the works of the all-perfect Lord.

Some in this place read " meditate " or " muse " instead of " talk ; " it is singular that the words should be so near of kin, and yet it is right that they should be, for none but foolish people will talk without thinking. If we read the passage in this sense, we take it to mean that in proportion as David understood the word of God he would meditate upon it more and more. It is usually so ; the thoughtless care not to know the inner meaning of the Scriptures, while those who know them best are the very men who strive after a greater familiarity with them, and therefore give themselves up to musing upon them.

Observe the third verse of the last eight (19), and see how the sense is akin to this. There he was a stranger in the earth, and here he prays to know his way ; there, too, he prayed that the word might not be hid from himself, and here he promises that he will not hide it from others.

28. " *My soul melteth for heaviness.*" He was dissolving away in tears. The solid strength of his constitution was turning to liquid as if molten by the furnace-heat of his afflictions. Heaviness of heart is a killing thing, and when it abounds it threatens to turn life into a long death, in which a man seems to drop away in a perpetual drip of grief. Tears are the distillation of the heart ; when a man weeps he wastes away his soul. Some of us know what great heaviness means, for we have been brought under its power again and again, and often have we felt ourselves to be poured out like water, and near to being like water spilt upon the ground, never again to be gathered up. There is one good point in this downcast state, for it is better to be melted with grief than to be hardened by impenitence.

" *Strengthen thou me according unto thy word.*" He had found out an ancient promise that the saints shall be strengthened, and here he pleads it. His hope in his state of depression lies not in himself, but in his God ; if he may be strengthened from on high he will yet shake off his heaviness and rise to joy again. Observe how he pleads the promise of the word, and asks for nothing more than to be dealt with after the recorded manner of the Lord of mercy. Had not Hannah sung, " He shall give strength unto his King, and exalt the horn of his anointed ? " God strengthens us by infusing grace through his word : the word which creates can certainly sustain. Grace can enable us to bear the constant fret of an abiding sorrow, it can repair the decay caused by the perpetual tear-drip, and give to the believer the garment of praise for the spirit of heaviness. Let us always resort to prayer in our desponding times, for it is the surest and shortest way out of the depths. In that prayer let us plead nothing but the word of God ; for there is no plea like a promise, no argument like a word from our covenant God.

Note how David records his inner soul-life. In verse 20 he says, " My soul breaketh ; " in verse 25, " My soul cleaveth to the dust ; " and here, " My soul melteth." Further on, in verse 81, he cries, " My soul fainteth ; " in 109, " My soul is continually in my hand ; " in 167, " My soul hath kept thy testimonies ; and lastly, in 175, " Let my soul live." Some people do not even know that they have a soul, and here is David all soul. What a difference there is between the spiritually living and the spiritually dead.

29. " *Remove from me the way of lying.*" This is the way of sin, error, idolatry, folly, self-righteousness, formalism, hypocrisy. David would not only be kept from that way, but have it kept from him ; he cannot endure to have it near him, he would have it swept away from his sight. He desired to be right and upright, true and in the truth ; but he feared that a measure of falsehood would cling to him unless the Lord took it away, and therefore he earnestly cried for its removal. False motives may at times sway us, and we may fall into mistaken notions of our own spiritual condition before God, which erroneous conceits may be kept up by a natural prejudice in our own favour, and so we may be confirmed in a delusion, and abide under error unless grace comes to the rescue. No true heart can rest in a false view of itself ; it finds no anchorage, but is tossed to and fro till it gets into the truth and the truth into it. The true-born child of heaven sighs out and cries against a lie, desiring to have it taken away as much as a man desires to be set at a distance from a venomous serpent or a raging lion.

" *And grant me thy law graciously.*" He is in a gracious state who looks upon the law itself as a gift of grace. David wishes to have the law opened up to his understanding, engraved upon his heart, and carried out in his life ; for this he seeks the Lord, and pleads for it as a gracious grant. No doubt he viewed this as the only mode of deliverance from the power of falsehood : if the law be not in our hearts the lie will enter. David would seem to have remembered those times when, according to the eastern fashion, he had practised deceit for his own preservation, and he saw that he had been weak and erring on that point ; therefore he was bowed down in spirit and begged to be quickened and delivered from transgressing in that manner any more. Holy men cannot review their sins without tears, nor weep over them without entreating to be saved from further offending.

There is an evident opposition between falsehood and the gracious power of God's law. The only way to expel the lie is to accept the truth. Grace also has a clear affinity to truth : no sooner do we meet with the sound of the word "graciously" than we hear the footfall of truth : " I have chosen the way of truth." Grace and truth are ever linked together, and a belief of the doctrines of grace is a grand preservative from deadly error.

In the fifth of the preceding octave (21) David cries out against pride, and here against lying—these are much the same thing. Is not pride the greatest of all lies ?

30. " I have chosen the way of truth." As he abhorred the way of lying, so he chose the way of truth : a man must choose one or the other, for there cannot be any neutrality in the case. Men do not drop into the right way by chance ; they must choose it, and continue to choose it, or they will soon wander from it. Those whom God has chosen in due time choose his way. There is a doctrinal way of truth which we ought to choose, rejecting every dogma of man's devising ; there is a ceremonial way of truth which we should follow, detesting all the forms which apostate churches have invented ; and then there is a practical way of truth, the way of holiness, to which we must adhere whatever may be our temptation to forsake it. Let our election be made, and made irrevocably. Let us answer to all seducers, " I have chosen, and what I have chosen I have chosen." O Lord, by thy grace lead us with a hearty free-will to choose to do thy will ; thus shall thine eternal choice of us bring forth the end which it designs.

" Thy judgments have I laid before me." What he had chosen he kept in mind, laying it out before his mind's eye. Men do not become holy by a careless wish : there must be study, consideration, deliberation, and earnest enquiry, or the way of truth will be missed. The commands of God must be set before us as the mark to aim at, the model to work by, the road to walk in. If we put God's judgments into the background we shall soon find ourselves departing from them.

Here again the sixth stanzas of the third and fourth octaves ring out a similar note. " I have kept thy testimonies " (22), and " Thy judgments have I laid before me," This is a happy confession, and there is no wonder that is is repeated.

31. " I have stuck unto thy testimonies,"—or I have cleaved, for the word is the same as in verse 25. Though cleaving to the dust of sorrow and of death, yet he kept fast hold of the divine word. This was his comfort, and his faith stuck to it, his love and his obedience held on to it, his heart and his mind abode in meditation upon it. His choice was so heartily and deliberately made that he stuck to it for life, and could not be removed from it by the reproaches of those who despised the way of the Lord. What could he have gained by quitting the sacred testimony ? Say rather, what would he not have lost if he had ceased to cleave to the divine word ? It is pleasant to look back upon past perseverance and to expect grace to continue equally steadfast in the future. He who has enabled us to stick to him will surely stick to us.

"O LORD, put me not to shame." This would happen if God's promises were unfulfilled, and if the heart of God's servant were suffered to fail. This we have no reason to fear, since the Lord is faithful to his word. But it might also happen through the believer's acting in an inconsistent manner, as David had himself once done, when he fell into the way of lying, and pretended to be a madman. If we are not true to our profession we may be left to reap the fruit of our folly, and that will be the bitter thing called " shame." It is evident from this that a believer ought never to be ashamed, but act the part of a brave man who has done nothing to be ashamed of in believing his God, and does not mean to adopt a craven tone in the presence of the Lord's enemies. If we beseech the Lord not to put us to shame, surely we ought not ourselves to be ashamed without cause.

The prayer of this verse is found in the parallel verse of the next section (39) : " Turn away my reproach which I fear." It is evidently a petition which was often on the Psalmist's heart. A brave heart is more wounded by shame than by any weapon which a soldier's hand can wield.

32. " I will run the way of thy commandments." With energy, promptitude, and zeal he would perform the will of God, but he needed more life and liberty from the

hand of God. " *When thou shalt enlarge my heart.*" Yes, the heart is the master ; the feet soon run when the heart is free and energetic. Let the affections be aroused and eagerly set on divine things, and our actions will be full of force, swiftness, and delight. God must work in us first, and then we shall will and do according to his good pleasure. He must change the heart, unite the heart, encourage the heart, strengthen the heart, and enlarge the heart, and then the course of the life will be gracious, sincere, happy, and earnest ; so that from our lowest up to our highest state in grace we must attribute all to the free favour of our God. We must run ; for grace is not an overwhelming force which compels unwilling minds to move contrary to their will: our running is the spontaneous leaping forward of a mind which has been set free by the hand of God, and delights to show its freedom by its bounding speed.

What a change from verse 25 to the present, from cleaving to the dust to running in the way. It is the excellence of holy sorrow that it works in us the quickening for which we seek, and then we show the sincerity of our grief and the reality of our revival by being zealous in the ways of the Lord.

For the third time an octave closes with, " I will." These " I wills " of the Psalms are right worthy of being each one the subject of study and discourse.

Note how the heart has been spoken of up to this point : " whole heart " (2), " uprightness of heart " (7), "hid in mine heart" (11), " enlarge my heart." There are many more allusions further on, and these all go to show what heart-work David's religion was. It is one of the great lacks of our age that heads count for more than hearts, and men are far more ready to learn than to love, though they are by no means eager in either direction.

NOTES ON VERSES 25 TO 32.

The eight verses alphabetically arranged :—

25. Depressed to the dust is my soul : quicken thou me according to thy word.
26. Declared have I (to thee) my ways, and thou heardest me : teach me thy statutes.
27. Declare thou to me the way of thy precepts : so shall I talk of thy wondrous works.
28. Dropping (*marg.*) is my soul for heaviness : strengthen thou me according unto thy word.
29. Deceitful ways remove from me ; and grant me thy law graciously.
30. Determined have I upon the way of truth ; thy judgments have I laid before me.
31. Deliberately I have stuck unto thy testimonies : O Lord, put me not to shame.
32. Day by day I will run the way of thy commandments, when thou shalt enlarge my heart.

Theodore Kübler.

Verse 25.—*" My soul cleaveth unto the dust."* The Hebrew word for *" cleaveth "* signifies *" is joined," " has adhered," " has overtaken," "has taken hold," "has joined itself."* Our soul is a polypus : as the polypus readily adheres to the rocks, so does the soul cleave to the earth ; and hardly can it be torn from the place to which it has once strongly attached itself. Though thy soul be now more perfect, and escaping from the waters of sin has become a bird of heaven, be not careless ; earthly things are birdlime and glue ; if thou rubbest thy wings against these thou wilt be held, and joined to the earth.—*Thomas Le Blanc.*

Verse 25.—*" My soul cleaveth unto the dust,"* etc. The word rendered *" cleaveth "* means to be glued to ; to stick fast. It has the sense of adhering firmly to anything, so that it cannot easily be separated from it. The word *" dust "* here may mean either the earth, and earthly things, considered as low, base, unworthy, worldly ; or it may mean the grave, as if he were near to that, and in danger of dying. De Wette understands it in the latter sense. Yet the word *cleave* would hardly suggest this idea ; and the force of that word would be better represented by the idea that his soul, as it were, *adhered* to the things of earth ; that it seemed to be so fastened to them—*so glued* to them that it could not be detached from them ; that his affections were low, earthly, grovelling, so as to give him deep distress, and lead him to cry to God for life and strength that he might break away from them.—*Albert Barnes.*

Verse 25.—*" My soul cleaveth unto the dust,"* etc. The first clause seems intended to suggest two consistent but distinct ideas, that of deep degradation, as in Ps. xliv. 25, and that of death, as in Ps. xxii. 29. The first would be more obvious in itself, and in connection with the parallel referred to ; but the other seems to be indicated as the prominent idea by the correlative petition for quickening in the last clause. *" Quicken,"* i.e., save me alive, or restore me to life, the Hebrew word being a causative of the verb *to live.*—*Joseph Addison Alexander.*

Verse 25.—*" My soul cleaveth to the dust,"* etc. In this verse, David hath a complaint ; *" My soul cleaveth to the dust ; "* and a prayer ; *" Quicken thou me according to thy word."* The prayer, being well considered, shall teach us the meaning of the complaint ; that it was not, as some think, any hard bodily estate which grieved him, but a very sore spiritual oppression (as I may call it), bearing down his soul ; that where he should have mounted up toward heaven, he was pressed down to the earth, and was so clogged with earthly cogitations, or affections, or perturbations, that he could not mount up. His particular temptation he expresseth not: for the children of God many times are in that estate that they cannot tell their own griefs ; and sometimes so troubled ; that it is not expedient, albeit they might, to express them to others.

And hereof we learn, how that which the worldling counts wisdom, to the Christian is folly ; what is joy to the one, is grief to the other. The joy of a worldling is to cleave unto the earth ; when he gripes it surest, he thinks himself happiest, for it is his portion : to take heed to his worldly affairs, and have his mind upon them (in his estimation) is only wisdom. For the serpent's curse is upon him, he creeps on the earth, and licks the dust all the days of his life. This is the miserable condition of the wicked, that even their heavenly soul is become earthly. *Qui secundum corporis appetentiam vivit caro est, etiam anima eorum caro est ;* as the Lord spake of those who perished in the Deluge, that they were but flesh, no spirit in them ; that is, no spiritual or heavenly motion.

But the Christian, considering that his soul is from above, sets his affection also on those things which are above : he delights to have his conversation in heaven and it is a grief to him when he finds his motions and affections drawn down and entangled with the earth.   His life is to cleave to the Lord ; but it is death to him when the neck of his soul is bowed down to the yoke of the world.—*William Cowper.*

Verse 25.—*" My soul cleaveth to the dust."* " Look up now to the heavens." So once spake the Lord to Abraham his friend, and he speaketh thus to us also. Alas ! why must it be so always that, when we come to know ourselves even but a little, we are constantly answering with the mournful sigh, *" My soul cleaveth to the dust ? "* Ah ! that is indeed the *deepest pain* of a soul which has already tasted that the Lord is merciful, when, although desiring to soar on high, it sadly feels how impossible it is to rise.   There is much hidden pain in every heart of man even in the spiritual life ; but what can deeper grieve us than the perception that we are chained as with leaden weights to things concerning which we know that they may weary but cannot satisfy us ?   Nay, we could never have supposed, when we first heard the Psalm of the Good Shepherd, that it could issue from a heart that panteth after God, so often and so bitterly ; we could never have imagined that it could become so cold, so dry, so dark within a heart which at an earlier period had tasted so much of the power of that which is to come.   Have we not formerly, with this same Psalm, been able to vaunt, " I have rejoiced in the way of thy testimonies, as much as in all riches ? " But afterwards, or now perhaps. . . . Oh sad hours, when the beams of the sun within seem quenched, and nothing but a blood-red disc remains !   The fervency of the first love is cooled ; earthly cares and sins have, as it were, attached a leaden plummet to the wings of a soul which, God knows, would fain soar upwards. We would render thanks, and scarce can pray ; we would pray, and scarce can sigh. Our treasure is in heaven, but our soul cleaves to the earth ; at least earth cleaves on all sides so to it, and weighs it down, that the eye merely sees the clouds, the tongue can but breathe forth complaints.   Ah, so completely can the earth fetter us, that the heavens appear to be only a problem, and our old man is like the Giant of Mythology, who, cast to the ground in the exhausting combat, receives by contact with his mother earth fresh strength.   Oh, were it otherwise !   Shall it not at last, at last be altered ?

Dost thou really desire it, thou who out of the depths of thy soul so complainest, and canst scarcely find more tears to bewail the sorrow of thy heart ?   Well is it for thee if the pain thou sufferest teach thee to cry to God : " Quicken thou me, according to thy word."   Yea, this is the *best comfort* for him who too well knows what it is to be bowed together with pain ; this is the only hope for a heart which almost sinks in still despair.   There is an *atmosphere* of life, high above this dust, which streams to us from every side, and penetrates even the darkest dungeon. There is a *spring* of life by which the weary soul may be refeshed ; and the entrance to this spring stands open, in spite of all the clouds of dust which obscure this valley of shadows here.   There is a *power* of life which can even so completely make an end of our dead state, that we shall walk again before the face of the Lord in the land of the living, and, instead, of uttering lamentation, we shall bear a song of praise upon our lips.   Does not the Prince of life yet live in order also to repeat to us, " Awake and rejoice, thou that dwellest in the dust ; " and the Spirit, that bloweth whither he listeth, can, will, shall he not in his own good time, with his living breath, blow from our wings the dust that cleaveth to them ?   But, indeed, even the gnawing pain of the soul over so much want of spirituality and dulness is ever an encouraging sign that the good work is begun in our hearts : that which is really dead shivers no more at its own cold.   " *My soul cleaveth to the dust,*" sayest thou, with tears ? thus wouldest thou not speak except that already a higher hand between the soul and this dust had cleft a hollow which was unknown to it before.   No one has less cause for despair than he who has lost hope in himself, and really learns to seek in God that, which he deeply feels, he least of all can give himself.

Yes, this is the *way* from the deepest pain to procure the best consolation ; the humble, earnest, persevering prayer, that he who lives would also give life to our souls, and continue to increase it, till freed from all dryness and deadness of spirit, and unrooted from the earth, we ascend to the eternal mount of light, where at last we behold all earthly clouds beneath us.   This the God of life alone can work ; but he is willing—nay, we have his own word as pledge, that he promises and bestows on us true life.   Only, let us not forget that he who will quicken us *" according "* to his word, also performs this *through* his word.   Let us then draw from out the eternally-flowing fountain, and henceforth leave it unconditionally to him, how he will listen to our cry, even though he lead us through dark paths ! Even through means of death God can quicken us and keep us alive. . . . Lo, we are here ; Lord, do with us as seemeth good to thee ! Only, let our souls live, that they may praise thee, here and eternally !—*J. J. Van Oosterzee, in " The Year of Salvation,"* 1874.

Verse 25.—*" Cleaveth to the dust."* Is weighed down by the flesh, which itself is dust.—*James G. Murphy.*

Verse 25.—*" The dust "* is the place of the afflicted, the wounded, and the dead. *" Quicken me,"* viz., to life, peace, and joy.—*A. R. Fausset.*

Verse 25.—*" Quicken thou me,"* etc. Seeing he was alive, how prays he that God would quicken him ? I answer,—The godly esteem of life, not according to that they have in their body, but in their soul. If the soul lacks the sense of mercy, and a heavenly disposition to spiritual things, they lament over it, as a dead soul : for sure it is, temporal desertions are more heavy to the godly than temporal death. *" According to thy word."* This is a great faith, that where in respect of his present feeling he found himself dead, yet he hopes for life from God, according to his promise. Such was the faith of Abraham, who under hope, believed above hope. And truly, many times are God's children brought to this estate, that they have nothing to uphold them but the word of God ; no sense of mercy, no spiritual disposition ; but on the contrary, great darkness, horrible fears and terrors. Only they are sustained by looking to the promise of God, and kept in some hope that he will restore them to life again, because it is his praise to finish the work which he begins.—*William Cowper.*

Verse 25.—*" Quicken thou me."* This phrase occurs nine times, and only in this Psalm. It is of great importance, as it expresses the spiritual change by which a child of Adam becomes a child of God. Its source is God ; the instrument by which it is effected is the word, verse 50.—*James G. Murphy.*

Verse 25.—*" Quicken thou me according to thy word."* Where there is life there will be the endeavour to rise—the believer will not lie prone in his aspirations after God. From the lowest depths the language of faith is heard ascending to God most high, who performeth all things for the believer. The true child cannot but look towards the loving Father, who is the Almighty, All-sufficient One. Have you not found it so ? But will you mark the intelligence that shines around the believer's prayer ? He prays that the Lord may quicken him *according to his word.* The *word* may be regarded in the light of the standard after which he is to be fashioned ; or the Psalmist may have in view the requirements contained in the word regarding the believer's progress ; or he may be thinking of the promises found therein in behalf of the poor and needy when they apply. Indeed, all these significations may be wrapt up in the one expression—*" according to thy word "*—the standard of\perfection, the requirements of the word, and the promises concerning it. The great exemplar of the believer is Christ,—of old it was the Christ of prophecy. Then the requirements of the Lord's will were scattered through the word. The Psalmist, however, may be dwelling upon the large promises which the Lord hath given towards the perfecting of his people. You see after what the spiritual nature aspires. It is quite enough to the natural man or the formalist that he be as the generally well-behaved and esteemed among professors—the spiritual man aspires beyond—he aspires after being quickened according to God's word. Judge of yourselves.—*John Stephen.*

Verse 25.—*" Quicken thou me according to thy word."* By thy providence put life into my affairs, by thy grace put life into my affections; cure me of my spiritual deadness, and make me lively in my devotion.—*Matthew Henry.*

Verse 25.—*" Quicken thou me according to thy word."* Albeit the Lord suffer his own to lie so long low in their heavy condition of spirit, that they may seem dead ; yet by faith in his word he keepeth in them so much life as doth furnish unto them prayer to God for comfort : *" Quicken thou me according to thy word."*—*David Dickson.*

Verse 25.—*" Quicken thou me."* To whom shall the godly fly when life faileth but to that Well-spring of all life ? Even as to remove cold the next way is to draw near the fire, so to dispel any death, the next way is to look to him who is our root, by whom we live this natural life. All preservatives and restoratives are nothing, all colleges of physicians are vanity, if compared with him. Other things which have not life, give life as the instruments of him who is life, as fire burneth being the instrument of heat. " When heart and flesh fail, God is the strength of my heart." As a man can let a fire almost go out which had been kindled, and then blow it up, and by application of new fuel make it blaze as much as ever : so can God deal with this flame of life which he hath kindled.—*Paul Bayne.*

Verse 25.—" *According to thy word.*" The word removes deadness of conscience and hardness. Is not this word a hammer to soften the heart, and is not this the immortal seed by which we are begotten again ? Therefore David, finding his conscience in a dead frame, prayeth, " My soul cleaveth to the dust ; quicken thou me according to thy word." The *word* is the first thing by which conscience is purified and set right.—*John Sheffield, in " A Good Conscience the Strongest Hold,"* 1650.

Verse 25.—" *According to thy word.*" What word doth David mean ? Either the general promises in the books of Moses or Job ; which intimate deliverance to the faithful observers of God's law, or help to the miserable and distressed ; or some particular promise given to him by Nathan, or others. Chrysostom saith, " Quicken me according to thy word : but it is not a word of command, but a word of promise." Mark here,—he doth not say *secundum meritum meum,* but, *secundum verbum tuum;* the hope, or that help which we expect from God, is founded upon his word ; there is our security, in his promises, not in our deservings: *Promittendo se fecit debitorem, etc.*

When there was so little Scripture written, yet David could find out a word for his support. Alas ! in our troubles and afflictions, no promise occurreth to mind. As in outward things, many that have less live better than those that have abundance ; so here, now Scripture is so large, we are less diligent, and therefore, though we have so many promises, we are apt to faint, we have not a word to bear us up. This word did not help David, till he had lain so long under this heavy condition, that he seemed dead. Many, when they have a promise, think presently to enjoy the comfort of it. No, waiting and striving are first necessary. We never relish the comfort of the promises till the creatures have spent their allowance, and we have been exercised. God will keep his word, and yet we must expect to be tried.

In this his dead condition, faith in God's word kept him alive. When we have least feeling, and there is nothing left us, the word will support us : " And being not weak in faith, he considered not his own body now dead, when he was about an hundred years old, neither yet the deadness of Sarah's womb : he staggered not at the promise of God through unbelief ; but was strong in faith, giving glory to God " (Rom. iv. 19, 20). One way to get comfort is to plead the promise of God in prayer, *Chirographa tua injiciebat tibi Domine,* show him his handwriting ; God is tender of his word. These arguings in prayer, are not to work upon God, but ourselves.—*Thomas Manton.*

Verses 25—32.—One does not wonder at the fluctuations which occur in the feelings and experience of a child of God—at one time high on the mountain, near to God and communing with God, at another in the deep and dark valley. All, more or less, know these changes, and have their sorrowing as well as their rejoicing seasons. When we parted with David last, what was he telling us of his experience ? that God's testimonies were *his delight and his counsellors ;* but now what a different strain ! all joy is darkened, and *his soul cleaveth to the dust.* And there must have been seasons of deep depression and despondency in the heart of David—driven as a fugitive and wanderer from his home, hunted as a partridge upon the mountains, and holding, as he himself says, his life continually in his hands. Yet I think in this portion of the Psalm there is evidence of a deeper abasement and sorrow of heart than any mere worldly suffering could produce. He had indeed said, " I shall one day perish by the hand of Saul ; " but, even in that moment of weak and murmuring faith, he knew that he was God's anointed one to sit on the throne of Israel. But here there is indication of sin, of grievous sin which had laid his soul low in the dust ; and I think the petition in the 29th verse gives us some clue to what that sin had been : " *Remove me from the way of lying.*" Had David—you may well ask in wonder—had David ever lied ? had he ever deviated from the strait and honourable path of truth ? I am afraid we must own that he had at one time gone so near the confines of a falsehood, that he would be but a poor casuist and a worse moralist who should attempt to defend the Psalmist from the imputation. We cannot read the 27th chapter of the 1st of Samuel without owning into what a sad tissue of equivocation and deceit David was unhappily seduced. Well might his soul cleave to the dust as he reviewed that period of his career ; and though grace did for him what it afterwards did for Peter, and he was plucked as a brand out of the burning, yet one can well imagine that, like the Apostle afterwards, when he thought thereon he wept, and that bitterly.—*Barton Bouchier.*

Verse 26.—" *I have declared my ways,*" etc.   This verse contains a prayer, with a reason after this form :—O Lord, I have oft before declared unto thee the whole state and course of my life, my wanderings, my wants, my doubts, my griefs ; I hid nothing from thee, and thou, according to my necessity, didst always hear me : therefore now, Lord, I pray thee to teach me ; by thy light illuminate me that I may know thy statutes and receive grace to walk in them.   This is a good argument in dealing with the Lord,—I have gotten many mercies and favourable answers from thee ; therefore, Lord, I pray thee to give me more ; for whom he loves he loves to the end ; and where he begins to show mercy he ceaseth not till he crown his children with mercy.   And so gracious is the Lord, that he esteems himself to be honoured as oft as we give him the praise that we have found comfort in him, and therefore come to seek more.

Next, it is to be marked how he saith, " *I have declared my ways, and thou heardest me :* " these two go well together, Mercy and Truth : truth in the heart of man confessing ; mercy in God, hearing and forgiving : happy is the soul wherein these two meet together.   Many there are who are destitute of this comfort ; they cannot say, God hath heard me, and all because they deal not plainly and truly with the Lord in *declaring their ways* unto him.—*William Cowper.*

Verse 26.—" *I have declared my ways.*"   In verse 59 he *thinketh upon his ways,* that is, his inward imperfections and outward aberrations from the strait and straight ways of God ; and here he is not ashamed to *declare them,* that is, to acknowledge and confess that all this came upon him because he was forgetful to do God's will. Note the connection between this and the previous verse : My soul clave unto the dust, because I clave not to thee.—*Richard Greenham.*

Verse 26.—" *I have declared my ways.*"   ספרתי, *sipparti,* " I have remembered my ways ; " I have searched them out ; I have investigated them.   And that he had earnestly *prayed* for pardon of what was wrong in them, is evident ; for he adds, " *Thou heardest me.*"—*Adam Clarke.*

Verse 26.—" *I have declared my ways,*" etc.   Him whom thou hast heard in humble confessing of his sins, him thou must teach thy statutes.   The saints lay open to God what they find, both good and evil, seeking deliverance, supply, strengthening, directing : even as sick patients tell to their doctor both what good and what otherwise they perceive   or as clients lay bare their case to their counsel.

" *Declared.*"   As if he had read them out of a book.   The saints know their ways.   A man that hath light with him seeth the way, and can tell you all about it ; another is in darkness and knoweth nothing : the one taketh observation of his course, the other doth not.

" *Thou hast heard me.*"   God's goodness is seen in his hearing what we lay open before him.   If great ones let a poor man tell his tale at large we count it honourable patience ; but it is God's glory to hear our wants, our weakness through sin, the invincibleness of our evils, our utter impotency in ourselves even to seek redress. That mode of procedure would lose the favour of man, but it winneth favour with God.   The more humbly we confess all our wants, the more confident we may be that God will hear us.   *He teacheth the humble,* for the humble scholar will give to his master the honour of that he learneth.

I have rehearsed (said with myself) my ways ; and " thou hast heard my private confession."   " *I have declared* " to others what my way is, and " thou hast heard me " so discoursing ; wherefore " *teach me,*" seeing I communicate what I receive. It is a plea derived from his carefulness to learn, and from the use he had made of that he had learned.   The godly, like candles, light each other.—*Paul Bayne.*

Verse 26.—" *I have declared my ways.*"   They that would speed with God, should learn this point of Christian ingenuity, unfeignedly to lay open their whole case to him.   That is, to declare what they are about, the nature of their affairs, the state of their hearts, what of good or evil they find in themselves, their conflicts, supplies, distresses, hopes ; this is declaring our ways—the good and evil we are conscious of. As a sick patient will tell the physician how it is with him, so should we deal with God, if we would find mercy.   This declaring his ways may be looked upon, 1. As an act of faith and dependence.   2. As an act of holy friendship.   3. As an act of spiritual contrition, and brokenness of heart : for this declaring must be explained according to what David meant by the expression, " *My ways.*"

First, By his " *ways* " may be meant his businesses or undertakings : I have still made them known to thee, committing them to the direction of thy providence ;

and so it is an act of faith and dependence, consulting with God, and acquainting him with all our desires.

Secondly, By his " *ways* " may be meant, all his straits, sorrows, and dangers ; and so this declaration is an act of holy friendship, when a man comes as one friend to another, and acquaints God with his whole state, lays his condition before the Lord, in hope of pity and relief.

Thirdly, By " *ways* " is meant temptations and sins ; and so this declaring is an act of spiritual contrition or brokenness of heart. Sins are properly our ways, as Ezek. xviii. 25.—*Thomas Manton.*

Verses 26, 27, 29, 30.—" *The way of thy precepts.*"   " *My ways.*"   " The *way of lying.*"   " *The way of truth.*"   Here should be noticed the two contrasts by which the Prophet teaches what must be shunned both in life and in doctrine, and what embraced. The first respects *the life* of Christians, as the Prophet sets the way of God's commandments over against his own ways, verses 26, 27 ; and respecting these he confesses that they have pressed him down to the dust and have greatly distressed him ; but respecting those he declares that they have again raised him up. He means by his own ways a depraved nature, carnal desire, and the carnal mind which is enmity against God, Rom. viii. ; but by the ways of the Lord he denotes the will of God expressed in the Word. Therefore the boastings of the papists of the perfect obedience of the renewed are empty ; for David, assured by having been renewed, complains bitterly and with many tears that his soul, under the intolerable weight of sins, had been brought down to the dust of death and almost suffocated ; but that God had heard his prayers and brought him back to the way of his commandments. We here, also, gather that in this life all the saints experience the wrestling and contest of the flesh and the spirit, so that they are continually compelled to mourn that their flesh turns them aside from the way of the Lord into the by-paths of sin : just as Paul cries out, " I see another law in my members, warring against the law of my mind, etc. O wretched man that I am ! who shall deliver me from the body of this death ? " Rom. vii. 23, 24.

The second contrast concerneth the *doctrine ;* for David opposes the way of lying to the way of truth. We are taught by this contrast that we should eschew false doctrine, and steadfastly adhere to divine truth. To this applies the precept of Paul, Eph. iv. 25, " Wherefore, having put away the lie, speak truth each one with his neighbour." Further, we learn, if we hate our own ways, *i.e.*, confess our sins to the Lord, and, trusting in the Mediator, pray for forgiveness, that God is wont to hear and mercifully to forgive our sins ; as it is written, 1 John i. 9, " If we confess our sins, he is faithful and just to forgive us our sins, and to cleanse us from all unrighteousness."—*Solomon Gesner.*

Verse 26.—" *Thou heardest me.*" Past answers to prayer should encourage us to come the more boldly to the throne of grace.—Jacob never forgot the night he spent at Bethel.—*William S. Plumer.*

Verse 26.—" *Teach me thy statutes.*" The often repetition of this one thing in this Psalm argueth, 1. The necessity of this knowledge. 2. The desire he had to obtain it. 3. That such repetitions are not frivolous when they proceed from a sound heart, a zealous affection, and a consideration of the necessity of the thing prayed for. 4. That such as have most light have little in respect of what they should have. 5. As covetous men think they have never gold enough, so Christian men should think they have never knowledge enough.—*Richard Greenham.*

Verse 26.—" *Teach me.*" We can never do without *teaching*, even in old age. Unless the Spirit of God teaches us we learn in vain.—*Martin Geier.*

Verses 26, 27.—Here is David's earnest desire for the continuance of that intimacy that had been between him and his God ; not by visions and voices from heaven, but by the Word and Spirit in an ordinary way : " *Teach me thy statutes,*" that is, " *make me to understand the way of thy precepts.*" When he knew God had heard his declaration of his ways, he doth not say, Now, Lord, tell me my lot, and let me know what the event will be ; but, Now, Lord, tell me my duty, let me know what thou wouldest have me to do as the case stands. Note, Those that in all their ways acknowledge God, may pray in faith that he will direct their steps in the right way. And the surest way of keeping up our communion with God is, by learning his statutes, and walking diligently in the *way of his precepts.*—*Matthew Henry.*

Verse 27.—" *Make me to understand.*" Natural blindness is an obstinate disease, and hardly cured : therefore again and again we had need to pray, "Open mine eyes ; " " Teach me thy statutes ; " "*Make me to understand the way of thy precepts.*" Our ignorance is great even when it is cured in part. The clouds of temptation and carnal affection cause it to return upon us, so that we know not what we know. Therefore he cries, " open my eyes ; cause me to understand." Yea, the more we know the more is our ignorance discovered to us : " Surely I am more brutish than any man, and have not the understanding of a man. I neither learned wisdom, nor have the knowledge of the holy " (Prov. xxx. 2, 3). " I have heard of thee by the hearing of the ear, but now mine eye seeth thee; wherefore I abhor myself, and repent in dust and ashes " (Job xlii. 5, 6). Alas, a poor, little, hearsay knowledge availeth not ; they abhor themselves when they have more intimate acquaintance. None so confident as a young professor that knoweth a few truths, but in a weak and imperfect manner : the more we know indeed, the more sensible we are of our ignorance, and how liable to this mistake and that, so that we dare not trust ourselves for an hour.—*Thomas Manton.*

Verse 27.—"*Understand the way . . . so shall I talk.*" We can talk with a better grace of God's " *wondrous works,*" the wonders of providence, and especially the wonders of redeeming love, when we understand *the way* of God's precepts, and walk in that way.—*Matthew Henry.*

Verse 27.—"*The way of thy precepts.*" He desireth that God would, partly by his Spirit, partly by his ministers, partly by affliction, partly by study and labour, make him to have a right and sound understanding, not only of his *statutes,* but of the *way* of his statutes, that is, after what sort and order he may live and direct his life, according to those things which God hath commanded him in his law. Learn here how hard a thing it is for man, overweening himself in his own wisdom, to know God's will till God *make* him to know.—*Richard Greenham.*

Verse 27.—"*So shall I talk of thy wondrous works.*" He that is sensible of the wondrous things that are in God's word, will be talking of them. 1. It will be so. 2. It should be so.

1. *It will be so.* When the heart is deeply affected, the tongue cannot hold, but will run out in expressions of it ; " for out of the abundance of the heart the mouth speaketh." When cheered and revived in their afflictions saints are transported with the thought of the excellency of God. " Come, and I will tell you what God hath done for my soul " (Ps. lxvi. 15). The woman, when she had found the lost groat, calleth her neighbours to rejoice with her. He that hath but a cold knowledge, will not be so full of good discourse.

2. *It should be so* in a threefold respect : for the honour of God ; the edification of others ; and for our own profit.

(1). For the honour of God, to whom we are so much indebted, to bring him into request with those about us. Experience deserveth praise ; when you have found the Messiah, call another to him : " Andrew calleth Peter, and saith unto him, We have found the Messias : and Philip called Nathanael and saith unto him, We have found him, of whom Moses in the law, and the prophets, did write, Jesus of Nazareth, the son of Joseph " (John i. 41—45).

(2). For the edification of others : " And thou, being converted, strengthen thy brethren " (Luke xxii. 32). True grace is communicative as fire, etc.

(3). For our own profit. He that useth his knowledge, shall have more. Whereas on the contrary, full breasts, if not sucked, become dry. In the dividing, the loaves increased. All gifts, but much more spiritual, which are the best, are improved by exercise.—*Thomas Manton.*

Verse 27.—"*So shall I talk,*" etc. Desire of knowledge should not be for satisfying of curiosity, or for ostentation, or for worldly gain, but to edify ourselves and others in wisdom. . . . "*Thy wondrous works.*" The works of creation, redemption and providence, either set down in Scripture, or observed in our own experience, transcend our capacity, and cannot but draw admiration from them that see them well.—*David Dickson.*

Verse 27.—"*So shall I talk.*" It is a frequent complaint with Christians, that they are straitened in religious conversation, and often feel unable to speak " to the use of edifying, that they may minister grace to the hearers," Eph. iv. 29. Here, then, is the secret disclosed, by which we shall be kept from the danger of dealing in unfelt truths, for " out of the abundance of the heart our mouths shall speak," Matt. xii. 34. Seek to have the heart searched, cleansed, filled with the graces of the Spirit. Humility, teachableness, simplicity, will bring light unto the understanding, influence the heart, "open the lips," and unite every member that we have in the service and praise of God.—*Charles Bridges.*

Verse 27.—" *I shall talk of.*"   There is a close affinity between all the duties of religion.   The same word is rendered *pray, meditate,* and *talk of.*   We think of God's excellent majesty ; we cry to him in humble prayer ; we study his word until our souls are filled with gladness and admiration ; and then how can we but *talk of his wondrous works ?—William S. Plumer.*

Verse 28.—" *My soul melteth for heaviness.*"   In the original the word signifies, "droppeth away."   The Septuagint hath it thus : "My soul fell asleep through weariness."   Probably by a fault of the transcribers, putting one word for another. My soul droppeth.   It may relate (1) to the plenty of his tears, as the word is used in Scripture : "My friends scorn me : but mine eye poureth out tears unto God " (Job xvi. 20), or droppeth to God, the same word ; so it notes his deep sorrow and sense of his condition.   The like allusion is in Joshua vii. 5 : "The heart of the people melted, and became as water."   Or (2) it relates to his languishing under the extremity of his sorrow ; as an unctuous thing wasteth by dropping, so was his soul even dropping away.   Such a like expression is used in Psalm cvii. 26 : "Their soul is melted because of trouble ; " and of Jesus Christ, whose strength was exhausted by the greatness of his sorrows, it is said, Psalm xxii. 14, " I am poured out like water and all my bones are out of joint : my heart is like wax ; it is melted in the midst of my bowels."   Be the allusion either to the one or to the other ; either to the dropping of tears, or to the melting and wasting away of what is fat or unctuous, it notes a vehement sorrow, and brokenness of heart.   So much is clear, his soul was even melting away, and unless God did help, he could hold out no longer.—*Thomas Manton.*

Verse 28.—" *My soul melteth.*"   The oldest versions make it mean *to slumber* (LXX. ἐνύσταθεν, Vulg. *dormitavit*), which would make the clause remarkably coincident with Luke xxii. 45.—*Joseph Addison Alexander.*

Verse 28.—" *Heaviness.*"   There is nothing may comfort a natural man but David had it ; yet cannot all these keep him from that heaviness whereunto, as witnesseth S. Peter, the children of God are subject in this life, through their manifold temptations.   The men of the world are so far from this disposition, that if they have health and wealth, they marvel what it is should make a man heavy : they are not acquainted with the exercise of a feeling conscience ; they know not the defects of the spiritual life, and are not grieved at them : being dead in sin they feel not that they want life ; all their care is to eat and drink and make merry.   But miserable are they ; for in their best estate they are as oxen fed for the slaughter.   Woe be to them who laugh now, they shall mourn ; but blessed are they who mourn now, for they shall be comforted.—*William Cowper.*

Verse 28.—" *Strengthen thou me according unto thy word.*"   Strengthen me to do the duties, resist the temptations, and bear up under the burdens of an afflicted state, that the spirit may not fail.—*Matthew Henry.*

Verse 28.—" *Strengthen thou me according unto thy word.*"   What is that word which David pleaded ? "As thy days, so shall thy strength be," Deut. xxxiii. 25. "Will he plead against me," said Job, " with his great power ? No ; but he will put strength in me," Job xxiii. 6.—*Charles Bridges.*

Verse 28.—" *Strengthen thou me.*"   Gesenius translates this, " *Keep me alive,*" Thus, קימני, in this verse, answers to חיני, in the first verse.   This prayer for new strength, or life, is an entreaty that the waste of life through tears might be restored by the life-giving word.—*Frederick G. Marchant.*

Verse 29.—It says, " *Remove from me the way,*" and not me from the way ; because that way of iniquity is within us, for we are born children of wrath, and the passions innate in us run to the lie, and make the wretched way of crimes in our souls.— *Thomas Le Blanc.*

Verse 29.—" *Remove from me the way of lying.*"   Here he acknowledgeth that although he were already exercised in the law of God and in his knowledge, and that although he were a prophet to teach others, nevertheless he was subject to a number of wicked thoughts and imaginations which might always wickedly lead him from the right way, except God had held him with his mighty and strong hand.   And this is a point which we ought here rightly to note ; for we see how men greatly abuse themselves.   When any of us shall have had a good beginning, we straightway think that we are at the highest ; we never bethink us to pray any more to God, when once he hath showed us favour enough to serve our turns ; but if we have done any small deed, we by-and-by lift up ourselves and wonder at our great virtues, thinking straightway that the Devil can win no more of us.   This foolish arrogancy causeth God to let us go astray, so that we fall mightily, yea, that we break both arms and legs, and are in great hazard of breaking our necks.   I speak not now of our natural body, but of our soul.   Let us look upon David himself ; for he it is that hath made proof hereof.   It came to pass that he villainously and wickedly erred when he took Bathsheba the wife of his subject, Uriah, to play the whoremonger with her, that he was the cause of so execrable a murder, yea, and that of many ; for he did as much as in him lay, to cause the whole army of the Lord and all the people of Israel to be utterly overthrown.   See, then, the great negligence and security into which David fell ; and see also wherefore he saith, " Alas, my good God, I beseech thee so to guide me, that I may forsake the way of lying."—*John Calvin.*

Verse 29.—" *Lying.*"   A sin that David, through diffidence, fell into frequently. See 1 Sam. xxi. 2, 8, where he roundly telleth three or four lies ; and the like he did, 1 Sam. xxvii. 8, 10 : this evil he saw by himself, and here prayeth against it.—*John Trapp*

Verse 29.—" *The way of lying,*" etc.   Lying ways are all ways, except the ways of God's commandments : reason, sense, example, custom, event, deceivable lusts, these tell a man he is safe, or that he shall repent of them, and take no hurt in the end, and they promise ease and blessedness, but perform it not.   Such as desire to obey God must be kept from evil ways : we are not so sanctified but that temptation will injure our graces.   As a fire in kindling, not throughly alight, may be quenched by a little water, so may our holiness be damped by temptation.   We find within us a proneness to false ways, as candles new blown out are soon blown in again.   Therefore as burnt children dread the fire, so do we fear the way of lying.   God doth not suffer temptations to come into the presence of some ; and in others God maketh the heart averse from sin when temptation is present.   We must come out of the ways of sin, ere we can walk in the ways of God.—*Paul Bayne.*

Verse 29.—" *The way of lying.*"   The whole life of sin is a *lie* from beginning to end.   The word " *lying* " occurs *eight* times in this Psalm.—*William S. Plumer.*

Verse 29.—" *The way of lying.*"   By *the way of lying* is to be understood all that is in man's nature, nót agreeable to the word, whether it be counsels, or conclusions of the heart, or external actions ; and it is called a lying way, because nature promises a good to be gotten by sin which man shall not find in it.—*William Cowper.*

Verse 29.—" *The way of lying.*"   The prophet here desireth to be confirmed by God against all corruptions in doctrine, and disorder of conversation, which Satan by his witty and wily instruments doth seek to set abroach in the world.   These are called " *the way of lying.*"   1. Because they are invented by Satan, the father of lies. 2. They are countenanced by man's wit, the storehouse of lies.   3. They seem to be that which they are not, which is of the nature of lies.   4. They are contrary to God and his truth, the discoverers of lies.—*Richard Greenham.*

Verse 29.—" *Grant me thy law graciously.*"   He opposes the law of God to the way of lying.   First, because it is the only rule of all truth, both in religion and manners : that which is not agreeable to it is but a lie which shall deceive man. Secondly, it destroys and shall at length utterly destroy all contrary errors.   As the rod of Aaron devoured the rods of the enchanters ; so the word, which is the rod of the mouth of God, shall, in the end, eat up and consume all untruths whatsoever. Thirdly, according to the sentence of this word, so shall it be unto every man ; it deceives none.   Men shall find by experience it is true : he who walks in a way condemned by the word, shall come to a miserable end.   And on the contrary, it cannot but be well with them who live according to this rule.—*William Cowper.*

Verse 29.—" *Grant me thy law graciously.*"   David had ever the book of the law ; for every king of Israel was to have it always by him, and the Rabbis say, written with his own hand.   But, " *Grant me thy law graciously ;* " that is, he desires he might have it not only written by him, but upon him, to have it imprinted upon his heart, that he might have a heart to observe and keep it.   That is the blessing he begs for, " *the law ;* " and this is begged " *graciously,*" or upon terms of grace, merely according to thine own favour, and good pleasure.   Here is,—I. The sin deprecated, " *Remove from me the way of lying.*"   II. The good supplicated and asked, " *Grant me thy law graciously.*"   In the first clause you have his malady, David had been enticed to a course of lying.   In the second we have his remedy, and that is the law of God.—*Thomas Manton.*

Verse 30.—" *I have chosen the way of truth."* Here you have the working of a gracious soul. This is more than sitting and hearing the word—having no objection to what you hear. Such hearing is all that can be affirmed of the generality of gospel hearers, except we add, that none are more ready to be caught by false and easy ways of salvation, for they assent to all they hear. The man of God strikes a higher and more spiritual note—he goes into the *choice* of the thing ; he chooses the way of truth ; and he cannot but choose it ; it is the bent of his renewed nature, the effect indeed of all he has been pleading. How act we? The way of truth is all that God has revealed concerning his Son Jesus. The willing heart chooses this way, and all of it ; the bitterness of it, the self-denial of it, as well as the comfort of it ; a Saviour from sin as well as a Saviour from hell ; a Saviour whose Spirit can lead from prayerfulness to godliness, from idleness upon the Sabbath-day to a holy keeping of that day, from self-seeking to the seeking of Christ, from slack, inconsistent conduct to a careful observance of all the Lord's will. Where God's people meet, there such will delight to be. O for such to abound among us !—*John Stephen.*

Verse 30.—" *I have chosen the way of truth."* Religion is not a matter of chance, but of choice. Have we weighed things in the balance, and, upon mature deliberation, made an election,—" We will have God upon any terms ? " Have we sat down and reckoned the cost,—or what religion *must* cost us,—the parting with our lusts ; and what it *may* cost us,—the parting with our lives ? Have we resolved, through the assistance of grace, to own Christ when the swords and staves are up ? and to sail with him, not only in a pleasure-boat, but in a man-of-war ? This choosing God speaks him to be ours : hypocrites profess God out of worldly design, not religious choice.—*Thomas Watson, in " The Morning Exercises."*

Verse 30.—" *I have chosen the way of truth."* The choice which David makes here of God's truth proceeds from that choice and election whereby the Lord before all time made choice of David, in Christ, to be one of his elect. For as it is true of love " Herein is love, not that we loved God, but that he loved us "—we could never have loved him, if first he had not loved us ; so is it true of election ; if he before time had not chosen us to be his people, we could never in time have chosen him to be our God. And this I mark in them who love the word of God, and delight in it, who can say out of a good heart, that the Lord is their portion and the joy of their soul : this is a sure seal of their election, imprinted by the finger of God in their heart.—*William Cowper.*

Verse 30.—In all our religious exercises, let deliberation precede our resolution, and consideration usher in determination. David did so ; and therefore he says here, " *I have chosen the way of truth : thy judgments have I laid before me."* Indeed, he cannot but resolve upon, and make choice of, the way of piety, who layeth before him the goodness, the rectitude and pleasantness of the way. When the prodigal considereth with himself how well his father's servants fared, he thinketh of, yea, determineth to go home ; " I will arise and go to my father."—*Abraham Wright,* 1661.

Verse 30.—" *I have chosen."* No man ever served the Lord but he first made choice of him to be his Master. Every man when he comes to years of discretion so as to be master of himself, adviseth with himself what course he shall take, whether he will serve God or the world. Now all the saints of God have made this distinct choice ; we will serve the Lord, and no other. Moses when both stood before him, the pleasures of Egypt on the one hand, and God and his people with their afflictions on the other, he chose the latter before the former, Heb. xi. 25. So David saith he did, " *I have chosen the way of truth : thy judgments have I laid before me ;"* for to choose is, when a thing lies before a man, and he considers and takes it. So Joshua, " I and my house will serve the Lord."—*John Preston* (1587—1628) *in " The Golden Sceptre held forth to the Humble."* 1638.

Verse 30.—" *Truth."* There are three kinds of truth ; truth in heart, truth in word, truth in deed (2 Kings xx. 3 ; Zech. viii. 16 ; Heb. x. 22).—*Ayguan. From " The Preacher's Storehouse," by J. E. Vaux.*

Verse 30.—" *Thy judgments."* God's word is called his judgment, because it discerns good from evil ; and is not a naked sentence ; but, as it points out evil, so it pronounceth plagues against it, which shall be executed according to the sentence thereof.—*William Cowper.*

Verses 30, 31.—" *I have chosen ;" " I have stuck."* The choosing Christian is likely to be the sticking Christian ; when those that are Christians by chance tack about if the wind turn.—*Matthew Henry.*

Verse 30.—"*Thy judgments have I laid before me."* The solid consideration that God's word is God's decree or judgment may guard a believer against mental terrors and allurements, and fix him in his right choice, as here.—*David Dickson.*

Verse 30.—*"Thy judgments have I laid before me."* Men that mean to travel the right way will lay before them a map : so David, as his will had resolved upon the ways of truth, so he setteth before his eyes the map of the law, which did manifest this unto him, as the ship-man hath his card with the compass.—*Paul Bayne.*

Verse 31.—*"I have stuck unto thy testimonies."* It is not a little remarkable, that while the Psalmist says (verse 25), " My soul *cleaveth* to the dust," he should say here, *"I have cleaved unto thy testimonies"*; for it is the same original word in both verses. The thing is altogether compatible with the experience of the believer. Without there is the body of indwelling sin, and within there is the undying principle of divine grace. There is the contest between them—" the flesh lusteth against the spirit and the spirit against the flesh " (Gal. v. 17), and the believer is constrained to cry out, " O wretched man that I am " (Rom. vii. 24). It is the case ; and all believers find it so. While the soul is many times felt cleaving to the dust, the spirit strives to cleave unto God's testimonies. So the believer prays, Cause that I be not put to shame. And keeping close to Christ, brethren, you shall not be put to shame, world without end.—*John Stephen.*

Verse 31.—*"I have stuck unto thy testimonies."* He adhered to them when momentary interests might have dictated a different line of conduct, when unbelief would have been ready to shrink from the path of duty, when outward appearances were greatly discouraging to fidelity, when all were ready to deride his preposterous determination.—*John Morison.*

Verse 31.—*"I have stuck."* True godliness evermore wears upon her head the garland of perseverance.—*William Cowper.*

Verse 31.—*"Put me not to shame."* Forasmuch as David, in a good conscience, endeavoured to serve God, he craves that the Lord would not confound him. This is two ways done ; either when the Lord forsakes his children, so that in their trouble they feel not his promised comforts, and great confusion of mind and perturbation is upon them ; or otherwise when he leaves them as a prey to their enemies, who scorn them for their godly and sincere life, and exult over them in their time of trouble ; when they see that all their prayer and other exercises of religion cannot keep them out of their enemies' hands. " He trusted in God : let him deliver him." From this shame and contempt he desires the Lord would keep him, and that he should never be like unto them, who, being disappointed of that wherein they trusted, are ashamed.—*William Cowper.*

Verse 32.—*"I will run in the way of thy commandments when,"* etc. You must remember that the speaker, the Psalmist, is not an unconverted man, but one who had long before been brought under the dominion of religion. He is not, therefore, soliciting the first entrance, but the after and multiplied workings of a principle of grace ; and he states his desire in an expression which is singularly descriptive of the outgoing of an influence from the heart over the rest of the man. His wish is that his heart might be enlarged ; and this wish amounted to a longing that the whole of himself might act in unison with the heart, so that he might become, as it were, all heart, and thus the heart in the strictest sense be enlarged, through the spreading of itself over the body and soul, expanding itself till it embraced all the powers of both. If there be the love of God in the heart, then gradually the heart, possessed and actuated by so noble and stirring a principle, will bring over to a lofty consecration all the energies, whether mental or corporeal, and will be practically the same as though the other departments of man were thus the result turned into heart, and he became, according to the phrase which we are accustomed to employ when describing a character of unwonted generosity and warmth, " all heart." So that the desire after an enlarged heart you may fairly consider tantamount to a desire that every faculty might be brought into thorough subjection to God, and that just as God himself is love—love being rather the Divine essence than a Divine attribute, and therefore love mingling itself with all the properties of Godhead, so the man having love in the heart might become all heart, the heart throwing itself into all his capacities, pervading but not obliterating the characteristics of his nature. And exactly in accordance with this view of the enlargement of heart which the Psalmist desired is the practical result which was to follow on its attainment. He was already walking in the way of God's commandments ; but what he proposed to himself was the *running* that way : *"I will run the way of thy commandments, when thou shalt enlarge my heart."* A quickened pace, a more rapid progress, a greater alacrity, a firmer constancy, a more resolute and unflinching obedience, these were the results which the Psalmist looked for from the enlargement of his heart. And truly if all the faculties of mind and body be dedicated to God, with a constant and vigorous step will man press on in the way that leadeth to heaven. So long as the dedication is at best only partial, the world retaining some fraction of its empire, notwithstanding the setting up of the kingdom of God, there can be nothing but a slow and impeded progress, a walking interrupted by repeated haltings, if not backslidings, by much of loitering, if not of actual retreat ; but if the man be all heart, then he will be all life, all warmth, all zeal, all energy, and the consequence of this complete surrender to God will be exactly that which is prophetically announced by Isaiah : " They that wait upon the Lord shall renew their strength ; they shall mount up with wings as eagles ; they shall run, and not be weary ; and they shall walk, and not faint."—*Henry Melvill*, 1798—1871.

Verse 32.—"*I will run.*" By running is meant cheerful, ready, and zealous observance of God's precepts : it is not go, or walk, but *run*. They that would come to their journey's end, must run in the way of God's commandments. It noteth a speedy or a ready obedience, without delay. We must begin with God betimes. Alas ! when we should be at the goal, we have many of us scarce set forth. And it noteth earnestness ; when a man's heart is set upon a thing, he thinks he can never do it soon enough. And this is running, when we are vehement and earnest upon the enjoyment of God and Christ in the way of obedience. And it notes again, that the heart freely offereth itself to God.

This running is the fruit of effectual calling. When the Lord speaks of effectual calling, the issue of it is running ; when he speaks of the conversion of the Gentiles, " Nations that know not thee shall run unto thee " ; and, " Draw me, and we will run after thee." When God draws there is a speedy, earnest motion of the soul.

This running, as it is the fruit of effectual calling, so it is very needful ; for cold and faint motions are soon overborne by difficulty and temptation : " Let us run with patience the race that is set before us " (Heb. xii. 1). When a man hath a mind to do a thing, though he be hindered and jostled, he takes it patiently, he goes on and cannot stay to debate the business. A slow motion is easily stopped, whereas a swift one bears down that which opposeth it ; so is it when men run and are not tired in the service of God. Last of all, the prize calls for running : " So run that ye may obtain " (1 Cor. ix. 24).—*Thomas Manton.*

Verse 32.—"*I will run.*" It was not the *walking* " the way of God's commandments," but the *running* " the way of God's commandments," to which David aspired. The text has no connection with the case of one who habitually pursues the opposite path ; it has exclusive reference to the pace at which the line of duty is to be traversed. . . . . It may not unnaturally excite surprise, that " the sweet singer of Israel "—he who was emphatically declared to be " a man after God's own heart "—should, nevertheless, in the words of the text, seem to imply that *he* was not yet " running the way of God's commandments." But, dear brethren, the greater an individual's comparative holiness, the more intense will be his longing for absolute holiness. To others, David might appear to be speeding marvellously along the path of life ; and yet he himself deemed his movements to be far less rapid. His humility was one of the evidences of his holiness.—*Hugh B. Moffat*, 1871.

Verse 32.—"*I will run the way.*" His intended course in this way he expresses by running. It is good to be in this way even in the slowest motions ; love will creep where it cannot walk. But if thou art so indeed, then thou wilt long for a swifter motion ; if thou do but creep, creep on, desire to be enabled to go. If thou goest, but yet haltingly and lamely, yet desire to be strengthened to walk straight ; and if thou walkest, let not that satisfy thee, desire to run. So here, David did walk in this way ; but he earnestly wishes to mend his pace ; he would willingly run, and for that end he desires an enlarged heart.

Some dispute and descant too much whether they go or no, and childishly tell their steps, and would know at every step whether they advance or no, and how much they advance, and thus amuse themselves, and spend the time of doing and going in questioning and doubting. Thus it is with many Christians ; but it were a more wise and comfortable way to be endeavouring onwards, and if thou make little progress, at least to be desiring to make more ; to be praying and walking, and praying that thou mayest walk faster, and that in the end thou mayest run, not satisfied with anything attained. Yet by that unsatisfiedness we must not be so dejected as to sit down, or to stand still, but rather we must be excited to go on.—*Robert Leighton.*

Verse 32.—*"Enlarged my heart,"* or dilated it, namely, with joy. It is obvious to remark the philosophical propriety with which this expression is applied : since the heart is dilated, and the pulse by consequence becomes strong and full, from the exultation of joy as well as of pride. (See Parkhurst on רחב.)—*Richard Mant.*

Verse 32.—*"Thou wilt enlarge my heart."* God would enlarge the very seat of life, and thus give his weak servant more strength ; such strength that he need no longer lie prone on the dust struggling to arise ; but strength to enable him to run in the way of truth. Thus, he who prays, *"O Lord, put me not to shame,"* finds for himself the truth of an earlier song : " They looked unto him, and were lightened, and their faces were not ashamed."—*Frederick G. Marchant.*

Verse 32.—*"Enlarge my heart."* It is said of Solomon, that he had " a large heart (the same word that is used here), as the sand of the sea shore : " that is a vast, comprehensive spirit, that could fathom much of nature, both its greater and lesser things. Thus, I conceive, the enlargement of the heart compriseth the enlightening of the understanding. There arises a clearer light there to discern spiritual things in a more spiritual manner ; to see the vast difference betwixt the vain things the world goes after, and the true, solid delight that is in the way of God's commandments ; to know the false blush of the pleasures of sin, and what deformity is under that painted mask, and not be allured by it ; to have enlarged apprehensions of God, his excellency, and greatness and goodness ; how worthy he is to be obeyed and served ; this is the great dignity and happiness of the soul ; all other pretensions are low and poor in respect of this. Here then is enlargement to see the purity and beauty of his law, how just and reasonable, yea, how pleasant and amiable it is ; that his commandments are not grievous, that they are beds of spices ; the more we walk in them, still the more of their fragrant smell and sweetness we find.—*Robert Leighton.*

Verse 32.—Narrow is the way unto life, but no man can run in it save with widened heart.—*Prosper, of Aquitaine* (403—463), *quoted by Neale and Littledale.*

Verse 32.—*"Enlarged."* Surely a temple for the great God (such as our hearts should be) should be fair and ample. If we would have God dwell in our hearts, and shed abroad his influences, we should make room for God in our souls, by a greater largeness of faith and expectation. The rich man thought of enlarging his barns, when his store was increased upon him (Luke xii.), so should we stretch out the curtains of Christ's tent and habitation, have larger expectations of God, if we would receive more from him. The vessels failed before the oil failed. We are not straitened in God, but in ourselves ; by the scantiness of our thoughts, we do not make room for him, nor greaten God : " My soul doth magnify the Lord " (Luke i. 46). Faith doth greaten God. How can we make God greater than he is ? As to the declarative being, we can have greater and larger apprehensions of his greatness, goodness, and truth.

1. There needs a large heart, because the command is exceedingly broad : " I have seen an end of all perfection ; but thy commandment is exceeding broad " (Ps. cxix. 96). A broad law and a narrow heart will never suit : we need love, faith, knowledge, and all to carry us through this work, which is of such a vast extent and latitude.

2. We need enlarged heart, because of the lets and hindrances within ourselves. There is lust drawing off from God to sensual objects : " Every man is tempted, when he is drawn away of his own lust, and enticed " (James i. 14). Therefore there needs something to draw us on, to carry us out with strength and life another way, to urge us in the service of God. Lust sits as a clog upon us, it is a weight of corruption (Heb. xii. 1), retarding us in all our flights and motions, thwarting, opposing, breaking the force of spiritual impulsions, if not hindering them altogether (Gal. v. 17). Well then, lust drawing so strongly one way, God needs to draw us more strongly the other way. When there is a weight to poise us to worldly and sensual objects, we need a strength to carry us on with vigorous and lively motions of soul towards God, an earnest bent upon our souls, which is this enlargement of heart.—*Thomas Manton.*

Verse 32.—*"My heart."* The great Physician knows at once where to look for the cause, when he sees anything amiss in the outward life of his people. He well knows that all spiritual disease is heart disease, and it is the heart remedies that he must apply.   At one time, our Physician sees symptoms which are violent in their nature ;   at another, he sees symptoms of languor and debility ;   but he knows that both come from the heart ;   and so, it is upon the heart that he operates, when he is about to perform a cure.

The strong action of the heart in all holy things comes from the blessed operation of the Spirit upon it ;   then only can we " *run* " the way of God's commandments, when he has enlarged our heart.

Heartiness in action is the subject to which the reader's attention is here directed, and it is one of considerable importance.

There are many believers, who for want of enlargement of heart are occupying a poor position in the church of God.   They are trusting to Jesus for life eternal, and he will doubtless not disappoint them ;   he will be true to his word, that " he that believeth shall be saved ; " but they are still, alas ! to a deplorable degree, shut up in self ;   they have contracted hearts ;   still do they take narrow views of God's claim, and their own privileges, and the position in which they are set in the world ;   and however much they might be said to stand, or sit, or walk in the way of God's commandments, they cannot be said to "*run* " in it.   Running is a strong and healthy action of the body ;   it requires energy, it is an exercise that needs a sound heart ;   none can run in the way of God's commandments, except in strength and vigour imparted by him.   The *running* Christians are comparatively few ;   walking and sitting Chrsitians are comparatively common ;   but the running Christian is so uncommon as often to be thought almost mad.

Let us, for the sake of order, classify our observations on this subject under the following heads :—

I. *What heartiness is.*   The heartiness spoken of here under the term, " enlargement of the heart," is cheerfulness in doing God's will—love for that will—a drawing out of the affections towards it—an interest in it ;   all this it is, and a great deal more, which it is not easy to describe or define.

II. *What heartiness does.*   Where there is enlargement of the heart by God, there is an outgoing beyond all the limits which fallen selfishness assigns.   The heart contracted at the fall ;   it shrank when sin entered into it ;   it became unequal to containing great and generous thoughts ;   it became a bondaged heart.   True ! the responsibilities of duty could not be escaped, not could the directions of conscience ;   but the affections are voluntary, and the fallen heart drew in its affections from God ;   it felt that it had the power of withholding them from him and his commandments, and it rejoiced to shew its enmity in withholding its sympathy, where it could not withhold its obedience. . . . .

III. *Whence heartiness comes.*   Now, as we have already said, where the heart is operated on by the Spirit, and all its natural evil overruled, it has outgoings which are entirely beyond the limits that fallen selfishness assigns.   Love is inwrought with it :   the union of sentiment, the identity of interest which love inspires, pervade it, in all belonging to God, for it has received these from God ;   the heart becomes unbondaged from mere rules, or perhaps to speak more correctly, it rises above them, and it feels—not merely it *knows*, but it *feels*—so much of the beauty of God's commandments, that it delights to "*run* " in them ;   it loves to be hearty in them ;   its interests, its affections are in them.—*Philip Bennet Power, in "The 'I Wills' of the Psalms,"* 1862.

Verse 32.—Disquiets of heart unfit us for duty, by hindering our activity in the prosecution of duty.   The whole heart, soul, and strength should be engaged in all religious services ;   but these troubles are as clogs and weights to hinder motion.   Joy is the dilatation of the soul, and widens it for anything which it undertakes ;   but grief contracts the heart, and narrows all the faculties.   Hence doth David beg an " enlarged heart," as the principle of activity :   "*I will run the way of thy commandments, when thou shalt enlarge my heart*" ;   for what else can be expected when the mind is so distracted with fear and sorrow, but that it should be uneven, tottering, weak, and confused ?   so that if it do set itself to anything, it acts troublesomely, drives on heavily, and doth a very little with a great deal ado ;   and yet, the unfitness were less, if that little which it can do were well done ;   but the mind is so interrupted in its endeavours that sometimes in prayer the man begins, and then is presently at a stand, and dares not proceed, his words are swallowed up, " he is so troubled that he cannot speak," Ps. lxxvii. 4.—*Richard Gilpin,* (1625—1699), *in* "*Dæmonologia Sacra.*"

EXPOSITION OF VERSES 33 TO 40.

TEACH me, O LORD, the way of thy statutes ; and I shall keep it *unto* the end.

34 Give me understanding, and I shall keep thy law ; yea, I shall observe it with *my* whole heart.

35 Make me to go in the path of thy commandments ; for therein do I delight.

36 Incline my heart unto thy testimonies, and not to covetousness.

37 Turn away mine eyes from beholding vanity ; *and* quicken thou me in thy way.

38 Stablish thy word unto thy servant, who *is devoted* to thy fear.

39 Turn away my reproach which I fear : for thy judgments *are* good.

40 Behold, I have longed after thy precepts : quicken me in thy righteousness.

A sense of dependence and a consciousness of extreme need pervade this section, which is all made up of prayer and plea. The former eight verses trembled with a sense of sin, quivering with a childlike sense of weakness and folly, which caused the man of God to cry out for the help by which alone his soul could be preserved from falling back into sin.

33. *"Teach me, O LORD, the way of thy statutes."* Child-like, blessed words, from the lips of an old, experienced believer, and he a king, and a man inspired of God. Alas, for those who will never be taught. They dote upon their own wisdom ; but their folly is apparent to all who rightly judge. The Psalmist will have the Lord for his teacher ; for he feels that his heart will not learn of any less effectual instructor. A sense of great slowness to learn drives us to seek a great teacher. What condescension it is on our great Jehovah's part that he deigns to teach those who seek him. The lesson which is desired is thoroughly practical ; the holy man would not only learn the *statutes*, but the w*a*y of them, the daily use of them, their tenor, spirit, direction, habit, tendency. He would know that path of holiness which is hedged in by divine law, along which the commands of the Lord stand as sign-posts of direction and mile-stones of information, guiding and marking our progress. The very desire to learn this way is in itself an assurance that we shall be taught therein, for he who made us long to learn will be sure to gratify the desire.

"And I shall keep it unto the end." Those who are taught of God never forget their lessons. When divine grace sets a man in the true way he will be true to it. Mere human wit and will have no such enduring influence : there is an end to all perfection of the flesh, but there is no end to heavenly grace except its own end, which is the perfecting of holiness in the fear of the Lord. Perseverance to the end is most certainly to be predicted of those whose beginning is in God, and with God, and by God ; but those who commence without the Lord's teaching soon forget what they learn, and start aside from the way upon which they professed to have entered. No one may boast that he will hold on his way in his own strength, for that must depend upon the continual teaching of the Lord : we shall fall like Peter, if we presume on our own firmness as he did. If God keeps us we shall keep his way ; and it is a great comfort to know that it is the way with God to keep the feet of his saints. Yet we are to watch as if our keeping of the way depended wholly on ourselves ; for, according to this verse, our perseverance rests not on any force or compulsion, but on the teaching of the Lord, and assuredly teaching; whoever be the teacher, requires learning on the part of the taught one : no one can teach a man who refuses to learn. Earnestly, then, let us drink in divine instruction, that so we may hold fast our integrity, and to life's latest hour follow on in the path of uprightness ! If we receive the living and incorruptible seed of the word of God we must live : apart from this we have no life eternal, but only a name to live.

The " *end* " of which David speaks is the end of life, or the fulness of obedience. He trusted in grace to make him faithful to the utmost, never drawing a line and saying to obedience, " Hitherto shalt thou go, but no further." The end of our keeping the law will come only when we cease to breathe ; no good man will think of marking a date and saying, " It is enough, I may now relax my watch, and live after the manner of men." As Christ loves us to the end, so must we serve him to the end. The end of divine teaching is that we may persevere to the end.

The portions of eight show a relationship still. GIMEL begins with prayer for life, that he may keep the word (17) ; DALETH cries for more life, according to that word (25) ; and now HE opens with a prayer for teaching, that he may keep the way of God's statutes. If a keen eye is turned upon these verses a closer affinity will be discerned.

34. *"Give me understanding, and I shall keep thy law."* This is the same prayer enlarged, or rather it is a supplement which intensifies it. He not only needs teaching, but the power to learn : he requires not only to understand, but to obtain *an understanding.* How low has sin brought us; for we even lack the faculty to understand spiritual things, and are quite unable to know them till we are endowed with spiritual discernment. Will God in very deed give us understanding ? This is a miracle of grace. It will, however, never be wrought upon us till we know our need of it ; and we shall not even discover that need till God gives us a measure of understanding to perceive it. We are in a state of complicated ruin, from which nothing but manifold grace can deliver us. Those who feel their folly are by the example of the Psalmist encouraged to pray for understanding : let each man by faith cry, " Give *me* understanding." Others have had it, why may it not come to *me ?* It was a gift to them ; will not the Lord also freely bestow it upon *me ?*

We are not to seek this blessing that we may be famous for wisdom, but that we may be abundant in our love to the law of God. He who has understanding will learn, remember, treasure up, and obey the commandment of the Lord. The gospel gives us grace to keep the law ; the free gift leads us to holy service ; there is no way of reaching to holiness but by accepting the gift of God. If God gives, we keep ; but we never keep the law in order to obtaining grace. The sure result of regeneration, or the bestowal of understanding, is a devout reverence for the law and a resolute keeping of it in the heart. The spirit of God makes us to know the Lord and to understand somewhat of his love, wisdom, holiness, and majesty ; and the result is that we honour the law and yield our hearts to the obedience of the faith.

"Yea, I shall observe it with my whole heart." The understanding operates upon the affections ; it convinces the heart of the beauty of the law, so that the soul loves it with all its powers ; and then it reveals the majesty of the lawgiver, and the whole nature bows before his supreme will. An enlightened judgment heals the divisions of the heart, and bends the united affections to a strict and watchful observance of the one rule of life. He alone obeys God who can say, " My Lord, I would serve thee, and do it with all my heart"; and none can truly say this till they have received as a free grant the inward illumination of the Holy Ghost. To observe God's law with all our heart at all times is a great grace, and few there be that find it ; yet it is to be had if we will consent to be taught of the Lord.

Observe the parallel of verses 2 and 10 where the *whole* heart is spoken of in reference to seeking, and in 58 in pleading for mercy ; these are all second verses in their octonaries. The frequent repetition of the phrase shows the importance of undivided love : the heart is never whole or holy till it is whole or united. The heart is never one with God till it is one within itself.

35. *"Make me to go in the path of thy commandments ; for therein do I delight."* " To will is present with me ; but how to perform that which is good I find not." Thou hast made me to love the way, now make me to move in it. It is a plain path, which others are treading through thy grace ; I see it and admire it ; cause me to travel in it. This is the cry of a child that longs to walk, but is too feeble ; of a pilgrim who is exhausted, yet pants to be on the march ; of a lame man who pines to be able to run. It is a blessed thing to delight in holiness, and surely he who gave us this delight will work in us the yet higher joy of possessing and practising it. Here is our only hope ; for we shall not go in the narrow path till we are made to do so by the Maker's own power. O thou who didst once make me, I pray thee make me again : thou hast made me to know ; now make me to go. Certainly I shall never be happy till I do, for my sole delight lies in walking according to thy bidding.

The Psalmist does not ask the Lord to do for him what he ought to do for himself: he wishes himself to "go" or tread in the path of the command. He asks not to be carried while he lies passive ; but to be made "to go." Grace does not treat us as stocks and stones, to be dragged by horses or engines, but as creatures endowed with life, reason, will, and active powers, who are willing and able to go of themselves if once made to do so. God worketh in us, but it is that we may both will and do according to his good pleasure. The holiness we seek after is not a forced compliance with command, but the indulgence of a whole-hearted passion for goodness, such as shall conform our life to the will of the Lord. Can the reader say, "*therein do I delight*"? Is practical godliness the very jewel of your soul, the coveted prize of your mind ? If so, the outward path of life, however rough will be clean, and lead the soul upward to delight ineffable. He who delights in the law should not doubt but what he will be enabled to run in its ways, for where the heart already finds its joy the feet are sure to follow.

Note that the corresponding verse in the former eight (35) was "Make me to understand," and here we have "Make me to go." Remark the order, first understanding and then going ; for a clear understanding is a great assistance towards practical action.

During the last few octaves the fourth has been *the heart* verse : see 20, 28, and now 36. Indeed in all the preceeding fourths great heartiness is observable. This also marks the care with which this sacred song was composed.

36. "*Incline my heart unto thy testimonies.*" Does not this prayer appear to be superfluous, since it is evident that the Psalmist's heart was set upon obedience ? We are sure that there is never a word to spare in Scripture. After asking for active virtue it was meet that the man of God should beg that his heart might be in all that he did. What would his goings be if his heart did not go ? It may be that David felt a wandering desire, an inordinate leaning of his soul to wordly gain,— possibly it even intruded into his most devout meditations, and at once he cried out for more grace. The only way to cure a wrong leaning is to have the soul bent in the opposite direction. Holiness of heart is the cure for covetousness. What a blessing it is that we may ask the Lord even for an inclination. Our wills are free, and yet without violating their liberty, grace can incline us in the right direction. This can be done by enlightening the understanding as to the excellence of obedience, by strengthening our habits of virtue, by giving us an experience of the sweetness of picty, and by many other ways. If any one duty is irksome to us it behoves us to offer this prayer with special reference thereto : we are to love all the Lord's testimonies, and if we fail in any one point we must pay double attention to it. The leaning of the heart is the way in which the life will lean : hence the force of the petition, "*Incline my heart.*" Happy shall we be when we feel habitually inclined to all that is good. This is not the way in which a carnal heart ever leans ; all its inclinations are in opposition to the divine testimonies.

"*And not to covetousness.*" This is the inclination of nature, and grace must put a negative upon it. This vice is as injurious as it is common ; it is as mean as it is miserable. It is idolatry, and so it dethrones God ; it is selfishness, and so it is cruel to all in its power ; it is sordid greed, and so it would sell the Lord himself for pieces of silver. It is a degrading, grovelling, hardening, deadening sin, which withers every-thing around it that is lovely and Christlike. He who is covetous is of the race of Judas, and will in all probability turn out to be himself a son of perdition. The crime of covetousness is common, but very few will confess it ; for when a man heaps up gold in his heart the dust of it blows into his eyes, and he cannot see his own fault. Our hearts must have some object of desire, and the only way to keep out worldly gain is to put in its place the testimonies of the Lord. If we are inclined or bent one way, we shall be turned *from* the other ; the negative virtue is most surely attained by making sure of the positive grace which inevitably produces it.

37. "*Turn away mine eyes from beholding vanity.*" He had prayed about his heart, and one would have thought that the eyes would so surely have been influenced by the heart that there was no need to make them the objects of a special petition ; but our author is resolved to make assurance doubly sure. If the eyes do not see, perhaps the heart may not desire ; at any rate, one door of temptation is closed when we do not even look at the painted bauble. Sin first entered man's mind by the eye, and it is still a favourite gate for the incoming of Satan's allurements ; hence the need of a double watch upon that portal. The prayer is not so much that the eyes may be shut as "*turned away ;*" for we need to have them open, but directed to right objects. Perhaps we are now gazing upon folly, we need to have our eyes

turned away ; and if we are beholding heavenly things we shall be wise to beg that our eyes may be kept away from vanity.   Why should we look on vanity ?—it melts away as a vapour.   Why not look upon things eternal ?   Sin is vanity, unjust gain is vanity, self-conceit is vanity, and, indeed, all that is not of God comes under the same head.   From all this we must turn away.   It is a proof of the sense of weakness felt by the Psalmist and of his entire dependence upon God that he even asks to have his eyes turned for him ; he meant not to make himself passive, but he intended to set forth his own utter helplessness apart from the grace of God.   For fear he should forget himself and gaze with a lingering longing upon forbidden objects, he entreats the Lord speedily to make him turn away his eyes, hurrying him off from so dangerous a parley with iniquity.   If we are kept from looking on vanity we shall be preserved from loving iniquity.

" *And quicken thou me in thy way.*"   Give me so much life that dead vanity may have no power over me.   Enable me to travel so swiftly in the road to heaven that I may not stop long enough within sight of vanity to be fascinated thereby.   The prayer indicates our greatest need—more life in our obedience.   It shows the preserving power of increased life to keep us from the evils which are around us, and it, also, tells us where that increased life must come from, namely, from the Lord alone. Vitality is the cure of vanity.   When the heart is full of grace the eyes will be cleansed from impurity.   On the other hand, if we would be full of life as to the things of God we must keep ourselves apart from sin and folly, or the eyes will soon captivate the mind, and, like Samson, who could slay his thousands, we may ourselves be overcome through the lusts which enter by the eye.

This verse is parallel to verses 21 and 29 in the previous eights : " rebuke," " remove," " turn away ; " or " proud," " lying," " vanity."

38. " *Stablish thy word unto thy servant.*"   Make me sure of thy sure word : make it sure to me and make me sure of it.   If we possess the spirit of service, and yet are troubled with sceptical thoughts we cannot do better than pray to be established in the truth.   Times will arise when every doctrine and promise seems to be shaken, and our mind gets no rest : then we must appeal to God for establishment in the faith, for he would have all his servants to be well instructed and confirmed in his word.   But we must mind that we are the Lord's servants, for else we shall not long be sound in his truth.   Practical holiness is a great help towards doctrinal certainty : if we are God's servants he will confirm his word in our experience.   " If any man will do his will, he shall know of the doctrine ; " and so know it as to be fully assured of it.   Atheism in the heart is a horrible plague to a God-fearing man, it brings more torment with it than can well be described and nothing but a visitation of grace can settle the soul after it has been violently assailed thereby.   Vanity or falsehood is bad for the eyes, but it is even worse when it defiles the understanding and casts a doubt upon the word of the living God.

" *Who is devoted to thy fear,*" or simply—" *to thy fear.*"   That is, make good thy word to godly fear wherever it exists ; strengthen the whole body of reverent men. Stablish thy word, not only to me, but to all the godly ones under the sun.   Or, again, it may mean—" Stablish thy word to thy fear," namely, that men may be led to fear thee ; since a sure faith in the divine promise is the fountain and foundation of godly fear.   Men will never worship a God in whom they do not believe.   More faith will lead to more godly fear.   We cannot look for the fulfilment of promises in our experience unless we live under the influence of the fear of the Lord : establishment in grace is the result of holy watchfulness and prayerful energy.   We shall never be rooted and grounded in our belief unless we daily practise what we profess to believe.   Full assurance is the reward of obedience.   Answers to prayer are given to those whose hearts answer to the Lord's command.   If we are devoted to God's fear we shall be delivered from all other fear.   He has no fear as to the truth of the word who is filled with fear of the Author of the word.   Scepticism is both the parent and the child of impiety ; but strong faith both begets piety and is begotten of it. We commend this whole verse to any devout man whose tendency is to scepticism : it will be an admirable prayer for use in seasons of unusually strong misgivings.

39. " *Turn away my reproach which I fear.*"   He feared just reproach, trembling lest he should cause the enemy to blaspheme through any glaring inconsistency. We ought to fear this, and watch that we may avoid it.   Persecution in the form of calumny may also be prayed against, for it is a sore trial, perhaps the sorest of trials to men of sensitive minds.   Many would sooner bear burning at the stake than the trial of cruel mockings.   David was quick tempered, and he probably had all the

greater dread of slander because it raised his anger, and he could hardly tell what he might not do under great provocation. If God turns away our eyes from falsehood, we may also expect that he will turn away falsehood from injuring our good name. We shall be kept from lies if we keep from lies.

"*For thy judgments are good.*" Therefore he is anxious that none may speak evil of the ways of God through hearing an ill report about himself. We mourn when we are slandered ; because the shame is cast rather upon our religion than ourselves. If men would be content to attribute evil *to us*, and go no further, we might bear it, for we are evil ; but our sorrow is that they cast a slur upon the word and character of God, who is so good, that there is none good in comparison with him. When men rail at God's government of the world it is our duty and privilege to stand up for him, and openly to declare before him, " thy judgments are good ; " and we should do the same when they assail the Bible, the gospel, the law, or the name of our Lord Jesus Christ. But we must take heed that they can bring no truthful accusation against us, or our testimony will be so much wasted breath.

This prayer against reproach is parallel to verse 31, and in general to many other of the seventh verses in the octaves, which usually imply opposition from without and a sacred satisfaction within. Observe the things which are good : "*thy judgments are good ;*" "thou art good and doest good " (68) ; " good for me to have been afflicted " (71) ; " teach me good judgment " (66).

40. "*Behold, I have longed after thy precepts.*" He can at least claim sincerity. He is deeply bowed down by a sense of his weakness and need of grace ; but he does desire to be in all things conformed to the divine will. Where our longings are, there are we in the sight of God. If we have not attained perfection, it is something to have hungered after it. He who has given us to desire, will also grant us to obtain. The precepts are grievous to the ungodly, and therefore when we are so changed as to long for them we have clear evidence of conversion, and we may safely conclude that he who has begun the good work will carry it on. "*Quicken me in thy righteousness.*" Give me more life wherewith to follow thy righteous law ; or give me more life because thou hast promised to hear prayer, and it is according to thy righteousness to keep thy word. How often does David plead for quickening ! But never once too often. We need quickening every hour of the day for we are so sadly apt to become slow and languid in the ways of God. It is the Holy Spirit who can pour new life into us ; let us not cease crying to him. Let the life we already possess show itself by longing for more.

The last verses of the octaves have generally exhibited an onward look of resolve, hope, and prayer. Here past fruits of grace are made the plea for further blessing. Onward is the heavenly life is the cry of this verse.

SPECIAL NOTES ON VERSES 33 TO 40.

Upon this Octonary the Notes furnished by Mr. Marchant, one of the Tutors of the Pastors' College, are so excellent that we give them entire.

SECTION ה, HE.

SUBJECT : THE LAW OF JEHOVAH TO BE SET BEFORE THE EYES, THE MIND, THE FEET, AND THE HEART.

Key phrase : הָקֵם לְעַבְדְּךָ אִמְרָתֶךָ.   " *Set up before thy servant thy word* " (ver. 38).

Verse 33.—THE WORD SET UP BEFORE THE EYES. " *Teach me ; "* literally, " *point out,*" " *indicate to me.*"   יָרָה, as used here, means " *to send out the hand,*" especially in the sense of pointing out. Hence " to show," " to indicate," " to teach." The Psalmist here prays for direction in its more superficial form. Many paths were before his eyes, leading down to death : one path was before him, leading unto life. He here asks to be shown *which* is Jehovah's way. If the Lord will ever show his eyes which way is the right way, then he will keep it unto the end. Here is light wanted for the eyes. As the Indian pursues his trail with unerring eye and unfaltering step, so, watching for every deviation which might take us astray, we should pursue the way which leadeth unto life.

Verse 34.—THE WORD SET BEFORE THE MIND. " *Give me understanding.*" The word used here refers to mental comprehension, as distinguished from the mere direction, or pointing out, asked for in the previous verse. Here the prayer is, " *Make me to discern,*" " *Cause me to perceive,*" *i.e.*, with the understanding. " Faith cometh by hearing, and hearing by the word of God." The outer senses must first see the way, then the mind must understand it, then, with faith and love, the heart should follow it. Thus, too, the Psalmist, if God will cause him to understand the law, will keep it with all his heart. Still, the heart is prone to lean to things earthly and sinful, and divine help has presently to be invoked for that also.

Verse 35.—THE WORD SET BEFORE THE FEET. The word הַדְרִיכֵנִי is from דָּרַךְ " *to tread with the feet,*" " *to trample.*" Hence, " *Make me to go,*" alludes here to the very act of walking in the divine way, in distinction from mere perception of the way with the eyes and with the understanding. It is in this matter of practical walking that the actual difficulties of the way seem to come more forcibly into sight ; hence we no longer have דֶּרֶךְ used (as in verse 33) which may mean a broad open way, but נָתִיב, which (says Gesenius) " never denotes a public and royal road, such as was raised up and formed by art, but always a footpath." So the younger Buxtorf renders the word by *Semita.* When the feet really come to tread it, the way of truth is ever found to be " the narrow way."

Verse 36.—THE WORD SET BEFORE THE HEART. " *Incline my heart unto thy testimonies.*" It is nothing for the eyes to see, for the mind to understand, nor even for the feet to be made to go in the way of truth, if the heart be not inclined thereunto also. It is with the heart that man believeth unto righteousness. To be without love is, according to 1 Cor. xiii., to be without everything.

Thus the sense of these four methodical petitions in this section is as follows : Make me to see, make me to understand, make me to go in, and make me to love to go in, the beaten and narrow path of thy testimonies. So far as I gather, Luther gives almost the exact sense of the foregoing exposition ; for he translates the opening words of verses 33, 34, 35, and 36 by terms signifying respectively, " Point out to me," " Explain to me," " Lead me," and " Incline (bend, slope) my heart," etc.

Verse 37.—" *Turn away mine eyes,*" etc. Literally, " *Make mine eyes to pass from seeing vanity ; "* as though he would pray, Whatever is of vanity, make me to pass without seeing it. The sentiment is strikingly like that in our Lord's prayer : " Lead us not into temptation." Having prayed for what he wanted to see, the Psalmist here prays for the hiding of what he would not see.

Verse 38.—*" Stablish thy word unto thy servant."* In view of the exposition of the previous verses of the section this would be more correctly rendered, *" Hold up thy word before thy servant ; "* i.e., hold it up to my eyes, to my mind, to my steps, and to my heart. Make all that is vain to pass, so that I see it not ; but let thy word be so set up before my whole being that I shall always see it, and thus, by it, see my way to thee.

Verse 39.—*" Turn away my reproach which I fear."* " Cause to pass my reproach which *I feared."* This also, like the vanity spoken of in verse 37, the Psalmist prays that he may not see. He would have the gaze of his whole manhood bent only on the word. The reproach which he feared is that to which he had already referred in verses 21, 22, and perhaps again in verse 31. The proud had erred from the commandments, and had inherited rebuke ; it was the reproach and shame which were theirs that the Psalmist would have to be turned aside, so that they should not be seen. *" For thy judgments are good."* This is given as a reason why the reproach should be thus turned aside. The proud had thought lightly and contemptuously on the divine judgments, hence their reproach ; the Psalmist held those judgments to be good, and thus hoped that he might not see reproach.

Verse 40.—*" Behold, I have longed after,"* etc. This is given as an intenser form of the statement which he had just made, that he esteemed the judgments to be good. They were so good that he longed after them. Not only so, but he desired to long after them even more. Thus he prays for even more life and vigour in pursuing the path which they pointed out—*" Quicken me in thy righteousness."* He who really longs after divine truth, mourns that he does not long more. When the heart has no love, the mind has no light, and can only judge the precepts erroneously. " The pure in heart " see better with the mind than can the impure. " Unto the upright there ariseth light in the darkness." Love so enlarges discernment that he who really loves often finds that his judgment of the blessedness of truth has outstripped even his longing for it. Hence it is the quick who cry, " *Quicken me ;* " it is those who have living desires who pray for yet more life in the way of righteousness.

NOTES ON VERSES 33 TO 40.

Verses 33—40.—In this Octonarius, now and again, the same prayer is repeated, of which several times mention has before been made. For he prays that he may be divinely taught, governed, strengthened, and defended against the calumnies, reproaches, and threatenings of his enemies. And the prayer is full of the most ardent longings, which is manifest from the same resolve being so frequently repeated. For the more he knows the ignorance, obscurity, doubts, and the imbecility of the human mind, and sees how men are impelled by a slight momentum, so that they fall away from the truth and embrace errors repugnant to the divine word, or fall into great sins, the more ardently and strongly does he ask in prayer that he may be divinely taught, governed, and strengthened, lest he should cast away acknowledged truth, or plunge himself into wickedness. And by his example he teaches that we, also, against blindness born with us, and the imbecility of our flesh, and also against the snares and madnesses of devils should fortify ourselves with those weapons ; namely, with the right study and knowledge of the divine Word, and with constant prayer. For if so great a man, who had made such pre-eminent attainments, prayed for this, how much more ought they to do so, who are but novices and ignorant beginners. This is the sum of this Octonarius.—*D. H. Mollerus.*

Verses 33—40.—In this part, nine times does the Psalmist send up his petition to his God, and six of these he accompanies with a reason for being heard. . . . These petitions are the utterances of a renewed heart ; the man of God could not but give utterance to them—such was the new refining process that had taken place upon him. . . . . The outline runs thus :—Petitions are offered for Instruction (33) and Understanding (34), and likewise for Spiritual Ability (35) and Inclination (36). These are followed by petitions for Exemption from the Spirit of Vanity (37), and for Divine Quickening (37). The Lord is besought to make good his Word of Promise to his servant (38), and to deliver him from Feared Reproach. Last of all, the man of God places his prayer for quickening upon the ground of the Divine Righteousness (40). May the Divine Spirit teach us to compare ourselves with what we find here, as we would see the salvation of our God !—*John Stephen.*

Verses 33—40.—I observe that in this one octonary which is not to be found in any of the rest, namely, that in every several verse there is a several prayer. In the first whereof he prayeth to be taught, and then promiseth to take in that which God shall teach him. He had before resolved to run in this way ; but he felt forthwith his own natural aberrations, and therefore he cometh to this guide to be taught. —*Richard Greenham.*

Verse 33.—" *Teach me, O* LORD, *the way of thy statutes,*" etc. Instruction from above is necessary for the children of God, while they continue in this world. The more we know, the more we shall desire to know ; we shall beg a daily supply of grace, as well as of bread ; and a taste of " the cluster of Eshcol " will make us long after the vintage of Canaan (Numb. xiii. 23). Religion is the art of holy living, and then only known when it is practised ; as he is not a master of music who can read the notes which compose it, but he who has learnt to take a lesson readily from the book, and play it on his instrument ; after which the pleasure it affords will be sufficient motive for continuing so to do.—*George Horne.*

Verse 33.—" *Teach me, O* LORD, *the way of thy statutes,*" etc. In the sincerity of your hearts go to God for his teaching. God is pleased with the request. " Give therefore thy servant an understanding heart to judge thy people, that I may discern between good and bad : for who is able to judge this thy so great a people ? And the speech pleased the Lord, that Solomon had asked this thing " (1 Kings iii. 9, 10). Oh, beg it of God, for these three reasons—1. The way of God's statutes is worthy to be found by all. 2. It is hard to be found and kept by any. 3. It is so dangerous to miss it, that this should quicken us to be earnest with God.—*Thomas Manton.*

Verse 33.—" *Teach me, O* LORD," etc. " He who is his own pupil," remarks S. Bernard, " has a fool for his master." A soldier who enters on a march does not settle for himself the order of his going, nor begin the journey at his own will, nor yet choose pleasant short-cuts, lest he should fall out of rank, away from the standards, but gets the route from his general, and keeps to it ; advances in a prescribed order, walks armed, and goes straight on to the end of his march, to find there the supplies provided by the commissariat. If he goes by any other road, he gets no rations, and finds no quarters ready, because the general's orders are that all things of this kind shall be prepared for those who follow him, and turn not aside to the right hand or the left. And thus he who follows his general does not break down, and that for good reasons; for the general consults not for his own convenience, but for the capability of his whole army. And this, too, is Christ's order of march, as he leads his great host out of the spiritual Egypt to the eternal Land of Paradise.—*Ambrose, quoted by Neale and Littledale.*

Verse 33.—" *Teach me, O LORD, the way,*" etc. It should never be forgotten, as this fifth section teaches us, that there is a way marked out by God's own appointment for all his people to walk in, and in which to persevere. Others lay down a path each for himself, and keeping to it think they are safe. David did not trust to anything of this kind; he was only desirous of being found in the way of God's ordinance, and to be so taught of God as to keep it to the end; or as the original reads, keep it the end, the end of his profession, the salvation of his soul.—*W. Wilson.*

Verse 33.—" *Teach me, O LORD, the way of thy statutes; and I shall keep it,*" etc. If thou continue a teacher of me, saith David, I shall continue a servant to thee. Perseverance cannot be, unless continual light and grace be furnished to us from the Lord. As the tree which hath not sap at the root may flourish for a while, but cannot continue; a man, whose heart is not watered with the dew of God's grace continually, may for a time make a fair show of godliness, but in the end he will fall away. We bear not the root, but the root bears us: let us tremble and fear. If we abide not in our Lord, we become withered branches, good for nothing but the fire. Let us alway pray that he would ever abide with us, to inform us by his light, and lead us by his power, in that way which may bring us to himself.—*William Cowper.*

Verse 33.—" *Statutes,*" from a word signifying to *mark, trace out, describe* and *ordain;* because they *mark out* our way, *describe* the line of conduct we are to pursue, and *order* or *ordain* what we are to observe.—*Adam Clarke.*

Verse 33.—God's " *statutes* " declare his authority and power of giving us laws.—*Matthew Pool,* 1624—1679.

Verse 33.—" *Unto the end,*" or, *by way of return,* or *reward,* or *gratitude* to thee; God's mercy in *teaching* being in all reason to be *rewarded* or answered by our *observing* and taking exact care of what he teaches. Or else by analogy with Psalm xix. 11, where the *keeping* his *commandments* brings *great reward* with it: it may here be rendered עקב (understanding the preposition ל) *for the reward,* meaning the present joy of it, verse 32, not excluding the future crown.—*H. Hammond.*

Verse 33.—" *Unto the end.*" *Quite through;* the Hebrew is, *to the heel.* The force of the words seems to be " Quite through, from head to foot."—*Zachary Mudge,* 1744.

Verses 33, 34.—" *Unto the end.*" He will be no *temporizer;* he will keep it " *to the end.*" He will be no *hypocrite;* he will keep it " *with his whole heart.*"—*Adam Clarke.*

Verse 34.—" *Give me understanding.*" The Psalmist goes to the root of the matter; he is taught to do so by the Spirit of all teaching. He would not merely be taught, as a master would teach, but he would have his mind remoulded and informed as only the Creator could do. The words imply as much. " *Give me understanding* "—make me to understand. Not merely did he want to know a thing—the general nature of it; but he wished to understand the beginning, the outgoing and the end of it. He wanted to attain the power of distinction between right and wrong—spiritual discernment that so he might discern the right, and, at the same time, all that was contrary to it; he wanted understanding, that so he might know, and discern, and prize the truth, the true way of God, carefully avoiding all that would be aside from it.—*John Stephen.*

Verse 34.—" *Give me understanding.*" This is that which we are indebted to Christ for; for " the Son of God is come, and hath given us an understanding (1 John v. 20).—*Matthew Henry.*

Verse 34.—" *Understanding.*" The understanding is the pilot and guide of the whole man; that faculty which sits at the stern of the soul: but as the most expert guide may mistake in the dark, so may the understanding, when it wants the light of knowledge. " Without knowledge the mind cannot be good " (Prov. xix. 2); nor the life good; nor the external condition safe (Eph. iv. 18). " My people are destroyed for the lack of knowledge " (Hosea iv. 6).

It is ordinary in Scripture to set profaneness, and all kinds of miscarriages, upon the score of ignorance. Diseases in the body have many times their rise from distempers in the *head ;* and exorbitances in practice, from errors in the judgment. And, indeed. in every sin, there is something both of ignorance and error at the bottom : for did sinners truly know what they do in sinning, we might say of every sin what the Apostle speaks concerning that great sin, " Had they known him, they would not have crucified the Lord of glory " (1 Cor. ii. 8).   Did they truly know that every sin is a provoking the Lord to jealousy, a proclaiming war against heaven, a crucifying the Lord Jesus afresh, a treasuring up wrath afresh unto themselves against the day of wrath ; and that if ever they be pardoned, it must be at no lower a rate than the price of his blood—*it were scarce possible* but sin, instead of alluring, should affright, and instead of tempting, scare.—*From the " Recommendatory Epistle prefixed to the Westminster Confession and Catechisms."*

Verse 34.—*" My whole heart."*   The whole man is God's by every kind of right and title ; and therefore, when he requireth the whole heart, he doth but require that which is his own.   God gave us the whole by creation, preserveth the whole, redeemeth the whole, and promiseth to glorify the whole.   If we had been mangled in creation we would have been troubled ; if born without hands or feet.   If God should turn us off to ourselves to keep that part to ourselves which we reserved from him, or if he should make such a division at death, take a part to heaven, or if Christ had bought part : " Ye are bought with a price : therefore glorify God in your body, and in your spirit, which are God's."   (1 Cor. vi. 20).   If you have had any good work upon you, God sanctified the whole in a gospel-sense, that is every part : " And the very God of peace sanctify you wholly ; and I pray God your whole spirit and soul and body be preserved blameless unto the coming of our Lord Jesus Christ."   (1 Thess. v. 23).   Not only conscience, but will and affections, appetite and body.   And you have given all to him for his use : " I am my beloved's ! " not a part, but the whole.   He could not endure Ananias that kept back part of the price ; all is his due.   When the world, pleasure, ambition, pride, desire of riches. unchaste love, desire a part in us, we may remember we have no affections to dispose of without God's leave.   It is all his, and it is sacrilege to rob or detain any part from God.   Shall I alienate that which is God's to satisfy the world, the flesh, and the Devil ?—*Thomas Manton.*

Verses 34, 35.—*"Give me understanding."* *"Make me to go."*   The understanding which he seeks leads to going, and is sought to that end.   God's teaching begets obedience ; he showeth us the path of life, and he maketh us to go in it.   It is such instruction as giveth strength, that exciteth the sluggish will, and breaketh the force of corrupt inclinations ; it removeth the darkness which corruption and sin have brought upon the mind, and maketh us pliable and ready to obey ; yea, it giveth not only the will, but the deed ; in short, it engageth us in a watchful, careful, uniform, and constant obedience.—*Thomas Manton.*

Verse 35.—*"Make me to go in the path of thy commandments."*   David, in the former verses, had begged for light, now for strength to walk according to this light.   We need not only light to know our way, but a heart to walk in it.   Direction is necessary because of the blindness of our minds ; and the effectual impulsions of grace are necessary because of the weakness of our hearts.   It will not answer our duty to have a naked notion of truths, unless we embrace and pursue them. So, accordingly, we need a double assistance from God ; the mind must be enlightened, the will moved and inclined.   The work of a Christian lies not in depth of speculation, but in the height of practice.   The excellency of Divine grace consisteth in this,—That God doth first teach what is to be done, and then make us to do what is taught : *"Make me to go in the path of thy commandments."*—*Thomas Manton.*

Verse 35.—*"The path of thy commandments."*   They are termed *"the paths,"* because paths are narrow, short, straight, clean passages for people on foot only, and not for horses and carriages ; and such is the way of the Lord, as compared with that of the flesh and of the world, all the ways of which are broad, filthy, and crooked, trodden by the brute beasts, the type of carnal, animal man.   He assigns a reason for being heard when he says, *"For this same I have desired" ;* because, through God's grace, I have chosen this path, and desired to walk in it, and it is only meet that he who gives the will should give the grace to accomplish, as St. Paul says, " Who worketh in you both to will and to do."—*Robert Bellarmine.*

Verse 35.—*"The path"* is *"the path of thy commandments."*   Not any new way, but the old and pathed way wherein all the servants of God have walked before him, and for which the Grecians (as Euthymius noteth) called it τριβον, *quasi viam tritam*. But howsoever this way be pathed, by the walking and treading of many in it, yet he acknowledgeth it is but one, yea, and a narrow and difficult path to keep, and therefore seeks he to be guided into it.—*William Cowper*.

Verse 35.—*"The path."* It is a *"path,"* not a public road ; a path where no *beast* goes, and *men* seldom.—*Adam Clarke*.

Verses 35, 37.—*"The path." "Thy way."* The Hindus call *panth* or *way* the line of doctrine of any sect followed, in order to attain to *mukti*, or deliverance from sin. *Way* signifies the chief means to an end, and is applied to the Scriptures, Ps. cxix. 27, to God's counsels, to God's works. This spiritual way is—(1) *easy* to find, Isa. xxxv. 8 ; (2) *clean*, no mud of sin ; (3) never out of *repair*—Christ the same as 6,000 years ago ; (4) no *lion* or wild beasts on ; (5) *costly*, the blood of Christ made it ; (6) not *lonely*, many believers on it, Heb. xii. 1 ; (7) no *toll*, all may come ; (8) *wide*. The way to the cities of refuge was forty-eight feet wide. The map of the Bible shows this path ; (9) the *end* pleasant—Heaven.—*J. Long, in " Eastern Proverbs and Maxims illustrating old Truths,"* 1881.

Verses 35, 36.—*"Therein do I delight. Incline my heart unto thy testimonies."* A child of God hath not the bent of his heart so perfectly fixed towards God but it is ever and anon returning to its old bent and bias again. The best may find that they cannot keep their affections as loose from the world when they have houses, and lands, and all things at their will, as they could when they are kept low and bare. The best may find that their love to heavenly things is on the wane as worldly things are on the increase. It is reported of Pius Quintus that he should say of himself that, when he first entered into orders, he had some hopes of his salvation ; when he came to be a cardinal, he doubted of it ; but since he came to be pope, he did even almost despair. Many may find a very great change in themselves, much decay of zeal for God's glory, and love to and relish of God's word, and mindfulness of heavenly things, as it fares better with them in the world. Now it is good to observe this before the mischief increaseth. Look, as jealousy and caution are necessary to prevent the entrance and beginning of this mischief, so observation is necessary to prevent the increase of it. When the world doth get too deep an interest in our hearts, when it begins to insinuate and entice us from God, and weaken our delight in the ways of God and zeal for his glory, then we need often to tell you how hard it is for a rich man to enter into the kingdom of heaven.—*Thomas Manton*.

Verse 36.—*"Incline my heart unto thy testimonies, and not to covetousness."* We must be convinced that covetousness, I mean that our covetousness, is a vice ; for it holds something of a virtue, of frugality, which is not to waste that which one hath : and this makes us entertain thoughts that it is no vice ; and we often say that it is good to be a little worldly ; a little covetousness we like well ; which shows that we do not indeed and in heart, hold it to be a sin. For if sin be naught, a little of sin cannot be good. As good say, a little poison were good, so it be not too much. And so we find, that men will rate at their children for spending, and are ready to turn them out of doors, if they be given unto waste ; but if they be near and pinching then we like that too much ; and I scarce know a man who doth use to call upon his children that they spare not, save not. I know youth is rather addicted the other way, and is more subject to waste and consume, by reason that the natural heat is quick and active in them ; and therefore indeed there is more fear and danger that they prove prodigal and turn wasters, and therefore the more may be said and done that way to youth. But the thing I press is, that in case we see our children in their youth to begin to be covetous and worldly, we call them good husbands, and are but too glad to see it so, and are too much pleased with them for it. Little do they think that worldliness is a most guiltful sin in respect of God, and most hurtful in respect of men. Hark what the word of God saith of it, Ephesians v. 5 : *It is idolatry*, and idolatry is the first sin of the first table. *It is the root of all evils*, 1 Tim. vi. 10. There is no evil but a worldly man will do it to save his purse. Thus David : *"Incline my heart unto thy testimonies, and not to covetousness" :* he saith not, this or that testimony, but (as including all the laws of God) he saith *"testimonies" ;* to show us that covetousness draws us away, not from some only, but from all God's commandments. So St. Paul : where covetousness is, there are " many lusts," 1 Tim. vi. 9, and " many sorrows," 1 Tim. vi. 10. " It drowns men in perdition and destruction," 1 Tim. vi. 9. And the Greek word signifies such a drowning as is almost past all hope and recovery. It is the bane of all society : men cry out of it, because they would have none covetous, none rich but themselves. A hater he is of mankind ; he hates all poor, because they would beg something of him ; and all rich, because they have riches which he would have. A covetous man would have all that all have. Thus speaks a noble father.* Such believe not the word, they trust neither God nor man. For he that trusts not God, cannot trust man. It robs God of that confidence we should have in him, and dependence we owe unto him ; it turns a man from all the commandments. Hence the prophet David prays God to turn his heart to his commandments, *"and not to covetousness."* For not only we *ought* not, but as the phrase is, " we *cannot* serve God and mammon," Luke xvi. 13.—*Richard Capel, in "Tentations : their Nature, Danger, Cure."* 1655.

Verse 36.—*"Incline my heart unto thy testimonies, and not to covetousness."* Without a restraining hand the heart is prone to turn aside into the byeways of petty love of pelf. The remedy must be from above. Heavenly aid is therefore sought.—*Henry Law.*

Verse 36.—*"Incline my heart."* Were we naturally and spontaneously inclined to the righteousness of the law, there would be no occasion for the petition of the Psalmist, *"Incline my heart."* It remains, therefore, that our hearts are full of sinful thoughts, and wholly rebellious until God by his grace change them.—*John Calvin.*

Verse 36.—*"Incline my heart."* In the former verses David had asked understanding and direction to know the Lord's will ; now he asketh an inclination of heart to do the Lord's will. The understanding needs not only to be enlightened, but the will to be moved and changed. Man's heart is of its own accord averse from God and holiness, even then when the wit is most refined, and the understanding is stocked and stored with high notions about it : therefore David doth not only say, " Give me understanding," but, *"Incline my heart."* We can be worldly of ourselves, but we cannot be holy and heavenly of ourselves ; that must be asked of him who is the Father of lights, from whom cometh down every good and perfect gift. They that plead for the power of nature, shut out the use of prayer. But Austin hath said well, *Natura vera confessione non falsa defensione opus habet :* we need rather to confess our weakness, than defend our strength. Thus doth David, and so will every broken-hearted Christian that hath had an experience of the inclinations of his own soul, he will come to God, and say, *"Incline my heart unto thy testimonies, and not to covetousness."*—*Thomas Manton.*

Verse 36.—*"Incline."* Then shall I not decline.—*James G. Murphy.*

Verse 36.—*"Unto thy testimonies."* The contrast is most striking. There are the *divine testimonies* on the one hand, and there is *"covetousness"* on the other. God stands on one side, the world on the other. The renewed man chooses between the two ; he does not require long to think, and God is his choice.—*John Stephen.*

Verse 36.—*"Not to covetousness."* He prays in particular that his heart may be diverted from covetousness, which is not only an evil, but as saith the Apostle, " the root of all evil." David here opposes it as an adversary to all the righteousness of God's testimonies : it inverts the order of nature, and makes the heavenly soul earthly. It is a handmaid of all sins ; for there is no sin which a covetous man will not serve for his gain. We should beware of all sins, but specially of mother-sins.—*William Cowper.*

Verse 36.—*"Covetousness,"* or rather, " gain unjustly acquired." . . . . The Hebrew word בְצַע can only mean *plunder, rapine, unjust gain.*—*J. J. Stewart Perowne.*

Verse 36.—*"Covetousness."*—S. Bonaventura, on our Psalm, says *Covetousness* must be hated, shunned, put away : must be hated, because it attacks the life of nature : must be shunned, because it hinders the life of grace : must be put away, because it obstructs the life of glory. Clemens Alexandrinus says that covetousness is the citadel of the vices, and Ambrose says that it is the loss of the soul.—*Thomas Le Blanc.*

Verse 36.—*"Covetousness."* I would observe to the reader, and desire him duly and seriously to consider, that although this commandment, " Thou shalt not covet," is placed the last in number, yet it is too often the first that is broken, man's covetous heart leading the van in transgression.—*William Crouch, in "The Enormous Sin of Covetousness detected,"* 1708.

---

* Chrysostom.

Verse 36.—"*Covetousness*" is an immoderate desire of riches, in which these vices concur. *First*, An excessive love of riches, and the fixing of our hearts upon them. *Secondly*, A resolution to become rich, either by lawful or unlawful means, 1 Tim. vi. 9. *Thirdly*, Too much haste in gathering riches, joined with impatience of any delay, Prov. xxviii. 20, 22, and xx. 21. *Fourthly*, An insatiable appetite, which can never be satisfied ; but when they have too much, they still desire more, and have never enough, Eccles. iv. 8. Like the horseleech, Prov. xxx. 15 ; the dropsy, and hell itself, Prov. xxvii. 20. *Fifthly*, Miser-like tenacity, whereby they refuse to communicate their goods, either for the use of others, or themselves. *Sixthly*, Cruelty. Prov. i. 18, 19, exercised both in their unmercifulness and oppression of the poor. Covetousness is a most heinous vice ; for it is idolatry, and the root of all evil, Col. iii. 5 ; 1 Tim. vi. 10 ; a pernicious thorn, that stifles all grace and choketh the seed of the word, Matt. xiii. 22, and pierceth men through with many sorrows, 1 Tim. vi. 10, and drowneth them in destruction and perdition.— *James Usher,* 1580—1655.

Verse 37.—"*Turn away mine eyes,*" etc. Having prayed for his heart, he now prayeth for his eyes also. *Omnia à Deo petit, docens illum omnia efficere.* By the eyes oftentimes, as by windows, death enters into the heart ; therefore to keep the heart in a good estate three things are requisite, First, a careful study of the senses, specially of the eyes ; for it is a righteous working of the Lord, *ut qui exteriori oculo negligenter utitur, interiori non injusté cæcetur ;* that he who negligently useth the external eye of his body, should be punished with blindness in the internal eye of his mind. And for this cause Nazianzen, deploring the calamities of his soul, wished that a door might be set before his eyes and ears, to close them when they opened to anything that is not good ; *malis autem sua sponte utrumque clauderetur.* The second thing is, a subduing of the body by discipline. And the third is, continuance in prayer.—*William Cowper.*

Verse 37.—"*Turn away mine eyes from beholding vanity.*" Notice this, that he does not say, I will turn away mine eyes ; but, "*Turn away mine eyes.*" This shows that it is not possible for us sufficiently to keep our eyes by our own caution and diligence ; but there must be divine keeping. For, first, wheresoever in this world you turn yourself provocations to evil are met with. Secondly, with the unwary, and with far different persons, the eyes, the servants of a corrupt heart, wander after the things which are vanities. Thirdly, before you are aware, the evil contracted through the eyes creeps in to the inmost recesses of the heart, and casts in the seeds of perdition. This the Psalmist himself had experienced, not without the greatest trouble both of heart and condition.—*Wolfgang Musculus,* 1497—1563.

Verse 37.—"*Turn away mine eyes from beholding vanity.*" It may seem a strange prayer of David, to say, "*Turn away mine eyes from seeing vanity ;* " as though God meddled with our looking ; or that we had not power in ourselves to cast our eyes upon what objects we list. But is it not, that what we delight in, we delight to look upon ? and what we love, we love to be seeing ? and so to pray to God, that our eyes may not see vanity, is as much as to pray for grace, that we be not in love with vanity. For, indeed, vanity hath of itself so graceful an aspect, that it is not for a natural man to leave looking upon it ; unless the fairer aspect of God's grace draw our eyes from vanity, to look upon itself ; which will always naturally be looking upon the fairest. And as David here makes his prayer in the particular, against temptations of prosperity, so Christ teacheth us to make our prayer in the general, against the temptations, both of prosperity and adversity, and very justly. For many can bear the temptations of one kind, who are quickly overcome by temptations of the other kind. So David could bear persecution without murmuring, but when he came to prosperity he could not turn away his eyes from vanity.— *Sir Richard Baker.*

Verse 37.—"*Turn away mine eyes from beholding vanity.*" An ugly object loses much of its deformity when we look often upon it. Sin follows this general law, and is to be avoided altogether, even in its contemplation, if we would be safe. A man should be thankful in this world that he has eyelids ; and as he can close his eyes, so he should often do it.—*Albert Barnes.*

Verse 37.—"*Turn away,*" then "*quicken,*" etc. The first request is for the removing the impediments of obedience, the other for the addition of new degrees of grace. These two are fitly joined, for they have a natural influence upon one another ; unless we turn away our eyes from vanity, we shall soon contract deadness of heart.   Nothing causeth it so much as an inordinate liberty in carnal vanities ; when our affections are alive to other things, they are dead to God, therefore the less we let loose our hearts to these things, the more lively and cheerful in the work of obedience.   On the other side, the more the vigour of grace is renewed, and the habits of it quickened into actual exercise, the more is sin mortified and subdued. Sin dieth, and our senses are restored to their proper use.—*Thomas Manton.*

Verse 37.—*"Turn away mine eyes from beholding vanity."*   That sin may be avoided we must avoid whatsoever leads to or occasions it.   As this caused Job (ch. xxxi. 1) to covenant strongly with his eyes, so it caused David to pray earnestly about his eyes.   *"Turn away mine eyes* (or as the Hebrew may be rendered, *make them to pass,) from beholding vanity."*   The eye is apt to make a stand, or fix itself, when we come in view of an ensnaring object ; therefore it is our duty to hasten it away, or to pray that God would make it pass off from it. . . He that feareth burning must take heed of playing with fire : he that feareth drowning must keep out of deep waters.   He that feareth the plague must not go into an infected house. Would they avoid sin who present themselves to the opportunities of it ?—*Joseph Caryl.*

Verse 37.—*"Turn away mine eyes."*   Lest looking cause liking and lusting : 1 John ii. 16.   In Hebrew the same word signifieth both an *eye* and a *fountain ;* to show that from the eye, as from a fountain, floweth much mischief ; and by that window Satan often winds himself into the soul.   This David found by experience, and therefore prays here, *"Turn away,"* transfer, make to pass *"mine eyes,"* etc. He knew the danger of irregular glancing and inordinate gazing.—*John Trapp.*

Verse 37.—*"Turn away mine eyes from beholding vanity."*   It is a most dangerous experiment for a child of God to place himself within the sphere of seductive temptations.   Every feeling of duty, every recollection of his own weakness, every remembrance of the failure of others, should induce him to hasten to the greatest possible distance from the scene of unnecessary conflict and danger.— *John Morison.*

Verse 37.—*"Turn away mine eyes from beholding vanity."*   From gazing at the delusive *mirages* which tempt the pilgrim to leave the safe highway.—*William Kay.*

Verse 37.—Is it asked—" What will most effectually turn my eyes from vanity ? " Not the seclusion of contemplative retirement—not the relinquishment of our lawful connexion with the world—but the transcendent beauty of Jesus unveiled to our eyes, and fixing our hearts.—*Charles Bridges.*

Verse 37.—*"Turn away mine eyes,"* etc.   The fort-royal of your souls is in danger of a surprise while the outworks of your senses are unguarded.   Your eyes, which may be floodgates to pour out tears, should not be casements to let in lusts. A careless eye is an index to a graceless heart.   Remember, the whole world died by a wound in the eye.   The eyes of a Christian should be like sunflowers, which are opened to no blaze but that of the sun.—*William Secker,* 1660.

Verse 37.—*"Vanity,"* in Hebrew usage, has often special reference to idols and the accompaniments of idol worship.   The Psalmist prays that he may never be permitted even to see such tempting objects.—*Henry Cowles.*

Verse 37.—*"Quicken thou me."*   Every saint is very apt to be a sluggard in the way and work of God.   *"Quicken me,"* says one of the chiefest and choicest of saints, *"in thy way";* and it is as much as if he should say in plain terms, "Ah, Lord !   I am a dull jade, and have often need of thy spur, thy Spirit."   This prayer of David seems proof enough to this point ; but if you desire farther confirmation, I shall produce an argument *instar omnium,* " that none shall dare to deny, nor be able to disapprove " ; and that is drawn from the topic of your own experience ; and this is *argumentum lugubre,* like a funeral anthem, " very sad and sorrowful." Do you not feel and find, to the grief of your own souls, that, whereas you should weep as if you wept not, rejoice as if you rejoiced not, and buy as if you were possessed not ; *inverso ordine,* [" inverting this order,"] you weep for losses as if you would weep out your eyes ; you rejoice in temporal comforts as if you were in heaven ; and you buy as if it were for ever a day (Ps. xlix. 11).   But *e contrario,* [" on the contrary,"] you pray as if you prayed not ; hear as if you heard not ; work for God as if you worked not.   Now, we know, *experto credas,** a man that sticks fast in a ditch needs no reason to prove he is in, but remedies to pull him out.   Your best course will be to propose the case how you may get rid of this unwelcome guest,

---

* " You may yield credence to that of which you have made trial."

spiritual sloth : it is a case we are all concerned in. *Asini aures quis non habet ?**
Every man and mortal hath some of the ass's dulness and sloth in him.—*Mr. Simmons
in "The Morning Exercises,"* 1661.

Verse 37.—*"Quicken thou me."* Another quickening ordinance is *prayer.* How
often doth David pray for quickening grace ? five or six times in one Psalm. He
begins many a prayer with a heavy heart, and before he hath done he is full of life.
Therefore, pray much, because all life is from God, and he quickens whom he will.
Only let me add this caution, before I let this pass,—Be sure thy understanding
and affection go along together in every ordinance, and in every part of the ordinance,
as thou wouldst have it a quickening ordinance.—*Matthew Lawrence, in "The Use
and Practice of Faith,"* 1657.

Verse 37.—*"Thy way,"* by way of emphasis, in opposition to and exaltation of,
above, all other ways. There is a fourfold way :—1. *Via mundi,* the way of the
world ; and that is *spinosa,* thorny. 2. *Via carnis,* the way of the flesh ; and
that is *insidiosa,* treacherous. 3. *Via Satana,* the way of the devil ; and that is
tenebricosa, darksome. 4. *Via Domini,* the way of God ; and that is *gratiosa,*
gracious.—*Simmons.*

Verses 37, 38.—Prayer is nothing but the promise reversed, or God's word formed
into an argument, and retorted by faith upon God again. Know, Christian, thou
hast law on thy side. Bills and bonds must be paid. David prays against the
sins of a wanton eye and a dead heart : *"Turn away mine eyes from beholding vanity ;
and quicken thou me in thy way";* and see how he urgeth his argument in the next
words,—*"Stablish thy word unto thy servant."* A good man is as good as his word,
and will not a good God be so ? But where finds David such a word for help against
these sins ? Surely in the covenant. It is in the magna charta. The first promise
held forth thus much,—" The seed of the woman shall bruise the serpent's head."
—*William Gurnall.*

Verse 38.—*"Stablish thy word unto thy servant,"* etc.—Well, but here is a strange
thing—a man who is a true *"servant of God," "devoted to his fear,"* praying for what
he surely must already have, else how could he be a servant ? or be living in Jehovah's
fear ? He seems to assume, clearly and without any doubt, his own personal consecration, and then he prays for that which must surely be, at least in considerable
measure, assumed and comprehended in the very idea of a true personal consecration.
Unless God's word is made sure to a man he will never become his servant. If he
is his servant, why should he pray, *"Stablish thy word" ?* Why, too, should he say
in the thirty-fifth verse, *"Make me to go in the path of thy commandments ; for therein
do I delight" ?* " Therein do I delight. It is the way of my choice, of my joy ! "
And yet, " Make me to go in it," as if I were unwilling. This apparent contradiction
or discrepancy is easily solved in a true experience, and can be, in fact, solved in no
other way. Is not this the very condition of many and many a one ? *"Stablished,"*
yet moved ; *"devoted,"* yet uncertain ; *"serving"* God truly, yet looking and longing
for clear warrant, and higher sanction, and more inward grace, to make the service
better ; " believing," yet crying, sometimes, " with tears, Help thou mine unbelief ! "
—*Alexander Raleigh.*

Verse 38.—*"Stablish thy word unto thy servant."* Why doth David pray thus,
"Stablish thy word to me ; " since God's word is most certain and so stable in itself
that it cannot be more so ? (2 Pet. i. 19). " We have a more sure," or a more
stable, " word of prophecy," as the word signifies. How can the word be more
stable than it is ? I answer, it is sure in regard of God from whom it comes, and
in itself. In regard of the things propounded it cannot be more or less stable, it
cannot be fast and loose : but in regard of us, it may be more or less established.
And that two ways,—1. By the inward assurance of the Spirit increasing our faith.
2. By the outward performance of what is promised.

1st, By the inward assurance of the Spirit, by which our faith is increased. Great
is the weakness of our faith, as appears by our fears, doubts, distrusts, so that we
need to be assured more and more. We need say with tears as he doth in the gospel :
" Lord, I believe ; help thou mine unbelief " (Mark ix. 24) ; and to cry out with
the apostles, " Lord, increase our faith " (Luke xvii. 5). There is none believeth so,
but he may yet believe more. And in this sense the word is more established,
when we are confirmed in the belief of it, and look upon it as sure ground for faith

---

* " Where is the man who hath not the ears of an ass ? "

to rest upon.   2ndly, By actual performance, when the promise is made good for us. Every event which falls out according to the word is a notable testimony of the truth of it, and a seal to confirm and strengthen our faith.   Three ways may this be made good.

1. The making good of some promises at one time strengthens our faith in expecting the like favour at another.   Christ was angry with his disciples for not remembering the miracle of the loaves, when they fell into a like strait again.   " Do ye not yet understand, neither remember the five loaves ? " (Matt. xvi. 9).   We are to seek upon every difficulty ; whereas former experience in the same kind should be a means of establishment to us : " He hath delivered, and doth deliver : in whom we trust that he will yet deliver us " (2 Cor. i. 10).   In teaching a child to spell we are angry, if, when we have showed him a letter once, twice, and a third time, yet when he meets with it again still he misseth : so, God is angry with us when we have had experience of his word in this, that, and the other providence, yet still our doubts return upon us.

2. The accomplishment of one promise confirms another ; for God, that keepeth touch at one time, will do so at another : " I was delivered out of the mouth of the lion.   And the Lord shall deliver me from every evil work, and will preserve me unto his heavenly kingdom " (2 Tim. iv. 17, 18).   In such a strait God failed not, and surely he that hath been true hitherto will not fail at last.

3. When the word is performed in part, it assureth us of the performance of the whole.   It is an earnest given us of all the rest : " For all the promises of God in him are yea, and in him amen " (2 Cor. i. 20).   A Christian hath a great many promises, and they are being performed daily ; God is delivering, comforting, protecting him, speaking peace to his conscience ; but the greater part are yet to be performed.   Present experiences do assure us of what is to come.   Thus, *"Stablish thy word,"* that is, make it good by the event, that I may learn to trust another time either for the same, or other promises or accomplishments of thy whole word.— *Thomas Manton.*

Verse 38.—"Stablish thy word unto thy servant."   Confirm it ; make it *seem* firm and true ; let not my mind be vacillating or sceptical in regard to thy truth. This seems to be a prayer against the influence of doubt and scepticism ; a prayer that doubts might not be suffered to spring up in his mind, and that the objections and difficulties of scepticism might have no place there.   There is a class of men whose minds are naturally sceptical and unbelieving, and for such men such a prayer is peculiarly appropriate.   For none can it be improper to pray that the word of God may always seem to them to be true ; that their minds may never be left to the influence of doubt and unbelief.—*Albert Barnes.*

Verse 38.—"Who is devoted to thy fear."   The word may be rendered either which or who ; as relating either to thy word or to thy servant.   1. Thy word ; for in the original Hebrew the posture of the verse is thus, " Stablish to thy servant thy word, which is to the fearing of thee," or, " which is given that thou mayest be feared ; " there being in the word of God the greatest arguments and induce- ments to fear, to reverence, and to obey him.   The word of God was appointed to plant the fear of God in our hearts, and to increase our reverence of God ; not that we may play the wantons with promises, and feed our lusts with them.   2. I rather take our own translation, and it hath such a sense as that passage, " But I give myself unto prayer " (Psalm cxix. 4).   In the original it is, " But I prayer."   So in this place it may be read, Stablish thy word to thy servant, " Who is to thy fear." Our translators add, to make the sense more full, addicted, or " devoted to thy fear," that is, who makes it his business, care, and desire to stand in the fear of God.

Now this is added as a true note and description of God's servants, as being a main thing in religion, " The fear of the Lord is the beginning of wisdom" (Psalm cxi. 10), it is the first in point of order, and it is the first thing when we begin to be wise, to think of God, to have awful thoughts of God, it is a chief point of wisdom, the great thing that makes us wise to salvation.   And it is added as an argument of prayer, " O Lord, let thine ear be attentive to the prayer of thy servants, who desire to fear thy name " (Neh. i. 11).   The more any are given to the fear of God, the more assurance they have of God's love, and of his readiness to hear them at the throne of grace.—*Thomas Manton.*

Verse 38.—"Who is devoted to thy fear."   He who hath received from the Lord grace to fear him may be bold to seek any necessary good thing from him ; because the fear of God hath annexed the promises of all other blessings with it.—*William Cowper.*

Verse 38.—He that chooses God, devotes himself to God as the vessels of the sanctuary were consecrated and set apart from the common to holy uses, so he that has chosen God to be his God, has dedicated himself to God, and will no more be devoted to profane uses.—*Thomas Watson.*

Verse 39.—"*Turn away my reproach,*" etc. In these words you have,—1. A request, "*Turn away my reproach.*" 2. A reason to enforce it. "*For thy judgments are good.*"

First, for the request. "*Turn away,*" roll from upon me, so it signifies. He was clothed with reproach ; now roll from me "*my reproach.*" Some think he means God's condemnatory sentence, which would turn to his reproach, or some remarkable rebuke from God, because of his sin. Rather, I think, the calumnies of his enemies ; and he calls it "*my reproach,*" either as deserved by himself, or as having personally lighted upon him, the reproach which was like to be his lot and portion in the world, through the malice of his enemies : "*the reproach which I fear,*" that is, which I have cause to expect, and am sensible of the sad consequences of it.

Secondly, for the reason by which this is enforced: "*for thy judgments are good.*" There are different opinions about the form of this argument. Some take the reason thus : Let me not suffer reproach for adhering to thy word, thy word which is so good. But David doth not speak here of suffering reproach for righteousness' sake, but such reproach as was likely to befall him because of his own infirmities and failings. Reproaches for righteousness' sake are to be "rejoiced in;" but he saith, this I "*fear,*" and therefore I suppose this doth not hit the reason. Neither do I accept the other sense,—Why should I be looked upon as an evil-doer as long as I keep thy law, and observe thy statutes ? Others judge badly of me, but I appeal to thy good judgment.

By "*judgments*" we may understand God's dealings. Thou dost not deal with men according to their desert. Thy dispensations are kind and gracious. Better still : by "*judgments*" are meant the ways, statutes, and ordinances of God called judgments, because all our words, works, thoughts are to be judged according to the sentence of the word : now these, it is a pity they should suffer in my reproach and ignominy. This is that I fear more than anything else that can happen to me. I think the reason will better run thus : Lord, there is in thy law, word, covenant, many promises to encourage thy people, and therefore rules to provide for the due honour and credit of thy people.—*Thomas Manton.*

Verse 39.—"*Turn away my reproach.*" In the Hebrew it is, "*Take away my rebuke*"; as if he should have said, O Lord, I may commit some such evil against thy good law, yea, some such notorious transgression, as may tend to my shame ; I beseech thee, take it away. Or else he meaneth, I have already, O Lord, by divers sins, and by name through adultery and murder brought shame and rebuke upon myself among men ; I entreat thee to remove this shame and rebuke.

Out of the first exposition we learn, First, that the godly are subject unto notorious sins. Secondly, that those sins will cause shame in them, though the wicked will not be ashamed. Thirdly, that God only can take away this shame. Fourthly, that we may pray for the removing of shame even amongst men, especially that which may bring with it some dishonour to God. Fifthly, that the godly are most jealous over themselves. Sixthly, the way to avoid sin is ever to be afraid lest we should sin.

Out of the second exposition note, that the remembrance of our former sins must draw out of us prayers unto God, that for them we may not be rebuked in displeasure in this life, nor confounded and abashed in the life to come.—*Richard Greenham.*

Verse 39.—"*My reproach*" is the reproach which the world casts on the God-fearing. This is dreaded as a great temptation to apostasy.—*James G. Murphy.*

Verse 39.—"*For thy judgments are good.*" One would have expected him to say—For thou art merciful—Cause my reproach which I fear to pass over from me, for thou art merciful. No, he does not add this as his present reason, but "*Thy judgments are good.*" We should catch the meaning at once, were the words these —For thy judgments are *awful*—" Turn away my reproach which I fear," for thy judgments are awful. But as the words are—" For thy judgments are *good,*" we find he verily takes refuge in the " judgments "—viz., that the Lord would vindicate him against all the unjust judgments of men; and as to judgment with God, since he took refuge in the atonement which the Lord had appointed, the Lord would vindicate him there also.—*John Stephen.*

Verse 39.—*"For thy judgments are good."* The judgments of the wicked are bad judgments, but the judgments of God are good ; I pray against those, I appeal to these : I fear the one, I approve the other. Now the judgments which God pronounceth in his word, be they threatenings in the law, or consolations in the Gospel, yea, and those also which he executeth in the world, whether upon the godly or godless, they must needs be good. 1. Because God is goodness itself. 2. He cannot be deceived. 3. He will not be bribed. 4. He alone is no respecter of persons, but judgeth according to every man's work.—*Richard Greenham.*

Verse 39.—The " *reproach* " which the poet fears in this verse is not the reproach of confessing, but of denying God.—*Franz Delitzsch.*

Verse 39.—*"For thy judgments are good."* This reason shows he feared God's rebuke. Man's " *reproach* " comes from a corrupt judgment, he condemns where God will absolve, I pass not for it ; but I know thy rebuke is always deserved, " *for thy judgments are good.*"—*William Nicholson.*

Verse 40.—*"I have longed after thy precepts."* We are sometimes unconsciously led to " *long* " after the promises, more than " *after the precepts*" of God ; forgetting that it is our privilege and safety to have an equal regard to both—to obey his precepts in dependence on his promises, and to expect the accomplishment of the promises in the way of obedience to the precepts.—*Charles Bridges.*

Verse 40.—*"Precepts,"* from a word which means to *place in trust*, mean something entrusted to man, " that which is committed to thee " ; appointments of God, which consequently have to do with the conscience, for which man is responsible as an intelligent being. The precepts are not so obviously apprehended as the law and the testimonies. They must be sought out. *"Behold, my desire is for thy precepts"* (ver. 40). *"Thy precepts I seek"* (ver. 45). *"Thy precepts I have sought"* (ver. 94). . . . They are a law of liberty : *"And I will walk at liberty : for I seek thy precepts"* (ver. 45).—*John Jebb.*

Verse 40.—*"Quicken me in thy righteousness."* He said before, " Quicken me in thy word," here, " in thy righteousness " ; all is one ; for the word of God is the righteousness of God, in which is set down the will of righteousness. In this the prophet desires to be quickened, that is, to be confirmed, that in cheerfulness and gladness of spirit he might rely upon the word of God.—*Richard Greenham.*

Verse 40.—*"Quicken me in thy righteousness."* The petition is for liveliness in the knowledge and practice of holiness, according to the tenor of God's word and by its operation on the heart. If any prefer by " *righteousness* " to understand the faithfulness or justice of God, whereby he has bound himself to give grace to those who trust in him, there is no objection to such an interpretation. It is in fact implied in the others. Whoever can truly use the language of this verse is regenerate. Before renewing grace the law was a dead letter. It was more ; it was a hated letter. The carnal mind is not subject to the law of God, neither indeed can be. A sinner desires no restraint from the divine precepts.—*William S. Plumer.*

EXPOSITION OF VERSES 41 TO 48.

LET thy mercies come also unto me, O LORD, *even* thy salvation, according to thy word.

42 So shall I have wherewith to answer him that reproacheth me : for I trust in thy word.

43 And take not the word of truth utterly out of my mouth ; for I have hoped in thy judgments.

44 So shall I keep thy law continually for ever and ever.

45 And I will walk at liberty : for I seek thy precepts.

46 I will speak of thy testimonies also before kings, and will not be ashamed.

47 And I will delight myself in thy commandments, which I have loved.

48 My hands also will I lift up unto thy commandments, which I have loved ; and I will meditate in thy statutes.

In these verses holy fear is apparent and prominent. The man of God trembles lest in any way or degree the Lord should remove his favour from him. The eight verses are one continued pleading for the abiding of grace in his soul, and it is supported by such holy arguments as would only suggest themselves to a spirit burning with love to God.

41. "*Let thy mercies come also unto me, O LORD.*" He desires *mercy* as well as teaching, for he was guilty as well as ignorant. He needed much mercy and varied mercy, hence the request is in the plural. He needed mercy from God rather than from man, and so he asks for "thy mercies." The way sometimes seemed blocked, and therefore he begs that the mercies may have their way cleared by God, and may "come" to him. He who said, "Let there be light," can also say, "Let there be mercy." It may be that under a sense of unworthiness the writer feared lest mercy should be given to others, and not to himself ; he therefore cries, "Bless me, even me also, O my Father." Viewed in this light the words are tantamount to our well-known verse—

> "Lord, I hear of showers of blessing
> Thou art scattering, full and free ;
> Showers, the thirsty land refreshing ;
> Let some droppings fall on me,
> Even me."

Lord, thine enemies come to me to reproach me, let thy mercies come to defend me ; trials and troubles abound, and labours and sufferings not a few approach me ; Lord, let thy mercies in great number enter by the same gate, and at the same hour ; for art thou not the God of my mercy ?

"*Even thy salvation.*" This is the sum and crown of all mercies—deliverance from all evil, both now and for ever. Here is the first mention of salvation in the Psalm, and it is joined with mercy : "By grace are ye saved." Salvation is styled "thy salvation," thus ascribing it wholly to the Lord : "He that is our God is the God of salvation." What a mass of mercies are heaped together in the one salvation of our Lord Jesus ! It includes the mercies which spare us before our conversion, and lead up to it. Then comes calling mercy, regenerating mercy, converting mercy, justifying mercy, pardoning mercy. Nor can we exclude from complete salvation any of those many mercies which are needed to conduct the believer safe to glory. Salvation is an aggregate of mercies incalculable in number, priceless in value, incessant in application, eternal in endurance. To the God of our mercies be glory, world without end.

"*According to thy word.*" The way of salvation is described in the word, salvation itself is promised in the word, and its inward manifestation is wrought by the word ; so that in all respects the salvation which is in Christ Jesus is in accordance with the word. David loved the Scriptures, but he longed experimentally to know the salvation contained in them : he was not satisfied to read the word, he longed to experience its inner sense. He valued the field of Scripture for the sake of the treasure which he had discovered in it.   He was not to be contented with chapter and verse, he wanted mercies and salvation.

Note that in the first verse of HE (33) the Psalmist prayed to be taught to keep God's word, and here in VAU he begs the Lord to keep his word.   In the first case he longed to come to the God of mercies, and here he would have the Lord's mercies come to him : there he sought grace to persevere in faith, and here he seeks the end of his faith, even the salvation of his soul.

42.   "*So shall I have wherewith to answer him that reproacheth me.*"   This is an unanswerable answer.   When God, by granting us salvation, gives to our prayers an answer of peace, we are ready at once to answer the objections of the infidel, the quibbles of the sceptical, and the sneers of the contemptuous.   It is most desirable that revilers should be answered, and hence we may expect the Lord to save his people in order that a weapon may be put into their hands with which to rout his adversaries.   When those who reproach *us* are also reproaching God, we may ask him to help us to silence them by sure proofs of his mercy and faithfulness.

"*For I trust in thy word.*"   His faith was seen by his being trustful while under trial, and he pleads it as a reason why he should be helped to beat back reproaches by a happy experience.   Faith is our argument when we seek mercies and salvation ; faith in the Lord who has spoken to us in his word.   "I trust in thy word" is a declaration more worth the making than any other ; for he who can truly make it has received power to become a child of God, and so to be the heir of unnumbered mercies.   God hath more respect to a man's trust than to all else that is in him ; for the Lord hath chosen faith to be the hand into which he will place his mercies and his salvation.   If any reproach us for trusting in God, we reply to them with arguments the most conclusive when we show that God has kept his promises, heard our prayers, and supplied our needs.   Even the most sceptical are forced to bow before the logic of facts.

In this second verse of this eight the Psalmist makes a confession of faith, and a declaration of his belief and experience.   Note that he does the same in the corresponding verses of the sections which follow.   See 50, "Thy word hath quickened me"; 58, "I entreated thy favour"; 66, "I have believed thy commandments"; 74, "I have hoped in thy word."   A wise preacher might find in these a series of experimental discourses.

43.   "*And take not the word of truth utterly out of my mouth.*"   Do not prevent my pleading for thee by leaving me without deliverance ; for how could I continue to proclaim thy word if I found it fail me ? such would seem to be the run of the meaning.   The word of truth cannot be a joy to our mouths unless we have an experience of it in our lives, and it may be wise for us to be silent if we cannot support our testimonies by the verdict of our consciousness.   This prayer may also refer to other modes by which we may be disabled from speaking in the name of the Lord : as, for instance, by our falling into open sin, by our becoming depressed and despairing, by our labouring under sickness or mental aberration, by our finding no door of utterance, or meeting with no willing audience.   He who has once preached the gospel from his heart is filled with horror at the idea of being put out of the ministry ; he will crave to be allowed a little share in the holy testimony, and will reckon his dumb Sabbaths to be days of banishment and punishment.

"*For I have hoped in thy judgments.*"   He had expected God to appear and vindicate his cause, that so he might speak with confidence concerning his faithfulness.   God is the author of our hopes, and we may most fittingly entreat him to fulfil them.   The judgments of his providence are the outcome of his word ; what he says in the Scriptures he actually performs in his government ; we may therefore look for him to show himself strong on the behalf of his own threatenings and promises, and we shall not look in vain.

God's ministers are sometimes silenced through the sins of their people, and it becomes them to plead against such a judgment ; better far that they should suffer sickness or poverty than that the candle of the gospel should be put out among them, and that thus they should be left to perish without remedy.   The Lord save us, who are his ministers, from being made the instruments of inflicting such a penalty.   Let us exhibit a cheerful hopefulness in God, that we may plead it in prayer with him when he threatens to close our lips.

In the close of this verse there is a declaration of what the Psalmist had done in reference to the word of the Lord, and in this the thirds of the octaves are often alike. See 35, "therein do I delight"; 43, "I have hoped in thy judgments"; 51, "yet have I not declined from thy law"; 59, "I turned my feet to thy testimonies"; and verses 67, 83, 99, etc. These verses would furnish an admirable series of meditations.

44. "*So shall I keep thy law continually for ever and ever.*" Nothing more effectually binds a man to the way of the Lord than an experience of the truth of his word, embodied in the form of mercies and deliverances. Not only does the Lord's faithfulness open our mouths against his adversaries, but it also knits our hearts to his fear, and makes our union with him more and more intense. Great mercies lead us to feel an inexpressible gratitude which, failing to utter itself in time, promises to engross eternity with praises. To a heart on flame with thankfulness, the "always, unto eternity and perpetuity" of the text will not seem to be redundant; yea, the hyperbole of Addison in his famous verse will only appear to be solid sense :—

> " Through all eternity to thee
> A joyful song I'll raise ;
> But oh ! eternity's too short
> To utter all thy praise."

God's grace alone can enable us to keep his commandments without break and without end ; eternal love must grant us eternal life, and out of this will come everlasting obedience. There is no other way to ensure our perseverance in holiness but by the word of truth abiding in us, as David prayed it might abide with him.

The verse begins with "So," as did verse 42. When God grants his salvation we are *so* favoured that we silence our worst enemy and glorify our best friend. Mercy answereth all things. If God doth but give us salvation we can conquer hell and commune with heaven, answering reproaches and keeping the law, and that to the end, world without end.

We may not overlook another sense which suggests itself here. David prayed that the word of truth might not be taken out of his mouth, and so would he keep God's law : that is to say, by public testimony as well as by personal life he would fulfil the divine will, and confirm the bonds which bound him to his Lord for ever. Undoubtedly the grace which enables us to bear witness with the mouth is a great help to ourselves as well as to others : we feel that the vows of the Lord are upon us, and that we cannot run back.

45. "*And I will walk at liberty : for I seek thy precepts.*" Saints find no bondage in sanctity. The Spirit of holiness is a free spirit ; he sets men at liberty and enables them to resist every effort to bring them under subjection. The way of holiness is not a track for slaves, but the King's highway for freemen, who are joyfully journeying from the Egypt of bondage to the Canaan of rest. God's mercies and his salvation, by teaching us to love the precepts of the word, set us at a happy rest ; and the more we seek after the perfection of our obedience the more shall we enjoy complete emancipation from every form of spiritual slavery. David at one time of his life was in great bondage through having followed a crooked policy. He deceived Achish so persistently that he was driven to acts of ferocity to conceal it, and must have felt very unhappy in his unnatural position as an ally of Philistines, and captain of the body guard of their king. He must have feared lest through his falling into the crooked ways of falsehood the truth would no longer be on his tongue, and he therefore prayed God in some way to work his deliverance, and set him at liberty from such slavery. By terrible things in righteousness did the Lord answer him at Ziklag : the snare was broken, and he escaped.

The verse is united to that which goes before, for it begins with the word " And," which acts as a hook to attach it to the preceding verses. It mentions another of the benefits expected from the coming of mercies from God. The man of God had mentioned the silencing of his enemies (42), power to proceed in testimony (43), and perseverance in holiness ; now he dwells upon liberty, which next to life is dearest to all brave men. He says, " I shall walk," indicating his daily progress through life ; " at liberty," as one who is out of prison, unimpeded by adversaries, unencumbered by burdens, unshackled, allowed a wide range, and roaming without fear. Such liberty would be dangerous if a man were seeking himself or his own lusts ; but when the one object sought after is the will of God, there can be no need to restrain the searcher. We need not circumscribe the man who can say, "I seek thy precepts." Observe, in the preceding verse he said he would keep the law ;

but here he speaks of seeking it. Does he not mean that he will obey what he knows, and endeavour to know more ? Is not this the way to the highest form of liberty,—to be always labouring to know the mind of God and to be conformed to it ? Those who *keep* the law are sure to *seek* it, and bestir themselves to keep it more and more.

46. *"I will speak of thy testimonies also before kings, and will not be ashamed."* This is part of his liberty ; he is free from fear of the greatest, proudest, and most tyrannical of men. David was called to stand before kings when he was an exile ; and afterwards, when he was himself a monarch, he knew the tendency of men to sacrifice their religion to pomp and statecraft ; but it was his resolve to do nothing of the kind. He would sanctify politics, and make cabinets know that the Lord alone is governor among the nations. As a king he would speak to kings concerning the King of kings. He says, " *I will speak* " : prudence might have suggested that his life and conduct would be enough, and that it would be better not to touch upon religion in the presence of royal personages who worshipped other gods, and claimed to be right in so doing. He had already most fittingly preceded this resolve by the declaration, " I will walk," but he does not make his personal conduct an excuse for sinful silence, for he adds, " I will speak." David claimed religious liberty, and took care to use it, for he spoke out what he believed, even when he was in the highest company. In what he said he took care to keep to God's own word, for he says, " I will speak of *thy testimonies*." No theme is like this, and there is no way of handling that theme like keeping close to the book, and using its thought and language. The great hindrance to our speaking upon holy topics in all companies is shame, but the Psalmist will *"not be ashamed"*; there is nothing to be ashamed of, and there is no excuse for being ashamed, and yet many are as quiet as the dead for fear some creature like themselves should be offended. When God gives grace, cowardice soon vanishes. He who speaks for God in God's power, will not be ashamed when beginning to speak, nor while speaking, nor after speaking ; for his theme is one which is fit for kings, needful to kings, and beneficial to kings. If kings object, we may well be ashamed of *them*, but never of our Master who sent us, or of his message, or of his design in sending it.

47. " *And I will delight myself in thy commandments, which I have loved.*" Next to liberty and courage comes delight. When we have done our duty, we find a great reward in it. If David had not spoken for his Master before kings, he would have been afraid to think of the law which he had neglected ; but after speaking up for his Lord he feels a sweet serenity of heart when musing upon the word. Obey the command, and you will love it ; carry the yoke, and it will be easy, and rest will come by it. After speaking of the law the Psalmist was not wearied of his theme, but he retired to meditate upon it ; he discoursed and then he delighted, he preached and then repaired to his study to renew his strength by feeding yet again upon the precious truth. Whether he delighted others or not when he was speaking, he never failed to delight himself when he was musing on the word of the Lord. He declares that he loved the Lord's commands, and by this avowal he unveils the reason for his delight in them : where our love is, there is our delight. David did not delight in the courts of kings, for there he found places of temptation to shame, but in the Scriptures he found himself at home ; his heart was in them, and they yielded him supreme pleasure. No wonder that he spoke of keeping the law, which he loved ; Jesus says, " If a man love me, he will keep my words." No wonder that he spoke of walking at liberty, and speaking boldly, for true love is ever free and fearless. Love is the fulfilling of the law ; where love to the law of God reigns in the heart the life must be full of blessedness. Lord, let thy mercies come to us that we may love thy word and way, and find our whole delight therein.

The verse is in the future, and hence it sets forth, not only what David had done, but what he would do ; he would in time to come delight in his Lord's commands. He knew that they would neither alter, nor fail to yield him joy. He knew also that grace would keep him in the same condition of heart towards the precepts of the Lord, so that he should throughout his whole life take a supreme delight in holiness. His heart was so fixed in love to God's will that he was sure that grace would always hold him under its delightful influence.

All the Psalm is fragrant with love to the word, but here for the first time love is expressly spoken of. It is here coupled with delight, and in verse 165 with " great peace." All the verses in which love declares itself in so many words are worthy of note. See verses 47, 97, 113, 119, 127, 140, 159, 163, 165, 167.

48. *"My hands also will I lift up unto thy commandments, which I have loved."* He will stretch out towards perfection as far as he can, hoping to reach it one day ; when his hands hang down he will cheer himself out of languor by the prospect of glorifying God by obedience , and he will give solemn sign of his hearty assent and consent to all that his God commands. The phrase " lift up my hands " is very full of meaning, and doubtless the sweet singer meant all that we can see in it, and a great deal more. Again he declares his love ; for a true heart loves to express itself ; it is a kind of fire which must send forth its flames. It was natural that he should reach out towards a law which he delighted in, even as a child holds out its hands to receive a gift which it longs for. When such a lovely object as holiness is set before us, we are bound to rise towards it with our whole nature, and till that is fully accomplished we should at least lift up our hands in prayer towards it. Where holy hands and holy hearts go, the whole man will one day follow.

"And I will meditate in thy statutes." He can never have enough of meditation upon the mind of God. Loving subjects wish to be familiar with their sovereign's statutes, for they are anxious that they may not offend through ignorance. Prayer with lifted hands, and meditation with upward-glancing eyes will in happy union work out the best inward results. The prayer of verse 41 is already fulfilled in the man who is thus struggling upward and studying deeply. The whole of this verse is in the future, and may be viewed not only as a determination of David's mind, but as a result which he knew would follow from the Lord's sending him his mercies and his salvation. When mercy comes down, our hands will be lifted up ; when God in favour thinks upon us, we are sure to think of him. Happy is he who stands with hands uplifted both to receive the blessing and to obey the precept ; he shall not wait upon the Lord in vain.

NOTES ON VERSES 41 TO 48.

Verses 41—48.—This commences a new portion of the Psalm, in which each verse begins with the letter *Vau,* or *v.*   There are almost no words in Hebrew that begin with this letter, which is properly a conjunction, and hence in each of the verses in this section the beginning of the verse is in the original a conjunction,—*vau.*— *Albert Barnes.*

Verses 41—48.—This whole section consists of petitions and promises.   The petitions are two ; verses 41, 43.   The promises are six.   This, among many, is a difference between godly men and others : all men seek good things from God, but the wicked so seek that they give him nothing back again, nor yet will promise any sort of return.   Their prayers must be unprofitable, because they proceed from love of themselves, and not of the Lord.   If so be they obtain that which is for their necessity, they care not to give to the Lord that which is for his glory : but the godly, as they seek good things, so they give praise to God when they have gotten them, and return the use of things received, to the glory of God who gave them. They love not themselves for themselves, but for the Lord ; what they seek from him they seek it for this end, that they may be the more able to serve him.   Let us take heed unto this ; because it is a clear token whereby such as are truly religious are distinguished from counterfeit dissemblers.—*William Cowper.*

Verse 41.—"*Let thy mercies come also unto me.*"   The way was blocked up with sins and difficulties, yet mercy could clear all, and find access to him, or make its own way : "*Let it come,*" that is, let it be performed or come to pass, as it is rendered : " Now let thy words come to pass " (Judg. xiii. 12)—Hebrew, " Let it come."   Here we read, let it come home *to me,* for my comfort and deliverance.   David elsewhere saith, " Goodness and mercy shall follow me all the days of my life " (Psalm xxiii. 6) ; go after him, find him out in his wanderings.   So, " What shall I render to the Lord for all his benefits *toward me ?* " (Psalm cxvi. 12).   They found their way to him though shut up with sins and dangers.—*Thomas Manton.*

Verse 41.—"*Let thy mercies come also unto me, O Lord.*"   The mercies of God everywhere meet the man whom God *quickens* (verse 40).   David understood that God blesses the soul, the body, the household, the ordinances, and all things else that belong to his servants ; the whole of which blessing is from mercy, without merit, bestowed largely, wonderfully, etc.—*Martin Geier.*

Verse 41.—"*Let thy mercies come also unto me, O Lord,*" etc.   Ministers of the Word and students of Theology are reminded by this prayer that they ought not only to preach to others the true way of attaining everlasting salvation, but that they should also with earnest prayers cry unto God that they might themselves be made partakers of the Divine mercies, and receive " the end of their faith, the salvation of their souls."   Paul, indeed, was greatly anxious respecting this matter, and was constrained to write, that he kept his body under, and brought it into subjection, lest after preaching to others he should himself be a castaway.—*Solomon Gesner.*

Verse 41.—"*Thy mercies.*"   " *Thy word.*"   We should consider here the way in which the Prophet seeks salvation from God.   In this prayer he conjoins two things, as those which uphold his confidence, viz., the mercy of God and his Word. These are to the man of faith the two strongest pillars of his hope.—*Wolfgang Musculus.*

Verse 41.—"*Even thy salvation,*" etc.   It is not any sort of delivery by any means, which the servant of God being in straits doth call for, or desire, but such a deliverance as God will allow, and be pleased to give in a holy way.   "*Let thy salvation come.*"   As the word of promise is the rule of our petition, so is it a pawn of the thing promised, and must be held fast till the performance come : "*Let thy mercies come also unto me, O Lord, even thy salvation, according to thy word*"; and this is one reason of the petition.—*David Dickson.*

Verse 42.—"*So shall I have,*" etc.   I shall have something by which I may reply to those who calumniate me.   So the Saviour replied to the suggestions of the tempter almost wholly by passages of Scripture (Matthew iv. 4, 7, 10) ; and so, in many cases, the best answer that can be given to reproaches on the subject of religion will be found in the very words of Scripture.   A man of little learning, except that which he has derived from the Bible, may often thus silence the cavils and reproaches of the learned sceptic; a man of simple-hearted, pure piety, with no weapon but the word of God, may often thus be better armed than if he had all the arguments of the schools at his command. Comp. Eph. vi. 17.—*Albert Barnes.*

Verse 42.—*"So shall I have wherewith to answer,"* etc. When the heart realizes assured salvation, it is supplied with abundant answers to those who sneer at the delights of faith.—*Henry Law.*

Verse 42.—*"So shall I have wherewith to answer,"* etc. Hugo Cardinalis observeth that there are three sorts of blasphemers of the godly,—the devils, heretics, and slanderers. The devil must be answered by the internal word of humility; heretics by the external word of wisdom; slanderers by the active word of a good life.—*Richard Greenham.*

Verse 42.—*"So shall I have,"* etc. For I should give them a short answer, and a true one,—*that I trust in thy word;* I put my confidence in thee, who canst make good thy promises, because thou art omnipotent; and wilt, because thou art merciful.—*William Nicholson.*

Verse 42.—*"So shall I have wherewith to answer,"* etc. This follows the phrase, *"according to thy word."* Christians should learn from the example of David what to oppose to the reproaches and false accusations of the enemies of the truth. Nothing is done by railing; but weapons should be taken from the word of God; and these are strong through faith in God for the overturning of both the Devil himself and his instruments. For truly with weapons of this kind the Saviour himself discomfited Satan in the wilderness (Matt. iv.); and Paul (Ephes. vi.) puts on himself, and commends to the Christian soldier, the girdle of Divine truth, the breast-plate of righteousness, the shoes of the Gospel, the shield of faith, and the sword of the Spirit, which is the Word of God.—*Solomon Gesner.*

Verse 42.—*"Wherewith to answer,"* etc. It is not forbidden to believers, modestly and fully, *to answer* those that reproach them, and to rebut the lie. See Prov. xxvi. 5, xxvii. 11. But to be able to answer them is received as a blessing from God.—*Martin Geier.*

Verses 42, 43.—In verse 42 there is a play upon the two senses of the term *"word,"* thus: " and I will answer my revilers a word, for I have trusted in thy word." Having trusted in thy word of promise, I shall have a word of reply to make to them when thou shalt graciously hear this prayer. *"Take not thy word of truth "* (*i.e.,* of promise) *"out of my mouth";* let me have it still to speak of before my enemies and to rest upon for my own soul. If God were to fail in fulfilling his word of promise, it would, in the sense here contemplated, be quite taken out of his mouth.—*Henry Cowles.*

Verse 43.—*"Take not the word of truth,"* etc. It is well known that men do, when persecution threatens, either altogether deny the truth, or weakly and luke-warmly confess it; but lest this should happen to him, David therefore prays here, *"O Lord, take not the word of truth utterly out of my mouth,"* i.e., make me, with an intrepid spirit, always to confess the avowed truth boldly and manfully. In the Hebrew text it is עַד מְאֹד, *"very." "very much."* or, as Augustine renders it, *"wholly and altogether";* and he thinks that David prayed for this, that, if through human weakness it should happen to him to fall, and at some time or other not steadfastly to confess the word, yet that God would not allow him to continue in that sin, but again restore and establish him; and he illustrates this by the example of Peter. Further, David adds the reason which has impelled him thus to pray: *"Because I hope for,"* and even with great desire, as the Hebrew verb יָחַל signifies, *"thy judgments,"* with which in the last day thou wilt openly pass sentence on heretics, fanatics, and all tyrants.—*Solomon Gesner.*

Verse 43.—*"Take not the word of truth utterly out of my mouth."* The word is taken out of the mouth, when it is said to the sinner, *"Wherefore dost thou declare my statutes ? "* And eloquence itself becomes dumb if the conscience be evil. The birds of heaven come and take the word out of thy mouth, even as they took the seed of the word from off the rock lest it should bring forth fruit.—*Ambrose.*

Verse 43.—*The word is also taken out of our mouth* when in strong temptations all things, as it were, fail, neither can we discover where we may make a stand: Psalm lxix. 2.—*Martin Geier.*

Verse 43.—*"Take not the word of truth utterly out of my mouth."* Sometimes we are afraid to speak for the Saviour, lest we should incur the charge of hypocrisy. At other times we are ashamed to speak, from the absence of that only constraining principle—" the love of Christ." And thus *the word of truth is taken out of our mouths.*" Often have we wanted a word to speak for the relief of the Lord's tempted people, and have not been able to find it ; so that the recollection of precious lost opportunities may well give utterance to the prayer—*"Take not the word of truth utterly out of my mouth."* Not only do not take it out of my heart ; but let it be ready in my mouth for a confession of my Master. Some of us know the painful trial of the indulgence of worldly habits and conversation, when a want of liberty of spirit has hindered us from standing up boldly for our God. We may perhaps allege the plea of bashfulness or judicious caution in excuse for silence ; which however, in many instances, we must regard as a self-deceptive covering for the real cause of restraint—the want of apprehension of the mercy of God to the soul.—*Charles Bridges.*

Verse 43.—*"Take not the word of truth utterly out of my mouth."* Oh, what service can a dumb body do in Christ's house ! Oh, I think the word of God is imprisoned also ! Oh, I am a dry tree ! Alas, I can neither plant nor water ! Oh, if my Lord would make but dung of me, to fatten and make fertile his own corn-ridges in Mount Zion ! Oh, if I might but speak to three or four herd-boys of my worthy Master, I would be satisfied to be the meanest and most obscure of all the pastors in this land, and to live in any place, in any of Christ's basest outhouses ! But he saith, " Sirrah, I will not send you ; I have no errands for you there away." My desire to serve him is sick of jealousy, lest he be unwilling to employ me. . . . I am very well every way, all praise to him in whose books I must stand for ever as his debtor ! Only my silence paineth me. I had one joy out of heaven, next to Christ my Lord, and that was to preach him to this faithless generation ; and they have taken that from me. It was to me as the poor man's one eye, and they have put out that eye.—*Samuel Rutherford.*

Verse 43.—*"For I have hoped in thy judgments,"* the word משפט, *judgment,* signifieth either the law, or the execution of the sentence thereof.

1. The law or whole word of God ; so that, *"I have hoped in thy judgments,"* is no more, but in thy word do I hope ; as it is, " I wait for the Lord, my soul doth wait, and in his word do I hope " (Ps. cxxx. 5).

2. Answerable execution of the law, when the promise or threatening is fulfilled. (1) When the promise is fulfilled : that is judgment in a sense when God accomplisheth what he hath promised for our salvation and deliverance. Thus God is said to judge his people, when he righteth and saveth them according to his word : " O Lord, thou hast seen my wrong : judge thou my cause " (Lam. iii. 59). (2) But the more usual notion of judgment is the execution of the threatening on wicked men ; which being a benefit to God's faithful servants, and done in their favour, David might well be said to hope for it. Their " judgment " is our obtaining the promise.—*Thomas Manton.*

Verses 43, 44.—Lord, let me have the word of truth in *"my mouth "* that I may commit that sacred *depositum* to the rising generation (2 Tim. ii. 22), and by them it may be transmitted to succeeding ages ; so shall *"thy law "* be kept *"for ever and ever,"* i.e., from one generation to another, according to that promise (Isa. lix. 21) : " My words in thy mouth shall not depart out of the mouth of thy seed, nor out of the mouth of thy seed's seed."—*Matthew Henry.*

Verse 44.—*"So shall I keep thy law continually,"* etc. The Lord's keeping our heart in faith, and our mouth and outward man in the course of confession and obedience, is the cause of our perseverance.—*David Dickson.*

Verse 44.—*"So shall I keep."* Mark, the promise of obedience is brought in by way of argument ; *"So shall I keep," "so,"* that is, this will encourage me, this will enable me.

1st. The granting of his requests would give him encouragement : when God answers our hope and expectation, gratitude should excite and quicken us to give all manner of obedience. If he will give us a heart, and a little liberty to confess his name, and serve him, we should not be backward or uncertain, but walk closely with him.

2ndly. This would give him assistance and strength. If God do daily give assistance, we shall stand ; if not, we fall and falter ; this will be a means of his perseverance, not only to engage and oblige him, but to help him to hold on to the end.

Then mark the constancy of this obedience, *"Continually, and for ever and ever."* David would not keep it for a fit, or for a few days, or a year, but always, even to the end of his life. Here are three words to the same sense : *"continually," "for ever," "and ever."* And the Septuagint expresses it thus : " I shall keep thy law always, and for ever, and for ever, and ever ; " four words there. This heaping of words is not in vain.

1. It shows the difficulty of perseverance : unless believers do strongly persist in the resistance of temptation, they will soon be turned out of the way ; therefore David binds his heart firmly : we must do it now, yea, always, unto the end.

2. He expresseth his vehemence of affection : those that are deeply affected with anything are wont to express themselves as largely as they can. As Paul, who had a deep sense of God's power : " Exceeding greatness of his power, according to the working of his mighty power " (Eph. i. 19). He heaps up several words, because his sense of them was so great : so David here doth heap up words—*"continually, and for ever, and ever, and ever."*

3. Some think the words are so many, that they may express not only this life, but that which is to come. I will keep them continually, and for ever, and ever ; that is, all the days of my life, and in the other world. So Chrysostom, " I will keep them continually," etc., points out the other life, where there will be pure and exact keeping of the law of God. Here we are every hour in danger, but then we shall be put out of all danger, and without fear of sinning, we shall remain in a full and perfect righteousness ; we hope for that which we have not attained unto, and this doth encourage us for the present : so would he make David express himself.

4. If we must distinguish these words, I suppose they imply the continuity and perpetuity of obedience ; the continuity of obedience, that he would serve God continually, without intermission ; and the perpetuity of obedience, that he would serve God for ever and ever, without defection or revolt, at all times, and to the end. Constancy and perseverance in obedience is the commendation of it.—*Thomas Manton.*

Verse 44.—*"So shall I keep thy law continually."* That is, if thou wilt not take the word of thy truth out of my mouth, *"I will alway keep thy law."* *"Yea, unto age, and age of age : "* he showeth what is meant by *alway.* For sometimes by *"alway "* is meant, as long as we live here ; but this is not, *"unto age, and age of age."* For it is better thus translated than as some copies have, *"to eternity, and to age of age,"* since they could not say, and to eternity of eternity. That law therefore should be understood, of which the apostle saith, " Love is the fulfilling of the law." For this will be kept by the saints, from whose mouth the word of truth is not taken, that is, by the church of Christ herself, not only during this world, that is, until this world is ended ; but for another world which is styled *world without end.* For we shall not there receive the commandments of the law, as here, to keep them, but we shall keep the fulness of the law itself without any fear of sinning ; for we shall love God the more fully when we shall have seen him ; and our neighbour too ; for " God will be all in all " ; nor will there be room for any false suspicion concerning our neighbour, where no man will be hidden to any.—*Augustine.*

Verse 44.—*"Continually, for ever and ever."* The language of this verse is very emphatic. Perfect obedience will constitute a large proportion of heavenly happiness to all eternity ; and the nearer we approach to it on earth, the more we anticipate the felicity of heaven.—*Note in Bagster's Comprehensive Bible.*

Verse 45.—*"I will walk at liberty."* Wherever God pardons sin, he subdues it (Micah vii. 19). Then is the condemning power of sin taken away, when the commanding power of it is taken away. If a malefactor be in prison, how shall he know that his prince hath pardoned him ? If a jailer come and knock off his chains and fetters, and lets him out of prison, then he may know he is pardoned : so, how shall we know God hath pardoned us ? If the fetters of sin be broken off, and we walk at liberty in the ways of God, this is a blessed sign we are pardoned.—*Thomas Watson.*

Verse 45.—*"I will walk at liberty : for I seek thy precepts."* As he who departs from confessing of God's truth doth cast himself in straits, in danger and bonds ; so he that beareth out the confession of the truth doth walk as a free man ; the truth doth set him free.—*David Dickson.*

Verse 45.—*"I will walk at liberty : for I seek thy precepts."* When the Bible says that a man led by the Spirit is not under the law, it does not mean that he is free because he may sin without being punished for it ; but it means that he is free because being taught by God's Spirit to love what his law commands he is no longer conscious of acting from restraint. The law does not drive him, because the Spirit leads him. . . . There is a state, brethren, when we recognize God, but do not love God in Christ. It is that state when we admire what is excellent, but are not able to perform it. It is a state when the love of good comes to nothing, dying away in a mere desire. That is a state of nature, when we are under the law, and not converted to the love of Christ. And then there is another state, when God writes his law upon our hearts by love instead of fear. The one state is this, " I cannot do the things that I would ; " the other state is this, " I will walk at liberty, for I seek thy commandments."—*Frederick William Robertson*, 1816—1853.

Verse 45.—"*I will walk at liberty.*" The Psalmist's mind takes in the enlargement of his position. A little while ago, and he felt like a man straitened—hemmed in by rocks, in a narrow dangerous pass—who could not make his way out. You know the characteristics of Canaan, and you can easily conceive of the position of a traveller exploring his dreaded way through one of the mountain passes. The traveller before us has attained to tread upon secure ground. Now, all at once, favoured of the Most High, and conscious of being in his way, he finds himself in a spacious place, and he walks at large : "*And I will walk at liberty ; for I seek thy precepts.*" He had made diligent enquiry into all that the Lord had enjoined, and seeking conformity thereto, he felt that he could walk with comfort. He recreates himself in his spiritual emancipation. The secret evil-doer of fair profession cannot know this spiritual liberty at all. As long as a man finds himself to be wrong, and especially a man of a tender conscience, he feels hampered on all sides, depressed in mind, and evilly circumstanced. To what expansion of mind does a man awake when he becomes conscious of being in the appointed way of God ! And he is actually at liberty ; for the good providence of God is around him, and his grace supports him.—*John Stephen.*

Verse 45.—He who goes the beaten and right path will have no brambles hit him across the eyes.—*Saxon proverb.*

Verses 45—48.—Five things David promiseth himself here in the strength of God's grace. 1. That he should be free and easy in his duty : "*I will walk at liberty :*" freed from that which is evil, not hampered with the fetters of my own corruptions, and free to that which is good. 2. That he should be bold and courageous in his duty : "*I will speak of thy testimonies before kings.*" 3. That he should be cheerful and pleasant in his duty : "*I will delight myself in thy commandments,*" in conversing with them, in conforming to them. 4. That he should be diligent and vigorous in his duty : "*I will lift up my hands unto thy commandments ;*" which notes not only a vehement desire towards them, but a close application of mind to the observance of them. 5. That he should be thoughtful and considerate in his duty : "*I will meditate in thy statutes.*"—*Matthew Henry.*

Verses 45—48.—In these four verses he explains, *seriatim*, in what the observance of the law consists ; a thing he promised, when he said in the fourth verse of this division, that he would observe God's law in his heart, in his words, in his mind, and in his acts ; and the prophet seems all at once, as having been heard, to have changed his mode of speaking, for he says, "*And I walked at large.*" When God's mercy visited me, I did not walk in the narrow ways of fear, but in the wide one of love ; that is to say, I observed the law willingly, joyfully, with all the affections of my heart, "*because I have sought after thy commandments*" as a thing of great value, and most important to come at ; "*and I spoke*" openly and fearlessly on the justice of his most holy law, even "*before kings, and I was not ashamed*"; and I constantly turned the law in my mind, and made its mysteries the subject of my meditation, "*and I lifted up my hands,*" to carry out his high and sublime commands ; that is, his extremely perfect and arduous commands. Finally, in all manner of ways, in heart, mind, word, and deed, "*I was exercised in thy justifications.*"—*Robert Bellarmine.*

Verse 46.—"*I will speak of thy testimonies also before kings.*" In these words he seems to believe that he is in possession of that which he formerly prayed for. He had said, " Take not the word of truth out of my mouth," and now, as if he had obtained what he requested, he rises up, and maintains that he would not be dumb, even were he called upon to speak in the presence of kings. He affirms that he would willingly stand forward in vindication of the glory of God in the face of the whole world.—*John Calvin.*

Verse 46.—"*I will speak of thy testimonies also before kings.*" The terror of kings and of men in power is an ordinary hindrance of free confession of God's truth in time of persecution ; but faith in the truth sustained in the heart by God is able to bring forth a confession at all hazards.—*David Dickson.*

Verse 46.—"*I will speak of thy testimonies also before kings.*" Before David came to the crown kings were sometimes his *judges,* as Saul and Achish ; but if he were called before them to give a reason of the hope that was in him, he would speak of God's testimonies, and profess to build his hope upon them, and make them his council, his guard, his crown, his all. We must never be afraid to own our religion, though it should expose us to the wrath of kings, but speak of it as that which we will live and die by, like the three children before Nebuchadnezzar, Dan. iii. 16, Acts iv. 20. After David came to the crown kings were sometimes his *companions,* they visited him, and he returned their visits ; but he did not, in complaisance to them, talk of everything but religion for fear of affronting them, and making his converse uneasy to them : no, God's testimonies shall be the principal subject of his discourse with the kings, not only to show that he was not ashamed of his religion, but to instruct them in it, and bring them over to it. It is good for kings to hear of *God's testimonies,* and it will adorn the conversation of princes themselves to speak of them.—*Matthew Henry.*

Verse 46.—"*I will speak of thy testimonies also before kings.*" Men of greatest holiness have been men of greatest boldness ; witness Nehemiah, the three children, Daniel, and all the holy prophets and apostles : Prov. xxviii. 1, " The wicked flee when no man pursueth : but the righteous are bold as a lion," yea, as a young lion, as the Hebrew has it, one that is in his hot blood and fears no colours, and that is more bold than any others. Holiness made Daniel not only as bold as a lion, but also to daunt the lions with his boldness. Luther was a man of great holiness, and a man of great boldness : witness his standing out against all the world ; and when the emperor sent for him to Worms, and his friends dissuaded him from going, as sometimes Paul's did him, " Go," said he, " I will surely go, since I am sent for, in the name of our Lord Jesus Christ ; yea, though I knew that there were as many devils in Worms to resist me as there be tiles to cover the houses, yet I would go." And when the same author and his associates were threatened with many dangers from opposers on all hands, he lets fall this heroic and magnanimous speech : " Come, let us sing the 46th Psalm, and then let them do their worst." Latimer was a man of much holiness, counting the darkness and profaneness of those times wherein he lived, and a man of much courage and boldness ; witness his presenting to King Henry the Eighth, for a New Year's gift, a New Testament, wrapped up in a napkin, with this posie or motto about it, " Whoremongers and adulterers God will judge."—*Thomas Brooks.*

Verse 46.—Note that in this verse we are taught to shun four vices. First, overmuch silence : hence he says, "*I will speak.*" Secondly, useless talkativeness : "*of thy testimonies.*" The Hebrew doctors say that ten measures of speaking had descended to the earth,—that nine had been carried off by the women, but one left for all the rest of the world. Hieronymus rightly exhorts all Christians : " Consecrate thy mouth to the Gospel : be unwilling to open it with trifles or fables." Thirdly, we are taught to shun cowardice : "*before kings.*" For, as it is said (Prov. xxix. 25), "*The fear of man bringeth a snare.*" Fourthly, and lastly, we are taught to shun cowardly bashfulness : "*and will not be ashamed.*"—*Thomas Le Blanc.*

Verse 46.—"*I will not be ashamed.*" That is, I shall not be cast down from my position or my hope ; I shall not be afraid ; nor will I, from fear of danger or reproach, shun or renounce the confession ; nor shall I be overcome by terrors or threats.—*D. H. Mollerus.*

Verses 46, 47, 48. In these three last verses David promiseth a threefold duty of thankfulness. First, the service of his tongue. Next, the service of his affections. Thirdly, the service of his actions. A good conscience renders always great consolation ; and an honest life makes great boldness to speak without fear or shame, as ye see in David towards Saul, in Elias to Ahab, in Paul to Agrippa, to Festus, and to Felix.—*William Cowper.*

Verse 47.—"*I will delight myself in thy commandments.*" It is but poor comfort to the believer to be able to talk well to others upon the ways of God, and even to " bear the reproach " of his people, when his own heart is cold, insensible, and dull. He longs for "*delight*" in these ways ; and he shall delight in them. —*Charles Bridges.*

Verse 47.—He who would preach boldly to others must himself "*delight*" in the practice of what he preacheth.   If there be in us a new nature, it will *"love the commandments of God"* as being congenial to it ; on that which we love we shall continually be *"meditating,"* and our meditation will end in action ; we shall "lift up the hands which hang down" (Heb. xii. 12), that they may "work the works of God whilst it is day, because the night cometh when no man can work." (John ix. 4).—*George Horne.*

Verse 47.—"Thy commandments, which I have loved."   On the word *"loved,"* the Carmelite quotes two sayings of ancient philosophers, which he commends to the acceptance of those who have learnt the truer philosophy of the Gospel.   The first is Aristotle's answer to the question of what profit he had derived from philosophy : "I have learnt to do without constraint that which others do from fear of the law." The second is a very similar saying of Aristippus : "If the laws were lost, all of us would live as we do now that they are in force."   And for us the whole verse is summed up in the words of a greater Teacher than they : "If a man love me, he will keep my words" : John xiv. 23.—*Neale and Littledale.*

Verses 47, 48.—What is in the word a law of precept, is in the heart a law of love ; what is in the one a law of command, is in the other a law of liberty.   "Love is the fulfilling of the law," Gal. v. 14.   The law of love in the heart, is the fulfilling the law of God in the Spirit.   It may well be said to be written in the heart, when a man doth love it.   As we say, a beloved thing is in our hearts, not physically, but morally, as Calais was said to be in Queen Mary's heart.   They might have looked long enough before they could have found there the map of the town ; but grief for the loss of it killed her.   It is a love that is inexpressible.   David delights to mention it in two verses together : *"I will delight myself in thy commandments, which I have loved.   My hands also will I lift up unto thy commandments, which I have loved,"* and often in the Psalm resumes the assertion.   Before the new creation, there was no affection to the law : it was not only a dead letter, but a devilish letter in the esteem of a man : he wished it razed out of the world, and another more pleasing to the flesh enacted.   He would be a law unto himself ; but when this is written within him, he is so pleased with the inscription, that he would not for all the world be without that law, and the love of it ; whereas what obedience he paid to it before was out of fear, now out of affection ; not only because of the authority of the lawgiver, but of the purity of the law itself.   He would maintain it with all his might against the power of sin within, and the powers of darkness without him.   He loves to view this law ; regards every lineament of it, and dwells upon every feature with delightful ravishments.   If his eye be off, or his foot go away, how doth he dissolve in tears, mourn and groan, till his former affection hath recovered breath, and stands upon its feet !—*Stephen Charnock.*

Verse 48.—"My hands also will I lift up unto thy commandments," etc.   The duty that David promiseth God here, is the service of his actions, that he will lift up his hands to the practice of God's commandments.   The kingdom of God is not in word, but in power ; we are the disciples of that Master, who first began to do and then to teach.   But now the world is full of mutilated Christians ; either they want an ear and cannot hear God's word, or a tongue and cannot speak of it ; or if they have both, they want hands and cannot practise it.—*William Cowper.*

Verse 48.—"My hands also will I lift up."   To lift up the hands is taken variously and it signifies :—1. *To pray :* as in Psalm xxviii. 2 ; Lam. ii. 19 ; Hab. iii. 10.— 2. *To bless* others : as Levit. ix. 22 ; Ps. cxxxiv. 2.—3. *To swear :* as Gen. xiv. 22 ; Exod. vi. 8.—4. *To set about some important matter :*   as Gen. xli. 44 ;   "without thee shall no man lift up his hand ;" *i.e.* shall attempt anything, or shall accomplish ; Psalm x. 12, "lift up thine hand," viz., effectively, to bring help : Heb. xii. 12, "lift up the hands," etc. ; *i.e.* strongly stimulate Christians.   Perhaps all these may be accommodated to the present passage ; for it is possible to be either, 1. Prayer for Divine grace for the doing of the precepts : or, 2. Blessing, *i.e.* praise of God because of them, and the advantages which have thence accrued to us : which the Syriac translator approves, who adds, "and I will glory in thy faithfulness :"— or, 3. Vow, or oath of constant obedience, etc. :—or, 4. Active and earnest undertaking of them ; which, also, appears to be here chiefly meant.—*Henry Hammond in Synopsis Poli.*

Verse 48.—"My hands also will I lift up unto thy commandments ;" vowing obedience to them : Genesis xiv. 22.—*William Kay.*

Verse 48.—"My hands also will I lift up."   I will present every victim and sacrifice which the law requires. I will make prayer and supplication before thee, lifting up holy hands without wrath and doubting.—*Adam Clarke.*

Verse 48.—"*My hands also will I lift up.*" Aben Ezra explains, (and perhaps rightly,) that the metaphor, in this place, is taken from the action of those who receive any one whom they are glad or proud to see.—*Daniel Cresswell, 1776—1844.*

Verse 48.—" I will lift up my hands *in admiration of* thy precepts, And meditate on thy statutes."—*W. Green, in "A New Translation of the Psalms," 1762.*

Verse 48.—To lift up the hand is a gesture importing readiness, and special intention in doing a thing. *"My hands* (saith David) *also will I lift up unto thy commandments " ;* as a man that is willing to do a thing and addresseth himself to the doing of it, lifts up his hand ; so a godly man is described as lifting up his hand to fulfil the commands of God.—*Joseph Caryl.*

Verse 48.—"*Thy commandments.*" By *commandments* he understandeth the word of God, yet it is more powerful than so ; it is not, I have loved thy *word ;* but, I have loved that part of thy word that is thy "*commandments,*" the *mandatory* part. There are some parts of the will and word of God that even ungodly men will be content to love. There is the *promissory* part ; all men gather and catch at the promises, and show love to these. The reason is clear ; there is pleasure, and profit, and gain, and advantage in the promises ; but a pious soul doth not only look to the promises, but to the *commands.* Piety looks on Christ as a *Lawgiver,* as well as a *Saviour,* and not only on him as a *Mediator,* but as a *Lord* and *Master ;* it doth not only live by *faith,* but it liveth by *rule ;* it makes indeed the *promises* the stay and *staff* of a Christian's life, but it makes the commandments of God the *level.* A pious heart knows that some command is implied in the qualification and condition of every promise ; it knows that as for the fulfilling of the promises, it belongs to God ; but the fulfilling of the commands belongs to us. Therefore it looks so, upon the enjoying of that which is promised that it will first do that which is commanded. There is no hope of attaining comfort in the promise but in keeping of the precept ; therefore he pitcheth the emphasis, " I have loved thy *word,*" that is true, and *all* thy word, and this part, the *mandatory* part : " I have loved thy *commandments.*"

Observe the number, " thy commandments " ; it is plural, that is, *all* thy commandments without exception ; otherwise even ungodly men will be content to love *some* commandments, if they may choose them for themselves.—*Richard Holdsworth* (1590—1649), *in "The Valley of Vision."*

Verse 48.—"*Which I love,*" or "*have loved,*" as in verse 47, the terms of which are studiously repeated with a fine rhetorical effect, which is further heightened by the *and* at the beginning, throwing both verses, as it were, into one sentence. As if he had said : I will derive my happiness from thy commandments, which I love and have loved, and to these commandments, which I love and have loved, I will lift up my hands and heart together.—*Joseph Addison Alexander.*

Verse 48.—"*I will meditate.*" It is in holy meditation on the word of God that all the graces of the Spirit are manifested. What is the principle of faith but the reliance of the soul upon the promises of the word ? What is the sensation of godly fear but the soul trembling before the threatenings of God ? What is the object of hope but the apprehended glory of God ? What is the excitement of desire or love but longing, endearing contemplations of the Saviour, and of his unspeakable blessings ? So that we can scarcely conceive of the influences of grace separated from spiritual meditation in the word.—*Charles Bridges.*

Verse 48.—The Syriac has an addition to verse 48, which I am surprised has not been noticed. The addition is, *"and I will glory in thy faithfulness."* Dathe in a note says, THE SEVENTY seem to have read some such addition, although not exactly the same.—*Edward Thomas Gibson, 1819—1880.*

EXPOSITION OF VERSES 49 TO 56.

REMEMBER the word unto thy servant, upon which thou hast caused me to hope.

50 This *is* my comfort in my affliction: for thy word hath quickened me.

51 The proud have had me greatly in derision: *yet* have I not declined from thy law.

52 I remembered thy judgments of old, O LORD, and have comforted myself.

53 Horror hath taken hold upon me because of the wicked that forsake thy law.

54 Thy statutes have been my songs in the house of my pilgrimage.

55 I have remembered thy name, O LORD, in the night, and have kept thy law.

56 This I had, because I kept thy precepts.

This octrain deals with the comfort of the word. It begins by seeking the main consolation, namely, the Lord's fulfilment of his promise, and then it shows how the word sustains us under affliction, and makes us so impervious to ridicule that we are moved by the harsh conduct of the wicked rather to horror of their sin than to any submission to their temptations. We are then shown how the Scripture furnishes songs for pilgrims, and memories for night-watchers; and the Psalm concludes by the general statement that the whole of this happiness and comfort arises out of keeping the statutes of the Lord.

49. *"Remember the word unto thy servant."* He asks for no new promise, but to have the old word fulfilled. He is grateful that he has received so good a word, he embraces it with all his heart, and now entreats the Lord to deal with him according to it. He does not say, " remember my service to thee," but " thy word to me." The words of masters to servants are not always such that servants wish their lords to remember them; for they usually observe the faults and failings of the work done, inasmuch as it does not tally with the word of command. But we who serve the best of masters are not anxious to have one of his words fall to the ground, since the Lord will so kindly remember his word of command as to give us grace wherewith we may obey, and he will couple with it a remembrance of his word of promise, so that our hearts shall be comforted. If God's word to us as his servants is so precious, what shall we say of his word to us as his sons?

The Psalmist does not fear a failure in the Lord's memory, but he makes use of the promise as a plea, and this is the form in which he speaks, after the manner of men when they plead with one another. When the Lord remembers the sins of his servant, and brings them before his conscience, the penitent cries, Lord, remember thy word of pardon, and therefore remember my sins and iniquities no more. There is a world of meaning in that word *"remember,"* as it is addressed to God; it is used in Scripture in the tenderest sense, and suits the sorrowing and the depressed. The Psalmist cried, " Lord, remember David, and all his afflictions " : Job also prayed that the Lord would appoint him a set time, and remember him. In the present instance the prayer is as personal as the " Remember me " of the thief, for its essence lies in the words—" unto thy servant." It would be all in vain for us if the promise were remembered to all others if it did not come true to ourselves; but there is no fear, for the Lord has never forgotten a single promise to a single believer.

"Upon which thou hast caused me to hope." The argument is that God, having given grace to hope in the promise, would surely never disappoint that hope. He cannot have caused us to hope without cause. If we hope upon his word we have a sure basis: our gracious Lord would never mock us by exciting false hopes. Hope deferred maketh the heart sick, hence the petition for immediate remembrance of the cheering word. Moreover, it is the hope of a servant, and it is not possible that a great and good master would disappoint his dependent; if such a master's word were not kept it could only be through an oversight, hence the anxious cry, " Remember." Our great Master will not forget his own servants, nor disappoint

the expectation which he himself has raised : because we are the Lord's, and endeavour to remember his word by obeying it, we may be sure that he will think upon his own servants, and remember his own promise by making it good.

This verse is the prayer of love fearing to be forgotten, of humility conscious of insignificance and anxious not to be overlooked, of penitence trembling lest the evil of its sin should overshadow the promise, of eager desire longing for the blessing, and of holy confidence which feels that all that is wanted is comprehended in the word. Let but the Lord remember his promise, and the promised act is as good as done.

50. *"This my comfort in my affliction : for thy word hath quickened me."* He means,—Thy word is my comfort, or the fact that thy word has brought quickening to me is my comfort. Or he means that the hope which God had given him was his comfort, for God had quickened him thereby. Whatever may be the exact sense, it is clear that the Psalmist had affliction,—affliction peculiar to himself which he calls *"my* affliction"; that he had comfort in it,—comfort specially his own, for he styles it *"my* comfort"; and that he knew what the comfort was, and where it came from, for he exclaims—*"this is* my comfort." The worldling clutches his money-bag, and says, " this is my comfort "; the spendthrift points to his gaiety and shouts, " this is my comfort"; the drunkard lifts his glass and sings, " this is my comfort"; but the man whose hope comes from God feels the life-giving power of the word of the Lord, and he testifies, " this is my comfort." Paul said, " I know whom I have believed." Comfort is desirable at all times ; but comfort in affliction is like a lamp in a dark place. Some are unable to find comfort at such times ; but it is not so with believers, for their Saviour has said to them, " I will not leave you comfortless." Some have comfort and no affliction, others have affliction and no comfort ; but the saints have comfort in their affliction.

The word frequently comforts us by increasing the force of our inner life ; " this is my comfort ; thy word hath quickened me." To quicken the heart is to cheer the whole man. Often the near way to consolation is sanctification and invigoration. If we cannot clear away the fog, it may be better to rise to a higher level, and so to get above it. Troubles which weigh us down while we are half dead become mere trifles when we are full of life. Thus have we often been raised in spirit by quickening grace, and the same thing will happen again, for the comforter is still with us, the Consolation of Israel ever liveth, and the very God of peace is evermore our Father. On looking back upon our past life there is one ground of comfort as to our state—the word of God has made us alive, and kept us so. We were dead, but we are dead no longer. From this we gladly infer that if the Lord had meant to destroy he would not have quickened us. If we were only hypocrites worthy of derision, as the proud ones say, he would not have revived us by his grace An experience of quickening is a fountain of good cheer.

See how this verse is turned into a prayer in verse 107. " Quicken me, O Lord, according unto thy word." Experience teaches us how to pray, and furnishes arguments in prayer.

51. *"The proud have had me greatly in derision."* Proud men never love gracious men, and as they fear them they veil their fear under a pretended contempt. In this case their hatred revealed itself in ridicule, and that ridicule was loud and long. When they wanted sport they made sport of David because he was God's servant. Men must have strange eyes to be able to see farce in faith, and a comedy in holiness ; yet it is sadly the case that men who are short of wit can generally provoke a broad grin by jesting at a saint. Conceited sinners make footballs of godly men. They call it roaring fun to caricature a faithful member of " The Holy Club"; his methods of careful living are the material for their jokes about " the Methodist"; and his hatred of sin sets their tongues a-wagging at long-faced Puritanism, and strait-laced hypocrisy. If David was greatly derided, we may not expect to escape the scorn of the ungodly. There are hosts of proud men still upon the face of the earth, and if they find a believer in affliction they will be mean enough and cruel enough to make jests at his expense. It is the nature of the son of the bondwoman to mock the child of the promise.

"Yet have I not declined from thy law." Thus the deriders missed their aim : they laughed, but they did not win. The godly man, so far from turning aside from the right way, did not even slacken his pace, or in any sense fall off from his holy habits. Many would have declined, many have declined, but David did not do so. It is paying too much honour to fools to yield half a point to them. Their

unhallowed mirth will not harm us if we pay no attention to it, even as the moon suffers nothing from the dogs that bay at her.   God's law is our highway of peace and safety, and those who would laugh us out of it wish us no good.

From verse 61 we note that David was not overcome by the spoiling of his goods any more than by these cruel mockings.   See also verse 157, where the multitude of persecutors and enemies were baffled in their attempts to make him decline from God's ways.

52. *"I remembered thy judgments of old, O LORD ; and have comforted myself."* He had asked the Lord to remember, and here he remembers God and his judgments. When we see no present display of the divine power it is wise to fall back upon the records of former ages, since they are just as available as if the transactions were of yesterday, seeing the Lord is always the same.   Our true comfort must be found in what our God works on behalf of truth and right, and as the histories of the olden times are full of divine interpositions it is well to be thoroughly acquainted with them.   Moreover, if we are advanced in years we have the providences of our early days to review, and these should by no means be forgotten or left out of our thoughts. The argument is good and solid : he who has shown himself strong on behalf of his believing people is the immutable God, and therefore we may expect deliverance at his hands.   The grinning of the proud will not trouble us when we remember how the Lord dealt with their predecessors in bygone periods ; he destroyed them at the deluge, he confounded them at Babel, he drowned them at the Red Sea, he drove them out of Canaan : he has in all ages bared his arm against the haughty, and broken them as potters' vessels.   While in our own hearts we humbly drink of the mercy of God in quietude, we are not without comfort in seasons of turmoil and derision ; for then we resort to God's justice, and remember how he scoffs at the scoffers : " He that sitteth in the heavens doth laugh, the Lord doth have them in derision."

When he was greatly derided the Psalmist did not sit down in despair, but rallied his spirits.   He knew that comfort is needful for strength in service, and for the endurance of persecution, and therefore he comforted himself.   In doing this he resorted not so much to the sweet as to the stern side of the Lord's dealings, and dwelt upon his judgments.   If we can find sweetness in the divine justice, how much more shall we perceive it in divine love and grace.   How thoroughly must that man be at peace with God who can find comfort, not only in his promises, but in his judgments.   Even the terrible things of God are cheering to believers. They know that nothing is more to the advantage of all God's creatures than to be ruled by a strong hand which will deal out justice.   The righteous man has no fear of the ruler's sword, which is only a terror to evil doers.   When the godly man is unjustly treated he finds comfort in the fact that there is a Judge of all the earth who will avenge his own elect, and redress the ills of these disordered times.

53. *"Horror hath taken hold upon me because of the wicked that forsake thy law."* He was horrified at their action, at the pride which led them to it, and at the punishment which would be sure to fall upon them for it.   When he thought upon the ancient judgments of God he was filled with terror at the fate of the godless ; as well he might be.   Their laughter had not distressed him, but he was distressed by a foresight of their overthrow.   Truths which were amusement to them caused amazement to him.   He saw them utterly turning away from the law of God, and leaving it as a path forsaken and overgrown from want of traffic, and this forsaking of the law filled him with the most painful emotions : he was astonished at their wickedness, stunned by their presumption, alarmed by the expectation of their sudden overthrow, amazed by the terror of their certain doom.

See verses 106 and 158, and note the tenderness which combined with all this. Those who are the firmest believers in the eternal punishment of the wicked are the most grieved at their doom.   It is no proof of tenderness to shut one's eyes to the awful doom of the ungodly.   Compassion is far better shown in trying to save sinners than in trying to make things pleasant all round.   Oh that we were all more distressed as we think of the portion of the ungodly in the lake of fire ! The popular plan is to shut your eyes and forget all about it, or pretend to doubt it ; but this is not the way of the faithful servant of God.

54. *"Thy statutes have been my songs in the house of my pilgrimage."*   Like others of God's servants, David knew that he was not at home in this world, but a pilgrim through it, seeking a better country.   He did not, however, sigh over this fact, but he sang about it.   He tells us nothing about his pilgrim sighs, but

speaks of his pilgrim songs. Even the palace in which he dwelt was but *"the house of his pilgrimage,"* the inn at which he rested, the station at which he halted for a little while. Men are wont to sing when they come to their inn, and so did this godly sojourner ; he sang the songs of Zion, the statutes of the great King. The commands of God were as well known to him as the ballads of his country, and they were pleasant to his taste and musical to his ear. Happy is the heart which finds its joy in the commands of God, and makes obedience its recreation. When religion is set to music it goes well. When we sing in the ways of the Lord it shows that our hearts are in them. Ours are pilgrim Psalms, songs of degrees ; but they are such as we may sing throughout eternity ; for the statutes of the Lord are the psalmody of heaven itself.

Saints find horror in sin, and harmony in holiness. The wicked shun the law, and the righteous sing of it. In past days we have sung the Lord's statutes, and in this fact we may find comfort in present affliction. Since our songs are so very different from those of the proud, we may expect to join a very different choir at the last, and sing in a place far removed from their abode.

Note how in the sixth verses of their respective octaves we often find resolves to bless God, or records of testimony. In verse 46 it is, " I will speak," and in 62, " I will give thanks," while here he speaks of songs.

55. *"I have remembered thy name, O LORD, in the night."* When others slept I woke to think of thee, thy person, thy actions, thy covenant, thy *name*, under which last term he comprehends the divine character as far as it is revealed. He was so earnest after the living God that he woke up at dead of night to think upon him. These were David's Night Thoughts. If they were not Sunny Memories they were memories of the Sun of Righteousness. It is well when our memory furnishes us with consolation, so that we can say with the Psalmist,—Having early been taught to know thee, I had only to remember the lessons of thy grace, and my heart was comforted. This verse shows not only that the man of God had remembered, but that he still remembered the Lord his God. We are to hallow the name of God, and we cannot do so if it slips from our memory.

"And have kept thy law." He found sanctification through meditation ; by the thoughts of the night he ruled the actions of the day. As the actions of the day often create the dreams of the night, so do the thoughts of the night produce the deeds of the day. If we do not keep the name of God in our memory we shall not keep the law of God in our conduct. Forgetfulness of minds leads up to forgetfulness of life.

When we hear the night songs of revellers we have in them sure evidence that they do not keep God's law ; but the quiet musings of gracious men are proof positive that the name of the Lord is dear to them. We may judge of nations by their songs, and so we may of men ; and in the case of the righteous, their singing and their thinking are both indications of their love to God : whether they lift up their voices, or sit in silence, they are still the Lord's. Blessed are the men whose " night-thoughts " are memories of the eternal light ; they shall be remembered of their Lord when the night of death comes on. Reader, are your thoughts in the dark full of light, because full of God ? Is his name the natural subject of your evening reflections ? Then it will give a tone to your morning and noonday hours. Or do you give your whole mind to the fleeting cares and pleasures of this world ? If so, it is little wonder that you do not live as you ought to do. No man is holy by chance. If we have no memory for the name of Jehovah we are not likely to remember his commandments : if we do not think of him secretly we shall not obey him openly.

56. *"This I had, because I kept thy precepts."* He had this comfort, this remembrance of God, this power to sing, this courage to face the enemy, this hope in the promise, because he had earnestly observed the commands of God, and striven to walk in them. We are not rewarded for our works, but there is a reward *in* them. Many a comfort is obtainable only by careful living : we can surely say of such consolations, " This I had because I kept thy precepts." How can we defy ridicule if we are living inconsistently ? how can we comfortably remember the name of the Lord if we live carelessly ? It may be that David means that he had been enabled to keep the law because he had attended to the separate precepts : he had taken the commands in detail, and so had reached to holiness of life. Or, by keeping certain of the precepts he had gained spiritual strength to keep others : for God gives more grace to those who have some measure of it, and those who improve

their talents shall find themselves improving.   It may be best to leave the passage open just as our version does ; so that we may say of a thousand priceless blessings, " these came to us in the way of obedience."   All our possessions are the gifts of grace, and yet some of them come in the shape of reward ; yet even then the reward is not of debt, but of grace.   God first works in us good works, and then rewards us for them.

Here we have an apt conclusion to this section of the Psalm, for this verse is a strong argument for the prayer with which the section commenced.   The sweet singer had evidence of having kept God's precepts, and therefore he could the more properly beg the Lord to keep his promises.   All through the passage we may find pleas, especially in the two *remembers*.   " I have remembered thy judgments," and " I have remembered thy name " ;   " Remember thy word unto thy servant."

NOTES ON VERSES 49 TO 56.

Verse 49.—"Remember the word unto thy servant," etc. Those that make God's promises their portion, may with humble boldness make them their plea. God gave the promise in which the Psalmist hoped, and the hope by which he embraced the promise.—*Matthew Henry.*

Verse 49.—"Remember the word unto thy servant," etc. When we hear any promise in the word of God, let us turn it into a prayer. God's promises are his bonds. Sue him on his bond. He loves that we should wrestle with him by his promises. Why, Lord, thou hast made this and that promise, thou canst not deny thyself, thou canst not deny thine own truth ; thou canst not cease to be God, and thou canst as well cease to be God, as deny thy promise, that is thyself. *" 'Lord, remember thy word.'* I put thee in mind of thy promise, *'whereon thou hast caused me to hope.'* If I be deceived, thou hast deceived me. Thou hast made these promises, and caused me to trust in thee, and ' thou never failest those that trust in thee, therefore keep thy word to me.' "—*Richard Sibbes.*

Verse 49.—"Remember the word unto thy servant," etc. God promiseth salvation before he giveth it, to excite our desire of it, to exercise our faith, to prove our sincerity, to perfect our patience. For these purposes he seemeth sometimes to have forgotten his word, and to have deserted those whom he had engaged to succour and relieve ; in which case he would have us, as it were, to remind him of his promise, and solicit his performance of it. The Psalmist here instructeth us to prefer our petition upon these grounds : first that God cannot prove false to his own word : *"Remember thy word ; "* secondly, that he will never disappoint an expectation which himself hath raised : *" upon which thou hast caused me to hope."* —*George Horne.*

Verses 49, 52, 55.—"Remember." *"I remembered."* As David beseecheth the Lord to remember his promise, so he protests, in verse 52, that he remembered the judgments of God, and was comforted ; and in verse 55, that he remembered the name of the Lord in the night. It is but a mockery of God, to desire him to remember his promise made to us, when we make no conscience of the promise we have made to him. But alas, how often we fail in this duty, and by our own default diminish that comfort we might have of God's promises in the day of our trouble.—*William Cowper.*

Verse 49.—"Thy servant." Be sure of your qualification ; for David pleadeth here, partly as a servant of God, and partly as a believer. First, " Remember the word unto thy servant ; " and then, " upon which thou hast caused me to hope." There is a double qualification : with respect to the precept of subjection, and the promise of dependence. The precept is before the promise. They have right to the promises, and may justly lay hold upon them, who are God's servants ; they who apply themselves to obey his precepts, these only can rightly apply his promises to themselves. None can lay claim to rewarding grace but those who are partakers of sanctifying grace. Make it clear that you are God's servants, and then these promises which are generally offered are your own, no less than if your name were inserted in the promise, and written in the Bible.—*Thomas Manton.*

Verse 49.—"Thou hast caused me to hope." Let us remember, first, that the promises made to us are of God's free mercy ; that the grace to believe, which is the condition of the promise, is also of himself ; for " faith is the gift of God"; thirdly, that the arguments by which he confirms our faith in the certainty of our salvation are drawn from himself, not from us.—*William Cowper.*

Verse 50.—"This is my comfort," etc. The word of promise was David's comfort because the word had quickened him to receive comfort. The original is capable of another modification of thought—*"This is my consolation that thy word hath quickened me."* He had the happy experience within him ; he felt the reviving, restoring, life-giving power of the word, as he read, as he dwelt upon it, as he meditated therein, and as he gave himself up to the way of the word. The believer has all God's unfailing promises to depend upon, and as he depends he gains strength by his own happy experiences of the faithfulness of the word.—*John Stephen.*

Verse 50.—"My comfort." *"Thy word."* God hath given us his Scriptures, his word ; and the comforts that are fetched from thence are strong ones, because they are his comforts, since they come from his word.   The word of a prince comforts, though he be not there to speak it.   Though it be by a letter, or by a messenger, yet he whose word it is, is one that is able to make his word good.   He is Lord and Master of his word.   The word of God is comfortable, and all the reasons that are in it, and that are deduced from it, upon good ground and consequence, are comfortable, because it is God's word.   Those comforts in God's word, and reasons from thence, are wonderful in variety.   There is comfort from the liberty of a Christian, that he hath free access to the throne of grace ; comfort from the prerogatives of a Christian, that he is the child of God, that he is justified, that he is the heir of heaven, and such like ; comforts from the promises of grace, of the presence of God, of assistance by his presence.—*Richard Sibbes.*

Verse 50.—"*Comfort.*"   *Nechamah,* consolation ; whence the name of Nehemiah was derived.   The word occurs only in Job vi. 9.

Verse 50.—"*Comfort.*"   The Hebrew verb rendered *to comfort* signifies, first, to repent, and then to comfort.   And certainly the sweetest joy is from the surest tears.   Tears are the breeders of spiritual joy.   When Hannah had wept, she went away, and was no more sad.   The bee gathers the best honey from the bitterest herbs.   Christ made the best wine of water. . . .

Gospel comforts are, first, unutterable comforts, 1 Pet. i. 8 ; Philip. iv. 4. Secondly, they are real, John xiv. 27 ; all others are but seeming comforts, but painted comforts.   Thirdly, they are holy comforts, Isa. lxiv. 5 ; Ps. cxxxviii. 5 ; they flow from a Holy Spirit, and nothing can come from the Holy Spirit but that which is holy.   Fourthly, they are the greatest and strongest comforts, Eph. vi. 17. Few heads and hearts are able to bear them, as few heads are able to bear strong wines.   Fifthly, they reach to the inward man, to the soul, 2 Thess. ii. 17, the noble part of man.   " My soul rejoiceth in God my Saviour."   Our other comforts only reach the face ; they sink not so deep as the heart.   Sixthly, they are the most soul-filling and soul-satisfying comforts, Ps. xvi. 11, Cant. ii. 3.   Other comforts cannot reach the soul, and therefore they cannot fill nor satisfy the soul.   Seventhly, they comfort in saddest distresses, in the darkest night, and in the most stormy day, Ps. xciv. 19, Hab. iii. 7, 8.   Eighthly, they are everlasting, 2 Thess. ii. 16. The joy of the wicked is but as a glass, bright and brittle, and evermore in danger of breaking ; but the joy of the saints is lasting.—*Thomas Brooks.*

Verse 50.—"*Thy word hath quickened me.*"   It is a reviving comfort which quickeneth the soul.   Many times we seem to be dead to all spiritual operations, our affections are damped and discouraged ; but the word of God puts life into the dead, and relieveth us in our greatest distresses.   Sorrow worketh death, but joy is the life of the soul.   Now, when dead in all sense and feeling, " the just shall live by faith " (Hab. ii. 4), and the hope wrought in us by the Scriptures is " a lively hope " (1 Pet. i. 3).   Other things skin the wound, but our sore breaketh out again, and runneth ; faith penetrateth into the inwards of a man, doth good to the heart ; and the soul reviveth by waiting upon God, and gets life and strength.—*Thomas Manton.*

Verse 50.—"*Thy word hath quickened me.*"   Here, as is evident from the mention of " affliction "—and indeed throughout the Psalm—the verb "*quicken*" is used not merely in an external sense of " preservation from death " (Hupfeld), but of " reviving the heart," " imparting fresh courage," etc.—*J. J. Stewart Perowne.*

Verse 50.—"*Thy word hath quickened me.*"   It made me alive when I was dead in sin ; it has many a time made me lively when I was dead in duty ; it has quickened me to that which is good, when I was backward and averse to it ; and it has quickened me in that which is good, when I was cold and indifferent.—*Matthew Henry.*

Verse 50.—(*Second Clause*).   Adore God's distinguishing grace, if you have felt the power and authority of the word upon your conscience ; if you can say as David, "*Thy word hath quickened me.*"   Christian, bless God that he has not only given thee his word to be a rule of holiness, but his grace to be a principle of holiness. Bless God that he has not only written his word, but sealed it upon thy heart, and made it effectual.   Canst thou say it is of divine inspiration, because thou hast felt it to be of lively operation ?   Oh free grace !   That God should send out his word, and heal thee ; that he should heal thee and not others !   That the same Scripture which to them is a dead letter, should be to thee a savour of life.—*Thomas Watson.*

Verse 51.—"*The proud have had me greatly in derision.*"   The saints of God have complained of this in all ages : David of his busy mockers ; the abjects jeered him.

Job was disdained of those children whose fathers he would have scorned to set with the dogs of his flock, Job xxx. 1. Joseph was nicknamed a dreamer, Paul a babbler, Christ himself a Samaritan, and with intent of disgrace a carpenter. . . . Michal was barren, yet she hath too many children, that scorn the habit and exercises of holiness. There cannot be a greater argument of a foul soul, than the deriding of religious services. Worldly hearts can see nothing in those actions, but folly and madness ; piety hath no relish, but is distasteful to their palates.—*Thomas Adams.*

Verse 51.—*"The proud,"* etc. Scoffing proceedeth from pride. Prov. iii. 34, with 1 Peter v. 5.—*John Trapp.*

Verse 51. *"Greatly."* The word noteth " continually," the Septuagint translates it by αφόδρα, the vulgar Latin by *usque valde,* and *usque longe.* They derided him with all possible bitterness ; and day by day they had their scoffs for him, so that it was both a grievous and a perpetual temptation.—*Thomas Manton.*

Verse 51.—*"Derision."* David tells that he had been jeered for his religion, but yet he had not been jeered out of his religion. They laughed at him for his praying and called it cant, for his seriousness and called it mopishness, for his strictness and called it needless preciseness.—*Matthew Henry.*

Verse 51.—It is a great thing in a soldier to behave well under fire ; but it is a greater thing for a soldier of the cross to be unflinching in the day of his trial. It does not hurt the Christian to have the dogs bark at him.—*William S. Plumer.*

Verses 50, 51.—The life and vigour infused into me by the promise which *"quickened me,"* caused me *"not to decline from thy law,"* even though *"the proud did iniquitously altogether"*; doing all in their power, through their jeerings at me, to deter me from its observance.—*Robert Bellarmine.*

Verse 52.—*"I remembered thy judgments of old."* It is good to have a number of examples of God's dealings with his servants laid up in the storehouse of a sanctified memory, that thereby faith may be strengthened in the day of affliction ; for so are we here taught.—*David Dickson.*

Verse 52.—*"I remembered thy judgments."* He remembered that at the beginning Adam, because of transgression of the divine command, was cast out from dwelling in Paradise ; and that Cain, condemned by the authority of the divine sentence, paid the price of his parricidal crime ; that Enoch, caught up to heaven because of his devotion, escaped the poison of earthly wickedness ; that Noah, because of righteousness the victor of the deluge, became the survivor of the human race ; that Abraham, because of faith, diffused the seed of his posterity through the whole earth ; that Israel, because of the patient bearing of troubles, consecrated a believing people by the sign of his own name ; that David himself, because of gentleness, having had regal honour conferred, was preferred to his elder brothers.—*Ambrose.*

Verse 52.—*"I remembered,"* etc. Jerome writes of that religious lady Paula, that she had got most of the Scriptures by heart. We are bid to have the " word dwell in " us : Col. iii. 16. The word is a jewel that adorns the hidden man ; and shall we not remember it ? " Can a maid forget her ornaments ? " Jer. ii. 32. Such as have a disease they call *lienteria,* in which the meat comes up as fast as they eat it, and stays not in the stomach, are not nourished by it. If the word stays not in the memory, it cannot profit. Some can better remember a piece of news than a line of Scripture : their memories are like those ponds, where frogs live, but fish die.—*Thomas Watson, in "The Morning Exercises."*

Verse 52.—*"I remembered thy judgments, and have comforted myself."* A case of conscience may be propounded : how could David be comforted by God's judgments, for it seemeth a barbarous thing to delight in the destruction of any ? it is said, " He that is glad at calamities shall not be unpunished " (Prov. xvii. 5).

1. It must be remembered that judgment implies both parts of God's righteous dispensation, the deliverance of the godly, and the punishment of the wicked. Now, in the first sense there is no ground of scruple, for it is said, " Judgment shall return unto righteousness " (Ps. xciv. 15) ; the sufferings of good men shall be turned into the greatest advantages, as the context showeth that God will not cast off his people, but judgment shall return unto righteousness. 2. Judgment, as it signifieth punishment of the wicked, may yet be a comfort, not as it importeth the calamity of any, but either,—

(1) When the wicked is punished, the snare and allurement to sin is taken away, which is the hope of impunity ; for by their punishment men see that it is dangerous to sin against God : " When thy judgments are in the earth, the inhabitants

of the world will learn righteousness " (Isai. xxvi. 9) ; the snare is removed from many a soul.

(2) Their derision and mockage of godliness ceaseth, they do no longer vex and pierce the souls of the godly, saying, " Aha, aha " (Ps. xl. 15) ; it is as a wound to their heart when they say, " Where is thy God ? " (Ps. xlii. 10). Judgment slayeth this evil.

(3) The impediments and hindrances of worshipping and serving God are taken away : when the nettles are rooted up, the corn hath the more room to grow.

(4) Opportunity of molesting God's servants is taken away, and they are prevented from afflicting the church by their oppressions ; and so way is made for the enlarging of Christ's kingdom.

(5) Thereby also God's justice is manifested : When it goeth well with the righteous, the city rejoiceth : and when the wicked perish, there is shouting " (Prov. xi. 10) ; " The righteous also shall see, and fear, and shall laugh at him : lo this is the man that made not God his strength " (Ps. lii. 6, 7) ; rejoice over Babylon, " ye holy apostles and prophets, for God hath avenged you on her " (Rev. xviii. 20). When the word of God is fulfilled, surely then we may rejoice that his justice and truth are cleared.—*Thomas Manton.*

Verse 52.—The word *mishphatim*, *"judgments,"* is used in Scripture either for laws enacted, or judgments executed according to those laws. The one may be called the judgments of his mouth, as, " Remember his marvellous works that he hath done ; his wonders, and the judgments of his mouth " (Ps. cv. 5), the other, the judgments of his hand. As both will bear the name of judgments, so both may be said to be *"of old."* His decrees and statutes which have an eternal equity in them, and were graven upon the heart of man in innocency, may well be said to be of old : and because from the beginning of the world God hath been punishing the wicked, and delivering the godly in due time, his judiciary dispensations may be said to be so also. The matter is not much, whether we interpret it of either his statutes or decrees, for they both contain matter of comfort, and we may see the ruin of the wicked in the word, if we see it not in providence. Yet I rather interpret it of those righteous acts recorded in Scripture, which God as a just judge hath executed in all ages, according to the promises and threatenings annexed to his laws. Only in that sense I must note to you, judgments imply his mercies in the deliverance of his righteous servants, as well as his punishments on the wicked : the seasonable interpositions of his relief for the one in their greatest distresses, as well as his just vengeance on the other notwithstanding their highest prosperities.—*Thomas Manton.*

Verses 52, 55.—*"I remembered thy judgments," "thy name in the night."* Thomas Fuller thus writes in his " David's Heartie Repentance " :—

> " For sundry duties he did dayes devide,
> Making exchange of worke his recreation ;
> For prayer he set the precious morne aside,
> The mid-day he bequeathed to meditation :
> Sweete sacred stories he reserved for night,
> To reade of Moses' meeknes, Sampson's might :
> These were his joy, these onely his delight."

Verse 53.—*"Horror hath taken hold upon me because of the wicked."* I have had clear views of *eternity ;* have seen the blessedness of the *godly,* in some measure ; and have longed to share their happy state ; as well as been comfortably satisfied that through grace I shall do so ; but, oh, what anguish is raised in my mind, to think of an *eternity* for those who are *Christless,* for those who are mistaken, and who bring their false hopes to the grave with them ! The sight was so dreadful I could by no means bear it : my thoughts recoiled, and I said, (under a more affecting sense than ever before,) " Who can dwell with everlasting burnings ? "—*David Brainerd,* 1718—1747.

Verse 53.—*"Horror hath taken hold upon me,"* etc. Oh who can express what the state of a soul in such circumstances is ! All that we can possibly say about it gives but a very feeble, faint representation of it ; it is inexpressible and inconceivable ; for who knows the power of God's anger ?

How dreadful is the state of those that are daily and hourly in danger of this great wrath and infinite misery ! But this is the dismal case of every soul in this congregation that has not been born again, however moral and strict, sober and religious, they may otherwise be. Oh that you would consider it, whether you be

young or old !   There is reason to think, that there are many in this congregation
now hearing this discourse, that will actually be the subjects of this very misery to
all eternity.   We know not who they are, or in what seats they sit, or what thoughts
they now have.   It may be they are now at ease, and hear all these things without
much disturbance, and are now flattering themselves that they are not the persons,
promising themselves that they shall escape.   If we knew that there was one person,
and but one, in the whole congregation, that was to be the subject of this misery,
what an awful thing would it be to think of !   If we knew who it was, what an awful
sight would it be to see such a person !   How might all the rest of the congregation
lift up a lamentable and bitter cry over him !   But, alas ! instead of one, how many
is it likely will remember this discourse in hell !—*Jonathan Edwards, in a Sermon
entitled, "Sinners in the Hands of an angry God."*

Verse 53.—"*Horror.*" ולעפה, *zilàphah*, properly signifies the pestilential burning
wind called by the Arabs simoon (see Ps. xi. 6) ; and is here used in a figurative
sense for the *most horrid mental distress ;* and strongly marks the idea the Psalmist
had of the corrupting, pestilential, and destructive nature of sin.—*Note in Bagster's
Comprehensive Bible.*

Verse 53.—"*Horror.*"   The word for "*horror* " signifieth also a tempest or storm.
Translations vary ; some read it, as Junius, " a storm overtaking one " ; Ainsworth,
" a burning horror hath seized me," and expoundeth it a storm of terror and dismay.
The Septuagint, ἀθυμία κατέχε μὲ, " faintness and dejection of mind hath possessed
me " ; our own translation, " I am horribly afraid " ; all translations, as well as
the original word, imply a great trouble of mind, and a vehement commotion ; like
a storm, it was matter of disquiet and trembling to David.—*Thomas Manton.*

Verse 53.—"*Because of the wicked that forsake thy law.*"   David grieved, not
because he was himself attacked ; but because the law of God was forsaken ; and
he bewailed the condemnation of those who so did, because they are lost to God.
Just as a good father in the madness of his son, when he is ill-used by him, mourns
not his own but the misery of the diseased ; and he grieves at the contumely, not
because it is cast on himself, but because the diseased person knows not what he
does in his madness : so a good man, when he sees a sinner neither reverence nor
honour the grey hairs of a parent, that to his face he can insult him, that he does
not know in the madness of sinning what unbecoming and shameful things he does,
grieves for him as one on the point of death, laments him as one despaired of by the
physicians.   As a good physician in the first place advises, then, even if he receive
hard words, though he be beaten, nevertheless as the man is ill he bears with him ;
and if he be cursed he does not leave ; and any medicine that may be applied he
does not refuse ; nor does he go away as from a stubborn fellow, but strives with
all diligence to heal him as one that has deserved well from him, exercising not only
the skill of science but also benignity of disposition.   Even so, a righteous man,
when he is treated with contempt, does not turn away, but when he is calumniated
he regards it as madness, not as depravity ; and desires rather to apply his own
remedy to the wound, and sympathises, and grieves not for himself, but for him
who labours under an incurable disease.—*Ambrose.*

Verse 53.—"*The wicked that forsake thy law*" ; not only transgress the law of
the Lord, as every man does, more or less ; but wilfully and obstinately despise it,
and cast it behind their backs, and live in a continued course of disobedience to it ;
or who apostatize from the doctrine of the word of God ; wilfully deny the truth,
after they have had a speculative knowledge of it, whose punishment is very grievous
(Heb. x. 26—29) ; and now partly because of the daring impiety of wicked men,
who stretch out their hands against God, and strengthen themselves against the
Almighty, and run upon him, even on the thick bosses of his bucklers : because of
the shocking nature of their sin, the sad examples thereby set to others, the detriment
they are to themselves, and the dishonour they bring to God ; and partly because
of the dreadful punishment that shall be inflicted on them here, and especially
hereafter, when a horrible tempest of wrath will come upon them.   Hence such
trembling seized the Psalmist : and often so it is, that good men tremble more for
the wicked than they do for themselves : see verse 120.—*John Gill.*

Verse 54.—"*Thy statutes have been my songs.*"   The Psalmist rejoiced, doubtless,
as the good do now, 1. In law itself ; law, as a rule of order ; law as a guide of
conduct ; law, as a security for safety.   2. In *such* a law as that of God—so pure,
so holy, so fitted to promote the happiness of man.   3. In the stability of that law

as constituting his own personal security, the ground of his hope.   4. In law in its influence on the universe, preserving order and securing harmony.—*Albert Barnes.*

Verse 54.—"*Thy statutes have been my songs.*"   In the early ages it was customary to versify the laws, that the people might learn them by heart, and sing them.—*Williams.*

Verse 54.—"*Thy statutes have been my songs.*"   God's statutes are here his "*songs*," which give him spiritual refreshing, sweeten the hardships of the pilgrimage, and measure and hasten his steps.—*Franz Delitzsch.*

Verse 54.—"*Songs.*"   Travellers sing to deceive the tediousness of the way; so did David; and hereby he solaced himself under that horror which he speaks of in verse 53.   Great is the comfort that cometh in by singing of Psalms with grace in our hearts.—*John Trapp.*

Verse 54.—"*Songs.*"

> " Such songs have power to quiet
> The restless pulse of care,
> And come like the benediction
> That follows after prayer.

> " And the night shall be filled with music,
> And the cares that infest the day
> Shall fold their tents like the Arabs,
> And as silently steal away."
> *Henry Wadsworth Longfellow.*

Verse 54.—"*Songs in the house of my pilgrimage.*"   Wherefore is everything like warmth in religion branded with the name of enthusiasm ?   Warmth is expected in the poet, in the musician, in the scholar, in the lover—and even in the tradesman it is allowed, if not commended—why then is it condemned in the concerns of the soul—a subject which, infinitely above all others, demands and deserves all the energy of the mind ?   Would a prisoner exult at the proclamation of deliverance, and is the redeemed sinner to walk forth from his bondage, unmoved, unaffected, without gratitude or joy ?   No, " Ye shall go out with joy, and be led forth with peace : the mountains and the hills shall break forth before you into singing, and all the trees of the field shall clap their hands."   Shall the condemned criminal feel I know not what emotions, when instead of the execution of the sentence he receives a pardon ? and is the absolved transgressor to be senseless and silent ?   No.   " Being justified by faith, we have peace with God through our Lord Jesus Christ : by whom also we have access by faith into this grace wherein we stand, and rejoice in hope of the glory of God.   And not only so, but we glory in tribulations also : and not only so, but we also joy in God through our Lord Jesus Christ, by whom we have now received the atonement."

Other travellers are accustomed to relieve the tediousness of their journey with a song.   The Israelites, when they repaired from the extremities of the country three times a year to Jerusalem to worship, had songs appointed for the purpose, and travelled singing as they went.   And of the righteous it is said, " They shall sing in the ways of the Lord.   The redeemed of the Lord shall return, and come to Zion with songs ; and everlasting joy shall be upon their heads."—*William Jay.*

Verse 54.—"*Songs in the house of my pilgrimage.*"   See how the Lord in his wise dispensation attempers himself to our infirmities.   Our life is subject to many changes, and God by his word hath provided for us also many instructions and remedies.   Every cross hath its own remedy, and every state of life its own instruction.   Sometimes our grief is so great that we cannot sing ; then let us pray : sometimes our deliverance so joyful that we must break out in thanksgiving ; then let us sing. " If any man among you be afflicted, let him pray ; if he be merry, let him sing." Prayers for every cross, and psalms for every deliverance, hath God by his own Spirit penned for us ; so that now we are more than inexcusable if we fail in this duty.—*William Cowper.*

Verse 54.—"*In the house of my pilgrimage.*"   According to the original, "*the house of my pilgrimages*"; that is, whatever places I have wandered to during Saul's persecution of me.—*Samuel Burder.*

Verse 54.—"*In the house of my pilgrimage.*"   Vatablus expounds this of his banishment amongst the Philistines ; that when he was put from his native country and kindred, and all other comforts failed him, the word of the Lord furnished matter of joy to him. And indeed, the banishment of God's servants may cast them far from their kindred and acquaintance ; but it chaseth them nearer to the Lord, and the Lord nearer to them. Proof of this in Jacob, when he was banished and lay without, all night in the fields, he found a more familiar presence of God than he did when he slept in the tent with father and mother.

But we may rather, with Basil, refer it to the whole time of David's mortal life : *omnem vitam suam peregrinationem vocare arbitror.* So Jacob acknowledgeth to Pharaoh, that his life was a pilgrimage ; and Abraham and Isaac dwelt in the world as strangers.

S. Peter therefore teacheth us as pilgrims to abstain from the lusts of the flesh ; and S. Paul, to use this world as if we used it not ; for the fashion thereof goeth away. Many ways are we taught this lesson ; but slow are we to learn it. Alas, what folly is this, that a man should desire to dwell in the earth, when God calleth him to be a citizen of heaven ! Yet great is the comfort we have of this, that the houses wherein we lodge upon earth are but *houses of our pilgrimage.* The faithful Israelites endured their bondage in Egypt the more patiently, because they knew they were to be delivered from it. If the houses of our servitude were eternal mansions, how lamentable were our condition ! But God be thanked, they are but wayfaring cottages, and houses of our pilgrimage. Such a house was the womb of our mother : if we had been enclosed there for ever, what burden had it been to her, what bondage to ourselves ! Such a house will be the grave ; of the which we must all say with Job, " The grave shall be my house, and I shall make my bed in the dark." If we were there to abide for ever, how comfortless were our estate. But, God be praised, our mansion house is above ; and the houses we exchange here on earth are but the houses of our pilgrimage ; and happy is he who can so live in the world as esteeming himself in his own house, in his own bed, yea, in his own body, to be but a stranger, in respect of his absence from the Lord.—*William Cowper.*

Verse 54.—*"My pilgrimage."* If men have been termed pilgrims, and life a journey, then we may add that the Christian pilgrimage far surpasses all others in the following important particulars :—in the goodness of the road, in the beauty of the prospects, in the excellence of the company, and in the vast superiority of the accommodation provided for the Christian traveller when he has finished his course.— *H. G. Salter, in "The Book of Illustrations," 1840.*

Verse 55.—*"I have remembered thy name, O LORD, in the night,"* etc. As the second clause of the verse depends on the first, I consider the whole verse as setting forth one and the same truth ; and, therefore, the prophet means that he was induced, by the remembrance he had of God, to keep the law. Contempt of the law originates in this, that few have any regard for God ; and hence, the Scripture, in condemning the impiety of men, declares that they *have forgotten* God (Psalm l. 22 ; lxxviii. 11 ; cvi. 21) . . . .

The word *"night"* is not intended by him to mean the remembering of God merely for a short time, but a perpetual remembrance of him ; he, however, refers to that season in particular, because then almost all our senses are overpowered with sleep. " When other men are sleeping, God occurs to my thoughts during my sleep." He has another reason for alluding to the night-season,—that we may be apprised, that though there was none to observe him, and none to put him in remembrance of it ; yea, though he was shrouded in darkness, yet he was as solicitous to cherish the remembrance of God as if he occupied the most public and conspicuous place.—*John Calvin.*

Verse 55.—*"I have remembered thy name in the night,"* and therefore I *"have kept thy law "* all day.—*Matthew Henry.*

Verse 55.—*"I have remembered thy name, O LORD, in the night."* This verse contains a new protestation of his honest affection toward the word of God. Wherein, first, let us mark his *sincerity ;* he was religious not only in public, but in private ; for private exercises are the surest trials of true religion. In public, oftentimes hypocrisy carries men to simulate that which they are not ; it is not so in the private devotion ; for then, either doth a man, if he make no conscience of God's worship, utterly neglect it, because there is no eye of man to see him ; or otherwise, if he be indeed religious, even in private he presents his heart to God, seeking it to be approved by him ; for his " praise is not of man, but of God."

Again, this argueth his *fervency* in religion : for as elsewhere he protests that he loved the word more than his appointed food ; so here he protests that he gave up his night's rest that he might meditate in the word.   But now, so far is zeal decayed in professors, that they will not forego their superfluities, far less their needful refreshment, for love of the word of God.—*William Cowper.*

Verse 55.   *"Thy name, O Lord."*   The *"name"* of the Lord is his character, his nature, his attributes, the manifestations he hath made of his holiness, his wisdom, goodness and truth.—*John Stephen.*

Verse 55.—*"In the night."*   First, that is, *continually*, because he remembered God in the day also.   Secondly, *sincerely*, because he avoided the applause of men. Thirdly, *cheerfully*, because the heaviness of natural sleep could not overcome him. All these show that he was *intensely* given to the word ; as we see men of the world will take some part of the night for their delights.   And in that he did keep God's testimonies in the night, he showeth that he was the same in secret that he was in the light ; whereby he condemned all those that will cover their wickedness with the dark.   Let us examine ourselves whether we have broken our sleeps to call upon God, as we have to fulfil our pleasures.—*Richard Greenham.*

Verse 55.—*"In the night."*   Pastor Harms of Hermansburg used to preach and pray and instruct his people for nine hours on the Sabbath.   And then when his mind was utterly exhausted, and his whole body was thrilling with pain, and he seemed almost dying for the want of rest, he could get no sleep.   But he used to say that he loved to lie awake all night in the silence and darkness and think of Jesus.   The night put away everything else from his thoughts, and left his heart free to commune with the One whom his soul most devoutly loved, and who visited and comforted his weary disciple in the night watches.   And so God's children have often enjoyed rare seasons of communion with him in the solitude of exile, in the deep gloom of the dungeon, in the perpetual night of blindness, and at times when all voices and instructions from the world have been most completely cut off, and the soul has been left alone with God.—*Daniel March, in "Night unto Night."*   1880.

Verse 55.—*"In the night."*   There is never a time in which it is not proper to turn to God and think on his name.   In the darkness of midnight, in the darkness of mental depression, in the darkness of outward providences, God is still a fitting theme.—*William S. Plumer.*

Verse 55.—*"The night."*—

> " Dear night ! this world's defeat ;
> The stop to busy fools ; Care's check and **curb ;**
> The day of spirits ; my soul's calm retreat
> Which none disturb !
> Christ's progress, and his prayer time ;
> The hours to which high heaven doth chime.
>
> " God's silent, searching flight ;
> When my Lord's head is filled with dew, and all
> His locks are wet with the clear drops of night ;
> His still, soft call ;
> His knocking time ; the soul's dumb watch,
> When spirits their fair kindred catch."
>
> *Henry Vaughan, 1621—1695.*

Verse 55.—*"And have kept thy law"* ; though imperfectly, yet spiritually, sincerely, heartily, and from a principle of love and gratitude, and with a view to the glory of God, and without mercenary, sinister ends.—*John Gill.*

Verse 55.—*"And have kept thy law."*   Hours of secret fellowship with God must issue in the desire of increased conformity to his holy will.   It is the remembrance of God that leads to the keeping of his laws, as it is forgetfulness of God that fosters every species of transgression.—*John Morison.*

Verse 55.—*"And have kept."*   The verb is in the future, and perhaps is better so rendered, thus making it the expression of a solemn, deliberate purpose to continue, his obedience.—*William S. Plumer.*

Verses 55, 56.—He that delights to keep God's law, God will give him more grace to keep it, according to that remarkable text, *"I have remembered thy name, O LORD, in the night, and have kept thy law.   This I had, because I kept thy precepts."*   What had David for keeping God's precepts ?   He had power to keep his law ; that is, to grow and increase in keeping of it.   As the prophet (Hosea vi. 3) speaks of the knowledge of God : " Then shall we know, if we follow on to know the Lord"; that is, if we industriously labour to know God, we shall have this reward, to be made able to know him more. So may I say of the grace of God : he that delights to keep God's law shall have his reward,—to be enabled to keep it more perfectly. A true delight in God's word is grace increasing. Grace is the mother of all true joy (Isai. xxxii. 17), and joy is as the daughter, and the mother and daughter live and die together.—*Edmund Calamy* (1600—1666), *in "The Godly Man's Ark."*

Verse 56.—*"This I had, because I kept thy precepts."* As sin is a punishment of sin, and the wicked waxeth ever worse and worse ; so godliness is the recompense of godliness. The right use of one talent increaseth more, and the beginnings of godliness are blessed with a growth of godliness. David's good exercises here held him in memory of his God, and the memory of God made him more godly and religious.—*William Cowper.*

Verse 56.—*"This I had,"* etc. The Rabbins have an analogous saying,—*The reward of a precept is a precept ;* or, *A precept draws a precept.* The meaning of which is, that he who keeps one precept, to him God grants, as if by way of reward, the ability to keep another and more difficult precept. The contrary to this is that other saying of the Rabbins, that *the reward of a sin is a sin ;* or, *Transgression draws transgression.*—*Simon de Muis,* 1587—1644.

Verse 56.—*"This I had,"* that is, this happened to me, etc. I experienced many evils and adversities ; but, on the other hand, I drew sweetest consolations from the word, and I was crowned with many blessings from God.

Others thus render it, This is my business, This I care for and desire, to keep thy commandments ; *i.e.*, to hold fast the doctrine incorrupt with faith and a good conscience.—*D. H. Mollerus.*

Verse 56.—*"This I had,"* etc. I had the comfort of keeping thy law *because I kept it.* God's work is its own wages.—*Matthew Henry.*

Verse 56.—*"This I had,"* etc. What is that ? This comfort I had, this supportation I had in all my afflictions, this consolation I had, this sweet communion with God I had. Why ? *"Because I kept thy precepts,"* I obeyed thy will. Look, how much obedience is yielded to the commands of God, so much comfort doth flow into the soul : God usually gives in comforts proportionably to our obedience. O the sweet, soul-satisfying consolation a child of God finds in the ways of God, and in doing the will of God, especially when he lies on his death-bed ; then it will be sweeter to him than honey and the honeycomb ; then will he say with good king Hezekiah, when he lay upon his death-bed, " Lord, remember how I have walked before thee in truth, and with a perfect heart, and have done that which was good in thy sight." O the sweet satisfaction that a soul shall find in God, when he comes to appear before God !—*James Nalton,* 1664.

Verse 56.—*"This I had,"* etc. Or, " This was my *consolation*, that I kept thy precepts ;" which is nearly the reading of the Syriac, and renders the sense more complete.—*Note in Bagster's Comprehensive Bible.*

Verse 56.—*"This I had,"* etc. When I hear the faithful people of God telling of his love, and saying—*"This I had,"* must I not, if unable to join their cheerful acknowledgment, trace it to my unfaithful walk, and say—" This I had not "—because I have failed in obedience to thy precepts ; because I have been careless and self-indulgent ; because I have slighted thy love ; because I have " grieved thy Holy Spirit," and forgotten to " ask for the old paths, that I might walk therein, and find rest to my soul "? Jer. vi. 16.—*Charles Bridges.*

Verse 56.—David saith indefinitely, " *This I had*"; not telling us what good or privilege it was ; only in the general, it was some benefit that accrued to him in this life. He doth not say, This I hope for ; but, *"This I had ;"* and therefore he doth not speak of the full reward in the life to come. In heaven we come to receive the full reward of obedience ; but a close walker, that waiteth upon God in an humble and constant obedience, shall have sufficient encouragement even in this life. Not only he shall be blessed, but he is blessed ; he hath something on hand as well as in hope : as David saith in this the 119th Psalm, not only he shall be blessed, but he is blessed ; as they that travelled towards Zion, they met with a well by the way : " Who passing through the valley of Baca make it a well ; the rain also filleth the pools " (Ps. lxxxiv. 6). In a dry and barren wilderness, through which they were to pass, they were not left wholly comfortless, but met with a well or a cistern ; that is, they had some comfort vouchsafed to them before they came to enjoy God's presence in Zion ; some refreshments they had by the way. As servants, that, besides their wages, have their veils ; so, besides the recompense of reward hereafter, we have our present comforts and supports during our course of service, which are enough to counterbalance all worldly joys, and outweigh the greatest pleasures that men can expect in the way of sin. In the benefits that believers find by walking with God in a course of obedience every one can say, *"This I had, because I kept thy precepts."*—Thomas Manton.

EXPOSITION OF VERSES 57 TO 64.

*T*HOU *art* my portion, O LORD : I have said that I would keep thy words.

58 I intreated thy favour with *my* whole heart : be merciful unto me according to thy word.

59 I thought on my ways, and turned my feet unto thy testimonies.

60 I made haste, and delayed not to keep thy commandments.

61 The bands of the wicked have robbed me : *but* I have not forgotten thy law.

62 At midnight I will rise to give thanks unto thee because of thy righteous judgments.

63 I *am* a companion of all *them* that fear thee, and of them that keep thy precepts.

64 The earth, O LORD, is full of thy mercy : teach me thy statutes.

In this section the Psalmist seems to take firm hold upon God himself ; appropriating him (57), crying out for him (58), returning to him (59), solacing himself in him (61, 62), associating with his people (63), and sighing for personal experience of his goodness (64). Note how the first verse of this octave is linked to the last of the former one, of which indeed it is an expanded repetition. " This I had because I kept thy precepts. Thou art my portion, O Lord : I have said that I would keep thy words."

57. "*Thou art my portion, O LORD.*" A broken sentence. The translators have mended it by insertions, but perhaps it had been better to have left it alone, and then it would have appeared as an exclamation,—" My portion, O Lord ! " The poet is lost in wonder while he sees that the great and glorious God is all his own ! Well might he be so, for there is no possession like Jehovah himself. The form of the sentence expresses joyous recognition and appropriation,—" My portion, O Jehovah ! " David had often seen the prey divided, and heard the victors shouting over it ; here he rejoices as one who seizes his share of the spoil ; he chooses the Lord to be his part of the treasure. Like the Levites, he took God to be his portion, and left other matters to those who coveted them. This is a large and lasting heritage, for it includes all, and more than all, and it outlasts all ; and yet no man chooses it for himself until God has chosen and renewed him. Who that is truly wise could hesitate for a moment when the infinitely blessed God is set before him to be the object of his choice ? David leaped at the opportunity, and grasped the priceless boon. Our author here dares exhibit the title-deeds of his portion before the eye of the Lord himself, for he addresses his joyful utterance directly to God whom he boldly calls his own. With much else to choose from, for he was a king, and a man of great resources, he deliberately turns from all the treasures of the world, and declares that the Lord, even Jehovah, is his portion.

"*I have said that I would keep thy words.*" We cannot always look back with comfort upon what we have said, but in this instance David had spoken wisely and well. He had declared his choice : he preferred the word of God to the wealth of worldlings. It was his firm resolve to keep—that is, treasure up and observe— the words of his God, and as he had aforetime solemnly expressed it in the presence of the Lord himself, so here he confesses the binding obligation of his former vow. Jesus said, " If a man love me, he will keep my words," and this is a case which he might have quoted as an illustration ; for the Psalmist's love to God as his portion led to his keeping the words of God. David took God to be his Prince as well as his Portion. He was confident as to his interest in God, and therefore he was resolute in his obedience to him. Full assurance is a powerful source of holiness. The very words of God are to be stored up ; for whether they relate to doctrine, promise, or precept, they are most precious. When the heart is determined to keep these words, and has registered its purpose in the court of heaven, it is prepared for all the temptations and trials that may befall it ; for, with God as its heritage, it is always in good case.

58. "*I intreated thy favour with my whole heart.*" A fully assured possession of God does not set aside prayer, but rather urges us to it ; he who knows God to

be his God will seek his face, longing for his presence. Seeking God's presence is the idea conveyed by the marginal reading, " thy face," and this is true to the Hebrew. The presence of God is the highest form of his favour, and therefore it is the most urgent desire of gracious souls : the light of his countenance gives us an antepast of heaven. O that we always enjoyed it ! The good man entreated God's smile as one who begged for his life, and the entire strength of his desire went with the entreaty. Such eager pleadings are sure of success ; that which comes from our heart will certainly go to God's heart. The whole of God's favours are ready for those who seek them with their whole hearts.

" *Be merciful unto me according to thy word.*" He has entreated favour, and the form in which he most needs it is that of mercy, for he is more a sinner than anything else. He asks nothing beyond the promise, he only begs for such mercy as the word reveals. And what more could he want or wish for ? God has revealed such an infinity of mercy in his word that it would be impossible to conceive of more. See how the Psalmist dwells upon favour and mercy, he never dreams of merit. He does not demand, but entreat ; for he feels his own unworthiness. Note how he remains a suppliant, though he knows that he has all things in his God. God is his portion, and yet he begs for a look at his face. The idea of any other standing before God than that of an undeserving but favoured one never entered his head. Here we have his " Be merciful unto me " rising with as much intensity of humble pleading as if he still remained among the most trembling of penitents. The confidence of faith makes us bold in prayer, but it never teaches us to live without prayer, or justifies us in being other than humble beggars at mercy's gate.

59. "*I thought on my ways, and turned my feet unto thy testimonies.*" While studying the word he was led to study his own life, and this caused a mighty revolution. He came to the word, and then he came to himself, and this made him arise and go to his father. Consideration is the commencement of conversion : first we think and then we turn. When the mind repents of ill ways the feet are soon led into good ways ; but there will be no repenting until there is deep, earnest thought. Many men are averse to thought of any kind, and as to thought upon their ways, they cannot endure it, for their ways will not bear thinking of. David's ways had not been all that he could have wished them to be, and so his thoughts were sobered o'er with the pale cast of regret ; but he did not end with idle lamentations, he set about a practical amendment ; he turned and returned, he sought the testimonies of the Lord, and hastened to enjoy once more the conscious favour of his heavenly friend. Action without thought is folly, and thought without action is sloth : to think carefully and then to act promptly is a happy combination. He had entreated for renewed fellowship, and now he proved the genuineness of his desire by renewed obedience. If we are in the dark, and mourn an absent God, our wisest method will be not so much to think upon our sorrows as upon our ways : though we cannot turn the course of providence, we can turn the way of our walking, and this will soon mend matters. If we can get our feet right as to holy walking, we shall soon get our hearts right as to happy living. God will turn to his saints when they turn to him ; yea, he has already favoured them with the light of his face when they begin to think and turn.

60. "*I made haste, and delayed not to keep thy commandments.*" He made all speed to get back into the royal road from which he had wandered, and to run in that road upon the King's errands. Speed in repentance and speed in obedience are two excellent things. - We are too often in haste to sin ; O that we may be in a greater hurry to obey. Delay in sin is increase of sin. To be slow to keep the commands is really to break them. There is much evil in a lagging pace when God's command is to be followed. A holy alacrity in service is much to be cultivated. It is wrought in us by the Spirit of God, and the preceding verses describe the method of it : we are made to perceive and mourn our errors, we are led to return to the right path, and then we are eager to make up for lost time by dashing forward to fulfil the precept.

Whatever may be the slips and wanderings of an honest heart, there remains enough of true life in it to produce ardent piety when once it is quickened by the visitations of God. The Psalmist entreated for mercy, and when he received it he became eager and vehement in the Lord's ways. He had always loved them, and hence when he was enriched with grace he displayed great vivacity and delight in them. He made double speed ; for positively he " made haste," and negatively he refused to yield to any motive which suggested procrastination,—he " delayed not." Thus he made rapid advances and accomplished much service, fulfilling thereby the vow which is recorded in the 57th verse : " I said that I would keep thy words." The commands which he was so eager to obey were not ordinances of man, but precepts of the Most High. Many are zealous to obey custom and society, and yet they are slack in serving God. It is a crying shame that men should be served post-haste, and that God's work should have the go-by, or be performed with dreamy negligence.

61. *"The bands of the wicked have robbed me."* Aforetime they derided him, and now they have defrauded him. Ungodly men grow worse, and become more and more daring, so that they go from ridicule to robbery. Much of this bold opposition arose from their being banded together : men will dare to do in company what they durst not have thought of alone. When firebrands are laid together there is no telling what a flame they will create. It seems that whole bands of men assailed this one child of God, they are cowardly enough for anything ; though they could not kill him, they robbed him ; the dogs of Satan will worry saints if they cannot devour them. David's enemies did their utmost : first the serpents hissed, and then they stung. Since words availed not, the wicked fell to blows. How much the ungodly have plundered the saints in all ages, and how often have the righteous borne gladly the spoiling of their goods !

"But I have not forgotten thy law." This was well. Neither his sense of injustice, nor his sorrow at his losses, nor his attempts at defence diverted him from the ways of God. He would not do wrong to prevent the suffering of wrong, nor do ill to avenge ill. He carried the law in his heart, and therefore no disturbance of mind could take him off from following it. He might have forgotten himself if he had forgotten the law : as it was, he was ready to forgive and forget the injuries done him, for his heart was taken up with the word of God. The bands of the wicked had not robbed him of his choicest treasure, since they had left him his holiness and his happiness.

Some read this passage, " The bands of the wicked environ me." They hemmed him in, they cut him off from succour, they shut up every avenue of escape, but the man of God had his protector with him ; a clear conscience relied upon the promise, and a brave resolve stuck to the precept. He could not be either bribed or bullied into sin. The cordon of the ungodly could not keep God from him, nor him from God : this was because God was his portion, and none could deprive him of it either by force or fraud. That is true grace which can endure the test : some are barely gracious among the circle of their friends, but this man was holy amid a ring of foes.

62. *"At midnight I will rise to give thanks unto thee because of thy righteous judgments."* He was not afraid of the robbers ; he rose, not to watch his house, but to praise his God. Midnight is the hour for burglars, and there were bands of them around David, but they did not occupy his thoughts ; these were all up and away with the Lord his God. He thought not of thieves, but of thanks ; not of what *they* would steal, but of what *he* would give to his God. A thankful heart is such a blessing that it drives out fear and makes room for praise. Thanksgiving turns night into day, and consecrates all hours to the worship of God. Every hour is canonical to a saint.

The Psalmist observed posture ; he did not lie in bed and praise. There is not much in the position of the body, but there is something, and that something is to be observed whenever it is helpful to devotion and expressive of our diligence or humility. Many kneel without praying, some pray without kneeling ; but the best is to kneel and pray : so here. it would have been no virtue to rise without giving thanks, and it would have been no sin to give thanks without rising ; but to rise and give thanks is a happy combination. As for the season, it was quiet, lonely, and such as proved his zeal. At midnight he would be unobserved and undisturbed ; it was his own time which he saved from his sleep, and so he would be free from the charge of sacrificing public duties to private devotions. Midnight ends one day and begins another, it was therefore meet to give the solemn moments to communion with the Lord. At the turn of the night he turned to his God. He had thanks to give for mercies which God had given : he had on his mind the truth of verse fifty-seven, " Thou art my portion," and if anything can make a man sing in the middle of the night that is it.

The *righteous* doings of the great Judge gladdened the heart of this godly man.

His *judgments* are the terrible side of God, but they have no terror to the righteous; they admire them, and adore the Lord for them : they rise at night to bless God that he will avenge his own elect. Some hate the very notion of divine justice, and in this they are wide as the poles asunder from this man of God, who was filled with joyful gratitude at the memory of the sentences of the Judge of all the earth. Doubtless in the expression, " thy righteous judgments," David refers also to the written judgments of God upon various points of moral conduct ; indeed, all the divine precepts may be viewed in that light ; they are all of them the legal decisions of the Supreme Arbiter of right and wrong. David was charmed with these judgments. Like Paul, he could say, " I delight in the law of God after the inward man." He could not find time enough by day to study the words of divine wisdom, or to bless God for them, and so he gave up his sleep that he might tell out his gratitude for such a law and such a Law-giver.

This verse is an advance upon the sense of verse fifty-two, and contains in addition the essence of fifty-five. Our author never repeats himself : though he runs up and down the same scale, his music has an infinite variety. The permutations and combinations which may be formed in connection with a few vital truths are innumerable.

63. *"I am a companion of all them that fear thee."* The last verse said, " I will," and this says, " I am " We can hardly hope to be right in the future unless we are right now. The holy man spent his nights with God and his days with God's people. Those who fear God love those who fear him, and they make small choice in their company so long as the men are truly God-fearing. David was a king, and yet he consorted with *"all "* who feared the Lord, whether they were obscure or famous, poor or rich. He was a fellow-commoner of the College of All-saints.

He did not select a few specially eminent saints and leave ordinary believers alone. No, he was glad of the society of those who had only the beginning of wisdom in the shape of " the fear of the Lord": he was pleased to sit with them on the lower forms of the school of faith. He looked for inward godly fear, but he also expected to see outward piety in those whom he admitted to his society ; hence he adds, *"and of them that keep thy precepts."* If they would keep the Lord's commands the Lord's servant would keep their company. David was known to be on the godly side, he was ever of the Puritanic party : the men of Belial hated him for this, and no doubt despised him for keeping such unfashionable company as that of humble men and women who were strait-laced and religious ; but the man of God is by no means ashamed of his associates ; so far from this, he even glories to avow his union with them, let his enemies make what they can of it. He found both pleasure and profit in saintly society ; he grew better by consorting with the good, and derived honour from keeping right honourable company. What says the reader ? Does he relish holy society ? Is he at home among gracious people ? If so, he may derive comfort from the fact. Birds of a feather flock together. A man is known by his company. Those who have no fear of God before their eyes seldom desire the society of saints ; it is too slow, too dull for them. Be this our comfort, that when we are let go by death we shall go to our own company, and those who loved the saints on earth shall be numbered with them in heaven.

There is a measure of parellelism between this seventh of its octave and the seventh of Teth (71) and of Jod (79) ; but, as a rule, the similarities which were so manifest in earlier verses are now becoming dim. As the sense deepens, the artificial form of expression is less regarded.

64. *"The earth, O LORD, is full of thy mercy."* David had been exiled, but he had never been driven beyond the range of mercy, for he found the world to be everywhere filled with it. He had wandered in deserts and hidden in caves, and there he had seen and felt the lovingkindness of the Lord. He had learned that far beyond the bounds of the land of promise and the race of Israel the love of Jehovah extended, and in this verse he expressed that large-hearted idea of God which is so seldom seen in the modern Jew. How sweet it is to us to know that not only is there mercy all over the world, but there is such an abundance of it that the earth is " full " of it. It is little wonder that the Psalmist, since he knew the Lord to be his portion, hoped to obtain a measure of this mercy for himself, and so was encouraged to pray, *"teach me thy statutes."* It was to him the *beau-ideal* of mercy to be taught of God, and taught in God's own law. He could not think of a greater mercy than this. Surely he who fills the universe with his grace will

grant such a request as this to his own child. Let us breathe the desire to the All-merciful Jehovah, and we may be assured of its fulfilment.

The first verse of this eight is fragrant with full assurance and strong resolve, and this last verse overflows with a sense of the divine fulness, and of the Psalmist's personal dependence. This is an illustration of the fact that full assurance neither damps prayer nor hinders humility. It would be no error if we said that it creates lowliness and suggests supplication. "Thou art my portion, O Lord," is well followed by "teach me"; for the heir of a great estate should be thoroughly educated, that his behaviour may comport with his fortune. What manner of disciples ought we to be whose inheritance is the Lord of hosts? Those who have God for their Portion long to have him for their Teacher. Moreover, those who have resolved to obey are the most eager to be taught. "I have said that I would keep thy words" is beautifully succeeded by "teach me thy statutes." Those who wish to keep a law are anxious to know all its clauses and provisions lest they should offend through inadvertence. He who dares not care to be instructed of the Lord has never honestly resolved to be holy.

NOTES ON VERSES 57 TO 64.

This begins a new division of the Psalm, indicated by the Hebrew letter *Cheth*, which may be represented in English by *hh.—Albert Barnes.*

Verses 57—64.—In this section David laboureth to confirm his faith, and to comfort himself in the certainty of his regeneration, by eight properties of a sound believer, or eight marks of a new creature. The first whereof is his choosing of God for his portion. Whence learn, 1. Such as God hath chosen and effectually called, they get grace to make God their choice, their delight, and their portion ; and such as have chosen God for their portion have an evidence of their regeneration and election also ; for here David maketh this a mark of his regeneration : *"Thou art my portion."* 2. It is another mark of regeneration, after believing in God, and choosing him for our portion, to resolve to bring forth the fruits of faith in new obedience, as David did : *"I have said that I would keep thy words."* 3. As it is usual for God's children, now and then because of sin falling out, to be exercised with a sense of God's displeasure, so it is a mark of a new creature not to lie stupid and senseless under this exercise, but to deal with God earnestly, for restoring the sense of reconciliation, and giving new experience of his mercy, as the Psalmist did ; *"I intreated thy favour with my whole heart;"* and this is the evidence of a new creature. 4. The penitent believer hath the word of grace and the covenant of God for his assurance to be heard when he seeketh mercy : *"Be merciful unto me according to thy word."* 5. The searching in what condition we are in, and examination of our ways according to the word, and renewing of repentance, with an endeavour of amendment, is a fourth mark of a new creature : *"I thought on my ways, and turned my feet unto thy testimonies."* 6. When we do see our sin we are naturally slow to amend our doings ; but the sooner we turn us to the way of God's obedience, we speed the better, and the more speedy the reforming of our life be, the more sound mark is it of a new creature : *"I made haste, and delayed not to keep thy commandments."* 7. Enduring of persecution and spoiling of our goods, for adhering to God's word, without forsaking of his cause, is a fifth mark of a new creature : *"The bands of the wicked have robbed me : but I have not forgotten thy law."* 8. As it is the lot of God's children who resolve to be godly, to suffer persecution, and to be forced either to lose their temporal goods or else to lose a good cause and a good conscience ; so it is the wisdom of the godly to remember what the Lord's word requireth of us and speaketh unto us, and this shall comfort our conscience more than the loss of things temporal can trouble our minds : *"The bands of the wicked have robbed me : but I have not forgotten thy law."* 9. A sixth mark of a new creature is, to be so far from fretting under hard exercise as to thank God in secret cheerfully for his gracious word, and for all the passages of his providence, where none seeth us, and where there is no hazard of ostentation : *"At midnight I will rise to give thanks unto thee because of thy righteous judgments."* 10. A seventh mark of a renewed creature is, to associate ourselves and keep communion with such as are truly gracious, and do fear God indeed, as we are able to discern them : *"I am a companion of all them that fear thee."* 11. The fear of God is evidenced by believing and obeying the doctrine and direction of the Scripture, and no other ways : *"I am a companion of all them that fear thee, and of them that keep thy precepts."* 12. The eighth mark of a new creature is, not to rest in any measure of renovation, but earnestly to deal with God for the increase of saving knowledge, and fruitful obedience of it ; for, *"Teach me thy statutes,"* is the prayer of the man of God, in whom all the former marks are found. 13. As the whole of the creatures are witnesses of God's bounty to man, and partakers of that bounty themselves, so are they pawns of God's pleasure to bestow upon his servants greater gifts than these, even the increase of sanctification, in further illumination of mind and reformation of life : for this the Psalmist useth for an argument to be more and more sanctified : *"The earth, O LORD, is full of thy mercy : teach me thy statutes."—David Dickson.*

Verse 57.—*"Thou art my portion, O LORD."* The sincerity of this claim may be gathered, because he speaks by way of address to God. He doth not say barely, "He is my portion" ; but challengeth God to his face : *"Thou art my portion, O LORD."* Elsewhere it is said, "The Lord is my portion, saith my soul" (Lam. iii. 24). There he doth not speak it by way of address to God, but he adds, "saith my soul " ; but here to God himself, who knows the secrets of the heart. To speak thus of God to God, argues our sincerity, when to God's face we avow our trust and choice ; as Peter, " Lord, thou knowest all things ; thou knowest that I love thee " (John xxi. 17).—*Thomas Manton.*

Verse 57.—"*Thou art my portion, O LORD.*" Luther counsels every Christian to answer all temptations with this short saying, "*Christianus sum,*" I am a Christian ; and I would counsel every Christian to answer all temptations with this short saying, " The Lord is my portion." O Christian, when Satan or the world shall tempt thee with honours, answer, " The Lord is my portion" ; when they shall tempt thee with riches, answer, " The Lord is my portion" ; when they shall tempt thee with preferments, answer, "The Lord is my portion " ; and when they shall tempt thee with the favours of great ones, answer, " The Lord is my portion " ; yea, and when this persecuting world shall threaten thee with the loss of thy estate, answer, " The Lord is my portion" ; and when they shall threaten thee with the loss of thy liberty, answer, " The Lord is my portion " ; and when they shall threaten thee with the loss of friends, answer, " The Lord is my portion ; " and when they shall threaten thee with the loss of life, answer, " The Lord is my portion." O sir, if Satan should come to thee with an apple, as once he did to Eve, tell him that " the Lord is your portion" ; or with a grape, as once he did to Noah, tell him that " the Lord is your portion " ; or with a change of raiment, as once he did to Gehazi, tell him that " the Lord is your portion" ; or with a wedge of gold, as once he did to Achan, tell him that " the Lord is your portion" ; or with a bag of money, as once he did to Judas, tell him that " the Lord is your portion " ; or with a crown, a kingdom, as once he did to Moses, tell him that " the Lord is your portion."—*Thomas Brooks.*

Verse 57.—"*Thou art my portion, O LORD.*" God is all sufficient ; get him for your "*portion,*" and you have all ; then you have infinite wisdom to direct you, infinite knowledge to teach you, infinite mercy to pity and save you, infinite love to care and comfort you, and infinite power to protect and keep you. If God be yours ; all his creatures, all his works of providence, shall do you good, as you have need of them. He is an eternal, full, satisfactory portion. He is an ever-living, ever-loving, ever-present friend ; and without him you are a cursed creature in every condition, and all things will work against you.—*John Mason*—1694.

Verse 57.—"*Thou art my portion, O LORD.*" If there was a moment in the life of David in which one might feel inclined to envy him, it would not be in that flush of youthful victory, when Goliath lay prostrate at his feet, nor in that hour of even greater triumph, when the damsels of Israel sang his praise in the dance, saying, " Saul hath slain his thousands, and David his ten thousands" ; it would not be on that royal day, when his undisputed claim to the throne of Israel was acknowledged on every side and by every tribe ; but it would be in that moment when, with a loving and trustful heart, he looked up to God and said, "*Thou art my portion.*" In a later Psalm (cxlii.), which bears with it as its title. " A prayer of David, when he was in the cave," we have the very same expression : " I said, Thou art my refuge and my portion in the land of the living." It adds immeasurably to such an expression, if we believe it to have been uttered at a time when every other possession and inheritance was taken from him, and the Lord alone was his portion.—*Barton Bouchier.*

Verse 57.—He is an exceedingly covetous fellow to whom God is not sufficient ; and he is an exceeding fool to whom the world is sufficient. For God is an inexhaustible treasury of all riches, sufficing innumerable men ; while the world has mere trifles and fascinations to offer, and leads the soul into deep and sorrowful poverty. —*Thomas Le Blanc.*

Verse 57.—They who are without an ample patrimony in this life, may make to themselves a portion in heavenly blessedness.—*Solomon Gesner.*

Verse 57.—"*I have said that I would keep thy words.*" This he brings in by way of proving that which he said in the former words. Many will say with David, that God is their portion ; but here is the point ; how do they prove it ? If God were their portion they would love him ; if they loved him they would love his word ; if they loved his word they would live by it and make it the rule of their life.—*William Cowper.*

Verse 57.—"*I have said that I would keep thy words.*" He was resolved to keep his commandments, lay up his promises, observe his ordinances, profess and retain a belief in his doctrines.—*John Gill.*

Verse 58.—*"I intreated thy favour,"* or ; I seek thy face.   To seek the face is to come into the presence.   Thus the Hebrews speak when desirous of expressing that familiar intercourse to which God admits his people when he bids them make known their requests.   It is truly the same as speaking face to face with God.— *Franciscus Vatablus,* 1545.

Verse 58.—*"I intreated thy favour with my whole heart."*   I have often remarked how graciously and lovingly the Lord delights to return an answer to prayer in the very words that have gone up before him, as if to assure us that they have reached his ear, and been speeded back again from him laden with increase.   *"I intreated thy favour with my whole heart."*   Hear the Lord's answer to his praying people : " I will rejoice over them to do them good, assuredly *with my whole heart and with my whole soul."—Barton Bouchier.*

Verse 58.—*"With my whole heart."*   The Hebrew expresses great earnestness and humility in supplication.—*A. R. Fausset.*

Verse 58.—*"With my whole heart."*   Prayer is chiefly a heart-work.   God heareth the heart without the mouth, but never heareth the mouth acceptably without the heart.—*Walter Marshall.*

Verse 58.—*"Be merciful unto me,"* etc.   He protested before that he sought the Lord with his whole heart, and now he prayeth that he may find mercy.   So indeed it shall be ; boldly may that man look for mercy at God's hand who seeks him truly.   Mercy and truth are wont to meet together, and embrace one another : where truth is in the soul to seek, there cannot but be mercy in God to embrace. If truth be in us to confess our sins and forsake them, we shall find mercy in God to pardon and forgive them.—*William Cowper*

Verse 58.—*"According to thy word."*   He prayeth not for what he lusteth after, but for that which the Lord promised ; for St. James saith, " You pray and have not," etc., and this is the cause, that we have not the thing we pray for, because we pray not according to the word.   His word must be the rule of our prayers, and then we shall receive ; as Solomon prayed and obtained.   God hath promised forgiveness of sins, the knowledge of his word, and many other blessings.   If we have these, let not our hearts be set on other things.—*Richard Greenham.*

Verse 58.—*"According to thy word."*   The Word of God may be divided into three parts ; into commandments, threatenings, and promises ; and though a Christian must not neglect the commanding and threatening word, yet if ever he would make the Word a channel for Divine comfort, he must study the promising word ; for the promises are a Christian's magna charta for heaven.   All comfort must be built upon a Scripture promise, else it is presumption, not true comfort. The promises are *pabulum fidei, et anima fidei,* the food of faith, and the soul of faith.   As faith is the life of a Christian, so the promises are the life of faith : faith is a dead faith if it hath no promise to quicken it. As the promises are of no use without faith to apply them, so faith is of no use without a promise to lay hold on.—*Edward Calamy.*

Verse 58.—The rule and ground of confidence is, *"according to thy word."*   God's word is the rule of our confidence ; for therein is God's stated course.   If we would have favour and mercy from God, it must be upon his own terms.   God will accept of us in Christ, if we repent, believe, and obey, and seek his favour diligently : he will not deny those who seek, ask, knock.   Many would have mercy, but will not observe God's direction.   We must ask according to God's will, not without a promise, nor against a command.   God is made a voluntary debtor by his promise. These are notable props of faith, when we are encouraged to seek by the offer, and urged to apply by the promise.   We thrive no more in a comfortable sense of God's love, because we take not this course.—*Thomas Manton.*

Verse 59.—*"I thought on my ways, and turned my feet unto thy testimonies."*   The transition which is made in the text from the occasion of this alteration, *"I thought on my ways,"* to the change itself, is very lofty and elegant.   He does not tell us that, after a review of them, he saw the folly and danger of sin, the debasedness of its pleasures, and the poison of its delights ; or that, upon a search into God's law, he was convinced that what he imagined so severe, rigid, and frightful before, was now all amiable and lovely ; no, but immediately adds, *"I turned my feet unto thy testimonies";*   than which I can conceive nothing more noble or strong ; for it emphatically says, that there was no need to express the appearance his ways had when once he thought upon them. What must be the consequence of his deliberation was so plain, namely, that sin never prevails but where it is masked over with some false beauties, and the inconsiderate, foolish sinner credulously gives ear to its enchantments, and is not at pains and care to enquire into them ; for a deep, thorough search would soon discover that its fairest appearances are but lying vanities, and that he who is captivated with that empty show is in the same circumstances with a person in a dream, who can please himself with his fancy only while asleep, and that his awakening out of it no sooner or more certainly discovers the cheat, than a serious thinking upon the ways of iniquity and rebellion against God will manifest the fatal madness of men in ever pursuing them.—*William Dunlop*, 1692—1720.

Verse 59.—"*I thought on my ways, and turned my feet unto thy testimonies.*" Some translate the original, I looked on both sides upon my ways, I considered them every way, " and turned my feet unto thy testimonies." I considered that I was wandering like a lost sheep, and then I returned.—*George Swinnock.*

Verse 59.—"*I thought on my ways,*" etc. The Hebrew word חשב that is here used for thinking, signifies to think on a man's ways accurately, advisedly, seriously, studiously, curiously. This holy man of God thought exactly and curiously on all his purposes and practices, on all his doings and sayings, on all his words and works, and finding too many of them to be short of the rule, yea, to be against the rule, he turned his feet to God's testimonies ; having found out his errors, upon a diligent search, a strict scrutiny, he turned over a new leaf, and framed his course more exactly by rule. O Christians ! you must look as well to your spiritual wants as to your spiritual enjoyments ; you must look as well to your layings out as to your layings up ; you must look as well forward to what you should be, as backward to what you are. Certainly that Christian will never be eminent in holiness that hath many eyes to behold a little holiness, and never an eye to see his further want of holiness.—*Thomas Brooks.*

Verse 59.—"*I thought on my ways.*" The word signifies a fixed, abiding thought. Some make it an allusion to those that work embroidery ; that are very exact and careful to cover the least flaw ; or to those that cast accounts. Reckon with yourselves, What do I owe ? what am I worth ? "*I thought*" not only on my wealth, as the covetous man, Ps. xlix. 11 ; but "*on my ways*" ; not what I have, but what I do ; because what we do will follow us into another world, when what we have must be left behind. Many are critical enough in their remarks upon other people's ways that never think of their own, but " let every man prove his own work."

This account which David here gives of himself may refer either to his constant practice every day ; he reflected on his ways at night, directed his feet to God's testimonies in the morning, and what his hand found to do that was good he did it without delay : or it may refer to his first acquaintance with God and religion, when he began to throw off the vanity of childhood and youth, and to remember his Creator ; that blessed change was by the grace of God thus wrought. Note, 1. Conversion begins in serious consideration ; Ezek. xviii. 28 ; Luke xv. 17. 2. Consideration must end in a sound conversion. To what purpose have we thought on our ways, if we do not turn our feet with all speed to God's testimonies ?—*Matthew Henry.*

Verse 59.—"*I thought on my ways.*" Be frequent in this work of serious consideration. If daily you called yourselves to an account, all acts of grace would thrive the better. Seneca asked of Sextius, *Quod hodie malum sanasti ? cui vitio obstitisti ?* You have God's example in reviewing every day's work, and in dealing with Adam before he slept. The man that was unclean was to wash his clothes at eventide.—*Thomas Manton.*

Verse 59.—"*I thought on my ways,*" etc. Poisons may be made medicinable. Let the thoughts of old sins stir up a commotion of anger and hatred. We feel shiverings in our spirits, and a motion in our blood, at the very thought of a bitter potion we have formerly taken. Why may we not do that spiritually, which the very frame and constitution of our bodies doth naturally, upon the calling a loathsome thing to mind ? The Romans' sins were transient, but the shame was renewed every time they reflected on them : Rom. vi. 21, " Whereof ye are now ashamed." They reacted the detestation instead of the pleasure : so should the revivings of old sins in our memories be entertained with our sighs, rather than with joy. We should also manage the opportunity, so as to promote some further degrees of our conversion : "*I thought on my ways, and turned my feet unto thy testimonies.*" There is not the most hellish motion, but we may strike some sparks from it, to kindle our love to God, renew our repentance, raise our thankfulness, or quicken our obedience.—*Stephen Charnock.*

Verse 59.—*"And turned my feet unto thy testimonies."* Mentioning this passage, Philip Henry observed, that the great turn to be made in heart and life is, from all other things to the word of God. Conversion turns us to the word of God, as our touch-stone, to examine ourselves, our state, our ways, spirits, doctrines, worships, customs ; as our glass, to dress by, James i. ; as our rule to walk and work by, Galatians vi. 16 ; as our water, to wash us, Psalm cxix. 9 ; as our fire to warm us, Luke xxiv. ; as our food to nourish us, Job xxiii. 12 ; as our sword to fight with, Ephesians vi. ; as our counsellor, in all our doubts, Ps. cxix. 24 ; as our cordial, to comfort us ; as our heritage, to enrich us.

Verse 59.—*"And turned my feet unto thy testimonies."* No itinerary to the heavenly city is simpler or fuller than the ready answer made by an English prelate to a scoffer who asked him the way to heaven ; " First turn to the right, and keep straight on."—*Neale and Littledale.*

Verse 59.—*"And turned."* Turn to God, and he will turn to you ; then you are happy, though all the world turn against you.—*John Mason.*

Verse 60.—*"I made haste, and delayed not,"* etc. Duty discovered should instantly be discharged. There is peril attending every step which is taken in the indulgence of any known sin, or in the neglect of any acknowledged obligation. A tender conscience will not trifle with its convictions, lest the heart should be hardened through the deceitfulness of sin. It is unsafe, it is unreasonable, it is highly criminal to hesitate to carry that reformation into effect which conscience dictates. He who delays when duty calls may never have it in his power to evince the sincerity of his contrition for past folly and neglect. *"I made haste,"* said the Psalmist, *"and delayed not to keep thy commandments"*; that is, being fully convinced of the necessity and excellency of obedience, I instantly resolved upon it, and immediately put it into execution.—*John Morison.*

Verse 60.—*"I made haste, and delayed not to keep thy commandments."* We often hear the saying, " Second thoughts are best." This does not hold in the religious life. In the context the Psalmist says, " I thought on my ways, and turned my feet unto thy testimonies," that is, I did not wait to think again. In religion it may be a deadly habit to take time to reflect. Make haste.—*Henry Melvill.*

Verse 60.—*"I made haste, and delayed not."* When anyone is lawfully called either to the study of theology, or to the teaching it in the church, he ought not to hesitate, as Moses, or turn away, as Jonah ; but, leaving all things, he should obey God who calls him ; as David says, *"I made haste, and delayed not."* Matt. iv. 20 ; Luke ix. 62.—*Solomon Gesner.*

Verse 60.—*"I made haste, and delayed not."* Sound faith is neither suspicious, nor curious ; it believes what God says, without sight, without examining. For since it is impossible for God to lie (for how should truth lie ?) it is fit his word be credited for itself's sake. It must not be examined with hows and whys. That which the Psalmist says of observing the law, that must the Christian say of receiving the gospel. התמהמהתי לא, *"I disputed not,"* saith David ; I argued not *with God.* The word is very elegant in the original tongue, derived in the Hebrew from the pronoun מה, which signifieth *quid.* Faith reasons not with God, asketh no *quids,* no *quares,* no *quomodos,* no whats, no hows, no wherefores : it moveth no questions. It meekly yields assent, and humbly says *Amen* to every word of God. This is the faith at which our Saviour wondered in the centurion's story.—*Richard Clerke.*—1634.

Verse 60.—*"I made haste, and delayed not."* The original word, which we translate *"delayed not,"* is amazingly emphatical. התמהמהתי ולא, *velo hithmahmahti,* I did not stand *what-what-whating ;* or, as we used to express the same sentiment, *shilly-shallying* with myself : I was *determined,* and so set out. The Hebrew word as well as the English, strongly marks indecision of mind, positive action being suspended, because the mind is so unfixed as not to be able to make a choice.—*Adam Clarke.*

Verse 60.—Take heed of delays and procrastination, of putting it off from day to day, by saying there will be time enough hereafter ; it will be time enough for me to look after heaven when I have got enough of the world ; if I do it in the last year of my life, in the last month of the last year, in the last week of the last month, it will serve. O take heed of delays ; this putting off repentance hath ruined thousands of souls ; shun that pit into which many have fallen, shun that rock upon which many have suffered shipwreck ; say with David, *"I made haste, and delayed not to keep thy commandments."*—*James Nalton,* 1664.

Verse 60.—*"I made haste, and delayed not,"* etc. In the verse immediately preceding, the man of God speaks of repentance as the fruit of consideration and self-examining : " I thought on my ways, and turned my feet unto thy testimonies." But when did he turn ? for, though we see the evil of our ways, we are naturally slow to get it redressed. Therefore David did not only turn to God, but he did it speedily : we have an account of that in this verse, *"I made haste,"* etc. This readiness in the work of obedience is doubly expressed ; affirmatively and negatively. Affirmatively, *"I made haste"*; negatively, *"I delayed not."* This double expression increaseth the sense according to the manner of the Hebrews ; as, " I shall not die, but live " (Ps: cxviii. 17) ; that is, surely live ; so here, *"I made haste, and delayed not ; "* that is, I verily delayed not a moment ; as soon as he had thought of his ways, and taken up the resolution to walk closely with God, he did put it into practice. The Septuagint read the words thus, " I was ready, and was not troubled or diverted by fear of danger." Indeed, besides our natural slowness to good, this is one usual ground of delays ; we distract ourselves with fears ; and, when God hath made known his will to us in many duties, we think of tarrying till the times are more quiet, and favourable to our practice, or till our affairs are in a better posture. A good improvement may be made of that translation ; but the words run better, as they run more generally, with us, *"I made haste, and delayed not,"* etc.

David *delayed not.* When we dare not flatly deny, then we delay. *Non vacat,* that is the sinner's plea, " I am not at leisure " ; but, *Non placet,* there is the reality. They which were invited to the wedding varnished their denial over with an excuse (Matt. xxii. 5). Delay is a denial ; for, if they were willing, there would be no excuse. To be rid of importunate and troublesome creditors, we promise them payment another time : though we know our estate will be more wasted by that time, it is but to put them off : so this delay and putting off of God is but a shift. Here is the misery, God always comes unseasonably to a carnal heart. It was the devils that said, "Art thou come hither to torment us before the time ? " (Matt. viii. 29). Good things are a torment to a carnal heart ; and they always come out of time. Certainly, that is the best time when the word is pressed upon thy heart with evidence, light, and power, and when God treats with thee about thine eternal peace.—*Thomas Manton.*

Verse 60.—*"Delayed."* *Hithmahmah ;* the word used of Lot's lingering, in Genesis xix. 16.—*William Kay.*

Verse 60.—Delay in the Lord's errands is next to disobedience, and generally springs out of it, or issues in it. " God commanded me to make haste " (2 Chron. xxxv. 21). Let us see to it that we can say, *"I made haste, and delayed not to keep thy commandments."*—*Frances Ridley Havergal.*

Verse 60.—Avoid all delay in the performance of this great work of believing in Christ. Until we have performed it we continue under the power of sin and Satan, and under the wrath of God ; and there is nothing between hell and us besides the breath of our nostrils. It is dangerous for Lot to linger in Sodom, lest fire and brimstone come down from heaven upon him. The manslayer must fly with all haste to the city of refuge, lest the avenger of blood pursue him, while his heart is hot, and slay him. We should make haste, and not delay to keep God's commandments.—*Walter Marshall.*

Verse 60.—If convictions begin to work, instantly yield to their influence. If any worldly or sinful desire is touched, let this be the moment for its crucifixion. If any affection is kindled towards the Saviour, give immediate expression to its voice. If any grace is reviving, let it be called forth into instant duty. This is the best, the only, expedient to fix and detain the motion of the Spirit now striving in the heart ; and who knoweth but the improvement of the present advantage may be the moment of victory over difficulties hitherto found insuperable, and may open our path to heaven with less interruption and more steady progress ?—*Charles Bridges.*

Verse 61.—*"The bands of the wicked have robbed me."* Two readings remain, either of which may be admitted : *The cords of the wicked have caught hold of me,* or, *The companies of the wicked have robbed me.* Whether we adopt the one or the other of these readings, what the prophet intends to declare is, that when Satan assailed the principles of piety in his soul, by grievous temptations, he continued with undeviating steadfastness in the love and practice of God's law. *Cords* may, however, be understood in two ways ; either, first, as denoting the deceptive allurements by which the wicked endeavoured to get him entangled in their society ; or, secondly, the frauds which they practised to effect his ruin.—*John Calvin.*

Verse 61.—"*The bands of the wicked have robbed me.*"—Some have it, " Cords of wicked men have entwined me." Others, " Snares of wicked men surround me." The meaning is that wicked men by their plots and contrivances had beset him, as men would ensnare a wild beast in their toils. They might, indeed, hem him round about in the wilderness, but they could not enthral the free mind ; he would still feel at liberty in spirit, he would not forget God's law.—*John Stephen.*

Verse 61.—"*The bands of the wicked have robbed me.*" They set upon his goods, and spoiled him of them, either by plunder in the time of war, or by fines and confiscations under colour of law. Saul (it is likely) seized his effects ; Absalom his palace ; the Amalekites rifled Ziklag.—*Matthew Henry.*

Verse 61.—The friendship of the wicked must be shunned. First, because it binds us, as they are bound together—"*bands of the wicked.*" Every sinner is a gladiator with net and sword, going down into the arena, and endeavouring to enmesh any one who comes near him. A second reason for shunning the friendship of the wicked, which may be taken from the Hebrew word, is their cruelty and barbarity ; for not only do the wicked bind their friends, but they make a spoil and a prey of them : "*have robbed me.*" They are decoying thieves, journeying with an unwary traveller, until they have led him into thick and dark woods, where they strip him of heavenly riches.—*Thomas Le Blanc.*

Verses 61.—"*The bands of the wicked have robbed me.*" Then said *Christian* to his fellow, Now I call to remembrance that which was told me of a thing that happened to a good man hereabout. The name of the man was *Little-Faith*, but a good man, and he dwelt in the town of *Sincere.* The thing was this ; at the entering in of this passage there comes down from *Broadway-gate* a lane called *Dead-man's-lane ;* so called because of the murders that are commonly done there. And this *Little-Faith* going on pilgrimage, as we do now, chanced to sit down there and slept. Now there happened, at that time, to come down that lane from *Broad-way-gate* three sturdy rogues, and their names were *Faint-heart*, *Mistrust*, and *Guilt*, (three brothers,) and they espying *Little-Faith* where he was came galloping up with speed. Now the good man was just awaked from his sleep, and was getting up to go on his journey. So they came all up to him, and with threatening language bid him *stand.* At this, *Little-Faith* looked as white as a clout, and had neither power to *fight* nor *flie.* Then said *Faint-heart*, Deliver thy purse ; but he making no haste to do it, (for he was loth to lose his money,) *Mistrust* ran up to him, and thrusting his hand into his pocket, pulled out thence a bag of silver. Then he cried out, Thieves ! Thieves ! With that *Guilt*, with a great club that was in his hand, struck *Little-Faith* on the head, and with that blow felled him flat to the ground, where he lay bleeding as one that would bleed to death. . . . The place where his jewels were they never ransacked, so those he kept still ; but, as I was told, the good man was much afflicted for his loss. For the thieves got most of his spending money. That which they got not (as I said) were jewels, also he had a little odd money left, but scarce enough to bring him to his journey's end ; nay, (if I was not misinformed,) he was forced to beg as he went, to keep himself alive (for his jewels he might not sell). But beg, and do what he could he went (as we say) with many a hungry belly, the most part of the rest of the way.—*John Bunyan.*

Verse 61.—"*Bands.*" Howsoever, to strengthen themselves in an evil course, the wicked go together by bands and companies, yet shall it not avail them, nor hurt us. Babel's builders ; Moab, Ammon, Edom, conspiring in one, may tell us, " Though hand join in hand, the wicked shall not escape unpunished." The wicked are like thorns before the fire ; their multitude may well embolden the flame, but cannot resist it.—*William Cowper.*

Verse 61.—It is a salutary reflection to bear in mind, that thousands of spiritual adversaries are ever watching to make us their prey.—*John Morison.*

Verse 62.—"*At midnight I will rise to give thanks.*" Though we cannot enforce the particular observance upon you, yet there are many notable lessons to be drawn from David's practice.

1. The ardency of his devotion, or his earnest desire to praise God : "*at midnight,*" when sleep doth most invade men's eyes, then he would rise up. His heart was so

set upon the praising of God, and the sense of his righteous providence did so affect him, and urge and excite him to this duty, that he would not only employ himself in this work in the daytime, and so show his love to God, but he would rise out of his bed to worship God and celebrate his praise. That which hindereth the sleep of ordinary men, is either the cares of this world, the impatient resentment of injuries, or the sting of an evil conscience : these keep others waking, but David was awaked by a desire to praise God. No hour is unseasonable to a gracious heart : he is expressing his affection to God when others take their rest. Thus we read of our Lord Christ, that he spent whole nights in prayer (Luke vi. 12). It is said of the glorified saints in heaven, that they praise God continually : "Therefore are they before the throne of God, and serve him day and night in his temple : and he that sitteth on the throne shall dwell among them" (Rev. vii. 15). Now, holy men, though much hindered by their bodily necessities, will come as near to continual praise as present frailty will permit. Alas, we oftentimes begin the day with some fervency of prayer and praise, but we faint ere the evening comes.

2. His sincerity, seen in his secrecy. David would profess his faith in God when he had no witness by him ; *"at midnight,"* when there was no hazard of ostentation. It was a secret cheerfulness and delighting in God : when alone he could have no respect to the applause of men, but only to approve himself to God who seeth in secret. See Christ's direction : " But thou, when thou prayest, enter into thy closet, and when thou hast shut thy door, pray to thy Father which is in secret ; and thy Father which seeth in secret shall reward thee openly " (Matt. vi. 6). Note also Christ's own practice : " Rising up a great while before day, he went out, and departed into a solitary place, and there prayed " (Mark i. 35) : before day he went into a desert to pray ; both time and place implied secrecy.

3. We learn hence the preciousness of time : it was so to David ; see how he spendeth the time of his life. We read of David, when he lay down at night, he watered his couch with his tears, after the examination of his heart (Psalm vi. 6) ; at midnight he rose to give thanks ; in the morning he prevented the morning watches ; and seven times a-day he praised God : morning, noon, and night he consecrated. These are all acts of eminent piety. We should not content ourselves with so much grace as will merely serve to save us. Alas ! we have much idle time hanging upon our hands : if we would give that to God, it were well.

4. The value of godly exercises above our natural refreshings. The word is sweeter than appointed food : " I have esteemed the words of his mouth more than my necessary food " (Job xxiii. 12). David preferreth the praises of God before his sleep and rest in the night. Surely, this should shame us for our sensuality. We can dispense with other things for our vain pleasures : we have done as much for sin, for vain sports, etc. ; and shall we not deny ourselves for God ?

5. The great reverence to be used in secret adoration. David did not only raise up his spirits to praise God, but rise up out of his bed, to bow the knee to him. Secret duties should be performed with solemnity, not slubbered over. Praise, a special act of adoration, requireth the worship of body and soul.—*Thomas Manton.*

Verse 62.—*"At midnight I will rise to give thanks."* He had praised God in the courts of the Lord's house, and yet he will do it in his bed-chamber. Public worship will not excuse us from secret worship.—*Matthew Henry.*

Verse 62.—*"At midnight I will rise to give thanks unto thee."* Was he not ready also to praise God at midday ? Certainly ; but he says, *"at midnight,"* that he may express the ardour and longing of his soul. We are wont to assure our friends of our good will by saying that we will rise at midnight to consult about their affairs.— *Wolfgang Musculus.*

Verse 62.—*"At midnight I will rise to give thanks,"* etc. In these words observe three things :—1. David's holy employment, or the duty promised, giving thanks to God. 2. His earnestness and fervency implied in the time mentioned, " At midnight I will rise " ; he would rather interrupt his sleep and rest, than God should want his praise. 3. The cause or matter of his thanksgiving, " because of thy righteous judgments " : whereby he meaneth the dispensations of God's providence in delivering the godly and punishing the wicked, according to his word.—*Thomas Manton.*

Verse 62.—*"At midnight I will rise to give thanks."* Cares of this world, impatience of wrongs, a bad conscience, keep awake the ungodly and disturb their sleep (*Rivetus*) ; but what I awake for is to give thanks to thee.—*A. R. Faussett.*

Verse 63.—"I am a companion," etc. He said in the first verse of this section that God was his portion ; now he saith, that all the saints of God are his companions. These two go together—the love of God and the love of his saints. He that loveth not his brother, made in God's image, whom he seeth, how shall he love God whom he hath not seen ? Seeing our goodness extends not to the Lord ; if it be showed to his saints and excellent ones upon earth, for his sake, it shall be no small argument of our loving affection towards himself.

Godly David, when Jonathan was dead, made diligent inquisition, Is there none of Jonathan's posterity to whom I may show kindness for Jonathan's sake ? and at length he found a silly, lame Mephibosheth. So if we enquire diligently, Is there none upon earth to whom I may show kindness for Christ's sake who is in heaven ? we shall ever find some, to whom whatsoever we do shall be accepted as done to himself.

His great modesty is to be marked. He saith not, I am companion of all that follow thee, but of all that fear thee. The fear of God is the beginning of wisdom. He places himself among novices in humility, though he excelled ancients in piety.— *William Cowper.*

Verse 63.—"I am a companion of all them that fear thee." How weak is human nature ! Verily there are times when the presence of one so great as the Almighty becomes oppressive, and we feel our need of one like ourselves to sympathize with us. . . . And there have been provided for us by the way many kind, sympathizing friends, like Jesus. As we pass on, we get the human supports which the Lord hath provided. We get them for fellowship too.—*John Stephen.*

Verse 63.—"I am a companion of all them that fear thee." Birds of a feather will flock together. Servants of the same Lord, if faithful, will join with their fellows, and not with the servants of his enemy. When a man comes to an inn you may give a notable guess for what place he is bound by the company he enquires after. His question,—" Do you know of any travelling towards London ? I should be heartily glad of their company," will speak his mind and his course. If he hear of any bound for another coast he regards them not ; but if he know of any honest passengers that are to ride in the same road, and set out for the same city with himself, he sends to them, and begs the favour of their good company. This world is an inn, all men are in some sense pilgrims and strangers, they have no abiding-place here. Now the company they enquire after, and delight in, whether those that walk in the " broad way " of the flesh, or those who walk in the " narrow way " of the Spirit, will declare whether they are going towards heaven or towards hell. A wicked man will not desire the company of them who walk in a contrary way, nor a saint delight in their society who go cross to his journey. " Can two walk together except they be agreed ? " The young partridges hatched under a hen go for a time along with her chickens, and keep them company, scraping in the earth together ; but when they are grown up, and their wings fit for the purpose, they mount up into the air, and seek for birds of their own nature. A Christian, before his conversion, is brought up under the prince of darkness, and walks in company with his cursed crew, according to the course of this world ; but when the Spirit changes his disposition, he quickly changes his companions, and delights only in the saints that are on earth.—*George Swinnock.*

Verse 63.—"I am a companion of all them that fear thee." 1. The person speaking. The disparity of the persons is to be observed. David, who was a great prophet, yea, a king, yet saith, *"I am a companion of all them that fear thee."* Christ himself called them his " fellows ": " Thy God hath anointed thee with the oil of gladness above thy fellows " (Ps. xlv. 7) ; and therefore David might well say, *"I am a companion."*

2. The persons spoken of. David saith of *"all them that fear thee."* The universal particle is to be observed ; not only some, but *"all"*: when any lighted upon him, or he upon any of them, they were welcome to him. How well would it be for the world, if the great potentates of the earth would thus think, speak, and do, *"I am a companion of all that fear thee."* Self-love reigneth in most men : we love the rich and despise the poor, and so have the faith of our Lord Jesus Christ with respect of persons (James ii. 1) : therefore this universality is to be regarded. Hearing of your faith and love to all the saints (Eph. i. 15), to the mean as well as the greatest. Meanness doth not take away church relations (1 Cor. xi. 20). There are many differences in worldly respects between one Christian and another ; yea, in spiritual gifts, some weaker, some stronger ; but we must love all ; for all are children

of one Father, all owned by Christ : " He is not ashamed to call them brethren " (Heb. ii. 11).

This, I say, is observable, the disparity of the persons : on the one side, David, on the other, all the people of God.—*Thomas Manton.*

Verse 63.—"*I am a companion,*" etc. : as if he would say, This is a sign to me that I belong to thy family ; because "*I am the companion of all those fearing thee* " with a filial fear, and keeping "*thy precepts.*"—*Paulus Palanterius.*

Verse 63.—"*A companion,*" properly is such an one as I do choose to walk and converse with ordinarily in a way of friendship ; so that company keeping doth imply three things ; first, it is a matter of choice, and therefore relations, as such, are not properly said to be our companions ; secondly, it implies a constant walking and converse with another, and so it is expressed, Job xxxiv. 8 ; Prov. xiii. 20. And, thirdly, this ordinary converse or walking with another, must be in a way of friendship.—*William Bridge,* 1600—1670.

Verse 63.—Shun the company that shuns God, and keep the company that God keeps. Look on the society of the carnal or profane as infectious, but reckon serious, praying persons the excellent ones of the earth. Such will serve to quicken you when dead, and warm you when cold. Make the liveliest of God's people your greatest intimates, and see that their love and likeness to Christ be the great motive of your love to them, more than their love or likeness to you.—*John Willison,* 1680—1750.

Verse 64.—"*The earth, O* LORD, *is full of thy mercy.*" The humble and devoted servant of God does not look with a jaundiced eye upon that scene through which he is passing to his eternal home. Amidst many sorrows and privations, the necessary fruits of sin, he beholds all nature and providence shining forth in the rich expression of God's paternal benignity and mercy to the children of men.—*John Morison.*

Verse 64.—"*The earth, O* LORD, *is full of thy mercy.*" The molten sea, the shew-bread, the sweet incense, the smoke of the sacrifices, Aaron's breastplate, the preaching of the cross, the keys of the kingdom of heaven : do not all these proclaim mercy ? Who could enter a sanctuary, search conscience, look up to heaven, pray or sacrifice, call upon God, or think of the tree of life in the midst of the paradise of God, if there were no mercy ? Do not all visions, covenants, promises, messages, mysteries, legal purifications, evangelical pacifications, confirm this ? Yes, mercy is in the air which we breathe, the daily light which shines upon us, the gracious rain of God's inheritance ; it is the public spring for all the thirsty, the common hospital for all the needy ; all the streets of the church are paved with these stones. What would become of the children if there were not these breasts of consolation ? How should the bride, the Lamb's wife, be trimmed, if her bridegroom did not deck her with these habiliments ? How should Eden appear like the Garden of God, if it were not watered by these rivers ? It is mercy that takes us out of the womb, feeds us in the days of our pilgrimage, furnishes us with spiritual provisions, closes our eyes in peace, and translates us to a secure resting-place. It is the first petitioner's suit, and the first believer's article, the contemplation of Enoch, the confidence of Abraham, the burden of the Prophetic Songs, the glory of all the apostles, the plea of the penitent, the ecstacies of the reconciled, the believer's hosannah, the angel's hallelujah. Ordinances, oracles, altars, pulpits, the gates of the grave, and the gates of heaven, do all depend upon mercy. It is the load-star of the wandering, the ransom of the captive, the antidote of the tempted, the prophet of the living, and the effectual comfort of the dying :—there would not be one regenerate saint upon earth, nor one glorified saint in heaven, if it were not for mercy.—*From G. S. Bowes's "Illustrative Gatherings,"* 1869.

Verse 64.—"*The earth, O* LORD, *is full of thy mercy.*"

> " Why bursts such melody from tree and bush,
>   The overflowing of each songster's heart,
> So filling mine that it can scarcely hush
>   Awhile to listen, but would take its part ?
> 'Tis but one song I hear where'er I rove,
> Though countless be the notes, that God is Love.

" Why leaps the streamlet down the mountain-side ?
　　Hasting so swiftly to the vale beneath,
To cheer the shepherd's thirsty flock, or glide
　　Where the hot sun has left a faded wreath,
Or, rippling, aid the music of a grove ?
Its own glad voice replies, that God is **Love**

" Is it a fallen world on which I gaze ?
　　Am I as deeply fallen as the rest,
Yet joys partaking, past my utmost **praise,**
　　Instead of wandering forlorn, unblest ?
It is as if an unseen spirit strove
To grave upon my heart, that God is Love ! "

Thomas Davis, 1864.

EXPOSITION OF VERSES 65 TO 72.

THOU hast dealt well with thy servant, O LORD, according unto thy
　　word.

66 Teach me good judgment and knowledge : for I have believed thy
commandments.

67 Before I was afflicted I went astray : but now have I kept thy word.

68 Thou *art* good, and doest good ; teach me thy statutes.

69 The proud have forged a lie against me : *but* I will keep thy precepts
with *my* whole heart.

70 Their heart is as fat as grease ; *but* I delight in thy law.

71 *It is* good for me that I have been afflicted ; that I might learn thy
statutes.

72 The law of thy mouth *is* better unto me than thousands of gold and
silver.

In this ninth section the verses all begin with the letter Teth. They are the
witness of experience, testifying to the goodness of God, the graciousness of his
dealings, and the preciousness of his word. Especially the Psalmist proclaims the
excellent uses of adversity, and the goodness of God in afflicting him. The sixty-fifth
verse is the text of the entire octave.

65. "*Thou hast dealt well with thy servant, O LORD, according unto thy word.*"
This is the summary of his life, and assuredly it is the sum of ours. The Psalmist
tells the Lord the verdict of his heart ; he cannot be silent, he must speak his gratitude
in the presence of Jehovah, his God. From the universal goodness of God in nature,
in verse 64, it is an easy and pleasant step to a confession of the Lord's uniform
goodness to ourselves personally. It is something that God has *dealt* at all with
such insignificant and undeserving beings as we are, and it is far more that he has
dealt *well* with us, and so well, so wondrously well. He hath done all things well :
the rule has no exception. In providence and in grace, in giving prosperity and
sending adversity, in everything Jehovah hath dealt well with us. It is dealing
well on our part to tell the Lord that we feel that he hath dealt well with us ; for
praise of this kind is specially fitting and comely. This kindness of the Lord is,
however, no chance matter : he promised to do so, and he has done it according to
his word. It is very precious to see the word of the Lord fulfilled in our happy
experience ; it endears the Scripture to us, and makes us love the Lord of the Scripture. The book of providence tallies with the book of promise : what we read in
the page of inspiration we meet with again in the leaves of our life-story. We may
not have thought that it would be so, but our unbelief is repented of now that we
see the mercy of the Lord to us, and his faithfulness to his word ; henceforth we are
bound to display a firmer faith both in God and in his promise. He has spoken
well, and he has dealt well. He is the best of Masters ; for it is to a very unworthy
and incapable *servant* that he has acted thus blessedly : does not this cause us to
delight in his service more and more ? We cannot say that we have dealt well with
our Master ; for when we have done all, we are unprofitable servants ; but as for
our Lord, he has given us light work, large maintenance, loving encouragement, and
liberal wages. It is a wonder that he has not long ago discharged us, or at least
reduced our allowances, or handled us roughly ; yet we have had no hard dealings,
all has been ordered with as much consideration as if we had rendered perfect

obedience. We have had bread enough and to spare, our livery has been duly supplied, and his service has ennobled us and made us happy as kings. Complaints we have none. We lose ourselves in adoring thanksgiving, and find ourselves again in careful thanks-living.

66. *"Teach me good judgment and knowledge."* Again he begs for teaching, as in verse 64, and again he uses God's mercy as an argument. Since God had dealt well with him, he is encouraged to pray for judgment to appreciate the Lord's goodness. Good judgment is the form of goodness which the godly man most needs and most desires, and it is one which the Lord is most ready to bestow. David felt that he had frequently failed in judgment in the matter of the Lord's dealings with him : from want of knowledge he had misjudged the chastening hand of the heavenly Father, and therefore he now asks to be better instructed, since he perceives the injustice which he had done to the Lord by his hasty conclusions. He means to say—Lord, thou didst deal well with me when I thought thee hard and stern, be pleased to give me more wit, that I may not a second time think so ill of my Lord. A sight of our errors and a sense of our ignorance should make us teachable. We are not able to judge, for our knowledge is so sadly inaccurate and imperfect ; if the Lord teaches us knowledge we shall attain to good judgment, but not otherwise. The Holy Ghost alone can fill us with light, and set the understanding upon a proper balance : let us ardently long for his teachings, since it is most desirable that we should be no longer mere children in knowledge and understanding.

"For I have believed thy commandments." His heart was right, and therefore he hoped his head would be made right. He had faith, and therefore he hoped to receive wisdom. His mind had been settled in the conviction that the precepts of the word were from the Lord, and were therefore just, wise, kind, and profitable ; he believed in holiness, and as that belief is no mean work of grace upon the soul, he looked for yet further operations of divine grace. He who believes the commands is the man to know and understand the doctrines and the promises. If in looking back upon our mistakes and ignorances we can yet see that we heartily loved the precepts of the divine will, we have good reason to hope that we are Christ's disciples, and that he will teach us and make us men of good judgment and sound knowledge. A man who has learned discernment by experience, and has thus become a man of sound judgment, is a valuable member of a church, and the means of much edification to others. Let all who would be greatly useful offer the prayer of this verse : " Teach me good judgment and knowledge."

67. *"Before I was afflicted I went astray."* Partly, perhaps, through the absence of trial. Often our trials act as a thorn hedge to keep us in the good pasture, but our prosperity is a gap through which we go astray. If any of us remember a time in which we had no trouble, we also probably recollect that then grace was low, and temptation was strong. It may be that some believer cries, " O that it were with me as in those summer days before I was afflicted." Such a sigh is most unwise, and arises from a carnal love of ease : the spiritual man who prizes growth in grace will bless God that those dangerous days are over, and that if the weather be more stormy it is also more healthy. It is well when the mind is open and candid, as in this instance : perhaps David would never have known and confessed his own strayings if he had not smarted under the rod. Let us join in his humble acknowledgments, for doubtless we have imitated him in his strayings. Why is it that a little ease works in us so much disease ? Can we never rest without rusting ? Never be filled without waxing fat ? Never rise as to one world without going down as to another ? What weak creatures we are to be unable to bear a little pleasure ! What base hearts are those which turn the abundance of God's goodness into an occasion for sin.

"But now have I kept thy word." Grace is in that heart which profits by its chastening. It is of no use to plough barren soil. When there is no spiritual life affliction works no spiritual benefit ; but where the heart is sound trouble awakens conscience, wandering is confessed, the soul becomes again obedient to the command, and continues to be so. Whipping will not turn a rebel into a child ; but to the true child a touch of the rod is a sure corrective. In the Psalmist's case the medicine of affliction worked a change—*"but"* ; an immediate change—*"now"*; a lasting change—*"have I"* ; an inward change—*"have I kept"* ; a change Godward—*"thy word."* Before his trouble he wandered, but after it he kept within the hedge of the word, and found good pasture for his soul : the trial tethered him to his proper place ; it kept him, and then he kept God's word. Sweet are the uses of adversity,

and this is one of them, it puts a bridle upon transgression and furnishes a spur for holiness.

68. *"Thou art good, and doest good."* Even in affliction God is good, and does good. This is the confession of experience. God is essential goodness in himself, and in every attribute of his nature he is good in the fullest sense of the term ; indeed, he has a monopoly of goodness, for there is none good but one, that is God. His acts are according to his nature : from a pure source flow pure streams. God is not latent and inactive goodness ; he displays himself by his doings, he is actively beneficent, he does good. How much good he does no tongue can tell ! How good he is no heart can conceive ! It is well to worship the Lord as the poet here does by describing him. Facts about God are the best praise of God. All the glory we can give to God is to reflect his own glory upon himself. We can say no more good of God than God is and does. We believe in his goodness, and so honour him by our faith ; we admire that goodness, and so glorify him by our love ; we declare that goodness, and so magnify him by our testimony.

"Teach me thy statutes." The same prayer as before, backed with the same argument. He prays, " Lord be good, and do good to me that I may both be good and do good through thy teaching." The man of God was a learner, and delighted to learn : he ascribed this to the goodness of the Lord, and hoped that for the same reason he would be allowed to remain in the school and learn on till he could perfectly practise every lesson. His chosen class-book was the royal statutes, he wanted no other. He knew the sad result of breaking those statutes, and by a painful experience he had been led back to the way of righteousness ; and therefore he begged as the greatest possible instance of the divine goodness that he might be taught a perfect knowledge of the law, and a complete conformity to it. He who mourns that he has not kept the word longs to be taught it, and he who rejoices that by grace he has been taught to keep it is not less anxious for the like instruction to be continued to him.

In verse 12, which is the fourth verse of Beth, we have much the same sense as in this fourth verse of Teth.

69. *"The proud have forged a lie against me."* They first derided him (51), then defrauded him (61), and now they have defamed him. To injure his character they resorted to falsehood, for they could find nothing against him if they spoke the truth. They forged a lie as a blacksmith beats out a weapon of iron, or they counterfeited the truth as men forge false coin. The original may suggest a common expression—" They have patched up a lie against me." They were not too proud to lie. Pride is a liar, and when a proud man utters lies " he speaketh of his own." Proud men are usually the bitterest opponents of the righteous : they are envious of their good fame and are eager to ruin it. Slander is a cheap and handy weapon if the object is the destruction of a gracious reputation ; and when many proud ones conspire to concoct, exaggerate, and spread abroad a malicious falsehood, they generally succeed in wounding their victim, and it is no fault of theirs if they do not kill him outright. O the venom which lies under the tongue of a liar ! Many a happy life has been embittered by it, and many a good repute has been poisoned as with the deadliest drug. It is painful to the last degree to hear unscrupulous men hammering away at the devil's anvil forging a new calumny ; the only help against it is the sweet promise, " No weapon that is formed against thee shall prosper, and every tongue that riseth against thee in judgment thou shalt condemn."

"But I will keep thy precepts with my whole heart." My one anxiety shall be to mind my own business and stick to the commandments of the Lord. If the mud which is thrown at us does not blind our eyes or bruise our integrity it will do us little harm. If we keep the precepts, the precepts will keep us in the day of contumely and slander. David renews his resolve—*"I will keep"* ; he takes a new look at the commands, and sees them to be really the Lord's—*"thy precepts " ;* and he arouses his entire nature to the work—*"with my whole heart."* When slanders drive us to more resolute and careful obedience they work our lasting good ; falsehood hurled against us may be made to promote our fidelity to the truth, and the malice of men may increase our love to God. If we try to answer lies by our words we may be beaten in the battle ; but a holy life is an unanswerable refutation of all calumnies. Spite is balked if we persevere in holiness despite all opposition.

70. *"Their heart is as fat as grease."* They delight in fatness, but I delight in thee. Their hearts, through sensual indulgence, have grown insensible, coarse, and grovelling ; but thou hast saved me from such a fate through thy chastening hand

Proud men grow fat through carnal luxuries, and this makes them prouder still. They riot in their prosperity, and fill their hearts therewith till they become insensible, effeminate, and self-indulgent. A greasy heart is something horrible; it is a fatness which makes a man fatuous, a fatty degeneration of the heart which leads to feebleness and death. The fat in such men is killing the life in them. Dryden wrote—

> " O souls ! In whom no heavenly fire is found,
> Fat minds and ever grovelling on the ground."

In this condition men have no heart except for luxury, their very being seems to swim and stew in the fat of cookery and banqueting. Living on the fat of the land, their nature is subdued to that which they have fed upon ; the muscle of their nature has gone to softness and grease.

"But I delight in thy law." How much better is it to joy in the law of the Lord than to joy in sensual indulgences ! This makes the heart healthy, and keeps the mind lowly. No one who loves holiness has the slightest cause to envy the prosperity of the worldling. Delight in the law elevates and ennobles, while carnal pleasure clogs the intellect and degrades the affections. There is and always ought to be a vivid contrast between the believer and the sensualist, and that contrast is as much seen in the affections of the heart as in the actions of the life : *their* heart is as fat as grease, and our heart is delighted with the law of the Lord. Our delights are a better test of our character than anything else : as a man's heart is, so is the man. David oiled the wheels of life with his delight in God's law, and not with the fat of sensuality. He had his relishes and dainties, his festivals and delights, and all these he found in doing the will of the Lord his God. When law becomes delight, obedience is bliss. Holiness in the heart causes the soul to eat the fat of the land. To have the law for our delight will breed in our hearts the very opposite of the effects of pride ; deadness, sensuality, and obstinacy will be cured, and we shall become teachable, sensitive, and spiritual. How careful should we be to live under the influence of the divine law that we fall not under the law of sin and death.

71. *"It is good for me that I have been afflicted."* Even though the affliction came from bad men, it was overruled for good ends ; though it was bad as it came from them it was good for David. It benefited him in many ways, and he knew it. Whatever he may have thought while under the trial, he perceived himself to be the better for it when it was over. It was not good to the proud to be prosperous, for their hearts grew sensual and insensible ; but affliction was good for the Psalmist. Our worst is better for us than the sinner's best. It is bad for sinners to rejoice, and good for saints to sorrow. A thousand benefits have come to us through our pains and griefs, and among the rest is this—that we have thus been schooled in the law. *"That I might learn thy statutes."* These we have come to know and to keep by feeling the smart of the rod. We prayed the Lord to teach us (66), and now we see how he has already been doing it. Truly he has dealt well with us, for he has dealt wisely with us. We have been kept from the ignorance of the greasy-hearted by our trials, and this, if there were nothing else, is just cause for constant gratitude. To be larded by prosperity is not good for the proud ; but for the truth to be learned by adversity is good for the humble. Very little is to be learned without affliction. If we would be scholars we must be sufferers. As the Latins say, *Experientia docet*, experience teaches. There is no royal road to learning the royal statutes ; God's commands are best read by eyes wet with tears.

72. *"The law of thy mouth."* A sweetly expressive name for the word of God. It comes from God's own mouth with freshness and power to our souls. Things written are as dried herbs ; but speech has a liveliness and dew about it. We do well to look upon the word of the Lord as though it were newly spoken into our ear ; for in very truth it is not decayed by years, but is as forcible and sure as though newly uttered. Precepts are prized when it is seen that they come forth from the lips of our Father who is in heaven. The same lips which spoke us into existence have spoken the law by which we are to govern that existence. Whence could a law so sweetly proceed as from the mouth of our covenant God ? Well may we prize beyond all price that which comes from such a source.

"Is better unto me than thousands of gold and silver." If a poor man had said this, the world's witlings would have hinted that the grapes are sour, and that men who have no wealth are the first to despise it ; but this is the verdict of a man who owned his thousands, and could judge by actual experience of the value of

money and the value of truth. He speaks of great riches, he heaps it up by thousands, he mentions the varieties of its forms,—" gold and silver " ; and then he sets the word of God before it all, as better *to him*, even if others did not think it better to them. Wealth is good in some respects, but obedience is better in all respects. It is well to keep the treasures of this life ; but far more commendable to keep the law of the Lord. The law is better than gold and silver, for these may be stolen from us, but not the word ; these take to themselves wings, but the word of God remains ; these are useless in the hour of death, but then it is that the promise is most dear. Instructed Christians recognize the value of the Lord's word, and warmly express it, not only in their testimony to their fellow-men, but in their devotions to God. It is a sure sign of a heart which has learned God's statutes when it prizes them above all earthly possessions ; and it is an equally certain mark of grace when the precepts of Scripture are as precious as its promises. The Lord cause us thus to prize the law of his mouth.

See how this portion of the Psalm is flavoured with goodness. God's dealings are good (65), holy judgment is good (66), affliction is good (67), God is good (68), and here the law is not only good, but better than the best of treasure. Lord, make us good through thy good word. Amen.

NOTES ON VERSES 65 TO 72.

TETH.—In the original each stanza begins with T, and in our own version it is so in all but verses 67 and 70, which can easily be made to do so by reading, " 'Till I was afflicted," and " 'Tis good for me that I have been afflicted."—*C. H. S.*

Verse 65.—"Thou hast dealt well with thy servant, O Lord."

1. The party dealing is God himself : all good is to be referred to God as the author of it.

2. The benefit received is generally expressed, *"Thou hast dealt well."* Some translate it out of the Hebrew, *Bonum fecisti,* thou hast done good with thy servant ; the Septuagint, Χρηστότητα ἐποίησας μετα του δουλου σου, thou hast made goodness to or with thy servant ; out of them, the Vulgate, *Bonitatem fecisti.* Some take this cause generally, " Whatever thou dost for thy servants is good " : they count it so, though it be never so contrary to the interest of the flesh : sickness is good, loss of friends is good ; and so are poverty and loss of goods, to an humble and thankful mind. But surely David speaketh here of some supply and deliverance wherein God had made good some promise to him. The Jewish rabbies understand it of his return to the kingdom ; but most Christian writers understand it of some spiritual benefit ; that good which God had done to him. If anything may be collected from the subsequent verses, it was certainly some spiritual good. The Septuagint repeat χρηστότητα twice in this and the following verse, as if he acknowledged the benefit of that good judgment and knowledge of which there he beggeth an increase. It was in part given him already, and that learned by afflictions, as we see, in the third verse of this portion : " Before I was afflicted, I went astray, but now have I kept thy word." His prayer is—Now, then, go on to increase this work, this goodness which thou hast shown to thy servant.

3. The object, *"thy servant"* : it is an honourable, comfortable style ; David delighted in it. God is a bountiful and a gracious master, ready to do good to his servants, rewarding them with grace here, and crowning that grace with glory hereafter : " He that cometh to God, must believe that he is, and that he is a rewarder of them that diligently seek him " (Heb. xi. 6).—*Thomas Manton.*

Verse 65.—"Thou hast dealt well." If the children of God did but know what was best for them, they would perceive that God did that which was best for them. —*John Mason.*

Verse 65.—"Thou hast dealt well with thy servant." He knew that God's gifts are without repentance, and that he is not weary of well-doing, but will finish the thing he hath begun ; and therefore he pleads past favours. Nothing is more forcible to obtain mercy than to lay God's former mercies before him. Here are two grounds, First. If he dealt well with him when he was not regenerate, how much more will he now ? and Secondly, all the gifts of God shall be perfectly finished, therefore he will go on to deal well with his servant. Here is a difference between faith and an accusing conscience : the accusing conscience is afraid to ask more, because it hath abused the former mercies : but faith, assuring us that all God's benefits are tokens of his love bestowed on us according to his word, is bold to ask for more.—*Richard Greenham.*

Verse 65.—"Thou hast dealt well with thy servant." " No doubt," said the late Rev. J. Brown, of Haddington, Scotland, " I have met with trials as well as others ; yet so kind has God been to me, that I think if he were to give me as many years as I have already lived in the world, I should not desire one single circumstance in my lot changed, except that I wish I had less sin. It might be written on my coffin, ' Here lies one of the cares of Providence, who early wanted both father and mother, and yet never missed them.' "—*Arvine's Anecdotes.*

Verse 65.—"Thou hast dealt well with thy servant, O Lord, according unto thy word." The expression, *"according to thy word,"* is so often repeated in this Psalm, that we are apt to overlook it, or to give it only the general meaning of " because of thy promise." But in reality it implies much more. Had God dealt *"well"* with David according to man's idea ? If so, what mean such expressions as these —" O forsake me not utterly " (ver. 8)—" I am a stranger in the earth " (ver. 19)— " My soul cleaveth unto the dust " (ver. 25)—" My soul melteth for heaviness " (ver. 28)—" Turn away my reproach which I fear " (ver. 39)—" The proud have had me greatly in derision " (ver. 51)—" Horror hath taken hold upon me " (ver. 53) ?

In view of such passages as these, can it be said that God " dealt *well* " with David, according to man's idea ? David's experience was one of very great and very varied trial. There is not a phase of our feelings in sorrow which does not find ample expression in his Psalms. And yet he says, " Thou hast dealt well with thy servant, *according to thy word.*"

How, then, are we to interpret the expression, so often repeated here, in accordance with the facts of David's spiritual life ?

God dealt well with him " according to his word," in the sense of dealing with him *according to what his word explained was the true good*—not delivering him from all trial, but sending him such trial as he specially required. He felt truly that God had dealt *well* with him when he could say (ver. 67), " Before I was afflicted I went astray, but now have I kept thy word." Again (ver. 71), " It is good for me that I have been afflicted, that I might learn thy statutes." Such dealing was hard for flesh and blood to bear, but it was indeed "*well*," in the sense of accomplishing most blessed results.

It was " according to his word " too, in the sense of being *in accordance with his revealed manner of dealing with his people*, who are chastened for their profit.

Again, God had " dealt well " with David *according to his word or covenant;* the present fulfilment (even if in itself bitter) being a sure earnest of his final perfecting of his work, and glorifying himself in the entire fulfilment of his word, in the completed salvation of his servant.

According to thy word, O Lord, thou hast dealt well with thy servant. Thy word is the light and lamp that shows things in their true aspect, and teaches us to know that all things work together for good to thy people ; that thou doest all things well. " Open thou mine eyes, O Lord, that I may see wondrous things out of thy law." What can be more wonderful than such views to our eyes ?

" According to thy word ": not only " because of thy promise," but in such a manner and measure as thy word declares. See how such an understanding of the expression opens out the idea of " Be merciful to me according to thy word " (ver. 58). All the sweet promises and declarations of God's infinite mercy rise before us, and make it a vast request. Again, " Quicken thou me," and " strengthen thou me according to thy word "—*up to the full measure of what thou hast promised and provided for thy people.* See the fulness in this view, of ver. 76, " Let, I pray thee, thy merciful kindness be for my comfort, *according to thy word.*" Again, ver. 169, " Give me understanding *according to thy word*"; ver. 170, " Deliver me *according to thy word.*" In each of these we are to feel that the request includes the thought of all that the word teaches on the subject.

Let our prayer then for mercy, and strength, and comfort, and understanding, and deliverance, ever be a prayer for these, in the full measure in which they are revealed and promised in the word of God.—*Mary B. M. Duncan* (1835—1865) *in "Under the Shadow."*

Verse 66.—"*Teach me good judgment,*" etc. David, who discovered a holy taste (Ps. xix. 10; civ. 34; cxix. 103); and recommended it to others (xxxiv. 8), requests in our text to have it increased. For the word rendered "*judgment,*" properly signifies *taste*, and denotes that relish for divine truth, and for the divine goodness and holiness, which is peculiar to true saints. I propose therefore to consider the nature and objects of that spiritual taste which is possessed by every gracious soul, and which all true saints desire to possess in a still greater degree.

The original word, which is often applied to those objects of sense which are distinguished by the palate, is here used in a metaphorical sense, as the corresponding term frequently is in our own language. " Doth not the ear try words, and the mouth taste meat ? " (Job xii. 11). Our translators in this place render it, "*judgment,*" which is nearly the same thing ; yet as the terms are applied among us, there is a difference between them. Taste is that which enables a man to form a more compendious judgment. Judgment is slower in its operations than taste ; it forms its decisions in a more circuitous way. So we apply the term *taste* to many objects of mental decision, to the beauty of a poem, to excellence of style, to elegance of dress or of deportment, to painting, to music, etc., in which a good taste will lead those who possess it, to decide speedily, and yet accurately, on the beauty, excellence, and propriety of the objects with which it has long been conversant without laborious examination.

Just so, true saints have a power of receiving pleasure from the beauty of holiness, which shines forth resplendently in the word of God, in the divine character, in the law, in the gospel, in the cross of Christ, in the example of Christ, and in the conduct of all his true followers, so far as they are conformed to his lovely image. I do not mean by this that they are influenced by a blind instinct, for which they can assign no sufficient reason : the genuine feelings of a true Christian can all of them be justified by the soundest reason : but those feelings which were first produced by renewing grace, are so strengthened by daily communion with God, and by frequent contemplation of spiritual things, that they acquire a delicacy and readiness of perception, which no one can possess who has never tasted how gracious the Lord is. You cannot touch, as it were, a certain string, but the renewed heart must needs answer to it. Whatever truly tends to exalt God, to bring the soul near to him, and to insure his being glorified and enjoyed, will naturally attract the notice, excite the affections and influence the conduct of one who is born of God. " Sweeter also than honey, and the honeycomb." " My meditation of thee shall be sweet." " How sweet are thy words to my taste ! sweeter than honey to my mouth." " O taste and see that the Lord is good."—*John Ryland,* 1753—1825.

Verse 66.—"*Teach me good judgment and knowledge,*" etc. Literally it may be rendered thus,—Teach me goodness, discernment and knowledge ; for I have believed or confided in thy commandments. In our system of divine things, we might be inclined to place knowledge and discernment first, as begetting the " goodness." But it is a well ascertained fact, that the intellectual and moral powers are reciprocal—that the moral also give strength to the intellectual. Moreover, it is only the spiritual man that discerns the things of God. The state of being spiritually minded, and also conversant with divine things, gives a vigour and breadth to the intellect itself, that remarkably appears in the lives of eminent men. And if you remark that some have been eminent who were devoid of spiritual qualities, the reply might be—How much more eminent would they have been had they possessed these qualities. The petition is, "*Teach me goodness, discernment and knowledge.*" The principle of pleasing God may be within, and yet the mind may require to be enlightened in all duty ; and again, though all duty be known, we may require spiritual discernment to see and feel it aright.—*John Stephen.*

Verse 66.—"*Teach me good judgment.*" In a lecture of Sir John Lubbock's [on the fertilization of flowers by the agency of insects], a striking distinction is noted in regard to this operation between beautiful and hideous plants. Bees, it would appear, delight in pleasant odours and bright colours, and invariably choose those plants which give pleasure to man. If we watch the course of these insects on their visit to a garden, we shall observe them settling upon the rose, the lavender, and all other similar agreeable flowers of brilliant hues or sweet scent. In marked contrast with this is the conduct of flies, which always show a preference for livid yellow or dingy red plants, and those which possess an unpleasant smell. The bee is a creature of fine and sensitive tastes. The fly is " a species of insectoid vulture," naturally turning to such vegetable food as resembles carrion. Let two plates be placed on a lawn, at a little distance apart, the one containing that ill-scented under-ground fungus, the Stink-horn, and the other a handful of moss roses, and this difference will be immediately discerned. The foul-odoured and unsightly fungus will soon be covered with flies, while the bees will resort to the plate of roses. To this love of bees for fine colours and fragrant perfumes we are indebted for our choicest flowers. For by taking the pollen dust of some conspicuous flower to the stigma of another, they have by this union produced the seed of a still richer variety. Thus, age after age, many blossoms have been growing increasingly beautiful. On the other hand, strange to say, through a similar process, a progress in the opposite direction has taken place in those plants which are frequented by flies, and their unwholesome and repulsive qualities have become intensified.

So is it with the two great classes into which mankind may be divided—the men of this world, and the men of the next. While the purified affections of the one centre continually on " whatsoever things are honest, whatsoever things are just, whatsoever things are pure, whatsoever things are lovely, whatsoever things are of good report," so the earthward and vile affections of the other fasten on corruption. Not more surely does the laborious bee fly from one beautiful flower to another, than does the Christian seek of set purpose all that is fairest, sweetest, and best on earth. His prayer is that of David, in Psalm cxix. 66, "*Teach me good taste* " (which is the literal translation) ; and " if there be any virtue, and if there be any praise," he thinks on these things.—*James Neil, in "Rays from the Realms of Nature,"* 1879.

Verse 66.—"Good judgment and knowledge." No blessings are more suitable than *"good judgment and knowledge"*—*"knowledge"* of ourselves, of our Saviour, of the way of obedience—and *"good judgment"* to direct and apply this knowledge to some valuable end. These two parts of our intellectual furniture have a most important connexion and dependence upon each other. *"Knowledge"* is the speculative perception of general truth. *"Judgment"* is the practical application of it to the heart and conduct.—*Charles Bridges.*

Verse 66.—"For I have believed thy commandments." These words deserve a little consideration, because believing is here joined to an unusual object. Had it been, " for I have believed thy promises," or, " obeyed thy commandments," the sense of the clause had been more obvious to every vulgar apprehension. To believe commandments, sounds as harsh to a common ear, as to see with the ear, and hear with the eye ; but, for all this, the commandments are the object ; and of them he saith, not, " I have obeyed "; but, *"I have believed."*

To take off the seeming asperity of the phrase, some interpreters conceive that *"commandments"* is put for the word in general ; and so promises are included, yea, they think, principally intended, especially those promises which encouraged him to look to God for necessary things, such as good judgment and knowledge are. But this interpretation would divert us from the weight and force of these significant words. Therefore let us note,—

1. Certainly there is a faith in the commandments, as well as in the promises. We must believe that God is their author, and that they are the expressions of his commanding and legislative will, which we are bound to obey. Faith must discern the sovereignty and goodness of the law-maker and believe that his commands are holy, just and good ; it must also teach us that God loves those who keep his law and is angry with those who transgress, and that he will see to it that his law is vindicated at the last great day.

2. Faith in the commandments is as necessary as faith in the promises ; for, as the promises are not esteemed, embraced, and improved, unless they are believed to be of God, so neither are the precepts ; they do not sway the conscience, nor incline the affections, except as they are believed to be divine.

3. Faith in the commands must be as lively as faith in the promises. As the promises are not believed with a lively faith, unless they draw off the heart from carnal vanities to seek that happiness which they offer to us ; so the precepts are not believed rightly, unless we be fully resolved to acquiesce in them as the only rule to guide us in obtaining that happiness, and unless we are determined to adhere to them, and obey them. As the king's laws are not kept as soon as they are believed to be the king's laws, unless also, upon the consideration of his authority and power, we subject ourselves to them ; so this believing noteth a ready alacrity to hear God's voice and obey it, and to govern our hearts and actions according to his counsel and direction in the word.—*Thomas Manton.*

Verse 66.—"For I have believed thy commandments." The commandments of God are not alone ; but they have promises of grace on the right hand, and threatenings of wrath on the left : upon both of these faith exercises itself, and without such faith no one will be able to render obedience to God's commands.— *Wolfgang Musculus.*

Verse 67.—"Before I was afflicted I went astray," etc. Not that he wilfully, wickedly, maliciously, and through contempt, departed from his God ; this he denies (Ps. xviii. 21) ; but through the weakness of the flesh, the prevalence of corruption, and the force of temptation, and very much through a careless, heedless, and negligent frame of spirit, he got out of the right way, and wandered from it before he was well aware. The word is used of erring through ignorance (Lev. v. 18). This was in his time of prosperity, when, though he might not, like Jeshurun, wax fat and kick, and forsake and lightly esteem the Rock of his salvation ; or fall into temptations and hurtful lusts, and err from the faith, and be pierced with many sorrows ; yet he might become inattentive to the duties of religion, and be negligent of them, which is a common case.—*John Gill.*

Verse 67.—"Before I was afflicted." The Septuagint and Latin Vulgate, " Before I was humbled." The Hebrew word has the general sense of being afflicted, and may refer to any kind of trial.—*Albert Barnes.*

Verse 67.—*"Before I was afflicted."* Prosperity is a more refined and severe test of character than adversity, as one hour of summer sunshine produces geater corruption than the longest winter day.—*Eliza Cook.*

Verse 67.—*"I was afflicted."* God in wisdom deals with us as some great person would do with a disobedient son, that forsakes his house, and riots among his tenants. His father gives orders that they should treat him ill, affront, and chase him from them, and all, that he might bring him back. The same doth God : man is his wild and debauched son ; he flies from the commands of his father, and cannot endure to live under his strict and severe government. He resorts to the pleasures of the world, and revels and riots among the creatures. But God resolves to recover him, and therefore commands every creature to handle him roughly. " Burn him, fire ; toss him, tempests, and shipwreck his estate ; forsake him, friends ; designs, fail him ; children, be rebellious to him, as he is to me ; let his supports and dependencies sink under him, his riches melt away, leave him poor, and despised, and destitute." These are all God's servants, and must obey his will. And to what end is all this, but that, seeing himself forsaken of all, he may at length, like the beggared prodigal, return to his father ?—*Ezekiel Hopkins,* 1633—1690.

Verse 67.—*"I was afflicted."* As men clip the feathers of fowls, when they begin to fly too high or too far ; even so doth God diminish our riches, etc., that we should not pass our bounds, and glory too much of such gifts.—*Otho Wermullerus.*

Verse 67.—*"But now have I kept thy word."*

Affliction brings Man Home.

" Man like a silly sheep doth often stray,
  Not knowing of his way,
Blind deserts and the wilderness of sin
  He daily travels in ;
There's nothing will reduce him sooner than
  Afflictions to his pen.
He wanders in the sunshine, but in rain
  And stormy weather hastens home again.

" Thou, the great Shepherd of my soul, O keep
  Me, thy unworthy sheep
From gadding : or if fair means will not do it,
  Let foul, then, bring me to it.
Rather then I should perish in my error,
  Lord bring me back with terror ;
Better I be chastizèd with thy rod
  And Shepherd's staff, than stray from thee, my God.

" Though for the present stripes do grieve me sore,
  At last they profit more,
And make me to observe thy word, which I
  Neglected formerly ;
Let me come home rather by weeping cross
  Then still be at a loss.
For health I'd rather take a bitter pill,
  Then eating sweet-meats to be always ill."

Thomas Washbourne, 1606—1687.

Verse 67.—From the countless throng before the throne of God and the Lamb, we may yet hear the words of the Psalmist, *"Before I was afflicted I went astray : but now I have kept thy word."* There is many an one who will say, " Behold, happy is the man whom God correcteth " (Job v. 17). One would tell you that his worldly undoing was the making of his heavenly prospects ; and another that the loss of all things was the gain of All in All. There are multitudes whom God has afflicted with natural blindness that they might gain spiritual sight ; and those who under bodily infirmities and diseases of divers sorts have pined and wasted away this earthly life, gladly laying hold on glory, honour, and immortality instead.—*William Garrett Lewis,* in *"Westbourne Grove Sermons,"* 1872.

Verse 67.—By affliction God separates the sin which he hates from the soul which he loves.—*John Mason.*

Verse 68.—*"Thou art good, and doest good."* There is a good God set before us, that we may not take up with any low pattern of goodness. He is represented to us as all goodness. He is good in his nature ; and his work is agreeable to his nature ; nothing is wanting to it, or defective in it. Nothing can be added to it to make it better. Philo saith, "'O ὄντως ὢν το πρῶτον αγαθόν " : the first being must needs be the first good. As soon as we conceive that there is a God, we presently conceive that he is good, He is good of himself, good in himself, goodness itself, and both the fountain and the pattern of all the good that is in the creatures.

1. As to his NATURE, he is originally "good," good in himself, and good to others ; as the sun hath light in himself, and giveth light to all other things. Essentially good ; not only good, but goodness itself. Goodness in us is an accessory quality or superadded gift ; but in God it is not a quality, but his essence. In a vessel that is gilded with gold the gilding or lustre is a superadded quality ; but in a vessel all of gold, the lustre and the substance is the same. God is infinitely good ; the creatures' good is limited, but there is nothing to limit the perfection of God, or give it any measure. He is an ocean of goodness without banks or bottom. Alas ! what is our drop to this ocean ! God is immutably good ; his goodness can never be more or less than it is ; as there can be no addition to it, so no subtraction from it. Man in his innocency was *peccabilis*, or liable to sin, afterwards *peccator*, or an actual sinner ; but God ever was and is good. Now this is the pattern propounded to us, but his nature is a great deep. Therefore—

2. As to his WORK, "*he doeth good.*" What hath God been acting upon the great theatre of the world but goodness for these six thousand years ? Acts xiv. 17, " Nevertheless he left not himself without witness, in that he did good, and gave us rain from heaven, and fruitful seasons, filling our hearts with food and gladness." He left not himself without a witness, ἀγαθοποιῶν, not by taking vengeance of their idolatries, but by distributing benefits. This is propounded to our imitation, that our whole life may be nothing else but doing good : Matt. v. 48, " Be ye therefore perfect, even as your Father which is in heaven is perfect." Well, therefore, doth the Psalmist say, "*Teach me thy statutes.*"—*Thomas Manton.*

Verse 68.—"*Thou art good, and doest good.*" We should bless the Lord at all times, and keep up good thoughts of God on every occasion, especially in the time of affliction. Hence we are commanded to glorify God in the fires (Isai. xxiv. 15) ; and this the three children did in the hottest furnace. . . . . I grant, indeed, we cannot give thanks for affliction as affliction, but either as it is the means of some good to us, or as the gracious hand of God is some way remarkable therein toward us. In this respect there is no condition on this side of hell but we have reason to praise God in it, though it be the greatest of calamities. Hence it was that David, when he speaks of his affliction, adds presently, "*Thou art good, and doest good* " ; and he declares (ver. 65), "*Thou hast dealt well with thy servant, O LORD, according unto thy word.*" Hence Paul and Silas praised God when they were scourged and imprisoned. —*John Willison, 1680—1750.*

Verse 68.—"*Thou art good.*" The blessed effects of chastisement, as a special instance of the Lord's goodness, might naturally lead to an acknowledgment of his general goodness, in his own character, and in his unwearied dispensations of love. Judging in unbelieving haste of his providential and gracious dealings, feeble sense imagines a frown, when the eye of faith discerns a smile upon his face ; and therefore in proportion as faith is exercised in the review of the past, and the experience of the present, we shall be prepared with the ascription of praise—"*Thou art good.*"—*Charles Bridges.*

Verse 69.—"*The proud have forged a lie against me.*" If in the present day the enemies of the truth in their lying writings rail against the orthodox teachers in the Church, that is a very old artifice of the Devil, since David complains that in his day it happened unto him.—*Solomon Gesner.*

Verse 69.—"*The proud have forged a lie.*" They trim up lies with shadows of truth and neat language ; they have mints to frame their lies curiously in, and presses to print their lies withal.—*William Greenhill, 1591—1677.*

Verse 69.—"*The proud.*" Faith humbleth, and infidelity maketh proud. Faith humbleth, because it letteth us see our sins, and the punishments thereof, and that we have no dealing with God but through the mediation of Christ ; and that we can do no good, nor avoid evil, but by grace. But when men know not this, then they think much of themselves, and therefore are proud. Therefore all ignorant men, all heretics, and worldlings are proud. They that are humbled under God's hands, are humble to men ; but they that despise God do also persecute his servants. —*Richard Greenham.*

Verse 69.—*"Forged a lie."* Vatablus translates it, *concinnarunt mendacia.* So Tremellius : *they have trimmed up lies.* As Satan can transform himself into an angel of light, so he can trim up his lies under coverings of truth, to make them the more plausible unto men. And indeed this is no small temptation, when lies made against the godly are trimmed up with the shadows of truth, and wicked men cover their unrighteous dealings with appearances of righteousness. Thus, not only are the godly unjustly persecuted, but simple ones are made to believe that they have most justly deserved it. In this case the godly are to sustain themselves by the testimony of a good conscience.—*William Cowper.*

Verse 69.—*"Forged"* expresses the essential meaning of the Hebrew word, but not its figurative form, which seems to be that of sewing, analogous to that of weaving, as applied to the same thing, both in Hebrew and in other languages. We may also compare our figurative phrase, *to patch up,* which, however, is not so much suggestive of artifice or skill as of the want of it. The connection of the clauses is, that all the craft and malice of his enemies should only lead him to obey God with a more undivided heart than ever.—*Joseph Addison Alexander.*

Verse 69.—*"Forged."* The metaphor may be like the Greek (ῥάπτειν δόλους), from sewing or patching up : or, from *smearing,* or *daubing* (Delitzsch, Moll, etc.), a wall, so as to hide the real substance. The Psalmist remains true to God despite the faslehoods with which the proud smear and hide his true fidelity.—*The Speaker's Commentary.*

Verse 69.—*"A lie."*—Satan's two arms by which he wrestles against the godly are violence and lies : where he cannot or dare not, use violence, there be sure he will not fail to fight with lies. And herein doth the Lord greatly show his careful providence, in fencing his children against Satan's malice and the proud brags of his instruments, in such sort, that their proudest hearts are forced to forge lies ; their malice being so great that they must do evil ; and yet their power so bridled that they cannot do what they would.—*William Cowper.*

Verse 69.—*"I will keep thy precepts with my whole heart."* Let the word of the Lord come, let it come ; and if we had six hundred necks, we would submit them all to its dictates.—*Augustine.*

Verse 70.—*"Their heart is as fat as grease."* The word טפש occurs nowhere else in Scripture, but with the Chaldees טפש signifies *to fatten, to make fat ;* also *to make stupid and doltish,* because such the fat ofttimes are . . . . For this reason the proud, who are mentioned in the preceding verse, are described by their fixed resolve in evil, because they are almost insensible ; as is to be seen in pigs, who pricked through the skin with a bodkin, and that slowly, as long as the bodkin only touches the fat, do not feel the prick until it reaches to the flesh. Thus the proud, whose great prosperity is elsewhere likened to fatness, have a heart totally insusceptible, which is insensible to the severe reproofs of the Divine word, and also to its holy delights and pleasures, by reason of the affluence of carnal things ; aye, more, is altogether unfitted for good impulses ; just as elsewhere is to be seen with fat animals, how slow they are and unfit for work, when, on the contrary, those are agile and quick which are not hindered by this same fatness.—*Martin Geier.*

Verse 70.—*"Their heart is as fat as grease."* This makes them—1. *Senseless* and secure ; they are past feeling : thus the phrase is used (Isa. vi. 10) : " Make the heart of the people fat." They are not sensible of the teaching of the word of God, or his rod. 2. *Sensual* and voluptuous : " Their eyes stand out with fatness " (Psa. lxxiii. 7) : they roll themselves in the pleasures of sense, and take up with them as their chief good ; and much good may it do them : I would not change conditions with them ; *"I delight in thy law."*—*Matthew Henry.*

Verse 70.—*"Their heart is as fat as grease ; but I delight in thy law ; "* as if he should say, My heart is a lean heart, a hungry heart, my soul loveth and rejoiceth in thy word. I have nothing else to fill it but thy word, and the comforts I have from it ; but their hearts are fat hearts ; fat with the world, fat with lust ; they hate the word. As a full stomach loatheth meat and cannot digest it ; so wicked men hate the word, it will not go down with them, it will not gratify their lusts.—*William Fenner.*

Being anxious to know the medical significance of fatty heart, I applied to an eminent gentleman who is well known as having been President of the College of Physicians. His reply shows that the language is rather figurative than literal. He kindly replied to me as follows :—

There are two forms of so-called " fatty heart." In the one there is an excessive amount of fatty tissue covering the exterior of the organ, especially about the base. This may be observed in all cases where the body of the animal is throughout over fat, as in animals fattened for slaughter. It does not necessarily interfere with the action of the heart, and may not be of much importance in a medical point of view. The second form is, however, a much more serious condition. In this, the muscular structure of the heart, on which its all-important function, as the central propelling power, depends, undergoes a degenerative change, by which the contractile fibres of the muscles are converted into a structure having none of the properties of the natural fibres, and in which are found a number of fatty, oily globules, which can be readily seen by means of the microscope. This condition, if at all extensive, renders the action of the heart feeble and irregular, and is very perilous, not infrequently causing sudden death. It is found in connection with a general unhealthy condition of system, and is evidence of general mal-nutrition. It is brought about by an indolent, luxurious mode of living, or, at all events, by neglect of bodily exercise and those hygienic rules which are essential for healthy nutrition. It cannot, however, be said to be incompatible with mental vigour, and certainly is not necessarily associated with stupidity. But the heart, in this form of disease, is literally " greasy," and may be truly described as " fat as grease." So much for physiology and pathology. May I venture on the sacred territory of biblical exegesis without risking the charge of fatuousness ? Is not the Psalmist contrasting those who lead an animal, self-indulgent, vicious life, by which body and mind are incapacitated for their proper uses, and those who can *run* in the way of God's commandments, *delight* to do his will, and *meditate* on his precepts ? Sloth, fatness, and stupidity, *versus* activity, firm muscles, and mental vigour. Body *versus* mind. Man become as a beast *versus* man retaining the image of God.—*Sir James Risdon Bennett*, 1881.

Verse 71.—"*It is good for me*," etc. I am mended by my sickness, enriched by my poverty, and strengthened by my weakness, and with S. Bernard desire, *Irascaris mihi Domine*, O Lord, be angry with me. For if thou chidest me not, thou considerest me not ; if I taste no bitterness, I have no physic ; if thou correct me not, I am not thy son. Thus was it with the great-grandchild of David, Manasseh, when he was in affliction, " He besought the Lord his God " : even that king's iron was more precious to him than his gold, his jail a more happy lodging than his palace, Babylon a better school than Jerusalem. What fools are we, then, to frown upon our afflictions ! These, how crabbed soever, are our best friends. They are not indeed for our pleasure, they are for our profit ; their issue makes them worthy of a welcome. What do we care how bitter that potion be that brings health.—*Abraham Wright.*

Verse 71.—"*It is good for me that I have been afflicted.*" Saints are great gainers by affliction, because " godliness," which is " great gain," which is " profitable for all things," is more powerful than before. The rod of correction, by a miracle of grace, like that of Aaron's, buds and blossoms, and brings forth the fruits of righteousness, which are most excellent. A rare sight it is indeed to see a man coming out of a bed of languishing, or any other furnace of affliction, more like to angels in purity, more like to Christ who was holy, harmless, undefiled, and separate from sinners ; more like unto God himself, being more exactly righteous in all his ways, and more exemplarily holy in all manner of conversation.—*Nathanael Vincent,*—1697.

Verse 71.—"*It is good for me that I have been afflicted.*" If I have no cross to bear to-day, I shall not advance heavenwards. A cross (that is anything that disturbs our peace), is the spur which stimulates, and without which we should most likely remain stationary, blinded with empty vanities, and sinking deeper into sin. A cross helps us onwards, in spite of our apathy and resistance. To lie quietly on a bed of down, may seem a very sweet existence ; but pleasant ease and rest are not the lot of a Christian : if he would mount higher and higher, it must be by a rough road. Alas ! for those who have no daily cross ! Alas ! for those who repine and fret against it !—*From "Gold Dust,"* 1880.

Verse 71.—"*It is good for me,*" etc. There are some things good but not pleasant, as *sorrow* and *affliction.* Sin is pleasant, but unprofitable ; and sorrow is profitable, but unpleasant. As waters are purest when they are in motion, so saints are generally holiest when in affliction. Some Christians resemble those children who will learn their books no longer than while the rod is on their backs. It is well known that by the greatest affliction the Lord has sealed the sweetest instruction. Many are not bettered by the judgments they see, when they are by the judgments they have felt. The purest gold is the most pliable. That is the best blade which bends well without retaining its crooked figure.—*William Secker*, 1660.

Verse 71.—*"It is good for me,"* etc. Piety hath a wondrous virtue to change all things into matter of consolation and joy. No condition in effect can be evil or sad to a pious man : his very sorrows are pleasant, his infirmities are wholesome, his wants enrich him, his disgraces adorn him, his burdens ease him ; his duties are privileges, his falls are the grounds of advancement, his very sins (as breeding contrition, humility, circumspection, and vigilance), do better and profit him : whereas impiety doth spoil every condition, doth corrupt and embase all good things, doth embitter all the conveniences and comforts of life.—*Isaac Barrow*, 1630—1677.

Verse 71.—*"It is good for me that I have been afflicted."* In Miss E. J. Whately's very interesting Life of her Father, the celebrated Archbishop of Dublin, a fact is recorded, as told by Dr. Whately, with reference to the introduction of the larch-tree into England. When the plants were first brought, the gardener, hearing that they came from the south of Europe, and taking it for granted that they would require warmth,—forgetting that they might grow near the snow-line,—put them into a hot-house. Day by day they withered, until the gardener in disgust threw them on a dung-heap outside; there they began to revive and bud, and at last grew into trees. They needed the cold.

The great Husbandman often saves his plants by throwing them out into the cold. The nipping frosts of trial and affliction are ofttimes needed, if God's larches are to grow. It is under such discipline that new thoughts and feelings appear. The heart becomes more dead to the world and self. From the night of sorrow rises the morning of joy. Winter is the harbinger of spring. From the crucifixion of the old man comes the resurrection of the new, as in nature life is the child of death

> " The night is the mother of the day,
> And winter of the spring ;
> And ever upon old decay,
> The greenest mosses spring."

James Wareing Bardsley in "Illustrated Texts and Texts Illustrated," 1876.

Verse 71.—*"It is good for me that I have been afflicted."* It is a remarkable circumstance that the most brilliant colours of plants are to be seen on the highest mountains, in spots that are most exposed to the wildest weather. The brightest lichens and mosses, the loveliest gems of wild flowers, abound far up on the bleak, storm-scalped peak. One of the richest displays of organic colouring I ever beheld was near the summit of Mount Chenebettaz, a hill about 10,000 feet high, immediately above the great St. Bernard Hospice. The whole face of an extensive rock was covered with a most vivid yellow lichen, which shone in the sunshine like the golden battlement of an enchanted castle. There, in that lofty region, amid the most frowning desolation, exposed to the fiercest tempest of the sky, this lichen exhibited a glory of colour such as it never showed in the sheltered valley. I have two specimens of the same lichen before me while I write these lines, one from the great St. Bernard, and the other from the wall of a Scottish castle, deeply embosomed among sycamore trees ; and the difference in point of form and colouring between them is most striking. The specimen nurtured amid the wild storms of the mountain peak is a lovely primrose hue, and is smooth in texture and complete in outline ; while the specimen nurtured amid the soft airs and the delicate showers of the lowland valley is of a dim rusty hue, and is scurfy in texture, and broken in outline. And is it not so with the Christian who is afflicted, tempest-tossed, and not comforted ? Till the storms and vicissitudes of God's providence beat upon him again and again, his character appears marred and clouded by selfish and worldly influences. But trials clear away the obscurity, perfect the outlines of his disposition, and give brightness and blessings to his piety.

> " Amidst my list of blessings infinite
> Stands this the foremost, that my heart has bled ;
> For *all* I bless thee, *most* for the *severe*."

                                                                    —*Hugh Macmillan.*

Verse 71.—*"That I might learn thy statutes."* He speaks not of that learning which is gotten by hearing or reading of God's word ; but of the learning which he had gotten by experience ; that he had felt the truth and comfort of God's word more effectual and lively in trouble than he could do without trouble ; which also made him more godly, wise, and religious when the trouble was gone.—*William Cowper.*

Verse 71.—*"That I might learn."* " I had never known," said Martin Luther's wife, " what such and such things meant, in such and such Psalms, such complaints and workings of spirit ; I had never understood the practice of Christian duties, had not God brought me under some affliction." It is very true that God's rod is as the schoolmaster's pointer to the child, pointing out the letter, that he may the better take notice of it ; thus he pointeth out to us many good lessons which we should never otherwise have learned.—*From John Spencer's "Things New and Old,"* 1658.

Verse 71.—*"That I might learn."* As prosperity blindeth the eyes of men, even so doth adversity open them. Like as the salve that remedieth the disease of the eyes doth first bite and grieve the eyes, and maketh them to water, but yet afterward the eyesight is clearer than it was ; even so trouble doth vex men wonderfully at the first, but afterwards it lighteneth the eyes of the mind, that it is afterward more reasonable, wise and circumspect. For trouble bringeth experience, and experience bringeth wisdom.—*Otho Wermullerus,* 1551.

Verse 71.—*"Learn thy statutes."* The Christian has reason to thank God that things have not been accommodated to his wishes. When the mist of tears was in his eyes, he looked into the word of God and saw magnificent things. When Jonah came up from the depths of ocean, he showed that he had learned the statutes of God. One could not go too deep to get such knowledge as he obtained. Nothing now could hinder him from going to Nineveh. It is just the same as though he had brought up from the deep an army of twelve legions of the most formidable troops. The word of God, grasped by faith, was all this to him, and more. He still, however, needed further affliction ; for there were some statutes not yet learned. Some gourds were to wither. He was to descend into a further vale of humiliation. Even the profoundest affliction does not, perhaps, teach us everything ; a mistake we sometimes make. But why should we compel God to use harsh measures with us ? Why not sit at the feet of Jesus and learn quietly what we need to learn ?—*George Bowen, in "Daily Meditations,"* 1873.

Verse 71.—*"Statutes."* The verb from which this word is formed means to engrave or inscribe. The word means a definite, prescribed, written law. The term is applied to Joseph's law about the portion of the priests in Egypt, to the law about the passover, etc. But in this Psalm it has a more internal meaning ; that moral law of God which is engraven on the fleshy tables of the heart ; the inmost and spiritual apprehension of his will ; not so obvious as the law and the testimonies, and a matter of more direct spiritual communication than his precepts ; the latter being more elaborated by the efforts of the mind itself, divinely guided indeed, but perhaps more instrumentally, and less passively, employed. They are continually spoken of as things yet to be learned, either wholly or in part, not objectively apprehended already, like God's law . . . . They are learned, not suddenly, but by experience, and through the means of trials mercifully ordained by God ; lessons therefore which are deeply engraven on the heart. " Good is it for me that I have been in trouble, that I might learn thy statutes." " I have more understanding than my teachers, because thy statutes I have observed."—*John Jebb.*

Verse 72.—*"The law of thy mouth is better unto me,"* etc. Highly prize the Scriptures. Can he make a proficiency in any art, who doth slight and deprecate it ? Prize this book above all other books. St. Gregory calls the Bible " the heart and soul of God." The rabbins say, that a mountain of sense hangs upon every apex and tittle of Scripture. " The law of the Lord is perfect " : Ps. xix. 7. The Scripture is the library of the Holy Ghost ; it is a pandect of divine knowledge, an exact model and platform of religion. The Scripture contains in it the *credenda,* " the things which we are to believe," and the *agenda,* " the things which we are to practise." It is " able to make us wise unto salvation " : 2 Tim. iii. 15. The Scripture is the standard of truth, the judge of controversies ; it is the pole-star to direct us to heaven : Isai. viii. 20. " The commandment is a lamp " : Prov. vi. 23.   The Scripture is the compass by which the rudder of our will is to be steered ; it is the field in which Christ, the Pearl of price, is hid ; it is a rock of diamonds ; it is a sacred collyrium, or eye-salve ; it mends their eyes that look upon it ; it is a spiritual optic-glass in which the glory of God is resplendent ; it is the panacy, or universal medicine for the soul.   The leaves of Scripture are like the " leaves of the tree of life, for the healing of the nations " : Rev. xxii. 2. The Scripture is both the breeder and feeder of grace.   How is the convert born, but by " the word of truth " ?   James i. 18.   How doth he grow, but by " the sincere milk of the word " ?   1 Pet. ii. 2.   The word written is the book out of which our evidences for heaven are fetched ; it is the sea-mark which shows us the rocks of sin to avoid ; it is the antidote against error and apostasy, the two-edged sword which wounds the old serpent.   It is our bulwark to withstand the force of lust ; like the Capitol of Rome, which was a place of strength and ammunition.   The Scripture is the " tower of David," wherein the shields of our faith hang : Cant. iv. 4.   " Take away the word and you deprive us of the sun," said Luther.   The word written is above an angelic embassy, or voice from heaven.   " This voice which came from heaven we heard.   .   .   .   We have also a more sure word " : 2 Pet. i. 18, 19.   O, prize the word written ; prizing is the way to profiting.   If Cæsar so valued his commentaries, that for preserving them he lost his purple robe, how should we estimate the sacred oracles of God ?   " I have esteemed the words of his mouth more than my necessary food."—*Thomas Watson, in "The Morning Exercises."*

Verse 72.—"*The law of thy mouth is better unto me.*"   The sacred Scriptures are the treasures and pleasures of a gracious soul : to David they were better than thousands of gold and silver.   A mountain of transparent pearls, heaped as high as heaven, is not so rich in treasure as these ; hence that good man chose these as his heritage for ever, and rejoiced in them as in all riches.   A covetous miser could not take such delight in his bags, nor a young heir in a large inheritance, as holy David did in God's word.

The word *law* comes from a root that signifies to try as merchants that search and prove the wares that they buy and lay up ; hence also comes the word for gems and jewels that are tried, and found right.   The sound Christian is the wise merchant, seeking goodly pearls ; he tries what he reads or hears by the standard or touchstone of Scripture, and having found genuine truths he lays them up to the great enriching of this supreme and sovereign faculty of the understanding.— *Oliver Heywood.*

Verse 72.—The word of God must be nearer to us than our friends, dearer to us than our lives, sweeter to us than our liberty, and pleasanter to us than all earthly comforts.—*John Mason.*

Verse 72.—One lesson, taught by sanctified affliction, is, the love of *God's word.* " This is my *comfort,* in my affliction : thy word hath quickened me."   In reading a part of the one hundred and nineteenth Psalm to Miss Westbrook, who died, she said, " Stop, sir, I never said so much to you before—I never could ; but now I *can* say, ' The word of thy mouth is dearer to me, than *thousands* of gold and silver.' What can gold and silver do for me *now* ? "—*George Redford, in "Memoirs of the late Rev. John Cooke, 1828."*

Verse 72.—"*Thousands of gold and silver.*"   Worldly riches are gotten with labour, kept with care, lost with grief.   They are false friends, farthest from us when we have most need of comfort ; as all worldlings shall find to be true in the hour of death.   For then, as Jonah's gourd was taken from him in a morning, when he had most need of it against the sun ; so is it with the comfort of worldlings.   It is far otherwise with the word of God ; for if we will lay it up in our hearts, as Mary did, the comfort thereof shall sustain us, when all other comfort shall fail us.

This it is that makes us rich unto God, when our souls are storehouses, filled with the treasures of his word.   Shall we think it poverty to be scant of gold and silver ?   *An ideo angelus pauper est, quia non habet jumenta,* etc.*   Shall we esteem the angels poor, because they have not flocks of cattle ?   or that S. Peter was poor, because he had not gold nor silver to give unto the cripple ?   No, he had store of grace, by infinite degrees more excellent than it.

Let the riches of gold be left unto worldlings : these are not current in Canaan, not accounted of in our heavenly country.   If we would be in any estimation

---

*Chrysostom.

there, let us enrich our souls with spiritual graces, which we have in abundance in the mines and treasures of the word of God.—*William Cowper.*

Verse 72.—The Scripture is an ever-overflowing fountain that cannot be drawn dry, and an inexhausted treasure that cannot be emptied. To this purpose tend those resemblances of the law made use of by David in this Psalm, and no less justly applicable to the gospel ; it is not only better than *"gold and silver,"* which are things of value, but *"thousands,"* which implieth abundance. In another verse he compares it to all riches and great spoil, both which contain in them *multiplex genus,* all sorts of valuable commodities, sheep, oxen, lands, houses, garments, goods, moneys, and the like : thus are all sorts of spiritual riches, yea, abundance of each sort, to be had in the gospel. And therefore the Greek fathers compare Scripture verities to precious stones, and our Saviour to a pearl of great price. A minister, in this respect, is called a merchant of invaluable jewels ; for, indeed, gospel truths are choice and excellent, as much worth as our souls, as heaven, as salvation is. Nay, should I go higher, look what worth there is in the riches of God's grace, the precious blood of Christ, that may secondarily be applied to the gospel, which discovereth and offereth both to us.—*Abraham Wright.*

Verses 72, 127.—When David saw how some make void the law of God, he saith, *"Therefore I love thy commandments above gold : yea, above fine gold."* As if he had said, I love thy law all the more because I see some men esteem and reckon it as if it were dross, and throw it up as void and antiquated, or taking the boldness, as it were, to repeal and make it void, that they may set up their own lusts and vain imaginations. Because I see both profane and superstitious men thus out of love with thy law, therefore my love is more enflamed to it, *"I love it above gold,"* which leads the most of men away captives in the love of it ; and I esteem it more than that which is most esteemed by men, and gains men most esteem in this world, *"fine gold" ;* yea, as he said (Ps. xix. 10) *"more than much fine gold."*—*Joseph Caryl.*

Verse 72.—You that are gentlemen, remember what Hierom reports of Nepotianus, a young gentleman of Rome, *qui longa et assidua meditatione Scripturarum pectus suum fecerat bibliothecam Christi,* who by long and assiduous meditation of the Scriptures, made his breast the library of Christ. Remember what is said of King Alfonsus, that he read over the Bible fourteen times, together with such commentaries as those times afforded.

You that are scholars, remember Cranmer and Ridley ; the former learned the New Testament by heart in his journey to Rome, the latter in Pembroke-hall walks in Cambridge. Remember what is said of Thomas-à-Kempis,—that he found rest nowhere *nisi in angulo, cum libello,* but in a corner with this Book in his hand. And what is said of Beza,—that when he was above fourscore years old he could say perfectly by heart any Greek chapter in Paul's Epistles.

You that are women, consider what Hierom saith of Paula, Eustochiam, and other ladies, who were singularly versed in the Holy Scriptures.

Let all men consider that hyperbolical speech of Luther, that he would not live in Paradise without the Word ; and with it he could live well enough in hell. This speech of Luther must be understood *cum grano salis.*—*Edmund Calamy.*

EXPOSITION OF VERSES 73 TO 80.

THY hands have made me and fashioned me : give me understanding, that I may learn thy commandments.

74 They that fear thee will be glad when they see me ; because I have hoped in thy word.

75 I know, O LORD, that thy judgments *are* right, and *that* thou in faithfulness hast afflicted me.

76 Let, I pray thee, thy merciful kindness be for my comfort, according to thy word unto thy servant.

77 Let thy tender mercies come unto me, that I may live : for thy law *is* my delight.

78 Let the proud be ashamed ; for they dealt perversely with me without a cause : *but* I will meditate in thy precepts.

79 Let those that fear thee turn unto me, and those that have known thy testimonies.

80 Let my heart be sound in thy statutes ; that I be not ashamed.

We have now come to the tenth portion, which in each stanza begins with Jod, but it certainly does not treat of jots and titles and other trifles. Its subject would seem to be personal experience and its attractive influence upon others. The prophet is in deep sorrow, but looks to be delivered and made a blessing. Endeavouring to teach, the Psalmist first seeks to be taught (verse 73), persuades himself that he will be well received (74), and rehearses the testimony which he intends to bear (75). He prays for more experience (76, 77), for the baffling of the proud (78), for the gathering together of the godly to him (79), and for himself again that he may be fully equipped for his witness-bearing and may be sustained in it (80). This is the anxious yet hopeful cry of one who is heavily afflicted by cruel adversaries, and therefore makes his appeal to God as his only friend.

73. *"Thy hands have made me and fashioned me."* It is profitable to remember our creation, it is pleasant to see that the divine hand has had much to do with us, for it never moves apart from the divine thought. It excites reverence, gratitude, and affection towards God when we view him as our Maker, putting forth the careful skill and power of his hands in our forming and fashioning. He took a personal interest in us, making us with his own hands ; he was doubly thoughtful, for he is represented both as making and moulding us. In both giving existence and arranging existence he manifested love and wisdom ; and therefore we find reasons for praise, confidence, and expectation in our being and well-being. *"Give me understanding, that I may learn thy commandments."* As thou hast made me, teach me. Here is the vessel which thou hast fashioned ; Lord, fill it. Thou hast given me both soul and body ; grant me now thy grace that my soul may know thy will, and my body may join in the performance of it. The plea is very forcible ; it is an enlargement of the cry, " Forsake not the work of thine own hands." Without understanding the divine law and rendering obedience to it we are imperfect and useless ; but we may reasonably hope that the great Potter will complete his work and give the finishing touch to it by imparting to it sacred knowledge and holy practice. If God had roughly made us, and had not also elaborately fashioned us, this argument would lose much of its force ; but surely from the delicate art and marvellous skill which the Lord has shown in the formation of the human body, we may infer that he is prepared to take equal pains with the soul till it shall perfectly bear his image.

A man without a mind is an idiot, the mere mockery of a man ; and a mind' without grace is wicked, the sad perversion of a mind. We pray that we may not be left without a spiritual judgment : for this the Psalmist prayed in verse 66, and he here pleads for it again ; there is no true knowing and keeping of the commandments without it. Fools can sin ; but only those who are taught of God can be holy. We often speak of gifted men ; but he has the best gifts to whom God has given a sanctified understanding wherewith to know and prize the ways of the Lord. Note well that David's prayer for understanding is not for the sake of speculative knowledge, and the gratification of his curiosity : he desires an enlightened judgment that he may learn God's commandments, and so become obedient and holy. This is the best of learning. A man may abide in the College where this science is taught all his days, and yet cry out for ability to learn more. The commandment of God is exceeding broad, and so it affords scope for the most vigorous and instructed mind : in fact, no man has by nature an understanding capable of compassing so wide a field, and hence the prayer, "give me under- standing " ;—as much as to say—I can learn other things with the mind I have, but thy law is so pure, so perfect, spiritual and sublime, that I need to have my mind enlarged before I can become proficient in it. He appeals to his maker to do this, as if he felt that no power short of that which made him could make him wise unto holiness. We need a new creation, and who can grant us that but the Creator himself ? He who made us to live must make us to learn ; he who gave us power to stand must give us grace to understand. Let us each one breathe to heaven the prayer of this verse ere we advance a step further, for we shall be lost even in these petitions unless we pray our way through them, and cry to God for understanding.

74. *"They that fear thee will be glad when they see me : because I have hoped in thy word."* When a man of God obtains grace for himself he becomes a blessing to others, especially if that grace has made him a man of sound understanding and holy knowledge. God-fearing men are encouraged when they meet with ex- perienced believers. A hopeful man is a God-send when things are declining or in danger. When the hopes of one believer are fulfilled his companions are cheered and established, and led to hope also. It is good for the eyes to see a man whose witness is that the Lord is true ; it is one of the joys of saints to hold converse with their more advanced brethren. The fear of God is not a left-handed grace, as some have called it ; it is quite consistent with gladness ; for if even the sight of a comrade gladdens the God-fearing, how glad must they be in the presence of the Lord himself ! We do not only meet to share each others' burdens, but to partake in each others' joys, and some men contribute largely to the stock of mutual gladness. Hopeful men bring gladness with them. Despondent spirits spread the infection of depression, and hence few are glad to see them, while those whose hopes are grounded upon God's word carry sunshine in their faces, and are welcomed by their fellows. There are professors whose presence scatters sadness, and the godly quietly steal out of their company : may this never be the case with us.

75. *"I know, O Lord, that thy judgments are right."* He who would learn most must be thankful for what he already knows, and be willing to confess it to the glory of God. The Psalmist had been sorely tried, but he had continued to hope in God under his trial, and now he avows his conviction that he had been justly and wisely chastened. This he not only thought but knew, so that he was positive about it, and spoke without a moment's hesitation. Saints are sure about the rightness of their troubles, even when they cannot see the intent of them. It made the godly glad to hear David say this, *"And that thou in faithfulness hast afflicted me."* Because love required severity, therefore the Lord exercised it. It was not because God was unfaithful that the believer found himself in a sore strait, but for just the opposite reason : it was the faithfulness of God to his covenant which brought the chosen one under the rod. It might not be needful that others should be tried just then ; but it was necessary to the Psalmist, and therefore the Lord did not withhold the blessing. Our heavenly Father is no Eli : he will not suffer his children to sin without rebuke, his love is too intense for that. The man who makes the confession of this verse is already progressing in the school of grace, and is learning the commandments. This third verse of the section corresponds to the third of Teth (67), and in a degree to several other verses which make the thirds in their octaves.

76. *"Let, I pray thee, thy merciful kindness be for my comfort, according to thy word unto thy servant."* Having confessed the righteousness of the Lord, he now appeals to his mercy, and while he does not ask that the rod may be removed, he earnestly begs for comfort under it. Righteousness and faithfulness afford us no consolation if we cannot also taste of mercy, and, blessed be God, this is promised us in the word, and therefore we may expect it. The words " merciful kindness," are a happy combination, and express exactly what we need in affliction : mercy to forgive the sin, and kindness to sustain under the sorrow. With these we can

be comfortable in the cloudy and dark day, and without them we are wretched indeed ; for these, therefore, let us pray unto the Lord, whom we have grieved by our sin, and let us plead the word of his grace as our sole reason for expecting his favour. Blessed be his name, notwithstanding our faults we are still his servants, and we serve a compassionate Master. Some read the last clause, " according to thy saying unto thy servant " ; some special saying of the Lord was remembered and pleaded : can we not remember some such " faithful saying," and make it the groundwork of our petitioning ? That phrase, " according to thy word," is a very favourite one ; it shows the motive for mercy and the manner of mercy. Our prayers are according to the mind of God when they are according to the word of God.

77. *"Let thy tender mercies come unto me, that I may live."* He was so hard pressed that he was at death's door if God did not succour him. He needed not only mercy, but " mercies," and these must be of a very gracious and considerate kind, even " tender mercies," for he was sore with his wounds. These gentle favours must be of the Lord's giving, for nothing less would suffice ; and they must " come " all the way to the sufferer's heart, for he was not able to journey after them ; all he could do was to sigh out, " Oh that they would come." If deliverance did not soon come, he felt ready to expire, and yet he told us but a verse or so ago that he hoped in God's word : how true it is that hope lives on when death seems written on all besides. A heathen said, " dum spiro spero," while I breathe I hope; but the Christian can say, " dum expiro spero," even when I expire I still expect the blessing. Yet no true child of God can live without the tender mercy of the Lord ; it is death to him to be under God's displeasure. Notice, again, the happy combination of the words of our English version. Was there ever a sweeter sound than this— " tender mercies " ? He who has been grievously afflicted, and yet tenderly succoured is the only man who knows the meaning of such choice language.

How truly we live when tender mercy comes to us. Then we do not merely exist, but live ; we are lively, full of life, vivacious, and vigorous. We know not what life is till we know God. Some are said to die by the visitation of God, but we live by it.

"For thy law is my delight." O blessed faith ! He is no mean believer who rejoices in the law even when its broken precepts cause him to suffer. To delight in the word when it rebukes us, is proof that we are profiting under it. Surely this is a plea which will prevail with God, however bitter our griefs may be ; if we still delight in the law of the Lord he cannot let us die, he must and will cast a tender look upon us and comfort our hearts.

78. *"Let the proud be ashamed."* He begged that the judgments of God might no longer fall upon himself, but upon his cruel adversaries. God will not suffer those who hope in his word to be put to shame, for he reserves that reward for haughty spirits : they shall yet be overtaken with confusion, and become the subjects of contempt, while God's afflicted ones shall again lift up their heads. Shame is for the proud, for it is a shameful thing to be proud. Shame is not for the holy, for there is nothing in holiness to be ashamed of.

"For they dealt perversely with me without a cause." Their malice was wanton, he had not provoked them. Falsehood was employed to forge an accusation against him ; they had to bend his actions out of their true shape before they could assail his character. Evidently the Psalmist keenly felt the malice of his foes. His consciousness of innocence with regard to them created a burning sense of injustice, and he appealed to the righteous Lord to take his part and clothe his false accusers with shame. Probably he mentioned them as " the proud," because he knew that the Lord always takes vengeance on proud men, and vindicates the cause of those whom they oppress. Sometimes he mentions the proud, and sometimes the wicked, but he always means the same persons ; the words are interchangeable : he who is proud is sure to be wicked, and proud persecutors are the worst of wicked men.

"But I will meditate in thy precepts." He would leave the proud in God's hands, and give himself up to holy studies and contemplations. To obey the divine precepts we have need to know them, and think much of them, hence this persecuted saint felt that meditation must be his chief employment. He would study the law of God and not the law of retaliation. The proud are not worth a thought. The worst injury they can do us is to take us away from our devotions ; let us baffle them by keeping all the closer to our God when they are most malicious in their onslaughts.

In a similar position to this we have met with the proud in other octaves, and shall meet them yet again. They are evidently a great plague to the Psalmist but he rises above them.

79. *"Let those that fear thee turn unto me, and those that have known thy testimonies."* Perhaps the tongue of slander had alienated some of the godly, and probably the actual faults of David had grieved many more. He begs God to turn to him, and then to turn his people towards him. Those who are right with God are also anxious to be right with his children. David craved the love and sympathy of gracious men of all grades,—of those who were beginners in grace, and of those who were mature in piety—" those that fear thee," and " those that have known thy testimonies." We cannot afford to lose the love of the least of the saints, and if we have lost their esteem we may most properly pray to have it restored. David was the leader of the godly party in the nation, and it wounded him to the heart when he perceived that those who feared God were not as glad to see him as aforetime they had been. He did not bluster and say that if they could do without *him* he could very well do without *them ;* but he so deeply felt the value of their sympathy, that he made it a matter of prayer that the Lord would turn their hearts to him again. Those who are dear to God, and are instructed in his word, should be very precious in our eyes, and we should do our utmost to be upon good terms with them.

David has two descriptions for the saints, they are God-fearing and God-knowing. They possess both devotion and instruction ; they have both the spirit and the science of true religion. We know some believers who are gracious, but not intelligent ; and, on the other hand, we also know certain professors who have all head and no heart : he is the man who combines devotion with intelligence. We neither care for devout dunces nor for intellectual icebergs. When fearing and knowing walk hand in hand they cause men to be thoroughly furnished unto every good work. If these are my choice companions I may hope that I am one of their order. Let such persons ever turn to me because they find in me congenial company.

80. *"Let my heart be sound in thy statutes ; that I be not ashamed."* This is even more important than to be held in esteem by good men. This is the root of the matter. If the heart be sound in obedience to God, all is well, or will be well. If right at heart we are right in the main. If we be not sound before God, our name for piety is an empty sound. Mere profession will fail, and undeserved esteem will disappear like a bubble when it bursts ; only sincerity and truth will endure in the evil day. He who is right at heart has no reason for shame, and he never shall have any ; hypocrites ought to be ashamed now, and they shall one day be put to shame without end ; their hearts are rotten, and their names shall rot. This eightieth verse is a variation of the prayer of the seventy-third verse ; there he sought sound understanding, here he goes deeper, and begs for a sound heart. Those who have learned their own frailty by sad experience, are led to dive beneath the surface, and cry to the Lord for truth in the inward parts. In closing the consideration of these eight verses, let us join with the writer in the prayer, " Let my heart be sound in thy statutes."

NOTES ON VERSES 73 TO 80.

In this section each verse begins with the Hebrew letter *Jod*, or **i**, the smallest letter in the Hebrew alphabet, called in Matthew v. 18, *jot;* one jot or tittle shall in no wise pass from the law.—*Albert Barnes.*

Verses 73—80.—The usual account of this section, as given by the mediæval theologians, is that it is the prayer of man to be restored to his state of original innocence and wisdom by being conformed to the image of Christ.   And this squares with the obvious meaning, which is partly a petition for divine grace and partly an assertion that the example of piety and resignation in trouble is attractive enough to draw men's hearts on towards God, a truth set forth at once by the Passion, and by the lives of all those saints who have tried to follow it.—*Neale and Littledale.*

Verse 73.—*"Thy hands have made me and fashioned me,"* etc.   This verse hath a petition for understanding and a reason with it :   I am the workmanship of thine hands, therefore give me understanding.   There is no man but favours the works of his hands.   And shall not the Lord much more love his creatures, especially man, his most excellent creature ?   whom, if ye consider according to the fashion of his body, ye shall find nothing on earth more precious than he ;   but in that which is not seen, namely, his soul, he is much more beautiful.   So you see, David's reasoning is very effectual ;   all one as if he should say as he doth elsewhere, " Forsake not, O Lord, the work of thine hands" ;   thou art my author and maker ;   thine help I seek, and the help of none other.

No man can rightly seek good things from God, if he consider not what good the Lord hath already done to him.   But many are in this point so ignorant, that they know not how wonderfully God did make them ;   and therefore can neither bless him, nor seek from him, as from their Creator and Conserver.   But this argument, drawn from our first creation, no man can rightly use, but he who is through grace partaker of the second creation ;   for all the privileges of our first creation we have lost by our fall.   So that now by nature it is no comfort to us, nor matter of our hope, that God did make us ;   but rather matter of our fear and distrust, that we have mismade ourselves, have lost his image, and are not now like unto that which God created us in the beginning.—*William Cowper.*

Verse 73.—*"Thy hands have made me and fashioned me,"* etc.   Mark here two things :   first, that in making his prayer for holy understanding, he justly accuseth himself and all others of blindness, which proceeded not from the Creator, but from man corrupted.   Secondly, that even from his creation he conceived hope that God would continue his work begun in him, because God leaveth not his work, and therefore he beggeth God to bestow new grace upon him, and to finish that which he had begun in him.—*Thomas Wilcocks,* 1586.

Verse 73.—Hugo ingeniously notices in the different verbs of this verse the particular vices to be shunned :   ingratitude, when it is said, *"Thy hands have made me"* ;   pride, *"and fashioned me"* ;   confidence in his own judgment, *"give me understanding"* ;   prying inquisitiveness, *"that I may learn thy commandments."*

Verse 73.—*"Thy hands."*   Hilary and Ambrose think that by the plural *"hands"* is intimated that there is a more exact and perfect workmanship in man, and as if it were with greater labour and skill he had been formed by God, because *after the image and likeness of God :*   and that it is not written that any other thing but man was made by God with both hands, for he saith in Isaiah, " Mine hand also hath laid the foundation of the earth " :   Isa. xlviii. 13.*—*John Lorinus,* 1569—1634.

Verse 73.—*"Thy hands."*   Oh, look upon the *wounds* of thine hands, and forget not the *work* of thine hands :   so Queen Elizabeth prayed.—*John Trapp.*

Verse 73.—Some refer the verb עשׂה, " made," to the soul, פּוּכך, *"fashioned,"* to the body.—*D. H. Mollerus.*

Verse 73.—*"Made me and fashioned me : give me understanding."*   The greatness of God is no hindrance to his intercourse with us, for one special part of the divine greatness is to be able to condescend to the littleness of created beings, seeing that

---

* This, however, is an error, as Augustine notes ;   for it is written, " The heavens are the work of thine hands."   Ps. cii. 25.—C. H. S.

creaturehood must, from its very nature, have this littleness; inasmuch as God must ever be God, and man must ever be man : the ocean must ever be the ocean, the drop must ever be the drop. The greatness of God compassing our littlenesses about, as the heavens the earth, and fitting into it on every side, as the air into all parts of the earth, is that which makes the intercourse so complete and blessed : " In his hand is the soul of every living thing, and the breath of all mankind " (Job xii. 10). Such is his nearness to, such is his intimacy with, the works of his hands.

It is nearness, not distance, that the name Creator implies ; and the simple fact of his having *made* us is the assurance of his desire to bless us and to hold intercourse with us. Communication between the thing made and its maker is involved in the very idea of creation. *"Thy hands have made me and fashioned me : give me understanding, that I may learn thy commandments."* " Faithful Creator " is his name (1 Pet. iv. 19), and as such we appeal to him, " Forsake not the work of thine own hands " (Ps. cxxxviii. 8).—*Horatius Bonar, in "The Rent Veil,"* 1875.

Verse 73. — *" Give me understanding,"* etc. The book of God is like the apothecary's shop, there is no wound but therein is a remedy ; but if a stranger come unto the apothecary's shop, though all these things be there, yet he cannot tell where they are, but the apothecary himself knoweth ; so in the Scriptures, there are cures for any infirmities ; there is comfort against any sorrows, and by conferring chapter with chapter, we shall understand them. The Scriptures are not wanting to us, but we to ourselves ; let us be conversant in them, and we shall understand them, when great clerks who are negligent remain in darkness.—*Richard Stock.*

Verse 73.—*"Give me understanding."* Let us pray unto God that he would open our understandings ; that as he hath given us consciences to guide us, so also he would give eyes to these guides that they may be able to direct us aright. The truth is, it is God only that can soundly enlighten our consciences ; and therefore let us pray unto him to do it. All our studying, and hearing, and reading, and conferring will never be able to do it ; it is only in the power of him who made us to do it. He who made our consciences, he only can give them this heavenly light of true knowledge and right understanding ; and therefore let us seek earnestly to him for it.—*William Fenner,* 1600—1640.

Verse 73.—*"That I may learn thy commandments."* That he might *learn* them so as to know the sense and meaning of them, their purity and spirituality ; and so as to do them from a principle of love, in faith, and to the glory of God : for it is not a bare learning of them by heart or committing them to memory, nor a mere theory of them, but the practice of them in faith and love, which is here meant.—*John Gill.*

Verses 73, 74.—From these verses, learn, 1. Albeit nothing can satisfy unbelief, yet true faith will make use of the most common benefit of creation to strengthen itself : *"Thine hands have made me and fashioned me."* 2. It is a good way of reasoning with God, to ask another gift, because we have received one ; and because he hath given common benefits, to ask that he would give us also saving graces : *"Thy hands have made me and fashioned me : give me understanding, that I may learn thy commandments."* 3. Seeing that God is our Creator, and that the end of our creation is to serve God, we may confidently ask whatsoever grace may enable us to serve him, as the Psalmist's example doth teach us. . . . 4. It should be the joy of all believers to see one of their number sustained and borne up in his sufferings ; for in the proof and example of one sufferer a pawn is given to all the rest, that God will help them in like case : *"They that fear thee will be glad when they see me."*—*David Dickson.*

Verse 74.—*"They that fear thee will be glad,"* etc. They who *"fear God"* are naturally *"glad when they see"* and converse with one like themselves ; but more especially so, when it is one whose faith and patience have carried him through troubles, and rendered him victorious over temptations; one who hath *" hoped in God's word,"* and hath not been disappointed. Every such instance affordeth fresh encouragement to all those, who, in the course of their welfare, are to undergo like troubles, and to encounter like temptations. In all our trials let us, therefore, remember, that our brethren, as well as ourselves, are deeply interested in the event, which may either strengthen or weaken the hands of the multitudes.—*George Horne.*

Verse 74.—*"They that fear thee will be glad when they see me,"* etc. How comfortable it is for the heirs of promise to see one another, or meet together : *aspectus boni viri delectat,* the very look of a good man is delightful : it is a pleasure to converse with those that are careful to please God, and fearful to offend him. How much affected they are with one another's mercies : *" they will be glad when they see me,"* since I have obtained an event answerable to my hope.   They shall come and look upon me as a monument and spectacle of the mercy and truth of God.   But what mercy had he received ?   The context seemeth to carry it for grace to obey God's commandments ; that was the prayer immediately preceding, to be instructed and taught in God's law (ver. 73).   Now they will rejoice to see my holy behaviour, how I have profited and glorified God in that behalf.   The Hebrew writers render the reason, " Because then I shall be able to instruct them in those statutes, when they shall see me, their king, study the law of God.'   It may be expounded of any other blessing or benefit God had given according to his hope ; and I rather understand it thus, they will be glad to see him sustained, supported, and borne out in his troubles and sufferings.   " They will be glad when they shall see in me a notable example of the fruit of hoping in thy grace."—*Thomas Manton.*

Verse 74.—*"Because I have hoped in thy word."*   And have not been disappointed. The Vulgate rendereth it *supersp, I* have over-hoped ; and then Aben-Ezra glosseth, *"I have hoped in all thy decree"* ; even that of afflicting me, as in the next verse.—*John Trapp.*

Verse 75.—*"I know, O LORD, that thy judgments are right."*   In very early life the tree of knowledge seemed a very fine, a glorious tree in my sight ; but how many mistakes have I made upon that subject !   And how many are the mistakes which yet abound upon that which we are pleased to call knowledge, in common speech. He that hath read the classics ; he that hath dipped into mathematical science ; he that is versed in history, and grammar, and common elocution ; he that is apt and ready to solve some knotty question, and versed in the ancient lore of learning, is thought to be a man of knowledge ; and so he is, compared with the ignorant mass of mankind.   But what is all this compared with the knowledge in my text ? Knowledge of which few of the learned, as they are called, have the least acquaintance with at all.

"I know "—What, David ? what do you know ?—" I know, O Lord, that thy judgments are right, and that thou in faithfulness hast afflicted me."

Fond as I may yet be of other speculations, I would rather, much rather, possess the knowledge of this man in this text, than have the largest acquaintance with the whole circle of the sciences, as it is proudly called. . . . I am apprehensive that, in the first clause, the Psalmist speaks, in general, of the ordinances, appointments, providences, and judgments of God ; and the assertion is, he doth know that they are right, that they are equitable, that they are wise, that they are fair, and that they are not to be found fault with ; and that though men, through folly, bring themselves into distress, and then their hearts fret against God.   He was blessed with superior understanding.   He excepts nothing : " I know that *all* thy judgments are right."   Then, in the latter part of the text, he makes the matter personal. It might be said, it is an easy thing for you so to think when you see the revolutions of kingdoms, the tottering of thrones, the distresses of some mortals, and the pains of others, that they are all right.   " Yes," saith he, " but I have the same persuasion about all my own sorrows ; I do know that in faithfulness thou hast afflicted *me*."— *From a Sermon by John Martin,* 1817.

Verse 75.—*"I know, O LORD, that thy judgments are right,"* etc.   The text is in the form of an address to God.   We often find this in David, that, when he would express some deep feeling, or some point of spiritual experience, he does so in this way—addressing himself to God.   Those who love God delight to hold communion with him ; and there are some feelings which the spiritual mind finds peculiar comfort and pleasure in telling to God himself.   *"I know, O LORD, that thy judgments are right."*   God orders all things, and his *"judgments"* here mean his general orderings, decisions, dealings—not afflictions only, though including them.   And when the Psalmist says, *"thy judgments,"* he means especially God's judgments towards *him,* God's dealings with him, and thus all that had happened to him, or should happen to him.   For in the Psalmist's creed there was no such thing as chance. God ordered all that befell him, and he loved to think so   He expresses a sure and happy confidence in all that God did, and would do, with regard to him. He trusted fully in God's wisdom, God's power, God's love. "*I know thy judgments are right*"—quite right, right in every way, without one single point that might have been better, perfectly wise and good. He shows the firmest persuasion of this. "*I know*," he says, not merely, "I think." But these very words, "*I know*," clearly show that this was a matter of faith, not of sight. For he does not say, "I can *see* that thy judgments are right," but "*I know*." The meaning plainly is, "Though I cannot see all—though there are some things in thy dealings which I cannot fully understand—yet I believe, I am persuaded, and thus I *know*, O Lord, that thy judgments are right."

"*Thy judgments*." Not some of them, but all. He takes into view all God's dealings with him, and says of them without exception, "*I know, O LORD, that thy judgments are right*." When the things that happen to us are plainly for our comfort and good, as many of them are, then we thankfully receive what God thus sends to us, and own him as the Giver of all, and bless him for his gracious dealing; and this is right. But all the faith required for this (and some faith there is in it) is to own God as dealing with us, instead of thanklessly receiving the gifts with no thought of the Giver. It is a far higher degree of faith, that says of *all* God's dealings, even when seemingly not for our happiness, "*I know that thy judgments are right*."

Yet this is the meaning here, or certainly the chief meaning. For though the word "*judgments*" does mean God's dealings of every kind, yet *here* the words that follow make it apply especially to God's afflictive dealings, that is, to those dealings of his that do not seem to be for our happiness; "*I know, O LORD, that thy judgments are right, and that thou in faithfulness hast afflicted me*." The judgments which the Psalmist chiefly had in view, and which he felt so sure were right, were not joys, but sorrows; not things bestowed, but things taken away; those blessings in disguise, those veiled mercies, those gifts clad in the garb of mourning, which God so often sends to his children. The Psalmist knew, and knew against all appearance to the contrary, that these judgments were "*right*." Whatever they might be—losses, bereavements, disappointments, pain, sickness—they were right; as right as the more manifest blessings which went before them; quite right, perfectly right; so right that they could not have been better; just what were best; and all because they were God's judgments. That one thing satisfied the Psalmist's mind, and set every doubt at rest. The dealings in themselves he might have doubted, but not him whose dealings they were. "*Thy* judgments." That settled all. "*And that thou in faithfulness hast afflicted me*." This means that, in appointing trouble as his lot, God had dealt with him in faithfulness to his word, faithfulness to his purposes of mercy, with a faithful, not a weak love. He had sent him just what was most for his good, though not always what was most pleasing; and in this he had shown himself faithful. Gently and lovingly does the Lord deal with his children. He gives no unnecessary pain; but that which is needful he will not withhold.—*Francis Bourdillon*, 1881.

Verse 75.—"*Thy judgments*." There are *judicia oris*, and there are *judicia operis*; the judgments of God's mouth, and the judgments of God's hands. Of the former there is mention at verse 13: "With my lips have I declared all the judgments of thy mouth." And by these "*judgments*" are meant nothing else but the holy law of God, and his whole written word; which everywhere in this Psalm are indifferently called his "statutes," his "commandments," his "precepts," his "testimonies," his "judgments." And the laws of God are therefore, amongst other reasons, called by the name of "*judgments*," because by them we come to have a right judgment whereby to discern between good and evil. We could not otherwise with any certainty judge what was meet for us to do, and what was needful for us to shun. *A lege tua intellexi*, at verse 104: "By the law have I gotten understanding." St. Paul confesseth (Rom. vii.), that he had never rightly known what sin was if it had not been for the law; and he instanceth in that of lust, *which he had not known to be a sin if the law* had not said, "thou shalt not covet." And no question but these "*judgments*," these *judicia oris*, are all "*right*" too; for it were unreasonable to think that God should make that a rule of right to us, which were itself not right. We have both the name (that of "*judgments*;") and the thing too, (that they are "*right*") in the 19th Psalm; where having highly commended the law of God, under the several appellations of the "law," testimonies, statutes and commandments, verses 7 and 8, the prophet then concludeth under this name of " judgments," verse 9 : " The judgments of the Lord are true and righteous altogether."

Besides these *judicia oris,* which are God's judgments of *direction,* there are also *judicia operis,* which are his judgments for *correction.* And these do ever include *aliquid pænale,* something inflicted upon us by Almighty God, as it were by way of punishment ; something that breedeth in us trouble or grief. The apostle saith (Heb. xii.) that every chastening is grievous ; and so it is, more or less ; or else it could be to us no punishment. And these, again, are of two sorts ; yet not distinguished so much by the things themselves that are inflicted, as by the condition of the persons on whom they are inflicted, and especially by the affection and intention of God that inflicteth them. For all, whether public calamities that light upon whole nations, cities, or other greater or lesser societies of men (such as are pestilences, famine, war, inundations, unseasonable weather, and the like ;) or private afflictions, that light upon particular families or persons, (as sickness, poverty disgrace, injuries, death of friends, and the like ;) all these, and whatsoever other of either kind, may undergo a twofold consideration ; in either of which they may not unfitly be termed the judgments of God, though in different respects.

Now we see the several sorts of God's judgments : which of all these may we think is here meant ? If we should take them all in, the conclusion would hold them, and hold true too. *Judicia oris,* and *judicia operis ;* public and private judgments ; those plagues wherewith in fury he punisheth his enemies, and those rods wherewith in mercy he correcteth his children : most certain it is they are all " *right.*" But yet I conceive those *judicia oris* not to be so properly meant in this place ; for the exegesis in the latter part of the verse (wherein what are here called *judgments* are there expounded by *troubles*) seemeth to exclude them, and to confine to the text in the proper intent thereof to these *judicia operis* only ; but yet to all them of what sort soever ; public or private, plagues or corrections. Of all which he pronounceth that they are " *right ; *" which is the predicate of the conclusion : "*I know, O Lord, that thy judgments are right.*"—*Robert Sanderson.*

Verse 75.—"*Thou in faithfulness hast afflicted me.*" Mark the emphasis : he doth not barely acknowledge that God was faithful, though notwithstanding he had afflicted him, but faithful in sending the afflictions. Affliction and trouble are not only consistent with God's love plighted in the covenant of grace ; but they are parts and branches of the new-covenant administration. God is not only faithful notwithstanding afflictions, but faithful in sending them. There is a difference between these two : the one is like an exception to the rule, *quæ firmat regulam in non exceptis :* the other makes it a part of the rule, God cannot be faithful without doing all things that tend to our good and eternal welfare. The conduct of his providence is one part of the covenant engagement ; as to pardon our sins, and sanctify us, and give us glory at the last, so to suit his providence as our need and profit require in the way to heaven. It is an act of his sovereign mercy which he hath promised to his people, to use such discipline as conduceth to their safety. In short, the cross is not an exception to the grace of the covenant, but a part of the grace of the covenant.

The cause of all afflictions is sin, therefore justice must be acknowledged : their end is repentance, and therefore faithfulness must be acknowledged. The end is not destruction and ruin, so afflictions would be acts of justice, as upon the wicked ; but that we may be fit to receive the promises, and so they are acts of faithfulness. —*Thomas Manton.*

Verse 75.—"*Thou in faithfulness hast afflicted me.*" That is with a sincere intention of doing me good. God thoroughly knows our constitution, what is noxious to our health, and what may remedy our distempers ; and therefore accordingly disposeth to us

Pro jucundis aptissima quæque *

Instead of pleasant honey, he sometimes prescribes wholesome wormwood for us. We are ourselves greatly ignorant of what is conducible to our real good, and, were the choice of our condition wholly permitted to us, should make very foolish, very disadvantageous elections.

We should (be sure) all of us embrace a rich and plentiful estate ; when, as God knows, that would make us slothful and luxurious, swell us with pride and

---

* Juv. Sat. x. 349.

haughty thoughts, encumber us with anxious cares and expose us to dangerous temptations ; would render us forgetful of ourselves and neglectful of him. Therefore he wisely disposeth poverty unto us ; poverty, the mother of sobriety, the nurse of industry, the mistress of wisdom ; which will make us understand ourselves and our dependence on him, and force us to have recourse unto his help. And is there not reason we should be thankful for the means by which we are delivered from those desperate mischiefs, and obtain these excellent advantages ?

We should all (certainly) choose the favour and applause of man : but this, God also knows, would corrupt our minds with vain conceit, would intoxicate our fancies with spurious pleasure, would tempt us to ascribe immoderately to ourselves, and sacrilegiously to deprive God of his due honour. Therefore he advisedly suffers us to incur the disgrace and displeasure, the hatred and contempt of men ; that so we may place our glory only in the hopes of his favour, and may pursue more earnestly the purer delights of a good conscience. And doth not this part of divine providence highly merit our thanks ?

We would all climb into high places, not considering the precipices on which they stand, nor the vertiginousness of our own brains : but God keeps us safe in the humble valleys, allotting to us employments which we are more capable to manage.

We should perhaps insolently abuse power, were it committed to us : we should employ great parts on unwieldy projects, as many do, to the disturbance of others, and their own ruin : vast knowledge would cause us to overvalue ourselves and contemn others : enjoying continual health, we should not perceive the benefit thereof, nor be mindful of him that gave it. A suitable mediocrity therefore of these things the divine goodness allotteth unto us, that we may neither starve for want, nor surfeit with plenty.

In fine, the advantages arising from afflictions are so many, and so great, that it were easy to demonstrate that we have great reason, not only to be contented with, but to rejoice in, and to be very thankful for, all the crosses and vexations we meet with ; to receive them cheerfully at God's hand, as the medicines of our soul, and the condiments of our fortune ; as the arguments of his goodwill, and the instruments of virtue ; as solid grounds of hope, and comfortable presages of future joy unto us.—*Isaac Barrow.*

Verse 75.—*"Thou in faithfulness hast afflicted me."* When a father disowns and banishes a child, he corrects him no more. So God may let one whom he intends to destroy go unchastened ; but never one with whom he is in covenant.— *William S. Plumer.*

Verse 75.—*"I know, O Lord,"* etc.

> Yet, Lord, in memory's fondest place
>   I shrine those seasons sad,
> When, looking up, I saw thy face
>   In kind austereness clad.
>
> I would not miss one sigh or tear,
>   Heart-pang, or throbbing brow ;
> Sweet was the chastisement severe,
>   And sweet its memory now.
>
> Yes ! let the fragrant scars abide,
>   Love-tokens in thy stead,
> Faint shadows of the spear-pierced side,
>   And thorn-encompassed head.
>
> And such thy tender force be still,
>   When self would swerve or stray,
> Shaping to truth the froward will
>   Along thy narrow way.
>
>   —*John Henry Newman,* 1829.

Verse 76.—*"Let, I pray thee, thy merciful kindness be for my comfort."* In the former verse he acknowledged that the Lord had afflicted him ; now in this he prayeth the Lord to comfort him. This is strange that a man should seek comfort at the same hand that strikes him : it is the work of faith ; nature will never teach us to do it. " Come, and let us return unto the Lord ; for he hath spoiled, and he will heal us : he hath wounded, and he will bind us up." Again, we see that the crosses which God lays on his children, are not to confound, not to consume them ; only to prepare them for greater consolations. With this David sustained himself against Shimei's cursing ; " The Lord will look on my affliction, and do me good for this evil " : with this our Saviour comforts his disciples ; " Your mourning shall be turned into joy." As the last estate of Job was better than his first ; so shall the Lord render more to his children at the last than now at the first he takes from them : let us therefore bear his cross, as a preparative to comfort.—*William Cowper.*

Verse 76.—*"Let thy merciful kindness be for my comfort."* Several of the pre- ceding verses have spoken of affliction (verses 67, 71, 75). The Psalmist now presents his petition for alleviation under it. But of what kind ? He does not ask to have it removed. He does not " beseech the Lord, that it might depart from him " : 2 Cor. xii. 8. No. His repeated acknowledgments of the supports vouchsafed under it, and the benefits he had derived from it, had reconciled him to commit its measure and continuance to the Lord. All that he needs, and all that he asks for, is a sense of his *" merciful kindness "* upon his soul. Thus he submits to his justice in his accumulated trials, and expects consolation under them solely upon the ground of his free favour.—*Charles Bridges.*

Verse 76.—*"Let thy merciful kindness,"* etc. Let me derive my comfort and happiness from a diffusion of thy love and mercy, הסדך, *chasdecha,* thy exuberant goodness through my soul.—*Adam Clarke.*

Verse 76.—*"According to thy word unto thy servant."* If his promise did not please him, why did he make it ? If our reliance on the promise did not please him, why did his goodness work it ? It would be inconsistent with his goodness to mock his creature, and it would be the highest mockery to publish his word, and create a temper in the heart of his supplicant suited to his promise, which he never intended to satisfy. He can as little wrong his creature as wrong himself, and therefore he can never disappoint that faith which after his own methods casts itself into the arms of his kindness, and is his own workmanship, and calls him author. That goodness which imparted itself so freely to the irrational creation will not neglect those nobler creatures that put their trust in him. This renders God a fit object for trust and confidence.—*Stephen Charnock.*

Verse 76.—*"According to thy word."* David had a particular promise of a particular benefit ; to wit, the kingdom of Israel. And this promise God performed unto him ; but his comfort stood not in it ; for Saul before him had the kingdom, but the promises of mercy belonged not to him, and therefore, when God forsook him. his kingdom could not sustain him. But David here depends upon the general promises of God's mercy made to his children ; wherein he acknowledgeth a particular promise of mercy made to him. For the general promises of mercy and grace made in the gospel are by faith made particular to every believer.— *William Cowper.*

Verse 76.—*"Thy word unto thy servant."* Here we may use the eunuch's question : " Of whom speaketh the prophet this, of himself or of some other man ? " Of himself questionless, under the denomination of God's servant. But then the question returneth,—Is it a word of promise made to himself in particular, or to God's servants in the general ? Some say the former, the promises brought to him by Nathan. I incline to the latter, and it teacheth us these three truths :— 1st. That God's servants only are capable of the sweet effects of his mercy and the comforts of his promises. Who are God's servants ? (1) Such as own his right and are sensible of his interest in them : " God, whose I am, and whom I serve " (Acts xxviii. 23). (2) Such as give up themselves to him, renouncing all other masters. Renounce we must, for we were once under another master (Rom. vi. 17 ; Matt. vi. 24 ; Rom. vi. 13 ; 1 Chron. xxx. 8). (3) Such as accordingly frame themselves to do his work sincerely : " serve with my spirit " (Rom. i. 9) ; and, " in newness of spirit " (Rom. vii. 6), even as becomes those who are renewed by the Spirit : diligently (Acts xxvi. 7), and universally (Luke i. 74, 75), and wait upon him for grace to do so (Heb. xii. 28). These are capable of comfort. The book of God speaketh no comfort to persons that live in sin, but to God's servants, such as do not live as if they were at their own disposal, but at God's beck. If he say go, they go. They give up themselves to be and do what God will have them to be and do.

2ndly. If we have the benefit of the promise, we must thrust in ourselves under one title or other among those to whom the promise is made ; if not as God's children, yet as God's servants. Then the promise is as sure to us as if our name were in it.

3rdly. All God's servants have common grounds of comfort : every one of God's servants may plead with God as David doth. The comforts of the word are the common portion of God's people.—*Thomas Manton.*

Verse 76.—*"Thy word unto thy servant."* Our Master has passed his word to all his servants that he will be kind to them, and they may plead it with him.—*Matthew Henry.*

Verse 77.—*"Let thy tender mercies come unto me, that I may live."* If we mark narrowly we shall find that David here seeks another sort of mercy than he sought before. For first he sought mercy to forgive his sins ; then he sought mercy to comfort him in his troubles ; now he seeks mercy to live, and sin no more. Alas, many seek the first mercy, of remission ; and the second mercy of consolation in trouble, who are altogether careless of the third mercy, to live well. It is a great mercy of God to amend thy life : where this is not, let no man think he hath received either of the former. It is a great mercy of God, which not only pardons evil that is done, but strengthens us also to further good that we have not done ; and this is the mercy which here David seeks.—*William Cowper.*

Verse 77.—*"Let thy tender mercies come unto me,"* etc. The mercies of God are *" tender mercies,"* they are the mercies of a father to his children, nay, tender as the compassion of a mother over the son of her womb. They *"come unto"* us, when we are not able to go to them. By them alone we *" live "* the life of faith, of love, of joy and gladness. And to such as *" delight"* in his law, God will grant these mercies, and this life ; he will give them pardon, and, by so doing, he will give them life from the dead.—*George Horne.*

Verse 77.—*"Let thy tender mercies,"* etc. Taking the more literal rendering, the words express high confidence—*"* Thy tender mercies *shall* come unto me, and I shall live ; for thy law is my delight.*"* Had the believer nothing but his own deserts to support his plea at the throne of grace, he could never rise into this high confidence. He goes upon the foundation of the divine goodness, manifested through the anointed One, and he goes surely.—*John Stephen.*

Verse 77.—*"Come."* Coming to him noteth a personal and effectual application. 1st. A personal application, as in the 41st verse of this Psalm : " Let thy mercies come also unto me, O Lord, even thy salvation, according to thy word." David would not be forgotten, or left out or lost in the throng of mankind, when mercy was distributing the blessing to them. 2ndly. Effectual application : which signifieth, 1. The removal of obstacles and hindrances ; 2. The obtaining the fruits and effects of this mercy.

First. The removing of obstacles. Till there be a way made, the mercy of God cannot come at us ; for the way is barricaded and shut up by our sins : as the Lord maketh a way for his anger (Ps. lxxviii. 50), by removing the hindrances, so the Lord maketh way for his mercy, or mercy maketh way for itself, when it removeth the obstruction. Sin is the great hindrance of mercy. We ourselves raise the mists and the clouds which intercept the light of God's countenance ; we build up the partition wall which separates between God and us ; yet mercy finds the way.

Secondly. The obtaining the fruits of mercy . . . . It is not enough to hear somewhat of God's saving mercies ; but we should beg that they may come unto us, be effectually and sensibly communicated unto us, that we may have experience of them in our own souls. A man that hath read of honey, or heard of honey, may know the sweetness of it by guess and imagination ; but a man that hath tasted of honey knoweth the sweetness of it in truth : so, by reading and hearing of the grace and mercy of God in Christ, we may guess that it is a sweet thing ; but he that hath had an experimental proof of the sweet effects and fruits of it in his own heart perceives that all which is spoken of God's pardoning and comforting of sinners is verified in himself.—*Thomas Manton.*

Verse 77.—*"Thy law is my delight."* A child of God, though he cannot serve the Lord perfectly, yet he serves him willingly ; his will is in the law of the Lord ; he is not a pressed soldier, but a volunteer. By the beating of this pulse we may judge whether there be spiritual life in us or no. David professeth that God's law was his delight ; he had his crown to delight in, he had his music to delight in ; but the love he had to God's law did drown all other delights ; as the joy of harvest and vintage exceeds the joy of gleaning.—*Thomas Watson.*

Verse 78.—*"Let the proud be ashamed,"* etc.   Here is the just recompense of his pride.   He would fain have honour and pre-eminence, but God will not give them unto him : he flies shame and contempt, but God shall pour them upon him. *"For they dealt perversely with me without a cause."*   David complains of the wicked and false dealing of his enemies against him ; and his prayer is written to uphold us in the like temptation.   For Satan is alway like himself, hating them whom the Lord loveth.   He can scarce be worse, he can never be better ; and therefore with restless malice stirs he up all his cursed instruments in whom he reigns, to persecute those who are loved and protected of the Lord.   *"But I will meditate in thy precepts."* David's enemies fought against him with the weapons of the flesh, wickedness and falsehood : he withstands them by the armour of the Spirit ; not meeting wickedness with wickedness, and falsehood with falsehood.   For if we fight against Satan with Satan's weapons he will soon overcome us ; but if we put upon us the complete armour of God to resist him, he shall flee from us.—*William Cowper.*

Verse 78.—*"Let the proud be ashamed."*   That is, that they may not prosper or succeed in their attempts ; for men are ashamed when they are disappointed. All their endeavours for the extirpation of God's people are vain and fruitless, and those things which they have subtilely devised have not that effect which they propounded unto themselves.   *"For they dealt perversely with me without a cause."* The Septuagint have it ἀδίκως, unjustly.   Ainsworth readeth, " With falsehood they have depraved me."   It implieth two things : first, that they pretended a cause ;   but, secondly, David avoucheth his innocency to God ;   and so, without any guilt of his, they accused, defamed, condemned his actions, as is usual in such cases.   When the proud are troublesome and injurious to God's people the saints may boldly commend their cause to God. . . . The Lord may be appealed unto upon a double account ;   partly, as he is an enemy to the proud, and as a friend to the humble (James iv. 6 ;   Ps. cxxxviii. 6) ;   partly, as he is the portion of the afflicted and oppressed (Ps. cxl. 12).   When Satan stirreth up his instruments to hate those whom the Lord loveth, the Lord will stir up his power to help and defend them.   Is not this a revengeful prayer ?

Answer, No.   1st. Because those who pray it are seeking their own deliverance, that they may more freely serve God by consequence.   Indeed, by God's showing mercy to his people, the pride of wicked ones is suppressed (verse 134) ;   but mercy is the main object of the prayer.

2ndly. As it concerneth his enemies, he expresseth it in mild terms—that they may " be ashamed";   that is, disappointed, in their counsels, hopes, machinations, and endeavours.   And therefore it is not against the persons of his enemies, but their plots and enterprises.   In such cases shame and disappointment may even do them good.   They think to bring in the total suppression of God's people, but that would harden them in their sins ;   therefore God's people desire that he would not let their innocency be trampled upon, but disappoint their adversaries, that the proud may be ashamed in the failing of their attempts.

3rdly. The prayers of the righteous for the overthrow of the wicked, are a kind of prophecies ;   so that, in praying, David doth in effect foretell, that such as dealt perversely should soon be ashamed, since a good cause will not always be oppressed : " But he shall appear to your joy, and they shall be ashamed " (Isa. lxvi. 5).

4thly. Saints have a liberty to imprecate vengeance, but such as must be used sparingly and with great caution :   " Let them be confounded and consumed that are adversaries to my soul " (Ps. lxxi. 13).   Malicious enemies may be expressly prayed against.—*Thomas Manton.*

Verse 78.—*"Let the proud be ashamed."*   This suggests a word to the wicked. Take heed that by your implacable hatred to the truth and church of God you do not engage her prayers against you.   These imprecatory prayers of the saints, when shot at the right mark, and duly put up, are murdering pieces, and strike dead where they light.   " Shall not God avenge his own elect, which cry day and night unto him, though he bear long with them ?   I tell you that he will avenge them speedily."   Luke xviii. 7, 8.   They are not empty words—as the imprecations of the wicked poured into the air, and there vanishing with their breath—but are received into heaven, and shall be sent back with thunder and lightning upon the pates of the wicked.   David's prayer unravelled Ahithophel's fine-spun policy, and twisted his halter for him.   The prayers of the saints are more to be feared—as once a great person said and felt—than an army of twenty thousand men in the field. Esther's fast hastened Haman's ruin, and Hezekiah's against Sennacherib brought his huge host to the slaughter, and fetched an angel from heaven to do the execution in one night upon them.—*William Gurnall.*

Verse 78.—*"The proud."* The wicked, especially the persecutors of God's people, are usually characterized by this term in this Psalm, *"the proud"* (verses 51, 69, 122). Pride puts wicked men upon being troublesome and injurious to the people of God. But why are the persecutors and the injurious called *"the proud"*? 1. Because wicked men shake off the yoke of God, and will not be subject to their Maker, and therefore desist not from troubling his people : " Who is the Lord, that I should obey his voice to let Israel go"? (Exod. v. 2). What was in his tongue, is in all men's hearts ; they contemn God and his laws. Every sin hath a degree of pride, and a depreciation of God included in it, (2 Sam xii. 9). 2. Because they are drunk with worldly felicity, and never think of changes. " Our soul is exceedingly filled with the scorning of those that are at ease, and with the contempt of the proud " (Ps. cxxiii. 4). When men go on prosperously, they are apt wrongfully to trouble others, and then to flout at them in their misery, and to despise the person and cause of God's people, which is a sure effect of great arrogancy and pride. They think they may do what they please : " They have no changes ; therefore they fear not God," and put forth their hands against such as be at peace with them (Ps. lv. 19, 20) : whilst they go on prosperously and undisturbedly, they cannot abstain from violence and oppression. 3. Because they effect a life of pomp, and ease, and carnal greatness, and so despise the affliction, and meanness, and simplicity of God's people. The false church hath usually the advantage of worldly power and external glory ; and the true church is known by the Divine power, gifts and graces, and the lustre of holiness. 4. They are called *" proud,"* because of their insolent carriage towards the Lord's people ; partly in their laws and injunctions, requiring them to give them more honour, respect, and obedience, than in conscience can be afforded them ; as Haman would have Mordecai to devote himself to him after the manner of the Persians (Esther iii. 5).—*Condensed from Manton.*

Verse 78.—" When any of you," says Cæsarius, " is singing the verse of the Psalm wherein it is said, '*Let the proud be put to shame,*' let him be earnest to avoid pride, that he may escape everlasting shame."—*William Kay.*

Verse 78.—*"But I will meditate in thy precepts."* He repeateth the same thing often, and surely if the world could not contain the books that might be written of Christ, and yet for our infirmity the Lord hath comprised them in such a few books, and yet one thing in them is often repeated, it showeth that the matter is weighty, and of us duly and often to be considered. And again we are taught that this is a thing that none do so carefully look unto as they ought. And he showeth that as his enemies sought by evil means to hurt him ; so he sought to keep a good conscience, that so they might not hurt him. Then we must not set policy against policy nor *cretizare cum Cretensibus ;* but let us always tend to the word, and keep within the bounds of that, and fight with the weapons that it lendeth us. . . . . If we would give over ourselves to God and his word, and admit nothing but that which agreeth to the word, then should we be made wiser than our enemies. —*Richard Greenham.*

Verse 78.—*"I will meditate in thy precepts."* The verb אשיח, *asiach*, in the second clause of the verse, may be rendered, "*I will speak of,*" as well as, "*I will meditate upon*" ; implying that, when he had obtained the victory, he would proclaim the goodness of God, which he had experienced. *To speak of God's statutes,* is equivalent to declaring out of the law how faithfully he guards his saints, how securely he delivers them, and how righteously he avenges their wrongs.—*John Calvin.*

Verse 78.—*"Meditate."* Truths lie hid in the heart without efficacy or power, till improved by deep, serious, and pressing thoughts . . . . A sudden carrying a candle through a room, giveth us not so full a survey of the object, as when you stand a while beholding it. A steady contemplation is a great advantage.—*Thomas Manton.*

Verse 79.—*"Let those that fear thee turn unto me."* Some think it intimates that when David had been guilty of that foul sin in the murder of Uriah, though he was a king, they that feared God grew strange to him, and turned from him, for they were ashamed of him ; this troubled him, and therefore he prays, Lord, let them *"turn to me"* again.   He desires especially the company of those that were not only honest but intelligent, *"that have known thy testimonies,"* have good heads as well as good hearts, and whose conversation will be edifying.   It is desirable to have an intimacy with such.—*Matthew Henry.*

Verse 79.—*"Let those that fear thee turn unto me,"* etc.   As he had not his own flesh to fight against only, but the world also, so he did not only himself fight, but he seeketh the help of others.   When many see that religion cannot be truly professed but danger will come of it, because many set themselves against it, they flee from it, and go to the greater part, which is the wicked.   If we will avoid this, let us join ourselves to God's children, and they will help us with counsel and advice; for one may be strong when we are weak, another may have counsel when we shall not know what to do; therefore by them we shall be kept from many evil things.   So Paul (2 Tim. i. 16), after he had complained of the wrong that many had done unto him, he straightway giveth thanks for the family of Onesiphorus, which refreshed him more than all his enemies could discourage him; so that he durst oppose this one household to the whole rabble of the wicked.—*Richard Greenham.*

Verse 79.—*"Let those that fear thee,"* etc.   You must go to God and beseech him to choose your company for you.   Mark what David said and did; in verse 63 he saith, *"I am a companion of all them that fear the Lord";* yet in this verse he goes to God, and prayeth, saying, *Let those that fear thee, O Lord, turn unto me, and those that have known thy testimonies.*   As if he should say, "Of a truth, Lord, I am a companion of all that do fear thee; but it is not in my power to bend their hearts unto me; the hearts of all men are in thy hands, now therefore *"let those that fear thee turn unto me."*   So do you go to God, and say likewise: Lord, do thou choose my company for me; oh, do thou bow and incline their hearts to be my companions. —*William Bridge.*

Verse 79.—*"Those that fear." "Those that have known."*   Fear and knowledge do make up a godly man.   Knowledge without fear breedeth presumption; and fear without knowledge breedeth superstition; and blind zeal, as a blind horse, may be full of mettle, but is ever and anon stumbling.   Knowledge must direct fear, and fear must season knowledge; then it is a happy mixture and composition.— *Thomas Manton.*

Verse 79.—One great means to restore a good understanding among God's people is prayer.   David goeth to God about it: *"Lord, let them turn to me."*   The Lord governeth hearts and interests, both are in his hands, and he useth their alienation or reconciliation, either for judgment or mercy.   God, when he pleaseth, can divert from us the comfort of godly friends; and when he pleaseth, he can bring them back again to us.   The feet of God's children are directed by God himself; if they come to us, it is a blessing of God; if not, it is for a correction.   He made Jacob and Laban meet peaceably (Gen. xxx.), and in the next chapter, Jacob and Esau.— *Thomas Manton.*

Verse 80.—*"Let my heart be sound."*   What is a sound heart?   It noteth reality and solidity in grace.   The Septuagint hath it, *Let my heart be without spot and blemish.*   It implieth the reality of grace, opposed to the bare form of godliness, or the fair shows of hypocrites, and the sudden and vanishing motions of temporaries. If you would have me unfold what this sound heart is, there is required these four things:—

1. An enlightened understanding; that is, the directive part of the soul; and it is sound when it is kept free from the leaven and contagion of error: "A man of understanding walketh uprightly," Prov. xv. 21.   A sound mind is a good help to a sound heart.

2. There is required an awakened conscience, that warneth us of our duty, and riseth up in dislike of sin upon all occasions: "When thou goest, it shall lead thee; when thou sleepest, it shall keep thee; and when thou awakest, it shall talk with thee" (Prov. vi. 22): to have a constant monitor in our bosoms to put us in mind of God, when our reins preach to us in the night season (Ps. xvi. 7): there is a secret spy in our bosoms that observes all that we do, and think, and speak; a domestic chaplain, that is always preaching to us.   His heart is his Bible.

3. There is required a rightly disposed will, or a steadfast purpose to walk with God in all conditions, and to do what is good and acceptable in his sight: "He exhorted them all that with purpose of heart they would cleave unto the Lord," Acts xi. 23.   Many have light inclinations, or wavering resolutions; but their

hearts are not fixedly, habitually bent to please God ; therein chiefly lieth this sound heart, that it doth inseparably cleave to God in all things.

4. There is required that the affections be purged and quickened : these are the vigorous motions of the will, and therefore this must be heedfully regarded ; purged they must be from that carnality and fleshliness that cleaveth to them. This is called in Scripture the circumcision of the heart (Deut. xxx. 6).—*Condensed from Manton.*

Verse 80.—*"Let my heart be sound."* " A sound mind in a sound body," was the prayer of a heathen, and his desire was according to the extent of his knowledge ; but a heart sound in God's statutes, sound to the very core, with no speck, nor spot, nor wrinkle, nor any such thing, and like the king's daughter, " all glorious within," this is what the Psalmist prays for, this is what every child of God aims at, and prays for too,—" Even as He is pure."—*Barton Bouchier.*

Verse 80.—*"Let my heart be sound."*

> True-hearted, whole-hearted, faithful and loyal,
> King of our lives, by thy grace will we be !
> Under thy standard, exalted and royal,
> Strong in thy strength, we will battle for thee !
>
> True-hearted, whole-hearted ! Fullest allegiance
> Yielding henceforth to our glorious King ;
> Valiant endeavour and loving obedience
> Freely and joyously now would we bring.
>
> True-hearted, Saviour, thou knowest our story ;
> Weak are the hearts that we lay at thy feet,
> Sinful and treacherous ! yet for thy glory,
> Heal them, and cleanse them from sin and deceit
>
> Whole-hearted ! Saviour, belovèd and glorious,
> Take thy great power, and reign thou alone,
> Over our wills and affections victorious,
> Freely surrendered, and wholly thine own.
>
> Half-hearted ! false-hearted ! Heed we the warning !
> Only the whole can be perfectly true ;
> Bring the whole offering, all timid thought scorning,
> True-hearted only if whole-hearted too.
>
> Half-hearted ! Saviour, shall aught be withholden,
> Giving thee part who hast given us all ?
> Blessings outpouring, and promises golden
> Pledging, with never reserve or recall.
>
> Half-hearted ! Master, shall any who know thee
> Grudge thee their lives, who hast laid down thine own ?
> Nay ; we would offer the hearts that we owe thee,—
> Live for thy love and thy glory alone.
>
> Sisters, dear sisters, the call is resounding,
> Will ye not echo the silver refrain,
> Mighty and sweet, and in gladness abounding,—
> " True-hearted, whole-hearted ! " ringing again ?
>
> Jesus is with us, his rest is before us,
> Brightly his standard is waving above.
> Brothers, dear brothers, in gathering chorus,
> Peal out the watchword of courage and love !
>
> Peal out the watchword, and silence it never,
> Song of our spirits rejoicing and free !
> " True-hearted, whole-hearted, now and for ever,
> King of our lives, by thy grace we will be ! "

Frances Ridley Havergal (1836—1879) in "Loyal Responses."

Verse 80.—*"Let my heart be sound,"* etc. This is a plain difference between a sound heart and a false heart ; in the receiving of Christ the sound heart receives him as a favourite receives a prince, he gives up all to him, and lets him have the command of all. A mere innkeeper entertains him that comes next to him ; he will take any man's money, and will give welcome to any man ; if it be the worst man that comes he cares not, for he loves gain above all things. Not so the good heart ; he welcomes Christ alone, and resigns up all to Christ. Whatsoever is pleasing to Christ he will do it, and whatsoever comes from Christ he will welcome.— *Thomas Hooker* (1586—1647) *in "The Soules Implantation."*

Verse 80.—"*Be sound.*" Heb. *Be perfect;* as the word from the same root is rendered in Job i. 1. Dr. R. Young gives as the meaning of the word as used by the Psalmist, *whole, complete, plain.*

Verse 80.—"*Sound in thy statutes,*" etc. Though an *orthodox creed* does not constitute true religion, yet it is the basis of it, and it is a great blessing to have it.— *Nicolson, quoted by W. S. Plumer.*

Verse 80.—If you would be faithful to Christ, be sincere in your profession of him, make David's prayer and desire to be yours : "*Let my heart be sound in thy statutes ; that I be not ashamed.*" Religion which is begun in hypocrisy will certainly end in apostasy, and this always carries with it reproach and ignominy.—*William Spurstow* (—1666).

Verse 80.—"*Ashamed.*" We may be ashamed either before God or men, ourselves or others.

1. Before God : either in our addresses to him at the throne of grace or when summoned to appear at the last day before the tribunal of his justice. (1) If you understand it of our approach to him, we cannot come into his presence with confidence if we have not a sound heart. " If our heart condemn us not, then have we confidence toward God " : 1 John iii. 21. We lose that holy familiarity and cheerfulness, when we are unbosoming ourselves to our heavenly Father, when our hearts are not sound. (2) When we are summoned to appear before the tribunal of his justice. Many, now, with a bold impudence, will obtrude themselves upon the worship of God, because they see him not, and have not a due sense of his majesty ; but the time will come, when the most impudent and outbraving sinners will be astonished, even then when the secrets of all hearts shall be laid open and made manifest, and hidden things brought to light (1 Cor. iv. 5) ; and every one is to receive his judgment from God according to what he hath done, either good or evil.

2. Before men a man may be ashamed, and so before ourselves and others. (1) Ourselves. It was a saying of Pythagoras, Reverence thyself ; be not ashamed of thyself. God hath a spy and deputy within us, and taketh notice of our conformity and unconformity to his will, and, after sin committed, lasheth the soul with the sense of its own guilt and folly, as the body is lashed with stripes : " What fruit had ye then in those things whereof ye are now ashamed ? " Rom. vi. 21. (2) Before others. And so our shame may be occasioned by our scandals, or our punishments ; it is hard to say which is intended here.—*Condensed from Manton.*

EXPOSITION OF VERSES 81 TO 88.

MY soul fainteth for thy salvation : *but* I hope in thy word.

82 Mine eyes fail for thy word, saying, When wilt thou comfort me ?

83 For I am become like a bottle in the smoke ; *yet* do I not forget thy statutes.

84 How many *are* the days of thy servant ? when wilt thou execute judgment on them that persecute me ?

85 The proud have digged pits for me, which *are* not after thy law.

86 All thy commandments *are* faithful : they persecute me wrongfully : help thou me.

87 They had almost consumed me upon earth ; but I forsook not thy precepts.

88 Quicken me after thy lovingkindness ; so shall I keep the testimony of thy mouth.

This portion of the gigantic Psalm sees the Psalmist *in extremis*. His enemies have brought him to the lowest condition of anguish and depression ; yet he is faithful to the law and trustful in his God. This octave is the midnight of the Psalm, and very dark and black it is. Stars, however, shine out, and the last verse gives promise of the dawn. The strain will after this become more cheerful ; but meanwhile it should minister comfort to us to see so eminent a servant of God so hardly used by the ungodly : evidently in our own persecutions, no strange thing has happened unto us.

81. "*My soul fainteth for thy salvation.*" He wished for no deliverance but that which came from God : his one desire was for " thy salvation." But for that divine deliverance he was eager to the last degree,—up to the full measure of his strength, yea, and beyond it till he fainted. So strong was his desire that it produced prostration of spirit. He grew weary with waiting, faint with watching, sick with urgent need. Thus the sincerity and the eagerness of his desires were proved. Nothing else could satisfy him but deliverance wrought out by the hand of God, his inmost nature yearned and pined for salvation from the God of all grace, and he must have it or utterly fail. "*But I hope in thy word.*" Therefore he felt that salvation would come, for God cannot break his promise, nor disappoint the hope which his own word has excited : yea, the fulfilment of his word is near at hand when our hope is firm and our desire fervent. Hope alone can keep the soul from fainting by using the smelling-bottle of the promise. Yet hope does not quench desire for a speedy answer to prayer ; it increases our importunity, for it both stimulates ardour and sustains the heart under delays. To faint for salvation, and to be kept from utterly failing by the hope of it, is the frequent experience of the Christian man. We are " faint yet pursuing." Hope sustains when desire exhausts. While the grace of desire throws us down, the grace of hope lifts us up again.

82. "*Mine eyes fail for thy word, saying, When wilt thou comfort me ?*" His eyes gave out with eagerly gazing for the kind appearance of the Lord, while his heart in weariness cried out for speedy comfort. To read the word till the eyes can no longer see is but a small thing compared with watching for the fulfilment of the promise till the inner eyes of expectancy begin to grow dim with hope deferred. We may not set times to God, for this is to limit the Holy One of Israel ; yet we may urge our suit with importunity, and make fervent enquiry as to why the promise tarries. David sought no comfort except that which comes from God ; his question is, " When wilt *thou* comfort me ? " If help does not come from heaven it will never come at all : all the good man's hopes look that way, he has not a glance to

dart in any other direction. This experience of waiting and fainting is well-known by full-grown saints, and it teaches them many precious lessons which they would never learn by any other means. Among the choice results is this one—that the body rises into sympathy with the soul, both heart and flesh cry out for the living God, and even the eyes find a tongue, " saying, When wilt thou comfort me ? " It must be an intense longing which is not satisfied to express itself by the lips, but speaks with the eyes, by those eyes failing through intense watching. Eyes can speak right eloquently ; they use both mutes and liquids, and can sometimes say more than tongues. David says in another place, " The Lord hath heard the voice of my weeping " (Ps. vi. 8). Specially are our eyes eloquent when they begin to fail with weariness and woe. A humble eye lifted up to heaven in silent prayer may flash such flame as shall melt the bolts which bar the entrance of vocal prayer, and so heaven shall be taken by storm with the artillery of tears. Blessed are the eyes that are strained in looking after God. The eyes of the Lord will see to it that such eyes do not actually fail. How much better to watch for the Lord with aching eyes than to have them sparkling at the glitter of vanity.

83. *"For I am become like a bottle in the smoke."* The skins used for containing wine, when emptied, were hung up in the tent, and when the place reeked with smoke the skins grew black and sooty, and in the heat they became wrinkled and worn. The Psalmist's face through sorrow had become dark and dismal, furrowed and lined ; indeed, his whole body had so sympathized with his sorrowing mind as to have lost its natural moisture, and to have become like a skin dried and tanned. His character had been smoked with slander, and his mind parched with persecution ; he was half afraid that he would become useless and incapable through so much mental suffering, and that men would look upon him as an old worn-out skin bottle, which could hold nothing and answer no purpose. What a metaphor for a man to use who was certainly a poet, a divine, and a master in Israel, if not a king, and a man after God's own heart ! It is little wonder if we, commoner folk, are made to think very little of ourselves, and are filled with distress of mind. Some of us know the inner meaning of this simile, for we, too, have felt dingy, mean, and worthless, only fit to be cast away. Very black and hot has been the smoke which has enveloped us ; it seemed to come not alone from the Egyptian furnace, but from the bottomless pit ; and it had a clinging power which made the soot of it fasten upon us and blacken us with miserable thoughts.

"Yet do I not forget thy statutes." Here is the patience of the saints and the victory of faith. Blackened the man of God might be by falsehood, but the truth was in him, and he never gave it up. He was faithful to his King when he seemed deserted and left to the vilest uses. The promises came to his mind, and, what was a still better evidence of his loyalty, the statutes were there too : he stuck to his duties as well as to his comforts. The worst circumstances cannot destroy the true believer's hold upon his God. Grace is a living power which survives that which would suffocate all other forms of existence. Fire cannot consume it, and smoke cannot smother it. A man may be reduced to skin and bone, and all his comfort may be dried out of him, and yet he may hold fast his integrity and glorify his God. It is, however, no marvel that in such a case the eyes which are tormented with the smoke cry out for the Lord's delivering hand, and the heart heated and faint longs for the divine salvation.

84. *"How many are the days of thy servant ? "* I cannot hope to live long in such a condition, thou must come speedily to my rescue or I shall die. Shall all my short life be consumed in such destroying sorrows ? The brevity of life is a good argument against the length of an affliction. Perhaps the Psalmist means that his days seemed too many when they were spent in such distress. He half wished that they were ended, and therefore he asked in trouble, " How many are the days of thy servant ? " Like a hired servant, he had a certain term to serve, and he would not complain ; but still the time seemed long because his griefs were so heavy. No one knows the appointed number of our days except the Lord, and therefore to him the appeal is made that he would not prolong them beyond his servant's strength. It cannot be the Lord's mind that his own servant should always be treated so unjustly ; there must be an end to it ; when would it be ?

"When wilt thou execute judgment on them that persecute me ? " He had placed his case in the Lord's hands, and he prayed that sentence might be given and put into execution. He desired nothing but justice, that his character might be cleared and his persecutors silenced. He knew that God would certainly avenge his own

elect, but the day of rescue tarried, the hours dragged heavily along, and the perse-cuted one cried day and night for deliverance.

85. *"The proud have digged pits for me, which are not after thy law."* As men who hunt wild beasts are wont to make pitfalls and snares, so did David's foes endeavour to entrap him. They went laboriously and cunningly to work to ruin him, " they digged *pits";* not one, but many. If one would not take him, perhaps another would, and so they digged again and again. One would think that such haughty people would not have soiled their fingers with digging ; but they swallowed their pride in hopes of swallowing their victim. Whereas they ought to have been ashamed of such meanness, they were conscious of no shame, but, on the contrary, were proud of their cleverness ; proud of setting a trap for a godly man. *"Which are not after thy law."* Neither the men nor their pits were according to the divine law : they were cruel and crafty deceivers, and their pits were contrary to the Levitical law, and contrary to the command which bids us love our neighbour. If men would keep to the statutes of the Lord, they would lift the fallen out of the pit, or fill up the pit so that none might stumble into it ; but they would never spend a moment in working injury to others. When, however, they become proud, they are sure to despise others ; and for this reason they seek to circumvent them, that they may afterwards hold them up to ridicule.

It was well for David that his enemies were God's enemies, and that their attacks upon him had no sanction from the Lord. It was also much to his gain that he was not ignorant of their devices, for he was thus put upon his guard, and led to watch his ways lest he should fall into their pits. While he kept to the law of the Lord he was safe, though even then it was an uncomfortable thing to have his path made dangerous by the craft of wanton malice.

86. *"All thy commandments are faithful."* He had no fault to find with God's law, even though he had fallen into sad trouble through obedience to it. Whatever the command might cost him it was worth it ; he felt that God's way might be rough, but it was right ; it might make him enemies, but still it was his best friend. He believed that in the end God's command would turn out to his own profit, and that he should be no loser by obeying it.

"They persecute me wrongfully." The fault lay with his persecutors, and neither with his God nor with himself. He had done no injury to anyone, nor acted other-wise than according to truth and justice ; therefore he confidently appeals to his God, and cries, *"Help thou me."* This is a golden prayer, as precious as it is short. The words are few, but the meaning is full. Help was needed that the persecuted one might avoid the snare, might bear up under reproach, and might act so prudently as to baffle his foes. God's help is our hope. Whoever may hurt us, it matters not so long as the Lord helps us ; for if indeed the Lord help us, none can really hurt us. Many a time have these words been groaned out by troubled saints, for they are such as suit a thousand conditions of need, pain, distress, weakness, and sin. " Help, Lord," will be a fitting prayer for youth and age, for labour and suffering, for life and death. No other help is sufficient, but God's help is all-sufficient and we cast ourselves upon it without fear.

87. *"They had almost consumed me upon earth."* His foes had almost destroyed him so as to make him altogether fail. If they could they would have eaten him, or burned him alive ; anything so that they could have made a full end of the good man. Evidently he had fallen under their power to a large extent, and they had so used that power that he was well nigh consumed. He was almost gone from off the earth ; but almost is not altogether, and so he escaped by the skin of his teeth. The lions are chained : they can rage no further than our God permits. The Psalmist perceives the limit of their power : they could only touch his earthly life and earthly goods. Upon earth they almost ate him up, but he had an eternal portion which they could not even nibble at. *"But I forsook not thy precepts."* Nothing could drive him from obeying the Lord. If we stick to the precepts we shall be rescued by the promises. If ill-usage could have driven the oppressed saint from the way of right the purpose of the wicked would have been answered, and we should have heard no more of David. If we are resolved to die sooner than forsake the Lord, we may depend upon it that we shall not die, but shall live to see the overthrow of them that hate us.

88. *"Quicken me after thy lovingkindness."* Most wise, most blessed prayer ! If we are revived in our own personal piety we shall be out of reach of our assailants. Our best protection from tempters and persecutors is more life. Lovingkindness

itself cannot do us greater service than by making us to have life more abundantly. When we are quickened we are able to bear affliction, to baffle cunning, and to conquer sin.   We look to the lovingkindness of God as the source of spiritual revival, and we entreat the Lord to quicken us, not according to our deserts, but after the boundless energy of his grace.   What a blessed word is this " lovingkindness."   Take it to pieces, and admire its double force of love.   *"So shall I keep the testimony of thy mouth."*   If quickened by the Holy Ghost we shall be sure to exhibit a holy character. We shall be faithful to sound doctrine when the Spirit visits us and makes us faithful. None keep the word of the Lord's mouth unless the word of the Lord's mouth quickens them.   We ought greatly to admire the spiritual prudence of the Psalmist, who does not so much pray for freedom from trial as for renewed life that he may he supported under it.   When the inner life is vigorous all is well.   David prayed for a sound heart in the closing verse of the last octave, and here he seeks a revived heart ; this is going to the root of the matter, by seeking that which is the most needful of all things.   Lord let it be heart-work with us, and let our hearts be right with thee.

NOTES ON VERSES 81 TO 88.

The whole eight verses, 81—89.—The eleventh letter, *Caph*, signifies the *hollowed hand.* The expositors, however, looking only to the meaning *curved*, which is but half of its import, explain the section as signifying the act of bowing down in penitence or as noting that the fathers of the Old Testament were like veteran soldiers, stooping with years and toil, and bowed down yet further by the heavy weight of the law, only removable by that coming of Christ for which they prayed. Others extend the notion to the saints of the church, weighed down by the sorrows and cares of this life and therefore desiring to be dissolved and to be with Christ. The true meaning is to be sought in the full interpretation of the word ; for the hand is hollowed either in order to retain something which actually lies in it, or to receive something about to be placed in it by another. Thus the hand may be God's, as the giver of bounty, or man's, as the receiver of it ; and the whole scope of the section, as a prayer for speedy help, is that man holds out his hand as a beggar, supplicating the mercy of God.—*Jerome, Ambrose, and others, in Neale and Littledale.*

Verse 81.—*"My soul fainteth for thy salvation."* The word here rendered *"fainteth"* is the same that in Ps. lxxiii. 26 is translated *"faileth"* : " My flesh and my heart *faileth."* The idea is, that his strength gave way ; he had such an intense *desire* for salvation that he became weak and powerless. Any strong emotion *may* thus prostrate us ; and the love of God, the desire of his favour, the longing for heaven may be so intense as to produce this result.—*Albert Barnes.*

Verse 81.—*"My soul fainteth."* Fainting is proper to the body, but here it is ascribed to the soul ; as also in many other places. The Apostle saith, " Lest ye be wearied and faint in your minds" (Heb. xii. 3); where two words are used, weariness and fainting, both taken from the body. Weariness is a lesser, fainting is a higher degree of deficiency : in weariness, the body requireth some rest or refreshment, when the active power is weakened, and the vital spirits and principles of motion are dulled ; but, in fainting, the vital power is contracted, and retireth, and leaveth the outward parts lifeless and senseless. When a man is wearied, his strength is abated ; when he fainteth, he is quite spent. These things, by a metaphor, are applied to the soul, or mind. A man is weary, when the fortitude of his mind, his moral or spiritual strength, is broken, or begins to abate, when his soul sits uneasy under sufferings ; but when he sinketh under the burden of grievous, tedious, or long affliction, then he is said to faint, when all the reasons and grounds of his comfort are quite spent and he can hold out no longer.—*Thomas Manton.*

Verse 81.—*"My soul fainteth."* What is this fainting but the lofty state of raptured contemplation in which the strength of heavenly affections weakens those of earth. Just as the ascent into the highest mountains causes a new respiration, as when Daniel had a great vision from God, he tells us " he fainted and was sick certain days."—*E. Paxton Hood*, 1871.

Verse 81.—*"My soul fainteth for thy salvation ; but I hope."* Believe under a cloud, and wait for him when there is no moonlight nor starlight. Let faith live and breathe, and lay hold of the sure salvation of God, when clouds and darkness are about you, and appearance of rotting in the prison before you. Take heed of unbelieving hearts, which can father lies upon Christ. Beware of " Doth his promise fail for evermore ? " for it was a man, and not God said it. Who dreameth that a promise of God can fail, fall aswoon, or die ? Who can make God sick, or his promises weak ? When we are pleased to seek a plea with Christ, let us plead that we hope in him. O stout word of faith, " Though he slay me, yet will I trust in him ! " O sweet epitaph, written upon the grave-stone of a departed believer, namely, " I died hoping, and my dust and ashes believe in life ! " Faith's eyes, that can see through a mill-stone, can see through a gloom* of God, and under it read God's thoughts of love and peace. Hold fast Christ in the dark ; surely ye shall see the salvation of God. Your adversaries are ripe and dry for the fire. Yet a little while, and they shall go up in a flame ; the breath of the Lord, like a river of brimstone, shall kindle about them.—*Samuel Rutherford*, 1600—1661.

Verse 81.—*"For thy salvation."* Understood in a higher sense, the holy man longs for the coming of the Saviour in the flesh.—*Cornelius Jansen.*

---

* Frown.

Verse 81.—"*Thy salvation.*" A believer in God, how afflicted so ever he be, seeketh not to be delivered but in a way allowed by God ; "*My soul fainteth for thy salvation*"; or, till thou deliver me in thy good way.—*David Dickson.*

Verse 81.—"*I hope in thy word.*" David knew where he moored his ship. Hope without a promise is like an anchor without ground to hold by ; but David's hope fixed itself upon the divine word.—*William Gurnall.*

Verse 81.—"*I hope in thy word :*" i.e. I hope beyond anything I understand, and beyond anything I can possibly do, and beyond anything I deserve, and beyond all carnal and spiritual consolations, for I desire and look for Thee only. I seek Thee, not Thine : I long to hear "*Thy word,*" that I may obey it in patience and meekness.—*Le Blanc.*

Verses 81, 83.—It is good in all times of persecution or affliction to have an eye both on the promises and on the precepts ; for the looking to the promise doth encourage to hope, and the eyeing of the precepts doth prove the hope to be sound. The Psalmist *hoped in the word* (verse 81), and (verse 83), *he forgot not the statutes.* —*David Dickson.*

Verse 82.—"*Mine eyes fail for thy word.*" Has a mother promised to visit her son or daughter ? should she not be able to go, the remark of the son or daughter will be : "Alas ! my mother promised to come to me : how long have I been looking for her ? But a speck has grown on my eye." "I cannot see, my eyes have failed me " ; that is, by looking so intensely for her coming.—*Joseph Roberts.*

Verse 82.—"*Mine eyes fail for thy word.*" He was continuously lifting the eyes to heaven, looking for help from God. He was so perpetually doing this, that at length the eyes themselves became dim.

"*When wilt thou comfort me ?*" He was saying this in his heart ; he was saying this with his mouth ; he was saying the same thing with his eyes perpetually looking up to heaven.—*Wolfgang Musculus.*

Verse 82.—"*For thy word.*" The children of God make more of a promise than others do ; and that upon a double account : partly, because they value the blessing promised ; partly, because they are satisfied with the assurance given by God's word ; so that, whereas others pass by these things with a careless eye, their souls are lifted up to the constant and earnest expectation of the blessing promised. It is said of the hireling, that he must have his wages before the sun go down, because he is poor and hath set his heart upon it (Deut. xxiv. 15) ; or, as it is in the Hebrew, lifted up his soul to it, meaning thereby both his desire and hope. He esteemeth his wages ; for it is the solace of his labours, and the maintenance of his life ; and he assuredly expecteth it, upon the promise and covenant of him who setteth him awork. So it is with the children of God ; they esteem the blessings promised, and God's word giveth them good assurance that they do not wait upon him in vain.—*Thomas Manton.*

Verse 82.—"*Saying, When.*" The same spirit of faith which teaches a man to cry earnestly, teaches him to wait patiently ; for as it assures him that mercy is in the Lord's hand, so it assures him, it will come forth in the Lord's time.—*John Mason*, 1688.

Verse 82.—"*When wilt thou comfort me ?*" It is a customable manner of God's working with his children, to delay the answer to their prayers, and to suspend the performance of his promises : not because he is unwilling to give, but because he will have them better prepared to receive. *Tardius dando quod pettimus instantia nobis orationis indicit :* * he is slow to give that which we seek, that we should not seek slowly, but may be awakened to instancy and fervency in prayer, which he knows to be the service most acceptable unto him, and most profitable unto ourselves. —*William Cowper.*

Verse 82.—"*When wilt thou comfort me ?*" Let us complain not *of* God, but *to* God. Complaints of God give a vent to murmuring ; but complaints to God, to faith, hope, and patience.—*Thomas Manton.*

Verse 82.—The prophet, to prevent it from being supposed that he was too effeminate and faint-hearted, intimates that his fainting was not without cause. In asking God, "*When wilt thou comfort me ?*" he shows, with sufficient plainness, that he was for a long time, as it were, cast off and forsaken.—*John Calvin.*

Verse 82.—"*When wilt thou comfort me ?*" The people of God are sometimes

† Chrysostom.

very disconsolate, and need comforting, through the prevalence of sin, the power of Satan's temptations, the hidings of God's face, and a variety of afflictions, when they apply to God for comfort, who only can comfort them, and who has set them to do it ; but they are apt to think it long, and enquire, as David here, when it will be.—*John Gill.*

Verse 82.—*"When wilt thou comfort me ? "* A poor woman had been long time questioning herself, and doubting of her salvation ; when at last the Lord made it good unto her soul that Christ was her own, then her minister said unto her, The Lord will not always give his children a cordial, but he hath it ready for them when they are fainting.—*Thomas Hooker.*

Verse 82.—*"When wilt thou comfort me ? "* Comfort is necessary because a great part of our temptations lies in troubles, as well as allurements. Sense of pain may discompose us as well as pleasure entice us. The world is a persecuting as well as a tempting world. The flesh troubleth as well as enticeth. The Devil is a disquieting as well as an ensnaring Devil. But yet comfort, though necessary, is not so necessary as holiness : therefore, though comfort is not to be despised, yet sincere love to God is to be preferred, and, though it be not dispensed so certainly, so constantly, and in so high a degree in this world, we must be contented. The Spirit's comforting work is oftener interrupted than the work of holiness ; yet so much as is necessary to enable us to serve God in this world we shall assuredly receive.—*Thomas Manton.*

Verse 83.—*"A bottle in the smoke."* Sleep was out of the question, for I was . . . almost smothered with the smoke from a wood fire, for there was no chimney. I was indeed *"like a bottle in the smoke,"* turned black and dried almost to cracking ; for this was something of what the Psalmist had in view. The bottles being of leather, and being hung up in rooms with large fires of wood, and without chimneys, they became smoke-dried, shrivelled, and unfit for use.—*From "My Wanderings," by John Gadsby,* 1860.

Verse 83.—*"Like a bottle in the smoke."* The tent of a common Arab is so smoky a habitation, that I consider the expression of *a bottle in the smoke,* to be equivalent to that of *a bottle in the tent of an Arab.* There was a fire, we find, in that Arab tent to which Bishop Pococke was conducted when he was going to Jerusalem. How smoky must such an habitation be, and how black all its utensils ! Le Bruyn in going from Aleppo to Scanderoon was made sufficiently sensible of this : for being obliged to pass a whole night in a hut of reeds, in the middle of which there was a fire, to boil a kettle of meat that hung over it, and to bake some bread among the ashes, he found the smoke intolerable, the door being the only place by which it could get out of the hut.

To the *blackness* of a goat-skin bottle. in a tent. but to the *meanness* also of such a drinking-vessel, the Psalmist seems to refer, and it was a most natural image for him to make use of, driven from among the vessels of silver and gold in the palace of Saul, to live as the Arabs do and did, and consequently often obliged to drink out of a smoked leather-bottle.—*Thomas Harmer,* 1719—1788.

Verse 83.—*"For I am become like a bottle in the smoke."* A bottle in the smoke has very little inflation, fatness, moisture, beauty. Thus God wastes away, debases, and empties his people, while he exercises them with tribulations and the disquiet of hoping and waiting. The glory and eagerness of the flesh must be emptied, that the Divine gifts may find room, and the remembrance of the commandments of God may be restrained, which cannot be well kept in bottles which are swollen, inflated, and filled.—*Wolfgang Musculus.*

Verse 83.—*"A bottle in the smoke."* One object amongst the ancients of such exposure was to mellow the wine by the gradual ascent of the heat and smoke from the fire over which the skin was suspended ; and thus the words teach us the uses of affliction in ripening and improving the soul.—*Rosenmüller, quoted in Neale and Littledale.*

Verse 83.—*"For I am become like a bottle in the smoke,"* etc. Satan can afflict the *body* by the *mind.* For these two are so closely bound together that their good and bad estate is shared between them. If the heart be merry the countenance is cheerful, the strength is renewed, the bones do flourish like an herb. If the heart be troubled, the health is impaired, the strength is dried up, the marrow of the bones wasted, etc. Grief in the heart is like a moth in the garment, it insensibly consumeth the body and disordereth it. This advantage of weakening the body falls into Satan's hands by necessary consequence, as the prophet's ripe figs, that fell into the mouth of the eater.   And surely he is well pleased with it, as he is an enemy both to body and soul.   But 'tis a greater satisfaction to him, in that as he can make the sorrows of the mind produce the weakness and sickness of the body ; so can he make the distemper of the body (by a reciprocal requital) to augment the trouble of the mind.   How little can a sickly body do ?   it disables a man for all services ;   he cannot oft pray, nor read, nor hear.   Sickness takes away the sweetness and comfort of religious exercises ;   this gives occasion for them to think the worse of themselves ;   they think the soul is weary of the ways of God when the body cannot hold out.—*Richard Gilpin, in "A Treatise of Satan's Temptations," 1677.*

Verse 83.—*"Like a bottle in the smoke."*   In this did the afflicted Psalmist find a striking emblem of his own spiritual state.   He waited for the Lord to come.   In spirit he was dried up by pressure upon him ;   and he still waited for the Lord to come, declaring his shrivelled condition.   Perhaps his outward man partook of the same sad qualities at this time. . . .   The outward appearance of the man of God, to which he may be alluding, was, however, but the semblance of his spiritual nature at this period, whatever may have been the visible effects.   David was exposed to the calumnious reports of evil-minded men, and to the hot persecution of relent-less enemies, till the effect upon his mind was such that his whole spiritual nature resembled, in his own mind, a skin hung up in the smoke for a length of time.   Not only was he shrivelled in public estimation, but also in his own mind ;   not indeed because at this time, and on the ground of the charges made against him, he felt that he deserved it ;   but because so incessant and multifarious was the bitter invasion of his spirit, that even with all his faith in God, he well-nigh literally sunk under it.   The term given in our translation to the original would imply, that he bore himself well notwithstanding—*"For I am become like a bottle in the smoke ; yet do I not forget thy statutes."*   Whereas the words rendered more literally would convey the import that all this happened to him even while he was in the very way of duty :   *"I am become like a bottle in the smoke—I do not forget thy statutes."*   He was directly in the way of the Lord's appointments for all salvation ;   yet trouble came.   It is sad when our spiritual man becomes shrivelled and dried up because of our falling into sin, or because of guilty omissions ;   but here seems to be a falling off of the spiritual man, and of the physical man, while the believer is conscious that he is not forgetting the statutes of his gracious God.—*John Stephen.*

Verse 83.—Observe here the difference between the beauty and strength of the body and of the soul :   the beauty of the soul groweth fairer by afflictions, whereas that of the body is blasted.   David was a bottle shrivelled and shrunk up ;   yet the holy frame of his soul was not altered :   his beauty was gone, but not his grace.—*Thomas Manton.*

Verse 83.—*"I am become like a bottle in the frost"* (so the Seventy translate it).   When spiritual desires burn, carnal desires without doubt cool :   on this account followeth, *"Since I am become like a bottle in the frost I do not forget thy righteousness."*   Truly he desireth this mortal flesh to be understood by the bottle, the heavenly blessing by the frost, whereby the lusts of the flesh as it were by the binding of the frost become sluggish :   and hence it ariseth that the righteousnesses of God do not slip from the memory so long as we do not meditate apart from them ;   since what the apostle saith (Rom. xiii. 14) is brought to pass :   " Make not provision for the flesh, to fulfil the lusts thereof."   Therefore when he had said, *"For I have become like a bottle in the frost,"* he added, *"and I do not forget thy righteousnesses,"* that is, I forget them not, because I have become such.   For the fervour of lust had cooled, that the memory of love might glow.—*Augustine.*

Verse 84.—*"How many are the days of thy servant ? "* etc.   Some read the two clauses apart, as if the first were a general complaint of the brevity of human life, such as is to be met with in other Psalms, and more frequently in the book of Job ;   and next in their opinion, there follows a special prayer of the Psalmist that God would take vengeance upon his enemies.   But I rather prefer joining the two clauses together, and limit both to David's afflictions ;   as it it had been said, Lord, how long hast thou determined to abandon thy servant to the will of the ungodly ?   when wilt thou set thyself in opposition to their cruelty and outrage, in order to take vengeance upon them ?   The Scriptures often use the word *"days"* in this sense. . . .   By the use of the plural number is denoted a determinate portion of time, which, in other places, is compared to the " days of an hireling " :   Job xiv. 6 ;

Isaiah xvi. 14. The Psalmist does not, then, bewail in general the transitory life of man, but he complains that the time of his state of warfare in this world had been too long protracted ; and, therefore, he naturally desires that it might be brought to a termination. In expostulating with God about his troubles, he does not do so obstinately, or with a murmuring spirit ; but still, in asking how long it will be necessary for him to suffer, he humbly prays that God would not delay to succour him.—*John Calvin.*

Verse 84.—*"When wilt thou execute judgment on them that persecute me ?"* He declares that he does not doubt but that there will be at some period an end to his afflictions, and that there will be a time in which his haters and enemies will be judged and punished. He assumes the fact and therefore enquires the date. Thus in the saints their very impatience of delay does itself prove their confidence of future salvation and deliverance.—*Wolfgang Musculus.*

Verse 84.—*"When wilt thou execute judgment,"* etc. This is an ordinary prayer, not against any certain persons, but rather generally against God's enemies, and their evil courses. For the Lord executeth judgment upon his children for their conversion, as Paul (Acts ix.), and upon the wicked for their confusion. He prayeth against them that belonged not to God, and yet not so much against their persons as against their evil causes ; and no otherwise against their persons than as they are joined with the evil causes. Thus we may pray for the confusion of God's enemies ; otherwise we cannot.—*R. Greenham.*

Verse 84.—In this verse there is none of the ten words used in reference to God's law.—*Adam Clarke.* [Is not judgment one of them ?—C. H. S.]

Verse 85.—*"Pits."* Hajji said he would tell me a tale or two about crocodiles, and he would begin by telling me how they catch them sometimes. A deep pit, he said, is dug by the side of the river, and then covered with doura straw. The crocodiles fall into these pits, and cannot get out again. . . . . There can be no doubt that formerly pits were dug for the crocodiles, as Hajji described, as is the case still in some parts of the world for other animals. To this custom allusion is made in Ps. vii. 15 ; ix. 15 ; x. 2 ; xxxv. 8 ; cxli. 10 ; Prov. xxvi. 27 ; Eccles. x. 8 : etc. " He made a pit and digged it, and is fallen into the ditch which he made." Probably also this was the kind of pit referred to in Exod. xxi. 33 : " If a man shall dig a pit, and not cover it"; *i.e.,* not cover it effectually ; " and an ass or an ox fall therein," etc.

Prisoners were sometimes shut up in pits, and left without water, literally to die of thirst. What a dreadful death ! It is said that nothing can be more terrible. How dreadful must be their groans !—*John Gadsby.*

Verse 85.—*"The proud have digged pits."* It seems strange that a proud man should be a digger of pits ; but so it is ; for pride for a time can submit itself to gain a greater vantage over him whom it would tread under foot. " The wicked is so proud that he seeks not God, yet he croucheth and boweth, to cause heaps of the poor to fall by his might," Ps. x. 4, 10. So proud Absalom abased himself to meanest subjects that so he might prepare a way to usurpation over his king and father. But mark, he saith not that he had fallen into the pits which his enemies had digged. No, no : in God's righteous judgments, the wicked are snared in the work of their own hands, while the good escape free. " He made a pit, and digged it, and is fallen into the ditch which he made. His mischief shall return upon his own head, and his violent dealing shall come down upon his own pate." Ps. viii. 15, 16. Thus Haman hanselled the gallows which he raised for Mordecai ; and Saul when he thought by subtlety to slay David with the Philistine's sword (when he sent him out to seek two hundred of their foreskins in a dowry) was disappointed of his purpose ; but he himself at length was slain by the sword.—*William Cowper.*

Verse 85.—Let men beware how they *dig pits* for others. All God's word testifies against such wickedness. How many tests are invented simply for the purpose of entangling men's consciences and furnishing ground for persecution.—*William S. Plumer.*

Verse 85.—*"Which are not after thy law."* Hebrew, Not after thy law. It may refer to the men or to the practice. The men walk not according to thy law, and their fraudulent practices are not agreeable to thy law. The law of God condemned pits for tame beasts : Exodus xxi. 33, 34. Though it was lawful for hunters to take wild beasts, yet they were to take heed that a tame beast fell not therein, at their peril.—*Thomas Manton.*

Verse 85.—*"Which are not after thy law."* After God's law they could not be while they were doing such things. Perhaps he refers to the deed more than to the men : " The proud have digged pits for me, which is not after thy law "—which is against thy law ; and they would seem to do it because it is against thy law— delighting in wickedness as they do. Such men would seem to imbibe the foul spirit which Milton ascribes to the fallen archangel : " Evil, be thou my good." Obviously, however, the words contain this sentiment,—The proud have sought to overthrow me, because they are not obedient to thy law. Hereupon he sets their conduct in the light of God's holy commandments, that the comparison may be made : *"All thy commandments are faithful : they persecute me wrongfully."* Whatever the Lord did was done in truth ; these men acted against his servant without cause, and in so doing they also acted in defiance of his known will.—*John Stephen.*

Verse 85.—*"The wicked have told me fables, but not as thy law"* (So the Septuagint). The special reason why he desires to be freed from the company of the wicked is, because they always tempt the pious by relating the pleasures of the world, which are nothing but fables, filthy, fleeting pleasures, more fallacious than real—nothing like the grand and solid pleasure that always flows from a pious observance of the law of the Lord.—*Robert Bellarmine.*

Verse 86.—*"All thy commandments are faithful."* David setteth down here three points. The one is that God is true ; and after that he addeth a protestation of his good conduct and guidance, and of the malice of his adversaries : thirdly, he calleth upon God in his afflictions. Now as concerning the first, he showeth us that although Satan to shake us, and in the end utterly to carry us away, subtilly and cunningly goeth about to deceive us, we must, to the contrary, learn how to know his ambushes, and to keep us from out of them. So often then as we are grieved with adversity and affliction, where must we begin ? See Satan how he pitcheth his nets and layeth his ambushes to induce and persuade us to come into them, what sayeth he ? Dost thou not see thyself forsaken of thy God ? Where are the promises whereunto thou didst trust ? Now here thou seest thyself to be a wretched, forlorn creature. So then thou right well seest that God hath deceived thee, and that the promises whereunto thou trustedst appertain nothing at all unto thee. See here the subtlety of Satan. What is now to be done ? We are to conclude with David and say, yet God is true and faithful. Let us, I say, keep in mind the truth of God as a shield to beat back whatsoever Satan is able to lay unto our charge. When he shall go about to cause us to deny our faith, when he shall lie about us to make us believe that God thinketh no more of us, or else that it is in vain for us to trust unto his promises ; let us know the clean contrary and believe that it is very plain and sound truth which God saith unto us. Although Satan casteth at us never so many darts, although he have never so exceeding many devices against us, although now and then by violence, sometimes with subtility and cunning, it seemeth in very deed to us that he should overcome us ; nevertheless he shall never bring it to pass, for the truth of God shall be made sure and certain in our hearts.—*John Calvin.*

Verse 86.—*"All thy commandments are faithful."* The Hebrew is *Faithfulness ;* that is to say, they are true, sure, equal, infallible. *"They have persecuted me wrongfully :"* no doubt for asserting God's truths and commands, and adhering thereto.—*John Trapp.*

Verse 86.—*"They persecute me wrongfully."* There is a stress on the word *falsely* (or wrongfully) ; for that is a true saying of a martyr saint,* " The cause, not the pain, makes the martyr." Wherefore the apostle teaches us, " Let none of you suffer as a murderer or as a thief, or as an evil-doer, or as a busybody in other men's matters. Yet if any man suffer as a Christian, let him not be ashamed ; but let him glorify God on this behalf."—*Neale and Littledale.*

Verse 86.—*"Help thou me,"* " God help me " is an excellent, comprehensive prayer ; it is a pity it should ever be used lightly and as a bye-word.—*Matthew Henry.*

Verse 87.—*"Almost consumed."* The lives of good men are full of narrow escapes. The righteous are scarcely saved. Many a time their feet do almost

---

* Cyprian.

slip.   Yet he, who has redeemed them, will not let them so fall that they can rise no more.   One of their greatest perils is, a temptation to use unlawful means for terminating their trials.—*William S. Plumer.*

Verse 87.—It should be noticed that he says *"upon the earth:"* for it shows, that even if his enemies had taken away his life on earth, he nevertheless confidently looked for another life in heaven, and that already he had by faith entered into heaven, and was living a heavenly life; so that if the life of the body should be taken away, it was not to be regarded as an evil.   They who live such a life speedily recover from despair.—*D. H. Mollerus.*

Verse 88.—*"Quicken me after thy lovingkindness."*   Finally, the man of God appears entreating to be quickened, that so he may be enabled to keep the divine testimony. . . . Here is a last resort, but it is a sure one.   Let the living principles of divine grace be imparted to the soul, and the believer will be raised above dismay at the face of men.   How does the spiritual mind triumph over even the infirmities of the body!   We may behold this from the death-bed of the believer, and we may recall this in the lives and deaths of many eminent ones.   The man of pure mind goes right to the fountain of life.   He goes, with understanding, for he takes in the character in which the Lord hath spoken of himself: *"Quicken me after thy lovingkindness."*   All at once he lays aside thought of his enemies; he is present with his God.   His desire is to rise into higher spiritual existence, that he may hold closer communion with the Father of lights with whom there is no variableness. —*John Stephen.*

Verse 88.—*"Quicken me,"* etc.   He had prayed before, " Quicken me in thy righteousness " (verse 40); but here " Quicken me after thy lovingkindness." The surest token of God's good-will towards us is his good work in us.—*Matthew Henry.*

Verse 88.—*"Quicken me."*   Many a time in this Psalm doth David make this petition; and it seems strange that so often he should acknowledge himself a dead man, and desire God to quicken him.   But so it is unto the child of God: every desertion and decay of strength is a death.   So desirous are they to live unto God, that when they fail in it, and find any inability in their souls to serve God as they would, they account themselves but dead, and pray the Lord to quicken them.— *William Cowper.*

Verse 88.—*"The testimony of thy mouth."*   The title here given to the directory of our duty—*"The testimony of God's mouth,"* gives increasing strength to our obligations.   Thus let every word we read or hear be regarded as coming directly from the " mouth of God " (John vi. 63).   What reverence!   what implicit submission does it demand!   May it ever find us in the posture of attention, humility, and faith!   each one of us ready to say, " Speak Lord, for thy servant heareth."—*Charles Bridges.*

EXPOSITION OF VERSES 89 TO 96.

FOR ever, O LORD, thy word is settled in heaven.

90 Thy faithfulness *is* unto all generations : thou hast established the earth, and it abideth.

91 They continue this day according to thine ordinances : for all *are* thy servants.

92 Unless thy law *had been* my delights, I should then have perished in mine affliction.

93 I will never forget thy precepts : for with them thou hast quickened me.

94 I *am* thine, save me ; for I have sought thy precepts.

95 The wicked have waited for me to destroy me : *but* I will consider thy testimonies.

96 I have seen an end of all perfection : *but* thy commandment *is* exceeding broad.

89. *"For ever, O Lord, thy word is settled in heaven."* The strain is more joyful, for experience has given the sweet singer a comfortable knowledge of the word of the Lord, and this makes a glad theme. After tossing about on a sea of trouble the Psalmist here leaps to shore and stands upon a rock. Jehovah's word is not fickle nor uncertain ; it is settled, determined, fixed, sure, immovable. Man's teachings change so often that there is never time for them to be settled ; but the Lord's word is from of old the same, and will remain unchanged eternally. Some men are never happier than when they are unsettling everything and everybody ; but God's mind is not with them. The power and glory of heaven have confirmed each sentence which the mouth of the Lord has spoken, and so confirmed it that to all eternity it must stand the same,—settled in heaven, where nothing can reach it. In the former section David's soul fainted, but here the good man looks out of self and perceives that the Lord fainteth not, neither is weary, neither is there any failure in his word.

The verse takes the form of an ascription of praise : the faithfulness and immutability of God are fit themes for holy song, and when we are tired with gazing upon the shifting scene of this life, the thought of the immutable promise fills our mouth with singing. God's purposes, promises, and precepts are all settled in his own mind, and none of them shall be disturbed. Covenant settlements will not be removed, however unsettled the thoughts of men may become ; let us therefore settle it in our minds that we abide in the faith of our Jehovah as long as we have any being.

90. *"Thy faithfulness is unto all generations."* This is an additional glory : God is not affected by the lapse of ages ; he is not only faithful to one man throughout his lifetime, but to his children's children after him, yea, and to all generations so long as they keep his covenant and remember his commandments to do them. The promises are ancient things, yet they are not worn out by centuries of use, for the divine faithfulness endureth for ever. He who succoured his servants thousands of years ago still shows himself strong on the behalf of all them that trust in him. *"Thou hast established the earth, and it abideth."* Nature is governed by fixed laws ; the globe keeps its course by the divine command, and displays no erratic movements : the seasons observe their predestined order, the sea obeys the rule of ebb and flow, and all things else are marshalled in their appointed order. There is an analogy between the word of God and the works of God, and specially

in this, that they are both of them constant, fixed, and unchangeable. God's word which established the world is the same as that which he has embodied in the Scriptures ; by the word of the Lord were the heavens made, and specially by him who is emphatically THE WORD. When we see the world keeping its place and all its laws abiding the same, we have herein assurance that the Lord will be faithful to his covenant, and will not allow the faith of his people to be put to shame. If the earth abideth the spiritual creation will abide ; if God's word suffices to establish the world surely it is enough for the establishment of the individual believer.

91. *"They continue this day according to thine ordinances."* Because the Lord has bid the universe abide, therefore it stands, and all its laws continue to operate with precision and power. Because the might of God is ever present to maintain them, therefore do all things continue. The word which spake all things into existence has supported them till now, and still supports them both in being and in well-being. God's ordinance is the reason for the continued existence of creation. What important forces these ordinances are ! *"For all are thy servants."* Created by thy word they obey that word, thus answering the purpose of their existence, and working out the design of their Creator. Both great things and small pay homage to the Lord. No atom escapes his rule, no world avoids his government. Shall we wish to be free of the Lord's sway and become lords unto ourselves ? If we were so, we should be dreadful exceptions to a law which secures the well-being of the universe. Rather while we read concerning all things else—they continue and they serve, let us continue to serve, and to serve more perfectly as our lives are continued. By that word which is settled may we be settled ; by that voice which establishes the earth may we be established ; and by that command which all created things obey may we be made the servants of the Lord God Almighty.

92. *"Unless thy law had been my delights, I should then have perished in mine affliction."* That word which has preserved the heavens and the earth also preserves the people of God in their time of trial. With that word we are charmed ; it is a mine of delight to us. We take a double and treble delight in it, and derive a multiplied delight from it, and this stands us in good stead when all other delights are taken from us. We should have felt ready to lie down and die of our griefs if the spiritual comforts of God's word had not uplifted us ; but by their sustaining influence we have been borne above all the depressions and despairs which naturally grow out of severe affliction. Some of us can set our seal to this statement. Our affliction, if it had not been for divine grace, would have crushed us out of existence, so that we should have perished. In our darkest seasons nothing has kept us from desperation but the promise of the Lord : yea, at times nothing has stood between us and self-destruction save faith in the eternal word of God. When worn with pain until the brain has become dazed and the reason well-nigh extinguished, a sweet text has whispered to us its heart-cheering assurance, and our poor struggling mind has reposed upon the bosom of God. That which was our delight in prosperity has been our light in adversity ; that which in the day kept us from presuming has in the night kept us from perishing. This verse contains a mournful supposition —*"unless"*; describes a horrible condition—*"perished in mine affliction"*; and implies a glorious deliverance, for he did not die, but lived to proclaim the honours of the word of God.

93.—*"I will never forget thy precepts : for with them thou hast quickened me."* When we have felt the quickening power of a precept we never can forget it. We may read it, learn it, repeat it, and think we have it, and yet it may slip out of our minds ; but if it has once given us life or renewed that life, there is no fear of its falling from our recollection. Experience teaches, and teaches effectually. How blessed a thing it is to have the precepts written on the heart with the golden pen of experience, and graven on the memory with the divine stylus of grace. Forgetfulness is a great evil in holy things ; we see here the man of God fighting against it, and feeling sure of victory because he knew the life-giving energy of the word in his own soul. That which quickens the heart is sure to quicken the memory.

It seems singular that he should ascribe quickening to the precepts, and yet it lies in them and in all the words of the Lord alike. It is to be noted that when the Lord raised the dead he addressed to them the word of command. He said, "Lazarus, come forth," or, "Maid, arise." We need not fear to address gospel precepts to dead sinners, since by them the Spirit gives them life. Remark that the Psalmist does not say that the precepts quickened him, but that the Lord quickened him by their means : thus he traces the life from the channel to the source, and places the glory where it is due. Yet at the same time he prized the instruments of the blessing, and resolved never to forget them. He had already remembered them when he likened himself to a bottle in the smoke, and now he feels that whether in the smoke or in the fire the memory of the Lord's precepts shall never depart from him.

94. *"I am thine, save me."* A comprehensive prayer with a prevailing argument. Consecration is a good plea for preservation. If we are conscious that we are the Lord's we may be confident that he will save us. We are the Lord's by creation, election, redemption, surrender, and acceptance ; and hence our firm hope and assured belief that he will save us. A man will surely save his own child : Lord, save *me*. The need of salvation is better seen by the Lord's people than by any others, and hence their prayer—" save me " ; they know that only God can save them, and hence they cry to him alone ; and they know that no merit can be found in themselves, and hence they urge a reason fetched from the grace of God,—" I am thine." *"For I have sought thy precepts."* Thus had he proved that he was the Lord's. He might not have attained to all the holiness which he desired, but he had studiously aimed at being obedient to the Lord, and hence he begged to be saved even to the end. A man may be seeking the doctrines and the promises, and yet be unrenewed in heart ; but to seek the precepts is a sure sign of grace ; no one ever heard of a rebel or a hypocrite seeking the precepts. The Lord had evidently wrought a great work upon the Psalmist, and he besought him to carry it on to completion. Saving is linked with seeking, " save me, for I have sought " ; and when the Lord sets us seeking he will not refuse us the saving. He who seeks holiness is already saved ; if we have sought the Lord we may be sure that the Lord has sought us, and will certainly save us.

95.—*"The wicked have waited for me to destroy me : but I will consider thy testimonies."* They were like wild beasts crouching by the way, or highwaymen waylaying a defenceless traveller ; but the Psalmist went on his way without considering them, for he was considering something better, namely, the witness or testimony which God has borne to the sons of men. He did not allow the malice of the wicked to take him off from his holy study of the divine word. He was so calm that he could " consider " ; so holy that he loved to consider the Lord's " testimonies " ; so victorious over all their plots that he did not allow them to drive him from his pious contemplations. If the enemy cannot cause us to with-draw our thoughts from holy study, or our feet from holy walking, or our hearts from holy aspirations, he has met with poor success in his assaults. The wicked are the natural enemies of holy men and holy thoughts ; if they could, they would not only damage us but destroy us, and if they cannot do this to-day they will wait for further opportunities, ever hoping that their evil designs may be compassed. They have waited hitherto in vain, and they will have to wait much longer yet ; for if we are so unmoved that we do not even give them a thought their hope of destroying us must be a very poor one.

Note the double waiting,—the patience of the wicked who watch long and carefully for an opportunity to destroy the godly, and then the patience of the saint who will not quit his meditations, even to quiet his foes. See how the serpent seed lie in wait as an adder that biteth at the horse's heels ; but see how the chosen of the Lord live above their venom, and take no more notice of them than if they had no existence.

96.—*"I have seen an end of all perfection."* He had seen its limit, for it went but a little way ; he had seen its evaporation under the trials of life, its detection under the searching glance of truth, its exposure by the confession of the penitent. There is no perfection beneath the moon. Perfect men, in the absolute sense of the word, live only in a perfect world. Some men see no end to their own perfection, but this is because they are perfectly blind. The experienced believer has seen an end of all perfection in himself, in his brethren, in the best man's best works. It would be well if some who profess to be perfect could even see the beginning of perfection, for we fear they cannot have begun aright, or they would not talk so exceeding proudly. Is it not the beginning of perfection to lament your imperfec-tion ? There is no such thing as perfection in anything which is the work of man. *"But thy commandment is exceeding broad."* When the breadth of the law is known the notion of perfection in the flesh vanishes : that law touches every act, word, and thought, and is of such a spiritual nature that it judges the motives, desires, and emotions of the soul. It reveals a perfection which convicts us for shortcomings as well as for transgressions, and does not allow us to make up for deficiencies in one direction by special carefulness in others. The divine ideal of holiness is far too broad for us to hope to cover all its wide arena, and yet it is no broader than it ought to be. Who would wish to have an imperfect law? Nay, its perfection is its glory; but it is the death of all glorying in our own perfection. There is a breadth about the commandment which has never been met to the full by a corresponding breadth of holiness in any mere man while here below; only in Jesus do we see it fully embodied. The law is in all respects a perfect code; each separate precept of it is far-reaching in its hallowed meaning, and the whole ten cover all, and leave no space wherein to please our passions. We may well adore the infinity of divine holiness, and then measure ourselves by its standard, and bow before the Lord in all lowliness, acknowledging how far we fall short of it.

NOTES ON VERSES 89 TO 96.

LAMED.—*Verse* 89.—Here the climax of the delineation of the suppliant's pilgrimage is reached. We have arrived at the centre of the Psalm, and the thread of the connexion is purposely broken off. The substance of the first eleven strophes has evidently been : "Hitherto hath the Lord brought me : shall it be that I now perish ? " To this the eleven succeeding strophes make answer, "The Lord's word changeth not ; and in spite of all evil forebodings, the Lord will perfect concerning me the work that he hath already begun."—*Joseph Francis Thrupp*, 1860.

Verse 89.—*"For ever, O* LORD, *thy word is settled in heaven."* These words are usually rendered as making but one proposition ; but the accent *athnab* showeth there are two branches ; the one asserting the eternity of God ; the other, the constancy and permanency of his word. Thus, 1. *"For ever* [*art thou*] *O* LORD." 2. *"Thy word is settled in heaven."* So the Syriac readeth it ; and Geierus, and, after him, others prove and approve this reading. And so this verse and the following do the better correspond one with the other, if we observe beginning and ending : As thou art "for ever, O Lord," and "thy faithfulness is unto all generations," which are exactly parallel. And so also will the last clauses agree : "Thy word is settled in heaven," and, "thou hast established the earth, and it abideth."

It implieth that as God is eternal, so is his word, and that it hath a fit representation both in heaven and in earth : in heaven, in the constant motion of the heavenly bodies ; in earth, in the consistency and permanency thereof ; that as his word doth stand fast in heaven, so doth his faithfulness on earth, where the afflictions of the godly seem to contradict it.—*Thomas Manton.*

Verse 89.—*"For ever, O* LORD, *thy word is settled in heaven."* When Job considers his body turned to dust and worms (Job xix. 19, 25), yet by faith he says, "My Redeemer lives," etc. Even when patience failed in Job, yet *faith* failed not. Though God kill all other graces and comforts, and my soul too, yet he shall not kill my faith, says he. If he separate my soul from my body, yet not faith from my soul. And therefore the just lives by faith, rather than by other graces, because when all is gone, yet faith remains, and faith remains because the *promise* remains : *"For ever, O* LORD, *thy word is settled in heaven."* And this is the proper and principal meaning of this place.—*Matthew Lawrence.*

Verse 89.—*"For ever, O* LORD, *thy word is settled in heaven."* If we look at God's word of promise, as it is in our unsettled hearts, we dream that it's as ready to waver as our hearts are ; as the shadow of the sun and moon in the water seems to shake as much as the water doth which it shines upon. Yet for all this seeming shaking here below, the sun and moon go on in a steadfast course in heaven. So the Psalmist tells us that however our hearts stagger at a promise through unbelief ; nay, and our unbelief makes us believe that the promise often is shaken ; yet *God's word is settled*, though not *in our hearts*, yet *"in heaven"* ; yea, and there *"for ever,"* as settled as heaven itself is ; yea, more than so ; for " heaven and earth may pass," but "not one jot or tittle of the law (and therefore of the gospel) shall fail " : Luke xvi. 17.—*Anthony Tuckney*, 1599—1670.

Verse 89.—*"Settled."* J. M. Good translates the verse as follows—" For ever, O Jehovah, hath thy word given array to the heavens," and observes that the Hebrew word נצב is a military term, and applies to arraying and marshalling the divisions of an army in their proper stations when taking the field. The hosts of heaven are here supposed to be arrayed or marshalled with a like exact order ; and to maintain for ever the relative duties imposed on them : while the earth, like the heavens, has as established a march prescribed to it, which it equally fulfils ; for all are the servants of the great Creator ; and hence, as they change, produce the beautiful regularity of the seasons, the rich returns of harvest, and daily declare the glory of the Lord.

Verse 89.—*"In heaven."* Whenever you look to heaven, remember that within you have a God, who hath fixed his residence and shown his glory there, and made it the seat both of his mercy and justice.   You have also there a Saviour, who, after he had died for our sins, sat down at the right hand of Majesty, to see his promises accomplished, and by his word to subdue the whole world.   There are angels that " do his commandment, hearkening to the voice of his word " : Ps. ciii. 20. There are glorified saints, who see God face to face, and dwell with him for evermore, and came thither by the same covenant which is propounded to us, as the charter of our peace and hope.   In the outer region of heaven we see the sun and moon, and all the heavenly bodies, move in that fixed course and order wherein God hath set them ; and will God show his constancy in the course of nature, and be fickle and changeable in the covenant of grace, wherein he hath disposed the order and method of his mercies ?—*Thomas Manton.*

Verses 89, 91.—In these verses there is affirmed to be an analogy between the word of God and the works of God.   It is said of his *"word,"* that it is *"settled in heaven,"* and that it sustains its faithfulness from one generation to another.   It is said of his *"works,"* and more especially of those that are immediately around us, even of the earth which we inhabit, that as it was established at the first so it abideth afterwards.   And then, as if to perfect the assimilation between them, it is said of both in the 91st verse, *"They continue this day according to thine ordinances : for all are thy servants"*; thereby identifying the sureness of that word which proceeded from his lips, with the unfailing constancy of that Nature which was formed and is upholden by his hands.

The constancy of Nature is taught by universal experience, and even strikes the popular eye as the most characteristic of those features which have been impressed upon her.   It may need the aid of philosophy to learn how unvarying Nature is in all her processes—how even the seeming anomalies can be traced to a law that is inflexible —how what appears at first to be the caprices of her waywardness, are, in fact, the evolutions of a mechanism that never changes—and that the more thoroughly she is sifted and put to the test by the interrogations of the curious, the more certainly will they find that she walks by a rule which knows no abatement, and perseveres with obedient footstep in that even course from which the eye of strictest scrutiny has never yet detected one hair-breadth of deviation.   It is no longer doubted by men of science, that every remaining semblance of irregularity in the universe is due, not to the fickleness of Nature, but to the ignorance of man—that her most hidden movements are conducted with a uniformity as rigorous as *Fate*—that even the fitful agitations of the weather have their law and their principle—that the intensity of every breeze, and the number of drops in every shower, and the formation of every cloud, and all the occurring alternations of storm and sunshine, and the endless shiftings of temperature, and those tremulous varieties of the air which our instruments have enabled us to discover but have not enabled us to explain—that still, they follow each other by a method of succession, which, though greatly more intricate, is yet as absolute in itself as the order of the seasons, or the mathematical courses of astronomy.   This is the impression of every philosophical mind with regard to Nature, and it is strengthened by each new accession that is made to science. . . . . But there is enough of patent and palpable regularity in Nature to give also to the popular mind the same impression of her constancy.   There is a gross and general experience that teaches the same lesson, and that has lodged in every bosom a kind of secure and steadfast confidence in the uniformity of her processes.   The very child knows and proceeds upon it.   He is aware of an abiding character and property in the elements around him, and has already learned as much of the fire, and the water, and the food that he eats, and the firm ground that he treads upon, and even of the gravitation by which he must regulate his postures and his movements, as to prove that, infant though he be, he is fully initiated in the doctrine, that Nature has her laws and her ordinances, and that she continueth therein, and the proofs of this are ever multiplying along the journey of human observation ; insomuch that when we come to manhood, we read of Nature's constancy throughout every department of the visible world. It meets us wherever we turn our eyes. . . . . God has so framed the machinery of my perceptions, as that I am led irresistibly to expect that everywhere events will follow each other in the very train in which I have ever been accustomed to observe them ; and when God so sustains the uniformity of Nature, that in every instance it is rigidly so, he is just manifesting the faithfulness of his character.   Were it otherwise, he would be practising a mockery on the expectation which he himself had inspired.   God may be said to have promised to every human being that Nature will be constant—if not by the whisper of an inward voice to every heart, at least by the force of an uncontrollable bias which he has impressed on every constitution. So that, when we behold Nature keeping up its constancy, we behold the God of Nature keeping up his faithfulness ; and the system of visible things with its general laws, and its successions which are invariable, instead of an opaque materialism to intercept from the view of mortals the face of the Divinity, becomes the mirror which reflects upon the truth that is unchangeable, the ordination that never fails. . . . . And so it is, that in our text there are represented together, as if there was a tie of likeness between them—that the same God who is fixed as to the ordinances of Nature, is faithful as to the declarations of his word ; and as all experience proves how firmly he may be trusted for the one, so is there an argument as strong as experience, to prove how firmly he may be trusted for the other.   By his work in us he hath awakened the expectation of a constancy in Nature, which he never disappoints.   By his word to us, should he awaken the expectation of a certainty in his declarations, this he will never disappoint.   It is because Nature is so fixed, that we apprehend the God of Nature to be so faithful.   He who never falsifies the hope that hath arisen in every bosom, from the instinct which he himself hath communicated, will never falsify the hope that shall arise in any bosom from the express utterance of his voice.   Were he a God in whose hand the processes of nature were ever shifting, then might we conceive him a God from whose mouth the proclamations of grace had the like characters of variance and vacillation.   But it is just because of our reliance on the one that we feel so much of repose in our dependence upon the other ; and the same God who is so unfailing in the ordinances of his creation, we hold to be equally unfailing in the ordinances of his word.—*Thomas Chalmers.*

Verse 90.—*"Thy faithfulness is unto all generations."*   As he gathered the certainty of God's word from the endurance of heaven, so now he confirms it by considering the foundation of the earth.   Since the foundation of the earth, made by the word of God, abides sure, shall we not think that the foundation of our salvation, laid in Jesus Christ, is much more sure ?   Though the creatures cannot teach us the way of our salvation (for that we must learn by the word), yet do they confirm that which the word saith, " Thus saith the LORD, which giveth the sun for a light by day, and the ordinances of the moon and of the stars for a light by night, which divideth the sea when the waves thereof roar ; the LORD of hosts is his name : if those ordinances depart from before me, saith the LORD, then the seed of Israel also shall cease from being a nation before me for ever : " Jerem. xxxi. 35, 36.   As there Jeremy gathers the stability of the church from the stability of the creatures ; so here David confirms the certainty of our salvation by the most certain and unchangeable course of creation ; and both of them are amplified by Christ Jesus : " Heaven and earth may pass away, but one jot of God's word shall not fall to the ground."   Let us therefore be strengthened in faith and give glory to God.—*William Cowper.*

Verse 90.—*"Thou hast established the earth, and it abideth."*   Every time we set foot on the ground, we may remember the stability of God's promises, and it is also a confirmation of faith.   Thus,—

1. The stability of the earth is the effect of God's word ; this is the true pillar upon which the earth standeth ; for he upholdeth all things by the word of his power ;   " For he spake, and it was done ; he commanded, and it stood fast " : Ps. xxxiii. 9.   Now, his word of power helpeth us to depend upon his word of promise.

2. Nothing appeareth whereon the globe of the earth should lean and rest : " He stretcheth out the north over the empty place, and hangeth the earth upon nothing : " Job xxvi. 7.   Now, that this vast and ponderous body should lean upon the fluid air as upon a firm foundation, is matter of wonder ; the question is put in the book of Job : " Whereupon are the foundations thereof fastened ? or who laid the corner-stone thereof ? " ch. xxxviii. 6.   Yet firm it is, though it hang as a ball in the air. . . . Now, since his word beareth up such a weight, and all the church's weight, and our own burden leaneth on the promise of God, he can, by the power of his word, bear up all without visible means.   Therefore his people may trust his providence ; he is able to support them in any distresses, when no way of help appeareth.

3. The firmness and stability offereth itself to our thoughts.   The earth abideth in the same seat and condition wherein God left it, as long as the present course

and order of nature is to continue : Ps. civ. 5.   God's truth is as immovable as the earth : Ps. cxvii. 2.   Surely if the foundation of the earth abideth sure, the foundation of our salvation, laid by Jesus Christ, is much more sure.

4. The stability remains in the midst of changes : Eccles. i. 4.   All things in the world are subject to many revolutions, but God's truth is one and the same.

5. In upholding the frame of the world, all those attributes are seen, which are a firm stay to a believer's heart, such as wisdom, power, and goodness.   The covenant of grace is as sure as the covenant made after the deluge.   We cannot look upon this earth without seeing therein a display of those same attributes which confirm our faith, in waiting upon God till his promises be fulfilled to us.—*Condensed from T. Manton.*

Verse 90.—"It abideth."   Creation is as the mother, and Providence the nurse which preserveth all the works of God.   God is not like man ; for man, when he hath made a work, cannot maintain it : he buildeth a ship, and cannot save it from shipwreck ; he edifies a house, but cannot keep it from decay.   It is otherwise with God ; we daily see his conserving power, upholding his creatures ; which should confirm us that he will not cast us off, nor suffer us to perish (since we are the works of his hands) if we so depend upon him, and give him glory as our Creator, Conserver, and Redeemer.—*William Cowper.*

Verse 91.—"They continue this day according to thine ordinances," etc.   Which of the works of God are not pervaded by a beautiful *order ?*   Think of the succession of day and night.   Think of the revolution of the seasons.   Think of the stars as they walk in their majestic courses,—one great law of harmony " binding the sweet influence of the Pleiades, ... and guiding Arcturus with his sons " : Job xxxviii. 31, 32.   Look upwards, amid the magnificence of night, to that crowded concave,— worlds piled on worlds—and yet see the calm grandeur of that stately march ;— not a discordant note there to mar the harmony, though wheeling at an inconceivable velocity in their intricate and devious orbits !   These heavenly sentinels all keep their appointed watch-towers.   These Levites in the upper firmament, light their altar fires " at the time of the evening incense," and quench them again, when the sun, who is appointed to rule the day, walks forth from his chamber.   " These wait all upon thee" : Ps. civ. 27.   *"They continue this day according to thine ordinances : for all are thy servants."—J. R. Macduff, in "Sunsets on the Hebrew Mountains,"* 1862.

Verse 91.—"They continue this day according to thine ordinances."   Man may destroy a plant, but he is powerless to force it into disobedience to the laws given it by the common Creator.   " If," says one, " man would employ it for his use, he must carefully pay attention to its wants and ways, and bow his own proud will to the humblest grass at his feet.   Man may forcibly obstruct the path of a growing twig, but it turns quietly aside, and moves patiently and irresistibly on its appointed way."   Do what he may, turf will not grow in the tropics, nor the palm bear its fruit in a cold climate.   Rice refuses to thrive out of watery swamps, or cotton to form its fleece of snowy fibres where the rain can reach them.   Some of the handsomest flowers in the world, and stranger still, some of the most juicy and succulent plants with which we are acquainted, adorn the arid and desolate sands of the Cape of Good Hope, and will not flourish elsewhere.   If you twist the branch of a tree so as to turn the under surface of its leaves towards the sky, in a very little while all those leaves will turn down and assume their appointed position.   This process will be performed sooner or later, according to the heat of the sun and the flexibility of the leaves, but none the less it will surely take place. You cannot induce the Sorrowful tree of India to bloom by day, or cause it to cease all the year round from loading the night air with the rich perfume of its orange- like flowers.   The philosopher need not go far to find the secret of this.   The Psalmist declares it when, speaking of universal nature, he traces the true cause of its immutable order.   God he says, " hath established them for ever and ever : He hath made a decree which shall not pass ; " or, as it is in the Prayer-book version, " hath given them a law which shall not be broken " : Psalm cxlviii. 6.   Truly is it said in another Psalm (cxix. 91), *"They continue this day according to thine ordinances : for all are thy servants."*   Wilful man may dare to defy his Maker, and set at nought his wise and merciful commands ; but not so all nature besides. Well, indeed, is it for us that his other works have not erred after the pattern of our rebellion ; that seed-time and harvest, cold and heat, summer and winter, day and night, with all their accompanying provision, have not ceased ! To the precepts imposed upon vegetation when first called into being on creation's third day, it still yields implicit submission, and the tenderest plant will die rather than transgress.   What an awful contrast to this is the conduct of man, God's noblest work, endowed with reason and a never-dying soul, yet too often ruining his health, wasting and destroying his mental power, defiling his immortal spirit, and, in a word, madly endeavouring to frustrate every purpose for which he was framed.— *James Neil, in "Rays from the Realms of Nature,"* 1879.

Verse 91.—All creatures punctually observe the law he hath implanted on their nature, and in their several capacities acknowledge him their sovereign ; they move according to the inclinations he imprinted on them.   The sea contains itself in its bounds, and the sun steps not out of his sphere ; the stars march in their order : *"They continue this day according to thine ordinances : for all are thy servants."* If he orders things contrary to their primitive nature they obey him.   When he speaks the word, the devouring fire becomes gentle, and toucheth not the hair of the children he will preserve ; the hunger-starved lions suspend their ravenous nature when so good a morsel as Daniel is set before them ; and the sun, which had been in perpetual motion since its creation, obeys the writ of ease God sent in Joshua's time, and stands still.—*Stephen Charnock.*

Verse 91.—*"All are thy servants."*   We should consider how great is that perversity by which man only, formed in the image of God, together with reprobate angels, has fallen away from obedience to God ; so that what is said of all other creatures cannot be said of him, unless renewed by singular grace.—*Wolfgang Musculus.*

Verse 91.—*"For all are thy servants."*   Since all creatures must serve God, therefore we ought neither to use them for any other purpose, nor turn them to the service of sin.   The creature by the sin of our first parents has been made subject to vanity, and groans and longs to be delivered, Rom. viii. : Christians, therefore, who use the creature and the world, should use as not abusing, 1 Cor. vii. ; but enjoy them with praise of the divine majesty and goodness, 1 Tim. iv.—*Solomon Gesner.*

Verse 91.—*"All are thy servants."*

> Say not, my soul, " From whence
> Can God relieve my care ? "
> Remember that Omnipotence
> Has servants everywhere.
>
> *Thomas T. Lynch,* 1855.

Verse 92.—*"Unless thy law had been my delights,"* etc.   This text sets out the great benefit and comfort which David found in the law of God in the time of his affliction.   It kept him from perishing : *"Had not thy law been my delights, I had perished in my affliction "* . . . . David speaks this (saith Musculus) of the distressful condition he was in when persecuted by Saul, forced to fly to the Philistines, and sometimes to hide himself in the rocks and caves of the earth.   It is very likely (saith he) that he had the book of God's law with him, by the reading of which he mitigated and allayed his sorrows, and kept himself pure from communicating with the heathen in their superstitions.   The Greek scholiasts say that David uttered these words when driven from Saul, and compelled to live among the Philistines, etc.   For he would have been allured to have communicated with them in their impieties had he not carried about him the meditation of the word of God. The word of God delighted in is the afflicted saint's antidote against ruin and destruction.   The word of God is the sick saint's salve, the dying saint's cordial, a precious medicine to keep God's people from perishing in time of affliction.   This upheld Jacob from sinking, when his brother Esau came furiously marching to destroy him (Gen. xxxii. 12).   He pleaded, " And thou saidst, I will surely do thee good," etc.   Thus the promise of God supported him.   This also upheld Joshua and enabled him courageously to fight the Lord's battles, because God had said, " He would never leave him nor forsake him " (Josh. i. 5).   Melancthon saith that the Landgrave of Hesse told him at Dresden that it had been impossible for him to have borne up under the manifold miseries of so long an imprisonment, *Nisi habuisset consolationem verbo divino in suo corde,* but for the comfort of the Scriptures in his heart.—*Edmund Calamy* (1600—1666), *in "The Godly Man's Ark."*

Verse 92.—Certainly the reading of most part of the Scriptures must needs be a very comfortable thing ; and I think a godly heart (disposed as it ought to be) can hardly tell how to be sad while it does it. For what a comfort is it for a man to read an earthly father's letters sent to him, though they were written long ago ? With what care do we keep such letters in our chests ? With how much delight do we ever and anon take them out and look upon them ? and with how much sorrow do we lose them ? Is my love to my *earthly* father so great, and shall my love to my *heavenly* Father be less ? Can my heart choose but rejoice and my bones flourish like an herb, as oft as I look upon my Redeemer's last will and testament, whereby I know that he gave me so much, and that he doth so much for me continually, and that I shall be ever with him ?

How is David ever and anon talking of his *delight in the law of God*, and in his statutes and testimonies. It was to him instead of all other delights ; standing by him when all delights else left him ; *"Unless thy law had been my delight* (or, *my very great delight*), *I should then have perished in mine affliction,"* ver. 92. Let *princes sit and speak* against him never so much ; yet will he meditate in God's statutes, ver. 23. Let him have never so many *persecutors and enemies ;* yet will he not decline from God's testimonies, ver. 157. Let him be in a strange place, there shall God's statutes be his song, ver. 54. Let him be a *stranger in the earth* all his life ; so that he be not a stranger to God's commandments he cares not, ver. 19. Although he should have never so much *contempt* cast upon him, yet will he not forget God's precepts, ver. 141. Although his *soul* should be *continually in his hand*, yet that should not make him forget God's law. Yea, although he became like *a bottle in the smoke*, yet will he not forget God's precepts, ver. 83. And therefore was it that he rejoiced, because he had been *afflicted* upon this account, that it made him learn God's statutes. He cared for no other *wealth*. *"Thy testimonies have I taken as an heritage for ever : for they are the rejoicing of my heart,"* ver. 111. Neither cared he much for *life*, but only to keep God's word, ver. 17. Whatever he had said before, or meant to say next, he still cries, *"Teach me thy statutes,"* and, *"I have longed for thy precepts,"* etc. ; or some such expression or other. He could not forbear to speak of them, for they were still before him, ver. 30. No wonder, then, that he meditated upon them so often, as he saith he did. *"O how I love thy law ! it is my meditation all the day,"* ver. 97. And *"Thy testimonies are my meditation,"* ver. 99. God's commandments were to David sweeter in his mouth than honey, to talk and discourse of them, ver. 103.—*Zachary Bogan*, 1653.

Verse 92.—The persons to whose *delight* the word of God actually conduces are the children of God, and none else. None but they are prepared to take in the consolation of the word.

1. As they only are spiritually enlightened to discern the great and comfortable things contained in it, enlightened in a manner in which no others are : " The natural man receiveth not the things of the Spirit of God, for they are foolishness unto him : neither can he know them, because they are spiritually discerned " (1 Cor. ii. 14).

2. As they have the highest value for the word of God, this prepares them for receiving consolation from it.

3. As they have their hearts and ways suited to the word of God, this is another reason of the delight they fetch from it. " For they that are after the flesh do mind the things of the flesh," and take pleasure in them ; " but they that are after the Spirit the things of the Spirit " (Rom. viii. 5). The comforts of the word are spiritual ; and only the spiritual heart, as it is renewed by grace, can taste and relish them. The delight which the people of God have from the word, is a privilege peculiar to themselves : and this word hath enough to give delight to all of their number.—*Daniel Wilcox*, 1676—1733.

Verse 92.—*"My delights."* The word signifieth delights in the plural number. Many were the sorrows of David's life ; but against them all he found as many comforts and delectations in God's word. With such variety of holy wisdom hath God penned his word, that it hath convenient comfort for every state of life, and therefore the children of God account nothing so dear as it ; they prefer it to their appointed food.—*William Cowper.*

Verse 92.—*"Thy law . . . my delights . . . in mine affliction."* I happened to be standing in a grocer's shop one day in a large manufacturing town in the west of Scotland, when a poor, old, frail widow came in to make a few purchases. There never was, perhaps, in that town a more severe time of distress. Nearly every loom was stopped. Decent and respectable tradesmen who had seen better days, were obliged to subsist on public charity. So much money per day (but a trifle at most) was allowed to the really poor and deserving. The poor widow had received her daily pittance, and she had now come into the shop of the grocer to lay it out to the best advantage. She had but a few coppers in her withered hands. Carefully did she expend her little stock—a pennyworth of this and the other necessary of life nearly exhausted all she had. She came to the last penny, and with a singular expression of heroic contentment and cheerful resignation on her wrinkled face, she said, " Now I must buy oil with this, that I may see to read my Bible during these long dark nights, for it is my only comfort now when every other comfort has gone away."—*Alexander Wallace, in "The Bible and the Working Classes,"* 1853.

Verse 92.—This verse I may call a Perfume against the Plague ; The Sick Man's Salve ; The Afflicted Man's Consolation ; and a blessed Triumph, in and over all troubles.—*Richard Greenham.*

Verse 93.—"*I will never forget thy precepts,*" etc. *Forgetfulness* must be striven against in every possible way, lest it should gradually creep in, through ingratitude, old age, weakness of mind, or other overwelming cares. See verses 16, 61, 83.—*Martin Geier.*

Verse 93.—"*I will never forget thy precepts,*" etc. This afflicted good man is now comforted ; his comfort came from his delight in God's law ; he thinks of it, he feels the force of it, and therefore to the end that he might ever receive the like comforts, he will bind himself by a promise to the Lord that he will never forget his precepts ; adding a reason, namely, that they were to him spirit and life. "*With them hast thou quickened me.*" Quickened he was, as he saith, by God, but yet also by the word, soundly preached, savingly understood, and particularly applied to the conscience. Thus then doth the power of Christ's death make us to walk on in newness of life. No *aqua vitæ,* or *celestis,* like unto this, by which we have inward peace of conscience, and an outward obedience to God's commandments. David rejoiced in this blessing, so ought we : we desire to be ever quick, and cheerful to all good duties ; it is only God, by his Spirit, in the word, that can give it.—*Richard Greenham.*

Verse 93.—"*With them thou hast quickened me.*" The quickening Spirit delights to work by means of the word ; but though the word be the means, yet the benefit comes from God : " For with them *thou* hast quickened me." Life comes from the fountain of life. The gospel is a sovereign plaster ; but it is God's hand that must apply it, and make it stick ; make it to be peace, comfort, and quickening to our souls. There is a double quickening, when, from dead, we are made living ; or when, from cold, we are made lively . . . . and so not only have life, but enjoy it more abundantly, according to Christ's gracious promise (John x. 10) ; that they may be living, lively, kept still in vigour. Now, this second quickening may be taken, either more largely, for the vitality of grace ; or, strictly, for actual comfort. Largely taken ; so God quickens by increasing the life of grace ; either internally, by promising the life of grace ; or morally and externally, by promising the life of glory. More strictly, his quickening may be taken for comfort and support in his affliction ; so it is likely to be taken here : he had said immediately before, " Unless thy law had been my delights, I should then have perished in my affliction"; and now, " I will never forget thy precepts, for with them thou hast quickened me." It was great comfort and support to him ; and therefore he should prize the word as long as he lived.—*Thomas Manton.*

Verse 93.—"*Thou hast quickened me.*" Leave not off reading the Bible till you find your hearts warmed. Read the word, not only as a history, but labour to be affected with it. Let it not only inform you, but inflame you. " Is not my word like a fire ? saith the Lord " : Jer. xxiii. 29. Go not from the word till you can say as those disciples, " Did not our hearts burn within us ? " Luke xxiv. 32.—*Thomas Watson.*

Verse 94.—"*I am thine, save me.*" David, a man after God's own heart, would be saved, but not after the manner of the men of this world, that would be saved to be their own and to enjoy themselves at their own will ; but he in being saved would be God's, and at his disposing : "*I am thine, save me.*"
There is a threefold strength in this argument.
1. The *law of nature,* which obligeth a father to be good to his child, the husband to his wife, etc., and God hath subjected himself more unto the law of nature, he

lies more under it, than any of these ; and doth more perfectly, fully, and gloriously fulfil this law of nature than any ; there is no father like him, no friend, no husband like him. " Can a woman forget her sucking child ? yet will I not forget thee : " Isai. xlix. 15. A mother can hardly do it ; nature teacheth her to have bowels, and a merciful remembrance towards her child ; much more will I, saith God.

2. When we can say to God, "*I am thine*," we plead *the covenant which God hath made with us*, wherein he is become our father and friend : and this is that which was pleaded in Isai. lxiii. 16 : " Doubtless thou art our father, though Abraham be ignorant of us, and Israel acknowledge us not (because they are gone, and so have no cognizance of us now) ; yet thou, O Lord, art our Father, our Redeemer ; thy name is from everlasting." See what a conclusion here is made ; doubtless thou art our Father, and therefore we call to thee for help.

3. There is this encouragement and strength that the spirit of a man receives in thus arguing with God, *that if he can say in truth, "I am thine," God much more will say to the creature, "I am thine."* If we have so much love to offer ourselves to God, to become his ; much more will the love of God make him to become ours ; for God loves first, and most, and surest. If mine heart rise toward God, much more is the heart of God toward me ; because there love is in the fountain. Never did a spouse speak to her husband, whom her soul loved to the highest, more willingly, and say, "*I am thine*," than the spirit of an upright man saith to God, "*Lord, I am thine*." And he loves him with a *love of thankfulness*. Hast thou given thyself to me, saith he, and shall I then withhold myself from thee ? Hast thou, who art so great, done all this for me, and shall I stand out against thee ? The gracious man will willingly acknowledge himself to be the Lord's. The saints often do this : David above twenty times comes with this acknowledgment in this Psalm, and in Psalm cxvi. 16 : "*I am thy servant ; I am thy servant*." To say it once was not enough ; he saith it again, to show the sincerity of his spirit, and to witness that his heart was fully pleased with this, that he was not his own, but the Lord's. The knowledge of our interest in God doth much further our approaches to God. When a man is once assured, and can say with a clear spirit, "*I am thine*," he will naturally cry, "*Save me*." Such a man is a man of prayer, he is much in addresses to God, and conversing with him.—*Joseph Symonds*, 1653.

Verse 94.—"I am thine." This is an excellent motive to draw from the Lord help in trouble,—"*I am thine*." Thine by *creation*, I was made by thee ; thine by *adoption*, I was assigned over to thee ; thine by *donation*, I was given to thee ; thine by *marriage*, I was espoused to thee ; thine by *redemption*, I was purchased by thee ; thine by *stipulation*, I have vowed myself unto thee.—*Richard Greenham*.

Verse 94.—"For I have sought thy precepts." See here how David qualifies his protestation : from his earnest affection to the word of God, he proves that he was God's man and not his own servant. It is not words, but affections and actions which must prove us to be the Lord's. *Tuus sum, quia id solum quod tuum est quæsivi :* I am thine because I sought nothing but that which is thine, and how I might please thee. *Mihi in tuis justificationibus est omne patrimonium :* in the observance of thy precepts is all my patrimony.—*William Cowper*.

Verse 95.—"The wicked have waited for me to destroy me." Two things again he notes in his enemies ; diligence, in waiting all occasions whereby to do him evil ; and cruelty without mercy, for their purpose was to destroy him : wherein, still we see how restless and insatiable is the malice of the wicked against the godly. Daniel's preservation in the lions' den was a great miracle ; but it is no less a marvellous work of God, that the godly who are the flock of Christ, are daily preserved in the midst of the wicked, who are but ravening wolves, and thirst for the blood of the saints of God, having a cruel purpose in their heart if they might perform it, utterly to destroy them.—*William Cowper*.

Verse 95.—"But I will consider thy testimonies." It was a grievous temptation to be sought for to be given up to slaughter, but a greater mercy to consider God's testimonies, even then when his life was sought for. Had it not been for the consideration of God's testimonies, a thousand to one he had fallen away.—*Richard Greenham*.

Verse 96.—"I have seen an end of all perfection," etc. These words are variously rendered and understood by interpreters, who in this variety do very much conspire and agree in the same sense. The *Chaldee* Paraphrase renders the words thus, "*I have seen an end of all things about which I have employed my care ; but thy commandment is very large.*" The *Syriac* version thus, "*I have seen an end of all regions and countries* " (that is, I have found the compass of the habitable world to be finite and limited) "*but thy commandment is of a vast extent.*" Others explain it thus, "*I have seen an end of all perfection,*" that is, of all the things of this world which men value and esteem at so high a rate ; of all worldly wisdom and knowledge, of wealth, and honour, and greatness, which do all perish and pass away ; "*but thy law is eternal, and still abideth the same*" ; or, as the Scripture elsewhere expresses it, " The word of the Lord endureth for ever."—*John Tillotson,* 1630—1694.

Verse 96.—"*I have seen an end of all perfection.*" Poor perfection which one sees an end of ! Yet such are all those things in this world which pass for perfections. David in his time had seen Goliath, the strongest, overcome ; Asahel, the swiftest, overtaken ; Ahithophel, the wisest, befooled ; Absalom, the fairest, deformed.— *Matthew Henry.*

Verse 96.—"*I have seen an end of all perfection,*" etc. The Psalmist's words offer us a double comfort and encouragement. We may read them in two ways : (1) " I have seen an end of all perfection ; *for* thy commandment is exceeding broad " ; and (2) " I have seen an end of all perfection, *but* thy commandment is exceeding broad."

Read in the first way, they suggest the animating thought, that our haunting consciousness of imperfection springs from the bright and awful perfection of the Law we are bent on obeying, of the ideal we have set before us. It is not because we are worse than those who are without law, or who are a law unto themselves, that we are restless and dissatisfied with ourselves ; but because we measure both ourselves and our fellows by the lofty standard of God's commandment. It is because that commandment is so broad, that we cannot embrace it ; it is because it is so high, that we cannot attain to it ; it is because it is so perfect, that we cannot perfectly obey it.

But we may read the verse in another way, and still derive comfort and encouragement from it. We may say : " I have seen an end of all perfection in myself, and in the world ; *but* thy commandment is exceeding broad : *that* is perfect, though *I* am imperfect, and in its perfection I find the promise of my own." For shall God give a law for human life, and that law remain for ever unfulfilled ! Impossible ! " The gifts of God are without repentance "—irreversible, never to be lessened or withdrawn. His purpose is not to be made of none effect by our weaknesses and sins. In the Law he has shown us what he would have us to be. And shall we never become what he would have us to be ? Can the Law remain for ever without any life that corresponds to it and fulfils it ? Nay, God will never take back the fair and perfect ideal of human life depicted in his Law, never retract his purpose to raise the life of man till it touches and fulfils its ideal. And so the very Law which is our despair is our comfort also ; for if *that* be perfect *we* must become perfect ; its perfection is the pledge of ours.—*From "The Expositor,"* 1876.

Verse 96.—"*I have seen an end of all perfection.*" David's natural eye had seen the end of many human perfections, and the eye of his understanding saw the end of them all. He had seen some actually end, and he saw that all must end. Adam did not continue in that perfection which had no imperfection in it ; how then shall any of his children continue in what is at best an imperfect perfection ?— *Abraham Wright.*

Verse 96.—"*I have seen an end,*" etc. The laws of Lycurgus among the Grecians, and of Numa among the Romans, had somewhat of good in them, but not all ; prohibited somewhat that was evil, but not all that was evil. But the Christian religion is of a larger extent, both in its precepts and prohibitions : "*I have seen an end of all perfection : but thy commandment is exceeding broad.*" A man with the eye of his body may behold an end of many worldly perfections, of many fair estates, great beauties, large parts, hopeful families ; but a man with the eye of his soul (or by faith) may see an end of all earthly perfections. He may see the world in a flame, and all its pomp and pride, and glory, and gallantry, and crowns and sceptres, and riches, and treasures, turned into ashes. He may see the heavens passing away like a scroll, and the elements melting with fervent heat, and the earth, with the things thereon, consumed ; and all its perfections, which men doated so much on, vanished into smoke and nothing. It is easy to see to the end of all terrene perfections, but it is difficult, yea, impossible, to see to the end of divine precepts : *"But thy commandments are exceeding broad,"* of a vast latitude, beyond our apprehension. They are so deep that none can fathom them, Ps. xxxvi. 6, so high that they are established in heaven, Ps. cxix. 48 ; so long that they endure for ever. 2 Pet. i. , and so broad, that none can measure them. They are not only *"broad,"* but *"exceeding* broad " : " higher than heaven, longer than the earth, broader than the sea." The commands of God reach the inward parts, the most secret motions and retired recesses of the soul. They reach all the privy thoughts, they pierce even to the dividing asunder of soul and spirit, and of the joints and marrow, and discern the thoughts and intents of the heart, Heb. iv. 12. They reach to all our actions ; to those that seem smallest and of less concernment, as well as to those that are greater and of more concernment.—*George Swinnock.*

Verse 96.—"Thy commandment is exceeding broad." As there is more mercy in the gospel than we are able to comprehend, so there is more holiness in the law than we are able to comprehend. No man ever saw into the depths of that righteousness. There is an infinite holiness in the law. *"I have seen an end of all perfection : but thy commandment is exceeding broad."* He speaks not in the concrete, I have seen an end of *perfect things,* but in the abstract, " an end of *perfection,"* I have come to the outside or to the very bottom of all (a man may soon travel through all the perfections that are in the world, and either see their end, or see that they end) ; *"but thy commandment is exceeding broad,"* that is, it is exceedingly broader than any of these perfections ; I cannot see the end of it, and I know it shall never have an end. There is a vastness of purity and spiritualness in the law.—*Joseph Caryl.*

Verse 96.—"Thy commandment is exceeding broad." It is so by the comprehensive applicableness of its grand, simple rules. " Thou shalt love the Lord thy God with all thy heart, and soul, and strength, and thy neighbour as thyself." It is so by the ample order of its special injunctions. Where is there a spot without a signal of the divine will ? It is so by laying an authoritative hand on the first principles and origin from which any thing can proceed, in human spirit and action ; then it reaches to all things that do or can proceed thence. It asserts a jurisdiction over all thought and inward affection. All language is uttered under this same jurisdiction. All that the world and each man is in action about. And even over what is not done it maintains its authority, and pronounces its dictates and judgments. It is a positive thing with respect to what is negative, omission, non-existence. Like the divine government in the material world, over the wastes, deserts, and barren sands. And from these spaces of nothing (as it were) it can raise up substantial forms of evil, of sin, in evidence against men. As at the resurrection men will rise from empty wastes, where it would not have been suspected that any were concealed. Let a man look back on all his omissions, and think what the divine law can raise from them against him. Thus the law in its exceeding breadth, is vacant nowhere ; it is not stretched to this wide extent by chasms and void spaces. If a man could find one such, he might there take his position for sin with impunity, if not with innocence.—*John Foster,* 1768—1843.

Verse 96.—"Thy commandment is exceeding broad." In the popular religious literature of the present times, the terms " broad " and " free " are of frequent occurrence. The fascination that surrounds them is enhanced by the use, at the same time, of their opposites, " narrow " and " bigoted." By an adroit manipulation of these terms and their equivalents, the heterodoxy of the day is labouring to stamp out the doctrine and spirit of the evangelical faith, and to allure the Christian multitude within the influence of the spreading rationalistic drift. Going to the market where the heterodox wares are exhibited with labels so attractive, the unsuspecting purchaser soon discovers that " their vine is of the vine of Sodom, and of the fields of Gomorrah : their grapes are grapes of gall, their clusters are bitter." Is the time not come when the adherents of the true faith should make an effort to wrest from their opponents the monopoly in the use of these terms, which they seem desirous of establishing for themselves ? Those who, in the spirit of their Master, abide most closely by, and contend most tenaciously for, the whole faith that has been delivered to the saints, must be the most liberal-minded and catholic ; and those who forsake the " old paths " must, in proportion to the extent of their departures, become contracted in their mental grasp, and narrow in their soul. Is not the Bible—the whole Bible—the only manual of Broad-churchism in its truest and highest sense ? Is not the revelation of God's Son in us, the great soul-expanding power ? " If the Son shall make you free, ye shall be free indeed."

Must we not infer, from the words of Christ, " Ye shall know the truth, and the truth shall make you free," that the mind which apprehends the truth is a home of mental liberty ?   Does not strict conformity of the life to God's law produce real breadth of character ?   For "*Thy commandment is exceeding broad.*"   Is not the gospel system the only true Broad-churchism—" the perfect law of liberty " ?   Is not the believer—and the more so in proportion to the strength of his faith—the only true Broad-churchman, "increasing with the increase of God," "filled with all the fulness of God " ?—*James Kerr, in "The Modern Scottish Pulpit,"* 1880.

Verse 96.—"*Exceeding broad.*" Notwithstanding many things do show the way of life to be narrow, yet unto the godly man it is a way of great breadth ; though not for sin, yet for duty and delight. He makes haste and progress in it.—*Robert Trail,* 1642—1716.

Verse 96.—Take notice that the law, which is your mark, is *exceeding broad.* And yet not the more easy to be hit ; because you must aim to hit it, in every duty of it, with a performance of equal breadth, or else you cannot hit it at all.—*Stephen Marshall.*

EXPOSITION OF VERSES 97 TO 104.

O HOW love I thy law ! it *is* my meditation all the day.

98 Thou through thy commandments hast made me wiser than mine enemies : for they *are* ever with me.

99 I have more understanding than all my teachers : for they testimonies *are* my meditation.

100 I understand more than the ancients, because I keep thy precepts.

101 I have refrained my feet from every evil way, that I might keep thy word.

102 I have not departed from thy judgments : for thou hast taught me.

103 How sweet are thy words unto my taste ! *yea, sweeter* than honey to my mouth !

104 Through thy precepts I get understanding : therefore I hate every false way.

97. *"O how love I thy law !"* It is a note of exclamation. He loves so much that he must express his love, and in making the attempt he perceives that it is inexpressible—and therefore cries, " O how I love ! " We not only reverence but love the law, we obey it out of love, and even when it chides us for disobedience we love it none the less. The law is God's law, and therefore it is our love. We love it for its holiness, and pine to be holy ; we love it for its wisdom, and study to be wise ; we love it for its perfection, and long to be perfect. Those who know the power of the gospel perceive an infinite loveliness in the law as they see it fulfilled and embodied in Christ Jesus. *"It is my meditation all the day."* This was both the effect of his love and the cause of it. He meditated in God's word because he loved it, and then loved it the more because he meditated in it. He could not have enough of it, so ardently did he love it : all the day was not too long for his converse with it. His matin prayer, his noonday thought, his evensong were all out of Holy Writ ; yea, in his worldly business he still kept his mind saturated with the law of the Lord. It is said of some men that the more you know them the less you admire them ; but the reverse is true of God's word. Familiarity with the word of God breeds affection, and affection seeks yet greater familiarity. When " thy law," and " my meditation " are together all the day, the day grows holy, devout, and happy, and the heart lives with God. David turned away from all else ; for in the preceding verse he tells us that he had seen an end of all perfection ; but he turned in unto the law and tarried there the whole day of his life on earth, growing henceforth wiser and holier.

98. *"Thou through thy commandments hast made me wiser than mine enemies."* The commands were his book, but God was his teacher. The letter can make us knowing, but only the divine Spirit can make us wise. Wisdom is knowledge put to practical use. Wisdom comes to us through obedience : " If any man will do his will he shall know of the doctrine." We learn not only from promise, and doctrine, and sacred history, but also from precept and command ; in fact, from the commandments we gather the most practical wisdom, and that which enables us best to cope with our adversaries. A holy life is the highest wisdom and the surest defence. Our enemies are renowned for subtlety, from the first father of them, the old serpent, down to the last cockatrice that has been hatched from the egg ; and it would be vain for us to try to be a match with them in the craft and mystery of cunning, for the children of this world are in their generation wiser than the children of light. We must go to another school and learn of a different instructor, and then by uprightness we shall baffle fraud, by simple truth we shall vanquish deep-laid scheming, and by open candour we shall defeat slander. A thoroughly straightforword man, devoid of all policy, is a terrible puzzle to diplomatists ; they suspect him of a subtle duplicity through which they cannot see, while he, indifferent to their suspicions, holds on the even tenor of his way, and baffles all their arts. Yes, " honesty is the best policy." He who is taught of God has a practical wisdom such as malice cannot supply to the crafty ; while harmless as a dove he also exhibits more than the serpent's wisdom.

"For they are ever with me." He was always studying or obeying the command-ments ; they were his choice and constant companions. If we wish to become proficient we must be indefatigable. If we keep the wise law ever near us we shall become wise, and when our adversaries assail us we shall be prepared for them with that ready wit which lies in having the word of God at our fingers' ends. As a soldier in battle must never lay aside his shield, so must we never have the word of God out of our minds ; it must be ever with us.

99. *"I have more understanding than all my teachers."* That which the Lord had taught him had been useful in the camp, and now he finds it equally valuable in the schools. Our teachers are not always to be trusted ; in fact, we may not follow any of them implicitly, for God holds us to account for our personal judgments. It behoves us then to follow closely the chart of the Word of God, that we may be able to save the vessel when even the pilot errs. If our teachers should be in all things sound and safe, they will be right glad for us to excel them, and they will ever be ready to own that the teaching of the Lord is better than any teaching which they can give us. Disciples of Christ who sit at his feet are often better skilled in divine things than doctors of divinity. *"For thy testimonies are my meditation."* This is the best mode of acquiring understanding. We may hear the wisest teachers and remain fools, but if we meditate upon the sacred word we must become wise. There is more wisdom in the testimonies of the Lord than in all the teachings of men if they were all gathered into one vast library. The one book outweighs all the rest.

David does not hesitate to speak the truth in this place concerning himself, for he is quite innocent of self-consciousness. In speaking of his understanding he means to extol the law and the Lord, and not himself. There is not a grain of boasting in these bold expressions, but only a sincere childlike desire to set forth the excellence of the Lord's word. He who knows the truths taught in the Bible will be guilty of no egotism if he believes himself to be possessed of more important truth than all the agnostic professors buried and unburied.

100. *"I understand more than the ancients, because I keep thy precepts."* The men of old age, and the men of old time, were outdone by the holier and more youthful learner. He had been taught to observe in heart and life the precepts of the Lord, and this was more than the most venerable sinner had ever learned, more than the philosopher of antiquity had so much as aspired to know. He had the word with him, and so outstripped his foes ; he meditated on it, and so outran his friends ; he practised it, and so outshone his elders. The instruction derived from Holy Scripture is useful in many directions, superior from many points of view, unrivalled everywhere and in every way. As our soul may make her boast in the Lord, so may we boast in his word. "There is none like it : give it me," said David as to Goliath's sword, and we may say the same as to the word of the Lord. If men prize antiquity they have it here. The ancients are had in high repute, but what did they all know compared with that which we perceive in the divine precepts ? "The old is better" says one : but the oldest of all is the best of all, and what is that but the word of the Ancient of days.

101. *"I have refrained my feet from every evil way, that I might keep thy word."* There is no treasuring up the holy word unless there is a casting out of all unholiness : if we keep the good word we must let go the evil. David had zealously watched his steps and put a check upon his conduct,—he had refrained his feet. No one evil way could entice him, for he knew that if he went astray but in one road he had practically left the way of righteousness, therefore he avoided every false way. The by-paths were smooth and flowery, but he knew right well that they were evil, and so he turned his feet away, and held on along the straight and thorny pathway which leads to God. It is a pleasure to look back upon self-conquests,—" I have refrained," and a greater delight still to know that we did this out of no mere desire to stand well with our fellows, but with the one motive of keeping the law of the Lord. Sin avoided that obedience may be perfected is the essence of this verse ; or it may be that the Psalmist would teach us that there is no real reverence for the book where there is not carefulness to avoid every transgression of its precepts. How can we keep God's word if we do not keep our own works from becoming vile ?

102. *"I have not departed from thy judgments : for thou hast taught me."* They are well taught whom God teaches. What we learn from the Lord we never forget. God's instruction has a practical effect,—we follow his way when he teaches us ;

and it has an abiding effect,—we do not depart from holiness. Read this verse in connection with the preceding and you get the believer's " I have," and his " I have not " : he is good both positively and negatively. What he did, namely, " refrained his feet," preserved him from doing that which otherwise he might have done, namely, " departed from thy judgments." He who is careful not to go an inch aside will not leave the road. He who never touches the intoxicating cup will never be drunk. He who never utters an idle word will never be profane. If we begin to depart a little we can never tell where we shall end. The Lord brings us to persevere in holiness by abstinence from the beginning of sin ; but whatever be the method he is the worker of our perseverance, and to him be all the glory.

103. *"How sweet are thy words unto my taste ! "* He had not only heard the words of God, but fed upon them : they affected his palate as well as his ear. God's words are many and varied, and the whole of them make up what we call " the word ": David loved them each one, individually, and the whole of them as a whole ; he tasted an indescribable sweetness in them. He expresses the fact of their sweetness, but as he cannot express the degree of their sweetness he cries, " How sweet ! " Being God's words they were divinely sweet to God's servant ; he who put the sweetness into them had prepared the taste of his servant to discern and enjoy it. David makes no distinction between promises and precepts, doctrines and threatenings; they are all included in God's words, and all are precious in his esteem. Oh for a deep love to all that the Lord has revealed, whatever form it may take.

"Yea, sweeter than honey to my mouth." When he did not only eat but also speak the word, by instructing others, he felt an increased delight in it. The sweetest of all temporal things fall short of the infinite deliciousness of the eternal word : honey itself is outstripped in sweetness by the word of the Lord. When the Psalmist fed on it he found it sweet ; but when he bore witness of it it became sweeter still. How wise it will be on our part to keep the word on our palate by meditation and on our tongue by confession. It must be sweet to our taste when we think of it, or it will not be sweet to our mouth when we talk of it.

104. *"Through thy precepts I get understanding."* God's direction is our instruction. Obedience to the divine will begets wisdom of mind and action. As God's way is always best, those who follow it are sure to be justified by the result. If the Lawgiver were foolish his law would be the same, and obedience to such a law would involve us in a thousand mistakes ; but as the reverse is the case, we may count ourselves happy to have such a wise, prudent, and beneficial law to be the rule of our lives. We are wise if we obey and we grow wise by obeying !

" Therefore I hate every false way," Because he had understanding, and because of the divine precepts, he detested sin and falsehood. Every sin is a falsehood ; we commit sin because we believe a lie, and in the end the flattering evil turns a liar to us and we find ourselves betrayed. True hearts are not indifferent about falsehood, they grow warm in indignation ; as they love the truth, so they hate the lie. Saints have a universal horror of all that is untrue, they tolerate no falsehood or folly, they set their faces against all error of doctrine or wickedness of life. He who is a lover of one sin is in league with the whole army of sins ; we must have neither truce nor parley with even one of these Amalekites, for the Lord hath war with them from generation to generation, and so must we. It is well to be a good hater. And what is that ? A hater of no living being, but a hater of " every false way." The way of self-will, of self-righteousness, of worldliness, of pride, of unbelief, of hypocrisy,—these are all false ways, and therefore not only to be shunned, but to be abhorred.

This final verse of the strophe marks a great advance in character, and shows that the man of God is growing stronger, bolder, and happier than aforetime. He has been taught of the Lord, so that he discerns between the precious and the vile, and while he loves the truth fervently he hates falsehood intensely. May all of us reach this state of discrimination and determination, so that we may greatly glorify God.

NOTES ON VERSES 97 TO 104.

Verse 97.—*"O how love I thy law !"* He speaketh not of his knowing, reading, hearing, speaking, or outward practising of the law, but of *love* to the law : this is more than all the former : all the former may be without this, but this cannot be without the former. We may know, read, hear, speak, yea, preach the law, and all God's word, as also outwardly perform outward works prescribed and commanded by the law, and yet not love it ; but where this love is there cannot but be all the former. Love is the principal affection of all other ; like a queen commanding and overruling all the rest : all the rest depend upon it ; yea, sometimes also the judgment itself. As the love is set, whether rightly or wrongly, towards good or evil, so are all the affections swayed ; yea, judgment itself sometimes blinded by love, erreth, as the love itself erreth ; and so words and all actions are accordingly. Doth not daily experience daily teach the truth hereof ? Moreover, besides this observation of this word, in respect of other, and in a kind of opposition unto other ; let us observe two other things therein : 1. The first person ; 2. The present tense. He saith not, O how is thy word to be loved, namely, by others ; but O, how do *I myself* love thy law or thy word ! Neither doth he say, O, how have I loved thy law in times past, or, how will I love it hereafter, how unfeignedly do I purpose to love it, when I shall be advanced unto and settled in my kingdom ; or, how would I love it if I were so advanced and settled, or were I in this or that estate, or had this or that which I yet have not, or that others have ; the prophet, I say, speaketh not in such manner ; but he speaketh, as in the first person, so also in the present tense, saying, O how do I (now, such as I am) love thy law ! Both these things are very worthy of our observation, and they be in the greater in respect of the person of the prophet ; for albeit the name of the writer of this Psalm be not expressed in the title thereof (as in many other Psalms), yet the stream of most interpreters carrieth it to David. The matter also and style of the Psalm, compared with the matter and style of other Psalms which are David's, do both savour of David, and argue it was written by David. . . . . Whether David were now in full and quiet possession of his kingdom (though not without many adversaries), or whether he was only known to be the heir-apparent, appointed to succeed Saul (as most do think), or whether he were for a time in flight from the cruel and rebellious insurrection of his unnatural son Absalom, yet is it a great matter that here he speaketh of his great love towards the law of God. If he were in full and quiet possession of his kingdom, then had he many other things that he might have loved, and wherewith the hearts of such princes are commonly taken up, yea, also stolen away from those things that are much more worthy of love. What need I speak of the daily experience, whereby the truth hereof is manifest in far more mean persons than princes are ? If David were in exile or flight, a man would think that his wife, and children, and other friends, as also his country, would have so occupied and fully possessed his heart, that there should have been little place for other things therein ; but that rather he should have said, Oh, how love I those things ! Oh, how is my heart troubled with thoughts of them, and care for them in my great love towards them ! Moreover, that neither any troubles on the one side, wherewith David was continually exercised ; nor his honours, riches, or pleasures either in possession or in hope on the other side, did extinguish, or cool, or abate his love, is it not a thing of great note ?

The next word to be observed is that word *"how"*: " Oh *how* love I thy law ! " This noteth the manner or measure of his love. It is a word of admiration, or a note of comparison ; so is it taken in divers other places . . . . . it noteth a kind of excess or excellency, even such as cannot be well expressed. The prophet seemeth to speak with a kind of sighing, as being so ravished with love towards the law of God, that he was even sick of love, as the church saith (Cant. ii. 5 ; v. 8), she was sick of love towards Christ : so seemeth the prophet to be sick of love towards the word of God. This word *"how,"* also importeth a comparison, and noteth a greater love in David towards the word than towards riches or any other thing ; in which respect he saith afterward in this very Psalm (ver. 127), that he loveth the Lord's commandments " above gold, yea, above fine gold " ; yea, as whosoever so loveth not Christ, that in respect of Christ, and for Christ's sake, he forsaketh father, and mother, and brethren, and sisters, wife and children, and his own life also (much more riches and other things not to be compared to life) is not worthy of him ; so he that doth not love the word above all other things ; yea, he that hateth not all other things below here, in respect of the word, is not worthy of the word. Christ himself loved the word of God more than he loved any riches ; for did he not for the performance of the word submit himself to such want, that the foxes had holes, and the birds had nests, but he had not whereon to lay his head ? and that, although he were the heir of all things, yet he was ministered unto by certain women ? He loved the word of God more than he loved his mother, brethren, and sisters . . . . . Yea, Christ loved the word of God more than he loved his own life ; for did he not lay down his life to fulfil the word of God ? . . . . If Christ Jesus himself loved the word more than all other things, yea, more than his life, which was more than the life of all angels, was there not great reason why David should love it in like manner ? had not David as much need of it as Christ ? . . . .

"*It is my meditation.*" The noun "*meditation*" seemeth to be more than if he had said only that he meditated. For he seemeth to mean that though he did often think upon other matters, yet he made nothing his "meditation" but that which he here speaketh of, and that this was his only, or his chief and principal meditation and set study.

The object of David's meditation is not only to be understood of the bare letter of the word, as if he did always meditate of some text or other of the word before written ; but also of the matters contained in the word ; as of the justice, power, wisdom, mercy and goodness of God ; of the frailty, corruption, and wickedness that is in man naturally, of the sins that God forbiddeth, and of the virtues that God commandeth in the word, and other the like. For he that meditateth of these things, though he meditate not of any one text of the word, yet he may be truly said to meditate of the word.

"*All the day.*" We are not to imagine that the prophet did nothing else but meditate on the word ; but this, first of all ; that no day passed over his head wherein he did not meditate on the word ; yea, that he took every occasion of meditating on the word. He was never weary of meditating. Though he had many other things wherein to employ himself, yet he forgot not the meditation of the word. His mind was not by any other employment alienated from the meditation of the word, but the more thereby provoked thereunto. As a man that hath laboured never so much one day in his calling, is not to be wearied thereby, but that he laboureth afresh the next day, and so day after day : so was it with the prophet touching this act of meditation. Secondly, when he saith he meditated on the word continually, or all the day, he meaneth that he did nothing at any time of the day without meditation on the word for doing thereof. Therefore we may safely say that continual meditation is more necessary than continual praying, as being necessary before the doing of everything, and in the very doing of everything ; yea, even before the said duty of prayer, and in the very act thereof, this work of meditation of the word is always necessary ; as without which, we know not either for what to pray, or in what sort and manner to pray : it is God's word only that can and must teach us both to pray for and also how to pray.—*Thomas Stoughton, in "Two Profitable Treatises,"* 1616.

Verse 97.—"*O how love I thy law!*" Who without love attempts anything in the law of God, does it coldly, and quickly gives it up. For the mind cannot give itself earnestly and perseveringly to things which are not loved. Only he who loves the law makes it his meditation all the day.—*Wolfgang Musculus.*

Verse 97.—"*O how love I thy law!*" Were I to enjoy Hezekiah's grant, and to have fifteen years added to my life, I would be much more frequent in my applications to the throne of grace. Were I to renew my studies, I would take my leave of those accomplished trifles—the historians, the orators, the poets of antiquity —and devote my attention to the Scriptures of truth. I would sit with much greater assiduity at my Divine Master's feet, and desire to know nothing but " Jesus Christ, and him crucified." This wisdom, whose fruits are peace in life, consolation in death, and everlasting salvation after death—this I would trace—this I would seek—this I would explore through the spacious and delightful fields of the Old and New Testament.—*James Hervey,* 1713-14—1758.

Verse 97.—This most precious jewel is to be preferred above all treasures. If thou be hungry, it is meat to satisfy thee ; if thou be thirsty, it is drink to refresh thee ; if thou be sick, it is a present remedy ; if thou be weak, it is a staff to lean unto ; if thine enemy assault thee, it is a sword to fight withal ; if thou be in darkness, it is a lanthorn to guide thy feet ; if thou be doubtful of the way, it is a bright shining

star to direct thee ; if thou be in displeasure with God, it is the message of reconciliation ; if thou study to save thy soul, receive the word engrafted, for that is able
to do it : it is the word of life.   Whoso loveth salvation will love this word, love
to read it, love to hear it ; and such as will neither read nor hear it, Christ saith
plainly, they are not of God.   For the spouse gladly heareth the voice of the bridegroom ; and " my sheep hear my voice," saith the Prince of pastors (John x. 27).—
Edwin Sandys, 1519—1587.

Verse 97.—"*O how love I thy law !* "   As faith worketh by love unto God, so
it worketh by love unto his word.   Love me, love my word : love a king, love
his laws.   So it did on David ; so it should do on us : " O how love I thy law ! "
saith David.   "*O how love I thy law !* " should every one of us say ; not only because
it is a good law, but chiefly because it is God's law.—*Richard Capel*, 1586—1656.

Verse 97.—"*O how love I thy law !* "   He calls God himself to be judge of his
love to the word ; witnessing thereby that it was no counterfeit love, but complete
and sincere love which he bore unto it.   The like protestation was used by S. Peter :
" Thou knowest, O Lord, that I love thee ! "—*William Cowper.*

Verse 97.—"*Thy law.*"   In every one of these eight verses the Bible is spoken
of as the Lord's, as, indeed, all through the Psalm.   Who is the author of Scripture ?
God.   What is the matter of Scripture ? God ; it was not fit that any should write
of God, but God himself.   What is the end of Scripture ? God.   Why was the
Scripture written, but that we might everlastingly enjoy the blessed God ?   As
Cæsar wrote his own commentaries ; so God, when there was none above him of
whom he could write, he wrote of himself ; by histories, laws, prophecies, and
promises, and many other doctrines, hath he set himself forth to be the Creator,
Preserver, Deliverer, and Glorifier of mankind ; and all this is done in a perfect
manner.—*Thomas Manton.*

Verse 97.—"*It is my meditation.*"   Holy Scripture is not a book for the slothful ;
it is not a book which can be interpreted without, and apart from, and by the deniers
of, that Holy Spirit by whom it came.   Rather is it a field, upon the surface of
which, if sometimes we gather manna easily and without labour, and given, as it
were, freely to our hands, yet of which also, many portions are to be cultivated
with pains and toil ere they will yield food for the use of man.   This bread of life
also is to be eaten in the wholesome sweat of our brow.—*Richard Chenevix French*,
1807—.

Verse 98.—"*Thou through thy commandments hast made me wiser than mine
enemies.*"   Now he praiseth the word for the singular profit and fruit which he reaped
by it ; to wit, that he learned wisdom by it.   And this he amplifies, by comparing
himself with three sorts of men ; his enemies, his teachers, and the ancients.   And
this he doth, not of vain glory (for bragging is far from him who is governed by
the Spirit of grace) ; but to commend the word of the Lord, and to allure others
to love it, by declaring to them what manifold good he found in it.

"*Wiser than mine enemies.*"   But how can this be, seeing that our Saviour
saith that the men of this world are wiser in their own generation than the children
of God ?   The answer is, our Saviour doth not call worldlings wise men simply ;
but *wiser in their own generation ;* that is, wise in things pertaining to this life.   Or
as Jeremy calls them, " wise to do evil " ; and when they have so done, wise to
conceal and cloak it.   All which in very deed is but folly ; and therefore David,
who by the light of God's word saw that it was so, could not be moved to follow
their course.   Well ; there is a great controversy between the godly and the wicked :
either of them in their judgment accounts the other to be fools ; but it is the light
of God's word which must decide it.—*William Cowper.*

Verse 98.—"*Wiser than mine enemies.*"   They are wiser than their enemies
as to security against their attempts, and that enmity and opposition that they
carry on against them ; they are far more safe by walking under the covert of God's
protection than their enemies can possibly be, who have all manner of worldly
advantages.   A godly-wise man is careful to keep in with God : he is more prepared
and furnished, can have a higher hope, more expectation of success, than others
have ; or, if not, he is well enough provided for, though all things fall out never
so cross to his desires.   As to success, who hath made wiser provision, think you,
he that hath made God his friend, or he that is borne up with worldly props and
dependences ?   they that are guided by the Spirit of God, or they that are guided
by Satan ?   those that make it their business to walk with God step by step, or those

that not only forsake him, but provoke him to his face ? those that break with men, and keep in with God, or those that break with God ? Surely, a child of God hath more security by piety than his enemies can have by secular policy, whereby they think to overreach and ruin him. The safety of a child of God lieth in two things : 1. God is his friend. 2. As long as God hath work for him to do, he will maintain him, and bear him out in it.—*Thomas Manton.*

Verse 98.—*"They are ever with me."* The meaning of the last clause is not merely, *"it is ever with me,"* but *"it is for ever to me,"* i.e., mine, my inalienable, indefeasible possession.—*Joseph Addison Alexander.*

Verse 98.—*"They are ever with me."* God gives knowledge to whom he pleaseth ; but those that meditate most, thrive most. This may imply also that the word should be a ready help. Such as derive their wisdom from without cannot have their counsellers always with them to give advice. But, when a man hath gotten the word in his heart, he finds a ready help : he hath a seasonable word to direct him in all difficulties, in all straits, and in all temptations, to teach him what to do against the burden of the present exigence ; to teach him what to do and what to hope for.—*Thomas Manton.*

Verse 98.—*"They are ever with me."* A good man, wherever he goes, carries his Bible along with him, if not in his hands, yet in his head and in his heart.—*Matthew Henry.*

Verses 98, 99, 100.—Three sorts of men he mentioneth, *"enemies," "teachers," "ancients"* ; the enemies excel in policy, teachers in doctrine, and ancients in counsel ; and yet by the word was David made wiser than all these. Malice sharpens the wit of enemies, and teacheth them the arts of opposition ; teachers are furnished with learning because of their office ; and ancients grow wise by experience ; yet David, by the study of the word, excelled all these.—*Thomas Manton.*

Verse 99.—*"I have more understanding than all my teachers."* Even where the preacher is godly, partaker of that grace himself, whereof he is an ambassador to others, it falls out oftentimes that greater measure of light and grace is communicated by his ministry to another than is given to himself ; as Augustine first illuminated and converted by Ambrose did far excel, both in knowledge and spiritual grace, him that taught him. And herein God wonderfully shows his glory, that, whoever be the instrument, he is the dispenser of light and glory, giving more by the instrument than it hath in itself. And this is so far from being to a godly teacher a matter of grief, that it is rather a matter of glory.—*William Cowper.*

Verse 99.—*"I have more understanding than all my teachers."* It is no reflection upon my teachers, but rather an honour to them, for me to improve so as to excel them, and no longer to need them. By *meditation* we preach to ourselves, and so we come to *understand more than our teachers*, for we come to understand our hearts, which they cannot.—*Matthew Henry.*

Verse 100.—*"I understand . . . because I keep."* Would we know the Lord ? let us keep his commandments. " By thy precepts," saith David, that is, by the observance of thy precepts, " I get understanding." " If any man do my will " (saith our blessed Saviour, John vii. 17), " he shall know my doctrine." Βούλει θεόλογος γενέσθαι? τὰς εντογάς φυλασσε, saith Nazienzen : Wouldst thou be a divine ? do the commandments ; for action is (as it were) the basis of contemplation. It is St. Gregory's observation concerning the two disciples who, whilst Christ talked with them, knew him not ; but in performing an act of hospitality towards him, to wit, breaking bread with him, they knew him, that they were enlightened, not by hearing him, but by doing divine precepts, *Quisquis ergo vult audita intelligere ; festinet ea quæ jam audire potuit, opere implere,* Whosoever therefore will understand, let him first make haste to do what he heareth.—*Nathanael Hardy,* 1618—1670.

Verse 100.—*"I understand more than the ancients."* The ordinary answer of ignorant people is, " What ! must we be wiser than our forefathers ? " And yet those same people would be richer than their forefathers were. The *maximum quod sic* of a Christian is this,—he must grow in grace, till his head reach up to heaven, till grace is perfected in glory.—*Christopher Love,* 1618—1651.

Verse 100.—*"More than the ancients."* Understanding gotten by the precepts of the word is better than understanding gotten by long experience. It is better in four regards. First, It is *more exact.* Our experience reacheth but to a few things ; but the word of God reacheth to all cases that concern true happiness.

The word is the result of God's wisdom, who is the Ancient of days ; therefore exceeds the wisdom of the ancients, or experience of any men, or all men.   Secondly, as it is more exact, so a *more sure* way of learning wisdom, whereas experience is more uncertain.   Many have much experience, yet have not a heart to see and to gather wisdom from what they feel : Deut. xxix. 2—4.   Thirdly, It is a *safer and cheaper* way of learning, to learn by rule, than to come home by weeping cross, and to learn wisdom by our own smart.   Experience is too expensive a way ; and, if we had nothing else to guide us, into how many thousand miseries should we run ?   Fourthly, It is *shorter.*   The way by age and experience is a long way ; and so, for a long time, all a man's younger age must needs be miserable and foolish. Now, here you may come betimes to be wise by studying the word of God.   It concerns a man, not only to be wise at length, but to be wise betimes.   The foolish virgins were wise too late ; but never were any wise too soon.—*Condensed from Thomas Manton.*

Verse 100.—If this way [the Word of God] were thus perfect in David's time, what is it by the addition of so many parcels of Scripture since ?   If it then gave wisdom to the simple (Ps. xix. 7) ; if it made David, being brought up but as a shepherd, *wiser than* his enemies, than *his ancients,* than his teachers ;   as an angel of God in discerning right from wrong (2 Sam. xiv. 17) ;   able to guide the people by the skilfulness of his hands (Ps. lxxviii. 72) ;   what kind of wisdom is there which we may not now gather from thence ?   What depth of natural philosophy have we in Genesis and Job !   what flowers of rhetoric in the prophets !   what force of logic in Saint Paul's epistles !   what art of poetry in the Psalms !   what excellent moral precepts, not only for private life, but for the regulation of families and commonwealths in the Proverbs and Ecclesiastes !   to which may be added in a second rank as very useful, though apocryphal, the Book of Wisdom and Ecclesiasticus. What reasonable and just laws have we in Leviticus and Deuteronomy, which moved the great Ptolemy to hire the Septuagints to translate them into Greek : what unmatchable antiquity, variety, and wonderful events, and certainty of story, in the books of Moses, Joshua, the Judges, Samuel, the Kings, and Chronicles, together with Ruth and Esther, Ezra and Nehemiah, and, since Christ, in the sacred Gospels and Acts of the Apostles.   And, lastly, what profound mysteries have we in the prophecies of Ezekiel and Daniel, and the Revelation of Saint John.   But in this it infinitely exceeds the wisdom of all human writings, that it is alone " able to make a man wise unto salvation " (2 Tim. iii. 15).   Upon these considerations, Charles the Fifth of France, surnamed *The Wise,* not only caused the Bible to be translated into French, but was himself very studious in the Holy Scriptures.   And Alphonsus, King of Arragon, is said to have read over the whole Bible fourteen several times, with Lyra's notes upon it ;   though he were otherwise excellently well learned, yet was the law of God his delight, " more desired of him than gold, yea, than much fine gold, sweeter also than honey and the honeycomb."—*George Hakewell,* 1579—1649.

Verse 101.—"*I have refrained my feet,*" etc.   1. We have David's practice : "*I have refrained my feet from every evil way.*"   2. His end or motive :   "*That I might keep thy word ;*" that he might be exact and punctual with God in a course of obedience.

First, In his practice.   You may note the seriousness of it :   "*I have refrained my feet.*"   By the *feet* are meant the affections :   " Keep thy foot when thou goest to the house of God," Eccl. v. 1.   Our affections which are the rigorous bent of the soul, do engage us to practice ; therefore fitly resembled by the feet, by which we walk to any place that we do desire : so that, "*I have refrained my feet,*" the meaning is, I keep a close and strict hand over my affections, that they might not lead me to sin.   Then you may note the extent of it ; he doth not only say, I refrained from evil, but universally, "*from every evil way.*"   But how could David say this is truth of heart, if conscious of his offence in the matter of Uriah ?   Answer : This was the usual frame and temper of his soul, and the course of his life ; and such kind of assertions concerning the saints are to be interpreted, *voce et canatu, licet non semper eventu.*   This was his errand and drift, his purpose and endeavour, his usual course, though he had his failings.

Secondly, What was his end and motive in this ?   " That I might keep thy word " ; that I might be exact and punctual with God in a course of obedience, and adhere to his word universally, impartially.—*Thomas Manton.*

Verse 101.—"*I have refrained my feet*," etc. Where there is real holiness, there is a holy hatred, detestation, and indignation against all ungodliness and wickedness, and that upon holy accounts : " *I have refrained my feet from every evil way*." But why ? "*That I may keep thy word*." " Through thy precepts I get understanding ; therefore I hate every false way ; " ver. 104. The good that he got by divine precepts stirred up his hatred against every false way : verse 128, " Therefore I esteem all thy precepts concerning all things to be right ; and I hate every false way." His high esteem of every precept raised up in him a holy indignation against every evil way. A holy man knows that all sin strikes at the holiness of God, the glory of God, the nature of God, the being of God, and the law of God ; and therefore his heart rises against all ; he looks upon every sin as the Scribes and Pharisees that accused Christ ; and as that Judas that betrayed Christ ; and as that Pilate that condemned Christ ; and as those soldiers that scourged Christ ; and as those spears that pierced Christ ; and therefore his heart cries out for justice upon all.— *Thomas Brooks.*

Verse 101.—"*Refrained . . that I might keep*." By doing what is right we come both to know right and to be better able to do it.—"*Plain Commentary*."

Verse 101.—"*I have refrained my feet*," etc. The word "*refrained*" warns us that we are naturally borne by our feet into the path of every kind of sin, and are hurried along it by the rush of human passions, so that even the wise and understanding need to check, recall, and retrace their steps, in order that they may keep God's word, and not become castaways. And further note that the Hebrew verb here translated "*refrained*" is even stronger in meaning, and denotes, " I *fettered*, or *imprisoned*, my feet," whereby we may learn that no light resistance is enough to prevent them from leading us astray.—*Agellius and Genebrardus, in Neale and Littledale.*

Verse 102.—By *misphalim*, "*judgments*," is meant God's law ; for thereby he will judge the world. And the word "*departed not*" intimateth both his exactness and constancy : his exactness, that he did not go a hair's-breadth from his direction ; " Ye shall observe to do therefore as the Lord your God hath commanded you : ye shall not turn aside to the right hand or to the left " (Deut. v. 32) ; and his constancy is implied in it, for then we are said to depart from God and his law, when we fall off from him in judgment and practice. Jer. xxxii. 40.—*Thomas Manton.*

Verse 102.—"*Thou hast taught me*." God teacheth two ways :—1. By common illumination. 2. By special operation.

1. By common illumination, barely enlightening the mind to know or understand what he propoundeth by his messengers : so God showed it to the heathen : Rom. i. 20.

But then, 2. By way of special operation, effectually inclining the will to embrace and prosecute duties so known : " I will put my law in their inward parts, and write it in their hearts " : Jer. xxxi. 33. This way of teaching is always effectual and persuasive. Now, in this sense they are taught of God, so that they do not only get an ear to hear, but a heart to understand, learn, and practise.

This teaching is the ground of constancy, because, (1) They that are thus taught of God see things more clearly than others do ; God is the most excellent teacher. (2) They know things more surely, and with certainty of demonstration, whereas others have but dubious conjectures, and loose and wavering opinions about the things of God. (3) This teaching is so efficacious and powerful, as that the effect followeth : " Teach me thy way, O Lord, I will walk in thy truth " (Ps. lxxxvi. 11.) (4) God reneweth this teaching, and is always at hand to guide us, and give counsel to us, which is the cause of our standing.—*Thomas Manton.*

Verse 102.—"*For thou hast taught me*." Lest it should seem that David ascribed the praise of godliness to himself, or that it came from any goodness in him that he did refrain his feet from every evil way, he gives here all the glory to God, protesting, that because God did teach him, therefore he declined not. Wherefrom we learn, that if at any time we stand, or if when we have fallen we rise and repent, it is ever to be imputed to God that teacheth us ; for there is no evil so abominable, but it would soon become plausible to us, if God should leave us to ourselves. David was taught by his ordinary teachers, and he did reverence them ; but that he profited by them he ascribes unto God. Paul may plant, and Apollos water ; God must give the increase.—*William Cowper.*

Verse 103.—*"How sweet are thy words unto my taste!"* Even the words of a fellow-creature of earth, how inexpressibly sweet sometimes, how beyond all calculation precious! All gold and silver would be despised in comparison with them. They come freighted with love, and the heart is enriched with them as though the breath of God had come into it. But does not this rainbow of earthly joy die gradually out ? Do not the enrapturing words sooner or later become exsiccated in the memory, and may they not meet with contemptuous treatment as remembrancers of an earthly illusion ? Indeed they do ; indeed they may.

Nevertheless the heart may find its happiness, its true and undying happiness, *in words.* At this moment there is nothing in the whole world so much to be desired as certain words. Words of love. Words expressive of infinite love. Treasures, pleasures, honours, of earth, what are they ? My unsatisfied soul cries out, Give me words. Words whereby I may know the love that God has towards me. Words declaring the unchangeable attachment of the Saviour. Words purifying my heart. Emboldening me in prayer. Exhibiting to me the blissful future. Words that shall give life to my dead powers, and change me from glory to glory, as by the Spirit of the Lord.—*George Bowen, in "Daily Meditations,"* 1873.

Verse 103.—*"How sweet are thy words unto my taste!"* etc. There is given to the regenerated a new, supernatural sense, a certain divine, spiritual taste. This is in its whole nature diverse from any of the other five senses, and something is perceived by a true saint in the exercise of this new sense of mind, in spiritual and divine things, as entirely different from any thing that is perceived in them by natural men, as the sweet taste of honey is diverse from the ideas men get of honey by looking on it or feeling of it. Now the beauty of holiness is that which is perceived by this spiritual sense, so diverse from all that natural men perceive in them ; or, this kind of beauty is the quality that is the immediate object of this spiritual sense ; this is the sweetness that is the proper object of this spiritual taste. The Scripture often represents the beauty and sweetness of holiness as the grand object of a spiritual taste and a spiritual appetite. This was the sweet food of the holy soul of Jesus Christ, John iv. 32, 34. "I have meat to eat that ye know not of . . . My meat is to do the will of him that sent me, and to finish his work." I know of no part of the Holy Scriptures where the nature and evidence of true and sincere godliness are so fully and largely insisted on and delineated, as in the 119th Psalm. The Psalmist declares his design in the first verses of the Psalm, keeps his eye on it all along, and pursues it to the end. The excellency of holiness is represented as the immediate object of a spiritual taste and delight. *God's law,* that grand expression and emanation of the holiness of God's nature, and prescription of holiness to the creature, is all along represented as the great object of the love, the complacence, and rejoicing of the gracious nature, which prizes God's commandments *above gold, yea, the finest gold,* and to which they are *sweeter than honey, and the honey-comb ;* and that upon account of their holiness. The same Psalmist declares that this is the sweetness that a spiritual taste relishes in God's law : Ps. xix. 7—10.—*Jonathan Edwards,* 1703—1758.

Verse 103.—*"How sweet are thy words unto my taste!"* Why does he not rather say, How pleasant are thy words to my ears ? than that they are sweet to his taste and his mouth ? I answer : It is most meet that when God speaks by the mouth of his ministers we should be hearers, and the words of God should be the most joyous of all to our ears. But it is also the practice of the godly to converse about the words of God, and their words are so sweet to their own taste that they are more pleased and delighted than by any honey from the comb. And this is most necessary when either there is a scarcity of teachers, as with David in the wilderness or dwelling among the Philistines ; or when those who hold the office of teaching, adulterate and vitiate the pure word of God.—*Wolfgang Musculus.*

Verse 103.—That which is here called, *"word,"* I take rather for *"judgments,"* partly because in the proper tongue the word is left out, and partly because he had used this word *"judgments"* in the verse immediately going before. But some will say, How can the judgments of God be *"sweet,"* which are so troublesome, fearful, and grievous ? I answer, that the godly have no greater joy than when they feel either the mercies of God accomplished towards them that fear him, or his judgments showered upon the reprobates.—*Richard Greenham.*

Verse 103.—*"Unto my taste." "To my mouth."* That is, I take as great pleasure in talking, conferring, and persuading, thy judgments, as my mouth, or the mouth of any that loveth honey, delighteth therewith.—*Richard Greenham.*

Verse 103.—*"Sweeter."* As there are always among violets some that are very much sweeter than others, so among texts there are some that are more precious to us than others.—*Henry Ward Beecher*, 1879.

Verse 103.—An affectionate wife often says, " My husband ! your words are sweeter to me than honey ; yea, they are sweeter than the sugar-cane." " Alas ! my husband is gone," says the widow : " how sweet were his words ! Honey dropped from his mouth : his words were ambrosia."—*Joseph Roberts*.

Verse 104.—*"Through thy precepts I get understanding : therefore I hate every false way."* In this sentence the prophet seems to invert the order set down in verse 101. He had said, " I have refrained my feet from every evil way, that I might keep thy word," where the avoiding of evil is made the means of profiting by the word ; here his profiting by the word is made the cause of avoiding evil. In the one verse you have an account of his beginning with God ; in the other, of his progress.—*Thomas Manton*.

Verse 104.—*"I hate every false way,"* David saith, *"I hate every false way"*; I hate not only the way, when I have been misled into it, but I hate to go in it ; and he professeth at the 163rd verse, *"I hate and abhor lying, but thy law do I love."* To abstain from and forbear lying is a sign of a gracious heart, much more to hate and abhor it. A godly man not only doth that which is good, but he delights to do it, his soul cleaves to it ; he is in his element when he is doing it, nothing comes more suitably to him than the business of his duty, he loveth to do it, yea, he loveth it when he cannot do it ; Rom. vii. 22. Paul complained much that his corruptions clogged, hindered and shackled him ; he was in lime twigs as to the doing of good, yet (saith he) " I delight in the law of God after the inward man " ; that is, the inward man delightfully moves after the law of God, when I am basely moved by my corrupt heart, and stirred by temptation against it. Now, as a godly man not only chooseth to do the holy will of God, but delights and rejoiceth to do it, and hath sweet content in doing it ; so likewise a godly man not only refuseth to do the will of the flesh, or to follow the course of the world, but hates to do it, and is never so discontented with himself as when through carelessness and neglect of his watch he hath been overtaken and hath fallen. A carnal man may forbear the doing of evil, and do what is materially good, but he never abhors what is evil, nor delights in what is good. Though he abstain from acting those things which God forbids, yet he doth not say, with Job, " God forbid, I should act them." . . . . To delight in good is better than the doing of it, and to abhor evil is better than abstaining from it. And if we compare the nature of sin with the new nature of a godly man, we may see clear grounds why his abstinence from sin is joined with an abhorrence of it.—*Joseph Caryl*.

Verse 104.—*"Through thy precepts I get understanding."* Spiritual understanding is connected with the taste of spiritual sweetness. (Compare Proverbs ii. 10, 11.) " The sweetness of the lips "—as the wise man observes—" increaseth learning. The heart of the wise teacheth his mouth, and addeth learning to his lips." Prov. xvi. 21, 23. Thus having learned " the principles of the doctrine of Christ," we are encouraged to " go on to perfection "—" growing *in grace* and in the knowledge of Christ." For the connexion between " grace and knowledge " is clearly manifested.—*Charles Bridges*.

Verse 104.—*"I hate every false way."* Universality in this is a sure sign of sincerity. Herod spits out some sins, when he rolls others as sweet morsels in his mouth. A hypocrite ever leaves the devil some nest-egg to sit upon, though he take many away. Some men will not buy some commodities, because they cannot have them at their own price, but they lay out the same money on others ; so hypocrites forbear some sins, yea, are displeased at them, because they cannot have them without disgrace or disease, or some other disadvantage ; but they lay out the same love upon other sins which will suit better with their designs. Some affirm that what the sea loseth in one place it gaineth in another ; so what ground the corruption of the unconverted loseth one way, it gaineth another. There is in him some one lust especially which is his favourite ; some king sin, like Agag, which must be spared when others are destroyed. " In this the Lord be merciful to thy servant," saith Naaman. But now the regenerate laboureth to cleanse himself from all pollutions, both of flesh and spirit. 2 Cor. vii. 1.—*George Swinnock*.

Verse 104.—*"I hate."* The Scriptures place religion very much in the affection of *love ;* love to God, and the Lord Jesus Christ ; love to the people of God, and to mankind. The texts in which this is manifest, both in the Old Testament and the New, are innumerable. The contrary affection of *hatred* also, as having sin for its object, is spoken of in Scripture as no inconsiderable part of true religion. It is spoken of as that by which true religion may be known and distinguished. Prov. viii. 13. " The fear of the Lord is to hate evil." Accordingly, the saints are called upon to give evidence of their sincerity by this, Psalm xcvii. 10. " Ye that love the Lord, *hate* evil." And the Psalmist often mentions it as an evidence of his sincerity : Ps. ci. 2, 3, " I will walk within my house with a perfect heart. I will set no wicked thing before mine eyes ; I *hate* the work of them that turn aside." So Ps. cxix., verse 128, and the present place. Again, Ps. cxxxix. 21 : " Do not I *hate* them, O Lord, that hate thee ? "—*Jonathan Edwards.*

Verse 104.—"*I hate.*" Hatred is a stabbing, murdering affection, it pursues sin with a hot heart to death, as an avenger of blood, that is to say, of the blood of the soul which sin would spill, and of the blood of Christ which sin hath shed. Hate sin perfectly and perpetually and then you will not spare it but kill it presently. Till sin be hated it cannot be mortified ; you will not cry against it, as the Jews did against Christ, Crucify it ! Crucify it ! but shew indulgence to it as David did to Absalom and say, Deal gently with the young man,—with this or that lust, for my sake. Mercy to sin is cruelty to the soul.—*Edward Reyner*, 1600—1670.

Verse 104.—"*False way.*" It is not said, " evil way," but " false way " : or, as it is in the original, every path of lying and falsehood. Falsehood is either in point of opinion or practice. If you take it in the first sense, for falsehood in opinion or error in judgment, or false doctrine, or false worship, this sentence holds good. Those that get understanding by the word are established against error, and not only established against error, or against the embracing or possession of it, but they hate it.—*Thomas Manton.*

Verse 104.—"*False way.*" All sin is a *lie.* By it we attempt to cheat God. By it we actually cheat our souls : Prov. xiv. 12. There is no delusion like the folly of believing that a course of sin will conduce to our happiness.—*William S. Plumer.*

EXPOSITION OF VERSES 105 TO 112.

THY word *is* a lamp unto my feet, and a light unto my path.

106 I have sworn, and I will perform *it*, that I will keep thy righteous judgments.

107 I am afflicted very much : quicken me, O LORD, according unto thy word.

108 Accept, I beseech thee, the freewill offerings of my mouth, O LORD, and teach me thy judgments.

109 My soul *is* continually in my hand : yet do I not forget thy law.

110 The wicked have laid a snare for me : yet I erred not from thy precepts.

111 Thy testimonies have I taken as an heritage for ever : for they *are* the rejoicing of my heart.

112 I have inclined mine heart to perform thy statutes alway, *even unto* the end.

105. *"Thy word is a lamp unto my feet."* We are walkers through the city of this world, and we are often called to go out into its darkness ; let us never venture there without the light-giving word, lest we slip with our feet. Each man should use the word of God personally, practically, and habitually, that he may see his way and see what lies in it. When darkness settles down upon all around me, the word of the Lord, like a flaming torch, reveals my way. Having no fixed lamps in eastern towns, in old time each passenger carried a lantern with him that he might not fall into the open sewer, or stumble over the heaps of ordure which defiled the road. This is a true picture of our path through this dark world : we should not know the way, or how to walk in it, if the Scripture, like a blazing flambeau, did not reveal it. One of the most practical benefits of Holy Writ is guidance in the acts of daily life ; it is not sent to astound us with its brilliance, but to guide us by its instruction. It is true the head needs illumination, but even more the feet need direction, else head and feet may both fall into a ditch. Happy is the man who personally appropriates God's word, and practically uses it as his comfort and counsellor,—a lamp to his own feet. *"And a light unto my path."* It is a lamp by night, a light by day, and a delight at all times. David guided his own steps by it, and also saw the difficulties of his road by its beams. He who walks in darkness is sure, sooner or later, to stumble ; while he who walks by the light of day, or by the lamp of night, stumbleth not, but keeps his uprightness. Ignorance is painful upon practical subjects ; it breeds indecision and suspense, and these are uncomfortable : the word of God, by imparting heavenly knowledge, leads to decision, and when that is followed by determined resolution, as in this case, it brings with it great restfulness of heart.

This verse converses with God in adoring and yet familiar tones. Have we not something of like tenor to address to our heavenly Father ?

Note how like this verse is to the first verse of the first octave, and the first of the second and other octaves. The seconds also are often in unison.

106. *"I have sworn, and I will perform it, that I will keep thy righteous judgments."* Under the influence of the clear light of knowledge he had firmly made up his mind and solemnly declared his resolve in the sight of God. Perhaps mistrusting his own fickle mind, he had pledged himself in sacred form to abide faithful to the determinations and decisions of his God. Whatever path might open before him, he was sworn to follow that only upon which the lamp of the word was shining. The Scriptures are God's judgments, or verdicts, upon great moral questions ; these are all righteous, and hence righteous men should be resolved to keep them at all hazards, since it must always be right to do right. Experience shows that the less of covenanting and swearing men formally enter upon the better, and the genius of our Saviour's teaching is against all supererogatory pledging and swearing ; and yet under the gospel we ought to feel ourselves as much bound to

obey the word of the Lord as if we had taken an oath so to do. The bonds of love are not less sacred than the fetters of law. When a man has vowed he must be careful to " perform it," and when a man has not vowed in so many words to keep the Lord's judgments, yet is he equally bound to do so by obligations which exist apart from any promise on our part,—obligations founded in the eternal fitness of things, and confirmed by the abounding goodness of the Lord our God. Will not every believer own that he is under bonds to the redeeming Lord to follow his example, and keep his words ? Yes, the vows of the Lord are upon us, especially upon such as have made profession of discipleship, have been baptized into the thrice-holy name, have eaten of the consecrated memorials, and have spoken in the name of the Lord Jesus. We are enlisted, and sworn in, and are bound to be loyal soldiers all through the war. Thus having taken the word into our hearts by a firm resolve to obey it, we have a lamp within our souls as well as in the Book, and our course will be light unto the end.

107. "I am afflicted very much." According to the last verse he had been sworn in as a soldier of the Lord, and in this next verse he is called to suffer hardness in that capacity. Our service of the Lord does not screen us from trial, but rather secures it for us. The Psalmist was a consecrated man, and yet a chastened man ; nor were his chastisements light ; for it seemed as if the more he was obedient the more he was afflicted. He evidently felt the rod to be cutting deep, and this he pleads before the Lord. He speaks not by way of murmuring, but by way of pleading ; from the very much affliction he argues for very much quickening.

"Quicken me, O LORD, according unto thy word." This is the best remedy for tribulation ; the soul is raised above the thought of present distress, and is filled with that holy joy which attends all vigorous spiritual life, and so the affliction grows light. Jehovah alone can quicken : he has life in himself, and therefore can communicate it readily ; he can give us life at any moment, yea, at this present instant ; for it is of the nature of quickening to be quick in its operation. The Lord has promised, prepared, and provided this blessing of renewed life for all his waiting servants : it is a covenant blessing, and it is as obtainable as it is needful. Frequently the affliction is made the means of the quickening, even as the stirring of a fire promotes the heat of the flame. In their affliction some desire death, let us pray for life. Our forebodings under trial are often very gloomy, let us entreat the Lord to deal with us, not according to our fears, but according to his own word. David had but few promises to quote, and probably these were in his own Psalms, yet he pleads the word of the Lord; how much more should we do so, since to us so many holy men have spoken by the Spirit of the Lord in that wonderful library which is now our Bible. Seeing we have more promises, let us offer more prayers.

108. "Accept, I beseech thee, the freewill offerings of my mouth, O LORD." The living praise the living God, and therefore the quickened one presents his sacrifice. He offers prayer, praise, confession, and testimony—these, presented with his voice in the presence of an audience, were the tribute of his mouth unto Jehovah. He trembles lest these should be so ill uttered as to displease the Lord, and therefore he implores acceptance. He pleads that the homage of his mouth was cheerfully and spontaneously rendered ; all his utterances were freewill offerings. There can be no value in extorted confessions : God's revenues are not derived from forced taxation, but from freewill donation. There can be no acceptance where there is no willingness ; there is no work of free grace where there is no fruit of free will. Acceptance is a favour to be sought from the Lord with all earnestness, for without it our offerings are worse thon useless. What a wonder of grace that the the Lord will accept anything of such unworthy ones as we are !

"And teach me thy judgments." When we render unto the Lord our best, we become all the more concerned to do better. If, indeed, the Lord shall accept us, we then desire to be further instructed, that we may still be more acceptable. After quickening we need teaching : life without light, or zeal without knowledge, would be but half a blessing. These repeated cries for teaching show the humility of the man of God, and also discover to us our own need of similar instruction. Our judgment needs educating till it knows, agrees with, and acts upon, the judgments of the Lord. Those judgments are not always so clear as to be seen at once ; we need to be taught in them till we admire their wisdom and adore their goodness as soon as ever we perceive them.

109. "My soul is continually in my hand." He lived in the midst of danger. He had to be always fighting for existence—hiding in caves, or contending in

battles. This is a very uncomfortable and trying state of affairs, and men are apt to think any expedient justifiable by which they can end such a condition : but David did not turn aside to find safety in sin, for he says, "*Yet do I not forget thy law.*" They say that all things are fair in love and war ; but the holy man thought not so : while he carried his life in his hand, he also carried the law in his heart. No danger of body should make us endanger our souls by forgetting that which is right. Trouble makes many a man forget his duty, and it would have had the same effect upon the Psalmist if he had not obtained quickening (verse 107) and teaching (verse 108). In his memory of the Lord's law lay his safety ; he was certain not to be forgotten of God, for God was not forgotten of him. It is a special proof of grace when nothing can drive truth out of our thoughts, or holiness out of our lives. If we remember the law even when death stares us in the face, we may be well assured that the Lord is remembering us.

110. "*The wicked have laid a snare for me.*" Spiritual life is the scene of constant danger : the believer lives with his life in his hand, and meanwhile all seem plotting to take it from him, by cunning if they cannot by violence. We shall not find it an easy thing to live the life of the faithful. Wicked spirits and wicked men will leave no stone unturned for our destruction. If all other devices fail, and even hidden pits do not succeed, the wicked still persevere in their treacherous endeavours, and, becoming craftier still, they set snares for the victim of their hate. The smaller species of game are usually taken by this method, by gin, or trap, or net, or noose. Wicked men are quite indifferent as to the manner in which they can destroy the good man—they think no more of him than if he were a rabbit or a rat : cunning and treachery are always the allies of malice, and everything like a generous or chivalrous feeling is unknown among the graceless, who treat the godly as if they were vermin to be exterminated. When a man knows that he is thus assailed, he is too apt to become timorous, and rush upon some hasty device for deliverance, not without sin in the endeavour ; but David calmly kept his way, and was able to write, "*Yet I erred not from thy precepts.*" He was not snared, for he kept his eyes open, and kept near his God. He was not entrapped and robbed for he followed the King's highway of holiness, where God secures safety to every traveller. He did not err from the right, and he was not deterred from following it, because he referred to the Lord for guidance, and obtained it. If we err from the precepts, we part with the promises ; if we get away from God's presence, we wander into the wilds where the fowlers freely spread their nets. From this verse let us learn to be on our guard, for we, too, have enemies both crafty and wicked. Hunters set their traps in the animals' usual runs, and our worst snares are laid in our own ways. By keeping to the ways of the Lord we shall escape the snares of our adversaries, for his ways are safe and free from treachery.

111. "*Thy testimonies have I taken as an heritage for ever.*" He chose them as his lot, his portion, his estate ; and what is more, he laid hold upon them and made them so,—taking them into possession and enjoyment. David's choice is our choice. If we might have our desire, we would desire to keep the commands of God perfectly. To know the doctrine, to enjoy the promise to practise the command,—be this a kingdom large enough for me. Here we have an inheritance which cannot fade and cannot be alienated ; it is for ever, and ours for ever, if we have so taken it. Sometimes, like Israel at the first coming into Canaan, we have to take our heritage by hard fighting, and, if so, it is worthy of all our labour and suffering ; but always it has to be taken by a decided choice of the heart and grip of the will. What God gives we must take. "*For they are the rejoicing of my heart.*" The gladness which had come to him through the word of the Lord had caused him to make an unalterable choice of it. All the parts of Scripture had been pleasing to David, and were so still, and therefore he stuck to them, and meant to stick to them for ever. That which rejoices the heart is sure to be chosen and treasured. It is not the head-knowledge but the heart-experience which brings the joy.

In this verse, which is the seventh of its octave, we have reached the same sweetness as in the last seventh (103) : indeed, in several of the adjoining sevenths, delight is evident. How good a thing it is when experience ripens into joy, passing up through sorrow, prayer, conflict, hope, decision, and holy content into rejoicing ! Joy fixes the spirit : when once a man's heart rejoices in the divine word, he greatly values it, and is for ever united to it.

112. "*I have inclined mine heart to perform thy statutes alway, even unto the end.*"

He was not half inclined to virtue, but heartily inclined to it. His whole heart was bent on practical, persevering godliness. He was resolved to keep the statutes of the Lord with all his heart, throughout all his time, without erring or ending. He made it his end to keep the law unto the end, and that without end. He had by prayer, and meditation, and resolution made his whole being lean towards God's commands ; or as we should say in other words—the grace of God had inclined him to incline his heart in a sanctified direction. Many are inclined to preach, but the Psalmist was inclined to practise ; many are inclined to perform ceremonies, but he was inclined to perform statutes ; many are inclined to obey occasionally, but David would obey alway ; and, alas, many are inclined for temporary religion, but this godly man was bound for eternity, he would perform the statutes of his Lord and King even unto the end. Lord, send us such a heavenly inclination of heart as this : then shall we show that thou hast quickened and taught us. To this end create in us a clean heart, and daily renew a right spirit within us, for only so shall we incline in the right direction.

NOTES ON VERSES 105 TO 112.

Verse 105.—*"Thy word is a lamp unto my feet, and a light,"* etc. David was a man of very good wit and natural understanding ; but he gives to God the glory of his wisdom, and owns that his best light was but darkness when he was not lightened and ruled by the word of God. Oh that we would consider this, that in all our ways wherein the word of God shines not unto us to direct us, we do but . walk in darkness, and our ways without it can lead us to none other end but utter darkness. If we hearken not to the word of God, if we walk not by the rule thereof, how is it possible we can come to the face of God ?—*William Cowper.*

Verse 105.—*"Thy word is a lamp unto my feet, and a light unto my path."* The use of a *lamp* is by night, while the *light* of the sun shineth by day. Whether it be day or night with us, we clearly understand our duty by the Word of God. The *night* signifieth adversity, and the *day* prosperity. Hence we may learn how to behave ourselves in all conditions. The word " *path* " noteth our general choice and course of life ; the word " *feet* " our particular actions. Now whether the matter, wherein we would be informed, concerneth our choice of the way that leadeth to true happiness, or our dexterous prosecution of the way, still the word of God will direct a humble and well-disposed mind.—*Thomas Manton.*

Verse 105.—*"Thy word is a lamp unto my feet,"* etc. Basil the Great, interpreting the " *word* " as God's will revealed in Holy Scriptures, observes that the Old Testament, and in especial the Law, was only a *lantern* (*lamp* or *candle*) because an artificial light, imperfectly illumining the darkness, whereas the Gospel, given by the Lord Jesus himself, is a *light* of the Sun of Righteousness, giving brightness to all things. Ambrose, going yet deeper, tells us that Christ is himself both *lamp* and *light.* He, the Word of God, is a great light to some, to others he is a lamp. To me he is a lamp ; to angels a light, He was a light to Peter, when the angel stood by him in the prison, and the light shined about him. He was a light to Paul when the light from heaven shined round about him, and he heard Christ saying to him, " Saul, Saul, why persecutest thou me ? " And Christ is truly a lamp to me when I speak of him with my mouth. He shineth in clay, he shineth in a potter's vessel : he is that treasure which we bear in earthen vessels.—*Neale and Littledale.*

Verse 105.—*"Thy word is a lamp . . . and a light."* Except the " *lamp*" be lighted—except the teaching of the Spirit accompany the word—all is " darkness, gross darkness " still. Did we more habitually wait to receive, and watch to improve, the light of the word, we should not so often complain of the perplexity of our path.—*Charles Bridges.*

Verse 105.—*"Thy word is a lamp unto my feet,"* etc. What we all want, is not to see wonders that daze us, and to be rapt in ecstatic visions and splendours, but a little light on the dark and troubled path we have to tread, a lamp that will burn steadfastly and helpfully over the work we have to do. The stars are infinitely more sublime, meteors infinitely more superb and dazzling ; but the lamp shining in a dark place is infinitely closer to our practical needs.—*From "The Expositor,"* 1864.

Verse 105.—*"Thy word is a lamp unto my feet."* Going two miles into a neighbourhood where very few could read, to spend an evening in reading to a company who were assembled to listen, and about to return by a narrow path through the woods where paths diverged, I was provided with a torch of light wood, or " pitch pine." I objected ; it was too small, weighing not over half a pound. *"It will light you home,"* answered my host. I said, " The wind may blow it out." He said, " It will light you home." " But if it should rain ? " I again objected. " It will light you home," he insisted.

Contrary to my fears, it gave abundant light to my path all the way home, furnishing an apt illustration, I often think, of the way in which doubting hearts would be led safely along the " narrow way." If they would take the Bible as their guide, it would be a lamp to their feet, leading to the heavenly home. One man had five objections to the Bible. If he would take it as a lamp to his feet, it would " light him home." Another told me he had two faults to find with the Bible. I answered him in the words of my good friend who furnished the torch, " It will light you home."—*From the American Messenger,"* 1881.

Verse 105.—*"A lamp unto my feet,"* etc. All depends on our way of using the lamp. A man tells that when a boy he was proud to carry the lantern for his Sabbath school teacher. The way to their school led through unlit, muddy streets. The boy held the lantern far too high, and both sank in the deep mud. " Ah ! you must hold the lamp lower," the teacher exclaimed, as they gained a firm footing on the farther side of the slough. The teacher then beautifully explained our text, and the man declares that he never forgot the lesson of that night. You may easily hold the lamp too high ; but you can hardly hold it too low.—*James Wells, in "Bible Images,"* 1882.

Verse 105.—*"Light."*

> Lead, kindly light, amid the encircling gloom,
>   Lead thou me on.
> The night is dark, and I am far from home,
>   Lead thou me on.
> Keep thou my feet ; I do not ask to see
> The distant scene ; one step enough for me.
>
> *John Henry Newman* (1801—).

Verses 105, 106.—*"A light unto my path. I have sworn, and I will perform it,"* etc. I have looked upon thy word as a lamp to my own feet, as a thing nearly concerning myself, and then I have sworn, and I will perform it, that I will keep thy righteous judgments. It is a mighty means to stir up a man's spirit and quicken him to obedience, to look upon the word as written to himself, as a lamp and a light for him. When you come to hear out of God's Word, and God directs the minister so that you apprehend the truth as spoken to you, it will stir and awaken you, and you will say, " Oh methought this day every word the minister spoke was directed to me ; I must take heed thereto." And so every word in the Scripture that concerns thee, God writes to thee ; and if thou wilt take it so, it will be a mighty means to stir thee up to obedience.—*Jeremiah Burroughs,* 1599—1646.

Verse 106.—*"I have sworn,"* etc. Patrick's paraphrase is, " I have solemnly resolved and bound myself by the most sacred ties, which I will never break, but do now confirm."

Verse 106.—*"I have sworn."* I would now urge you to make a solemn surrender of yourself unto the service of God. Do not only form such a purpose in your heart, but expressly declare it in the Divine presence. Such solemnity in the manner of doing it is certainly very reasonable in the nature of things ; and sure it is highly expedient, for binding to the Lord such a treacherous heart, as we know our own to be. It will be pleasant to reflect upon it, as done at such and such a time, with such and such circumstances of place and method, which may serve to strike the memory and the conscience. The sense of the vows of God which are upon you will strengthen you in an hour of temptation ; and the recollection may encourage your humble boldness and freedom in applying to him under the character and relation of your covenant God and Father, as future exigencies may require.

Do it therefore, but do it deliberately. Consider what it is that you are to do : and consider how reasonable it is that it should be done, and done cordially and cheerfully, " not by constraint, but willingly " ; for in this sense, and every other, " God loveth a cheerful giver." . . . . . .

Let me remind you that this surrender must be perpetual. You must give yourself up to God in such a manner, as never more to pretend to be your own ; for the rights of God are, like his nature, eternal and immutable ; and with regard to his rational creatures, are the same yesterday, to-day, and for ever.

I would further advise and urge, that this dedication may be made with all possible solemnity. Do it in express words. And perhaps it may be in many cases most expedient, as many pious divines have recommended, to do it in writing. Set your hand and seal to it, " that on such a day of such a month and year, and at such a place, on full consideration and serious reflection, you came to this happy resolution, that whatever others might do, you would serve the Lord."—*Philip Doddridge* (1702—1751) *in "The Rise and Progress of Religion in the Soul."*

Verse 106.—Frequently renew settled and holy resolutions. A soldier unresolved to fight may easily be defeated. True and sharpened courage tread down those difficulties which would triumph over a cold and wavering spirit. Resolution in a weak man will perform more than strength in a coward. The weakness of our graces, the strength of our temptations, and the diligence of our spiritual enemies, require strong resolutions. We must be " steadfast and unmoveable," and this will make us " abound in the work of the Lord " : 1 Cor. xv. 58. Abundant exercise in God's work will strengthen the habit of grace, increase our skill in the contest, and make the victory more easy and pleasant to us. Let us frame believing, humble resolutions in the strength of God's grace, with a fear of ourselves, but a confidence in God. David bound himself to God with a hearty vow, depending upon his strength : *"I have sworn, and I will perform it, that I will keep thy righteous judgments."* This was not in his own strength, for, ver. 107, he desires God to quicken him, and to "accept the freewill offerings of his mouth," ver. 108, namely, the oath which proceeded from a free and resolved will. God will not slight, but strengthen the affectionate resolutions of his creature. We cannot keep ourselves from falling unless we first keep our resolutions from flagging.—*Stephen Charnock.*

Verse 106.—*"I have sworn, and I will perform it."* Theodoricus, Archbishop of Cologne, when the Emperor Sigismund demanded of him the directest and most compendious way how to attain true happiness, made answer in brief, thus : " Perform when thou art well what thou promisedst when thou wast sick." David did so ; he made vows in war, and paid them in peace ; and thus should all good men do ; not like the cunning devil, of whom the epigrammatist writeth :

" The devil was sick, the devil a monk would be ;
The devil was well, the devil a monk was he."

Nor like unto many now-a-days, that, if God's hand do but lie somewhat heavy upon them, oh, what promises, what engagements are there for amendment of life ! How like unto marble against rain do they seem to sweat and melt but still retain their hardness ! Let but the rod be taken off their backs, or health restored, then, as their bodies live, their vows die ; all is forgotten : nay, many times it so falleth out, that they are far worse than ever they were before.—*From John Spencer's "Things New and Old,"* 1658.

Verse 106.—*"Thy righteous judgments."* So David styles the word of God, because it judgeth most righteously between right and wrong, truth and falsehood. And, secondly, because according to the judgment given therein, God will act towards men. Let us take heed unto it ; for the word contains God's judgment of men and hath a catalogue of such as shall not inherit the kingdom of God, and another of such as shall dwell in God's tabernacle : let us read and see in which of the two catalogues our two selves are ; for according to that word will the judgment go.—*William Cowper.*

Verse 107.—*"I am afflicted very much,"* etc. Whence learn, 1. It is no strange thing for the most holy men to be acquainted with the saddest sort of affliction, bodily and spiritual : *"I am afflicted very much."* 2. From whence soever affliction doth come, faith goeth to God only for comfort, as here : *"Quicken me, O Lord."* 3. When God is pleased to make the word of promise lively, or to perform what the promise alloweth us to expect, such a consolation is a sufficient antidote to the heaviest affliction : *"Quicken me, O Lord, according unto thy word."*—*David Dickson.*

Verse 107.—*"I am afflicted very much."* We can recommend so persuasively the cheerful drinking of the cup of sorrow when in the hand of others, but what wry faces we make when it is put into our own.—*Alfred John Morris,* 1814—1869.

Verse 107.—*"I am afflicted . . . quicken me."* The Christian lives in the midst of crosses, as the fish lives in the sea.—*Jean-Baptiste-Marie Vianney,* 1786—1859.

Verse 107.—*"Quicken me, O Lord."* How doth God quicken us ? By reviving our suffering graces, such as our hope, patience, and faith. Thus he puts life into us again, that we may go on cheerfully in our service, by infusion of new comforts. He revives the heart of his contrite ones, so the prophet saith (Isai. lvii. 15). This is very necessary, for the Psalmist saith elsewhere, " Quicken us, and we will call upon thy name " (Ps. lxxx. 18). Discomfort and discouragement weaken our hands in calling upon God. Until the Lord cheers us again we have no life in prayer. By two things especially doth God quicken us in affliction, by reviving our sense of his love, and by reviving our hope of glory.—*Thomas Manton.*

Verse 107.—*"According unto thy word."* David goes often over with that phrase, which imports that David lay under the sense of some promise which God had made for the quickening of his heart when it was out of frame, and acordingly he recounts the gracious influence of God's Spirit, and professeth that he will never forget his precepts, because by them he had quickened him : ver. 93.

Thus, lay your dead hearts at Christ's feet, and plead in this manner : Lord, my heart is exceedingly dull and distracted ; I feel not these enlarging, melting influences which thy saints have felt ; but are they not chief material mercies of the covenant ? dost thou not promise a spirit of illumination, conviction, and humiliation ? is not holiness of heart and life a main branch of it ? dost thou not promise therein to write thy law in my heart ? to give me oneness of heart, to put thy fear within me, to subdue my corruptions, to help my infirmities in prayer ? Now, Lord, these are the mercies my soul wants and waits for, fill my soul with these animating influences, revive thy work of grace in my soul, draw out my heart towards thee, increase my affection for thee, repair thine image, call forth grace into lively exercise. Doth not that gracious word intend such a mercy when thou sayest thou wilt not only give a new heart, but " put a new spirit within me " (Ezek. xxxvi. 26), to make my soul lively, active, and spiritual in duties and exercises ? Dear Lord, am not I in covenant with thee ? and are not these covenant mercies ? why, then, my God, is my heart thus hardened from thy fear ? why dost thou leave me in all this deadness and distraction ? Remember thy word unto thy servant in which thou hast caused me to hope, and which thou hast helped me to plead ; O quicken my dull heart, according to thy word.—*Oliver Heywood.*

Verse 107.—*"According unto thy word."* David, when he begs for quickening, he is encouraged so to do by a promise. The question is, where this promise should be ? Some think it was that general promise of the law, if thou do these things thou shalt live in them (Lev. xviii. 5), and that from thence David drew this particular conclusion, that God would give life to his people. But rather, it was some other promise, some word of God he had, to bear him out in this request. The Lord has made many promises to us of sanctifying our affliction. The fruit of all shall be the taking away of sin (Isa. xxvii. 9) ; of bettering and improving us by it (Heb. ii. 10), of moderating our affliction, that he will stay his rough wind in the day of the east wind (Isa. xxvii. 8) ; that he will lay no more upon us than he will enable us to bear (1 Cor. x. 13). He hath promised he will moderate our affliction so that we shall not be tempted above our strength. He hath promised he will deliver us from it, that the rod of the wicked shall not always rest on the lot of the righteous (Ps. cxxv. 3) ; that he will be with us in it, and never fail us (Heb. xiii. 5). Now, I argue thus : if the people of God could stay their hearts upon God's word, when they had but such obscure hints to work upon that we do not know where the promise lies, ah ! how should our hearts be stayed upon God, when we have so many promises ! When the Scriptures are enlarged for the comfort and enlarging of our faith, surely we should say now as Paul, when we got a word, " I believed God " (Acts xxvii. 25) ; I may expect God will do thus for me, when his word speaks it everywhere.—*Thomas Manton.*

Verse 108.—*"The freewill offerings of the mouth,"* may be the offerings which the mouth had promised and vowed. And who can lay claim to these as the Lord ? His are all things.—*John Stephen.*

Verse 108.—*"The freewill offerings of my mouth."* This place makes known that species of sacrifices, which neither tribulations nor poverty of means can hinder, and which does not require an external temple, but in desert places and among heathen may be offered by a godly man. And these sacrifices of the mouth God himself makes more of than if all the flocks of the whole earth had been offered to him, and all the treasures of gold, and of silver, and of precious stones.—*Wolfgang Musculus.*

Verse 108.—*"Freewill offerings."* This expression is often used in the law (Lev. xxii. 18 ; Numb. xxix. 39 ; 2 Chron. xxxi. 14 ; Amos iv. 5). What are these freewill offerings ? They are distinguished from God's stated worship, and distinguished from that service which fell under a vow. Besides the stated peace-offerings, there were certain sacrifices performed upon certain occasions, to testify God's general goodness, and upon receipt of some special mercy ; and you will find these sacrifices to be expressly distinguished from such services as men bound themselves to by vow (Lev. vii. 16) . . . . These serve to teach us two things. 1st. They are to teach us how ready we should be to take all occasions of thankfulness and spiritual worship ; for, besides their vowed services and instituted sacrifices, they had their freewill offerings, offered to God in thankfulness for some special blessing received, or for deliverance from danger. 2ndly. It shows with what voluntariness and cheerfulness we should go about God's worship in the Gospel, and what a free disposition of heart there should be, and edge upon our affections, in all things that we offer to God ; in this latter sense our offerings to God—prayer and praise —should be freewill offerings, come from us not like water out of a still forced by the fire, but like water out of a fountain with native freeness, readily and freely.— *Thomas Manton.*

Verse 108.—*"Offerings."* All God's people are made priests unto God ; for every offering supposeth a priest : so it is said, that Christ Jesus hath made us kings and priests (Rev. i. 6). All Christians have a communion with Christ in all his offices ; whatever Christ was, that certainly they are in some measure and degree.— *Thomas Manton.*

Verse 108.—*"Accept . . . . . the freewill offerings of my mouth, O Lord."* It is a great grace that the Lord should accept anything from us, if we consider these three things : First, who the Lord is ; next, what we are ; thirdly, what it is we have to give unto him.

As for the Lord, he is all-sufficient, and stands in need of nothing we can give him. Our goodness extends not to the Lord (Ps. xvi).

As for us, we are poor creatures, living by his liberality ; yea, begging from all the rest of his creatures ; from the sun and moon ; from the air, the water, and the earth ; from fowls and fishes ; yea, from the worms : some give us light, some meat, some clothes ; and are such beggars as we meet to give to a king ?

And, thirdly, if we well consider, What is it that we give ? Have we anything to give but that which we have received from him ? and whereof we may say with David, " O Lord, all things are of thee, and of thine own have we given thee again " (1 Chron. xxix. 14). Let this humble us, and restrain us from that vain conceit of meriting at God's hand.

David at this time, in his great necessity, having no other sacrifice to offer unto the Lord, offers him the calves of his lips ; but no doubt, when he might, he offered more.

There is nothing so small, but if it come from a good heart, God will accept it : the widow's mite, a cup of cold water ; yea, and the praise of our lips, although it has no other external oblation joined with it : but where men may do more, and will not, it is an argument that their heart is not sincerely affected toward him, and their praises are not welcome to him.—*William Cowper.*

Verse 108.—*"Accept . . . . the freewill offerings of my mouth, O Lord, and teach me thy judgments."* Two things we are here taught to pray for in reference to our religious performances.

1. Acceptance of them : this we must aim at in all we do in religion, that whether present or absent we may be accepted of the Lord. That which David here earnestly prays for the acceptance of is " *the freewill offerings*," not of his purse, but of his " *mouth*," his prayers and praises ; " the calves of our lips " (Hosea xiv. 2) ; " the fruit of our lips " (Heb. xiii. 15) ; these are the spiritual offerings which all Christians, as spiritual priests, must offer to God ; and they must be " *freewill offerings ;* " for we must offer them abundantly and cheerfully ; and it is this willing mind that is accepted. The more there is of freeness and willing-ness in the service of God, the more pleasing it is to him.

2. Assistance in them : *"Teach me thy judgments."* We cannot offer anything to God which we have reason to think he will accept of, but what he is pleased to instruct us in the doing of ; and we must be earnest for the grace of God in us as for the favour of God toward us.—*Matthew Henry.*

Verse 108.—*"Teach me thy judgments."* As if the man of God should say, This is one thing whereunto I will give over myself, even to see how thou dost punish the wicked, and conduct thy children. So that we must learn, that as it is necessary to understand the law and the gospel, so is it requisite to discern God's judgments. For as we cannot learn the one without observing God's mercy ; so we cannot attain to the other without marking his vengeance. We must see always by the peculiar teaching of God's Spirit, how the Lord punisheth in justice, and yet in mercy ; in wrath, and yet in love ; in rigour and hatred of our sin, humbling us with one hand ; in pity and compassion to our salvation, comforting us with the other hand. We see then how the prophet prayeth, both to see them and to mark them : we need teach this often, because we dream so much of fatal necessity, and of the connections of natural causes, or else because we cannot discern between the crosses of the godly and the ungodly . . . This is then a singular gift of God, to discern how by the self-same means the Lord both humbleth the good and over-throweth the wicked.—*Richard Greenham.*

Verse 109.—*"My soul is continually in my hand."* He had his soul in his hand, ready to give whenever God should take it. And this is to be observed, that there is no trouble so ready to take away the life of God's children, as they are ready to give it. As Elijah came out to the mouth of his cave to meet with the Lord ; and Abraham stood in the door of his tent to speak to the angel ; so the soul of the godly stands ready in the door of the tabernacle of this body to remove when the Lord shall command it ; whereas the soul of the wicked lies back, hiding itself, as Adam among the bushes, and is taken out of the body perforce ; as was the soul of that worldling ; " This night thy soul shall be required of thee ; " but they never sacrifice their souls willingly to the Lord.—*William Cowper.*

Verse 109.—*"My soul is continually in my hand."* If any one carry in the hand a fragile vessel, made of glass or any other similar material, filled with a precious liquor, especially if the hand be weak, or if from other causes dangers be threatening, he will scarcely be able to avoid the breaking of the vessel and the running out of the liquor. Such is the condition of my life, which I, set upon by various enemies, carry as it were in my hand ; which, therefore, is exposed to such a great danger, as that I always have death present before my sight, my life hanging on the slenderest thread.—*Andreas Rivetus,* 1572—1651.

Verse 109.—*"My soul is continually in my hand."* The believer is always in the very jaws of death. He lives with wings outstretched to fly away. Paul testified, " I die daily." In the extremity of persecution, the fervent desire was to know what God would have him to do.—*Henry Law.*

Verse 109.—*"My soul is continually in my hand."* I make no more of life than a child doth of his bird which he carrieth in the palm of his hand held open.—*John Trapp.*

Verse 109.—*"My soul is continually in my hand,"* etc. Why doth David say, " My soul is in mine hand"; had he called it out of the hand of God, and taken the care of it upon himself ? Nothing less. His meaning is only this,—I walk in the midst of dangers and among a thousand deaths continually ; I am in deaths often, my life is exposed to perils every day, yet do I not forget thy law : I keep close to thee, and will keep close to thee whatsoever comes of it. Augustine upon that place doth ingeniously confess that he understood not what David meant, by having his soul in his hands ; but Jerome, another of the ancients, teacheth us, that it is an Hebraism, signifying a state of extremest peril. The Greeks also have drawn it into a proverb speaking the same thing.

But why doth the holding or putting the life in the hand signify the exposing of the life to peril ? There is a twofold reason of it.

First. Because those things which are carried openly in the hand are apt to fall out of the hand, and being carried in sight, they are apt to be snatched or wrested out of the hand. And, therefore, though to be in the hand of God signifies *safety*, because his hand is armed with irresistible power to protect us ; yet for a man to carry a thing in his own hand is to carry it in danger, because his hand is weak, and there are safer ways of carrying or conveying a thing than openly in the hand. If a man be to ride a long journey with any treasure about him, he doth not carry it in his hand, but puts it in some secret and close place where it may be hidden, and so be more secure. The Chaldee paraphrast, to express the elegancy of that place forecited out of the Psalm, gives it thus, *"My life is in as much danger as if it stood upon the very superficies or outside of my hand,"* as if he had no hold of it, but it stood barely upon his hand ; for that which is set upon the palm of the hand, and not grasped, is in greater danger. Things safe kept are hidden or held fast.

Secondly. There is another reason of that speech, because when a man is about to deliver a thing or to give it up, he takes it in his hand. They that put themselves upon great perils and dangers for God and his people, deliver up their lives and their all to God. Hence that counsel of the Apostle (1 Pet. iv. 19) : " Let them that suffer according to the will of God commit the keeping of their souls to him in well doing, as unto a faithful Creator." So here, the life of men in danger is said to be put in the hand, because such are, as it were, ready to deliver and commit their lives unto God, that he would take care of their lives to preserve them from the danger, or to take them to himself if they lose them in his service.—*Joseph Caryl.*

Verse 110.—*"The wicked."* He calls them *wicked men ;* which importeth three things. First, they work wickedness. Secondly, they love it. Thirdly, they persevere in it.—*William Cowper.*

Verse 110.—*"A snare."* One manner of catching wild animals, such as lions, bears, jackals, foxes, hart, roebuck, and fallow-deer, was by a trap (*pach*), which is the word used in this place ; this was set under ground (Job xviii. 10), in the run of the animal (Prov. xxii. 5), and caught it by the leg (Job xviii. 9).—*William Latham Bevan, in Smith's Dictionary of the Bible,* 1863.

Verse 110.—*"The wicked have laid a snare for me."* In eating, he sets before us gluttony ; in love he impels to lust ; in labour, sluggishness ; in conversing, envy ; in governing, covetousness ; in correcting, anger ; in honour, pride ; in the heart, he sets evil thoughts ; in the mouth, evil words ; in actions, evil works ; when awake, he moves us to evil actions ; when asleep, to filthy dreams.—*Girolamo Savonarola,* 1452—1498.

Verse 110.—*"Laid a snare for me : yet I erred not,"* etc. It is not the laying the bait hurts the fish, if the fish do not bite.—*Thomas Watson.*

Verse 111.—*"Thy testimonies have I taken,"* etc. The Scripture is called " testimonies " in respect to God himself, because it doth give a testimony to him, and makes God known to us : it gives a testimony of all those attributes that are himself, of his wisdom, of his power, of his justice, of his goodness, of his truth. The declaration of these, we have them all in the various books of the Scriptures : there is never a book, but there is a testification of these attributes. In the book of Genesis we have a testimony of his *power* in making the world, of his *justice* in drowning the world, and of his *goodness* in saving Noah. In the book of Exodus we have a testimony of his *providence* in leading the people of Israel through the Red Sea, in bringing them out of Egypt ; we have a testimony of his *wisdom* in giving them his law. What should I name more ? In the *New* Testament, in the Gospel, all is testimony. As the *Old* gave testimony to *God,* so the *New* to *Christ :* " To him gave all the prophets witness ; " not only the *Old,* but the *New :* " These are they that testify of me." Everywhere there is testimony of Christ,— of his *humility,* in taking our nature ; of his *power,* in working miracles ; of his *wisdom,* in the parables that he spoke ; of his *patience* and *love,* in the torments that he suffered for us. Both Law and Gospel—the whole book of Scripture, and every part of it in these regards is fitly called " *the testimonies of the Lord."* And the holy Psalmist made choice of this name when he was to speak to the honour and glory of it ; because it was that name from which he sucked a great deal of comfort, because it was the testimony of God's *truth* and *goodness* and *wisdom* and *power* to him ; thereupon he makes so precious esteem of it as to account it his " *heritage."—Richard Holdsworth* (1590—1649), *in "The Valley of Vision."*

Verse 111.—*"Thy testimonies."* By " *testimonies* " is meant the covenant between God and his people ; wherein he bindeth himself to them, and them to him. Some think that the excellency of the word is here set out by many names ; but we must look to the propriety of every word : as before by " judgments," so by this word " *testimonies,*" is meant the covenant : not the commandments, because they cannot be an inheritance, for they cannot comfort us, because we cannot fulfil them, but fail in them, and cannot therefore take comfort in them. It is the gospel that bringeth peace and comfort. *"The law,"* when it is taken generally, containeth all the word, particularly the commandments ; so " *the word* " generally containeth both law and gospel, but particularly the promises, as Rom. x. So likewise by the " *testimonies,*" when they are opposed to the law, is meant the promise of the covenant, as Isaiah viii., and this testimony is confirmed to us by the sacraments, as to them by sacrifices.—*Richard Greenham.*

Verse 111.—*"As an heritage."* Why the divine testimonies should be called by the Psalmist an *inheritance ;* why he brings them within the compass of this notion, may not so easily be understood ; for the word of God points out the inheritance, but it is not the inheritance itself. Yes, there is good reason to be given for the expression, were there no more than this, that we consider the inestimable comfort, and heavenly treasure that is to be found in the word of God ; it is a rich mine of all celestial treasure, it is a storehouse of all good things, of all saving knowledge.

All privileges whatsoever they are that we can expect on earth or heaven, they are all contained in the word of God : here is ground enough why it is called an *inheritance ;* he hath a good *heritage* that hath all these.

Yet there is a better reason than this ; for if it be so that heaven is our inheritance, then the word of God is ; because it is the word that points out heaven, that gives the *assurance* of heaven : we have in the word of God all the evidences of heaven. Whatsoever *title* any saint hath to heaven, he hath it in and out of the word of God.   There are the evidences in the word of God ; both the evidence of *discovery,* it is the holy terrier of the celestial Canaan, and the evidence of *assurance,* it is as a sacred bond or indenture between God and his creature.   St. Gregory said wittily, when he called it God's epistle that he sent to man for the declaration of his will and pleasure, he might as well have called it God's deed of gift, whereby he makes over and conveys to us all those hopes that we look for in heaven.   Whatsoever interest we have in God, in Christ, whatsoever hope of bliss and glory, whatsoever comfort of the Spirit, whatsoever proportion of grace, all are made over to us in the promises of the gospel, in the word of God.

Now put this together, look as in human affairs, *evidences,* though they be not properly the inheritance itself, yet they are called the inheritance, and are the inheritance, though not actually, yet virtually so ; because all the title we have to an inheritance is in the deeds and evidences ; therefore evidences are precious things.   Though it be but a piece of paper, or parchment full of dust and worm-eaten, yet it is as much worth sometimes as a county, as much worth as all a man's possessions besides.   So likewise it is with the Scriptures ; they are not actually and properly the inheritance itself, but they are *via,* the way to the kingdom.   It is called the gospel of the kingdom, nay more, the kingdom itself : " The kingdom of God is come among you," or " to you."   Why the kingdom ?   Why the inheritance ?   By the same reason, both, because here we have the *conveyance,* here we have the *deed,* here we have the *assurance* of whatsoever title or claim we make to heaven.—*Richard Holdsworth.*

Verse 111.—*"They are the rejoicing of my heart."*   He saith not that God's testimonies bring joy, but that they are joy, there is no other joy but the delight in the law of the Lord.   For all other joy, the wise king said of laughter, " thou art mad," and of joy, " what is it that thou dost ? "   Eccles. ii.   True joy is the earnest which we have of heaven, it is the treasure of the soul, and therefore should be laid up in a safe place ; and nothing in this world is safe to place it in.   And therefore with the spouse we say, " We will be glad in thee, we will remember thy love more than wine."   Let others seek their joy in wine, in society, in conversation, in music ; for me, thou hast put gladness in my heart, more than in the time that their corn and their wine increased.   These indeed are the precious fruits of the earth, but they seal not up special favour ; a man may have together with them, an empty, husky, and chaffy soul.   And therefore these are not the joys of the saints ; they must have God, or else they die for sorrow ; his law is their life.—*Abraham Wright.*

Verse 112.—*"I have inclined my heart to perform thy statutes alway,"* etc.   In the former verse he showed his faith, and his joy which came thereof ; now he showeth that here in this joy he will keep the commandments ; whereby he showeth that this was a true joy, because it wrought a care to do good.   For if we believe the promises truly, then we also love the commandments, otherwise faith is vain ; a care to live a godly life nourisheth faith in God's promises.   Here is the cause then why many regard not the word and sacraments ; or if they do a little, it is to no purpose, because they labour not to keep the commandments.   For unless they have care to do this, the word of God to them cannot be profitable, nor the sacraments sacred.—*Richard Greenham.*

Verse 112.—*"I have inclined my heart to perform,"* etc.   Observe.   In the 36th verse he prayed to God, saying, *"Incline my heart unto thy testimonies."*   And here he speaks about himself, saying, *"I have inclined mine heart to perform thy statutes alway even unto the end."*   What need, then, was there to ask from God that which he in another place glories to have done himself ?   I answer : These things are not contrary the one to the other.   God inclines, and the godly man inclines.   Man inclines by striving ; God inclines by effecting.   Neither is that which the man attempts, nor that which he by striving achieves goodwards, from the man, but from God, who gives, ' *both to will and to do of his good pleasure :* " Phil. ii. 13.—*Wolfgang Musculus.*

Verse 112.—The sinful heart of itself will run any way ; upon earthly things, upon evil things, or upon impertinent and unseasonable things ; but it will not come to or keep upon that which it should mind ; therefore it must be taken as by strong hand, and set upon spiritual things, set on musing and meditation of heavenly things. A carnal heart is like the loadstone, it cleaves to nothing but steel or iron, and both of them easily unite : but the heart must be of another property, and act in a higher way. And a good heart, though it thinks too much earthward, and runs often wrong, yet it will set itself in its thinkings on right objects, and make itself and them to meet and unite. David tells us how he did ; he *inclined his heart to God's commandments*, both to keep them and to meditate on them. He took and *bent his heart*, as a thing bending too much to other things ; set his mind on musing on it. He found his heart and the law of God too far asunder, and so would continue, unless he brought them together and made them one. If he had not brought his heart to the word, he had never meditated : the object cannot apply itself to the mind, but the mind must bring itself to the object. No holy duties will come to us, we must come to them.—*Nathanael Ranew, in "Solitude Improved by Divine Meditation,"* 1670.

Verse 112.—"*I have inclined mine heart to perform*," etc. In this work he was determined to *continue*. 1. "*I have inclined my heart.*" The counsel of the soul is like a balance ; and the mind, which hath the commanding power over the affections, inclines the balance to that which it judges best. 2. It was to *perform it*, that he thus *inclined his heart*. 3. And this not for a *time*, or some *particular occasion*, but *always*, and unto *the end*. Then *the end of life* would be the *beginning of glory*.—*Adam Clarke.*

Verse 112.—"*I have inclined my heart.*" The prophet, in order briefly to define what it is to serve God, asserts that he applied not only his hands, eyes, or feet, to the keeping of the law, but that he began with the affection of the heart.—*John Calvin.*

Verse 112.—"*Unto the end.*" Our life on earth is a race ; in vain begins he to run swiftly, that fainteth, and gives over before he come to the end. And this was signified (saith Gregory) when in the law the tail of the beast was sacrificed with the rest : perseverance crowneth all. It is good we have begun to do well ; let us also strive to persevere to the end.—*William Cowper.*

EXPOSITION OF VERSES 113 TO 120.

I HATE *vain* thoughts : but thy law do I love.

114 Thou *art* my hiding place and my shield : I hope in thy word.

115 Depart from me, ye evildoers : for I will keep the commandments of my God.

116 Uphold me according unto thy word, that I may live : and let me not be ashamed of my hope.

117 Hold thou me up, and I shall be safe : and I will have respect unto thy statutes continually.

118 Thou hast trodden down all them that err from thy statutes : for their deceit *is* falsehood.

119 Thou puttest away all the wicked of the earth *like* dross : therefore I love thy testimonies.

120 My flesh trembleth for fear of thee ; and I am afraid of thy judgments.

Verse 113. "*I hate vain thoughts : but thy law do I love.*"   In this paragraph the Psalmist deals with thoughts and things and persons which are the opposite of God's holy thoughts and ways.   He is evidently in great fear of the powers of darkness, and of their allies, and his whole soul is stirred up to stand against them with a determined opposition.   Just as he began the octave, verse 97, with " O how I love thy law," so here he begins with a declaration of hatred against that which breaks the law.   The opposite of the fixed and infallible law of God is the wavering, changing opinion of men : David had an utter contempt and abhorrence for this ; all his reverence and regard went to the sure word of testimony. In proportion to his love to the law was his hate of men's inventions.   The thoughts of men are vanity ; but the thoughts of God are verity.   We hear much in these days of " men of thought," " thoughtful preachers," and " modern thought " : what is this but the old pride of the human heart ?   Vain man would be wise.   The Psalmist did not glory in his thoughts ; and that which was called " thought " in his day was a thing which he detested.   When man thinks his best, his highest thoughts are as far below those of divine revelation as the earth is beneath the heavens.   Some of our thoughts are specially vain in the sense of vain-glory, pride, conceit, and self-trust ; others in the sense of bringing disappointment, such as fond ambition, sinful dreaming, and confidence in man ;   in the sense of emptiness and frivolity, such as the idle thoughts and vacant romancings in which so many indulge ;   and, yet once more, too many of our thoughts are vain in the sense of being sinful, evil, and foolish.   The Psalmist is not indifferent to evil thoughts as the careless are ; but upon them he looks with a hate as true as was the love with which he clung to the pure thoughts of God.

The last octave was practical, this is thoughtful ; there the man of God attended to his feet, and here to his heart : the emotions of the soul are as important as the acts of the life, for they are the fountain and spring from which the actions proceed. When we love the law it becomes a law of love, and we cling to it with our whole heart.

114. "*Thou art my hiding place and my shield.*"   To his God he ran for shelter from vain thoughts ; there he hid himself away from their tormenting intrusions, and in solemn silence of the soul he found God to be his hiding-place.   When called into the world, if he could not be alone with God as his hiding-place, he could have the Lord with him as his shield, and by this means he could ward off the attacks of wicked suggestions.   This is an experimental verse, and it testifies to that which the writer knew of his own personal knowledge : he could not fight with his own thoughts, or escape from them, till he flew to his God, and then he found deliverance. Observe that he does not speak of God's word as being his double defence, but he ascribes that to God himself.   When we are beset by very spiritual assaults, such as those which arise out of vain thoughts, we shall do well to fly distinctly to the person of our Lord, and to cast ourselves upon his real presence.   Happy is he who can truly say to the triune God, " Thou art my hiding-place."   He has beheld

God under that glorious covenant aspect which ensures to the beholder the surest consolation. *"I hope in thy word."* And well he might, since he had tried and proved it : he looked for protection from all danger, and preservation from all temptation to him who had hitherto been the tower of his defence on former occasions. It is easy to exercise hope where we have experienced help. Sometimes when gloomy thoughts afflict us, the only thing we can do is to hope, and, happily, the word of God always sets before us objects of hope and reasons for hope, so that it becomes the very sphere and support of hope, and thus tiresome thoughts are overcome. Amid fret and worry a hope of heaven is an effectual quietus.

115. *"Depart from me, ye evildoers."* Those who make a conscience of their thoughts are not likely to tolerate evil company. If we fly to God from vain thoughts, much more shall we avoid vain men. Kings are all too apt to be surrounded by a class of men who flatter them, and at the same time take liberty to break the laws of God : David purged his palace of such parasites ; he would not harbour them beneath his roof. No doubt they would have brought upon him an ill name, for their doings would have been imputed to him, since the acts of courtiers are generally set down as acts of the court itself ; therefore the king sent them packing bag and baggage, saying,—" Depart from me." Herein he anticipated the sentence of the last great day, when the Son of David shall say, " Depart from me, ye workers of iniquity." We cannot thus send all malefactors out of our houses, but it will often become a duty to do so where there is right and reason for it. A house is all the better for being rid of liars, pilferers, lewd talkers, and slanderers. We are bound at all hazards to keep ourselves clear of such companions as come to us by our own choice if we have any reason to believe that their character is vicious. Evildoers make evil counsellors. Those who say unto God, " Depart from us," ought to hear the immediate echo of their words from the mouths of God's children, " Depart from us. We cannot eat bread with traitors."

"For I will keep the commandments of my God." Since he found it hard to keep the commandments in the company of the ungodly, he gave them their marching orders. He *must* keep the commandments, but he did not need to keep their company. What a beautiful title for the Lord this verse contains ! The word *God* only occurs in this one place in all this lengthened Psalm, and then it is attended by the personal word " my "—" my God."

> " My God ! how charming is the sound !
> How pleasant to repeat !
> Well may that heart with pleasure bound,
> Where God hath fix'd his seat."

Because Jehovah is our God therefore we resolve to obey him, and to chase out of our sight those who would hinder us in his service. It is a grand thing for the mind to have come to a point, and to be steadfastly fixed in the holy determination, —" I will keep the commandments." God's law is our pleasure when the God of the law is our God.

116. *"Uphold me according unto thy word, that I may live."* It was so necessary that the Lord should hold up his servant, that he could not even live without it. Our soul would die if the Lord did not continually sustain it, and every grace which makes spiritual life to be truly life would decay if he withdrew his upholding hand. It is a sweet comfort that this great necessity of upholding is provided for in the word, and we have not to ask for it as for an uncovenanted mercy, but simply to plead for the fulfilment of a promise, saying, " Uphold me according to thy word." He who has given us eternal life hath in that gift secured to us all that is essential thereto, and as gracious upholding is one of the necessary things we may be sure that we shall have it. *"And let me not be ashamed of my hope."* In verse 114 he had spoken of his hope as founded on the word, and now he begs for the fulfilment of that word that his hope might be justified in the sight of all. A man would be ashamed of his hope if it turned out that it was not based upon a sure foundation ; but this will never happen in our case. We may be ashamed of our thoughts, and our words, and our deeds, for they spring from ourselves ; but we never shall be ashamed of our hope, for that springs from the Lord our God. Such is the frailty of our nature that unless we are continually upheld by grace, we shall fall so foully as to be ashamed of ourselves, and ashamed of all those glorious hopes which are now the crown and glory of our life. The man of God had uttered the most positive resolves, but he felt that he could not trust in his own solemn determination : hence

these prayers. It is not wrong to make resolutions, but it will be useless to do so unless we salt them well with believing cries to God. David meant to keep the law of the Lord, but he first needed the Lord of the law to keep him.

117. *"Hold thou me up"*: as a nurse holds up a little child. *"And I shall be safe,"* and not else ; for unless thou hold me up I shall be falling about like an infant that is weak upon its knees. We are saved by past grace, but we are not safe unless we receive present grace. The Psalmist had vowed to keep the Lord's commands, but here he pleads with the Lord to keep him : a very sensible course of procedure. Our version reads the word " uphold," and then " hold up ; " and truly we need this blessing in every shape in which it can come, for in all manner of ways our adversaries seek to cast us down. To be safe is a happy condition ; there is only one door to it, and that is to be held up by God himself ; thank God, that door is open to the least among us. *"And I will have respect unto thy statutes continually."* In obedience is safety ; in being held up is obedience. No man will outwardly keep the Lord's statutes for long together unless he has an inward respect for them, and this will never be unless the hand of the Lord perpetually upholds the heart in holy love. Perseverance to the end, obedience continually, comes only through the divine power ; we start aside as a deceitful bow unless we are kept right by him that first gave us grace. Happy is the man who realizes this verse in his life ; upheld through his whole life in a course of unswerving integrity, he becomes a safe and trusted man, and maintains a sacred delicacy of conscience which is unknown to others. He feels a tender respect for the statutes of the Lord, which keeps him clear of inconsistencies and conformities to the world that are so common among others, and hence he is a pillar in the house of the Lord. Alas, we know some professors who are not upright, and therefore they lean to sin till they fall over, and though they are restored they are never safe or reliable, neither have they that sweet purity of soul which is the charm of the more sanctified who have been kept from falling into the mire.

118. *"Thou hast trodden down all them that err from thy statutes."* There is no holding up for them ; they are thrown down and then trodden down, for they choose to go down into the wandering ways of sin. Sooner or later God will set his foot on those who turn their foot from his commands : it has always been so, and it always will be so to the end. If the salt has lost its savour, what is it fit for but to be trodden under foot ? God puts away the wicked like dross, which is only fit to be cast out as road-metal to be trodden down.

"For their deceit is falsehood." They call it far-seeing policy, but it is absolute falsehood, and it shall be treated as such. Ordinary men call it clever diplomacy, but the man of God calls a spade a spade, and declares it to be falsehood, and nothing less, for he knows that it is so in the sight of God. Men who err from the right road invent pretty excuses with which to deceive themselves and others, and so quiet their consciences and maintain their credits ; but their mask of falsehood is too transparent. God treads down falsehoods ; they are only fit to be spurned by his feet, and crushed into the dust. How horrified must those be who have spent all their lives in contriving a confectionery religion, and then see it all trodden upon by God as a sham which he cannot endure !

119. *"Thou puttest away all the wicked of the earth like dross."* He does not trifle with them, or handle them with kid gloves. No, he judges them to be the scum of the earth, and he treats them accordingly by putting them away. He puts them away from his church, away from their honours, away from the earth, and at last away from himself. " Depart," saith he, " ye cursed." If even a good *man* feels forced to put away the evil-doers from him, much more must the thrice holy God put away the wicked. They looked like precious metal, they were intimately mixed up with it, they were laid up in the same heap; but the Lord is a refiner, and every day he removes some of the wicked from among his people, either by making a shameful discovery of their hypocrisy or by consuming them from off the earth. They are put away as dross, never to be recalled. As the metal is the better for losing its alloy, so is the church the better for having the wicked removed. These wicked ones are " of the earth,"—" the wicked of the earth," and they have no right to be with those who are not of the world ; the Lord perceives them to be out of place and injurious, and therefore he puts them away, *all* of them, leaving none of them to deteriorate his church. The process will one day be perfect ; no dross will be spared, no gold will be left impure. Where shall we be when that great work is finished ?

" *Therefore I love thy testimonies.*" Even the severities of the Lord excite the love of his people. If he allowed men to sin with impunity, he would not be so fully the object of our loving admiration; he is glorious in holiness because he thus rids his kingdom of rebels, and his temple of them that defile it. In these evil days, when God's punishment of sinners has become the butt of proud sceptical contentions, we may regard as a mark of the true man of God that he loves the Lord none the less, but a great deal the more, because of his condign judgment of the ungodly.

120. *"My flesh trembleth for fear of thee."* Such was his awe in the presence of the Judge of all the earth, whose judgment he had just now been considering, that he did exceedingly fear and quake. Even the grosser part of his being,—his flesh felt a solemn dread at the thought of offending one so good and great, who would so effectually sever the wicked from among the just. Alas, poor flesh, this is the highest thing to which thou canst attain! *"And I am afraid of thy judgments."* God's words of judgment are solemn, and his deeds of judgment are terrible; they may well make us afraid. At the thought of the Judge of all,—his piercing eye, his books of record, his day of assize, and the operations of his justice,—we may well cry for cleansed thoughts, and hearts, and ways, lest his judgments should light on us. When we see the great Refiner separating the precious from the vile, we may well feel a godly fear, lest we should be put away by him, and left to be trodden under his feet.

Love in the previous verse is quite consistent with fear in this verse: the fear which hath torment is cast out, but not the filial fear which leads to reverence and obedience.

NOTES ON VERSES 113 TO 120.

The fifteenth letter, SAMECH, denotes a *prop* or *pillar*, and this agrees well with the subject matter of the strophe, in which God is twice implored to uphold his servant (verses 16, 17), while the utter destruction of those who make light of his law, or encourage scepticism regarding it, may be compared to the fate of the Philistine lords, on whom Samson brought down the roof of the house where they were making merry, by overthrowing the pillars which supported it.—*Neale and Littledale.*

Verses 112, 113.—When David had an inclination in his heart to God's statutes, the immediate effect of it was to *"hate vain thoughts."* We read, *"I have inclined mine heart to perform thy statutes";* and it follows, *"I hate vain thoughts."* The vanity of his heart was a burden to him. A new creature is as careful against wickedness in the head or heart, as in the life. A godly man would be purer in the sight of God than in the view of man. He knows none but God can see the wanderings of his heart or the thoughts of his head, yet he is as careful that sins should not rise up as that they should not break out.—*Stephen Charnock.*

Verse 113.—*"I hate vain thoughts,"* or, the evil devices; or, the double-hearted imaginations; or, the intermeddling, counter-coursing thoughts: that is to say, that kind of practice of some men, that sail with every wind, and seek still to have two strings to their bow. The Hebrew word doth properly signify boughs or branches, which shoot up perplexedly or confusedly in a tree.—*Theodore Haak,* 1618—1657.

Verse 113.—*"I hate vain thoughts."* In those vacant hours which are spared from business, pleasure, company, and sleep, and which are spent in solitude, at home or abroad; unprofitable, proud, covetous, sensual, envious, or malicious imaginations, occupy the minds of ungodly men, and often infect their very dreams. These are not only sinful in themselves, indicating the state of their hearts, and as such will be brought into the account at the day of judgment; but they excite the dormant corruptions, and lead to more open and gross violations of the holy law. The carnal mind welcomes and delights to dwell upon these congenial imaginations, and to solace itself by ideal indulgences, when opportunity of other gratification is not presented, or when a man dares not commit the actual transgression. But the spiritual mind recoils at them; such thoughts will intrude from time to time, but they are unwelcome and distressing, and are immediately thrust out; while other subjects, from the word of God, are stored up in readiness to occupy the mind more profitably and pleasantly during the hours of leisure and retirement. There is no better test of our true character, than the habitual effect of *"vain thoughts"* upon our minds—whether we love and indulge them, or abhor, and watch and pray against them.—*Thomas Scott,* 1747—1821.

Verse 113.—*"I hate vain thoughts."* A godly man may have roving thoughts in duty. Sad experience proves this; the thoughts will be dancing up and down in prayer. The saints are called stars; but many times in duty they are wandering stars. The heart is like quicksilver which will not fix. It is hard to tie two good thoughts together; we cannot lock our hearts so close, but that distracting thoughts, like wind, will get in. Hierom complains of himself; "Sometimes," saith he, "when I am about God's service, I am walking in the galleries, or casting up accounts." But these wandering thoughts are not allowed: *"I hate vain thoughts,"* they come as unwelcome guests, which are no sooner spied, but turned out of doors.—*Thomas Watson.*

Verse 113.—*"I hate."* Every dislike of evil is not sufficient; but perfect hatred is required of us against all sorts and degrees of sin.—*David Dickson.*

Verse 113.—*"Vain thoughts."* The word is used for the *opinions* of men; and may be applied to all heterodox opinions, human doctrines, damnable heresies; such as are inconsistent with the perfections of God, derogate from his grace, and from the person and offices of Christ; and are contrary to the word, and which are therefore rejected and abhorred by good men.—*John Gill.*

Verse 113.—*"Vain thoughts."* Hebrew, *seäphim,* haltings between two opinions. See 1 Kings xviii. 21. Hence it signifies *sceptical doubts.*—*Christopher Wordsworth.*

Verse 113.—*"Vain thoughts."* Our thoughts are set upon trifles and frivolous things, neither tending to our own profit nor the benefit of others : " The heart of the wicked is little worth ; " all their debates, conceits, musings, are of no value : for all their thoughts are taken up about childish vanity and foolish conceits. " The thought of foolishness is sin " (Prov. xxiv. 9) ; not only the thought of wickedness, but foolishness. Thoughts are the first-born of the soul, the immediate issues of the mind ; yet we lavish them away upon every trifle. Follow men all the day long, and take account of their thoughts. Oh ! what madness and folly are in all the musings they are conscious of : " The Lord knoweth the thoughts of man, that they are vanity " (Ps. xciv. 11). If we did judge as God judges, all the thoughts, reasonings, discourses of the mind, if they were set down in a table, we might write at the bottom, Here is the sum and total account of all,—nothing but vanity.

The sins that do most usually engross and take up our thoughts are,

1st. Uncleanness. Speculative wickedness makes way for active : " Hath committed adultery . . . . in his heart " (Matt. v. 28). There is a polluting ourselves by our thoughts, and this sin usually works that way.

2ndly. Revenge. Liquors are soured when long kept ; so, when we dwell upon discontents, they turn to revenge. Purposes of revenge are most sweet and pleasant to carnal nature : " Frowardness is in his heart, he deviseth mischief continually " (Prov. vi. 14), that is to say, he is full of revengeful and spiteful thoughts.

3rdly. Envy. It is a sin that feeds upon the mind. Those songs of the women, that Saul had slain his thousands, but David his ten thousands, they ran in Saul's mind, therefore he hated David (1 Sam. xviii. 9). Envy is an evil disease that dwelleth in the heart, and betrays itself mostly in thoughts.

4thly. Pride. Either pride in the desires or pride in the mind, either vain-glory or self-conceit ; this is entertaining our hearts with whispers of vanity : there-fore it is said, " He hath scattered the proud in the imagination of their hearts " (Luke i. 51) : proud men are full of imaginations.

5thly. Covetousness, which is nothing but vain musings and exercises of the heart : " A heart they have exercised with covetous practices " (2 Peter ii. 14). And it withdraws the heart in the very time of God's worship : " Their heart goeth after their covetousness " (Ezek. xxxiii. 31).

6thly. Distrust is another thing which usually takes up our thoughts—distracting motions against God's providence.—*Thomas Manton.*

Verse 113.—*"Vain thoughts."* Let us see what *vanity* is. Take it in all the acceptations of it, it is true of our thoughts that they are *"vain."*

1. It is taken for *unprofitableness.* So, Eccles. i. 2, 3, " All is vain," because there is " no profit in them under the sun." Such are our thoughts by nature ; the wisest of them will not stand us in any stead in time of need, in time of temptation, distress of conscience, day of death or judgment : 1 Cor. ii. 6, " All the wisdom of the wise comes to nought " ; Prov. x. 20, " The heart of the wicked is little worth," not a penny for them all.

2. Vanity is taken for *lightness.* " Lighter than vanity " is a phrase used, Ps. lxii. 9 ; and whom is it spoken of ? Of men ; and if anything in them be lighter than other, it is their *thoughts,* which swim in the uppermost parts, float at the top, are as the scum of the heart. When all the best, and wisest, and deepest, and solidest thoughts in Belshazzar, a prince, were weighed, they were found too light, Dan. v. 27.

3. Vanity is put for *folly.* So, Prov. xii. 11, " vain men " is made all one with men " void of understanding." Such are our thoughts. Among other evils which are said to " come out of the heart " (Mark vii. 22), ἀφροσύνη is reckoned as one, " foolishness " ; that is, thoughts that are such as madmen have, and fools—nothing to the purpose of which there can be made no use.

4. Vanity is put for *inconstancy* and frailty ; therefore vanity and a shadow are made synonymous, Ps. cxliv. 4. Such are our thoughts, flitting and perishing, as bubbles : Ps. cxlvi. 4, " All their thoughts perish."

5. Lastly, they are *wicked and sinful.* Vanity is [Jer. iv. 14] yoked with wicked-ness, and vain men and sons of Belial are all one, 2 Chron. xiii. 7. And such are our thoughts by nature : Prov. xxiv. 9, " The thought of foolishness is sin." And therefore a man is to be humbled for a proud thought.—*Thomas Goodwin.*

Verse 113.—*"But thy law do I love."* Ballast your heart with a love to God. Love will, by a pleasing violence, bind down our thoughts : if it doth not establish our minds, they will be like a cork, which, with a light breath, and a short curl of water, shall be tossed up and down from its station. Scholars that love learning will be continually hammering upon some notion or other which may further their progress, and as greedily clasp it as the iron will its beloved loadstone. He that is "winged with a divine love" to Christ will have frequent glances and flights toward him, and will start out from his worldly business several times in a day to give him a visit. Love, in the very working, is a settling grace ; it increaseth our delight in God, partly by the sight of his amiableness, which is cleared to us in the very act of loving ; and partly by the recompences he gives to the affectionate carriage of his creature ; both which will prevent the heart's giving entertainment to such loose companions as evil thoughts.—*Stephen Charnock.*

Verses 113, 114.—When David was able to vouch his love to the command, he did not question his title to the promise. Here he asserts his sincere affection to the precepts : *"I hate vain thoughts : but thy law do I love."* Mark, he doth not say he is *free* from vain thoughts, but he "hates" them, he likes their company no better than one would a pack of thieves that break into his house. Neither saith he that he *fully kept* the law, but he *"loved"* the law even when he failed of exact obedience to it. Now from this testimony his conscience brought in for his love to the law, his faith acts clearly and strongly on the promise in the next words, *"Thou art my hiding place and my shield : I hope in thy word."*—*William Gurnall.*

Verse 114.—*"Thou art my hiding place and my shield,"* etc. From vain thoughts and vain persons the Psalmist teaches us to fly, by prayer, to God, as our Refuge and Protector. This course a believer will as naturally take, in the hour of temptation and danger, as the offspring of the hen, on perceiving a bird of prey hovering over their heads, retire to their *"hiding-place,"* under the wings of the dam ; or as the warrior opposeth his *"shield"* to the darts which are aimed at him.—*George Horne.*

Verse 114.—*"Thou art my hiding place."* Christ hath all qualifications that may fit him for this work [of being a *hiding-place* to believers].

1. He hath *strength*. A hiding-place must be *locus munitissimus*. Paper houses will never be good hiding-places. Houses made of reeds or rotten timber will not be fit places for men to hide themselves in. Jesus Christ is a place of strength. He is the Rock of Ages : His name is " the Mighty God," Isaiah ix. 6.

2. He hath *height*. A hiding-place must be *locus excelsissimus*. Your low houses are soon scaled. Jesus Christ is a high place ; he is as high as heaven. He is the Jacob's ladder that reacheth from earth to heaven : Gen. xxviii. 12. He is too high for men, too high for devils ; no creature can scale these high walls.

3. He hath *secret places*. A hiding-place must be *locus abditissimus*. The more secret, the more safe. Now, Jesus Christ hath many secret chambers that no creatures can ever find : Cant. ii. 14, " O my dove, that art in the secret places of the stairs ! " As Christ hath hidden comforts which no man knows but he that receiveth them ; so he hath hidden places of secresy which none can find out but he that dwells in them. " Come, my people, enter into thy chambers, and shut the doors upon thee " (Isaiah xxvi. 20).

4. Christ is *faithful*. He that will hide others had need be very faithful. A false-hearted protector is worse than an open pursuer. " Will the men of Keilah deliver me up ? " saith David ; " They will deliver thee up," saith the Lord. But now Christ is faithful : Rev. iii. 14, he is " the faithful witness ; " he cannot be bribed to surrender up any creature that comes to hide himself with him. Christ will die before he will betray his trust.

5. Christ is *diligent*. Diligence is as necessary in those that will hide others, as faithfulness. A sleepy guard may betray a castle or garrison as well as a faithless guard. But Jesus Christ is very diligent and watchful, he hath his intelligencers abroad ; yea, his own eyes run to and fro in the earth, to see what contrivances are made and set on foot against those who are hid with him : Ps. cxxi. 3, 4, " He that keepeth Israel neither slumbereth nor sleepeth."—*Ralph Robinson* (1614—1655) *in "Christ All in All."*

Verse 114.—*"Hiding place."* The first word in the verse means properly a secret, or a secret place.—*Joseph Addison Alexander.*

Verse 114.—*"My shield."* Good people are safe under God's protection ; he is their " strength and their shield " ; their " shield and their great reward " ; and here, their *"hiding place and their shield."*—*Matthew Henry.*

Verse 114.—*"Shield."* The excellency and properties of a shield lie in these things :—1. In the largeness and breadth of it, in that it hides and covers the person that weareth it from all darts that are flung at him, so as they cannot reach him : Thou, Lord, wilt bless the righteous ; with favour wilt thou compass him as with a shield (Ps. v. 12). 2. The excellence of a shield lies in that it is hard and impenetrable. So this answers to the invincible power of God's providence, by which he can break the assaults of all enemies ; and such a shield is God to his people : " My shield, and he in whom I trust " (Ps. cxliv. 2). 3. Shall I add one thing more ? Stones and darts flung upon a hard shield are beaten back upon him that flings them ; so God beats back the evil upon his enemies and the enemies of his people : " Bring them down, O Lord, our shield " (Ps. lix. 11).—*Thomas Manton.*

Verse 114.—"*I hope in thy word.*" Of all the ingredients that sweeten the cup of human life, there is none more rich or powerful than *hope*. Its absence embitters the sweetest lot ; its presence alleviates the deepest woe. Surround me with all the joys which memory can awaken or possession bestow,—without hope it is not enough. In the absence of hope there is sadness in past and present joys—sadness in the thought that the past is past, and that the present is passing too. But though you strip me of all the joys the past or the present can confer, if the morrow shineth bright with hope, I am glad amid my woe. Of all the busy motives that stir this teeming earth, hope is the busiest. It is the sweetest balm that soothes our sorrows, the brightest beam that gilds our pleasures. Hope is the noblest offspring, the first born, the last buried child of foreseeing and forecasting man. Without it the unthinking cattle may be content amid present plenty. But without it reflecting man should not, cannot be truly happy.—*William Grant* (1814—1876), in "*Christ our Hope, and other Sermons.*"

Verses 114, 115.—"*Thou art my hiding place.*" "*Depart from me, ye evil-doers.*" Safe and quiet in his hiding-place, David deprecates all attempts to disturb his peace. The society, therefore, of the ungodly is intolerable to him, and he cannot forbear frowning them from his presence. He had found them to be opposed to his best interests ; and he feared their influence in shaking his determination of obedience to his God. Indeed, when have the Lord's people failed to experience such society to be a prevailing hindrance alike to the enjoyment and to the service of God ?—*Charles Bridges.*

Verse 115.—"*Depart from me, ye evildoers,*" etc. As if he had said, Talk no more of it, save your breath, I am resolved on my course, I have sworn, and am steadfastly purposed to keep the commandments of my God ; with God's help, there will I hold me, and all the world shall not wrest me from it.—*Robert Sanderson,* 1587—1662-3.

Verse 115.—"*Depart from me, ye workers of iniquity,*" etc. It is common to sin for company, and that cup usually goeth round, and is handed from one to another. It is therefore wise to quit the company which is infected by sin. It can bring thee no benefit. At least evil company will abate the good in thee. The herb of grace will never thrive in such a cold soil. How poorly doth the good corn grow which is compassed about with weeds ! Cordials and restoratives will do little good to the natural body, whilst it aboundeth with ill-humours. Ordinances are little effectual to souls which are distempered with such noxious inmates. It is said of the mountain Kadish, that whatsoever vine be planted near it, it causeth it to wither and die : it is exceeding rare for saints to thrive near such pull-backs. It is difficult, even to a miracle, to keep God's commandments and evil company too ; therefore when David would marry himself to God's commands, to love them, and live with them, for better for worse, all his days, he is forced to give a bill of divorce to wicked companions, knowing that otherwise the match could never be made : "*Depart from me, ye workers of iniquity, for I will keep the commandments of my God.*" As if he had said, Be it known unto you, O sinners, that I am striking a hearty covenant with God's commands ; I like them so well, that I am resolved to give myself up to them, and to please them well in all things, which I never do unless ye depart ; ye are like a strumpet, which will steal away the love from the true wife. I cannot, as I ought, obey my God's precepts, whilst ye abide in my presence ; therefore depart from me, ye workers of iniquity, for I will keep the commandments of my God.—*George Swinnock.*

Verse 115.—"*Depart from me, ye evildoers.*" Woe be to the wicked man, and woe to those who adhere to him and associate with him, saith *Ben Sira.* And even the pagans of ŏld thought that a curse went along with those who kept evil company.

To inhabit, or to travel with an impious man, and one not beloved of the gods, was held by them to be unlucky and unfortunate.

> Vetabo qui Cereris sacrum
> Vulgavit, sub isdem
> Sit trabibus, fragilemque mecum
> Solvat phaselum,

as Horace speaks.*

To dwell under the same roof, or to sail in the same yacht or pleasure-boat with profane persons was deemed unsafe and dangerous by men of Pagan principles. How much more, then, ought Christians to be thoroughly persuaded of the mischief and danger of conversing with wicked men ? It can no ways be safe to hold correspondence with them.   Yea, we are in great danger all the while we are with them.   You have heard, I suppose, who it was that would not stay in the bath so long as an arch-heretic was there.   It was St. John the Evangelist ; he would not (as *Irenæus* acquaints us) remain in that place because *Cerinthus*, who denied the divinity of Christ, was then present there.   That holy man thought no place was safe where such persons are.

Therefore be mindful of the Apostle's exhortation, and " Come out from among them " (2 Cor. vi. 17) ; listen to that voice from heaven : " Come out, that ye be not partakers of their sins, and that ye receive not of their plagues." Separate yourselves from them, lest you not only indamage your souls, but your bodies, lest some remarkable judgment arrest you here, and lest the divine vengeance more furiously assault you hereafter.   The fanciful poets tell us that *Theseus* and *Perithous* (a pair of intimate friends) loved one another so well that they went down to hell together.   I am sure it is no poetical fiction that many do thus ; that is to say, that they perish together, and descend into the bottomless pit for company's sake.—*John Edwards* (1637—1716), *in "Theologia Reformata."*

Verse 115.—Depart from them that depart from God.—*T. Manton*.

Verse 115.—"*Of my God.*"   As a man can esteem of anything which he knows is his own ; so if once he know that God is his, he cannot but love him, and carefully obey him : neither is it possible that any man can give to God hearty and permanent service, who is not persuaded to say with David, *He is my God*.   All the pleasures, all the terrors of the world cannot sunder that soul from God, who can truly say, *The Lord is my God.—W. Cowper*.

Verse 116.—"*Uphold me.*"   A kite soaring on high is in a situation quite foreign to its nature ; as much as the soul of man is when raised above this lower world to high and heavenly pursuits.   A person at a distance sees not how it is kept in its exalted situation : he sees not the wind that blows it, nor the hand that holds it, nor the string by whose instrumentality it is held.   But all of these powers are necessary to its preservation in that preternatural state.   If the wind were to sink it would fall.   It has nothing whatever in itself to uphold itself ; it has the same tendency to gravitate towards the earth that it ever had ; and if left for a moment to itself it would fall.   Thus it is with the soul of every true believer.   It has been raised by the Spirit of God to a new, a preternatural, a heavenly state ; and in that state it is upheld by an invisible and Almighty hand, through the medium of faith. And upheld it shall be, but not by any power in itself.   If left for a moment it would fall as much as ever.   Its whole strength is in God alone ; and its whole security is in the unchangeableness of his nature, and in the efficacy of his grace.   In a word, " It is kept by the power of God, through faith, unto salvation."—*From "The Book of Illustrations," by H. G. Salter*, 1840.

Verse 116.—"*That I may live.*"   The life of a Christian stands in this, to have his soul quickened by the spirit of grace.   For as the presence of the soul quickens the body, and the departure thereof brings instant death ; and the body without it is but a dead lump of clay : so it is the presence of God's Spirit which giveth life to the soul of man.   And this life is known by these two notable effects ; for first, it brings a joyful sense of God's mercy ; and next, a spiritual disposition to spiritual exercises.   And without this, pretend a man what he will, he is but the image of a Christian, looking somewhat like him, but not quickened by his life.— *William Cowper*.

---

*   They who mysteries reveal
Beneath my roof shall never live,
Shall never hoist with me the doubtful sail.

Verse 116.—*"That I may live."*   The children of God think they have no life if they live not in God's life.   For if we think we are alive, because we see, so do the brute beasts ; if we think we are alive because we hear, so do the cattle ; if we think we are alive because we eat and drink, or sleep, so do beasts ; if we think we live because we do reason and confer, so do the heathen.   The life of God's children is the death of sin ; for where sin is alive, there that part is dead unto God. . . . . God's children, finding themselves dull and slow to good things, when they cannot either rejoice in the promises of God, or find their inward man delighted with the law of God, think themselves to be dead.—*Richard Greenham.*

Verse 117.—*"Hold thou me up, and I shall be safe."*   Not only the consciousness of my weakness, but the danger of the slippery path before me, reminds me, that the safety of every moment depends upon the upholding power of my faithful God. The ways of temptation are so many and imperceptible—the influence of it so appalling—the entrance into it so deceitful, so specious, so insensible—and my own weakness and unwatchfulness are so unspeakable—that I can do nothing but go on my way, praying at every step, *"Hold thou me up, and I shall be safe."*—*Charles Bridges.*

Verse 117.—*"Hold thou me up."*   Three things made David afraid.   First, great temptation without ; for from every air the wind of temptation blows upon a Christian.   Secondly, great corruption within.   Thirdly, examples of other worthy men that had fallen before him, and are written for us : not that we should learn to fall, but to fear lest we fall.   These three should alway hold us humble, according to that warning, " Let him that thinketh he standeth take heed lest he fall."—*William Cowper.*

Verse 117.—*"Up,"* up above the littlenesses in which I have lived too long,—above the snares which have so often caught me,—above the stumbling-blocks upon which I have so often fallen,—above the world,—above myself,—higher than I have ever reached yet,—above the level of my own mortality : worthy of thee,—worthy of the blood, with which I have been bought,—nearer to heaven,—nearer to thee,—" *hold thou me up.*"

God's methods of holding his people up are many.   Sometimes it is by the preacher's word, when the word comes fitly spoken to the heart and conscience. May God, in his infinite condescension, enable his servants in this church so to hold you up.   Sometimes it is by the ordained means and sacraments which his grace commanded.   Sometimes it is by the efficacy of the Holy Scriptures, when some passages in your own room strikes the mind, just in season ; or the stay of some sweet promise comes in sustainingly to your spirit.   Sometimes by the simple inworking of the Holy Ghost in a man's own thoughts, as he will work,—" Uphold me with thy free Spirit."   Sometimes by the ministration of angels,—" They shall hold thee up in their hands, lest thou dash thy foot against a stone."   Sometimes by putting you very low indeed, making you feel that the safe place is the valley. There is no elevation like the elevation of abasement.   Sometimes by severe discipline to brace up the heart, and strengthen it, and make it independent of external things.   Sometimes by heavy affliction, which is the grasp of his hand, that he may hold you tighter.   Sometimes by putting into your heart to think the exact thing that you need,—to pray the very prayer which he intends at the moment to grant.   Sometimes by appearing to let you go, and forsake you, while at the same time—like the Syro-Phœnician woman—he is giving you the wish to hold on that he may give you the more at the last.—*James Vaughan, of Brighton,* 1877.

Verse 117.—*"I will have respect unto thy statutes continually."*   I will employ myself, so some ; I will delight myself, so others ; in thy statutes.   If God's right hand uphold us, we must in his strength go on in our duty, both with diligence and with pleasure.—*Matthew Henry.*

Verse 118.—*"Thou hast trodden down,"* etc.   David here, by a new meditation, confirms himself in the course of godliness : for considering the judgments of God, executed according to his word in all ages upon the wicked, he resolves so much the more to fear God and keep his testimonies.   Thus the judgments of God, executed on others, should be awe-bands to keep us from sinning after their similitude.

The Lord in chastening his own children takes them in hand like a father to correct them ; but when his wrath is kindled against the wicked he tramples them under his feet, as vile creatures which are no account with him.—*William Cowper.*

Verse 118.—"*Thou hast trodden down.*" The Septuagint, ἐξουδένωσας, *ad nihil deduxisti ;* thou hast brought to nothing ; Aquila, *confixisti,* thou hast stricken through : Symmachus, ἀπήλεγξας, *reprobasti,* thou hast disproved ; the Vulgate, *sprevisti,* thou hast contemned ; Apollinarius, ἀθέριξας, *parvi pependisti,* thou hast little esteemed : all to the same purpose. The phrase of treading under foot, used by us, implies, 1. A full punishment ; 2. A disgraceful one. 1. A full punishment. God will pull them down from their altitudes, even to the dust, though never so high and proudly exalting themselves against God. A full conquest of enemies is thus often expressed in Scripture. The Assyrian is said " to take the prey, and to tread them down like the mire of the streets " (Isa. x. 6). 2. It implies a disgraceful punishment : " Until I make thine enemies thy footstool " (Ps. cx. 1) ; an expression used to show the ignominy and contempt God will put upon them. Thus Sapores, the king of Persia, trampled upon Valentinian the emperor, and Tamerlane made Bajazet his footstool. The meaning is, God will not only bring them under, but reduce them to an abject and contemptible condition. So Chrysostom on the text expoundeth this phrase, that God will make them ἐπονειδίστους καὶ καταγελάστους, ignominious and contemptible. They shall not go off honourably, but with scorn and confusion of face, miserably broken.—*Thomas Manton.*

Verse 118.—"*Thou hast trodden down,*" etc. There is a disposition to merge all the characterictics of the Divinity into one ; and while with many of our most eminent writers, the exuberant goodness, the soft and yielding benignity, the mercy that overlooks and makes liberal allowance for the infirmities of human weakness, have been fondly and most abundantly dwelt upon—there has been what the French would call, if not a studied, at least an actually observed *reticence,* on the subject of his truth and purity and his hatred of moral evil. There can be no government without a law ; and the question is little entertained—how are the violations of that law to be disposed of ? Every law has its sanctions—the hopes of proffered reward on the one hand, the fears of threatened vengeance on the other. Is the vengeance to be threatened only, but never to be executed ? Is guilt only to be dealt with by proclamations that go before, but never by punishments that are to follow ? . . . . Take away from jurisprudence its penalties, or, what were still worse, let the penalties only be denounced but never exacted ; and we reduce the whole to an unsubstantial mockery. The fabric of moral government falls to pieces ; and, instead of a great presiding authority in the universe, we have a subverted throne and a degraded Sovereign. . . . . If there is only to be the parade of a judicial economy, without any of its power or its performance ; if the truth is only to be kept in the promises of reward, but as constantly to be receded from in the threats of vengeance ; if the judge is thus to be lost in the overweening parent —there is positively nothing of a moral government over us but the name, we are not the subjects of God's authority ; we are the fondlings of his regard. Under a system like this, the whole universe would drift, as it were, into a state of anarchy ; and, in the uproar of this wild misrule, the King who sitteth on high would lose his hold on the creation that he had formed.—*Thomas Chalmers.*

Verse 118.—"*For their deceit is falsehood.*" The true sense of the passage is, " for their cunning hath been fallacious," that is, it hath deceived themselves and brought on their ruin.—*Samuel Horsley,* 1733—1806.

Verse 118.—"*Their deceit is falsehood.*" He means not here of that deceit whereby the wicked deceive others, but that whereby they deceive themselves. And this is two-fold : first, in that they look for a good in sin, which sin deceitfully promiseth, but they shall never find. Next, that they flatter themselves with a vain conceit to escape judgment, which shall assuredly overtake them.—*William Cowper.*

Verse 119.—"*Thou puttest away all the wicked of the earth like dross.*" The godly and the wicked live together in the visible Church, as dross and good metal ; but God, who is the purger of his church, will not fail by diversity of trials and judgments to put difference between them, and at last will make a perfect separation of them, and cast away the wicked as refuse.—*David Dickson.*

Verse 119.—God's judgments upon others may be a necessary act of love to us. They are purged out as "*dross,*" that they may not infect us by their example, or molest us by their persecutions or oppressions. Now, the more we are befriended in this kind, the more we are bound to serve God cheerfully : " That we being delivered out of the hand of our enemies might serve him without fear, in holiness and righteousness before him all the days of our life " : Luke i. 74, 75. The world is one of those enemies, or the wicked of the earth ; therefore we should serve him faithfully.—*Thomas Manton.*

Verse 119.—*"Thou puttest away all the wicked."* Many ways are wicked men taken away ; sometime by the hand of other men, sometime by their own hand. The Philistines slew not Saul, but forced him to slay himself ; yet the eye of faith ever looks to the finger of God, and sees that the fall of the wicked is the work of God.—*William Cowper.*

Verse 119.—*"The wicked of the earth."* Why are they thus characterized ? Because here they flourish ; their names " shall be written in the earth " (Jer. xvii. 13) ; they grow great and of good reckoning and account here. Judas had the bag ; they prosper in the world : " Behold, these are the ungodly, who prosper in the world " (Ps. lxxiii. 12). Here they are respected : " They are of the world, therefore speak they of the world, and the world heareth them " (1 John iv. 5). Their hearts and minds are in the world (Matt. vi. 19, 20). It is their natural frame to be worldly, they only savour the things of the world ; preferment, honour, greatness, it is their *unum magnum ;* here is their pleasure, and here is their portion, their hope, and their happiness. A child of God looketh for another inheritance, immortal and undefiled.—*Thomas Manton.*

Verse 119.—*"Like dross."* The men of this world esteem God's children as the offscourings of the earth ; so Paul (a chosen vessel of God) was disesteemed of men ; but ye see here what the wicked are, in God's account, but dross indeed, which is the refuse of gold and silver. Let this confirm the godly against the contempt of men : only the Lord hath in his own hand the balance which weigheth men according as they are.—*William Cowper.*

Verse 119.—*"Dross."* 1. The *dross* obscures the lustre and glory of the metal, yea, covers it up, so that it appears not ; rust and filth compass and hide the gold, so that neither the nature nor lustre of it can be seen. 2. *Dross* is a deceiving thing. It is like metal, but is not metal ; the dross of silver is like it, and so the dross of gold is like gold, but the dross is neither silver nor gold. 3. *Dross* is not bettered by the fire : put it into the fire time after time, it abides so still. 4. *Dross* is a worthless thing. It is of no value—base, vile, contemptible. 5. It is useless, and to be rejected. 6. *Dross* is an offensive thing : rust eats into the metal, endangers it, and makes the goldsmith to kindle the fire, to separate it from the gold and silver.—*Condensed from William Greenhill.*

Verse 119.—*"Thy testimonies."* So, very frequently, he calleth God's word, wherein there are both commands and promises : the commandments of God appertain to all, his testimonies belong to his children only ; whereby more strictly, I understand his promises containing special declarations of his love and favour toward his own in Christ Jesus.—*William Cowper.*

Verse 120.—*"My flesh trembleth for fear of thee."* Instead of exulting over those who fell under God's displeasure he humbleth himself. What we read and hear of judgments of God upon wicked people should make us (1) Te reverence his terrible majesty, and to stand in awe of him. Who is able to stand before this holy Lord God ? 1 Sam. vi. 20. (2) To fear lest we offend him, and become obnoxious to his wrath. Good men have need to be restrained from sin by the terrors of the Lord ; especially when judgment begins at the house of God, and hypocrites are discovered, and put away as dross.—*Matthew Henry.*

Verse 120.—*"My flesh trembleth for fear of thee,"* etc. At the presence of Jehovah, when he appeareth in judgment, the earth trembled and is still. His best servants are not exempted from an awful dread, upon such occasions ; scenes of this kind, shown in vision to the prophets, cause their flesh to quiver, and all their bones to shake. Encompassed with a frail body, and a sinful world, we stand in need of every possible tie ; and the affections both of fear and love must be employed, to restrain us from transgression ; we must, at the same time, " love God's testimonies, and fear his judgments."—*George Horne.*

Verse 120.—*"My flesh trembleth for fear of thee,"* etc. In prayer, in the evening, I had such near and terrific views of God's judgments upon sinners in hell, that my flesh trembled for fear of them. . . . . I flew trembling to Jesus Christ as if the flames were taking hold of me ! Oh ! Christ will indeed save me or else I perish. —*Henry Martyn,* 1781—1812.

Verse 120.—*"My flesh trembleth for fear of thee."* Familiarity with men breeds contempt ; familiarity with God, not so : none reverence the Lord more than they who know him best and are most familiar with him.—*William Cowper.*

Verse 120 with 116.—*"My flesh trembleth for fear of thee ; I am afraid."* . . . . *"Let me not be ashamed of my hope."* True religion consists in a proper mixture of *fear* of God, and of *hope* in his mercy ; and wherever either of these is entirely wanting, there can be no true religion. God has joined these things, and we ought by no means to put them asunder. He cannot take pleasure in those who fear him with a slavish fear, without hoping in his mercy, because they seem to consider him as a cruel and tyrannical being, who has not mercy or goodness in his nature ; and, besides, they implictly charge him with falsehood, by refusing to believe and hope in his invitations and offers of mercy. On the other hand, he cannot be pleased with those who pretend to hope in his mercy without fearing him ; for they insult him by supposing that there is nothing in him which ought to be feared ; and, in addition to this, they make him a liar, by disbelieving his awful threatenings denounced against sinners, and call in question his authority, by refusing to obey him. Those only who both fear him and hope in his mercy, give him the honour that is due to his name.—*Edward Payson.*

Verse 120.—*"Trembleth"* or shuddereth, strictly used of the hair as standing erect in terror (comp. Job iv. 15).—*J. J. Stewart Perowne.*

EXPOSITION OF VERSES 121 TO 128.

I HAVE done judgment and justice : leave me not to mine oppressors.

122 Be surety for thy servant for good : let not the proud oppress me.

123 Mine eyes fail for thy salvation, and for the word of thy righteousness.

124 Deal with thy servant according unto thy mercy, and teach me thy statutes.

125 I *am* thy servant ; give me understanding, that I may know thy testimonies.

126 *It is* time for *thee*, LORD, to work : *for* they have made void thy law.

127 Therefore I love thy commandments above gold ; yea, above fine gold.

128 Therefore I esteem all *thy* precepts *concerning* all *things to be* right ; *and* I hate every false way.

121. "*I have done judgment and justice.*" This was a great thing for an Eastern ruler to say at any time, for these despots mostly cared more for gain than justice. Some of them altogether neglected their duty, and would not even do judgment at all, preferring their pleasures to their duties ; and many more of them sold their judgments to the highest bidders by taking bribes, or regarding the persons of men. Some rulers gave neither judgment nor justice, others gave judgment without justice, but David gave judgment and justice, and saw that his sentences were carried out. He could claim before the Lord that he had dealt out even-handed justice, and was doing so still. On this fact he founded a plea with which he backed the prayer—"*Leave me not to mine oppressors.*" He who, as far as his power goes, has been doing right, may hope to be delivered from his superiors when attempts are made by them to do him wrong. If I will not oppress others, I may hopefully pray that others may not oppress me. A course of upright conduct is one which gives us boldness in appealing to the Great Judge for deliverance from the injustice of others. Nor is this kind of pleading to be censured as self-righteous : when we are dealing with God as to our shortcomings, we use a very different tone from that with which we face the censures of our fellow-men ; when they are in the question, and we are guiltless towards them, we are justified in pleading our innocence.

122. "*Be surety for thy servant for good.*" Answer for me. Do not leave thy poor servant to die by the hand of his enemy and thine. Take up my interests and weave them with thine own, and stand for me. As my Master, undertake thy servants' cause, and represent me before the faces of haughty men till they see what an august ally I have in the Lord my God.

"*Let not the proud oppress me.*" Thine interposition will answer the purpose of my rescue : when the proud see that thou art my advocate they will hide their heads. We should have been crushed beneath our proud adversary the devil if our Lord Jesus had not stood between us and the accuser, and become a surety for us. It is by his suretiship that we escape like a bird from the snare of the fowler. What a blessing to be able to leave our matters in our Surety's hands, knowing that all will be well, since he has an answer for every accuser, a rebuke for every reviler.

Good men dread oppression, for it makes even a wise man mad, and they send up their cries to heaven for deliverance ; nor shall they cry in vain, for the Lord will undertake the cause of his servants, and fight their battles against the proud. The word " servant " is wisely used as a plea for favour for himself, and the word " proud " as an argument against his enemies. It seems to be inevitable that proud men should become oppressors, and that they should take most delight in oppressing really gracious men.

123. "*Mine eyes fail for thy salvation.*" He wept, waited, and watched for God's saving hand, and these exercises tried the eyes of his faith till they were almost ready to give out. He looked to God alone, he looked eagerly, he looked long, he looked till his eyes ached. The mercy is, that if our eyes fail, God does not fail, nor do *his* eyes fail. Eyes are tender things, and so are our faith, hope and expectancy : the Lord will not try them above what they are able to bear. "*And for the word of thy righteousness :*" a word that would silence the unrighteous words

of his oppressors. His eyes as well as his ears waited for the Lord's word : he looked to see the divine word come forth as a fiat for his deliverance. He was " waiting for the verdict "—the verdict of righteousness itself. How happy are we if we have righteousness on our side ; for then that which is the sinners' terror is our hope, that which the proud dread is our expectation and desire. David left his reputation entirely in the Lord's hand, and was eager to be cleared by the word of the Judge rather than by any defence of his own. He knew that he had done right, and, therefore, instead of avoiding the supreme court, he begged for the sentence which he knew would work out his deliverance. He even watched with eager eyes for the judgment and the deliverance, the word of righteousness from God which meant salvation to himself.

124. *"Deal with thy servant according unto thy mercy."* Here he recollects himself : although before men he was so clear that he could challenge the word of righteousness, yet before the Lord, as his servant, he felt that he must appeal to mercy. We feel safest here. Our heart has more rest in the cry, " God be merciful to me," than in appealing to justice. It is well to be able to say, " I have done judgment and justice," and then to add in all lowliness, yet " deal with thy servant according unto thy mercy." The title of servant covers a plea ; a master should clear the character of his servant if he be falsely accused, and rescue him from those who would oppress him ; and, moreover, the master should show mercy to a servant, even if he deal severely with a stranger. The Lord condescendingly deals, or has communications with his servants, not spurning them, but communing with them ; and this he does in a tender and merciful way, for in any other form of dealing we should be crushed into the dust. *"And teach me thy statutes."* This will be one way of dealing with us in mercy. We may expect a master to teach his own servant the meaning of his own orders. Yet since our ignorance arises from our own sinful stupidity, it is great mercy on God's part that he condescends to instruct us in his commands. For our ruler to become our teacher is an act of great grace, for which we cannot be too grateful. Among our mercies this is one of the choicest.

125. *"I am thy servant."* This is the third time he has repeated this title in this one section : he is evidently fond of the name, and conceives it to be a very effective plea. We who rejoice that we are sons of God are by no means the less delighted to be his servants. Did not the firstborn Son assume the servant's form and fulfil the servant's labour to the full ? What higher honour can the younger brethren desire than to be made like the Heir of all things ?

"Give me understanding, that I may know thy testimonies." In the previous verse he sought teaching ; but here he goes much further, and craves for understanding. Usually, if the instructor supplies the teaching, the pupil finds the understanding ; but in our case we are far more dependent, and must beg for understanding as well as teaching : this the ordinary teacher cannot give, and we are thrice happy that our Divine Tutor can furnish us with it. We are to confess ourselves fools, and then our Lord will make us wise, as well as give us knowledge. The best understanding is that which enables us to render perfect obedience and to exhibit intelligent faith, and it is this which David desires,—" understanding, that I may know thy testimonies." Some would rather not know these things ; they prefer to be at ease in the dark rather than possess the light which leads to repentance and diligence. The servant of God longs to know in an understanding manner all that the Lord reveals of man and to man ; he wishes to be so instructed that he may apprehend and comprehend that which is taught him. A servant should not be ignorant concerning his master, or his master's business ; he should study the mind, will, purpose, and aim of him whom he serves, for so only can he complete his service ; and as no man knows these things so well as his master himself, he should often go to him for instructions, lest his very zeal should only serve to make him the greater blunderer.

It is remarkable that the Psalmist does not pray for understanding through acquiring knowledge, but begs of the Lord first that he may have the gracious gift of understanding, and then may obtain the desired instruction. All that we know before we have understanding is apt to spoil us and breed vanity in us ; but if there be first an understanding heart, then the stores of knowledge enrich the soul, and bring neither sin nor sorrow therewith. Moreover, this gift of understanding acts also in the form of discernment, and thus the good man is preserved from hoarding up that which is false and dangerous : he knows what are and what are not the testimonies of the Lord.

126. *"It is time for thee, Lord, to work: for they have made void thy law."* David was a servant, and therefore it was always his time to work : but being oppressed by a sight of man's ungodly behaviour, he feels that his Master's hand is wanted, and therefore he appeals to him to work against the working of evil. Men make void the law of God by denying it to be his law, by promulgating commands and doctrines in opposition to it, by setting up tradition in its place, or by utterly disregarding and scorning the authority of the lawgiver. Then sin becomes fashionable, and a holy walk is regarded as a contemptible puritanism ; vice is styled pleasure, and vanity bears the bell. Then the saints sigh for the presence and power of their God : Oh for an hour of the King upon the throne and the rod of iron ! Oh for another Pentecost with all its wonders, to reveal the energy of God to gainsayers, and make them see that there is a God in Israel ! Man's extremity, whether of need or sin, is God's opportunity. When the earth was without form and void, the Spirit came and moved upon the face of the waters ; should he not come when society is returning to a like chaos ? When Israel in Egypt were reduced to the lowest point, and it seemed that the covenant would be void, then Moses appeared and wrought mighty miracles ; so, too, when the church of God is trampled down, and her message is derided, we may expect to see the hand of the Lord stretched out for the revival of religion, the defence of the truth, and the glorifying of the divine name. The Lord can work either by judgments which hurl down the ramparts of the foe ; or by revivals which build up the walls of his own Jerusalem. How heartily may we pray the Lord to raise up new evangelists, to quicken those we already have, to set his whole church on fire, and to bring the world to his feet. God's work is ever honourable and glorious ; as for our work, it is as nothing apart from him.

127. *"Therefore I love thy commandments above gold ; yea, above fine gold."* As it was God's time to work so it was David's time to love. So far from being swayed by the example of evil men, so as to join them in slighting the Scriptures, he was the rather led into a more vehement love of them. As he saw the commandments slighted by the ungodly, his heart was in sympathy with God, and he felt a burning affection for his holy precepts. It is the mark of a true believer that he does not depend upon others for his religion, but drinks water out of his own well, which springs up even when the cisterns of earth are all dried. Our holy poet amid a general depreciation of the law felt his own esteem of it rising so high that gold and silver sank in comparison. Wealth brings with it so many conveniences that men naturally esteem it, and gold as the symbol of it is much set by ; and yet, in the judgment of the wise, God's laws are more enriching, and bring with them more comfort than all the choicest treasures. The Psalmist could not boast that he always kept the commands ; but he could declare that he loved them ; he was perfect in heart, and would fain have been perfect in life. He judged God's holy commands to be better than the best earthly thing, yea, better than the best sort of the best earthly thing ; and this esteem was confirmed and forced into expression by those very oppositions of the world which drive hypocrites to forsake the Lord and his ways.

> " The dearer, for their rage,
> Thy words I love and own,—
> A wealthier heritage
> Than gold and precious stone "

128. *"Therefore I esteem all thy precepts concerning all things to be right."* Because the ungodly found fault with the precepts of God, therefore David was all the more sure of their being right. The censure of the wicked is a certificate of merit ; that which they sanction we may justly suspect, but that which they abominate we may ardently admire. The good man's delight in God's law is unreserved, he believes in all God's precepts concerning all things.

"And I hate every false way." Love to truth begat hatred of falsehood. This godly man was not indifferent to anything, but that which he did not love he hated. He was no chip in the porridge without flavour ; he was a good lover or a good hater, but he was never a waverer. He knew what he felt, and expressed it. He was no Gallio, caring for none of the things. His detestation was as unreserved as his affection ; he had not a good word for any practice which would not bear the light of truth. The fact that such large multitudes follow the broad road had no influence upon this holy man, except to make him more determined to avoid every form of error and sin. May the Holy Spirit so rule in our hearts that our affections may be in the same decided condition towards the precepts of the word.

NOTES ON VERSES 121 TO 128.

Verse 121.—This commences a new division of the Psalm indicated by the Hebrew letter *Ain*—a letter which cannot well be represented in the English alphabet, as there is, in fact, no letter in our language exactly corresponding with it.   It would be best represented probably by what are called "*breathings*" in Greek. —*Albert Barnes.*

Verse 121.—"*I have done judgment*" against the wicked, "*and justice*" towards the good.—*Simon de Muis, 1587—1644.*

Verse 121.—"*I have done judgment and justice.*"—Here the view of David in his judicial capacity might present itself to us ; and if so, we have David in the midst of large experiences ; for the words would take in a large portion of his life. How blessed were their reflections, if, after a long reign, all sovereign rulers could thus appeal unto God.   It should be so ; for to him all shall be accountable at last. Even although we only conceive of David as speaking in the character of a private man, the sentiment is worthy of all consideration. . . . . For parents to say this of their dealings with their children, masters of servants, a man of his neighbours, is very excellent.—*John Stephen.*

Verse 121.—"*Judgment*" and "*justice*" are often put in Scripture for the same, and when put together, the latter is as an epithet to the former. "*I have done judgment and justice,*" that is, I have done judgment *justly,* exactly, to a hair.— *Joseph Caryl.*

Verse 121.—

> Do right and be a king,
> Be this thy brazen bulwark of defence,
> Still to preserve thy conscious innocence,
> Nor e'er turn pale with guilt.
>
> —*Francis's Horace.*

Verse 121.—" If our heart condemn us not, then have we confidence before God : " 1 John iii. 21.   This " testimony of conscience " has often been " the rejoicing " of the Lord's people, when suffereng under unmerited reproach or "proud oppression." They have been enabled to plead it without offence in the presence of their holy, heart-searching God ; nay, even when, in the near prospect of the great and final account, they might well have been supposed to shrink from the strict and unerring scrutiny of their Omniscient Judge.   Perhaps, however, we are not sufficiently aware of the importance of moral integrity in connexion with our spiritual comfort. Mark the boldness which it gave David in prayer : "*I have done judgment and justice : leave me not to mine oppressors.*"—*Charles Bridges.*

Verse 121.—"*Leave me not to mine oppressors.*"   That is, maintain me against those who would wrong me, because I do right ; interpose thyself between me and my enemies, as if thou wert my pledge.   Impartial justice upon oppressors sometimes lays judges open to oppression ; but yet they who run greatest hazards in zeal for God shall find God ready to be their surety, when they pray, " *be surety for thy servant,*" as in the next verse.—*Abraham Wright.*

Verses 121, 122.—"*I have done judgment and justice ;* " but, that I may always do it, and never fail in doing it, "*uphold thy servant unto good,*" by directing him, so that he may always relish what is good, and then the consequence will be that " *the proud will not calumniate me ;* " for he that is well established " *unto good,*" and so made up that nothing but what is good and righteous will be agreeable to him, he will so persevere that he will have no reason for fearing " *the proud that calumniate him.*"—*Robert Bellarmine.*

Verse 122.—"*Be surety for thy servant for good.*"   What David prays to God to be for him, that Christ is for all his people : Heb. vii. 22.   He drew nigh to God, struck hands with him, gave his word and bond to pay the debts of his people ; put himself in their law-place and stead, and became responsible to law and justice for them ; engaged to make satisfaction for their sins, to bring in everlasting righteousness for their justification, and to preserve and keep them, and bring them safe to eternal glory and happiness ; and this was being *a surety for them for good.* —*John Gill.*

Verse 122.—"*Be surety for thy servant for good.*"   There are three expositions of this clause, as noting the end, the cause, the event.   1. Undertake for me, *ut sim bonus et justus,* so Rabbi Arama on the place ; " Be surety for me *that I may be good.*" Theodoret expounds it, " Undertake that I shall make good my resolution of keeping thy law." He that joineth, undertaketh ; though we have precepts and promises, without God's undertaking we shall never be able to perform our duty. 2. Undertake for me to help me *in doing good ;* so some read it : God would not take his part in an evil cause. To commend a wrong cause to God's protection, is to provoke him to hasten our punishment, to make us serve under our oppressors ; but, when we have a good cause, and a good conscience, he will own us. We cannot expect he should maintain us and bear us out in the Devil's service, wherein we have entangled ourselves by our own sin.

3. *Be with me for good :* so it is often rendered : " Shew me a token for good " (Ps. lxxxvi. 17) ; " Pray not for this people for good " (Jer. xiv. 11) ; so, " Remember me, O my God, for good " (Neh. xiii. 31). So here ; *"Be surety for thy servant for good."—Thomas Manton.*

Verse 122.—"Be surety for thy servant for good." It is the prayer of Hezekiah in his trouble, " O Lord, I am oppressed, undertake for me " (Isa. xxxviii. 14) ; it is the prayer of Job for a " daysman " to stand between him and God (Job ix. 33) ; it is the cry of the church before the Incarnation for the appearance of a Divine Mediator ; it is the confidence of every faithful soul since that blessed time in the perpetual intercession of our great High Priest in heaven, which is to us the pledge of future blessedness.—*Agellius and Cocceius, in Neale and Littledale.*

Verse 122.—"Be surety for thy servant for good." His meaning is, Lord, thou knowest how unjustly I am calumniated and evil spoken of in many parts : where I am not present or where I may not answer for myself, Lord, answer thou for me.—*William Cowper.*

Verse 122.—"Be surety for thy servant for good." The keen eye of the world may possibly not be able to affix any blot upon my outward profession ; but, " if thou, Lord, shouldst mark iniquities ; O Lord, who shall stand ? " The debt is continually accumulating, and the prospect of payment as distant as ever. I might well expect to be " left to my oppressors," until I should pay all that was due unto my Lord. But behold ! " Where is the fury of the oppressor ? " Isa. li. 13. The surety is found—the debt is paid—the ransom is accepted—the sinner is free. There was a voice heard in heaven—" Deliver him from going down to the pit : I have found a ransom," Job xxxiii. 24. The Son of God himself became " Surety for a stranger," and " smarted for it," Prov. xi. 15. At an infinite cost—the cost of his own precious blood—he delivered me from *" mine oppressors "*—sin—Satan —the world—death—hell.—*Charles Bridges.*

Verse 122.—Some observe that this is the only verse throughout the whole Psalm wherein the Word is not mentioned under the name of " law," " judgments," " statutes," or the like terms, and they make this note upon it,—" Where the Law faileth, there Christ is a surety of a better testament." There are that render the words thus,—*"Dulcify, or, delight thy servant in good,"* that is, make him joyful and comfortable in the pursuit and practice of that which is good.—*John Trapp.*

Verse 123.—"Mine eyes fail for thy salvation." In times of great sorrow, when the heart is oppressed with care, and when danger threatens on every side, the human eye expresses with amazing accuracy the distressed and anguished emotions of the soul. The posture here described is that of an individual who perceives himself surrounded with enemies of the most formidable character, who feels his own weakness and insufficiency to enter into conflict with them, but who is eagerly looking for the arrival of a devoted and powerful friend who has promised to succour him in the hour of his calamity. As his friend delays the hour of his coming, his fears and anxieties multiply, till he finds himself in the condition of one whose eyes fail and grow dim in looking for the approach of his great deliverer. In this condition was the suppliant here described,—his enemies were ready to swallow him up, and except from heaven he had no hope of final extrication. To the promises of God he betook himself, and while waiting their accomplishment, and looking with the utmost eagerness to the word of God's righteousness, he gives utterance to the desponding sentiment, *"Mine eyes fail for thy salvation."* O for such warm and anxious desires for that great salvation, which will realize the victory over all our spiritual enemies, and enable us to shout triumphantly through all eternity in the name of our almighty Deliverer !—*John Morison.*

Verse 123.—"Mine eyes fail . . . . . for the word of thy righteousness." Albeit the words of promise be neither performed, nor the like to be performed, yet faith should justify the promise, for true and faithful.—*David Dickson.*

Verse 123.—*"For the word of thy righteousness."* This would be the word of promised salvation, which the Lord had given in righteousness. What an amazing plea—God on the ground of his own righteousness appealed to for deliverance—and yet how true! Or this might be the word of his justice, the issuing of justice, the exercising of a righteous decision between him and his oppressors. He looked for the Lord to interpose between them, and so to fulfil all he had promised on behalf of the believer. The Lord will vindicate his own. Are any in great difficulty; and are they waiting for the Lord to interpose, to whom they have committed their concerns ? . . . . Wait on ; he will not disappoint a gracious hope.—*John Stephen.*

Verse 123.—*"For the word of thy righteousness,"* or, *"* the word of thy *justice ;"* that is to say, for the sentence of justice on my oppressors, as the first part of the verse teaches ; for the passing this sentence will be equivalent to the granting the salvation which the Psalmist so earnestly desired.—*George Phillips.*

Verse 124.—*"Deal with thy servant according unto thy mercy."* If I am a *"* servant *"* of God, I can bring my services before him only upon the ground of *"* mercy *"* ; feeling that for my best performances I need an immeasurable world of mercy—pardoning—saving—everlasting mercy ; and yet I am emboldened by the blood of Jesus to plead for my soul—*"Deal with thy servant according unto thy mercy."*

But then I am ignorant as well as guilty ; and yet I dare not pray for divine teaching, much and hourly as I need it, until I have afresh obtained mercy. *"Mercy"* is the first blessing, not only in point of importance, but in point of order. I must seek the Lord, and know him as a Saviour, before I can go to him with any confidence to be my teacher. But when once I have found acceptance to my petition—*"Deal with thy servant according unto thy mercy "*—my way will be opened to follow on my petition—*"Teach me thy statutes. Give me understanding, that I may know thy testimonies "*—that I may know, walk, yea, *"* run in the way of thy commandments *"* with an enlarged heart, ver. 32. My plea is the same as I have urged with acceptance (ver. 94)—*"I am thy servant."*—*Charles Bridges.*

Verse 124.—*"Thy mercy."* All the year round, every hour of every day, God is richly blessing us ; both when we sleep and when we wake, his mercy waits upon us. The sun may leave off shining, but our God will never cease to cheer his children with his love. Like a river, his loving-kindness is always flowing, with a fulness inexhaustible as his own nature, which is its source. Like the atmosphere which always surrounds the earth, and is always ready to support the life of man, the benevolence of God surrounds all his creatures ; in it, as in their element, they live, and move, and have their being. Yet as the sun on summer days appears to gladden us with beams more warm and bright than at other times, and as rivers are at certain seasons swollen with the rain, and as the atmosphere itself on occasions is fraught with more fresh, more bracing, or more balmy influences than heretofore, so is it with the mercy of God ; it hath its golden hours, its days of overflow, when the Lord magnifieth his grace and lifteth high his love before the sons of men.—*C. H. S.*

Verse 124.—*"Teach me."* David had Nathan and Gad the prophets ; and beside them, the ordinary Levites to teach him. He read the word of God diligently, and did meditate in the law night and day ; but he acknowledgeth all this was nothing unless God speaks to the heart : so Paul preached to Lydia, but God opened her heart. Let us pray for this grace.—*William Cowper.*

Verse 125.—*"I am thy servant ; give me understanding,"* etc. I am not a stranger to thee, but thine own domestic servant ; let me want no grace which may enable me to serve thee.—*William Cowper.*

Verse 125.—*"I am thy servant."* That thou art the servant *of God,* thou shouldst regard as thy chiefest glory and blessedness.—*Martin Geier.*

Verse 126.—*"It is time for thee, LORD, to work."* Was ever vessel more hopelessly becalmed in mid-ocean ? or did crew ever cry with more frenzy for some favouring breeze than those should cry who man the Church of the living God ? If God work not, it is certain there is nothing before the Church but the prospect of utter discomfiture and overthrow. Greater is the world than the Church if God be not in her. But if God be in her, she shall not be moved. May he help her, and that right early !

When he arises to work we know not what may be the form and fashion of his operations. He worketh according to the counsel of his own will ; and who knows but that when once he awakes, and puts on his strength, it may not be confined in its results to the immediate and exclusive quickening of the spiritual life of the Church ; but may be associated with providential upheavals and convulsions which will fill the heart of the world with astonishment and dismay. His spiritual kingdom does not stand in isolation. It has relations which closely involve it with the material universe, and with human society and national life. There have been times when God has worked, and the signs of his presence have been seen, in terrible shakings of the nations, in the ploughing up from their foundations of hoary injustice, in the smiting of grinding tyrannies, and in the emancipation of peoples whose life had been a long and hopeless moan. There have been times, too, and many, when he has worked through the elements of nature —through blasting and mildew, through floods and famine, through locust, caterpillar and palmer-worm ; through flagging commerce, with its machinery rusting in the mill and its ships rotting in the harbour. All these things are his servants. Sometimes the sleep of the world, and the Church too, is so profound that it can be broken only by agencies like the wind, or fire, or earthquake, which made the prophet shiver at the mouth of the cave, and without which the voice that followed, so still, so small and tender, would have lost much of its melting and subduing power. When society has become drugged with the Circean cup of wordliness, and the voices that come from eternity are unheeded, if not unheard, even terror has its merciful mission. The frivolous and superficial hearts of men have to be made serious, their idols have to be broken, their nests have to be stoned, or tossed from the trees where they had been made with so much care, and they have to be taught that if this life be all, it is but a phantom and a mockery. When the day of the Lord shall come, in which he shall begin to work, let us not marvel if it " shall be upon every one that is proud and lofty, and upon every one that is lifted up ; and he shall be brought low ; and upon all the cedars of Lebanon, that are high and lifted up, and upon every high tower, and upon every fenced wall, and upon all the ships of Tarshish, and upon all the pleasant pictures. And the loftiness of man shall be bowed down, and the haughtiness of men shall be made low : and the Lord alone shall be exalted in that day." But this working of God will also take other shapes. Will it not be seen in the inspiration of the Church with faith in its own creed, so far as that creed has the warrant of the Divine word ? Does the Church believe its creed ? It writes it, sets it forth, sings it, defends it ; but does it believe it, at least with a faith which begets either enthusiasm in itself, or respect from the world ? Have not the truths which form the methodized symbols of the Church become propositions instead of living powers ? Do they not lie embalmed with superstitious reverence in the ark of tradition, tenderly cherished for what they have been and done ? But is it not forgotten that if they be truths they are not dead and cannot die ? They are true now, or they were never true ; living now, or they never lived. Time cannot touch them, nor human opinion, nor the Church's sluggishness or unbelief, for they are emanations from the Divine essence, instinct with his own undecaying life. They are not machinery which may become antiquated and obsolete and displaced by better inventions ; they are not methods of policy framed for conditions which are transient, and vanishing with them ; they are not scaffolding within which other and higher truth is to be reared from age to age. They are like him who is the end of our conversation, " Jesus Christ, the same yesterday, to-day, and for ever." There is not one of them which, if the faith it awakens were but commensurate with its intrinsic worth, would not clothe the Church with a new and wondrous power. But what would be that power if that faith were to grasp them all ? It would be life from the dead.—*Enoch Mellor* (1823 —1881), *in "The Hem of Christ's Garment, and other Sermons."*

Verse 126.—*"It is time for thee, Lord, to work."* עת expresses emphatically *the proper time* for the Lord to do his own work ; as if the Psalmist had said, " It is not for us to prescribe the time and occasion for God to exercise his power, and to vindicate the authority of his own law ; he does every thing at the proper time, and he will at the proper season punish those *' who have made void his law,'* and who have become notorious for their impiety and wickedness."—*George Phillips.*

Verse 126.—"*It is time to work,*" just as when the attack of some illness is becoming more severe, you hurry to the physician, that he may come more quickly, lest he should later be unable to do any good. So when the prophet saw in the Holy Spirit the rebellion of the people, their luxury, pleasures, deceits, frauds, avarice, drunkenness, he runs, for our help, to Christ, whom he knew to be alone able to remedy, such sins; implores him to come, and admits of no delay.—*Ambrose, in Neale and Littledale.*

Verse 126.—"*It is time for thee, Lord, to work.*"—Infidelity was never more subtle, more hurtful, more plausible, perhaps more successful, than in the day in which we live. It has left the low grounds of vulgarity, and coarseness and ribaldry, and entrenched itself upon the lofty heights of criticism, philology, and even science itself. It pervades to a fearful extent our popular literature; it has invested itself with the charms of poetry, to throw its spell over the public mind; it has endeavoured to enweave itself with science; and he must be little acquainted with the state of opinion in this land, who does not know that it is espoused by a large portion of the cultivated mind of this generation. " It is time for thee, Lord, to work." —*John Angell James,* 1785—1859.

Verse 126.—"*It is time for thee, Lord, to work,*" etc. To send the Messiah, to work by righteousness, to fulfil the law and vindicate the honour of it, broken by men. It was always a notion of the Jews that the time of the Messiah's coming would be when it was a time of great wickedness in the earth; and which seems to agree with the word of God, and was true in fact. See Mal. ii. 17, and iii. 1, 2, 3, 15, 16, and iv. 2.—*John Gill.*

Verse 126.—"*It is time for thee, Lord, to work,*" etc. True it is, Lord, that we are not to appoint thee thy times and limits, for thou art the Ancient of Days, Time's Creator and destinator. Neither do we presume to press in at the portal of thy privy chamber, to " know the times and seasons" which thou our Father hast reserved in thine own power; yet, Lord, thou hast taught us, as to discern the face of the sky, so to descry the signs of the times, and from the cause to expect the effect which necessarily doth ensue. " Thou art a God full of compassion and mercy, slow to anger, and of great kindness " (Ps. ciii. 8); and thou dost sustain many wrongs of the sons of men, being crushed with their sins as a cart is laden with sheaves: but if still they continue to load thee, thou wilt ease thyself of that burden, and cast it on the ground of confusion. Thou art " slow to anger, but great in power, and wilt not surely clear the wicked " (Nahum i. 3). Thou dost for a long space hold thy peace at men's sins, and art still, and dost restrain thyself. But if men will not turn, thou wilt whet thy sword and bend thy bow, and make it ready. Patient thou art, and for a long time dost forbear thine hand; but when the forehead of sin beginneth to lose the blush of shame, when the beadroll of transgressions doth grow in score from East to West, when the cry of them pierceth above the clouds, when the height of wickedness is come unto the top, and the fruits thereof are ripe and full, then it is time for thee, Lord, to take notice of it, to awake like a giant, and to put to thine all-revenging hand.

But our sins are already ripe, yea, rotten ripe, the measure of our iniquities is full up to the brim. Doubtless our land is sunken deep in iniquity; our tongues and works have been against the Lord, to provoke the eyes of his glory; the trial of our countenance doth testify against us (Isaiah iii. 8, 9), yea, we declare our sins as Sodom; we hide them not, the cry of our sins is exceeding grievous, the clamours of them pierce the skies, and with a loud voice roar, saying: " How long, Lord, holy and true? How long ere thou come to avenge thyself on such a nation as this ? " Rev. vi. 10; Jer. ix. 9.—*George Webbe, in "A Posie of Spiritual Flowers,"* 1610.

Verse 126.—"*It is time for thee, Lord.*" Some read it, and the original will bear it, "*It is time to work for thee, O Lord;* " it is time for every one in his place to appear on the Lord's side, against the threatening growth of profaneness and immorality. We must do what we can for the support of the sinking interests of religion, and after all, we must beg of God to take the work into his own hands. —*Matthew Henry.*

Verse 126.—"*They have made void thy law.*" In the second verse of this section he complained that the proud would oppress him, now he complaineth that they destroyed the law of God. Who, then, are David's enemies, who seek to oppress him ? Only such as are enemies to God, and seek to destroy his law. A great comfort have we in this, that if we love the Lord, and study in a good conscience to serve him, we can have no enemies but such as are enemies to God.—*William Cowper.*

Verse 126.—"*They have made void thy law.*" As if they would not only sin against the Law, but sin away the Law, not only withdraw themselves from the obedience of it, but drive it out of the world ; they would make void and repeal the holy acts of God, that their own wicked acts might not be questioned ; and lest the Law should have a power to punish them, they will deny it a power to rule them ; that's the force of the simple word here used, as applied to highest transgressing against the Law of God.—*Joseph Caryl.*

Verses 126, 127.—Everything betters a saint. Not only ordinances, word, sacraments, holy society, but even sinners and their very sinning. Even these draw forth their graces into exercise, and put them upon godly, broken-hearted mourning. A saint sails with every wind. As the wicked are hurt by the best things, so the godly are bettered by the worst. Because " *they have made void thy law, therefore do I love thy commandments.*" Holiness is the more owned by the godly, the more the world despiseth it. The most eminent saints were those of Cæsar's (Nero's) house (Phil. iv. 22) ; they who kept God's name were they who lived where Satan's throne was (Rev. ii. 13). Zeal for God grows the hotter by opposition ; and thereby the godly most labour to give the glory of God reparation.—*William Jenkyn* (1612 —1685), *in "The Morning Exercises."*

Verse 127.—"*Therefore I love thy commandments above gold,*" etc. Partly, because it is one evidence of their excellency, that they are disliked by the vilest of men. Partly, out of just indignation and opposition against my sworn enemies ; and partly, because the great and general apostasy of others makes this duty more necessary to prevent their own and other men's relapses.—*Matthew Pool.*

Verse 127.—"*I love thy commandments above gold ; yea, above fine gold.*" The image employed brings before us the picture of the miser ; his heart and his treasure are in his gold. With what delight he counts it ! with what watchfulness he keeps it ! hiding it in safe custody, lest he should be despoiled of that which is dearer to him than life. Such should Christians be, spiritual misers, counting their treasure which is " *above fine gold* " ; and " hiding it in their hearts," in safe keeping, where the great despoiler shall not be able to reach it. Oh, Christians ! how much more is your portion to you than the miser's treasure ! Hide it ; watch it ; retain it. You need not be afraid of covetousness in spiritual things : rather "covet earnestly" to increase your store ; and by living upon it and living in it, it will grow richer in extent, and more precious in value.—*Charles Bridges.*

Verse 127.—"*I love thy commandments.*" He professeth not that he fulfilled them, but that he *loved* them ; and truly it is a great progress in godliness, if we become thus far, as from our heart to love them. The natural man hates the commandments of God ; they are so contrary to his corruption ; but the regenerate man, as he hates his own corruption, so he loves the word, because according to it he desires to be reformed. And here is our comfort, that, albeit we cannot do what is commanded, yet if we love to do it, it is an argument of grace received. "*Above gold,*" etc. It is lawful to love those creatures which God hath appointed for our use ; with these conditions : the one is, that the first seat in our affection of love be reserved to God ; and any other thing we love, that we love it in him and for him, and give it only the second room. Thus David, being a natural man, loved his natural food ; but he protesteth he loved the law of the Lord more than his appointed food ; and here he loves the commandments of God above all gold.—*William Cowper.*

Verse 128.—"*I esteem all thy precepts concerning all things to be right.*" It is no compromising testimony to the integrity and value of the Lord's precepts with which the Psalmist concludes, "*I esteem all thy precepts concerning all things to be right*"—every command, however hard ; every injunction, however distasteful ; every precept, however severe ; even cut off thy right hand, pluck out thy right eye ; forget thine own people and thy father's house ; take up thy cross daily ; sell all that thou hast—yea, Lord, even so, " *all* thy precepts concerning ALL things are right." What a blessed truth to arrive at, and find comfort in !—*Barton Bouchier.*

Verse 128.—"*I esteem all thy precepts,*" etc. We must not only respect all God's commandments, but also respect them all alike, and give them all the like respect.

Obedience must be universal.—*R. Mayhew, in "The death of Death in the Death of Christ,"* 1679.

Verse 128.—*"All."* The many *alls* in this verse used (not unlike that in Ezekiel xliv. 30) showeth the integrity and universality of his obedience. *"All"* is but a little word, but of large extent.—*John Trapp.*

Verse 128.—*"All thy precepts concerning all things to be right."* He had a high estimate of God's precepts ; he thought them just in all things ; just, because they prescribe nothing but that which is exactly just ; and just, because they bring a just punishment on the transgressors, and a reward to the righteous.—*William Nicholson.*

Verse 128.—The upright man squares all his actions by a right rule : carnal reason cannot bias him, corrupt practice cannot sway him, but God's sacred word directs him. Hence it is that his respect is universal to all divine precepts, avoiding all evil, performing all good without exception. Thus David's upright man here *esteems God's precepts concerning all things to be right,* and therefore is careful to observe them. Hence it is, that he is the same man at all times, in all places ; because at all times, and in all societies, he acts by one and the same rule. 'Tis a good saying of S. Cyprian, *ea non est religio, sed dissimulatio, quæ per omnia non constat sibi,* that is not piety, but hypocrisy, that is not in all things like itself, since the upright man measures every action by the straight line of divine prescript. —*Abraham Wright.*

Verse 128.—*"I hate every false way."* The best trial of our love to God and his word is the contrary—hatred of sin and impiety : " Ye that love the Lord, hate evil." He that loves a tree, hates the worm that consumes it ; he that loves a garment, hates the moth that eats it ; he that loveth life, abhorreth death ; and he that loves the Lord hates every thing that offends him. Let men take heed to this, who are in love of their sins : how can the love of God be in them ?

Religion binds us not only to hate one way of falsehood, but all the ways of it. As there is nothing good, but in some measure a godly man loves it ; so there is nothing evil, but in some measure he hates it. And this is the perfection of the children of God ; a perfection not of degrees ; for we neither love good nor hate evil as we should ; but a perfection of parts ; because we love every good, and we hate every evil in some measure.—*William Cowper.*

Verse 128.—*"And I hate."* The Being who loves the good with infinite intensity must hate evil with the same intensity. So far from the incompatibility between this love and this hatred, they are the counterparts of each other,—opposite poles of the same moral emotion.—*John W. Haley, in "An Examination of the alleged Discrepancies of the Bible,"* 1875.

Verse 128.—*"I hate every false way."* If Satan get a grip of thee by any one sin, is it not enough to carry thee to damnation ? As the butcher carries the beast to the slaughter, sometime bound by all the four feet, and sometime by one only ; so it is with Satan. Though thou be not a slave to all sin ; if thou be a slave to one, the grip he hath of thee, by that one sinful affection, is sufficient to captive thee.—*William Cowper.*

EXPOSITION OF VERSES 129 TO 136.

THY testimonies *are* wonderful : therefore doth my soul keep them.

130 The entrance of thy words giveth light ; it giveth understanding unto the simple.

131 I opened my mouth, and panted : for I longed for thy commandments.

132 Look thou upon me, and be merciful unto me, as thou usest to do unto those that love thy name.

133 Order my steps in thy word : and let not any iniquity have dominion over me.

134 Deliver me from the oppression of man : so will I keep thy precepts.

135 Make thy face to shine upon thy servant ; and teach me thy statutes.

136 Rivers of waters run down mine eyes, because they keep not thy law.

129. *"Thy testimonies are wonderful."* Full of wonderful revelations, commands and promises. Wonderful in their nature, as being free from all error, and bearing within themselves overwhelming self-evidence of their truth ; wonderful in their effects as instructing, elevating, strengthening, and comforting the soul. Jesus the eternal Word is called Wonderful, and all the uttered words of God are wonderful in their degree. Those who know them best wonder at them most. It is wonderful that God should have borne testimony at all to sinful men, and more wonderful still that his testimony should be of such a character, so clear, so full, so gracious, so mighty. *"Therefore doth my soul keep them."* Their wonderful character so impressed itself upon his mind that he kept them in his memory : their wonderful excellence so charmed his heart that he kept them in his life. Some men wonder at the words of God, and use them for their speculation ; but David was always practical, and the more he wondered the more he obeyed. Note that his religion was soul work ; not with head and hand alone did he keep the testimonies ; but his soul, his truest and most real self, held fast to them.

130. *"The entrance of thy words giveth light."* No sooner do they gain admission into the soul than they enlighten it : what light may be expected from their prolonged indwelling ! Their very entrance floods the mind with instruction, for they are so full, so clear ; but, on the other hand, there must be such an " entrance," or there will be no illumination. The mere hearing of the word with the external ear is of small value by itself, but when the words of God enter into the chambers of the heart then light is scattered on all sides. The word finds no entrance into some minds because they are blocked up with self-conceit, or prejudice, or indifference ; but where due attention is given, divine illumination must surely follow upon knowledge of the mind of God. Oh, that thy words, like the beams of the sun, may enter through the window of my understanding, and dispel the darkness of my mind ! *"It giveth understanding unto the simple."* The sincere and candid are the true disciples of the word. To such it gives not only knowledge, but understanding. These simple-hearted ones are frequently despised, and their simplicity has another meaning infused into it, so as to be made the theme of ridicule ; but what matters it ? Those whom the world dubs as fools are among the truly wise if they are taught of God. What a divine power rests in the word of God, since it not only bestows light, but gives that very mental eye by which the light is received —" It giveth understanding." Hence the value of the words of God to the simple, who cannot receive mysterious truth unless their minds are aided to see it and prepared to grasp it.

131. *"I opened my mouth, and panted."* So animated was his desire that he looked into the animal world to find a picture of it. He was filled with an intense longing, and was not ashamed to describe it by a most expressive, natural, and yet singular symbol. Like a stag that has been hunted in the chase, and is hard pressed, and therefore pants for breath, so did the Psalmist pant for the entrance of God's word into his soul. Nothing else could content him. All that the world

could yield him left him still panting with open mouth. *"For I longed for thy commandments."* Longed to know them, longed to obey them, longed to be conformed to their spirit, longed to teach them to others. He was a servant of God, and his industrious mind longed to receive orders ; he was a learner in the school of grace, and his eager spirit longed to be taught of the Lord.

132. *"Look thou upon me."* A godly man cannot long be without prayer. During the previous verses he had been expressing his love to God's word, but here he is upon his knees again. This prayer is specially short, but exceedingly sententious, " Look thou upon me." While he stood with open mouth panting for the commandments, he besought the Lord to look upon him, and let his condition and his unexpressed longings plead for him. He desires to be known of God, and daily observed by him. He wishes also to be favoured with the divine smile which is included in that word—" look." If a look from us to God has saving efficacy in it, what may we not expect from a look from God to us. *"And be merciful unto me."* Christ's look at Peter was a look of mercy, and all the looks of the heavenly Father are of the same kind. If he looked in stern justice his eyes would not endure us, but looking in mercy he spares and blesses us. If God looks and sees us panting, he will not fail to be merciful to us. *"As thou usest to do unto those that love thy name."* Look on me as thou lookest on those who love thee ; be merciful to me as thou art accustomed to be towards those who truly serve thee. There is a use and wont which God observes towards them that love him, and David craved that he might experience it. He would not have the Lord deal better or worse with him than he was accustomed to deal with his saints—worse would not save him, better could not be. In effect he prays, " I am thy servant ; treat me as thou treatest thy servants. I am thy child ; deal with me as with a son." Especially is it clear from the context that he desired such an entering in of the word, and such a clear understanding of it as God usually gives to his own, according to the promise, " All thy children shall be taught of the Lord."

Reader, do you love the name of the Lord ? Is his character most honourable in your sight ? most dear to your heart ? This is a sure mark of grace, for no soul ever loved the Lord except as the result of love received from the Lord himself.

133. *"Order my steps in thy word."* This is one of the Lord's customary mercies to his chosen,—" He keepeth the feet of his saints." By his grace he enables us to put our feet step by step in the very place which his word ordains. This prayer seeks a very choice favour, namely, that every distinct act, every step, might be arranged and governed by the will of God. This does not stop short of perfect holiness, neither will the believer's desires be satisfied with anything beneath that blessed consummation. *"And let not any iniquity have dominion over me."* This is the negative side of the blessing. We ask to do all that is right, and to fall under the power of nothing that is wrong. God is our sovereign, and we would have every thought in subjection to his sway. Believers have no choice, darling sins to which they would be willing to bow. They pant for perfect liberty from the power of evil, and being conscious that they cannot obtain it of themselves, they cry unto God for it.

134. *"Deliver me from the oppression of man."* David had tasted all the bitterness of this great evil. It had made him an exile from his country, and banished him from the sanctuary of the Lord : therefore he pleads to be saved from it. It is said that oppression makes a wise man mad, and no doubt it has made many a righteous man sinful. Oppression is in itself wicked, and it drives men to wickedness. We little know how much of our virtue is due to our liberty ; if we had been in bonds under haughty tyrants we might have yielded to them, and instead of being confessors we might now have been apostates. He who taught us to pray, " Lead us not into temptation," will sanction this prayer, which is of much the same tenor, since to be oppressed is to be tempted. *"So will I keep thy statutes."* When the stress of oppression was taken off he would go his own way, and that way would be the way of the Lord. Although we ought not to yield to the threatenings of men, yet many do so ; the wife is sometimes compelled by the oppression of her husband to act against her conscience : children and servants, and even whole nations have been brought into the same difficulty. Their sins will be largely laid at the oppressor's door, and it usually pleases God ere long to overthrow those powers and dominions which compel men to do evil. The worst of it is that some persons, when the pressure is taken off from them, follow after unrighteousness of their own accord. These give evidence of being sinners in grain. As for the righteous, it happens

to them as it did to the apostles of old, "Being let go, they went to their own company."
When saints are freed from the tyrant they joyfully pay homage to their king.

135. *"Make thy face to shine upon thy servant."* Oppressors frown, but do thou
smile. They darken my life, but do thou shine upon me, and all will be bright.
The Psalmist again declares that he is God's servant, and he seeks for no favour
from others, but only from his own Lord and Master. *"And teach me thy statutes."*
This is the favour which he considers to be the shining of the face of God upon
him. If the Lord will be exceeding gracious, and make him his favourite, he will
ask no higher blessing than still to be taught the royal statutes. See how he craves
after holiness; this is the choicest of all gems in his esteem. As we say among
men that a good education is a great fortune, so to be taught of the Lord is a gift
of special grace. The most favoured believer needs teaching; even when he walks
in the light of God's countenance he has still to be taught the divine statutes or he
will transgress.

136. *"Rivers of waters run down mine eyes, because they keep not thy law."* He
wept in sympathy with God to see the holy law despised and broken. He wept
in pity for men who were thus drawing down upon themselves the fiery wrath of
God. His grief was such that he could scarcely give it vent; his tears were not
mere drops of sorrow, but torrents of woe. In this he became like the Lord Jesus
who beheld the city, and wept over it; and like unto Jehovah himself, who hath
no pleasure in the death of him that dieth, but that he turn unto him and live. The
experience of this verse indicates a great advance upon anything we have had before:
the Psalm and the Psalmist are both growing. That man is a ripe believer who
sorrows because of the sins of others. In verse 120 his flesh trembled at the presence
of God, and here it seems to melt and flow away in floods of tears. None are so
affected by heavenly things as those who are much in the study of the word, and
are thereby taught the truth and essence of things, Carnal men are afraid of brute
force, and weep over losses and crosses; but spiritual men feel a holy fear of the
Lord himself, and most of all lament when they see dishonour cast upon his holy
name.

> "Lord, let me weep for nought but sin,
> And after none but thee,
> And then I would, O that I might!
> A constant weeper be."

NOTES ON VERSES 129 TO 136.

All the verses of this section begin with the seventeenth letter of the Hebrew alphabet ; but each verse with a different word.—*William S. Plumer.*

This seventeenth letter is the letter P. The section is precious, practical, profitable, powerful : peculiarly so.—*C. H. S.*

Verse 129.—*"Thy testimonies are wonderful."* The Scriptures are *" wonderful,"* with respect to the matter which they contain, the manner in which they are written, and the effects which they produce. They contain the sublimest spiritual truths, veiled under external ceremonies and sacraments, figurative descriptions, typical histories, parables, similitudes, etc. When properly opened and enforced, they terrify and humble, they convert and transform, they console and strengthen. Who but must delight to study and to " observe " these " testimonies " of the will and the wisdom, the love and the power of God Most High ! While we have these holy writings, let us not waste our time, mis-employ our thoughts, and prostitute our admiration, by doating on human follies, and wondering at human trifles.—*George Horne.*

Verse 129.—*"Thy testimonies are wonderful."* God's testimonies are " wonderful " (1) in their *majesty* and *composure*, which striketh reverence into the hearts of those that consider ; the Scripture speaketh to us at a God-like rate. (2) It is " wonderful " for the *matter* and *depth of mystery*, which cannot be found elsewhere, concerning God, and Christ, the creation of the world, the souls of men, and their immortal and everlasting condition, the fall of man, etc. (3) It is " wonderful " for *purity* and *perfection*. The Decalogue in ten words compriseth the whole duty of man, and reacheth to the very soul, and all the motions of the heart. (4) It is " wonderful " for the *harmony* and *consent* of all the parts. All religion is of a piece, and one part doth not interfere with another, but conspireth to promote the great end, of subjection of the creature to God. (5) It is " wonderful " for the *power* of it. There is a mighty power which goeth along with the word of God, and astonisheth the hearts of those that consider it and feel it. 1 Thess. i. 5.—*Thomas Manton.*

Verse 129.—*"Thy testimonies are wonderful."* The Bible itself is an astonishing and standing miracle. Written fragment by fragment, through the course of fifteen centuries, under different states of society, and in different languages, by persons of the most opposite tempers, talents, and conditions, learned and unlearned, prince and peasant, bond and free ; cast into every form of instructive composition and good writing ; history, prophecy, poetry, allegory, emblematic representation, judicious interpretation, literal statement, precept, example, proverbs, disquisition, epistle, sermon, prayer—in short, all rational shapes of human discourse, and treating, moreover, on subjects not obvious, but most difficult ; its authors are not found like other men, contradicting one another upon the most ordinary matters of fact and opinion, but are at harmony upon the whole of their sublime and momentous scheme.—*J. Maclagan,* 1853.

Verse 129.—Highly prize the Scriptures, or you will not obey them. David said, *" therefore doth my soul keep them ";* and why was this, but that he counted them to be wonderful ? Can *he* make a proficiency in any art, who doth slight and deprecate it ? Prize this book of God above all other books. St. Gregory calls the Bible " the heart and soul of God." The rabbins say, that there is a mountain of sense hangs upon every *apex* and tittle of Scripture. " The law of the Lord is perfect " (Ps. xix. 7). The Scripture is the library of the Holy Ghost ; it is a pandect of divine knowledge, an exact model and platform of religion. The Scripture contains in it the *credenda*, " the things which we are to believe," and the *agenda*, " the things which we are to practise." It is " able to make us wise unto salvation" 2 Tim. iii. 15. " The Scripture is the standard of truth," the judge of controversies ; it is the pole-star to direct us to heaven (Isa. viii. 20). " The commandment is a lamp " : Prov. vi. 23. The Scripture is the compass by which the rudder of our will is to be steered ; it is the field in which Christ, the Pearl of price, is hid ; it is a rock of diamonds, it is a sacred *collyrium*, or " *eye-salve ;* " it mends *their* eyes *that* look upon it ; it is a spiritual optic-glass in which the glory of God is resplendent ; it is the panacea or " universal medicine " for the soul. The leaves of Scripture are like the leaves of the tree of life, " for the healing of the nations " : Rev. xxii. 2. The Scripture is both the breeder and feeder of grace. How is the

convert born, but by "the word of truth"?   James i. 18.   How doth he grow,
but by "the sincere milk of the word"?   1 Pet. ii. 2.   The word written is the
book out of which our evidences for heaven are fetched ; it is the sea-mark which
shows us the rocks of sin to avoid ; it is the antidote against error and apostasy,
the two-edged sword which wounds the old serpent.   It is our bulwark to withstand the force of lust ; like the Capitol of Rome, which was a place of strength and
ammunition.   The Scripture is the "tower of David," whereon the shields of our
faith hang : Canticles iv. 4.   "Take away the word, and you deprive us of the
sun," said Luther.   The word written is above an angelic embassy, or voice from
heaven.   "This voice which came from heaven we heard.   We have also," βεβαιότερον
λογον "a more sure word" : 2 Peter i. 18, 19.   O, prize the word written ; prizing
is the way to profiting.   If Cæsar so valued his Commentaries, that for preserving
them he lost his purple robe, how should we estimate the sacred oracles of God ?
" I have esteemed the words of his mouth more than any necessary food ": Job
xxiii. 12.   King Edward the Sixth, on the day of his coronation, had presented
before him three swords, signifying that he was monarch of three kingdoms.   The
king said, there was one sword wanting ; being asked what that was, he answered,
"The Holy Bible, which is the sword of the Spirit, and is to be preferred before
these ensigns of royalty."   Robert King of Sicily did so prize God's word, that,
speaking to his friend Petrarcha, he said, " I protest, the Scriptures are dearer
to me than my kingdom ; and if I must be deprived of one of them, I had rather
lose my diadem than the Scriptures."—*Thomas Watson, in "The Morning Exercises."*

Verse 129.—The word contains matter to exercise the greatest minds.   Many
men cannot endure to spend their thoughts and time about trivial matters ; whereas
others think it happiness enough if they can, by the meanest employments, procure
subsistence.   Oh, let all those of high aspirations exercise themselves in the law
of God ; here are objects fit for great minds, yea, objects that will elevate the
greatest :   and indeed none in the world are truly great but the saints, for they
exercise themselves in the great counsels of God.   We account those men the greatest
that are employed in state affairs :   now the saints are lifted up above all things
in the world, and regard them all as little and mean, and are exercised in the great
affairs of the kingdom of Jesus Christ.   Hence the Lord would have the kings and
the judges to have the book of the law written, Deut. xvii. 18, 19 ; and it is reported
of Alphonsus, king of Arragon, that in midst of all his great and manifold occupations,
he read over the Scriptures fourteen times with commentaries.   How many have
we, men of great estates, and claiming to be of great minds, that scarce regard the
law of God : they look upon his law as beneath them.   Books of history and war
they will peruse with diligence ; but for the Scripture, it is a thing that has little
in it.   It is a special means to obedience to have high thoughts of God's law.   That
is the reason why the prophet speaks thus, " I have written to him the great things
of my law, but they were counted as a strange thing " : Hos. viii. 12.   As if he
should say, if they had had the things of my law in their thoughts, they would
never so have acted.   Ps. cxix. 129, *"Thy testimonies are wonderful, therefore doth
my soul keep them."*   He saith not, therefore do I keep them ; but, therefore doth
my soul keep them ; my very soul is in this, in keeping thy testimonies, for I look
upon them as wonderful things.   It is a good sign that the spirit of the great God
is in a man, when it raises him above other things, to look upon the things of his
word as the only great things in the world.   " All flesh is grass, and all the good-
liness thereof is as the flower of the field :   the grass withereth, the flower fadeth :
but the word of our God shall stand for ever : " Isa. xl. 6, 8.   There is a vanity in
all things of the world ; but in that which the word reveals, in that there is an
eternity :   we should therefore admire at nothing so as at the word, and we should
greatly delight in God's commandments ;   an ordinary degree of admiration or
delight is not sufficient, but great admiration and great delight there should be in
the law of God.   And all arguments drawn from God's law should powerfully prevail with you.—*Jeremiah Burroughs.*

Verse 129.—*"Thy testimonies are wonderful."*   Wonders will never cease.   Air,
earth, water, the world above, the world beneath, time, eternity, worms, birds,
fishes, beasts, men, angels are all full of wonders.   The more all things are studied,
the more do wonders appear.   It is idle, therefore, to find fault with the mysteries
of Scripture, or to deny them.   Inspiration glories in them.   He who rejects the
mysteries of love, grace, truth, power, justice and faithfulness of God's word, rejects
salvation.   It has marvels in itself, and marvels in its operation.   They are good

cause of love, not of offence ; of *keeping*, not of breaking God's precepts.—*William S. Plumer.*

Verse 129.—*"My soul,"* not merely I, but I with all my heart and soul.—*Joseph Addison Alexander.*

Verse 129.—I have completed reading the whole Bible through since January last. I began it on the first day of the present year, and finished it on the the 26th of October. I have read it in that space four times, and not without real profit to myself. I always find in it something new ; it being, like its Author, infinite and inexhaustible.—*Samuel Eyles Pierce*, 1841.

Verse 129.—What do I not owe to the Lord for permitting me to take a part in the translation of his word ? Never did I see such wonders, and wisdom, and love, in the blessed book, as since I have been obliged to study every expression ; and it is a delightful reflection, that death cannot deprive us of the pleasure of studying its mysteries.—*Henry Martyn.*

Verse 130.—*"The opening of thy words enlightens, making the simple understand."* The common version of the first word (*entrance*) is inaccurate, and the one here given, though exact, is ambiguous. The clause does not refer to the mechanical opening of the book by the reader, but to the spiritual opening of its true sense by divine illumination, to the mind which naturally cannot discern it.—*Joseph Addison Alexander.*

Verse 130.—*"Entrance,"* lit. *opening, i.e.* unfolding or unveiling.—*J. J. Stewart Perowne.*

Verse 130.—*"The entrance of thy words giveth light."* The first entrance, or vestibule : for the Psalmist wishes to point out that only the beginnings are apprehended in this life ; and that these beginnings are to be preferred to all human wisdom.—*Henricus Mollerus.*

Verse 130.—*"The entrance of thy words giveth light,"* etc. The beginning of them ; the first three chapters in Genesis, what light do they give into the origin of all things ; the creation of man, his state of innocence ; his fall through the temptations of Satan, and his recovery and salvation by Christ, the seed of the woman ! The first principles of the oracles of God, the rudiments of religion, the elements of the world, the rites of the ceremonial law gave great light unto the Gospel mysteries.—*John Gill.*

Verse 130.—*"The entrance of thy words giveth light."* A profane shopman crams into his pocket a leaf of a Bible, and reads the last words of Daniel : " Go thou thy way, till the end be, for thou shalt rest and stand in thy lot at the end of the days," and begins to think what his own lot will be when days are ended. A Göttingen Professor opens a big printed Bible to see if he has eyesight enough to read it, and alights on the passage, "I will bring the blind by a way that they knew not," and in reading it the eyes of his understanding are enlightened. Cromwell's soldier opens his Bible to see how far the musket-ball has pierced, and finds it stopped at the verse : " Rejoice, O young man, in thy youth, and let thy heart cheer thee in the days of thy youth ; and walk in the ways of thine heart and the sight of thine eyes ; but know thou that for all these things God will bring thee into judgment." And in a frolic the Kentish soldier opens the Bible which his broken-hearted mother had sent him, and the first sentence that turns up is the text so familiar in boyish days : " Come unto me, all ye that labour and are heavy laden," and the weary profligate repairs for rest to Jesus Christ.—*James Hamilton*, 1814—1867.

Verse 130.—He amplifies his praise of the word of God when he saith that the entrance thereof, the first opening of the door of the word, gives light : for if the first entrance to it give light, what will the progress and continuance thereof do ? This accuseth the age wherein we live, who now of a long time hath been taught by the word of God so clearly, that in regard of time they might have been teachers of others, yet are they but children in knowledge and understanding. But to whom doth the word give understanding ? David saith to the *" simple "* : not to such as are high-minded, or double in heart, or wise in their own eyes, who will examine the mysteries of godliness by the quickness of natural reason. No : to such as deny themselves, as captive their natural understanding, and like humble disciples submit themselves, not to ask, but to hear ; not to reason, but to believe. And if for this cause, naturalists who want this humility cannot profit by the word ; what marvel that Papists far less become wise by it, who have their hearts so full of prejudices concerning it, that they spare not to utter blasphemies against it, calling it not unprofitable, but pernicious to the simple and to the idiots.

And again, where they charge it with difficulty, that simple men and idiots should not be suffered to read it, because it is obscure ; all these frivolous allegations of men are annulled by this one testimony of God, that *it gives light to the simple.*— *William Cowper.*

Verse 130.—*"Light."* This *"light"* hath excellent properties. 1. It is *lux manifestans*, it manifesteth itself and all things else. How do I see the sun, but by the sun, by its own light ? How do I know the Scripture to be the word of God, but by the light that shineth in it, commending itself to my conscience ! So it manifests all things else ; it layeth open all the frauds and impostures of Satan, the vanity of wordly things, the deceits of the heart, the odiousness of sin 2. It is *lux dirigens*, a directing light, that we may see our way and work. As the sun lighteth man to his labour, so doth this direct us in all our conditions : verse 105. It directs us how to manage ourselves in all conditions. 3. It is *lux vivificans*, a quickening light. " I am the light of the world : ·he that followeth me shall not walk in darkness, but shall have the light of life " : John viii. 12. "Awake thou that sleepest, and arise from the dead, and Christ shall give thee light " : Eph. v. 14. That light was the life of men : so is this spiritual life ; it not only discovereth the object, but helpeth the faculty, filleth the soul with life and strength. 4. It is *lux exhilarans*, a comforting, refreshing, cheering light ; and that in two respects. (1) Because it presents us with excellent grounds of comfort. (2) Because it is a soul-satisfying light.—*Condensed from Manton.*

Verse 130.—*"It giveth understanding."* If all the books in the world were assembled together, the Bible would as much take the lead in disciplining the under-standing as in directing the soul. It will not make astronomers, chemists, or linguists, but there is a great difference between strengthening the mind and storing it with information.—*Henry Melvill.*

Verse 130.—*"It giveth understanding to the simple."* There are none so knowing that God cannot blind ; none so blind and ignorant whose mind and heart his spirit cannot open. He who, by his incubation upon the waters at the creation, hatched that rude mass into the beautiful form we now see, and out of that dark chaos made the glorious heavens, and garnished them with so many orient stars, can move upon thy dark soul and enlighten it, though it be as void of knowledge as the evening of the world's first day was of light. The schoolmaster sometimes sends home the child, and bids his father to put him to another trade, because not able, with all his art, to make a scholar of him ; but if the Spirit of God be master, thou shalt learn, though a dunce : *"The entrance of thy word giveth light, it giveth understanding to the simple."* No sooner is the soul entered into the Spirit's school, than he becomes a proficient.—*William Gurnall.*

Verse 130.—*"To the simple."* He does not say, *" giveth understanding "* to the wise and prudent, to learned men, and to those skilled in letters ; but to the " simple."—*Wolfgang Musculus.*

Verse 130.—*"To the simple."* This is one great characteristic of the word of God,—however incomprehensible to the carnal mind, it is adapted to every grade of enlightened intelligence.—*W. Wilson.*

Verse 130.—*"To the simple."* The word is used sometimes in a good sense, and sometimes in a bad sense. It is used in a good sense, First, for the sincere and plain-hearted : " The Lord preserveth the simple : I was brought low, and he helped me " : Ps. cxvi. 6. " For our rejoicing is this, the testimony of our conscience, that in simplicity and godly sincerity, not with fleshly wisdom, but by the grace of God, we have had our conversation in the world, and more abundantly to you-ward " : 2 Cor. i. 12. Secondly, for those that do not oppose the presumption of carnal wisdom to the pure light of the word : so we must all be simple, or fools, that we may be wise : " If any man among you seemeth to be wise in this world, let him become a fool, that he may be wise " (1 Cor. iii. 18) ; that is, in simplicity of heart submitting to God's conduct, and believing what he hath revealed.—*Thomas Manton.*

Verse 131.—*"I opened my mouth, and panted."* By this manner of speech, David expresses, as Basil thinks, *animi propensionem*, that the inclination of his soul was after God's word. For, this opened mouth, Ambrose thinks, is *os interioris hominis*, the mouth of the inward man, which in effect is his heart ; and the speech notes *vehementem animi intensionem*, a vehement intension of his spirit, saith Euthymius. Yet shall it not be amiss to consider here how the mind of the godly earnestly affected moves the body also.   The speech may be drawn from travellers, who being very desirous to attain to their proposed ends, enforce their strength thereunto ;   and finding a weakness in their body to answer their will, they pant and open their mouth, seeking refreshment from the air to renew their strength : or as Vatablus thinks, from men exceeding hungry and thirsty, who open their mouth as if they would draw in the whole air, and then pant and sigh within themselves when they find no full refreshment by it.   So he expresseth it :   " My heart burns with so ardent a longing for thy commandments, that I am forced ever and anon to gasp by reason of my painful breathing."

However it be, it lets us see how the hearing, reading, or meditating of God's word wakened in David a most earnest affection to have the light, joy, grace, and comfort thereof communicated to his own heart.   For in the godly, knowledge of good increaseth desires ;   and it cannot be expressed how vehemently their souls long to feel that power and comfort which they know is in the word ;   and how sore they are grieved and troubled when they find it not.

And happy were we, if we could meet the Lord with this like affection ;   that when he opens his mouth, we could also open our heart to hear. as David here doth. *Christus aperit os, ut daret aliis spiritum ; David aperuit ut acciperet ;* offering his heart to receive the spirit of grace, when God openeth his mouth in his word to give it.   For it is his promise to us all—" Open thy mouth wide, and I will fill it."   Let us turn it into a prayer, that the Lord, who opened the heart of Lydia, would open our heart to receive grace when he offers by his word to give it.—*William Cowper.*

Verse 131.—"*I opened my mouth, and panted,*" etc.   There are two ways in which these words may be understood.   They may be considered as expressing the very earnest longing of the Psalmist for greater acquaintance with God in spiritual things ;   and then, in saying, "*I opened my mouth, and panted,*" he merely asserts the vehemence of his desire.   Or you may separate the clauses :   you may regard the first as the utterance of a man utterly dissatisfied with the earth and earthly things, and the second as the expression of a consciousness that God, and God only, could meet the longings of his soul.   "*I opened my mouth, and panted.*"   Out of breath, with chasing shadows, and hunting after baubles, I sit down exhausted, as far off as ever from the happiness which has been earnestly but fruitlessly sought.   Whither, then, shall I turn ?   Thy commandments, O Lord, and these alone, can satisfy the desires of an immortal being like myself;   and on these, therefore, henceforward shall my longings be turned.—*Henry Melvill.*

Verse 131.—"*I opened my mouth, and panted.*"   A metaphor taken from men scorched and sweltered with heat, or from those that have run themselves out of breath in following the thing which they would overtake.   The former metaphor expressed the vehemency of his love ;   the other the earnestness of his pursuit ;   he was like a man gasping for breath, and sucking in the cool air.—*Thomas Manton.*

Verse 131.—"*I longed for thy commandments.*"   This is a desire which God will satisfy.   " Open thy mouth wide, and I will fill it " :   Ps. lxxxi. 10.—*Thomas Manton.*

Verse 132.—"*Look thou upon me, and be merciful unto me,*" etc.   "*Look upon me,*" stripped by thieves of my virtues, and then wounded with sins, and "*be merciful unto me,*" showing compassion on me, taking care of me in the inn of the Church universal, that I fall not again among thieves, nor be harmed by the wolves which howl about this fold, but dare not enter in.   "*Look upon me,*" no longer worthy to be called thy son, and "*be merciful unto me,*" not as the jealous elder brother would treat me, but let me join the glad song and banquet of them that love thy name.   Look upon me the publican, standing afar off in thy temple the Church, and be merciful unto me, not after the Pharisee's judgment, but "*as thou usest to do unto them that love thy name,*" which is the gracious God.   Look on me as on weeping Peter, and be merciful unto me as thou wast to him, who so loved thy name as by his triple confession of love to wash out his threefold denial, saying, " Lord, thou knowest that I love thee."   "*Look upon me,*" as on the sinful woman, penitent and weeping, and be merciful unto me, not according to the judgment of the Pharisee who murmured at her, as Judas who was indignant at her, but forgiving me as thou didst her, " because she loved much," telling me also, " Thy faith hath saved thee, go in peace."—*Neale and Littledale.*

Verse 132.—"*Look thou upon me.*"   Lord !   since our looks to thee are often so slight, so cold, so distant, that no impression is made upon our hearts, do thou condescend continually to look upon us with mercy and with power. Vouchsafe us such a look, as may bring us to ourselves, and touch us with tenderness and contrition in the remembrance of that sin, unbelief, and disobedience, which pierced the hands, the feet, the heart of our dearest Lord and Saviour. Comp. Luke xxii. 61. —*Charles Bridges.*

Verse 132.—*"As thou usest to do,"* etc. David would not lose any privilege that God hath by promise settled on his children. Do with me, saith he, *"as thou usest to do."* This is no more than family fare, what thou promisest to do for all that love thee ; and let me not go worse clad than the rest of my brethren.—*William Gurnall.*

Verse 132.—*"As thou usest to do unto those,"* etc. We should be content if God deals with us as he has always dealt with his people. While he could not be satisfied with anything less than their portion, David asks for nothing better ; he implores no singular dispensation in his favour, no deviation from the accustomed methods of his grace. . . . It is always a good proof that your convictions and desires are from the operation of the Spirit when you are willing to conform to God's order. What is this order ? It is to dispense his blessings connectedly. It is never to justify without sanctifying ; never to give a title to heaven without a meetness for it. Now the man that is divinely wrought upon will not expect nor desire the one without the other. Therefore he will not expect the blessing of God without obedience ; because it is always God's way to connect the comforts of the Holy Ghost with the fear of the Lord ; and if his children transgress his laws, to visit their transgressions with a rod. Therefore he will neither expect nor desire his blessing without exertion ; for it has always been God's way to crown only those that run the race that is set before them, and fight the good fight of faith. Therefore he will not expect nor desire the Divine blessing without prayer ; for it has always been God's way to make his people sensible of their wants, and to give an answer to prayer. Therefore he will not expect nor desire to reach heaven without difficulties ; for his people have always had to deny themselves, and take up their cross. If they have not been chosen in the furnace of affliction, they have been purified. God had one Son without sin, but he never had one without sorrow : " he scourgeth every son whom he receiveth." " Yes," says the suppliant before us, " secure me their everlasting portion, and I am willing to drink of the cup they drank of, and to be baptized with the baptism they were baptized with. I want no new, no by-path to glory. I am content to keep the King's high road. *'Be merciful unto me, as thou usest to do unto those that love thy name.'* I ask no more."— *William Jay, 1769—1853.*

Verse 133.—*"Order my steps in thy word."* As before he sought mercy, so now he seeks grace. There are many that seek mercy to forgive sin, who seek not grace to deliver them from the power of sin : this is to abuse God's mercy, and turn his grace into wantonness. He that prayeth for mercy to forgive the guilt of sin only, seeks not that by sin he should not offend God ; but that he may sin and not hurt himself : but he who craves deliverance also from the commanding power and deceit of sin, seeks not only a benefit to himself, but grace also to please and serve the Lord his God. The first is but a lover of himself ; the second is a lover of God, more than of himself. And truly he never knew what it was to seek mercy for sin past, who with it also earnestly sought not grace to keep him from sin in time to come. These benefits cannot be divided : he who hath not the second (howsoever he flatter himself) may be assured that he hath not gotten the first.—*William Cowper.*

Verse 133.—*"Order my steps in thy word."* It is written of Boleslaus, one of the kings of Poland, that he still carries about him the picture of his father, and when he was to do any great work or set upon any design extraordinary, he would look on the picture and pray that he might do nothing unworthy of such a father's name. Thus it is that the Scriptures are the picture of God's will, therein drawn out to the very life. Before a man enter upon or engage himself in any business whatsoever, let him look there, and read there what is to be done ; what to be undone ; and what God commands, let that be done ; what he forbids, let that be undone ; let the balance of the sanctuary weigh all, the oracles of God decide all, the rule of God's word be the square of all, and his glory the ultimate of all intendments whatsoever.—*From Spencer's "Things New and Old."*

Verse 133.—*"Order my steps."* הכן *hachen*, make them *firm ;* let me not walk with a halting or unsteady step.—*Adam Clarke.*

Verse 133.—*"Order my steps,"* etc. The people of God would not only have their path right, but their *steps ordered;* as not their general course wrong (as those who walk in the way of everlasting perdition), so not a step awry ; they would not miss the way to heaven, either in whole or in part.—*Thomas Manton.*

Verse 133.—*"My steps."* Speaking of the steps of the Temple, Bunyan says, " These steps, whether cedar, gold, or stone, yet that which added to their adornment, was the wonderment of a Queen. And whatever they were made of, to be sure, they were a shadow of those steps, which we should take to, and in the house of God. ' Steps of God,' Ps. lxxxv. 13. ' Steps ordered by him,' Ps. xxxvii. 23. ' Steps ordered in his word,' Ps. cxix. 133. ' Steps of faith,' Rom. iv. 12. ' Steps of the spirit,' 2 Cor. xii. 18. ' Steps of truth,' 3 John 4. ' Steps washed with butter,' Job xxix. 6. ' Steps taken before, or in the presence of God.' Steps butted and bounded by a divine rule. These are steps indeed."—*John Bunyan, in "Solomon's Temple Spiritualized."*

Verse 133.—*"Let not any iniquity,"* etc. True obedience to God is inconsistent with the dominion of any one lust, or corrupt affection. I say, though a man out of some slender and insufficient touch of religion upon his heart, may go right for a while, and do many things gladly ; yet that corruption which is indulged, and under the power of which a man lieth, will at length draw off from God ; and therefore no one sin should have dominion over us. When doth sin reign, or have dominion over us ? When we do not endeavour to mortify it, and to cut off the provisions that may feed that lust. Chrysostom's observation is, the apostle does not say, let it not tyrannize over you, but, let it not reign over you ; that is, when you suffer it to have a quiet reign in your hearts.—*Thomas Manton.*

Verse 133.—*"Let not any iniquity have dominion over me."* I had rather be a prisoner to man all my life than be a bondage to sin one day. He says not, Let not this and the other man rule over me ; but " let not *sin* have dominion over me." Well said ! There is hope in such a man's condition as long as it is so.— *Michael Bruce,* 1666.

Verse 134.—*"Deliver me from the oppression of man."* 1. *"Man"* by way of *distinction.* There is the oppression and tyranny of the Devil and sin ; but the Psalmist doth not mean that now : *Hominum non dæmonum,* saith Hugo. 2. *"Man"* by way of *aggravation. Homo homini lupus :* no creatures so ravenous and destructive to one another as man. It is a shame that one man should oppress another. Beasts do not usually devour those of the same kind; but, usually, a man's enemies are those of his own household : Matt. x. 36. The nearer we are in bonds of alliance, the greater the hatred. 3. *"Man"* by way of *diminution.* And to lessen the fear of this evil, this term Adam is given them, to show their weakness in comparison of God. Thou art God ; but they that are so ready and forward to oppress and injure us are but men : thou canst easily overrule their power and break the yoke. I think this consideration chiefest, because of other places. " Who art thou, that thou shouldst be afraid of a man that shall die, and of the son of man which shall be made as grass ; and forgettest the Lord thy maker, that hath stretched forth the heavens, and laid the foundations of the earth ; and hast feared continually every day because of the fury of the oppressor, as if he were ready to destroy ? and where is the fury of the oppressor ? " Isa. li. 12, 13.— *Thomas Manton.*

Verse 134.—*"From the oppression of man."* Some render it, *"from the oppression of Adam ; "* as Jarchi observes ; and Arama interprets it of the sin of Adam, and as a prayer to be delivered or redeemed from it ; as the Lord's people are by the blood of Christ.—*John Gill.*

Verse 135.—*"Make thy face to shine upon thy servant."* The face of God shines upon us, when, in his providence, we are guided and upheld ; also when we are made to share in the good things of his providence, and when we are placed in a position wherein we can do much good. Much more does the face of God shine upon us, when we are favoured with tokens of his gracious favour ; for then we grow under the consciousness of a loving God, with rich supplies of his grace and Spirit. —*John Stephen.*

Verse 135.—*"Make thy face to shine upon thy servant."* Oftentimes the wrongful dealings of men, of others, and of ourselves, like a cloud of smoke arising from the earth and obscuring the face of the sun, hide from us for a while the light of the countenance of God : but he soon clears it all away, and looks down upon us in loving mercy as before, lighting for us the path of obedience, and brightening our way unto himself.—*"Plain Commentary,"* 1859.

Verse 135.—*"Make thy face to shine upon thy servant."* The believer's incessant cry is, Let me see "the King's face." This is a blessing worth praying for. It is his heart's desire, his present privilege, and what is infinitely better, his sure, everlasting prospect—*"They shall see his face."* Rev. xxii. 4.—*Charles Bridges.*

Verse 135.—*"Make thy face to shine . . . and teach me."* Blessed is the man whom eternal Truth teacheth, not by obscure figures and transient sounds, but by direct and full communication. The perceptions of our senses are narrow and dull, and our reason on those perceptions frequently misleads us. He whom the eternal Word condescendeth to teach is disengaged at once from the labyrinth of human opinions. For "of one word are all things"; and all things without voice or language speak of him alone : he is that divine principle which speaketh in our hearts, and without which there can be neither just apprehension nor rectitude of judgment.

O God, who art the truth, make me one with thee in everlasting life ! I am often weary of reading, and weary of hearing ; in thee alone is the sum of my desire ! Let all teachers be silent, let the whole creation be dumb before thee, and do thou only speak unto my soul !

Thy ministers can pronounce the words, but cannot impart the spirit ; they may entertain the fancy with the charms of eloquence, but if thou art silent they do not inflame the heart. They administer the letter, but thou openest the sense ; they utter the mystery, but thou revealest its meaning ; they point out the way of life, but thou bestowest strength to walk in it ; they water, but thou givest the increase. Therefore do thou, O Lord my God, Eternal Truth ! speak to my soul ! lest, being outwardly warmed, but not inwardly quickened, I die, and be found unfruitful. "Speak, Lord, for thy servant heareth." "Thou only hast the words of eternal life."—*Thomas à Kempis,* 1380—1471.

Verse 135.—*"Make thy face to shine . . . . teach me,"* etc. God hath many ways of teaching ; he teaches by book, he teaches by his fingers, he teaches by his rod ; but his most comfortable and effectual teaching is by the light of his eye : *"O send out thy light and thy truth ; let them lead me : let them bring me unto thy holy hill : "* Ps. xlii. 3.—*Richard Alleine* (1611—1681), *in "Heaven Opened."*

Verse 135.—*"Make thy face to shine . . . . teach me thy statutes."* God's children, when they beg comfort, also beg grace to serve him acceptably. For by teaching God's statutes is not meant barely a giving us a speculative knowledge of God's will ; for so David here ; *"Make thy face to shine"; and "Teach me thy statutes."*—*Thomas Manton.*

Verse 136.—*"Rivers of waters run down my eyes."* Most of the easterns shed tears much more copiously than the people of Europe. The Psalmist said *rivers of waters* ran down his eyes ; and though the language is beautifully figurative, I have no doubt it was also literally true. I have myself seen Arabs shed tears like streams.—*John Gadsby.*

Verse 136.—*"Rivers of waters run down mine eyes,"* etc. Either *because mine eyes keep not thy law,* so some. The eye is the inlet and outlet of a great deal of sin, and therefore it ought to be a weeping eye. Or rather, *they, i.e., those about me :* ver. 139. Note, the sins of sinners are the sorrows of saints. We must mourn for that which we cannot mend.—*Matthew Henry.*

Verse 136.—*"Rivers of waters run down mine eyes,"* etc. David's afflictions drew not so many tears from him as the sins of others ; not his banishment by his son, as the breach of God's law by the wicked. Nothing went so to his heart as the dishonour of God, whose glory shining in his word and ordinances, is dearer to the godly than their lives. Elijah desired to die when he saw God so dishonoured by Ahab and Jezebel. The eye is for two things, sight and tears : if we see God dishonoured, presently our eyes should be filled with tears.—*William Greenhill,* 1591—1677.

Verse 136.—*"Rivers of waters run down mine eyes,"* etc. Godly men are affected with deep sorrow for the sins of the ungodly.

Let us consider the *nature* of this affection. 1. It is not a stoical apathy, and affected carelessness ; much less a delightful partaking with sinful practices. 2. Not a proud setting off of their own goodness, with marking the sin of others as the

Pharisee did in the gospel.   3. Not the derision and mocking of the folly of men, with that " laughing philosopher " : it comes nearer to the temper of the *other* who *wept* always for it.   4. It is not a bitter, bilious anger, breaking forth into railings and reproaches, nor an upbraiding insultation.   5. Nor is it a vindictive desire of punishment, venting itself in curses and imprecations, which is the rash temper of many, but especially of the vulgar sort.   The disciples' motion to Christ was far different from that way, and yet he says to them, " Ye know not of what spirit ye are."   They thought they had been of Elijah's spirit, but he told them they were mistaken, and did not know of what a spirit they were in that motion.   Thus heady zeal often mistakes and flatters itself.   We find not here a desire of fire to come down from heaven upon the breakers of the law, but such a grief as would rather bring water to quench it, if it were falling on them.   *"Rivers of waters run down mine eyes."*—*Robert Leighton.*

Verse 136.—*"Rivers of waters run down mine eyes,"* etc.   The Lord requireth this [mourning bitterly for other men's sins] to keep our hearts the more tender and upright ; it is an act God useth to make us more careful of our own souls, to be troubled at the sins of others, at sin in a third person.   It keepeth us at a great distance from temptation.   This is like quenching of fire in a neighbour's house : before it comes near thee, thou runnest with thy bucket.   There is no way to keep us free from the infection, so much as mourning.   The soul will never agree to do that which it grieved itself to see another do.   And, as it keepeth us upright, so also humble, fearful of Divine judgment, tender lest we ourselves offend, and draw down the wrath of God.   He that shruggeth when he seeth a snake creeping upon another, will much more be afraid when it cometh near to himself.   In our own sins we have the advantage of conscience scourging the soul with remorse and shame ; in bewailing the sins of others, we have only the reasons of duty and obedience.   They that fight abroad out of love to valour and exploits, will certainly fight at home out of love to their own safety.—*Thomas Manton.*

Verse 136.—*"Rivers of waters run down mine eyes,"* etc.   Thus uniformly is the character of God's people represented—not merely as those who are *free from* —but as *" those that sigh and cry for—all the abominations that are done in the midst of the land"* : Ezek. ix. 4.   And who does not see what an enlarged sphere still presents itself on every side for the unrestrained exercise of Christian compassion ?   The appalling spectacle of a world apostatized from God, of multitudes sporting with everlasting destruction—as if the God of heaven were " a man that he should lie " is surely enough to force *"rivers of waters "* from the hearts of those that are concerned for his honour.   What a mass of sin ascends as a cloud before the Lord, from a single heart !   Add the aggregate of a village—a town—a country—a world !   every day—every hour—every moment.   Well might the *"rivers of waters "* rise to an overflowing tide, ready to burst its barriers.—*Charles Bridges.*

Verse 136.—*"Rivers of waters run down mine eyes, because they keep not thy law."* —The vices of the religious are the shame of religion : the sight of this hath made the stoutest champions of Christ melt into tears.   David was one of those great worthies of the world, not matchable in his times ; yet he weeps.   Did he tear in pieces a bear like a kid ?   Rescue a lamb with the death of a lion ?   Foil a mighty giant, that had dared the whole army of God ?   Did he like a whirlwind, bear and beat down his enemies before him ; and now, does he, like a child or a woman, fall a-weeping ?   Yes, he had heard the name of God blasphemed, seen his holy rites prophaned, his statutes vilipended, and violence offered to the pure chastity of that holy virgin, religion ; this resolved that valiant heart into tears : *"Rivers of waters run down mine eyes."*—*Thomas Adams.*

Verse 136.—My soul frequently spent itself in such breathings after conformity to the law of God as the one hundred and nineteenth Psalm is filled with throughout : " O that my ways were directed to keep thy statutes !   My heart breaketh through the longing it hath to thy commands at all times ; incline my heart that I may keep them alway unto the end," and the like.   This appeared further in a fixed dislike of the least inconformity to the law, either in myself or others.   Now ; albeit I was always suitably affected with my own or others' breaches, yet this was my burden ; I wished always that rivers of tears might run down mine eyes, because I, or other transgressors, kept not God's law.—*Thomas Halyburton, 1674—1712.*

Verse 136.—If we grieve not for others, their sin may become ours.   Ezek. ix. 8 ; 1 Cor. v. 2.—*William Nicholson.*

EXPOSITION OF VERSES 137 TO 144.

RIGHTEOUS *art* thou, O LORD, and upright *are* thy judgments.

138 Thy testimonies *that* thou hast commanded *are* righteous and very faithful.

139 My zeal hath consumed me, because mine enemies have forgotten thy words.

140 Thy word *is* very pure : therefore thy servant loveth it.

141 I *am* small and despised : *yet* do not I forget thy precepts.

142 Thy righteousness *is* an everlasting righteousness, and thy law *is* the truth.

143 Trouble and anguish have taken hold on me : *yet* thy commandments *are* my delights.

144 The righteousness of thy testimonies *is* everlasting : give me understanding, and I shall live.

This passage deals with the perfect righteousness of Jehovah and his word, and expresses the struggles of a holy soul in reference to that righteousness. The initial letter with which every verse commences sounds like the Hebrew word for *righteousness :* our keynote is righteousness.

137. "*Righteous art thou, O LORD.*" The Psalmist has not often used the name of Jehovah in this vast composition. The whole Psalm shows him to have been a deeply religious man, thoroughly familiar with the things of God ; and such persons never use the holy name of God carelessly, nor do they even use it at all frequently in comparison with the thoughtless and the ungodly. Familiarity begets reverence in this case. Here he uses the sacred name in worship. He praises God by ascribing to him perfect righteousness. God is always right, and he is always actively right, that is, righteous. This quality is bound up in our very idea of God. We cannot imagine an unrighteous God. "*And upright are thy judgments.*" Here he extols God's word, or recorded judgments, as being right, even as their Author is righteous. That which comes from the righteous God is itself righteous. Jehovah both saith and doth that which is right, and that alone. This is a great stay to the soul in time of trouble. When we are most sorely afflicted, and cannot see the reason for the dispensation, we may fall back upon this most sure and certain fact, that God is righteous, and his dealings with us are righteous too. It should be our glory to sing this brave confession when all things around us appear to suggest the contrary. This is the richest adoration—this which rises from the lips of faith when carnal reason mutters about undue severity, and the like.

138. "*Thy testimonies that thou hast commanded are righteous and very faithful.*" All that which God hath testified in his word is right and truthful. It is righteous, and may be relied upon for the present ; it is faithful, and may be trusted in for the future. About every portion of the inspired testimonies there is a divine authority, they are issued and published by God's *command*, and they bear the impress of the royal style which carries omnipotence about it. Not only the precepts but the promises also are commanded of the Lord, and so are all the teachings of Scripture. It is not left to our choice whether we will accept them or no ; they are issued by royal command, and are not to be questioned. Their characteristic is that they are like the Lord who has proclaimed them, they are the essence of justice and the soul of truth. God's word is righteous and cannot be impeached ; it is faithful and cannot be questioned ; it is true from the beginning, and it will be true unto the end.

Dwell upon that sweet word—"*very faithful.*" What a mercy that we have a God to deal with who is scrupulously faithful, true to all the items and details of his promises, punctual to time, steadfast during all time. Well may we risk all upon a word which is " ever faithful, ever sure."

139. In the last two verses David spoke concerning his God and his law ; here he speaks of himself, and says, "*My zeal hath consumed me, because mine enemies have forgotten thy words*" : this was no doubt occasioned by his having so clear a sense of the admirable character of God's word. His zeal was like a fire burning ·

within his soul. The sight of man's forgetfulness of God acted as a fierce blast to excite the fire to a more vehement flame, and it blazed until it was ready to consume him. David could not bear that men should forget God's words. He was ready to forget himself, ay, to consume himself, because these men forgot God. The ungodly were David's enemies : his enemies because they hated him for his godliness ; his enemies, because he abhorred them for their ungodliness. These men had gone so far in iniquity that they not only violated and neglected the commands of God, but they appeared actually to have forgotten them. This put David into a great heat ; he burned with indignation. How dare they trample on sacred things ! How could they utterly ignore the commands of God himself ! He was astonished, and filled with holy anger.

140. *"Thy word is very pure."* It is truth distilled, holiness in its quintessence. In the word of God there is no admixture of error or sin. It is pure in its sense, pure in its language, pure in its spirit, pure in its influence, and all this to the very highest degree—*"very* pure." *"Therefore thy servant loveth it,"* which is a proof that he himself was pure in heart, for only those who are pure love God's word because of its purity. His heart was knit to the word because of its glorious holiness and truth. He admired it, delighted in it, sought to practise it, and longed to come under its purifying power.

141. *"I am small and despised : yet do not I forget thy precepts."* That fault of forgetfulness which he condemned in others (verse 139) could not be charged upon himself. His enemies made no account of him, regarded him as a man without power or ability, and therefore looked down upon him. He appears to accept the situation and humbly take the lowest room, but he carries God's word with him. How many a man has been driven to do some ill action in order to reply to the contempt of his enemies : to make himself conspicuous he has either spoken or acted in a manner which he could not justify. The beauty of the Psalmist's piety was that it was calm and well-balanced, and as he was not carried away by flattery, so was he not overcome by shame. If small, he the more jealously attended to the smaller duties ; and if despised, he was the more in earnest to keep the despised commandments of God.

142. *"Thy righteousness is an everlasting righteousness."* Having in a previous verse ascribed righteousness to God, he now goes on to declare that that righteousness is unchanging and endures from age to age. This is the joy and glory of the saints, that what God is he always will be, and his mode of procedure towards the sons of men is immutable : having kept his promise, and dealt out justice among his people, he will do so world without end. Both the righteousnesses and the unrighteousnesses of man come to an end, but the righteousness of God is without end. *"And thy law is the truth."* As God is love, so his law is the truth, the very essence of truth, truth applied to ethics, truth in action, truth upon the judgment-seat. We hear great disputes about, " What is truth ? " The holy Scriptures are the only answer to that question. Note, that they are not only true, but the truth itself. We may not say of them that they contain the truth, but that they are the truth : " thy law is the truth." There is nothing false about the law or preceptory part of Scripture. Those who are obedient thereto shall find that they are walking in a way consistent with fact, while those who act contrary thereto are walking in a vain show.

143. *"Trouble and anguish have taken hold on me."* This affliction may have arisen from his circumstances, or from the cruelty of his enemies, or from his own internal conflicts, but certain it is that he was the subject of much distress, a distress which apprehended him, and carried him away a captive to its power. His griefs, like fierce dogs, had taken hold upon him ; he felt their teeth. He had double trouble : trouble without and anguish within, as the apostle Paul put it, " without were fightings and within were fears." *"Yet thy commandments are my delights."* Thus he became a riddle ; troubled, and yet delighted ; in anguish, and yet in pleasure. The child of God can understand this enigma, for well he knows that while he is cast down on account of what he sees within himself he is all the more lifted up by what he sees in the word. He is delighted with the commandments, although he is troubled because he cannot perfectly obey them. He finds abundant light in the commandments, and by the influence of that light he discovers and mourns over his own darkness. Only the man who is acquainted with the struggles of the spiritual life will understand the expression before us. Let the reader herein find a balance in which to weigh himself. Does he find even when he is begirt with

sorrow that it is a delightful thing to do the will of the Lord ? Does he find more joy in being sanctified than sorrow in being chastised ? Then the spot of God's children is upon him.

144. *"The righteousnesss of thy testimonies is everlasting."* First he had said that God's testimonies were righteous, then that they were everlasting, and now that their righteousness is everlasting. Thus he gives us a larger and more detailed account of the word of God the longer he is engaged in writing upon it. The more we say in praise of holy writ, the more we may say and the more we can say. God's testimonies to man cannot be assailed, they are righteous from beginning to end ; and though ungodly men have opposed the divine justice, especially in the plan of salvation, they have always failed to establish any charge against the Most High. Long as the earth shall stand long as there shall be a single intelligent creature in the universe it will be confessed that God's plans of mercy are in all respects marvellous proofs of his love of justice : even that he may be gracious Jehovah will not be unjust. *"Give me understanding and I shall live."* This is a prayer which he is constantly praying, that God would give him understanding. Here he evidently considers that such a gift is essential to his living. To live without understanding is not to live the life of a man, but to be dead while we live. Only as we know and apprehend the things of God can we be said to enter into life. The more the Lord teaches us to admire the eternal rightness of his word, and the more he quickens us to the love of such rightness, the happier and the better we shall be. As we love life, and seek many days that we may see good, it behoves us to seek immortality in the everlasting word which liveth and abideth for ever, and to seek good in that renewal of our entire nature which begins with the enlightenment of the understanding and passes on to the regeneration of the entire man. Here is our need of the Holy Spirit, the Lord and giver of life, and the guide of all the quickened ones, who shall lead us into all truth. O for the visitations of his grace at this good hour !

NOTES ON VERSES 137 TO 144.

S. Jerome, whom most of the mediævalists follow, explains *Tsaddi* as meaning *justice* or *righteousness*, which, however, is צָדֵק, *tsedek*. But he is so far right that there is a play in this strophe on the sound of the initial letter, as in the case of *Gemol ;* for the very first word, righteous, is צַדִּיק, *tsaddik*, and the whole scope of the strophe is the strong grasp which even the young and inexperienced soul can have of righteousness amidst the troubles of the world.—*Neale and Littledale.*

All these verses begin wth *Tzaddi*, the eighteenth letter of the Hebrew alphabet ; 137, 142, 144, with some form of the word which we render *righteous*, or *righteousness ;* each of the remainder with a wholly different word.—*William S. Plumer.*

Verse 137.—"*Righteous art thou, O* LORD," etc. Here David, sore troubled with grief for the wickedness of his enemies, yea, tempted greatly to impatience and distrust, by looking to their prosperous estate, notwithstanding their so gross impiety, doth now show unto us a three-fold ground of comfort, which in this dangerous temptation upheld him. The first is, a considerstion of that which God is in himself ; namely, just and righteous : the second, a consideration of the equity of his word ; the third, a view of his constant truth, declared in his working and doing according to his word. When we find ourselves tempted to distrust by looking to the prosperity of the wicked, let us look up to God, and consider his nature, his word, his works, and we shall find comfort.

"*Righteous art thou.*" This is the first ground of comfort—a meditation of the righteousness of God's nature ; he alters not with times, he changes not with persons, he is, alway and unto all, one and the same righteous and holy God. Righteousness is essential to him, it is himself ; and he can no more defraud the godly of their promised comforts, nor let the wicked go unpunished in their sins, than he can deny himself to be God, which is impossible.—*William Cowper.*

Verse 137.—"*Righteous art thou, O* LORD," etc. Essentially, originally, and of himself ; naturally, immutably and universally, in all his ways and works of nature and grace ; in his thoughts, purposes, counsels, and decrees ; in all the dispensations of his providence ; in redemption, in the justification of a sinner, in the pardon of sin, and in the gift of eternal life through Christ. "*And upright are thy judgments.*" They are according to the rules of justice and equity. He refers to the precepts of the word, the doctrines of the gospel, as well as the judgments of God inflicted on wicked men, and all the providential dealings of God with his people, and also the final judgment.—*John Gill.*

Verse 137.—"*Righteous art thou, O* LORD," etc. Here is much to keep the children of God in awe. The Lord is a righteous God : though they have found mercy and taken sanctuary in his grace, the Lord is impartial in his justice. God that did not spare the angels when they sinned, nor his Son when he was a sinner by imputation, will not spare you, though you are the dearly beloved of his soul : Prov. xi. 31. The sinful courses of God's children occasion bitterness enough ; they never venture upon sin, but with great loss. If Paul give way to a little pride, God will humble him. If any give way to sin, their pilgrimage will be made uncomfortable. Eli falls into negligence and indulgence, then is the ark of God taken, his two sons are slain in battle, his daughter-in-law dies, he himself breaks his neck. Oh ! the wonderful tragedies that sin works in the houses of the children of God ! David, when he intermeddled with forbidden fruit, was driven from his palace, his concubines defiled, his own son slain ; a great many calamities did light upon him. Therefore the children of God have cause to fear ; for the Lord is a just God, and they will find it so. Here upon earth he hath reserved liberty to visit their iniquity with rods, and their transgression with scourges. I must press you to imitate God's righteousness : " If ye know that he is righteous, ye know that every one that doeth righteousness is born of him " : 1 John ii. 29. You have a righteous God ; and this part of his character you should copy out.—*Thomas Manton.*

Verse 137.—David's great care, when he was under the afflicting hand of God, was to clear the Lord of injustice. Oh ! Lord, saith he, there is not the least show, spot, stain, blemish, or mixture of injustice, in all the afflictions thou hast brought upon me. I desire to take shame to myself, and to set to my seal, that the Lord is righteous, and that there is no injustice, no cruelty, nor no extremity in all that the Lord hath brought upon me. He sweetly and readily subscribes unto the righteousness of God in those sharp and smart afflictions that God exercised him with. *"Righteous art thou, O Lord, and upright are thy judgments."* God's judgments are always just ; he never afflicts but in faithfulness. His will is the rule of justice ; and therefore a gracious soul dares not cavil nor question his proceedings. —*Thomas Brooks.*

Verse 137.—The hundred and thirty-seventh verse, like the twenty-fifth, is associated with the sorrows of an Imperial penitent.* When the deposed and captive Emperor Maurice was led out for execution by the usurper Phocas, his five sons were previously murdered one by one in his presence ; and at each fatal blow he patiently exclaimed, *"Righteous art thou, O Lord, and upright are thy judgments."*— *Neale and Littledale.*

Verse 138.—*"Thy testimonies that thou hast commanded are righteous and very faithful."* The force of this expression is much feebler than that of the original, which literally may be rendered, " Thou hast commanded righteousness, thy testimonies, and truth exceedingly." So the Septuagint hath it. Righteousness and truth were his testimonies ; the testimonies were one with his righteousness and truth. The English translation gives *the quality of the testimonies ;* the Hebrew gives *that which is commanded ;* as if we might say, Thou hast enjoined righteousness to be thy testimonies, and truth exceedingly.—*John Stephen.*

Verse 138.—*"Thy testimonies."* The word of God is called his *testimony,* both because it testifies his will, which he will have us to do ; as also because it testifies unto men truly what shall become of them, whether good or evil. Men by nature are curious to know their end, rather than careful to mend their life ; and for this cause seek answers where they never get good : but if they would know, let me go to the word and testimony ; they need not to seek any other oracle. If the word of God testify good things unto them, they have cause to rejoice ; if otherwise it witnesseth evil unto them, let them haste to prevent it, or else it will assuredly overtake them.—*William Cowper.*

Verse 138.—*"Righteous and very faithful."* Literally, " faithfulness exceedingly." Harsh and severe as they may seem, they are all thoroughly for man's highest good.—*William Kay.*

Verse 139.—*"My zeal hath consumed me."* "Zeal" is a high degree of love ; and when the object of that love is ill treated, it venteth itself in a mixture of grief and indignation which are sufficient to wear and " consume " the heart. This will be the case where men rightly conceive of that dishonour which is continually done to God by creatures whom he hath made and redeemed. But never could the verse be uttered with such fulness of truth and propriety by any one as by the Son of God, who had such a sense of his Father's glory, and of man's sin, as no person else ever had. And, accordingly, when his zeal had exerted itself in purging the temple, St. John tells us, " his disciples remembered that it was written, The zeal of thine house hath eaten me up." The place where it is so written is Psalm lxix. 9, and the passage is exactly parallel to this before us.— *George Horne.*

Verse 139.—*"My zeal hath consumed me,"* etc. Zeal is the heat or intension of the affections ; it is a holy warmth, whereby our love and anger are drawn out to the utmost for God, and his glory. Now, our love to God and his ways, and our hatred of wickedness, should be increased, because of ungodly men. Cloudy and dark colours in a table, make those that are fresh and lively to appear more beautiful ; others' sin should make God and godliness more amiable in thine eyes. Thy heart should take fire by striking on such cold flints. David by a holy antiperistasis did kindle from others' coldness : *"My zeal hath consumed me, because mine enemies have forgotten thy words."* Cold blasts make a fire to flame the higher, and burn the hotter.—*George Swinnock.*

Verse 139.—*"My zeal hath consumed me."* The fire of zeal, like the fire which consumed Solomon's sacrifice, cometh down from heaven ; and true zealots are not those salamanders that always live in the fire of hatred and contention ; but seraphims, burning with the spiritual fire of divine love. And there true zeal inflames the desires and affections of the soul. If it be true zeal, then tract of time, multitude of discouragements, falseness of men deserting the cause, strength of oppositions, will not tire out a man's spirit. Zeal makes men resolute, difficulties are but whetstones to their fortitude, it steels men's spirits with an undaunted resolution.

---

* Gibbon. Decline and Fall ; ch. xlvi.

This was the zeal that burned in the disciples (Luke xxiv.), that consumed David here, and dried up the very marrow of Christ : John ii. 17.—*Abraham Wright.*

Verse 139.—*"My zeal hath consumed me."* There are divers kinds of zeal : there is a zeal of the world, there is a zeal of the flesh, there is a zeal of false religion, there is a zeal of heresy, and there is a zeal of the true word of God. First, we see the zeal of the world maketh men to labour day and night to get a transitory thing. The zeal of the flesh tormenteth men's minds early and late for a momentary pleasure. The zeal of heresy maketh men travel and compass sea and land, for the maintaining and increasing of their opinion. Thus we see every man is eaten up with some kind of zeal. The drunkard is consumed with drunkenness, the whore-monger is spent with his whoredom, the heretic is eaten up with heresies. Oh, how ought this to make us ashamed, who are so little eaten, spent, and consumed with the zeal of the word ! And so much the rather, because godly zeal leaveth in us an advantage and a recompence, which the worldly and carnally zealous men have not. For when they have spent all the strength of their bodies, and powers of their mind, they have no gain or comfort left, but torment of conscience ; and when they are outwardly spent, they are inwardly never the better : whereas the godly being concerned for a good thing, and eaten up with the zeal of God's glory, have this notable privilege and profit, that howsoever their outward man perisheth and decayeth, yet their inward man is still refreshed and nourished to everlasting life. Oh, what a benefit it is to be eaten up with the love and zeal of a good thing !— *Richard Greenham.*

Verse 139.—*"Have forgotten thy words."* A proper phrase to set forth those in the bosom of the visible church who do not wholly deny and reject the word and rule of Scripture, but yet live on as though they had forgotten it : they do not observe it ; as if God had never spoken any such thing, or given them any such rule. They that reject and condemn such things as the word enforceth, surely do not remember to do them.—*Thomas Manton.*

Verse 140.—*"Thy word is very pure."* In the original, " tried, refined, purified, like gold in the furnace," absolutely perfect, without the dross of vanity and fallibility, which runs through human writings. The more we try the promises, the surer we shall find them. Pure gold is so fixed, that Boerhaave informs us of an ounce of it set in the eye of a glass furnace for two months, without losing a single grain.—*George Horne.*

Verse 140.—*"Thy word is very pure ; therefore,"* etc. The word of God is not only *"pure,"* free from all base admixture, but it is a *purifier ;* it cleanses from sin and guilt every heart with which it comes into contact. " Now ye are clean," said Jesus Christ to his disciples, " by the word which I have spoken unto you " : John xv. 3. It is this its pure quality combined with its tendency to purify every nature that yields to its holy influence, that endears it to every child of God. Here it is that he finds views of the divine character, those promises, those precepts, those representations of the deformity of sin, of the beauty of holiness, which lead him, above all things, to seek conformity to the divine image. A child of God in his best moments does not wish the word of God brought down to a level with his own imperfect character, but desires rather that his character may be gradually raised to a conformity to that blessed word. Because it is altogether pure, and because it tends to convey to those who make it their constant study a measure of its own purity, the child of God loves it, and delights to meditate in it day and night.— *John Morison.*

Verse 140.—*"Thy word is very pure."* Before I knew the word of God in spirit and in truth, for its great antiquity, its interesting narratives, its impartial biography, its pure morality, its sublime poetry, in a word, for its beautiful and wonderful variety, I preferred it to all other books ; but since I have entered into its spirit, like the Psalmist, I love it above all things for its purity ; and desire, whatever else I read, it may tend to increase my knowledge of the Bible, and strengthen my affection for its divine and holy truths.—*Sir William Jones,* 1746—1794.

Verse 140.—*"Thy word."* Let us refresh our minds and our memories with some of the Scripture adjuncts connected with " the word," and realize, in some degree at least, the manifold relations which it bears both to God and our souls. It is called " the word of Christ," because much of it was given by him, and it all bears testimony to him . . . . It is called " the word of his grace," because the glorious theme on which it loves to expatiate is *grace,* and especially grace as it is seen in Christ's dying love for sinful men. It is called ὁ λόγος τοῦ σταυροῦ, "the word of the cross" (1 Cor. i. 18), because in the crucifixion of the divine Redeemer we see eternal mercy in its brightest lustre. It is called "the word of the gospel," because it brings glad tidings of great joy to all nations. It is called "the word of the kingdom," because it holds out to all believers the hope of an everlasting kingdom of righteousness and peace. It is called "the word of salvation," because the purpose for which it was given is the salvation of sinners. It is called "the word of truth," because, as Chillingworth says, it has God for its author, salvation for its end, and truth without mixture of error for its contents. And we will only add, it is called "the word of life," because it reveals to a sinful, perishing world the doctrines of life and immortality.—*W. Graham, in "A Commentary on the First Epistle of John,"* 1857.

Verse 140.—*"Therefore thy servant loveth it."* Love in God is the fountain of all his benefits extended to us; and love in man is the fountain of all our service and obedience to God. He loved us first to do us good; and hereof it comes that we have grace to love him next to do him service. Love is such a duty that the want thereof cannot be excused in any; for the poorest both may and should love God: yet without it all the rest thou canst do in his service is nothing; nay, not if thou shouldst give thy goods to the poor, and offer thy body to be burned. Small sacrifices, flowing from faith and love, are welcome to him, where greater without these are but abomination to him. Proofs of both we have in the widow's mite and Cain's rich oblation; whereof the one was rejected, the other received. Happy are we though we cannot say, "We have done as God commands," if out of a good heart we can say,—"We love to do what he commands."—*William Cowper.*

Verse 140.—*"Therefore thy servant loveth it."* Of all our grounds and reasons of love to the word of God, the most noble and excellent is to love the word for its purity. This showeth indeed that we are made partakers of the Divine nature: 2 Pet. i. 4. For I pray you mark, when we hate evil as evil, and love good as good, we have the same love and hatred that God hath. When once we come to love things because they are pure, it is a sign that we have the same love that God hath.—*Thomas Manton.*

Verse 140.—*"Thy servant loveth it."* Otherwise, indeed, the Psalmist would not have been the Lord's servant at all. But he glories in the title because he delights in the pure service.—*John Stephen.*

Verses 140, 141.—God's own utterance is indeed without spot, and therefore not to be carped at; it is pure, fire-proved, noblest metal, therefore he loves it, and does not, though young and lightly esteemed, care for the remonstrances of his proud opponents who are older and more learned than himself.—*Franz Delitzsch.*

Verse 141.—*"I am small and despised,"* or, *I have been.* Some versions render it *young*; as if it had respect to the time of his anointing by Samuel, when he was overlooked and despised in his father's family (1 Sam. xvi. 11, and xvii. 28); but the word here used is not expressive of age, but of state, condition, and circumstances; and the meaning is, that he was little in his own esteem, and in the esteem of men, and was despised; and that on account of religion, in which he was a type of Christ (Ps. xxii. 6, and Isa. liii. 3), and which is the common lot of good men, who are treated by the world as the filth of it, and the offscouring of all things.—*John Gill.*

Verse 141.—*"I am small."* They that love God may be reduced to a mean, low, and afflicted condition; the Lord seeth it meet for divers reasons: 1. That they may know their happiness is not in this world, and so the more long for heaven, and delight in heavenly things. 2. It is necessary to cut off the provisions of the flesh and the fuel of their lusts. A rank soil breedeth weeds; and when we sail with a full stream we are apt to be carried away with it. 3. That they may be more sensible of his displeasure against their sins and scandalous carriage by which they have dishonoured him, and provoked the pure eyes of his glory. 4. That they may learn to live upon the promises, and learn to exercise suffering graces; especially dependence upon God, who can support us without a temporal, visible interest. 5. That God may convince the enemies that there is a people that do sincerely serve him, and not for carnal, selfish ends: Job i. 6. That his glory may be more seen in their deliverance; and therefore, before God doth appear for his children, he bringeth them very low.—*Thomas Manton.*

Verse 141.—*"Small."* This applies to David in his early days of trouble and persecution. It is difficult to find any other individual to whom it is so suitable.—*James G. Murphy.*

Verse 141.—A notable example to the shame of them, that perhaps will serve and praise God in their prosperity, and when they are increased; but let affliction or want come, and then they have little heart to do it.—*Abraham Wright.*

Verse 141.—"*Yet do not I forget thy precepts.*" God observeth what we do in our trouble: "If we have forgotten the name of our God, or stretched out our hands to a strange god; shall not God search this out? for he knoweth the secrets of the heart"; Ps. xliv. 20, 21. If we slacken our service to God, or fall off to any degree of apostasy, the Judge of hearts knoweth all: God knoweth whether we would have depraved and corrupt doctrine, worship, or ordinances; or whether we will faithfully adhere to him, to his word, and worship, and ordinances, whatever it cost us.

In our poor and despicable condition we see more cause to love the word than we did before; because we experience supports and comforts which we have thereby: "Knowing that tribulation worketh patience," etc. (Rom. v. 3); "For as the sufferings of Christ abound in us, so our consolation also aboundeth by Christ": 2 Cor. i. 5. God hath special consolations for his afflicted and despised people, and makes their consolation by Christ to run parallel with, and keep pace with, their sufferings for Christ.—*Thomas Manton.*

Verse 141.—"*Yet do not I forget thy precepts.*" We see by experience that our affection leaves anything from the time it goes out of our remembrance. We cease to love when we cease to remember; but earnest love ever renews remembrance of that which is beloved. The first step of defection is to forget what God hath commanded, and what we are obliged in duty to do to him; and upon this easily follows the offending of God by our transgression. Such beasts as did not chew their cud, under the law were accounted unclean, and not meet to be sacrificed unto God: that was but a figure, signifying unto us that a man who hath received good things from God, and doth not think upon them, cannot feel the sweetness of them, and so cannot be thankful to God.—*William Cowper.*

Verse 142.—"*Thy righteousness is an everlasting righteousness.*" Here the law of God is honoured by the additional encomium, that it is everlasting righteousness and truth; as if it had been said, that all other rules of life, with whatever attractions they may appear to be recommended, are but a shadow, which quickly vanishes away. The Psalmist, no doubt, indirectly contrasts the doctrine of the law with all the human precepts which were ever delivered, that he may bring all the faithful in subjection to it, since it is the school of perfect wisdom. There may be more of plausibility in the refined and subtle disquisitions of men; but there is in them nothing firm or solid at bottom, as there is in God's law. This firmness of the divine law he proves in the following verse from one instance—the continual comfort he found in it when grievously harassed with temptations. And the true test of the profit we have reaped from it is, when we oppose to all the distresses of whatever kind which may straiten us, the consolation derived from the word of God, that thereby all sadness may be effaced from our minds. David here expresses something more than he did in the preceding verse; for there he only said that he reverently served God, although from his rough and hard treatment he might seem to lose his labour; but now when distressed and tormented, he affirms that he finds in the law of God the most soothing delight, which mitigates all griefs, and not only tempers their bitterness, but also seasons them with a certain sweetness. Assuredly when this taste does not exist to afford us delight, nothing is more natural than for us to be swallowed up of sorrow.—*John Calvin.*

Verse 142.—"*Thy righteousness is an everlasting righteousness.*" Not only righteous at the first giving out, but righteous in all ages and times; and should we slight this rule that will hold for ever? In the world new lords, new laws; men vary and change their designs and purposes; privileges granted to-day may be repealed to-morrow; but this word will hold true for ever. Our justification by Christ is irrevocable; that part of righteousness is everlasting. Be sure you are justified now upon terms of the gospel, and you shall be justified for ever: your forgiveness is an everlasting forgiveness, and your peace is an everlasting peace: "I will remember their sin no more": Jer. xxxi. 34. So the other righteousness of sanctification, it is for ever; approve yourselves to God now, and you will approve yourselves at the day of judgment.—*Thomas Manton.*

Verse 142.—"*Thy righteousness is an everlasting righteousness,*" etc. The original is better expressed thus, " Thy righteousness is righteousness everlastingly, and thy law is truth." So the Septuagint. The English translation expresses the *perpetuity* of the righteousness, the original expresses also the *character* of it. . . . God's righteousness is essentially and eternally righteousness. The expressions are absolute ; there is only this righteousness, and only this truth.—*John Stephen.*

Verse 142.—"*Thy law is the truth.*" 1. It is the *chief* truth. There is some truth in the laws of men and the writings of men, even of heathens ; but they are but sorry fragments and scraps of truth, that have escaped since the fall. 2. It is the *only* truth ; that is, the only revelation of the mind of God that you can build upon. It is the rule of truth. 3. It is the *pure* truth. In it there is nothing but the truth, without the mixture of falsehood ; every part is true as truth itself. It is true in the promises, threatenings, doctrines, histories, precepts, prohibitions. 4. It is *the whole* truth. It containeth all things necessary for the salvation of those that yield up themselves to be instructed by it.—*Thomas Manton.*

Verse 143.—"*Trouble and anguish have taken hold on me : yet thy commandments are my delights.*" This is strange, that in the midst of anguish David had *delight :* but indeed the sweetness of God's word is best perceived under the bitterness of the cross. The joy of Christ and the joy of the world cannot consist together. A heart delighted with worldly joy cannot feel the consolations of the Spirit ; the one of these destroys the other ; but in sanctified trouble, the comforts of God's word are felt and perceived in a most sensible manner. Many a time hath David protested this delight of his in the word of God ; and truly it is a great argument of godliness, when men come not only to reverence it, but to love it, and delight in it. Let this be considered by those unhappy men who hear it of custom, and count it but a weariness.—*Abraham Wright.*

Verse 143.—"*Trouble and anguish have taken hold on me,*" or "*found me,*" etc. We need not take pains, as many do, " to find trouble and anguish ; " for they will, one day, " find us." In that day the revelations of God must be to us instead of all worldly " delights " and pleasures, which will then have forsaken us ; and how forlorn and desolate will be our state if we should have no other delights, no other pleasures, to succeed them, and to accompany us into eternity ! Let our study be then in the Scriptures, if we expect our comfort in them in time to come.—*George Horne.*

Verse 143.—"*Trouble and anguish have taken hold on me.*" You may conceive a bold figure here, as if Trouble and Anguish were being sent out against the helpless sons of men. These, like enemies, were going round. Instead of seizing upon the wicked, they had found the righteous man. So it was by the ordering of God. I suppose many of us have remarked, that the believer is never long at ease. He is in the world ; he is in the flesh ; there is indwelling sin ; there are enemies around ; there is the great enemy ; besides all this, the Lord, for wise purposes, hides his face. Then the believer is in trouble and anguish.—*John Stephen.*

Verse 143.—"*Have taken hold on me.*" Hebrew, *found me.* Like dogs tracking out a wild beast hiding or fleeing.—*A. R. Fausset.*

Verse 143.—"*Thy commandments are my delights.*" Delight in moral things (saith Aquinas) is the rule by which we may judge of men's goodness or badness. *Delectatio est quies voluntatis in bono.* Men are good and bad, as the objects of their delight are : they are good who delight in good things, and they are evil who delight in evil things.—*Thomas Manton.*

Verse 144.—"*The righteousness of thy testimonies is everlasting.*" Thy *moral law* was not made for one people, or for one particular time ; it is as imperishable as thy nature, and of endless obligation. It is that law by which all the children of Adam shall be judged. "*Give me understanding.*" To know and practise it. "*And I shall live.*" Shall glorify thee, and live eternally ; not for the *merit* of having done it, but because thou didst fulfil the work of the law in my heart, having saved me from condemnation by it.—*Adam Clarke.*

Verse 144.—"*Give me understanding, and I shall live.*" I read it in connection with the preceding clause ; for although David desires to have his mind enlightened by God, yet he does not conceive of any other way by which he was to obtain an enlightened understanding than by his profiting aright in the study of the law. Further, he here teaches that men cannot, properly speaking, be said to live when they are destitute of the light of heavenly wisdom ; and as the end for which men are created is not that, like swine or asses, they may stuff their bellies, but that they may exercise themselves in the knowledge and service of God, when they turn away from such employment their life is worse than a thousand deaths. David therefore protests that for him to live was not merely to be fed with meat and drink, and to enjoy earthly comforts, but to aspire after a better life, which he could not do save under the guidance of faith. This is a very necessary warning ; for although it is universally acknowledged that man is born with this distinction, that he excels the lower animals in intelligence, yet the great bulk of mankind, as if with deliberate purpose, stifle whatever light God pours into their understandings. I indeed admit that all men desire to be sharp-witted ; but how few aspire to heaven, and consider that the fear of God is the beginning of wisdom. Since, then, meditation upon the celestial life is buried by earthly care, men do nothing else than plunge into the grave, so that while living to the world, they die to God. Under the term life, however, the prophet denotes the utmost he could wish. Lord, as if he had said, although I am already dead, yet if thou art pleased to illumine my mind with the knowledge of heavenly truth, this grace alone will be sufficient to revive me.—*John Calvin.*

Verse 144.—*"Give me understanding, and I shall live."* The saving knowledge of God's testimonies is the only way to live. There is a threefold life. 1. Life natural. 2. Life spiritual, and, 3. Life eternal. In all these considerations may the point be made good.

First. Life is taken for the *life of nature,* or the life of the body, or life temporal, called " this life " in Scripture : 1 Cor. xv. 19 ; 1 Tim. iv. 8. Life is better preserved in a way of obedience than by evil-doing ; that provoketh God to cast us off, and exposes us to dangers. It is not in the power of the world to make us live or die a day sooner or longer than God pleaseth. If God will make us happy, they cannot make us miserable : therefore, *"Give me understanding, and I shall live" ;* that is, lead a comfortable and happy life for the present. Prevent sin, and you prevent danger. Obedience is the best way to preserve life temporal : as great a paradox as it seems to the world, it is a Scripture truth, " Keep my commandments, and live " (Prov. iv. 4) ; and, " Take fast hold of instruction ; let her not go : keep her ; for she is thy life " (verse 13) ; and, " Length of days is in her right hand ; and in her left hand riches and honour " (Prov. iii. 16) ; and, " She is a tree of life " (verse 18). The knowledge and practice of the word is the only means to live comfortably and happily here, as well as for ever hereafter.

Secondly. *Life spiritual ;* that is twofold, the life of justification, and the life of sanctification.

1. The life of justification : " The free gift came upon all men unto justification of life " : Rom. v. 18. He is dead, not only on whom the hangman hath done his work, but also he on whom the judge hath passed sentence, and the law pronounceth him dead. In this sense we were all dead, and justification is called justification to life ; there is no living in this sense without knowledge : " By his knowledge shall my righteous servant justify many " : Isa. liii. 11. We live by faith, and faith cometh by hearing, and hearing doeth no good unless the Lord giveth understanding ; as meats nourish not unless received and digested.

2. The life of sanctification : " And you hath he quickened, who were dead in trespasses and sins " : Eph. ii. 1. And men live not properly till they live the life of grace ; they live a false, counterfeit life, not a blessed, happy, certain, and true life. Now this life is begun and carried on by saving knowledge : " The new man which is renewed in knowledge": Col. iii. 10. Again, men are said to be " alienated from the life of God through the ignorance that is in them : " Eph. iv. 18. They that are ignorant are dead in sin : life spiritual cometh by knowledge. Hence beginneth the change of the inward man, and thenceforth we live. *"Give me understanding," ut vere in te vivam,* that the true life begun in me may grow and increase daily, but never be quenched by sin.

Thirdly. *Life everlasting,* or our blessed estate in heaven. So it is said of the saints departed, they all live unto God : Luke xx. 38. And this is called the water of life, the tree of life, the crown of life ; properly this is life. What is the present life in comparison of everlasting life ? The present life, it is *mors vitalis,* a living death ; or *mortalis vita,* a dying life, a kind of death ; it is always *in fluxu,* like a stream : it runneth from us as fast as it cometh to us: " He fleeth also as a shadow and continueth not " : Job. xiv. 2. We die as fast as we live: it differeth but as the point from the line where it terminateth. It is not one and the same, no permanent thing; it is like the shadow of a star in a flowing stream. Its contentments are base and low, called " the life of thine hand " : Isa. lvii. 10. It is patched up of several creatures, fain to ransack the storehouses of nature to support a ruinous fabric. And compare it with the life of grace here, it doth not exempt us from sin, nor miseries. Our capacities are narrow. We are full of fears, and doubts, and dangers ; but in the life of glory we shall neither sin nor sorrow any more. This is meant here : *"The righteousness of thy testimonies is everlasting : give me understanding and I shall live "* ; it is chiefly meant of the life of glory. This is the fruit of saving knowledge, when we so know God and Christ as to come to God by him.—*Thomas Manton.*

Verse 144.—*"I shall live."* I shall be kept from those sins which deserve and bring death.—*Matthew Pool.*

EXPOSITION OF VERSES 145 TO 152.

I CRIED with *my* whole heart ; hear me, O LORD : I will keep thy statutes.

146 I cried unto thee ; save me, and I shall keep thy testimonies.

147 I prevented the dawning of the morning, and cried : I hoped in thy word.

148 Mine eyes prevent the *night* watches, that I might meditate in thy word.

149 Hear my voice according unto thy lovingkindness : O LORD, quicken me according to thy judgment.

150 They draw nigh that follow after mischief : they are far from thy law.

151 Thou *art* near, O LORD ; and all thy commandments *are* truth.

152 Concerning thy testimonies, I have known of old that thou hast founded them for ever.

This section is given up to memories of prayer. The Psalmist describes the time and the manner of his devotions, and pleads with God for deliverance from his troubles. He who has been with God in the closet will find God with him in the furnace. If we have cried we shall be answered. Delayed answers may drive us to importunity ; but we need not fear the ultimate result, since God's promises are not uncertain, but are " founded for ever." The whole passage shows us : How he prayed (verse 145). What he prayed for (146). When he prayed (147). How long he prayed (148). What he pleaded (149). What happened (150). How he was rescued (151). What was his witness as to the whole matter (152).

145.—"*I cried with my whole heart.*" His prayer was a sincere, plaintive, painful, natural utterance, as of a creature in pain. We cannot tell whether at all times he used his voice when he thus cried ; but we are informed of something which is of much greater consequence, he cried with his heart. Heart-cries are the essence of prayer. He mentions the unity of his heart in this holy engagement. His whole soul pleaded with God, his entire affections, his united desires all went out towards the living God. It is well when a man can say as much as this of his prayers : it is to be feared that many never cried to God with their whole heart in all their lives. There may be no beauty of elocution about such prayers, no length of expression, no depth of doctrine, nor accuracy of diction ; but if the whole heart be in them they will find their way to the heart of God. "*Hear me, O* LORD." He desires of Jehovah that his cries may not die upon the air, but that God may have respect to them. True supplicants are not satisfied with the exercise itself, they have an end and object in praying, and they look out for it. If God does not hear prayer we pray in vain. The term " hear " is often used in Scripture to express attention and consideration. In one sense God hears every sound that is made on earth, and every desire of every heart ; but David meant much more ; he desired a kindly, sympathetic hearing, such as a physician gives to his patient when he tells him his pitiful story. He asked that the Lord would draw near, and listen with friendly ear to the voice of his complaint, with the view of pitying him and helping him. Observe, that his whole-hearted prayer goes to the Lord alone ; he has no second hope or help. " Hear me, O LORD," is the full range of his petition and expectation. "*I will keep thy statutes.*" He could not expect the Lord to hear him if he did not hear the Lord, neither would it be true that he prayed with his whole heart unless it was manifest that he laboured with all his might to be obedient to the divine will. His object in seeking deliverance was that he might be free to fulfil his religion and carry out every ordinance of the Lord. He would be a free man that he might be at liberty to serve the Lord. Note well that a holy resolution goes well with an importunate supplication : David is determined to be holy, his whole heart goes with that resolve as well as with his prayers. He will keep God's statutes in his memory, in his affections, and in his actions. He will not wilfully neglect or violate any one of the divine laws.

146.—*"I cried unto thee."* Again he mentions that his prayer was unto God alone. The sentence imports that he prayed vehemently, and very often ; and that it had become one of the greatest facts of his life that he cried unto God. *"Save me."* This was his prayer ; very short, but very full. He needed saving, none but the Lord could save him, to him he cried, " Save me " from the dangers which surround me, from the enemies that pursue me, from the temptations which beset me, from the sins which accuse me. He did not multiply words, and men never do so when they are in downright earnest. He did not multiply objects, and men seldom do so when they are intent upon the one thing needful : " save me " was his one and only prayer. *"And I shall keep thy testimonies."* This was his great object in desiring salvation, that he might be able to continue in a blameless life of obedience to God, that he might be able to believe the witness of God, and also to become himself a witness for God. It is a great thing when men seek salvation for so high an end. He did not ask to be delivered that he might sin with impunity ; his cry was to be delivered from sin itself. He had vowed to keep the statutes or laws, here he resolves to keep the testimonies or doctrines, and so to be sound of head as well as clean of hand. Salvation brings all these good things in its train. David had no idea of a salvation which would allow him to live in sin, or abide in error : he knew right well that there is no saving a man while he abides in disobedience and ignorance.

147.—*"I prevented the dawning of the morning, and cried."* He was up before the sun, and began his pleadings before the dew began to leave the grass. Whatever is worth doing is worth doing speedily. This is the third time that he mentions that he cried. He cried, and cried, and cried again. His supplications had become so frequent, fervent, and intense, that he might hardly be said to be doing anything else from morning to night but crying unto his God. So strong was his desire after salvation that he could not rest in his bed ; so eagerly did he seek it that at the first possible moment he was on his knees. *"I hoped in thy word."* Hope is a very powerful means of strengthening us in prayer. Who would pray if he had no hope that God would hear him ? Who would not pray when he has a good hope of a blessed issue to his entreaties ? His hope was fixed upon God's word, and this is a sure anchorage, because God is true, and in no case has he ever run back from his promise, or altered the thing that has gone forth from his mouth. He who is diligent in prayer will never be destitute of hope. Observe that as the early bird gets the worm, so the early prayer is soon refreshed with hope.

148.—*"Mine eyes prevent the night watches."* Or rather, *the watches.* Before the watchman cried the hour, he was crying to God. He did not need to be informed as to how the hours were flying, for every hour his heart was flying towards heaven. He began the day with prayer, and he continued in prayer through the watches of the day, and the watches of the night. The soldiers changed guard, but David did not change his holy occupation. Specially, however, at night did he keep his eyes open, and drive away sleep, that he might maintain communion with his God. He worshipped on from watch to watch as travellers journey from stage to stage. *"That I might meditate in thy word."* This had become meat and drink to him. Meditation was the food of his hope, and the solace of his sorrow : the one theme upon which his thoughts ran was that blessed " word " which he continually mentions, and in which his heart rejoices. He preferred study to slumber ; and he learned to forego his necessary sleep for much more necessary devotion. It is instructive to find meditation so constantly connected with fervent prayer : it is the fuel which sustains the flame. How rare an article is it in these days.

149.—*"Hear my voice according unto thy lovingkindness."* Men find it very helpful to use their voices in prayer ; it is difficult long to maintain the intensity of devotion unless we hear ourselves speak ; hence David at length broke through his silence, arose from his quiet meditations, and began crying with voice as well as heart unto the Lord his God. Note, that he does not plead his own deservings, nor for a moment appeal for payment of a debt on account of merit ; he takes the free-grace way, and puts it, " according unto thy lovingkindness." When God hears prayer according to his lovingkindness he overlooks all the imperfections of the prayer, he forgets the sinfulness of the offerer, and in pitying love he grants the desire though the suppliant be unworthy. It is according to God's lovingkindness to answer speedily, to answer frequently, to answer abundantly, yea, exceeding abundantly above all that we ask or even think. Lovingkindness is one of the sweetest words in our language. Kindness has much in it that is most precious, but lovingkindness is doubly dear ; it is the cream of kindness. *"O LORD, quicken me according to thy judgment."* This is another of David's wise and ardent prayers. He first cried, " Save me ; " then, " Hear me ; " and now, " Quicken me." This is often the very best way of delivering us from trouble,—to give us more life that we may escape from death ; and to add more strength to that life that we may not be overloaded with its burdens. Observe, that he asks to receive quickening according to God's judgment, that is, in such a way as should be consistent with infinite wisdom and prudence. God's methods of communicating greater vigour to our spiritual life are exceedingly wise ; it would probably be in vain for us to attempt to understand them ; and it will be our wisdom to wish to receive grace, not according to our notion of how it should come to us, but according to God's heavenly method of bestowing it. It is his prerogative to make alive as well as to kill, and that sovereign act is best left to his infallible judgment. Hath he not already given us to have life more and more abundantly ? " Wherein he hath abounded toward us in all wisdom and prudence."

150.—*"They draw nigh that follow after mischief."* He could hear their footfalls close behind him. They are not following him for his benefit, but for his hurt, and therefore the sound of their approach is to be dreaded. They are not prosecuting a good object, but persecuting a good man. As if they had not enough mischief in their own hearts, they are hunting after more. He sees them going a steeple-chase over hedge and ditch in order to bring mischief to himself, and he points them out to God, and entreats the Lord to fix his eyes upon them, and deal with them to their confusion. They were already upon him, and he was almost in their grip, and therefore he cries the more earnestly. *"They are far from thy law."* A mischievous life cannot be an obedient one. Before these men could become persecutors of David they were obliged to get away from the restraints of God's law. They could not hate a saint and yet love the law. Those who keep God's law neither do harm to themselves nor to others. Sin is the greatest mischief in the world. David mentions this to the Lord in prayer, feeling some kind of comfort in the fact that those who hated him hated God also, and found it needful to get away from God before they could be free to act their cruel parts towards himself. When we know that our enemies are God's enemies, and ours because they are his, we may well take comfort to ourselves.

151. *"Thou art near, O LORD."* Near as the enemy might be, God was nearer : this is one of the choicest comforts of the persecuted child of God. The Lord is near to hear our cries, and to speedily afford us succour. He is near to chase away our enemies, and to give us rest and peace. *"And all thy commandments are truth."* God neither commands a lie, nor lies in his commands. Virtue is truth in action, and this is what God commands. Sin is falsehood in action, and this is what God forbids. If all God's commands are truth, then the true man will be glad to keep near to them, and therein he will find the true God near him. This sentence will be the persecuted man's protection from the false hearts that seek to do him mischief: God is near and God is true, therefore his people are safe. If at any time we fall into danger through keeping the commands of God we need not suppose that we have acted unwisely : we may, on the contrary, be quite sure that we are in the right way ; for God's precepts are right and true. It is for this very reason that wicked men assail us : they hate the truth, and therefore hate those who do the truth. Their opposition may be our consolation ; while God's presence upon our side is our glory and delight.

152. *"Concerning thy testimonies, I have known of old that thou hast founded them for ever."* David found of old that God had founded them of old, and that they would stand firm throughout all ages. It is a very blessed thing to be so early taught of God that we know substantial doctrines even from our youth. Those who think that David was a young man when he wrote this Psalm will find it rather difficult to reconcile this verse with the theory ; it is much more probable that he was now grown grey, and was looking back upon what he had known long before. He knew at the very first that the doctrines of God's word were settled before the world began, that they had never altered, and never could by any possibility be altered. He had begun by building on a rock, by seeing that God's testimonies

were " founded," that is, grounded, laid as foundations, settled and established ;
and that with a view to all the ages that should come, during all the changes that
should intervene. It was because David knew this that he had such confidence
in prayer, and was so importunate in it. It is sweet to plead immutable promises
with an immutable God. It was because of this that David learned to hope : a
man cannot have much expectation from a changing friend, but he may well have
confidence in a God who cannot change. It was because of this that he delighted
in being near the Lord, for it is a most blessed thing to keep up close intercourse
with a Friend who never varies. Let those who choose follow at the heels of the
modern school and look for fresh light to break forth which will put the old light
out of countenance ; we are satisfied with the truth which is old as the hills and
as fixed as the great mountains. Let " cultured intellects " invent another god, more
gentle and effeminate than the God of Abraham ; we are well content to worship
Jehovah, who is eternally the same. Things everlastingly established are the joy
of established saints. Bubbles please boys, but men prize those things which are
solid and substantial, with a foundation and a bottom to them which will bear the
test of ages.

NOTES ON VERSES 145 TO 152.

Verse 145.—*"I cried with my whole heart."* As a man cries most loudly when he cries with all his mouth opened ; so a man prays most effectually when he prays with his whole heart. Neither doth this speech declare only the fervency of his affection ; but it imports also that it was a great thing which he sought from God. And thou, when thou prayest, pray for great things ; for things enduring, not for things perishing : pray not for silver, it is but rust ; nor for gold, it is but metal ; nor for possessions, they are but earth. Such prayer ascends not to God. He is a great God, and esteems himself dishonoured when great things with great affection are not sought from him.—*William Cowper.*

Verse 145.—*" I cried with my whole heart."* In all your closet duties God looks first and most to your *hearts*: " My son, give me thine heart ": Prov. xxiii. 26. It is not a piece, it is not a corner of the heart, that will satisfy the Maker of the heart ; the heart is a treasure, a bed of spices, a royal throne wherein he delights. God looks not at the elegancy of your prayers, to see how neat they are ; nor yet at the geometry of your prayers, to see how long they are ; nor yet at the arithmetic of your prayers, to see how many they are ; nor yet at the music of your prayers, nor yet at the sweetness of your voice, nor yet at the logic of your prayers ; but at the sincerity of your prayers, how hearty they are. There is no prayer acknowledged, approved, accepted, recorded, or rewarded by God, but that wherein the heart is sincerely and wholly. The true mother would not have the child divided. God loves a broken and a contrite heart, so he loathes a divided heart : Ps. li. 17 ; James i. 8. God neither loves halting nor halving ; he will be served truly and totally. The royal law is, " Thou shalt love and serve the Lord thy God with all they heart, and with all thy soul." Among the heathens, when the beasts were cut up for sacrifice, the first thing the priest looked upon was the heart, and if the heart was naught, the sacrifice was rejected. Verily, God rejects all those sacrifices wherein the heart is not. Prayer without the heart is but as sounding brass or a tinkling cymbal. Prayer is only lovely and weighty, as the heart is in it, and no otherwise. It is not lifting up of the voice, nor the wringing of the hands, nor the beating of the breasts, nor an affected tone, nor studied motions, nor seraphical expressions, but the strings of the heart, that God looks at in prayer. God hears no more than the heart speaks. If the heart be dumb, God will certainly be deaf. No prayer takes with God, but that which is the travail of the heart.—*Thomas Brooks.*

Verse 146.—*"I cried unto thee."* The distressed soul expresses itself in strong cries and tears. Of old they cried unto the Lord, and he heard them in their distress. So Israel at the Red Sea. The men of the Reformation thus expressed themselves in earnest prayer, and found relief. Luther at the Diet of Worms, when remanded for another day, spent the long night in the loud utterance of prayer that he might appear for his Lord before an august earthly assembly. Our reading of the covenanting times will remind us of many instances of the same. We may think of John Welch, going into his garden night after night, in a night covering, and crying to the Lord to grant him Scotland. The expression of prayer, however, is manifold as the frame of the spirit. Intense feeling will beget strong cries in prayer ; but prayer that is uttered under realizing views of our gracious God will be mild, and often delivered as it were in whispers. So was Alexander Peden accustomed to pray, as if he had been engaged in calm converse with a friend. . . . . But when the feeling is intense, when wrath lies heavy upon us, when danger is apprehended as near, when the Lord is conceived to be at a distance, or when there is eager desire after immediate attainment—in all these cases there will be the strong cries. Such seems to have been the state of the Psalmist's mind when he poured forth the expressive utterance of this part.—*John Stephen.*

Verse 146.—Brief as are the petitions, the whole compass of language could not make them more comprehensive. *"Hear me."* The Soul is in earnest, *the whole heart* is engaged in the " cry." *"Save me "*—includes a sinner's whole need—pardon, acceptance, access, holiness, strength, comfort, heaven,—all in one word—Christ. The way of access *is not indeed mentioned* in these short ejaculations. But *it is always implied* in every moment's approach and address to the throne of grace. *"Hear me "* in the name of my all-prevailing Advocate. *"Save me "* through him, whose name is Jesus the Saviour.—*Charles Bridges.*

Verse 146.—*"I cried unto thee."* A crying prayer pierces the depths of heaven. We read not a word that Moses spake, but God was moved by his cry. Exod. xiv. 15. It means not an obstreperous noise, but melting moans of heart. Yet sometimes the sore and pinching necessities and distresses of spirit extort even vocal cries not displeasant to the inclined ears of God. " I cried unto God with my voice," says David, " and he heard me out of his holy hill " : Ps. iii. 4. And this encourages to a fresh onset : " Hearken unto the voice of my cry, my King, and my God " : Ps. v. 2. " Give ear unto my cry : hold not thy peace at my tears " : Ps. xxxix. 12. Another time he makes the cave echo with his cries. " I cried, I cried. Attend unto my cry, for I am brought very low."—*Samuel Lee* (1625—1691), *in* " *The Morning Exercises."*

Verse 146.—*" I cried unto thee ; save me."* In our troubles, we must have recourse to God, and sue to him by prayer and supplication for help and deliverance in due time ; because he is the author of our trouble. In mercies and afflictions, our business lieth not with men, but God ; by humble dealing with him we stop wrath at the fountain-head : he that bindeth us must loose us ; he is at the upper end of causes, and whoever be the instruments of our trouble, and how malicious soever, God is the party with whom we are to make our peace ; for he hath the absolute disposal of all creatures, and will have us to acknowledge the dominion of his providence and our dependence upon him. In treaties of peace between two warring parties, the address is not made to private soldiers, but to their chief : " The Lord hath taken away," saith Job ; " When he giveth quietness, who then can make trouble ? " Job. xxxiv. 29.—*Thomas Manton.*

Verse 146.—*"Save me, and I shall keep thy testimonies."* The servants of God regard life itself as chiefly desirable on account of the opportnuity which it affords for serving God : " *Save me that I might keep thy testimonies,*" is the prayer of the believer in the day of trouble and conflict. " To me to live," says he, " is Christ, and to die is gain." How unlike is this to the wicked ! Their whole desire in the day of trouble is expended on the wish to escape calamity ; they have no desire to be delivered from sin, no wish to be conformed to God !—*John Morison.*

Verse 146.—*"Save me."* From my sins, my corruptions, my temptations, all the hindrances that lie in my way, that I may *"keep thy testimonies."* We must cry for salvation, not that we may have the ease and comfort of it, but that we may have the opportunity of serving God the more cheerfully.—*Matthew Henry.*

Verse 146.—God hears us, that we should hear him.—*Thomas Manton.*

Verse 147.—*"I prevented the dawning of the morning."* The manner of speech is to be marked. He saith he prevented the morning watch, thereby declaring that he lived, as it were, in a strife with time, careful that it should nor overrun him. He knew that time posts away, and in running by wearieth man to dust and ashes. But David pressed to get before it, by doing some good in it, before that it should spur away from him. And this care which David had of every day, alas, how may it make them ashamed who have no care of a whole life ! He was afraid to lose a day ; they take no thought to lose months and years without doing good in them : yea, having spent the three ages of their life in vanity and licentiousness, scarce will they consecrate their old and decrepit age to the Lord.—*William Cowper.*

Verse 147.—*"I prevented the dawning of the morning,"* etc. Those that make a business of prayer will use great vigilancy and diligence therein. I say, that make a business of prayer ; others that use it as a compliment and customary formality, will not be thus affected ; they do it as a thing by-the-by, or a work that might well be spared, and do not look upon it as a necessary duty ; but if a man's heart be in it, he will be early at work, and follow it close, morning and night : his business is to maintain communion with God, his desires will not let him sleep, and he gets up early to be calling upon God. " But unto thee have I cried, O Lord : and in the morning shall my prayer prevent thee." Ps. lxxxviii. 13. Thus will good men even break their sleep to give themselves to prayer, and calling upon the name of God.—*Thomas Manton.*

Verse 147.—*"I prevented the dawning of the morning."* It is a grievous thing if the rays of the rising sun find thee lazy and ashamed in thy bed, and the bright light strike on eyes still weighed down with slumbering sloth. Knowest thou not, O man, that thou owest the daily first-fruits of thy heart and voice to God? Thou hast a daily harvest, a daily revenue. The Lord Jesus remained all night in prayer, not that he needed its help, but putting an example before thee to imitate. He spent the night in prayer for thee, that thou mightest learn how to ask for thyself. Give him again, therefore, what he paid for thee.—*Ambrose.*

Verse 147.—*"I prevented the dawning of the morning."* David was a good husband, up early at it : at night he was late at this duty : " At midnight will I rise to give thanks unto thee " : verse 62. This surely was his meaning when he said he should dwell in the house of the Lord for ever ; he would be ever in the house of prayer. . . . . I wish that when I first open my eyes in the morning, I may then, in soul ejaculatory prayer, open my heart to my God, that at night prayer may make my bed soft, and lay my pillow easy ; that in the day-time prayer may perfume my clothes, sweeten my food, oil the wheels of my particular vocation, keep me company upon all occasions, and gild over all my natural, civil, and religious actions. I wish that, after I have poured out my prayer in the name of Christ, according to the will of God, having sowed my seed, I may expect a crop, looking earnestly for the springing of it up, and believing assuredly that I shall reap in time if I faint not.—*George Swinnock.*

Verse 147. *"I prevented the dawning of the morning."* Early prayers are undisturbed by the agitating cares of life, and resemble the sweet melody of those birds which sing loudest and sweetest when fewest ears are open to listen to them. O my soul, canst thou say that thou hast thus *"prevented the dawning of the morning"* in thy approaches to God ? Has the desire of communion with heaven raised thee from thy slumbers, shaken off thy sloth, and carried thee to thy knees ?—*John Morison.*

Verse 147.—*"And cried."* Here is a repetition of the same prayer, *"I cried"* ; yea, again I cried, and a third time, " I prevented the dawning of the morning, and cried." We use to knock at a door thrice, and then depart. Our Lord Jesus " prayed the third time, saying the same words " (Matt. xxvi. 44), " Father, if it be possible, let this cup pass from me." So the apostle Paul : " For this thing I besought the Lord thrice, that it might depart from me " : 2 Cor. xii. 8. So, " And he stretched himself upon the child three times, and cried unto the Lord, and said, O Lord my God, I pray thee, let this child's soul come into him again " : 1 Kings xvii. 21. This, it seemeth, was the time in which they expected an answer in weighty cases ; and yet I will not confine it to that number ; for here we are to reiterate our petitions for one and the same thing as often as occasion requireth, till it be granted.—*Thomas Manton.*

Verse 147.—Poets have delighted to sing of the morning as " Mother of the Dews," " sowing the earth with orient pearl" ; and many of the saints upstarting from their beds at the first blush of dawn have found the poetry of nature to be the reality of grace as they have felt the dews of heaven refreshing their spirit. Hence morning exercises have ever been dear to the enlightened, heaven-loving souls, and it has been their rule, never to see the face of man till they have first seen the face of God. The breath of morn redolent of the smell of flowers is incense offered by earth to her Creator, and living men should never let the dead earth excel them ; truly living men tuning their hearts for song, like the birds, salute the radiant mercy which reveals itself in the east. The first fresh hour of every morning should be dedicated to the Lord whose mercy gladdens it with golden light. The eye of day openeth its lids, and in so doing opens the eyes of hosts of heaven-protected slumberers ; it is fitting that those eyes should first look up to the great Father of Lights, the fount and source of all the good upon which the sunlight gleams. It augurs for us a day of grace when we begin betimes with God ; the sanctifying influence of the season spent upon the mount operates upon each succeeding hour. Morning devotion anchors the soul so that it will not very readily drift far away from God during the day ; it perfumes the heart so that it smells fragrant with piety until nightfall ; it girds up the soul's garments so that it is less apt to stumble, and feeds all its powers so that it is not permitted to faint. The morning is the gate of the day, and should be well guarded with prayer. It is one end of the thread on which the day's actions are strung, and should be well knotted with devotion. If we felt more the majesty of life we should be more careful of its mornings. He who rushes from his bed to his business and waiteth not to worship, is as foolish as though he had not put on his clothes, or cleansed his face, and as unwise as though he dashed into battle without arms or armour. Be it ours to bathe in the softly flowing river of communion with God, before the heat of the wilderness and the burden of the way begin to oppress us.—*C. H. S.*

Verse 147.—"*I hoped in thy word.*" Even if there should not be actual enjoyment, at least let us honour God by the spirit of expectancy.—*Charles Bridges.*

Verses 147, 148.—The student of theology and the minister of the word should begin the day with prayer, and this chiefly to seek from God, that he may rightly understand the word of God, and be able to teach others.—*Solomon Gesner.* Brethren, note this !—*C. H. S.*

Verses 147, 148.—See here : 1. That David was an early riser, which perhaps contributed to his eminency. He was none of those that say, " Yet a little sleep." 2. That he began the day with God ; the first thing he did in the morning, before he admitted any business, was to pray ; when his mind was most fresh and in the best frame. If our first thoughts in the morning be of God, it will help to keep us in his fear all the day long. 3. That his mind was so full of God and the cares and delights of his religion, that a little sleep served his turn, even in "*the night-watches,*" when he awaked from his first sleep, he would rather meditate and pray, than turn him and go to sleep again. He esteemed the words of God's mouth more than his necessary repose, which we can as ill want as our food : Job xxiii. 21. 4. That he would redeem time for religious exercises ; he was full of business all day, but that will excuse no man from secret devotion ; it is better to take time from sleep, as David did, than not find time for prayer. And this is our comfort when we pray in the night, that we can never come unseasonably to the throne of grace, if we may have access to it at all hours. Baal may be asleep, but Israel's God never slumbers, nor are there any hours in which he may not be spoken with.—*Matthew Henry.*

Verse 148.—"*Mine eyes prevent the night watches, that I might meditate in thy word.*" You will all admit that this is the language of an ardent, earnest, and painstaking student. David represents himself as " rising early, and late taking rest," on purpose that he might employ himself in the study of God's word. " He *meditates* in this word," the expression implying close and patient thought ; as if there were much in the word which was not to be detected by a cursory glance, and which required the strictest application both of the head and the heart.

The Bible is a book in which we may continually meditate, and yet not exhaust its contents. When David expressed himself in the language of our text, Holy Writ—the word of God—was of course a far smaller volume than it now is, though, even now, the Bible is far from a large book. Yet David could not, so to speak, get to the end of the book. He might have been studying the book for years,—nay, we are sure that he had been,—and yet, as though he were just entering on a new course of reading, with volume upon volume to peruse, he must rise before day to prosecute the study. "*Mine eyes prevent the night watches, that I might meditate in thy word.*"

The same remark may be made upon precepts which enjoin continued study of the Bible. Is there material for that study ? Unless there be, the precepts will become out of place ; the Scriptural student will have exhausted the Scriptures ; and what is he to do then ? He can no longer obey the precepts, and the precepts will prove that they cannot have been made for perpetuity—for the men of all ages and all conditions. . . . . .

Here is a servant of God, who, from his youth upward, has been diligent in the study of the Bible. Year after year he has devoted to that study, and yet the Bible is but a single volume, and that not a large volume. " Well, then," you might be inclined to say, " the study must surely by this time have exhausted the book ! There can be nothing new for him to bring out ; nothing which he has not investigated and fathomed." Ah, how you mistake the Bible ! What a much larger book it must be than it seems ! In place of having exhausted it, the royal student speaks as though there were more work before him than he knew how to compass. "*Mine eyes prevent the night watches, that I might mediate in thy word.*"—*Henry Melvill.*

Verse 148.—"*Mine eyes prevent the night watches.*" The Hebrew word means *a watch*—a part of the night, so called from military watches, or a dividing of the night to keep guard. The idea of the Psalmist here is, that he *anticipated* these regular divisions of the night in order that he might engage in devotion. Instead of waiting for their return, he arose for prayer before they recurred ; so much did his heart delight in the service of God. The language would seem to be that of one who was accustomed to pray in these successive "*watches*" of the night ; the early, the middle, and the dawn.   This may illustrate what occurs in the life of all who love God.   They will have regular seasons of devotion, but they will often *anticipate* those seasons.   They will be in a state of mind which prompts them to pray ;   when nothing will meet their state of mind *but* prayer ;   and when they cannot wait for the regular and ordinary season of devotion ;   like a hungry man, who cannot wait for the usual and regular hour of his meals.   The meaning of the phrase, *"Mine eyes* prevent," is that he awoke before the usual time for devotion.— *Albert Barnes.*

Verse 148.—*"Mine eyes prevent the night watches,"* etc.   His former purpose is yet continued, declaring his indefatigable perseverance in prayer.   Oh, that we could learn of him to use our time well !   At evening he lay down with prayers and tears ;   at midnight he rose to give thanks ;   he got up before the morning light to call upon the Lord.   This is to imitate the life of angels, who ever are delighted to behold the face of God, singing alway a new song without wearying.   This is to begin our heaven upon earth :   Oh, that we could alway remember it !—*William Cowper.*

Verse 148.—*"Night watches."*   The Jews, like the Greeks and Romans, divided the night into military watches instead of hours, each watch representing the period for which sentinels or pickets remained on duty.   The proper Jewish reckoning recognised only three such watches, entitled the first, or " beginning of the watches " (Lam. ii. 19), " the middle watch " (Judg. vii. 19), and " the morning watch " (Exod. xiv. 24 ;   1 Sam. xi. 11).   These would last respectively from sunset to 10 p.m. ;   from 10 p.m. to 2 a.m. ;   and from 2 a.m. to sunrise.   It has been contended by Lightfoot that the Jews really reckoned four watches, three only of which were in the dead of the night, the fourth being in the morning.   This, however, is rendered improbable by the use of the term " middle," and is opposed to Rabbinical authority. Subsequently to the establishment of Roman supremacy, the number of watches was increased to four, which were described either according to their numerical order, as in the case of the " fourth watch " (Matt. xiv. 25), or by the terms " even, midnight, cock-crowing, and morning " (Mark xiii. 35),   These terminated respectively at 9 p.m., midnight, 3 a.m., and 6 a.m.   Conformably to this, the guard of soldiers was divided into four relays (Acts xii. 4), showing that the Roman régime was followed in Herod's army.   Watchmen appear to have patrolled the streets of the Jewish towns (Cant. iii. 3 ; v. 7 ; Ps. cxxvii. 1, where for " maketh " we should substitute " watcheth " ;   Ps.   cxxx.   6).—*William Latham Bevan, in Smith's Dictionary of the Bible,* 1863.

Verse 149.—*"Quicken me."*   By *quickening* some understand restitution to happiness ;   for a calamitous man is as one dead and buried under deep and heavy troubles, and his recovery is a life from the dead, or a reviving from the grave :   so quickening seemeth to be taken in Psalm lxxi. 20 : " Thou, which hast shewed me great and sore troubles, shalt quicken me again and shalt bring me up again from the depths of the earth."

Others understand by *quickening,* the renewing and increasing in him the vigour of his spiritual life.   That he beggeth that God would revive, increase, and preserve that life, which he had already given, that it might be perfected and consummated in glory.   That he might be ever ready to bring forth the habits of grace into acts. —*Thomas Manton.*

Verse 149.—*"Judgment "* is sometimes taken for the execution of God's threatenings against transgressors ;   and this David declares : " Enter not into judgment with thy servant " :   Ps. cxliii. 2.   Sometime it is taken for the performance of his promises, according to his word ;   and this David desires as in this verse.—*William Cowper.*

Verse 150.—*"They are far from thy law."*   Truly it should greatly comfort all the godly, to remember that such as are their enemies are God's enemies also. Since they are far from the obedience of God's law, what marvel they be also far from the duty of love which they owe us ?   It may content us to want that comfort in men which otherwise we might and would have, when we consider that God wants his glory in them.   Let this sustain us when we see that godless men are enemies unto us.—*William Cowper.*

Verse 150.—If we can get a carnal pillow and bolster under our heads, we sleep and dream many a golden dream of ease and safety.   Now, God, who is jealous

of our trust, will not let us alone, and therefore will put us upon sharp trials. **It**
is not faith, but sense, we live upon before ; that is faith, if we can depend upon God
when " they draw near that follow after mischief : " " I will not be afraid of ten
thousands of people, that have set themselves against me round about " : Ps. iii. 6.
A danger at a distance is but imagined, it worketh otherwise when it is at hand.
Christ himself had other thoughts of approaching danger than danger at a distance :
" Now is my soul troubled " : John xii. 27.   This vessel of pure water was troubled,
though he discovered no dross.—*Thomas Manton.*

Verses 150, 151.—Our spiritual enemies, like David's earthly persecutors, are
ever present and active. The devouring " lion," or the insinuating " serpent "
is *"nigh to follow after mischief"* ; and so much the more dangerous, as his approaches
are invisible.   Nigh also is a tempting ensnaring world ; and nearer still, a lurking
world of sin within, separating us from communion with our God. But in turning
habitually and immediately to our stronghold, we can enjoy the confidence—*"Thou
art near, O Lord."* Though " the High and Lofty One, whose name is Holy "—
though the just and terrible God, yet art thou made nigh to thy people, and they to
thee, " by the blood of the cross." And thou dost manifest thy presence to them
in " the Son of thy love."—*Charles Bridges.*

Verses 150, 151.—They are *"nigh"* to persecute and destroy me ; thou art
nigh, O Lord, to help me.—*J. J. Stewart Perowne.*

Verses 150, 151.—*"They draw nigh."* . . . *"Thou art near."*   From the meditation
of his enemies' malice he returns again to the meditation of God's mercy ; and so
it is expedient for us to do, lest the number and greatness and maliciousness of
our enemies make us to faint when we look unto them.   It is good that we should
cast our eyes upward to the Lord ; then shall we see that they are not so near to
hurt us as the Lord our God is near to help us ; and that there is no evil in them
which we have cause to fear, but we shall find in our God a contrary good sufficient
to preserve us.   Otherwise we could not endure, if when Satan and his instruments
come near to pursue us, the Lord were not near to protect us.—*William Cowper.*

Verse 151.—*"Thou art near, O Lord."*—How sweetly and how often has this
thought been brought home to some forsaken and forgotten one ! " When my
father and my mother forsake me, the Lord will take me up," was the comfort
of one in that deep affliction. And in the first outbreaking of the heart, how
sweetly has the conviction come, like some whisper of peace, " I am with thee ! "
And I have no doubt that many and many a time in those hours of solitary prayer,
when before the dawning of the morning, and before the night watches, or the Psalmist
arose at midnight to commune with God, when no voice broke on the stillness, and
every sound was hushed save the beating of his own heart, then had David heard the
whisper of God's Holy Spirit, *"I am near,"* " Fear not, I am with thee."—*Barton
Bouchier.*

Verse 151.—*"Thou art near, O Lord."*   This was *once* man's greatest blessing,
and source of sweetest consolation.   It was the fairest flower which grew in Paradise ;
but sin withered it, the flower faded, it drooped, it died.   Gen. iii. 8 ; iv. 16.   It
must be so *once more ;* the flower must once again bloom, again it must revive ;
even upon earth must it blossom, or in heaven it will never put forth its fragrance.

"Thou art near."   Even in thy works of *creation,* in the sun in his glory, in the
moon in her softness, gleaming in the firmament, I see thee.   In the balm of this
fragrant air, in the light of this cheerful day, in the redolence of these shrubs around
me, whose flowery tops, as they drink in the soft and gentle shower as it falls, seem
to breathe forth a fresh perfume in gratitude to him who sends it.   In the melody
of these birds which fill the air with their songs, thou, O Lord, art near.   I perceive
thee not with my bodily eyes, although by these I discern thy workmanship, and
with the eye of the mind behold thee in thy works, *a present God.*

"Thou art near."   Even in the book of thy providence, dark and mysterious
though it be, I see thee.   There do I read thy *wisdom,* as developed in thy world,
thy church, thy saints, thy servant before thee ; the wisdom that guides, the
wisdom that guards, the wisdom that bestows, the wisdom that encourages, the
wisdom that corrects, that kills and makes alive.   There do I read thy *power,* thy
justice, thy *faithfulness,* thy *holiness,* thy *love.*

But it is in thy *Son,* thy beloved Son, that I most clearly and distinctly see
thee as near.   If in creation, if in providence, thou art near, in him thou art very
near, O Lord.   Near as a sin-forgiving God.   Rom. viii. 1.   Near as a promise-

keeping God. 2 Cor. i. 20. Near as a prayer-hearing God. John xvi. 20 ; Ps. cxlv. 18. Near as a covenant-keeping God. Heb. viii. 10. Near as a gracious, tender Father. John xx. 17.

"*Thou art near, O Lord.*" O that I might live in the constant sense of thy nearness to me ! How often, far too often, alas, do I seem quite to forget it !

Art thou near ? Then may I realizingly remember, that *by the blood of thy dear Son,* and by that alone, have I been brought nigh (Eph. ii. 13) ; that it required nothing less than the stoop of Deity, and the sufferings and death of his perfect humanity, to remove those hindrances which interposed between a holy God and an unholy creature. Oh, to walk before thee with a grateful spirit, and with a broken, contrite heart !

Art thou near ? Then may I walk as before thee, *as seeing thee,* in holy fear, in filial love, in simple faith, in child-like confidence. Gen. xvii. 1. When *sin* would tempt and solicit indulgence, when the *world* presents some new allurement, when *Satan* would take advantage of constitution, society, circumstances, oh, that I may ever remember "*Thou art near.*"

If my dearest comforts droop and die, if friends are cool, if the bonds once the firmest, the closest, the tenderest, are torn asunder, and dissevered, yet may I still remember, "*Thou* art near, O Lord," and not afar off. And when the solemn moment shall come, when heart and flesh shall fail, when all earthly things are seen with a dying eye, when I hear thee say, " Thou must die, and not live," then, oh then may I remember, with all the composedness of faith, and all the liveliness of hope, and all the ardour of love, "*Thou art near, O Lord.*"—*James Harrington Evans,* 1785—1849.

Verse 151.—"*All thy commandments are truth.*" His meaning is,—Albeit, O Lord, the evil will of wicked men follows me because I follow thee ; yet I know thy commandments are true, and that it is not possible that thou canst desert or fail thy servants who stand to the maintenance of thy word. Then, ye see, David's comfort in trouble was not in any presumptuous conceit of his own wisdom or strength but in the truth of God's promises, which he was persuaded could not fail him. And here also he makes a secret opposition between the word of the Lord and the word of his enemies. Sometimes men command, but without reason ; sometimes they threaten, but without effect. Herod's commanding, Rabshakeh's railing, Jezebel's proud boasting against Elijah, may prove this. But as to the Lord our God he is alway better than his word, and his servants shall find more in his performance hereafter than now they can perceive in his promise : like as his enemies should find more weight in his judgments than now they can apprehend in his threatenings. —*William Cowper.*

Verse 152.—This portion of our Psalm endeth with the triumph of faith over all dangers and temptations. "*Concerning thy testimonies,*" the revelations of thy will, thy counsels for the salvation of thy servants, "*I have known of old,*" by faith, and by my own experience, as well as that of others, "*that thou hast founded them for ever*" ; they are unalterable and everlasting as the attributes of their great Author, and can never fail those who rely upon them, in time or in eternity.—*George Horne.*

Verse 152.—"*I have known of old.*" It was not a late persuasion, or a thing that he was now to learn ; he always knew it since he knew anything of God, that God had owned his word as the constant rule of his proceedings with creatures, in that God had so often made good his word to him, not only by present and late, but by old and ancient experiences. Well, then, David's persuasion of the truth and unchangeableness of the word was not a sudden humour or a present fit, or a persuasion of a few days' standing ; but he was confirmed in it by long experience. One or two experiences had been no trial of the truth of the word, they might seem but a good hit ; but his word ever proveth true, not once or twice, but always ; what we say " of old," the Septuagint reads κατ αρχὰς, " from the beginnings " ; that is, either—1. From my tender years. Timothy knew the Scriptures from a child (2 Tim. iii. 15) ; so David very young was acquainted with God and his truth. 2. Or, from the first time that he began to be serious, or to mind the word in good earnest, or to be a student either in God's word or works, by comparing providences and promises, he found concerning his testimonies that "*God had founded them for ever.*" 3. Lastly, "*of old*" may be what I have heard of all foregoing ages, their experience as well as mine : " Our fathers trusted in thee : they trusted, and thou didst deliver them. They cried unto thee, and were delivered: they trusted in thee, and were not confounded:" Ps. xxii. 4, 5.—*Thomas Manton.*

Verse 152.—Let us mark this eternal basis of "the testimonies of God." The whole plan of redemption was emphatically *"founded for ever"*: the Saviour was *"foreordained before the foundation of the world."* The people of God were *"chosen in Christ before the world began!"* The great Author *"declares the end from the beginning,"* and thus clears his dispensations from any charge of mutability or contingency. Every event in the church is fixed, permitted, and provided for—not in the passing moment of time, but in the counsels of eternity. When, therefore, the testimonies set forth God's faithful engagements with his people of old, the recollection that they are *"founded for ever"* gives us a present and unchangeable interest in them. And when we see that they are grounded upon the oath and promise of God—the two " immutable things, in which it is impossible for God to lie "—we may truly " have strong consolation " in venturing every hope for eternity upon this rock ; nor need we be dismayed to see all our earthly dependencies— " the world, and the lust, and the fashion of it—passing away " before us.—*Charles Bridges.*

EXPOSITION OF VERSES 153 TO 160.

CONSIDER mine affliction, and deliver me : for I do not forget thy law.

154 Plead my cause, and deliver me : quicken me according to thy word.

155 Salvation *is* far from the wicked : for they seek not thy statutes.

156 Great *are* thy tender mercies, O LORD : quicken me according to thy judgments.

157 Many *are* my persecutors and mine enemies ; *yet* do I not decline from thy testimonies.

158 I beheld the transgressors, and was grieved ; because they kept not thy word.

159 Consider how I love thy precepts : quicken me, O LORD, according to thy lovingkindness.

160 Thy word *is* true *from* the beginning : and every one of thy righteous judgments *endureth* for ever.

In this section the Psalmist seems to draw still nearer to God in prayer, and to state his case and to invoke the divine help with more of boldness and expectation. It is a pleading passage, and the key-word of it is, " Consider." With much boldness he pleads his intimate union with the Lord's cause as a reason why he should be aided. The special aid that he seeks is personal *quickening*, for which he cries to the Lord again and again.

153. *"Consider mine affliction, and deliver me."* The writer has a good case, though it be a grievous one, and he is ready, yea anxious, to submit it to the divine arbitration. His matters are right, and he is ready to lay them before the supreme court. His manner is that of one who feels safe at the throne. Yet there is no impatience : he does not ask for hasty action, but for consideration. In effect he cries—" Look into my grief, and see whether I do not need to be delivered. From my sorrowful condition judge as to the proper method and time for my rescue." The Psalmist desires two things, and these two things blended : first, a full considera- tion of his sorrow ; secondly, deliverance ; and, then, that this deliverance should come with a consideration of his affliction. It should be the desire of every gracious man who is in adversity that the Lord should look upon his need, and relieve it in such a way as shall be most for the divine glory, and for his own benefit. The words, " mine affliction," are picturesque ; they seem to portion off a special spot of woe as the writer's own inheritance : he possesses it as no one else had ever done, and he begs the Lord to have that special spot under his eye : even as a husbandman looking over all his fields may yet take double care of a certain selected plot. His prayer is eminently practical, for he seeks to be delivered ; that is, brought out of the trouble and preserved from sustaining any serious damage by it. For God to consider is to act in due season : men consider and do nothing ; but such is never the case with out God. *"For I do not forget thy law."* His affliction was not sufficient, with all its bitterness, to drive out of his mind the memory of God's law ; nor could it lead him to act contrary to the divine command. He forgot prosperity, but he did not forget obedience. This is a good plea when it can be honestly urged. If we are kept faithful to God's law we may be sure that God will remain faithful to his promise. If we do not forget his law the Lord will not forget us. He will not long leave that man in trouble whose only fear in trouble is lest he should leave the way of right.

154.—*"Plead my cause, and deliver me."* In the last verse he had prayed, " Deliver me," and here he specifies one method in which that deliverance might be vouchsafed, namely, by the advocacy of his cause. In providence the Lord has many ways of clearing the slandered of the accusations brought against them. He can make it manifest to all that they have been belied, and in this way he can practically plead their cause. He can, moreover, raise up friends for the godly who will leave no stone unturned till their characters are cleared ; or he can smite their enemies with such fearfulness of heart that they will be forced to confess their falsehood, and thus the righteous will be delivered without the striking of a blow. Alexander reads it, " Strive my strife, and redeem me "—that is, stand in my stead, bear my burden, fight my fight, pay my price, and bring me out to liberty. When we feel ourselves dumb before the foe, here is a prayer made to our hand. What a comfort that if we sin we have an advocate, and if we do *not* sin the same pleader is engaged on our side. *"Quicken me."* We had this prayer in the last section, and we shall have it again and again in this. It is a desire which cannot be too often felt and expressed. As the soul is the centre of everything, so to be quickened is the central blessing. It means more love, more grace, more faith, more courage, more strength, and if we get these we can hold up our heads before our adversaries. God alone can give this quickening ; but to the Lord and giver of life the work is easy enough, and he delights to perform it. *"According to thy word."* David had found such a blessing among the promised things, or at least he perceived that it was according to the general tenor of God's word that tried believers should be quickened and brought up again from the dust of the earth ; therefore he pleads the word, and desires the Lord to act to him according to the usual run of that word. What a mighty plea is this—" according to thy word." No gun in all our arsenals can match it.

155.—*"Salvation is far from the wicked."* By their perseverance in evil they have almost put themselves out of the pale of hope. They talk about being saved, but they cannot have known anything of it or they would not remain wicked. Every step they have taken in the path of evil has removed them further from the kingdom of grace : they go from one degree of hardness to another till their hearts become as stone. When they fall into trouble it will be irremediable. Yet they talk big, as if they either needed no salvation or could save themselves whenever their fancy turned that way. *"For they seek not thy statutes."* They do not endeavour to be obedient, but quite the reverse ; they seek themselves, they seek evil, and therefore they never find the way of peace and righteousness. When men have broken the statutes of the Lord their wisest course is by repentance to seek forgiveness, and by faith to seek salvation : then salvation is near them, so near them that they shall not miss it ; but when the wicked continue to seek after mischief, salvation is set further and further from them. Salvation and God's statutes go together : those who are saved by the King of grace love the statutes of the King of glory.

156. This verse is exceedingly like verse one hundred and forty-nine, and yet it is no vain repetition There is such a difference in the main idea that the one verse stands out distinct from the other. In the first case he mentions his prayer, but leaves the method of its accomplishment with the wisdom or judgment of God ; while here he pleads no prayer of his own, but simply the mercies of the Lord, and begs to be quickened by judgments rather than to be left to spiritual lethargy. We may take it for granted that an inspired author is never so short of thought as to be obliged to repeat himself : where we think we have the same idea in this Psalm we are mislead by our neglect of careful study. Each verse is a distinct pearl. Each blade of grass in this field has its own drop of heavenly dew. *"Great are thy tender mercies, O LORD."* Here the Psalmist pleads the largeness of God's mercy, the immensity of his tender love ; yea, he speaks of *mercies*—mercies many, mercies tender, mercies great ; and with the glorious Jehovah he makes this a plea for his one leading prayer, the prayer for quickening. Quickening is a great and tender mercy ; and it is many mercies in one. Shall one so greatly good permit his servant to die ? Will not one so tender breathe new life into him ? *"Quicken me according to thy judgments."* A measure of awakening comes with the judgments of God ; they are startling and arousing ; and hence the believer's quickening thereby. David would have every severe stroke sanctified to his benefit, as well as every tender mercy. The first clause of this verse may run, " Many," or, " manifold are thy compassions, O Jehovah." This he remembers in connection with the " many persecutors " of whom he will speak in the next verse. By all these many mercies he pleads for enlivening grace, and thus he has many strings to his bow. We shall never be short of arguments if we draw them from God himself, and urge both his mercies and his judgments as reasons for our quickening.

157.—"*Many are my persecutors and mine enemies.*" Those who actually assail me, or who secretly abhor me, are many. He sets this over against the many tender mercies of God. It seems a strange thing that a truly godly man, as David was, should have many enemies ; but it is inevitable. The disciple cannot be loved where his Master is hated. The seed of the serpent must oppose the seed of the woman : it is their nature. "*Yet do I not decline from thy testimonies.*" He did not deviate from the truth of God, but proceeded in the straight way, however many adversaries might endeavour to block up his path. Some men have been led astray by one enemy, but here is a saint who held on his way in the teeth of many persecutors. There is enough in the testimonies of God to recompense us for pushing forward against all the hosts that may combine against us. So long as they cannot drive or draw us into a spiritual decline our foes have done us no great harm, and they have accomplished nothing by their malice. If we do not decline they are defeated. If they cannot make us sin they have missed their mark. Faithfulness to the truth is victory over our enemies.

158.—"*I beheld the transgressors.*" I saw the traitors ; I understood their character, their object, their way, and their end. I could not help seeing them, for they pushed themselves into my way. As I was obliged to see them I fixed my eyes on them, to learn what I could from them. "*And was grieved.*" I was sorry to see such sinners. I was sick of them, disgusted with them, I could not endure them. I found no pleasure in them, they were a sad sight to me, however fine their clothing or witty their chattering. Even when they were most mirthful a sight of them made my heart heavy ; I could not tolerate either them or their doings. "*Because they kept not thy word.*" My grief was occasioned more by their sin against God than by their enmity against myself. I could bear their evil treatment of my words, but not their neglect of thy word. Thy word is so precious to me that those who will not keep it move me to indignation ; I cannot keep the company of those who keep not God's word. That they should have no love for me is a trifle ; but to despise the teaching of the Lord is abominable.

159.—"*Consider,*" or see, "*how I love thy precepts.*" A second time he asks for consideration. As he said before, " Consider mine affliction," so now he says, " Consider mine affection." He loved the precepts of God—loved them unspeakably —loved them so as to be grieved with those who did not love them. This is a sure test : many there are who have a warm side towards the promises, but as for the precepts, they cannot endure them. The Psalmist so loved everything that was good and excellent that he loved all God had commanded. The precepts are all of them wise and holy, therefore the man of God loved them extremely, loved to know them, to think of them, to proclaim them, and principally to practise them. He asked the Lord to remember and consider this, not upon the ground of merit, but that it should serve as an answer to the slanderous accusations which at this time were the great sting of his sorrow. "*Quicken me, O LORD, according to thy lovingkindness.*" Here he comes back to his former prayer, " Quicken me " (v. 154), " quicken me " (v. 156). " Quicken me." He prays again the third time, using the same words. We may understand that David felt like one who was half stunned with the assaults of his foes, ready to faint under their incessant malice. What he wanted was revival, restoration, renewal ; therefore he pleaded for more life, O thou who didst quicken me when I was dead, quicken me again that I may not return to the dead ! Quicken me that I may outlive the blows of my enemies, the faintness of my faith, and the swooning of my sorrow. This time he does not say, " Quicken me according to thy judgments," but " Quicken me, O Lord, according to thy lovingkindness." This is the great gun which he brings up last to the conflict : it is his ultimate argument, if this succeed not he must fail. He has long been knocking at mercy's gate, and with this plea he strikes his heaviest blow. When he had fallen into great sin this was his plea, " Have mercy upon me, O God, according to thy lovingkindness," and now that he is in great trouble he flies to the same effectual reasoning. Because God is love he will give us life ; because he is kind he will again kindle the heavenly flame within us.

160. The sweet singer finishes up this section in the same way as the last by dwelling upon the sureness of the truth of God. It will be well for the reader to note the likeness between verses 144, 152, and the present one. "*Thy word is true.*" Whatever the transgressors may say, God is true, and his word is true. The ungodly are false, but God's word is true. They charge us with being false, but our solace is that God's true word will clear us. "*From the beginning.*" God's word has been

true from the first moment in which it was spoken, true throughout the whole of history, true to us from the instant in which we believed it, ay, true to us before we were true to it. Some read it, " Thy word is true from the head ; " true as a whole, true from top to bottom. Experience had taught David this lesson, and experience is teaching us the same. The Scriptures are as true in Genesis as in Revelation, and the five books of Moses are as inspired as the four Gospels. *"And every one of thy righteous judgments endureth for ever."* That which thou hast decided remains irreversible in every case. Against the decisions of the Lord no writ of error can be demanded, neither will there ever be a repealing of any of the acts of his sovereignty. There is not one single mistake either in the word of God or in the providential dealings of God. Neither in the book of revelation nor of providence will there be any need to put a single note of *errata.* The Lord has nothing to regret or to retract, nothing to amend or to reverse. All God's judgments, decrees, commands, and purposes are righteous, and as righteous things are lasting things, every one of them will outlive the stars. " Till heaven and earth pass, one jot or one tittle shall in no wise pass from the law, till all be fulfilled." God's justice endureth for ever. This is a cheering thought, but there is a much sweeter one, which of old was the song of the priests in the temple ; let it be ours, " His mercy endureth for ever."

NOTES ON VERSES 153 TO 160.

Verse 153.—*"Consider mine affliction, and deliver me."* God looks upon or considers man in various ways, and for different ends. To give him light ; for " as Jesus passed by, he saw a man which was blind from his birth " (John ix. 1). To convert him ; " He saw a man, named Matthew, sitting at the receipt of custom : and he saith unto him, Follow me " (Matt. ix. 9). To restore him ; " And the Lord turned, and looked upon Peter " (Luke xxii. 61). To deliver him ; " I have surely seen the affliction of my people which are in Egypt " (Exod. iii. 7). To advance him ; " He hath regarded the low estate of his handmaiden " (Luke i. 48) : and to reward him ; " The Lord had respect unto Abel and to his offering " (Gen. iv. 4).—*Hugo (circa* 1120), *in Neale and Littledale.*

Verse 153.—*"Consider mine affliction, and deliver me."* We must pray that God will help and deliver us, not after the device of our own brains, but after such wise as seemeth best unto his tender wisdom, or else that he will mitigate our pain, that our weakness may not utterly faint. Like as a sick person, although he doubt nothing of the faithfulness and tenderness of his physician, yet, for all that, desireth him to handle his wound as tenderly as possible, even so may we call upon God, that, if it be not against his honour and glory, he will vouchsafe to give some mitigation of the pain.—*Otho Wermullerus.*

Verse 153.—*"Consider mine affliction."* These prayers of David are penned with such heavenly wisdom that they are convenient for the state of the whole church, and every member thereof. The church is the bush that burneth with fire, but cannot be consumed ; every member thereof beareth a part of the cross of Christ ; they are never without some affliction, for which they have need to pray with David, *"Behold mine affliction."*

We know that in afflictions it is some comfort to us to have our crosses known to those of whom we are assured that they love us : it mitigates our dolour when they mourn with us, albeit they be not able to help us. But the Christian hath a more solid comfort ; to wit, that in all his troubles the Lord beholds him ; like a king, rejoicing to see his own servant wrestle with the enemy. He looks on with a merciful eye, pitying the infirmity of his own, when he sees it ; and with a powerful hand ready to help them. But because many a time the cloud of our corruption cometh between the Lord and us, and lets us not see his helping hand, nor his loving face looking upon us, we have need to pray at such times with David, *"Behold mine affliction."*—*William Cowper.*

Verse 154.—*"Plead my cause, and deliver me,"* etc. Albeit the godly under persecution have a good cause, yet they cannot plead it except God the Redeemer show himself as Advocate for them ; therefore prayeth the Psalmist, *"Plead my cause."*

When God the Redeemer pleadeth a man's cause, he doth it to purpose and effectually : *"Plead my cause, and deliver me."*

Except the Lord's clients shall find new influence from God from time to time in their troubles, they are but as dead men in their exercise ; for, *"Quicken me"* importeth this.

Till we find lively encouragement given to us in trouble we must adhere to the word of promise : *"Quicken me according to thy word."*

What the believer hath need of, that God hath not only a will to supply, but also an office to attend it, and power to effectuate it, as here he hath the office of an Advocate and of a powerful Redeemer also, wherein the believer may confidently give him daily employment, as he needeth : *"Plead my cause, and deliver me : quicken me according to thy word."*—*David Dickson.*

Verse 154.—*"Plead my cause, and deliver me,"* etc. He now supposes himself to be arraigned before the tribunal of men, as he certainly was in their general charges against him ; arraigned, too, in his helplessness, without a name, without state ; in such way as one disowned would be arraigned. He prays the Lord to come in and plead his cause ; so should he be redeemed ; for this is the import of the original. As it were, he regards himself as one sold to corrupt judges, or at all events, as one that has lost his standing in society in the estimation of men. But if the Lord will come, and maintain the cause of his servant, his servant shall be redeemed indeed. There is good confidence in this prayer ; the man of God is acquainted with the way of the Lord, and he makes his believing application.   O how much do we need to know the Lord's righteous character in our seasons of great distress !   Now the Lord pleads the cause of his own by the power of the truth ; he pleads it also in his providences of divers kinds ; he acts upon the hearts, and the hopes, and the fears of men ; and in many wondrous ways he pleads his people's cause.   He redeems his saints from all evil ; and if not altogether from all evil in this world, certainly from all evil as concerns the world to come.—*John Stephen.*

Verse 154.—*"Plead my cause, and deliver me,"* etc.   In this verse are three requests, and all backed with one and the same argument.   In the first, he intimateth the right of his cause, and that he was unjustly vexed by wicked men ; therefore, as burdened with their calumnies, he desireth God to undertake his defence : *"Plead my cause."*   In the second, he representeth the misery and helplessness of his condition ; therefore, as oppressed by violence, he saith, *"Deliver me ; "* or, as the words will bear, Redeem me.   In the third, his own weakness, and readiness to faint under this burden ; therefore he saith, *"Quicken me."*

Or, in short, with respect to the injustice of his adversaries, *"Plead my cause ; "* with respect to the misery of his condition, *"Deliver me ; "* with respect to the weakness and imbecility of his own heart, *"Quicken me."* . . .

The reason and ground of asking, *"According to thy word."*   This last clause must be applied to all the branches of the prayer : " Plead my cause," " according to thy word ; " " deliver me," " according to thy word ; " " quicken me," " according to thy word : " for God in his word engageth for all : to be advocate, Redeemer, and fountain of life.   The word that David buildeth upon was found either in the general promises made to them that kept the law, or in some particular promise made to himself by the prophets of that time.—*Thomas Manton.*

Verse 154.—*"Plead my cause, and deliver me."*   A wicked woman once brought against Dr. Payson an accusation, under circumstances which seemed to render it impossible that he should escape.   She was in the same packet, in which, many months before, he had gone to Boston.   For a time, it seemed almost certain that his character would be ruined.   He was cut off from all resource except the throne of grace.   He felt that his only hope was in God ; and to him he addressed his fervent prayer.   He was heard by the Defender of the innocent.   A " compunctious visiting " induced the wretched woman to confess that the whole was a malicious slander.—*From Asa Cummings' Memoir of Edward Payson.*

Verse 154.—*"Plead my cause."*   I do not know that David meant, by calling upon God to plead his cause, anything more than that he should vindicate his innocence, and make it manifest to all, by delivering him out of the hand of all his enemies ; but whether he had an ulterior reference or no, the word powerfully and sweetly recalls to every Christian heart him who was indeed to be the Advocate for poor sinners, even Jesus Christ the righteous, who is the propitiation for our sins.—*Barton Bouchier.*

Verse 154.—*"Plead my cause."*   The children of this world are wiser in their generation than the children of God.   Which made David here pray to God that *he* would *plead his cause,* and be his Advocate against all their policies.   He trusted not to the equity of his own cause, but to the Lord.   From whence we gather, that the cause why our oppressors prevail oft against us is, because we trust too much in our own wits, and lean too much upon our own inventions ; opposing subtilty to subtilty, one evil device to another, matching and maintaining policy by policy, and not committing our cause to God.— *Abraham Wright.*

Verse 154.—*"Deliver."*   Not as in verse 153, but a word meaning to *redeem* or to *save by avenging.*   The corresponding particle is rendered redeemer, avenger, revenger, kinsman, near kinsman, next kinsman.—*William S. Plumer.*

Verse 154.—*"Quicken me."*   Here, again, we are called to consider the bearing of the pious mind.   Ever and anon, the great desire of the man of God is to advance in the divine life.   He makes spiritual gain of everything.   He seeks his goodly pearls out of strange conditions ; the reason is, his heart is in these things. Deliverance from temporal evil, deliverance from spiritual evil, both were sought ; but along with these, ever does the man of God take up the prayer to be quickened. Certainly we may understand him as seeking life.   Such is the import of the phraseology ; but in a man like David, the life he seeks must be the highest.   He desires spiritual life above all things ; he wants to get more into a blessed assimilation to God, that so he may enjoy the highest good.   So pants the heaven-born soul. . . . Give the believer this, and this will set him above all the ills of life.   And this and all good had been promised in the word. So he prays, *"Quicken me according to thy word."* He goes upon the word for everything ; he cannot be self-deceived there. Judge of yourselves, my brethren, by your spiritual aspirations. Nothing less will prove you to be of the Lord's redeemed.—*John Stephen.*

Verses 154, 156, 159.—*"Quicken me."* Pray to be *quickened*, as the Psalmist often does, and look unto Jesus, who is a quickening spirit : 1 Cor. xv. 45. " The first man Adam was made a living soul ; the last Adam was made a quickening spirit." As he has given you life, so he is ready to give it more and more abundantly ; this will make you to live to him, and to be unweariedly active for him.— *Nathanael Vincent, in "A Present for such as have been Sick and Recovered,"* 1693.

Verse 155.—*"Salvation is far from the wicked."* The Lord is almighty to pardon ; but he will not use it for thee an impenitent sinner. Thou hast not a friend on the bench, not an attribute in all God's name will speak for thee. Mercy itself will sit and vote with the rest of its fellow-attributes for thy damnation. God is able to save and help in a time of need, but upon what acquaintance is it that thou art so bold with God, as to expect his saving arm to be stretched forth for thee ? Though a man rise at midnight to let in a child that cries and knocks at his door, yet he will not take so much pains for a dog that lies howling there. This presents thy condition, sinner, sad enough, yet this is to tell thy story fairest ; for that almighty power of God which is engaged for the believer's salvation, is as deeply obliged to bring thee to thy execution and damnation. What greater tie than an oath ? God himself is under an oath to be the destruction of every impenitent soul. That oath which God sware in his wrath against the unbelieving Israelites, that they should not enter into his rest, concerns every unbeliever to the end of the world. In the name of God consider, were it but the oath of a man, or a company of men that, like those in the Acts, should swear to be the death of such an one, and thou wert the man, would it not fill thee with fear and trembling, night and day, and take away the quiet of thy life, till they were made thy friends ? What then are their pillows stuffed with, who can sleep so soundly without any horror or amazement, though they be told that the almighty God is under an oath of damning them body and soul, without timely repentance ?—*William Gurnall.*

Verse 155.—*"Salvation" !* What music is there in that word, music that never tires, but is always new, that always rouses yet always rests us ! It holds in itself all that our hearts would say. It is sweet vigour to us in the morning, and in the evening it is contented peace. It is a song that is always singing itself deep down in the delighted soul. Angelic ears are ravished by it up in heaven ; and our Eternal Father himself listens to it with adorable complacency. It is sweet even to him out of whose mind is the music of a thousand worlds. To be saved ! What is it to be saved in the fullest and utmost meaning ? Who can tell ? Eye hath not seen, nor ear heard. It is a rescue, and from such a shipwreck ! It is a rest, and in such an unimaginable home ! It is to lie down for ever in the bosom of God, in an endless rapture of insatiable contentment.—*Frederick William Faber,* 1853.

Verses 155, 156.—*"Salvation is far from the wicked."* *"Great are thy tender mercies, O Lord."* When the godly do think and speak of the damnable condition of the wicked, they should not be senseless of their own ill deserving, nor of God's grace which hath made the difference between the wicked and them.—*David Dickson.*

Verse 156.—*"Great are thy tender mercies, O Lord."* Two epithets he ascribes to God's mercies ; first, he calls them *"great,"* and then he calls them *"tender"* mercies. They are great in many respects : for continuance, they endure for ever ; for largeness, they reach unto the heavens, and are higher than they ; yea, they are above all the works of God. And this is for the comfort of poor sinners, whose sins are many and great : let them not despair ; his mercies are greater and more ; for since they are greater than all his works, how much more greater than thou and all thy sinful works ! . . . . . The other epithet he gives them is, that they are *"tender"* mercies ; because the Lord is easy to be entreated ; for he is slow unto wrath, but ready to show mercy. S. James saith that the wisdom which is from above is "gentle, peaceable, easy to be entreated." If his grace in his children make them gentle and easy to be entreated, what shall we think of himself ? Since he will have such pity in us poor creatures, that seventy times seven times in the day he will have us to forgive the offences of our brethren ; Oh, what pity and compassion abound in himself! Thus we see our comfort is increased; that as his mercies are great, so are they tender; easily obtained, where they are earnestly craved.—*William Cowper.*

Verse 156.—The Psalmist, when speaking of the wretched condition of "*the wicked*," is naturally led to adore the mercies of the Lord which had " made him to differ." For indeed to this source alone must we trace the distinction between us and them.—*Charles Bridges.*

Verse 157.—"*Persecutors.*" A participle from the verb rendered *pursue, chase.* "*Enemies*," as in verse 139, the authors of my distress. Until men are hunted and hounded by many enemies, who for the time have power, and are withal fierce and to some extent unscrupulous, they can have but a faint conception of the anguish of the prophet when he experienced the evils noted in this verse. Yet they did not move him from his constancy and integrity.—*William S. Plumer.*

Verse 158.—"*I beheld the trangressors, and was grieved.*" Celerinus in Cyprian's Epistles, acquaints a friend with his great grief for the apostasy of a woman through fear of persecution; which afflicted him so much, that at the feast of Easter (the Queen of feasts in the primitive church) he wept night and day, and resolved never to know a moment's delight, till through the mercy of God she should be recovered. —*Charles Bridges.*

Verse 158.—"*I beheld the transgressors, and was grieved.*" Oh, if you have the hearts of Christians or of men in you, let them yearn towards your poor ignorant, ungodly neighbours. Alas, there is but a step betwixt them and death and hell: many hundred diseases are waiting ready to seize on them, and if they die unregenerate they are lost for ever. Have you hearts of rock, that cannot pity men in such a case as this? If you believe not the word of God, and the danger of sinners, why are you Christians yourselves? If you do believe it, why do you not bestir yourself to the helping of others? Do you not care who is damned, so you be saved? If so, you have sufficient cause to pity yourselves, for it is a frame of spirit utterly inconsistent with grace: should you not rather say, as the lepers of Samaria, Is it not a day of glad tidings, and do we sit still and hold our peace? 2 Kings vii. 9. Hath God had so much mercy on you, and will you have no mercy on your poor neighbours? You need not go far to find objects for your pity: look but into your streets, or into the next house to you, and you will probably find some. Have you never an ignorant, an unregenerate neighbour that sets his heart on things below, and neglecteth eternity? What blessed place do you live in, where there is none such? If there be not some of them in thine own family, it is well; and yet art thou silent? Dost thou live close by them, or meet them in the streets, or labour with them, or travel with them, or sit and talk with them, and say nothing to them of their souls, or the life to come? If their houses were on fire, thou wouldst run and help them; and wilt thou not help them when their souls are almost at the fire of hell? If thou knewest but a remedy for their diseases thou wouldst tell it them, or else thou wouldst judge thyself guilty of their death.—*Richard Baxter* (1615—1691), *in "The Saints' Everlasting Rest."*

Verse 158.—"*Grieved, because they kept not thy law.*" I never thought the world had been so wicked, when the Gospel began, as now I see it is; I rather hoped that every one would have leaped for joy to have found himself freed from the filth of the Pope, from his lamentable molestations of poor troubled consciences, and that through Christ they would by faith obtain the celestial treasure they sought after before with such vast cost and labour, though in vain. And especially I thought the bishops and universities would with joy of heart have received the true doctrines; but I have been lamentably deceived. Moses and Jeremiah, too, complained they had been deceived.—*Martin Luther.*

Verse 158.—"*Grieved.*" The word that is here translated "*grieved* " is from *katat,* that signifies to loathe, abhor, and contend. I beheld the transgressors, and I loathed them; I beheld the transgressors, and I abhorred them; I beheld the transgressors, and I contended with them; but not so much because they were mine enemies, as because they were thine.—*Thomas Brooks.*

Verse 158.—The day when I first met Colonel Gardiner at Leicester, I happened to preach a lecture from Ps. cxix. 158: "*I beheld the transgressors, and was grieved; because they kept not thy word.*" I was large in describing that mixture of indignation and grief, strongly expressed by the original word there, with which a good man looks on the varying transgressors of the divine law; and in tracing the causes of that grief, as arising from a regard to the divine honour, and the interest of a Redeemer, and a compassionate concern for the misery such offenders bring on themselves, and for the mischief they do to the world about them. I little thought how exactly I was drawing Colonel Gardiner's character under each of those heads; and I have often reflected upon it as a happy providence, which opened a much speedier way than I could have expected, to the breast of one of the most amiable and useful friends which I ever expect to find upon earth. We afterwards sung a hymn, which brought over again some of the leading thoughts in the sermon, and struck him so strongly, that on obtaining a copy of it, he committed it to his memory, and used to repeat it with so forcible an accent, as showed how much every line expressed of his very soul. In this view the reader will pardon my inserting it; especially as I know not when I may get time to publish a volume of these serious though artless compositions, which I sent him in manuscript some years ago, and to which I have since made very large additions :—

> Arise, my tenderest thoughts, arise,
> To torrents melt my streaming eyes;
> And thou, my heart, with anguish feel
> Those evils which thou canst not heal.
>
> See human nature sunk in shame;
> See scandals pour'd on Jesu's name;
> The Father wounded through the Son;
> The world abused, and souls undone.
>
> See the short course of vain delight
> Closing in everlasting night;
> In flames that no abatement know,
> Though briny tears for ever flow.
>
> My God, I feel the mournful scene;
> My bowels yearn o'er dying men,
> And fain my pity would reclaim,
> And snatch the firebrands from the flame.
>
> But feeble my compassion proves,
> And can but weep where most it loves;
> Thy own all-saving arm employ,
> And turn these drops of grief to joy.

Philip Doddridge, in "The Life of Colonel Gardiner."

Verse 159.—"*Consider how I love thy precepts.*" Search me. Behold the evidence of my attachment to thy law. This is the confident appeal of one who was conscious that he was truly attached to God; that he really loved his law. It is similar to the appeal of Peter to the Saviour (John xxi. 17), " Lord, thou knowest all things; thou knowest that I love thee." A man who truly loves God *may* make this appeal without impropriety. He may be so confident, so certain, that he has true love for the character of God, that he may make a solemn appeal to him on the subject, as he might appeal to a friend, to his wife, to his son, to his daughter, with the utmost confidence that he loved them. A man *ought* to have such love for *them*, that he could affirm this without hesitation or doubt; a man *ought* to have such love for *God*, that he could affirm this with equal confidence and propriety.—*Albert Barnes.*

Verse 159.—"*Consider how I love thy precepts.*" He saith not, consider how I *perform* thy precepts; but how I *love* them. The comfort of a Christian militant, in this body of sin, is rather in the sincerity and fervency of his affections than in the absolute perfection of his actions. He fails many times in his obedience to God's precepts, in regard of his action; but love in his affection still remains; so that both before the temptation to sin, and after it, there is a grief in his soul, that he should find in himself any corrupt will or desire, contrary to the holy will of the Lord his God; and this proves an invincible love in him to the precepts of God.—*William Cowper.*

Verse 159.—"*Consider,*" etc. Translate (the Hebrew being the same as in verse 158) "*Behold* how I love thy precepts," as is evinced in that when " I *beheld* the transgressors I was grieved." He begs to God to behold this, not as meritorious of grace, but as a distinctive mark of a godly man.—*A. R. Fausset.*

Verse 159.—*"I love thy precepts: quicken me."* The love wherewith he loved God came from that love wherewith God first loved him. For by seeing the great love wherewith God loved him, he was moved and inforced to love God again. So that his meaning is thus much: Thou seest, Lord, that I am an enemy to sin in myself, for I forget not thy law; thou seest that I am an enemy to sin in others, for I am grieved to see them transgress thy law; wherefore, O Lord, *"quicken me,"* and let thy loving mercy whereby thou hast created me and redeemed me in Christ, whereby thou hast delivered me from so many troubles, and enriched me with so many and continual benefits, renew, revive, quicken, and restore me.—*Richard Greenham.*

Verse 159.—*"Quicken me."* Often as the Psalmist had repeated his prayer for quickening grace,* it was not a *"vain repetition,"* or an empty sound. Each time was it enlivened with abundant faith, intense feeling of his necessity, and the vehemency of most ardent affection. If the consciousness of the faintness of our strength and the coldness of our affections should lead us to offer this petition a hundred times a day in this spirit, it would never fail of acceptance.—*Charles Bridges.*

Verse 159.—*"According to thy lovingkindness."* We need not desire to be quickened any further than God's lovingkindness will quicken us.—*Matthew Henry.*

Verse 160.—*"Thy word is true from the beginning."* Literally, "The beginning of thy word is truth," in antithesis to the "enduring for ever," in the future, in the next clause. Cocceius and Hengstenberg take it, "The *sum* of thy word is true," as in Numbers xxvi. 2; xxxi. 26. But the antithesis noticed above in the English version is thus lost; and the old versions support the English version. Also, if it were *"the sum,"* the plural ought to follow, viz., "of thy *words*," not *"word."*—*A. R. Fausset.*

Verse 160.—*"Thy word is true from the beginning,"* etc. As if he should say, I believe that thou wilt thus quicken me, because the very beginning of thy word is most just and true; and when thou didst enter into covenant with me, I did find that thou didst not deceive me, nor beguile me. And when by thy Spirit thou madest me believe thy covenant, thou meanedst truth; and I know that as thou didst promise, thou wilt perform, for thou art no more liberal in promising than faithful and just in performing, and thy judgment will be as righteous as thy promise is true. I know that as soon as thou speakest, truth proceedeth from thee; and even so I know thou wilt defend and preserve me, that thy judgments may shine as righteous in thee.—*Richard Greenham.*

Verse 160.—*"Thy word is true from the beginning,"* etc. God's commandment and promise is exceeding broad, reaching to all times. Was a word of command "the guide of thy youth"? I assure thee it will be as good a staff of thine age. A good promise is a good nurse, both to the young babe and to the decrepid old man. Your apothecaries' best cordials in time will lose their spirits, and sometimes the stronger they are, the sooner. But hath a promise cheered thee, say, twenty, thirty, forty years ago? Taste it but now afresh, and thou shalt find it as fresh, and as full of refreshment as ever. If it hath been thy greatest joy in thy joyful youth, I tell thee, it hath as much joy in it for thy sad old age. That may be said of God's word, which the prophet saith of God himself (Isa. xlvi. 4): "And even to your old age I am he; and even to hoar hairs will I carry you." Doth not the Psalmist say as much here, *"Thy word is true from the beginning"*? It's well, it begins well. But will it last as well? Yes: he adds, *"and every one of thy righteous judgments endureth for ever."* Answerable to which is that other expression (verse 152), *"Concerning thy testimonies, I have known of old that thou hast founded them for ever."* "For ever," and "founded for ever." O sweet expression! O grounded comfort! Brethren, get acquainted with God's word and promise as soon as you can, and maintain that acquaintance everlastingly; and your knowledge of it shall not either go before, or go beyond its truth. Know it as soon and as long as you will or can, and you shall never find it tripping or failing; but you may after long experience of God say of it, *"I have known of old that thou hast founded it for ever."*—*Anthony Tuckney,* 1599—1670.

---

* Nine times is this petition urged, verses 25, 37, 40, 88, 107, 149, 154, 156, 159.

EXPOSITION OF VERSES 161 TO 168.

PRINCES have persecuted me without a cause : but my heart standeth in awe of thy word.

162 I rejoice at thy word, as one that findeth great spoil.

163 I hate and abhor lying : *but* thy law do I love.

164 Seven times a day do I praise thee because of thy righteous judgments.

165 Great peace have they which love thy law : and nothing shall offend them.

166 LORD, I have hoped for thy salvation, and done thy commandments.

167 My soul hath kept thy testimonies ; and I love them exceedingly.

168 I have kept thy precepts and thy testimonies ; for all my ways *are* before thee.

161. "*Princes have persecuted me without a cause.*" Such persons ought to have known better ; they should have had sympathy with one of their own rank. A man expects a fair trial at the hand of his peers : it is ignoble to be prejudiced. Moreover, if honour be banished from all other breasts it should remain in the bosom of kings, and honour forbids the persecution of the innocent. Princes are appointed to protect the innocent and avenge the oppressed, and it is a shame when they themselves become the assailants of the righteous. It was a sad case when the man of God found himself attacked by the judges of the earth, for eminent position added weight and venom to their enmity. It was well that the sufferer could truthfully assert that this persecution was without cause. He had not broken their laws, he had not injured them, he had not even desired to see them injured, he had not been an advocate of rebellion or anarchy, he had neither openly nor secretly opposed their power, and therefore, while this made their oppression the more inexcusable, it took away a part of its sting, and helped the brave-hearted servant of God to bear up. "*But my heart standeth in awe of thy word.*" He might have been overcome by awe of the princes had it not been that a greater fear drove out the less, and he was swayed by awe of God's word. How little do crowns and sceptres become in the judgment of that man who perceives a more majestic royalty in the commands of his God. We are not likely to be disheartened by persecution, or driven by it into sin, if the word of God continually has supreme power over our minds.

162. "*I rejoice at thy word, as one that findeth great spoil.*" His awe did not prevent his joy ; his fear of God was not of the kind which perfect love casts out, but of the sort which it nourishes. He trembled at the word of the Lord, and yet rejoiced at it. He compares his joy to that of one who has been long in battle, and has at last won the victory and is dividing the spoil. This usually falls to the lot of princes, and though David was not one with them in their persecutions, yet he had his victories, and his spoil was equal to their greatest gains. The profits made in searching the Scriptures were greater than the trophies of war. We too have to fight for divine truth ; every doctrine costs us a battle, but when we gain a full understanding of it by personal struggles it becomes doubly precious to us. In these days godly men have a full share of battling for the word of God ; may we have for our spoil a firmer hold upon the priceless word. Perhaps, however, the Psalmist may have rejoiced as one who comes upon hidden treasure for which he had not fought, in which case we find the analogy in the man of God who, while reading the Bible, makes grand and blessed discoveries of the grace of God laid up for him,—discoveries which surprise him, for he looked not to find such a prize. Whether we come by the truth as finders or as warriors fighting for it, the heavenly treasure should be equally dear to us. With what quiet joy does the ploughman steal home with his golden find ! How victors shout as they share the plunder ! How glad should that man be who has discovered his portion in the promises of holy writ, and is able to enjoy it for himself, knowing by the witness of the Holy Spirit that it is all his own.

163. "*I hate and abhor lying.*" A double expression for an inexpressible loathing.

Falsehood in doctrine, in life, or in speech, falsehood in any form or shape, had become utterly detestable to the Psalmist. This was a remarkable state for an Oriental, for generally lying is the delight of Easterns, and the only wrong they see in it is a want of skill in its exercise so that the liar is found out. David himself had made much progress when he had come to this. He does not, however, alone refer to falsehood in conversation ; he evidently intends perversity in faith and teaching. He set down all opposition to the God of truth as lying, and then he turned his whole soul against it in the intensest form of indignation. Godly men should detest false doctrine even as they abhor a lie. *"But thy law do I love,"* because it is all truth. His love was as ardent as his hate. True men love truth, and hate lying. It is well for us to know which way our hates and loves run, and we may do essential service to others by declaring what are their objects. Both love and hate are contagious, and when they are sanctified the wider their influence the better.

164. *"Seven times a day do I praise thee because of thy righteous judgments."* He laboured perfectly to praise his perfect God, and therefore fulfilled the perfect number of songs. Seven may also intend frequency. Frequently he lifted up his heart in thanksgiving to God for his divine teachings in the word, and for his divine actions in providence. With his voice he extolled the righteousness of the Judge of all the earth. As often as ever he thought of God's ways a song leaped to his lips. At the sight of the oppressive princes, and at the hearing of the abounding falsehood around him, he felt all the more bound to adore and magnify God, who in all things is truth and righteousness. When others rob us of our praise it should be a caution to us not to fall into the same conduct towards our God, who is so much more worthy of honour. If we praise God when we are persecuted our music will be all the sweeter to him because of our constancy in suffering. If we keep clear of all lying, our song will be the more acceptable because it comes out of pure lips. If we never flatter men we shall be in the better condition for honouring the Lord. Do we praise God seven times a day ? Do we praise him once in seven days ?

165. *"Great peace have they which love thy law."* What a charming verse is this ! It deals not with those who perfectly keep the law, for where should such men be found ? but with those who love it, whose hearts and hands are made to square with its precepts and demands. These men are ever striving, with all their hearts, to walk in obedience to the law, and though they are often persecuted they have peace, yea, *great* peace ; for they have learned the secret of the reconciling blood, they have felt the power of the comforting Spirit, and they stand before the Father as men accepted. The Lord has given them to feel his peace, which passed all understanding. They have many troubles, and are likely to be persecuted by the proud, but their usual condition is that of deep calm—a peace too great for this little world to break. *"And nothing shall offend them,"* or, " shall really injure them." " All things work together for good to them that love God, to them who are the called according to his purpose." It must needs be that offences come, but these lovers of the law are peacemakers, and so they neither give nor take offence. That peace which is founded upon conformity to God's will is a living and lasting one, worth writing of with enthusiasm, as the Psalmist here does.

166. *"Lord, I have hoped for thy salvation, and done thy commandments."* Here we have salvation by grace, and the fruits thereof. All David's hope was fixed upon God, he looked to him alone for salvation ; and then he endeavoured most earnestly to fulfil the commands of his law. Those who place least reliance upon good works are very frequently those who have the most of them ; that same divine teaching which delivers us from confidence in our own doings leads us to abound in every good work to the glory of God. In times of trouble there are two things to be done, the first is to hope in God, and the second is to do that which is right. The first without the second would be mere presumption : the second without the first mere formalism. It is well if in looking back we can claim to have acted in the way which is commanded of the Lord. If we have acted rightly towards God we are sure that he will act kindly with us.

167. *"My soul hath kept thy testimonies."* My outward life has kept thy precepts, and my inward life—my soul, has kept thy testimonies. God has borne testimony to many sacred truths, and these we hold fast as for life itself. The gracious man stores up the truth of God within his heart as a treasure exceedingly dear and precious —he keeps it. His secret soul, his inmost self, becomes the guardian of these divine teachings which are his sole authority in soul matters. *"And I love them exceedingly."* This was why he kept them, and having kept them this was the result of the keeping.

He did not merely store up revealed truth by way of duty, but because of a deep, unutterable affection for it. He felt that he could sooner die than give up any part of the revelation of God. The more we store our minds with heavenly truth, the more deeply shall we be in love with it : the more we see the exceeding riches of the Bible the more will our love exceed measure, and exceed expression.

168. *"I have kept thy precepts and thy testimonies."* Both the practical and the doctrinal parts of God's word he had stored up, and preserved, and followed. It is a blessed thing to see the two forms of the divine word, equally known, equally valued, equally confessed : there should be no picking and choosing as to the mind of God. We know those who endeavour to be careful as to the precepts, but who seem to think that the doctrines of the gospel are mere matters of opinion, which they may shape for themselves. This is not a perfect condition of things. We have known others again who are very rigid as to the doctrines, and painfully lax with reference to the precepts. This also is far from right. When the two are "kept" with equal earnestness then have we the perfect man. *"For all my ways are before thee."* Probably he means to say that this was the motive of his endeavouring to be right both in head and heart, because he knew that God saw him, and under the sense of the divine presence he was afraid to err. Or else he is thus appealing to God to bear witness to the truth of what he has said. In either case it is no small consolation to feel that our heavenly Father knows all about us, and that if princes speak against us, and worldlings fill their mouths with cruel lies, yet he can vindicate us, for there is nothing secret or hidden from him.

We are struck with the contrast between this verse, which is the last of its octave, and verse 176, which is similarly placed in the next octave. This is a protest of innocence, " I have kept thy precepts," and that a confession of sin, " I have gone astray like a lost sheep." Both were sincere, both accurate. Experience makes many a paradox plain, and this is one. Before God we may be clear of open fault and yet at the same time mourn over a thousand heart-wanderings which need his restoring hand.

NOTES ON VERSES 161 TO 168.

Verse 161.—"Princes have persecuted me." The evil is aggravated from the consideration that it is the very persons who ought to be as bucklers to defend us, who employ their strength in hurting us. Yea, when the afflicted are stricken by those in high places, they in a manner think that the hand of God is against them. There was also this peculiarity in the case of the prophet, that he had to encounter the grandees of the chosen people—men whom God had placed in such honourable stations, to the end they might be the pillars of the Church.—*John Calvin.*

Verse 161.—"Without a cause." I settle it as an established point with me, that the more diligently and faithfully I serve Christ, the greater reproach and the more injury I must expect. I have drank deep of the cup of slander and reproach of late, but I am in no wise discouraged ; no, nor by, what is much harder to bear, the unsuccessfulness of my endeavours to mend this bad world.—*Philip Doddridge.*

Verse 161.—"Without a cause." We know what persecutions the body of Christ, that is, the holy Church, suffered from the kings of the earth. Let us therefore here also recognize the words of the Church : *"Princes have persecuted me without a cause."* For how had the Christians injured the kingdoms of the earth ? Although their King promised them the kingdom of heaven, how, I ask, had they injured the kingdoms of earth ? Did their King forbid his soldiers to pay and to render due service to the kings of the earth ? Saith he not to the Jews who were striving to calumniate him, " Render therefore unto Cæsar the things which are Cæsar's ; and unto God the things that are God's " ? Matt. xxii. 21. Did he not even in his own person pay tribute from the mouth of a fish ? Did not his forerunner, when the soldiers of this kingdom were seeking what they ought to do for their everlasting salvation, instead of replying, " Loose your belts, throw away your arms, desert your king, that ye may wage war for the Lord," answer, " Do violence to no man, neither accuse any falsely ; and be content with your wages " ? Luke iii. 14. Did not one of his soldiers, his most beloved companion, say to his fellow soldiers, the provincials, so to speak, of Christ, " Let every soul be subject unto the higher powers " ? and a little lower he addeth, " Render therefore to all their dues : tribute to whom tribute is due ; custom to whom custom ; fear to whom fear ; honour to whom honour. Owe no man anything, but to love one another." Rom. xiii. 1, 7, 8. Does he not enjoin the Church to pray even for kings themselves ? How, then, have the Christians offended against them ? What due have they not rendered ? In what have not Christians obeyed the monarchs of earth ? The kings of the earth therefore have persecuted the Christians *without a cause.—Augustine.*

Verse 161.—"But my heart standeth in awe of thy word." If there remains any qualm of fear on thy heart, fear from the wrath of bloody men threatening thee for thy profession of the truth, then to a heart inflamed with the love of truth, labour to add a heart filled with the fear of that wrath which God hath in store for all that apostatize from the truth. When you chance to burn your finger, you hold it to the fire, which being a greater fire draws out the other. Thus, when thy thoughts are scorched, and thy heart scared with the fire of man's wrath, hold them a while to hell fire, which God hath prepared for the fearful (Rev. xxi. 8), and all that run away from truth's colours (Heb. x. 39), and thou wilt lose the sense of the one for fear of the other. *Ignosce imperator*, saith the holy man, *tu carcerem, Deus gehennam minatur ;* " Pardon me, O Emperor, if I obey not thy command ; thou threatenest a prison, but God a hell." Observable is that of David : " Princes have persecuted me without a cause : but my heart standeth in awe of thy word." He had no cause to fear them that had no cause to persecute him. One threatening out of the word, that sets the point of God's wrath to his heart, scares him more than the worst that the greatest on earth can do to him. Man's wrath, when hottest, is but a temperate climate to the wrath of the living God. They who have felt both have testified as much. Man's wrath cannot hinder the access of God's love to the creature, which hath made the saints sing in the fire, in spite of their enemies' teeth. But the creature under God's wrath is like one shut up in a close oven, no crevice is open to let any of the heat out, or any refreshing in to him.—*William Gurnall.*

Verse 161.—"My heart standeth in awe of thy word." There is an *awe* of the word, not that maketh us shy of it, but tender of violating it, or doing anything contrary to it. This is not the fruit of slavish fear, but of holy love ; it is not afraid of the word, but delighteth in it, as it discovereth the mind of God to us ; as in the next verse it is written, " I rejoice at thy word." This awe is called by a proper name, reverence, or godly fear ; when we consider whose word it is, namely, the word of the Lord, who is our God, and hath a right to command what he pleaseth ; to whose will and word we have already yielded obedience, and devoted ourselves to walk worthy of him in all well-pleasing ; who can find us out in all our failings, as knowing our very thoughts afar off (Ps. cxxxix. 2), and having all our ways before him, and being one of whom we read,—" He is a holy God ; he is a jealous God ; he will not forgive your transgressions nor your sins " (Josh. xxiv. 19), that is to say, if we impenitently continue in them. Considering these things we receive the word with that trembling of heart which God so much respects.—*Thomas Manton.*

Verse 161.—"*In awe of thy word.*" I would advise you all, that come to the reading or hearing of this book, which is the word of God, the most precious jewel, and most holy relic that remaineth upon earth, that ye bring with you the fear of God, and that ye do it with all due reverence, and use your knowledge thereof, not to vain glory of frivolous disputation, but to the honour of God, increase of virtue, and edification both of yourselves and others.—*Thomas Cranmer*, 1489—1555.

Verse 161.—"*Awe of thy word.*" They that tremble at the convictions of the word may triumph in the consolations of it.—*Matthew Henry.*

Verse 162.—"*I rejoice at thy word, as one that findeth great spoil.*" He never came to an ordinance but as a soldier to the spoil, after a great battle, as having a constant warfare with his corruptions that fought against his soul. Now he comes to see what God will say to him, and he will make himself a saver [or gainer], and get a booty out of every commandment, promise, or threatening he hears.—*John Cotton* (1585—1652), *in "The way of life."*

Verse 162.—"*I rejoice at thy word.*" " Euripides," saith the orator, " hath in his well-composed tragedies more sentiments than sayings ; " and Thucydides hath so stuffed every syllable of his history with substance, that the one runs parallel along with the other ; Lysias's works are so well couched that you cannot take out the least word but you take away the whole sense with it ; and Phocion had a special faculty of speaking much in a few words. The Cretians, in Plato's time (however degenerated in St. Paul's), were more weighty than wordy ; Timanthes was famous in this, that in his pictures more things were intended than deciphered ; and of Homer it is said that none could ever peer him for poetry. Then how much more apt and apposite are these high praises to the book of God, rightly called *the Bible* or *the book*, as if it were, as indeed it is, both for fitness of terms and fulness of truth, the only book to which (as Luther saith) all the books in the world are but waste paper. It is called *the word*, by way of eminency, because it must be the butt and boundary of all our words ; and *the scripture*, as the lord paramount above all other words or writings of men collected into volumes, there being, as the Rabbins say, a mountain of sense hanging upon every tittle of it, whence may be gathered flowers and phrases to polish our speeches with, even sound words, that have a healing property in them, far above all filed phrases of human elocution.—*Thomas Adams.*

Verse 162.—"*As one that findeth great spoil.*" This expressive image may remind us of the inward conflict to be endured in acquiring the spoils of this precious word. It is so contrary to our natural taste and temper, that habitual self-denial and struggle with the indisposition of the heart can alone enable us to "*find the spoil.*" But what "*great spoil*" is divided as the fruit of the conflict ! How rich and abundant is the recompense of the " good soldier of Jesus Christ," who is determined through the power of the Spirit to " endure hardness," until he overcome the reluctance of his heart to this spiritual duty. He shall "*rejoice*" in "*finding great spoil.*" Sometimes—as the spoil with which the lepers enriched themselves in the Syrian camp—it may be found unexpectedly. Sometimes we see the riches and treasures contained in a passage or doctrine, long before we can make it our own. And often when we gird ourselves to the conflict with indolence, and wanderings, under the weakness of our spiritual perceptions and the power of unbelief, many a prayer, and many a sigh is sent up for Divine aid, before we are crowned with victory, and are enabled, as the fruit of our conquest joyfully to appropriate the word to our present need and distress.—*Charles Bridges.*

Verse 163.—"*I hate and abhor lying,*" etc. One sees here how the light on David's soul was increasing more and more unto the perfect day. In the earlier part of this Psalm, David in the recollection of his own sin had prayed, " Remove from me the way of lying," and the Lord had indeed answered his prayer, for he now declares his utter loathing of every false way : *"I hate and abhor lying."* And we see, in some measure, the instrument by which the Holy Spirit wrought the change : *"Thy law do I love"* ; nay, as he adds in a later verse, " I love them exceedingly." And so it ever must be, the heart must have some holier object of its affection to fill up the void, or there will be no security against a relapse into sin. I might talk for ever on the sin, the disgrace, and the danger of lying, and though at the time and for a time my words might have some influence, yet, unless the heart be filled with the love of God and of God's law, the first temptation would prove too powerful. The Bible teaches us this in a variety of ways. God says to Israel, not only " cease to do evil," but, " learn to do well." And still more pointedly does the apostle, when he was warring against drunkenness, say, " Be not drunk with wine, wherein is excess,—but be filled with the Spirit."—*Barton Bouchier.*

Verse 163.—*"I hate and abhor lying."* *"Lying,"* according to Scripture usage, not only signifies speaking contrary to what one thinks, but also thinking contrary to the truth of things, and, particularly, the giving to any other of that worship and glory which are due to the true God alone. It is to think and act aside from God's truth. The men who persecuted that godly man thought of earthly prosperity and power as they should not have thought ; they judged God's servant falsely, and they thought wickedly of God himself. The man of God took a view of these things ; he saw the wickedness and the vileness of them, and he continued—*"False-hood I hate and abhor : thy law do I love."* From all the false and delusive ways of men, from all the pride and pomp that surround courts, from the sinful pleasures and pursuits of worldly men, as well as from the ostentatious idolatry of heathen nations, he could turn with heart delight to the contemplation of Jehovah, in that wonderful ritual which manifested the divine mercy in vicarious sacrifices, and observances, and festivals ; and to that holy law which was given as man's rule of duty and grateful obedience, and all these he loved as the manifestations of God's grace.—*John Stephen.*

Verse 163.—*"I hate and abhor lying"* : not only *"hate"* it, nor simply I *"abhor"* it, but *"hate and abhor,"* to strengthen and increase the sense, and make it more vehement. Where the enmity is not great against the sin, the matter may be compounded and taken up ; but David will have nothing to do with it, for he saith,— I loathe and abhor it, and hate it with a deadly hatred. Slight hatred of a sinful course is not sufficient to guard us against it.—*Thomas Manton.*

Verse 163.—Sin seemeth to have its name from the Hebrew word *sana, to hate,* the word here used, because it is most of all to be hated, as the greatest evil, as that which setteth us furthest from God the greatest good. None can hate it but those that love the law of God ; for all hatred comes from love. A natural man may be angry with his sin, but hate it he cannot ; nay, he may leave it, but not loathe it ; if he did, he would loathe all sin as well as any one sin.—*Abraham Wright.*

Verse 163.—*"Lying."* All injustice is abominable : to do any sort of wrong is a heinous crime, but lying is that crime which, above all others, tendeth to the dissolution of society and disturbance of human life ; which God therefore doth most loathe, and men have reason especially to detest. Of this the slanderer is most deeply guilty. "A witness of Belial scorneth judgment, and the mouth of the wicked devoureth iniquity," saith the wise man : Prov. xix. 28 He is indeed, according to just estimation. guilty of all kinds of injury, breaking all the second table of commands respecting our neighbour. Most distinctly he beareth false witness against his neighbour : he doth covet his neighbour's goods, for 'tis constantly out of such an irregular desire, for his own presumed advantage, to dispossess his neighbour of some good, and transfer it on himself, that the slanderer uttereth his tale : he is also a thief and robber of his good name, a deflowerer and defiler of his reputation, an assassin and murderer of his honour. So doth he violate all the rules of justice, and perpetrateth all sorts of wrong against his neighbour.—*Isaac Barrow.*

Verse 164.—*"Seven times a day do I praise thee."* Affections of the soul cannot long be kept secret ; if they be strong they will break forth in actions. The love of God is like a fire in the heart of man, which breaks forth, and manifests itself in the obedience of his commandments, and praising him for his benefits ; and this is it which David now protests, that the love of God was not idle in his heart, but made him fervent and earnest in praising God, so that *"seven times a day"* he did praise God. For by this number the carefulness of holy devotion is expressed, and the fervency of his love. In praising God he could not be satisfied, saith Basil.—*William Cowper.*

Verse 164.—*"Seven times a day do I praise thee."* "As every grace," says Sibbes, "increaseth by exercise of itself, so doth the grace of prayer. By prayer we learn to pray." And thus it was with the Psalmist; he oftentimes anticipated the dawning of the morning for his exercise of prayer; and at midnight frequently arose to pour out his soul in prayer; now he adds that *"seven times in a day,"* or as we might express it, "at every touch and turn," he finds opportunity for and delight in praise. Oh for David's spirit and David's practice!—*Barton Bouchier.*

Verse 164.—*"Seven times a day do I praise thee."* A Christian ought to give himself up eminently to this duty without limits.—*Walter Marshall.*

Verse 164.—*"Seven times a day do I praise thee."* Not as if he, had seven set hours for this duty every day, as the Papists would have it, to countenance their seven canonical hours, but rather a definite number is put for an indefinite, and so amounts to this,—he did very often in a day praise God; his holy heart taking the hint of every providence to carry him to heaven on this errand of prayer and praise.—*William Gurnall.*

Verse 164.—*"Seven times a day."* Some of the Jewish Rabbis affirm that David is here to be understood literally, observing, that the devout Hebrews were accustomed to praise God twice in the morning, before reading the ten commandments, and once after; twice in the evening before reading the same portion of inspiration, and twice after; which makes up the number of seven times a day.—*James Anderson's note to Calvin in loc.*

Verse 165.—*"Great peace have they which love thy law."* Amidst the storms and tempests of the world, there is a perfect calm in the breasts of those, who not only do the will of God, but *"love"* to do it. They are at peace with God, by the blood of reconciliation; at peace with themselves, by the answer of a good conscience, and the subjection of those desires which war against the soul; at peace with all men, by the spirit of charity; and the whole creation is so at peace with them that all things work together for their good. No external troubles can rob them of this *"great peace,"* no "offences" or stumbling blocks, which are thrown in their way by persecution, or temptation, by the malice of enemies, or by the apostasy of friends, by anything which they see, hear of, or feel, can detain, or divert them from their course. Heavenly love surmounts every obstacle, and runs with delight the way of God's commandments.—*George Horne.*

Verse 165.—*"Great peace have they which love thy law."* There have been Elis trembling for the ark of God, and Uzzahs putting out their hand in fear that it was going to fall; but in the midst of the deepest troubles through which the church has passed, and the fiercest storms that have raged about it, there have been true, faithful men of God who have never despaired. In every age there have been Luthers and Latimers, who have not only held fast their confidence, but whose peace has deepened with the roaring of the waves. The more they have been forsaken of men, the closer has been their communion with God. And with strong hold of him and of his promises, and hearts that could enter into the secret place of the Most High, although there has been everything without to agitate, threaten, and alarm, they have been guided into perfect peace.—*James Martin, in "The Christian Mirror, and other Sermons,"* 1878.

Verse 165.—*"Great peace have they which love thy law."* Clearness of conscience is a help to comfortable thoughts. Yet observe, that peace is not so much affected as preserved by a good conscience and conversation; for though joy in the Holy Ghost will make its nest nowhere but in a holy soul, yet the blood of Christ only can speak peace; "being justified by faith, we have peace:" Rom. v. 1. An exact life will not make, but keep conscience quiet; an easy shoe does not heal a sore foot, but it keeps a sound one from hurt. Walking with God according to gospel rules hath peace entailed upon it, and that peace is such a treasure, as thereby a Christian may have his rejoicing from himself. Gal. vi. 4, 16. His own heart sings him a merry tune, which the threats and reproaches of the world cannot silence. The treasure of comfort is not expended in affliction; death itself doth not exhaust but increase and advance it to an eternal triumph. O the excellency and necessity of it! Paul laid it up for a death-bed cordial: "Our rejoicing is this, the testimony of our conscience:" 2 Cor. i. 12. And Hezekiah dares hold it up to God, as well as cheer himself up with it on approaching death. A conscience good in point of integrity will be good also in point of tranquillity: "The righteous are bold as a lion ": they have great peace that love and keep God's commandments : Prov. xxviii. 1 ; Ps. cxix. 165. And saith the apostle, "If our heart condemn us not, then have we confidence towards God " (1 John iii. 2), and I may add also, towards men. Oh ! what comfort and solace hath a clear conscience ! A conscientious man hath something within to answer accusations without ; he hath such a rich treasure as will not fail in greatest straits and hazards. I shall conclude this with a notable saying of Bernard :—" The pleasures of a good conscience are the Paradise of souls, the joy of angels, a garden of delights, a field of blessing, the temple of Solomon, the court of God, the habitation of the Holy Spirit."—*Oliver Heywood.*

Verse 165.—"*Great peace.*" Note that for "*peace*" the Hebrew word is שלום *shâlom :* it signifies not only "*peace,*" but also *perfection, wholeness, prosperity, tranquillity, healthfulness, safety,* the *completion* and *consummation* of every good thing, and so it is frequently taken by the Hebrews ; hence in salutations wishing one the other well, they say, שלום לך, *shâlom lekha, i.e.,* "peace be with thee"; as if one should say, "may all things be prosperous with thee."—*Thomas Le Blanc.*

Verse 165.—"*They which love thy law.*" To *love* a law may seem strange ; but it is the only true divine life. To keep it because we are afraid of its penalties is only a form of fear or prudential consideration. To keep it to preserve a good name may be propriety and respectability. To keep it because it is best for society may be worldly self-interest. To keep it because of physical health may be the policy of epicurean philosophy. To keep it because we love it is to show that it is already part of us—has entered into the moral texture of our being. Sin then becomes distasteful, and temptations lose their power.—*W. M. Statham, quoted in "A Homiletic Commentary on the Psalms,"* 1879.

Verse 165.—"*And nothing shall offend them.*" Hebrew, "they shall have no *stumblingblock.*" 1 John ii. 10, "There is none *occasion of stumbling* in him " who abides in the *light,* which makes him to see and avoid such stumblingblocks. Wealth, tribulation, temptation, which are the occasion to many of falling (Isa. viii. 14, 15 ; Ezek. iii. 20 ; vii. 19 ; xiv. 3, 4, 7), are not so to him.—*A. R Fausett.*

Verse 165.—Learn the true wisdom of those of you who are new creatures, and who love God's holy law. All of you who are really brought to Christ are changed into his image, so that you love God's holy law. " I delight in the law of God after the inward man." " The statutes of the Lord are right, rejoicing the heart ": Ps. xix. The world says : What a slave you are ! you cannot have a little amusement on the Sabbath—you cannot take a Sabbath walk, or join a Sabbath tea-party ; you cannot go to a dance or a theatre ; you cannot enjoy the pleasures of sensual indulgence—you are a slave. I answer : Christ had none of these pleasures. He did not want them ; nor do we. He knew what was truly wise, and good, and happy, and he chose God's holy law. He was the freest of all beings, and yet he knew no sin. Only make me free as Christ is free—this is all I ask. " Great peace have they which love thy law : and nothing shall offend them."—*Robert Murray M'Cheyne,* 1813—1843.

Verse 165.—"*Nothing shall offend them.*" They that have this character of God's children, will not be stumbled at God's dispensations, let them be never so cross to their desires, because they have a God to fly unto in all their troubles, and a sure covenant to rest upon. Therefore the reproaches cast upon them, and on the way of God, do not scandalize them ; for they have found God in that very way which others speak evil of ; they are not so offended by anything that attends the way of God, as to dislike or forsake that way. Nevertheless we must take heed that we be not offended.—*John Bunyan.*

Verse 166.—"*Lord, I have hoped for thy salvation,*" etc. This is the true posture in which all the servants of God should desire to be found—hoping in his mercy, and doing his commands. How easy were it to demonstrate the connection between the mental feeling here recognized, and the obedience with which it is here associated ! It is the hope of salvation which is the great and pervading motive to holiness, and it is the consciousness of obedience to the will of God which strengthens our hope of interest in the divine mercy.—*John Morison.*

Verse 166.—"*Lord, I have hoped for thy salvation.*" This saying he borrowed from good old Jacob. Gen. xlix. 18.—*John Trapp.*

Verse 166.—"*I have done thy commandments.*" Set upon the practice of what you read. A student in physic doth not satisfy himself to read over a system or body of physic, but he falls upon practising physic : the life-blood of religion lies in the practical part. Christians should be walking Bibles. Xenophon said, " Many read Lycurgus's laws, but few observe them." The word written is not only a rule of knowledge, but a rule of obedience ; it is not only to mend our sight, but to mend our pace. David calls God's word " a lamp unto his feet " (verse 105). It was not only a light to his eyes to see by, but to his feet to walk by. By practice we trade with the talent of knowledge, and turn it to profit. This is a blessed reading of Scripture, when we fly from the sins which the word forbids, and espouse the doctrines which the word commands. Reading without practice will be but a torch to light men to hell.—*Thomas Watson.*

Verses 166, 167, 168.—He that casts the commands behind his back is very presumptuous in applying the promises to himself. That hope which is not accompanied with obedience will make a man ashamed. He that has learned the word of God knows that the law is not made void by faith, but established : Rom. iii. 31. Christ the Church's Head and Prophet, in his sermon upon the mount shows the extent of the law, requiring purity in the heart and thoughts, as well as in the life and actions, and condemns them " who shall break the least of these commands and shall teach men so "; but " those that teach and do them," he owns as great in his kingdom : Matt. v. 19. The law spoken on Mount Sinai is established by the Legislator Christ in Mount Zion as a rule of righteousness. And they who are rightly instructed, " which walk according to this rule," will have both heart and conversation ordered according to his direction, and " peace and mercy will be upon them," and hereby they will show themselves to be indeed the Israel of God.—*Nathanael Vincent.*

Verse 167.—*My soul hath kept thy testimonies ; and I love them exceedingly.*" Should he not have said, first, I have loved thy commandments, and so have kept them ? Doubtless he did so ; but he ran here in a holy and most heavenly circle, I have kept them and loved them, and loved them and kept them. If we love Christ, we shall also live the life of love in our measure, and his commandments will be most dear when himself is most precious.—*Thomas Shepard, in "The Sound Believer,"* 1671.

Verse 167.—*"My soul."* It is a usual phrase among the Hebrews, when they would express their affection to anything, to say, *"My soul" :* as Ps. ciii. 1 and civ. 1, *"My soul,* praise thou the Lord," and Luke i. *"My soul* doth magnify the Lord."—*Richard Greenham.*

Verse 167.—*"I love them exceedingly."* It is only a reasonable return to God ; for the Father loved me so *exceedingly* as not to spare his own Son, but to give him up for me ; and the Son loved me so *exceedingly* that he gave himself to me, and gave me back to myself when I was lost in my sins, original and actual.—*Gerhohus* (1093—1169), *in Neale and Littledale.*

Verses 167, 168.—Let not our consciousness of daily failures make us shrink from this strong expression of confidence. It is alleged as an evidence of grace, not as a claim of merit, and therefore the most humble believer need not hesitate to adopt it as the expression of Christian sincerity before God. David aspired to no higher character than that of a poor sinner : but he was conscious of spirituality of obedience, " *exceeding love* " to the divine word, and an habitual walk under the eye of his God—the evidences of a heart (often mentioned in the Old Testament) " perfect with him."—*Charles Bridges.*

Verse 168.—*"I have kept thy precepts, for all my ways are before thee."* When men are some way off in a king's eye they will be comely in their carriage ; but when they come into his presence-chamber to speak with him they will be most careful. Because saints are always in God's sight, their constant deportment must be pious and seemly.—*George Swinnock.*

Verse 168.—*"I have kept thy precepts,* etc. The Hebrew word שמר, *shamar,* that is here rendered *" kept,"* signifies to keep carefully, diligently, studiously, exactly. It signifies to keep as men keep prisoners, and to keep as a watchman keeps the city or the garrison ; yea, to keep as a man would keep his very life. But now mark what was the reason that David kept the precepts and the testimonies of the Lord so carefully, so sincerely, so diligently, so studiously, and so exactly. Why, the reason you have in the latter part of the verse, *" for all my ways are before thee."* O sirs ! it is as necessary for him that would be eminent in holiness, to set the Lord always before him, as it is necessary for him to breathe. In that 31st of Job you have a very large narrative of that height and perfection of holiness that Job had attained to, and the great reason that he gives you, for this is in the 4th verse, " Doth not he see my way, and count all my steps ? " The eye of God had so strong an influence upon his heart and life, that it wrought him up to a very high pitch of holiness.—*Thomas Brooks.*

Verse 168.—*"All my ways are before thee."* That God seeth the secrets of our heart, is a point terrible to the wicked but joyful to the godly. The wicked are sorry that their heart is so open : it is a boiling pot of all mischief, a furnace and forge-house for evil. It grieveth them that man should hear and see their words and actions ; but what a terror is this—that their Judge, whom they hate, seeth their thought ! If they could deny this, they would. But so many of them as are convinced and forced to acknowledge a God, are shaken betimes with this also—that he is All-seeing. Others proceed more summarily, and at once deny the Godhead in their heart, and so destroy this conscience of his All-knowledge. But it is in vain : the more they harden their heart by this godless thought, the more fear is in them ; while they choke and check their conscience that it crow not against them it checketh them with foresight of fearful vengeance, and for the present convinceth them of the omniscience of God, the more they press to suppress it. But the godly rejoice herein ; it is to them a rule to square their thoughts by ; they take no liberty of evil thinking, willing, wishing, or affecting, in their hearts. Where that candle shineth, all things are framed as worthy of him and of his sight, whom they know to be seeing their heart.—*William Struther*, 1633.

Verse 168.—*"All my ways are before thee."* Walk Christian, in the view of God's omniscience ; say to thy soul, *cave, videt Deus ;* take heed God seeth. It is under the rose, as the common phrase is, that treason is spoken, when subjects think they are far enough from their king's hearing ; but did such know the prince to be under the window, or behind the hangings, their discourse would be more loyal. This made David so upright in his walking : *"I have kept thy precepts, for all my ways are before thee."* If Alexander's empty chair, which his captains, when they met in counsel, set before them, did awe them so as to keep them in good order ; how helpful would it be to set before ourselves the fact that God is looking upon us ! The Jews covered Christ's face, and then buffeted him : Mark xiv. 65. So does the hypocrite ; he first says in his heart, God sees not, or at least forgets that he sees, and then he makes bold to sin against him ; like that foolish bird, which runs her head among the reeds, and thinks herself safe from the fowler, as if because she did not see her enemy, therefore he could not see her. *Te mihi abscondam, non me tibi* (Augustine). I may hide thee from my eye, but not myself from thine eye.—*William Gurnall.*

NOTES ON VERSES 169 TO 176.

LET my cry come near before thee, O LORD : give me understanding according to thy word.

170 Let my supplication come before thee : deliver me according to thy word.

171 My lips shall utter praise, when thou hast taught me thy statutes.

172 My tongue shall speak of thy word : for all thy commandments *are* righteousness.

173 Let thine hand help me ; for I have chosen thy precepts.

174 I have longed for thy salvation, O LORD ; and thy law *is* my delight.

175 Let my soul live, and it shall praise thee ; and let thy judgments help me.

176 I have gone astray like a lost sheep ; seek thy servant : for I do not forget thy commandments.

The Psalmist is approaching the end of the Psalm, and his petitions gather force and fervency; he seems to break into the inner circle of divine fellowship, and to come even to the feet of the great God whose help he is imploring. This nearness creates the most lowly view of himself, and leads him to close the Psalm upon his face in deepest self-humiliation, begging to be sought out like a lost sheep.

169. *"Let my cry come near before thee, O LORD."* He is tremblingly afraid lest he should not be heard. He is conscious that his prayer is nothing better than the cry of a poor child, or the groan of a wounded beast. He dreads lest it should be shut out from the ear of the most High, but he very boldly prays that it may come before God, that it may be in his sight, under his notice, and looked upon with his acceptance ; yea, he goes further, and entreats, " Let my cry come near before thee, O Lord." He wants the Lord's attention to his prayer to be very close and considerate. He uses a figure of speech and personifies his prayer. We may picture his prayer as Esther, venturing into the royal presence, entreating an audience, and begging to find favour in the sight of the blessed and only Potentate. It is a very sweet thing to a suppliant when he knows of a surety that his prayer has obtained audience, when it has trodden the sea of glass before the throne, and has come even to the footstool of the glorious seat around which heaven and earth adore. It is to Jehovah that this prayer is expressed with trembling earnestness —our translators, filled with holy reverence, translate the word, " O LORD." We crave audience of none else, for we have confidence in none beside. *" Give me understanding according to thy word."* This is the prayer about which the Psalmist is so exceedingly anxious. With all his gettings he would get understanding, and whatever he misses he is resolved not to miss this priceless boon. He desires spiritual light and understanding as it is promised in God's word, as it proceeds from God's word, and as it produces obedience to God's word. He pleads as though he had no understanding whatever of his own, and asks to have one given to him. " Give me understanding." In truth, he had an understanding according to the judgment of men, but what he sought was an understanding according to God's word, which is quite another thing. To understand spiritual things is the gift of God. To have a judgment enlightened by heavenly light and conformed to divine truth is a privilege which only grace can give. Many a man who is accounted wise after the manner of this world is a fool according to the word of the Lord. May we be among those happy children who shall all be taught of the Lord.

170. *" Let my supplication come before thee."* It is the same entreaty with a slight change of words. He humbly calls his cry a supplication, a sort of beggar's petition ; and again he asks for audience and for answer. There might be hindrances in the way to an audience, and he begs for their removal—let it come. Other believers are heard—let my prayer come before thee. *" Deliver me according to thy word."* Rid me of mine adversaries, clear me of my slanderers, preserve me from my tempters, and bring me up out of all my afflictions even as thy word has led me to expect thou wilt do. It is for this that he seeks understanding. His enemies would succeed through his folly, if they succeeded at all ; but if he exercised a sound discretion they would be baffled, and he would escape from them. The

Lord in answer to prayer frequently delivers his children by making them wise as serpents as well as harmless as doves.

171. "*My lips shall utter praise, when thou hast taught me thy statutes.*" He will not always be pleading for himself, he will rise above all selfishness, and render thanks for the benefit received. He promises to praise God when he has obtained practical instruction in the life of godliness : this is something to praise for, no blessing is more precious. The best possible praise is that which proceeds from men who honour God, not only with their lips, but in their lives. We learn the music of heaven in the school of holy living. He whose life honours the Lord is sure to be a man of praise. David would not only be grateful in silence, but he would express that gratitude in appropriate terms : his lips would utter what his life had practised. Eminent disciples are wont to speak well of the master who instructed them, and this holy man, when taught the statutes of the Lord, promises to give all the glory to him to whom it is due.

172. "*My tongue shall speak of thy word.*" When he had done singing he began preaching. God's tender mercies are such that they may be either said or sung. When the tongue speaks of God's word it has a most fruitful subject ; such speaking will be as a tree of life, whose leaves shall be for the healing of the people. Men will gather together to listen to such talk, and they will treasure it up in their hearts. The worst of us is that for the most part we are full of our own words, and speak but little of God's word. Oh, that we could come to the same resolve as this godly man, and say henceforth, "My tongue shall speak of thy word." Then should we break through our sinful silence ; we should no more be cowardly and half-hearted, but should be true witnesses for Jesus. It is not only of God's works that we are to speak, but of his word. We may extol its truth, its wisdom, its preciousness, its grace, its power ; and then we may tell of all it has revealed, all it has promised, all it has commanded, all it has effected. The subject gives us plenty of sea-room ; we may speak on for ever : the tale is for ever telling, yet untold. "*For all thy commandments are righteousness.*" David appears to have been mainly enamoured of the preceptive part of the word of God, and concerning the precept his chief delight lay in its purity and excellence. When a man can speak this from his heart, his heart is indeed a temple of the Holy Ghost. He had said aforetime (verse 138), "Thy testimonies are righteous," but here he declares that they are righteousness itself. The law of God is not only the standard of right, but it is the essence of righteousness. This the Psalmist affirms of each and every one of the precepts without exception. He felt like Paul—"The law is holy, and the commandment holy and just good." When a man has so high an opinion of God's commandments it is little wonder that his lips should be ready to extol the ever-glorious One.

173. "*Let thine hand help me.*" Give me practical succour. Do not entrust me to my friends or thy friends, but put thine own hand to the work. Thy hand has both skill and power, readiness and force : display all these qualities on my behalf. I am willing to do the utmost that I am able to do ; but what I need is thine help, and this is so urgently required that if I have it not I shall sink. Do not refuse thy succour. Great as thy hand is, let it light on me, even me. The prayer reminds us of Peter walking on the sea and beginning to sink ; he, too, cried, "Lord, help me," and the hand of his Master was stretched out for his rescue. "*For I have chosen thy precepts.*" A good argument. A man may fitly ask help from God's hand when he has dedicated his own hand entirely to the obedience of the faith. "I have chosen thy precepts." His election was made, his mind was made up. In reference to all earthly rules and ways, in preference even to his own will, he had chosen to be obedient to the divine commands. Will not God help such a man in holy work and sacred service ? Assuredly he will. If grace has given us the heart with which to will, it will also give us the hand with which to perform. Whenever, under the constraints of a divine call, we are engaged in any high and lofty enterprise, and feel it to be too much for our strength, we may always invoke the right hand of God in words like these.

174. "*I have longed for thy salvation, O Lord.*" He speaks like old Jacob on his deathbed ; indeed, all saints, both in prayer and in death, appear as one, in word, and deed, and mind. He knew God's salvation, and yet he longed for it ; that is to say, he had experienced a share of it, and he was therefore led to expect something yet higher and more complete. There is a salvation yet to come, when we shall be clean delivered from the body of this death, set free from all the turmoil

and trouble of this mortal life, raised above the temptations and assaults of Satan, and brought near unto our God, to be like him and with him for ever and ever. "I have longed for thy salvation, O Jehovah; *and thy law is my delight.*" The first clause tells us what the saint longs for, and this informs us what is his present satisfaction.   God's law, contained in the ten commandments, gives joy to believers. God's law, that is, the entire Bible, is a well-spring of consolation and enjoyment to all who receive it. Though we have not yet reached the fulness of our salvation, yet we find in God's word so much concerning a present salvation that we are even now delighted.

175. *"Let my soul live."* Fill it full of life, preserve it from wandering into the ways of death, give it to enjoy the indwelling of the Holy Ghost, let it live to the fulness of life, to the utmost possibilities of its new-created being. *"And it shall praise thee."* It shall praise thee for life, for new life, for thou art the Lord and Giver of Life. The more it shall live, the more it shall praise, and when it shall live in perfection it shall praise thee in perfection.   Spiritual life is prayer and praise. *"And let thy judgments help me."* While I read the record of what thou hast done, in terror or in love, let me be quickened and developed. While I see thy hand actually at work upon me, and upon others, chastening sin, and smiling upon righteousness, let me be helped both to live aright and to praise thee. Let all thy deeds in providence instruct me, and aid me in the struggle to overcome sin and to practise holiness. This is the second time he has asked for help in this portion; he was always in need of it, and so are we.

176. This is the *finale*, the conclusion of the whole matter : *"I have gone astray like a lost sheep"*—often, wilfully, wantonly, and even hopelessly, but for thine interposing grace. In times gone by, before I was afflicted, and before thou hadst fully taught me thy statutes, "I went astray" from the practical precepts, from the instructive doctrines, and from the heavenly experiences which thou hadst set before me.   I lost my road, and I lost myself. Even now I am apt to wander. and, in fact, have roamed already; therefore, Lord, restore me. *"Seek thy servant."* He was not like a dog, that somehow or other can find its way back; but he was like a lost sheep, which goes further and further away from home; yet still he was a sheep, and the Lord's sheep, his property, and precious in his sight, and therefore he hoped to be sought in order to be restored. However far he might have wandered he was still not only a sheep, but God's "servant," and therefore he desired to be in his Master's house again, and once more honoured with commissions for his Lord. Had he been only a lost sheep he would not have prayed to be sought; but being also a "servant" he had the power to pray. He cries, "Seek thy servant," and he hopes to be not only sought, but forgiven, accepted, and taken into work again by his gracious Master.

Notice this confession; many times in the Psalm David has defended his own innocence against foul-mouthed accusers, but when he comes into the presence of the Lord his God he is ready enough to confess his transgressions. He here sums up, not only his past, but even his present life, under the image of a sheep which has broken from its pasture, forsaken the flock, left the shepherd, and brought itself into the wild wilderness, where it has become as a lost thing.   The sheep bleats, and David prays, "Seek thy servant." His argument is a forcible one,— *"for I do not forget thy commandments."* I know the right, I approve and admire the right, what is more, I love the right, and long for it. I cannot be satisfied to continue in sin, I must be restored to the ways of righteousness. I have a home-sickness after my God, I pine after the ways of peace; I do not and I cannot forget thy commandments, nor cease to know that I am always happiest and safest when I scrupulously obey them, and find all my joy in doing so.   Now, if the grace of God enables us to maintain in our hearts the loving memory of God's commandments it will surely yet restore us to practical holiness. That man cannot be utterly lost whose heart is still with God. If he be gone astray in many respects, yet still, if he be true in his soul's inmost desires, he will be found again, and fully restored. Yet let the reader remember the first verse of the Psalm while he reads the last: the major blessedness lies not in being restored from wandering, but in being upheld in a blameless way even to the end. Be it ours to keep the crown of the causeway, never leaving the King's highway for By-path Meadow, or any other flowery path of sin. May the Lord uphold us even to the end. Yet even then we shall not be able to boast with the Pharisee, but shall still pray with the publican, "God be merciful to me a sinner;" and with the Psalmist, "Seek thy servant."

EXPOSITION OF VERSES 169 TO 176.

This commences a new division of the Psalm, indicated by the last letter of the Hebrew alphabet, the letter *Tau*, corresponding to our *t*, or *th.—Albert Barnes.*

Verse 169.—*"Let my cry come near before thee, O LORD."* That is, as some will have it, Let this whole preceding Psalm, and all the petitions (whereof we have here a repetition) therein contained, be highly accepted in heaven.—*John Trapp.*

Verse 169.—*"Let my cry come near before thee, O LORD."* We are now come to the last section of this Psalm, wherein we see David more fervent in prayer than he was in the first, as ye shall easily observe by comparing them both together. The godly, the longer they speak to God, are the more fervent and earnest to speak to him ; so that unless necessity compel them, they desire never to intermit conference with him.

Many prayers hath he made to God in this Psalm : now in the end he prays for his prayers, that the Lord would let them come before him. Some men send out prayers, but God turns them into sin, and puts them away back from him : therefore David seeks favour to his prayers.—*William Cowper.*

Verse 169.—*"Give me understanding."* This was the prayer of Solomon (1 Kings iii. 9), and we are told that it pleased the Lord, and as a reward he added temporal prosperity, which the young king had not asked. Yet Solomon meant less by his prayer than his father David did ; for we see in him little trace of the deep devotion for which his father was so remarkable. The Psalmist here prays a deep prayer which can only be answered by the Holy Ghost himself enlightening the soul. The understanding is a most important member of our spiritual frame. Conscience is the understanding exercised upon moral questions, and if that be not right, where shall we be ? Our understanding of the word of God comes by teaching, but also through experience : we understand hardly anything till we experience it. Such an enlightening experience is the gift of God, and to him we must look for it in prayer.—*C H. S.*

Verse 169.—*"Give me understanding."* The especial work of the Holy Spirit in the illumination of our minds unto the understanding of the Scripture is called *"understanding."* The Psalmist prays *"Give me understanding, and I shall keep thy law"* (verse 34). So the apostle speaks to Timothy : " Consider what I say ; and the Lord give thee understanding in all things " 2 Tim. ii. 7. Besides his own consideration of what was proposed unto him, which includes the due and diligent use of all outward means, it was moreover necessary that God *should give him understanding* by an inward effectual work of his Spirit, that he might comprehend the things wherein he was instructed. And the desire hereof, as of that without which there can be no saving knowledge of the word, nor advantage by it, the Psalmist expresseth emphatically, with great fervency of spirit in verse 144 : " The righteousness of thy testimony is everlasting : give me understanding, and I shall live." Without this he knew that he could have no benefit by the everlasting righteousness of the testimonies of God. All understanding, indeed, however it be abused by the most, is the work and effect of the Holy Ghost , for " the inspiration of the Almighty giveth understanding " : Job xxxii. 8. So is this spiritual understanding in an especial manner the gift of God. In this " understanding " both the ability of our mind and the due exercise of it is included. This one consideration, that the saints of God have with so much earnestness prayed that God would *give them understanding* as to his mind and will as revealed in the word, with his reiterated promises that he would so do, is of more weight with me than all the disputes of men to the contrary. No farther argument is necessary to prove that men do not understand the mind of God in the Scripture in a due manner, than their supposal and confidence that so they can do without the communication of a spiritual understanding unto them by the Holy Spirit. This self-confidence is directly contrary unto the plain, express testimonies of the word.—*John Owen.*

Verse 169.—*"Give me understanding."* Why should the man of God here pray for *understanding ?* Had he not often prayed for it before ? Was he a novice in knowledge, being a prophet ? Doth not our Saviour Christ reprehend repetitions and babbling in prayer ? True it is our Saviour Christ doth reprehend that babbling which is without faith and knowledge and a feeling of our wants ; but he speaketh not against those serious repetitions which proceed from a plentiful knowledge, abundant faith, and lively feeling of our necessities. Again, although it cannot be denied but he was a man of God, and had received great grace, yet God giveth knowledge to his dearest saints in this life but in part, and the most which we see and know is but little. Besides, when we have knowledge, and knowledge must be brought into practice, we shall find such difficulties, such waywardness, such forgetfulness, such wants, that although we have had with the prophet a very good direction in the general things of the word, which are universal and few, yet we shall find many distractions in our practices, which must be particular and many ; and we shall either fail in memory by forgetfulness, or in judgment by blindness, or in affection by dulness. So easily may we slip when we think we may hold our journey on. Wherefore the man of God, through that examination which he took of his heart and affections, seeing those manifold straits and difficulties, prayeth in the verse following, not for the renewing of men in general in their troubles, but for the considering of his own particular condition.—*Richard Greenham.*

Verse 169.—*"According to thy word."* David here seeks understanding not carnally, for the wisdom of the flesh is death : but he seeks understanding *according to God's word.* Without this the wisdom of man is foolishness ; and the more subtil he seems to be in his ways, the more deeply he involves himself in the snare of the devil. " They have rejected the word of the Lord ; and what wisdom is in them ? " Jer. viii. 9. But seeing he was an excellent prophet, and protested before that he had more understanding than the ancients, yea, than his teachers ; how is it that he still prays for understanding ? In answer to this we are to know, that there is a great difference between the gifts of nature and grace. Nature ofttimes gives to man very excellent gifts, as rare memory, knowledge, quick wit, strength, external beauty ; but therewithal it teacheth not man to consider that in which he is wanting ; whereof it comes to pass, that he waxeth proud of that which he hath. This is a common thing to men in the state of nature, that of small gifts they conceive a great pride : but grace, as it gives to man more excellent gifts than nature can afford, so it teacheth him to look unto that which he wants, that he be not puffed up by considering that which he hath, but carried in all humility of heart to pray for that which he wants.—*Abraham Wright.*

Verse 170.—*"Let my supplication come before thee,"* etc. The sincere worshipper cannot be contented with anything short of actual intercourse with God. The round of duty cannot please where the spirit of grace and supplication has not been vouchsafed. A filial disposition will pour itself forth in earnest longings after communion with God. Nor will the hope of gracious audience be founded on any other plea save that of the sure word of Jehovah's promise. It is in accordance with that word, and not in opposition to it, that the child of God expects to be heard. All his deliverance he feels to be from the Lord, and all that he looks for from heaven he anticipates in answer to prayer. O for more of that faith which makes its appeal to the divine veracity, and which looks with steadfast eye to the promise of a covenant-keeping God.—*John Morison.*

Verse 170.—*"Let my supplication come before thee."* Observe the order of the words here and in the preceding verse. First we had, " Let my cry come near ; " then " Give me understanding," and that " according to thy word," and now we have "*Let my prayer enter in* (LXX., Syr., Arb., Vulg.,) *before thee."* Just so, if you wish for an interview with a man of very high rank, first you come near his house, then you ask for information and instruction as to his intentions, then you ask permission to enter, lest you should be driven away and refused admittance. Knock therefore at the door of the heavenly palace : knock, not with your bodily hand, but with the right hand of prayer. For the voice can knock as well as the hand, as it is written, " It is the voice of my Beloved that knocketh " : Cant. v. 2. And when you have knocked, see how you go in, lest after entering you should not get the sight of the King. For there are many who make their way into palaces, and do not at once get an audience of an earthly sovereign, but have to watch constantly to obtain an interview at last. Nor have they the choice of the opportunity, they come when they are sent for, and then present their petition, if they wish to be favourably received.—*Ambrose, in Neale and Littledale.*

Verse 171.—*"My lips shall utter praise."* You have stood at the fountain head of a stream of water, and admired while it bubbled up, and ran down in a clear rivulet, till at length it swelled the mighty river. Such is the allusion here.

The heart taught of God cannot contain itself, but breaks out in praise and singing. This would be the effect of divine illumination, and this would be felt to be a privilege, yea, and a high duty. Have you not found so, believers, specially on communion occasions ? Be assured, such utterances are the sign of a renewed heart ; yea, of a heart filled with all gratitude of right feeling.—*John Stephen.*

Verse 171.—*"My lips shall utter praise,"* etc.

> O make me, Lord, thy statutes learn !
>   Keep in thy ways my feet,
> Then shall my lips divinely burn ;
>   Then shall my songs be sweet.
>
> Each sin I cast away shall make
>   My soul more strong to soar ;
> Each deed of holiness shall wake
>   A strain divine the more.
>
> My voice shall more delight thine ear
>   The more I wait on thee ;
> Thy service bring my song more near
>   The angelic harmony.

T. H. Gill, in "Breathings of the Better Life" [1881].

Verse 172.—*"My tongue shall speak of thy word."* One duty of thankfulness promised by David is, *to speak of God's words* for the edification of others. Every Christian man, as he is a priest to offer sacrifice unto God, so is he a prophet to teach his brethren ; for unto us all stands that commandment, " Edify one another in their most holy faith." But, alas, ye shall see many Christians now, who at their tables, and in their companies, can speak freely upon any subject ; only for spiritual matters, which concern the soul, there they are dumb, and cannot say with David, *"My tongue shall speak of thy word."—William Cowper.*

Verse 173.—*"Let thine hand help me."* David having before made promises of thankfulness, seeks now help from God, that he may perform them. Our sufficiency is not of ourselves, but of God ; to will and to do are both from him. In temporal things men ofttimes take great pains with small profit ; first, because they seek not to make their conscience good ; next, because they seek not help from God : therefore they speed no better than Peter, who fished all night and got nothing till he cast his net in the name of the Lord. But in spiritual things we may far less look to prosper, if we call not for God's assistance : the means will not profit us unless God's blessing accompany them. There is preaching, but for the most part without profit ; there is prayer, but it prevails not ; there is hearing of the word, but without edifying ; and all because in spiritual exercises instant prayer is not made unto God, that his hand may be with us to help us.—*Abraham Wright.*

Verse 173.—*"I have chosen thy precepts."* Hath God given you a heart to make choice of his ways ? O bless God ! There was a time when you went on in giving pleasure to the flesh, and you saw then no better thing than such a kind of life, and the Lord hath been pleased to discover better things to you, so as to make you renounce your former ways, and to make choice of another way, in which your souls have found other manner of comforts, and satisfactions, and contentments than ever you did before. Bless God as David did : " Blessed be the Lord who hath given me counsel " . . . . Seeing God hath thus inclined your heart to himself, be for ever established in your *choice :* seeing God hath shown to you his ways, as Pilate said in another case, " That I have written I have written " : so say you, " That I have chosen I have chosen."—*Jeremiah Burroughs, in "Moses his Choice."*

Verses 173, 174.—*"I have chosen."* *"My delight."* Cheerfulness accompanies election of a thing. Lumpishness is a sign we never chose it, but were forced to it. Such cheerfulness in service procures cheerfulness in mercies : Isa. lxiv. 5, " Thou meetest him that rejoiceth and worketh righteousness." He puts to his hand to help such an one. Christ loves not melancholy and phlegmatic service ; such a temper in acts of obedience is a disgrace to God and to religion : to God, it betrays us to have jealous thoughts of God, as though he were a hard master ; to religion it makes others think duties are drudgeries, and not privileges.—*Stephen Charnock.*

Verse 174.—"*I have longed for thy salvation, O LORD,*" etc. The thing which we learn hence out of David's joining these two together, *I long for salvation,* and *thy law is my delight,* is this, that it is not enough for a man to say, he longs and desires to be saved, unless he makes a conscience to use the appointed means to bring him thereunto. It had been but hypocrisy in David to say he longed for salvation, if his conscience had not been able to witness with him that *the law was his delight.* It is mere mockery for a man to say he longeth for bread, and prayeth to God every day to give him his daily bread, if he yet walk in no calling, or else seek to get it by fraud and rapine, not staying himself at all upon God's providence. Who will imagine that a man wisheth for health, who either despiseth or neglecteth the means of his recovery ? God hath in his own wisdom appointed a lawful means for every lawful thing ; this means, being obediently used, the comfortable obtaining of the end may be confidently looked for ; the means being not observed, to think to attain to the end is mere presumption. God will deliver Noah from the flood, but Noah must be "*moved with reverence,*" and "*prepare the ark*" (Heb. xi. 7), or else he could not have escaped. He would save Lot from Sodom, but yet Lot must hie him out quickly, and not look behind him till he have entered Zoar : Gen. xix. 17. He was pleased to cure Hezekiah of the plague, but yet Hezekiah must take " a lump of figs, and lay it upon his boil : " Isa. xxxviii. 21. He vouchsafed to preserve Paul and company at sea, yet the sailors must " abide in the ship," else ye cannot be saved, saith Paul : Acts xxvii. 31.—*Samuel Hieron,* 1572—1617.

Verse 174.—"*I have longed for thy salvation.*" It is God's salvation proper that he must desire—"*thy salvation*"—for nothing else could satisfy his pure mind— perfect peace with God, perfect purity and perfect hope. Now if you ask what was God's way of delivering, and what was his way of salvation, the answer is, it was set forth in his word, and was what the Psalmist calls his "*law.*" God's salvation and his law were discerned to be one. "*I have longed for thy salvation, O LORD ; and thy law is my delight.*"—*John Stephen.*

Verse 174.—"*I have longed for thy salvation, O Lord.*" "*Salvation,*" by the " hand," or arm of Jehovah (which is often in scripture a title of Messiah), hath been the object of the hopes, the desires, and " longing " expectations of the faithful, from Adam to this hour, and will continue so to be until he, who hath already visited us in great humility, shall come again in glorious majesty to complete our redemption and take us to himself.—*George Horne.*

Verse 174.—"*I have longed for thy salvation, O LORD.*" For a present salvation from the guilt and power of sin, and for future salvation, in the full and everlasting enjoyment of God in heaven. David had the happiness to be a partaker, both of pardoning mercy and of sanctifying grace ; yet still he longed for more of this salvation, that is, for a more assured faith of pardoning mercy, and larger measures of sanctifying grace. A gracious soul is insatiable ; the more it hath received, the more it desires to receive. Enjoyment, instead of surfeiting, sharpens the appetite. Nay, so sweet is the relishing of spiritual things, that every renewed taste of them quenches the thirst for other things.

"*Thy law is my delight.*" Here David chooses the term "*law*" for denoting the whole revelation of God's will, to remind us of the inseparable connexion between privilege and duty, faith and obedience, holiness and comfort ; and to teach us that we ought to be thankful to God for the direction he hath given us in the road to heaven no less than for the promises by which we are assured of the possession of it.— *Robert Walker,* 1716—1783.

Verse 174.—"*Thy law is my delight.*" Religion will decay or flourish as it is our *duty* or our *delight.* The mind is incapable of continued exertion *for duty ;* but it readily falls in *with* "*delight.*" Thus our duties become our privileges, while Christ is their source and life. Every step of progress is progress in happiness. This verse (of which experience is the best interpreter) is the believer's language in his lively, as well as in his fainting state. For the more he knows and enjoys of the Divine presence, the more he longs to know and enjoy it.—*Charles Bridges.*

Verse 174.—"*Delight,*" in the plural, " *delights,*" as in verses 24, 77, 92, 143. God's word is an abundant source of pleasure to his people.—*William S. Plumer.*

Verse 175.—"*Let my soul live, and it shall praise thee,*" etc. This verse containeth three things, 1st. David's petition for life : "*Let my soul live.*" "*My soul ; *" that is, myself : the soul is put for the whole man. The contrary : " Let me die with the Philistines," said Samson (Judges xxi. 30) ; Hebrew, margin, " Let my soul die." His life was sought after by the cruelty of his enemies ; and he desireth God to keep him alive.

2ndly. His argument from the aim of his life ; *"And it shall praise thee."* The glorifying of God was his aim. The fruit of all God's benefits is to profit us, and praise God. David professeth that all the days of his life he would live in the sense and acknowledgment of such a benefit.

3rdly. The ground of his hope and confidence in the last clause : *"And let thy judgments help me."* Our hopes of help are grounded on God's judgments, whereby is meant his word. There are judgments decreed, and judgments executed ; doctrinal judgments, and providential judgments. That place intimateth the distinction : "Because sentence against an evil work is not executed speedily, therefore the heart of the sons of men is fully set in them to do evil : " Eccl. viii. 11. There is *sententia lata et dilata.* Here God's judgments are put for the sentence pronounced ; and chiefly for one part of them, the promises of grace. As also, "I have hoped in thy judgments : " Ps. cxix. 43. Promises are the objects of hope.—*Thomas Manton.*

Verse 175.—*"Let my soul live."* What is the life that the Psalmist is now praying for, but the salvation for which he had just expressed his longing ? The taste that he has received makes him hunger for a higher and more continued enjoyment—not for selfish gratification, but that he might employ himself in the praise of his God. Indeed, as we have drawn towards the close of this Psalm, we cannot but have observed that character of praise to pervade his experience, which has been generally remarked in the concluding Psalms of this sacred book. Much do we lose of spiritual strength for want of occupying ourselves more in the exercise of praise.—*Charles Bridges.*

Verse 175.—*"Live and praise."* The saint improves his earthly things for an heavenly end. Where layest thou up thy treasure ? Dost thou bestow it on thy voluptuous appetite, thy hawks and thy hounds ; or lockest thou it up in the bosom of Christ's poor members ? What use makest thou of thy honour and greatness ? To strengthen the hands of the godly or the wicked ? And so of all thy other temporal enjoyments. A gracious heart improves them for God ; when a saint prays for these things, he hath an eye to some heavenly end. If David prays for life, it is not that he may live, but *"live and praise God."* When he was driven from his regal throne by the rebellious arms of Absalom, see what his desire and hope were, 2 Sam. xv. 25 : " The king said unto Zadok, Carry back the ark of God into the city : if I shall find favour in the eyes of the LORD, he will bring me again, and shew me both it, and his habitation." Mark, not shew me my crown, my palace, but the ark, the house of God.—*William Gurnall.*

Verse 175.—*"Live and praise."* Liveliness of soul is the Spirit's gift, and it will show itself in abounding praises.—*Henry Law.*

Verse 175.—*"Let thy judgments help me."* In the second clause it would be harsh to understand the word *"judgments"* of the commandments, to which it does not properly belong to give help. It seems, then, that the prophet, perceiving himself liable to numberless calamities—even as the faithful, by reason of the unbridled license of the wicked, dwell in this world as sheep among wolves,—calls upon God to protect him in the way of restraining, by his secret providence, the wicked from doing him harm. It is a very profitable doctrine, when things in the world are in a state of great confusion, and when our safety is in danger amidst so many and varied storms, to lift up our eyes to the judgments of God, and to seek a remedy in them.—*John Calvin.*

Verses 175, 176—

> Though like a sheep estranged I stray,
> Yet have I not renounced thy way.
> Thine hand extend ; thine own reclaim ;
> Grant me to live, and praise thy name.
>
> *Richard Mant.*

Verse 176.—*"I have gone astray like a lost sheep."* Though a sheep go astray, yet it is soon called back by the voice of the shepherd : " My sheep hear my voice." Thus David when he went against Nabal was called back by the Lord's voice in a woman ; and when he had slain Uriah he was brought again by Nathan. And therefore if we will be sheep, then though we sometimes go astray, yet we must be easily reclaimed.—*Richard Greenham.*

Verse 176.—"*I have gone astray like a lost sheep,*" driven out by storm, or dark day, or by the hunting of the dogs chased out from the rest of the flock.—*David Dickson.*

Verse 176.—"*I have gone astray like a lost sheep,*" etc. And this is all the conclusion—"*a lost sheep*"! This long Psalm of ascriptions, praises, avowals, resolves, high hopes, ends in this, that he is a perishing sheep. But, stay, there is hope—"*Seek thy servant.*" "*I have gone astray like a lost sheep.*" The original is of the most extensive range, comprehending all time past, and also the habitual tendencies of the man. The believer feels that he had gone astray when the grace of God found him ; that he had gone astray many times, had not the grace of God prevented it. He feels that he went astray on such and such unhappy occasions. He also feels that he hath gone astray in all that he hath done ; and indeed that he is astray now. But the word expresses the habitual tendency likewise—I go astray like a lost sheep, and this rendering is in keeping with the prayer, "*Seek thy servant.*" The third member is also properly rendered in keeping with it : " I go astray like a lost sheep ; seek thy servant ; for I do not forget thy commandments." All this is descriptive of the remaining corruption that is in the believer. He is not unmindful of the Lord ; he has the root of the matter in him, the seed of divine life ; yet he does go astray ; whence the necessity of the prayer : "*Seek thy servant.*" Isaiah's description of men, although conveyed in the same terms, is evidently more sweeping as the context words show : " All we like sheep have gone astray ; we have turned every one to his own way ; and the Lord hath laid on him the iniquity of us all." This would seem to apply to the race of man. Rather is the experience of the Psalmist similar to that described by the apostle Paul : " I find a law, that when I would do good, evil is present with me. For I delight in the law of God, after the inward man : But I see another law in my members, warring against the law of my mind, and bringing me into captivity to the law of sin which is in my members." And the Psalmist had the same remedy at the early period, as had the apostle in the later times ; for God's salvation is one. The Psalmist's remedy was, "*Seek thy servant ;*" the apostle's, " O wretched man that I am ! who shall deliver me from the body of this death ? I thank God through Jesus Christ our Lord."—*John Stephen.*

Verse 176.—"*I have gone astray.*" The original word signifies either the turning of the foot, or the turning of the heart, or both, out of the way. "*I have gone astray like a lost sheep ;*" that is, I have been deceived, and so have gone out of the way of thy holy commandments. Satan is an ill guide, and our hearts are no better : he that follows either, quickly loseth himself ; and until God seeketh us (as David prays in the next words), we cannot find our way when we are once out of it.—*Joseph Caryl.*

Verse 176.—"*I have gone astray.*" Gotthold one day saw a farmer carefully counting his sheep as they came from the field. Happening at the time to be in an anxious and sorrowful mood, he gave vent to his feelings and said : Why art thou cast down, my soul ? and why disquieted with vexing thoughts ? Surely thou must be dear to the Most High as his lambs are to this farmer. Art thou not better than many sheep ? Is not Jesus Christ thy shepherd ? Has not he risked his blood and life for thee ? Hast thou no interest in his words : " I give unto my sheep eternal life, and they shall never perish, neither shall any pluck them out of my hand " ? John x. 28. This man is numbering his flock ; and thinkest thou that God does not also count and care for his believing children and elect, especially as his beloved Son has averred, that the very hairs of our head are all numbered ? Matt. x. 30. During the day, I may perhaps have gone out of the way, and heedlessly followed my own devices ; still, at the approach of evening, when the faithful Shepherd counts his lambs, he will mark my absence, and graciously seek and bring me back. Lord Jesus, "*I have gone astray like a lost sheep ; seek thy servant ; for I do not forget thy commandments.*"—*Christian Scriver* (1629—1693), *in Gotthold's Emblems.*

Verse 176.—"*I have gone astray,*" etc. Who is called " the man after God's own heart " ? David, the Hebrew king, had fallen into sins enough—blackest crimes—there was no want of sin. And, therefore, unbelievers sneer, and ask, " Is this your man after God's own heart ? " The sneer, it seems to me, is but a shallow one. What are faults, what are the outward details of a life, if the inner secret of it, the remorse, temptations, the often-baffled, never-ended struggle of it, be forgotten ? . . . . David's life and history, as written for us in those Psalms of his, I consider to be the truest emblem ever given us of a man's moral progress and warfare here below. All earnest souls will ever discover in it the faithful struggle of an earnest human soul towards what is good and best. Struggle often baffled—sore baffled—driven as into entire wreck ; yet a struggle never ended, ever with tears, repentance, true unconquerable purpose begun anew.—*Thomas Carlyle* (1795—1881), *in "Heroes and Hero-Worship."*

Verse 176.—*"For I do not forget thy commandments."* In all my wandering ; with my consciousness of error ; with my sense of guilt ; I still *do* feel that I love thy law, thy service, thy commandments. They are the joy of my heart, and I desire to be recalled from all my wanderings, that I may find perfect happiness in thee and in thy service evermore. Such is the earnest wish of every regenerated heart. For as such a one may have wandered from God, yet he is conscious of true attachment to him and his service ; he desires and earnestly prays that he may be " sought out," brought back, and kept from wandering any more.—*Albert Barnes.*

Verses 176.—*"For I do not forget thy commandments."* The godly never so fall but there remains in them some grace, which reserves a hope of medicine to cure them : so David here. Albeit he transgressed some of God's commandments, yet he fell not into any full oblivion of them.—*William Cowper.*

Verse 176.—I do not think that there could possibly be a more appropriate conclusion of such a Psalm as this, so full of the varied experience and the ever-changing frames and feelings even of a child of God, in the sunshine and the cloud, in the calm and in the storm, than this ever-clinging sense of his propensity to wander, and the expression of his utter inability to find his way back without the Lord's guiding hand to restore him ; and at the same time with it all, his fixed and abiding determination never to forget the Lord's commandments. What an insight into our poor wayward hearts does this verse give us—not merely liable to wander, but ever wandering, ever losing our way, ever stumbling on the dark mountains, even while cleaving to God's commandments ! But at the same time what a prayer does it put into our mouths, *"Seek thy servant,"*—" I am thine, save me." Yes, blessed be God ! there is One mighty to save. " Kept by the power of God through faith unto salvation."—*Barton Bouchier.*

As far as I have been able, as far as I have been aided by the Lord, I have treated throughout, and expounded, this great Psalm. A task which more able and learned expositors have performed, or will perform better ; nevertheless, my services were not to be withheld from it on that account, when my brethren earnestly required it of me.—*Augustine.*

HINTS TO PREACHERS.

OUTLINES UPON KEYWORDS OF THE PSALM, BY PASTOR C. A. DAVIS.

A good memory.—I. What it should retain: God's *"name"* (ver. 55); God's *"word"* (ver. 16); God's *"law"* (ver. 109). The law is dilated upon under various names, *"statutes"* (ver. 83); *"precepts"* (ver. 141); *"commandments"* (ver. 176); *"judgments"* (ver. 52). II. How its retentive power may be fostered. By effort of will (ver. 16; 93). By delight in the theme (ver. 16). By a consideration of blessings received (ver. 93). III. Hindrances that must be overcome. Such as arise from severe affliction (ver. 83); from personal danger (ver. 109); and from insignificance and relative contempt (ver. 141). IV. Reasons for its cultivation. Former blessings derived (ver. 93). It furnishes ground of appeal to God (ver. 153; 176). V. The good that will spring from it. Consistent fidelity (ver. 55); or, if necessary, restoration from backsliding (ver. 176). Divine consideration (ver. 153); comfort (ver. 52); delight (ver. 16). And now the believer may appeal to the remembrance of God (ver. 49).

The believer in affliction.—I. His distress (ver. 92). II. His support (ver. 92). III. His submission (ver. 75). IV. His prayer (ver. 107; 153). V. Its answer (ver. 50). VI. His review (ver. 71).

Spiritual understanding.—I. Is the gift of God. Jehovah (the only wise), 169. Creator (who has endowed us with our other faculties, therefore with this), 73. Master (who allots our service and therefore our qualification), 125. II. Must be sought from God. With deep sense of need, 169. With faith, 169. With perseverance and importunity, 27, 34, 73, 125, 144, 169. III. Pleas to be used in the prayer for understanding. That I may *learn*, 73, and *know* thy commandments, 125. That thus I may live, 144. Hating every false way, 104. Rendering whole-hearted obedience, 34, and engaging in godly conversation, 27. IV. When obtained it must be improved by exercise in the Word of God. The entrance of the word into the heart is its dawn, 130. It increases by meditation in the word, 99. Is brought to perfection by faithful observance of the precepts of the word, 100. John vii. 17.

The Ten Titles of the Word of God.—" Way" (ver. 1, etc.). " Law" (ver. 1). " Testimonies" (ver. 2). " Precepts" (ver. 4). " Statutes" (ver. 5). " Commandments" (ver. 6). " Judgments" (ver. 7). " Word" (ver. 9). " Truth" (ver. 30). " Righteousness" (ver. 40).
Show the particular shade of meaning in each of these titles, and the light they cast on the divine law and on the duty of the believer.

Holy meditation.—I. Its theme: The revealed will of God in its varied aspects; *i.e.* " precepts "; " statutes "; " law "; " testimonies "; " word." II. The spirit which prompts it: Love (vers. 48 and 97). Love to God will induce meditation. Neglect of meditation argues want of love. III. Its times: By " day " (ver. 97). By " night " (ver. 148); when maltreated by the world (ver. 78); when falsely accused (ver. 23). IV. Its results: A holy walk (ver. 15). Proficiency in understanding (ver. 99). Support in trial (ver. 23, 78).
If you would gladden your nights and days and your times of trial, if you would excel in heavenly wisdom, and hallow your life, abundantly occupy yourself with sacred meditation.

THE PSALM TREATED IN ITS SECTIONS, BY C. A. DAVIS.

The subject of each portion is indicated in its first verse. Each section may serve as the subject for a discourse.
Verses 1—8.—The undefiled; described, in vers. 1—3. Such a life commanded by God is prayed for in ver. 5, and with its attendant happiness is anticipated in ver. 6—7, and resolved upon in ver. 8.

Verses 9—16.—Sanctification by the word, declared generally (ver. 9) ; sought personally (ver. 10—12) ; published to others (ver. 13) ; personally rejoiced in (ver. 14—16).

Verses 17—24.—Divine bounties desired. Life, for godly service (ver. 17). Illumination (ver. 18). Guidance homeward for the stranger (" thy command-ments ") (ver. 19—20), and, glancing at the proud who err from this guidance (ver. 21), the Psalmist prays for removal of the " reproach " entailed by fidelity to God (ver. 22—24).

Verses 25—32.—Quickening. Prayed for with confession (ver. 25, 26). When obtained shall be talked of (ver. 27). Desired for the sake of strength (ver. 28), of truthfulness (ver. 29—31), and of activity (ver. 32).

Verses 33—40.—Faithfulness secured by divine inworking. Prayer for divine teaching, understanding, constraint, and control of heart and eyes, to ensure persevering and whole-hearted faithfulness (ver. 33—37). The Psalmist, thus established in the word, prays for the establishment of the word to himself (ver. 38) ; deprecates the reproach of unfaithfulness (ver. 39) ; and enforces the whole prayer by the vehemence of the desire which prompts it (ver. 40).

Verses 41—48.—Promised mercies. Desired (ver. 41), as an answer to " him that reproacheth " (ver. 42, 43) ; as a means of faithfulness (ver. 44) ; liberty (ver. 45) ; boldness (ver. 46) ; delight (ver. 47), and eager longing (ver. 48).

Verses 49—56.—Hope in affliction. It arises from God's word (ver. 49). It produces comfort (ver. 50), even in trouble caused by the wicked (ver. 51—53). It gladdens the believer's pilgrimage and his holy night-seasons (ver. 54—56).

Verses 57—64.—The believer's portion. The Lord is the believer's portion (ver. 57) ; heartily sought (ver. 58—60) ; remaining though all else be taken away (ver. 61) ; causing joy even at midnight (ver. 62), and the selection of congenial company (ver. 63, 64).

Verses 65—72.—The Lord's dealings. Gratefully acknowledged (ver. 65), and their instructiveness still desired (ver. 66), even affliction from him is " good " (ver. 67, 68), and with its beneficial result is preferred to the prosperity of the wicked (ver. 69—72).

Verses 73—80.—Natural and spiritual creation. The Psalmist prays to the Creator for spiritual life or " understanding " (ver. 73), he will then be welcomed by the spiritual (ver. 74). He submissively receives affliction for spiritual training (vers. 75—77), deprecates the hostility of the proud (ver. 78), craves the company of the spiritual (ver. 79), and prays for heart-soundness (ver. 80).

Verses 81—88.—Hope in depression. In the depression arising from mortal frailness (ver. 81—84), and from unjust persecution (ver. 85—87), the word of God is the source of joy and comfort.

Verses 89—96.—The immutable word of God. Is enthroned in heaven (ver. 89), and on earth (ver. 90, 91), is the salvation of the believer in affliction (ver. 92—94), his resource in danger (ver. 95), and the embodiment of perfection (ver. 96).

Verses 97—104.—The profitableness of holy meditation. Its theme—" thy law " (ver. 97), its effect—" wisdom " (ver. 98—100), practically shown in daily life (ver. 101, 102), its sweetness (ver. 103), and hallowing influence (ver. 104).

Verses 105—112.—The word a lamp. For guidance (ver. 105, 106). For life in affliction (ver. 107). For preservation in peril of enemies (ver. 109, 110). For joy of heart (ver. 111, 112).

Verses 113—120.—Vain thoughts contrasted with God's law. The believer takes sides (ver. 113—115) ; prays for upholding in the law (ver. 116, 117) ; contemplates the fate of the followers of vain thoughts (ver. 118, 119) ; and expresses the godly fear thereby inspired (ver. 120).

Verses 121—128.—The just man's prayer against injustice. Out of the prison of oppression he appeals to God to be his surety (ver. 121, 122) ; utters his weary longing for deliverance (ver. 123—125) ; points to the " time " (ver. 126) ; and professes his supreme love for God's law in contrast to the oppressors' contempt of it (ver. 127, 128).

Verses 129—136.—The wonderfulness of God's testimonies. Declared (ver. 129), instanced as light-giving (ver. 130), pantingly longed for (ver. 131). An appeal for divine ordering in the word (ver. 132—135). Grief at its rejection by others (ver. 136).

Verses 137—144.—The righteousness of God and his word. Declared (ver. 137, 138). Indignation at the forgetfulness of the enemies (ver. 139). The purity of the word (ver. 140, 141). This righteousness of God and of his testimonies is everlasting (ver. 142—144).

Verses 145—152.—The believer's cry. The reiterated cry (ver. 145—148). An appeal for audience (ver. 149). The nearness of the enemy perceived (ver. 150). But, in response to the cry, God is also near (ver. 151).

Verses 153—160.—Divine consideration besought. " Consider my affliction " (ver. 153) ; my cause (ver. 154) ; " for thy mercies' sake " (ver. 156). Consider my persecutors (ver. 157—158), and my love to thy precepts (ver. 160), and act accordingly.

Verses 161—168.—What the word is to the believer. The object of awe (ver. 161), joy (ver. 162), love (ver. 163), praise (ver. 164), the producer of peace (ver. 165), and hope (166) ; therefore exceedingly loved (ver. 167), and faithfully kept (ver. 168).

Verses 169—176.—The concluding cry. Bespeaking audience for his cry, the Psalmist asks for understanding and deliverance (ver. 169, 170) ; promises to praise God (ver. 171), and to speak of God (ver. 172), and again cries for help (ver. 173), salvation (ver. 174), life (ver. 175), and restoration (ver. 176).

HINTS TO PREACHERS.

Verse 1.—"*Blessed.*" True blessedness lies in—I. Defilement avoided by the word. II. Delight experienced in the word.

Verse 1.—Spiritual pedestrians are often mentioned in this Psalm. Model travellers are described in this passage. Observe,—I. *Their Character :* " Undefiled." They are so (1) *in Christ :* found in him ; complete ; accepted. They are so (2) *by Christ :* His spirit, truth, and grace are in them. " Chosen generation," " peculiar people." II. *Their path :* " the law of the Lord." This path is (1) *Conspicuous*—high, visible, distinguished from every other. (2) *Ancient.* The old path. Holiness is older than sin, wisdom than folly, life than death, joy than sorrow. (3) *Safe.* Christ has repaired it. Apart from his work none can pass safely over. He has brought down mountains, raised up valleys, made crooked places straight, and rough places smooth. He has driven away the lion. (4) *Narrow.* It has a fence of commands on one side, and of prohibitions on the other. It is entered by a strait gate, which renders it necessary for the great to become as little children. III. *Their progress :* " walk." Not only talk, but step in the footprints of Jesus. Follow the law-fulfiller. They proceed in the exercise of his graces, in the exhibition of his virtues, in the fulfilment of his injunctions, and in the enjoyment of his favours. IV. *Their happiness :* " Blessed." They have unfailing help, suitable company, animating prospects on the way.—*W. Jackson,* 1882.

Verses 1, 2, 3.—I. Positive and Negative Beatitudes of Being.—II. Six Conditions of Peace with God. 1. Purity. 2. Obedience. 3. Fidelity. 4. Seeking. 5. Integrity. 6. Following.—*William Durban,* 1882.

Verse 2.—"*Blessed are they that keep his testimonies, and that seek him with the whole heart.*" I. *The sacred Quest :* " Seek him." He has been sought among the trees, the hills, the planets, the stars. He has been sought in his own defaced image, man. He has been sought amid the mysterious wheels of Providence. But these quests have often been prompted simply by intellect, or compelled by conscience, and have therefore resulted but in a cold, faint light. He has been sought in the word which this Psalm so highly extols, when it has led up the smoke-covered and gleaming peaks of Sinai. It has been followed, when it has led beneath the olives of Gethsemane to witness a mysterious struggle in blood-sweating and anguish ; to Calvary, where, in the place of a skull, life and immortality are brought to light. The sacred quest but there begins. II. *The Conduct of the Quest.* Seekers might be mistakenly dejected by so literal an interpretation of the " whole heart." We do not hesitate to say a stream is in its whole volume flowing toward sea while there are little side creeks in which the water eddies backward ; or to say the tide is coming despite receding waves ; or that spring is upon us despite hail-storm and biting wind. Indication of, 1. Unity. 2. Intensity. 3. Determination. No one conducts this quest aright who is not prompted to or sustained in it by the gracious Spirit. III. *Blessedness both in the pursuit and issue.* 1. Blessedness in the bitterness of penitence. The door-handle touched by him drops of myrrh. The rising sun sends kindling beams upon the highest peaks. 2. Blessedness in the gladsome findings of salvation and adoption. 3. Blessedness in the perpetual pursuit.—*William Anderson,* 1882.

Verse 2.—The double blessing. I. On keeping the testimonies. II. On seeking the Lord.

Verse 2.—"*That seek him with the whole heart.*" I. Seek what ? God himself. No peace until he is found. II. Seek where ? In his testimonies. 1. By studying them. 2. By keeping to them. III. Seek how ? With the whole heart.—*George Rogers.*

Verse 2. — *Seeking for God.* I. The Psalmist's way of seeking God. 1. He sought God *with the heart.* Only the heart can find God. Sight fails. " The scientific method " fails. All reason fails. Only love and trust can succeed. Love sees much where all other perception finds nothing. Faith generally goes with discovery, and nowhere so much as in finding God. 2. He sought God *with all his heart.* (1) Half-heartedness seldom finds anything worth having. (2) Half-heartedness shows contempt for God. (3) God will not reveal himself to half-heartedness. It would be putting the highest premium possible upon indifference. II. The Psalmist's plea in seeking God : " Let me not wander from thy commandments." 1. God's commandments lead, presently, into his own presence. If we take even the moral law, every one of the ten commandments leads away from the world, and sin, into that seclusion of holiness in which he hides. It is thus with all the commandments of the Scriptures. 2. The earnestness of the soul's search for God becomes, in itself, a plea with God that he will be found of us. God, who loves importunity in prayer, loves it no less when it takes the form of searching with all the heart. He who seeks with all the heart finds special encouragement to pray : " Let me not wander from thy commandments."—*F. G. Marchant.*

Verse 2.—*"That seek him."* We must remember six conditions required in them who would seek the Lord rightly. I. We must seek him in Christ the Mediator. John xiv. 6. II. We must seek him in truth. Jer. x. 10 ; John iv. 24 ; Ps. vii. 6. III. We must seek him in holiness. 2 Tim. ii. 19 ; Heb. xii. 14 ; 1 John iii. IV. We must seek him above all things and for himself. V. We must seek him by the light of his own word. VI. We must seek him diligently and with perseverance, never resting till we find him, with the spouse in the Canticles.—*William Cowper.*

Verses 2, 4, 5, 8.—" Blessed are they that *keep.*" " Thou hast commanded us to *keep.*" " O that my ways were directed to *keep.*" " I will *keep.*" The blessedness of *keeping* God's precepts—displayed (2), commanded (4), prayed for (5), resolved upon (8).—*C. A. D.*

Verse 3.—*"They also do no iniquity."* They work no iniquity with—1. Purpose of heart ; 2. Delight ; 3. Perseverance ; 4. Nor at all when the heart is fully sanctified unto God ; Christ dwelling in it by faith, and casting out sin.—*Adam Clarke.*

Verse 3.—The relation between negative and positive virtue. Or walking with God the best preventive of iniquity.

Verse 4.—I. Take notice of the law-giver : " Thou." Not thy equal, or one that will be baffled, but the great God. II. He hath interposed his authority : " hast commanded." III. The nature of this obedience, or the thing commanded : " To keep thy precepts."—*T. Manton.*

Verse 4.—*The supplementary commandment.* God having ordained the moral law, supplements it with a commandment prescribing the manner of keeping it. Hence : I. God is not indifferent to men's treatment of his law—whether they observe, neglect, or defy it. II. When observed, God discriminates the spirit of its observance, whether slavish, partial, careless, or diligent. III. There is but one spirit of obedience, whether slavish, partial, careless, or diligent. III. There is but one spirit of obedience which satisfies God's requirements. " Diligently " implies an obedience which is,—careful to ascertain the law—prompt to fulfil it (ver. 60)—unreserved—love-inspired (" diligently," old meaning, through the Latin, " lovingly," ver. 47, 97, 113). IV. Does our obedience come up to this standard ?—*C. A. D.*

Verse 4.—Not only is service commanded, but the manner of it. Heartiness, care, perseverance required, because without these it will not be true, uniform, or victorious over difficulty.

Verse 4.—How to obey : *"Diligently."* 1. Not partially, but fully. 2. Not doubtfully, but confidently. 3. Not reluctantly, but readily. 4. Not slovenly, but carefully. 5. Not coldly, but earnestly. 6. Not fitfully, but regularly.—*W. J.*

Verses 4, 5, 6.—A willing recognition (ver. 4). An ardent aspiration (ver. 5). A happy consequence (ver. 6).—*W. D.*

Verse 5.—The prayer of the gracious. I. Suggested by each preceding clause of blessing. II. By a consciousness of failure. III. By a loving clinging to the Lord.

Verse 5.—I. The end desired : " To keep thy statutes." Not to be safe merely, or happy, but holy. II. The help implored. 1. To understand the divine precepts. 2. To keep them.—*G. R.*

Verse 5.—Longing to obey. 1. *It is a noble aspiration.* There is nothing grander than the desire to do this except the doing of it. 2. *It is a spiritual aspiration.* Not the offspring of our carnal nature. It is the heart of God in the new creature. 3. *It is a practicable aspiration.* We sometimes sigh for the impossible. But this may be attained by divine grace. 4. *It is an intense aspiration.* It is the " Oh ! " of a burning wish. 5. *It is an influential aspiration.* It does not evaporate in sighs. It is a mighty incentive implanted by grace which will not let us rest without holiness.—*W. J.*

Verse 6.—See " Spurgeon's Sermons," No. 1443 : " A Clear Conscience."

Verse 6.—Holy confidence the offspring of universal obedience.

Verse 6.—*The armour of proof.* I. Universal obedience will give unabashed confidence—1. Before the criticising world. 2. In the court of conscience. 3. At the throne of grace. 4. In the day of judgment. II. But our obedience is far from universal, and leaves us open to—1. The world's shafts. 2. The rebukes of conscience. 3. It paralyses our prayers, and, 4. It dares not appear for us at the bar of God. III. Then let us by faith wrap ourselves in the perfect righteousness of Christ. Our answer to the world's cavil. We are not faultless, and for salvation we rest wholly on another. This righteousness is—1. The salve of our wounded conscience. 2. Our mighty plea in prayer. 3. Our triumphant vindication in the judgment day.—*C. A. D.*

Verse 6.—Topic :—Self-respect depends on respect for one greater than self.— *W. D.*

Verse 7.—The best of praise, the best of learning, the best of blendings, viz., praise and holiness.

Verse 7.—I. The professor of sacred music : " I will praise." II. The subject of his song : " Thee." III. The instrument : " Heart." IV. The instrument tuned : " Uprightness of heart." V. The musician's training academy : " Judgments."—*W. D.*

Verse 7.—Learning and praising. I. They are *two spiritual exercises.* It is possible for learners and singers to be carnal and sensual ; but in this case they are employed about the righteous ends, works, and ways of the Lord. II. They are *two appropriate exercises.* What can be more seemly than to learn of God and to praise him? III. They are *two profitable exercises.* The expectations of the most utilitarian are surpassed. The pleasure and the profit yield abundant reward. Heart, head, life are all benefited. IV. They are *two mutually-assisting exercises.* In the one we are receptive, and in the other communicative. By the one we are fitted to do the other. By the former we are stimulated to do the latter. How wonderfully the lesson is turned into a song, and the learner into a singer.—*W. J.*

Verse 7.—I. Deficiency confessed : " When I shall have learned." This is essential to growth. It is an admission all can truly make. II. Progress anticipated. He gave his heart to the work of learning. He sought divine help. III. Praise promised. He promised it to God alone. He vowed it should be sincere : " with upright heart."—*W. Williams,* 1882.

Verse 8.—I. A hopeful resolve for life. II. A dreadful fear. III. A series of considerations removing the fear.

Verse 8.—I. The resolution : " I will keep," etc. II. The petition : " O forsake me not utterly." 1. Filial submission. I deserve it occasionally. 2. Filial confidence. " Not utterly." III. The connection between the two. Obedience without prayer and prayer without obedience are equally in vain. To make headway both oars must be applied. God cannot abide lazy beggars, who while they can get anything by asking will not work.—*G. R.*

Verse 8.—"*O forsake me not utterly.*" Divine desertion deprecated. I. The anguished prayer. 1. Sovereign forsakings. Sovereignty is not arbitrariness or capriciousness ; perhaps its right definition is mysterious kingly love ; unknown now, but justified when revealed. 2. Vicarious forsakings. 3. Forsakings on account of sin. David, Jonah, and Peter. The seven churches of Asia ; the Jews. But to know what "*utter*" both in regard to degree and time means, we must go to hell. Like one trembling on the very verge of hell, he prays. Like belated traveller, in vast wood and surrounded by beasts of prey, sighs at day's departure. Like the watch on the raft, seeing the sail that he has shouted himself hoarse to stop fading away in the sky line. II. Its doctrinal foundation. Where he condescendeth to dwell, his abode is perpetual. He can only utterly forsake us because he was deceived in us. He can only utterly forsake because baffled. Both imply blasphemy. Thou who hatest putting away, thou who hast never yet *utterly* forsaken any saint, make not me the solitary exception. III. Historical certainty of answer. The saint and the church in all time delivered. It may tarry till " eventide," as in Cowper's case. His face bore after death an expression of delighted surprise.—*W. A.*

Verse 9.—I. The young man's question. II. The wise man's reply.

Verse 9.—In the word of God, when applied to the heart by the Spirit of God, there is, I. A sufficiency of light to discover to men the need of cleansing their way. II. Sufficiency of energy for the cleansing their way. III. A sufficiency of pleasure to encourage them to choose to cleanse their way. IV. A sufficiency of support to sustain them in their cleansed way.—*Theophilus Jones, in a "Sermon to the Young,"* 1829.

Verse 9.—The word of God provides for the cleansing of the way, I. By pointing out to the young man the evil of the way. II. By discovering an infallible remedy for the disorders of his nature—the salvation that is by Jesus Christ. III. By becoming a directory in all the paths of duty to which he may be called.—*Daniel Wilson*, 1828.

Verse 9.—The Psalmist's rules for the attainment of holiness deduced from his own experience. 1. Seek God with thy " whole heart " (ver. 2). Be truly sensible of your wants. 2. Keep and remember what God says (ver. 11): "Thy word have I hidden," etc. 3. Reduce all this to practice (ver. 11): "That I might not sin against thee." 4. Bless God for what he has given (ver. 12): "Blessed art thou," etc. 5. Ask more (ver. 12): "Teach me thy statutes." 6. Be ready to communicate his knowledge to others (ver. 13): "With my lips have I declared." 7. Let it have a due effect on thy own heart (ver. 14): " I have rejoiced," etc. 8. Meditate frequently upon them (ver. 15): " I will meditate," etc. 9. Deeply reflect on them (ver. 16): " I will have respect," etc. As food undigested will not nourish the body, so the word of God not considered with deep meditation and reflection will not feed the soul. 10. Having pursued the above course he should continue in it, and then his happiness would be secured (ver. 16): " I will not forget thy word : I will (in consequence) delight myself in thy statutes."—*Adam Clarke.*

Verse 9.—A question and answer for the young. The Bible is a book for young people. Here it intimates, I. That the young man's way *needs to be cleansed*. His way of thinking, feeling, speaking, acting. II. That *he must take an active part in the work*. The efficient cause in the operation is God. Other good influences are also at work. But the young man must be in hearty and practical sympathy with the work. III. That *he must use the Bible for the purpose*. This records facts, presents incitations, enjoins precepts, utters promises, and sets up examples, all which are adapted to make a young man holy. By reading, studying, and imitating the Scriptures in a lowly and prayerful spirit the young shall escape pollution and ornament society.—*W. J.*

Verse 9.—A word to the young. I. Show how the young man is in special danger of defiling his way. Through, 1. His strong passions. 2. His immature judgment. 3. His inexperience. 4. His rash self-sufficiency. 5. His light companions, and, 6. His general heedlessness. II. The circumspection he should use to cleanse his way. *"Taking heed,"* 1. Of his evil propensities. 2. Of his companions. 3. Of his pursuits. 4. Of the tendencies of all he does. III. The infallible guide by which his circumspection is to be regulated : *"according to thy word "*—that is to say, 1. Its precepts. 2. Its examples. 3. Its motives. 4. Its warnings. 5. Its allurements.—*C. A. D.*

Verse 10.—I. A grateful review. II. An anxious forecast. III. A commendable prayer.

Verse 10.—The believer's two great solicitudes. 1. What he is anxious to find : " I have sought thee." 2. What he is afraid of losing : " Thy commandments."— *W. D.*

Verse 10.—*Sincerity not self-sufficiency.* I. The believer must be conscious of whole-heartedness in seeking God. II. But consciousness of sincerity does not warrant self-sufficiency. III. The most whole-hearted seeker must still look to divine grace to keep him from wandering.—*C. A. D.*

Verse 11.—The best thing, in the best place, for the best of purposes.

Verse 12.—The blessedness of God, and the mode of entering into it.

Verse 12.—I. David gives glory to God : *"Blessed art thou, O LORD."* II. He asks grace from God.—*Matthew Henry.*

Verse 12.—I. What it is, or how God doth teach us. 1. God doth teach us outwardly ; by his ordinances, by the ministry of men. 2. Inwardly ; by the inspiration and work of the Holy Ghost. II. The necessity of his teaching. III. The benefit and utility of it.—*T. Manton.*

Verse 12.—*Desire for Divine Teaching excited by the Recognition of Divine Blessedness.* I. Unveil in some inadequate degree the happiness of the ever blessed God, arising from his purity, benevolence, love. II. Show the way in which man may become partaker of that blessedness by conformity to his precepts. III. Utter the prayer of the text.—*C. A. D.*

Verse 13.—Speech fitly employed. It is occupied with a choice subject, a full subject, a subject profitable to men, and glorifying to God.

Verse 14.—Practical religion, the source of a comfort surpassing riches. It gives a man ease of mind, independence of carriage, weight of influence, and other matters supposed to arise out of wealth.

Verse 14.—I. The subject of rejoicing. Not the " testimonies " merely, but their observances, " the way of," etc. II. The rejoicing in that subject. 1. In its inward peace. 2. In its external consequences. III. The degree of the rejoicing : " as much as," etc.—*G. R.*

Verse 14.—*The two scales of the balance.* Whatever riches are good for, God's testimonies are good for. I. Riches are desirable as the means of procuring the necessaries of life ; but God's testimonies supply the necessities of the soul. II. Riches are desirable as a means of procuring personal enjoyment ; but God's testimonies produce the highest joy. III. Riches are desirable as a means of attaining personal improvement ; but God's testimonies are the highest educators. IV. Riches are desirable as a means of doing good ; but God's testimonies work the highest good.—*C. A. D.*

Verse 15.—The contemplative and active life ; their common food, object, and reward.

Verse 16.—I. What there is to be delighted in. II. What comes of such delight : ' I will never forget." III. What comes of such memory—more delight.

Verse 17.—I. A bountiful master. II. A needy servant—begging for very life. III. A suitable recompense : " and keep thy word."

Verse 17.—We are here taught, I. That we owe our lives to God's mercy. II. That therefore we ought to spend our lives in God's service.—*Matthew Henry.*

Verse 18.—I. The precious casket : " thy law." II. The invisible treasure : " wondrous things." III. The miraculous eyesight : " that I may behold." IV. The divine oculist : " Open thou mine eyes."

Verse 18.—*The hidden wonders of the gospel.* There are many hidden things in nature ; many in our fellow men ; so there are many in the Bible. The things of the Bible are hidden because of the blindness of man. I. *The blind man's sorrow :* " Open mine eyes." I cannot see. I have eyes and see not. The pain of this conscious blindness when a man really feels it. II. *The blind man's conviction :* " That I may behold wondrous," etc. There are wondrous things there to be seen. I am sure of it. There is a wonderful view,—(1) of sin ; (2) of hell, as its desert ; (3) of One ready to save ; (4) of perfect pardon ; (5) of God's love ; (6) of all-sufficient grace ; (7) of heaven. III. *The blind man's wisdom.* The fault is in my eyes, not in thy word. " Open my eyes," and all will be well. The reason for not seeing is because the eyes are blinded by sin. There is nothing wanting in the Bible. IV. *The blind man's prayer :* " Open *thou* mine eyes." 1. I cannot open them. 2. My dearest friends cannot. 3. Only thou canst. " Lord, I pray thee, now open them." Many seek to stop such praying. Be like Bartimeus who *"cried so much the more."* V. *The blind man's anticipation :* " That I may behold." 1. The joy of a cured blind man when he is about to behold, for the first time, the beauties of nature. 2. The joy of the spiritually healed when they begin " looking unto Jesus." 3. The personal character of the joy : " Open thou *mine* eyes, that I may behold." I have hitherto had to see through the eyes of others. I would depend on other eyes no longer. The glad anticipation of Job : " Whom I shall see for myself, and mine eyes shall behold, and not another."—*Frederick G. Marchant,* 1882.

Verse 18.—God's word suited to man's sense of wonder. I. We shall make some remarks on the sense of wonder in man, and what generally excites it. One of the first causes of wonder is the *new or unexpected.* The second source is to be found in things *beautiful and grand.* A third source is the *mysterious* which surrounds man— there are things *unknowable.* II. God has made provision for this sense of wonder in his revealed word. The Bible addresses our sense of wonder by constantly presenting the *new and unexpected* to us ; it sets before us things *beautiful and grand.* If we come to the third source of wonder, that which raises it to *awe,* it is the peculiar province of the Bible to deal with this. III. The means we are to use in order to have God's word thus unfolded—the prayer of the Psalmist may be our guide— " Open mine eyes, that I may behold wondrous things out of thy law."— *John Ker, of Glasgow,* 1877.

Verse 18.—*Wondrous sights for opened eyes.* I. The wondrous things in God's law. A wondrous rule of life. A wondrous curse against transgression. A wondrous redemption from the curse shadowed forth in the ceremonial law. II. Special eyesight needed to behold them. They are spiritual things. Men are spiritually blind. 1 Cor. ii. 14. III. Personal prayer to the Great Opener of eyes.—*C. A. D.*

Verse 19.—An insight into the divine will, the best assistance in our journey through the earth. Or, what I am; where I am; where I am going; how am I to get there?

Verse 19 (first clause).—The stranger in the earth. I. A short exposition. The text means,—1. That the saint is not born of the earth. 2. That the saint is not known on earth. 3. The saint's portion is not upon the earth. 4. The saint is compassed with sorrows and trials upon earth. 5. The saint is soon to leave the earth. II. A short application. 1. Do not be like the world. 2. Be prepared to be a sufferer on the earth. 3. Sit loose to the world. 4. Correspond with home. 5. Cherish brotherly love for your fellow-strangers on the earth. 6. Hasten home. 7. Press others to come with you.—*Duncan Macgregor's Sermon in "The Shepherd in Israel,"* 1869.

Verse 19.—*The stranger's prayer.* I. How he came to be a stranger in the earth. He was born again. He learned the manners of his foreign home. He spoke the language of his Fatherland; and so was misunderstood and rejected on earth. II. How he longed after everything homelike. Home rules: " thy commandments." Home teaching: " hide not." Specially his Father's voice. III. How in his loneliness he solaced himself by communication with his Father. IV. Would you not like to be a stranger?—*C. A. D.*

Verse 20.—I. The word sought, and sought at all times. II. The word sought, and sought with intense desire. III. The word sought, and sought the more intensely the more it is found. It was because he had found so much in the word of the Lord already, that the soul of the Psalmist was breaking to find more. Those who have been once admitted to " the secret of the Lord " find their highest joy in knowing that secret still more fully. It is to those who know that secret that the promise is given: " He will shew them his covenant:" Ps. xxv. 14.—*F. G. M.*

Verse 20.—One of the best tests of character and prophecies of what a man will be, are his longings. I. The saint's absorbing object: " Thy judgments." The word here is synonymous with the " word " of God. 1. The Psalmist greatly reverenced the word. 2. He intensely desired to know its contents. 3. He wishes to feed upon God's word. 4. He longed to obey it. 5. He longed to feel the power of God's judgments in his own heart. II. The saint's ardent longings. 1. They constitute a living experience. 2. The expression used in the text represents a humble sense of imperfection. 3. It indicates an advanced experience. 4. It is an experience which we may term a bitter sweet. 5. These longings may become very wearying to a man's soul. III. Cheering reflections. 1. God is at work in your soul. 2. The result of God's work is very precious. 3. It is leading on to something more precious. 4. The desire itself is doing you good. 5. It makes Christ precious. See " Spurgeon's Sermons," No. 1586 : " Holy Longings."

Verse 21.—I. The character of the proud. II. God's dealings with them. III. Our own relation to them.

Verse 21.—I. The sin; " Err from the commandments." 1. By neglect; or, 2. By abuse of them. II. Its origin—pride : pride of reason, of heart, of life. III. Its punishment. 1. Rebuke. 2. Condemnation.—*G. R.*

Verse 23.—Meditation. I. Our best employment while others slander. II. Our best comfort under their falsehood. III. Our best preservative from a spirit of revenge. IV. Our best mode of showing our superiority to their attacks.

Verse 24.—I. He reverenced them as God's testimonies. II. He revelled in them as his delight. III. He referred to them as his counsellors.

Verse 25.—I. Nature and its tendency. II. Grace and its mode of operation. III. Both truths in their personal application.

Verse 25.—"*Quicken thou me,*" etc. I. There are many reasons why we should seek quickening. 1. Because of the deadening influence of the world. " My soul cleaveth," etc. 2. The influence of vanity (see ver. 37). 3. Because we are surrounded by deceivers (see ver. 87, 88). 4. Because of the effect of seasons of affliction upon us (see ver. 7). II. Some of the motives for seeking quickening. 1. Because of what you are—a Christian ; life seeks more life. 2. Because of what you ought to be. 3. Because of what we shall be. 4. In order to obedience (see ver. 88). 5. For your comfort (ver. 107 and 50). 6. As the best security against the attacks of enemies (ver. 87 and 88). 7. To invigorate our memories (ver. 93). 8. Consider (as a motive to seek this quickening) the terrible consequences of losing spiritual life or, in other words, lacking it in its manifest display. III. Some of the ways in which the quickening may be brought to us. 1. It must be by the Lord himself.

" Quicken me, O Lord." 2. By the turning of the eyes (ver. 37). 3. By the word (ver. 50). 4. By the precepts (ver. 93). 5. By affliction (ver. 107). 6. By divine comforts. IV. Enquire where are our pleas when we come before God to ask for quickening. 1. Our necessity (ver. 107, etc.). 2. Our earnest desire (ver. 40). 3. Appeal to God's righteousness (ver. 40). 4. To his lovingkindness (ver. 88, 149, 156). 5. The plea in the text : " according to thy word " (ver. 28 and 107). See " Spurgeon's Sermons," No. 1350 : " Enlivening and Invigorating."

Verse 26.—Confession. Absolution. Instruction.

Verse 26.—I. The duty : " I have declared my ways "—made known my experience of thy word to others. II. Its notice by God : " Thou heardest me." III. Its reward. More knowledge will be given : " Teach me," etc.—*G. R.*

Verse 27.—I. A student's prayer. 1. It deals with the main subject of the conversation which is to be that student's occupation—" the way of God's precepts." 2. A confession is implied : " Make me," etc. 3. A great boon is asked—to understand, to know, thy statutes. 4. The Fountain of all wisdom is applied to. II. The occupation of the instructed man. 1. He testifies of God's works—his wondrous works—Christ's work for us ; the Holy Spirit's work in us. The wonderful character of these works of God, a wide field for devout study. 2. He speaks very plainly : " I will talk," etc. 3. He will speak very frequently : " I will talk." 4. He will speak to the point : " So "—*i.e.*, according to understanding. III. The intimate relation between the prayer of the student and the pursuit that he subsequently followed. See " Spurgeon's Sermons," No. 1344 : " The Student's Prayer."

Verse 27.—Education for the ministry. I. The student at college : " Make me to understand." His lesson. His instructor. His application. II. The preacher at his work : " So shall I talk," etc. His qualification. His theme. His manner.— *C. A. D.*

Verse 28.—Heaviness, its cause, curse, and cure.

Verse 29.—The way of lying. I. Describe the way of lying. Various paths, *e.g.*, erroneous views of doctrine : false grounds of faith : looseness of practice : shrinking from the daily cross. II. Show why it is thus named. It does not furnish its promised pleasures. It does not lead to its professed goal. It lies through the territory of the father of lies. III. Notice the peculiarity in the prayer against it. Not remove me from, but remove from me : for the way of lying is within us. IV. Our deliverance from the way of lying lies with God.—*C. A. D.*

Verses 29, 30.—I. The way of lying, our wish to have it removed, and the method of answer. II. The way of truth, our choice, and the method of carrying it out.

Verse 31.—Reasons for sticking to the Divine testimonies.

Verse 31.—A wholesome mixture. I. Sturdy fidelity. II. Self-distrust, and, III. Importunate prayer.—*C. A. D.*

Verse 32.—The Fettered Racer set free. I. The course that invited him. II. The shackles that bound him. III. The impatience that prompted him. IV. The Lord that freed him. V. Now let him go.—*C. A. D.*

Verse 32.—I. Liberty desired. II. Liberty rightly used. Or, the effect of the heart upon the feet.

Verse 32.—The text will give us occasion to speak, 1. Of the benefit of an enlarged heart. The necessary precedency of this work on God's part, before there can be any serious bent or motion of heart towards God on our part. 3. The subsequent resolution of the saints to engage their hearts to live to God. 4. With what earnestness, alacrity and vigour of spirit this work is to be carried on : " I will run."— *T. Manton.*

Verse 32.—I. The way of obedience : " Thy commandments." II. The duty of obedience : " I will run "—not stand still—not loiter—not creep—not walk, but run. III. The life of obedience. 1. Where it lies—in the heart. 2. Whence it comes : " When thou shalt," etc. 3. What it does—enlarges the heart.—*G. R.*

Verse 33.—In this prayer for grace observe, 1. The person to whom he prays : "*O Lord.*" 2. The person for whom : " teach *me.*" 3. The grace for which he prayeth : to be taught. 4. The object of this teaching : " The way of thy statutes." The teaching which he beggeth, is not speculative, but practical, to learn how to walk in the way of God.—*T. Manton.*

Verse 33.—The superior efficacy of divine teaching : it secures holy practice and insures its perpetuity.

Verses 33, 34.—*Light from above.* I. The blinding power of sin. " Teach me," *i.e.*, " point out to me." " Give me understanding." Whatever may have been the original amount of light which came from eating from the tree of knowledge of good and evil, that light has long been insufficient. 1. Men need light to discern the right way from the wrong. 2. Men need light to understand the beauties of the right way. Such beauties line the way of truth on either hand, but only the God-taught mind appreciates them. Even Jesus, who is the way, the truth, and the life, is as a root out of a dry ground, till the mind is taught of the Lord. Sin is the cause of this blindness. The farther any man walks in the way of sin, the less can he see of the beauties of holiness. II. The enlightening grace of the Lord. " Teach me." " Give me understanding." This grace, 1. May be boldly asked : " If any man lack wisdom let him ask of God." 2. Will be freely given. " Who giveth to all men liberally." " Ask, and it shall be given." 3. Will be amply sufficient. " I shall keep it unto the end." " I shall keep Thy law." To see is to follow. III. The stimulating power of clearly revealed truth. " I shall observe it with my whole heart." To see is not only to follow, but to follow with love and gladness. It is written of the light which will come before the throne, " We shall be like him, *for* we shall see him as he is." " O thou, that dwellest between the Cherubim, shine forth," even here, on the way that leads to thy presence.—*F. G. M.*

Verses 33—35.—Alpha and Omega. I. God, the giver of spiritual instruction : ver. 33. II. Of spiritual understanding, without which this instruction is in vain : ver. 34. III. Of grace for practical obedience when thus instructed : ver. 35. IV. For whole-hearted obedience : ver. 34. V. For final perseverance : ver. 33.—*C. A. D.*

Verses 33—36.—Human Dependence on Divine help. I. There can be no steady keeping in the way of the Lord without the Lord's guidance : ver. 33. II. There can be no observing of the way with the heart without Divine light for the mind : ver. 34. III. There can be no diligent pursuit of the way till divine energy be given to the will : ver. 35. IV. There can be no true love of the way unless the heart be constrained by the love of God : ver. 36. He who said, " Without me ye can do nothing," is necessary for us to see the way, to understand the way, to walk in the way, and to love the way.—*F. G. M.*

Verse 34.—The influence of the understanding upon the heart, and the united power of understanding and heart over the life.

Verse 34.—Seeing and loving. I. When men see they love (the whole verse). II. When men love they see. Only the loving heart would have seen enough to write such a verse.—*F. G. M.*

Verse 35.—The prayer of a child, and the delight of a child. Or, Our pleasure in holiness a plea for grace.

Verse 35.—I. Delight avowed. II. Disinclination implied. III. Constraint implored.—*W. W.*

Verse 36.—Holiness a cure for covetousness.

Verses 36, 112.—The Co-operation of the Divine and the Human in Salvation. I. It is God that worketh in you : ver. 36. II. Therefore work out your own salvation with fear and trembling : ver. 112.—*C. A. D.*

Verse 37.—"Quicken thou me in thy way." This brief prayer—1. Deals with the believer's frequent need. II It directs us to the sole worker of quickening : " Thou." III. It describes the sphere of renewed vigour : " in thy way." IV. It denotes that there may be special reasons and special seasons for this prayer—times of temptation : ver. 37 ; seasons of affliction : ver. 107 ; when called to some extraordinary service. See " Spurgeon's Sermons," No. 1073 : " A Honeycomb."

Verse 37.—Here is, I. Conversion *from*—" vanity." II. Conversion *to*—" thy way. III. Conversion *by*—" Quicken thou me."—*G. R.*

Verse 37.—David prays, (1) for *restraining* grace that he might be prevented and kept back from that which would hinder him in the way of his duty : " Turn away mine eyes from beholding vanity." He prays (2) for *constraining* grace, that he might not only be kept from everything that would obstruct his progress heaven-ward, but that he might have that grace which was necessary to forward him in that progress : " Quicken thou me in thy way."—*M. Henry.*

Verse 38.—Confirmation. What ? " Thy word established." To whom ? " Unto thy servant." Why ? " Who is devoted," etc.

Verse 38.—Fear of God evidences itself, 1. By a dread of his displeasure. 2. Desire of his favour. 3. Regard for his excellencies. 4. Submission to his will. 5. Gratitude for his benefits. 6. Conscientious obedience to his commands.—*Charles Buck.*

Verse 38.—The four kinds of fear. 1. The fear of man, by which we are led rather to do wrong than to suffer evil. 2. Servile fear, through which we are induced to avoid sin only from the dread of hell. 3. Initial fear, in which we avoid sin partly from the fear of hell, but partly also from the love of God, which is the fear of ordinary Christians. 4. Filial fear, when we are afraid to disobey God only and altogether from the love we bear him. Jer. xxxii. 40.—*Ayguan, in J. Edward Vaux's "Preacher's Storehouse,"* 1878.

Verse 39.—I. Man's judgment dreaded. II. God's judgment approved.

Verse 39.—*The reproach of inconsistency.* I. The dishonour caused by it (2 Sam. xii. 14). II. The danger of incurring it. III. The prayer against it.—*C. A. D.*

Verse 40.—I. Gracious longings experienced. II. Great necessity felt—more life needed. III. Wise petition offered.

Verse 41.—See " Spurgeon's Sermons," No. 1524 : " Your Personal Salvation."

Verse 41.—I. God's mercies come to us unsought continually. His sparing mercies, temporal mercies, etc. II. The chief outcome of God's mercies is his salvation. It is our greatest need ; it is his greatest gift. III. We should have a personal interest in this salvation : " Let thy mercies come also unto me." IV. When we seek God's salvation, we may plead his promise : " according to thy word."—*Horatio Wilkins,* 1882.

Verse 41.—" Even me." I. In me there is need of mercy. II. To me mercy can come. III. Thy salvation suits me. IV. Special difficulties would daunt me. V. Thy word encourages me.

Verse 41.—I. Salvation is all of mercy. II. All mercies are in salvation. III. All men should be anxious for salvation to come to them. IV. It can only come according to God's word.—*W. W.*

Verses 41—43.—*A Comprehensive Prayer.* I. The possession of salvation, ver. 41. II. Is the power for defence : ver. 42. III. And the qualification for usefulness : ver. 43.—*C. A. D.*

Verse 42.—Faith's answer to reproach found in the fact that she trusts God's word.

Verses 42, 43, 47.—Faith, hope, and love. " I trust." " I have hoped." " I have loved." Faith warring, hope testifying, love obeying.

Verse 43.—How the true preacher could be silenced, and his plea that he may not be so.

Verse 44.—The perpetuity of gracious living. On what it is conditioned : " So." How entirely it is consistent with free agency : " I keep." How continuous it is, and how eternal.

Verse 44.—*Heaven begun below.* I. The present life of the believer—keeping God's law. II. The continual care of the believer—to keep God's law. III. The eternal prospect of the believer—keeping God's law for ever and ever.—*C. A. D.*

Verses 45—47.—Liberty of walk. Liberty of speech. Liberty of heart.

Verses 45—48.—The true freeman enjoys—1. *Free walk* with God. 2. *Free talk* about God. 3. *Free love* unto God. 4. *Free exercise* of soul, (1) in holy practice ; (2) in heavenly meditation.—*W. Durban.*

Verses 45—48.—Five things the Psalmist promiseth himself here in the strength of God's grace. 1. That he should be free and easy in his duty : " I will walk at liberty." 2. That he should be bold and courageous in his duty : " I will speak of thy testimonies also before kings." 3. That he should be cheerful and pleasant in his duty : " I will delight myself in thy commandments." 4. That he should be diligent and vigorous in his duty : " I will delight myself in thy commandments." 5. That he should be thoughtful and considerate in his duty : " I will meditate in thy statutes."—*M. Henry.*

Verses 46—48.—*Lips, heart, and hands.* I. Public profession of God's word (" I will speak," ver. 46) must be warranted by—II. Private delight in God's word (" I will delight myself," ver. 47), which must result in—III. Practical obedience to God's word (" I will lift up my hands," ver. 48).

Verse 46.—I. The truly earnest must speak. II. They are at no loss for good subjects : " Thy testimonies." The range is boundless—the variety endless. III. They never fear any audience : " before kings."—*W. W.*

Verse 48.—I. Love renewing its activity. II. Love refreshing itself with spiritual food.

Verse 48.—I. Scripture in the hand for reading. Often in the hand. II. In the mind for meditation: " I will meditate," etc. III. In the heart for love: " Which I have loved."—*G. R.*

Verse 48.—Religion engaged the whole manhood of David : hands, heart, head. I. The uplifted hands. 1. *Taking an oath of allegiance to God's word.* Gen. xiv. 22 ; Ezek. xx. 28. To receive its doctrines, obey its precepts, regard its warnings, uphold its honour. 2. *Imploring a blessing upon God's word.* Gen. xlviii. 14 ; Lev. ix. 22 ; Luke xxiv. 50. That its light might spread : " Fly abroad, thou mighty gospel ; " that its influence may become universal. II. The loyal heart. 1. *This accounts for uplifted hands.* He had loved the word himself. Religion is inward first, then outward. We must love it before we are anxious to spread it. 2. *But what accounts for the loyal heart ?* The word had brought him salvation, yielded him sustenance, afforded him guidance. We love the word for its joyous effects upon ourselves. III. The studious mind. 1. Devout meditation the best employment. 2. The word of God affords a grand field for it. 3. To meditate in it learn to love it : " have loved," " will meditate."—*W. W.*

Verse 48.—I. God's commandments loved. We love the law when we love the Lawgiver. We love his will only when our hearts are reconciled and renewed. Hence the need of spiritual renewal. II. God's commandments the subject of prayer : " My hands also will I lift up." Perowne says, " The expression denotes the act of prayer." We may pray for a fuller knowledge, a deeper experience, a readier and more perfect obedience. III. A theme for meditation. Amidst the hurry of outward activities we must not forget the need of quiet meditation. —*H. W.*

Verse 49.—I. The personality of the word : " the word unto thy servant." II. The application of the word : " upon which thou hast caused me to hope." III. The pleading of the word : " Remember the word," etc.

Verse 49.—*The word of hope.* I. God's word the foundation of human hope. (The fact of a revelation. The substance of the revelation.) II. Particular words of God which have been found peculiarly hope-enkindling. III. The pleading of such words at the throne of grace.—*C. A. D.*

Verse 50.—Each man has his own affliction and his own consolation. Quickened piety the best comfort. The word the means of it.

Verse 50.—I. The need of consolation. II. The consolation needed.—*G. R.*

Verse 51.—The proud man's contumely, and the gracious man's constancy.

Verse 51.—*Fidelity in the face of contempt.* I. The proud deride the believer's subjection to God's law. II. They ridicule the believer's delight in God's service. III. They are met by the believer's resolution to cleave to God. 2 Sam. vi. 20, 22. —*C. A. D.*

Verse 52.—Comfort derived from a review of the ancient doings of the Lord towards the wicked and his people.

Verse 52.—I. The dead speaking to the living. II. The living listening to the dead.—*G. R.*

Verse 52.—*Sweet water from a dark well.* I. God's judgments are calculated to inspire terror. II. But they prove God's superintending care over the world. III. They are ever against sin, and for holiness. IV. In all times of judgment God delivers his people. Noah, Lot, etc. V. Therefore God's judgments are a source of comfort to the believer.—*C. A. D.*

Verse 53.—The sensations of godly men at the sight of sinners : horror at their crime, their perseverance in it, their rejection of grace, and their end.

Verse 53.—*Horror-stricken.* I. The guilt and danger of impenitent sinners. II. The horror and concern of godly spectators. III. The prayer and labour which such concern should dictate.—*C. A. D.*

Verse 54.—Here is—I. Light in darkness. II. Companionship in solitude. III. Activity in rest : " house of pilgrimage."—*G. R.*

Verse 54.—*The cheerful pilgrim.* I. A good man views his residence in this world as only the house of his pilgrimage. II. The situation, however disadvantageous, admits of cheerfulness. III. The sources of his joy are derived from the Scriptures.—*W. Jay.*

Verse 54.—See " Spurgeon's Sermons," No. 1652 : " The Singing Pilgrim."

Verse 55 with 49.—" Remember." " I have remembered."

Verse 55.—Night memories. Day duties. How they act and react upon each other.

Verse 55.—Dark nights. Bright memories. Right results.—*C. A. D.*

Verse 55.—I. Happy though restless night. II. Happy though busy day.—*W. D.*

Verse 56.—The gains of godliness ; or, what a man gets through holy living.

Verse 56.—I. The duty : " I kept thy precepts." II. Its reward : " This I had," etc. Protection : " this I had." Guidance : " this I had." Prosperity : " this I had." Consolation : " this I had."—*G. R.*

Verse 57.—I. The infinite possession : " Thou art my portion, O LORD." Notice—1. A clear distinction made by the Psalmist between his portion and that of the ungodly here and hereafter : See Ps. lxxiii. 2. A positive claim : " Thou art my portion, O LORD." This " portion " is boundless, abiding, appropriate, satisfying, elevating, all of grace. II. The appropriate resolution : " I have said that I would keep thy words." 1. Notice the preface : " I have said." 2. The link between the portion possessed and the resolution made. 3. The work of keeping God's words. Keep him who is the *Word*—Christ Jesus. Keep the word of the gospel—doctrines, precepts, promises (kept in the heart to comfort the believer). This blessed subject suggests a solemn contrast. See the portion of that servant who did not keep his Lord's word : Matt. xxix. 48—51. See "Spurgeon's Sermons," No. 1372 : " God our Portion, and his Word our Treasure."

Verse 57 (*first clause*).—The believer's portion. I. Show the validity of his claim : " my." 1. A gift by covenant : Heb. viii. 10—13. 2. Involved in joint heirship with Christ : Rom. viii. 17. 3. Confirmed by the experience of faith. II. Survey. the superlative value of his possession : " The Lord." 1. Absolutely good. 2. Infinitely precious. 3. Inexhaustibly full. 4. Everlastingly sure. III. Suggest a method of deriving the greatest *present* advantage from it. 1. Meditate much upon God, under the conviction that he is your portion. 2. Carry all cares to him, and cast every burden on him. 3. Refer every temptation to the word of his law, and every doubt to the word of his promise. 4. Draw largely upon his riches to meet every need as it arises.—*John Field,* 1882.

Verses 57, 58.—The believer's estate, profession, and petition.

Verse 58.—*The soul's sunshine.* I. God's favour the one thing needful. II. Whole-heartedness the one mode of entreating it. III. Covenant mercy the one plea for obtaining it.—*C. A. D.*

Verse 58.—We may learn how a seeker may come to enjoy saving favour, by a careful study of—I. The Profession : " I intreated thy favour with my whole heart." 1. What he did : " I intreated." *Heb.* " I painfully sought thy face." Earnest desire. Importunate supplication. Painful sorrow for sin. 2. How he did it : " With my whole heart." The intellect, affections, will, all engaged and concentrating effort. Otherwise, seeking is solemn trifling. This only worthy of our purpose, pleasing to God, and successful. 3. The evidence that we are doing it. Frequent prayer, searching the word, often enquiring. The first and main business —Giving up for Christ. II. The Petition : " Be merciful unto me." 1. God's favour to be expected on the terms of mercy only. 2. Happily, this is a prayer every sinner can and should use. 3. Blessedly true it is, that it never fails. III. The Plea : " According to thy word." 1. A plea that cannot be gainsaid is a great thing in an entreaty. 2. The promise of God is just such a plea. 3. Seek it out, lay hold of it, and urge it.—*J. F.*

Verse 59.—I. Self-examination : " I thought on " my private " ways "—my social ways—my sacred ways—my public ways. II. Its advantages : " And turned my feet," etc.—*G. R.*

Verse 59.—I. Unthinking and straying. II. Thinking and turning.—*C. A. D.*

Verse 59.—I. Conviction. II. Conversion.—*W. D.*

Verse 59.—*Thinking on our own ways.* Enquire, I. Why so generally neglected ? 1. Want of courage. 2. Occupied too much. 3. Unpleasant, and therefore the chief care of many is to banish it. II. When is it wisely conducted ? 1. When honestly engaged in. 2. When thoroughly carried out. 3. When Scripture is made the referee and standard. 4. When Divine help is sought. III. What end will it serve ? 1. Turn us from our own ways with shame and penitence. 2. Turn us to God's testimonies with earnestness, reverence, and hopefulness.—*J. F.*

Verse 59.—I. Right thinking : " I thought on my ways." 1. That this thought upon his ways caused the Psalmist dissatisfaction is evident. 2. Right thinking upon our ways will suggest a practical change. 3. The retrospect we take of our life should suggest that any turn we make should be Godward : " Unto thy testimonies." 4. Right thinking also suggests that such a turning is possible. II. Right turning. The turn was—1. Complete. 2. Practical. 3. Spiritual.

4. Immediate. 5. It must be a divine work. See "Spurgeon's Sermons," No. 1181: "Thinking and Turning."

Verse 60.—The dangers of delay. The reasons for prompt action.

Verse 60.—*A sermon to loiterers.* I. Reflection. Keeping God's commandments is my duty ; is my welfare. Commandments delayed may be never kept. Delay is in itself disobedience. Alacrity is the soul of obedience. II. Resolve. I will make haste and delay not.—*C. A. D.*

Verse 60.—I. Quick. II. Sure.—*W. D.*

Verse 60.—Procrastination considered in its most important application ; that is, to religion. I. This procrastination is irrational. II. It is unpleasant, disagreeable, painful. II. It is disgraceful. IV. It is sinful, and that is the highest degree. V. It is dangerous.—*John Angell James.*

Verse 61.—I. Spiritual highway-robbery. II. The traveller keeping his road. Or, what enemies can do, and what they cannot do.

Verse 62.—I. The duty of gratitude : "give thanks." II. The subject for gratitude : "thy righteous judgments." III. The season for gratitude : at night as well as in the day.—*G. R.*

Verse 62.—Up in the night. Singing in the night. Reasons for such singular conduct.

Verse 62.—*The nightingale.* I. A natural association of thought : "midnight" and "judgments." Exod. xii., etc. II. An incongruous association of feeling : "thanks" and "judgments." III. A full justification of this apparent incongruity : "*thanks* because of thy *righteous* judgments." IV. A vigorous performance of an incumbent duty : "at midnight I will rise to give thanks."—*C. A. D.*

Verse 63.—I. True religion is friendly. II. Our friendliness should be catholic. II. Our friendliness should be discriminating. IV. Such friendliness is most useful.

Verse 63.—Of good and bad company. How to avoid the one, and improve the other. See W. Bridge's Sermon, in his works, vol. v., p. 90. Tegg's edition, 1845.

Verse 63.—The believer's choice of companions. I. Ought to be decided by their piety : "Them that fear thee." II. Is directed by their conduct : "Them that keep thy precepts." III. Should be extended as far as possible : "All." IV. Involves reciprocal obligation : "I am a companion."—*J. F.*

Verse 64.—The sum and substance of this verse will be comprised in these five propositions :—I. That saving knowledge is a benefit that must be asked of God. II. That this benefit cannot be too often or sufficiently enough asked : it is his continual request. III. In asking, we are encouraged by the bounty or mercy of God. IV. That God is merciful all his creatures declare. V. That his goodness to all his creatures should confirm us in hoping for saving grace or spiritual good things—*T. Manton.*

Verse 64.—I. Observations in the school of nature. II. Supplications to enter the school of grace.

Verse 64.—The mercy of God in nature and his mercy as revealed in the word. I. The one excellent ; the other super-excellent. II. The one easily given ; the other coming through a great sacrifice. III. The one may be enjoyed, and even increase condemnation ; the other, if enjoyed, is sure salvation. IV. The one should lead to repentance ; the other is specially adapted for the penitent's restoration to holiness.—*J. F.*

Verse 65.—The servant giving his master a character ; or, experience tallying with Scripture : two fruitful themes.

Verse 65.—I. Experience confirmed by the word. II. The word confirmed by experience.—*G. R.*

Verse 65.—A servant's story. I. Although he knew my faults he engaged me. II. Although I am so far beneath him, yet he familiarly teaches me. III. Although I am always ailing, he is very kind to me in my afflictions. IV. Although I am one of the meanest of his servants, he permits me to feast at his own table. V. Although I do little work, he will pay me good wages. VI. Although I am to have such great wages, I have very many perquisites. VII. Although my Master is all this to me (can you believe it ?) I murmur and repine at him if he crosses me in anything. Application :—1. Does not the word "servant" sound like a misnomer ?—"not servants. . . . . but I have called you friends." 2. Though he calls me "friend," I shall never cease to call him "Master."—*Richard Andrew Griffin, in "Stems and Twigs."*

Verse 66.—I. Singular faith : " I have believed thy commandments."
II. Special petition based upon it : " Teach me."

Verse 66.—The value of a good judgment to sound knowledge.   I. It carefully
discriminates between truth and error.   II. It puts each truth in its proper relation
to other truths.   III. It holds every truth firmly, but has the greater care for the
more important.   IV. It rather avoids the curious and the speculative, but really
loves the plain and useful.   V. Knowing that truths are rightly held only, when
applied, it turns all to practical account.   VI. Knowing also, that good food may,
under some circumstances, become poisonous, it is careful in its selection and use
of truths.—*J. F.*

Verse 67.—I. The dangers of prosperity.   II. The benefits of adversity.
—*G. R.*

Verse 67.—The restraining power of affliction.

Verses 67, 71, 75.—*Affliction thrice viewed and thrice blessed.*   I. Before affliction :
straying.   II. In affliction : learning.   III. After affliction : knowing.—*C. A. D.*

Verse 68.—The double plea for a choice blessing.   The goodness of God the
hope of our ignorance.

Verse 68.—*"Thou art good and doest good."*   The nature and work of God are
manifest in nature, providence, grace, and glory.   They are morally good ; bene-
ficially good ; perfectly good ; immeasurably good ; immutably good ; experimentally
good ; satisfactorily good.—*W. J.*

Verse 68 (*first clause*).—A sermon on God's goodness.   I. The perfectness of it.
II. The proofs of it.   III. The power it should have over us.—*J. F.*

Verse 69.—Whole-hearted obedience the best solace under slander ;   the best
answer to it ;   and the best way of converting the slanderers.

Verse 70.—I. Fatty degeneration of the heart.   II. Thorough regeneration of
the heart.

Verse 70.—*A fatty heart.*   I. The diagnosis of the disease.   II. Its symptoms.
Pride ;   no delight in God, nor in his law ;   dislike to his people ;   readiness to lie :
ver. 69.   III. Its fatal character.   IV. Its only cure.   Psa. li. 10 ;   Ezek. xxxvi. 26.
—*C. A. D.*

Verse 71.—I. David knew what was good for him.   II. David learned what is
good essentially.   Active obedience is learned by passive obedience.

Verse 71.—Affliction an instructor.   I. Never welcomed :   " Have been."
II. Often impatiently endured.   III. Always gratefully remembered :   " It is
good," etc.   IV. Efficient for a perverse scholar :   " That I might learn."   V. Indispensable in the education of all.—*J. F.*

Verse 71.—*The school of affliction.*   I. The reluctant scholar sent to school.
II. The scholar's hard lesson.   III. The scholar's blessed learning.   IV. The
scholar's sweet reflection.—*C. A. D.*

Verse 72.—The advantages of riches far excelled by the blessings of the word.

Verse 72.—*A valuation.*   I. The saints' high estimate of God's law.   II. Show
when it was formed :   in affliction :   ver. 71.   III. Vindicate its truth—by illustrating
the hollowness of riches, and the satisfaction found in godliness.—*C. A. D.*

Verse 72.—The word, better than gold and silver.   I. It gives what gold and
silver cannot purchase.   II. Without what it gives, gold and silver may be a curse.
III. Without gold and silver, it may yield its treasure more freely and fully than
with them.   IV. The word and what it gives shall rejoice the heart when gold
and silver shall be useless to their disappointed worshippers.—*J. F.*

Verse 72.—*"The law of thy mouth is better,"* etc.   I. It is more refining, and
makes me a better man.   II. It is more enriching, and makes me a wealthier man.
III. It is more distinguishing, and makes me a greater man.   IV. It is more
sustaining, and makes me a stronger man.   V. It is more preserving, and makes
me a safer man.   VI. It is more satisfying and makes me a happier man.   VII. It
is more lasting, and better suited to me as an immortal man.—*W. J.*

Verse 73.—I. Consider the Lord's great care in our creation.   II. See in it a
reason for his perfecting the new creation within us.   III. Observe the method of
this perfecting.

Verse 74.—I. The encouraging influence of good men upon others.   II. The
instructive influence of others upon them.—*G. R.*

Verse 74.—Converse with a tried but steadfast believer is a source of gladness
to the children of God.   I. He has a thrilling tale of experience to tell.   II. He
has valuable counsels and cautions to give.   III. He is a monument of God's

faithfulness, confirming the hope of others. IV. He is an epistle of Christ, written expressly to illustrate the preciousness and the power of the gospel.—*J. F.*

Verse 75.—Experimental knowledge: positive, personal, glorifying to God, consoling to the saints.

Verse 76.—Comfort. I. May be a matter of prayer. II. Is provided for in the Lord. III. Is promised in the word. IV. Is of great value to the believer.

Verse 76.—I. The need of comfort. II. The source of comfort: " Thy merciful kindness " III. The rule of comfort: " According to thy word."—*G. R.*

Verse 77.—I. Visitors invited. II. Boon expected. III. Welcome guaranteed: " for thy law," etc.

Verse 77.—*Divine life*—it is born, sustained, increased, by God's tender mercies. —*W. W.*

Verse 78.—I. A hard thing—to make the proud ashamed. II. A cruel thing— " they dealt perversely with me," etc. III. A wise thing—" but I will meditate," etc.

Verse 79.—Restoration to church fellowship. I. Good men may be in such a case as to need to be restored. II. They should not be ashamed to seek it. III. They should pray about it.

Verse 79.—*Select society.* I. Sociableness is an instinct of human nature. II. Sociableness is helpful to a wholesome Christian life. III. The choice of society should be a subject of prayer.—*C. A. D.*

Verse 80.—I. David's prayer for sincerity—that his heart might be brought to God's statutes, and that it might be sound in them, not rotten or deceitful. II. His dread of the consequences of hypocrisy: " that I be not ashamed." Shame is the portion of hypocrites, here or hereafter.—*M. Henry.*

Verse 80.—I. The heart in religion. II. The necessity of its being sound in it. III. The result of such sound-heartedness.

Verse 81.—Text suitable for a missionary sermon. I. The condition of the heathen world, enough to make the Christian faint for the salvation of God to visit it. 1. The grossness of its darkness. 2. Its wide area. 3. Its long continuance. 4. The limited character and effort of mission labour. 5. The opposing influences. II. This condition, though exceedingly sad, is not hopeless. Because—1. Of the intention, adaptation, and universal call of the gospel. 2. Of Christ's commission to his church. 3. Of the compassionate character of the spiritually enlightened, produced by their faith in the word. 4. Of the prophecies and promises. Thus, there is hope in the word. III. If Christians are fainting for the salvation, but hoping in the word, their interest in mission work will be intense, and will show itself. 1. In earnest prayer for more labourers, and greater results. 2. In devoting themselves, if possible, to the work. 3. In free and generous giving, to help on the work.—*J. F.*

Verse 81.—*"My soul fainteth,"* etc. Men faint for health, provision, rest, promotion, success, and in some instances for salvation. David fainted. I. For his own salvation. 1. From guilt: " Deliver me from all my transgressions ; " " from bloodguiltiness." 2. From defilement: " Create in me a clean heart." " Wash me." 3. From formality: " Let the words of my mouth," etc. 4. From darkness: " Why hidest thou thyself ? " " Lift up," etc. " Say unto my soul," etc. 5. From unhappiness: " Out of the depths," etc. II. For the salvation of others. 1. He talked about it: " Time for thee to work, Lord." 2. He prayed for it: " Oh that the salvation," etc. " Let thy work," etc. " God be merciful unto us: " " Save now, I beseech thee." 3. He laboured for it: " I will make mention of thy righteousness : " " I will teach transgressors thy ways."—*W. J.*

Verse 81.—I. Eagerness of expectation. II. Energy of hope. III. Establishment of promise: " in thy word."

Verse 81.—*"Salvation,"* in Scripture, hath divers acceptations: it is put— 1. For that temporal deliverance which God giveth, or hath promised to give to his people: so it is taken. Exod. xiv. 13. 2. For the exhibition of Christ in the flesh. Ps. xcviii. 2, 3 ; Luke ii. 29, 30. 3. For the benefits which we have by Christ on this side of heaven ; as the pardon of sin, and the renovation of our natures. Matt. i. 21; Titus iii. 5; Ps. li. 12. 4. For everlasting life: " Receiving the end of your faith, even the salvation of your souls " (1 Pet. i. 9) ; meaning thereby our final reward.—*T. Manton.*

Verse 81.—I. Faint. II. Pursuing.—*W. D.*

Verse 82.—Answer to the enquiry—" When wilt thou comfort me ? " 1. When your grief has answered its purpose. 2. When you believe. 3. When you leave sin. 4. When you obey. 5. When you submit to my will. 6. When you seek my glory.

Verse 82.—I. How longingly the believer turns to God for comfort in his affliction : " W. en wilt thou comfort me ? " II. How intently he gazes upon the Divine promises : " My eyes fail for thy word." III. How the weariness of waiting cannot wear out his patience, while hope increases his importunity : " When wilt thou ? " —*J. F.*

Verse 82.—*The pleading of the eyes.* I. How the eyes speak. By " expression " of the moods of the soul, as—longing, Isa. viii. 17 ; faith, Isa. xlv. 22 ; Heb. xii. 2 ; expectation, Ps. v. 3 ; Phil. iii. 20 ; Tit. ii. 13 ; love, 2 Cor. iii. 18 ; John i. 14. II. What the eyes say. " When wilt *thou* comfort me ? Brushing aside all other comforters, thou art my sun : my life : my love : my all." III. How the pleading eyes shall meet the responsive Eye of the Lord : Heb. ix. 18. In the look of the recognition of grief, Ex. ii. 25 ; in the look of pardon, Luke xxiii. 61 ; of strength-giving, Jud. vi. 14 ; of complacent love, Isa. lxvi. 2.—*C. A. D.*

Verse 83.—I. The outward man in ill case. II. Character blackened. III. Constantly exposed to discomfort. IV. Contents maturing.

Verse 83.—"*A bottle in the smoke.*" I. God's people have their trials. 1. From the poverty of their condition. 2. Our trials frequently result from our comforts. 3. The ministry hath made much smoke with it. 4. The poor bottle in the smoke keeps there for a long time, till it gets black. II. Christian men feel their troubles ; they are like " bottles " in the smoke. 1. The trial that we do not feel is no trial at all. 2. Trials which are not felt are unprofitable trials. A bottle in the smoke gets very black, becomes very useless, is an empty bottle. III. Christians do not, in their troubles, forget God's statutes of command, the statutes of promise. Why was it that David still held fast by God's statutes ? 1. He was not a bottle in the fire, or he would have forgotten them. 2. Jesus Christ was in the smoke with him, and the statutes were in the smoke with him too. 3. The statutes were in the soul, where the smoke does not enter.—*From "Spurgeon's Sermons,"* No. 71.

Verse 84.—A solemn question pointing to the shortness of life, the severity of sorrow, the necessity of industry, the nearness of the reward.

Verse 85.—Pits ; or, the secret schemes of wicked men against the godly.

Verse 86 (last clause).—A prayer for all occasions. See the many cases in which it is used in Scripture.

Verse 87.—I. What the good man loses by gaining. II. What he gains by losing.—*G. R.*

Verse 87.—I. "Almost," but not altogether. II. The saving clause : " I forsook not thy precepts."

Verse 87.—Passing through fires, and the asbestos covering.

Verse 88.—I. New life is the cause of new obedience. II. New obedience is the effect of new life.—*G. R.*

Verse 88.—Quickening. I. Our greatest need. II. God's most gracious boon. III. The guarantee of our steadfastness ; and so, IV. The promotor of God's glory.

Verse 88.—1. He closes with a frequent petition : "*Quicken thou me*—make me alive." All true religion consists in the LIFE *of God* in the SOUL *of man.* 2. The *manner* in which he wishes to be quickened : "*After thy lovingkindness.*" He wishes not to be raised from the *death of sin by God's thunder*, but by the *loving voice* of a *tender Father.* 3. The *effect* it should have upon him : "*So shall I keep the testimony of thy mouth.*" Whatever thou *speakest* I will *hear, receive, love, and obey.*—*Adam Clarke.*

Verses 89—92.—The Psalmist here tells us the prescription which soothed his pains and sustained his spirits. Here we have strong consolation. I. In certain facts which he remembered. 1. The eternal existence of God. 2. The immutability of his word. 3. The faithfulness of the fulfilment of that word. 4. The perpetuity of the word in nature. 5. The perpetuity of the word in experience. II. The delights which he experienced in the time of his trouble. In bereavements ; when everything seemed shifting and inconstant ; when his own faith failed him ; when all helpers failed him ; he fell back upon the eternal settlements : " O Lord, thy word is settled," etc. See " Spurgeon's Sermons," No. 1656 : " My Solace in my Affliction."

Verse 89.—Eternal settlements, or, heavenly certainties.

Verse 89.—God's eternal calm (in contrast with earth's mutations) imaged in the starry heavens.—*William Bickle Haynes*, 1882.

Verse 89.—Consider, I. The term, " thy word." 1. A word is a revealed thought. The Scriptures are just this : the thoughts and purposes of God made intelligible to man. 2. But a " word " also marks specially unity (it is one word) and wholeness or completeness, a word, not a syllable. The Scriptures are one and complete. II. The statement, " for ever settled in heaven." 1. " Settled in heaven " before it came to earth; therefore it could come as a continuous unfolding, through various dispensations, without the shadow of hesitation or contradiction manifest in it. 2. Abides " settled in heaven," for its central revelation ; the atonement is a completed fact, and Christ is now in heaven a perfected Saviour ; thus the word is unalterable. 3. " For ever settled in heaven." Not only because God in heaven is of one mind and cannot be turned ; but because righteousness itself, the righteousness of heaven, demands that an atonement by suffering shall be fully and everlastingly answered by its due reward. III. The lessons. 1. If settled in heaven, men on earth can never unsettle it. 2. The wicked may not indulge a future hope arising from any new dispensation beyond the grave ; God's present word to us cannot then be unsettled. 3. The godly may rely on a settled word amidst the unsettled experiences and feelings incident to earth.—*J. F.*

Verse 90.—The stability of the earth a present picture of everlasting faithfulness.

Verses 90, 91.—Consider, I. The steadfastness of nature as dependent upon the divine decree : " according to thy ordinances." II. The subserviency of nature to the divine will : " for all are thy servants." III. The fixedness of nature's laws, together with their subserviency to God's purposes, as a confirmation of the Christian's faith in the written word, in the care of a divine providence, and in the sureness of spiritual and heavenly things. " Thy faithfulness is," etc.—*J. F.*

Verse 91.—Our starry monitors. They teach us, I. To serve : though we cannot shine with their brightness. II. To do all with strict regard to God's will. III. To " continue "—" according to thine ordinances."—*W. B. H.*

Verse 91.—The service of nature. I. Universal : " all are thy servants." II. Obedient : " according to thy ordinances." III. Perpetual : " they continue." IV. Derived : " thou hast established the earth."

Verse 92.—The sustaining power of joy in God.

Verse 92.—The word of God as a sustaining power amid the greater sorrows of life. I. Its necessity. 1. For want of it, men have become drunkards to drown their sorrows, have become suicides because life was unbearable, have become broken and hopeless because they had no strength to struggle against misfortune, have become atheists in creed as, alas, they were before in practice ; all, in fact, become subject to sorrow's worst bitterness and calamity's worst effects. 2. Nothing can supply the place of God's word. Nature throws no light on the mystery of suffering. Human philosophy is at best cold comfort, and when most needed most fails. II. Its efficiency. Proved—1. In the experience of those who have tried it. 2. By the character of its promises. 3. By the discovery it makes of a beneficent providence working through calamity and sorrow. 4. By the revelation it gives of the pity of God and the sympathy of Christ. 5. By its record of the " Man of sorrows," who through suffering wrought out man's salvation, and entered into glory. 6. By its teaching concerning the Incarnate Word ; thus showing a suffering God, which may well be a solace to suffering men. 7. By displaying the glory of heaven and the eternal felicity awaiting those who overcome through the blood of the Lamb.—*J. F.*

Verse 92.—The Godly Man's Ark ; or, City of Refuge in the day of his Distress. Discovered in divers (five) Sermons . . . . By Edmund Calamy, B. D. . . . . Eighteenth edition. 1709. 12mo.

Verse 92.—We have here set before us by the Psalmist, I. The case which he had been in, and which he now refers to—one sad and sinking. He was under such affliction that he was ready to perish ; which seems to include inward and outward trouble at once ; trials without and pressure within. II. What it was that gave him relief, and this when nothing else could, etc., the law of God. III. How he looked back upon this relief received, namely, with thankfulness to God, to whom he speaks, and records it for the encouragement and direction of others : " Unless thy law had been my delights, I should then have perished in mine affliction."— *Daniel Wilcox*, 1676—1733.

Verse 92.—*The life-buoy.* Under the form of the narrative of a shipwrecked mariner, describe the experience of the soul struggling in the sea of affliction; almost overwhelmed : yet buoyed up over each successive billow : and finally saved by clinging to the Word of God.—*C. A. D.*

Verse 92.—The Psalmist's shudder at recollected danger. I. Sore peril : affliction tending to despair and ruin. II. Fearful crisis : "then." III. Many-handed help : "thy law my delights."—*W. B. H.*

Verse 93.—Experience fixes the word upon the memory.

Verse 93.—I. A good resolve : "I will never forget thy precepts." 1. The precepts are worth remembering. 2. Safety lies in remembering them. 3. Fidelity to God cannot be without remembering them. 4. Not to remember them is shameful ingratitude. II. An excellent reason for making it : "For with them thou hast quickened me." 1. A reason founded upon personal experience : "me." 2. A reason appreciative of the benefit received : "quickened." 3. A reason indicative of gratitude to God : "thou."—*J. F.*

Verse 93.—"Never forget "; an often-uttered phrase. Here golden. I. Something that *could* not be forgotten : life and pardon received. How could it ? II. Something that *should* not be forgotten : the precious instrumentality.—*W. B. H.*

Verse 93.—I. The instrumental power of truth. 1. Used by God in our regeneration : James i. 18 ; Ps. xix. 7. 2. Used in our liberation : John viii. 32. 3. Used in our sanctification : John xvii. 7. II. Our consequent affection for it. We cannot forget. 1. Our past obligations to it. 2. Our present dependence upon it. 3. Our future needs of it.—*W. W.*

Verse 94.—1. David claims relation to God : " I am thine "—devoted to thee, and owned by thee, thine in covenant. 2. He proves his claim : " I am thine, save me ; for I have sought thy precepts " ; *i.e.*, I have carefully enquired concerning my duty, and diligently endeavoured to do it. 3. He improves his claim : " I am thine, save me." Save me from sin, save me from ruin.—*M. Henry.*

Verse 94.—I. A great prayer : "Save me." II. A grand prayer : "I am thine." III. A gracious experience : " I have sought," etc.

Verse 94.—I. Relation : " I am thine." II. Preservation : " save me." III. Obligation : " I have sought," etc.—*G. R.*

Verse 94.—God's child humbly points out to him his responsibility : " I am thine." II. Ventures to urge his own sincerity : he has at least " sought." III. With these two hands extended, he utters a sharp cry for help : " save me."—*W. B. H.*

Verse 94.—*Multum in parvo.* I. A profession. II. A prayer. III. A plea.—*C. A. D.*

Verse 94.—I. God's interest in us. II. Our interest in God.—*W. D.*

Verse 94.—The characteristics of personal religion. I. Personal devotedness to God : " I am thine." II. Personal obedience rendered : " I have sought thy precepts." III. Personal expectation cherished ; " save me."—*J. F.*

Verse 94.—The courage obedience gives. I. It emboldens us to a firm assurance : " I am thine, for I have," etc. 1. We become God's by faith alone. 2. But the assurance of being his cannot exist without obedience ; obedience proves the faith to ourselves ; satisfies us concerning grace received. 3. Poor obedience always interferes with assurance. II. It emboldens us to pray, and in prayer : " Save me." 1. The Christian's prayers are only of faith and offered in faith. 2. Yet disobedience makes him shrink from approaching God in prayer, and renders him feeble in petitioning. 3. Obedience is humble but bold. The middle clause of the text applies equally to the first and third clauses.—*J. F.*

Verse 95.—Wicked men patient in carrying out their evil designs. Good men patient in considering the ways of the Lord.

Verse 95.—The hatred of the wicked towards the righteous. I. Show that it ever has been, and still is. 1. Select Scriptural instances, beginning with Abel. 2. Notice the persecutions of the church. 3. Treatment in the workshop. 4. Often in the home. 5. The contemptuous manner the " saints " are spoken of, etc. II. Enquire as to why it is so. 1. The enmity of the carnal heart to God. 2. The jealousy excited by the Christian's assurance of eternal blessedness. 3. The consciousness of being rebuked by a holy life. 4. Excited to it by Satan. 5. The restless mischievousness of sin which, if it cannot hinder holiness, will maliciously hurt its advocates. III. Direct how to act when exposed to it : " I will consider thy testimonies." That means—1. Be the more obedient to God. 2. Have the more watchful control over words and feelings. 3. Love your enemies. 4. Pray for those who hate you.   5. Do good to them on every opportunity.   6. Be thankful that you are among the hated and not the haters.   7. Especially consider the holy testimony of Christ's forbearing patience.—*J. F.*

Verse 95.—Waiting counterwrought by waiting.   I. Temptations in ambush. II. The saint with his Lord.—*W. B. H.*

Verse 95.—*Immunity.*   I. I am in danger.   II. I will attend to my duty.   III. I will trust thee to deliver me.—*C. A. D.*

Verse 96.—I. An end :—" seen " ; seen by one man where it should not have been ; seen where there was no end of boasting ; seen in *all* perfection.   II. No end :—to the extent, spirituality, perpetuity, and perfectness of the law.

Verse 96.—I. The Finite explored.   II. The Infinite unexplored.—*W. D.*

Verse 96.—Perfectionism disproved by experience and inspiration.—*W. B. H.*

Verse 96.—*Perfection—perfect and imperfect.*   I. Loud professions of perfection arise from ignorance (of self, or of God's requirements).   II. Are peculiarly liable to collapse : " I have seen an end."   III. Are best corrected by a survey of the breadth of the divine law.—*C. A. D.*

Verse 97.—I. Unusual Exclamation.   II. Unusual Application.—*W. D.*

Verse 97.—Indescribable love and insatiable thought.   The action and reaction of affection and meditation.

Verse 97.—I. The object of love : " thy law."   II. The degree of that love : " oh, how love I," etc.   III. The evidence of that love : " it is my meditation," etc.—*G. R.*

Verse 97.—*Love to the law.*   I. An ardent confession of love.   II. An unanswerable evidence of love.—*C. A. D.*

Verse 97 (*first clause*).—Vehemency of love for God's word.   I. Its recognisable marks.   1. Profound reverence for the authority of the word.   2. Admiration for its holiness.   3. Jealousy for its honour ; God's servant feels acute pain when men show it any slight.   4. Respect for its wholeness ; he would not divorce precepts from promises, nor ignore a single statement in it.   5. Indefatigability in its study. 6. Eager desire to obey it.   7. Forwardness in praising it.   8. Activity in spreading it abroad.   II. Its reasonableness.   1. The word well deserves it.   2. It is a proof of true intelligence.   3. It is not less than a regard for our own interest demands. III. Its requisiteness to the true worship of God.   Men sneeringly call such an affection bibliolatry, as though it were the worship of a book.   In truth, it is an essential element in the due worship of God.   For—1. Without it there cannot be the faith which honours God.   2. It is involved in that love to God which constitutes the very essence of worship.   3. It is itself an act of homage that a worshipper dare not withhold.—*J. F.*

Verses 97—100.—*Spiritual wisdom.*   I. God's word the source of surpassing wisdom—excelling that of " mine enemies," " my teachers," " the ancients." II. The three methods of acquiring this wisdom—love, meditation, practice. III. The one Giver of this wisdom : " Thou : " ver. 98.—*C. A. D.*

Verse 98.—Constant communion with truth the student's road to proficiency.

Verses 98, 99, 100.—The truly wise man.   1. *The source of his wisdom.*   The word of " the only wise God," here described as (1) Thy commandments.   (2) Thy testimonies.   (3) Thy precepts.   2. *The increase of his wisdom.*   It arises from (1) The abiding indwelling of the word : " ever with me," ver. 98.   (2) Meditation upon the word, ver. 99.   (3) Obedience to the word, ver. 100.   3. *The measure of his wisdom.*   (1) Wiser than his enemies, whose wisdom was " not from above, but earthly, sensual, devilish."   (2) Wiser than his teachers, whose wisdom was " of this world."   (3) Wiser than the ancients, whose wisdom was that of unsanctified age and experience.—*W. H. J. Page,* 1882.

Verse 99.—The surest way to excellence.   I. A good subject : " thy testimonies." II. A good method : " are my meditations."

Verse 100.—Antiquity no security for truth as contrasted with revelation : old age no proof of wisdom as contrasted with holy living : open confession no evidence of boasting as contrasted with sullen pride.

Verse 100.—Obedience the high road to understanding.—*W. B. H.*

Verse 100.—Obedience the key of knowledge.   John vii. 17.

Verse 100.—Self-restraint needful to piety.

Verse 102.—Divine teaching necessary to secure perseverance, and effectual to that end.

Verse 102.—Consider,—I. The path appointed for men to walk in : " Thy judgments." 1. Right path. 2. Clean path. 3. Pleasant path. 4. Safe path. 5. The end—eternal glory. II. The persistent pursuit of it : " I have not departed." 1. Persecution would drive from it. 2. Pleasures would allure from it. 3. The flesh would weary in it. 4. But the true believer determines to hold on his way to the end. 5. And carefully watches his steps lest they depart. III. The preserving power that holds the traveller to it : " For thou hast taught me." 1. The traveller walks with God, and receives instruction by the special illumination of the Holy Spirit. 2. The choice property of this teaching is, not only that it makes wise, but that it captivates the soul, strengthens it, and holds it to a holy obedience.—*J. F.*

Verse 103.—Experience in religion the source of enjoyment in it ; or, I. Tasting the word : its sweetness. II. Declaring the word with the mouth : its greater sweetness.

Verse 103.—I. The word is positively sweet : " sweet to my taste." II. Comparatively sweet : " sweeter than honey." III. Superlatively sweet : " how sweet," etc.—*G. R.*

Verse 103.—The comparison, setting forth the precious property of sweetness in the word : " Sweeter than honey." " Better than honey," would not do as well. It is—1. The purest sweetness ; even precepts and rebukes. 2. Uncloying sweetness. 3. Always a beneficial sweetness. 4. A specially grateful sweetness— in affliction, in the hour of death.—*J. F.*

Verse 103.—*Spiritual delicacy.* I. The taste needed to relish it. II. The life that alone is nourished by it. III. The rare enjoyment derived from it.—*C. A. D.*

Verse 103.—I. It is sweet. II. Let us enjoy it. III. The best effects will follow. George Herbert says :—

> " O Book ! infinite sweetness ! let my heart
> Suck every letter, and a honey gain,
> Precious for any grief in any part ;
> To clear the breast, to mollify all pain."

Verse 103.—If we would taste the honey of God, we must have the palate of faith.—*A. R. Fausset.*

Verse 104.—The influence of the precepts. I. Upon the understanding. II. Upon the affections. III. Upon the life.

Verse 104.—I. The intellectual effect of the Scriptures : " I get understanding." II. Their moral effect : " I hate," etc.—*G. R.*

Verse 104.—The understanding derived from God's precepts begets holy hatred, I. To the false ways of conventional morality. II. To the false ways of a formal religiousness. III. To the false ways of an erring theology. IV. To the false ways of hypocritical practice. V. To the false ways of sinful suggestions. VI. To the false ways of one's own deceitful heart.—*J. F.*

Verses 105—108.—I. Illumination (ver. 105). II. Decision (ver. 106). III. Testing : " I am afflicted " (ver. 107). IV. Consecration (ver. 108). V. Education : " teach me," etc. (ver. 108).

Verse 105.—The practical, personal, everyday use of the word of God.

Verse 105.—*Lamp-light.* I. The believer's dangerous night-journey through the world. II. The lamp that illumines his path. III. The eternal day towards which he travels (when the lamp will be laid aside : Rev. xxii. 5).—*C. A. D.*

Verse 106.—Decision for God, and fit modes of expressing it.

Verse 106.—I. Veneration for the word. II. Consecration to the word. III. Fidelity to the word.—*G. R.*

Verse 106.—*Swearing and performing.* I. The usefulness of religious vows. To quicken perception ; to rouse conscience ; (seen in Jewish nation : Ex. xxiv. 37 ; 2 Chr. xv. 12—15 ; Neh. x. 28, 29 ; in Scottish nation—Solemn League and Covenant). II. The danger of religious vows. A vow unfulfilled, or receded from, is a moral injury : Eccl. v. 4—7. III. The safeguard of religious vows : dependence on the Spirit of God : Ezek. xi. 19, 20 ; 2 Cor. iv. 5.—*C. A. D.*

Verse 107.—I. A good man greatly afflicted. II. A sure cure for the ills of affliction : " Quicken me." III. A safe rule to pray by when afflicted : " according unto thy word."

Verse 107.—I. The " very much " afflicted. 1. The world has such—widows, orphans, etc, etc. 2. Most take their turn. II. But there is " very much " grace. 1. God's word promises the needed quickening. 2. Himself very much greater than all our needs. 3. Christ tried " in all points " has all help. III. Therefore bring "very much" faith, as the Psalmist here. 1. Keen-eyed for promises. 2. Fervent in pleading them. 3. Strong in expectation.—*W. B. H.*

Verse 108.—Consider,—I. The instructive title given to prayer and praise: "The free-will offerings of my mouth." 1. It shows the believer to be a priest: "offerings." 2. It shows the peculiarity of his service: "free-will." 3. It implies whole-hearted consecration. II. The humility portrayed in the prayer: "Accept, I beseech thee." 1. Here is no pharisaic boasting. 2. Even the free-will offering is felt to need an "I beseech thee." III. The longing desire for further instruction in order to a more perfect obedience: "Teach me thy judgments."—*J. F.*

Verse 108.—Free will seeking free grace.—*W. D.*

Verse 108.—Work for Free-willers. I. Offerings of Prayer—for each of the blessings of salvation. II. Offerings of Repudiation—of all claim to unassisted good. III. Offerings of Praise—for sovereign grace.—*W. B. H.*

Verse 109.—The soul's life in jeopardy. The life of the soul secured.

Verses 109, 110.—Here is—I. David in danger of losing his life. There is but a step between him and death; for "the wicked have laid a snare" for him. Wherever he was he found some design or other laid against him; which made him say, "My soul is continually in my hand." It was not so only as a man—it is true of us all that we are exposed to the strokes of death—but as a man of war, and especially as "a man after God's own heart." II. David in no danger of losing his religion through this peril; for, 1. He "doth not forget the law," and therefore is likely to persevere. 2. He hath not yet erred from God's precepts, and therefore it is to be hoped he will not.—*M. Henry.*

Verse 110.—Various kinds of snares, and the one way of escaping them.

Verse 110.—Consider,—I. Some of the snares set for saints by sinners. 1. Doctrinal snares, by intellectual sinners. 2. False accusations, by malignant sinners. 3. False flatteries, by deceitful sinners. 4. False charity, by a large number of sinners nowadays. II. The secure safeguard for a saint's safety: "I erred not from thy precepts." Obedience to God gives security, because—1. The snares are then suspected and watched against. 2. The feet cannot become entangled by them. 3. God keeps him who keeps his word.—*J. F.*

Verse 111.—I. Estate. II. Entering upon it. III. Entail upon it. IV. Enjoyment of it.

Verse 111.—Notice,—I. How rich the Psalmist was determined to be: "Thy testimonies have I taken as a heritage." Rich,—1. In knowledge. 2. In holiness. 3. In comfort. 4. In companionship, for God's company goes with his word. 5. In hope. II. How he clung to his wealth: "For ever." 1. He hurt none by so doing; he could give generously his portion, and yet not waste. 2. He was right; for he had the only wealth of which an everlasting possession is possible. 3. He was wise. III. How he rejoiced in his wealth: "They are the rejoicing of my heart." 1. Here is internal and deep joy; not always possible to the possession of wealth. 2. Pure, unalloyed joy; it is never so with other wealth. 3. Safe joy; other joy is dangerous. 4. Unlosable joy.—*J. F.*

Verse 112.—Heart-leanings. Personality, pressure, inclination, performance, constancy, perpetuity.

Verse 112.—The godly man's obedience. I. Its reality. 1. "To perform"; not words or feelings merely; but deeds. 2. "Thy statutes"; not human inventions, nor self conceits, nor conventional maxims. II. Its cordiality: "inclined my heart." 1. Heart inclination is requisite for pleasing a heart-searching God. 2. And to make obedience easy and even delightful. 3. "I have," he says; was it therefore his doing? Yes. Was it his work alone? No. See verse 36. 4. The proofs. (1) Universality: "statutes," the whole of them. (2) Uniformity: "alway." III. Its constancy: "even unto the end." 1. Though a man should be cautious when planning for the future, yet this life-long purpose is right, wise, and safe. 2. Nor can he purpose less, if holy fervency fill the heart. 3. It is no more than what God and consistency demand.—*J. F.*

Verse 113.—The thought of the age, and the truth of all ages.

Verse 113.—I. The object of hatred. II. The object of love. Or—I. Love the cause of hatred. II. Hatred the effect of love.—*G. R.*

Verse 113.—"*Vain thoughts.*" What they are. Whence they arise. The mischief they cause. How they should be treated.—*W. H. J. P.*

Verse 113.—How the believer—1. Is troubled by vain thoughts. A frequent and painful experience. 2. Does not tolerate vain thoughts. Some suffer them to lodge within; he is anxious to expel them. 3. Triumphs over vain thoughts. By his love to the law of God. His prayer is—

> "With thoughts of Christ and things divine,
> Fill up this foolish heart of mine."
>
> *W. H. J. P.*

Verse 114. — Our protection *from* danger—"hiding-place"; *in* danger — "shield"; *before* danger—"I hope."

Verse 114.—"*Hiding-place.*" Secrecy to conceal us. Capacity to hold us. Safety. Comfort.—*T. Manton.*

Verse 114.—*Hiding and hoping.* I. A hiding-place needed. II. A hiding-place provided (Isa. xxv. 14; xxxii. 2). III. A hiding-place used.—*C. A. D.*

Verse 114.—I. The refuge provided: "Thou art," etc. II. The refuge revealed: "In thy word." III. The refuge found: "I hope," etc.—*G. R.*

Verse 114.—"*Thou art my hiding place.*" I. In thy grace, from condemnation. II. In thy compassion, from sorrow. III. In thy succour, from temptation. IV. In thy power, from opposition. V. In thy fulness, from want.—*W. J.*

Verse 115.—I. Ill company hinders piety. II. Piety quits ill company. III. Piety, in compelling this departure, acts as God will do at the last.

Verse 115.—Evil companionships incompatible with genuine righteousness. I. They necessitate concealment and compromise. II. They destroy the capability of communion with God, and the relish for spiritual things. III. They blunt the sensitiveness of conscience. IV. They involve deliberate disobedience to God.— *J. F.*

Verse 116.—I. Upholding promised. II. Needful for holy living. III. The preventive of shameful acts.

Verse 116.—"*Uphold me according unto thy word,*" etc. 1. The Psalmist pleads the promise of God, his dependence upon the promise, and his expectation from it: "*Uphold me according unto thy word,*" which word I hope in, and if it be not performed I shall be "ashamed of my hope." 2. He pleads the great need he had of God's grace, and the great advantage it would be to him: "Uphold me, that I may live"; intimating that he could not live without the grace of God.—*M. Henry.*

Verse 117.—I. Upholding—God's holding us up. It implies a danger, and that danger takes many forms. The believer's life may be described as walking in uprightness; he is a pilgrim. He needs upholding, for—1. The way is slippery. 2. Our feet make the danger as well as the way. 3. Cunning foes seek to trip us up. 4. Sometimes the difficulty is not caused by the way, but by the height to which God may elevate us. 5. The prayer is all the more needful because the most of people do not keep upright. II. Two blessed things that come out of this holding up. 1. We shall be safe for ourselves, as examples, and as pillars of the church. 2. We shall be watchful and sensitive: "I will have respect unto thy statutes continually." Without this no man is safe. See "Spurgeon's Sermons," No. 1657: "My Hourly Prayer."

Verse 117.—"*Hold thou me up,*" etc. I. The good man is up. II. The good man wishes to keep up. III. The good man prays to be held up. IV. The good man knows that divine support is abundantly sufficient.—*W. J.*

Verse 117.—I. Dependence for the future: "Hold," etc. II. Resolution for the future: "I will have," etc.—*G. R.*

Verse 118.—Sin and falsehood: their connection, punishment, and cure.

Verse 118.—I. Hearken to the tramp of God's armies. In nature; providence; angelic hosts of last day. II. The mangled victims. Cunning deceivers specially obnoxious to God. Examples: Balaam, Pharaoh, Rome, the deceiver of the nations. III. The warnings to us of this Aceldama. Repent. Avoid deceit. Mind God's landmarks. Hide in Christ.—*W. B. H.*

Verse 118.—God's punishment of the wicked though awfully severe is just and necessary. I. It is due as the merited wages of iniquity. II. It is demanded by the position of God as moral governor, and by his character as righteous. III. It is necessary to mark the real worth of righteousness and its reward. If the wicked are not punished, the full worth of righteousness cannot appear. IV. In the nature of the case, it is absolutely unavoidable, except upon one condition, namely, the gift of genuine repentance and holiness after death; *that* no man has any right to expect, nor has God given the slightest intimation that he will bestow it. V. Hell lies in the bosom of sin ; and if the wicked were taken to heaven, they would carry hell thither.   Heaven supplies not the things in which the wicked delight while it abounds in those they can neither understand nor sympathise with.—*J. F.*

Verse 118 (*second clause*).—The deceits of the wicked are all falsehoods.   I. The world they embrace is a false Delilah.   II. The pleasure they enjoy is a Satanic snare.   III. Their formal religiousness is a vain delusion.   IV. Their conceits of God are self-invented lies.—*J. F.*

Verses 118—120.—*Saved by fear.*   I. The wrath of God revealed against sin. II. The judgment of God executed upon sinners.   III. The fear of God created in the heart.—*C. A. D.*

Verse 119.—The saint's acquiescence in God's judgments.—*W. B. H.*

Verse 119.—I. Comparison of the wicked to dross.   II. Comparison of their doom to the putting away of dross.   III. The saint's admiration of divine justice as seen in the rejection of the wicked.

Verse 119.—God's putting away the wicked like dross.   I. God's judgments are a searching and separating fire.   II. The final judgment of the great day will complete the separating process.   III. The great result will be, the true metal and the dross, each gathered to its *own* place.—*J. F.*

Verse 120.—The judgments of God on the wicked cause in the righteous, I. Love. II. Awe.   III. Fear.

Verse 120.—I. Describe the true character of the fear.   1. It is the fear of reverence for God's authority and power.   2. It is the fear of horror against sin as meriting judgment.   II. Show its compatibility with filial love.   1. The more we love God the more firmly we believe in the certainty and awfulness of his judgments.   2. The more we love God the more will we fear to arouse his chastising rod against ourselves.   3. In fact, if we love not God, we shall have no fear lest sin should involve us in judgment.   III. Commend it.   1. As it proves a just sense of sin's desert.   2. As it shows a true appreciation of God's righteousness.   3. As it is not a fear that hath torment, but a fear which increases watchfulness, and walks hand in hand with perfect confidence in saving grace.—*J. F.*

Verses 121, 122.—*The double appeal.*   I. Of conscious integrity : " I have done judgment," etc.   II. Of conscious deficiency : " Be surety for thy servant for good."—*C. A. D.*

Verse 122.—I. Suretyship entreated.   II. Good expected.   III. Obligation acknowledged : " thy servant."

Verse 122 (*first clause*).—After explaining the Psalmist's meaning as shown in the preceding verse, this sentence may be used for a sermon upon the Suretyship of Christ, by a reference to Heb. vii. 22.   I. A Surety for good wanted—the deeply felt, though, perhaps, undefined want of a sin-burdened soul.   1. The mere statement of a gratuitous pardon on the part of God is not thoroughly believable to such a soul, nor, if it could be believed in, would it give peace to the conscience.   For, on the one hand, the pardon could not be perceived as just, nor as consistent with God's necessary hatred of sin, yet the conscience demands this perception ; on the other hand, mere pardon does not show how the obligation to a perfect fulfilment of God's law, as righteousness, can be met, yet the conscience demands to see this before it can be satisfied to realize peace.   Luther's experience.   2. Now the Scriptures tell us that God " justifies the ungodly," and that his " righteousness " is declared in his justifying sinners : Rom. iii. 25.   He can forgive sins with justice. He can treat sinners as righteous persons, and yet be righteous in doing so.   How ? By a Surety.   Therefore, a Surety is the real want.   II. A Surety existent.   Jesus is the Surety.   1. He undertook to bear our obligation to the law's penalty, and fulfilled it in death.   Thus pardon, though mercy to us, is an act of justice to Christ. 2. He undertook our obligation to a perfect obedience, and satisfied for that in his fulfilment of the law ; thus for God to treat us as righteous is only just to Christ. 3. God has shown his satisfaction with the office of Christ, and with his work, by the resurrection and glorification of Christ.   Hence a well-accredited and efficient Surety exists.   III. A Surety nigh at hand.   1. In the gospel, Christ as Surety comes to the sinner as truly as though he himself left his throne and came in his own person.   2. Thus, he is so close that a sinner has but to receive the gospel into his heart and he receives Christ.   3. Christ received as a Surety is the Surety for whosoever receives him.—*J. F.*

Verse 123.—Holy expectation—long maintained, in danger of failing ; this fact pleaded ; reasons for never renouncing it.

Verses 124, 125.—*The servant of God.* I. Making profession : " I am thy servant." II. Making confession—of guilt, dulness, ignorance. III. Making petition—for mercy, understanding, and teaching.—*C. A. D.*

Verse 124.—Heavenly instruction a great mercy.

Verse 124.—I. His confidence in divine mercy. II. His submission to divine authority. III. His prayer for divine teaching.—*G. R.*

Verse 124.—A Perfect Prayer, I. As to the matter of it. 1. Here is nothing superfluous ; no petition for wealth, nor for honours, nor for anything the worldling covets. 2. Here is nothing wanting ; " Deal with thy servant according to thy mercy " comprehends everything the guilty soul needs ; " Teach me thy statutes " comprehends all a saint needs to be anxious for. II. As to the manner of it. 1. It is direct and definite. 2. It is simple and fervent. 3. It is reverent yet bold. III. As to the spirit of it. 1. " Deal with thy *servant* "; a sense of obligation; a feeling of devotedness ; a spirit of consecration to holy work. 2. " Deal . . . . according to thy mercy " ; a sense of unworthiness ; becoming humility ; submissiveness to the divine will as to what form the mercy shall take ; great faith in the mercy, its freeness and sufficiency. 3. " Teach me thy statutes." Longing for holiness, sense of ignorance, of weakness, of dependence upon special divine spiritual influence.—*J. F.*

Verse 125.—I. An office accepted. II. Fitness requested. III. Discernment desired.

Verse 125.—I. A cheerful acknowledgment : " I am thy servant." II. A desire implied—to serve more perfectly. III. A need recognized—Divine instruction in holy service. IV. A plea urged : " I am thy servant," therefore " Teach me," etc.—*W. H. J. P.*

Verses 126—128.—I. A terrible fact : " They have made void thy law " : ver. 126. II. Two blessed inferences : " Therefore," " Therefore," etc : verses 127, 128.

Verses 126.—They make void the law, by denying inspiration, by exalting tradition, by antinomianism, by scepticism, by indifference, etc.

Verse 126.—1. There are times when sin is specially active and dominant. 2. Such times reveal the dependence of the church upon God. 3. Such times awaken the desires of the church for the intervention of God. 4. Such times are the times when God does arise to plead his own cause.—*W. H. J. P.*

Verse 126.—I. The work anticipated—the vindication of the divine law. II. The work delayed. III. The work executed : " It is time," etc.—*G. R.*

Verse 127.—The world's assault upon the truth a reason for our loving it.

Verse 127.—I. The object of love : " Thy commandments." II. The degree of love : " above gold," etc. III. The reason of this love : " therefore," etc., because its object must ultimately prevail.—*G. R.*

Verse 127.—God's will *versus* the golden idol. I. God's commandments are better than gold. II. The love of them is proportionably nobler. III. The unmeasurable superiority of character they produce.—*W. B. H.*

Verse 128 (*first clause*).—This view should be taken of all divine precepts in their bearing, I. Christ-ward. II. Self-ward. III. World-ward. IV. Church-ward. V. Heaven-ward.—*W. J.*

Verse 128.—The Bible right. I. Its science is correct. II. Its history is true. III. Its promises are genuine. IV. Its morality is perfect. V. Its doctrines are divine.—*W. W.*

Verse 128.—Learn four lessons,—I. It is a good thing when wicked men do not praise the truth they cannot love. II. It is a suspicious circumstance when they are found speaking well of any part of it ; it is a Judas' kiss in order to betray its interests. III. It must be right to accept and love what the wicked oppose. IV. It is always safe to be on the opposite side to them.—*J. F.*

Verses 129—136.—In this division the Psalmist—I. Praises God's word. II. Shows his affection to it. III. Prays for grace to keep it. IV. Mourns for those who do not.—*Adam Clarke.*

Verse 129.—The wonderful character of the word a reason for obedience. So wonderfully pure, just, balanced, elevating. So much for our own benefit, for the good of society, and for the divine glory.

Verse 129.—I. What is wonderful in God's word should be believed. II. What is believed should be obeyed.—*G. R.*

Verse 129.—"*Thy testimonies are wonderful.*" 1. The *facts* which they record are wonderful—so wonderful, that if the book recording them were now published for the first time, there would be no bounds to the avidity and curiosity with which it would be sought and perused.   2. The *morality* which they inculcate is wonderful. 3. If you turn from the morality to the *doctrines* of the Bible, your admiration will rather increase than diminish at the contents of the singular book.   4. These testimonies are wonderful for *the style* in which they are written.   5. They are wonderful for *their preservation* in the world.   6. They are wonderful for the *effects* which they have produced.—*Hugh Hughes,* 1838.

Verse 129.—*"Thy testimonies are wonderful."*   The *ceremonial law* is wonderful, because the mystery of our redemption by the blood of Christ is pointed out in it. 2. The *prophecies* are wonderful, as predicting things, humanly speaking, so uncertain, and at such great distance of time, with so much accuracy.   3. The *decalogue* is wonderful, as containing in a very few words all the principles of justice and charity. 4. Were we to go to the *New Testament,* here wonders rise on wonders !   All is astonishing ;   but the Psalmist could not have had this in view.—*Adam Clarke.*

Verse 129 *(first clause).*—I. Let us look at five of the wonders of the Bible. 1. Its authority.   It prefaces every statement with a " Thus saith the Lord." 2. Its light.   3. Its power—it has a convincing, awakening, drawing, life-giving power.   4. Its depth.   5. Its universal adaptation.   II. Indicate three practical uses.   1. Study the Bible daily.   2. Pray for the Spirit to grave it on your heart with a pen of iron.   3. Practise it daily.—*D. Macgregor.*

Verse 129.—To whom and in what respects are God's testimonies wonderful ? I. To whom ?   To those, and those only, who through grace do know, believe, and experience the truth and power of them for themselves.   II. In what respects wonderful, *i.e.,* astonishingly pleasing, delightful, and profitable (see ver. 174). 1. In respect of the Author and origin of them, whose they are and from whence they come.   2. In respect of the subject matter of them, which they contain and reveal.   3. In respect of the manner of language in which they are revealed and declared.   4. In respect of the multitude and variety of them suited to every case. 5. In respect of the usefulness of them, and the great benefit and advantage he received from them.   6. In the respect of the pleasure and delight he finds in them (see ver. 111).   7. In respect of the final design, intent, and end of them : viz., eternal life, salvation, and glory.—*Samuel Medley,* 1738—1799.

Verse 130.—I. The essential light of the word.   II. The dawn of it in the soul. III. The great benefit of its advancing day.

Verse 130.—I. The source of divine light to man : " Thy words."   II. Its force.   It forces an entrance into the heart.   III. Its direction : " unto the simple." IV. Its effect : " it giveth understanding."—*G. R.*

Verse 130.—*A Bible Society Sermon.*   I. Evidence from history and from personal experience that God's word has imparted the light of civilization, liberty, holiness.   II. Argument drawn from hence for the further spread of the word of God.—*C. A. D.*

Verse 130.—The Self-evidencing Virtue of God's Word.   I. Prove it.   " The entrance of thy word giveth light."   If this be true, God's word is light ; for only light can give light.   But light is self-evidencing ; it needs nothing to show its presence and its value but itself ; so the word of God, to show its own truth and divinity to the believer.   I. His conscience proves it ; in its conviction of sin ; in its peace through the atoning blood.   2. His heart proves it ; in its outgoings of love to the God, the Christ, and the righteousness revealed.   3. His experience in affliction and temptation proves it ; in the solace and in the strength given by the word.   II. Answer an objection.   " If God's word were self-evidencing as light is, then everyone would acknowledge it to be truth."   Answer, No ; for the law holds good in universal experience, that the " entrance " only of light gives light.   Light cannot enter a blind man.   1. The Scriptures teach that men by nature are blind.   2. If all men did perceive, by merely reading and hearing the word, that it was light and truth, paradoxical as it may seem, the word would not be truth. 3. Hence the want of universal acknowledgment is not an objection, but a confirmation. III. Show its importance.   1. It makes the believer independent of church authority for his faith.   2. He need not trouble to examine books of evidence ; his faith is valid enough without them.   3. He who receives the word into his soul shall be satisfied of its truth and value.—*J. F.*

Verse 131.—Panting for holiness.   A rare hunger ; the evidence of much grace, and the pledge of glory.

Verse 132.—I. Look. II. Love. III. Use and wont.

Verse 132.—Fellowship with the righteous. I. There are some who love God's name. II. His mercy is the source of all the goodness they experience. III. The Lord has been always accustomed to deal mercifully with them. IV. His mercy towards them should encourage us to implore mercy for ourselves. V. We should be anxious to secure the mercy that is peculiar to them. VI. We should be content if God deals with us as he has always dealt with his people.—*W. Jay.*

Verse 132.—*Divine use and wont.* I. God is accustomed to look upon and be merciful toward his people. II. We are stirred up to specially desire such merciful dealings in time of affliction. III. Love to God qualifies us for these loving looks and merciful dealings.—*C. A. D.*

Verse 132.—Notice,—I. The mark of true believers: "Those that love thy name." II. God's custom of dealing with them: "Be merciful as thou usest to do." III. Their individual and earnest solicitude: "Look thou upon me." —*J. F.*

Verse 133.—I. A holy life is no work of chance, it is a masterpiece of *order*— the order of conformity to the prescribed rule; there is arithmetical and geometrical order: the proportional order; the order of relation; an order of period: holiness, as to the order, is seasonable, suitable. II. The rule of this order: "in thy word." III. The director chosen. See "Spurgeon's Sermons," No. 878: "A Well-ordered Life."

Verse 133.—I. Order in outward life desired. II. Order according to the divine idea. III. Order in the government within.

Verse 133.—I. Help needed. 1. To avoid sin. 2. To be holy. II. Help sought. 1. From below: "thy word." 2. From above: "order," etc., and "let not," etc.—*G. R.*

Verse 133.—Sin's sway in the soul. I. Fervently deprecated. 1. Realization of the horrors of its rule. 2. Recognition of the better power. 3. Thorough exclusion sought. II. Wisely combated. 1. Practicalness as well as prayerfulness. 2. Regard had to little "steps." 3. Steps to be governed by divine rule. 4. System not trusted apart from God.—*W. B. H.*

Verse 133.—Notice,—I. The right path for human feet: "In thy word." II. The needed help to control the steps: "Order my steps." III. The perverting power of a dominant sin: "Let not any," etc.—*J. F.*

Verse 134.—What sins may be produced by oppression. What obedience ought to come from those who are set free.

Verse 134.—I. The course to be pursued: "thy precepts." II. The opposition to that course: "the oppression of men." 1. Human opinions. 2. Human examples. 3. Human sympathies. 4. Interests. 5. Persecutions. III. The resistance to that opposition: "Deliver me, so will I," etc.—*G. R.*

Verse 134.—*Hindrances removed.* I. The impeding influence of persecution. II. The prayer of the persecuted one. III. The conduct of the delivered one (Luke i. 74, 75).—*C. A. D.*

Verse 134.—I. How some men oppress their fellows. By the laws they make— as statesmen. By the books they write—as authors. By the tyranny they exercise —as masters. By the lives they live—as professors. By the sermons they deliver —as *ministers!* II. How the prayer of the oppressed may be answered. By the gift of wise and good statesmen. By increase of sound literature. By the conversion or removal of hard masters. By a baptism of the Spirit on the church.—*W. W.*

Verse 135.—I. A choice position: "thy servant." II. A choice delight: "thy face to shine." III. A choice privilege: "teach me thy statutes."

Verse 135.—I. God *in* the word: "Thy word." II. God *for* the word: "Teach me," etc. III. God *with* the word: "Make thy face," etc.—*G. R.*

Verse 135 —*Sunshine.* I. The light in which we can best learn our lessons —God's favour shown in pardon, justification, adoption, assurance, etc. II. The lessons we should learn in the light—grace is productive of holiness.—*C. A. D.*

Verse 135.—I. A rich historic promise (Num. vi. 25). Its sublime origin and associations. II. The *new* prayer born of it. 1. Looks up for the face Divine; the same in its majestic sweetness that has watched generations decay since the word was first spoken. 2. Asks to know its shinings. Light of fatherhood, etc.

III. The *old* prayer repeated: "Teach me thy statutes." Last time in the Psalm. 1. Our need of teaching—oft-repeated prayer. 2. The intimate connection between obedience and the shinings of God's face.—*W. B. H.*

Verse 136.—Abundant sorrow for abounding sin. Other men's sins the saint's own sorrows. He thinks of the good God provoked, of the sinners themselves debased, of their death, and their perdition.

Verse 136.—I. Occasion of his grief : " they keep not thy law." II. Extent of his grief : " rivers," etc. See examples in Jeremiah, Ezra, Paul, Christ himself. III. Effect of his grief. To warn, teach, invite, and exhort them—as in his Psalms. —*G. R.*

Verse 136.—*Sacred tears.* I. The world sinning. II. The church weeping. III. It is time the world began to weep for itself.—*C. A. D.*

Verse 136.—I weep, because, 1. Of the dishonour done to the Law-giver. 2. Of the injury done to the law-breaker. 3. Of the wrong done to the law-abiding.

" That kingly prophet, that wept so plentifully for his own offences (Psalm vi. 6), had yet floods of tears left to bewail his people's " (Psalm cxix. 136).—*Thomas Adams.* " Bendetti, a Franciscan monk, author of the *Stabat Mater,* one day was found weeping, and when asked the reason of his tears, he exclaimed, ' I weep because Love goes about unloved.' "—*W. H. J. P.*

Verses 137, 138.—*Solemn contemplation.* I. The contemplation of the deep and awful display of the divine character is good for the soul. II. It will lead to a conviction of the righteousness of God's character and administration. III. It will result in loyal submission.—*C. A. D.*

Verse 137.—A consideration of divine righteousness. Convinces us of sin, reconciles us to trying providences, excites a desire to imitate, arouses to reverent adoration.

Verse 137.—God is righteous. I. In his commands. II. In his threatenings. III. In his chastisements. IV. In his judgments. V. In his promises.—*G. R.*

Verse 138.—*"Very faithful."* Based on a faithful covenant ; confirmed by faithful promises ; carried out by a faithful Redeemer ; enjoyed hitherto ; relied on for the future. " Though we believe not, yet he abideth faithful."

Verse 139.—*"Zeal."* I. Consuming self. II. Inflamed by that which would naturally quench it. III. Fed upon God's words.

Verse 139.—*"Zeal."* I. Flourishing in an uncompromising atmosphere. II. Attaining an astonishing growth. III. Accomplishing a blessed work—the consumption of self.—*C. A. D.*

Verse 139.—I. The object of his zeal: " Thy words." II. The occasion of his zeal : " Mine enemies," etc. III. The fervour of his zeal : " My zeal hath consumed me."—*G. R.*

Verse 140.—I. An awakened sinner adoring the holy law. II. A saint loving it because the pure love the pure. III. A saint among sinners loving the law all the more for its contrast.

Verse 140.—I. The crystal stream. 1. Flows from under the throne. 2. Mirrors heaven. 3. Undefiled through the ages. 4. Nourishes holiness as it flows. II. The enraptured pilgrim. 1. Keeping by its brink. 2. Delighted with its lucid depths. 3. Pleased with its mirrored revelations—self, heaven, God. 4. Cleansed and refreshed by its waters.—*W. B. H.*

Verse 140.—I. *The purity of God's word.* 1. It proceeds from a perfectly pure source : *"Thy* word." 2. It reveals a purity otherwise unknown. 3. It treats impure subjects with absolute purity. 4. It inculcates the most perfect purity. 5. It produces such purity in those who are subject to its power. II. *The love which its purity inspires in gracious souls.* 1. They love it because, while it reveals their natural impurity, it shows them how to escape from it. 2. They love it because it conforms them to its own purity. 3. They love it because to a pure heart the purity of the word is one of its chief commendations. III. *The evidences of this love to the pure word.* 1. Desire to possess it in its purity. 2. Subjection to its spirit and teachings. 3. Zeal for its honour and diffusion.—*W. H. J. P.*

Verses 141—144.—*A mournful song and a joyful refrain.* Stanza I. " I am small and despised." Refrain. The everlasting righteousness of God. Stanza II. " Trouble and anguish have seized me." Refrain. The everlasting righteousness of God.—*C. A. D.*

Verse 141.—Here is—1. David pious, and yet poor. He was a man after God's own heart, and yet " small and despised " in his own account and in account of many others. 2. David poor and yet pious ; " small and despised " for his strict and serious godliness ; yet his conscience can witness for him, that he " did not forget God's precepts."—*M. Henry.*

Verse 141.—I. The source of man's littleness is in himself. II. The source of his greatness is in the Divine word. Hence the greatest philosopher is a small man compared with the most uneducated whose delight is in the law of God, and who meditates, etc.—*G. R.*

Verse 141.—I. A little scholar. II. A quick learner. III. A firm remembrancer.

Verse 141.—"*Unknown, yet well known.*" I. The estimate formed of the believer by the world. II. The estimate formed of the believer by himself. III. The profession made by the believer to God. IV. On a review, a revised estimate of the believer : 1 Cor. i. 27 ; James ii. 5.—*C. A. D.*

Verse 142.—Righteousness, immutability, and truth combined in the revelation of God.

Verse 143.—Mingled emotions.

Verse 143.—I. The dark cloud. Trouble, etc. II. His silver lining. Yet, etc.

Verse 143.—I. The saint cast into prison. 1. The jailers : "Trouble and anguish." 2. Their proceeding : "take hold" and make him fast. II. Songs in the night. 1. Blessed theme : "thy commandments." 2. Ecstatic melodies : "delights." III. Let the prisoners hear them. 1. Pain-held, sin-held, despair held. 2. It is matter and melody to open prisons.—*W. B. H.*

Verse 143.—Consider,—I. The excellency of the word, in that it gives delight when trouble and anguish oppress. II. The great kindness of God in so framing his word that it can give delight at such a time, and under such circumstances. III. The disposition of the believer to resort to the word for delight, when others give themselves over to vain grief and despondency. IV. The blessed position of the believer, in that he need never be without joy.—*J. F.*

Verse 144.—Everlasting righteousness revealed in the word, and producing everlasting life in believers.

Verse 144.—I. Eternal truths. II. Eternal life dependent upon them. III. A cry from amid these everlasting hills.—*W. B. H.*

Verse 144 (*last clause*).—I. Consider the prayer in its simplicity. 1. It is suitable for the awakened sinner. 2. For the Christian struggling against temptation. 3. For the suffering believer. 4. For the worker. 5. For aspiring minds in the church of God. 6. For expiring saints. II. The prayer more fully opened up. 1. Here is want confessed. 2. The prayer is evidently put upon the footing of free grace : "Give." III. Lay bare the argument in the prayer. 1. The word of God, when practically and experimentally understood, is a pledge of life. 2. The word of God is the incorruptible "seed" which liveth and abideth for ever. 3. It is the food of life. 4. It is the very flower and crown and glory of true life. 5. It is righteous. 6. It is everlasting. See "Spurgeon's Sermons," No. 1572 : "Alive."

Verses 145—148.—*The cry.* I. Whence it came : from my heart. II. Whither it went : to the Lord. III. When it was heard : at dawn and dark. IV. What it sought : hearing, salvation. V. What it promised : obedience. VI. How it was sustained : by hope in God's word.—*C. A. D.*

Verses 145, 146.—The soul's cry. I. The depth from which it rose. II. The height it reached.

Verses 145, 146.—*Childlike prayer.* I. In its ring : "I cried." II. In its directness : "to thee." III. In its outburst : "whole heart." IV. In its outcries : "hear me"; "save me." V. In its promise of better behaviour : "I *will* keep thy statutes."—*W. B. H.*

Verse 145.—I. The model of prayer : "I cried with my whole heart." II. The object of prayer : "Hear me, O Lord." III. The accompaniment of prayer : "I will keep thy statutes."

Verse 146.—I. Prayer remembered. II. Prayer continued : "Save me." III. Prayer yielding fruit : "I shall keep," etc.

Verse 146.—*Salvation.* I. A likely path to it—prayer : cry on. II. The proper place for it : "unto thee"; not man, not the heart. III. A sound view of it : "keep thy testimonies." Not to escape hell, or gain heaven, but to please and love God.—*W. B. H.*

Verses 147, 148.—I. The heavenly companions : prayer and meditation. Inseparable. Mutually helpful. II. Their favourite seasons : times of stillness ; night ; the hour before day. III. Their volume and night-lamp : "Thy word ;" "Hope." Or—I. A grand plea : "Thy lovingkindness." Who can match it ?

Who can measure it? Who can mar it? II. An insignificant pleader: "my voice." What can "my voice" ever say to keep step with "thy lovingkindness"? Asking too much out of the question. III. A clever petition ("according to thy judgment"); requesting life; stolen from God's mouth. God's lovingkindness is matched by God's own promise.—*W. B. H.*

Verse 147.—Observe in this David's diligence. I. That it was a personal, closet, or secret prayer; "I cried"; I alone, with thee in secret. II. That it was an early morning prayer: "I prevented the dawning of the morning." III. That it was a vehement and earnest prayer; for it is expressed by crying.— *T. Manton.*

Verse 147.—*Early rising commended.* I. A fit time for prayer. II. For reading the word. III. For indulging the emotions excited by it: "I hoped in thy word."

Verse 148.—"The Inexhaustibleness of the Bible." A sermon by Harry Melvill, at "The Golden Lecture." 1850.

Verse 148.—*Meditation.* Appropriate time, and fruitful subject.

Verse 148.—Meditation in the word well worth self-denial and care on the part of the Christian. I. Without meditation reading is a waste of time and an indignity offered to the word. II. Meditation with prayer, but not prayer without meditation, will discover the sense of the word, when all other means fail; and it has this advantage, that the meaning sinks into the mind. III. Meditation extracts sweetness from the promises, and nourishment from the whole truth. IV. Meditation makes a wise teacher and an efficient worker of one who has little natural skill or learning. V. Meditation subjects the soul to the sanctifying power of the word. VI. Meditation is an invitation to the Holy Spirit to bless the soul, for he is closely associated with the truth, and delights to see the truth honoured. —*J. F.*

Verse 149.—Prayer—hearing the result of love; prayer—answering ruled by wisdom.

Verse 149.—*Quickening.* I. A prayer of unquestionable necessity: "quicken me." II. Twin pleas of irresistible power: "thy lovingkindness:" "thy judgment."—*C. A. D.*

Verse 149.—The two accordings. I. The "according," to which a believer hopes to be heard by God: "Hear my voice according unto thy lovingkindness." 1. The believer is fully aware of his own unworthiness, and the imperfections of his prayers, therefore he would have God to accept him and interpret them after the rule of his own lovingkindness. 2. Nor does he hope in vain; God's lovingkindness overlooks the imperfections, and supplies the omissions. 3. What a blessed thing it is, that while the Holy Spirit helps our infirmities, the groanings that cannot be uttered are read in their true meaning by divine lovingkindness! II. The "according" to which he expects to be answered by God: "Quicken me according to thy judgment." "Judgment" here may mean the revealed word. Then—1. He expects to be answered certainly. 2. He expects to be answered wisely. 3. He expects to be answered fully, as all his needs require. 4. He expects that every answer should quicken spiritual life, making him holy.—*J. F.*

Verses 150, 151.—*Against mischief-makers.* I. They press as near as they can to harm us. II. They get far from right to get more liberty to injure us. III. The Lord is nearer than they. IV. God's truth is our shield and sword.

Verses 150, 151.—*Foes near: the Friend nearer.* I. The believer viewing with alarm the *approach* of his foes: "They draw near." II. The believer viewing with comfort the *presence* of his friend: "Thou art near:" Gen. xv. 1; 2 Kings vi. 14—17.—*C. A. D.*

Verses 150, 151.—Two beleaguering hosts. I. The host of evil: NEAR— 1. Demons, godless men, spiritual foes of world and heart. 2. Mischief in their van. 3. Law and truth left far behind. 4. Seeking to narrow their lines. 5. Thus are all saints beset. II. The host of God: NEARER—Jehovah, his angels, and battalions of truths holy and immortal: "Thou and all thy commandments. 1. Entrenched in the reason: "are truth." 2. Camped in the heart's pavilion: "near." 3. Forming impregnable lines within those of the foe.—*W. B. H.*

Verse 150.—Consider—I. Whether the description here given does not apply, more or less, to all believers in Christ: "They that follow after mischief." 1. Some men undoubtedly and of set purpose do follow after mischief; they make themselves the tempters of others, and delight in it. 2. Others, who do not delight in it, yet cannot help the mischievous effect of their example. 3. The very morality of many unbelievers enables them to carry the pernicious influence of their unbelief where the immorally wicked cannot come. 4. Even regular attendants at public worship may by their indecision encourage others in delay. II. The dangerous position of all to whom the description, in any measure, belongs : " They are far from thy law." 1. They are so, in that they are unbelievers ; for " this is his commandment, that we shall believe," etc. 2. They are so, in that they are a cause of evil to others ; for we are commanded to love and do good. 3. To be far from God's law is to be nigh unto God's righteous wrath. 4. For the sake of others, as well as their own, men should believe in Christ, and through faith become sanctified.—*J. F.*

Verse 151 (*last clause*).—The commandments of the Lord are true in principle ; they lead to true living, if carried out ; they truly reward the obedient ; they never lead to falsehood, nor cause to be deluded.

Verse 152.—Knowledge of the word. I. It is well to know it as God's own word. II. As founded in truth. III. As founded for ever. IV. The earlier we know this the better.

Verses 153—159.—The two considers. The subjects, the prayers, the arguments.

Verses 153, 154—Here—I. David prays for succour in distress. " Is any afflicted ? let him pray " ; let him pray as David doth here. 1. He hath an eye to God's pity and prays, "*Consider mine affliction*" ; take it unto thy thoughts, and all the circumstances, and sit not by as one unconcerned. God is never unmindful of his people's afflictions, but he will have us to " put him in remembrance " (Isa. xliii. 26), to spread our case before him, and then leave it to his compassionate consideration to do in it as in his wisdom he shall think fit, in his own time and way. 2. He has an eye to God's power, and prays, "*Deliver me*," and again, "*Deliver me.*" Consider my troubles and bring me out of them. God has promised deliverance (Ps. l. 15), and we may pray for it with submission to his will, and with regard to his glory, that we may serve him the better. 3. He has an eye to God's righteousness, and prays, "*Plead my cause*" : be thou my patron and advocate, and take me for thy client. David had a just cause, but his adversaries were many and mighty, and he was in danger of being run down by them: he therefore begs of God to clear his integrity, and silence their false accusations. If God do not plead his people's cause, who will ? He is righteous, and they commit themselves to him, and therefore he will do it, and do it effectually : Isa. li. 22 ; Jer. i. 34. 4. He has an eye to God's grace, and prays, "*Quicken me.*" Lord, I am weak, and unable to bear my troubles ; my spirit is apt to droop and sink : Oh, that thou wouldst revive and comfort me, till the deliverance is wrought ! II. He pleads his dependence upon the word of God, and his devotedness to his conduct. "*Quicken*" and "*deliver me according to thy word*" of promise ; "*for I do not forget thy precepts.*" The closer we cleave to the word of God, both as our rule and as our stay, the more assurance we may have of deliverance in due time.—*M. Henry.*

Verse 153.—*The sick man's prayer.* I. The medicine remembered. II. The physician sent for. III. The physician considering the case. IV. The healing wrought.—*C. A. D.*

Verse 153.—I. Lord, do not forget my sorrow. II. I do not forget thy law.

Verses 154, 156, 159.—The threefold quickening. A capital subject, if the contexts are carefully considered.

Verse 154.—Intercession, deliverance, quickening, and all in faithfulness to the word.

Verse 154.—A prayer. I. For promisd defence. II. For promised deliverance. III. For promised revival.—*G. R.*

Verse 154.—*The advocate.* I. The soul hard-pressed by the accuser—in the conscience (1 John iii. 20) ; before the world ; at the throne of grace (Zech. iii.) ; at the bar of judgment. II. The accused soul commiting its case to the Advocate : 1 John ii. 2 ; 2 Tim. i. 12. III. How the case will go. He never lost one yet. —*C. A. D*.

Verse 155.—I. An awful distance. II. A distance never decreased by seeking. III. A distance increased by sinning.

Verse 155.—I. When salvation is far off. II. When it is near. Or—I. When the word is far off salvation is far off. II. When the word is near salvation is near.—*G. R.*

Verse 155.—*How to avoid salvation.* I. Salvation is inseparable from conformity to God's law: Lev. xviii. 5; Luke x. 25—28; Matt. xix. 17. II. Salvation is brought to law-breakers by the Law-giver condescending to become the Law-keeper and the Law-victim. Salvation is avoided by those who refuse to be conformed to the eternal law or will of God. They perish themselves: their own sin punishes them: necessity punishes them.—*C. A. D.*

Verse 155.—A syllogism on salvation. I. Salvation and obedience go together. 1. Have a common centre—God, his *arm* and his *lips.* 2. A mutual relation: we are saved in order to obedience. In obeying we are being saved. Without obedience there is no salvation. 3. An identical aim—our good and God's glory. 4. Obedience and salvation are inseparable for ever. II. The godless are far from obedience. 1. Commands avoided. 2. Submission excluded. III. Therefore they are far from salvation. They *will* not have the one; they *cannot* have the other.—*W. B. H.*

Verse 156.—I. A great need. II. Laid before a great Lord. III. Great favours pleaded. IV. A great mercy sought: " Quicken me."

Verse 156.—*Just, and the Quickener.* I. Spiritual life is the gift of God's mercy. II. Its continuance depends on the exercise of God's power. III. We may therefore plead for quickening on the ground of God's justice.—*C. A. D.*

Verse 156.—The saint, I. Lost in admiration. 1. Of God's tender mercies. 2. He cries out at their greatness. They are numerous. Greatly tender. Great *and* tender; (exquisite combination!). II. Filled with animation. The child of his admiration. 1. The arrow-like prayer: " Quicken me." To be like, to be true to, such a God. 2. The bow in the hand: " according to thy judgments." —*W. B. H.*

Verse 156.—I. The tenderness of God's greatness. II. The greatness of God's tenderness. III. The stimulus to life found in his great and tender presence.

Verse 157.—I. A word of multitude: "many." II. A tendency of dread, viz., a tendency to decline. III. A note of consolation: "yet do I not decline."

Verse 158.—*A grievous sight.* I. Transgressors beyond God's bounds. II. Bounds so kindly set: "thy word." III. Transgressions so wantonly ungrateful, so terribly dangerous, so fatal.

Verse 158.—*Sorrow over sinners.* I. A sight we cannot avoid seeing. II. A sorrow we ought not to avoid feeling. (See Lot: 2 Pet. ii. 7, 8. Moses: Deut. ix. 18, 19. Samuel: 1 Sam. xv. 11; Jeremiah ix. 1. Paul: Phil. iii. 18. Christ: Luke xix. 41.) III. A reason we will not avoid endorsing.

Verse 158.—A righteous man cannot but be grieved at the sins of the wicked. He sees in them,—I. The violation of the divine law which he loves. II. Ungrateful rebellion against the God he worships. III. Contempt for the gospel of salvation and the blood of Christ. IV. The dominion of Satan, the enemy of his God. V. The degradation of souls which might have been sacred temples. VI. Prophetic signs of an awful, everlasting retribution.—*J. F.*

Verse 159.—I. His own love avowed. II. God's love pleaded. III. Renewed life implored.

Verse 159.—I. Attention invited: " Consider how." II. Profession made: " I love thy precepts." III. Petition offered: " Quicken me," etc. IV. Plea suggested: " according to," etc.—*G. R.*

Verse 159.—*My love and thy lovingkindness.* The saint's love. I. Avowed. " Thou knowest all things," etc. II. Submitted. In humble insistance on its sincerity. In sense of its insufficiency. In prayer to God not to overlook it. III. Lost sight of in the sudden glory of God's lovingkindness. Where is my love now? IV. Recovered and humbly brought for quickening. Lord, I'll say no more about it: " Quicken me."—*W. B. H.*

Verse 159.—*Quicken me for love's sake.* I. A prayer for quickened life. II. Awakened by love to the divine rule of life. III. Enforced by the plea of that love. IV. Addressed to the God of love.—*C. A. D.*

Verse 159.—Consider,—I. The holy unsatisfiedness of the believer: " Quicken me " etc. 1. A prayer frequently occurring in the Psalm, and always urged with great earnestness. 2. Its importunity proves the possession of spiritual life; in fact, none but the living ones crave quickening. 3. The most earnest feel the most acutely their indwelling sin, and appreciate most highly thorough sanctification. 4. Thus, this is, perhaps, the only unsatisfiedness perfectly pure in its character. II. The assuring Divine attribute to which he can appeal: " According to thy lovingkindness." 1. An attribute, not only made known in the word, but made manifest to us in our experience of its gentle dealing. 2. An attribute that covers sin, and is touched with a feeling of our infirmities. 3. An attribute that must be affected with the cry for quickening grace. III. The consideration he ought to be able to lay before God : " Consider how I love thy precepts." 1. Because from the word he learnt of the lovingkindness, and through it received life. 2. Without it the prayer cannot be genuine. 3. It is a good reason for expecting more grace ; for " whosoever hath, to him shall be given," etc.—*J. F.*

Verse 160.—I. Early : " true from the beginning." II. Late : " endureth for ever." Or, Truth and immutability the believer's Jachin and Boaz.

Verses 161, 162.—God's word, the object of godly fear and godly joy. 1. It makes the heart quake by its purity and power. 2. It makes the heart rejoice by its grace and truth.—*W. H. J. P.*

Verse 161.—I. Wrong without cause. II. Right with abundant cause.

Verse 161 (*second clause*).—Awe of God's word—its propriety, its hallowed influence, the evil of its absence.

Verse 161.—*Restrained by awe.* I. The causelessness of persecution. II. The temptations to evil occasioned thereby—to revenge : to apostasy. III. The safeguard against falling : awe of God's word. 1 Sam. xxiv. 6 ; Dan. iii. 16—18 ; Acts iv. 19 ; v. 29.—*C. A. D.*

Verse 162.—I. The treasure hid : " great spoil " hidden in the divine word. II. The treasure found : " as one that findeth," etc. 1. By reading. 2. By meditation. 3. By prayer. III. The treasure enjoyed : " I rejoice," etc.—*G. R.*

Verse 162.—David's joy over God's word he compares to the joy of the warrior when he finds great spoil. I. This great joy is sometimes aroused by the fact that there is a word of God. 1. The Scriptures are a revealing of God. 2. The guide of our life. 3. A sure pledge of mercy. 4. The beginning of communion with God. 5. The instrument of usefulness. II. Frequently the joy of the believer in the word arises out of his having had to battle to obtain a grasp of it. 1. We have had to fight over certain doctrines before we could really come at them. 2. The same may be said of the promises. 3. Of the precepts. 4. Of the threatenings. 5. Even about the word which reveals Christ. III. At times the joy of the believer lies in enjoying God's word without any fighting at all : " One that findeth." IV. There is a joy arising out of the very fact that Holy Scripture may be considered to be a spoil. 1. A spoil is the end of uncertainty. 2. It is the weakening of the adversary for any future attacks. 3. It gives a sense of victory. 4. There is, in dividing the spoil, profit, pleasure, and honour. 5. The spoiling of the enemy is a prophecy of rest. See " Spurgeon's Sermons," No. 1641 : " Great Spoil."

Verse 163.—*Opposite poles of the Christian character.* I. Why I hate lying, because it comes from the devil (Pro. viii. 44, Acts v. 3) : it leads to the devil (Rev. xxi. 8, xxii. 15) : it is base, dangerous, degrading (Prov. xix. 5, 1 Tim. iv. 2, 2 Tim. iii. 13) : it is hated by the Lord (Prov. vi. 16, 17, xii. 22). II. Why I love the law. Because it emanates from God ; is the reflection of his character ; is the ideal of my character. III. How I came thus to hate and love. By the grace of God : ver. 29.—*C. A. D.*

Verse 163.—I. Opposite things. II. Opposite feelings.

Verse 164.—Praise rendered. Frequently, statedly, heartily, intelligently.

Verse 164.—*Perpetual praise.* I. True praise is ever warranted. II. True praise is ever welcome. III. True praise is never weary.—*C. A. D.*

Verse 164.—1. Some never praise thee ; but, " seven times a day," etc. ; for I delight to do so. " Thy righteous judgments " are a terror to them, a joy to me. 2. Some feebly and coldly praise thee, while, " seven times," etc. My warm devotion must frequently express itself in praise. 3. Some are content with occasionally praising thee, but, " seven times," etc. They think it enough to begin and end the day with praise, while all the day long I am in the spirit of praise. 4. Some soon cease to praise thee, but, " seven times," etc. Not seven times only, but " unto seventy times seven." Even without ceasing, will I praise thee.—*W. H. J. P.*

Verse 165.—I. Great love to a great law. II. Great peace under great disquietude. III. Great upholding from all stumbling blocks.

Verse 165.—*Perfect peace.* I. The law of God should be regarded with love. II. Love to the law is productive of great peace. Peace with God through the blood of reconciliation : peace with self by good conscience and suppression of evil desires : peace with men by charity. III. The peace which springs from love to the law is a security against stumbling : " nothing shall offend them ; " neither the daily cross (Mark x. 21, 22) ; nor the fiery trial (Mark iv. 7) ; nor the humbling doctrine (John vi. 60, 66, etc.).—*C. A. D.*

Verse 165.—I. The characters described : " they which love thy law." II. The blessing they enjoy : " great peace." III. The evils they escape : " nothing shall offend them."—*G. R.*

Verse 165.—The peace and security of the godly. I. *Their peace.* It arises from—1. Freedom from an accusing conscience. 2. Conformity to the requirements of the law. 3. Enjoyment of the privileges revealed in the law. 4. Assurance of divine approval and benediction. II. *Their security.* 1. They are prepared for every duty. 2. They are proof against every temptation. 3. They are pledged to final perseverance. 4. They have the promise of divine protection.—*W. H. J. P.*

Verse 165.—I. An honourable title : " They which love thy law." II. A good possession : " Great peace have they." III. A blessed immunity : " Nothing shall offend them."—*J. F.*

Verse 166.—I. A hope which is not ashamed. II. A life which is not ashamed. III. A God of whom he is not ashamed.

Verse 166.—*A good hope through grace.* I. Salvation is God's gift : " thy salvation." II. Is apprehended by hope : " I have hoped." III. Is accompanied by obedience : " and done thy commandments." Heb. vi. 9.—*C. A. D.*

Verse 167.—Past and present.

Verse 167.—I. The more we keep God's testimonies the more we shall love them. II. The more we love them the more we shall keep them.—*G. R.*

Verse 167.—I. The jewels : " Thy testimonies." 1. Rare ; none like them. 2. Rich ; surpassing valuation. 3. Beautifying those who wear them. 4. Glittering with an internal and essential splendour, in the darkness of this world. 5. Realising in truth the old superstitions regarding precious stones having medicinal and magic virtues. II. The cabinet : " My soul." 1. Exactly made to receive the jewels. 2. A wonderful piece of divine workmanship ; but all ruined and marred unless applied to the use designed. 3. The only receptacle out of which the genuine beauty of God's testimonies can so shine as to excite the admiration of beholders. III. The lock that keeps all safe : " I love them exceedingly." 1. Love is the strongest holdfast in the universe. 2. It is needed, for ten thousand thieves prowl around to steal from us the treasure. 3. A love " exceedingly " is a heavenly patent ; no ingenuity can pick it ; it is fire-proof and burglar-proof against hell itself.—*J. F.*

Verse 168.—I. The claim of God's word upon our utmost obedience. " I have kept thy precepts and thy testimonies." He does not mean that he had kept them perfectly ; for that were to contradict other expressions in the Psalm. He means that he kept them sincerely and strove to keep them perfectly, as one who realized their claim upon him. 1. The whole word is divine : an equal authority pervades every precept ; no distinction should be made of more or less obligation. 2. The whole word is pure and right ; expediency, or making the measure and manner of obedience suitable to our own purpose, is a false principle ; to be carefully distinguished from righteous expediency, which is the foregoing of a personal right in consideration of another's benefit. 3. The moral code of the word is a unity ; obedience is like a connected chain, a wilful flaw in one link renders all useless. II. The consciousness which greatly helps obedience : " For all my ways are before thee." 1. " Are before thee," as plainly seen by thee. 2. " Are before thee," constantly observed. 3. " Are before thee ; " deliberately placed before thee by me, that they may be corrected and directed.—*J. F.*

Verse 168.—"*All my ways are before thee.*" I. The saint's delight. II. The sinner's distress.—*W. W.*

Verse 168 (*second clause*).—1. *Necessarily so :* for thou art the omniscient God : Psalm cxxxix. 3. 2. *Voluntarily so :* for I choose to walk in thy sight. See Psalm cxvi. 9. 3. *Consciously and blessedly so :* for the light of thy countenance inspires and gladdens me. See Psalm lxxxix. 15.—*W. H. J. P.*

Verse 168 (*second clause*).—Living in the sight of God. Actually the case with all ; designedly the case of the godly ; happily the case of the favoured ; preeminently the case of those who abide in fellowship.

Verse 168.—I. The practical and doctrinal teachings of God before us. II. All our ways before him. III. The sort of conduct which these two causes will produce.

Verses 169, 170.—I. The singular dignity of prayer. We are on earth, but our prayers pass the seraphim and " come near before God." II. The powerful right of prayer—to urge with God his own word : " according to thy word." III. The triumphant possibilities of prayer. Blessing us in mind and estate. For time and eternity. " Give me understanding." " Deliver me." IV. The amazing license accorded to prayer. To double and reiterate its requests (as here).—*W. B. H.*

Verse 169.—I. Admission to the royal court. II. Instruction from the royal throne. III. Reliance on the royal word.

Verses 170—174.—The pleader : ver. 170. The singer : ver. 171. The preacher : ver. 172. The worker : ver. 173. The waiter : ver. 174.

Verse 170.—I. Access sought. II. Answer entreated. III. Argument employed.

Verse 171.—Taught ; taught to praise ; praising ; praising for being taught.

Verse 171.—Learning to sing by learning to obey.

Verse 171.—*The Happy Scholar.* I. He rejoices in the lesson he has learnt. II. In the Teacher who has taught him. III. Looks forward to the end of his lesson as the time for the full singing of his song.—*C. A. D.*

Verse 171.—Lessons in Praise.—I. It is saints' work. II. It is sacred work, not to be hurriedly rushed into. III. It needs Spirit-instructed singers.—*W. B. H.*

Verse 172.—I. The orator : " My tongue shall speak." II. His chosen theme : " of thy word." III. His inward impulse : " for all thy commandments are righteousness."

Verse 172.—*Savoury Speech.* I. A resolution all believers should make. II. The qualification all believers should seek (Psalm xlv. 1 ; Mat. xii. 34, 35). III. The edification believers would thus secure.—*C. A. D.*

Verse 173.—I. " To will is present with me." II. " How to perform that which I would, I find not." III. " Help, Lord."

Verse 173.—I. Help needed to keep the divine precepts. II. Help sought : " Let thy hand," etc. We should choose nothing and do nothing in which we cannot ask help from God.—*G. R.*

Verse 173.—I. God's Hand. 1. Its warm hold (John x. 29). 2. Its wealth of contents (Ps. civ. 28). 3. Its heavy blow (Ps. xxxix. 10). 4. Its weight (1 Sam. v. 11). 5. Its saving reach (Isa. lix. 1). 6. Its sweet shadow (Isa. xlix. 2), etc. II. The saint plucks him by the sleeve : " Let thy hand help me." 1. His humble representation. 2. His down-drawing of the hand of God.—*W. B. H.*

Verse 173.—*"Let thy hand help me."* I. Thy reconciling hand : " stretched out." II. Thy comforting hand ; like that which touched Daniel and John. III. Thy supplying hand. " Thou openest thy hand," etc. IV. Thy protecting hand : " all his saints are in thy hand": Deut. xxxiii. 3. " Great Shepherd of the sheep." V. Thy supporting hand : " I will uphold thee." VI. Thy governing hand : " all my times are in thy hand." VII. Thy chastening hand : " thy hand was heavy upon me." VIII. Thy prospering hand : " the hand of the Lord was with," etc.—*W. J.*

Verse 174.—I. Jacob's longings. II. Moses' choice.

Verse 174.—God's servant drinking at salvation's well, but unsated. I. Longing yielding to delight. 1. At God's salvation. 2. At the rich Scripture inventory. II. Delight bringing forth further longing. 1. For deeper discoveries in the word. 2. Richer experiences in the life. 3. Heaven's consummation.—*W. B. H.*

Verse 174.—I. Sighings for heaven. Holiness, happiness, God. II. Sips by the way. The word of God, the will of God, service of God, the God in all.—*W. B. H.*

Verse 174.—*"I have longed for thy salvation."* Thy holy salvation. Thy full salvation. Thy free salvation. Thy present salvation. Thy permanent salvation.—*W. J.*

Verse 174.—*"I have longed,"* etc. This longing arises, 1. From a painful consciousness of the need of salvation. 2. From a perception of the glories of God's salvation. 3. From the promises which give assurance of the possibility of obtaining this salvation. 4. From the gracious promptings of the Holy Ghost.—*W. H. J. P.*

Verse 175.—I. The highest life. II. The highest occupation. III. Both dependent on the highest aid.

Verse 175.—*Praise.* I. The noblest employment of life—to praise God. II. The noblest presentation of praise—the holy life. III. The noblest application of divine judgments—to inspire praise.

Verse 176.—I. My confession : " I have gone astray." II. My profession : " thy servant." III. My petition : " seek thy servant." IV. My plea : " for I do not forget," etc.

Verse 176.—I. The confession : " I have gone astray." II. The petition : " Seek thy servant." III. The plea : " For I do not," etc.—*G. R.*

Verse 176.—The last verse *as such. The closing minor cadence.* I. The highest flights of human devotion must end in confession of sin : " I have gone astray." II. The sincerest professions of human fidelity must give place to the acknowledgment of helplessness : " seek thy servant." III. The loftiest human declarations of love to God's law must come down to the mournful acknowledgment that we have only not forgotten it.—*C. A. D.*

INDEX

OF AUTHORS QUOTED OR REFERRED TO

THE
TREASURY OF DAVID

VOLUME THREE
(PART 2)
PSALM CXX to CL

PREFACE.

At the end of all these years the last page of this Commentary is printed, and the final preface is requested. The demand sounds strangely in my ears. A preface when the work is done ? It can be only nominally a preface, for it is really a farewell. I beg to introduce my closing volume, and then to retire with many apologies for having trespassed so much upon my reader's patience.

A tinge of sadness is on my spirit as I quit " The Treasury of David," never to find on this earth a richer storehouse, though the whole palace of revelation is open to me. Blessed have been the days spent in meditating, mourning, hoping, believing, and exulting with David ! Can I hope to spend hours more joyous on this side of the golden gate. Perhaps not ; for the seasons have been very choice in which the harp of the great poet of the sanctuary has charmed my ears. Yet the training which has come of these heavenly contemplations may haply go far to create and sustain a peaceful spirit which will never be without its own happy psalmody, and never without aspirations after something higher than it yet has known. The Book of Psalms instructs us in the use of wings as well as words : it sets us both mounting and singing. Ofter have I ceased my commenting upon the text, that I might rise with the Psalm, and gaze upon visions of God. If I may only hope that these volumes will be as useful to other hearts in the reading as to mine in the writing, I shall be well rewarded by the prospect.

The former volumes have enjoyed a singular popularity. It may be questioned if in any age a commentary so large, upon a single book of the Bible, has enjoyed a circulation within measurable distance of that which has been obtained by this work. Among all orders of Christians " The Treasury " has found its way unrestrained by sectarian prejudice—another proof of the unity of the spiritual life, and the oneness of the food upon which it delights to feed. The author may not dare to be proud of the generous acknowledgments which he has received from men of all sections of the church ; but, on the other hand, he cannot pass over them in ungrateful silence. Conscious as he is of his many literary sins of omission and of commission in these volumes, he is yet glad to have been permitted to do his best, and to have received abundant encouragement in the doing of it. Of all its good the glory is the Lord's ; of all its weakness the unworthy author must bear the blame.

This last portion of the Psalms has not been the easiest part of my gigantic task. On the contrary, with the exception of *The Songs of Degrees*, and one or two other Psalms, these later hymns and hallelujahs have not been largely expounded, nor frequently referred to, by our great divines. Failing the English, a larger use has been made of the Latin authors ; and my esteemed friend, W. Durban, B.A., has rendered me great service in their translation. It would astonish our readers if they could see what tomes have been read, what folios have been covered with translations, and in the end what tiny morsels have been culled from the vast mass for incorporation with this Treasury. Heaps of earth have been sifted and washed, and have yielded only here and there a little " dust of gold." No labour has been spared ; no difficulty has been shirked. May the good Lord accept my service, and enrich his church by it this day, and when I am gathered to my fathers !

My friend and amanuensis, Mr. J. L. KEYS, has continued to search the British Museum and public Libraries for me ; and to him and many other kind friends I owe many a quotation which else might have been overlooked. Of the extracts I am editor in chief, and not much more ; for brethren such as Mr. HENSON, of Kingsgate Street, have at sundry times, of their own accord, sent me material more or less useful. In the homiletical department my obligations are exceedingly great, and are duly acknowledged under initials. My venerable friend, the Rev. GEORGE ROGERS, leads the way ; but several other brethren, hailing from the Pastors' College, follow with almost equal steps. Thanks are hereby tendered to them all, and to the multitude of authors from whom I have gathered flowers and fruits, fragrant and nourishing.

And now the colossal work is done ! To God be all glory. More than twenty years have glided away while this pleasant labour has been in the doing ; but the wealth of mercy which has been lavished upon me during that time my grateful heart is unable to measure. Surely goodness and mercy have followed me all those years, and made my heart to sing new Psalms for new mercies. There is none like the God of Jeshurun. To him be all glory for ever and ever.

In these busy days, it would be greatly to the spiritual profit of Christian men if they were more familiar with the Book of Psalms, in which they would find a complete armoury for life's battles, and a perfect supply for life's needs. Here we have both delight and usefulness, consolation and instruction. For every condition there is a Psalm, suitable and elevating. The Book supplies the babe in grace with penitent cries, and the perfected saint with triumphant songs. Its breadth of experience stretches from the jaws of hell to the gate of heaven. He who is acquainted with the marches of the Psalm-country knows that the land floweth with milk and honey, and he delights to travel therein. To such I have aspired to be a helpful companion.

Reader, I beseech David's God to bless thee ; and I pray thee, when it is well with thee, breathe a like prayer for

Thine heartily,

C. H. Spurgeon

THE

SONGS OF DEGREES,

OR,

THE GRADUAL PSALMS.

PSALM CXX. TO CXXXIV.

THE SONGS OF DEGREES AS A WHOLE.

This little Psalter within the Psalter consists of fifteen brief songs. Why they are grouped together and what is meant by their generic name it would be hard to tell. The conjectures are very many, but they are mere suppositions. Out of them all the conjecture of Dr. Jebb best commends itself to my own mind, though it would be quite consistent with this suggestion to believe that the series of songs arranged by David became the Pilgrim Psalms of after ages, and were chanted by the Lord's people as they went up to the temple. They are " Songs of the Goings Up ; " so some read the word. Those who delight to spiritualize everything find here Ascents of the Soul, or language fitted to describe the rising of the heart from the deepest grief to the highest delight. I have thought it well to indicate the methods by which learned men have tried to explain the term " Songs of Degrees," but the reader must select his own interpretation.—*C. H. S.*

In the thirteenth chapter of the First Book of Chronicles, it is related, that David brought up the Ark from Kirjath-jearim to the house of Obed-edom. The word (עלמה) used in the seventh verse, for " bringing up " the Ark, is of the same etymology with, and cognate to that which is translated *"degrees."* And upon this occasion the great event was celebrated by the accompaniment of sacred music. " Anα David and all Israel played before God with all their might, and with singing, and with harps, and with psalteries, and with timbrels, and with cymbals, and with trumpets." Again, in the fifteenth chapter of the same book, in the fourteenth verse, the same term is employed for bringing up the Ark to Jerusalem ; and the choral services of the Levites are mentioned in immediate connection. And in the fifth chapter of the Second Book of Chronicles (fifth verse), we are told that Solomon assembled the people at the dedication of the Temple, to bring up the Ark from Sion to the Temple of the Lord.—*John Jebb.*

I abide in the simple and plain sense as much as I may, and judge that these Psalms are called The Psalms of Degrees because the Levites or priests were wont to sing them upon the stairs or some high place ; even as with us he that beginneth the Psalms or preacheth, standeth in a place above the rest, that he may be the better seen and heard. For it seemeth not that these Psalms were sung of the multitude which were in the Temple, or of the rest of the choir, but of certain which were appointed to sing them, or at least to begin them on the stairs to the rest, and so have their name ; like as some other of the Psalms have their name and title from the singer. But how should a man know all their rites and ceremonies, especially after so long a time, whereby they are now clean worn out of the memory of all men ? Seeing therefore among such a multitude of Psalms, when the law was yet in his full force and power, some were wont to be sung with one manner of ceremony, and some with another, according to the time and place, as the use and custom then was, let this suffice us to think that this title pertaineth to no point of doctrine, but only to the ceremony of the singers, what manner of ceremony soever it was.—*Martin Luther, in "A Commentarie upon the Psalmes of Degrees,"* 1577.

There were *fifteen steps* by which the priests ascended into the Temple, on each of which they sang one of these *fifteen* Psalms.—*David Kimchi.*

Whatever view of the *Songs of Degrees* you may take besides, you cannot leave out some association of them with the steps, without ignoring the unanimous belief about them handed down from time immemorial amongst the people who gave them to us ; without, in fact, implying that at some epoch or other this strange association of the steps with the Psalms was gratuitously invented, and, being invented, secured general acceptance in the sacred literature of the Hebrew nation. It is quite impossible to believe such a thing, when we are dealing with a people so jealous of precedent and authority in religion as the Hebrews have always been. I see, in fact, no sufficient reason why we should not follow the leading of the Mischna and feel that Songs of Degrees, Songs of the Steps, is as much as to say Songs in the sacred Orchestra.—*H. T. Armfield, in "The Gradual Psalms,"* 1874.

The great Carmelite expositor, Michael Ayguan, alleges that the fifteen Psalms were divided by the Jews into three portions of five, with prayers intercalated, much as the Gregorian division of matins into three nocturns ; and that each of the three grades of advance in the spiritual life is betokened by each quinary ; the beginners, the progressors, and the perfect ; or, in other terms, those who are severally in the purgative, the illuminative, and the unitive way. And thus it will be noticed that in Psalms cxx.—cxxiv. there is constant reference to trouble and danger ; in cxxv.—cxxix. to confidence in God ; in cxxx.—cxxxiv. to direct communion with him in his house. And Genebrardus, a later commentator, defines the fifteen degrees of going up out of the valley of weeping to the presence of God to be (1) affliction, (2) looking to God, (3) joy in communion, (4) invocation, (5) thanksgiving, (6) confidence, (7) patient waiting for deliverance, (8) God's grace and favour, (9) fear of the Lord, (10) martyrdom, (11) hatred of sins, (12) humility, (13) desire for the coming of Christ, (14) concord and charity, (15) constant blessing of God.—*Neale and Littledale.*

No trace in history, or authentic tradition, can be found of these *steps*, which owe their construction solely to the accommodating fancy of the Rabbins, who, as usual, imagined facts, in order to support their preconceived theories.—*John Jebb.*

It is an additional objection to this Rabbinical conceit, that David, whose name several of these Psalms bear—and others of which have evident reference to his time and circumstances—lived in the time of the tabernacle which had no steps.—*James Anderson's Note to Calvin in loc.*

In the version of Theodotian, executed in the early part of the second century, with the express view of correcting the errors of the Septuagint, as well as in the translations by Aquila and by Symmachus, these Psalms are rightly described as songs for the journeys up, and are thus at once referred to the stated pilgrimages to the Temple. The expressions, " Thou shalt *go up* to appear before the Lord thy God thrice in the year " (Exod. xxxiv. 24), " If this people *go up* to do sacrifice " (1 Kings xii. 27)—a form of expression constantly employed as often as these sacred journeys are mentioned—is precisely that which the Psalms themselves exhibit : " I was glad when it was said unto me, Go up unto the house of the Lord "; and while we may well adopt this view, for the additional reason that it is in harmony with the whole spirit and sentiment which they breathe throughout, we shall find these Psalms to form at the same time one of the most admirable and instructive manuals of devotion with which the love of our heavenly Father, through the grace of the Holy Spirit, has been pleased to bless us.—*Robert Nisbet, in "The Songs of the Temple Pilgrims,"* 1863.

If the traditionary interpretation of the title, Song of Degrees, be accepted, that they were sung by devout pilgrims on their way to Jerusalem to keep the great feasts of the Lord, we may suppose that companies toiling up this long ascent would relieve the tedium of the way by chanting some of them.

From the customs of Orientals still prevalent, I think it highly probable that such an explanation of the title may be substantially correct. Nothing is more common than to hear individuals and parties of natives, travelling together through the open country and along mountain-paths, especially during the night, break out into singing some of their favourite songs. Once, descending from the top of Sunnîn, above Beirût, with a large company of natives, they spontaneously began to sing in concert. The moon was shining brightly in the clear sky, and they kept up their chanting for a long time. I shall not soon forget the impression made by that moonlight concert, as we wound our way down the eastern side of Lebanon to the Bukâ'a, on the way to Ba'albek. Through the still midnight air of that lofty region the rough edge of their stentorian voices, softened into melody, rang out full and strong, waking the sleeping echoes far and wide down the rocky defiles of the mountain. Something like this may have often rendered vocal this dreary ascent to Jerusalem. It is common in this country to travel in the night during the summer, and we know that the Hebrew pilgrims journeyed in large companies. On his ascent along this road from Jericho to the Holy City, Jesus was attended not only by the twelve apostles, but by others, both men and women ; and it would be strange indeed if sometimes they did not seek relief from this oppressive solitude by singing the beautiful songs of Zion.—*William M. Thomson, in "The Land and the Book,"* 1881.

When we consider the place in the Psalter which these *"Songs of Degrees,* or *of the goings up "* occupy, we see good reason to accept the statement (of the Syriac version, and of S. Chrysostom, Theodoret, Euthymius, and other Fathers, and also of Symmachus, Aquila, and of Hammond, Ewald, and many moderns), that these Psalms describe the feelings of those Israelites who *went up* with Zerubbabel and Jeshua, and afterwards with Ezra, and still later with Nehemiah, from the land of their captivity and dispersion at Babylon, Susa, and other regions of the East, to the home of their fathers, Jerusalem. Hence, in some of the foregoing Psalms, we have seen a reference to the dedication of the Second Temple (Ps. cxviii.), and of the walls of Jerusalem (Ps. cii.), and to the building up of the nation itself on the old foundation of the law of God, given to their fathers at Sinai (Ps. cxix.)—*Christopher Wordsworth.*

Gesenius has the merit of having first discerned the true meaning of the questioned inscription, inasmuch as first in 1812, and frequently since that time, he has taught that the fifteen songs have their name from the step-like progressive rhythm of their thoughts, and that consequently the name, like the triolet (roundelay) in Western poetry, does not refer to the liturgical usage, but to the technical structure. The correctness of this view has been duly appraised more particularly by De Wette, who adduces this rhythm of steps or degrees, too, among the more artificial rhythms. The songs are called Songs of Degrees or Gradual Psalms as being songs that move onward towards a climax, and that by means of πλοκή (ἐπιπλοκή), *i.e.*, a taking up again of the immediately preceding word by way of giving intensity to the expression ; and they are placed together on account of this common characteristic, just like the *Michtammim*, which bear that name from a similar characteristic.—*Franz Delitzsch.*

" Go up, go up, my soul ! " must be the motto of one who would enter into the meaning of these Psalms. They are a Jacob's ladder whose foot is fixed on the earth, but the top reaches up to the " heavenly Jerusalem."

The rhythmical structure of these Psalms (in which one line is built up upon another stair-wise) is a suitable outward accompaniment of the interior character of the Psalms. Short, pointed lines fall in well with the flow of mystico-allegorical thought :—as in " Nearer, my God, to thee," or, " Jerusalem the golden."—*William Kay.*

We may notice the following characteristics of nearly all these Psalms : sweetness and tenderness ; a sad pathetic tone ; brevity ; an absence generally of the ordinary parallelism ; and something of a quick, trochaic rhythm.—*"The Speaker's Commentary."*

Though it may be they are so called because of their excellency ; a song of degrees being an *excellent* song, as an excellent man is called a man of high degree (1 Chron. xvii. 17) ; these being excellent ones for the matter of them, their manner of composure, and the brevity of them.—*John Gill.*

This being a matter of small moment, I am not disposed to make it the subject of elaborate investigation ; but the probable conjecture is, that this title was given to these Psalms because they were sung on a higher key than others. The Hebrew word for *degrees* being derived from the word, צלה, *tsalah, to ascend* or *go up,* I agree with those who are of opinion that it denotes the different musical notes rising in succession.—*John Calvin.*

Hezekiah liveth, these fifteen years, in safety and prosperity, having humbled himself before the Lord for his pride to the ambassadors of Babel. The degrees of the sun's reversing, and the fifteen years of Hezekiah's life prolonging, may call to our minds the fifteen Psalms of Degrees ; viz. from Psalm cxx. and forward. There were Hezekiah's songs that were sung to the stringed instruments in the house of the Lord (Isa. xxxviii. 20) : whether these were picked out by him for that purpose may be left to conjecture.—*John Lightfoot,* 1602—1675.

PSALM CXX.

Suddenly we have left the continent of the vast Hundred and Nineteenth Psalm for the islands and islets of the Songs of Degrees. It may be well to engage in protracted devotion upon a special occasion, but this must cast no slur upon the sacred brevities which sanctify the godly life day by day. He who inspired the longest Psalm was equally the author of the short compositions which follow it.

TITLE.—A SONG OF DEGREES.—*We have already devoted a sufficient space to the consideration of this title in its application to this Psalm and the fourteen compositions which succeed it. These appear to us to be Pilgrim Psalms, but we are not sure that they were always sung in company ; for many of them are in the first person singular. No doubt there were solitary pilgrims as well as troops who went to the house of God in company, and for these lonely ones hymns were prepared.*

SUBJECT.—*A certain author supposes that this hymn was sung by an Israelite upon leaving his house to go up to Jerusalem. He thinks that the good man had suffered from the slander of his neighbours, and was glad to get away from their gossip, and spend his time in the happier engagements of the holy feasts. It may be so, but we hope that pious people were not so foolish as to sing about their bad neighbours when they were leaving them for a few days. If they wished to leave their houses in safety, and to come home to kind surroundings, it would have been the height of folly to provoke those whom they were leaving behind by singing aloud a Psalm of complaint against them. We do not know why this ode is placed first among the Psalms of Degrees, and we had rather hazard no conjecture of our own. We prefer the old summary of the translators—" David prayeth against Doeg "—to any far-fetched supposition : and if this be the scope of the Psalm, we see at once why it suggested itself to David at the station where the ark abode, and from which he had come to remove it. He came to fetch away the ark, and at the place where he found it he thought of Doeg, and poured out his plaint concerning him. The author had been grievously calumniated, and had been tortured into bitterness by the false charges of his persecutors, and here is his appeal to the great Arbiter of right and wrong, before whose judgment-seat no man shall suffer from slanderous tongues.*

EXPOSITION.

IN my distress I cried unto the LORD, and he heard me.

2 Deliver my soul, O LORD, from lying lips, *and* from a deceitful tongue.

3 What shall be given unto thee ? or what shall be done unto thee, thou false tongue ?

4 Sharp arrows of the mighty, with coals of juniper.

5 Woe is me, that I sojourn in Mesech, *that* I dwell in the tents of Kedar !

6 My soul hath long dwelt with him that hateth peace.

7 I *am for* peace : but when I speak, they *are* for war.

1. "*In my distress.*" Slander occasions distress of the most grievous kind. Those who have felt the edge of a cruel tongue know assuredly that it is sharper than the sword. Calumny rouses our indignation by a sense of injustice, and yet we find ourselves helpless to fight with the evil, or to act in our own defence. We could ward off the strokes of a cutlass, but we have no shield against a liar's tongue. We do not know who was the father of the falsehood, nor where it was born, nor where it has gone, nor how to follow it, nor how to stay its withering influence. We are perplexed, and know not which way to turn. Like the plague of flies in Egypt, it baffles opposition, and few can stand before it. Detraction touches us in the tenderest point, cuts to the quick, and leaves a venom behind which it is difficult to extract. In all ways it is a sore distress to come under the power of " slander, the foulest whelp of sin." Even in such distress we need not hesitate to cry unto the Lord. Silence to man and prayer to God are the best cures for the evil of slander.

"*I cried unto the LORD*" (or Jehovah). The wisest course that he could follow. It is of little use to appeal to our fellows on the matter of slander, for the more we stir in it the more it spreads ; it is of no avail to appeal to the honour of the slanderers, for they have none, and the most piteous demands for justice will only increase their malignity and encourage them to fresh insult. As well plead with panthers and wolves as with black-hearted traducers. However, when cries to man would be our weakness, cries to God will be our strength. To whom should children cry but to their father ? Does not some good come even out of that vile thing, falsehood, when it drives us to our knees and to our God ? *"And he heard me."* Yes, Jehovah hears. He is the living God, and hence prayer to him is reasonable and profitable. The Psalmist remembered and recorded this instance of prayer-hearing, for it had evidently much affected him ; and now he rehearses it for the glory of God and the good of his brethren. " The righteous cry and the Lord heareth them." The ear of our God is not deaf, nor even heavy. He listens attentively, he catches the first accent of supplication ; he makes each of his children confess,—" he heard *me.*" When we are slandered it is a joy that the Lord knows us, and cannot be made to doubt our uprightness : he will not hear the lie against us, but he will hear our prayer against the lie.

If these Psalms were sung at the ascent of the ark to Mount Zion, and then afterwards by the pilgrims to Jerusalem at the annual festivals and at the return from Babylon, we shall find in the life of David a reason for this being made the first of them. Did not this servant of God meet with Doeg the Edomite when he enquired of the oracle by Abiathar, and did not that wretched creature belie him and betray him to Saul ? This made a very painful and permanent impression upon David's memory, and therefore in commencing the ark-journey he poured out his lament before the Lord, concerning the great and monstrous wrong of " that dog of a Doeg," as Trapp wittily calls him. The poet, like the preacher, may find it to his advantage to " begin low," for then he has the more room to rise : the next Psalm is a full octave above the present mournful hymn. Whenever we are abused it may console us to see that we are not alone in our misery : we are traversing a road upon which David left his footprints.

2. *"Deliver my soul, O Lord, from lying lips."* It will need divine power to save a man from these deadly instruments. Lips are soft ; but when they are *lying* lips they suck away the life of character and are as murderous as razors. Lips should never be red with the blood of honest men's reputes, nor salved with malicious falsehoods. David says, " Deliver my soul " : the soul, the life of the man, is endangered by lying lips ; cobras are not more venomous, nor devils themselves more pitiless. Some seem to lie for lying sake, it is their sport and spirit : their lips deserve to be kissed with a hot iron ; but it is not for the friends of Jesus to render to men according to their deserts. Oh for a dumb generation rather than a lying one ! The faculty of speech becomes a curse when it is degraded into a mean weapon for smiting men behind their backs. We need to be delivered from slander by the Lord's restraint upon wicked tongues, or else to be delivered out of it by having our good name cleared from the liar's calumny. *"And from a deceitful tongue."* This is rather worse than downright falsehood. Those who fawn and flatter, and all the while have enmity in their hearts, are horrible beings ; they are the seed of the devil, and he worketh in them after his own deceptive nature. Better to meet wild beasts and serpents than deceivers : these are a kind of monster whose birth is from beneath, and whose end lies far below. It should be a warning to liars and deceivers when they see that all good men pray against them, and that even bad men are afraid of them. Here is to the believer good cause for prayer. " Deliver us from evil," may be used with emphasis concerning this business. From gossips, talebearers, writers of anonymous letters, forgers of newspaper paragraphs, and all sorts of liemongers, good Lord deliver us !

3. *"What shall be given unto thee ?"* What is the expected guerdon of slander ? It ought to be something great to make it worth while to work in so foul an atmosphere and to ruin one's soul. Could a thousand worlds be bribe enough for such villainous deeds ? The liar shall have no welcome recompense : he shall meet with his deserts ; but what shall they be ? What punishment can equal his crime ? The Psalmist seems lost to suggest a fitting punishment. It is the worst of offences—this detraction, calumny, and slander. Judgment sharp and crushing would be measured out to it if men were visited for their transgressions. But what punishment could be heavy enough ? What form shall the chastisement take ? O liar, " what shall be given unto thee ? "

"Or what shall be done unto thee, thou false tongue ?" How shalt thou be visited ?

The law of retaliation can hardly meet the case, since none can slander the slanderer, he is too black to be blackened ; neither would any of us blacken him if we could. Wretched being ! He fights with weapons which true men cannot touch. Like the cuttlefish, he surrounds himself with an inky blackness into which honest men cannot penetrate. Like the foul skunk, he emits an odour of falsehood which cannot be endured by the true ; and therefore he often escapes, unchastised by those whom he has most injured. His crime, in a certain sense, becomes his shield ; men do not care to encounter so base a foe. But what will God do with lying tongues ? He has uttered his most terrible threats against them, and he will terribly execute them in due time.

4. *"Sharp arrows of the mighty."* Swift, sure, and sharp shall be the judgment Their words were as arrows, and so shall their punishment be. God will see to it that their punishment shall be comparable to an arrow keen in itself, and driven home with all the force with which a mighty man shoots it from his bow of steel,— " sharp arrows of the mighty." Nor shall one form of judgment suffice to avenge this complicated sin. The slanderer shall feel woes comparable to *coals of juniper,* which are quick in flaming, fierce in blazing, and long in burning. He shall feel sharp arrows and sharper fires. Awful doom ! All liars shall have their portion in the lake which burneth with fire and brimstone. Their worm dieth not, and their fire is not quenched. Juniper-coals long retain their heat, but hell burneth ever, and the deceitful tongue may not deceive itself with the hope of escape from the fire which it has kindled. What a crime is this to which the All-merciful allots a doom so dreadful ! Let us hate it with perfect hatred. It is better to be the victim of slander than to be the author of it. The shafts of calumny will miss the mark, but not so the arrows of God : the coals of malice will cool, but not the fire of justice. Shun slander as you would avoid hell.

5. *"Woe is me, that I sojourn in Mesech, that I dwell in the tents of Kedar ! "* Gracious men are vexed with the conversation of the wicked. Our poet felt himself to be as ill-at-ease among lying neighbours as if he had lived among savages and cannibals. The traitors around him were as bad as the unspeakable Turk. He cries " Woe is me ! " Their sin appalled him, their enmity galled him. He had some hope from the fact that he was only a sojourner in Mesech ; but as years rolled on the time dragged heavily, and he feared that he might call himself a dweller in Kedar. The wandering tribes to whom he refers were constantly at war with one another ; it was their habit to travel armed to the teeth ; they were a kind of plundering gipsies, with their hand against every man and every man's hand against them ; and to these he compared the false-hearted ones who had assailed his character. Those who defame the righteous are worse than cannibals ; for savages only eat men after they are dead, but these wretches eat them up alive.

> " Woe's me that I in Mesech am
> A sojourner so long ;
> That I in tabernacles dwell
> To Kedar that belong.
>
> My soul with him that hateth peace
> Hath long a dweller been ;
> I am for peace ; but when I speak,
> For battle they are keen.
>
> My soul distracted mourns and pines
> To reach that peaceful shore,
> Where all the weary are at rest,
> And troublers vex no more."

6. *"My soul hath long dwelt with him that hateth peace."* Long, long enough, too long had he been an exile among such barbarians. A peace-maker is a blessing, but a peace-hater is a curse. To lodge with such for a night is dangerous, but to dwell with them is horrible. The verse may apply to any one of the Psalmist's detractors : he had seen enough of him and pined to quit such company. Perhaps the sweet singer did not at first detect the nature of the man, for he was a deceiver ; and when he did discover him he found himself unable to shake him off, and so was compelled to abide with him. Thoughts of Doeg, Saul, Ahithophel, and the sons of Zeruiah come to our mind,—these last, not as enemies, but as hot-blooded soldiers who were often too strong for David. What a change for the man of God from the quietude

of the sheepfold to the turmoil of court and the tumult of combat ! How he must have longed to lay aside his sceptre, and to resume his crook. He felt the time of his dwelling with quarrelsome spirits to be long, too long ; and he only endured it because, as the Prayer-book version has it, he was *constrained* so to abide.

7. *"I am for peace."* Properly, " I am peace " ; desirous of peace, peaceful, forbearing,—in fact, peace itself. *"But when I speak, they are for war."* My kindest words appear to provoke them, and they are at daggers drawn at once. Nothing pleases them ; if I am silent they count me morose, and if I open my mouth they cavil and controvert. Let those who dwell with such pugilistic company console themselves with the remembrance that both David and David's Lord endured the same trial. It is the lot of the saints to find foes even in their own households. Others besides David dwelt in the place of dragons. Others besides Daniel have been cast into a den of lions. Meanwhile, let those who are in quiet resting-places and peaceful habitations be greatly grateful for such ease. *Deus nobis hæc otia fecit :* God has given us this tranquillity. Be it ours never to inflict upon others that from which we have been screened ourselves.

EXPLANATORY NOTES AND QUAINT SAYINGS.

Title.—"A Song of Degrees." A most excellent song, Tremellius rendereth it ; and so indeed this and the fourteen following are, both for the matter, and for the form or manner of expression, which is wondrous short and sweet, as the very epigrams of the Holy Ghost himself, wherein each verse may well stand for an oracle. And in this sense, *adam hammahalah,* or, a man of degrees, is put for an eminent or excellent man : 1 Chron. xvii. 17. Others understand it otherwise ; wherein they have good leave to abound in their own sense ; an error here is not dangerous.—*John Trapp.*

Whole Psalm.—In the interpretation of these Psalms, which sees in them the " degrees " of Christian virtues, this Psalm aptly describes the first of such steps— the renunciation of the evil and vanity of the world. It thus divides itself into two parts. 1. The Psalmist, in the person of one beginning the grades of virtue, finds many opponents in the shape of slanderers and ill advisers. 2. He laments the admixture of evil—" Woe is me."—*H. T. Armfield.*

Whole Psalm.—It is a painful but useful lesson which is taught by this first of the Pilgrim Psalms, that all who manifest a resolution to obey the commands and seek the favour of God, may expect to encounter opposition and reproach in such a course. . . . This these worshippers of old found when preparing to seek the Lord in his Temple. They were watched in their preparation by malignant eyes ; they were followed to the house of prayer by the contempt and insinuations of bitter tongues. But their refuge is in him they worship ; and, firmly convinced that he never can forsake his servants, they look up through the cloud of obloquy to his throne, and implore the succour which they know that his children shall ever find there. *"O LORD, in this my trouble deliver my soul."*—*Robert Nisbet.*

Whole Psalm.—The pilgrims were leaving home ; and lying lips commonly attack the absent. They were about to join the pilgrim caravan ; and in the excitements of social intercourse their own lips might easily deviate from truth. The Psalm, moreover, breathes an intense longing for peace ; and in this world of strife and confusion, when is that longing inappropriate ? Is it any marvel that a Hebrew, with a deep spiritual longing for peace, should cry as he started for the Temple, " Let me get out of all *that*, at least for a time. Let me be quit of this fever and strain, free from the vain turbulence and conflicting noises of the world. Let me rest and recreate myself a while in the sacred asylum and sanctuary of the God of peace. God of peace, grant me thy peace as I worship in thy presence ; and let me find a bettered world when I come back to it, or at least bring a bettered and more patient heart to its duties and strifes."—*Samuel Cox.*

Verse 1.—"In my distress I cried unto the LORD," etc. See the wondrous advantage of trouble,—that it makes us call upon God ; and again see the wondrous readiness of mercy, that when we call he heareth us ! Very blessed are they that mourn while they are travelling the long upward journey from the Galilee of the Gentiles of this lower world to the heavenly Jerusalem, the high and holy city of the saints of God.— *J. W. Burgon, in "A Plain Commentary."*

Verse 1.—*"In my distress."* God's help is seasonable; it comes when we need it. Christ is a seasonable good. . . . For the soul to be dark, and for Christ to enlighten it ; for the soul to be dead, and Christ to enliven it ; for the soul to be doubting, and for Christ to resolve it ; and for the soul to be distressed, and for Christ to relieve it ; is not this in season ? For a soul to be hard, and for Christ to soften it ; for a soul to be haughty, and for Christ to humble it ; for a soul to be tempted, and for Christ to succour it ; and for a soul to be wounded, and for Christ to heal it ? Is not this in season ?—*R. Mayhew,* 1679.

Verse 1.—*"Cried." "Heard."* The verbs are in the past tense, but do not refer merely to a past occasion. Past experience and present are here combined. From the past he draws encouragement for the present.—*J. J. Stewart Perowne.*

Verse 1.—*"And he heard me."* The effectual fervent prayer of a righteous man availeth much : James v. 16 ; Zech. xiii. 9. He that prayeth ardently, speedeth assuredly (Ps. xci. 15) ; and the unmiscarrying return of prayer should be carefully observed and thankfully improved : Ps. lxvi. 20.—*John Trapp.*

Verse 2.—*"Deliver my soul, O LORD, from lying lips,"* etc. An unbridled tongue is *vehiculum Diaboli,* the chariot of the Devil, wherein he rides in triumph. Mr. Greenham doth describe the tongue prettily by contraries, or diversities : " It is a little piece of flesh, small in quantity, but mighty in quality ; it is soft, but slippery ; it goeth lightly, but falleth heavily ; it striketh soft, but woundeth sore ; it goeth out quickly, but burneth vehemently ; it pierceth deep, and therefore not healed speedily ; it hath liberty granted easily to go forth, but it will find no means easily to return home ; and being once inflamed with Satan's bellows, it is like the fire of hell." The course of an unruly tongue is to proceed from evil to worse, to begin with foolishness, and go on with bitterness, and to end in mischief and madness. See Eccles. x. 13. The Jew's conference with our Saviour began with arguments : " We be Abraham's seed," said they, etc. ; but proceeded to blasphemies : " Say we not well that thou art a Samaritan, and hast a devil ? " and ended in cruelty : " Then took they up stones to cast at him." John viii. 33, 48, 59. This also is the base disposition of a bad tongue to hate those whom it afflicts : Prov. xxvi. 28. The mischief of the tongue may further appear by the mercy of being delivered from it, for, 1. So God hath promised it (Job v. 15, 21). " God saveth the poor from the sword, from their mouth, and from the hand of the mighty," and " thou shalt be hid from the scourge of the tongue," or from being betongued, as some render it, that is, from being, as it were, caned or cudgelled with the tongues of others. " Thou shalt hide them in the secret of thy presence from the pride of man : thou shalt keep them secretly in a pavilion from the strife of tongues " (Ps. xxxi. 20) ; that is, from all calumnies, reproaches, evil speakings of all kinds. God will preserve the good names of his people from the blots and bespatterings of malicious men, as kings protect their favourites against slanders and clamours. 2. So the saints have prayed for it, as David : *"Deliver my soul, O LORD, from lying lips, and from a deceitful tongue."*—*Edward Reyner.*

Verse 2.—*"Deliver my soul, O LORD, from lying lips,"* etc. In the drop of venom which distils from the sting of the smallest insect, or the spike of the nettle-leaf, there is concentrated the quintessence of a poison so subtle that the microscope cannot distinguish it, and yet so virulent that it can inflame the blood, irritate the whole constitution, and convert day and night into restless misery ; so it is sometimes with the words of the slanderer.—*Frederick William Robertson.*

Verse 2.—*"Lying lips"* bore false witness against him, or with a *"deceitful tongue"* tried to ensnare him, and to draw something from him, on which they might ground an accusation.—*George Horne.*

Verse 3.—*"What shall be given unto thee ? or what shall be done unto thee, thou false tongue ? "* What dost thou expect, *"thou false tongue,"* in pleading a bad cause ? What fee or reward hast thou for being an accuser instead of an advocate ? What shall it profit thee (as we put it in the margin) ; what shalt thou gain by thy deceitful tongue ? or (as our margin hath it again), *"What shall the deceitful tongue give unto thee,"* that thou goest about slandering thy brother, and tearing his good name ? Hath thy deceitful tongue houses or lands to give thee ? hath it any treasures of gold and silver to bestow upon thee ?   Surely, as itself is, so it gives only *"Sharp arrows of the mighty, with coals of juniper,"* as the next verse intimates. . . . The tongue indeed will speak often in these cases *gratis*, or without a fee ; but it never doth without danger and damage to the speaker.   As such speakers shoot arrows, like the arrows of the mighty, and as they scatter coals, like the coals of juniper, so they usually get an arrow in their own sides, and not only burn their fingers, but heap coals of fire upon their own heads.   Ungodly men will do mischief to other men purely for mischief's sake : yet when once mischief is done it proves most mischievous to the doers of it ; and while they hold their brethren's heaviness a profit, though they are never the better, they shall feel and find themselves in a short time much the worse.—*Joseph Caryl.*

Verses 3, 4.—*"What shall be given ? "*   Intimating that his enemy expected some great reward for his malice against David ; but, saith the Psalmist, he shall have *"sharp arrows of the Almighty, with coals of juniper"*; as if he had said, " Whatever reward he have from men, this shall be his reward from God."—*John Jackson, in "The Morning Exercises,"* 1661.

Verses 3, 4.—The victim of slander, in these heavy complaints he has just uttered, may be indulging in excess, which pious friends are represented as coming forward to reprove by reminding him how little a true servant of God can be really injured by slander.   Hence, as in the margin of our Bibles, the Psalm assumes the dramatic form, and represents his fellow-worshippers as asking the complainer : What evil, O servant of God, *can the false tongue give to thee !* Nursling of Omnipotence, *what can it do to thee !* . . . . The answer of suffering nature and bleeding peace still returns : *"It is like the sharp arrows of the mighty, like coals of juniper."* An arrow from the bow of a mighty warrior, that flies unseen and unsuspected to its mark, and whose presence is only known when it quivers in the victim's heart, not unaptly represents the silent and deadly flight of slander ; while the fire which the desert pilgrim kindles on the sand, from the dry roots of the juniper, a wood which, of all that are known to him, throws out the fiercest and most continued heat, is not less powerfully descriptive of the intense pain and the lasting injury of a false and malicious tongue.—*Robert Nisbet.*

Verses 3, 4.—*"Coals of juniper,"* these *"shall be given unto thee."* As if he had said, thou shalt have the hottest coals, such coals as will maintain heat longest, implying that the hottest and most lasting wrath of God should be their portion. Some naturalists say that coals of juniper raked up in the ashes will keep fire a whole year ; but I stay not upon this.—*Joseph Caryl.*

Verse 4.—*"Sharp arrows of the mighty, with coals of juniper."* The world's sin is the world's punishment.   A correspondence is frequently observed between the transgression and the retribution. . . . This law of correspondence seems to be here indicated.   Similar figures are employed to express the offence and the punishment of the wicked.   *"They bend their tongue like a bow for lies."*   *"Who whet their tongue like a sword, and bend their bows to shoot in secret at the perfect."* But let the slanderer be upon his guard.   There is another bow besides that in his possession.   The arrows are sharp and burning ; and when they are sent from the bow by the arm of Omnipotence, nothing can resist their force, and in mortal agony his enemies bite the dust.   " He hath bent his bow, and made it ready.   He hath also prepared for him the instruments of death : he ordaineth his arrows against the persecutors."   " God shall shoot at them with an arrow ; suddenly shall they be wounded ; so shall they make their own tongue fall upon themselves."   This train of thought is also pursued in the illustration of fire.   James compares the tongue of slander to fire.   " And the tongue is a fire, a world of iniquity : so is the tongue among the members, that it defileth the whole body, and setteth on fire the course of nature ; and it is set on fire of hell."   Such is the tongue, and here is the punishment : *"Coals of juniper,"* remarkable for their long retention of heat.   And yet what a feeble illustration of the wrath of God, which burns down to the lowest hell !   " His lips are full of indignation, and his tongue as a devouring fire."   Liars are excluded from heaven by a special enactment of the Sovereign ; and all of them "shall have their part in the lake which burneth with fire and brimstone, which is the second death."   " Who among us shall dwell with the devouring fire ?   Who among us shall dwell with everlasting burnings ? "   With what solemn awe should we not cry out to the Lord,

" Gather not my soul with sinners, nor my life with bloody men ! "—*N. McMichael, in "The Pilgrim Psalms,"* 1860.

Verse 4.—*"Sharp arrows of the mighty."* He compareth wicked doctrine to an *arrow* which is not blunt, but *sharp ;* and moreover which is cast, not of him that is weak and feeble, but that is strong and *mighty ;* so that there is danger on both sides, as well of the arrow which is sharp and able to pierce, as also of him which with great violence hurleth the same.—*Martin Luther.*

Verse 4.—*"Arrows." "Coals of juniper."* When the *tongue* is compared to "*arrows,*" there is a reference (according to the Midrash), to the irrevocableness of the tongue's work. Even the lifted sword may be stayed, but the shot arrow may not. The special point to be drawn out in the mention of " coals of *juniper,*" is the unextinguishableness of such fuel. There is a marvellous story in the Midrash which illustrates this very well. Two men in the desert sat down under a juniper tree, and gathered sticks of it wherewith they cooked their food. After a year they passed over the same spot where was the dust of what they had burned ; and remarking that it was now twelve months since they had the fire, they walked fearlessly upon the dust, and their feet were burned by the " coals " beneath it, which were still unextinguished.—*H. T. Armfield.*

Verse 4.—*"Coals of juniper."* The fire of the *rothem* burns for a very long time covered with its ashes ; like malignant slander. But the secret malignity becomes its own terrible punishment.—*William Kay.*

Verse 4.—*"Coals of juniper."* We here [at Wádí Kinnah] found several Bedouins occupied in collecting brushwood, which they burn into charcoal for the Cairo market ; they prefer for this purpose the thick roots of the shrub Retham, *Genista rætam* of Forskal, which grows here in abundance.—*Johann Ludwig Burckhardt,* 1784—1817.

Verse 4.—*"Coals of juniper."* At this time we spoke four " ships of the desert," bound for Cairo, and loaded with *"coals of juniper,"* or, in other words, with charcoal made from the roots or branches of the *ratam,* or white broom of the desert, the identical bush referred to by the sacred writer.—*John Wilson, in "The Lands of the Bible visited and described,"* 1847.

Verse 4.—By *"coals of juniper,"* we understand arrows made of this wood, which when heated possesses the property of retaining the heat for a long time : and consequently, arrows of this kind, after having been placed in the fire, would in the hands of the warrior do terrible execution.

Some persons think that this verse is not to be understood as a figurative description of calumny, but rather of the punishment which God will inflict upon the calumniator. They therefore regard this as an answer to the question in the preceding verse : *"What shall he give ? "* etc.—*George Phillips.*

Verse 5.—*"Woe is me, that I sojourn in Mesech, that I dwell in the tents of Kedar ! "* Mesech was a son of Japheth ; and the name here signifies his descendants, the Mosques, who occupied that wild mountain region which lies between the Caspian Sea and the Black Sea. Kedar, again, was a son of Ishmael ; and the name here signifies his descendants, the wandering tribes, whose " hand is against every man, and every man's hand against them." There is no geographical connection between those two nations : the former being upon the north of Palestine, and the latter upon the south. The connection is a moral one. They are mentioned together, because they were fierce and warlike barbarians. David had never lived on the shores of the Caspian Sea, or in the Arabian wilderness ; and he means no more than this, that the persons with whom he now dwelt were as savage and quarrelsome as Mesech and Kedar. After a similar fashion, we call rude and troublesome persons Turks, Tartars, and Hottentots. David exclaims, I am just as miserable among these haters of peace, as if I had taken up my abode with those savage and treacherous tribes.—*N. McMichael.*

Verse 5.—*"Woe is me, that I sojourn in Mesech,"* etc. David exclaims, *Alas for me !* because, dwelling amongst false brethren and a bastard race of Abraham, he was wrongfully molested and tormented by them, although he had behaved himself towards them in good conscience. Since then, at the present day, in the church of Rome, religion is dishonoured by all manner of disgraceful imputations, faith torn in pieces, light turned into darkness, and the majesty of God exposed to the grossest mockeries, it will certainly be impossible for those who have any feeling of true piety within them to lie in the midst of such pollutions without great anguish of spirit.—*John Calvin.*

Verse 6.—The Arabs are naturally thievish and treacherous; and it sometimes happens, that those very persons are overtaken and pillaged in the morning who were entertained the night before with all the instances of friendship and hospitality. Neither are they to be accused for plundering strangers only, and attacking almost every person whom they find unarmed and defenceless, but for those many implacable and hereditary animosities which continually subsist among them; literally fulfilling the prophecy of Hagar, that " Ishmael should be a wild man; his hand should be against every man, and every man's hand against him."—*Thomas Shaw*, 1692—1751.

Verse 6.—Our Lord was with the wild beasts in the wilderness. There are not a few who would rather face even these than the angry spirits which, alas, are still to be found even in Christian Churches.—*Wesleyan Methodist Magazine*, 1879.

Verses 6, 7.—What holy and gentle delight is associated with the very name of *peace !* Peace resting upon our bosom, and soothing all its cares : peace resting upon our households, and folding all the members in one loving embrace : peace resting upon our country, and pouring abundance from her golden horn : peace resting upon all nations, and binding them together with the threefold cord of a common humanity, a common interest, and a common religion ! The man who hates peace is a dishonour to the race, an enemy to his brother, and a traitor to his God. He hates Christ, who is the Prince of peace. He hates Christians, who are men of peace.—*N. McMichael.*

Verse 7.—"*I am for peace*," etc. Jesus was a man of peace ; he came into our world, and was worshipped at his nativity as the Prince of peace : there was universal peace throughout the world at the time of his birth ; he lived to make peace " by the blood of his cross : " he died to complete it. When he was going out of the world, he said to his disciples, " Peace I leave with you, my peace I give unto you : not as the world giveth, give I unto you. Let not your heart be troubled, neither let it be afraid " : John xiv. 27. When he was risen from the dead, and made his first appearance to his disciples, he said unto them, " Peace be unto you " : he is the peace-maker : the Holy Ghost is the peace-maker : his gospel is the gospel of peace ; it contains the peace of God which passeth all understanding. "*I am for peace : but when I speak, they are for war.*" The bulk of the Jewish nation abhorred Christ, they were for putting him to death ; to avenge which, the Lord brought the Roman army against them, and many of them were utterly destroyed. So David literally was for peace with Saul ; yet, when opportunities made way for any negotiations, it was soon discovered Saul was for war, instead of peace, with him.

May we see how this, which is the introductory Psalm to those fourteen which follow, styled *Songs of Degrees*, hath a concern with our Lord Jesus Christ ; and that David the son of Jesse was in many cases a type of him, and several of his enemies, sorrows, and griefs, forerunning figures of what would befall Messiah, and come upon him. Amen.—*Samuel Eyles Pierce.*

Verse 7.—"*I am for peace.*" Good men love peace, pray for it, seek it, pursue it, will give anything but a good conscience for it. Compare Matt. v. 9 ; Heb. xii. 14 : *W. S. Plumer.* " It is a mark of a pious man, as far as in him is, to seek peace " : *Amesius.* " I would not give one hour of brotherly love for a whole eternity of contention."—*Dr. Ruffner.*

Verse 7.—"*When I speak, they are for war.*" He spoke with all respect and kindness that could be ; proposed methods of accommodation ; spoke reason, spoke love ; but they would not so much as hear him patiently ; but cried out, To arms ! To arms ! so fierce and implacable were they, and so bent on mischief. Such were Christ's enemies : for his love they were his adversaries ; and for his good words and good works they stoned him ; and if we meet with such enemies we must not think it strange, nor love peace the less for our seeking it in vain. " Be not overcome of evil," no, not of such evil as this ; " but," even when thus tried, still try to " overcome evil with good."—*Matthew Henry.*

HINTS TO PREACHERS.

Verse 1.—A reminiscence. I. It is threefold ; distress, prayer, deliverance. II. It has a threefold bearing : it excites my hope, stimulates my petitions, and arouses my gratitude.

*Verse 1.—*I. Special trouble : " In my distress." II. Special prayer : " I cried unto the Lord." III. Special favour : " He heard me."—*G. R.*

*Verse 2.—*The unjustly slandered have, besides the avenging majesty of their God to protect them, many other consolations, as—1. The consciousness of innocence to sustain them. 2. The promise of divine favour to support them : " I will hide thee from the scourge of the tongue." 3. There is the consideration to soothe : " Blessed are ye when men shall revile you and persecute you," etc. 4. That a lie has not usually a long life. 5. There is, lastly, for comfort, the repairing influence of time.—*R. Nisbet.*

Verse 2.—A prayer against slander. We are liable to it ; it would do us great injury and cause us great pain ; yet none but the Lord can protect us from it, or deliver us out of it.

Verse 3.—The rewards of calumny. What can they be ? What ought they to be ? What have they been ?.

*Verse 3.—*I. What the reviler does for others. II. What he does to himself. III. What God will do with him.

*Verse 4.—*The nature of slander and the punishment of slander.

*Verse 4.—*I. The tongue is sharper than an arrow. 1. It is shot in private. 2. It is tipped with poison. 3. It is polished with seeming kindness. 4. It is aimed at the tenderest part. II. The tongue is more destructive than fire. Its scandals spread with greater rapidity. They consume that which other fires cannot touch, and they are less easily quenched. " The tongue," says an Apostle, " is a fire . . . and setteth on fire the course of nature ; and it is set on fire of hell." A fiery dart of the wicked one.—*G. R.*

Verse 5.—Bad lodgings. Only the wicked can be at home with the wicked. Our dwelling with them is trying, and yet it may be useful (1) to them, (2) to us : it tries our graces, reveals our character, abates our pride, drives us to prayer, and makes us long to be home.

*Verse 5.—*I. None but the wicked enjoy the company of the wicked. II. None but the worldly enjoy the company of worldlings. III. None but the righteous enjoy the company of the righteous.—*G. R.*

*Verse 6.—*I. Trying company. II. Admirable behaviour. III. Undesirable consequences : " When I speak they are for war."

Verse 7.—The character of the man of God. He is at peace. He is for peace. He is peace. He shall have peace.

*Verse 7.—*I. Piety and peace are united. II. So are wickedness and war.—*G. R.*

PSALM CXXI.

TITLE, ETC.—*This bears no other title than " A song of degrees."* *It is several steps in advance of its predecessor, for it tells of the peace of God's house, and the guardian care of the Lord, while Psalm cxx. bemoans the departure of peace from the goodman's abode, and his exposure to the venomous assaults of slanderous tongues. In the first instance his eyes looked around with anguish, but here they look up with hope. From the constant recurrence of the word* keep, *we are led to name this song " a Psalm to the keeper of Israel." Were it not placed among the Pilgrim Psalms we should regard it is a martial hymn, fitted for the evensong of one who slept upon the tented field. It is a soldier's song as well as a traveller's hymn. There is an ascent in the Psalm itself which rises to the greatest elevation of restful confidence.*

EXPOSITION.

I WILL lift up mine eyes unto the hills, from whence cometh my help.

2 My help *cometh* from the LORD, which made heaven and earth.

3 He will not suffer thy foot to be moved : he that keepeth thee will not slumber.

4 Behold, he that keepeth Israel shall neither slumber nor sleep.

5 The LORD *is* thy keeper : the LORD *is* thy shade upon thy right hand.

6 The sun shall not smite thee by day, nor the moon by night.

7 The LORD shall preserve thee from all evil : he shall preserve thy soul.

8 The LORD shall preserve thy going out and thy coming in from this time forth, and even for evermore.

1. *"I will lift up mine eyes unto the hills, from whence cometh my help."* It is wise to look to the strong for strength. Dwellers in valleys are subject to many disorders for which there is no cure but a sojourn in the uplands, and it is well when they shake off their lethargy and resolve upon a climb. Down below they are the prey of marauders, and to escape from them the surest method is to fly to the strongholds upon the mountains. Often before the actual ascent the sick and plundered people looked towards the hills and longed to be upon their summits. The holy man who here sings a choice sonnet looked away from the slanderers by whom he was tormented to the Lord who saw all from his high places, and was ready to pour down succour for his injured servant. Help comes to saints only from above, they look elsewhere in vain : let us lift up our eyes with hope, expectancy, desire and confidence. Satan will endeavour to keep our eyes upon our sorrows that we may be disquieted and discouraged ; be it ours firmly to resolve that we will look out and look up, for there is good cheer for the eyes, and they that lift up their eyes to the eternal hills shall soon have their hearts lifted up also. The purposes of God ; the divine attributes ; the immutable promises ; the covenant, ordered in all things and sure ; the providence, predestination, and proved faithfulness of the Lord—these are the hills to which we must lift our eyes, for from these our help must come. It is our resolve that we will not be bandaged and blindfolded, but will lift up our eyes.

Or is the text in the interrogative ? Dose he ask, " Shall I lift up mine eyes to the hills ? " Does he feel that the highest places of the earth can afford him no shelter ? Or does he renounce the idea of recruits hastening to his standard from the hardy mountaineers ? and hence does he again enquire, " Whence cometh my help ? " If so, the next verse answers the question, and shows whence all help must come.

2. *"My help cometh from the LORD, which made heaven and earth."* What we need is help,—help powerful, efficient, constant : we need a very present help in trouble. What a mercy that we have it in our God. Our hope is in Jehovah, for our help comes from him. Help is on the road, and will not fail to reach us in due time, for he who sends it to us was never known to be too late. Jehovah who created all things is equal to every emergency ; heaven and earth are at the disposal of him who made them, therefore let us be very joyful in our infinite helper. He

will sooner destroy heaven and earth than permit his people to be dstroyed, and the perpetual hills themselves shall bow rather than he shall fail whose ways are everlasting. We are bound to look beyond heaven and earth to him who made them both : it is vain to trust the creatures : it is wise to trust the Creator.

3. *"He will not suffer thy foot to be moved."* Though the paths of life are dangerous and difficult, yet we shall stand fast, for Jehovah will not permit our feet to slide ; and if he will not suffer it we shall not suffer it. If our foot will be thus kept we may be sure that our head and heart will be preserved also. In the original the words express a wish or prayer,—" May he not suffer thy foot to be moved." Promised preservation should be the subject of perpetual prayer ; and we may pray believingly ; for those who have God for their keeper shall be safe from all perils of the way. Among the hills and ravines of Palestine the literal keeping of the feet is a great mercy ; but in the slippery ways of a tried and afflicted life, the boon of upholding is of priceless value, for a single false step might cause us a fall fraught with awful danger. To stand erect and pursue the even tenor of our way is a blessing which only God can give, which is worthy of the divine hand, and worthy also of perennial gratitude. Our feet shall move in progress, but they shall not be moved to their overthrow. *"He that keepeth thee will not slumber,"*—or " thy keeper shall not slumber." We should not stand a moment if our keeper were to sleep ; we need him by day and by night ; not a single step can be safely taken except under his guardian eye. This is a choice stanza in a pilgrim song. God is the convoy and body-guard of his saints. When dangers are awake around us we are safe, for our Preserver is awake also, and will not permit us to be taken unawares. No fatigue or exhaustion can cast our God into sleep ; his watchful eyes are never closed.

4. *"Behold, he that keepeth Israel shall neither slumber nor sleep."* The consoling truth must be repeated : it is too rich to be dismissed in a single line. It were well if we always imitated the sweet singer, and would dwell a little upon a choice doctrine, sucking the honey from it. What a glorious title is in the Hebrew— *"The keeper of Israel,"* and how delightful to think that no form of unconsciousness ever steals over him, neither the deep slumber nor the lighter sleep. He will never suffer the house to be broken up by the silent thief ; he is ever on the watch, and speedily perceives every intruder. This is a subject of wonder, a theme for attentive consideration, therefore the word *"Behold"* is set up as a waymark. Israel fell asleep, but his God was awake. Jacob had neither walls, nor curtains, nor body-guard around him ; but the Lord was in that place though Jacob knew it not, and therefore the defenceless man was safe as in a castle. In after days he mentioned God under this enchanting name—" The God that led me all my life long " : perhaps David alludes to that passage in this expression. The word *" keepeth "* is also full of meaning : he keeps us as a rich man keeps his treasures, as a captain keeps a city with a garrison, as a royal guard keeps his monarch's head. If the former verse is in strict accuracy a prayer, this is the answer to it ; it affirms the matter thus, " Lo, he shall not slumber nor sleep—the Keeper of Israel." It may also be worthy of mention that in verse three the Lord is spoken of as the personal keeper of one individual, and here of all those who are in his chosen nation, described as Israel : mercy to one saint is the pledge of blessing to them all, Happy are the pilgrims to whom this Psalm is a safe-conduct ; they may journey all the way to the celestial city without fear.

5. *"The LORD is thy keeper."* Here the preserving One, who had been spoken of by pronouns in the two previous verses, is distinctly named—Jehovah is thy keeper. What a mint of meaning lies here : the sentence is a mass of bullion, and when coined and stamped with the king's name it will bear all our expenses between our birthplace on earth and our rest in heaven. Here is a glorious person— *Jehovah*, assuming a gracious office and fulfilling it in person,—Jehovah is thy *keeper*, in behalf of a favoured individual—*thy* and a firm assurance of revelation that it is even so at this hour—Jehovah *is* thy keeper. Can we appropriate the divine declaration ? If so, we may journey onward to Jerusalem and know no fear ; yea, we may journey through the valley of the shadow of death and fear no evil. *"The LORD is thy shade upon thy right hand."* A shade gives protection from burning heat and glaring light. We cannot bear too much blessing even divine goodness, which is a right-hand dispensation, must be toned down and shaded to suit our infirmity, and this the Lord will do for us. He will bear a shield before us, and guard the right arm with which we fight the foe. That member which

has the most of labour shall have the most of protection. When a blazing sun pours down its burning beams upon our heads the Lord Jehovah himself will interpose to shade us, and that in the most honourable manner, acting as our right-hand attendant, and placing us in comfort and safety. "The Lord at thy right hand shall smite through kings." How different this from the portion of the ungodly ones who have Satan standing at their right hand, and of those of whom Moses said "their defence has departed from them." God is as near us as our shadow, and we are as safe as angels.

6. "*The sun shall not smite thee by day, nor the moon by night.*" None but the Lord could shelter us from these tremendous forces. These two great lights rule the day and the night, and under the lordship of both we shall labour or rest in equal safety. Doubtless there are dangers of the light and of the dark, but in both and from both we shall be preserved—literally from excessive heat and from baneful chills; mystically from any injurious effects which might follow from doctrine bright or dim; spiritually from the evils of prosperity and adversity; eternally from the strain of overpowering glory and from the pressure of terrible events, such as judgment and the burning of the world. Day and night make up all time : thus the ever-present protection never ceases. All evil may be ranked as under the sun or the moon, and if neither of these can smite us we are indeed secure. God has not made a new sun or a fresh moon for his chosen, they exist under the same outward circumstances as others, but the power to *smite* is in their case removed from temporal agencies; saints are enriched, and not injured, by the powers which govern the earth's condition; to them has the Lord given "the precious things brought forth by the sun, and the precious things put forth by the moon," while at the same moment he has removed from them all bale and curse of heat or damp, of glare or chill.

7. "*The LORD shall preserve thee from all evil*," or *keep* thee from all evil. It is a great pity that our admirable translation did not keep to the word *keep* all through the Psalm, for all along it is one. God not only keeps his own in all evil times but from all evil influences and operations, yea, from evils themselves. This is a far-reaching word of covering : it includes everything and excludes nothing : the wings of Jehovah amply guard his own from evils great and small, temporary and eternal. There is a most delightful double personality in this verse : Jehovah keeps the believer, not by agent, but by himself; and the person protected is definitely pointed out by the word *thee*,—it is not our estate or name which is shielded, but the proper personal man. To make this even more intensely real and personal another sentence is added, "*The LORD shall preserve thee from all evil : he shall preserve thy soul*,"—or Jehovah will keep thy soul. Soul-keeping is the soul of keeping. If the soul be kept all is kept. The preservation of the greater includes that of the less so far as it is essential to the main design : the kernel shall be preserved, and in order thereto the shell shall be preserved also. God is the sole keeper of the soul. Our soul is kept from the dominion of sin, the infection of error, the crush of despondency, the puffing up of pride; kept from the world, the flesh and the devil; kept for holier and greater things; kept in the love of God; kept unto the eternal kingdom and glory. What can harm a soul that is kept of the Lord ?

8. "*The LORD shall preserve thy going out and thy coming in from this time forth, and even for evermore.*" When we go out in the morning to labour, and come home at eventide to rest, Jehovah shall keep us. When we go out in youth to begin life, and come in at the end to die, we shall experience the same keeping. Our exits and our entrances are under one protection. Three times have we the phrase, "Jehovah shall keep," as if the sacred Trinity thus sealed the word to make it sure: ought not all our fears to be slain by such a threefold flight of arrows ? What anxiety can survive this triple promise ? This keeping is eternal; continuing from this time forth, even for evermore. The whole church is thus assured of everlasting security : the final perseverance of the saints is thus ensured, and the glorious immortality of believers is guaranteed. Under the ægis of such a promise we may go on pilgrimage without trembling, and venture into battle without dread. None are so safe as those whom God keeps; none so much in danger as the self-secure. To goings out and comings in belong peculiar dangers, since every change of position turns a fresh quarter to the foe, and it is for these weak points that an especial security is provided : Jehovah will keep the door when it opens and closes, and this he will perseveringly continue to do so long as there is left a single man that trusteth in him, as long as a danger survives, and, in fact, as long as time

endures.   Glory be unto the Keeper of Israel, who is endeared to us under that title, since our growing sense of weakness makes us feel more deeply than ever our need of being kept.   Over the reader we would breathe a benediction, couched in the verse of Keble.

> " God keep thee safe from harm and sin,
> Thy spirit keep ; the Lord watch o'er
> Thy going out, thy coming in,
> From this time, evermore."

EXPLANATORY NOTES AND QUAINT SAYINGS.

Title, "*A song of degrees.*"—It has been ingeniously pointed out that these "*degrees*" or " *steps* " consist in the reiteration of a word or thought occurring in one clause, verse, or stanza, which in the next verse or stanza is used, as it were, as a *step* (or degree) by which to ascend to another and higher truth.   Thus in our Psalm, the idea of " *my help,*" expressed in verse 1, is repeated in verse 2.   This has now become a step by which in verse 3 we reach the higher truth or explanation of " *my help,*" as : "*He that keepeth thee will not slumber,*" the same idea being with slight modification re-embodied in verse 4.   Another " degree " is then reached in verse 5, when " He who *slumbers* not " is designated as *Jehovah*, the same idea once more enlarged upon being (the *word* occurring twice in verse 5) in verse 6.   The last and highest degree of this song is attained in verse 7, when the truth implied in the word *Jehovah* unfolds itself in its application to our *preservation,* which, with further enlargement, is once more repeated in verse 8.   *Perhaps* some internal connexion might be traced between all the fifteen Psalms of Degrees.   At any rate, it will not be difficult to trace the same structure in each of the Psalms "of Degrees," making allowance for occasional devotions and modifications.—*Alfred Edersheim, in "The Golden Diary,"* 1877.

Whole Psalm.—According to verse 1 this Psalm was designed to be sung in view of the mountains of Jerusalem, and is manifestly an evening song for the sacred band of pilgrims, to be sung in the last night-watch, the figures of which are also peculiarly suitable for a pilgrim song ; and with Ps. cxxii. which, according to the express announcement in the introduction, was sung, when the sacred pilgrim trains had reached the gates of Jerusalem, and halted for the purpose of forming in order, for the solemn procession into the Sanctuary, Ps. cxxxiv. . . . .

The idea is a very probable one, that the Psalm was the evening song of the sacred pilgrim band, sung on retiring to rest upon the last evening, when the long wished-for termination of their wandering, the mountains of Jerusalem, had come into view in the distance.   In this we obtain a suitable connection with the following Psalm, which would be sung *one* station further on when the pilgrims were at the gates of Jerusalem.   In this case we find an explanation of the fact, that in the middle point of the Psalm there stands the Lord as the " *keeper* " of Israel, with reference to the declaration, " I keep thee," which was addressed to the patriarch as he slept on his pilgrimage : and in this case also " he neither slumbereth nor sleepeth " is seen in its true light.—*E. W. Hengstenberg.*

It has been said Mr. Romaine read this Psalm every day ; and sure it is, that every word in it is calculated to encourage and strengthen our faith and hope in God.—*Samuel Eyles Pierce.*

Verse 1.—"*I will lift up mine eyes,*" etc.   Since we, being burthened with the effects of worldly pleasures, and also with other cares and troubles, can by no means ascend to thee that art on the top of so high a mountain, accompanied with so many legions of angels that still attend upon thee, we have no remedy, but with thy prophet David now to lift up the eyes of our hearts and minds toward thee, and to cry for help to come down from thee to us, thy poor and wretched servants.—*Sir Anthony Cope, in "Meditations on Twenty Select Psalms,"* 1547.

Verse 1.—"*I will lift up mine eyes,*" etc.   In thy agony of a troubled conscience always look upwards unto a gracious God to keep thy soul steady ; for looking downward on thyself thou shalt find nothing but what will increase thy fear, infinite sins, good deeds few, and imperfect: it is not thy faith, but God's faithfulness thou must rely upon; casting thine eyes downwards on thyself, to behold the great distance betwixt what thou deservest and what thou desirest, is enough to make thee giddy, stagger, and reel into despair. Ever therefore *lift up thine eyes unto the hills, from whence cometh thy help,* never viewing the deep dale of thy own un-worthiness, but to abate thy pride when tempted to presumption.—*Thomas Fuller* (1608—1661), *in "The cause and Cure of a Wounded Conscience."*

Verse 1.—*"The hills."* There can be no doubt that in Palestine we are in the "Highlands" of Asia. This was the more remarkable in connection with the Israelites, because they were the only civilized nation then existing in the world, which dwelt in a mountainous country. . . . . The Hebrew people was raised above the other ancient states, equally in its moral and in its physical relations. From the Desert of Arabia to Hebron is a continual ascent, and from that ascent there is no descent of any importance, except to the plains of the Jordan, Esdraelon, and the coast. From a mountain sanctuary, as it were, Israel looked over the world. . . . . It was to the "mountains" of Israel that the exile lifted up his eyes, as the place *from whence his help came.—Arthur Penrhyn Stanley.*

Verse 1.—*"The hills, from whence cometh my help."* See no riches but in grace, no health but in piety, no beauty but in holiness, no treasure but in heaven, no delight but in "the things above."—*Anthony Farindon.*

Verse 1.—*"From whence cometh my help."* The natives of India used to say that when Sir Henry Lawrence looked twice to heaven and then to earth he knew what to do.

> To Heaven I lift mine eye,
> To Heaven, Jehovah's throne,
> For there my Saviour sits on high,
> And thence shall strength and aid supply
> To all He calls His own.
>
> He will not faint nor fail,
> Nor cause thy feet to stray:
> For him no weary hours assail,
> Nor evening darkness spreads her veil
> O'er his eternal day.
>
> Beneath that light divine
> Securely shalt thou move;
> The sun with milder beams shall shine.
> And eve's still queen her lamp incline
> Benignant from above.
>
> For he, thy God and Friend,
> Shall keep thy soul from harm,
> In each sad scene of doubt attend,
> And guide thy life, and bless thy end,
> With his almighty arm.
>
> *John Bowdler,* 1814.

Verses 1, 2.—Faint at the close of life's journey, a Christian pilgrim repeated the line,—

> "Will he not his help afford?"

She quoted it several times, trying to recall the song in which it occurs, and asked that the once familiar hymn, part of the voice of which she caught, might be all fetched home to her mind again; and she was greatly refreshed and comforted when we read at her bedside Charles Wesley's spirited paraphrase, beginning,—

> "To the hills I lift mine eyes,
> The everlasting hills;
> Streaming thence in fresh supplies,
> My soul the Spirit feels.
>
> Will he not his help afford?
> Help, while yet I ask, is given:
> God comes down; the God and Lord
> That made both earth and heaven."

Edward Jewitt Robinson, in "The Caravan and the Temple," 1878

Verses 1—3.—

Look away to Jesus,
Look away from all !
Then we need not stumble,
Then we shall not fall.
From each snare that lureth,
Foe or phantom grim,
Safety this ensureth,
Look away to him !

Frances Ridley Havergal.

Verse 2.—*"My help cometh from the Lord."* I require to remember that my *help cometh from the Lord,* not only when seemingly there is no *outward* help from men or otherwise, but also and especially when all seems to go well with me,—when abundance of friends and help are at hand. For then, surely, I am most in danger of making an arm of flesh my trust, and thus reaping its curse ; or else of saying to my soul, " Take thine ease," and finding the destruction which attends such folly.—*Alfred Edersheim.*

Verse 2.—*"Maker of heaven and earth,"* and therefore mighty to help.—*James G. Murphy.*

Verse 3.—*"He will not suffer thy foot to be moved."* The sliding of the foot is a frequent description of misfortune, for example, Ps. xxxviii. 16, lxvi. 9, and a very natural one in mountainous Canaan, where a single slip of the foot was often attended with great danger. The language here naturally refers to complete, lasting misfortune.—*E. W. Hengstenberg.*

Verse 3.—*"He will not suffer thy foot to be moved."* A man cannot go without moving his feet ; and a man cannot stand whose feet are moved. The foot by a *synechdoche* is put for the whole body, and the body for the whole outward estate ; so that, *" he will not suffer thy foot to be moved,"* is, he will not suffer thee or thine to be moved or violently cast down. The power of thine opposers shall not prevail over thee, for the power of God sustains thee. Many are striking at thy heels, but they cannot strike them up while God holds thee up. If the will of thine enemies might stand, thou shouldst quickly fall ; but God *" will not suffer thy foot to be moved."* —*Joseph Caryl.*

Verses 3—8.—There is something very striking in the assurance that the Lord will not suffer the foot even of the most faint and wearied one to be moved. The everlasting mountains stand fast, and we feel as if, like Mount Zion, they could not be removed for ever ; but the step of man—how feeble in itself, how liable to stumble or trip even against a pebble in the way ! Yet that foot is as firm and immoveable in God's protection as the hills themselves. It is one of his own sweet promises, that he will give his angels charge over every child of his, that he come to no harm by the way. But, oh, how immeasurably beyond even the untiring wings of angels is the love promised here ! that love which engages to protect from every danger, as a hen gathereth her chickens under her wings. In the hours of occupation and hurry, in the conflicts and perils of the day, in the helplessness of sleep, in the glare and heat of the noon-day, amid the damps and dews of night, that unslumbering eye is still over every child for his good. Man, indeed, goeth forth to his work and to his labour till the evening ; but alike as he goes forth in the morning, and as he returns in the evening, the Lord still holds him up in all his goings forth and his comings in ; no manner of evil shall befall him. And oh ! what a sweet addition is it to the promise. " He shall preserve *thy soul."* It is the very argument of the apostle, and the very inference he draws, " The eyes of the Lord are upon the righteous, and his ears are open unto their cry,"—" He neither slumbereth nor sleepeth,"— and then he asks, " Who is he that will harm you, if ye be followers of that which is good ? " From the very dawn of life to its latest close, even for evermore, " He will preserve thee from all evil ; he will preserve thy soul."—*Barton Bouchier.*

Verses 3, 4, 5.—A great practical difficulty is to find a " keeper " who will remain *awake during the whole night.* The weariness of those who keep a faithful watch, and their longing for day during the tedious lonely hours of darkness, is alluded to in a graphic and beautiful figure of the Psalmist—

" My soul waiteth for the Lord
More than keepers for the morning,
More than keepers for the morning."

The usual method adopted to secure due vigilance is to require the man to call out loudly, or to blow a whistle, every quarter of an hour. . . . . Yet, notwithstanding all precautions, as soon as sleep falls on the tired camp, it is too often the case that the hireling keeper lies down on the ground, wraps around him his thick *abaiyeh*, or cloak, and, careless of his charge, or overcome with weariness, yields himself up to his drowsy propensities.

Viewed in the light of these facts, how full of condescension and cheer is the assurance of God's never-ceasing care—

" He who keepeth thee will not slumber.
Behold, he who keepeth Israel
Doth not slumber or sleep.
Jehovah is thy keeper."

While the services of the keeper constitute at all times a marked feature of life in Palestine, they are perhaps more needed when travelling through the country than at any other time. Then, when the moving camp is nightly pitched in strange fields, it becomes absolutely necessary to apply to the nearest authorities for a nocturnal guardian, before one can safely lie down to rest. Now this Psalm cxxi. being one of " the Songs of Degrees," was probably composed to be sung on the way to Jerusalem, as a pilgrim hymn, when the Israelites were coming up annually to keep the three great feasts. As a journeying Psalm, it would therefore have peculiar significance in its allusion to *the keeper by night.—James Neil, in "Palestine Explored,"* 1882.

Verses 3, 4.—When one asked Alexander how he could sleep so soundly and securely in the midst of danger, he told him that Parmenio watched. Oh, how securely may they sleep over whom *he* watcheth that never slumbers nor sleeps !— *From "The Dictionary of Illustrations,"* 1873.

Verses 3, 4.—A poor woman, as the Eastern story has it, came to the Sultan one day, and asked compensation for the loss of some property. " How did you lose it ? " said the monarch. " I fell asleep," was the reply, " and a robber entered my dwelling." " Why did you fall asleep ? " " I fell asleep because I believed that you were awake." The Sultan was so much delighted with the answer of the woman, that he ordered her loss to be made up. But what is true, only by a legal fiction, of human governments, that they never sleep, is true in the most absolute sense with reference to the divine government. We can sleep in safety because our God is ever awake. We are safe because he never slumbers. Jacob had a beautiful picture of the ceaseless care of Divine Providence on the night when he fled from his father's house. The lonely traveller slept on the ground, with the stones for his pillow, and the sky for his canopy. He had a wondrous vision of a ladder stretching from earth to heaven, and on which angels were seen ascending and descending. And he heard Jehovah saying to him, " Behold, I am with thee, and will keep thee in all places whither thou goest."—*N. McMichael.*

Verse 4.—It is necessary, observes S. Bernard, that *"he who keepeth Israel"* should *" neither slumber nor sleep,"* for he who assails Israel neither slumbers nor sleeps. And as the One is anxious about us, so is the other to slay and destroy us, and his one care is that he who has once been turned aside may never come back.— *Neale and Littledale.*

Verse 4.—"Slumber." "Sleep." There is no climax in these words, as some have supposed. Etymologically, the first is the stronger word, and it occurs in Ps. lxxvi. 5 [6] of the sleep of death. In this instance there is no real distinction between the two. Possibly there may be an allusion to the nightly encampment, and the sentries of the caravan.—*J. J. Stewart Perowne.*

Verse 4.—"He . . . shall neither slumber nor sleep." This form of expression, *he will not slumber nor sleep,* would be improper in other languages, according to the idiom of which it should rather be, *He will not sleep, yea, he will not slumber :* but when the Hebrews invert this order, they argue from the greater to the less. The sense then is, that as God never slumbers even in the smallest degree, we need not be afraid of any harm befalling us while he is asleep.—*John Calvin.*

Verse 4.—"He that keepeth Israel." With an allusion to Jacob, who slept at Bethel, and to whom the promise of God took this form, " And, behold, I am with thee, and will *keep* thee in all places whither thou goest " : Gen. xxviii. 15.—*Aben Ezra, quoted by H. T. Armfield.*

Verse 4.—*"Shall neither slumber nor sleep."* Man sleeps ; a sentinel *may* slumber on his post by inattention, by long-continued wakefulness, or by weariness ; a pilot *may* slumber at the helm ; even a mother *may* fall asleep by the side of the sick child ; but God is never exhausted, is never weary, is never inattentive. He never closes his eyes on the condition of his people, on the wants of the world.— *Albert Barnes.*

Verse 4.—A number of years ago Captain D. commanded a vessel sailing from Liverpool to New York, and on one voyage he had all his family with him on board the ship.

One night, when all were quietly asleep, there arose a sudden squall of wind, which came sweeping over the waters until it struck the vessel, and instantly threw her on her side, tumbling and crashing everything that was moveable, and awaking the passengers to a consciousness that they were in imminent peril.

Everyone on board was alarmed and uneasy, and some sprang from their berths and began to dress, that they might be ready for the worst.

Captain D. had a little girl on board, just eight years old, who, of course, awoke with the rest.

"What's the matter ? " said the frightened child.

They told her a squall had struck the ship.

" Is father on deck ? " said she.

" Yes ; father's on deck."

The little thing dropped herself on her pillow again without a fear, and in a few moments was sleeping sweetly in spite of winds or waves.

> Fear not the windy tempests wild,
> Thy bark they shall not wreck ;
> Lie down and sleep, O helpless child !
> Thy Father's on the deck.

"The Biblical Treasury," 1873.

Verses 4, 5.—The same that is the protector of the church in general, is engaged for the preservation of every particular believer ; the same wisdom, the same power, the same promises. *"He that keepeth Israel"* (verse 4), *"is thy keeper"* (verse 5). The Shepherd of the flock is the Shepherd of every sheep, and will take care that not one, even of the little ones, shall perish.—*Matthew Henry.*

Verse 5.—*"The Lord is thy keeper."* Two principal points are asserted in these previous words. 1. Jehovah, and Jehovah alone, the omnipotent and self-existent God, is the Keeper, and Preserver of his people. 2. The people of God are kept, at all times and in all circumstances, by his mighty power unto everlasting salvation ; they are preserved even " for evermore." In the first particular, the divinity of the great Keeper is declared ; and, in the second, the eternal security of his people through his omnipotence and faithfulness. This was the Psalmist's gospel. He preached it to others, and he felt it himself. He did not speculate upon what he did not understand ; but he had a clear evidence, and a sweet perception, of these two glorious doctrines, which he delivered to the people. . . . This character, under the name of Jehovah, is the character of Christ. Just such a one is Jesus, the Shepherd of Israel. He says of himself to the Father, " Those that thou gavest me *I have kept*, and *none of them is lost*, but the Son of Perdition, that the Scripture might be fulfilled." . . . . From what has been premised, it seems evident, that the keeper of the faithful is no other than Jehovah. This the Psalmist has proved. It appears equally evident that Christ is their Keeper and Preserver. This he hath declared himself ; and his apostles have repeatedly declared it of him. It follows, therefore, that Christ is truly and essentially Jehovah. All the sophistry in the world cannot elude this conclusion ; nor all the heretics in the world destroy the premises. And, if Christ be Jehovah, he is all that supreme, eternal, omnipotent being, which Arians, Socinians, and others deny him to be.—*Ambrose Serle, in "Horæ Solitariæ,"* 1815.

Verse 5.—" *Keeper.*" "*Shade.*" The titles of God are virtually promises— when he is called a sun, a shield, a strong tower, a hiding-place, a portion. The titles of Christ, light of the world, bread of life, the way, the truth, and life ; the titles of the Spirit, the Spirit of truth, of holiness, of glory, of grace, and supplication, the sealing, witnessing Spirit ; faith may conclude as much out of these as out of promises. Is the Lord a sun? then he will influence me, etc. Is Christ life? then he will enliven me, etc.—*David Clarkson,* 1621—1686.

Verse 5.—*"Thy shade upon thy right hand."* That is, always present with thee ; or, as the Jewish Arab renders it, " Nigher than thy shadow at, or from thy right hand."—*Thomas Fenton, in "Annotations on the Book of Job and the Psalms," 1732.*

Verse 5.—*"Thy shade."* In eastern countries the sun's burning rays are often arrows by which premature death is inflicted ; and when the Psalmist speaks of Jehovah as a shady covert for the righteous, that imagery suggests the idea of the " coup de soleil" or sunstroke as the evil avoided.—*J. F., in "The Baptist Magazine," 1831.*

Verse 5.—*"Shade."* The Hebrew word is צל, *tsel,* " a shadow," and hence it has been supposed that the words, " thy shadow at thy right hand," are a figurative expression, referring to the protection afforded by the shade of a tree against the scorching rays of the sun or to the custom which prevails in tropical climates especially, of keeping off the intense heat of the sun by a portable screen, such as an umbrella or parasol. The word is often put for *defence* in general. Compare Num. xiv. 9 ; Isaiah xxx. 2 ; Jer. xlviii. 45.—*James Anderson.*

Verses 5—8.—How large a writ or patent of protection is granted here ! No time shall be hurtful, neither *"day nor night,"* which includes all times. Nothing shall hurt, neither *sun nor moon,* nor heat nor cold. These should include all annoyances. Nothing shall be hurt, *"Thy soul shall be preserved, thy outgoings and thy comings in shall be preserved."* These include the whole person of man, and him in all his just affairs and actions. Nothing of man is safe without a guard, and nothing of man can be unsafe which is thus guarded. They should be kept who can say, " The Lord is our keeper " ; and they cannot be kept, no, not by legions of angels, who have not the Lord for their keeper. None can keep us but he, and he hath promised to keep us " for evermore."—*Joseph Caryl.*

Verse 6.—*"The sun shall not smite thee."* הכּה of the sun signifies to smite injuriously (Isa. xlix. 10), plants, so that they wither (Ps. cii. 5), and the head (Jonah iv. 8), so that symptoms of sunstroke (2 Kings iv. 19 ; Judith viii. 2 seq.) appear. The transferring of the word to the moon is not zeugmatic. Even the moon's rays may become insupportable, may affect the eyes injuriously, and (more particularly in the equatorial regions) produce fatal inflammation of the brain. From the hurtful influences of nature that are round about him the promise extends in verses 7, 8 in every direction. Jahve, says the poet to himself, will keep (guard) thee against all evil, of whatever kind it may be and whencesoever it may threaten ; he will keep thy soul, and thereafter thy life both inwardly and outwardly ; he will keep thy going out and coming in, *i.e.,* all thy business and intercourse of life . . . . . . everywhere and at all times ; and that from this time forth even for ever.—*Franz Delitzsch.*

Verse 6.—*"The sun shall not smite thee by day,"* etc. A promise made with allusion unto, and application of that care which God had over his people, when he brought them out of Egypt through the wilderness, when he guarded them from the heat of the sun by a cloud by day, and from the cold and moistness of the night and moon by a pillar of fire by night.—*David Dickson.*

Verse 6.—*"Nor the moon by night."*

> The moon, the governess of floods,
> Pale in her anger, washes all the air,
> That rheumatic diseases do abound.

William Shakespeare (1564—1616), *in "The Midsummer Night's Dream."*

Verse 6.—Joseph Hart in one of his hymns speaks of some who " travel much by night." To such this promise is precious.—*"Biblical Treasury."*

Verse 6.—*"Nor the moon by night."* The effect of the moonlight on the eyes in this country is singularly injurious. . . . The moon here really strikes and affects the sight, when you sleep exposed to it, much more than the sun, a fact of which I had a very unpleasant proof one night, and took care to guard against it afterwards ; indeed, the sight of a person who should sleep with his face exposed at night would soon be utterly impaired or destroyed.—*John Carne, in " Letters from the East," 1826.*

Verse 6.—*"Nor the moon by night."* In the cloudless skies of the East, where the moon shines with such exceeding clearness, its effects upon the human frame have been found most injurious. The inhabitants of these countries are most careful in taking precautionary measures before exposing themselves to its influence. Sleeping much in the open air, they are careful to cover well their heads and faces. It has been proved beyond a doubt that the moon smites as well as the sun, causing blindness for a time, and even distortion of the features.

Sailors are well aware of this fact ; and a naval officer relates that he has often, when sailing between the tropics, seen the commanders of vessels waken up young men who have fallen asleep in the moonlight. Indeed, he witnessed more than once the effects of a moonstroke, when the mouth was drawn on one side and the sight injured for a time. He was of opinion that, with long exposure, the mind might become seriously affected. It is supposed that patients suffering under fever and other illnesses are affected by this planet, and the natives of India constantly affirm that they will either get better or worse, according to her changes.—*C. W., in "The Biblical Treasury."*

Verse 7.—*"The LORD shall preserve thee from all evil."* Lawyers, when they are drawing up important documents, frequently conclude with some general terms to meet any emergency which may possibly occur. They do this on the principle, that what is not in may be supposed to be intentionally left out. In order to guard against this inference, they are not content with inserting a number of particular cases ; they conclude with a general statement, which includes everything, whether expressed or not. A similar formula is inserted here. It is of great importance that the feet of travellers be kept from sliding, as they pursue their journey. It is of great importance that they be preserved from heat by day, and from cold by night. But other dangers await them, from which they require protection ; and lest the suspicion be entertained, that no provision is made for these being surmounted, they are all introduced in the saving and comprehensive clause. No matter what may be their character, no matter from what quarter they may appear, no matter when they may come, and no matter how long they may continue, the declaration covers them all. Divine grace changes the nature of everything it handles, and transforms everything it touches into gold. Afflictions are overruled for good ; and the virtues of the Christian life are developed with unusual lustre. *"The LORD shall preserve thee from all evil."*—*N. McMichael.*

Verse 7.—*"The LORD shall preserve thee from all evil,"* etc. It is an absolute promise, there are no conditions annexed ; it honours God for us simply to believe it, and rest on the Lord for the performance of it. As we view it, what have we to fear ? The mouth of the Lord hath spoken it, his word is immutable. Jesus preserves body and soul, he is the Saviour of the body as well as of the soul.—*Samuel Eyles Pierce.*

Verses 7, 8.—The threefold expression, *"shall keep thee . . . thy soul . . . thy going out* and *thy coming in,"* marks the completeness of the protection vouchsafed, extending to all that the man is and that he does.—*J. J. Stewart Perowne.*

Verses 7, 8.—It is of importance to mark the reason why the prophet repeats so often what he had so briefly and in one word expressed with sufficient plainness. Such repetition seems at first sight superfluous ; but when we consider how difficult it is to correct our distrust, it will be easily perceived that he does not improperly dwell upon the commendation of the divine providence. How few are to be found who yield to God the honour of being a *"keeper,"* in order to their being thence assured of their safety, and led to call upon him in the midst of their perils ! On the contrary, even when we seem to have largely experienced what this protection of God implies, we yet instantly tremble at the noise of a leaf falling from a tree, as if God had quite forgotten us. Being then entangled in so many unholy misgivings, and so much inclined to distrust, we are taught from the passage that if a sentence couched in a few words does not suffice us, we should gather together whatever may be found throughout the whole Scriptures concerning the providence of God, until this doctrine—*"That God always keeps watch for us"*—is deeply rooted in our hearts ; so that, depending upon his guardianship alone, we may bid adieu to all the vain confidences of the world.—*John Calvin.*

Verse 8.—*"The LORD shall preserve."* The word *shamar* imports a most tender preservation ; from it comes *shemuroth*, signifying the eyelids, because they are the keepers of the eve, as the Lord is called in the verse preceding—*shomer Ishrael, "the keeper of Israel."* If the lids of the eye open, it is to let the eye see ; if they close, it is to let it rest, at least to defend it ; all their motion is for the good of the eye. O, what a comfort is here! The Lord calleth his Church "the apple of his eye": "he that toucheth you, touches the apple of mine eye." The Church is the apple of God's eye, and the Lord is the covering of it. O, how well are they kept whom "the keeper of Israel" keepeth! The Lord was a buckler to Abraham, none of his enemies could harm him; for his buckler covered him throughly. The Lord was a hedge unto Job; Satan himself confessed he could not get through it, howsoever many a time he assayed it, to have done evil unto Job. . . . . . .

But seeing this same promise of preservation was made before (for from the third verse to the end of the Psalm, six sundry times, is the word of keeping or preserving repeated), why is it now made over again? Not without cause; for this doubling and redoubling serves, first, for a remedy of our ignorance. Men, if they be in any good estate, are ready to "sacrifice to their own net," or "to cause their mouth to kiss their own hand," as if their own hand had helped them: thus to impute their "deliverance" to their "calf," and therefore often is this resounded, "The Lord," "The Lord." Is thy estate advanced? The Lord hath done it. Hast thou been preserved from desperate dangers? Look up to the Lord, thy help is from on high, and to him let the praise be returned. Secondly, it is for a remedy for our natural diffidence: the word of the Lord in itself is as sure when it is spoken, as when it is sworn; as sure spoken once, as when it is oftener repeated; yet is not the Lord content to speak only, but to swear also; nor to speak once, but often, one and the selfsame thing. The reason is showed us by the apostle, that hereby he may "declare to the heirs of promise the stability of his counsel." Heb. vi.; Gen. xxi. 32. As Joseph spake of Pharaoh his vision, "It was doubled, because the thing is established by God, and God hasteth to perform it"; so is it with every word of the Lord, when it is repeated; it is because it is established, and God hastens to perform it.—*From a Sermon by Bishop Cowper, entitled "His Majesties Comming in," 1623.*

Verse 8.—*"The Lord shall preserve thy going out and thy coming in."* All actions being comprehended under one of these two sorts, *"going out"* to more public, and *"coming in"* to more private affairs; or again, *"going out"* to begin, and *"coming in"* at the end of the work. But by this expression may here perhaps be more particularly signified that God would protect David, even to the end of his days, whenever he marched out with his armies, or brought them home.—*Thomas Fenton.*

Verse 8.—*"From this time forth and even for evermore."* He has not led me so tenderly thus far to forsake me at the very gate of heaven.—*Adoniram Judson.*

HINTS TO PREACHERS.

Verse 1.—The window opened towards Jerusalem. I. The hills we look to. II. The help we look for. III. The eyes we look with.

Verse 1.—*"Whence cometh my help?"* A grave question; for, I. I need it, greatly, in varied forms, constantly, and now. II. In few directions can I look for it, for men are feeble, changeable, hostile, etc. III. I must look above. To Providence, to Grace, to my God.

Verse 2.—The Creator the creature's helper.

Verse 2.—I. God is his people's "help." II. He helps them in proportion as they feel their need of his help. III. His help is never in vain. "My help cometh," not from the earth merely, or the skies, but "from the Lord, which made heaven and earth." Isa. xl. 26—31.—*G. R.*

Verse 3 (first clause).—The preservation of saintly character the care of the Creator.

Verse 3.—Comfort for a pilgrim along the *mauvais pas* of life. We have a Guide omniscient, omnipotent, unsleeping, unchanging.

Verse 3.—*"He that keepeth thee will not slumber."* I. The Lord's care is personal in its objects. The keeper of Israel is the keeper of the individual. God deals with us individually. 1. This is implied in his care of the church, which is composed of individuals. 2. It is involved in the nature of our religion, which is a personal thing. 3. It is affirmed in Scripture. Examples; promises; experiences. "He loved *me*," etc., etc. 4. It is confirmed by experience. II. The Lord's care is unwearied in its exercise: "Will not slumber." 1. He is never unacquainted with our condition. 2. He is never indifferent to it. 3. He is never weary of helping us. We sometimes think he sleeps, but this is our folly.—*Frederick J. Benskin,* 1882.

Verse 4.—I. The suspicion—that God sleeps. II. The denial. III. The implied opposite—he is ever on the watch to bless.

Verse 4.—He keepeth Israel, 1. As his chief treasure, most watchfully. 2. As his dearest spouse, most tenderly. 3. As the apple of his eye, most charily and warily.—*Daniel Featly,* 1582—1645.

Verse 5.—The Lord Keeper. I. Blessings included in this title. II. Necessities which demand it. III. Offices which imply it,—Shepherd, King, Husband, Father, etc. IV. Conduct suggested by it.

Verse 5 (*last clause*).—God as near us, and as indivisible from us as our shadow.

Verse 5.—"*The LORD is thy keeper,*" not angels. I. He is *able* to keep thee. He has infinite knowledge, power, etc. II. He has *engaged* to keep thee. III. He *has* kept thee. IV. He *will* keep thee. In his love; in his covenant, etc., as his sheep, his children, his treasures, as the apple of his eye, etc.—*F. J. B.*

Verse 5.—"*The LORD is thy keeper.*" I. Wakeful: "Will not slumber." II. Universal: "Thy going out and thy coming in:" "From all evil." III. Perpetual: "Day:" "night:" "evermore." IV. Special: "Thy:" "Israel."—*W. J.*

Verse 6.—The highest powers, under God, prevented from hurting believers, and even made to serve them.

Verse 6.—Our Horoscope. I. Superstitious fears removed. II. Sacred assurances supplied.

Verse 7.—I. Personal agency of God in providence. II. Personal regard of providence to the favoured individual. III. Special care over the centre of the personality—"thy soul."

Verse 8.—Who? "The Lord." What? "Shall preserve thee." When? "Going out and coming in from this time forth." How long? "For evermore." What then? "I will lift up mine eyes."

Verse 8.—I. Changing—going out and coming in. II. Unchanging—"The Lord shall preserve," etc.

PSALM CXXII.

TITLE AND SUBJECT.—*This brief but spirited Psalm is entitled "A Song of Degrees of David," and thus we are informed as to its author, and the occasion for which it was designed: David wrote it for the people to sing at the time of their goings up to the holy feasts at Jerusalem. It comes third in the series, and appears to be suitable to be sung when the people had entered the gates, and their feet stood within the city. It was most natural that they should sing of Jerusalem itself, and invoke peace and prosperity upon the Holy City, for it was the centre of their worship, and the place where the Lord revealed himself above the mercy-seat. Possibly the city was not all built in David's day, but he wrote under the spirit of prophecy, and spoke of it as it would be in the age of Solomon: a poet has license to speak of things, not only as they are, but as they will be when they come to their perfection. Jerusalem, or the Habitation of Peace, is used as the key-word of this Psalm, wherein we have in the original many happy allusions to the salem, or peace, which they implored upon Jerusalem. When they stood within the triple walls, all things around the pilgrims helped to explain the words which they sang within her ramparts of strength. One voice led the Psalm with its personal "I," but ten thousand brethren and companions united with the first musician and swelled the chorus of the strain.*

EXPOSITION.

I WAS glad when they said unto me, Let us go into the house of the LORD.

2 Our feet shall stand within thy gates, O Jerusalem.

3 Jerusalem is builded as a city that is compact together:

4 Whither the tribes go up, the tribes of the LORD, unto the testimony of Israel, to give thanks unto the name of the LORD.

5 For there are set thrones of judgment, the thrones of the house of David.

6 Pray for the peace of Jerusalem: they shall prosper that love thee.

7 Peace be within thy walls, *and* prosperity within thy palaces.

8 For my brethren and companions' sakes, I will now say, Peace *be* within thee.

9 Because of the house of the LORD our God I will seek thy good.

1. "*I was glad when they said unto me, Let us go into the house of the LORD.*" Good children are pleased to go home, and glad to hear their brothers and sisters call them thither. David's heart was in the worship of God, and he was delighted when he found others inviting him to go where his desires had already gone: it helps the ardour of the most ardent to hear others inviting them to a holy duty. The word was not "go," but "let us go"; hence the ear of the Psalmist found a double joy in it. He was glad *for the sake of others:* glad that they wished to go themselves, glad that they had the courage and liberality to invite others. He knew that it would do them good; nothing better can happen to men and their friends than to love the place where God's honour dwelleth. What a glorious day shall that be when many people shall go and say, "Come ye, and let us go up to the mountain of the Lord, to the house of the God of Jacob, and he will teach us of his ways, and we will walk in his paths." But David was glad *for his own sake:* he loved the invitation to the holy place, he delighted in being called to go to worship in company, and, moreover, he rejoiced that good people thought enough of him to extend their invitation to him. Some men would have been offended, and would have said, "Mind your own business. Let my religion alone;" but not so King David, though he had more dignity than any of us, and less need to be reminded of his duty. He was not teased but pleased by being pressed to attend holy services. He was glad to go into the house of the Lord, glad to go in holy company, glad

to find good men and women willing to have him in their society. He may have been sad before, but this happy suggestion cheered him up : he pricked up his ears, as the proverb puts it, at the very mention of his Father's house. Is it so with us ? Are we glad when others invite us to public worship, or to church fellowship ? Then we shall be glad when the spirits above shall call us to the house of the Lord not made with hands, eternal in the heavens.

> " Hark ! they whisper : angels say,
> Sister spirit, come away."

If we are glad to be called by others to our Father's house, how much more glad shall we be actually to go there. We love our Lord, and therefore we love his house, and pangs of strong desire are upon us that we may soon reach the eternal abode of his glory. An aged saint, when dying, cheered herself with this evidence of grace, for she cried, " I have loved the habitation of thine house, and the place where thine honour dwelleth," and therefore she begged that she might join the holy congregation of those who for ever behold the King in his beauty. Our gladness at the bare thought of being in God's house is detective as to our character, and prophetic of our being one day happy in the Father's house on high. What a sweet Sabbath Psalm is this ! In prospect of the Lord's day, and all its hallowed associations, our soul rejoices. How well, also, may it refer to the church ! We are happy when we see numerous bands ready to unite themselves with the people of God. The pastor is specially glad when many come forward and ask of him assistance in entering into fellowship with the church. No language is more cheering to him than the humble request, " Let us go into the house of the Lord."

2. *"Our feet shall stand within thy gates, O Jerusalem ;"* or, better, " our feet are standing." The words imply present and joyous standing within the walls of the city of peace ; or perhaps the pilgrims felt so sure of getting there that they antedated the joy, and spoke as if they were already there, though they were as yet only on the road. If we are within the church we may well triumph in the fact. While our feet are standing in Jerusalem our lips may well be singing. Outside the gates all is danger, and one day all will be destruction ; but within the gates all is safety, seclusion, serenity, salvation, and glory. The gates are opened that we may pass in, and they are only shut that our enemies may not follow us. The Lord loveth the gates of Zion, and so do we when we are enclosed within them. What a choice favour, to be a citizen of the New Jerusalem ! Why are *we* so greatly favoured ? Many feet are running the downward road, or kicking against the pricks, or held by snares, or sliding to an awful fall ; but our feet, through grace divine, are " standing "—an honourable posture, " within thy gates, O Jerusalem "—an honourable position, and there shall they stand for ever—an honourable future.

3. *"Jerusalem is builded as a city that is compact together."* David saw in vision the city built ; no more a waste, or a mere collection of tents, or a city upon paper, commenced but not completed. God's mercy to the Israelitish nation allowed of peace and plenty, sufficient for the uprise and perfecting of its capital : that city flourished in happy times, even as the church is only built up when all the people of God are prospering. Thanks be to God, Jerusalem is builded : the Lord by his glorious appearing has built up Zion. Furthermore, it is not erected as a set of booths, or a conglomeration of hovels, but as a city, substantial, architectural, designed, arranged, and defended. The church is a permanent and important institution, founded on a rock, builded with art, and arranged with wisdom. The city of God had this peculiarity about it, that it was not a long, straggling street, or a city of magnificent distances (as some mere skeleton places have been styled), but the allotted space was filled, the buildings were a solid block, a massive unity : this struck the dwellers in villages, and conveyed to them the idea of close neighbourhood, sure standing, and strong defence. No quarter could be surprised and sacked while other portions of the town were unaware of the assault : the ramparts surrounded every part of the metropolis, which was singularly one and indivisible. There was no flaw in this diamond of the world, this pearl of cities. In a church one of the most delightful conditions is the compactness of unity : " one Lord, one faith, one baptism." A church should be one in creed and one in heart, one in testimony and one in service, one in aspiration and one in sympathy. They greatly injure our Jerusalem who would build dividing walls within her ; she needs compacting, not dividing. There is no joy in going up to a church which is rent with internal dissension : the gladness of holy men is aroused by the adhesiveness

of love, the unity of life ; it would be their sadness if they saw the church to be a house divided against itself. Some bodies of Christians appear to be periodically blown to fragments, and no gracious man is glad to be in the way when the explosions take place : thither the tribes do not go up, for strife and contention are not attractive forces.

4. *"Whither the tribes go up, the tribes of the LORD."* When there is unity within there will be gatherings from without : the tribes go up to a compact centre. Note that Israel was one people, but yet it was in a sense surface divided by the mere surface distinction of tribes ; and this may be a lesson to us that all Christendom is essentially one, though from various causes we are divided into tribes. Let us as much as possible sink the tribal individuality in the national unity, so that the church may be many waves, but one sea ; many branches, but one tree ; many members, but one body. Observe that the tribes were all of them the Lord's ; whether Judah or Benjamin, Manasseh or Ephraim, they were all the Lord's. Oh that all the regiments of the Christian army may be all and equally the Lord's own, alike chosen, redeemed, accepted, and upheld by Jehovah. *"Unto the testimony of Israel."* They went up to the holy city to hear and to bear testimony. Everything in the temple was a testimony unto the Lord, and the annual journeys of the tribes to the hallowed shrine partook of the same testifying character, for these journeys were Israel's open avowal that Jehovah was their God, and that he was the one only living and true God. When we assemble on the Sabbath a large part of our business is giving out and receiving testimony : we are God's witnesses ; all the tribes of the one church of Jesus Christ bear witness unto the Lord. *"To give thanks unto the name of the LORD."* Another part of our delightful duty is to praise the Lord. Sacred praise is a chief design of the assembling of ourselves together. All Israel had been fed by the fruit of the field, and they went up to give thanks unto the name of their great Husbandman : we, too, have countless mercies, and it becomes us unitedly in our solemn gatherings to magnify the name of our loving Lord. Testimony should be mingled with thanks, and thanks with testimony, for in combination they bless both God and man, and tend to spread themselves over the hearts of our companions ; who, seeing our joyful gratitude, are the more inclined to hearken to our witness-bearing.

Here, then, was part of the cause of the gladness of the pious Israelite when he had an invitation to join the caravan which was going to Zion : he would there meet with representatives of all the clans of his nation, and aid them in the double object of their holy assemblies, namely, testimony and thanksgiving. The very anticipation of such delightful engagements filled him to overflowing with sacred gladness.

5. *"For there are set thrones of judgment."* If discontented with the petty judgments of their village lords, the people could bring their hard matters to the royal seat, and the beloved King would be sure to decide aright ; for the judgment-thrones were *"The thrones of the house of David."* We who come to the church and its public worship are charmed to come to the throne of God, and to the throne of the reigning Saviour.

> " He reigns ! Ye saints, exalt your strains :
> Your God is King, your Father reigns :
> And he is at the Father's side,
> The Man of love, the Crucified."

To a true saint the throne is never more amiable than in its judicial capacity : righteous men love judgment, and are glad that right will be rewarded and iniquity will be punished. To see God reigning in the Son of David and evermore avenging the just cause is a thing which is good for weeping eyes, and cheering for disconsolate hearts. They sang of old as they went towards the throne, and so do we. " The Lord reigneth, let the earth rejoice." The throne of judgment is not removed, but firmly *"set,"* and there it shall remain till the work of justice is accomplished, and truth and right are set on the throne with their King. Happy people to be under so glorious a rule.

6. *"Pray for the peace of Jerusalem."* Peace was her name, pray that her condition may verify her title. Abode of Peace, peace be to thee. Here was a most sufficient reason for rejoicing at the thought of going up to the house of the Lord, since that sacred shrine stood in the centre of an area of peace : well might Israel pray that such peace should be continued. In a church peace is to be desired,

expected, promoted, and enjoyed. If we may not say " Peace at any price," yet we may certainly cry " Peace at the highest price." Those who are daily fluttered by rude alarms are charmed to reach their nest in a holy fellowship, and abide in it. In a church one of the main ingredients of success is internal peace : strife, suspicion, party-spirit, division,—these are deadly things. Those who break the peace of the church deserve to suffer, and those who sustain it win a great blessing. Peace in the church should be our daily prayer, and in so praying we shall bring down peace upon ourselves ; for the Psalmist goes on to say, *"They shall prosper that love thee."* Whether the passage be regarded as a promise or as a prayer matters not, for prayer pleads the promise, and the promise is the ground of prayer. Prosperity of soul is already enjoyed by those who take a deep interest in the church and cause of God : they are men of peace, and find peace in their holy endeavours : God's people pray for them, and God himself delights in them. Prosperity of worldly condition often comes to the lovers of the church if they are able to bear it : many a time the house of Obed-edom is blessed because of the ark of the Lord. Because the Egyptian midwives feared the Lord, therefore the Lord made them houses. No man shall ever be a permanent loser by the house of the Lord : in peace of heart alone, if in nothing else, we find recompense enough for all that we can do in promoting the interests of Zion.

7. *"Peace be within thy walls."* See how the poet personifies the church, and speaks to it ; his heart is with Zion, and therefore his conversation runs in that direction. A second time is the sweet favour of peace earnestly sought after : " There is none like it, give it me." Walls were needed to keep out the foe, but it was asked of the Lord that those walls might prove sufficient for her security. May the munitions of rock so securely defend the city of God that no intruder may ever enter within her enclosure. May her ramparts repose in safety. Three walls environed her, and thus she had a trinity of security. *"And prosperity within thy palaces,"* or " Repose within thy palaces." Peace is prosperity ; there can be no prosperity which is not based on peace, nor can there long be peace if prosperity be gone, for decline of grace breeds decay of love. We wish for the church rest from internal dissension and external assault : war is not her element, but we read of old, " Then had the churches rest ; and walking in the fear of the Lord, and in the comfort of the Holy Ghost, were multiplied." The bird of Paradise is not a stormy petrel : her element is not the hurricane of debate, but the calm of communion.

Observe that our Jerusalem is a city of palaces : kings dwell within her walls, and God himself is there. The smallest church is worthy of higher honour than the greatest confederacies of nobles. The order of the New Jerusalem is of more repute in heaven than the knights of the Golden Fleece. For the sake of all the saintly spirits which inhabit the city of God we may well entreat for her the boons of lasting peace and abounding prosperity.

8. *"For my brethren and companions' sakes, I will now say, Peace be within thee."* It is to the advantage of all Israel that there should be peace in Jerusalem. It is for the good of every Christian, yea, of every man, that there should be peace and prosperity in the church. Here our humanity and our common philanthropy assist our religious prayer. By a flourishing church our children, our neighbours, our fellow-countrymen are likely to be blest. Moreover, we cannot but pray for a cause with which our dearest relatives and choicest friends are associated : if they labour for it, we must and will pray for it. Here peace is mentioned for the third time. Are not these frequent threes some hint of the Trinity ? It would be hard to believe that the triple form of so many parts of the Old Testament is merely accidental. At least, the repetition of the desire displays the writer's high valuation of the blessing mentioned ; he would not again and again have invoked peace had he not perceived its extreme desirableness.

9. *"Because of the house of the LORD our God I will seek thy good."* He prays for Jerusalem because of Zion. How the church salts and savours all around it. The presence of Jehovah, our God, endears to us every place wherein he reveals his glory. Well may we seek her good within whose walls there dwells God who alone is good. We are to live for God's cause, and to be ready to die for it. First we love it (verse 6) and then we labour for it, as in this passage : we see its good, and then seek its good. If we can do nothing else we can intercede for it. Our covenant relation to Jehovah as our God binds us to pray for his people,—they are " the house of the Lord our God." If we honour our God we desire the prosperity of the church which he has chosen for his indwelling.

Thus is the poet glad of an invitation to join with others in the Lord's service. He goes with them and rejoices, and then he turns his delight into devotion, and intercedes for the city of the great King. O church of the living God, we hail thine assemblies, and on bended knee we pray that thou mayest have peace and felicity. May our Jehovah so send it. Amen.

EXPLANATORY NOTES AND QUAINT SAYINGS.

Whole Psalm.—Foxe, in his "Acts and Monuments," relates of Wolfgang Schuch, the martyr, of Lothareng in Germany, that upon hearing the sentence that he was to be burned pronounced upon him, he began to sing the hundred and twenty-second Psalm, *Lætus sum in his quæ dicta sunt mihi,* etc.

Whole Psalm.—An introduction of two verses stands instead of a *Title,* announcing the object of the Psalm. The preceding Psalm was intended to be sung in sight of Jerusalem, and this one at the gates of the city, where the pilgrim train had halted for the purpose of arranging the solemn procession to the sanctuary.—*E. W. Hengstenberg.*

Verse 1.—"*I was glad when they said unto me,*" etc. Gregory Nazianzen writeth that his father being a heathen, and often besought by his wife to become a Christian, had this verse suggested unto him in a dream, and was much wrought upon thereby. —*John Trapp.*

Verse 1.—"*I was glad when they said,*" etc. These words seem to be very simple, and to contain in them no great matter ; but if you look into the same with spiritual eyes, there appeareth a wonderful great majesty in them ; which because our Papists cannot see, they do so coldly and negligently pray, read, and sing this Psalm and others, that a man would think there were no tale so foolish or vain, which they would not either recite or hear with more courage and delight. These words, therefore, must be unfolded and laid before the eyes of the faithful : for when he saith, "*We will go into the house of the Lord,*" what notable thing can we see in these words, if we only behold the stones, timber, gold, and other ornaments of the material temple ? But to go into the house of the Lord signifieth another manner of thing ; namely, to come together where we may have God present with us, hear his word, call upon his holy name, and receive help and succour in our necessity. Therefore it is a false definition of the temple which the Papists make ; that it is a house built with stones and timber to the honour of God. What this temple is they themselves know not ; for the temple of Solomon was not therefore beautiful because it was adorned with gold and silver, and other precious ornaments ; but the true beauty of the temple was, because in that place the people heard the word of the Lord, called upon his name, found him merciful, giving peace and remission of sins, etc. This is rightly to behold the temple, and not as the visored bishops behold their idolatrous temple when they consecrate it.—*Martin Luther.*

Verse 1.—"*I was glad when they said unto me, Let us (or, We will) go,*" etc. You have here, I. David's delight. II. The object or reason of it. I. In the object there are circumstances enough to raise his joy to the highest note. First, *A company,* either a tribe or many of, or all, the people : " They said unto me." So, in another place, he speaketh of " walking to the house of God in company : " Ps. lv. 14. A glorious sight, a representation of heaven itself, of all the angels crying aloud, the Seraphim to the Cherubim, and the Cherubim echoing back again to the Seraphim, " Holy, holy, holy, Lord God of Sabaoth." Secondly, *Their resolution* to serve the Lord : *Dixerunt,* " They said it : " and " to say " in Scripture is to resolve. " We will go," is either a lie, or a resolution. Thirdly, *Their agreement* and joint consent : " We." This is as a circle, and taketh in all within its compass. If there be any dissenting, unwilling person, he is not within this circumference, he is none of the " We." A Turk, a Jew, and a Christian cannot say, " We will serve the Lord ; " and the schismatic or separatist shutteth himself out of the house of the Lord. " We " is a bond of peace, keepeth us at unity, and maketh many as one. Fourthly, *Their cheerfulness* and alacrity. They speak like men going out of a dungeon into the light, as those who had been long absent from what they loved, and were now approaching unto it, and in fair hope to enjoy what they most earnestly desired : " We will go ; " we will make haste, and delay no longer. *Ipsa festinatio tarda est ;* " Speed itself is but slow paced." We cannot be there soon enough. Fifthly and lastly : *The place where they will serve God :* not one of their own choosing ; not the groves, or hills, or high places ; no oratory which pride, or malice, or faction had erected ; but a place appointed and set apart by God himself. *Servient Domino in domo suâ :* " They will serve the Lord in his own house." They said unto me, " We will go into the house of the Lord."—*Anthony Farindon.*

Verse 1.—*"Let us go into the house of the* Lord." *"Let us go,"* spoken by one hundred men in any city to those over whom they have influence, would raise a monster meeting. . . . But who among those who thus single out the working classes, have gone to them and said, " Let us go—let us go together into the house of the Lord " ? The religious adviser, standing at a distance from the multitude, has advised, and warned, and pleaded, saying " Go, or you will not escape perdition ; " " Why don't you go ? " The Christian visitor has likewise used this kind of influence ; but how few have taken the working man by the hand, and said, " Let us go together " ? You can *bring* multitudes whom you never can send. Many who would never come alone would come most willingly under the shadow of your company. Then, brethren, to your non-attending neighbours say, " Let us go"; to reluctant members of your own family say, " Let us go " ; to those who once went to the house of God in your company, but who have backslidden from worship say, " Let us go " ; to all whose ear, and mind, and heart, you can command for such a purpose say, " Let us go—let us go together into the house of the Lord."— *Samuel Martin (1817—1878), in a Sermon entitled " Gladness in the Prospect of Public Worship."*

Verse 1.—*"I was glad when they said unto me,"* etc. Such in kind, but far greater in degree, is the gladness, which the pious soul experiences when she is called hence ; when descending angels say unto her, Thy labour and sorrow are at an end, and the hour of thy enlargement is come ; put off immortality and misery at once ; quit thy house of bondage, and the land of thy captivity ; fly forth, and " let us go together into the house of the Lord, not made with hands, eternal in the heavens."—*George Horne.*

Verses 1, 2.—This is a mutual exhortation. The members of the church invite each other : " Let us go into the house of the Lord." It is not enough to say, Go you to church, and I shall stop at home. That will never do. We must invite by example as well as by precept. Mark the plural forms : " Let *us* go into the house of God. *Our* feet shall stand within thy gates, O Jerusalem." We are to speak as Moses did to Hobab, his brother-in-law, " Come thou with us, and we will do thee good ; for the Lord hath spoken good concerning Israel." The same duty is binding upon us, with regard to those who make no profession of religion, and whose feet never stand in the house of God. Zechariah, in an animated picture of the future glories of the church, describes the new-born zeal of the converts as taking this direction. They cannot but speak of what they have seen and heard, and others must share in their joy. " And the inhabitants of one city shall go to another, saying, Let us go speedily to pray before the Lord, and to seek the Lord of hosts : I will go also."—*N. M'Michael.*

Verse 2.—With what a blessed hope do they, while they are here in this mortal life, lift up their affections, desires, and thoughts to the heavenly country, because they are able to say with the prophet, *"Our feet stand within thy gates, O Jerusalem."* Like those who haste to any place, they are said to be always thinking as if they were already there, and in reality they are there in mind though not in body, and are able greatly to comfort others. What wonder, if a righteous man, wishing to comfort others, should thus speak, *"Our feet stand,"* i.e., our desires, our contemplations, shall be fixed and stable in thy courts, O Jerusalem ; i.e., in the mansions of the heavenly kingdom, so that our conversation shall be in heaven, and all our works be done in relation to eternal life, for which we long with greatest intensity of desire. This is not that Jerusalem which killed the prophets and stoned those that were sent unto her, but that where the perfect vision of peace reigns.—*Paulus Palanterius.*

Verse 2.—*"Our feet shall stand within thy gates, O Jerusalem."* Dr. Clarke, in his travels, speaking of the companies that were travelling from the East to Jerusalem, represents the procession as being very long, and, after climbing over the extended and heavy ranges of hills that bounded the way, some of the foremost at length reached the top of the last hill, and, stretching up their hands in gestures of joy, cried out, " The Holy City! The Holy City ! "—and fell down and worshipped ; while those who were behind pressed forward to see. So the dying Christian, when he gets on the last summit of life, and stretches his vision to catch a glimpse of the heavenly city, may cry out of its glories, and incite those who are behind to press forward to the sight.—*Edward Payson, 1783—1827.*

Verse 2.—*"O Jerusalem."* The celestial city is full in my view. Its glories beam upon me, its breezes fan me, its odours are wafted to me, its sounds strike upon my ears, and its spirit is breathed into my heart. Nothing separates me from it but the river of death, which now appears but as an insignificant rill, that may be crossed at a single step, whenever God shall give permission. The Sun of Righteousness has been gradually drawing nearer and nearer, appearing larger and brighter as he approached, and now he fills the whole hemisphere ; pouring forth a flood of glory, in which I seem to float like an insect in the beams of the sun ; exulting, yet almost trembling, while I gaze on this excessive brightness, and wondering, with unutterable wonder, why God should deign thus to shine upon a sinful worm.—*Edward Payson's dying experience.*

Verse 2.—*"O Jerusalem "*—

> Lo, towered Jerusalem salutes the eyes !
> A thousand pointing fingers tell the tale ;
> " Jerusalem ! " a thousand voices cry,
> " All hail, Jerusalem ! " hill, down, and dale
> Catch the glad sounds, and shout " Jerusalem, all hail."

Torquato Tasso, 1544—1595.

Verse 3.—*"Jerusalem is builded as a city that is compact together."* The deep depressions which secured the city must have always acted as its natural defence. But they also determined its natural boundaries. The city, wherever else it spread, could never overleap the valley of the Kedron or of Hinnom ; and those two fosses, so to speak, became accordingly, as in the analogous case of the ancient towns of Etruria, the Necropolis of Jerusalem. . . . The compression between these valleys probably occasioned the words of the Psalmist : *"Jerusalem is built as a city that is at unity in itself."* It is an expression not inapplicable even to the modern city, as seen from the east. But it was still more appropriate to the original city, if, as seems probable, the valley of Tyropœon formed in earlier times a fosse within a fosse, shutting in Zion and Moriah into one compact mass not more than half a mile in breadth.—*Arthur Penrhyn Stanley (1815—1881), in "Sinai and Palestine."*

Verse 3.—*"Jerusalem."* It matters not how wicked or degraded a place may have been in former times, when it is sanctified to the use and service of God it becomes honourable. Jerusalem was formerly Jebus—a place where the Jebusites committed their abominations, and where were all the miseries of those who hasten after another God. But now, since it is devoted to God's service, it is a city— *"compact together," "the joy of the whole earth."—William S. Plumer.*

Verse 3.—*"Compact."* Jerusalem was compactly built ; every rood of ground, every foot of frontage, was valuable ; house was joined to house ; those who had gardens had them beyond the city walls, among the " paradises " of the valley of Jehoshaphat.—*Samuel Cox.*

Verse 3.—*"Compact together."* Methinks Philadelphia, the name of one of the seven golden candlesticks (Rev. i.), is a very proper fitting name for a church, which signifies brotherly love ; and every congregation ought to be in a good sense the family of love. Breaches and divisions, distractions and heart-burnings, may happen in other kingdoms which are without God in the world and strangers to the covenant of grace ; yet let Jerusalem, the Church of God, be always like a city which is at unity within itself.—*John Pigot, 1643.*

Verse 3.—*"As a city that is compact together."* Can we say of the great universal church throughout the world, what the pilgrims said of Jerusalem when gazing on its splendour, from the surrounding hills, that it is built *"as a city that is compact together "* ? A stately capital, throned on a base of rock, its spacious streets and noble edifices, beautiful in themselves, deriving added splendour from the taste and regularity of their arrangement, appears, both to the scoffing unbeliever and grieving Christian, a singularly inappropriate emblem of the divided and distracted, the jarring and warring church. If the church may be compared to a city in respect of magnitude, it is one in which every one builds on his own plan ; in which the various masses which should embellish and support each other are studiously kept apart, suggesting less the idea of a compact and united capital than of detached and isolated forts, held by persons who keep themselves jealously aloof from each other, save when mutual hatred and heart-burnings bring them together for conflict. There is some truth in the picture ; alas ! for the proud, foolish builders who give occasion to it, and who, instead of praying for and seeking the peace of Jerusalem, rejoice in exhibiting, perpetuating, and fomenting strife ! But, blessed be God, there is yet more of falsehood than truth in it. With all our divisions the Christian Jerusalem *is compact in itself together.* What occupies the hearts and tongues of the myriads of worshippers that assemble themselves weekly in the sanctuaries of our beloved land, and of the millions that assemble beyond the Atlantic billows, but the one glorious gospel of the grace of God ? Leave out from the computation the priest with his mass-book, the cold Socinian without his Saviour, and the deluded orthodox professor who holds the truth in unrighteousness ; still yonder and yonder and yonder, whatever their name, their place, or their outward worship, are myriads of true hearts, beating with one pulse, gazing on one hope, possessed of one conviction, and praying and pressing forward to one blessed home.—*Robert Nisbet.*

Verses 3, 4.—He commendeth Jerusalem, the figure of the church of God and of the corporation of his people. First, as a city for a community. Secondly, as the place of God's public assemblies for religious worship. Thirdly, as the place of public judicature, for governing the Lord's people under David, the type of Christ. Whence learn, 1. The church of God is not without cause compared to a city, and especially to Jerusalem, because of the union, concord, community of laws, mutual commodities, and conjunction of strength which should be among God's people : *"Jerusalem is builded as a city that is compact together."* 2. That which commendeth a place most of anything is the erecting of the Lord's banner of love in it, and making it a place for his people to meet together for his worship : *"Jerusalem is a city whither the tribes go up."* 3. Whatsoever civil distinction God's children have among themselves, and howsoever they dwell scattered in several places of the earth, yet as they are the Lord's people, they should entertain a communion and conjunction among themselves as members of one universal church, as the signification of the peoples meeting thrice in the year at Jerusalem did reach : *"Whither the tribes did go up, the tribes of the Lord."* 4. As the tribes, so all particular churches, how far soever scattered, have one Lord, one covenant, one law and Scripture, signified by the tribes going up to *" the testimony of Israel,"* or to the Ark of the Covenant or testimony where the whole ordinances of God were to be exercised. 5. The end of the ordinances of God, of holy covenanting and communion, and joining in public worship, is to acknowledge the grace and goodness of God, and to glorify him ; for the tribes did go up *" to give thanks unto the name of the Lord."*—*David Dickson.*

Verse 4.—*"The tribes "* are " the tribes of the Lord," as being the keepers of his commandments.—*H. T. Armfield.*

Verse 4.—*"Unto the testimony of Israel, and to give thanks unto the name of the Lord."* These two mean nothing else than that in Jerusalem was the appointed place where the word was to be taught and prayer offered. But these ought to be written in golden letters, because David says nothing about the other services, but only of these two. He does not say that the Temple was divinely appointed, that there the victims should be sacrificed ; that there incense should be offered ; that oblations and sacrifices should be brought ; that each one should by his gifts show his gratitude. He says nothing about these things, although only in the Temple were they commanded to be done. He makes mention only of prayer and of thanksgiving.—*Martin Luther.*

Verse 4.—*"The testimony of Israel."* The object which is represented in the Psalm as having power to attract all hearts, and command the ready attendance of the tribes, is *" the testimony of Israel,"* the revelation, in other words, which God made to that people of his character, feelings, and purposes, as most holy, yet ready to forgive, a just God and the Saviour. This discovery of the nature of that great Being before whom all must appear, is justly regarded as a ground of joy.—*Robert Nisbet.*

Verses 4, 5.—Observe what a goodly sight it was to see *" the testimony of Israel "* and the "*tnrones of judgment*" such near neighbours ; and they are good neighbours, which may greatly befriend one another. Let "*the testimony of Israel*" direct the "*thrones of judgment*," and the "*thrones of judgment*" protect "*the testimony of Israel.*" —*Matthew Henry.*

Verse 5.—"*Thrones of judgment.*" On a throne of ivory, brought from Africa or India, the throne of many an Arabian legend, the kings of Judah were solemnly seated on the day of their accession. From its lofty seat, and under that high gateway, Solomon and his successors after him delivered their solemn judgments. That " porch " or " gate of justice," still kept alive the likeness of the old patriarchal custom of sitting in judgment at the gate ; exactly as the Gate of Justice still recalls it to us at Granada, and the Sublime Porte—" the Lofty Gate " at Constantinople. He sate on the back of a golden bull, its head turned over its shoulder, probably the ox or bull of Ephraim ; under his feet, on each side of the steps, were six golden lions, probably the lions of Judah. This was " the seat of judgment." This was the throne of the house of David.—*Arthur Penrhyn Stanley, in "Lectures on the History of the Jewish Church."*

Verse 5.—It was a worthy commendation that David uttered in the praise of Jerusalem when he said, "*There is the seat for judgment ;*" the which appointing of that seat for judgment was an argument that they loved justice. And first, the place wherein it was set assureth us hereof, for it was set in the gate, where-through men might have passage to and from the judgment seat. Secondly, the manner of framing the seat in the gate, namely, that the judges of force must sit with their faces towards the rising of the sun, in token that then judgment should be as pure from corruption, as the sun was clear in his chiefest brightness. Oh happy house of David, whose seat was set so conveniently, whose causes were heard so carefully, and matters judged so justly !—*Henry Smith, 1560—1591.*

Verse 6.—"*Pray for the peace of Jerusalem.*" By praying for Jerusalem's peace is meant such serene times wherein the people of God might enjoy his pure worship without disturbance. The Church has always had her vicissitudes, sometimes fair, and sometimes foul weather ; but her winter commonly longer than her summer ; yea, at the same time that the Sun of peace brings day to one part of it, another is wrapped up in the night of persecution. Universal peace over all the churches is a great rarity.—*William Gurnall.*

Verse 6.—"*Pray for the peace of Jerusalem.*" When the Wesleyan Methodists opened a chapel at Painswick, near his own meeting, the late excellent Cornelius Winter prayed three times publicly the preceding Sabbath for their encouragement and success. When Mr. Hoskins, of Bristol, the Independent minister of Castle-green, opened a meeting in Temple Street ; what did the incomparable Easterbrooke, the Vicar of the parish ? The morning it was opened, he was almost the first that entered it. He seated himself near the pulpit. When the service was over, he met the preacher at the foot of the stairs, and shaking him with both hands, said aloud : " I thank you cordially, my dear brother, for coming to my help—here is room enough for us both ; and work enough for us both ; and much more than we can both accomplish : and I hope the Lord will bless our co-operation in this good cause."—*William Jay.*

Verse 6.—"*Pray* (with this princely prophet) *for the peace of Jerusalem.*" I wish I could express the incomparable sweetness of this little *hemistichium.* I guess, the Holy Ghost was pleased to let the Psalmist play the poet here : the Psalms are holy poetry. The original words have such elegancy here, as (I think) all the Scripture cannot parallel this verse. It is in English unexpressible. For the point in hand only, he bids us pray for the peace of *Jerusalem. Peace* denominates *Jerusalem,* 'tis the etymon of the word, it means *the vision of peace.* David by that term most sweetly alludes to the name of the city, yet conceals his wit ; which could have been made more open : he said, שַׁאֲלוּ שְׁלוֹם, "*Pray for the peace of Salem.*" For so it was called too, called first so, called still so (Ps. lxxvi.) : " At Salem is his tabernacle." That word merely sounds *peace :* God would have his Church the house of peace ; and his temple there David might not build because he was a man of war ; but Solomon his son, who had his name of peace, must build it. Christ, whose the church is, she his spouse, would not be born in Julius Cæsar's reign ; he was a warrior too : but in Augustus's days, who reigned in peace. And this may be a reason too,

If you please, why David bids pray but for peace only, an earthly blessing. That word most fitted his art here, and sounded best. But under that word, by poetical *synecdoche*, lie couched all heavenly blessings.—*Richard Clerke*, 1634.

Verse 6.—*"Pray,"* etc. Our praying for the church giveth us a share in all the church's prayers ; we have a venture in every ship of prayer that maketh a voyage for heaven, if our hearts be willing to pray for the church ; and if not, we have no share in it.

Let no man flatter himself : they that *pray not* for the church of God *love not* the church of God. *"Let them prosper that love thee"*; that is, that *pray* for thee, the one is the counterpart of the other. If we do not love it, we will not pray for it ; and if we do not pray for it, we do not love it. Yea, if we pray not for the church, *we lose* our share in the prayers of the church. You will say that man hath a great estate that hath a part in every ship at sea ; and yet to have an adventure in all the prayers that are made to heaven is better than all the world. All the church's prayers are for all the living members of it, viz.—the blessings will be to them, for a man to have a venture in every ship of prayer of all the churches throughout all the world. I would not (for my part) leave my share in it for all the world ; and that man hath no share in it that will not afford a prayer for the church.—*John Stoughton*, 1640.

Verse 6.—*"They shall prosper that love thee."* The word *"prosper"* conveys an idea which is not in the original. The Hebrew word means *to be secure, tranquil, at rest,* spoken especially of one who enjoys quiet prosperity : Job iii. 26 ; xii. 6. The essential idea is that of quietness or rest ; and the meaning here is, that those who love Zion *will* have peace ; or, that the tendency of that love is to produce peace. See Rom. v. 1. The prayer was for " peace " ; the thought in connexion with that was naturally that those who loved Zion *would* have peace. It is indeed true, in general, that they who love Zion, or who serve God, *will* " prosper " ; but that is not the truth taught here. The idea is that they will have *peace :*—peace with God ; peace in their own consciences ; peace in the prospect of death and of the future world ; peace amidst the storms and tempests of life ; peace in death, in the grave, and for ever.—*Albert Barnes.*

Verse 6.—*"They shall prosper that love thee."* Seeing they prosper that love and bear affection to Jerusalem, let men learn to show good will unto Christ's church, though as yet they be no ripe scholars themselves in Christ's school : though they be not grown to perfection let them express a good affection. A good will and inclination, where strength yet faileth, is accepted, and a ready disposition is not rejected : though thou be not yet of the saints, yet love the saints. If thou likest and lovest that thou wouldst be, thou must be that hereafter which yet thou art not. The little bird before she flieth fluttereth with her wings in the nest : the child creepeth before he goeth : so religion beginneth with affection, and devotion proceedeth from desire. A man must first love that he would be, before he can be that which he loveth. It is a good sign when a man affecteth that which he expecteth, and doth favour that which he would more fully favour. He that loveth Sion shall prosper : he that loveth virtue shall increase and prosper in it. The day of small things shall not be despised (Zech. iv. 10), neither shall the smoking flax be quenched (Matt. xii. 20) ; but the smoke shall bring forth fire, and fire shall break forth into a flame.—*Andrew Willett* (1562—1621), *in "Certaine Fruitfull Meditations upon the 122. Psalme."*

Verse 6.—*"They shall prosper that love thee."* The reverse is also true. " None ever took a stone out of the Temple, but the dust did fly into his eyes."—*Jewish Proverb.*

Verses 6—9.—In this cordial and even impassioned invocation, it is curious to find one of those puns, or plays on words, which are characteristic of Hebrew poetry. The leading words of the strophe are *"peace"* and *"prosperity."* Now the Hebrew word for *"peace"* is shâlôm, and the Hebrew word for *"prosperity"* is shalvah, while the Hebrew form of " Jerusalem," which means " City of Peace," is Yeru-*shalaim.* So that, in effect, the poet wishes shâlôm and shalvah on shalaim—" peace " and " prosperity " on " the City of Peace." Such an use of words may not strike us as indicating any very subtle or profound sense of humour, or any remarkable artistic skill. But we must always remember that it is always difficult for one race to appreciate the humour, or wit, of another race. We must also remember that this art of playing on words and the sound of words—an art of which we are growing weary—was very novel and surprising to men not surfeited with it as we are, and who were themselves for the most part quite incapable of the simplest dexterities of speech.—*Samuel Cox*

Verse 7.—*"Peace be within thy walls."* The Church is a war-town, and a walled-town, which is situated among enemies, and may not trust them who are without, but must be upon its keeping, as the type thereof, Jerusalem, with her walls and towers, did shadow forth.—*David Dickson.*

Verse 7.—*"Within thy walls."* Or, *To thy outward wall.* Josephus tells us (Book V.) that there were at Jerusalem three ranges or rows of walls. The sense here is, Let no enemy approach so much as to thy out-works to disturb thee.—*Thomas Fenton.*

Verse 8.—*"For my brethren and companions' sakes."* Because they dwell there or, because they go up there to worship ; or, because they love thee, and find their happiness in thee ; or, because they are unconverted, and all my hope of their salvation is to be derived from thee,—from the church, from the influence of religion.—*Albert Barnes.*

Verse 8.—*"My brethren."* On another occasion, an elderly native, formerly a cannibal, addressing the Church members, said, " Brethren ! " and, pausing for a moment, continued, " Ah ! that is a new name ; we did not know the true meaning of that word in our heathenism. It is the ' Evangelia a Jesu ' that has taught us the meaning of ' brethren.' "—*William Gill, in "Gems from the Coral Islands,"* 1869.

Verse 9.—*"Because of the house of the Lord."* The city that was the scene of so immense assemblies had necessarily a peculiar character of its own. It existed for them, it lived by them. There were priests needed for the conduct of the worship, twenty-four courses of them and 20,000 men. There were Levites, their servants, in immense numbers, needed to watch, maintain, clean the temple—to do the menial and ministering work necessary to its elaborate service and stupendous acts of worship. There were scribes needed for the interpretation of the law, men skilled in the Scriptures and tradition, with names like Gamaliel, so famed for wisdom as to draw young men like Saul from distant Tarsus, or Apollos from rich Alexandria. There were synagogues, 480 of them at least, where the rabbis read and the people heard the word which God had in past times spoken unto the fathers by the prophets. The city was indeed in a sense the religion of Israel, incorporated and localized, and the man who loved the one turned daily his face toward the other, saying, " My soul longeth, yea, even fainteth for the courts of Jahveh."—*A. M. Fairbairn, in "Studies in the Life of Christ,"* 1881.

Verse 9.—*"I will seek thy good."* It is not a cold wish ; it is not a careless, loose seeking after it, that is the phrase in my text—*"I will seek thy good."* It is not a careless, loose seeking after it, almost as indifferently as a woman seeks after a pin which she has dropped ; no, no ; effort is implied. *"I will seek"*; I will throw my energies into it ; my powers, my faculties, my property, my time, my influence, my connections, my family, my house, all that I have under my command shall, as far as I have power to command, and as far as God gives me ability to turn them to such a use, be employed in an effort to promote the interests of Zion.—*Joseph Irons,* 1786—1852.

HINTS TO PREACHERS.

Whole Psalm.—Observe, I. The joy with which they were to go up to Jerusalem : verses 1, 2. II. The great esteem they were to have of Jerusalem : verses 3—5. III. The great concern they were to have for Jerusalem, and the prayers they were to put up for its welfare.—*M. Henry.*

Verse 1.—I. David was glad to go to the house of the Lord. It was the house of the Lord, therefore he desired to go. He preferred it to his own house. II. He was glad when others said to him, " Let us go." The distance may be great, the weather may be rough, still, " Let us go." III. He was glad to say it to others, " Let us go," and to persuade others to accompany him.—*G. R.*

Verse 1.—I. Joy in prospect of religious worship. 1. Because of the instruction we receive. 2. Because of the exercises in which we engage. 3. Because of the society in which we mingle. 4. Because of the sacred interests we promote. II. Joy in the invitation to religious worship. 1. Because it shows others are interested in the service of God. 2. Because it shows their interest in us. 3. Because it furthers the interests of Zion.—*F. J. B.*

Verse 1.—Gladness of God's house. Are you " glad when," etc. ? Why glad ? I. That I have a house of the Lord to which I may go. II. That any feel enough interest in me to say, " Let us go," etc. III. That I am able to go to God's house. IV. That I am disposed to go.—*J. G. Butler, in "The Preacher's Monthly,"* 1882.

Verse 1.—"*I was glad,*" etc. So says, I. *The devout worshipper,* who is glad to be invited *to God's earthly house.* It is his home, his school, his hospital, his bank. II. *The adhesive Christian, who is glad to be invited to God's spiritual house.* Church is builded together, etc. There would he find a settled rest. Has no sympathies with religious gipsies, or no-church people. III. *The dying saint, who is glad to be invited to God's heavenly house.* Simeon—Stephen—Peter—Paul.—*W. J.*

Verse 1.—1. The duty of attending the services of God's house. 2. The duty of exciting one another to go. 3. The benefit of being thus excited.—*F. J. B.*

Verse 2. — Here is, I. Personal attendance : "*My* feet shall stand," etc. II. Personal security : " My feet shall *stand.*" III. Personal fellowship : " O Jerusalem."—*G. R.*

Verse 2.—The inside of the church. The honour, privilege, joy, and fellowship of standing there.

Verse 3. — I. A type of the New Jerusalem. 1. As chosen by God. 2. As founded upon a rock. 3. As taken from an enemy. II. A type of its prosperity : " Builded as a city." III. A type of its perfection : " Compact together."—*G. R.*

Verse 3.—The unity of the church. 1. Implied in all covenant dealings. 2. Suggested by all Scriptural metaphors. 3. Prayed for by our Lord. 4. Promoted by the gifts of the Spirit. 5. To be maintained by us all.

Verses 3, 4.—The united church the growing church.

Verse 4.—I. The duty of public worship. 1. In one place : "*Whither* the tribes go up." 2. In one company, though of many tribes : " Whither the *tribes* go up." II. The design. 1. For instruction : " Unto the testimony of Israel." 2. For praise : " To give thanks unto the name of the Lord."—*G. R.*

Verse 5.—I There are thrones of judgment in the sanctuary. Men are judged there. 1. By the law. 2. By their own consciences. 3. By the gospel. II. There are thrones of grace : " Of the house of David." 1. Of David's Son in the hearts of his people. 2. Of his people in David's Son.—*G. R.*

Verse 6.—I. The prayer. 1. " For Jerusalem : " not for ourselves merely, or for the world ; but for the church. For the babes in grace ; for the young men, and for the fathers. For the pastors, with the deacons and elders. 2. For the " peace " of Jerusalem. Inward peace and outward peace. II. The promise. 1. To whom given : " They that love thee." 2. The promise itself : " They shall prosper "—individually and collectively. Or, I. Love to Jerusalem is the effect of true piety. II. Prayer for Jerusalem is the effect of that love. III. The peace of Jerusalem is the effect of that prayer ; and, IV. The prosperity of Jerusalem is the effect of that peace.—*G. R.*

Verse 6.—God has connected giving and receiving, scattering and increasing, sowing and reaping, praying and prospering. I. What we must do if we would prosper—" Pray for the peace of Jerusalem." 1. Comprehensively : " Peace "— spiritual, social, ecclesiastical, national. 2. Supremely : " Prefer Jerusalem above," etc. 3. Practically : " Let peace rule in your hearts." " Seek peace and pursue it." II. What we shall gain if we pray thus—" Prosperity." 1. Temporal prosperity may thus come. God turned again the captivity of Job when he prayed for his friends. 2. Spiritual prosperity shall thus come. Affairs of soul—holy exercises and services. 3. Numerical prosperity will thus come. " Increased with men as a flock."—*W. J.*

Verses 6—9.—I. The blessings desired for the church. 1. Peace. 2. Prosperity. Notice the order and connection of these two. II. The way to secure them. 1. Prayer : " Pray for the peace of Jerusalem." 2. Delight in the service of God : " I was glad," etc. 3. Practical effort : " I will seek thy good." III. Reasons for seeking them. 1. For our own sake : " They shall prosper," etc. 2. For our " companions' " sake. 3. For the sake of the " house of the Lord."—*F. J. B.*

Verse 7.—I. Where peace is most desirable : "Within thy walls." Within town walls, within house walls, but principally within temple walls. II. Where prosperity is most desirable. 1. In the closet. 2. In the church. These are the palaces of the Great King ; "The ivory palaces whereby they have made thee glad."—*G. R.*

Verse 7.—The connection between peace and prosperity.

Verse 7.—"*Thy walls.*" 1. Enquire why the church needs walls. 2. Enquire what are the walls of a church. 3. Enquire on which side of them we are.

Verse 7.—The church a palace. 1. Intended for the great King. 2. Inhabited by the royal family. 3. Adorned with regal splendour. 4. Guarded by special power. 5. Known as the court of the blessed and only potentate.

Verses 8, 9.—Two great principles are here laid down why we should pray for the church,—I. Love to the brethren : " For my brethren and companions' sakes." II. Love to God : " Because of the house of the Lord our God I will seek thy good."— *N. M'Michael.*

Verse 9.—"*I will seek thy good.*" 1. By prayer for the church. 2. By service in the church. 3. By bringing others to attend. 4. By keeping the peace. 5. By living so as to commend religion.

PSALM CXXIII.

TITLE.—A Song of degrees. *We are climbing.* *The first step (Ps. cxx.) saw us lamenting our troublesome surroundings, and the next saw us lifting our eyes to the hills and resting in assured security; from this we rose to delight in the house of the Lord; but here we look to the Lord himself, and this is the highest ascent of all by many degrees. The eyes are now looking above the hills, and above Jehovah's footstool on earth, to his throne in the heavens.* Let us know it as " the Psalm of the eyes." *Old authors call it Oculus Sperans, or the eye of hope. It is a short Psalm, written with singular art, containing one thought, and expressing it in a most engaging manner. Doubtless it would be a favourite song among the people of God. It has been conjectured that this brief song, or rather sigh, may have first been heard in the days of Nehemiah, or under the persecutions of Antiochus. It may be so, but there is no evidence of it; it seems to us quite as probable that afflicted ones in all periods after David's time found this Psalm ready to their hand. If it appears to describe days remote from David, it is all the more evident that the Psalmist was also a prophet, and sang what he saw in vision.*

UNTO thee will I lift up mine eyes, O thou that dwellest in the heavens.

2 Behold, as the eyes of servants *look* unto the hand of their masters, *and* as the eyes of a maiden unto the hand of her mistress; so our eyes *wait* upon the LORD our God, until that he have mercy upon us.

3 Have mercy upon us, O LORD, have mercy upon us: for we are exceedingly filled with contempt.

4 Our soul is exceedingly filled with the scorning of those that are at ease, *and* with the contempt of the proud.

EXPOSITION.

1. *"Unto thee lift I up mine eyes."* It is good to have some one to look up to. The Psalmist looked so high that he could look no higher. Not to the hills, but to the God of the hills he looked. He believed in a personal God, and knew nothing of that modern pantheism which is nothing more than atheism wearing a figleaf. The uplifted eyes naturally and instinctively represent the state of heart which fixes desire, hope, confidence, and expectation upon the Lord. God is everywhere, and yet it is most natural to think of him as being above us, in that glory-land which lies beyond the skies. *"O thou that dwellest in the heavens,"* just sets forth the unsophisticated idea of a child of God in distress; God is, God is in heaven, God resides in one place, and God is evermore the same, therefore will I look to him. When we cannot look to any helper on a level with us it is greatly wise to look above us; in fact, if we have a thousand helpers, our eyes should still be toward the Lord. The higher the Lord is the better for our faith, since that height represents power, glory, and excellence, and these will be all engaged on our behalf. We ought to be very thankful for spiritual eyes; the blind men of this world, however much of human learning they may possess, cannot behold our God, for in heavenly matters they are devoid of sight. Yet we must use our eyes with resolution, for they will not go upward to the Lord of themselves, but they incline to look downward, or inward, or anywhere but to the Lord: let it be our firm resolve that the heavenward glance shall not be lacking. If we cannot see God, at least we will look towards him. God is in heaven as a king in his palace; he is there revealed, adored, and glorified: thence he looks down on the world and sends succours to his saints as their needs demand; hence we look up, even when our sorrow is so great that we can do **no**

more. It is a blessed condescension on God's part that he permits us to lift up our eyes to his glorious high throne ; yea, more, that he invites and even commands us so to do. When we are looking to the Lord in hope, it is well to tell him so in prayer : the Psalmist uses his voice as well as his eye. We need not speak in prayer : a glance of the eye will do it all ; for—

> " Prayer is the burden of a sigh,
> The falling of a tear,
> The upward glancing of an eye
> When none but God is near."

Still, it is helpful to the heart to use the tongue, and we do well to address ourselves in words and sentences to the God who heareth his people. It is no small joy that our God is always at home : he is not on a journey, like Baal, but he dwells in the heavens. Let us think no hour of the day inopportune for waiting upon the Lord ; no watch of the night too dark for us to look to him.

2. *"Behold"*—for it is worthy of regard among men, and O that the Majesty of heaven would also note it, and speedily send the mercy which our waiting spirits seek. See, O Lord, how we look to thee, and in thy mercy look on us. This *Behold* has, however, a call to us to observe and consider. Whenever saints of God have waited upon the Lord their example has been worthy of earnest consideration. Sanctification is a miracle of grace ; therefore let us behold it. For God to have wrought in men the spirit of service is a great marvel, and as such let all men turn aside and see this great sight. *"As the eyes of servants* (or slaves) *look unto the hand of their masters."* They stand at the end of the room with their hands folded watching their lord's movements. Orientals speak less than we do, and prefer to direct their slaves by movements of their hands ; hence, the domestic must fix his eyes on his master, or he might miss a sign, and so fail to obey it : even so, the sanctified man lifts his eyes unto God, and endeavours to learn the divine will from every one of the signs which the Lord is pleased to use. Creation, providence, grace ; these are all motions of Jehovah's hand, and from each of them a portion of our duty is to be learned ; therefore should we carefully study them, to discover the divine will. *"And as the eyes of a maiden unto the hand of her mistress ; "* this second comparison may be used because Eastern women are even more thorough than the men in the training of their servants. It is usually thought that women issue more commands, and are more sensitive of disobedience, than the sterner sex. Among the Roman matrons female slaves had a sorry time of it, and no doubt it was the same among the generality of Eastern ladies. *"Even so our eyes wait upon the LORD our God."* Believers desire to be attentive to each and all of the directions of the Lord ; even those which concern apparently little things are not little to us, for we know that even for idle words we shall be called to account, and we are anxious to give in that account with joy, and not with grief. True saints, like obedient servants, look to the Lord their God *reverentially :* they have a holy awe and inward fear of the great and glorious One. They watch, *obediently,* doing his commandments, guided by his eye. Their constant gaze is fixed *attentively* on all that comes from the Most High ; they give earnest heed, and fear lest they should let anything slip through inadvertence or drowsiness. They look *continuously,* for there never is a time when they are off duty ; at all times they delight to serve in all things. Upon the Lord they fix their eyes *expectantly,* looking for supply, succour, and safety from his hands, waiting that he may have mercy upon them. To him they look *singly,* they have no other confidence, and they learn to look *submissively,* waiting patiently for the Lord, seeking both in activity and suffering to glorify his name. When they are smitten with the rod they turn their eyes *imploringly* to the hand which chastens, hoping that mercy will soon abate the rigour of the affliction. There is much more in the figure than we can display in this brief comment ; perhaps it will be most profitable to suggest the question—Are we thus trained to service ? Though we are sons, have we learned the full obedience of servants ? Have we surrendered self, and bowed our will before the heavenly Majesty ? Do we desire in all things to be at the Lord's disposal ? If so, happy are we. Though we are made joint-heirs with Christ, yet for the present we differ little from servants, and may be well content to take them for our model.

Observe the covenant name, *"Jehovah our God" :* it is sweet to wait upon a covenant God. Because of that covenant he will show mercy to us ; but we may have to wait for it. *"Until that he have mercy upon us : "* God hath his time and

season, and we must wait *until* it cometh.   For the trial of our faith our blessed
Lord may for awhile delay, but in the end the vision will be fulfilled.   Mercy is that
which we need, that which we look for, that which our Lord will manifest to us.
Even those who look to the Lord, with that holy look which is here described, still
need mercy, and as they cannot claim it by right they wait for it till sovereign grace
chooses to vouchsafe it.   Blessed are those servants whom their Master shall find
so doing.   Waiting upon the Lord is a posture suitable both for earth and heaven :
it is, indeed, in every place the right and fitting condition for a servant of the Lord.
Nor may we leave the posture so long as we are by grace dwellers in the realm of
mercy.   It is a great mercy to be enabled to wait for mercy.

3. *"Have mercy upon us, O Lord, have mercy upon us."*   He hangs upon the
word " mercy," and embodies it in a vehement prayer :   the very word seems to
hold him, and he harps upon it.   It is well for us to pray about everything, and turn
everything into prayer ;   and especially when we are reminded of a great necessity
we should catch at it as a keynote, and pitch our tune to it.   The reduplication of
the prayer before us is meant to express the eagerness of the Psalmist's spirit and
his urgent need :   what he needed speedily he begs for importunately.   Note that
he has left the first person singular for the plural.   All the saints need mercy ; they
all seek it ;   they shall all have it, therefore we pray—" have mercy upon *us*."   A
slave when corrected looks to his master's hand that the punishment may cease,
and even so we look to the Lord for mercy, and entreat for it with all our hearts.   Our
contemptuous opponents will have no mercy upon us ;   let us not ask it at their
hands, but turn to the God of mercy, and seek his aid alone.

"For we are exceedingly filled with contempt," and this is an acid which eats into
the soul.   Observe the emphatic words.   *Contempt* is bitterness, wormwood mingled
with gall ;   he that feels it may well cry for mercy to his God.   *Filled* with contempt,
as if the bitter wine had been poured in till it was up to the brim.   This had become
the chief thought of their minds, the peculiar sorrow of their hearts.   Excluding all
other feelings, a sense of scorn monopolized the soul and made it unutterably wretched.
Another word is added adverbially—*exceedingly* filled.   Filled even to running over,
as if pressed down and then heaped up.   A little contempt they could bear, but
now they were satiated with it, and weary of it.   Do we wonder at the threefold
mention of mercy when this master evil was in the ascendant ?   Nothing is more
wounding, embittering, festering than disdain.   When our companions make little
of us we are far too apt to make little of ourselves and of the consolations prepared
for us.   Oh to be filled with communion, and then contempt will run off from us,
and never be able to fill us with its biting vinegar.

4. *"Our soul is exceedingly filled with the scorning of those that are at ease."*   Knowing
no troubles of their own, the easy ones grow cruel and deride the people of the Lord.
Having the godly already in secret contempt, they show it by openly scorning them.
Note those who do this :   they are not the poor, the humble, the troubled, but those
who have a merry life of it. and are self-content.   They are in easy circumstances ;
they are easy in heart through a deadened conscience and so they easily come to
mock at holiness ;   they are easy from needing nothing, and from having no severe
toil exacted from them ;   they are easy as to any anxiety to improve, for their conceit
of themselves is boundless.   Such men take things easily, and therefore they scorn the
holy carefulness of those who watch the hand of the Lord.   They say, Who is the
Lord that we should obey his voice ?   and then they turn round with a contemptuous
look and sneer at those who fear the Lord.   Woe unto them that are at ease in
Zion ;   their contempt of the godly shall hasten and increase their misery.   The
injurious effect of freedom from affliction is singularly evident here.   Place a man
perfectly at ease and he derides the suffering godly, and becomes himself proud in
heart and conduct.   *"And with the contempt of the proud."*   The proud think so
much of themselves that they must needs think all the less of those who are better
than themselves.   Pride is both contemptible and contemptuous.   The contempt
of the great ones of the earth is often peculiarly acrid :   some of them, like a well-
known statesman, are " masters of gibes and flouts and sneers," and never do they
seem so much at home in their acrimony as when a servant of the Lord is the victim
of their venom.   It is easy enough to write upon this subject, but to be selected as
the target of contempt is quite another matter.   Great hearts have been broken
and brave spirits have been withered beneath the accursed power of falsehood, and
the horrible blight of contempt.   For our comfort we may remember that our divine
Lord was despised and rejected of men, yet he ceased not from his perfect service

till he was exalted to dwell in the heavens. Let us bear our share of this evil which still rages under the sun, and let us firmly believe that the contempt of the ungodly shall turn to our honour in the world to come : even now it serves as a certificate that we are not of the world, for if we were of the world the world would love us as its own.

EXPLANATORY NOTES AND QUAINT SAYINGS.

Whole Psalm.—This Psalm (as ye see) is but short, and therefore a very fit example to show the force of prayer not to consist in many words, but in fervency of spirit. For great and weighty matters may be comprised in a few words, if they proceed from the spirit and the unspeakable groanings of the heart, especially when our necessity is such as will not suffer any long prayer. Every prayer is long enough if it be fervent and proceed from a heart that understandeth the necessity of the saints.—*Martin Luther.*

Whole Psalm.—The change of performers in this Psalm is very evident ; the pronoun in the first distich is in the first person *singular*, in the rest of Psalm the first *plural* is used.—*Stephen Street.*

Whole Psalm.—This Psalm has one distinction which is to be found in " scarcely any other piece in the Old Testament." In the Hebrew it has many rhymes. But these rhymes are purely accidental. They result simply from the fact that many words are used in it with the same inflexions, and therefore with the same or similar terminations. Regularly recurring and intentional rhymes are not a characteristic of Hebrew poetry, any more than they were of Greek or Latin poetry.—*Samuel Cox.*

Verse 1.—*"Unto thee lift I up mine eyes."* He who previously lifted his eyes unto the hills, now hath raised his heart's eyes to the Lord himself.—*The Venerable Bede* (672—735), *in Neale and Littledale.*

Verse 1.—*"Unto thee lift I up mine eyes,"* etc. This is the sigh of the pilgrim who ascendeth and loveth, and ascendeth because he loveth. He is ascending from earth to heaven, and while he is ascending, unto whom shall he lift his eyes, but unto him that dwelleth in heaven ? We ascend to heaven each time we think of God. In that ascent lies all goodness : if we would repent, we must look not on ourselves, but on him ; if we would be humble, we must look not on ourselves, but on him ; if we would truly love, we must look not on ourselves, but on him who dwelleth in the heavens. If we would have him turn his eyes from our sins, we must turn our eyes unto his mercy and truth.—*"Plain Commentary."*

Verse 1.—*"Unto thee lift I up mine eyes."* Praying by the glances of the eye rather than by words ; mine afflictions having swollen my heart too big for my mouth.—*John Trapp.*

Verse 1.—*"Unto* THEE *do I lift up mine eyes."* You feel the greatness of the contrast these words imply. Earth and heaven, dust and deity ; the poor, weeping sinful children of mortality, the holy, ever-blessed, eternal God : how wide is the interval of separation between them ! But over the awful chasm, broader than ocean though it be, love and wisdom in the person of Jesus Christ, have thrown a passage, by which the most sinful may repair unterrified to his presence, and find the shame and the fears of guilt exchanged for the peace of forgiveness and the hope that is full of immortality.—*Robert Nisbet.*

Verse 1.—There are many testimonies in *the lifting up of the eyes to heaven* 1. It is the testimony of a *believing*, humble heart. *Infidelity* will never carry a man above the earth. *Pride* can carry a man no higher than the earth either. 2. It is the testimony of an *obedient* heart. A man that lifts up his eye to God, he acknowledgeth thus much,—Lord, I am thy servant. 3. It is the testimony of a *thankful* heart ; acknowledging that every good blessing, every perfect gift, is from the hand of God. 4. It is the testimony of a *heavenly* heart. He that lifts up his eye to heaven acknowledgeth that he is weary of the earth ; his heart is not there ; his hope and desire is above. 5. It is the testimony of a *devout* heart : there is no part of the body besides the tongue that is so great an agent in prayer as the *eye*.—*Condensed from Richard Holdsworth.*

Verse 1.—*"O thou that dwellest in the heavens." "That sittest."* The Lord is here contemplated as enthroned in heaven, where he administers the affairs of the universe executes judgment, and hears prayer.—*James G. Murphy.*

Verses 1, 2.—The lifting up the eyes, implies faith and confident persuasion that God is ready and willing to help us. The very lifting up of the bodily eyes towards heaven is an expression of this inward trust : so David in effect saith, From thee, Lord, I expect relief, and the fulfilling of thy promises. So that there is faith in it, that faith which is the evidence of things not seen. How great soever the darkness of our calamities be, though the clouds of present troubles thicken about us, and hide the Lord's care and loving-kindness from us, yet faith must look through all to his power and constancy of truth and love. The eye of faith is a clear, piercing, eagle eye : Moses " endured, as seeing him who is invisible : " Heb. xi. 27. . . . Faith seeth things afar off in the promises (Heb. xi. 13), at a greater distance than the eye of nature can reach to. Take it either for the eye of the body, or the mind, faith will draw comfort not only from that which is invisible, but also from that which is future as well as invisible ; its supports lie in the other world, and in things which are yet to come.—*Thomas Manton.*

Verses 1, 2.—In the first strophe the poet places himself before us as standing in the presence of the Majesty of Heaven, with his eyes fixed on the hand of God, absorbed in watchful expectation of some sign or gesture, however slight, which may indicate the Divine will. He is like a slave standing silent but alert, in the presence of the Oriental " lord," with hands folded on his breast, and eyes fixed on his master, seeking to read, and to anticipate, if possible, his every wish. He is like a maiden in attendance on her mistress, anxiously striving to see her mind in her looks, to discover and administer to her moods and wants. The grave, reserved Orientals, as we know, seldom speak to their attendants, at least on public occasions. They intimate their wishes and commands by a wave of the hand, by a glance of the eye, by slight movements and gestures which might escape notice were they not watched for with eager attention. Their slaves *"hang"* upon their faces ; " they *"fasten* their eyes " on the eyes of their master ; they watch and obey every turn of his hand, every movement of his finger. Thus the Psalmist conceives of himself as waiting on God, looking to him alone, watching for the faintest signal bent on catching and obeying it.—*Samuel Cox.*

Verse 2.—*"Behold."* An ordinary word, but here it hath an extraordinary position. Ordinarily it is a term of *attention*, used for the awakening of man, to stir up their admiration and audience ; but here it is a word not only prefixed for the exciting of men, but of God himself. David is speaking to God in his meditations. " Behold," saith he. As we take it with respect to God, so it is a *precatory* particle : he beseecheth God to look *down* upon him, while he looks *up* unto God : Look on us, as we look to thee ; *"Behold, Lord, as the eyes of servants,"* etc. If we take it as it hath respect to *man*, so it is an *exemplary* particle, to stir them up to do the like. *"Behold"* what we do, and do likewise ; let your eyes be like ours. " Behold, as the eyes of servants are to the hand of their masters, so are our eyes to the Lord our God." Let yours have the same fixing. So it is a word that draws all eyes after it to imitation.—*Richard Holdsworth.*

Verse 2.—*"Behold, as the eyes of servants look,"* etc. For direction, defence, maintenance, mercy in time of correction, help when the service is over-hard, etc., *" so do our eyes wait upon the Lord our God,"* viz., for direction and benediction. —*John Trapp.*

Verse 2.—*"Eyes of servants unto the hand,"* etc. Our eyes ought to be to the hand of the Lord our God :—First, that we may admire his works. Secondly, that we may show that our service is pleasant to us ; and to show our dependence on such a benign, mighty, and bountiful hand. Thirdly, that we may evince to him our love, and devoted willingness to do all things which he shall command by the slightest movement of a finger. Fourthly, that from him we may receive food, and all things necessary for sustenance. Fifthly, that he may be a defence for us against the enemies that molest us, either by smiting them with the sword, or by shooting of arrows ; or by repelling others by the movement of a finger ; or, at least, by covering us with the shield of his good-will. Sixthly and lastly, that, moved by mercy, he would cease from chastisement.—*Condensed from Le Blanc.*

Verse 2.—*"As the eyes of servants look unto the hand of their masters,"* etc. A traveller says, " I have seen a fine illustration of this passage in a gentleman's house at Damascus. The people of the East do not speak so much or so quick as those in the West, and a sign of the hand is frequently the only instructions given to the servants in waiting. As soon as we were introduced and seated on the divan, a wave of the master's hand indicated that sherbet was to be served. Another wave brought coffee and pipes ; another brought sweetmeats. At another signal dinner was made ready. The attendants watched their master's eye and hand, to know his will and do it instantly." Such is the attention with which we ought to wait upon the Lord, anxious to fulfil his holy pleasure,—our great desire being, " Lord, what wilt thou have me to do ? " An equally pointed and more homely illustration may be seen any day, on our own river Thames, or in any of our large seaport towns, where the call-boy watches attentively the hand of the captain of the boat, and conveys his will to the engine-men.—"*The Sunday at Home.*"

Verse 2.—"*As the eyes of slaves,*" watching anxiously the least movement, the smallest sign of their master's will. The image expresses complete and absolute dependence. Savary (in his *Letters on Egypt,* p. 135), says, " The slaves stand silent at the bottom of the rooms with their hands crossed over their breasts. *With their eyes fixed upon their master* they seek to anticipate every one of his wishes." . . . . In the Psalm the eye directed to the hand of God is the *oculus sperans,* the eye which waits, and hopes, and is patient, looking only to him and none other for help.—*J. J. Stewart Perowne.*

Verse 2.—"*As the eyes of servants,*"etc. The true explanation, I should apprehend, is this : As a slave, ordered by a master or mistress to be chastised for a fault, turns his or her imploring eyes to that superior, till that motion of the hand appears that puts an end to the bitterness that is felt ; so our eyes are up to thee, our God, till thy hand shall give the signal for putting an end to our sorrows : for our enemies, O Lord, we are sensible, are only executing thy orders, and chastening us according to thy pleasure.—*Thomas Harmer.*

Verse 2.—"*Servants.*" Note how humbly the faithful think of themselves in the sight of God. They are called and chosen to this dignity, to be the heirs and children of God, and are exalted above the angels, and yet, notwithstanding, they count themselves no better in God's sight than "*servants.*" They say not here, Behold, like as children look to the hand of their fathers, but " as servants " to the hand of their masters. This is the humility and modesty of the godly, and it is so far off that hereby they lose the dignity of God's children, to the which they are called, that by this means it is made to them more sure and certain.—*Martin Luther.*

Verse 2.—From the everyday conduct of domestic servants we should learn our duty Godwards. Not without cause did our Saviour take his parables from common, everyday things, from fields, vines, trees, marriages, etc., that thus we might have everywhere apt reminders.—*Martin Geier.*

Verse 2.—"*Servants.*" "*A maiden.*" Consider that there be two sorts of servants set down here, man-servants and maid-servants ; and this is to let us know that both sexes may be confident in God. Not only may men be confident in the power of God, but even women also, who are more frail and feeble. Not only may women mourn to God for wrongs done to them, and have repentance for sin, but they may be confident in God also. And therefore see, in that rehearsal of believers and cloud of witnesses, not only is the faith of men noted and commended by the Spirit of God, but also the faith of women : and among the judges, Deborah, Jael, etc., are commended as worthies, and courageous in God. And the women also in the New Testament are noted for their following of Christ—even when all fled from him, then they followed him.—*From a sermon by Alexander Henderson,* 1583—1646.

Verse 2.—"*Servants.*" "*A maiden.*" We know how shamefully servants were treated in ancient times, and what reproaches must be cast upon them, whilst yet they durst not move a finger to repel the outrage. Being therefore deprived of all means of defending themselves, the only thing which remained for them to do was, what is here stated, to crave the protection of their masters. The same explanation is equally applicable to the case of *handmaids.* Their condition was indeed shameful and degrading ; but there is no reason why we should be ashamed of, or offended at, being compared to slaves, provided God is our defender, and takes our lives under his guardianship ; God, I say, who purposely disarms us and strips us of all worldly aid, that we may learn to rely upon his grace, and to be contented with it alone. It having been anciently a capital crime for bondmen to carry a sword or any other weapon about them, and as they were exposed to injuries of every description, their masters were wont to defend them with so much the more spirit, when anyone causelessly did them violence. Nor can it be doubted that God, when he sees us placing an exclusive dependence upon his protection, and renouncing all confidence in our own resources, will, as our defender, encounter and shield us from all the molestation that shall be offered to us.—*John Calvin*.

Verse 2.—"Hand." With the *hand* we demand, we promise, we call, dismiss, threaten, entreat, supplicate, deny, refuse, interrogate, admire, reckon, confess, repent; express fear, express shame, express doubt; we instruct, command, unite, encourage, swear, testify, accuse, condemn, acquit, insult, despise, defy, disdain, flatter, applaud, bless, abase, ridicule, reconcile, recommend, exalt, regale, gladden, complain, afflict, discomfort, · discourage, astonish; exclaim, indicate silence, and what not? with a variety and a multiplication that keep pace with the tongue.—*Michael de Montaigne*, 1533—1592.

Verse 2.—"Masters." It is said of Mr. George Herbert, that divine poet, that, to satisfy his independency upon all others, and to quicken his diligence in God's service, he used in his ordinary speech, when he made mention of the blessed name of Jesus, to add, " my Master." And, without any doubt, if men were unfeignedly of his mind, their respects would be more to Christ's command, to Christ's will, to Christ's pleasure.—*From Spencer's "Things New and Old."*

Verse 2.—"Our eyes wait." Here the Psalmist uses another word : it is the eye *waiting*. What is the reason of the second word ? Now he leaves the similitude in the first line ; for in the first line it is thus,—"As the eyes of servants *look*, and the eyes of a maiden *look* " ; here it is the eye *waits*. There is good reason : to *wait* is more than to *look :* to *wait* is to look constantly, with patience and submission, by subjecting our affections and wills and desires to God's will ; that is to *wait*. David in the second part, in the second line, gives a *better* word, he betters his copy. There is the duty of a Christian, to better his example ; the eyes of servants *look*, David's eyes shall *wait : "So our eyes wait."* It is true indeed this word is not in the original, therefore you may observe it is in a small letter in your Bibles, to note that it is a word of necessity, added for the supply of the sense, because the Holy Ghost left it not imperfect, but more perfect, that he put not in the verb ; because it is left to every man's heart to supply a verb to his own comfort, and a better he cannot than this. And that this word must be added appears by the next words : *" until that he have mercy upon us."* To look till he have mercy on us is to *wait ;* so there is good reason why this word is added. If we look to the thing begged—*" mercy"*—it is so precious that we may *wait* for it. It was " servants " that he mentioned, and it is their duty to *wait* upon their masters ; they wait upon their trenchers at meat ; they wait when they go to bed and when they rise ; they wait in every place. Therefore, because he had mentioned the first word, he takes the proper duty ; there is nothing more proper to servants than waiting, and if we are the servants of God we must *wait*. There is good reason in that respect, because it is a word so significant, therefore the Spirit of God varies it ; he keeps not exactly to the line, " So do our eyes *look*," but he puts it, " So do our eyes *wait*." —*Richard Holdsworth*.

Verse 3.—"Have mercy upon us, O LORD, have mercy upon us !" Note how a godly man speaks. He does not say, *"Have mercy upon me, O LORD, have mercy upon me !* because I am disgraced;" but, *"Have mercy upon us, O LORD, for we are filled with contempt !"* The godly man is not so grieved for his own and individual contempt as he is for the general contempt of the good and faithful. There is an accord of the godly, not only in the cross, but also in groanings, and in the invocation of divine grace.—*Wolfgang Musculus*.

Verse 3.—"For we are exceedingly filled." The Hebrew word here used means " *to be saturated* "; to have the appetite fully satisfied—as applied to one who is hungry or thirsty. Then it comes to mean to be entirely full, and the idea here is, that as much contempt had been thrown upon them as could be ; they could experience no more.—*Albert Barnes*.

Verse 3.—"We are exceedingly filled with contempt." Men of the world regard the Temple Pilgrims and their religion with the quiet smile of disdain, wondering that those who have so much to engage them in a present life should be weak enough to concern themselves about frames and feelings, about an unseen God, and unknown eternity; and this is a trial they find hard to bear. *Their soul, too, is filled exceedingly with the scorning of those that are at ease.* The prosperous of their neighbours declare that they have found the world a generous and happy scene to all who deserve its gifts. Poverty and sorrow they attribute to unworthiness alone. " Let them exert themselves," is the unfeeling cry ; " let them bestir themselves instead of praying, and with them as with us it will soon be well;" and these words of harsh and unfeeling ignorance are like poison to the wounds of the bleeding heart. They have further " *the contempt of the proud* " to mourn ; of those who give expression to their fierce disdain by assailing them with words of contumely, and who seek to draw them by reproaches both from peace and from piety. These are still the trials of Zion's worshippers : silent contempt, open misrepresentation, fierce opposition. Religion, their last comfort, is despised ; peace, their first desire, is denied. Anxious to devote themselves in the spirit of humble and earnest piety to the duties of their appointed sphere, they find enemies in open outcry and array against them. But God is their refuge, and to him they go.—*Robert Nisbet.*

Verses 3, 4.—The second strophe takes up the " have mercy upon us," as it were in echo. It begins with a *Kyrie eleison*, which is confirmed in a *crescendo* manner after the form of steps.—*Franz Delitzsch.*

Verse 4.—"*Exceedingly filled,*" or perhaps, "*has long been filled.*" (Compare cxx. 6). This expression, together with the earnestness of the repeated prayer, " Be gracious unto us," shows that the " scorn " and " contempt " have long pressed upon the people, and their faith has accordingly been exposed to a severe trial. The more remarkable is the entire absence of anything like impatience in the language of the Psalm.—*J. J. Stewart Perowne.*

Verse 4.—"*The scorning of those that are at ease.*" When men go on prosperously, they are apt wrongfully to trouble others, and then to shout at them in their misery, and to despise the person and cause of God's people. This is the sure effect of great arrogancy and pride. They think they may do what they please ; they have no changes, therefore they fear not God, but put forth their hands against such as be at peace with them (Ps. lv. 19, 20) ; whilst they go on prosperously and undisturbedly, they cannot abstain from violence and oppression. This is certainly pride, for it is a lifting up of the heart above God and against God and without God. And they do not consider his providence, which alternately lifts up and casts down, that adversity may not be without a cordial, nor prosperity without a curb and bridle. When men sit fast, and are well at ease, they are apt to be insolent and scornful. Riches and worldly greatness make men insolent and despisers of others, and not to care what burdens they impose upon them ; they are intrenched within a mass of wealth and power and greatness, and so think none can call them to an account.—*Thomas Manton.*

Verse 4.—"*Those that are at ease.*" The word always means such as are recklessly at their ease, *the careless ones,* such as those whom Isaiah bids, " rise up, tremble, be troubled ; " for " many days and years shall ye be troubled " (ch. xxxii. 9—11). It is that luxury and ease which sensualize the soul, and make it dull, stupid, hard-hearted.—*Edward Bouverie Pusey* (1800—), *in "The Minor Prophets."*

Verse 4.—"*Those that are at ease,*" who are regardless of the troubles of others, and expect none of their own.—*James G. Murphy.*

HINTS TO PREACHERS.

Whole Psalm.—We have here, I. The prayer of *dependence,* verse 2. II. The prayer of *apprehension :* " Unto *thee,*" etc. III. The spirit of *obedience :* " As the eyes of servants," etc. IV. The *patience* of the saints : ''*Until* he have mercy upon us."—*R. Nisbet.*

Whole Psalm.—Eyes and no eyes. I. EYES. 1. *Upward,* in confidence, in prayer, in thought. 2. "*Unto,*" in reverence, watchfulness, obedience. 3. *Inward,* producing a cry for mercy. II. No EYES. 1. No sight of the excellence of the godly. 2. No sense of their own danger : " at ease." 3. No humility before God : " proud." 4. No uplifted eyes in hope, prayer, expectation.

Verse 1.—The eyes of faith. I. Need uplifting. II. See best upward. III. Have always something to see upward. IV. Let us look up, and so turn our eyes from too much introspection and retrospection.

Verse 1.—I. The language of Adoration: "Thou that dwellest in the heavens." II. The language of Confession. 1. Of need. 2. Of helplessness. III. The language of Supplication: "Unto thee," etc. IV. The language of Expectation; as shown in verse 2.—*G. R.*

Verse 2.—(Psalm cxxi. 4 with this verse.) Two beholds. I. God's watchful eye over us. II. The saint's watchful eye upon God.

Verse 2.—"Our eyes wait upon the Lord our God." I. What it is to wait with the eye. II. What peculiar aspect of the Lord suggests such waiting: "Jehovah our God." The covenant God is the trusted God. III. What comes of such waiting —" mercy."

Verse 2.—The guiding hand. I. A beckoning hand—to go near. II. A directing hand—to go here and there. III. A quiescent hand—to remain where we are. —*G. R.*

Verse 2.—Homely metaphors, or what may be learned from maids and their mistresses.

Verse 3 (first portion).—The Sinner's Litany. The Saint's Entreaty.

Verse 3 (second portion).—The world's contempt, the abundance of it, the reason of it, the bitterness of it, the comfort under it.

Verses 3, 4.—I. The occasion of the prayer: the contempt of men. This is often the most difficult to bear. 1. Because it is most unreasonable. Why ridicule men for yielding to their own convictions of what is right? 2. Most undeserved. True religion injures no man, but seeks the good of all. 3. Most profane. To reproach the people of God because they are his people is to reproach God himself. II. The subject of the prayer. 1. The prayer: is not for justice, which might be desired, but for mercy. 2. The plea: "For we are," etc. The reproaches of men are an encouragement to look for special help from God. The harp hung upon the willows sends forth its sweetest tones. The less it is in human hands the more freely it is played upon by the Spirit of God.—*G. R.*

Verse 4.—"Those that are at ease." I. Explain their state: "at ease." II. Show their ordinary state of mind: "proud." III. Denounce their frequent sin: scorn of the godly. IV. Exhibit their terrible danger.

PSALM CXXIV.

TITLE.—*A Song of degrees of David. Of course the superfine critics have pounced upon this title as inaccurate, but we are at liberty to believe as much or as little of their assertions as we may please. They declare that there are certain ornaments of language in this little ode which were unknown in the Davidic period. It may be so ; but in their superlative wisdom they have ventured upon so many other questionable statements that we are not bound to receive this dictum. Assuredly the manner of the song is very like to David's, and we are unable to see why he should be excluded from the authorship. Whether it be his composition or no, it breathes the same spirit as that which animates the unchallenged songs of the royal composer.*

DIVISION.—*This short Psalm contains an acknowledgment of favour received by way of special deliverance (1—5), then a grateful act of worship in blessing Jehovah (6, 7), and, lastly, a declaration of confidence in the Lord for all future time of trial. May our experience lead us to the same conclusion as the saints of David's time. From all confidence in man may we be rescued by a holy reliance upon our God.*

EXPOSITION.

IF *it had not been* the LORD who was on our side, now may Israel say :

2 If *it had not been* the LORD who was on our side, when men rose up against us :

3 Then they had swallowed us up quick, when their wrath was kindled against us :

4 Then the waters had overwhelmed us, the stream had gone over our soul :

5 Then the proud waters had gone over our soul.

1. *"If it had not been the LORD who was on our side, now may Israel say."* The opening sentence is abrupt, and remains a fragment. By such a commencement attention was aroused as well as feeling expressed : and this is ever the way of poetic fire—to break forth in uncontrollable flame. The many words in italics in our authorized version will show the reader that the translators did their best to patch up the passage, which, perhaps, had better have been left in its broken grandeur, and it would then have run thus :—

> " Had it not been Jehovah ! He was for us, oh let Israel say !
> Had it not been Jehovah ! He who was for us when men rose against us.

The glorious Lord became our ally ; he took our part, and entered into treaty with us. If Jehovah were not our protector where should we be ? Nothing but his power and wisdom could have guarded us from the cunning and malice of our adversaries ; therefore, let all his people say so, and openly give him the honour of his preserving goodness. Here are two " ifs," and yet there is no " if " in the matter. The Lord was on our side, and is still our defender, and will be so from henceforth, even for ever. Let us with holy confidence exult in this joyful fact. We are far too slow in declaring our gratitude, hence the exclamation which should be rendered, " O let Israel say." We murmur without being stirred up to it, but our thanksgiving needs a spur, and it is well when some warm-hearted friend bids us say what we feel. Imagine what would have happened if the Lord had left us, and then see what has happened because he has been faithful to us. Are not all the materials of a song spread before us ? Let us sing unto the Lord.

2. *"If it had not been the LORD who was on our side, when men rose up against us."* When all men combined, and the whole race of men seemed set upon stamping out the house of Israel, what must have happened if the covenant Lord had not interposed ? When they stirred themselves, and combined to make an assault upon our quietude and safety, what should we have done in their rising if the Lord had not also risen ? No one who could or would help was near, but the bare arm

of the Lord sufficed to preserve his own against all the leagued hosts of adversaries. There is no doubt as to our deliverer, we cannot ascribe our salvation to any second cause, for it would not have been equal to the emergency ; nothing less than omnipotence and omiscience could have wrought our rescue. We set every other claimant on one side, and rejoice because the Lord was on our side.

3. *"Then they had swallowed us up quick when their wrath was kindled against us."* They were so eager for our destruction that they would have made only one morsel of us, and have swallowed us up alive and whole in a single instant. The fury of the enemies of the church is raised to the highest pitch, nothing will content them but the total annihilation of God's chosen. Their wrath is like a fire which is kindled, and has taken such firm hold upon the fuel that there is no quenching it. Anger is never more fiery than when the people of God are its objects. Sparks become flames, and the furnace is heated seven times hotter when God's elect are to be thrust into the blaze. The cruel world would make a full end of the godly seed were it not that Jehovah bars the way. When the Lord appears, the cruel throats cannot swallow, and the consuming fires cannot destroy. Ah, if it were not Jehovah, if our help came from all the creatures united, there would be no way of escape for us : it is only because the Lord liveth that his people are alive.

4. *"Then the waters had overwhelmed us."* Rising irresistibly, like the Nile, the flood of opposition would soon have rolled over our heads. Across the mighty waste of waters we should have cast an anxious eye, but looked in vain for escape. The motto of a royal house is, " Tossed about but not submerged " : we should have needed an epitaph rather than an epigram, for we should have been driven by the torrent and sunken, never to rise again. *"The stream had gone over our soul."* The rushing torrent would have drowned our soul, our hope, our life. The figures seem to be the steadily-rising flood, and the hurriedly-rushing stream. Who can stand against two such mighty powers ? Everything is destroyed by these unconquerable forces, either by being submerged or swept away. When the world's enmity obtains a vent it both rises and rushes, it rages and rolls along, and spares nothing. In the great water-floods of persecution and affliction who can help but Jehovah ? But for him where would we be at this very hour ? We have experienced seasons in which the combined forces of earth and hell must have made an end of us had not omnipotent grace interfered for our rescue.

5. *"Then the proud waters had gone over our soul."* The figure represents the waves as proud, and so they seem to be when they overleap the bulwarks of a frail bark, and threaten every moment to sink her. The opposition of men is usually embittered by a haughty scorn which derides all our godly efforts as mere fanaticism or obstinate ignorance. In all the persecutions of the church a cruel contempt has largely mingled with the oppression, and this is overpowering to the soul. Had not God been with us our disdainful enemies would have made nothing of us, and dashed over us as a mountain torrent sweeps down the side of a hill, driving everything before it. Not only would our goods and possessions have been carried off, but our soul, our courage, our hope would have been borne away by the impetuous assault, and buried beneath the insults of our antagonists. Let us pause here, and as we see what might have been, let us adore the guardian power which has kept us in the flood, and yet above the flood. In our hours of dire peril we must have perished had not our Preserver prevailed for our safe keeping.

6 Blessed *be* the LORD, who hath not given us *as* a prey to their teeth.

7 Our soul is escaped as a bird out of the snare of the fowlers : the snare is broken, and we are escaped.

6. *"Blessed be the LORD, who hath not given us as a prey to their teeth."* Leaving the metaphor of a boiling flood, he compares the adversaries of Israel to wild beasts who desired to make the godly their prey. Their teeth are prepared to tear, and they regard the godly as their victims. The Lord is heartily praised for not permitting his servants to be devoured when they were between the jaws of the raging ones. It implies that none can harm us till the Lord permits : we cannot be their prey unless the Lord gives us up to them, and that our loving Lord will never do. Hitherto he has refused permission to any foe to destroy us, blessed be his name. The more imminent the danger the more eminent the mercy which would not permit the soul to perish in it. God be blessed for ever for keeping us from the curse. Jehovah be praised for checking the fury of the foe, and saving his own. The

verse reads like a merely negative blessing, but no boon can be more positively precious. He has given us to his Son Jesus, and he will never give us to our enemies.

7. *"Our soul is escaped as a bird out of the snare of the fowlers."* Our soul is like a bird for many reasons; but in this case the point of likeness is weakness, folly, and the ease with which it is enticed into the snare. Fowlers have many methods of taking small birds, and Satan has many methods of entrapping souls. Some are decoyed by evil companions, others are enticed by the love of dainties; hunger drives many into the trap, and fright impels numbers to fly into the net. Fowlers know their birds, and how to take them; but the birds see not the snare so as to avoid it, and they cannot break it so as to escape from it. Happy is the bird that hath a deliverer strong, and mighty, and ready in the moment of peril; happier still is the soul over which the Lord watches day and night to pluck its feet out of the net. What joy there is in this song, " our soul is escaped." How the emancipated one sings and soars, and soars and sings again. Blessed be God many of us can make joyous music with these notes, " our soul is escaped." Escaped from our natural slavery; escaped from the guilt, the degradation, the habit, the dominion of sin; escaped from the vain deceits and fascinations of Satan; escaped from all that can destroy; we do indeed experience delight. What a wonder of grace it is! What a miraculous escape that we who are so easily misled should not have been permitted to die by the dread fowler's hand. The Lord has heard the prayer which he taught us to pray, and he hath delivered us from evil. *"The snare is broken, and we are escaped."* The song is worth repeating; it is well to dwell upon so great a mercy. The snare may be false doctrine, pride, lust, or a temptation to indulge in policy, or to despair, or to presume; what a high favour it is to have it broken before our eyes, so that it has no more power over us. We see not the mercy while we are in the snare; perhaps we are so foolish as to deplore the breaking of the Satanic charm; the gratitude comes when the escape is seen, and when we perceive what we have escaped from, and by what hand we have been set free. Then our Lord has a song from our mouths and hearts as we make heaven and earth ring with the notes, " the snare is broken, and we are escaped." We have been tempted, but not taken; cast down, but not destroyed; perplexed, but not in despair; in deaths oft, but still alive: blessed be Jehovah!

This song might well have suited our whole nation at the time of the Spanish Armada, the church in the days of the Jesuits, and each believer among us in seasons of strong personal temptation.

8 Our help *is* in the name of the LORD, who made heaven and earth.

8. *"Our help,"* our hope for the future, our ground of confidence in all trials present and to come. *"Is in the name of the LORD."* Jehovah's revealed character is our foundation of confidence, his person is our sure fountain of strength. *"Who made heaven and earth."* Our Creator is our preserver. He is immensely great in his creating work; he has not fashioned a few little things alone, but all heaven and the whole round earth are the works of his hands. When we worship the Creator let us increase our trust in our Comforter. Did he create all that we see, and can he not preserve us from evils which we cannot see? Blessed be his name, he that has fashioned us will watch over us; yea, he has done so, and rendered us help in the moment of jeopardy. He is our help and our shield, even he alone. He will to the end break every snare. He made heaven for us, and he will keep us for heaven; he made the earth, and he will succour us upon it until the hour cometh for our departure. Every work of his hand preaches to us the duty and the delight of reposing upon him only. All nature cries, " Trust ye in the Lord for ever, for in the Lord Jehovah there is everlasting strength." " Wherefore comfort one another with these words."

The following versification of the sense rather than the words of this Psalm is presented to the reader with much diffidence :—

> Had not the Lord, my soul may cry,
> Had not the Lord been on my side;
> Had he not brought deliverance nigh,
> Then must my helpless soul have died.
>
> Had not the Lord been on my side,
> My soul had been by Satan slain;
> And Tophet, opening large and wide,
> Would not have gaped for me in vain.

Lo, floods of wrath, and floods of hell,
In fierce impetuous torrents roll ;
Had not the Lord defended well,
The waters had o'erwhelm'd my soul.

As when the fowler's snare is broke,
The bird escapes on cheerful wings ;
My soul, set free from Satan's yoke,
With joy bursts forth, and mounts, and sings.

She sings the Lord her Saviour's praise ;
Sings forth his praise with joy and mirth ;
To him her song in heaven she'll raise,
To him that made both heaven and earth.

EXPLANATORY NOTES AND QUAINT SAYINGS.

Title.—The title informs us that this sacred march was composed by king David ; and we learn very clearly from the subject, that the progression referred to was the triumphant return of the king and his loyal army to Jerusalem, upon the overthrow of the dangerous rebellion to which the great mass of the people had been excited by Absalom and his powerful band of confederates.—*John Mason Good.*

Whole Psalm.—This Psalm is ascribed to David. No reference is made to any specific danger and deliverance. There is a delightful universality in the language which suits it admirably for an anthem of the redeemed, in every age and in every clime. The people of God still live in a hostile territory. Traitors are in the camp, and there are numerous foes without. And the church would soon be exterminated, if the malice and might of her adversaries were not restrained and defeated by a higher power. Hence this ode of praise has never become obsolete. How frequently have its strains of adoring gratitude floated on the breeze ! What land is there, in which its outbursting gladness has not been heard ! It has been sung upon the banks of the Jordan and the Nile, the Euphrates and the Tigris. It has been sung upon the banks of the Tiber and the Rhine, the Thames and the Forth. It has been sung upon the banks of the Ganges and the Indus, the Mississippi and the Irraway. And we anticipate a period when the church, surmounting all her difficulties, and victory waving over her banners, shall sing this Psalm of praise in every island and continent of our globe. The year of God's redeemed must come. The salvation of Christ shall extend to the utmost extremities of earth. And when this final emancipation takes place, the nations will shout for joy, and praise their Deliverer in Psalms, and hymns, and spiritual songs.—*N. McMichael.*

Whole Psalm.—In the year 1582, this Psalm was sung on a remarkable occasion in Edinburgh. An imprisoned minister, John Durie, had been set free, and was met and welcomed on entering the town by two hundred of his friends. The number increased till he found himself in the midst of a company of two thousand, who began to sing, as they moved up the long High Street, "*Now Israel may say,*" etc. They sang in four parts with deep solemnity, all joining in the well-known tune and Psalm. They were much moved themselves, and so were all who heard ; and one of the chief persecutors is said to have been more alarmed at this sight and song than at anything he had seen in Scotland.—*Andrew A. Bonar, in "Christ and His Church in the Book of Psalms,"* 1859.

Verse 1. "The Lord *. . . on our side."* Jehovah is on the side of his people in a spiritual sense, or otherwise it would be bad for them. God the Father is on their side ; his love and relation to them engage him to be so ; hence all those good things that are provided for them and bestowed on them ; nor will he suffer any to do them hurt, they being as dear to him as the apple of his eye ; hence he grants them his gracious presence, supports them under all their trials and exercises, supplies all their wants, and keeps them by his power, and preserves them from all their enemies ; so that they have nothing to fear from any quarter. Christ is on their side ; he is the Surety for them, the Saviour of them ; has taken their part against all their spiritual enemies, sin, Satan, the world, and death ; has engaged with them and conquered them ; he is the Captain of their salvation, their King at the head of them, that protects and defends them here, and is their friend in the court of heaven ; their Advocate and interceding High-priest there, who pleads their cause against Satan, and obtains every blessing for them.   The Spirit of Jehovah is on their side, to carry on his work in them ; to assist them in their prayers and supplications ; to secure them from Satan's temptations ; to set up a standard for them when the enemy comes in like a flood upon them ; and to comfort them in all their castings down ; and to work them up for, and bring them safe to heaven : but were this not the case, what would become of them ?—*John Gill.*

Verse 1.—*"Israel."*   The *"Israel"* spoken of in this Psalm may be Israel in the house of Laban, in whose person the Midrash Tehillim imagines the Psalm to be said.   There are certainly some of its phrases which acquire an appropriate meaning from being interpreted in this connection.—*H. T. Armfield.*

Verses 1—4.—Such abrupt and unfinished expressions in the beginning of the Psalm indicate the great joy and exultation that will not suffer the speaker to finish his sentences.—*Robert Bellarmine.*

Verses 1, 2.—The somewhat paraphrastic rendering of these verses (with the unnecessary interpolation of the words in italics in the Authorised Version) greatly weaken their force and obscure their meaning.   There is far more meant and expressed than simply that God gave the Israelites the victory over their enemies. The Psalm is typico-prophetic.   It sets forth the condition of the church in this world, surrounded by enemies, implacable in their hatred, maddened by rage, and bent on her destruction.   It gives assurance of her preservation, and continuous triumph, because Jehovah is her God.   It foretells the future, full, and final destruction of all her enemies.   It re-echoes the song sung on the shores of the Red Sea. In it are heard the notes of the New Song before the great white throne.   The praise and thanksgiving are to יְהוָֹה, the revealed אֱלֹהִים, whose *"eternal power and Godhead are understood by the things that are made :"*—to יְהוָֹה, the revealed אֵל שַׁדַּי, whom the fathers knew as the Almighty, from the great things which he did for them :—to יְהוָֹה, the God who has made a covenant with his people, the Redeemer.   It is יִשְׂרָאֵל, the chosen people of God, the holy nation, the peculiar treasure to him above all peoples, and thus become as the Rabbins say, *"Odium generis humani,"* against whom אָדָם (not *men,* but *man* collectively) rose up, and sought to destroy.   It is יִשְׂרָאֵל, God's chosen, the people of the covenant, that with the " full delight of a personal ' my,' " joys in God and sings, *"But that Jehovah* was לָנוּ, ours ! "   Tame and frigid is the rendering—*"was on our side."*   Jehovah was theirs : *that,* their safety : *that,* their blessedness : *that,* their joy.—*Edward Thomas Gibson,* 1818—1880.

Verses 1, 2.—1. God was on our side ; he took our part, espoused our cause and appeared for us.   He was our helper, and a very present help, a help on our side, nigh at hand.   He was with us ; not only for us, but among us, and commander-in-chief of our forces. 2. That God was Jehovah ; there the emphasis lies. " If it had not been Jehovah himself, a God of infinite power and perfection, that had undertaken our deliverance, our enemies would have overpowered us. Happy the people therefore whose God is Jehovah, a God all-sufficient.   Let Israel say this to his honour, and resolve never to forsake him.—*Matthew Henry.*

Verses 1, 2, 8.—These three things will I bear on my heart, O Lord : " The Lord *was* on our side," this for the *past ;* " The snare is broken," for the *present ;* " Our help is in the name of the Lord," this for the *future.*   I will not and I cannot be fainthearted, whether in my contest with Satan, in my intercourse with the world, or in the upheavings of my wicked heart, so long as I hold this " threefold cord " in my hand, or rather, am held by it.—*Alfred Edersheim.*

Verse 2.—*"If it had not been the* LORD,"* etc.   This repetition is not in vain.   For whilst we are in danger, our fear is without measure ; but when it is once past, we imagine it to have been less than it was indeed.   And this is the delusion of Satan, to diminish and obscure the grace of God.   David therefore with this repetition stirreth up the people to more thankfulness unto God for his gracious deliverance, and amplifieth the dangers which they had passed.   Whereby we are taught how to think of our troubles and afflictions past, lest the sense and feeling of God's grace vanish out of our minds.—*Martin Luther.*

Verse 2.—*"Men rose up against us."*   It may seem strange that these wicked and wretched enemies, monsters rather than men, should be thus moderately spoken of, and have no other name than this of *men* given them, which of all others they least deserved, as having in them nothing of man but outward show and shape, being rather beasts, yea, devils in the form and fashion of men, than right men. But hereby the church would show that she did leave the further censuring of them unto God their righteous Judge ; and would also further amplify their wickedness, who being men, did yet in their desires and dispositions bewray a more than beastly immanity and inhumanity.—*Daniel Dyke* (—1614 ?) *in "Comfortable Sermons upon the cxxiiii. Psalme,"* 1617.

Verse 3.—*" Then they had swallowed us up quick."* The metaphor may be taken from famished wild beasts attacking and devouring men (comp. v. 5) ; or the reference may be to the case of a man shut up alive in a sepulchre (Prov. i. 12) and left there to perish, or (Numb. xvi. 30) swallowed up by an earthquake.—*Daniel Cresswell.*

Verse 3.—*"Then they had swallowed us up."* The word implieth eating with insatiable appetite ; every man that eateth must also swallow ; but a glutton is rather a swallower than an eater. He throws his meat whole down his throat, and eats (as we may say) without chewing. The rod of Moses, turned into a serpent, " swallowed up " the rods of the Egyptian sorcerers. The word is often applied to express oppression (Ps. xxxv. 25) : " Let them not say in their hearts, Ah, so would we have it : let them not say, We have swallowed him up " : that is, we have made clear riddance of him ; he is now a gone man for ever. The ravenous rage of the adversary is described in this language.—*Joseph Caryl.*

Verse 3.—*"Quick."* Not an adverb, *"quickly,"* but an adjective, *alive.* As greedy monsters, both of the land and of the deep, sometimes swallow their food before the life is out of it, so would the enemies of the Church have destroyed her as in a moment, but for divine interposition.—*William S. Plumer.*

Verse 3.—Objection. But what may the reason thereof be ? May a man say, thus the godly shall always prevail and be never overthrown by their enemies, but overcome them rather ? Experience doth teach us that they are fewer in number than the wicked are, that they are weaker for power and strength, that they are more simple for wit and policy, and that they are more careless for diligence and watchfulness than their adversaries be: how, then, comes it to pass that they have the upper hand ?

Answer. The Prophet Esay doth declare it unto us in the 8th chapter of his prophecy, and the 10th verse thereof, it is in few words " because the Lord is with them and for them."

For, first, he is stronger than all, being able to resist all power that is devised against him and his, and to do whatsoever he will both in heaven and in earth.

2. He is wiser than all, knowing how to prevent them in all their ways, and also how to bring matters to pass for the good of his people.

3. He is diligenter than all, to stand, as it were, upon the watch, and to take his advantage when it is offered him, for " He that keepeth Israel doth neither slumber nor sleep."

4. Lastly, he is happier than all to have good success in all his enterprizes, for he doth prosper still in all things which he doth take in hand and none can resist a thought of his ; yea, the very " word which goeth out of his mouth doth accomplish that which he wills, and prosper in the thing whereunto he doth send it." In war, all these four things are respected in a captain that will still overcome : first, that he be strong ; secondly, that he be wise ; thirdly, that he be diligent ; and, lastly, that he be fortunate ; for the victory goeth not always with the strong, nor always with the wise, nor always with the diligent, nor always with the fortunate ; but sometimes with the one of them, and sometimes with the other : but look, where all four do concur together there is always the victory, and therefore seeing all of them are in God, it is no marvel though those whose battles he doth fight, do always overcome and get the victory.—*Thomas Stint,* 1621.

Verses 4, 5.—A familiar, but exceedingly apt and most significant figure. Horrible is the sight of a raging conflagration ; but far more destructive is a river overflowing its banks and rushing violently on : for it is not possible to restrain it by any strength or power. As, then, he says, a river is carried along with great impetuosity, and carries away and destroys whatever it meets with in its course ;

thus also is the rage of the enemies of the church, not to be withstood by human strength. Hence, we should learn to avail ourselves of the protection and help of God. For what else is the church but a little boat fastened to the bank, which is carried away by the force of the waters ? or a shrub growing on the bank, which without effort the flood roots up ? Such was the people of Israel in the days of David compared with the surrounding nations. Such in the present day is the church compared with her enemies. Such is each one of us compared with the power of the malignant spirit. We are as a little shrub, of recent growth and having no firm hold : but he is like the Elbe, overflowing, and with great force overthrowing all things far and wide. We are like a withered leaf, lightly holding to the tree ; he is like the north wind, with great force rooting up and throwing down the trees. How, then, can we withstand or defend ourselves by our own power ?—*Martin Luther.*

Verses 4, 5.—First the *"waters"*; then *"the stream"* or *torrent;* then *" the proud waters,"* lifting up their heads on high. First the waters overwhelm us ; then the torrent goes over our soul ; and then the proud waters go over our soul. What power can resist the rapid floods of waters, when they overspread their boundaries, and rush over a country ? Onward they sweep with resistless force, and men and cattle, and crops and houses, are destroyed. Let the impetuous waters break loose, and, in a few minutes, the scene of life, and industry, and happiness, is made a scene of desolation and woe. Perhaps, there is an allusion here to the destruction of the Egyptians in the Red Sea. The floods fell upon them, the depths covered them : they sank into the bottom as a stone. Had God not stretched forth his hand to rescue the Israelites, their enemies would have overwhelmed them. Happy they who, in seasons of danger, have Jehovah for a hiding-place.—*N. McMichael.*

Verse 5.—*"Then the proud waters had gone over our soul."* The same again, to note the greatness both of the danger and of the deliverance. And it may teach us not lightly to pass over God's great blessings, but to make the most of them.— *John Trapp.*

Verse 5.—

" When winds and seas do rage,
    And threaten to undo me,
Thou dost their wrath assuage,
    If I but call unto thee.

A mighty storm last night
    Did seek my soul to swallow
But by the peep of light
    A gentle calm did follow.

What need I then despair
    Though ills stand round about me ;
Since mischiefs neither dare
    To bark or bite without thee ? "

Robert Herrick, 1591—1674.

Verses 6, 7.—Two figures are again employed, in order to show how imminent was the destruction, had there been no divine interposition. The first is that of a savage beast, which was formerly used. But an addition is made, to describe the urgency of the danger. The wild beast was not only lying in wait for them ; he was not merely ready to spring upon his prey, he had already leaped upon it : he had actually seized it : it was even now between his teeth. What a graphic description ! A moment's delay, and all help would have been in vain. But Jehovah appears on the ground. He goes up to the ferocious beast, and takes out the trembling prey from between his bloody jaws. The danger is imminent ; but nothing is too hard for the Lord. " My soul is among lions." " What time I am afraid I will trust in thee." " He shall send from heaven, and save me from the reproach of him that would swallow me up." The second figure is that of a fowler. The fowler has prepared his snare in a skilful manner. The bird enters it, unconscious of danger : the net is thrown over it ; and in an instant its liberty is lost. There it lies, the poor bird, its little heart throbbing wildly, and its little wings beating vainly against the net. It is completely at the mercy of the fowler, and escape is impossible. But again the Lord appears, and his presence is safety. He goes up to the net, lifts it from the ground ; the bird flies out, lights on a neighbouring tree, and sings among the branches. " Surely he shall deliver thee from the snare of the fowler." God rescues his people from the craft and subtlety of their enemies, as he does from their open violence.—*N. McMichael.*

Verses 6, 7.—We were delivered, 1. Like a *lamb* out of the very jaws of a beast of prey : God *"hath not given us as a prey to their teeth";* intimating that they had no power against God's people, but what was given them from above. They could not be a prey to their teeth unless God gave them up, and therefore they were rescued, because God would not suffer them to be ruined. 2. Like *"a bird,"* a *little* bird, the word signifies a sparrow, *"out of the snare of the fowler."* The enemies are very subtle and spiteful, they lay snares for God's people, to bring them into sin and trouble, and to hold them there. Sometimes they seem to have prevailed so far as to gain their point, the children of God are taken in the snare, and are as unable to help themselves out as any weak and silly bird is ; and then is God's time to appear for their relief ; when all other friends fail, then God breaks the snare, and turns the counsel of the enemies into foolishness : *"The snare is broken, and so we are delivered."*—*Matthew Henry.*

Verse 7.—*"Our soul is escaped as a bird out of the snare of the fowlers,"* etc. Various snares are placed for birds, by traps, bird-lime, guns, etc. : who can enumerate all the dangers of the godly, threatening them from Satan, and from the world ? Psalm xci. 3 : Hosea v. 1. — *"We are delivered,"* not by our own skill or cunning, but by the grace and power of God only : so that every device is made vain, and freedom is preserved.—*Martin Geier.*

Verse 7.—*"Our soul is escaped as a bird out of the snare of the fowlers,"* etc. I am quite sure that there is not a day of our lives in which Satan does not lay some snare for our souls, the more perilous because unseen ; and if seen, because perhaps unheeded and despised. And of this, too, I am equally sure, that if any one brings home with him at night a conscience void of offence towards God and man, it is in no might nor strength of his own, and that if the Lord had not been his guide and preserver he would have been given over, nay, he would have given himself over, as a prey to the devourer's teeth. I believe there are few even of God's saints who have not had occasion, in some season of sore temptation, when Satan has let loose all his malice and might, and poured in suggestion upon suggestion and trial upon trial, as he did on Job, and they have been ready to faint, if not to fall by the way—then, perhaps, in a moment when they looked not for it, Satan has departed, foiled and discomfited, and with his prey snatched out of his hands, and they, too, have had gratefully to own, *"Our soul is escaped as a bird out of the snare of the fowlers ; the snare is broken, and we are escaped."* Yes ! depend upon it, our best and only hope *"is in the name of the Lord, who made heaven and earth."*—*Barton Bouchier.*

Verse 7.—*"Our soul is escaped as a bird."* The snare of the fowler was the lime-twigs of this world ; our soul was caught in them by the feathers, our affections : now, indeed, we are escaped ; but the Lord delivered us.—*Thomas Adams.*

Verse 7.—*"As a bird out of the snare of the fowlers."* The soul is surrounded by many dangers. 1. *It is ensnared by worldliness.* One of the most gigantic dangers against which God's people have specially to guard—an enemy to all spirituality of thought and feeling. 2. *It is ensnared by selfishness*—a foe to all simple-hearted charity, to all expansive generosity and Christian philanthropy. 3. *It is ensnared by unbelief*—the enemy of prayer, of ingenuous confidence, of all personal Christian effort. These are not imaginary dangers. We meet them in everyday life. They threaten us at every point, and often have we to lament over the havoc they make in our hearts.—*George Barlow, in a "Homiletic Commentary on the Book of Psalms,"* 1879.

Verse 7.—*"The snare is broken."* It is as easy for God to deliver his people out of their enemies' hands, even when they have the godly in their power, as to break a net made of thread or yarn, wherewith birds are taken.—*David Dickson.*

Verse 7.—*"The snare is broken, and we are escaped."* Our life lieth open always to the snares of Satan, and we as silly birds are like at every moment to be carried away, notwithstanding the Lord maketh a way for us to escape ; yea, when Satan seemeth to be most sure of us, by the mighty power of God the snares are broken and we are delivered. Experience we have hereof in those who are inwardly afflicted and with heaviness of spirit grievously oppressed, that when they seem to be in utter despair, and ready now, as you would say, to perish, yet even at the last pinch, and in the uttermost extremity cometh the sweet comfort of God's Holy Spirit and raiseth them up again. When we are most ready to perish, then is God most ready to help. " Except the Lord had holpen me," saith David, " my soul had almost dwelt in silence." And this again do we mark for the comfort of the weak conscience. It is Satan's subtlety whereby commonly he disquiets many, that because carnal corruption is in them he would therefore bear them in hand that they are none of Christ's. In this he plays the deceiver ; he tries us by the wrong rule of perfect sanctification ; this is the square that ought to be laid to Christ's members triumphant in heaven, and not to those who are militant on earth. Sin remaining in me will not prove that therefore I am not in Christ, otherwise Christ should have no members upon earth ; but grace working that new disposition which nature could never effect proves undoubtedly that we are in Christ Jesus.—*Thomas Stint.*

Verse 8.—*"Our help is in the name of the* LORD, *who made heaven and earth."*
He hath made *the earth* where the snare lies, so that he can rightfully destroy the snare as laid unlawfully in his domain ; he hath made the *heaven,* the true sphere of the soaring wings of those souls which he has delivered, so that they may fly upwards from their late prison, rejoicing. He came down to earth himself, the Lord Jesus in whose name is our help, that he might break the snare ; he returned to heaven, that we might fly " as the doves to their windows " (Isa. lx. 8), following where he showed the way.—*Richard Rolle, of Hampole* (1340), *in "Neale and Little-dale."*

Verse 8.—*"Our help is in the name of the* LORD." The fairest fruits of our by-past experience is to glorify God by confidence in him for time to come, as here.—*David Dickson.*

Verse 8.—*"The* LORD *who made heaven and earth."* As if the Psalmist had said, As long as I see heaven and earth I will never distrust. I hope in that God which made all these things out of nothing ; and therefore as long as I see those two great standing monuments of his power before me, heaven and earth, I will never be discouraged. So the apostle : 1 Peter iv. 19, " Commit the keeping of your souls to him in well-doing, as unto a faithful Creator." O Christian ! remember when you trust God you trust an almighty Creator, who is able to help, let your case be never so desperate. God could create when he had nothing to work *upon*, which made one wonder ; and he could create when he had nothing to work *with*, which is another wonder. What is become of the tools wherewith he made the world ? Where is the trowel wherewith he arched the heaven ? and the spade wherewith he digged the sea ? What had God to work upon, or work withal when he made the world ? He made it out of nothing. Now you commit your souls to the same faithful Creator.—*Thomas Manton.*

Verse 8.—The Romans in a great distress were put so hard to it, that they were fain to take the weapons out of the temples of their gods to fight with them ; and so they overcame. And this ought to be the course of every good Christian, in times of public distress, to fly to the weapons of the church, prayers and tears. The Spartans' walls were their spears, the Christians' walls are his prayers. His help standeth in the name of the Lord who hath made both heaven and earth.—*Edmund Calamy.*

Verse 8.—The French Protestants always begin their public worship with the last verse of this Psalm, and there is no thought more encouraging and comfortable. —*Job Orton,* 1717—1783.

Verse 8.—*"Our help is in the name of the* LORD," etc. These are the words of a triumphing and victorious faith, *"Our help standeth in the name of the* LORD, *which made heaven and earth "* : as if he said, the Maker of heaven and earth is my God and my helper. Ye see whither he flieth in his great distress. He despaireth not, but crieth unto the Lord, as one yet hoping assuredly to find relief and comfort. Rest thou also in this hope, and do as he did. David was not tempted to the end he should despair ; think not thou, therefore, that thy temptations are sent unto thee that thou shouldest be swallowed up with sorrow and desperation : if thou be brought down to the very gates of hell, believe that the Lord will surely raise thee up again. If so thou be bruised and broken, know it is the Lord that will help thee again. If thy heart be full of sorrow and heaviness, look for comfort from him, who said, that a troubled spirit is a sacrifice unto him: (Ps. li. 17.) Thus he setteth the eternal God, the Maker of heaven and earth, against all troubles and dangers, against the floods and overflowings of all temptations, and swalloweth up, as it were, with one breath all the raging furies of the whole world, and of hell itself, even as a little drop of water is swallowed up by a mighty flaming fire: and what is the world with all its force and power, in respect of him that made heaven and earth!—*Thomas Stint.*

HINTS TO PREACHERS.

Verse 1.—"*The Lord who was on our side.*" Who is he? Why on our side? How does he prove it? What are we bound to do?

Verses 1—3.—Regard the text, I. From the life of Jacob or Israel. II. From the history of the nation. III. From the annals of the church. IV. From our personal biography.

Verses 1—5.—I. What might have been. II. Why it has not been.

Verses 1—5.—I. What the people of God would have been if the Lord had not been on our side. 1. What if left to their enemies? verses 2, 3. Israel left to Pharaoh and his host in the time of Moses: left to the Canaanites in the time of Joshua: to the Midianites in the time of Gideon: Judah to the Assyrians in the time of Hezekiah: "Then they had swallowed us up," etc. 2. What if left to themselves? "The stream had gone over our soul": verses 4, 5. II. What the people of God are with the Lord on their side. 1. All the designs of their enemies against them are frustrated. 2. Their inward sorrow is turned into joy. 3. Both their inward and their outward troubles work together for their good.—*G. R.*

Verses 2, 3.—I. To swallow us alive—the desire of our wrathful enemies. II. To save us alive—the work of our faithful God.

Verses 4, 5.—Perils of waters: a number of thoughts may be worked out from the likeness between afflictions and torrents.

Verse 6.—I. The Lamb. II. The Lion. III. The Lord.

Verse 6.—I. They would gladly devour us. II. They cannot devour unless the Lord will. III. God is to be praised since he does not permit them to injure us.

Verse 6.—I. The ill-will of men against the righteous. 1. For their spoliation. 2. For their destruction: "As a prey to their teeth." II. The goodwill of God. "Blessed be the Lord," etc. 1. What it supposes—that good men, in a measure and for a time, may be given into the hands of the wicked. 2. What it affirms—that they are not given entirely into their hands—*G. R.*

Verse 7.—I. The soul ensnared. 1. By whom? Wicked men are fowlers. By Satan.

> "Satan, the fowler, who betrays
> Unguarded souls a thousand ways."

2. How? By temptations—to pride, worldliness, drunkenness, error, or lust, according to the tastes and habits of the individual. II. The soul escaped: "Our soul is escaped," etc. "The snare is broken," not by ourselves, but by the hand of God.—*G. R.*

Verse 7.—I. A bird. II. A snare. III. A capture. IV. An escape.

Verse 8.—Our Creator, our Helper. Special comfort to be drawn from creation in this matter.

Verse 8.—I. The Helper: "The Lord, who made heaven and earth," who in his works has given ample proofs of what he can do. II. The helped. "Our help" is, 1. Promised in his name. 2. Sought in his name: these make it ours. —*G. R.*

Verse 8.—I. We have help. As troubled sinners, as dull scholars, as trembling professors, as inexperienced travellers, as feeble workers. II. We have help in God's name. In his perfections—"They shall put my name upon the children of Israel." In his gospel—"A chosen vessel to bear my name." In his authority —"In the name of Jesus Christ rise up," etc. III. Therefore we exert ourselves. —*W. J.*

PSALM CXXV.

TITLE.—*A Song of Degrees. Another step is taken in the ascent, another station in the pilgrimage is reached : certainly a rise in the sense is here perceptible, since full assurance concerning years to come is a higher form of faith than the ascription of former escapes to the Lord. Faith has praised Jehovah for past deliverances, and here she rises to a confident joy in the present and future safety of believers. She asserts that they shall for ever be secure who trust themselves with the Lord. We can magine the pilgrims chanting this song when perambulating the city walls.*

We do not assert that David wrote this Psalm, but we have as much ground for doing so as others have for declaring that it was written after the captivity. It would seem probable that all the Pilgrim Psalms were composed, or, at least, compiled by the same writer, and as some of them are certainly by David, there is no conclusive reason for taking away the rest from him.

DIVISION.—*First we have a song of holy confidence* (1, 2) ; *then a promise*, 3 ; *followed by a prayer*. 4 ; *and a note of warning*.

EXPOSITION.

THEY that trust in the LORD *shall be* as mount Zion, *which* cannot be removed, *but* abideth for ever.

2 *As* the mountains *are* round about Jerusalem, so the LORD *is* round about his people from henceforth even for ever.

3 For the rod of the wicked shall not rest upon the lot of the righteous ; lest the righteous put forth their hands unto iniquity.

4 Do good, O LORD, unto *those that be* good, and to *them that are* upright in their hearts.

5 As for such as turn aside unto their crooked ways, the LORD shall lead them forth with the workers of iniquity : *but* peace *shall be* upon Israel.

1. *"They that trust in the LORD shall be as mount Zion."* The emphasis lies upon the object of their trust, namely, Jehovah the Lord. What a privilege to be allowed to repose in God ! How condescending is Jehovah to become the confidence of his people ! To trust elsewhere is vanity ; and the more implicit such misplaced trust becomes the more bitter will be the ensuing disappointment ; but to trust in the living God is sanctified common sense which needs no excuse, its result shall be its best vindication. There is no conceivable reason why we should not trust in Jehovah, and there is every possible argument for so doing ; but, apart from all argument, the end will prove the wisdom of the confidence. The result of faith is not occasional and accidental ; its blessing comes, not to some who trust, but to all who trust in the Lord. Trusters in Jehovah shall be as fixed, firm, and stable as the mount where David dwelt, and where the ark abode. To move mount Zion was impossible : the mere supposition was absurd. *"Which cannot be removed, but abideth for ever."* Zion was the image of eternal steadfastness,—this hill which, according to the Hebrew, " sits to eternity," neither bowing down nor moving to and fro. Thus doth the trusting worshipper of Jehovah enjoy a restfulness which is the mirror of tranquillity ; and this not without cause, for his hope is sure, and of his confidence he can never be ashamed. As the Lord sitteth King for ever, so do his people sit enthroned in perfect peace when their trust in him is firm. This is, and is to be our portion ; we are, we have been, we shall be as steadfast as the hill of God. Zion cannot be removed, and does not remove ; so the people of God can neither be moved passively nor actively, by force from without or fickleness from within. Faith in God is a settling and establishing virtue ; he who by his strength setteth fast the mountains, by that same power stays the hearts of them that trust in him. This steadfastness will endure " for ever," and we may be assured

therefore that no believer shall perish either in life or in death, in time or in eternity. We trust in an eternal God, and our safety shall be eternal.

2. "*As the mountains are round about Jerusalem, so the* LORD *is round about his people from henceforth even for ever.*" The hill of Zion is the type of the believer's constancy, and the surrounding mountains are made emblems of the all-surrounding presence of the Lord. The mountains around the holy city, though they do not make a circular wall, are, nevertheless, set like sentinels to guard her gates. God doth not enclose his people within ramparts and bulwarks, making their city to be a prison ; but yet he so orders the arrangements of his providence that his saints are as safe as if they dwelt behind the strongest fortifications. What a double security the two verses set before us ! First, we are established, and then entrenched : settled, and then sentinelled : made like a mount, and then protected as if by mountains. This is no matter of poetry, it is so in fact ; and it is no matter of temporary privilege, but it shall be so for ever. Date when we please, " from henceforth " Jehovah encircles his people : look on us as far as we please, the protection extends " even for ever." Note, it is not said that Jehovah's power or wisdom defends believers, but he himself is round about them : they have his personality for their protection, his Godhead for their guard. We are here taught that the Lord's people are those who trust him, for they are thus described in the first verses : the line of faith is the line of grace, those who trust in the Lord are chosen of the Lord. The two verses together prove the eternal safety of the saints : they must abide where God has placed them, and God must for ever protect them from all evil. It would be difficult to imagine greater safety than is here set forth.

3. "*For the rod of the wicked shall not rest upon the lot of the righteous.*" The people of God are not to expect immunity from trial because the Lord surrounds them, for they may feel the power and persecution of the ungodly. Isaac, even in Abraham's family, was mocked by Ishmael. Assyria laid its sceptre even upon Zion itself. The graceless often bear rule and wield the rod ; and when they do so they are pretty sure to make it fall heavily upon the Lord's believing people, so that the godly cry out by reason of their oppressors. Egypt's rod was exceeding heavy upon Israel, but the time came for it to be broken. God has set a limit to the woes of his chosen : the rod may light on their portion, but it shall not *rest* upon it. The righteous have a lot which none can take from them, for God has appointed them heirs of it by gracious entail : on that lot the rod of the wicked may fall, but over that lot it cannot have lasting sway. The saints abide for ever, but their troubles will not. Here is a good argument in prayer for all righteous ones who are in the hands of the wicked.

"*Lest the righteous put forth their hands unto iniquity.*" The tendency of oppression is to drive the best of men into some hasty deed for self-deliverance or vengeance. If the rack be too long used the patient sufferer may at last give way ; and therefore the Lord puts a limit to the tyranny of the wicked. He ordained that an Israelite who deserved punishment should not be beaten without measure : forty stripes save one was the appointed limit. We may therefore expect that he will set a bound to the suffering of the innocent, and will not allow them to be pushed to the uttermost extreme. Especially in point of time he will limit the domination of the persecutor, for length adds strength to oppression, and makes it intolerable : hence the Lord himself said of a certain tribulation, " except those days should be shortened, there should no flesh be saved ; but for the elect's sake those days shall be shortened."

It seems that even righteous men are in peril of sinning in evil days, and that it is not the will of the Lord that they should yield to the stress of the times in order to escape from suffering. The power and influence of wicked men when they are uppermost are used to lead or drive the righteous astray ; but the godly must not accept this as an excuse, and yield to the evil pressure ; far rather must they resist with all their might till it shall please God to stay the violence of the persecutor, and give his children rest. This the Lord here promises to do in due time.

4. "*Do good, O* LORD, *unto those that be good, and to them that are upright in their hearts.*" Men to be good at all must be good at heart. Those who trust in the Lord are good ; for faith is the root of righteousness, and the evidence of uprightness. Faith in God is a good and upright thing, and its influence makes the rest of the man good and upright. To such God will do good : the prayer of the text is but another form of promise, for that which the Lord prompts us to ask he virtually promises to give. Jehovah will take off evil from his people, and in the place thereof

will enrich them with all manner of good.   When the rod of the wicked is gone his
own rod and staff shall comfort us.   Meanwhile it is for us to pray that it may be
well with all the upright who are now among men.   God bless them, and do them
good in every possible form.   We wish well to those who do well.   We are so plagued
by the crooked that we would pour benedictions upon the upright.

5. *"As for such as turn aside unto their crooked ways, the LORD shall lead them
forth with the workers of iniquity."*   Two kinds of men are always to be found, the
upright and the men of crooked ways.   Alas, there are some who pass from one
class to another, not by a happy conversion, turning from the twisting lanes of
deceit into the highway of truth, but by an unhappy declension leaving the main
road of honesty and holiness for the bypaths of wickedness.   Such apostates have
been seen in all ages, and David knew enough of them ; he could never forget Saul,
and Ahithophel, and others.   How sad that men who once walked in the right way
should turn aside from it !   Observe the course of the falsehearted : first, they
look out for crooked ways ; next, they choose them and make them *"their* crooked
ways " ;   and then they turn aside into them.   They never intend to go back unto
perdition, but only to make a curve and drop into the right road again.   The straight
way becomes a little difficult, and so they make a circumbendibus, which all along
aims at coming out right, though it may a little deviate from precision.   These
people are neither upright in heart, nor good, nor trusters in Jehovah, and therefore
the Lord will deal otherwise with them than with his own people :   when execution
day comes these hypocrites and time-servers shall be led out to the same gallows
as the openly wicked.   All sin will one day be expelled the universe, even as criminals
condemned to die are led out of the city ;   then shall secret traitors find themselves
ejected with open rebels.   Divine truth will unveil their hidden pursuits, and lead
them forth, and to the surprise of many they shall be set in the same rank with
those who avowedly wrought iniquity.

"But peace shall be upon Israel."   In fact the execution of the deceivers shall
tend to give the true Israel peace.   When God is smiting the unfaithful not a blow
shall fall upon the faithful.   The chosen of the Lord shall not only be like Salem,
but they shall have salem, or peace.   Like a prince, Israel has prevailed with God,
and therefore he need not fear the face of man ;   his wrestlings are over, the blessing
of peace has been pronounced upon him.   He who has peace with God may enjoy
peace concerning all things.   Bind the first and last verses together :   Israel trusts
in the Lord (verse 1), and Israel has peace (verse 5).

EXPLANATORY NOTES AND QUAINT SAYINGS.

Whole Psalm.—In the degrees of Christian virtue, this Psalm represents the
sixth step—the confidence which the Christian places in the Lord.   " It teacheth
us, while we ascend and raise our minds unto the Lord our God in loving charity and
piety, not to fix our gaze upon men who are prosperous in the world with a false
happiness."*—*H. T. Armfield, in "The Gradual Psalms,"* 1874.

Whole Psalm.—This short Psalm may be summed up in those words of the prophet
(Isaiah iii. 10, 11), " Say ye to the righteous, that it shall be well with him.   Woe
unto the wicked !   it shall be ill with him."   Thus are life and death, the blessing
and the curse, set before us often in the Psalms, as well as in the law and in the
prophets.—*Matthew Henry,* 1662—1714.

Verse 1.—*"They that trust in the LORD."*   Note how he commandeth no work
here to be done, but only speaketh of trust.   In popery in the time of trouble men
were taught to enter into some kind of religion, to fast, to go on pilgrimage, and
to do such other foolish works of devotion, which they devised as an high service
unto God, and thereby thought to make condign satisfaction for sin and to merit
eternal life.   But here the Psalmist leadeth us the plain way unto God, pronouncing
this to be the chiefest anchor of our salvation,—only to hope and trust in the Lord ;

---

* Augustine.

and declaring that the greatest service that we can do unto God is to trust him. For this is the nature of God—to create all things of nothing. Therefore he createth and bringeth forth in death, life ; in darkness, light. Now to believe this is the essential nature and most special property of faith. When God then seeth such a one as agreeth with his own nature, that is, which believeth to find in danger help, in poverty riches, in sin righteousness, and that for God's own mercy's sake in Christ alone, him can God neither hate nor forsake.—*Martin Luther* (1483—1546), *in "A Commentary on the Psalms of Degrees."*

Verse 1.—*"They that trust in the* LORD." All that deal with God must deal upon trust, and he will give comfort to those only that give credit to him, and make it appear they do so by quitting other confidences, and venturing to the utmost for God. The closer our expectations are confined to God, the higher our expectations may be raised.—*Matthew Henry.*

Verse 1.—*"They that trust,"* etc. Trust, therefore, in the Lord, *always, altogether, and for all things.*—*Robert Nisbet, in "The Songs of the Temple Pilgrims,"* 1863.

Verse 1.—*"Shall be as mount Zion."* Some persons are like the sand—ever shifting and treacherous. See Matthew vii. 26. Some are like the sea—restless and unsettled. See Isaiah lvii. 20 ; James i. 6. Some are like the wind—uncertain and inconstant. See Ephesians iv. 14. Believers are like a mountain—strong, stable, and secure. To every soul that trusts him the Lord says, " Thou art Peter."—*W. H. J. Page,* 1883.

Verse 1.—*"As mount Zion,"* etc.—Great is the stability of a believer's felicity.—*John Trapp,* 1601—1669.

Verse 1.—*"Mount Zion, which cannot be removed,"* etc. Lieutenant Conder, reviewing Mr. Maudslay's important exploration, says, " It is especially valuable as showing that, however the masonry may have been destroyed and lost, we may yet hope to find indications of the ancient enceinte *in the rock scarps which are imperishable."* This is very true ; for, while man can destroy what man has made, the everlasting hills smile at his rage. Yet who can hear of it without perceiving the force and sublimity of that glorious description of the immobility of believers.

" They that trust in Jehovah are as mount Zion,
Which shall not be moved, it abideth for ever."

James Neil, in "Palestine Explored," 1882.

Verse 1.—*"Cannot be removed,"* etc. They can never be removed from the Lord, though they may be removed from his house and ordinances, as sometimes David was ; and from his gracious presence, and sensible communion with him ; and out of the world by death : yet never from his heart's love, nor out of the covenant of his grace, which is sure and everlasting ; nor out of his family, into which they are taken ; nor from the Lord Jesus Christ, nor out of his hands and arms, nor from off his heart ; nor from off him, as the foundation on which they are laid ; nor out of a state of grace, either regeneration or justification ; but such abide in the love of God, in the covenant of his grace, in the hands of his Son, in the grace wherein they stand, and in the house of God for evermore.—*John Gill,* 1697—1771.

Verse 1.—*"Abideth for ever."* So surely as *"Mount Zion"* shall never be *"removed,"* so surely shall the church of God be preserved. Is it not strange that wicked and idolatrous powers have not joined together, dug down this mount, and carried it into the sea, that they might nullify a promise in which the people of God exult ! Till ye can carry Mount Zion into the Mediterranean Sea, the church of Christ shall grow and prevail. Hear this, ye murderous Mohammedans !—*Adam Clarke,* 1760—1832.

Verse 1.—*"Abideth."* Literally, *sitteth ;* as spoken of a mountain, " lieth " or " is situated " ; but here with the following *"for ever,"* used in a still stronger sense.—*J. J. Stewart Perowne,* 1868.

Verses 1, 2.—That which is here promised the saints is a perpetual preservation of them in that condition wherein they are ; both on the part of God, " he is round about them from henceforth even for ever"; and on their parts, *"they shall not be removed,"*—that is, from the condition of acceptation with God wherein they are supposed to be,—but they shall abide for ever, and continue therein immovable unto the end. This is a plain promise of their continuance in that condition wherein they are, with their safety from thence, and not a promise of some other good thing provided that they continue in that condition. Their being compared to mountains, and their stability, which consists in their being and continuing so, will admit no other sense. As mount Zion abides in its condition, so shall they ; and as the mountains about Jerusalem continue, so doth the Lord continue his presence unto them.

That expression which is used, verse 2, is weighty and full to this purpose, *"The LORD is round about his people from henceforth even for ever."* What can be spoken more fully, more pathetically ? Can any expression of men so set forth the safety of the saints ? The Lord is round about them, not to save them from this or that incursion, but from all ; not from one or two evils, but from every one whereby they are or may be assaulted. He is with them, and round about them on every side that no evil shall come nigh them. It is a most full expression of universal preservation, or of God's keeping his saints in his love and favour, upon all accounts whatsoever ; and that not for a season only, but it is *"henceforth,"* from his giving this promise unto their souls in particular, and their receiving of it, throughout all generations, *"even for ever."*—*John Owen*, 1616—1683.

Verse 2.—*"As the mountains cre round about Jerusalem."* This image is not realised, as most persons familiar with our European scenery would wish and expect it to be realised. Jerusalem is not literally shut in by mountains, except on the eastern side, where it may be said to be enclosed by the arms of Olivet, with its outlying ridges on the north-east and south-west. Anyone facing Jerusalem westward, northward, or southward, will always see the city itself on an elevation higher than the hills in its immediate neighbourhood, its towers and walls standing out against the sky, and not against any high back-ground such as that which encloses the mountain towns and villages of our own Cumbrian or Westmoreland valleys. Nor, again, is the plain on which it stands enclosed by a continuous though distant circle of mountains, like that which gives its peculiar charm to Athens and Innspruck. The mountains in the neighbourhood of Jerusalem are of unequal height, and only in two or three instances—Neby-Samwil, Er-Rain, and Tuleil el-Ful—rising to any considerable elevation. Even Olivet is only a hundred and eighty feet above the top of Mount Zion. Still they act as a shelter : they must be surmounted before the traveller can see, or the invader attack, the Holy City ; and the distant line of Moab would always seem to rise as a wall against invaders from the remote east. It is these mountains, expressly including those beyond the Jordan, which are mentioned as " standing round about Jerusalem," in another and more terrible sense, when, on the night of the assault of Jerusalem by the Roman armies, they " echoed back " the screams of the inhabitants of the captured city, and the victorious shouts of the soldiers of Titus.*—*Arthur Penrhyn Stanley* (1815—1881), *in "Sinai and Palestine."*

Verse 2.—*"As the mountains are round about Jerusalem."* Jerusalem is situated in the centre of a mountainous region, whose valleys have drawn around it in all directions a perfect net-work of deep ravines, the perpendicular walls of which constitute a very efficient system of defence.—*William M. Thomson, in "The Land and the Book,"* 1881.

Verse 2.—*"As the mountains are round about Jerusalem,"* etc. The mountains most emphatically stand *"round about Jerusalem,"* and in doing so must have greatly safeguarded it in ancient times. We are specially told that when Titus besieged the city, he found it impossible to invest it completely until he had built a wall round the entire sides of these mountains, nearly five miles long, with thirteen places at intervals in which he stationed garrisons, which added another mile and a quarter to these vast earthworks. " The whole was completed," says the Jewish historian, " in three days ; so that what would naturally have required some months was done in so short an interval as is incredible."† Assaults upon the city, even then, could only be delivered effectively upon its level corner to the north-west, whence every hostile advance was necessarily directed in all its various sieges. To those familiar with these facts, beautifully bold, graphic, and forceful is the Psalmist's figure of the security of the Lord's people—

> " The mountains are round about Jerusalem ;
> And Jehovah is round about his people,
> Henceforth, even for evermore."

---

* Josephus. Bell. Jud. vi. 5, 1.
† Josephus. Wars of the Jews. Book v. chap xli. section 2.

These words must have been in Hebrew ears as sublime as they were comforting, and, when sung on the heights of Zion, inspiring in the last degree.—*James Neil.*

Verse 2.—*"The LORD is round about his people."* It is not enough that we are compassed about with fiery walls, that is, with the sure custody, the continual watch and ward of the angels ; but the Lord himself is our wall : so that every way we are defended by the Lord against all dangers. Above us is his heaven, on both sides he is as a wall, under us he is as a strong rock whereupon we stand : so are we everywhere sure and safe. Now if Satan through these munitions casts his darts at us, it must needs be that the Lord himself shall be hurt before we take harm. Great is our incredulity if we hear all these things in vain.—*Martin Luther.*

Verse 2.—*"From henceforth, even for ever."* This amplification of the promise, taken from time or duration, should be carefully noted ; for it shows that the promises made to the people of Israel pertain generally to the Church in every age, and are not to expire with that polity. Thus it expressly declares, that the Church will continuously endure in this life ; which is most sweet consolation for pious minds, especially in great dangers and public calamities, when everything appears to threaten ruin and destruction.—*D. H. Mollerus,* 1639.

Verse 3.—*"The rod of the wicked."* It is *their* rod, made for them ; if God scourge his children a little with it, he doth but borrow it from the immediate and natural use for which it was ordained ; their rod, their judgment. So it is called their cup : " This is the portion " and potion " of their cup." Ps. xi. 6.—*Thomas Adams, in "An Exposition of the Second Epistle of Peter,"* 1633.

Verse 3.—*"For the rod of the wicked,"* etc. According to Gussetius, this is to be understood of a measuring rod ; laid not on persons, but on lands and estates ; and best agrees with the lot, inheritance, and estate of the righteous ; and may signify that though wicked men unjustly seize upon and retain the farms, possessions, and estates of good men, as if they were assigned to them by the measuring line ; yet they shall not hold them long, or always.—*John Gill.*

Verse 3.—*"For the rod of the wicked shall not rest upon the lot of the righteous."* No tyranny, although it appear firm and stable, is of long continuance : inasmuch as God does not relinquish the sceptre. This is manifest from the example of Pharaoh, of Saul, of Sennacherib, of Herod, and of others. Rightly, therefore, says Athanasius of Julian the Apostate, " That little cloud has quickly passed away." And how quickly beyond all human expectation the foundations of the ungodly are overthrown is fully declared in Psalm xxxvii.—*Solomon Gesner,* 1559—1605.

Verse 3.—*"Shall not rest,"* that is to say, " lie heavy," so as to oppress, as in Isa. xxv. 10, with a further sense of *continuance* of the oppression.—*J. J. Stewart Perowne.*

Verse 3.—*"Shall not rest,"* etc. The wrath of man, like water turned upon a mill, shall come on them with no more force than shall be sufficient for accomplishing God's gracious purposes on their souls : the rest, however menacing its power may be, shall be made to pass off by an opened sluice. Nevertheless the trouble shall be sufficient to try every man, and to prove the truth and measure of his integrity.— *Charles Simeon* (1759—1836) *in "Horæ Homileticæ."*

Verse 3.—*"The lot of the righteous."* There is a fourfold lot belonging to the faithful. 1. The lot of the saints is the sufferings of the saints. " All that will live godly in Christ Jesus shall suffer persecution : " 2 Tim. iii. 12. 2. The lot of the saints is also that light and happiness they have in this world. The lot is " fallen unto me in pleasant places ; yea, I have a goodly heritage : " Ps. xvi. 6. When David sat at the sheepfold, which was his lot, he was thus prepared for the kingdom of Israel which was given him by lot from God. 3. But more specially faith, grace, and sanctification ; which give them just right and title to the inheritance of glory. Heaven is theirs now ; though not in possession, yet in succession. They have the earnest of it ; let them grow up to stature and perfection, and take it. 4. Lastly, they have the lot of heaven. Hell is the lot of the wicked : " Behold at eveningtide trouble ; and before the morning he is not. This is the portion of them that spoil us, and the lot of them that rob us " ; Isa. xvii. 14. Therefore it is said of Judas, that he went " to his own place " : Acts i. 25. " Upon the wicked he shall rain snares, fire and brimstone, and an horrible tempest ; this shall be the portion of their cup " : Ps. xi. 6. But the lot of the righteous is faith, and the end of their faith the salvation of their souls. God gives them heaven, not for any foreseen worthiness in the receivers, for no worthiness of our own can make us our father's heirs ; but for his own mercy and favour in Christ, preparing heaven for us, and us for heaven. So that upon his decree it is allotted to us ; and unless heaven could lose God, we cannot lose heaven.

Here, then, consider how the lottery of Canaan may shadow out to us that blessed land of promise whereof the other was a type.—*Thomas Adams.*

Verse 3.—*"Lest the righteous put forth their hands unto iniquity."* Lest overcome by impatiency, or drawn aside by the world's *allurements* or *affrightments*, they should yield and comply with the desires of the wicked, or seek to help themselves out of trouble by sinister practices. God (saith Chrysostom) acts like a lutanist, who will not let the strings of his lute be too slack, lest it mar the music, nor suffer them to be too hard stretched or screwed up, lest they break.—*John Trapp*, 1601—1669.

Verse 3.—*"Lest the righteous put forth their hands,"* etc. The trial is to prove faith, not to endanger it by too sharp a pressure ; *lest*, overcome by this, even the faithful put forth a hand (as in Gen. iii. 22), to forbidden pleasure ; or (as in Exod. xxii. 8), to contamination : through force of custom gradually persuading to sinful compliance, or through despair of good, as the Psalmist (see Ps. xxxvii. and lxxiii.) describes some in his day who witnessed the prosperity of wicked men.—*The Speaker's Commentary*, 1871—1881.

Verse 4.—*"Do good, O LORD, unto those that be good."* The Midrash here calls to mind a Talmudic riddle :—There came a good one (Moses, Ex. ii. 2) and received a good thing (the Tôra, or Law, Prov. iv. 2) from the good One (God, Ps. cxlv. 9) for the good ones (Israel, Ps. cxxv. 4).—*Franz Delitzsch*, 1871.

Verse 4.—*"Do good, O LORD, unto those that be good."* A favourite thought with Nehemiah. See Nehemiah ii. 8, 18 ; v. 19 ; xiii. 14, 31 : " Remember me, O my God, for *good*," the concluding words of his book.—*Christopher Wordsworth*, 1872.

Verse 4.—*"Do good, O LORD, unto those that be good."* They consult their own good best, who do most good. I may say these three things of *those who do good* (and what is serving God but doing of good ? or what is doing good but serving God ?). First, they shall receive true good. Secondly, they shall for ever hold the best good, the chief good ; they shall not only spend their days and years in good ; but when their days and years are spent, they shall have good, and a greater good than any they had, in spending the days and years of this life. They shall have good in death, they shall come to a fuller enjoyment of God, *the chief good*, when they have left and let fall the possession of all earthly goods. Thirdly, they that do good shall find all things working together for their good ; if they have a loss they shall receive good by it ; if they bear a cross, that cross shall bear good to them.—*Joseph Caryl*, 1602—1673.

Verse 4.—*"Do good, O LORD, unto those that be good,"* etc. Perhaps it may not prove unprofitable to enquire, with some minuteness, who are the persons for whom prayer is presented, and who have an interest in the Divine promises. They are brought before us under different denominations. In the first verse, they are described as trusting in the Lord : in the second verse, they are described as the Lord's people : in the third verse, they are called the righteous : in the fourth verse, they are called good and upright in heart : and in the fifth verse, they are called Israel. Let us collect these terms together, and endeavour to ascertain from them, what is their true condition and character, for whose security the Divine perfections are pledged. And while a rapid sketch is thus drawn, let each breathe the silent prayer, " Search me, O God, and know my heart ; try me, and know my thoughts ; and see if there be any wicked way in me, and lead me in the way everlasting."—*N. M'Michael, in "The Pilgrim Psalms,"* 1860.

Verse 4.—*" Do good, O LORD, unto those that be good."* Believers are described as *"good."* The name is explained by the Spirit as implying the indwelling of the Holy Ghost and of faith. It is proof that no guile is harboured in their hearts. Prayer is made that God would visit them with goodness. This prayer indited by the Spirit amounts to a heavenly promise that they shall receive such honour.—*Henry Law, in "Family Devotion,"* 1878.

Verse 4.—*"Them that be good."* Oh, brethren, the good in us is God in us. The inwardness makes the outwardness, the godliness the beauty. It is indisputable that it is Christ in us that makes all our Christianity. Oh, Christians who have no Christ in them—such Christians are poor, cheap imitations, and hollow shams—

and Christ will, with infinite impatience, even infinite love, fling them away.—
Charles Stanford, in a Sermon preached before the Baptist Union, 1876.

Verse 4.—*"Upright in their hearts."* All true excellence has its seat here. It
is not the good action which makes the good man : it is the good man who does
the good action. The merit of an action depends entirely upon the motives which
have prompted its performance ; and, tried by this simple test, how many deeds,
which have wrung from the world its admiration and its glory, might well be described
in old words, as nothing better than splendid sins. When the heart is wrong, all
is wrong. When the heart is right, all is right.—*N. M'Michael.*

Verse 4.—*"Upright."* Literally, *straight,* straightforward, as opposed to all
moral obliquity whatever.—*Joseph Addison Alexander* (1809—1860), *in "The Psalms
Translated and Explained."*

Verse 5.—*"Such as turn aside unto their crooked ways."* This is the anxiety of
the pastor in this pilgrim song. The shepherd would keep his sheep from straggling.
His distress is that all in Israel are not true Israelites. Two sorts of people, described
by the poet, have ever been in the church. The second class, instead of being at
the trouble to " withstand in the evil day," will " put forth their hands unto iniquity."
Rather than feel, they will follow the rod of the wicked. They will " turn aside
unto their crooked ways," sooner than risk temporal and material interests.—
Edward Jewitt Robinson, in "The Caravan and the Temple," 1878.

Verse 5.—*"Such as turn aside unto their crooked ways."* All the ways of sin are
called *"crooked ways,"* and they are our own ways. The Psalmist calls them " *their*
crooked ways " ; that is, the ways of their own devising ; whereas the way of holiness
is the Lord's way. To exceed or do more ; to be deficient or do less, than God
requires, both these are *"crooked ways."* The way of the Lord lies straight forward,
right before us. " Whoso walketh uprightly shall be saved ; but he that is perverse
(or *crooked*) in his ways shall fall at once": Prov. xxviii. 18. The motion of a
godly man is like that of the kine that carried the ark : "Who took the straight
way to the way of Beth-shemesh, and went along the highway, lowing as they went,
and turned not aside to the right hand or to the left ": 1 Sam. vi. 12.—*Joseph Caryl.*

Verse 5.—*"Crooked ways."* The ways of sinners are *"crooked "* ; they shift
from one pursuit to another, and turn hither and thither to deceive ; they wind
about a thousand ways to conceal their base intentions, to accomplish their iniquitous
projects, or to escape the punishment of their crimes ; yet disappointment, detection,
confusion, and misery, are their inevitable portion.—*Thomas Scott,* 1747—1821.

Verse 5.—*The LORD shall lead them forth with the workers of iniquity."* They
walked according to the prince of the air, and they shall go where the prince of the
air is. God will bring forth men from their hiding-places. Though they walk among
the drove of his children, in procession now, yet if they also walk in by-lanes of sin,
God will rank them at the latter day, yea, often in this world, with the workers
of iniquity. They walk after workers of iniquity here before God, and God will
make manifest that it is so before he hath done with them. The reason, my brethren,
why they are to be reckoned among workers of iniquity, and as walkers among them,
though they sever themselves from them in respect of external conversation, is,
because they agree in the same internal principle of sin. They walk in their lusts :
every unregenerate man doth so. Refine him how you will, it is certain he doth
in heart pursue *"crooked ways."*—*Thomas Goodwin,* 1600—1679.

Verse 5.—Sometimes God takes away a barren professor by permitting him to
fall into open profaneness. There is one that hath taken up a profession of the
worthy name of the Lord Jesus Christ, but this profession is only a cloak ; he secretly
practiseth wickedness ; he is a glutton, or a drunkard, or covetous, or unclean.
Well, saith God, I will loose the reins of this professor, I will give him up to his vile
affections. I will loose the reins of his sins before him, he shall be entangled with
his filthy lusts, he shall be overcome of ungodly company. Thus they that turn
aside to their own crooked ways, *"the Lord shall lead them forth with the workers of
iniquity."*—*John Bunyan,* 1628—1688.

Verse 5.—*"But peace shall be upon Israel."* Do you ask, What is the peace upon
Israel ? I answer :—First, the peace of Israel, that is, of a believing and holy soul,
is *from above,* and is higher than all the disturbances of the world ; it rests upon
him, and makes him calm and peaceful, and lifts him above the world : for upon
him rests the Holy Spirit, who is the Comforter ; who is essential love and uncreated
peace. Secondly, the peace of a believing and holy soul is *internal ;* for it is sent

down from heaven upon his head, flows into his heart, and dwells there, and stills all agitations of mind. Thirdly, the peace of a believing and holy soul, is also *external*. It is a fountain of Paradise watering all the face of the earth ; Gen. ii. 6 : you see it in the man's face and life. Fourthly, the peace of a believing and holy soul is *divine :* for chiefly, it maintains peace with God. Fifthly, the peace of a believing and holy soul is *universal :* to wit, with neighbours, with God, with himself : in the body, in the eyes, in the ears, in tasting, smelling, feeling, in all the members, and in all the appetites. This peace is not disturbed by devils, the world, and the flesh, setting forth their honours, riches, pleasures. Sixthly, the peace of a believing and holy soul is peace *eternal* and never interrupted ; for it flows from an eternal and exhaustless fountain, even from God himself.—*Condensed from Le Blanc*, 1599 —1669.

Verse 5.—"*Israel.*" The Israelites derived their joint names from the two chief parts of religion : Israelites, from Israel, whose prayer was his " strength " (Hosea xii. 3), and Jews, from Judah, whose name means " praise."—*George Seaton Bowes, in "Illustrative Gatherings,"* 1869.

HINTS TO PREACHERS.

Whole Psalm.—I. The mark of the covenant : " They that trust." II. The security of the covenant (verses 1, 2). III. The rod of the covenant (verse 3). IV. The tenor of the covenant (verse 4). V. The spirit of the covenant,—" peace."

Verse 1.—See " Spurgeon's Sermons," No. 1,450 : " The Immortality of the Believer."

Verses 1, 2.—I. The believer's singularity : he trusts in Jehovah. II. The believer's stability : " abideth for ever." III. The believer's safety : " As the mountains," etc.

Verse 2.—The all-surrounding presence of Jehovah the glory, safety, and eternal blessedness of his people. Yet this to the wicked would be hell.

Verse 2.—See " Spurgeon's Sermons," Nos. 161-2 : " The Security of the Church."

Verse 2.—The endurance of mercy : " From henceforth even for ever."

Verse 2.—Saints hemmed-in by infinite love. I. *The City and the Girdle*, or *the symbols separated.* 1. Jerusalem imaging God's people. Anciently chosen ; singularly honoured ; much beloved ; the shrine of Deity. 2. The Mountain Girdle setting forth Jehovah : Strength ; All-sidedness ; Sentinel through day and night. II. *The City within the Girdle*, or *the symbols related.* 1. Delightful Entanglement. The view from the windows ! (Jehovah " round about.") To be lost must *break through God !* Sound sleep and safe labour. 2. Omnipotent Circumvallation, suggesting—God's determination ; Satan's dismay. This mountain ring immutable. —*W. B. Haynes.*

Verse 3.—Observe, I. The Permission implied. The rod of the wicked may come upon the lot of the righteous. Why ? 1. That wickedness may be free to manifest itself. 2. That the righteous may be made to hate sin. 3. That the righteousness of God's retribution may be seen. 4. That the consolations of the righteous may abound. 2 Cor. i. 5. II. The Permanency denied : " The rod . . . shall *not* rest," etc. Illustrate by history of Job, Joseph, David, Daniel, Christ, martyrs, etc. III. The Probity tried and preserved : " Lest the righteous put forth," etc., by rebelling, sinful compromise, etc. 1. God will have it tried, to prove its worth, beauty, etc. 2. But no more than sufficiently tried.—*John Field.*

Verses 3, 4.—I. The good defined : " The upright in heart ; " such as do not " turn aside," and are not " workers of iniquity." II. The good distressed : by " the rod of the wicked." III. The good delivered : " Do good"; fulfil thy promise (verse 3).—*W. H. J. Page.*

Verse 4.—I. What it is to be good. II. What it is for God to do us good.

Verse 5.—Temporary Professors. I. The crucial test : " They turn aside." II. The crooked policy : they make crooked ways their own. III. The crushing doom : " led forth with workers of iniquity."

Verse 5.—Hypocrites. I. Their ways : " crooked." 1. Like the way of a winding stream, seeking out the fair level, or the easy descent. 2. Like the course of a tacking ship, which skilfully makes every wind to drive her forward. 3. Ways constructed upon no principle but that of pure selfishness. II. Their conduct under trial. They " turn aside." 1. From their religious profession. 2. From their former companions. 3. To become the worst scorners of spiritual things, and the most violent calumniators of spiritually-minded men. III. Their doom : " The Lord shall," etc. 1. In the judgment they shall be classed with the most flagrant sinners ; " with the workers of iniquity." 2. They shall be exposed by an irresistible power : " The Lord shall lead them forth." 3. They shall meet with terrible execution with the wicked in hell.—*J. Field.*

Verse 5 (*last clause*).—To whom peace belongs. To " Israel " ; the chosen, the once wrestler, the now prevailing prince. Consider Jacob's life after he obtained the name of Israel ; note his trials, and his security under them as illustrating this text. Then take the text as a sure promise.

Verse 5 (*last clause*).—Enquire, I. Who are the Israel ? 1. Covenanted ones. 2. Circumcised in heart. 3. True worshippers. II. What is the peace ? 1. Peace of conscience. 2. Of friendship with God. 3. Of a settled and satisfied heart. 4. Of eternal glory, in reversion. III. Why the certainty (" shall be ") ? 1. Christ has made peace for them. 2. The Holy Spirit brings peace to them. 3. They walk in the way of peace.—*J. Field.*

PSALM CXXVI.

TITLE.—*A Song of Degrees. This is the seventh step, and we may therefore expect to meet with some special perfection of joy in it; nor shall we look in vain. We see here not only that Zion abides, but that her joy returns after sorrow. Abiding is not enough, fruitfulness is added. The pilgrims went from blessing to blessing in their Psalmody as they proceeded on their holy way. Happy people to whom every ascent was a song, every halt a hymn. Here the truster becomes a sower : faith works by love, obtains a present bliss, and secures a harvest of delight.*

There is nothing in this Psalm by which we can decide its date, further than this,— that it is a song after a great deliverance from oppression. "Turning captivity" by no means requires an actual removal into banishment to fill out the idea ; rescue from any dire affliction or crushing tyranny would be fitly described as "captivity turned." Indeed, the passage is not applicable to captives in Babylon, for it is Zion itself which is in captivity, and not a part of her citizens : the holy city was in sorrow and distress ; though it could not be removed, the prosperity could be diminished. Some dark cloud lowered over the beloved capital, and its citizens prayed " Turn again our captivity, O Lord."

This Psalm is in its right place and most fittingly follows its predecessor, for as in Psalm cxxv. we read that the rod of the wicked shall not rest upon the lot of the righteous, we here see it removed from them to their great joy. The word " turn " would seem to be the key-note of the song ; it is a Psalm of conversion—conversion from captivity ; and it may well be used to set forth the rapture of a pardoned soul when the anger of the Lord is turned away from it. We will call it, "Leading captivity captive."

The Psalm divides itself into a narrative (1, 2), *a song* (3), *a prayer* (4), *and a promise* (5 and 6).

EXPOSITION.

WHEN the LORD turned again the captivity of Zion, we were like them that dream.

2 Then was our mouth filled with laughter, and our tongue with singing : then said they among the heathen, The LORD hath done great things for them.

3 The LORD hath done great things for us ; *whereof* we are glad.

4 Turn again our captivity, O LORD, as the streams in the south.

5 They that sow in tears shall reap in joy.

6 He that goeth forth and weepeth, bearing precious seed, shall doubtless come again with rejoicing, bringing his sheaves *with him.*

1. "*When the* LORD *turned again the captivity of Zion, we were like them that dream.*" Being in trouble, the gracious pilgrims remember for their comfort times of national woe which were succeeded by remarkable deliverances. Then sorrow was gone like a dream, and the joy which followed was so great that it seemed too good to be true, and they feared that it must be the vision of an idle brain. So sudden and so overwhelming was their joy that they felt like men out of themselves, ecstatic, or in a trance. The captivity had been great, and great was the deliverance ; for the great God himself had wrought it : it seemed too good to be actually true : each man said to himself,—

> " Is this a dream ? O if it be a dream,
> Let me sleep on, and do not wake me yet."

It was not the freedom of an individual which the Lord in mercy had wrought, but of all Zion, of the whole nation ; and this was reason enough for overflowing gladness. We need not instance the histories which illustrate this verse in connection with literal Israel ; but it is well to remember how often it has been true to ourselves. Let us look to the prison-houses from which we have been set free. Ah, me, what captives we have been ! At our first conversion what a turning again of captivity we experienced. Never shall that hour be forgotten. Joy! Joy! Joy! Since then, from multiplied troubles, from depression of spirit, from miserable backsliding, from grievous doubt, we have been emancipated, and we are not able to describe the bliss which followed each emancipation.

> " When God reveal'd his gracious name
> And changed our mournful state,
> Our rapture seem'd a pleasing dream,
> The grace appeared so great."

This verse will have a higher fulfilment in the day of the final overthrow of the powers of darkness when the Lord shall come forth for the salvation and glorification of his redeemed. Then in a fuller sense than even at Pentecost our old men shall see visions, and our young men shall dream dreams : yea, all things shall be so wonderful, so far beyond all expectation, that those who behold them shall ask themselves whether it be not all a dream. The past is ever a sure prognostic of the future ; the thing which has been is the thing that shall be : we shall again and again find ourselves amazed at the wonderful goodness of the Lord. Let our hearts gratefully remember the former lovingkindnesses of the Lord : we were sadly low, sorely distressed, and completely past hope, but when Jehovah appeared he did not merely lift us out of despondency, he raised us into wondering happiness. The Lord who alone turns our captivity does nothing by halves : those whom he saves from hell he brings to heaven. He turns exile into ecstasy, and banishment into bliss.

2. *"Then was our mouth filled with laughter, and our tongue with singing."* So full were they of joy that they could not contain themselves. They must express their joy and yet they could not find expression for it. Irrepressible mirth could do no other than laugh, for speech was far too dull a thing for it. The mercy was so unexpected, so amazing, so singular that they could not do less than laugh ; and they laughed much, so that their mouths were full of it, and that because their hearts were full too. When at last the tongue could move articulately, it could not be content simply to talk, but it must needs sing ; and sing heartily too, for it was full of singing. Doubtless the former pain added to the zest of the pleasure : the captivity threw a brighter colour into the emancipation. The people remembered this joy-flood for years after, and here is the record of it turned into a song. Note the *when* and the *then.* God's *when* is our *then.* At the moment when he turns our captivity, the heart turns from its sorrow ; when he fills us with grace we are filled with gratitude. We were made to be as them that dream, but we both laughed and sang in our sleep. We are wide awake now, and though we can scarcely realize the blessing, yet we rejoice in it exceedingly.

"Then said they among the heathen, The LORD hath done great things for them." The heathen heard the songs of Israel, and the better sort among them soon guessed the cause of their joy. Jehovah was known to be their God, and to him the other nations ascribed the emancipation of his people, reckoning it to be no small thing which the Lord had thus done ; for those who carried away the nations had never in any other instance restored a people to their ancient dwelling-place. These foreigners were no dreamers ; though they were only lookers-on, and not partakers in the surprising mercy, they plainly saw what had been done, and rightly ascribed it to the great Giver of all good. It is a blessed thing when saints set sinners talking about the lovingkindness of the Lord : and it is equally blessed when the saints who are hidden away in the world hear of what the Lord has done for his church, and themselves resolve to come out from their captivity and unite with the Lord's people. Ah, dear reader, Jehovah has indeed done marvellous things for his chosen, and these " great things " shall be themes for eternal praise among all intelligent creatures.

3. *"The LORD hath done great things for us ; whereof we are glad."* They did not deny the statement which reflected so much glory upon Jehovah : with exultation they admitted and repeated the statement of Jehovah's notable dealings with them. To themselves they appropriated the joyful assertion ; they said " The Lord hath done great things *for us,*" and they declared their gladness of the fact. It is a poor modesty which is ashamed to own its joy in the Lord. Call it rather a robbery of God. There is so little of happiness abroad that if we possess a full share of it we ought not to hide our light under a bushel, but let it shine on all that are in the house. Let us avow our joy, and the reason of it, stating the " whereof " as

well as the fact. None are so happy as those who are newly turned and returned from captivity; none can more promptly and satisfactorily give a reason for the gladness that is in them. The Lord himself has blessed us, blessed us greatly, blessed us individually, blessed us assuredly; and because of this we sing unto his name. I heard one say the other day in prayer "whereof we desire to be glad." Strange dilution and defilement of Scriptural language! Surely if God has done great things for us we are glad, and cannot be otherwise. No doubt such language is meant to be lowly, but in truth it is loathsome.

4. *"Turn again our captivity, O Lord."* Remembering the former joy of a past rescue they cry to Jehovah for a repetition of it. When we pray for the turning of our captivity, it is wise to recall former instances thereof: nothing strengthens faith more effectually than the memory of a previous experience. "The Lord hath done" harmonizes well with the prayer, "Turn again." The text shows us how wise it is to resort anew to the Lord who in former times has been so good to us. Where else should we go but to him who has done such great things for us? Who can turn again our captivity but he who turned it before?

"As the streams in the south." Even as the Lord sends floods adown the dry beds of southern torrents after long droughts, so can he fill our wasted and wearied spirits with floods of holy delight. This the Lord can do for any of us, and he can do it at once, for nothing is too hard for the Lord. It is well for us thus to pray, and to bring our suit before him who is able to bless us exceeding abundantly. Do not let us forget the past, but in the presence of our present difficulty let us resort unto the Lord, and beseech him to do that for us which we cannot possibly do for ourselves,—that which no other power can perform on our behalf. Israel did return from the captivity in Babylon, and it was even as though a flood of people hastened to Zion. Suddenly and plenteously the people filled again the temple courts. In streams they shall also in the latter days return to their own land, and replenish it yet again. Like mighty torrents shall the nations flow unto the Lord in the day of his grace. May the Lord hasten it in his own time.

5. *"They that sow in tears shall reap in joy."* Hence, present distress must not be viewed as if it would last for ever: it is not the end, by any means, but only a means to the end. Sorrow is our sowing, rejoicing shall be our reaping. If there were no sowing in tears there would be no reaping in joy. If we were never captives we could never lead our captivity captive. Our mouth had never been filled with holy laughter if it had not been first filled with the bitterness of grief. We must sow: we may have to sow in the wet weather of sorrow; but we shall reap, and reap in the bright summer season of joy. Let us keep to the work of this present sowing time, and find strength in the promise which is here so positively given us. Here is one of the Lord's shalls and wills; it is freely given both to workers, waiters, and weepers, and they may rest assured that it will not fail: "in due season they *shall* reap."

This sentence may well pass current in the church as an inspired proverb. It is not every sowing which is thus insured against all danger, and guaranteed a harvest; but the promise specially belongs to sowing *in tears*. When a man's heart is so stirred that he weeps over the sins of others, he is elect to usefulness. Winners of souls are first weepers for souls. As there is no birth without travail, so is there no spiritual harvest without painful tillage. When our own hearts are broken with grief at man's transgression we shall break other men's hearts: tears of earnestness beget tears of repentance: "deep calleth unto deep."

6. *"He."* The general assurance is applied to each one in particular. That which is spoken in the previous verse in the plural—"they," is here repeated in the singular—"he." *"He that goeth forth and weepeth, bearing precious seed, shall doubtless come again with rejoicing, bringing his sheaves with him."* He leaves his couch to go forth into the frosty air and tread the heavy soil; and as he goes he weeps because of past failures, or because the ground is so sterile, or the weather so unseasonable, or his corn so scarce, and his enemies so plentiful and so eager to rob him of his reward. He drops a seed and a tear, a seed and a tear, and so goes on his way. In his basket he has seed which is precious to him, for he has little of it, and it is his hope for the next year. Each grain leaves his hand with anxious prayer that it may not be lost: he thinks little of himself, but much of his seed, and he eagerly asks, "Will it prosper? shall I receive a reward for my labour?" Yes, good husbandman, *doubtless* you will gather sheaves from your sowing. Because the Lord has written *doubtless*, take heed that you do not doubt. No

reason for doubt can remain after the Lord has spoken. You will return [to this field—not to sow, but to reap; not to weep, but to rejoice: and after awhile you will go home again with nimbler step than to-day, though with a heavier load, for you shall have sheaves to bear with you. Your handful shall be so greatly multiplied that many sheaves shall spring from it; and you shall have the pleasure of reaping them and bringing them home to the place from which you went out weeping.

This is a figurative description of that which was literally described in the first three verses. It is the turning of the worker's captivity, when, instead of seed buried beneath black earth, he sees the waving crops inviting him to a golden harvest.

It is somewhat singular to find this promise of fruitfulness in close contact with return from captivity; and yet it is so in our own experience, for when our own soul is revived the souls of others are blessed by our labours. If any of us, having been once lonesome and lingering captives, have now returned home, and have become longing and labouring sowers, may the Lord, who has already delivered us, soon transform us into glad-hearted reapers, and to him shall be praise for ever and ever. Amen.

EXPLANATORY NOTES AND QUAINT SAYINGS.

Title.—Augustine interprets the title, " A Song of Degrees, i.e. a Song of drawing upwards," of the drawing (going) up to the heavenly Jerusalem. This is right, inasmuch as the deliverance from the captivity of sin and death should in an increased measure excite those feelings of gratitude which Israel must have felt on being delivered from their corporeal captivity; in this respect again is the history of the outward theocracy a type of the history of the church.—*Augustus F. Tholuck*, 1856.

Whole Psalm.—In its Christian aspect the Psalm represents the seventh of the " degrees " in our ascent to the Jerusalem that is above. The Christian's exultation at his deliverance from the spiritual captivity of sin.—*H. T. Armfield.*

Whole Psalm.—In mine opinion they go near to the sense and true meaning of the Psalm who do refer it to that great and general captivity of mankind under sin, death and the devil, and to the redemption purchased by the death and blood-shedding of Christ, and published in the Gospel. For this kind of speech which the Prophet useth here is of greater importance than that it may be applied only to Jewish particular captivities. For what great matter was it for these people of the Jews, being, as it were, a little handful, to be delivered out of temporal captivity, in comparison of the exceeding and incomparable deliverance whereby mankind was set at liberty from the power of their enemies, not temporal but eternal, even from death, Satan and hell itself? Wherefore we take this Psalm to be a prophecy of the redemption that should come by Jesus Christ, and the publishing of the gospel, whereby the kingdom of Christ is advanced, and death and the devil with all the powers of darkness are vanquished.—*Thomas Stint, in An Exposition on Psalms cxxiv—cxxvi*, 1621.

Whole Psalm.—I believe this Psalm is yet once more to be sung in still more joyous strain; once more will the glad tidings of Israel's restoration break upon her scattered tribes, like the unreal shadow of a dream; once more will the inhabitants of the various lands from among whom they come forth exclaim in adoring wonder, " The Lord hath done great things for them," when they see Israelite after Israelite and Jew after Jew, as on that wondrous night of Egypt, with their loins girded, their shoes on their feet, and their staff in their hand, hasting to obey the summons that recalls them to their own loved land !—*Barton Bouchier* (1794—1865), *in "Manna in the Heart."*

Whole Psalm.—

When, her sons from bonds redeeming,
God to Zion led the way,
We were like to people dreaming
Thoughts of bliss too bright to stay.

Fill'd with laughter, stood we gazing,
　　Loud our tongues in rapture sang;
Quickly with the news amazing
　　All the startled nations rang.

" See Jehovah's works of glory !
　　Mark what love for them he had ! "
" Yes, FOR US ! Go tell the story.
　　This was done, and we are glad."

Lord ! thy work of grace completing
　　All our exiled hosts restore,
As in thirsty channels meeting
　　Southern streams refreshing pour.

They that now in sorrow weeping
　　Tears and seed commingled sow,
Soon, the fruitful harvest reaping,
　　Shall with joyful bosoms glow.

Tho' the sower's heart is breaking,
　　Bearing forth the seed to shed,
He shall come, the echoes waking,
　　Laden with his sheaves instead.

William Digby, in *"The Hebrew Psalter. A New Metrical Translation,"* 1882.

Verse 1.—*"When the Lord turned again the captivity."* As by the Lord's permission they were led into captivity, so only by his power they were set at liberty. When the Israelites had served in a strange land four hundred years, it was not Moses, but Jehovah, that brought them out of the land of Egypt, and out of the house of bondage. In like manner it was he and not Deborah that freed them from Jabin after they had been vexed twenty years under the Canaanites. It was he and not Gideon that brought them out of the hands of the Midianites, after seven years' servitude. It was he and not Jephthah that delivered them from the Philistines and Amorites after eighteen years' oppression. Although in all these he did employ Moses and Deborah, Gideon and Jephthah, as instruments for their deliverance; and so it was not Cyrus's valour, but the Lord's power; not his policy, but God's wisdom, that, overthrowing the enemies, gave to Cyrus the victory, and put it into his heart to set his people at liberty; for he upheld his hands to subdue nations. He did weaken the loins of kings, and did open the doors before him, he did go before him and made the crooked places straight; and he did break the brazen doors, and burst the iron bars. Isaiah xlv. 1, 2.—*John Hume, in "The Jewes Deliverance,"* 1628.

Verse 1.—*"In Jehovah's turning (to) the turning of Zion."* Meaning to return to the return, or meet those returning, as it were, half way. The Hebrew noun denotes *conversion*, in its spiritual sense, and the verb God's gracious condescension in accepting or responding to it.—*Joseph Addison Alexander.*

Verse 1.—*"The captivity of Zion."* I ask, first, Why of *Zion?* why not the captivity of Jerusalem, Judah, Israel? Jerusalem, Judah, Israel, were led away captives, no less than Zion. They, the greater and more general; why not *the captivity* of them, but of *Zion?* It should seem there is more in Zion's captivity than in the rest, that choice is made of it before the rest. Why? what was Zion? We know it was but a hill in Jerusalem, on the north side. Why is that hill so honoured? No reason in the world but this,—that upon it the Temple was built; and so, that Zion is much spoken of, and much made of, it is only for the Temple's sake. For whose sake it is (even for his church), that " the Lord loveth the gates of Zion more than all the dwellings of Jacob " (Ps. lxxxvii. 2); loveth her more, and so her captivity goeth nearer him, and her deliverance better pleaseth him, than all Jacob besides. This maketh *Zion's captivity* to be mentioned chiefly, as chiefly regarded by God, and to be regarded by his people. As we see it was: when they sat by the waters of Babylon, that which made them weep was, " When we remembered thee, O Zion "; that was their greatest grief. That their greatest grief, and this their greatest joy; *Lætati sumus*, when news came (not, saith the Psalm, *in domos nostras*, We shall go everyone to his own house, but) in *domum Domini ibimus*, "We shall go to the house of the Lord, we shall appear before the God of gods in Zion."—*Lancelot Andrewes*, 1555—1626.

Verse 1.—"We were like them that dream." That is, they thought it was but mere fantasy and imagination.—*Sydrach Simpson,* 1658.

Verse 1.—"We were like them that dream." Here you may observe that God doth often send succour and deliverance to the godly in the time of their affliction, distress, and adversity ; that many times they themselves do doubt of the truth thereof, and think that in very deed they are not delivered, but rather that they have dreamed. Peter, being imprisoned by Herod, when he was delivered by an angel, for all the light that did shine in the prison ; though the angel did smite him on the side and raised him up ; though he caused the chains to fall off his hands ; though he spake to him three several times, *Surge, cinge, circunda ;* "Arise quickly, gird thyself, and cast thy garment about thee"; though he conducted him safely by the watches ; and though he caused the iron gates to open willingly ; yet for all this he was like unto them that dream. "For he wist not that it was true which was done by the angel; but thought he saw a vision": Acts xii. 9. When old Jacob was told by his sons that his son Joseph was alive, his heart failed, and he believed them not ; but when he had heard all that Joseph had said, and when he saw the chariots that Joseph had sent, then, as it were, raised from a sleep, and awakened from a dream, his spirit revived, then, and, rejoicing, he cried out, "I have enough ; Joseph my son is yet alive."

Lorinus seems to excuse this their distrust, because they were so over-ravished with joy, that they misdoubted the true cause of their joy : like the Apostles, who having Christ after his resurrection standing before them, they were so exceedingly joyed, that rejoicing they wondered and doubted ; and like the two Marys, when the angel told them of our Saviour Christ's resurrection, they returned from the sepulchre rejoicing, and yet withal fearing. It may be they feared the truth of so glad news, and doubted lest they were deceived by some apparition.—*John Hume.*

Verse 1.—"We were like them that dream." We thought that we were dreaming ; we could hardly believe our eyes, when at the command of Cyrus, king of the Persians, we had returned to our own land. The same thing happened to the Greeks, when they heard that their country, being conquered by the Romans, had been made free by the Roman consul, P. Quinctius Flaminius. Livy says that when the herald had finished there was more good news than the people could receive all at once. They could scarcely believe that they had heard aright. They were looking on each other wonderingly, like sleepers on an empty dream.—*John Le Clerc [Clericus],* 1657—1736.

Verse 1.—"We were like them that dream," etc. In the lapse of seventy years the hope of restoration to their land, so long deferred, had mostly gone out in despair, save as it rested (in some minds) on their faith in God's promise. The policy of those great powers in the East had long been settled, viz., to break up the old tribes and kingdoms of Western Asia ; take the people into far eastern countries, and *never let them return.* No nation known to history, except the Jews, ever did return to rebuild their ancient cities and homes. Hence this joyous surprise.—*Henry Cowles, in "The Psalms ; with Notes."* 1872.

Verse 1.—"Like them that dream." It was no dream ; it was Jacob's dream become a reality. It was the promise, "I will bring thee back into this land" (Gen. xxviii. 15), fulfilled beyond all their hope.—*William Kay, in "The Psalms, with Notes, chiefly exegetical,"* 1871.

Verse 1.—"We were like them that dream." The words should rather be translated, *"We are like unto those that are restored to health."* The Hebrew word signifies to recover, or, to be restored to health. And so the same word is translated in Isa. xxxviii., when Hezekiah recovered, he made a Psalm of praise, and said, "O Lord, by these things men live, and in all these things is the life of my spirit : so wilt thou recover me, and make me to live." It is the same word that is used here. Thus Cajetan, Shindler, and others would have it translated here ; and it suits best with the following words, "Then were our mouths filled with laughter, and our tongues with praise." When a man is in a good dream, his mouth is not filled with laughter, nor his tongue with praise : if a man be in a bad dream, his mouth is not filled with laughter, nor his tongue with praise ; but when a man is restored to health after a great sickness, it is so.—*William Bridge,* 1600—1670.

Verse 2.—"Then was our mouth filled with laughter," etc. We must earnestly endeavour to learn this practice, or at least to attain to some knowledge thereof ; and we must raise up ourselves with this consideration—that the gospel is nothing

74   EXPOSITIONS OF THE PSALMS.

else but laughter and joy. This joy properly pertaineth to captives, that is, to those that feel the captivity of sin and death ; to the fleshy and tender hearts, terrified with the feeling of the wrath and judgment of God. These are the disciples in whose hearts should be planted laughter and joy, and that by the authority of the Holy Ghost, which this verse setteth forth. This people was in Zion, and, after the outward show of the kingdom and priesthood, did mightily flourish ; but if a man consider them according to the spirit, he shall see them to be in miserable captivity, and that their tongue is full of heaviness and mourning, because their heart is terrified with the sense of sin and death. This is Moses' tongue or Moses' mouth, full of wormwood and of bitterness of death ; wherewith he designs to kill none but those which are too lively and full of security. But they who feel their captivity shall have their mouths filled with laughter and joy : that is, redemption and deliverance from sin and death shall be preached unto them. This is the sense and meaning of the Holy Ghost, that the mouth of such shall be filled with laughter, that is, their mouth shall show forth nothing else but great gladness through the inestimable consolations of the gospel, with voices of triumph and victory by Christ, overcoming Satan, destroying death, and taking away sins. This was first spoken unto the Jews ; for this laughter was first offered to that people, then having the promises. Now he turneth to the Gentiles, whom he calleth to the partaking of this laughter.—*Martin Luther.*

Verse 2.—*"Then was our mouth filled with laughter,"* etc. It was thus in the valley of Elah, where Goliath fell, and Philistia fled. It was thus at Baal-Perazim. It was thus when one morning, after many nights of gloom, Jerusalem arose at dawn of day, and found Sennacherib's thousands a camp of the dead. And it has all along been the manner of our God.

" The Lord has wrought mightily
In what he has done for us ;
And we have been made glad."

Ever do this till conflict is over ! Just as thou dost with the streams of the south, year by year, so do with us—with all, with each. And we are confident thou wilt ; we are sure that we make no vain boast when we sing this Psalm as descriptive of the experience of all thy pilgrims and worshippers.—*Andrew A. Bonar, in "Christ and his Church in the Book of Psalms,"* 1859.

Verse 2.—*"Then was our mouth filled with laughter."*—They that were laughed at, now laugh, and a new song is put into their mouths. It was a laughter of joy in God, not scorn of their enemies.—*Matthew Henry.*

Verse 2.—*"Mouth"; "tongue."* Lorinus, the Jesuit, hath observed that the Psalmist nominates the *mouth* and *tongue* in the singular, not *mouths* and *tongues* in the plural ; because all the faithful and the whole congregation of the Jews *univocè*, with one voice, with one consent, and, as it were, with one mouth, did praise and glorify the Lord.—*John Hume.*

Verse 2.—*"And our tongue with singing."* Out of the abundance of the heart the mouth speaks ; and if the heart be glad the tongue is glib. Joy cannot be suppressed in the heart, but it must be expressed with the tongue.—*John Hume.*

Verse 2.—*"Then said they among the heathen."* And what is it they said ? It is to the purpose. In this (as in many others) the heathens' saying cannot be mended. This they say : 1. That they were no quotidian, or common things ; but " *great.*" 2. Then, these great things they ascribe not to *chance ;* that they *happened* not, but were " *done.*" 3. Then, " done " *by God himself :* they see God in them. 4. Then, not done by God at random, without any particular aim ; but *purposely* done *for them.* 5. And yet, there is more in *magnificavit facere* (if we look well). For, *magna fecit* would have served all this ; but in saying *magnificavit facere,* they say *magnificit illos, ut magna faceret pro illis.* He magnified them, or set greatly by them. for whom he would bring to pass so great a work. This said they among the " heathen."

And it is a pity the " *heathen* " said it, and that the Jews themselves spake not these words first. But now, finding the " *heathen* " so saying ; and finding it was all true that they said, they must needs find themselves bound to say at least as much ; and more they could not say ; for more cannot be said. So much then, and no less than they. And this addeth a degree to the *dicebant,*—that the sound of it was so great among *the heathen* that it made an *echo* even in Jewry itself.—*Lancelot Andrewes.*

Verse 2.—*"The LORD hath done great things."* He multiplied to do great things ;

so the Chaldee, Syriac, and Arabic versions render it; and the history of this deliverance makes it good.—*Thomas Hodges, in a Sermon entitled "Sion's Hallelujah,"* 1660.

Verses 2, 3.—There is this great difference between the praise which the heathen are forced to give to God, and that which the Lord's people heartily offer unto him : the one doth speak as having no interest nor share in the mercy ; the other do speak as they to whom the mercy is intended, and wherein they have their portion with others : *"He hath done great things for them,"* say the heathen : but, *" he hath done great th*ings *for us,"* say the Lord's people.—*David Dickson,* 1583—1662.

Verse 3.—*"The* LORD *hath done great things for us,"* etc. This verse is the marrow of the whole Psalm, occasioned by the return of God's people out of Babel's captivity into their own country. Their deliverance was so great and incredible that when God brought it to pass they were *as men in a dream,* thinking it rather a dream, and a vain imagination, than a real truth. 1. Because it was so great a deliverance from so great and lasting a bondage, it seemed too good to be true. 2. It was sudden and unexpected, when they little thought or hoped for it. . . . . 3. All things seemed desperate, nothing more unlikely, or impossible rather. 4. The manner was so admirable (without the counsel, help, or strength of man : nay, it was beyond and against all human means) ; that they doubt whether these things be not the dreams of men that are awake.—*Thomas Taylor* (1576—1632) *in "A Mappe of Rome."*

Verse 3.—*"For us."* What were we, might Sion say (who were glad to lick the dust of the feet of our enemies), that the Lord of heaven and earth should look so graciously upon us ? The meanness of the receiver argueth the magnificence of the giver. " Who am I, that the mother of my Lord should visit me ? " this was a true and religious compliment of devout Elizabeth. The best of men are but the children of dust, and grand-children of nothing. And yet for the Lord to do *" great things "* for us ! this yet *greatens* those *"great things."* Was it because *we were his church ?* It was his superabounding grace to select us out of others, as it was our greater gracelessness, above all others, so to provoke him, as to force him to throw us into captivity. Or was it because *our humiliation,* in that disconsolate condition, did move him to so great compassion ? Alas ! there was a choice of nations whom he might have taken in our room, that might have proved far more faithful than we have been for the one half of those favours we have enjoyed.

Or was it for *his covenant's sake* with our forefathers ? Alas ! we had forfeited that long since, again and again, we know not how often. Wherefore, when we remember ourselves, we cannot but make this an aggravation of God's *"great things,"* that he should do them *for us,* FOR US, so very, very unworthy.—*Malachiah [or Matthew] Harris, in a Sermon entitled "Brittaines Hallelujah,"* 1639.

Verse 4.—*"Turn again our captivity, O* LORD.*"* A prayer for the perfecting of their deliverance. Let those that are returned to their own land be eased of their burdens which they are yet groaning under. Let those that remain in Babylon have their hearts stirred up, as ours were, to take the benefit of the liberty granted. The beginnings of mercy are encouragements to us to pray for the completing of it. While we are here in this world, there will still be matter for prayer, even when we are most furnished with matter for praise. When we are free, and in prosperity ourselves, we must not be unmindful of our brethren that are in trouble and under restraint.—*Matthew Henry.*

Verse 4.—*"Turn again our captivity."* As Israel of old prayed that he would bring all their brethren scattered abroad in captivity back to their own land in one full stream, multitudinous, joyous, mighty, like the waters of Nile or Euphrates pouring over the parching fields of the south in the hot, dry summer-tide ; so now should the members of Christ's church ever pray " that all that profess and call themselves Christians may be led into the way of truth, and hold the faith in unity of spirit, in the bond of peace, and in righteousness of life."—*J. W. Burgon, in "A Plain Commentary,"* 1859.

Verse 4.—The Psalmist cries—

> " Turn our captivity, O Jehovah,
> As aqueducts in the Negeb."

This Negeb, or South Country, the region stretching below Hebron, being comparatively dry and waterless, was doubtless irrigated by a system of small artificial channels. The words of the Psalmist imply that it is as easy for God to turn Israel back from Babylonian bondage to their own land, as for the horticulturist to direct the waters of the spring to any part of the land he chooses along the channels of the aqueducts.—*James Neil.*

Verse 4.—*"As the streams in the south."* Then shall our captivity be perfectly changed even as *the rivers* or *waters in the south*, which by the mighty work of God were dried up and utterly consumed. Whether ye understand here the Red Sea, or else the river of Jordan, it mattereth little. The similitude is this: Like as by thy mighty hand thou broughtest to pass miraculously that the waters were dried up and consumed, so dry up, O Lord, and bring to nothing all our captivity. Some do interpret this verse otherwise; that is, Turn our captivity, O Lord, as the rivers in the south, which in the summer are dried up in the desert places by the heat of the sun, but in the winter are filled up again with plenty of water.—*Martin Luther.*

Verse 4.—*"Streams."* The Hebrew word for *"streams"* means strictly a river's bed, the channel which holds water when water is there, but is often dry. Naturally there is joy for the husbandmen when those valley-beds are filled again with flowing waters. So, the prayer is, let thy people return joyfully to their father-land.—*Henry Cowles.*

Verse 4.—*"As the streams in the south."* Some render it, *As the mighty waters in the south.* Why would they have their captivity turned like those mighty floods in the south? The reason is this, because the south is a dry country, where there are few springs, scarce a fountain to be found in a whole desert. What, then, are the waters they have in the south, in those parched countries? They are these mighty strong torrents, which are caused by the showers of heaven: so the meaning of that prayer in the Psalm is, that God would suddenly turn their captivity. Rivers come suddenly in the south: where no spring appears, nor any sign of a river, yet in an hour the water is up and the streams overflow. As when Elijah sent his servant toward the sea, in the time of Ahab, he went and looked, and said, " there is nothing "; that is, no show of rain, not the least cloud to be seen; yet presently the heavens grew black, and there was a great rain: 1 Kings xviii. 44. Thus let our captivity be turned thus speedily and suddenly, though there be no appearance of salvation, no more than there is of a fountain in the sandy desert, or of rain in the clearest of heavens, yet bring salvation for us. We used to say of things beyond our supply, Have we a spring of them? or can we fetch them out of the clouds? So though no ground appears whence such rivers should flow, yet let our salvation be as rivers in the south, as rivers fetched out of the clouds, and dropped in an instant immediately from the heavens.—*Joseph Caryl*, 1602 —1673.

Verses 4, 5, 6.—The saints are oft feeding their hopes on the carcases of their slain fears. The time which God chose and the instrument he used to give the captive Jews their gaol delivery and liberty to return home were so incredible to them when it came to pass (like Peter whom the angel had carried out of prison, Acts xii.), it was some time before they could come to themselves and resolve whether it was real truth, or but a pleasing dream. Now see, what effect this strange disappointment of their fears had upon their hope for afterward. It sends them to the throne of grace for the accomplishment of what was so marvellously begun. " The Lord hath done great things for us; whereof we are glad. Turn again our captivity, O Lord ": verses 3, 4. They have got a hand-hold by this experiment of his power and mercy, and they will not now let him go till they have more; yea, their hope is raised to such a pitch of confidence, that they draw a general conclusion from this particular experience for the comfort of themselves or others in any future distress: " They that sow in tears shall reap in joy," etc., verses 5, 6.— *William Gurnall*, 1617—1679.

Verse 5.—*"They that sow in tears."* I never saw people sowing in tears exactly, but have often known them to do it in fear and distress sufficient to draw them from any eye. In seasons of great scarcity, the poor peasants part in sorrow with every measure of precious seed cast into the ground. It is like taking bread out of the mouths of their children; and in such times many bitter tears are actually shed over it. The distress is frequently so great that government is obliged to furnish seed, or none would be sown. Ibrahim Pasha did this more than once within my remembrance, copying the example, perhaps, of his great predecessor in Egypt when the seven years' famine was ended.

The thoughts of this Psalm may likewise have been suggested by the extreme danger which frequently attends the farmer in his ploughing and sowing. The calamity which fell upon the husbandmen of Job when the oxen were ploughing, and the asses feeding beside them, and the Sabeans fell upon them and took them away, and slew the servants with the edge of the sword (Job i. 14, 15), is often repeated in our day. To understand this you must remember what I have just told you about the situation of the arable lands in the open country; and here again we meet that verbal accuracy: the sower *"goes forth"*—that is, from the village. The people of Ibel and Khiem, in Merj' Aiyûn, for example, have their best grain-growing fields down in the 'Ard Hûleh, six or eight miles from their homes, and just that much nearer the lawless border of the desert. When the country is disturbed, or the government weak, they cannot sow these lands except at the risk of their lives. Indeed, they always *go forth* in large companies, and completely armed, ready to drop the plough and seize the musket at a moment's warning; and yet, with all this care, many sad and fatal calamities overtake the men who must thus sow in tears. And still another origin may be found for the thoughts of the Psalm in the extreme difficulty of the work itself in many places. The soil is rocky, impracticable, overgrown with sharp thorns; and it costs much painful toil to break up and gather out the rock, cut and burn the briars, and to subdue the stubborn soil, especially with their feeble oxen and insignificant ploughs. Join all these together, and the sentiment is very forcibly brought out, that he who labours hard, in cold and rain, in fear and danger, in poverty and in want, casting his precious seed into the ground, will surely come again, at harvest-time, with rejoicing, and bearing his sheaves with him.—*W. M. Thomson.*

Verse 5.—*"They that sow in tears shall reap in joy,"* etc. This promise is conveyed under images borrowed from the instructive scenes of agriculture. In the sweat of his brow the husbandman tills his land, and casts the seed into the ground, where for a time it lies dead and buried. A dark and dreary winter succeeds, and all seems to be lost; but at the return of spring universal nature revives, and the once desolate fields are covered with corn which, when matured by the sun's heat, the cheerful reapers cut down, and it is brought home with triumphant shouts of joy. Here, O disciple of Jesus, behold an emblem of thy present labour and thy future reward! Thou "sowest," perhaps, in "tears"; thou doest thy duty amidst persecution, and affliction, sickness, pain, and sorrow; thou labourest in the Church, and no account is made of thy labours, no profit seems likely to arise from them. Nay, thou must thyself drop into the dust of death, and all the storms of that winter must pass over thee, until thy form shall be perished, and thou shalt see corruption. Yet the day is coming when thou shalt "reap in joy," and plentiful shall be thy harvest. For thus thy blessed Master "went forth weeping," a man of sorrows and acquainted with grief, "bearing precious seed" and sowing it around him, till at length his own body was buried, like a grain of wheat, in the furrow of the grave. But he arose, and is now in heaven, from whence he shall "doubtless come again with rejoicing," with the voice of the archangel and the trump of God, "bringing his sheaves with him." Then shall every man receive the fruit of his works, and have praise of God.—*George Horne* (1730—1792), *in "A Commentary on the Psalms."*

Verse 5.—*"They that sow in tears shall reap in joy."* They sow *in faith;* and God will bless that seed: it shall grow up to heaven, for it is sown in the side of Jesus Christ who is in heaven. "He that believeth on God," this is the seed; "shall have everlasting life" (John v. 24); this is the harvest. *Qui credit quod non videt, videbit quod credit,*—he that believes what he doth not see; this is the seed: shall one day see what he hath believed; this is the harvest.

They sow *in obedience:* this is also a blessed seed, that will not fail to prosper wheresoever it is cast. "If ye keep my commandments"; this is the seed: "ye shall abide in my love" (John xv. 10); this is the harvest. (Rom. vi. 22), "Ye are become servants to God, and have your fruit unto holiness"; this is the sowing: "and the end everlasting life"; this is the reaping. *Obedientia in terris, regnabit in cælis,*—he that serves God on earth, and sows the seed of obedience, shall in heaven reap the harvest of a kingdom.

They sow *in repentance;* and this seed must needs grow up to blessedness. . . . Many saints have now reaped their crop in heaven, that sowed their seed in tears. David, Mary Magdalene, Peter; as if they had made good the proverb, "No coming to heaven with dry eyes." Thus nature and God differ in their proceedings. To have a good crop on earth, we desire a fair seedtime; but here a wet time of sowing shall bring the best harvest in the barn of heaven. "Blessed are they that mourn"; this is the seeding: "for they shall be comforted" (Matt. v. 4); this is the harvest.

They sow *in renouncing the world,* and adherence to Christ; and they reap a great harvest. "Behold," saith Peter to Christ, "we have forsaken all, and followed thee" (Matt. xix. 27); this is the seeding. "What shall we have therefore?" What? "You shall sit on twelve thrones, judging the twelve tribes of Israel" (verses 28, 29); all that you have lost shall be centupled to you: "and you shall inherit everlasting life"; this is the harvest. "Sow to yourselves in righteousness and reap in mercy": Hos. x. 12.

They sow *in charity.* He that sows this seed shall be sure of a plentiful crop. "Whosoever shall give to drink to one of these little ones a cup of cold water only"— a little refreshing—"in the name of a disciple; verily I say unto you, he shall in no wise lose his reward:" Matt. x. 42. But if he that giveth a little shall be thus recompensed, then "he that soweth bountifully shall reap bountifully": 2 Cor. ix. 6. Therefore sparse abroad with a full hand, like a seedsman in a broad field, without fear. Doth any think he shall lose by his charity? No worldling, when he sows his seed, thinks he shall lose his seed; he hopes for increase at harvest. Darest thou trust the ground and not God? Sure God is a better paymaster than the earth: grace doth give a larger recompense than nature. Below thou mayest receive forty grains for one; but in heaven, (by the promise of Christ,) a hundred-fold: a "measure heapen, and shaken, and thrust together, and yet running over." "Blessed is he that considereth the poor"; this is the seeding: "the Lord shall deliver him in the time of trouble" (Ps. xli. 1); this is the harvest.—*Thomas Adams.*

Verse 5.—"*They that sow in tears,*" etc. Observe two things here. I. That the afflictions of God's people are as sowing in tears. 1. In sowing ye know there is great pains. The land must be first tilled and dressed; and there is pains in casting the seed into it; and then it takes a great dressing all the year, before it be set in the barn-yard. 2. It requires great charges, too, and therefore it is called "precious seed." For ye know that seed corn is aye dearest. 3. There is also great hazard; for corn, after it is sown, is subject to many dangers. And so it is with the children of God in a good cause. II. Then after the seed-time follows the harvest, and that comes with joy. There be three degrees of the happiness of God's children, in reaping of fruits. 1. In the first-fruits. Even when they are enduring anything for the Gospel of Christ, it carries contentment and fruit with it. 2. After the first-fruits, then come sheaves to refresh the husbandman, and to assure him that the full harvest is coming. The Lord now and then gives testimony of a full deliverance to his own people, especially of the deliverance of Sion, and lets them taste of the sheaves which they have reaped. 3. And lastly, they get the full harvest; and that is gotten at the great and last day. Then we get peace without trouble, joy without grief, profit without loss, pleasure without pain; and then we have a full sight of the face of God.—*Alexander Henderson.*

Verse 5.—"*They that sow in tears shall reap in joy.*" Gospel tears are not lost; they are seeds of comfort: while the penitent doth pour out tears, God pours in joy. If thou wouldst be cheerful, saith Chrysostom, be sad. It was the end of Christ's anointing and coming into the world, that he might comfort them that mourn: Isaiah lxi. 3. Christ had the oil of gladness poured on him, as Chrysostom saith, that he might pour it on the mourner; well then might the apostle call it "a repentance not to be repented of": 2 Cor. vii. 10. . . . Here is sweet fruit from a bitter stock: Christ caused the earthen vessels to be filled with water, and then turned the water into wine: John ii. 9. So when the eye, that earthen vessel, hath been filled with water brim full, then Christ will turn the water of tears into the wine of joy. Holy mourning, saith St. Basil, is the seed out of which the flower of eternal joy doth grow.—*Thomas Watson* (—1690 ?), *in "The Beatitudes."*

Verse 5.—"*They that sow in tears shall reap.*" We must take notice of the reapers: "*They* shall reap." Which *they?* They that did sow; they shall, and none but they shall. They shall; and good reason they should, because it was they that did sow. And though some that have sown in tears do complain of the lateness or thinness of the harvest, that they have not reaped in joy, as is here promised; know that some grounds are later than others, and in some years the harvest falleth later than in others, and that God, who is the Lord of the harvest, in his good time will ripen thy joy, and thou shalt reap it: and in the meantime, if we try it narrowly, we shall find the cause in ourselves, both of the lateness of our joy, because we were too late in sowing our tears; and of the thinness of our joy, because we did sow our tears too thin. And if after our sowing of tears we find no harvest of joy at all, we may be well assured that either our seed was not good, or else some of the mischances are come upon them, which came upon the seed that came to no good in the thirteenth of Matthew.—*Walter Balcanqual, in "a Sermon preached at St. Maries Spittle,"* 1623.

Verse 5.—*"They that sow in tears,"* etc. I saw in seedtime a husbandman at plough in a very rainy day. Asking him the reason why he would not rather leave off than labour in such foul weather, his answer was returned me in their country rhythm :—

> " Sow beans in the mud,
> And they'll come up like a wood.'

This could not but remind me of David's expression, *"They that sow in tears shall reap in joy,"* etc.—*Thomas Fuller* (1608—1661), *in "Good Thoughts in Worse Times."*

Verse 5.—*"Sow in tears."* There are tears which are themselves the seed that we must sow ; tears of sorrow for sin, our own and others' ; tears of sympathy with the afflicted church ; and tears of tenderness in prayer and under the word.—*Matthew Henry.*

Verse 5.—*"Shall reap in joy."* This spiritual harvest comes not alike soon to all, no more than the other which is outward doth. But here's the comfort, whoever hath a seed-time of grace pass over his soul shall have his harvest-time also of joy : this law God hath bound himself to as strongly as to the other, which " is not to cease while the earth remaineth " (Gen. viii. 22) ; yea, more strongly ; for that was to the world in general, not to every country, town, or field in particular, for some of these may want a harvest, and yet God may keep his word : but God cannot perform his promise if any one particular saint should everlastingly go without his reaping time. And therefore you who think so basely of the gospel and the professors of it, because at present their peace and comfort are not come, should know that it is on the way to them, and comes to stay everlastingly with them ; whereas your peace is going from you every moment, and is sure to leave you without any hope of returning to you again. Look not how the Christian begins, but ends. The Spirit of God by his convictions comes into the soul with some terrors, but it closeth with peace and joy. As we say of the month of March, it enters like a lion, but goes out like a lamb. " Mark the perfect man, and behold the upright : for the end of that man is peace " : Psalm xxxvii. 37.—*William Gurnall.*

Verses 5, 6.—In my little reading and small experience, I have found that corn sown in dear years and times of scarcity hath yielded much more increase than at other times ; so that presently after much want, there hath followed great plenty of grain, even beyond expectation.—*Humphrey Hardwick, in a Sermon entitled "The Difficulty of Sion's Deliverance and Reformation,"* 1644.

Verses 5, 6.—Mind we the undoubted certainty of our harvest verified by divers absolute positive asseverations in the text : " *he shall reap* " ; *"he shall come again "* ; *"he shall bring his sheaves with him."* Here's no item of contingency or possibility, but all absolute affirmations ; and you know heaven and earth shall pass away, but a jot of God's word shall not fail. Nothing shall prevent the harvest of a labourer in Sion's vineyard.—*Humphrey Hardwick.*

Verses 5, 6.—In a fuller, deeper sense, the sower in tears is the Man of sorrows himself. Believers know him thus. He has accomplished, in the sore travail of his soul, the seed time of affliction which is to bear its satisfying harvest when he shall again appear as the reaper of his own reward. He will fill his bosom with sheaves in that day of joy. The garner of his gladness will be filled to overflowing. By how much his affliction surpassed the natural measure of human grief, when he underwent for our sakes the dread realities of death and judgment ; by so much shall the fulness of his pure delight as the eternal blesser of his people excel their joy (yet what a measure, too, is there !) whose sum of blessedness is to be for ever with the Lord.—*Arthur Pridham, in "Notes and Reflections on the Psalms,"* 1869.

Verse 6.—*"He that goeth forth and weepeth, bearing precious seed,"* etc. This is very expressive of a gospel minister's life ; he goeth forth with the everlasting gospel which he preaches ; he sows it as precious seed in the church of God ; he waters it with tears and prayers ; the Lord's blessing accompanies it ; the Lord crowns his labours with success ; he has seals to his ministry ; and at the last day he shall doubtless come again with joy from the grave of death *"bringing his sheaves with him"*; and will, in the new Jerusalem state, be addressed by his Lord with, "Well done, good and faithful servant, enter thou into the joy of thy Lord."—*Samuel Eyles Pierce* (1746—1829 ?), *in "The Book of Psalms, an Epitome of the Old Testament Scripture."*

Verse 6.—*"He may go forth, he may go forth, and weep, bearing (his) load of seed. He shall come, he shall come with singing, bearing sheaves."* The emphatic combination of the finite tense with the infinitive is altogether foreign from our idiom, and very imperfectly represented, in the ancient and some modern versions, by the active participle (*venientes venient*, coming they shall come), which conveys neither the peculiar form nor the precise sense of the Hebrew phrase. The best approximation to the force of the original is Luther's repetition of the finite tense, *he shall come, he shall come*, because in all such cases the infinitive is really defined or determined by the term which follows, and in sense, though not in form, assimilated to it.— *Joseph Addison Alexander.*

Verse 6.—

> " Though he go, though he go, and be weeping,
>   While bearing some handfuls of seed ;
> He shall come, he shall come with bright singing,
>   While bearing his plentiful sheaves."

Ben-Tehillim, in "The Book of Psalms, in English Blank Verse," **1883.**

Verse 6.—*"Goeth forth."* The church must not only keep this seed in the storehouse, for such as come to enquire for it ; but must send her sowers forth to cast it among those who are ignorant of its value, or too indifferent to ask it at her hands. She must not sit weeping because men will not apply to her, but must go forth and bear the precious seed to the unwilling, the careless, the prejudiced, and the profligate. —*Edwin Sidney, in "The Pulpit,"* 1840.

Verse 6.—*Weeping* must not hinder sowing : when we suffer ill we must be doing well.—*Matthew Henry.*

Verse 6.—*"Precious seed."* Seed-corn is always dearest ; and when other corn is dear, then it is very dear ; yet though never so dear, the husbandman resolves that he must have it ; and he will deprive his own belly, and his wife and children of it, and will sow it, going out *"weeping"* with it. There is also great hazard ; for corn, after it is sown, is subject to many dangers. And so is it, indeed, with the children of God in a good cause. Ye must resolve to undergo hazards also, in life, lands, moveables, or whatsoever else ye have in this world : rather hazard all these before either religion be in hazard, or your own souls.—*Alexander Henderson.*

Verse 6.—*"Precious seed."* Aben Ezra, by the words rendered *precious seed,* or, as they may be, *a draught of seed,* understands the vessel in which the sower carries his seed, the seed basket, from whence he draws and takes out the seed, and scatters it ; see Amos ix. 13 : so the Targum, " bearing a tray of sowing corn."— *John Gill.*

Verse 6.—*"Precious seed."* Faith is called *"precious seed"* : *quod rarum est charum est.* Seed was accounted precious when all countries came unto Egypt to buy corn of Joseph, and that faith must needs be precious, seeing that when Christ comes he shall hardly "find faith upon the earth " : Luke xviii. 8. The necessity of faith is such, that therefore it must need be precious ; for as the material seed is the only instrumental means to preserve the life of man ; for all the spices, honey, myrrh, nuts, and almonds, gold and silver, that were in Canaan, were not sufficient for Jacob and his children's sustenance ; but they were forced to repair unto Egypt for corn, that they might live and not die ; even so, without faith the soul is starved ; it is the food of it ; for, " the just man liveth by his faith " : Gal. iii. 11.—*John Hume.*

Verse 6.—*"Sheaves."* The Psalm which begins with " dream " and ends with " sheaves " invites us to think of Joseph ; Joseph, " in whom," according to S. Ambrose's beautiful application, " there was revealed the future resurrection of the Lord Jesus, to whom both his eleven disciples did obeisance when they saw him gone into Galilee, and to whom all the saints shall on their resurrection do obeisance, bringing forth the fruit of good works, as it is written, ' He shall doubtless come again with rejoicing, bringing his sheaves with him.' "—*H. T. Armfield.*

HINTS TO PREACHERS.

Verse 1.—I. Sunny memories of what the Lord did, " he turned again the captivity," etc. II. Singular impressions,—we could not believe it to be true. III. Special discoveries—it was true, abiding, etc.

Verse 1.—A comparison and a contrast. I. The saved like them that dream. 1. In the strangeness of their experience. 2. In the ecstasy of their joy. II. The saved unlike them that dream. 1. In the reality of their experience. Dreams are unsubstantial things, but " the Lord turned "—an actual fact. 2. In their freedom from disappointment. No awakening to find it " but a dream " : see Isaiah xxix. 8. 3. In the endurance of their joy. The joy of dreams is soon forgotten, but this is " everlasting joy."—*W. H. J. P.*

Verse 2.—Saintly laughter. What creates it, and how it is justified.

Verse 2.—*Recipe for holy laughter.*—1. Lie in prison a few weeks. 2. Hear the Lord turning the key. 3. Follow him into the high-road. 4. Your sky will burst with sunshine, and your heart with song and laughter. 5. If this recipe is thought too expensive, try *keeping in the high-road.*—*W. B. H.*

Verses 2, 3.—I. Reports of God's doings. II. Experience of God's doings.

Verses 2, 3.—I. The Lord does great things for his people. II. These great things command the attention of the world. III. They inspire the joyful devotion of the saints.—*W. H. J. P.*

Verse 3.—"*The* LORD *hath done great things for us.*" In this acknowledgment and confession there are three noteworthy points of thankfulness. I. That they were "*great things* " which were done. II. Who it was who did them : "*the Lord.*" III. That they are done, not *against* us, but "*for* us."—*Alexander Henderson,* 1583—1646.

Verse 4.—Believers, rejoicing in their own deliverance, solicitous for a flood of prosperity to overflow the church. See the connection, verses 1—3. Remark, I. The doubting and despondent are too concerned about themselves, and too busy seeking comfort, to have either solicitude or energy to spare for the church's welfare ; but the joyful heart is free to be earnest for the church's good. II. Joyful believers, other things being equal, know more of the constraining power of Christ's love, which makes them anxious for his glory and the success of his cause. III. The joyful can appreciate more fully the contrast of their condition to that of the undelivered, and for their sake cannot fail to be anxious for the church through whose ministry their deliverance comes. IV. The joyful are, in general, the most believing and the most hopeful ; their expectation of success leads them to prayer, and impels them to effort.—*J. F.*

Verse 4.—I. The dried-up Christian. II. His unhappy condition. III. His one hope. IV. Result when realized.

Verse 5. — *The Christian Husbandman.* I. Illustrate the metaphor. The husbandman has a great variety of work before him ; every season and every day brings its proper business. So the Christian has duties in the closet, in the family, in the church, in the world, etc., etc. II. Whence it is that many Christians sow in tears. 1. It may be owing to the badness of the soil. 2. The inclemency of the season. 3. The malice and opposition of enemies. 4. Past disappointments. III. What connection there is between sowing in tears and reaping in joy. 1. A joyful harvest, by God's blessing, is the natural consequence of a dripping seed-time. 2. God, who cannot lie, hath promised it. IV. When this joyful harvest may be expected. It must not be expected in our wintry world, for there is not sun enough to ripen it. Heaven is the Christian's summer. When you come to reap the fruits of your present trials, you will bless God who made you sow in tears. *Improvement.* 1. How greatly are they to blame who in this busy time stand all the day idle ! 2. How greatly have Christians the advantage of the rest of the world ! 3. Let the hope and prospect of this joyful harvest support us under all the glooms and distresses of this vale of tears.—*Outline of a Sermon by Samuel Lavington,* 1726—1807.

Verse 5.—Two pictures. The connecting "*shall.*"

Verse 5.—I. There must be sowing before reaping. II. What men sow they will reap. If they sow precious seed, they will reap precious seed. III. In proportion as they sow they will reap. " He that soweth sparingly," etc. IV. The sowing may be with sorrow, but the reaping will be with joy. V. In proportion to the sorrow of sowing will be the joy of reaping.—*G. R.*

Verse 6.—In the two parts of this verse we may behold a threefold antithesis or opposition ; in the *progress,* 1. A sojourning : " He that now goeth on his way." 2. A sorrowing : " weeping." 3. A sowing : " and beareth forth good seed." In the *regress* there are three opposites unto these. 1. Returning : " He shall doubtless come again." 2. A Rejoicing : " with joy." 3. A Reaping : " and bring his sheaves with him."—*John Hume.*

Verse 6.—"*Doubtless.*" Or the reasons why our labour cannot be in vain in the Lord.

Verse 6.—"*Bringing his sheaves with him.*" The faithful sower's return to his Lord. Successful, knowing it, personally honoured, abundantly recompensed.

Verse 6.—See " Spurgeon's Sermon," No. 867 : " Tearful Sowing and Joyful Reaping."

Verse 6.—I. The sorrowful sower. 1. His activity—" he goeth forth." 2. His humility—" and weepeth." 3. His fidelity—" bearing precious seed." II. The joyful reaper. 1. His certain harvest-time—" shall doubtless come again." 2. His abundant joy—" with rejoicing." 3. His rich rewards—" bringing his sheaves with him."—*W. H. J. P.*

PSALM CXXVII.

Title.—*A Song of Degrees for Solomon.* *It was meet that the builder of the holy house should be remembered by the pilgrims to its sacred shrine. The title probably indicates that David wrote it for his wise son, in whom he so greatly rejoiced, and whose name Jedidiah, or "beloved of the Lord," is introduced into the second verse. The spirit of his name, "Solomon, or peaceable," breathes through the whole of this most charming song. If Solomon himself was the author, it comes fitly from him who reared the house of the Lord. Observe how in each of these songs the heart is fixed upon Jehovah only. Read the first verses of these Psalms, from Psalm cxx. to the present song, and they run thus : "I cried unto the Lord," "I will lift up mine eyes to the hills," " Let us go unto the house of the Lord," "Unto thee will I lift up mine eyes," "If it had not been the Lord," "They that trust in the Lord," "When the Lord turned again the captivity." The Lord and the Lord alone is thus lauded at each step of these songs of the ascents. O for a life whose every halting-place shall suggest a new song unto the Lord !*

Subject.—*God's blessing on his people as their one great necessity and privilege is here spoken of. We are here taught that builders of houses and cities, systems and fortunes, empires and churches all labour in vain without the Lord ; but under the divine favour they enjoy perfect rest. Sons, who are in the Hebrew called "builders," are set forth as building up families under the same divine blessing, to the great honour and happiness of their parents. It is* THE BUILDER'S PSALM. *"Every house is builded by some man, but he that built all things is God," and unto God be praise.*

EXPOSITION.

EXCEPT the LORD build the house, they labour in vain that build it : except the LORD keep the city, the watchman waketh *but* in vain.

2 *It is* vain for you to rise up early, to sit up late, to eat the bread of sorrows : *for* so he giveth his beloved sleep.

3 Lo, children *are* an heritage of the LORD : *and* the fruit of the womb *is his* reward.

4 As arrows *are* in the hand of a mighty man ; so *are* children of the youth.

5 Happy *is* the man that hath his quiver full of them : they shall not be ashamed, but they shall speak with the enemies in the gate.

1. "*Except the LORD build the house, they labour in vain that build it.*" The word *vain* is the key-note here, and we hear it ring out clearly three times. Men desiring to build know that they must labour, and accordingly they put forth all their skill and strength ; but let them remember that if Jehovah is not with them their designs will prove failures. So was it with the Babel builders ; they said, " Go to, let us build us a city and a tower "; and the Lord returned their words into their own bosoms, saying, " Go to, let us go down and there confound their language." In vain they toiled, for the Lord's face was against them. When Solomon resolved to build a house for the Lord, matters were very different, for all things united under God to aid him in his great undertaking : even the heathen were at his beck and call that he might erect a temple for the Lord his God. In the same manner God blessed him in the erection of his own palace ; for this verse evidently refers to all sorts of house-building. Without God we are nothing. Great houses have been erected by ambitious men ; but like the baseless fabric of a vision they have passed away, and scarce a stone remains to tell where once they stood. The wealthy builder of a Non-such Palace, could he revisit the glimpses of the moon, would be perplexed to find a relic of his former pride : he laboured in vain, for the place of his travail knows not a trace of his handiwork. The like may be said of the builders of castles and abbeys : when the mode of life indicated by these piles ceased to be

endurable by the Lord, the massive walls of ancient architects crumbled into ruins, and their toil melted like the froth of vanity. Not only do we now spend our strength for nought without Jehovah, but all who have ever laboured apart from him come under the same sentence. Trowel and hammer, saw and plane are instruments of vanity unless the Lord be the Master-builder.

"Except the LORD keep the city, the watchman waketh but in vain." Around the wall the sentinels pace with constant step ; but yet the city is betrayed unless the unsleeping Watcher is with them. We are not safe because of watchmen if Jehovah refuses to watch over us. Even if the guards are wakeful, and do their duty, still the place may be surprised if God be not there. " I, the Lord, do keep it," is better than an army of sleepless guards. Note that the Psalmist does not bid the builder cease from labouring, nor suggest that watchmen should neglect their duty, nor that men should show their trust in God by doing nothing : nay, he supposes that they will do all that they can do, and then he forbids their fixing their trust in what they have done, and assures them that all creature effort will be in vain unless the Creator puts forth his power, to render second causes effectual. Holy Scripture endorses the order of Cromwell—" Trust in God, and keep your powder dry " : only here the sense is varied, and we are told that the dried powder will not win the victory unless we trust in God. Happy is the man who hits the golden mean by so working as to believe in God, and so believing in God as to work without fear.

In Scriptural phrase a dispensation or system is called a house. Moses was faithful as a servant over all his house ; and as long as the Lord was with that house it stood and prospered ; but when he left it, the builders of it became foolish and their labour was lost. They sought to maintain the walls of Judaism, but sought in vain : they watched around every ceremony and tradition, but their care was idle. Of every church, and every system of religious thought, this is equally true : unless the Lord is in it, and is honoured by it, the whole structure must sooner or later fall in hopeless ruin. Much can be done by man ; he can both labour and watch ; but without the Lord he has accomplished nothing, and his wakefulness has not warded off evil.

2. *"It is vain for you to rise up early, to sit up late, to eat the bread of sorrows."* Because the Lord is mainly to be rested in, all carking care is mere vanity and vexation of spirit. We are bound to be diligent, for this the Lord blesses ; we ought not to be anxious, for that dishonours the Lord, and can never secure his favour. Some deny themselves needful rest ; the morning sees them rise before they are rested, the evening sees them toiling long after the curfew has tolled the knell of parting day. They threaten to bring themselves into the sleep of death by neglect of the sleep which refreshes life. Nor is their sleeplessness the only index of their daily fret ; they stint themselves in their meals, they eat the commonest food, and the smallest possible quantity of it, and what they do swallow is washed down with the salt tears of grief, for they fear that daily bread will fail them. Hard earned is their food, scantily rationed, and scarcely ever sweetened, but perpetually smeared with sorrow ; and all because they have no faith in God, and find no joy except in hoarding up the gold which is their only trust. Not thus, not thus, would the Lord have his children live. He would have them, as princes of the blood, lead a happy and restful life. Let them take a fair measure of rest and a due portion of food, for it is for their health. Of course the true believer will never be lazy or extravagant ; if he should be he will have to suffer for it ; but he will not think it needful or right to be worried and miserly. Faith brings calm with it, and banishes the disturbers who both by day and by night murder peace.

"For so he giveth his beloved sleep." Through faith the Lord makes his chosen ones to rest in him in happy freedom from care. The text may mean that God gives blessings to his beloved in sleep, even as he gave Solomon the desire of his heart while he slept. The meaning is much the same : those whom the Lord loves are delivered from the fret and fume of life, and take a sweet repose upon the bosom of their Lord. He rests them ; blesses them while resting ; blesses them more in resting than others in their moiling and toiling. God is sure to give the best thing to his beloved, and we here see that he gives them sleep—that is a laying aside of care, a forgetfulness of need, a quiet leaving of matters with God : this kind of sleep is better than riches and honour. Note how Jesus slept amid the hurly-burly of a storm at sea. He knew that he was in his Father's hands, and

therefore he was so quiet in spirit that the billows rocked him to sleep : it would be much oftener the same with us if we were more like HIM.

It is to be hoped that those who built Solomon's temple were allowed to work at it steadily and joyfully. Surely such a house was not built by unwilling labourers. One would hope that the workmen were not called upon to hurry up in the morning nor to protract their labours far into the night ; but we would fain believe that they went on steadily, resting duly, and eating their bread with joy. So, at least, should the spiritual temple be erected ; though, truth to tell, the workers upon its walls are all too apt to grow cumbered with much serving, all too ready to forget their Lord, and to dream that the building is to be done by themselves alone. How much happier might we be if we would but trust the Lord's house to the Lord of the house ! What is far more important, how much better would our building and watching be done if we would but confide in the Lord who both builds and keeps his own church !

3. *"Lo, children are an heritage of the* LORD.*"* This points to another mode of building up a house, namely, by leaving descendants to keep our name and family alive upon the earth. Without this what is a man's purpose in accumulating wealth ? To what purpose does he build a house if he has none in his household to hold the house after him ? What boots it that he is the possessor of broad acres if he has no heir ? Yet in this matter a man is powerless without the Lord. The great Napoleon, with all his sinful care on this point, could not create a dynasty. Hundreds of wealthy persons would give half their estates if they could hear the cry of a babe born of their own bodies. Children are a heritage which Jehovah himself must give, or a man will die childless, and thus his house will be unbuilt.

"And the fruit of the womb is his reward," or a reward from God. He gives children, not as a penalty nor as a burden, but as a favour. They are a token for good if men know how to receive them, and educate them. They are " doubtful blessings " only because we are doubtful persons. Where society is rightly ordered children are regarded, not as an incumbrance, but as an inheritance ; and they are received, not with regret, but as a reward. If we are over-crowded in England, and so seem to be embarrassed with too large an increase, we must remember that the Lord does not order us to remain in this narrow island, but would have us fill those boundless regions which wait for the axe and the plough. Yet even here, with all the straits of limited incomes, our best possessions are our own dear offspring, for whom we bless God every day.

4. *"As arrows are in the hand of a mighty man ; so are children of the youth."* Children born to men in their early days, by God's blessing become the comfort of their riper years. A man of war is glad of weapons which may fly where he cannot : good sons are their father's arrows speeding to hit the mark which their sires aim at. What wonders a good man can accomplish if he has affectionate children to second his desires, and lend themselves to his designs ! To this end we must have our children in hand while they are yet children, or they are never likely to be so when they are grown up ; and we must try to point them and straighten them, so as to make arrows of them in their youth, lest they should prove crooked and unserviceable in after life. Let the Lord favour us with loyal, obedient, affectionate offspring, and we shall find in them our best helpers. We shall see them shot forth into life to our comfort and delight, if we take care from the very beginning that they are directed to the right point.

5. *"Happy is the man that hath his quiver full of them."* Those who have no children bewail the fact ; those who have few children see them soon gone, and the house is silent, and their life has lost a charm ; those who have many gracious children are upon the whole the happiest. Of course a large number of children means a large number of trials ; but when these are met by faith in the Lord it also means a mass of love, and a multitude of joys. The writer of this comment gives it as his own observation, that he has seen the most frequent unhappiness in marriages which are unfruitful ; that he has himself been most grateful for two of the best of sons ; but as they have both grown up, and he has no child at home, he has without a tinge of murmuring, or even wishing that he were otherwise circumstanced, felt that it might have been a blessing to have had a more numerous family : he therefore heartily agrees with the Psalmist's verdict herein expressed. He has known a family in which there were some twelve daughters and three sons, and he never expects to witness upon earth greater domestic felicity than fell to the lot of their parents, who rejoiced in all their children, as the children also rejoiced

in their parents and in one another. When sons and daughters are arrows, it is well to have a quiver full of them ; but if they are only sticks, knotty and useless, the fewer of them the better. While those are blessed whose quiver is full, there is no reason to doubt that many are blessed who have no quiver at all ; for a quiet life may not need such a warlike weapon. Moreover, a quiver may be small and yet full ; and then the blessing is obtained. In any case we may be sure that a man's life consisteth not in the abundance of children that he possesseth.

"*They shall not be ashamed, but they shall speak with the enemies in the gate.*" They can meet foes both in law and in fight. Nobody cares to meddle with a man who can gather a clan of brave sons about him. He speaks to purpose whose own sons make his words emphatic by the resolve to carry out their father's wishes. This is the blessing of Abraham, the old covenant benediction, " Thy seed shall possess the gate of his enemies"; and it is sure to all the beloved of the Lord in some sense or other. Doth not the Lord Jesus thus triumph in his seed ? Looked at literally, this favour cometh of the Lord : without his will there would be no children to build up the house, and without his grace there would be no good children to be their parent's strength. If this must be left with the Lord, let us leave every other thing in the same hands. He will undertake for us and prosper our trustful endeavours, and we shall enjoy a tranquil life, and prove ourselves to be our Lord's beloved by the calm and quiet of our spirit. We need not doubt that if God gives us children as a reward he will also send us the food and raiment which he knows they need.

He who is the father of a host of spiritual children is unquestionably happy. He can answer all opponents by pointing to souls who have been saved by his means. Converts are emphatically the heritage of the Lord, and the reward of the preacher's soul travail. By these, under the power of the Holy Ghost, the city of the church is both built up and watched, and the Lord has the glory of it.

EXPLANATORY NOTES AND QUAINT SAYINGS.

Title.—"*A Song of Degrees for Solomon.*" This Psalm has Solomon's name prefixed to the title, for the purpose that the very builder of the Temple may teach us that he availed nothing to build it without the help of the Lord.—*The Venerable Bede* (672-3—735), *in Neale and Littledale.*

Whole Psalm.—Viewed as one of the " Degrees " in Christian virtue, the ninth, the Psalm is directed against self-reliance.—*H. T. Armfield.*

Whole Psalm.—The steps or degrees in this Psalm, though distinctly marked, are not so regular as in some others. The twice repeated *"in vain"* of verse 1 may be regarded as the motto or " degree " for verse 2. The correspondence between the two clauses in verse 1 is also very striking. It is as if, on entering on some spiritual undertaking, or even in referring to the present state of matters, the Psalmist emphatically disclaimed as *vain* every other interposition or help than that of Jehovah. And of this *"in vain"* it is well constantly to remind ourselves, especially in seasons of activity and in times of peace ; for then we are most liable to fall into the snare of this *vanity.* The next " degree " is that of success and prosperity (verses 3, 4), which is ascribed to the same Jehovah whose help and protection constituted the commencement and continuance, as now the completion of our well-being. Hence also verse 5 goes not beyond this, but contemplates the highest symbol of full security, influence, and power, in the figurative language of the Old Testament, which St. Augustine refers to " spiritual children, shot forth like arrows into all the world."—*Alfred Edersheim, in "The Golden Diary of Heart Converse with Jesus in the Book of Psalms,"* 1877.

Whole Psalm.—Solomon, the wisest and richest of kings, after having proved, both from experience and careful observation, that there was nothing but vanity in the life and labours of man, comes to this conclusion, that there is nothing better for a man in this life than that he should moderate his cares and labours, enjoy what he has, and fear God and keep his commandments : to this end he directs all that is debated in the Book of Ecclesiastes. Very similar are the argument and intention of the Psalm ; the authorship of which is ascribed to Solomon in the Inscription, and which there is no reason to doubt. Nor would it be safe, either to call in doubt any inscription without an urgent reason, or to give any other sense to the letter ל than that of *authorship*, unless it be meant that all the inscriptions are uncertain. Again, if the collectors of the Psalms added *titles* according to their own opinion and judgment, there would be no reason why they should have left so many Psalms without any title. This Psalm, therefore, is *Solomon's*, with whose genius and condition it well agrees, as is clear from *Ecclesiastes*, with which it may be compared, and from many *proverbs* on the same subject. . . . The design is, to drawn men away from excessive labours and anxious cares ; and to excite godliness and faith in Jehovah. To this the Psalm manifestly tends : for since men, desirous of the happiness and stability of their houses, are unable to secure this by their own endeavours, but need the blessing of God, who gives prosperity with even lighter labours to those that fear him ; it is their duty to put a limit to their labours and cares, and to seek the favour of God, by conforming their life and conduct to his will, and confiding in him.—*Herman Venema*, 1697—1787.

Verse 1.—"*Except the* LORD *build.*" It is a fact that בן, *ben, a son,* and בת, *bath, a daughter,* and בית, *beith, a house,* come from the same root, בנה, *banah, to build ;* because sons and daughters build up a household, or constitute a *family,* as much and as really as stones and timber constitute a *building.* Now it is true that unless the good hand of God be upon us we cannot prosperously build a place of worship for his name. Unless we have his blessing, a dwelling-house cannot be comfortably erected. And if his blessing be not on our children, the house (the family) may be built up ; but instead of its being the house of God, it will be the synagogue of Satan. All marriages that are not under God's blessing will be a private and public curse.—*Adam Clarke.*

Verse 1.—"*Except the* LORD *build the house,*" etc. He does not say, Unless the Lord consents and is willing that the house should be built and the city kept : but, " Unless the Lord *build ;* unless he *keep.*" Hence, in order that the building and keeping may be prosperous and successful, there is necessary, not only the consent of God, but also his working is required : and that working without which nothing can be accomplished, that may be attempted by man. He does not say, Unless the Lord help ; but unless the Lord build, unless he keep ; *i.e.,* Unless he do all himself. He does not say, To little purpose he labours and watches ; but to no purpose he labours, both the builder and the keeper. Therefore, all the efficacy of labours and cares is dependent on the operation and providence of God ; and all human strength, care, and industry is in itself vain.

It should be noticed, that he does not say, Because the Lord builds the house he labours in vain who builds it, and, because the Lord keeps the city the watchman waketh in vain : but, If the Lord do not build the house, if he do not keep the city ; he labours in vain who builds the house ; he waketh in vain who keeps the city. He is far from thinking that the care and human labour, which is employed in the building of houses and keeping of cities, is to be regarded as useless, because the Lord builds and keeps ; since it is then the more especially useful and effectual when the Lord himself is the builder and keeper. The Holy Spirit is not the patron of lazy and inert men ; but he directs the minds of those who labour to the providence and power of God.—*Wolfgang Musculus,* 1497—1563.

Verse 1.—"*Except the* LORD *build the house.*" On the lintel of the door in many an old English house, we may still read the words, *Nisi Dominus frustra*—the Latin version of the opening words of the Psalm. Let us also trust in him, and inscribe these words over the portal of " the house of our pilgrimage "; and beyond a doubt all *will* be well with us, both in this world and in that which is to come.—*Samuel Cox, in "The Pilgrim Psalms,"* 1874.

Verse 1.—"*Except the* LORD *build the house,*" etc. In the beginning of the contest with Britain, when we were sensible of danger, we had daily prayers in this room for the Divine protection. Our prayers, sir, were heard, and they were graciously answered. All of us who were engaged in the struggle must have observed frequent instances of a superintending Providence in our favour. To that kind Providence we owe this happy opportunity of consulting in peace on the means of establishing our future national felicity. And have we now forgotten this powerful Friend ?

or do we imagine we no longer need his assistance ?   I have lived for a long time
[81 years] ; and the longer I live the more convincing proofs I see of this truth,
that God governs in the affairs of man.   And if a sparrow cannot fall to the ground
without his notice, is it probable that an empire can rise without his aid ?   We
have been assured, sir, in the sacred writings, that " Except the LORD build the
house, they labour in vain that build it."   I firmly believe this ; and I also believe
that without his concurring aid we shall proceed in this political building no better
than the builders of Babel : we shall be divided by our little, partial, local interests ;
our prospects will be confounded ; and we ourselves shall become a reproach and
a by-word down to future ages.   And what is worse, mankind may hereafter, from
this unfortunate instance, despair of establishing government by human wisdom,
and leave it to chance, war, or conquest.   I therefore beg leave to move that henceforth prayers, imploring the assistance of Heaven and its blessings on our delibera-
tions, be held in this assembly every morning before we proceed to business ; and
that one or more of the clergy of this city be requested to officiate in that service.—
*Benjamin Franklin : Speech in Convention for forming a Constitution for the United
States*, 1787.

   Verse 1.—Note, how he puts first the building of the house, and then subjoins
the keeping of the city.   He advances from the part to the whole ; for the city
consists of houses.—*Wolfgang Musculus.*

   Verse 1.—"*Except the LORD keep the city,*" etc.   Fires may break out in spite
of the watchmen ; a tempest may sweep over it ; bands of armed men may assail
it ; or the pestilence may suddenly come into it, and spread desolation through
its dwellings.—*Albert Barnes* (1798—1870), *in "Notes on the Psalms."*

   Verse 1.—One important lesson which Madame Guyon learned from her temptations and follies was that of her entire dependence on Divine grace.   " I became,"
she says, " deeply assured of what the prophet hath said, '*Except the LORD keep
the city, the watchman waketh but in vain.*'   When I looked to thee, O my Lord !
thou wast my faithful keeper ; thou didst continually defend my heart against
all kinds of enemies.   But, alas ! when left to myself, I was all weakness.   How
easily did my enemies prevail over me !   Let others ascribe their victories to their
own fidelity : as for myself, I shall never attribute them to anything else than thy
paternal care.   I have too often experienced, to my cost, what I should be without
thee, to presume in the least on any wisdom or efforts of my own.   It is to thee,
O God, my Deliverer, that I owe everything !   And it is a source of infinite satisfaction, that I am thus indebted to thee."—*From the Life of Jeanne Bouvier de la
Moihe Guyon*, 1648—1717.

   Verse 1.—

> If God build not the house, and lay
>   The groundwork sure—whoever build,
> It cannot stand one stormy day.
> If God be not the city's shield,
> If he be not their bars and wall,
> In vain is watch-tower, men, and all.
>
> Though then thou wak'st when others rest,
>   Though rising thou prevent'st the sun,
> Though with lean care thou daily feast,
>   Thy labour's lost, and thou undone ;
> But God his child will feed and keep,
> And draw the curtains to his sleep.

Phineas Fletcher, 1584—1350.

   Verse 2.—"*It is vain for you to rise up early, to sit up late,*" etc.   The Psalmist
is exhorting to give over undue and anxious labour to accomplish our designs.   The
phrases in the Hebrew are " making early to rise " and " making late to sit "—
not " up," but *down*.   This means an artificial lengthening of the day.   The law
of work is in our nature.   The limitations of effort are set forth in nature.   In
order that all may be accomplished by the human race which is necessary to be
done for human progress, all men must work.   But no man should work beyond
his physical and intellectual ability, nor beyond the hours which nature allots.
No net result of good to the individual or to the race comes of any artificial
prolonging of the day at either end.   Early rising, eating one's breakfast by
candlelight, and prolonged vigils, the scholar's " midnight oil," are a delusion and

a snare. Work while it is day. When the night comes, rest. The other animals do this, and, as races, fare as well as this anxious human race.

"The bread of sorrows" means the bread of toil, of wearisome effort. Do what you ought to do, and the Lord will take care of that which you cannot do. Compare Prov. x. 22 : " The blessing of the Lord, it maketh rich, and he addeth no sorrow with it," which means, " The blessing of Jehovah maketh rich, and toil can add nothing thereto." Compare also Matt. vi. 25 : " Take no thought [be not anxious] for your life," etc.

"For so he giveth his beloved sleep." The *"for"* is not in the original. *"So"* means "with just the same result" or " all the same," or "without more trouble." That is the signification of the Hebrew word as it occurs. *"His beloved"* may work and sleep ; and what is needed will be provided just as certainly as if they laboured unduly, with anxiety. It has been suggested that the translation should be *"in sleep."* While they are sleeping, the Heavenly Father is carrying forward his work for them. Or, while they wake and work, the Lord giveth to them, and so he does when they rest and sleep.—*Charles F. Deems, in "The Study," 1879.*

Verse 2.—The Lord's Temple was built without any looking unto or dependence on man ; all human wisdom and confidence was rejected on the whole ; the plan was given by the Lord God himself ; the model of it was in Solomon's possession ; nothing was left to the wit or wisdom of men ; there was no reason to rise up early, to sit up late, to eat the bread of sorrows, whilst engaged in the good work ; no, I should conceive it was a season of grace to such as were employed in the building ; somewhat like what it was with you and me when engaged in God's holy ordinances. I should conceive the minds of the workmen at perfect peace, their conversation together much on the grand subject of the Temple, and its intention as referring to the glorious Messiah, its grand and glorious antitype. I should conceive their minds were wholly disencumbered from all carking cares. They did not rise early without being refreshed in body and mind ; they did not sit up late as though they wanted ; they were not careful how they should provide for their families ; they were, as the beloved of the Lord, perfectly contented ; they enjoyed sweet sleep and refreshment by it, this was from the Lord ; he giveth his beloved ones sleep.— *Samuel Eyles Pierce.*

Verse 2.—*"It is vain,"* etc. Some take this place in a more particular and restrained sense ; as if David would intimate that all their agitations to oppose the reign of Solomon, though backed with much care and industry, should be fruitless ; though Absalom and Adonijah were tortured with the care of their own ambitious designs, yet God would give Jedidiah, or his beloved, rest ; that is, the kingdom should safely be devolved upon Solomon, who took no such pains to court the people, and to raise himself up into their esteem as Absalom and Adonijah did. The meaning is, that though worldly men fare never so hardly, beat their brains, tire their spirits, rack their consciences, yet many times all is for nothing ; either God doth not give them an estate, or not the comfort of it. But his beloved, without any of these racking cares, enjoy contentment ; if they have not the world, they have sleep and rest ; with silence submitting to the will of God, and with quietness waiting for the blessing of God. Well, then, acknowledge the providence that you may come under the blessing of it : labour *without God* cannot prosper ; *against God* and against his will in his word, will surely miscarry.—*Thomas Manton, 1620— 1677.*

Verse 2.—*"It is vain for you to rise up early, to sit up late, to eat the bread of sorrows : for so he giveth his beloved sleep."* No prayer without work, no work without prayer.—

By caring and fretting,
By agony and fear,
There is of God no getting,
But prayer he will hear.

From J. P. Lange's Commentary on James, 1862.

Verse 2.—*"Eat the bread of sorrows."* Living a life of misery and labours, fretting at their own disappointments, eaten up with envy at the advancement of others, afflicted overmuch with losses and wrongs. There is no end of all their labours. Some have died of it, others been distracted and put out of their wits ; so that you are never like to see good days as long as you cherish the love of the world, but will still lie under self-tormenting care and trouble of mind, by which a man grateth on his own flesh.—*Thomas Manton.*

Verse 2.—*"So he giveth his beloved sleep."* כֵּן יִתֵּן לִידִידוֹ שֵׁנָה. These latter words are variously rendered, and sufficiently obscurely, because all take this כֵּן as a particle of comparison, which does not seem to be in place here : some even omit it altogether. But כֵּן also signifies *"well," "rightly" :* 2 Kings vii. 9 ; Num. xxvii. 7. Why should we not render it here, *"He giveth to His beloved to sleep well" : i.e.,* While those who, mistrusting God, attribute all things to their own labour, do not sleep well ; for truly they *"rise early and sit up late" ;* he gives to his beloved this grace, that reposing in his fatherly care and goodness, they fully enjoy their sleep, as those who know that such anxious labour is not necessary for them : or, *"Truly, he giveth to his beloved sleep ;" as* כֵּן may be the same as אָכֵן. But שֵׁנָה may be taken for בְּשֵׁנָה, and rendered, *"Truly, he giveth to his beloved in sleep ;"* viz., that he should be refreshed by this means.—*Louis De Dieu,* 1590—1642.

Verse 2 (last clause).—The sentence may be read either, *he will give sleep to his beloved,* or, *he will give in sleeping ;* that is, he will give them those things which unbelievers labour to acquire by their own industry. The particle כֵּן, *ken, thus,* is put to express certainty ; for with the view of producing a more undoubted persuasion of the truth—that God gives food to his people without any great care on their part—which seems incredible and a fiction, Solomon points to the thing as it were with the finger. He indeed speaks as if God nourished the slothfulness of his servants by his gentle treatment ; but as we know that men are created with the design of their being occupied, and as in the subsequent Psalm we shall find that the servants of God are accounted happy when they eat the labour of their hands, it is certain that the word *sleep* is not to be understood as implying slothfulness, but a placid labour, to which true believers subject themselves by the obedience of faith. Whence proceeds this so great ardour in the unbelieving, that they move not a finger without a tumult or bustle, in other words, without tormenting themselves with superfluous cares, but because they attribute nothing to the providence of God ! The faithful, on the other hand, although they lead a laborious life, yet follow their vocations with composed and tranquil minds. Thus their hands are not idle, but their minds repose in the stillness of faith, as if they were asleep.— *John Calvin,* 1509—1564.

Verse 2.—*"He giveth his beloved sleep."* It is *a peculiar rest,* it is a rest peculiar to sons, to saints, to heirs, to beloved ones. "So he gives *his beloved* rest," or as the Hebrew hath it, dearling, or dear beloved, quiet rest, without care or sorrow. The Hebrew word שֵׁנָא, *shena,* is written with א, a quiet, dumb letter, which is not usual, to denote the more quietness and rest. This rest is a crown that God sets only upon the head of saints ; it is a gold chain that he only puts about his children's necks ; it is a jewel that he only hangs between his beloved's breasts ; it is a flower that he only sticks in his darlings' bosoms. This rest is a tree of life that is proper and peculiar to the inhabitants of that heavenly country ; it is children's bread, and shall never be given to dogs.—*Thomas Brooks,* 1608—1680.

Verse 2 (last clause).—As the Lord *gave* a precious gift to his *beloved,* the first Adam, while he *slept,* by taking a rib from his side, and by *building* therefrom a woman, Eve his bride, the Mother of all living ; so, while Christ, the Second Adam, the true Jedidiah, the Well-beloved Son of God, was sleeping in death on the cross, God formed for him, in his death, and by his death,—even by the life-giving streams flowing from his own precious side,—the Church, the spiritual Eve, the Mother of all living ; and gave her to him as his bride. Thus he *built* for him in his *sleep* the spiritual Temple of his Church.—*Christopher Wordsworth.*

Verse 2.—Quiet sleep is the gift of God, and it is the love of God to give quiet sleep.

1. *'Tis God's gift* when we have it : quiet sleep does revive nature as the dew or small rain does refresh the grass. Now, as the prophet speaks (Jer. xiv. 22), " Are there any of the gods of the heathen can cause rain, or can the heavens give showers ? " so it may be said : Are there any of the creatures in earth or heaven that can give sleep ? That God which gives showers of rain must give hours of rest : peaceable repose is God's peculiar *gift.*

2. *'Tis God's love* when he gives it, *"for so he giveth his beloved sleep ";* that is, sleep with quietness : yea, the Hebrew word, *shena,* being with *aleph,* a quiet or resting letter, otherwise than is usual, it signifies the greater quietness in time of sleep. And whereas some apply the peace only to Solomon, who was called Jedidiah, the beloved of the Lord, to whom God gave sleep ; the Septuagint turns the Hebrew word plurally, *"so God giveth his beloved ones sleep ";* to his saints in general God

gives quiet sleep as a token of his love ; yea, in the times of their greatest peril. Thus Peter in prison when he was bound with chains, beset with soldiers, and to die the next day, yet see how fast he was found asleep (Acts xii. 6, 7) : " The same night Peter was sleeping, and behold the angel of the Lord came upon him, and a light shined in the prison," yet Peter slept till the angel smote him on the side and raised him up : so God " gives his beloved sleep," and let his beloved give him the honour ; and the rather because *herein God answers our prayer, herein God fulfils his promise.*

Is it not *our prayer* that God would prevent affrighting, and afford refreshing sleep ? and is it not God's answer when in sleep he doth sustain us ? " I cried (says David) unto the Lord with my voice, and he heard me out of his holy hill. I laid me down and slept, for the Lord sustained me " : Ps. iii. 4, 5.

Is it not *God's promise* to vouchsafe sleep free from frights ? " When thou liest down, thou shalt not be afraid : yea, thou shalt lie down, and thy sleep shall be sweet " : Prov. iii. 24. Hence God's servants while they are in the wilderness and woods of this world, they sleep safely, and devils as wild beasts can do them no harm. Ezek. xxxiv. 25. Have we through God's blessing this benefit, let us abundantly give praise and live praise unto God hereupon. Yea, large praise belongs to the Lord for quiet sleep from men of all sorts.—*Philip Goodwin, in "The Mystery of Dreams,"* 1658.

Verse 2.—*"So he giveth his beloved sleep."* The world would give its favourites power, wealth, distinction ; God gives *"sleep."* Could he give anything better? To give sleep when the storm is raging ; to give sleep when conscience is arraying a long catalogue of sins ; to give sleep when evil angels are trying to overturn our confidence in Christ ; to give sleep when death is approaching, when judgment is at hand—oh ! what gift could be more suitable ? what more worthy of God ? or what more precious to the soul ?

But we do not mean to enlarge upon the various senses which might thus be assigned to the gift. You will see for yourselves that sleep, as denoting repose and refreshment, may be regarded as symbolising " the rest which remaineth for the righteous," which is the gift of God to his chosen. " Surely he giveth his beloved sleep," may be taken as parallel to what is promised in Isaiah—" Thou wilt keep him in perfect peace whose mind is stayed on thee." Whatever you can understand by the " peace " in the one case, you may also understand by the *"sleep "* in the other. But throughout the Old and New Testaments, and especially the latter, sleep, as you know, is often put for death. " He slept with his fathers " is a common expression in the Jewish Scriptures. To " sleep in Jesus " is a common way of speaking of those who die in the faith of the Redeemer.

Suppose, then, we take the *"sleep "* in our text as denoting death, and confine our discourse to an illustration of the passage under this one point of view. ' *Surely he giveth his beloved sleep."* What an aspect will this confer on death—to regard it as God's gift—a gift which he vouchsafes to those whom he loves !

It is not " he *sendeth* his beloved sleep," which might be true whilst God himself remained at a distance ; it is " he *giveth* his beloved sleep " ; as though God himself brought the sleep, and laid it on the eyes of the weary Christian warrior. And if God himself have to do with the dissolution, can we not trust him that he will loosen gently the silver cord, and use all kindness and tenderness in " taking down the earthly house of this tabernacle " ? I know not more comforting words than those of our text, whether for the being uttered in the sick-room of the righteous, or breathed over their graves. They might almost take the pain from disease, as they certainly do the dishonour from death. What is bestowed by God as a " gift on his beloved " will assuredly occupy his care, his watchfulness, his solicitude ; and I conclude, therefore, that he is present, in some special and extraordinary sense when the righteous lie dying ; ay, and that he sets his seal, and plants his guardianship where the righteous lie dead. "O death, where is thy sting ? O grave, where is thy victory?" Let the saint be but constant in the profession of godliness, and his last hours shall be those in which Deity himself shall stand almost visibly at his side, and his last resting-place that which he shall shadow with his wings. Sickness may be protracted and distressing ; " earth to earth, ashes to ashes, dust to dust," may be plaintively breathed over the unconscious dead ; but nothing in all this lengthened struggle, nothing in all this apparent defeat, can harm the righteous man—nay, nothing can be other than for his present good and his eternal glory, seeing that death with all its accompaniments is but joy—God's gift to his beloved. Dry your tears, ye that stand around the bed of the dying believer, the parting moment is almost at hand—a cold damp is on the forehead— the eye is fixed—the pulse too feeble to be felt—are you staggered at such a spectacle ? Nay ! let faith do its part ! The chamber is crowded with glorious forms ; angels are waiting there to take charge of the disembodied soul ; a hand gentler than any human is closing those eyes ; and a voice sweeter than any human is whispering— *"Surely the Lord giveth his beloved sleep."*—*Henry Melvill* (1798—1871), *in a Sermon entitled "Death the Gift of God."*

Verse 2.—*"For so he giveth his beloved sleep."* One night I could not rest, and in the wild wanderings of my thoughts I met this text, and communed with it : *"So he giveth his beloved sleep."* In my reverie, as I was on the border of the land of dreams, methought I was in a castle. Around its massive walls there ran a deep moat. Watchmen paced the walls both day and night. It was a fine old fortress, bidding defiance to the foe ; but I was not happy in it. I thought I lay upon a couch ; but scarcely had I closed my eyes, ere a trumpet blew, " To arms ! To arms ! " and when the danger was overpast, I lay me down again. " To arms ! To arms ! " once more resounded, and again I started up. Never could I rest. I thought I had my armour on, and moved about perpetually clad in mail, rushing each hour to the castle top, aroused by some fresh alarm. At one time a foe was coming from the west ; at another from the east. I thought I had a treasure somewhere down in some deep part of the castle, and all my care was to guard it. I dreaded, I feared, I trembled lest it should be taken from me. I awoke, and I thought I would not live in such a tower as that for all its grandeur. It was the castle of discontent, the castle of ambition, in which man never rests. It is ever, " To arms ! To arms ! " There is a foe here, or a foe there. His dear-loved treasure must be guarded. Sleep never crossed the drawbridge of the castle of discontent. Then I thought I would supplement it by another reverie. I was in a cottage. It was in what poets call a beautiful and pleasant place, but I cared not for that. I had no treasure in the world, save one sparkling jewel on my breast : and I thought I put my hand on that and went to sleep, nor did I wake till morning light. That treasure was a quiet conscience and the love of God—" the peace that passeth all understanding." I slept, because I slept in the house of content, satisfied with what I had. Go, ye overreaching misers ! Go, ye grasping, ambitious men ! I envy not your life of inquietude. The sleep of statesmen is often broken ; the dream of the miser is always evil ; the sleep of the man who loves gain is never hearty ; but God *"giveth,"* by contentment, *" his beloved sleep."*—*C. H. S.*

Verse 2.—*"He giveth his beloved sleep."*

> Of all the thoughts of God that are
> Borne inward unto souls afar,
> Along the Psalmist's music deep,
> Now tell me if that any is,
> For gift or grace surpassing this—
> *"He giveth his beloved sleep."*

Elizabeth Barrett Browning, 1809—1861.

Verse 3.—*"Lo, children are an heritage of the Lord."* There is no reason, there- fore, why you should be apprehensive for your families and country ; there is no reason why you should weary yourselves with such great and such restless labour. God will be with you and your children, since they are his heritage.—*Thomas Le Blanc.*

Verse 3.--*"Lo, children are an heritage of the LORD."* That is, to many God gives children in place of temporal good. To many others he gives houses, lands, and thousands of gold and silver, and with them the womb that beareth not ; and these are their inheritance. The poor man has from God a number of children, without lands or money ; these are his inheritance ; and God shows himself their father, feeding and supporting them by a chain of miraculous providences. Where is the *poor man* who would give up his *six children* with the prospect of having *more,* for the *thousands* or *millions* of him who is the *centre* of his *own existence,* and has neither *root* nor *branch* but his forlorn solitary self upon the face of the earth ? Let the fruitful family, however poor, lay this to heart · *"Children are an heritage of the Lord : and the fruit of the womb is his reward."* And he who gave them will feed them ; for it is a fact, and the *maxim* formed on it has never failed, " Wherever God sends mouths, he sends meat." " Murmur not," said an Arab to his friend,

" because thy family is large ; know that it is for *their sakes* that God feeds *thee*."— *Adam Clarke.*

Verse 3.—"*Children are an heritage of the Lord.*" The Hebrew seems to imply that children are an heritage belonging to the Lord, and not an heritage given by the Lord, as most English readers appear to take it. The Targum likewise bears this out.—*H. T. Armfield.*

Verse 3.—"*Children are an heritage of the LORD,*" etc. The Psalmist speaks of what children are unto godly and holy parents, for unto such only is any blessing given by God as a reward, and the Psalmist expressly speaks of blessings which God gives his beloved ones, and this blessing of children he makes to be the last and greatest. It is also as certain that he speaks of children as supposed to be holy and godly ; for otherwise they are not a reward, but a curse, and a sorrow to him that begat them. The Psalm was made, as appears by the title of it, "*of or for Solomon,*" and therefore, as it is more than probable, was penned, as that other Psalm, the 72nd, which bears the same title, by David the father, of and for Solomon his son, who was, for his father's sake, " the beloved of God " (2 Sam. xii. 24, 25), and upon whom the sure covenant and mercies of David were entailed, together with his kingdom. And what is said in this Psalm, in the verse before, fitly agrees to him, for he it was who was to build God's house, to keep, and preserve Jerusalem the city, and the kingdom in peace, and to have rest, or as the Psalmist calls it (verse 3), quiet sleep given him by God, from all his enemies round about him. And for this, compare the prophecy of him (1 Chron. xxii. 9, 10) with the instructions here given him in the three first verses of this Psalm, and ye will see how fitly this Psalm concerns him.—*Thomas Goodwin.*

Verse 3.—"*Children are an heritage of the Lord.*" Hence note, 'tis one of the greatest outward blessings to have a family full of dutiful children. To have many children is the next blessing to much grace. To have many children about us is better than to have much wealth about us. To have store of these olive plants (as the Psalmist calls them) round about our table is better than to have store of oil and wine upon our table. We know the worth of dead, or rather lifeless treasures, but who knows the worth of living treasures ? Every man who hath children hath not a blessing in them, yet children are a blessing, and some have many blessings in one child. Children are chiefly a blessing to the children of God. "*Lo, children are an heritage of the LORD : and the fruit of the womb is his reward.*" But are not houses and lands, gold and silver, an heritage bestowed by the Lord upon his people ? Doubtless they are, for the earth is his, and the fulness of it, and he gives it to the children of men. But though all things are of God, yet all things are not alike of him : children are more of God than houses and lands.—*Joseph Caryl.*

Verse 3.—Children !—might one say as the word was uttered—I left mine in my distant home, in poverty, their wants and numbers increasing, with the means of providing for their comfort daily narrowing. Even should my life be prolonged, they will be children of want, but with sickness and warnings of death upon me, they will soon be helpless and friendless orphans. Yes ! but will God be neglectful of his own heritage ? will he turn a gift into a sorrow ? Poor as thou art, repine not at the number of thy children. Though lions lack thou shalt not, if thou seekest him ; and know that it may be even for their sakes that he feedeth thee. If even thou wouldst not part with one of them for thousands of gold and silver, believe that he who is the fountain of all tenderness regards them with yet deeper love, and will make them now, in thy hour of trial, a means of increasing thy dependence on him, and soon thy support and pride.

Children !—might another say, as the Psalm referred to them—on their opening promise the breath of the destroyer has been poured. They are ripening visibly for the grave, and their very smile and caress cause my wounded heart to bleed anew. Yes, mourner ; but *God's heritage !* may he not claim his own ? They are in safe keeping when in his, and will soon be restored to thee in the better land, where death will make them ministering angels at his throne ; nay, they will be the first to welcome thee to its glories, to love and worship with thee throughout eternity.

Children ! this word to a third, of an even sadder and more anxious spirit, might seem like the planting of a dagger in his heart. His children have forsaken their father's God. Their associates were the vain and vicious ; their pleasures were the pleasures of folly and shame ; their lives barren of all promise, their souls destitute of all purpose, and steeled against all reproof. True, but *the heritage of the Lord still.* Hast thou, sorrowing parent, asked him for wisdom to keep it for him ?

Have due thought, prayer, watchful and holy living been expended on that heritage of God ? No culture, no harvest in the soil ; no prayer, no blessing from the soul. " Train up a child in the way he should go, and when he is old he will not depart from it," is a promise that though sometimes, yet but seldom has missed fulfilment. Bring them to Jesus, and, unchanged in his tenderness, he will still lay his hands upon them and bless them.—*Robert Nisbet.*

Verse 3.—*"The fruit of the womb is his reward."* John Howard Hinton's daughter said to him as she knelt by his death-bed :—" There is no greater blessing than for children to have godly parents." "And the next," said the dying father, with a beam of gratitude, " for parents to have godly children."—*Memoir in Baptist Handbook,* 1875.

Verse 4.—*"As arrows."* Well doth David call children *"arrows"*; for if they be well bred, they shoot at their parents' enemies ; and if they be evil bred, they shoot at their parents.—*Henry Smith,* 1560—1591.

Verse 4.—*"As arrows."* Children are compared to *"arrows."* Now, we know that sticks are not by nature arrows ; they do not grow so, but they are made so ; by nature they are knotty and rugged, but by art they are made smooth and handsome. So children by nature are rugged and untoward, but by education are refined and reformed, made pliable to the divine will and pleasure.—*George Swinnock,* 1627—1673.

Verse 4.—*"As arrows."* " Our children are what we make them. They are represented '*As arrows in the hand of a mighty man,*' and *arrows* go the way we aim them."

Verse 4.—*"As arrows."* In a collection of *Chinese Proverbs and Apophthegms,* subjoined to *Hau Kiou Choaan,* or, *The Pleasing History,* I find a proverb cited from *Du Halde,* which seems full to our purpose. It is this :—" When a son is born into a family, a bow and arrow are hung before the gate." To which the following note is added : " As no such custom appears to be literally observed, this should seem to be a metaphorical expression, signifying that a new protector is added to the family," equivalent to that of the Psalms,—*"as arrows,"* etc.—*James Merrick* (1720—1769), *in "Annotations on the Psalms."*

Verse 4.—*"Children of the youth "* are *"arrows in the hand,"* which, with prudence, may be directed aright to the mark, God's glory, and the service of their generation ; but afterwards, when they are gone abroad in the world, they are arrows out of the hand ; it is too late to bend them then. But these *"arrows in the hand "* too often prove arrows in the heart, a constant grief to their godly parents, whose grey hairs they bring with sorrow to the grave.—*Matthew Henry.*

Verse 4.—*"Children of the youth."* Sons of youth, *i.e.,* born while their parents are still young. See Gen. xxxvii. 2 ; Isa. liv. 6. The allusion is not only to their vigour (Gen. xlix. 3), but the value of their aid to the parent in declining age.— *Joseph Addison Alexander.*

Verse 4.—*"Children of the youth."* If the right interpretation is commonly given to this phrase, this Psalm greatly encourages early marriages. It is a growing evil of modern times that marriages are so often deferred till it is highly improbable that in the course of nature the father can live to mould his offspring to habits of honour and virtue.—*William Swan Plumer* (1802—1880), *in "Studies in the Book of Psalms."*

Verse 5.—*"Happy is the man that hath his quiver full of them."* Dr. Guthrie used to say, " I am rich in nothing but children." They were eleven in number.

Verse 5.—*"Quiver full."* Many children make many prayers, and many prayers bring much blessing.—*German Proverb.*

Verse 5.—The Rev. Moses Browne had twelve children. On one remarking to him, " Sir, you have just as many children as Jacob," he replied, " Yes, and I have Jacob's God to provide for them."—*G. S. Bowes.*

Verse 5.—I remember a great man coming into my house, at Waltham, and seeing all my children standing in the order of their age and stature, said, " These are they that make rich men poor." But he straight received this answer, " Nay, my lord, these are they that make a poor man rich ; for there is not one of these whom we would part with for all your wealth." It is easy to observe that none are so gripple and hardfisted as the childless ; whereas those, who, for the maintenance of large families, are inured to frequent disbursements, find such experience of Divine providence in the faithful management of their affairs, as that they lay out with more cheerfulness what they receive. Wherein their care must be abated when God takes it off from them to himself ; and, if they be not wanting to themselves, their faith gives them ease in casting their burden upon him, who hath more power and more right to it, since our children are more his than our own. He that feedeth the young ravens, can he fail the best of his creatures ?—*Joseph Hall*, 1574—1656.

Verse 5.—"*They shall not be ashamed,*" etc. Able enough he shall be to defend himself, and keep off all injuries, being fortified by his children ; and if it happen that he hath a cause depending in the gate, and to be tried before the judges, he shall have the patronage of his children, and not suffer in his plea for want of advocates ; his sons will stand up in a just cause for him.—*William Nicholson* (——1671), *in "David's Harp Strung and Tuned."*

Verse 5.—"*But they shall speak.*" "*But destroy*" is the marginal version, and is here much more emphatical than the rendering "*speak.*" For this sense see 2 Chron. xxii. 10. Others refer it to litigation, when they shall successfully defend the cause of their parents. But as I do not see how their number or vigour could add weight to their evidence in a judicial cause, I prefer the sense given.—*Benjamin Boothroyd*, 1768—1836.

Verse 5.—"*With the enemies in the gate.*" Probably the Psalmist alludes here to the defence of a besieged city ; the gate was very commonly the point of attack, and the taking of it rendered the conquest of the place easy : compare Gen. xxii. 17 ; xxiv. 60.—*Daniel Cresswell* (1776—1844), *in "The Psalms . . . . with Critical and Explanatory Notes,"* 1843.

Verse 5.—

> This is the pride, the glory of a man,
> To train obedient children in his house,
> Prompt on his enemies t' avenge his wrongs,
> And with the father's zeal in honour high
> To hold his friends.
>
> *Sophocles' "Antigone." R. Potter's Translation.*

HINTS TO PREACHERS.

Verse 1.—I. The human hand without the hand of God is in vain. II. The human eye without the eye of God is in vain. Or, I. God is to be acknowledged in all our works. 1. By seeking his direction before them. 2. By depending upon his help in them. 3. By giving him the glory of them. II. In all our cares. 1. By owning our short sight. 2. By trusting to his foresight.—*G. R.*

Verse 1 (first part).—Illustrate the principles : I. In building up character. II. In constructing plans of life and of work. III. In framing schemes of happiness. IV. In rearing a hope of eternal life. V. In raising and enlarging the church.—*J. F.*

Verses 1, 2.—I. What we may not expect : namely, God to work without our building, watching, etc. II. What we may expect : Failure if we are without God. III. What we should not do : Fret, worry, etc. IV. What we may do : So trust as to rest in peace.

Verse 2 (with Psalm cxxvi. 2).—The labour of the law contrasted with the laughter of the gospel.

Verse 2.—"*The bread of sorrows.*" I. When God sends it, it is good to eat it. II. When we bake it ourselves, it is vain to eat it. III. When the devil brings it, it is deadly meat.

Verse 2 (last clause).—Blessings that come to us in sleep. 1. Renewed health and vigour of body. 2. Mental repose and refreshment. 3. Sweeter thoughts and holier purposes. 4. Providential gifts. The rains fall, the fruits of the earth grow and ripen, the mill wheel goes round, the ship pursues her voyage, etc., while we slumber. Often when we are doing nothing for ourselves God is doing most.—*W. H. J. P.*

Verse 2 (last clause).—See "Spurgeon's Sermons," No. 12: "The Peculiar Sleep of the Beloved."

Verse 3.—Sermon by Thomas Manton. Works: vol. xviii. pp. 84—95. [Nichol's Edition.]

Verses 3—5.—Children. Consider: I. The effects of receiving them as a heritage from the Lord. 1. Parents will trust in the Lord for their provision and safety. 2. Will regard them as a sacred trust from the Lord of whose care they must render an account. 3. Will train them up in the fear of the Lord. 4. Will often consult God concerning them. 5. Will render them up uncomplainingly when the Lord calls them to himself by death. II. The effects of their right training. 1. They become the parents' joy. 2. The permanent record of the parents' wisdom. 3. The support and solace of the parents' old age. 4. The transmitters of their parents' virtues to another generation; for well-trained children become, in their turn, wise parents.—*J. F.*

Verse 4.—The spiritual uses of children. I. When they die in infancy, awakening parents. II. When they go home from Sunday-school carrying holy influences. III. When they become converted. IV. When they grow up and become useful men and women.

Verses 4, 5.—I. The dependence of children upon parents. 1. For safety. They are in their quiver. 2. For direction. They are sent forth by them. 3. For support. They are in the hands of the mighty. II. The dependence of parents upon children. 1. For defence. Who will hear a parent spoken against? 2. For happiness. "A wise son maketh," etc. Children elicit some of the noblest and tenderest emotions of human nature. Happy is the Christian minister who with a full quiver can say, "Here am I, and the children which thou hast given me."—*G. R.*

Verse 6.—"The Reward of Well-doing Sure." Sermon by Henry Melvill, in "The Pulpit," 1856.

PSALM CXXVIII.

TITLE.—A Song of Degrees. *There is an evident ascent from the last Psalm : that did but hint at the way in which a house may be built up, but this draws a picture of that house built, and adorned with domestic bliss through the Lord's own benediction. There is clearly an advance in age, for here we go beyond children to children's children ; and also a progress in happiness, for children which in the last Psalm were arrows are here olive plants, and instead of speaking "with the enemies in the gate" we close with "peace upon Israel." Thus we rise step by step, and sing as we ascend.*

SUBJECT.—*It is a family hymn,—a song for a marriage, or a birth, or for any day in which a happy household has met to praise the Lord. Like all the songs of degrees, it has an eye to Zion and Jerusalem, which are both expressly mentioned, and it closes like Psalms cxxv., cxxx., and cxxxi., with an allusion to Israel. It is a short Psalm, but exceedingly full and suggestive. Its poetry is of the highest order. Perhaps in no country can it be better understood than in our own, for we above all nations delight to sing of "Home, sweet home."*

EXPOSITION.

BLESSED *is* everyone that feareth the LORD ; that walketh in his ways.

2 For thou shalt eat the labour of thine hands : happy *shalt* thou *be,* and *it shall be* well with thee.

3 Thy wife *shall be* as a fruitful vine by the sides of thine house : thy children like olive plants round about thy table.

4 Behold, that thus shall the man be blessed that feareth the LORD.

5 The LORD shall bless thee out of Zion : and thou shalt see the good of Jerusalem all the days of thy life.

6 Yea, thou shalt see thy children's children, *and* peace upon Israel.

1. *"Blessed is every one that feareth the LORD."* The last Psalm ended with a blessing,—for the word there translated " happy " is the same as that which is here rendered "blessed": thus the two songs are joined by a catch-word. There is also in them a close community of subject. The fear of God is the corner-stone of all blessedness. We must reverence the ever-blessed God before we can be blessed ourselves. Some think that this life is an evil, an infliction, a thing upon which rests a curse ; but it is not so ; the God-fearing man has a present blessing resting upon him. It is not true that it would be to him " something better not to be." He is happy now, for he is the child of the happy God, the ever-living Jehovah ; and he is even here a joint-heir with Jesus Christ, whose heritage is not misery, but joy. This is true of every one of the God-fearing, of all conditions, in all ages : each one and every one is blessed. Their blessedness may not always be seen by carnal reason, but it is always a fact, for God himself declares that it is so ; and we know that those whom he blesses are blessed indeed. Let us cultivate that holy filial fear of Jehovah which is the essence of all true religion ;—the fear of reverence, of dread to offend, of anxiety to please, and of entire submission and obedience. This fear of the Lord is the fit fountain of holy living : we look in vain for holiness apart from it : none but those who fear the Lord will ever walk in his ways.

"That walketh in his ways." The religious life, which God declares to be blessed, must be practical as well as emotional. It is idle to talk of fearing the Lord if we act like those who have no care whether there be a God or no. God's ways will be our ways if we have a sincere reverence for him : if the heart is joined unto God, the feet will follow hard after him. A man's heart will be seen in his walk, and the blessing will come where heart and walk are both with God. Note that the first Psalm links the benediction with the walk in a negative way, " Blessed is the man that walketh *not,*" etc. ; but here we find it in connection with the positive form of our conversation. To enjoy the divine blessing we must be active, and walk ;

we must be methodical, and walk in certain ways ; and we must be godly, and walk in the Lord's ways. God's ways are blessed ways ; they were cast up by the Blessed One, they were trodden by him in whom we are blessed, they are frequented by the blessed, they are provided with means of blessing, they are paved with present blessings, and they lead to eternal blessedness : who would not desire to walk in them ?

2. *"For thou shalt eat the labour of thine hands."* The general doctrine of the first verse here receives a personal application : note the change to the second person : *"thou* shalt eat," etc. This is the portion of God's saints,—to work, and to find a reward in so doing. God is the God of labourers. We are not to leave our worldly callings because the Lord has called us by grace : we are not promised a blessing upon romantic idleness or unreasonable dreaming, but upon hard work and honest industry. Though we are in God's hands we are to be supported by our own hands. He will give us daily bread, but it must be made our own by labour. All kinds of labour are here included ; for if one toils by the sweat of his brow, and another does so by the sweat of his brain, there is no difference in the blessing ; save that it is generally more healthy to work with the body than with the mind only. Without God it would be vain to labour ; but when we are labourers together with God a promise is set before us. The promise is that labour shall be fruitful, and that he who performs it shall himself enjoy the recompense of it. It is a grievous ill for a man to slave his life away and receive no fair remuneration for his toil : as a rule, God's servants rise out of such bondage and claim their own, and receive it : at any rate, this verse may encourage them to do so. "The labourer is worthy of his hire." Under the Theocracy the chosen people could see this promise literally fulfilled ; but when evil rulers oppressed them their earnings were withheld by churls, and their harvests were snatched away from them by marauders. Had they walked in the fear of the Lord they would never have known such great evils. Some men never enjoy their labour, for they give themselves no time for rest. Eagerness to get takes from them the ability to enjoy. Surely, if it is worth while to labour, it is worth while to eat of that labour. *"Happy shalt thou be,"* or, *Oh, thy happiness.* Heaped up happinesses in the plural belong to that man who fears the Lord. He is happy, and he shall be happy in a thousand ways. The context leads us to expect family happiness. Our God is our household God. The Romans had their Lares and Penates, but we have far more than they in the one only living and true God. *"And it shall be well with thee,"* or *good for thee.* Yes, good is for the good ; and it shall be well with those who do well.

> "What cheering words are these !
> Their sweetness who can tell ?
> In time, and to eternal days,
> 'Tis with the righteous well."

If we fear God we may dismiss all other fear. In walking in God's ways we shall be under his protection, provision, and approval ; danger and destruction shall be far from us : all things shall work our good. In God's view it would not be a blessed thing for us to live without exertion, nor to eat the unearned bread of dependence : the happiest state on earth is one in which we have something to do, strength to do it with, and a fair return for what we have done. This, with the divine blessing, is all that we ought to desire, and it is sufficient for any man who fears the Lord and abhors covetousness. Having food and raiment, let us be therewith content.

3. *"Thy wife."* To reach the full of earthly felicity a man must not be alone. A helpmeet was needed in Paradise, and assuredly she is not less necessary out of it. He that findeth a wife findeth a good thing. It is not every man that feareth the Lord who has a wife ; but if he has, she shall share in his blessedness and increase it.

"Shall be as a fruitful vine." To complete domestic bliss children are sent. They come as the lawful fruit of marriage, even as clusters appear upon the vine. For the grapes the vine was planted ; for children was the wife provided. It is generally well with any creature when it fulfills its purpose, and it is so far well with married people when the great design of their union is brought about. They must not look upon fruitfulness as a burden, but as a blessing. Good wives are also fruitful in kindness, thrift, helpfulness, and affection : if they bear no children, they are by no means barren if they yield us the wine of consolation and the clusters

of comfort.   Truly blessed is the man whose wife is fruitful in those good works which are suitable to her near and dear position.

"By the sides of thine house."   She keeps to the house : she is a home bird.   Some imagine that she is like a vine which is nailed up to the house wall ; but they have no such custom in Palestine, neither is it pleasant to think of a wife as growing up by a wall, and as bound to the very bricks and mortar of her husband's dwelling. No, she is a fruitful vine, and a faithful house-keeper ; if you wish to find her, she is within the house : she is to be found both inside and outside the home, but her chief fruitfulness is in the inner side of the dwelling, which she adorns. Eastern houses usually have an open square in the centre, and the various rooms are ranged around the sides,—there shall the wife be found, busy in one room or another, as the hour of the day demands.   She keeps at home, and so keeps the home.   It is her husband's house, and she is her husband's ; as the text puts it—" thy wife," and " thy house " ; but by her loving care her husband is made so happy that he is glad to own her as an equal proprietor with himself, for he is hers, and the house is hers too.

"Thy children like olive plants round about thy table."   Hundreds of times have I seen the young olive plants springing up around the parent stem, and it has always made me think of this verse.   The Psalmist never intended to suggest the idea of olive plants round a table, but of young people springing up around their parents, even as olive plants surround the fine, well-rooted tree.   The figure is very striking, and would be sure to present itself to the mind of every observer in the olive country. How beautiful to see the gnarled olive, still bearing abundant fruit, surrounded with a little band of sturdy successors, any one of which would be able to take its place should the central olive be blown down, or removed in any other way.   The notion of a table in a bower may suit a cockney in a tea-garden, but would never occur to an oriental poet ; it is not the olive plants, but the children, that are round about the table.   Moreover, note that it is not olive *branches*, but *plants*,—a very different thing.   Our children gather around our table to be fed, and this involves expenses : how much better is this than to see them pining upon beds of sickness, unable to come for their meals !   What a blessing to have sufficient to put upon the table !   Let us for this benefit praise the bounty of the Lord.   The wife is busy all over the house, but the youngsters are busiest at meal-times ; and if the blessing of the Lord rest upon the family, no sight can be more delightful.   Here we have the vine and the olive blended—joy from the fruitful wife, and solid comfort from the growing family ; these are the choicest products earth can yield : our families are gardens of the Lord.   It may help us to value the privileges of our home if we consider where we should be if they were withdrawn.   What if the dear partner of our life were removed from the sides of our house to the recesses of the sepulchre ? What is the trouble of children compared with the sorrow of their loss ?   Think, dear father, what would be your grief if you had to cry with Job, " Oh that I were as in months past, as in the days when God preserved me ; when my children were about me."

4. *"Behold, that thus shall the man be blessed that feareth the LORD."*   Mark this. Put a *Nota Bene* against it, for it is worthy of observation.   It is not to be inferred that all blessed men are married, and are fathers ; but that this is the way in which the Lord favours godly people who are placed in domestic life.   He makes their relationships happy and profitable.   In this fashion does Jehovah bless God-fearing households, for he is the God of all the families of Israel.   We have seen this blessing scores of times, and we have never ceased to admire in domestic peace the sweetest of human felicity.   Family blessedness comes from the Lord, and is a part of his plan for the preservation of a godly race, and for the maintence of his worship in the land.   To the Lord alone we must look for it.   The possession of riches will not ensure it ; the choice of a healthy and beautiful bride will not ensure it ; the birth of numerous comely children will not ensure it : there must be the blessing of God, the influence of piety, the result of holy living.

Verse 5. *"The LORD shall bless thee out of Zion."*   A spiritual blessing shall be received by the gracious man, and this shall crown all his temporal mercies. He is one among the many who make up God's inheritance ; his tent is part and parcel of the encampment around the tabernacle ; and therefore when the benediction is pronounced at the centre it shall radiate to him in his place.   The blessing of the house of God shall be upon his house.   The priestly benediction which is recorded in Numbers vi. 24—26, runs thus : " The Lord bless thee, and keep thee : the

Lord make his face shine upon thee, and be gracious unto thee : the Lord lift up his countenance upon thee, and give thee peace." This is it which shall come upon the head of the God-fearing man. Zion was the centre of blessing, and to it the people looked when they sought for mercy : from the altar of sacrifice, from the mercy-seat, from the Shekinah-light, yea, from Jehovah himself, the blessing shall come to each one of his holy people. "*And thou shalt see the good of Jerusalem all the days of thy life.*" He shall have a patriot's joy as well as a patriarch's peace. God shall give him to see his country prosper, and its metropolitan city flourish. When tent-mercies are followed by temple-mercies, and these are attended by national mercies,—the man, the worshipper, the patriot is trebly favoured of the Lord. This favour is to be permanent throughout the good man's life, and that life is to be a long one, for he is to see his sons' sons. Many a time does true religion bring such blessings to men ; and when these good things are denied them, they have a greater reward as a compensation.

6. "*Yea, thou shalt see thy children's children.*" This is a great pleasure. Men live their young lives over again in their grandchildren. Does not Solomon say that " children's children are the crown of old men " ? So they are. The good man is glad that a pious stock is likely to be continued ; he rejoices in the belief that other homes as happy as his own will be built up wherein altars to the glory of God shall smoke with the morning and evening sacrifice. This promise implies long life, and that life rendered happy by its being continued in our offspring. It is one token of the immortality of man that he derives joy from extending his life in the lives of his descendants.

"*And peace upon Israel.*" With this sweet word Psalm cxxv. was closed. It is a favourite formula. Let God's own heritage be at peace, and we are all glad of it. We count it our own prosperity for the chosen of the Lord to find rest and quiet. Jacob was sorely tossed about ; his life knew little of peace ; but yet the Lord delivered him out of all his tribulations, and brought him to a place of rest in Goshen for a while, and afterwards to sleep with his fathers in the cave of Machpelah. His glorious Seed was grievously afflicted and at last crucified ; but he has risen to eternal peace, and in his peace we dwell. Israel's spiritual descendants still share his chequered conditions, but there remains a rest for them also, and they shall have peace from the God of peace. Israel was a praying petitioner in the days of his wrestling, but he became a prevailing prince, and therein his soul found peace. Yes, all around it is true—" Peace upon Israel ! Peace upon Israel."

EXPLANATORY NOTES AND QUAINT SAYINGS.

Whole Psalm.—Psalm cxxviii. follows Psalm cxxvii. for the same reason as Psalm ii. follows Psalm i. In both instances they are Psalms placed together, of which one begins with *ashrè* (happy, very happy), and the other ends with *ashrè*. In other respects Psalms cxxviii. and cxxvii. supplement one another. They are related to one another much as the New Testament parables of the treasure in the field and the one pearl are related. That which makes man happy is represented in Psalm cxxvii. as a gift coming as a blessing, and in Psalm cxxviii. as a reward coming as a blessing, that which is briefly indicated in the word שכר, *sakar, reward*, in cxxvii. 3 being here expanded and unfolded. There it appears as a gift of grace in contrast to the God-estranged self-activity of man ; here as a fruit of the *ora et labora.—Franz Delitzsch.*

Whole Psalm.—It is to be observed, that here all men are spoken to as wedded ; because this is the ordinary estate of most people. See 1 Cor. vii. 1, 2. At this day every Jew is bound to marry at about eighteen years of age, or before twenty ; else he is accounted as one that liveth in sin.—*John Trapp.*

Whole Psalm.—This Psalm is an ἐπιθαλαμιος λογος, written for the commendation, instruction, and consolation of those who are either already married or are about to enter on that kind of life. It enumerates, therefore, at the commencement, as is usual in songs of this kind, all those things which are regarded as burdens in the married life, such as the labours in seeking to provide for the whole family ;

the spouse, and that marriage bond, which, as it were, binds a man and seems to make him a slave, just as that character says in the comedy, " I have taken a wife ; I have sold my liberty : " lastly, the education of the children, which certainly is most laborious, and requires the largest expenditure. To lighten the burden of all these things, there is added to each a blessing, or a promise, so that they might appear slight. And at the close, it subjoins in general, a spiritual promise, which easily makes light of all the labours and disquiets of the married life ; even if they should be the very heaviest. The blessing comes from Zion or the Church : for there is nothing so burdensome and difficult, but what it can be easily borne by those who are members of the true Church, and know the sources of true consolation.—*D. H. Mollerus.*

Verse 1.—*"Blessed is every one that feareth the LORD," etc.* Here we have the living fountain of the blessing which rests upon the conjugal and domestic state. When worldly prudence attempts to choose a wife and form a household, it can apply its hand only to so much of the work as has its seat upon earth, and is visible to the eye of sense. It builds, so to speak, the first and the second story, adds cornice and pediment, and the fabric presents a fair appearance—but it has no foundation. Whenever you see the household of a married pair continuing to defy every storm, you may be sure that it rests upon a sure foundation, lying beyond the reach of human sense, and that that foundation is *the fear of the Lord.* To the fear of the Lord, therefore, the holy Psalmist has wisely given a place in front of this beautiful Psalm. which celebrates the blessing that descends upon conjugal and domestic life.—*Augustus F. Tholuck, in "Hours of Christian Devotion,"* 1870.

Verse 1.—*"Blessed is every one that feareth the LORD."* There is a fear of the Lord which hath terror in it and not blessedness. The apprehension with which a warring rebel regards his triumphant and offended soverign, or the feelings of a fraudulent bankrupt towards a stern creditor, or, a conscience-striken criminal to a righteous judge, are frequently types of men's feelings in regard to God. This evidently cannot be the fear which the " *blessed* " of this Psalm feel. Nor can theirs, on the other hand, be the tormenting fear of self-reproach.

Their fear is that which the believed revelations given of him in his Word produce. It is the fear which a child feels towards an honoured parent,—a fear to offend : it is that which they who have been rescued from destruction feel to the benefactor who nobly and at the vastest sacrifice interposed for their safety,—a fear to act unworthily of his kindness : it is that which fills the breast of a pardoned and grateful rebel in the presence of a venerated sovereign at whose throne he is permitted to stand in honour,—a fear lest he should ever forget his goodness, and give him cause to regret it. Such is the fear of the Christian now : a fear which reverence for majesty, gratitude for mercies, dread of displeasure, desire of approval, and longing for the fellowship of heaven, inspire ; the fear of angels and the blessed Son ; the fear not of sorrow but of love, which shrinks with instinctive recoil from doing aught that would tend to grieve, or from denying aught that would tend to honour. Religion is the grand and the only wisdom ; and since the beginning, the middle, and the end of it, is the fear of the Lord, blessed is every man that is swayed by it.—*Robert Nisbet, in "The Songs of the Temple Pilgrims,"* 1863.

Verse 1.—*"Blessed is every one that feareth the LORD."* Let us take a little of the character of the blessed man. Who is it that is undaunted ? *"The man that feareth God."* Fear sounds rather contrary to blessedness ; hath an air of misery ; but add whom. He that feareth *the LORD";* that touch turns it into gold. He that so fears, fears not : he shall not be afraid ; all petty fears are swallowed up in this great fear ; and this great fear is as sweet and pleasing as little fears are anxious and vexing. Secure of other things, he can say—" If my God be pleased, no matter who is displeased ; no matter who despise me, if he account me his. Though all forsake me, though my dearest friends grow estranged, if he reject me not, that is my only fear ; and for that I am not perplexed, I know he will not." A believer hath no fear but of the displeasure of heaven, the anger of God to fall upon him ; he accounts that only terrible ; but yet he doth not fear it, doth not apprehend it will fall on him, is better persuaded of the goodness of God. So this fear is still joined with trust :—" Behold the eye of the Lord is upon them that fear him, upon them that hope in his mercy " ; Ps. xxxiii. 18.—*Robert Leighton,* 1611—1684.

Verse 1.—*"Blessed is every one,"* etc. There is a stress on *all* (" *every one* "), teaching that no disparity of sex or condition, of rank or wealth, affects the **degree** of happiness granted by God to every one of his true servants in their several stations. It is to be observed, further, that whenever the fear of the Lord is mentioned in Holy Writ, it is never set by itself, as though sufficient for the consummation of our faith, but always has something added or prefixed, by which to estimate its due proportion of perfection, according as it is stated by Solomon in the Proverbs (ii. 3—5).—*J. M. Neale and R. F. Littledale, in "A Commentary on the Psalms from Primitive and Mediæval Writers," 1860.*

Verse 1.—*"Blessed is every one"* etc. It is a precious promise, but perhaps thou art tempted to say in thy heart, not meant for everyone. Wilt thou answer against the Lord ? Hear him speak in the song. He says, " *every one."* " *Blessed is every one that feareth the LORD."* None are excluded but those who will not walk in his ways.—*Edward Jewitt Robinson.*

Verse 1.—*"Blessed,"* etc. The adage, " That it is best not to be born at all, or to die as soon as possible," has certainly been long since received by the common consent of almost all men. Carnal reason judges either that all mankind without exception are miserable, or that fortune is more favourable to ungodly and wicked men than to the good. To the sentiment that those are blessed who fear the Lord, it has an entire aversion. So much the more requisite, then, is it to dwell upon the consideration of this truth. Farther, as this blessedness is not apparent to the eye, it is of importance, in order to our being able to apprehend it, first to attend to the definition which will be given of it by-and-bye ; and secondly, to know that it depends chiefly upon the protection of God. Although we collect together all the circumstances which seem to contribute to a happy life, surely nothing will be found more desirable than to be kept hidden under the guardianship of God. If this blessing is, in our estimation, to be preferred, as it deserves, to all other good things, whoever is persuaded that the care of God is exercised about the world and human affairs, will at the same time unquestionably acknowledge that what is here laid down is the chief point of happiness.—*John Calvin.*

Verse 1.—*"That feareth the LORD ; that walketh in his ways."* The fear of the Lord is the internal principle ; but unless there be a corresponding expression in the outward life, what reason is there to suppose that it has any existence at all ?

Observe also, that there is no walking in the ways of the Lord, until his fear be established in the heart. There can be no genuine morality apart from the fear of God. How can a man obey God while his affections are alienated from him ? —*N. M'Michael.*

Verse 1.—*"That walketh in his ways."* God makes blessed those that walk in his ways, because he himself walks with them. This is said concerning David, and it is explained how that companionship blessed him, 2 Sam. v. 10 : " And David went on, and grew great, and the Lord God of hosts was with him " : where the " and " may be taken as the causal particle " because." That God does indeed join himself to those who walk in his ways as companion and leader we have in 2 Chron. xvii. 3, 4 : " And the Lord was with Jehoshaphat, because he walked in the first ways of his father David, and sought not unto Baalim ; but sought to the Lord God of his father."—*Thomas Le Blanc.*

Verse 2.—*"For thou shalt eat the labour of thine hands,"* etc. There is a fourfold literal sense here : Thou shalt live by honest, peaceful labour, not by rapine and violence on that produced by the toil of others, nor yet indolently and luxuriously ; thou shalt *"eat,"* and not penuriously stint thyself and others ; thy crops shall not be blighted, but shall bring forth abundantly ; and no enemy shall destroy or carry off thy harvest. And these two latter interpretations accord best with the converse punishments threatened to the disobedient by Moses. *"Thou shalt eat the labour of thine hands."* But he who hates labour does not eat of it, nor can he say, " My meat is to do the will of him that sent me, and to finish his work " : John iv. 34. On the other hand, he to whom such labour is a delight, does not merely look forward in hope to the future fruits or rewards of labour, but even here and now finds sustenance and pleasure in toiling for God ; so that it is *"well"* with him in the world, even amidst all its cares and troubles, and he *" shall be happy"* in that which is to come, whence sorrow is banished for ever, as it is written in the gospel : " Blessed is he that shall eat bread in the kingdom of God " : Luke xiv. 15.—*Neale and Littledale.*

Verse 2.—*"Thou shalt eat the labour of thine hands,"* etc. This must they learn also which are married, that they must labour. For the law of nature requireth that the husband should sustain and nourish his wife and his children.   For after that man and wife do know that they ought to fear God their Creator, who not only made them, but gave his blessing also unto his creature ; this secondly must they know, that something they must do that they consume not their days in ease and idleness.   Hesiod, the poet, giveth his counsel, that first thou shouldst get thee a house, then a wife, and also an ox to till the ground. . . . For albeit that our diligence, care, and travail is not able to maintain our family, yet God useth such as a means by the which he will bless us.—*Martin Luther.*

Verse 2.—*"Thou shalt eat the labour of thine hands."*   Men have dreamed fascinating dreams of removing the disabilities and limitations of the world and the evils of life, without sorrow.   Poets have pictured earthly paradises, where life would be one long festival,—

" Summer isles of Eden lying in dark purple spheres of sea."

But vain are all such dreams and longings.   They are of human, not of Divine origin, and spring from a root of selfishness and not of holiness.   They cannot be realized in a fallen world, full of sorrow because full of sin.   All blessings in man's economy are got from pains.   Happiness is the flower that grows from a thorn of sorrow transformed by man's cultivation.   The beautiful myth which placed the golden apples of the Hesperides in a garden guarded by dragons, is an allegory illustrative of the great human fact, that not till we have slain the dragons of selfishness and sloth can we obtain any of the golden successes of life.   Supposing it were possible that we could obtain the objects of our desire without any toil or trouble, we should not enjoy them.   To benefit us really, they must be the growths of our own self-denial and labour.   And this is the great lesson which the miracles of our Lord, wrought in the manner in which they were, unfolded.   They teach us that, in both temporal and spiritual things, we should not so throw ourselves upon the providence or grace of God as to neglect the part we have ourselves to act,—that God crowns every honest and faithful effort of man with success : *"Blessed is every one that feareth the* LORD ; *that walketh in his ways.   For thou shalt eat the labour of thine hands : happy shalt thou be, and it shall be well with thee."*—*Hugh Macmillan, in "The Ministry of Nature,"* 1871.

Verse 2 *(first clause)*.—

Labour, the symbol of man's punishment ;
Labour, the secret of man's happiness.
James Montgomery, 1771—1854.

Verse 2.—*"Happy shalt thou be."*   Oh trust in the Lord for happiness as well as for help !   All the springs of happiness are in him.   Trust " in him who giveth us all things richly to enjoy " ; who, of his own rich and free mercy, holds them out to us, as in his own hand, that, receiving them as his gifts, and as pledges of his love, we may enjoy all that we possess.   It is his love gives a relish to all we taste, puts life and sweetness into all ; while every creature leads us up to the great Creator, and all earth is a scale to heaven.   He transfuses the joys that are at his own right hand into all that he bestows on his thankful children, who, having fellowship with the Father and his Son Jesus Christ, enjoy him in all and above all.—*John Wesley,* 1703—1791.

Verse 2.—*"Happy shalt thou be."*   Mr. Disraeli puts these remarkable words into the mouth of one of his characters :—" Youth is a blunder ; manhood a struggle ; old age a regret."   A sad and cheerless view of life's progress that !   It may be true, in measure, of a life separated from godliness ; it certainly is not true of a life allied with godliness.   Let there be " life and godliness," and then youth is not a blunder, but a wise purpose and a glowing hope ; manhood is not a struggle only, but a conquest and a joy ; old age is not a regret, but a rich memory and a glorious prospect.—*R. P. Macmaster, in "The Baptist Magazine,"* 1878.

Verse 3.—*"Thy wife shall be as a fruitful vine,"* etc.   The comparison would perhaps be brought out more clearly by arranging the verse as follows :—

" Thy wife shall be in the inner part of thy house
        Like a fruitful vine ;
    Thy children round about thy table
        Like the shoots of the olive."

In the inner part, literally, "*the sides of thy house*," as in Amos vi. 10, *i.e.*, the women's apartments, as marking the proper sphere of the wife engaged in her domestic duties, and also to some extent her seclusion, though this was far less amongst the Jews than amongst other Orientals.

The "*vine*" is an emblem chiefly of *fruitfulness*, but perhaps also of dependence, as needing support ; the "*olive*," of vigorous, healthy, joyous life. The same figure is employed by Euripides, *Herc. Fur.*, 839. *Med.* 1098.—*J. J. Stewart Perowne.*

Verse 3.—"*Thy wife shall be as a fruitful vine*," etc. We do not remember to have met with a single instance, in the East, of vines trained *against the walls of a house*, or of olives near or about a house. Neither have we read of such instances. The passage doubtless derives its figures from the fertility of the vine, and from the appearance of the olive, or the order in which olive trees are planted. The construction would then be : " Thy wife, in the sides (interior apartments) of thy house, shall be as the fruitful vine, and thy children round about thy table, like olive plants."—*John Kitto (1804—1854), in "The Pictorial Bible."*

Verse 3.—"*Thy wife shall be as a fruitful vine by the sides of thine house.*" The wife is likened not to thorns or briers, nor even to oaks or to other fruits and trees, but to the vine ; and also to a vine neither in a vineyard nor in a garden, but set by the walls of the house ; also not barren, but fertile and fruit-bearing. This admonishes husbands as well as wives of their duties. For as the walls support the vine, and defend it against the force of winds and tempests, so ought husbands, as far as is in their power, to defend their wives by their godly conversation and wholesome teachings and institutions against the pestilential wind of the old serpent; also against the injuries of evil-disposed men. " He that loveth his wife loveth himself. For no man ever yet hated his own flesh ; but nourisheth and cherisheth it, even as the Lord the Church " : Ephes. v. 28, 29.

Further, the vine is exceedingly fragile wood, and not meet for any work, Ezek. xv. 4. Husbands, therefore, should remember that they ought to behave towards their wives patiently and prudently, as with the weaker vessel ; not keeping in mind the fragility of the wood, but the abundance and sweetness of the fruit. If husbands observe this, that will happen to them which Scripture says concerning the peaceful time of Solomon, " And Judah and Israel dwelt safely, every man under his vine and under his fig-tree " : 1 Kings iv. 25. Such was the married life of Abraham with Sarah, Isaac with Rebecca, Jacob with Leah and Rachel.—*Solomon Gesner.*

Verse 3.—"*A fruitful vine by the sides of thine house.*" It does not say *on* the sides of the house, but *by* the sides. The passage probably refers to the trellissed bowers which often lead up to the houses, and are covered with vines, the grapes hanging over head. Sitting in these bowers is sitting under our own vines : Micah iv. 4. I have seen in Constantinople grapes hanging over the people's heads in the principal streets, the vines being trained from one side of the street to the other.—*John Gadsby, in "My Wanderings,"* 1860.

Verse 3.—"*By the sides of thine house.*" Not on the roof, nor on the floor ; the one is too high, she is no ruler ; the other too low, she is no slave : but in the sides, an equal place between both.—*Thomas Adams.*

Verse 3.—"*By the sides of thine house.*" The house is her proper place ; for she is " the beauty of the house " ; there her business lies, there she is safe. The ancients painting them with a snail under their feet, and the Egyptians denying their women shoes, and the Scythians burning the bride's chariot axle-tree at her door, when she was brought to her husband's house, and the angel's asking Abraham where Sarah was (though he knew well enough), that it might be observed, she was " in the tent," do all intimate, that, by the law of nature, and by the rules of religion, the wife ought to keep at home, unless urgent necessity do call her abroad.—*Richard Steele (—1692), in "The Morning Exercises."*

Verse 3.—As it is visible that the good man's sons being " *like olive plants round about his table*," means not that they should be like the olive plants which grew round his table, it being, I presume, a thought in Bishop Patrick that will not be defended, that the Psalmist refers to a table spread in an arbour composed of young olive trees, for we find no such arbours in the Levant, nor is the tree very proper for such a purpose ; so in like manner the first clause must signify, thy wife *shall be in the sides*, or private apartments, *of thy house, fruitful as a thriving vine :* the place here mentioned (the sides of the house) referring to the wife, not to the vine ; as the other (the table) refers to the children, not to the olives.   Nor is this a new thought, it is a remark that Musculus and other interpreters have made.

The Hebrew word, translated *sides*, is very well known to signify the more *private apartments* of a house, as they have also remarked ; and he that reads Dr. Shaw's description of an Eastern house, must immediately see the propriety of calling the private apartments *its sides*.   Such a house consists of a square court, which the doctor observes, is called *the midst* of the house : and private apartments round it, which may as properly be called *its sides* in consequence : into this middle of the house, or this quadrangle, company, he tells us, are sometimes received, in which *other authors* tell us their *wives* remain concealed at such times.—*Thomas Harmer,* 1719—1788.

Verse 3.—*"Thy children like olive plants,"* etc.   Follow me into the grove, and I will show you what may have suggested the comparison.   Here we have hit upon a beautiful illustration.   This aged and decayed tree is surrounded, as you see, by several young and thrifty shoots, which spring from the root of the venerable parent.   They seem to uphold, protect, and embrace it, we may even fancy that they now bear that load of fruit which would otherwise be demanded of the feeble parent.   Thus do good and affectionate children gather round the table of the righteous.   Each contributes something to the common wealth and welfare of the whole—a beautiful sight, with which may God refresh the eyes of every friend of mine.—*W. M. Thomson.*

Verse 3.—Man by nature, uninfluenced by grace, is " a wild olive tree"; and the object of most parents is merely to cultivate this wild olive tree.   What anxiety is there about accomplishments which, how attractive soever, are but the dying blossoms of this wild olive tree !—*Richard Cecil,* 1748—1810.

Verse 3.—Although the world is carried away by irregular desires after various objects, between which it is perpetually fluctuating in its choice, God gives us in this Psalm a description of what he considers to be a blessing beyond all riches, and therefore we ought to hold it in high estimation.   If a man has a wife of amiable manners as the companion of his life, let him set no less value upon this blessing than Solomon did, who, in Prov. xix. 14, affirms that it is God alone who gives a good wife.   In like manner, if a man be a father of a numerous offspring, let him receive that goodly boon with a thankful heart.—*John Calvin.*

Verse 3.—Before the fall Paradise was man's home ; since the fall home has been his Paradise.—*Augustus William Hare* (1792—1834), *and Julius Charles Hare* (1795—1855), *in "Guesses at Truth."*

Verse 4.—As Haman caused it to be proclaimed (Esther vi. 9), " Thus shall it be done to the man whom the king delighteth to honour "; so here, *"Behold, that thus shall the man be blessed that feareth the LORD."*   He shall be blessed in his wife, and blessed in his children ; so blessed in both that the Psalmist calls all to behold it, as a rare, beautiful, yea, wonderful sight : *"Behold, thus shall the man be blessed."* And yet the man fearing God shall be blessed more than *thus :* his blessing shall come in the best way (verse 5) : *"The LORD shall bless thee out of Zion";* his temporal mercies shall come in a spiritual way, yea, he shall have spiritual blessings : *"He shall bless thee out of Zion";* and he shall have blessings beyond his own walls : *"Thou shalt see the good of Jerusalem all the days of thy life.   Yea, thou shalt see thy children's children, and peace upon Israel."*   Sometimes a good man can take no content in his family mercies because of the church's afflictions ; he *"prefers Jerusalem above his chief joy "* (Ps. cxxxvii. 6), and while that is mourning he cannot but be sorrowing, though his own house be full of joy.   Sometimes a man's own family is so afflicted, and his house so full of sorrow, that he cannot but mourn, even when Jerusalem rejoiceth and Zion is glad.   But when a good man looks home to his own house and sees good there ; when also he looks abroad to Jerusalem and sees good there too, how full is his joy ! how complete is his blessedness ! and, *"Behold, thus the man is blessed that feareth the LORD."*—*Joseph Caryl.*

Verse 4.—*"Behold, that thus shall the man be blessed,"* etc.   It is asserted with a note commanding attention : *behold* it by faith in the promise ; *behold* it by observation in the performance of the promise ; *behold* it with assurance that it shall be so, for God is faithful ; and with admiration that it should be so ; for we merit no favour, no blessing from him.—*Matthew Henry.*

Verse 5.—*"Thou shalt see the good of Jerusalem,"* etc.   What is added concerning *"the good of Jerusalem "* is to be regarded as enjoining upon the godly the duty not only of seeking their own individual welfare, or of being devoted to their own peculiar interests ; but rather of having it as their chief desire to see the church of God in a flourishing condition. It would be a very unreasonable thing for each member to desire what may be profitable for itself, while in the meantime the body was neglected. From our extreme proneness to err in this respect, the prophet, with good reason, recommends solicitude about the public welfare ; and he mingles together domestic blessings and the common benefits of the church in such a way as to show us that they are things joined together, and which it is unlawful to put asunder.—*John Calvin.*

Verse 6.—Lord, let thy blessing so accompany my endeavours in their breedings, that all my sons may be Benaiahs, the Lord's building, and then they will all be Abners, their father's light ; and that all my daughters may be Bethias, the Lord's daughters, and then they will all be Abigails, their father's joy.—*George Swinnock.*

Verse 6.—Religion is as favourable for long life as for happiness. She promotes long life by destroying those evils, the tendency of which is to limit the duration of human existence. War sweeps millions into a premature grave. Men live longer in Christian than in heathen countries. They live longer in Protestant than in Roman Catholic countries. The direct effect of true religion is to increase the period of human life. "Length of days is in her right hand."—*N. M'Michael.*

Verse 6.—Connecting this with the next Psalm we find the following in a famous Scotch divine :—"'*Peace upon Israel.*' The great blessing of peace, which the Lord hath promised to his people even in this life, (for where the Lord gives mercy to any, he gives them peace also, peace and grace are inseparably joined together,) this peace, I say, does not consist in this, that the people of God shall have no enemies ; no, for there is an immortal and endless enmity against them. Neither does their peace consist in this, that their enemies shall not assault them ; neither does it consist in this, that their enemies shall not molest or afflict them. We do but deceive ourselves if so be that we imagine, so long as we are in this our pilgrimage, and in our warfare here, if we promise to ourselves a peace of this kind ; for while we live in this world, we shall still have enemies, and these enemies shall assault us, and persecute and afflict us."—*Alexander Henderson.*

HINTS TO PREACHERS.

Verse 1.—The universality of the blessedness of God-fearing men. Circumstances, personal or relative, cannot alter the blessing ; nor age, nor public opinion, nor even their own sense of unworthiness.

Verse 1.—Consider : I. The union of a right fear with a right walk. 1. There is a wrong fear, because slavish ; this never can lead to genuine obedience, which must be willingly and cheerfully rendered. 2. But the fear of reverence and filial love will surely turn the feet to God's ways, keep them steadfast therein, and wing them with speed. II. The blessedness of him in whom they are united. 1. It is blessedness of life ; for that is prospered. 2. It is blessedness of domestic happiness ; for where the head of a family is holy, the family is the home of peace. 3. It is the blessedness of a holy influence in every sphere of his activity. 4. It is deep-felt heart-blessedness in walking with God. 5. And all is but a prelude to the everlasting blessedness of heaven.—*J. F.*

Verse 2.—The blessednesses of the righteous are first generalized, then particularized. Here they are divided into three particulars. I. The fruit of past labours. II. Present enjoyment. III. Future welfare : "It shall be well with thee." Well in time ; well in death ; well at the last judgment ; well for ever.—*G. R.*

Verse 2.—I. Labour a blessing to him who fears God. II. The fruits of labour the result of God's blessing. III. The enjoyment of the fruits of labour a further blessing from God.—*W. H. J. P.*

Verse 2 (first clause).—Success in life. I. Its source—God's blessing. II. Its channel—our own labour. III. The measure in which it is promised—as much as we can eat. More is above the promise. IV. The enjoyment. We are permitted to eat or enjoy our labour.

Verse 2 (second clause).—Godly happiness. I. Follows upon God's blessing. II. Grows out of character: "feareth the Lord." III. Follows labour: see preceding sentence. IV. It is supported by well-being: see following sentence.

Verse 2 (last clause).—I. It shall be well with thee while thou livest. II. It shall be better with thee when thou diest. III. It shall be best of all with thee in eternity.—*Adapted from Matthew Henry.*

Verse 3.—The blessing of children. I. They are round our table—expense, anxiety, responsibility, pleasure. II. They are like olive plants—strong, planted in order, coming on to succeed us, fruitful for God—as the olive provided oil for the lamp.

Verse 3.—A complete family picture. Here are the husband, the wife, the children, the house, the rooms in the side, the table. We should ask a blessing upon each, bless God for each, and use each in a blessed manner.

Verse 4.—Domestic happiness the peculiar blessing of piety. Show how it produces and maintains it.

Verse 5.—The blessing out of Zion. See Numbers vi. 24—26.

Verse 5.—Two priceless mercies. I. The house of God a blessing to our house. It is connected with our own salvation, edification, consolation, etc. It is our hope for the conversion of our children and servants, etc. It is the place of their education, and for the formation of helpful friendship, etc. II. Our house a blessing to God's house. Personal interest in the church, hospitality, generosity, service, etc. Children aiding holy work. Wife useful, etc.

Verse 6.—Old age blessed when—I. Life has been spent in the fear of God. II. When it is surrounded to its close by human affection. III. When it maintains its interest in the cause of God.—*W. H. J. P.*

Verse 6 (last clause).—Church peace—its excellence, its enemies, its friends, its fruits.

PSALM CXXIX.

TITLE.—A Song of Degrees. *I fail to see how this is a step beyond the previous Psalm ; and yet it is clearly the song of an older and more tried individual, who looks back upon a life of affliction in which he suffered all along, even from his youth. Inasmuch as patience is a higher, or at least more difficult, grace than domestic love, the ascent or progress may perhaps be seen in that direction. Probably if we knew more of the stations on the road to the Temple we should see a reason for the order of these Psalms ; but as that information cannot be obtained, we must take the songs as we find them, and remember that, as we do not now go on pilgrimages to Zion, it is our curiosity and not our necessity which is a loser by our not knowing the cause of the arrangement of the songs in this Pilgrim Psalter.*

AUTHOR, ETC.—*It does not seem to us at all needful to ascribe this Psalm to a period subsequent to the captivity : indeed, it is more suitable to a time when as yet the enemy had not so far prevailed as to have carried the people into a distant land. It is a mingled hymn of sorrow and of strong resolve. Though sorely smitten, the afflicted one is heart-whole, and scorns to yield in the least degree to the enemy. The poet sings the trials of Israel, verses 1—3 ; the interposition of the Lord, verse 4 ; and the unblessed condition of Israel's foes, verses 5—8. It is a rustic song, full of allusions to husbandry. It reminds us of the books of Ruth and Amos.*

EXPOSITION.

MANY a time have they afflicted me from my youth, may Israel now say :

2 Many a time have they afflicted me from my youth : yet they have not prevailed against me.

3 The plowers plowed upon my back : they made long their furrows.

4 The LORD is righteous : he hath cut asunder the cords of the wicked.

5 Let them all be confounded and turned back that hate Zion.

6 Let them be as the grass *upon* the housetops, which withereth afore it groweth up :

7 Wherewith the mower filleth not his hand ; nor he that bindeth sheaves his bosom.

8 Neither do they which go by say, The blessing of the LORD *be* upon you : we bless you in the name of the LORD.

1. *"Many a time have they afflicted me from my youth, may Israel now say."* In her present hour of trial, she may remember her former afflictions and speak of them for her comfort, drawing from them the assurance that he who has been with her for so long will not desert her in the end. The song begins abruptly. The poet has been musing, and the fire burns, therefore speaks he with his tongue : he cannot help it, he feels that he must speak, and therefore " may now say " what he has to say. The trials of the church have been repeated again and again, times beyond all count : the same afflictions are fulfilled in us as in our fathers. Jacob of old found his days full of trouble ; each Israelite is often harassed ; and Israel as a whole has proceeded from tribulation to tribulation. " Many a time," Israel says, because she could not say how many times. She speaks of her assailants as " they," because it would be impossible to write or even to know all their names. They had straitened, harassed, and fought against her from the earliest days of her history—from her youth ; and they had continued their assaults right on without ceasing. Persecution is the heirloom of the church, and the ensign of the elect. Israel among the nations was peculiar, and this peculiarity brought against her many restless foes, who could never be easy unless they were warring against the people of God. When in Canaan, at the first, the chosen household was often severely tried ; in

Egypt it was heavily oppressed ; in the wilderness it was fiercely assailed ; and in the promised land it was often surrounded by deadly enemies. It was something for the afflicted nation, that it survived to *say*, " Many a time have they afflicted me." The affliction began early—" from my youth " ; and it continued late. The earliest years of Israel and of the church of God were spent in trial. Babes in grace are cradled in opposition. No sooner is the man-child born than the dragon is after it. " It is," however, " good for a man that he bear the yoke in his youth," and he shall see it to be so when in after days he tells the tale.

2. *"Many a time have they afflicted me from my youth."* Israel repeats her state-ment of her repeated afflictions. The fact was uppermost in her thoughts, and she could not help soliloquizing upon it again and again. These repetitions are after the manner of poetry : thus she makes a sonnet out of her sorrows, music out of her miseries. *" Yet they have not prevailed against me."* We seem to hear the beat of timbrels and the clash of cymbals here : the foe is derided ; his malice has failed. That *"yet"* breaks in like the blast of trumpets, or the roll of kettledrums. " Cast down, but not destroyed," is the shout of a victor. Israel has wrestled, and has overcome in the struggle. Who wonders ? If Israel overcame the angel of the covenant, what man or devil shall vanquish him ? The fight was oft renewed and long protracted : the champion severely felt the conflict, and was at times fearful of the issue ; but at length he takes breath, and cries, " Yet they have not prevailed against me." " Many a time ; " yes, " many a time," the enemy has had his opportunity and his vantage, but not so much as once has he gained the victory.

3. *"The plowers plowed upon my back."* The scourgers tore the flesh as ploughmen furrow a field. The people were maltreated like a criminal given over to the lictors with their cruel whips ; the back of the nation was scored and furrowed by oppression. It is a grand piece of imagery condensed into few words. A writer says the metaphor is muddled, but he is mistaken : there are several figures, like wheel within wheel, but there is no confusion. The afflicted nation was, as it were, lashed by her adversaries so cruelly that each blow left a long red mark, or perhaps a bleeding wound, upon her back and shoulders, comparable to a furrow which tears up the ground from one end of the field to the other. Many a heart has been in like case ; smitten and sore wounded by them that use the scourge of the tongue; so smitten that their whole character has been cut up and scored by calumny. The true church has in every age had fellowship with her Lord under his cruel flagellations : his sufferings were a prophecy of what she would be called hereafter to endure, and the foreshadowing has been fulfilled. Zion has in this sense been ploughed as a field.

"They made long their furrows : "—as if delighting in their cruel labour. They missed not an inch, but went from end to end of the field, meaning to make thorough work of their congenial engagement. Those who laid on the scourge did it with a thoroughness which showed how hearty was their hate. Assuredly the enemies of Christ's church never spare pains to inflict the utmost injury : they never do the work of the devil deceitfully, or hold back their hand from blood. They smite so as to plough into the man ; they plough the quivering flesh as if it were clods of clay ; they plough deep and long with countless furrows ; until they leave no portion of the church unfurrowed or unassailed. Ah me ! Well did Latimer say that there was no busier ploughman in all the world than the devil : whoever makes short furrows, he does not. Whoever baulks and shirks, he is thorough in all that he does. Whoever stops work at sundown, he never does. He and his children plough like practised ploughmen ; but they prefer to carry on their pernicious work upon the saints behind their backs, for they are as cowardly as they are cruel.

4. *"The LORD is righteous."* Whatever men may be, Jehovah remains just, and will therefore keep covenant with his people and deal out justice to their oppressors. Here is the hinge of the condition : this makes the turning point of Israel's distress. The Lord bears with the long furrows of the wicked, but he will surely make them cease from their ploughing before he has done with them. *"He hath cut asunder the cords of the wicked."* The rope which binds the oxen to the plough is cut ; the cord which bound the victim is broken ; the bond which held the enemies in cruel unity has snapped. As in Psalm cxxiv. 7 we read, " the snare is broken ; we are escaped," so here the breaking of the enemies' instrument of oppression is Israel's release. Sooner or later a righteous God will interpose, and when he does so, his action will be most effectual ; he does not unfasten, but cuts asunder, the harness which the ungodly use in their labour of hate. Never has

God used a nation to chastise his Israel without destroying that nation when the chastisement has come to a close : he hates those who hurt his people even though he permits their hate to triumph for a while for his own purpose. If any man would have his harness cut, let him begin to plough one of the Lord's fields with the plough of persecution. The shortest way to ruin is to meddle with a saint : the divine warning is, " He that toucheth you toucheth the apple of his eye."

5. *"Let them all be confounded and turned back that hate Zion."* And so say we right heartily : and in this case *vox populi* is *vox Dei,* for so it shall be. If this be an imprecation, let it stand ; for our heart says " Amen " to it. It is but justice that those who hate, harass, and hurt the good should be brought to naught. Those who confound right and wrong ought to be confounded, and those who turn back from God ought to be turned back. Loyal subjects wish ill to those who plot against their king.

> " Confound their politics,
> Frustrate their knavish tricks,"

is but a proper wish, and contains within it no trace of personal ill-will. We desire their welfare as men, their downfall as traitors. Let their conspiracies be confounded, their policies be turned back. How can we wish prosperity to those who would destroy that which is dearest to our hearts ? This present age is so flippant that if a man loves the Saviour he is styled a fanatic, and if he hates the powers of evil he is named a bigot. As for ourselves, despite all objectors, we join heartily in this commination ; and would revive in our heart the old practice of Ebal and Gerizim, where those were blessed who bless God, and those were cursed who make themselves a curse to the righteous. We have heard men desire a thousand times that the gallows might be the reward of the assassins who murdered two inoffensive men in Dublin, and we would never censure the wish ; for justice ought to be rendered to the evil as well as to the good. Besides, the church of God is so useful, so beautiful, so innocent of harm, so fraught with good, that those who do her wrong are wronging all mankind and deserve to be treated as the enemies of the human race. Study a chapter from the " Book of Martyrs," and see if you do not feel inclined to read an imprecatory Psalm over Bishop Bonner and Bloody Mary. It may be that some wretched nineteenth century sentimentalist will blame you : if so, read another *over him.*

6. *"Let them be as the grass upon the housetops, which withereth afore it groweth up."* Grass on the housetop is soon up and soon down. It sprouts in the heat, finds enough nutriment to send up a green blade, and then it dies away before it reaches maturity, because it has neither earth nor moisture sufficient for its proper development. Before it grows up it dies ; it needs not to be plucked up, for it hastens to decay of itself. Such is and such ought to be the lot of the enemies of God's people. Transient is their prosperity ; speedy is their destruction. The height of their position, as it hastens their progress, so it hurries their doom. Had they been lower in station they had perhaps been longer in being. " Soon ripe, soon rotten," is an old proverb. Soon plotting and soon rotting, is a version of the old adage which will suit in this place. We have seen grass on the rustic thatch of our own country cottages which will serve for an illustration almost as well as that which comes up so readily on the flat roofs and domes of eastern habitations. The idea is—they make speed to success, and equal speed to failure. Persecutors are all sound and fury, flash and flame ; but they speedily vanish—more speedily than is common to men. Grass in the field withers, but not as speedily as grass on the housetops. Without a mower the tufts of verdure perish from the roofs, and so do opposers pass away by other deaths than fall to the common lot of men ; they are gone, and none is the worse. If they are missed at all, their absence is never regretted. Grass on the housetop is a nonentity in the world : the house is not improverished when the last blade is dried up : and, even so, the opposers of Christ pass away, and none lament them. One of the fathers said of the apostate emperor Julian, " That little cloud will soon be gone " ; and so it was. Every sceptical system of philosophy has much the same history ; and the like may be said of each heresy. Poor, rootless things, they are and are not : they come and go, even though no one rises against them. Evil carries the seeds of dissolution within itself. So let it be.

7. *"Wherewith the mower filleth not his hand ; nor he that bindeth sheaves his bosom."* When with his sickle the husbandman would cut down the tufts, he found

nothing to lay hold upon : the grass promised fairly enough, but there was no fulfilment, there was nothing to cut or to carry, nothing for the hand to grasp, nothing for the lap to gather. Easterns carry their corn in their bosoms, but in this case there was nothing to bear home. Thus do the wicked come to nothing. By God's just appointment they prove a disappointment. Their fire ends in smoke ; their verdure turns to vanity ; their flourishing is but a form of withering. No one profits by them, least of all are they profitable to themselves. Their aim is bad, their work is worse, their end is worst of all.

8. *"Neither do they which go by say, The blessing of the* LORD *be upon you : we bless you in the name of the* LORD.*"* In harvest times men bless each other in the name of the Lord ; but there is nothing in the course and conduct of the ungodly man to suggest the giving or receiving of a benediction. Upon a survey of the sinner's life from beginning to end, we feel more inclined to weep than to rejoice, and we feel bound rather to wish him failure than success. We dare not use pious expressions as mere compliments, and hence we dare not wish God-speed to evil men lest we be partakers of their evil deeds. When persecutors are worrying the saints, we cannot say, " The blessing of the Lord be upon you." When they slander the godly and oppose the doctrine of the cross, we dare not bless them in the name of the Lord. It would be infamous to compromise the name of the righteous Jehovah by pronouncing his blessing upon unrighteous deeds.

See how godly men are roughly ploughed by their adversaries, and yet a harvest comes of it which endures and produces blessing ; while the ungodly, though they flourish for a while and enjoy a complete immunity, dwelling, as they think, quite above the reach of harm, are found in a short time to have gone their way and to have left no trace behind. Lord, number me with thy saints. Let me share their grief if I may also partake of their glory. Thus would I make this Psalm my own, and magnify thy name, because thine afflicted ones are not destroyed, and thy persecuted ones are not forsaken.

EXPLANATORY NOTES AND QUAINT SAYINGS.

Whole Psalm.—In the " degrees " of Christian virtue the Psalm corresponds to the tenth step, which is patience in adversity.—*H. T. Armfield.*

Whole Psalm.—The following incident in connection with the glorious return of the Vaudois under Henri Arnaud is related in Muston's " Israel of the Alps " :— " After these successes the gallant patriots took an oath of fidelity to each other, and celebrated divine service in one of their own churches, for the first time since their banishment. The enthusiasm of the moment was irrepressible ; they chanted the seventy-fourth Psalm to the clash of arms ; and Henri Arnaud, mounting the pulpit with a sword in one hand and a Bible in the other, preached from the Hundred and twenty-ninth Psalm, and once more declared, in the face of heaven, that he would never resume his pastoral office in patience and peace, until he should witness the restoration of his brethren to their ancient and rightful settlements."

Verse 1.—*"Many a time have they afflicted me from my youth."* 1. How *old* these afflictions are : *"From my youth."* Ay, from my infancy, birth and conception. 2. There is the *frequency* and *iteration* of these afflictions. They were *oft* and *many :* *"many a time."* 3. There is the *grievousness* of these afflictions, expressed by a comparison. " The plowers plowed upon my back : they made long their furrows." So these were *old* afflictions—*from her youth.* They were *many a time :* more times than can be numbered. And then they were *grievous,* even like iron ploughs, drawing deep and long furrows on their back.—*Alexander Henderson.*

Verse 1.—*"Many a time have they afflicted me,"* etc. God had one Son, and but one Son, without sin ; but never any without sorrow. We may be God's children, and yet still under persecution ; his Israel, and afflicted from our youth up. We may feel God's hand as a Father upon us when he strikes us as well as when he strokes us. When he strokes us, it is lest we faint under his hand ; and when he strikes us, it is that we should know his hand.—*Abraham Wright* (1611—1690), *in "A Practical Commentary upon the Psalms."*

Verse 1.—"*They.*" The persecutors deserve not a name. The rich man is not named (as Lazarus is) because not worthy : Luke xvi. " They shall be written in the earth" : Jeremiah xvii. 13.—*John Trapp.*

Verse 1.—"*They.*" In speaking of the enemies of Israel simply by the pronoun "*they,*" without being more specific, the Psalmist aggravates the greatness of the evil more than if he had expressly named the Assyrians or the Egyptians. By not specifying any particular class of foes, he tacitly intimates that the world is filled with innumerable bands of enemies, whom Satan easily arms for the destruction of good men, his object being that new wars may arise continually on every side. History certainly bears ample testimony that the people of God had not to deal with a few enemies, but that they were assaulted by almost the whole world ; and further, that they were molested not only by external foes, but also by those of an internal kind, by such as professed to belong to the Church.—*John Calvin.*

Verse 1.—"'*They afflicted me.*" Why are these afflictions of the righteous ? Whence is it that he who has given up his Son to death for them, should deny them earthly blessings ? Why is faith a mourner so frequently here below, and with all that heroic firmness in her aspect, and hope of glory in her eye, why needs she to be painted with so deep a sorrow on her countenance, and the trace of continual tears on her cheek ? First, we reply, *for her own safety.* Place religion out of the reach of sorrow, and soon she would pine and perish. God is said to choose his people in the furnace, because they oftenest choose him there.

It is ever from the cross that the most earnest "My God" proceeds, and never is the cry heard but he speeds forth at its utterance, who once hung there, to support, to comfort, and to save.

As it is only in affliction God is *sought,* so by many it is only in affliction God is *known.* This, one of the kings of these worshippers of the Temple found. " When Manasseh was brought to affliction, *then* he knew that the Lord he was God " : 2 Chronicles xxxiii. 12, 13.

But, further, it is only by affliction *we ourselves are known.* What is the source of that profound and obstinate indifference to divine truth which prevails among men of the world, except the proud conviction that they may dispense with it ? It is only when they are crushed as the worm they are made to feel that the dust is their source ; only when earthly props are withdrawn will they take hold of that arm of omnipotence which Jesus offers, and which he has offered so long in vain.

While men know themselves, they *know their sin* also in affliction. What is the natural course and experience of the unbelieving of mankind ? Transgression, remorse, and then forgetfulness ; new transgression, new sorrow, and again forgetfulness. How shall this carelessness be broken ? How convince them that they stand in need of a Saviour as the first and deepest want of their being, and that they can only secure deliverance from wrath eternal by a prompt and urgent application to him ? By nothing so effectually as by affliction. God's children, who had forgotten him, arise and go to their Father when thus smitten by the scourge of sorrow ; and no sooner is the penitent "*Father, I have sinned*" spoken, than they are clasped in his arms, and safe and happy in his love.

It is, further, by affliction that the *world* is known to God's children. God's great rival is the world. The lust of the flesh, pleasure ; the lust of the eye, desire ; the pride of life, the longing to be deemed superior to those about us,—comprise everything man naturally covets. Give us ease, honour, distinction, and all life's good will seem obtained. *But what wilt thou do, when he shall judge thee ?* This is a question fitted to alarm the happiest of the children of prosperity.

What so frequently and effectually shows the necessity of piety as the sharp teachings of affliction ? They show what moralists and preachers never could, that riches profit not in the day of death, that pleasures most fully enjoyed bring no soothing to the terrors which nearness to eternity presents, and that friends, however affectionate, cannot plead for and save us at the bar of God. " Miserable comforters are they all," and it is for the very purpose of inspiring this conviction, along with a belief that it is Jesus alone who can comfort in the hour of need, that affliction is sent to God's children.—*Robert Nisbet.*

Verse 1.—"*From my youth.*" The first that ever died, died for religion ; so early came martyrdom into the world.—*John Trapp.*

Verses 1, 2.—1. The visible Church from the beginning of the world is one body, and, as it were, one man, growing up from infancy to riper age ; for so speaketh the church here : "*Many a time have they afflicted me from my youth.*" 2. The wicked enemies of the church, they also are one body, one adverse army, from the beginning of the world continuing war against the church : *"Many a time have they afflicted me from my youth."* 3. As the former injuries done to the church are owned by the church, in after-ages, as done against the same body, so also the persecution of former enemies is imputed and put upon the score of present persecutors : *"Many a time have they afflicted me from my youth, may Israel now say."* 4. New experience of persecution, when they call to mind the exercise of the church in former ages, serves much for encouragement and consolation in troubles : *"Many a time have they afflicted me from my youth, may Israel now say."* 5. Albeit this hath been the endeavour of the wicked in all ages to destroy the church, yet God hath still preserved her from age to age : *"Yet they have not prevailed."*—*David Dickson.*

Verses 1, 2.—When the prophet says twice, *"They have afflicted me,"* *"they have afflicted me,"* the repetition is not superfluous, it being intended to teach us that the people of God had not merely once or twice to enter the conflict, but that their patience had been tried by continual exercises.—*John Calvin.*

Verse 2.—*"Many a time,"* etc. The Christian Church may adopt the language of the Hebrew Church : " Many a time have they afflicted me from my youth : yet they have not prevailed against me." What afflictions were endured by the Christian Church from her youth up ! How feeble was that youth ! How small the number of the apostles to whom our Lord gave his gospel in charge ! How destitute were they of human learning, of worldly influence, of secular power ! To effect their destruction, and to frustrate their object—the glory of God and the salvation of men—the dungeon and the mine, the rack and the gibbet, were all successively employed. The ploughers ploughed their back, and made long their furrows. Their property was confiscated ; their persons were imprisoned ; their civil rights were taken from them ; their heads rolled on the scaffold ; their bodies were consumed at the burning pile ; they were thrown, amidst the ringing shouts of the multitude, to the wild beasts of the amphitheatre. Despite, however, of every opposition, our holy religion took root and grew upward. Not all the fury of ten persecutions could exterminate it from the earth. The teeth of wild beasts could not grind it to powder ; the fire could not burn it ; the waters could not drown it ; the dungeon could not confine it. Truth is eternal, like the great God from whose bosom it springs, and therefore it cannot be destroyed. And because Christianity is the truth, and no lie, her enemies have never prevailed against her.—*M. M'Michael.*

Verse 2.—*"Yet they have not prevailed against me."* The words are the same as in Gen. xxxii. 28. The blessing won by Jacob, when he wrestled with the angel, remained on his descendants. During the long night of the Captivity the faithful had wrestled in faithful prayer ; now the morning had appeared, and Israel was raised to a higher stage of privilege.—*W. Kay.*

Verse 2.—*"Yet they have not prevailed against me."* Israel prevailed with God in wrestling with him, and therefore it is that he prevails with men also. If so be that we will wrestle with God for a blessing, and prevail with him, then we need not to fear but we shall wrestle the enemies out of it also. If we be the people of God, and persist in wrestling against his enemies, we need not fear but that we shall be victorious.—*Alexander Henderson.*

Verse 3.—*"The plowers plowed,"* etc. There does not seem to be any need to look for an interpretation of this in scourging or any other bodily infliction of pain ; it seems to be " a figurative mode of expressing severe oppression." Roberts informs us that when, in the East, a man is in much trouble through oppressors, he says, " How they plough me and turn me up."—*Ingram Cobbin,* 1839.

Verse 3.—*"The plowers plowed,"* etc. The great Husbandman who owns this plough (at least by whose permission this plough goes), is God. Not only is it God who makes your common ploughs to gang, and sends the gospel into a land, but it is God also who disposes and overrules this same plough of persecution. For without his licence the plough cannot be yoked ; and being yoked, cannot enter to gang till he direct ; and he tempers the irons, so that they cannot go one inch deeper than he thinks meet. When he thinks it time to quit work, then presently he cuts their cords, so that they cannot go once about after he thinks it time to quit work. Albeit when they yoke, they resolve to have all the land upside down, yet he will let them plough no more of it than he sees meet. Now for the ploughmen of this plough, they are Satan and the evil angels ; they hold the plough, and are goad-men to it ; and they yoke in the oxen into the plough, and drive them up with their goads. And they have a sort of music also, which they whistle into their ears, to make them go the faster ; and that is the allurements and provocations of the world. And for the oxen who draw into this plough, it may be princes when they turn persecutors of the kirk ; it may be prelates ; it may be politicians in the world : these are the oxen, Satan and the ill spirits inciting them, and stirring them up to go forward in their intended course. Then consider here that the plough and the ploughmen and oxen go about as God thinks meet ; but what is it that they are doing in the meantime ? Nothing else but preparing the ground for seed, and so the Lord employs them to prepare his people better to receive the seed of his word and of his Spirit.—*Alexander Henderson.*

Verse 3.—God fails not to sow blessings in the furrows, which the plowers plow upon the back of the church.—*Jeremy Taylor, 1613—1667.*

Verse 3.—"*The plowers plowed upon my back : they made long their furrows.*" When the Lord Jesus Christ was in his suffering state, and during his passion, these words here predicted of him were most expressly realized. Whilst he remained in the hands of the Roman soldiers they stript him of his raiment ; they bound him with cords to a pillar ; they flogged him. This was so performed by them, that they made ridges in his back and sides ; they tore skin and flesh, and made him bare even to the bone, so that his body was like a ploughed field ; the gashes made in it were like ridges made in a ploughed field ; these were on his back. "*The plowers plowed upon my back : they made long their furrows.*" Whilst every part of our Lord's sorrows and sufferings is most minutely set forth in the sacred hymns, Psalms, and songs, contained in what we style the Book of Psalms, yet we shall never comprehend what our most blessed Lord, in every part of his life, and in his passion and death, underwent for us : may the Lord the Spirit imprint this fresh expression used on this subject effectually upon us. Our Lord's words here are very expressive of the violence of his tormentors and their rage against him, and of the wounds and torments they had inflicted on him.

What must the feelings of our Lord have been when they made such furrows on his back, that it was all furrowed and welted with such long wounds, that it was more like a ploughed field than anything else. Blessings on him for his grace and patience, it is " with his stripes we are healed."—*Samuel Eyles Pierce.*

Verse 3.—"*They made long their furrows.*" The apparent harshness of this figure will disappear if it be considered to refer to severe public scourgings. To those who have been so unhappy as to witness such scourgings this allusion will then appear most expressive. The long weals or wounds which the scourge leaves at each stroke may most aptly be compared either to *furrows* or (as the original admits) to the *ridges between the furrows.* The *furrows* made by the plough in the East are very superficial, and (although straight) are usually carried to a great length, the fields not being enclosed as in this country.—*John Kitto, in "The Pictorial Bible."*

Verse 4.—"*The LORD is righteous : he hath cut asunder the cords of the wicked ;*" *i.e.,* he has put an end to their domination and tyranny over us. In the Hebrew word which is rendered "*cords*" there is a reference to the *harness* with which the oxen were fastened to the plough ; and so to the *involved machinations* and *cruelties* of the enemy. The Hebrew word properly denotes thick *twisted cords*; figuratively, intertwined wickedness ; Micah vii. 3. "*The cords of the wicked,*" therefore, signify their *power, dominion, tyranny,* wickedness, and violence. These cords God is said "*to have cut,*" so that *he should have made an end ;* and, therefore, "*to have cut*" *for ever,* so that they should never be reunited.—*Hermann Venema.*

Verse 4.—"*He hath cut asunder the cords of the wicked.*" The enemies' power has been broken ; *God has cut asunder the cords of the wicked,* has cut their gears, their traces, and so spoiled their ploughing ; has cut their scourges, and so spoiled their lashing ; has cut the bands of union, by which they were combined together ; he has cut the bands of captivity, in which they held God's people. God has many ways of disabling wicked men to do the mischief they design against his church, and shaming their counsels.—*Matthew Henry.*

Verse 4.—"*He hath cut asunder the cords of the wicked.*" He repeateth the same praise of God in delivering his church from oppression of the enemy, under the similitude of cutting the cords of the plough, which tilleth up another man's field. Whence learn, 1. The enemies of the church do no more regard her than they do the earth under their feet, and do seek to make their own advantage of her, as usurpers use to do in possessing and labouring of another man's field. *"The plowers plowed upon my back."* 2. The Lord useth to suffer his enemies to break up the fallow ground of his people's proud and stiff hearts with the plough of persecution, and to draw deep and long furrows on them : *"They made long their furrows."* 3. What the enemies do against the church the Lord maketh use of for manuring the church, which is his field, albeit they intend no good to God's church, yet they serve in God's wisdom to prepare the Lord's people for receiving the seed of God's word ; for the similitude speaketh of their tilling of the church, but nothing of their sowing, for that is reserved for the Lord himself, who is owner of the field. 4. When the wicked have performed so much of God's husbandry as he thinketh good to suffer them, then he stoppeth their design, and looseth their plough. *"He hath cut asunder the cords of the wicked."—David Dickson.*

Verse 5.—If any one be desirous to accept these words, *"Let them be confounded and turned backward,"* as they sound, he will devoutly explain the imprecation : that is to say, it may be an imprecation of good confusion, which leads to repentance, and of turning to God from sin ; thus Bellarmine. There is a confounding by bringing grace, glory, and turning from the evil way. Thus some enemies and persecutors of the Christians have been holily confounded and turned to the faith of Christ ; as St. Paul, who full of wrath and slaughter was going to Damascus that he might afflict the believers, but was graciously confounded on the road.—*Thomas Le Blanc.*

Verse 5.—*"Let them all be confounded."* Mr. Emerson told a convention of rationalists once, in this city, that the morality of the New Testament is scientific and perfect. But the morality of the New Testament is that of the Old. " Yes," you say ; " but what of the imprecatory Psalms ? " A renowned professor, who, as Germany thinks, has done more for New England theology than any man since Jonathan Edwards, was once walking in this city with a clergyman of a radical faith, who objected to the doctrine that the Bible is inspired, and did so on the ground of the imprecatory Psalms. The replies of the usual kind were made ; and it was presumed that David expressed the Divine purpose in praying that his enemies might be destroyed, and that he gave utterance only to the natural, righteous indignation of conscience against unspeakable iniquity. But the doubter would not be satisfied. The two came at last to a newspaper bulletin, on which the words were written,—" Baltimore to be shelled at twelve o'clock." " I am glad of it," said the radical preacher ; " I am glad of it." " And so am I," said his companion, " but I hardly dare say so, for fear you should say that I am uttering an imprecatory Psalm."—*Joseph Cook, in Boston Monday Lectures. "Transcendentalism."*

Verse 5.—*"And turned back ; "* from pursuing their designs and accomplishing them ; as the Assyrian monarch was, who had a hook put into his nose, and a bridle in his lips, and was turned back by the way he came : Isaiah xxxvii. 29. —*John Gill.*

Verse 5.—*"All those who hate Zion."* Note that he does not say, All who hate *me ;* but *" all who hate Zion."* Thus the saints are not led to this from the desire of revenge, but from zeal for the people of God, so that they pray for the confusion and repression of the ungodly.—*Wolfgang Musculus.*

Verse 6.—*" Let them be as the grass upon the housetops."* They are rightly compared to *"grass on the housetops ; "* for more contemptuously the Holy Ghost could not speak of them. For this grass is such, that it soon withereth away before the sickle be put into it. Yea, no man thinketh it worthy to be cut down, no man regardeth it, every man suffereth it to brag for a while, and to show itself unto men from the housetops as though it were something when it is nothing. So the wicked persecutors in the world, which are taken to be mighty and terrible according to the outward show, are of all men most contemptible. For Christians do not once think of plucking them up or cutting them down ; they persecute them not, they revenge not their own injuries, but suffer them to increase, to brag and glory as much as they list. For they know that they cannot abide the violence of a vehement wind. Yea, though all things be in quietness, yet as grass upon the housetops, by little and little, withereth away through the heat of the sun, so tyrannies upon small occasions do perish and soon vanish away. The faithful, therefore, in suffering do prevail and overcome ; but the wicked in doing are overthrown, and miserably perish, as all the histories of all times and ages do plainly witness.—*Martin Luther.*

Verse 6.—*"Like grass upon the housetops."* The flat roofs of the Eastern houses " are plastered with a composition of mortar, tar, ashes, and sand," in the crevices of which grass often springs. The houses of the poor in the country were formed of a plaster of mud and straw, where the grass would grow still more freely : as all the images are taken from country life, it is doubtless to country dwellings that the poet refers.—*J. J. Stewart Perowne.*

Verse 6.—*"Like grass upon the housetops."* The enemies of Zion may have an elevated position in the nation, they may seem to promise growth, but having no root in themselves, like the hearers on the stony ground, give no promise of fruit. Their profession dies away and leaves no benefit to the church, as it claims no blessing from others.—*William Wilson* (1783—1873), *in "The Book of Psalms, with an Exposition."*

Verse 6.—*"Grass upon the housetops."* In the morning the master of the house laid in a stock of earth, which was carried up, and spread evenly on the top of the house, which is flat. The whole roof is thus formed of mere earth, laid on and rolled hard and flat. On the top of every house is a large stone roller, for the purpose of hardening and flattening this layer of rude soil, so that the rain may not penetrate ; but upon this surface, as may be supposed, grass and weeds grow freely, but never come to maturity. It is to such grass the Psalmist alludes as useless and bad.—*William Jowett, in "Christian Researches in Syria and the Holy Land,"* 1825.

Verse 7.—*"The mower filleth not his hand,"* etc. The grain was rather pulled than cut, and as each handful was taken the reaper gave it a flourishing swing up into his bosom.—*Mrs. Finn, in "Home in the Holy Land,"* 1866.

Verse 7.—*"He that bindeth sheaves his bosom."* A practice prevails in hot climates of sending out persons into the woods and other wild places to collect the grass, which would otherwise be wasted ; and it is no uncommon thing in the evening to see groups of grass-cutters in the market, waiting to dispose of their bundles or sheaves, which are often so large that one is disposed to wonder how they could have been conveyed from the woods upon one man's shoulders.—*Maria Calcott, in "A Scripture Herbal,"* 1842.

Verse 8.—The latter expressions are most refreshingly Arabic. Nothing is more natural than for them, when passing by a fruit-tree or corn-field loaded with a rich crop to exclaim, *"Barak Allah !"* God bless you ! We bless you in the name of the *Lord !*—*W. M. Thomson.*

HINTS TO PREACHERS.

Verse 1.—Affliction as it comes to saints from men of the world. I. Reason for it—enmity of the serpent's seed. II. Modes of its display—persecution, ridicule, slander, disdain, etc. III. Comfort under it. So persecuted they the prophets: so the Master. It is their nature. They cannot kill the soul. It is but for a time, etc.

Verses 1 and 2.—I. How far persecution for righteousness' sake may go. 1. It may be great : " afflicted " " afflicted." 2. It may be frequent : " Many a time." 3. It may be early : " From my youth." II. How far it cannot go. 1. It may seem to prevail. 2. It may prevail in some degree. 3. It cannot ultimately prevail. 4. It shall cause that to which it is opposed increasingly to prevail.—*G. R.*

Verses 1—4.—Israel persecuted but not forsaken. Persecution. I. Whence it came : " they." II. How it came : " Many a time," " from my youth," severely : " afflicted," " ploughed." III. Why it came. Human and Satanic hatred, and Divine permission. IV. What came of it : " not prevailed "—to destroy, to drive to despair, to lead to sin. God's righteousness manifested in upholding his people, baffling their foes, etc.

Verses 1—4. The enemies of God's church. I. Their violence : " The plowers plowed," etc. II. Their persistency : " Many a time . . . . from my youth." III. Their failure : " Yet they have not prevailed." IV. Their great opponent : " The Lord . . . . hath cut asunder."—*J. F.*

Verse 3.—I. Literally fulfilled. 1. In Christ. Matt. xxvii. 26 ; xx. 19 ; Mark xv. 15 ; Luke xviii. 33 ; John xix. 1. 2. In his followers. Matt. x. 17 ; Acts xvi. 23 ; 2 Cor. vi. 5 ; xi. 23, 24 ; Heb. xi. 36. And frequently in subsequent persecutions. II. Figuratively. In secret calumnies both in Christ and his followers.—*G. R.*

Verse 4.—Israel's song of triumph. I. The Lord is righteous in permitting these afflictions to come upon his people. II. He is righteous in keeping his promise of deliverance to his people. III. He is righteous in visiting the enemies of his people with judgment.—*W. H. J. P.*

Verse 5.—I. An inexcusable hatred described : " hate Zion," God's church and cause. For, 1. Her people are righteous. 2. Her faith is a gospel. 3. Her mission is peace. 4. Her very existence is the world's preservation. II. An inveterate sinfulness indicated : " Them that hate Zion." For, whatever moral virtues they may boast of, they must be, 1. Enemies to the human race. 2. In defiant opposition to God. 3. Perversely blind, as Saul, or radically vile. 4. Devil-like. III. An instinctive feeling of a good man expressed : " Let them all be," etc. Prompted by, 1. His love to God. 2. Love to man. 3. Love to righteousness. Hence, its existence is in itself a pledge that the righteous God will respect and comply with it.—*J. F.*

Verses 5—8.—I. The characters described. 1. They do not love Zion. They say not, " Lord, I have loved the habitation of thine house," etc. 2. They hate Zion—both its King and its subjects. II. Their prosperity : " As the grass," etc. III. Their end. 1. Shame : " Let them be confounded." 2. Loss : " Turned back." 3. Disappointment. No mowing ; no reaping. 4. Dishonour. Unblessed by others as well as in themselves.—*G. R.*

Verses 6—9.—The wicked flourishing and perishing. I. Eminent in position. II. Envied in prosperity. III. Evanescent in duration. IV. Empty as to solidity. V. Excepted from blessing.

PSALM CXXX.

TITLE.—A Song of Degrees. *It would be hard to see any upward step from the preceding to the present Psalm, and therefore it is possible that the steps or ascents are in the song itself : certainly it does rise rapidly out of the depths of anguish to the heights of assurance. It follows well upon cxxix. : when we have overcome the trials which arise from man we are the better prepared to meet those sharper sorrows which arise out of our matters towards God. He who has borne the scourges of the wicked is trained in all patience to wait the dealings of the Holy Lord. We name this the* DE PROFUNDIS PSALM *: "Out of the depths" is the leading word of it : out of those depths we cry, wait, watch, and hope. In this Psalm we hear of the pearl of redemption, verses 7 and 8 : perhaps the sweet singer would never have found that precious thing had he not been cast into the depths. "Pearls lie deep."*

DIVISION.—*The first two verses reveal an intense desire ; and the next two are a humble confession of repentance and faith, verses 3 and 4. In verses 5 and 6 waiting watchfulness is declared and resolved upon ; and in the last two verses joyful expectation, both for himself and all Israel, finds expression.*

EXPOSITION.

OUT of the depths have I cried unto thee, O LORD.

2 Lord, hear my voice : let thine ears be attentive to the voice of my supplications.

3 If thou, LORD, shouldest mark iniquities, O Lord, who shall stand ?

4 But *there is* forgiveness with thee, that thou mayest be feared.

5 I wait for the LORD, my soul doth wait, and in his word do I hope.

6 My soul *waiteth* for the Lord more than they that watch for the morning : *I say, more than* they that watch for the morning.

7 Let Israel hope in the LORD : for with the LORD *there is* mercy, and with him *is* plenteous redemption.

8 And he shall redeem Israel from all his iniquities.

1. *"Out of the depths have I cried unto thee, O LORD."* This is the Psalmist's statement and plea : he had never ceased to pray even when brought into the lowest state. The depths usually silence all they engulf, but they could not close the mouth of this servant of the Lord ; on the contrary, it was in the abyss itself that he cried unto Jehovah. Beneath the floods prayer lived and struggled ; yea, above the roar of the billows rose the cry of faith. It little matters where we are if we can pray ; but prayer is never more real and acceptable than when it rises out of the worst places. Deep places beget deep devotion. Depths of earnestness are stirred by depths of tribulation. Diamonds sparkle most amid the darkness. Prayer *de profundis* gives to God *gloria in excelsis*. The more distressed we are, the more excellent is the faith which trusts bravely in the Lord, and therefore appeals to him, and to him alone. Good men may be in the depths of temporal and spiritual trouble ; but good men in such cases look only to their God, and they stir themselves up to be more instant and earnest in prayer than at other times. The depth of their distress moves the depths of their being ; and from the bottom of their hearts an exceeding great and bitter cry rises unto the one living and true God. David had often been in the deep, and as often had he pleaded with Jehovah, his God, in whose hand are all deep places. He prayed, and remembered that he had prayed, and pleaded that he had prayed ; hoping ere long to receive an answer. It would be dreadful to look back on trouble and feel forced to own that we did not cry unto the Lord in it ; but it is most comforting to know that whatever we did not do, or could not do, yet we did pray, even in our worst times. He that prays in the depth will not sink out of his depth. He that cries out of the depths shall soon sing in the heights.

2. *"Lord, hear my voice."* It is all we ask ; but nothing less will content us. If the Lord will but hear us we will leave it to his superior wisdom to decide whether he will answer us or no. It is better for our prayer to be heard than answered. If the Lord were to make an absolute promise to answer all our requests it might be rather a curse than a blessing, for it would be casting the responsibility of our lives upon ourselves, and we should be placed in a very anxious position : but now the Lord hears our desires, and that is enough ; we only wish him to grant them if his infinite wisdom sees that it would be for our good and for his glory. Note that the Psalmist spoke audibly in prayer : this is not at all needful, but it is exceedingly helpful ; for the use of the voice assists the thoughts. Still, there is a voice in silent supplication, a voice in our weeping, a voice in that sorrow which cannot find a tongue : that voice the Lord will hear if its cry is meant for his ear. *"Let thine ears be attentive to the voice of my supplication."* The Psalmist's cry is a beggar's petition ; he begs the great King and Lord to lend an ear to it. He has supplicated many times, but always with one voice, or for one purpose ; and he begs to be noticed in the one matter which he has pressed with so much importunity. He would have the King hearken, consider, remember, and weigh his request. He is confused, and his prayer may therefore be broken, and difficult to understand ; he begs therefore that his Lord will give the more earnest and compassionate heed to the voice of his many and painful pleadings. When we have already prayed over our troubles it is well to pray over our prayers. If we can find no more words, let us entreat the Lord to hear those petitions which we have already presented. If we have faithfully obeyed the precept by praying without ceasing, we may be confident that the Lord will faithfully fulfil the promise by helping us without fail. Though the Psalmist was under a painful sense of sin, and so was in the depth, his faith pleaded in the teeth of conscious unworthiness ; for well he knew that the Lord's keeping his promise depends upon his own character and not upon that of his erring creatures.

3. *"If thou, LORD, shouldest mark iniquities, O Lord, who shall stand ?"* If JAH, the all-seeing, should in strict justice call every man to account for every want of conformity to righteousness, where would any one of us be ? Truly, he does record all our transgressions ; but as yet he does not act upon the record, but lays it aside till another day. If men were to be judged upon no system but that of works, who among us could answer for himself at the Lord's bar, and hope to stand clear and accepted ? This verse shows that the Psalmist was under a sense of sin, and felt it imperative upon him not only to cry as a suppliant but to confess as a sinner. Here he owns that he cannot stand before the great King in his own righteousness, and he is so struck with a sense of the holiness of God, and the rectitude of the law, that he is convinced that no man of mortal race can answer for himself before a Judge so perfect, concerning a law so divine. Well does he cry, " O Lord, who shall stand ? " None can do so : there is none that doeth good, no, not one. Iniquities are matters which are not according to equity : what a multitude we have of these ! Jehovah, who sees all, and is also our *Adonai*, or Lord, will assuredly bring us into judgment concerning those thoughts, and words, and works which are not in exact conformity to his law. Were it not for the Lord Jesus, could we hope to stand ? Dare we meet him in the dread day of account on the footing of law and equity ? What a mercy it is that we need not do so, for the next verse sets forth another way of acceptance to which we flee.

4. *"But there is forgiveness with thee."* Blessed *but.* Free, full, sovereign pardon is in the hand of the great King : it is his prerogative to forgive, and he delights to exercise it. Because his nature is mercy, and because he has provided a sacrifice for sin, therefore forgiveness is with him for all that come to him confessing their sins. The power of pardon is permanently resident with God : he has forgiveness ready to his hand at this instant. *"That thou mayest be feared."* This is the fruitful root of piety. None fear the Lord like those who have experienced his forgiving love. Gratitude for pardon produces far more fear and reverence of God than all the dread which is inspired by punishment. If the Lord were to execute justice upon all, there would be none left to fear him ; if all were under apprehension of his deserved wrath, despair would harden them against fearing him : it is grace which leads the way to a holy regard of God, and a fear of grieving him.

5. *"I wait for the LORD, my soul doth wait."* Expecting him to come to me in love, I quietly wait for his appearing ; I wait *upon* him in service, and *for* him in faith. For God I wait and for him only : if he will manifest himself I shall have nothing more to wait for ; but until he shall appear for my help I must wait on,

hoping even in the depths. This waiting of mine is no mere formal act, my very soul is in it,—" my soul doth wait."   I wait and I wait—mark the repetition! " My soul waits," and then again, " My soul waits " ; to make sure work of the waiting.   It is well to deal with the Lord intensely.   Such repetitions are the reverse of vain repetitions.   If the Lord Jehovah makes us wait, let us do so with our whole hearts ; for blessed are all they that wait for him.   He is worth waiting for.   The waiting itself is beneficial to us : it tries faith, exercises patience, trains submission, and endears the blessing when it comes.   The Lord's people have always been a waiting people : they waited for the First Advent, and now they wait for the Second. They waited for a sense of pardon, and now they wait for perfect sanctification. They waited in the depths, and they are not now wearied with waiting in a happier condition.   They have cried and they do wait ; probably their past prayer sustains their present patience.

"*And in his word do I hope.*"   This is the source, strength, and sweetness of waiting.   Those who do not hope cannot wait ; but if we hope for that we see not, then do we with patience wait for it.   God's word is a true word, but at times it tarries ; if ours is true faith it will wait the Lord's time.   A word from the Lord is as bread to the soul of the believer ; and, refreshed thereby, it holds out through the night of sorrow expecting the dawn of deliverance and delight.   Waiting, we study the word, believe the word, hope in the word, and live on the word ; and all because it is "*his* word,"—the word of him who never speaks in vain.   Jehovah's word is a firm ground for a waiting soul to rest upon.

6. "*My soul waiteth for the Lord more than they that watch for the morning.*"   Men who guard a city, and women who wait by the sick, long for daylight.   Worshippers tarrying for the morning sacrifice, the kindling of the incense and the lighting of the lamps, mingle fervent prayers with their holy vigils, and pine for the hour when the lamb shall smoke upon the altar.   David, however, waited more than these, waited longer, waited more longingly, waited more expectantly.   He was not afraid of the great Adonai before whom none can stand in their own righteousness, for he had put on the righteousness of faith, and therefore longed for gracious audience with the Holy One.   God was no more dreaded by him than light is dreaded by those engaged in a lawful calling.   He pined and yearned after his God.   "*I say, more than they that watch for the morning.*"   The figure was not strong enough, though one can hardly think of anything more vigorous : he felt that his own eagerness was unique and unrivalled.   Oh to be thus hungry and thirsty after God !   Our version spoils the abruptness of the language ; the original runs thus—" My soul for the Lord more than those watching for the morning—watching for the morning." This is a fine poetical repeat.   We long for the favour of the Lord more than weary sentinels long for the morning light which will release them from their tedious watch. Indeed this is true.   He that has once rejoiced in communion with God is sore tried by the hidings of his face, and grows faint with strong desire for the Lord's appearing,

> " When wilt thou come unto me, Lord ?
> Until thou dost appear,
> I count each moment for a day,
> Each minute for a year."

7. "*Let Israel hope in the* LORD."   Or, " Hope thou, Israel, in Jehovah."   Jehovah is Israel's God ; therefore, let Israel hope in him.   What one Israelite does he wishes all Israel to do.   That man has a just right to exhort others who is himself setting the example.   Israel of old waited upon Jehovah and wrestled all the night long, and at last he went his way succoured by the Hope of Israel : the like shall happen to all his seed.   God has great things in store for his people ; they ought to have large expectations.   "*For with the* LORD *there is mercy.*"   This is in his very nature, and by the light of nature it may be seen.   But we have also the light of grace, and therefore we see still more of his mercy.   With us there is sin ; but hope is ours, because " with the Lord there is mercy."   Our comfort lies not in that which is with us, but in that which is with our God.   Let us look out of self and its poverty to Jehovah and his riches of mercy.   "*And with him is plenteous redemption.*"   He can and will redeem all his people out of their many and great troubles ; nay, their redemption is already wrought out and laid up with him, so that he can at any time give his waiting ones the full benefit thereof.   The attribute of mercy, and the fact of redemption, are two most sufficient reasons for hoping in Jehovah ; and the fact that there is no mercy or deliverance elsewhere should effectually wean the

soul from all idolatry. Are not these deep things of God a grand comfort for those who are crying out of the depths ? Is it not better to be in the deeps with David, hoping in God's mercy, than up on the mountain-tops, boasting in our own fancied righteousness ?

8. *" And he shall redeem Israel from all his iniquities."* Our iniquities are our worst dangers : if saved from these, we are saved altogether; but there is no salvation from them except by redemption. What a blessing that this is here promised in terms which remove it out of the region of question : the Lord shall certainly redeem his believing people from all their sins. Well may the redemption be plenteous since it concerns all Israel and all iniquities ! Truly, our Psalm has ascended to a great height in this verse : this is no cry out of the depths, but a chorale in the heights. Redemption is the top of covenant blessings. When it shall be experienced by all Israel, the latter-day glory shall have come, and the Lord's people shall say, " Now, Lord, what wait we for ? " Is not this a clear prophecy of the coming of our Lord Jesus the first time? and may we not now regard it as the promise of his second and more glorious coming for the redemption of the body ? For this our soul doth wait : yea, our heart and our flesh cry out for it with joyful expectation.

EXPLANATORY NOTES AND QUAINT SAYINGS.

Whole Psalm.—The Psalm is the eleventh in the order of the gradual Psalms, and treats of the eleventh step in the spiritual ascent, viz., penitential prayer.— *H. T. Armfield.*

Whole Psalm.—Of the Psalms which are called Penitential this is the chiefest. But, as it is the most excellent, so it has been perverted to the most disgraceful abuse in the Popedom : *e.g.*, that it should be mumbled in the lowest voice by slow bellies, in the sepulchral vigils for their liberation of souls from purgatory : as if David were here treating of the dead, when he has not even spoken a word about them ; but says that he himself, a living man, was calling upon God ; and exhorts the Israelites, living men also, to do the same. But leaving the buffooneries of the Papists we will rather consider the true meaning and use of the Psalm. It contains the most ardent prayer of a man grievously distressed by a sense of the Divine anger against sin : by earnest turning to God and penitence, he is seeking the forgiveness of his iniquities.—*Solomon Gesner.*

Whole Psalm.—The Holy Ghost layeth out here two opposite passions most plainly—*fear*, in respect of evil-deserving sins, and *hope*, in regard of undeserved mercies.—*Alexander Roberts*, 1610.

Whole Psalm.—The passionate earnestness of the Psalm is enhanced by the repetition eight times in it of the Divine Name.—*The Speaker's Commentary*, 1873.

Whole Psalm.—This Psalm, perhaps more than any other, is marked by its mountings : depth ; prayer ; conviction ; light ; hope ; waiting ; watching ; longing ; confidence ; assurance ; universal happiness and joy. . . . Just as the barometer marks the rising of the weather, so does this Psalm, sentence by sentence, record the progress of the soul. And you may test yourself by it, as by a rule or measure, and ask yourself at each line, " Have I reached to this ? Have I reached to this ? " and so take your spiritual gauge.—*James Vaughan, in "Steps to Heaven,"* 1878.

Whole Psalm.—Whosoever he was that wrote this Psalm, he maketh mention and rehearsal of that prayer that he made to his God in the time of his great danger, and this he doth to the fifth verse ; then finding in experience a comfortable answer, and how good a thing it was to pray to God, and to wait on him, he professeth, that, as before, he had awaited on him, so still in time coming he would await on him, and this he doeth to the seventh verse. In the third and last part, he turneth him to Israel, to the church, and exhorteth them to await on God, as he had done, promising them mercy and redemption from all their iniquities if they would await on him.—*Robert Rollock*, 1555—1599.

Whole Psalm.—Luther being once asked which were the best Psalms, replied, *Psalmi Paulini ;* and when his companions at table pressed him to say which these were, he answered : Psalms xxxii., li., cxxx., and cxliii.—*Franz Delitzsch.*

Whole Psalm.—Luther, when he was buffeted by the devil at Coburg, and in great affliction, said to those about him, *Venite, in contemptum Diaboli, Psalmum, De Profundis, quatuor vocibus cantemus;* " Come, let us sing that Psalm, ' Out of the depths,' etc., in derision of the devil."—*John Trapp.*

Whole Psalm.—The circumstances in which Dr. John Owen's Exposition of Psalm cxxx. originated are peculiarly interesting. Dr. Owen himself, in a statement made to Mr. Richard Davis, who ultimately became pastor of a church in Rowel, Northamptonshire, explains the occasion which led him to a very careful examination of the fourth verse in the Psalm. Mr. Davis, being under religious impressions, had sought a conference with Owen. In the course of the conversation, Dr. Owen put the question, " Young man, pray in what manner do you think to go to God?" " Through the Mediator, sir," answered Mr. Davis. " That is easily said," replied the doctor, " but I assure you it is another thing to go to God through the Mediator than many who make use of the expression are aware of. I myself preached Christ," he continued, " some years, when I had but very little, if any, experimental acquaintance with access to God through Christ; until the Lord was pleased to visit me with sore affliction, whereby I was brought to the mouth of the grave, and under which my soul was oppressed with horror and darkness; but God graciously relieved my spirit by a powerful application of Psalm cxxx. 4, '*But there is forgiveness with thee, that thou mayest be feared,*' from whence I received special instruction, peace and comfort, in drawing near to God through the Mediator, and preached thereupon immediately after my recovery."—*William H. Goold, editor of Owen's Collected Works,* 1851.

Verse 1.—"*Out of the depths have I cried unto thee, O LORD.*" Is there not a depth of sin, and a depth of misery by reason of sin, and a depth of sorrow by reason of misery? In all which, both David was, and I, God help me, am deeply plunged; and are not these depths enough out of which to cry? And yet, perhaps, none of these depths is that which David means; but there are depths of danger—a danger of body and a danger of soul, and out of these it seems that David cried; for the danger of his body was so deep that it had brought him to death's door, and the danger of his soul so deep that it had almost brought him to the gates of despair; and had he not just cause then to say, "*Out of the depths have I cried to thee, O God*"? And yet there is a depth besides these that must help to lift us out of these—a depth of devotion, without which depth our crying out of other depths will never be heard. For devotion is a fire that puts a heat into our crying, and carries it up into *cœlum empyræum*—the heaven of fire, where God himself is. And now join all these depths together—the depth of sin, of misery, of sorrow, the depth of danger, and the depth of devotion,—and then tell me if David had not, if I have not, as just cause as ever Jonah had to say, " Out of the depths have I cried to thee, O God." Indeed, to cry out of the depths hath many considerable circumstances to move God to hear: it acknowledgeth his infinite power when no distance can hinder his assistance; it presents our own faith when no extremity can weaken our hope; it magnifies God's goodness when he, the Most High, regards the most low; it expresseth our own earnestness, seeing crying out of depths must needs be a deep cry; and if each of these singly, and by itself, be motive sufficient to move God to hear, how strong must the motive needs be when they are all united? and united they are all in crying out of the depths; and therefore now that I cry to thee out of the depths, be moved, O God, in thy great mercy to "*hear my voice.*"

It is cause enough for God not to hear some because they do not cry—cause enough not to hear some that cry because not out of the depths; but when crying and out of the depths are joined together, it was never known that ever God refused to hear; and therefore now that I cry to thee out of the depths, be pleased, O God, in thy great mercy to hear my voice.—*Sir Richard Baker, in "Meditations and Disquisitions upon the Three last Psalmes of David,"* 1639.

Verse 1.—"*Out of the depths.*" By the deep places (as all the ancients consent) is meant the deep places of afflictions, and the deep places of the heart troubled for sin. Afflictions are compared to deep waters. Ps. xviii. 16: " He drew me out of many waters." " Save me, O God, for the waters are come in unto my soul." And surely God's children are often cast into very desperate cases, and plunged into deep miseries, to the end that they may send out of a contrite and feeling heart such prayers as may mount aloft and pierce the heavens. When we are in prosperity our prayers come from our lips; and therefore the Lord is forced to cast us down, that our prayers may come from our hearts, and that our senses may be wakened from the security in which they are lying. Albeit the throne of God be most high, yet he delighteth to hear the petition of hearts that are most low, that are most cast down by the sight of sin. There is no affliction, neither any place so low (yea, if as low as the belly of the whale wherein Jonah lay) which can separate us from the love of the Lord, or stay our prayers from coming before him. Those that are farthest cast down, are not farthest from God, but are nearest unto him. God is near to a contrite heart, and it is the proper seat where his Spirit dwelleth: Isai. lxvi. 2. And thus God dealeth with us, as men do with such houses that they are minded to build sumptuously and on high; for then they dig deep grounds for the foundation. Thus God purposing to make a fair show of Daniel, and the three children in Babel; of Joseph in Egypt; of David in Israel; he first threw them into the deep waters of afflictions. Daniel is cast into the den of lions; the three children are thrown into the fiery furnace; Joseph is imprisoned; David exiled. Yet all those he exalted and made glorious temples to himself. Mark hereby the dulness of our nature, that is such, that God is forced to use sharp remedies to awaken us. Jonah lay sleeping in the ship, when the tempest of God's wrath was pursuing him: God therefore threw him into the belly of the whale, and the bottom of the deep, that from those deep places he might cry to him.

When, therefore, we are troubled by heavy sickness, or poverty, or oppressed by the tyranny of men, let us make profit and use thereof, considering that God hath cast his best children into such dangers for their profit; and that it is better to be in deep dangers praying, than on high mountains of vanity playing.—*Archibald Symson, in "A Sacred Septenarie."* 1638.

Verse 1.—*"Out of the depths."* "Depths!" oh! into what *"depths"* men can sink! How far from happiness, glory, and goodness men can fall.

There is the depth of *poverty.* A man can become utterly stripped of all earthly possessions and worldly friends! Sometimes we come upon a man, still living, but in such abject circumstances, that it strikes us as a marvel that a human being can sink lower than the beasts of the field.

Then there is the depth of *sorrow.* Billow after billow breaks over the man, friend after friend departs, lover and friend are put into darkness. All the fountains of his nature are broken up. He is like a water-logged ship, from the top waves plunging down as if into the bottom of the sea. So often in such depths, sometimes like Jonah in the whale's belly, the monster carrying him down, down, down, into darkness.

There are depths after depths of *mental darkness*, when the soul becomes more and more sorrowful, down to that very depth which is just this side of *despair.* Earth hollow, heaven empty, the air heavy, every form a deformity, all sounds discord, the past a gloom, the present a puzzle, the future a horror. One more step down, and the man will stand in the chamber of despair, the floor of which is blisteringly hot, while the air is biting cold as the polar atmosphere. To what depths the spirit of a man may fall!

But the most horrible depth into which a man's soul can descend is *sin.* Sometimes we begin on gradual slopes, and slide so swiftly that we soon reach great depths; depths in which there are horrors that are neither in poverty, nor sorrow, nor mental depression. It is sin, it is an outrage against God and ourselves. We feel that there is no bottom. Each opening depth reveals a greater deep. This is really the bottomless pit, with everlasting accumulations of speed, and perpetual lacerations as we descend. Oh, depths below depths! Oh, falls from light to gloom, from gloom to darkness! Oh, the hell of sin!

What can we do? We can simply cry, CRY, CRY! But, let us cry to God. Useless, injurious are other cries. They are mere expressions of impotency, or protests against imaginary fate. But the cry of the spirit to the Most High is a manful cry. Out of the depths of all poverty, all sorrow, all mental depression, all sin, *cry unto God!—From "The Study and the Pulpit,"* 1877.

Verse 1.—*"Out of the depths have I cried."*

> Up from the deeps, O God, I cry to thee!
> Hear my soul's prayer, hear thou her litany,
> O thou who sayest, "Come, wanderer, home to me."
>
> Up from the deeps of sorrow, wherein lie
> Dark secrets veil'd from earth's unpitying eye,
> My prayers, like star-crown'd angels, Godward fly.

From the calm bosom when in quiet hour
God's Holy Spirit reigns with largest power,
Then shall each thought in prayer's white blossom flower.

Not from life's shallows, where the waters sleep,
A dull, low marsh where stagnant vapours creep,
But ocean-voiced, deep calling unto deep.

As he of old, King David, call'd to thee,
As cries the heart of poor humanity,
" Clamavi, Domine, exaudi me ! "

C. S. Fenner.

Verse 1.—But when he crieth from the deep, he riseth from the deep, and his very cry suffereth him not to be long at the bottom.—*Augustine.*

Verse 1.—It has been well said that the verse puts before us six conditions of true prayer : it is lowly, *"out of the deep"*; fervent, *"have I called"*; direct to God himself, *"unto thee"*; reverent, *"O Lord"*; awed, *"Lord,"* a solemn title, is again used ; one's very own, *"hear my voice."*—*Neale and Littledale.*

Verse 1.—*"Have I cried."* There are many kinds and degrees of prayer in the world ; from the coldest form to the intensest agony. Every one prays ; but very few "cry." But of those who do "cry to God," the majority would say,— *"I owe it to the depths. I learnt it there. I often prayed before ; but never—till I was carried down very deep— did I cry."* "Out of the depths have I cried unto thee, O Lord." It is well worth while to go down into any "depth" to be taught to "cry."

It is not too much to say that we do not know what prayer may be till we have "cried." And we seldom rise till we have gone very deep. "I die ! I perish ! I am lost ! Help, Lord ! Help me ! Save me now ! Do it *now*, Lord, or I am lost. O Lord, hear ! O Lord, forgive ! O Lord, hearken and do ; defer not, for thine own sake, O my God ! "

In mid-day, if you are taken from the bright and sunny scenes of light, and go down into the bottom of a pit, you may see the stars, which were invisible to you in the upper air. And how many could say that things they knew not in life's noon, they have found in life's midnight, and that they owe their glimpses of glory, and their best avenues of thought, and the importunacy of prayer, and the victories of faith, to seasons when they walked in very dark places. *"Out of the depths* have I cried unto thee, O Lord."—*James Vaughan.*

Verse 1.—*"Have I cried unto thee, Jehovah."* God gave out that name Jehovah to his people to confirm their faith in the stability of his promises : Exod. iii. He who is Being himself will assuredly give being and subsistence to his promises. Being to deal with God about the promises of grace, he makes his application to him under this name : *"I call upon thee, Jehovah."*—*John Owen, in "A practical Exposition upon Psalm cxxx."*

Verse 2.—*"Lord, hear my voice,"* etc. Every prayer should have its reverent invocation, as every temple its porch. The two greatest prayers in the Old Testament—Solomon's prayer and Daniel's prayer—both have it very emphatically. And it is a very distinct part of our own perfect model : " Our Father, which art in heaven, hallowed be thy name." On our part it is deferential, and puts the mind into its proper form ; while it places the great God, whom it addresses, where he ought to be,—in the awe of his glory ; in the magnitude of his power ; in the infinitude of his wisdom and love.

Never think little of that part of your prayer : never omit, never hurry over the opening address. Do not go into his presence without a pause, or some devout ascription. *"Lord, hear my voice : let thine ears be attentive to the voice of my supplications."* True, he is always listening and waiting for his children's "cry," —far more prepared to answer, than we are to ask. And the very fact that we are praying is a proof of his attention,—for who but he put it into our hearts to make that prayer ? Nevertheless, it becomes us, and honours him, to establish, at the outset, the right relationship between a creature and his Creator ; between a child and his father : "Lord, hear my voice : let thine ears be attentive to the voice of my supplication."—*James Vaughan.*

Verse 2.—*"Lord."* Hebrew, *Adonai.* As *Jehovah* marks his unchangeable faithfulness to his promises of delivering his people, so *Adonai* his *Lordship* over all hindrances in the way of his delivering them.—*Andrew Robert Fausset, in "A Commentary, Critical, Experimental and Practical,"* 1866.

Verse 2.—*"Lord, hear my voice,"* etc. The expressions are metaphorical, and borrowed from the carriage of a parent to a child, and upon the matter his suit is this,—Lord, notice me when I pray, as a parent will notice his distressed child's cry when he is like to ruin. *"Let thine ears be attentive to the voice of my supplications;"* that goes a little further; that as a parent knowing a child to be in hazard, he will listen and hearken attentively if he can here him cry, and notice and ponder that cry, and what he cries for; so he pleaded with God, that he would be waiting on and attentive, to see and hear if a cry should come from him, and that he would affectionately ponder and notice it when he hears it.—*George Hutcheson,*—1678.

Verse 3.—*"If thou, Lord, shouldest mark iniquities,"* etc. But doth not the Lord mark iniquity? Doth not he take notice of every sin acted by any of the children of men, especially by his own children? Why, then, doth the Psalmist put it upon an *if? "If thou, Lord, shouldest mark iniquity."* 'Tis true, the Lord marks all iniquity to know it, but he doth not mark any iniquity in his children to condemn them for it: so the meaning of the Psalm is, that if the Lord should mark sin with a strict and severe eye, as a judge, to charge it upon the person sinning, no man could bear it.

The word rendered *to mark* notes, first, to watch, or to observe with strictest diligence, and is therefore in the noun rendered *a watch-tower,* upon which a man is placed to take observation of all things that are done, and of all persons that pass by, or approach and come near. A watchman placed upon a high tower is bound industriously and critically to observe all passengers and passages, all that his eye can reach. So saith the text, —If thou shouldst mark as a watchman, and eye with rigour everything that passeth from us, *" who will stand?"* that is, make good his cause in the day of his judgment and trial before thee?

Secondly, the word signifieth to keep in mind, to lay up, to have, as it were, a store and stock, a memorial or record, of such and such things by us. In that sense it is said (Gen. xxxvii. 11), " Joseph's brethen envied him; but his father observed the saying ": he marked what Joseph spake about his dreams, he laid it up, and did not let it pass away as a dream, or as a vision of the night. Thus, by *"If the Lord should mark iniquity,"* we understand—if he should treasure up our sins in his memory, and keep them by him, *" who were able to stand when accounted with?"* The Lord, in a way of grace, seeth as if he saw not, and winks at us oftentimes when we do amiss.—*Joseph Caryl.*

Verse 3.—Let thine ears be attentive to the voice of my supplication, but let not thine eyes be intentive to the stains of my sin; for *"If thou, Lord, shouldest mark iniquities, O Lord, who shall stand ?"* or who shall be able to abide it? Did not the angels fall when thou markedst their follies? Can flesh, which is but dust, be clean before thee, when the stars, which are of a far purer substance, are not? Can anything be clean in thy sight which is not as clean as thy sight? and can any cleanness be equal to thine? Alas! O Lord, we are neither angels nor stars, and how then can we stand when those fell? how can we be clean when these be impure? If thou shouldest mark what is done amiss, there would be marking-work enough for thee as long as the world lasts; for what action of man is free from stain of sin, or from defect of righteousness? Therefore, mark not anything in me, O God, that I have done, but mark that only in me which thou hast done thyself. Mark in me thine own image; and then thou mayest look upon me, and yet say still, as once thou saidst, *Et erant omnia valde bona* [" And all things were very good "].—*Sir Richard Baker.*

Verse 3 (whole verse).—We are introduced at once into all the solemnities of a criminal court. The judge is seated on the bench: the culprit is standing at the bar, charged with a capital offence: the witnesses are giving their evidence against him. The judge is listening attentively to everything which is said; and in order to assist his memory, he takes notes of the more important parts. If the Lord were to try us after this fashion, what would be the result? Suppose him seated on his throne of inflexible righteousness, taking notes, with a pen in his hand, of the transgressions which are proven against us. Nothing is omitted. Every sin is marked down with its peculiar aggravations. There is no possibility of escape from the deserved condemnation. The evidence against us is clear, and copious, and overwhelming. A thousandth part of it is sufficient to determine our doom.

The judge has no alternative but to pronounce the awful sentence. We must die a felon's death. *"If thou, Lord, shouldest mark iniquities, O Lord, who shall stand ?"* —N. M'Michael.

Verse 3.—*"If thou, Lord, shouldest mark."* If thou shouldst inquire and scrutinize, and then shouldst retain and impute : (for the Hebrew word imports both :) if thou shouldst inquire, thou wouldst find something of iniquity in the most righteous of mankind : and when thou hast found it, if thou shouldst retain it, and call him to an account for it, he could by no means free himself of the charge, or expiate the crime. Inquiring, thou wouldst easily find iniquity ; but the sinner by the most diligent inquiry will not be able to discover a ransom, and therefore will be unable to stand, will have no place on which to rest his foot, but will fall by the irresistible judgments of thy law, and the sentence of thy justice.—*Robert Leighton.*

Verse 3.—*"If thou, Lord."* He here fixes on another name of God, which is Jah : a name, though from the same root as the former, yet seldom used but to intimate and express the terrible majesty of God : " He rideth on the heavens, and is extolled by his name Jah : " Ps. lxviii. 4. He is to deal now with God about the guilt of sin : and God is represented to the soul as great and terrible, that he may know what to expect and look for, if the matter must be tried out according to the demerit of sin,—*John Owen.*

Verse 3.—*"If thou, Lord . . . O Lord."* Mark here that in this third verse he two times nameth God by *the Lord* (as he doth also in the ninth verse), showing to us hereby his earnest desire to take hold of God with both his hands. He nameth not only *Adonai*, but also *Jah* (which two signify his nature and power) ; all the qualities of God must be conjoined and concur together for us : although he be *Adonai*, yet if he be not also *Jah* we are undone.—*Archibald Symson.*

Verse 3.—*"Lord . . . Lord."* If God should show himself as Jah, no creature would be able to stand before him, who is *Adonai*, and can therefore carry out his judicial will or purpose.—*Franz Delitzsch.*

Verse 3.—*"Iniquities."* The literal meaning of the word *" iniquity "* is " a thing which is not equal," or " not fair." Whatever breaks a command of God is " not equal," It does not match with what man is, nor with what God is. It does not keep the high level of the law. It is altogether out of proportion to all that God has done. It destroys the harmony of creation. It does not rise even to the height of conscience. Still more, it mars and makes a flaw in the divine government. Therefore sin is an unequal thing, fitting nothing, disarranging everything. And it is *not fair.* It is not fair to that God upon whose empire it is a tresspass. It is not fair to your fellow-creatures, to whom it may be a very great injury. It is not fair to yourself, for your happiness lies in obedience. Therefore we call sin *" iniquity "* Or, as the Prayer-Book Version expresses the same idea, "a thing amiss," missing its proper mark. " If thou shouldest be extreme to mark what is *done amiss."*—*James Vaughan.*

Verse 3.—*"O Lord, who shall stand ?"* As soon as God manifests signs of anger, even those who appear to be the most holy adopt this language. If God should determine to deal with them according to justice, and call them to his tribunal, not one would be able to stand ; but would be compelled to fly for refuge to the mercy of God. See the confessions of Moses, Job, David, Nehemiah, Isaiah, Daniel, Paul, and others of the apostles. Hear Christ teaching his disciples to cry to the Father who is in heaven, *"Forgive us our trespasses ! "* If before God the Patriarchs, Prophets, and Apostles, although possessing unusual holiness, nevertheless fell down, and as suppliants prayed for forgiveness, what shall be done with those who add sin to sin ?—*D. H. Mollerus.*

Verses 3, 4.—These two verses contain the sum of all the Scriptures. In the third is the form of repentance, and in the fourth the mercies of the Lord. These are the two mountains, Gerizim and Ebal, mentioned in Deut. xxvii. 12, 13. These are the pillars in Solomon's Temple (1 Kings vii. 21), called Jachin and Boaz. We must, with Paul, persuade ourselves that we are come from Mount Sinai to Mount Zion, where mercy is, although some sour grapes must be eaten by the way. Jeremy tasted in his vision first a bitter fig out of one basket, then a sweet fig out of the other. In the days of Moses the waters were first bitter, then sweetened by the sweet wood. And Elisha cast in salt into the pottage of the sons of the prophets, then it became wholesome.—*Archibald Symson.*

Verses 3, 4.—As I was thus in musing and in my studies, considering how to love the Lord, and to express my love to him, that saying came in upon me : *"If thou, LORD, shouldest mark iniquities, O Lord, who shall stand ? But there is forgiveness with thee, that thou mayest be feared."* These were good words to me, especially the latter part thereof ; to wit, that there is forgiveness with thee that thou mayest be feared ; that is, as then I understood it, that he might be loved and had in reverence ; for it was thus made out to me, that the great God did set so high an esteem upon the love of his poor creatures, that rather than he would go without their love he would pardon their transgressions.—*John Bunyan.*

Verse 4.—*"But there is forgiveness with thee, that thou mayest be feared."* One would think that punishment should procure fear, and forgiveness love ; but *nemo majus diligit, quam qui maxime veretur offendere*—no man more truly loves God than he that is most fearful to offend him. " Thy mercy reacheth to the heavens, and thy faithfulness to the clouds "—that is, above all sublimities. God is glorious in all his works, but most glorious in his works of mercy ; and this may be one reason why St. Paul calls the gospel of Christ a " glorious gospel " : 1 Tim. i. 11. Solomon tells us, " It is the glory of a man to pass by an offence." Herein is God most glorious, in that he passeth by all the offences of his children. Lord, who can know thee and not love thee, know thee and not fear thee ? We fear thee for thy justice, and love thee for thy mercy ; yea, fear thee for thy mercy, and love thee for thy justice ; for thou art infinitely good in both.—*Thomas Adams.*

Verse 4.—*"But there is forgiveness with thee, that thou mayest be feared."* But is this not a mistaking in David to say, There is mercy with God, that he may be feared ; all as one to say, There is severity with him, that he may be loved ? for if we cannot love one for being severe, how should we fear him for being merciful ? Should it not, therefore, have been rather said, There is justice with thee, that thou mayest be feared ? seeing it is justice that strikes a terror and keeps in awe ; mercy breeds a boldness, and boldness cannot stand with fear, and therefore not fear with mercy. But is there not, I may say, an active fear, not to offend God, as well as a passive fear for having offended him ? and with God's mercy may well stand the active fear, though not so well, perhaps, the passive fear which is incident properly to his justice.

There is a common error in the world, to think we may be the bolder to sin because God is merciful ; but, O my soul, take heed of this error, for God's mercy is to no such purpose ; it is not to make us bold, but to make us fear : the greater his mercy is, the greater ought our fear to be, for there is mercy with him that he may be feared. Unless we fear, he may choose whether he will be merciful or no ; or rather, we may be sure he will not be merciful, seeing he hath mercy for none but for them that fear him ; and there is great reason for this, for to whom should mercy show itself but to them that need it ? and if we think we need it we will certainly fear. Oh, therefore, most gracious God, make me to fear thee ; for as thou wilt not be merciful to me unless I fear thee, so I cannot fear thee unless thou first be merciful unto me.—*Sir Richard Baker.*

Verse 4.—*"But there is forgiveness with thee, that thou mayest be feared."* Even Saul himself will lift up his voice and weep when he seeth a clear testimony of the love and undeserved kindness of David. Hast thou never beheld a condemned prisoner dissolved in tears upon the unexpected and unmerited receipt of a pardon, who all the time before was as hard as a flint ? The hammer of the law may break the icy heart of man with terrors and horrors, and yet it may remain ice still, unchanged ; but when the fire of love kindly thaweth its ice, it is changed and dissolved into water—it is no longer ice, but of another nature.—*George Swinnock.*

Verse 4.—*"But there is forgiveness with thee, that thou mayest be feared."* The Evangelical doctrine of the gratuitous forgiveness of sins does not of itself beget carelessness, as the Papists falsely allege ; but rather a true and genuine fear of God ; like as the Psalmist here shows that this is the final cause and effect of the doctrine.—*Solomon Gesner.*

Verse 4.—*"But there is forgiveness with thee,"* etc. His judgments and his wrath may make us astonished and stupefied ; but, if there be no more, they will never make us to come to God. Then if this be not sufficient, what more is requisite ? Even a sight of the Lord's mercy, for that is most forcible to allure, as the prophet saith here, and as the church of God sayeth (Cant. i. 3), "Because of the savour of thy good ointments, therefore the virgins love thee." This only is forcible to allure the sinner : for all the judgments of God, and curses of the law, will never allure him. What was the chief thing that moved the prodigal son to return home to his father ? Was it chiefly the distress, the disgrace and poverty wherewith he was burdened, or the famine that almost caused him to starve ? No, but the chief thing was this, he remembered that he had a loving father. That maketh him to resolve with an humble confession to go home. Luke xv. Even so it is with the sinner ; it is not terrors and threatenings that chiefly will move him to come to God, but the consideration of his manifold and great mercies.—*Robert Rollock.*

Verse 4.—*"But."* How significant is that word *"but!"* As if you heard justice clamouring, "Let the sinner die," and the fiends in hell howling, "Cast, him down into the fires," and conscience shrieking, "Let him perish," and nature itself groaning beneath his weight, the earth weary with carrying him, and the sun tired with shining upon the traitor, the very air sick with finding breath for cne who only spends it in disobedience to God. The man is about to be destroyed, to be swallowed up quick, when suddenly there comes this thrice-blessed *" but,"* which stops the reckless course of ruin, puts forth its strong arm bearing a golden shield between the sinner and destruction, and pronounces these words, *"But there is forgiveness with God, that he may be feared."*—*C. H. S.*

Verse 4.—*"There is a propitiation with thee,"* so some read it : Jesus Christ is the great propitiation, the ransom which God has found ; he is ever with him, as advocate for us, and through him we hope to obtain forgiveness.—*Matthew Henry.*

Verse 4.—*"Forgiveness,"* Hebrew, *selichah,* a word used only here and by Daniel once (ix. 9), and by Nehemiah (ix. 17).—*Christopher Wordsworth.*

Verse 4.—*"That thou mayest be feared."* This forgiveness, this smile of God, binds the soul to God with a beautiful fear. Fear to lose one glance of love. Fear to lose one word of kindness. Fear to be carried away from the heaven of his presence by an insidious current of wordliness. Fear of slumber. Fear of error. Fear of not enough pleasing him. Our duty, then, is to drink deep of God's forgiving love. To be filled with it is to be filled with purity, fervency, and faith. Our sins have to hide their diminished heads, and slink away through crevices, when forgiveness—when Christ—enters the soul.—*George Bowen, in "Daily Meditations,"* 1873.

Verses 4, 5, 7, 8.—David puts his soul out of all fear of God's taking this course [reckoning strictly] with poor penitent souls, by laying down this comfortable conclusion, as an indubitable truth : *"But there is forgiveness with thee, that thou mayest be feared."* That is, there is forgiveness in thy nature, thou carriest a pardoning heart in thy bosom ; yea, there is forgiveness in thy promise ; thy merciful heart doth not only incline thee to thoughts of forgiving ; but thy faithful promise binds thee to draw forth the same unto all that humbly and seasonably lay claim thereunto. Now, this foundation laid, see what superstructure this holy man raiseth (verse 5) : *"I wait for the* Lord, *my soul doth wait, and in his word do I hope."* As if he had said, Lord, I take thee at thy word, and am resolved by thy grace to wait at the door of thy promise, never to stir thence till I have my promised dole (forgiveness of my sins) sent out unto me. And this is so sweet a morsel, that he is loth to eat it alone, and therefore he sends down the dish, even to the lower end of the table, that every godly person may taste with him of it (verses 7, 8) : *"Let Israel hope in the* Lord : *for with the* Lord *there is mercy, and with him is plenteous redemption. And he shall redeem Israel from all his iniquities."* As if he had said, That which is a ground of hope to me, notwithstanding the clamour of my sins, affords as solid and firm a bottom to any true Israelites or sincere soul in the world, did he but rightly understand himself, and the mind of God in his promise. Yea, I have as strong a faith for such as [for] my own soul, and I durst pawn the eternity of my happiness upon this principle,—that God should redeem every sincere Israelite from all his iniquities.—*William Gurnall.*

Verse 5.—*"I wait for the* Lord," etc. We pronounce this a most blessed posture of the believer. It runs counter to everything that is natural, and, therefore, it is all the more a supernatural grace of the gracious soul. In the first place it is *the posture of faith.* Here is the gracious soul hanging in faith upon God in Christ Jesus ; upon the veracity of God to fulfil his promise, upon the power of God to help him in difficulty, upon the wisdom of God to counsel him in perplexity, upon the omniscience of God to guide him with his eye, and upon the omnipresence of God to cheer him with his presence, at all times and in all places, his sun and shield. Oh, have faith in God.

It is also a *prayerful posture.* The soul waiting *for* God, is the soul waiting *upon* God. The Lord often shuts us up to this waiting for his interposition on our behalf, that he may keep us waiting and watching at the foot of his cross, in earnest, believing, importunate prayer. Oh, it is the waiting *for* the Lord that keeps the soul waiting *upon* the Lord !

It is also *the posture of a patient waiting* for the Lord. There is not a more God-honouring grace of the Christian character than *patience*—a patient waiting on and for the Lord. It is that Christian grace, the fruit of the Spirit which will enable you to bear with dignity, calmness, and submission the afflictive dealings of your Heavenly Father, the rebuke of the world, and the wounding of the saints.

It is *the posture of rest.* A soul-waiting for the Lord is a soul-resting in the Lord. Waiting and resting ! Wearied with traversing in vain the wide circle of human expedients ; coming to the end of all your own wisdom, strength, and resources ; your uneasy, jaded spirit is brought into this resting posture of waiting on, and waiting for, the Lord ; and thus folds its drooping wings upon the very bosom of God. Oh, how real and instant is the rest found in Jesus ! Reposing in him, however profound the depth of the soul, however dark the clouds that drape it, or surging the waters that overwhelm it, all is sunshine and serenity within.— *Condensed from "Soul-Depths and soul-heights," by Octavius Winslow,* 1874.

Verse 5.—"*I wait for the Lord.*" *Waiting* is a great part of life's discipline, and therefore God often exercises the grace of waiting. *Waiting* has four purposes. It practises the patience of faith. It gives time for preparation for the coming gift. It makes the blessing the sweeter when it arrives. And it shows the sovereignty of God,—to give just *when* and just *as* he pleases. It may be difficult to define exactly what the Psalmist had in his mind when he said, " I wait *for the Lord,* my soul doth wait, and in his word do I hope. My soul waiteth *for the Lord* more than they that watch for the morning." It may have been the Messiah, whose coming was a thing close at hand to the mind of the ancient Jews, just as the Second Advent is to us.

It may have been some special interposition of divine Providence. But more probably, looking at the place which it occupies, and at the whole tenor of the Psalm, and its line of thought, " The Lord " he waited for so intently was that full sense of safety, peace, and love which God's felt presence gives, and which is, indeed, nothing else but the coming of the Lord most sensibly and palpably into an anxious and longing heart.

The picture of *the waiting man* is a striking one. It is as one on the ridge of a journey, looking onward on his way, standing on tiptoe, and therefore needing something to lean on, and to support him. "*I wait for the Lord,*"—spiritually, with my deepest thoughts—in the very centre of my being—"*I wait for the Lord, my soul doth wait.*" And I rest, I stay myself on what thou, O Lord, hast said, " My soul doth wait, and *in his word* do I hope."

In all your *waitings* remember two things : Let it not be so much the event which you wait for, as the Lord *of* the event ; the Lord *in* the event. And take care that you have a promise underneath you.—" In his word do I hope,"—else " waiting " will be too much for you, and after all it may be in vain.—*James Vaughan.*

Verse 5.—"*I wait . . . I hope.*" Waiting and hoping ever attend the same thing. No man will wait at all for that which he hath no hope of, and he who hath hope will wait always. He gives not over waiting, till he gives over hoping. The object of hope is some future good, but the act of hoping is a present good, and that is present pay to bear our charges in waiting. The word implies both a patient waiting and a hopeful trusting. So Christ expounds it (Matt. xii. 21), rendering that of the prophet (Isa. xlii. 4), " The isles shall wait for his law," thus, " In his name shall the Gentiles trust."—*Joseph Caryl.*

Verses 5, 6.—In these two verses he doth four times make mention of his hope, and attendance upon God and his word, to let us see how sure a hold we should take on God, and with how many temptations our faith is assaulted, when we can see no reason thereof. Nothing will bear us up but hope. *Spero meliora.* What encourageth husbandmen and mariners against the surges and waves of the sea, and evil weather, but hope of better times ? What comforteth a sick man in time of sickness, but hope of health ? or a poor man in his distress, but hope of riches ? or a prisoner, but hope of liberty ? or a banished man, but hope to come home ? All these hopes may fail, as oftentimes wanting a warrant. Albeit a physician may encourage a sick man by his fair words, yet he cannot give him an assurance of his recovery, for his health dependeth on God : friends and courtiers may promise poor men relief, but all men are liars; only God is faithful who hath promised. Therefore let us fix our faith on God, and our hope in God ; for he will stand by his promise. No man hath hoped in him in vain, neither was ever any disappointed of his hope.—*Archibald Symson.*

Verses 5, 7.—Faith doth ultimately centre in the Deity. God himself in his glorious nature, is the ultimate object whereunto our faith is resolved. The promise, simply considered, is not the object of trust, but God in the promise ; and from the consideration of that we ascend to the Deity, and cast our anchor there. " Hope in the word " is the first act, but succeeded by hoping in the Lord : *"In his word do I hope"* : that is not all ; but, *"Let Israel hope in the Lord."* That is the ultimate object of faith, wherein the essence of our happiness consists, and that is God. God himself is the true and full portion of the soul.—*Stephen Charnock, 1628—1680.*

Verse 6.—*"My soul waiteth for the LORD."* And now, my soul, what do I live for but only to wait upon God, and to wait for God ? To wait upon him, to do him service, to wait for him, to be enabled to do him better service ; to wait upon him, as being Lord of all ; and to wait for him, as being the rewarder of all ; to wait upon him whose service is better than any other command, and to wait for him whose expectation is better than any other possession. Let, others, therefore, wait upon the world, wait for the world ; I, O God, will wait upon thee, for thee, seeing I find more true contentment in this waiting than all the world can give me in enjoying ; for how can I doubt of receiving reward by my waiting for thee when my waiting for thee is itself the reward of my waiting upon thee ? And therefore my soul waiteth ; for if my soul did not wait, what were my waiting worth ? no more than I were worth myself, if I had not a soul ; but my soul puts a life into my waiting, and makes it become a living sacrifice. Alas, my frail body is very unfit to make a waiter : it rather needs to be waited upon itself : it must have so much resting, so often leave to be excused from waiting, that if God should have no other waiters than bodies, he would be left oftentimes to wait upon himself ; but my soul is *Divinæ particula auræ* [a portion of the Divine breath], endued with all qualities fit for a waiter ; and hath it not received its abilities, O God, from thee ? And therefore my soul waiteth, and is so intentive in the service that it waits *"more than they that watch for the morning."*—*Sir Richard Baker.*

Verse 6.—*Hammond* thus renders the verse :—" My soul hasteneth to the Lord from the guards in the morning, the guards in the morning."

Verse 6.—*"More than they that watch for the morning."* Look, as the weary sentinel that is wet and stiff with cold and the dews of the night, or as the porters that watched in the Temple, the Levites, were waiting for the daylight, so " more than they that watch for the morning " was he waiting for some glimpse of God's favour. Though he do not presently ease us of our smart or gratify our desires, yet we are to wait upon God. In time we shall have a good answer. God's delays are not denials. Day will come at length, though the weary sentinel or watchman counts it long first ; so God will come at length ; he will not be at our beck. We have deserved nothing, but must wait for him in the diligent use of means ; as Benhadad's servants watched for the word " brother," or anything of kindness to drop from the king of Israel.—*Thomas Manton.*

Verse 6.—*"More than they that watch for the morning."* How many in the hallowed precincts of the Temple turned with anxious eye to the east, for the first red streak over Moab's mountains that gave intimation of approaching day ; yet it was not for deliverance they waited, but for the accustomed hour when the morning sacrifice could be offered, and the soul relieved of its gratitude in the hymn of thanksgiving, and of the burden of its sorrows and sins by prayer, and could draw that strength from renewed intercourse with heaven, that would enable it in this world to breathe the spirit and engage in the beneficent and holy deeds of a better.—*Robert Nisbet.*

Verse 6.—*"I say, more than they that watch for the morning,"* for must there not be a proportion between the cause and effect ? If my cause of watching be more than theirs, should not my watching be more than theirs ? They that watch for the morning have good cause, no doubt, to watch for it, that it may bring them the light of day ; but have not I more cause to watch, who wait for the light that lighteth every one that comes into the world ? They that watch for the morning wait but for the rising of the sun to free them from darkness, that hinders their sight ; but I wait for the rising of the Sun of righteousness to dispel the horrors of darkness that affright my soul.   They watch for the morning that they may have light to walk by ; but I wait for the Dayspring from on High to give light to them that sit in darkness and in the shadow of death, and to guide our feet into the way of peace.   But though there may be question made of the intentiveness of our watching, yet of the extensiveness there can be none, for they that watch for the morning watch at most but a piece of the night ; but I have watched whole days and whole nights, and may I not then justly say, I wait *more* than they that watch for the morning ?— *Sir Richard Baker.*

Verse 6.—Holy men like Simeon, and devout priests like Zacharias, there were, amidst this seething people, who, brooding, longing, waiting, chanted to themselves day by day the words of the Psalmist, "*My soul waiteth for the Lord more than they that watch for the morning.*"   As lovers that watch for the appointed coming, and start at the quivering of a leaf, the flight of a bird, or the humming of a bee, and grow weary of the tense strain, so did the Jews watch for their Deliverer.   It is one of the most piteous sights of history, especially when we reflect that he came,—and they knew him not.—*Henry Ward Beecher, in his "Life of Jesus the Christ."*

Verse 6.—"*Watch.*"   We do injustice to that good and happy word, "*watch,*" when we take it as watching against ; against a danger ; against a coming evil.   It will bear that interpretation ; but it is a far higher, and better, and more filial thing to watch *for* a coming good than to watch *against* an approaching evil.

So, "*watching for,*" we send up our arrows of prayer, and then look trustingly to see where they are coming down again.   So, "*watching for,*" we listen, in silence, for the familiar voice we love.   So, "*watching for,*" we expect the Bridegroom !

Take care, that as one always standing on the eve,—not of danger, but of happiness,—your "*watch*" be the "*watch*" of love, and confidence, and cheerful hope.— *James Vaughan.*

Verse 6.—In the year 1830, on the night preceding the 1st of August, the day the slaves in our West Indian Colonies were to come into possession of the freedom promised them, many of them, we are told, never went to bed at all.   Thousands, and tens of thousands of them, assembled in their places of worship, engaging in devotional duties, and singing praises to God, waiting for the first streak of the light of the morning of that day on which they were to be made free.   Some of their number were sent to the hills, from which they might obtain the first view of the coming day, and, by a signal, intimate to their brethren down in the valley the dawn of the day that was to make them men, and no longer, as they had hitherto been, mere goods and chattels,—men with souls that God had created to live for ever. How eagerly must these men have watched for the morning.—*T. W. Aveling, in "The Biblical Museum,"* 1872.

Verse 7.—"*Let Israel hope in the Lord.*"   This title is applied to all the Lord's people ; it sets forth *their dignity*—they are PRINCES ; it refers to *their experience*— they wrestle with God in prayer, and they prevail.   Despondency does not become a prince, much less a Christian.   Our God is " THE GOD OF HOPE"; and we should hope in him.   Israel should hope in his mercy, in his patience, in his provision, in his plenteous redemption.   They should hope for light in darkness ; for strength in weakness ; for direction in perplexity ; for deliverance in danger ; for victory in conflict ; and for triumph in death.

They should hope in God confidently, because he hath promised ; prayerfully, for he loves to hear from us ; obediently, for his precepts are to be observed by us ; and constantly, for he is always the same.—*James Smith* (1802—1862), *in "The Believer's Daily Remembrancer."*

Verse 7.—"*Let Israel hope in the Lord.*"   Whereas, in all preceding verses of the Psalm, the thoughts, the sorrows, the prayer, the penitence, the awe, the waiting, the watching, were all personal and confined to himself ; here a great change has taken place, and it is no longer "*I,*" but "*Israel*"; all Israel.   " Let *Israel* hope in the Lord : for with the Lord there is mercy, and with him is plenteous redemption. And he shall redeem *Israel* from all his iniquities."   This is as it always ought to be. . . . It is the genius of our religion to go forth to multitudes.—*James Vaughan.*

Verse 7.—"*For with the Lord there is mercy.*"   Mercy has been shown to us, but it dwells in God.   It is one of his perfections.   The exercise of it is his delight. There is mercy with the Lord in all its *fulness ;* he never was more merciful than now, neither will he ever be.   There is mercy with the Lord in all its *tenderness,* he is full of compassion, his bowels are troubled for us, his tender mercies are over us. There is mercy with him in all its *variety*, it suits every case.

Here is mercy that receives sinners, mercy that restores backsliders, mercy that keeps believers. Here is the mercy that pardons sin, that introduces to the enjoyment of all gospel privileges, and that blesses the praying soul far beyond its expectations. With the Lord there is mercy, and he loves to display it, he is ready to impart it, he has determined to exalt and glorify it.

There is mercy with the Lord ; this should encourage the miserable to approach him ; this informs the fearful that they need bring nothing to induce him to bless them ; this calls upon backsliders to return to him ; and this is calculated to cheer the tried Christian, under all his troubles and distresses. Remember, mercy is like God, it is infinite and eternal. Mercy is always on the throne. Mercy may be obtained by any sinner.—*James Smith.*

Verse 7.—*"With him is plenteous redemption."* This plenteous redemption leaves behind it no more relics of sin than Moses left hoofs of beasts behind him in Egypt. It redeems not only from the fault, but from the punishment ; not only *a tanto*, but *a toto* [not only from such, but also from all sin and penalty] ; not only from the sense but from the fear of pain ; and in the fault, not only from the guilt, but from the stain ; not only from being censured, but from being questioned. Or is it meant by a plenteous redemption that not only he leads captivity captive, but gives gifts unto men ? For what good is it to a prisoner to have his pardon, if he be kept in prison still for not paying his fees ? but if the prince, together with the pardon, sends also a largess that may maintain him when he is set at liberty, this, indeed, is a plenteous redemption ; and such is the redemption that God's mercy procures unto us. It not only delivers us from a dungeon, but puts us in possession of a palace ; it not only frees us from eating bread in the sweat of our brows, but it restores us to Paradise, where all fruits are growing of their own accord ; it not only clears us from being captives, but endears us to be children ; and not only children, but heirs ; and not only heirs, but co-heirs with Christ ; and who can deny this to be a plenteous redemption ? Or is it said a plenteous redemption in regard of the price that was paid to redeem us ? for we are redeemed with a price, not of gold or precious stones, but with the precious blood of the Lamb slain before the foundation of the world. For God so loved the world that he gave his only Son to be a ransom for us ; and this I am sure is a plenteous redemption.—*Sir Richard Baker.*

Verse 7.—*"Plenteous redemption,"* or more literally, " redemption plenteously." He calls it plenteous, as Luther says, because such is the straitness of our heart, the slenderness of our hopes, the weakness of our faith, that it far exceeds all our capacity, all our petitions and all our desires.—*J. J. Stewart Perowne.*

Verses 7, 8.—This Psalm containeth an evident prophecy of the Messias ; in setting forth his plentiful redemption, and that he should redeem Israel, that is, the Church, from all their sins. Which words in their full sense were used by an angel to Joseph, in telling him that the child's name should be JESUS, " because he should save his people from their sins " : Matt. i. 21.—*Sir John Hayward* (1560—1627), *in "David's Tears."* 1623.

Verse 8.—*"He will redeem."* HE emphatic, He alone, for none other can.—*J. J. Stewart Perowne.*

Verse 8.—*"From his iniquities."* Not only from the punishment (as Ewald and Hupfeld). The redemption includes the forgiveness of sins, the breaking of the power and dominion of sin, and the setting free from all the consequences of sin.—*J. J. Stewart Perowne.*

Verse 8.—*"Iniquities."* Iniquities of *eye*—has conscience no voice there ? Is no iniquity ever practised by your eye ? Let conscience speak. Iniquity of *ear*—is there no iniquity that enters into your heart through the ear ? You cannot listen to a conversation in the street without iniquity entering into your heart through what Bunyan calls " Ear-gate." Iniquity of *lip*—do you always keep your tongue as with a bridle ? Do your lips never drop anything unbecoming the gospel ? Is there no carnal conversation, no angry word at home, no expression that you would not like the saints of God to hear ? What ! your lips always kept so strictly that there is never a single expression dropped from them which you would be ashamed to utter before an assembly of God's people ? Iniquity of *thought*—If your eyes, ears, and lips are clean, is there no iniquity of thought ? What ! in that workshop within, no iniquitous suggestions, no evil workings? Oh, how ignorant must we be of ourselves, if we feel that we have no iniquity of thought! Iniquity of *imagination*—does not fancy sometimes bring before you scenes of sensuality in which your carnal nature is vile enough to revel? Iniquity of *memory*—does not memory sometimes bring back sins you formerly committed, and your evil nature is perhaps base enough to desire they had been greater? Iniquity of *feeling*—no enmity against God's people ever working? no pride of heart? no covetousness? no hypocrisy? no self-righteousness? no sensuality? no base thought that you cannot disclose even to your bosom friend? But here is the blessed promise—a promise only suited to Israel: for all but Israel lose sight of their iniquities, and justify themselves in self-righteousness. None but Israel feel and confess their iniquities, and therefore to Israel is the promise of redemption limited: "He shall redeem *Israel* from all his iniquities." What! all? Yes. Not *one* left? No, not a trace, not a shade, not the shadow of a shade; all buried, all gone, all swallowed up, all blotted out, all freely pardoned, all cast behind God's back.—*Joseph C. Philpot*, 1802—1869.

Verse 8.—What a graceful and appropriate conclusion of this comprehensive and instructive Psalm! Like the sun, it dawns veiled in cloud, it sets bathed in splendour; it opens with soul-depth, it closes with soul-height. Redemption from all iniquity! It baffles the most descriptive language, and distances the highest measurement. The most vivid imagination faints in conceiving it, the most glowing image fails in portraying it, and faith droops her wing in the bold attempt to scale its summit. *"He shall redeem Israel from all his iniquities."* The verse is a word-painting of man restored, and of Paradise regained.—*Octavius Winslow.*

HINTS TO PREACHERS.

Verse 1.—The assertion of an experienced believer. I. I have cried—that is, I have earnestly, constantly, truthfully prayed. II. I have cried only unto thee. Nothing could draw me to other confidences, or make me despair of thee. III. I have cried in distress. At my worst, temporally or spiritually, I have cried out of the depths. IV. I therefore infer—that I am thy child, no hypocrite, no apostate; and that thou hast heard and wilt hear me evermore.

Verse 1.—I. What we are to understand by "the depths." Great misery and distress. II. How men get into "the depths." By sin and unbelief. III. What gracious souls do when in "the depths." Cry unto the Lord. IV. How the Lord lifts praying souls out of "the depths": "He shall redeem," etc., verse 8.—*W. H. J. P*

Verse 1.—I. In the pit. II. The morning-star seen: "Thee, O Lord." III. Prayer flutters up "out of the depths."—*W. B. H.*

Verses 1, 2.—I. The depths from which prayer may rise. 1. Of affliction. 2. Of conviction. 3. Of desertion. II. The height to which it may ascend. 1. To the hearing of God. 2. To a patient hearing. "Hear my voice." 3. To an attentive hearing.

Or, I. We should pray at all times II. We should pray that our prayers may be heard. III. We should pray until we know we are heard. IV. We should pray in faith that when heard we have the thing we have asked. "That which thou hast prayed to me against the King of Assyria I have heard." God had heard. That was enough. It was the death of Sennacherib and the overthrow of his host.—*G. R.*

Verses 1, 2.—Consider, I. The Psalmist's condition in the light of a warning. Evidently, through sin, he came into the depths; see verses 3 and 4. Learn, 1. The need of watchfulness on the part of all. 2. That backsliding will, sooner or later, bring great trouble of soul. II. His sometime continuance in that condition, in the light of a Divine judgment: "I *have* cried." Certainly his first cry had not brought deliverance. 1. The realization of pardon is a Divine work, dependent upon God's pleasure. Ps. lxxxv. 8. 2. But he will not always nor often speak pardon at the first asking; for He will make His people reverence his holiness, feel

the bitterness of sinning, learn caution, etc.   III. His conduct while in that condition
in the light of a direction.   He, 1. Seeks deliverance only of God.   2. Is intensely
earnest in his application : " I cried."   3. Is importunate in his pleading : " Hear
my voice," etc.—*J. F.*

Verse 2.—Attention from God to us—how to gain it.   I. Let us plead the name
which commands attention.   II. Let us ourselves pay attention to God's word.
III. Let us give earnest attention to what we ask, and how we ask.   IV. Let us
attentively watch for a reply.

Verse 2.—"*Lord, hear my voice.*"   I. Though it be faint by reason of distance—
hear it.   II. Though it be broken because of my distress—hear it.   III. Though
it be unworthy on account of my iniquities—hear it.—*W. H. J. P.*

Verse 3.—I. The supposition : " If thou, Lord, shouldst mark iniquities."
1. It is scriptural.   2. It is reasonable.   If God is not indifferent towards men, he
must observe their sins.   If he is holy, he must manifest indignation against sin.
If he is the Creator of conscience, he must certainly uphold its verdict against sin.
If he is not wholly on the side of sin, how can he fail to avenge the mischiefs and
miseries sin has caused ?   II. The question it suggests : " Who shall stand ?"   A
question, 1. Not difficult to answer.   2. Of solemn import to all.   3. Which ought
to be seriously pondered without delay.   III. The possibility it hints at.   " If thou,
Lord."   The " if " hints at the possibility that God may not mark sin.   The
possibility, 1. Is reasonable, providing it can be without damage to God's righteousness ; for the Creator and Preserver of men cannot delight in condemning and
punishing.   2. Is a God-honouring reality, through the blood of Christ, Rom.
iii. 21—26.   3. Becomes a glorious certainty in the experience of penitent and
believing souls.—*J. F.*

Verses 3, 4.—I. The Confession.   He could not stand.   II. The Confidence.
" There is forgiveness."   III. The Consequence.   " That thou mayest be feared."

Verses 3, 4.—I. The fearful supposition.   II. The solemn interrogation.   III. The
Divine consolation.—*W. J.*

Verse 4. — *Forgiveness with God.*   I. The proofs of it.   1. Divine declarations.
2. Invitations and promises, Isa. i. 18.   3. The bestowment of pardon so effectually
as to give assurance and joy.   2 Sam. xii. 13.   Ps. xxxii. 5.   Luke vii. 47-8.   1 John
ii. 12.   II. The reason of it.   1. In God's nature there is the desire to forgive ;
the gift of Christ is sufficient evidence for it.   2. But, the text speaks not so much
of a desire as it asserts the existence of a forgiveness being " with " God, therefore
ready to be dispensed.   The blood of Christ is the reason (Col. i. 14) ; by it the
disposition to forgive righteously manifests itself in the forgiving act ; Rom. iii. 25, 26.
3. Hence, forgiveness for all who believe is sure : Rom. iii. 25 ; 1 John ii. 1, 2.
III. The result of its realization : " That thou mayest be feared " : with a reverential
fear, and spiritual worship.   1. The possibility of forgiveness begets in an anxious
soul true penitence, as opposed to terror and despair.   2. The hope of receiving it
begets earnest seeking and prayerfulness.   3. A believing reception of it gives peace
and rest, and, exciting grateful love, leads to spiritual worship and filial service.—
J. F.

Verse 4.—"*There is forgiveness.*"   I. It is needed.   II. God alone can give it.
III. It may be had.   IV. We may know that we have it.

Verse 4.—I. A most cheering announcement : " There is forgiveness with thee."
1. A fact certain.   2. A fact in the present tense.   3. A fact which arises out of
God himself.   4. A fact stated in general terms.   5. A fact to be meditated upon
with delight.   II. A most admirable design : " That thou mayest be feared."
1. Very contrary to the abuse made of it by rebels, triflers, and procrastinators.
2. Very different from the pretended fears of legalists.   3. No pardon, no fear of
God—devils, reprobates.   4. No pardon, none survive to fear him.   5. But the
means of pardon encourage faith, repentance, prayer ; and the receipt of pardon
creates love, suggests obedience, inflames zeal.

Verse 4.—See " Spurgeon's Sermons," No. 351 : " Plenteous Redemption."

Verse 4.—Tender Light.   I. The Angel by the Throne : " Forgiveness with
Thee."   II. The shadow that enhances his sweet majesty : " If," " But."   III. The
homage resultant from his ministry ; universal from highest to least.—*W. B. H.*

Verses 5, 6.—Three postures : Waiting, Hoping, Watching.

Verses 5, 6.—1. The seeking sinner.   2. The Christian mourner.   3. The loving
intercessor.   4. The spiritual labourer.   5. The dying believer.—*W. J.*

Verses 5, 6.—I. We are to wait on God.   1. By faith : " In his word do I hope."

2. By prayer. Prayer can wait when it has a promise to rest upon. II. We are to wait for God : " I wait for the Lord." " My soul waiteth for the Lord more," etc. 1. Because he has his own time for giving. 2. Because what he gives is worth waiting for.—*G. R.*

Verse 6.—"*More than they.*" I. For the darker sorrow his absence causes. II. For the richer splendour his coming must bring. III. For the greater might of our indwelling love.—*W. B. H.*

Verse 6.—I. A long, dark night : The Lord absent. II. An eager, hopeful watcher : Waiting the Lord's return. III. A bright, blessed morning : The time of the Lord's appearing.—*W. H. J. P.*

Verse 7.—Redeeming grace the sole hope of the holiest.—*W. B. H.*

Verse 7.—I. A divine exhortation : " Let Israel hope in the LORD." II. A spiritual reason : "For with the LORD there is mercy," etc. III. A gracious promise : " He shall redeem Israel from all his iniquities."—*J. C. Philpot.*

Verses 7, 8.—It is our wisdom to have personal dealings with God. I. The first exercise of faith must be upon the Lord himself. This is the natural order, the necessary order, easiest, wisest, and most profitable order. Begin where all begins. II. Exercises of faith about other things must still be in connection with the Lord. Mercy—" with the Lord." Plenteous redemption " with him." III. Exercises of faith, whatever their object, must *all* settle on him. " HE shall redeem," etc.

Verse 8.—I. The Redemption : " From all iniquities." II. The Redeemer : "The Lord." See Titus ii. 14. III. The Redeemed : " Israel."—*W. H. J. P.*

PSALM CXXXI.

TITLE.—A Song of Degrees of David. *It is both by David and of David: he is the author and the subject of it, and many incidents of his life may be employed to illustrate it. Comparing all the Psalms to gems, we should liken this to a pearl: how beautifully it will adorn the neck of patience. It is one of the shortest Psalms to read, but one of the longest to learn. It speaks of a young child, but it contains the experience of a man in Christ. Lowliness and humility are here seen in connection with a sanctified heart, a will subdued to the mind of God, and a hope looking to the Lord alone. Happy is the man who can without falsehood use these words as his own; for he wears about him the likeness of his Lord, who said, "I am meek and lowly in heart." The Psalm is in advance of all the Songs of Degrees which have preceded it; for lowliness is one of the highest attainments in the divine life. There are also steps in this Song of Degrees: it is a short ladder, if we count the words; but yet it rises to a great height, reaching from deep humility to fixed confidence. Le Blanc thinks that this is a song of the Israelites who returned from Babylon with humbled hearts, weaned from their idols. At any rate, after any spiritual captivity let it be the expression of our hearts.*

EXPOSITION.

LORD, my heart is not haughty, nor mine eyes lofty: neither do I exercise myself in great matters, or in things too high for me.

2 Surely I have behaved and quieted myself, as a child that is weaned of his mother: my soul *is* even as a weaned child.

3 Let Israel hope in the LORD from henceforth and for ever.

1. *"LORD, my heart is not haughty."* The Psalm deals with the Lord, and is a solitary colloquy with him, not a discourse before men. We have a sufficient audience when we speak with the Lord, and we may say to him many things which were not proper for the ears of men. The holy man makes his appeal to Jehovah, who alone knows the heart: a man should be slow to do this upon any matter, for the Lord is not to be trifled with; and when anyone ventures on such an appeal he should be sure of his case. He begins with his heart, for that is the centre of our nature, and if pride be there it defiles everything; just as mire in the spring causes mud in all the streams. It is a grand thing for a man to know his own heart so as to be able to speak before the Lord about it. It is beyond all things deceitful and desperately wicked, who can know it? Who can know it unless taught by the Spirit of God? It is a still greater thing if, upon searching himself thoroughly, a man can solemnly protest unto the Omniscient One that his heart is not haughty: that is to say, neither proud in his opinion of himself, contemptuous to others, nor self-righteous before the Lord; neither boastful of the past, proud of the present, nor ambitious for the future. *"Nor mine eyes lofty."* What the heart desires the eyes look for. Where the desires run the glances usually follow. This holy man felt that he did not seek after elevated places where he might gratify his self-esteem, neither did he look down upon others as being his inferiors. A proud look the Lord hates; and in this all men are agreed with him; yea, even the proud themselves hate haughtiness in the gestures of others. Lofty eyes are so generally hateful that haughty men have been known to avoid the manners natural to the proud in order to escape the ill-will of their fellows. The pride which apes humility always takes care to cast its eyes downward, since every man's consciousness tells him that contemptuous glances are the sure ensigns of a boastful spirit. In Psalm cxxi. David lifted up his eyes to the hills; but here he declares that they were not lifted up in any other sense. When the heart is right, and the eyes are right, the whole man is on the road to a healthy and happy condition. Let us take care that we do not use the language of this Psalm unless, indeed, it be true as to ourselves; for there is no worse pride than that which claims humility when it does not possess it.

"Neither do I exercise myself in great matters." As a private man he did not usurp the power of the king or devise plots against him : he minded his own business, and left others to mind theirs. As a thoughtful man he did not pry into things unrevealed ; he was not speculative, self-conceited or opinionated. As a secular person he did not thrust himself into the priesthood as Saul had done before him, and as Uzziah did after him. It is well so to exercise ourselves unto godliness that we know our true sphere, and diligently keep to it. Many through wishing to be great have failed to be good : they were not content to adorn the lowly stations which the Lord appointed them, and so they have rushed at grandeur and power; and found destruction where they looked for honour. *"Or in things too high for me."* High things may suit others who are of greater stature, and yet they may be quite unfit for us. A man does well to know his own size. Ascertaining his own capacity, he will be foolish if he aims at that which is beyond his reach, straining himself, and thus injuring himself. Such is the vanity of many men that if a work be within their range they despise it, and think it beneath them : the only service which they are willing to undertake is that to which they have never been called, and for which they are by no means qualified. What a haughty heart must he have who will not serve God at all unless he may be trusted with five talents at the least ! His looks are indeed lofty who disdains to be a light among his poor friends and neighbours here below, but demands to be created a star of the first magnitude to shine among the upper ranks, and to be admired by gazing crowds. It is just on God's part that those who wish to be everything should end in being nothing. It is a righteous retribution from God when every matter turns out to be too great for the man who would only handle great matters, and every thing proves to be too high for the man who exercised himself in things too high for him. Lord, make us lowly, keep us lowly, fix us for ever in lowliness. Help us to be in such a case that the confession of this verse may come from our lips as a truthful utterance which we dare make before the Judge of all the earth.

2. *"Surely I have behaved and quieted myself."* The original bears somewhat of the form of an oath, and therefore our translators exhibited great judgment in introducing the word "surely"; it is not a literal version, but it correctly gives the meaning. The Psalmist had been upon his best behaviour, and had smoothed down the roughnesses of his self-will ; by holy effort he had mastered his own spirit, so that towards God he was not rebellious, even as towards man he was not haughty. It is no easy thing to quiet yourself : sooner may a man calm the sea, or rule the wind, or tame a tiger, than quiet himself. We are clamorous, uneasy, petulant ; and nothing but grace can make us quiet under afflictions, irritations, and disappointments. *"As a child that is weaned of his mother."* He had become as subdued and content as a child whose weaning is fully accomplished. The Easterns put off the time of weaning far later than we do, and we may conclude that the process grows none the easier by being postponed. At last there must be an end to the suckling period, and then a battle begins : the child is denied his comfort, and therefore frets and worries, flies into pets, or sinks into sulks. It is facing its first great sorrow, and it is in sore distress. Yet time brings not only alleviations, but the ending of the conflict ; the boy ere long is quite content to find his nourishment at the table with his brothers, and he feels no lingering wish to return to those dear fountains from which he once sustained his life. He is no longer angry with his mother, but buries his head in that very bosom after which he pined so grievously : he is weaned *on* his mother rather than *from* her.

> " My soul doth like a weanling rest,
>   I cease to weep ;
> So mother's lap, though dried her breast,
>   Can lull to sleep."

To the weaned child his mother is his comfort though she has denied him comfort. It is a blessed mark of growth out of spiritual infancy when we can forego the joys which once appeared to be essential, and can find our solace in him who denies them to us : then we behave manfully, and every childish complaint is hushed. If the Lord removes our dearest delight we bow to his will without a murmuring thought ; in fact, we find a delight in giving up our delight. This is no spontaneous fruit of nature, but a well-tended product of divine grace : it grows out of humility and lowliness, and it is the stem upon which peace blooms as a fair flower. *"My soul is even as a weaned child"*; or it may be read, "as a weaned child on me my soul," as if his soul leaned upon him in mute submission, neither boasting nor complaining. It is not every child of God who arrives at this weanedness speedily. Some are sucklings when they ought to be fathers; others are hard to wean, and cry, and fight, and rage against their heavenly parent's discipline. When we think ourselves safely through the weaning, we sadly discover that the old appetites are rather wounded than slain, and we begin crying again for the breasts which we had given up, It is easy to begin shouting before we are out of the wood, and no doubt hundreds have sung this Psalm long before they have understood it. Blessed are those afflictions which subdue our affections, which wean us from self-sufficiency, which educate us into Christian manliness, which teach us to love God not merely when he comforts us, but even when he tries us. Well might the sacred poet repeat his figure of the weaned child; it is worthy of admiration and imitation; it is doubly desirable and difficult of attainment. Such weanedness from self springs from the gentle humility declared in the former verse, and partly accounts for its existence. If pride is gone, submission will be sure to follow; and, on the other hand, if pride is to be driven out, self must also be vanquished.

3. "*Let Israel hope in the* LORD *from henceforth and for ever.*" See how lovingly a man who is weaned from self thinks of others! David thinks of his people, and loses himself in his care for Israel. How he prizes the grace of hope! He has given up the things which are seen, and therefore he values the treasures which are not seen except by the eyes of hope. There is room for the largest hope when self is gone, ground for eternal hope when transient things no longer hold the mastery of our spirits. This verse is the lesson of experience: a man of God who had been taught to renounce the world and live upon the Lord alone, here exhorts all his friends and companions to do the same. He found it a blessed thing to live by hope, and therefore he would have all his kinsmen do the same. Let all the nation hope, let all their hope be in Jehovah, let them at once begin hoping " from henceforth," and let them continue hoping "for ever." Weaning takes the child out of a temporary condition into a state in which he will continue for the rest of his life: to rise above the world is to enter upon a heavenly existence which can never end. When we cease to hanker for the world we begin hoping in the Lord. O Lord, as a parent weans a child, so do thou wean me, and then shall I fix all my hope on thee alone.

EXPLANATORY NOTES AND QUAINT SAYINGS.

Whole Psalm.—This little song is inscribed לְדָוִד because it is like an echo of the answer (2 Sam. vi. 21 sq.) with which David repelled the mocking observation of Michal when he danced before the Ark in a linen ephod, and therefore not in kingly attire, but in the common raiment of the priests. *I esteem myself still less than I now show it, and I appear base in mine own eyes.* In general David is the model of the state of mind which the poet expresses here. He did not push himself forward, but suffered himself to be drawn forth out of seclusion. He did not take possession of the throne violently; but after Samuel has anointed him, he willingly and patiently traverses the long, thorny, circuitous way of deep abasement, until he receives from God's hand that which God's promise had assured to him. The persecution by Saul lasted about ten years, and his kingship in Hebron, at first only incipient, seven years and a half. He left it entirely to God to remove Saul and Ishbosheth. He let Shimei curse. He left Jerusalem before Absalom. Submission to God's guidance, resignation to his dispensations, contentment with that which was allotted to him, are the distinguishing traits of his noble character. —*Franz Delitzsch.*

Whole Psalm.—Psalm cxxx. is a Song of Forgiveness; Psalm cxxxi. is a Song of Humility: the former celebrates the blessedness of the man whose transgressions are pardoned; the latter celebrates the blessedness of the man who is of a meek and lowly spirit. Forgiveness *should* humble us. Forgiveness implies sin; and should not the sinner clothe himself with humility? and when not for any desert of his, but simply by the free grace of Heaven, his sins have been pardoned, should he not bind the garments of humility still more closely about him? The man who is of a nature at once sincere and sweet, will be even more humbled by the sense of an undeserved forgiveness than by the memory of the sins from which it has cleansed him. Very fitly, therefore, does the Psalm of humility follow the Psalm which sings of the Divine lovingkindness and tender mercy.—*Samuel Cox.*

Whole Psalm.—This Psalm, which records the meek and humble spirit of those who are the true worshippers of the Temple, doubtless belongs, as its title announces, to the time of David. It is exactly in the spirit of that humble thanksgiving made by him, after the divine revelation by Nathan of the future blessings of his posterity (1 Chron. xxii. 9—11); and forms a most appropriate introduction to the following Psalm, the theme of which is evidently the dedication of the Temple.—*John Jebb.*

Verse 1.—*"Lord, my heart is not haughty."* For the truth of his plea he appealeth to God; and from all those who are affected like David, God will accept of the appeal.

Firstly. He could in truth of heart appeal to God: *"Lord, my heart is not haughty."* He appealeth to him who knoweth all things. "Lord, from whom nothing is hid, thou knowest that this is the very disposition of my soul. If I have anything, it is from thee; it is thy providence which brought me from following the ewes great with young to feed and govern thy people." Such a holy man would not rashly invoke God, and take his holy name in vain; but knowing his integrity, durst call God to witness. The saints are wont to do so upon like occasions; as Peter (John xxi. 17); "Lord, thou knowest all things; thou knowest that I love thee." They know they have a God that will not be deceived with any shows, and that he knoweth and approveth them for such as he findeth them to be.

Secondly. From those that are affected like David, God will accept the appeal; for in the account of God we are that which we sincerely desire and endeavour to be, and that which is the general course and tenor of our lives, though there be some intermixture of failing. David saith, *"Lord, my heart is not haughty";* and yet he was not altogether free from pride. His profession respecteth his sincere purpose and constant endeavour, and the predominant disposition of his soul. God himself confirmeth such appeals by his own testimony: 1 Kings xv. 5, "My servant David did that which was right in the eyes of the Lord, neither departed from all that which he had commanded him, save only in the matter of Uriah" . . . . . By all this it is shown that the plea of sincerity is allowed by God, though there be some mixture of failings and weaknesses.

Thirdly. Is not this boasting like the Pharisee? Luke xviii. 9, "God, I thank thee, I am not like other men." If David were thus humble, why doth he speak of it? Is he not guilty of pride while he seemeth to speak against pride?

This is spoken either as, (1) A necessary vindication; or (2) A necessary instruction. 1. As a necessary vindication against the censures and calumnies of his adversaries. Saul's courtiers accused him as aspiring after the kingdom; yea, his own brother taxed him with pride when he came first abroad: 1 Sam. xvii. 28, "I know thy pride, and the naughtiness of thine heart; for thou art come down that thou mightest see the battle." If his brother would calumniate his actions, much more might others. Now it is for the honour of God that his children, as they would not commit a fault, so they should not be under the suspicion of it; therefore he appealeth to God. 2. A necessary instruction; for whatsoever David said or wrote here, he said or wrote by the inspiration of the Holy Ghost, that Israel may learn how to hope in God. Herein David is a notable pattern of duty both to superiors and inferiors.—*Thomas Manton.*

Verse 1.—*"My heart is not haughty."* Albeit pride is a common vice, which attendeth vain man in every degree of excellency and supposed worth in him, yet the grace of God is able to keep humble a wise, rich, and potent man, yea, to keep humble a king and conqueror; for it is no less a person than David who saith here, *"Lord, my heart is not haughty."*—*David Dickson.*

Verse 1.—*"Nor mine eyes lofty."* Pride has its seat in the heart; but its principal expression is in the eye. The eye is the mirror of the soul; and from it mental and moral characteristics may be ascertained, with no small degree of precision. What a world of meaning is sometimes concentrated in a single glance! But of all the passions, pride is most clearly revealed in the eyes. There can scarcely be a mistake here. We are all familiar with a class of phrases, which run in pairs. We speak of sin and misery; holiness and happiness; peace and prosperity; war and desolation. Among these may be numbered, the proud heart and the haughty look. " There is a generation, Oh, how lofty are their eyes ! and their eyelids are lifted up." " Him that hath an high look and a proud heart I will not suffer." . . . A proud look is one of the seven things which are an abomination unto the Lord. It is said of him, " Thou wilt save the afflicted people ; but wilt bring down high looks." And hence David makes the acknowledgment : Lord, thou knowest all things ; thou knowest that pride has no existence in my heart. Thou knowest that no pride flashes forth from mine eyes.—*N. M'Michael.*

Verse 1.—"*Nor mine eyes lofty.*" He had neither a scornful nor an aspiring look. "*My eyes are not lofty,*" either to look with envy upon those that are above me, or to look with disdain upon those that are below me. Where there is a proud heart, there is commonly a proud look (Prov. vi. 17) ; but the humble publican will not so much as lift up his eyes.—*Matthew Henry.*

Verse 1.—"*Neither have I occupied myself,*" etc. One cannot admire enough the prayer of Anselm, a profound divine of our own country, in the eleventh century. " I do not seek, O Lord, to penetrate thy depths. I by no means think my intellect equal to them : but I long to understand in some degree thy truth, which my heart believes and loves. For I do not seek to understand that I may believe ; but I believe, that I may understand."—*N. M'Michael.*

Verse 1.—"*Great matters . . . things too high for me.*" The great and wonderful things meant are God's secret purposes, and sovereign means for their accomplishment, in which man is not called to co-operate, but to acquiesce. As David practised this forbearance by the patient expectation of the kingdom, both before and after the death of Saul, so he here describes it as a characteristic of the chosen people.— *Joseph Addison Alexander.*

Verses 1, 2.—Our Father is our superior ; it is fit therefore that we be resigned to his will. " Honour thy father and thy mother " (Exod. xx. 12) ; how much more our heavenly Father ! (Heb. xii. 9). See David's spirit in the case : "*LORD, my heart is not haughty,*" etc. : Ps. cxxxi. 1, 2. As if he had said, " I will keep within my own sphere ; I will not stretch beyond my line, in prescribing to God ; but submit to his will, '*as a weaned child,*' taken from its dear breasts" : intimating that he would wean himself from whatever God removed from him. How patiently did Isaac permit himself to be bound and sacrificed by Abraham ! Gen. xxii. 9. And yet he was of age and strength sufficient to have struggled for his life, being twenty-five years old ; but that holy young man abhorred the thought of striving with his father. And shall not we resign ourselves to our God and Father in Christ Jesus ?—*John Singleton (— 1706), in "The Morning Exercises."*

Verses 1, 2.—It has always been my aim, and it is my prayer, to have no plan as regards myself ; well assured as I am that the place where the Saviour sees meet to place me must ever be the best place for me.—*Robert Murray M'Cheyne,* 1813—1843.

Verse 2.—"*Surely I have behaved and quieted myself,*" etc. Oh, how sapless and insipid doth the world grow to the soul that is making meet for heaven ! " I am crucified to the world, and this world to me." Gal. vi. 14. In vain doth this harlot think to allure me by her attractions of profit and pleasure. " Surely I have behaved and quieted myself, as a child that is weaned of his mother : my soul is even as a weaned child." There is no more relish in these gaudy things to my palate, than in the white of an egg ; everything grows a burden to me, were it not my duty to follow my calling, and be thankful for my enjoyments. Methinks, I have my wife, husband, and dearest relations, as if I had none ; I weep for outward losses, as if I wept not ; rejoice in comforts below as if I rejoiced not (1 Cor. vii. 29, 30) ; my thoughts are taken up with other objects. The men of the world slight me, many seem to be weary of me, and I am as weary of them. It is none of these earthly things that my heart is set upon ; my soul is set on things above, my treasure is in heaven, and I would have my heart there also : I have sent before me all my goods into another country, and am shortly for removing ; and when I look about me, I see a bare, empty house, and am ready to say with Monica, What do I here ? my father, husband, mother (Jerusalem above), my brethren, sisters, best friends are above. Methinks, I grudge the world any portion of my heart, and think not these temporal visible things worth a cast of my eye compared with things invisible and eternal : 2 Cor. iv. 18.—*Oliver Heywood,* 1629—1702.

Verse 2 (*first clause*).—"*If I have not restrained,*" or quieted, and compelled to silence, "*my soul.*" It is a Hebrew phrase of asseveration and of swearing : as if he would say, I have thoroughly imposed silence on my soul, that it should be tranquil, and should bear patiently the divinely imposed cross. Just as in the following Psalm we hear a like form of asseveration : " If I will come into the tabernacle of my house," meaning " I will not come," etc.—*Solomon Gesner.*

Verse 2.—"*I have behaved and quieted myself, as a child that is weaned.*" Weaned from what ? Self-sufficiency, self-will, self-seeking. From creatures and the things of the world—not, indeed, as to their use, but as to any dependence upon them for his happiness and portion. . . . . Yet this experience is no easy attainment. The very form of expression—" I have behaved and *quieted* myself," reminds us of some risings which were with difficulty subdued. There is a difference here between Christ and Christians. In him the exercise of grace encountered no adverse principles ; but in them it meets with constant opposition. The flesh lusteth against the spirit ; and when we would do good, evil is present with us ; hence the warfare within. So it is with "the child that is weaned." The task to the mother is trying and troublesome. The infant cries, and seems to sob out his heart. He thinks it very hard in her, and knows not what she means by her seeming cruelty, and the mother's fondness renders all her firmness necessary to keep her at the process ; and sometimes she also weeps at the importunity of his dear looks, and big tears, and stretched-out hands. But it must be done, and therefore, though she pities, she perseveres ; and after a while he is soothed and satisfied, forgets the breast, and no longer feels even a hankering after his former pleasure. But how is the weaning of the child accomplished ? By embittering the member to his lips ; by the removal of the object in the absence and concealment of the mother ; by the substitution of other food ; by the influence of time. So it is with us. We love the world, and it deceives us. We depend on creatures, and they fail us, and pierce us through with many sorrows. We enter forbidden paths, and follow after our lovers ; and our way is hedged up with thorns ; and we then say, " Return unto thy rest, O my soul ; and now, Lord, what wait I for ? My hope is in thee." The enjoyment of a greater good subdues the relish of a less. What are the indulgences of sin, or the dissipations of the world to one who is abundantly satisfied with the goodness of God's house, and is made to drink of the river of his pleasures ? —*William Jay* (1769—1853), *in "Evening Exercises for the Closet."*

Verse 2.—"*As a child that is weaned of his mother.*" Though the weaned child has not what it would have, or what it naturally most desireth, the milk of the breast—yet it is contented with what the mother giveth—it rests upon her love and provision. So are we to be content with what providence alloweth us : Heb. xiii. 5, " Let your conversation be without covetousness, and be content with such things as ye have"; and Phil. iv. 11, " I have learned, in whatsover state I am, therewith to be content." Whatever pleaseth our heavenly Father should please us. The child that is put from the breast to a harder diet is yet contented at last. The child doth not prescribe what it will eat, drink or put on. Children are in no care for enlarging possessions, heaping up riches, aspiring after dignities and honours ; but meekly take what is provided for them. The child, when it has lost the food which nature provideth for it, is not solicitous, but wholly referreth itself to the mother, hangeth upon the mother. So for everything whatsoever should we depend upon God, refer ourselves to God, and expect all things from him : Ps. lxii. 5, " My soul, wait thou only upon God ; for my expectation is from him." With such a simplicity of submission should we rest and depend upon God. Let us take heed of being over wise and provident for ourselves, but let us trust our Father which is in heaven, and refer ourselves to his wise and holy government.— *Thomas Manton.*

Verse 2.—"*As a child that is weaned of his mother.*" Weaned from the world, the riches, honours, pleasures, and profits of it ; as well as from nature, from self, from his own righteousness, and all dependence upon it ; and as a child that is weaned from the breast wholly depends on its nurse for sustenance, so did he wholly depend upon God, his providence, grace, and strength ; and as to the kingdom, he had no more covetous desires after it than a weaned child has to the breast, and was very willing to wait the due time for the enjoyment of it. The Targum has it, " as one weaned on the breasts of its mother, I am strengthened in the law." This is to be understood not of a child whilst weaning, when it is usually peevish, fretful, and froward, but when it is weaned, and is quiet and easy in its mother's arms without the breast.—*John Gill.*

Verse 2.—"*My soul is even as a weaned child.*" In its *nature*, weanedness of

soul differs essentially from that disgust with the world, to which its ill-usage and
meanness sometimes give rise.   It is one thing to be angry with the world, or ashamed
of it, and another to be weaned from it.   Alter the world, ennoble it, and many a
proud mind that now despises, would court it.   It is different also from that weariness
of spirit which generally follows a free indulgence in earthly enjoyments.   There
is such a thing as wearing out the affections.   Solomon appears to have done this
at one period of his life.   " I have not a wish left," said a well-known sensualist
of our own country, who had drunk as deeply as he could drink of the world's cup.
" Were all the earth contains spread out before me, I do not know a thing I would
take the trouble of putting out my hand to reach."

This weanedness of soul presupposes a power left in the soul of loving and
desiring.   It is not the destruction of its appetite, but the controlling and changing
of it.   A weaned child still hungers, but it hungers no more after the food that
once delighted it ; it is quiet without it ; it can feed on other things : so a soul
weaned from the world, still pants as much as ever for food and happiness, but it
no longer seeks them in worldly things, or desires to do so.   There is nothing in the
world that it feels necessary for its happiness.   This thing in it it loves, and that
thing it values ; but it knows that it can do without them, and it is ready to do
without them whenever God pleases.

Let us inquire now into *the sources of this frame of mind*—how we get it.   One
thing is certain—it is not our work.   We do not bring ourselves to it.   No infant
weans itself.   The truth is, it is God that must wean us from the world.   We shall
never leave it of our own accord.   It is God's own right hand that must draw us
from it.   And how ?   The figure in the text will partly tell us.   1. *By embittering
the world to us.*   2. At other times *the Lord removes from us the thing we love.*   3. But
he weans us most from the earth *by giving us better food.*—*Condensed from a Sermon
by Charles Bradley, entitled "Weanedness of Soul,"* 1836.

Verse 2.—*"As a weaned child."*   That is, meek, modest, humble, submissive,
simple, etc.   See Matt. xviii. 1, 2, 3, 4.—*Henry Ainsworth,* —1622.

Verse 2.—Here is David's picture of himself . . . Observe, the *"child"*—which
is drawn for us to copy—is *"weaned":* the process is complete ; it has been truly
disciplined ; the lesson is learned ; and now it rests in its " weaning."   The whole
image expresses a repose which follows a struggle.   *"Surely I have behaved and
quieted myself, as a child that is weaned of his mother";* or, more literally, *"on* his
mother"; now content to lie still on the very place of its privation,—*"* as a child
that is weaned on his mother."

That obedience would be a tame and valueless thing, which was not the
consequence of quiet control.   A mere apathetic state is the very opposite of obedience
that may be truly so called.   But this is the point of the similitude,—there has
been a distress, and a battle, and a self-victory ; and now the stilled will is hushed
into submission and contentment ; ready to forego what is most liked, and to take
just whatever is given it—*"a weaned child."*

I do not believe that it was ever the intention of God that any man should so
merge and lose his will in the Divine, that he should have no distinct will of his
own.   There have been many who have tried to attain this annihilation of will ;
and they have made it the great aim and end of life.   But the character of the
dispensation does not allow it.   I do not believe it to be a possible thing ; and if it
were possible, I do not believe that it would be after the mind of God.   It is not
man's present relation to his Maker.   None of the saints in the Bible did more
than submit a strong existing will.   The Lord Jesus Christ himself did no more.
" What shall I say ?   Father, save me from this hour ; but for this cause came
I unto this hour.   Father, glorify thy name.   Not my will, but thine be done."
Evidently two things—" My will," " Thy will."   It was an instantly and perfectly
subjugated will,—nevertheless, a will.

And this is what is required of us ; and what the nature of our manhood, and the
provisions of our religion have to assume.   A will, decidedly a will : the more
decided the will, the stronger the character, and the greater the man.   But a will
that is always being given up, separated, conformed, constantly, increasingly
conformed.   The unity of the two wills is heaven.—*Condensed from a Sermon by
James Vaughan.*

Verse 3.—*"Let Israel hope in the* LORD."   After the example, therefore, of the
King of Israel, who thus demeaned himself in his afflictions, lowly, contented, and

resigned, casting all his care upon the Father who cared for him, and patiently waiting his time for deliverance and salvation ; after this their example and pattern, let his faithful people hope and trust, not in themselves, their wisdom, or their power, but in Jehovah alone, who will not fail to exalt them, as he hath already exalted their Redeemer, if they do but follow his steps.—*George Horne.*

Verse 3.—*"Let Israel hope in the* LORD." Though David could himself wait patiently and quietly for the crown designed him, yet perhaps Israel, the people whose darling he was, would be ready to attempt something in favour of him before the time ; he therefore endeavours to quiet them too, and bids them " *hope in the* LORD " that *they* should see a happy change of the face of affairs in due time. Thus " it is good to hope, and quietly to wait for the salvation of the Lord."—*Matthew Henry.*

Verse 3.—*"Let Israel hope in the* LORD," etc. Remember that he is *Jehovah.* 1. Wise to plan. 2. Good to purpose. 3. Strong to execute, and that he will withhold no good thing from them that walk uprightly. 4. Trust *"from henceforth."* If you have not begun before, begin now. 5. And do not be weary ; trust *"for ever."* Your case can never be out of the reach of God's power and mercy.—*Adam Clarke.*

HINTS TO PREACHERS.

Verse 1.—*Humility.* I. A profession which ought to befit every child of God. II. A profession which nevertheless many children of God cannot truthfully make. Point out the prevalence of pride and ambition even in the church. III. A profession which can only be justified through the possession of the spirit of Christ (Matt. xi. 29, 30 ; xviii. 1—5).—*C. A. D.*

Verse 2.—The soul is as a weaned child : I. In conversion. II. In sanctification, which is a continual weaning from the world and sin. III. In bereavement. IV. In affliction of every kind. V. In death.—*G. R.*

Verse 2.—I. The soul has to be weaned as well as the body. 1. It is first nourished by others. 2. It is afterwards thrown upon its own resources. II. The soul is weaned from one thing by giving its attention to another. 1. From worldly things by heavenly. 2. From self-righteousness by the righteousness of another. 3. From sin to holiness. 4. From the world to Christ. 5. From self to God.—*G. R.*

Verse 2.—I. A desirable condition : " As a weaned child." II. A difficult task—to subdue and quiet self. III. A delightful result : " Surely . . . . my soul is as a weaned child."—*W. H. J. P.*

Verse 2. — I. Soul - fretfulness : weak, dishonourable, rebellious. II. Soul-government ; throne often abdicated ; God gives each the sceptre of self-rule ; necessary to successful life. III. Soul-quiet ; its sweetness ; its power. Come, Holy Spirit, breathe it upon us !—*W. B. H.*

Verse 2.—See " Spurgeon's Sermons," No. 1,210 : " The Weaned Child."

Verses 2, 3.—The weaned child hoping in the Lord : I. The first weaning of the soul, the grand event of a man's history. II. The joy in the Lord that springs up in every weaned soul : " My soul is even as a weaned child ; let Israel hope in the Lord from henceforth and for ever." III. The daily weaning of the soul through life. IV. The earnest desires and the fruitful work of every weaned soul. —*A. Moody Stuart.*

Verse 3.—I. The encouragement to hope in God. 1. As a covenant God, " the God of Israel." 2. As a covenant-keeping God : " From henceforth," etc. II. The effect of this hope. 1. The humility and dependence in the first verse. 2. The contentment and weaning in the second verse. Would Israel be thus humble and obedient as a little child ? " Let Israel hope," etc.—*G. R.*

Verse 3.—*The Voice of Hope heard in the Calm.* I. Calmed souls appreciate God. Quiet favours contemplation. God's majesty, perfection, and praise so discovered. II. Calmed souls confide in God ; seen to be so worthy of trust. III. Calmed souls look fearlessly into eternity ; " from henceforth and for ever."—*W. B. H.*

Verse 3.—*Hope on, hope ever.* I. For the past warrants such confidence. II. For the present demands such confidence. III. For the future will justify such confidence.—*W. H. J. P.*

PSALM CXXXII.

TITLE.—A Song of Degrees. *A joyful song indeed: let all pilgrims to the New Jerusalem sing it often. The degrees or ascents are very visible; the theme ascends step by step from " afflictions " to a " crown," from " remember David," to "I will make the horn of David to bud." The latter half is like the over-arching sky bending above " the fields of the wood " which are found in the resolves and prayers of the former portion.*

DIVISION.—*Our translators have rightly divided this Psalm. It contains a statement of David's anxious care to build a house for the Lord (verses 1 to 7); a prayer at the removal of the ark (verses 8 to 10); and a pleading of the divine covenant and its promises (verses 11 to 18).*

EXPOSITION.

LORD, remember David, *and* all his afflictions:

2 How he sware unto the LORD, *and* vowed unto the mighty *God* of Jacob;

3 Surely I will not come into the tabernacle of my house, nor go up into my bed;

4 I will not give sleep to mine eyes, *or* slumber to mine eyelids,

5 Until I find out a place for the LORD, an habitation for the mighty *God* of Jacob.

6 Lo, we heard of it at Ephratah; we found it in the fields of the wood.

7 We will go into his tabernacles; we will worship at his footstool.

1. *"LORD, remember David, and all his afflictions."* With David the covenant was made, and therefore his name is pleaded on behalf of his descendants, and the people who would be blessed by his dynasty. Jehovah, who changes not, will never forget one of his servants, or fail to keep his covenant; yet for this thing he is to be entreated. That which we are assured the Lord will do must, nevertheless, be made a matter of prayer. The request is that the Lord would *remember*, and this is a word full of meaning. We know that the Lord remembered Noah, and assuaged the flood; he remembered Abraham, and sent Lot out of Sodom; he remembered Rachel, and Hannah, and gave them children; he remembered his mercy to the house of Israel, and delivered his people. That is a choice song wherein we sing, " He *remembered us* in our low estate: for his mercy endureth for ever "; and that is a notable prayer, " Lord, remember me." The plea is urged with God that he would bless the family of David for the sake of their progenitor; how much stronger is our master-argument in prayer that God would deal well with us for Jesus' sake ! David had no personal merit; the plea is based upon the covenant graciously made with him : but Jesus has deserts which are his own, and of boundless merit—these we may urge without hesitation. When the Lord was angry with the reigning prince, the people cried, " Lord, remember David "; and when they needed any special blessing, again they sang, " Lord, remember David." This was good pleading, but it was not so good as ours, which runs on this wise, " Lord, remember *Jesus*, and all his afflictions."

The *afflictions* of David here meant were those which came upon him as a godly man in his endeavours to maintain the worship of Jehovah, and to provide for its decent and suitable celebration. There was always an ungodly party in the nation, and these persons were never slow to slander, hinder, and molest the servant of the Lord. Whatever were David's faults, he kept true to the one, only, living, and true God; and for this he was a speckled bird among monarchs. Since he zealously delighted in the worship of Jehovah, his God, he was despised and ridiculed by those who could not understand his enthusiasm. God will never forget what his people suffer for his sake. No doubt innumerable blessings descend upon families and nations through the godly lives and patient sufferings of the saints. We cannot be saved by the merits of others, but beyond all question we are benefited by their virtues. Paul saith, " God is not unrighteous to forget your work and labour of love, which ye have showed toward his name." Under the New Testament dispensation, as well as under the Old, there is a full reward for the righteous. That reward frequently comes upon their descendants rather than upon themselves : they sow, and their successors reap. We may at this day pray—Lord, remember the martyrs and confessors of our race, who suffered for thy name's sake, and bless our people and nation with gospel grace for our fathers' sakes.

2. *"How he sware unto the* LORD, *and vowed unto the mighty God of Jacob."* Moved by intense devotion, David expressed his resolve in the form of a solemn vow, which was sealed with an oath. The fewer of such vows the better under a dispensation whose great Representative has said, " swear not at all." Perhaps even in this case it had been wiser to have left the pious resolve in the hands of God in the form of a prayer ; for the vow was not actually fulfilled as intended, since the Lord forbade David to build him a temple. We had better not swear to do anything before we know the Lord's mind about it, and then we shall not need to swear. The instance of David's vow shows that vows are allowable, but it does not prove that they are desirable. Probably David went too far in his words, and it is well that the Lord did not hold him to the letter of his bond, but accepted the will for the deed, and the meaning of his promise instead of the literal sense of it. David imitated Jacob, that great maker of vows at Bethel, and upon him rested the blessing pronounced on Jacob by Isaac, " God Almighty bless thee " (Gen. xxviii. 3), which was remembered by the patriarch on his death-bed, when he spoke of " the mighty God of Jacob." God is mighty to hear us, and to help us in performing our vow. We should be full of awe at the idea of making any promise to the Mighty God : to dare to trifle with him would be grievous indeed. It is observable that affliction led both David and Jacob into covenant dealings with the Lord : many vows are made in anguish of soul. We may also remark that if the votive obligations of David are to be remembered of the Lord, much more are the suretiship engagements of the Lord Jesus before the mind of the great Lord, to whom our soul turns in the hour of our distress.

Note, upon this verse, that Jehovah was the God of Jacob, the same God evermore ; that he had this for his attribute, that he is mighty—mighty to succour his Jacobs who put their trust in him, though their afflictions be many. He is, moreover, specially *the Mighty One* of his people ; he is the God of Jacob in a sense in which he is not the God of unbelievers. So here we have three points concerning our God :—*name,* Jehovah ; *attribute,* mighty ; *special relationship,* "mighty God of Jacob." He it is who is asked to remember David and his trials, and there is a plea for that blessing in each one of the three points.

3. *"Surely I will not come into the tabernacle of my house, nor go up into my bed."* Our translators give the meaning though not the literal form, of David's vow, which ran thus, " If I go "—" If I go up," etc. This was an elliptical form of imprecation, implying more than it expressed, and having therefore about it a mystery which made it all the more solemn. David would not take his ease in his house, nor his rest in his bed, till he had determined upon a place for the worship of Jehovah. The ark had been neglected, the Tabernacle had fallen into disrespect ; he would find the ark, and build for it a suitable house ; he felt that he could not take pleasure in his own palace till this was done. David meant well, but he spake more than he could carry out. His language was hyperbolical, and the Lord knew what he meant : zeal does not always measure its terms, for it is not thoughtful of the criticisms of men, but is carried away with love to the Lord, who reads the hearts of his people. David would not think himself housed till he had built a house for the Lord, nor would he reckon himself rested till he had said, " Arise, O Lord, into thy rest." Alas, we have many around us who will never carry their care for the Lord's worship too far ! No fear of their being indiscreet ! They are housed and bedded, and as for the Lord, his people may meet in a barn, or never meet at all, it will be all the same to them. Observe that Jacob in his vow spoke of the stone being God's house, and David's vow also deals with a house for God.

4. *"I will not give sleep to mine eyes, or slumber to mine eyelids."* He could not enjoy sleep till he had done his best to provide a place for the ark. It is a strong expression, and it is not to be coolly discussed by us. Remember that the man was all on fire, and he was writing poetry also, and therefore his language is not

that which we should employ in cold blood. Everybody can see what he means, and how intensely he means it. Oh, that many more were seized with sleeplessness because the house of the Lord lies waste! They can slumber fast enough and not even disturb themselves with a dream, though the cause of God should be brought to the lowest ebb by their covetousness. What is to become of those who have no care about divine things, and never give a thought to the claims of their God?

5. "*Until I find out a place for the* LORD, *an habitation for the mighty God of Jacob.*" He resolved to find a place where Jehovah would allow his worship to be celebrated, a house where God would fix the symbol of his presence, and commune with his people. At that time, in all David's land, there was no proper place for that ark whereon the Lord had placed the mercy-seat, where prayer could be offered, and where the manifested glory shone forth. All things had fallen into decay, and the outward forms of public worship were too much disregarded; hence the King resolves to be first and foremost in establishing a better order of things.

Yet one cannot help remembering that the holy resolve of David gave to a place and a house much more importance than the Lord himself ever attached to such matters. This is indicated in Nathan's message from the Lord to the king—" Go and tell my servant David, Thus saith the Lord, Shalt thou build me an house for me to dwell in? Whereas I have not dwelt in any house since the time that I brought up the children of Israel out of Egypt, even to this day, but have walked in a tent and in a tabernacle. In all the places wherein I have walked with all the children of Israel, spake I a word with any of the tribes of Israel, whom I commanded to feed my people Israel, saying, Why build ye not me an house of cedar?" Stephen in his inspired speech puts the matter plainly: "Solomon built him an house. Howbeit the Most High dwelleth not in temples made with hands." It is a striking fact that true religion never flourished more in Israel than before the temple was built, and that from the day of the erection of that magnificent house the spirit of godliness declined. Good men may have on their hearts matters which seem to them of chief importance, and it may be acceptable with God that they should seek to carry them out; and yet in his infinite wisdom he may judge it best to prevent their executing their designs. God does not measure his people's actions by their wisdom or want of wisdom, but by the sincere desire for his glory which has led up to them. David's resolution, though he was not allowed to fulfil it, brought a blessing upon him: the Lord promised to build the house of David, because he had desired to build the house of the Lord. Moreover, the King was allowed to prepare the treasure for the erection of the glorious edifice which was built by his son and successor. The Lord shows the acceptance of what we desire to do by permitting us to do something else which his infinite mind judges to be fitter for us, and more honourable to himself.

6. Meanwhile, where was the habitation of God among men? He was wont to shine forth from between the cherubim, but where was the ark? It was like a hidden thing, a stranger in its own land. "*Lo, we heard of it at Ephratah.*" Rumours came that it was somewhere in the land of Ephraim, in a temporary lodging; rather an object of dread than of delight. Is it not wonderful that so renowned a symbol of the presence of the Lord should be lingering in neglect—a neglect so great that it was remarkable that we should have heard of its whereabouts at all? When a man begins to think upon God and his service it is comforting that the gospel is heard of. Considering the opposition which it has encountered it is marvellous that it should be heard of, and heard of in a place remote from the central city; but yet we are sorrowful that it is only in connection with some poor despised place that we do hear of it. What is Ephratah? Who at this time knows where it was? How could the ark have remained there so long?

David instituted a search for the ark. It had to be hunted for high and low; and at last at Kirjath-jearim, the forest-city, he came upon it. How often do souls find Christ and his salvation in out-of-the-way places! What matters where we meet with him so long as we do behold him, and find life in him? That is a blessed Eureka which is embedded in our text—" *we found it.*" The matter began with hearing, led on to a search, and concluded in a joyful find. "*We found it in the fields of the wood.*" Alas that there should be no room for the Lord in the palaces of kings, so that he must needs take to the woods. If Christ be in a wood he will yet be found of those who seek for him. He is as near in the rustic home, embowered among the trees, as in the open streets of the city; yea, he will answer prayer offered from the heart of the black forest where the lone traveller seems out of all hope of hearing. The text presents us with an instance of one whose heart was set upon finding the place where God would meet with him ; this made him quick of hearing, and so the cheering news soon reached him. The tidings renewed his ardour, and led him to stick at no difficulties in his search ; and so it came to pass that, where he could hardly have expected it, he lighted upon the treasure which he so much prized.

7. *"We will go into his tabernacles."* Having found the place where he dwells we will hasten thereto. He has many dwellings in one in the various courts of his house, and each of these shall receive the reverence due : in each the priest shall offer for us the appointed service ; and our hearts shall go where our bodies may not enter. David is not alone, he is represented as having sought for the ark with others, for so the word *"we"* implies ; and now they are glad to attend him in his pilgrimage to the chosen shrine, saying, *"We* found it, *we* will go." Because these are the Lord's courts we will resort to them. *"We will worship at his footstool."* The best ordered earthly house can be no more than the footstool of so great a King. His ark can only reveal the glories of his feet, according to his promise that he will make the place of his feet glorious : yet thither will we hasten with joy, in glad companionship, and there will we adore him. Where Jehovah is, there shall he be worshipped. It is well not only to go to the Lord's house, but to *worship* there : we do but profane his tabernacles if we enter them for any other purpose.

Before leaving this verse let us note the ascent of this Psalm of degrees—" we heard. . . . we found . . . we will go . . . we will worship."

8 Arise, O LORD, into thy rest ; thou, and the ark of thy strength.

9 Let thy priests be clothed with righteousness ; and let thy saints shout for joy.

10 For thy servant David's sake turn not away the face of thine anointed.

8. In these three verses we see the finders of the ark removing it to its appointed place, using a formula somewhat like to that used by Moses when he said, " Rise up, Lord," and again, " Return, O Lord, unto the many thousands of Israel." The ark had been long upon the move, and no fit place had been found for it in Canaan, but now devout men have prepared a temple, and they sing, *"Arise, O LORD, into thy rest ; thou, and the ark of thy strength."* They hoped that now the covenant symbol had found a permanent abode—a rest, and they trusted that Jehovah would now abide with it for ever. Vain would it be for the ark to be settled if the Lord did not continue with it, and perpetually shine forth from between the cherubim. Unless the Lord shall rest with us there is no rest for us ; unless the ark of his strength abide with us we are ourselves without strength. The ark of the covenant is here mentioned by a name which it well deserved ; for in its captivity it smote its captors, and broke their gods, and when it was brought back it guarded its own honour by the death of those who dared to treat it with disrespect. The power of God was thus connected with the sacred chest. Reverently, therefore did Solomon pray concerning it as he besought the living God to consecrate the temple by his presence. It is the Lord and the covenant, or rather say the covenant Jehovah whose presence we desire in our assemblies, and this presence is the strength of his people. Oh that the Lord would indeed abide in all the churches, and cause his power to be revealed in Zion.

9. *"Let thy priests be clothed with righteousness."* No garment is so resplendent as that of a holy character. In this glorious robe our great High-priest is evermore arrayed, and he would have all his people adorned in the same manner. Then only are priests fit to appear before the Lord, and to minister for the profit of the people, when their lives are dignified with goodness. They must ever remember that they are God's priests, and should therefore wear the livery of their Lord, which is holiness : they are not only to have righteousness, but to be clothed with it, so that upon every part of them righteousness shall be conspicuous. Whoever looks upon God's servants should see holiness if they see nothing else. Now, this righteousness of the ministers of the temple is prayed for in connection with the presence of the Lord ; and this instructs us that holiness is only to be found among those who commune with God, and only comes to them through his visitation of their spirits. God will dwell among a holy people : and on the other hand, where God is the people become holy.

"And let thy saints shout for joy." Holiness and happiness go together ; where the one is found, the other ought never to be far away. Holy persons have a right

to great and demonstrative joy : they may shout because of it. Since they are saints, and thy saints, and thou hast come to dwell with them, O Lord, thou hast made it their duty to rejoice, and to let others know of their joy. The sentence, while it may read as a permit, is also a precept : saints are commanded to rejoice in the Lord. Happy religion which makes it a duty to be glad ! Where righteousness is the clothing, joy may well be the occupation.

10. *"For thy servant David's sake turn not away the face of thine anointed."* King Solomon was praying, and here the people pray for him that his face may not be turned away, or that he may not be refused an audience. It is a dreadful thing to have our face turned away from God, or to have his face turned away from us. If we are anointed of the Spirit the Lord will look upon us with favour. Specially is this true of HIM who represents us, and is on our behalf the *Christ*—the truly anointed of the Lord. Jesus is both our David and God's anointed ; in him is found in fulness that which David received in measure. For his sake all those who are anointed in him are accepted. God blessed Solomon and succeeding kings, for David's sake ; and he will bless us for Jesus' sake. How condescending was the Son of the Highest to take upon himself the form of a *servant*, to be anointed for us, and to go in before the mercy-seat to plead on our behalf ! The Psalm sings of the ark, and it may well remind us of the going in of the anointed priest within the veil : all depended upon his acceptance, and therefore well do the people pray, " Turn not away the face of thine anointed."

Thus, in these three verses, we have a prayer for the temple, the ark, the priests, the Levites, the people, and the king : in each petition there is a fulness of meaning well worthy of careful thought. We cannot plead too much in detail ; the fault of most prayers is their indefiniteness. In God's house and worship everything needs a blessing, and every person connected therewith needs it continually. As David vowed and prayed when he was minded to house the ark, so now the prayer is continued when the temple is consecrated, and the Lord deigns to fill it with his glory. We shall never have done praying till we have done needing.

11 The LORD hath sworn *in* truth unto David ; he will not turn from it ; Of the fruit of thy body will I set upon thy throne.

12 If thy children will keep my covenant and my testimony that I shall teach them, their children shall also sit upon thy throne for evermore.

13 For the LORD hath chosen Zion ; he hath desired *it* for his habitation.

14 This *is* my rest for ever : here will I dwell ; for I have desired it.

15 I will abundantly bless her provision : I will satisfy her poor with bread.

16 I will also clothe her priests with salvation : and her saints shall shout aloud for joy.

17 There will I make the horn of David to bud : I have ordained a lamp for mine anointed.

18 His enemies will I clothe with shame : but upon himself shall his crown flourish.

11. Here we come to a grand covenant pleading of the kind which is always prevalent with the Lord. *"The LORD hath sworn in truth unto David."* We cannot urge anything with God which is equal to his own word and oath. Jehovah swears that our faith may have strong confidence in it : he cannot forswear himself. He swears *in truth*, for he means every word that he utters ; men may be perjured, but none will be so profane as to imagine this of the God of truth. By Nathan this covenant of Jehovah was conveyed to David, and there was no delusion in it. *"He will not turn from it."* Jehovah is not a changeable being. He never turns from his purpose, much less from his promise solemnly ratified by oath. He turneth never. He is not a man that he should lie, nor the son of man that he should repent. What a rock they stand upon who have an immutable oath of God for their foundation ! We know that this covenant was really made with Christ, the spiritual seed of David, for Peter quotes it at Pentecost, saying, " Men and brethen, let me freely speak unto you of the patriarch David, that he is both dead and buried, and his sepulchre is with us unto this day. Therefore being a prophet, and knowing that God had sworn with an oath to him, that of the fruit of his

loins, according to the flesh, he would raise up Christ to sit on his throne ; he seeing this before spake of the resurrection of Christ." Christ therefore sits on a sure throne for ever and ever, seeing that he has kept the covenant, and through him the blessing comes upon Zion, whose poor are blessed in him. *"Of the fruit of thy body will I set upon thy throne."* Jesus sprang from the race of David, as the evangelists are careful to record ; he was " of the house and lineage of David " : at this day he is the King of the Jews, and the Lord has also given him the heathen for his inheritance. He must reign, and of his kingdom there shall be no end. God himself has set him on the throne and no rebellion of men or devils can shake his dominion. The honour of Jehovah is concerned in his reign, and therefore it is never in danger ; for the Lord will not suffer his oath to be dishonoured.

12. *"If thy children will keep my covenant and my testimony that I shall teach them."* There is a condition to the covenant so far as it concerned kings of David's line before the coming of the true Seed ; but *he* has fulfilled that condition, and made the covenant indefeasible henceforth and for ever as to himself and the spiritual seed in him. Considered as it related to temporal things it was no small blessing for David's dynasty to be secured the throne upon good behaviour. These monarchs held their crowns from God upon the terms of loyalty to their superior Sovereign, the Lord who had elevated them to their high position. They were to be faithful to the covenant by obedience to the divine law, and by belief of divine truth. They were to accept Jehovah as their Lord and their Teacher, regarding him in both relations as in covenant with him. What a condescension on God's part to be their teacher ! How gladly ought they to render intelligent obedience ! What a proper, righteous, and needful stipulation for God to make that they should be true to him when the reward was the promise, *"Their children shall also sit upon thy throne for evermore."* If they will sit at his feet God will make them sit on a throne ; if they will keep the covenant they shall keep the crown from generation to generation.

The kingdom of Judah might have stood to this day had its kings been faithful to the Lord. No internal revolt or external attack could have overthrown the royal house of David : it fell by its own sin, and by nothing else. The Lord was continually provoked, but he was amazingly long-suffering, for long after seceding Israel had gone into captivity, Judah still remained. Miracles of mercy were shown to her. Divine patience exceeded all limits, for the Lord's regard for David was exceeding great. The princes of David's house seemed set on ruining themselves, and nothing could save them ; justice waited long, but it was bound at last to unsheathe the sword and strike. Still, if in the letter man's breach of promise caused the covenant to fail, yet in spirit and essence the Lord has been true to it, for Jesus reigns, and holds the throne for ever. David's seed is still royal, for he was the progenitor according to the flesh of him who is King of kings and Lord of lords.

This verse shows us the need of family piety. Parents must see to it that their children know the fear of the Lord, and they must beg the Lord himself to teach them his truth. We have no hereditary right to the divine favour : the Lord keeps up his friendship to families from generation to generation, for he is loth to leave the descendants of his servants, and never does so except under grievous and long-continued provocation. As believers we are all in a measure under some such covenant as that of David : certain of us can look backward for four generations of saintly ancestors, and we are now glad to look forward to see our children, and our children's children, walking in the truth. Yet we know that grace does not run in the blood, and we are filled with holy fear lest in any of our seed there should be an evil heart of unbelief in departing from the living God.

13. *"For the* LORD *hath chosen Zion."* It was no more than any other Canaanite town till God chose it, David captured it, Solomon built it, and the Lord dwelt in it. So was the church a mere Jebusite stronghold till grace chose it, conquered it, rebuilt it, and dwelt in it. Jehovah has chosen his people, and hence they are his people. He has chosen the church, and hence it is what it is. Thus in the covenant David and Zion, Christ and his people, go together. David is for Zion, and Zion for David : the interests of Christ and his people are mutual. *"He hath desired it for his habitation."* David's question is answered. The Lord has spoken : the site of the temple is fixed : the place of the divine manifestation is determined. Indwelling follows upon election, and arises out of it : Zion is chosen, chosen for a habitation of God. The desire of God to dwell among the people whom he has

chosen for himself is very gracious and yet very natural : his love will not rest apart from those upon whom he has placed it. God desires to abide with those whom he has loved with an everlasting love ; and we do not wonder that it should be so, for we also desire the company of our beloved ones. It is a double marvel, that the Lord should choose and desire such poor creatures as we are : the indwelling of the Holy Ghost in believers is a wonder of grace parallel to the incarnation of the Son of God. God in the church is the wonder of heaven, the miracle of eternity, the glory of infinite love.

14. *"This is my rest for ever."* Oh, glorious words ! It is God himself who here speaks. Think of rest for God ! A Sabbath for the Eternal and a place of abiding for the Infinite. He calls Zion *my rest.* Here his love remains and displays itself with delight. " He shall rest in his love." And this *for ever.* He will not seek another place of repose, nor grow weary of his saints. In Christ the heart of Deity is filled with content, and for his sake he is satisfied with his people, and will be so world without end. These august words declare a distinctive choice—*this* and no other ; a certain choice—*this* which is well known to me ; a present choice—*this* which is here at this moment. God has made his election of old, he has not changed it, and he never will repent of it : his church was his rest and *is* his rest still. As he will not turn from his oath, so he will never turn from his choice. Oh, that we may enter into *his* rest, may be part and parcel of his church, and yield by our loving faith a delight to the mind of him who taketh pleasure in them that fear him, in them that hope in his mercy. *"Here will I dwell ; for I have desired it."* Again are we filled with wonder that he who fills all things should dwell in Zion—should dwell in his church. God does not unwillingly visit his chosen ; he desires to dwell with them ; he desires them. He is already in Zion, for he says *here,* as one upon the spot. Not only will he occasionally come to his church, but he will dwell in it, as his fixed abode. He cared not for the magnificence of Solomon's temple, but he determined that at the mercy-seat he would be found by suppliants, and that thence he would shine forth in brightness of grace among the favoured nation. All this, however, was but a type of the spiritual house, of which Jesus is foundation and cornerstone, upon which all the living stones are builded together for an habitation of God through the Spirit. Oh, the sweetness of the thought that God *desires* to dwell in his people and rest among them ! Surely if it be his desire he will cause it to be so. If the desire of the righteous shall be granted much more shall the desire of the righteous God be accomplished. This is the joy of our souls, for surely we shall rest in God, and certainly our desire is to dwell in him. This also is the end of our fears for the church of God ; for if the Lord dwell in her, she shall not be moved ; if the Lord desire her, the devil cannot destroy her.

15. *"I will abundantly bless her provision."* It must be so. How can we be without a blessing when the Lord is among us ? We live upon his word, we are clothed by his charity, we are armed by his power : all sorts of provision are in him, and how can they be otherwise than blessed ? The provision is to be *abundantly blessed ;* then it will be abundant and blessed. Daily provision, royal provision, satisfying provision, overflowingly joyful provision the church shall receive ; and the divine benediction shall cause us to receive it with faith, to feed upon it by experience, to grow upon it by sanctification, to be strengthened by it to labour, cheered by it to patience, and built up by it to perfection. *"I will satisfy her poor with bread."* The citizens of Zion are poor in themselves, poor in spirit, and often poor in pocket, but their hearts and souls shall dwell in such abundance that they shall neither need more nor desire more. Satisfaction is the crown of experience. Where God rests his people shall be satisfied. They are to be satisfied with what the Lord himself calls " *bread,*" and we may be sure that he knows what is really bread for souls. He will not give us a stone. The Lord's poor shall " have food convenient for them " : that which will suit their palate, remove their hunger, fill their desire, build up their frame, and perfect their growth. The bread of earth is " the bread that perisheth," but the bread of God endureth to life eternal. In the church where God rests his people shall not starve ; the Lord would never rest if they did. He did not take rest for six days till he had prepared the world for the first man to live in ; he would not stay his hand till all things were ready ; therefore, we may be sure if the Lord rests it is because " it is finished," and the Lord hath prepared of his goodness for the poor. Where God finds his desire his people shall find theirs ; if he is satisfied, they shall be.

Taking the two clauses together, we see that nothing but an abundant blessing in the church will satisfy the Lord's poor people : they are naked and miserable till that comes. All the provision that Solomon himself could make would not have satisfied the saints of his day : they looked higher, and longed for the Lord's own boundless blessing, and hungered for the bread which came down from heaven. Blessed be the Lord, they had in this verse two of the " I wills " of God to rest upon, and nothing could be a better support to their faith.

16. More is promised than was prayed for. See how the ninth verse asks for the priests to be clad in righteousness, and the answer is, "*I will also clothe her priests with salvation.*" God is wont to do exceeding abundantly, above all that we ask or even think. Righteousness is but one feature of blessing, salvation is the whole of it. What cloth of gold is this ! What more than regal array ! Garments of salvation ! we know who has woven them, who has dyed them, and who has given them to his people. These are the best robes for priests and preachers, for princes and people ; there is none like them ; give them me. Not every priest shall be thus clothed, but only *her* priests, those who truly belong to Zion, by faith which is in Christ Jesus, who hath made them priests unto God. These are clothed by the Lord himself, and none can clothe as he does. If even the grass of the field is so clothed by the Creator as to outvie Solomon in all his glory, how must his own children be clad ? Truly he shall be admired in his saints ; the liveries of his servants shall be the wonder of heaven. "*And her saints shall shout aloud for joy.*" Again we have a golden answer to a silver prayer. The Psalmist would have the " saints shout for joy." " That they shall do," saith the Lord, " and *aloud* too "; they shall be exceedingly full of delight ; their songs and shouts shall be so hearty that they shall sound as the noise of many waters, and as great thunders. These joyful ones are not, however, the mimic saints of superstition, but *her* saints, saints of the Most High, " sanctified in Christ Jesus." These shall be so abundantly blessed and so satisfied, and so apparelled that they can do no otherwise than shout to show their astonishment, their triumph, their gratitude, their exultation, their enthusiasm, their joy in the Lord. Zion has no dumb saints. The sight of God at rest among his chosen is enough to make the most silent shout. If the morning stars sang together when the earth and heavens were made, much more will all the sons of God shout for joy when the new heavens and the new earth are finished, and the New Jerusalem comes down out of heaven from God, prepared as a bride for her husband. Meanwhile, even now the dwelling of the Lord among us is a perennial fountain of sparkling delight to all holy minds. This shouting for joy is guaranteed to Zion's holy ones : God says they *shall* shout aloud, and depend upon it they will : who shall stop them of this glorying ? The Lord hath said by his Spirit, " let them shout," and then he has promised that " they shall shout aloud " : who is he that shall make them hold their peace ? The Bridegroom is with them, and shall the children of the bride-chamber fast ? Nay, verily, we rejoice, yea and will rejoice.

17. "*There will I make the horn of David to bud.*" In Zion David's dynasty shall develop power and glory. In our notes from other authors we have included a description of the growth of the horns of stags, which is the natural fact from which we conceive the expression in the text to be borrowed. As the stag is made noble and strong by the development of his horns, so the house of David shall advance from strength to strength. This was to be by the work of the Lord—" there will I make," and therefore it would be sure and solid growth. When God makes us to bud none can cause us to fade. When David's descendants left the Lord and the worship of his house, they declined in all respects, for it was only through the Lord, and in connection with his worship that their horn would bud.

"*I have ordained a lamp for mine anointed.*" David's name was to be illustrious, and brilliant as a lamp ; it was to continue shining like a lamp in the sanctuary ; it was thus to be a comfort to the people, and an enlightenment to the nations. God would not suffer the light of David to go out by the extinction of his race : his holy ordinances had decreed that the house of his servant should remain in the midst of Israel. What a lamp is our Lord Jesus ! A light to lighten the Gentiles, and the glory of his people Israel. As the anointed—the true Christ, he shall be the light of heaven itself. Oh for grace to receive our illumination and our consolation from Jesus Christ alone.

18. "*His enemies will I clothe with shame.*" They shall be utterly defeated, they shall loathe their evil design, they shall be despised for having hated the Ever Blessed One. Their shame they will be unable to hide, it shall cover them : God

will array them in it for ever, and it shall be their convict dress to all eternity. *"But upon himself shall his crown flourish."* Green shall be his laurels of victory. He shall win and wear the crown of honour, and his inherited diadem shall increase in splendour. Is it not so to this hour with Jesus? His kingdom cannot fail, his imperial glories cannot fade. It is *himself* that we delight to honour ; it is to himself that the honour comes, and upon himself that it flourishes. If others snatch at his crown their traitorous aims are defeated ; but he in his own person reigns with ever growing splendour.

> "Crown him, crown him,
> Crowns become the victor's brow."

EXPLANATORY NOTES AND QUAINT SAYINGS.

Whole Psalm.—Lightfoot ascribes this Psalm to David, and supposes it to have been composed on the second removal of the ark from the house of Obed-edom : 1 Chron. xv. 4, etc. But the mention of David's name in the tenth verse in the third person, and the terms there employed, militate against his being the author. Others ascribe it to Solomon, who, they think, wrote it about the time of the removing of the ark into the Temple which he had built for it : 2 Chron. v. 2, etc. Others are of opinion, that it was composed by Solomon for the solemn services that were celebrated at the dedication of the Temple.—*James Anderson's note to Calvin in loc.*

Whole Psalm.—The Psalm is divided into four stanzas of ten lines, each of which contains the name of David. The first part begins with speaking of David's vow to the Lord ; the third with the Lord's promise to David.—*William Kay.*

Whole Psalm.—The parallelisms need to be traced with some care. Verses 1, 2, 3, 4, 5, 6 are answered by verse 12 ; verse 7 by verse 13 ; verse 8 by verse 14 ; verse 9 by verses 15, 16 ; verse 10 by verses 17, 18.

An attention to these parallelisms is often necessary to bring out the meaning of Scripture.—*Joseph Angus, in "The Bible Handbook,"* 1862.

Verse 1.—*" LORD, remember."* It is a gracious privilege to be permitted to be God's remembrancers. Faith is encouraged to remind him of his covenant, and of his precious promises. There is, indeed, no forgetfulness with him. The past, as also the future, is a present page before his eye. But by this exercise we impress on our own minds invaluable lessons.—*Henry Law.*

Verse 1.—*"Remember David, and all his afflictions."* Solomon was a wise man, yet pleads not any merit of his own ;—I am not worthy, for whom thou shouldst do this, but, *" LORD, remember David,"* with whom thou madest the covenant ; as Moses prayed (Exod. xxxii. 13), *"Remember Abraham,"* the first trustee of the covenant ; remember *"all his afflictions,"* all the troubles of his life, which his being anointed was the occasion of ; or his care and concern about the ark, and what an uneasiness it was to him that the ark was in curtains (2 Sam. vii. 2). *Remember all his humility and weakness,* so some read it ; all that pious and devout affection with which he had made the following vow.—*Matthew Henry.*

Verse 1.—*"Remember . . . all his afflictions."* The sufferings of believers for the cause of truth are not meritorious, but neither are they in vain ; they are not forgotten by God. Matt. v. 11, 12.—*Christopher Starke,* 1740.

Verse 1.—*"Afflictions."* The Hebrew word for *"afflictions"* is akin to the word for " trouble " in 1 Chron. xxii. 14 : " Now, behold, in my *trouble* I have prepared for the house of the Lord an hundred thousand talents of gold."—*H. T. Armfield.*

Verses 1, 2.—If the Jew could rightly appeal to God to show mercy to his church and nation for the sake of that shepherd youth whom he had advanced to the kingdom, much more shall we justly plead our cause in the name of David's son (called *David* four times in the prophets), and of *all his trouble,* all the sorrows of his birth and infancy, his ministry and passion and death, which he bore as a consequence of his self-dedication to his Father's will, when his priesthood, foreordained from all eternity, was confirmed with an oath, " for those [Levitical] priests were made without [swearing] an oath ; but this with an oath by him that said unto him, The

Lord sware and will not repent, Thou art a priest for ever after the order of Melchizedek " : Heb. vii. 21 ; Ps. cx. 4.—*Theodoret and Cassiodorus, in Neale and Littledale.*

Verse 2.—"*And vowed.*" The history does not record the time nor the occasion of this vow ; but history does record how it was ever in David's thoughts and on David's heart. David, indeed, in the first verse, asks of God to remember his afflictions, and then records his vow ; and you may, perhaps, think that the vow was the consequence of his afflictions, and that he made it contingent on his deliverance. . . . It is far more consistent with the character of David to look upon the affliction to which he alludes as resulting from the Lord's not permitting him to carry out his purpose of erecting an earthly habitation for the God of heaven, inasmuch as he had shed blood abundantly. And if, as is more than probable, amid that blood which he had shed, David's conscience recalled the blood of Uriah as swelling the measure, he could not but be deeply afflicted, even while he acknowledged the righteousness of the sentence.

But though not permitted of God to execute his purpose, we cannot but feel and own that it was a noble resolution which David here makes ; and though recorded in all the amplification of Oriental imagery, it expresses the holy determination of the Psalmist to forego every occupation and pursuit, and not to allow a single day to elapse till he had at least fixed on the site of the future temple.—*Barton Bouchier.*

Verse 2.—"*He vowed.*" He who is ready to vow on every occasion will break his vow on every occasion. It is a necessary rule, that " we be as sparing in making our vows as may be " ; there being many great inconveniences attending frequent and multiplied vows. It is very observable, that the Scripture mentioneth very few examples of vows, compared with the many instances of very great and wonderful providences ; as if it would give us some instances, that we might know what we have to do, and yet would give us but few, that we might know we are not to do it often. You read Jacob lived seven score and seven years (Gen. xlvii. 28) ; but you read, I think, but of one vow that he made. Our extraordinary exigencies are not many ; and, I say, our vows should not be more. Let this, then, be the first necessary ingredient of a well-ordered vow. Let it be no oftener made than the pressing greatness of an evil to be removed, or the alluring excellency of a blessing extraordinary to be obtained, will well warrant. Jephthah's vow was so far right ; he had just occasion ; there was a great and pressing danger to be removed ; there was an excellent blessing to be obtained : the danger was, lest Israel should be enslaved ; the blessing was victory over their enemies. This warranted his vow, though his rashness marred it. It was in David's troubles that David sware, and vowed a vow to the Most High ; and Jacob forbare to vow until his more than ordinary case bade him vow, and warranted him in so doing : Gen. xxviii. 20. Let us do as he did,—spare to vow, until such case puts us on it.—*Henry Hurst (1629 ?—1690), in "The Morning Exercises."*

Verse 2.—"*Vowed unto the mighty God of Jacob.*" The first holy votary that ever we read of was Jacob here mentioned in this text, who is therefore called the father of vows : and upon this account some think David mentions God here under the title of "*the mighty God of Jacob,*" rather than any other, because of his vow.—*Abraham Wright.*

Verse 2.—"*The mighty God of Jacob.*" The title *strong one of Jacob*, by which God is here designated, first used by Jacob himself, Gen. xlix. 24, and thence more generally used as is clear from Isaiah i. 24, xlix. 26, and other places, here sets forth God both as the *most mighty* who is able most severely to punish perjury, and with whom no one may dare to contend, and also as the *defender* and most mighty vindicator of Israel, such as Jacob had proved him, and all his descendants, in particular David, who frequently rejoiced and gloried in this mighty one and defender. Such a mighty one of Jacob was worthy to have a temple built for him, and was so great that he would not suffer perjury.—*Hermann Venema.*

Verse 2.—Where the interpreters have translated, "*the God of Jacob,*" it is in the Hebrew, "*the mighty in Jacob.*" Which name is sometimes attributed unto the angels, and sometimes it is also applied to other things wherein are great strength and fortitude ; as to a lion, an ox, and such like. But here it is a singular word of faith, signifying that God is the power and strength of his people ; for only faith ascribeth this unto God. Reason and the flesh do attribute more to riches, and such other worldly helps as man seeth and knoweth. All such carnal helps are very

Idols, which deceive men, and draw them to perdition ; but this is the strength and fortitude of the people, to have God present with them. . . . So the Scripture saith in another place : " Some trust in chariots, and some in horses, but we will remember the name of the Lord." Likewise Paul saith : " Be strong in the Lord, and in the power of his might." For this power is eternal, and deceiveth not. All other powers are not only deceitful, but they are transitory, and continue but for a moment.— *Martin Luther.*

Verse 3.—*"Surely I will not come into the tabernacle of my house,"* etc. To avoid the absurdity of thinking that David should make such a rash and unwarrantable vow as this might seem to be, that till he had his desire satisfied in that which is afterwards expressed he would abide in the open air, and never go within his doors, nor ever take any rest, either by day or by night, some say that David spake this with reference to his purpose of taking the fort of Zion from the Jebusites (2 Sam. v. 6), where by revelation he knew that God meant to have the ark settled, and which he might probably think would be accomplished within some short time. And then others again say, that he meant it only of that stately cedar house, which he had lately built for himself at Jerusalem (2 Sam. vii. 1, 2), to wit, that he would not go into that house ; and so also that he would not go up unto his bed, nor (verse 4) give any sleep to his eyes, nor slumber to his eyelids, to wit, in that house. But neither of these expositions give me any satisfaction. I rather take these to be hyperbolical expressions of the continual, exceeding great care wherewith he was perplexed about providing a settled place for the ark to rest in, like that in Prov. vi. 4, 5 : " Give not sleep to thine eyes, nor slumber to thine eyelids ; deliver thyself as a roe from the hand of the hunter," etc. Neither is it any more in effect than if he had said, I will never lay by this care to mind myself in anything whatsoever : I shall never with any content abide in mine own house, nor with any quiet rest in my bed, until, etc.—*Arthur Jackson,* 1593—1666.

Verse 3.—*"Surely I will not come into the tabernacle of my house,"* etc. When he had built himself a palace (1 Chron. xv. 1), it appears by the context, that he did not *bless* it (ch. xvi. 43), nor consequently live in it (for that he might not do till it were blest) until he had first prepared a place, and brought up the ark to it.— *Henry Hammond.*

Verse 3.—*"Surely I will not come,"* etc. Our translation of the verse is justified by Aben Ezra, who remarks that אם is here to be translated not in its usual sense of " if,"—" if I shall come "—but as introducing a vow, " I will not come." This idiom, it may be observed, is more or less missed by our existing translation of Hebrews iv. 5 : " And in this place again, If they shall enter into my rest "—a translation which is the more curious from the fact that the idiom in the present Psalm is hit off exactly in the preceding chapter, Hebrews iii. 11 : " So I sware in my wrath, They shall not enter into my rest."—*H. T. Armfield.*

Verse 3.—*"I will not come into the tent which is my house."* What does this singular form of expression denote ? Is it " an instance of the way in which the associations of the old patriarchal tent life fixed themselves in the language of the people," as Perowne suggests ? or does David deliberately select it to imply that even his palace is but a tent as compared with the house that he will rear for God ?— *Samuel Cox.*

Verse 3.—*"Nor go up into my bed."* From the expression of the Psalmist it would seem that a lofty bed was not only a necessary luxury, but a sign of superior rank. This idea was very prevalent in the period of the revival of the arts on the Continent, where the state bed, often six feet high, always stood on a dais in an alcove, richly curtained off from the saloon. In the East the same custom still continues, and a verse in the Koran declares it to be one of the delights of the faithful in paradise that " they shall repose themselves on lofty beds " (Cap. 56, " The Inevitable "). Frequently these state beds were composed of the most costly and magnificent materials. The prophet Amos speaks of ivory beds (Amos vi. 4); Nero had a golden one ; that of the Mogul Aurungzeebe was jewelled ; and, lastly, in the privy purse expenses of our own profligate Charles II., we read of a " silver bedstead for Mrs. Gwynn." And to this day the state bedsteads in the viceregal palace at Cairo are executed in the same metal, and are supposed to have cost upwards of £3,000 each.—*From "The Biblical Museum,"* 1879.

Verses 3—5.—*"Surely I will not come,"* etc. These were all types and figures of Christ, the true David, who, in his desire of raising a living temple, and an everlasting tabernacle to God, spent whole nights in prayer, and truly, neither entered his house, nor went up into his bed, nor gave slumber to his eyelids, nor rest to his temples, and presented to himself " a glorious church, not having spot, nor wrinkle, nor any such thing," nor built " with corruptible gold or silver," but with his own precious sweat and more precious blood ; it was with them he built that city in heaven that was seen by St. John in the Apocalypse, and " was ornamented with all manner of precious stones." Hence, we can all understand the amount of care, cost, and labour we need to erect a becoming temple in our hearts to God.—*Robert Bellarmine* (1542—1621), *in "A Commentary on the Book of Psalms."*

Verses 3—5.—This admirable zeal of this pious king condemns the indifference of those who leave the sacred places which are dependent upon their care in a condition of shameful neglect, while they lavish all their care to make for themselves sumptuous houses.—*Pasquier Quesnel* (1634—1719), *dans "Les Pseaumes, avec des Reflexions,"* 1700.

Verse 5.—*"An habitation for the mighty God of Jacob."* Jacob " vowed a vow," when he declared, " this . . . shall be God's house " : Gen. xxviii. 20—22. David accordingly preserved a reminiscence of the fact, when he vowed a vow in connection with a similar object.—*H. T. Armfield.*

Verse 6.—*"We heard of it at Ephratah."* This is commonly understood of Bethlehem, as that place had this name. But the ark never was at Bethlehem, at least we read of no such thing. There was a district called by this name, or one closely resembling it, where Elkanah, Samuel's father, lived, and whence Jeroboam came, both of whom are called Ephrathites. 1 Sam. i. 1 ; 1 Kings xi. 26. This was in the tribe of Ephraim, and is probably the place meant by the Psalmist. Now the ark had been for a long series of years at Shiloh, which is in Ephraim, when it was taken to be present at the battle with the Philistines, in which Hophni and Phinehas, the sons of Eli, were slain, and when thirty thousand of the Israelites lost their lives, together with the capture of the ark. The frightful report of this calamity was brought to Eli, and occasioned his instant death. This appears to be the event referred to in the words, *"We heard of it at Ephratah"* ; and a grievous report it was, not likely to be soon forgotten.

"We found it in the fields of Jaar." After the ark had been for some time in the land of the Philistines, they sent it away, and it came to Bethshemesh, in the tribe of Judah. 1 Sam. vi. 12. In the immediate vicinity of this place was also Kirjath-jearim, i.e. the city of Jaar, to which the ark was removed ; for the Bethshemites were afraid to retain it, as many thousands of them had lost their lives, for the violation of the sanctity of the ark, by looking into it. As this slaughter took place close by, if not in the fields of Jaar, the Psalmist, with reference to it, says, *"We found it in the fields of Jaar."* Having glanced at these two afflictive and memorable events, he goes on with his direct design, of encouraging the people to perform due honour to the ark, and to the temple, by contrasting with the sad occurrences to which he had adverted their present joy and prosperity.—*William Walford, in "The Book of Psalms. A New Translation, with Notes."* 1837.

Verse 6.—*"We heard of it at Ephratah,"* etc. Either of the ark which David and others had heard of, that it formerly was at Shiloh (Josh. xviii. 1), here called Ephratah, as some think ; so the Ephraimites are called Ephrathites (Jud. xii. 5) ; and Elkanah of Ramathaim-zophim, of Mount Ephraim, is said to be an Ephrathite (1 Sam. i. 1) ; but this tribe the Lord chose not, but the tribe of Judah, for his habitation ; and rejected the tabernacle of Shiloh, and removed it from thence (Ps. lxxviii. 60, 67, 68). *"We found it in the fields of the wood ;"* at Kirjath-jearim, which signifies *the city of woods ;* being built among woods, and surrounded with them : here the ark was twenty years, and here David found it ; and from hence he brought it to the house of Obed-edom, and from thence to Zion.

Christ has been *found in the fields of the wood ;* in a low, mean, abject state, as this phrase signifies : Ezek. xvi. 5. The shepherds found him rejected from being in the inn, there being no room for him, and lying in a manger (Luke ii. 7, 16) ; the angels found him in the wilderness, among the wild beasts of the field (Mark i. 13) ; nor had he the convenience even of foxes and birds of the air ; he had no habitation or place where to lay his head : Matt. viii. 20. And he is to be found in the field of the Scriptures, where this rich treasure and pearl of great price lies hid : Matt. xiii. 44.—*John Gill.*

Verse 6.—"*We heard of it at Ephratah.*" The only explanation, equally agreeable to usage and the context, is that which makes Ephratah the ancient name of Bethlehem (Gen. xlviii. 7), here mentioned as the place where David spent his youth, and where he used to hear of the ark, although he never saw it till long afterwards, when he found it in the fields of the wood, in the neighbourhood of *Kirjath-jearim*, which name means Forest-town, or City of the Woods. Compare 1 Sam vii. 1 with 2 Sam. vi. 3, 4.—*Joseph Addison Alexander.*

Verse 6.—"*We heard of it at Ephratah,*" etc. Having prepared a sumptuous tabernacle, or tent, for the ark on Mount Zion, in the "City of David," a great national assembly was summoned, at which all the tribes were invited to attend its removal to this new sanctuary. The excitement spread over all Israel. "We heard men say at Ephratah [Bethlehem], in the south of the land, and we found them repeat it in the woody Lebanon," sings the writer of the 132nd Psalm, according to Ewald's rendering. "Let us go into his tabernacle; let us worship at his footstool." The very words of the summons were fitted to rouse the deepest feelings of the nation, for they were to gather at Baalah, of Judah, another name for Kirjath-jearim, to "bring up thence" to the mountain capital "the Ark of God, called by the name, the name of Jehovah of Hosts that dwelleth between the cherubim": 2 Sam. vi. 2. It "had not been enquired at in the days of Saul": but, when restored, the nation would have their great palladium once more in their midst, and could "appear before God in Zion," and be instructed and taught in the way they should go.—*Cunningham Geikie, in "Hours with the Bible,"* 1881.

Verse 6.—"*Ephratah.*" The Psalmist says, that David himself, even when a youth in Bethlehem-Ephratah, heard of the sojourn of the ark in Kirjath-jearim, and that it was a fond dream of David's boyhood to be permitted to bring up the ark to some settled habitation, which he desired *to find* (verse 5).—*Christopher Wordsworth.*

Verse 6.—"*We found it.*" The church can never long be hid. The sun reappears after a short eclipse.—*Henry Law.*

Verse 6.—It is not always where we first seek God that he is to be found. "We *heard* of it at Ephratah: we *found* it in the fields of the wood." We must not be governed by hearsay in seeking for God in Christ; but seek for ourselves until we find. It is not in every house of prayer that God in Christ can be found: after seeking him in gorgeous temples we may find him "in the fields of the woods." "If any man shall say unto you, Lo, here is Christ, or lo, there; believe it not" upon his own testimony, but seek him for yourselves.—*George Rogers,* 1883.

Verse 7.—"*We will go . . . we will worship.*" Note their agreement and joint consent, which is visible in the pronoun "*we*": "*We will go.*" "*We*" taketh in a whole nation, a whole people, the whole world, and maketh them one. "*We*" maketh a commonwealth; and "*we*" maketh a church. We go up to the house of the Lord together, and we hope to go to heaven together. Note their alacrity and cheerfulness in going. Their long absence rendered the object more glorious. For, what we love and want, we love the more and desire the more earnestly. When Hezekiah, having been "sick unto death," had a longer lease of life granted him, he asketh the question, "What is the sign" (not, *that I shall live,* but) "that I shall go up to the house of the Lord?" Isaiah xxxviii. 1—22. Love is on the wing, cheerful to meet its object; yea, it reacheth it at a distance, and is united to it while it is afar off. . . . "*We will go.*" We long to be there. We will hasten our pace. We will break through all difficulties in the way.—*Condensed from Anthony Farindon.*

Verse 7 (first clause).—"*Tabernacles*" are spoken of in the plural number, and this it may be (though we may doubt whether the Psalmist had such minute distinctions in his eye) because there was in the Temple an inner sanctuary, a middle apartment, and then the court. It is of more importance to attend to the epithet which follows, where the Psalmist calls the Ark of the Covenant *God's footstool,* to intimate that the sanctuary could never contain the immensity of God's essence, as men were apt absurdly to imagine. The mere outward Temple with all its majesty being no more than his footstool, his people were called upon to look upwards to the heavens, and fix their contemplations with due reverence upon God himself.—*John Calvin.*

Verse 7.—The Lord's "*footstool*" here mentioned was either *the Ark of the Testimony* itself, or the place at least where it stood, called *Debir,* or the *Holy of*

Holies, towards which the Jews in their temple used to worship. The very next words argue so much : *"Arise, O LORD, into thy rest ; thou, and the ark of thy strength " ;* and it is plain out of 1 Chron. xxviii. 2, where David saith concerning his purpose to have built God an house, " I had in mine heart to build an house of rest for the ark of the covenant of the Lord, and for the *footstool* of our God," where the conjunction *and* is exegetical, and the same with *that is.* According to this expression the prophet Jeremy also, in the beginning of the second of his Lamentations, bewaileth that " the Lord had cast down the beauty of Israel " (that is, his glorious Temple), " and remembered not his *footstool* " (that is, the Ark of the Covenant), " in the day of his wrath " ; as Isaiah lx. 7, and lxiv. 11 ; Ps. xcvi. 6.

That this is the true and genuine meaning of this phrase of *worshipping the Lord towards his footstool,* besides the confessed custom of the time, is evidently confirmed by a parallel expression of this worshipping posture (Ps. xxviii. 2) : " Hear the voice of my supplications when I cry unto thee, when I lift up mine hands אֶל־דְּבִיר קָדְשֶׁ‎ towards thy *holy oracle" ;* that is, towards the Most Holy place where the ark stood, and from whence God gave his answers. For that דביר *Debir,* which is here translated *"oracle,"* was the *Sanctum Sanctorum* or Most Holy place, is clear out of the sixth and eighth chapters of the First Book of Kings ; where in the former we read (verse 19) that " Solomon prepared the *oracle* or *Debir,* to set the ark of the covenant of the Lord there " : in the latter (verse 6), that " the priests brought in the ark of the covenant of the Lord unto his place, into the oracle of the house, to the most holy place, even under the wings of the cherubims." Wherefore the authors of the translation used in our Liturgy rendered this passage of the Psalm, " When I hold up my hands toward the mercy seat of thy holy temple " ; namely, having respect to the meaning thereof. Thus you see that one of the two must needs be this *scabellum pedum,* or *"footstool"* of God, either *the ark* or *mercy-seat* itself, or the *adytum Templi,* the Most Holy place, where it stood. For that it is not the whole Temple at large (though it might be so called), but some thing or part of those that are within it, the first words of my text (*"We will go into his tabernacles "*) do argue. If, then, it be *the ark* (whose *cover* was that which we call the *mercy-seat*), it seems to have been so called in respect of God's sitting upon the cherubims, under which the ark lay, as it were his footstool : whence sometimes it is described, " The ark of the covenant of the Lord of Hosts, which sitteth upon the cherubims " : 1 Sam iv. 4. If the *ark,* with the *cover* thereof (*the mercy-seat*), be considered as God's *throne,* then the place thereof, the *Debir,* may not unfitly be termed his *"footstool."* Or, lastly, if we consider heaven to be the throne of God, as indeed it is, then whatsoever place or monument of presence he hath here on earth is in true esteem no more than his *"footstool."*—*Joseph Mede,* 1586—1638.

Verse 8.—*"Arise, O LORD, into thy rest ; thou, and the ark of thy strength."* Whenever the camp was about to move, Moses used the language found in the first part of this verse. *"Arise* (or rise up), *O Jehovah."*—*William Swan Plumer.*

Verse 8.—*"Thou, and the ark of thy strength."* " Both he that sanctifieth and they who are sanctified are all of one " : Heb. ii. 11. Now Christ, our Great High Priest, is gone up into the holy resting-place. Of him it is said, " Arise " : for he arose from the dead, and ascended into heaven. And to his *"ark,"* the church, it is said, " Arise " : because he lives, all in him shall live also.—*Edward Simms, in "A Spiritual Commentary on the Book of Psalms,"* 1882.

Verse 8.—*"The ark of thy strength."* The historical records of the ark are numerous, and deeply interesting. Miracles were often wrought at its presence. At the passage of the Jordan, no sooner were the feet of the priests which bare this holy vessel dipped in the brim of the river, than the waters rose up upon an heap, and the people of God passed over on dry ground—" clean over Jordan " : Joshua iii. 14—17. At the siege of Jericho, the ark occupied a most prominent position in the daily procession of the tribes around the doomed city. . . . It was, however, captured by the Philistines, and Hophni and Phineas, Eli's wicked sons, in whose care it was placed, slain. Thus the Lord " delivered his strength into captivity and his glory into the enemy's hand " : Ps. lxxviii. 61.—*Frank H. White, in "Christ in the Tabernacle,"* 1877.

Verse 9 (first clause).—The chief badge and cognizance of the Lord's minister is the true doctrine of justification and obedience of faith in a holy conversation : *"Let thy priests be clothed with righteousness."*—*David Dickson.*

Verse 9.—*"Let thy priests be clothed with righteousness."*

> Holiness on the head,
> Light and perfections on the breast,
> Harmonious bells below, raising the dead
> To lead them unto life and rest.
> Thus are true *Aarons* drest, etc.

George Herbert, 1593—1633.

Verse 9.—*"Saints."* If the very names given by God's prophets to his people are such as *saints, gracious ones, merciful ones,* surely his professed people ought to see to it that they are not cruel, untender, or *unholy.*—*William Swan Plumer.*

Verses 9, 16.—Let us notice the prayer, verse 9, with the answer, verse 16. The prayer asks in behalf of the priests *"righteousness" :* the answer is, " I will clothe her priests with *salvation,"* i.e., with what shows forth God's *gracious character.* Caring for the interest of God, the worshipper finds his own interest fully cared for. And now, after spreading the Lord's pledged word (verses 11, 12) before him, the worshipper hears the Lord himself utter the reply, *q.d.,* " I will do all that has been sought."—*A. A. Bonar.*

Verse 10.—*" For thy servant David's sake."* Solomon's plea for the divine blessing to rest upon him as king, *"For thy servant David's sake,"* was justified in its use by God: Is. xxxvii. 35. It gives no countenance to the idea of intercession on the part of deceased saints ; for it is not a prayer to David, but a pleading with God for the sake of David. Nor does it support the idea of works of supererogation on the part of David ; it only implies a special divine delight in David, on account of which God was pleased to honour David's name during succeeding generations ; and if the delight itself is pure grace, the expression of it, in any way, must be grace. Nor does it even give countenance to the idea that God's converting and saving grace may be expected by any man because his parents or ancestors were delighted in by God ; for a plea of this character is in Scripture strictly confined to two instances, Abraham and David, with both of whom a special covenant was made, including their descendants, and it was just this covenant that authorised the use of the plea by those who by promise were specially interested, and by none others, and for the ends contemplated by the covenant. But it did prefigure the great Christian plea, " For Christ Jesus' sake " ; just as God's selection of individual men and making them centres of revelation and religion, in the old time, prefigured " The man Christ Jesus " as the centre and basis of religion for all time. Hence in the plea, " For Christ's sake," the old pleas referred to are abolished, as the Jewish ritual is abolished. Christ bids us use His name : John xiv. 13, 14 ; xvi. 26, etc. To believe the false notions mentioned above, or to trust in any other name for divine, gracious favour, is to dishonour the name of Christ. " For Christ's sake " is effective on account of the great covenant, the merits of Christ, and his session in heaven.—*John Field,* 1883.

Verse 10.—*"For thy servant David's sake."* The frequency with which God is urged to hear and answer prayer *for David's sake* (1 Kings xi. 12, 13 ; xv. 4 ; 2 Kings viii. 19, etc.), is not to be explained by making *David* mean the promise to David, nor from the personal favour of which he was the object, but for his historical position as the great theocratical model, in whom it pleased God that the old economy should reach its culminating point, and who is always held up as the type and representative of the Messiah, so that all the intervening kings are mere connecting links, and their reigns mere repetitions and continuations of the reign of David, with more or less resemblance as they happened to be good or bad. Hence the frequency with which his name appears in the later Scriptures, compared with even the last of his successors, and the otherwise inexplicable transfer of that name to the Messiah himself.—*Joseph Addison Alexander.*

Verse 10.—*"For thy servant David's sake."* When Sennacherib's army lay around Jerusalem besieging it, God wrought deliverance for Israel partly out of regard to the prayer of the devout Hezekiah, but partly also out of respect for the pious memory of David, the hero-king, the man after God's own heart. The message sent through Isaiah to the king concluded thus : " Therefore thus saith the Lord concerning the king of Assyria, he shall not come into this city, nor shoot an arrow there, not come before it with shield, nor cast a bank against it. By the way that he came, by the same shall he return, and shall not come into this city, saith the Lord. For I will defend this city, to save it, for mine own sake, and for my servant

David's sake " : 2 Kings xix. 32—4.   What a respect is shown to David's name by its being thus put on a level with God !   *Mine own sake, and David's sake.—Alexander Balmain Bruce, in "The Galilean Gospel,"* 1882.

Verse 10.—*"Turn not away the face,"* etc.   As if in displeasure, or in forgetfulness.—*Albert Barnes.*

Verse 10.—*"Thine anointed."*   What is meant by *"thine anointed"?*   Is it David himself ; or some definite king among his merely human descendants ; or does it apply to each or any of them as they come into office to bear the responsibilities of this line of anointed kings ?   I incline to the latter construction, under which the petition is applicable to any one or to all the anointed successors of David.   For David's sake let every one of them be admitted to free audience before thee, and his prayer be evermore availing.   The context contemplates a long line of kings descended from David.   It was pertinent to make them all the subjects of this prayer.—*Henry Cowles.*

Verse 11.—*"The* LORD *hath sworn."*   The most potent weapon with God is his own word.   They remind him, therefore, as did Ethan in Psalm lxxxix. 20, etc., of the solemn words which he had spoken by Nathan, and which must at that time have been still fresh in the memory of all.   Solomon, too, made mention of those glorious words of comfort in his prayer at the dedication of the temple.—*Augustus F. Tholuck.*

Verses 11, 12.—This Psalm is one of those fifteen which are called Psalms of Degrees ; of which title whatsoever reason can be given fitting the rest, surely if we consider the argument of this, it may well import the excellency thereof, and why ? It is nothing else but a sacred emulation, wherein God and a king contend ;   the king in piety, God in bounty.   The king declares himself to be a most eminent pattern of zeal, and God himself to be a most magnificent rewarder of his servants. The king debarreth himself of all worldly content, while he is busily providing to entertain God ; and God, who filleth heaven and earth, vouchsafeth to lodge in that place which was provided by the king.   The king presents his supplication not only for himself, but also for his charge, the priests, the people ; and God restraineth not his blessing to the king, but also at his suit enlargeth it to church and commonweal. Finally, the king bindeth himself to make good his duty with a votive oath, and God restipulateth with an oath that which he promised both to king and kingdom : to the kingdom in the words that follow ; but to the king in those that I have now read to you.

This speech, then, is directed unto the king, unto David ; but it containeth a blessing which redounds unto his issue, *"the fruit of his body."*   This blessing is no less than a royal succession in the throne of David : David's sons shall inherit it, but it is God that states them in it.   They shall sit, but *I will set* them, yea, so set them that they shall never fall ; they shall sit for ever ; the succession shall be perpetual.   And hitherto the promise runs absolute : it is qualified in that which followeth.

The king was busy to build God's house ; and see how God answers him, promising the building of the king's house !   God requites a building with a building.   There is a very apt allusion in the word, upon which the son of Syrach also plays, when he saith, that children and the building of a city make a perpetual name ; how much more if they be a royal offspring, that are destined to sit upon a throne ?   And God promiseth David sons for this honourable end—*"to sit upon his throne."—Arthur Lake,* —1626.

Verse 12.—*"If thy children will keep my covenant,"* etc.   Lest David's sons, if they be left without law, should live without care, they must know that the succession shall be perpetual ; but the promise is conditional ; if David's sons conform themselves to God, *"if thou keep my covenant,"* whereof they cannot pretend ignorance. And they have an authentical record : the record, *"my testimonies " ;* authentical, *"I myself will teach them."*   You see the king's blessing, it is very great ; but lest the promise thereof be thought too good to be true, God secures the king with a most unchangeable warrant.   The warrant is his oath, *"The Lord sware" ;* and this warrant is, 1. Unchangeable, because sincere ; he swore in truth.   2. Stable, *he will not turn from it.*   And what could king David desire more for his own house than a promise of such a blessing, and such a warrant of that promise ?   Yes, he might, and no doubt he did desire [more] ; and God also intended to him more than the letter of this promise doth express, even the accomplishment of the truth whereof this was but a type. And what is that ? The establishment of the kingdom of Jesus Christ.—*Arthur Lake.*

Verse 12.—*"That I shall teach them."* Here is to be noted that he addeth, *"which I will teach them";* for he will be the teacher and will be heard. He wills not that church councils should be heard, or such as teach that which he hath not taught. . . . God giveth no authority unto man above the word. So should he set man, that is to say, dust and dung, above himself ; for what is the word, but God himself ? This word they that honour, obey, and keep, are the true church indeed, be they never so contemptible in the world : but they which do not, are the church of Satan, and accursed of God. And this is the cause why it is expressly set down in the text, *"The testimonies which I will teach them."* For so will God use the ministry of teachers and pastors in the church, that he notwithstanding will be their chief Pastor, and all other ministers and pastors whatsoever, yea, the church itself, shall be ruled and governed by the word.—*Martin Luther.*

Verse 12.—*"Their children shall also sit upon thy throne for evermore."* As if he had said, this promise as touching Christ will I accomplish, and will undoubtedly establish the throne unto my servant David ; but do not ye, which in the meantime sit on this throne, and govern this kingdom, presume upon the promise, and think that you cannot err, or that I will wink at your errors, and not rather condemn and severely punish them. Therefore either govern your kingdom according to my word, or else I will root you out and destroy you for ever. This promise he now amplifieth, and setteth forth more at large.—*Martin Luther.*

Verse 13.—*"For the* LORD *hath chosen Zion,"* etc. The Lord's pitching upon any place to dwell there cometh not of the worthiness of the place, or persons, but from God's good pleasure alone. The Lord having chosen his church, resteth in his love to her : he smelleth a sweet savour of Christ, and this maketh his seat among his people steadfast.—*David Dickson.*

Verse 13.—*" For the* LORD *hath chosen Zion."* Here, of a singular purpose, he useth the same word which Moses used (Deut. xvi. 6) : " As the place which the Lord thy God *shall choose* to place his name in." For at the beginning there was no certain place appointed wherein the tabernacle should remain ; but it wandered, not only from place to place, but also from tribe to tribe, as Ephraim, Manasseh, Dan, etc.

Moreover, by the word, *" hath chosen,"* he overthroweth all kinds of worship and religion of men's own devising and choosing, whereof there was an infinite number among the Jews. Election or choice belongeth not unto us ; but we must yield obedience to the voice of the Lord. Else shall that happen unto us which Jeremiah threateneth : " That they have chosen will I reject." These things destroy and confound the inventions, the devices and devotions, the false and counterfeit religions, which we have seen in the papacy. . . . God is not served but when that is done which he hath commanded. Wherefore election or choice pertaineth not to us, so that what God hath commanded, that we must do.—*Martin Luther.*

Verse 14.—*"This is my rest for ever."* Of the Christian church we may affirm with undoubted certainty, that it is *God's rest for ever :* after this dispensation of his will, there will never succeed another ; Christianity closes and completes the Divine communication from God to man ; nothing greater, nothing better can or will be imparted to him on this side eternity ; and even in heaven itself we shall, through an everlasting duration, be employed in contemplating and adoring the riches of that grace, the brightest glories of which have been realized in the consummations of Calvary, the ascension of the Messiah, the breaking down of all national peculiarity, and the gift and mission of the Divine Spirit. Let the argument of the apostle to the Hebrews be fully weighed, and the conclusion of every mind must be, that God has " removed those things that are shaken, as of things that are made, that those things which cannot be shaken may remain : " Heb. xii. 27.— *John Morison, in "An Exposition of the Book of Psalms," 1829.*

Verse 14.—*"This is my rest for ever."* The heart of the saints is the dwelling-place of God. He rests in those who rest in him. He rests when he causes us to rest.— *Pasquier Quesnel.*

Verse 14.—*"Dwell."* The word translated *"dwell"* means originally to *sit,* and especially to sit enthroned, so that this idea would be necessarily suggested with the other to a Hebrew reader.—*Joseph Addison Alexander.*

Verses 14—18.—Now that he might apparently see how near the Lord is to all them that call upon him in faithfulness and truth, he waiteth not long for an answer, but carries it away with him before he departs. For to David's petition, *"Return, O* LORD, *unto thy resting-place, thou, and the ark of thy strength";* God's answer is this,—" This shall be my resting-place, here will I dwell, for I have a delight therein. I will bless her victuals with increase, and will satisfy her poor with bread." To David's petition, *"Let thy priests be clothed with righteousness, and let thy saints sing with joyfulness,"* God's answer is this : " I will clothe her priests with salvation : and her saints shall rejoice and sing." Lastly, to David's petition, *"For thy servant David's sake turn not away the face of thine anointed,"* God's answer is this : " There will I make the horn of David to flourish : I have ordained a light for mine anointed. As for his enemies, I will clothe them with shame ; but upon himself shall his crown flourish." As if he should have said,—Turn away the face of mine anointed ? Nay, that will I never do ; I will indeed turn away the face of the enemies of mine anointed ; their face shall be covered with confusion, and clothed with shame. But contrariwise, I have ordained a light for mine anointed. He shall even have a light in his face and a crown upon his head. " As for his enemies, I will clothe them with shame ; but upon himself shall his crown flourish."—*Thomas Playfere,* 1633.

Verse 15.—*"I will abundantly bless her provision,"* etc. The *provision* of Zion, the church of God, the word and ordinances, of which Christ is the sum and substance ; the gospel is milk for babes, and meat for strong men ; the ordinances are a feast of fat things ; Christ's flesh is meat indeed, and his blood drink indeed ; the whole provision is spiritual, savoury, salutary, strengthening, satisfying, and nourishing, when the Lord blesses it ; as he does to those who hunger and thirst after it, and feed upon it by faith ; so that their souls grow thereby, and they become fat and flourishing ; grace increases in them, and they are fruitful in every good work ; and this the Lord promises to do *abundantly*, in a very large way and manner ; or *certainly*, for it is, in the original text, " in blessing I will bless," that is, will surely bless, as this phrase is sometimes rendered.

"I will satisfy her poor with bread." Zion has her poor ; persons may be poor and yet belong to Zion, belong to Zion and yet be poor ; there are poor in all the churches of Christ ; our Lord told his disciples that they had the poor, and might expect to have them, always with them ; and particular directions are given to take care of Zion's poor under the gospel dispensation, that they may not want bread in a literal sense : though by the *poor* are chiefly designed the Lord's afflicted and distressed ones ; or those who in a spiritual sense are poor, sensible of their spiritual poverty, and seeking after the true riches ; or are poor in spirit, to whom the kingdom of heaven belongs ; these the Lord promises to satisfy, to fill them to the full with the bread of the gospel, made of the finest of the wheat, of which there is enough and to spare in his house ; and with Christ the bread of life, of which those that eat shall never die, but live for ever.—*John Gill.*

Verse 15.—*"Her provision I will bless, I will bless."* The repetition of the verb may express either certainty or fulness. *I will surely bless,* or *I will bless abundantly.* —*Joseph Addison Alexander.*

Verse 15.—*"I will abundantly bless her provision."* Believe it, a saint hath rare fare, gallant cheer, and rich diet, and all at free cost. He is feasted all the day long ; he is brought oft into the banqueting-house, and hath the rarest, the costliest, the wholesomest diet, that which is most hearty and strengthening, that which is most dainty and pleasant, and the greatest variety, and nothing is wanting, that may make his state happy, except a full enjoyment of glory itself. The Lord gives him all the experiences of his power and goodness to his Church in former ages to feed his hopes upon ; nay, many choice providences, many answers of prayer, many foretastes of glory, many ordinances, especially that great one of the Lord's Supper, at which Christ and all his benefits are served up in a royal dish to refresh and feast the faith, hope, and love of the saints. And that which sweetens all this—he knows that all this is but a little to what he shall shortly live upon when he comes to the marriage-supper ; then he shall always be feasted and never surfeited. And beside all this, he hath the sweet and refreshing incomes of the Spirit, filling him with such true pleasure, that he can easily spare the most sumptuous banquet, the noblest feast, and highest worldly delights, as infinitely short of one hour's treatment in his

Friend's chamber. And, if this be his entertainment in the inn, what shall he have at the court ? If this heavenly manna be his food in the wilderness, at what rate is he like to live when he comes into Canaan ? If this be the provision of the way, what is that of the country ?—*John Janeway, about* 1670.

Verse 15.—*"I will satisfy her poor with bread."* Christ is a satisfying good. A wooden loaf, a silver loaf, a golden loaf will not satisfy a hungry man ; the man must have bread. The dainties and dignities of the world, the grandeur and glory of the world, the plenty and prosperity of the world, the puff and popularity of the world, will not satisfy a soul sailing by the gates of hell, and crying out of the depths ; it must be a Christ. " Children, or I die," was the cry of the woman ; a Christ, or I die—a Christ, or I am damned, is the doleful ditty and doleful dialect of a despairing or desponding soul. " He that loveth silver shall not be satisfied therewith ; nor he that loveth abundance with increase : " Eccles. v. 10. It is a good observation that the world is round, but the heart of man is triangular. Now, all the globe of the world will not fill the triangular heart of man. What of the world and in the world can give quietness, when Christ, the Sun of Righteousness, goes down upon the soul ? The heart is a three-square, and nothing but a trinity in unity and a unity in trinity will satisfy this. Not riches, nor relations, nor barns, nor bags, will satisfy a convinced and deserted soul. This person can say concerning his bags as a great person upon a sick, if not a dying, bed, did concerning his bags,—Away, and away for ever. Though there be bag upon bag, yet they are altogether insignificant in a dying hour ; these bags, they are but as so many ciphers before a figure. This is the cry of despairing and desponding souls : " O satisfy us early with thy mercy ; that we may rejoice and be glad all our days : " Ps. xc. 14.—*Richard Mayhew,* 1679.

Verse 15.—*"I will satisfy her poor with bread."* Dainties I will not promise them ; a *sufficiency,* but not a *superfluity :* poor they may be, but not destitute ; bread they shall have, and of that *God's plenty,* as they say ; enough to bring them to their Father's house, " where there is bread enough." Let not, therefore, the poor Israelite fear to bring his offerings, or to disfurnish himself for God's worship, etc.— *John Trapp.*

Verse 16.—*"I will clothe her priests with salvation."* Their salvation shall be evident and conspicuous, just as a garment is.—*Aben-Ezra.*

Verse 16.—God's presence is an earnest of all good ; for all this follows upon " here will I dwell." By it he giveth meat to the hungry, and comfort to the poor, even the Bread of Life to the believing and repenting soul ; by it he himself is the sanctification of his priests, and his righteousness and salvation is their most glorious vesture ; and by his presence he maketh his elect ever glad, filling their hearts with joy and their mouths with songs.—*J. W. Burgon.*

Verse 16.—*"Her saints shall shout aloud for joy."* It would astonish and amuse a European stranger to hear these natives sing. They have not the least idea either of harmony or melody ; noise is what they best understand, and he that sings the loudest is considered to sing the best. I have occasionally remonstrated with them on the subject ; but the reply I once received silenced me for ever after. " Sing softly, brother," I said to one of the principal members. " Sing softly ! " he replied, " is it you, our father, who tells us to sing softly ? Did you ever hear us sing the praises of our Hindoo gods ? how we threw our heads backward, and with all our might shouted out the praises of those who are no gods ! And now do you tell us to *whisper* the praises of Jesus ? No, sir, we cannot—we must express in loud tones our gratitude to him who loved us, and died for us ! " And so they continued to sing with all their might, and without further remonstrance.— *G. Gogerly, in "The Pioneers : a Narrative of the Bengal Mission,"* 1870.

Verse 17.—*" There will I make the horn of David to bud,"* etc. A metaphor taken from those goodly creatures, as stags, and such like ; whose chiefest beauty and strength consisteth in their horns, especially when they bud and branch abroad. —*Thomas Playfere.*

Verse 17.—*" The horn of David."* This image of *a horn* is frequent in the Old Testament. . . The explanation must be found neither in the horns of the altar on which criminals sought to lay hold, nor in the horns with which they ornamented their helmets ; the figure is taken from the horns of the bull, in which the power of this animal resides. It is a natural image among an agricultural people. . . .

Just as the strength of the animal is concentrated in its horn, so all the delivering power granted to the family of David for the advantage of the people will be concentrated in the Messiah.—*F. Godet, in " A Commentary on the Gospel of St. Luke,"* 1875.

Verse 17.—*" Make the horn to bud."* In the beginning of the month of March the common stag, or red deer, is lurking in the sequestered spots of his forest home, harmless as his mate, and as timorous. Soon a pair of prominences make their appearance on his forehead, covered with a velvety skin. In a few days these little prominences have attained some length, and give the first indication of their true form. Grasp one of these in the hand and it will be found burning hot to the touch, for the blood runs fiercely through the velvety skin, depositing at every touch a minute portion of bony matter. More and more rapidly grow the horns, the carotid arteries enlarging in order to supply a sufficiency of nourishment, and in the short period of ten weeks the enormous mass of bony matter has been completed. Such a process is almost, if not entirely, without parallel in the history of the animal kingdom.—*J. G. Wood, in " The Illustrated Natural History,"* 1861.

Verse 17.—*" The horn."* My friend, Mr. Graham, of Damascus, says, concerning the horns worn by eastern women, " This head-dress is of dough, tin, silver, or gold, according to the wealth of the different classes. The rank is also indicated by the length of it. The nobler the lady, the longer the horn. Some of them are more than an English yard." I procured at Damascus an ancient gem, representing a man wearing the horn. In the present day, its use is confined to the women.—*John Wilson, in " The Lands of the Bible,"* 1847.

Verse 17.—*" I have ordained a lamp for mine anointed."* This clause contains an allusion to the law, which cannot be preserved in any version. The word translated " lamp " is used to designate the several burners of the golden candlesticks (Ex. xxv. 37 ; xxxv. 14 ; xxxvii. 23 ; xxxix. 37), and the verb here joined with it is the one applied to the ordering or tending of the sacred lights by the priests (Ex. xxvii. 21 ; Lev. xxvii. 3). The meaning of the whole verse is, that the promise of old made to David and to Zion should be yet fulfilled, however dark and inauspicious present appearances.—*Joseph Addison Alexander.*

Verse 17.—*"I have ordained a lamp for mine anointed."* We here remark, 1. The designation given unto Christ by God his Father ; he is *"mine anointed."* Though he be despised and rejected of men ; though an unbelieving world see no form or comeliness in him, why he should be desired, yet I own him, and challenge him as mine Anointed, the Prophet, Priest, and King of my church. " I have found David my servant : with my holy oil have I anointed him : with whom my hand shall be established : mine arm also shall strengthen him " : Ps. lxxxix. 20, 21.

2. The great means of God's appointment for manifesting the glory of Christ to a lost world ; he has provided *" a lamp "* for his Anointed. The use of a lamp is to give light to people in the darkness of the night ; so the word of God, particularly the gospel, is a light shining in a dark place, until the day of glory dawn, when the Lord God and the Lamb will be the light of the ransomed for endless evermore.

3. The authority by which this lamp is lighted and carried through this dark world ; it is *"ordained"* of God ; and by his commandment it is that we preach and spread the light of the gospel (Mark xvi. 15, 20).—*Ebenezer Erskine,* 1680—.

Verse 17.—*"I have ordained a lamp for mine anointed."* That is, I have ordained prosperity and blessings for him ; blessings upon his person, and especially the blessing of posterity. Children are as a *lamp* or *candle* in their father's house, making the name of their ancestors conspicuous ; hence in Scripture a child given to succeed his father is called a *lamp.* When God by Ahijah the prophet told Jeroboam that God would take the kingdom out of the hand of Solomon's son, and give it unto him, even ten tribes ; he yet adds (1 Kings xi. 36), " And unto his son will I give one tribe, that David my servant may have a light (*lamp* or *candle*) alway before me in Jerusalem, the city which I have chosen to put my name there." And again (1 Kings xv. 4), when Abijam the son of Rehoboam proved wicked, the text saith, " Nevertheless for David's sake did the Lord his God give him a *lamp* (or *candle*) in Jerusalem, to set up his son after him."—*Joseph Caryl.*

Verses 17, 18.—God having chosen David's family, he here promiseth to bless that also with suitable blessings.

1. Growing power : *"There* (in Zion) *will I make the horn of David to bud."* The royal dignity should increase more and more, and constant additions be made to the lustre of it. Christ is the "horn of salvation," noting a plentiful and powerful

salvation, which God hath raised up and made to bud " in the house of his servant David." David had promised to use his power for God's glory, to cut off the horns of the wicked, and to exalt the horns of the righteous (Ps. lxxv. 10) ; and in recompense for it, God here promises to make his horn to bud ; for to them that have power and use it well, more shall be given.

2. Lasting honour : *"I have ordained a lamp for mine anointed."* Thou wilt " light my candle " (Ps. xviii. 28) : that lamp is likely to burn brightly which God ordains. A lamp is a successor ; for when a lamp is almost out, another may be lighted by it : it is a succession ; for by this means David shall not want a man to stand before God. Christ is the lamp and the light of the world.

3. Complete victory. *"His enemies,"* that have formed designs against him, *"will I clothe with shame,"* when they shall see their designs baffled. Let the enemies of all good governors expect to be clothed with shame, and especially the enemies of the Lord Jesus and his government, who shall rise in the last great day " to everlasting shame and contempt."

4. Universal prosperity : *"Upon himself shall his crown flourish,"* i.e., his government shall be more and more his honour. This was to have its full accomplishment in Christ Jesus, whose crown of honour and power shall never fade, nor the flowers of it wither. The crowns of earthly princes " endure not to all generations " (Prov. xxvii. 24) ; but Christ's crown shall endure to all eternity, and the crowns reserved for his faithful subjects are such as " fade not away."— *Matthew Henry.*

Verse 18.—*"His enemies will I clothe with shame."* That is, *shame* shall so inseparably cover them, that as wheresoever a man goeth, he carrieth his clothes with him ; so wheresoever they go they shall carry their *shame* with them. And that which is strangest of all, they which are ashamed use to clothe or cover their shame, and then think themselves well enough ; but David's enemies shall be so ashamed, that even the very covering of their shame shall be a discovering of it ; and the clothing or cloaking of their ignominy shall be nothing else but a girding of it more closely and more inseparably unto them.—*Thomas Playfere.*

Verse 18.—*"Upon himself shall the crown flourish."* This idea seems to be taken from the nature of the ancient crowns bestowed upon conquerors. From the earliest periods of history, the laurel, olive, ivy, etc., furnished crowns to adorn the heads of heroes, who had conquered in the field of battle, gained the prize in the race or performed some other important service to the public. These were the dear bought rewards of the most heroic exploits of antiquity. This sets the propriety of the phrase in full view. The idea of a crown of gold and jewels flourishing, is at least unnatural ; whereas, flourishing is natural to laurels, oaks, etc. These were put upon the heads of the victors in full verdure, and their merit seemed to make them flourish on their heads, in fresher green. The literal crown which Jesus wore was also of the vegetable kind, and the thorn of sorrow never flourished in such vigour as on his head. Now he has got the crown of life, which shall not fade away, like the perishing verdure of the crowns of other heroes. It shall flourish for ever, with all the vigour of immortality, and bring forth all the olive-fruits of peace for his people. Its branches shall spread, and furnish crowns for all the victors in the spiritual warfare.—*Alexander Pirie,* —1804.

HINTS TO PREACHERS.

Verse 1.—I. The Lord remembers Jesus, our David : he loves him, he delights in him, he is with him. II. In that memory his griefs have a prominent place— " all his afflictions." III. Yet the Lord would be put in remembrance by his people.

Verses 1, 2.—Concerning his people, I. The Lord remembers, 1. Their persons. 2. Their afflictions. 3. Their vows. II. The Lord remembers them, 1. To accept them. 2. To sympathise with them. 3. To assist them.

Verses 1, 2.—I. God remembers his people, each one : " Remember David."

The Spirit maketh intercession within us according to the will of God. II. He remembers their afflictions : " David and all his afflictions." " I know thy works and thy tribulation." III. He remembers their vows, especially, 1. Those which relate to his service. 2. Those which are solemnly made. 3. Those which are faithfully performed.—*G. R.*

Verses 1—5.—Notice, I. How painfully David felt what he conceived to be a dishonouring of God, which he thought he might be able to remedy. Consider " his afflictions,"—because the ark dwelt within curtains, while he himself dwelt in a house of cedar : 2 Sam. vii. 2. Consider, 1. Its singularity. Most find affliction in personal losses ; very few suffer from a cause like this. 2. The little sympathy such a feeling meets with from the most of men. " If God means to convert the heathen, he can do it without you, young man," was said to Dr., then Mr. Carey, when heathenism was an affliction to him. 3. Its fittingness to a really God-fearing man. 4. Its pleasingness to God : 1 Sam. ii. 30. II. How earnestly he set himself to remedy the evil he deplored : " He sware," etc. There cannot be the least doubt that he would have foregone the enjoyment of temporal luxuries until he had accomplished the work dear to his heart, if he had been permitted of God. Remark, 1. There is little zeal for God's honour when self-denial is not exercised for the sake of his cause. 2. Were a like zeal generally shown by God's people, there would be more givers and more liberal gifts ; more workers, and the work more heartily and better done. 3. It would be well to astonish the world, and deserve the commendations of the righteous by becoming enthusiasts for the honour of God.—*J. F.*

Verses 3—5.—I. We should desire a habitation for God more than for ourselves. God should have the best of everything. " See, now, I dwell in a house of cedar, but the ark of God dwelleth within curtains." II. We should be guided by the house of God in seeking a house for ourselves : " Surely I will not come," etc. III. We should labour for the prosperity of God's house even more than of our own. Nothing should make sleep more sweet to us than when the church of God prospers; nothing keep us more awake then when it declines : " I will not give sleep," etc. (verse 4) ; " Is it time for you, O ye, to dwell in your ceiled houses, and this house lie waste ? "—*G. R.*

Verse 5.—Something to live for—to find fresh habitations for God. I. The Condescension implied : God *with us.* II. The Districts explored : hearts, homes, " dark places of the earth." III. The Royalty of the Work. It makes King David busy, and is labour worthy of a king.—*W. B. H.*

Verse 5.—"*A place for the* LORD." In the heart, the home, the assembly, the life. Everywhere we must find or make a place for the Lord.

Verse 5.—"*The mighty God of Jacob.*" I. Mighty, and therefore he joined heaven and earth at Bethel. II. Mighty, and therefore brought Jacob back from Mesopotamia. III. Mighty, and yet wrestled with him at Jabbok. IV. Mighty, and yet allowed him to be afflicted. V. Mighty and therefore gave him full deliverance.

Verses 6, 7.—We shall use this for practical purposes. A soul longing to meet with God. God has appointed a meeting place. I. *We know what it is.* A mercy-seat, a throne of grace, a place of revealed glory. Within it the law preserved. Heavenly food—pot of manna. Holy rule—Aaron's rod. II. *We desire to find it.* Intensely. Immediately. Reverently. Longing to receive it. III. *We heard of it.* In our young days. We almost forget where. From ministers, from holy men, from those who loved us. IV. *We found it.* Where we least expected it. In a despised place. In a lonely place. Where we lost ourselves. Very near us— where we hid like Adam among the trees. V. *We will go.* To God in Christ. For all he gives. To dwell with him. To learn of him. VI. *We will worship.* Humbly. Solemnly. Gratefully. Preparing for heaven.

Verse 7.—I. The Place : " His tabernacles." 1. Built for God. 2. Accepted by God : present everywhere, he is especially present here. II. The Attendance : " We will go," etc. There God is present to meet us, and there we should be present to meet him. III. The Design : 1. For adoration. 2. For self-consecration : " We will worship at his footstool."—*G. R.*

Verses 8, 9.—I. The Presence of God desired—1. That it may be signally manifested : " Arise " and enter. 2. That it may be gracious : " Thou and the ark "—that he may be present on the mercy-seat. 3. That it may be felt : accompanied with power : " The ark of thy strength." 4. That it may be abiding :

" Arise into thy rest." II. The reasons for this desire. 1. With respect to the priests or ministers : " Let thy priests," etc. : not their own righteousness, but as a clothing : let them speak of " garments of salvation " and " robes of righteousness." 2. With respect to the worshippers : " And let thy saints," etc. Let ministers preach the gift of righteousness ; not that which grows out of man's nature, but that which is " unto all and upon all them that believe," and saints will shout for joy.—*G. R.*

Verse 9.—Consider, I. The importance of a righteous ministry in the church. II. The connection between such a ministry and a joyous people. III. The dependence of both on the gracious working of God.—*J. F.*

Verse 9 (second clause).—I. Saints. II. Shouting. III. Explaining—" for joy." IV. Encouraging—" Let thy saints shout."

Verse 9 (second clause).—The connection between holiness and joy.

Verses 9, 16.—*The Spiritual Vestry.* I. The Vestments : 1. Righteousness ; for which the costliest stole is a poor substitute. 2. Salvation : learning, oratory, etc., of small account in comparison. II. The Procuring of the vestments : 1. Must be from God. 2. Earnest prayer should constantly arise from all saints. III. The Robing : 1. By God's own hand ! 2. Their beauty and power who are so invested. 3. The persons are " thy priests."—*W. B. H.*

Verses 9, 16.—I. Priests and Saints. II. Vestments. III. " Hymns Ancient and Modern." IV. The Real Presence : God giving the garments and the joy.

Verse 10.—I. An evil to be deprecated : " Turn not away the face "—so that he cannot see thee, or be seen of thee, or accepted, or allowed to hope. II. A plea to be employed, " for thy servant David's sake "—thy covenant with him, his zeal, his consecration, his afflictions, his service. Good gospel pleading, such as may be used on many occasions.

Verse 11.—I. The divine oath. II. Its eternal stability. III. The everlasting Kingship.

Verse 11 (middle clause).—Our confidence : " He will not turn from it." He is not a changing God. He foreknew everything. He is able to carry out his purpose. His honour is bound up in it. His oath can never be broken.

Verse 12.—Family favour may be perpetual, but the conditions must be observed.

Verse 13.—I. Sovereign choice. II. Condescending indwelling. III. Eternal rest. IV. Gracious reason—" I have desired it."

Verse 14.—I. *God finding rest in his church.* 1. The three persons honoured. 2. The divine nature exercised. 3. Eternal purposes fulfilled. 4. Almighty energies rewarded. 5. Tremendous sacrifices remembered. 6. Glorious attributes extolled. 7. Dearest relationships indulged. II. *This rest enduring for ever.* 1. There will always be a church. 2. That church will always be such as God can rest in. 3. That church will therefore be secure on earth. 4. That church will be glorified eternally in heaven.

Verse 15.—I. Blessed provision. II. Satisfied people—" satisfy her poor." III. Glorified God—" I will." IV. Happy place—Zion.

Verses 16, 18.—Two forms of clothing : salvation and shame, prepared for his priests and his enemies. Which will you wear ?

Verse 17.—A Lamp ordained for God's Anointed. Being the Substance of Two Sermons, by Ebenezer Erskine. [Works, Vol. 3, pp. 3—41.]

Verses 17, 18.—I. The budding horn of growing power. II. The perpetual lamp of constant brightness. III. The sordid array of defeated foes. IV. The unfading wreath of glorious sovereignty.

Verse 18.—I. *His enemies clothed.* 1. Who are they ? The openly profane. The moral but irreligious. The self-righteous. The hypocritical. 2. How clothed with shame ? In repentance, in disappointment, in remorse, in destruction. Sin detected. Self defeated. Hopes scattered. 3. Who clothes them ? The Lord. He will shame them thoroughly. II. *Himself crowned.* 1. His crown : his dominion and glory. 2. Its flourishing. Glory extending. Subjects increasing. Wealth growing. Foes fearing, etc.

Verse 18 (last clause).—The **Lord** Jesus himself the source, sustenance, and centre of the prosperity of his kingdom.

PSALM CXXXIII.

TITLE.—*A Song of Degrees of David. We see no reason for depriving David of the authorship of this sparkling sonnet. He knew by experience the bitterness occasioned by divisions in families, and was well prepared to celebrate in choicest psalmody the blessing of unity for which he sighed. Among the " songs of degrees," this hymn has certainly attained unto a good degree, and even in common literature it is frequently quoted for its perfume and dew. In this Psalm there is no wry word, all is " sweetness and light,"—a notable ascent from Psalm cxx. with which the pilgrims set out. That is full of war and lamentation, but this sings of peace and pleasantness. The visitors to Zion were about to return, and this may have been their hymn of joy because they had seen such union among the tribes who had gathered at the common altar. The previous Psalm, which sings of the covenant, had also revealed the centre of Israel's unity in the Lord's anointed and the promises made to him. No wonder that brethren dwell in unity when God dwells among them, and finds his rest in them. Our translators have given to this Psalm an admirable explanatory heading, " The benefit of the communion of saints." These good men often hit off the meaning of a passage in a few words.*

EXPOSITION.

BEHOLD, how good and how pleasant *it is* for brethren to dwell together in unity !

2 *It is* like the precious ointment upon the head, that ran down upon the beard, *even* Aaron's beard : that went down to the skirts of his garments ;

3 As the dew of Hermon, *and as the dew* that descended upon the mountains of Zion : for there the LORD commanded the blessing, *even* life for evermore.

1. *"Behold."* It is a wonder seldom seen, therefore behold it ! It may be seen, for it is the characteristic of real saints,—therefore fail not to inspect it ! It is well worthy of admiration ; pause and gaze upon it ! It will charm you into imitation, therefore note it well ! God looks on with approval, therefore consider it with attention. *"How good and how pleasant it is for brethren to dwell together in unity ! "* No one can tell the exceeding excellence of such a condition ; and so the Psalmist uses the word " how " twice ;—Behold how good ! and how pleasant ! He does not attempt to measure either the good or the pleasure, but invites us to behold for ourselves. The combination of the two adjectives " good " and " pleasant," is more remarkable than the conjunction of two stars of the first magnitude : for a thing to be " good " is good, but for it also to be pleasant is better. All men love pleasant things, and yet it frequently happens that the pleasure is evil ; but here the condition is as good as it is pleasant, as pleasant as it is good, for the same *" how "* is set before each qualifying word.

For *brethren* according to the flesh to dwell together is not always wise ; for experience teaches that they are better a little apart, and it is shameful for them to dwell together in disunion. They had much better part in peace like Abraham and Lot, than dwell together in envy like Joseph's brothers. When brethren can and do dwell together *in unity*, then is their communion worthy to be gazed upon and sung of in holy psalmody. Such sights ought often to be seen among those who are near of kin, for they are brethren, and therefore should be united in heart and aim ; they dwell together, and it is for their mutual comfort that there should be no strife ; and yet how many families are rent by fierce feuds, and exhibit a spectacle which is neither good nor pleasant !

As to brethren in spirit, they ought to dwell together in church fellowship, and in that fellowship one essential matter is unity. We can dispense with uniformity if we possess unity : oneness of life, truth, and way ; oneness in Christ Jesus ; oneness of object and spirit—these we must have, or our assemblies will be synagogues of contention rather than churches of Christ. The closer the unity the better; for the more of the good and the pleasant there will be. Since we are imperfect beings, somewhat of the evil and the unpleasant is sure to intrude; but this will readily be neutralized and easily ejected by the true love of the saints, if it really exists. Christian unity is good in itself, good for ourselves, good for the brethren, good for our converts, good for the outside world; and for certain it is pleasant; for a loving heart must have pleasure and give pleasure in associating with others of like nature. A church united for years in earnest service of the Lord is a well of goodness and joy to all those who dwell round about it.

2. "*It is like the precious ointment upon the head.*" In order that we may the better behold brotherly unity David gives us a resemblance, so that as in a glass we may perceive its blessedness. It has a *sweet perfume* about it, comparable to that precious ointment with which the first High Priest was anointed at his ordination. It is *a holy thing*, and so again is like the oil of consecration which was to be used only in the Lord's service. What a sacred thing must brotherly love be when it can be likened to an oil which must never be poured on any man but on the Lord's high-priest alone! It is a *diffusive* thing: being poured on his head the fragrant oil flowed down upon Aaron's head, and thence dropped upon his garments till the utmost hem was anointed therewith; and even so doth brotherly love extend its benign power and bless all who are beneath its influence. Hearty concord brings a benediction upon all concerned; its goodness and pleasure are shared in by the lowliest members of the household; even the servants are the better and the happier because of the lovely unity among the members of the family. *It has a special use* about it; for as by the anointing oil Aaron was set apart for the special service of Jehovah, even so those who dwell in love are the better fitted to glorify God in his church. The Lord is not likely to use for his glory those who are devoid of love; they lack the anointing needful to make them priests unto the Lord. "*That ran bown upon the beard, even Aaron's beard.*" This is a chief point of comparison, that as the oil did not remain confined to the place where it first fell, but flowed down the High Priest's hair and bedewed his beard, even so brotherly love descending from the head distils and descends, anointing as it runs, and perfuming all it lights upon. "*That went down to the skirts of his garments.*" Once set in motion it would not cease from flowing. It might seem as if it were better not to smear his garments with oil, but the sacred unguent could not be restrained, it flowed over his holy robes; even thus does brotherly love not only flow over the hearts upon which it was first poured out, and descend to those who are an inferior part of the mystical body of Christ, but it runs where it is not sought for, asking neither leave nor license to make its way. Christian affection knows no limits of parish, nation, sect or age. Is the man a believer in Christ? Then he is in the one body, and I must yield him an abiding love. Is he one of the poorest, one of the least spiritual, one of the least lovable? Then he is as the skirts of the garment, and my heart's love must fall even upon him. Brotherly love comes from the head, but falls to the feet. Its way is downward. It "ran down," and it "went down": love for the brethren condescends to men of low estate, it is not puffed up, but is lowly and meek. This is no small part of its excellence: oil would not anoint if it did not flow down, neither would brotherly love diffuse its blessing if it did not descend.

3. "*As the dew of Hermon, and as the dew that descended upon the mountains of Zion.*" From the loftier mountains the moisture appears to be wafted to the lesser hills: the dews of Hermon fall on Zion. The Alpine Lebanon ministers to the minor elevation of the city of David; and so does brotherly love descend from higher to the lower, refreshing and enlivening in its course. Holy concord is as dew, mysteriously blessed, full of life and growth for all plants of grace. It brings with it so much benediction that it is as no common dew, but as that of Hermon which is specially copious, and far-reaching. The proper rendering is, "As the dew of Hermon that descended upon the mountains of Zion," and this tallies with the figure which has been already used; and sets forth by a second simile the sweet descending diffusiveness of brotherly unity. "*For there the Lord commanded the blessing, even life for evermore.*" That is, in Zion, or better still, in the place where brotherly love abounds. Where love reigns God reigns. Where love wishes blessing, there God commands the blessing. God has but to command, and it is done. He is so pleased to see his dear children happy in one another that he fails not to make them happy in himself. He gives especially his best blessing of eternal life, for love is life; dwelling together in love we have begun the enjoyments of eternity,

and these shall not be taken from us. Let us love for evermore, and we shall live for evermore. This makes Christian brotherhood so good and pleasant ; it has Jehovah's blessing resting upon it, and it cannot be otherwise than sacred like "the precious ointment," and heavenly like " the dew of Hermon."

O for more of this rare virtue !   Not the love which comes and goes, but that which dwells ; not that spirit which separates and secludes, but that which dwells together ; not that mind which is all for debate and difference, but that which dwells together in unity.   Never shall we know the full power of the anointing till we are of one heart and of one spirit ; never will the sacred dew of the spirit descend in all its fulness till we are perfectly joined together in the same mind ; never will the covenanted and commanded blessing come forth from the Lord our God till once again we shall have " one Lord, one faith, one baptism."   Lord, lead us into this most precious spiritual unity, for thy Son's sake. Amen.

EXPLANATORY NOTES AND QUAINT SAYINGS.

Whole Psalm.—This Psalm is an effusion of holy joy occasioned by the sight of the gathering of Israel as one great household at the yearly feasts. . . . There might likewise be an allusion to the previous jealousies and alienations in the family of Israel, which seemed to be exchanged for mutual concord and affection, on David's accession to the throne of the whole nation.—*Joseph Addison Alexander.*

Verse 1.—"*Behold how good and how pleasant it is,*" etc.   There are three things wherein it is very pleasant to behold the people of God joining in one.

1. When they join or are *one in opinion* and judgment, when they all think the same thing, and are of one mind in the truth.

2. When they join together and are *one in affection*, when they are all of one heart, though possibly they are not all of one mind ; or, when they meet in affection, though not in opinion.   When David had spoken admiringly of this goodly sight, he spoke declaratively concerning the goodness of it (verse 2) : "*It is like the precious ointment upon the head.*"   'Tis so, first, for the sweetness of it ; 'tis so, secondly· for the diffusiveness of it (as followeth), "*that ran down upon the beard, even Aaron's beard : that went down to the skirts of his garments.*"

3. It is a blessed thing to see them joining *together in duty,* either as duty is considered—First, *in doing that which is good ;* or, when, as the apostle's word is (2 Cor. vi. 1), they are, among themselves, " workers together " in any good work : we say (to fill up the text), " workers together with God."   That's a blessed sight indeed, when we join with God, and God joineth with us in his work.   It is also a blessed sight when all the ministers of Jesus Christ, and many as members of Jesus Christ, join in any good work, in this especially, to beseech all we have to do with " that they receive not the grace of God in vain."   Secondly, *in turning from evil,* and putting iniquity far from them ; in praying for the pardon of sin, and making their peace with God.   'Tis a good work to turn away from evil, especially when all who are concerned in it join in it . . . . As to join in sin, and to be brethren in iniquity, is the worst of unions, indeed, a combination against God ; so to join as brethren in mourning for sin and repenting of our iniquities is a blessed union, and highly pleasing to God.—*Joseph Caryl.*

Verse 1.—"*How good and how pleasant it is,*" etc.   The terms of this praise and commendation, or the particulars whereof it consists, is taken from a twofold qualification.

1. Brotherly concord and the improvement of it in all occasional expressions is a very great good.   This is, and will appear to be so in sundry considerations.

As, *First,* in regard of the *Author* and *owner* of it, which is *God Himself,* who lays special claim hereunto.   Therefore in Scripture we find him to be from hence denominated and intitled. 1 Cor. xiv. 33.   " God is not the author of confusion (or of unquietness), but the author of peace. 2 Cor. xiii. 11.   " The God of peace and love."   Peace is called " the peace of God : " Phil. iv. 7.   And God is called the " God of peace ; " each of which expressions does refer it and reduce it to him, and does thereby advance it. Look, then, how far forth God himself is said to be good, so far forth is this dwelling in unity good also, as it is commanded and owned by him, as it appears thus to be.

Secondly. It is good in the *nature* of it ; it is good, as any grace is good. It is good morally. Love is a fruit of the Spirit : Gal. v. 22. And so to dwell in love and unity one with another is a goodness reducible thereunto. It is good spiritually ; it is not only such a good as is taught by moral philosophy, and practised by the students thereof, but it is taught by the *Holy Ghost himself*, and is a part of the work of regeneration and of the new creature in us, especially if we take it in the full latitude and extent of it, as it becomes us to do.

Thirdly. It is good in the *effects* and *consequences* and *concomitants* of it : it has much good. It is *bonum utile*. A great deal of advantage comes by brethren's dwelling together in unity, especially *spiritual advantage*, and for the doing and receiving of good.

2. The second qualification is, the sweetness of it, because it is *"pleasant:"* it is not only *bonum utile*, and *bonum honestum*, but it is also *bonum jucundum;* it has a great deal of pleasure in it. Pleasure is such a kind of goodness, especially to some kind of persons, as that they care not almost what they do or part with to obtain it, and all other good besides is nothing to them, if it be devoid of this. Therefore for the further commendation of this fraternal unity to us, there is this also to be considered, that it is *"pleasant."* Thus it is with respect to all sorts of persons whatsoever, that are made sensible of it.

First. It is *pleasant to God*, it is such as is very acceptable to him ; it is that which he much delights in, wheresoever he observes it ; being himself a God of peace, he does therefore so much the more delight in peaceable Christians, and such as do relate to himself. How much do natural parents rejoice in the agreement of their children, to see them loving and friendly and kind and courteous to one another, oh, it pleases them and joys them at their very heart ! and so it is likewise with God to those who are truly his.

Secondly. This brotherly unity is also *pleasant to ourselves*, who accordingly shall have so much the greater pleasure in it and from it.

Thirdly. It is also *pleasing to others*, indeed to all men else besides, that are standers-by and spectators of it. *"Behold, how pleasant it is,"* etc. It is pleasant to all beholders : "He that in these things serveth Christ is acceptable to God, and approved of men," says the apostle : Rom. xiv. 18.—*Thomas Horton,*—1673.

Verse 1.—*"Pleasant."* It is a pleasant thing for the saints and people of God to agree together ; for the same word which is used here for *"pleasant,"* is used also in the Hebrew for a harmony of music, such as when they rise to the highest strains of the viol, when the strings are all put in order to make up a harmony ; so pleasant is it, such pleasantness is there in the saints' agreement. The same word is used also in the Hebrew for the pleasantness of a corn field. When a field is clothed with corn, though it be cut down, yet it is very pleasant, oh, how pleasant is it ; and such is the saints' agreement. The same word in the Psalmist is used also for the sweetness of honey, and of sweet things in opposition to bitter things. And thus you see the pleasantness of it, by its being compared to the harmony of music, to the corn field, to the sweetness of honey, to the precious ointment that ran down Aaron's beard, and to the dew that fell upon Hermon and the hills of Zion : and all this to discover the pleasantness, profitableness, and sweetness of the saints' agreement. It is a pleasant thing to behold the sun, but it is much more pleasant to behold the saints' agreement and unity among themselves.—*William Bridge.*

Verse 1.—*"Brethren."* Abraham made this name, *"brethren,"* a mediator to keep peace between Lot and him : " Are we not brethren ? " saith Abraham. As if he should say, Shall brethren fall out for trifles, like infidels ? This was enough to pacify Lot, for Abraham to put him in mind that they were brethren ; when he heard the name of brethren, straight his heart yielded, and the strife was ended. So this should be the lawyer to end quarrels between Christians, to call to mind that they are brethren. And they which have spent all at law have wished that they had taken this lawyer, to think, with Lot, whether it were meet for brethren to strive like enemies.—*Henry Smith.*

Verse 1.—*"Brethren."* Some critics observe that the Hebrew word for a *brother* is of near brotherhood or alliance with two other words, whereof the first signifies *one*, and the other *alike* or *together*, to show that *"brethren"* ought to be as one, and *alike,* or *together ;* which latter is by an elegant *paranomasia* joined with it : " Behold, how good and how pleasant it is for *brethren to dwell together in unity,"* or, as we put it in the margin, *"to dwell even together."* So then, the very word whereby *" brethren"* are expressed notes that there ought to be a *nearness,* a *similitude,* yea, a *oneness* (if I may so speak) between them in their affections and actions.— *Joseph Caryl.*

Verse 1.—*To dwell* is a word of residence, and abode, and continuation. There is also pertaining to the love and concord of brethren a perseverance and persistency in it ; not only to be together, or to come together, or to meet together for some certain time ; but *to dwell* together in unity, this is which is here so extolled and commended unto us. It seems to be no such great matter, nor to carry any such great difficulty in it, for men to command themselves to some expresions of peace and friendship for some short space of time (though there are many now and then who are hardly able to do that) ; but to hold out in it, and to continue so long, this endurance is almost impossible to them. Yet this is that which is required of them as *Christians* and as *"brethren"* one to another, even to *"dwell together in unity ; "* to follow peace, and love, and concord, and mutual agreement, not only upon some occasional meetings, but all along the whole course of their lives, whilst they converse and live together.—*Thomas Horton.*

Verse 1.—*"Together in unity."* If there be but one God, as God is one, so let them that serve him be one. This is what Christ prayed so heartily for. " That they may be one" : John xvii. 21. Christians should be one, 1. *In judgment.* The apostle exhorts to be all of one mind. 1 Cor. i. 10. How sad is it to see religion wearing a coat of divers colours ; to see Christians of so many opinions, and going so many different ways ! It is Satan that has sown these tares of division. Matt. xiii. 39. He first divided men from God, and then one man from another. 2. One *in affection.* They should have one heart. " The multitude of them that believed were of one heart and of one soul " : Acts iv. 32. As in music, though there be several strings of a viol, yet all make one sweet harmony ; so, though there are several Christians, yet there should be one sweet harmony of affection among them. There is but one God, and they that serve him should be one. There is nothing that would render the true religion more lovely, or make more proselytes to it, than to see the professors of it tied together with the heart-strings of love. If God be one, let all that profess him be of one mind, and one heart, and thus fulfil Christ's prayer, " that they all may be one."—*Thomas Watson.*

Verse 2.—*"Precious ointment upon the head."* Though every priest was anointed, yet only the high priest was anointed on the *head,* and there is a tradition that this rite was omitted after the Captivity, so that there is a special stress on the name of Aaron.—*Neale and Littledale.*

Verse 2.—*"The precious ointment . . . that ran down upon the beard . . . that went down to the skirts of his garments."* Magnificence, misnamed by churls extravagance and waste, is the invariable attribute of all true love. David recognised this truth when he selected the profuse anointing of Aaron with the oil of consecration at his installation into the office of High Priest as a fit emblem of brotherly love. There was waste in that anointing, too, as well as in the one which took place at Bethany. For the oil was not *sprinkled* on the head of Aaron, though that might have been sufficient for the purpose of a mere ceremony. The vessel was emptied on the High Priest's person, so that its contents flowed down from the head upon the beard, and even to the skirts of the sacerdotal robes. In that very waste lay the point of the resemblance for David. It was a feature that was very likely to strike his mind, for he, too, was a wasteful man in his way. He had loved God in a manner which exposed him to the charge of extravagance. He had danced before the Lord, for example, when the ark was brought up from the house of Obededom to Jerusalem, forgetful of his dignity, exceeding the bounds of decorum, and, as it might seem, without excuse, as a much less hearty demonstration would have served the purpose of a religious solemnity.—*Alexander Balmain Bruce, in* "*The Training of the Twelve,"* 1877.

Verse 2.—*"The precious ointment . . . that ran down."* Of the Hebrew perfumes an immense quantity was annually manufactured and consumed, of which we have a very significant indication in the fact that the holy anointing oil of the tabernacle and temple was never made in smaller quantities than 750 ounces of solids compounded with five quarts of oil, and was so profusely employed that when applied to Aaron's head it flowed down over his beard and breast, to the very skirts of his garments.—*Hugh Macmillan, in "The Ministry of Nature,"* 1871.

Verse 2.—*"That ran down . . . . that went down,"* etc. Christ's grace is so diffusive of itself, that it conveys holiness to us, " running down from the head to the skirts," to all his members. He was not only anointed himself, but he is our anointer. Therefore it is called " the oil of gladness," because it rejoiceth our hearts, by giving us spiritual gladness, and peace of conscience.—*Thomas Adams.*

Verse 2.—*"Down upon the beard, even Aaron's beard : that went down to the skirts of his garments."* Not the extremity of them, as our version inclines to ; for not so great a quantity of oil was poured upon him ; nor would it have been decent to have his clothes thus greased from top to bottom ; but the upper part of his garment, the top of his coat, on which the beard lay, as Zarchi ; the neck or collar of it, as Kimchi and Ben Melech ; the hole in which the head went through when it was put on, about which there was a band, that it might not be rent : Exod. xxviii. 32, and xxxix. 23 ; where the Septuagint use the same word as here.—*John Gill.*

Verses 2, 3.—In this prayer and song of the unity of the church, it is noteworthy how, commencing with the fundamental idea of *"brethren,"* we rise to the realization of the Elder Brother, who is our common anointed High Priest. It is the bond of his priesthood which joins us together as brethren. It is the common anointing which flows down even to the skirts of the garment of our High Priest which marks our being brethren. Whether we dwell north or south, meeting in Zion, and sharing in the blessings of that eternal Priesthood of Christ, we form in reality, and before our Father, but one family—" the whole family in earth and heaven." Our real bond of union consists in the " flowing down," the " running down," or " descending" of the common blessing, which marks the steps in this Psalm of Degrees (verses 2, 3). And if " the dew of Hermon " has descended upon " the mountains of Zion," long after the sun has risen shall gladsome fruit appear—in some twenty, in some thirty, and in some a hundredfold.—*Alfred Edersheim.*

Verse 3.—*"As the dew of Hermon,"* etc. " What we read in the 133rd Psalm of the dew of Hermon descending upon the mountains of Zion," says Van de Velde in his " Travels " (Bd. i. S. 97), " is now become quite clear to me. Here as I sat at the foot of Hermon, I understood how the water-drops which rose from its forest-mantled heights, and out of the highest ravines, which are filled the whole year round with snow, after the sun's rays have attenuated them and moistened the atmosphere with them, descend at evening-time as a heavy dew upon the lower mountains which lie round about as its spurs. One sought to have seen Hermon with its white-golden crown glistening aloft in the blue sky, in order to be able rightly to understand the figure. Nowhere in the whole country is so heavy a dew perceptible as in the districts near to Hermon." To this dew the poet likens brotherly love. This is *"as the dew of Hermon" :* of such pristine freshness and thus refreshing, possessing such pristine power and thus quickening, thus born from above (cx. 3), and in fact like the dew of Hermon which comes down upon the mountains of Zion— a feature in the picture which is taken from the natural reality ; for an abundant dew, when warm days have preceded, might very well be diverted to Jerusalem by the operation of the cold current of air sweeping down from the north over Hermon. We know, indeed, from our own experience how far off a cold air coming from the Alps is perceptible, and produces its effects. The figure of the poet is therefore as true to nature as it is beautiful. When brethren bound together in love also meet together in one place, and, in fact, when brethren of the north unite with brethren in the south in Jerusalem, the city which is the mother of all, at the great Feasts, it is as when the dew of Mount Hermon, which is covered with deep, almost eternal snow, descends upon the bare, unfruitful—and therefore longing for such quickening—mountains round about Zion. In Jerusalem must love and all that is good meet.—*Franz Delitzsch.*

Verse 3.—*"As the dew of Hermon,"* etc. As touching this similitude, I think the prophet useth the common manner of speaking. For whereas the mountains oftentimes seem to those that behold them afar off, to reach up even unto heaven, the dew which cometh from heaven seemeth to fall from the high mountains unto the hills which are under them. Therefore he saith that the dew descendeth from Hermon unto the mount Sion, because it so seemeth unto those that do behold it afar off.—*Martin Luther.*

Verse 3.—*"As the dew of Hermon."* The dews of the mists that rose from the watery ravines, or of the clouds that rested on the summit of Hermon, were perpetual witnesses of freshness and coolness—the sources, as it seemed, of all the moisture, which was to the land of Palestine what the fragrant oil was to the garments of the High Priest ; what the influence of brotherly love was to the whole community.— *Arthur Penrhyn Stanley (1815–1881), in "Sinai and Palestine."*

Verse 3.—"Dew of Hermon." We had sensibly proof at Rasheiya of the copiousness of the *"dew of Hermon,"* spoken of in Ps. cxxxiii. 3, where " Zion " is only another name for the same mountain. Unlike most other mountains which gradually rise from lofty table-lands and often at a distance from the sea, Hermon starts at once to the height of nearly ten thousand feet, from a platform scarcely above the sea level. This platform, too—the upper Jordan valley, and marshes of Merom— is for the most part an impenetrable swamp of unknown depth, whence the seething vapour, under the rays of an almost tropical sun, is constantly ascending into the upper atmosphere during the day. The vapour, coming in contact with the snowy sides of the mountain, is rapidly congealed, and is precipitated in the evening in the form of a dew, the most copious we ever experienced. It penetrated everywhere, and saturated everything. The floor of our tent was soaked, our bed was covered with it, our guns were dripping, and dewdrops hung about everywhere. No wonder that the foot of Hermon is clad with orchards and gardens of such marvellous fertility in this land of droughts.—*Henry Baker Tristram*, 1867.

Verse 3.—"As the dew of Hermon that descended upon the mountain of Zion."—

> So the dews on Hermon's hill
> Which the summer clouds distil,
> Floating southward in the night,
> Pearly gems on Zion light.
>
> *William Digby Seymour.*

Verse 3.—" There the Lord *commanded the blessing."* God commands his blessing where peace is cultivated ; by which is meant, that he testifies how much he is pleased with concord amongst men, by showering down blessings upon them. The same sentiment is expressed by Paul in other words, (2 Cor. xiii. 11 ; Phil. iv. 9) " Live in peace, and the God of peace shall be with you."—*John Calvin.*

Verse 3.—"The Lord *commanded the blessing."* By a bare word of command he blesseth : *" there he commands the blessing,"* that blessing of blessings, *"even life for evermore" ;* like as it is said, " he commanded, and they were created ": Ps. cxlviii. 5. So he commands and we are blessed."—*Thomas Goodwin.*

Verse 3.—"The Lord *commanded the blessing."* It is an allusion possibly to great persons, to a general, or an emperor : " Where the word of a king is, there is power." The centurion said, " I say to one soldier, Go, and he goeth ; to another, Come, and he cometh ; to a third, Do this, and he doth it." So God commandeth one ordinance, " Go and build up such a saint," and it goeth ; he saith to another ordinance, " Come, and call home such a sinner," and it doth it ; God's words and work go together. Men cannot enable others, or give them power to obey them ; they may bid a lame man walk, or a blind man see ; but they cannot enable them to walk or see : God with his word giveth strength to do the thing commanded ; as in the old, so in the new creation, " He spake, and it was done ; he commanded, and it stood fast : " Ps. xxxiii. 9. But there the Lord commands his blessing, *" even life for evermore."* The stream of regeneration, or a spiritual life, which shall never cease, but still go forward and increase, till it swell to, and be swallowed up in the ocean of eternal life, *"even life for evermore."*—*George Swinnock.*

HINTS TO PREACHERS.

Verse 1.—Christian unity. I. Its admirable excellences. II. The signs of its existence. III. The causes of its decay. IV. The means of its renewal.

Verse 1.—The saints are here contemplated, I. In their brotherhood. II. In their concord. III. In their felicity.—*W. J.*

Verses 1—3.—Six blessings which dwell with unity. 1. Goodness. 2. Pleasure. 3. Anointing. 4. Dew. 5. God's blessing. 6. Eternal life.

Verses 1—3.—I. The contemplation: brethren dwelling together in unity. 1. In a family. 2. In a Christian church. 3. Brethren of the same denomination. 4. Of different denominations. II. Its commendation. 1. Literally: " good and pleasant." 2. Figuratively: fragrant as the priestly anointing; fruitful as the dew on Hermon. 3. Spiritually, it has a blessing from God, that gives life, and continues for evermore !—*G. R.*

Verses 1—3.—On Christians dwelling together in unity as a church. 1. *Its propriety,* on account of fraternal relationship: *"For brethren."* The Christian brotherhood is so unique, sacred and lasting, that a lack of unity is a disgrace. They are brethren, 1. Because born of God, who is " the God of peace." Their claim to the brotherhood is dependent upon likeness to Him: Matt. v. 9. 2. Because united to Christ, who as elder brother desires unity: John xvii. 20, 21. Not to seek it is virtually to disown Him. 3. Because " by one Spirit are we all baptized into one body " (1 Cor. xii. 13), wherein unity must be kept: Eph. iv. 3. 4. Because destined to " dwell together in unity," for ever in heaven; therefore we should aim at it here. II. *Its peculiar excellency :* both " good and pleasant." 1. Good, in respect of church work and influence; of mutual edification and growth in grace (2 Cor. xiii. 11); of the success of prayer (Mat. xviii. 19); of recommending the gospel to others. 2. Pleasant, as productive of happiness: as pleasing to God. III. *Its promotion* and maintenance. 1. Seeking the glory of God unites; in opposition to self-honour which divides. 2. Love to Christ as a constraining power unites each to the other as it binds all closely to Christ. 3. Activity in ministering to others, rather than desiring to be ministered unto, binds heart to heart.—*J. F.*

Verse 2.—There must have been special reasons why a priestly anointing should be selected for the comparison, and why that of Aaron, rather than of any other of the high priests. They are these—I. *The ointment was "holy,"* prepared in accordance with the Divine prescription : Ex. xxx. 23—25. Church union is sacred. It must spring from the love commanded by God; be based on the principles laid down by God; and exist for the ends appointed of God. II. *The anointing was from God through Moses,* who acted on behalf of God in the matter. Church unity is of the Holy Spirit (1 Cor. xiii. 13), through Jesus as Mediator. Therefore it should be prayed for, and thankfully acknowledged. III. *By the anointing, Aaron became consecrated,* and officially qualified to act as priest. By unity the Church, as a whole, lives its life of consecration, and effectively ministers in the priesthood assigned it. IV. *The oil was diffusive ;* it rested not on Aaron's head, but flowed down to the skirts of his garments. Unity will, in time, make its way from a few to the whole, especially from the leaders in a church to the rest of its members. Hence, it is a personal matter. Each should realize it, and by love and wise conduct diffuse it.—*J. F.*

Verses 2, 3.—Christian love scatters blessing by the way of down-coming : " ran down," " went down," " descended." I. God to his saints. II. Saint to saint. III. Saint to sinner.

Verse 3.—The chosen place for blessing. A church ; a church united, a church bedewed of the Spirit. What a blessing for the world that there is a commanded place of blessing !

Verse 3 (*first clause*).—This should be rendered, " As the dew of Hermon, that cometh down on the mountains of Zion." From the snows upon the lofty Hermon, the moisture raised by the sun is carried in the form of vapour, by the wind towards the lesser elevations of Zion, upon which it falls as a copious dew. Thus, Christian concord in church-fellowship—I. Despises not the little ones, *i.e.* the mean, poor, and less gifted. It, 1. Recognises that God is the Father, and Christ is the Redeemer of all believers alike. 2. Acknowledges oneness of faith as the true basis of fellowship ; not wealth, social position or talent. 3. Believes that the least member is essential to the completeness of Christ's body. 4. Realises that everything which renders one in any way superior to another is the gift of God.   II. Distributes of its abundance to the needy : Acts iv. 32—37.   1. The wealthy to the poor : 1 John iii. 17.   2. The learned to the ignorant.   3. The joyful to the sorrowing.   4. The steadfast to the erring : Jas. v. 19.   III. Displays its value more by loving generosity, than by a conspicuous appearance before the world.   As Hermon was more valuable to Zion for its dew than for its adornment of the landscape.   1. A generous activity exhibits and requires more real grace than showy architecture or ornate worship does.   2. Through it, godliness flourishes more than by a vaunted respectability.   Zion was fertilized by the dew, not by the grandeur of Hermon. 3. By it the heart of Christ is touched and his reward secured : Mark ix. 40, 42.— J. F.

Verse 3.—*Commanded Mercy.* Elsewhere goodness is bestowed, but in Zion it is commanded.   I. Commanded mercy implies that it must necessarily be given. II. Commanded mercy attends commanded unity.   III. Commanded mercy secures life more abundantly, " life for evermore."—*W. B. H.*

PSALM CXXXIV.

TITLE.—A Song of Degrees. *We have now reached the last of the Gradual Psalms. The Pilgrims are going home, and are singing the last song in their Psalter. They leave early in the morning, before the day has fully commenced, for the journey is long for many of them. While yet the night lingers they are on the move. As soon as they are outside the gates they see the guards upon the temple wall, and the lamps shining from the windows of the chambers which surround the sanctuary ; therefore, moved by the sight, they chant a farewell to the perpetual attendants upon the holy shrine. Their parting exhortation arouses the priests to pronounce upon them a blessing out of the holy place : this benediction is contained in the third verse. The priests as good as say, "You have desired us to bless the Lord, and now we pray the Lord to bless you."*

The Psalm teaches us to pray for those who are continually ministering before the Lord, and it invites all ministers to pronounce benedictions upon their loving and prayerful people.

EXPOSITION.

BEHOLD, bless ye the LORD, all *ye* servants of the LORD, which by night stand in the house of the LORD.

2 Lift up your hands *in* the sanctuary, and bless the LORD.

3 The LORD that made heaven and earth bless thee out of Zion.

1. *"Behold."* By this call the pilgrims bespeak the attention of the night-watch. They shout to them—Behold ! The retiring pilgrims stir up the holy brotherhood of those who are appointed to keep the watch of the house of the Lord. Let them look around them upon the holy place, and everywhere " behold " reasons for sacred praise. Let them look above them at night and magnify him that made heaven and earth, and lighted the one with stars and the other with his love. Let them see to it that their hallelujahs never come to an end. Their departing brethren arouse them with the shrill cry of " Behold ! " Behold !—see, take care, be on the watch, diligently mind your work, and incessantly adore and bless Jehovah's name.

"Bless ye the LORD." Think well of Jehovah, and speak well of him. Adore him with reverence, draw near to him with love, delight in him with exultation. Be not content with praise, such as all his works render to him ; but, as his saints, see that ye " bless " him. He blesses you ; therefore, be zealous to bless him. The word " bless " is the characteristic word of the Psalm. The first two verses stir us up to bless Jehovah, and in the last verse Jehovah's blessing is invoked upon the people. Oh to abound in blessing ! May *blessed* and *blessing* be the two words which describe our lives. Let others flatter their fellows, or bless their stars, or praise themselves ; as for us, we will bless Jehovah, from whom all blessings flow. *"All ye servants of the LORD."* It is your office to bless him ; take care that you lead the way therein. Servants should speak well of their masters. Not one of you should serve him as of compulsion, but all should bless him while you serve him ; yea, bless him for permitting you to serve him, fitting you to serve him, and accepting your service. To be a servant of Jehovah is an incalculable honour, a blessing beyond all estimate. To be a servant in his temple, a domestic in his house, is even more a delight and a glory : if those who are ever with the Lord, and dwell in his own temple, do not bless the Lord, who will ? *"Which by night stand in the house of the LORD."* We can well understand how the holy pilgrims half envied those consecrated ones who guarded the temple, and attended to the necessary offices thereof through the hours of night. To the silence and solemnity of night there was added the awful glory of the place where Jehovah had ordained that his worship should be celebrated ; blessed were the priests and Levites who were ordained to a service so sublime. That these should bless the Lord throughout

their nightly vigils was most fitting : the people would have them mark this, and never fail in the duty. They were not to move about like so many machines, but to put their hearts into all their duties, and worship spiritually in the whole course of their duty. It would be well to watch, but better still to be " watching unto prayer " and praise.

When night settles down on a church the Lord has his watchers and holy ones still guarding his truth, and these must not be discouraged, but must bless the Lord even when the darkest hours draw on. Be it ours to cheer them, and lay upon them this charge—to bless the Lord at all times, and let his praise be continually in their mouths.

2. *"Lift up your hands in the sanctuary."* In the holy place they must be busy, full of strength, wide-awake, energetic, and moved with holy ardour. Hands, heart, and every other part of their manhood must be upraised, elevated, and consecrated to the adoring service of the Lord. As the angels praise God day without night, so must the angels of the churches be instant in season and out of season. *"And bless the Lord."* This is their main business. They are to bless men by their teaching, but they must yet more bless Jehovah with their worship. Too often men look at public worship only from the side of its usefulness to the people ; but the other matter is of even higher importance : we must see to it that the Lord God is adored, extolled, and had in reverence. For a second time the word " bless " is used, and applied to Jehovah. Bless the Lord, O my soul, and let every other soul bless him. There will be no drowsiness about even midnight devotion if the heart is set upon blessing God in Christ Jesus, which is the gospel translation of God in the sanctuary.

3. This last verse is the answer from the temple of the pilgrims preparing to depart as the day breaks. It is the ancient blessing of the high-priest condensed, and poured forth upon each individual pilgrim. " *The Lord that made heaven and earth bless thee out of Zion.*" Ye are scattering and going to your homes one by one ; may the benediction come upon you one by one. You have been up to Jehovah's city and temple at his bidding ; return each one with such a benediction as only he can give—divine, infinite, effectual, eternal. You are not going away from Jehovah's works or glories, for he made the heaven above you and the earth on which you dwell. He is your Creator, and he can bless you with untold mercies ; he can create joy and peace in your hearts, and make for you a new heaven and a new earth. May the Maker of all things make you to abound in blessings.

The benediction comes from the City of the Great King, from his appointed ministers, by virtue of his covenant, and so it is said to be " out of Zion." To this day the Lord blesses each one of his people through his church, his gospel, and the ordinances of his house. It is in communion with the saints that we receive untold benisons. May each one of us obtain yet more of the blessing which cometh from the Lord alone. Zion cannot bless us ; the holiest ministers can only wish us a blessing ; but Jehovah can and will bless each one of his waiting people. So may it be at this good hour. Do we desire it ? Let us then bless the Lord ourselves. Let us do it a second time. Then we may confidently hope that the third time we think of blessing we shall find ourselves conscious receivers of it from the Ever-blessed One. Amen.

EXPLANATORY NOTES AND QUAINT SAYINGS.

Whole Psalm.—It is a beautiful little ode, equally full of sublimity and simplicity. It is commonly supposed to be the work of David. With what admiration should we contemplate the man whose zeal in the cause of religion thus urged him to embrace every opportunity that could occur to him, among the lowest as well as the highest ranks of life, of promoting the praise and glory of his Creator ; now composing penitential hymns for his own closet ; now leading the temple service in national eulogies of the sublimest pitch to which human language can reach ; and now descending to the class of the watchman and patrol of the temple and the city, and tuning their lips to a reverential utterance of the name and the service of God !—*John Mason Good* (1764—1827), *in "An Historical Outline of the Book of Psalms."*

Whole Psalm.—This Psalm consists of a greeting, verses 1, 2, and the reply thereto. The greeting is addressed to those priests and Levites who have the night-watch in the Temple ; and this antiphon is purposely placed at the end of the collection of Songs of Degrees in order to take the place of a final beracha.* In this sense Luther styles the Psalm *epiphonema superiorum.*† It is also in other respects an appropriate finale.—*Franz Delitzsch.*

Whole Psalm.—The last cloud of smoke from the evening sacrifice has mixed with the blue sky, the last note of the evening hymn has died away on the ear. The watch is being set for the night. The twenty-four Levites, the three priests, and the captain of the guard, whose duty it was to keep ward from sunset to sunrise over the hallowed precincts, are already at their several posts, and the multitude are retiring through the gates, which will soon be shut, to many of them to open no more. But they cannot depart without one last expression of the piety that fills their hearts ; and turning to the watchers on tower and battlement, they address them in holy song, in what was at once a brotherly admonition and a touching prayer : *"Behold, bless ye the Lord, all ye servants of the Lord, which by night stand in the house of the Lord. Lift up your hands in the sanctuary, and bless the Lord."* The pious guard are not unprepared for the appeal, and from their lofty heights, in words that float over the peopled city and down into the quiet valley of the Kedron, like the melody of angels, they respond to each worshipper who thus addressed them with a benedictory farewell : *"The Lord bless thee out of Zion, even he who made heaven and earth."*—*Robert Nisbet.*

Whole Psalm.—The tabernacle and temple were served by priests during the *night* as well as the day. Those priests renewed the altar fire, fed the lamps, and guarded the sacred structure from intrusion and from plunder. The Psalm before us was prepared for the priests who served the sacred place by night. They were in danger of slumbering ; and they were in danger of idle reverie. Oh, how much time is wasted in mere reverie—in letting thought wander, and wander, and wander ! The priests were in danger, we say, of slumbering, of idle reverie, of vain thoughts, of useless meditation, and of profitless talk ; and therefore it is written,—*"Behold, bless ye the Lord, all ye servants of the Lord, which by night stand in the house of the Lord."* Is it your duty to spend the night in watching ? then spend the night in worship. Do not let the time of watching be idle, wasted time ; but when others are slumbering and sleeping, and you are necessarily watchful, sustain the praises of God's house ; let there be praise in Zion—still praise by night as well as by day ! *"Lift up your hands in the sanctuary, and bless the Lord."*

We may suppose these words to be addressed to the sacred sentinels, by the head of their course, or by the captain of the guard, or even by the high priest. We can imagine the captain of the guard coming in during the night watches, and saying to the priests who were guarding the temple, *"Behold, bless ye the Lord, all ye servants of the Lord, which by night stand in the house of the Lord."* Or we could imagine the high priests, when the watch was set for the first part of the night, going to the priests who were under his control, and addressing to them these same soul-stirring words. Now our text is the response of these sacred sentinels. As they listened to the captain of the guard, or to the high priest, telling them to worship by night in the courts of the Lord—to lift up their hands in the sanctuary, and bless the Lord—they answered him, *"The Lord that made heaven and earth bless thee out of Zion."* So that here you have brought before you the interesting and instructive subject of mutual benediction—the saints blessing each other.—*Samuel Martin,* 1817—1878.

Verse 1.—The Targum explains the first verse of the Temple watch. " The custom in the Second Temple appears to have been this. After midnight the chief of the door-keepers took the key of the inner Temple, and went with some of the priests through the small postern of the Fire Gate. In the inner court this watch divided itself into two companies, each carrying a burning torch ; one company turned west, the other east, and so they compassed the court to see whether all

---

* Blessing.

† " I take this Psalm to be a conclusion of those things which were spoken of before."—*Luther.*

were in readiness for the Temple service on the following morning. In the bake-house, where the *Mincha* (' meat-offering ') of the High Priest was baked, they met with the cry, ' All well.' Meanwhile the rest of the priests arose, bathed them-selves, and put on their garments. They then went into the stone chamber (one half of which was the hall of session of the Sanhedrim), and there, under the superintendence of the officer who gave the watchword, and one of the Sanhedrim, surrounded by the priests clad in their robes of office, their several duties for the coming day were assigned to each of the priests by lot. Luke i. 9."—*J. J. Stewart Perowne.*

Verse 1.—*"Behold."* The Psalm begins with the demonstrative adverb *Behold!* setting the matter of their duty before their eyes, for they were to be stimulated to devotion by looking constantly to the Temple. We are to notice the Psalmist's design in urging the duty of praise so earnestly upon them. Many of the Levites, through the tendency which there is in all men to abuse ceremonies, considered that nothing more was necessary than standing idly in the Temple, and thus over-looked the principal part of their duty. The Psalmist would show that merely to keep nightly watch over the Temple, kindle the lamps, and superintend the sacrifices, was of no importance, unless they served God spiritually, and referred all outward ceremonies to that which must be considered the main sacrifice—the celebration of God's praises. You may think it a very laborious service, as if he had said, to stand at watch in the Temple, while others sleep in their own houses ; but the worship which God requires is something more excellent than this, and demands of you to sing his praises before all the people.—*John Calvin.*

Verse 1.—*"Behold."* The first word in this verse, *"Behold,"* seemeth to point at the reasons which the priests in the Temple had to bless Jehovah ; as if it had been said, Behold, the house of God is built, the holy services are appointed, and the Lord hath given you rest from your enemies, that you may serve him acceptably ; set about it, therefore, with gratitude and alacrity. We read (1 Chron. ix. 33) that the Levitical singers were " employed in their work day and night "; to the end, doubtless, that the earthly sanctuary might bear some resemblance to that above, where St. John tells us, the redeemed " are before the throne of God, and serve him day and night in his temple ": Rev. vii. 15.—*George Horne.*

Verse 1.—*"Behold, bless ye the LORD, all ye servants of the LORD."* From the exhortation to the Lord's ministers, learn, that the public worship of God is to be carefully looked unto ; and all men, but especially ministers, had need to be stirred up to take heed to themselves, and to the work of God's public worship, when they go about it ; for so much doth " *behold* " in this place import.—*David Dickson.*

Verse 1.—*"By night."* Even by night the Lord is to be remembered, and his praises are to be rehearsed.—*Martin Geier, 1614—1681.*

Verse 1.—*"Stand in the house of the LORD."* The Rabbins say, that the high priest only sat in the sanctuary (as did Eli, 1 Sam. i. 9) ; the rest stood, as ready pressed to do their office.—*John Trapp.*

Verse 1.—*"Which stand in the house of the LORD."* You who have now a per-manent house, and no longer, like pilgrims, have to dwell in tents.—*Robert Bellarmine.*

Verse 1.—*"Which stand in the house of the LORD."* Let not this your frequent being in his presence breed in you contempt ; as the saying is, " Too much familiarity breedeth contempt ; " but bless him always, acknowledge, and with reverence praise his excelllency.—*John Mayer, 1653.*

Verse 2.—*"Lift up your hands,"* etc. The lifting up of the hands was a gesture in prayer, it was an intimation of their expectation of receiving blessings from the Lord, and it was also an acknowledgment of their having received the same.—*Samuel Eyles Pierce.*

Verse 2.—*"In the sanctuary."* The Hebrew word signifying *holiness* as well as the *holy place* may here be taken in the former sense, the latter having been sufficiently expressed (verse 1) by " the house of the Lord " . . . . The priests (which are here spoken to) before their officiating, which is here expressed by *lifting up* their *hands*, were obliged to wash their hands.—*Henry Hammond.*

Verse 3.—*"The LORD that made heaven and earth bless thee out of Zion."* He doth not say, the Lord that made the earth bless thee out of heaven ; nor, the Lord that made heaven bless thee out of heaven ; but *"bless thee out of Zion."* As if he would teach us that all blessings come as immediately and primarily from heaven, so mediately and secondarily from *Zion*, where the Temple stood. If ever, therefore, we would have blessings outward, inward, private, public, secular, spiritual ; if ever we would have blessing in our estate, blessing in our land, blessing in our souls, we must pray for it, and pray for it here, in *Zion*, in God's house : for from the piety there exercised all blessings flow, as from a fountain that can never be drawn dry.—*Abraham Wright.*

Verse 3.—*"The* Lord *that made heaven and earth,"* etc. The priestly benediction brings God before us in a twofold character. He is described first as the Creator of the universe. He is described, in the second place, as dwelling "in Zion." In the first aspect, he is represented as the God of nature; in the second, as the God of grace. When I contemplate him as the Creator of the universe, there is abundant proof that he *can* bless me. When I contemplate him as dwelling in the Church, there is abundant proof that he *will* bless me. Both of these elements are essential to our faith.—*N. M'Michael.*

Verse 3.—*"The* Lord *that made heaven and earth,"* etc. As the priests were called upon to bless God in behalf of the people, so here they bless the people in behalf of God. Between the verses we may suppose the previous request to be complied with. The priests, having blessed God, turn and bless the people. The obvious allusion to the sacerdotal blessing (Num. vi. 23—27), favours the optative construction of this verse, which really includes a prediction—the Lord will bless thee.—*Joseph Addison Alexander.*

Verse 3.—*"The* Lord *bless thee."* All men lie under the curse, till God brings them into the fellowship of his church, and pronounce them blessed by his word, as *"The* Lord *bless thee "* doth import.—*David Dickson.*

Verse 3.—*"The* Lord *bless thee out of Zion."* The Church is the conservator of Divine revelation ; the Church is the offerer on earth of true worship ; it consists of a company of priests, a royal priesthood, part of whose mission is " to offer up spiritual sacrifices acceptable to God by Jesus Christ." The Church is the heritor of the covenants. God's covenants are made with his Church, and his promises are addressed chiefly to his Church. The Church is the scene of special Divine ministrations, God shows himself to his Church as he does not to that which is called the world. It is also the scene of special heavenly influences : and in a sense next to that in which God is said to reside in heaven, the Church is the dwelling-place of the Most High. Now, what is it to be *blessed out of Zion?* It is surely to be blessed with Zion's blessings, and to have Zion's endowments and gifts rendered sources of advantage and profit to us.—*Samuel Martin.*

Verse 3.—*"Bless thee."* The singular instead of the plural " bless *you*," because the words are taken from the form used by the High Priest in blessing the people. Num. vi. 24.—*J. J. Stewart Perowne.*

Verse 3.—*"Bless thee."* It is addressed to the church as one person, and to each individual in this united, unit-like church.—*Franz Delitzsch.*

HINTS TO PREACHERS.

Whole Psalm.—There are two things in this Psalm. I. Our blessing God : verses 1, 2. 1. How ? By gratitude, by love, by obedience, by prayer, by praise. 2. Where ? " In the house of the Lord," " in the sanctuary." 3. When ? Not in the day merely, but at night. Some of old spent the whole night, others part of the night, in the temple, praising God. As Christ spent whole nights in prayer for his people, they should not think it too much occasionally to spend whole nights in praise of him. Evening services should not be neglected on the Sabbath, nor on other days of the week.

II. God blessing us : verse 3. 1. The persons blessed : " bless thee "—every one who blesses him. 2. The condition : " out of Zion." In the fulfilment of religious duties, not in the neglect of them. 3. The blessing itself : of the Lord. They are blessed whom he blesses.—*G. R.*

Whole Psalm.—I. God—Jehovah—the fountain of blessing. II. The heavens and the earth, evidence of divine capacity to bless. III. The church, a channel of blessing. IV. The saints, the means of spreading blessing, through the spirit of blessing. V. The riches involved in the divine benediction.—*Samuel Martin.*

Whole Psalm.—I. Unique service : temple watching, night-sentinelship. II. Sublime society : the awful things of the sanctuary. III. Holy uplifting : hands, hearts, eyes. IV. Praise in the darkness heard far up in the light. V. Response from the stars fulfilling the prayer : " The Creator Lord bless *thee*."—*W. B. H.*

Verse 1.—I. Night settles on the holy place : dark periods of church story. II. But God has his guards : Wycliffe and his band watching for the Reformation ; Waldenses, etc. Never a night so dark but God is praised and served. III. Be it night or day, let the Levites fulfil their courses.—*W. B. H.*

Verse 1.—The Lord's servants exhorted to be, 1. Devout and joyful in their service. Sing at your work, though it be in the dark. 2. Zealous to employ every season of service aright. " By night," as by day, " bless the Lord." 3. Careful to avoid all hindrances to devotion in their service. When tempted to indolence and drowsiness, say—

> " Wake, and lift up thyself, my heart,
> And with the angels bear thy part,
> Who all night long, unwearied, sing
> High praise to the Eternal King."

W. H. J. P.

Verse 1.—Directions for worship. I. It should be with great care : " Behold." II. With grateful joy : " Bless ye the Lord." III. Unanimously : " all ye." IV. With holy reverence, as by " servants of the Lord." V. With unflagging constancy : " stand by night."

Verse 1.—" Ye that stand by night." The night-watchman of the Lord's house, their value, their obscurity, their danger-slumber, their consolation, their dignity, their reward.

Verse 2.—Ingredients of worship. I. Uplifted hands. Energy, courage, prayer, aspiration. II. Uplifted hearts. Thank, praise, adore, and love the Lord.

Verse 3.—The Divine Benediction. I. From the Creator : ample, new, varied, boundless, enduring—all illustrated by his making heaven and earth. II. From the Redeemer : blessings most needful, rich, effectual, abiding,—all illustrated and guaranteed by his dwelling among men, purchasing a church, building an abode, revealing his glory, reigning on his throne

and the earth, evidence of divine ownership to them.	17. The church, a channel
of blessing, IV. The saints, the means of spreading blessing through the Spirit
of blessing, V. The church involved in the divine benediction.—Samuel Martin.

Whole Psalm.—I. Unique service: temple worship, night service-ship. II.
Sublime society: the saints (ver. 1). III. Holy callings: hands
hearts, eyes. IV. Praise in all places: temple and the Lord. V. Response
from the risen blessing the saints—in the temple and the—J. W. B.

PSALM CXXXV.

GENERAL REMARKS.—*This Psalm has no title. It is mainly made up of selections
from other Scriptures. It has been called a mosaic, and compared to a tessellated
pavement. At the outset, its first two verses are taken from Ps. cxxxiv; while the
latter part of verse 2 and the commencement of verse 3 put us in mind of Ps. cxvi. 19;
and verse 4 suggests Deut. vii. 6. Does not verse 5 remind us of Ps. xcv. 3 ? As for
verse 7, it is almost identical with Jer. x. 13, which may have been taken from it. The
passage contained in verse 13 is to be found in Ex. iii. 15, and verse 14 in Deut. xxxii.
36. The closing verses, 8 to 12, are in Ps. cxxxvi. From verse 15 to the end the strain
is a repetition of Ps. cxv. This process of tracing the expressions to other sources might
be pushed further without straining the quotations ; the whole Psalm is a compound
of many choice extracts, and yet it has all the continuity and freshness of an original
poem. The Holy Spirit occasionally repeats himself ; not because he has any lack
of thoughts or words, but because it is expedient for us that we hear the same things
in the same form. Yet, when our great Teacher uses repetition, it is usually with
instructive variations, which deserve our careful attention.*

DIVISION.—*The first fourteen verses contain an exhortation to praise Jehovah
for his goodness (verse 3), for his electing love (verse 4), his greatness (5—7), his
judgments (8—12), his unchanging character (13), and his love towards his people.
This is followed by a denunciation of idols (verses 15 to 18), and a further exhortation
to bless the name of the Lord. It is a song full of life, vigour, variety, and devotion.*

EXPOSITION.

PRAISE ye the LORD. Praise ye the name of the LORD ; praise *him*,
O ye servants of the LORD.

2 Ye that stand in the house of the LORD, in the courts of the house of
our God,

3 Praise the LORD ; for the LORD *is* good : sing praises unto his name ;
for *it is* pleasant.

4 For the LORD hath chosen Jacob unto himself, *and* Israel for his peculiar
treasure.

5 For I know that the LORD *is* great, and *that* our Lord *is* above all gods.

6 Whatsoever the LORD pleased, *that* did he in heaven, and in earth,
in the seas, and all deep places.

7 He causeth the vapours to ascend from the ends of the earth ; he
maketh lightnings for the rain ; he bringeth the wind out of his treasuries.

8 Who smote the firstborn of Egypt, both of man and beast.

9 *Who* sent tokens and wonders into the midst of thee, O Egypt, upon
Pharaoh, and upon all his servants.

10 Who smote great nations, and slew mighty kings ;

11 Sihon king of the Amorites, and Og king of Bashan, and all the
kingdoms of Canaan ;

12 And gave their land *for* an heritage, an heritage unto Israel his people.

13 Thy name, O LORD, *endureth* for ever ; *and* thy memorial, O LORD,
throughout all generations.

14 For the LORD will judge his people, and he will repent himself concerning his servants.

1. *"Praise ye the LORD,"* or, *Hallelujah.* Let those who are themselves full
of holy praise labour to excite the like spirit in others. It is not enough for us

to praise God ourselves, we are quite unequal to such a work ; let us call in all our friends and neighbours, and if they have been slack in such service, let us stir them up to it with loving exhortations. *"Praise ye the name of the LORD."* Let his character be extolled by you, and let all that he has revealed concerning himself be the subject of your song ; for this is truly his *name.* Specially let his holy and incommunicable name of " Jehovah " be the object of your adoration. By that name he sets forth his self-existence, and his immutability ; let these arouse your praises of his Godhead. Think of him with love, admire him with heartiness, and then extol him with ardour. Do not only magnify the Lord because he is God ; but study his character and his doings, and thus render intelligent, appreciative praise. *"Praise him, O ye servants of the LORD."* If others are silent, you must not be ; you must be the first to celebrate his praises. You are " servants," and this is part of your service ; his " name " is named upon you, therefore celebrate his name with praises ; you know what a blessed Master he is, therefore speak well of him. Those who shun his service are sure to neglect his praise ; but as grace has made you his own personal servants, let your hearts make you his court-musicians. Here we see the servant of the Lord arousing his fellow-servants by three times calling upon them to praise. Are we then, so slow in such a sweet employ ? Or is it that when we do our utmost it is all too little for such a Lord ? Both are true. We do not praise enough ; we cannot praise too much. We ought to be always at it ; answering to the command here given—Praise, Praise, Praise. Let the three-in-one have the praises of our spirit, soul, and body. For the past, the present, and the future, let us render three-fold hallelujahs.

2. *"Ye that stand in the house of the LORD, in the courts of the house of our God."* You are highly favoured ; you are the domestics of the palace, nearest to the Father of the heavenly family, privileged to find your home in his house ; therefore you must, beyond all others, abound in thanksgiving. You " stand," or abide in the temple ; you are constant occupants of its various courts ; and therefore from you we expect unceasing praise. Should not ministers be celebrated for celebrating the praises of Jehovah? Should not church-officers and church-members excel all others in the excellent duty of adoration ? Should not all of every degree who wait even in his outer courts unite in his worship ? Ought not the least and feeblest of his people to proclaim his praises, in company with those who live nearest to him ? Is it not a proper thing to remind them of their obligations ? Is not the Psalmist wise when he does so in this case and in many others ? Those who can call Jehovah *"our God"* are highly blessed, and therefore should abound in the work of blessing him. Perhaps this is the sweetest word in these two verses. " This God is our God for ever and ever." " Our God " signifies possession, communion in possession, assurance of possession, delight in possession. Oh the unutterable joy of calling God our own !

3. *"Praise the LORD."* Do it again ; continue to do it ; do it better and more heartily ; do it in growing numbers ; do it at once. There are good reasons for praising the Lord, and among the first is this—*" for the LORD is good."* He is so good that there is none good in the same sense or degree. He is so good that all good is found in him, flows from him, and is rewarded by him. The word God is brief for good ; and truly God is the essence of goodness. Should not his goodness be well spoken of ? Yea, with our best thoughts, and words, and hymns let us glorify his name. *"Sing praises unto his name ; for it is pleasant."* The adjective may apply to the singing and to the name—they are both pleasant. The vocal expression of praise by sacred song is one of our greatest delights. We were created for this purpose, and hence it is a joy to us. It is a charming duty to praise the lovely name of our God. All pleasure is to be found in the joyful worship of Jehovah ; all joys are in his sacred name as perfumes lie slumbering in a garden of flowers. The mind expands, the soul is lifted up, the heart warms, the whole being is filled with delight when we are engaged in singing the high praises of our Father, Redeemer, Comforter. When in any occupation goodness and pleasure unite, we do well to follow it up without stint : yet it is to be feared that few of us sing to the Lord at all in proportion as we talk to men.

4. *"For the LORD hath chosen Jacob unto himself."* Jehovah hath chosen Jacob. Should not the sons of Jacob praise him who has so singularly favoured them ? Election is one of the most forcible arguments for adoring love. Chosen ! chosen unto himself !—who can be grateful enough for being concerned in this privilege ? " Jacob have I loved," said Jehovah, and he gave no reason for his love except that

he chose to love. Jacob had then done neither good nor evil, yet thus the Lord determined, and thus he spake. If it be said that the choice was made upon foresight of Jacob's character, it is, perhaps, even more remarkable; for there was little enough about Jacob that could deserve special choice. By nature Jacob was by no means the most lovable of men. No, it was sovereign grace which dictated the choice. But, mark, it was not a choice whose main result was the personal welfare of Jacob's seed : the nation was chosen by God *unto himself*, to answer the divine ends and purposes in blessing all mankind. Jacob's race was chosen to be the Lord's own, to be the trustees of his truth, the maintainers of his worship, the mirrors of his mercy. Chosen they were; but mainly for this end, that they might be a peculiar people, set apart unto the service of the true God.

"*And Israel for his peculiar treasure.*" God's choice exalts; for here the name is changed from Jacob, the supplanter, to Israel, the prince. The love of God gives a new name and imparts a new value; for the comparison to a royal treasure is a most honourable one. As kings have a special regalia, and a selection of the rarest jewels, so the Lord deigns to reckon his chosen nation as his wealth, his delight, his glory. What an honour to the spiritual Israel that they are all this to the Lord their God ! We are a people near and dear unto him; precious and honourable in his sight. How can we refuse our loudest, heartiest, sweetest music ? If *we* did not extol him, the stones in the street would cry out against us.

5. "*For I know that the* Lord *is great, and that our Lord is above all gods.*" The greatness of God is as much a reason for adoration as his goodness, when we are once reconciled to him. God is great positively, great comparatively, and great superlatively—"above all gods." Of this the Psalmist had an assured personal persuasion. He says positively, "I know." It is knowledge worth possessing. He knew by observation, inspiration, and realization; he was no agnostic, he was certain and clear upon the matter. He not only knows the greatness of Jehovah, but that as the Adonai, or Ruler, "our Lord" is infinitely superior to all the imaginary deities of the heathen, and to all great ones besides.

> " Let princes hear, let angels know,
> How mean their natures seem ;
> Those gods on high, and gods below,
> When once compared with him."

Many have thought to worship Jehovah, and other gods with him ; but this holy man tolerated no such notion. Others have thought to combine their religion with obedience to the unrighteous laws of tyrannical princes ; this, also, the sweet singer of Israel denounced ; for he regarded the living God as altogether above all men, who as magistrates and princes have been called gods. Observe here the fourth of the five "fors." Verses 3, 4, 5, and 14 contain reasons for praise, each set forth with "for." A fruitful meditation might be suggested by this.

6. "*Whatsoever the* Lord *pleased, that did he in heaven, and in earth, in the seas, and all deep places.*" His will is carried out throughout all space. The king's warrant runs in every portion of the universe. The heathen divided the great domain ; but Jupiter does not rule in heaven, nor Neptune on the sea, nor Pluto in the lower regions ; Jehovah rules over all. His decree is not defeated, his purpose is not frustrated : in no one point is his good pleasure set aside. The word "whatsoever" is of the widest range and includes all things, and the four words of peace which are mentioned comprehend all space ; therefore the declaration of the text knows neither limit nor exception. Jehovah works his will : he pleases to do, and he performs the deed. None can stay his hand. How different this from the gods whom the heathen fabled to be subject to all the disappointments, failures, and passions of men ! How contrary even to those so-called Christian conceptions of God which subordinate him to the will of man, and make his eternal purposes the football of human caprice. Our theology teaches us no such degrading notions of the Eternal as that he can be baffled by man. " His purpose shall stand, and he will do all his pleasure." No region is too high, no abyss too deep, no land too distant, no sea too wide for his omnipotence : his divine pleasure travels post over all the realm of nature, and his behests are obeyed.

7. "*He causeth the vapours to ascend from the ends of the earth.*" Here we are taught the power of God in creation. The process of evaporation is passed by unnoticed by the many, because they see it going on all around them ; the usual ceases to be wonderful to the thoughtless, but it remains a marvel to the instructed.

When we consider upon what an immense scale evaporation is continually going on, and how needful it is for the existence of all life, we may well admire the wisdom and the power which are displayed therein. All around us from every point of the horizon the vapour rises, condenses into clouds, and ultimately descends as rain. Whence the vapours originally ascended from which our showers are formed it would be impossible to tell ; most probably the main part of them comes from the tropical regions, and other remote places at " the ends of the earth." It is the Lord who causes them to rise, and not a mere law. What is law without a force at the back of it ? "*He maketh lightnings for the rain.*" There is an intimate connection between lightning and rain, and this would seem to be more apparent in Palestine than even with ourselves ; for we constantly read of thunderstorms in that country as attending heavy down-pours of rain. Lightning is not to be regarded as a lawless force, but as a part of that wonderful machinery by which the earth is kept in a fit condition : a force as much under the control of God as any other, a force most essential to our existence. The ever-changing waters, rains, winds, and electric currents circulate as if they were the life-blood and vital spirits of the universe. "*He bringeth the wind out of his treasuries.*" This great force which seems left to its own wild will is really under the supreme and careful government of the Lord. As a monarch is specially master of the contents of his own treasure, so is our God the Lord of the tempest and hurricane ; and as princes do not spend their treasure without taking note and count of it, so the Lord does not permit the wind to be wasted, or squandered without purpose. Everything in the material world is under the immediate direction and control of the Lord of all. Observe how the Psalmist brings before us the personal action of Jehovah : " he causeth," " he maketh," " he bringeth." Everywhere the Lord worketh all things, and there is no power which escapes his supremacy. It is well for us that it is so : one bandit force wandering through the Lord's domains defying his control would cast fear and trembling over all the provinces of providence. Let us praise Jehovah for the power and wisdom with which he rules clouds, and lightnings, and winds, and all other mighty and mysterious agencies.

8. "*Who smote the firstborn of Egypt, both of man and beast.*" Herein the Lord is to be praised ; for this deadly smiting was an act of justice against Egypt, and of love to Israel. But what a blow it was ! All the firstborn slain in a moment ! How it must have horrified the nation, and cowed the boldest enemies of Israel ! Beasts because of their relationship to man as domestic animals are in many ways made to suffer with him. The firstborn of beasts must die as well as the firstborn of their owners, for the blow was meant to astound and overwhelm, and it accomplished its purpose. The firstborn of God had been sorely smitten, and they were set free by the Lord's meting out to their oppressors the like treatment.

9. "*Who sent tokens and wonders into the midst of thee, O Egypt, upon Pharaoh, and upon all his servants.*" The Lord is still seen by the Psalmist as sending judgments upon rebellious men ; he keeps before us the personal action of God, " who sent tokens, etc." The more distinctly God is seen the better. Even in plagues he is to be seen, as truly as in mercies. The plagues were not only terrible wonders which astounded men, but forcible tokens or signs by which they were instructed. No doubt the plagues were aimed at the various deities of the Egyptians, and were a grand exposure of their impotence : each one had its own special significance. The judgments of the Lord were no side blows, they struck the nation at the heart ; he sent his bolts " into the midst of thee, O Egypt ! " These marvels happened in the centre of the proud and exclusive nation of Egypt, which thought itself far superior to other lands ; and many of these plagues touched the nation in points upon which it prided itself. The Psalmist addresses that haughty nation, saying, " O Egypt," as though reminding it of the lessons which it had been taught by the Lord's right hand. Imperious Pharaoh had been the ringleader in defying Jehovah, and he was made personally to smart for it ; nor did his flattering courtiers escape, upon each one of them the scourge fell heavily. God's servants are far better off than Pharaoh's servants : those who stand in the courts of Jehovah are delivered, but the courtiers of Pharaoh are smitten all of them, for they were all partakers in his evil deeds. The Lord is to be praised for thus rescuing his own people, and causing their cruel adversaries to bite the dust. Let no true Israelite forget the song of the Red Sea, but anew let us hear a voice summoning us to exulting praise : " Sing unto the Lord, for he hath triumphed gloriously."

10. "*Who smote great nations, and slew mighty kings.*" The nations of Canaan

joined in the desperate resistance offered by their monarchs, and so they were smitten ; while their kings, the ringleaders of the fight, were slain. Those who resist the divine purpose will find it hard to kick against the pricks. The greatness of the nations and the might of the kings availed nothing against the Lord. He is prepared to mete out vengeance to those who oppose his designs : those who dream of him as too tender to come to blows have mistaken the God of Israel. He intended to bless the work through his chosen people, and he would not be turned from his purpose : cost what it might, he would preserve the candle of truth which he had lighted, even though the blood of nations should be spilt in its defence. The wars against the Canaanite races were a price paid for the setting up of a nation which was to preserve for the whole world the lively oracles of God.

11. "*Sihon king of the Amorites, and Og king of Bashan.*" These two kings were the first to oppose, and they were among the most notable of the adversaries : their being smitten is therefore a special object of song for loyal Israelites. The enmity of these two kings was wanton and unprovoked, and hence their overthrow was the more welcome to Israel. Sihon had been victorious in his war with Moab, and thought to make short work with Israel, but he was speedily overthrown : Og was of the race of the giants, and by his huge size inspired the tribes with dread ; but they were encouraged by the previous overthrow of Sihon, and soon the giant king fell beneath their sword. "*And all the kingdoms of Canaan.*" Many were these petty principalities, and some of them were populous and valiant ; but they all fell beneath the conquering hand of Joshua, for the Lord was with him. Even so shall all the foes of the Lord's believing people in these days be put to the rout : Satan and the world shall be overthrown, and all the hosts of sin shall be destroyed, for our greater Joshua leads forth our armies, conquering and to conquer.

Note that in this verse we have the details of matters which were mentioned in the bulk in the previous stanza : it is well when we have sung of mercies in the gross to consider them one by one, and give to each individual blessing a share in our song. It is well to preserve abundant memorials of the Lord's deliverance, so that we not only sing of mighty kings as a class, but also of " Sihon king of the Amorites, and Og king of Bashan " as distinct persons.

12. "*And gave their land for an heritage, an heritage unto Israel his people.*" Jehovah is Lord Paramount, and permits men to hold their lands upon lease, terminable at his pleasure. The nations of Canaan had become loathsome with abominable vices, and they were condemned by the great Judge of all the earth to be cut off from the face of the country which they defiled. The twelve tribes were charged to act as their executioners, and as their fee they were to receive Canaan as a possession. Of old the Lord had given this land to Abraham and his seed by a covenant of salt, but he allowed the Amorites and other tribes to sojourn in it till their iniquity was full, and then he bade his people come and take their own out of the holders' hands. Canaan was their heritage beeause they were the Lord's heritage, and he gave it to them actually because he had long before given it to them by promise.

The Lord's chosen still have a heritage from which none can keep them back. Covenant blessings of inestimable value are secured to them ; and, as surely as God has a people, his people shall have a heritage. To them it comes by gift, though they have to fight for it. Often does it happen when they slay a sin or conquer a difficulty that they are enriched by the spoil : to them even evils work for good, and trials ensure triumphs. No enemy shall prevail so as to really injure them, for they shall find a heritage where once they were opposed by " all the kingdoms of Canaan."

13. "*Thy name, O Lord, endureth for ever.*" God's name is eternal, and will never be changed. His character is immutable ; his fame and honour also shall remain to all eternity. There shall always be life in the name of Jesus, and sweetness and consolation. Those upon whom the Lord's name is named in verity and truth shall be preserved by it, and kept from all evil, world without end. Jehovah is a name which shall outlive the ages, and retain the fulness of its glory and might for ever. "*And thy memorial, O Lord, throughout all generations.*" Never shall men forget thee, O Lord. The ordinances of thine house shall keep thee in men's memories, and thine everlasting gospel and the grace which goes therewith shall be abiding remembrancers of thee. Grateful hearts will for ever beat to thy praise, and enlightened minds shall continue to marvel at all thy wondrous works. Men's memorials decay, but the memorial of the Lord abideth evermore. What a comfort

to desponding minds, trembling for the ark of the Lord! No, precious Name, thou shalt never perish! Fame of the Eternal, thou shalt never grow dim!

This verse must be construed in its connection, and it teaches us that the honour and glory gained by the Lord in the overthrow of the mighty kings would never die out. Israel for long ages reaped the benefit of the *prestige* which the divine victories had brought to the nation. Moreover, the Lord in thus keeping his covenant which he made with Abraham, when he promised to give the land to his seed, was making it clear that his memorial contained in promises and covenant would never be out of his sight. His name endures in all its truthfulness, for those who occupied Israel's land were driven out that the true heirs might dwell therein in peace.

14. *"For the LORD will judge his people."* He will exercise personal discipline over them, and not leave it to their foes to maltreat them at pleasure. When the correction is ended he will arise and avenge them of their oppressors, who for a while were used by him as his rod. He may seem to forget his people, but it is not so; he will undertake their cause and deliver them. The judges of Israel were also her deliverers, and such is the Lord of hosts: in this sense—as ruling, preserving, and delivering his chosen—Jehovah will judge his people. *"And he will repent himself concerning his servants."* When he has smitten them, and they lie low before him, he will pity them as a father pitieth his children, for he doth not afflict willingly. The Psalm speaks after the manner of men: the nearest description that words can give of the Lord's feeling towards his suffering servants is that he repents the evil which he inflicted upon them. He acts as if he had changed his mind and regretted smiting them. It goes to the heart of God to see his beloved ones oppressed by their enemies: though they deserve all they suffer, and more than all, yet the Lord cannot see them smart without a pang. It is remarkable that the nations by which God has afflicted Israel have all been destroyed as if the tender Father hated the instruments of his children's correction. The chosen nation is here called, first, " his people," and then " his servants: " as his people he judges them, as his servants he finds comfort in them, for so the word may be read. He is most tender to them when he sees their service; hence the Scripture saith, " I will spare them, as a man spareth his own son that serveth him." Should not the " servants " of God praise him? He plagued Pharaoh's servants; but as for his own he has mercy upon them, and returns to them in love after he has in the truest affection smitten them for their iniquities. " Praise him, O ye servants of the Lord."

Now we come to the Psalmist's denunciation of idols, which follows most naturally upon his celebration of the one only living and true God.

15 The idols of the heathen *are* silver and gold, the work of men's hands.

16 They have mouths, but they speak not; eyes have they, but they see not;

17 They have ears, but they hear not; neither is there *any* breath in their mouths.

18 They that make them are like unto them: *so is* every one that trusteth in them.

15. *"The idols of the heathen are silver and gold, the work of men's hands."* Their essential material is dead metal, their attributes are but the qualities of senseless substances, and what of form and fashion they exhibit they derive from the skill and labour of those who worship them. It is the height of insanity to worship metallic manufactures. Though silver and gold are useful to us when we rightly employ them, there is nothing about them which can entitle them to reverence and worship. If we did not know the sorrowful fact to be indisputable, it would seem to be impossible that intelligent beings could bow down before substances which they must themselves refine from the ore, and fashion into form. One would think it less absurd to worship one's own hands than to adore that which those hands have made. What great works can these mock deities perform for man when they are themselves the works of man? Idols are fitter to be played with, like dolls by babes, than to be adored by grown-up men. Hands are better used in breaking than in making objects which can be put to such an idiotic use. Yet the heathen love their abominable deities better than silver and gold: it were well if we could say that some professed believers in the Lord had as much love for *him*.

16. *"They have mouths."* For their makers fashioned them like themselves. An opening is made where the mouth should be, and yet it is no mouth, for they eat not, *they speak not.* They cannot communicate with their worshippers; they are dumb as death. If they cannot even speak, they are not even so worthy of worship as our children at school. Jehovah speaks, and it is done; but these images utter never a word. Surely, if they could speak, they would rebuke their votaries. Is not their silence a still more powerful rebuke? When our philosophical teachers deny that God has made any verbal revelation of himself they also confess that their god is dumb.

"Eyes have they, but they see not." Who would adore a blind man—how can the heathen be so mad as to bow themselves before a blind image? The eyes of idols have frequently been very costly; diamonds have been used for that purpose; but of what avail is the expense, since they see nothing? If they cannot even see us, how can they know our wants, appreciate our sacrifices, or spy out for us the means of help? What a wretched thing, that a man who can see should bow down before an image which is blind! The worshipper is certainly physically in advance of his god, and yet mentally he is on a level with it; for assuredly his foolish heart is darkened, or he would not so absurdly play the fool.

17. *"They have ears,"* and very large ones too, if we remember certain of the Hindoo idols. *"But they hear not."* Useless are their ears; in fact, they are mere counterfeits and deceits. Ears which men make are always deaf: the secret of hearing is wrapped up with the mystery of life, and both are in the unsearchable mind of the Lord. It seems that these heathen gods are dumb, and blind, and deaf— a pretty bundle of infirmities to be found in a deity! *"Neither is there any breath in their mouths;"* they are dead, no sign of life is perceptible; and breathing, which is of the essence of animal life, they never know. Shall a man waste his breath in crying to an idol which has no breath? Shall life offer up petitions to death? Verily, this is a turning of things upside down.

18. *"They that make them are like unto them:"* they are as blockish, as senseless, as stupid as the gods they have made, and, like them they are the objects of divine abhorrence, and shall be broken in pieces in due time. *"So is every one that trusteth in them."* The idol-worshippers are as bad as the idol-makers; for if there were none to worship, there would be no market for the degrading manufacture. Idolaters are spiritually dead, they are the mere images of men, their best being is gone, they are not what they seem. Their mouths do not really pray, their eyes see not the truth, their ears hear not the voice of the Lord, and the life of God is not in them. Those who believe in their own inventions in religion betray great folly, and an utter absence of the quickening Spirit. Gracious men can see the absurdity of forsaking the true God and setting up rivals in his place; but those who perpetrate this crime think not so: on the contrary, they pride themselves upon their great wisdom, and boast of " advanced thought " and " modern culture." Others there are who believe in a baptismal regeneration which does not renew the nature, and they make members of Christ and children of God who have none of the spirit of Christ, or the signs of adoption. May we be saved from such mimicry of divine work lest we also become like our idols.

19 Bless the LORD, O house of Israel : bless the LORD, O house of Aaron :

20 Bless the LORD, O house of Levi : ye that fear the LORD, bless the LORD.

21 Blessed be the LORD out of Zion, which dwelleth at Jerusalem. Praise ye the LORD.

19. *"Bless the LORD, O house of Israel."* All of you, in all your tribes, praise the one Jehovah. Each tribe, from Reuben to Benjamin, has its own special cause for blessing the Lord, and the nation as a whole has substantial reasons for pouring out benedictions upon his name. Those whom God has named " the house of Israel," a family of prevailing princes, ought to show their loyalty by thankfully bowing before their sovereign Lord. *"Bless the LORD, O house of Aaron."* These were elected to high office and permitted to draw very near to the divine presence; therefore they beyond all others were bound to bless the Lord. Those who are favoured to be leaders in the church should be foremost in adoration. In God's house the house of Aaron should feel bound to speak well of his name before all the house of Israel.

20. *"Bless the Lord, O house of Levi."* These helped the priests in other things, let them aid them in this also. The house of Israel comprehends all the chosen seed ; then we come down to the smaller but more central ring of the house of Aaron, and now we widen out to the whole tribe of Levi. Let reverence and adoration spread from man to man until the whole lump of humanity shall be leavened. The house of Levi had choice reasons for blessing God : read the Levite story and see. Remember that the whole of the Levites were set apart for holy service, and supported by the tribes allotted to them ; therefore they were in honour bound above all others to worship Jehovah with cheerfulness.

"Ye that fear the Lord, bless the Lord." These are the choicer spirits, the truly spiritual : they are not the Lord's in name only, but in heart and spirit. The Father seeketh such to worship him. If Aaron and Levi both forget and fail, these will not. It may be that this verse is intended to bring in God-fearing men who were not included under Israel, Aaron, and Levi. They were Gentile proselytes, and this verse opens the door and bids them enter. Those who fear God need not wait for any other qualification for sacred service ; godly fear proves us to be in the covenant with Israel, in the priesthood with Aaron, and in the service of the Lord with Levi. Filial fear, such as saints feel towards the Lord, does not hinder their praise ; nay, it is the main source and fountain of their adoration.

21. *"Blessed be the Lord out of Zion, which dwelleth at Jerusalem."* Let him be most praised at home. Where he blesses most, let him be blessed most. Let the beloved mount of Zion, and the chosen city of Jerusalem echo his praises. He remains among his people : he is their dwelling-place, and they are his dwelling-place : let this intimate communion ensure intense gratitude on the part of his chosen. The temple of holy solemnities which is Christ, and the city of the Great King, which is the church, may fitly be regarded as the head-quarters of the praises of Jehovah, the God of Israel. *"Praise ye the Lord."* Hallelujah. Amen, and Amen.

EXPLANATORY NOTES AND QUAINT SAYINGS.

Whole Psalm.—This glorious Psalm of universal praise, placed at the end of the " Songs of Up-goings," which flow into it, and find their response in it, may be likened to a large and beautiful lake, into which rivers discharge their waters, and lose themselves in its calm expanse.—*Chr. Wordsworth.*

Whole Psalm.—This Psalm differs from that which went before. Its drift is not only to stir up the priests and Levites, as it was in the former, to this duty of praising God, but *the people* also :   and that, 1. Because the arguments which here he brings to press this duty, did in common concern both priests and people ; and, 2. Because that clause, which is here added, " *in the courts of the house of our God,*" may be extended to the people, as well as to the priests, seeing there were some courts in the Temple which were for the people to worship God in.—*Arthur Jackson.*

Whole Psalm.—This is a song of praise to the Lord for his goodness as the Lord of creation, in seven verses ; for his grace as the deliverer of his people, in seven more : and for his unity as the only true and living God, in seven more.—*James G. Murphy.*

Whole Psalm.—This seems to have been the morning hymn which the Levites were called upon to sing at the opening of the gates of the Temple ; and, as some think, the one before was used at shutting them in the evening.—*John Kitto, in "The Pictorial Bible."*

Verse 1.—This verse and the following are word for word with the first verse of the last Psalm, and are now repeated, with the view of keeping up the praise then and there commenced.—*Robert Bellarmine.*

Verse 1.—*"Praise ye the Lord."* *Hallelujah* is the Hebrew word. It signifies " *Praise ye the Lord.*" By this the faithful do provoke one another to give thanks unto God, and they cheer up their hearts and tune their spirits to perform this duty in the best manner, by making this preface as it were thereunto. True joy of the

Holy Ghost will not endure to be kept and cooped up in any one man's breast and bosom, but it striveth to get companions both for the pouring out and imparting of itself unto them, that they may be filled and refreshed out of this spring of joy ; as also that itself may be the more increased and inflamed by the united rejoicing of many good hearts together, that are all baptized in one spirit, and are thereby made able to inflame and to edify one another.—*Thomas Brightman* (1557—1607), *in "The Revelation of St. John Illustrated."*

Verse 1.—*"Praise ye the name of the LORD."* That is, the Lord himself, and the perfections of his nature; his greatness, goodness, grace, and mercy; his holiness, justice, power, truth, and faithfulness. Also his word, by which he makes known himself : this is a distinguishing blessing to his people, for which he is to be praised : see Ps. xlviii. 1, and Ps. cxlvii. 19, 20.—*John Gill.*

Verse 1.—*"The name of the LORD."*—The first discovery of the name I AM, which signifies the Divine eternity, as well as immutability, was for the comfort of the oppressed Israelites in Egypt : Exodus iii. 14, 15. It was then published from the secret place of the Almighty, as the only strong cordial to refresh them. It hath not yet, it shall not ever, lose its virtue in any of the miseries that have or shall successively befall the church. 'Tis as durable as the God whose name it is : he is still I AM and the same to the church as he was then to his Israel. His spiritual Israel have a greater right to the glories of it than the carnal Israel could have. No oppression can be greater than theirs ; what was a comfort suited to that distress hath the same suitableness to every other oppression. It was not a temporary name, but a name for ever, his " memorial to all generations " (verse 15), and reacheth to the church of the Gentiles, with whom he treats as the God of Abraham, ratifying that covenant by the Messiah, which he made with Abraham the father of the faithful.—*Stephen Charnock.*

Verse 1.—*"The name of the LORD."* Jehovah is called *"the name"* as far exceeding all other names, and as being proper and peculiar only to the true God. Other things are sometimes called gods, but nothing is or can be called Jehovah but only the Almighty Creator of the world. " That men may know," saith David, " that thou, whose name is Jehovah, art the Most High over all the earth " : Ps. lxxxiii. 18. From his calling himself JEHOVAH the LORD, we may easily gather what kind of thoughts he would have us, his creatures, entertain in our minds concerning him. When we think of him, we must raise our thoughts above all things else, and think of him as the Universal Being of the world, that gives essence and existence to all things in it : as Jehovah, the Being in whom we particularly, as well as other things, live and move, and have our being : as Jehovah, the Lord paramount over the whole world, to whom all angels and archangels in heaven, with all the kings and kingdoms upon earth, are entirely subject : as Jehovah, in whom all perfections are so perfectly united that they are all but one infinite perfection : as Jehovah, knowledge itself, always actually knowing all things that ever were, or are, or will be, or can be known : as Jehovah, wisdom itself, always contriving, ordering, and disposing of all, and everything, in the best order, after the best manner, and to the best possible end : as Jehovah, power, omnipotence itself, continually doing what he wills, only by willing it should be done, and always working either with means or without means, as he himself sees good : as Jehovah, light and glory itself, shining forth in and by and through everything that is made or done in the whole world. as Jehovah, holiness, purity, simplicity, greatness, majesty, eminency, super-eminency itself, infinitely exalted above all things else, existing in, and of himself, and having all things else continually subsisting in him : as Jehovah, goodness itself, doing and making all things good, and so communicating his goodness to all his creatures as to be the only fountain of all the goodness that is in any of them : as Jehovah, justice and righteousness itself, giving to all their due, and exacting no more of any man than what is absolutely due to him : as Jehovah, mercy itself, pardoning and forgiving all the sins that mankind commit against him, as soon as they repent and turn to him : as Jehovah, patience and longsuffering itself, bearing a long time, even with those who continue in their rebellions against him, waiting for their coming to a due sense of their folly and madness, that he may be gracious and merciful to them ; as Jehovah, love and kindness, and bounty itself, freely distributing his blessings among all his creatures, both good and bad, just and unjust, those that love him, and those that love him not : as Jehovah, truth and faithfulness itself, always performing what he promiseth to his people : as Jehovah, infinitude, immensity itself, in all things, to all things, beyond all things, everywhere, wholly, essentially, continually present : as Jehovah, constancy, immutability, eternity itself, without any variableness, or shadow of change ; yesterday, to-day, and for ever the same. In a word, when we think of the Most High God, Father, Son, and Holy Ghost, we should think of him as Jehovah, Unity in Trinity, Trinity in Unity, Three Persons, One Being, One Essence, One Lord, One Jehovah, blessed for ever. This is that glorious, that Almighty being, which the Psalmist here means when he saith, *"Praise ye the name of the* LORD*."*— *William Beveridge,* 1636—1708.

Verse 1.—*"Praise him, O ye servants of the* LORD*."* For ye will do nothing out of place by praising your Lord *as servants.* And if ye were to be for ever only servants, ye ought to praise the Lord ; how much more ought those servants to praise the Lord who have obtained the privilege of sons ?—*Augustine.*

Verse 1.—*"Praise," "praise," "praise."* When duties are thus inculcated, it noteth the necessity and excellency thereof ; together with our dulness and back-wardness thereunto.—*John Trapp.*

Verses 1, 2, 21.—*"Praise."* To prevent any feeling of weariness which might arise from the very frequent repetition of this exhortation to praise God, it is only necessary to remember that there is no sacrifice in which he takes greater delight than in the expression of praise. Thus (Ps. l. 14), " Sacrifice unto the Lord thanks-giving, and pay thy vows unto the Most High ; " and (Ps. cxvi. 12, 13), " What shall I render unto the LORD for all his benefits toward me ? I will take the cup of salvation, and call upon the name of the LORD." Particular attention is to be paid to those passages of Scripture which speak in such high terms of that worship of God which is spiritual ; otherwise we may be led, in the exercise of a misguided zeal, to spend our labour upon trifles, and in this respect imitate the example of too many who have wearied themselves with ridiculous attempts to invent additions to the service of God, while they have neglected what is of all other things most important. That is the reason why the Holy Spirit so repeatedly inculcates the duty of praise. It is that we may not undervalue, or grow careless in this devotional exercise. It implies, too, an indirect censure of our tardiness in proceeding to the duty ; for he would not reiterate the admonition were we ready and active in the discharge of it.—*John Calvin.*

Verses 1, 2, 3.—As *Gotthold* was one day passing a tradesman's house, he heard the notes of a Psalm, with which the family were concluding their morning meal. He was deeply affected, and, with a full heart, said to himself : O my God, how pleasing to my ears is the sound of thy praise, and how comforting to my soul the thought that there are still a few who bless thee for thy goodness. Alas, the great bulk of mankind have become brutalized, and resemble the swine, which in harvest gather and fatten upon the acorns beneath the oak, but show to the tree, which bore them, no other thanks than rubbing off its bark, and tearing up the sod around it. In former times, it was the law in certain monasteries, that the chanting of the praise of God should know no interruption, and that one choir of monks should, at stated intervals, relieve another in the holy employment. To the superstition and trust in human works, of which there may have been here a mixture, we justly assign a place among the wood, hay, and stubble (1 Cor. iii. 12). At the same time it is undeniably right that thy praise should never cease ; and were men to be silent, the very stones would cry out. We must begin eternal life here below, not only in our conscience, but also with our praise. Our soul ought to be like a flower, not merely receiving the gentle influence of heaven, but, in its turn, and as if in gratitude, exhaling also a sweet and pleasant perfume. It should be our desire, as it once was that of a pious man, that our hearts should melt and dissolve like incense in the fire of love, and yield the sweet fragrance of praise ; or we should be like the holy martyr who professed himself willing to be consumed, if from his ashes a little flower might spring and blossom to the glory of God. We should be ready to give our very blood to fertilize the garden of the church, and render it more pro-ductive of the fruit of praise.

Well, then, my God, I will praise and extol thee with heart and mouth to the utmost of my power. Oh, that without the interruptions which eating, and drinking, and sleep require, I could apply myself to this heavenly calling ! Every mouthful of air which I inhale is mixed with the goodness which preserves my life ; let every breath which I exhale be mingled at least with a hearty desire for thy honour and praise.

Hallelujah ! Ye holy angels, ye children of men, and all ye creatures, praise the Lord with me, and let us exalt his name together.—*Christian Scriver [Gotthold]*, 1629—1693.

Verse 3.—*"Praise the LORD." Hallelujah* (praise to Jah !) *for good (is) Jehovah, Make music to his name, for it is lovely.* The last words may also be translated, *he is lovely,* i.e. an object worthy of supreme attachment.—*Joseph Addison Alexander.*

Verse 3.—*"Praise the LORD ; for the LORD is good."* That is, originally, transcendently, effectively ; he is good, and doeth good (Ps. cxix. 68), and is therefore to be praised with mind, mouth, and practice.—*John Trapp.*

Verse 3.—*"Sing praises unto his name ; for it is pleasant."* The work of praising God hath a sort of reward joined with it. When we praise God most we get much benefit by so doing : it is so comely in itself, so pleasant unto God, and profitable to the person that offereth praises, so fit to cheer up his spirit, and strengthen his faith in God, whose praises are the pillars of the believer's confidence and comfort, that a man should be allured thereunto : *"Sing praises unto his name ; for it is pleasant ; "* and this is the second motive or reason to praise God [the first being that " the Lord is good "].—*David Dickson.*

Verse 4.—*"For the LORD hath chosen,"* etc. God's distinguishing grace should make his elect lift up many a humble, joyful, and thankful heart to him.—*John Trapp.*

Verse 4.—*"Jacob," "Israel."* Praise the Lord for enrolling you in this company. To quicken you in this work of praise, consider what you were ; you were not a people, God raised you up from the very dunghill to this preferment ; remember your past estate. Look, as old Jacob considered what he had been when God preferred him (Gen. xxxii. 10) ; " With my staff I passed over this Jordan, and now I am become two bands ; " so do you say, I am a worthless creature, it is God that hath taken me into his grace, praised be the Lord that hath chosen me. Then consider how many are left to perish in the wide world. Some live out of the church's pale that never heard of Christ, and many others have only a loose general form of Christianity. Oh ! blessed be God that hath chosen me to be of the number of his peculiar people. It is said (Zech. xiii. 8), " And it shall come to pass in all the land, saith the Lord, that two parts shall be cut off and die, but the third shall be left therein." We pass through many bolters before we come to be God's peculiar people, as the corn is ground, bolted, searched before it comes to be fine flour. Many have not the knowledge of God, and others live in the church but are carnal ; and for me to be one of his peculiar people, a member of Christ's mystical body, oh ! what a privilege is this ! And then what moved him to all this ? Nothing but his own free grace. Therefore praise the Lord.—*Thomas Manton.*

Verse 4.—*"His peculiar treasure."* The Hebrew word *segullah* signifieth God's special jewels, God's proper ones, or God's secret ones, that he keeps in store for himself, and for his own special service and use. Princes lock up with their own hands in secret their most precious and costly jewels ; and so doth God his : *"For the LORD hath chosen Jacob unto himself, and Israel for his peculiar treasure,"* or for his secret gain.—*Thomas Brooks.*

Verse 4.—*"His peculiar treasure."* Will not a man that is not defective in his prudentials secure his jewels ? " They shall be mine in that day when I make up my jewels, and I will spare them as a father his son that serveth him : " Malachi iii. 17. If a house be on fire, the owner of it will first take care of his wife and children, then of his jewels, and last of all, of his lumber and rubbish. Christ secures first his people, for they are his jewels ; the world is but lumber and rubbish.—*Richard Mayhew.*

Verse 5.—*"For I know."* The word *"I"* is made emphatic in the original. Whatever may be the case with others, I have had personal and precious experience of the greatness of Jehovah's power, and of his infinite supremacy above all other gods. The author of the Psalm may either speak for all Israel as a unit, or he may have framed his song so that every worshipper might say this for himself as his own testimony.—*Henry Cowles.*

Verse 5.—*"For I know that the LORD is great,"* etc. On what a firm foundation does the Psalmist plant his foot—*"I know ! "* One loves to hear men of God speaking in this calm, undoubting, and assured confidence, whether it be of the Lord's goodness or of the Lord's greatness. You may perhaps say, that it required no great stretch of faith or knowledge, or any amount of bravery, to declare that God was great ; but I think that not many wise nor mighty had in the Psalmist's days attained unto his knowledge or made his confession, that Jehovah, the God of Israel, was "*above all gods.*"   Baal and Chemosh, and Milcom and Dagon, claimed the fealty of the nations round about ; and David, in the Court of Achish, would have found his declaration as unwelcome, as it would have been rejected as untrue. Moses once carried a message from Jehovah to the king of Egypt, and his reply was, " Who is the Lord, that I should obey his voice ? I know not the Lord ; " and even of Jehovah's peculiar treasure, all were not Israel that were of Israel.

There is a knowledge that plays round the head, like lightning on a mountain's summit, that leaves no trace behind ; and there is a knowledge that, like the fertilizing stream, penetrates into the very recesses of the heart, and issues forth in all the fruits of holiness, of love, and peace, and joy for evermore.—*Barton Bouchier.*

Verse 6.—"*Whatsoever the* LORD *pleased, that did he,*" etc. He was not forced to make all that he made, but *all that he willed he made.* His will was the cause of all things which he made. Thou makest a house, because if thou didst not make it thou wouldest be left without a habitation : necessity compels thee to make a home, not free-will. Thou makest a garment, because thou wouldest go about naked if thou didst not make it ; thou art therefore led to making a garment by necessity, not by free-will. Thou plantest a mountain with vines, thou sowest seed, because if thou didst not do so, thou wouldest not have food ; all such things thou doest of necessity. God has made all things of his goodness. He needed nothing that he made ; and therefore he hath made all things that he willed.

He did whatsoever he willed in the heaven and earth : dost thou do all that thou willest even in thy field ? Thou willest many things, but canst not do all thou wishest in thy own house. Thy wife, perchance, gainsays thee, thy children gainsay thee, sometimes even thy servant contumaciously gainsays thee, and thou doest not what thou willest. But thou sayest, I do what I will, because I punish the disobedient and gainsayer. Even this thou doest not when thou willest.—*Augustine.*

Verse 6.—"*Whatsoever the* LORD *pleased, that did he,*" etc. God's will obtains and hath the upper hand everywhere. Down man, down pope, down devil ; you must yield ; things shall not be as you will, but as God will ! We may well say, " Who hath resisted his will ? " Rom. ix. 19. Many, indeed, disobey, and sin against the will of his precept ; but none ever did, none ever shall, frustrate or obstruct the will of his purpose ; for he will do all his pleasure, and in his way mountains shall become a plain.—*William Slater* (—1704), *in "The Morning Exercises."*

Verse 6.—Upon the Arminian's plan (if absurdity can deserve the name of a plan), the glorious work of God's salvation, and the eternal redemption of Jesus Christ, are not complete, unless a dying mortal lends his arm ; that is, unless he, who of himself can do nothing, vouchsafe to begin and accomplish that which all the angels in heaven cannot do ; namely, to convert the soul from Satan to God. How contrary is all this to the language of Scripture—how repugnant to the oracles of truth ! " Whatsoever the Lord pleased, that did he in heaven and in earth."—*Ambrose Serle* (—1815), *in "Horæ Solitariæ."*

Verse 6.—"*In heaven and in the earth,*" etc. His power is infinite. He can do what he will do everywhere ; all places are there named but purgatory ; perhaps he can do nothing there, but leaves all that work for the Pope.—*Thomas Adams.*

Verse 6.—"*In the seas, and all deep places.*" He did wonders in the mighty waters : more than once he made the boisterous sea a calm, and walked upon the surface of it ; and as of old he broke up the fountains of the great deep, and drowned the world ; and at another time dried up the sea, and led his people through the depths, as through a wilderness ; so he will hereafter bind the old serpent, the devil, and cast him into the abyss, into the great deep, the bottomless pit, where he will continue during the thousand years' reign of Christ with his saints.—*John Gill.*

Verse 6.—The word "*pleaseth*" limits the general note or particle "*all*" unto all works which in themselves are good, or else serve for good use, and so are pleasing to the Lord for the use sake. He doth not say that the Lord doth all things which are done, but all things which he pleaseth, that is, he doth not make men sinful and wicked, neither doth he work rebellion in men, which is displeasing unto him ;

but he doth whatsoever is pleasing, that is, all things which are agreeable to his nature. And whatsoever is according to his will and good pleasure, that he doth, for none can hinder it. This is the true sense and meaning of the words.—*George Walker, in "God made visible in his Works," 1641.*

Verse 6.—*"Whatsover the Lord pleased, that did he,"* etc. With reference to the government of Providence, it is said of God, that " he doeth according to his will in the army of heaven, and among the inhabitants of the earth." Even insensible matter is under his control. Fire and hail, snow and vapour, and stormy wind, fulfil his word : and with reference to intelligent agents, we are told that he maketh the most refractory, even the wrath of man, to praise him, and the remainder of wrath he restrains. The whole Bible exhibits Jehovah as so ordering the affairs of individuals, and of nations, as to secure the grand purpose he had in view in creating the world,—viz., the promotion of his own glory, in the salvation of a multitude which no man can number, of all nations, and kindreds, and tribes, and peoples, and tongues. One of the most prominent distinctions between divine revelation and ordinary history is, that when the same general events are narrated, the latter exhibits—(it is its province so to do—it is not able indeed to do more,) the agency of man, the former, the agency of God. Profane history exhibits the instruments by which Jehovah works ; the finger of divine revelation points to the unseen but almighty hand which wields and guides the instrument, and causes even Herod and Pontius Pilate, together with the Jews and the people of Israel, to do what the hand and the counsel of God determined before to be done.—*George Payne, in "Lectures on Christian Theology," 1850.*

Verse 7.—*"He causeth the vapours to ascend,"* etc. Dr. Halley made a number of experiments at St. Helena as to the quantity of water that is daily evaporated from the sea, and he found that ten square inches of the ocean's surface yielded one cubic inch of water in twelve hours—a square mile therefore yields 401,448,960 cubic inches, or 6,914 tons of water. From the surface of the Mediterranean Sea during a summer's day there would pass off in invisible vapour five thousand millions of tons of water. This being only for one day, the quantity evaporated in a year would be 365 times greater, and in two thousand years it would amount to four thousand billions of tons, which evaporation would in time empty the Mediterranean Sea ; but we have good reason for believing that there is as much water there now as in the time of the Romans, therefore the balance is kept up by the downpour of rain, the influx of the rivers, and the currents from the Atlantic.

Now let us consider the amount of power required for all this evaporation. Mr. Joule, whose experiments have given to the world so much valuable information, says that if we had a pool of water one square mile and six inches in depth to be evaporated by artificial heat, it would require the combustion of 30,000 tons of coal to effect it ; therefore to evaporate all the water that ascends from the earth it would take 6,000,000,000,000 (six billion) tons, or more than all the coal that could be stowed away in half-a-dozen such worlds as this ; and yet silently and surely has the process of evaporation been going on for millions of years.—*Samuel Kinns, in "Moses and Geology," 1882.*

Verse 7.—*"He causeth the vapours to ascend,"* etc. There is no physical necessity that the boiling-point of water should occur at two hundred and twelve degrees of the Fahrenheit scale. As far as we know, it might have been the same with the boiling-points of oil of turpentine, alcohol or ether. We shall see the benevolence of the present adjustment by noticing some of the consequences which would follow if any change were made.

The amount of vapour given off at ordinary temperatures by any liquid depends on the temperature at which it boils. If the boiling-point of water were the same as that of alcohol, the vapour given off by the ocean would be two and a half times as much as at present. Such an excess of aqueous vapour would produce continual rains and inundations, and would make the air too damp for animal, and too cloudy for vegetable life. If water boiled at the same temperature as ether, the vapour rising from the ocean would be more than twenty-five times as much as at present. In such a state of things no man could see the sun on account of the clouds ; the rain would be so excessive as to tear up the soil and wash away plants ; inundations would be constant, and navigation would be impossible in the inland torrents which would take the place of our rivers. In winter the snow of one day might bury the houses. If, on the other hand, water boiled at the same temperature with oil of turpentine, the vapour given off by the ocean would be less than one-fourth of its present amount.   In this case rain would be a rarity, like an eclipse of the sun, the dryness of the desert of Sahara would be equalled in a large part of the globe, which would, therefore, be bare of vegetation, and incapable of sustaining animal life.   Plants would be scorched by unclouded sunshine, springs and rivulets would be dry, and inland navigation would cease ; for nearly all the rain would be absorbed by the porous earth.

We see, then, that the boiling-point of water has been adjusted to various relations.   It is adjusted to the capacity of space to contain aqueous vapour in a transparent state ; if it were higher than two hundred and twelve degrees, the earth would be scorched by an unclouded sun ; if it were lower, it would droop under continual shade.   It is suited to the demand of plants for water ; if it were higher, they would suffer from drought ; if it were lower, they would be torn up by floods. It is in harmony with the texture of the soil ; if it were higher, the earth would absorb all the rain which falls ; if it were lower, the soil would often be washed away by the surface torrents after a shower.   It is adapted to the elevation of the continents above the sea ; if it were higher, rivers with their present inclination would be so shallow as to be often dry ; if it were lower, most rivers would be so deep as to be torrents, while the land would be covered with floods.—*Professor Hemholtz.*

Verse 7.—"To ascend from the ends of the earth."   Rains in England are often introduced by a south-east wind.   " Vapour brought to us by such a wind must have been generated in countries to the south and east of our island.   It is therefore, probably, in the extensive valleys watered by the Meuse, the Moselle, and the Rhine, if not from the more distant Elbe, with the Oder and the Weser, that the water rises, in the midst of sunshine, which is soon afterwards to form *our* clouds, and pour down *our* thunder-showers."   " Drought and sunshine in one part of Europe may be necessary to the production of a wet season in another."*—*William Whewell (1795—1866), in "The Bridgwater Treatise " [Astronomy and General Physics],* 1839.

Verse 7.—"From the surface of the earth raising the vapours."   The whole description is beautifully exact and picturesque.   Not " the ends," or even " the summits " or " extreme mountains," for the original is in the singular number (קצה), but from the whole of the *extreme layer*, the *superficies* or *surface* of the earth ; from every point of which the great process of exhalation is perpetually going on to supply the firmament with refreshing and fruitful clouds.—*John Mason Good.*

Verse 7.—"He maketh lightnings for the rain."   When the electrical clouds are much agitated, the rain generally falls heavily, and if the agitation is excessive, it hails.   As the electricity is dissipated by the frequent discharges the cloud condenses and there comes a sudden and heavy rain ; but the greater the accumulation of electricity, the longer is the rain delayed.   Thus connected as the electrical phenomena of the atmosphere are with clouds, vapour, and rain, how forcibly are we struck with these appropriate words in the Scriptures.—*Edwin Sidney, in "Conversations on the Bible and Science,"* 1866.

Verse 7.—"He maketh lightnings for the rain."   Dr. Russell, in his description of the weather at Aleppo, in September, tells us, that seldom a night passes without much *lightning* in the north-west quarter, but not attended with *thunder ;* and that when this *lightning* appears in the west or south-west points, it is a *sure sign* of the approaching rain, which is *often followed* with thunder.   This last clause, which is not perfectly clear, is afterwards explained in his more enlarged account of the weather of the year 1746, when he tells us that though it began to be cloudy on the 4th of September, and continued so for a few days, and *even thundered*, yet no rain fell till the 11th, which shows that his meaning was, that the *lightning* in the west or south-west points, which is often followed with thunder, is a sure sign of the approach of rain.   I have before mentioned that a squall of wind and clouds of dust are the usual forerunners of these first rains.   Most of these things are taken notice of in Ps. cxxxv. 7 ; Jer. x. 13 ; li. 16 ; and serve to illustrate them.   Russell's account determines, I think, that the Nesiim, which our translators render *vapours*, must mean, as they elsewhere translate the word, *clouds*.   It shows that God "*maketh lightnings for the rain*," they, in the west and south-west points, being at Aleppo the sure *prognostics* of rain.   The squalls of wind bring on these refreshing

---

* Howard on the Climate of London.

showers, and are therefore " precious things " of the " treasuries " of God.—
Thomas Harmer.

Verse 7.—*"He maketh lightnings for the rain."* The Psalmist mentions it as
another circumstance calling for our wonder, that *lightnings are mixed with rain,*
things quite opposite in their nature one from another. Did not custom make us
familiar with the spectacle, we would pronounce this mixture of fire and water to
be a phenomenon altogether incredible. The same may be said of the phenomena
of the winds. Natural causes can be assigned for them, and philosophers have
pointed them out ; but the winds, with their various currents, are a wonderful
work of God. He does not merely assert the power of God, be it observed, in the
sense in which philosophers themselves grant it, but he maintains that not a drop
of rain falls from heaven without a divine commission or dispensation to that effect.
All readily allow that God is the author of rain, thunder, and wind, in so far as he
originally established the order of things in nature ; but the Psalmist goes farther
than this, holding that when it rains, this is not effected by a blind instinct of nature,
but is the consequence of the decree of God, who is pleased at one time to darken
the sky with clouds, and at another to brighten it again with sunshine.—*John Calvin.*

Verse 7.—*"He maketh lightnings for the rain."* It is a great instance of the
divine wisdom and goodness, that lightning should be accompanied by rain, to
soften its rage, and prevent its mischievous effects. Thus, in the midst of judgment, does God remember mercy. The threatenings in his word against sinners
are like lightning ; they would blast and scorch us up, were it not for his promises
made in the same word to penitents, which, as a gracious rain, turn aside their fury,
refreshing and comforting our affrighted spirits.—*George Horne.*

Verse 7.—*"He bringeth the wind out of his treasuries."* That is, say some, out
of the caves and hollow places of the earth ; but I rather conceive that because
the wind riseth many times on a sudden, and as our Saviour saith (John iii. 8), "we
cannot tell whence it cometh," therefore God is said here to bring it forth, as if he
had it locked up in readiness in some secret and hidden treasuries or storehouses.—
Arthur Jackson.

Verse 7.—*"He bringeth the wind."* The winds are with great beauty, represented
as laid up by him as jewels in a treasure house. Indeed, few verses better express
creative control, than those in which the winds, which make sport of man's efforts
and defy his power, are represented as thus ready to spring forth at God's bidding
from the quarters where they quietly sleep. The occasion comes, the thoughts
of Jehovah find expression in his providence, and his ready servants leap suddenly
forth : *"He bringeth the winds out of his treasuries."* But this bringing forth is not
for physical purposes only ; it is for great moral and spiritual ends also. Take
one illustration out of many. His people were on the edge of deepest and most
brutish idolatry. They were ready to fall into a most degraded form of idol worship,
when he offered to them that ever yearning heart of Fatherly love : " Thus saith
the Lord, Learn not the way of the heathen." Their God is only " the tree cut
out of the forest," silvered over, or decked with gold ; " upright as the palm tree,
but speaks not ; the stock is a doctrine of vanities ; but the Lord is the true God ;
he maketh lightnings with rain ; he bringeth the wind out of his treasures." Jer.
x. 2—16. Thus, too, the words of Agur to Ithiel and Ucal, " He hath gathered
the wind in his fists." Prov. xxx. 4.—*John Duns, in "Science and Christian Thought,"*
1868.

Verse 8.—*"Who smote the firstborn of Egypt."* The firstborn only were smitten ;
these were singled out in every family with unerring precision, the houses of the
Israelites, wherever the blood of the lamb was sprinkled on the door-posts, being
passed over. The death of all those thousands, both of man and beast, took place
at the same instant—" at midnight."

Is God unrighteous, then, that taketh vengeance ? No ; this is an act of
retribution. The Egyptians had slain the children of the Israelites, casting their
infants into the river. Now the affliction is turned upon themselves ; the delight
of their eyes is taken from them ; all their firstborn are dead, from the firstborn
of Pharaoh that sat upon his throne, unto the the firstborn of the captive that was
in the dungeon.—*Thomas S. Millington, in "Signs and Wonders in the Land of Ham,"*
1873.

Verse 8.—*"And beast."* The Egyptians worshipped many animals, and when
the firstborn of the sacred animals died the circumstance greatly increased the

impressiveness of the plague as an assault upon the gods of Egypt.—*C. H. S. Suggested by Otto Von Gerlach.*

Verses 8, 9, 10—12.—Worthy is Jahve to be praised, for he is the Redeemer out of Egypt. Worthy is he to be praised, for he is the Conqueror of the Land of Promise.—*Franz Delitzsch.*

Verse 9.—*"Who sent tokens and wonders."*—*"Tokens,"* that is, signs or evidences of the Divine power. *"Wonders,"* things fitted to impress the mind with awe; things outside of the ordinary course of events; things not produced by natural laws, but by the direct power of God. The allusion here is, of course, to the plagues of Egypt, as recorded in Exodus.—*Albert Barnes.*

Verse 10.—*"Who smote great nations,"* etc. It is better that the wicked should be destroyed a hundred times over than that they should tempt those who are as yet innocent to join their company. Let us but think what might have been our fate, and the fate of every other nation under heaven at this hour, had the sword of the Israelites done its work more sparingly. Even as it was, the small portions of the Canaanites who were left, and the nations around them, so tempted the Israelites by their idolatrous practices that we read continually of the whole people of God turning away from his service. But, had the heathen lived in the land in equal numbers, and, still more, had they intermarried largely with the Israelites, how was it possible humanly speaking, that any sparks of the light of God's truth should have survived to the coming of Christ? Would not the Israelites have lost all their peculiar character; and if they had retained the name of Jehovah as of their God, would they not have formed as unworthy notions of his attributes, and worship him with a worship as abominable as that which the Moabites paid to Chemosh or the Philistines to Dagon?

But this was not to be, and therefore the nations of Canaan were to be cut off utterly. The Israelites, sword, in its bloodiest executions, wrought a work of mercy for all the countries of the earth to the very end of the world. They seem of very small importance to us now, these perpetual contests with the Canaanites, and the Midianites, and the Ammonites, and the Philistines, with which the Books of Joshua and Judges and Samuel are almost filled. We may half wonder that God should have interferred in such quarrels, or have changed the course of nature, in order to give one of the nations of Palestine the victory over another. But in these contests, on the fate of one of these nations of Palestine the happiness of the human race depended. The Israelites fought not for themselves only, but for us. It might follow that they should thus be accounted the enemies of all mankind, —it might be that they were tempted by their very distinctness to despise other nations; still they did God's work,—still they preserved unhurt the seed of eternal life, and were the ministers of blessing to all other nations, even though they themselves failed to enjoy it.—*Thomas Arnold, 1795—1842.*

Verse 10.—*"Who smote great nations,"* etc. Let us not stand in fear of any enemies that rise up against us, and conspire to hinder the peace of the church, and stop the passage of the gospel; when God beginneth to take the cause of his people into his own hand, and smitteth any of his enemies on the jaw-bone, the rest are reserved to the like destruction. For wherefore doth God punish his adversaries, and enter into judgment with them? Wherefore doth he visit them, and strike them down with his right hand! Is it only to take vengeance, and to show his justice in their confusion? No, it serveth for the comfort and consolation of his servants, that howsoever God be patient, yet in the end they shall not escape.— *William Attersoll, 1618.*

Verse 11.—*"Sihon king of the Amorites, and Og."* Notice is taken of two kings, Sihon and Og, not as being more powerful than the rest, but because shutting up the entrance to the land in front they were the most formidable enemies met with, and the people, besides, were not as yet habituated to war.—*John Calvin.*

Verse 11.—*"Sihon king of the Amorites."* When Israel arrived on the borders of the promised Land they encountered Sihon. (Numb. xxi. 21.) He was evidently a man of very great courage and audacity. Shortly before the time of Israel's arrival he had dispossessed the Moabites of a splendid territory, driving them south of the natural bulwark of the Arnon with great slaughter and the loss of a great number of captives (xxi. 26—29). When the Israelite host appears, he does not hesitate or temporize like Balak, but at once gathers his people together and attacks them. But the battle was his last. He and all his host were destroyed, and their district from Arnon to Jabbok became at once the possession of the conqueror.

Josephus (Ant. iv. 5, § 2) has preserved some singular details of the battle, which have not survived in the text either of the Hebrew or LXX. He represents the Amorite army as containing every man in the nation fit to bear arms. He states that they were unable to fight when away from the shelter of their cities, and that being especially galled by the slings and arrows of the Hebrews, and at last suffering severely from thirst, they rushed to the stream and to the recesses of the ravine of the Arnon. Into these recesses they were pursued by their active enemy and slaughtered in vast numbers.

Whether we accept these details or not, it is plain, from the manner in which the name of Sihon fixed itself in the national mind, and the space which his image occupies in the official records, and in the later poetry of Israel, that he was a truly formidable chieftain.—*George Grove, in Smith's Dictionary of the Bible,* 1863.

Verse 11.—*Sihon,* although conqueror of Moab, and much more formidable than the Canaanites whom Israel had feared at Kadesh, fell easily because Israel fought in faith. There is no adversary that can really offer any effectual opposition to our onward march if assailed in the strength of Christ with a cheerful courage.

Og the king of Bashan was much more formidable even than *Sihon,* but he seems to have fallen yet more easily, judging from the brief notice of the conquest. Even so, when once we have overcome a difficulty or conquered an evil habit in the strength of faith, other conquests open out before us readily and naturally which we should not have dared to contemplate before. It is most true in religion that " nothing succeeds like success."—*R. Winterbotham, in "The Pulpit Commentary,"* 1881.

Verse 11.—*"Og king of Bashan."* The task was not an easy one, for Edrei— " the strong "—Og's capital, was in ordinary circumstances almost unassailable, since it was, strange to say, built in a hollow artificially scooped out of the top of a hill, which the deep gorge of the Hieromax isolates from the country round. Its streets may be still seen running in all directions beneath the present town of Adraha. But Kenath, in the district called Argob—" the stony "—was still stronger, for it was built in the crevices of a great island of lava which has split, in cooling, into innumerable fissures, through whose labyrinth no enemy could safely penetrate. In these were its streets and houses, some of which, of a later date, with stone doors, turning on hinges of stone, remain till this day. . . . . Nor were these the only fastnesses. No fewer than sixty cities " fenced with high walls, gates, and bars " (Deut. iii. 5), had to be taken ; but they all fell, sooner or later, before the vigorous assaults of the invaders, and, long afterwards, there might be seen, in the capital of their allies, the Ammonites, one of the trophies of the campaign— the gigantic iron bedstead of King Og, or as some think, the huge sarcophagus he had prepared for himself, as was the custom with Canaanite kings.—*Cunningham Geikie, in "Hours with the Bible,"* 1881.

Verse 12.—*"Their land for an heritage."* The land was given to them to be transmitted from father to son, by hereditary right and succession.—*Joseph Addison Alexander.*

Verse 13. — *"Thy name, O* LORD, *endureth for ever,"* etc. Immutability is a glory belonging to all the attributes of God. It is not a single perfection of the Divine nature, nor is it limited to particular objects thus and thus disposed. Mercy and justice have their distinct objects and distinct acts : mercy is conversant about a penitent, justice about an obstinate sinner. In our conceptions of the Divine perfections, his perfections are different. The wisdom of God is not his power, nor his power his holiness ; but immutability is the centre wherein they all unite. There is not one perfection which may not be said to be, and truly is, immutable ; none of them will appear so glorious about this beam, the sun of immutability, which renders them highly excellent, without the least shadow of imperfection. How cloudy would his blessedness be, if it were changeable ; how dim his wisdom, if it might be obscured ; how feeble his power, if it were capable of becoming sickly and languishing ; how would mercy lose much of its lustre, if it could change into wrath, and justice much of its dread, if it could be turned into mercy ; while the object of justice remains unfit for mercy, and one that hath need of mercy continues only fit for the Divine fury? But unchangeableness is the thread that runs through the whole web; it is the enamel of all the rest; none of them without it could look with a triumphant aspect.—*Stephen Charnock.*

Verse 13.—*"Thy name, O Lord, endureth for ever."* God is, and will be always the same to his church, a gracious, faithful, wonder-working God; and his church is, and will be the same to him, a thankful, praising people; and thus his name *endures for ever.—Matthew Henry.*

Verse 13.—*"Thy memorial, O Lord, throughout all generations;"* or, *the remembrance of them to generation and generation;* to every age. The love of Christ is remembered by his people in every age, as they enjoy the blessings of his grace in redemption, justification, pardon, etc. It cannot be forgotten as long as the gospel is preached, the ordinances of Baptism and the Lord's Supper administered, and the Lord has a people in the world; all which will be as long as the sun and moon endure, and there will therefore always be a memorial of him.—*John Gill.*

Verse 14.—*"For the Lord will judge his people,"* etc. Is it so, that all providence is for the good of the church? This is comfort in the low estate of the church at any time. God's eye is upon his people even whilst he seems to have forsaken them. If he seems to be departed, it is but in some other part of the earth, to show himself strong for them; wherever his eye is fixed in any part of the world, his church hath his heart, and his church's relief is his end. Though the church may sometimes lie among the pots in a dirty condition, yet there is a time of resurrection, when God will restore it to its true glory, and make it as white as a dove with its silver wings: Ps. lxviii. 13. The sun is not always obscured by a thick cloud, but it will be freed from the darkness of it. *"God will judge his people, and he will repent himself concerning his servants"* [the original is, *Comfort himself*]. It is a comfort to God to deliver his people, and he will do it when it shall be most comfortable to his glory and to their hearts.—*Stephen Charnock.*

Verse 14.—*"He will repent himself."* The original word *" repent himself"* here has a very extensive signification, which cannot be expressed by any one English rendering. It implies taking compassion upon them, with the intention of being comforted in their future, and of taking vengeance on their oppressors. Such are the several meanings in which the word is used. Language fails to express the mind of God toward his faithful people. How dear ought his counsels to be to us, and the consideration of all his ways! This reflection was continually urged upon the nation of Israel, so liable as they were to fall away to idolatory.—*W. Wilson.*

Verse 15.—*"The idols of the heathen."* The shrines on the hill-tops were very rude affairs, enclosures formed by rough stone walls, and containing ragamuffin gods—stocks of weather-beaten wood, blocks of battered stone, and lumps of rusty old iron. The carved wooden gods were so much the worse for the weather, that their features, if they ever had any, were altogether defaced. One, not made of a single piece, like the rest, but built together by joiner work, had fared worse than its more humble neighbours. His arms were gone, and his breast, heart, and stomach had all fallen out; strange to say, his head remained, and it was laughable to see such a hollow mockery stare at you with a solemn face. The stone images were sadly battered by tumbling about among the rubbish, and the cast-metal gods mostly had their heads broken off and set carefully on again, to stand there till the next storm would send them rolling. Thus God is not only robbed in the valley, but men climb up as near to heaven as they can, and insult him to his face. —*James Gilmour, in "Among the Mongols,"* 1883.

Verse 15.—*"The idols,"* etc. Herodotus telleth us that Amasis had a large laver of gold, wherein both he and his guests used to wash their feet. This vessel he brake and made a god of it, which the Egyptians devoutly worshipped. And the like idolomania is at this day found among Papists, what distinction soever they would fain make betwixt an *idol* and an *image*, which indeed (as they use them) are all one.—*John Trapp.*

Verse 15.—*"Silver and gold."* By singling out these metals, the most precious materials of which the idols were framed, and pouring contempt upon even these costly images, the Psalmist heightens the scorn which he implies for such as were of inferior price, and which had not the one element of costliness in their favour. And when we bear in mind the Apostles saying that covetousness is idolatry we shall be warned that we, too, may need this lesson against worshipping silver and gold, or the worldly wisdom and specious eloquence which may be compared to these metals.—*Neale and Littledale.*

Verse 15.—*"The work of men's hands."* Therefore they should rather, if it were possible, worship man, as their creator and lord, than be worshipped by him.—*Matthew Pool, 1624—1679.*

Verses 15, 16, 17.—The Rev. John Thomas, a missionary in India, was one day travelling alone through the country, when he saw a great number of people waiting near an idol temple. He went up to them, and as soon as the doors were opened, he walked into the temple. Seeing an idol raised above the people, he walked boldly up to it, held up his hand, and asked for silence. He then put his fingers on its eyes, and said, " It has eyes, but it cannot see ! It has ears, but it cannot hear ! It has a nose, but it cannot smell ! It has hands, but it cannot handle ! It has a mouth, but it cannot speak ! Neither is there any breath in it ! " Instead of doing injury to him for affronting their god and themselves, the natives were all surprised ; and an old Brahmin was so convinced of his folly by what Mr. Thomas said, that he also cried out, " It has feet, but cannot run away ! " The people raised a shout, and being ashamed of their stupidity, they left the temple, and went to their homes—*From "The New Cyclopædia of Illustrative Anecdote,"* 1875.

Verses 16, 17.—*"Mouths," " eyes," " ears."* So many members as the images have, serving to represent perfections ascribed to them, so many are the lies.—*David Dickson.*

Verses 16—17.—They can neither *speak* in answer to your prayers and enquiries, nor *see* what you do or what you want, nor *hear* your petitions, nor *smell* your incenses and sacrifices, nor use their *hands* either to take anything from you, or to give anything to you ; nor so much as *mutter,* nor give the least sign of apprehending your condition or concerns.—*Matthew Pool.*

Verses 16—17.—*"Mouths, but they speak not :" " ears, but they hear not."*

> A heated fancy or imagination
> May be mistaken for an inspiration.
> True ; but is this conclusion fair to make
> That inspiration must be all mistake ?
> A pebble-stone is not a diamond : true ;
> But must a diamond be a pebble too ?
> *To own a God who does not speak to men,*
> *Is first to own, and then disown again ;*
> *Of all idolatry the total sum*
> *Is having gods that are both deaf and dumb.*
>
> John Byrom, 1691—1763.

Verse 18.—*"Like them shall be those making them, every one who (is) trusting in them."* If the meaning had been simply, those who make them *are* like them, Hebrew usage would have required the verb to be suppressed. Its insertion, therefore, in the future form (ﬠﬢﬨ) requires it to be rendered strictly *shall be,* i.e., in fate as well as character. Idolaters shall perish with their perishable idols. See Isa. i. 31.—*Joseph Addison Alexander.*

Verse 18.—People never rise above the level of their gods, which are to them their better nature.—*Andrew Robert Faussett.*

Verse 18.—*"They that make them are like unto them."* Idolatry is a benumbing sin, which bereaveth the idolater of the right use of his senses.—*David Dickson.*

Verse 18.—*"They that make them,"* etc. Teacheth us, that the idol, the idol-maker, and all such also as serve idols, are not only beastly and blockish before men, but shall before God, in good time, come to shame and confusion.—*Thomas Wilcocks, 1549—1608.*

Verse 18.—*"Like unto them."* A singular phenomenon, known as the Spectre of the Brocken, is seen on a certain mountain in Germany. The traveller who at dawn stands on the topmost ridge beholds a colossal shadowy spectre. But in fact it is only his own shadow projected upon the morning mists by the rising sun ; and it imitates, of course, every movement of its creator. So heathen nations have mistaken their own image for Deity. Their gods display human frailties and passions and scanty virtues, projected and magnified upon the heavens, just as the small figures on the slide of a magic-lantern are projected, magnified, and illuminated upon a white sheet.—*From Elan Foster's New Cyclopædia of Illustrations, 1870.*

Verse 18.—*"Like unto them."* How many are like idol-images, when they have eyes, ears, and mouths as though they had none : that is, when they do not use them when and how they should !—*Christoph Starke.*

Verse 19.—*"Bless the LORD."* Blessing of God is to wish well to, and speak well of God, out of good-will to God himself, and a sense of his goodness to ourselves. God loves your good word, that is, to be spoken of well by you ; he rejoiceth in your well-wishes, and to hear from you expressions of rejoicings in his own independent blessedness. Though God hath an infinite ocean of all blessedness, to which we can add nothing, and he is therefore called by way of eminency, "The Blessed One" (Mark xiv. 61), a title solely proper and peculiar to him, yet he delights to hear the *amen* of the saints, his creatures, resounding thereto ; he delights to hear us utter our "so be it."—*Thomas Goodwin.*

Verse 19.—*"Bless the LORD."* And not an idol (Isa. lxvi. 3), as the Philistines, did their Dagon and as Papists still do their he-saints and she-saints.—*John Trapp.*

Verse 20.—*"Bless the LORD, O house of Levi."* In Ps. cxv. the exhortation given is to *trust* or *hope* in the Lord ; here, to *bless* him. The *Levites* are mentioned in addition to the house of Aaron, there being two orders of priesthood. Everything else in the two Psalms is the same, except that, in the last verse, the Psalmist here joins himself, along with the rest of the Lord's people, in blessing God.—*Franz Delitzsch.*

Verse 20.—*"Ye that fear the LORD, bless the LORD."* These are distinct from the Israelites, priests, and Levites, and design the proselytes among them of other nations that truly feared God, as Jarchi notes ; and all such persons, whoever and wherever they are, have reason to bless the Lord for the fear of him they have, which is not from nature but from grace ; and for the favours shown them, the blessings bestowed upon them, the good things laid up for them, and the guard that is about them, which the Scriptures abundantly declare, and experience confirms.—*John Gill.*

Verse 20.—*"Ye that fear the LORD, bless the LORD."* In Scripture it is quite common to find this *"fear"* put for holiness itself, or the sum of true religion. It is not, therefore, such a fear as seized the hearts of our first parents when, hearing the voice of the Lord God, they hid themselves amongst the trees of the garden ; nor such as suddenly quenched the noise of royal revelry in the night of Babylon's overthrow ; nor such as, on some day yet future, shall drive desparing sinners to the unavailing shelter of the mountains and rocks. It is not the fear of guilty distrust, or of hatred, or of bondage—that fear which hath torment, and which perfect love casteth out ; but a fear compatible with the highest privileges, attainments, and hopes of the Christian life. It is the fear of deep humility and reverence, and filial subjection, and adoring gratitude ; the fear which "blesseth the Lord," saying, *"His mercy endureth for ever."*—*John Lillie (1812—1867), in "Lectures on the Epistles of Peter."*

Verse 21.—The conclusion, verse 21, alludes to the conclusion of the preceding Psalm. There, the Lord blesses thee out of Zion ; here, let him be blessed out of Zion. The praise proceeds from the same place from which the blessing issues. For Zion is the place where the community dwells with God.—*E. W. Hengstenberg.*

Verse 21.—*"Praise ye the LORD."* When the song of praise is sung unto God, the work of his praise is not ended, but must be continued, renewed, and followed still : *"Praise ye the LORD."*—*David Dickson.*

Verse 21.—*"Bless," "Praise."* We are not only to bless God, but to praise him : "All thy works shall praise thee, O LORD ; and thy saints shall bless thee." Blessing relateth to his benefits, praise to his excellencies. We bless him for what he is to us, we praise him for what he is in himself. Now, whether we bless him, or praise him ; it is still to increase our love to him, and delight in him ; for God is not affected with the flattery of empty praises ; yet this is an especial duty, which is of use to you, as all other duties are. It doth you good to consider him as an infinite and eternal Being, and of glorious and incomprehensible majesty. It is pleasant and profitable to us.—*Thomas Manton.*

HINTS TO PREACHERS.

Verses 1—4.—I. The Employment. Praise three times commended, and in three respects. 1. With respect to God : not his works merely, but himself. 2. With respect to ourselves : it is pleasant and profitable. 3. With respect to others : it best recommends our religion to all who hear it. All others are religions of fear, ours of joy and praise. II. The Persons : servants in attendance at his house, who stand there by appointment, ready to hear, ready to obey. III. The Motives. 1. In general. It is due to God, because he is good ; and it is pleasant to us : verse 3. 2. In particular. Those who are specially privileged by God should specially praise him : verse 4. " This people have I formed for myself; they shall show forth my praise."—*G. R.*

Verse 1.—" *Praise ye the* LORD." I. The Lord ought to be praised. II. He ought to be praised *by you.* III. He ought to be praised *now :* let us remember his present favours. IV. He ought to be praised in everything for ever.

Verse 1.—"*Praise him, O ye servants of the* LORD." I. Praise him for the privilege of serving him. II. Praise him for the power to serve him. III. Praise him for the acceptance of your service. IV. Praise him as the chief part of your service. V. Praise him that others may be induced to engage in his service.—*W. H. J. P.*

Verse 2.—What is at this day " the house of the Lord " ? Who may be said to stand in it ? What special reasons have they for praise ?

Verse 2.—The nearer to God, the dearer to God ; and the better our place, the sweeter our praise.—*W. B. H.*

Verses 2—5.—" *Our* God," " *Our* Lord." Sweet subject. See our Exposition.

Verse 3.—Praise the Lord, I. For the excellence of his nature. II. For the revelation of his name. III. For the pleasantness of his worship.

Verse 4.—It is a song of praise, and therefore election is mentioned because it is a motive for song. I. *The Choice*—" The Lord hath chosen." Divine. Sovereign. Gracious. Immutable. II. *The Consecration*—" Chosen Jacob to himself." To know him. To preserve his truth. To maintain his worship. To manifest his grace. To keep alive the hope of the Coming One. III. *The Separation* —implied in the special choice. By being taken into covenant : Abraham and his seed. By receiving the covenant inheritance : Canaan. By redemption. By power and by blood out of Egypt. Wilderness separation. Settled establishment in their own land. IV. *The Elevation.* In name—from Jacob to Israel. In value—from worthless to precious. In purpose and use—crown jewels. In preser vation—kept as treasures. In delight—God rejoices in his people as his heritage.

Verse 5.—"*I know that the* LORD *is great.*" I. By observing nature and providence. II. By reading his word. III. By my own conversion, comfort, and regeneration. IV. By my after-experience. V. By my overpowering com- munion with him.

Verse 5.—Delicious dogmatism. "*I know,*" etc. I. What I know. 1. The Lord. 2. That he is great. 3. That he is above all. II. Why I know it. 1. Because he is " our Lord." 2. By his operations in nature, providence, and grace (vers. 6—13) III. My incorrigible obstinacy in this regard is proof against worshippers of all other gods : which gods are effeminate ; without sovereignty ; no god, or any god.—*W. B. H.*

Verse 6.—"*Whatsoever the* LORD *pleased, that did he.*" *God's good pleasure in the work of grace.* Seen, *not* in the death of the wicked, Ezek. xxxiii. 11 ; but in the election of his people, 1 Sam. xii. 22 ; in the infliction of suffering on the substitute, Isa. liii. 10 ; in the provision of all fulness for his people in Christ, Col. i. 19, in the arrangement of salvation by faith in Christ, John vi. 39 ; in instituting preaching as the means of salvation, 1 Cor. i. 21 ; in the adoption of believers as his children, Eph. i. 5 ; in their sanctification, 1 Thess. iv. 3 ; in their ultimate triumph and reign, Luke xii. 32.—*C. A. D.*

Verse 6 (*last words*).—The power of God in places of trouble, change, and danger —*seas ;* and in conditions of sin, weakness, despair, perplexity—in all *deep places.*

Verses 6—12.—The Resistless Pleasure of Jehovah. I. Behold it as here exemplified : 1. Ruling all nature. 2. Overturning a rebellious nation. 3. Making sport of kings and crowns. 4. Laying a fertile country at the feet of the chosen. II. Be wise in view thereof. 1. Submit to it : it sweeps the seas, and lays hands on earth and heaven. 2. Think not to hide from it : the " ends of the earth " and " all deep places " are open to it ; it is swifter than its own lightnings. 3. Be awed by its majesty : God's way is strewn with crowns and the bones of kings. 4. Seek its protection : its mightiest efforts are in defence of those it favours. 5. Let the Lord's people fear not with so great a God, and so exhaustless an armoury.— W. B. H.

Verse 13.—*"Thy name, O Lord, endureth for ever."* I. As *the embodiment of perfection :* God's attributes and glory. II. As *the object of veneration :* " Holy and reverend is his name." III. As *the cause of salvation :* " For my name's sake," etc. IV. As *the centre of attraction :* " In his name shall the Gentiles trust." " Our desire is to the remembrance of thy name." " Where two or three are gathered in my name," etc. V. As *a plea in supplication :* " For thy name's sake, pardon," etc. " Hitherto ye have asked nothing in my name." VI. As *a warrant for action :* " Whatsoever ye do, do all in the name," etc. VII. As *a refuge in tribulation :* " The name of the Lord is a strong tower : the righteous runneth into it, and is safe." " I have kept them in thy name." VIII. As *a mark of glorification :* " I will write upon him the name of my God." IX. As *a terror to transgressors :* " My name is dreadful among the heathen."—*W. J.*

Verse 14.—*"The Lord will judge his people."* Others would like to do it, but must not. The world has seven judgment-days in every week, but shall not be able to condemn the saints. He himself will judge. How will he judge them ? 1. Their persons, as to whether they are in or out of Christ. 2. Their principles, as to whether they are genuine or spurious. 3. Their prayers, as to whether they are availing or useless. 4. Their profession, as to whether it is true or false. 5. Their procedure, as to whether it is good or bad.—*W. J.*

Verse 14.—I. The position of believers—" his people," " his servants." II. The discipline of God's family. III. The tenderness of the Lord to them. IV. The safety of believers : they are still the Lord's.

Verse 15.—*"Silver and gold."* These are idols in our own land, among world-lings, and with some professors. Show the folly and wickedness of loving riches, and the evils which come of it.

Verses 16, 17.—The Portrait of many. I. *"Mouths, but they speak not."* No prayer, praise, confession. II. *"Eyes, but they see not."* Discern not, understand not, take no warning ; do not look to Christ. III. *"Ears, but they hear not.'* Attend no ministry, or are present but unaffected ; hear not God. IV. *"Neither is there any breath in their mouths."* No life, no tokens of life, no prayer and praise which are the breath of spiritual life.

Verse 18.—I. Men make idols like themselves. II. The idols make their makers like themselves. Describe both processes.

Verse 19.—*"House of Israel."* The Lord's great goodness to all his people, perceived and proclaimed, and the Lord praised for it.

Verse 19.—*"House of Aaron."* God's blessing on Aaron's house typical of his grace to those who are priests unto God.

Verses 19—21.—I. The Exhortation. 1. To bless the Lord. 2. To bless him in his own house. II. To whom it is addressed. 1. To the house of Israel, or the whole church. 2. To the house of Aaron, or ministers of the sanctuary. 3. To the house of Levi, or the attendants upon ministers, and assistants in the services. 4. To all who fear God, wherever they may be. Even they who fear God are invited to praise him, which is a sure sign that he delighteth in mercy.—*G. R.*

Verse 20.—The Levites, their history, duties, rewards, and obligations to bless God.

Verse 20 (second clause).—I. The fear of God includes all religion. II. The fear of the Lord suggests praise. III. The fear of the Lord renders praise acceptable.

Verse 21.—I. The double fact. 1. Blessing perpetually ascending from Zion to God. 2. God perpetually blessing his people by dwelling with them in Zion. II. The double reason for praise, which is found in the double fact, and concerns every member of the church.

PSALM CXXXVI.

We know not by whom this Psalm was written, but we do know that it was sung in Solomon's temple (2 Chron. vii. 3, 6), and by the armies of Jehoshaphat when they sang themselves into victory in the wilderness of Tekoa. From the striking form of it we should infer that it was a popular hymn among the Lord's ancient people. Most hymns with a solid, simple chorus become favourites with congregations, and this is sure to have been one of the best beloved. It contains nothing but praise. It is tuned to rapture, and can only be fully enjoyed by a devoutly grateful heart.

It commences with a three-fold praise to the Triune Lord (1—3), then it gives us six notes of praise to the Creator (4—9), six more upon deliverance from Egypt (10—15), and seven upon the journey through the wilderness and the entrance into Canaan. Then we have two happy verses of personal gratitude for present mercy (23 and 24), one (verse 25) to tell of the Lord's universal providence, and a closing verse to excite to never-ending praise.

EXPOSITION.

O GIVE thanks unto the LORD ; for *he is* good : for his mercy *endureth* for ever.

2 O give thanks unto the God of gods : for his mercy *endureth* for ever.

3 O give thanks to the Lord of lords : for his mercy *endureth* for ever.

1. *"O give thanks unto the LORD."* The exhortation is intensely earnest : the Psalmist pleads with the Lord's people with an " O," three times repeated. Thanks are the least that we can offer, and these we ought freely to give. The inspired writer calls us to praise Jehovah for all his goodness to us, and all the greatness of his power in blessing his chosen. We thank our parents, let us praise our heavenly Father ; we are grateful to our benefactors, let us give thanks unto the Giver of all good. *"For he is good."* Essentially he is goodness itself, practically all that he does is good, relatively he is good to his creatures. Let us thank him that we have seen, proved, and tasted that he is good. He is good beyond all others ; indeed, he alone is good in the highest sense ; he is the source of good, the good of all good, the sustainer of good, the perfecter of good, and the rewarder of good. For this he deserves the constant gratitude of his people. *"For his mercy endureth for ever."* We shall have this repeated in every verse of this song, but not once too often. It is the sweetest stanza that a man can sing. What joy that there is mercy, mercy with Jehovah, enduring mercy, mercy enduring for ever. We are ever needing it, trying it, praying for it, receiving it : therefore let us for ever sing of it.

" When all else is changing within and around,
In God and his mercy no change can be found."

2. *"O give thanks unto the God of gods,"* If there be powers in heaven or on earth worthy of the name of gods he is the God of them ; from him their dominion comes, their authority is derived from him, and their very existence is dependent upon his will. Moreover, for the moment assuming that the deities of the heathen were gods, yet none of them could be compared with our Elohim, who is infinitely beyond what they are fabled to be. Jehovah is our God, to be worshipped and adored, and he is worthy of our reverence to the highest degree. If the heathen cultivate the worship of their gods with zeal, how much more intently should we seek the glory of the God of gods—the only true and real God. Foolish persons have gathered from this verse that the Israelites believed in the existence of many gods, at the same time believing that their Jehovah was the chief among them ; but this is an absurd inference, since gods who have a God over them cannot possibly be gods themselves. The words are to be understood after the usual manner of human speech, in which things are often spoken of not as they really are, but as they profess to be. God as God is worthy of our warmest thanks, *"for his mercy endureth*

for ever." Imagine supreme Godhead without everlasting mercy ! It would then have been as fruitful a source of terror as it is now a fountain of thanksgiving. Let the Highest be praised in the highest style, for right well do his nature and his acts deserve the gratitude of all his creatures.

> Praise your God with right good will,
> For his love endureth still.

3. *"O give thanks to the Lord of lords."* There are lords many, but Jehovah is the Lord of them. All lordship is vested in the Eternal. He makes and administers law, he rules and governs mind and matter, he possesses in himself all sovereignty and power. All lords in the plural are summed up in this Lord in the singular : he is more lordly than all emperors and kings condensed into one. For this we may well be thankful, for we know the superior Sovereign will rectify the abuses of the underlings who now lord it over mankind. He will call these lords to his bar, and reckon with them for every oppression and injustice. He is as truly the Lord of lords as he is Lord over the meanest of the land, and he rules with a strict impartiality, for which every just man should give heartiest thanks. *"For his mercy endureth for ever."* Yes, he mingles mercy with his justice, and reigns for the benefit of his subjects. He pities the sorrowful, protects the helpless, provides for the needy, and pardons the guilty ; and this he does from generation to generation, never wearying of his grace, " because he delighteth in mercy." Let us arouse ourselves to laud our glorious Lord ! A third time let us thank him who is our Jehovah, our God, and our Lord ; and let this one reason suffice us for three thanksgivings, or for three thousand—

> For his mercy shall endure,
> Ever faithful, ever sure.

4 To him who alone doth great wonders : for his mercy *endureth* for ever.

5 To him that by wisdom made the heavens : for his mercy *endureth* for ever.

6 To him that stretched out the earth above the waters : for his mercy *endureth* for ever.

7 To him that made great lights : for his mercy *endureth* for ever :

8 The sun to rule by day : for his mercy *endureth* for ever :

9 The moon and stars to rule by night : for his mercy *endureth* for ever

4. " *To him who alone doeth great wonders."* Jehovah is the great Thaumaturge, the unrivalled Wonderworker. None can be likened unto him, he is alone in wonderland, the Creator and Worker of true marvels, compared with which all other remarkable things are as child's play. His works are all great in wonder even when they are not great in size ; in fact, in the minute objects of the microscope we behold as great wonders as even the telescope can reveal. All the works of his unrivalled skill are wrought by him alone and unaided, and to him, therefore, must be undivided honour. None of the gods or the lords helped Jehovah in creation, or in the redemption of his people : his own right hand and his holy arm wrought for him these great deeds. What have the gods of the heathen done ? If the question be settled by doings, Jehovah is indeed " alone." It is exceedingly wonderful that men should worship gods who can do nothing, and forget the Lord who alone doeth great wonders. Even when the Lord uses men as his instruments, yet the wonder of the work is his alone ; therefore let us not trust in men, or idolize them, or tremble before them. Praise is to be rendered to Jehovah, *"for his mercy endureth for ever."* The mercy of the wonder is the wonder of the mercy ; and the enduring nature of that mercy is the central wonder of that wonder. The Lord causes us often to sit down in amazement as we see what his mercy has wrought out and prepared for us : " wonders of grace to God belong," yea, great wonders and unsearchable. Oh the depth ! Glory be to his name world without end !

> Doing wondrous deeds alone,
> Mercy sits upon his throne.

5. *"To him that by wisdom made the heavens."* His goodness appears in creating the upper regions. He set his wisdom to the task of fashioning a firmament, or

an atmosphere suitable for a world upon which mortal men should dwell. What a mass of wisdom lies hidden in this one creating act ! The discoveries of our keenest observers have never searched out all the evidences of design which are crowded together in this work of God's hands. The lives of plants, animals, and men are dependent upon the fashioning of our heavens : had the skies been other than they are we had not been here to praise God. Divine foresight planned the air and the clouds, with a view to the human race. *"For his mercy endureth for ever."* The Psalmist's details of mercy begin in the loftiest regions, and gradually descend from the heavens to " our low estate " (verse 23) ; and this is an ascent, for mercy becomes greater as its objects become less worthy. Mercy is far-reaching, long-enduring, all-encompassing. Nothing is too high for its reach, as nothing is beneath its stoop.

> High as heaven his wisdom reigns,
> Mercy on the throne remains.

6. *"To him that stretched out the earth above the waters."* Lifting it up from the mingled mass, the dank morass, the bottomless bog, of mixed land and sea ; and so fitting it to be the abode of man. Who but the Lord could have wrought this marvel ? Few even think of the divine wisdom and power which performed all this of old ; yet, if a continent can be proved to have risen or fallen an inch within historic memory, the fact is recorded in the " transactions " of learned societies, and discussed at every gathering of philosophers. *"For his mercy endureth for ever,"* as is seen in the original upheaval and perpetual upstanding of the habitable land, so that no deluge drowns the race. By his strength he sets fast the mountains and consolidates the land upon which we sojourn.

> From the flood he lifts the land :
> Firm his mercies ever stand.

7. *"To him that made great lights."* This also is a creating miracle worthy of our loudest thanks. What could men have done without light ? Though they had the heavens above them, and dry land to move upon, yet what could they see, and where could they go without light ? Thanks be to the Lord, who has not consigned us to darkness. In great mercy he has not left us to an uncertain, indistinct light, floating about fitfully, and without order ; but he has concentrated light upon two grand luminaries, which, as far as we are concerned, are to us " great lights." The Psalmist is making a song for common people, not for your critical savans,—and so he sings of the sun and moon as they appear to us,—the greatest of lights. These the Lord created in the beginning ; and for the present age of man made or constituted them light-bearers for the world. *"For his mercy endureth for ever."* Mercy gleams in every ray of light, and it is most clearly seen in the arrangement by which it is distributed with order and regularity from the sun and moon.

> Lamps he lit in heaven's heights,
> For in mercy he delights.

8. *"The sun to rule by day."* We cannot be too specific in our praises ; after mentioning great lights, we may sing of each of them, and yet not outwear our theme. The influences of the sun are too many for us to enumerate them all, but untold benefits come to all orders of beings by its light, warmth, and other operations. Whenever we sit in the sunshine, our gratitude should be kindled. The sun is a great ruler, and his government is pure beneficence, because by God's mercy it is moderated to our feebleness ; let all who rule take lessons from the sun which rules to bless. By day we may well give thanks, for God gives cheer. The sun rules because God rules ; it is not the sun which we should worship, like the Parsees ; but the Creator of the sun, as he did who wrote this sacred song. *"For his mercy endureth for ever."* Day unto day uttereth speech concerning the mercy of the Lord ; every sunbeam is a mercy, for it falls on undeserving sinners who else would sit in doleful darkness, and find earth a hell. Milton puts it well :

> He, the golden tressèd sun
> Caused all day his course to run;
> For his mercy shall endure
> Ever faithful, ever sure.

9. *"The moon and stars to rule by night."* No hour is left without rule. Blessed be God, he leaves us never to the doom of anarchy. The rule is one of light and

benediction. The moon with her charming changes, and the stars in their fixed spheres gladden the night. When the season would be dark and dreary because of the absence of the sun, forth come the many minor comforters. The sun is enough alone ; but when he is gone a numerous band cannot suffice to give more than a humble imitation of his radiance. Jesus, the Sun of Righteousness, alone, can do more for us than all his servants put together. He makes our day. When he is hidden, it is night, and remains night, let our human comforters shine at their full. What mercy is seen in the lamps of heaven gladdening our landscape at night ! What equal mercy in all the influences of the moon upon the tides, those life-floods of the earth ! The Lord is the Maker of every star, be the stars what they may ; he calleth them all by their names, and at his bidding each messenger with his torch enlightens our darkness. *"For his mercy endureth for ever."* Let our thanks be as many as the stars, and let our lives reflect the goodness of the Lord, even as the moon reflects the light of the sun. The nightly guides and illuminators of men on land and sea are not for now and then, but for all time. They shone on Adam, and they shine on us. Thus they are tokens and pledges of undying grace to men ; and we may sing with our Scotch friends—

> For certainly
> His mercies dure
> Most firm and sure
> Eternally.

10 To him that smote Egypt in their firstborn : for his mercy *endureth* for ever :

11 And brought out Israel from among them : for his mercy *endureth* for ever :

12 With a strong hand, and with a stretched out arm : for his mercy *endureth* for ever.

13 To him which divided the Red sea into parts : for his mercy *endureth* for ever :

14 And made Israel to pass through the midst of it : for his mercy *endureth* for ever :

15 But overthrew Pharaoh and his host in the Red sea : for his mercy *endureth* for ever.

10. We have heard of the glory of the world's creation, we are now to praise the Lord for the creation of his favoured nation by their Exodus from Egypt. Because the monarch of Egypt stood in the way of the Lord's gracious purposes it became needful for the Lord to deal with him in justice ; but the great design was mercy to Israel, and through Israel mercy to succeeding ages, to all the world. *"To him that smote Egypt in their firstborn."* The last and greatest of the plagues struck all Egypt to the heart. The sorrow and the terror which it caused throughout the nation it is hardly possible to exaggerate. From king to slave each one was wounded in the tenderest point. The joy and hope of every household was struck down in one moment, and each family had its own wailing. The former blows had missed their aim compared with the last ; but that " smote Egypt." The Lord's firstborn had been oppressed by Egypt, and at last the Lord fulfilled his threatening, " I will slay thy son, even thy firstborn." Justice lingered but it struck home at last. *"For his mercy endureth for ever."* Yes, even to the extremity of vengeance upon a whole nation the Lord's mercy to his people endured. He is slow to anger, and judgment is his strange work ; but when mercy to men demands severe punishments he will not hold back his hand from the needful surgery. What were all the firstborn of Egypt compared with those divine purposes of mercy to all generations of men which were wrapt up in the deliverance of the elect people ? Let us even when the Lord's judgments are abroad in the earth continue to sing of his unfailing grace.

> For evermore his love shall last
> For ever sure, for ever fast.

11. *"And brought out Israel from among them."* Scattered as the tribes were up and down the country, and apparently held in a grasp which would never be

relaxed, the Lord wrought their deliverance, and severed them from their idolatrous task-masters. None of them remained in bondage. The Lord brought them out; brought them out at the very hour when his promise was due; brought them out brought them all out; despite their being mingled among the Egyptians; brought them out never to return. Unto his name let us give thanks for this further proof of his favour to the chosen ones, *"For his mercy endureth for ever."* Once the Israelites did not care to go out, but preferred to bear the ills they had rather than risk they knew not what; but the Lord's mercy endured that test also, and ceased not to stir up the nest till the birds were glad to take to their wings. He turned the land of plenty into a house of bondage, and the persecuted nation was glad to escape from slavery. The unfailing mercy of the Lord is gloriously seen in his separating his elect from the world. He brings out his redeemed, and they are henceforth a people who show forth his praise.

> For God doth prove
> Our constant friend;
> His boundless love
> Shall never end.

12. *"With a strong hand, and with a stretched out arm."* Not only the matter but the manner of the Lord's mighty acts should be the cause of our praise. We ought to bless the Lord for adverbs as well as adjectives. In the Exodus the great power and glory of Jehovah were seen. He dashed in pieces the enemy with his right hand. He led forth his people in no mean or clandestine manner. " He brought them forth also with silver and gold, and there was not one feeble person in all their tribes." Egypt was glad when they departed. God worked with great display of force, and with exceeding majesty; he stretched out his arm like a workman intent on his labour, he lifted up his hand as one who is not ashamed to be seen. Even thus was it in the deliverance of each one of us from the thraldom of sin: " according to the working of his mighty power which he wrought in Christ when he raised him from the dead and set him at his own right hand in the heavenly places." *"For his mercy endureth for ever "*—therefore his power is put forth for the rescue of his own. If one plague will not set them free there shall be ten; but free they shall all be at the appointed hour; not one Israelite shall remain under Pharaoh's power. God will not only use his hand but his arm—his extraordinary power shall be put to the work sooner than his purpose of mercy shall fail.

> See he lifts his strong right hand,
> For his mercies steadfast stand.

13. *"To him which divided the Red sea into parts."* He made a road across the sea-bottom, causing the divided waters to stand like walls on either side. Men deny miracles; but, granted that there is a God, they become easy of belief. Since it requires me to be an atheist that I may logically reject miracles, I prefer the far smaller difficulty of believing in the infinite power of God. He who causes the waters of the sea ordinarily to remain as one mass can with equal readiness divide them. He who can throw a stone in one direction can with the same force throw it another way: the Lord can do precisely what he wills, and he wills to do anything which is for the deliverance of his people. *"For his mercy endureth for ever,"* and therefore it endures through the sea as well as over the dry land. He will do a new thing to keep his old promise. His way is in the sea, and he will make a way for his people in the same pathless region.

> Lo, the Red Sea he divides
> For his mercy sure abides.

14. *"And made Israel to pass through the midst of it."* He gave the people courage to follow the predestined track through the yawning abyss, which might well have terrified a veteran host. It needed no little generalship to conduct so vast and motley a company along a way so novel and apparently so dangerous. He made them to pass, by the untrodden road; he led them down into the deep and up again on the further shore in perfect order, keeping their enemies back by the thick darkness of the cloudy pillar. Herein is the glory of God set forth, as all his people see it in their own deliverance from sin. By faith we also give up all reliance upon works and trust ourselves to pass by a way which we have not known, even by the way of reliance upon the atoning blood: thus are we effectually sundered from

the Egypt of our former estate, and our sins themselves are drowned. The people marched dry shod through the heart of the sea. Hallelujah ! *"For his mercy endureth for ever."* Mercy cleared the road, mercy cheered the host, mercy led them down, and mercy brought them up again. Even to the depth of the sea mercy reaches,— there is no end to it, no obstacle in the way of it, no danger to believers in it, while Jehovah is all around. " Forward ! " be *our* watchword as it was that of Israel of old, for mercy doth compass us about.

> Through the fire or through the sea
> Still his mercy guardeth thee.

15. *"But overthrew Pharaoh and his host in the Red sea."* Here comes the thunder-clap. Though we hear them sounding peal upon peal, yet the judgments of the Lord were only loud-mouthed mercies speaking confusion to the foe, that the chosen might tremble before him no longer. The chariots were thrown over, the horses were overthrown. The King and his warriors were alike overwhelmed ; they were hurled from their chariots as locusts are tossed to and fro in the wind. Broken was the power and conquered was the pride of Egypt. Jehovah had vanquished the enemy. " Art thou not it which cut Rahab and wounded the crocodile ? " None are too great for the Lord to subdue, none too high for the Lord to abase. The enemy in his fury drove after Israel into the sea, but there his wrath found a terrible recompense beneath the waves. *"For his mercy endureth for ever."* Yes, mercy continued to protect its children, and therefore called in the aid of justice to fulfil the capital sentence on their foes. Taken red-handed, in the very act of rebellion against their sovereign Lord, the audacious adversaries met the fate which they had themselves invited. He that goes down into the midst of the sea asks to be drowned. Sin is self-damnation. The sinner goes downward of his own choice, and if he finds out too late that he cannot return, is not his blood upon his own head ? The finally impenitent, however terrible their doom, will not be witnesses against mercy ; but rather this shall aggravate their misery, that they went on in defiance of mercy, and would not yield themselves to him whose mercy endureth for ever. To the Israelites as they sung this song their one thought would be of the rescue of their fathers from the fierce oppressor. Taken like a lamb from between the teeth of the lion, Israel justly praises her Deliverer and chants aloud :

> Evermore his love shall reign ;
> Pharaoh and his host are slain.

16 To him which led his people through the wilderness : for his mercy *endureth* for ever.

17 To him which smote great kings : for his mercy *endureth* for ever :

18 And slew famous kings : for his mercy *endureth* for ever :

19 Sihon king of the Amorites : for his mercy *endureth* for ever :

20 And Og the king of Bashan : for his mercy *endureth* for ever :

21 And gave their land for an heritage : for his mercy *endureth* for ever :

22 *Even* an heritage unto Israel his servant : for his mercy *endureth* for ever.

16. *"To him which led his people through the wilderness."* He led them into it, and therefore he was pledged to lead them through it. They were " his people," and yet they must go into the wilderness, and the wilderness must remain as barren as ever it was ; but in the end they must come out of it into the promised land. God's dealings are mysterious, but they must be right, simply because they are his. The people knew nothing of the way, but they were led ; they were a vast host, yet they were all led ; there were neither roads nor tracks, but being led by unerring wisdom they never lost their way. He who brought them out of Egypt, also led them through the wilderness. By Moses, and Aaron, and Jethro, and the pillar of cloud he led them. What a multitude of mercies are comprehended in the conduct of such an enormous host through a region wherein there was no provision even for single travellers ; yet the Lord by his infinite power and wisdom conducted a whole nation for forty years through a desert land, and their feet did not swell, neither did their garments wax old in all the journey. *"For his mercy endureth for ever."* Their conduct in the wilderness tested his mercy most severely, but it bore the

strain ; many a time he forgave them ; and though he smote them for their transgressions, yet he waited to be gracious and speedily turned to them in compassion.
Their faithfulness soon failed, but *his* did not : the fiery, cloudy pillar which never
ceased to lead the van was the visible proof of his immutable love—

> For his mercy, changing never,
> Still endureth, sure for ever.

17. *"To him which smote great kings."* Within sight of their inheritance Israel
had to face powerful enemies. Kings judged to be great because of the armies at
their back blocked up their road. This difficulty soon disappeared, for the Lord
smote their adversaries, and a single stroke sufficed for their destruction. He who
had subdued the really mighty ruler of Egypt made short work of these petty
sovereigns, great though they were in the esteem of neighbouring princes. *"For
his mercy endureth for ever."* Mercy, which had brought the chosen tribes so far,
would not be baulked by the opposition of boastful foes. The Lord who smote
Pharaoh at the beginning of the wilderness march, smote Sihon and Og at the close
of it. How could these kings hope to succeed when even mercy itself was in arms
against them.

> Evermore his mercy stands
> Saving from the foeman's hands.

18. *"And slew famous kings."* What good was their fame to them ? As they
opposed God they became infamous rather than famous. Their deaths made the
Lord's fame to increase among the nations while their fame ended in disgraceful
defeat. *"For his mercy endureth for ever."* Israelitish patriots felt that they could
never have too much of this music ; God had protected their nation, and they
chanted his praises with unwearied iteration.

> Kings he smote despite their fame,
> For his mercy's still the same.

19. *"Sihon king of the Amorites."* Let the name be mentioned that the mercy
may be the better remembered. Sihon smote Moab, but he could not smite Israel,
for the Lord smote *him*. He was valiant and powerful, so as to be both great and
famous ; but as he wilfully refused to give a peaceful passage to the Israelites, and
fought against them in malice, there was no choice for it but to let him run into
that destruction which he courted. His fall was speedy and final, and the chosen
people were so struck with it that they sung of his overthrow in their national songs.
"For his mercy endureth for ever." His mercy is no respecter of persons, and neither
the greatness nor the fame of Sihon could protect him after he had dared to attack
Israel. The Lord will not forsake his people because Sihon blusters.

> Come what may
> By night or day,
> Still most sure,
> His love shall dure.

20. *"And Og the king of Bashan."* He was of the race of the giants, but he was
routed like a pigmy when he entered the lists with Israel's God. The Lord's people
were called upon to fight against him, but it was God who won the victory. The
fastnesses of Bashan were no defence against Jehovah. Og was soon ousted from
his stronghold when the captain of the Lord's host led the war against him. He
had to exchange his bedstead of iron for a bed in the dust, for he fell on the battlefield. Glory be to the divine conqueror, *"for his mercy endureth for ever."*

> Giant kings before him yield,
> Mercy ever holds the field.

If Sihon could not turn the Lord from his purpose we may be sure that Og could
not. He who delivers us out of one trouble will rescue us out of another, and fulfil
all the good pleasure of his grace in us.

21. *"And gave their land for an heritage."* As Lord of the whole earth he transferred his estate from one tenant to another. The land did not become the property
of the Israelites by their own sword and bow, but by a grant from the throne. This
was the great end which all along had been aimed at from Egypt to Jordan. He
who brought his people out also brought them in. He who had promised the and

to the seed of Abraham also saw to it that the deed of gift did not remain a dead letter. Both our temporal and our spiritual estates come to us by royal charter. What God gives us is ours by the best of titles. Inheritance by God's gift is a tenure which even Satan cannot dispute. *"For his mercy endureth for ever."* Faithful love endures without end, and secures its own end. " Thou wilt surely bring them in," said the prophet poet ; and here we see the deed complete.

> Till they reach the promised land
> Mercy still the same must stand.

22. *"Even an heritage unto Israel his servant."* Repetitions are effective in poetry, and the more so if there be some little variation in them, bringing out into fuller light some point which else had not been noticed. The lands of the heathen kings were given to " Israel," the name by which the chosen seed is here mentioned for the third time in the Psalm, with the addition of the words, " his servant." The leasehold of Canaan to Israel after the flesh was made dependent upon suit and service rendered to the Lord-of-the-manor by whom the lease was granted. It was a country worth singing about, richly justifying the two stanzas devoted to it. The division of the country by lot, and the laws by which the portions of ground were reserved to the owners and their descendants for a perpetual inheritance were fit subjects for song. Had other nations enjoyed land-laws which ensured to every family a plot of ground for cultivation, much of the present discontent would never have arisen, beggary would soon have become uncommon, and poverty itself would have been rare. *"For his mercy endureth for ever."* Yes, mercy fights for the land, mercy divides the spoil among its favoured ones, and mercy secures each man in his inheritance. Glory be to God the faithful One.

> For his mercy full and free,
> Wins us full felicity.

23 Who remembered us in our low estate : for his mercy *endureth* for ever :

24 And hath redeemed us from our enemies : for his mercy *endureth* for ever.

23. *"Who remembered us in our low estate."* Personal mercies awake the sweetest song—" he remembered *us."* Our prayer is, " Lord remember me," and this is our encouragement—he has remembered us. For the Lord even to think of us is a wealth of mercy. Ours was a sorry estate,—an estate of bankruptcy and mendicancy. Israel rested in its heritage, but we were still in bondage, groaning in captivity : the Lord seemed to have forgotten us, and left us in our sorrow ; but it was not so for long : he turned again in his compassion, bethinking himself of his afflicted children. Our state was once so low as to be at hell's mouth ; since then it has been low in poverty, bereavement, despondency, sickness, and heart-sorrow, and we fear, also, sinfully low in faith, and love, and every other grace ; and yet the Lord has not forgotten us as a dead thing out of mind ; but he has tenderly remembered us still. We thought ourselves too small and too worthless for his memory to burden itself about us, yet he remembered us. *"For his mercy endureth for ever."* Yes, this is one of the best proofs of the immutability of his mercy, for if he could have changed towards any, it would certainly have been towards us who have brought ourselves low, kept ourselves low, and prepared ourselves to sink yet lower. It is memorable mercy to remember us in our low estate : in our highest joys we will exalt Jehovah's name, since of this we are sure,—he will not now desert us—

> For his mercy full and free
> Lasteth to eternity.

24. *"And hath redeemed us from our enemies."* Israel's enemies brought the people low ; but the Lord intervened, and turned the tables by a great redemption. The expression implies that they had become like slaves, and were not set free without price and power ; for they needed to be " *redeemed.*" In our case the redemption which is in Christ Jesus is an eminent reason for giving thanks unto the Lord. Sin is our enemy, and we are redeemed from it by the atoning blood ; Satan is our enemy, and we are redeemed from him by the Redeemer's power ; the world is our

enemy, and we are redeemed from it by the Holy Spirit. We are ransomed, let us enjoy our liberty ; Christ has wrought our redemption, let us praise his name.

"*For his mercy endureth for ever.*" Even to redemption by the death of his Son did divine mercy stretch itself. What more can be desired ? What more can be imagined ? Many waters could not quench love, neither could the floods drown it.

> E'en to death upon the tree
> Mercy dureth faithfully.

25 Who giveth food to all flesh : for his mercy *endureth* for ever.

25. "*Who giveth food to all flesh.*" Common providence, which cares for all living things, deserves our devoutest thanks. If we think of heavenly food, by which all saints are supplied, our praises rise to a still greater height ; but meanwhile the universal goodness of God in feeding all his creatures is as worthy of praise as his special favours to the elect nation. Because the Lord feeds all life therefore we expect him to take special care of his own family. "*For his mercy endureth for ever.*" Reaching downward even to beasts and reptiles, it is, indeed, a boundless mercy, which knows no limit because of the meanness of its object.

> All things living he doth feed,
> His full hand supplies their need ;
> For his mercy shall endure,
> Ever faithful, ever sure.

26 O give thanks unto the God of heaven : for his mercy *endureth for* ever.

26. "*O give thanks unto the God of heaven.*" The title is full of honour. The Lord is God in the highest realms, and among celestial beings. His throne is set in glory, above all, out of reach of foes, in the place of universal oversight. He who feeds ravens and sparrows is yet the glorious God of the highest realms. Angels count it their glory to proclaim his glory in every heavenly street. See herein the greatness of his nature, the depth of his condescension, and the range of his love. Mark the one sole cause of his bounty—"*For his mercy endureth for ever.*" He hath done all things from this motive ; and because his mercy never ceases, he will continue to multiply deeds of love world without end. Let us with all our powers of heart and tongue give thanks unto the holy name of Jehovah for ever and ever.

> Change and decay in all around I see,
> O thou who changest not, abide with me.

EXPLANATORY NOTES AND QUAINT SAYINGS.

Whole Psalm.—This Psalm was very probably composed by David, and given to the Levites to sing every day : 1 Chron. xvi. 41. Solomon his son followed his example, and made use of it in singing at the dedication of the Temple (2 Chron. vii. 3—6) ; as Jehoshaphat seems to have done when he went out to war against his enemies (2 Chron. xx. 21).—*John Gill.*

Whole Psalm.—The grand peculiarity of form in this Psalm . . . . is the regular recurrence, at the close of every verse, of a burden or *refrain*. . . . It has been a favourite idea with interpreters that such repetitions necessarily imply alternate or responsive choirs. But the other indications of this usage in the Psalter are extremely doubtful, and every exegetical condition may be satisfied by simply supposing that the singers, in some cases, answered their own questions, and that in others, as in that before us, the people united in the burden or chorus, as they were wont to do in the Amen.—*Joseph Addison Alexander.*

Whole Psalm.—The Psalm is called by the Greek church *Polyeleos*, from its continual mention of the mercy of God.—*Neale and Littledale.*

Whole Psalm.—In the liturgical language this Psalm is called *par excellence* the great Hallel, for according to its broadest compass the great Hallel comprehends Ps. cxx. to cxxxvi., whilst the Hallel which is absolutely so called extends from Ps. cxiii. to cxviii.—*Franz Delitzsch.*

Whole Psalm.—"*Praise ye* (הוֹדוּ) *Jehovah* "; not as in Ps. cxxxv. 1, " Hallelujah," but varying the words,—" Be ye *Judahs* to the Lord ! "
Praise him for what he is (ver. 1—3).
Praise him for what he is able to do (ver. 4).
Praise him for what he has done in creation (ver. 5—9).
Praise him for what he did in redeeming Israel from bondage (ver. 10—15).
Praise him for what he did in his providence toward them (ver. 16—22).
Praise him for his grace in times of calamity (ver. 23, 24).
Praise him for his grace to the world at large (ver. 25).
Praise him at the remembrance that this God is the God of heaven (ver. 26).—*Andrew A. Bonar.*

Whole Psalm.—When, in the time of the Emperor Constantius, S. Athanasius was assaulted by night in his church at Alexandria by Syrianus and his troops, and many were wounded and murdered, the Bishop of Alexandria sat still in his chair, and ordered the deacon to begin this Psalm, and the people answered in prompt alternation, "*For his mercy endureth for ever.*"—*Christopher Wordsworth.*

Verse 1.—"*O give thanks unto the* LORD." When we have praised God for reasons offered unto us in one Psalm, we must begin again, and praise him for other reasons ; and even when we have done this, we have not overtaken our task, the duty lieth still at our door, to be discharged afresh, as this Psalm doth show.—*David Dickson.*
Verse 1.—"*For he is good.*" Observe what we must give thanks for : not as the Pharisee that made all his thanksgivings terminate in his own goodness—" God, I thank thee " that I am so and so—but directing them all to God's glory : "*for he is good.*"—*Matthew Henry.*
Verse 1.—"*His mercy endureth for ever.*" This appears four times in Ps. cxviii. 1—4. This sentence is the wonder of Moses, the sum of revelation, and the hope of man.—*James G. Murphy.*
Verse 1.—"*His mercy.*" Many sweet things are in the word of God, but the name of mercy is the sweetest word in all the Scriptures, which made David harp upon it twenty-six times in this Psalm : "*For his mercy endureth for ever.*" It was such a cheerful note in his ears when he struck upon mercy, that, like a bird that is taught to pipe, when he had sung it, he sang it again, and when he had sung it again, he recorded it again, and made it the burden of his song : "*For his mercy endureth for ever.*" Like a nightingale which, when she is in a pleasant vein, quavers and capers, and trebles upon it, so did David upon his mercy : "*For his mercy endureth for ever.*"—*Henry Smith.*
Verse 1.—"*Mercy.*" By "*mercy* " we understand the Lord's disposition to compassionate and relieve those whom sin has rendered miserable and base ; his readiness to forgive and to be reconciled to the most provoking of transgressors, and to bestow all blessings upon them ; together with all the provision which he has made for the honour of his name, in the redemption of sinners by Jesus Christ.—*Thomas Scott.*
Verse 1.—"*His mercy endureth for ever.*" It is everlasting. Everlastingness, or eternity, is a perfect possession, all at once, of an endless life (saith Boëthius). Everlasting mercy, then, is perfect mercy, which shuts out all the imperfections of time, beginning, end, succession, and such is God's mercy. First, his *essential mercy* is everlastingness itself ; for it is himself, and God hath not, but *is*, things. He is beginning, end, being ; and that which is of himself and even himself is eternity itself. Secondly, his *relative mercy* (which respects us, and makes impression on us), is everlasting, too, in a sense ; for the creatures, ever since they had being in him, or existence in their natural causes, ever did and ever will need mercy, either preserving or conserving. Preventing or continuing mercy in the first sense is *negatively endless*, that is, incapable of end, because unboundable for being : in the second sense, it is *privatively endless*, it shall never actually take end, though in itself it may be, and in some ways is, bounded ; the first is included in the latter, but the latter is chiefly here intended ; and therefore the point arises to be this,—*God's mercy* (*chiefly to his church*) *is an endless mercy ;* it knows no end, receives no interruption. Reasons hereof from the word are these (for as touching testimony this Psalm shall be our security), first, from *God's nature,* "*he is good.*" Mercy pleaseth him. It is

no trouble for him to exercise mercy. It is his delight: we are never weary of receiving, therefore he cannot be of giving; for it is a more blessed thing to give than to receive; so God takes more content in the one than we in the other.— *Robert Harris*, 1578—1658.

Verse 1.—*"His mercy endureth for ever."* God's goodness is a fountain; it is never dry. As grace is from the world's beginning (Ps. xxv. 6), so it is to the world's end, *à seculo in seculum*, from one generation to another. Salvation is no termer; grace ties not itself to times. Noah as well as Abel, Moses as well as Jacob, Jeremy as well as David, Paul as well as Simeon hath part in this salvation. God's gracious purpose the Flood drowned not, the smoke of Sinai smothered not, the Captivity ended not, the ends of the world (Saint Paul calls them so) determined not. For Christ, by whom it is, was slain from the beginning,—Saint John saith so. He was before Abraham, he himself saith so. And *Clemens Alexandrinus* [tom. v. page 233] doth Marcion wrong, though otherwise an heretic, in blaming him for holding that Christ saved those also that believed in him before his incarnation. The blood of the beasts under the law was a type of his. And the scars of his wounds appear yet still, and will for ever, till he cometh to judgment. The Apostle shall end this: he is *heri*, and *hodi*, and *semper idem*: Christ is the same yesterday and to-day and for ever.—*Richard Clerke*,—1634.

Verses 1—3.—The three first verses of this Psalm contain the three several names of the Deity, which are commonly rendered *Jehovah*, *God*, and *Lord*, respectively; the first having reference to his essence as *self-existent*, and being his proper name; the second designating him under the character of *a judge* or of an all-powerful being, if Aleim be derived from *Al*; and the third, *Adondi*, representing him as *exercising rule.*—*Daniel Cresswell.*

Verses 1—3.—*"O give thanks."*

What! give God thanks for everything,
　Whatever may befall—
Whatever the dark clouds may bring?
　Yes, give God thanks for all;
For safe he leads thee, hand in hand,
To thy blessèd Fatherland.

What! thank him for the lonely way
　He to me hath given—
For the path which, day by day
　Seems farther off from heaven?
Yes, thank him, for he holds thy hand
And leads thee to thy Fatherland.

Close, close he shields thee from all harm;
　And if the road be steep,
Thou know'st his everlasting arm
　In safety doth thee keep,
Although thou canst not understand
The windings to thy Fatherland.

What blessing, thinkest thou, will he,
　Who knows the good and ill,
Keep back, if it is good for thee,
　While climbing up the hill?
Then trust him, and keep fast his hand,
He leads thee to thy Fatherland.
　　　　　B. S., in "The Christian Treasury," 1865.

Verses 1—9.—Like the preceding Psalm, this Psalm allies itself to the Book of Deuteronomy. The first clauses of verses 2 and 3 (*"God of gods"* and *"Lord of lords"*) are taken from Deut. x. 17; verse 12, first clause (*"with a strong hand and stretched out arm"*) from Deut. iv. 34, and v. 15. Verse 16, first clause, is like Deut. viii. 15 (cf. Jer. ii. 6).—*Franz Delitzsch.*

Verses 1—26.—All repetitions are not vain, nor is all length in prayer to be accounted babbling. For repetitions may be used, 1. When they express *fervency* and *zeal*: and so we read, Christ prayed over the same prayer thrice (Matt. xxvi. 44); " O my Father, if it be possible, let this cup pass from me." And another evangelist showeth that he did this out of special fervency of spirit (Luke xxii. 44); " Being in an agony, he prayed more earnestly." 2. This repetition is not to be disapproved when there is *a special emphasis*, and spiritual elegancy in it, as in Psalm cxxxvi. you have it twenty-six times repeated, *"For his mercy endureth for ever,"* because there was a special reason in it, the Psalmist's purpose there being to show the unweariedness, and the unexhausted riches of God's free grace ; that notwithstanding all the former experiences they had had, God is where he was at first.   We waste by giving, our drop is soon spent ; but God is not wasted by bestowing, but hath the same mercy to do good to his creatures, as before.   Though he had done all those wonders for them, yet his mercy was as ready to do good to them still.   All along God saved and blessed his people, *"For his mercy endureth for ever."—Thomas Manton.*

Verse 2.—*"The God of gods."*   *"God of gods "* is an Hebrew superlative, because he is far above all gods, whether they be so reputed or deputed.—*Robert Harris.*

Verse 2.—*"The God of gods."*   One, as being Creator, infinitely higher than all others, his creatures, who have at any time been regarded as gods.—*French and Skinner,* 1842.

Verses 2, 3.—Before proceeding to recite God's works, the Psalmist declares his supreme Deity, and dominion : not that such comparative language implies that there is anything approaching Deity besides him, but there is a disposition in men, whenever they see any part of his glory displayed, to conceive of a God separate from him, thus impiously dividing the Godhead into parts, and even proceeding so far as to frame gods of wood and stone.   There is a depraved tendency in all to take delight in a multiplicity of gods.   For this reason, apparently, the Psalmist uses the plural number not only in the word *Elohim* but in the word *Adonim,* so that it reads literally, *Praise ye the Lords of lords :* he would intimate, that the fullest perfection of all dominion is to be found in the one God.—*John Calvin.*

Verse 3.—*"The Lord of lords."*   The meaning of the title *"Lord,"* as distinct from " Jehovah " and " God," is " Governor."   And in this view also he is eminently entitled to praise and thanksgiving, in that his rule and government of the world are also eminently marked by *"mercy "* and *"goodness : "* not the display of power only, but of power declared chiefly in showing mercy and pity : as again all subject to that rule are witnesses.   Such is God *in himself.*   Nor is it without intention that the doxology is threefold, indicating, doubtless, like the threefold invocation of the Name of the Lord in the blessing of the people (Num. vi. 24—26)—God in Trinity, " Father, Son, and Holy Ghost," as now fully revealed.—*William De Burgh.*

Verse 4.—*"To him who alone doeth great wonders."*   God hath preserved to himself the power of miracles, as his prerogative : for the devil does no miracles ; the devil and his instruments do but hasten nature or hinder nature, antedate nature or postdate nature, bring things sooner to pass or retard them ; and however they pretend to oppose nature, yet still it is but upon nature and by natural means that they work.   Only God shakes the whole frame of nature in pieces, and in a miracle proceeds so, as if there were no creation yet accomplished, no course of nature yet established.   *Facit mirabilia magna solus,* says David here.   There are *mirabilia parva,* some lesser wonders, that the devil and his instruments, Pharaoh's sorcerers, can do ; but when it comes to *mirabilia magna,* great wonders, so great that they amount to the nature of a miracle, *facit solus,* God and God only does them.—*Abraham Wright.*

Verse 4.—*"To him who alone doeth great wonders."*   Does he *"alone "* do great wonders ? that means, he does so by himself, unaided, needing nothing from others, asking no help from his creatures.   As the Nile from Nubia to the Mediterranean rolls on 1,300 miles in solitary grandeur, receiving not one tributary, but itself alone dispensing fertility and fatness wherever it comes ; so our God " alone " does wonders. (See Deut. xxxii. 12 ; Ps. lxxii. 18, etc.)   No prompter, no helper ; spontaneously he goes forth to work, and all he works is worthy of God.   Then we have no need of any other ; we are independent of all others ; all our springs are in him.—*Andrew A. Bonar.*

Verse 4.—*"Who alone doeth great wonders."*   There are three things here declared of God ; that he doeth *wonders,* that the wonders he doeth are *great ;* that he *only* doeth them.—*Augustine, in Neale and Littledale.*

Verse 4.—*"Who alone doeth great wonders."*   Whatsoever instruments the Lord is pleased to use in any of his wonderful works, he alone is the worker, and will not share the glory of the work with any creature.—*David Dickson.*

Verse 4.—It becomes the great God to grant great things. *"To him who alone doeth great wonders."* When you ask great things, you ask such as it becomes God to give, *"* whose mercy is great above the heavens ! *"* Nothing under heaven can be too great for him to give. The greater things he bestows, the greater glory redounds to his Name.—*David Clarkson,* 1622—1686.

Verse 4.—Christians should not be ashamed of the mysteries and *miracles* of their religion. Sometimes of late years there has been manifested a disposition to recede from the defence of the supernatural in religion. This is a great mistake. Give up all that is miraculous in true religion and there is nothing left of power sufficient to move any heart to worship or adore ; and without worship there is no piety.—*William Swan Plumer.*

Verse 4.—The longer I live, O my God, the more do I wonder at all the works of thy hands. I see such admirable artifice in the very least and most despicable of all thy creatures, as doth every day more and more astonish my observation. I need not look so far as heaven for matter of marvel, though therein thou art infinitely glorious ; while I have but a spider in my window, or a bee in my garden, or a worm under my feet : every one of these overcomes me with a just amazement : yet can I see no more than their very outsides ; their inward form, which gives their being and operations, I cannot pierce into. The less I can know, O Lord, the more let me wonder ; and the less I can satisfy myself with marvelling at thy works, the more let me adore the majesty and omnipotence of thee, that wroughtest them.—*Joseph Hall.*

Verse 5.—*"To him that by wisdom made the heavens."* We find that God has built the heavens in wisdom, to declare his glory, and to show forth his handiwork. There are no iron tracks, with bars and bolts, to hold the planets in their orbits. Freely in space they move, ever changing, but never changed ; poised and balancing ; swaying and swayed ; disturbing and disturbed, onward they fly, fulfilling with unerring certainty their mighty cycles. The entire system forms one grand complicated piece of celestial machinery ; circle within circle, wheel within wheel, cycle within cycle ; revolutions so swift as to be completed in a few hours ; movements so slow, that their mighty periods are only counted by millions of years.—*From "The Orbs of Heaven,"* 1859.

Verse 5.—*"To him that by wisdom made the heavens."* Not only the firmament, but the third heavens, too, where all is felicity, where is the throne of glory. Then, I infer, that if the *mercy* which visits earth is from the same Jehovah who built that heaven and filled it with glory, there must be in his *mercy* something of the same *"understanding"* or *"wisdom."* It is wise, prudent mercy ; not rashly given forth ; and it is the mercy of him whose love has filled that heaven with bliss. The same architect, the same skill, the same love !—*Andrew A. Bonar.*

Verse 6.—*"Stretched out the earth above the waters."* The waters of the great deep (Gen. vii. 11) are meant ; above which the crust of the earth is outspread. In Prov. viii. 27 the great deep encircles the earth.—*"Speaker's Commentary."*

Verse 7.—*"Great lights."* The luminaries of heaven are unspeakable blessings to the children of men. The sun, in the greatness of his strength, measures their day, and exerts an influence over animal and vegetable life, which surrounds them with innumerable comforts ; and the moon and stars walking forth in their brightness, give direction to them amidst the sable hours of night, and both by land and sea proclaim the wisdom, and benignity, and gracious arrangement of the adorable Creator. By these luminaries, day and night, heat and cold, summer and winter are continually regulated ; so that God's covenant with the earth is maintained through their medium. How truly, then, may we exclaim, " His mercy endureth for ever ! "—*John Morison.*

Verse 7.—*"To him that made great lights."* Light is the life and soul of the universe, the noblest emblem of the power and glory of God, who, in the night season, leaves not himself without witness, but gives us some portion of that light reflected, which by day we behold flowing from its great fountain in the heart of heaven. Thy church and thy saints, O Lord, " are the moon and the stars," which, by the communication of doctrine, and the splendour of example, guide our feet, while we travel on in the night that hath overtaken us, waiting for the dawn of everlasting day. Then we shall behold thy glory, and see thee as thou art.—*George Horne.*

Verse 8.—*"The sun to rule by day."* This verse showeth that the sun shineth in the day, by the order which God hath set, and not for any natural cause alone, as some imagine and conjecture.—*Thomas Wilcocks.*

Verse 8.—*"The Sun."* The *lantern of the world* (*lucerna Mundi*), as Copernicus names the sun, enthroned in the centre—according to Theon of Smyrna, the all-vivifying, pulsating *heart of the universe,* is the primary source of light and of radiating heat, and the generator of numerous terrestrial, electro-magnetic processes, and indeed of the greater part of the organic vital activity upon our planet, more especially that of the vegetable kingdom. In considering the expression of solar force, in its widest generality, we find that it gives rise to alterations on the surface of the earth, —partly by gravitative attraction,—as in the ebb and flow of the ocean (if we except the share taken in the phenomenon by lunar attraction), partly by light and heat-generating transverse vibrations of ether, as in the fructifying admixture of the aerial and aqueous envelopes of our planet, from the contact of the atmosphere with the vaporizing fluid element in seas, lakes, and rivers. The solar action operates, moreover, by differences of heat, in exciting atmospheric and oceanic currents ; the latter of which have continued for thousands of years (though in an inconsiderable degree) to accumulate or waste away alluvial strata, and thus change the surface of the inundated land ; it operates in the generation and maintenance of the electro-magnetic activity of the earth's crust, and that of the oxygen contained in the atmosphere ; at one time calling forth calm and gentle forces of chemical attraction, and variously determining organic life in the endosmose of cell-walls and in tissue of muscular and nervous fibres ; at another time evoking light processes in the atmosphere, such as the coloured coruscations of the polar light, thunder and lightning, hurricanes and waterspouts.

Our object in endeavouring to compress in one picture the *influences of solar action,* in as far as they are independent of the orbit and the position of the axis of our globe, has been clearly to demonstrate, by an exposition of the connection existing between great, and at first sight heterogeneous, phenomena, how physical nature may be depicted in the *History of the Cosmos* as a whole, moved and animated by internal and frequently self-adjusting forces. But the waves of light not only exert a decomposing and combining action on the corporeal world ; they not only call forth the tender germs of plants from the earth, generate the green colouring matter (chlorophyll) within the leaf, and give colour to the fragrant blossom—they not only produce myriads of reflected images of the Sun in the graceful play of the waves, as in the moving grass of the field—but the rays of celestial light, in the varied gradations of their intensity and duration, are also mysteriously connected with the inner life of man, his intellectual susceptibilities, and the melancholy or cheerful tone of his feelings. This is what Pliny the elder referred to in these words, *"Cæli tristram discutit sol, et humani nubila animi serenat."* ["The sun chases sadness from the sky, and dissipates the clouds which darken the human heart."]—*F. H. Alexander Von Humboldt* (1769—1859), *in "Cosmos."*

Verse 8.—*"The sun."*

> O sun ! what makes thy beams so bright ?
> The word that said, " Let there be light."
>   *James Montgomery.*

Verse 9.—*"The moon and stars to rule by night."* While the apparent revolution of the sun marks out the year and the course of the seasons, the revolution of the moon round the heavens marks out our months ; and by regularly changing its figure at the four quarters of its course, subdivides the months into two periods of weeks, and thus exhibits to all the nations of the earth a " watch-light," or signal, which every seven days presents a form entirely new, for marking out the shorter periods of duration. By its nearness to the earth, and the consequent increase of its gravitating power, it produces currents in the atmosphere, which direct the course of the winds, and purify the aerial fluid from noxious exhalations ; it raises the waters of the ocean, and perpetuates the regular returns of ebb and flow, by which the liquid element is preserved from filth and putrefaction. It extends its sway even over the human frame, and our health and disorders are sometimes partially dependent on its influence. Even its eclipses, and those it produces of the sun, are not without their use. They tend to arouse mankind to the study of astronomy, and the wonders of the firmament; they serve to confirm the deductions of chronology, to direct the navigator, and to settle the geographical position of towns and countries; they assist the astronomer in his celestial investigations, and exhibit an agreeable variety of phenomena in the scenery of the heavens. In short, there are terrestrial scenes presented in moon-light, which, in point of solemnity, grandeur, and picturesque beauty, far surpass in interest, to a poetic imagination, all the brilliancy and splendours of noon-day. Hence, in all ages, a moonlight scene has been regarded, by all ranks of men, with feelings of joy and sentiments of admiration. The following description of Homer, translated into English verse by Pope, has been esteemed one of the finest night-pieces in poetry :—

> " Behold the moon, refulgent lamp of night,
> O'er Heaven's clear azure spreads her sacred light,
> When not a breath disturbs the deep serene,
> And not a cloud o'ercasts the solemn scene ;
> Around her throne the vivid planets roll,
> And stars unnumbered gild the glowing pole ;
> O'er the dark trees a yellower verdure shed,
> And tip with silver every mountain's head ;
> Then shine the vales ; the rocks in prospect rise ;
> A flood of glory bursts from all the skies ;
> The conscious swains, rejoicing in the sight,
> Eye the blue vault, and bless the useful light."

Without the light of the moon, the inhabitants of the polar regions would be for weeks and months immersed in darkness. But the moon, like a kindly visitant, returns at short intervals, in the absence of the sun, and cheers them with her beams for days and weeks together. So that, in this nocturnal luminary, as in all the other arrangements of nature, we behold a display of the paternal care and beneficence of that Almighty Being who ordained " the moon and the stars to rule by night," as an evidence of his superabundant goodness, and of " his mercy which endureth for ever."—*Thomas Dick* (1774—1857), *in "Celestial Scenery."*

Verse 9.—*"Stars to rule by night."* The purpose of the sacred narrative being to describe the adaptation of the earth to the use of man, no account is taken of the nature of the stars, as suns or planets, but merely as signs in the heavens.—*"Speaker's Commentary."*

Verse 9.—*"Stars."* The stars not only adorn the roof of our sublunary mansion, they are also in many respects *useful* to man. Their influences are placid and gentle. Their rays, being dispersed through spaces so vast and immense, are entirely destitute of heat by the time they arrive at our abode ; so that we enjoy the view of a numerous assemblage of luminous globes without any danger of their destroying the coolness of the night or the quiet of our repose. They serve to guide the traveller both by sea and land ; they direct the navigator in tracing his course from one continent to another through the pathless ocean. They serve " for signs and for seasons, and for days and years." They direct the labours of the husbandman, and determine the return and conclusion of the seasons. They serve as a magnificent " time piece," to determine the true length of the day and of the year, and to mark with accuracy all their subordinate divisions. They assist us in our commerce, and in endeavouring to propagate religion among the nations, by showing us our path to every region of the earth. They have enabled us to measure the circumference of the globe, to ascertain the *density* of the materials of which it is composed, and to determine the exact position of all places upon its surface. They cheer the long nights of several months in the polar regions, which would otherwise be overspread with impenetrable darkness. Above all, they open a prospect into the regions of other worlds, and tend to amplify our views of the Almighty Being who brought them into existence by his power, and " whose kingdom ruleth over all." In these arrangements of the stars in reference to our globe, the Divine wisdom and goodness may be clearly perceived. We enjoy all the advantages to which we have alluded as much as if the stars had been created solely for the use of our world, while, at the same time, they serve to diversify the nocturnal sky of other planets, and to diffuse their light and influence over ten thousands of other worlds with which they are more immediately connected, so that, in this respect, as well as in every other, the Almighty produces the most sublime and diversified effects by means the most simple and economical, and renders every part of the universe subservient to another, and to the good of the whole.—*Thomas Dick.*

Verse 9.—*"Stars."* When the First Consul crossed the Mediterranean on his Egyptian expedition, he carried with him a cohort of *savans*, who ultimately did good service in many ways. Among them, however, as might be expected at that era, were not a few philosophers of the Voltaire-Diderot school. Napoleon, for his own instruction and amusement on shipboard, encouraged disputation among these gentlemen ; and on one occasion they undertook to show, and, according to their own account, *did* demonstrate, by infallible logic and metaphysic, that there is no God. Bonaparte, who hated all idealogists, abstract reasoners, and logical demonstrators, no matter what they were demonstrating, would not fence with these subtle dialecticians, but had them immediately on deck, and, pointing to the stars in the clear sky, replied, by way of counter-argument, " Very good, messieurs ! but who made all these ? "—*George Wilson, in "Religio Chemici,"* 1862.

Verse 10.—*"To him that smote Egypt in their first-born."* The Egyptians are well said to have been *smitten in their first-born ;* because they continued in their outrageous obstinacy under the other plagues, though occasionally terrified by them, but were broken and subdued by this last plague, and submitted.—*John Calvin.*

Verse 10.—*"To him that smote Egypt in their first-born, for his mercy,"* etc. Remember his sovereign grace, when righteousness would show itself upon the guilty. There was mercy even then to Israel—drops of that mercy that for ever endureth—at the very time when judgment fell on others. Should not this give emphasis to our praises ? The dark background makes the figures in the foreground more prominent.—*Andrew A. Bonar.*

Verse 11.—*"And brought out Israel from among them."* Such an emigration as this the world never saw. On the lowest computation, the entire multitude must have been above two millions, and in all probability the number exceeded three millions. Is the magnitude of this movement usually apprehended ? Do we think of the emigration of the Israelites from Egypt as of the emigration of a number of families twice as numerous as the population of the principality of Wales, or considerably more than the whole population of the British Metropolis (in 1841), with all their goods, property, and cattle ? The collecting together of so immense a multitude—the arranging the order of their march—the provision of the requisite food even for a few days, must, under the circumstances, have been utterly impossible, unless a very special and overruling Providence had graciously interfered to obviate the difficulties of the case. To the most superficial observer it must be evident, that no man, or number of men, having nothing but human resources, could have ventured to undertake this journey. Scarcely any wonder, wrought by Divine power in Egypt, appears greater than this emigration of a nation, when fairly and fully considered.—*George Smith, in "Sacred Annals,"* 1850.

Verse 12.—*"With a stretched out arm."* The figure of *an outstretched arm* is appropriate, for we stretch out the arm when any great effort is required ; so that this implies that God put forth an extraordinary and not a common or slight display of his power in redeeming his people.—*John Calvin.*

Verse 13.—*"Divided the Red Sea into parts."* The entire space between the mountains of Ataka and Abon Deradj was dry. At the former point the gulf is eight miles across, at the latter more than double that distance. The waters that had filled this broad and deep chasm stood in two huge mounds on the right hand and on the left. The light of God shone brightly on the astonished multitude. The word was given, they advanced abreast ; awe-stricken, but quiet and confident. . . . " Then the Egyptians pursued and went in after them into the midst of the sea, all Pharaoh's horses, even his chariots and his fleet horses " : Exod. xiv. 23.— *William Osburn, in "Israel in Egypt,"* 1856.

Verse 14.—*"And made Israel to pass through the midst of it,"* etc. Willingly, without reluctance ; with great spirit and courage, fearless of danger, and with the utmost safety, so that not one was lost in the passage ; see Ps. lxxviii. 53 ; and thus the Lord makes his people willing to pass through afflictions, he being with them ;

and able to bear them, he putting underneath the everlasting arms, even when in the valley of the shadow of death. He carries them safely through them, so that they are not hurt by them ; the waters do not overflow them, nor the flames kindle upon them ; nor are any suffered to be lost : but all come safe to land.—*John Gill.*

Verse 14.—*"And made Israel to pass through the midst of it."* It is a work of no less mercy and power to give his people grace to make use of an offered means of delivery, than to prepare the deliverance for them ; but the constancy of God's mercy doth not only provide the means, but also giveth his people grace to make use thereof in all ages.—*David Dickson.*

Verse 14.—*"And made Israel to pass through the midst of it."* It is many times *hail* with the saints, when *ill* with the wicked. Abraham from the hill seeth Sodom on fire.—*John Trapp.*

Verse 15.—*"But overthrew Pharaoh,"* etc. Thus fell Sethos II. It was his terrible destiny to leave to after-times the strongest exemplification of daring wickedness and mad impiety in his life, and of the vengeance of God in his death, that ever was enacted on the earth. Never had such a judgment befallen any nation, as his reign in Egypt. Accordingly the memory of this fearful event has never departed from among men. The gulf in which he perished is named Bahr-Kolzoum, " the sea of destruction," to this day.

The memory and name of Sethos II. were infamous in Egypt. His tomb was desecrated, and his sarcophagus publicly and judicially broken. The vault seems to have been used as a burying-place for slaves. The distinctive title of his name, *Sethos,* has been mutilated on all the monuments of Egypt. In Lower Egypt the mutilation has even been extended to the same title in the rings of his great-grand-father (Sethos I.), such was the deep abhorrence in which the name had fallen, after it had been borne by this wicked king. His is the only one in the whole range of the kings of Egypt which has suffered this mark of public infamy.—*William Osburn.*

Verse 15.—*"But overthrew Pharaoh,"* etc. Margin, as in Hebrew, *shaked off.* The word is applicable to a tree shaking off its foliage, Isa. xxxiii. 9. The same word is used in Ex. xiv. 27 : " And the Lord overthrew (Margin, *shook off*) the Egyptians in the midst of the sea." He shook them off as if he would no longer protect them. He left them to perish.—*Albert Barnes.*

Verse 15.—*"But shook off Pharaoh."* This translation gives an image of locusts. They fell into the sea like a swarm of locusts.—*Zachary Mudge*—1769.

Verse 15.—*"But overthrew Pharaoh,"* etc. I know that the Gospel is a book of mercy ; I know likewise that in the prophets there are many expressions of mercy ; I know likewise that in the ten commandments, which are the ministration of death, there is made express mention of mercy, " I will have mercy on thousands ": yet, notwithstanding all this, if every leaf, and every line, and every word in the Bible were nothing but mercy, it would nothing avail the presumptuous sinner. Our God is not an impotent God with one arm ; but as he is slow to anger, so is he great in power. And therefore though in this Psalm there is nothing but *"his mercy endureth for ever,"* which is twenty-six times in twenty-six verses : yet mark what a rattling thunder-clap is here in this verse. In our addresses therefore unto God, let us so look upon him as a just God as well as a merciful ; and not either despair of or presume upon his mercy.—*Abraham Wright.*

Verse 16.—*"Led his people through the wilderness."*

> When Israel, of the Lord beloved,
> Out of the land of bondage came,
> Her father's God before her moved,
> An awful guide, in smoke and flame.
> By day, along the astonished lands,
> The cloudy pillar glided slow ;
> By night Arabia's crimsoned sands
> Returned the fiery column's glow.

Sir Walter Scott, 1711—1832.

Verse 16.—*"He led his people through the wilderness."* It was an astonishing miracle of God to support so many hundreds of thousands of people in a wilderness totally deprived of all necessaries for the life of man, and that for the space of forty years.—*Adam Clarke.*

Verse 16.—*"He led his people through the wilderness,"* etc. It is a very sweet truth which is enunciated in this verse, and one which I think we need very much to realize. His own people, his peculiar people, his chosen, loved, and favoured ones, whom he cherished as the apple of his eye, who were graven on the palms of his hands, and loved with an everlasting love, even these he led through the wilderness ; and all this *because* " His mercy endureth for ever." In another Psalm it is said, " He leadeth them beside the still waters, he maketh them to lie down in green pastures " ; but the barren wilderness has no green pastures, the parched and arid desert has no still waters. And yet " in the wilderness shall waters break out, and streams in the desert, and an highway shall be there ; and the ransomed of the Lord shall return, and come to Zion with songs and everlasting joy upon their heads." " Who is this that cometh up from the wilderness, leaning upon her beloved ? " It is one of the Lord's sweet truths that so perplex those that are without, but which are so full of consolation to his own children, that the wilderness and mercy are linked together of God in indissoluble union here. " I will allure her," saith the Lord, " and bring her into the wilderness, and speak comfortably unto her."— *Barton Bouchier.*

Verse 16.—*"Who led his people."* Note that in what precedes this, in this verse itself, and in what follows, God's three ways of leading are set forth. He leads *out*, he leads *through*, and he leads *into ;* out of sin, through the world, into heaven ; out by faith, through by hope, into by love.—*Michael Ayguan* (1416), *in Neale and Littledale.*

Verse 17.—*"Great kings."* Great, as those times accounted them, when every small city almost had her king. Canaan had thirty and more of them. *Great* also in regard of their stature and strength ; for they were of the giants' race. Deut. iii. ; Amos ii.—*John Trapp.*

Verses 18, 20.—The profane of our times may hence learn to take heed how they wrong the faithful. God is " wise in heart and mighty in strength : " Job ix. 4. Who ever waxed fierce against his people and hath prospered ? For their sakes he hath destroyed great kings and mighty, *"Sihon king of the Amorites, and Og the king of Bashan."* He can pluck off thy chariot wheels, strike thee in the hinder parts, cause thy heart to fail thee for fear, and in a moment fetch thy soul from thee : better were it for thee to have a millstone hanged about thy neck, and thou to be cast into the bottom of the sea, than to offend the least of these faithful ones ; they are dear in his sight, tender to him, as the apple of his eye.—*John Barlow*, 1632.

Verse 19.—*"Sihon"* occupied the whole district between the Arnon and Jabbok, through which the approach to the Jordan lay. He had wrested it from the predecessor of Balak, and had established himself, not in the ancient capital of Moab-Ar, but in the city still conspicuous to the modern traveller from its wide prospect and its cluster of stone pines—Heshbon. The recollection of his victory survived in a savage war-song, which passed into a kind of proverb in after-times :—

> " Come home to Heshbon ;
> Let the city of Sihon be built and prepared,
> For there is gone out a fire from Heshbon,
> A flame from the city of Sihon.
> It hath consumed Ar of Moab,
> And the lords of the high places of Arnon :
> Woe to thee, Moab ; thou art undone, thou people of Chemosh !
> He hath given his sons that escaped, and his daughters, into captivity
> To the king of the Amorites, Sihon."*

The decisive battle between Sihon and his new foes took place at Jahaz, probably on the confines of the rich pastures of Moab and the desert whence the Israelites emerged. It was the first engagement in which they were confronted with the future enemies of their nation. The slingers and archers of Israel, afterwards so renowned, now first showed their skill. Sihon fell ; the army fled † (so ran the later tradition), and devoured by thirst, like the Athenians in the Assinarus on their flight from Syracuse, were slaughtered in the bed of one of the mountain streams. The memory of this battle was cherished in triumphant strains, in which, after reciting, in bitter

---

* Num. xxi. 27–29, repeated, as is well known, in Jer. xlviii. 45, 46.
† Joseph. Ant. iv. 5; § 2.

irony, the song just quoted of the Amorites' triumph, they broke out into an exulting contrast of the past greatness of the defeated chief and his present fall :—

> " We have shot at them : Heshbon is perished :
> We have laid them waste : even unto Nophah :
> With fire : even unto Medeba."*

Arthur Penrhyn Stanley, in "The History of the Jewish Church."

Verse 20.—*"Og the king of Bashan."* There is continued victory. The second hindrance disappears after the first. *"Og, king of Bashan,"* last of the giants (Deut. iii. 11), fared no better for all his strength than *Sihon.* It was not some peculiar weakness of Sihon that overthrew him. All enemies of God, however different in resource they may appear when they measure themselves among themselves, are alike to those who march in the strength of God. The power by which the Christian conquers one foe will enable him to conquer all. And yet because *Og* did *look* more formidable than Sihon, God gave his people special encouragement in meeting him : Numb. xxi. 34. God remembers that even the most faithful and ardent of his people cannot get entirely above the deceitfulness of outward appearances.—*Pulpit Commentary.*

Verse 20.—When *"Og king of Bashan"* took the field—a giant, a new and more terrific foe—he, too, fell. And the *mercy* that thus dealt with enemies so great, enemies so strong, one after another, *"endureth for ever."* When Antichrist raises up his hosts in the latter days, one after another—when the great, the famous, the mighty, the noble, the gigantic men, in succession assail the Church, they shall perish : " For his *mercy* endureth for ever.—*Andrew A. Bonar.*

Verse 22.—*"Israel his servant."* He speaks of all that people as of one man, because they were united together in one body, in the worship of one and the same God. Thus God calleth them all his " first-born " : Exod. iv. 22.—*Matthew Pool.*

Verse 23.—*"Who remembered us."* We should echo in our thankfulness the first intimation that God gives in his providence of an approaching mercy. If you do but hear when the king is on his road towards your town you raise your bells to ring him in, and stay not till he be entered the gates. The birds rise betimes in the morning, and are saluting the rising sun with their sweet notes in the air. Thus should we strike up our harps in praising God at the first appearance of a mercy.—*William Gurnall.*

Verse 23.—*"Who remembered us."* The word *" remembered "* is a pregnant word, it bears twins twice told, it is big of a six-fold sense, as so many degrees of mercy in it. 1. *To remember* signifies to think upon, in opposition to forgetfulness. We may dwell in man's thoughts and not be the better for it, but we cannot be in God's remembering thoughts but we shall be the better for it. 2. To remember (as the second degree of the mercy) signifies to take notice of a thing, in opposition to neglect ; so it is used in Exod. xx. 8 : *"Remember* the Sabbath-day, to keep it holy : "take notice, that is, neglect it not, " remember " to keep holy the Sabbath-day. So God " *remembered* " us in our low estates : how ? Why, he did not barely think upon us, but he did observe and take notice of us, and considered what our case was. But, 3. It signifies (as the third degree of mercy), to lay to heart, to pity and compassionate persons in such a case. What am I better for anybody's thinking of me, if he do not take notice of me, so as to pity me in my low estate ? So God doth, as in Jer. xxxi. 20. 4. *To remember,* signifies yet more (as the fourth degree of mercy) to be well pleased with a person in such a case, to accept of a person in such a case ; so the word is used in Ps. xx. 3 : " The Lord *remember* all thy offerings, and accept thy burnt sacrifice "; remember, that is accept. 5. *To remember* signifies (as the fifth degree of mercy) to hear and to grant a request ; so it is used in 1 Sam. i. 19, 20, 27 : " God *remembered* Hannah," and the next word is, " He gave her what she asked." 6. *To remember* signifies (as the sixth degree of mercy) to help and succour, or to redeem and deliver from that which we were appointed to, from the low estate ; and so it is in Gal. ii. 10 : " Only they would that we should *remember* the poor." Remembering the poor is not barely a thought, but a relieving thought ; therefore saith the Psalmist in the following verse, " who hath redeemed us from our enemies : " this was the *remembrance* of God, *redemption* from enemies.

---

* Numb. xxi. 30.

I might draw considerations [for thanksgiving] from the *Author* of the mercy, *God;* a God that was offended by us, a God that needed us not, and a God that gains nothing by us ; and yet this God remembered us in our low estate ; that should engage us.   I might also draw obligations from *the objects*, and that is *us* that were not only an undeserving but an ill-deserving, and are not a suitable returning people. I might draw arguments from *the mercy*, itself,—that God *remembered* us. . . . and I might draw arguments from *the season*, " in our low estate," and from *the excellency of the duty* of thanksgiving ; 'tis a comely thing ; it makes us like the angels, whose whole employment and liturgy is to give and live praise to God.   And from this also I might enlarge the discoveries of the obligation, that " *his mercy endureth for ever.*"

"*For his mercy endureth for ever.*"   There is no reason to be given for grace but grace ; there is no reason to be given for mercy but mercy ; who remembered us : " *for his mercy endureth for ever.*"—*Ralph Venning* (1620—1673), *in "Mercies Memorial.*"

Verse 24.—"*And.*"   If the end of one mercy were not the beginning of another, we were undone.—*Philip Henry*, 1631—1696.

Verse 24.—"*And hath redeemed us.*"   Or, *broken us off*, pulled us away, as by violence ; for they would never else have loosed us.—*John Trapp.*

Verse 25.—"*Who giveth food to all flesh,*" etc.   The very air we breathe in, the bread we eat, our common blessings, be they never so mean, we have them all from grace, and all from the tender mercy of the Lord.   Ps. cxxxvi. 25, you have there the story of the notable effects of God's mercy, and he concludes it thus : "*Who giveth food to all flesh : for his mercy endureth for ever.*"   Mark, the Psalmist doth not only ascribe those mighty victories, those glorious instances of his love and power, to his unchangeable mercy, but he traces our daily bread to the same cause. In eminent deliverances of the church we will acknowledge mercy ; yea, but we should do it in every bit of meat we eat ; for the same reason is rendered all along. What is the reason his people smote Sihon king of the Amorites, and Og the king of Bashan, and that they were rescued so often out of danger ?   " For his mercy endureth for ever."   And what is the reason he giveth food to all flesh ?   " For his mercy endureth for ever."   It is not only mercy which gives us Christ, and salvation by Christ, and all those glorious deliverances and triumphs over the enemies of the church ; but it is mercy which furnisheth our tables, it is mercy that we taste with our mouths and wear at our backs.   It is notable, our Lord Jesus, when there were but five barley loaves and two fishes (John vi. 11), " He lift up his eyes and gave thanks."   Though our provision be never so homely and slender, yet God's grace and mercy must be acknowledged.—*Thomas Manton.*

Verse 25.—"*Who giveth food to all flesh.*"   We might fancy that they who have so much to sing of in regard to themselves, so much done for their own souls, would have little care for others.   We might fear that they would be found selfish.   But not so ; the love of God felt by a man makes the man feel as God does toward men ; and as God's love is ever going forth to others, so is the heart of the man of God. We see how it is even as to patriotism—a man's intensest patriotic feelings do not necessarily make him indifferent to the good of other countries, but rather make him wish all countries to be like his own ; so it is, much more certainly and truly, with the Lord's people in their enjoyment of blessing.   Their heart expands towards others ; they would fain have all men share in what they enjoy.   They therefore cannot close their song without having this other clause—Praise him who is " *the giver of bread to all flesh.*"   Not to Israel only does he give blessing. Israel had their manna ; but, at the same time, the earth at large has its food. So in spiritual things.   Israel's God is he who giveth himself as the Bread of Life to the world.   Perhaps at this point the Psalmist's eye may be supposed to see *earth in its state of blessedness*, after Israel is for the last time redeemed from all enemies, and become " life from the dead " to the world—when Christ reigns and dispenses the bread of life to the New Earth, as widely as he gave common food—" the feast of fat things to all nations," (Isa. xxv. 6.) ; for his mercy will not rest till this is accomplished.—*Andrew A. Bonar.*

Verse 25.—"*Who giveth food to all flesh.*"   In the close the Psalmist speaks of the paternal providence of God as extending not only to all mankind, but to every living creature, suggesting that we have no reason to feel surprise at his sustaining the character of a kind and provident father to his own people, when he condescends to care for the cattle, and the asses of the field, and the crow, and the sparrow. Men are much better than brute beasts, and there is a great difference between some men and others, though not in merit, yet as regards the privilege of the divine adoption, and the Psalmist is to be considered as reasoning from the less to the greater and enhancing the incomparably superior mercy which God shows to his own children.—*John Calvin.*

Verse 25.—*"Who giveth food to all flesh."* Of Edward Taylor, better known as "Father Taylor," the Sailor Preacher of Boston, it is said that his prayers were more like the utterances of an Oriental, abounding in imagery, than a son of these colder western climes. The Sunday before he was to sail for Europe, he was entreating the Lord to care well for his church during his absence. All at once he stopped and ejaculated, "What have I done? Distrust the providence of heaven! A God that gives a whale a ton of herrings for a breakfast, will he not care for my children?" and then went on, closing his prayer in a more confiding strain.— *C. H. Spurgeon, in "Eccentric Preachers," 1880.*

Verse 26.—*"The God of heaven."* The phrase *"God of heaven"* is not found in the earlier Scriptures. We meet it nowhere else in the Psalms; but we meet it in 2 Chron. xxxvi. 23; Ezra i. 2; v. 11, 12; vi. 9; vii. 12, 23; Neh. i. 4; ii. 4; Dan. ii. 18, 19, 44; Jonah i. 9. It is twice found in the Apocalypse, Rev. xi. 13; xvi. 11. It is a sublime and appropriate designation of the true God, expressive of his glorious elevation above the passions and perturbations of earth. To him all flesh should give thanks, for all receive his mercy in many forms and ways. His favours come down on generation after generation, and to his willing, obedient people they shall flow on during eternal ages.—*William Swan Plumer.*

Verse 26.—My brethen, God's mercies are from everlasting; and it is a treasure that can never be spent, never exhausted, unto eternity. In Isa. lxiv. 5, we read, "In thy mercy is continuance." If God will but continue to be merciful to me, will a poor soul say, I have enough. Why, saith he, "in his mercies is continuance, and we shall be saved." Hath God pardoned thee hitherto? but hast thou sinned again? Can he stretch his goodness and mercy a little further? Why, he will stretch them out unto eternity, unto everlasting; and if one *everlasting* be not enough, there are twenty-six everlastings in this one Psalm. In Isa. liv. 8, "In a little wrath I hid my face from thee, but with everlasting kindness will I have mercy on thee."—*Thomas Goodwin.*

Verse 26.—*"O give thanks unto the God of heaven."* His mercy in providing heaven for his people is more than all the rest.—*John Trapp.*

HINTS TO PREACHERS.

Verse 1.—I. Consider his name—"Jehovah." II. Carry out your joyful duty: "O give thanks." III. Contemplate the two reasons given—goodness and enduring mercy.

Verse 1.—I. Many subjects for praise. 1. For the goodness of God: "He is good" (verse 1). 2. For his supremacy: "God of gods; Lord of lords" (verses 2, 3). 3. For his works in general (verse 4). 4. For his works of creation in particular (verses 5—9). 5. For his works of Providence (verses 10—26). II. The chief subject for praise:—"For his mercy endureth for ever." 1. For mercy. This is the sinner's principal need. 2. For mercy in God. This is the sinner's attribute, and is as essential to God as justice. 3. For mercy enduring for ever. If they who have sinned need mercy for ever, they must exist for ever; and their guilt must be for ever.—*G. R.*

Verse 1.—*"The LORD is good."* God is originally good—good of himself. He is infinitely good. He is perfectly good, because infinitely good. He is immutably good.—*Charnock.*

Verses 1—3.—I. The triplet of names: "Jehovah," "the God of gods," "the Lord of lords." II. The threefold adjuration, "O give thanks." III. The irrepressible attribute and argument—"for his mercy," etc.—*W. B. H.*

Verses 1—26.—" For his mercy endureth for ever." See " Spurgeon's Sermons," No. 787 : " A Song, a Solace, a Sermon, and a Summons."

Verse 4.—I. The Lord does great wonders of mercy. II. He does them unaided. III. He does them as none else can do. IV. He should have unique praise.

Verse 4.—*The great lone Wonderworker.* I. God was alone in the wonderwork of Creation : Gen. i. II. Alone in the wonderwork of redemption : Isa. lxiii. 5. III. Is alone in the wonderwork of Providence : Ps. civ. 27, 28. IV. Alone in the wonderwork of Sanctification : 1 Thess. v. 23, 24. V. Will be alone in the wonderwork of Universal Triumph : 1 Cor. xv. 25.—*C. A. D.*

Verse 4.—The merciful in the wonderful. The wonderful in the merciful.

Verse 7.—The mercy which dwells in the creation and distribution of light.

Verses 7—9.—I. The constancy of rule. II. The association of light with rule. III. The perpetuity of mercy in this matter.

Verses 8, 9.—I. The glory of the day of joy. II. The comforts of the night of sorrow. III. The hand of God in each.

Verse 10.—Mercy and judgment. In the stroke that filled Egypt with anguish there was conspicuous mercy.—I. Even to Egypt ; the sharp stroke should have wrought repentance. So God still strives with men. II. Evidently to Israel ; they being thus delivered ; their firstborn saved. III. Emphatically to the whole world : power made known, Christ foreshadowed, an important link in the chain of redemption.—*W. B. H.*

Verse 11.—The bringing out of God's people from their natural state, from their misery, and from association with the ungodly, a great marvel of everlasting mercy.

Verse 11.—Effectual calling ; the intervention at the determined moment of the mercy of infinite ages.—*W. B. H.*

Verse 12.—Displays of divine power in the history of the saints a reason for song.

Verses 13, 14.—God to be praised not only, I. For clearing our way ; but also, II. For giving faith to traverse it. The last as great a mercy as the first.

Verses 13—15.—Mercy queen of the Exodus. I. Her sceptre upon the sea. What cannot Love divine conquer for its chosen ! II. Her standard in the van. Whither shall saints fear to follow her ? III. Her frown upon the pursuers ; life to the beloved, fatal to the foe. IV. To her let there be brought the chaplet of our praises.—*W. B. H.*

Verse 15.—Final victory. I. Battalions of evil annihilated. II. Love unharmed mounting immortal above the wave : " for his mercy endureth for ever." III. Heaven resonant with the song of Moses and the Lamb, to him give thanks. —*W. B. H.*

Verse 16.—I. Personal care : " To him which led." II. Peculiar interest : " His people." III. Persevering goodness : " Through the wilderness."

Verse 16.—*Led through the wilderness.* I. God's people must enter the wilderness for trial, for self knowledge, for development of graces, for preparation for Canaan. II. God leads his people while in the wilderness. Their route, their provision, their discipline, their protection. III. God will bring his people out of the wilderness.—*C. A. D.*

Verses 17—22.—See " Spurgeon's Sermons," No. 1285 : " Sihon and Og ; or, Mercies in Detail."

Verse 21.—I. Our portion, a heritage. II. Our title-deed, a royal grant : " And gave." III. Our praise, due to enduring mercy.

Verse 23.—Prayer of the dying thief turned into a song.

Verses 23, 24.—The gracious remembrance and the glorious redemption.— *C. A. D.*

Verse 24.—Our enemies, our accomplished redemption, the author of it, and his reason for effecting it.

Verse 24.—The multiplied redemptions of the Christian life, and their inexhaustible spring.—*W. B. H.*

Verse 25.—Divine housekeeping. I. The Royal Commissariat. II. Its spiritual counterpart : God's august provisioning for our immortal nature. III. The queenly grace that hath the keeping of the keys : " for his mercy," etc.—*W. B. H.*

Verse 26.—Consider, I. How he rules in heaven. II. How he rules earth from heaven. III. How mercy is the eternal element of that rule, and therefore he is the eternal object of praise.

PSALM CXXXVII.

This plaintive ode is one of the most charming compositions in the whole Book of Psalms for its poetic power. If it were not inspired it would nevertheless occupy a high place in poesy, especially the former portion of it, which is tender and patriotic to the highest degree. In the later verses (7, 8, 9), we have utterances of burning indignation against the chief adversaries of Israel,—an indignation as righteous as it was fervent. Let those find fault with it who have never seen their temple burned, their city ruined, their wives ravished, and their children slain ; they might not, perhaps, be quite so velvet-mouthed if they had suffered after this fashion. It is one thing to talk of the bitter feeling which moved captive Israelites in Babylon, and quite another thing to be captives ourselves under a savage and remorseless power, which knew not how to show mercy, but delighted in barbarities to the defenceless. The song is such as might fitly be sung in the Jews' wailing-place. It is a fruit of the Captivity in Babylon, and often has it furnished expression for sorrows which else had been unutterable. It is an opalesque Psalm within whose mild radiance there glows a fire which strikes the beholder with wonder.

EXPOSITION.

BY the rivers of Babylon, there we sat down, yea, we wept, when we remembered Zion.

2 We hanged our harps upon the willows in the midst thereof.

3 For there they that carried us away captive required of us a song ; and they that wasted us *required of us* mirth, *saying*, Sing us *one* of the songs of Zion.

4 How shall we sing the LORD's song in a strange land ?

5 If I forget thee, O Jerusalem, let my right hand forget *her cunning.*

6 If I do not remember thee, let my tongue cleave to the roof of my mouth ; if I prefer not Jerusalem above my chief joy.

1. *"By the rivers of Babylon, there we sat down."* Water-courses were abundant in Babylon, wherein were not only natural streams but artificial canals : it was a place of broad rivers and streams. Glad to be away from the noisy streets, the captives sought the river side, where the flow of the waters seemed to be in sympathy with their tears. It was some slight comfort to be out of the crowd, and to have a little breathing room, and therefore they sat down, as if to rest a while and solace themselves in their sorrow. In little groups they sat down and made common lamentation, mingling their memories and their tears. The rivers were well enough, but, alas, they were the rivers of Babylon, and the ground whereon the sons of Israel sat was foreign soil, and therefore they wept. Those who came to interrupt their quiet were citizens of the destroying city, and their company was not desired. Everything reminded Israel of her banishment from the holy city, her servitude beneath the shadow of the temple of Bel, her helplessness under a cruel enemy ; and therefore her sons and daughters sat down in sorrow.

"Yea, we wept, when we remembered Zion." Nothing else could have subdued their brave spirits ; but the remembrance of the temple of their God, the palace of their king, and the centre of their national life, quite broke them down. Destruction had swept down all their delights, and therefore they wept—the strong men wept, the sweet singers wept ! They did not weep when they remembered the cruelties of Babylon ; the memory of fierce oppression dried their tears and made their hearts burn with wrath : but when the beloved city of their solemnities came into their minds they could not refrain from floods of tears. Even thus do true believers mourn when they see the church despoiled, and find themselves unable to succour her : we could bear anything better than this. In these our times the

Babylon of error ravages the city of God, and the hearts of the faithful are grievously wounded as they see truth fallen in the streets, and unbelief rampant among the professed servants of the Lord. We bear our protests, but they appear to be in vain ; the multitude are mad upon their idols. Be it ours to weep in secret for the hurt of our Zion : it is the least thing we can do ; perhaps in its result it may prove to be the best thing we can do. Be it ours also to sit down and deeply consider what is to be done. Be it ours, in any case, to keep upon our mind and heart the memory of the church of God which is so dear to us. The frivolous may forget, but Zion is graven on our hearts, and her prosperity is our chief desire.

2. *"We hanged our harps upon the willows in the midst thereof.* The drooping branches appeared to weep as we did, and so we gave to them our instruments of music ; the willows could as well make melody as we, for we had no mind for minstrelsy. In the midst of the willows, or in the midst of the rivers, or in the midst of Babylon, it matters little which, they hung their harps aloft—those harps which once in Zion's halls the soul of music shed. Better to hang them up than to dash them down : better to hang them on willows than profane them to the service of idols. Sad indeed is the child of sorrow when he grows weary of his harp, from which in better days he had been able to draw sweet solaces. Music hath charms to give unquiet spirits rest ; but when the heart is sorely sad it only mocks the grief which flies to it. Men put away their instruments of mirth when a heavy cloud darkens their souls.

3. *"For there they that carried us away captive required of us a song."* It was ill to be a singer at all when it was demanded that this talent should go into bondage to an oppressor's will. Better be dumb than be forced to please an enemy with forced song. What cruelty to make a people sigh, and then require them to sing ! Shall men be carried away from home and all that is dear to them, and yet chant merrily for the pleasure of their unfeeling captors ? This is studied torture : the iron enters into the soul. It is indeed " woe to the conquered " when they are forced to sing to increase the triumph of their conquerors. Cruelty herein reached a refinement seldom thought of. We do not wonder that the captives sat them down to weep when thus insulted. *"And they that wasted us required of us mirth."* The captives must not only sing but smile, and add merriment to their music. Blind Samson in former days must be brought forth to make sport for Philistines, and now the Babylonians prove themselves to be loaves of the same leaven. Plundered, wounded, fettered, carried into captivity and poverty, yet must the people laugh as if it were all a play, and they must sport as if they felt no sorrow. This was wormwood and gall to the true lovers of God and his chosen land. *"Saying, Sing us one of the songs of Zion."* Nothing would serve their turn but a holy hymn, and a tune sacred to the worship of Jehovah. Nothing will content the Babylonian mockers but one of Israel's Psalms when in her happiest days she sang unto the Lord whose mercy endureth for ever : this would make rare fun for their persecutors, who would deride their worship and ridicule their faith in Jehovah. In this demand there was an insult to their God, as well as a mockery of themselves, and this made it the more intensely cruel. Nothing could have been more malicious, nothing more productive of grief. These wanton persecutors had followed the captives into their retirement, and had remarked upon their sorrowful appearance, and " there " and then they bade the mourners make mirth for them. Could they not let the sufferers alone ? Were the exiles to have no rest ? The daughter of Babylon seemed determined to fill up her cup of iniquity, by torturing the Lord's people. Those who had been the most active agents of Israel's undoing must needs follow up their ferocities by mockeries. " The tender mercies of the wicked are cruel." Worse than the Egyptians, they asked not labour which their victims could have rendered, but they demanded mirth which they could not give, and holy songs which they dared not profane to such a purpose.

4. *"How shall we sing the* LORD'S *song in a strange land ?"* How shall they sing at all ? sing in a strange land ? sing Jehovah's song among the uncircumcised ? No, that must not be ; it shall not be. With one voice they refuse, but the refusal is humbly worded by being put in the form of a question. If the men of Babylon were wicked enough to suggest the defiling of holy things for the gratification of curiosity, or for the creation of amusement, the men of Zion had not so hardened their hearts as to be willing to please them at such a fearful cost. There are many things which the ungodly could do, and think nothing of the doing thereof, which gracious men cannot venture upon. The question " How can I ? " or " How shall

we ? " comes of a tender conscience and denotes an inability to sin which is greatly to be cultivated.

5. *"If I forget thee, O Jerusalem, let my right hand forget her cunning."* To sing Zion's songs for the pleasure of Zion's foes, would be to forget the Holy City. Each Jew declares for himself that he will not do this ; for the pronoun alters from " we " to " I." Individually the captives pledge themselves to fidelity to Jerusalem, and each one asserts that he had sooner forget the art which drew music from his harp-strings than use it for Babel's delectation. Better far that the right hand should forget its usual handicraft, and lose all its dexterity, than that it should fetch music for rebels out of the Lord's instruments, or accompany with sweet skill a holy Psalm desecrated into a common song for fools to laugh at. Not one of them will thus dishonour Jehovah to glorify Belus and gratify his votaries. Solemnly they impre-cate vengeance upon themselves should they so false, so faithless prove.

6. *"If I do not remember thee, let my tongue cleave to the roof of my mouth."* Thus the singers imprecate eternal silence upon their mouths if they forget Jerusalem to gratify Babylon. The players on instruments and the sweet songsters are of one mind : the enemies of the Lord will get no mirthful tune or song from them. *"If I prefer not Jerusalem above my chief joy."* The sacred city must ever be first in their thoughts, the queen of their souls ; they had sooner be dumb than dishonour her sacred hymns, and give occasion to the oppressor to ridicule her worship. If such the attachment of a banished Jew to his native land, how much more should we love the church of God of which we are children and citizens. How jealous should we be of her honour, how zealous for her prosperity. Never let us find jests in the words of Scripture, or make amusement out of holy things, lest we be guilty of forgetting the Lord and his cause. It is to be feared that many tongues have lost all power to charm the congregations of the saints because they have forgotten the gospel, and God has forgotten *them.*

7 Remember, O LORD, the children of Edom in the day of Jerusalem ; who said, Rase *it*, rase *it, even* to the foundation thereof.

8 O daughter of Babylon, who art to be destroyed ; happy *shall he be,* that rewardeth thee as thou hast served us.

9 Happy *shall he be,* that taketh and dasheth thy little ones against the stones.

7. *"Remember, O LORD, the children of Edom in the day of Jerusalem."* The case is left in Jehovah's hands. He is a God of recompenses, and will deal out justice with impartiality. The Edomites ought to have been friendly with the Israelites, from kinship ; but there was a deep hatred and cruel spite displayed by them. The elder loved not to serve the younger, and so when Jacob's day of tribulation came, Esau was ready to take advantage of it. The captive Israelites being moved by grief to lodge their plaints with God, also added a prayer for his visitation of the nation which meanly sided with their enemies, and even urged the invaders to more than their usual cruelty. *"Who said, Rase it, rase it, even to the foundation thereof."* They wished to see the last of Jerusalem and the Jewish state ; they would have no stone left standing, they desired to see a clean sweep of temple, palace, wall, and habitation. It is horrible for neighbours to be enemies, worse for them to show their enmity in times of great affliction, worst of all for neighbours to egg others on to malicious deeds. Those are responsible for other men's sins who would use them as the tools of their own enmity. It is a shame for men to incite the wicked to deeds which they are not able to perform themselves. The Chaldeans were ferocious enough without being excited to greater fury ; but Edom's hate was insatiable. Those deserve to be remembered by vengeance who in evil times do not remember mercy ; how much more those who take advantage of calamities to wreak revenge upon sufferers. When Jerusalem's day of restoration comes Edom will be remembered and wiped out of existence.

8. *"O daughter of Babylon, who art to be destroyed."* Or the destroyer, let us accept the word either way, or both ways : the destroyer would be destroyed, and the Psalmist in vision saw her as already destroyed. It is usual to speak of a city as a virgin daughter. Babylon was in her prime and beauty, but she was already doomed for her crimes. *"Happy shall he be that rewardeth thee as thou hast served us."* The avenger would be fulfilling an honourable calling in overthrowing a power so brutal, so inhuman. Assyrian and Chaldean armies had been boastfully

brutal in their conquests ; it was meet that their conduct should be measured back into their own bosoms. No awards of punishment can be more unanswerably just than those which closely follow the *lex talionis*, even to the letter. Babylon must fall, as she caused Jerusalem to fall ; and her sack and slaughter must be such as she appointed for other cities. The patriot-poet sitting sorrowfully in his exile, finds a solace in the prospect of the overthrow of the empress city which holds him in bondage, and he accounts Cyrus right happy to be ordained to such a righteous work. The whole earth would bless the conqueror for ridding the nations of a tyrant ; future generations would call him blessed for enabling men to breathe again, and for once more making liberty possible upon the earth.

We may rest assured that every unrighteous power is doomed to destruction, and that from the throne of God justice will be measured out to all whose law is force, whose rule is selfishness, and whose policy is oppression. Happy is the man who shall help in the overthrow of the spiritual Babylon, which, despite its riches and power, is " to be destroyed." Happier still shall he be who shall see it sink like a millstone in the flood, never to rise again. What that spiritual Babylon is none need enquire. There is but one city upon earth which can answer to the name.

9. "*Happy shall he be, that taketh and dasheth thy little ones against the stones.*" Fierce was the heart of the Jew who had seen his beloved city the scene of such terrific butchery. His heart pronounced like sentence upon Babylon. She should be scourged with her own whip of wire. The desire for righteous retribution is rather the spirit of the law than of the gospel ; and yet in moments of righteous wrath the old fire will burn ; and while justice survives in the human breast it will not lack for fuel among the various tyrannies which still survive. We shall be wise to view this passage as a prophecy. History informs us that it was literally fulfilled : the Babylonian people in their terror agreed to destroy their own offspring, and men thought themselves happy when they had put their own wives and children to the sword. Horrible as was the whole transaction, it is a thing to be glad of if we take a broad view of the world's welfare ; for Babylon, the gigantic robber, had for many a year slaughtered nations without mercy, and her fall was the rising of many people to a freer and safer state. The murder of innocent infants can never be sufficiently deplored, but it was an incident of ancient warfare which the Babylonians had not omitted in their massacres, and, therefore, they were not spared it themselves. The revenges of providence may be slow, but they are ever sure ; neither can they be received with regret by those who see God's righteous hand in them. It is a wretched thing that a nation should need an executioner ; but yet if men will commit murder tears are more fitly shed over their victims than over the assassins themselves. A feeling of universal love is admirable, but it must not be divorced from a keen sense of justice.

The captives in Babylon did not make music, but they poured forth their righteous maledictions, and these were far more in harmony with their surroundings than songs and laughter could have been. Those who mock the Lord's people will receive more than they desire, to their own confusion : they shall have little enough to make mirth for them, and more than enough to fill them with misery. The execrations of good men are terrible things, for they are not lightly uttered, and they are heard in heaven. " The curse causeless shall not come ; " but is there not a cause ? Shall despots crush virtue beneath their iron heel and never be punished ? Time will show.

EXPLANATORY NOTES AND QUAINT SAYINGS.

Whole Psalm.—Observe that this very Psalm in which the question is asked, " How can we sing ? " is itself a song, one of the Lord's songs, still. Nothing can be more sad, more desponding. It speaks of weeping in the remembrance of Zion ; it speaks of harps hung upon the willows by exiles who have no heart to use them ; and yet the very telling of these sorrows, of this incapacity for song, is a song still.

We chant it in our congregations now, hundreds and thousands of years after its composition, as one of the Church's melodies, as one of the Lord's songs. It gives us a striking example of the variety, of the versatility of worship, even in that department which might seem to be all joyous, all praise. The very refusal to sing may be itself a song. Any real utterance of good thoughts, whether they be thoughts of gladness or thoughts of sorrow, may be a true hymn, a true melody for the congregation, even though it may not breathe at every moment the very thought of all the worshippers. " How shall we sing ? " is itself a permanent hymn, an inspired song, for all the churches.—*C. J. Vaughan.*

Whole Psalm.—This Psalm is composed of two parts. The first is, an heavy complaint of the church, unto verse 7. The other is an heavy imprecation and a prophetical denunciation against the enemies of the church, unto the end of the Psalm.—*Robert Rollock.*

Whole Psalm.—What a wonderful mixture is the Psalm of soft melancholy and fiery patriotism ! The hand which wrote it must have known how to smite sharply with the sword, as well as how to tune the harp. The words are burning words of a heart breathing undying love to his country, undying hate to his foe. The poet is indeed

> " Dower'd with the hate of hate, the scorn of scorn,
> The love of love."

J. J. Stewart Perowne.

Whole Psalm.—Several of the Psalms obviously refer to the time of the Babylonian captivity . . . . The captives' mournful sentiments of pensive melancholy and weary longing during its long and weary continuance constitute the burden of the hundred and thirty-seventh. It was probably written by some gifted captive Levite at the time. Some suppose it to have been composed by Jeremiah, the prophet of tears, and sent to his countrymen in the land of their exile, in order to awaken fond memories of the past and sustain a lively hope for the future ; and certainly the ode is worthy even of his pen, for it is one of the sweetest, most plaintive, and exquisitely beautiful elegies in any language. It is full of heart-melting, tear-bringing pathos. The moaning of the captive, the wailing of the exile, and the sighing of the saints are heard in every line.—*W. Ormiston, in "The Study," 1874.*

Whole Psalm.—Here, I. The melancholy captives cannot enjoy themselves, verses 1, 2. II. They cannot humour their proud oppressors, verses 3, 4. III. They cannot forget Jerusalem, verses 5, 6. IV. They cannot forget Edom and Babylon, verses 7, 8, 9.—*Matthew Henry.*

Verse 1.—*"By the rivers of Babylon."* The canals of Babylon itself, probably (comp. verse 2).—*William Kay.*

Verse 1.—*"By the rivers."* Euphrates, Tigris, Chaboras, etc., and the canals which intersected the country. The exiles would naturally resort to the banks of the streams as shady, cool and retired spots, where they could indulge in their sorrowful remembrances. The prophets of the exile saw their visions by the river. Ezek. i. 1 ; Dan. viii. 2 ; x. 4.—*"Bibliotheca Sacra and Theological Review," 1848.*

Verse 1.—*"By the rivers."* The bank of a river, like the seashore, is a favourite place of sojourn of those whom deep grief drives forth from the bustle of men into solitude. The boundary line of the river gives to solitude a safe back ; the monotonous splashing of the waves keeps up the dull, melancholy alternation of thoughts and feelings ; and at the same time the sight of the cool, fresh water exercises a soothing influence upon the consuming fever within the heart.—*Franz Delitzsch.*

Verse 1.—*"By the rivers."* The peculiar reason for the children of Israel being represented as sitting at the streams is the *weeping.* An internal reference of the weeping to the streams, must therefore have been what gave rise to the representation of the sitting. Nor is this reference difficult to be discovered. All languages know of brooks, or streams of tears, compare in Scripture, Lam. ii. 18 ; " Let tears run down like a river day and night "; iii. 48 ; also Job xxviii. 11, where inversely the gushing of the floods is called *weeping* (Marg.). The children of Israel placed themselves beside the streams of Babel because they saw in them the image and symbol of their floods of tears.—*E. W. Hengstenberg.*

Verse 1.—*"We sat down."* Among the poets, sitting on the ground is a mark of misery or captivity.

Multos illa dies incomtis mœsta capillis
Sederat.—*Propertius.*

With locks unkempt, mournful, for many days
She sat.

O utinam ante tuos sedeam captiva penates.—*Propertius.*
O might I sit a captive at thy gate !

You have the same posture in an old coin that celebrates a victory of Lucius Verus over the Parthians.

We find Judea on several coins of Vespasian and Titus in the posture that denotes sorrow and captivity.—*From Joseph Addison's Dialogues on Medals.*

Verse 1.—*"Sat down"* implies that the burst of grief was a long one, and also that it was looked on by the captives as some relaxation and repose.—*Chrysostom.*

Verse 1.—*"We wept when we remembered Zion."* A godly man lays to heart the miseries of the church. I have read of certain trees, whose leaves if cut or touched, the other leaves contract and shrink up themselves, and for a space hang down their heads ; such a spiritual sympathy is there among Christians ; when other parts of God's church suffer, they feel themselves, as it were, touched in their own persons. Ambrose reports, that when Theodosius was sick unto death, he was more troubled about the church of God than about his own sickness. When Æneas would have saved Anchises' life, saith he, " Far be it from me that I should desire to live when Troy is buried in its ruins." There are in music two unisons ; if you strike one, you shall perceive the other to stir, as if it were affected : when the Lord strikes others a godly heart is deeply affected, Isa. xv. 11 : " My bowels shall sound like an harp." Though it be well with a child of God in his own particular, and he dwells in an house of cedar, yet he grieves to see it go ill with the public. Queen Esther enjoyed the king's favour, and all the delights of the court, yet when a bloody warrant was signed for the death of the Jews she mourns and fasts, and ventures her own life to save theirs.—*Thomas Watson.*

Verse 1.—For *Sion* only they wept, unlike many who weep with the weeping and rejoice with the joy of Babylon, because their whole interests and affections are bound up in the things of this world.—*Augustine.*

Verse 1.—Let us weep, because in this life we are forced to sit by the waters of Babylon, and are yet strangers and as it were banished and barred from being satisfied with the pleasures of that river which gladdeth the city of God. Alas, if we did consider that our country were heaven, and did apprehend this place here below to be our prison, or place of banishment, the least absence from our country would draw tears from our eyes and sighs from our hearts, with David (Ps. cxx. 5) : " Woe is me that I sojourn in Mesech, and am constrained to dwell in the tents of Kedar."⁴

Do you remember how the Jews behaved themselves in the time of their exile and captivity, while they sat by the rivers and waters of Babylon ? They wept, would not be comforted ; hanged up their harps and instruments. What are the waters of Babylon but the pleasures and delights of the world, the waters of confusion, as the word signifies ? Now when the people of God sit by them, that is to say, do not carelessly, but deliberately, with a settled consideration, see them slide by and pass away, and compare them with Sion, that is to say, with the inconceivable rivers of pleasure, which are permanent in the heavenly Jerusalem ; how can they choose but weep, when they see themselves sitting by the one, and sojourning from the other ? And it is worthy your observing, that notwithstanding the Jews had many causes of tears, the Chaldeans had robbed them of their goods, honours, countries, liberty, parents, children, friends : the chief thing, for all this, that they mourn for is their absence from Sion,—*"We wept when we remembered thee, O Sion"* —for their absence from Jerusalem. What should we then do for our absence from another manner of Jerusalem ? Theirs was an earthly, old, robbed, spoiled, burned, sacked Jerusalem ; ours a heavenly, new one, into which no arrow can be shot, no noise of the drum heard, nor sound of the trumpet, nor calling unto battle : who would not then weep, to be absent from hence ? "—*Walter Balcanqual, in "A Sermon Preached at St. Maries Spittle," 1623.*

Verse 1.—*"We remembered Zion."* It necessarily implies they had *forgot,* else how could they now remember ? In their peace and plenty they had but little regard of Zion then.—*John Whincop, in a Sermon entitled, "Israel's Tears for Distressed Zion," 1645.*

Verse 1.—Nothing could present a more striking contrast to their native country than the region into which the Hebrews were transplanted. Instead of their irregular and picturesque mountain city, crowning its unequal heights, and looking down into its deep and precipitous ravines, through one of which a scanty stream wound along, they entered the vast, square, and level city of Babylon, occupying both sides of the broad Euphrates ; while all around spread immense plains, which were intersected by long, straight canals, bordered by rows of willows. How unlike their national temple—a small but highly finished and richly adorned fabric, standing in the midst of its courts on the brow of a lofty precipice—the colossal temple of the Chaldean Bel, rising from the plain, with its eight stupendous stories or towers, one above the other, to the perpendicular height of a furlong : The palace of the Babylonian kings was more than twice the size of their whole city ; it covered eight miles, with its hanging gardens built on arched terraces, each rising above the other, and rich in all the luxuriance of artificial cultivation. How different from the sunny cliffs of their own land, where the olive and the vine grew spontaneously, and the cool, shady, and secluded valleys, where they could always find shelter from the heat of the burning noon ! No wonder then that, in the pathetic words of their own hymn, *"by the waters of Babylon they sat down and wept, when they remembered thee, O Zion."* Of their general treatment as captives we know little. The Psalm above quoted seems to intimate that the Babylonians had taste enough to appreciate the poetical and musical talent of the exiles, and that they were summoned occasionally to amuse the banquets of their masters, though it was much against their will that they sang the songs of Zion in a strange land. In general it seems that the Jewish exiles were allowed to dwell together in considerable bodies, not sold as household or personal or prædial slaves, at least not those of the better order of whom the Captivity chiefly consisted. They were colonists rather than captives, and became by degrees possessed of considerable property. They had taken the advice of the prophet Jeremiah (who gave them no hopes of speedy return to their homes) : they had built houses, planted gardens, married and brought up children, submitted themselves as peaceful subjects to the local authorities : all which implies a certain freedom, a certain degree of prosperity and comfort. They had free enjoyment of their religion, such at least as adhered faithfully to their belief in Jehovah. We hear of no special and general religious persecution.—*Henry Hart Milman* (1791—1868), *in "The History of the Jews."*

Verse 1.—They sat in silence ; they remembered in silence ; they wept in silence. —*J. W. Burgon.*

Verses 1—6.—Israel was a typical people. 1. They were typical of God's church in all ages of the world. And, 2. They were typical of the soul of every individual believer.

This Psalm is composed for Israel in her captivity. Let us go over it, taking its typical meaning.

I. *When a believer is in captivity he has a sorrowful remembrance of Zion.* So it was with God's ancient people : " By the rivers of Babylon, there we sat down, yea, we wept, when we remembered Zion " (verse 1). In the last chapter of 2 Chron. (14—20,) we find the melancholy tale of Judah's captivity. Many of their friends had been slain by the sword—the house of God was burned—the walls of Jerusalem were broken down—and they themselves were captives in a foreign land. No wonder that they sat down and wept when they remembered Zion.

So it is often with the believer when led captive by sin—he sits down and weeps when he remembers Zion. Zion is the place where God makes himself known. When a poor awakened sinner is brought to know the Saviour, and to enter through the rent veil into the holiest of all, then he becomes one of the people of Zion : " A day in thy courts is better than a thousand." He dwells in Zion ; and the people that dwell therein are forgiven their iniquity. But when a believer falls into sin he falls into darkness—he is carried a captive away from Zion. No more does he find entrance within the veil ; no more is he glad when they say to him, " Let us go up to the house of the Lord." He sits down and weeps when he remembers Zion.

II. *The world derides the believer in his captivity.* So it was with ancient Israel. The Chaldeans were cruel conquerors. God says by his prophet,—" I was but a little displeased, and they helped forward the affliction." Not only did they carry them away from their temple, their country, and their homes, but they made a mock of their sorrows. When they saw them sit down to shed bitter tears by the rivers of Babylon, they demanded mirth and a song, saying, " Sing us one of the songs of Zion."

So is it with the world and the captive Christian. There are times when the world does not mock at the Christian. Often the Christian is filled with so strange a joy that the world wonders in silence. Often there is a meek and quiet spirit in the Christian, which disarms opposition. The soft answer turneth away wrath ; and his very enemies are forced to be at peace with him. But stop till the Christian's day of darkness comes—stop till sin and unbelief have brought him into captivity —stop till he is shut out from Zion, and carried afar off, and sits and weeps ; then will the cruel world help forward the affliction—then will they ask for mirth and song ; and when they see the bitter tear trickling down the cheek, they will ask with savage mockery, " Where is your Psalm-singing now ? " " Sing us one of the songs of Zion." Even Christ felt this bitterness when he hung upon the cross.

III. *The Christian cannot sing in captivity.* So it was with ancient Israel. They were peculiarly attached to the sweet songs of Zion. They reminded them of the times of David and Solomon—when the temple was built, and Israel was in its greatest glory. They reminded them, above all, of their God, of their temple, and the services of the sanctuary. Three times a year they came up from the country in companies, singing these sweet songs of Zion—lifting their eyes to the hills whence came their help. But now, when they were in captivity, they hanged their harps upon the willows ; and when their cruel spoilers demanded mirth and a song, they said : " How shall we sing the Lord's song in a strange land ? " So is it with the believer in darkness. He hangs his harp upon the willows, and cannot sing the song of the Lord. Every believer has got a harp. Every heart that has been made new is turned into a harp of praise. The mouth is filled with laughter—the tongue with divinest melody. Every true Christian loves praise—the holiest Christians love it most. But when the believer falls into sin and darkness, his harp is on the willows, and he cannot sing the Lord's song, for he is in a strange land.

1. *He loses all sense of pardon.* It is the sense of pardon that gives its sweetest tones to the song of the Christian. But when a believer is in captivity he loses this sweet sense of forgiveness, and therefore cannot sing.

2. *He loses all sense of the presence of God.* It is the sweet presence of God with the soul that makes the believer sing. But when that presence is away, the Lord's house is but a howling wilderness ; and you say, " How can we sing the Lord's song in a strange land ? "

3. *He loses sight of the heavenly Canaan.* The sight of the everlasting hills draws forth the heavenly melodies of the believing soul. But when a believer sins, and is carried away captive, he loses this hope of glory. He sits and weeps—he hangs his harp upon the willows, and cannot sing the Lord's song in a strange land.

4. *The believer in darkness still remembers Zion, and prefers it above his chief joy.* He often finds, when he has fallen into sin and captivity, that he has fallen among worldly delights and worldly friends. A thousand pleasures tempt him to take up his rest here ; but if he be a true child of Zion he will never settle down in a strange land. He will look over all the pleasures of the world and the pleasures of sin, and say, " A day in thy courts is better than a thousand "—" If I forget thee, O Jerusalem, let my right hand forget her cunning."—*Condensed from Robert Murray M'Chayne,* 1813—1843.

Verses 1, 2.—The Psalm is universally admired. Indeed, nothing can be more exquisitely beautiful. It is written in a strain of sensibility that must touch every soul that is capable of feeling. It is remarkable that Dr. Watts, in his excellent versification, has omitted it. He has indeed some verses upon it in his Lyrics ; and many others have written on this ode. We have seen more than ten productions of this kind ; the last, and perhaps the best, of which is Lord Byron's. But who is satisfied with any of these attempts ? Thus it begins : " By the rivers of Babylon, there we sat down, yea, we wept, when we remembered Zion." These rivers were probably some of the streams branching off from the Euphrates and Tigris. Here it is commonly supposed these captive Jews were placed by their task-masters, to preserve or repair the water-works. But is it improper to conjecture that the Psalmist refers to their being here ; not constantly, but occasionally ; not by compulsion, but choice ? Hither I imagine their retiring, to unbend their oppressed minds in solitude. " Come," said one of these pious Jews to another, " come, let us for a while go forth, from this vanity and vileness. Let us assemble together by ourselves under the refreshing shade of the willows by the watercourses. And let us take our harps with us, and solace ourselves with some of the songs of Zion." But as soon as they arrive, and begin to touch the chords, the notes—such is the power of association—awaken the memory of their former privileges and pleasures. And, overwhelmed with grief, they sit down on the grass ; and weep when they remember Zion ; their dejected looks, averted from each other, seeming to say, " If I forget thee, O Jerusalem, let my right hand forget her cunning. If I do not remember thee, let my tongue cleave to the roof of my mouth ; if I prefer not Jerusalem above my chief joy." But what do they with their harps ? The voice of mirth is heard no more, and all the daughters of music are brought low. Melody is not in season to a distressed spirit. " Is any afflicted ? Let him pray. Is any merry ? Let him sing Psalms." " As he that taketh away a garment in cold weather, and as vinegar upon nitre, so is he that singeth songs to a heavy heart." They did not, however, break them to pieces, or throw them into the stream—but *hanged* them up only. They hoped that what they could not use at present they might be able to resume at some happier period. To be cast down is not to be destroyed. Distress is not despondency.

> " Beware of desperate steps : the darkest day,
> Live till to-morrow, will have passed away."

"We hanged our harps upon the willows in the midst thereof." Let us pass from the Jew to the Christian ; and let us survey the Christian in his SPIRITUAL SORROWS. He who would preach well, says Luther, must distinguish well. It is peculiarly necessary to discriminate, when we enter upon the present subject. For all the sorrows of the Christian are not of the same kind or descent. Let us consider four sources of his moral sadness.

I. The first will be *physical*. II. The second will be *criminal*. III. The third will be *intellectual*. IV. The fourth will be *pious*.—*William Jay, in "The Christian Contemplated."*

Verse 2.—*"Our harps."* Many singers were carried captives : Ezra ii. 41. These would of course carry their instruments with them, and be insulted, as here. Their songs were sacred, and unfit to be sung before idolaters.—*From "Anonymous Notes" in James Merrick's Annotations,* 1768.

Verse 2.—*"Willows."* All the flat, whereon Babylon stood, being by reason of so many rivers and canals running through it made in many places marshy, especially near the said rivers and canals, this caused it to abound much in *willows,* and therefore it is called in Scripture the " Valley of Willows " ; for so the words in Isaiah xv. 7, which we translate " the brook of the willows," ought to be rendered. —*Humphrey Prideaux* (1648—1724), *in "The Old and New Testament Connected," etc.*

Verse 2.—*"Willows."* The *Weeping Willow* of Babylon will grow to be a large tree ; its branches being long, slender, and pendulous, makes it proper to be planted upon the banks of rivers, ponds, and over springs ; the leaves, also, are long and narrow ; and when any mist or dew falls, a drop of water is seen hanging at their extremities, which, together with their hanging branches, cause a most lugubrious appearance. Lovers' garlands are said to have been made of a species of this willow, the branches of which are very slender and pliable ; and the plant itself has always been sought after for ornamental plantations, either to mix with others of the like growth in the largest quarters, or to be planted out singly over springs, or in large opens, for the peculiar variety occasioned by its mournful look.—*John Evelyn* (1620— 1706), *in "Silva ; or, A Discourse of Forest-Trees."*

Verse 2.—*"Willows."* It is a curious fact, that during the Commonwealth of England, when Cromwell, like a wise politician, allowed them to settle in London and to have synagogues, the Jews came hither in sufficient numbers to celebrate the feast of Tabernacles in booths, among the *Willows* on the borders of the Thames. The disturbance of their comfort from the innumerable spectators, chiefly London apprentices, called for some protection from the local magistrates. Not that any insult was offered to their persons, but a natural curiosity, excited by so new and extraordinary a spectacle, induced many to press too closely round their camp, and perhaps intrude upon their privacy.—*Maria Callcott* (1788–1842), *in "A Scripture Herbal,"* 1842.

Verse 2.—*"Willows."* There is a pretty story told about the way in which the

Weeping Willow was introduced into England.* Many years ago, the well-known poet, Alexander Pope, who resided at Twickenham, received a basket of figs as a present from Turkey. The basket was made of the supple branches of the Weeping Willow, the very same species under which the captive Jews sat when they wept by the waters of Babylon. *"We hanged our harps upon the willows."* The poet valued highly the small slender twigs as associated with so much that was interesting, and he untwisted the basket, and planted one of the branches on the ground. It had some tiny buds upon it, and he hoped he might be able to rear it, as none of this species of willow was known in England. Happily the willow is very quick to take root and grow. The little branch soon became a tree, and drooped gracefully over the river, in the same manner that its race had done over the waters of Babylon. From that one branch all the Weeping Willows in England are descended.—*Mary and Elizabeth Kirby, in "Chapters on Trees,"* 1873.

Verse 2.—*"In the midst thereof."* This is most naturally understood of the *city* of Babylon ; which was nearly as large as Middlesex, and had parks and gardens inside it.—*William Kay.*

Verse 3.—*"They that carried us away captive required of us a song"* ; or rather, as it should be rendered, *"the words* of a song." They see no inconsistency in a religion which freely mixes with the world. In their ignorance they only require *"the words* of a song"; its heavenly strain they have never caught. " They that *wasted us* required of us mirth." Remember, it is this worldly element which wasteth, or lays on heaps, whether so far as our own hearts or the church of God is concerned. But, true to his spiritual instincts, the child of God replies, " How shall we sing *Jehovah's* song in the land of a *stranger ?* " and then, so far from being utterly cast down or overcome, rises with fresh outburst of resolution and intenseness of new vigour, to utter the vows of verses 5 and 6. For, after having passed through such a spiritual conflict, we come forth, not wearied, but refreshed ; not weaker, but stronger. It is one of the seeming contradictions of the gospel, that the cure of weariness, and the relief of heavy-ladenness, lies in this—*to take the cross upon ourselves.* After the night-long conflict of Israel, " as he passed over Peniel, *the sun rose upon him,"* and that though " he halted upon his thigh."—*Alfred Edersheim.*

Verse 3.—*"Sing us one of the songs of Zion."* It is variously set down as simple curiosity to hear something of the famous melodies of the Hebrew people ; as well-meaning counsel to the exiles to reconcile themsleves to their inevitable situation, and to resume their former habits in social harmony with the inhabitants of the land ; or, most generally as a fresh aggravation of their misery, in requiring them to make sport for their new masters.—*Genebrardus, Chrysostom, and Cocceius, in Neale and Littledale.*

Verse 3.—*"Sing us one of the songs of Zion."* No music will serve the epicures in the prophet but temple music: Amos. vi. 5, " They invent to themselves instruments of music like David." As choice and excellent as David was in the service of the temple, so would they be in their private feasts. Belshazzar's draughts are not half so sweet in other vessels as in the utensils of the temple : Dan. v. 2, " He commanded to bring forth the golden and silver vessels that were taken out of the house of God." So the Babylonian humour is pleased with nothing so much as with " *one of the songs of Zion ;"* not an ordinary song, but " Sing us *one of your songs of Zion."* No jest relisheth with a profane spirit so well as when Scripture is abused, and made to lackey to their sportive jollity. Vain man thinketh he can never put honour enough upon his pleasures, and scorn enough upon God and holy things.—*Thomas Manton.*

Verse 3.—*"Sing us one of the songs of Zion."* The insulting nature of the demand will become the more conspicuous, if we consider, that the usual subjects of these songs were the omnipotence of Jehovah, and his love towards his chosen people.— *William Keatinge Clay,* 1839.

Verse 3.—The Babylonians asked them in derision for one of the songs of Zion. They loaded with ridicule their pure and venerable religion, and aggravated the sufferings of the weary and oppressed exiles by their mirth and their indecency. We are sorry to say that the resemblance still holds betwixt the Jews in a state of captivity and the Christians in the state of their pilgrimage. We have also

---

* The two preceding extracts would seem to prove that this story is not true ; at least Evelyn's willow is evidently the weeping willow, and would seem to have long been known.

to sustain the mockery of the profane and the unthinking. Ridicule and disdain are often the fate of sincere piety in this world. Fashion and frivolity and false philosophy have made a formidable combination against us ; and the same truth, the same honesty, the same integrity of principle, which in any other cause would be esteemed as manly and respectable, is despised and laughed at when attached to the cause of the gospel and its sublime interests.—*Thomas Chalmers.*

Verses 3, 4.—St. John Chrysostom observes the improvement such tribulation effected in the Jews, who previously derided, nay, even put to death, some of the prophets ; but now that they were captives in a foreign land, they would not attempt to expose their sacred hymns to the ridicule of the Gentiles.—*Robert Bellarmine.*

Verse 4.—"*How shall we sing the* LORD'S *song in a strange land ?*" Now, is it not true that, in many senses, we, like the Jewish exiles, have to sing the Lord's song in a strange land ? If not a land strange to *us,* then, all the more strange to *it*—a land foreign, so to say, and alien to the Lord's song. The very life which we live here in the body is a life of sight and sense. Naturally we walk by sight ; and to sing the Lord's song is possible only to faith. Faith is the soul's sight : faith is seeing the Invisible : this comes not of nature, and without this we cannot sing the Lord's song, because we are in a land strange to it.

Again, the feelings of the present life are often adverse to praise. The exiles in Babylon could not sing because they were in heaviness. God's hand was heavy upon them. He had a controversy with them for their sins. Now the feelings of many of us are in like manner adverse to the Lord's song. Some of us are in great sorrow. We have lost a friend ; we are in anxiety about one who is all to us ; we know not which way to turn for to-morrow's bread or for this day's comfort. How can we sing the Lord's song ?

And there is another kind of sorrow, still more fatal, if it be possible, to the lively exercise of adoration. And that is, a weight and burden of unforgiven sin. Songs may be heard from the prison-cell of Philippi ; songs may be heard from the calm death-bed, or by the open grave ; but songs cannot be drawn forth from the soul on which the load of God's displeasure, real or imagined, is lying, or which is still powerless to apprehend the grace and the life for sinners which is in Christ Jesus. That, we imagine, was *the* difficulty which pressed upon the exile Israelite ; that certainly is an impediment now, in many, to the outburst of Christian praise. And again, there is a land yet more strange and foreign to the Lord's song even than the land of unforgiven guilt—and that is the land of unforsaken sin.—*Condensed from C. J. Vaughan.*

Verse 4.—"*The Lord's song—in a strange land.*" It was the contrast, it was the incongruity which perplexed them. The captives in Babylon—that huge, unwieldy city, with its temple of the Chaldean Bel towering aloft on its eight stupendous stories to the height of a furlong into the sky—the Israelite exiles, bidden there to an idolatrous feast, that they might make sport for the company by singing to them one of the far-famed Hebrew melodies, for the gratification of curiosity or the amusement of the ear—how could it be done ? *The Lord's song*— one of those inspired compositions of Moses or David, in which the saintly soul of the king or the prophet poured itself forth in lowliest, loftiest adoration, before the one Divine Creator, Redeemer, and Sanctifier—how *could* it be sung, they ask, in a scene so incongruous ? The words would languish upon the tongue, the notes would refuse to sound upon the disused harp. Such Psalmody requires its accompaniment and its adaptation—if not actually in the Temple-courts of Zion, yet at least in the balmy gales of Palestine and the believing atmosphere of Israel.— *C. J. Vaughan, in "The Family Prayer and Sermon Book."*

Verse 4.—"*The Lord's song.*" These songs of old, to distinguish them from heathenish songs, were called God's songs, the Lord's songs ; because taught by him, learned of him, and commanded by him to be sung to his praise.—*John Bunyan.*

Verse 4.—Many were the sad thoughts which the remembrance of Zion would call up : the privileges they had there enjoyed ; the solemn feasts and happy meetings of their tribes to worship there before the Lord ; the Temple—" the beautiful house where their fathers had worshipped "—now laid waste.

But the one embittering thought that made them indeed heavy at heart, silenced their voices, and unstrung their harps, was the cause of this calamity—their sin. Paul and Silas could sing in a dungeon, but it was not their sin brought them there :

and so the saints suffering for the name of Christ could say, " we are exceeding joyful in all our tribulation." There is no real sorrow in any circumstances into which God brings us, or where he leads and goes with us ; but where sin is, and suffering is felt to be—not persecution, but—judgment, there is and can be no joy ; the soul refuses to be comforted. Israel cannot sing beside the waters of Babylon.— *William De Burgh.*

Verse 4.—There is a distinction between us and God's ancient people ; for at that time the worship of God was confined to one place ; but now he has his temple wherever two or three are met together in Christ's name, if they separate themselves from all idolatrous profession, and maintain purity of Divine worship.—*John Calvin.*

Verse 4.—It is one of the pathetic touches about the English captivity of King John II. of France, that once sitting as a guest to see a great tournament held in his honour, he looked on sorrowfully, and being urged by some of those about him to be cheerful and enjoy the splendid pageant, he answered with a mournful smile, *"How shall we sing the* LORD'S *song in a strange land ? "*—*Polydore Virgil,* —1555.

Verse 5.—*"If I forget thee, O Jerusalem."* Calvary, Mount of Olives, Siloam, how fragrant are ye with the Name that is above every name ! *"If I forget thee, O Jerusalem ! "* Can I forget where he walked so often, where he spake such gracious words, where he died ? Can I forget that his feet shall stand on that " Mount of Olives, which is before Jerusalem, on the east ? " Can I forget that there stood the Upper Room, and there fell the showers of Pentecost ?—*Andrew A. Bonar.*

Verse 5.—*"Let my right hand forget her cunning."* There is a striking and appropriate point in this, which has been overlooked. It is, that, as it is customary for people in the East to swear by their professions, so one who has no profession —who is poor and destitute, and has nothing of recognized value in the world— swears by his right hand, which is his sole stake in society, and by the *"cunning"* of which he earns his daily bread. Hence the common Arabic proverb (given by Burckhardt) reflecting on the change of demeanour produced by improved circumstances :—" He was wont to swear ' by the cutting off of his right hand ! ' He now swears ' by the giving of money to the poor.' " The words, " *her cunning,"* are supplied by the translators, in whose time *cunning* (from the Saxon *cannan,* Dutch *konnen,* " to know ") meant " skill ; " and a cunning man was what we should now call a skilful man. In the present case the skill indicated is doubtless that of playing on the harp, in which particular sense it occurs so late as Prior :—

> " When Pedro does the lute command,
> She guides the cunning artist's hand."

Modern translators substitute " skill ; " but perhaps a term still more general would be better—such as, " May my right hand lose its power."—*John Kitto, in "The Pictorial Bible."*

Verse 5.—*"Let my right hand forget."* Something must be supplied from the context . . . . the playing on the stringed instrument, verse 2, whether the right hand should be applied to the purpose or not, was the point in question. Then, the punishment also perfectly accords with the misdeed, as in Job xxxi. 22 : If I, misapplying my right hand to the playing of joyful strains on my instrument, forget thee, Jerusalem, let my right hand, as a punishment, forget the noble art ; and then also verse 6 fits admirably to what goes before : May my misemployed hand lose its capacity to play, and my tongue, misemployed in singing cheerful songs, its capacity to sing.—*E. W. Hengstenberg.*

Verse 6.—*"If I do not remember thee."* Either our beds are soft, or our hearts hard, that can rest when the church is at unrest, that feel not our brethren's hard cords through our soft beds.—*John Trapp.*

Verse 6.—*"If I prefer not Jerusalem above my chief joy."* Literally, *"if I advance not Jerusalem above the head of my joy."* If I set not Jerusalem as a diadem on the head of my rejoicing, and crown all my happiness with it.—*Christopher Wordsworth.*

Verse 7.—*"Remember, O* LORD, *the children of Edom,"* etc. The Jews were their brethren : Obad. 10 ; Amos i. 11. They were their neighbours, Idumea and Judea bordered upon one another : Mark iii. 8. They were confederates with the Jews (Jer. xxvii. 3 : an Edomitish ambassador was at Jerusalem), who, together with the ambassadors of the other kings there mentioned, were strengthening themselves with Zedekiah against Nebuchadnezzar; see Obad. 7. For them, therefore, to revenge themselves for former wrongs done them upon the Jews, and that in the day of their calamity, this made their sin exceeding sinful.—*William Greenhill*, 1591—1677.

Verse 7.—*"Remember, O Lord, the children of Edom,"* etc. Of all kinds of evil speaking against our brother, this sin of Edom, to sharpen an enemy against our brother in the day of his sorrow and distress, this opening of the mouth wide against him, to insult over him in his calamity, is most barbarous and unchristian. . . . Observe how the cruelty of the Edomites is aggravated by the time; the wofullest time that ever Jerusalem had, called therefore *"the day of Jerusalem."* When all things conspired to make their sorrow full, then, in the anguish and fit of their mortal disease, then did Edom arm his eye, his tongue, his heart, his hand, and join all those with the enemy against his brother. Learn, that God taketh notice not only *what* we do against another, but *when;* for he will set these things in order before us; for the God of mercy cannot abide cruelty.—*Edward Marbury*, 1649.

Verse 7.—*"Remember, O Lord, the children of Edom."* Edom shall be remembered for the mischievous counsel he gave; and the daughter of Babylon shall be for ever razed out of memory for razing Jerusalem to the ground. And let all the secret and open enemies of God's church take heed how they employ their tongues and hands against God's secret ones: they that presume to do either may here read their fatal doom written in the *dust* of Edom, and in the *ashes* of Babylon.—*Daniel Featley* (1582—1645), *in "Clavis Mystica."*

Verse 7.—In Herod, the Idumean, Edom's hatred found its concentrated expression. *His* attempt was to destroy him whom God had laid in Zion as the " sure foundation."—*William Kay.*

Verse 7.—It may be observed that the Jews afterward acted the same part toward the Christian church which the Edomites had acted toward them, encouraging and stirring up the Gentiles to persecute and destroy it from off the face of the earth. And God " remembered " them for the Christians' sakes, as they prayed him to " remember Edom " for their sakes. Learn we hence, what a crime it is, for Christians to assist the common enemy, or call in the common enemy to assist them, against their brethren.—*George Horne.*

Verse 7.—We are not to regard the imprecations of this Psalm in any other light than as prophetical. They are grounded on the many prophecies which had already gone forth on the subject of the destruction of Babylon, if, as we may admit, the Psalm before us was written after the desolation of Jerusalem. But these prophecies have not yet been fulfilled in every particular, and remain to be accomplished in mystic Babylon, when the dominion of Antichrist shall be for ever swept away, and the true church introduced into the glorious liberty of the sons of God, at the appearing of their Lord and Saviour Jesus Christ in his own kingdom.—*William Wilson.*

Veres 7.—Edom's hatred was the hatred with which the carnal mind in its natural enmity against God always regards whatever is the elect object of his favour. Jerusalem was the city of God. " Rase it, rase it even to the ground," is the mischievous desire of every unregenerate mind against every building that rests on the elect Stone of Divine foundation. For God's election never pleases man until, through grace, his own heart has become an adoring receiver of that mercy which while in his natural state he angrily resented and refused to own in its effects on other men. From Cain to Antichrist this solemn truth holds always good.—*Arthur Pridham.*

Verse 7—9.—I do not know if the same feeling has occurred to others, but I have often wished the latter verses of this Psalm had been disjoined from this sweet and touching beginning. It sounds as if one of the strings on their well-tuned harps was out of melody, as if it struck a jarring note of discord. And yet I know the feeling is wrong, for it is no more than what the Lord himself had foretold and declared should be the final desolation of proud Babylon itself : yet one longs more intensely for the period when the nations of the earth shall learn war no more; and every harp and every voice, even those of the martyred ones beneath God's altar loudest and sweetest of all, shall sing the Lord's songs, the song of Moses, and the Lamb, in that pleasant land, where no sighing and no tears are seen.—*Barton Bouchier.*

Verse 8.—"O daughter of Babylon, who art to be destroyed." In the beginning of the fifth year of Darius happened the revolt of the Babylonians which cost him the trouble of a tedious siege again to reduce them . . . . he besieged the city with all his forces . . . . As soon as the Babylonians saw themselves begirt by such an army as they could not cope with in the field, they turned their thoughts wholly to the supporting of themselves in the siege ; in order whereto they took a resolution, the most desperate and barbarous that ever any nation practised. For to make their provisions last the longer, they agreed to cut off all unnecessary mouths among them, and therefore drawing together all the women and children, they strangled them all, whether wives, sisters, daughters, or young children useless for the wars, excepting only that every man was allowed to save one of his wives, which he best loved, and a maid-servant to do the work of the house.—*Humphrey Prideaux.*

Verse 8.—"Who art to be destroyed." הַשְּׁדוּדָה has been explained in a variety of ways. Seventy: ἡ ταλαίπωρος ; Vulg. *misera :* others, *destroyer, powerful, violent,* or *fierce.* Perhaps it best suits the context to regard it as expressing what is already accomplished : it is so certain, in the view of the Psalmist, that the ruin will come, that he uses the past participle, as if the work were now completed. " O daughter of Babylon, the destroyed ! "—*"Bibliotheca Sacra and Theological Review."*

*Verse 8.—*He that sows evil shall reap evil ; he that soweth the evil of sin, shall reap the evil of punishment. So Eliphaz told Job that he had seen (Job iv. 8), " they that plough iniquity, and sow wickedness, reap the same." And that either in kind or quality, proportion or quantity. In kind, the very same that he did to others shall be done to him ; or in proportion, a measure answerable to it. So he shall reap what he hath sown, in quality or in quantity ; either in portion the same, or in proportion the like. The prophet cursing Edom and Babel saith thus, " O daughter of Zion, happy shall he be that rewardeth thee as thou hast served us." The original is, " that recompenseth to thee thy deed which thou didst to us." . . . Thus is wickedness recompensed *suo genere,* in its own kind. So often the transgressor is against the transgressor, the thief robs the thief, *proditoris proditor ;* as in Rome many unchristened emperors, and many christened popes, by blood and treason got the sovereignty, and by blood and treason lost it. Evil men drink of their own brewing, are scourged with their own rod, drowned in the pit which they digged for others, as Haman was hanged on his own gallows, Perillus tormented in his own engine !—*Thomas Adams.*

*Verses 8, 9.—*The subject of these two verses is the same with that of many chapters in Isaiah and Jeremiah ; namely, the vengeance of heaven executed upon Babylon by Cyrus, raised up to be king of the Medes and Persians, united under him for that purpose. The meaning of the words, *"Happy shall he be,"* is, He shall go on and prosper, for the Lord of hosts shall go with him, and fight his battles against the enemy and oppressor of his people, empowering him to recompense upon the Chaldeans the works of their hands, and to reward them as they served Israel.—*George Horne.*

*Verses 8, 9.—*It needs no record to tell us that, in the siege and carrying away of Jerusalem, great atrocities were committed by the conquerors. We may be quite sure that

> " Many a childing mother then
> And new-born baby died."

for the wars of the old world were always attended by such barbarous cruelties. The apostrophe of verses 8, 9, consequently merely proclaims the certainty of a just retribution—of the same retribution that the prophets had foretold (Isa. xiii. 16 ; xlvii. ; Jer. l. ; compare, " who art to be destroyed, verse 8), and the happiness of those who should be its ministers ; who should mete out to her what she had measured to the conquered Jew. It was the decree of Heaven that their " children " should " be dashed to pieces before their eyes." The Psalmist simply recognizes the decree as just and salutary ; he pronounces the terrible vengeance to have been deserved. To charge him with vindictiveness, therefore, is to impugn the justice and mercy of the Most High. And there is nothing to sustain the charge, for his words are simply a prediction, like that of the prophet, " As thou hast done, it shall be done unto thee : thy reward shall return upon thine own head : " Obad. 15. —*Joseph Hammond, in "The Expositor,"* 1876.

Verse 9.—*"Happy shall he be that taketh,"* etc. That is, so oppressive hast thou been to all under thy domination, as to become universally hated and detested; so that those who may have the last hand in thy destruction, and the total extermination of thy inhabitants, shall be reputed *"happy"*—shall be *celebrated* and *extolled* as those who have rid the world of a curse so grievous. These prophetic declarations contain no excitement to any person or persons to commit acts of cruelty and barbarity; but are simply *declarative* of what would take place in the order of the retributive providence and justice of God, and the general opinion that should in consequence be expressed on the subject; therefore *praying for the destruction of our enemies* is totally out of the question.—*Adam Clarke.*

Verse 9.—*"Happy shall he be,"* etc. With all possible might and speed oppose the very first risings and movings of the heart to sin; for these are the buds that produce the bitter fruit; and if sin be not nipped in the very bud, it is not imaginable how quickly it will shoot forth. . . . Now these sins, though they may seem small in themselves, yet are exceedingly pernicious in their effects. These little foxes destroy the grapes as much or more than the greater, and therefore are to be diligently sought out, hunted, and killed by us, if we would keep our hearts fruitful. We should deal with these first streamings out of sin as the Psalmist would have the people of God deal with the brats of Babylon: *"Happy shall he be, that taketh and dasheth thy little ones against the stones."* And without doubt most happy and successful will that man prove in his spiritual welfare, who puts on no bowels of pity even to his infant corruptions, but slays the small as well as the great; and so not only conquers his enemies by opposing their present force, but also by extinguishing their future race. The smallest children, if they live, will be grown men; and the first motions of sin, if they are let alone, will spread into great, open, and audacious presumptions.—*Robert South,* 1633—1716.

Verse 9.—*"Against the stones."* That סֶלַע signifies *a rock,* is undubitable, from the concurrent testimony of all the best Hebrew lexicographers Hence it follows, because there is no rock, nor mountain, nor hill, either in the city or in the province of ancient Babylonia, that the locality, against which the malediction of this Psalm is hurled, cannot be the metropolis of the ancient Assyrian empire, but must be apocalyptic Babylon, or Papal Rome, built upon seven hills, one of which is the celebrated Tarpeian Rock. But the eighth verse emphatically declares that the retributive justice of God will visit upon apocalyptic Babylon, the same infliction which Assyrian Babylon, and also Pagan Rome, inflicted upon Jerusalem. As therefore Nebuchadnezzar as well as Titus "burnt the house of the Lord, and the king's house, and all the houses of Jerusalem, and every great man's house burnt he with fire" (2 Kings xxv. 9) so "the ten horns shall hate the whore, and shall make her desolate and naked, and shall eat her flesh, and burn her with fire; and she shall be utterly burned with fire" (Rev. xvii. 16; xviii. 8). When the Canaanites had filled up the measure of their iniquity, Israel received a divine commission to exterminate the guilty nation. When Papal Rome shall have filled up the measure of her iniquity, then "a mighty angel will take up a stone, like a great millstone, and will cast it into the sea, saying, Thus with violence shall that great city Babylon be thrown down": "For her sins have reached unto heaven, and God hath remembered her iniquities. Reward her even as she rewarded you, and double unto her double according to her works: in the cup which she hath filled fill to her double" (Rev. xviii. 5, 6). Then shall issue the divine proclamation: "Rejoice over her, thou heaven, and ye holy apostles and prophets; for God hath avenged you on her" (Rev. xviii. 20).—*John Noble Coleman, in "The Book of Psalms, with Notes,"* 1863.

Verse 9.—*"He that taketh and dasheth thy little ones against the stones."*

> My heroes slain, my bridal bed o'erturned,
> My daughters ravish'd, and my city burn'd,
> My bleeding infants dash'd against the floor;
> These have I yet to see, perhaps yet more.

Homer's Iliad, Pope's Translation, Book xxii. 89—91.

HINTS TO PREACHERS.

Verse 1.—I. A duty once the source of joy : " remember Zion." II. Circumstances which make the remembrances sorrowful. III. Peculiar persons who feel this joy or sorrow : " we."

Verse 1.—I. Zion forsaken in prosperity. Its services neglected ; its priests demoralized ; the worship of Baal and of Ashtaroth preferred to the worship of the true God. II. Zion remembered in adversity. In Babylon more than in Jerusalem ; on the banks of the Euphrates more than on the banks of Jordan ; with tears when they might have remembered it with joy. " I spake unto thee in thy prosperity, and thou saidst, I will not hear." " Lord, in trouble they have visited thee. They poured out a prayer when thy chastening was upon them."— G. R.

Verse 2.—I. Harps—or capacities for praise. II. Harps on willows, or song suspended. III. Harps retuned, or joys to come.

Verse 2.—I. A confession of joy being turned into sorrow : " we hanged," etc. The moaning of their harps upon weeping willows better harmonized with their feelings than any tunes which they had been accustomed to play. II. A hope of sorrow being turned into joy. They took their harps with them into captivity, and hung them up for future use.—G. R.

Verse 2.—"*We hanged our harps*," etc. I. In remembrance of lost joys. Their harps were associated with a glorious past. They could not afford to forget that past. They kept up the good old custom. There are always means of remembrance at hand. II. In manifestation of present sorrow. They could not play on account of, 1. Their sinfulness. 2. Their circumstances. 3. Their home. III. In anticipation of future blessing. They did not dash their harps to pieces. Term of exile limited. Return expressly foretold. We shall want our harps in the good times coming. Sinners play their harps now, but must soon lay them aside for ever.— W. J.

Verse 3 (*last clause*).—Taken away from the text this is a very pleasant and praiseworthy request. Why do we wish for such a song ? 1. It is sure to be pure. 2. It will certainly be elevating. 3. It will probably be gladsome. 4. It will comfort and enliven us. 5. It will help to express our gratitude.

Verses 3, 4.—I. The cruel demand. 1. A song when we are captives. 2. A song to please our adversaries. 3. A holy song for unholy purposes. II. The motive for it. Sometimes mere ridicule ; at others, mistaken kindness seeking by sharpness to arouse us from despondency ; often mere levity. III. The answer to it, " How can ? " etc.

Verses 3, 4.—I. When God calls for joy we ought not to sorrow. The songs of Zion should be sung in Zion. II. When God calls for sorrow we ought not to rejoice. " How shall we sing ? " etc. See Is. v. 12.—G. R.

Verses 3, 4.—I. The unreasonable request : " Sing us one of the songs of Zion." This was—1. A striking testimony to the joyful character of Jehovah's worship. Even the heathen had heard of " the songs of Zion." 2. A severe trial of the fidelity of captive Israel. It might have been to their present advantage to have complied with the request. 3. A cruel taunt of the sad and desponding condition of the captives. II. The indignant refusal. " How shall we sing the Lord's song in a strange land ? " There is no singing this song by true Israelites—1. When the heart is out of tune, as it must necessarily be when in " a strange land." 2. In uncongenial society—amongst unsympathetic strangers. 3. For unsanctified purposes—to make mirth for the heathen. Many so-called sacred concerts pain devout Christians as much as the demand to sing the Lord's song did the devout Israelites. The Lord's song must be sung only " to the Lord;"—W. H. J. P.

Verses 3, 4.—The burlesque of holy things. I. The servants of God are in an unsympathetic world. II. The demand to be amused and entertained. Temple songs to pass an idle hour ! Such the popular demand to-day. Men would have us burlesque religion to tickle them. III. The justly indignant reply of all true men, " How shall we ? " Christian workers have more serious if less popular business on hand.—W. B. H.

Verse 5.—The person who remembers ; the thing remembered ; the solemn imprecation.

Verse 5.—No harp but for Jesus.
I. The harp consecrated.   At conversion.

> " One sword, at least, thy rights shall guard,
>   One faithful harp shall praise thee."

II. The harp silent :

> " Thy songs were made for the brave and free,
>   They shall never sound in slavery."

III. The harp re-strung above :

> " And I heard the voice of harpers
>   Harping with their harps."

W. B. H.

Verses 5, 6.—I. To rejoice with the world is to forget the church.   II. To love the church we must prefer her above everything.   III. To serve the church we must be prepared to suffer anything.

Verse 7.—The hatred of the ungodly to true religion.   I. Its cause.   II. Its extent.   "Rase it," etc.   III. Its season for display : " in the day of Jerusalem "—trouble, etc.   IV. Its reward : " Remember, O Lord."

PSALM CXXXVIII.

TITLE.—A Psalm of David. *This Psalm is wisely placed. Whoever edited and arranged these sacred poems, he had an eye to apposition and contrast; for if in Ps. cxxxvii. we see the need of silence before revilers, here we see the excellence of a brave confession. There is a time to be silent, lest we cast pearls before swine; and there is a time to speak openly, lest we be found guilty of cowardly non-confession. The Psalm is evidently of a Davidic character, exhibiting all the fidelity, courage, and decision of that King of Israel and Prince of Psalmists. Of course the critics have tried to rend the authorship from David on account of the mention of the temple, though it so happens that in one of the Psalms which is allowed to be David's the same word occurs. Many modern critics are to the word of God what blow-flies are to the food of men: they cannot do any good, and unless relentlessly driven away they do great harm.*

DIVISION.—*In full confidence David is prepared to own his God before the gods of the heathen, or before angels or rulers (1—3); he declares that he will instruct and convert kings and nations, till on every highway men shall sing the praises of the Lord (4 and 5). Having thus spoken, he utters his personal confidence in Jehovah, who will help his lowly servant, and preserve him from all the malice of wrathful foes.*

EXPOSITION.

I WILL praise thee with my whole heart: before the gods will I sing praise unto thee.

2 I will worship toward thy holy temple, and praise thy name for thy lovingkindness and for thy truth: for thou hast magnified thy word above all thy name.

3 In the day when I cried thou answeredst me, *and* strengthenedst me *with* strength in my soul.

1. *"I will praise thee with my whole heart."* His mind is so taken up with God that he does not mention his name: to him there is no other God, and Jehovah is so perfectly realized and so intimately known, that the Psalmist, in addressing him, no more thinks of mentioning his name than we should do if we were speaking to a father or a friend. He sees God with his mind's eye, and simply addresses him with the pronoun "thee." He is resolved to praise the Lord, and to do it with the whole force of his life, even with his whole heart. He would not submit to act as one under restraint, because of the opinions of others; but in the presence of the opponents of the living God he would be as hearty in worship as if all were friends and would cheerfully unite with him. If others do not praise the Lord, there is all the more reason why we should do so, and should do so with enthusiastic eagerness. We need a broken heart to mourn our own sins, but a whole heart to praise the Lord's perfections. If ever our heart is whole and wholly occupied with one thing, it should be when we are praising the Lord. *"Before the gods will I sing praise unto thee."* Why should these idols rob Jehovah of his praises? The Psalmist will not for a moment suspend his songs because there are images before him, and their foolish worshippers might not approve of his music. I believe David referred to the false gods of the neighbouring nations, and the deities of the surviving Canaanites. He was not pleased that such gods were set up; but he intended to express at once his contempt of *them,* and his own absorption in the worship of the living Jehovah by continuing most earnestly to sing wherever he might be. It would be paying these dead idols too much respect to cease singing because they were perched aloft. In these days when new religions are daily excogitated, and

new gods are set up, it is well to know how to act. Bitterness is forbidden, and controversy is apt to advertise the heresy ; the very best method is to go on personally worshipping the Lord with unvarying zeal, singing with heart and voice his royal praises. Do they deny the Divinity of our Lord ? Let us the more fervently adore him. Do they despise the atonement ? Let us the more constantly proclaim it. Had half the time spent in councils and controversies been given to praising the Lord, the church would have been far sounder and stronger than she is at this day. The Hallelujah Legion will win the day. Praising and singing are our armour against the idolatries of heresy, our comfort under the depression caused by insolent attacks upon the truth, and our weapons for defending the gospel. Faith when displayed in cheerful courage, has about it a sacred contagion : others learn to believe in the Most High when they see his servant

> " Calm 'mid the bewildering cry,
> Confident of victory."

2. "*I will worship toward thy holy temple*," or the place of God's dwelling, where the ark abode. He would worship God in God's own way. The Lord had ordained a centre of unity, a place of sacrifice, a house of his indwelling; and David accepted the way of worship enjoined by revelation. Even so, the true-hearted believer of these days must not fall into the will-worship of superstition, or the wild worship of scepticism, but reverently worship as the Lord himself prescribes. The idol gods had their temples ; but David averts his glance from them, and looks earnestly to the spot chosen of the Lord for his own sanctuary. We are not only to adore the true God, but to do so in his own appointed way : the Jew looked to the temple, we are to look to Jesus, the living temple of the Godhead. "*And praise thy name for thy lovingkindness and for thy truth.*" Praise would be the main part of David's worship ; the name or character of God the great object of his song ; and the special point of his praise the grace and truth which shone so conspicuously in that name. The person of Jesus is the temple of the Godhead, and therein we behold the glory of the Father, " full of grace and truth." It is upon these two points that the name of Jehovah is at this time assailed—his grace and his truth. He is said to be too stern, too terrible, and therefore " modern thought " displaces the God of Abraham, Isaac, and Jacob, and sets up an effeminate deity of its own making. As for us, we firmly believe that God is love, and that in the summing up of all things it will be seen that hell itself is not inconsistent with the beneficence of Jehovah, but is, indeed, a necessary part of his moral government now that sin has intruded into the universe. True believers hear the thunders of his justice, and yet they do not doubt his lovingkindness. Especially do we delight in God's great love to his own elect, such as he showed to Israel as a race, and more especially to David and his seed when he entered into covenant with him. Concerning this there is abundant room for praise. But not only do men attack the lovingkindness of God, but the truth of God is at this time assailed on all sides ; some doubt the truth of the inspired record as to its histories, others challenge the doctrines, many sneer at the prophecies ; in fact, the infallible word of the Lord is at this time treated as if it were the writing of imposters, and only worthy to be carped at. The swine are trampling on the pearls at this time, and nothing restrains them ; nevertheless, the pearls are pearls still, and shall yet shine about our Monarch's brow. We sing the lovingkindness and truth of the God of the Old Testament,—" the God of the whole earth shall he be called." David before the false gods first sang, then worshipped, and then proclaimed the grace and truth of Jehovah ; let us do the same before the idols of the New Theology.

"*For thou hast magnified thy word above all thy name.*" The word of promise made to David was in his eyes more glorious than all else that he had seen of the Most High. Revelation excels creation in the clearness, definiteness, and fulness of its teaching. The name of the Lord in nature is not so easily read as in the Scriptures, which are a revelation in human language, specially adapted to the human mind, treating of human need, and of a Saviour who appeared in human nature to redeem humanity. Heaven and earth shall pass away, but the divine word will not pass away, and in this respect especially it has a pre-eminence over every other form of manifestation. Moreover, the Lord lays all the rest of his name under tribute to his word : his wisdom, power, love, and all his other attributes combine to carry out his word. It is his word which creates, sustains, quickens, enlightens, and comforts. As a word of command it is supreme ; and in the person of the incarnate Word it is set above all the works of God's hands. The sentence in the text is wonderfully full of meaning. We have collected a vast mass of literature upon it, but space will not allow us to put it all into our notes. Let us adore the Lord who has spoken to us by his word, and by his Son ; and in the presence of unbelievers let us both praise his holy name and extol his holy word.

3. *"In the day when I cried thou answeredst me."* No proof is so convincing as that of experience. No man doubts the power of prayer after he has received an answer of peace to his supplication. It is the distinguishing mark of the true and living God that he hears the pleadings of his people, and answers them ; the gods hear not and answer not, but Jehovah's memorial is—"the God that heareth prayer." There was some special day in which David cried more vehemently than usual ; he was weak, wounded, worried, and his heart was wearied ; then like a child he "cried,"—cried unto his Father. It was a bitter, earnest, eager prayer, as natural and as plaintive as the cry of a babe. The Lord answered it ; but what answer can there be to a cry ?—to a mere inarticulate wail of grief ? Our heavenly Father is able to interpret tears, and cries, and he replies to their inner sense in such a way as fully meets the case. The answer came in the same day as the cry ascended : so speedily does prayer rise to heaven, so quickly does mercy return to earth. The statement of this sentence is one which all believers can make, and as they can substantiate it with many facts, they ought boldly to publish it, for it is greatly to God's glory. Well might the Psalmist say, " I will worship " when he felt bound to say " thou answeredst me." Well might he glory before the idols and their worshippers when he had answers to prayer to look back upon. This also is our defence against modern heresies : we cannot forsake the Lord, for he has heard our prayers.

"And strengthenedst me with strength in my soul." This was a true answer to his prayer. If the burden was not removed, yet strength was given wherewith to bear it, and this is an equally effective method of help. It may not be best for us that the trial should come to an end ; it may be far more to our advantage that by its pressure we should learn patience. Sweet are the uses of adversity, and our prudent Father in heaven will not deprive us of those benefits. Strength imparted to the soul is an inestimable boon ; it means courage, fortitude, assurance, heroism. By his word and Spirit the Lord can make the trembler brave, the sick whole, the weary bright. This soul-might will continue : the man having been strengthened for one emergency remains vigorous for life, and is prepared for all future labours and sufferings ; unless, indeed, he throw away his force by unbelief, or pride, or some other sin. When God strengthens, none can weaken. Then is our soul strong indeed when the Lord infuses might into us.

4 All the kings of the earth shall praise thee, O LORD, when they hear the words of thy mouth.

5 Yea, they shall sing in the ways of the LORD : for great *is* the glory of the LORD.

4. *"All the kings of the earth shall praise thee, O LORD, when they hear the words of thy mouth."* Kings have usually small care to hear the word of the Lord ; but King David feels assured that if they do hear it they will feel its power. A little piety goes a long way in courts ; but brighter days are coming, in which rulers will become hearers and worshippers : may the advent of such happy times be hastened. What an assembly !—" all the kings of the earth ! " What a purpose ! Gathered to hear the words of Jehovah's mouth. What a preacher ! David himself rehearses the words of Jehovah. What praise ! when they all in happy union lift up their songs unto the Lord. Kings are as gods below, and they do well when they worship the God above. The way of conversion for kings is the same as for ourselves : faith to them also cometh by hearing, and hearing by the word of God. Happy are those who can cause the word of the Lord to penetrate palaces ; for the occupants of thrones are usually the last to know the joyful sounds of the gospel. David, the king, cared for kings' souls, and it will be wise for each man to look first after those who are of his own order. He went to his work of testimony with full assurance of success : he meant to speak only the words of Jehovah's mouth, and he felt sure that the kings would hear and praise Jehovah.

5. *"Yea, they shall sing in the ways of the LORD."* Here is a double wonder— kings in God's ways, and kings singing there. Let a man once know the ways of

Jehovah, and he will find therein abundant reason for song ; but the difficulty is to bring the great ones of the earth into ways so little attractive to the carnal mind. Perhaps when the Lord sends us a King David to preach, we shall yet see monarchs converted and hear their voices raised in devout adoration. *"For great is the glory of the Lord."* This glory shall overshadow all the greatness and glory of all kings : they shall be stirred by a sight of it to obey and adore. O that Jehovah's glory were revealed even now ! O that the blind eyes of men could once behold it, then their hearts would be subdued to joyful reverence. David, under a sense of Jehovah's glory, exclaimed, " I will sing " (verse 1), and here he represents the kings as doing the same thing.

6 Though the Lord *be* high, yet hath he respect unto the lowly : but the proud he knoweth afar off.

7 Though I walk in the midst of trouble, thou wilt revive me : thou shalt stretch forth thine hand against the wrath of mine enemies, and thy right hand shall save me.

8 The Lord will perfect *that which* concerneth me : thy mercy, O Lord, *endureth* for ever : forsake not the works of thine own hands.

6. *"Though the Lord be high."* In greatness, dignity, and power, Jehovah is higher than the highest. His nature is high above the comprehension of his creatures, and his glory even exceeds the loftiest soarings of imagination. *"Yet hath he respect unto the lowly."* He views them with pleasure, thinks of them with care, listens to their prayers, and protects them from evil. Because they think little of themselves he thinks much of them. They reverence him, and he respects them. They are low in their own esteem, and he makes them high in his esteem. *"But the proud he knoweth afar off."* He does not need to come near them in order to discover their utter vanity : a glance from afar reveals to him their emptiness and offensiveness. He has no fellowship with them, but views them from a distance ; he is not deceived, but knows the truth about them, despite their blustering ; he has no respect unto them, but utterly abhors them. To a Cain's sacrifice, a Pharaoh's promise, a Rabshakeh's threat, and a Pharisee's prayer, the Lord has no respect. Nebuchadnezzar, when far off from God, cried, " Behold this great Babylon which I have builded ; " but the Lord knew him, and sent him grazing with cattle. Proud men boast loudly of their culture and " the freedom of thought," and even dare to criticize their Maker : but he knows them from afar, and will keep them at arm's length in this life, and shut them up in hell in the next.

7. *"Though I walk in the midst of trouble, thou wilt revive me."* If I am walking there now, or shall be doing so in years to come, I have no cause for fear ; for God is with me, and will give me new life. When we are somewhat in trouble it is bad enough, but it is worse to penetrate into the centre of that dark continent and traverse its midst : yet in such a case the believer makes progress, for he walks ; he keeps to a quiet pace, for he does no more than walk ; and he is not without the best of company, for his God is near to pour fresh life into him. It is a happy circumstance that, if God be away at any other time, yet he is pledged to be with us in trying hours : " when thou passest through the rivers I will be with thee." He is in a blessed condition who can confidently use the language of David,—" thou wilt revive me." He shall not make his boast of God in vain : he shall be kept alive, and made more alive than ever. How often has the Lord quickened us by our sorrows ! Are they not his readiest means of exciting to fulness of energy the holy life which dwells within us ? If we receive reviving, we need not regret affliction. When God revives us, trouble will never harm us. *"Thou shalt stretch forth thine hand against the wrath of mine enemies, and thy right hand shall save me."* This is the fact which would revive fainting David. Our foes fall when the Lord comes to deal with them ; he makes short work of the enemies of his people,—with one hand he routs them. His wrath soon quenches their wrath ; his hand stays their hand. Adversaries may be many, and malicious, and mighty ; but our glorious Defender has only to stretch out his arm and their armies vanish. The sweet singer rehearses his assurance of salvation, and sings of it in the ears of the Lord, addressing him with this confident language. He will be saved,—saved dexterously, decidedly, divinely ; he has no doubt about it. God's right hand cannot forget its cunning ; Jerusalem is his chief joy, and he will defend his own elect.

8. *"The LORD will perfect that which concerneth me."*   All my interests are safe in Jehovah's hands.

> " The work which his goodness began,
> The arm of his strength will complete ;
> His promise is yea and Amen,
> And never was forfeited yet."

God is concerned in all that concerns his servants.   He will see to it that none of their precious things shall fail of completion ; their life, their strength, their hopes, their graces, their pilgrimage, shall each and all be perfected.   Jehovah himself will see to this ; and therefore it is most sure.   *"Thy mercy, O LORD, endureth for ever."* The refrain of the former Psalm is in his ears, and he repeats it as his own personal conviction and consolation.   The first clause of the verse is the assurance of faith, and this second one reaches to the full assurance of understanding.   God's work in us will abide unto perfection because God's mercy towards us thus abideth. *"Forsake not the works of thine own hands."*   Our confidence does not cause us to live without prayer, but encourages us to pray all the more.   Since we have it written upon our hearts that God will perfect his work in us, and we see it also written in Scripture that his mercy changeth not, we with holy earnestness entreat that we may not be forsaken.   If there be anything good in us, it is the work of God's own hands : will he leave it ?   Why has he wrought so much in us if he means to give us up ?—it will be a sheer waste of effort.   He who has gone so far will surely persevere with us to the end.   Our hope for the final perseverance of the believer lies in the final perseverance of the believer's God.   If the Lord begins to build, and does not finish, it will not be to his honour.   He will have a desire to the work of his hands, for he knows what it has cost him already, and he will not throw away a vessel upon which he has expended so much of labour and skill.   Therefore do we praise him with our whole heart, even in the presence of those who depart from his Holy Word, and set up another God and another gospel ; which are not another, but there be some that trouble us.

EXPLANATORY NOTES AND QUAINT SAYINGS.

Psalms cxxxviii.—cxlv.—These eight Psalms are composed in the *first* person, and they follow very happily after the fifteen " Songs of Up-goings," and the three Psalms of praise uttered by the chorus of those who have *gone up* to Sion.   Those Psalms were the united utterances of national devotion.   These eight Psalms are the devout Israelite's Manual of *private* prayer and praise.—*Christopher Wordsworth.*

Whole Psalm.—This is the first of a series of eight Psalms (cxxxviii.—cxlv.), probably the last composed by David, a kind of commentary on the great Messianic promise in 2 Sam. vii.   They are found in this part of the Psalter, in consequence of having been made the basis, or rather the body, of a system or series (cxxxv.— cxlvi.) by a later writer.—*Joseph Addison Alexander.*

Whole Psalm.—If this Psalm refers to the promise in 2 Sam. vii., there can be no doubt of the correctness of the superscription, which ascribes it to David.   For he, on whom the promise has been conferred, himself stands forth as the speaker. Proof also of David's authorship is found in the union, so characteristic of him, of bold courage, see especially verse 3, and deep humility, see verse 6.   And in proof of the same comes, finally, the near relationship in which it stands with the other Psalms of David, especially those which likewise refer to the promise of the everlasting kingdom ; and with David's thanksgiving in 2 Sam. vii., the conclusion of which remarkably agrees with the conclusion of our Psalm : " And now, Lord God, the word which thou hast spoken upon thy servant and upon his house, that fulfil even to eternity, and do as thou hast spoken."—*E. W. Hengstenberg.*

Verse 1.—*"I* will praise *thee with my whole heart."*   It is a part of our thankfulness to engage our heart to praise God in time to come, since we find that all the thanks we can give for the present are short of our duty or desire to praise him : *"I will praise thee,"* saith David.   Sometimes the believer will find his heart set at liberty in God's worship, which at another time he will find to be in bands, and then he should take the opportunity of an enlarged heart to run in the way of God's service, as David doth here : *"I will praise thee with my whole heart."*—*David Dickson.*

Verse 1.—*"I will praise thee."* Up, dear soul ! What though thou hast once complained like Israel of thy captivity in Babylon, Ps. cxxxvii. 1, yet now sing once more a song of joy to the Lord. Thou hast been pressed like a cluster of grapes, now give forth thy ripe juice.—*Christoph Starke.*

Verse 1.—*"I will praise thee."* Alas, for that capital crime of the Lord's people— barrenness in praises ! Oh, how fully I am persuaded that a line of praises is worth a leaf of prayer, and an hour of praises is worth a day of fasting and mourning !— *John Livingstone,* 1603—1672.

Verse 1.—*"With my whole heart."* This expression, as in Ps. ix. 1, points to the surpassing greatness of the benefit received, which filled the whole heart with thankfulness, and did not proceed, as it were, from some particular corner of it. It corresponds also to the greatness of the benefaction, in the expression, *"before the gods,"*—demanding of these, whether they would verify their godhead by pointing to any such boon conferred by them on their servants. The benefit which could afford such a demonstration, and give occasion and ground for raillery, must have been a surpassingly great one.—*E. W. Hengstenberg.*

Verse 1.—*"Before the gods."* There is much diversity in the meaning assigned to *"gods"* in this verse. It may mean literally in an idolatrous country, in the very temples of false gods, as so many Christian martyrs bore testimony to the faith. The LXX., Vulgate, Ethiopic, and Arabic translate *angels.* The Chaldee has *judges,* the Syriac *kings,* and the earlier Greek fathers explain it as a reference to the choirs of *Priests and Levites* in the Temple.—*Zigabenus, in Neale and Littledale.*

Verse 1.—*"Before the gods."* Some (LXX., Luther, Calvin, etc.) interpret these words of the angels, and compare Ps. xxix. 1 ; but it is doubtful if the Hebrew word Elohim, used nakedly and without any explanation, can have this meaning : it is also, as it would seem, in this connection, pointless : others (Rabbins, Flamin., Delitzsch, etc.) interpret " the great ones of the earth," and compare verse 4 below, and Pss. lxxxii. 1, cxix. 46, etc. ; but this interpretation, too, seems to give no special force to the passage. Probably (Aq., Symm., Jer., etc.) the meaning is, " Before, or in the presence of, the gods of the heathen, *i.e.,* in scorn of, in sight of, the idols, who can do nothing, I will praise Jehovah, who does miracles for me and his people." For a similar expression, see Ps. xxiii. 5, Heb. : see also Pss. xcv. 3, xcvi. 5, for places in which the Hebrew word *"gods"* is used probably for idols.— *Speaker's Commentary.*

Verse 1.—*"Before the gods,"* etc. The Vulgate hath, *in conspectu angelorum,* " before the angels " ; their presence should awe men and women, and keep them from all dishonesty, evil words, acts, gestures, secret grudging, all discontents and distempers. For as they are rejoiced to discern a good frame of spirit in you, to see you keep that order God hath set in the church and state, to walk as Christians to the honour of God ; so they are grieved to see the contrary, and you must answer for your sins against these great officers in the great family of heaven and earth.— *William Greenhill.*

Verse 2.—*"I will worship toward thy holy temple."* The holy temple was a type and figure of the Lord Jesus Christ. Therefore we find Daniel opening his windows toward the temple, where he prayed three times a day ; and we find Jonah saying, " Yet will I look again toward thy holy temple." So looking to Jesus, he is our temple. There is no acceptable worship except through him ; but we can offer spiritual sacrifices acceptable to God through Jesus Christ. Then, set the Lord Jesus Christ before your eyes, that you may worship God and draw near to the footstool of mercy through him, that you may offer an acceptable sacrifice, and praise his name for his lovingkindness and for his truth.—*Joseph C. Philpot,* 1802— 1869.

Verse 2.—*"Thy holy temple."* This Psalm is entitled " a Psalm of David," and Calvin considers him to be its author agreeably to the title ; but the mention of " the temple " in this verse seems to render such an opinion doubtful. If, however, we translate this word by " mansion," which is the proper rendering of the original— *"the mansion of thy sanctity,"*—this objection to its composition by David falls to the ground.—*James Anderson's Note to Calvin in loc.*

Verse 2.—*"I will . . . . praise thy name for thy lovingkindness."* There are two beautiful thoughts brought out here ; one is, " God's condescension in thought ; " the other, " his tenderness in action." These are both included in *"lovingkindness."* And both of these are shown by God to his own people. He humbleth himself to behold the things of the children of men ; he condescends to men of low estate. Of the blessed Jesus it is said, that " though he was rich, yet for your sakes he became poor, that ye through his poverty might be rich : " 2 Cor. viii. 9. Who can tell the depths to which God condescends in loving thought ? We are told that the very hairs of our head are all numbered ; and if the hairs of our head, then surely all else beside. God, as the Heavenly Father, takes an interest in everything about his people ; he takes this interest in matters which they think beneath his notice, or of which they, from their ignorance, do not know the importance. The mother may draw whole stores of comfort from a realization of the *condescending thoughtfulness of God.* He will be interested about her babe ; if she commit it to him, he who made the universe will, with his infinite mind, think upon her cradle and the helpless creature that is rocked to sleep therein. The sick man may draw whole stores of comfort from the same source, for he can believe the ONE by whom the body was fearfully and wonderfully made will think over the sufferings of that body, and alleviate them, or give strength for the endurance of them if they must be borne. Condescension of thought marks all the dealings of God with his people. And hard following upon it comes *tenderness in action.* Now this " tenderness in action " is a great part of the lovingkindness of God ; it is meet that a thoughtful mind and tender hand should go together in the perfection of love. God is not only energetic, but tender also in action ; he is the God of the dew-drops, as well as the God of the thunder showers ; the God of the tender grass blade, as much as of the mountain oak. We read of great machines, which are able to crush iron bars, and yet they can touch so gently as not to break the shell of the smallest egg ; as it is with them, so is it with the hand of the Most High ; he can crush a world, and yet bind up a wound. And great need have we of tenderness in our low estate ; a little thing would crush us : we have such bruised and feeble souls, that unless we had One who would deal tenderly with us we must soon be destroyed.—*Philip Bennett Power, in "The 'I Wills' of the Psalms,"* 1861.

Verse 2.—*"Thou hast magnified thy word above all thy name."* His *"word"* being here annexed to *"lovingkindness* and *truth,"* must needs be that part of his word to which these two are applicable, *i.e.,* his promise, the matter whereof is *mercy* or *lovingkindness,* and in the performance of which is *truth* or *fidelity.* And then to " magnify " this " word " of promise seems to signify two things ; 1, the making very great and excellent promises, and then, 2, the performing them most punctually ; and the doing it *above all his name* is promising and performing most superlative mercies above all that is famed or spoken or believed of God. Then thus it will run ; *I will worship,* etc., *and praise thy name above thy lovingkindness and above thy truth ;* i.e., it will be too low, too short a compellation, to call thee merciful or veracious, or style thee after any other of thy attributes ; thou art all these, and more than so, " *thou hast magnified thy word,"* given and performed most glorious promises, *"above all thy name,"* above all that men have apprehended or spoken of thee.

This verse and Psalm may easily be interpreted of God's mercies in Christ, so far above what could be famed, or said, or believed, or apprehended of him.—*Condensed from H. Hammond.*

Verse 2.—*"Thou hast magnified thy word above all thy name."* Beyond all question there are higher and clearer manifestations of himself, of his being, of his perfection, of his purposes in the volume of revelation, than any which his works have disclosed or can disclose. There are very many points in relation to God, of the highest interest to mankind, on which the disclosures of science shed no light ; there are many things which it is desirable for man to know, which cannot be learned in the schools of philosophy ; there are consolations which man needs in a world of trouble which cannot be found in nature ; there is especially a knowledge of the method by which sin may be pardoned, and the soul saved, which can never be disclosed by the blow-pipe, the telescope, or the microscope. These things, if learned at all, must be learned from revelation, and these are of more importance to man as a traveller to another world than all the learning which can be acquired in the schools of philosophy—valuable as that learning is.—*Albert Barnes.*

Verse 2.—*"For thou hast magnified thy word above all thy name,"* etc. This is a dark sentence at the first view, but as a judicious expositor upon the place well observes, the words may be thus read, and will better agree with the Hebrew; "*thou hast magnified thy name above all things, in thy word,*" that is, in fulfilling thy word thou hast magnified thy name above all things, in that thou hast fulfilled thy word. What thou freely promisedst, thou hast faithfully performed ; what thou hast spoken with thy mouth thou hast fulfilled with thy hand ; for which thy name is wonderfully to be magnified.—*James Nalton,* 1664.

Verse 2.—"*Thou hast magnified thy word above all thy name.*" Every creature bears the name of God ; but in his word and truth therein contained it is written at length, and therefore he is more choice of this than of all his other works ; he cares not much what becomes of the world and all in it, so that he keeps his word, and saves his truth. Ere long we shall see the world in flames ; the heavens and earth shall pass away, " but the word of the Lord endures for ever." When God will, he can make more such worlds as this ; but he cannot make another truth, and therefore he will not lose one jot thereof. Satan, knowing this, sets all his wits on work to deface this and disfigure it by unsound doctrine. The word is the glass in which we see God, and seeing him are changed into his likeness by his Spirit. If this glass be cracked, then the conceptions we have of God will misrepresent him unto us ; whereas the word, in its native clearness, sets him out in all his glory unto our eye.—*William Gurnall.*

Verse 2.—"*Thou hast magnified thy word above all thy name.*" Thou hast bestowed the promise of perpetuity to my house and to my kingdom, which rises in grandeur and goodness above all thy past manifestations of thyself in behalf of thy people (2 Sam. vii. 10, 12, 13, 15, 16, 21, 22, 24—26, 29 : ver. 21 especially, " For thy *Word's* sake . . . hast thou done all these *great* things " ; ver. 26, " And let thy name be *magnified* for ever "—an undesigned coincidence of language between the history and the Psalm). In the Messiah alone the greatness of the promise finds, and shall hereafter more fully find, its realization for Israel and the whole world.—*Andrew Robert Fausset.*

Verse 2.—"*Thou hast magnified thy word above all thy name.*" God has sent his word to us,

1. As *a mirror,* to reflect his glory. " The heavens declare the glory of God ; and the firmament sheweth his handy-work " ; from them may his eternal power and Godhead be clearly seen. Ps. xix. 1, 3, 4. In his providential dealings, also, is much of his wisdom and goodness exhibited. But of his perfections, generally, we can form no idea from these things ; of his purposes we can know nothing. The state of the Heathen world clearly attests this ; for they behold the wonders of Creation and Providence, as well as we : " There is no speech nor language where *their* voice is not heard. Their line is gone out through all the earth, and their words to the end of the world " : Ps. xix. 3, 4. But in the sacred volume all the glory of the Godhead shines : there we are admitted, so to speak, even to the council-chamber of the Most High ; to hear the covenant entered into between the Father and the Son ; the Father engaging to give to him a seed, whom he should have for his inheritance, if he, on his part, would " make his soul an offering for their sins," and in their nature, expiate the guilt of their iniquities. This mysterious transaction having taken place in the incarnation and death of the Lord Jesus Christ, we behold all the perfections of God united and harmonizing in a way that they never did, or could, by any other means : we see justice more inexorable, than if it had executed vengeance on the whole human race ; and mercy more abundant, than if it had spared the whole human race without any such atonement. There, as it is well expressed, " Mercy and truth are met together ; righteousness and peace have kissed each other " : Ps. lxxxv. 10. Of this great mystery we find not a trace in the whole creation besides : but in the word it is reflected, as in a mirror (2 Cor. iii. 18) ; and it shines so brightly, that the very angels around the throne are made wiser by the revelation of it to the Church : Eph. iii. 10.

2. As *a standard,* to which everything may be referred. Of God's will we know nothing, but from the word : " we know neither good nor evil from all that is before us." What God requires of us, nothing in Creation or Providence can inform us : what he will do for us, we cannot ascertain : how he will deal with us, we cannot ascertain. But, in the sacred volume, all is written as with a sunbeam. There is nothing which God expects us to do for him, which is not there most explicitly declared : nothing which he engages to do for us, that does not form the subject of a distinct promise. The whole of his procedure in the day of judgment is there laid open : the laws by which we shall be judged ; the manner in which the testimony,

whether against us or in our favour, shall be produced ; the grounds on which the sentence of condemnation or acquittal shall be passed ; yea, the very state to which every person, either as acquitted or condemned, shall be consigned ; all is so clearly made known, that every person, who will judge himself with candour now, may assuredly anticipate his fate. There is nothing left to conjecture. Every man has a standard to which he may refer, for the rectifying of his judgment in every particular : so that nothing can be added for the instruction of our minds, or the regulation of our future expectations.

3. As *a fountain*, from whence all his blessings emanate. Great blessings, beyond all doubt, flow down to us through the works of Creation and Providence : in fact, they are incessantly administering to our welfare ; for " God opens his hands, and fills all things living with plenteousness." Still, however, the benefits derived from them are only temporal ; whereas those which the inspired volume imparts are spiritual and eternal ; from whence we derive all our knowledge of Divine truth, and all our hopes of everlasting salvation. Nor is it the knowledge only of truth that we obtain, but the operation and efficacy of it on our souls. There is in Divine truth, when applied by the Holy Spirit, a power to wound, to sanctify, to save : Ps. xix. 7—11. When it comes to the soul with power, the stoutest heart in the universe is made to tremble : when it is poured out as balm, the most afflicted creature under heaven is made to leap for joy. Look over the face of the globe, and see how many, who were once under the unrestrained dominion of sin, are now transformed into the image of their God. And then ascend to heaven, and behold the myriads of the redeemed around the throne of God, uniting their hallelujahs to God and to the Lamb ; to this state were they all brought by that blessed word, which alone could ever prevail for so great a work. Thus it is that God has magnified his word ; and thus it is that he *will* magnify it, to the end of time ; yea, through eternity will it be acknowledged as the one source of all blessings that shall ever be enjoyed.—*Charles Simeon, in Horæ Homileticæ.*

Verse 2.—"For thou hast magnified thy word above all thy name." This is one of those expressions of Scripture that seem so comprehensive, and yet so amazing. To my mind it is one of the most remarkable expressions in the whole book of God. *"Thou hast magnified thy word above all thy name."* The *name* of God includes all the perfections of God ; everything that God is, and which God has revealed himself as having—his justice, majesty, holiness, greatness, and glory, and whatever he is in himself, that is God's name. And yet he has *"magnified"* something *"above his name "*—his *word*—his *truth*. This may refer to the Incarnate Word, the Son of God, who was called *"the Word."* " There are three that bear record in heaven, the Father, the *Word*, and the Holy Ghost, and these three are one " 1 John v. 7, " In the beginning was the *Word*, and the *Word* was with God " : John i. 1. You may take the words either as meaning that God has magnified his *Word*, his eternal Son—above all his great name, that is, he has set Jesus on high above all the other perfections of his majesty ; or take it as meaning his written word, which is written in the sacred Scriptures. So, in that case, not only the Incarnate *Word* in the person of Jesus ; but also the written word in the Scriptures of truth. He has magnified it above all his name in the fulfilment of it : God's faithfulness being so dear to him, he has exalted his faithfulness above all his other perfections. We see this in nature. Here is a man so to be depended upon, so faithful to his word, that he will sacrifice anything sooner than depart from it : that man will give up his property, or life itself, rather than forfeit his word. So God has spoken of magnifying his word above all his name. He would sooner allow all his other perfections to come to naught, than for his faithfulness to fail. He has so magnified his faithfulness, that his love, his mercy, his grace, would all sooner fail than his faithfulness—the word of his mouth and what he has revealed in the Scripture. What a firm salvation, then, is ours, which rests upon his word, when God has magnified that word above all his name ! What volumes of blessedness and truth are contained therein ! so that, if God has revealed his truth to your soul, and given you faith to anchor in the word of promise, sooner than that should fail, he would suffer the loss of all ; for, he has magnified his word above all his name.— *Joseph C. Philpot.*

Verse 2.—"Thou hast magnified thy word above all thy name." God has a *greater* regard unto the words of his mouth, than to the works of his hand : heaven and earth shall pass away, but one jot or tittle of what he hath spoken shall never fall to the ground. Some do understand this of Christ the essential Word, in whom he has set his name, and whom he has so highly exalted, that he has given him " a name above every name."—*Ebenezer Erskine*, 1680—1754.

Verse 2.—"*Thou hast magnified thy word above all thy name.*" Meaning that his word or promise shall have, as it were, and exercise a kind of sovereignty over all his prerogatives and attributes, wisdom, justice, power, etc. So that men need not fear that any of them shall at any time, or in any case whatsoever, move in the least contrariety thereunto.—*John Goodwin*, 1593—1665.

Verse 2.—"*Thou hast magnified thy word above all thy name.*" It may be when there are some extraordinary works of God in the world, thunder and lightning, etc., we are ready to be afraid, and oh ! the great God that doth appear in these great works ! Were our hearts as they ought to be when we read the *Word*, we would tremble at that more than at any manifestation of God since the world began in all his works ; and if so be thou dost not see more of the glory of God in his *Word* than in his works, it is because thou hast little light in thee.—*Jeremiah Burroughs*, 1599—1646.

Verse 2.—"*Thou hast magnified thy word above all thy name.*" " By the word of the Lord were the heavens made, and all the host of them by the breath of his mouth." But mightier far is the word by which a lost world is redeemed. This is the "*word* " that he hath "*magnified above all his name*," as displaying at once the exceeding greatness of his power, the resources of his manifold wisdom, and the blended glories of holiness and love.—*John Lillie.*

Verse 2.—It is not with the truth merely excogitated, but with the truth expressed, that we have any concern ; not with the truth as seen by our inspired teacher, but with the truth as by him spoken to us. It is not enough that the Spirit hath made him to see it aright—this is not enough if he have not also made him to speak it aright. A pure influx into the mind of an apostle is no sufficient guarantee for the instruction of the world, unless there be a pure efflux also ; for not the doctrine that has flowed in, but the doctrine that has flowed out, is truly all that we have to do with. Accordingly, it is to the doctrine in efflux, that is to the *word*, that we are bidden to yield ourselves. It is the word that is a light unto our feet and a lamp unto our path ; it is his word that God hath exalted above all his name ; it is the word that he hath settled fast in heaven, and given to it a stability surer and more lasting than to the ordinances of nature. We can take no cognizance of the doctrine that is conveyed from heaven to earth, when it has only come the length of excogitation in the mind of an apostle ; and it is not till brought the farther length of expression, either by speech or by writing, that it comes into contact with us. In short our immediate concern is with, not what apostles conceive inwardly, but what they bring forth outwardly not with the schemes or the systems which they have been made to apprehend, but with the books which they have written ; and had the whole force and effect of this observation been sufficiently pondered, we feel persuaded that the advocates of a mitigated inspiration would not have dissevered, as they have done, the inspiration of sentiment from the inspiration of language.—*Thomas Chalmers.*

Verse 2.—"*Thy word,*" or "*Thy promise.*" So great are God's promises, and so faithful and complete is his performance of them, as even to surpass the expectations which the greatness of his name has excited.—*Annotated Paragraph Bible.*

Verse 3.—"*In the day when I cried,*" etc. God granted him a speedy answer : for it was in the very day that he cried that he was heard : and it was a spiritual answer ; he was *strengthened with strength in his soul.* Would you have soul strength for the work you have in view ? then cry unto him who is the " strength of Israel " for it ; for " he giveth power to the faint, and he increaseth strength to them that have no might."—*Ebenezer Erskine.*

Verse 3.—"*In the day when I cried thou answeredst me,*" etc. That part of an army which is upon action in the field is sure to have their pay, if their masters have any money in their purse, or care of them ; yea, sometimes when their fellows left in their quarters are made to wait. I am sure there is more gold and silver (spiritual joy, I mean, and comfort) to be found in Christ's camp, among his suffering ones, than their brethren at home in peace and prosperity ordinarily can show. What are the promises but vessels of cordial wine, tunned on purpose against a groaning hour, when God usually broacheth them ! " Call upon me," saith God, " in the day of trouble." Ps. l. 15. And may we not do so in the day of peace ? Yes ; but he would have us most bold with him in the day of trouble. None find such quick despatch at the throne of grace as suffering saints. *"In the day that I cried,"* said David, *"thou answeredst me, and strengthenedst me with strength in my soul."* He was now in a strait, and God comes in haste to him. Though we may keep a well friend waiting should he send for us, yet we will give a sick friend leave to call us up at midnight. In such extremities we usually go with the messenger that comes for us ; and so doth God with the prayer. Peter knocked at their gate, who were assembled to seek God for him, almost as soon as their prayer knocked at heaven gate in his behalf. And truly it is no more than needs, if we consider the temptations of our afflicted condition ; we are prone then to be suspicious that our best friends forget us, and to think every stay a delay, and neglect of us ; therefore God chooseth to show himself most kind at such a time. *"As the sufferings of Christ abound in us, so our consolation also aboundeth by Christ :"* 2 Cor. i. 5. As man laid on trouble, so Christ laid in consolation : both tides rose and fell together ; when it was spring-tide with him in affliction, it was so with him in his joy. We relieve the poor as their need increaseth ; so Christ comforts his people as their troubles multiply. And now, Christian, tell me, doth not thy dear Lord deserve a ready spirit in thee to meet any suffering with, for, or from him, who gives his sweetest comforts where his people are put to bear their saddest sorrows ? Well may the servant do his work, cheerfully when his master is so careful of him as with his own hands to bring him his breakfast into the fields. The Christian stays not till he comes to heaven for all his comfort. There indeed shall be the full supper, but there is a breakfast, Christian, of previous joys, more or less, which Christ brings to thee into the field, to be eaten on the place where thou endurest thy hardship.—*William Gurnall.*

Verse 3.—*"Thou answeredst me, and strengthenedst me with strength in my soul."* It is one gracious way of answering our prayers when God doth bestow upon us spiritual strength in our souls ; if he do not give the things we desire, yet if he gives us strength in our souls, he graciously answers our prayers. What is this spiritual strength ? I answer, it is a work of the Spirit of God, enabling a man to do and suffer what God would have him without fainting or backsliding.—*James Nalton.*

Verse 3.—*"Thou strengthenedst me with strength in my soul."* Other masters cut out work for their servants, but do not help them in their work ; but our Master in heaven doth not only give us work, but strength. God bids us serve him, and he will enable us to serve him, Ezek. xxxvi. 27 : " I will cause you to walk in my statutes." The Lord doth not only fit work for us, but fits us for our work ; with his command he gives power.—*Thomas Watson.*

Verse 3.—*"Thou makest me brave in my soul (with) strength."* The common version of this clause (*"strengthenedst me with strength in my soul "*) contains a paronomasia not in the original, where the verb and noun have not even a letter in common. The verb is by some translated *made me proud, i.e.,* elated me, not with a vain or selfish pride, but with a lofty and exhilarating hope.—*Joseph Addison Alexander.*

Verse 4.—*"All the kings of the earth shall praise thee."* In a sense sufficiently striking this promise was fulfilled to David, and to the nation of Israel, as surrounding monarchs beheld the wonderful dispensations of divine providence which attended their steps (2 Sam. v. 11 ; viii. 10) ; but in its completest sense, it shall realize its accomplishment in the future conquests of Messiah, when the princes and potentates of the earth receive his word, learn by divine grace to celebrate the glorious methods of his love, and see in the light of faith the greatness of Jehovah's glory as the God of salvation. *"All the kings of the earth "* shall yet praise the Lord, and shall hasten with their numerous subjects to hail the triumphs of his grace.—*John Morison.*

Verse 5.—*"Yea, they shall sing in the ways of the LORD."* There will come a time when the praise of Jahve, which according to cxxxvii. 4 was obliged to be dumb in the presence of the heathen, will be sung by the kings of the heathen themselves.—*Franz Delitzsch.*

Verse 5.—*"Yea, they shall sing in the ways of the LORD."* Walking with God is a pleasant walk : the ways of wisdom are called " ways of pleasantness " : Prov. iii. 17. Is not the light pleasant ? Ps. lxxxix. 15 : " They shall walk, O LORD, in the light of thy countenance." Walking with God is like walking among beds of spices, which send forth a fragrant perfume. This is it which brings peace,

Acts ix. 31 : " Walking in the fear of the Lord, and in the comfort of the Holy Ghost." While we walk with God, what sweet music doth the bird of conscience make in our breast ! *"They shall sing in the ways of the Lord."—Thomas Watson.*

Verse 6.—"Though the LORD *be high."* We have here God's transcendent greatness ; he is the *high Lord*, or Jehovah : he is " the high and lofty One, who inhabits eternity, and who dwells in the high and lofty place, to which no man can approach." Who can think or speak of his highness in a suitable manner ? It dazzles the eyes of sinful mortal worms to behold " the place where his honour dwells." Oh how infinite is the distance between him and us ! " There are none of the sons of the mighty that can be compared unto him ; " yea, " the inhabitants of the earth are before him but as the drop in the bucket, and the small dust in the balance." He is not only *"high"* above men, but above angels : cherubims and seraphims are his ministering spirits. He is *"high"* above the heavens ; for " the heaven, yea, the heaven of heavens cannot contain him " ; and he " humbleth himself " when " he beholds things that are in heaven." Oh, sirs, study to entertain high and admiring thoughts and apprehensions of the glorious majesty of God ; for " honour and majesty are before him ; strength and beauty are in his sanctuary." —*Ebenezer Erskine.*

Verse 6.—"The LORD *hath respect unto the lowly."* God has such a respect unto the lowly, not as if this frame of soul were meritorious of any good at his hand, but because,—

1. This is a disposition that best serves God's great design of lifting up and glorifying his free grace. What think you, sirs, was God's design in election, in redemption, in the whole of the gospel dispensation, and in all the ordinances thereof ? His grand design in all was to rear up a glorious high throne, from which he might display the riches of his free and sovereign grace ; this is that which he will have magnified through eternity above all his other name. Now, this lowliness and humility of spirit suits best unto God's design of exalting the freedom of his grace. It is not the legalist, or proud Pharisee, but the poor humble publican, who is smiting on his breast, and crying, " God be merciful to me, a sinner," that submits to the revelation of grace.

2. God has such respect unto the humble soul because it is a fruit of the Spirit inhabiting the soul, and an evidence of the soul's union with the Lord Jesus Christ, in whom alone we are accepted.

3. This is a disposition that makes the soul like Christ ; and the like that a person is to Christ, God loves him ay the better. We are told that Christ was " meek and lowly " ; " he did not cry, nor lift up, nor cause his voice to be heard in the streets " ; though he was " the brightness of his Father's glory," yet he was content to appear " in the form of a servant"; though he was rich, yet he was content to become poor, that we through his poverty might be rich. Now, the humble soul, being the image of Christ, who is the express image of his Father, God cannot but have a regard unto him.—*Ebenezer Erskine.*

Verse 6.—"He hath respect unto the lowly." Give me the homely vessel of humility, which God shall preserve, and fill with the wine of his grace ; rather than the varnished cup of pride, which he will dash in pieces, like a potter's vessel. Where humility is the corner stone, there glory shall be the topstone.—*William Secker, in "The Nonsuch Professor in his Meridian Splendour,"* 1660.

Verse 6.—"The proud he knoweth afar off." He that meets a spectacle or person which he cannot endure to look upon, avoids it, or turns from it while he is yet afar off ; whereas, if the object be delightful, he draweth near and comes as close as he can. When therefore it is said, *the Lord knoweth a proud man afar off*, it shows his disdain of him : he will scarce touch him with a pair of tongs (as we say) ; he cannot abide to come near him. He knows well enough how vile he is even at the greatest distance.—*Joseph Caryl.*

Verse 6.—"The proud he knoweth afar off." By punishing them in hell.—*Richard Rolle,* 1340.

Verse 7.—"Though I walk in the midst of trouble, thou wilt revive me." So as to the three youths in the fiery furnace, their persecutor, Nebuchadnezzar, said, " Lo, I see four men loose, *walking in the midst of the fire*, and they have no hurt, and the form of the fourth is like the Son of God."—*Andrew Robert Fausset.*

Verse 7.—"In the midst of trouble thou wilt revive me." The wisdom of God is seen in helping in desperate cases. God loves to show his wisdom when human help and wisdom fail. Exquisite lawyers love to wrestle with niceties and difficulties in the law, to show their skill the more. God's wisdom is never at a loss ; but when providences are darkest, then the morning star of deliverance appears. Sometimes God melts away the spirits of his enemies. Josh. ii. 24. Sometimes he finds them other work to do, and sounds a retreat to them, as he did to Saul when he was pursuing David. " The Philistines are in the land." " In the mount God will be seen." When the church seems to be upon the altar, her peace and liberty ready to be sacrificed, then the angel comes.—*Thomas Watson.*

Verse 7.—*"Thou shalt stretch forth thine hand,"* etc. Thou shalt interpose thine help betwixt me and them, and save me harmless ; as the poets feign their gods did those whom they favoured. *Thou shalt strike them with thy left hand, and save me with thy right ;* so Tremellius senseth it.—*John Trapp.*

Verse 8.—*"The LORD will perfect,"* etc. God's work is perfect, man's is clumsy and incomplete. God does not leave off till he has finished. When he rests, it is because, looking on his work, he sees it all " very good." His Sabbath is the Sabbath of an achieved purpose, of a fulfilled counsel. The palaces which we build are ever like that in the story, where one window remains dark and unjewelled, while the rest blaze in beauty. But when God builds none can say, " He was not able to finish." In his great palace he makes her " windows of agates," and *all* her " borders of pleasant stones."

I suppose that if the mediæval dream had ever come true, and an alchemist had ever turned a grain of lead into gold, he could have turned all the lead in the world, in time, and with crucibles and furnaces enough. The first step is all the difficulty, and if you and I have been changed from enemies into sons, and had one spark of love to God kindled in our hearts, that is a mightier change than any that yet remains to be effected in order to make us perfect. One grain has been changed, the whole mass will be in due time.—*Alexander Maclaren, Sermon in " Wesleyan Methodist Magazine,"* 1879.

Verse 8.—*"Forsake not the works of thine own hands."* When we are under such afflictions as threaten to ruin us, 'tis seasonable to tell the Lord he made us. David strengthens prayer upon this argument : *"Forsake not the works of thine own hands."* All men love their own works, many dote upon them : shall we think God will forsake his ? See how the people of God plead with God in greatest distress. (Isa. lxiv. 8) : " But now, O LORD, thou art our father ; we are the clay, and thou our potter ; and we are all the work of thy hand. Be not wroth very sore, O LORD." —*Joseph Cary.*

Verse 8.—*"Forsake not the works of thine own hands."* Look upon the wounds of thine hands, and forsake not the works of thine hands, prayed Queen Elizabeth. And Luther's usual prayer was, Confirm, O God, in us that thou hast wrought, and perfect the work that thou hast begun in us, to thy glory. So be it.—*John Trapp.*

Verse 8.—*"Forsake not the works of thine own hands."* Behold in me thy work, not mine : for mine, if thou seest, thou condemnest ; thine, if thou seest, thou crownest. For whatever good works there be of mine, from thee are they to me ; and so they are more thine than mine. For I hear from thine apostle, " By grace are ye saved through faith ; and that not of yourselves : it is the gift of God : Not of works, lest any man should boast. For we are his workmanship, created in Christ Jesus : " Eph. ii. 8—10.—*Augustine.*

Verse 8.—*"Thine own hands."* His creating hands formed our souls at the beginning ; his nail-pierced hands redeemed them on Calvary ; his glorified hands will hold our souls fast and not let them go for ever. Unto his hands let us commend our spirits, sure that even though the works of our hands have made void the works of his hands, yet his hands will again make perfect all that our hands have unmade. —*J. W. Burgon.*

HINTS TO PREACHERS.

Verses 1, 2, 3.—David vexed with rival gods, as we are with rival gospels. How will he act ? I. *Sing with whole-hearted praise.* 1. It would generously show his contempt of the false. 2. It would evince his strong faith in the true. 3. It would declare his joyful zeal for God. 4. It would shield him from evil from those about him. II. *Worship by the despised rule.* 1. Quietly ignoring all will-worship. 2. Looking to the person of Christ, which was typified by the temple. 3. Trusting in sacrifice. 4. Realizing God himself, for it is to God he speaks. III. *Praise the questioned attributes.* 1. Lovingkindness in its universality, in its speciality. Grace in everything. 2. Truth. Historic accuracy. Certainty of promises. Correctness of prophecies. Assured of the love of God and the truth of his word, let us cling the closer to these. IV. *Reverence the honoured word.* It is beyond all revelation by creation and providence, for it is—1. More clear. 2. More sure. 3. More sovereign. 4. More complete, unique. 5. More lasting. 6. More glorifying to God. V. *Prove it by experience.* 1. By offering prayer. 2. By narrating the answer. 3. By exhibiting the strength in soul which was given in answer to prayer.

Verse 2.—The Christward position. I. Worship and praise are to be blended. II. They are to be presented with an eye to God in Christ, for he is the temple : the place of divine indwelling, sacrifice, intercession, priesthood, oracle, and manifestation.

Verse 2 (*first clause*).—I. The soul's noblest attitude : " Toward thy holy temple." II. The soul's noblest exercise : " worship," " praise."—*W. W.*

Verse 2.—I. *The worshipper's contemplation.* Gaze fixed on Holy Temple. Material temple not yet built. Christ the sanctuary. Heb. viii. 2. All worship through him. Eye of worshippers fixed on him. II. *The worshipper's song.* Love and truth. Note the combination. Truth by Moses. Grace and truth by Jesus Christ. III. *The worshipper's argument.* Because Christ " The Word " is the embodiment and most glorious manifestation of God. Heb. i. 2, 3.—*Archibald G. Brown.*

Verse 3.—I. Prayer answered *in* the day. II. Prayer answered by giving strength *for* the day. See 2 Cor. xii. 8, 9.—*A. G. B.*

Verse 3.—I. Answers to prayer should be noted and acknowledged : " Thou answeredst me." II. Speedy answers should have special praise : " In the day when I cried, thou," etc. III. A strengthened soul is sometimes the best answer to prayer : " Strengthened me with strength."—*J. F.*

Verse 3.—Remarkable answer to prayer. I. The prayer : feeble, earnest, sorrowful, inarticulate. II. The answer : prompt, divine, effectual, certain. III. The praise deserved by such grace. See preceding verses.

Verse 3.—I. A special day. II. A specific form of prayer : " I cried." III. A special method of response.—*W. W.*

Verse 4.—I. A royal audience. II. A royal orchestra.

Verses 4, 5.—I. They who hear the words of God will know God. II. They who know God will praise him, however exalted they may be amongst men : " All the kings," etc. III. They who praise God will walk in his ways. IV. They who walk in the ways of the Lord will glorify him, and he will be glorified in them.—*G. R.*

Verse 5.—See " Spurgeon's Sermons," No. 1615 : " Singing in the Ways of the Lord."

Verse 5.—This is spoken of kings, but it is true of the humblest pilgrims. The Lord hath respect unto the lowly, and will make them sing. I. *They shall sing in the ways.* 1. They take pleasure in them. 2. They do not go out of them to find pleasure. 3. They sing as they proceed in service, in worship, in holiness, in suffering. 4. They are in a case for singing. They have strength, safety, guidance, provision, comfort. II. *They sing of the ways of the Lord.* 1. Of God's ways to them. 2. Of their way to God. They know whence they came out. They know where they are going. It is a good road ; prophets went by it, and the Lord of the prophets. Therein we have good company, good accommodation, good prospects, good daylight. III. *They sing of the Lord of the way.* His lovingkindness. His truth. Answers to prayer. His condescension. His reviving us in trouble. His delivering us. His perfecting us. His everlasting mercy. IV. *They shall sing to the Lord of the way.* 1. To his honour. 2. To the extending of that honour. 3. As a preparation to eternally honouring him.

Verse 6.—Divine inversions. I. Lowliness honoured to its great surprise.
II. Pride passed by to its eternal mortification.—*W. B. H.*

Verse 7 (*first clause*).—I. The Psalmist's dismal excursion : walking " in the
midst of trouble ; " this is not a spectator, but one assailed. Troubles—personal,
social, ecclesiastical, national. II. His cheering anticipation—of revival, defence,
deliverance.—*W. J.*

Verse 7.—I. Good men are sometimes in the midst of troubles : these are many,
and continue long. II. They interfere not with their progress. They " walk in
the midst " of them ; faint, yet pursuing ; sometimes they " run with patience,"
etc. III. They have comfort in them : " Though I walk," etc., " thou wilt revive
me." IV. They are benefited by them. 1. Their enemies are overthrown. 2. Their
deliverance is complete.—*G. R.*

Verse 7.—The child of God often revived *out* of trouble ; more frequently *in*
trouble ; not seldom *through* trouble. Delivered from, sustained in, sanctified
through, trouble.—*A. G. B.*

Verse 7.—An incident of the road to the city. I. Pilgrim beset by thieves and
struck down. II. The arrival of Greatheart and flight of the enemy. III. The
flask to the lips : " thou wilt revive me." Sweet awakening to know the beauty
of his face and strength of his hand !—*W. B. H.*

Verse 7 (*third clause*).—Right-hand salvation. I. It shall be wrought of God.
II. He shall throw his strength into the deed. III. His utmost dexterity shall be
displayed.

Verse 8 (*first clause*).—I. A wide subject—" That which concerneth me." Not
necessarily that which gives me concern. II. A promise that covers it : " the Lord
will perfect."—*A. G. B.*

Verse 8 (*first and last clauses*).—Faith in divine purpose no hindrance to prayer,
but rather an encouragement in it : " The Lord will perfect." " Forsake not."—
A. G. B.

Verse 8.—See " Spurgeon's Sermons," Nos. 231 and 1506 : " Faith in Perfection,"
and, " Choice Comfort for a Young Believer."

Verse 8.—The grace of God makes a man thoughtful, and leads him to concern
about himself, his life, his future, and the completeness of the work of grace. This
might lead us to sadness and despair, but the Lord worketh in us for other ends.
I. *He fills us with assurance.* 1. That the Lord will work for us. 2. That he will
complete his work. 3. That he will do this in providence ; if it be properly a
concern of ours. 4. That he will do this within us. Our graces shall grow. Our
soul shall become Christly. Our whole nature perfect. 5. That he will do this
with our work for him. II. *He gives us rest in his mercy.* 1. Thou wilt forgive
my sins. 2. Thou wilt bear with my nature. 3. Thou wilt support me in suffering.
4. Thou wilt supply me in need. 5. Thou wilt succour me in death. III. *He puts
prayer into our hearts.* 1. That he will not forsake me. 2. That he will not leave
his own work in me undone. 3. Nor his work by me unfinished. Why did he
begin ? Why carry so far ? Why not complete ?

Verse 8.—I. Faith's full assurance : " The Lord will perfect that which concerneth me." II. Faith's firm foundation : " Thy mercy, O Lord, endureth for
ever." III. Faith's fervent prayer : " Forsake not the works of thine own hands."
—*W. H. J. P.*

PSALM CXXXIX.

One of the most notable of the sacred hymns. It sings the omniscience and omnipresence of God, inferring from these the overthrow of the powers of wickedness, since he who sees and hears the abominable deeds and words of the rebellious will surely deal with them according to his justice. The brightness of this Psalm is like unto a sapphire stone, or Ezekiel's "terrible crystal"; it flames out with such flashes of light as to turn night into day. Like a Pharos, this holy song casts a clear light even to the uttermost parts of the sea, and warns us against that practical atheism which ignores the presence of God, and so makes shipwreck of the soul.

TITLE.—To the Chief Musician. *The last time this title occurred was in Psalm cix. This sacred song is worthy of the most excellent of the singers, and is fitly dedicated to the leader of the Temple psalmody, that he might set it to music, and see that it was devoutly sung in the solemn worship of the Most High.* A Psalm of David. *It bears the image and superscription of King David, and could have come from no other mint than that of the son of Jesse. Of course the critics take this composition away from David, on account of certain Aramaic expressions in it. We believe that upon the principles of criticism now in vogue it would be extremely easy to prove that Milton did not write Paradise Lost. We have yet to learn that David could not have used expressions belonging to "the language of the patriarchal ancestral house." Who knows how much of the antique speech may have been purposely retained among those nobler minds who rejoiced in remembering the descent of their race? Knowing to what wild inferences the critics have run in other matters, we have lost nearly all faith in them, and prefer to believe David to be the author of this Psalm, from internal evidences of style and matter, rather than to accept the determination of men whose modes of judgment are manifestly unreliable.*

EXPOSITION.

O LORD, thou hast searched me, and known *me*.

2 Thou knowest my downsitting and mine uprising, thou understandest my thought afar off.

3 Thou compassest my path and my lying down, and art acquainted *with* all my ways.

4 For *there is* not a word in my tongue, *but*, lo, O LORD, thou knowest it altogether.

5 Thou hast beset me behind and before, and laid thine hand upon me.

6 *Such* knowledge *is* too wonderful for me; it is high, I cannot *attain* unto it.

1. *"O Lord, thou hast searched me, and known me."* He invokes in adoration Jehovah the all-knowing God, and he proceeds to adore him by proclaiming one of his peculiar attributes. If we would praise God aright we must draw the matter of our praise from himself—"O Jehovah, thou hast." No pretended god knows aught of us; but the true God, Jehovah, understands us, and is most intimately acquainted with our persons, nature, and character. How well it is for us to know the God who knows us! The divine knowledge is extremely thorough and searching; it is as if he had searched us, as officers search a man for contraband goods, or as pillagers ransack a house for plunder. Yet we must not let the figure run upon all fours, and lead us further than it is meant to do: the Lord knows all things naturally and as a matter of course, and not by any effort on his part. Searching ordinarily implies a measure of ignorance which is removed by observation; of course this is not the case with the Lord; but the meaning of the Psalmist is, that the Lord knows us as thoroughly as if he had examined us minutely, and had pried into the most secret corners of our being. This infallible knowledge has always existed—" Thou hast searched me"; and it continues unto this day, since God

cannot forget that which he has once known.   There never was a time in which we were unknown to God, and there never will be a moment in which we shall be beyond his observation.   Note how the Psalmist makes his doctrine personal : he saith not, " O God, thou knowest all things "; but, " thou hast known *me*."   It is ever our wisdom to lay truth home to ourselves.   How wonderful the contrast between the observer and the observed !   Jehovah and me !   Yet this most intimate connection exists, and therein lies our hope.   Let the reader sit still a while and try to realize the two poles of this statement,—the Lord and poor puny man—and he will see much to admire and wonder at.

2. *"Thou knowest my downsitting and mine uprising."   Me* thou knowest, and all that comes of me.   I am observed when I quietly sit down, and marked when I resolutely rise up.   My most common and casual acts, my most needful and necessary movements, are noted by thee, and thou knowest the inward thoughts which regulate them.   Whether I sink in lowly self-renunciation, or ascend in pride, thou seest the motions of my mind, as well as those of my body.   This is a fact to be remembered every moment : sitting down to consider, or rising up to act, we are still seen, known, and read by Jehovah our Lord.   *"Thou understandest my thought afar off."* Before it is my own it is foreknown and comprehended by thee.   Though my thought be invisible to the sight, though as yet I be not myself cognizant of the shape it is assuming, yet thou hast it under thy consideration, and thou perceivest its nature, its source, its drift, its result.   Never dost thou misjudge or wrongly interpret me : my inmost thought is perfectly understood by thine impartial mind.   Though thou shouldst give but a glance at my heart, and see me as one sees a passing meteor moving afar, yet thou wouldst by that glimpse sum up all the meanings of my soul, so transparent is everything to thy piercing glance.

3. *"Thou compassest my path and my lying down."*   My path and my pallet, my running and my resting, are alike within the circle of thine observation.   Thou dost surround me even as the air continually surrounds all creatures that live. I am shut up within the wall of thy being ; I am encircled within the bounds of thy knowledge.   Waking or sleeping I am still observed of thee.   I may leave thy path, but thou never leavest mine.   I may sleep and forget thee, but thou dost never slumber, nor fall into oblivion concerning thy creature.   The original signifies not only surrounding, but winnowing and sifting.   The Lord judges our active life and our quiet life ; he discriminates our action and our repose, and marks that in them which is good and also that which is evil.   There is chaff in all our wheat, and the Lord divides them with unerring precision.   *"And art acquainted with all my ways."* Thou art familiar with all I do ; nothing is concealed from thee, nor surprising to thee, nor misunderstood by thee.   Our paths may be habitual or accidental, open or secret, but with them all the Most Holy One is well acquainted.   This should fill us with awe, so that we sin not ; with courage, so that we fear not ; with delight, so that we mourn not.

4. *"For there is not a word in my tongue, but lo, O LORD, thou knowest it altogether."* The unformed word, which lies within the tongue like a seed in the soil, is certainly and completely known to the Great Searcher of hearts.   A negative expression is used to make the positive statement all the stronger : not a word is unknown is a forcible way of saying that every word is well known.   Divine knowledge is perfect, since not a single word is unknown, nay, not even an unspoken word, and each one is " altogether " or wholly known.   What hope of concealment can remain when the speech with which too many conceal their thoughts is itself transparent before the Lord ?   O Jehovah, how great art thou !   If thine eye hath such power, what must be the united force of thine whole nature !

5. *"Thou hast beset me behind and before."*   As though we were caught in an ambush, or besieged by an army which has wholly beleaguered the city walls, we are surrounded by the Lord.   God has set us where we be, and beset us wherever we be.   Behind us there is God recording our sins, or in grace blotting out the remembrance of them ; and before us there is God foreknowing all our deeds, and providing for all our wants.   We cannot turn back and so escape him, for he is behind ; we cannot go forward and outmarch him, for he is before.   He not only beholds us, but he besets us ; and lest there should seem any chance of escape, or lest we should imagine that the surrounding presence is yet a distant one, it is added,—*"And laid thine hand upon me."*   The prisoner marches along surrounded by a guard, and gripped by an officer.   God is very near ; we are wholly in his power ; from that power there is no escape.   It is not said that God *will* thus beset

us and arrest us, but it is done—" Thou hast beset me." Shall we not alter the
figure, and say that our heavenly Father has folded his arms around us, and caressed
us with his hand ? It is even so with those who are by faith the children of the
Most High.

6. *"Such knowledge is too wonderful for me."* I cannot grasp it. I can hardly
endure to think of it. The theme overwhelms me. I am amazed and astounded
at it. Such knowledge not only surpasses my comprehension, but even my imagination. *"It is high, I cannot attain unto it."* Mount as I may, this truth is too lofty
for my mind. It seems to be always above me, even when I soar into the loftiest
regions of spiritual thought. Is it not so with every attribute of God ? Can we
attain to any idea of his power, his wisdom, his holiness ? Our mind has no line
with which to measure the Infinite. Do we therefore question ? Say, rather, that
we therefore believe and adore. We are not surprised that the Most Glorious God
should in his knowledge be high above all the knowledge to which we can attain :
it must of necessity be so, since we are such poor limited beings ; and when we
stand a-tip-toe we cannot reach to the lowest step of the throne of the Eternal.

7 Whither shall I go from thy spirit ? or whither shall I flee from thy
presence ?

8 If I ascend up into heaven, thou *art* there : if I make my bed in hell,
behold, thou *art there*.

9 *If* I take the wings of the morning, *and* dwell in the uttermost parts
of the sea ;

10 Even there shall thy hand lead me, and thy right hand shall hold me.

11 If I say, Surely the darkness shall cover me ; even the night shall be
light about me.

12 Yea, the darkness hideth not from thee ; but the night shineth as
the day : the darkness and the light *are* both alike *to thee*.

Here omnipresence is the theme,—a truth to which omniscience naturally leads
up. *"Whither shall I go from thy spirit ?"* Not that the Psalmist wished to go
from God, or to avoid the power of the divine life ; but he asks this question to
set forth the fact that no one can escape from the all-pervading being and observation
of the Great Invisible Spirit. Observe how the writer makes the matter personal
to himself—" Whither shall *I* go ? " It were well if we all thus applied truth to
our own cases. It were wise for each one to say—The spirit of the Lord is ever
around *me :* Jehovah is omnipresent *to me.* *"Or whither shall I flee from thy
presence ?"* If, full of dread, I hastened to escape from that nearness of God which
had become my terror, which way could I turn ? " Whither ? " " Whither ? "
He repeats his cry. No answer comes back to him. The reply to his first
" Whither ? " is its echo,—a second " Whither ? " From the sight of God he
cannot be hidden, but that is not all,—from the immediate, actual, constant presence
of God he cannot be withdrawn. We must be, whether we will it or not, as near
to God as our soul is to our body. This makes it dreadful work to sin ; for we
offend the Almighty to his face, and commit acts of treason at the very foot of his
throne. *Go* from him, or *flee* from him we cannot : neither by patient travel nor
by hasty flight can we withdraw from the all-surrounding Deity. His mind is in
our mind ; himself within ourselves. His spirit is over our spirit ; our presence
is ever in his presence.

8. *"If I ascend up into heaven, thou art there."* Filling the loftiest region with
his yet loftier presence, Jehovah is in the heavenly place, at home, upon his throne.
The ascent, if it were possible, would be unavailing for purposes of escape ; it
would, in fact, be a flying into the centre of the fire to avoid the heat. There would
he be immediately confronted by the terrible personality of God. Note the abrupt
words—" THOU, THERE." *"If I make my bed in hell, behold, thou art there."*
Descending into the lowest imaginable depths among the dead, there should we
find the Lord. THOU ! says the Psalmist, as if he felt that God was the one great
Existence in all places. Whatever Hades may be, or whoever may be there,
one thing is certain, *Thou, O* Jehovah, art there. Two regions, the one of glory
and the other of darkness, are set in contrast, and this one fact is asserted of both
—" thou art there." Whether we rise up or lie down, take our wing or make our

bed, we shall find God near us. A *"behold"* is added to the second clause, since it seems more a wonder to meet with God in hell than in heaven, in Hades than in Paradise. Of course the presence of God produces very different effects in these places, but it is unquestionably in each ; the bliss of one, the terror of the other. What an awful thought, that some men seem resolved to take up their night's abode in hell, a night which shall know no morning.

9. *"If I take the wings of the morning, and dwell in the uttermost parts of the sea."*—If I could fly with all swiftness, and find a habitation where the mariner has not yet ploughed the deep, yet I could not reach the boundaries of the divine presence. Light flies with inconceivable rapidity, and it flashes far afield beyond all human ken ; it illuminates the great and wide sea, and sets its waves gleaming afar ; but its speed would utterly fail if employed in flying from the Lord. Were we to speed on the wings of the morning breeze, and break into oceans unknown to chart and map, yet there we should find the Lord already present. He who saves to the uttermost would be with us in the uttermost parts of the sea.

10. *"Even there shall thy hand lead me."* We could only fly from God by his own power. The Lord would be leading, covering, preserving, sustaining us even when we were fugitives from him. *"And thy right hand shall hold me."* In the uttermost parts of the sea my arrest would be as certain as at home : God's right hand would there seize and detain the runaway. Should we be commanded on the most distant errand, we may assuredly depend upon the upholding right hand of God as with us in all mercy, wisdom, and power. The exploring missionary in his lonely wanderings is led, in his solitary feebleness he is held. Both the hands of God are with his own servants to sustain them, and against rebels to overthrow them ; and in this respect it matters not to what realms they resort, the active energy of God is around them still.

11. *"If I say, Surely the darkness shall cover me."* Dense darkness may oppress me, but it cannot shut me out from thee, or thee from me. Thou seest as well without the light as with it, since thou art not dependent upon light, which is thine own creature, for the full exercise of thy perceptions. Moreover, thou art present with me whatever may be the hour ; and being present thou discoverest all that I think, or feel, or do. Men are still so foolish as to prefer night and darkness for their evil deeds ; but so impossible is it for anything to be hidden from the Lord that they might just as well transgress in broad daylight.

> Darkness and light in this agree ;
> Great God, they're both alike to thee.
> Thine hand can pierce thy foes as soon
> Through midnight shades as blazing nocn.

A good man will not wish to be hidden by the darkness, a wise man will not expect any such thing. If we were so foolish as to make sure of concealment because the place was shrouded in midnight, we might well be alarmed out of our security by the fact that, as far as God is concerned, we always dwell in the light ; for even the night itself glows with a revealing force,—*"even the night shall be light about me."* Let us think of this if ever we are tempted to take license from the dark—it is light about us. If the darkness be light, how great is that light in which we dwell ! Note well how David keeps his song in the first person ; let us mind that we do the same as we cry with Hagar, " Thou God seest *me*."

12. *"Yea,"* of a surety, beyond all denial. *"The darkness hideth not from thee ;"* it veils nothing, it is not the medium of concealment in any degree whatever. It hides from men, but not from God. *"But the night shineth as the day :"* it is but another form of day : it shines, revealing all ; it " shineth as the day,"—quite as clearly and distinctly manifesting all that is done. *"The darkness and the light are both alike to thee."* This sentence seems to sum up all that went before, and most emphatically puts the negative upon the faintest idea of hiding under the cover of night. Men cling to this notion, because it is easier and less expensive to hide under darkness than to journey to remote places ; and therefore the foolish thought is here beaten to pieces by statements which in their varied forms effectually batter it. Yet the ungodly are still duped by their grovelling notions of God, and enquire, " How doth God know ? " They must fancy that he is as limited in his powers of observation as they are, and yet if they would but consider for a moment they would conclude that he who could not see in the dark could not be God, and he who is not present everywhere could not be the Almighty Creator. Assuredly

God is in all places, at all times, and nothing can by any possibility be kept away from his all-observing, all-comprehending mind. The Great Spirit comprehends within himself all time and space, and yet he is infinitely greater than these, or aught else that he has made.

13 For thou hast possessed my reins : thou hast covered me in my mother's womb.

14 I will praise thee ; for I am fearfully *and* wonderfully made : marvellous *are* thy works ; and *that* my soul knoweth right well.

15 My substance was not hid from thee, when I was made in secret, *and* curiously wrought in the lowest parts of the earth.

16 Thine eyes did see my substance, yet being unperfect ; and in thy book all *my members* were written, *which* in continuance were fashioned, when *as yet there was* none of them.

17 How precious also are thy thoughts unto me, O God ! how great is the sum of them !

18 *If* I should count them, they are more in number than the sand : when I awake, I am still with thee.

13. *"For thou hast possessed my reins."* Thou art the owner of my inmost parts and passions : not the indweller and observer only, but the acknowledged lord and possessor of my most secret self. The word " reins " signifies the kidneys, which by the Hebrews were supposed to be the seat of the desires and longings ; but perhaps it indicates here the most hidden and vital portion of the man ; this God doth not only inspect, and visit, but it is his own ; he is as much at home there as a landlord on his own estate, or a proprietor in his own house. *"Thou hast covered me in my mother's womb."* There I lay hidden—covered by thee. Before I could know thee, or aught else, thou hadst a care for me, and didst hide me away as a treasure till thou shouldst see fit to bring me to the light. Thus the Psalmist describes the intimacy which God had with him. In his most secret part—his reins, and in his most secret condition—yet unborn, he was under the control and guardianship of God.

14. *"I will praise thee :"* a good resolve, and one which he was even now carrying out. Those who are praising God are the very men who *will* praise him. Those who wish to praise have subjects for adoration ready to hand. We too seldom remember our creation, and all the skill and kindness bestowed upon our frame : but the sweet singer of Israel was better instructed, and therefore he prepares for the chief musician a song concerning our nativity and all the fashioning which precedes it. We cannot begin too soon to bless our Maker, who began so soon to bless us : even in the act of creation he created reasons for our praising his name. *"For I am fearfully and wonderfully made."* Who can gaze even upon a model of our anatomy without wonder and awe ? Who could dissect a portion of the human frame without marvelling at its delicacy, and trembling at its frailty ? The Psalmist had scarcely peered within the veil which hides the nerves, sinews, and blood-vessels from common inspection ; the science of anatomy was quite unknown to him ; and yet he had seen enough to arouse his admiration of the work and his reverence for the Worker. *"Marvellous are thy works."* These parts of my frame are all *thy* works ; and though they be home works, close under my own eye, yet are they wonderful to the last degree. They are works within my own self, yet are they beyond my understanding, and appear to me as so many miracles of skill and power. We need not go to the ends of the earth for marvels, nor even across our own threshold ; they abound in our own bodies.

"And that my soul knoweth right well." He was no agnostic—he knew ; he was no doubter—his soul knew ; he was no dupe—his soul knew right well. Those know indeed and of a truth who first know the Lord, and then know all things in him. He was made to know the marvellous nature of God's work with assurance and accuracy, for he had found by experience that the Lord is a master-worker, performing inimitable wonders when accomplishing his kind designs. If we are marvellously wrought upon even before we are born, what shall we say of the Lord's dealings with us after we quit his secret workshop, and he directs our pathway through the pilgrimage of life ? What shall we not say of that new birth which

is even more mysterious than the first, and exhibits even more the love and wisdom of the Lord.

15. *"My substance was not hid from thee."* The substantial part of my being was before thine all-seeing eye ; the bones which make my frame were put together by thine hand. The essential materials of my being before they were arranged were all within the range of thine eye. I was hidden from all human knowledge, but not from thee : thou hast ever been intimately acquainted with me. *"When I was made in secret."* Most chastely and beautifully is here described the formation of our being before the time of our birth. A great artist will often labour alone in his studio, and not suffer his work to be seen until it is finished ; even so did the Lord fashion us where no eye beheld us, and the veil was not lifted till every member was complete. Much of the formation of our inner man still proceeds in secret ; hence the more of solitude the better for us. The true church also is being fashioned in secret, so that none may cry, " Lo, here ! " or " Lo, there ! " as if that which is visible could ever be identical with the invisibly growing body of Christ. *"And curiously wrought it in the lowest parts of the earth."* " Embroidered with great skill," is an accurate poetical description of the creation of veins, sinews, muscles, nerves, etc. What tapestry can equal the human fabric ? This work is wrought as much in private as if it had been accomplished in the grave, or in the darkness of the abyss. The expressions are poetical, beautifully veiling, though not absolutely concealing, the real meaning. God's intimate knowledge of us from the beginning, and even before it, is here most charmingly set forth. Cannot he who made us thus wondrously when we were not, still carry on his work of power till he has perfected us, though we feel unable to aid in the process, and are lying in great sorrow and self-loathing, as though cast into the lowest parts of the earth ?

16. *"Thine eyes did see my substance, yet being unperfect."* While as yet the vessel was upon the wheel the Potter saw it all. The Lord knows not only our shape, but our substance : this is substantial knowledge indeed. The Lord's observation of us is intent and intentional,—" Thine eyes did see." Moreover, the divine mind discerns all things as clearly and certainly as men perceive by actual eye-sight. His is not hearsay acquaintance, but the knowledge which comes of sight. *"And in thy book all my members were written, which in continuance were fashioned, when as yet there was none of them."* An architect draws his plans, and makes out his specifications ; even so did the great Maker of our frame write down all our members in the book of his purposes. That we have eyes, and ears, and hands, and feet, is all due to the wise and gracious purpose of heaven : it was so ordered in the secret decree by which all things are as they are. God's purposes concern our limbs and faculties. Their form, and shape, and everything about them were appointed of God long before they had any existence. God saw us when we could not be seen, and he wrote about us when there was nothing of us to write about. When as yet there were none of our members in existence, all those members were before the eye of God in the sketch-book of his foreknowledge and predestination.

This verse is an exceedingly difficult one to translate, but we do not think that any of the proposed amendments are better than the rendering afforded us by the Authorized Version. The large number of words in italics will warn the English reader that the sense is hard to come at, and difficult to express, and that it would be unwise to found any doctrine upon the *English* words ; happily there is no temptation to do so.

The great truth expressed in these lines has by many been referred to the formation of the mystical body of our Lord Jesus. Of course, what is true of man, as man, is emphatically true of Him who is the representative man. The great Lord knows who belong to Christ ; his eye perceives the chosen members who shall yet be made one with the living person of the mystical Christ. Those of the elect who are as yet unborn, or unrenewed, are nevertheless written in the Lord's book. As the form of Eve grew up in silence and secrecy under the fashioning hand of the Maker, so at this hour is the Bride being fashioned for the Lord Jesus ; or, to change the figure,—a body is being prepared in which the life and glory of the indwelling Lord shall for ever be displayed. The Lord knoweth them that are his : he has a specially familiar acquaintance with the members of the body of Christ ; he sees their substance, unperfect though they be.

17. *"How precious also are thy thoughts unto me, O God ! "* He is not alarmed at the fact that God knows all about him ; on the contrary, he is comforted, and even feels himself to be enriched, as with a casket of precious jewels. That God

should think upon him is the believer's treasure and pleasure. He cries, "How costly, how valued are thy thoughts, how dear to me is thy perpetual attention!" He thinks upon God's thoughts with delight; the more of them the better he is pleased. It is a joy worth worlds that the Lord should think upon us who are so poor and needy: it is a joy which fills our whole nature to think upon God; returning love for love, thought for thought, after our poor fashion. *"How great is the sum of them!"* When we remember that God thought upon us from old eternity, continues to think upon us every moment, and will think of us when time shall be no more, we may well exclaim, "How great is the sum!" Thoughts such as are natural to the Creator, the Preserver, the Redeemer, the Father, the Friend, are evermore flowing from the heart of the Lord. Thoughts of our pardon, renewal, upholding, supplying, educating, perfecting, and a thousand more kinds perpetually well up in the mind of the Most High. It should fill us with adoring wonder and reverent surprise that the infinite mind of God should turn so many thoughts towards us who are so insignificant and so unworthy! What a contrast is all this to the notion of those who deny the existence of a personal, conscious God! Imagine a world without a thinking, personal God! Conceive of a grim providence of machinery!—a fatherhood of law! Such philosophy is hard and cold. As well might a man pillow his head upon a razor edge as seek rest in such a fancy. But a God always thinking of us makes a happy world, a rich life, a heavenly hereafter.

18. *"If I should count them, they are more in number than the sand."* This figure shows the thoughts of God to be altogether innumerable; for nothing can surpass in number the grains of sand which belt the main ocean and all the minor seas. The task of counting God's thoughts of love would be a never-ending one. If we should attempt the reckoning we must necessarily fail, for the infinite falls not within the line of our feeble intellect. Even could we count the sands on the sea-shore, we should not then be able to number God's thoughts, for they are " more in number than the sand." This is not the hyperbole of poetry, but the solid fact of inspired statement: God thinks upon us infinitely: there is a limit to the act of creation, but not to the might of divine love.

"When I am awake I am still with thee." Thy thoughts of love are so many that my mind never gets away from them, they surround me at all hours. I go to my bed, and God is my last thought; and when I wake I find my mind still hovering about his palace-gates; God is ever with me, and I am ever with him. This is life indeed. If during sleep my mind wanders away into dreams, yet it only wanders upon holy ground, and the moment I wake my heart is back with its Lord. The Psalmist does not say, "When I awake, I return to thee," but, " I am still with thee"; as if his meditations were continuous, and his communion unbroken. Soon we shall lie down to sleep for the last time: God grant that when the trumpet of the archangel shall waken us we may find ourselves still with him.

19 Surely thou wilt slay the wicked, O God: depart from me therefore, ye bloody men.

20 For they speak against thee wickedly, *and* thine enemies take *thy name* in vain.

21 Do not I hate them, O LORD, that hate thee? and am not I grieved with those that rise up against thee?

22 I hate them with perfect hatred: I count them mine enemies.

23 Search me, O God, and know my heart: try me, and know my thoughts.

24 And see if *there be any* wicked way in me, and lead me in the way everlasting.

19. *"Surely thou wilt slay the wicked, O God."* There can be no doubt upon that head, for thou hast seen all their transgressions, which indeed have been done in thy presence; and thou hast long enough endured their provocations, which have been so openly manifest before thee. Crimes committed before the face of the Judge are not likely to go unpunished. If the eye of God is grieved with the presence of evil, it is but natural to expect that he will remove the offending object. God who sees all evil will slay all evil. With earthly sovereigns sin may go unpunished for lack of evidence, or the law may be left without execution from lack of vigour in the judge; but this cannot happen in the case of God, the living God. He beareth not the sword in vain. Such is his love of holiness and hatred of wrong,

that he will carry on war to the death with those whose hearts and lives are wicked. God will not always suffer his lovely creation to be defaced and defiled by the presence of wickedness : if anything is sure, this is sure, that he will ease him of his adversaries. *"Depart from me therefore, ye bloody men."* Men who delight in cruelty and war are not fit companions for those who walk with God. David chases the men of blood from his court, for he is weary of those of whom God is weary. He seems to say—If God will not let you live with him I will not have you live with me. You would destroy others, and therefore I want you not in my society. You will be destroyed yourselves, I desire you not in my service. Depart from me, for you depart from God. As we delight to have the holy God always near us, so would we eagerly desire to have wicked men removed as far as possible from us. We tremble in the society of the ungodly lest their doom should fall upon them suddenly, and we should see them lie dead at our feet. We do not wish to have our place of intercourse turned into gallows of execution, therefore let the condemned be removed out of our company.

20. *"For they speak against thee wickedly."* Why should I bear their company when their talk sickens me ? They vent their treasons and blasphemies as often as they please, doing so without the slighest excuse or provocation ; let them therefore begone, where they may find a more congenial associate than I can be. When men speak against God they will be sure to speak against us, if they find it serve their turn ; hence godless men are not the stuff out of which true friends can ever be made. God gave these men their tongues, and they turn against their Benefactor, wickedly, from sheer malice, and with great perverseness. *"And thine enemies take thy name in vain."* This is their sport : to insult Jehovah's glorious name is their amusement. To blaspheme the name of the Lord is a gratuitous wickedness in which there can be no pleasure, and from which there can be no profit. This is a sure mark of the " enemies " of the Lord, that they have the impudence to assail his honour, and treat his glory with irreverence. How can God do other than slay them ? How can we do other than withdraw from every sort of association with them ? What a wonder of sin it is that men should rail against so good a Being as the Lord our God ! The impudence of those who talk wickedly is a singular fact, and it is the more singular when we reflect that the Lord against whom they speak is all around them, and lays to heart every dishonour which they render to his holy name. We ought not to wonder that men slander and deride us, for they do the same with the Most High God.

21. *"Do not I hate them, O LORD, that hate thee ? "* He was a good hater, for he hated only those who hated good. Of this hatred he is not ashamed, but he sets it forth as a virtue to which he would have the Lord bear testimony. To love all men with benevolence is our duty ; but to love any wicked man with complacency would be a crime. To hate a man for his own sake, or for any evil done to us, would be wrong ; but to hate a man because he is the foe of all goodness and the enemy of all righteousness, is nothing more nor less than an obligation. The more we love God the more indignant shall we grow with those who refuse him their affection. " If any man love not the Lord Jesus Christ let him be Anathema Maranatha." Truly, " jealousy is cruel as the grave." The loyal subject must not be friendly to the traitor. *"And am not I grieved with those that rise up against thee ? "* He appeals to heaven that he took no pleasure in those who rebelled against the Lord ; but, on the contrary, he was made to mourn by a sight of their ill behaviour. Since God is everywhere, he knows our feelings towards the profane and ungodly, and he knows that so far from approving such characters the very sight of them is grievous to our eyes.

22. *"I hate them with perfect hatred."* He does not leave it a matter of question. He does not occupy a neutral position. His hatred to bad, vicious, blasphemous men is intense, complete, energetic. He is as whole-hearted in his hate of wickedness as in his love of goodness. *"I count them mine enemies."* He makes a personal matter of it. They may have done him no ill, but if they are doing despite to God, to his laws, and to the great principles of truth and righteousness, David proclaims war against them. Wickedness passes men into favour with unrighteous spirits ; but it excludes them from the communion of the just. We pull up the drawbridge and man the walls when a man of Belial goes by our castle. His character is a *casus belli ;* we cannot do otherwise than contend with those who contend with God.

23. *"Search me, O God, and know my heart."* David is no accomplice with traitors. He has disowned them in set form, and now he appeals to God that he

does not harbour a trace of fellowship with them. He will have God himself search him, and search him thoroughly, till every point of his being is known, and read, and understood; for he is sure that even by such an investigation there will be found in him no complicity with wicked men. He challenges the fullest investigation, the innermost search: he had need be a true man who can put himself deliberately into such a crucible. Yet we may each one desire such searching; for it would be a terrible calamity to us for sin to remain in our hearts unknown and undiscovered. "*Try me, and know my thoughts.*" Exercise any and every test upon me. By fire and by water let me be examined. Read not alone the desires of my heart, but the fugitive thoughts of my head. Know with all-penetrating knowledge all that is or has been in the chambers of my mind. What a mercy that there is one being who can know us to perfection! He is intimately at home with us. He is graciously inclined towards us, and is willing to bend his omniscience to serve the end of our sanctification. Let us pray as David did, and let us be as honest as he. We cannot hide our sin: salvation lies the other way, in a plain discovery of evil, and an effectual severance from it.

24. "*And see if there be any wicked way in me.*" See whether there be in my heart, or in my life, any evil habit unknown to myself. If there be such an evil way, take me from it, take it from me. No matter how dear the wrong may have become, nor how deeply prejudiced I may have been in its favour, be pleased to deliver me therefrom altogether, effectually, and at once, that I may tolerate nothing which is contrary to thy mind. As I hate the wicked in their way, so would I hate every wicked way in myself. "*And lead me in the way everlasting.*" If thou hast introduced me already to the good old way, be pleased to keep me in it, and conduct me further and further along it. It is a way which thou hast set up of old, it is based upon everlasting principles, and it is the way in which immortal spirits will gladly run for ever and ever. There will be no end to it world without end. It lasts for ever, and they who are in it last for ever. Conduct me into it, O Lord, and conduct me throughout the whole length of it. By thy providence, by thy word, by thy grace, and by thy Spirit, lead me evermore.

EXPLANATORY NOTES AND QUAINT SAYINGS.

Whole Psalm.—Aben Ezra observes, that this is the most glorious and excellent Psalm in all the book: a very excellent one it is; but whether the most excellent, it is hard to say.—*John Gill.*

Whole Psalm.—There is one Psalm which it were well if Christians would do by it as Pythagoras by his Golden Precepts,—every morning and evening repeat it. It is David's appeal of a good conscience unto God, against the malicious suspicions and calumnies of men, in Psalm cxxxix.—*Samuel Annesley* (1620—1696), *in "The Morning Exercises."*

Whole Psalm.—This Psalm is one of the sublimest compositions in the world. How came a shepherd boy to conceive so sublime a theme, and to write in so sublime a strain? Holy men of God spake as they were moved by the Holy Ghost. What themes are more sublime than the Divine attributes? And which of these attributes is more sublime than Omnipresence? Omniscience, spirituality, infinity, immutability and eternity are necessarily included in it.—*George Rogers.*

Whole Psalm.—Let the modern wits, after this, look upon the honest shepherds of Palestine as a company of *rude and unpolished clowns;* let them, if they can, produce from profane authors thoughts that are more sublime, more delicate, or better turned; not to mention the sound divinity and solid piety which are apparent under these expressions.—*Claude Fleury,* 1640—1723.

Whole Psalm.—Here the poet inverts his gaze, from the blaze of suns, to the strange atoms composing his own frame. He stands shuddering over the precipice of himself. Above is the All-encompassing Spirit, from whom the morning wings cannot save; and below, at a deep distance, appears amid the branching forest of his animal frame, so fearfully and wonderfully made, the abyss of his spiritual existence, lying like a dark lake in the midst. How, between mystery and mystery his mind, his wonder, his very reason, seem to rock like a little boat between the sea and sky. But speedily does he regain his serenity ; when he throws himself, with childlike haste and confidence, into the arms of that Fatherly Spirit, and murmurs in his bosom, " How precious also are thy thoughts unto *me*, O God ; how great is the sum of them " ; and looking up at last in his face, cries—" Search me, O Lord. I cannot search thee ; I cannot search myself ; I am overwhelmed by those dreadful depths ; but search me as thou only canst ; see if there be any wicked way in me, and lead me in the way everlasting."—*George Gilfillan* (1813—1878), *in "The Bards of the Bible."*

Whole Psalm.—The Psalm has an immediately practical aim, which is unfolded near the close. It is not an abstract description of the Divine attributes, with a mere indirect purpose in view. If God is such a being, if his vital agency reaches over all his creation, pervades all objects, illumines the deepest and darkest recesses ; if his knowledge has no limits, piercing into the mysterious processes of creation, into the smallest and most elemental germs of life ; if his eye can discern the still more subtle and recondite processes of mind, comprehending the half-formed conception, the germinating desire " afar off " ; if, anterior to all finite existence, his predetermining decree went forth ; if in those ancient records of eternity man's framework, with all its countless elements and organs, in all the ages of his duration, were inscribed—then for his servant, his worshipper on earth, two consequences follow, most practical and momentous : *first*, the ceasing to have or feel any complacency with the wicked, any sympathy with their evil ways, any communion with them as such ; and, *secondly*, the earnest desire that God would search the Psalmist's soul, lest in its unsounded depths there might be some lurking iniquity, lest there might be, beyond the present jurisdiction of his conscience, some dark realm which the Omniscient eye only could explore.—*Bela B. Edwards* (1802–1852), *in H. C. Fish's "Masterpieces of Pulpit Eloquence."*

Whole Psalm.—

Searcher of hearts ! to thee are known
   The inmost secrets of my breast ;
At home, abroad, in crowds, alone,
   Thou mark'st my rising and my rest,
My thoughts far off, through every maze,
Source, stream, and issue—all my ways.

How from thy presence should I go,
   Or whither from thy Spirit flee,
Since all above, around, below,
   Exist in thine immensity ?
If up to heaven I take my way,
I meet thee in eternal day.

If in the grave I make my bed
   With worms and dust, lo ! thou art there !
If, on the wings of morning sped,
   Beyond the ocean I repair,
I feel thine all-controlling will,
And thy right hand upholds me still.

" Let darkness hide me," if I say,
   Darkness can no concealment be ;
Night, on thy rising, shines like day ;
   Darkness and light are one with thee :
For thou mine embryo-form didst view,
Ere her own babe my mother knew.

In me thy workmanship display'd,
   A miracle of power I stand :
Fearfully, wonderfully made,
   And framed in secret by thine hand ;
I lived, ere into being brought,
Through thine eternity of thought.

How precious are thy thoughts of peace,
   O God, to me ! how great the sum !
New every morn, they never cease ;
   They were, they are, and yet shall come,
In number and in compass more
Than ocean's sands or ocean's shore.

Search me, O God! and know my heart,
Try me, my inmost soul survey;
And warn thy servant to depart
From every false and evil way:
So shall thy truth my guidance be
To life and immortality.
James Montgomery.

Whole Psalm.—The Psalm may be thus summarized. Verse 1. "*O LORD, thou hast searched me, and known me.*"—As though he said, " O LORD, thou art the heart-searching God, who perfectly knowest all the thoughts, counsels, studies, endeavours, and actions of all men, and therefore mine." Verse 2. "*Thou knowest my downsitting and mine uprising, thou understandest my thought afar off.*"—As if he had said, " Thou knowest my rest and motion, and my plodding thoughts of both." Verse 3. "*Thou compassest my path and my lying down, and art acquainted with all my ways.*"—As if he had said, " Thou fannest and winnowest me," that is, " Thou discussest and triest me to the utmost." Verse 4. "*For there is not a word in my tongue, but, lo, O LORD, thou knowest it altogether.*"—As if he had said, "I cannot speak a word, though never so secret, obscure, or subtle, but thou knowest what, and why, and with what mind it was uttered." Verse 5. " *Thou hast beset me behind and before, and laid thine hand upon me.*"—As if he had said, " Thou keepest me within the compass of thy knowledge, like a man that will not let his servant go out of his sight. I cannot break away from thee." Verse 6. " *Such knowledge is too wonderful for me ; it is high, I cannot attain unto it.*"—As if he had said, " The knowledge of thy great and glorious majesty and infiniteness is utterly past all human comprehension." Verse 7. " *Whither shall I go from thy spirit ? or whither shall I flee from thy presence ?* "—As if he had said, " Whither can I flee from thee, whose essence, presence, and power is everywhere ? " Verse 8. "*If I ascend up into heaven, thou art there : if I make my bed in hell, behold, thou art there.*"—As if he had said, " There is no height above thee, there is no depth below thee." Verse 9. "*If I take the wings of the morning, and dwell in the uttermost parts of the sea.*"—As if he had said, " If I had wings to fly as swift as the morning light, from the east to the west, that I could in a moment get to the furthest parts of the world." Verse 10. "*Even there shall thy hand lead me, and thy right hand shall hold me.*"—As if he had said, " Thence shall thy hand lead me back, and hold me fast like a fugitive." Verse 11. "*If I say, Surely the darkness shall cover me ; even the night shall be light about me.*"—As if he had said, " Though darkness hinders man's sight, it doth not thine." In a word, look which way you will, there is no hiding-place from God. " For his eyes are upon the ways of man, and he seeth all his goings. There is no darkness nor shadow of death, where the workers of iniquity may hide themselves " : Job xxxiv. 21, 22. Therefore, Christians, do nothing but what you are willing God should take notice of ; and judge in yourselves whether this be not the way to have a good and quiet conscience.—*Samuel Annesley.*

Whole Psalm.—In this Aramaizing Psalm what the preceding Psalm says in verse 6 comes to be carried into effect, viz. : "*For Jahve is exalted and he seeth the lowly, and the proud he knoweth from afar.*" This Psalm has manifold points of contact with its predecessor.—*Franz Delitzsch.*

" *To the Chief Musician.*"—As a later writer could have no motive for prefixing the title, " *To the Chief Musician,*" it affords an incidental proof of antiquity and genuineness.—*Joseph Addison Alexander.*

"*A Psalm of David.*"—How any critic can assign this Psalm to other than David I cannot understand. Every line, every thought, every turn of expression and transition, is his, and his only. As for the arguments drawn from the two Chaldaisms which occur, this is really nugatory. These Chaldaisms consist merely in the substitution of one letter for another, very like it in shape, and easily to be mistaken by a transcriber, particularly by one who had been used to the Chaldee idiom ; but the moral arguments for David's authorship are so strong as to overwhelm any such verbal, or rather *literal* criticism, were even the objections more formidable than they actually are.—*John Jebb.*

Verse 1.—"*O* LORD, *thou hast searched me, and known* (me)." There is no " *me* " after " *known* " in the Hebrew ; therefore it is better to take the object after " *known* " in a wider sense. The omission is intentional, that the believing heart of all who use this Psalm may supply the ellipsis. Thou hast known and knowest *all that concerns the matter in question,* as well whether I and mine are guilty or innocent

(Ps. xliv. 21) ; also my exact circumstances, my needs, my sorrows, and the precise time when to relieve me.—*A. R. Fausset.*

Verse 1.—"*O Lord, thou hast searched me, and known me.*" The godly may sometimes be so overclouded with calumnies and reproaches as not to be able to find a way to clear themselves before men, but must content and comfort themselves with the testimony of a good conscience and with God's approbation of their integrity, as here David doth.—*David Dickson.*

Verse 1.—"*O Lord, thou hast searched me, and known me.*" David here lays down the great doctrine, that God has a perfect knowledge of us, First, *in the way of an address to God :* he saith it to him, acknowledging it to him, and giving him the glory of it. Divine truths look full as well when they are prayed over as when they are preached over : and much better than when they are disputed over. When we speak of God to him himself, we find ourselves concerned to speak with the utmost degree both of sincerity and reverence, which will be likely to make the impressions the deeper. Secondly, he lays it down *in a way of application to himself :* not thou hast known all, but " thou hast known *me* " ; that is it which I am most concerned to believe, and which it will be most profitable for me to consider. Then we know things for our good when we know them for ourselves. Job v. 27. . . . David was a king, and " the hearts of kings are unsearchable " to their subjects (Prov. xxv. 3), but they are not so to their sovereign.—*Matthew Henry.*

Verse 1.—"*O Lord, thou hast searched me.*" I would have you observe how thoroughly in the very first verse he brings home the truth to his own heart and his own conscience : " O Lord, thou hast searched *me.*" He does not slur it over as a general truth, in which such numbers shared that he might hope to escape or evade its solemn appeal to himself ; but it is, " Thou hast searched *me.*"—*Barton Bouchier.*

Verse 1.—"*Searched.*" The Hebrew word originally means *to dig,* and is applied to the search for precious metals (Job xxviii. 3), but metaphorically to a moral inquisition into guilt.—*Joseph Addison Alexander.*

Verses 1—5.—God knows everything that passes in our inmost souls better than we do ourselves : he reads our most secret thoughts : all the cogitations of our hearts pass in review before him ; and he is as perfectly and entirely employed in the scrutiny of the thoughts and actions of an individual, as in the regulation of the most important concerns of the universe. This is what we cannot comprehend ; but it is what, according to the light of reason, must be true, and, according to revelation, is indeed true. God can do nothing imperfectly ; and we may form some idea of his superintending knowledge, by conceiving what is indeed the truth, that all the powers of the Godhead are employed, and solely employed, in the observation and examination of the conduct of one individual. I say, this is indeed the case, because all the powers of the Godhead are employed upon the least as well as upon the greatest concerns of the universe ; and the whole mind and power of the Creator are as exclusively employed upon the formation of a grub as of a world. God knows everything perfectly, and he knows everything perfectly at once. This, to a human understanding, would breed confusion ; but there can be no confusion in the Divine understanding, because confusion arises from imperfection. Thus God, without confusion, beholds as distinctly the actions of every man, as if that man were the only created being, and the Godhead were solely employed in observing him. Let this thought fill your mind with awe and with remorse.—*Henry Kirke White,* 1785—1806.

Verses 1—12.—

> O Lord, in me there lieth nought
> But to thy search revealed lies ;
>   For when I sit
>   Thou markest it ;
> No less thou notest when I rise ;
> Yea, closest closet of my thought
> Hath open windows to thine eyes.
>
> Thou walkest with me when I walk,
> When to my bed for rest I go,
>   I find thee there,
>   And everywhere :
> Not youngest thought in me doth grow,
> No, not one word I cast to talk
> But, yet unuttered, thou dost know.

If forth I march, thou goest before ;
If back I turn, thou com'st behind :
     So forth nor back
     Thy guard I lack ;
Nay, on me, too, thy hand I find.
Well, I thy wisdom may adore,
     But never reach with earthy mind.

To shun thy notice, leave thine eye,
O whither might I take my way ?
     To starry sphere ?
     Thy throne is there.
To dead men's undelightsome stay ?
There is thy walk, and there to lie
     Unknown, in vain I should assay.

O sun, whom light nor flight can match !
Suppose thy lightful flightful wings
     Thou lend to me,
     And I could flee
As far as thee the evening brings :
Ev'n led to west he would me catch,
     Nor should I lurk with western things.

Do thou thy best, O secret night,
In sable veil to cover me :
     Thy sable veil
     Shall vainly fail :
With day unmasked my night shall be ;
For night is day, and darkness light,
     O Father of all lights, to thee.

                     Sir Philip Sidney, 1554—1586.

     Verse 2.—"*Thou.*" David makes the personal pronoun the very frontispiece of the verse, and so says expressly and distinctly to Jehovah, "*Thou* knowest ;" thus marking the difference between God and all others, as though he said, " Thou, and thou alone, O God, in all the universe, knowest altogether all that can be known concerning me, even to my inmost thought, as well as outward act."—*Martin Geier.*

     Verse 2.—"*Thou knowest my downsitting and mine uprising.*" Does God care ? Is he our Friend ? Even in such little matters as these, does he watch over us " to do us good " ? . . . When we " sit down " he sees ; when we rise up he is there. Not an action is lost or a thought overlooked. No wonder that, as these tiny miracles of care are related by David, he adds the words, "*Such knowledge is too wonderful for me ; it is high, I cannot attain unto it.*" We get accustomed to the thought that God made the sun and sky, the " moon and stars which he hath ordained," and we bow to the fact that they are " the work of his fingers." Let us go further ! The "*coming in*" and "*going out*" of the Christian is mentioned several times in Scripture as though it were very important. So much hinges on these little words. " David went out and came in before the people. And David behaved himself wisely in all his ways ; and the Lord was with him ": 1 Sam. xviii. 13, 14. " The LORD shall preserve thy going out and thy coming in from this time forth, and even for evermore " : Ps. cxxi. 8. David was given both *preservation* and *wisdom* in his " goings out " and " comings in." Perhaps the latter was both cause and effect of the first. It was needed, for many eyes were upon him, and many eyes are upon us : are they not ? Perhaps more than we think.—*Lady Hope, in "Between Times," 1884.*

     Verse 2.—"*Downsitting and uprising.*" "*Uprising*" following "*downsitting*" is in the order of right sequence ; for action ought to follow meditation. Jacob saw the angels ascending to God before they descended to service among mortals. Hence we are taught first to join ourselves to God by meditation, and afterwards to repair to the aid of our fellows.—*Thomas Le Blanc.*

     Verse 2.—"*Uprising*" may respect either rising *from bed*, when the Lord knows whether the heart is still with him (ver. 18) ; what sense is had of the Divine protection and sustentation, and what thankfulness there is for the mercies of the night past ; and whether the voice of prayer and praise is directed to him in the morning, as it should be (Ps. iii. 5 ; v. 3) ; or else rising *from the table*, when the Lord knows whether a man's table has been his snare, and with what thankfulness he rises from it for the favours he has received. The Targum interprets this of rising up to go to war ; which David did, in the name and strength, and by the direction of the Lord.— *John Gill.*

Verse 2.—*"Thou understandest my thought afar off." "My thought :"* that is, every thought, though innumerable thoughts pass through me in a day. The divine knowledge reaches to their source and fountain, before they are our thoughts. If the Lord knows them before their existence, before they can be properly called ours, much more doth he know them when they actually spring up in us ; he knows the tendency of them, where the bird will alight when it is in flight ; he knows them exactly ; he is therefore called a " discerner " or criticiser of the heart : Heb. iv. 2.— *Stephen Charnock.*

Verse 2.—*"Thou understandest my thought afar off."* Not that God is at a distance from our thoughts ; but he understands them while they are far off from us, from our knowledge, while they are potential, as gardeners know what weeds such ground will bring forth, when nothing appears. Deut. xxxi. 21. " I know their imagination which they go about, even now, before I have brought them into the land which I sware " : God knew their thoughts before they came into Canaan, what they would be there. And how can it be, but that God should know all our thoughts, seeing he made the heart, and it is in his hand (Prov. xxi. 1), seeing, " we live, and move, and have our being " in God (Acts xvii. 28) ; seeing he is through us all, and in us all (Eph. iv. 6). Look well to your hearts, thoughts, risings, whatever comes into your mind ; let no secret sins, or corruptions, lodge there ; think not to conceal anything from the eye of God.—*William Greenhill.*

Verse 2.—*"Thou understandest my thought afar off."* Though my thoughts be never so foreign and distant from one another, thou understandest the chain of them, and canst make out their connexion, when so many of them slip my notice that I myself cannot.—*Matthew Henry.*

Verse 2.—*"My thought."* The רֵעַ, *rea,* which we have rendered *"thought,"* signifies also a *friend* or *companion,* on which account some read—*thou knowest what is nearest me afar off,* a meaning more to the point than any other, if it could be supported by example. The reference would then be very appropriately to the fact that the most distant objects are contemplated as near by God. Some for *"afar off"* read *beforehand,* in which signification the Hebrew word is elsewhere taken ; as if he had said, O Lord, every thought which I conceive in my heart is already known to thee beforehand.—*John Calvin.*

Verse 2.—*"Thought."* In all affliction, in all business, a man's best comfort is this, that all he does and even all he thinks, God knows. In the Septuagint we read διαλογισμοὺς, that is, " reasonings." God knows all our inner ratiocination, all the dialogues, all the colloquies of the soul with itself.—*Thomas Le Blanc.*

Verse 2.—*"Thou understandest my thought."* Before men we stand as opaque bee-hives. They can see the thoughts go in and out of us, but what work they do inside of a man they cannot tell. Before God we are as glass bee-hives, and all that our thoughts are doing within us he perfectly sees and understands.—*Henry Ward Beecher.*

Verse 2.—*"Thou understandest my thought afar off."*

> Man may not see thee do an impious deed ;
> But God thy very inmost thought can read."
>
> *Plutarch.*

Verse 2.—*"Afar off."* This expression is, as in Ps. cxxxviii. 6, to be understood as contradicting the delusion (Job xxii. 12—14) that God's dwelling in heaven prevents him from observing mundane things.—*Lange's Commentary.*

Verse 2.—*"Afar off."* Both in distance, however far off a man may seek to hide his thoughts from God ; and in time, for God knows the human thought before man conceives it in his heart, in his eternal prescience. The Egyptians called God the " eye of the world."—*Thomas Le Blanc.*

Verses 2—4.—Do not fancy that your demeanour, posture, dress, or deportment are not under God's providence. You deceive yourself. Do not think that your thoughts pass free from inspection. The Lord understands them afar off. Think not that your words are dissipated in the air before God can hear. Oh, no ! He knows them even when still upon your tongue. Do not think that your ways are so private and concealed that there is none to know or censure them. You mistake. God knows all your ways.—*Johann David Frisch,* 1731.

Verse 3.—"*Thou compassest my path and my lying down,*" etc. The words that I have read unto you, seem to be a metaphor, taken from soldiers surrounding the ways with an ambush, or placing scouts and spies in every corner, to discover the enemy in his march ; "*Thou compassest my path*" *:* thou hast (as it were) thy spies over me, wheresoever I go. By "*path*" is meant the outward actions and carriage of his ordinary conversation. By "*lying down*" is signified to us the private and close actions of his life ; such as were attended only by darkness and solitude. In Ps. xxxvi. verse 4, it is said of the wicked that "he deviseth mischief upon his bed," to denote not only his perverse diligence, but also his secresy in it : and God is said to "hide his children in the secret of his pavilion," so that these places of rest and lying down are designed for secresy and withdrawing. When a man retires into his chamber, he does in a manner, for a while, shut himself out of the world. And that this is the fine sense of that expression of *lying down* appears from the next words, "*Thou art acquainted with all my ways*"; where he collects in one word what he had before said in two ; or, it may come in by way of entrance and deduction, from the former. As if he should say, Thou knowest what I do in my ordinary converse with men, and also how I behave myself when I am retired from them ; therefore thou knowest *all* my actions, since a man's actions may be reduced either to his public or private deportment. By the other expression of "*my ways*" is here meant the total of a man's hehaviour before God, whether in thoughts, words, or deeds, as is manifest by comparing this with other verses.—*Robert South.*

Verse 3.—"*Thou compassest my path.*" This is a metaphor either from huntsmen watching all the motions and lurking-places of wild beasts, that they may catch them ; or from soldiers besieging their enemies in a city, and setting round about them.—*Matthew Pool.*

Verse 3.—"*Thou compassest,*" or *fannest,* or *winnowest,* "*my path*" ; that is, discussest or triest out to the utmost, even tracing the footsteps, as the Greek signifieth. Compare Job xxxi. 4.—*Henry Ainsworth.*

Verse 3.—"*Thou art acquainted with all my ways.*" God takes notice of every step we take, every right step, and every by-step. He knows what rule we walk by, what end we walk toward, what company we walk with.—*Religious Tract Society's Commentary.*

Verse 3.—"*Art acquainted,*" as by most familiar intercourse, as if thou hadst always lived with me [Hebrew] and thus become entirely familiar with my ways.—*Henry Cowles.*

Verse 3.—The Psalmist mentions four modes of human existence ; *stationis, sessionis, itionis, cubationis ;* because man never stayeth long in one mood, but in every change the eyes of the Lord cease not to watch him.—*Geier.*

Verse 4.—"*For there is not a word in my tongue,*" etc. The words admit a double meaning. Accordingly some understand them to imply that God knows what we are about to say before the words are formed on our tongue ; others, that though we speak not a word, and try by silence to conceal our secret intentions, we cannot elude his notice. Either rendering amounts to the same thing, and it is of no consequence which we adopt. The idea meant to be conveyed is, that while the tongue is the index of thought to man, being the great medium of communication, God, who knows the heart, is independent of words. And use is made of the demonstrative particle *lo !* to indicate emphatically that the innermost recesses of our spirit stand present to his view.—*John Calvin.*

Verse 4.—"*For there is not a word in my tongue,*" etc. How needful it is to set a watch before the doors of our mouth, to hold that unruly member of ours, the tongue, as with bit and bridle. Some of you feel at times that you can scarcely say a word, and the less you say the better. Well, it may be as well ; for great talkers are almost sure to make slips with their tongue. It may be a good thing that you cannot speak much ; for in the multitude of words there lacketh not sin. Wherever you go, what light, vain, and foolish conversations you hear ! I am glad not to be thrown into circumstances where I can hear it. But with you it may be different. You may often repent of speaking, you will rarely repent of silence. How soon angry words are spoken ! How soon foolish expressions drop from the mouth ! The Lord knows it all, marks it all, and did you carry about with you a more solemn recollection of it you would be more watchful than you are.—*Joseph C. Philpot.*

Verse 4.—*"When there is not a word in my tongue, O LORD, thou knowest all;"* so some read it; for thoughts are words to God.—*Matthew Henry.*

Verse 4.—*"Thou knowest it."* The gods know what passes in our minds without the aid of eyes, ears, or tongues; on which divine omniscience is founded the feeling of men that, when they wish in silence, or offer up a prayer for anything, the gods hear them.—*Cicero.*

Verse 5.—*"Thou hast beset me behind and before,"* etc. There is here an insensible transition from God's omniscience to his omnipresence, out of which the Scriptures represent it as arising. *"Behind and before,"* i.e. on all sides. The idea of *above* and *below* is suggested by the last clause. *"Beset,"* besiege, hem in, or closely surround. *"Thy hand,"* or the palm of thy hand, as the Hebrew word strictly denotes.—*Joseph Addison Alexander.*

Verse 5.—*"Thou hast beset me behind and before."* What would you say if, wherever you turned, whatever you were doing, whatever thinking, whether in public or private, with a confidential friend telling your secrets, or alone planning them—if, I say, you saw an eye constantly fixed on you, from whose watching, though you strove ever so much, you could never escape. . . . that could perceive your every thought? The supposition is awful enough. There is such an Eye.—*De Vere.*

Verse 5.—*"Thou hast beset me behind and before."* One who finds the way blocked up turns back; but David found himself hedged in *behind* as well as *before*. —*John Calvin.*

Verse 5.—*"Thou hast . . . . laid thine hand upon me."* As by an arrest; so that I am thy prisoner, and cannot stir a foot from thee.—*John Trapp.*

Verse 5.—*"And laid thine hand upon me."* To make of me one acceptable to thyself. To rule me, to lead me, to uphold me, to protect me; to restore me; in my growth, in my walk, in my failures, in my affliction, in my despair.—*Thomas Le Blanc.*

Verse 6.—*"Such knowledge is too wonderful for me,"* etc. When we are about to look upon God's perfections, we should observe our own imperfections, and thereby learn to be the more modest in our searching of God's unsearchable perfection: *"Such knowledge,"* saith David, *"is too high for me, I cannot attain unto it."* Then do we see most of God, when we see him incomprehensible, and do see ourselves swallowed up in the thoughts of his perfection, and are forced to fall in admiration of God, as here. *"Such knowledge is too wonderful for me; it is high, I cannot attain unto it."*—*David Dickson.*

Verse 6.—*"Such knowledge is too wonderful for me."* Compared with our stinted knowledge, how amazing is the knowledge of God! As he made all things, he must be intimately acquainted, not only with their properties, but with their every essence. His eye, at the same instant, surveys all the works of his immeasurable creation. He observes, not only the complicated system of the universe, but the slightest motion of the most microscopic insect;—not only the sublimest conception of angels, but the meanest propensity of the most worthless of his creatures. At this moment he is listening to the praises breathed by grateful hearts in distant worlds, and reading every grovelling thought which passes through the polluted minds of the fallen race of Adam. . . . At one view, he surveys the past, the present, and the future. No inattention prevents him from observing; no defect of memory or of judgment obscures his comprehension. In his remembrance are stored not only the transactions of this world, but of all the worlds in the universe; not only the events of the six thousand years which have passed since the earth was created, but of a duration without beginning. Nay, things to come, extending to a duration without end, are also before him. An eternity past and an eternity to come are, at the same moment, in his eye; and with that eternal eye he surveys infinity. How amazing! How inconceivable!—*Henry Duncan* (1774—1846), *in "Sacred Philosophy of the Seasons."*

Verse 6.—*" Such knowledge is too wonderful for me."* There is a mystery about the Divine Omnipresence, which we do not learn to solve, after years of meditation. As God is a simple spirit, without dimensions, parts, or susceptibility of division, he is equally, that is, fully, present at all times in all places. At any given moment he is not present partly here and partly in the utmost skirt of the furthest system which revolves about the dimmest telescopic star, as if like a galaxy of perfection he stretched a sublime magnificence through universal space, which admitted of separation and partition; but he is present, with the totality of his glorious properties in every point of space. This results undeniably from the simple spirituality of the Great Supreme. All that God is in one place he is in all places. All there is of God is in every place. Indeed, his presence has no dependence on space or matter. His attribute of essential presence were the same if universal matter were blotted out. Only by a figure can God be said to be in the universe; for the universe is comprehended by him. All the boundless glory of the Godhead is essentially present at every spot in his creation, however various may be the manifestations of this glory at different times and places.

Here we have a case which ought to instruct and sober those, who, in their shallow philosophy, demand a religion without mystery. It would be a religion without God; for "who by searching can find out God?"—*James W. Alexander, in "The [American] National Preacher,"* 1860.

Verse 7.—*"Whither shall I go from thy spirit?"* By the *"spirit of God"* we are not here, as in several other parts of Scripture, to conceive of his power merely, but his understanding and knowledge. In man the spirit is the seat of intelligence, and so it is here in reference to God, as is plain from the second part of the sentence, where by *"the face of God"* is meant his knowledge or inspection.—*John Calvin.*

Verse 7.—*"Whither shall I go from thy spirit?"* That is, either from thee, who art a spirit, and so canst pierce and penetrate me; be as truly and essentially in the very bowels and marrow of my soul, as my soul is intimately and essentially in my body: *"from thy spirit;"* that is, from thy knowledge and thy power; thy knowledge to detect and observe me, thy power to uphold or crush me.—*Ezekiel Hopkins,* 1633—1690.

Verse 7.—We may elude the vigilance of a human enemy and place ourselves beyond his reach. God fills all space—there is not a spot in which his piercing eye is not on us, and his uplifted hand cannot find us out. Man must strike soon if he would strike at all; for opportunities pass away from him, and his victim may escape his vengeance by death. There is no passing of opportunity with God, and it is this which makes his longsuffering a solemn thing. God can wait, for he has a whole eternity before him in which he may strike. "All things are open and naked to him with whom we have to do."—*Frederick William Robertson,* 1816—1853.

Verse 7.—*"Whither shall I go,"* etc. A heathen philosopher once asked, "Where is God?" The Christian answered, "Let me first ask you, Where is he not?"—*John Arrowsmith,* 1602—1659.

Verse 7.—*"Whither shall I flee from thy presence?"* That exile would be strange that could separate us from God. I speak not of those poor and common comforts, that in all lands and coasts it is his sun that shines, his elements of earth or water that bear us, his air we breathe; but of that special privilege, that his gracious presence is ever with us; that no sea is so broad as to divide us from his favour; that wheresoever we feed, he is our host; wheresoever we rest, the wings of his blessed providence are stretched over us. Let my soul be sure of this, though the whole world be traitors to me.—*Thomas Adams.*

Verse 7.—*"Whither shall I flee?"* etc. Surely no whither: they that attempt it, do but as the fish which swimmeth to the length of the line, with a hook in the mouth.—*John Trapp.*

Verse 7.—*"Thy presence."* The presence of God's glory is in heaven; the presence of his power on earth; the presence of his justice in hell; and the presence of his grace with his people. If he deny us his powerful presence, we fall into nothing; if he deny us his gracious presence, we fall into sin; if he deny us his merciful presence, we fall into hell.—*John Mason.*

Verse 7.—*"Thy presence."* The celebrated Linnæus testified in his conversation, writings, and actions, the greatest sense of God's presence. So strongly indeed was he impressed with the idea, that he wrote over the door of his library: *"Innocuè vivite, Numen adest—Live innocently: God is present."*—*George Seaton Bowes, in "Information and Illustration,"* 1884.

Verses 7—11.—You will never be neglected by the Deity, though you were so small as to sink into the depths of the earth, or so lofty as to fly up to heaven; but you will suffer from the gods the punishment due to you, whether you abide here, or depart to Hades, or are carried to a place still more wild than these.—*Plato.*

Verses 7—12.—The Psalm was not written by a Pantheist. The Psalmist speaks of God as a Person everywhere present in creation, yet distinct from creation. In these verses he says, *"Thy spirit . . . thy* presence . . . *thou* art there . . . *thy* hand . . . *thy* right hand . . . darkness hideth not from *thee."* God is everywhere, but he is not everything.—*William Jones, in "A Homiletic Commentary on the Book of Psalms,"* 1879.

Verse 8.—*"If I make my bed."* Properly, " If I strew or spread my couch." If I should seek that as a place to lie down.—*Albert Barnes.*

Verse 8.—*"Hell "* in some places in Scripture signifies the lower parts of the earth, without relation to punishment : *"If I ascend up into heaven, thou art there ; if I make my bed in hell, behold, thou art there."* By *"heaven "* he means the upper region of the world, without any respect to the state of blessedness ; and *"hell "* is the most opposite and remote in distance, without respect to misery. As if he had said, Let me go whither I will, thy presence finds me out.—*Joseph Caryl.*

Verse 8.—*"Thou art there."* Or, more emphatically and impressively in the original, *"Thou ! "* That is, the Psalmist imagines himself in the highest heaven, or in the deepest abodes of the dead,—and lo ! God is there also ; he has not gone from *him !* he is still in the presence of the same God !—*Albert Barnes.*

Verse 8.—*"Thou art there."* This is not meant of his knowledge, for that the Psalmist had spoken of before : verses 2, 3, " Thou understandest my thought afar off : thou art acquainted with all my ways." Besides, " thou art there " not thy wisdom or knowledge, but *thou,* thy essence, not only thy virtue. For having before spoken of his omniscience, he proves that such knowledge could not be in God unless he were present in his essence in all places, so as to be excluded from none. He fills the depths of hell, the extension of the earth, and the heights of the heavens. When the Scripture mentions the power of God only, it expresseth it by hand or arm ; but when it mentions the spirit of God, and doth not intend the third person of the Trinity, it signifies the nature and essence of God ; and so here, when he saith, *"Whither shall I go from thy spirit ? "* he adds exegetically, *"whither shall I flee from thy presence ? "* or Hebrew, *"face" ;* and the face of God in Scripture signifies the essence of God : Exod. xxxiii. 20, 23, " Thou canst not see my face," and " my face shall not be seen"; the effects of his power, wisdom, providence, are seen, which are his back-parts, but not his face. The effects of his power and wisdom are seen in the world, but his essence is invisible, and this the Psalmist elegantly expresseth.—*Stephen Charnock.*

Verse 9.—*"The wings of the morning,"* is an elegant metaphor ; and by them we may conjecture is meant the sunbeams, called *"wings "* because of their swift and speedy motion, making their passage so sudden and instantaneous, as that they do prevent the observation of the eye ; called *"the wings of the morning "* because the dawn of the morning comes flying in upon these wings of the sun, and brings light along with it ; and, by beating and fanning of these wings, scatters the darkness before it. " Now," saith the Psalmist, " if I could pluck these wings of the morning," the sunbeams, if I could imp [graft] my own shoulders with them, if I should fly as far and as swift as light, even in an instant, to the uttermost parts of the sea ; yea, if in my flight I should spy out some solitary rock, so formidable and dismal as if we might almost call in question whether ever a Providence had been there, if I could pitch there on the top of it, where never anything had made its abode, but coldness, thunders, and tempests ; yet there shall thy hand lead me, and thy right hand shall hold me."—*Ezekiel Hopkins.*

Verse 9.—*"The wings of the morning."* This figure to a Western is not a little obscure. For my part, I cannot doubt that we are to understand certain beautiful light clouds as thus poetically described. I have observed invariably, that in the late spring-time, in summer, and yet more especially in the autumn, white clouds are to be seen in Palestine. They only occur at the earliest hours of morning, just previous to and at the time of sunrise. It is the total absence of clouds at all other parts of the day, except during the short period of the winter rains, that lends such striking solemnity and force to those descriptions of the Second Advent where our Lord is represented as coming in the clouds. This feature of his majesty loses all its meaning in lands like ours, in which clouds are of such common occurrence that they are rarely absent from the sky. The morning clouds of summer and autumn are always of a brilliant silvery white, save at such times as they are dyed with the delicate opal tints of dawn. They hang low upon the mountains of Judah, and produce effects of undescribable beauty, as they float far down in the valleys, or rise to wrap themselves around the summit of the hills. In almost every instance, by about seven o'clock the heat has dissipated these fleecy clouds, and to the vivid Eastern imagination morn has folded her outstretched wings.—*James Neil.*

Verse 9.—"*If I take the wings of the morning.*" The point of comparison appears to be the incalculable velocity of light.—*Joseph Addison Alexander.*

Verses 9, 10.—When we think that we fly from God, in running out of one place into another, we do but run from one hand to the other ; for there is no place where God is not, and whithersoever a rebellious sinner doth run, the hand of God will meet with him to cross him, and hinder his hoped-for good success, although he securely prophesieth never so much good unto himself in his journey. What ! had Jonah offended the winds or the waters, that they bear him such enmity ? The winds and the waters and all God's creatures are wont to take God's part against Jonah, or any rebellious sinner. For though God in the beginning gave power to man over all creatures to rule them, yet when man sins, God giveth power and strength to his creatures to rule and bridle man. Therefore even he that now was lord over the waters, now the waters are lord over him.—*Henry Smith.*

Verses 9, 10.—

> Should fate command me to the farthest verge
> Of the green earth, to distant barbarous climes,
> Rivers unknown to song ; where first the sun
> Gilds Indian mountains, or his setting beam
> Flames on the Atlantic isles ; 'tis nought to me :
> Since GOD is ever present, ever felt,
> In the void waste as in the city full ;
> And where he vital breathes, there must be joy,
> When e'en at last the solemn hour shall come,
> And wing my mystic flight to future worlds,
> I cheerful will obey ; there with new powers,
> Will rising wonders sing : I cannot go
> Where universal love smiles not around,
> Sustaining all yon orbs, and all their sons :
> From seeming evil still deducing good,
> And better thence again, and better still,
> In infinite progression.

James Thomson, 1700—1748.

Verse 11.—"*If I say, Surely the darkness shall cover me,*" etc. The foulest enormities of human conduct have always striven to cover themselves with the shroud of night. The thief, the counterfeiter, the assassin, the robber, the murderer, and the seducer, feel comparatively safe in the midnight darkness, because no human eye can scrutinize their actions. But what if it should turn out that sable night, to speak paradoxically, is an unerring photographist ! What if wicked men, as they open their eyes from the sleep of death, in another world, should find the universe hung round with faithful pictures of their earthly enormities, which they had supposed for ever lost in the oblivion of night ! What scenes for them to gaze at for ever ! They may now, indeed, smile incredulously at such a suggestion ; but the disclosures of chemistry may well make them tremble. Analogy does make it a scientific probability that every action of man, however deep the darkness in which it was performed, has imprinted its image on nature, and that there may be tests which shall draw it into daylight, and make it permanent so long as materialism endures.—*Edward Hitchcock, in "The Religion of Geology,"* 1851.

Verse 12.—"*The darkness hideth not from thee.*" Though the place where we sin be to men as dark as Egypt, yet to God it is as light as Goshen.—*William Secker.*

Verse 13.—"*Thou hast possessed my reins.*" From the sensitiveness to pain of this part of the body, it was regarded by the Hebrews as the seat of sensation and feeling, as also of desire and longing (Ps. lxxii. 21 ; Job xvi. 13 ; xix. 27). It is sometimes used of the inner nature generally (Ps. xvi. 7 ; Jer. xx. 12), and specially of the judgment or direction of reason (Jer. xi. 20 ; xii. 2).—*William Lindsay Alexander, in Kitto's Cyclopædia.*

Verse 13.—"*Thou hast possessed my reins.*" The *reins* are made specially prominent in order to mark them, the seat of the tenderest, most secret emotions, as the work of him who trieth the heart and the reins.—*Franz Delitzsch.*

Verse 13.—"*Thou hast covered me in my mother's womb.*" The word here rendered *cover* means properly to interweave ; to weave ; to knit together, and the literal translation would be, " Thou hast *woven* me in my mother's womb," meaning that God had put his parts together, as one who weaves cloth, or who makes a basket. So it is rendered by De Wette and by Gesenius (*Lex.*). The original word has however, also the idea of protecting, as in a booth or hut, woven or knit together, —to wit, of boughs and branches. The former signification best suits the connection ; and then the sense would be, that as God had made him—as he had formed his members, and united them in a bodily frame and form before he was born— he must be able to understand all his thoughts and feelings. As he was not concealed from God before he saw the light, so he could not be anywhere.—*Albert Barnes.*

Verse 14.—"*I will praise thee,*" etc. All God's works are admirable, man wonderfully wonderful. " Marvellous are thy works ; and that my soul knoweth right well." What infers he on all this ? Therefore "*I will praise thee.*" If we will not praise him that made us, will he not repent that he made us ? Oh that we knew what the saints do in heaven, and how the sweetness of that doth swallow up all earthly pleasures ! They sing honour and glory to the Lord. Why ? Because he hath created all things : Rev. iv. 11. When we behold an exquisite piece of work, we presently enquire after him that made it, purposely to commend his skill : and there is no greater disgrace to an artist, than having perfected a famous work, to find it neglected, no man minding it, or so much as casting an eye upon it. All the works of God are considerable, and man is bound to this contemplation. " When I consider the heavens," etc., I say, " What is man ? " Ps. viii. 3, 4. He admires the heavens, but his admiration reflects upon man. *Quis homo ?* There is no workman but would have his instruments used, and used to that purpose for which they were made . . . . Man is set like a little world in the midst of the great, to glorify God ; this is the scope and end of his creation.—*Thomas Adams.*

Verse 14.—"*I am fearfully and wonderfully made.*" The term "*fearful*" is sometimes to be taken subjectively, for our being possessed of fear. In this sense it signifies the same as timid. Thus the prophet was directed to say to them that were of a " fearful heart, be strong." At other times it is taken objectively, for that property in an object the contemplation of which excites fear in the beholder. Thus it is said of God that he is " fearful in praises," and that it is " a fearful thing to fall into the hands of the living God." In this sense it is manifestly to be understood in the passage now under consideration. The human frame is so admirably constructed, so delicately combined, and so much in danger of being dissolved by innumerable causes, that the more we think of it the more we tremble, and wonder at our own continued existence.

> " How poor, how rich, how abject, how august;
> How complicate, how wonderful is man !
> How passing wonder he who made him such,
> Who mingled in our make such strange extremes
> Of different natures, marvellously mixed !
> Helpless immortal, insect infinite,
> A worm, a god—I tremble at myself ! "

To do justice to the subject, it would be necessary to be well acquainted with anatomy. I have no doubt that a thorough examination of that " substance which God hath curiously wrought " (verse 15), would furnish abundant evidence of the justness of the Psalmist's words ; but even those things which are manifest to common observation may be sufficient for this purpose. In general it is observable that the human frame abounds with avenues at which enter every thing conducive to preservation and comfort, and every thing that can excite alarm. Perhaps there is not one of these avenues but what may become an inlet to death, nor one of the blessings of life but what may be the means of accomplishing it. We live by inhalation, but we also die by it. Diseases and death in innumerable forms are conveyed by the very air we breathe. God hath given us a relish for divers aliments, and rendered them necessary to our subsistence : yet, from the abuse of them, what a train of disorders and premature deaths are found amongst men ! And, when there is no abuse, a single delicious morsel may, by the evil design of another, or even by mere accident, convey poison through all our veins, and in one hour reduce the most athletic form to a corpse.

The elements of fire and water, without which we could not subsist, contain properties which in a few moments would be able to destroy us ; nor can the utmost circumspection at all times preserve us from their destructive power. A single stroke on the head may divest us of reason or of life. A wound or a bruise of the spine may instantly deprive the lower extremities of all sensation. If the vital parts be injured, so as to suspend the performance of their mysterious functions, how soon is the constitution broken up ! By means of the circulation of the blood, how easily and suddenly are deadly substances diffused throughout the frame ! The putridity of a morbid subject has been imparted to the very hand stretched out to save it. The poisoned arrow, the envenomed fang, the hydrophobic saliva, derive from hence their fearful efficacy. Even the pores of the skin, necessary as they are to life, may be the means of death. Not only are poisonous substances hereby admitted, but, when obstructed by surrounding damps, the noxious humours of the body, instead of being emitted, are retained in the system, and become productive of numerous diseases, always afflictive, and often fatal to life.

Instead of wondering at the number of premature deaths that are constantly witnessed, there is far greater reason to wonder that there are no more, and that any of us survive to seventy or eighty years of age.

> " Our life contains a thousand springs,
>   And dies if one be gone :
> Strange that a harp of thousand strings
>   Should keep in tune so long."

Nor is this all. If we are *"fearfully made"* as to our animal frame, it will be found that we are much more so considered as moral and accountable beings. In what relates to our animal nature, we are in most instances constructed like other animals ; but, in what relates to us as moral agents, we stand distinguished from all the lower creation. We are made for eternity. The present life is only the introductory part of our existence. It is that, however, which stamps a character on all that follows. How fearful is our situation ! What innumerable influences is the mind exposed to from the temptations which surround us ! Not more dangerous to the body is the pestilence that walketh in darkness than these are to the soul. Such is the construction of our nature that the very word of life, if heard without regard, becomes a savour of death unto death. What consequences hang upon the small and apparently trifling beginning of evils ! A wicked thought may issue in a wicked purpose, this purpose in a wicked action, this action in a course of conduct, this course may draw into its vortex millions of our fellow-creatures, and terminate in perdition, both to ourselves and them. The whole of this process was exemplified in the case of Jeroboam, the son of Nebat. When placed over the ten tribes, he first *said in his heart,* " If this people go up to sacrifice at Jerusalem, their hearts will turn to Rehoboam ; and thus shall the kingdom return to the house of David." 1 Kings xii. 26—30. On this he took counsel, and made the calves of Dan and Bethel. This engaged him in a course of wickedness, from which no remonstrances could reclaim him. Nor was it confined to himself ; for he " made all Israel to sin." The issue was, not only their destruction as a nation, but, to all appearance, the eternal ruin of himself, and great numbers of his followers. Such were the fruits of an evil thought !

Oh, my soul, tremble at thyself ! Tremble at the fearfulness of thy situation ; and commit thine immortal all into his hands " who is able to keep thee from falling, and to present thee faultless before the presence of his glory with exceeding joy."—*Andrew Fuller.*

Verse 14.—*"I am fearfully and wonderfully made."* Never was so terse and expressive a description of the physical conformation of man given by any human being. So *"fearfully"* are we made, that there is not an action or gesture of our bodies, which does not, apparently, endanger some muscle, vein, or sinew, the rupture of which would destroy either life or health. We are so *"wonderfully"* made, that our organization infinitely surpasses, in skill, contrivance, design, and adaptation of means to ends, the most curious and complicated piece of mechanism, not only ever executed " by art and man's device," but ever conceived by human imagination.—*Richard Warner*, 1828.

Verse 14.—"*I am wonderfully made.*" Take notice of the curious frame of the body. David saith, "*I am wonderfully made*"; *acu pictus sum*, so the Vulgate rendereth it, " painted as with a needle," like a garment of needlework, of divers colours, richly embroidered with nerves and veins. What shall I speak of the eye, wherein there is such curious workmanship, that many upon the first sight of it have been driven to acknowledge God ? Of the hand made to open and shut, and to serve the labours and ministries of nature without wasting and decay for many years ? If they should be of marble or iron, with such constant use they would soon wear out ; and yet now they are of flesh they last so long as life lasteth. Of the head ? fitly placed to be the seat of the senses, to command and direct the rest of the members. Of the lungs ? a frail piece of flesh, yet, though in continual action, of a long use. It were easy to enlarge upon this occasion ; but I am to preach a sermon, not to read an anatomy lecture. In short, therefore, every part is so placed and framed, as if God had employed his whole wisdom about it. But as yet we have spoken but of the casket wherein the jewel lieth. The soul, that divine spark of blast, how quick, nimble, various, and indefatigable in its motions ! how comprehensive in its capacities ! how it animateth the body, and is like God himself, all in every part ! Who can trace the flights of reason ? What a value hath God set upon the soul ! He made it after his image, he redeemed it with Christ's blood.—*Thomas Manton.*

Verse 14.—What is meant by saying that the soul is *in* the body, any more than saying that a thought or a hope is in a stone or a tree ? *How* is it joined to the body ? what keeps it one with the body ? what keeps it in the body ? what prevents it any moment from separating from the body ? When two things which we see are united, they are united by some connexion which we can understand. A chain or cable keeps a ship in its place ; we lay the foundation of a building in the earth, and the building endures. But what is it which unites soul and body ? how do they touch ? how do they keep together ? how is it we do not wander to the stars or the depths of the sea, or to and fro as chance may carry us, while our body remains where it was on earth ? So far from its being wonderful that the body one day dies, how is it that it is made to live and move at all ? how is it that it keeps from dying a single hour ? Certainly it is as uncomprehensible as anything can be, how soul and body can make up one man ; and, unless we had the instance before our eyes, we should seem in saying so to be using words without meaning. For instance, would it not be extravagant and idle to speak of time as deep or high, or of space as quick or slow ? Not less idle, surely, it perhaps seems to some races of spirits to say that thought and mind have a body, which in the case of man they have, according to God's marvellous will.—*John Henry Newman, in Parochial Sermons,* 1839.

Verse 14.—Moses describes the creation of man (Gen. ii. 7) : " The Lord God formed man of the dust of the ground, and breathed into his nostrils the breath of life ; and man became a living soul." Now what God did then immediately, he doth still by means. Do not think that God made man at first, and that ever since men have made one another. No (saith Job), " he that made me in the womb made him : " ch. xxxi. 15. David will inform us : "*I am fearfully and wonderfully made : marvellous are thy works,*" etc. As if he had said, Lord, I am wonderfully made, and thou hast made me. I am a part or parcel of thy marvellous works, yea, the breviate or compendium of them all. The frame of the body (much more the frame of the soul, most of all the frame of the new creature in the soul) is God's work, and it is a wonderful work of God. And therefore David could not satisfy himself in the bare affirmation of this, but enlargeth in the explication of it in verses 15 and 16. David took no notice of father or mother, but ascribed the whole efficiency of himself to God. And indeed David was as much made by God as Adam ; and so is every son of Adam. Though we are begotten and born of our earthly parents, yet God is the chief parent and the only fashioner of us all. Thus graciously spake Jacob to his brother Esau, demanding, " Who are those with thee ? And he said, The children which God hath graciously given thy servant " : Gen. xxxiii. 5. Therefore, as the Spirit of God warns, " Know ye that the Lord he is God : it is he that hath made us, and not we ourselves " (Ps. c. 3) ; which as it is true especially of our spiritual making, so 'tis true also of our natural.—*Joseph Caryl.*

Verse 14.—Those who were skilful in Anatomy among the ancients, concluded, from the outward and inward make of a human body, that it was the work of a Being transcendently wise and powerful. As the world grew more enlightened in this art, their discoveries gave them fresh opportunities of admiring the conduct of Providence in the formation of a human body. Galen was converted by his dissections, and could not but own a Supreme Being upon a survey of this his handiwork. There are, indeed, many parts, of which the old anatomists did not know the certain use; but as they saw that most of those which they examined were adapted with admirable art to their several functions, they did not question but those whose uses they could not determine, were contrived with the same wisdom for respective ends and purposes. Since the circulation of the blood has been found out, and many other great discoveries have been made by our modern anatomists, we see new wonders in the human frame, and discern several important uses for those parts, which uses the ancients knew nothing of. In short, the body of man is such a subject as stands the utmost test of examination. Though it appears formed with the nicest wisdom upon the most superficial survey of it, it still mends upon the search, and produces our surprise and amazement in proportion as we pry into it.—*The Spectator.*

Verses 14—16.—The subject, from the 14th verse to the 16th inclusive, might have been much more particularly illustrated; but we are taught, by the peculiar delicacy of expression in the Sacred Writings, to avoid, as in this case, the entering too minutely into *anatomical* details.—*Adam Clarke.*

Verse 15.—"*My substance was not hid from thee,*" etc. What deeper solitude, what state of concealment more complete, than that of the babe as yet unborn? Yet the Psalmist represents the Almighty as present even there. "*My substance was not hid from thee, when I was made in secret, and curiously wrought in the lowest parts of the earth.*" The whole image and train of thought is one of striking beauty. We see the wonderful work of the human body, with all its complex tissue of bones, and joints, and nerves, and veins, and arteries growing up, and fashioned, as it had been a piece of rich and curious embroidery under the hand of the manufacturer. But it is not the work itself that we are now called on to admire. The contexture is indeed fearful and wonderful; but how much more when we reflect that the divine Artificer wrought within the dark and narrow confines of the womb. Surely the darkness is no darkness with him who could thus work. Surely the blackest night, the closest and most artificial recess, the subtlest disguises and hypocrisies are all seen through, are all naked and bare before him whose "*eyes did see our substance yet being imperfect.*" The night is as clear as the day; and secret sins are set in the light of his countenance, no less than those which are open and scandalous, committed before the sun or on the house-top. And if " in his book all our members are written, which day by day were fashioned, when as yet there was none of them," surely the actions of these members, now that they are grown, or growing, to maturity, and called upon to fulfil the functions for which they were created, shall be all noted down; and none be contrived so secretly, but that when the books are opened at the last day, it shall be found written therein to justify or to condemn us. Such is the main lesson which David himself would teach us in this Psalm,—the *omnipresence* and *omniscience* of Almighty God. My brethren, let us reflect for a little upon this deep mystery; that he, " the High and Lofty One that inhabiteth eternity," is about our path and about our bed, and spieth out all our ways; that go whither we will he is there; that say what we will, there is not a word on our tongue but he knoweth it altogether. The reflection is, indeed, mysterious, but it is also most profitable.—*Charles Wordsworth, in "Christian Boyhood,"* 1846.

Verse 15.—"*My substance was not hid from thee.*" Should an artizan intend commencing a work in some dark cave where there was no light to assist him, how would he set his hand to it? in what way would he proceed? and what kind of workmanship would it prove? But God makes the most perfect work of all in the dark, for he fashions man in the mother's womb.—*John Calvin.*

Verse 15.—"*When I was made in secret,*" etc. The author uses a metaphor derived from the most subtle art of the Phrygian workman:

" When I was formed in the secret place,
When I was wrought with a needle in the depths of the earth.

Whoever observes this (in truth he will not be able to observe it in the common translations), and at the same time reflects upon the wonderful mechanism of the human body ; the various implications of the veins, arteries, fibres, and membranes; the "undescribable texture" of the whole fabric—may, indeed, feel the beauty and gracefulness of this well-adapted metaphor, but will miss much of its force and sublimity, unless he be apprised that the art of designing in needlework was wholly dedicated to the use of the sanctuary, and, by a direct precept of the divine law, chiefly employed in furnishing a part of the sacerdotal habit, and the vails for the entrance of the Tabernacle. Exod. xxviii. 39 ; xxvi. 36 ; xxvii. 16. Thus the poet compares the wisdom of the divine Artificer with the most estimable of human arts—that art which was dignified by being consecrated altogether to the use of religion ; and the workmanship of which was so exquisite, that even the sacred writings seem to attribute it to a supernatural guidance. See Exod. xxxv. 30—35.—*Robert Lowth* (1710—1787), *in "Lectures on the Sacred Poetry of the Hebrews."*

Verse 15.—"*Curiously wrought in the lowest parts of the earth*," that is, in the womb : as curious workmen, when they have some choice piece in hand, they perfect it in private, and then bring it forth to light for men to gaze at. What a wonderful piece of work is man's head (God's masterpiece in this little world), the chief seat of the soul, that *cura Divini ingenii*, as Favorinus calls it. Many locks and keys argue the value of the jewel that they keep, and many papers wrapping the token within them, the price of the token. The tables of the testament, first laid up in the ark, secondly, the ark bound about with pure gold ; thirdly, over-shadowed with cherubim's wings ; fourthly, enclosed within the vail of the Tabernacle ; fifthly, with the compass of the Tabernacle ; sixthly, with a court about all ; seventhly, with a treble covering of goats' rams', and badgers' skins above all ; they must needs be precious tables. So when the Almighty made man's head (the seat of the reasonable soul) and overlaid it with hair, skin, and flesh, like the threefold covering of the Tabernacle, and encompassed it with a skull and bones like boards of cedar, and afterwards with divers skins like silken curtains ; and lastly, enclosed it with the yellow skin that covers the brain (like the purple veil), he would doubtless have us to know it was made for some great treasure to be put therein. How and when the reasonable soul is put into this curious cabinet philosophers dispute many things, but can affirm nothing of certainty.—*Abraham Wright.*

Verse 15.—"*In the lowest parts of the earth.*" From this remarkable expression which, in the original, and as elsewhere used, denotes the region of the dead—*Sheol*, or *Hades*—it would appear that it is not only his formation in the womb the Psalmist here contemplates, but also—regarding the region of the dead as the womb of resurrection life—the refashioning of the body hereafter, and its new birth to the life immortal, which will be no less " marvellous " a work, but rather more so, than the first fashioning of man's " substance." Confirmed by the words of verse 18—"When I awake, I am still with thee "—the same language before employed to express the resurrection hope, Ps. xvii. 15 : when there shall be a further illustration of God's mindfulness of his purposes and " precious counsels " with respect to his redeemed, in anticipation of which they may repeat this Psalm with renewed feelings of wonder and admiration.—*William De Burgh.*

Verses 15, 16.—The word "*substance*" represents different words in these verses. In verse 15 it is " my strength," or " my bones ; " in verse 16 the word is usually rendered " embryo " : but " clew " (life a ball yet to be unwound) finds favour with great scholars.

"*In the lowest parts of the earth*" denotes no subterranean limbo or workshop ; but is a poetical parallel to " in secret."

"*Which in continuance were fashioned*" is wrong. The margin, though also wrong, indicates the right way : " my days were determined before one of them was."—*David M'Laren, in "The Book of Psalms in Metre,"* 1883.

Verse 16.—"*Thine eyes did see my substance, yet being unperfect,*" etc. From whence we may learn, first, not to be proud of what we are ; all's the work of God. How beautiful or comely, how wise or holy soever you are, 'tis not of yourselves. What hath any man, either in naturals or supernaturals, which he hath not received ? Secondly, despise not what others are or have, though they are not such exact pieces, though they have not such excellent endowments as yourselves ; yet they are what God hath made them. Thirdly, despise not what yourselves are. Many are ashamed to be seen as God made them ; few are ashamed to be seen what the devil hath made them. Many are troubled at small defects in the outward man ; few are troubled at the greatest deformities of the inward man : many buy artificial beauty to supply the natural ; few spiritual, to supply the defects of the super-natural beauty of the soul.—*Abraham Wright.*

Verse 16.—*"My substance yet being unperfect."* One word in the original, which means strictly anything *rolled together* as a ball, and hence is generally supposed to mean here the fœtus or embryo. Hupfeld, however, prefers to understand it of the ball of life, as consisting of a number of different threads (" the days " of verse 16—see margin) which are first a compact mass as it were, and which are then unwound as life runs on.—*J. J. Stewart Perowne.*

Verse 16.—A skilful architect before he builds draws a model, or gives a draught of the building in his book, or upon a table ; there he will show you every room and contrivance : in his book are all the parts of the building written, while as yet there are none of them, or before any of them are framed and set up. In allusion to architects and other artisans, David speaks of God, *"In thy book all my members were written";* that is, Thou hast made me as exactly as if thou hadst drawn my several members and my whole proportion with a pen or pencil in a book, before thou wouldst adventure to form me up. The Lord uses no book, no pen to decipher his work. He had the perfect idea of all things in himself from everlasting ; but he may well be said to work as by pattern, whose work is the most perfect pattern. —*Joseph Caryl.*

Verse 17.—*"How precious also are thy thoughts unto me,"* etc. So far from thinking it a hardship to be subject to this scrutiny, he counts it a most valuable privilege. However others may regard this truth, *"to me,"* my judgment and my feelings, *"how costly,"* valuable *"are thy thoughts,"* i.e. thy perpetual attention to me.—*Joseph Addison Alexander.*

Verse 17.—*"How precious also are thy thoughts unto me, O God !"* How cold and poor is *our* warmest thoughts towards God ! How unspeakably loving and gloriously rich are *his* thoughts towards us ! Compare Eph. i. 18 : " The riches of the glory of his inheritance in the saints."—*A. R. Fausset.*

Verse 17.—*"How precious . . . how great is the sum of them !"* Our comforts vie with the number of our sorrows, and win the game. The mercies of God passed over in a gross sum breed no admiration ; but cast up the particulars, and then arithmetic is too dull an art to number them. As many dusts as a man's hands can hold, is but his handful of so many dusts ; but tell them one by one, and they exceed all numeration. It was but a crown which king Solomon wore ; but weigh the gold, tell the precious stones, value the richness of them, and what was it then ? —*Thomas Adams.*

Verses 17, 18.—Behold David's love to God ; sleeping and waking his mind runs upon him. There needs no arguments to bring those to our remembrance whom we love. We neglect ourselves to think upon them. A man in love wastes his spirits, vexes his mind, neglects his meat, regards not his business, his mind still feeds on that he loves. When men love that they should not, there is more need of a bridle to keep them from thinking of it, than of spurs to keep them to it. Try thy love of God by this. If thou thinkest not often of God, thou lovest him not. If thou canst not satisfy thyself with profits, pleasures, friends, and other worldly objects, but thou must turn other businesses aside, that thou mayest daily think of God, then thou lovest him.—*Francis Taylor, in "God's Glory in Man's Happiness,"* 1654.

Verses 17, 18.—Mercies are either ordinary or extraordinary—our common necessaries, or the remarkable supplies which we receive now and then at the hand of God. Thou must not only praise him for some extraordinary mercy, that comes with such pomp and observation that all thy neighbours take notice of it with thee, as the mercy which Zacharias and Elizabeth had in their son, that was noised about all the country (Luke i. 65) ; but also for ordinary, every-day mercies : for first, we are unworthy of the least mercy (Gen. xxxii. 10), and therefore God is worthy of praise for the least, because it is more than he owes us. Secondly, these common, ordinary mercies are many. Thus David enhanceth the mercies of this kind,— *"O God, how great is the sum of them !* If I should count them, they are more in number than the sand ; when I wake I am still with thee." As if he had said,

There is not a point of time wherein thou art not doing me good ; as soon as I open my eyes in the morning I have a new theme, in some fresh mercies given since I closed them over-night, to employ my praiseful meditations. Many little items make together a great sum. What is lighter than a grain of sand, yet what is heavier than the sand upon the sea-shore ? As little sins (such as vain thoughts and idle words), because of their multitude, arise to a great guilt, and will bring in a long bill, a heavy reckoning at last ; so, ordinary mercies, what they want in their size of some other great mercies, have compensated it in their number. Who will not say that a man shows greater kindness in maintaining one at his table with ordinary fare all the year than in entertaining him at a great feast twice or thrice in the same time ?—*William Gurnall.*

Verse 18.—*"They are more in number than the sand."* Pindar says, that sand flies number (*Olymp. Ode* 2). The Pythian oracle indeed boastingly said, I know the number of the sand, and the measure of the sea (*Herodot. Clio.* 1. i. c. 47). It is to this that Lucan may refer when he says, measure is not wanting to the ocean, or number to the sand (*Pharsal.* 1. 5, v. 182).—*Samuel Burder.*

Verse 18.—*"If I should count them, they are more in number than the sand."*

> If all his glorious deeds my song would tell,
> The shore's unnumbered stones I might recount as well.
>
> *Pindar,* B.C. 518—442.

Verse 18.—*"When I awake, I am still with thee."* It is the great advantage of a Christian, which he has above other men, that he has his friends always about him, and (if the fault be not his own) need never to be absent from them. In the friendship and converse of the world, we use to say, " Friends must part," and those who have delight and satisfaction in one another's society must be content to leave it, and to be taken off from it. But this is the privilege of a believer that undertakes communion with God, that it is possible for him always to be with him. Again, in human converse and society we know it is ordinary for friends to dream that they are in company with one another ; but when they awake they are a great way off. But a Christian that converses with God, and has his thoughts fastened upon him, when he awakes he is still with him, which is that which is here exhibited to us in the example of the prophet David.

A godly soul should fall asleep in God's arms, like a child in the mother's lap ; it should be sung and lulled to sleep with " songs of the night." And this will make him the fitter for converse with God the next day after. This is the happiness of a Christian that is careful to lie down with God, that he finds his work still as he left it, and is in the same disposition when he rises as he was at night when he lay down to rest. As a man that winds up his watch over night, he finds it going the next morning ; so is it also, as I may say, with a Christian that winds up his heart. This is a good observation to be remembered, especially in the evening afore the Sabbath.—*Thomas Horton,* —1673.

Verse 18.—*"When I awake, I am still with thee."* It is no small advantage to the holy life to " begin the day with God." The saints are wont to leave their hearts with him over night, that they may find them with him in the morning. Before earthly things break in upon us, and we receive impressions from abroad, it is good to season the heart with thoughts of God, and to consecrate the early and virgin operations of the mind before they are prostituted to baser objects. When the world gets the start of religion in the morning, it can hardly overtake it all the day ; and so the heart is habituated to vanity all the day long. But when we begin with God, we take him along with us to all the business and comforts of the day ; which, being seasoned with his love and fear, are the more sweet and savoury to us.—*Thomas Case* (1598—1682), *in the Epistle Dedicatory to "The Morning Exercise."*

Verse 18.—*"When I awake."* Accustom yourself to a serious meditation every morning. Fresh airing our souls in heaven will engender in us a purer spirit and nobler thoughts. A morning seasoning will secure us for all the day. Though other necessary thoughts about our calling will and must come in, yet when we have dispatched them, let us attend to our morning theme as our chief companion. As a man that is going with another about some considerable business, suppose to Westminster, though he meets with several friends on the way, and salutes some, and with others with whom he has some affairs he spends some little time, yet he quickly returns to his companion, and both together go to their intended stage.

Do thus in the present case. Our minds are active and will be doing something, though to little purpose; and if they be not fixed upon some noble object, they will, like madmen and fools, be mightily pleased in playing with straws. The thoughts of God were the first visitors David had in the morning. God and his heart met together as soon as he was awake, and kept company all the day after.—*Stephen Charnock.*

Verse 19.—*"Depart from me therefore, ye bloody men."* The expression, *"bloody men,"* or *"men of blood,"* includes not only homicides, who shed human blood, but all other wicked and evil doers, who injure, or seek to injure others, or who slay their own souls by sin, or the souls of others by scandal; all of whom may be truly called homicides; for hatred may be called the mainspring of homicide, and thus St. John says, "Whoso hateth his brother is a homicide."—*Robert Bellarmine.*

Verse 19.—*"Therefore."* When we have a controversy with the wicked we should take heed that private spleen do not rule us, but that only our interest in God's quarrel with them doth move us, as the Psalmist doth here.—*David Dickson.*

Verse 20.—*"Thine enemies take thy name in vain."* In every action three things are considerable,—the *end*, the *agent*, the *work*. These three duly weighed, we shall soon see what it is to take God's name in vain.

I. That which hath no end proposed, or is done to no end, may truly be said to be done in vain. As the sowing of seed without reaping the fruit, the planting a vineyard without a vintage, or feeding a flock without eating the milk of it. These are labours in vain. So he that taketh the name of God to no end, neither to God's glory, nor the private or public good, taketh it in vain. *Cui bono?* is a question in all undertakings. If to no good, as good and better not undertaken at all; it is to no end, it is in vain. If a man have well-fashioned legs, and they be lame, *frustra pulchras habet tibia claudus*, the lame man hath them in vain. The chief end, therefore, in taking this name must be, 1. The glory of God, otherwise we open our mouths in vain, as it is in Job. God is willing to impart all his blessings to us, and requires nothing of us again but glory, which if we return not, he may say, as David did of Nabal, for whom he had done many good turns, in securing his shepherds and flocks, etc.; and when he desired nothing but a little meat for the young men he denied it: All that I have done for this fellow is in vain; in vain have I kept all he hath. So, God having done so much for us, and expecting nothing but the glory of his name, if we be defective herein, he may well say all that he hath done for us is in vain.

2. Next to God's glory is the good of ourselves and others; and so to take God's name without reference to this end, if we neither promote our own good nor the good of others, it is in vain, *ex privatione finis*, because it wants a right end; therefore Saint Paul rejoiced, having by his preaching laboured for the saving of souls, I rejoice, saith he, that I have not run in vain, neither laboured in vain.

II. In the *agent* the heart and soul is to be considered, which in the person acting is the chief mover. If the soul be *Rachah*, vain and light, as when we take God's name without due advice and reverence, though we propound a right end, yet we take his name in vain. Therefore the wise man advises "not to be rash with our mouth" (Eccl. v. 2); and the Psalmist professeth that his heart was fixed when he praised God (Ps. lvii. 7): the heart ought to be fixed and stablished by a due consideration of God's greatness when we speak of him. This is opposed to rashness, inconstancy, and lightness, such as are in chaff and smoke, which are apt to be carried away with every blast, and such as are so qualified do take God's name in vain.

III. In the *work* itself may be a twofold vanity, which must be avoided. Firstly, Falsehood. Secondly, Injustice.

1. If it be *false*, then is it also vain, as theirs in Isaiah (ch. xxviii. 15): "We have made a covenant with death, and with hell are we at agreement; when the overflowing scourge shall pass through, it shall not come unto us: for we have made lies our refuge, and under falsehood have we hid ourselves." And this is that *actio erroris*, work of error, of which Jeremiah speaketh. *Vanitas opponitur veritati*, vanity is opposed to verity and truth; therefore a thing is said to be vain when it is false or erroneous. "They are vanity, the work of errors," saith the prophet (Jer. x. 15); and as there is truth in natural things, so is there a truth in moral things, which if it be wanting, our speech is vain.

2. If *unjust* it is vain too. " If I be wicked, why then labour I in vain ? " saith holy Job (ch. ix. 29) ; " The very hope of unjust men perisheth," saith the wise man (Prov. xi. 7) ; and, " They walk in a vain shadow, and disquiet themselves in vain " (Ps. xxxix. 6). If justice be wanting in our actions, or truth in our assertions and promises, they are vain ; and to use God's name in either is to take his name in vain. So that if either we take the name of God to no end, but make it common, and take it up as a custom till it come to a habit, not for any good end ; or if our hearts be not stable or fixed, but light and inconstant when we take it ; or if we take it to colour or bolster up any falsehood or any unjust act, we take it in vain, and break the commandment.—*Lancelot Andrews.*

Verse 21.—"*Do not I hate them, O Lord, that hate thee ?* " The simple future in the first clause comprehends several distinct shades of meaning. Do I not, may I not, must I not, hate those hating thee ? Hate them, not as man hates, but as God hates.—*Joseph Addison Alexander.*

Verse 21.—"*Do not I hate them, O Lord, that hate thee ?* " Can he who thinks good faith the holiest thing in life, avoid being an enemy to that man who, as quæstor, dared to despoil, desert, and betray ? Can he who wishes to pay due honours to the immortal gods, by any means avoid being an enemy to that man who has plundered all their temples ?—*Cicero.*

Verse 21.—"*And am not I grieved with those that rise up against thee ?* " The expression here—"*grieved* "—explains the meaning of the word "*hate* " in the former member of the verse. It is not that hatred which is followed by malignity or ill-will ; it is that which is accompanied with grief, pain of heart, pity, sorrow. So the Saviour looked on men : Mark iii. 5 : " And when he had looked round about on them with *anger*, being *grieved* for the hardness of their hearts." The Hebrew word used here, however, contains *also* the idea of being disgusted with ; of loathing ; of nauseating. The feeling referred to is anger—conscious disgust—at such conduct ; grief, pain, sorrow, that men should evince such feelings towards their Maker.—*Albert Barnes.*

Verse 21.—"*Am not I grieved ?* " etc. Acted upon by mingled feelings of sorrow for them, and loathing at their evil practices. Thus our Lord " looked round about on them with *anger*, being *grieved* for the hardness of their hearts " : Mark iii. 5.— *French and Skinner.*

Verse 21.—It is said that Adam Smith disliked nothing more than that moral apathy—that obtuseness of moral perception—which prevents man from not only seeing clearly, but feeling strongly, the broad distinction between virtue and vice, and which, under the pretext of liberality, is all indulgent even to the blackest crimes. At a party at Dalkeith Palace, where Mr. ——, in his mawkish way, was finding palliations for some villainous transactions, the doctor waited in patient silence until he was gone, then exclaimed : " Now I can breathe more freely. I cannot bear that man ; he has no indignation in him."

Verses 21, 22.—A faithful servant hath the same interests, the same friends, the same enemies, with his master, whose cause and honour he is, upon all occasions, in duty bound to support and maintain. A good man hates, as God himself doth ; he hates not the persons of men, but their sins ; not what God made them, but what they have made themselves. We are neither to hate the men, on account of the vices they practise ; nor to love the vices, for the sake of the men who practise them. He who observeth invariably this distinction, fulfilleth the perfect law of charity, and hath the love of God and of his neighbour abiding in him.—*George Horne.*

Verses 21, 22.—First, we must hate the company and society of manifest and obstinate sinners, who will not be reclaimed. Secondly, all their sins, not communicating with any man in his sin, we must have no fellowship (as with the workers so) with the unfruitful works of darkness. Thirdly, all occasions and inducements unto these sins. Fourthly, all appearances of wickedness (1 Thess. v. 22), that is, which men in common judgment account evil ; and all this must proceed from a good ground, even from a good heart hating sin perfectly, that is all sin, as David, "*I hate them with perfect hatred ;* " and not as some, who can hate some sin, but cleave to some other : as many can hate pride, but love covetousness or some other darling sin : but we must attain to the hatred of all, before we can come to the practice of this precept [Jude 23] ; besides that, all sins are hateful even in themselves.—*William Perkins*, 1558—1602.

Verses 21, 24.—The temper of mourning for public sins, for the sins of others, is the greatest note of sincerity. When all other signs of righteousness may have their exceptions, this temper is the utmost term, which we cannot go beyond in our self-examination. The utmost prospect David had of his sincerity, when he was upon a diligent enquiry after it, was his anger and grief for the sin of others. When he had reached so far, he was at a stand, and knew not what more to add: "Am not I grieved with those that rise up against thee? I hate them with perfect hatred: I count them mine enemies. Search me, O God, and know my heart: try me, and know my thoughts: and see if there be any wicked way in me." If there be anything that better can evidence my sincerity than this, Lord, acquaint me with it; "know my heart," *i.e.*, make me to know it. He whose sorrow is only for matter confined within his own breast, or streams with it in his life, has reason many times to question the truth of it; but when a man cannot behold sin as sin in another without sensible regret, it is a sign he hath savingly felt the bitterness of it in his own soul. It is a high pitch and growth, and a consent between the Spirit of God and the soul of a Christian, when he can lament those sins in others whereby the Spirit is grieved; when he can rejoice with the Spirit rejoicing, and mourn with the Spirit mourning. This is a clear testimony that we have not self-ends in the service of God; that we take not up religion to serve a turn; that God is our aim, and Christ our beloved.—*Stephen Charnock.*

Verse 22.—"*I hate them with perfect hatred.*" What is "*with a perfect hatred*"? I hated in them their iniquities, I loved thy creation. This it is to hate with a perfect hatred, that neither on account of the vices thou hate the men, nor on account of the men love the vices. For see what he addeth, "*They became my enemies.*" Not only as God's enemies but as his own too doth he now describe them. How then will he fulfil in them both his own saying, "*Have not I hated those that hated thee, Lord,*" and the Lord's command, "*Love your enemies*"? How will he fulfil this, save with that perfect hatred, that he hate in them that they are wicked, and love that they are men? For in the time even of the Old Testament, when the carnal people was restrained by visible punishments, how did Moses, the servant of God, who by understanding belonged to the New Testament, how did he hate sinners when he prayed for them, or how did he not hate them when he slew them, save that he "*hated them with a perfect hatred*"? For with such perfection did he hate the iniquity which he punished, as to love the manhood for which he prayed.—*Augustine.*

Verse 23.—"*Try me.*" True faith is precious; it is like gold, it will endure a trial. Presumption is but a counterfeit, and cannot abide to be tried: 1 Pet. i. 7. A true believer fears no trial. He is willing to be tried by God. He is willing to have his faith tried by others, he shuns not the touchstone. He is much in testing himself. He would not take anything upon trust, especially that which is of such moment. He is willing to hear the worst as well as the best. That preaching pleases him best which is most searching and distinguishing: Heb. iv. 12. He is loath to be deluded with vain hopes. He would not be flattered into a false conceit of his spiritual state. When trials are offered, he complies with the apostle's advice, 2 Cor. xiii. 5.—*David Clarkson.*

Verse 23.—What fearful dilemma have we here? The Holiest changeth not when he comes a visitant to a human heart. He is the same there that he is in the highest heaven. He cannot look upon sin; and how can a human heart welcome him into its secret chambers? How can the blazing fire welcome the quenching water? It is easy to commit to memory the seemly prayer of an ancient penitent, "*Search me, O God, and know my heart; try me, and know my thoughts.*" The dead letters, worn smooth by frequent use, may drop freely from callous lips, leaving no sense of scalding on the conscience; and yet, truth of God, though they are, they may be turned into a lie in the act of utterance. The prayer is not true, although it is borrowed from the Bible, if the suppliant invite the All-seeing in, and yet would give a thousand worlds, if he had them, to keep him out for ever.

Christ has declared the difficulty, and solved it: "I am the way, the truth, and the life: no man cometh unto the Father, but by me." When the Son has made the sinner free, he is free indeed. The dear child, pardoned and reconciled, loves and longs for the Father's presence. What! is there neither spot nor wrinkle now upon the man, that he dares to challenge inspection by the Omniscient, and to offer his heart as Jehovah's dwelling-place ? He is not yet so pure ; and well he knows it. The groan is bursting yet from his broken heart : " O wretched man that I am ! who shall deliver me from the body of this death ? " Many stains defile him yet ; but he loathes them now, and longs to be free. The difference between an unconverted and a converted man is not that the one has sins, and the other has none ; but that the one takes part with his cherished sins against a dreaded God, and the other takes part with a reconciled God against his hated sins. He is out with his former friends, and in with his former adversary. Conversion is a turning, and it is one turning only ; but it produces simultaneously and necessarily two distinct efforts. Whereas his face was formerly turned away from God, and toward his own sins ; it is now turned away from his own sins, and toward God. This one turning, with its twofold result, is in Christ the Mediator, and through the work of the Spirit.

As long as God is my enemy, I am his. I have no more power to change that condition than the polished surface has to refrain from reflecting the sunshine that falls upon it. It is God's love, from the face of Jesus shining into my dark heart, that makes my heart open to him, and delight to be his dwelling-place. The eyes of the just Avenger I cannot endure to be in this place of sin ; but the eye of the compassionate Physician I shall gladly admit into this place of disease ; for he comes from heaven to earth that he may heal such sin-sick souls as mine. When a disciple desires to be searched by the living God, he does not thereby intimate that there are no sins in him to be discovered : he intimates rather that his foes are so many and so lively, that nothing can subdue them except the presence and power of God.— *William Arnot* (—1875), *in "Laws from Heaven for Life on Earth."*

Verses 23, 24.—There are several things worthy of notice in the Psalmist's appeal, in the words before us. First, notice *the Psalmist's intrepidity.* Here is a man determined to explore the recesses of his own heart. Did Buonaparte, did Nelson, did Wellington, ever propose to do this ? Were all the renowned heroes of antiquity present, I would ask them all if they ever had courage to enter into their own hearts. David was a man of courage. When he slew a lion in the way, when he successfully encountered a bear, when he went out to meet the giant Goliath, he gave undoubted proofs of courage ; but never did he display such signal intrepidity as when he determined to look into his own heart. If you stood upon some eminence, and saw all the ravenous and venomous creatures that ever lived collected before you, it would not require such courage to combat them as to combat with your own heart. Every sin is a devil, and each may say, " My name is Legion, for we are many." Who knows what it is to face himself ? And yet, if we would be saved, this must be done.

Secondly, notice *the Psalmist's integrity.* He wished to know all his sins, that he might be delivered from them. As every individual must know his sins at some period, a wise man will seek to know them here, because the present is the only time in which to glorify God, by confessing, by renouncing, by overcoming them. One of the attributes of sin is to hide man from himself, to conceal his deformity, to prevent him from forming a just conception of his true condition. It is a solemn fact, that there is not an evil principle in the bosom of the devil himself which does not exist in ours, at the present moment, unless we are fully renewed by the power of the Holy Spirit. That these evil principles do not continually develop themselves, in all their hideous deformity, is entirely owing to the restraining and forbearing mercy of God.

Thirdly, notice *the Psalmist's wisdom.* He presents his prayer to God himself. God is the only Being in the universe that knows himself—that peruses himself in his own light. In the same light he sees all other beings ; and hence it follows that, if other beings see themselves truly, it must be in the light of God. If the sun were an intelligent being, I would ask him, " How do you see yourself ? In your own light ? " And he would reply, " Yes." " And how do you see the planets that are continually revolving around you ? " " In my own light also, for all the light that is in them is borrowed from me."

You will observe that the Psalmist begins with his principles : his desire is to have these tried by a competent judge, and to have every thing that is evil removed from them. This is an evidence of his wisdom. The heart and its thoughts must be made right, before the actions of the life can be set right. Those who are most eminent for piety are most conversant with God ; and, for this reason, they become most conversant with themselves. David says, elsewhere, " Who can understand his errors ? Cleanse THOU me from *secret* faults." And Job says, " If I wash myself with snow water, and make me never so clean, yet shalt THOU plunge me in the ditch, and mine own clothes shall abhor me." When these holy men perused themselves in God's light, they saw their sins of omission and commission, and prayed earnestly to be delivered from all.—*William Howels*, 1832.

Verses 23, 24.—The text is a prayer, and it indicates, as we think, three great facts in regard to the suppliant : the first, that David thoroughly wished to become acquainted with himself ; the second, that he felt conscious that God could see through all disguises ; and the third, that he desired to discover, in order that by Divine help he might correct, whatsoever was wrong in his conduct.

Now, the first inference which we draw from the text, when considered as indicating the feelings of the petitioner is, that he was thoroughly honest, that it was really his wish to become acquainted with his own heart. And is there, you may say, anything rare or remarkable in this ? Indeed we think there is. It would need, we believe, a very high degree of piety to be able to put up with sincerity the prayers of our text. For, will you tell me that it does not often happen, that even whilst men are carrying on a process of self-examination, there is a secret wish to remain ignorant of certain points, a desire not to be proved wrong when interest and inclination combine in demanding an opposite verdict ? . . . In searching into yourselves, you know where the tender points are, and those points you will be apt to avoid, so as not to put yourselves to pain, nor make it evident how much you need the caustic and the knife. Indeed, we may be sure that we state nothing but what experience will prove, when we declare it a high attainment in religion to be ready to know how bad we are. . . . And this had evidently been reached by the Psalmist, for he pleads very earnestly with God that he would leave no recess of his spirit unexplored, that he would bring the heart and all its thoughts, the life and all its ways, under a most searching examination, so that no form and no degree of evil might fail to be detected.—*Henry Melvill.*

Verses 23, 24.—Self-examination is not the simple thing which, at first sight, it might appear. No Christian who has ever really practised it has found it easy. Is there any exercise of the soul which any one of us has found so unsatisfactory, so almost impossible, as self-examination ? The fact is this, that the heart is so exceedingly complicated and intricate, and it is so very near the eye which has to investigate it, and both it and the eye are so restless and so shifting, that its deep anatomy baffles our research. Just a few things, here and there, broad and open, and floating upon the surface, a man discovers ; but there are chambers receding within chambers, in that deepest of all deep things, a sinner's heart, which no mere human investigation ever will reach, . . . it is the prerogative of God alone to *"search"* the human heart.

To the child of God—the most intimate with himself in all the earth—I do not hesitate to say—" There are sins latent at this moment in you, of which you have no idea ; but it only requires a larger measure of spiritual illumination to impress and unfold them. You have no idea of the wickedness that is now in you." But while I say this, let every Christian count well the cost before he ventures on the bold act of asking God to " search " him. For be sure of this, if you do really and earnestly ask God to *"search"* you, he will do it. And he will search you most searchingly ; and if you ask him to *"try"* you, he will try you,—and the trial will be no light matter !

I am persuaded that we often little calculate what we are doing—what we are asking God to do—when we implore him to give us some spiritual attainment, some growth in grace, some increase in holiness, or peace. To all these things there is a condition, and that condition lies in a discipline, and that discipline is generally proportionate to the strength and the measure of the gift that we ask.

I do not know what may have been the state of the Psalmist at the period when he indited this Psalm ; but I should think either one of Saul's most cruel persecutions, or the rebellion of his son Absalom, followed quick upon the traces of that prayer,—"Search me, O God, and know my heart : try me, and know my thoughts," etc.

Still, whatever his attainment, every child of God will desire, at any sacrifice, to know his own exact state before God ; for, as he desires in all things to have a mind conformed to the mind of God, so he is especially jealous lest he should, by any means, be taking a different view, or estimate, of his own soul from that which God sees it.—*Condensed from James Vaughan.*

Verses 23, 24.—Hypocrisy at the fashionable end of the town is very different from hypocrisy in the city. The modish hypocrite endeavours to appear more vicious than he really is, the other kind of hypocrite more virtuous. The former is afraid of everything that has the show of religion in it, and would be thought engaged in many criminal gallantries and amours which he is not guilty of. The latter assumes a face of sanctity, and covers a multitude of vices under a seeming religious deportment.

But there is another kind of hypocrisy, which differs from both these ; I mean that hypocrisy by which a man does not only deceive the world, but very often imposes on himself ; that hypocrisy which conceals his own heart from him, and makes him believe he is more virtuous than he really is, and either not attend to his vices, or mistake even his vices for virtues. It is this fatal hypocrisy and self-deceit which is taken notice of in those words, " Who can understand his errors ? cleanse thou me from secret faults."

These two kinds of hypocrisy, namely, that of deceiving the world, and that of imposing on ourselves, are touched with wonderful beauty in the hundred and thirty-ninth Psalm. The folly of the first kind of hypocrisy is there set forth by reflections on God's omniscience and omnipresence, which are celebrated in as noble strains of poetry as any other I ever met with, either sacred or profane. The other kind of hypocrisy, whereby a man deceives himself, is intimated in the two last verses, where the Psalmist addresses himself to the great Searcher of hearts in that emphatical petition ; " Try me, O God, and seek the ground of my heart : prove me, and examine my thoughts. Look well if there be any way of wickedness in me, and lead me in the way everlasting."—*Joseph Addison* (1672—1719), *in "The Spectator."*

Verses 23, 24.—How beautiful is the humility of David ! He cannot speak of the wicked but in terms of righteous indignation ; he cannot but hate the haters of his God ; yet, he seems immediately to recollect, and to check himself—" Try *me*, O Lord, and seek the ground of *my* heart." Precisely in the same spirit of inward humility and self-recollection, Abraham, when pleading before God in prayer for guilty depraved Sodom, fails not to speak of *himself*, as being dust and ashes : Gen. xviii. 27.—*James Ford*, 1871.

Verses 23, 24.—Why did David pray thus to God, "*Search me, O God, and know my heart,*" having said before, in the first verse, "*Thou hast searched me, and known me*" ? Seeing David knew that God had searched him, what needed he to pray that God would search him ? why did he beg God to do that which he had done already ? The answer is at hand. David was a diligent self-searcher, and therefore he was so willing to be searched, yea, he delighted to be searched by God ; and that not (as was said) because himself had done it already, but also because he knew God could do it better. He knew by his own search that he did not live in any way of wickedness against his knowledge, and yet he knew there might be some way of wickedness in him that he knew not of. And therefore he doth not only say, "*Search me, O God, and know my thoughts*"; but he adds, "*See if there be any wicked way* (or *any way of pain and grief*) *in me*"; (the same word signifies both, because wicked ways lead in the end to pain and grief) ; "*and lead me in the way everlasting.*" As if he had said, Lord, I have searched myself, and can see no wicked way in me ; but, Lord, thy sight is infinitely clearer than mine, and if thou wilt but search me thou mayest see some wicked way in me which I could not see, and I would fain see and know the worst of myself, that I might amend and grow better ; therefore, Lord, if there be any such way in me, cause me to know it also. O take that way out of me, and take me out of that way ; "*lead me in the way everlasting.*" David had tried himself, and he would again be tried by God, that he, being better tried, might become yet better. He found himself gold upon his own trial, and yet he feared there might be some dross in him that he had not found ; and now he would be re-tried that he might come forth purest gold. Pure gold fears neither the furnace nor the fire, neither the test nor the touchstone ; nor is weighty gold afraid of the balance. He that is weight will be weight, how often soever he is weighed ; he that is gold will be gold, how often soever he is tried, and the oftener he is tried the purer gold he will be ; what he is he will be, and he would be better than he is.—*Joseph Caryl.*

Verse 24.—"*See if there be any wicked way in me.*" This is a beautiful and impressive *prayer* for the commencement of every day. It is, also, a great sentiment to *admonish* us at the beginning of each day.

There is the way of *unbelief* within, to which we are very prone. There is the way of *vanity* and pride, to which we often accustom ourselves. There is the way of *selfishness* in which we frequently walk. There is the way of *worldliness* we often pursue—empty pleasures, shadowy honours, etc. There is the way of *sluggishness*. What apathy in prayer, in the examination and application of God's Word, we manifest! There is the way of *self-dependence*, by which we often dishonour God and injure ourselves. There is, unhappily, the way of *disobedience*, in which we often walk. At any rate, our obedience is cold, reluctant, uncertain—not simple, entire, fervent.

How necessary is it, then, to go to God at once, and earnestly to prefer the petition, *"Lord, see if there be any wicked way in me."* Let nothing that is wrong, that is opposed to thy character, repugnant to thy word, or injurious and debasing to ourselves, remain, or be harboured within us.—*Condensed from T. Wallace, in "Homiletic Commentary."*

Verse 24.—*"See if there be any wicked way in me."* To what a holiness must David have attained ere he could need, if we may so speak, Divine scrutiny, in order to his being informed of errors and defects! Is there one of us who can say that he has corrected his conduct up to the measure of his knowledge, and that now he must wait the being better informed before he can do more towards improving his life? I do not know how to define a higher point in religious attainment than supposing a man warranted in offering up the prayer of our text. I call upon you to be cautious in using this prayer. It is easy to mock God, by asking him to search you whilst you have made but little effort to search yourselves, and perhaps still less to act upon the result of the scrutiny.—*Henry Melvill.*

Verse 24.—*"See if there be any wicked way in me,"* etc.—

> Think and be careful what thou art within,
> For there is sin in the desire of sin :
> Think and be thankful, in a different case,
> For there is grace in the desire of grace.
>
> *John Byrom, 1691—1763.*

Verse 24.—*"The way everlasting."* *Way of eternity,* or *of antiquity, the old way,* as Jer. vi. 16 ; meaning the way of faith and godliness, which God taught from the beginning, and which continueth for ever ; contrary to " the way of the wicked," which perisheth : Ps. i. 6.—*Henry Ainsworth.*

HINTS TO PREACHERS.

Verses 1 and 23.—A matter of fact made a matter of prayer.

Verse 1.—1. A cheering thought for sinners. If God knew them not perfectly, how could he have prepared a perfect salvation for them? 2. A comfortable truth for saints. " Your heavenly Father knoweth that ye have need of all these things."—*G. R.*

Verses 1—5.—In these verses we have God's Omniscience, I. Described. 1. As observing minute and comparatively unimportant actions : " My downsitting and uprising." 2. As taking note of our thoughts and the motives behind them : " Understandest my thought." 3. As investigating all our ways : " Thou compassest," etc. ; better rendered, " Thou triest my walking and lying down," *i.e.,* my activities and restings. 4. Accurately estimating every word at the instant of its utterance : " For there is not a word," etc. 5. As being " behind " men, remembering their past, and " before " men, acquainted with their future : " Thou hast beset me," etc. 6. As every instant holding men under watchful scrutiny : " And laid," etc. II. Personally realized and pondered : " Thou hast searched *me.*" *Me* and *my* run through the whole set of statements. Thus felt and used, the fact of God's omniscience. 1. Begets reverence. 2. Inspires confidence. 3. Produces carefulness of conduct.—*J. F.*

Verses 2—4.—The knowledge of God extends, I. To our movements, our " downsitting and uprising "—when we sit down to read, write, or converse, and when we rise up to active service. II. To our thoughts : " Thou understandest my thoughts afar off." What they have been, what they now are, what they will be, what under all circumstances they would have been. He who made minds knows what their thoughts will be at all times, or he could not predict future events, or govern the world. He can know our thoughts without being the Author of them. III. To our actions: verse 3. Every step we take by day, and all we purpose to do in wakeful hours of the night: all our private, social, and public ways, are compassed or sifted by him, to distinguish the good from the bad, as wheat from the chaff. IV. To our words: verse 4. It has been said that the words of all men and from all time are registered in the atmosphere, and may be faithfully recalled. Whether it be so or not, they are phonographed in the mind of God.—*G. R.*

Verse 2 (first clause).—The importance of the commonest acts of life.

Verse 2 (second clause).—The serious nature of thoughts. Known to God; seen through, their drift perceived; and attention given to them while as yet in the distance.

Verse 3.—The encircling Presence, in our activities, meditations, secrecies, and movements.

Verse 4.—I. Words on the tongue first *in* it, and in that stage known to God. II. Words on the tongue very numerous, yet all known. III. Words on the tongue have wide meaning, yet known "altogether." Lesson: Take heed of your words not yet spoken.

Verse 5.—A soul captured. Stopped, overtaken, arrested. What has it done? What shall it do?

Verse 6.—I. God imperfectly known to man. II. Man perfectly known to God. It has been said that wise men never wonder; to us it appears they are always wondering.—*G. R.*

Verse 6.—Theme: the facts of our religion, too wonderful to understand, are just those in which we have most reason to rejoice. I. Prove it. 1. The incomprehensible attributes of God give unspeakable value to his promises. 2. The Incarnation is at once the most complete and most endearing manifestation of God we possess, yet it is the most inexplicable. 3. Redemption by the death of Christ is the highest guarantee of salvation we can conceive; but who can explain it? 4. Inspiration makes the Bible the word of God, though none can give an account of its mode of operation in the minds of those "moved by the Holy Ghost." 5. The resurrection of the body, and its glorification, satisfy the deepest yearning of our soul (Rom. viii. 23; 2 Cor. v. 2—4); but none can conceive the how. II. Apply its lessons. 1. Let us not stumble at doctrines simply because they are mysterious. 2. Let us be thankful God has not kept back the great mysteries of our religion simply because there would be some offended at them. 3. Let us readily receive all the joy which the mysteries bring, and calmly wait the light of heaven to make them better understood.—*J. F.*

Verses 7—10.—I. God is wherever I am. I fill but a small part of space; he fills all space. II. He is wherever I shall be. He does not move with me, but I move in him. "In him we live, and move," etc. III. God is wherever I could be. "If I ascend to heaven," etc. "If I descend to Sheol," etc. If I travel with the sunbeams to the most distant part of the earth, or heavens, or the sea, I shall be in thy hand. No mention is here made of annihilation, as though that were possible; which would be the only escape from the Divine Presence; for he is not the God of the dead, of the annihilated, in the Sadducean meaning of the word, but of the living. Man is always somewhere, and God is always everywhere.—*G. R.*

Verse 8.—The glory of heaven and the terror of hell: "THOU."

Verses 9, 10.—I. The greatest security and encouragement to a sinner supposed. 1. The place—the remotest part of the sea; by which you are to understand the most obscure nook in the creation. 2. His swift and speedy flight after the commission of sin, to this supposed refuge and sanctuary: "If I take the wings of the morning." II. This supposed security and encouragement is utterly destroyed (verse 10).—*See Flavel's "Seaman's Preservative in Foreign Countries."*

Verses 11, 12.—Darkness and light are both alike to God. I. Naturally. "I form the light, and I create the darkness." II. Providentially. Providential dispensations that are dark to us are light to him. We change with respect to him, not he to us. III. Spiritually. "Let him that walketh in darkness," etc. "Yea, though I walk," etc. He went before them in a pillar of cloud to guide them by day, and a pillar of fire to guide them by night. It was the same God in the day-cloud and in the night-light.—*G. R.*

Verse 14.—" I am fearfully and wonderfully made." This is true of man in his fourfold state. I. In his primitive integrity. II. In his deplorable depravity. III. In his regeneration. IV. In his fixed state in hell or heaven.—*W. W.*

Verses 17, 18.—The Psalm dilates upon the omniscience of God. In no mournful manner, but the reverse. I. *God's thoughts of us.* 1. How certain. 2. How numerous. 3. How condescending. 4. How tender. 5. How wise. 6. How practical. 7. How constant. II. *Our thoughts upon his thoughts.* 1. How rare and yet how due to the subject. 2. How delightful. 3. How consoling. 4. How strengthening to faith. 5. How arousing to love. III. *Our thoughts upon God himself.* 1. They place us near God. 2. They keep us near God. 3. They restore us to him. We are with God when we awake from sleep, from lethargy, from death.

Verses 17, 18.—I. The saint precious to God. He thinks of him tenderly ; in countless ways ; perpetually. II. God precious to the saints. Noting God's loving-kindnesses, numbering them, newly awakening to them. III. The mingling of these loves : " I am still with thee."—*W. B. H.*

Verse 18.—"*When I awake I am still with thee.*" Awaking is sometimes, yea, most commonly, taken in the *natural signification*, for the recovery from bodily sleep. 2. *Morally,* for recovery from sin. 3. *Mystically ;* " when I shall awake," that is, from the sleep of death.—*T. Horton.*

Verse 18.—" A Christian on Earth still in Heaven " [an Appendix to " A Christian on the Mount ; or, A Treatise concerning Meditation "], by *Thomas Watson,* 1660.

Verse 18.—"*I am still with thee.*" 1. By way of meditation. 2. In respect to communion. 3. In regard of action, and the businesses which are done by us.—*T. Horton.*

Verse 19.—I. The doctrine of punishment the necessary outcome of omniscience. II. Inevitable judgment an argument for separation from sinners.—*W. B. H.*

Verse 20.—Two scandalous offences against God. I. To speak slanderously of him. II. To speak irreverently of him. These are committed only by his enemies.

Verses 21, 22.—I. Such hatred one need not be ashamed of. II. Such hatred one should be able to define : " grieved." III. Such hatred one must labour to keep right. " Perfect hatred " is a form of hate consistent with all the virtues.

Verses 23, 24.—The language, I. Of self-examination. 1. As in the sight of God. 2. With a desire for the help of God : verse 23. Look me through and through, and tell me what thou thinkest of me. II. Of self-renunciation : " See if," etc. (verse 24) ; any sin unpardoned, any evil disposition unsubdued, any evil habit unrestrained, that I may renounce it. III. Of self-dedication : " Lead me," etc. : a submission entirely to divine guidance in the future.—*G. R.*

Verse 24.—I. The evil way. Naturally in us ; may be of different kinds ; must be removed ; removal needs Divine help. II. The everlasting way. There is but one, we need leading in it. It is the good old way, it does not come to an end ; it leads to blessedness without end.

Verse 24 (*last clause*).—See " Spurgeon's Sermons," No. 903 : " The Way Everlasting."

PSALM CXL.

This Psalm is in its proper place, and so fitly follows cxxxix. that you might almost read right on, and make no break between the two. Serious injury would follow to the whole Book of Psalms if the order should be interferred with as certain wiseacres propose. It is THE CRY OF A HUNTED SOUL, *the supplication of a believer incessantly persecuted and beset by cunning enemies, who hungered for his destruction. David was hunted like a partridge upon the mountains, and seldom obtained a moment's rest. This is his pathetic appeal to Jehovah for protection, an appeal which gradually intensifies into a denunciation of his bitter foes. With this sacrifice of prayer he offers the salt of faith; for in a very marked and emphatic manner he expresses his personal confidence in the Lord as the protector of the oppressed, and as his own God and Defender. Few short Psalms are so rich in the jewelry of precious faith.*

" To the Chief Musician."—The writer wished this experimental hymn to be under the care of the chief master of song, that it might neither be left unsung, nor chanted in a slovenly manner. Such trials and such rescues deserved to be had in remembrance, and to be set up among the choicest memorials of the Lord's goodness. We too, have our songs which are of no ordinary kind, and these must be sung with our best powers of heart and tongue. We will offer them to the Lord by no other hand than that of " the Chief Musician."

" A Psalm of David."—The life of David wherein he comes in contact with Saul and Doeg is the best explanation of this Psalm; and surely there can be no reasonable doubt that David wrote it, and wrote it in the time of his exile and peril. The tremendous outburst at the end has in it the warmth which was so natural to David, who was never lukewarm in anything; yet it is to be noticed that concerning his enemies he was often hot in language through indignation, and yet he was cool in action, for he was not revengeful. His was no petty malice, but a righteous anger: he foresaw, foretold, and even desired the just vengeance of God upon the proud and wicked, and yet he would not avail himself of opportunities to revenge himself upon those who had done him wrong. It may be that his appeals to the great King cooled his anger, and enabled him to leave his wrongs unredressed by any personal act of violence. "Vengeance is mine; I will repay, saith the Lord "; and David when most wounded by undeserved persecution and wicked falsehood was glad to leave his matters at the foot of the throne, where they would be safe with the King of kings.

EXPOSITION.

DELIVER me, O LORD, from the evil man: preserve me from the violent man;

2 Which imagine mischiefs in *their* heart; continually are they gathered together *for* war.

3 They have sharpened their tongues like a serpent; adders' poison *is* under their lips. Selah.

1. *"Deliver me, O* LORD, *from the evil man."* It reads like a clause of the Lord's prayer, " Deliver us from evil." David does not so much plead against an individual as against the species represented by him, namely, the being whose best description is— " the evil man." There are many such abroad; indeed we we shall not find an unregenerate man who is not in some sense an evil man, and yet all are not alike evil. It is well for us that our enemies are evil: it would be a horrible thing to have the good against us. When " the evil man " bestirs himself against the godly he is as terrible a being as a wolf, or a serpent, or even a devil. Fierce, implacable, unpitying, unrelenting, unscrupulous, he cares for nothing but the indulgence of his malice. The persecuted man turns to God in prayer; he could not do a wiser thing. Who can meet the evil man and defeat him save Jehovah himself, whose infinite goodness is more than a match for all the evil in

the universe ? We cannot of ourselves baffle the craft of the enemy, but the Lord knoweth how to deliver his saints. He can keep us out of the enemy's reach, he can sustain us when under his power, he can rescue us when our doom seems fixed, he can give us the victory when defeat seems certain ; and in any and every case, if he do not save us from the man he can keep us from the evil. Should we be at this moment oppressed in any measure by ungodly men, it will be better to leave our defence with God than to attempt it ourselves.

"*Preserve me from the violent man.*" Evil in the heart simmers in malice, and at last boils in passion. Evil is a raging thing when it getteth liberty to manifest itself ; and so "the evil man" soon develops into "the violent man." What watchfulness, strength, or valour can preserve the child of God from deceit and violence ? There is but one sure Preserver, and it is our wisdom to hide under the shadow of his wings. It is a common thing for good men to be assailed by enemies : David was attacked by Saul, Doeg, Ahithophel, Shimei, and others ; even Mordecai sitting humbly in the gate had his Haman ; and our Lord, the Perfect One, was surrounded by those who thirsted for his blood. We may not, therefore, hope to pass through the world without enemies, but we may hope to be delivered out of their hands, and preserved from their rage, so that no real harm shall come of their malignity. This blessing is to be sought by prayer, and expected by faith.

2. "*Which imagine mischiefs in their heart.*" They cannot be happy unless they are plotting and planning, conspiring and contriving. They seem to have but one heart, for they are completely agreed in their malice ; and with all their heart and soul they pursue their victim. One piece of mischief is not enough for them ; they work in the plural, and prepare many arrows for their bow. What they cannot actually do they nevertheless like to think over, and to rehearse on the stage of their cruel fancy. It is an awful thing to have such a heart-disease as this. When the imagination gloats over doing harm to others, it is a sure sign that the entire nature is far gone in wickedness. "*Continually are they gathered together for war.*" They are a committee of opposition in permanent session : they never adjourn, but perpetually consider the all-absorbing question of how to do the most harm to the man of God. They are a standing army always ready for the fray : they not only go to the wars, but dwell in them. Though they are the worst of company, yet they put up with one another, and are continually in each other's society, confederate for fight. David's enemies were as violent as they were evil, as crafty as they were violent, and as persistent as they were crafty. It is hard dealing with persons who are only in their element when they are at daggers-drawn with you. Such a case calls for prayer, and prayer calls on God.

3. "*They have sharpened their tongues like a serpent.*" The rapid motion of a viper's tongue gives you the idea of its sharpening it ; even thus do the malicious move their tongues at such a rate that one might suppose them to be in the very act of wearing them to a point, or rubbing them to a keen edge. It was a common notion that serpents inserted their poison by their tongues, and the poets used the idea as a poetical expression, although it is certain that the serpent wounds by his fangs and not by his tongue. We are not to suppose that all authors who used such language were mistaken in their natural history any more than a writer can be charged with ignorance of astronomy because he speaks of the sun's travelling from east to west. How else can poets speak but according to the appearance of things to an imaginative eye. The world's great poet puts it in "King Lear" :

> "She struck me with her tongue,
> Most serpent-like, upon the very heart."

In the case of slanderers, they so literally sting with their tongues, which are so nimble in malice, and withal so piercing and cutting, that it is by no means unjust to speak of them as sharpened. "*Adders' poison is under their lips.*" The deadliest of all venom is the slander of the unscrupulous. Some men care not what they say so long as they can vex and injure. Our text, however, must not be confined in its reference to some few individuals, for in the inspired epistle to the Romans it is quoted by the apostle as being true of us all. So depraved are we by nature that the most venomous creatures are our fit types. The old serpent has not only inoculated us with his venom, but he has caused us to be ourselves producers of the like poison : it lies under our lips, ready for use, and, alas, it is all too freely used when we grow angry, and desire to take vengeance upon any who have caused us vexation. It is sadly wonderful what hard things even good men will say when provoked ; yea, even such as call themselves " perfect " in cool blood are not quite as gentle as doves when their claims to sinlessness are bluntly questioned. This poison of evil-speaking would never fall from our lips, however much we might be provoked, if it were not there at other times ; but by nature we have as great a store of venomous words as a cobra has of poison. O Lord, take the poison-bags away, and cause our lips to drop nothing but honey. *"Selah."* This is heavy work. Go up, go up, my heart! Sink not too low. Fall not into the lowest key. Lift up thyself to God.

4 Keep me, O Lord, from the hands of the wicked ; preserve me from the violent man ; who have purposed to overthrow my goings.

5 The proud have hid a snare for me, and cords ; they have spread a net by the wayside ; they have set gins for me. Selah.

4. *"Keep me, O Lord, from the hands of the wicked."* To fall into their hands would be a calamity indeed. David in his most pitiable plight chose to fall into the hand of a chastising God rather than to be left in the power of men. No creature among the wild beasts of the wood is so terrible an enemy to man as man himself when guided by evil, and impelled by violence. The Lord by providence and grace can keep us out of the power of the wicked. He alone can do this, for neither our own watchfulness nor the faithfulness of friends can secure us against the serpentine assaults of the foe. We have need to be preserved from the smooth as well as the rough hands of the ungodly, for their flatteries may harm us as much as their calumnies. The hands of their example may pollute us, and so do us more harm than the hands of their oppression. Jehovah must be our keeper, or evil hands will do what evil hearts have imagined and evil lips have threatened. *"Preserve me from the violent man."* His intense passion makes him terribly dangerous. He will strike anyhow, use any weapon, smite from any quarter : he is so furious that he is reckless of his own life if he may accomplish his detestable design. Lord, preserve us by thine omnipotence when men attack us with their violence. This prayer is a wise and suitable one. *"Who have purposed to overthrow my goings."* They resolve to turn the good man from his resolve, they would defeat his designs, injure his integrity, and blast his character. Their own goings are wicked, and therefore they hate those of the righteous, seeing they are a standing rebuke to them. This is a forcible argument to use in prayer with God : he is the patron of holiness, and when the pure lives of his people are in danger of overthrow, he may be expected to interpose. Never let the pious forget to pray, for this is a weapon against which the most determined enemy cannot stand.

5. *"The proud have hid a snare for me."* Proud as they are, they stoop to this mean action : they use a snare, and they hide it away. that their victim may be taken like a poor hare who is killed without warning—killed in its usual run, by a snare which it could not see. David's enemies wished to snare him in his path of service, the usual way of his life. Saul laid many snares for David, but the Lord preserved him. All around us there are snares of one sort or another, and he will be well kept, ay, divinely kept, who never falls into one of them. *"And cords."* With these they pull the net together and with these they bind their captive. Thus fowlers do, and trappers of certain large animals. The cords of love are pleasant, but the cords of hate are cruel as death itself. *"They have spread a net by the wayside."* Where it will be near their prey ; where the slightest divergence from the path will bring the victim into it. Surely the common wayside ought to be safe : men who go out of the way may well be taken in a net, but the path of duty is proverbially the path of safety ; yet it is safe nowhere when malicious persons are abroad. Birds are taken in nets, and men are taken by deceit. Satan instructs his children in the art of fowling, and they right speedily learn how to spread nets : perhaps they have been doing that for us already ; let us make our appeal to God concerning it. *"They have set gins for me."* One instrument of destruction is not enough ; they are so afraid of missing their prey that they multiply their traps, using differing devices, so that one way or another they may take their victim. Those who avoid the snare and the net may yet be caught in a gin, and accordingly gins are placed in all likely places. If a godly man can be cajoled, or bribed, or cowed, or made angry, the wicked will make the attempt. Ready are they to twist his words, misread his intentions, and misdirect his efforts ; ready to fawn, and lie, and make themselves mean to the last degree so that they

may accomplish their abominable purpose. *"Selah."* The harp needs tuning after such a strain, and the heart needs lifting up towards God.

6 I said unto the LORD, Thou *art* my God : hear the voice of my supplications, O LORD.

7 O GOD the Lord, the strength of my salvation, thou hast covered my head in the day of battle.

8 Grant not, O LORD, the desires of the wicked : further not his wicked device ; *lest* they exalt themselves. Selah.

6. *"I said unto the LORD, thou art my God."* Here was David's stay and hope. He was assured that Jehovah was his God, he expressed that assurance, and he expressed it before Jehovah himself. That had need be a good and full assurance which a man dares to lay before the face of the heart-searching Lord. The Psalmist when hunted by man, addressed himself to God. Often the less we say to our foes, and the more we say to our best Friend the better it will fare with us : if we say anything, let it be said unto the Lord. David rejoiced in the fact that he had already said that Jehovah was his God : he was content to have committed himself, he had no wish to draw back. The Lord was David's own by deliberate choice, to which he again sets his seal with delight. The wicked reject God, but the righteous receive him as their own, their treasure, their pleasure, their light and delight. *"Hear the voice of my supplications, O LORD."* Since thou art mine, I pray thee hear my cries. We cannot ask this favour of another man's god, but we may seek it from our own God. The prayers of saints have a voice in them ; they are expressive pleadings even when they sound like inarticulate moanings. The Lord can discern a voice in our wailings, and he can and will hearken thereto. Because he is God he can hear us ; because he is *our* God he will hear us. So long as the Lord doth but hear us we are content : the answer may be according to his own will, but we do entreat to be heard : a soul in distress is grateful to any one who will be kind and patient enough to hearken to its tale, but specially is it thankful for an audience with Jehovah. The more we consider his greatness and our insignificance, his wisdom and our folly, the more shall we be filled with praise when the Lord attends unto our cry.

7. *"O GOD the Lord, the strength of my salvation, thou hast covered my head in the day of battle."* When he looked back upon past dangers and deliverances, the good man felt that he should have perished had not the Lord held a shield over his head. In the day of the clash of arms, or of putting on of armour (as some read it), the glorious Lord had been his constant protector. Goliath had his armour-bearer, and so had Saul, and these each one guarded his master ; yet the giant and the king both perished, while David, without armour or shield, slew the giant and baffled the tyrant. The shield of the Eternal is better protection than a helmet of brass. When arrows fly thick and the battle-axe crashes right and left, there is no covering for the head like the power of the Almighty. See how the child of providence glorifies his Preserver ! He calls him not only his salvation, but the strength of it, by whose unrivalled force he had been enabled to outlive the cunning and cruelty of his adversaries. He had obtained a deliverance in which the strength of the Omnipotent was clearly to be seen. This is a grand utterance of praise, a gracious ground of comfort, a prevalent argument in prayer. He that has covered our head aforetime will not now desert us. Wherefore let us fight a good fight, and fear no deadly wound : the Lord God is our shield, and our exceeding great reward.

8. *"Grant not, O LORD, the desires of the wicked."* Even they are dependent upon thee ; they can do no more than thou dost permit. Thou dost restrain them ; not a dog of them can move his tongue without thy leave and license. Therefore I entreat thee not to let them have their way. Even though they dare to pray to thee, do not hear their prayers against innocent men. Assuredly the Lord Jehovah will be no accomplice with the malevolent ; their desires shall never be his desires ; if they thirst for blood he will not gratify their cruelty. *"Further not his wicked device."* They are so united as to be like one man in their wishes ; but do not hear their prayers. Though hand join in hand, and they desire and design as one man, yet do not thou lend them the aid of thy providence. Do not permit their malicious schemes to succeed. The Lord may allow success to attend the policy of the wicked

for a time for wise reasons unknown to us, but we are permitted to pray that it be not so.   The petition " Deliver us from evil " includes and allows such supplication.   *"Lest they exalt themselves."*   If successful, the wicked are sure to grow proud, and insult the righteous over whom they have triumphed, and this is so great an evil, and so dishonouring to God, that the Psalmist uses it in his pleading as an argument against their being allowed to prosper.   The glory of the wicked is opposed to the glory of God.   If God seems to favour them they grow too high for this world, and their heads strike against the heavens.   Let us hope that the Lord will not suffer this to be.   *"Selah."*   Here let us exalt our thoughts and praises high over the heads of self-exalting sinners.   The more they rise in conceit the higher let us rise in confidence.

9 *As for* the head of those that compass me about, let the mischief of their own lips cover them.

10 Let burning coals fall upon them; let them be cast into the fire; into deep pits, that they rise not up again.

11 Let not an evil speaker be established in the earth: evil shall hunt the violent man to overthrow *him*.

9.   *"As for the head of those that compass me about, let the mischief of their own lips cover them."*   To the Lord who had covered his head amid the din of arms the Psalmist appeals against his foes, that their heads may be covered in quite another sense—covered with the reward of their own malice.   David's foes were so many that they hemmed him in, encircling him as hunters do their prey.   It is little wonder that he turns to the Lord in his dire need.   The poet represents his adversaries as so united as to have but one head ; for there is often a unanimity among evil spirits which makes them the more strong and terrible for their vile purposes.   The *lex talionis*, or law of retaliation, often brings down upon violent men the evil which they planned and spoke of for others : their arrows fall upon themselves.   When a man's lips vent curses they will probably, like chickens, come home to roost.   A stone hurled upward into the air is apt to fall upon the thrower's head.

David's words may be read in the future as a prophecy ; but in this verse, at any rate, there is no need to do so in order to soften their tone.   It is so just that the mischief which men plot and the slander which they speak should recoil upon themselves that every righteous man must desire it : he who does not desire it may wish to be considered humane and Christlike, but the chances are that he has a sneaking agreement with the wicked, or is deficient in a manly sense of right and wrong.   When evil men fall into pits which they have digged for the innocent we believe that even the angels are glad ; certainly the most gentle and tender of philanthropists, however much they pity the sufferers, must also approve the justice which makes them suffer.   We suspect that some of our excessively soft-spoken critics only need to be put into David's place, and they would become a vast deal more bitter than he ever was.

10.   *"Let burning coals fall upon them."*   Then will they know that the scattering of the firebrands is not the sport they thought it to be.   When hailstones and coals of fire descend upon them, how will they escape ?   Even the skies above the wicked are able to deal out vengeance upon them.   *"Let them be cast into the fire."*   They have kindled the flames of strife, and it is fair that they should be cast therein.   They have heated the furnace of slander seven times hotter than it was wont to be heated, and they shall be devoured therein.   Who would have pitied Nebuchadnezzar if he had been thrown into his own burning fiery furnace ?   *"Into deep pits, that they rise not up again."*   They made those ditches or fosses for the godly, and it is meet that they should themselves fall into them and never escape.   When a righteous man falls he rises again ; but when the wicked man goes down " he falls like Lucifer, never to hope again."   The Psalmist in this passage graphically depicts the Sodom of the wicked persecutor : fire falls upon him from heaven ; the city blazes, and he is cast into the conflagration ; the vale of Siddim is full of slime-pits, and into these he is buried.   Extraordinary judgment overtakes the extraordinary offender : above, around, beneath, all is destruction.   He would have consumed the righteous, and now he is consumed himself.   So shall it be : so let it be.

11. *"Let not an evil speaker be established in the earth."* For that would be an established plague, a perpetual curse. Men of false and cruel tongues are of most use when they go to fatten the soil in which they rot as carcasses: while they are alive they are the terror of the good, and the torment of the poor. God will not allow the specious orators of falsehood to retain the power they temporarily obtain by their deceitful speaking. They may become prominent, but they cannot become permanent. They shall be disendowed and disestablished in spite of all that they can say to the contrary. All evil bears the element of decay within itself; for what is it but corruption? Hence the utmost powers of oratory are insufficient to settle upon a sure foundation the cause which bears a lie within it. *"Evil shall hunt the violent man to overthrow him."* He hunted the good, and now his own evil shall hunt him. He tried to overthrow the goings of the righteous, and now his own unrighteousness shall prove his overthrow. As he was violent, so shall he be violently assaulted and hunted down. Sin is its own punishment; a violent man will need no direr doom than to reap what he has sown. It is horrible for a huntsman to be devoured by his own hounds; yet this is the sure fate of the persecutor.

12 I know that the LORD will maintain the cause of the afflicted, *and* the right of the poor.

13 Surely the righteous shall give thanks unto thy name : the upright shall dwell in thy presence.

12. *"I know that the LORD will maintain the cause of the afflicted, and the right of the poor."* All through the Psalm the writer is bravely confident, and speaks of things about which he had no doubt : in fact, no Psalm can be more grandly positive than this protest against slander. The slandered saint knew Jehovah's care for the afflicted, for he had received actual proofs of it himself. " I will maintain it " is the motto of the great Defender of the rights of the needy. What confidence this should create within the bosoms of the persecuted and poverty-stricken ! The prosperous and wealthy can maintain their own cause, but those who are otherwise shall find that God helps those who cannot help themselves. Many talk as if the poor had no rights worth noticing, but they will sooner or later find out their mistake when the judge of all the earth begins to plead with them.

13. *"Surely the righteous shall give thanks unto thy name."* The former Psalm had its " surely," but this is a more pleasing one. As surely as God will slay the wicked he will save the oppressed, and fill their hearts and mouths with praises. Whoever else may be silent, the righteous will give thanks ; and whatever they may suffer, the matter will end in their living through the trial, and magnifying the Lord for his delivering grace. On earth ere long, and in heaven for ever, the pure heart shall sing unto the Lord. How loud and sweet will be the songs of the redeemed in the millennial age, when the meek shall inherit the earth, and delight themselves in the abundance of peace !

"The upright shall dwell in thy presence." Thus shall they give thanks in the truest and fullest manner. This abiding before the Lord shall render to him " songs without words," and therefore all the more spiritual and true. Their living and walking with their God shall be their practical form of gratitude. Sitting down in holy peace, like children at their father's table, their joyful looks and language shall speak their high esteem and fervent love to him who has become their dwelling-place. How high have we climbed in this Psalm—from being hunted by the evil man to dwelling in the divine presence ; so doth faith upraise the saint from the lowest depths to heights of peaceful repose. Well might the song be studded with Selahs, or uplifters.

EXPLANATORY NOTES AND QUAINT SAYINGS.

Whole Psalm.—Another Psalm " *of David,*" to be sung by all saints, even as it was used by their Head, David's Son. In it we have (verses 1—3) the *picture of the wicked*, with a "*Selah*," that bids us pause over its dark colours. Then we have (verses 4, 5) *a view of the snares spread by the wicked*, with another " Selah "-pause. Thereafter, we see a soul in *the attitude of faith* (verses 6—8). They are laying the snares, but calm as Elisha beholding the Syrian host assembling (2 Kings v. 15), the stayed soul sings—

"I have said to the Lord, My God art thou ; "

and then he prays, putting a "*Selah*" at the close, that we may again pause and survey the scene.—*Andrew A. Bonar.*

Whole Psalm.—There is no doubt that this Psalm expresses the feelings of David on the first intelligence of Saul's setting out *anew* in pursuit of him (comp. verse 2). And then, in Psalm cxli. we have his supplication at the time when this danger was ever approaching nearer. Various things are said in this Psalm (according to the Hebrew) primarily of a single person, (Saul:) thus *e.g.*, verses 1, 4 ; and the numerous tongues of which David complains (verse 3) are just the tongues of traitors who again informed Saul of this new place of residence in the wilderness of Engedi, where he might have imagined himself so secure. The laying of snares (verse 5) agrees perfectly in part with this treachery, and in part with the search after David by Saul and his numerous army, mentioned in 1 Sam. xxiv. 2. In the same way might the burning coals, spoken of in verse 10, and likewise the deep pits (German, floods) mentioned there, have suggested themselves most naturally to David upon the rocks of Engedi, where he had the Dead Sea just before him. Verse 10 seems also to allude to the events which happened on the night before the destruction of Sodom.—*T. C. Barth, in "The Bible Manual."*

Whole Psalm.—As in Psalm cxxxviii. David set before his seed God's promise as the anchor of hope (2 Sam. vii.) ; and in Psalm cxxxix., God's omniscience as our consolation in danger and motive for shunning evil ; so in this Psalm he sets forth the danger from calumnious enemies, and our only safety in Jehovah, our strength.—*Andrew Robert Fausset.*

Verses 1, 4, 6, 8.—Good men live by prayer. He who gets to the throne of grace is covered by the cloud of glory, through which no sun can smite by day, nor moon by night.—*William Swan Plumer.*

Verses 1, 7—11.—On the first reading of this Psalm one is inclined to think that there is somewhat of fierceness and bitterness in it, which is hardly consistent with the character of a child of God, and therefore unbecoming in David . . . . And yet I really think that a little more examination of the language of this Psalm will lead us to believe that we are doing David wrong in affixing anything like a meaning or desire of vindictiveness to his words.

Assuredly we can find no fault with one who takes his wrongs in prayer to God ; who, like Hezekiah, takes the roll of his cares, and sorrows, and trials, and spreads it before the Lord. And this is what David does in the very first verse: "*Deliver me, O LORD, from the evil man ; preserve me from the violent man.*" I do not think a person who does this, who, when smarting under a sense of injury and wrong, goes at once to God and lays open his heart to him, is likely to go very far wrong ; for even though he may have begun in somewhat of an unkindly spirit, yet prayer opens before us such a sight and sense of our own guiltiness and wrongs towards God, and thereby exercises such an abasing, as well as healing and soothing, influence over our feelings towards others, that we might almost be assured that he whose prayer might begin even with a vehement enumeration of his own wrongs, would end with something very like a determination to bless them that cursed, and to do good to them that hated him.

You will observe, too, how, from first to last, David leaves his cause in God's hands ; it is not " my sword and my bow that shall help me ; " he counted them vain things to help a man ; and therefore, as he had so often said in other Psalms ; " The Lord was his shield and his defence," and as God had already shielded his head in the day of battle, so he prays for the same protection against his enemies now.—*Barton Bouchier.*

Verses 1, 11.—Three special forms of Satanic energy are individualized. The *evil* or wicked man, the *violent* man, and the *man of tongue* are severally appealed from by the suppliant speaker of the prayer of faith.—*Arthur Pridham.*

Verse 2.—"*Continually are they gathered together for war.*" Literally, this clause reads, " *who gather wars,*" and so some understand it. But it is well known that the prepositions are often omitted in the Hebrew, and no doubt he means that they stirred up general enmity by their false information which acted as a trumpet sounding to battle.—*John Calvin.*

Verses 2, 3.—The wicked assault the righteous with three weapons—with the heart, by conspiracy ; with the tongue, by lying ; and with the hand, by violence. —*John Lorinus*, 1569—1634.

Verse 3.—*They have sharpened their tongues like a serpent.*" To sharpen or whet the tongue imports the keenest and extremest kind of talkativeness, much more to sharpen the tongue " *like a serpent.*" Naturalists tell us that no living creature stirs his tongue so swiftly as a serpent, and serpents are therefore said to have a treble tongue, because, moving their tongues so fast, they seem to have three tongues. The Psalmist means—the wicked speak thick and threefold, they sting and poison me with their tongues.—*Joseph Caryl.*

Verse 3.—"*They have sharpened their tongues like a serpent.*" This is an exact description of the way in which a serpent darts out his tongue before he inflicts the wound. See him : his head is erect, and his piercing eye is wildly and fiercely fixed on the object ; the tongue rapidly appears and disappears, as if by that process it would be sharpened for the contest. Thus were the enemies of David making sharp their tongues for his destruction.—*Joseph Roberts, in "Oriental Illustrations of the Sacred Scriptures,*" 1835.

Verse 3.—"*They have sharpened their tongues like a serpent,*" etc. Is it not a fact, that there are many men, the very existence of whom is a baneful poison, as it were ? They dart their livid tongue like the tongue of a serpent ; and the venom of their disposition corrodes every object upon which it concentrates itself ; ever vilifying and maligning, like the ill-omened bird of night.—*Pliny.*

Verse 3.—"*They have sharpened their tongues like a serpent.*" As the adder skilfully prepares herself for her work of death, so do the unhappy children of slander and falsehood prepare themselves, by every possible effort, for injuring their unoffending victims.—*John Morison.*

Verse 3.—In St. James's day, as now, it would appear that there were idle men and idle women, who went about from house to house, dropping slander as they went, and yet you could not take up that slander and detect the falsehood there. You could not evaporate the truth in the slow process of the crucible, and then show the residuum of falsehood glittering and visible. You could not fasten upon any word or sentence, and say that it was calumny ; for in order to constitute slander, it is not necessary that the word spoken should be false—half-truths are often more calumnious than whole falsehoods. It is not even neccessary that a word should be distinctly uttered ; a dropped lip, an arched eyebrow, a shrugged shoulder, a significant look, an incredulous expression of countenance, nay, even an emphatic silence, may do the work ; and when the light and trifling thing which has done the mischief has fluttered off, the venom is left behind, to work and rankle, to inflame hearts, to fever human existence, and to poison human society at the fountain springs of life. Very emphatically was it said by one whose whole being had smarted under such affliction, "*Adders' poison is under their lips.*" —*Frederick Wiliam Robertson.*

Verse 3.—Slander and calumny must always precede and accompany ᵢerse-cution, because malice itself cannot excite people against a good man, as such ; to do this, he must first be represented as a bad man. What can be said of those who are busied in this manner, but that they are a " generation of vipers," the brood of the old " Serpent," that grand accuser and calumniator of the brethren, having under their tongues a bag of " poison." conveying instant death to the reputation on which they fasten. Thus David was hunted as a rebel, Christ was crucified as a blasphemer, and the primitive Christians were tortured as guilty of incest and murder.—*George Horne.*

Verse 3.—Man consists of soul and body ; the body is but the shadow, or at best but the bearer of the soul : it's the soul that bears God's image ; it's the soul especially for which Christ died. Now, by how much the soul is more precious than the body, by so much are the helps more excellent, and the enemies more dangerous than the body's. The body is fed with meat; but it is perishing meat (1 Cor. vi. 13); but the food of the soul is the heavenly manna (John vi. 27). Answerably, the enemies are more hurtful, for that that hurts or kills the body toucheth not the soul; but what hurts or kills the soul kills the body with it, and destroys the whole man. The conclusion is, that therefore the bane or poison of the soul is much more hideous, horrible and hateful than that of the body; and of that poison speaks the present Scripture: "*adders' poison is under their lips.*"

A strange text some may say, and 'tis true; but it is the fitter for these strange times, wherein the poison both of soul and body so far prevails. The words do describe in part the malignant and malicious nature of the unregenerate and sinful man; and to that purpose are they cited by the apostle to the Romans (ch. iii. 13). The *asp* is but a little creature; but not a little poisonful. So little a creature hath been the bane and death of many a great person; let one suffice for all. That royal and renowned Cleopatra, queen of Egpyt, chose rather to die by the biting of two asps than to be carried in triumph at Rome by Augustus. The manner of their poisoning is this,—he that is bitten by the asp falls forthwith into a gentle sweat and a sweet sleep, and his strength and vital spirits decay and weaken by little till he die; thus the present pain is little, but the stroke is deadly. And even such stings are the tongues, and such swords the words of wicked men. And no marvel; for what can come but poisonful words and actions from them whose very inward nature is all poison within!

The poison of the soul is only *sin*, and this is like to poison in many respects. Poison, wherever it enters, stays not there, but diffuseth itself all over the body, and never ceaseth till it has infected all. Such is the nature of sin; enter where it will it creeps from one member of the body to another, and from the body to the soul, till it has infected the whole man; and then from man to man, till the whole family; and stays not there, but runs like a wildfire, from family to family, till it has poisoned a whole town, and so a whole country, and a whole kingdom. Woeful experience proves this true, both for Popish opinions, idle fashions, vain customs, and ill-examples of all sorts, which once set on foot, spread themselves over the politic body of church and commonwealth, like a gangrene or a leprosy over the natural body or like a poison through all the blood. Poison, having entered anywhere, as it seeks to creep presently over all, so desires it especially to seize upon the heart; such a malice and pride lies in the malignant nature of it, that it aspires to the heart; and such a craft and cunning lurks in it, that having once entered, it creeps closely and unfelt till it gets to the heart; but having possessed itself of that sovereign part of man, then like a tyrant it reigns and rages, and infecting first the vital blood and noble parts, it diffuseth itself over all and every part. And such is the nature of sin, the spiritual poison of the soul; enter where it will, it is the heart it aims at, and it will never stay till it come there. The truth of this is so clear that proofs are needless; for who knows not that the senses are but the doors or windows, but the heart is the throne, and the soul itself the seat of sin: and hence it is that Solomon adviseth,—"My son, keep thy heart with all diligence": Prov. iv. 23. —*William Crashaw, in "The Parable of Poyson,"* 1618.

Verse 3.—"*Adders' poison is under their lips.*" The word rendered "*adder*," עַכְשׁוּב, *achsub*, occurs here only; and it is perhaps impossible to determine what species is intended. As the word, in its proper signification, seems to express coiling, or bending back—an act common to most serpents—the name has perhaps no determinate reference; or it may be another name for the *pethen*, mentioned under Job xx.; which seems also to have been the opinion of the Seventy, as they render both words by ἀσπίς, and are followed by the Vulgate (*aspis*).

As to the *poison*, it will be observed, that in the venomous serpents there is a gland under the eye secreting the poisonous matter, which is conveyed, in a small tube or canal, to the end of a fang which lies concealed at the roof of the mouth. This fang is moveable at the pleasure of the serpent, and is protruded when it is about to strike at an antagonist. The situation of this poison, which is, in a manner, behind the upper lip, gives great propriety to the expression, "*adders' poison is under their lips.*" The usage of the Hebrew language renders it by no means improbable that the fang itself is called לָשׁוֹן *lashon*, a tongue, in the present text; and a serpent might then be said to sharpen its tongue, when, in preparing to strike, it protruded its fangs. We do not see any explanation by which a more consistent meaning may be extracted from the expression here employed.—*John Kitto, in the "Pictorial Bible."*

Verse 3.—Often the tongue of the serpent is spoken of as the seat of its venom. This is popular, not scientific language.—*William Swan Plumer.*

Verse 3.—*"Adder."* The word *acshub* (pronounced ăk-shoob), only occurs in this one passage. The precise species represented by this word, is unknown. Buxtorf, however, explains the word as the Spitter, "illud genus quod venenum procul exspuit." Now, if we accept this derivation, we must take the word *acshub* as a synonym for *pethen*. We have already identified the Pethen with the Naja haje, a snake which has the power of expelling the poison to some distance, when it is out of reach of its enemy. Whether the snake really intends to eject the poison, or whether it is merely flung from the hollow fangs by the force of the sudenly-checked stroke, is uncertain. That the Haje cobra can expel its poison is an acknowledged fact, and the Dutch colonists of the Cape have been so familiarly acquainted with this habit, that they have called this reptile by the name of Spuugh-Slange, or Spitting-Snake, a name which, if we accept Buxtorf's etymology, is precisely equivalent to the word *acshub.*—*J. G. Wood, in "Bible Animals."*

Verses 3, 5, 8.—*"Selah."* We meet with Selah here for the first time since Psalm lxxxix. From Psalm xc. to Psalm cxl. no *Selah* occurs. Why omitted in these fifty we cannot tell any more than why so often recurring in others. However, there are only about forty Psalms in all in which it is used.—*Andrew A. Bonar.*

Verse 4.—*"Keep me,"* etc. From doing as they do, or as they would have me do, or as they promise themselves I will do.—*Matthew Henry.*

Verse 4.—*"Preserve me from the violent man."* The second clause of the first versicle of this verse is the same as the second versicle of verse 1, which seems the burden of the song.—*"Speaker's Commentary."*

Verse 4.—*"To overthrow my goings."* To take my feet from under me, to destroy the basis of belief, the power of advance in good works, that we may turn back from the way of salvation, or fall upon it, or, at any rate, may go very slowly along it.—*Neale and Littledale.*

Verse 5.—*"The proud have hid a snare for me, and cords."* The following story illustrates how *cords* have been used by thieves so lately as the year 1822 :—" Two skilful leaders of Dacoits, having collected some forty followers, and distributed among them ten matchlocks, ten swords, and twenty-five spears, waylaid a treasure going from the native Collector's treasury at Budrauna to Goruckpore. The prize consisted of £1,200, and was guarded by a Naik, or corporal, with four sepoys and five troopers. It had to pass through a dense jungle, and it was settled—said one of them in after years—' that the attack should take place there ; that we should have strong ropes tied across the road in front and festooned to trees on both sides, and, at a certain distance behind, similar ropes festooned to trees on one side, and ready to be fastened on the other, as soon as the escort of horse and foot should get well in between them.' Having completed these preparations the gang laid down on either side of the road patiently awaiting their prey. ' About five in the morning,' continued the narrator, ' we heard a voice as if calling upon the name of God (Allah), and one of the gang started up at the sound and said, " Here comes the treasure ! " We put five men in front with their matchlocks loaded—not with ball but shot, that we might, if possible, avoid killing anybody. When we got the troopers, infantry, and treasure all within the space, the hind ropes were run across the road, and made fast to the trees on the opposite side, and we opened a fire in upon the party from all sides. The foot soldiers got into the jungle at the sides of the road, and the troopers tried to get over the ropes at both ends, but in vain.' The corporal and a horse were killed ; two troopers wounded, and the treasure carried off in spite of a hot pursuit."—*From James Hutton's "Popular Account of the Thugs and Dacoits of India,"* 1857.

Verse 5.—*"The proud have hid a snare for me, and cords."* There was " a trap hidden for him with cords ;" a trap being sunk into some frequented path, and always covered over with grass or brushwood, and having long cords attached to each side, by which the hunter, lurking at a little distance, might close it whenever he saw the game stepping on the spot. But the net spread for him by his enemies extended to the very " side of the encampment," which indicates, that even among the soldiers lying around him, there were some who had been bribed and persuaded to watch and betray him.—*Benjamin Weiss, in "A New Translation of the Psalms, with Notes," 1858.*

Verse 5.—*"Snare." "Net." "Gins."* The several uses to which the contrivances denoted by the Hebrew words thus rendered were respectively applied, do not appear to be well ascertained. In general the Psalmist alludes to the artifices employed for capturing birds or beasts. It is, however, a curious circumstance, as noticed by Thevenot, that artifices of this kind are literally employed against men as well as other animals by some of the Orientals. " The cunningest robbers in the world," says he, " are in this country. They use a certain slip with a running noose, which they cast with so much sleight about a man's neck when they are within reach of him, that they never fail, so that they strangle him in a trice."— *Richard Mant.*

Verse 6.—*"The voice of my supplications."* The one safety for simple and unlearned people when assailed by the crafty arguments of heretics and infidels is not controversy, but prayer, a weapon their adversaries seldom use, and cannot understand—*Bruno of Aste, 1123.*

Verse 7.—*"Thou hast covered my head in the day of battle."* Hebrew, *of armour.* For David had never indeed any battle with Saul, but declined it ; but Saul often armed against him ; but then God's providence covered him as a shield : but the *head* is only spoken of to set forth his whole body, because that is chiefly aimed at by the enemy, as where the life principally lieth.—*John Meyer.*

Verse 7.—*"Thou hast covered my head,"* etc. That is, I had no other helmet or armour but thy Almighty power in the day when I fought with Goliath. 1 Sam. xvii. 39, 40. 50.—*Thomas Fenton.*

Verse 7.—*"Thou hast covered my head in the day of battle."* A captain or prince had always beside him in battle an armour-bearer, whose duty it was " to cover his master's head," that is, to ward off with the shield the blows aimed at his head, and which, in the heat of the fight, had escaped his own notice.—*Benjamin Weiss.*

Verse 8.—*"His wicked device"* ; which is to destroy me. *"Exalt themselves"* ; not only against me, but against thee also, as if by their power and policy they had frustrated thy design and promise made to me.—*M. Pool.*

Verse 9.—*"As for the head of those that compass me about,"* etc. God, he saith, had covered his head in the day of battle : now contrariwise he showeth what should cover the head of his enemies, viz., it should come to them as with their lips they had maliciously spoken against him ; for it may be thus rendered—"The head of my besieger, let the trouble of his lips cover it " : for cursing, let him be covered with cursing as with a cloak.—*John Mayer.*

Vere 9.—*"Those that compass me about."* For an explanation of this expression we would refer the reader to " The Treasury of David," vol. i., p. 343—344, where he will find two very pertinent extracts from J. Stevenson and Dr. Shaw.

Verse 9.—*"The mischief of their own lips."* The pride and hauteur of the Jews in our Lord's day brought the Roman arms upon them, and caused them to fall into irremediable ruin. They evoked their own fate by exposing themselves to an invasion from Rome at all ; but they did it still more in that terrific cry—" His blood be upon us and on our children."—*William Hill Tucker, in "The Psalms, with Notes, shewing their Prophetic and Christian Character," 1840.*

Verses 9, 10.—Such passages admit of translation in the future, and are rather predictions than imprecations.—*Ingram Cobbin, 1839.*

Verses 9—11.—The prophet, in these three verses, predicted those just judgments which heaven will inflict on the slanderers and persecutors of the righteous. Their lips, which uttered mischief against others, shall be the means of covering themselves with confusion, when out of their own mouths they shall be judged. Those tongues which have contributed to set the world on fire, shall be tormented with the hot burning coals of eternal vengeance : and they, who, with so much eagerness and diligence have prepared pits for the destruction of their brethren, shall be cast into a deep and bottomless pit, out of which they will not rise up again any more for ever. Evil speakers and false accusers shall gain no lasting establishment, but punishment shall hunt sin through all its doubles, and seize it at last as its legal prey. Let these great truths be firmly rooted in our hearts, and they will keep us steady in the worst of times.—*George Horne.*

Verse 10.—*"Let burning coals fall upon them,"* etc. The Psalmist seems here to allude to the destruction of the Sodomites. In these imprecations he considered his enemies as the enemies of God, rather than as his own ; and he thus cursed them, as knowing, in the quality of a prophet, that God himself had cursed them : and therefore these sorts of imprecations do not authorize other persons to curse their enemies.—*Thomas Fenton.*

Verse 10.—*"Let burning coals fall upon them,"* etc. An imprecation which (with the similar previous one, Psalm ix. 6, etc.), is a prophecy ; and one which, while it has had no fulfilment in the case of David's enemies, or any persecutors of the church in times past, brings again vividly before the mind the fiery judgment of the Lord's coming, and the awful sentence already pronounced against " the beast and false prophet," the leaders of the confederation of the kings of the earth and their armies, then " gathered together to make war against him "—" these were cast alive into the lake of fire burning with brimstone"; Rev. xix. 19, 20. So before, Psalm lv. 15 ; lxiii. 9.—*William De Burgh.*

Verse 11.—*"Let not an evil speaker [a man full of tongue] be established,"* etc. The man given to talk, the liar, the flatterer, the detractor, the scold, the brawler, *"shall not be established in the earth,"* for such people are abhorred by the wicked as well as by the good.—*Robert Bellarmine.*

Verse 11.—*"Let not an evil speaker be established,"* etc. The positions laid down in this verse will find abundant illustration in every age of the church. *"An evil speaker,"* who takes delight in wounding the reputation of others, is seldom established or prospered in the earth. Providence fights against such an unhappy wretch. *"The violent man,"* the Ishmaelite whose hand is against every man, is in general overthrown by the very same weapons which he wields against others.—*John Morison.*

Verse 11.—*"An evil speaker."* By " a man of the tongue," as the original has it, the Hebrews express a *detractor* or *sycophant ;* one who gives his tongue the liberty to vent what mischief he pleases. The Chaldee here expresses it by *a delator* or vile informer with a *threefold* or *three-forked tongue ;* because such a man wounds *three* at once ; the receiver, the sufferer, and himself.—*Thomas Fenton.*

Verse 11.—*"Evil shall hunt the violent man to overthrow him."* 'Tis an allusion to hounds that are of a quick scent, and pursue the game with pleasure ; they do not see the deer or the hare, yet they follow upon the scent ; and though they have sometimes a very cold and dead scent, yet they will follow and work it out. Thus *"evil shall hunt the violent man to overthrow him";* and though sometimes he hath, as it were, got out of the view or sight of evil, and thinks himself under covert, yet these evils, like a company of greedy hounds, will pursue till they have overtaken and overthrown him.—*Joseph Caryl.*

Verse 12.—*"I know."* For I have a promise of it, and that's infallible.—*John Trapp.*

Verses 12, 13.—*"I know that the LORD will maintain the cause,"* etc. Why, how comes the Psalmist so confident ? *"Surely the righteous shall give thanks unto thy name " :* as if he had said, Thou hast a name for a gracious and faithful God in thy promise, and this thou wilt never suffer to be blotted by failing in thy word. Christian, thou mayest venture all thou art worth on the public faith of Heaven : " His words are pure, as silver tried seven times in a furnace." He that will not suffer a liar or covenant-breaker to set foot on his holy hill, will much less suffer any one thought of falseness or unfaithfulness to enter into his own most holy heart.—*William Gurnall.*

Verse 13.—*"Surely the righteous shall give thanks unto thy name,"* etc. Teacheth us two things, first, that it becometh the godly to show themselves continually thankful, because God is continually merciful to them ; secondly, what is the excellent estate and condition of God's children, which, though it do not yet appear, yet shall it in the end break forth with fulness of glory."—*Thomas Wilcocks.*

Verse 13.—*"The upright shall dwell in thy presence."* *"Sit in thy presence,"* as thy friends or guests or favoured servants. Perhaps it may mean *sit (enthroned) before thee.* Compare Matt. xix. 28. Some understand the sense to be *shall dwell* (in the land) *before thee,* i.e., under thy protection and inspection.—*Joseph Addison Alexander.*

HINTS TO PREACHERS.

Verses 1—5.—I. The particular source of David's affliction : it was from men. In this he was a type of Christ. 1. Their wickedness : " the evil man." 2. Their violence : " the violent man." 3. Their malicious designs : " which imagine mischiefs in their heart." 4. Their confederacy : " continually are they gathered together for war." 5. Their false accusations : " They have sharpened their tongues like a serpent," etc. (verse 3). 6. Their avowed design : " they have purposed to overthrow my goings " (verse 4). 7. Their intrigues (verse 5). II. His universal remedy : " Deliver me, O LORD " ; " preserve " and help me. His defence is, 1. In God. 2. In prayer to God.—*G. R.*

Verses 1—5.—In our position, age, and country, we are not in danger of violence from men, as was David ; still, no man is absolutely safe from the danger. I. Mention some cases not yet impossible. 1. A Christian workman, because he cannot comply with unrighteous customs, excites the animosity of his fellow workers. They will do him mischief, spoil his work, steal his tools, speak evil of him, until his employer discharges him to restore peace in the factory. 2. A Christian clerk or shop assistant, because his presence is a check upon his sinful companions, may have snares laid for him, etc. II. Suggest advice, useful, should such a case arise. 1. Resort to God with a " Deliver me," and a " Preserve me." 2. Maintain integrity and uprightness. 3. Should the mischievous ones succeed, still trust in God, who can make their mischief lead to your profit, and make his goodness outwit their devices.—*J. F.*

Verse 3.—The depraved state of the natural man as to his speech.

Verse 4 (first clause).—A wise prayer. The wicked will slander, and oppress, or mislead, flatter and defile. No one can keep us but the Lord.

Verse 5.—The Dangers of Society. I. The secrecy of the attacks of the ungodly : " hid a snare." II. The variety of their weapons : " and cords." III. The cunning choice of position : " by the wayside." IV. The object of their designs : " for me " : they desire to destroy the man himself.

Verse 5.—" The Net by the Wayside," or, covert temptations ; temptations brought near, and made applicable to daily life.

Verse 6.—I. The language of assurance. II. The plea for acceptance in prayer.

Verses 6, 7.—David comforted himself, 1. In his interest in God : " I said . . . thou art my God." 2. In his access to God : he had leave to speak to him, and might expect an answer of peace : " Hear," etc. 3. In the assurance he had of help from God, and happiness in him (verse 7). 4. In the experience he had formerly of God's care of him : " Thou hast covered my head in the day of battle."—*Matthew Henry.*

Verses 6—8.—Three arguments to be pleaded in a prayer for protection. I. The believer's covenanted property in God. " I said . . . thou art my God." II. The past mercies of God. " Thou hast covered," etc. III. The impropriety of the wicked being encouraged in their wickedness, ver. 8.—*J. F.*

Verses 6, 7—12.—The Consolations of the Believer in Time of Trouble. I. What he can say. II. What he can remember. III. What he is assured of.

Verses 6, 7, 12, 13.—Times of Assault, Slander, and Temptation should be special times of Prayer and Faith. David here makes prominent five things. I. *Possession asserted.* 1. The Possession : " My God." Opposed to idols. Beloved by self. 2. The Claim published. 3. The Witness selected. Secret. Sacred. Searching. 4. The Occasion chosen. II. *Petition presented.* 1. His prayers were frequent. 2. His prayers were full of meaning. 3. His prayers were meant for God. 4. His prayers needed divine attention. III. *Preservation experienced.* 1. God had been his Armour-bearer. 2. God had guarded his most vital part. 3. God had saved him. 4. God's strength had been displayed. IV. *Protection expected.* 1. God is a righteous Judge. 2. God is a compassionate Friend. 3. God is a well-known Guardian. V. *Praise predicted.* 1. Praise assured by gratitude. 2. Praise expressed by words. 3. Praise implied in confidence. 4. Praise practised by communion.

Verse 9.—How the sin of evil-speakers comes home to them.—*W. B. H.*

Verse 11 (first clause).—I. Notice a few varieties of evil speakers, 1. Liars the common liar, the trade liar, the stock-exchange liar, the political liar, etc. 2. Scandal-mongers. 3. Blasphemers and swearers. 4. Libertines and seducers.

5. Sceptics and new theology inventors.   II. The propriety of the prayer.   1. Because evil speaking is intrinsically an evil thing.   2. It is an extensively injurious thing. 3. He who would have God's truth established must needs desire that evil speaking must fail.   III. The limitation of the prayer : " In the earth."   1. It is certain an evil speaker cannot be established in heaven, nor in hell.   2. The earth is the only sphere of his influence ; but, alas ! men on the earth are too prone to be influenced by him.   3. Then, become righteous and true, by faith in the Righteous One and the " Truth."—*J. F.*

Verse 11 (second clause).—The Cruel Hunter pursued by his own Dogs.

Verse 11 (second clause).—Theme—Sins committed, and not repented of, pursue men to their ruin.   I. Illustrate.   1. They may raise a force of opposition from men.   Tarquin, Napoleon, etc.   2. They may precipitate ruin, as Haman was hunted by his own sin to the gallows.   3. They may arouse destructive remorse, as in Judas.   4. Certainly they will pursue to the judgment-seat, and hunt the soul into hell.   II. Apply.   1. How fearful a thing must sin be.   2. The more terrible because self-created.   3. Flee from the avenging pursuers to Christ, the only and safe refuge.—*J. F.*

Verse 11 (second clause).—The hunt and pursuit of the violent sinner.   I. The progress of the chase.   1. At first the victim is ignorant of it.   2. But ere long he finds Scripture, conscience, God, Death, at his heels.   3. His own sins cry loudest after him.   II. The issue of the hunt.   Hemmed in, overthrown, lost for ever, unless he repent.   III. Another Huntsman.   " The Son of man is come to seek and save that which was lost."—*W. B. H.*

Verse 12.—I. The known fact.   II. The reasons for being so assured of it. III. The conduct arising out of the knowledge.

Verse 12.—Something worth knowing.   I. By the afflicted and the poor who trust in the Lord.   II. By the oppressors who afflict and do the wrong.   III. By all men, that they may trust in the Lord, and praise him for his compassion towards the needy, and for his even-handed justice.—*J. F.*

Verses 12, 13.—I. Trust under all circumstances (verse 12).   II. Gratitude for all things : " The righteous shall give thanks unto thy name."   III. Safety at all times : " The upright shall dwell in thy presence."—*G. R.*

Verse 13.—One of the noblest forms of praise,—dwelling in the presence of God. Or, reverent regard to God's presence, holy communion with the Lord, confiding rest in God's dealings, obedient doing of the heavenly will—the best way of giving thanks to God.

Verse 13.—Two assertions beyond contradiction.   I. The righteous are sure to give thanks to God, let others be as thankless as they will.   For, 1. They recognise all their good as coming from God.   2. They realise themselves as unworthy of the good they receive.   3. They are anxious to do right, because they are righteous ; and that involves thanksgiving.   4. Thankfulness is a part of the joy derived from what they enjoy.   II. The upright are sure to dwell in God's presence.   1. In the sense of setting the Lord before them.   2. In the sense of an abiding, present fellowship with God.   3. In the sense of enjoying God's approval.   4. In the sense of dwelling in heaven for ever —*J. F.*

PSALM CXLI.

TITLE.—A Psalm of David.   *Yes, David under suspicion, half afraid to speak lest he should speak unadvisedly while trying to clear himself; David slandered and beset by enemies; David censured even by saints, and taking it kindly; David deploring the condition of the godly party of whom he was the acknowledged head; David waiting upon God with confident expectation.   The Psalm is one of a group of four, and it bears a striking likeness to the other three.   Its meaning lies so deep as to be in places exceedingly obscure, yet even upon its surface it has dust of gold.   In its commencement the Psalm is lighted up with the evening glow as the incense rises to heaven; then comes a night of language whose meaning we cannot see; and this gives place to morning light in which our eyes are unto the Lord.*

DIVISION.—*The Psalmist cries for acceptance in prayer (verses 1, 2); then he begs to be kept as to his speech, preserved in heart and deed, and delivered from every sort of fellowship with the ungodly.   He prefers to be rebuked by the gracious rather than to be flattered by the wicked, and consoles himself with the confident assurance that he will one day be understood by the godly party, and made to be a comfort to them (verses 3—6). In the last verses the slandered saint represents the condition of the persecuted church, looks away to God and pleads for rescue from his cruel enemies, and for the punishment of his oppressors.*

EXPOSITION.

LORD, I cry unto thee: make haste unto me;   give ear unto my voice, when I cry unto thee.

2 Let my prayer be set forth before thee *as* incense;   *and* the lifting up of my hands *as* the evening sacrifice.

1. "*LORD, I cry unto thee.*"   This is my last resort: prayer never fails me.   My prayer is painful and feeble, and worthy only to be called a cry; but it is a cry unto Jehovah, and this ennobles it.   I have cried unto thee, I still cry to thee, and I always mean to cry to thee.   To whom else could I go?   What else can I do? Others trust to themselves, but I cry unto thee.   The weapon of all prayer is one which the believer may always carry with him, and use in every time of need.   "*Make haste unto me.*"   His case was urgent, and he pleaded that urgency.   God's time is the best time, but when we are sorely pressed we may with holy importunity quicken the movements of mercy.   In many cases, if help should come late, it would come too late; and we are permitted to pray against such a calamity.   "*Give ear unto my voice, when I cry unto thee.*"   See how a second time he talks of crying: prayer had become his frequent, yea, his constant exercise: twice in a few words he says, "I cry; I cry."   How he longs to be heard, and to be heard at once! There is a voice to the great Father in every cry, and groan, and tear of his children: he can understand what they mean when they are quite unable to express it.   It troubles the spirit of the saints when they fear that no favourable ear is turned to their doleful cries: they cannot rest unless their "unto thee" is answered by an "unto me."   When prayer is a man's only refuge, he is deeply distressed at the bare idea of his failing therein.

> "That were a grief I could not bear,
> Didst thou not hear and answer prayer;
> But a prayer-hearing, answering God
> Supports me under every load."

2. "*Let my prayer be set forth before thee as incense.*"   As incense is carefully prepared, kindled with holy fire, and devoutly presented unto God, so let my prayer

be. We are not to look upon prayer as easy work requiring no thought, it needs to be " set forth " ; what is more, it must be set forth " before the Lord," by a sense of his presence and a holy reverence for his name : neither may we regard all supplication as certain of divine acceptance, it needs to be set forth before the Lord " as incense," concerning the offering of which there were rules to be observed, otherwise it would be rejected of God. *"And the lifting up of my hands as the evening sacrifice."* Whatever form his prayer might take his one desire was that it might be accepted of God. Prayer is sometimes presented without words by the very motions of our bodies : bended knees and lifted hands are the tokens of earnest, expectant prayer. Certainly work, or the lifting up of the hands in labour, is prayer if it be done in dependence upon God and for his glory : there is a hand-prayer as well as a heart-prayer, and our desire is that this may be sweet unto the Lord as the sacrifice of eventide. Holy hope, the lifting up of hands that hang down, is also a kind of worship : may it ever be acceptable with God. The Psalmist makes a bold request : he would have his humble cries and prayers to be as much regarded of the Lord as the appointed morning and evening sacrifices of the holy place. Yet the prayer is by no means too bold, for, after all, the spiritual is in the Lord's esteem higher than the ceremonial, and the calves of the lips are a truer sacrifice than the calves of the stall.

So far we have a prayer about prayer ; we have a distinct supplication in the two following verses.

3 Set a watch, O LORD, before my mouth ; keep the door of my lips.

4 Incline not my heart to *any* evil thing, to practise wicked works with men that work iniquity : and let me not eat of their dainties.

5 Let the righteous smite me ; *it shall be* a kindness : and let him reprove me ; *it shall be* an excellent oil, *which* shall not break my head : for yet my prayer also *shall be* in their calamities.

6 When their judges are overthrown in stony places, they shall hear my words ; for they are sweet.

3. *"Set a watch, O LORD, before my mouth."* That mouth had been used in prayer, it would be a pity it should ever be defiled with untruth, or pride, or wrath ; yet so it will become unless carefully watched, for these intruders are ever lurking about the door. David feels that with all his own watchfulness he may be surprised into sin, and so he begs the Lord himself to keep him. When Jehovah sets the watch the city is well guarded : when the Lord becomes the guard of our mouth the whole man is well garrisoned. *"Keep the door of my lips."* God has made our lips the door of the mouth, but we cannot keep that door of ourselves, therefore do we entreat the Lord to take the rule of it. O that the Lord would both open and shut our lips, for we can do neither the one nor the other aright if left to ourselves. In times of persecution by ungodly men we are peculiarly liable to speak hastily, or evasively, and therefore we should be specially anxious to be preserved in that direction from every form of sin. How condescending is the Lord ! We are ennobled by being door-keepers for him, and yet he deigns to be a door-keeper for us.

4. *"Incline not my heart to any evil thing."* It is equivalent to the petition, " Lead us not into temptation." O that nothing may arise in providence which would excite our desires in a wrong direction. The Psalmist is here careful of his heart. He who holds the heart is lord of the man ; but if the tongue and the heart are under God's care all is safe. Let us pray that he may never leave us to our own inclinations, or we shall soon decline from the right.

"To practise wicked works with men that work iniquity." The way the heart inclines the life soon tends : evil things desired bring forth wicked things practised. Unless the fountain of life is kept pure the streams of life will soon be polluted. Alas, there is great power in company : even good men are apt to be swayed by association ; hence the fear that we may practise wicked works when we are with wicked workers. We must endeavour not to be with them lest we sin with them. It is bad when the heart goes the wrong way alone, worse when the life runs in the evil road alone ; but it is apt to increase unto a high degree of ungodliness when the backslider runs the downward path with a whole horde of sinners around him. Our practice will be our perdition if it be evil ; it is an aggravation of sin rather than an excuse for it to say that it is our custom and our habit. It is God's practice to

punish all who make a practice of iniquity.   Good men are horrified at the thought of sinning as others do ; the fear of it drives them to their knees.   Iniquity, which, being interpreted, is a want of equity, is a thing to be shunned as we would avoid an infectious disease.   *"And let me not eat of their dainties."*   If we work with them we shall soon eat with them.   They will bring out their sweet morsels, and delicate dishes, in the hope of binding us to their service by the means of our palates.   The trap is baited with delicious meats that we may be captured and become meat for their malice.   If we would not sin with men we had better not sit with them, and if we would not share their wickedness we must not share their wantonness.

5.   *"Let the righteous smite me ; it shall be a kindness."*   He prefers the bitters of gracious company to the dainties of the ungodly.   He would rather be smitten by the righteous than feasted by the wicked.   He gives a permit to faithful admonition, he even invites it—" let the righteous smite me."   When the ungodly smile upon us their flattery is cruel ; when the righteous smite us their faithfulness is kind.   Sometimes godly men rap hard ; they do not merely hint at evil, but hammer at it ; and even then we are to receive the blows in love, and be thankful to the hand which smites so heavily.   Fools resent reproof ; wise men endeavour to profit by it.   *"And let him reprove me ; it shall be an excellent oil, which shall not break my head."*   Oil breaks no heads, and rebuke does no man any harm ; rather, as oil refreshes and perfumes, so does reproof when fitly taken sweeten and renew the heart.   My friend must love me well if he will tell me of my faults : there is an unction about him if he is honest enough to point out my errors.   Many a man has had his head broken at the feasts of the wicked, but none at the table of a true-hearted reprover.   The oil of flattery is not excellent ; the oil so lavishly used at the banquet of the reveller is not excellent ; head-breaking and heart-breaking attend the anointings of the riotous ; but it is otherwise with the severest censures of the godly : they are not always sweet, but they are always excellent ; they may for the moment bruise the heart, but they never break either it or the head.   *"For yet my prayer also shall be in their calamities."*   Gracious men never grow wrathful with candid friends so as to harbour an ill-feeling against them ; if so, when they saw them in affliction, they would turn round upon them and taunt them with their rebukes.   Far from it ; these wisely grateful souls are greatly concerned to see their instructors in trouble, and they bring forth their best prayers for their assistance.   They do not merely pray for them, but they so closely and heartily sympathize that their prayers are " in their calamities," down in the dungeon with them.   So true is Christian brotherhood that we are with our friends in sickness or persecution, suffering their griefs ; so that our heart's prayer is in their sorrows.   When we can give good men nothing more, let us give them our prayers, and let us do this doubly to those who have given us their rebukes.

6.   This is a verse of which the meaning seems far to seek.   Does it refer to the righteous among the Israelites ?   We think so.   David surely means that when their leaders fell never to rise again, they would then turn to him and take delight in listening to his voice.   *"When their judges are overthrown in stony places, they shall hear my words ; for they are sweet."*   And so they did : the death of Saul made all the best of the nation look to the son of Jesse as the Lord's anointed ; his words became sweet to them.   Many of those good men who had spoken severely of David's quitting his country, and going over to the Philistines, were nevertheless dear to his heart for their fidelity, and to them he returned nothing but good-will, loving prayers, and sweet speeches, knowing that by-and-by they would overlook his faults, and select him to be their leader.   They smote him when he erred, but they recognized his excellences.   He, on his part, bore no resentment, but loved them for their honesty.   He would pray for them when their land lay bleeding at the feet of their foreign enemies ; he would come to their rescue when their former leaders were slain ; and his words of courageous hopefulness would be sweet in their ears.   This seems to me to be a good sense, consistent with the context.   At the same time, other and more laboured interpretations have their learned admirers, and to these we will refer in our notes from other authors.

7 Our bones are scattered at the grave's mouth, as when one cutteth and cleaveth *wood* upon the earth.

8 But mine eyes *are* unto thee, O GOD the Lord : in thee is my trust ; leave not my soul destitute.

9 Keep me from the snares *which* they have laid for me, and the gins of the workers of iniquity.

10 Let the wicked fall into their own nets, whilst that I withal escape.

7. David's case seemed hopeless : the cause of God in Israel was as a dead thing, even as a skeleton broken, and rotten, and shovelled out of the grave, to return as dust to its dust. *"Our bones are scattered at the grave's mouth."* There seemed to be no life, no cohesion, no form, order, or headship among the godly party in Israel : Saul had demolished it, and scattered all its parts, so that it did not exist as an organized whole. David himself was like one of these dried bones, and the rest of the godly were in much the same condition. There seemed to be no vitality or union among the holy seed ; but their cause lay at death's door. *"As when one cutteth and cleaveth wood upon the earth."* They were like wood divided and thrown apart : not as one piece of timber, nor even as a bundle, but all cut to pieces, and thoroughly divided. Leaving out the word "wood," which is supplied by the translators, the figure relates to cleaving upon the earth, which probably means ploughing, but may signify any other form of chopping and splitting, such as felling a forest, tearing up bushes, or otherwise causing confusion and division. How often have good men thought thus of the cause of God ! Wherever they have looked, death, division, and destruction have stared them in the face. Cut and cloven, hopelessly sundered ! Scattered, yea, scattered at the grave's mouth ! Split up and split for the fire ! Such the cause of God and truth has seemed to be. " Upon the earth " the prospect was wretched ; the field of the church was ploughed, harrowed, and scarified : it had become like a wood-chopper's yard, where everything was doomed to be broken up. We have seen churches in such a state, and have been heart-broken. What a mercy that there is always a place above the earth to which we can look ! There lives One who will give a resurrection to his cause, and a reunion to his divided people. He will bring up the dead bones from the grave's mouth, and make the dried faggots live again. Let us imitate the Psalmist in the next verse, and look up to the living God.

8. *"But mine eyes are unto thee, O GOD the Lord."* He looked upward and kept his eyes fixed there. He regarded duty more than circumstances ; he considered the promise rather than the external providence ; and he expected from God rather than from men. He did not shut his eyes in indifference or despair, neither did he turn them to the creature in vain confidence, but he gave his eyes to his God, and saw nothing to fear. Jehovah his Lord is also his hope. Thomas called Jesus Lord and God, and David here speaks of his God and Lord. Saints delight to dwell upon the divine names when they are adoring or appealing. *"In thee is my trust."* Not alone in thine attributes or in thy promises, but in thyself. Others might confide where they chose, but David kept to his God : in him he trusted always, only, confidently, and unreservedly. *"Leave not my soul destitute"* ; as it would be if the Lord did not remember and fulfil his promise. To be destitute in circumstances is bad, but to be destitute in soul is far worse ; to be left of friends is a calamity, but to be left of God would be destruction. Destitute of God is destitution with a vengeance. The comfort is that God hath said, " I will never leave thee nor forsake thee."

9. *"Keep me from the snares which they have laid for me."* He had before asked, in verse 3, that the door of his mouth might be kept ; but his prayer now grows into " Keep *me.*" He seems more in trouble about covert temptation than concerning open attacks. Brave men do not dread battle, but they hate secret plots. We cannot endure to be entrapped like unsuspecting animals ; therefore we cry to the God of wisdom for protection. *"And the gins of the workers of iniquity."* These evil workers sought to catch David in his speech or acts. This was in itself a piece of in-equity, and so of a piece with the rest of their conduct. They were bad themselves, and they wished either to make him like themselves, or to cause him to seem so. If they could not catch the good man in one way, they would try another ; snares and gins should be multiplied, for anyhow they were determined to work his ruin. Nobody could preserve David but the Omniscient and Omnipotent One : he also will preserve us. It is hard to keep out of snares which you cannot see, and to escape gins which you cannot discover. Well might the much-hunted Psalmist cry, " Keep me."

10. *"Let the wicked fall into their own nets, whilst that I withal escape."* It may not be a Christian prayer, but it is a very just one, and it takes a great deal of grace

to refrain from crying *Amen* to it ; in fact, grace does not work towards making us wish otherwise concerning the enemies of holy men. Do we not all wish the innocent to be delivered, and the guilty to reap the result of their own malice ? Of course we do, if we are just men. There can be no wrong in desiring that to happen in our own case which we wish for all good men. Yet is there a more excellent way.

EXPLANATORY NOTES AND QUAINT SAYINGS.

Whole Psalm.—This Psalm, like the one before it, is distinguished by a pregnant brevity and the use of rare expressions, while at the same time it is full of verbal and real coincidences with the other Psalms of David. These indications are so clear and undeniable, that a sceptical critic of great eminence (De Wette) pronounces it one of the oldest Psalms in the collection.—*Joseph Addison Alexander.*

Whole Psalm.—Few Psalms in so small a compass crowd together so many gems of precious and holy truth.—*Barton Bouchier.*

Whole Psalm.—Many commentators are strongly of opinion that this Psalm was written as a memorial of that very interesting scene in the life of David recorded in 1 Sam. xxiv., relating to his generous treatment of Saul. Though he had an opportunity of putting his cruel persecutor to death in the cave of Engedi, yet he spared his life, only cutting off his skirt, and not suffering his followers to touch him ; and when Saul had gone out of the cave, David, going out after him, remonstrated with him from some distance in the gentlest and most respectful language in regard to the injustice of his conduct towards him. It is thought that the sixth verse contains so express a reference to this very remarkable occurrence in David's history, as to leave little doubt that it was the occasion on which the Psalm was composed.—*James Anderson's Note to Calvin, in loc.*

Whole Psalm.—The imagery and allusions of the Psalm are in keeping ; viz., the oil which had lately anointed him ; and the watch before his mouth, etc., suggested by the watching at the mouth of the cave, though ultimately referring to the tabernacle service.—*John Jebb.*

Verse 1.—*"Lord, I cry unto thee."* Misbelief doth seek many ways for delivery from trouble ; but faith hath but one way,—to go to God, to wit, by prayer, for whatsoever is needful.—*David Dickson.*

Verse 1.—*"Lord, I cry unto thee."* No distress or danger, how great soever, shall stifle my faith or stop my mouth, but it shall make me more earnest, and my prayers, like strong streams in narrow straits, shall bear down all before them.—*John Trapp.*

Verse 1.—*"Unto thee . . . . unto me."* Our prayer and God's mercy are like two buckets in a well ; while the one ascends, the other descends.—*Ezekiel Hopkins.*

Verse 1.—Note that the difference of tense, *"I have cried"* (Heb., LXX., and Vulgate) followed by *"when I cry,"* signifies the earnest perseverance of the saint in prayer, never ceasing, so long as trouble lasts. And trouble does last so long as we are in the world ; wherefore the apostle teaches us to " Pray without ceasing."—*Augustine and Bruno, in Neale and Littledale.*

Verses 1—5.—That the Psalmist was now in some distress, whereof he was deeply sensible, is evident from the vehemency of his spirit, which he expresseth in the reiteration of his request or supplication (verse 1) ; and by his desire that his " prayer might come before the Lord like incense, and the lifting up of his hands as the evening sacrifice " (verse 2). The Jewish expositors guess, not improbably, that in that allusion he had regard unto his present exclusion from the holy services of the tabernacle, which in other places he deeply complains of.

For the matter of his prayer in this beginning of the Psalm, it respecteth himself, and his deportment under his present condition, which he desireth may be harmless and holy, becoming himself, and useful to others. And whereas he was two ways liable to miscarry ; first, by too high an exasperation of spirit against his oppressors and persecutors ; and, secondly, by a fraudulent and pusillanimous compliance with them in their wicked courses ;—which are the two extremes which men are apt sinfully to run into in such conditions : he prays earnestly to be delivered from them both. The first he hath respect unto in verse 3, *"Set a watch, O LORD, before my mouth ; keep the door of my lips"*: namely, that he might not, under those great provocations which were given him, break forth into an unseemly intemperance of speech against his unjust oppressors, which sometimes fierce and unreasonable cruelties will wrest from the most sedate and moderate spirits. But it was the desire of this holy Psalmist, as in like cases it should be ours, that his heart might be always preserved in such a frame, under the conduct of the Spirit of God, as not to be surprised into an expression of distempered passion in any of his words or sayings. The other he regards in his earnest supplication to be delivered from it, verse 4 : *"Incline not my heart to any evil thing, to practise wicked works with men that work iniquity : and let me not eat of their dainties."* There are two parts of his request unto the purpose intended. 1. That by the power of God's grace influencing his mind and soul, his heart might not be inclined unto any communion or society with his wicked adversaries in their wickedness. 2. That he might be preserved from a liking of, or a longing after those things, which are the baits and allurements whereby men are apt to be drawn into societies and conspiracies with the workers of iniquity ; *"And let me not eat of their dainties."* See Prov. i. 10—14. For he here describeth the condition of men prospering for a season in a course of wickedness ; they firstly give up themselves unto the practice of iniquity, and then together solace themselves in those satisfactions of their lusts, with which their power and interest in the world do furnish them.

These are the *"dainties,"* for which an impotent longing and desire do betray the minds of unstable persons unto a compliance with ways of sin and folly : for I look on these *"dainties"* as comprising whatever the lust of the eyes, the lust of the flesh, or the pride of life can afford. All these David prays to be delivered from any inclination unto ; especially when they are made the allurements of a course of sin. In the enjoyment of these *"dainties,"* it is the common practice of wicked men to soothe up, and mutually encourage one another in the way and course wherein they are engaged. And this completes that poor felicity which in this world so many aspire unto, and whereof alone they are capable. The whole of it is but a society in perishing sensual enjoyments, without control, and with mutual applauses from one another. This the Psalmist had a special regard unto when casting his eye towards another communion and society which he longed after (verse 5). He saw there not dainties but rebukes : he discerned that which is most opposite unto those mutual applauses and rejoicings in one another, which is the salt and cement of all evil societies, for he noticed rebukes and reproofs for the least miscarriages that shall be observed. Now whereas the dainties which some enjoy in a course of prosperous wickedness, are that alone which seems to have anything in it amongst them that is desirable, and on the other side rebukes and reproofs are those alone which seem to have any sharpness, or matter of uneasiness and dislike in the society of the godly, David balanceth that which seemeth to be sharpest in the one society, against that which seems to be sweetest in the other, and, without respect unto other advantages, prefers the one above the other. Hence, some read the beginning of the words, " Let the righteous *rather* smite me," meaning, " rather than that I should eat of the dainties of the ungodly." —*John Owen.*

Verse 2.—*"Let my prayer be set forth before thee."* Margin, *directed.* The Hebrew word means to fit ; to establish ; to make firm. The Psalmist desires that his prayer should not be like that which is feeble, languishing, easily dissipated ; but that it should be like that which is firm and secure.—*Albert Barnes.*

Verse 2.—*"Let my prayer be set forth before thee as incense."* Literally, Let my prayer, incense, be set in order before Thee,—implying that prayer was in the reality what incense was in the symbol. . . . Passing to New Testament Scripture, though still only to that portion which refers to Old Testament times, we are told of the people without being engaged in prayer, while Zacharias was offering incense within the Sanctuary (Luke i. 10) ; they were in spirit going along with the priestly service. And in the book of Revelation the prayers of saints are once and again identified with the offering of incense on the golden altar before the throne. Rev. v. 8 ; viii. 3, 4.—*Patrick Fairbairn, in "The Typology of Scripture."*

Verse 2.—*"Set forth."* Prayer is knowing work, believing work, thinking work, searching work, humbling work, and nothing worth if heart and hand do not join in it.—*Thomas Adam*, 1701—1784.

Verse 2.—*"Set forth before thee as incense,"* whose fragrant smoke still ascends upwards. But many times in the very ascent, whilst it strives up higher and higher, *infimo phantasmate verberatur*, saith Gregory, "it is beaten back again by earthly imaginations which intervene," and then is extenuated by degrees, and vanisheth to nothing. Therefore the prophet prays *ut dirigatur oratio*, "that his prayer may be set before God," *ut stabiliatur ;* so some render it out of the Hebrew, "that it may be established," that it may neither evaporate itself nor be whiffed about with the wind of vain and contrary imaginations, which come *ab extrinseco* [from without], and may corrupt it.—*Anthony Farindon.*

Verse 2.—*"As incense."* That in general by *incense* prayer is signified, the Scripture expressly testifieth. And there is a fourfold resemblance between them : 1. In that *it was beaten and pounded* before it was used. So doth acceptable prayer proceed from a broken and contrite heart : Ps. li. 17. 2. *It was of no use until fire was put under it*, and that taken from the altar. Nor is that prayer of any virtue or efficacy which is not kindled by the fire from above, the Holy Spirit of God, which we have from our altar, Christ Jesus. 3. *It naturally ascended upwards towards heaven*, as all offerings in the Hebrew are called נים, "ascensions," risings up. And this is the design of prayer, to ascend unto the throne of God : "I will direct unto thee, and will look up " ; that is, pray : Ps. v. 3. 4. *It yielded a sweet savour ;* which was one end of it in temple services, wherein there was so much burning of flesh and blood. So doth prayer yield a sweet savour unto God ; a savour of rest, wherein he is well pleased.—*John Owen.*

Verse 2.—*"As incense . . . . as the evening sacrifice."* Though this address of mine must necessarily want all that solemnity of preparation required in the service of thy holy Tabernacle, the cloud of incense and perfume, etc., the mincha or oblation of fine flour, etc., yet let the purity and fervour of my heart, and the innocency of my hands, now lifted up to thee in this sad hour of my distress, be accepted instead of all these, and prevail for deliverance and a safe retreat to me and my companions.—*Charles Peters (—1777), in "A Critical Dissertation on the Book of Job,"* 1751.

Verse 2.—*"As the evening sacrifice."* This should be our daily service, as a lamb was offered up morning and evening for a sacrifice. But, alas ! how dull and dead are our devotions ! Like Pharaoh's chariots, they drive on heavily. Some, like Balaam's ass, scarce ever open their mouths twice.—*Thomas Adams.*

Verse 2.—*"My hands."* Spreading forth our hands in believing and fervent prayer is the only way of grasping mercy.—*F. E., in "The Saints Ebenezer,"* 1667.

Verse 2.—In the gorgeous ceremonial worship of the Hebrews, none of the senses were excluded from taking part in the service. . . . . The sense of smell occupied, perhaps, the most prominent place ; for the acceptance of the worship was always indicated by a symbol borrowed from this sense : "The Lord smelled a sweet savour." The prayer of the people ascended as incense, and the lifting up of their hands as the evening sacrifice. The offering of incense formed an essential part of the religious service. The altar of incense occupied one of the most conspicuous and honoured positions in the tabernacle and temple. . . . On this altar a censer full of incense poured forth its fragrant clouds every morning and evening ; and yearly, as the day of atonement came round, when the high priest entered the holy of holies, he filled a censer with live coals from the sacred fire on the altar of burnt-offerings, and bore it into the sanctuary, where he threw upon the burning coals the "sweet incense beaten small," which he had brought in his hand. Without this smoking censer he was forbidden, on pain of death, to enter into the awful shrine of Jehovah. Notwithstanding the washing of his flesh, and the linen garments with which he was clothed, he dare not enter the holiest of all with the blood of atonement, unless he could personally shelter himself under a cloud of incense.

It has been supposed by some writers that incense was invented for the purpose of concealing or neutralizing the noxious effluvia caused by the number of beasts slaughtered every day in the sanctuary. Other writers have attached a mystical import to it, and believed that it was a symbol of the breath of the world arising in praise to the Creator, the four ingredients of which it was composed representing the four elements. While a third class, looking upon the tabernacle as the palace of God, the theocratic King of Israel, and the ark of the covenant as his throne, regarded the incense as merely corresponding to the perfume so lavishly employed about the person and appointments of an Oriental monarch. It may doubtless have been intended primarily to serve these purposes and convey these meanings, but it derived its chief importance in connection with the ceremonial observances of the Mosaic ritual from the fact of its being the great symbol of prayer. It was offered at the time when the people were in the posture and act of devotion; and their prayers were supposed to be presented to God by the priest, and to ascend to him in the smoke and odour of that fragrant offering. Scripture is full of allusions to it, understood in this beautiful symbolical sense. Acceptable, prevailing prayer was a sweet-smelling savour to the Lord; and prayer that was unlawful, or hypocritical, or unprofitable, was rejected with disgust by the organ of smell.

Doubtless the Jews felt, when they saw the soft white clouds of fragrant smoke rising slowly from the altar of incense, as if the voice of the priest were silently but eloquently pleading in that expressive emblem in their behalf. The association of sound was lost in that of smell, and the two senses were blended in one. And this symbolical mode of supplication, as Dr. George Wilson has remarked, has this one advantage over spoken or written prayer, that it appealed to those who were both blind and deaf, a class that are usually shut out from social worship by their affliction. Those who could not hear the prayers of the priest could join in devotional exercises symbolized by incense, through the medium of their sense of smell; and the hallowed impressions shut out by one avenue were admitted to the mind and heart by another.

The altar of incense stood in the closest connection with the altar of burnt-offerings. The blood of the sin-offering was sprinkled on the horns of both on the great day of annual atonement. Morning and evening, as soon as the sacrifice was offered, the censer poured forth its fragrant contents, so that the perpetual incense within ascended simultaneously with the perpetual burnt-offering outside. Without the live coals from off the sacrificial altar, the sacred incense could not be kindled; and without the incense previously filling the holy place, the blood of atonement from the altar of burnt-offering could not be sprinkled on the mercy-seat. Beautiful and expressive type of the perfect sacrifice and the all-prevailing intercession of Jesus—of intercession founded upon atonement, of atonement preceded and followed by intercession! Beautiful and expressive type, too, of the prayers of believers kindled by the altar-fire of Christ's sacrifice, and perfumed by his merits!—*Hugh Macmillan, in "The Ministry of Nature,"* 1871.

Verse 3.—*"Set a watch, O LORD, before my mouth,"* etc. 1. A man would never use this language without a conviction of *the importance of the subject.* . . . Everything is transacted by speech, in natural, civil, and religious concerns: how much, therefore, depends on the good or evil management of the tongue! What an ardour of holy love and friendship, or of anger and malice, may a few words fan into a flame! The tongue is the principal instrument in the cause of God; and it is the chief engine of the devil; give him this, and he asks no more—there is no mischief or misery he will not accomplish by it. The use, the influence of it, therefore, is inexpressible; and words are never to be considered only as *effects*, but as *causes*, the operation of which can never be fully imagined. Let us suppose a case, I fear, but too common. You drop, in the thoughtlessness of conversation, or for the sake of argument or wit, some irreligious, sceptical expression—it lodges in the memory of a child, or a servant—it takes root in a soil favourable to such seed—it gradually springs up, and brings forth fruit, in the profanation of the Sabbath; the neglect of the means of grace; in the reading of improper books; in the choice of dangerous companions;—who can tell where it will end? But there is a Being who knows where it began. It will be acknowledged that some have it in their power, by reason of their office, talents, and influence, to do much more injury than others; but none are so insignificant as to be harmless.

2. A man would never use this language without a conviction that *he is in danger of transgression.* And if David was conscious of a liableness to err, shall we ever presume on our safety? Our danger arises from the depravity of our nature. "The heart is deceitful above all things, and desperately wicked"; and "who can bring a clean thing out of an unclean?" Our danger arises from the contagion of example. There is nothing in which mankind are more universally culpable than in the disorders of speech. Yet with these we are constantly surrounded; and to these we have been accustomed from our impressible infancy. We are in danger from the frequency of speech. "In the multitude of words there wanteth not sin."

We must of necessity speak often ; but we often speak without necessity. **Duty** calls us to intermingle much with our fellow-creatures ; but we are too little in the closet, and too much in the crowd—and when we are in company we forget the admonition, " Let every man be swift to hear, and slow to speak."

3. A man would never use this language without a conviction of *inability to preserve himself.* The Bible teaches us this truth, not only doctrinally, but historically. The examples of good men, and men eminent in godliness, confirm it in the very article before us. Moses, the meekest man in the earth, " spake unadvisedly with his lips." You have heard of the patience of Job, but he " cursed the day of his birth " ; and Jeremiah, the prophet of the Lord, did the same. Peter said, " Though all men should be offended because of thee, I will never be offended ; though I should die with thee, yet will I not deny thee." But how did he use his tongue a few hours after ? Then " began he to curse and to swear, saying, I know not the man ! "

4. A man would never use this language without a conviction of *the wisdom of applying to God for the assistance he needs.* Prayer is the effect of our weakness, and the expression of our dependence. It confesses the agency of God. 1. In the first place—God is equal to our preservation. 2. His succours are not to be obtained without prayer. 3. Prayer always brings the assistance it implores.— *Condensed from W. Jay's Sermon on "The Regulation of the Tongue."*

Verse 3.—*"Set a watch, O LORD, before my mouth,"* etc. Watching and prayer are often joined together. We are best kept when recommended into God's hand. I do observe here, First, That unadvised and passionate speeches do easily drop from us in our troubles, especially in our persecution. Secondly, That a godly, conscientious man is very tender of these, as of all evil. He that would live in communion with God for the present, and hope to appear with comfort before him hereafter, is sensible of the least thing that tends to God's displeasure, and God's dishonour : this is the true spirit of one that will be owned by Christ at the last day. Thirdly, There is no way to prevent being provoked to impatience and rashness of speech, or any evil, but by keeping a watch, and renewing our obligations to God. Fourthly, Whoever would keep a watch must call in the aid and assistance of God's grace ; *"Lord, set a watch before my mouth."—Thomas Manton.*

Verse 3.—*"Set a watch, O LORD, before my mouth,"* etc. Thus holy men have kept the sessions at home, and made their hearts the foremen of the jury, and examined themselves as we examine others. The fear of the Lord stood at the door of their souls, to examine every thought before it went in, and at the door of their lips, to examine every word before it went out, whereby they escaped a thousand sins which we commit, as though we had no other work.—*Henry Smith.*

Verse 3.—*"Set a watch, O LORD, before my mouth."* Nature having made my lips to be a door to my words, let grace keep that door, that no word may be suffered to go out which may any way tend to the dishonour of God, or the hurt of others.— *Matthew Henry.*

Verse 3.—*"Set a watch,"* etc. Let a seal for words not to be spoken lie on the tongue. A watch over words is better than over wealth.—*Lucian.*

Verse 3.—*"Keep the door of my lips."* That it move not creaking and complaining, as on rusty hinges, for want of the oil of joy and gladness. David had somewhat to do with his tongue, as we see (Ps. xxxix. 1, 3) ; and when he had carted the ark, how untowardly he spake, as if the fault were more in God than himself, that there was such a breach made in Uzzah (1 Chron. xiii. 12). It was but need thus to pray. —*John Trapp.*

Verse 4.—*"Incline not my heart to any evil thing,"* etc. The present pleasure and commodity of sin is in high estimation with the sinner, and much sweeter to him than what he may lawfully enjoy ; the pleasures of sin are his delicates. No man can keep himself from being taken with the allurements of a sinful course, except the Lord preserve him : *"Let me not eat of their dainties."* The holiest men in Scripture have been most sensible of the impotency of their own free will, and of their inability to resist temptations, or to bring the principles of grace into action ; most diffident of themselves, most dependent upon God, most careful to make use of means, and conscientious in following of ordinances, as their prayers do testify : *"Incline not my heart to any evil thing,"* etc.—*David Dickson.*

Verse 4.—*"Incline not my heart."* Heb. Let not be inclined my heart.— *John Jebb.*

Verse 4.—*"My heart."* That man is like Esau which had an inheritance, which had a heart but now he hath not possession of his own ; therefore, give God thy heart, that he may keep it ; and not a piece of thy heart, not a room in thy heart, but thy heart. The heart divided, dyeth. God is not like the mother which would have the child divided, but like the natural mother, which said, rather than it should be divided, let her take all. Let the devil have all, if he which gave it be not worthy of it. God hath no cope-mate, therefore he will have no parting of stakes, but all or none ; and therefore he which asks here thy heart, in the sixth of Deuteronomy and the fifth verse, asketh " all thy heart, all thy soul, and all thy strength " ; thrice he requireth *all*, lest we should keep a thought behind. Yet it is *thy* heart, that is, a vain heart, a barren heart, a sinful heart, until thou give it unto God, and then it is the spouse of Christ, the temple of the Holy Ghost, and the image of God, so changed, and formed, and refined, that God calls it a new heart.

There is such strife for the heart as there was for Moses's body. " Give it me," saith the Lord ; " give it me," saith the tempter ; " give it me," saith the pope ; " give it me," saith riches ; " give it me," saith pleasure ; as though thou must needs give it to some one. Now here is the choice, whether thou wilt give it to God or the devil ; God's heart or the devil's heart ; whose wilt thou be ?—*Henry Smith.*

Verse 4.—"*Let me not eat of their dainties.*" Sin is not only meat, but sweet meat ; not only bread, but pleasant bread to an evil heart. Daniel for some weeks ate no pleasant bread ; he ate bread to keep life and soul together, but he forbare feasting or good cheer. Sin is a feast to a carnal man, it is his good cheer, yea, it is "*dainties*" to him. David, speaking of wicked men says, "*Incline not my heart to any evil thing, to practise wicked works with men that work iniquity : and let me not eat of their dainties.*" These "*dainties*" may be expounded either for the prosperity that comes in by wicked practices (some by wicked ways get not only their ordinary food but "*dainties* ") ; or those "*dainties* " are sin itself : they feasted themselves in doing evil : "*Lord, let me not eat of their dainties.*" If that be their food I had rather starve than eat with them.—*Joseph Caryl.*

Verse 4.—"*Their dainties.*" The enemies of David were sensual and luxurious ; and they would have gladly admitted him to share in their banquets, if his character had resembled their own. He entreats to be preserved from inducement so to do.—*William Walford.*

Verse 5.—"*Let the righteous smite me,*" etc. This verse is so obscure as to be almost unintelligible. According to the English versions, it expresses his willingness to be rebuked by good men for his benefit. But this sense is not only hard to be extracted from the words, but foreign from the context. Of the many contradictory interpretations which have been proposed the most probable is that which makes the sentence mean, that the sufferings endured by the good man, even at the hand of the wicked, are chastisements inflicted by a righteous God in justice and with mercy, and as such may be likened to a festive ointment, which the head of the sufferer should not refuse, as he will still have need of consolation and occasion to invoke God, in the midst of trials and of mischiefs yet to be experienced.—*Joseph Addison Alexander.*

Verse 5.—"*Let the righteous smite me.*" The word הָלַם is seldom used in Scripture but to signify a severe stroke which shakes the subject smitten, and causeth it to tremble ; see Prov. xxiii. 35 ; 1 Sam. xiv. 16 ; Ps. lxxiv. 6 ; and it is used for the stroke of the hammer on the anvil in fashioning of the iron (Isa. xli. 7). Wherefore the word חֶסֶד following may be taken adverbially, as a lenitive of that severity which this word importeth : " Let him smite me, but " *leniter, benignè, misericorditer,* " gently, kindly, friendly, mercifully : " and so some translations read the words, " Let the righteous smite me friendly, or kindly."—*John Owen.*

Verse 5.—"*Let the righteous smite me ; it shall be a kindness,*" etc. Grace will teach a Christian to take those potions which are wholesome, though they be not toothsome. Faithful reproof is a token of love, and therefore may well be esteemed a kindness. Such wounding of a friend is healing, and so David might well call it " *an excellent oil.*" And he did not only say so, which is easy and ordinary, but acted accordingly. He did not as the papists, who highly commend holy water, but turn away their faces when it comes to be sprinkled on them. When he had by sin, and continuance in it, so gangrened his flesh, and corrupted himself, that he was in danger of death, he suffered his sores to be thoroughly searched without regret. Nathan was the chirurgeon whom God employed to search that wound which had divers mouths for festering in his soul; and truly he did not dally with his patient, though he were a prince, but thrust his instrument to the bottom; yet whatever pain it put him to, he took it patiently, and was so far from being angry with the prophet, that he made him one of his privy council. It is a sign of a polluted nature for a man, like a serpent, if he be but touched, to gather poison and vomit it up at the party. "Rebuke a wise man, and he will love thee": Prov. ix. 8. —*George Swinnock.*

Verse 5.—"*Let the righteous smite me,*" etc. If the righteous smite us by reproofs, it must be taken as a kindness, and as a precious balsam, which doth not break our head, but heal us. Not that we are bound to belie ourselves in compliance with every man's censorious humour that will accuse us; but we must be readier to censure ourselves than others, and readier to confess a fault than to expect a confession from others whom we reprove. Sincerity and serious repentance will be honourable in that person who is most careful to avoid sin, and most ready penitently to confess it when he hath been overcome, and truly thankful to those that call him to repentance; as being more desirous that God and his laws and religion should have the glory of their holiness, than that he himself should have the undue glory of innocency, and escape the deserved shame of sin.

It is one of the most dangerous diseases of professors, and one of the greatest scandals of this age, that persons taken for eminently religious are more impatient of pain, though just, reproof than many a drunkard, swearer, or fornicator; and when they have spent hours or days in the seeming earnest confession of their sin, and lament before God and man that they cannot do it with more grief and tears, yet they take it for a heinous injury in another that will say half so much against them, and take him for a malignant enemy of the godly who will call them as they call themselves.—*Richard Baxter* (1615—1691), *in "The Morning Exercises."*

Verse 5.—"*Let the righteous smite me.*" If a righteous or a right-wise man smite and reprove, he will do it, 1. *Sine felle,* without gall, without bitterness. 2. *Sine publicatione,* without publishing, divulging, or telling it to the world. 3. *Sine contumelia,* without disgrace—to reform his friend, not to disgrace him. 4. *Sine adulatione,* without flattery. 5. *Non sine Deo,* not without God.—*John Gore, in a Sermon entitled "Unknowne Kindnesse,"* 1635.

Verse 5.—"*The righteous,*" etc. The minister cannot be always preaching; two or three hours, may be, in a week, he spends among his people in the pulpit, holding the glass of the gospel before their faces; but the lives of professors, these preach all the week long: if they were but holy and exemplary, they would be as a repetition of the preacher's sermon to their families and neighbours among whom they converse, and keep the sound of his doctrine continually ringing in their ears. This would give Christians an amiable advantage in doing good to their carnal neighbours by counsel and reproof, which now is seldom done, and when done it proves to little purpose, because not backed with their own exemplary walking. "It behoves him," saith Tertullian, "that would counsel or reprove another, to guard his speech with the authority of his own conversation, lest, wanting that, what he says puts himself to the blush." We do not love one that hath a stinking breath to come very near us; such, therefore, had need have a sweet-scented life.

Reproofs are a good physic, but they have an unpleasant reception; it is hard for men not to throw them back on the face of them that gives them. Now nothing is more powerful to keep a reproof from thus coming back than the holiness of the person that reproves. "*Let the righteous smite me.*" saith David, "*it shall be a kindness: and let him reprove me; it shall be an excellent oil, which shall not break my head.*" See how well it is taken from such a hand, from the authority that holiness carries with it. None but a vile wretch will smite a righteous man with reproach for smiting him with a reproof, if softly laid on, and like oil fomented, and wrought into him, as it should, with compassion and love to his soul! Thus we see how influential the power of holiness would be unto the wicked, neither would it be less upon our brethren and fellow-Christians. Holy David professed he would take it as a kindness for the righteous to smite him; yea, as kindly as if he broke a box of precious oil upon his head, which was amongst the Jews a high expression of love.—*William Gurnall.*

Verse 5.—"*It shall be a kindness*" 1. It is a kindness *reducere erratum,* to bring back the wandering. 2. *Sanare ægrotum,* to recover the sick. 3. *Suscitare lethargum,* to awake, to stir up the lethargic, the sleepy. 4. *Ligare insanum,* to bind a madman. **5.** *Liberare perditum*, to save a lost man, one in imminent danger.—*John Gore.*

Verse 5.—*"It shall be an excellent oil, which shall not break my head."* Some persons pride themselves on being blunt, or, as they call it, " honest " ; but very blunt people do little good to others, and get little love to themselves. The Scriptures recommend gentleness and kindness. Reproof should fall like the dew, and not like the rushing hail-storm. The *" oil "* insinuates itself ; the stone wounds and then rebounds. Christians should take heed of getting fond of the work of " rebuking." Such " spiritual constables " do a great deal of mischief without intending it. They are in a church what a very witty and sarcastic person is in society, or what a tell-tale is in school ; and approximate very closely to that class which the apostle terms " busybodies in other men's matters." Our manner must be tender and winning. The nail of reproof, says an old writer, must be well oiled in kindness before it is driven home. Meddling with the faults of others is like attempting to move a person afflicted with the rheumatic gout : it must be done slowly and tenderly, nor must we be frightened by an outcry or two. The great thing is to show the person that you really love him ; and if you manifest this in the sight of God, he will bless your efforts, and give you favour in the sight of an erring brother.—*Christian Treasury.*

Verse 5.—*"It shall be an excellent oil."* Certain oils are said to have a most salutary effect on the head ; hence in fevers, or any other complaints which effect the head, the medical men always recommend oil. I have known people who were deranged, cured in a very short time by nothing more than the application of a peculiar kind of oil to the head. There are, however, other kinds which are believed, when thus applied, to produce delirium. Thus the reproofs of the righteous were compared to *" excellent oil,"* which produced a most salutary effect on the head. So common is this practice of anointing the head, that all who can afford it do it every week.

But, strange as it may appear, the crown of their heads is the place selected for the chastisement ; thus owners of slaves, or husbands, or schoolmasters, beat the heads of the offenders with their knuckles. Should an urchin come late to school, or forget his lesson, the pedagogue says to some of the other boys, " Go, beat his head!" " Begone, fellow ! or I will beat thy head." Should a man be thus chastised by an inferior, he quotes the old proverb : " If my head is to be beaten, let it be done with the fingers that have rings on " ; meaning a man of rank. " Yes, yes ; let a holy man smite my head ! and what of that ? it is an excellent oil." " My master has been beating my head, but it has been good oil for me."—*Joseph Roberts.*

Verse 5.—*"Oil, which shall not break my head."* When I first took this text in hand, this seemed unto me a very strange and uncouth expression. If the Psalmist had said, It shall be a stone that shall not break my head, etc., we had easily understood him ; but to speak of an oil, or a balm, which we know to be so soft, so supple, so lithe and gentle an ointment, that he should speak of breaking his head with oil, it is strange. I confess it troubled me a while, till at length I conceived it might be spoken by contraries ; as when a physician gives a patient some pectoral, or cordial, and saith, Take this, it will not hurt you ; his meaning is, it will help and do him good. So this oil *shall not break my head ;* that is, it shall heal it, being broken by my own corruption, by Satan's temptations, and by the evil influence of such as flatter me in my sins.—*John Gore.*

Verse 5.—If David could say of his enemy that cursed him, " Let him alone, for God hath bidden him to curse " ; much more safely mayest thou say of thy friend that reproves thee, " Let him alone, for God hath bidden him to smite." And as the apostle saith of ministers, that God " doth entreat you by us "; so persuade yourselves that God doth reprove you by them.—*John Gore.*

Verse 5.—It was the saying of a heathen, though no heathenish saying, " That he who would be good, must either have a faithful friend to instruct him, or a watchful enemy to correct him." Should we murder a physician because he comes to cure us ; or like him worse, because he would make us better ? The flaming sword of *reprehension* is but to keep us from the forbidden fruit of *transgression.* *"Let the righteous smite me ; it shall be a kindness : and let him reprove me ; it shall be an excellent oil, which shall not break my head."* Let him smite me as with a *hammer,* for so the word signifies. A Boanerges is as necessary as a Barnabas, —*William Secker.*

Verse 5.—*"Yet my prayer also shall be in their calamities."* That is, if ever they who are my reprovers fall into calamity, though they may think they provoked me so by reproving me, that they have lost my love, and have cast themselves out of my prayers, or that I will never speak well of them or for them again; yet I will pray for them with all my heart, as their matter shall require. I will pray for them when they have most need of prayer, even *" in their calamities."* Some heighten the sense thus,—The more they sharpen their reproof, the more I think myself bound to pray for them. It shows an excellent spirit, not to be hindered from doing good to others by anything they do or speak against us, nor their sharpest (though perhaps mistaken) reproofs of us. Thus it was that that good man Job *" prayed for his friends,"* who had spoken much against him, and not only reproved him without cause, but reproached him without charity.—*Joseph Caryl.*

Verse 6.—*"When their judges are overthrown,"* etc. When the judgments in reserve for the leaders of my enemies shall come upon them, they will perceive too late how reasonble are my words, and wish that they had hearkened to them sooner. —*Joseph Addison Alexander.*

Verse 6.—*"Overthrown."* The verb rendered *" overthrown"* is used of Jezebel in 2 Kings ix. 33; " Throw her down. So they threw her down."—*Speaker's Commentary.*

Verse 6.—*"They shall hear my words ; for they are sweet."* This is especially true of all the words which David spake by inspiration, or the Spirit of God spake to him; particularly in his book of Psalms, concerning the Messiah, the covenant of grace, and the blessings of it; of the rich experiences of grace he had, and the several doctrines of the gospel declared by him; which were sweet, delightful, and entertaining to those who have ears to hear such things; or those ears are opened to hear them, so as to understand them and distinguish them, but to others not. —*John Gill.*

Verse 6.—*"They shall hear my words ; for they are sweet."* Those that slighted the word of God before, will relish it and be glad of it when they are in affliction; for that opens the ear to instruction. When the world is bitter the word is sweet. Oppressed innocency cannot gain a hearing with those that live in pomp and pleasure; but when they come to be overthrown themselves, they will have more compassionate thoughts of the afflicted.—*Matthew Henry.*

Verse 6.—*"For they are sweet."* They shall be pleasant; mild; gentle; equitable; just. After the harsh and severe enactments of Saul, after enduring his acts of tyranny, the people will be glad to welcome me, and to live under the laws of a just and equal administration. The passage, therefore, expresses confidence that Saul and his hosts would be overthrown, and that the people of the land would gladly hail the accession to the throne of one who had been anointed to reign over them.—*Albert Barnes.*

Verses 6, 7.—The mild and dutiful behaviour of David towards Saul and his friends are set together by way of contrast, in the strongest light, from the instances of each sort here produced. The first is, David's humanity towards Saul, in giving him his life at two several times, when he had it in his power to destroy him as he pleased. *"Their judges have been dismissed in the rocky places ; and have heard my words that they are sweet " ;* that is, " Their princes have been dismissed in safety, when I had them at an advantage in those rocky deserts ; and only heard me expostulate with them in the gentlest words."

The other is, Saul's barbarity and cruelty towards David (or his friends, which is much the same) in the horrid massacre of Ahimelech and the priests, by the hand of Doeg the Edomite, done in such a savage manner, that he compares it to the chopping and cleaving wood ; *"Like as when one cutteth and cleaveth, so have our bones been scattered on the earth at the command of Saul " ;* for so I read the Hebrew words, *le-pi Saul, at the mouth,* that is, the command *of Saul.*

Should we suppose this passage to refer to the first time of David's sparing Saul, viz., when he had him in his power in the cave of *Engedi* (here called *jedé selay*), the sides of the rock, or the rocky places, the speech he made on this occasion when he called after Saul (and which is recorded in 1 Sam. xxiv., from the eighth to the sixteenth verse) might well be called *sweet* or *pleasant words.* For they set his own innocence and the king's unjust behaviour to him in so strong a light, and with all that gentleness and mildness, and even this hard-hearted prince could not forbear being greatly affected with it for the present ; and we are told (verses 16, 17) that "he lifted up his voice and wept."—*Charles Peters.*

Verse 7.—*"Our bones are scattered at the grave's mouth,"* etc. The primary reference may be to the slaughter of the priests by the command of Saul, 1 Sam. xxii. 16—19. The language, however, may be illustrative of the many massacres like that on the eve of St. Bartholomew, so numerous as to be scattered on the face of the earth, marking the passage of pious martyrs from this world to a better, and testifying where the blood of the slain shall be disclosed for the judgment of their murderers.—*W. Wilson.*

Verse 7.—*"Our bones are scattered at the grave's mouth,"* etc. Assuming the very extreme, it is a look of hope into the future : should his bones and the bones of his followers be even scattered about the mouth of Sheôl (cf. the Syrian picture of Sheôl : "the dust upon its threshold, *'al-escûfteh,"* *Deutsche Morgenländ. Zeitschrift,* xx. 513), their soul below, their bones above—it would nevertheless be only as when one in ploughing cleaves the earth ; *i.e.*, they do not lie there in order that they may continue lying, but that they may rise up anew, as the seed that is sown sprouts up out of the upturned earth.—*Franz Delitzsch.*

Verse 7.—*"Our bones are scattered at the grave's mouth."* That is to say, I and my company are in a dying condition, free among the dead ; yea, if taken we should be put to most cruel deaths, hewn in pieces, or pulled limbmeal, and left unburied ; and our dead bodies mangled by a barbarous inhumanity, as wood-cleavers make the shivers fly hither and thither. This is the perilous case of me and my partisans.—*John Trapp.*

Verse 7.—*"Our bones are scattered at the grave's mouth."*—This seems to be strong eastern painting, and almost figurative language ; but that it may be strictly true, the following extract demonstrates : " At five o'clock we left Garigana, our journey being still to the eastward of north ; and, at a quarter past six in the evening, arrived at the village of that name, whose inhabitants had all perished with hunger the year before; their wretched bones being all unburied, and scattered upon the surface of the ground, where the village formerly stood. We encamped among the bones of the dead, as no space could be found free from them ; and on the 23rd, at six in the morning, full of horror at this miserable spectacle, we set out for Teawa."—*(James Bruce's Travels.)* To the Jews such a spectacle must have been very dreadful, as the want of burial was esteemed one of the greatest calamities which could befall them.—*Burder's "Oriental Customs."*

Verse 7.—*"Like one ploughing and cleaving in the earth."* This clause may be explained not of cleaving wood but ploughing, to which the first verb is applied in Arabic. *Like (one) ploughing and cleaving* (making furrows) *in the earth,* not for the sake of mangling its surface, but to make it fruitful and productive, (so) *our bones are scattered at the mouth of hell,* as the necessary means of a glorious resurrection.—*Joseph Addison Alexander.*

Verse 7.—Who can attend the digging of a grave, .and view the ruins then disclosed, without exclaiming, *"Our bones are scattered at the grave's mouth, as when one cutteth and cleaveth wood upon the earth"* ?—*George Horne.*

Verse 8.—*"Mine eyes are unto thee, O GOD the Lord."* If you would keep your mind fixed in prayer, keep your *eye* fixed. Much vanity comes in at the eye. When the eyes wander in prayer the heart wanders. To think to keep the heart fixed in prayer, and yet let the eyes gaze abroad, is as if one should think to keep his house safe, yet let the windows be open.—*Thomas Watson.*

Verse 8.—*"Leave not my soul destitute."* The literal Hebrew is, *Pour not out my soul,* but keep it in thy cup of salvation.—*Agellius.* [Compare Isa. liii. 12 : " He hath poured out his soul unto death."]

Verse 8.—*"Leave not my soul destitute,"* or, *"Cast not out my soul."* That is, cast not my life away, as water, which is of no account, is cast out of a vessel containing it.—*Daniel Cresswell.*

Verse 8.—*"Leave not my soul destitute."* His soul knew what it was to be " destitute" ; he had known the misery of spiritual beggary and soul poverty. It was not with him as natural poverty is with the rich, a matter of speculation, a mere matter of theory ; but a matter of personal and painful experience. . . . It is in the margin *"Make not my soul bare"* ; Strip me not of every hope ; leave me not completely naked ; abandon me not to nature's beggary and misery ; let me not go down into the pit with all my sins upon my head ; leave not my soul destitute of pardon and peace.—*Joseph C. Philpot.*

Verses 8—10.—

> O pour not out my soul, I pray,
> From the dark snare preserve my way,
> The chambers of the blind entangling net,
> Which by my path the powers of evil set.
>
> Behold them laid, the godless crew,
> Low in the toils they darkly drew :
> The while, with gathering heart and watchful eye,
> I wait mine hour to pass victorious by.
>
> *John Keble.*

Verse 9. 10.—*"Snares," "Gins," "Nets."* The usual method of capturing or killing the lion in Palestine was by pitfalls or nets, to both of which there are many references in the Scriptures. The mode of hunting the lion with the nets was identical with that which is practised in India at the present time. The precise locality of the lion's dwelling-place having been discovered, a circular wall of net is arranged round it, or if only a few nets can be obtained, they are set in a curved form, the concave side being towards the lion. They then send dogs into the thicket, hurl stones and sticks at the den, shoot arrows into it, fling burning torches at it, and so irritate and alarm the animal that it rushes against the net, which is so made that it falls down and envelops the animal in its folds. If the nets be few, the drivers go to the opposite side of the den, and induce the lion to escape in the direction where he sees no foes, but where he is sure to run against the treacherous net. Other large and dangerous animals were also captured by the same means. Another and more common, because an easier and a cheaper method, was, by digging a deep pit, covering the mouth with a slight covering of sticks and earth, and driving the animal upon the treacherous covering. It is an easier method than the net, because after the pit is once dug, the only trouble lies in throwing the covering over its mouth. But it is not so well adapted for taking beasts alive, as they are likely to be damaged, either by the fall into the pit, or by the means used in getting them out again. Animals, therefore, that are caught in pits are generally, though not always, killed before they are taken out. The net, however, envelops the animal so perfectly, and renders it so helpless, that it can be easily bound and taken away, The hunting net is very expensive, and requires a large staff of men to work it, so that none but a rich man could use the net in hunting.

Besides the net, several other modes of bird-catching were used by the ancient Jews, just as is the case at the present day. Boys, for example, who catch birds for their own consumption, and not for the market, can do so by means of various traps, most of which are made on the principle of the noose, or snare. Sometimes a great number of hair-nooses are set in places to which the birds are decoyed, so that in hopping about, many of them are sure to be entangled in the snares. Sometimes the noose is ingeniously suspended in a narrow passage which the birds are likely to traverse, and sometimes a simple fall-trap is employed.—*J. G. Wood.*

Verse 10.—*"Into their own nets."* The word rendered " *nets* " occurs only in this place, as the closely corresponding word in Ps.cxl. 10, which is rendered " *deep pits*," occurs there only.—*Speaker's Commentary.*

HINTS TO PREACHERS.

Verse 1.—I. The Perpetuity of Prayer : " I cry, I cry." II. The Personality : " unto thee," " unto me." II. The Practicalness : " Make haste ; give ear."

Verse 1.—Holy haste. I. The saint hasting to God. II. The saint hastening God. III. God's sure hastening to his help.—*W. B. H.*

Verses 1, 2.—I. Prayer put forth : 1. With urgency : " Make haste unto me." 2. With fervency : " Give ear," etc. II. Prayer set forth : " Let my prayer be set forth," etc. When hearing is obtained there is composure and order in prayer.

When the fire is kindled the incense rises. III. Prayer held forth : " The lifting up of my hands as the evening sacrifice," as constant and accepted.—*G. R.*

Verse 2.—True prayer acceptable as incense and as the evening sacrifice. It is spiritual, solemn, ordained of God, brings Christ to remembrance.

Verse 3.—I. The mouth a door. II. A watchman needed. III. The Lord fulfilling that office.

Verse 4.—Total abstinence from evil desires, practices, and delights.

Verse 4.—A prayer, I. For the repression of every evil tendency in the heart : " Incline not my heart," etc. II. For the prevention of any association with the wicked in their sinful works : " To practise," etc. III. For a holy contempt of the temporal pleasure or profit placed in our way through the sin of others : " Let me not eat," etc. Note, many who will not engage in a wicked act do not object to participate in its gains.—*J. F.*

Verse 4.—Deprecation of, I. Devil's desires. II. Devil's deeds. III. Devil's dainties.—*W. B. H.*

Verse 5.—Rebukes of good men. I. Invited. II. Appreciated : " it shall be a kindness." III. Utilized : " an excellent oil." IV. Cheerfully endured : " not break my head." V. Repaid, by our prayers for them in time of trouble.

Verse 5 (*last clause*).—" Intercessory Prayer." See " Spurgeon's Sermons," No. 1,049,

Verse 6.—I. Times of trouble will come to the careless. II. Then they will be more ready to hear the gospel. III. Then they will find sweetness in that which they formerly refused.

Verse 6.—A Desert Oasis. I. The world is a stony place, hard, barren. II. Often pride and self-trust suffer overthrowing there. III. Then words of God by his sent servant make an oasis in the desert.—*W. B. H.*

Verses 7, 8.—A cemetery scene. I. Dry bones of the dead about the grave. II. Weary bones of the aged and sick around the grave. III. all bones being from day to day made ready for the grave. IV. Bones finding rest in God : " mine eyes are unto thee, O God," etc.

Verse 8.—Expectation. Supplication.

Verse 9.—The snares. Who lay them ? Why ? Who so many ? How are we to escape ? " Keep me."

Verses 9, 10.—David prays, 1. That he may see God in his deliverance from his enemies, and 2. That they may see God in the frustration of their designs.—*G. R.*

Verse 10.—Great pains to little purpose. I. The making of nets, etc. II. The taking of God's antagonists in their own nets. III. The invariable escape of God's friends. Lesson : Nothing can prosper sin, or hurt godliness.—*W. B. H.*

PSALM CXLII.

TITLE.—**Maschil of David.** *This Maschil is written for our instruction. It teaches us principally by example how to order our prayer in times of distress. Such instruction is among the most needful, practical, and effectual parts of our spiritual education. He who has learned how to pray has been taught the most useful of the arts and sciences. The disciples said unto the Son of David, "Lord, teach us to pray"; and here David gives us a valuable lesson by recording his own experience as to supplication from beneath a cloud.*

A Prayer when he was in the cave. He was in one of his many lurking places, either Engedi, Adullam, or some other lone cavern wherein he could conceal himself from Saul and his bloodhounds. Caves make good closets for prayer; their gloom and solitude are helpful to the exercise of devotion. Had David prayed as much in his palace as he did in his cave, he might never have fallen into the act which brought such misery upon his later days.

SUBJECT.—*There can be little doubt that this song dates from the days when Saul was sorely persecuting David, and David himself was in soul-trouble, probably produced by that weakness of faith which led him to associate with heathen princes. His fortunes were evidently at their lowest, and, what was worse, his repute had fearfully fallen; yet he displayed a true faith in God, to whom he made known his pressing sorrows. The gloom of the cave is over the Psalm, and yet as if standing at the mouth of it the prophet-poet sees a bright light a little beyond.*

EXPOSITION.

I CRIED unto the LORD with my voice; with my voice unto the LORD did I make my supplication.

2 I poured out my complaint before him; I shewed before him my trouble.

3 When my spirit was overwhelmed within me, then thou knewest my path. In the way wherein I walked have they privily laid a snare for me.

4 I looked on *my* right hand, and beheld, but *there was* no man that would know me: refuge failed me; no man cared for my soul.

5 I cried unto thee, O LORD: I said, Thou *art* my refuge *and* my portion in the land of the living.

6 Attend unto my cry; for I am brought very low: deliver me from my persecutors; for they are stronger than I.

7 Bring my soul out of prison, that I may praise thy name: the righteous shall compass me about; for thou shalt deal bountifully with me.

1. "*I cried unto the LORD with my voice.*" It was a cry of such anguish that he remembers it long after, and makes a record of it. In the loneliness of the cave he could use his voice as much as he pleased; and therefore he made its gloomy vaults echo with his appeals to heaven. When there was no soul in the cavern seeking his blood, David with all his soul was engaged in seeking his God. He felt it a relief to his heart to use his voice in his pleadings with Jehovah. There was a voice *in* his prayer when he used his voice *for* prayer: it was not *vox et præterea nihil*. It was a prayer *vivo corde* as well as *vivâ voce*. "*With my voice unto the LORD did I make my supplication.*" He dwells upon the fact that he spoke aloud in prayer; it was evidently well impressed upon his memory, hence he doubles the word and says, " with my voice; with my voice." It is well when our supplications are such that we find pleasure in looking back upon them. He that is cheered by the memory of his prayers will pray again. See how the good man's appeal was to Jehovah only: he did not go round about to men, but he ran straight forward to Jehovah, his God. What true wisdom is here! Consider how the Psalmist's prayer grew into shape as he proceeded with it. He first poured out his natural longings,—

" I cried ; " and then he gathered up all his wits and arranged his thoughts,—" I made supplication." True prayers may differ in their diction, but not in their direction : an impromptu cry and a preconceived supplication must alike ascend towards the one prayer-hearing God, and he will accept each of them with equal readiness. The intense personality of the prayer is noteworthy : no doubt the Psalmist was glad of the prayers of others, but he was not content to be silent himself. See how everything is in the first person,—"*I* cried with *my* voice ; with *my* voice did *I* make *my* supplication." It is good to pray in the plural—" Our Father," but in times of trouble we shall feel forced to change our note into " Let this cup pass from *me*."

2. "*I poured out my complaint before him.*" His inward meditation filled his soul : the bitter water rose up to the brim ; what was to be done ? He must pour out the wormwood and the gall, he could not keep it in ; he lets it run away as best it can, that so his heart may be emptied of the fermenting mixture. But he took care *where* he outpoured his complaint, lest he should do mischief, or receive an ill return. If he poured it out before man he might only receive contempt from the proud, hard-heartedness from the careless, or pretended sympathy from the false ; and therefore he resolved upon an outpouring before God alone, since *he* would pity and relieve. The word is scarcely " complaint " ; but even if it be so we may learn from this text that our complaint must never be of a kind that we dare not bring before God. We may complain *to* God, but not *of* God. When we complain it should not be before men, but before God alone. "*I shewed before him my trouble.*" He exhibited his griefs to one who could assuage them : he did not fall into the mistaken plan of so many who publish their sorrows to those who cannot help them. This verse is parallel with the first ; David first pours out his complaint, letting it flow forth in a natural, spontaneous manner, and then afterwards he makes a more elaborate show of his affliction ; just as in the former verse he began with crying, and went on to " make supplication." Praying men pray better as they proceed. Note that we do not show our trouble before the Lord that *he* may see *it*, but that *we* may see *him*. It is for *our* relief, and not for his information that we make plain statements concerning our woes : it does us much good to set out our sorrow in order, for much of it vanishes in the process, like a ghost which will not abide the light of day ; and the rest loses much of its terror, because the veil of mystery is removed by a clear and deliberate stating of the trying facts. Pour out your thoughts and you will see what they are ; show your trouble and the extent of it will be known to you : let all be done before the Lord, for in comparison with his great majesty of love the trouble will seem to be as nothing.

3. "*When my spirit was overwhelmed within me, then thou knewest my path.*" The bravest spirit is sometimes sorely put to it. A heavy fog settles down upon the mind, and the man seems drowned and smothered in it ; covered with a cloud, crushed with a load, confused with difficulties, conquered by impossibilities. David was a hero, and yet his spirit sank : he could smite a giant down, but he could not keep himself up. He did not know his own path, nor feel able to bear his own burden. Observe his comfort : he looked away from his own condition to the ever-observant, all-knowing God ; and solaced himself with the fact that all was known to his heavenly Friend. Truly it is well for us to know that God knows what we do not know. We lose our heads, but God never closes his eyes : our judgments lose their balance, but the eternal mind is always clear.

"*In the way wherein I walked have they privily laid a snare for me.*" This the Lord knew at the time, and gave his servant warning of it. Looking back, the sweet singer is rejoiced that he had so gracious a Guardian, who kept him from unseen dangers. Nothing is hidden from God ; no secret snare can hurt the man who dwells in the secret place of the Most High, for he shall abide under the shadow of the Almighty. The use of concealed traps is disgraceful to our enemies, but they care little to what tricks they resort for their evil purposes. Wicked men must find some exercise for their malice, and therefore when they dare not openly assail they will privately ensnare. They watch the gracious man to see where his haunt is, and there they set their trap ; but they do it with great caution, avoiding all observation, lest their victim being forewarned should escape their toils. This is a great trial, but the Lord is greater still, and makes us to walk safely in the midst of danger, for he knows us and our enemies, our way and the snare which is laid in it. Blessed be his name.

4. "*I looked on my right hand and beheld, but there was no man that would know*

me." He did not miss a friend for want of looking for him, nor for want of looking in a likely place. Surely some helper would be found in the place of honour ; some one would stand at his right hand to undertake his defence. He looked steadily, and saw all that could be seen, for he " beheld " ; but his anxious gaze was not met by an answering smile. Strange to say, all were strange to David. He had known many, but none would know him. When a person is in ill odour it is wonderful how weak the memories of his former friends become : they quite forget, they refuse to know. This is a dire calamity. It is better to be opposed by foes than to be forsaken by friends. When friends look for us they affect to have known us from our birth, but when we look for friends it is wonderful how little we can make them remember : the fact is that in times of desertion it is not true that no man did know us, but no man *would* know us. Their ignorance is wilful. *"Refuge failed me."* Where in happier days I found a ready harbour I now discovered none at all. My place of flight had taken to flight. My refuge gave me a refusal. *"No man cared for my soul."* Whether I lived or died was no concern of anybody's. I was cast out as an outcast. No soul cared for my soul. I dwelt in No-man's land, where none cared to have me, and none cared about me. This is an ill-plight—no place where to lay our head, and no head willing to find us a place. How pleased were his enemies to see the friend of God without a friend ! How sad was he to be utterly deserted in his utmost need ! Can we not picture David in the cave, complaining that even the cave was not a refuge for him, for Saul had come even there ? Hopeless was his looking out, we shall soon see him looking up.

5. *"I cried unto thee, O LORD."* As man would not regard him, David was driven to Jehovah, his God. Was not this a gain made out of a loss ? wealth gained by a failure ? Anything which leads us to cry unto God is a blessing to us. This is the second time that in this short Psalm we find the same record, " I cried unto thee, O LORD ": the saintly man is evidently glad to remember his cry and its results. We hear often of the bitter cry of outcast London, here is another bitter cry, and it comes from an outcast, in wretched lodgings, forgotten by those who should have helped him. *"I said, Thou art my refuge and my portion in the land of the living."* There is a sort of progressive repetition all through this sacred song ; he *cried* first, but he *said* afterwards : his cry was bitter, but his saying was sweet ; his cry was sharp and short, but his saying was fresh and full. It gives a believer great pleasure to remember his own believing speeches : he may well desire to bury his unbelieving murmurings in oblivion, but the triumphs of grace in working in him a living faith, he will not dream of forgetting. What a grand confession of faith was this ! David spoke to God, and of God—" THOU art my refuge." Not thou hast provided me a refuge, but thou, thyself, art my refuge. He fled to God alone ; he hid himself beneath the wings of the Eternal. He not only believed this, but said it, and practised it. Nor was this all ; for David, when banished from his portion in the promised land, and cut off from the portion of goods which he by right inherited, found his portion in God, yea, God *was* his portion. This was so not only in reference to a future state, but here among living men. It is sometimes easier to believe in a portion in heaven than in a portion upon earth : we could die more easily than live, at least we think so. But there is no living in the land of the living like living upon the living God. For the man of God to say these precious things in the hour of his dire distress was a grand attainment. It is easy to prate bravely when we dwell at ease, but to speak confidently in affliction is quite another matter.

Even in this one sentence we have two parts, the second rising far above the first. It is something to have Jehovah for our refuge, but it is everything to have him for our portion. If David had not *cried* he would not have *said ;* and if the Lord had not been his *refuge* he would never have been his *portion.* The lower step is as needful as the higher ; but it is not necessary always to stop on the first round of the ladder.

6. *"Attend unto my cry."* Men of God look upon prayer as a reality, and they are not content without having an audience with God ; moreover, they have such confidence in the Lord's condescending grace, that they hope he will even attend to that poor broken prayer which can only be described as a cry. *"For I am brought very low,"* and therefore all the prayer I can raise is a mournful cry. This is his argument with God : he is reduced to such a sad condition that if he be not rescued he will be ruined. Gracious men may not only be low, but very low ; and this should not be a reason for their doubting the efficacy of their prayers, but rather a plea

with the Lord why they should have special attention. *"Deliver me from my persecutors."* If he did not get out of their hands, they would soon kill him out of hand, and as he could not himself effect an escape, he cried to God, " deliver me." *"For they are stronger than I."* As he before found a plea in his sadness, so now in his feebleness : Saul and his courtiers were in power, and could command the aid of all who sought royal favour ; but poor David was in the cave, and every Nabal girded at him. Saul was a monarch, and David a fugitive ; Saul had all the forms of law on his side, while David was an outlaw : so that the prayer before us comes from the weak, who proverbially go to the wall,—a good place to go to if they turn their faces to it in prayer, as Hezekiah did in his sickness. The Lord is wont to take the side of the oppressed, and to show his power by baffling tyrants ; David's supplication was therefore sure to speed. In these sentences we see how explicitly the man of God described his case in his private communings with his Lord : in real earnest he poured out his complaint before him, and showed before him his trouble.

7. *"Bring my soul out of prison, that I may praise thy name."* That God may be glorified is another notable plea for a suppliant. Escaped prisoners are sure to speak well of those who give them liberty. Soul-emancipation is the noblest form of liberation, and calls for the loudest praise : he who is delivered from the dungeons of despair is sure to magnify the name of the Lord. We are in such a prison that only God himself can bring us out of it, and when he does so he will put a new song into our mouths. The cave was not half such a dungeon to David's body as persecution and temptation made for his soul. To be exiled from the godly is worse than imprisonment, hence David makes it one point of his release that he would be restored to church fellowship—*"The righteous shall compass me about."* Saints gather around a child of God when his Father smiles upon him ; they come to hear his joyful testimony, to rejoice with him, and to have their own faith encouraged. All the true believers in the twelve tribes were glad to rally to David's banner when the Lord enlarged his spirit ; they glorified God for him and with him and through him. They congratulated him, consorted with him, crowned him, and championed him. This was a sweet experience for righteous David, who had for awhile come under the censure of the upright. He bore their smiting with patience, and now he welcomes their sanction with gratitude. *"For thou shalt deal bountifully with me."* God's bountiful dealing is sure to bring with it the sympathy and alliance of all the favourites of the Great King. What a change from looking for a friend and finding none to this enthusiastic concourse of allies around the man after God's own heart ! When we can begin a Psalm with crying, we may hope to close it with singing. The voice of prayer soon awakens the voice of praise.

EXPLANATORY NOTES AND QUAINT SAYINGS.

Title.—He calls this prayer *Maschil,* " a Psalm of instruction," because of the good lessons he had himself learned in the cave, learned on his knees, and so learned that he desired to teach others.—*Matthew Henry.*

Title.—*"A prayer when he was in the cave."* Every part of this Psalm shows the propriety of its inscription or title. He expressly mentions his being in a place where he was entirely shut up, where he saw no possible method of escaping, as having no friends that dared to own him and appear for his deliverance, and when every one seemed to desert him, and to have abandoned all care of his safety and life. This he pathetically describes, and in such terms as cannot fail to move the tender affections of every one who considers them. On the first sense of his danger, shut up in a cave, surrounded by three thousand chosen soldiers, closely observed by a watchful enemy who would spare no art or pains to apprehend him, he seems almost to have despaired of himself, and declares that his spirit is quite overwhelmed with the greatness of his distress. At length, recollecting his principles, and the promises that God had made him, he earnestly supplicates the protection of God, and assures himself that he should yet praise God for his deliverance, and that good men should share his joy, and encompass the altar of God with thanksgiving for the mercy that he had shown him.—*Samuel Chandler.*

Title.—*"The cave."* Leaving our horses in charge of some Arabs, and taking one for our guide, we started for the cave now known as Mughâret Khureitûn, which is believed to be the cave Adullam, having a fearful gorge below, gigantic cliffs above, and the path winding along a narrow shelf of the rock. At length, from a great rock hanging on the edge of the shelf, we entered by a long leap a low window which opened into the perpendicular face of the cliff. We were then within the traditional hold of David, and, creeping half doubled through a narrow crevice for a few rods, we stood beneath the dark vault of the first grand chamber of this mysterious and oppressive cavern, 1 Sam. xxii. 1, 2 ; 2 Sam. xxiii. 13—17. Our whole collection of lights did little more than make the damp darkness visible. After groping about as long as we had time to spare, we returned to the light of day, fully convinced that, with David and his lion-hearted followers inside, all the strength of Israel under Saul could not have forced an entrance—would not have even attempted it.—*William M. Thompson.*

Verse 1.—*"I cried unto the LORD."* Thou hast posted me over to no deputy for the hearing of my prayer, neither dost thou require that I should bring a spokesman for the presenting of it ; but thou hast commanded me to come myself, and to come to thee thyself.—*Sir Richard Baker on the Lord's Prayer.*

Verse 1.—*"With my voice."* The Lord needs not the tongue to be an interpreter between him and the hearts of his children. He that hears without ears can interpret prayers though not uttered by the tongue. Our desires are cries in the ears of the Lord of hosts. The vehemency of the affections may sometimes cause the outcrying of the voice ; but alas ! without this it is but a tinkling cymbal . . . . There is a use of words in prayer, to excite, and convey, and give vent to, affection : Hosea xiv. 2, " Take with you words, and turn to the LORD : say unto him, Take away all iniquity, and receive us graciously." The prophet doth not only prescribe that they should take affections, but take with them words.—*Thomas Manton.*

Verse 2.—*"I poured out my complaint before him."* Literally, my meditation ; that is—what so much occupied my thoughts at the time I expressed aloud. The word *"complaint"* does not express the idea. The meaning is, not that he *complained* of God or of man ; but that his mind *meditated* on his condition.—*Albert Barnes.*

Verse 2.—*"I poured out,"* etc. I did it fully, and fervently, and confidently.—*Matthew Henry.*

Verse 2.—*"Poured out . . . before him."* Those words teach us that in prayer we should not try to keep anything back from God, but should show him all that is in our hearts, and that in his presence in our closet, with the door shut, but not before men. The Carmelite adds that there is much force in the words *"with my voice,"* twice repeated (as in Heb., A.V., Vulgate, etc.) to show us that we ought to pray to God directly for ourselves, and in person, and not to be contented with an *Ora pro me* addressed to some one else.—*Cassiodorus and Ayguan, in Neale and Littledale.*

Verse 2.—*"I shewed before him my trouble."* Be very particular in secret prayer, both as to sins, wants, and mercies . . . Be not ashamed to open out all thy necessities. David argues because he is " poor and needy ; " four several times he presses his wants and exigencies before God, like an earnest but holy beggar (Ps. xl. 17 ; lxx. 5 ; lxxxvi. 1 ; cix. 22). He *"shewed before him"* his trouble. He presents *"before"* God his ragged condition, and spreads open his secret wounds ; as Job said, he " would order " his " cause before him " : Job xxiii. 4. . . . Before God we may speak out our minds fully, and name the persons that afflict, affront, and trouble us ; and woe to them that a child of God upon a mature judgment names in prayer ! I find not that such a prayer in Scripture ever returned empty . . . A great reason why we reap so little benefit in prayer, is because we rest too much in generals ; and if we have success, it is but dark, so that often we cannot tell what to make of the issues of prayer. Besides, to be particular in our petitions would keep the spirit much from wandering when we are intent upon a weighty cause, and the progress of the soul in grace would manifest its gradual success in prayer.—*Samuel Lee* (1625 —1691), *in "The Morning Exercises."*

Verse 2.—The committing of our cause to God is at once our duty, our safety, and our ease.—*Abraham Wright.*

Verse 3.—*"When my spirit was overwhelmed within me."* *"When even my spirit* (the higher faculty) *is wrapped in darkness upon me ; "* that is, when even my spirit (*ruach*), which ought to elevate my *soul* (*nephesh*) falls heavily upon me, as in a swoon.

> " When heavy, like a veil of woe,
> My spirit on me lay."

What is here said of the *spirit*, is oftener predicated of the *soul*, the seat of the passions. See Psalms xlii. 6; xliii. 5; cxxxi. 2. The dejection of the *spirit* represents a still more sorrowful and downcast condition, than the fainting of the *soul*. See Psalm cxliii. 3, 4, and compare our Lord's words, " My *soul* is troubled " (John xii. 27) with the Evangelist's statement, " Jesus was troubled in **spirit** " (John xiii. 21; xi. 33).—*Christopher Wordsworth*.

Verse 3.—"*When my spirit was overwhelmed within me.*" Literally, *in the muffling upon me of my spirit.* When my spirit was so wrapped in trouble and gloom, so " muffled round with woe," that I could not see the path before me, was distracted and unable to choose a line of conduct, "*Thou* (emphatic) knewest my path.*"— A. S. Aglen, in "An Old Testament Commentary for English Readers," 1884.*

Verse 3.—I wish you much comfort from David's thought : "*When my spirit was overwhelmed within me, then thou knewest my path.*" The Lord is not withdrawn to a great distance, but his eye is upon you. He sees you not with the indifference of a mere spectator ; but he observes with attention, he knows, he considers your path : yea, he appoints it, and every circumstance about it is under his direction. Your trouble began at the hour he saw best,—it could not come before ; and he has marked the degree of it to a hair's breadth, and its duration to a minute. He knows likewise how your spirit is affected ; and such supplies of grace and strength, and in such seasons as he sees needful, he will afford in due season. So that when things appear darkest, you shall still be able to say, Though chastened, not killed. Therefore hope in God, for you shall yet praise him.—*John Newton* (1725—1807), *in "Cardiphonia."*

Verse 3.—"*Thou knewest.*"

> From human eyes 'tis better to conceal
> Much that I suffer, much I hourly feel ;
> But, oh, this thought can tranquillize and heal,
> All, all is known to thee.

> Nay, all by thee is ordered, chosen, planned,
> Each drop that fills my daily cup, thy hand
> Prescribes for ills, none else can understand,
> All, all is known to thee.
>
> *Charlotte Elliott.*

Verse 3.—Although we as Christians possess the full solution of the problem of suffering, yet we frequently find ourselves in the position of Job, in regard to this or that particular affliction. There are sorrows so far reaching, so universal ; there are losses so absolute, and blows so terrible and inexplicable, that it seems for a time as if we were wrapped in thickest gloom, and as if the secret of the Lord had not been revealed. Why was this man stricken, and that man spared ? Why was such and such a being, in whom so many hopes centred, or who had already realised so many pleasant expectations, why was he withdrawn ? Why was that other person left, a useless encumbrance to earth ? Why was that voice, which found echo in so many hearts, suddenly silenced ? Why have I been smitten ? Why have I lost that which rendered my moral life beautiful and useful ? Oftentimes the soul seems lost for awhile in thoughts which overwhelm it, it loses its foothold, it tumbles about helplessly amid the deep waters of affliction. It seems as if all were over. Do not believe it. Remember Job ; you cannot go to greater lengths of despair than he, and yet God had pity on him. There is much comfort for you in this example of indescribable suffering, exasperated to the highest degree, and yet pardoned and consoled. Cling to the memory of this blessed fact as to a cable of deliverance, a board or a plank amidst the shipwreck. And then remember that affliction forms part of God's plan, and that he also asks you to manifest ready and absolute confidence in him.—*E. De Pressensé, D.D., in "The Mystery of Suffering," 1869.*

Verse 3.—"*They have privily laid a snare for me.*" Snares on the right hand, and snares on the left : snares on the right hand, worldly prosperity ; snares on the left hand, worldly adversity ; snares on the right hand, flattery ; snares on the left hand, alarm. Do thou walk in the midst of the snares : depart not from the way : let neither flattery ensnare thee, nor alarm drive thee off it.—*Augustine.*

Verse 4.—"*I looked on my right hand, and beheld.*" The first two verbs must be translated as imperatives, as in the margin of the English Bible. [" Look on the right hand, and see."] The right hand is mentioned as the post of a protector.—*Joseph Addison Alexander.*

Verse 4.—"*I looked on my right hand.*" The allusion here, it is supposed, is to the observance of the ancient Jewish courts of judicature, in which the advocate, as well as the accuser, stood on the *right hand* of the accused (Psalm cx. 5). The Psalmist felt himself in the condition of one who had nobody to plead his cause, and to protect him in the dangerous circumstances in which he was placed.—*James Anderson's Note to Calvin in loc.*

Verse 4.—"*There was no man that would know me.*" The fact that David, although surrounded by a band of loyal subjects, confesses to having no true friend, is to be understood similarly to the language of Paul when he says in Phil. ii. 20 : " I have no man like-minded." All human love, since sin has taken possession of humanity, is more or less selfish, and all fellowship of faith and of love imperfect ; and there are circumstances in life in which these dark sides make themselves felt overpoweringly, so that a man seems to himself to be perfectly isolated, and turns all the more urgently to God, who alone is able to supply the soul's want of some object to love, whose love is absolutely unselfish, and unchangeable, and unbeclouded, to whom the soul can confide without reserve whatever burdens it, and who not only honestly desires its good, but is able also to compass it in spite of every obstacle. Surrounded by bloodthirsty enemies, and misunderstood, or at least not thoroughly understood by his friends, David feels himself broken off from all created beings.—*Franz Delitzsch.*

Verse 4.—"*There was no man that would know me.*" Teacheth us of what little estimation God's children be, with the world and worldly men.—*Thomas Wilcocks.*

Verse 4.—"*There was no man that would know me.*" Persecution from the side of our enemies presses sorely, but abandonment by our friends, who should have stood by one's side as helpers and defenders, presses more sorely still.—*Taube, in Lange's Commentary.*

Verse 4.—Observe the beautiful opposition between " Thou knewest " (verse 3) and " no man would know me." "*Refuge failed me,*"—literally "*perished*" from me (Jer. xxv. 35 ; Amos ii. 14). But " thou hast been my *refuge* in the day of my trouble " ; Ps. lix. 16.—*Andrew Robert Fausset.*

Verses 4, 5.—"*Refuge failed me. . . Thou art my refuge.*" Travellers tell us that they who are at the top of the Alps can see great showers of rain fall under them, but not one drop of it falls on them. They who have God for their portion are in a high tower, and thereby safe from all troubles and showers. A drift-rain of evil will beat in at the creature's windows, be they never so well pointed ; all the garments this world can make up cannot keep them that travel in such weather from being wet to the skin. No creature is able to bear the weight of its fellow-creature ; but as reeds, they break under the pressure, and as thorns, they run into the sides of those who lean on them. The bow drawn beyond its compass breaks in sunder, and the string wound above its strength snaps in pieces. Such are outward helps to all that trust to them in hardships.—*George Swinnock.*

Verses 4, 5.—"*Refuge failed me. . . Thou art my refuge.*" Are there any among us to whom the world's face is quite changed, and the brooks of comfort in it are dried up, and they are so tossed, chased, and harassed in it that they have forgotten their resting-place ? Are any of you " become a stranger unto your brethren and an alien unto your mother's children " ? Ps. lxix. 8. Is it grown such a strange world, that even " your own familiar friend, in whom you trusted, which did eat of your bread, hath lifted up his heel against you " ? (Ps. xli. 9) ; and that wherever you turn yourselves in it, to find rest and refuge, the door is shut in your face ? Here is refuge for you ; here is one open door ; come in, thou blessed of the Lord : " the Lord gathereth the outcasts of Israel " : Ps. cxlvii. 2. It seems the Lord minds to have you in : he is doing with you as a father with a stubborn son who ran away from his father's house, thinking to shift for himself among his friends, and not come back : the father sends peremptory word through them all, saying, " In whosesoever house my son is skulking, presently turn him out of doors, and let none of you take him in ; and if he come to you give him not one night's lodging, nay, let him not eat in your house." Wherefore is all this but just to get him back again to his father's house ?—*Thomas Boston*, 1676—1732.

Verses 4, 5.—When all slighted him, when none took care of him ; what doth David in this case ? The words in verse 5 tell us what. *"I cried unto thee, O Lord : I said, Thou art my refuge and my portion in the land of the living."* As if he had said, Upon these unkindnesses, disrespects, and slightings which I found in the world, I took occasion, yea, I was stirred in my spirit to cry unto thee, O Lord, and to say, *"Thou art my refuge,"* that is, then I made thee my refuge more than ever. Having made thee my choice in my best times, when men honoured and embraced me, I am much encouraged in these evil times when men regard me not, to shelter my weather-beaten self in thy name and power. When we have most friends in the world, then God is our best friend, but when the world hates us, and frowns upon us, especially when (as the prophet speaks of some, Isa. lxvi. 5) " our brethren hate us, and cast us out for the name's sake of God himself," saying, " Let the Lord be glorified," when 'tis thus with us (I say) our souls are even forced into the presence of God, to renew our interests in his love, and to assure our souls that we are accepted with him.—*Joseph Caryl.*

Verse 5.—*"I have cried unto thee, Jehovah, I have said,"* etc. I have cried and still cry ; I have said and still say.—*Joseph Addison Alexander.*

Verse 5.—*"I said."* This imports, I. A REMEMBRANCE OF THE SOLEMN TRANSACTION, Ps. ciii. 18. This is a deed never to be forgotten, but always to be kept in remembrance. But, O ye who have said this, remember, 1. *What* you said. You said that God in Christ should be your refuge, that under the shade of his wings you hid yourselves, and that, renouncing all other refuges, as refuges of lies, you did betake yourselves to the covert of Christ's righteousness, and that there ye would abide for your portion ; which was a formal acceptance of and laying hold on the covenant. 2. *To whom* you said it. To God in Christ speaking to you in the gospel-offer, and inviting you into the refuge. What men say to their superiors, they think themselves specially concerned to mind. And surely what ye have said to God, ye ought in a peculiar manner to remember, and awe your hearts with the consideration of the majesty of the party to whom ye said it, Ps. xvi. 2 : " O my soul, thou hast said unto the Lord, Thou art my Lord "; for he is not one with whom we may deal falsely. 3. *How* ye said it. Did ye not say it in your hearts, while God in Christ was held out as a refuge for you ? And the language of the heart is plain language with a heart-searching God. Did not some of you say it with your mouths ? and did not all communicants say it solemnly before the world, angels, and men, by their receiving the elements of bread and wine ? 4. *Upon what grounds* you said it. Did you not see a necessity of a refuge for you, and a necessity of taking God in Christ for your refuge ? Ye had rational grounds for it, and lasting grounds that can never fail ; so that ye can never have ground to retract, nor shift about for another refuge. Jer. ii. 31. 5. *Where* ye said it. Remember the spot of ground where ye said it in prayer, where ye said it at the communion-table. Ps. xlii. 6. The stones of the place will be witnesses of your saying it. Josh. xxiv. 27.

II. A STANDING TO IT, without regretting that we said it, remembering what is said, John vi. 66—69 ; " From that time many of his disciples went back, and walked no more with him. Then said Jesus unto the twelve, Will ye also go away ? Then Simon Peter answered him, Lord, to whom shall we go ? thou hast the words of eternal life. And we believe and are sure that thou art that Christ, the Son of the living God." Men often repent what they have said, and therefore will not own that they have said it. But gracious souls will not repent their saying this, but will abide by it. If they were to make their choice a thousand times, having chosen God in Christ for their refuge and portion, they would not alter ; Jer. iii. 19 : " I said, Thou shalt call me, My Father ; and shalt not turn away from me." Many alterations may be in men's circumstances in the world, but there can never be one that will afford ground for retracting this saying.

III. AN OWNING OF THE OBLIGATION OF IT : *"I said,"* and am obliged thereby to stand to it, " For I have opened my mouth unto the Lord, and I cannot go back," Judg. xi. 35. God in Christ is yours, and ye are his by his own consent ; ye are no more your own ; ye have said the word, and must own that it is binding on you ; and ye must beware that after vows ye make not enquiry. Whoever may pretend they have their choice yet to make of a refuge and portion to themselves, ye cannot :

ye are engaged already, and ye are not at liberty to hearken to any other proposals, any more than a woman who has already signed her contract with one man.

IV. A PROFESSING OF IT CONFIDENTLY without being ashamed of it : as though you should say, " I own it before all men, and am not ashamed of my choice." Antichrist allows some of his vassals to carry his mark in their right hand. Rev. xiii. 16. But all the followers of the Lamb have their mark on their foreheads, where it will not hide, Rev. xiv. 1. The world would put the people of God to shame on the head of their refuge and portion, as if they had made a foolish bargain of it, Psa. xiv. 6 : " Ye have shamed the counsel of the poor, because the LORD is his refuge." But sincerity will make men despise that shame as David said, " And I will yet be more vile than thus, and will be base in mine own sight."

V. A SATISFACTION OF HEART IN IT : as though you should say, " I said it, and, Oh, but I am well pleased that ever I said it ; it was the best saying I could ever say. Ps. xvi. 2, 5, 6, 7. And this is in effect to say it over again. And good reason there is for them who have sincerely said it to be well satisfied in their refuge, and to rejoice in their portion. The reflecting upon it may afford solid delight and content of heart. Ye who have taken the Lord for your refuge may with much satisfaction reflect upon what you have done.—*Thomas Boston.*

Verse 6.—*"Attend unto my cry."*—

Can I see another's woe,
And not be in sorrow too ?
Can I see another's grief,
And not seek for kind relief ?

Can I see a falling tear,
And not feel my sorrow's share ?
Can a father see his child
Weep, nor be with sorrow filled ?

Can a mother sit and hear
An infant groan, an infant fear ?
No, no ; never can it be !
Never, never can it be !

And can he, who smiles on all,
Hear the wren, with sorrows small—
Hear the small bird's grief and care,
Hear the woes that infants bear,

And not sit beside the nest,
Pouring pity in its breast ?
And not sit the cradle near,
Weeping tear on infant's tear ?

And not sit both night and day
Wiping all our tears away ?
Oh, no ! never can it be !
Never, never can it be !

He doth give his joy to all ;
He becomes an infant small ;
He becomes a man of woe ;
He doth feel the sorrow too.

Think not thou canst sigh a sigh,
And thy Maker is not by ;
Think not thou canst weep a tear,
And thy Maker is not near.

Oh ! he gives to us his joy,
That our grief he may destroy :
Till our grief is fled and gone,
He doth sit by us and moan.

William Blake (1757—1828), *in "Songs of Innocence," 1789.*

Verse 6.—*"I am brought very low,"* etc. However true this may have been of David lurking in a cave, while his enemy, Saul, was at the head of a powerful army, it is more literally true of Christ, who could truly say, "*I am brought very low*," because "he himself became obedient unto death, even to the death of the cross." He was also "*brought very low*," when he, that had the right of sitting on the cherubim, hung between two robbers. Truly also were his enemies "*stronger than he*" when "their hour came," and "power was given to darkness," so as to appear, for awhile, to eclipse the sun of justice itself.—*Robert Bellarmine.*

Verse 6.—"*For they are stronger than I.*" But they are not stronger than THOU. Thou canst make us "stronger than our enemies": Ps. cv. 24. He who is stronger than the strong man armed (Luke xi. 22), Israel's oppressor, and whose very "weakness is stronger than men" (1 Cor. i. 25), shall "ransom" her "from him that was stronger than" she: Jer. xxxi. 11; Ps. xviii. 17.—*Andrew Robert Fausset.*

Verse 7.—"*Bring my soul out of prison,*" etc. As if he should say, O Lord, I confess I am a poor prisoner to sin and Satan, I would fain be set at liberty to believe thy word, and to do thy will; but, alas, I cannot. I find many a door fast shut upon me in this prison, and many a lock upon the doors, many lets and impediments which I am never able to remove; and therefore, gracious Lord, do that for me, which neither I myself nor all the friends I can make are ever able to do for me; pay the debts of thy poor prisoner in my blessed Surety, and set open the prison doors: "*Bring my soul out of prison, O LORD, that I may praise thy name!*"—*Matthew Lawrence, in "The Use and Practice of Faith,"* 1657.

Verse 7.—"*The righteous shall compass me about.*" In a circle, like a crown, as the word signifies; when delivered they should flock to him and come about him to see him and look at him, as a miracle of mercy, whose deliverance was marvellous; and to congratulate him upon it, and to join with him in praise unto God for it. The Targum is, "For my sake the righteous will make to thee a crown of praise."—*John Gill.*

Verse 7.—"*For thou shalt deal bountifully with me.*" Others' mercies ought to be the matter of our praises to God; and others' praises to God on our behalf ought to be both desired and rejoiced in by us.—*Matthew Henry.*

HINTS TO PREACHERS.

Verse 1.—I. A vivid memory—of what he did, and how, and when. II. A public declaration; from which we infer that his prayer cheered him, brought him succour in trouble, and deliverance out of it. III. A reasonable inference: he prays again.

Verses 1, 2.—I. Special seasons for prayer: times of complaint and trouble. II. Special prayer on such occasions; "I cried," "I make my supplication." "I poured out my complaint," "I showed before him my trouble." Spread the whole case before God, as Hezekiah did the letter from Sennacherib.—*G. R.*

Verse 2.—I. The true place for prayer—"before him." II. The freedom of prayer—"poured out." III. The unveiling of the heart in prayer—"shewed before him my trouble."

Verse 3 (*first clause*).—I. When. II. Then.

Verse 3 (*latter clause*).—Temptations. I. What form they take?—"snares." II. Who lay them?—"they." III. How do they lay them? Secretly, craftily —"in the way," frequently. IV. What becomes of the tempted believer? He lives to tell the tale, to warn others to glorify God.

Verse 4 (*last clause*).—The soul considered of no value. I. Consider the worth of the soul. 1. The soul will continue for ever. 2. The righteous will grow more happy, and the wicked more miserable. 3. A great price has been paid for it. II. Contrast the care we take of our souls, and our anxiety about worldly objects. 1. The solicitude we manifest for riches. 2. Our care in educating the intellects of our children. 3. Eagerness in pursuit of business, honour—even trifles. 4. How anxious about a human life! Describe the search for a lost child. 5. Contrast our care for souls and our Saviour's care for them: Paul's, Luther's, Whitefield's. III. Remember some things which show that this care does not exist. 1. If you do not statedly observe secret prayer. 2. If your soul is not burdened with the souls of others. 3. If you neglect family prayer, or observe it as a mere form. 4. If you do not regularly go to prayer-meetings. Remark: The great responsibility resting upon every Christian.—*Jacob Knapp, in "The Homiletic Monthly," 1882.*

Verse 4 (last clause).—The burden of souls. I. What is meant by care for souls? 1. To have a firm conviction of their value 2. To cherish tender solicitude for their welfare. 3. To feel alarming apprehensions of their danger. 4. To make zealous exertions for their salvation. II. Who ought specially to exercise this care? 1. Parents. 2. Teachers. 3. Ministers. 4. Members. III. The criminality of neglect. 1. It is ungrateful. 2. It is cruel. 3. It is fatal.—*W. W. Wythe, in "The Pulpit Analyst,"* 1870.

Verses 4, 5.—I. A terrible plight; no friend, no helper, no pitying heart. II. A touching prayer. A cry and a saying.

Verses 4, 5.—I. Human help fails most when most needed. 1. In outward troubles: "I looked," etc. 2. In soul troubles: "No man cared for my soul." II. Divine help is most given when most needed. A refuge and a portion when all others fail. Man has many friends in prosperity, one only in adversity.—*G. R.*

Verses 4, 5.—I. Why the saints make God their refuge, and the object of their faith and hope in their greatest afflictions. 1. God has given himself to the saints, in the covenant of grace, to be their God, and has promised that they shall be his people. 2. God stands in a most near relation to the saints, and condescends to sustain many endearing characters of love, which he fulfils to their advantage. 3. The saints, through the power of God's grace upon their souls, have chosen him for their portion, and their highest felicity. II. What perfections there are in God that render him a safe refuge for the saints, and a proper object of their confidence. 1. God is infinite in mercy. 2. God is infallible in wisdom. 3. God is boundless in power. 4. God is omniscient and omnipresent. 5. God is a Being whose love never changes. 6. God is an independent Being, and the Governor and Director of all things. III. The many sweet advantages, arising to the saints, from this practice of making God their refuge, in their greatest troubles. 1. They have been preserved from fainting under their heavy burdens. 2. They have derived from God new and seasonable supplies of divine grace and strength for service. 3. God has refreshed his saints with divine consolations for the future.—*John Farmer,* 1744.

Verse 5.—The soul choosing God. I. Deliberately: "I cried unto thee, I said." II. For all in all: "refuge," "portion." III. Before every other "in the land of the living."—*W. B. H.*

Verse 5.—"How we may bring our Hearts to bear Reproofs." See John Owen's Sermon in "The Morning Exercises," vol. ii. page 600, etc.; and in his "Works," vol. xvi. p. 23, etc.

Verse 6.—Two petitions and two arguments.

Verses 6, 7.—I. The language of Despondency. "I am brought very low." "My enemies are stronger than I." "My soul is in prison." II. Of Prayer. "Attend unto me." "Deliver me." "Bring me out of prison." III. Of Praise. 1. For the congratulation of others. 2. For his own deliverance and prosperity. —*G. R.*

Verse 6.—Low and Lowly. Here is David, I. In a low place; the depth of a cave. II. In a low way: "very low"; "stronger than I." III. But see,— "with the lowly is wisdom" (Prov. xi. 2); he prays. IV. The Lord "hath respect to the lowly," Ps. cxxxviii. 6. He will not pray in vain.—*W. B. H.*

Verse 7.—A prisoner. A freed-man. A singer. A centre. A wonder.

Verse 7.—Prison Dreams. I. What we image in our fetters. 1. Christ's brow girt about with rare praise. 2. Christ's people compassing and companying us in costliest service. 3. A new life of bounty and blessing when we get out. II. How far do our dreamings come true? Before peril and after; under conviction, and after conversion; sick room, and active service. III. The duty of fidelity to prison vows and lessons.—*W. B. H.*

Verse 7 (middle clause).—A Queen Bee. An under-shepherd. A warm hearth. A Museum of wonders. Or, they shall surround me, interested in my story—"out of prison"; drawn by my song—"praise thy name"; attracted by likeness of character, and admiring the goodness of the Lord."

Verse 7 (last clause).—Take this with Ps. cxvi. 7. "The Lord hath dealt bountifully with thee." Infer the future from the past.

PSALM CXLIII.

TITLE.—*A Psalm of David. It is so much like other Davidic Psalms that we accept the title without a moment's hesitation. David's history illustrates it, and his spirit breathes in it. Why it has been set down as one of the seven Penitential Psalms we can hardly tell; for it is rather a vindication of his own integrity, and an indignant prayer against his slanderers, than a confession of fault. It is true the second verse proves that he never dreamed of justifying himself before the Lord; but even in it there is scarcely the brokenness of penitence. It seems to us rather martial than penitential, rather a supplication for deliverance from trouble than a weeping acknowledgment of transgression. We suppose that seven penitentials were needed by ecclesiastical rabbis, and therefore this was impressed into the service. In truth, it is a mingled strain, a box of ointment composed of divers ingredients, sweet and bitter, pungent and precious. It is the outcry of an overwhelmed spirit, unable to abide in the highest state of spiritual prayer, again and again descending to bewail its deep temporal distress; yet evermore struggling to rise to the best things. The singer moans at intervals; the petitioner for mercy cannot withhold his cries for vindication. His hands are outstretched to heaven, but at his girdle hangs a sharp sword, which rattles in its scabbard as he closes his Psalm.*

DIVISION.—*This Psalm is divided by the Selah. We prefer to follow the natural cleavage, and therefore have made no other dissection of it. May the holy Spirit lead us into its inner meaning.*

EXPOSITION.

HEAR my prayer, O LORD, give ear to my supplications: in thy faithfulness answer me, *and* in thy righteousness.

2 And enter not into judgment with thy servant: for in thy sight shall no man living be justified.

3 For the enemy hath persecuted my soul; he hath smitten my life down to the ground; he hath made me to dwell in darkness, as those that have been long dead.

4 Therefore is my spirit overwhelmed within me; my heart within me is desolate.

5 I remember the days of old; I meditate on all thy works; I muse on the work of thy hands.

6 I stretch forth my hands unto thee: my soul *thirsteth* after thee, as a thirsty land. Selah.

1. "*Hear my prayer, O LORD, give ear to my supplication.*" In the preceding Psalm he began by declaring that he had cried unto the Lord; here he begs to be favourably regarded by Jehovah the living God, whose memorial is that he heareth prayer. He knew that Jehovah did hear prayer, and therefore he entreated him to hear his supplication, however feeble and broken it might be. In two forms he implores the one blessing of gracious audience:—" hear " and " give ear." Gracious men are so eager to be heard in prayer that they double their entreaties for that boon. The Psalmist desires to be heard and to be considered; hence he cries, " hear," and then " give ear." Our case is difficult, and we plead for special attention. Here it is probable that David wished his suit against his adversaries to be heard by the righteous Judge; confident that if he had a hearing in the matter whereof he was slanderously accused, he would be triumphantly acquitted. Yet while somewhat inclined thus to lay his case before the Court of King's Bench, he prefers rather to turn it all into a petition, and present it before the Court of Requests, hence he cries rather " hear my prayer " than " hear my suit." Indeed David is specially earnest that he himself, and the whole of his life, may not become the

subject of trial, for in that event he could not hope for acquittal. Observe that he offered so much pleading that his life became one continual *prayer;* but that petitioning was so varied in form that it broke out in many *supplications.*

"*In thy faithfulness answer me, and in thy righteousness.*" Saints desire to be answered as well as heard : they long to find the Lord faithful to his promise and righteous in defending the cause of justice. It is a happy thing when we dare appeal even to righteousness for our deliverance ; and this we can do upon gospel principles, for " if we confess our sins he is faithful and just to forgive us our sins." Even the sterner attributes of God are upon the side of the man who humbly trusts, and turns his trust into prayer. It is a sign of our safety when our interests and those of righteousness are blended. With God's faithfulness and righteousness upon our side we are guarded on the right hand and on the left. These are active attributes, and fully equal to the answering of any prayer which it would be right to answer. Requests which do not appeal to either of these attributes it would not be for the glory of God to hear, for they must contain desires for things unpromised, and unrighteous.

2. "*And enter not into judgment with thy servant.*" He had entreated for audience at the mercy-seat, but he has no wish to appear before the judgment-seat. Though clear before men, he could not claim innocence before God. Even though he knew himself to be the Lord's servant, yet he did not claim perfection, or plead merit ; for even as a servant he was unprofitable. If such be the humble cry of a servant, what ought to be the pleading of a sinner ? "*For in thy sight shall no man living be justified.*" None can stand before God upon the footing of the law. God's sight is piercing and discriminating; the slightest flaw is seen and judged; and therefore pretence and profession cannot avail where that glance reads all the secrets of the soul. In this verse David told out the doctrine of universal condemnation by the law long before Paul had taken his pen to write the same truth. To this day it stands true even to the same extent as in David's day : no man living even at this moment may dare to present himself for trial before the throne of the Great King on the footing of the law. This foolish age has produced specimens of a pride so rank that men have dared to claim perfection in the flesh ; but these vain-glorious boasters are no exception to the rule here laid down : they are but men, and poor specimens of men. When their lives are examined they are frequently found to be more faulty than the humble penitents before whom they vaunt their superiority.

3. "*For the enemy hath persecuted my soul.*" He has followed me up with perseverance, and has worried me as often as I have been within his reach. The attack was upon the soul or life of the Psalmist : our adversaries mean us the worst possible evil, their attacks are no child's play, they hunt for the precious life. "*He hath smitten my life down to the ground.*" The existence of David was made bitter by the cruelty of his enemy ; he was as one who was hurled down and made to lie upon the ground, where he could be trampled on by his assailant. Slander has a very depressing effect upon the spirits ; it is a blow which overthrows the mind as though it were knocked down with the fist. "*He hath made me to dwell in darkness, as those that have been long dead.*" The enemy was not content with felling his life to the ground—he would lay him lower still, even in the grave ; and lower than that if possible, for the enemy would shut up the saint in the darkness of hell if he could. David was driven by Saul's animosity to haunt caverns and holes, like an unquiet ghost ; he wandered out by night, and lay hid by day like an uneasy spirit which had long been denied the repose of the grave. Good men began to forget him, as though he had been long dead ; and bad men made ridicule of his rueful visage, as though it belonged not to a living man, but was dark with the shadow of the sepulchre. Poor David ! He was qualified to bless the house of the living, but he was driven to consort with the dead ! Such may be our case, and yet we may be very dear to the Lord. One thing is certain, the Lord who permits us to dwell in darkness among the dead, will surely bring us into light, and cause us to dwell with those who enjoy life eternal.

4. "*Therefore is my spirit overwhelmed within me ; my heart within me is desolate.*" David was no stoic : he felt his banishment, and smarted under the cruel assaults which were made upon his character. He felt perplexed and overturned, lonely and afflicted. He was a man of thought and feeling, and suffered both in spirit and in heart from the undeserved and unprovoked hostility of his persecutors. Moreover, he laboured under the sense of fearful loneliness ; he was for a while forsaken of his God, and his soul was exceeding heavy, even unto death. Such

words our Lord Jesus might have used : in this the Head is like the members, and the members are as the Head.

5. "*I remember the days of old.*" When we see nothing new which can cheer us, let us think upon old things. We once had merry days, days of deliverance, and joy and thanksgiving ; why not again ? Jehovah rescued his people in the ages which lie back, centuries ago ; why should he not do the like again ? We ourselves have a rich past to look back upon ; we have sunny memories, sacred memories, satisfactory memories, and these are as flowers for the bees of faith to visit, from whence they may make honey for present use. "*I meditate on all thy works.*" When my own works reproach me, thy works refresh me. If at the first view the deeds of the Lord do not encourage us, let us think them over again, ruminating and considering the histories of divine providence. We ought to take a wide and large view of *all* God's works ; for as a whole they work together for good, and in each part they are worthy of reverent study. "*I muse on the work of thy hands.*" This he had done in former days, even in his most trying hours. Creation had been the book in which he read of the wisdom and goodness of the Lord. He repeats his perusal of the page of nature, and counts it a balm for his wounds, a cordial for his cares, to see what the Lord has made by his skilful hands. When the work of our own hand grieves us, let us look to the work of God's hands. Memory, meditation, and musing are here set together as the three graces, ministering grace to a mind depressed and likely to be diseased. As David with his harp played away the evil spirit from Saul, so does he here chase away gloom from his own soul by holy communion with God.

6. "*I stretch forth my hands unto thee.*" He was eager for his God. His thoughts of God kindled in him burning desires, and these led to energetic expressions of his inward longings. As a prisoner whose feet are bound extends his hands in supplication when there is hope of liberty, so does David. "*My soul thirsteth after thee, as a thirsty land.*" As the soil cracks, and yawns, and thus opens its mouth in dumb pleadings, so did the Psalmist's soul break with longings. No heavenly shower had refreshed him from the sanctuary : banished from the means of grace, his soul felt parched and dry, and he cried out, " My soul to thee " ; nothing would content him but the presence of his God. Not alone did he extend his hands, but his heart was stretched out towards the Lord. He was athirst for the Lord. If he could but feel the presence of his God he would no longer be overwhelmed or dwell in darkness ; nay, everything would turn to peace and joy.

Selah.—It was time to pause, for the supplication had risen to agony point. Both harp-strings and heart-strings were strained, and needed a little rest to get them right again for the second half of the song.

7 Hear me speedily, O LORD : my spirit faileth : hide not thy face from me, lest I be like unto them that go down into the pit.

8 Cause me to hear thy lovingkindness in the morning ; for in thee do I trust : cause me to know the way wherein I should walk ; for I lift up my soul unto thee.

9 Deliver me, O LORD, from mine enemies : I flee unto thee to hide me.

10 Teach me to do thy will ; for thou *art* my God : thy spirit *is* good ; lead me into the land of uprightness.

11 Quicken me, O LORD, for thy name's sake : for thy righteousness' sake bring my soul out of trouble.

12 And of thy mercy cut off mine enemies, and destroy all them that afflict my soul : for I *am* thy servant.

7. "*Hear me speedily, O LORD : my spirit faileth.*" If long delayed, the deliverance would come too late. The afflicted suppliant faints, and is ready to die. His life is ebbing out ; each moment is of importance ; it will soon be all over with him. No argument for speed can be more powerful than this. Who will not run to help a suppliant when his life is in jeopardy ? Mercy has wings to its heels when misery is in extremity. God will not fail when our spirit fails, but the rather he will hasten his course and come to us on the wings of the wind. "*Hide not thy face from me, lest I be like unto them that go down into the pit.*" Communion with God is so dear to a true heart that the withdrawal of it makes the man

feel as though he were ready to die and perish utterly. God's withdrawals reduce the heart to despair, and take away all strength from the mind. Moreover, his absence enables adversaries to work their will without restraint; and thus, in a second way, the persecuted one is like to perish. If we have God's countenance we live, but if he turns his back upon us we die. When the Lord looks with favour upon our efforts we prosper, but if he refuses to countenance them we labour in vain.

8. *"Cause me to hear thy lovingkindness in the morning; for in thee do I trust."* Lord, my sorrow makes me deaf,—cause me to hear: there is but one voice that can cheer me—cause me to hear thy lovingkindness; that music I would fain enjoy at once—cause me to hear it in the morning, at the first dawning hour. A sense of divine love is to the soul both dawn and dew; the end of the night of weeping, the beginning of the morning of joy. Only God can take away from our weary ears the din of our care, and charm them with the sweet notes of his love. Our plea with the Lord is our faith; if we are relying upon him, he cannot disappoint us: " in thee do I trust" is a sound and solid argument with God. He who made the ear will cause us to hear: he who is love itself will have the kindness to bring his lovingkindness before our minds. *"Cause me to know the way wherein I should walk; for I lift up my soul unto thee."* The Great First Cause must cause us to hear and to know. Spiritual senses are dependent upon God, and heavenly knowledge comes from him alone. To know the way we ought to take is exceedingly needful, for how can we be exact in obedience to a law with which we are not acquainted? or how can there be an ignorant holiness? If we know not the way, how shall we keep in it? If we know not wherein we should walk, how shall we be likely to follow the right path? The Psalmist lifts up his soul; faith is good at a dead lift: the soul that trusts will rise. We will not allow our hope to sink, but we will strive to get up and rise out of our daily griefs. This is wise. When David was in any difficulty as to his way he lifted his soul towards God himself, and then he knew that he could not go very far wrong. If the soul will not rise of itself we must lift it, lift it up unto God. This is good argument in prayer: surely the God to whom we endeavour to lift up our soul will condescend to show us what he would have us to do. Let us attend to David's example, and when our heart is low, let us heartily endeavour to lift it up, not so much to comfort as to the Lord himself.

9. *"Deliver me, O LORD, from mine enemies."* Many foes beset us, we cannot overcome them, we cannot even escape from them; but Jehovah can and will rescue us if we pray to him. The weapon of all-prayer will stand us in better stead than sword and shield. *"I flee unto thee to hide me."* This was a good result from his persecutions. That which makes us flee to our God may be an ill wind, but it blows us good. There is no cowardice in such flight, but much holy courage. God can hide us out of reach of harm, and even out of sight of it. He is our hiding-place; Jesus has made himself the refuge of his people: the sooner, and the more entirely we flee to him the better for us. Beneath the crimson canopy of our Lord's atonement believers are completely hidden; let us abide there and be at rest. In the seventh verse our poet cried, " Hide not thy face," and here he prays, " Hide me." Note also how often he uses the words " unto thee "; he is after his God; he must travel in that direction by some means, even though he may seem to be beating a retreat; his whole being longs to be near the Lord. It is possible that such thirstings for God will be left unsupplied? Never, while the Lord is love.

10. *"Teach me to do thy will."* How childlike—" teach me "! How practical —" Teach me to do "! How undivided in obedience—" to do thy will "! To do all of it, let it be what it may. This is the best form of instruction, for its source is God, its object is holiness, its spirit is that of hearty loyalty. The man is hidden in the Lord, and spends his peaceful life in learning the will of his Preserver. A heart cannot long be desolate which is thus docile. *"For thou art my God."* Who else can teach me as thou canst? Who else will care to do it but my God? Thou hast given me thyself, thou wilt surely give me thy teaching. If I have thee, may I not ask to have thy perfect mind? When the heart can sincerely call Jehovah " my God," the understanding is ready to learn of him, the will is prepared to obey him, the whole man is eager to please him. *"Thy spirit is good."* God is all spirit and all good. His essence is goodness, kindness, holiness: it is his nature to do good, and what greater good can he do to us than to hear such a prayer as that which follows—*"Lead me into the land of uprightness"*? David would fain he among

the godly, in a land of another sort from that which had cast him out. He sighed for the upland meadows of grace, the table-lands of peace, the fertile plains of communion. He could not reach them of himself ; he must be led there. God, who is good, can best conduct us to the goodly land. There is no inheritance like a portion in the land of promise, the land of precept, the land of perfectness. He who teaches us must put us into leading-strings, and guide and conduct us to his own dwelling-place in the country of holiness. The way is long, and steep, and he who goes without a divine leader will faint on the journey ; but with Jehovah to lead, it is delightful to follow, and there is neither stumbling nor wandering.

11. *"Quicken me, O LORD, for thy name's sake."* Oh for more life as well as more light ! Teaching and leading call for invigoration, or we shall be dull scholars and slow pilgrims. Jehovah, the Lord and giver of life, is the only one from whom life can come to renew and revive us ;—hence, the prayer is to him only. Perchance a servant might teach and lead, but only the Master can enliven. We are often near to death, and hence each one may fitly cry, " Quicken *me* " ; but what is there in us which we can plead as a reason for such a favour ? Nothing, literally nothing. We must beg it for his name's sake. He must quicken us because he is the living God, the loving God, the Lord who delighteth in mercy. What blessed arguments lie clustered together in his glorious name ! We need never cease praying for want of acceptable pleas ; and we may always fall back upon the one before us —" thy name's sake." It will render the name of Jehovah the more glorious in the eyes of men if he creates a high degree of spiritual life in his servants ; and this is a reason for his doing so, which we may urge with much confidence.

"For thy righteousness' sake bring my soul out of trouble." Let men see that thou art on the side of the right, and that thou wilt not allow the wicked to ride rough-shod over those who trust in thee. Thou hast promised to succour thy people ; thou art not unrighteous to forget their work of faith ; thou art, on the contrary, righteous in answering sincere prayer, and in comforting thy people. David was heavily afflicted. Not only was there trouble in his soul, but his soul was in trouble ; plunged in it as in a sea, shut up in it as in a prison. God could bring him out of it, and especially he could at once lift up his soul or spirit out of the ditch. The prayer is an eager one, and the appeal a bold one. We may be sure that trouble was soon over when the Lord heard such supplications.

12. *"And of thy mercy cut off mine enemies, and destroy all them that afflict my soul."* He believes that it will be so, and thus prophesies the event ; for the words may be read as a declaration, and it is better so to understand them. We could not *pray* just so with our Christian light ; but under Old Testament arrangements the spirit of it was congruous to the law. It is a petition which justice sanctions, but the spirit of love is not at home in presenting it. *We*, as Christians, turn the petition to spiritual use only. Yet David was of so generous a mind, and dealt so tenderly with Saul, that he could hardly have meant all that his words are made in our version to say. *"For I am thy servant ; "* and therefore I hope that my Master will protect me in his service, and grant me victory while I fight his battles. It is a warrior's prayer, and smells of the dust and smoke of battle. It was heard, and therefore it was not asking amiss. Still there is a more excellent way.

EXPLANATORY NOTES AND QUAINT SAYINGS.

Whole Psalm.—This Psalm of David most aptly answereth to that Psalm which precedeth it ; for in Ps. cxlii. he showeth that he prayed, repeating it twice (verse 1) ; and here he twice saith, " Hear my prayer, give ear to my supplication." In Psalm cxlii. (verse 3) he saith, " When my spirit was overwhelmed within me "; here (verse 4), " My spirit is overwhelmed within me."—*John Mayer.*

Whole Psalm.—The promise referred to throughout this octave of Psalms [cxxxviii—cxlv.] is that recorded in 2 Sam. vii. 12, etc., " When thy days be fulfilled . . . . . I will set up thy seed after thee . . . . . and I will establish his kingdom . . . . . If he commit iniquity, I will chasten him . . . . . But my mercy shall not depart away from him ; and thine house and thy kingdom shall be established for ever." What fixes the connection of the Psalm with the history is the frequent application of the term *"Thy* (Jehovah's) *servant,"* by David to himself in the latter, as in verses 2 and 12 of the former. Jehovah had first used it of David, " Tell to my servant, to David ; " David therefore fastens on it as his plea again and again (2 Sam. vii. 5, 9—21, 25—29). David's plea, " For I am thy servant," is no boast of his service, but a magnifying of God's electing grace : " Who am I, O Lord God ? and what is my house, that thou hast brought me hitherto ? " 2 Sam. vii. 18.

The cry (verse 6) *"My soul thirsteth after thee as a thirsty land,"* answers to David's own words in Psalm lxiii. 1, when he was fleeing from Absalom, and still in the wilderness of Judah (title, Ps. lxiii.) on the near side of Jordan : " My soul *thirsteth* for thee." The history here again is an undesigned agreement with the Psalm : (2 Sam. xvi. 2, 14,) " The King, and all the people with him, came *weary,* and refreshed themselves " with Ziba's fruits ; also xvii. 2. The Hebrew for *"thirsty "* in Psalm cxliii. is the same as for *"weary "* in lxiii. 1, and in 2 Sam. xvi. 14, and means " panting," " weary," " thirsting."—*Andrew Robert Fausset, in "Studies in the CL. Psalms,"* 1876.

Whole Psalm.—At the making of this Psalm (as it plainly appeareth) David was cast into some desperate danger ; whether by Saul when he was forced to flee into the cave, as in the former Psalm, or by Absalom his son, or by any other, it is uncertain. Howsoever, in this he complaineth grievously to God of the malice of his enemies, and desireth God to hear his prayers, he acknowledgeth that he suffereth those things by God's just judgment, most humbly craving mercy for his sins ; desiring not only to be restored, but also to be governed by God's Spirit, that he may dedicate and consecrate the rest of his life to God's service. This worthy Psalm, then, containeth these three things. First, a confession of his sins. Secondly, a lamentation over his injuries. Thirdly, a supplication for temporal deliverance and spiritual graces.—*Archibald Symson.*

Whole Psalm.—It is not without some use to observe in this Psalm how the heart of its devout composer turned alternately from spiritual to temporal, and again from temporal to spiritual subjects. He first complains of *his sins,* and begs for *mercy ;* then of *his enemies,* and prays for *deliverance.* Then he laments his darkness and pleads for the light of God's countenance, and for wisdom, and understanding. After this, the thought of his enemies rushes in again upon his soul, and he flees to God for protection. Lastly, he again puts up his prayer for wisdom and holiness : " Teach me to do thy will ; for thou art my God : thy spirit is good ; lead me into the land of uprightness." This is a peculiarly important petition : before he had prayed to know the way in which he should walk, he now prays that he may walk in it.—*John Fawcett,* 1769—1851.

Whole Psalm.—This is appointed by the Church for Ash-Wednesday, and is the seventh and last of the Penitential Psalms. These seven Penitential Psalms are also sometimes called " the Special Psalms," and have long been used in the Church as the completest and most spiritual acts of repentance which she possesses. They have sometimes been considered as directed against the seven deadly sins ; as, for instance, Psalm vi. against Wrath ; Ps. xxxii. against Pride ; Ps. xxxviii. against Gluttony ; Ps. li. against Impurity ; Ps. cii. against Covetousness ; Ps. cxxx. against Envy ; and the present Psalm against Indifference, or Carelessness.— *J. W. Burgon.*

Verse 1.—*"Hear my prayer, O Lord,"* etc. Alas, O Lord, if thou hear not my prayer, I were as good not pray at all ; and if thou hear it, and give not ear unto it, it were as good thou didst not hear it at all. O, therefore, *"hear my prayer, O God, and give ear to my supplications ";* that neither my praying may be lost for want of thy hearing it, nor thy hearing it be lost for want of thy attending it. When I only make a prayer to God, it seems enough that he hear it ; but when I make a supplication, it requires that he give ear unto it ; for seeing a supplication hath a greater intention in the setting out, it cannot without a greater attention be entertained.

But what niceness of words is this ? as though it were not all one *" to hear "* and *" to give ear "* ? or as though there were any difference between a prayer and a supplication ? Is it not perhaps so indeed ? for hearing sometimes may be only passive, where giving ear is always active ; and seeing Christ, we doubt not, heard the woman of Canaan's first cry, while it was a prayer ; but gave no ear till her second cry, when it was grown to a supplication. However it be, as thy hearing, O God, without giving ear would be to no purpose, so thy giving ear without giving answer would do me no good; O, therefore, "*answer me*," O God; for if thou answer not my prayer, how canst thou answer my expectation? My prayer is but the seed; it is thy answer that makes the harvest. If thou shouldst not answer me at all, I could not hope for any harvest at all; and if thou shouldst answer me, and not "*in thy righteousness*," that would be a harvest indeed, but nothing but of blasted corn. Therefore, answer me, O God, but "in thy righteousness"; for thy righteousness never made an unpleasing answer. It was an answer in thy righteousness which thou madest to Noah: " My spirit shall not always strive with man; for the imagination of man's heart is evil from his infancy." It was an answer in thy righteousness which thou madest to Abraham: " Fear not; I will be thy shield, and thy exceeding great reward." It was an answer in thy righteousness which thou madest to the thief upon the cross : " This day thou shalt be with me in paradise." Oh, then, answer me also in thy righteousness, O God, and then the harvest of my hope will be as plentiful as the seven years of plenty foretold by Joseph.—*Sir Richard Baker.*

Verse 1.—"*Hear my prayer*," . . . "*give ear to my supplications*," . . . "*answer me.*" He doth here three times repeat his earnest desire to be heard, as in the fifth Psalm four times he doubleth and ingeminateth this same suit to be heard. . . . When he doubleth his request of hearing, he would have God hear him with both his ears, that is, most attentively and readily: so instant is a troubled mind that he desireth the prayer he putteth up to be remembered, as was said by the angel to the centurion : " Thy prayer and almsdeeds are come up before God": Acts x. 4. —*Archibald Symson.*

Verse 1.—"*In thy faithfulness answer me, and in thy righteousness.*" It was thy righteousness that thou didst make the promise, but it is thy faithfulness that thou wilt keep thy promise: and seeing I am certain of thy making it, how can I be doubtful of thy keeping it ? If thou shouldst not answer me in thy righteousness, yet thou shouldst be righteous still; but if thou shouldst not answer me in thy faithfulness, thou shouldst not be faithful still.—*Sir Richard Baker.*

Verse 1.—"*Answer me in thy righteousness.*" Forgiveness is not inconsistent with the truth or righteousness, and the pardon which in mercy God bestows upon the sinner is bestowed in justice to the well-beloved Son who accepted and discharged the sinner's obligations. This is an infinitely precious truth, and the hearts of thousands in every age have been sustained and gladdened by it. A good old Christian woman in humble life so fully realized this, that when a revered servant of God asked her, as she lay on her dying pillow, the ground of her hope for eternity, she replied, with great composure, " I rely on the justice of God"; adding, however, when the reply excited surprise, " justice, not to me, but to my Substitute, *in whom I trust.—Robert Macdonald, in "From Day to Day ; or, Helpful Words for Christian Life,"* 1879.

Verse 2.—"*Enter not into judgment with thy servant.*" The Divine justice has just been invoked in the first verse ; and now the appellant suddenly seems to deprecate it. These verses really sum up the apparent paradox of the Book of Job (See Job iv. 17, ix. 2, 32, xiv. 3, *seq.*, xv. 14, xxii. 4, etc.) In one breath Job frequently pours forth pathetic protestations of his innocence, and a dread lest God should take him at his word, and arraign him for trial. The godly man, in his desire to have his character vindicated before man, appeals to the just Judge, but instantly falls back with a guilty sense that before his tribunal none can stand :

" For merit lives from man to man,
And not from man, O Lord, to thee."
A. S. Aglen.

Verse 2.—He doth not pray absolutely that God " would not enter into judgment with him," for this were to forego his government of the world ; but that he would not do so on account of his own duties and obedience. But if so be these duties and obedience did answer, in any sense or way, what is required of us as a righteousness unto justification, there was no reason why he should deprecate a trial by them, or upon them.—*John Owen.*

Verse 2.—He doth not say, " with an enemy, a rebel, a traitor, an impenitent sinner ; " but " *with thy servant*," one that is devoted to thy fear, one that is consecrated to thy service, one that is really and indeed "wholly thine, as much and as fully as he can be." As if he had said, " Lord, if the holiest, purest, best of men should come and stand before thee in judgment, or plead with thee, they must needs be cast in their cause. ' If thou, Lord, shouldest mark iniquities,' alas ! ' O Lord, who shall stand ? ' " Psalm cxxx. 3.—*Thomas Lye* (1621—1684), *in "The Morning Exercises."*

Verse 2.—*"Enter not into judgment with thy servant,"* for thou hast already entered into judgment with thy Son, and laid upon him the iniquity of us all. *"Enter not into judgment with thy servant,"* for thy servant enters into judgment with himself ; and " if we will judge ourselves we shall not be judged."—*Matthew Henry.*

Verse 2.—Not the proudest philosopher among the Gentiles, nor the most precise Pharisee among the Jews ; we may go yet further and say, not the holiest saint that ever lived, can stand righteous before that bar. God hath nailed that door up, that none can for ever enter by a law-righteousness into life and happiness. This way to heaven is like the northern passage to the Indies, whoever attempts it is sure to be frozen up before he gets half way thither.—*William Gurnall.*

Verse 2.—*"Enter not into judgment,"* &c. Some years ago I visited a poor young woman dying with consumption. She was a stranger in our town, and had been there a few weeks before, some time in her girlhood, and had attended my Sabbath-school class. What did I find was her only stay, and hope, and comfort in the view of the dark valley of the shadow of death, which was drawing down upon her ? One verse of a Psalm she had learned at the class, and never forgot. She repeated it with clasped hands, piercing eyes, and thin voice trembling from her white lips :

> " Thy servant also bring thou not
> In judgment to be tried :
> Because no living man can be
> In thy sight justify'd."

No—no sinner can endure sight of thee, O God, if he tries to be self-justified. —*James Comper Gray, in "The Biblical Museum,"* 1879.

Verse 2.—*"Enter not into judgment with thy servant."* We read of a certain Dutch divine, who being to die, was full of fears and doubts. And when some said to him, " You have been so active and faithful, why should you fear ? " Oh, said he, the judgment of man and the judgment of God are different.—*John Trapp.*

Verse 2.—*"Enter not into judgment."* A metaphor taken from the course pursued by those who seek to recover the very utmost to which they are entitled by strict legal process. Compare Job xxii. 4, 5. In a similar sense we are commanded to pray to God that he will forgive us our debts.—*Daniel Cresswell.*

Verse 2.—There is probably here a tacit reference to the great transgression, the consequences of which followed David all his days.—*William Walford.*

Verse 2.—*"Thy servant."* A servant is one who obeys the will of another. . . . . There were these four ways in which one might come to be a servant,—by birth, by purchase, by conquest, and by voluntary engagement. Some were servants in one of the ways, and some in another. There were servants who were born in the master's house, servants who were bought with the master's money, servants who were the captives of his sword and bow, and servants who had freely engaged themselves to do his work. . . . In the case of the believer there is something that is peculiar and remarkable. He is God's servant by birth. But he is more—he is God's servant by purchase. And that is not all : he is God's servant by conquest. Yes, and by voluntary engagement too. He is the servant of God, not in some one of the four ways, but in all of them together.—*Andrew Gray* (1805—1861), *in "Gospel Contrasts and Parallels."*

Verse 2.—Not only the worst of my sins, but the best of my duties speak me a child of Adam.—*William Beveridge.*

Verse 2.—So far from being able to answer for my sins, I cannot answer even for my righteousness.—*Bernard of Clairvaux*, 1091—1153.

Verse 2.—A young man once said to me : " I do not think I am a sinner." I asked him if he would be willing his mother or sister should know all he had done, or said, or thought,—all his motions and all his desires. After a moment he said : " No, indeed, I should not like to have them know ; no, not for the world." " Then can you dare to say, in the presence of a holy God, who knows every thought of your heart, ' I do not commit sin ' ? "—*John B. Gough, in "Sunlight and Shadow,"* 1881.

Verse 3.—*"For the enemy,"* etc. If ever trouble be just cause for calling upon thee, how can mine but be most just, when *"the enemy hath persecuted my soul, hath smitten my life down to the ground, and hath made me to dwell in darkness, as those that have been long dead "* ? All this *" the enemy "* hath done unto me : but what enemy ? Is it not the enemy of all mankind, who hath singled me out, as it were to a duel ? And can *I* resist him myself alone, whom the whole army of mankind cannot ? But it is not the enemy of thyself, O God, who is but my enemy because I am thy servant ? And wilt thou see thy servants persecuted—in thy cause persecuted —and not protect them ? Shall I suffer, grievously suffer, for thy sake, and wilt thou forsake me ? Alas, O Lord ; if they were but some light evils that are inflicted upon me I would bear them without complaining, and never make my moan to thee about them ; but they are the three greatest miseries that can be thought of ; the greatest persecution, the greatest overthrow, and the greatest captivity. For what persecution so grievous as to be persecuted in my soul ? for he plays no less a game than for souls : he casts indeed at the body sometimes, and sometimes at goods, yet these are but the bye ; the main of his aim is at the soul ; for if he can otherwise win the soul he cares not much for either body or goods, but rather makes use of them to keep men in security ; for whatsoever he doth, whatsoever he leaves undone, it is all done but in persecution of the soul ; and he can persecute as well with prosperity as with adversity, and knows how to fit their several application. It seems as if he takes me for another Job ; he sees he can do no good upon me with fawning and clawing, and therefore falls now to quarrelling and striking ; and he strikes no light blows ; for *" he hath stricken my life down to the ground "* ; and lower would have struck it, if thou, God, hadst not broken his blow. He strikes me downward, to keep me from heaven, as much as he can : and now that he sees me down, he lets not me rest so neither ; but seizeth upon me, and being himself the prince of darkness, hath kept me in darkness ; not for a night or two, as men stay at their inn, but for a much longer time, as at their dwelling : and it is no ordinary darkness that he hath made me to dwell in, but even the darkness of dead men ; and that in the highest degree, as those that have been long dead. They that have been dead but a while are yet remembered sometimes, and sometimes talked of ; but they that have been long dead are as quite forgotten as if they had never been ; and such, alas, am I. So long have I been made to dwell in darkness, as if I had been dead many years ago, that he that would seek to find me out must be fain to look for me amongst the tombs and monuments. Indeed, to dwell in darkness is no better than the house of death : for as long as we are in life, if we want sometimes the light of the sun, yet the light of a candle will serve to supply it ; but I, alas, am kept in such darkness that neither the sunshine of thy gospel nor the lantern of thy law gives any light unto me. I cannot with confidence say, as once I did, " Thou, O Lord, shalt light my candle for me "; and as a body being dead grows cold and stiff, and is not to be bowed, so my soul with continuance in sinning is grown hardened, and, as it were, stiff in sin ; that it is as hard a matter to make me flexible to any goodness as to bring a body long dead to life again.—*Sir Richard Baker.*

Verse 3.—*"To dwell in darkness."* To seek my safety in holes and obscure places in the wilderness. See 2 Sam. xvii. 16. *"As those that have been long dead."* That is, where I seem to be buried alive, and to have no more hopes of being restored to a happy condition in this world than those that have been long dead have of living again in it.—*Thomas Fenton.*

Verse 4.—*"Therefore is my spirit overwhelmed,"* etc. David was not only a great saint, but a great soldier, and yet even he was sometimes ready to faint in the day of adversity. " Howl, fir trees, if the cedars be shaken."—*Matthew Henry.*

Verse 4 *(second clause).* — *"Within me "* — literally, *"in the midst of me"* ; implying how *deeply* the feeling had penetrated. *"Is desolate,"* or rather, *"is stupefied,"* in a similar sense to that of the Hebrew (Isa. lix. 16 ; lxiii. 5 ; Dan. viii. 27). So the Chaldaic, The LXX., Vulgate, Arabic, and Syriac, *"is agitated."* —*Andrew Robert Fausset.*

Verse 4.—*"Is desolate."* Or rather, " is full of amazement," literally, " astonies itself " ; seeks to comprehend the mystery of its sufferings, and is ever beaten back upon itself in its perplexity : such is the full force of the reflexive conjugation here employed.—*J. J. Stewart Perowne.*

Verses 4, 5.—How poor a man's judgment can be formed of a man's state from the considerations of comfort only. A holy man, we clearly see, may be void of comfort; his spirit may be overwhelmed, and his heart desolate. Nay, was it not so even with the holy Jesus himself? was he not very heavy, and his soul exceeding sorrowful even unto death? But never did the Saviour's faith and submission to his Father's will shine more brightly than in that hour of darkness. And David's faith also rises to meet the occasion. His trial is great, and his faith is great also. Hardly when he is on the mount of praise, and singing his songs of Zion in the most triumphant strain, does he appear more admirable than when struggling through this painful conflict. He is troubled on every side, yet not removed; perplexed, but not in despair; persecuted, but not forsaken; cast down, but not destroyed. He has no arm of flesh to trust to, and nothing within himself to support his hope; but with what simplicity, and energy of trust, does he betake himself to God, revolving in his memory past seasons of deliverance, and staying his mind on the power and truth of Jehovah! " I remember the days of old; I meditate on all thy works; I muse on the work of thy hands."—*John Fawcett.*

Verse 5.—"*I remember the days of old; I meditate,*" etc. This meditation gives an ease to the overwhelming of my spirits, a comfort to the desolateness of my heart; for I am thinking sometimes upon Jonah, how he was overwhelmed with waters and swallowed up of a whale, and yet at last delivered; sometimes I am thinking of Joseph, how he was bound and left desolate in a pit, and yet at last relieved; and then I meditate thus with myself,—Is God's power confined to persons? could he deliver them in their extremities, and can he not deliver me in mine?—*Sir Richard Baker.*

Verse 5.—"*I meditate on all thy works.*" Let us look for God in the future more earnestly than we have done in the past,—look for him in vineyards and orchards and harvest fields,—in the bright plumage of birds, and the delicate bloom of fruit, and the sweet gracefulness of flowers,—in the dense foliage of the forest, and the sparse heather of the moor,—in the rich luxuriance of fertile valleys, and the rugged grandeur of the everlasting hills,—in the merry dance of the rivulet, and the majestic tides of the ocean,—in the gay colours of the rainbow, and the splendour of the starry heavens,—in the gentle radiance of the moon, and the gorgeous light of setting suns,—in the clear azure sky, and the weird pageantry of clouds,—in the snow-mantled wintry landscape, and the brilliant effulgence of a summer's noon,—in the virgin loveliness of spring, and in the pensive fading beauty of autumn,—let us look for him with an earnest, eager, and unwearied gaze, till we see him to be a God of wisdom as well as power, of love as well as sovereignty, of beauty as well as glory.—*A. W. Momerie, in "The Origin of Evil, and other Sermons,"* 1881.

Verses 5, 6.—"*I meditate.*" "*I stretch forth my hands.*" Meditation is prayer's handmaid to wait on it, both before and after the performance of supplication. It is as the plough before the sower, to prepare the heart for the duty of prayer; and as the harrow after the sower, to cover the seed, when 'tis sown. As the hopper feeds the mill with grist, so does meditation supply the heart with matter for prayer. —*William Gurnall.*

Verse 6.—"*I stretch forth my hands unto thee.*" As a poor beggar for an alms. Beggary here is not the easiest and poorest trade, but the hardest and richest of all other.—*John Trapp.*

Verse 6.—"*I stretch forth my hands unto thee,*" as if I were in hope thou wouldst take me by the hand and draw me to thee.—*Sir Richard Baker.*

Verse 6.—"*My soul thirsteth after thee,*" etc. Alas! this thirst is rare to be found. Worldly thirsts there are in many: the drunkard's thirst, Deut. xxix. 19; the worldling's thirst, Hab. ii. 5; the epicure's thirst, whose belly is his god, Phil. iii. 19; the ambitious man's thirst—Diotrephes, 3 John 9; and the malicious man's thirst, the blood thirsty, Ps. v. 6. Thirst after these things doth keep away that thirst after grace without which we shall never escape Dives' thirst in hell, Luke xvi. 24. If we have a godly thirst, it will appear by diligence in frequenting the place and means of grace, Prov. viii. 34; brute beasts for want of water will break through hedges, and grace-thirsty souls will make their ways through all encumbrances to come where they may have satisfaction.—*Thomas Pierson,* 1570—1633.

Verse 6.—"*My soul thirsteth after thee, as a thirsty land.*" He declareth his vehement affection to God by a very pretty similitude, taken from the ground which is thirsty by the long drought of summer, wherein the earth, rent in pieces, as it were, and with open mouth through long thirst, seeketh drink from heaven. By which he showeth that he came to God as destitute of natural substance, and therefore seeketh from above that which he lacked. So in all his extremities he looked ever upward ; from above he seeketh help and comfort. Albeit we be in extremity, and as it were rent asunder, yet here is comfort,—there are waters in heaven which will refresh us, if we gape after them. Here is a blessing—those that thirst shall be satisfied. If we thirst for mercy, for deliverance, for spiritual or temporal comfort, we shall be satisfied therewith ; for if God heard the prayers of Hagar and Ishmael being athirst in the wilderness, and opened unto them a fountain (Gen. xxi. 17, 19), will he forsake Isaac, the child of promise ? If he heard Samson in the bitterness of his heart, when he said, " I die from thirst," and opened a spring out of the jawbone of an ass (Jud. xv. 19), will he forsake us in time of our distress, if we thirst aright ?—*Archibald Symson.*

Verse 6.—"*My soul thirsteth after thee, as a thirsty land.*" Sir John Chardin, in his MSS. says :—" The lands of the East, which the great dryness there causes to crack, are the ground of this figure, which is certainly extremely beautiful ; for these dry lands have chinks too deep for a person to see the bottom of : this may be observed in the Indies more than anywhere, a little before the rains fall, and wherever the lands are rich and hard."—*Harmer's Observations.*

Verse 6.—"*I stretch forth my hands unto thee,*" etc. It is not a strange thing, then, for the soul to find its life in God. This is its native air : God as the Environment of the soul has been from the remotest age the doctrine of all the deepest thinkers in religion. How profoundly Hebrew poetry is saturated with this high thought will appear when we try to conceive of it with this left out. True poetry is only science in another form. And long before it was possible for religion to give scientific expression to its greatest truths, men of insight uttered themselves in Psalms which could not have been truer to Nature had the most modern light controlled the inspiration. " As the hart panteth after the water-brooks, so panteth my soul after thee, O God." What fine sense of the natural analogy of the natural and spiritual does not underlie these words. As the hart after its environment, so man after his ; as the water-brooks are fitly designed to meet the natural wants, so fitly does God implement the spiritual need of man. It will be noticed that in the Hebrew poets the longing for God never strikes one as morbid, or unnatural to the men who uttered it. It is as natural for them to long for God as for the swallow to seek her nest. Throughout all their images no suspicion rises within us that they are exaggerating. We feel how truly they are reading themselves, their deepest selves. No false note occurs in all their aspiration. There is no weariness even in their ceaseless sighing, except the lover's weariness for the absent—if they would fly away, it is only to be at rest. Men who have no soul can only wonder at this. Men who have a soul, but with little faith, can only envy it. How joyous a thing it was to the Hebrews to seek their God ! How artlessly they call upon him to entertain them in his pavilion, to cover them with his feathers, to hide them in his secret place, to hold them in the hollow of his hand, or stretch around them the everlasting arms ! These men were true children of nature. As the humming-bird among its own palm-trees, as the ephemera in the sunshine of a summer evening, so they lived their joyous lives. And even the full share of the sadder experiences of life which came to all of them but drove them the further into the secret place, and led them with more consecration to make, as they expressed it, "*the Lord their portion.*" All that has been said since from Marcus Aurelius to Swedenborg, from Augustine to Schleiermacher, of a besetting God as the full complement of humanity is but a repetition of the Hebrew poets' faith. And even the New Testament has nothing higher to offer man than this. The Psalmist's " God is our refuge and strength " is only the earlier form, less defined, less practicable, but not less noble, of Christ's " Come unto me, and I will give you rest."—*Henry Drummond, in* "*Natural Law in the Spiritual World,*" 1884.

Verses 6, 7.—"*I stretch forth my hands. . . . Hear me,*" etc. So will the weary hands be raised yet again, through faith in him who stretched forth his hands upon the cross. So will the fainting soul wait and long for the outpouring of his grace, who upon the cross said, " I thirst." We shall thirst for our salvation, even as the parched-up fields and dying herbs seem to gasp and pant like living things for the sweet and cheering showers in the fierce heat of summer. So will the soul cry to be heard, and that soon, lest its faith grow faint with delay ; and the hiding of God's face, the denying of his smile of pardon, will press on the spirit like sickness, and weigh it down like the heaviness of death.—*J. W. Burgon.*

Verse 7.—*"Hear me speedily."* David is in trouble, and he betakes himself to prayer. Prayer is the sovereign remedy the godly fly to in all their extremities. The saints in sorrows have fled for comfort and healing unto prayers and supplications. Heaven is a shop full of all good things—there are stored up blessings and mercies ; this the children of God know who fly to this shop in their troubles, begging for help from this holy sanctuary. " In the day of my trouble I sought the Lord": Ps. lxxvii. 2. When any vexation makes our life grievous unto us, what should we seek but help ? of whom should we seek, but of the Lord ? how should we seek, but by prayer ? . . . . *"Speedily."* His request is not only for hearing, but for speedy hearing : *"Hear me, and hear me speedily ; "* answer, and answer quickly. This is the tone and tune of men in distress. Man in misery earnestly sues for speedy delivery. In our afflictions and troubles, deliverance, though it should come with wings, we never think it comes soon enough. Weak man cannot content himself to know he shall have help, unless it be present help.—*Thomas Calvert,* 1647.

Verse 7.—*"My spirit faileth."* This is David's first reason to move the Lord ; he is at the last cast and even giving up the ghost with long waiting for help : from his low condition we may see what is often the condition of God's children,—and the best of God's servants have waited for comfort and the feelings of his Spirit, to the very failing of their own spirit. David, a man after God's own heart, is yet brought low with the faintness and failing of his heart, in waiting for help from God. " In the sweat of thy face shalt thou eat bread " (Gen. iii. 19) ; this lies upon the sons of men. But here, not sweat of face only, that were but small ; but sighs and fainting of the heart lie upon the sons of God, in seeking and hungering after a taste of God's bread of life, inward comfort, assurance, and joy of the Holy Ghost. Thus the Church was brought to this sick bed ere her comfort came : " For these things I weep ; mine eye, mine eye runneth down with water, because the comforter that should relieve my soul is far from me : " Lam. i. 16. The disciples' spirits were even failing in the tempest, when Christ slept and seemed to neglect them, as if he cared not though they perished. How should our spirits do other but fail, when our Comforter sleeps, when our only friend seems to be our enemy ?

Failing of spirit is both a motive which God means to yield unto and to be won by withal ; and it is also his opportunity, when he usually helps. It is a strong motive in our prayers to move him, for he is pitiful, and will not let his children utterly fail and perish ; he is a pitiful Spirit to failing spirits. " I will not contend (saith the Lord) for ever, neither will I be always wroth ; " why ? we deserve his wrath should last and take fire for ever against us ; yea, but (saith the Lord) this is the reason, " The spirit should fail before me, and the souls which I have made " (Isaiah lvii. 16) : I love and pity the fainting souls and spirits of men ; I will help my children ; how can I see my creatures whom I made and do love, to perish for want of my help ? David knew the Lord's nature, and that this was a speeding argument in prayer, which made him here and elsewhere so often use it. A pitiful father will not see the spirit of his children utterly fail. It is his opportunity ; he usually helps when all other helps fail, that we may the more strongly cleave to him, and ground ourselves upon him, as knowing how infirm we are, if he confirm us not. When man's cruse of oil is dry, and fails, and can drop no more, then is God's time to prepare his. Thus helped he the Israelites at the Red Sea, when all man's strength and wisdom was at a stand. He loves to be seen in the mount, in extremities.—*Condensed from Thomas Calvert.*

Verse 7.—The prayer of David becomes, as he proceeds, both more spiritual and more fervent. In the sixth verse we find him thirsting after God ; and now that thirst is become so intense that it admits of no delay. In the beginning of the Psalm he was content to say, " Hear my prayer ; " but now he cries, " Hear me *speedily."* This is not the language of sinful impatience : it is, indeed, good that a man should both hope and quietly wait for the salvation of God ; yet a man may desire, not only an answer, but also a speedy answer, without incurring the charge of impatience. Whatever a man desires to have he desires to have soon ; nor can be be otherwise than grieved at anything which delays the accomplishment of his wishes. In such desire or grief there is nothing sinful, provided it do not lead to murmuring or distrust of God. Hence this petition for *speedy* relief, and manifestation of God's presence and favour is very frequent with the Psalmist. He often prays, " Make haste, O Lord, to deliver ; make haste to help me, O Lord." Nay, if a man does not desire the light of God's countenance soon, it is a certain proof that he does not desire it at all. If the natural language of his heart be not, " hear me speedily," delay is to him no exercise of patience. The very idea of patience implies that something is contrary to our wish ; and the stronger the desire is, the more difficult will that exercise of patience become.

" Hope deferred maketh the heart sick ; " and therefore David adds, " my spirit faileth." He believed verily to see the goodness of the Lord in the land of the living ; yet so intense was his desire, that faith could hardly keep his spirit from fainting, while the blessing, which he so eagerly pursued, seemed still distant, and fled before him. He is afraid lest if God should long delay, and withdraw himself, faith and hope could hold out no longer. He therefore pleads, " hide not thy face from me, lest I become like them that go down into the pit ; " and urges the failing of his spirit before him who " will not contend for ever, lest the spirit should fail before him."—*John Fawcett.*

Verses 7, 8, 10, 11.—Observe how David mixes together prayers for joy, for guidance, and for sanctification—" Hide not thy face from me." " Cause me to know the way wherein I should walk." " Teach me to do thy will." " Cause me to hear thy loving-kindness in the morning." " Quicken me, O Lord, for thy name's sake." Now this is exactly right : our prayers, as well as our other obedience, must be without partiality ; nay, we should desire comfort for the sake of holiness, rather than holiness for the sake of comfort.—*John Fawcett.*

Verse 8.—*"Cause me to hear thy lovingkindness."* Here he craveth God's favour and kindness, as he doth in many other Psalms. Because in his favour is life, wealth, and grace, all good things, and pleasure for evermore, so that if he look kindly to us we need be afraid of nothing. But how shall he be assured of his favour ? Even by *hearing* it, as he saith in the fifty-first Psalm : " Make me to hear joy and gladness." The voice which is heard is the word of God, which, being apprehended by faith, is able to comfort our souls in whatsoever temptation. It is no marvel that such atheists and papists who altogether refuse the word of God, live comfortless and die without comfort, because they refuse that instrument which should carry joy to them. Good reason they die athirst, since they reject that vessel, the word of God, by which they might be refreshed. Therefore since faith cometh by hearing of God's word, and all our comfort cometh by it, let us pray God to bore our ears and our hearts, that we may receive the glad tidings of reconciliation from God.

"Cause me to know the way wherein I should walk." The second petition ariseth very well from the first. For when we have obtained an assurance of God's favour, as he is reconciled to us in Jesus Christ, it followeth next that we should desire to conform our lives to the obedience of his commandments. For no man will frame himself to walk in God's ways till he be assured of God's favour. Therefore faith in God's promises is the most effectual cause to bring forth good works ; and an assurance of justification the surest means to produce sanctification.

"For I lift up my soul unto thee." Behold what a wonderful effect God worketh by afflictions : they depress and cast down the outward man, and our inward man by them is elevated and raised aloft ; yea, the more we are afflicted, the more we are stirred up. The oftener the messenger of Satan is sent to buffet us, the more earnestly (with Paul) we cry unto the Lord to be delivered (2 Cor. xii. 8). So if we be cast down to hell in our feelings, what the worse are we if by that we be raised up to heaven ?—*Archibald Symson.*

Verse 8.—*"Cause me to hear thy lovingkindness in the morning,"* etc. To hear thy lovingkindness in the morning makes my waking to be saluted, as it were, with music ; makes my troubles seem as if they were but dreams ; makes me find it true that though " weeping may endure for a night, yet joy cometh in the morning : " Ps. xxx. 5. . . . It may well be said we hear this lovingkindness in the morning, seeing it makes it morning to us whensoever we hear it.—*Sir Richard Baker.*

Verse 8.—*"Cause me to hear thy lovingkindness in the morning."* If evil fall upon us in the night, we would have it removed ere the morning ; if in the morning, we would not have it our bed-fellow in the evening. We would have the Lord's promise run thus,—Your sorrows shall not endure the whole night, your joy shall come long before the morning. The luxurious Emperor (? Smyndirides the Sybarite) and his drunken mates sat and drank all the night, and slept all the day, insomuch that it was said of them, they never saw sun-set nor sun-rise. Such would we have the evils we suffer—of so short continuance that neither sun-set nor sun-rise might see us in our misery. This makes me wonder at that strange Egyptian beast called Pharaoh, who being demanded of Moses when he would have God's plague of the frogs removed, answered, *"To-morrow."* Surely, here he spake not as a man, to whom one hour's trouble is accounted a day, a day a month, a month a year. For in leaving of two things we change our desires, and are much different.

1. In leaving of sin, then we procrastinate and put off ; and when God says, "To-day hear my voice," we answer, "To-morrow," and are like the Levite's wife's father (Judg. xix. 6), too kind hosts to such bad guests : saying to our sins "tarry till the morning." Our pace to repentance is slow, we are far from haste in that matter.

2. But for afflictions to leave us, then we wish they had feet like hinds' feet, to run away from us, or we the wings of a dove to fly away from them, and be at rest. . . . . What prisoner desires not to be presently set free, and that liberty's soft hand may loose his iron knots ? What mariner wishes a long storm ? What servant sighs not over his hard apprenticeship ? Yea, who is he, that if there were an appearance of an offering to take the cup of calamity from his mouth, saying, " Thou shalt drink no more," would answer, " This cup shall not yet pass from me, I delight to carouse and drink deeply of those bitter waters " ? Yea, this desire extends so far that it comes to the Son of Man, the blessed Seed of the woman, who was so clad with human weakness that he earnestly prayed for speedy help from his heavy anguish ; and that not once, but often,—" Oh, my Father, if it be possible," etc. ; and when his Father answers not, he cries like one ready to fall under the burden, " My God, my God, why hast thou forsaken me ? " The reason for Christ's thus complaining is to be fetched from thence, whence his flesh came ; even from us. It was our human flesh, not his Divine spirit, which was so weary of suffering ; his spirit was willing, it was our flesh that was so weak.— *Thomas Calvert.*

Verse 8.—*"Cause me to hear thy lovingkindness in the morning."* This is a short and sweet morning prayer. God hears early prayer, and lovingly responds to it. The smiles of his face, the sweetness of his voice, the gifts of his hand, bless the morning, bless all the day. Do we write and read experimentally ? Then we know the blessedness of divine love. The subject is truly pleasant and precious. *"Lovingkindness"* is a favourite expression, is a choice theme of David's. It is used more in the Book of Psalms than in any other book in the Scriptures. Lovingkindness is love showing kindness ; it is the sun of love shining with rays of kindness ; the river of love sending forth streams of kindness ; it is the heart of love uttering itself by words of kindness, doing deeds, and giving gifts of kindness.

Here it is the *voice* of the lovingkindness of the Lord that David desires to hear. This voice is the music of heaven, the joyful sound of the gospel, and it makes a jubilee in the Christian's heart. To him there is beauty, sweetness, fulness in the theme ; it is his joy and rejoicing. This is the voice that speaks *pardon.* Pardon is through Jesus the medium of this kindness. Apart from this there is no hope of forgiveness. We plead this and realize pardon. " Have mercy upon me, O God, according to thy lovingkindness : according unto the multitude of thy tender mercies blot out my transgressions ": Ps. li. 1. It is the Lord's lovingkindness that pardons me. This voice speaks *peace :* " The Lord will speak peace unto his people." Precious peace is the result of pardoning kindness. This voice also speaks *joy.* This is the alone and all-sufficient source of joy. It is sought elsewhere, but found only here. It sweetens every bitter, and makes sweeter every sweet. It is a balsam for every wound, a cordial for every fear. The present is but a taste, but a drop of the future fulness of joy. How sweetly refreshing is the joy of the Lord's lovingkindness. This voice speaks *hope.* With the sweet music of this voice falling upon our ears, the night of hopelessness passes away, and the morning of expectation opens upon us. It assures us of supplies for our wants, of safety in danger, of endurance to the end, and of a glorious portion in eternity.

"The morning" is the season in which David desires to hear the voice of the lovingkindness of the Lord. The morning is a season often mentioned by him, and as a time of devotion is much prized by him. " My voice shalt thou hear in the morning, O Lord ; in the morning will I direct my prayer unto thee, and will look up ": Ps. v. 3. *"Cause me to hear thy lovingkindness in the morning" :* let it engage my thoughts and affections. It is well to have a subject like this to occupy our waking thoughts, and to take hold of our first desires. If other thoughts get

into our hearts in the morning, we may not be able to turn them out all the day. Prayer and praise, reading and meditation, will be sweet with such a subject occupying and influencing our minds. They will be exercises of cheerfulness, freedom, and blessedness.

"*Cause me to hear*" this voice. It speaks every morning, but many ears are deaf to it. But while others are indifferent to it, cause me to hear it; let me not lose the opportunity: waken my ear morning by morning, so that I may hail the season and enjoy the privilege. And when the morning of eternity shall come, "cause me to hear the voice of thy lovingkindness" welcoming me to its joys.— *W. Abbot, in "The Baptist Messenger,"* 1870.

Verse 8.—"*Cause me to know the way wherein I should walk.*" The whole valley is surrounded by ranges of regal crags; but the mountain of the Gemmi, apparently absolutely inaccessible, is the last point to which you would turn for an outlet. A side gorge that sweeps up to the glaciers and snowy pyramids flashing upon you in the opposite direction is the route which you suppose your guide is going to take; and visions of pedestrians perilously scaling icy precipices, or struggling up to the middle through ridges of snow, begin to surround you, as the prospect of your own experience in this day's expedition. So convinced was I that the path *must* go in that direction, that I took a short cut, which I conceived would bring me again into the mule path at a point under the glaciers; but after scaling precipices and getting lost in a wood of firs in the valley, I was glad to rejoin my friend with the guide, and to clamber on in pure ignorance and wonder. . . . Now what a striking symbol is this of things that sometimes take place in our spiritual pilgrimage. We are often brought to a stand, hedged up and hemmed in by the providence of God so that there seems no way out. A man is sometimes thrown into difficulties in which he sits down beginning to despair, and says to himself, "Well, this time it is all over with me"; like Sterne's starling, or, worse, like Bunyan's man in the cage, he says, "I cannot get out." Then when God has drawn him from all self-confidence and self-resource, a door opens in the wall and he rises up, and walks at liberty, praising God.—*George Barrell Cheever,* 1807—.

Verses 8—10.—After thou hast prayed, observe what God doth towards thee; especially how he doth guide thy feet and heart after prayer; there is much in that. That which was the spirit of supplication in a man when he prayed, rests upon him as the spirit of obedience in his course. That dependence which he hath upon God for the mercy he seeks for is a special motive and means to keep him fearful of offending, and diligent in duty. He looks to his paths, and endeavours to behave himself as becomes a suitor, as well as to pray as a suitor. David walked by this principle when he said (Ps. lxvi. 18), "If I regard iniquity in my heart, the Lord will not hear me"; that consideration still came in as a curb unto sin. Therefore David, in these verses, when he was to pray, even as for his life, for deliverance from his enemies, he specially prays God to direct him and keep him, that he might not sin against him; for he knew that by sinning he should enervate and spoil all his prayers. He cries not only "*Hear me speedily,*" but also, "*Cause me to know the way wherein I should walk; teach me to do thy will.*" This he especially prays for, more than for deliverance, for else he knew God would not hear him. Therefore when thou art in treaty with God for any mercy, observe, doth God still after praying keep thee in a more obedient frame of spirit? If so, it is a sign he intends to answer thee. The same is true when he keeps thee from using ill means, etc. When he meant to give David the kingdom, he kept him innocent, and made his heart tender, so that it smote him but for cutting off the lap of Saul's garment.—*Thomas Goodwin.*

Verse 9.—"*Deliver me, O LORD, from mine enemies.*" In the former verse he desireth God's mercy and lovingkindness, and that he might be showed the way wherein he should walk: now he desireth to be free of temporal danger. This is a good method in prayer, first to seek the kingdom of God and spiritual graces, for then all other things shall be added to us. We seek in vain temporal deliverances of God if we neglect to seek spiritual graces, which are most necessary for us.

As for *enemies*, the church and her members neither have wanted nor shall want innumerable foes, against whom we can only oppose God's protection. In number, in power, in policy and subtilty they are ever above us. There is no help for us against them all but our gracious God. Esau came with four hundred against Jacob, a naked man, with his wife, children, and droves of cattle. But

Mahanaim was with him; he was guarded by God's angels. And, therefore, since the church of God in France, Germany, and elsewhere is in danger of the Leviathan and the sons of Anak, let us run to the Lord, and cry unto him,—O God Jehovah, who art one against all, deliver thy church from her enemies, who likewise are thy enemies.—*Archibald Symson.*

Verse 9.—*"I flee unto thee to hide me."* Is David's valour come to this, that he is come now to be glad to fly? Had he not done better to have died valiantly than to fly basely? O my soul, to fly is not always a sign of baseness; it is not always a point of valour to stand to it; but then to fly when we feel our own weakness, and to him to fly, in whom is our strength—this is, if not valour, at least wisdom, but it is, to say true, both wisdom and true valour. And now, O God, seeing I find my own weakness, and know thy strength, what should I do but fly, and whither fly but only to thee?—to thee, a strong fortress to all that build upon thee; to thee, a safe sanctuary to all that fly unto thee.—*Sir Richard Baker.*

Verse 9.—*"I flee unto thee to hide me."* This implies, 1. *Danger:* the Christian may be in danger from sin, self, foes. 2. *Fear:* his fears may be groundless, but they are often very painful. 3. *Inability*—to defend himself or overcome his opposers. 4. *Foresight:* he sees the storm in the distance, and looks out for the covert. 5. *Prudence:* he hides before the storm, ere the enemy comes upon him. 6. A laudable *concern* for safety and comfort. The believer, if wise, will at all times flee to Jehovah. Jacob flies to Laban; the manslayer to the refuge; the bird to his mountain; and the Christian to his God. Asa may seek to physicians; Ephraim to king Jareb; and Saul to the witch; but the believer looks to his God. The Lord receives, befriends, and secures him. Let us flee to him by prayer, in faith, with hope, for salvation; and he will receive us, shelter us, and be our refuge and strength. Flee from sin, from self, from the world; but flee to Jesus. His heart is ever toward us, his ear is open to us, and his hand is ready to help, protect, and deliver us. His throne is our asylum. His promise is our comfort, and his omnipotence is our guard.

> Happy soul, that, free from harms
> Rests within his Shepherd's arms!
> Who his quiet shall molest?
> Who shall violate his rest?
> He who found the wandering sheep,
> Loves, and still delights to keep.

James Smith, in "The Believer's Daily Remembrancer."

Verse 9.—*"I flee unto thee to hide me."* The Lord hid the prophets so that Ahab could not find them out: 1 Kings xviii. 13. If we will creep under his wings he will surely keep us.—*Archibald Symson.*

Verse 9.—*"I flee unto thee to hide me."* It may be rendered, *"With thee have I hid"*; that is, myself: so Arama gives the sense. *"I have hid myself with thee."* Jarchi, Aben Ezra, and Kimchi interpret it to this purpose, "I have hid my affairs, my straits and troubles, my difficulties and necessities, from men, and have revealed them unto thee, who alone can save." The Targum is, "I have appointed thy Word to be (my) Redeemer.—*John Gill.*

Verses 9, 10.—Be persuaded actually to hide yourselves with Jesus Christ. To have a hiding-place and not to use it is as bad as to want one: fly to Christ; run into the holes of this rock. Three things must be done by all those that would hide themselves with Christ.

1. You must put away sin by repentance. Jesus Christ will not be a sanctuary for rebels, he will not protect evil-doers. Christ will never hide the devil, nor any of his servants. Isa. lv. 6, 7: "Let the ungodly forsake his ways," etc. David knew this, therefore he prays that God would teach him to do his will: *"Deliver me, etc. I flee unto thee to hide me. Teach me to do thy will."* He that will not do the will of Christ shall receive no protection from Christ. *Protectio sequitur allegiantiam.* You must be his liege people if you will have him to defend you. Job xxii. 23, 25.

2. You must pray that he would hide you. The promise is made to prayer: Isa. lxv. 10, "Sharon shall be a fold of flocks, and the valley of Achor a place for the herds to lie down in, for my people that have sought me." He that prays most fervently is like to be hid most securely. And then,

3. You must believe in him. Faith is the key that opens the door of this

hiding-place, and locks it again.   One word in the Hebrew signifies to trust and to make a refuge. Ps. lvii. 1.   He that doth not make Christ his trust shall not have Christ for his hiding-place ;   he will hide none but those that commit themselves to him : " I will set him on high, because he hath known my name " : Ps. xci. 9, 14. —*Ralph Robinson.*

Verse 10.—*"Teach me to do thy will."*   He saith not, Teach me to *know* thy will, but to *do* thy will.   God teaches us in three ways.   First, by his word. Secondly, he illuminateth our minds by the Spirit.   Thirdly, he imprinteth it in our hearts, and maketh us obedient to the same ; for the servant who knoweth the will of his master, and doeth it not, shall be beaten with many stripes : Luke xii. 47.—*Archibald Symson.*

Verse 10.—*"Teach me to do thy will."*   We are to pray that God would teach us to know, and then teach us to do, his will.   Knowledge without obedience is lame, obedience without knowledge is blind ; and we must never hope for acceptance if we offer the blind and the lame to God.—*Vincent Alsop* (—1703), *in "The Morning Exercises."*

Verse 10.—*"Teach me to do thy will."*   The Lord doth no sooner call his people to himself, but as soon as ever he hath thus crowned them with these glorious privileges, and given them any sense and feeling of them, then they immediately cry out, O Lord, what shall I now do for thee ?   How shall I now live to thee ? They know now that they are no more their own, but his ; and therefore should now live to him.

It is true indeed, obedience to the law is not required of us now as it was of Adam ; it was required of him as a condition antecedent to life, but of those that be in Christ it is required only as a duty consequent to life, or as a rule of life, that seeing he hath purchased our lives in redemption, and actually given us life in vocation and sanctification, we should now live unto him, in all thankful and fruitful obedience, according to his will revealed in the moral law.   It is a vain thing to imagine that our obedience is to have no other rule but the Spirit, without an attendance to the law : the Spirit is indeed the efficient cause of our obedience, and hence we are said to be " led by the Spirit " (Rom. viii. 14) ; but it is not properly the rule of our obedience, but the will of God revealed in his word, especially in the law, is the rule ; the Spirit is the wind that drives us in our obedience ; the law is our compass, according to which it steers our course for us : the Spirit and the law, the wind and the compass, can stand well together.   *"Teach me to do thy will ; for thou art my God"* (there is David's rule, viz., God's will revealed) ; *"Thy Spirit is good"* (there is David's wind, that enabled him to steer his course according to it).   The Spirit of life doth free us from the law of sin and death ; but not from the holy, and pure, and good, and righteous law of God. Rom. viii. 1—3.—*Thomas Shepard, in "The Sound Believer,"* 1671.

Verse 10.—*"Teach me to do thy will,"* etc.   We are inclined and enabled [to good] by the sanctifying Spirit.   In the Christian religion, not only the precepts are good, but there goeth along with them the power of God to make us good.   *"Teach me to do thy will ; for thou art my God : thy Spirit is good."*   The Spirit's direction hath strength joined with it.   And he is a good Spirit, as he doth incline us to good. The Spirit is the only fountain of all goodness and holiness : Neh. ix. 20, " Thou gavest also thy good Spirit to instruct them."   Why is he so often called the good Spirit, but that all his operations tend to make men good and holy ? Eph. v. 9, " The fruit of the Spirit is in all goodness and righteousness and truth."—*Thomas Manton.*

Verse 10.—*"Thy Spirit is good ; lead me,"* says the Psalmist.   And therefore it is a usual phrase in Rom. viii. and Gal. iv., our being *led* by the Spirit.—*Thomas Goodwin.*

Verse 10.—*"Lead me into the land of uprightness,"* into the communion of saints, the pleasant land of the upright ; or into a settled course of holy living, which will lead to heaven, that land of uprightness, where holiness will be in perfection, and he that is holy will be holy still.   We should desire to be led and kept safe to heaven, not only because it is a land of blessedness, but because it is a land of uprightness ; it is the perfection of grace.—*Matthew Henry.*

Verse 10.—*"Lead me."*   Man by nature is as a cripple and blind, he cannot go upright unless he be led by a superior spirit ; yea, he must be carried as an eagle carrieth her little ones, or as a mother her tender child.   Think not that we can step one right step to heaven but by the conduct and convoy of God's Holy Spirit. Miserable are those who go without his conduction.—*Archibald Symson.*

Verse 10.—*"The land of uprightness."* Mishor is the name for the smooth upland downs of Moab (Deut. iii. 10 ; Josh. xiii. 17 ; xx. 8 ; Jer. xlviii. 8, 21). Derived from the root *yashar*, "even, level plain," it naturally came to be used figuratively for equity, right, righteous, and uprightness.   Mal. ii. 6 ;   Isa. xi. 4 ; Ps. xlv. 7 ; lxvii. 5 ; cxliii. 10.—*Cunningham Geikie, in "Hours with the Bible,"* 1884.

Verse 10.—*" The land of uprightness."* The land of plainness, a land where no wickedness of men, and malice of Satan, vex the soul from day to day ; a land where no rough paths and crooked turns lengthen out the traveller's weary journey (see verse 5); but where all is like the smooth pasture-lands of Reuben (Deut. iii. 10 ; Josh. xiii. 9), a fit place for flocks to lie down.—*Andrew A. Bonar.*

Verse 11.—*"Quicken me, O LORD, for thy name's sake."* For the sake of thine own glory, that thou mayest show thyself to be the God of lovingkindness and power which thou art esteemed to be.—*Andrew Robert Fausset.*

Verse 11.—*"For thy righteousness' sake."* It is worthy of observation that the Psalmist pleads God's righteousness as the foundation on which he bases his supplication for the deliverance of his soul from trouble, and God's lovingkindness or mercy as that on which he grounds his prayer, or his conviction, that God will destroy his enemies. This is not the language of a revengeful and bloodthirsty spirit.—*Speaker's Commentary.*

Verse 11.—*"Bring my soul out of trouble."* I can bring it in, but thou only canst bring it out.—*John Trapp.*

Verses 11, 12.—*"Thy name's sake . . . thy righteousness' sake . . . And of thy mercy."* Mark here, my soul, with what three cords David seeks to draw God to grant him his suits : for his name's sake, for his righteousness' sake, and for his mercy's sake,—three such motives, that it must be a very hard suit that God will deny, if either of them be used. But though all the three strong motives, yet as David riseth in his suits, so he may seem also to rise in his motives ; and by this account ; for his righteousness' sake will prove a motive of a higher degree than for his name's sake, and for his mercy's sake the highest of them all—as indeed his mercy-seat is the highest part of all his ark, if it be not rather that as the attributes of God, so these motives, that are drawn from the attributes, are of equal pre-eminence. But if the three motives be all of them so strong, being each of them single, how strong would they be if they were all united, and twisted, I may say, into one cord ? And united they are all, indeed, into a motive, which God hath more clearly revealed to us than he did to David (although it be strange, seeing it was his Lord ; and yet not strange, seeing it was his son) ; and this is the motive : for thy Son Christ Jesus' sake ; for he is the *verbum abbreviatum* [the Word in brief], in whom are included all the motives—all the powerful motives—that can be used to God for obtaining our suits.—*Sir Richard Baker.*

Verses 11, 12.—The verbs in these two last verses, as Dr. Hammond hath noted, should be rendered in the future ; *"Thou shalt quicken,"* etc., and then the Psalm will end, as usual, with an act of faith and assurance, that all those mercies, which have been asked, shall be obtained ; that God, for the sake of his " *name*," and his " *righteousness*," of his glory, and his faithfulness in the performance of his promises, will not fail to be favourable and gracious to his servants, " *quickening*" them, even when dead in trespasses and sins, and bringing them, by degrees, " *out of all their troubles* " : going forth with them to the battle against their spiritual " *enemies*," and enabling them to vanquish the authors of their " *affliction*" and misery, to mortify the flesh, and to overcome the world ; that so they may triumph with their Redeemer, in the day when he shall likewise quicken their mortal bodies, and put all enemies under their feet.—*George Horne.*

Verse 12.—*"Of thy mercy cut off mine enemies."* He desireth God to slay his enemies in his mercy, when rather their destruction was a work of his justice ? I answer that the destruction of the wicked is a mercy to the church. As God showed great mercy and kindness to his church by the death of Pharaoh, Sennacherib, Herod, and other troublers thereof.—*Archibald Symson.*

Verse 12.—*"Cut off mine enemies,"* etc. When you find these imprecations to be prophecies of events which the Psalmist himself could not understand ; but were to be fulfilled in persons whom the Psalmist could not know, as they were to live in distant future ages,—for instance, Judas, and the Romans, and leaders of the Jewish nation,—who would make these imprecations proofs of a revengeful spirit ?—*James Bennett* (1774—1862), *in "Lectures on the Acts of the Apostles,"* 1847.

Verse 12.—*"I am thy servant."* David the king professeth himself one of God's pensioners. Paul, when he would blaze his coat of arms, and set forth his best heraldry, he doth not call himself Paul, an Hebrew of the Hebrews, or Paul of the tribe of Benjamin, but Paul " a servant of Christ " : Rom. i. 1. Theodosius thought it a greater dignity to be God's servant than to be an emperor. Christ himself, who is equal with his Father, yet is not ashamed of the title *servant :* Isa. liii. 11. Every servant of God is a son, every subject a prince : it is more honour to serve God than to have kings to serve us : the angels in heaven are servitors to the saints.—*Thomas Watson.*

HINTS TO PREACHERS.

Verse 1.—Three threes. I. As to his devotions,—prayers, supplications, requests. II. As to his success,—hear, give ear, answer me. III. As to his argument,—because thou art Jehovah, faithful, righteous.

Verses 1, 2.—A suitable prayer for a believer who has reason to suppose that he is suffering chastening for sin. I. Here is earnest importunity, as of one depending entirely upon divine favour for a hearing. II. Here is believing fervency laying hold of divine faithfulness and justice ; see 1 John i. 9. III. Here is a deep consciousness of the vanity of self-justification pleading for pure mercy, ver. 2. —*J. F.*

Verse 2.—I. Who he is. " Thy servant." II. What he knows. " In thy sight shall no man living be justified." III. What he asks. " Enter not into judgment."

Verses 3—6.—Consider, I. The great lengths God may sometimes permit the enemy to go, ver 3. The case of Job a good illustration. II. The deep depression of spirit he may even permit his saints to experience, ver. 4. III. The good things he has provided for their meditation when even at their worst, ver. 5. IV. The two things his grace will never suffer to die, whose existence is a pledge of near approaching joy,—1. The thirsting after himself. 2. The practice of prayer. The whole is a good text for a lecture on the life and experience of Job.—*J. F.*

Verses 4, 5, 6.—I. Down in Despondency. II. Deep in Meditation. III. Determined in Supplication.

Verses 5, 6.—*"I muse on the work of thy hands. I stretch forth my hands unto thee."* Hand in hand : or the child of God admiring the work of God's hands, and praying with uplifted hands to be wrought upon by the like power.

Verse 5.—David's method. I. He gathered materials ; facts and evidence concerning God : " I remember." II. He thought out his subject and arranged his matter : " I meditate." III. He discoursed thereon, and was brought nearer to God : " I muse "—discourse. IV. Let us close by viewing all this as an example for preachers and others.—*W. B. H.*

Verse 6.—God alone the desire of his people.

Verse 6.—Deep calling to deep. I. The insatiable craving of the heart. II. The vast riches in glory. III. The rushing together of these as : " My soul is to thee." —*W. B. H.*

Verse 7.—Reasons for speedy answers.

Verse 7.—Never despair. I. Because you have the Lord to plead with. Because you may freely tell him the desperateness of your case. III. Because you may be urgent with him for deliverance.—*J. F.*

Verse 7.—Cordial for the swooning heart. I. God's beloved fainting. II. The best restorative ; her Lord's face. III. She has the presence of mind to call him as she falls.—*W. B. H.*

Verse 8.—The two prayers—*"Cause me to hear,"* and *"Cause me to know."* The two pleas—*"In thee do I trust,"* and *"I lift up my soul unto thee."*

Verse 8, Ps. cxlii. 3.—*"Thou knewest my path."* Ps. cxliii. 8.—*"Cause me to know the way."* I. Trusting Omniscience in everything. II. Following conscience in everything.

Verse 8.—On fixing a time for the answering of our prayer. I. By whom it may be done. Not by all believers, but by those who through dwelling with God have attained to a holy boldness. II. When it may be done. 1. When the case is specially urgent. 2. When God's honour is concerned. III. What renders it pleasing to God when done. Great faith. " For in thee do I trust."—*J. F.*

Verse 8.—Listening for Lovingkindness. I. Where to listen. At the gates of Scripture ; in the halls of meditation ; nigh the footsteps of Jesus. II. When to listen. " In the morning ; " as early and as often as possible. III. How to listen. In trustful dependence : " Cause me to hear thy lovingkindness in the morning, for in thee do I trust." IV. Why to listen. To " know the way wherein I should walk."—*W. B. H.*

Verse 9.—Admirable points in this prayer to be imitated by us. There is, I. A sense of danger. II. A confession of weakness. III. A prudent foresight. IV. A solid confidence : —he expects to be hidden from his foes.

Verse 9.—I. Looking up. II. Lying close.—*W. B. H.*

Verse 10.—Two childlike requests—" Teach me. . . . lead me."

Verse 10.—See " Spurgeon's Sermons," No. 1519, " At School,"

Verse 10 (first half).—I. The best instructions : " Teach me to do thy will." Not merely to know, but " to do." II. The only efficient Instructor. III. The best reason for asking and expecting instruction : " For thou art my God."—*J. F.*

Verse 10.—*"Teach me to do thy will."* We may call this sentence a description of David's school ; and it is a very complete one ; at least, it hath in it the three best things that belong to a school. I. The best teacher. II. The best scholar. III. The best lesson ; for who so good a teacher as God ? who so good a scholar as David ? what so good a lesson as to do God's will ?—*Sir Richard Baker.*

Verse 10 (latter half).—I. Utopia—" the land of uprightness." Describe it, and declare its glories. II. The difficult paths to that upland country. III. The divine Guide,—" thy Spirit is good."

Verse 11 (first clause).—I. What is this blessing ? " Quicken me." II. In what way will it glorify God, so that we may plead for the sake of his name ?

Verse 11 (second clause).—How is the righteousness of God concerned in our deliverance from trouble ?

Verse 12.—I. To the Master : " I am thy servant." II. For the servant : he seeks protection because he belongs to his master.

PSALM CXLIV.

Albeit that this Psalm is in some measure very similar to Psalm xviii., yet it is a new song, and in its latter portion it is strikingly so.   Let the reader accept it as a new Psalm, and not as a mere variation of an old one, or as two compositions roughly joined together.   It is true that it would be a complete composition if the passage from verse 12 to the close were dropped ; but there are other parts of David's poems which might be equally self-contained if certain verses were omitted ; and the same might be said of many uninspired sonnets.   It does not, therefore, follow that the latter part was added by another hand, nor even that the latter part was a fragment by the same author, appended to the first song merely with the view of preserving it.   It seems to us to be highly probable that the Psalmist, remembering that he had trodden some of the same ground before, felt his mind moved to fresh thought, and that the Holy Spirit used this mood for his own high purposes.   Assuredly the addendum is worthy of the greatest Hebrew poet, and it is so admirable in language, and so full of beautiful imagery, that persons of taste who were by no means overloaded with reverence have quoted it times without number, thus confessing its singular poetical excellence.   To us the whole Psalm appears to be perfect as it stands, and to exhibit such unity throughout that it would be a literary Vandalism, as well as a spiritual crime, to rend away one part from the other.

TITLE.—*Its title is " Of David," and its language is of David, if ever language can belong to any man.   As surely as we could say of any poem, This is of Tennyson, or of Longfellow, we may say, This is of David.   Nothing but the disease which closes the eye to manifest fact and opens it to fancy, could have led learned critics to ascribe this song to anybody but David.   Alexander well says, "The Davidic origin of this Psalm is as marked as that of any in the Psalter."*

It is to God the devout warrior sings when he extols him as his strength and stay (verses 1 and 2).   Man he holds in small account, and wonders at the Lord's regard for him (verses 3 and 4) ; but he turns in his hour of conflict to the Lord, who is declared to be " a man of war," whose triumphant interposition he implores (verses 5 to 8). He again extols and entreats in verses 9, 10, and 11 ; and then closes with a delightful picture of the Lord's work for his chosen people, who are congratulated upon having such a God to be their God.

EXPOSITION.

BLESSED *be* the LORD my strength, which teacheth my hands to war, *and* my fingers to fight :

2 My goodness, and my fortress ;   my high tower, and my deliverer ; my shield, and *he* in whom I trust ; who subdueth my people under me.

1. *"Blessed be the LORD my strength."*   He cannot delay the utterance of his gratitude, he bursts at once into a loud note of praise.   His best word is given to his best friend—" Blessed be Jehovah."   When the heart is in a right state it must praise God, it cannot be restrained ; its utterances leap forth as waters forcing their way from a living spring.   With all his strength David blesses the God of his strength.   We ought not to receive so great a boon as strength to resist evil, to defend truth, and to conquer error, without knowing who gave it to us, and rendering to him the glory of it.   Not only does Jehovah give strength to his saints, but he is their strength.   The strength is made theirs because God is theirs.   God is full of power, and he becomes the power of those who trust him.   In him our great strength lieth, and to him be blessings more than we are able to utter.   It may be read, *"My Rock,"* but this hardly so well consorts with the following words : *"Which teacheth my hands to war and my fingers to fight."*   The word *rock* is the Hebrew way of expressing strength : the grand old language is full of such suggestive symbols.   The Psalmist in the second part of the verse sets forth the Lord as teacher in the arts of war.   If we have strength we are not much the better unless we have skill also.   Untrained force is often an injury to the man who possesses it, and it even becomes a danger to those who are round about him ; and therefore the

Psalmist blesses the Lord as much for teaching as for strength. Let us also bless Jehovah if he has in anything made us efficient. The tuition mentioned was very practical, it was not so much of the brain as of the hands and fingers; for these were the members most needful for conflict. Men with little scholastic education should be grateful for deftness and skill in their handicrafts. To a fighting man the education of the hands is of far more value than mere book-learning could ever be; he who has to use a sling or a bow needs suitable training, quite as much as a scientific man or a classical professor. Men are too apt to fancy that an artisan's efficiency is to be ascribed to himself; but this is a popular fallacy. A clergyman may be supposed to be taught of God, but people do not allow this to be true of weavers or workers in brass; yet these callings are specially mentioned in the Bible as having been taught to holy women and earnest men when the tabernacle was set up at the first. All wisdom and skill are from the Lord, and for them he deserves to be gratefully extolled. This teaching extends to the smallest members of our frame: the Lord teaches fingers as well as hands; indeed, it sometimes happens that if the finger is not well trained the whole hand is incapable.

David was called to be a man of war, and he was eminently successful in his battles; he does not trace this to his good generalship or valour, but to his being taught and strengthened for the war and the fight. If the Lord deigns to have a hand in such unspiritual work as fighting, surely he will help us to proclaim the gospel and win souls; and then we will bless his name with even greater intensity of heart. We will be pupils, and he shall be our Master, and if we ever accomplish anything we will give our instructor hearty blessing.

This verse is full of personality; it is mercy shown to David himself which is the subject of grateful song. It has also a presentness about it; for Jehovah is now his strength, and is still teaching him; we ought to make a point of presenting praise while yet the blessing is on the wing. The verse is also pre-eminently practical, and full of the actual life of every day; for David's days were spent in camps and conflicts. Some of us who are grievously tormented with rheumatism might cry, " Blessed be the Lord, my Comforter, who teacheth my knees to bear in patience, and my feet to endure in resignation "; others who are on the look out to help young converts might say, " Blessed be God who teaches my eyes to see wounded souls, and my lips to cheer them "; but David has his own peculiar help from God, and praises him accordingly. This tends to make the harmony of heaven perfect when all the singers take their parts; if we all followed the same score, the music would not be so full and rich.

2. Now our royal poet multiplies metaphors to extol his God. *"My goodness, and my fortress."* The word for *goodness* signifies *mercy.* Whoever we may be, and wherever we may be, we need mercy such as can only be found in the infinite God. It is all of mercy that he is any of the other good things to us, so that this is a highly comprehensive title. O how truly has the Lord been mercy to many of us in a thousand ways ! He is goodness itself, and he has been unbounded goodness to us. We have no goodness of our own, but the Lord has become goodness to us. So is he himself also our *fortress* and safe abode: in him we dwell as behind impregnable ramparts and immovable bastions. We cannot be driven out, or starved out; for our fortress is prepared for a siege; it is stored with abundance of food, and a well of living water is within it. Kings usually think much of their fenced cities, but King David relies upon his God, who is more to him than fortresses could have been. *"My high tower, and my deliverer."* As from a lofty watch-tower the believer, trusting in the Lord, looks down upon his enemies. They cannot reach him in his elevated position; he is out of bow-shot; he is beyond their scaling ladders; he dwells on high. Nor is this all; for Jehovah is our Deliverer as well as our Defender. These different figures set forth the varied benefits which come to us from our Lord. He is every good thing which we can need for this world or the next. He not only places us out of harm's way full often, but when we must be exposed, he comes to our rescue, he raises the siege, routs the foe, and sets us in joyous liberty. *"My shield, and he in whom I trust."* When the warrior rushes on his adversary, he bears his targe upon his arm, and thrusts death aside; thus doth the believer oppose the Lord to the blows of the enemy, and finds himself secure from harm. For this and a thousand other reasons our trust rests in our God for everything; he never fails us, and we feel boundless confidence in him. *'Who subdueth my people under me."* He keeps my natural subjects subject, and my conquered subjects peaceful under my sway. Men who rule others should

thank God if they succeed in the task. Such strange creatures are human beings, that if a number of them are kept in peaceful association under the leadership of any one of the Lord's servants, he is bound to bless God every day for the wonderful fact. The victories of peace are as much worthy of joyful gratitude as the victories of war. Leaders in the Christian church cannot maintain their position except as the Lord preserves to them the mighty influence which ensures obedience and evokes enthusiastic loyalty. For every particle of influence for good which we may possess let us magnify the name of the Lord.

Thus has David blessed Jehovah for blessing him. How many times he has appropriated the Lord by that little word *My !* Each time he grasps the Lord, he adores and blesses him ; for the one word *Blessed* runs through all the passage like a golden thread. He began by acknowledging that his strength for fighting foreign enemies was of the Lord, and he concluded by ascribing his domestic peace to the same source. All round as a king he saw himself to be surrounded by the King of kings, to whom he bowed in lowly homage, doing suit and service on bended knee, with grateful heart admitting that he owned everything to the Rock of his salvation.

3 LORD, what *is* man, that thou takest knowledge of him ! *or* the son of man, that thou makest account of him !

4 Man is like to vanity : his days *are* as a shadow that passeth away.

3. *"LORD what is man, that thou takest knowledge of him !"* What a contrast between Jehovah and man ! The Psalmist turns from the glorious all-sufficiency of God to the insignificance and nothingness of man. He sees Jehovah to be everything, and then cries, " Lord, what is man ! " What is man in the presence of the Infinite God ? What can he be compared to ? He is too little to be described at all : only God, who knows the most minute object, can tell what man is. Certainly he is not fit to be the rock of our confidence : he is at once too feeble and too fickle to be relied upon. The Psalmist's wonder is that God should stoop to know him, and indeed it is more remarkable than if the greatest archangel should make a study of emmets, or become the friend of mites. God knows his people with a tender intimacy, a constant, careful observation : he foreknew them in love, he knows them by care, he will know them is acceptance at last. Why and wherefore is this ? What has man done ? What has he been ? What is he now that God should know him, and make himself known to him as his goodness, fortress, and high tower ? This is an unanswerable question. Infinite condescension can alone account for the Lord stooping to be the friend of man. That he should make man the subject of election, the object of redemption, the child of eternal love, the darling of infallible providence, the next of kin to Deity, is indeed a matter requiring more than the two notes of exclamation found in this verse.

"Or the son of man, that thou makest account of him !" The son of man is a weaker being still,—so the original word implies. He is not so much *man* as God made him, but man as his mother bore him ; and how can the Lord think of him, and write down such a cipher in his accounts ? The Lord thinks much of man, and in connection with redeeming love makes a great figure of him : this can be believed, but it cannot be explained. Adoring wonder makes us each one cry out, Why dost thou take knowledge of me ? We know by experience how little man is to be reckoned upon, and we know by observation how greatly he can vaunt himself, it is therefore meet for us to be humble and to distrust ourselves ; but all this should make us the more grateful to the Lord, who knows man better than we do, and yet communes with him, and even dwells in him. Every trace of the misanthrope should be hateful to the believer ; for if God makes account of man it is not for us to despise our own kind.

4. *"Man is like to vanity."* Adam is like to Abel. He is like that which is nothing at all. He is actually vain, and he resembles that unsubstantial empty thing which is nothing but a blown-up nothing,—a puff, a bubble. Yet he is not vanity, but only like it. He is not so substantial as that unreal thing ; he is only the likeness of it. Lord, what is a man ? It is wonderful that God should think of such a pretentious insignificance. *"His days are as a shadow that passeth away."* He is so short-lived that he scarcely attains to years, but exists by the day, like the ephemera, whose birth and death are both seen by the self-same sun. His life is only like to a shadow, which is in itself a vague resemblance, an absence of something

rather than in itself an existence. Observe that human life is not only as a shade, but as a shade which is about to depart. It is a mere mirage, the image of a thing which is not, a phantasm which melts back into nothing. How is it that the Eternal should make so much of mortal man, who begins to die as soon as he begins to live ?

The connection of the two verses before us with the rest of the Psalm is not far to seek : David trusts in God and finds him everything ; he looks to man and sees him to be nothing ; and then he wonders how it is that the great Lord can condescend to take notice of such a piece of folly and deceit as man.

5 Bow thy heavens, O LORD, and come down : touch the mountains, and they shall smoke.

6 Cast forth lightning, and scatter them : shoot out thine arrows, and destroy them.

7 Send thine hand from above ; rid me, and deliver me out of great waters, from the hand of strange children ;

8 Whose mouth speaketh vanity, and their right hand *is* a right hand of falsehood.

5. *"Bow thy heavens, O LORD, and come down."* The heavens are the Lord's own, and he who exalted them can bow them. His servant is struggling against bitter foes, and he finds no help in men, therefore he entreats Jehovah to come down to his rescue. It is, indeed, a coming down for Jehovah to interfere in the conflicts of his tried people. Earth cries to heaven to stoop ; nay, the cry is to the Lord of heaven to bow the heaven, and appear among the sons of earth. The Lord has often done this, and never more fully than when in Bethlehem the Word was made flesh and dwelt among us : now doth he know the way, and he never refuses to come down to defend his beloved ones. David would have the real presence of God to counterbalance the mocking appearance of boastful man : eternal verity could alone relieve him of human vanity. *"Touch the mountains, and they shall smoke."* It was so when the Lord appeared on Sinai ; the strongest pillars of earth cannot bear the weight of the finger of God. He is a consuming fire, and his touch kindles the peaks of the Alps, and makes them smoke. If Jehovah would appear, nothing could stand before him ; if the mighty mountains smoke at his touch, then all mortal power which is opposed to the Lord must end in smoke. How long-suffering he is to his adversaries, whom he could so readily consume. A touch would do it ; God's finger of flame would set the hills on fire, and consume opposition of every kind.

6. *"Cast forth lightning, and scatter them."* The Eternal can hurl his lightnings wheresoever he pleases, and effect his purpose instantaneously. The artillery of heaven soon puts the enemy to flight : a single bolt sets the armies running hither and thither in utter rout. *"Shoot out thine arrows, and destroy them."* Jehovah never misses the mark ; his arrows are fatal to his foes when he goes forth to war. It was no common faith which led the poet-king to expect the Lord to use his thunderbolts on behalf of a single member of that race which he had just now described as " like to vanity." A believer in God may without presumption expect the Almighty Lord to use on his behalf all the stores of his wisdom and power : even the terrible forces of tempest shall be marshalled to the fight, for the defence of the Lord's chosen. When we have once mastered the greater difficulty of the Lord's taking any interest in us, it is but a small thing that we should expect him to exert his great power on our behalf. This is far from being the only time in which this believing warrior had thus prayed : the eighteenth Psalm is specially like the present ; the good man was not abashed at his former boldness, but here repeats himself without fear.

7. *"Send thine hand from above."* Let thy long and strong arm be stretched out till thine hand seizes my foes, and delivers me from them. *"Rid me, and deliver me out of great waters."* Make a Moses of me,—one drawn out of the waters. My foes pour in upon me like torrents, they threaten to overwhelm me ; save me from their force and fury ; take them from me, and me from them. *"From the hand of strange children."* From foreigners of every race ; men strange to me and thee, who therefore must work evil to me, and rebellion against thyself. Those against whom he pleaded were out of covenant with God ; they were Philistines and Edomites ; or else they were men of his own nation of black heart and traitorous

spirit, who were real strangers, though they bore the name of Israel. Oh to be rid of those infidel, blaspheming beings who pollute society with their false teachings and hard speeches! Oh to be delivered from slanderous tongues, deceptive lips, and false hearts! No wonder these words are repeated, for they are the frequent cry of many a tried child of God ;—*"Rid me and deliver me."* The devil's children are strange to us : we can never agree with them, and they will never understand us, they are aliens to us, and we are despised by them. O Lord, deliver us from the evil one, and from all who are of his race.

8. *"Whose mouth speaketh vanity."* No wonder that men who are vanity speak vanity. "When he speaketh a lie, he speaketh of his own." They cannot be depended upon, let them promise as fairly as they may : their solemn declarations are light as the foam of the sea, in no wise to be depended upon. Good men desire to be rid of such characters : of all men deceivers and liars are among the most disgusting to true hearts. *"And their right hand is a right hand of falsehood."* So far their hands and their tongues agree, for they are vanity and falsehood. These men act as falsely as they speak, and prove themselves to be all of a piece. Their falsehood is right-handed, they lie with dexterity, they deceive with all their might. It is a dreadful thing when a man's expertness lies more in lies than in truth ; when he can neither speak nor act without proving himself to be false. God save us from lying mouths, and hands of falsehood.

9 I will sing a new song unto thee, O God : upon a psaltery *and* an instrument of ten strings will I sing praises unto thee.

10 *It is he* that giveth salvation unto kings : who delivereth David his servant from the hurtful sword.

11 Rid me, and deliver me from the hand of strange children, whose mouth speaketh vanity, and their right hand *is* a right hand of falsehood :

9. *"I will sing a new song unto thee, O God."* Weary of the false, I will adore the true. Fired with fresh enthusiasm, my gratitude shall make a new channel for itself. I will sing as others have done ; but it shall be a new song, such as no others have sung. That song shall be all and altogether for my God : I will extol none but the Lord, from whom my deliverance has come. *"Upon a Psaltery and an instrument of ten strings will I sing praises unto thee."* His hand should aid his tongue, not as in the case of the wicked, co-operating in deceit ; but his hand should unite with his mouth in truthful praise. David intended to tune his best instruments as well as to use his best vocal music : the best is all too poor for so great a God, and therefore we must not fall short of our utmost. He meant to use many instruments of music, that by all means he might express his great joy in God. The Old Testament dispensation abounded in types, and figures, and outward ritual, and therefore music dropped naturally into its place in the "worldly sanctuary" ; but, after all, it can do no more than represent praise, and assist our expression of it ; the real praise is in the heart, the true music is that of the soul. When music drowns the voice, and artistic skill takes a higher place than hearty singing, it is time that instruments were banished from public worship ; but when they are subordinate to the song, as here, it is not for us to prohibit them, or condemn those who use them, though we ourselves greatly prefer to do without them, since it seems to us that the utmost simplicity of praise is far more congruous with the spirit of the gospel than pomp of organs. The private worshipper, singing his solo unto the Lord, has often found it helpful to accompany himself on some familiar instrument, and of this David in the present Psalm is an instance, for he says, " I will sing praise unto thee,"—that is, not so much in the company of others as by himself alone. He saith not " we," but " I."

10. *"It is he that giveth salvation unto kings."* Those whom the Lord sets up he will keep up. Kings, from their conspicuous position, are exposed to special danger, and when their lives and their thrones are preserved to them they should give the Lord the glory of it. In his many battles David would have perished had not almighty care preserved him. He had by his valour wrought salvation for Israel, but he lays his laurels at the feet of his Lord and Preserver. If any men need salvation kings do, and if they get it the fact is so astonishing that it deserves a verse to itself in the Psalm of praise. *"Who delivereth David his servant from the hurtful sword."* He traces his escape from death to the delivering hand of God. Note, he speaks in the present tense—*delivereth,* for this was an act which covered

his whole life. He puts his name to the confession of his indebtness : it is David who owns without demur to mercy given to himself. He styles himself the Lord's servant, accepting this as the highest title he had attained or desired.

11. Because of what the Lord had done, David returns to his pleading. He begs deliverance from him who is ever delivering him. *"Rid me, and deliver me from the hand of strange children."* This is in measure the refrain of the song, and the burden of the prayer. He desired to be delivered from his open and foreign adversaries, who had broken compacts, and treated treaties as vain things. *"Whose mouth speaketh vanity, and their right hand is a right hand of falsehood."* He would not strike hands with those who carried a lie in their right hand : he would be quit of such at once, if possible. Those who are surrounded by such serpents know not how to deal with them, and the only available method seems to be payer to God for a riddance and deliverance. David in the seventh verse, according to the original, had sought the help of both the Lord's hands, and well he might for his deceitful enemies with remarkable unanimity, were with one mouth and one hand seeking his destruction.

12 That our sons *may be* as plants grown up in their youth ; *that* our daughters *may be* as corner stones, polished *after* the similitude of a palace :

13 *That* our garners *may be* full, affording all manner of store : *that* our sheep may bring forth thousands and ten thousands in our streets :

14 *That* our oxen *may be* strong to labour ; *that there be* no breaking in, nor going out ; that *there be* no complaining in our streets.

15 Happy *is that* people, that is in such a case : *yea*, happy *is that* people, whose God *is the* LORD.

Riddance from the wicked and the gracious presence of the Lord are sought with a special eye to the peace and prosperity which will follow thereupon. The sparing of David's life would mean the peace and happiness of a whole nation. We can scarcely judge how much of happiness may hang upon the Lord's favour to one man.

12. God's blessing works wonders for a people. *" That our sons may be as plants grown up in their youth."* Our sons are of first importance to the state, since men take a leading part in its affairs ; and what the young men are the older men will be. He desires that they may be like strong, well rooted, young trees, which promise great things. If they do not grow in their youth, when will they grow ? If in their opening manhood they are dwarfed, they will never get over it. O the joys which we may have through our sons ! And, on the other hand, what misery they may cause us ! Plants may grow crooked, or in some other way disappoint the planter, and so may our sons. But when we see them developed in holiness, what joy we have of them ! *"That our daughters may be as corner stones, polished after the similitude of a palace."* We desire a blessing for our whole family, daughters as well as sons. For the girls to be left out of the circle of blessing would be unhappy indeed. Daughters unite families as corner stones join walls together, and at the same time they adorn them as polished stones garnish the structure into which they are builded. Home becomes a palace when the daughters are maids of honour, and the sons are nobles in spirit ; then the father is a king, and the mother a queen, and royal residences are more than outdone. A city built up of such dwellings is a city of palaces, and a state composed of such cities is a republic of princes.

13. *"That our garners may be full, affording all manner of store."* A household must exercise thrift and forethought : it must have its granary as well as its nursery. Husbands should husband their resources ; and should not only furnish their tables but fill their garners. Where there are happy households. there must needs be plentiful provision for them, for famine brings misery even where love abounds. It is well when there is plenty, and that plenty consists of " all manner of store." We have occasionally heard murmurs concerning the abundance of grain, and the cheapness of the poor man's loaf. A novel calamity ! We dare not pray against it. David would have prayed for it, and blessed the Lord when he saw his heart's desire. When all the fruits of the earth are plentiful, the fruits of our lips should be joyful worship and thanksgiving. Plenteous and varied may our products be, that every form of want may be readily supplied. *"That our sheep may bring forth thousands and ten thousands in our streets,"* or rather in the open places, the fields, and

sheep-walks where lambs should be born. A teeming increase is here described. Adam tilled the ground to fill the garner, but Abel kept sheep, and watched the lambs. Each occupation needs the divine blessing. The second man who was born into this world was a shepherd, and that trade has ever held an important part in the economy of nations. Food and clothing come from the flock, and both are of first consideration.

14. *"That our oxen may be strong to labour ; "* so that the ploughing and cartage of the farm may be duly performed, and the husbandman's work may be accomplished without unduly taxing the cattle, or working them cruelly. *"That there be no breaking in, nor going out ; "* no irruption of marauders, and no forced emigration ; no burglaries and no evictions. *"That there be no complaining in our streets ; "* no secret dissatisfaction, no public riot ; no fainting of poverty, no clamour for rights denied, nor concerning wrongs unredressed. The state of things here pictured is very delightful : all is peaceful and prosperous ; the throne is occupied efficiently, and even the beasts in their stalls are the better for it. This has been the condition of our own country, and if it should now be changed, who can wonder ? for our ingratitude well deserves to be deprived of blessings which it has despised.

These verses may with a little accommodation be applied to a prosperous church, where the converts are growing and beautiful, the gospel stores abundant, and the spiritual increase most cheering. There ministers and workers are in full vigour, and the people are happy and united. The Lord make it so in all our churches evermore.

15. *"Happy is that people, that is in such a case."* Such things are not to be overlooked. Temporal blessings are not trifles, for the miss of them would be a dire calamity. It is a great happiness to belong to a people so highly favoured. *"Yea, happy is that people, whose God is the LORD."* This comes in as an explanation of their prosperity. Under the Old Testament Israel had present earthly rewards for obedience ; when Jehovah was their God they were a nation enriched and flourishing. This sentence is also a sort of correction of all that had gone before ; as if the poet would say—all these temporal gifts are a part of happiness, but still the heart and soul of happiness lies in the people being right with God, and having a full possession of him. Those who worship the happy God become a happy people. Then if we have not temporal mercies literally we have something better : if we have not the silver of earth we have the gold of heaven, which is better still.

In this Psalm David ascribes his own power over the people, and the prosperity which attended his reign, to the Lord himself. Happy was the nation which he ruled ; happy in its king, in its families, in its prosperity, and in the possession of peace ; but yet more in enjoying true religion and worshipping Jehovah, the only living and true God.

EXPLANATORY NOTES AND QUAINT SAYINGS.

Whole Psalm.—The Psalm, in its mingled tones of prayer and praise, is a fit connecting link between the supplicatory Psalms which go before, and the strains of thanksgiving which follow it.—*Speaker's Commentary.*

Whole Psalm.—After six Psalms of sorrowful prayer in distress, we have now a Psalm of praise and thanksgiving for God's gracious answer to supplications ; and also a Psalm of intercession. The present Psalm bears a strong resemblance to David's last song in 2 Sam. xxii. and to Ps. xviii. Here we have a vision of Christ rejoicing ;—after his passion—risen in glory, and having ascended in triumph, and pleading for us at the right hand of God.—*Christopher Wordsworth.*

Whole Psalm.—This Psalm is ruled by the numbers ten and seven. Ten verses complete the first part of the Psalm, which falls into two divisions. The first portion contains, in verses 1 and 2, ten attributes of God,—three and seven, the seven divided into four and three. In like manner it contains ten requests to God in verses 5—7, divided precisely as the attributes. To this significance of the number ten for the first part, allusion is pointedly made in verse 9. Seven blessings are prayed for in the second part, four in verses 12, 13 (valiant sons, beautiful daughters, full store-houses, numerous flocks), and three in verse 14 (labouring oxen, no breach and diminution, no cry). The whole contains, apart from the closing epiphonem, which, as usual, stands outside the formal arrangement, seven strophes, each of two verses.

An objection has been brought against the Davidic authorship from the " traces of reading " it contains. But one would require to consider more exactly, what sort of reading is here to be thought of. It is only the Psalms of David which form the ground-work of this new Psalm. But that it is one of David's peculiarities to derive from his earlier productions a foundation for new ones, is evident from a variety of facts, which, if any doubt must still be entertained on the subject, would obtain a firm ground to stand upon in this Psalm, which *can* only have been composed by David. The way and manner of the use made of such materials is to be kept in view. This is always of a spirited and feeling nature, and no trace anywhere exists of a dead borrowing. That we cannot think here of such a borrowing ; that the appropriation of the earlier language did not proceed from spiritual impotence, but rested upon deeper grounds, is manifest from the consideration of the second part, where the dependence entirely ceases, and where even the opponents of the Davidic authorship have not been able to overlook the strong poetical spirit of the time of David. They betake themselves to the miserable shift of affirming that the Psalmist borrowed this part of the Psalm from a much older poem now lost.—*E. W. Hengstenberg.*

Verse 1.—*"Blessed be the* Lord*."* A prayer for further mercy is fitly begun with a thanksgiving for former mercy ; and when we are waiting upon God to bless us, we should stir up ourselves to bless him.—*Matthew Henry.*

Verse 1.—*"The* Lord *my strength,"* etc. Agamemnon says to Achilles—

> If thou hast strength, 'twas heaven that strength bestowed ;
> For know, vain man ! thy valour is from God.
>
> *Homer.*

Verse 1.—*"My strength"* [Heb. " *my rock* "]. The climax should be noted ; the rock, or cliff, comes first as the place of refuge, then the fortress or *fastness*, as a place carefully fortified, then the personal deliverer, without whose intervention escape would have been impossible.—*Speaker's Commentary.*

Verse 1.—*"The* Lord *. . . teacheth " :* and not as man teacheth. Thus he taught Gideon to fight with the innumerable host of Midian by sending to their homes two-and-twenty thousand, and retaining but ten thousand of his soldiers : and then again by reducing that remnant to the little band of three hundred who lapped when brought down to the water. Thus he taught Samson by abstaining from strong drink, and by suffering no razor to pass over his head. Thus he taught the three kings in the wilderness to war against their enemies, not by any strength of their armies, but by making ditches in the desert. Thus he taught David himself by waiting for the sound of the going in the tops of the mulberry trees. And so he taught the arms of the True David to fight when stretched on the cross : nailed, to human sight, to the tree of suffering, but, in reality, winning for themselves the crown of glory : helpless in the eyes of scribes and Pharisees ; in those of archangels, laying hold of the two pillars, sin and death, whereon the house of Satan rested, and heaving them up from their foundation.—*Ayguan, in Neale and Littledale.*

Verse 1.—*" The* Lord *my strength, which teacheth my hands to war."* There were three qualities of a valiant soldier found in Christ, the Captain of our salvation, in his war against Satan, which his followers are bound to emulate : boldness in attack, skill in defence, steadiness in conflict, all which he teaches by his example (Matt. iv. 1, 4, 7, 10, 11). He was *bold in attack*, for he began the combat by going up into the wilderness to defy the enemy. So we, too, should be always beforehand with Satan : ought to fast, even if not tempted to gluttony, and be humble, though not assailed by pride, and so forth. He was *skilful in defence*, parrying every attack with Holy Writ ; where we, too, in the examples of the saints, may find lessons for the combat. He was *steadfast in conflict*, for he persevered to the end, till the devil left him, and angels came and ministered unto him ; and we, too, should not be content with repelling the first attack, but persevere in our resistance until evil thoughts are put to flight, and heavenly resolutions take their place.—*Neale and Littledale.*

Verse 1.—*"Teacheth my hands."* Used to the hook and harp, and not to the sword and spear ; but God hath apted and abled them to feats of arms and warlike exploits. It is God that giveth skill and success, saith Solomon (Prov. viii.) ; wisdom and ability, saith Daniel (chap. ii.). And as in the spiritual warfare, so here; our weapons are " mighty through God " (2 Cor. x. 4), who promiseth that no weapon formed against his people shall prosper (Isa. liv. 17).—*John Trapp.*

Verse 1.—*"To war, . . . to fight."* I want to speak of a great defect among us, which often prevents the realization of going " from strength to strength "; viz., the *not using, not trading with*, the strength given. We should not think of going to God for money only to keep it in the bank. But are we not doing this with regard to strength? We are constantly asking for strength for service; but if we are not putting this out in hearty effort, it is of no use to us. Nothing comes of hoarded strength.

" Blessed be the Lord my strength, *which teacheth my hands to war, and my fingers to fight."* David, you see, was looking for strength for a purpose. Some people seem to expect strength, but never attempt to put forth their hands to war, and their fingers to fight—there is so little venturing upon God, so little use of grace given, partly from fear of man, partly from indolence and worldly-mindedness . . . It is not for us to be merely luxuriating in the power which God supplies. Action strengthens, and before we have a right to ask for an increase, we must use that already given.—*Catherine Pennefather, in " Service,"* 1881.

Verse 1.—Is not the spiritual victory of every believer achieved by God? Truly it is he who teaches his *hands to war and his fingers to fight:* and when the final triumph shall be sung in heaven, the victor's song will be, " Not unto me, O Lord, not unto me, but unto thy name give glory, for thy mercy and for thy truth's sake."—*John Morison.*

Verse 1.—*"My hands for fight, my fingers for war."* *Fight* and *war* are both verbs and nouns in English, but the Hebrew words are nouns with the article prefixed. —*Joseph Addison Alexander.*

Verse 1.—*"My fingers to fight."* Probably the immediate reference here is to the use of the bow,—placing the arrow, and drawing the string.—*Albert Barnes.*

Verse 2.—*"My goodness,"* etc. This way of using the word in a passive sense, as in the Hebrew, sounds harshly; just as elsewhere (Ps. xviii. 50) he calls himself " God's king," not in the sense of his having dominion over God, but being made and appointed king by him. Having experienced God's kindness in so many ways, he calls him *"his goodness,"* meaning that whatever good he possessed flowed from him. The accumulation of terms, one upon another, which follows, may appear unnecessary, yet it tends greatly to strengthen faith. We know how unstable men's minds are, and especially how soon faith wavers, when they are assailed by some trial of more than usual severity.—*John Calvin.*

Verse 2.—*"My fortress."* David calls God by names connected with the chief deliverances of his life. The Psalms abound in local references and descriptive expressions, *e.g.* Ps. xviii. 2 [and in this place]. The word translated *"fortress"* is *metzudah* or *masada.* From 1 Sam. xxiii. 29, I have no doubt that he is speaking of Masada, an isolated peak 1,500 feet high, on which was a stronghold.—*James Wareing Bardsley, in "Glimpses through the Veil,"* 1883.

Verse 2.—*"My high tower."* Such *towers* were erected on mountains, on rocks, or on the walls of a city, and were regarded as safe places mainly because they were inaccessible. So the old castles in Europe,—as that at Heidelberg, and generally those along the Rhine,—were built on lofty places, and in such positions as not to be easily accessible.—*Albert Barnes.*

Verse 2.—*"My shield."* The Hebrew word signifies, not the huge shield which was carried by an armour-bearer, but the handy target with which heroes entered into hand-to-hand conflicts. A warrior took it with him when he used his bow or his sword. It was often made of metal, but still was portable, and useful, and was made to serve as an ornament, being brightened or anointed with oil. David had made abundant use of the Lord, his God, from day to day, in battles many and murderous.—*C. H. S.*

Verse 2.—*"Who subdueth my people under me."* David, accordingly, having ascribed the victories he had gained over foreign enemies to God, thanks him at the same time for the settled state of the kingdom. Raised indeed as he was from an obscure station, and exposed to hatred from calumnious charges, it was scarcely to have been believed that he would ever obtain a peaceable reign. The people had suddenly, and beyond expectation, submitted to him; and so surprising a change was eminently God's work.—*John Calvin.*

Verse 3.—"LORD, *what is man*," etc.

Now what is man, when grace reveals
The virtues of a Saviour's blood ?
Again a life divine he feels,
Despises earth, and walks with God.

And what in yonder realms above,
Is ransomed man ordained to be ?
With honour, holiness, and love,
No seraph more adorned than he.

Nearest the throne, and first in song,
Man shall his hallelujahs raise,
While wondering angels round him throng,
And swell the chorus of his praise.

John Newton, in Olney Hymns.

Verse 3.—"LORD, *what is man ?*" Take him in his four elements, of earth, air, fire, and water. In the *earth*, he is as fleeting dust ; in the *air*, he is as disappearing vapour ; in the *water*, he is as a breaking bubble ; and in the *fire*, he is as consuming smoke.—*William Secker, in "The Nonsuch Professor."*

Verses 3, 4.—"LORD, *what is man*," etc. There is no book so well worthy reading as this living one. Even now David spake as a king of men, of *people subdued under him !* now he speaks as a humble vassal to God : "LORD, *what is man that thou takest knowledge of him ?*" In one breath is both sovereignty and subjugation : an absolute sovereignty over his people ; "*My people are subdued under me*"; an humble subjection to the God of kings ; "LORD, *what is man ?*" Yea, in the very same word wherein is the profession of that sovereignty, there is an acknowledgment of subjection : "*Thou hast subdued my people.*" In that he had a people, he was a king : that they might be his people, a subjection was requisite ; and that subjugation was God's and not his own: "*Thou* hast subdued." Lo, David, had not subdued his people, if God had not subdued them for him. He was a great king, but they were a stiff people : the God that made them swayed them to a due subjection. The great conquerors of worlds could not conquer hearts, if he, that moulded hearts, did not temper them. " By me kings reign," saith the Eternal Wisdom ; and he that had courage enough to encounter a bear, a lion, Goliath, yet can say, "*Thou hast subdued my people.*"

Contrarily, in the lowliest subjection of himself, there is an acknowledgment of greatness. Though he abused himself with, "*What is man ?*" yet, withal he adds, "*Thou takest knowledge of him, thou makest account of him*": and this knowledge, this account of God, doth more exalt man than his own vanity can depress him. My text, then, ye see, is David's rapture, expressed in an ecstatical question of sudden wonder ; a wonder at God and at man : MAN'S VILENESS; "*What is man ?*" GOD'S MERCY AND FAVOUR, in his knowledge, in his estimation of man. Lo, there are but two lessons that we need to take out here, in the world, God and man ; man, in the notion of his wretchedness ; God, in the notion of his bounty.

Let us, if you please, take a short view of both ; and, in the one, see cause of our humiliation ; of our joy and thankfulness in the other : and if, in the former, there be a sad Lent of mortification ; there is, in the latter, a cheerful Easter of our raising and exaltation.

Many a one besides David wonders at himself : one wonders at his own honour ; and, though he will not say so, yet thinks, " What a great man am I ! Is not this great Babel, which I have built ? " This is Nebuchadnezzar's wonder. Another wonders at his person, and finds, either a good face, or a fair eye, or an exquisite hand, or a well-shaped leg, or some gay fleece, to admire in himself : this was Absalom's wonder. Another wonders at his wit and learning : " How came I by all this ? *Turba hæc !* This vulgar, that knows not the law, is accursed " : this was the Pharisee's wonder. Another wonders at his wealth ; " Soul, take thine ease " ; as the epicure in the gospel. David's wonder is as much above, as against all these : he wonders at his *vileness :* like as the Chosen Vessel would boast of nothing but his infirmities : "LORD, *what is man ?*"

How well this hangs together ! No sooner had he said, "*Thou hast subdued my people under me,*" then he adds, "LORD, *what is man ?*" Some vain heart would have been lifted up with a conceit of his own eminence ; " Who am I ? I am not as other men. I have people under me ; and people of my own, and people subdued to me ; " this is to be more than a man. I know who hath said, " I said ye are gods."—*Joseph Hall.*

Verse 3.—Dr. Hammond refers this Psalm to the slaying of Goliath, and thus understands the appellation "*son of man*,"—" David was but a young stripling, the youngest and most inconsiderable of all the sons of Jesse, who also was himself an ordinary man."

Verse 3.—"*Thou takest knowledge of him.*" It is a great word. Alas ! what knowledge do we take of the gnats that play in the sun ; or the ants, or worms, that are crawling in our grounds ? Yet the disproportion betwixt us and them is but finite ; infinite betwixt God and us. Thou, the Great God of Heaven, to take knowledge of such a thing as man ! If a mighty prince shall vouchsafe to spy and single out a plain homely swain in a throng, as the Great Sultan did lately a tankard-bearer ; and take special notice of him, and call him but to a kiss of his hand and nearness to his person ; he boasts of it as a great favour : for thee, then, O God, who abasest thyself to behold the things in heaven itself, to cast thine eye upon so poor a worm as man, it must needs be a wonderful mercy.—*Exigua pauperibus magna ;* as Nazianzen to his Amphilochius.—*Joseph Hall.*

Verse 4.—"*Man is like to vanity.*" As he that goeth to a fair, with a purse full of money, is devising and debating with himself how to lay it out—possibly thinking that such and such commodities will be most profitable, and bring him in the greatest gain—when on a sudden a cut-purse comes and easeth him both of his money and how to dispose of it. Surely thou mightst have taken notice how some of thy neighbours or countrymen, when they have been busy in their contrivances, and big with many plots and projects how to raise their estate and names and families, were arrested by death in a moment, returned to their earth, and in that day all their gay, their great thoughts perished, and came to nothing. The heathen historian could not but observe how Alexander the Great, when he had to carry on his great designs, summoned a parliament before him of the whole world, he was himself summond by death to appear in the other world. The Dutch, therefore, very wittily to express the world's vanity, picture at Amsterdam a man with a full-blown bladder on his shoulders, and another standing by pricking the bladder with a pin, with this motto, QUAM SUBITO, How soon is all blown down ! —*George Swinnock.*

Verse 4.—"*Man is like to vanity.*" When Cain was born, there was much ado about his birth ; " I have gotten a man-child from God," saith his mother ; she looked upon him as a great possession, and therefore called his name *Cain*, which signifies " a possession." But the second man that was born unto the world bare the title of the world, " *vanity* " ; his name was *Abel*, that is, " *vanity.*" A premonition was given in the name of the second man what would or should be the condition of all men. In Psalm cxliv. 4 there is an allusion unto those two names. We translate it, "*Man is like to vanity*" ; the Hebrew is, "*Adam is as Abel*"; *Adam*, you know, was the name of the first man, the name of Abel's faither ; but as Adam was the proper name of the first, so it is an appellative, or common to all men, now *Adam*, that is, man or all men, are *Abel*, vain, and walking in a vain show. —*Joseph Caryl.*

Verse 4.—"*Man is like to vanity,*" etc. The occasion of the introduction of these sentiments here is not quite clear. It may be the humility of the warrior who ascribes all success to God instead of to human prowess, or it may be a reflection uttered over the corpses of comrades, or, perhaps a blending of the two.—*A. S. Aglen.*

Verse 4.—"*Man is like to vanity,*" etc. With what idle dreams, what foolish plans, what vain pursuits, are men for the most part occupied ! They undertake dangerous expeditions and difficult enterprises in foreign countries, and they acquire fame ; but what is it ?—*Vanity !* They pursue deep and abstruse speculations, and give themselves to that " much study which is a weariness to the flesh," and they attain to literary renown, and survive in their writings ; but what is it ?— *Vanity !* They rise up early and sit up late, and eat the bread of anxiety and care, and thus they amass wealth ; but what is it ?—*Vanity !* They frame and execute plans and schemes of ambition—they are loaded with honours and adorned with titles—they afford employment for the herald, and form a subject for the historian ; but what is it ?—*Vanity !* In fact, all occupations and pursuits are worthy of no other epithet, if they are not preceded by, and connected with, a deep and paramount regard to the salvation of the soul, the honour of God, and the interests of eternity. . . . . Oh, then, what phantoms, what airy nothings are those things that wholly absorb the powers and occupy the days of the great mass of mankind around us! Their most substantial good perishes in the using, and their most enduring realities are but " the fashion of this world that passeth away."—*Thomas Raffles*, 1788—1863.

Verse 4.—*"A shadow that passeth away."* The shadows of the mountains are constanly shifting their position during the day, and ultimately disappear altogether on the approach of night : so is it with man, who is every day advancing to the moment of his final departure from this world.—*Bellarmine.*

Verse 5.—*"Bow thy heavens."* This expression is derived from the appearance of the clouds during a tempest : they hang low, so as to obscure the hills and mountains, and seem to mingle earth and heaven together, Such an appearance is figuratively used to depict the coming of God, to execute vengeance upon the enemies of his people. See Ps. xviii. 10, and other instances.—*William Walford.*

Verse 5.—*"Bow thy heavens, O Lord, and come down,"* etc. This was never so remarkably fulfilled as in the incarnation of Jesus Christ, when heaven and earth were, as it were, brought together. Heaven itself was, as it were, made to bow that it might be united to the earth. God did, as it were, come down and bring heaven with him. He not only came down to the earth, but he brought heaven down with him to men and for men. It was a most strange and wonderful thing. But this will be more remarkably fulfilled still by Christ's second coming, when he will indeed bring all heaven down with him—viz., all the inhabitants of heaven. Heaven shall be left empty of its inhabitants to come down to the earth ; and then the mountains shall smoke, and shall indeed flow down at his presence, as in Isa. lxiv. 1.—*Jonathan Edwards.*

Verse 5.—*"Touch the mountains, and they shall smoke."* The meaning is, when God doth but lay his hand upon great men, upon the mightiest of the world, he makes them smoke or fume, which some understand of their anger ; they are presently in a passion, if God do but touch them. Or we may understand it of their consumption. A *smoking* mountain will soon be a *burnt* mountain. In our language, to make a man smoke is a proverbial expression for destroying or subduing.—*Joseph Caryl.*

Verses 5, 6.—

> Bow thy heavens, Jehovah,
>   Come down in thy might ;
> Let the rays of thy glory
>   The mountain-tops light.
>
> With the bolts of thy thunder
>   Discomfit my foe,
> With the flash of thine arrows
>   Their force overthrow.

> *William Digby Seymour.*

Verse 6.—*"Cast forth lightning."* The Hebrew here is, " Lighten lightning ; " that is, Send forth lightning. The word is used as a verb nowhere else.—*Albert Barnes.*

Verse 7.—*"Send thine hand from above."* Hebrew, *hands*, both hands, all thy whole power, for I need it.—*John Trapp.*

Verse 7.—*"Rid me, and deliver me."* Away, you who theorize about suffering, and can do no more than descant upon it, away! for in the time of weeping we cannot endure your reasonings. If you have no means of delivering us, if you have nothing but sententious phrases to offer, put your hands on you mouths ; enwarp yourselves in silence ! It is enough to suffer ; but to suffer and listen ;o you is more than we can bear. If Job's mouth was nigh unto blasphemy, the blame fs yours, ye miserable comforters, who talked instead of weeping. If I must suffer, than I pray for suffering without fine talk !—*E. De Pressensé.*

Verse 7.—*"Rid me, and deliver me . . . from the hand of strange children."* We must remember that as the Grecians (conceiting themselves the best bred people in the world) called all other nations " barbarians ; " so the people of Israel, the stock of Abraham (being God's peculiar covenant people), called all other nations "aliens" or "*strangers;*" and because they were hated and maligned by all other nations, therefore they called all professed strangers *enemies;* so the word is used (Isa. i. 7), "Your land strangers shall devour"; that is, enemies shall invade and prevail over you. "*Deliver me out of the hand of strange children,*" or out of the hand of strangers; that is, out of the hand of mine enemies. The Latin word *alienus* is often put for *hostis,* and the Roman orator [Cicero] telleth us that "he who is now called a stranger was called an enemy by our ancestors." The reason was because strangers proved unkind to, yea, turned enemies against those that entertained them.—*Joseph Caryl.*

Verse 7.—"*Strange children.*" He calls them *strangers,* not in respect of generic origin, but character and disposition.—*John Calvin.*

Verse 7.—The "*strange children,*" now the enemies of David, shall be either won to willing subjection, or else shall be crushed under the triumphant Messiah (Ps. ii.). The Spirit by David spake things the deep significance of which reached further than even he understood (1 Pet. i. 11, 12).—*Andrew Robert Fausset.*

Verse 8.—"*Whose mouth speaketh vanity,*" etc. Two things go naturally together in the verse—the lying tongue and deceitful hand. The meaning is that upon the matter in hand nothing was to be looked for from any of their promises, since it was only to deceive that they flattered with their mouth and gave the hand.— *John Calvin.*

Verse 8.—"*Their right hand is a right hand of falsehood.*" The pledge of the right hand, which used to be a witness of good faith, was violated by treachery and wickedness.—*Cicero. Philip. xi. c.* 2.

Verse 9.—"*Psaltery—an instrument of ten strings.*" Nebel-azor. We are led to the conclusion that the *nebel* was the veritable *harp* of the Hebrews. It could not have been large, because it is so frequently mentioned in the Bible as being carried in processions. . . . The English translators render *nebel* (apparently without any special reason) by no less than four words; (1) Psaltery, (2) Psalm, (3) lute, (4) viol. The first of these is by far the most common in the Authorised Version, and is no doubt the most correct translation if the word be understood in its true sense as a *portable harp.* Nebels were made of fir-wood, and afterwards of almug, or algum, which was, perhaps, the red sandal-wood of India. . . . With *nebel* is often associated the word *azor,* which is traced to a root signifying *ten,* and which has therefore been rendered in the Septuagint by ἐν δεκαχόρδῳ or as ψαλτηριον δεκάχορδον (*psalterium decem chordarum*), or *in dechachordo psalterio* in the Vulgate. In the Chaldee, Syriac, and Arabic versions also are found words implying the existence of ten strings in the *nebel-azor.* The word *azor* may therefore be considered as qualifying or describing the special kind of *nebel* to be used, much in the same way as we now speak of a *trichord* pianoforte. It is in our English version always rendered by the words "*ten-stringed.*"—*John Stainer in "The Music of the Bible,*" 1882.

Verse 10.—"*It is he that giveth salvation unto kings.*" Ferdinand, king of Aragon, sending his son against the Florentines, thus bespake him: Believe me, son, victories are not gotten by art or subtlety, but given of God.—*John Trapp.*

Verse 10.—"*It is he that giveth salvation unto kings.*" What a doctrine this for the kings and great men of the earth to remember! Could they be brought to feel and acknowledge it, they would not trust to the sagacity of their own councils, nor to the strength of their own arm; but would ever remember that the Most High is the ruler among the nations, and that he putteth down one and raiseth up another according to the dictates of his own all-perfect will. Such remembrances as this would stain the pride of all human glory, and would lead men to feel that the Lord alone is to be exalted.—*John Morison.*

Verse 11.—This Psalm is the language of a prince who wished his people's prosperity: that their "garners might be full of all manner of stores"; that their "sheep might bring forth thousands and ten thousands in their streets"; that their "oxen" might be fat for slaughter, or "strong for labour"; that there might be neither robbery nor beggary in their streets: no oppressive magistrates, nor complaining people: and as if all these blessings were to be derived from the character of the people, and the character of the people from the education they had received, our text is a prayer for the youth of Judea.—*Robert Robinson* (1735—1790), *in "The Nature and Necessity of Early Piety."*

Verse 12.—The reminiscences or imitations of Ps. xvii. suddenly cease here, and are followed by a series of original, peculiar, and for the most part no doubt antique expressions. On the supposition that the title is correct in making David the author, this is natural enough. On any other supposition, it is unaccountable, unless by the gratuitous assumption, that this is a fragment of an older composition, a mode of reasoning by which anything may be either proved or disproved.—*Joseph Addison Alexander.*

Verse 12.—*"That our sons may be as plants,"* etc. They who have ever been employed in the cultivation of plants of any kind, are continually tempted to wish that the human objects of their care and culture would grow up as rapidly, as straight, as flourishingly, would as uniformly fulfil their specific idea and purpose, as abundantly reward the labour bestowed on them. . . . . If our sons are indeed to grow up as young plants, like our English oaks, which according to the analogies of Nature, furnish no inappropriate type of our national character, they must not be stunted or dwarfed or pollarded, for the sake of being kept under the shade of a stranger. They should grow up straight toward heaven, as God had ordained them to grow. . . . There is something so palpable and striking in this type, that five-and-twenty years ago, in speaking of the gentlemanly character, I was led to say, " If a gentleman is to grow up he must grow like a tree : there must be nothing between him and heaven."—*Julius Charles Hare, in a Sermon entitled "Education the Necessity of Mankind,"* 1851.

Verse 12.—*"That our sons may be as plants grown up in their youth,"* etc. Thus David prays for the rising generation. Metaphors seem generally unsuitable to prayer, but they do not wear this aspect in the prayers recorded in the Scriptures. The language of the text is tropical, but the metaphors are suitable and seasonable. *Roots* of vegetables are necessarily invisible. *Tender* plants are insignificant. A plant *grown up*, having height in its stem, width in its branches, abundance in its foliage, and fulness in its bloom, is conspicuous. David prays that the sons of that generation might be in their youth *"as plants grown up,"* that is, that their piety might not only live, but that their godliness might be fully expressed. The stones of a *foundation* are concealed. The stones in the *mid-wall* of a building are also necessarily hid. The stones on the *surface* of a wall are visible, but they are not distinguished. The *corner-stone* of buildings in that day was prominent and eminent. Placed at the angle of the structure, where two walls met, on the top of the walls, and being richly ornamented and polished, it attracted attention. David prays that the daughters of that day might make an open and lovely profession of religion—that both sons and daughters might not only *have* piety but *show* it.—*Samuel Martin, in "Cares of Youth."*

Verse 12.—*"Plants grown up." "Corner-stones polished."* These processes of growth and polish can be carried on in one place only, the church of Christ.—*Neale and Littledale.*

Verse 12.—*"That our daughters may be as corner stones,"* etc. *"The polished corners of the temple,"* rather *" the sculptured angles, the ornament, of a palace."* Great care and much ornament were bestowed by the ancients upon the angles of their splendid palaces. It is remarkable that the Greeks made use of pilasters, called Caryatides (carved after the figure of a woman dressed in long robes), to support the entablatures of their buildings.—*Daniel Cresswell.*

Verse 12.—*"That our daughters may be as corner stones, polished after the similitude of a palace "* or *temple.* By daughters families are united and connected to their mutual strength, as the parts of a building are by the corner-stones ; and when they are graceful and beautiful both in body and mind, they are then polished after the similitude of a nice and curious structure. When we see our daughters well established, and stayed with wisdom and discretion, as corner-stones are fastened in the building ; when we see them by faith united to Christ, as the chief corner-stone, adorned with the graces of God's Spirit, which are the polishing of that which is naturally rough, and " become women professing godliness " ; when we see them purified and consecrated to God as living temples, we think ourselves happy in them.—*Matthew Henry.*

Verse 12.—*"That our daughters may be as corner stones,"* etc. One might perhaps at the first glance have expected that the *daughters* of a household would be as the graceful ornament of the clustering foliage or the fruit-bearing tree, and the *sons* as the corner-stones upholding the weight and burden of the building, and yet it is the reverse here. And I think one may read the love and tenderness of the Lord in this apparently casual but intended expression, and that he meant the nations of the earth to know and understand how much of their happiness, their strength, and their security was dependent on the female children of a family. It has not been so considered in many a nation that knew not God : in polished Greece in times of old, and in some heathen nations even to this day, the female children of a family have been cruelly destroyed, as adding to the burdens and diminishing the resources of a household ; and alas ! too, even in Christian countries, if not destroyed, they are with equal pitiless and remorseless cruelty cut off from all the solace and ties and endearments of life, and immured in that living mockery of a grave, the cloister, that they may not prove incumbrances and hindrances to others ! How contrary all this to the loving purpose of our loving God ! whose Holy Spirit has written for our learning that sons and daughters are alike intended to be the ornament and grace, the happiness and blessing of every household.—*Barton Bouchier.*

Verse 12.—"*After the similitude of a palace.*" Most interpreters give the last word the vague sense of "*a palace.*" There is something, however, far more striking in the translation *temple*, found in the Prayer Book and the ancient versions. The omission of the article is a poetic license of perpetual occurrence. The temple was the great architectural model and standard of comparison, and particularly remarkable for the great size and skilful elaboration of its foundation-stones, some of which, there is reason to believe, have remained undisturbed since the time of Solomon.— *Joseph Addison Alexander.*

Verses 12—15.—In the former part of the Psalm he speaks of such things as concern *his own* happiness : " Blessed be the Lord my strength " (verse 1) ; " Send thine hand from above ; and deliver me out of great waters " (verse 7) ; " Rid me, and deliver me from the hand of strange children " (verse 11). And he might as easily have continued the same strain in the clauses following : " That *my* sons may grow up as plants, *my* daughters may be as the polished corners of the temple, *my* sheep fruitful, *my* oxen strong, *my* garners full and plenteous " ; and accordingly he might have concluded it also—" Happy shall *I* be, if *I* be in such a case." This, I say, he might have done ; nay, this he would have done, if his desires had reflected only upon himself. But being of a diffusive heart, and knowing what belonged to the neighbourhoods of piety, as loth to enjoy this happiness alone, he alters his style, and (being in the height of well-wishes to himself) he turns the singular into a plural—*our sheep, our oxen, our garners, our sons and daughters*, that he might compendiate all in this,—"*Happy are the people.*" Here is a true testimony both of a religious and generous mind, who knew in his most retired thoughts to look out of himself, and to be mindful of the public welfare in his privatest meditations. S. Ambrose observes it as a clear character of a noble spirit, to do what tends to the public good, though to his own disadvantage.—*Richard Holdsworth* (1590— 1649), *in "The Valley of Vision."*

Verses 12—15.—These words contain a striking picture of a prosperous and happy nation. We are presented with a view of the *masculine youth* of the nation by the oaks of the forest, become great in the early period of the vigour and excellency of the soil. They are represented in the distinguishing character of their sex, standing abroad the strength of the nation, whence its resources for action must be derived. On the other hand, the *young females* of a nation are exhibited under an equally just and proper representation of their position and distinguishing character. They are not exhibited by a metaphor derived from the hardier tenants of the forest, but they are shown to us by a representation taken from the perpetual accompaniments of the dwelling ; they are the supports and the ornaments of domestic life. *Plenty* of every kind is represented to us in possession and in reasonable expectation. "*No breaking in,*" no invasion by a furious foe, oppresses the inhabitants of this happy country with terror ; neither is there any "*going out.*" The barbarous practice employed by Sennacherib, and other ancient conquerors, of transporting the inhabitants of a vanquished country to some distant, unfriendly, and hated land, —the practice at this moment employed, to the scandal of the name and the sorrow of Europe—they dread not : they fear no "*going out.*" Under circumstances of such a nature causes of distress or complaint exist not ; or, if they do, they are capable of being so modified, and alleviated, and remedied, that *there is no*

complaining in the streets. "Happy, then, is that people, that is in such a case."—
John Pye Smith, 1775—1851.

Verse 13.—*"That our sheep may bring forth thousands,"* etc. The surprising
fecundity of the sheep has been celebrated by writers of every class. It has not
escaped the notice of the royal Psalmist, who, in a beautiful ascription of praise
to the living and the true God, entreats that the sheep of his chosen people might
" *bring forth thousands and ten thousands in our streets."* In another song of Zion,
he represents, by a very elegant metaphor, the numerous flocks covering like a
garment the face of the field :—" The pastures are clothed with flocks ; the valleys
also are covered over with corn ; they shout for joy, they also sing " : Ps. lxv.
13. The bold figure is fully warranted by the prodigious numbers of sheep which
whitened the extensive pastures of Syria and Canaan. In that part of Arabia
which borders on Judea, the patriarch Job possessed at first seven thousand, and
after the return of his prosperity, fourteen thousand sheep ; and Mesha, the king of
Moab, paid the king of Israel " a yearly tribute of a hundred thousand lambs, and
an equal number of rams with the wool ": 2 Kings iii. 4. In the war which the
tribe of Reuben waged with the Hagarites, the former drove away " two hundred
and fifty thousand sheep " : 1 Chron. v. 21. At the dedication of the temple,
Solomon offered in sacrifice " an hundred and twenty thousand sheep." At the
feast of the passover, Josiah, the king of Judah, " gave to the people, of the flock,
lambs and kids, all for the passover offerings, for all that were present, to the number
of thirty thousand, and three thousand bullocks : these were of the king's substance ":
2 Chron. xxxv. 7. The ewe brings forth her young commonly once a year, and
in more ungenial climes, seldom more than one lamb at a time. But twin lambs are
as frequent in the oriental regions, as they are rare in other places ; which accounts
in a satisfactory manner for the prodigious numbers which the Syrian shepherd
led to the mountains. This uncommon fruitfulness seems to be intimated by Solomon
in his address to the spouse :—" Thy teeth are like a flock of sheep that are even
shorn, which came up from the washing ; whereof every one bear twins, and none
is barren among them " : Cant. iv. 2.—*George Paxton (1762—1837), in "Illustrations
of Scripture."*
Verses 13, 14.—*"Streets,"* though not incorrect, is an inadequate translation
of the Hebrew word, which means external spaces, streets as opposed to the inside
of houses, fields or country as opposed to a whole town. Here it includes not only
roads but fields.—*Joseph Addison Alexander.*

Verse 14.—*"That our oxen may be strong to labour."* [Margin : *"able to bear
burdens,"* or, *loaded* with flesh]. As in the verse before he had ascribed the fruitfulness of the herds and flocks to God's goodness, so now the fattening of their oxen,
to show that there is nothing relating to us here which he overlooks.—*John Calvin.*
Verse 14.—*"That our oxen may be strong to labour."* Oxen were not only used
for ploughing, thrashing, and drawing, but also for bearing burdens ; compare
1 Chron. xii. 40, which passage is peculiarly fitted to throw light on the verse before
us. Laden oxen presuppose a rich abundance of produce.—*E. W. Hengstenberg.*
Verse 14.—*"That there be no complaining in our streets,"* etc. Rather, " and
no cry of sorrow " (comp. Isaiah xxiv. 11 ; Jer. xiv. 2 ; xlvi. 12) " in our open
places," *i.e.,* the places where the people commonly assembled near the gate of
the city (comp. 2 Chron. xxxii. 6 ; Neh. viii. 1). The word rendered " *complaining* "
does not occur elsewhere in the Psalter.—*Speaker's Commentary.*
Verse 14.—*"No complaining."* No outcries but " Harvest-homes."—*John
Trapp.*

Verse 15.—*"Happy is that people,"* etc. We have in the text happiness with
an echo, or ingemination ; " *happy* " and " *happy."* From this ingemination arise
the parts of my text ; the same which are the parts both of the greater world and
the less. As the heaven and earth in the one, and the body and soul in the other ;
so are the passages of this Scripture in the two veins of happiness. We may range
them as Isaac does the two parts of his blessing (Gen. xxvii. 28) ; the vein of civil
happiness, in " the fatness of the earth ; " and the vein of Divine happiness, in
" the fatness of heaven." Or (if you will have it out of the gospel), here's Martha's
portion in the " many things " of the body ; and Mary's better part in the *unum*

necessarium of the soul. To give it yet more concisely, here's the path of *prosperity* in outward comforts, *"Happy is that people that is in such a case"* ; and the path of *piety* in comforts spiritual : *"Yea, happy is that people, whose God is the* LORD." In the handling of the first, without any further subdivision, I will only show what it is the Psalmist treats of ; and that shall be by way of gradation, in these three particulars. It is *De* FELICITATE ; *De Felicitate* POPULI ; *De* HAC *Felicitate Populi :* of *happiness ;* of the *people's* happiness ; of the people's happiness, as *in such a case.*

Happiness is the general, and the first : a noble argument, and worthy of an inspired pen, especially the Psalmist's. Of all other there can be none better to speak of *popular* happiness than such a *king ;* nor of *celestial,* than such a *prophet.* Yet I mean not to discourse of it in the full latitude, but only as it hath a peculiar positure in this Psalm, very various and different from the order of other Psalms. In this Psalm it is reserved to the *end,* as the close of the foregoing meditations. In other Psalms it is set in the *front,* or first place of all ; as in the xxxii., in the cxii., in the cxix., and in the cxxviii. Again, in this the Psalmist ends with *our* happiness and begins with God's. " Blessed be the LORD my strength." In the 41st Psalm,. contrary, he makes his *exordium* from *man's ;* " Blessed is he that considereth the poor"; his *conclusion* with *God's ;* " Blessed be the LORD God of Israel." I therefore observe these variations, because they are helpful to the understanding both of the *essence* and *splendour* of true happiness. To the knowledge of the *essence* they help, because they demonstrate how our own happiness is enfolded in the glory of God, and subordinate unto it. As we cannot begin with *beatus* unless we end with *benedictus :* so we must begin with *benedictus* that we may end with *beatus.* The reason is this,—because the glory of God is as well the *consummation* as the *introduction* to a Christian's happiness. Therefore as in the other Psalm he begins below and ends upwards ; so in this, having begun from above with that which is principal, " Blessed be the LORD"; he fixeth his second thoughts upon the subordinate, " Blessed, or happy, are the people." He could not proceed in a better order : he first looks up to *God's* kingdom, then reflects upon his own, as not meaning to *take* blessedness before he had *given* it.—*Richard Holdsworth.*

Verse 15.—*"Happy is that people, that is in such a case,"* etc. The first part of this text hath relation to temporal blessings, *"Blessed is the people that be so"* : the second to spiritual, *"Yea, blessed is the people whose God is the* LORD." " His left hand is under my head," saith the spouse (Cant. ii. 6) ; that sustains me from falling into murmuring, or diffidence of his providence, because out of his left hand he hath given me a competency of his temporal blessings ; " But his right hand doth embrace me," saith the spouse there ; his spiritual blessings fill me, possess me so that no rebellious fire breaks out within me, no outward temptation breaks in upon me. So also Solomon says again, " In her left hand is riches and glory," (temporal blessings) " and in her right hand length of days " (Prov. iii. 16), all that accomplishes and fulfils the eternal joys of the saints of heaven. The person to whom Solomon attributes this right and left hand is Wisdom ; and a wise man may reach out his right and left hand, to receive the blessings of both sorts. And the person whom Solomon represents by Wisdom there, is Christ himself. So that not only a wordly wiseman, but a Christian wiseman may reach out both hands, to both kinds of blessings, right and left, spiritual and temporal.

Now, for this blessedness, as no philosophers could ever tell us amongst the Gentiles what true blessedness was, so no grammarian amongst the Jews, amongst the Hebrews, could ever tell us what the right signification of this word is, in which David expresses blessedness here ; whether *asherei,* which is the word, be a plural noun, and signify *beatitudines,* blessednesses in the plural, and intimate thus much, that blessedness consists not in any one thing, but in a harmony and consent of many ; or whether this *asherei* be an adverb, and signify *beate,* and so be an acclamation, O how happily, how blessedly are such men provided for that are so ; they cannot tell. Whatsoever it be, it is the very first word with which David begins his Book of Psalms ; *beatus vir ;* as the last word of that book is *laudate Dominum ;* to show that all that passes between God and man, from first to last, is blessings from God to man, and praises from man to God ; and that the first degree of blessedness is to find the print of the hand of God even in his temporal blessednesses, and to praise and glorify him for them in the right use of them. A man that hath no land to hold by it, nor title to recover by it, is never the better for finding, or buying, or having a fair piece of evidence, a fair instrument, fairly written, duly sealed, authentically testified ; a man that hath not the grace of God, and spiritual blessings too, is never the nearer happiness, for all his abundances of temporal blessedness. Evidences are evidences to them who have title.   Temporal blessings are evidences to them who have a testimony of God's spiritual blessings in the temporal.   Otherwise, as in his hands who hath no title, it is a suspicious thing to find evidences, and he will be thought to have embezzled and purloined them, he will be thought to have forged and counterfeited them, and he will be called to an account for them, how he came by them, and what he meant to do with them : so to them who have temporal blessings without spiritual, they are but useless blessings, they are but counterfeit blessings, they shall not purchase a minute's peace here, nor a minute's refreshing to the soul hereafter ; and there must be a heavy account made for them, both how they were got, and how they were employed.—*John Donne.*

Verse 15.—*"Happy is that people,"* etc.   It is only a narrow and one-sided religion that can see anything out of place in this beatitude of plenty and peace. If we could rejoice with the Psalms fully and without misgiving, in the temporal blessings bestowed by heaven, we should the more readily and sincerely enter into the depths of their spiritual experience.   And the secret of this lies in the full comprehension and contemplation of the beautiful and pleasant as the gift of God.—*A. S. Aglen.*

Verse 15.—*" Yea, happy is that people, whose God is the LORD."* *"Yea, happy."* This is the best wine, kept to the last, though all men be not of this opinion.   You shall hardly bring a worldly man to think so.   The world is willing enough to misconstrue the order of the words, and to give the priority to civil happiness, as if it were first in dignity, because 'tis first named : they like better to hear of the *cui sic* than the *cui Dominus.*   To prevent this folly, the Psalmist interposeth a caution in this corrective particle, " *yea, happy.*"   It hath the force of a revocation, whereby he seems to retract what went before, not simply and absolutely, but in a certain degree, lest worldly men should wrest it to a misinterpretation.   It is not an *absolute* revocation, but a *comparative ;* it does not simply deny that there is some part of popular happiness in these outward things, but it prefers the spirituals before them : " *Yea,*" that is, *Yea more,* or, *Yea rather ;* like that of Christ in the Gospel, when one in the company blessed the womb that bare him, he presently replies, " Yea, rather blessed are they that hear the word of God and keep it : " Luke xi. 28.   In like manner, the prophet David, having first premised the inferior part and outside of a happy condition ; fearing lest they should of purpose mistake his meaning, and, hearing the first proposition, should either there set up their rest, and not at all take up the second ; or if they take it in, do it preposterously, and give it the precedence before the second, according to the world's order, *Virtus post nummos.*   In this respect he puts in the clause of revocation, whereby he shows that these outward things, though *named* first, yet they are not to be *reputed* first. The particle *"Yea"* removes them to the second place ; it tacitly transposeth the order ; and the path of piety, which was *locally* after, it placeth *virtually* before. 'Tis as if he said, Did I call them *happy* who are in such a case ?   Nay, miserable are they if they be only in such a case : the temporal part cannot make them so without the spiritual.   Admit the windows of the visible heaven were opened, and all outward blessings poured down upon us ; admit we did perfectly enjoy whatsoever the vastness of the earth contains in it ; tell me, What will it profit to gain all and lose God ?   If the earth be bestowed upon us, and not heaven ; or the material heaven be opened, and not the beatifical ; or the whole world made ours, and God not ours ; we do not arrive at happiness.   All that is in the first proposition is nothing unless this be added, *"Yea, happy are the people which have the Lord for their God."*—*Richard Holdsworth.*

Verse 15.—

> Thrice happy nations, where with look benign
> Thine aspect bends ; beneath thy smile divine
> The fields are with increasing harvests crown'd,
> The flocks grow fast, and plenty reigns around,
> Nor sire, nor infant son, black death shall crave,
> Till ripe with age they drop into the grave ;
> Nor fell suspicion, nor relentless care,
> Nor peace-destroying discord enter there,
> But friends and brothers, wives and sisters, join
> The feast in concord and in love divine.
>
> *Callimachus.*

Verse 15.—David having prayed for many temporal blessings in the behalf of the people from verse 12 to verse 15, at last concludes, "*Blessed are the people that are in such a case*"; but presently he checks and corrects himself, and eats, as it were, his own words, but rather, "*happy is that people whose God is the Lord.*" The Syriac rendereth it question wise, "Is not the people [happy] that is in such a case?" The answer is, "*No,*" except they have God to boot: Ps. cxlvi. 5. Nothing can make that man truly miserable that hath God for his portion, and nothing can make that man truly happy that wants God for his portion. God is the author of all true happiness; he is the donor of all true happiness; he is the maintainer of all true happiness, and he is the centre of all true happiness; and, therefore, he that hath him for his God, and for his portion, is the only happy man in the world.—*Thomas Brooks.*

Verse 15.—"*Whose God is* JEHOVAH." A word or name well-known to us English, by our translators now often retaining that name in the mention of God in our English Bibles, and therefore we do well to retain it. *Lord* was a lower word, in common acceptation, than *God*. But JEHOVAH is a higher name than either, and more peculiar, incommunicable, and comprehensive. Exod. vi. 3: "I appeared" (saith the Lord) "unto Abraham, unto Isaac, and unto Jacob, by the name *God Almighty*, but by my name JEHOVAH was I not known to them."

To have God to be our *Jehovah* is the insurance of happiness to us. For of many, observe but these two things in the name *Jehovah*: First, God's absolute *independency*—that he is of himself omnipotent, Exod. iii. 14: "And God said, I AM THAT I AM." Secondly, God's *faithfulness*, that he cannot but be as good as his word, Exod. vi. 2, 3, 4, 6: "And I have also established my covenant with them; wherefore say unto the children of Israel, I am JEHOVAH (so in the Hebrew), and I will bring you out from under the burdens of the Egyptians." So that this name is our *security* of God's performance. Examine we therefore our bonds, and bills, that is, his promises to us; behold, they are all the promises of Jehovah; they must stand good, for they bear his name; they must reflect his name, and promote both our good and God's grand design.—*Nathanael Homes,* 1678.

With this prayer of Jehovah's anointed One end the prayers of the Book of Psalms. The remaining six Psalms consist exclusively of praise and high Hallelujahs.—*Lord Congleton, in "The Psalms: a new Version, with Notes,"* 1875.

HINTS TO PREACHERS.

Verse 1.—I. Two things needful in our holy war—strength and skill; for the hands and the fingers, for the difficult and the delicate. II. In what way God supplies us with both. He is the one, and teaches the other. Impartation and Instruction. The teaching comes by illumination, experience, distinct guidance.

Verse 1.—Things not to be forgotten by the Christian Soldier. I. The true source of his strength: "The Lord my strength." If remembered, 1. He will not be found trusting in self. 2. He will never be wanting in courage. 3. He will always anticipate victory. 4. He will never be worsted in the conflict. II. His constant need of instruction, and the Teacher who never forgets him: "Which teacheth my hands," etc. If remembered, 1. He will gird on the armour provided and commended by God. 2. He will select for his weapon the sword of the Spirit. 3. He will study the divinely-given text-book of military tactics and discipline, that he may learn (1) the devices of the enemy; (2) methods of attack and defence; (3) how to bear himself in the thick of the fight. 4. He will wait upon God for understanding. III. The praise due to God, both for victories won and skill displayed: "Blessed be," etc. If remembered, 1. He will wear his honours humbly. 2. Glorify the honour of his King. 3. Twice taste the sweets of victory in the happiness of gratitude.—*J. F.*

Verse 2.—Double flowers. I. Good preserved from evil: "goodness" and "fortress." II. Safety enlarged into liberty: "tower," "deliverer." III. Security attended with rest: "shield, in whom I trust." IV. Sufficiency to maintain superiority: "subdueth my people under me." View God as working all.

Verse 2.—A Group of Titles. **Notice, I.** Which comes first. "Goodness." *Heb.* "Mercy." 1. It is right and natural that a saved sinner should make the most of "mercy," and place it in the foreground. 2. Mercy is the ground and reason of the other titles named. For whatever God is to us, it is a special manifestation of his mercy. 3. It is a good thing to see a believer ripe in experience making mercy the leading note in his song of praise. II. Which comes last : "He in whom I trust." It suggests, 1. That what God is makes him worthy of trust. 2. That meditation upon what he is strengthens our trust. III. What peculiar force the word " my " gives to each. It makes, 1. A record of experience. 2. An ascription of praise. 3. A blessed boasting. 4. An incentive, enough to set others longing.—*J. F.*

Verse 3.—A note of interrogation, exclamation, and admiration.

Verse 3.—The question, I. Denies any right in man to claim the regard of God. II. Asserts the great honour God has nevertheless put upon him. III. Suggests that the true reason of God's generous dealings is the graciousness of his own heart. IV. Implies the becomingness of gratitude and humility. V. Encourages the most unworthy to put their confidence in God.—*J. F.*

Verse 3.—I. What was man as he came from the hands of his Creator ? 1. Rational. 2. Responsible. 3. Immortal. 4. Holy and happy. II. What is man in his present condition ? 1. Fallen. 2. Guilty. 3. Sinful. 4. Miserable, and helpless in his misery. III. What is man when he has believed in Christ ? 1. Restored to a right relation to God. 2. Restored to a right disposition toward God. 3. He enjoys the influences of the Holy Spirit. 4. He is in process of preparation for the heavenly world. IV. What shall man be when he is admitted into heaven ? 1. Free from sin and sorrow. 2. Advanced to the perfection of his nature. 3. Associated with angels. 4. Near to his Saviour and his God.— *George Brooks, in "The Homiletic Commentary,"* 1879.

Verse 3.—Worthless man much regarded by the mighty God. Sermon by Ebenezer Erskine. Works iii., pp. 141—162.

Verse 3.—It is a wonder above all wonders, that ever the great God should make such account of such a thing as man. I. It will appear if you consider what a great God the Lord is. II. What a poor thing man is. III. What a great account the great God hath of this poor thing, man.—*Joseph Alleine.*

Verse 4.—He is nothing, he pretends to be something, he is soon gone, he ends in nothing as to this life ; yet there is a light somewhere.

Verse 4.—The Shadow-World. I. Our lives are like shadows. II. But God's light casts these shadows. Our being is of God. The brevity and mystery of life are a part of providence. III. The destiny of the shadows ; eternal night ; or eternal light.—*W. B. H.*

Verse 4.—The brevity of our earthly life. 1. A profitable subject for meditation. II. A rebuke to those who provide for this life alone. III. A trumpet-call to prepare for eternity. IV. An incentive to the Christian to make the best of this life for the glory of God.—*J. F.*

Verse 5.—Condescension, visitation, contact, and conflagration.

Verses 7, 8, 11.—Repetitions, not vain. Repetitions in prayer are vain when they result from form, thoughtlessness, or superstition ; but not, *e.g.,* I. When they are the utterance of genuine fervour. II. When the danger prayed against is imminent. III. When the fear which prompts the prayer is urgent. IV. When the repetition is prompted by a new motive, verses 7, 8 ; by God's condescension, verses 3, 11 ; by God's former deliverance, verse 10 ; and by the results which will flow from the answer, verses 12—14.—*C. A. D.*

Verse 8.—What is " a right hand of falsehood " ? Ask the hypocrite, the schemer, the man of false doctrine, the boaster, the slanderer, the man who forgets his promise, the apostate.

Verse 9.—For God's Ear. I. The Singer. A grateful heart. II. The Song. Praiseful. New. III. The Accompaniment : " Psaltery." Helps to devotion. Give God the best. IV. The Auditor and Object of the eulogium : " Thee, O God."—*W. B. H.*

Verse 11.—Persons from whom it is a mercy to escape : those alien to God, vain in conversation, false in deed.

Verses 11, 12.—The Nature and Necessity of early Piety. A Sermon preached to a Society of Young People, at Willingham, Cambridgeshire, on the First Day of the Year M.DCC.LXXII.—*Robert Robinson.*

Verse 12.—Youth attended with development, stability, usefulness, and spiritual health.

Verse 12 (*first clause*).—To Young Men. Consider, 1. What is desired on your behalf : " Sons may be as plants," etc. 1. That you may be respected and valued. 2. That you may have settled principles and virtues. Plants are not blown hither and thither. 3. That you may be vigorous and strong in moral power. II. What is requisite on your part to the accomplishment of this desire. 1. A good rootage in Christ. 2. Constant nourishment from the word of God. 3. The dews of divine grace obtained by prayer. 4. A resolute tendency within to answer the God-appointed purpose of your existence.—*J. F.*

Verse 12 (*second clause*).—To Young Women. Consider, 1. The important position you may occupy in the social fabric : " As corner-stones." 1. The moral and religious tone of society is determined more by your character and influence than by those of men. 2. The complexion of home life will be a reflex of your conduct and character, either as daughters, sisters, or wives. 3. The moulding of the character of the next generation, remember, begins with the mother's influence. 4. Let these facts weigh with you as a motive in seeking the grace of God, without which you can never fulfil your mission worthily. II. The beauty which ought to belong to you in your position. " Polished after," etc. The beauty of, 1. Heart purity : " The King's daughter is all glorious within." 2. A noble and modest conduct : " wrought gold," no imitation ; real gold. 3. Gracious and gentle demeanour. III. How both the right position and right beauty are obtained. 1. By yielding yourselves to God. 2. By Christ dwelling in your heart. 3. By becoming living stones and polished stones under the workmanship of the Holy Spirit.—*J. F.*

Verse 14.—A prayer for our ministers, and for the security, unity, and happiness of the church.

Verse 14.—The prosperous Church. There—I. Labour is cheerfully performed. II. The enemy is kept without the gate. III. There are few or no departures. IV. Faith and content silence complaint. V. Pray that such may be our case as a church.—*W. B. H.*

Verse 15.—The peculiar happiness of those whose God is the Lord.

PSALM CXLV.

This is one of the alphabetical Psalms, composed with much art, and, doubtless, so arranged that the memory might be aided. The Holy Spirit condescends to use even the more artificial methods of the poet, to secure attention, and impress the heart.

TITLE.—DAVID'S PSALM OF PRAISE. *It is David's, David's very own, David's favourite. It is David's Praise just as another (Psalm lxxxvi.) is David's Prayer. It is altogether praise, and praise pitched in a high key. David had blessed God many a time in other Psalms, but this he regarded as his peculiar, his crown jewel of praise. Certainly David's praise is the best of praise, for it is that of a man of experience, of sincerity, of calm deliberation, and of intense warmth of heart. It is not for any one of us to render David's praise, for David only could do that ; but we may take David's Psalm as a model, and aim at making our own personal adoration as much like it as possible : we shall be long before we equal our model. Let each Christian reader present his own praise unto the Lord, and call it by his own name. What a wealth of varied praise will thus be presented through Christ Jesus !*

DIVISION.—*The Psalm does not fall into any marked divisions, but is one and indivisible. Our own translators have mapped out this song with considerable discernment. It is not a perfect arrangement, but it will suit our convenience in exposition. David praiseth God for his fame or glory (1—7), for his goodness (8—10), for his kingdom (11—13), for his providence (14—16), for his saving mercy (17—21).*

EXPOSITION.

I WILL extol thee, my God, O king ; and I will bless thy name for ever and ever.

2 Every day will I bless thee ; and I will praise thy name for ever and ever.

3 Great *is* the LORD, and greatly to be praised ; and his greatness *is* unsearchable.

4 One generation shall praise thy works to another, and shall declare thy mighty acts.

5 I will speak of the glorious honour of thy majesty, and of thy wondrous works.

6 And *men* shall speak of the might of thy terrible acts ; and I will declare thy greatness.

7 They shall abundantly utter the memory of thy great goodness, and shall sing of thy righteousness.

1. *"I will extol thee, my God, O king."* David as God's king adores God as his king. It is well when the Lord's royalty arouses our loyalty, and our spirit is moved to magnify his majesty. The Psalmist has extolled his Lord many a time before, he is doing so still, and he will do so in the future : praise is for all tenses. When we cannot express all our praise just now, it is wise to register our resolution to continue in the blessed work, and write it down as a bond, "I will extol thee." See how David testifies his devotion and adherence to his God by the pronoun "my," how he owns his allegiance by the title "king," and how he goes on to declare his determination to make much of him in his song.

"And I will bless thy name for ever and ever." David determined that his praise should rise to blessing, should intelligently spend itself upon the name or character of God, and should be continued world without end. He uses the word "bless" not merely for variation of sound, but also for the deepening and sweetening of the sense. To bless God is to praise him with a personal affection for him, and a wishing well to him ; this is a growingly easy exercise as we advance in experience and grow in grace. David declares that he will offer every form of praise, through every

form of existence. His notion of duration is a full one—"for ever" has no end, but when he adds another " ever " to it he forbids all idea of a close. Our praise of God shall be as eternal as the God we praise.

2. *"Every day will I bless thee."* Whatever the character of the day, or of my circumstances and conditions during that day, I will continue to glorify God. Were we well to consider the matter we should see abundant cause in each day for rendering special blessing unto the Lord. All before the day, all in the day, all following the day should constrain us to magnify our God every day, all the year round. Our love to God is not a matter of holy days : every day is alike holy to holy men. David here comes closer to God than when he said, " I will bless thy name ": it is now, " I will bless *thee.*" This is the centre and kernel of true devotion : we do not only admire the Lord's words and works, but himself. Without realizing the personality of God, praise is well-nigh impossible ; you cannot extol an abstraction. *"And I will praise thy name for ever and ever."* He said he would bless that name, and now he vows to praise it ; he will extol the Lord in every sense and way. Eternal worship shall not be without its variations ; it will never become monotonous. Heavenly music is not harping upon one string, but all strings shall be tuned to one praise. Observe the personal pronouns here : four times he says " *I* will": praise is not to be discharged by proxy : there must be your very self in it, or there is nothing in it.

3. *"Great is the* LORD, *and greatly to be praised."* Worship should be somewhat like its object—great praise for a great God. There is no part of Jehovah's greatness which is not worthy of great praise. In some beings greatness is but vastness of evil : in him it is magnificence of goodness. Praise may be said to be great when the song contains great matter, when the hearts producing it are intensely fervent, and when large numbers unite in the grand acclaim. No chorus is too loud, no orchestra too large, no Psalm too lofty for the lauding of the Lord of Hosts.

"And his greatness is unsearchable."

" Still his worth your praise exceeds,
Excellent are all his deeds."

Song should be founded upon search ; hymns composed without thought are of no worth, and tunes upon which no pains have been spent are beneath the dignity of divine adoration. Yet when we meditate most, and search most studiously, we shall still find ourselves surrounded with unknowable wonders, which will baffle all attempts to sing them worthily. The best adoration of the Unsearchable is to own him to be so, and close the eyes in reverence before the excessive light of his glory. Not all the minds of all the centuries shall suffice to search out the unsearchable riches of God: he is past finding out; and, therefore, his deserved praise is still above and beyond all that we can render to him.

4. *"One generation shall praise thy works to another."* There shall be a tradition of praise : men shall hand on the service, they shall make it a point to instruct their descendants in this hallowed exercise. We look back upon the experience of our fathers, and sing of it ; even thus shall our sons learn praise from the Lord's works among ourselves. Let us see to it that we praise God before our children, and never make them think that his service is an unhappy one. *"And shall declare thy mighty acts."* The generations shall herein unite : together they shall make up an extraordinary history. Each generation shall contribute its chapter, and all the generations together shall compose a volume of matchless character. David began with " I," but he has in this verse soon reached to an inconceivable multitude, comprehending all the myriads of our race of every age. The praise of the Lord enlarges the heart, and as it grows upon us our minds grow with it. God's works of goodness and acts of power make up a subject which all the eras of human story can never exhaust. A praiseful heart seems to live in all the centuries in delightful companionship with all the good. We are not afraid that the incense will ever cease to burn upon the altars of Jehovah : the priests die, but the adoration lives on. All glory be unto him who remains the same Lord throughout all generations.

5. *"I will speak of the glorious honour of thy majesty."* 'Tis fit a king should speak of the majesty of the King of kings. David cannot give over the worship of God into the hands of others, even though all generations should undertake to perpetuate it : he must have his own individual share in it, and so he saith, " I will speak." What a speaker ! for he no sooner begins than he heaps up words of honour—" the glorious honour of thy majesty," or " the beauty of the honour

of thy majesty." His language labours to express his meaning; he multiplies the terms by which he would extol Jehovah, his King. Everything which has to do with the Great King is majestic, honourable, glorious. His least is greater than man's greatest, his lowest is higher than man's highest. There is nothing about the infinite Lord which is unworthy of his royalty; and, on the other hand, nothing is wanting to the splendour of his reign: his majesty is honourable, and his honour is glorious: he is altogether wonderful.

"*And of thy wondrous works.*" All the works of God among men are Godlike, but certain of them are specially calculated to create surprise. Many works of power, of justice, of wisdom, are wonderful; and his work of grace is wondrous above all. This specially, and all the rest proportionately, should be spoken of by holy men, by experienced men, and by men who have the ability to speak with power. These things must not be permitted to pass away in silence; if others do not remember them, representative men like David must make a point of conversing upon them in private, and speaking of them in public. Let it be the delight of each one of us according to our position to speak lovingly of our Lord.

6. "*And men shall speak of the might of thy terrible acts.*" If unobservant of other matters these acts of judgment shall seize their attention and impress their minds so that they must talk about them. Did not men in our Saviour's day speak of the falling tower of Siloam and the slaughtered Galileans? Are there not rumours of wars, when there are not even whispers of other things? Horrible news is sure to spread: under mercies men may be dumb, but concerning miseries they raise a great outcry. The force of dread is a power which loosens the tongue of the multitude: they are sure to talk of that which makes the ear to tingle and the hair to stand upright.

While they are thus occupied with " fearsome facts," such as the drowning of a world, the destruction of the cities of the plain, the plagues of Egypt, the destruction at the Red Sea, and so forth, David would look at these affairs in another light, and sing another tune. "*And I will declare thy greatness.*" Those acts which were terrible deeds to most men were mighty deeds, or *greatnesses* to our holy poet: these he would publish like a herald, who mentions the titles and honours of his royal master. It is the occupation of every true believer to rehearse the great doings of his great God. We are not to leave this to the common converse of the crowd, but we are personally to make a declaration of what we have seen and known. We are even bound in deep solemnity of manner to warn men of the Lord's greatness in his terrible acts of justice: thus will they be admonished to abstain from provoking him. To fulfil this duty we are already bound by solemn obligations, and we shall do well to bind ourselves further by resolutions, " I will—God helping me, I will."

7. "*They shall abundantly utter the memory of thy great goodness.*" They shall pour forth grateful memories even as springs gush with water, plenteously, spontaneously, constantly, joyously. The Lord's redeemed people having been filled with his great goodness, shall retain the happy recollection of it, and shall be moved often and often to utter those recollections. Not content with a scanty mention of such amazing love, they shall go on to an abundant utterance of such abundant favour. It shall be their delight to speak with one another of God's dealings with them, and to compare notes of their experiences. God has done nothing stintedly; all his goodness is great goodness, all worthy to be remembered, all suggestive of holy discourse. Upon this subject there is no scarcity of matter, and when the heart is right there is no need to stop from want of facts to tell. Oh, that there were more of these memories and utterances, for it is not meet that the goodness of the living God should be buried in the cemetery of silence, in the grave of ingratitude.

"*And shall sing of thy righteouness.*" They shall say and then sing. And what is the theme which impels them to leave the pulpit for the orchestra? What do they sing of? They sing of that righteousness which is the sinner's terror, which even good men mention with deep solemnity. Righteousness received by gospel light is in reality the secret foundation of the believer's hope. God's covenant of grace is our strong consolation, because he who made it is righteous, and will not run back from it. Since Jesus died as our substitute, righteousness requires and secures the salvation of all the redeemed. This attribute is our best friend, and therefore we sing of it.

Modern thinkers would fain expunge the idea of righteousness from their notion of God; but converted men would not. It is a sign of growth in sanctification when we rejoice in the justice, rectitude, and holiness of our God. Even a rebel may rejoice in mercy, which he looks upon as laxity ; but a loyal subject rejoices when he learns that God is so just that not even to save his own elect would he consent to violate the righteousness of his moral government. Few men will shout for joy at the righteousness of Jehovah, but those who do so are his chosen, in whom his soul delighteth.

8 The LORD *is* gracious, and full of compassion ; slow to anger, and of great mercy.

9 The LORD *is* good to all : and his tender mercies *are* over all his works.

10 All thy works shall praise thee, O LORD ; and thy saints shall bless thee.

8. *"The LORD is gracious."* Was it not in some such terms that the Lord revealed himself to Moses ? Is not this Jehovah's glory ? To all living men this is his aspect : he is gracious, or full of goodness and generosity. He treats his creatures with kindness, his subjects with consideration, and his saints with favour. His words and ways, his promises and his gifts, his plans and his purposes all manifest his grace, or free favour. There is nothing suspicious, prejudiced, morose, tyrannical, or unapproachable in Jehovah,—he is condescending and kind. *"And full of compassion."* To the suffering, the weak, the foolish, the despondent, he is very pitiful : he feels for them, he feels with them : he does this heartily, and in a practical manner. Of this pitifulness he is full, so that he compassionates freely, constantly, deeply, divinely, and effectually. In God is fulness in a sense not known among men, and this fulness is all fragrant with sympathy for human misery. If the Lord be full of compassion there is no room in him for forgetfulness or harshness, and none should suspect him thereof. What an ocean of compassion there must be since the Infinite God is full of it. *"Slow to anger."* Even those who refuse his grace yet share in long-suffering. When men do not repent, but, on the contrary, go from bad to worse, he is still averse to let his wrath flame forth against them. Greatly patient and extremely anxious that the sinner may live, he " lets the lifted thunder drop," and still forbears. " Love suffereth long and is kind," and God is love. *"And of great mercy."* This is his attitude towards the guilty. When men at last repent, they find pardon awaiting them. Great is their sin, and great is God's mercy. They need great help, and they have it though they deserve it not ; for he is greatly good to the greatly guilty.

9. *"The LORD is good to all."* No one, not even his fiercest enemy, can deny this ; for the falsehood would be too barefaced, since the very existence of the lips which slander him is a proof that it is slander. He allows his enemies to live, he even supplies them with food, and smooths their way with many comforts ; for them the sun shines as brightly as if they were saints, and the rain waters their fields as plentifully as if they were perfect men. Is not this goodness to all ? In our own land the gospel sounds in the ears of all who care to listen ; and the Scriptures are within reach of the poorest child. It would be a wanton wresting of Scripture to limit this expression to the elect, as some have tried to do : we rejoice in electing love, but none the less we welcome the glorious truth, " Jehovah is good to all."

"And his tender mercies are over all his works." Not " his new-covenant works," as one read it the other day who was wise above that which is written, yea, contrary to that which is written. Kindness is a law of God's universe : the world was planned for happiness ; even now that sin has so sadly marred God's handiwork, and introduced elements which were not from the beginning, the Lord has so arranged matters that the fall is broken, the curse is met by an antidote, and the inevitable pain is softened with mitigations. Even in this sin-stricken world, under its disordered economy, there are abundant traces of a hand skilful to soothe distress and heal disease. That which makes life bearable is the tenderness of the great Father. This is seen in the creation of an insect as well as in the ruling of nations. The Creator is never rough, the Provider is never forgetful, the Ruler is never cruel. Nothing is done to create disease, no organs are arranged to promote misery ; the incoming of sickness and pain is not according to the original design, but a result of our disordered state. Man's body as it left the Maker's hand was neither framed for disease, decay, nor death, neither was the purpose of it discomfort and anguish ; far otherwise, it was framed for a joyful activity, and a peaceful enjoyment of God. Jehovah has in great consideration laid up in the world cures for our ailments, and

helps for our feebleness, and if many of these have been long in their discovery, it is because it was more for man's benefit to find them out himself, than to have them labelled and placed in order before his eyes. We may be sure of this, that Jehovah has never taken delight in the ills of his creatures, but has sought their good, and laid himself out to alleviate the distresses into which they have guiltily plunged themselves.

The duty of kindness to animals may logically be argued from this verse. Should not the children of God be like their Father in kindness ?

10. *"All thy works shall praise thee, O Lord."* There is a something about every creature which redounds to the honour of God. The skill, kindness, and power manifested in the formation of each living thing is in itself to the praise of God, and when observed by an intelligent mind the Lord is honoured thereby. Some works praise him by their being, and others by their well-being ; some by their mere existence, and others by their hearty volition. *"And thy saints shall bless thee."* These holy ones come nearer, and render sweeter adoration. Men have been known to praise those whom they hated, as we may admire the prowess of a warrior who is our foe ; but saints lovingly praise, and therefore are said to "bless." They wish well to God ; they would make him more blessed, if such a thing were possible ; they desire blessings upon his cause and his children, and invoke success upon his work and warfare. None but blessed men will bless the Lord. Only saints or holy ones will bless the thrice holy God. If we praise Jehovah because of his works around us, we must go on to bless him for his works within us. Let the two " shalls " of this verse be fulfilled, especially the latter one.

11 They shall speak of the glory of thy kingdom, and talk of thy power ;

12 To make known to the sons of men his mighty acts, and the glorious majesty of his kingdom.

13 Thy kingdom *is* an everlasting kingdom, and thy dominion *endureth* throughout all generations.

11. *"They shall speak of the glory of thy kingdom."* Excellent themes for saintly minds. Those who bless God from their hearts rejoice to see him enthroned, glorified, and magnified in power. No subject is more profitable for humility obedience, hope, and joy than that of the reigning power of the Lord our God. His works praise him, but they cannot crown him : this remains for holy hands and hearts. It is their high pleasure to tell of the glory of his kingdom in its justice, kindness, eternity, and so forth. Kingdoms of earth are glorious for riches, for extent of territory, for victories, for liberty, for commerce, and other matters ; but in all true glories the kingdom of Jehovah excels them. We have seen a palace dedicated " to all the glories of France " ; but time, eternity, and all space are filled with the glories of God : on these we love to speak. *"And talk of thy power."* This power supports the kingdom and displays the glory, and we are sure to talk of it when the glory of the divine kingdom is under discussion. God's power to create or to destroy, to bless or to punish, to strengthen or to crush, is matter for frequent rehearsal. All power comes from God. Apart from him the laws of nature would be inoperative. His power is the one source of force—mechanical, vital, mental, spiritual. Beyond the power of God which has been put forth, infinite force lies latent in himself. Who can calculate the reserve forces of the Infinite ? How, then, can his kingdom fail ? We hear talk of the five great powers, but what are they to the One Great Power ? The Lord is " the blessed and only Potentate." Let us accustom ourselves to think more deeply and speak more largely of th' power which ever makes for righteousness and works for mercy.

12. *"To make known to the sons of men his mighty acts."* These glorious deeds ought to be known to all mankind ; but yet few reckon such knowledge to be an essential part of education. As the State cannot teach these holy histories the people of God must take care to do it themselves. The work must be done for every age, for men have short memories in reference to their God, and the doings of his power. They inscribe the deeds of their heroes upon brass, but the glorious acts of Jehovah are written upon the sand, and the tide of time washes them from present memory ; therefore we must repeat the lesson, and yet again repeat it. The saints are the religious instructors of the race ; they ought to be not only the historians of the past, but the bards of the present, whose duty it is to keep the sons of men in memory of the great deeds which the Lord did in the days of their fathers

and in the old time before them. Note the contrast between the great deeds of God and the puny sons of Adam, who have even degenerated from their father, though he was as nothing compared with his Maker.

"*And the glorious majesty of his kingdom.*" What a grand subject! Yet this we are to make known ; the publication of it is left to us who bless the Lord. " The glory of the majesty of his reign." What a theme ! Jehovah's reign as sovereign Lord of all, his majesty in that dominion, and the glory of that majesty ! The threefold subject baffles the most willing mind. How shall we make this known to the sons of men ? Let us first labour to know it ourselves, and then let us make it a frequent subject of discourse, so shall men know it from us, the Holy Spirit attending our word.

13. "*Thy kingdom is an everlasting kingdom.*" His meditation has brought him near to God, and God near to him : he speaks to him in adoration, changing the pronoun from " his " to " thy." He sees the great King, and prostrates himself before 'him. It is well when our devotion opens the gate of heaven, and enters within the portal to speak with God face to face, as a man speaketh with his friend. The point upon which the Psalmist's mind rests is the eternity of the divine throne, —" thy reign is a reign of all eternities." The Lord's kingdom is without beginning, without break, without bound, and without end. He never abdicates his throne, neither does he call in a second to share his empire. None can overthrow his power, or break away from his rule. Neither this age, nor the age to come, nor ages of ages shall cause his sovereignty to fail. Herein is rest for faith. " The Lord sitteth King for ever." "*And thy dominion endureth throughout all generations.*" Men come and go like shadows on the wall, but God reigneth eternally. We distinguish kings as they succeed each other by calling them first and second ; but this King is Jehovah, the First and the Last. Adam in his generation knew his Creator to be King, and the last of his race shall know the same. All hail, Great God ! Thou art ever Lord of lords !

These three verses are a reverent hymn concerning " the kingdom of God " : they will be best appreciated by those who are in that kingdom in the fullest sense, and are most truly loyal to the Lord. It is, according to these verses, a kingdom of glory and power ; a kingdom of light which men are to know, and of might which men are to feel ; it is full of majesty and eternity ; it is the benediction of every generation. We are to speak of it, talk of it, and make it known, and then we are to acknowledge it in the homage directed distinctly to the Lord himself—as in verse thirteen.

14 The LORD upholdeth all that fall, and raiseth up all *those that be* bowed down.

15 The eyes of all wait upon thee ; and thou givest them their meat in due season.

16 Thou openest thine hand, and satisfiest the desire of every living thing.

In these three verses Jehovah is adored for his gracious providence towards men and all other creatures ; this fitly follows the proclamation of his royalty, for we here see how he rules his kingdom, and provides for his subjects.

14. "*The LORD upholdeth all that fall.*" Read this verse in connection with the preceding and admire the unexpected contrast : he who reigns in glorious majesty, yet condescends to lift up and hold up those who are apt to fall. The form of the verb shows that he is always doing this ; he is Jehovah upholding. His choice of the fallen, and the falling, as the subjects of his gracious help is specially to be noted. The fallen of our race, especially fallen women, are shunned by us, and it is peculiar tenderness on the Lord's part that such he looks upon, even those who are at once the chief of sinners and the least regarded of mankind. The falling ones among us are too apt to be pushed down by the strong : their timidity and dependence make them the victims of the proud and domineering. To them also the Lord gives his upholding help. The Lord loves to reverse things,—he puts down the lofty, and lifts up the lowly.

"*And raiseth up all those that be bowed down.*" Another deed of condescension. Many are despondent, and cannot lift up their heads in courage, or their hearts with comfort ; but these he cheers. Some are bent with their daily load, and these he strengthens. Jesus loosed a daughter of Abraham whom Satan had so bound that she was bowed down, and could by no means lift up herself. In this he proved himself to be the true Son of the Highest. Think of the Infinite bowing to lift up the bowed, and stooping to be leaned upon by those who are ready to fall. The two "alls" should not be overlooked: the Lord has a kindly heart towards the whole company of the afflicted.

15. *"The eyes of all wait upon thee."* They have learned to look to thee: it has become their nature to turn to thee for all they want. As children look to a father for all they need, so do the creatures look to God, the all-sufficient Provider. It were well if all men had the eye of faith, and if all waited therewith upon the Lord. *"And thou givest them their meat in due season."* They wait, and God gives. The thought of this brings God so near to our poet-prophet that he is again speaking with God after the style of thee and thou. Is it to be wondered at when the Lord is feeding the hungry all around us,—giving food to all creatures, and to ourselves among them? Like a flock of sheep the creatures stand around the Lord as their great Shepherd; all eyes are to his hand expecting to receive their food; nor are they disappointed, for when the hour comes suitable provender is ready for each creature. Observe the punctuality of the Lord in giving food at meal-time,—in the season when it is due. This he does for all, and each living thing has its own season, so that the Lord of heaven is feeding his great flock both by day and by night, during every moment of time.

16. *"Thou openest thine hand, and satisfiest the desire of every living thing."* Thou alone providest, O Jehovah! Thou doest it liberally, with open hand; thou doest it easily, as if it were only to open thine hand; thou doest this at once as promptly as if all supplies were ready to hand. Living things have needs, and these create desires; the living God has suitable supplies at hand, and these he gives till inward satisfaction is produced, and the creature sighs no longer. In spiritual things, when God has raised a desire, he always gratifies it; hence the longing is prophetic of the blessing. In no case is the desire of the living thing excited to produce distress, but in order that it may seek and find satisfaction.

These verses refer to natural providence; but they may equally well apply to the stores of grace, since the same God is king in both spheres. If we will but wait upon the Lord for pardon, renewing, or whatever else we need, we shall not wait in vain. The hand of grace is never closed while the sinner lives.

17 The LORD *is* righteous in all his ways, and holy in all his works.

18 The LORD *is* nigh unto all them that call upon him, to all that call upon him in truth.

19 He will fulfil the desire of them that fear him: he also will hear their cry, and will save them.

20 The LORD preserveth all them that love him: but all the wicked will he destroy.

21 My mouth shall speak the praise of the LORD: and let all flesh bless his holy name for ever and ever.

In these verses we behold our God in the realm of his free grace dealing well with his believing people.

17. *"The LORD is righteous in all his ways, and holy in all his works."* His ways and works are both worthy to be praised. Jehovah cannot be unjust or impure. Let his doings be what they may, they are in every case righteous and holy. This is the confession of the godly who follow his ways, and of the gracious who study his works. Whatever God is or does must be right. In the salvation of his people he is as righteous and holy as in any other of his ways and works: he has not manifested mercy at the expense of justice, but the rather he has magnified his righteousness by the death of his Son.

18. *"The LORD is nigh unto all them that call upon him."* Not only near by his omnipresence, but to sympathize and favour. He does not leave praying men, and men who confess his name, to battle with the world alone, but he is ever at their side. This favour is not for a few of those who invoke him; but for each one of the pious company. "All" who place themselves beneath the shield of his glorious name by calling themselves by it, and by calling upon it in supplication, shall find him to be a very present help in trouble. *"To all that call upon him in truth:"* for there are many whose formal prayers and false professions will never bring them into communion with the Lord. To pray in truth, we must have a true

heart, and the truth in our heart ; and then we must be humble, for pride is a falsehood ; and be earnest, or else prayer is a lie. A God of truth cannot be nigh to the spirit of hypocrisy ; this he knows and hates ; neither can he be far removed from a sincere spirit, since it is his work, and he forsakes not the work of his own hands.

19. *"He will fulfil the desire of them that fear him : "* that is, those who reverence his name and his law. Inasmuch as they have respect unto his will, he will have respect unto their will. They shall have their way for they have his way in their hearts. A holy heart only desires what a holy God can give, and so its desire is filled full out of the fulness of the Lord. *"He also will hear their cry, and will save them."* Divinely practical shall his nearness be, for he will work their deliverance. He will listen to their piteous cry, and then will send salvation from every ill. This he will do himself personally ; he will not trust them to angels or saints.

20. *"The Lord preserveth all them that love him."* They keep him in their love, and he keeps them by his love. See how these favoured ones have advanced from fearing the Lord and crying to him, even to loving him, and in that love they are secure from all danger. Mark the number of " alls " in these later verses of the Psalm. In each of these God is all in all. *"But all the wicked will he destroy."* Wickedness is an offence to all holy beings, and therefore those who are determined to continue in it must be weeded out. As good sanitary laws remove all creators of pest and plague, so does the moral government of God mark every evil thing for destruction ; it cannot be tolerated in the presence of a perfectly holy God. What ruins wicked men frequently become in this life ! What monuments of wrath will they be in the world to come ! Like Nineveh and Babylon, and other destroyed places, they shall only exist to declare how thoroughly God fulfils his threatenings.

21. *"My mouth shall speak the praise of the Lord."* Whatever others may do, I will not be silent in the praise of the Lord : whatever others may speak upon, my topic is fixed once for all : I will speak the praise of Jehovah. I am doing it, and I will do it as long as I breathe. *"And let all flesh bless his holy name for ever and ever."* Praise is no monopoly for one, even though he be a David ; others are debtors, let them also be songsters. All men of every race, condition, or generation should unite to glorify God. No man need think that he will be rejected when he comes with his personal note of praise ; all are permitted, invited, and exhorted to magnify the Lord. Specially should his holiness be adored : this is the crown, and in a certain sense the sum, of all his attributes. Only holy hearts will praise the holy name, or character of the Lord ; oh, that all flesh were sanctified, then would the sancity of God be the delight of all. Once let the song begin and there will be no end to it. It shall go on for ever and a day, as the old folks used to say. If there were two for-evers, or twenty for-evers, they ought all to be spent in the praises of the ever-living, ever-blessing, ever-blessed Jehovah. Blessed be the Lord for ever for having revealed to us his name, and blessed be that name as he has revealed it ; yea, blessed be he above all that we can know, or think, or say. Our hearts revel in the delight of praising him. Our mouth, our mind, our lip, our life shall be our Lord's throughout this mortal existence, and when time shall be no more.

EXPLANATORY NOTES AND QUAINT SAYINGS.

This has been happily characterized as the " new song " promised in Ps. cxliv. 9. In other words, it is the song of praise, corresponding to the didactic, penitential, and supplicatory Psalms of this series.—*Joseph Addison Alexander.*

The ancient Hebrews declare him happy whoever, in after times, utters this Psalm thrice each day with the mouth, heart, and tongue.—*Victorinus Bythner,—* 1670.

The last six or seven Psalms are the Beulah of the book, where the sun shineth night and day, and the voice of the turtle is heard in the land. Coming at the close after all the mournful, plaintive, penitential, prayerful, varying notes, they unconsciously typify the joy and rest of glory.—*George Gilfillan.*

Title.—The Praise of David. Psalms are the praises of God accompanied with song ; Psalms are songs containing the praise of God. If there be praise, but not of God, it is not a Psalm. If there be praise, and praise of God, if it is not sung, it is not a Psalm. To make a Psalm there go these three—praise, God's praise, and song.—*Augustine.*

Title.—It is observable concerning David's entitling the Psalm *"The Praise of David,"* that in the original no Psalm else beareth such a title. It is appropriated to it, because this wholly consists of praise ; he was elevated therein to a frame of spirit made up of the pure praise of God, without any touch of what was particular to himself. It was not thanks, but altogether praise, and wholly praise.—*Thomas Goodwin.*

Title.—This Psalm, which is designated a *Tehillah,* or a Psalm of *praise,*— a name which has passed from this Psalm to the whole Psalter, which is commonly called *Sepher Tehillim,* or *"Book of Praises,"*—is the last of the Psalms ascribed to David.

It is remarkable, that although that is the name given to the Psalter (which is entitled in Hebrew *Sepher Tehillim,* or *Book of Praises*), this is the only Psalm in the whole number which is designated in the title as a *Tehillah*—a word derived from the same root as *Hallelujah.* It seems as if this name *Tehillah* had been studiously reserved for the *last* of David's Psalms, in order to mark more emphatically that all his utterances are consummated in *praise.* And this view is more clearly manifested by the circumstance that the word *Tehillah* is introduced into the *last* verse of this Psalm, " My soul shall speak the *praise* " *(tehillah)* " of the Lord," (observe this preparation for Hallelujah, *Praise ye* the Lord) ; " and let all flesh bless his holy name for ever and ever." As much as to say, that though David's voice was now about to be hushed in this life, yet it would never be silent in the world to come, and would ever " praise the Lord " ; and as much, also, as to say that his last exhortation should be to all nations to praise him, " Let all flesh bless his holy name for ever and ever."—*Christopher Wordsworth.*

Title.—This Psalm is entitled *"David's praise."* For howsoever the prayers and the praises (all) in this book, are (for the most part) of David's penning : yet two there are he hath singled out from the rest, and set his own mark on them as proper to himself : the lxxxvi. Psalm, his *Tephilla, David's* own *Prayer ;* and there is here his *Tehilla,* his own *Praise* or thanksgiving. As if he had made the rest for all in common, but reserved these peculiarly for himself.—*Lancelot Andrewes.*

Whole Psalm.—In regard to its alphabetic structure, it has one peculiarity, *viz.,* the *nun* is omitted ; the reason of which may be, that (as we have seen in some others Psalms of this structure) by means of that or some other such omission, we might be kept from putting stress on the mere form of the composition.—*Andrew A. Bonar.*

Whole Psalm.—Cassiodorus quaintly remarks that the Psalms in which the alphabetital order is complete, are especially fitted for the righteous in the Church Triumphant, but those in which one letter is missing, are for the Church Militant here on earth, as still imperfect, and needing to be purified from defect.—*Neale and Littledale.*

Verse 1.—"I will extol thee, my God, O King." To extol is to set pre-eminently on high ; to exalt above all others ; it is the expression of the greatest possible admiration ; it is letting others know our high opinion of a person, and endeavouring to win them over to it. The man who has such a high opinion of another as to induce him to extol him, will not be likely to rest without bringing forth into prominent observation the object of his praise.—*Philip Bennett Power.*

Verse 1.—"O King "; or *the King,* by way of eminency ; the King of kings, the God by whom kings reign, and to whom I and all other kings owe subjection and obedience.—*Matthew Pool.*

Verse 1.—"O king." The Psalmist in rapt ecstasy seems as though he saw God incarnate in Christ present to inspire his praise. Christ is our God and King, to be extolled in the heart, with the mouth, and by the life.—*Thomas Le Blanc.*

Verse 1.—"King." God is King in verity ; others are called kings in vanity.— *Martin Geier.*

Verse 1.—"I will bless thy name for ever and ever." The name of God in Scripture is taken, first, for *God himself.* The name of a thing is put for the thing named, Ps. xliv. 5 : " Through thee will we push down our enemies : through thy name will we tread them under that rise up against us." " Through thy *name,*" that is, through *thee.* Secondly, the name of God is often in Scripture put for *the attributes of God.* Thirdly, the name of God is put for *his ordinances or worship.* " Go ye now unto my place which was in Shiloh, where I set my name at the first " (Jer. vii. 12), that is, where I first set up my public worship ; because, as a man is known by his proper name, so is God by his proper worship. Fourthly, the name of God is *that reverence, esteem and honour which angels and men give unto God.* As we know amongst us, the report and reputation that a man hath among men is a man's name ; what men speak of him, that is his name ; such an one hath a good name, we say ; such an one hath an ill name, that is, men speak or think well or ill of such persons. So Gen. vi. 4. When Moses describes the giants, he saith, " They were men of renown " ; the Hebrew is, " They were men of *name,*" because the name of a man is the character he hath amongst men ; as a man is esteemed, so his name is carried, and himself is accepted in the world. So the name of God is that high esteem, those honourable apprehensions, which angels and men have of God ; such as the thoughts and speeches of men are for the celebration of God's glory and praise, such is his name in the world.—*Joseph Caryl.*

Verse 1.—*"For ever and ever."* לְעוֹלָם וָעֶד, *leolam vaed, for ever and onward,* in this and the coming world. Expressions of this sort are very difficult to be translated, but they are, on the whole, well interpreted by those words of Mr. Addison :—

> " Through all eternity to thee
> A joyful song I'll raise ;
> But oh, eternity's too short
> To utter all thy praise ! "

Adam Clarke.

Verse 1.—*"For ever and ever."* Praise is the only part of duty in which we at present engage, which is lasting. We pray, but there shall be a time when prayer shall offer its last litany ; we believe, but there shall be a time when faith shall be lost in sight ; we hope, and hope maketh not ashamed, but there shall be a time when hope lies down and dies, lost in the splendour of the fruition that God shall reveal. But praise goes singing into heaven, and is ready without a teacher to strike the harp that is waiting for it, to transmit along the echoes of eternity the song of the Lamb. In the party-coloured world in which we live, there are days of various sorts and experiences, making up the aggregate of the Christian's life. There are waiting days, in which, because Providence fences us round, and it seems as if we cannot march, we cannot move, as though we must just wait to see what the Lord is about to do in us and for us ; and there are watching days, when it behoves us never to slumber, but to be always ready for the attacks of our spiritual enemy ; and there are warring days, when with nodding plume, and with ample armour, we must go forth to do battle for the truth ; and there are weeping days, when it seems as if the fountains of the great deep within us were broken up ; and as though, through much tribulation, we had to pass to heaven in tears. But these days shall all pass away by-and-by—waiting days all be passed, warring days all be passed, watching days all be passed ; but

> " Our days of praise shall ne'er be past
> While life, and thought, and being last,
> And immortality endures."

William Morley Punshon, 1824—1881.

Verse 1.—*"For ever and ever."* To praise God now does not satisfy devout aspiration, for in this age the worshipper's devotion is interrupted by sin, fear, sickness, etc. ; but in eternity praise will proceed in unbroken procession.—*John Lorinus.*

Verses 1, 2.—*"I will bless thee for ever and ever,"* and again, verse 2. This intimates, 1. That he resolved to continue in this work *to the end of his life,* throughout his " for ever " in this world. 2. That the Psalms he penned should be made use of in praising God by the church *to the end of time.* 2 Chron. xxix. 30. 3. That he hoped to be praising God *to all eternity* in the other world : they that make it their constant work on earth, shall have it their everlasting bliss in heaven.—*Matthew Henry.*

Verse 2.—*"Every day."* Then God is to be blessed and praised in dark as well as bright days.—*Johannes Paulus Palanterius*, 1600.

Verse 2.—*"Every day (in the week) will I bless thee,"* the Psalmist seems to signify. As there are " seven spirits " peculiarly existing in nearness to God, David holds the seven days of the week like seven stars in his hand, or like a seven-branched candlestick of gold, burning every day with his devotion. He calls the seven days to be as seven angels with trumpets.—*Thomas Le Blanc.*

Verse 2.—*"I will bless thee : I will praise thy name."* The repetition intimates the fervency of his affection to this work, the fixedness of his purpose to abound in it, and the frequency of his performances therein.—*Matthew Henry.*

Verse 2.—*"Praise."* If we are to define it in words, we may say that *praise* is thankful, lowly, loving worship of the goodness and majesty of God. And therefore we often find the word " praise " joined with " blessing " and " thanksgiving": but though all three are akin to each other, they are not all alike. They are steps in a gradual scale—a song of degrees. Thanksgiving runs up into blessing, and blessing ascends into praise ; for praise comprehends both, and is the highest and most perfect work of all living spirits.—*Henry Edward Manning*, 1850.

Verse 3.—*"Great is the Lord."* If *"great"* here be referred to God as a king, then a *great* king he is in respect of the breadth of his empire, for all creatures, from the highest angel to the poorest worm, are under him. " Great " for length ; for " his kingdom is an everlasting kingdom." " Great " for depth ; for he rules even in the hearts of kings, of all men, overrules their thoughts, affections, nothing is hid from him. And " great " again for height ; being " a great King above all gods," ruling by his own absolute power and authority ; whereas all other kings have their sword from him, and rule by a delegated and vicarious power.—*William Nicholson.*

Verse 3.—*"His greatness is unsearchable."* God is so great, that till Christ revealed the Father, Deity was lost in its own infinity to the perception of men. He who attempts to navigate an infinite ocean must come back to his starting point, never being able to cross. So the ancient philosophers, disputing as to the Divine Nature, were baffled by their own ingenuity, they had to confess that they comprehended nothing of God except that he was incomprehensible. Without Christ, men can only find out about God that they can never find him.—*Thomas Le Blanc.*

Verse 3 (last clause).—The Vulgate renders thus, " Of his greatness no *end."* The Hebrew is, " Of his greatness no investigation." As the classic Greeks would say, ἀνεξιχνίαστος, *not to be traced out.*—*Simon de Muis*, 1587—1644.

Verse 3.—God had searched David through and through (Ps. cxxxix. 1), but David proved he could not search God's greatness.—*Martin Geier.*

Verses 3—6.—Verses 3 and 4 contain the material of praise, and verses 5 and 6 the praise itself. Verse 3 states a proposition, and verse 4 gives the amplification. —*Hermann Venema.*

Verse 4.—*"One generation shall praise thy works to another,"* etc. Deut. iv. 9, and vi. 7. Fathers teaching their sons the goodness and glory of God. This was a legal ordinance. The church and its worshippers are *collecting praises* of successive generations for the final Hallelujah celebration.—*Martin Geier.*

Verse 4.—*"One generation shall praise thy works to another."* Singular is exchanged for plural in the Hebrew, One generation shall praise (sing) thy works to another, and shall declare (plural) thy mighty acts." Here is melody first, the antiphony of the choirs responding to each other ; then harmony ; all generations will burst into chorus together.—*Hermann Venema.*

Verse 4.—*"One generation to another."* The *tradition* of praise ! Each generation catches the strains from the last, echoes it, and passes it along to the next. One generation declares what it has seen, and passes on the praise to the generation which has not seen as yet the wonders celebrated.—*Simon de Muis.*

Verse 4.—*"One generation shall praise thy works to another,"* etc. Thus God provides for his Church. When Elijah is carried into heaven, Elisha must follow in the power and spirit of Elias. When one stream is slid and shed into the ocean, another circulates from the same ocean through the bowels of the earth into the springs under the mountains, and refreshes the scorched plains. When one star sets, another rises to guide the wandering traveller, and at length the bright morning lamp glitters in the east, and then the glorious Sun of Righteousness. While the Church sits fainting under a juniper-tree in the wilderness, there shall fly prophets to feed her till the blessed resurrection of the witnesses. It's our high duty to study present work, and prize present help, and greatly rejoice when the Lord sends forth, as once he did, both Boanerges and Barnabas together. Pray for the mantle, girdle, and blessing of Elijah, for the love of John, and the zeal of Paul, to twine hands together to draw souls to heaven; till the Beloved comes like a roe or a young hart upon the mountains of spices; till the shadows flee away; till the day dawn, and the Day-star arise in your hearts.—*Samuel Lee, in his Preface to Row's "Emmanuel,"* 1679.

Verse 4.—"*One generation shall praise thy works to another.*" There is no phenomenon of human life more solemn than its succession of generations. "One generation passeth away, another generation cometh." And, as if to put this in a light as affecting and indelible as possible, the Psalmist immediately adds, "but the earth abideth for ever." A thought that gleams like a lightning flash across this panorama of life, burning it into the beholder's brain for ever. Even the rude, gross, material earth, which we were created to subdue, and upon which we so proudly tread, is represented as having to the palpable sense this advantage over us. The abiding earth constitutes a little eternity, compared with the duration of its changing inhabitants. We come into it, and pass over it, obliterating, perhaps, some footprints in its dust by the impress of our own, to be in their turn effaced, and then leave it with amazing rapidity, as a hireling man accomplishes his days.—*Henry Allon,* 1852.

Verse 5.—"*I will speak of the glorious honour,*" etc. The word which we here translate "*speak,*" is considered by Hebrew critics to include also the idea of "expatiating," "speaking at large"; not merely "alluding to incidentally," but "entering into particulars"; as though one took delight in speaking upon the matter in hand. Now there is something very satisfactory in entering into particulars; we can often gather light upon a great truth by having had set before us some of the particulars connected with it; we can often understand what is too high for us, *in* itself and *by* itself, by some examples which bring it within reach of our dull understandings. We are like men who want to attain a height, who have not wings to fly up to it, but who can reach it by going up a ladder step by step. Particulars are often like the rounds of a ladder, little, it may be, in themselves, but very helpful to us; and to dwell upon particulars is often of use to ourselves; it certainly is to many with whom we converse.

Let us remember, that circumstanced as we are in our present state, we have no faculties for grasping in its simple grandeur the glorious honour of the majesty of God. We know most of God from what we know of his doings amongst the children of men. Hereafter, the Lord's people shall, no doubt, have much revealed to them of the glorious honour of the majesty of God, which they could now neither bear nor understand; meanwhile they have to know him chiefly by what he has said and done; and if only our eyes be open, we shall be at no loss to recognise in these the glorious honour of his majesty.—*Philip Bennett Power.*

Verse 5.—"*I will speak,*" etc. "I will *muse*" is better than "speak," as being the primary and more usual sense of the Hebrew word. It suggests that these glorious qualities of God's character and deeds should be not merely talked about and extolled in song, but be deeply pondered, laid close upon our very heart, so that the legitimate impression may be wrought into our very soul, and may mould our whole spirit and character into God's own moral image.—*Henry Cowles.*

Verse 5.—With what a cumulus of glowing terms does Holy Writ seek to display the excellence of Deity! By these descriptions, those attributes which are feebly imitated or reflected in what we call *good* among created things are declared to exist in God, infinitely, immutably, ineffably.—*Martin Geier.*

Verse 5.—"*Thy wonderful works.*"—Heb.: "*the words of thy wonderful works.*" Thus the Psalmist declares that the records left of God's olden doings in the history of Israel are very precious. He has heard them. Moses and Aaron and others spoke them. He delights in them; he will sing them again on his own harp.—*Hermann Venema.*

Verses 5 and 6.—Verse 5 speaks of God's *opera mirabilia;* verse 6 of his *opera terribilia.* The former delight his saints; the latter terrify the wicked.—*John Lorinus.*

Verse 6.—*"And men shall speak of the might of thy terrible acts."* When men do not mark his works of mercy and bounty, the Lord will show unto them works of justice, that is, terrible works, and give them matter of talking upon this account. —*David Dickson.*

Verse 6 (*last clause*).—To *"declare"* here means either in speech or song ; not merely to *predicate* as a fact, but to *proclaim* in praise. The Hebrew word has this width of meaning ; not merely to declare in cold utterance, concerning mere history.—*Hermann Venema.*

Verse 6.—*"Thy greatness."* All men are enamoured of greatness. Then they must seek it *in* God, and get it *from* God. David did both. All history shows the creature aspiring after this glory. Ahasuerus, Astyages, Cyrus, Cambyses, Nebuchadnezzar, were all called *the great.* Alexander the Great, when he came to the Ganges, ordered his statue to be made of more than life size, that posterity might believe him to have been of nobler stature. In Christ alone does man attain the greatness his heart yearns for—the glory of perfect goodness.—*Thomas Le Blanc.*

Verse 6.—*"Thy greatness."* Or, according to the written text, *greatnesses.* So Aquila and Jerome. The parallelism is decidedly in favour of the plural.— *A. S. Aglen.*

Verse 7.—There is an extensive and an intensive greatness, and both must be found in our praises of God. First, an extensive greatness in regard of their number ; we must be frequent and plentiful in the duty : we must *"Abundantly utter the memory of God's great goodness."* Secondly, there must be an intensive greatness in our praises, in regard of the degree, fervour and heat of them. They must be high, and vehement, fervent, flaming, zealous and affectionate, full of life and vigour ; our spirits must be raised, our hearts and tongues enlarged in the performance of this duty. God's glorious name, as it is in Nehem. ix. 5, " is exalted above all blessing and praise," above our devoutest and most zealous praises ; and therefore surely faint, heartless, and lifeless praises are so far from reaching him, as that they may seem to be meant of another, and a lower object. God then is not praised at all if he be not greatly praised. Weak and dull praises are dispraises ; for a person or thing is not honoured or praised, unless there be some proportion between the honour and praise and the worthiness of the person or thing honoured and praised.—*Henry Jeanes, in "The Works of Heaven upon Earth,"* 1649.

Verse 7.—*"Abundantly utter."* The word contains the idea of boiling or bubbling-up like a fountain. It signifies, a holy fluency about the mercy of God. We have quite enough fluent people about, but they are many of them idlers for whom Satan finds abundant work to do. The Lord deliver us from the noise of fluent women ; but it matters not how fluent men and women are if they will be fluent on the topic now before us. Open your mouths ; let the praise pour forth let it come, rivers of it. Stream away ! Gush away, all that you possibly can. *"They shall abundantly utter the memory of thy great goodness."* Do not stop the joyful speakers, let them go on for ever. They do not exaggerate, they cannot. You say they are enthusiastic, but they are not half up to the pitch yet ; bid them become more excited and speak yet more fervently. Go on, brother, go on ; pile it up ; say something greater, grander, and more fiery still ! You cannot exceed the truth. You have come to a theme where your most fluent powers will fail in utterance. The text calls for a sacred fluency, and I would exhort you liberally to exercise it when you are speaking on the goodness of God.—*C. H. S.*

Verse 7.—Too many witnesses of God's goodness are silent witnesses. Men do not enough speak out the testimonies that they might bear in this matter. The reason that I love the Methodists—good ones—is, that they have a tongue to their piety. They fulfil the command of God,—to be fervent in spirit.—*Henry Ward Beecher.*

Verse 7.—

> The thought of our past years in me doth breed
> Perpetual benedictions.

William Wordsworth, 1770—1805.

Verse 7.—*"They shall sing of thy righteousness,"* or *justice.* To sing of goodness, mercy, forgiveness, is natural ; but a *song of justice* is singular. Here is the beauty of David's praise, that he sees subject of delight as much in the righteousness of God as in his mercy.—*John Lorinus.*

Verse 7.—*"They shall sing of thy righteousness."* The righteousness of God, whereby he justifieth sinners, and sanctifieth the justified, and execu eth judgment for his reconciled people, is the sweetest object of the church's joy.—*David Dickson.*

Verse 7.—*"Thy righteousness"* (read in connection with next verse). It is an easy thing to conceive the glory of the Creator, manifested in the good of an innocent creature ; but the glory of the righteous Judge, manifested in the good of the guilty criminal, is the peculiar, mysterious wisdom of the Cross. It is easy to perceive God's righteousness declared in the punishment of sins ; the Cross alone declares " His righteousness for the remission of sins." It magnifies justice in the way of pardoning sin, and mercy in the way of punishing it.—*John M'Laurin,* 1693—1754.

Verse 8.—*"The Lord is gracious,"* etc. The proclamation of the Lord to Moses (Exod. xxxiv. 6) is the fountain-head of these epithets.—*James G. Murphy.*

Verse 8.—In God there is no passion, only compassion.—*Richard Rothe,* 1799—1867.

Verse 8.—*"Of great mercy."* Mercy hath misery for its object, and is that attribute towards which the eyes of a fallen world must necessarily be turned. The Psalmist hath, accordingly, introduced her last with great pomp and splendour, seated in her triumphal chariot, and invested with a supremacy over all the works of God. She is above the heavens, and over all the earth, so that the whole creation findeth that refuge under the shadow of her wings of which, by reason of man's transgression, it standeth in need.—*Samuel Burder.*

Verse 9.—*"The Lord is good to all,"* etc. According to the doctrine of Christianity, we are not the creatures of a God who takes no care of his beings, and leaves them to themselves ; not the offspring of a father who disowns his children, who does not concern himself about them, and is indifferent to their happiness and their misery. No ; never has God, according to that comfortable doctrine, left himself unwitnessed to man ; never withdrawn from him his fatherly providence and love ; never abandoned the fortunes of his feeble, helpless, untutored children, to blind chance or to their own ignorance. No ; from their first progenitor, to his latest posterity, he has himself provided for their support, their instruction, their guidance, their progress to higher attainments. He has constantly revealed himself to them in various ways ; constantly shed innumerable benefits on them ; sometimes lovingly correcting, and sometimes bountifully blessing them ; has constantly been nigh to them, and has left them in want of no means for becoming wiser and better.—*George Joachim Zollikofer,* 1730—1788.

Verse 9.—*"The Lord is good to all,"* etc. God's pity is not as some sweet cordial, poured in dainty drops from a golden phial. It is not like the musical water-drops of some slender rill, murmuring down the dark side of Mount Sinai. It is wide as the whole scope of heaven. It is abundant as all the air. If one had art to gather up all the golden sunlight that to-day falls wide over the continent, falling through every silent hour ; and all that is dispersed over the whole ocean, floating from every wave ; and all that is poured refulgent over the northern wastes of ice, and along the whole continent of Europe, and the vast outlying Asia and torrid Africa—if we could in any wise gather up this immense and incalculable outflow and treasure that falls down through the bright hours, and runs in liquid ether about the mountains, and fills all the plains, and sends innumerable rays through every secret place, pouring over and filling every flower, shining down the sides of every blade of grass, resting in glorious humility upon the humblest things—on sticks, and stones, and pebbles—on the spider's web, the sparrow's nest, the threshold of the young foxes' hole, where they play and warm themselves—that rests on the prisoner's window, that strikes radiant beams through the slave's tear, and puts gold upon the widow's weeds, that plates and roofs the city with burnished gold, and goes on in its wild abundance up and down the earth, shining everywhere and always, since the day of primal creation, without faltering, without stint, without waste or diminution ; as full, as fresh, as overflowing to-day as if it were the very first day of its outlay—if one might gather up this boundless, endless, infinite treasure, to measure it, then might he tell the height, and depth, and unending glory of the pity of God ! That light, and the sun, its source, are God's own figure of the immensity and copiousness of his mercy and compassion.—*Henry Ward Beecher,* 1873.

Verse 9.—Even the worst taste of God's mercy ; such as fight against God's mercy taste of it ; the wicked have some crumbs from mercy's table. *"The Lord is good to all."* Sweet dewdrops are on the thistle as well as on the rose. The diocese where mercy visits is very large. Pharaoh's head was crowned though his heart was hardened.—*Thomas Watson.*

Verse 9.—*"His tender Mercies are over all his works."* When the sensible sinner is seeking faith of God, he may plead the *largeness* of mercy. God's mercy is like the firmament spread over all this lower world ; and every infirm creature partakes more or less of its influence, according to its exigence and capacity. True, may he say, I have made myself, by sin, the vilest of all creatures ; I am become worse than the beasts that perish ; as vile as a worm, as loathsome as a toad, by reason of the venomous corruption that is in my heart, and my woeful contrariety to the nature of a holy God. But there is *" mercy over all,"* even over such vile and loathsome creatures as these ; there may be some over me, though wrath do now abide on me. Oh, let that mercy, whose glory it is to stretch itself over all, reach my soul also ! Oh, that the blessed and powerful influence thereof would beget faith in my ·heart !—*David Clarkson.*

Verse 9.—*"His tender mercies."* The nature and force of the word רחמים, is properly the *bowels ;* that is, there are *tender mercies in God* (so we term it in the *Benedictus*). Not of the ordinary sort, slight, and such as pierce not deep, come not far ; but such as come *de profundis,* from the very *bowels* themselves, that affect that part, make the *bowels* relent. And what *bowels ?* Not the *bowels* of the common man (for then מעים had been the right word,) but רחמם are the *bowels* of a *parent* (so, we said, the word signifies), and this adds much ; adds to *mercy* στοργὴ, *natural love ;* to one strong affection another as strong or stronger than it.

And what *parent ?* the more pitiful of the twain, the *mother.* For רחם (the singular of this word) is Hebrew for the *womb.* So as this, to the two former addeth the sex ; the sex holden to be the more compassionate. Of all mercies, those of the *bowels ;* and of the bowels, the bowels of a *parent ;* and of the two parents, those of the *mother :* such pity as the mother takes of the children of her womb. *Mercies* are in God ; *such mercies* are in God.

"Over all." It is good news for us that these mercies are in God ; but, better yet, that they are in him with a *super*—" over." But, best of all, that that *super* is a *super omnia*—" over all." Much is said in few words to mercy's praise when 'tis said, *super omnia. Nihil supra* were much, none above it : but it is written *super omnia, above all.* He that saith this, leaves no more to say : there is no higher degree ; *super omnia* is the superlative.

All that are *above* are not *over.* It is not *above* only, as an obelisk or Maypole, higher than all about them, but have neither shadow nor shelter ; no good they do ! Mercy hath a broad top, spreading itself *over* all. It is so *above* all, as it is *over* them, too. As the vault of this chapel is *over* us, and the great vault of the firmament *over* that ; the *super* of latitude and expansion, no less than of altitude and elevation. And this to the end that all may retire to it, and take covert : it *over* them, and they *under* it. Under it, under the *shadow* of it, as of Esay's " great rock in the wilderness," from the *heat :* under the *shelter* of it as of Daniel's " great tree," from the tempest. (Isa. xxxii. 2 ; Dan. iv, 11, 12).—*Lancelot Andrewes.*

Verse 10.—*"All thy works shall praise thee, O Lord."* It is a poor philosophy and a narrow religion which does not recognise God as all in all. Every moment of our lives, we breathe, stand, or move in the temple of the Most High ; for the universe is that temple. Wherever we go, the testimony to his power, the impress of his hand, are there. Ask of the bright worlds around us, as they roll in the everlasting harmony of their circles, and they shall tell you of him whose power launched them on their courses ; ask of the mountains, that lift their heads among and above the clouds, and the bleak summit of one shall seem to call aloud to the snow-clad top of another, in proclaiming their testimony to the Agency which has laid their deep foundations. Ask of ocean's waters ; and the roar of their boundless waves shall chant from shore to shore a hymn of ascription to that Being, who hath said, " Hitherto shall ye come and no further." Ask of the rivers ; and, as they roll onward to the sea, do they not bear along their ceaseless tribute to the ever-working Energy, which struck open their fountains and poured them down through the valleys ? Ask of every region of the earth, from the burning equator to the icy pole, from the rock-bound coast to the plain covered with its luxuriant vegetation ; and will you not find on them all the record of the Creator's presence ? Ask of the countless tribes of plants and animals : and shall they not testify to the action of the great Source of Life ? Yes, from every portion, from every department of nature, comes the same voice ; everywhere we hear thy name, O God ! everywhere we see thy love ! Creation, in all its length and breadth, in all its depth and height, is the manifestation of thy Spirit, and without thee the worlds were dark and dead. The universe is to us as the burning bush which the Hebrew leader saw : God is ever present in it, for it burns with his glory, and the ground on which we stand is always holy.—*"Francis" (Viscount Dillon).*

Verse 10.—Marvellous is it that man is not always praising, since everything amidst which he dwells is continually inviting praise.—*Gregory the Great.*

Verse 10.—*"All thy works shall praise thee, O LORD,"* etc. *"All"* God's *"works"* do *"praise"* him, as the beautiful building praiseth the builder, or the well-drawn picture praiseth the painter : but his *"saints bless"* him, as the children of prudent and tender parents rise up and call them blessed. Of all God's works, his saints, the workmanship of his grace, the first-fruits of his creatures, have most reason to bless him.—*Matthew Henry.*

Verse 10.—*"All thy works shall praise thee, O LORD,"* etc. There are two words by which our thankfulness to God is expressed, *praising* and *blessing.* What is the difference ? Praise respecteth God's excellences, and blessing respecteth God's benefits. We may praise a man that never hath done us good, if he be excellent and praiseworthy ; but blessing respecteth God's bounty and benefits ; yet they are often used promiscuously.—*Thomas Manton.*

Verse 10.—*"And thy saints shall bless thee."* The lily lifts itself upon its slender stem, and displays its golden petals and its glittering ivory leaves ; and by its very existence it praises God. Yonder deep and booming sea rolls up in storm and tempest, sweeping everything before it ; and every dash of its waves praises God. The birds in the morning, and some of them all through the night, can never cease from praising ; uniting with the ten thousand other voices which make ceaseless concert before the throne. But observe, neither the flower, nor the sea, nor the bird, praises with intent to praise. To them it is no exercise of intellect, for they do not know God, and cannot understand his worthiness ; nor do they even know that they are praising him. They exhibit his skill, and his goodness, and so forth, and in so doing they do much ; but we must learn to do more. When you and I praise God, there is the element of will, of intelligence, of desire, of intent ; and in the saints of God there is another element, namely, that love to him, of reverent gratitude towards him, and this turns the praise into blessing. A man is an eminent painter, and you exclaim, "His pencil is instinct with life." Still, the man is no friend of yours, you pronounce no blessings on his name. It may be that your feeling towards him is that of deep regret that such abilities should be united with so ill a character. A certain person is exceedingly skilful in his profession, but he treats you unjustly, and therefore, though you often praise him for his extraordinary performances, you cannot bless him, for you have no cause to do so. I am afraid that there might be such a feeling as that of admiration of God for his great skill, his wonderful power, his extraordinary justness, and yet no warmth of love in the heart towards him : but in the saints the praise is sweetened with love, and is full of blessing.—*C. H. S.*

Verses 10, 11.—If not only irrational, but inanimate creatures praise God by giving occasion for his praise ; then how much more should men set forth his praise, who are not only living, but reasonable creatures ! And if creatures without life and reason should provoke mankind in general, as having life and reason, to praise God ; how much more should godly men be provoked by them to sing his praise, they having not only life, which stars have not ; and reason, which birds and beasts have not ; but grace, which the most of men have not ! Among visible creatures, men have most reason (because they have reason) to praise God ; and among men gracious men have most reason to praise God, because they have grace. And therefore as soon as ever David had said, *"All thy works shall praise thee, O LORD,"* he adds in the next words, *"and thy saints shall bless thee. They shall speak of the glory of thy kingdom, and talk of thy power."* As if he had said, As all thy works, O Lord, praise thee, so saints (who are the choicest pieces of thy workmanship) have cause to do it above all : they cannot but be speaking and talking of thy kingdom and power, which are very glorious.—*Joseph Caryl.*

Verse 11.—*"They shall speak of the glory of thy kingdom,"* etc. The glory of a kingdom is synonymous with its power. The power of a kingdom consists in the number of its subjects, and the sufficiency of its revenues to maintain them. Now, the glory, or the power of God's kingdom, may be inferred from the difference between it and that of man.   There are four points of difference.   First, the kings of this world have but *few subjects*, with but little wealth,—not more than the population and riches of one kingdom, or one province, while God reigns over all angels, all men, all demons ; and all wealth on land, in the sea, or in the air, belongs to him.   There is another difference, that while the kings of this world rule their subjects, they are still ruled by them, they are *dependent on them*, could do nothing without them ; and, however abundant their revenues may be, they are generally in want, nay, even in debt, and, consequently, always calling for fresh tributes and taxes ; but God, while he governs all, is subject to none, because he needs nobody's help or assistance.   Instead of being in want, he abounds in everything, because he could, in one moment, bring from nothing much more than he now beholds or enjoys.   The third difference is a consequence of the second, while the kings of this world seem so to enjoy their honours and dignities, they are, at the same time, *suffering acutely from interior fears*, doubts, and cares, which have some- times been so burdensome, as to cause them to abdicate altogether.   God never suffers such pressure, is subject to no fear, no misgivings, but reigns absolutely in perfect tranquillity.   The fourth difference, an essential one, is, that the kings of the world *reign but for a time ;* but God reigneth for ever.—*Robert Bellarmine.*

Verse 11.—*"They shall speak . . . and talk."*   Joy and sorrow are hard to conceal ; as from the countenance, so from the tongue.   There is so much corres- pondence betwixt the heart and tongue that they will move at once : every man therefore speaks of his own pleasure and care ; the hunter and falconer of his game ; the ploughman of his team ; the soldier of his march and colours.   If the heart were as full of God, the tongue could not refrain from talking of him : the rareness of Christian communication argues the common poverty of grace.   If Christ be not in our hearts, we are godless ; if he be there without our joy, we are senseless ; if we rejoice in him and speak not of him, we are shamefully unthankful.   Every man taketh, yea, raiseth occasion, to bring in speech of what he liketh.   As I will think of thee always, O Lord, so it shall be my joy to speak of thee often ; and if I find not opportunity, I will make it,—*Joseph Hall.*

Verse 13.—The Kingdom of God is his government of the world.   The glory of it becomes especially conspicuous in this, that he raises the dominion of his anointed over all the kingdoms of the world : comp. Ps. lxxxix. 27.   *"Thy kingdom is a kingdom of all eternities "* (verse 13), and so must also the kingdom of thine anointed be an eternal one, and will survive all the transitory kingdoms of this world, however highly they may puff themselves up.—*E. W. Hengstenberg.*

Verse 13.—On the door of the old mosque in Damascus, which was once a Christian church, but for twelve centuries has ranked among the holiest of the Mahomedan sanctuaries, are inscribed these memorable words : " Thy kingdom, O Christ, is an everlasting kingdom, and thy dominion endureth throughout all generations."   Though the name of Christ has been regularly blasphemed, and the disciples of Christ regularly cursed for twelve hundred years within it, the inscription has, nevertheless, remained unimpaired by time, and undisturbed by man.   It was unknown during the long reign of Mahomedan intolerance and oppression ; but when religious liberty was partially restored, and the missionaries were enabled to establish a Christian church in that city, it was again brought to light, encouraging them in their work of faith and labour of love.—*From John Bate's "Cyclopædia of Illustrations,"* 1865.

Verses 13, 14.—What we admire in these verses, is their combining the mag- nificence of unlimited power with assiduity of unlimited tenderness.   It is this combination which men are apt to regard as well-nigh incredible, supposing that a Being so great as God can never concern himself with beings so inconsiderable as themselves.   Tell them that God lifteth up those that be bowed down, and they cannot imagine that his kingdom and dominion are unbounded ; or tell them, on the other hand, of the greatness of his empire, and they think it impossible that he should uphold all that fall.—*Henry Melvill.*

Verse 14.—*"The Lord upholdeth all that fall,"* etc.   It is noteworthy how the Psalmist proceeds to exhibit the mightiness of God's kingdom, not by its power " to break in pieces and bruise," like the iron legs of the statue in Nebuchadnezzar's vision (Dan. ii. 40), but by the King's readiness to aid the weak. Even a heathen could see that this was the noblest use of power.

Regia (crede mihi) res est succurrere lapsis.
Ovid., Ep. de Panto, ii. 9, 11.
It is a kingly thing to help the fallen.

Neale and Littledale.

Verse 14.—*"The* LORD *upholdeth all that fall,"* etc. נֹפְלִים, *nophelim,* the *falling,* or those who are not able to keep their feet; the weak. He *shores* them up; he is their *prop.* No man falls through his own weakness merely; if he rely on God, the strongest foe cannot shake him.—*Adam* Clarke.

Verse 14.—*"And raiseth up all those that be bowed down,"* incurvatos. Many who do not actually fall are reduced to distress that may be even more painful; for the struggling are greater sufferers than the actually passive. Men are *bowed down* physically by infirmity; mentally, by care; spiritually, by remorse; some are even crushed by all three burdens. For all such there is help in a Mighty One. But none can help themselves alone: none are raised but by supernatural interposition—*non nisi opitulante Domino.—Martin Geier.*

Verse 14.—*"The* LORD *upholdeth all that fall."* The word here used is a participle, literally, *"The Lord sustaining"*; that is, the Lord *is* a Sustainer or Upholder of all that fall.—*Albert Barnes.*

Verse 14.—*"And raiseth up all those that he bowed down."* Alphonsus, King of Arragon, is famous for helping with his own hand one of his subjects out of a ditch. Of Queen Elizabeth it is recorded, to her eternal praise, that she hated (no less than did Mithridates) such as sought to crush virtue forsaken of fortune. Christ bruiseth not the broken reed, but upholdeth it, he quencheth not the smoking wick, but cherisheth it.—*John Trapp.*

Verses 14—19.—The Psalmist sets up a splendid argument. Having praised the kingdom, he goes on to display *seven glories* peculiar to kings, and shows that in Jehovah these shine supremely. Verses 14 to 19 contain each a royal virtue.— *John Lorinus.*

Verse 15.—*"The eyes of all wait upon thee."* God cannot be overmastered by what is great and enormous, so neither can he overlook what is small and insignificant. God is that being to whom the only great thing is himself; and, therefore, when " the eyes of all wait upon him," the seraph gains not attention by his gaze of fire, and the insect loses it not through the feebleness of vision. Archangels, and angels, and men, and beasts of the field, and fowls of the air, and fish of the sea, draw equally the regard of him, who, counting nothing great but himself, the Creator, can pass over as small no fraction of the creature.—*Henry Melvill.*

Verse 15.—Doth not nature teach you to pray? Ask the brutes, the ravens, lions, etc. (Job xxxviii. 41; Ps. cxlvii. 9; civ. 27; cxlv. 15); not as if these unreasonable creatures could know and worship God, but because nature hath taught them so much of this duty as they are capable of and can bear; they have some sense of their burdens and wants, they groan and cry, and desire to be eased; and the Lord hearkeneth to this voice and saith, " Now the poor creature is crying to me, and I will pity it." Ah! shall the beasts in their own way cry to God, and wilt thou be silent? Hath the Lord elevated thee so far above these inferior creatures, and fitted thee for the immediate acts of his worship, and for a higher communion with himself, and wilt thou not serve him accordingly? Hath he given thee a heart and a spiritual soul, as he hath given the brutes a sensitive appetite and natural desires, and shall they cry to God with the one, and not thou with the other?—*Alexander Pitcairne,* 1664.

Verse 15.—*"Eyes . . . wait upon thee."* Many dumb beggars have been relieved at Christ's gate by making signs.—*William Secker.*

Verse 15.—In agony nature is no atheist, the mind which knows not where to fly, flies to God.—*Hannah More,* 1745—1833.

Verse 15.—The creatures are his, and therefore to be received with thanksgiving; this our Saviour performed with great vigour and zeal; thus teaching us, when " looking up to heaven," that *"the eyes of all"* ought, in the most literal sense, *"to wait"* upon that Lord *"who gives them their meat in due season."* . . . A secret sense of God's goodness is by no means enough. Men should make solemn and outward expressions of it, when they receive his creatures for their support;

a service and homage not only due to him, but profitable to themselves.—*George Stanhope, 1660—1728.*

Verse 15.—While atheism, in its strict signification, namely, that of total denial of God's existence, is scarcely, if at all, to be found on earth ; atheism, as regards the denial of God's providence, is the espoused creed of hundreds amongst us. . . . Providence, which is confessed in great things, is rejected in small things ; and even if you can work up men to an easy confession that God presideth over national concerns, you will find them withdrawing individuals from his scrutiny. We bring against this paring down of God's providence a distinct charge of atheism. If we confess the existence of a God at all, we read it in the workmanship of the tiniest leaf, as well as the magnificent pinnacles of Andes and Alps ; if we believe in the providence of God at all, we must confess that he numbers the hairs of our heads, as well as marshals the stars of the firmament ; and that providence is not universal, and therefore cannot be godlike, if a sparrow, any more than a seraph, flit away unregarded.

Now, the words before us set themselves most strenuously against this popular atheism. The whole creation is represented as fastening its gaze on the universal Parent, and as drawing from his fulness the supply of every necessity. *"The eyes of all wait upon thee ; and thou givest them their meat in due season."* There is made, you observe, no exception whatever ; the exhibition is simply that of every rank and order of beings looking to the Almighty, confessing dependence upon him, and standing environed by his guardianship. So that, in place of anything which approximates to the abandonment of our creation, the Psalmist asserts a ceaseless attention to its wants, the suspension of which for an instant would cause chill and darkness throughout the whole universe.—*Henry Melvill.*

Verse 15.—*"Thou givest them their meat in due season."* The meat which endures to everlasting life ; the flesh of Christ, which is meat indeed ; the doctrines of the gospel, which, as some of them are milk for babes, others are meat for strong men, or strong meat for experienced believers ; and these are given forth under Christ's direction, by his ministering servants, who are his wise and faithful stewards, that give to everyone of the family their portion of meat in due season, which is the word fitly spoken ; and, when it is so, how good it is ! Luke xii. 42 ; Prov. xv. 23. This is food convenient for them, given out *in his time*, as in the original ; either in the Lord's time, when he sees best, or in *their* time, as the Syriac version, when they most need it, and it will do them most good.—*John Gill.*

Verse 15.—*(second clause.)* It is said that God gives them *"their food,"* and *"in its season,"* for the very variety of it serves more to illustrate the providence of God. Each has its own way of feeding, and the different kinds of aliment are designed and adapted for different uses. David therefore speaks of the food which is particular to them. The pronoun is not in the plural, and we are not to read *in their* season, as if it applied to the animals. The food he notices as given in its season ; for here also we are to notice the admirable arrangements of divine providence, that there is a certain time appointed for harvest, vintage, and hay crop, and that the year is so divided into intervals, that the cattle are fed at one time on grass, at another on hay, or straw, or acorns, or other products of the earth. Were the whole supply poured forth at one and the same moment, it could not be gathered together so conveniently ; and we have no small reason to admire the seasonableness with which the different kinds of fruit and aliment are yearly produced.—*John Calvin.*

Verse 15.—Mr. Robertson told of a poor child who was accustomed to see unexpected provision for his mother's wants arrive in answer to prayer. The meal-barrel in Scotland is everything to a hungry boy: so he said, " Mither, I think God aye hears when we're scraping the bottom o' the barrel."—*"The Christian."*

Verses 15—17.—Who can fear that, because God's ways are unsearchable, they may not be all tending to the final good of his creatures, when he knows that with the tenderness of a most affectionate parent this Creator and Governor ministers to the meanest living thing ? Who can be disquieted by the mysteriousness of the Divine dealings when he remembers that they are those of one who never ceases for a solitary moment to consult the happiness of whatsoever he hath formed ? Who, in short, can distrust God because clouds and darkness are round about him, when there is light enough to show that he is the vigilant guardian of every tenant of this earth, that his hand upholds, and his breath animates, and his bounty nourishes, the teeming hordes of the city, and the desert, and the ocean ? It seems that there is thus a beautiful, though tacit process of reasoning in our text, and that the seventeenth verse is set in its proper connection. It is as though David had said, " Come, let us muse on the righteousness of God. He would not be God if he were not righteous in all his ways and holy in all his works ; and therefore we may be sure that whatsoever he does is the best that could be done, whether or not we can discover its excellence."

Yes, this may be true, but when we look on the divine dealings what an abyss of dark waters there is ! How unsearchable, how unfathomable are God's judgments ! We admit it ; but being previously convinced of God's righteousness, we ought not to be staggered by what is dark in his dispensations.

" True," you reply, " but the mind does not seem satisfied by this reasoning ; it may be convincing to the intellect, but it does not address itself to the feelings." Well, then, pass from what is dark in God's dealing to what is clear. He is about your path and about your bed ; he " preserveth man and beast " ; " his tender mercies are over all his works." Is this a God of whom to be suspicious ? Is this a God to mistrust ? Oh ! surely if you will fortify yourselves by such facts as these—" Thou, O Lord, satisfiest the desire of every living thing," "The eyes of all wait upon thee ; and thou givest them their meat in due season "—if, I say, you will fortify your minds by such facts as these, you will be able at all times and in all circumstances to join heartily in the acknowledgment of the Psalmist—"The Lord is righteous in all his ways and holy in all his works."—Henry Melvill.

Verse 16.—
Thou openest thy hand of grace
And thou dost satisfy
The wants of all in every place
Who for thy presence cry.

Thomas MacKellar, 1883.

Verse 16.—"Thou openest thy hand." This seems as if depicted from a house-keeper's habit of feeding a brood of chickens and other creatures. She flings abroad with full and open hand a large supply, not measuring to a grain just what might be enough.—Martin Geier.

Verse 16.—"Thou openest thy hand." What an idea does this convey of the paternal goodness of the great Father of his creation ! How opposite to the conduct of many of his creatures one to another, whose hands and hearts are shut ! What an idea also does it convey of the ease with which the wants of the whole creation are supplied ! Let me pause a moment and think of their wants. What a quantity of vegetable and animal food is daily consumed in one town : what a quantity in a large city like London : what a quantity in a nation : in the whole world ! But men do not compose a hundredth part of "every living thing" ! What innumerable wants throughout all animate nature ; in the earth, in the air, in the waters ! Whence comes their supply ? " Thou openest thy hand," and all are satisfied. And can all these wants be supplied by only the opening of his hand ? What then must sin be, and salvation from it ? That is a work of wonderful expense. God openeth his hand and satisfieth all creation, but he must purchase the Church with his blood. . . . . In what a variety of ways are our wants supplied. The earth is fruitful, the air is full of life, the clouds empty themselves upon the earth, the sun pours forth its genial rays ; but the operation of all these second causes is only the opening of his hand ! Nay further : look we to instruments as well as means ? Parents feed us in our childhood, and supply our youthful wants ; ways are opened for our future subsistence ; connexions are formed, which prove sources of comfort ; friends are kind in seasons of extremity ; supplies are presented from quarters that we never expected. What are all these but the opening of his hand ? If his hand were shut, what a world would this be ! The heavens brass, the earth iron ; famine, pestilence, and death must follow. See Ps. civ. 27—29.

Consider next the term "hand." There is a difference between the hand and the heart. God opens his hand, in the way of providence, towards his worst enemies. He gave Nebuchadnezzar all the kingdoms of the earth. But he opens his heart in the gospel of his Son. This is the better portion of the two. While we are thankful for the one, let us not rest satisfied in it : it is merely a hand portion. Rather let us pray with Jabez to be blessed indeed ; and that we might have a Joseph's portion ; not only the precious things of the earth and the fulness thereof, but " the good will of him that dwelt in the bush ! "

"Thou satisfiest the desire," etc. God does not give grudgingly. It seems to be a characteristic of the divine nature, both in the natural and moral world, to raise desires, not with a view to disappoint, but to satisfy them. O what a consoling thought is this ! If there be any desires in us which are not satisfied, it is through their being self-created ones, which is our own fault ; or through artificial scarcity from men's luxury, which is the fault of our species. God raises no desires as our Creator, but he gives enough to satisfy them ; and none as our Redeemer and Sanctifier but what shall be actually satisfied. O the wonderful munificence of God ! " How great is his goodness, and how great is his beauty ! "—*Andrew Fuller.*

Verse 16 (second clause).—The word רצון, *ratson,* some render *"desire,"* as though he meant that God supplies each kind of animal with food according to its wish. And a little afterwards we do indeed find it used in that sense. Others, however, refer it rather to God's feeding them of his mere good pleasure and kindness ; it is not enough to say that our food is given us by God, unless we add, as in the second clause of the verse, that his kindness is gratuitous, and that there is no extrinsic cause whatever moving him to provide so liberally for every living creature. In that case the cause is put for the effect ; the various kinds of provision being effects of his good pleasure—χαρισματα της χαριτος.—*John Calvin.*

Verse 17.—*"The LORD is righteous in all his ways,"* etc. The ground upon which praise is here ascribed to God may seem a common one, being in every one's mouth ; but in nothing is wisdom shown more than in holding fast the truth, that God is just in all his ways, so as to retain in our hearts an unabated sense of it amidst all troubles and confusions. Though all acknowledge God to be just, most men are no sooner overtaken by affliction than they quarrel with his severity : unless their wishes are immediately complied with, they are impatient, and nothing is more common than to hear his justice impeached. As it is everywhere abused by the wicked imputations men cast upon it, here it is very properly vindicated from such ungrateful treatment, and asserted to be constant and unfailing, however loudly the world may disparage it. It is expressly added, *"in all his ways and works"* ; for we fail to give God due honour unless we recognise a constant tenor of righteousness in the whole progress of his operation. Nothing is more difficult in the time of trouble, when God has apparently forsaken us, or afflicts us without cause, than to restrain our corrupt feelings from breaking out against his judgments ; as we are told of the Emperor Mauricius in a memorable passage of history, that seeing his sons murdered by the wicked and perfidious traitor Phocas, and being about to be carried out himself to death, he cried out—" Thou art righteous, O God, and just are thy judgments."—*John Calvin.*

Verse 17.—*"Holy in all his works."* God is good, the absolute and perfect ; and from good nothing can come but good : and therefore all which God has made is good, as he is ; and therefore if anything in the world seems to be bad, one of two things must be true of it.

Either it is *not* bad, though it seems so to us ; and God will bring good out of it in his good time, and justify himself to men, and show us that he is holy in all his works, and righteous in all his ways. Or else—

If the thing be really bad, then God did not make it. It must be a disease, a mistake, a failure, a man's making, or some person's making, but not of God's making. For all that he has made he sees eternally ; and behold, it is very good.—*Charles Kingsley, in "The Good News of God,"* 1878.

Verse 18.—*"The LORD is nigh."* The nearness or remoteness of a friend is very material and considerable in our troubles, distresses, wants, dangers, etc. I have such a friend and he would help me, but he lives so far off ; and I have another friend that has a great love for me, that is able to counsel me, and to speak a word in season to me, and that in my distress would stand close to me, but he is so remote. I have a special friend, that did he know how things stand with me would make my burdens his, and my wants his, and my sorrows his ; but he is in a far country, he is at the Indies, and I may be undone before I can hear from him. But it is not thus with you, O Christians ! who have a God so nigh unto you, who have the signal presence of God in the midst of you, yea, who have a God always standing by you, " The Lord stood by me," etc. : 2 Tim. iv. 17.—*Thomas Brooks.*

Verse 18.—*"Them that call upon him."* *To call upon the name of the Lord* implies *right faith,* to call upon him as he *is ; right trust* in him, leaning upon him, *right devotion,* calling upon him as he has appointed ; *right life,* ourselves who call upon him being, or becoming by his grace, what he wills. They *"call"* not *" upon the Lord,"* but upon some idol of their own imagining, who call upon him as other than he has revealed himself, or remaining themselves other than those whom he has declared that he will hear. For such *deny* the very primary attribute of God, his truth. *Their* God is not a God of truth.—*Edward Bouverie Pusey,* 1800—1882.

Verse 18.—*"To all that call upon him in truth."* Because there is a counterfeit and false sort of worshipping, and calling upon God, which is debarred from the benefit of this promise, to wit, when the party suppliant is not reconciled, nor seeking reconciliation through Christ the Mediator, or is seeking something not promised, or something for a carnal end, that he may bestow it on his lusts ; therefore he who hath right unto this promise must be a worshipper of God in faith, and sincere intention ; and to such the Lord will show himself *"nigh."*—*David Dickson.*

Verse 18.—To call upon God in truth is, first, to repose an implicit confidence in the faithfulness of his promise, and to look for unlimited answers to prayer from the riches of his grace in Christ Jesus. But it is also, in the next place, to feel our own urgent need of the things for which we supplicate, and to realize an earnest and unfeigned concern to obtain them. " What things ye desire when ye pray," said the Lord, " believe that ye receive them, and ye shall have them ; " and hence we gather, that the hearty desire, arising out of the consciousness of need, is an integral and inseparable part of genuine and effectual prayer.—*Thomas Dale,* 1853.

Verses 18, 19.—God's people are a praying people, a generation of seekers, and such commonly are speeders. God never said to the seed of Jacob, Seek ye my face in vain. They seek his face, righteousness and strength, and he is found of them. . . . The saints alone betake themselves to God and his help, run to him as their sanctuary ; others fly from God's presence, run to the rocks, and the tops of the ragged rocks, call to the hills and the mountains ; but a child of God goes only and tells his Father, and before him lays open his cause ; as good Hezekiah did, when Rabshakeh came out against him ; " O Lord, I am oppressed, undertake for me "; or the Church (Isa. xxxiii. 2), " Be thou our arm every morning, and our salvation in time of trouble." They only sensibly need, and so alone crave and implore divine succour ; and God will not suffer his people to lose the precious treasure of their prayers. *"The Lord is nigh unto all them that call upon him ; he will fulfil their desire, he will hear their cry,"* etc. That God who prepares his people's heart to pray, prepares also his own ear to hear ; and he that promiseth to hear before we call, will never deny to hearken when we cry unto him. As Calvin saith : " Oppressions and afflictions make man cry, and cries and supplications make God hear."—*F. E., in "The Saint's Ebenezer,"* 1667.

Verse 19.—*"He will fulfil the desire of them that fear him."* This is for comfort for all poor broken hearts in whom God hath ingendered the true desire of grace. Let such know that the first step to grace is to see they have no grace ; and the first degree of grace is the *desire* of grace. It is not with the body as with the soul, if you will be healed you shall be healed. A man may desire to be healed corporally, and yet his disease continue upon him ; but it is not so with the soul : if thou wilt say, " Christ heal me," thou shalt be made whole. If a man have but the true desire of grace it shall be given him : " Lord, thou hast heard the desire of the humble " (Ps. x. 17) : when the poor soul is humbled before God in the sense of the want of grace, and breathes and desires after it, the Lord will grant such desires : *"He will fulfil the desire of them that fear him : he also will hear their cry, and will save them."* One said, " The greatest part of Christianity is to desire to be a Christian." And another said, " The total sum of a man's religion in this life consists in the true desires of saving grace." This was the perfection Saint Paul attained unto (Rom. vii. 18) : " To will is present with me ; but how to perform that which is good I find not." Saint Paul we know was the child of God, and one dearly beloved of God ; yet that was the pitch of his godliness ; it consisted more in desire than accomplishment. Canst thou approve by evident and sound arguments that thou hast the true desires of grace ? Then know for thy comfort that the Lord's spirit of grace hath been moving and stirring in thee : " It is God that worketh in you both the will and the deed " (Phil. ii. 13), and that of his good pleasure, not only of his bounty, from whence he hath bestowed many graces, even upon such as he will damn afterwards for their accursed abuse of them, with the neglect of the power thereof. But if God hath set thy will, and the stream of thy affections and desires, to himself and to grace, it is an evidence of God's good pleasure from which he did at first elect thee, and gave his Son to redeem thee.—*William Fenner* (1560—1640), *in "The Riches of Grace."*

Verse 19.—*"He will fulfil the desire of them that fear him."* God will not grant us every desire, that is our mercy ; for, 1. Some of them are *sinful.* David desired to be revenged on Nabal and his innocent family. Jonah desired Nineveh's ruin. 2. Others would *not be for our good.* David desired the life of the child he had by Bathsheba ; David also desired the life of Jonathan; neither of which would have been for his good. Nay, not every *righteous* desire. It is a righteous desire for a minister to desire the salvation of those that hear him. So Paul declared, " I would to God that all that are here present were altogether such as I am "; Acts xxvi. 29. So again, " I could wish that myself were accursed from Christ for my brethren, my kinsmen according to the flesh " : Rom. ix. 1. David *desired* to build a house for God, and it was a righteous desire, for God took it well at his hands ; yet he did not grant it. Kings and prophets desired to see the Lord Messiah, and yet did not see him. How then are we to understand it ? Answer. The sum or substance of their desires shall be fulfilled. What is the main desire of a seaman ? that he may arrive at the haven. So saints will be brought to their desired haven. What of a pilgrim ? See Heb. xi. 16. So all the desires of a Christian are summed up in this, *That he may eternally enjoy God and be like him.* Doubtless there is great mystery in these things. However I think it is certain that, when God raises a spiritual desire in a person, it is *often*, though not *always*, with an intention to bestow the object desired.—*Andrew Fuller.*

Verse 19 (first clause).—God will fulfil the will of those who fear to disobey *his* will.—*Simon de Muis.*

Verse 19.—*"Desire"* is the largest and most comprehensive word that can be used ; it contains all things in it . . . . Nothing good, nothing necessary, nothing profitable, but comes under this word *"desire."* When God promises to *"fulfil the desires of them that fear him,"* he doth promise all good things ; desire comprehends all that can be desired.—*Ralph Robinson.*

Verse 19.—*"He will hear their cry,"* etc. A mark of a great king—he gives willing audience to suppliants.—*Johannes Paulus Palanterius.*

Verse 19.—*"He will hear and save."* How true a description of Christ in his constant office. He heard Mary Magdalene and saved her. He heard the Canaanitish woman, and saved her daughter. He heard the cry of the two blind men and enlightened them. He heard the lepers and cleansed them. He heard the cry of the dying thief and promised him Paradise. Never has one yet cried to King Jesus who has not been heard and delivered.—*Thomas Le Blanc.*

Verse 20.—*"The Lord preserveth,"* etc. God's mercy and God's justice ; he preserves and he destroys. Philip IV. of France, surnamed the Beautiful, on his escutcheon emblazoned a sword and an olive branch, with the motto, *Utrumque,* i.e. " one or the other." A truly great king is master of either art—war and peace. —*Thomas Le Blanc.*

Verse 20.—Those who were called " them that *fear* him " are now denominated " them that *love* him."—*Simon de Muis.*

Verse 20. — *"All the wicked will he destroy."* God has so many different, unsearchable ways of taking wicked men out of the world, and sending them to hell, that there is nothing to make it appear that God had need to be at the expense of a miracle, or go out of the ordinary course of his providence, to destroy any wicked man at any moment.—*Jonathan Edwards.*

Verse 20.—*"All the wicked will he destroy."* It must not be overlooked that this declaration occurs in a song of praise. The whole of the context is utterly inconsistent with the expression of emotions of anger or revenge.—*Speaker's Commentary.*

Verse 20.—*"All the wicked will he destroy."* [Prayer-Book Version, *"scattereth abroad."*] Like the ruins of a demolished building ; or rather, like an army, which the enemy has completely routed.—*William Keatinge Clay.*

Verse 20.—*"Preserveth"* . . . . *"destroy."* Notice this recurrent thought, that the guardianship of the good implies the destruction of the wicked.—*A. S. Aglen.*

HINTS TO PREACHERS.

Verses **1, 2.**—Praise. **1.** Personal Praise. **2.** Daily praise. **3.** Enthusiastic praise. **4.** Perpetual praise. Or : I. The attractive theme of the song. II. The increasing fulness of the song. III. The unending life of the singer.—*C. A. D.*

Verses **1 & 2.**—The four " I wills " of praise. Praise to the King ; praise to the divine character ; praise for all time ; praise for all eternity.

Verse **2.**—*Every day ; for ever.* I. Day by day for ever God and I will endure. II. Day by day for ever our present relations will continue. He the God, I the creature ; he the Father, I the child ; he the blessing, I the blest. III. Day by day for ever he shall have my homage.—*W. B. H.*

Verse **3.**—I. The dignity of man is here implied in his capacity for praising God greatly. II. His immortality in his capacity for praising his unsearchable greatness.—*G. R.*

Verse 3 (*last clause*).—The unsearchable greatness of God. Consider it, I. As a fact amply demonstrated. II. As a rebuke to despondency : see Isaiah xl. 28. III. As the stay of a soul oppressed by mysteries. IV. As indicating a subject for our everlasting study.—*J. F.*

Verse **4.**—I. Our obligation to past generations. II. Our duty to generations to come.—*G. R.*

Verses **5—7.**—The Antiphon. I. To praise God is a personal duty : " I will." II. Its right performance will excite others to engage in it ; " And men shall." III. The accompaniment of others in praise will re-act upon ourselves. " And I will " ; " And they shall abundantly," etc. IV. Such praise widens and expands as it rolls along. Beginning with God's majesty and works, it extends to his acts, greatness, goodness, and righteousness.—*C. A. D.*

Verses **5—7.**—I. Subjects for praise. 1. Divine majesty. 2. Divine works. 3. Divine judgments. 4. Divine greatness. 5. Divine goodness. 6. Divine righteousness. II. Of whom is it required. 1. Personal ; " I will speak." 2. Universal ; " men shall speak."—*G. R.*

Verses **6, 7.**—I. *The awe-struck talk.* Silent as to mercies and promises, men must speak when God's terrible acts are among them. II. *The bold avowal.* One individual declares God's greatness in power, wisdom, truth and grace. This leads others to the same conclusion, and hence—III. *The grateful outpouring.* Many bless the Lord's great goodness in a song fresh, free, constant, joyous, refreshing, abundant, like the gush of a spring. IV. *The select song.* They *utter* goodness but *sing* of righteousness. This is a noteworthy topic for a discourse.

Verse **7.**—See " Spurgeon's Sermons," No. 1468 : " The Philosophy and Propriety of Abundant Praise."

Verse **8.**—I. Grace to the unworthy. II. Compassion to the afflicted. II. Forbearance to the guilty. IV. Mercy to the penitent.—*G. R.*

Verse **9.**—The universal goodness of God in no degree a contradiction to the special election of grace.

Verse **10.**—See " Spurgeon's Sermons," No. 1796 : " Concerning Saints."

Verse **11.**—The glory of Christ's kingdom. The glory of this kingdom is manifested,—I. In its origin. II. In the manner and spirit of its administration. III. In the character of its subjects. IV. In the privileges that are attached to it.—*Robert Hall,*

Verses **11, 12.**—Talk transfigured. I. The faculty of talk is extensively possessed II. Is commonly misused. III. May be nobly employed. IV. Will then be gloriously useful.—*C. A. D.*

Verses **11—13.**—To show the greatness of God's kingdom, David observes, 1. *The pomp of it.* Would we by faith look within the veil, we should " speak of the glory of his kingdom " (verse 11) ; " and the glorious majesty of it " (verse 12). 2. *The power of it.* When " they speak of the glory of God's kingdom," they must " talk of his power," the extent of it, the efficacy of it. 3. *The perpetuity of it* (verse 13). The thrones of earthly princes totter, and the flowers of their crowns wither, monarchs come to an end ; but, Lord, " thy kingdom is an everlasting kingdom."—*Matthew Henry.*

Verse **14.**—The grace of God in his kindness to the undeserving and the miserable, who look to him for help. I. He " upholdeth all that fall." 1. A description, embracing (1) Sinners who have fallen lowest : (2) Backsliders who have tripped most foully. 2. An act implying (1) Pity which draws nigh ; (2) Power which places the fallen upon their feet ; (3) Preservation which keeps them standing. II. He " raiseth up all those that are bowed down." Consolation for those who are —1. Bowed down with shame and penitence. 2. Oppressed with perplexities and cares. 3. Weighed with a sense of weakness in the presence of onerous duties. 4. Depressed because of prevailing error and sin around them.—*J. F.*

Verse 14.—Help for the fallible. I. Whatever our present position we are liable to fall. Sickness. Loss. Friendlessness. Sin. II. However low we fall we are not below the reach of God's hand. III. Within the reach of God's hand we shall experience the action of God's love. " Upholdeth." " Raiseth up."— *C. A. D.*

Verses 15, 16.—Universal dependence and divine support. The Psalmist here teaches—I. The Universality of Dependence amongst creatures : " The eyes of all wait upon thee." We depend upon God for " life, and breath, and all things." Entire dependence should beget deep humility. II. The Infinitude of the Divine Resources : " And thou givest them their meat." His resources must be, 1. Infinitely vast. 2. Infinitely various. Both sufficient and adapted for all. III. The Timeliness of the Divine Communications : " In due season." A reason for patience if his gifts seem delayed. IV. The Sublime Ease of the Divine Communications : " Thou openest thine hand," and the countless needs of the universe are satisfied. An encouragement to believing prayer. V. The Sufficiency of the Divine Communications : " And satisfiest the desire of every living thing." " God giveth to all liberally." Our subject urges all men to, 1. Gratitude. Constant provision should lead to constant thankfulness and consecration. 2. Trust. (1) For temporal supplies. " Grace to help in time of need" will surely be given to all who look to him.—*William Jones, in "The Homiletic Quarterly,"* 1878.

Verse 17.—I. What God declares himself to be. II. What his people find him to be. III. What all creatures will ultimately acknowledge him to be.—*G. R.*

Verses 18—20.—Gather from these verses the character of God's people. I. They call upon God. II. They fear God. III. They have desires towards God. IV. They have answers from God. V. They love God.

Verse 18 (last clause).—True prayer, in what it differs essentially from mere formalism.

Verse 18.—At the palace gates. I. Directions to callers. 1. " Call upon *him*" ; let the repetition suggest pertinacity. 2. Call " in truth " ; sincerely, with promises, in appointed way. II. Encouragement for callers. Jehovah is nigh, with his ready ear, sympathizing heart, and helpful hand.—*W. B. H.*

Verses 18, 19.—The blessedness of prayer. I. Definition of prayer : " calling upon God." II. Variety in prayer : " call, desire. cry." III. Essential characteristic of prayer : " truth." IV. God's nearness in prayer. V. Assured success of prayer. " He will fu. l, hear, save."—*C. A. D.*

Verse 20.—Those who love God are preserved *from* excessive temptation, falling into sin, despair, apostasy, remorse, famishing ; preserved *in* trial, persecution, depression, death ; preserved *to* activity, holiness, victory, glory.

Verse 20.—Solemn Contrasts. 1. Between human characters. " Them that love him." " The wicked." 2. Between human destinies. " Preserveth." " Destroy."—*C. A. D.*

Verse 20.—How the love of God is the opposite of wickedness, and wickedness inconsistent with the love of God.

Verse 21.—Individual praise suggests the desire for universal praise. We like company in a good deed ; we perceive the inadequacy of our own song ; we desire others to be happy ; we long to see that done which is right and good.

PSALM CXLVI.

DIVISION, ETC.—*We are now among the Hallelujahs. The rest of our journey lies through the Delectable Mountains. All is praise to the close of the book. The key is high-pitched: the music is upon the high-sounding cymbals. O for a heart full of joyful gratitude, that we may run, and leap, and glorify God, even as these Psalms do.*

Alexander thinks that this song may be regarded as composed of two equal parts; in the first we see the happiness of those who trust in God, and not in man (1—5), while the second gives the reason drawn from the Divine perfections (5—10). This might suffice for our purpose; but as there is really no break at all, we will keep it entire. It is "one pearl," a sacred censer of holy incense, pouring forth one sweet perfume.

EXPOSITION.

PRAISE ye the LORD. Praise the LORD, O my soul.

2 While I live will I praise the LORD: I will sing praises unto my God while I have any being.

3 Put not your trust in princes, *nor* in the son of man, in whom *there is* no help.

4 His breath goeth forth, he returneth to his earth; in that very day his thoughts perish.

5 Happy *is* he that *hath* the God of Jacob for his help, whose hope *is* in the LORD his God:

6 Which made heaven, and earth, the sea, and all that therein *is*: which keepeth truth for ever:

7 Which executeth judgment for the oppressed: which giveth food to the hungry. The LORD looseth the prisoners:

8 The LORD openeth *the eyes of* the blind: the LORD raiseth them that are bowed down: the LORD loveth the righteous:

9 The LORD preserveth the strangers; he relieveth the fatherless and widow: but the way of the wicked he turneth upside down.

10 The LORD shall reign for ever, *even* thy God, O Zion, unto all generations. Praise ye the LORD.

1. *"Praise ye the LORD,"* or, Hallelujah. It is saddening to remember how this majestic word has been trailed in the mire of late. Its irreverent use is an aggravated instance of taking the name of Jehovah our God in vain. Let us hope that it has been done in ignorance by the ruder sort; but great responsibility lies with leaders who countenance and even copy this blasphemy. With holy awe let us pronounce the word HALLELUJAH, and by it summon ourselves and all others to adore the God of the whole earth. Men need to be called to praise; it is important that they should praise; and there are many reasons why they should do it at once. Let all who hear the word *Hallelujah* unite immediately in holy praise.

"Praise the LORD, O my soul." He would practise what he had preached. He would be the leader of the choir which he had summoned. It is a poor business if we solely exhort others, and do not stir up our own soul. It is an evil thing to say, "Praise ye," and never to add, "Praise, O my soul." When we praise God let us arouse our innermost self, our central life: we have but one soul, and if it be saved from eternal wrath, it is bound to praise its Saviour. Come heart, mind, thought! Come my whole being, my soul, my all, be all on flame with joyful adoration! Up, my brethren! Lift up the song! "Praise ye the Lord." But what am I at? How dare I call upon others, and be negligent myself? If ever man was under bonds to bless the Lord I am that man, wherefore let me put my

soul into the centre of the choir, and then let my better nature excite my whole manhood to the utmost height of loving praise. " O for a well-tuned harp ! " Nay, rather, O for a sanctified heart. Then if my voice should be of the poorer sort, and somewhat lacking in melody, yet my soul without my voice shall accomplish my resolve to magnify the Lord.

2. *"While I live I will praise the LORD."* I shall not live here for ever. This mortal life will find a finis in death ; but while it lasts I will laud the Lord my God. I cannot tell how long or short my life may be ; but every hour of it shall be given to the praises of my God. While I live I'll love ; and while I breathe I'll bless. It is but for a while, and I will not wile that time away in idleness, but consecrate it to that same service which shall occupy eternity. As our life is the gift of God's mercy, it should be used for his glory. *"I will sing praises unto my God while I have any being."* When I am no longer in being on earth, I hope to have a higher being in heaven, and there I will not only praise, but *sing* praises. Here I have to sigh and praise, but there I shall only sing and praise. This " while I have any being " will be a great while, but the whole of it shall be filled up with adoration ; for the glorious Jehovah is my God, my own God by covenant, and by blood relationship in Christ Jesus. I have no being apart from my God, therefore, I will not attempt to enjoy my being otherwise than by singing to his honour. Twice the Psalmist says " I will " ; here first thoughts and second thoughts are alike good. We cannot be too firm in the holy resolve to praise God, for it is the chief end of our living and being that we should glorify God and enjoy him for ever.

3. *"Put not your trust in princes."* If David be the author this warning comes from a prince. In any case it comes from the Spirit of the living God. Men are always far too apt to depend upon the great ones of earth, and forget the Great One above ; and this habit is the fruitful source of disappointment. Princes are only men, and men with greater needs than others ; why, then, should we look to them for aid ? They are in greater danger, are burdened with greater cares, and are more likely to be misled than other men ; therefore, it is folly to select them for our confidence. Probably no order of men have been so false to their promises and treaties as men of royal blood. So live as to deserve *their* trust, but not burden them with your trust. *"Nor the son of man, in whom there is no help."* Though you should select one son of man out of the many, and should imagine that he differs from the rest and may be safely depended on, you will be mistaken. There is none to be trusted, no, not one. Adam fell ; therefore lean not on his sons. Man is a helpless creature without God ; therefore, look not for help in that direction. All men are like the few men who are made into princes, they are more in appearance than in reality, more in promising than in performing, more apt to help themselves than to help others. How many have turned away heart-sick from men on whom they once relied ! Never was this the case with a believer in the Lord. He is a very present help in time of trouble. In man there is no help in times of mental depression, in the day of sore bereavement, in the night of conviction of sin, or in the hour of death. What a horror when most in need of help to read those black words, NO HELP !

4. *"His breath goeth forth, he returneth to his earth."* His breath goes from his body, and his body goes to the grave. His spirit goes one way, and his body another. High as he stood, the want of a little air brings him down to the ground, and lays him under it. Man who comes from the earth returns to the earth : it is the mother and sister of his body, and he must needs lie among his kindred as soon as the spirit which was his life has made its exit. There is a spirit in man, and when that goes the man goes. The spirit returns to God who gave it, and the flesh to the dust out of which it was fashioned. This is a poor creature to trust in : a dying creature, a corrupting creature. Those hopes will surely fall to the ground which are built upon men who so soon lie under ground.

"In that very day his thoughts perish." Whatever he may have proposed to do, the proposal ends in smoke. He cannot think, and what he had thought of cannot effect itself, and therefore it dies. Now that he has gone, men are ready enough to let his thoughts go with him into oblivion ; another thinker comes, and turns the thoughts of his predecessor to ridicule. It is a pitiful thing to be waiting upon princes or upon any other men, in the hope that they will think of us. In an hour they are gone, and where are their schemes for our promotion ? A day has ended their thoughts by ending *them* ; and our trusts have perished, for

their thoughts have perished. Men's ambitions, expectations, declarations, and boastings all vanish into thin air when the breath of life vanishes from their bodies. This is the narrow estate of man : his breath, his earth, and his thoughts ; and this is his threefold climax therein,—his breath goeth forth, to his earth he returns, and his thoughts perish. Is this a being to be relied upon ? Vanity of vanities, all is vanity. To trust it would be a still greater vanity.

5. *"Happy is he that hath the God of Jacob for his help."* Heaped up is his happiness. He has happiness indeed : the true and the real delight is with him. The God of Jacob is the God of the covenant, the God of wrestling prayer, the God of the tried believer ; he is the only living and true God. The God of Jacob is Jehovah, who appeared unto Moses, and led the tribes of Jacob out of Egypt, and through the wilderness. Those are happy who trust him, for they shall never be ashamed or confounded. The Lord never dies, neither do his thoughts perish : his purpose of mercy, like himself, endures throughout all generations. Hallelujah ! *"Whose hope is in the LORD his God."* He is happy in help for the present and in hope for the future, who has placed all his confidence in Jehovah, who is his God by a covenant of salt. Happy is he when others are despairing ! Happiest shall he be in that very hour when others are discovering the depths of agony. We have here a statement which we have personally tried and proved : resting in the Lord, we know a happiness which is beyond description, beyond comparison, beyond conception. O how blessed a thing it is to know that God is our present help, and our eternal hope. Full assurance is more than heaven in the bud, the flower has begun to open. We would not exchange with Cæsar ; his sceptre is a bauble, but our bliss is true treasure.

In each of the two titles here given, namely, " the God of Jacob," and " Jehovah his God," there is a peculiar sweetness. Either one of them has a fountain of joy in it ; but the first will not cheer us without the second. Unless Jehovah be his God no man can find confidence in the fact that he was Jacob's God. But when by faith we know the Lord to be ours, then we are " rich to all the intents of bliss."

6. *"Which made heaven, and earth, the sea, and all that therein is."* Wisely may we trust our Creator : justly may we expect to be happy in so doing. He who made heaven can make a heaven for us, and make us fit for heaven. He who made the earth can preserve us while we are on earth, and help us to make good use of it while we sojourn upon it. He who made the sea and all its mysteries can steer us across the pathless deeps of a troubled life, and make it a way for his redeemed to pass over. This God who still makes the world by keeping it in existence is assuredly able to keep us to his eternal kingdom and glory. The making of the worlds is the standing proof of the power and wisdom of that great God in whom we trust. It is our joy that he not only made heaven but the sea ; not only things which are bright and blessed, but things which are deep and dark. Concerning all our circumstances, we may say the Lord is there. In storms and hurricanes the Lord reigneth as truly as in that great calm which rules the firmament above. *"Which keepeth truth for ever."* This is a second and most forcible justification of our trust the Lord will never permit his promise to fail. He is true to his own nature, true to the relationships which he has assumed, true to his covenant, true to his Word, true to his Son. He keeps true, and is the keeper of all that is true. Immutable fidelity is the character of Jehovah's procedure. None can charge him with falsehood or vacillation.

7. *"Which executeth judgment for the oppressed."* He is a swift and impartial administrator of justice. Our king surpasses all earthly princes because he pays no deference to rank or wealth, and is never the respecter of persons. He is the friend of the down-trodden, the avenger of the persecuted, the champion of the helpless. Safely may we trust our cause with such a Judge if it be a just one : happy are we to be under such a Ruler. Are we " evil entreated " ? Are our rights denied us ? Are we slandered ? Let this console us, that he who occupies the throne will not only think upon our case, but bestir himself to execute judgment on our behalf. *"Which giveth food to the hungry."* Glorious King art thou, O Jehovah ! Thou dost not only mete out justice but thou dost dispense bounty ! All food comes from God ; but when we are reduced to hunger, and providence supplies our necessity, we are peculiarly struck with the fact. Let every hungry man lay hold on this statement, and plead it before the mercy-seat, whether he suffer bodily-hunger or heart-hunger. See how our God finds his special clients

among the lowest of mankind : the oppressed and the starving find help in the God of Jacob *"The LORD looseth the prisoners."* Thus he completes the triple blessing : justice, bread, and liberty. Jehovah loves not to see man pining in dungeons, or fretting in fetters ; he brought up Joseph from the round-house, and Israel from the house of bondage. Jesus is the Emancipator, spiritually, providentially, and nationally. Thy chains, O Africa ! were broken by his hand. As faith in Jehovah shall become common among men freedom will advance in every form, especially will mental, moral, and spiritual bonds be loosed, and the slaves of error, sin, and death shall be set free. Well might the Psalmist praise Jehovah, who is so kind to men in bonds ! Well may the loosened ones be loudest in the song !

8. *"The LORD openeth the eyes of the blind."* Jesus did this very frequently, and hereby proved himself to be Jehovah. He who made the eye can open it, and when he does so it is to his glory. How often is the mental eye closed in moral night ! And who can remove this dreary effect of the fall but the Almighty God ? This miracle of grace he has performed in myriads of cases, and it is in each case a theme for loftiest praise. *"The LORD raiseth them that are bowed down."* This also Jesus did literally, thus doing the work peculiar to God. Jehovah consoles the bereaved, cheers the defeated, solaces the despondent, comforts the despairing. Let those who are bowed to the ground appeal to him, and he will speedily upraise them. *"The LORD loveth the righteous."* He gives to them the love of complacency, communion, and reward. Bad kings affect the licentious, but Jehovah makes the upright to be his favoured ones. This is greatly to his glory. Let those who enjoy the inestimable privilege of his love magnify his name with enthusiastic delight. Loved ones, you must never be absent from the choir ! You must never pause from his praise whose infinite love has made you what you are.

9. *"The LORD preserveth the strangers."* Many monarchs hunted aliens down, or transported them from place to place, or left them as outlaws unworthy of the rights of man ; but Jehovah made special laws for their shelter within his domain. In this country the stranger was, a little while ago, looked upon as a vagabond, —a kind of wild beast to be avoided if not to be assaulted ; and even to this day there are prejudices against foreigners which are contrary to our holy religion. Our God and King is never strange to any of his creatures, and if any are left in a solitary and forlorn condition he has a special eye to their preservation. *"He relieveth the fatherless and widow."* These excite his compassion, and he shows it in a practical way by upraising them from their forlorn condition. The Mosaic law made provision for these destitute persons. When the secondary fatherhood is gone the child falls back upon the primary fatherhood of the Creator ; when the husband of earth is removed the godly widow casts herself upon the care of her Maker. *"But the way of the wicked he turneth upside down."* He fills it with crooked places ; he reverses it, sets it down, or upsets it. That which the man aimed at he misses, and he secures that for himself which he would gladly have avoided. The wicked man's way is in itself a turning of things upside down morally, and the Lord makes it so to him providentially : everything goes wrong with him who goes wrong.

10. *"The LORD shall reign for ever."* Jehovah is King, and his kingdom can never come to an end. Neither does he die, nor abdicate, nor lose his crown by force. Glory be to his name, his throne is never in jeopardy. As the Lord ever liveth, so he ever reigneth. *"Even thy God, O Zion, unto all generations."* Zion's God, the God of his worshipping people, is he who in every age shall reign. There will always be a Zion ; Zion will always have Jehovah for her King ; for her he will always prove himself to be reigning in great power. What should we do in the presence of so great a King, but enter into his courts with praise, and pay to him our joyful homage ? *"Praise ye the LORD."* Again they said Hallelujah. Again the sweet perfume arose from the golden vials full of sweet odours. Are we not prepared for an outburst of holy song ? Do not we also say—Hallelujah ? Here endeth this gladsome Psalm. Here endeth *not* the praise of the Lord, which shall ascend for ever and ever. Amen.

EXPLANATORY NOTES AND QUAINT SAYINGS.

Psalms cxlvi.—cxlviii.—At the dedication of the second Temple, in the beginning of the seventh year of Darius, Psalms cxlvii., cxlvi. and cxlviii., seem to have been sung ; for in the Septuagint Version they are styled the Psalms of Haggai and Zechariah, as if they had been composed by them for this occasion. This, no doubt, was from some ancient tradition ; but in the original Hebrew these Psalms have no such title prefixed to them, neither have they any other to contradict it.—*Humphrey Prideaux.*

Psalms cxlvi.—cl.—We do not know who put together these different sacred compositions, or whether they were arranged on any particular principle. This, however, is obvious,—that the last series, those that close the whole, are full of praise. Though we meet frequently with grief and shame and tears in the former part, a great deal that presses upon the spirit,—and in the centre a great many references to the various vicissitudes and fortunes through which the church or the individual has passed,—yet, as we get towards the end, and as the book closes, it is *Hallelujah—praise.* As the ancient church ceases to speak to us, as she lays down her lyre, and ceases to touch it, the last tones are tones of heaven ; as if the warfare were done, the conflict accomplished, and she were anticipating either the revelations which are to make her glorious here, the " new thing " which God is about to " create " when he places her under another dispensation, or as you and I (I trust) shall do when we come to die, anticipating the praise and occupation of that eternity and rest for which we hope in the bosom of God.—*Thomas Binney,* 1798—1874.

Whole Psalm.—This Psalm gives in brief the Gospel of Confidence. It inculcates the elements of Faith, Hope, and Thanksgiving.—*Martin Geier.*

Verse 1.—*"Praise ye the* LORD." The word here used is *Alleluia,* and this is very proper to be constantly used by us who are dependent creatures, and under such great obligations to the Father of mercies. We have often heard of prayer doing great wonders ; but instances also are not wanting of praise being accompanied with signal events. The ancient Britons, in the year 420, obtained a victory over the army of the Picts and Saxons, near Mold, in Flintshire, The Britons, unarmed, having Germanicus and Lupus at their head, when the Picts and Saxons came to the attack, the two commanders, Gideon-like, ordered their little army to shout *Alleluia* three times over, at the sound of which the enemy, being suddenly struck with terror, ran away in the greatest confusion, and left the Britons masters of the field. A stone monument to perpetuate the remembrance of this Alleluia victory, I believe, remains to this day, in a field near Mold.—*Charles Buck,* 1771—1815.

Verse 1.—*"Praise the* LORD, *O my soul."* The Psalmist calls upon the noblest element of his being to exercise its noblest function.—*Hermann Venema.*

Verse 2.—*"While I live will I praise the* LORD." Mr. John Janeway on his death-bed cried out thus,—" Come, help me with praises, yet all is too little. Come, help me, all ye mighty and glorious angels, who are so well skilled in the heavenly work of praise ! Praise him, all ye creatures upon earth ; let every thing that hath being help me to praise God. Hallelujah ! Hallelujah ! Hallelujah ! Praise is now my work, and I shall be engaged in this sweet work now and for ever. Bring the Bible ; turn to David's Psalms, and let us sing a Psalm of praise. Come, let us lift up our voices in the praises of the Most High. I will sing with you as long as my breath doth last, and when I have none, I shall do it better."

Verse 2.—*"While I live will I praise the* LORD."—George Carpenter, the Bavarian martyr, being desired by some godly brethren, that when he was burning in the fire he would give them some sign of his constancy, answered, " Let this be a sure sign unto you of my faith and perseverance in the truth, that so long as I am able to hold open my mouth, or to whisper, I will never cease to praise God, and to profess his truth " ; the which also he did, saith mine author ; and so did many other martyrs besides.—*John Trapp.*

Verse 2.—*"I will sing praises unto my God while I have my being."* He had consecrated his entire earthly existence to the exercise of praise. And not only so, but he adds, *"I will sing praises unto my God while I have any being."* In which expression we may fairly conclude that the Psalmist stretches his thoughts beyond the limits of time, and contemplates that scene of eternal praise which shall succeed the less perfect songs of the church below.—*John Morison.*

Verse 2.—*"Unto my God."* Then praise is most pleasant, when in praising God we have an eye to him as ours, whom we have an interest in, and stand in relation to.—*Matthew Henry.*

Verse 2.—*"While I have any being."* Praise God for deliverance constantly. Some will be thankful while the memory of a deliverance is fresh, and then leave off. The Carthaginians used, at first, to send the tenth of their yearly revenues to Hercules ; and then by degrees they grew weary, and left off sending ; but we must be constant in our eucharistic sacrifice, or thankoffering. The motion of our praise must be like the motion of our pulse, which beats as long as life lasts.—*Thomas Watson.*

Verse 3.—*"Put not your trust in princes,"* etc. Through some kind of weakness, the soul of man, whensoever it is in tribulation here, despaireth of God, and chooseth to rely on man. Let it be said to one when set in some affliction, " There is a great man by whom thou mayest be set free ; " he smileth, he rejoiceth, he is lifted up. But if it is said to him, " God freeth thee," he is chilled, so to speak, by despair. The aid of the mortal is promised, and thou rejoicest ; the aid of the Immortal is promised, and art thou sad ? It is promised thee that thou shalt be freed by one who needeth to be freed with thee, and thou exultest as at some great aid : thou art promised that great Liberator, who needeth none to free him, and thou despairest, as though it were but a fable. Woe to such thoughts : they wander far ; truly there is sad and great death in them.—*Augustine.*

Verse 3.—*"Put not your trust in princes."* The word rendered " princes " signifieth liberal, bountiful ones, ἐνεργέται, so princes would be accounted ; but there's no trusting to them without God, or against him.—*John Trapp.*

Verse 3.—*"Put not your trust in princes."* King Charles had given the Earl of Strafford a solemn pledge, on the word of a king, that he should not suffer in " life, honour, or fortune," yet with singular baseness and ingratitude, as well as short-sighted policy, gave his assent to the bill of attainder, On learning that this had been done, Strafford, laying his hand on his heart, and raising his eyes to heaven, uttered the memorable words, " Put not your trust in princes, nor in the sons of men, for in them there is no salvation."—*James Taylor, in the "Imperial Dictionary of Universal Biography,"* 1868.

Verse 3.—*"Put not your trust in princes."* Shakespeare puts this sentiment into Wolsey's mouth :—

> " O how wretched
> Is that poor man that hangs on princes' favour !
> There is, betwixt that smile we would aspire to,
> That sweet aspect of princes, and their ruin,
> More pangs and fears than wars and women have :
> And when he falls, he falls like Lucifer,
> Never to hope again."

Verse 3.—*"Put not your trust in princes,"* etc. True, may some say, it were a folly to trust in weak princes, to trust in them for help who have no power to help ; but we will apply to mighty princes ; we hope there is help in them. No ; those words, *"in whom there is no help,"* are not a distinction of weak princes from strong, but a conclusion that there is no help in the strongest. That's strange. What ? No help in strong princes ! If he had said, no help in mean men, carnal reason would have consented ; but when he saith, *"Trust not in princes, nor in any son of man,"* one or other, who can believe this ? Yet this is divine truth ; we may write *insufficiency, insufficiency,* and a third time, *insufficiency,* upon them all ; the close of this verse may be their motto, *"There is no help in them."*—*Joseph Caryl.*

Verse 3.—*"Princes."* Earthly princes offer baubles to allure the soul from the pursuit of an eternal prize. Princes themselves have pronounced their principality to be their own greatest peril. Pope Pius V. said, " When I was a monk I had hope of my salvation ; when I became Cardinal I began to fear ; when I was made Pope I all but despaired of eternity."—*Thomas Le Blanc.*

Verse 3.—*"Nor in the son of man."* All sons of man are like the man **they are** sprung of, who, being in honour, did not abide.—*Matthew Henry.*

Verse 3.—For one man to put confidence in another, is as if one beggar should ask an alms of another, or one cripple should carry another, or the blind lead the blind.—*Anthony Farindon.*

Verses 3, 4.—You see the first and the last, highest and lowest, of all the sons of Adam, they may be made honourable *"princes,"* but they are born sinful, *"the sons of men"* ; born weak, *"there is no help in them"*; born mortal, *"their breath departeth ;"* born corruptible, *"they return to their earth"* ; and lastly, the mortality and corruption is not only in their flesh, but in some part or remnant of their spirits, for *"their thoughts perish."* The prophet (if you mark it) climbeth up by degrees to the disabling of the best men amongst us, and in them of all the rest. For if princes deserve not confidence, the argument must needs hold by comparison, much less do meaner men deserve it. The order of the words is so set that the members following are evermore either the reason or some confirmation to that which went before. *"Trust not in princes."* Why ? Because they are *"the sons of men."* Why not in *"the sons of men"* ? Because there is *no help in them.* Why is there no help in them ? Because when *"their breath goeth forth, they turn again to their earth."* What if their flesh be corrupted ? Nay, *"their thoughts"* also *"come to nothing."*

For, first, this first order and rank which the prophet hath here placed, the princes and gods of the earth, are by birth *men ;* secondly, *weak* men, and such in whom *no help is ;* thirdly, not only weak, but *dying,* their breath goeth out ; fourthly, not only dying, but subject to dissolution, *they turn to the earth ;* fifthly, if their bodies only were dissolved, and their intentions and actions might stand, there were less cause to distrust them ; but their *thoughts* are as transitory as their bodies.—*John King* (1559 ?—1621), *in a Funeral Sermon.*

Verses 3, 4.—The Psalmist inscribes an antithesis. Princes, though masters of armies, possessors of riches, loaded with honours, revelling in pleasures, are at the mercy of a ruthless Black Prince. Death is tyrant over prince and peasant alike. The very pleasures which are envied are often ministers of death to voluptuous princes.—*Thomas Le Blanc.*

Verse 4.—*"He returneth to his earth."* The earth—the dust—*is* *"his."* 1. It is *"his"* as that from which he was made : he turns back to what he was, Genesis iii. 19. "Dust thou art, and unto dust shalt thou return." 2. The earth—the dust—the grave is *"his,"* and it is his home—the place where he will abide. 3. It is *"his"* as it is the only property which he has in reversion. All that a man— a prince, a nobleman, a monarch, a millionaire—will soon have will be his grave, his few feet of earth. *That* will be his by right of possession, by the fact that for the time being he will occupy it, and not another man ! But that, too, may soon become another man's grave, so that even there he is a tenant only for a time ; he has no permanent possession *even of a grave.*—*Albert Barnes.*

Verse 4.—*"His breath goeth forth."* There is the death's-head, the mortality of man indeed, that a breath is as much as his being is worth. Our soul, that *spiraculum vitarum* (breath of lives), the Lord inspired it, not into Adam's eye, or ear, or mouth, but into his nostrils, which may show to man his imbecility, *cujus anima in naribus,* whose soul is in his nostrils, and dependeth upon a breath, as it were ; for the very soul must away if but breath expires ; soul and breath go forth together.

Now hear this, all ye people, ponder it high and low ; your castle is built upon the very air, the subsistence is in your nostrils, in a breath that is gone in the twinkling of an eye. Wherefore David maketh a question, saying, " Lord, what is man ? " He answereth himself also : " Man is a vanishing shadow " (Ps. cxliv. 3, 4), a shadow of smoke, or the dream of a shadow rather, as the poet speaketh. Blessed therefore are the poor in spirit ; this advantage have all afflicted ones, that they have checks enough to call them home, and make them see they be but men. The curtain of honour, profit, or pleasure, hard it is and rare to draw aside when it is spread over us : " man in honour understandeth not " (Ps. xlix. 20). To great ones therefore be it spoken ; the Psalm intendeth it of very princes : *"His breath goeth forth."*

See we now the continuedness, *exit,* *"it goeth" ;* as if it were now presently in its passage : showing this, that *Homo vivens continue moritur,* that life is a continued death ; our candle lightens, consumes, and dies : as in the passing of an hour-glass, every minute some sand falleth, and the glass once turned, no creature can intreat the sands to stay, but they continue to fall till all are gone : so is our life, it shortens and dies every minute, and we cannot beg a minute of time back, and that which we call death is but the termination, or consummation of it.— *Thomas Williamson ; in a Sermon, entitled, "A Comfortable Meditation of Humane Frailtie and Divine Mercie,"* 1630.

Verse 4.—The primary idea of *breath* and the secondary one of *spirit* run into each other in the usage of the Hebrew word רוח, so that either may be expressed in the translation without entirely excluding the other.—*Joseph Addison Alexander.*

Verse 4.—*"His breath* (or spirit) *goeth forth."* Now I come to the liberty of the spirit, that it recedes inviolate ; 1. In Act ; *"it goeth :"* 2. In Essence ; *"it goeth forth."*

1. Our spirit is *free in the act ;* it is not snatched out, as it were ; *"it goeth."* A soul in life sealed to eternity by the first fruits of the Spirit hath its good issue, its free passing, its hopes even in death ; for let this breath fade, *fidelis Deus,* God who cannot lie, will stand nigh us in that exigency, and begin to help where man leaveth. The Holy Spirit, whose name is the Comforter, will not omit and leave off his own act or office in the great needs of death. Hence good Hilarion, having served the Lord Christ seventy years, checks his soul that it was so loth at the last to go forth, saying, *Egredere, O anima mea, egredere,* " Go forth, my soul, go forth." Devout Simeon sueth for a manumission : " Lord, now lettest thou thy servant depart in peace, according to thy word." The spirit goeth forth ; it passes freely ; because it taketh up or embraceth the cross of Christ, as he commandeth us to do. But is the act at our will and liberty ? Not simply. We may not *projicere animam,* thrust or cast forth our breath or spirit ; *spiritus exit,* it goeth forth. Strive, we must, to cast the world out of us ; we may not cast ourselves out of the world. Saint Paul dareth not dissolve himself, though he could wish to be dissolved : God must part that which he joins ; God giveth, and God taketh away ; and if God say, as he doth to Lazarus, *Exi foras,* Come forth ; with faithful Stephen we must resign our spirit and all into his hands. When God biddeth us yoke, he is the wisest man that yieldeth his neck most willingly. When our great Captain recalls us, we must take the retreat in good part. But it is heathenish to force out the soul ; for when the misdeeming flesh, amidst our disasters, will not listen with patience for God's call, but rather shake off the thought of divine providence quite, then are we ready to curse God, and die, and that is probably to leap *e fumo in flammam,* out of the sin of self-murder into hell. No, but God will have our spirits to pass forth upon good terms. *Spiritus exit, "the spirit goeth forth."*

2. Secondly, the spirit goeth *free or inviolate in essence ;* death is not the end, but the outgoing of the soul, a transmigration or journey from one place to another. *"It goeth forth ;"* so the character of our weakness we see in the issue ; it is an argument of our eternity ; for man indeed is perishing, but so is not his spirit. The phœnix goes forth or out of his ashes, " the spirit returneth to God who gave it " (Eccl. xii. 7) ; that is, it abides still ; and as in the body it pleased God to inclose the soul for a season, so it may as well exist elsewhere without it, if God will ; for it hath no rise at all from the clay, yea, it bears in it immortality, an image of that breast whence it is breathed. The separate and very abstract acts of the spirit, even while it is in the body, the wondrous visions of the Lord to his prophets, usually when their bodies were bound up in sleep ; Saint Paul's rapture when he knew not whether he was in the body or out of it ; the admirable inventions and arts of men, manifest the soul's self-consisting. Not Socrates, and Cato, and the civilised heathen only, but the very savages believe this, and so entertain death, *ut exitum, non ut exitium,* as a dissolution, not as a destruction : *spiritus exit, "his spirit goeth forth."* —*Thomas Williamson.*

Verse 4.—*"His breath goeth forth,"* etc. The Hebrew gives the idea not that the *spirit,* but the mortal part of man will return to the dust. " His *soul* (fem. רוח) goeth forth," *i.e.,* returneth to God : " returneth *he* (masc. שׁב) to his earth." As in Eccl. xii. 7 : *"He"* is the mortal man of clay, but " his *breath*" (soul) is the real immortal man.—*Simon de Muis.*

Verse 4.—*"He returneth to his earth."* Returning, in its proper notion, is a-going back to that place from whence we came, so that in this clause here is a threefold truth, implied, expressed, inferred.

1. That which is *implied* in this phrase of returning is, that man in respect of his body came from the earth ; and as it is here implied, so it is expressed concerning the first man by Moses (Gen. ii. 7). " The Lord God formed man " (that is, the *body* of man) " of the dust " ; or according to the Hebrew, " dust of the ground " ; and by St. Paul (1 Cor. xv. 47), where he saith, " The first man is of the earth, earthy." True it is, we are formed in our mother's womb ; but yet inasmuch as we all came from the first man, we are truly said to come from *the earth ;* only with this difference, that he immediately, we mediately are framed out of the earth. This truth was engraven in full characters upon the name of the first man, who is called *Adam,* from a word that signifieth *red earth,* and that very word is here used, perhaps to mind us of that earth whereof man was first made ; yea, according to the usual etymology, the name *homo,* which in the Latin is a common name to both sexes, is derived *ab humo,* from *the ground.* For this reason it is that the earth is called by the poet *magna parens,* the great parent of all mankind, and in the answer of the Oracle, *our mother ;* and in this respect we are said by Eliphaz " to dwell in houses of clay, whose foundation is in the dust," Job iv. 19.

2. That which is *expressed* is, that man (when he dieth) returneth to the earth, πάντες λυόμενοι κόνις ἐσμέν, saith the poet, " We are all dust when dissolved." As the white snow when melted is black water ; so flesh and blood when bereaved of the soul become dust and ashes : in which respect St. Paul giveth this epithet of " vile " to our bodies. Phil. iii. 21. Indeed, man's original being from the earth, he had a natural propensity to earth ; according to the maxim, *Omne principiatum sequitur naturam principiorum,* " Everything hath an aptitude of returning to the principle whence it cometh " ; but yet had he not *turned away* from God he had never actually *returned* thither. It is sin which hath brought upon man a necessity of dying, and that dying brings a necessity of returning to the earth : in which respect it is observable, that the threat, " thou shalt die the death" (Gen. ii. 17), which was denounced against man before his fall, being afterwards renewed (iii. 19), is explained (as to temporal death) by these words, " to dust thou shalt return " ; so that now the motion of the little world man is like that of the great, *Circulare ab eodem puncto ad idem,* from the same to the same ; and that as in his *soul* from God to God, so in his *body* from the earth to the earth. The rivers come from the sea, and they return thither. The sun ariseth out of the east, and thither it returneth. Man is formed of the earth, and into earth he is again transformed : with which agreeth that of the poet Lucretius :

Cedit item retro de terra quod fuit ante.

3. That which is *inferred* in the emphatical pronoun "*his,*" which is annexed to the noun "*earth,*" is that the earth to which man returneth is *his ;* this being that which ariseth out of both the former conclusions ; since it is therefore *his earth* because he cometh from and returneth to it. Earth is man's Genesis and Analysis, his composition and resolution, his Alpha and Omega, his first and last ; *Ortus pulvis, finis cinis ;* earth is his both originally and finally. So that our bodies can challenge no alliance with, or property in any thing so much as earth. For if we call those things *ours* which had only an external relation to us, as our friends, our horses, our goods, our lands ; much more may we call that *our earth* whereof we are made and into which we shall moulder ; no wonder it is here said to be "*his*"; so elsewhere he is said to *be earth,* as being called by that name.—*Nathanael Hardy, in a Funeral Sermon entitled,* "*Man's Last Journey to His Long Home,*" 1659.

Verse 4.—"*In that very day his thoughts perish.*" The thoughts which the Psalmist here, no doubt, especially intends are those *purposes* which are in the minds of great men of doing good to those who are under, and depend upon them. The Hebrew word here used is derived from a verb that signifieth *to be bright : cogitationes serenæ,* those candid, serene, benign, benevolent thoughts which they have of advancing their allies, friends and followers. These thoughts are said to "*perish* " in "*that day* " wherein they are conceived ; so Tremellius glosseth. In which sense the instability of great men's favour is asserted, whose smiles are quickly changed into frowns, love into hatred, and so in a moment their mind being changed, their well-wishing thoughts vanish. But more rationally, " their thoughts perish in that day " wherein their *persons die,* because there is no opportunity of putting their purposes into execution. They perish like the child which comes to the birth, and there is no strength to bring forth ; or like the fruit which is plucked off before it be ripe. Whilst they live we may be deceived in our expectations by the alteration of their minds ; but, however, their condition is mortal, and when that great change by death comes, their designs (how well soever meant) must want success.

From hence it followeth, which is by some looked upon as a part of the meaning of the words, that the *"thoughts"* or *hopes of them who trust in them perish.* It is a true apothegm, *Major pars hominum expectando moritur ;* the greatest part of men perish by expectation. And good reason, inasmuch as their expectation, being misplaced, perisheth. How strongly this argument serveth to press the Psalmist's caution against confidence in man, though never so great, is obvious. It is true, princes and nobles being invested with honour, wealth and authority, have power in their hands, and perhaps they may have thoughts in their hearts to do thee good ; but, alas, how uncertain is the execution of those intentions, and therefore how foolish is it to depend upon them. " Trust in the Lord Jehovah " (saith the prophet), " for with him is everlasting strength." Ay, and with him is unchangeable goodness. It is safe building upon the rock, trusting upon God, whose thoughts of mercy are (like himself) from everlasting to everlasting ; but nothing is more foolish than to build on the sand, trust to men, whose persons, together with their thoughts, perish in a moment. Therefore let our resolution be that of David : " It is better to trust in the Lord than to put confidence in man ; it is better to trust in the Lord than to put confidence in princes," Psalm cxviii. 8, 9.—*Nathanael Hardy.*

Verse 4.—*"In that very day his thoughts perish."* At death a man sees all those thoughts which were not spent upon God to be fruitless. All worldly, vain thoughts, in the day of death perish and come to nothing. What good will the whole globe of the world do at such a time ? Those who have revelled out their thoughts in impertinences will but be the more disquieted ; it will cut them to the heart to think how they have spun a fool's thread. A Scythian captain having, for a draught of water, yielded up a city, cried out : " What have I lost ? What have I betrayed ? " So will it be with that man when he comes to die, who hath spent all his meditations upon the world ; he will say, What have I lost ? What have I betrayed ? I have lost heaven, I have betrayed my soul. Should not the consideration of this fix our minds upon the thoughts of God and glory ? All other meditations are fruitless ; like a piece of ground which hath much cost laid out upon it, but it yields no crop.—*Thomas Watson.*

Verse 4.—I would have you take this passage and illustrate it as applying to purposes, projects, and intentions. That, I think now, is precisely the idea intended to be conveyed. *"In that very day his thoughts perish ";* his purposes, his projects— what he intended to do. These cherished thoughts are gone. My dear brethren, there is something here for us. You find many beautiful passages and instances in Scripture in which this idea is embodied and realised, sometimes with great beauty and poetic effect, in relation to the enemies of the church. " The enemy said, I will pursue, I will overtake, I will divide the spoil, my hand shall destroy them ; thou didst blow with thy wind, the sea covered them, they sank as lead in the mighty waters." In that very day their thoughts perished. " Have they not sped ? have they not divided the prey ? to every man a damsel or two ? to Sisera a prey of divers colours of needlework ? So let all thine enemies perish, O Lord." The sacred poet does not even suggest that they had perished ; but feeling that it was a fact, only lifts up her heart to God. " So let all thine enemies perish, O Lord." And so you will find in many parts of Scripture beautiful ideas like this concerning the purposes and intentions that were in men's hearts utterly " perishing " by God's just laying his hand upon them—the purposes that were in their hearts against the church.—*Thomas Binney.*

Verse 4.—*"In that very day his thoughts perish."* In the case of the rich fool (Luke xii. 16, 20), his "thoughts" of building larger barns, and of many years of ease and prosperity,—all his selfish and worldly schemes,—" perished " in that self-same night.—*John W. Haley, in "An Examination of the Alleged Discrepancies of the Bible,"* 1875.

Verse 4.—*"His thoughts perish."* The science, the philosophy, the statesmanship of one age is exploded in the next. The men who are the masters of the world's intellect to-day are discrowned to-morrow. In this age of restless and rapid change they may survive their own thoughts ; their thoughts do not survive them.—*J. J. Stewart Perowne.*

Verse 4.—*"His thoughts perish."* As the purposes of all about worldly things perish in the approaches of death, so do the purposes of some about spiritual and heavenly things. How many have had purposes to repent, to amend their lives and turn to God, which have been prevented and totally broken off by the extremity of pain and sickness, but chiefly by the stroke of death when they have (as they thought) " been about to repent," and (as we say) " turn over a new leaf " in their lives ; they have been turned into the grave by death, and into hell by the just wrath of God.—*Joseph Caryl.*

Verse 4.—*"His thoughts."* Rather, " his false, deceitful show"; literally, " his glitterings."—*Samuel Horsley, 1733—1806.*

Verse 4.—To trust man is to lean not on a pillar but on a little heap of dust. The proudest element in man is his thought. In the thoughts of his heart he is lifted up if nowhere else ; but, behold, even his proudest thoughts, says the Psalmist, will be degraded and perish in that dust to which he will return. Poor, perishing pride ! Who should trust it ?—*Johannes Paulus Palanterius.*

Verse 5.—*"Happy is he."* This is the last of the twenty-five places (or twenty-six, if Psalm cxxviii. 2 be included) in which the word *ashre*, with which the Psalter begins, is found.—*Speaker's Commentary.*

Verse 5.—Alas, how often do we trust when we should be afraid, and become afraid when we should trust !—*Lange's Commentary.*

Verse 5.—*"The God of Jacob."* A famous and significant description of God ; and that, First, *in respect of his nature*, or the verity and reality of his being and excellence. He is styled here by way of elegancy or emphasis, *"The God of Jacob,"* saith Mollerus, to discern and distinguish the true God of Israel from all Heathenish deities, and to explode all fictitious gods and all worships thereof. As the true God is the God of Jacob, so the God of Jacob is the true God. He is God alone, and there is no other besides him. . . . Secondly. This title or appellation serves also to describe him *in his special relation to his people.* We find him called by our Psalmist, "The mighty God of Jacob " : Ps. cxxxii. 5. He is indeed the God of the whole earth, but in a peculiar manner " the God of *Israel* " : Matt. xv. 31. . . . It is observable in Scripture that he styles not himself so frequently, in his revelations of himself to them, " the God of heaven and earth " (though that also is a title full of encouragement), but " the God of Abraham, Isaac, and Jacob " ; as if he had borne such choice goodwill, and had such a peculiar care for these three men, as to overlook all the world besides them. So near and intimate relation have God's people to him, that their interests are mutually involved, and twisted in a reciprocal and covenant bond. They are his, he is their portion ; their Beloved is theirs and they are his : they are called by his name, the saints are styled his " holy ones," and the Church is termed expressly " Christ." Yea, he condescends to be called by their name ; he assumes the name of *Jacob*, Ps. xxiv. 6 : " This is the generation of them that seek him, that seek thy face, O *Jacob*."—*From "The Saints' Ebenezer," by F. E.,* 1667.

Verse 5.—*"The God of Jacob."* This verse aptly warrants us to apply to all believers all the illustrations of *help* and *hope* furnished by Jacob in his exile when none but God could help him.—*Simon de Muis.*

Verses 5, 6.—*"The God of Jacob . . . . which made heaven and earth, the sea, and all that therein is."* It is a characteristic of these Psalms, to proclaim to all nations which worshipped idols that " the God of Jacob," " the God of Zion," is the Creator and Governor of all things ; and to make an appeal to all nations to turn to him. All these Psalms have a *missionary character* and an *evangelical function.* We may compare here the apostolic prayer at Jerusalem, after the descent of the Holy Ghost at Pentecost ; " They lifted up their voices to God with one accord, and said, Lord, thou art God, *that made heaven and earth, and the sea, and all that in them is* " (where the words are the same as in the Septuagint in this place) : " Who by the mouth of thy servant David hast said, Why do the heathen rage ? " Acts iv. 24, 25. The office of these Psalms is to declare to the universe, that Jehovah, and he alone, is *Elohim ;* and to invite all to worship him as such, by their oft repeated *Hallelujah.*—*Christopher Wordsworth.*

Verse 6.—*"Which keepeth truth for ever."* Stored in his inexhaustible treasury as the most costly jewel ever there. And that because the *truth* which he so keeps, and which is the sustaining power which preserves the fabric of creation, is the Eternal Word, his only begotten Son, Jesus Christ.—*Dionysius the Carthusian, and Ayguan, in Neale and Littledale.*

Verse 6.—*"Which keepeth truth for ever."* God does indeed keep the truth from age to age—how else would the Book of God have lived ?—*John Lorinus.*

Verses 6—9.—The LORD, is an *Almighty* God, as the Creator of the universe ; next, he is a *faithful* God " who keepeth truth for ever " ; further, he is a *righteous* God (verse 7), a *bountiful* God (*ib.*) a *gracious* God (verses 7—9).—*J. J. Stewart Perowne.*

Verse 7.—"*Giveth food to the hungry.*" We learn from this that he is not always so indulgent to his own as to load them with abundance, but occasionally withdraws his blessing, that he may succour them when reduced to hunger. Had the Psalmist said that God fed his people with abundance, and pampered them, would not any of those under want or in famine have immediately desponded ? The goodness of God is therefore properly extended farther to the feeding of the hungry.—*John Calvin.*

Verse 7.—"*Giveth food to the hungry.*" Now, that Jesus was that Lord of whom the Psalmist in this place, and in Ps. cxlv. 16, speaketh, was fully testified by the miracles which he wrought, in feeding many thousands with some few loaves and two small fishes, and in filling so many baskets with the fragments or relics of that provision wherewith he had filled thousands. From these miracles, the people which had seen him do them, and tasted of his bounty, did rightly infer that he was the prophet which was to come into the world, as you may read, John vi. 14 ; and being supposed to be the prophet, they consequently presumed that he was likewise to be the King of Israel ; and out of this concert or presumption they would have enforced him to be their king, verse 15.—*Thomas Jackson*, 1579—1640.

Verse 7.—"*The* LORD *looseth the prisoners.*" As in that place of Isaiah (lxi. 1) the phrase of " opening the prison to them that are bound," is by the learned thought to be a prophetic elegance, to signify the cure of those that are deaf and dumb, whose souls consequently were shut up from being able to express themselves, as language enables others to do ; so here also it may be used poetically, and then it will be directly parallel to that part of Christ's answer, " the deaf hear " (Matt. xi. 5). At the curing of such, Christ's form of speech was, Ephphatha, " be opened," as to the door of a prison, when those which were under restraint therein were to be let loose out of it, their fetters being shaken off from them. But then, 'tis further manifest, that those that were under any sore disease or lameness, etc., are said to be " bound by Satan " (Luke xiii. 16), and be " loosed " by Christ, when they were cured by him. So saith Christ (verse 12), " Woman, thou art loosed from thine infirmity : and immediately she was made straight." Her being " made straight " was her being loosed out of her restraint, or bonds, or prison. And in this latitude of the poetic or prophetic expression, the Lord's *loosing the prisoners* here will comprehend the walking of the lame, the lepers being cleansed, the hearing of the deaf, yea, and the raising up of the dead ; for those of all others are fastest bound, and so when they were raised, the style is as proper as to Lazarus in respect of the graveclothes, " loose them, and let him go."—*Henry Hammond.*

Verses 7, 8.—It ought not to pass without remark that the name Jehovah is repeated here five times in five lines, to intimate that it is an almighty power, that of Jehovah, that is engaged and exerted for the relief of the oppressed ; and that it is as much to the glory of God to succour them that are in misery, as it is to ride on the heavens by his name JAH, Ps. lxviii. 4.—*Matthew Henry.*

Verse 8.—"*Openeth the eyes of the blind.*" Literally, "*openeth the blind* "—*i.e.,* maketh them to see. The expression may be used figuratively, as a remedy applied either to physical helplessness, as Deut. xxviii. 29 ; Isa. lix. 9, 10 ; Job xii. 25 ; or to spiritual want of discernment, as Isa. xxix. 18 ; xlii. 7, 18 ; xliii. 8. Here the context favours the former.—*J. J. Stewart Perowne.*

Verse 8.—"*The* LORD *openeth the eyes of the blind.*" The Hebrew does not mention *the eyes* of the blind. Hilary renders it *sapientificat.* The Arabic version follows the same. Jehovah by his *wisdom illumines dark minds.* It is *mental* blindness which is the common affliction of men.—*John Lorinus.*

Verse 8.—"*The blind.*" The large number of blind persons to be seen feeling their way along the streets in Cairo and Alexandria has been noticed by Volney. " Walking in the streets of Cairo," he says, " out of a hundred persons whom I met, there were often twenty blind, eighteen one eyed, and twenty others with eyes red, purulent, or spotted. Almost every one wears bandages, indicating that they either have or are recovering from ophthalmia." Ophthalmia is, in fact, one of the scourges of Egypt, as all physicians know. Its prevalence must be attributed in a great degree to the sand which the wind blows into the eyes ; but one can understand how in Oriental countries in general the excessive heat of the sun must make blindness much commoner than it is with us.

It is not therefore surprising to any one who knows the East to find the blind so often mentioned in the gospel history, and to meet in Scripture with so many allusions to this infirmity. Of the twelve maledictions of the Levites there is one against him " who maketh the blind to go out of the way " : Deut. xxvii. 18. " The spirit of God hath anointed me," said Jesus, quoting from Isaiah, " to preach the gospel to the poor, and recovery of sight to the blind " : Luke iv. 19. " The Lord," says David, " setteth at liberty them that are bound ; the Lord giveth sight to the blind."—*Felix Bovet* (1824—), *in "Egypt, Palestine, and Phœnicia,"* 1882.

Verse 9.—"The LORD preserveth the strangers." God has peculiar love for wanderers and pilgrims (Deut. x. 18), and Jacob was a stranger in a strange land when God showed himself to be the God of Jacob as his elect servant.—*Thomas Le Blanc.*

Verse 9.—"The LORD preserveth the strangers." They who do not belong to Babylon, nor to this world, but the true pilgrims in a strange land.—*Robert Bellarmine.*

Verse 9.—"He relieveth the fatherless and widow." The olive tree is not to be twice shaken, the vineyard is not to be twice gathered, nor are the sheaves of corn left in the fields to be gleaned ; all that belongs to the poor, to the widow and the orphan. It was allowable to pluck with the hand the ears of corn while passing through a neighbour's field (Deut. xxiii. 25), though a sickle might not be used. The law cares most anxiously for widows and orphans, for " God is a father of the fatherless and a judge of the widows " (Ps. lxviii. 5). A widow's raiment might not be taken in pledge, and both widows and orphans were to be invited to their feasts. An institution specially designed for the protection and relief of the poor was the second tithe, the so-called poor's-tithe. The first tithe belonged to the Levites. What remained over was again tithed, and the produce of this second tithe, devoted in the first two years to a feast in the sanctuary at the offering of first-fruits, was devoted in the third year to a feast in the dwelling-house, to which the Levites and the strangers, the widows and the orphans, were invited (Deut. xiv. 28, 29; xxvi. 12, 13.)—*G. Uhlhorn, in "Christian Charity in the Ancient Church,"* 1883.

Verse 9.—"The way of the wicked he turneth upside down." He overturns their plans, defeats their schemes ; makes their purposes accomplish what they did not intend they should accomplish. The Hebrew word here means to bend, to curve, to make crooked, to distort ; then, to overturn, to turn upside down. The same word is applied to the conduct of the wicked, in Ps. cxix. 78 : " They dealt perversely with me." The idea here is that the path is not a straight path ; that God makes it a crooked way ; that they are diverted from their design ; that through them he accomplishes purposes which they did not intend ; that he prevents their accomplishing their own designs ; and that he will make their plans subservient to a higher and better purpose than their own. This is the eleventh reason why those who put their trust in God are happy. It is that God is worthy of confidence and love, because he has all the plans of wicked men entirely under his control.— *Albert Barnes.*

Verse 9.—"The way of the wicked he turneth upside down." As the potter's clay, when the potter hath spent some time and pains in tempering and forming it upon the wheel, and now the vessel is even almost brought to its shape, a man that stands by may, with the least push, put it clean out of shape, and mar all on a sudden that he hath been so long a-making : so is it that all the plots and contrivances of wicked men, all their turning of things upside down shall be but as the potter's clay ; for when they think they have brought all to maturity, ripeness, and perfection, when they look upon their business as good as done, all on a sudden all their labour is lost ; for God, who stands by all the while and looks on, will, with one small touch, with the least breath of his wrath, blast and break all in pieces.—*Edlin,* 1656.

Verse 9.—"The way of the wicked he turneth upside down." All the ten clauses preceding lift up the poor saint step by step, higher and higher. At one word suddenly, like Satan falling as lightning from heaven, the wicked are shown dashed down the whole way from the summit of pride to the depths of hell.—*Johannes Paulus Palanterius.*

Verse 9.—"The way of the wicked he turneth upside down." A striking illustration of the folly of counting God out of one's plans for life, is given in the course of William M. Tweed, whose death is recently announced. Here was a man who sought wealth and power, and who for a time seemed successful in their pursuit. Apparently he did not propose to obey God or to live for a life to come. What he wanted was worldly prosperity. He thought he had it. He went to congress. He gathered his millions. He controlled the material interests of the metropolis of his country. He openly defied public sentiment and courts of justice in the prosecution of his plans. He was a brilliant and therefore a dangerous example of successful villainy. But the promise of prosperity for the life which now is, is only to the godly. As William M. Tweed lay dying in a prison-house in the city he once ruled, his confession of bitter disappointment was, " My life has been a failure in everything. There is nothing I am proud of." If any young man wants to come to an end like this, the way to it is simple and plain. " The great God that formed all things both rewardeth the fool, and rewardeth transgressors." *"The way of the wicked he turneth upside down."—American Sunday School Times,* 1878.

HINTS TO PREACHERS.

Verse 1.—I. An exhortation : it is addressed to ourselves : " Praise ye the Lord." II. An example : the Psalmist cries to himself, " Praise the Lord." III. An echo : " Praise the Lord, O my soul." Let us say this to our own souls.

Verse 1.—Whom should I praise ? And why ? And when ? And how ?

Verse 1.—Public worship. I. Should be with a sense of fellowship : " Praise ye " : pleasures of communion in praise. II. Should never lose its individuality : " O my soul." God is only praised by individual hearts. Temptations to wandering in public services. III. Should be full of Jehovah's felt presence : each and all should worship *him* alone.—*W. B. H.*

Verse 2.—Work for here and hereafter. I. " While I live " ; or a period of uncertainty and mystery. II. " I will praise the Lord " ; or a service definite, determined, due, and delightful. Certainty amid uncertainty. III. " While I have any being " ; or an enthusiastic pre-engagement of eternity.—*W. B. H.*

Verse 3.—I. It dishonours God. II. It degrades you. III. It disappoints in every case.

Verse 4.—Decease, Decay, Defeat.

Verse 4 (*second clause*). The failure of man's projects, the disappearance of his philosophies, the disproving of his boastings.

Verse 5.—The secret of true happiness. I. *What it is not.* The man here mentioned has his work and warfare, for he needs help ; and he has not all he desires, for he is a man of hope. II. *What it is.* It lies in the *hath,* the *help,* and the *hope,* and these are all in God.

Verses 6, 7.—The God of our hope is, I. Creator. II. Truth-keeper. III. Vindicator. IV. Provider. V. Deliverer.

Verse 7 (*last clause*).—See " Spurgeon's Sermons," No. 484 : " The Lord—the Liberator."

Verse 7.—The People's Rights. I. Three rights of humanity. Justice, Bread, Freedom. II. God's interventions in their behalf. Revolutions, Reforms, Regenerations. Christ's war with Satan. III. The magnificent supply of the three blessings in Christ's kingdom. IV. The men who are fashioned and trained under this *régime.*—*W. B. H.*

Verse 8 (*first clause*).—Spiritual blindness, its curse, cause, and cure.

Verse 8 (*second clause*).—Who are the people ? Who raises them ? How he does it. And what then ?

Verse 8 (*third clause*).—God's love to the righteous. I. He made them righteous. II. They are like him. III. They love him. IV. Their purposes are one with his own.

Verse 9.—Observe the provision made in the Jewish law for the stranger. The way in which strangers were received by God. The truth that his chosen are strangers in the world. His design to gather in strangers in the latter days.

Verse 9 (*centre clause*).—The claims of orphans and widows upon the people of God.

Verse 9 (*last clause*).—Illustrated by Joseph's brethren, Haman, and others.

Verse 10.—I. A cause for praise—" The Lord shall reign for ever." II. A centre of praise : " O Zion." III. A cycle of praise : " all generations." IV. A call to praise : " Praise ye the Lord."

PSALM CXLVII.

SUBJECT.—*This is a specially remarkable song. In it the greatness and the condescending goodness of the Lord are celebrated. The God of Israel is set forth in his peculiarity of glory as caring for the sorrowing, the insignificant, and forgotten. The poet finds a singular joy in extolling one who is so singularly gracious. It is a Psalm of the city and of the field, of the first and the second creations, of the commonwealth and of the church. It is good and pleasant throughout.*

DIVISION.—*The song appears to divide itself into three portions. From 1 to 6, Jehovah is extolled for building up Zion, and blessing his mourners; from 7 to 11, the like praise is given because of his provision for the lowly, and his pleasure in them; and then, from 12 to 20, he is magnified for his work on behalf of his people, and the power of his word in nature and in grace. Let it be studied with joyful gratitude.*

EXPOSITION.

PRAISE ye the LORD : for *it is* good to sing praises unto our God ; for *it is* pleasant ; *and* praise is comely.

2 The LORD doth build up Jerusalem : he gathereth together the outcasts of Israel.

3 He healeth the broken in heart, and bindeth up their wounds.

4 He telleth the number of the stars ; he calleth them all by *their* names.

5 Great *is* our Lord, and of great power : his understanding *is* infinite.

6 The LORD lifteth up the meek : he casteth the wicked down to the ground.

1. *"Praise ye the LORD,"* or Hallelujah. The flow of the broad river of the Book of Psalms ends in a cataract of praise. The present Psalm begins and ends with Hallelujah. Jehovah and happy praise should ever be associated in the mind of a believer. Jove was dreaded, but Jehovah is beloved. To one and all of the true seed of Israel the Psalmist acts as choir-master, and cries, " Praise *ye* the Lord." Such an exhortation may fitly be addressed to all those who owe anything to the favour of God ; and which of us does not ? Pay him we cannot, but praise him we will, not only now, but for ever. *"For it is good to sing praises unto our God."* It is good because it is right ; good because it is acceptable with God, beneficial to ourselves, and stimulating to our fellows. The goodness of an exercise is good argument with good men for its continual practice. Singing the divine praises is the best possible use of speech : it speaks of God, for God, and to God, and it does this in a joyful and reverent manner. Singing in the heart is good, but singing with heart and voice is better, for it allows others to join with us. Jehovah is *our* God, our covenant God, therefore let him have the homage of our praise ; and he is so gracious and happy a God that our praise may best be expressed in joyful song.

"For it is pleasant ; and praise is comely." It is pleasant and proper, sweet and suitable to laud the Lord Most High. It is refreshing to the taste of the truly refined mind, and it is agreeable to the eye of the pure in heart : it is delightful both to hear and to see a whole assembly praising the Lord. These are arguments for song-service which men who love true piety, real pleasure, and strict propriety will not despise. Please to praise, for praise is pleasant : praise the Lord in the beauty of holiness, for praise is comely. Where duty and delight, benefit and beauty unite, we ought not to be backward. Let each reader feel that he and his family ought to constitute a choir for the daily celebration of the praises of the Lord.

2. *"The LORD doth build up Jerusalem."* God appears both in the material and spiritual world as a Builder and Maker, and therein he is to be praised. His grace, wisdom, and power are all seen in the formation and establishment of the chosen seat of his worship ; once a city with material walls, but now a church

composed of spiritual stones. The Jews rejoiced in the uprising of their capital from its ruins, and we triumph in the growth of the church from among a godless world. *"He gathereth together the outcasts of Israel"*; and thus he repairs the waste places, and causes the former desolations to be inhabited. This sentence may relate to Nehemiah and those who returned with him; but there is no reason why it should not with equal fitness be referred to David, who, with his friends, was once an outcast, but ere long became the means of building up Jerusalem. In any case, the Psalmist ascribes to Jehovah all the blessings enjoyed; the restoration of the city and the restoration of the banished he equally traces to the divine hand. How clearly these ancient believers saw the Lord present, working among them and for them! Spiritually we see the hand of God in the edification of the church, and in the ingathering of sinners. What are men under conviction of sin but outcasts from God, from holiness, from heaven, and even from hope? Who could gather them from their dispersions, and make citizens of them in Christ Jesus save the Lord our God? This deed of love and power he is constantly performing. Therefore let the song begin at Jerusalem our home, and let every living stone in the spiritual city echo the strain; for it is the Lord who has brought again his banished ones, and builded them together in Zion.

3. *"He healeth the broken in heart, and bindeth up their wounds."* This the Holy Spirit mentions as a part of the glory of God, and a reason for our declaring his praise : the Lord is not only a Builder, but a Healer; he restores broken hearts as well as broken walls. The kings of the earth think to be great through their loftiness; but Jehovah becomes really so by his condescension. Behold, the Most High has to do with the sick and the sorry, with the wretched and the wounded! He walks the hospitals as the good Physician! His deep sympathy with mourners is a special mark of his goodness. Few will associate with the despondent, but Jehovah chooses their company, and abides with them till he has healed them by his comforts. He deigns to handle and heal broken hearts : he himself lays on the ointment of grace, and the soft bandages of love, and thus binds up the bleeding wounds of those convinced of sin. This is compassion like a God. Well may those praise him to whom he has acted so gracious a part. The Lord is always healing and binding : this is no new work to him, he has done it of old; and it is not a thing of the past of which he is now weary, for he is still healing and still binding, as the original hath it. Come, broken hearts, come to the Physician who never fails to heal : uncover your wounds to him who so tenderly binds them up!

4. *"He telleth the number of the stars."* None but he can count the mighty host, but as he made them and sustains them he can number them. To Jehovah stars are as mere coins, which the merchant tells as he puts them into his bag. *"He calleth them all by their names."* He has an intimate acquaintance with each separate orb, so as to know its name or character. Indeed, he gives to each its appropriate title, because he knows its constitution and nature. Vast as these stars are, they are perfectly obedient to his bidding; even as soldiers to a captain who calls their names, and allots them their stations. Do they not rise, and set, and move, or stand, precisely according to his order? What a change is here from the preceding verse! Read the two without a break, and feel the full force of the contrast. From stars to sighs is a deep descent! From worlds to wounds is a distance which only infinite compassion can bridge. Yet he who acts a surgeon's part with wounded hearts, marshals the heavenly host, and reads the muster-roll of suns and their majestic systems. O Lord, it is good to praise thee as ruling the stars, but it is pleasant to adore thee as healing the broken in heart!

5. *"Great is our Lord."* Our Lord and King is great—magnanimous, infinite, inconceivably glorious. None can describe his majesty, or reckon up the number of his excellences. *"And of great power."* Doing as he wills, and willing to do mighty deeds. His acts reveal something of his might, but the mass of his power is hidden, for all things are possible with God, even the things impossible with men. *"His understanding is infinite."* There is no fathoming his wisdom, or measuring his knowledge. He is infinite in existence, in power, and in knowledge, as these three phrases plainly teach us. The gods of the heathen are nothing, but our God filleth all things. And yet how condescending! For this is he who so tenderly nurses the sick souls, and waits to be gracious to sinful men. He brings his boundless power and infinite understanding to bear upon human distress for its assuagement and sanctification. For all these reasons let his praise be great : even could it be infinite, it would not exceed his due. In the building of his church and the salvation of

souls, his greatness, power, and wisdom are all displayed : let him be extolled because of each of these attributes.

6. *"The* LORD *lifteth up the meek : he casteth the wicked down to the ground."* He reverses the evil order of things. The meek are down, and he lifts them up ; the wicked are exalted, and he hurls them down to the dust. The Lord loves those who are reverent to himself, humble in their own eyes, and gentle to their fellow-men : these he lifts up to hope, to peace, to power, to eternal honour. When God lifts a man, it is a lift indeed. Proud men are, in their own esteem, high enough already ; only those who are low will care to be lifted up, and only such will Jehovah upraise. As for the wicked, they must come down from their seats of vain glory. God is accustomed to overthrow such ; it is his way and habit. None of the wicked shall in the end escape. To the earth they must go ; for from the earth they came, and for the earth they live. It is one of the glories of our God for which his saints praise him, that he hath put down the mighty from their seats, and hath exalted them of low degree. Well may the righteous be lifted up in spirit and the wicked be downcast as they think of the judgments of the Lord God.

In this verse we see the practical outcome of that character of Jehovah, which leads him to count and call the stars as if they were little things, while he deals tenderly with sorrowful men, as if they were precious in his esteem. He is so great that nothing is great to him, and he is so condescending that nothing is little to him : his infinite majesty thus naturally brings low the lofty and exalts the lowly.

7 Sing unto the LORD with thanksgiving ; sing praise upon the harp unto our God :

8 Who covereth the heaven with clouds, who prepareth rain for the earth, who maketh grass to grow upon the mountains.

9 He giveth to the beast his food, *and* to the young ravens which cry.

10 He delighteth not in the strength of the horse : he taketh not pleasure in the legs of a man.

11 The LORD taketh pleasure in them that fear him, in those that hope in his mercy.

7. In this paragraph the contrast announced in the former section is enlarged upon from another point of view, namely, as it is seen in nature and in providence.

"Sing unto the LORD *with thanksgiving ;"* or rather, " respond to Jehovah." He speaks to us in his works, let us answer him with our thanks. All that he does is gracious, every movement of his hand is goodness ; therefore let our hearts reply with gratitude, and our lips with song. Our lives should be responses to divine love. Jehovah is ever engaged in giving, let us respond with thanksgiving.

"Sing praise upon the harp unto our God." Blend music with song. Under a dispensation of ritual the use of music was most commendable, and suitable in the great congregation : those of us who judge it to be less desirable for public worship, under a spiritual economy, because it has led to so many abuses, nevertheless rejoice in it in our privacy, and are by no means insensible to its charms. It seems a profanation that choice minstrelsy should so often be devoted to unworthy themes : the sweetest harmonies should be consecrated to the honour of the Lord. He is *our* God, and this fact is one choice joy of the song. We have chosen him because he has chosen us ; and we see in him peculiarities which distinguish him from all the pretended deities of those among whom we dwell. He is *our* God in covenant relationship for ever and ever, and to him be praise in every possible form.

8. *"Who covereth the heaven with clouds."* He works in all things, above as well as below. Clouds are not caused by accident, but produced by God himself, and made to assume degrees of density by which the blue firmament is hidden. A sky-scape might seem to be a mere fortuitous concourse of vapours, but it is not so : the Great Artist's hand thus covers the canvas of the heavens. *"Who prepareth rain for the earth."* The Lord prepares clouds with a view to rain, and rain with an eye to the fields below. By many concurrent circumstances all things are made ready for the production of a shower ; there is more of art in the formation of a rain-cloud and in the fashioning of a rain-drop, than appears to superficial observers. God is in the vapour, and in the pearly drop which is born of it. *"Who maketh grass to grow upon the mountains."* By the far-reaching shower he produces vegetation where the hand of man is all unknown. He cares not only for Goshen's fertile plains.

but for Carmel's steep ascents. God makes the heavens the servants of the earth, and the clouds the irrigators of the mountain meadows. This is a kind of evolution about which there can be no dispute. Nor does the Lord forget the waste and desolate places, but causes the lone hills to be the first partakers of his refreshing visitations. This is after the manner of our God. He not only causes rain to descend from the heavens to water the grass, and thus unites the skies and the herbs by a ministry of mercy ; but he also thinks of the rocky ledges among the hills, and forgets not the pastures of the wilderness. What a God is this !

> " Passing by the rich and great,
> For the poor and desolate."

9. *"He giveth to the beast his food."* By causing the grass to grow on the hills the Lord feeds the cattle. God careth for the brute creation. Men tread grass under foot as though it were nothing, but God causeth it to grow ; too often men treat their cattle with cruelty, but the Lord himself feedeth them. The great God is too good, and, indeed, too great to overlook things that are despised. Say not, " Doth God care for oxen ? " Indeed he does, and he permits himself to be here described as giving them their food as husbandmen are wont to do. *"And to the young ravens which cry."* These wild creatures, which seem to be of no use to man ; are they therefore worthless ? By no means ; they fill their place in the economy of nature. When they are mere fledgelings, and can only clamour to the parent birds for food, the Lord does not suffer them to starve, but supplies their needs. Is it not wonderful how such numbers of little birds are fed ! A bird in a cage under human care is in more danger of lacking seed and water than any one of the myriads that fly in the open heavens, with no owner but their Creator, and no provider but the Lord. Greatness occupied with little things makes up a chief feature of this Psalm. Ought we not all to feel special joy in praising One who is so specially remarkable for his care of the needy and the forgotten ? Ought we not also to trust in the Lord ? for he who feeds the sons of the raven will surely nourish the sons of God ! Hallelujah to him who both feeds the ravens and rules the stars ! What a God art thou, O Jehovah !

10. *"He delighteth not in the strength of the horse."* Not to great and strong animals doth the Creator in any measure direct his special thought ; but in lesser living things he has equal pleasure. If man could act the Creator's part, he would take peculiar delight in producing noble quadrupeds like horses, whose strength and speed would reflect honour upon their maker ; but Jehovah has no such feeling ; he cares as much for helpless birds in the nest as for the war-horse in the pride of its power. *"He taketh not pleasure in the legs of a man."* These are the athlete's glory, but God hath no pleasure in them. Not the capacities of the creature, but rather its weakness and necessity, win the regard of our God. Monarchs trust in their cavalry and infantry ; but the King of kings exults not in the hosts of his creatures as though they could lend power to him. Physical or material greatness and power are of no account with Jehovah ; he has respect to other and more precious qualities. Men who boast in fight the valour of gigantic might, will not find themselves the favourites of God : though earthly princes may feast their eyes upon their Joabs and their Abners, their Abishais and Asahels, the Lord of hosts has no pleasure in mere bone and muscle. Sinews and thews are of small account, either in horses or in men, with Him who is a spirit, and delights most in spiritual things. The expression of the text may be viewed as including all creature power, even of a mental or moral kind. God does not take pleasure in us because of our attainments, or potentialities : he respects character rather than capacity.

11. *"The Lord taketh pleasure in them that fear him, in those that hope in his mercy."* While the bodily powers give no content to God, spiritual qualities are his delight. He cares most for those emotions which centre in himself : the fear which he approves is fear *of him*, and the hope which he accepts is hope *in his mercy*. It is a striking thought that God should not only be at peace with some kinds of men, but even find a solace and a joy in their company. Oh ! the matchless condescension of the Lord, that his greatness should take pleasure in the insignificant creatures of his hand. Who are these favoured men in whom Jehovah takes pleasure ? Some of them are the least in his family, who have never risen beyond hoping and fearing. Others of them are more fully developed, but still they exhibit a blended character composed of fear and hope : they fear God with holy awe and filial reverence, and they also hope for forgiveness and blessedness because of the divine mercy. As a father takes pleasure in his own children, so doth the Lord solace himself in his own

beloved ones, whose marks of new birth are fear and hope. They fear, for they are sinners ; they hope, for God is merciful. They fear him, for he is great ; they hope in him, for he is good. Their fear sobers their hope ; their hope brightens their fear : God takes pleasure in them both in their trembling and in their rejoicing.

Is there not rich cause for praise in this special feature of the divine character ? After all, it is a poor nature which is delighted with brute force ; it is a diviner thing to take pleasure in the holy character of those around us. As men may be known by the nature of the things which give them pleasure, so is the Lord known by the blessed fact that he taketh pleasure in the righteous, even though that righteousness is as yet in its initial stage of fear and hope.

12 Praise the LORD, O Jerusalem ; praise thy God, O Zion.

13 For he hath strengthened the bars of thy gates ; he hath blessed thy children within thee.

14 He maketh peace *in* thy borders, *and* filleth thee with the finest of the wheat.

15 He sendeth forth his commandment *upon* earth : his word runneth very swiftly.

16 He giveth snow like wool : he scattereth the hoarfrost like ashes.

17 He casteth forth his ice like morsels : who can stand before his cold ?

18 He sendeth out his word, and melteth them : he causeth his wind to blow, *and* the waters flow.

19 He sheweth his word unto Jacob, his statutes and his judgments unto Israel.

20 He hath not dealt so with any nation : and *as for his* judgments, they have not known them. Praise ye the LORD.

12. *"Praise the LORD, O Jerusalem ; praise thy God, O Zion."* How the poet insists upon praise ; he cries *praise, praise,* as if it were the most important of all duties. A peculiar people should render peculiar praise. The city of peace should be the city of praise ; and the temple of the covenant God should resound with his glories. If nowhere else, yet certainly in Zion there should be joyful adoration of Zion's God. Note, that we are to praise the Lord in our own houses in Jerusalem as well as in his own house in Zion. The holy city surrounds the holy hill, and both are dedicated to the holy God, therefore both should ring with hallelujahs.

13. *"For he hath strengthened the bars of thy gates."* Her fortifications were finished, even to the fastenings of the gates, and God had made all sound and strong, even to her bolts and bars : thus her security against invading foes was guaranteed. This is no small mercy. Oh, that our churches were thus preserved from all false doctrine and unholy living ! This must be the Lord's doing ; and where he has wrought it his name is greatly to be praised. Modern libertines would tear down all gates and abolish all bars ; but so do not we, because of the fear of the Lord. *"He hath blessed thy children within thee."* Internal happiness is as truly the Lord's gift as external security. When the Lord blesses " thy sons in the midst of thee," thou art, O Zion, filled with a happy, united, zealous, prosperous, holy people, who dwell in communion with God, and enter into the joy of their Lord. When God makes thy walls salvation thy gates must be praise. It would little avail to fortify a wretched, starving city ; but when the walls are strengthened, it is a still greater joy to see that the inhabitants are blessed with all good gifts. How much our churches need a present and abiding benediction.

14. *"He maketh peace in thy borders."* Even to the boundaries quiet extends ; no enemies are wrangling with the borderers. If there is peace there, we may be sure that peace is everywhere. " When a man's ways please the Lord he maketh even his enemies to be at peace with him." Peace is from the God of peace. Considering the differing constitutions, conditions, tastes, and opinions of men, it is a work of God when in large churches unbroken peace is found year after year ; and it is an equal wonder if worldlings, instead of persecuting the godly, treat them with marked respect. He who builds Zion is also her Peace-maker, the Lord and Giver of peace. *"And filleth thee with the finest of the wheat."* Peace is attended with plenty,—plenty of the best food, and of the best sort of that food. It is a great reason for thanksgiving when men's wants are so supplied that they are filled :

it takes much to fill some men : perhaps none ever are filled but the inhabitants of Zion ; and they are only to be filled by the Lord himself. Gospel truth is the finest of the wheat, and those are indeed blessed who are content to be filled therewith, and are not hungering after the husks of the world. Let those who are filled with heavenly food fill their mouths with heavenly praise.

15. *"He sendeth forth his commandment upon the earth."* His messages fly throughout his dominions : upon earth his warrants are executed as well as in heaven. From his church his word goes forth ; from Zion he missions the nations with the word of life. *"His word runneth very swiftly "* : his purposes of love are speedily accomplished. Oriental monarchs laboured hard to establish rapid postal communication ; the desire, will, and command of the Lord flash in an instant from pole to pole, yea, from heaven to earth. We who dwell in the centre of the Lord's dominions may exceedingly rejoice that to the utmost extremity of the realm the divine commandment speeds with sure result, and is not hindered by distance or time. The Lord can deliver his people right speedily, or send them supplies immediately from his courts above. God's commands in nature and providence are fiats against which no opposition is ever raised ; say, rather, to effect which all things rush onward with alacrity. The expressions in the text are so distinctly in the present that they are meant to teach us the present mission and efficiency of the word of the Lord, and thus to prompt us to present praise.

16. Here follow instances of the power of God upon the elements. *"He giveth snow like wool."* As a gift he scatters the snow, which falls in flakes like fleecy wool. Snow falls softly, covers universally, and clothes warmly, even as wool covers the sheep. The most evident resemblance lies in the whiteness of the two substances ; but many other likenesses are to be seen by the observant eye. It is wise to see God in winter and in distress as well as in summer and prosperity. He who one day feeds us with the finest of the wheat, at another time robes us in snow : he is the same God in each case, and each form of his operation bestows a gift on men. *"He scattereth the hoarfrost like ashes."* Here again the Psalmist sees God directly and personally at work. As ashes powder the earth when men are burning up the rank herbage ; and as when men cast ashes into the air they cause a singular sort of whiteness in the places where they fall, so also does the frost. The country people talk of a black frost and a white frost, and the same thing may be said of ashes, for they are both black and white. Moreover, excessive cold burns as effectually as great heat, and hence there is an inner as well as an outer likeness between hoarfrost and ashes. Let us praise the Lord who condescends to wing each flake of snow and scatter each particle of rime. Ours is no absent or inactive deity : he worketh all things, and is everywhere at home.

17. *"He casteth forth his ice like morsels."* Such are the crumbs of hail which he casts forth, or the crusts of ice which he creates upon the waters. These morsels are *his* ice, and *he* casts them abroad. The two expressions indicate a very real presence of God in the phenomena of nature. *"Who can stand before his cold ? "* None can resist the utmost rigours of cold any more than they can bear the vehemence of heat. God's withdrawals of light are a darkness that may be felt, and his withdrawals of heat are a cold which is absolutely omnipotent. If the Lord, instead of revealing himself as a fire, should adopt the opposite manifestation of cold, he would, in either case, consume us should he put forth all his power. It is ours to submit to deprivations with patience, seeing the cold is *his* cold. That which God sends, whether it be heat or cold, no man can defy with impunity, but he is happy who bows before it with child-like submission. When we cannot stand before God we will gladly lie at his feet, or nestle under his wings.

18. *"He sendeth out his word, and melteth them."* When the frost is sharpest, and the ice is hardest, the Lord intervenes ; and though he doth no more than send his word, yet the rocks of ice are dissolved at once, and the huge bergs begin to float into the southern seas. The phenomena of winter are not so abundant in Palestine as with us, yet they are witnessed sufficiently to cause the devout to bless God for the return of spring. At the will of God snow, hoar-frost, and ice disappear, and the time of the opening bud and the singing of birds has come. For this let us praise the Lord as we sun ourselves amid the spring flowers. *"He causeth his wind to blow, and the waters flow."* The Lord is the great first cause of everything ; even the fickle, wandering winds are caused by him. Natural laws are in themselves mere inoperative rules, but the power emanates directly from the Ever-potent One. The soft gales from the south, which bring a general thaw, are from the Lord, as

were those wintry blasts which bound the streams in icy bonds. Simple but effectual are the methods of Jehovah in the natural world ; equally so are those which he employs in the spiritual kingdom ; for the breath of his Holy Spirit breathes upon frozen hearts, and streams of penitence and love gush forth at once.

Observe how these two sentences the word and the wind go together in nature. They attend each other in grace ; the gospel and the Holy Spirit co-operate in salvation. The truth which the Spirit breathed into prophets and apostles he breathes into dead souls, and they are quickened into spiritual life.

19. *"He sheweth his word unto Jacob, his statutes and his judgments unto Israel."* He who is the Creator is also the Revealer. We are to praise the Lord above all things for his manifesting himself to us as he does not unto the world. Whatever part of his mind he discloses to us, whether it be a word of instruction, a statute of direction, or a judgment of government, we are bound to bless the Lord for it. He who causes summer to come in the place of winter has also removed the coldness and death from our hearts by the power of his word, and this is abundant cause for singing unto his name. As Jacob's seed of old were made to know the Lord, even so are we in these latter days ; wherefore, let his name be magnified among us. By that knowledge Jacob is ennobled into Israel, and therefore let him who is made a prevailing prince in prayer be also a chief musician in praise. The elect people were bound to sing hallelujahs to their own God. Why were they so specially favoured if they did not, above all others, tell forth the glory of their God ?

20. *"He hath not dealt so with any nation."* Israel had clear and exclusive knowledge of God, while others were left in ignorance. Election is the loudest call for grateful adoration. *"And as for his judgments, they have not known them"*; or, *" and judgments, they had not known them,"* as if not knowing the laws of God, they might be looked upon as having no laws at all worth mentioning. The nations were covered with darkness, and only Israel sat in the light. This was sovereign grace in its fullest noontide of power. *"Praise ye the Lord."* When we have mentioned electing, distinguishing love, our praise can rise no higher, and therefore we close with one more hallelujah.

EXPLANATORY NOTES AND QUAINT SAYINGS.

Whole Psalm.—The whole Psalm is an invitation unto praising of God. Arguments therein are drawn, First, from God's *general goodness* to the world (verses 4, 8, 9, 16—18) : Secondly, from his *special mercy* to his Church. 1. In *restoring* it out of a sad and broken condition (verses 2, 3). 2. In *confirming* it in a happy and prosperous estate, both temporal, in regard of strength, peace, and plenty (verses 12—14) ; and spiritual, in regard of his word, statutes, and judgments, made known unto them (verses 19, 20). Lastly, these mercies are all commended by the *manner* of bestowing them—*powerfully* and *swiftly.* He doth it by a word of command, and by a word of speed : " He sendeth forth his commandment upon earth : his word runneth very swiftly " (verse 15).

The temporal part of this happy estate, together with the manner of bestowing it, is herein described, but we must by no means exclude the spiritual meaning. And what can be wanting to a nation which is " strengthened " with walls, " blessed " with multitudes, hath " peace " in the border, " plenty " in the field, and, what is all in all, God in the sanctuary : God the bar of the " gate," the Father of the children, the crown of the " peace," the staff of the " plenty " ? They have a " gate " restored, a" city " blessed, a " border " quieted, a " field " crowned, a " sanctuary " beautified with the oracles of God. What can be wanting to such a people, but a mouth filled, a heart enlarged, a spirit exalted in the praises of the Lord ? " Praise the Lord, O Jerusalem ; praise thy God, O Zion," etc. (verse 12).—*Edward Reynolds, in a Sermon entitled "Sion's Praises,"* 1657.

Whole Psalm.—The God of Israel, what he has done, what he does, what he can do—this is the *"Hallelujah"* note of his song. So gladsome is the theme, that in verse 1 we find a contribution for it levied on Ps. xxxiii. 1, xcii. 1, and cxxxv. 3 ; each must furnish its quota of testimony to the desirableness of giving praise to such a God.—*Andrew A. Bonar.*

Verse 1.—*"Praise ye the Lord."* Alleluia. An expression in sound very similar to this seems to have been used by many nations, who can hardly be supposed to have borrowed it from the Jews. Is it impossible that this is one of the most ancient expressions of devotion ? From the Greeks using ἐλελεῦ ἰὴ, as a solemn beginning and ending of their hymns to Apollo, it should seem that they knew it ; it is said to have been heard among the Indians in America, and *Alla, Alla,* as the name of God, is used in great part of the East : also in composition. What might be the primitive stock which has furnished such spreading branches ?—*Augustine Calmet,* 1672—1757.

Verse 1.—*"It is good to sing praises unto our God."* Singing is necessarily included and recognised in the praise of the Psalms. That the joyful should sing is as natural as that the afflicted should pray—rather more natural. Song as the expression of cheerfulness is something universal in human nature ; there were always, both in Israel and among all other nations, songs of joy. Hence it is constantly mentioned in the prophets, by whom joyous singing is used as a frequent figure, even as they threaten that God will take away the song of the bridegroom and the bride, and so forth. The *singing* of men is in itself good and noble. The same God who furnished the birds of heaven with the notes wherein they unconsciously praise their Creator, gave to man the power to sing. We all know how highly Luther, for example, estimated the gift and the art of song. Let him to whom it is granted rejoice therein ; let him who lacks it seek, if possible, to excite it ; for it is a good gift of the Creator. Let our children learn to sing in the schools, even as they learn to read. Our fathers sang more in all the affairs of life than we do ; our tunes are in this respect less fresh, and artless, and joyous. There are many among us who never sing, except when adding their voices to the voice of the church, —and therefore they sing so badly there. Not that a harsh song from a good heart is unacceptable to God ; but he should have our best. As David in his day took care that there should be practised singers for the sanctuary, we should also make provision for the church's service of song, that God may have in all respects a perfect offering. How gracious and lovely is the congregation singing with the heart acceptable songs !—*Rudolf Stier, in "The Epistle of James Expounded,"* 1859.

Verse 1.—The translation here is doubtful. It may either be rendered, " Praise the Lord for *he* is good," or, " for *it* (*praise*) is good." Why is it declared to be " *pleasant* " and " *comely* " to praise the Deity ? Not only because if we glorify him he will also glorify us, but because he is so infinitely glorious that we are infinitely honoured simply in being reckoned worthy to worship One so great.—*John Lorinus.*

Verse 1.—*"It is good to sing praises unto our God ; for it is pleasant ; and praise is comely."* These points are worthy of careful consideration.

I. To praise God is " *good* " for divers reasons. 1. That is good which God commands (Mic. vi. 8). So that thanksgiving is no indifferent action, no will-worship, but it is *cultus institutus*, not to be neglected. 2. It raiseth the heart from earth to heaven ; and being the work of angels and saints in heaven, joins us with that choir above. 3. It is good, again, because by it we pay, or at least acknowledge, a debt, and this is common justice. 4. Good, because for it we are like to receive a good and a great reward ; for if he that prays to God is like to be rewarded (Matt. vi, 6), much more that man who sings praises to him ; for in prayer we consult with our own necessities, in our praises we honour God, and bless him for his gifts.

II. To praise God is " *pleasant.*" 1. Because it proceeds out of love ; for nothing is more pleasant to him that loves, than to make sonnets in the praise of that party he loves. 2. Because it must needs please a man to perform that duty for which he was created ; for to that end God created men and angels, that they should praise him. 3. Because God is delighted with it, as the sweetest sacrifice (Ps. l. 23). 4. It is pleasant to God, because he is delighted with those virtues which are in us,—faith, hope, charity, religion, devotion, humility, etc., of all which our praises are a manifestation and exercise.

III. To praise God is " *comely*" ; for there is no greater stain than ingratitude ; it is made up of a lie and injustice. There is, then, all the decency in the world in praise, and it is comely that a man be thankful to his God, who freely gives him all things,—*William Nicholson.*

Verse 1.—David, to persuade all men to thankfulness, saith, *"It is a good and pleasant thing"* to be thankful. If he had said no more but " *good,*" all which love goodness are bound to be thankful ; but when he saith not only " *good*," but " *pleasant* " too, all which love pleasure are bound to be thankful ; and therefore, as Peter's mother-in-law, so soon as Christ healed her of a fever, rose up immediately to minister unto him (Matt. viii. 15), so we, so soon as Christ hath done anything for us, should rise up immediately to serve him.—*Henry Smith.*

Verse 1.—There is no heaven, either in this world, or the world to come, for people who do not praise God. If you do not enter into the spirit and worship of heaven, how should the spirit and joy of heaven enter into you ? Selfishness makes long prayers, but love makes short prayers, that it may continue longer in praise.—*John Pulsford,* 1857.

Verse 1.—"*Praise.*" There is one other thing which is a serious embarrassment to praising through the song-service of the Church, and that is, that we have so few hymns of praise. You will be surprised to hear me say so ; but you will be more surprised if you take a real specimen of praising and search for hymns of praise. You shall find any number of hymns that talk about praise, and exhort you to praise. There is no lack of hymns that say that God ought to be praised. But of hymns that praise, and say nothing about it, there are very few indeed. And for what there are we are almost wholly indebted to the old churches. Most of them came down to us from the Latin and Greek Churches . . . . There is no place in human literature where you can find such praise as there is in the Psalms of David. —*Henry Ward Beecher.*

Verse 2.—"*The Lord doth build up Jerusalem,*" etc. If this Psalm were written on occasion of the return from Babylon, and the rebuilding of the earthly city, the ideas are to be transferred, as in other Psalms of the same kind, to a more important restoration from a much worse captivity, and to the building up of the church under the gospel, when Christ " gathered together in one the children of God that were scattered abroad " (John xi. 52) ; that is, in the words of our Psalm, he "*gathered together the outcasts of Israel.*" So shall he again, at the resurrection, " gather together his elect from the four winds " (Matt. xxiv. 31), and " build up a Jerusalem," in which they shall serve and praise him for ever.—*George Horne.*

Verse 2.—"*The Lord doth build up Jerusalem,*" etc.

> Jerusalem ! Jerusalem ! the blessing lingers yet
> On the city of the chosen, where the Sabbath seal was set
> And though her sons are scattered, and her daughters weep apart,
> While desolation, like a pall, weighs down each faithful heart ;
> As the plain beside the waters, as the cedar on the hills,
> She shall rise in strength and beauty when the Lord Jehovah wills :
> He has promised her protection, and the holy pledge is good,
> 'Tis whispered through the olive groves, and murmured by the flood,
> As in the Sabbath stillness the Jordan's flow is heard,
> And by the Sabbath breezes the hoary trees are stirred.

Mrs. Hale, in "The Rhyme of Life."

Verse 2.—"*He gathereth together the outcasts of Israel.*" Wonder not that God calls together "*the outcasts,*" and singles them out from every corner for a return ; why can he not do this, as well as " tell the number of the stars, and call them all by their names " ? There are none of his people so despicable in the eye of man, but they are known and regarded by God. Though they are clouded in the world, yet they are the stars of the world ; and shall God number the inanimate stars in the heavens, and make no account of his living stars on the earth ? No ; wherever they are dispersed, he will not forget them : however they are afflicted, he will not despise them. The stars are so numerous that they are innumerable by man ; some are visible and known by men, others lie more hid and undiscovered in a confused light, as those in the milky way ; a man cannot see one of them distinctly. God knows all his people. As he can do what is above the power of man to perform, so he understands what is above the skill of man to discover.—*Stephen Charnock.*

Verse 2.—"*He gathereth together the outcasts of Israel.*" David might well have written feelingly about the "*outcasts,*" for he had himself been one ; and even from Jerusalem, in his age, when driven forth from thence by his unnatural son, he went up by the ascent of Olivet, weeping and barefooted, and other "*outcasts*" with him weeping also as they went.—*Barton Bouchier.*

Verse 3.—*"He healeth the broken in heart,"* etc.   Here are two things contained in this text ; the *patients* and the *physician.*   The patients are the broken in heart. The physician is Christ ; it is he who bindeth up their wounds.

The patients here are felt and discerned to have two wounds or maladies ; brokenness of heart, and woundedness : he binds up such.   Brokenness of heart presupposeth a former wholeness of heart.   Wholeness of heart is twofold ; either wholeness of heart *in sin*, or wholeness of heart *from sin.*   First, wholeness of heart *from sin* is when the heart is *without sin ;* and so the blessed angels have whole hearts, and so Adam and Eve, and we in them, before the fall, had whole hearts.   Secondly, wholeness of heart *in sin ;* so the devils have whole hearts, and all men since the fall, from their conception till their conversion, have whole hearts ; and these are they that our Saviour intends,—" The whole need not the physician, but they that are sick."

Brokenness of heart may be considered two ways ; first, *in relation to wholeness of heart in sin :* so brokenness of heart is not a malady, but the commencement of the cure of a desperate disease.   Secondly, *in relation to wholeness of heart from sin ;* and so it is a malady or sickness, and yet peculiar to one blood alone, namely, God's elect ; for though the heart be made whole in its desire towards God, yet it is broken for its sins.   As a man that hath a barbed arrow shot into his side, and the arrow is plucked out of the flesh, yet the wound is not presently healed ; so sin may be plucked out of the heart, but the scar that was made with plucking it out is not yet cured.   The wounds that are yet under cure are the plagues and troubles of conscience, the sighs and groans of a hungering soul after grace, the stinging poison that the serpent's fang hath left behind it ; these are the wounds.

Now the heart is broken three ways.   First, *by the law ;* as it breaks the heart of a thief to hear the sentence of the law, that he must be hanged for his robbery ; so it breaks the heart of the soul, sensibly to understand the sentence of the law,—Thou shalt not sin ; if thou do, thou shalt be damned.   If ever the heart come to be sensible of this sentence,—" Thou art a damned man," it is impossible to stand out under it, but it must break.   " Is not my word like a hammer, that breaketh the rock in pieces ? " (Jer. xxiii. 29).   Can any rock-heart hold out and not be broken with the blows of it ?   Indeed, thus far a man may be broken, and yet be a reprobate ; for they shall all be thus broken in hell, and therefore this breaking is not enough.

Secondly, *by the Gospel ;* for if ever the heart come to be sensible of the love of the Gospel, it will break all to shatters.   " Rend your heart ; for the Lord is gracious," etc. : Joel ii. 13.   When all the shakes of God's mercy come, they all cry " Rend."   Indeed, the heart cannot stand out against them, if it once feel them.   Beat thy soul upon the gospel : if any way under heaven can break it, this is the way.

Thirdly, the heart is broken *by the skill of the minister* in the handling of these two, the law and the gospel : God furnisheth him with skill to press the law home, and gives him understanding how to put the gospel, and by this means doth God break the heart : for, alas, though the law be never so good a hammer, and although the gospel be never so fit an anvil, yet if the minister lay not the soul upon it the heart will not break : he must fetch a full stroke with the law, and he must set the full power of the gospel at the back of the soul, or else the heart will not break.

"He healeth the broken in heart."   Hence observe, that *Christ justifies and sanctifies ;* for that is the meaning.

1. First, because *God hath given Christ grace to practise for the sake of the broken in heart ;* and therefore if this be his grace, to heal the broken-hearted, certainly he will heal them.   " The Spirit of the Lord is upon me," etc.   He hath sent me to heal the broken-hearted," etc. : Luke iv. 18.   If he be *created* master of this art, even for this purpose, to heal the broken in heart, he will verily heal them, and none but them.   He is not like Hosander and Hippocrates, whose father appointed them both to be physicians : he appointed his son Hippocrates to be a physician of horses, yet he proved a physician for men ; he appointed Hosander to be a physician for men, and he proved a physician for horses.   Jesus is not like these ; no, no ; he will heal those whom he was appointed to heal.

2. Because *Christ hath undertaken to do it.*   When a skilful physician hath undertaken a cure, he will surely do it : indeed, sometimes a good physician may fail, as Trajan's physician did, for he died under his hands ; on whose tomb this was written, " Here lies Trajan the emperor, that may thank his physician that he died."   But if Christ undertake it, thou mayest be sure of it ; for he tells thee that art broken in heart that he hath undertaken it, he hath felt thy pulse already.   Isa. lvii. 15.   He

doth not only undertake it, but he saith he will go *visit* his sick patient, he will come to thy bedside, yea, he will come and dwell with thee all the time of thy sickness ; thou shalt never want anything, but he will be ready to help thee : thou needest not complain and say, " Oh, the physician is too far off, he will not come at me." I dwell in the high places indeed, saith God, but yet I will come and dwell with thee that art of an humble spirit. Thou needest not fear, saying, " Will a man cure his enemies ? I have been an enemy to God's glory, and will he yet cure me ? " Yea, saith Christ, if thou be *broken in heart* I will bind thee up.

3. Thirdly, because *this is Christ's charge*, and he will look to his own calling : " The Lord hath sent me to bind up the broken-hearted " (Isa. lxi. 1). . . . Neither needest thou fear thine own poverty, because thou hast not a fee to give him ; for thou mayest come to him by way of begging ; he will look to thee for nothing for, " To him will I look that is poor," etc. : Isa. lxvi. 2.

4. Fourthly, *none but the broken in heart will take physic of Christ.* Now this is a physician's desire, that his patient would cast himself upon him ; if he will not, the physician hath no desire to meddle with him. Now none but the broken in heart will take such physic as Christ gives, and therefore he saith, " To him will I look that is of a broken heart, and trembles at my words": Isa. lxv. 2. When I bid him take such a purge, saith God, he trembles, and he takes it.—*William Fenner, in a Sermon entitled "The Sovereign Virtue of the Gospel,"* 1647.

Verse 3.—

> O thou who dry'st the mourner's tear,
>   How dark this world would be,
> If, when deceived and wounded here,
>   We could not fly to Thee !
> The friends, who in our sunshine live,
>   When winter comes are flown ;
> And he who has but tears to give
>   Must weep those tears alone.
> But Thou wilt heal that broken heart,
>   Which, like the plants that throw
> Their fragrance from the wounded part,
>   Breathes sweetness out of woe.
>
> When joy no longer soothes or cheers,
>   And e'en the hope that threw
> A moment's sparkle o'er our tears
>   Is dimmed and vanished too ;
> Oh ! who would bear life's stormy doom,
>   Did not thy wing of love
> Come, brightly waiting through the gloom
>   Our peace-branch from above ?
> Then sorrow, touched by Thee, grows bright
>   With more than rapture's ray ;
> As darkness shows us worlds of light
>   We never saw by day !
>
>   *Thomas Moore,* 1779—1852.

Verse 3.—*"He healeth the broken in heart."* The broken in heart is one whose heart is affected with the evil of sin, and weeps bitter tears on account of it ; one who feels sorrow, shame, and anguish, on the review of his past sinful life, and his base rebellion against a righteous God. Such a one has a broken heart. His heart is broken at the sight of his own ingratitude —the despite done by him to the strivings of the Holy Spirit. His heart is broken when he considers the numberless invitations made to him in the Scriptures, all of which he has wickedly slighted and despised. His heart is broken at the recollection of a thousand kind providences to him and to his family, by day and by night, all sent by God, and intended for his moral, spiritual, and eternal benefit, but by him basely and wantonly abused. His heart is broken at the consideration of the love and compassion of the adorable Redeemer ; the humiliation of his birth ; the devotedness of his life ; the reproach, the indignity of his sufferings ; the ignominy and anguish of his death. His heart is broken when his conscience assures him that all this humiliation, this suffering, this death, was for him, who had so deliberately and repeatedly refused the grace which the blood and righteousness of Christ has purchased. It is the sight of Calvary that fills him with anguish of spirit, that overwhelms him with confusion and self-abasement. While he contemplates the amazing scene, he stands, he weeps, he

prays, he smites upon his breast, he exclaims, " God be merciful to me a sinner ! "
And adds, " O wretched man that I am, who shall deliver me from the body of
this death ? "

The broken in heart must further be understood as one who seeks help from God
alone, and will not be comforted till he speaks peace to his soul.

The act of God, in the scripture before us, is the moral and spiritual health of
man—of man, who had brought disease on himself—of man, by his own rebellion
against his Creator—of man, who had, in ten thousand ways, provoked the justice
of heaven, and deserved only indignation and eternal wrath—the health of man,
whom, in an instant, he could hurl to utter destruction.   The saving health here
proposed is the removal of all guilt, however contracted, and of all pollution, however rooted.   It is the communication of God's favour, the riches of his grace, the
implantation of his righteousness.

To effect the healing of the broken heart, God has, moreover, appointed a
Physician, whose skill is infallible, whose goodness and care are equal to his skill.
That Physician is none other than the Son of God.   In that character he has been
made known to us.   " They that be whole need not a physician, but they that
be sick."   The prophet Isaiah introduces his advent in the most sublime language :
" He hath sent me to bind up the broken-hearted, to proclaim liberty to the captives,
and the opening of the prison to them that are bound."

The health, the moral and spiritual soundness of the soul, my brethen, is derived
from the atoning sacrifice of Christ.   The grace of God flows to the broken in heart
through his manhood, his godhead, his righteousness, his truth ; through his patience,
his humility, his death and passion ; through his victory over sin, his resurrection,
and ascension into heaven.   Here, thou broken in heart, thou sorrowing, watching
penitent ; here is the medicine, here the Physician, here the cure, here the health
thou art seeking.

The healing of the broken in heart must be further understood as effected through
the agency of the Holy Spirit.   It is done by the Spirit of God, that it may be done,
and that it may be well done ;   and that all the praise, the glory of that which is
done, may be ascribed to the plenitude, the freeness, the sovereignty of his grace.
The Spirit of God, however, uses means.   The means of grace are appointed expressly
for this purpose ;   the blessing of health is there applied.   There, under the sound
of the everlasting gospel, while looking by faith to Christ, and appropriating his
merits, he healeth the broken in heart.   There, while commemorating the dying
love of Christ, and applying its benefits by faith to the soul, he healeth the broken
in heart.   There, while the soul, sensible of his goodness, is offering up the song
of praise, and trusting alone in his mercy, he healeth the broken in heart.   There,
while prostrate at his footstool, supplicating his grace, resting on his finished
redemption, he healeth the broken in heart.   In the private acts of devotion the
Spirit of God also is near to bless and save.   There, while reading and believing
his holy Word, while meditating on its meaning ; there, while in secret, solemn
prayer, the soul takes hold on God in Christ Jesus ; he healeth the broken in heart.
—*Condensed from a Sermon by Thomas Blackley*, 1826.

Verse 3.—*"He healeth the broken in heart."*   I do indeed most sincerely sympathise
with you in this fresh sorrow.   " Thy breaking waves pass over me."   The trial,
so much the heavier that it is not the first breaking in, but the waters continuing
still, and continuing to rise, until deep calleth unto deep at the noise of God's
water-spouts, " Yea, and thy billows all."   In such circumstances we are greatly
tempted to wonder if it be true, of the Holy One in the midst of us, that a bruised
reed he will not break, that the smoking flax he will not quench.   We may not,
however, doubt it, nor even in the day of our grief and our desperate sorrow, are
we at liberty to call it in question.   Our God is the God of the broken heart.
The deeper such a heart is smitten, and the more it bleeds, the more precious
it is in his sight, the nearer he draws to it, the longer he stays there.   " I dwell
with him who is of a contrite heart."   The more abundantly will he manifest the
kindness and the glory of his power, in tenderly carrying it in his bosom, and at
last binding up its painful wounds.   " He healeth the broken in heart."   " O thou
afflicted, tossed with tempest, and not comforted, behold, I will lay thy stones
with fair colours, and lay thy foundations with sapphires."   Weeping Naomi said,
" Call me Mara, for the Lord hath dealt very bitterly with me."   Afterwards,
happy Naomi took the child of her own Ruth, and laid it in her bosom, and sweetly
found that the days of her mourning were ended.

My dear friend, this new gash of deep sorrow was prepared for you by the Ancient of Days. His Son—and that Son is love—watched over the counsels of old, to keep and to perform them to the minutest circumstance.—*John Jameson,* 1838.

Verse 4.—*"He telleth the number of the stars,"* etc. In which similitude he showeth, that albeit Abraham could not comprehend the multitude of the children, either of his faith or of his flesh, more than he could count the number of the stars ; yet the Lord knoweth every believer by name, as he knoweth every star and can call everyone by its name.—*David Dickson.*

Verse 4.—*"He telleth the number of the stars,"* etc. Among the heathen every constellation represented some God. But the Scriptures show Jehovah, not as one of many starry gods, but as the one God of all the stars. He is, too, as he taught his people by Abraham, the God of a firmament of nobler stars. His people are scattered and trodden as the sands of the sea-shore. But he turns dust and dirt to stars of glory. He will make of every saint a star, and Heaven is his people's sky, where broken-hearted sufferers of earth are glorified into glittering galaxies. —*Hermann Venema.*

Verse 4.—*"He calleth them all by their names."* Literally, " calleth names to all of them," an expression marking not only God's power in marshalling them all as a host (Isa. xl. 26), but also the most intimate knowledge and watchful care, as that of a shepherd for his flock. John x. 3.—*J. J. Stewart Perowne.*

Verse 4.—*"He calleth them all by their names."* They render a due obedience to him, as servants to their master. When he singles them out and calls them by name to do some official service, he calls them out to their several offices, as the general of an army appoints the station of every regiment in a battalion ; or, *" he calls them by name,"* i.e. he imposeth names upon them, a sign of dominion, the giving names to the inferior creatures being the first act of Adam's derivative dominion over them. These are under the sovereignty of God. The stars by their influences fight against Sisera (Jud. v. 20) ; and the sun holds in its reins, and stands stone-still to light Joshua to a complete victory : Josh. x. 12. They are all marshalled in their ranks to receive his word of command, and fight in close order, as being desirous to have a share in the ruin of the enemies of their sovereign. —*Stephen Charnock.*

Verse 4.—The immense distance at which the nearest stars are known to be placed, proves that they are bodies of a prodigious size, not inferior to our own sun, and that they shine, not by reflected rays, but by their own native light. But bodies encircled with such refulgent splendour, would be of little use in Jehovah's empire, unless surrounding worlds were cheered by their benign influence, and enlightened by their beams. Every star is therefore concluded to be a sun surrounded by planetary globes. Nearly a thousand of these luminaries may be seen in a clear winter's night by the naked eye. But these do not form the eighty-thousandth part of what may be descried by the help of telescopes. While Dr. Herschel was exploring the most crowded part of the milky way, in one quarter of an hour's time no less than 116,000 stars passed through the field of view of his telescope. It has been computed, that nearly one hundred millions of stars might be perceived by our most perfect instruments, if all the regions of the sky were thoroughly explored. But immeasurable regions of space lie beyond the utmost boundaries of human vision, even thus assisted, into which imagination itself can scarcely penetrate, but which are doubtless filled with operations of divine wisdom and divine omnipotence.—*Thomas Dick, in "The Christian Philosopher."*

Verse 5.—*"His understanding is infinite."* Hebrew : *"Of his understanding there is no number."* God is incomprehensible. In *place ;* in *time ;* in *understanding ;* in *love.* First, in *place ;* because no place, no space, can be imagined so great, but God exceeds it, and may be found beyond it. Secondly, in *time ;* because he exceeds all time : for he was before all time that can be conceived, and shall be after all time. Time is a created thing, to attend upon the creation and continuance of all things created and continued by God. Thirdly, in *understanding ;* because no created understanding can comprehend him so that nothing of God may be hid from it. Fourthly, in *love ;* because God doth exceed all love : no creature can love God according to his worth. All these ways of incomprehensibleness follow upon his infiniteness.—*Thomas Larkham in "The Attributes of God Unfolded, and Applied,"* —1656.

Verse 5.—"His understanding is infinite." The Divine wisdom is said to be *"without number"*; that is, the objects of which this wisdom of God can take cognisance are innumerable.—*Simon de Muis.*

Verse 5.—In this verse we have three of God's attributes, his greatness, his power, and his knowledge; and though only the last of these be expressly said to be *infinite,* yet is the same implied also of the two former; for all the perfections of God being essential to him, must need be infinite as he himself is; and therefore what is affirmed of one must, by a parity of reason, be extended to the rest.—*John Conant, 1608—1693.*

Verse 6.—"The LORD lifteth up the meek," etc. The meek need not envy the lofty who sweep the earth with their gay robes, any more than real royalty is jealous of the kingly hero who struts his hour upon the stage. They shall be princes and rulers long after these actors have laid aside their tinselled crowns.

How wonderful shall be the reversal when God shall place the last first and the first last! Moralists have often pointed us to the ruler of a hundred broad kingdoms lying down at last in six feet of imprisoning clay; but God shall show us the wayside cottager lifted into the inheritance of the universe.—*Evangelical Magazine.*

Verses 7—9.—God creates, and then fails not to supply. Analogically, the Lord buildeth Jerusalem, and provides for the wants of the inhabitants: by spiritual inference, the saints argue that Christ establishes his church and gives all the gracious gifts which are needed in that institution.—*John Lorinus.*

Verses 8, 9.—"Mountains . . . ravens." Wonderful Providence which takes cognisance of the mountainous and the minute alike. The All-Provider descends from august and sublime heights to save the meanest creature from starvation—extending constant care to the wants of even those abject little objects, the young ravens, Heb. " the sons of the raven."—*Martin Geier.*

Verse 8.—"Clouds . . . rain . . . grass." There is a mutual dependence and subordination between all second causes. The creatures are serviceable to one another by mutual ministries and supplies; the earth is cherished by the heat of the heavens, moistened by the water, and by the temperament of both made fruitful; and so sendeth forth innumerable plants for the comfort and use of living creatures, and living creatures are for the supply of man. It is wonderful to consider the subordination of all causes, and the proportion they bear to one another. The heavens work upon the elements, the elements upon the earth, and the earth yieldeth fruits for the use of man. The prophet taketh notice of this admirable gradation : " I will hear the heavens, and the heavens shall hear the earth ; and the earth shall hear the corn, and the wine, and the oil ; and the corn, and the wine, and the oil, shall hear Jezreel " (Hosea ii. 21, 22). We look to the fields for the supplies of corn, wine, and oil ; but they can do nothing without clouds, and the clouds can do nothing without God. The creatures are beholden to one another, and all to God. In the order of the world there is an excellent chain of causes, by which all things hang together, that so they may lead up the soul to the Lord.—*Thomas Manton.*

Verse 8.—"Who prepareth rain?" The rain-cloud parts with its contents only when God commands it, and *as* he commands, whether in the soft gentle shower or in the drenching downpour that floods the fields and obstructs the labours of the husbandman.—*Thomas Robinson, in "Homiletical Commentary on the Book of Job," 1876.*

Verse 8.—"Who maketh grass to grow upon the mountains." The wild grasses are taken, as it were, under the special providence of God. In the perennial verdure in regions above the zone of man's cultivation, we have a perpetual proof of God's care of the lower animals that neither sow nor reap. The mountain grasses grow spontaneously ; they require no culture but such as the rain and the sunshine of heaven supply. They obtain their nourishment directly from the inorganic soil, and are independent of organic materials. Nowhere is the grass so green and vigorous as on the beautiful slopes of lawn-like pasture high up in the Alps, radiant with the glory of wild flowers, and ever musical with the hum of grasshoppers, and the tinkling of cattle-bells. Innumerable cows and goats browse upon them ; the peasants spend their summer months in making cheese and hay from them for winter consumption in the valleys. This exhausting system of husbandry has been carried on during untold centuries ; no one thinks of manuring the Alpine pastures ; and yet no deficiency has been observed in their fertility, though the soil is but a thin covering spread over the naked rocks. It may be regarded as a part of the same wise and gracious arrangement of Providence, that the insects which devour the grasses on the *Kuh* and *Schaf Alpen*, the pasturages of the cows and sheep, are kept in check by a predominance of carnivorous insects. In all the mountain meadows it has been ascertained that the species of carnivorous are at least four times as numerous as the species of herb-eating insects. Thus, in the absence of birds, which are rare in Switzerland, the pastures are preserved from a terrible scourge. To one not aware of this check, it may seem surprising how the verdure of the Alpine pastures should be so rich and luxuriant considering the immense development of insect life. The grass, whenever the sun shines, is literally covered with them—butterflies of gayest hues, and beetles of brightest iridescence ; and the air is filled with their loud murmurs. I remember well the vivid feeling of God's gracious providence, which possessed me when passing over the beautiful Wengern Alp at the foot of the Jungfrau, and seeing, wherever I rested on the green turf, alive with its tiny inhabitants, the balance of nature so wonderfully preserved between the herb which is for man's food and the moth before which he is crushed. Were the herbivorous insects allowed to multiply to their full extent, in such favourable circumstances as the warmth of the air and the verdure of the earth in Switzerland produce, the rich pastures which now yield abundant food for upwards of a million and a half of cattle would speedily become bare and leafless deserts. Nor only in their power of growing without cultivation, but also in the peculiarities of their structure, the mountain grasses proclaim the hand of God. Many of them are viviparous. Instead of producing flowers and seed, as the grasses in the tranquil valleys do, the young plants spring from them perfectly formed. They cling round the stem and form a kind of blossom. In this state they remain until the parent stalk withers and falls prostrate on the ground, when they immediately strike root and form independent grasses. This is a remarkable adaptation to circumstances ; for it is manifest that were seeds instead of living plants developed in the ears of the mountain grasses, they would be useless in the stormy regions where they grow. They would be blown away far from the places they were intended to clothe, to spots foreign to their nature and habits, and thus the species would speedily perish.

The more we think of it, the more we are struck with the wise foresight which suggested the creative fiat, " Let the earth bring forth grass." It is the most abundant and the most generally diffused of all vegetation. It suits almost every soil and climate.—*Hugh Macmillan, in "Bible Teachings in Nature," 1868.*

Verses 8, 9.—The Hebrews had no notion of what we denominate " secondary laws," but believed that God acted directly upon matter, and was the immediate, efficient cause of the solemn order, and the varied and wonderful phenomena of nature. Dispensing thus with the whole machinery of cause and effect, as we employ those terms in philosophical language, their minds were brought into immediate contact with God in his manifold works, and this gave, both to devotion and the spirit of poetry, the liveliest inspiration and the freest scope of action. Heaven and earth were governed by his commands ; the thunder was his " voice," the lightning his " arrows." It is he who " causeth the vapour to ascend from the ends of the earth." When the famished city should call upon the corn, the wine, and the oil, and those should call upon the earth for nourishment, and the parched earth should call upon the heavens for moisture, and the heavens should call upon the Lord for permission to refresh the earth, then Jehovah would hear and supply. He gave the rain, and he sent the drought and famine. The clouds were not looked upon merely as sustained by a law of specific gravity, but God spread them out in the sky ; these clouds were God's chariot, the curtains of his pavilion, the dust of his feet. Snow and hail were fearful manifestations of God, often sent as the messengers of his wrath.—*F. G. Hubbard, in "Bate's Encyclopædia," 1865.*

Verses 8, 9.—God by his special providence prepares *"food"* for those who have no other care taken for them. *"Beasts"* that live among men are by men taken care of ; they enrich the ground with manure, and till the ground ; and that brings forth corn for the use of these cattle as well as men. But the *wild beasts* that live upon the *mountains*, and in woods and desert places, are fed only from the heavens : the *"rain"* that from thence distils enricheth those dry hills and *"maketh grass to grow"* there, which else would not, and so God giveth to these *wild beasts* their food after the same manner of Divine Providence as in the end of the verse he is said to provide for the *"young ravens."*—*Henry Hammond.*

Verse 9.—*"The young ravens cry."* The strange stories told by Jewish and Arabian writers, on the raven's cruelty to its young, in driving them out of their nests before they are quite able to provide for themselves, are entirely without foundation, as no bird is more careful of its young ones than the raven. To its habit of flying restlessly about in search of food to satisfy its own appetite and that of its young ones, may perhaps be traced the reason of its being selected by the sacred writers as an especial object of God's protecting care.—*W. Houghton, in "The Bible Educator."*

Verse 9.—*"The young ravens cry."* While still unfledged the young ravens have a strange habit of falling out of their nests, and flapping their wings heavily to the ground. Next morning they are found by the shepherds sitting croaking on the ground beneath their former homes, and are then captured and taken away with comparative ease.—*J. G. Wood, in "The Illustrated Natural History,"* 1869.

Verse 9.—*"The young ravens cry."* The evening proceedings and manœuvres of the rooks are curious and amusing in the autumn. Just before dusk they return in long strings from the foraging of the day, and rendezvous by thousands over Selbourne-down, where they wheel round in the air, and sport and dive in a playful manner, all the while exerting their voices, and making a loud cawing, which, being blended and softened by the distance that we at the village are below them, becomes a confused noise or chiding ; or rather a pleasing murmur, very engaging to the imagination, and not unlike the cry of a pack of hounds in hollow, echoing woods, or the rushing of the wind in tall trees, or the tumbling of the tide upon a pebbly shore. When this ceremony is over, with the last gleam of day, they retire for the night to the deep beechen woods of Tisted and Ropley. We remember a little girl, who, as she was going to bed used to remark on such an occurrence, in the true spirit of physico-theology, that the rooks were saying their prayers, and yet this child was much too young to be aware that the Scriptures had said of the Deity that " He feedeth the ravens that call upon him."—*Gilbert White (1720—1793), in "The Natural History of Selbourne."*

Verse 9.—

> Behold, and look away your low despair ;
> See the light tenants of the barren air :
> To them, nor stores, nor granaries belong,
> Nought but the woodlands and the pleasing song ;
> Yet, your kind heavenly Father bends his eye
> On the least wing that flits along the sky.
> To him they sing when Spring renews the plain ;
> To him they cry in Winter's pinching reign ;
> Nor is the music, nor their plaint, in vain.
> He hears the gay, and the distressful call,
> And with unsparing bounty fills them all.
> Will he not care for you, ye faithless, say ?
> Is he unwise ? Or, are ye less than they ?

James Thomson, 1700—1748.

Verse 9.—It is related of Edward Taylor, the sailor-preacher of Boston, that on the Sunday before he was to sail for Europe, he was entreating the Lord to care well for his church during his absence. All at once he stopped, and ejaculated, " What have I done ? Distrust the Providence of heaven ! A God that gives a whale a ton of herrings for a breakfast, will he not care for my children ? " and then went on, closing his prayer in a more confiding manner.—*From "Eccentric Preachers," by C. H. S.*

Verse 10.—The two clauses of this verse are probably intended to describe *cavalry* and *infantry*, as forming the military strength of nations. It is not to those who trust in such resources that Jehovah shows favour, but to those who rely on his protection (verse 11).—*Annotated Paragraph Bible.*

Verses 10, 11.—When a sinner is brought upon his knees, and becomes a suppliant, when as he is laid low by affliction, so he lieth low in prayer and supplication, then the Lord will be favourable to him, and show his delight in him. *"The Lord delighteth not in the strength of the horse ; he taketh not pleasure in the legs of a man."* No man is favoured by God because of his outward favour, because he hath a beautiful face, or strong, clean limbs ; yea, not only hath the Lord no pleasure in any man's legs, but not in any man's brains, how reaching soever, nor in any man's wit how quick soever, nor in any man's judgment how deep soever, nor in any man's tongue how eloquent or well spoken soever ; but *"The Lord taketh pleasure in them that fear him, in those that hope in his mercy,"* in those that walk humbly with him, and call upon him. . . All the beauties and rarities both of persons and things are dull and flat, yea, wearisome and loathsome to God, in comparison of a gracious, honest, humble soul. Princes have their favourites (Job. xxxiii. 26) : they are favourable to some above many, either because they are beautiful and goodly persons, or because they are men of excellent speech, prudence and deportment. All godly men are God's favourites ; he is favourable to them not only above many men in the world, but above all the men of this world, who have their portion in this life ; and he therefore favours them, because they are the purchase of his Son and the workmanship of his Spirit, convincing them of, and humbling them for, their sins, as also creating them after God in righteousness and true holiness. Such shall be his favourites. —*Joseph Caryl.*

Verse 11.—*"Them that fear him, those that hope in his mercy."* Patience and fear are the fences of hope. There is a beautiful relation between hope and fear. The two are linked in this verse. They are like the cork in a fisherman's net, which keeps it from sinking, and the lead, which prevents it from floating. Hope without fear is in danger of being too sanguine ; fear without hope would soon become desponding.—*George Seaton Bowes, in "In Prospect of Sunday,"* 1880.

Verse 11.—*"Them that fear him, those that hope in his mercy."* A sincere Christian is known by both these ; a fear of God, or a constant obedience to his commands, and an affiance, trust, and dependence upon his mercies. Oh, how sweetly are both these coupled, a uniform, sincere obedience to him, and an unshaken, constant reliance on his mercy and goodness ! The whole perfection of the Christian life is comprised in these two—believing God and fearing him, trusting in his mercy and fearing his name ; the one maketh us careful in avoiding sin, the other diligent to follow after righteousness ; the one is a bridle from sin and temptations, the other a spur to our duties. Fear is our curb, and hope our motive and encouragement ; the one respects our duty, the other our comfort ; the one allayeth the other. God is so to be feared, as also to be trusted ; so to be trusted, as also to be feared ; and as we must not suffer our fear to degenerate into legal bondage, but hope in his mercy, so our trust must not degenerate into carnal sloth and wantonness, but so hope in his word as to fear his name. Well, then, such as both believe in God and fear to offend him are the only men who are acceptable to God and his people. God will take pleasure in them, and they take pleasure in one another.—*Thomas Manton.*

Verse 11.—*"Fear"* and *"Hope"* are the great *vincula* of Old Testament theology, bracketing and including in their meaning all its ideas.—*Thomas Le Blanc.*

Verse 11.—*Fear* and *hope* are passions of the mind so contrary the one to the other, that with regard to the same object, it is strange they should meet in the same laudable character ; yet here we see they do so, and it is the praise of the same persons, that they both fear God, and hope in him. Whence we may gather this doctrine : That in every concern that lies upon our hearts, we should still endeavour to keep the balance even between hope and fear.

We know how much the health of the body depends upon a due temperament of the humours, such as preserves any one from being predominant above the rest ; and how much the safety and peace of the nations result from a due balance of trade and power, that no one grow too great for its neighbours ; and so necessary is it to the health and welfare of our souls, that there be a due proportion maintained between their powers and passions, and that the one may always be a check upon the other, to keep it from running into extremes ; as in these affections mentioned in the text. A holy fear of God must be check upon our hope, to keep that from swelling into presumption ; and a pious hope in God must be a check upon our fear, to keep that from sinking into despondency. This balance must, I say, by a wise and steady hand, be kept even in every concern that lies upon our hearts, and that we have thoughts about. I shall enumerate those that are of the greatest importance. We must keep up both hope and fear. 1. As to the concerns of our souls, and our spiritual and eternal state. 2. As to our outward concerns, relating to the body and the life that now is. 3. As to the public concerns of the church of God, and our own land and nation.

In reference to each of these, we must always study and strive to support that affection, whether it be hope or fear, which the present temper of our minds and circumstances of our case make necessary to preserve us from an extreme.—*Matthew Henry.*

Verse 12.—That all Creation must involuntarily praise the Lord, and that the primary duty of conscious intelligence is the willing praise of the same Deity, are the two *axioms* of the Psalmist's theology. He has in the first part of this Psalm been stating the first, and now he is about to announce the second.—*Martin Geier.*

Verse 13.—*"He hath strengthened the bars of thy gates."*—Blessed is the city whose gates God barreth up with his power, and openeth again with his mercy. There is nothing can defend where his justice will strike ; and there is nothing can offend where his goodness will preserve.—*Thomas Adams.*

Verses 13, 14.—The Psalmist recites four arguments from which he would have Zion sing praises. 1. Security and defence. 2. Benediction. 3. Peace. 4. Sustenance or provision.

1. *Security.* Jerusalem is a city secure, being defended by God : *"For he hath strengthened the bars of thy gates."* Gates and bars do well to a city, but then only is the city secure when God makes them strong. The true munition of a city is God's defence of it. Arms, laws, wealth, etc., are the bars, but God must put strength into them.

2. *Benediction.* Jerusalem is a happy city, for *"he hath blessed thy children within thee,"* thy kings, princes, magistrates, etc., with wisdom, piety, etc.

3. *Peace.* Jerusalem is a peaceable city. *"He maketh peace in thy borders,"* the very name intimates so much ; for Jerusalem interpreted is *visio pacis*—Vision of peace.

4. *Abundance.* Jerusalem is a city provided by God with necessary food and provision ; for *"He filleth thee with the finest of the wheat."*—*William Nicholson.*

Verse 14.—*"He maketh peace in thy borders,"* etc. There is a political peace—peace in city and country ; this is the fairest flower of a Prince's crown ; peace is the best blessing of a nation. It is well with bees when there is a noise ; but it is best with Christians when, as in the building of the Temple, there is no noise of hammer heard. Peace brings plenty along with it ; how many miles would some go on pilgrimage to purchase this peace ! Therefore the Greeks made Peace to be the nurse of Pluto, the God of wealth. Political plants thrive best in the sunshine of peace. *"He maketh peace in thy borders, and filleth thee with the finest of the wheat."* The ancients made the harp the emblem of peace : how sweet would the sounding of this harp be after the roaring of the cannon ! All should study to promote this political peace. The godly man, when he dies, " enters into peace " (Isa. lvii. 2) ; but while he lives, peace must enter into him.—*Thomas Watson.*

Verse 14.—*"He maketh peace."* The Hebrews observe that all the letters in the name of God are *literæ quiescentes*, letters of rest. God only is the centre were the soul may find rest : God only can speak peace to the conscience.—*John Stoughton,* —1639.

Verse 14.—*"Finest of the wheat."* If men give much it is in cheap and coarse commodity. Quantity and quality are only possible with human production *in inverse ratio ;* but the Lord gives the *most* and *best* of all supplies to his pensioners. How truly the believer under the gospel knows the inner spirit of the meaning here ! The Lord Jesus Christ says, " My peace I give unto you." And when he sets us at rest and all is reconciliation and peace, then he feeds us with *himself*—his body, the finest wheat, and his blood, the richest wine.—*Johannes Paulus Palanterius.*

Verse 15.—*"His word runneth very swiftly."* There is not a moment between the shooting out of the arrow and the fastening of it in the mark ; both are done in the very same atom and point of time. Therefore we read in the Scripture of the immediate effects of the word of Christ. Saith he to the leprous man, " Be thou clean. And immediately his leprosy was cleansed " : Matt. viii. 3. And to the blind man, " Go thy way ; thy faith hath made thee whole. And immediately ιe received his sight " : Mark x. 52. No arrow makes so immediate an impression in the mark aimed at as the arrow of Christ's word. No sooner doth Christ say to the soul, Be enlightened, be quickened, be comforted, but the work is done.—*Ralph Robinson.*

Verse 16.—"*He giveth snow like wool.*" There are three things considerable in snow, for which it is compared to wool. First, for the *whiteness* of it. Snow is white as wool ; snow is so exceeding white that the whiteness of a soul cleansed by pardoning grace, in the blood of Christ, is likened unto it (Isa. i. 18) ; and the latter part of the same verse intimates that the whiteness of snow bears resemblance to that of wool. The whiteness of snow is caused by the abundance of air and spirits that are in that pellucid body, as the naturalists speak. Any thing that is of a watery substance, being frozen or much wrought upon by cold, appears more white ; and hence it is that all persons inhabiting cold climates or countries, are of a whiter complexion than they who inhabit hot. Secondly, snow is like wool for *softness*, 'tis pliable to the hand as a lock or fleece of wool. Thirdly, snow is like wool (which may seem strange) with respect to the *warmness* of it. Though snow be cold in itself, yet it is to the earth as wool, or as a woollen cloth or blanket that keeps the body warm. Snow is not warm formally, yet it is warm effectively and virtually ; and therefore is it compared to wool.—*Joseph Caryl.*

Verse 16.—"*Like wool.*" Namely, curled and tufted, and as white as the snow in those countries. Isa. i. 18, Rev. i. 14.—*John Diodati.*

Verse 16.—"*Snow like wool.*" The ancients used to call snow εριωδες υδωρ, *woolly water* (Eustathius, in Dionys. Perieget. p. 91). Martial gives it the name of *densum vellus aquarum, a thick fleece of waters* (Epigram. l. iv. Ep. 3). Aristophanes calls clouds, *flying fleeces of wool* (Nubes, p. 146). Pliny calls it *the froth of the celestial waters* (Nat. His. lib. xvii. cap. 2).—*Samuel Burder.*

Verse 16.—"*He giveth snow like wool.*" In Palestine snow is not the characteristic feature of winter as it is in northern latitudes. It is merely an occasional phenomenon. Showers of it fall now and then in severer seasons on the loftier parts of the land, and whiten for a day or two the vineyards and cornfields : but it melts from the green earth as rapidly as its sister vapours vanish from the blue sky. . . . . But the Psalmist seized the occasional snow, as he seized the fleeting vapour, and made it a text of his spiritual meditations. Let us follow his example.

"*He giveth snow like wool,*" says the Psalmist. This comparison expressly indicates one of the most important purposes which the snow serves in the economy of nature. It covers the earth like a blanket during that period of winter sleep which is necessary to recruit its exhausted energies, and prepare it for fresh efforts in the spring ; and being, like wool, a bad conductor, it conserves the latent heat of the soil, and protects the dormant life of plant and animal hid under it from the frosty rigour of the outside air. Winter-sown wheat, when defended by this covering, whose under surface seldom falls much below 32° Fahr., can thrive even though the temperature of the air above may be many degrees below the freezing-point. Our country, enjoying an equable climate, seldom requires this protection ; but in northern climates, where the winter is severe and prolonged, its beneficial effects are most marked. The scanty vegetation which blooms with such sudden and marvellous loveliness in the height of summer, in the Arctic regions and on mountain summits, would perish utterly were it not for the protection of the snow that lies on it for three quarters of a year.

But it is not only to Alpine plants and hybernating animals that God gives snow like wool. The Esquimaux take advantage of its curious protective property, and ingeniously build their winter huts of blocks of hardened snow ; thus, strangely enough, by a homœopathic law, protecting themselves against cold by the effects of cold. The Arctic navigator has been often indebted to walls of snow banked up around his ship for the comparative comfort of his winter quarters, when the temperature without has fallen so low that even chloric ether became solid. And many a precious life has been saved by the timely shelter which the snow-storm itself has provided against its own violence. But while snow thus warms in cold regions, it also cools in warm regions. It sends down from the white summits of equatorial mountains its cool breath to revive and brace the drooping life of lands sweltering under a tropic sun ; and from its lofty, inexhaustible reservoirs it feeds perennial rivers that water the plains when all the wells and streams are white and silent in the baking heat. Without the perpetual snow of mountain regions the earth would be reduced to a lifeless desert.

And not only does the Alpine snow thus keep always full rivers that water the plains, but, by its grinding force as it presses down the mountains, it removes particles from the rocks, which are carried off by the rivers and spread over the plains. Such is the origin of a large part of the level land of Europe. It has been formed out of the ruins of the mountains by the action of snow. It was by the snow of far-off ages that our valleys and lake-basins were scooped out, the form of our landscapes sculptured and rounded, and the soil formed in which we grow our harvests. Who would think of such a connection ? And yet it is true ! Just as each season we owe the bloom and brightness of our summer fields to the gloom and blight of winter, so do we owe the present summer beauty of the world to the great secular winter of the glacial period. And does not God bring about results as striking by agencies apparently as contradictory in the human world ? He who warms the tender latent life of the flowers by the snow, and moulds the quiet beauty of the summer landscape, by the desolating glacier, makes the cold of adversity to cherish the life of the soul, and to round into spiritual loveliness the harshness and roughness of a carnal, selfish nature. Many a profitable Christian life owes its fairness and fruitfulness to causes which wrecked and wasted it for a time. God giveth snow like wool ; and chill and blighting as is the touch of sorrow, it has a protective influence which guards against greater evils ; it sculptures the spiritual landscape within into forms of beauty and grace, and deepens and fertilises the soil of the heart, so that in it may grow from God's own planting the peaceable fruits of righteousness.

And now let us look at the Giver of the snow. *"He* giveth snow like wool." " The snow-flake," as Professor Tyndall strikingly says, " leads back to the sun "—so intimately related are all things to each other in this wonderful universe. It leads further and higher still—even to him who is our sun and shield, the light and heat of all creation. The whole vast realm of winter, with its strange phenomena, is but the breath of God—the Creative Word—as it were, congealed against the blue transparency of space, like the marvellous frost-work on a window-pane. The Psalmist had not the shadow of a doubt that God formed and sent the annual miracle of snow, as he had formed and sent the daily miracle of manna in the desert. It was a common-place thing ; it was a natural, ordinary occurrence ; but it had the Divine sign upon it, and it showed forth the glory and goodness of God as strikingly as the most wonderful supernatural event in his nation's history. When God would impress Job with a sense of his power, it was not to some of his miraculous, but to some of his ordinary works that he appealed. And when the Psalmist would praise God for the preservation of Israel and the restoration of Jerusalem—as he does in the Psalm from which my subject is taken—it is not to the wonderful, miraculous events with which the history of Israel abounded that he directs attention, but to the common events of Providence and the ordinary appearances and processes of nature. He cannot think enough of the Omnipotent Creator and Ruler of the Universe entering into familiar relations with his people, and condescending to their humblest wants. It is the same God that " giveth snow like wool," who " shows his word unto Jacob, and his statutes and commandments unto Israel." And the wonder of the peculiarity is enhanced by thoughts borrowed from the wonders of nature. We know a thousand times more of the nature, formation, and purpose of the snow than the Psalmist did. But that knowledge is dearly earned if our science destroys our faith. What amount or precision of scientific knowledge can compensate us for the loss of the spiritual sensibility, which in all the wonders and beauties of the Creation brings us into personal contact with an infinitely wise mind and an infinitely loving heart ?—*Hugh Macmillan, in "Two Worlds are Ours,"* 1880.

Verse 16.—*"Snow."* It is worth pausing to think what wonderful work is going on in the atmosphere during the formation and descent of every snow shower ; what building power is brought into play ! and how imperfect seem the productions of human minds and hands when compared with those formed by the blind forces of nature ! But who ventures to call the forces of nature blind ? In reality, when we speak thus, we are describing our own condition. The blindness is ours ; and what we really ought to say, and to confess, is that our powers are absolutely unable to comprehend either the origin or the end of the operations of nature.—*John Tyndall, in "The Forms of Water,"* 1872.

Verses 16, 17.—The Lord takes the ice and frost and cold to be his ; it is not only *his* sun, but *his* ice, and *his* frost : " he scattereth *his hoar frost* like ashes." The frost is compared to ashes in a threefold respect. First, because the hoarfrost gives a little interruption to the sight. If you scatter ashes into the air, it darkens the light, so doth the hoar frost. Secondly, the hoary frost is like ashes because near in colour to ashes. Thirdly, 'tis like, because there is a kind of burning in it : frost burns the tender buds and blossoms, it nips them and dries them up. The hoar frost hath its denomination in the Latin tongue from *burning*, and it differs but very little from that word which is commonly used in Latin for a coal of fire. The cold frost hath a kind of scorching in it, as well as the hot sun. Unseasonable frosts in the spring scorch the tender fruits, which bad effect of frost is usually expressed by *carbunculation* or blasting.—*Joseph Caryl.*

Verse 17.—*"He casteth forth his ice like morsels."* Or, *shivers of bread.* It is a worthy saying of one from this text,—The ice is bread, the rain is drink, the snow is wool, the frost a fire to the earth, causing it inwardly to glow with heat; teaching us what to do for God's poor.—*John Trapp.*

Verse 17.—*"He casteth forth his ice like morsels."* The word here translated *"morsels,"* means, in most of the places where it occurs in the Bible, *pieces of bread,* exactly the LXX. ψωμούς ; for this very ice, this wintry cold, is profitable to the earth, to fit it for bearing future harvests, and thus it matures the *morsels of bread* which man will yet win from the soil in due season.—*Genebrardus, in Neale and Littledale.*

Verse 17.—*"Morsels."* Or, *crumbs.* Gen. xviii. 5 ; Judges xix. 5. Doubtless the allusion is to hail.—*A. S. Aglen.*

Verse 17.—" It is extremely severe," said his sister to Archbishop Leighton one day, speaking of the season. The good man only said in reply, " But thou, O God, hast made summer and winter."—*From J. N. Pearson's Life of Archbishop Leighton,* 1830.

Verse 18.—*"He sendeth out his word, and melteth them."* Israel in the captivity had been ice-bound, like ships of Arctic voyagers in the Polar Sea ; but God sent forth the vernal breeze of his love, and the water flowed, the ice melted, and they were released. God turned their captivity, and, their icy chains being melted by the solar beams of God's mercy, they flowed in fresh and buoyant streams, like " rivers of the south," shining in the sun. See Ps. cxxvi. 4.

So it was on the day of Pentecost. The winter of spiritual captivity was thawed and dissolved by the soft breath of the Holy Ghost, and the earth laughed and bloomed with spring-tide flowers of faith, love, and joy.—*Christopher Wordsworth.*

Verse 19.—Here we see God in compassion bending down, in order to communicate to the deeply fallen son of man something of a blessed secret, of which without his special enlightment, the eye would never have seen anything, nor the ear ever have heard.—*J. J. Van Oosterzee, on "The Image of Christ."*

Verses 19, 20.—If the publication of the law by the ministry of angels to the Israelites were such a privilege that it is reckoned their peculiar treasure—*"He hath shewed his statutes unto Israel ; he hath not dealt so with any nation "*—what is the revelation of the gosel by the Son of God himself? For although the law is obscured and defaced since the fall, yet there are some ingrafted notions of it in human nature ; but there is not the least suspicion of the gospel. The law discovers our misery, but the gospel alone shows the way to be delivered from it. If an advantage so great and so precious doth not touch our hearts ; and, in possessing it with joy, if we are not sensible of the engagements the Father of mercies hath laid upon us ; we shall be the ungratefulest wretches in the world.—*William Bates.*

Verses 19, 20.—That some should have more means of knowing the Creator, others less, it is all from the mercy and will of God. His church hath a privilege and an advantage above other nations in the world ; the Jews had this favour above the heathens, and Christians above the Jews ; and no other reason can be assigned but his eternal love.—*Thomas Manton.*

Verse 20.—*"He hath not dealt so with any nation . . . . Praise ye the Lord."* The sweet Psalmist of Israel, a man skilful in praises, doth begin and end this Psalm with *Hallelujah.* In the body of the Psalm he doth set forth the mercy of God, both towards all *creatures* in general in his common providence, and towards his *church* in particular. So in this close of the Psalm : " He sheweth his word unto Jacob, and his statutes to Israel. He hath not dealt so with any nation." In the original 'tis, " He hath not dealt so with *every nation :* " that is, with *any* nation.

In the text you may observe *a position* and *a conclusion*. *A position ;* and that is, that God deals in a singular way of mercy with his people above all other people. And then the *conclusion : "Praise ye the Lord."* Doctrine. That God deals in a singular way of mercy with his people, and therefore expects singular praises from his people.—*Joseph Alleine* (1663—1668), *in "A Thanksgiving Sermon."*

Verse 20.—See the wonderful goodness of God, who besides the light of nature, has committed to us the sacred Scriptures. The heathen are enveloped in ignorance. *"As for his judgments, they have not known them."* They have the oracles of the Sybils, but not the writings of Moses and the apostles. How many live in the region of death, where the bright star of Scripture has never appeared ! We have the blessed Book of God to resolve all our doubts, and to point out a way of life to us. " Lord, how is it thou wilt manifest thyself unto us, and not unto the world ? "—John xiv. 22.—*Thomas Watson.*

HINTS TO PREACHERS.

Verse 1.—Praise. Its profit, pleasure, and propriety.—*J. F.*

Verse 1.—The Reasonable Service. I. The methods of praise : by word, song, life ; individually, socially. II. The offerers of praise : " ye." III. The object of praise : " the Lord, our God." IV. The reasons for praise : it is " good," " pleasant," " becoming."—*C. A. D.*

Verses 1—3.—I. The Privilege of Praising God. 1. It is good. 2. Pleasant. 3. Becoming. II. The Duty of Praising God. 1. For gathering a church for himself among men : " The Lord doth build up Jerusalem." 2. For the materials of which it is composed : " The outcasts," etc. 3. For the preparation of those materials for his purpose : " He healeth," etc., verse 3.—*G. R.*

Verse 2.—The Lord is Architect, Builder, Sustainer, Restorer, and Owner of the Church. In each relation let him be praised.

Verse 2.—The Great Gatherer. I. Strange persons sought for. II. Special search and means made use of. III. Selected centre to which he brings them. IV. Singular exhibition of them for ever and ever in heaven.

Verse 2.—First the church built and then the sinners gathered into it. A prosperous state of the church within necessary to her increase from without.

Verse 2.—See " Spurgeon's Sermons," No. 1302 : " Good Cheer for Outcasts."

Verse 2.—Upbuilding and In gathering. I. The church may be in a fallen condition. II. Its upbuilding is the Lord's work. III. He accomplishes it by gathering together its outcast citizens.—*C. A. D.*

Verse 3.—See " Spurgeon's Sermons," No. 53 : " Healing for the Wounded."

Verse 3.—God a true physician, and a tender nurse.—*J. F.*

Verses 3, 4.—Heaven's Brilliants, and Earth's Broken Hearts. I. The Proprietor of the Stars with the Wounded. The stars left kingless for broken hearts. Jehovah ! with lint and liniment and a woman's hand. Who binds together the stars, shall bind firmly grieved hearts. II. The Gentle Heart-healer with the Stars. Be all power entrusted to such tenderness. Its comely splendour. God guides the stars with an eye on wounded hearts. The hopefulness of prayer. III. Hearts, Stars, and Eternity. Some hearts shall " shine as the stars." Some stars shall expire in "blackness of darkness." God's hand and eye are everywhere making justice certain. Trust and sing.—*W. B. H.*

Verses 3, 4.—God's Compassion and Power. I. Striking diversity of God's cares : " hearts " and " stars." II. Wonderful variety of God's operations. Gently caring for human hearts. Preserving the order, regularity, and stability of creation. III. Blessed results of God's work. Broken hearts healed ; wounds bound up. Light, harmony, and beauty in the heavens. IV. Mighty encouragement to trust in God. God takes care of the universe ; may I not entrust my life, my soul, to him ? Where he rules unquestioned there is light and harmony ; let me not resist his will in my life.—*C. A. D.*

Verse 5.—A contemplation of God's greatness. I. Great in his essential nature. II. Great in power. III. Great in wisdom. Let us draw inferences concerning the insignificance of man, &c.

Verse 6.—Reversal. I. In the estimate of the world the meek are cast down and the wicked lifted up.   II. In the judgment of heaven the meek are lifted up and the wicked cast down.   III. The judgment of heaven will, in the end, be found the true one.—*C. A. D.*

Verse 7.—The use and benefit of singing.

Verse 8.—God in all.   The unity of his plan ; the co-operation of divine forces ; the condescending mercy of the result.

Verse 9.—See " Spurgeon's Sermons," No. 672 : " The Ravens' Cry."

Verse 11.—The singularity of our God, and of his favour.   For which he is to be praised.   I. *The objects of that favour distinguished.*   1. From physical strength. 2. From mental vigour.   3. From self-reliance.   4. From mere capacity for service.   II. *The objects of that favour described.*   1. By emotions relating to God. 2. By the weakest forms of spiritual life.   3. By the highest degrees of it ;   for the maturest saint fears and hopes.   4. By the sacred blend of it.   Fear of our guilt, hope of his mercy.   Fear of self, confidence in God.   Hope of perseverance, fear of sinning.   Hope of heaven, fear of coming short.   Hope of perfection, mourning defects.   III. *The blessing of that favour implied.*   1. God loves to think of them. 2. To be with them.   3. To minister to them.   4. To meet them in their fears and their hopes.   5. To reward them for ever.

Verse 11.—He takes pleasure in their persons, emotions, desires, devotions, hopes, and characters.—*W. W.*

Verse 12.—I. The Lord whom we praise.   II. His praise in our houses—Jerusalem.   III. Our praise in his house—Zion.

Verse 13.—A Strong Church.   I. The utility and value of a strong church. II. The marks which distinguish it.   1. Gates well kept.   2. Increase of membership.   3. The converts blessed to others.   III. The important care of a strong church : to trace all blessing to Zion's God.—*W. B. H.*

Verses 14, 15.—See " Spurgeon's Sermons,'" No. 425 : " Peace at Home, and Prosperity Abroad."

Verses 14, 15.—Church blessings.   I. Peace.   II. Food.   III. Missionary energy. IV. The presence of God : the source of all blessing.

Verse 15 (second clause).—See " Spurgeon's Sermons," No. 1607 : " The Swiftly Running Word."

Verse 16.—The unexpected results of adversity : snow acting as wool.

Verses 16—18.—See " Spurgeon's Sermons," No. 670 : " Frost and Thaw."

Verse 19.—I. God's people.   II. God's Word.   III. God's revelation to the soul.   IV. God's praise for this special revelation.

Verse 20.—Electing Grace inspires the Heart with Praise.   I. God's love has chosen us.   Hallelujah.   II. God has entrusted us with his truth.   Hallelujah. III. God has made us almoners of his bounty.   Hallelujah.   IV. God through us is to save the world.   Hallelujah.—*W. B. H.*

PSALM CXLVIII.

The song is one and indivisible. It seems almost impossible to expound it in detail, for a living poem is not to be dissected verse by verse. It is a song of nature and of grace. As a flash of lightning flames through space, and enwraps both heaven and earth in one vestment of glory, so doth the adoration of the Lord in this Psalm light up all the universe and cause it to glow with a radiance of praise. The song begins in the heavens, sweeps downward to dragons and all deeps, and then ascends again, till the people near unto Jehovah take up the strain. For its exposition the chief requisite is a heart on fire with reverent love to the Lord over all, who is to be blessed for ever.

EXPOSITION.

PRAISE ye the LORD. Praise ye the LORD from the heavens : praise him in the heights.

2 Praise ye him, all his angels : praise ye him, all his hosts.

3 Praise ye him, sun and moon : praise him, all ye stars of light.

4 Praise him, ye heavens of heavens, and ye waters that *be* above the heavens.

5 Let them praise the name of the LORD : for he commanded, and they were created.

6 He hath also stablished them for ever and ever : he hath made a decree which shall not pass.

7 Praise the LORD from the earth, ye dragons, and all deeps :

8 Fire, and hail ; snow, and vapours ; stormy wind fulfilling his word :

9 Mountains, and all hills ; fruitful trees, and all cedars :

10 Beasts, and all cattle ; creeping things, and flying fowl :

11 Kings of the earth, and all people ; princes, and all judges of the earth :

12 Both young men, and maidens ; old men, and children :

13 Let them praise the name of the LORD : for his name alone is excellent ; his glory *is* above the earth and heaven.

14 He also exalteth the horn of his people, the praise of all his saints ; *even* of the children of Israel, a people near unto him. Praise ye the LORD.

1. *"Praise ye the* LORD.*"* Whoever ye may be that hear this word, ye are invited, entreated, commanded, to magnify Jehovah. Assuredly he has made you, and, if for nothing else, ye are bound, upon the ground of creatureship, to adore your Maker. This exhortation can never be out of place, speak it where we may ; and never out of time, speak it when we may. *"Praise ye the* LORD *from the heavens."* Since ye are nearest to the High and lofty One, be ye sure to lead the song. Ye angels, ye cherubim and seraphim, and all others who dwell in the precincts of his courts, praise ye Jehovah. Do this as from a starting-point from which the praise is to pass on to other realms. Keep not your worship to yourselves, but let it fall like a golden shower from the heavens on men beneath. *"Praise him in the heights."* This is no vain repetition ; but after the manner of attractive poesy the truth is emphasized by reiteration in other words. Moreover, God is not only to be praised *from* the heights, but *in* them : the adoration is to be perfected in the heavens from which it takes its rise. No place is too high for the praises of the most High. On the summit of creation the glory of the Lord is to be revealed, even as the tops of the highest Alps are tipped with the golden light of the same sun which glads the valleys. Heavens and heights become the higher and the more heavenly as they are made to resound with the praises

of Jehovah. See how the Psalmist trumpets out the word "PRAISE." It sounds forth some nine times in the first five verses of this song. Like minute-guns, exultant exhortations are sounded forth in tremendous force—*Praise! Praise! Praise!* The drum of the great King beats round the world with this one note—*Praise! Praise! Praise!* "Again they said, Hallelujah." All this praise is distinctly and personally for Jehovah. Praise not his servants nor his works; but praise HIM. Is he not worthy of all possible praise? Pour it forth before HIM in full volume; pour it only there!

2. "*Praise ye him all his angels.*" Living intelligences, perfect in character and in bliss, lift up your loudest music to your Lord, each one of you. Not one bright spirit is exempted from this consecrated service. However many ye be, O angels, ye are all *his* angels, and therefore ye are bound, all of you, to render service to your Lord. Ye have all seen enough of him to be able to praise him, and ye have all abundant reasons for so doing. Whether ye be named Gabriel, or Michael, or by whatever other titles ye are known, praise ye the Lord. Whether ye bow before him, or fly on his errands, or desire to look into his covenant, or behold his Son, cease not, ye messengers of Jehovah, to sound forth his praise while ye move at his bidding. "*Praise ye him, all his hosts.*" This includes angelic armies, but groups with them all the heavenly bodies. Though they be inanimate, the stars, the clouds, the lightnings, have their ways of praising Jehovah. Let each one of the countless legions of the Lord of hosts show forth his glory; for the countless armies are all *his*, his by creation, and preservation, and consequent obligation. Both these sentences claim unanimity of praise from those in the upper regions who are called upon to commence the strain—" all his angels, all his hosts." That same hearty oneness must pervade the whole orchestra of praising ones; hence, further on, we read of all stars of light, all deeps, all hills, all cedars, and all people. How well the concert begins when all angels, and all the heavenly host, strike the first joyful notes! In that concert our souls would at once take their part.

3. "*Praise ye him, sun and moon : praise him, all ye stars of light.*" The Psalmist enters into detail as to the heavenly hosts. As all, so each, must praise the God of each and all. The sun and moon, as joint rulers of day and night, are paired in praise : the one is the complement of the other, and so they are closely associated in the summons to worship. The sun has his peculiar mode of glorifying the Great Father of lights, and the moon has her own special method of reflecting his brightness. There is a perpetual adoration of the Lord in the skies : it varies with night and day, but it ever continues while sun and moon endure. There is ever a lamp burning before the high altar of the Lord. Nor are the greater luminaries allowed to drown with their floods of light the glory of the lesser brilliants, for all the stars are bidden to the banquet of praise. Stars are many, so many that no one can count the host included under the words, " all ye stars "; yet no one of them refuses to praise its Maker. From their extreme brilliance they are fitly named " stars of light"; and this light is praise in a visible form twinkling to true music. Light is song glittering before the eye instead of resounding in the ear. Stars without light would render no praise, and Christians without light rob the Lord of his glory. However small our beam, we must not hide it : if we cannot be sun or moon we must aim to be one of the " stars of light," and our every twinkling must be to the honour of our Lord.

4. "*Praise him, ye heavens of heavens.*" By these are meant those regions which are heavens to those who dwell in our heavens ; or those most heavenly of abodes where the most choice of spirits dwell. As the highest of the highest, so the best of the best are to praise the Lord. If we could climb as much above the heavens as the heavens are above the earth, we could still cry out to all around us, " Praise ye the Lord." There can be none so great and high as to be above praising Jehovah. "*And ye waters that be above the heavens.*" Let the clouds roll up volumes of adoration. Let the sea above roar, and the fulness thereof, at the presence of Jehovah, the God of Israel. There is something of mystery about these supposed reservoirs of water ; but let them be what they may, and as they may, they shall give glory to the Lord our God. Let the most unknown and perplexing phenomena take up their parts in the universal praise.

5. "*Let them praise the name of the* LORD ; *for he commanded, and they were created.*" Here is good argument : The Maker should have honour from his works, they should tell forth *his* praise ; and thus they should praise his *name*—by which his character is intended. The name of JEHOVAH is written legibly upon his works,

so that his power, wisdom, goodness, and other attributes are there made manifest to thoughtful men, and thus his name is praised. The highest praise of God is to declare what he is. We can invent nothing which would magnify the Lord : we can never extol him better than by repeating his name, or describing his character. The Lord is to be extolled as creating all things that exist, and as doing so by the simple agency of his word. He cretead by a command ; what a power is this ! Well may he expect those to praise him who owe their being to him. Evolution may be atheistic ; but the doctrine of creation logically demands worship ; and hence, as the tree is known by its fruit, it proves itself to be true. Those who were created by command are under command to adore their Creator. The voice which said " Let them be," now saith " Let them praise."

6. *"He hath also stablished them for ever and ever."* The continued existence of celestial beings is due to the supporting might of Jehovah, and to that alone. They do not fail because the Lord does not fail them. Without his will these things cannot alter ; he has impressed upon them laws which only he himself can change. Eternally his ordinances are binding upon them. Therefore ought the Lord to be praised because he is Preserver as well as Creator, Ruler as well as Maker. *"He hath made a decree which shall not pass."* The heavenly bodies are ruled by Jehovah's decree : they cannot pass his limit, or trespass against his law. His rule and ordination can never be changed except by himself, and in this sense his decree " shall not pass " : moreover, the highest and most wonderful of creatures are perfectly obedient to the statutes of the Great King, and thus his decree is not passed over. This submission to law is praise. Obedience is homage ; order is harmony. In this respect the praise rendered to Jehovah from the " bodies celestial " is absolutely perfect. His almighty power upholds all things in their spheres, securing the march of stars and the flight of seraphs ; and thus the music of the upper regions is never marred by discord, nor interrupted by destruction. The eternal hymn is for ever chanted ; even the solemn silence of the spheres is a perpetual psalm.

7. *"Praise the LORD from the earth."* The song descends to our abode, and so comes nearer home to us. We who are " bodies terrestrial," are to pour out our portion of praise from the golden globe of this favoured planet. Jehovah is to be praised not only *in* the earth but *from* the earth, as if the adoration ran over from this planet into the general accumulation of worship. In the first verse the song was " from the heavens " ; here it is going " from the earth " ; songs coming down from heaven are to blend with those going up from earth. The " earth " here meant is our entire globe of land and water : it is to be made vocal everywhere with praise. *"Ye dragons, and all deeps."* It would be idle to enquire what special sea-monsters are here meant ; but we believe all of them are intended, and the places where they abide are indicated by " all deeps." Terrible beasts or fishes, whether they roam the earth or swim the seas, are bidden to the feast of praise. Whether they float amid the teeming waves of the tropics, or wend their way among the floes and bergs of polar waters, they are commanded by our sacred poet to yield their tribute to the creating Jehovah. They pay no service to man ; let them the more heartily confess their allegiance to the Lord. About " dragons " and " deeps " there is somewhat of dread, but this may the more fitly become the bass of the music of the Psalm. If there be aught grim in mythology, or fantastic in heraldry, let it praise the incomprehensible Lord.

8. *"Fire and hail."* Lightning and hailstones go together. In the plagues of Egypt they co-operated in making Jehovah known in all the terrors of his power. Fire and ice-morsels are a contrast in nature, but they are combined in magnifying the Lord. *"Snow and vapours."* Offsprings of cold, or creations of heat, be ye equally consecrated to his praise. Congealed or expanded vapours, falling flakes or rising clouds, should, rising or falling, still reveal the praises of the Lord. *"Stormy winds fulfilling his word."* Though rushing with incalculable fury, the storm-wind is still under law, and moves in order due, to carry out the designs of God. It is a grand orchestra which contains such wind-instruments as these ! He is a great leader who can keep all these musicians in concert, and direct both time and tune.

9. *"Mountains and all hills."* Towering steeps and swelling knolls alike declare their Creator. " All hills " are to be consecrated ; we have no longer Ebal and Gerizim, the hill of the curse and the hill of the blessing, but all our Ebals are turned to Gerizims. Tabor and Hermon, Lebanon and Carmel, rejoice in the name of the Lord. The greater and the lesser mounts are one in their adoration. Not

only the Alps and the mountains of the Jura thunder out his praise ; but our own Cotswolds and Grampians are vocal with songs in his honour. *"Fruitful trees and all cedars."* Fruit trees and forest trees, trees deciduous or evergreen, are equally full of benevolent design, and alike subserve some purpose of love ; therefore for all and by all let the great Designer be praised. There are many species of cedar, but they all reveal the wisdom of their Maker. When kings fell them, that they may make beams for their palaces, they do but confess their obligation to the King of trees, and to the King of kings, whose trees they are. Varieties in the landscape are produced by the rising and falling of the soil, and by the many kinds of trees which adorn the land : let all, and all alike, glorify their one Lord. When the trees clap their hands in the wind, or their leaves rustle in the gentle breath of Zephyr, they do to their best ability sing out unto the Lord.

10. *"Beasts, and all cattle."* Animals fierce or tame ; wild beasts and domestic cattle ; let all these show forth the praises of Jehovah. Those are worse than beasts who do not praise our God. More than brutish are those who are wilfully dumb concerning their Maker. *"Creeping things, and flying fowl."* The multitudes that throng the earth and the air ; insects of every form and birds of every wing are called upon to join the universal worship. No one can become familiar with insect and bird life without feeling that they constitute a wonderful chapter in the history of divine wisdom. The minute insect marvellously proclaims the Lord's handiwork : when placed under the microscope it tells a wondrous tale. So, too, the bird which soars aloft displays in its adaptation for an aerial life an amount of skill which our balloonists have in vain attempted to emulate. True devotion not only hears the praises of God in the sweet song of feathered ministrels, but even discovers it in the croaking from the marsh or in the buzz of "the bluefly which singeth in the window-pane." More base than reptiles, more insignificant than insects, are songless men.

11. *"Kings of the earth, and all people : princes, and all judges of the earth."* Now the poet has reached our own race, and very justly he would have rulers and subjects, chieftains and magistrates, unite in worshipping the sovereign Lord of all. Monarchs must not disdain to sing, nor must their people refrain from uniting with them. Those who lead in battle and those who decide in courts must neither of them allow their vocations to keep them from reverently adoring the Chief and Judge of all. All people, and all judges, must praise the Lord of all. What a happy day it will be when it is universally acknowledged that through our Lord Jesus, the incarnate Wisdom, "kings reign and princes decree justice"! Alas, it is not so as yet! kings have been patrons of vice, and princes ringleaders in folly. Let us pray that the song of the Psalmist may be realized in fact.

12. *"Both young men, and maidens ; old men, and children."* Both sexes and all ages are summoned to the blessed service of song. Those who usually make merry together are to be devoutly joyful together : those who make up the ends of families, that is to say, the elders and the juveniles, should make the Lord their one and only end. Old men should by their experience teach children to praise ; and children by their cheerfulness should excite old men to song. There is room for every voice at this concert : fruitful trees and maidens, cedars and young men, angels and children, old men and judges—all may unite in this oratorio. None, indeed, can be dispensed with : for perfect Psalmody we must have the whole universe aroused to worship, and all parts of creation must take their parts in devotion.

13. *"Let them praise the name of the LORD."* All that is contained in the name or character of Jehovah is worthy of praise, and all the objects of his creating care will be too few to set it forth in its completeness. *"For his name alone is excellent."* It alone deserves to be exalted in praise, for alone it is exalted in worth. There is none like unto the Lord, none that for a moment can be compared unto him. His unique name should have a monopoly of praise. *"His glory is above the earth and heaven :"* it is therefore alone because it surpasses all others. His royal splendour exceeds all that earth and heaven can express. He is himself the crown of all things, the excellency of the creation. There is more glory in him personally than in all his works united. It is not possible for us to exceed and become extravagant in the Lord's praise : his own natural glory is infinitely greater than any glory which we can render to him.

14. *"He also exalteth the horn of his people."* He hath made them strong, famous, and victorious. His goodness to all his creatures does not prevent his having a

special favour to his chosen nation : he is good to all, but he is God to his people. He lifts up the down-trodden, but he in a peculiar manner lifts up his people. When they are brought low he raises up a horn for them by sending them a deliverer ; when they are in conflict he gives them courage and strength, so that they lift up their horn amid the fray ; and when all is peaceful around them, he fills their horn with plenty, and they lift it up with delight. *"The praise of all his saints."* He is their glory : to him they render praise ; and he by his mercy to them evermore gives them further reasons for praise, and higher motives for adoration. He lifts up their horn, and they lift up his praise. He exalts them, and they exalt him. The Holy One is praised by holy ones. He is their God, and they are his saints ; he makes them blessed, and they bless him in return. *"Even of the children of Israel."* The Lord knoweth them that are his. He knows the name of him with whom he made a covenant, and how he came by that name, and who his children are, and where they are. All nations are bidden in verse 11 to praise the Lord ; but here the call is specially addressed to his elect people, who know him beyond all others. Those who are children of privilege should be children of praise. *"A people near unto him,"* near by kin, and near by care ; near as to manifestation and near as to affection. This is a highly honourable description of the beloved race ; and it is true even more emphatically of the spiritual Israel, the believing seed. This nearness should prompt us to perpetual adoration. The Lord's elect are the children of his love, the courtiers of his palace, the priests of his temple, and therefore they are bound beyond all others to be filled with reverence for him, and delight in him. *"Praise ye the LORD,"* or, *Hallelujah.* This should be the Alpha and Omega of a good man's life. Let us praise God to the end, world without end. The field of praise which lies before us in this Psalm is bounded at beginning and end by landmarks in the form of Hallelujahs, and all that lieth between them is every word of it to the Lord's honour. Amen.

EXPLANATORY NOTES AND QUAINT SAYINGS.

Psalms cxlviii.—cl.—The last three Psalms are *a triad of wondrous praise,* ascending from praise to higher praise, until it becomes " joy unspeakable and full of glory "—exultation which knows no bounds. The joy overflows the soul, and spreads throughout the universe ; every creature is magnetized by it, and drawn into the chorus. Heaven is full of praise, the earth is full of praise, praises rise from under the earth, " every thing that hath breath " joins in the rapture. God is encompassed by a loving, praising creation. Man, the last in creation, but the first in song, knows not how to contain himself. He dances, he sings, he commands all the heavens, with all their angels, to help him, "beasts and all cattle, creeping things and flying fowl " must do likewise, even "dragons " must not be silent, and " all deeps " must yield contributions. He presses even dead things into his service, timbrels, trumpets, harps, organs, cymbals, high-sounding cymbals, if by any means, and by all means, he may give utterance to his love and joy.—*John Pulsford.*

Whole Psalm.—In this splendid anthem the Psalmist calls upon the whole creation, in its two great divisions (according to the Hebrew conception) of heaven and earth, to praise Jehovah : things with and things without life, beings rational and irrational, are summoned to join the mighty chorus. This Psalm is the expression of the loftiest devotion, and it embraces at the same time the most comprehensive view of the relation of the creature to the Creator. Whether it is exclusively the utterance of a heart filled to the full with the thought of the infinite majesty of God, or whether it is also an anticipation, a prophetic forecast, of the final glory of creation, when at the manifestation of the sons of God, the creation itself also shall be redeemed from the bondage of corruption (Rom. viii. 18—23), and the homage of praise shall indeed be rendered by all things that are in heaven and earth and under the earth, is a question into which we need not enter.—*J. J. Stewart Perowne.*

Whole Psalm.—Milton, in his Paradise Lost (Book V., line 153, etc.), has elegantly imitated this Psalm, and put it into the mouth of Adam and Eve as their morning hymn in a state of innocency.—*James Anderson.*

Whole Psalm.—Is this universal praise never to be realized? is it only the longing, intense desire of the Psalmist's heart, which will never be heard on earth, and can only be perfected in heaven? Is there to be no jubilee in which the mountains and the hills shall break forth into singing, and all the trees of the field shall clap their hands? If there is to be no such day, then is the word of God of none effect; if no such universal anthem is to swell the chorus of heaven, and to be re-echoed by all that is on earth, then is God's promise void. It is true, in this Psalm our translation presents it to us as a call or summons for everything that hath or hath not breath to praise the Lord—or as a petition that they may praise; but it is in reality a prediction that they *shall* praise. . . . This Psalm is neither more nor less than a glorious prophecy of that coming day, when not only shall the knowledge of the Lord be spread over the whole earth, as the waters cover the sea, but from every created object in heaven and in earth, animate and inanimate, from the highest archangel through every grade and phase of being, down to the tiniest atom—young men and maidens, old men and children, and all kings and princes, and judges of the earth, shall unite in this millennial anthem to the Redeemer's praise.—*Barton Bouchier.*

Verse 1.—*"Praise ye the LORD,"* etc. All things praise, and yet he says, *"Praise ye."* Wherefore doth he say, *"Praise ye,"* when they are praising? Because he delighteth in their praising, and therefore it pleaseth him to add, as it were, his own encouragement. Just as, when you come to men who are doing any good work with pleasure in their vineyard or in their harvest-field, or in some other matter of husbandry, you are pleased at what they are doing, and say, " Work on," " Go on " ; not that they may begin to work, when you say this, but, because you are pleased at finding them working, you add your approbation and encouragement. For by saying, " Work on," and encouraging those who are working, you, so to speak, work with them in wish. In this sort of encouragement, then, the Psalmist, filled with the Holy Ghost, saith this.—*Augustine.*

Verse 1.—The thrice-repeated exhortation, *"Praise . . Praise . . Praise,"* in this first verse is not merely imperative, nor only hortative, but it is an exultant hallelujah.—*Martin Geier.*

Verse 1.—*"From the heavens : praise him in the heights."* Or, high places. As God in framing the world begun above, and wrought downward, so doth the Psalmist proceed in this his exhortation to all creatures to praise the Lord.—*John Trapp.*

Verse 1.—*"Praise him in the heights."* The principle applied in this verse is this, that those who have been exalted to the highest honours of the created universe, should proportionately excel in their tribute of honour to him who has exalted them. —*Hermann Venema.*

Verse 1.—Bernard, in his sermon on the death of his brother Gerard, relates that in the middle of his last night on earth his brother, to the astonishment of all present, with a voice and countenance of exultation, broke forth in the words of the Psalmist—*"Praise the Lord of heaven, praise him in the heights !"*

Verse 2.—*"Praise ye him, all his angels."* Angels are first invoked, because they can praise God with humility, reverence, and purity. The highest are the humblest, the leaders of all created hosts are the most ready themselves to obey.— *Thomas Le Blanc.*

Verse 2.—*"Praise ye him, all his angels."* The angels of God were his first creatures ; it has even been thought that they existed prior to the inanimate universe. They were already praising their Maker before the light of day, and they have never ceased their holy song. Angels praise God best in their holy service. They praised Christ as God when they sang their *Gloria in Excelsis* at the Incarnation, and they praised him as man when they ministered to him after his temptation and before his crucifixion. So also now angels praise the Lord by their alacrity in ministering to his saints.—*John Lorinus.*

Verse 2.—*"Praise ye him, all his hosts."* That is, his creatures (those above especially which are as his *cavalry*) called his "hosts," for, 1, Their number ; 2, their order ; 3, their obedience.—*John Trapp.*

Verse 3.—*"Praise ye him, sun and moon,"* etc. How does the *sun* specially praise Jehovah? 1. By its beauty. Jesus son of Sirach calls it the " globe of beauty." 2. By its fulness. Dion calls it " the image of the Divine capacity."

3. By its exaltation. Pliny calls it *cæli rector*, " the ruler of heaven." 4. By its perfect brightness. Pliny adds that it is " the mind and soul of the whole universe." 5. By its velocity and constancy of motion. Martian calls it " the Guide of Nature." God the Supreme was depicted by the ancients holding in his hand a wreath of stars, to show the double conception, that they both obey and adorn him.— *Thomas Le Blanc.*

Verses 3, 4.—Let the sun, the fount of light, and warmth, and gladness, the greater light which rules the day, the visible emblem of the Uncreated Wisdom, the Light which lighteth every man, the centre round whom all our hopes and fears, our wants and prayers, our faith and love, are ever moving,—let the moon, the lesser light which rules the night, the type of the Church, which giveth to the world the light she gains from the Sun of Righteousness,—let the stars, so vast in their number, so lovely in their arrangement and their brightness, which God hath appointed in the heavens, even as he hath appointed his elect to shine for ever and ever,—let all the heavens with all their wonders and their worlds, the depths of space above, and the waters which are above the firmament, the images of God's Holy Scripture and of the glories and the mysteries contained therein,—let these ever praise him who made and blessed them in the beginning of the creation.— *J. W. Burgon.*

Verses 3, 4.—

> Praise him, thou golden-tressèd sun ;
> Praise him, thou fair and silver moon,
> And ye bright orbs of streaming light ;
> Ye floods that float above the skies,
> Ye heav'ns, that vault o'er vault arise,
> Praise him, who sits above all height.

Richard Mant.

Verse 4.—"*Praise him, ye heavens of heavens,*" etc. From the heavenly inhabitants the poetic strain passes in transition to the *heavens* themselves. There are orders of heavens, ranks and heights supreme, and stages and degrees of lower altitude. This verse sublimely traverses the immensities which are the home of the most exalted dignities who wait on Deity, and then it descends to the firmament where the meteors flash forth, and where the heavens stoop to lift the clouds that aspire from earth. And the idea sustained is that all these vast realms, higher and lower, are one temple of unceasing praise.—*Hermann Venema.*

Verse 4.—The ancients thought there was an ethereal and lofty ocean in which the worlds floated like ships in a sea.—*Thomas Le Blanc.*

Verses 5, 6.—This is the account of creation in a word—He spake ; it was done. When Jesus came, he went everywhere showing his Divinity by this evidence, that his word was omnipotent. These verses declare two miracles of God's Will and Word, viz., the creation and consolidation of the earth. Jehovah first produced matter, then he ordered and established it.—*John Lorinus.*

Verse 6.—"*He hath also stablished them for ever and ever,*" etc. Here two things are set before us, the permanence and the cosmic order of creation. Each created thing is not only formed to endure, in the type or the development, if not in the individual, but has its place in the universe fixed by Gods decree, that it may fulfil its appointed share of working out his will. They raise a question as to the words "*for ever and ever,*" how they can be reconciled with the prophecy, Isaiah lxv. 17 : " Behold, I create new heavens and a new earth : and the former shall not be remembered, nor come into mind " ; a prophecy confirmed by the Lord himself, saying, " Heaven and earth shall pass away," and seen fulfilled in vision by the beloved disciple. Matt. v. 18 ; Rev. xxi. 1. And they answer that just as man dies and rises again to incorruption, having the same personality in a glorified body, so will it be with heaven and earth. Their qualities will be changed, not their identity, in that new birth of all things.—*Neale and Littledale.*

Verse 6.—"*For ever and ever.*"

> My heart is awed within me, when I think
> Of the great miracle which still goes on,
> In silence, round me—the perpetual work
> Of thy creation, finished, yet renewed,
> For ever.

William Cullen Bryant, 1794—1878.

Verse 6.—"*He hath made a decree,*" etc. Rather, *He hath made an ordinance, and will not trangress it.* This is more obvious and natural than to supply a new subject to the second verb, "and none of them transgress it." This anticipates, but only in form, the modern scientific doctrine of the inviolability of natural order. It is the imperishable faithfulness of God that renders the law invariable.—*A. S. Aglen.*

Verse 7.—"*Dragons.*" The word *tanninim*, rendered "*dragons,*" is a word which may denote whales, sharks, serpents, or sea-monsters of any kind (Job vii. 1 ; Ezek. xxix. 3).—*John Morison.*

Verse 7.—"*Sea-monsters,*" in Revised Version. Fishes constrain our admiration, as a created wonder, by the perfection of their form, their magnitude, their adaptation to the element they inhabit, and their multitude. Thus their very nature praises the Creator.—*Thomas Le Blanc.*

Verses 7, 8.—He calls to the *deeps, fire, hail, snow, mountains, and hills,* to bear a part in this work of praise. Not that they are able to do it actively, but to show that man is to call in the whole creation to assist him passively, and should have so much charity to all creatures as to receive what they offer, and so much affection to God as to present to him what he receives from him. *Snow* and *hail* cannot bless and praise God, but man ought to bless God for those things, wherein there is a mixture of trouble and inconvenience, something to molest our sense, as well as something that improves the earth for fruit.—*Stephen Charnock.*

Verses 7—10.—Here be many things easy to be understood, they are clear to every eye ; as when David doth exhort " kings " and " princes," " old men " and " babes " to praise God ; that is easy to be done, and we know the meaning as soon as we look on it ; but here are some things again that are hard to be understood, dark and obscure, and they are two :—

First, in that David doth exhort *dumb, unreasonable, and senseless creatures* to praise God, such as cannot hear, at least cannot understand. Doth the Holy Ghost in the gospel bid us avoid impertinent speeches, and vain repetitions, and shall we think he will use them himself ? No, no. But,

Secondly, not only doth he call upon these creatures, but also he calls upon the "*deeps*" and the "*seas*" to praise God ; these two things are hard to be conceived. But to give you some reasons.

The first reason may be this, why David calls upon the unreasonable creatures to perform this duty,—*He doth his duty like a faithful preacher,* whether they will hear or no that he preaches to, yet he will discharge his soul : a true preacher, he speaks forth the truth, and calls upon them to hear, though his auditors sleep, are careless, and regard it not. So likewise doth David, in this sense, with these creatures ; he doth his duty, and calls upon them to do it, though they understand not, though they comprehend it not. And likewise he doth it to show his vehement desire for all creatures to praise God.

The second reason may be this : *he doth it craftily,* by way of policy, to incite others to perform this duty, that if such creatures as they ought to do this, then those that are above them in degree have more cause, and may be ashamed to neglect it ; as an ill-governed master, though he stay himself at home, yet he will send his servants to church : so David, being conscious of his own neglect, yet he calls upon others not to be slack and negligent : though he came infinitely short of that he should do, yet he shows his own desire for all creatures to perform this duty.

But if these reasons will not satisfy you, though they have done many others, a third reason may be this : *to set forth the sweet harmony that is among all God's creatures ;* to show how that all the creatures being God's family, do with one consent speak and preach aloud God's praise ; and therefore he calls upon some above him, some below him, on both sides, everywhere, to speak God's praise ; for every one in their place, degree, and calling, show forth, though it be in a dumb sense and way, their Creator's praise.

Or, fourthly, and lastly, which I think to be a good reason : *zeal makes men speak and utter things impossible ;* the fire of zeal will so transport him that it will make him speak things unreasonable, impossible, as Moses in his zeal desired God, for the safety of Israel, " to blot his name out of his book " ; and Paul wished himself " anathema," accursed or separate from Christ, for his brethren's salvation, which was a thing impossible, it could not be.—*John Everard, in "Some Gospel Treasures,"* 1653.

Verses 7—10.—The ox and the ass acknowledge their master. The winds and the sea obey him. It should seem that as there is a religion above man, the religion of angels, so there may be a religion beneath man, the religion of dumb creatures. For wheresoever there is a service of God, in effect it is a religion. Thus according to the several degrees and difference of states—the state of nature, grace, and glory —religion may likewise admit of degrees.—*G. G., in a sermon entitled "The Creatures Praysing God,"* 1662.

Verse 8.—This verse arrays in striking order three elements that are ever full of movement and power—*ignea, aquea, aërea ;* fire (or caloric), water (or vapour), and air (or wind). The first includes meteors, lightnings and thunders ; the second, snow, hoar-frost, dew, mist and rain; the third breezes, tempests and hurricanes. —*Hermann Venema.*

Verse 8.—*"Fire and hail."* These are contrasted with one another. *"Snow and mist."* The mist is the vapour raised by the heat of the sun, and therefore suitably contrasted with the snow, which is the effect of cold. *"Stormy wind"* (Ps. cvii. 25), which accompanies the changes of temperature in the air.—*James G. Murphy.*

Verse 8.—*"Snow."* As sure as every falling flake of winter's snow has a part in the great economy of nature, so surely has every Word of God which falls within the sanctuary its end to accomplish in the moral sphere. I have stood on a winter's day, and seen the tiny flakes in little clouds lose themselves one by one in the rushing river. They seemed to die to no purpose—to be swallowed up by an enemy which ignored both their power and their existence. And so have I seen the Word of God fall upon human hearts. Sent of God, from day to day and from year to year, I have seen it dropping apparently all resultless into the fierce current of unbelief—into the fiercer gulf-stream of worldliness which was sweeping through the minds and the lives of the hearers. But as I stood upon the river's bank and looked upon what seemed to be the death of the little fluttering crystal, a second thought assured me that it was but death into life, and that every tiny flake which wept its life away in the rushing waters, became incorporate with the river's being. So when I have seen the Word of God fall apparently fruitless upon the restless, seething, rushing current of human life, a recovered faith in the immutable declaration of God has assured me that what I looked upon was not a chance or idle death, but rather the falling of the soldier, after that he had wrought his life-force into the destiny of a nation and into the history of a world. And so it must ever be. The Word of God ever reaches unto its end.—*S. S. Mitchell, in a Sermon entitled "The Coming of the Snow and the Coming of the Word,"* 1884.

Verse 8.—The *"stormy wind"* is the swift messenger of God, Ps. cxlvii. 15. The hurricane fulfils the divine command. See Matt. viii. 27. " Even the winds and the sea obey him." The *"wind"* is the minister of judgment. See Ezek. xiii. 13. The words of this verse have special use ; for men are exceedingly apt to ascribe the violence of tempests to blind chance.—*Martin Geier.*

Verse 8.—The half-learned man is apt to laugh at the simple faith of the clown or savage, who tells us that rain comes from God. The former, it seems, has discovered that it is the product of certain laws of air, water, and electricity. But truly the peasant is the more enlightened of the two, for he has discovered the main cause, and the real Actor, while the other has found only the second cause, and the mere instrument. It is as if a friend were to send us a gift of ingenious and beautiful workmanship, and just as our gratitude was beginning to rise to the donor, some bystanders were to endeavour to damp it all, by telling us that the gift is the product of certain machinery he had seen.—*James MacCosh,* 1811.

Verse 9.—*"Mountains and all hills,"* etc.—The diversifying of the face of the earth with higher and lower parts, with mountains, hills, and valleys, and the adorning of the face thereof with trees of varied sorts, contributeth much to the praise of God. —*David Dickson.*

Verse 9.—*"Mountains and all hills."* What voices have the hills ! How solemn the sounds of the mountains from their sublime solitudes ! The mountains thunder, and the hills re-echo ; but they speak peace and send down plenty to the vales in running rivulets.—*Thomas Le Blanc.*

Verse 9.—*"Fruitful trees and all cedars."* The praise of God is in the rustling voices of the trees. They fulfil his purpose in giving fruit to refresh, and shelter and shadow for a covert, and their murmur is the soft cadence that chants mercy and grace. In India, the ancients reported that the trees were worshipped as divine, and death was a penalty awarded to those who cut them down. In classic mythology the groves were the homes of gods. Jehovah decreed that an ark of safety for man, and also a temple for himself, should be constructed of wood. Thus more than any other created things, the trees of the wood have redounded to his glory.—*Le Blanc.*

Verse 9.—*"Fruitful trees."* Rather *fruit trees;* the fruit-bearing tree being representative of one division of the vegetable world, planted and reared by man; the "cedars" of the other, which are (Ps. civ. 16) of God's own plantation. So in verse 10 we have *wild* animals and *domesticated* animals.—*A. S. Aglen.*

Verse 9.—*"Trees."*

> All creatures of the eternal God but man,
> In several sorts do glorify his name;
> Each tree doth seem ten thousand tongues to have,
> With them to laud the Lord omnipotent;
> Each leaf that with wind's gentle breath doth wave,
> Seems as a tongue to speak to that intent,
> In language admirably excellent.
> The sundry sorts of fragrant flowers do seem
> Sundry discourses God to glorify,
> And sweetest volumes may we them esteem;
> For all these creatures in their several sort
> Praise God, and man unto the same exhort.
>
> *Peter Pett,* 1599.

Verse 9.—*"All cedars."* Beautiful indeed is the pine forest in all seasons: in the freshness of spring, when the gnarled boughs are penetrated and mollified by the soft wind and the warm sun, and, thrilled with new life, burst out into fringes and tassels of the richest green, and cones of the tenderest purple; beautiful in the sultry summer, when among its cool, dim shadows the heated hours all day sing vespers, while the open landscape is palpitating in the scorching heat; beautiful in the sadness of autumn, when its unfading verdure stands out in striking relief amid changing scenes, that have no sympathy with anything earthly save sorrow and decay, and directs the thoughts to the imperishableness of the heavenly Paradise; beautiful exceedingly in the depth of winter, when the tiers of branches are covered with pure, unsullied wreaths of snow, sculptured by the wind into curves of exquisite grace. It is beautiful in calm, when the tree-tops scarce whisper to each other, and the twitter of the golden wren sounds loud in the expectant hush; it is more than beautiful in storm, when the wild fingers of the wind play the most mournful music on its great harp-strings, and its full diapason is sublime as the roar of the ocean on a rock-bound shore. I do not wonder that the northern imagination in heathen times should have invested it with awe and fear as the favourite haunt of Odin and Thor; or that, in after times, its long rows of trunks, vanishing in the dim perspective, should have furnished designs for the aisles of Christian temples, and the sunset, burning among its fretted branches, should have suggested the gorgeous painted window of the cathedral. It looks like a place made for worship, all its sentiments and associations seem of a sacred and solemn character. Nature, with folded hands, as Longfellow says, seems kneeling there in prayer. It certainly reminds us in various ways of the power, wisdom, and goodness of him who thus spake by the mouth of his prophet: "I will plant in the wilderness the cedar, the fir tree, and the pine, and the box tree together: that they may see, and know, and consider, and understand together, that the hand of the Lord hath done this, and the Holy One of Israel hath created it."—*Hugh Macmillan, in "Bible Teachings in Nature,"* 1867.

Verse 10.—*"Creeping things."* In public worship all should join. The little strings go to make up a concert, as well as the great.—*Thomas Goodwin.*

Verse 10.—*"Flying fowl."* Thus the air is vocal. It has a hallelujah of its own. The *"flying fowl"* praise him; whether it be "the stork that knoweth her appointed time" (Jer. viii. 7), or "the sparrow alone upon the housetop" (Ps. cii. 7), or "the raven of the valley" (Prov. xxx. 17), or the eagle "stirring up her nest, and fluttering over her young" (Deut. xxxii. 11), or the turtle making its voice to be heard in the land (Song. ii. 12), or the dove winging its way to the wilderness (Ps. lv. 6). This is creation's harp (truer and sweeter than Memnon's), which each sunrise awakens, "turning all the air to music."—*Horatius Bonar, in "Earth's Morning; or, Thoughts on Genesis," 1875.*

Verse 11.—*"Kings of the earth, and all people; princes."* As kings and princes are blinded by the dazzling influence of their station, so as to think the world was made for them, and to despise God in the pride of their hearts, he particularly calls them to this duty; and, by mentioning them first, he reproves their ingratitude in withholding their tribute of praise when they are under greater obligations than others. As all men originally stand upon a level as to condition, the higher persons have risen, and the nearer they have been brought to God, the more sacredly are they bound to proclaim his goodness. The more intolerable is the wickedness of kings and princes who claim exemption from the common rule, when they ought rather to inculcate it upon others, and lead the way. He could have addressed his exhortation at once summarily to all men, as indeed he mentions *people* in general terms; but by thrice specifying *princes* he suggests that they are slow to discharge the duty, and need to be urged to it.—*John Calvin.*

Verse 11.—*"Kings of the earth"; "judges of the earth";* these are not proud but humiliating titles; for *earthly* kings and *earthly* judges will not be kings and judges long.

Verse 12.—*"Both young men, and maidens; old men, and children."* The parties are mentioned by couples, being tied two and two together. *"Young men and maidens; old men and children."* And here is a double *caveat*; first, against presumption; and secondly, against despair. First, that the younger sort might desire to praise God, they are exhorted to address themselves to the service of God, to remember their Creator in the days of their youth. Secondly, for aged men, that they might not doubt of the acceptation of their service, our Prophet exhorts them also. For the first, you know, David calls upon the sun and the moon to praise God. Should the sun reply, I will not do it in the morning, or at noon time, but when I am about to set? or the moon reply, I will not in the full, but in the wane? or the tree, not in the spring time, or in the summer, but at the fall of the leaf? So likewise, thou young man, defer not the time of praising God: take the swing of thy youth, and do not defer to apply thyself to the service of God till thy old age; but remember that for all these things thou shalt come to judgment. He that styles himself by the title *I AM*, cares not for I will be, or I have been, but he that is at this present: take heed, therefore, thou strong and lusty young man: the Devil that holds thee now will every day tie a new cord about thee. Consider this, you that are yet young, whom the morning sun of light adorns with his glorious rays: everyone doth not live to be old. Let us not procrastinate in God's service; for the longer we defer to serve God, the farther God's grace is distant from us, and the dominion of Satan is more strengthened in our hearts; the more we delay, the more is our debt, the greater our sin, and the less our grace. I will commend this lesson unto all. He that doth not repent to-day hath a day more to repent of, and a day less to repent in. I shall conclude with a hearty exhortation for us all, of what sex, age, and degree soever; I could wish that all our lives might end like this book of Psalms, in blessing and praising Almighty God.—*Thomas Cheshire, in "A Sermon preached in Saint Paule's Church," 1641.*

Verse 12.—*"Old men."* Think not, ye who are now near the end of life, that your tongues may without blame be silent in the praises of the Lord, because you are come to those years in which men say, they "have no pleasure in them." Were you not frequently praising God when you were children and young men? Have you less, or have you not greater, reason now to praise God than in those early days of life?

Old men ought to be better qualified than young persons to show forth the glory both of the perfections and works of God, because they have enjoyed more time, and more abundant opportunities than their juniors, for attaining the knowledge of God, and of those glorious perfections and works which furnish us with endless materials for praise. "Days should speak, and the multitude of years should teach wisdom."

The heavens are constantly declaring "the glory of God, and the firmament showeth forth his handy work. Day unto day uttereth speech, and night unto night showeth knowledge." Have you, then, lived twenty thousand days and twenty thousand nights? What deep impressions ought to be made upon your spirits, of those wonders which have been preached in your ears or eyes, ever since you could use your bodily senses as ministers to your intellectual powers ! All the works of God praise him, by showing forth how wonderful in power, and goodness, and wisdom, the Creator is. Your tongues are indeed inexcusable, if they are silent in the praises of him whose glory is proclaimed by every object above or around them, and even by every member of their own bodies, and every faculty of their souls. But old men are doubly inexcusable, if they are inattentive to those precious instructions which are given them by all the works of God which they have seen, or of which they have been informed, every day since the powers of their rational natures began to operate.

But old men in this highly favoured land have been blessed with more excellent instructions than those which are given them by the mountains and fruitful valleys, by the dragons of the desert or the deep, or by the fowls of heaven and the beasts of the earth, or by the sun and stars of heaven. For many more years than young men or maidens you have been learners, or you are very blamable if you have not been at the school of Christ. You were' early taught to read the Word of God. In the course of fifty or sixty years, you have probably heard six thousand religious discourses from the ministers of Christ, not to mention other excellent means you have enjoyed for increasing in the knowledge of God. " For the time," says Paul to the Hebrew Christians, " ye might have been teachers." May I not say the same to all aged Christians, who have had the Bible in their possession, and have enjoyed opportunities of frequenting the holy assemblies from their earliest days ? May it not be expected that your hearts and your mouths will be filled with the praises of God, not only as your Maker, but as your Redeemer ?

But there are many things more especially relating to themselves, which should induce the aged to abound in this duty of praise to God.

Consider how long you have lived. Is not every day of life, and even every hour, and every moment, an undeserved mercy ? You might have been cut off from the breast and the womb, for you were conceived in iniquity and born in sin. How many of your race have been cut off before they could distinguish between their right hand and their left, before they could do good or evil ! Since you were moral agents, not a day has passed in which you were not chargeable with many sins. What riches of long-suffering is manifested in a life of sixty or seventy years ! If you have lived in a state of sin all that time, have you not reason to be astonished, that you are not already in a condition which would for ever render it impossible for you to utter the voice of praise ? Give glory, therefore, to that God who has still preserved you alive.

Consider with what mercies your days have been filled up. God's mercies have been new to you every morning, although every day you have sinned against him.

Reflections on your own conduct through life will suggest to you many reasons for praise and thanksgiving. But on this part of the subject it is proper to put you in mind of the two great classes into which men are divided : saints and sinners. If you belong to the former class, who is it that has made you to differ from others ? Give thanks to him who delivered you from the power of darkness, and translated you into the kingdom of his dear Son. Have you been enabled to do some good works in the course of your lives ? For every one of them bless God, who wrought " in you both to will and to do of his good pleasure." Have any of your endeavours been successful to bring about the reformation of any of your fellow-men, or to promote their spiritual welfare ? What sufficient thanks can you render to God for making you the humble ministers of his grace ?

But there are too many of the old who have no reason to think that they have yet passed from death to life. These, certainly, are very unfit to praise God, and will not be able to praise him with their hearts, unless that change pass upon them, without which no man shall ever enter into the kingdom of heaven. Yet, surely, they have great reason to praise the Lord ; and they may see good reason for it, although they cannot carry their knowledge into practice. You have, indeed, greater reason to praise God that you are in the land of the living than those who are in a better state ; because, if you were deprived of your present life, nothing is left for you but the terrors of eternal death. Bless God, ye who have lived fifty or sixty years in sin, and have been all along spared in a world so full of mercy. You are still called by the gospel to receive that salvation which you have long treated with contempt.—*Condensed from a Sermon by George Lawson* (1749—1820), *entitled, "The Duty of the Old to praise God."*

Verse 12.—"*Old men and children.*" It is interesting always to see a friendship between the old and the young. It is striking to see the aged one retaining so much of freshness and simplicity as not to repel the sympathies of boyhood. It is surprising to see the younger one so advanced and thoughtful, as not to find dull the society of one who has outlived excitability and passion.—*Frederick William Robertson.*

Verses 12, 13.—The Psalms are church songs, and all who belong to the church are to sing them. "*Both young men, and maidens; old men, and children; let them praise the name of the* LORD." The ripe believer who can triumph in the steadfast hope of God's glory, is to lend his voice to swell the song of the church when she cries to God out of the depths; and the penitent, who is still sitting in darkness, is not to refrain his voice when the church pours out in song her sense of God's love. The whole church has fellowship in the Psalms.—*William Binnie, in "The Psalms, their History, Teachings, and Use,"* 1870.

Verses 12, 13.—"*Old men . . . Let them praise the name of the* LORD." It is a favourite speculation of mine that if spared to sixty we then enter on the seventh decade of human life, and that this, if possible, should be turned into the Sabbath of our earthly pilgrimage and spent sabbatically, as if on the shores of an eternal world, or in the outer courts, as it were, of the temple that is above, the tabernacle in heaven.—*Thomas Chalmers.*

Verse 13.—"*Let them praise.*" Exactly as at the close of the first great division of the anthem (verse 5), and, in the same way as there, the reason for the exhortation follows in the next clause. But it is a different reason. It is no longer because he has given them a decree, bound them as passive, unconscious creatures by a law which they cannot transgress. (It is the fearful mystery of the reasonable will that it can transgress the law.) It is because his name is exalted, so that the eyes of men can see, and the hearts and tongues of men confess it; it is because he has graciously revealed himself to, and mightily succoured, the people whom he loves, the nation who are near to him. If it be said that what was designed to be a Universal Anthem is thus narrowed at its close, it must be remembered that, however largely the glory of God was written on the visible creation, it was only to the Jew that any direct revelation of his character had been made.—*J. J. Stewart Perowne.*

Verse 13.—"*The name of Jehovah.*" Jehovah is a name of great power and efficacy, a name that hath in it five vowels, without which no language can be expressed; a name that hath in it also three syllables, to signify the Trinity of Persons, the eternity of God, One in Three, and Three in One; a name of such dread and reverence amongst the Jews, that they tremble to name it, and therefore they use the name *Adonai* (Lord) in all their devotions. And thus ought every one to stand in awe, and sin not by taking the name of God in vain; but to sing praises, to honour, to remember, to declare, to exalt, and bless it; for holy and reverend, only worthy and excellent is his name.—*Rayment,* 1630.

Verse 14.—"*His people, the praise of all his saints.*" But among all, one class in particular is called on to praise him, for they have an additional motive for so doing, namely, "*his people,*" and "*his saints.*" As man above all the creatures, so among men his elect or chosen, who are the objects of his special grace, and, above all, of his redeeming love. "*He also exalteth the horn of his people*"—exalts them, one and all, from the death of sin to the life of righteousness, and consequent on this, from the dust of earth to the glory of heaven. "*The praise of all his saints*"; and, yet again, among them, of one people in particular—"*even of the children of Israel, a people near unto him.*" "*Near to him*" of old, and yet again to be—yea, nearest of all the peoples of the earth—when he recalls them from their dispersion, and again places his name and his throne among them. HALLELUJAH—PRAISE YE THE LORD.—*William De Burgh.*

Verse 14.—"*A people near unto him.*" Jesus took our nature, and became one with us; thus he is "*near*" unto us; he gives us his Holy Spirit, brings us into union with himself, and thus we are near to him. This is our highest honour, an unfailing source of happiness and peace. We are near to him in point of *relation,* being his children; near to him in point of *affection,* being loved with an everlasting love; we are near to him in point of *union,* being members of his body, of his flesh, and of his bones; we are near to him in point of *fellowship,* walking with him as a man walketh with his friend; we are near to him in point of *attention,* being the objects of his daily, hourly, tender care; we shall soon be near to him in point of *locality,* when our mansion is prepared, for we shall depart to be with Christ, which is far better. We are near to him when poor, and when deeply tried ; and if ever nearer at one time than another, we shall be nearest to him in death. If we are near unto him, he will sympathize with us in all our sorrows, assist us in all our trials, protect us in all our dangers, hold intercourse with us in all our lonely hours, provide for us in all seasons of necessity, and honourably introduce us to glory. Let us realize this fact daily—we are near and dear to our God.—*James Smith.*

HINTS TO PREACHERS.

Whole Psalm.—I. What is implied in the invitation to the natural creation to praise God. 1. That praise is due to God on its account. 2. That it is due from those for whose benefit it was created. 3. That it is a reproof to those who do not praise God who are actually capable of it. " If these should hold their peace, the stones would immediately cry out." II. What is implied in the invitation to innocent beings to praise God. " Praise ye the Lord from the heavens. Praise ye him all his angels, praise ye him all his hosts : " verses 1, 2.—1. That they owe their creation in innocence to God. 2. That they owe their preservation in innocence to him. 3. That they owe the reward of their innocence to him. III. What is implied in the invitation to fallen beings to praise God : " Kings of the earth and all people," etc. : verses 11—13.—1. That God is merciful and ready to forgive. " Not willing that any should perish," etc. They would not be called upon to praise God if they were irrecoverably lost. Our Lord would not when on earth accept praise from an evil spirit. 2. That means of restoration from the fall are provided by God for men. Without this they would have no hope, and could offer no praise. IV. What is implied in the invitation to the redeemed to praise God : verse 14.—1. That God is their God. 2. That all his perfections are engaged for their present and eternal welfare.—*G. R.*

Verse 1.—*"Praise ye the Lord."* I. The Voice—of Scripture. of nature, of grace, of duty. II. The Ear on which it rightly falls—of saints and sinners, old and young, healthy and sick. It falls on our ear. III. The Time when it is heard. Now, ever, yet also at special times. IV. The Response which we will give. Let us now praise with heart, life, lip.

Verse 1 (second and third clauses).—I. The character of the praises of heaven. II. How far they influence us who are here below. III. The hope which we have of uniting in them.

Verse 2.—I. The angels as praiseful servants. II. The other hosts of God, and how they praise him. III. The rule without exception : *"all—all."* Imagine one heavenly being living without praising the Lord !

Verse 3.—I. God's praise continual both day and night. II. Light the leading fountain of this praise. III. Life behind all, calling for the praise.

Verses 5, 6.—Creation and conversation, two chief reasons for praise.

Verse 7.—God's praise from dark, deep, and mysterious things.

Verse 8.—Canon Liddon preached in St. Paul's on Sunday afternoon, December 23, 1883, and took for his text Ps. cxlviii. 8, *"Wind and storm fulfilling his word."* He spoke of the divine use of destructive forces. I. In the physical world we see wind and storm fulfilling God's word. 1. The Bible occasionally lifts the veil, and shows us how destructive forces of Nature have been the servants of God. 2. Modern history illustrates this vividly. II. In the human, spiritual, and moral world, we find new and rich application of the words of the text. 1. In the State we see the storm of invasion and the storm of revolution fulfilling God's word. 2. In the Church we see the storm of persecution and the storm of controversy fulfilling God's word. 3. In the experience of individual life we see outward troubles, and inward storms of religious doubts fulfilling God's word.—*The Contemporary Pulpit*, 1884.

Verse 9.—*"Trees."* The glory of God as seen in trees.

Verse 10.—The wildest, the quietest, the most depressed, and the most aspiring should each have its song.

Verses 11—13.—I. The universal King. Alone in excelling. Supreme in glory.

II. The universal summons. Of all nations, ranks, classes and ages. Foreshadowing the Judgment. III. The universal duty : praise,—constant, emphatic, growing. —*W. B. H.*

Verse 12.—God to be served by strength and beauty, experience and expectation.

Verse 12.—"*And children.*" A Children's Address. I. Where the children are found (verses 11 and 12). In royal and distinguished society : yet not lost or overlooked. II. What they are called to. "Praise the Lord." Even they have abundant reason. III. What are the lessons of the subject ? 1. Children should come up with their parents on the Sabbath. 2. Children should unite in heart and voice in God's praises. 3. Children should seek fitness for this praise by believing in Christ.—*W. B. H.*

Verse 14.—The Favoured People and their God. I. What he does for them. II. What he makes them : "Saints." III. Who they are : "Children of Israel." IV. Where they are : "Near unto him." V. What they do for him : "Praise ye the Lord."

PSALM CXLIX.

We are almost at the last Psalm, and still among the Hallelujahs. This is "a new song," evidently intended for the new creation, and the men who are of new heart. It is such a song as may be sung at the coming of the Lord, when the new dispensation shall bring overthrow to the wicked and honour to all the saints. The tone is exceedingly jubilant and exultant. All through one hears the beat of the feet of dancing maidens, keeping time to the timbrel and harp.

EXPOSITION.

PRAISE ye the LORD. Sing unto the LORD a new song, *and* his praise in the congregation of saints.

2 Let Israel rejoice in him that made him : let the children of Zion be joyful in their King.

3 Let them praise his name in the dance : let them sing praises unto him with the timbrel and harp.

4 For the LORD taketh pleasure in his people : he will beautify the meek with salvation.

5 Let the saints be joyful in glory : let them sing aloud upon their beds.

6 *Let* the high *praises* of God *be* in their mouth, and a two-edged sword in their hand ;

7 To execute vengeance upon the heathen, *and* punishments upon the people ;

8 To bind their kings with chains, and their nobles with fetters of iron ;

9 To execute upon them the judgment written : this honour have all his saints. Praise ye the LORD.

1. *"Praise ye the LORD."* Specially you, ye chosen people, whom he has made to be his saints. You have praised him aforetime, praise him yet again ; yea, for ever praise him. With renewed zeal and fresh delight lift up your song unto Jehovah. *"Sing unto the Lord a new song."* Sing, for it is the fittest method for expressing reverent praise. Sing a hymn newly composed, for you have now a new knowledge of God. He is ever new in his manifestations ; his mercies are new every morning ; his deliverances are new in every night of sorrow ; let your gratitude and thanksgivings be new also. It is well to repeat the old ; it is more useful to invent the new. Novelty goes well with heartiness. Our singing should be " unto the Lord " ; the songs we sing should be of him and to him, " for of him, and to him, and through him are all things." Among our novelties there should be new songs : alas ! men are fonder of making new complaints than new Psalms. Our new songs should be devised in Jehovah's honour ; indeed all our newest thoughts should run towards him. Never can we find a nobler subject for a song than the Lord, nor one more full of fresh matter for a new song, nor one which we are personally so much bound to sing as a new song " unto the Lord." *"And his praise in the congregation of saints."* Saints are precious, and a congregation of saints is a treasure house of jewels. God is in the midst of saints, and because of this we may well long to be among them. They are so full of his praise that we feel at home among them when we are ourselves full of praise. The sanctuary is the house of praise as well as the house of prayer. All saints praise God : they would not be saints if they did not. Their praise is sincere, suitable, seasonable, and acceptable. Personal praise is sweet unto God, but congregated praise has a multiplicity of sweetnesses in it. When holy ones meet, they adore the Holy One. Saints do not gather to amuse themselves with music, nor to extol one another, but to sing his praise whose

saints they are. A congregation of saints is heaven upon earth : should not Jehovah, the Lord of saints, have all the praise that can come from such an assembly ? Yet at times even saintly conclaves need to be stirred up to thanksgiving ; for saints may be sad and apprehensive, and then their spirits require to be raised to a higher key, and stimulated to happier worship.

2. *"Let Israel rejoice in him that made him."* Here is that new creation which calls for the new song. It was Jehovah who made Israel to be Israel, and the tribes to become a great nation : therefore let the Founder of the nation be had in perpetual honour. Joy and rejoicing are evidently to be the special characteristics of the new song. The religion of the dead in sin is more apt to chant dirges than to sing hallelujahs ; but when we are made new in the spirit of our minds we joy and rejoice in him that made us. Our joy is in our God and King : we choose no lower delight. *"Let the children of Zion be joyful in their King."* Those who had seen the tribes formed into a settled kingdom as well as into a united nation should rejoice. Israel is the nation, Zion is the capital of the kingdom : Israel rejoices in her Maker, Zion in her King. In the case of our God we who believe in him are as glad of his Government as we are of his Creation : his reign is as truly the making of us as was his divine power. The children of Israel are happy to be made a people ; the children of Zion are equally happy to be ruled as a people. In every character our God is the source of joy to us : this verse issues a permit to our joy, yea it lays an injunction upon us to be glad in the Lord.

3. *"Let them praise his name in the dance : let them sing praises unto him with the timbrel and harp."* Thus let them repeat the triumph of the Red Sea, which was ever the typical glory of Israel. Miriam led the daughters of Israel in the dance when the Lord had triumphed gloriously ; was it not most fit that she should ? The sacred dance of devout joy is no example, nor even excuse, for frivolous dances, much less for lewd ones. Who could help dancing when Egypt was vanquished, and the tribes were free ? Every mode of expressing delight was bound to be employed on so memorable an occasion. Dancing, singing, and playing on instruments were all called into requisition, and most fitly so. There are unusual seasons which call for unusual expressions of joy. When the Lord saves a soul its holy joy overflows, and it cannot find channels enough for its exceeding gratitude : if the man does not leap, or play, or sing, at any rate he praises God, and wishes for a thousand tongues with which to magnify his Saviour. Who would wish it to be otherwise ? Young converts are not to be restrained in their joy. Let them sing and dance while they can. How can they mourn now that their Bridegroom is with them ? Let us give the utmost liberty to joy. Let us never attempt its suppression, but issue in the terms of this verse a double license for exultation. If any ought to be glad it is the children of Zion ; rejoicing is more fit for Israel than for any other people : it is their own folly and fault that they are not oftener brimming with joy in God, for the very thought of him is delight.

4. *"For the LORD taketh pleasure in his people ;"* and therefore they should take pleasure in him. If our joy be pleasing to him let us make it full. What condescension is this on Jehovah's part, to notice, to love, and to delight in his chosen ! Surely there is nothing in our persons, or our actions, which could cause pleasure to the Ever-blessed One, were it not that he condescends to men of low estate. The thought of the Lord's taking pleasure in us is a mine of joy never to be exhausted. *"He will beautify the meek with salvation."* They are humble, and feel their need of salvation ; he is gracious, and bestows it upon them. They lament their deformity and he puts a beauty upon them of the choicest sort. He saves them by sanctifying them, and thus they wear the beauty of holiness, and the beauty of a joy which springs out of full salvation. He makes his people meek, and then makes the meek beautiful. Herein is grand argument for worshipping the Lord with the utmost exultation : he who takes such a pleasure in us must be approached with every token of exceeding joy.

God taketh pleasure in all his children as Jacob loved all his sons ; but the meek are his Josephs, and upon these he puts the coat of many colours, beautifying them with peace, content, joy, holiness, and influence. A meek and quiet spirit is called " an ornament," and certainly it is " the beauty of holiness." When God himself beautifies a man, he becomes beautiful indeed and beautiful for ever.

The verse may be read, " He shall beautify the meek with salvation," or " He shall beautify the afflicted with deliverance," or, " He shall beautify the meek with victory " ; and each of these readings gives a new shade of meaning, well worthy of quiet consideration. Each reading also suggests new cause for joyful adoration. " O come, let us sing unto the Lord."

5. *"Let the saints be joyful in glory."* God has honoured them, and put a rare glory upon them ; therefore let them exult therein. Shall those to whom God is their glory be cast down and troubled ? Nay, let their joy proclaim their honourable estate. *"Let them sing aloud upon their beds."* Their exultation should express itself in shouts and songs, for it is not a feeling of which they have any need to be ashamed. That which is so fully justified by fact, may well be loudly proclaimed. Even in their quietest retreats let them burst into song ; when no one hears them, let them sing aloud unto God. If confined by sickness let them joy in God. In the night watches let them not lie awake and weep, but like nightingales let them charm the midnight hours. Their shouts are not now for the battlefield, but for the places of their rest : they can peacefully lie down and yet enjoy the victory with which the Lord has beautified them. Without fighting, faith wins and sings the victory. What a blessing to have our beds made into thrones, and our retirements turned into triumphs !

6. *"Let the high praises of God be in their mouth, and a two-edged sword in their hand."* It seems they are not always on their beds, but are ready for deeds of prowess. When called to fight, the meek are very hard to overcome ; they are just as steady in conflict as they are steadfast in patience. Besides, their way of fighting is of an extraordinary sort, for they sing to God but keep their swords in their hands. They can do two things at a time : if they do not wield the trowel and the sword, at least they sing and strike. In this Israel was not an example, but a type : we will not copy the chosen people in making literal war, but we will fulfil the emblem by carrying on spiritual war. We praise God and contend with our corruptions ; we sing joyfully and war earnestly with evil of every kind. Our weapons are not carnal, but they are mighty, and wound with both back and edge. The word of God is all edge ; whichever way we turn it, it strikes deadly blows at falsehood and wickedness. If we do not praise we shall grow sad in our conflict ; and if we do not fight we shall become presumptuous in our song. The verse indicates a happy blending of the chorister and the crusader.

Note how each thing in the believer is emphatic : if he sings, it is high praises, and praises deep down in his throat, as the original hath it ; and if he fights, it is with the sword, and the sword is two-edged. The living God imparts vigorous life to those who trust him. They are not of a neutral tint : men both hear them and feel them. Quiet is their spirit, but in that very quietude abides the thunder of an irresistible force. When godly men give battle to the powers of evil each conflict is high praise unto the God of goodness. Even the tumult of our holy war is a part of the music of our lives.

7. *"To execute vengeance upon the heathen, and punishments upon the people."* This was once literally the duty of Israel : when they came into Canaan they fulfilled the righteous sentence of the Lord upon guilty nations. At this hour, under the gentler dispensation of grace, we wrestle not with flesh and blood ; yet is our warfare none the less stern, and our victory none the less sure. All evil shall eventually be overthrown : the Lord shall display his justice against evil-doers, and in that warfare his servants shall play their parts. The saints shall judge the world. Both the conflict and the victory at the end of it shall cause glory to God, and honour to his holy ones.

8. *"To bind their kings with chains, and their nobles with fetters of iron."* Thus are the greatest enemies of Jehovah and his people reduced to shame, rendered helpless, and themselves punished. This was Israel's boast in actual fact, it is ours spiritually. The chief powers of evil shall be restrained and ultimately destroyed. Those who made captives of the godly shall themselves be made captive. The powers of evil cannot bind *our* King, but by his power *their* king shall be bound with a great chain, and shut up in the bottomless pit, that he may at length be trodden under the feet of saints.

9. *"To execute upon them the judgment written."* Israel as a nation had this to do, and did it, and then they rejoiced in the God who gave success to their arms. *We* praise our God after another fashion ; we are not executioners of justice, but heralds of mercy. It would be a sad thing for any one to misuse this text : lest any warlike believer should be led to do so, we would remind him that the execution must not go beyond the sentence and warrant ; and we have received no warrant of execution against our fellow men. Christians have no commission of vengeance ;

It is theirs to execute the command of mercy, and that alone. *"This honour have all his saints."* All the godly shared in the triumphs of the Lord when he smote Israel's foes. We have like honour, but it is shown in victories of another sort. All the holy ones are sent upon errands by their holy Lord. The honours described in this Psalm are common to all the family of grace; and such service as the Lord appoints is to be undertaken by every one of them, without exception. The Lord honours all his chosen here, and he will glorify them all hereafter : this rule is without exception. Surely in this we have the best argument for glorifying the Lord, wherefore we close our new song with another Hallelujah, *"Praise ye the Lord."*

EXPLANATORY NOTES AND QUAINT SAYINGS.

Whole Psalm.—The foregoing Psalm was a hymn of praise to the Creator; this is a hymn to the Redeemer.—*Matthew Henry.*

Whole Psalm.—The New Testament spiritual church cannot pray as the Old Testament national church here prays. Under the illusion that it must be used as a prayer without any spiritual transmutation, Psalm cxlix. has become the watchword of the most horrible errors. It was by means of this Psalm that Caspar Scloppius, in his *Classicum Belli Sacri*, which, as Bakius says, is written, not with ink, but with blood, inflamed the Roman Catholic princes to the Thirty Years' Religious War. And in the Protestant church Thomas Müntzer stirred up the War of the Peasants by means of this Psalm. We see that the Christian cannot make such a Psalm directly his own, without disavowing the apostolic warning, " The weapons of our warfare are not carnal " (2 Cor. x. 4). The praying Christian must therefore transpose the letter of this Psalm into the spirit of the New Covenant.—*Franz Delitzsch.*

Verse 1.—*"A new song"*; for this Psalm is a song of renovation. If Israel when restored and renewed had new cause for rejoicing, much more should the New Covenant Israel feel constrained to strike the new note of triumph. Infidels blaspheme, the ungrateful murmur, the thoughtless are silent, the mournful weep, all acting according to their. old nature; but new men take up a new mode, which is the divinely-inspired song of peace, charity, and joy in the Lord.—*Johannes Paulus Palanterius.*

Verse 1.—*"A new song."*—The old man hath an old song, the new man a new song. The Old Testament is an old song, the New Testament is a new song. . . . . Whoso loveth earthly things singeth an old song : let him that desireth to sing a new song love the things of eternity. Love itself is new and eternal; therefore is it ever new, because it never groweth old.—*Augustine.*

Verse 1.—*"Saints."*—A title not to be restricted to the godly of the first times, but common to all that are saved in all after-times also, as Eph. iv. 12. This name putteth mere morality and formal profession out of countenance, as the sun doth a glow-worm. Saintship is a matter of Divine workmanship, and therefore it is far more remarkable than human excellence. We should keep up the name of " saints," that the reality of the true religion be not lowered by avoiding this title; for in these times it is to be feared that the name is out of use, because holiness itself is out of fashion.—*Thomas Goodwin.*

Verse 2.—*"Let Israel rejoice,"* etc. Give us, oh, give us the man who sings at his work ! Be his occupation what it may, he is equal to any of those who follow the same pursuit in silent sullenness. He will do more in the same time—he will do it better—he will persevere longer. One is scarcely sensible of fatigue whilst he marches to music. The very stars are said to make harmony as they revolve in their spheres. Wondrous is the strength of cheerfulness, altogether past calculation its powers of endurance. Efforts to be permanently useful must be uniformly joyous—a spiritual sunshine—graceful from very gladness—beautiful because bright.—*Thomas Carlyle.*

Verse 2.—*"Rejoice in him that made him : let the children of Zion be joyful."*

You are never right until you can be heartily merry in the Lord, nor until you can enjoy mirth in connection with holiness.—*Walter Marshall.*

Verse 2.—"*Him that made him.*" Jehovah is called *Maker,* as one who formed Israel as a nation, and constituted the people a kingdom, though they had been a race of slaves. This is more than a general creation of men.—*Hermann Venema.*

Verse 2.—Literally the Hebrew here brings forward the mystic doctrine of the Trinity, for it reads, " Let Israel rejoice in God *his Makers.*"—*Simon de Muis.*

Verse 2.—"*Joyful in their King.*" I beg the reader to remark with me, here is nothing said of Israel being joyful in what their king had done for them. These things in their proper place, became sweet subjects of praise. But the subject of praise in which Israel is now to be engaged is Jesus himself. Reader, pause over this apparently small, but most important, distinction. The Lord is gracious in his gifts, gracious in his love, gracious in his salvation. Every thing he gives, it is from his mercy, and ever to be so acknowledged. But Jesus' gifts are not himself: I cannot be satisfied with his gifts, while I know that to others he gives his *Person.* It is JESUS himself I want. Though he give me all things that I need, yet if he be to me himself all things that I need, in him I have all things. Hence, therefore, let us see that Jesus not only gives us all, but that he is our all.—*Robert Hawker.*

Verse 3.—"*The dance*" was in early times one of the modes of expressing religious joy (Ex. xv. 20 ; 2 Sam. vi. 16). When from any cause men's ideas shall undergo such a revolution as to lead them to do the same thing for the same purpose, it will be time enough to discuss that matter. In our time, dancing has no such use, and cannot, therefore, in any wise be justified by pleading the practice of pious Jews of old.—*William Swan Plumer.*

Verse 3.—"*Let them sing praises unto him with the timbrel and harp.*" They who from hence urge the use of music in religious worship, must, by the same rule, introduce dancing, for they went together, as in David's dancing before the ark (Judges xxi. 21). But whereas many Scriptures in the New Testament keep up singing as a gospel ordinance, none provide for the keeping up of music and dancing; the gospel canon for Psalmody is to " sing with the spirit and with the understanding." —*Matthew Henry.*

Verse 2.—"*Timbrel.*" The *toph* was employed by David in all the festivities of religion (2 Sam. vi. 5). The occasions on which it was used were mostly joyful, and those who played upon it were generally females (Psalm lxviii. 25), as was the case among most ancient nations, and is so at the present day in the East. The usages of the modern East might adequately illustrate all the scriptural allusions to this instrument, but happily we have more ancient and very valuable illustration from the monuments of Egypt. In these we find that the tambourine was a favourite instrument, both on sacred and festive occasions. There were three kinds, differing, no doubt, in sound as well as in form ; one was circular, another square or oblong, and the third consisted of two squares separated by a bar. They were all beaten by the hand, and often used as an accomplishment to the harp and other instruments. The tambourine was usually played by females, who are represented as dancing to its sound without the accompaniment of any other instrument.—*John Kitto.*

Verse 3.—"*Harp.*" Of the *kinnor* the Scripture affords little further information than that it was composed of the sounding parts of good wood, and furnished with strings. Josephus asserts that it was furnished with ten strings, and played with a *plectrum ;* which, however, is not understood to imply that it never had any other number of strings, or was always played with the *plectrum.* David certainly played it with the hand (1 Sam. xvi. 23 ; xviii. 10 ; xix. 9) ; and it was probably used in both ways, according to its size. That this instrument was really a *harp* is now very generally denied (*Kitto*). The reader will, by this time, have balanced the probabilities as to the nature and construction of the *kinnor ;* and most likely he will be led to think that it was either a *guitar* or *lyre,* a belief which seems to be gaining ground, on account of the aptitude of such instruments for the uses to which the *kinnor* was devoted.—*J. Stainer.*

Verse 4.—"*For the Lord taketh pleasure in his people.*" In the text there are two causes assigned why the saints should be excited to praise the Lord, and to be joyful in their King.

I.—THE DELIGHT WHICH THE LORD HAS IN THE SAINTS. " He taketh pleasure in his people." In this statement there are three subjects for inquiry, namely: 1. *Who* are the Lord's people? 2. *Why* he takes pleasure in them? 3. *In what respects* he takes pleasure in them?

1. *Who are the Lord's people?* Many are the names and titles given to them in Scripture. We find one in the second clause of the text; but it equally belongs to the first. "He will beautify *the meek.*" The scriptural term "*meekness*" is one which singularly characterizes and distinguishes the true Christian. It, in fact, contains in itself a combination of graces, which are most evidently the fruit of the Spirit, and can grow on no other tree than on the Christian vine. *Meekness,* as a Christian grace, may be considered as it respects both God and man. As it respects God, it implies poverty of spirit; humiliation of heart arising from a sense of guilt and a feeling of corruption; submission to God's will; silence and patience under his rod; acquiescence with his dispensations; and a surrender of our own natural desires and inclinations to his overruling appointments. As it respects man, meekness comprehends lowliness of mind, and a readiness to prefer others before ourselves; gentleness of disposition and behaviour; forbearance under provocations; forgiveness of injuries; quietness of spirit, and moderation in pushing forward our own interest and benefit. These are the qualities which distinguish "*the meek.*" Are not these, my brethen, the graces and tempers and dispositions which characterize and adorn true Christians? *They* are, in an especial manner, "*the meek* upon earth." In fact, there are, and can be, no others to whom this title really belongs. No man in his natural state can be *meek*, in the Scriptural sense of the word.

2. But *why* does the Lord "take pleasure" in them? Is there anything in them of *their own*, which he can regard with complacency and delight? No: they know and feel that they have no pretensions of this kind. It is not for their sake, but for his own sake; for his name's, his truth's, and his mercy's sake, that he has now a favour unto them. The Lord "taketh pleasure in his people," because they are his people; those whom he has purchased by his blood, renewed by his Spirit, and redeemed by his power. He "taketh pleasure in them," because in them he is himself honoured and glorified; because he sees in them the travail of his soul, the fruit of his suffering and mediation; because of the work which he has already begun in them; because they already exhibit some traces of his own image, some transcript of that mind which was in him, who was "meek and lowly in heart."

3. *In what respects* the Lord takes pleasure in his people. First: the Lord takes pleasure in them, inasmuch as he delights in *the exercise of their graces towards him.* They all believe in him, and have faith in his word and promises; they rely on his truth and power; they hope in his mercy; they fear his displeasure; they love his person and name. Secondly: the Lord hath pleasure in *the services* of his people. It is true, that they can do but little for him, and that little is nothing worth. At the best they can but render to him of his own again. But he regards their services, not with an eye to their intrinsic value in themselves, but for the sake of the willing mind from which they flow. He takes pleasure in their poor attempts to please him, because they are attempts. He weighs not the worth or merit of the action, but the principle and motive from which it springs. Thirdly: the Lord hath pleasure in the *prosperity* of his people. His name is love; his nature is goodness; and can we doubt but that he loves to see his people happy? Nay, we are expressly told that "he rejoiceth over them with joy"; that "he rejoiceth over them to do them good." Even in those dispensations which in themselves are grievous and painful he is seeking their good, and in the end promoting their happiness. What consolations do these reflections furnish to the *meek* and suffering servants of the Lord!

II.—Let us now consider THE LORD'S GRACIOUS DESIGNS concerning his people: "*He will beautify them with salvation.*" He designs not only to save, but to adorn and honour his people. Those "whom he justifies, them he also glorifies." He "will *beautify* them with salvation"; a promise relating both to the present life and to the future one.

1. *To the present life.* It is the purpose of God to beautify his people with salvation in this world. There are many passages in the Scripture which intimate this purpose, and lead us to this view of the happy effects of religion, even in the present life. When the prodigal returned home to his father's house, contrite, penitent, and reformed, he was not only received with kindness, assured of forgiveness,

and welcomed as a son, but he was *adorned* and *beautified* (Luke xv. 22).   So in the forty-fifth Psalm, the Church, the bride of Christ, is thus described : " The king's daughter is all glorious within : her clothing is of wrought gold.   She shall be brought unto the king in raiment of needlework."   " So shall he greatly desire thy *beauty*."   See also Eph. v. 25—27.

But what is the glory, the beauty, which is here meant in these passages, with which Christ will adorn and beautify his people ?   It is " the beauty of holiness." We have already seen that the meek and quiet spirit by which the Christian is distinguished is an " ornament " to him ;   and we read in another place that he is " adorned " with good works.   It is the great object of the gospel to sanctify all who embrace it, to restore them to the image of God which they have lost through sin.

2. We may now consider this promise as it relates *to the future world*.   Lovely and glorious as are the saints on earth, their beauty falls far short of the perfection to which it will attain hereafter.   They are " predestinated to be conformed to the image of his Son " ;   and when they awake up in another world, it will be after his likeness, without any remaining blemish, defect or spot.   Carry forward your thoughts to the morning of the resurrection, when this corruption shall have put on incorruption, this mortal immortality ;   when the body, raised in honour and glory, shall be clothed in its beauteous apparel, and being made like unto Christ's glorious body, shall shine as the sun in the firmament ;   when now, once more united to its kindred and sanctified spirit, it shall no longer be a weight, and a clog, and a hindrance, but become a furtherer of its joy, and a sharer and a helper in its spiritual happiness.   This is the meaning of the text, this is the *beauty* which he has designed for his people, and for which he is now preparing them.   In the contemplation of these, with reason may it be said to them, " Praise ye the Lord." —*Condensed from a Sermon by Edward Cooper,* 1826.

Verse 4.—Here in *ratio propositionis*, the important reason of the proposed praising of the Lord.   Those who know that they are objects of Divine complacency are likely to act on the principle of reciprocity.   God takes pleasure in sanctifying, justifying and glorifying them ;   they must surely take pleasure in extolling him as Friend, Protector, Law-giver, Leader, King, God !—*Simon de Muis.*

Verse 4.—"*He will beautify the meek with salvation.*"   Meekness not only gives great peace of mind, but often adds a lustre to the countenance.   We only read of three in Scripture whose faces shone remarkably —viz., Christ, Moses, and Stephen —and they were eminent for meekness.—*Matthew Henry.*

Verse 4.—"*The meek.*"   In the Hebrew ענוים, *anavim*, means *poor and afflicted ones ;* but the term came afterwards to be applied to *merciful persons*, as bodily afflictions have a tendency to subdue pride, while abundance begets cruelty.— *John Calvin.*

Verse 5.—" *Let the saints be joyful,*" etc.   Here begins a beautiful exegesis of the former passage.   A protected people may rejoice with confidence.   An anxious and fearful people could not sing aloud on their couches of repose.—*Simon de Muis.*

Verse 5.—"*Let the saints be joyful in glory : let them sing aloud upon their beds.*" At what time soever God is pleased to inspire his grace and comfort into us, we ought to rejoice therein, and by night on the bed to seek him whom our soul loveth ; abridging that time of rest and ease, that it may become as beneficial unto us as the day itself.   David was not satisfied by offering the sacrifice of thanksgiving in the courts of the Lord's house, and paying his vows in the presence of all the people ;   but in the night also he would continue his song of God's mercy.   Like that excellent bird, the nightingale, which is never weary nor spent by continuing her delightful notes, so this sweet singer of Israel was incessant in praising the Lord ; not giving sleep to his eyes until he had blessed his holy name.   In time of affliction he made his bed to swim, praying unto the Lord to return and deliver his soul.   Now in prosperity he gives thanks for the blessings he doth receive.   When our bones are vexed, and our sleep departeth from us, we pray unto God to deal mercifully with us ;   but when our diseases are healed, we do not return thanks, being soon overtaken with heaviness and security.   And yet David did endeavour to watch in the night, that he might sing praise unto the Lord.   He did not then only meditate in the law of God, when he could not take any rest (as Ahasuerus had the book of the records of the Chronicles read before him, when he could not sleep) ;   for now he might lie down in peace, and sleep, when God made him to dwell in safety.

Much less did he intend to procure sleep by a sinister performance of any good duty, like those who, by singing, or reading, or hearing, or meditating will have an unworthy aim to bring themselves asleep. David saith, *"Let the saints sing aloud upon their beds"* : thereby to testify their cheerful devotion, and also to chase away the spirit of slumber.—*William Bloys, in "Meditations upon the xlii. Psalm,"* 1632.

Verse 5.—*"The saints in glory"* shall rest from their labours, but not from their praises.—*Robert Bellarmine.*

Verse 5.—*"Upon their beds,"* where before in the loneliness of night they consumed themselves with grief for their shame. Comp. Hosea vii. 14.—*E. W. Hengstenberg.*

Verse 5.—The saints of God know most of domestic joy and peace. As the word of Jesus in John xiv. records, they have sorrows in plenty, but the more of these, the greater will be their joy, because their sorrows are to be transmuted into joys. They are to sing aloud *" on their beds,"* or rather couches, for on these the Orientals not only sleep, but also dine, and feast. So this verse calls on the saints to hold a banquet, a feast of fat things. They are, as David sings in Ps. xxiii., to sit at the table prepared by the Lord in the presence of their enemies. —*Johannes Paulus Palanterius.*

Verse 5.—This verse has been fulfilled in solemn crises of saintly life. On beds of death, and at the scaffold and the stake, joy and glory have been kindled in the hearts of Christ's faithful witnesses.—*Thomas Le Blanc.*

Verse 5.—How I long for my bed ! Not that I may sleep—I lie awake often and long ! but to hold sweet communion with my God. What shall I render unto him for all his revelations and gifts to me ? Were there no historical evidence of the truth of Christianity, were there no well-established miracles, still I should believe that the religion propagated by the fishermen of Galilee is divine. The holy joys it brings to me must be from heaven Do I write this boastingly, brother ? Nay, it is with tears of humble gratitude that I tell of the goodness of the Lord. —*From a private letter from Bapa Padmanji, in "Feathers for Arrows,"* 1870.

Verse 6.—*"Let the high praises of God be in their mouth and a two-edged sword in their hand."* Praise and power go ever hand in hand. The two things act and react upon each other. An era of spiritual force in the Church is always one of praise ; and when there comes some grand outburst of sacred song, we may expect that the people of God are entering upon some new crusade for Christ. Cromwell's Ironsides were sneeringly called Psalm-singers ; but God's Psalm-singers are always Ironsides. He who has a " new song in his mouth " is ever stronger, both to suffer " and to labour, than the man who has a dumb spirit and a hymnless heart. When he sings at his work, he will both do more and do it better than he would without his song. Hence, we need not be surprised that all through its history the Church of God has travelled " along the line of music "—*William Taylor, in "The Study,"* 1873.

Verse 6.—*"The high praises of God."* This expression needs a little explication, because so variously rendered by most interpreters ; some rendering it only, exaltations of God ; others, praisings exalting God ; others, sublime praises of God ; others, prasies highly uttered unto God : the reason whereof is, because the word *romemoth* in the text signifies sometimes actively, and then it notes the height, exaltation, and lifting up of anything to the observation of others ; and sometimes passively, and then it notes the height, worth, excellency of the thing that is exalted, or lifted up, in itself. But the scope and nature of the duty prescribed in the text necessarily comprehends both—as well the high acts for which God is to be praised, as the high praises to be given unto God for those high acts ; but especially the latter, namely, the height and excellency of the duty of praise to be performed for those high acts of God. This appears from the whole argument of the Psalm, which is entirely laudatory, as also from the instrument wherewith these high praises are to be performed, namely, the " mouth," " *the high praises of God in their mouth"* ; showing that the height herein mentioned is a property of man's work in praising God, and not only for the work of God, for which he is to be praised. In my observations I shall comprehend both, and all the particulars in the duty prescribed besides, which is this—

The duty of praising God is a high duty, which must exalt and lift up the high God in it.

This truth I shall labour to demonstrate, 1. From the Object. 2. The Effect.

3. Their Price.   4. Their Performance ; or, to use the School terms, they are
" high " :   1. Objectivè.   2. Effectivè.   3. Appreciativè.   4. Perfectivè.

1. The praises of God are " *high* " in relation to their *Object*, which is none other
but the Most High God, and that in the consideration of his transcendent height and
sublimity over and above all other things or persons : so the Psalmist's resolution
intimates (Ps. vii. 17), " I will praise the LORD according to his righteousness,"
which he expresseth in the following words, " To sing praise to the name of the
Lord most high " ; and Ps. xcii. 1 : " It is a good thing to give thanks unto the
LORD, and to sing praises unto thy name, O most High." In which places, and
very many more in the Scriptures, it is evident that the Lord, considered in his highest
sublimity, is the object of high praise, and that by most special and peculiar appropriation of it unto himself, and none other (Isa. xlii. 8).

2. In the second place, the praises of God will appear to be of a high, sublime
nature, from the high *effect*, the genuine and proper fruit they produce, viz., that
although their object to whom they are peculiarly appropriate (I mean the Lord
himself) be in his own nature, and of himself, most infinitely high and transcendent,
yet by the attribution and performance of praise unto him, doth he account his
name, his power, his wisdom, and justice, and himself to be exalted thereby. What
else do those expressions in Scripture imply wherein it is asserted, that by this
high duty of praise the high Jehovah is exalted (Ps. cviii. 32) ; His sublime perfections
are extolled and lifted up (Ps. lxviii. 4) : His great Name is magnified (Luke i. 64) ;
His infinite majesty is glorified (Ps. l. 23) ? Oh how high must be that duty, that
adds height to the high God, that magnifies the great God, and glorifies the God
of glory, and makes him higher, greater, and more glorious than he was before !

3. Thirdly, the praises of God are of a high nature, *appreciativè*, in respect of
the high estimation the Lord himself hath of them, which appears two ways : (1) By
the high price wherewith he purchaseth them ; (2) By the high delight he takes
in them, after he hath procured them.

First. The *price* wherewith God is willing to purchase them is very high, for
not only the expense of all his wisdom, power, and goodness, put forth in creation,
not only the layings out of all his counsel, care, love, and faithfulness in providence
and preservation ; but also the rich treasure of his promises, covenant, grace, yea,
the precious blood of his own Son, in our redemption, is given freely, absolutely,
intentionally, and ultimately, for no other thing but the purchase of high praises to
God (Eph. i. 5, 6). All that God doth and giveth ; all that Christ doth and suffereth,
is for the praise of the glory of his grace. I confess, consider men's highest praises
of God, as they are man's performance, they are poor and inconsiderable things ;
but consider them as they are the testimonies and expressions of a believing heart,
declaring and making known the unspeakable wisdom, faithfulness, bounty, and
excellencies of God, exercised in his works ; in this notion the Scripture declares
the heart of God to be so taken with the desire of them, that he is willing to give
heaven, earth, Himself, and Son to poor men for the praises of their hearts, hands,
and tongues ; and accounts himself abundantly satisfied. Therefore, when his
people will speak good of his name, they speak of him in the dialect of angels' notes,
" the high praises of God."

Secondly. The high value that God hath of " high praises " will be evident by
the *high delight and pleasure* God takes in them thus purchased ; for skilful artists,
and high-principled, elevated understandings, never take pleasure or delight in any
thing or work which is not answerable to their highest principles, and proportionable
to their uttermost skill and desire. Now the Lord, who is of the most perfect understanding, and deepest skill and knowledge, declares himself to take infinite delight
in his people's praises. It is his solace and pleasure to be attended with them, either
in earth or in heaven, by men or angels ; and his soul is ravished with the thoughts
and contemplation of them.

4. In the fourth place, the praises of God are high, and of a high nature *perfectivè*,
that is, in respect of the high measure of grace they are to be attended withal in
their performance : the Lord requiring the duty of high praise to be performed with
a great measure of Scripture-light, with a high degree of effectual faith, and with
a more ample proportion of practical holiness than any other of the most solemn
exercises of his public worship.—*Condensed from a Sermon by Samuel Fairclough,
entitled "The Prisoner's Praise,"* 1650.

Verse 8.—*"To bind their kings with chains,"* etc. Agrippa was captive to Paul.

The word had him in bands like a prisoner, and made him confess against himself before Festus that he was " almost persuaded to be a Christian." Then it was verified which before was prophesied, *"They shall bind kings in chains, and nobles in fetters of iron."* Oh, the majesty and force of the word !—*Henry Smith.*

Verse 8.—It was once the saying of Pompey, that with one stamp of his foot he could raise all Italy up in arms ; and the mighty men of the world may have nations, kingdoms, and commonwealths at their command, but yet God is more powerful than they all. If he do but arise, they shall all of them fly before him. If he once fall to fettering of princes, it shall be done so sure, that no flesh shall be able to knock off their bolts again.—*Stephen Gosson,* 1554—1623.

Verse 9.—*"This honour have all his saints."* All other glories and honours are but feminine, weak, poor things to it. God is their glory ; honoured they are with his blessed presence, honoured with his sight, with his embraces ; they see him and enjoy him. This is the very glory of their honour, the height and pitch of all, for " in thy presence is joy, and at thy right hand there is pleasure for evermore," honour advanced into eternal glory ; and *"this honour"* also *"have all his saints"*; some *in spe,* and some *in re,* some *in hope,* and some *in deed ;* all either in promise or in possession.—*Mark Frank.*

Verse 9.—*"This honour have all his saints."* *"His* saints " emphatically ; Divine providence foreseeing that in after ages some would usurp the title of saintship to whom it did not belong. " His saints " exclusively ; casting out saint traitors, as Beckett and Garnet ; saint hypocrites, and many others ; who, in the same sense as *auri sacra fames,* may be termed *sacri,* or *sancti,* saints. But, what honour have all his saints ? Mark what went before—" as it is written " ; but by whom, and where ? Though chapters and verses be of later date, the Holy Spirit might have cited the book. O no ! He, to quicken our industry, refers us to the Word at large. However, " search the Scriptures," and therein we shall meet with many honours afforded to the saints ; both whilst they were living, and when they were dead.

Honour to their memories is sometimes paid them very abundantly, even by those who formerly were so niggardly and covetous as not to afford them a good word in their lifetime.

Many are made converts by the godly ends of good men ; as the centurion himself, who attended and ordered the crucifying of Christ, after his expiring broke forth into that testimony of him,—" Verily, this was the Son of God." So, such as rail at, revile, curse, condemn, persecute, execute pious people, speak other language of them when such men have passed the purgation of death, and confess them faithful and sincere servants of God.

The last *"honour"* is imitation of their virtuous examples. The Papists brag that Stapleton, their great controversial divine, was born on that very day whereon Sir Thomas More was put to death ; but Providence so ordereth it that out of the ashes of dead saints many living ones do spring and sprout, by following the pious precedents of such godly persons deceased.—*Thomas Fuller, in "Abel Redivivus."*

HINTS TO PREACHERS.

Verse 1.—*"Praise ye the Lord."* I. The one work of a life. II. The work of the truly living of all degrees. III. Their work in many and various forms. IV. A work for which there is abundant cause, reason, and argument.

Verse 1.—I. A wonderful gift—to be a saint. II. A wonderful people—who are saints. III. A wonderful assembly—a congregation of saints. IV. A wonderful God—the object of their song.

Verses 1, 2.—*The new song of the saints.* I. The saints are God's children by the new birth. II. The new birth has given them a new heart. III. The new heart utters itself in a new song.—*C. A. D.*

Verses 1, 5.—I. We must praise God in public, " in the congregation of the **saints** " : the more the better ; it is like to heaven. II. We must praise him in private. "Let the saints" be so transported with their joy in God as to "sing aloud upon their beds," when they awake in the night, as David ; Ps. cxix. 62. —*Matthew Henry.*

Verse 2.—The duty, reasonableness, and benefit of holy joy.

Verse 2.—A peculiar people, their peculiar God, and their peculiar joy in him.

Verse 2 (second clause).—Christ's people may well rejoice :—I. In the majesty of his person. II. In the righteousness of his rule. III. In the extent of his conquests. IV. In the protection they enjoy under him. V. In the glory to which he will raise them.—*From "The Homiletical Library,"* 1882.

Verses 2, 4.—The cause given to God's Israel for Praise. Consider, I. God's doings for them. They have reason to rejoice in God, and employ themselves in his service ; for it is he that " made " them. II. God's dominion over them. This follows upon the former : if he made them he is their King. III. God's delight in them. He is a King that rules by love, and therefore to be praised. IV. God's designs concerning them. Besides the present complacency he hath in them, he hath prepared for their future glory. " He will beautify the meek," etc.—*Matthew Henry.*

Verse 4.—The text bears other renderings. Read as in Authorized Version. I. *The character to be aimed at—" the meek."* 1. Submissive to God. To his truth. To his dealings. 2. Gentle towards men. Bearing with patience. Forgiving with heartiness. Loving with perseverance. 3. Lowly in ourselves. II. *The favour to be enjoyed—"beautify."* 1. The beauty of gentleness. 2. The beauty of peace. 3. The beauty of content. 4. The beauty of joy. 5. The beauty of holiness. 6. The beauty of respect and influence. III. *The good results to be expected.* 1. God will be glorified and Christ manifested. 2. Men will be attracted. 3. Heaven will be anticipated.

Verse 4 (first clause).—The Lord's taking pleasure in his people is, I. A wonderful evidence of his grace. II. The highest honour they can desire. III. Their security for time and eternity.—*J. F.*

Verse 5.—*Saintly joy.* I. The state to which God has lifted the saints : " glory," in contrast with sin, reproach, affliction. II. The emotion which accordingly befits the saints : " be joyful." III. The utterance of that emotion incumbent on the saints : " sing aloud."—*C. A. D.*

Verse 5 (second clause).—Let them praise God—I. Upon their beds of *rest,* upon their *nightly* couch. 1. Because of what God has done for them during the day. 2. Because sleep is the gift of God. 3. Because they have a bed to lie upon. 4. Because the Lord is their keeper (Psalm iv. 5, 8). II. Upon their beds of *sickness.* 1. Because it is God's will they should suffer. 2. Because affliction is often a proof of God's love. 3. Because, if sanctified, sickness is a great blessing. 4. Because praise offered upon a bed of sickness is a testimony to the power of religion. III. Upon their beds of *death.* 1. Because the sting of death is removed. 2. Because their Lord has passed through death. 3. Because Christ is with them while they suffer. 4. Because of what awaits them. 5. Because they have the glorious hope of resurrection.—*C. W. Townsend.*

Verse 6.—I. The Christian life a combination of adoration and conflict. II. In each case it should be at its best : " high praises," " two-edged sword." III. In each case holiness should be conspicuous : it is of saints that the text speaks.

Verse 8.—The restraining and subduing power of the gospel.

Verse 9.—The honour common to all saints.

PSALM CL.

We have now reached the last summit of the mountain chain of Psalms. It rises high into the clear azure, and its brow is bathed in the sunlight of the eternal world of worship. It is a rapture. The poet-prophet is full of inspiration and enthusiasm. He stays not to argue, to teach, to explain : but cries with burning words, "Praise him, Praise him, Praise ye the LORD."

EXPOSITION.

PRAISE ye the LORD. Praise God in his sanctuary : praise him in the firmament of his power.

2 Praise him for his mighty acts : praise him according to his excellent greatness.

3 Praise him with the sound of the trumpet : praise him with the psaltery and harp.

4 Praise him with the timbrel and dance : praise him with stringed instruments and organs.

5 Praise him upon the loud cymbals : praise him upon the high sounding cymbals.

6 Let everything that hath breath praise the LORD. Praise ye the LORD.

1. *"Praise ye the LORD."* Hallelujah ! The exhortation is to all things in earth or in heaven. Should they not all declare the glory of him for whose glory they are, and were created ? Jehovah, the one God, should be the one object of adoration. To give the least particle of his honour to another is shameful treason ; to refuse to render it to him is heartless robbery. *"Praise God in his sanctuary."* Praise El, or the strong one, in his holy place. See how power is mentioned with holiness in this change of names. Praise begins at home. " In God's own house pronounce his praise." The holy place should be filled with praise, even as of old the high-priest filled the *sanctum sanctorum* with the smoke of sweet-smelling incense. In his church below and in his courts above hallelujahs should be continually presented. In the person of Jesus God finds a holy dwelling or sanctuary, and there he is greatly to be praised. He may also be said to dwell in holiness, for all his ways are right and good ; for this we ought to extol him with heart and with voice. Whenever we assemble for holy purposes our main work should be to present praises unto the Lord our God. *"Praise him in the firmament of his power."* It is a blessed thing that in our God holiness and power are united. Power without righteousness would be oppression, and righteousness without power would be too weak for usefulness ; but put the two together in an infinite degree and we have God. What an expanse we have in the boundless firmament of divine power ! Let it all be filled with praise. Let the heavens, so great and strong, echo with the praise of the thrice holy Jehovah, while the sanctuaries of earth magnify the Almighty One.

2. *"Praise him for his mighty acts."* Here is a reason for praise. In these deeds of power we see himself. These doings of his omnipotence are always on behalf of truth and righteousness. His works of creation, providence, and redemption all call for praise ; they are his acts, and his acts of might, therefore let him be praised for them. *"Praise him according to his excellent greatness."* His being is unlimited, and his praise should correspond therewith. He possesses a multitude or a plenitude of greatness, and therefore he should be greatly praised. There is nothing little about God, and there is nothing great apart from him. If we were always careful to make our worship fit and appropriate for our great Lord how much better should we sing ! How much more reverently should we adore ! Such excellent deeds should have excellent praise.

3. *"Praise him with the sound of the trumpet."* With the loudest, clearest note

call the people together. Make all men to know that we are not ashamed to worship. Summon them with unmistakable sound to bow before their God. The sound of trumpet is associated with the grandest and most solemn events, such as the giving of the law, the proclamation of jubilee, the coronation of Jewish kings, and the raging of war. It is to be thought of in reference to the coming of our Lord in his second advent and the raising of the dead. If we cannot give voice to this martial instrument, at least let our praise be as decided and bold as if we could give a blast upon the horn. Let us never sound a trumpet before us to our own honour, but reserve all our trumpeting for God's glory. When the people have been gathered by blast of trumpet, then proceed to *"praise him with the psaltery and harp."* Stringed instruments are to be used as well as those which are rendered vocal by wind. Dulcet notes are to be consecrated as well as more startling sounds. The gospel meaning is that all powers and faculties should praise the Lord—all sorts of persons, under all circumstances, and with differing constitutions, should do honour unto the Lord of all. If there be any virtue, if there be any talent, if there be any influence, let all be consecrated to the service of the universal Benefactor. Harp and lyre—the choicest, the sweetest, must be all our Lord's.

4. *"Praise him with the timbrel and dance."* Associated with the deliverance at the Red Sea, this form of worship set forth the most jubilant and exultant of worship. The hands, and the feet were both employed, and the entire body moved in sympathy with the members. Are there not periods of life when we feel so glad that we would fain dance for joy ? Let not such exhilaration be spent upon common themes, but let the name of God stir us to ecstasy. Let us exult as we cry,—

> " In the heavenly Lamb thrice happy I am,
> And my heart it doth dance at the sound of his name."

There is enough in our holy faith to create and to justify the utmost degree of rapturous delight. If men are dull in the worship of the Lord our God they are not acting consistently with the character of their religion. *"Praise him with stringed instruments and organs."* We have here the three kinds of musical instruments : timbrels, which are struck, and strings, and pipes : let all be educated to praise the Lord. Nothing is common and unclean : all may be sanctified to highest uses. Many men, many minds, and these as different as strings and pipes ; but there is only one God, and that one God all should worship. The word translated " organs " signifies pipe—a simpler form of wind instrument than the more modern and more elaborate organ. Doubtless many a pious shepherd has poured out gracious pastorals from a reed or oaten pipe, and so has magnified his God.

5. *"Praise him upon the loud cymbals : praise him upon the high sounding cymbals."* Let the clash of the loudest music be the Lord's : let the joyful clang of the loftiest notes be all for him. Praise has beaten the timbrel, swept the harp, and sounded the trumpet, and now for a last effort, awakening the most heavy of slumberers, and startling the most indifferent of onlookers, she dashes together the disks of brass, and with sounds both loud and high proclaims the glories of the Lord.

6. *"Let everything that hath breath praise the LORD."* " Let all breath praise him " : that is to say, all living beings. He gave them breath, let them breathe his praise. His name is in the Hebrew composed rather of breathings than of letters, to show that all breath comes from him : therefore let it be used for him. Join all ye living things in the eternal song. Be ye least or greatest, withhold not your praises. What a day will it be when all things in all places unite to glorify the one only living and true God ! This will be the final triumph of the church of God.

"Praise ye the LORD." Once more, Hallelujah ! Thus is the Psalm rounded with the note of praise ; and thus is the Book of Psalms ended by a glowing word of adoration. Reader, wilt not thou at this moment pause a while, and worship the Lord thy God ? Hallelujah !

EXPLANATORY NOTES AND QUAINT SAYINGS.

Whole Psalm.—Each of the last five Psalms begins and ends with *Hallelujah!* —*"Praise ye the Lord."* And each Psalm increases in praise, love, and joy, unto the last, which is praise celebrating its ecstasy. The elect soul, the heir of God, becomes " eaten up " with the love of God. He begins every sentence with *Hallelujah;* and his sentences are very short, for he is in haste to utter his next *Hallelujah,* and his next, and his next. He is as one out of breath with enthusiasm, or as one on tiptoe, in the act of rising from earth to heaven. The greatest number of words between any two Hallelujahs is four, and that only once : in every other instance, between one Hallelujah and another there are but two words. It is as though the soul gave utterance to its whole life and feeling in the one word, *Hallelujah!* The words, " Praise ye the Lord ! " or, " Praise him ! " " Praise him ! " " Praise him ! " are reiterated no fewer than twelve times in a short Psalm of six short verses.—*John Pulsford, in "Quiet Hours,"* 1857.

Whole Psalm.—And now, in the last Psalm of all, we see an echo to the first Psalm. The first Psalm began with " Blessed," and it ended with " Blessed," —" Blessed are all they that meditate on God's law and do it." Such was the theme of the first Psalm ; and now the fruit of that blessedness is shown in this Psalm, which begins and ends with Hallelujah.—*Christopher Wordsworth.*

Whole Psalm.—In his *Cours de Littérature,* the celebrated Lamartine, probably regarding the last four Psalms (the Hallelujah Psalms) as one whole (as Hengstenberg also does), thus speaks :—" The last Psalm ends with a chorus to the praise of God, in which the poet calls on all people, all instruments of sacred music, all the elements, and all the stars to join. Sublime finale of that opera of sixty years sung by the shepherd, the hero, the king, and the old man ! In this closing Psalm we see the almost inarticulate enthusiasm of the lyric poet ; so rapidly do the words press to his lips, floating upwards towards God, their source, like the smoke of a great fire of the soul wafted by the tempest ! Here we see David, or rather the human heart itself with all its God-given notes of grief, joy, tears, and adoration—poetry sanctified to its highest expression ; a vase of perfume broken on the step of the temple, and shedding abroad its odours from the heart of David to the heart of all humanity ! Hebrew, Christian, or even Mohammedan, every religion, every complaint, every prayer has taken from this vase, shed on the heights of Jerusalem, wherewith to give forth their accents. The little shepherd has become the master of the sacred choir of the Universe. There is not a worship on earth which prays not with his words, or sings not with his voice. A chord of his harp is to be found in all choirs, resounding everywhere and for ever in unison with the echoes of Horeb and Engedi ! David is the Psalmist of eternity ; what a destiny—what a power hath poetry when inspired by God ! As for myself, when my spirit is excited, or devotional, or sad, and seeks for an echo to its enthusiasm, its devotion, or its melancholy, I do not open Pindar or Horace, or Hafiz, those purely Academic poets ; neither do I find within myself murmurings to express my emotion. I open the Book of Psalms, and there I find words which seem to issue from the soul of the ages, and which penetrate even to the heart of all generations. Happy the bard who has thus become the eternal hymn, the personified prayer and complaint of all humanity ! If we look back to that remote age when such songs resounded over the world ; if we consider that while the lyric poetry of all the most cultivated nations only sang of wine, love, blood, and the victories of coursers at the games of Elidus, we are seized with profound astonishment at the mystic accents of the shepherd prophet, who speaks to God the Creator as one friend to another, who understands and praises his great works, admires his justice, implores his mercy, and becomes, as it were, an anticipative echo of the evangelic poetry, speaking the soft words of Christ before his coming. Prophet or not, as he may be considered by Christian or sceptic, none can deny in the poet-king an inspiration granted to no other man. Read Greek or Latin poetry after a Psalm, and see how pale it looks."—*William Swan Plumer.*

Whole Psalm.—The first and last of the Psalms have both the same number of verses, are both short and very memorable ; but the scope of them is very different ; the first Psalm is an elaborate instruction in our duty, to prepare us for the comforts of our devotion ; this is all rapture and transport, and perhaps was penned on purpose to be the conclusion of those sacred songs, to show what is the design of them all, and that is, to assist us in praising God.—*Matthew Henry.*

Whole Psalm.—Thirteen hallelujahs, according to the number of the tribes (Levi, Ephraim and Manasseh making three), one for each.—*John Henry Michaëlis, 1668—1738.*

Whole Psalm.—Some say this Psalm was sung by the Israelites, when they came with the first fruits into the sanctuary, with the baskets on their shoulders. *Thirteen* times in this short Psalm is the word *praise* used ; not on account of thirteen perfections or properties in God, as Kimchi thinks ; but it is so frequently, and in every clause used, to show the vehement desire of the Psalmist that the Lord might be praised ; and to express his sense of things, how worthy he is of praise ; and that all ways and means to praise him should be made use of, all being little enough to set forth his honour and glory.—*John Gill.*

Whole Psalm.—There is an interesting association connected with this Psalm which deserves to be recorded : that in former times, when the casting of church bells was more of a religious ceremony, this Psalm was chanted by the brethren of the guild as they stood ranged around the furnace, and while the molten metal was prepared to be let off into the mould ready to receive it. One may picture these swarthy sons of the furnace with the ruddy glow of the fire upon their faces as they stand around, while their deep voices rung forth this Hymn of Praise.—*Barton Bouchier.*

Verse 1.—"*Praise ye the* LORD." Praise God with a strong faith ; praise him with holy love and delight ; praise him with an entire confidence in Christ ; praise him with a believing triumph over the powers of darkness ; praise him with an earnest desire towards him, and a full satisfaction in him ; praise him by a universal respect to all his commands ; praise him by a cheerful submission to all his disposals ; praise him by rejoicing in his love, and solacing yourselves in his great goodness ; praise him by promoting the interests of the kingdom of his grace ; praise him by a lively hope and expectation of the kingdom of his glory.—*Matthew Henry.*

Verse 1.—"*In his sanctuary.*" בְּקָדְשׁוֹ. Many have been the notions of the commentators as to the shade of meaning here ; for the word differs from the form in Ps. xx. 2. מִקֹּדֶשׁ (*from the sanctuary*). The Vulgate adopts the plural rendering, *in sanctis ejus,* " in his holy places." Campensis renders it, *ob insignem sanctitatem ipsius,* " because of his excellent holiness." Some see under the word an allusion to the holy tabernacle of Deity, the flesh of Christ. Luther, in his German version, translates thus *in seinem Heiligthum,* " in his holiness." The same harmony of comparative thought appears in the two clauses of this verse as in such passages as 1 Kings viii. 13, 49 ; Isa. lvii. 15. The place of worship where God specially hears prayer and accepts praise, and the firmament where angels fly at his command, and veil their faces in adoration, are each a sanctuary. The sanctuary is manifestly here looked at as the temple of grace, the firmament as the temple of power. So the verse proclaims both grace and glory.—*Martin Geier.*

Verse 1.— '*Praise God in his sanctuary.*" The Septuagint, Vulgate Latin, and the eastern versions, render it, "*in his holy ones*" ; among his saints, in the assembly of them, where he is to be feared and praised : it may be translated, "*in his holy One,*" and be understood of Christ, as it is by Cocceius. . . . Some render it, "*for*" or "*because of his holiness.*" The perfection of holiness in him ; in which he is glorious and fearful in the praises of, and which appears in all his works of providence and grace.—*John Gill.*

Verse 1.—"*Praise God.*" In many places we have the compound word, הללו־יה, *halelujah,* praise ye Jehovah ; but this is the first place in which we find, הללו־אל, *halelu-el,* praise God, or the strong God. Praise him who is Jehovah, the infinite and self-existent Being ; and praise him who is God, *El,* or *Elohim,* the great God in covenant with mankind, to bless and save them unto eternal life.—*Adam Clarke.*

Verse 1.—Psalm cl. gives the full praise to Jehovah in a double character, *the sanctuary and the firmament of his power,* for his ways which come from the firmament of his power were always according to the sanctuary in which he governed Israel, and made good the revelation of himself there.—*John Nelson Darby,* 1800—1882.

Verse 2.—"*Praise him for his mighty acts,*" etc. The reasons of that praise which it becomes all intelligent creatures, and especially redeemed men, to render to Jehovah, are here assigned. We are to praise Jehovah " in his sanctuary," in the place where his glory dwells, where his holiness shines forth with ineffable splendour ; we are to praise him in the wide expanse over which he has spread the tokens of his power, whether in the heaven above, or in the earth beneath ; we are to praise him for those omnipotent acts whereby he hath shown himself to be above all gods ; we are to praise him in a manner suited to the excellent majesty of a Being whom all the heavens adore, and who is wonderful in counsel and excellent in working. His holiness, the infinity of his operations, the miraculous power which he has displayed, the unspotted excellence of his administration, call for loudest songs of praise from all whose reason enables them to rise to the contemplation of the great Supreme.—*John Morison.*

Verse 2.—*"Praise him according to his excellent greatness."* There is required special understanding and knowledge of the nature and worth of the mercy for which the duty of praise is undertaken ; for God will not be praised confusedly, but distinctly and proportionably to his dispensation : *"Praise him according to his wondrous works";* which is to be the prime and proper matter of their high praises, even his more proper and peculiar high acts, then to be remembered, as is largely expressed in Moses' praise for the particular mercy of coming safe through the Red Sea (Exod. xv.) ; and Deborah's high praise for deliverance from the host of Sisera (Judges v.) ; where the chiefest and highest part of the celebration and exaltation of God in his praise consists in the declaration and commemoration of the particulars of God's special goodness in their present deliverance. Thus, you see, the first thing that God looks for is proportionable praise, great praise for a great God, doing great things, and high praises for a high God, doing high things. —*Samuel Fairclough.*

Verse 2.—*"Praise him according to his excellent greatness,"* or, as the words may bear, " according to his *muchness of greatness* " ; for when the Scripture saith " God is great," this positive is to be taken as a superlative. " God is great," that is, he is greatest, he is greater than all ; so great that all persons and all things are little, yea, nothing before him. Isaiah xl. 15 : " Behold, the nations are (to him but) as a drop of a bucket, and are counted as the small dust of the balance : behold, he taketh up the isles as a very little thing. And Lebanon is not sufficient to burn, nor the beasts thereof sufficient for a burnt offering. All nations before him are as nothing ; and they are counted to him less than nothing, and vanity." How great is God, in comparison of whom the greatest things are little things, yea, the greatest things are nothing !—*Joseph Caryl.*

Verse 3.—*Trumpets* and *horns* are the only instruments concerning which any directions are given in the law.—*James Anderson.*

Verse 3.—*"Trumpet."* Of natural horns and of instruments in the shape of horns the antiquity and general use are evinced by every extensive collection of antiquities. . . . The Hebrew word *shophar*, rendered " trumpet," seems, first to denote horns of the straighter kind, including, probably, those of neat-cattle, and all the instruments which were eventually made in imitation of and in improvement upon such horns. The name *shophar* means *bright* or *clear*, and the instrument may be conceived to have been so called from its clear and shrill sound, just as we call an instrument a " clarion," and speak of a musical tone as " brilliant " or " clear." In the service of God this *shophar* or *trumpet*, was only employed in making announcements, and for calling the people together in the time of the holy solemnities, of war, of rebellion, or of any other great occasion. The strong sound of the instrument would have confounded a choir of singers, rather than have elevated their music. (*John Kitto.*) The *shophar* is especially interesting to us as being the only Hebrew instrument whose use on certain solemn occasions seems to be retained to this day. Engel, with his usual trustworthy research, has traced out and examined some of those in modern synagogues. Of those shown in our engraving, one is from the synagogue of Spanish and Portugese Jews, Bevis Marks, and is, he says, one foot in length ; the other is one used in the Great Synagogue, St. James's place, Aldgate, twenty-one inches in length. Both are made of horn.—*James Stainer.*

Verse 3.— The *"Psaltery"* was a ten-stringed instrument. It is constantly mentioned with the " harp." The *Psaltery* was struck with a plectrum, the *harp* more gently with the fingers. *"Psaltery and harp"* speak to us in figure of " law and gospel."—*Thomas Le Blanc*

Verse 3.—On *"Psaltery"* (*nebel*) see Note on Ps. cxliv. 9, and on " harp " see Note on Ps. cxlix. 3.

Verses 3, 4, 5.—As St. Augustine says here, " No kind of faculty is here omitted.

All are enlisted in praising God." The breath is employed in blowing the trumpet; the fingers are used in striking the strings of the psaltery and the harp; the whole hand is exerted in beating the timbrel; the feet move in the dance; there are stringed instruments (literally *strings*); there is the organ (the *'ugab, syrinx*) composed of many pipes, implying *combination*, and the cymbals clang one upon another.— *C. Wordsworth.*

Verses 3, 4, 5.—The variety of musical instruments, some of them made use of in the camp, as trumpets; some of them more suitable to a peaceable condition, as psalteries and harps; some of them sounding by blowing wind in them; some of them sounding by lighter touching of them, as stringed instruments; some of them by beating on them more sharply, as tabrets, drums and cymbals; some of them sounding by touching and blowing also, as organs: all of them giving some certain sound, some more quiet, and some making more noise: some of them having a harmony by themselves; some of them making a concert with other instruments, or with the motions of the body in dancings, some of them serving for one use, some of them serving for another, and all of them serving to set forth God's glory, and to shadow forth the duty of worshippers, and the privileges of the saints. The plurality and variety (I say) of these instruments were fit to represent divers conditions of the spiritual man, and of the greatness of his joy to be found in God, and to teach what stirring up should be of the affections and powers of our soul, and of one another, unto God's worship; what harmony should be among the worshippers of God, what melody each should make in himself, singing to God with grace in his heart, and to show the excellency of God's praise, which no means nor instrument, nor any expression of the body joined thereunto, could sufficiently set forth in these exhortations to praise God with trumpet, psaltery, etc.—*David Dickson.*

Verses 3, 4, 5.—Patrick has an interesting note on the many instruments of music in Psalm cxlix., which we quote here: "The ancient inhabitants of Etruria used the trumpet; the Arcadians, the whistle; the Sicilians, the pectid; the Cretians, the harp; the Thracians, the cornet; the Lacedemonians, the pipe; the Egyptians, the drum; the Arabians, the cymbal. (Clem. Pædag. ii. 4.) May we not say that in this Psalm's enumeration of musical instruments, there is a reference to the variety which exists among men in the mode of expressing joy, and exciting to feeling?—*Andrew A. Bonar.*

Verse 4.—"*Stringed instruments.*" *Minnim* [which is derived from a root signifying "division," or "distribution," hence *strings*] occurs in Ps. xlv. 8, and cl. 4, and is supposed by some to denote a stringed instrument, but it seems merely a poetical allusion to the *strings* of any instrument. Thus, in Ps. xlv. 8, we would read, "Out of the ivory palaces *the strings* (*i.e.* concerts of music) have made thee glad"; and so in Ps.cl. 4, "Praise him with *strings* (stringed instruments), and *'ugabs.*"—*John Kitto.*

Verse 4.—"*Organs.*" עוּגָב, *'ugab* is the word rendered "organ" in our version. The Targum renders the word simply by אבובא, *a pipe;* the Septuagint varies, it has κιθάρα in Genesis, ψάλμος in Job, and ὄργανον in the Psalms. The last is the sense which the Arabic, Syriac, Latin, English, and most other versions have adopted. The *organon* simply denotes a double or manifold pipe, and hence, in particular, the Pandæan or shepherd's pipe, which is at this day called a "mouth organ," among ourselves. (*Kitto.*) A collection of tubes of different sizes, stopped at one end and blown at the other, forms the musical instrument, known as Pan's pipes, in the Greek *syrinx*, σῦρυγξ .... Was the *'ugab* a *syrinx* or an organ? As the former seems to have been the more ancient of the two, and as *'ugab* is included in the very first allusion to musical instruments in the Bible, it would seem reasonable to say at once that it was *syrinx*, especially as this instrument was, and is to this day, commonly met with in various parts of Asia. Yet it would, indeed, be strange if such an instrument were selected for use in divine worship; and that the *ugab* was so used is proved beyond a doubt by its mention in Ps. cl.: "Praise him with the *minnim* and *'ugab.* "Its mention here in antithesis to a collective name for stringed instruments, surely points to the fact of its being a more important instrument than a few river-reeds fixed together with wax. Let us not forget that we have but one and the same name for the single row of about fifty pipes, placed, perhaps, in a little room, and the mighty instrument of five thousand pipes, occupying as much space as an ordinary dwelling-house. ... Each is an organ. May it not have been the case that the *'ugab*, which in Gen. iv. 21 is mentioned as the simply-constructed *wind*-instrument, in contrast to the simple *stringed*-instrument, the *kinnor*, was a greatly inferior instrument to that which in Ps. cl. is thought worthy of mention by the side of a term for the whole string power ?— *J. Stainer.*

Verse 5.—"*Loud cymbals . . . . high-sounding cymbals.*" This important passage clearly points to two instruments under the same name, and leaves us to conclude that the Hebrews had both hand-cymbals and finger-cymbals (or castanets), although it may not in all cases be easy to say which of the two is intended in particular texts.—*John Kitto.*

Verse 5. (Prayer Book Version).—"*Praise him upon the well-tuned cymbals: praise him upon the loud cymbals.*" As I have heard these words read monthly in our churches, it has often come into my thoughts that when we intend to glorify God with our cymbals, it should not be our only care to have them loud enough, but our first care should be to have them well tuned, else the louder the worse. Zeal does very well—there is great, yea, necessary use for it in every part of God's service. The cymbal will be flat, it will have no life or spirit in it, it will not be loud enough without it. But if meekness, peaceableness, and moderation do not first put the cymbal into good tune, the loudness will but make it the more ungrateful in the player, the more ungrateful to the hearer.—*Robert Sanderson,* 1587—1662.

Verse 6.—"*Praise ye the LORD.*" As the life of the faithful, and the history of the church, so also the Psalter, with all its cries from the depths, runs out into a Hallelujah.—*E. W. Hengstenberg.*

Verse 6.—"*Praise ye the LORD.*" When we have said all we are able to say for God's praise, we are but to begin anew ; for this are we taught by the renewing of the exhortation, in the close of sundry Psalms, and here also at the end of all the Psalms : "*Praise ye the LORD.*"—*David Dickson.*

Verse 6.—"*Let all breath praise Jah ! Hallelujah.*" The very ambiguity of "*all breath*" gives extraordinary richness of meaning to this closing sentence. From the simple idea of wind instruments, mentioned in the context, it leads us, by a beautiful transition, to that of vocal, articulate, intelligent praise, uttered by the breath of living men, as distinguished from mere lifeless instruments. Then, lastly, by a natural association, we ascend to the idea expressed in the common version, "*everything that hath breath,*" not merely all that lives, but all that has a voice to praise God. There is nothing in the Psalter more majestic or more beautiful than this brief but most significant *finale*, in which solemnity of tone predominates, without however in the least disturbing the exhilaration which the close of the Psalter seems intended to produce, as if in emblematical allusion to the triumph which awaits the church and all its members, when through much tribulation they shall enter into rest.—*Joseph Addison Alexander.*

HINTS TO PREACHERS.

Verse 1.—"*Praise God in his sanctuary.*" I. In his personal holiness. II. In the person of his Son. III. In heaven. IV. In the assembly of saints. V. In the silence of the heart.

Verses 1—6.—God should be praised. Where ? (*verse 1*). Wherefore ? (*verse 2*). Wherewith ? (*verses 3—5*). By whom ? (*verse 6*).—*C. A. D.*

Verse 2.—"*His excellent greatness.*" Wherein the greatness of God is specially excellent, and where it is best seen.

Verse 2.—"*Praise him for his mighty acts.*" I. For us. Election. Redemption. Inspiration. II. In us. The work of enlightenment in the understanding ; purification in the heart ; quickening in the conscience, subjugation in the will. III. By us. Thought through us ; felt through us, spoken through us ; worked through us. To him be all the glory !—*W. J.*

Verse 2.—"*Praise him according to his excellent greatness.*" I. Reverently according to the greatness of his being. II. Gratefully, according to the greatness of his love. III. Retrospectively, according to the greatness of his gifts. IV. Prospectively, according to the greatness of his promises—*W. J.*

Verse 2.—What the exhortation requires. I. That men should study God's works, and observe the glory of God in them. II. That they should meditate on his greatness till they realize its excellence. III. That they should openly proclaim the honour due to him. IV. That they should not contradict in their life the praise they speak.—*J. F.*

Verse 3.—"*Praise him with the sound of the trumpet.*" I. When you fight. II. When you conquer. III. When you assemble. IV. When you proclaim his Word. V. When you welcome Jubilee.

Verses 3—6.—I. The variety of the ancient service of worship necessitating serious expenditure ; consecration of high talent ; hard and constant toil. II. The lessons of such service. 1. God should be worshipped loyally. 2. The efforts of the best genius are his rightful tribute. 3. All human ability cannot place a worthy offering at his feet. III. The soul and essential of true worship. IV. God's requirements as to worship in these present times.—*W. B. H.*

Verse 6.—I. The august Giver of " life, and breath, and all things." II. The due and true use of the gifts of life. III. The resultant swathing of earth in consecrated atmosphere, and millennial hallelujahs.—*W. B. H.*

Verse 6.—A fitting close to the Psalter, considered as a desire, a prayer, or an exhortation. I. As a desire, it realizes the glory due to God, the worship ennobling to man, the disposition of heart which would make all the world into a holy brotherhood. II. As a prayer, it seeks the downfall of every superstition, the universal spread of the truth, the conversion of every soul. III. As an exhortation it is plain, pertinent, pure in its piety, perfect in its charity.—*J. F.*

HALLELUJAH!

INDEX

OF AUTHORS QUOTED OR REFERRED TO